D1362159

AMERICAN WRITERS

AMERICAN WRITERS

JAY PARINI
Editor

SUPPLEMENT XXIV

CHARLES SCRIBNER'S SONS
A part of Gale, Cengage Learning

GALE
CENGAGE Learning

Detroit • New York • San Francisco • New Haven, Conn • Waterville, Maine • London

GALE
CENGAGE Learning

American Writers Supplement XXIV

Editor in Chief: Jay Parini

Project Editor: Lisa Kumar

Permissions: Sheila Spencer

Composition and Electronic Capture: Gary Leach

Manufacturing: Cynde Lentz

Publisher: Jim Draper

Manager, New Product: Philip J. Virta

© 2014 Charles Scribner's Sons, a part of Gale, Cengage Learning

For product information and technology assistance, contact us at
Gale Customer Support, 1-800-877-4253.
For permission to use material from this text or product,
submit all requests online at **www.cengage.com/permissions**
Further permissions questions can be emailed to
permissionrequest@cengage.com

While every effort has been made to ensure the reliability of the information presented in this publication, Gale, a part of Cengage Learning, does not guarantee the accuracy of the data contained herein. Gale accepts no payment for listing; and inclusion in the publication of any organization, agency, institution, publication, service, or individual does not imply endorsement of the editors or publisher. Errors brought to the attention of the publisher and verified to the satisfaction of the publisher will be corrected in future editions.

EDITORIAL DATA PRIVACY POLICY. Does this publication contain information about you as an individual? If so, for more information about our editorial data privacy policies, please see our Privacy Statement at www.gale.cengage.com

LIBRARY OF CONGRESS CATALOGING-IN-PUBLICATION DATA

American writers: a collection of literary biographies / Leonard Unger, editor in chief.
  p. cm.
  The 4-vol. main set consists of 97 of the pamphlets originally published as the University of Minnesota pamphlets on American writers; some have been rev. and updated. The supplements cover writers not included in the original series.
  Supplement 2, has editor in chief, A. Walton Litz; Retrospective suppl. 1, c. 1998, was edited by A. Walton Litz & Molly Weigel; Suppl. 5–7 have as editor-in-chief, Jay Parini.
  Includes bibliographies and index.
  Contents: v. 1. Henry Adams to T.S. Eliot — v. 2. Ralph Waldo Emerson to Carson McCullers — v. 3. Archibald MacLeish to George Santayana — v. 4. Isaac Bashevis Singer to Richard Wright — Supplement\[s\]: 1, pt. 1. Jane Addams to Sidney Lanier. 1, pt. 2. Vachel Lindsay to Elinor Wylie. 2, pt. 1. W.H. Auden to O. Henry. 2, pt. 2. Robinson Jeffers to Yvor Winters. — 4, pt. 1. Maya Angelou to Linda Hogan. 4, pt. 2. Susan Howe to Gore Vidal — Suppl. 5. Russell Banks to Charles Wright — Suppl. 6. Don DeLillo to W. D. Snodgrass — Suppl. 7. Julia Alvarez to Tobias Wolff — Suppl. 8. T.C. Boyle to August Wilson. — Suppl. 11 Toni Cade Bambara to Richard Yates.
  ISBN 978-1-4144-9609-2
  1. American literature—History and criticism. 2. American literature—Bio-bibliography. 3. Authors, American—Biography. I. Unger, Leonard. II. Litz, A. Walton. III. Weigel, Molly. IV. Parini, Jay. V. University of Minnesota pamphlets on American writers.

PS129 .A55
810'.9
\[B\]   73-001759

ISBN-13: 978-1-4144-9609-2
ISBN-10: 1-4144-9609-5

Charles Scribner's Sons an imprint of Gale, Cengage Learning
27500 Drake Rd.
Farmington Hills, MI, 48331-3535

Printed in Mexico
1 2 3 4 5 6 7 17 16 15 14 13

Acknowledgments

The editors wish to thank the copyright holders of the excerpted criticism included in this volume and the permissions managers of many book and magazine publishing companies for assisting us in securing reproduction rights. Following is a list of the copyright holders who have granted us permission to reproduce material in this volume of *American Writers*. Every effort has been made to trace copyright, but if omissions have been made, please let us know.

COPYRIGHTED EXCERPTS IN *AMERICAN WRITERS*, VOLUME 24, WERE REPRODUCED FROM THE FOLLOWING BOOKS:

ABRAHAM, PEARL. Dinitia Smith, "An Author's Hasidic Roots Become Her Inspiration," *New York Times*, Feb. 8, 2005. Copyright © 2005 by *New York Times*. All rights reserved. Reproduced by permission.

BERRIGAN, TED. Ron Padgett, "June 17, 1942," from *Ted: A Personal Memoir of Ted Berrigan*, The Figures, 1993, pp. 61-62. Copyright © 1993 by Ron Padgett. All rights reserved. Reproduced by permission. / Edward Dorn, "Trippin' with Ted," from *Nice to See You: Homage to Ted Berrigan*, Coffee House Press, 1991, p. 178. Copyright © 1991 by Edward Dorn. All rights reserved. Reproduced by permission. / Charles Bernstein, "Writing Against the Body," from *Nice to See You: Homage to Ted Berrigan*, Coffee House Press, 1991, pp. 154-155. Copyright © 1991 by Charles Bernstein. All rights reserved. Reproduced by permission. / Ted Berrigan, "Personal Poem #9," from *The Collected Poems of Ted Berrigan*, University of California Press, 2006, p. 118. Copyright © 2006 by Alice Notley. All rights reserved. Reproduced by permission. / Ted Berrigan, "Words of Love," from *The Collected Poems of Ted Berrigan*, University of California Press, 2006, p. 118. Copyright © 2006 by Alice Notley. All rights reserved. Reproduced by permission. / Ted Berrigan, "In the 51st State," from *The Collected Poems of Ted Berrigan*, University of California Press, 2006, p. 514. Copyright © 2006 by Alice Notley. All rights reserved. Reproduced by permission. / Ted Berrigan, "In the Land of Pygmies & Giants," from *The Collected Poems of Ted Berrigan*, University of California Press, 2006, p. 573. Copyright © 2006 by Alice Notley. All rights reserved. Reproduced by permission. / Ted Berrigan, "Interstices," from *The Collected Poems of Ted Berrigan*, University of California Press, 2006, p. 612. Copyright © 2006 by Alice Notley. All rights reserved. Reproduced by permission. / Ted Berrigan, "Autumn," from *The Collected Poems of Ted Berrigan*, University of California Press, 2006, p. 454. Copyright © 2006 by Alice Notley. All rights reserved. Reproduced by permission. / Ted Berrigan, "Look Fred, You're a Doctor, My Problem Is Something Like This:," from *The Collected Poems of Ted Berrigan*, University of California Press, 2006, p. 554. Copyright © 2006 by Alice Notley. All rights reserved. Reproduced by permission. /

ACKNOWLEDGEMENTS

Ted Berrigan, "Last Poem," from *The Collected Poems of Ted Berrigan,* University of California Press, 2006, p. 650. Copyright © 2006 by Alice Notley. All rights reserved. Reproduced by permission. / Ted Berrigan, untitled, from *The Collected Poems of Ted Berrigan,* University of California Press, 2006, p. 158. Copyright © 2006 by Alice Notley. All rights reserved. Reproduced by permission. / Ted Berrigan, "A Boke," from *The Collected Poems of Ted Berrigan,* University of California Press, 2006, p. 103. Copyright © 2006 by Alice Notley. All rights reserved. Reproduced by permission. / Ted Berrigan, "Cento: A Note on Philosophy," from *The Collected Poems of Ted Berrigan,* University of California Press, 2006, pp. 443-444. Copyright © 2006 by Alice Notley. All rights reserved. Reproduced by permission. / Ted Berrigan, "Anselm," from *The Collected Poems of Ted Berrigan,* University of California Press, 2006, p. 621. Copyright © 2006 by Alice Notley. All rights reserved. Reproduced by permission. / Ted Berrigan, "Train Ride," from *The Collected Poems of Ted Berrigan,* University of California Press, 2006, pp. 273-274. Copyright © 2006 by Alice Notley. All rights reserved. Reproduced by permission. / Ted Berrigan, "Memorial Day," from *The Collected Poems of Ted Berrigan,* University of California Press, 2006, pp. 300-301. Copyright © 2006 by Anne Waldman. All rights reserved. Reproduced by permission. / Ted Berrigan, "Train Dreams," from *The Collected Poems of Ted Berrigan,* University of California Press, 2006, p. 262. Copyright © 2006 by Alice Notley. All rights reserved. Reproduced by permission. / Ted Berrigan, "Poem," from *The Collected Poems of Ted Berrigan,* University of California Press, 2005, p. 568. Copyright © 2006 by Alice Notley. All rights reserved. Reproduced by permission. / Ted Berrigan, "Red Shift," from *The Collected Poems of Ted Berrigan,* University of California Press, 2005, pp. 515-516. Copyright © 2006 by Alice Notley. All rights reserved. Reproduced by permission.

BOYLE, KAY. "And Winter" from *Collected Poems of Kay Boyle.* Copyright © 1991 by Kay Boyle. Reprinted with the permission of The Permissions Company, Inc. on behalf of Copper Canyon Press, www.coppercanyonpress.org.

DUBUS, ANDRE III. Quentin D. Miller, interview with Andre Dubus, May 25, 2012. Copyright © 2012 by Andre Dubus. All rights reserved. Reproduced by permission.

DURANG, CHRISTOPHER. John M. Clum, interview with Christopher Durang, October 3, 2011. Copyright © 2011 by John M. Clum. All rights reserved. Reproduced by permission.

FERRY, DAVID. "At a Low Bar" from *On the Way to the Island* © 1960 by David Ferry. Reprinted by permission of Wesleyan University Press. www.wesleyan.edu/wespress. / *Strangers,* University of Chicago Press, 1983, back cover. Copyright © 1983 by David Ferry. All rights reserved. Reproduced by permission. / "A Night-Time River Road," from *Strangers,* University of Chicago Press, 1983, p. 8. Copyright © 1983 by University of Chicago Press. All rights reserved. Reproduced by permission. / "Rereading Old Writing," from *Strangers,* University of Chicago Press, 1983, p. 51. Copyright © 1983 by University of Chicago Press. All rights reserved. Reproduced by permission. / "To Sestius," from *Strangers,* University of Chicago Press, 1983, p. 31. Copyright © 1983 by University of Chicago Press. All rights reserved. Reproduced by permission. / Reprinted by permission of Farrar, Straus & Giroux, LLC: Excerpts from "Tablet X" from *Gilgamesh: A New Rendering In English Verse* by David Ferry. Copyright © 1992 by David Ferry. / David Ferry, "Mnemosyne," from *Of No Country I Know,* University of Chicago Press, 1999, p. 210. Copyright © 1999 by University of Chicago Press. All rights reserved. Reproduced by permission. / David Ferry, "In the Garden," from *Of No Country I Know,* University of Chicago Press, 1999, p. 201. Copyright © 1999 by University of Chicago Press. All rights reserved. Reproduced by permission. / David Ferry, "The License Plate," from *Of No Country I Know,* University of Chicago Press, 1999, p. 21. Copyright © 1999 by University of Chicago Press. All rights reserved. Reproduced by permission. / David Ferry, "The Guest Ellen at the Supper for Street

ACKNOWLEDGEMENTS

People," from *Of No Country I Know,* University of Chicago Press, 1993, p. 7. Copyright © 1999 by University of Chicago Press. All rights reserved. Reproduced by permission. / Reprinted by permission of Farrar, Straus & Giroux, LLC.: Excerpts from "Note on the Translations," "To Sestius," "To the Republic," "To Lydia," "To Lingurinus," and "To Virgil" from *The Odes Of Horace* translated by David Ferry. Translation copyright © 1997 by David Ferry. / Mcclatchy, J.D., Editor, *Horace, The Odes.* © 2002 Princeton University Press. Reprinted by permission of Princeton University Press. / Reprinted by permission of Farrar, Straus & Giroux, LLC.: Excerpt from "Third Ecologue" from *The Eclogues of Virgil* by David Ferry. Copyright © 1999 by David Ferry. / Rachel Hadas, "Reading David Ferry's Poems," *The New Criterion,* vol. 18, Feb. 2000, p. 30. Copyright © 2000 by Rachel Hadas. All rights reserved. Reproduced by permission. / Reprinted by permission of Farrar, Straus & Giroux, LLC.: Excerpts from *The Epistles of Horace: Bilingual Edition* by David Ferry. Copyright © 2001 by David Ferry. / Reprinted by permission of Farrar, Straus & Giroux, LLC.: Excerpt from "Fourth Georgic" from *The Georgics of Virgil: Bilingual Edition* by David Ferry. Copyright © 2006 by David Ferry. / Lloyd Schwartz, *Bewilderment: New Poems and Translations,* University of Chicago Press, 2012, back cover. Copyright © 2012 by Lloyd Schwartz. All rights reserved. Reproduced by permission. / David Ferry, "Reading Arthur Gold's 'Trolley Poem,'" from *Bewilderment: New Poems and Translations,* University of Chicago Press, 2012, p. 72. Copyright © 2012 by University of Chicago Press. All rights reserved. Reproduced by permission. / David Ferry, "Resemblance," from *Bewilderment: New Poems and Translations,* University of Chicago Press, 2012, pp. 108-110. Copyright © 2012 by University of Chicago Press. All rights reserved. Reproduced by permission. / David Ferry, "Soul," from *Bewilderment: New Poems and Translations,* University of Chicago Press, 2012, p. 209. Copyright © 2012 by University of Chicago Press. All rights reserved. Reproduced by permission. / David Ferry, "Virgill Aeneid VII," from *The Aeneid of Virgil,* Farrar, Straus & Giroux, forthcoming, pp. 362-484. Copyright © (forthcoming) by David Ferry. All rights reserved. Reproduced by permission.

GALLAGHER, TESS. Excerpt from "Kidnaper" from *Midnight Lantern: New and Selected Poems.* Copyright © 1976 by Tess Gallagher. Reprinted with the permission of The Permissions Company, Inc. on behalf of Graywolf Press, Minneapolis, Minnesota, www.graywolfpress.org. / Excerpt from "Instructions to the Double" from *Midnight Lantern: New and Selected Poems.* Copyright © 1976 by Tess Gallagher. Reprinted with the permission of The Permissions Company, Inc. on behalf of Graywolf Press, Minneapolis, Minnesota, www.graywolfpress.org. / Excerpt from "The Same Kiss After Many Years" from *Under Stars.* Copyright © 1978 by Tess Gallagher. Reprinted with the permission of The Permissions Company, Inc. on behalf of Graywolf Press, Minneapolis, Minnesota, www.graywolfpress.org. / Excerpt from "We're All Pharohs When We Die" from *Midnight Lantern: New and Selected Poems.* Copyright © 1992 by Tess Gallagher. Reprinted with the permission of The Permissions Company, Inc. on behalf of Graywolf Press, Minneapolis, Minnesota, www.graywolfpress.org. / Excerpt from "Barrie Cooke Painting" from *Midnight Lantern: New and Selected Poems.* Copyright © 2011 by Tess Gallagher. Reprinted with the permission of The Permissions Company, Inc. on behalf of Graywolf Press, Minneapolis, Minnesota, www.graywolfpress.org.

JONES, GAYL. "Song for Anninho," from *Song for Anninho,* Beacon Press, 1999, pp. 7, 10, 46. Copyright © 1999 by Beacon Press. All rights reserved. Reproduced by permission.

JULY, MIRANDA. George Saunders, *No One Belongs Here More Than You: Stories by Miranda July,* Simon & Schuster/Scribner, 2008, inside cover. Copyright © 2008 by George Saunders. All rights reserved. Reproduced by permission.

KRIEGEL, LEONARD. Richard F. Shepard, "End Papers," *New York Times,* May 7, 1964, p. 35. Copyright © 1964 by *New York Times.* All rights reserved. Reproduced by permission. /

ACKNOWLEDGEMENTS

Elizabeth Hanson, "Review of Flying Solo," *New York Times Book Review,* February 22, 1998, p. 20. Copyright © 1998 by *New York Times.* All rights reserved. Reproduced by permission. / Leonard Kriegel, "Wonder Woman in the Land of Good and Plenty," from *Flying Solo,* Beacon Press, 1998, p. 163. Copyright © 1998 by Beacon Press. All rights reserved. Reproduced by permission. / Leonard Kriegel, "Wheelchairs," from *Flying Solo,* Beacon Press, 1998, p. 41. Copyright © 1998 by Beacon Press. All rights reserved. Reproduced by permission. / Ed Peaco, "Flying Solo: Reimagining Manhood, Courage, and Loss," *The Antioch Review,* vol 57, Issue 1, Winter 1999, pp. 106-107. Copyright © 1999 by *The Antioch Review.* All rights reserved. Reproduced by permission. / Morris Dickstein, "Torn by Diverse Loyalties," *New York Times Book Review,* Nov. 19, 1972. Copyright © 1972 by *New York Times Book Review.* All rights reserved. Reproduced by permission.

MONSON, ANDER. Excerpt from "Transubstantiation" from *Vanishing Point.* Copyright © 2010 by Ander Monson. Reprinted with the permission of The Permissions Company, Inc. on behalf of Graywolf Press, Minneapolis, Minnesota, www.graywolfpress.org. / Excerpt from "Vanishing Point for Solo Voice" from *Vanishing Point.* Copyright © 2010 by Ander Monson. Reprinted with the permission of The Permissions Company, Inc. on behalf of Graywolf Press, Minneapolis, Minnesota, www.graywolfpress.org. / Exerpt from "Sermon Now Encrypted" from *The Available World.* Copyright © 2010 by Ander Monson. Reprinted with the permission of The Permissions Company, Inc. on behalf of Sarabande Books, Inc., www.sarabandebooks.org. / Exerpt from "Some of Us Have Fewer" from *The Available World.* Copyright © 2010 by Ander Monson. Reprinted with the permission of The Permissions Company, Inc. on behalf of Sarabande Books, Inc., www.sarabandebooks.org. / Exerpt from "Slow Dance with Icarus" from *The Available World.* Copyright © 2010 by Ander Monson. Reprinted with the permission of The Permissions Company, Inc. on behalf of Sarabande Books, Inc., www.sarabandebooks.org.

SILVER, NICKY. Lloyd Rose, "Free Will's Flip Sides: Frenentic Pain and Mirth at Woolly Mammoth," *Washington Post,* Jan. 19, 1993, C10. Copyright © 1993 by *Washington Post.* All rights reserved. Reproduced by permission. / Erik Piepenburg, "A New Play and Much Else to Worry About," *New York Times,* August 24, 2008, AR7. Copyright © 2008 by *New York Times.* All rights reserved. Reproduced by permission.

List of Subjects

Introduction   *xi*

List of Contributors   *xiii*

PEARL ABRAHAM   1
Terry Barr

GERTRUDE ATHERTON   17
Windy Counsell Petrie

TED BERRIGAN   33
John Steen

KAY BOYLE   49
Bridget T. Chalk

WILLIAM ELLERY CHANNING   67
Jacob Risinger

JUNOT DÍAZ   83
Allen Guy Wilcox

ANDRE DUBUS III   97
D. Quentin Miller

CHRISTOPHER DURANG   113
John M. Clum

JEFFREY EUGENIDES   131
Joseph Dewey

DAVID FERRY   147
Daniel Bosch

TESS GALLAGHER   165
Cheri Johnson

GAYL JONES   183
Tracie Church Guzzio

MIRANDA JULY   199
Elaine Roth

LEONARD KRIEGEL   213
Sanford Pinsker

ANDER MONSON   229
Amanda Fields

MARI SANDOZ   243
Bette S. Weidman

NICKY SILVER   263
Deirdre O'Leary

HUNTER S. THOMPSON   279
Jeffrey Bickerstaff

Cumulative Index   295

Introduction

Not everyone—myself included—would agree with the Nobel Prize-winning novelist William Faulkner, who wrote: "What a writer's obituary should read—he wrote the books, then he died." It's an amusing statement; but to follow it closely would leave us very little room for discussion in the case of any writer in our table of contents. What this series has put forward over several decades is the thesis that a writer's life is relevant to his or her writing in a variety of ways. We have tried to prove this over and again, drawing connections between the actual circumstances in a writer's life—including the political and social times in which this life unfolded—and the work itself, its tones, shape, and aesthetic contours. It is our contention that the more you know about a writer's life and times, taken as a whole, the more likely you are to understand this writer's work in its multiple dimensions.

In this twentieth-fourth volume of *American Writers,* we present substantial and lively articles on eighteen writers—their lives and times—from a wide array of genres, including poets, novelists, essayists and playwrights. They are all relatively well-known figures who have achieved a good deal in their writing lives, including degrees of fame; yet none of them has yet been featured in this series. It is our hope that readers will find many things here to attract and sustain them in their pursuit of these writers and their books, plays, or films: biographical, cultural, and historical context; close readings of major texts; and supplementary material designed to help with the close reading of the work itself.

This series itself has its origins in a series of critical and biographical monographs that appeared between 1959 and 1972. The *Minnesota Pamphlets on American Writers* achieved fame in their time; they were incisively written and informative, treating ninety-seven American writers in a format and style that attracted a devoted following of readers. The series proved invaluable to a generation of students and teachers, who found they could depend on these reliable and interesting critiques of major figures. The inspired idea of reprinting these essays occurred to Charles Scribner, Jr. (1921-1995). The series originally appeared in four volumes titled *American Writers: A Collection of Literary Biographies* (1974).

Since then, twenty-three supplements have appeared with regularity on a yearly basis, treating hundreds of well-known and less known American writers: poets, novelists, playwrights, screenwriters, essayists, and autobiographers, even a handful of literary critics who have managed to create texts that somebody might want to read in future years. The idea has been consistent with the original series: to provide informative essays aimed at the general reader or student. These essays often rise to a high level of craft and critical vision, but they are meant to introduce a body of work of some importance in the history of American literature, and to provide a sense of the scope and nature of the career under review. Each writer is told to keep in mind the general reader, not the specialist.

Supplement twenty-four treats a range of authors from the past and present. William Ellery Channing—a major author from the early nineteenth century and a key figure among the Transcendalist thinkers—has long needed acknowledgement in this series, as his ideas hugely influenced Emerson and others. The remaining writers discussed here are from the twentieth century, including Pearl Abraham, Gertrude Atherton, Ted Berrigan, Kay Boyle,

INTRODUCTION

Junot Díaz, Andre Dubus III, Christopher Du-rang, Jeffrey Eugenides, David Ferry, Tess Gal-lagher, Gayl Jones, Miranda July, Leonard Krie-gel, Ander Monson, Mari Sandoz, Nicky Silver, and Hunter S. Thompson. While each of these writers has been written about in journals and newspapers and some have won major prizes, including the Pulitzer, few of have had the kind of sustained critical attention they deserve, and we hope to provide a beginning here, as their work certainly merits close reading and rereading.

The rich amount of biographical and histori-cal detail included in each of these eighteen es-says will certainly make Faulkner's pronounce-ment seem shallow, if not comical. It's true: what matters in the end is the work itself. That goes without saying. Yet one can only begin to appreciate complex works of art—novels, poems, plays, films, and essays—when the full context of the production of the work is taken into account. Our critics do that here, exploring the career of each subject with clarity, taking into account the chronology of each life and the development of each individual body of writ-ing. The hope is that, in each case, the work itself will be given a fresh sense of its impor-tance in the tradition of American literature.

—JAY PARINI

Contributors

Terry Barr. Terry Barr is a Professor of Modern Literature and Creative Writing at Presbyterian College in Clinton, South Carolina. He lives in Greenville, SC with his wife and two daughters. His literary biography of Tova Mirvis appeared in *American Writers* Supplement XX, and he has had creative nonfiction essays published in the *Montreal Review, moonShine review, American Literary Review, Museum of Americana, Orange Quarterly,* and *Scissors and Spackle.* PEARL ABRAHAM

Jeffrey Bickerstaff. Jeffrey Bickerstaff received his Ph.D. from Miami University of Ohio. He currently teaches writing and literature at Johnson State College and the Community College of Vermont. His research interests include representations of American politics in literature and film. HUNTER S. THOMPSON

Daniel Bosch. Daniel Bosch is a poet, critic, and translator. He has taught at Boston University, Harvard University, and Tufts University. His book *Crucible* was published by Other Press in 2002. DAVID FERRY

Bridget T. Chalk. Bridget T. Chalk is an Assistant Professor of English at Manhattan College in the Bronx, specializing in twentieth-century British literature and transatlantic modernism. She is currently working on a manuscript about interwar modernism and the passport system, as well as an article about women writers and semi-public spaces. Her work has appeared in *jml: The Journal of Modern Literature, Twentieth-Century Literature,* and *The Journal of British Studies.* KAY BOYLE

John M. Clum. John M. Clum's books include *Still Acting Gay: Male Homosexuality in Mod-* *ern Drama* and Something for the Boys: Musical Theatre and Gay Culture, both from St. Martins Press; as well as *He's All Man: Learning Masculinity, Homosexuality and Love from American Movies* and *The Drama of Marriage: Gay Playwrights/Straight Unions from Oscar Wilde to the Present,* both from Palgrave Macmillan. He is the author of numerous essays on modern and contemporary British and American drama and musical theatre. Currently, he is the series editor for the Cambria Series on Contemporary Theatre and Drama (from Cambria Press) and editor of a two-volume collection of gay drama to be published in that series. His plays have been produced by a number of theatres around the United States and he has directed over seventy-five theatrical and operatic productions. He is Professor Emeritus of Theater Studies and English at Duke University. CHRISTOPHER DURANG

Joseph Dewey. Joseph Dewey is an Associate Professor of American Literature at the University of Pittsburgh. He is the author of *In a Dark Time: The Apocalyptic Temper of the American Novel in the Nuclear Age* (1990); *Novels from Reagan's America* (1997); *Understanding Richard Powers* (2001); and *Beyond Grief and Nothing: A Reading of Don DeLillo* (2006). In addition, Dewey has edited casebooks on the short fiction of Henry James, DeLillo's *Underworld,* and J. D. Salinger's *The Catcher in the Rye.* He is completing a manuscript on Michael Chabon. JEFFREY EUGENIDES

Amanda Fields. Amanda Fields' creative writing has been published in *Indiana Review, Brevity,* and other journals. She received an MFA from the University of Minnesota and is a Ph.D. candidate in Rhetoric and Composition at the

CONTRIBUTORS

University of Arizona, where she is a scholar with the Crossroads Collaborative, a Ford-funded project focusing on youth sexuality, health, and rights. ANDER MONSON

Tracie Church Guzzio. Tracie Church Guzzio is Professor of English at the State University of New York at Plattsburgh. She is the author of *All Stories Are True: History, Memory, and Trauma in the Work of John Edgar Wideman,* as well as several other short articles on African-American literature. Currently, she is at work on a study of trauma and the Gothic in the African-American literary tradition. GAYL JONES

Cheri Johnson. Cheri Johnson's fiction, poetry, and reviews have appeared in *Glimmer Train Stories, Pleiades, Puerto Del Sol, New South, The Rio Grande Review,* and *Provincetown Arts.* Her chapbook of poems, *Fun & Games,* was published in 2009 by Finishing Line Press, and she has won fellowships from The McKnight Foundation, The Bush Foundation, the Fine Arts Work Center in Provincetown, and the Minnesota State Arts Board. She studied writing at Augsburg College, Hollins University, and The University of Minnesota. Raised in northern Minnesota, she lives in Minneapolis. TESS GALLAGHER

D. Quentin Miller. D. Quentin Miller is Professor of English at Suffolk University in Boston where he teaches courses on contemporary American literature, African-American literature, and fiction writing. He is the author of a number of articles and books, most recently *"A Criminal Power": James Baldwin and the Law* (Ohio State UP, 2012). He is also the chief editor of the contemporary section (volume E) of *The Heath Anthology of American Literature.* ANDRE DUBUS III

Deirdre O'Leary. Deirdre O'Leary is an Assistant Professor of English at Manhattan College, where she teaches courses in American drama, Irish literary revival, literary studies, and contemporary British drama. She has

published essays and theatre reviews in *Theatre Journal, Theatre Survey, New England Theatre Journal, Foilsiu, Ecumenica, Irish Studies Review,* and *Nordic Irish Studies.* NICKY SILVER

Windy Counsell Petrie. Windy Counsell Petrie (Ph.D., University of Delaware, 2001) is Associate Professor and Chair of English at Colorado Christian University. Her research investigates the overlapping territories and techniques of autobiography and fiction. In 2006, she served as a Fulbright Scholar to Lithuania, where she lectured on representations of exile in nineteenth- and twentieth-century novels as well as on the roles of female and African-American authors in American literary history. Most recently, she has published and presented work which examines expatriatism and authorship in the early twentieth century. GERTRUDE ATHERTON

Sanford Pinsker. Sanford Pinsker is an emeritus professor at Franklin and Marshall College. He currently lives in south Florida where he continues to write articles and reviews about American literature. LEONARD KRIEGEL

Jacob Risinger. Jacob Risinger is a Ph.D. candidate and Teaching Fellow in the English Department at Harvard University. He is currently working on a dissertation about the flexible inheritance of stoic philosophy in British and American Romanticism. His work has been published in *Romanticism,* and is forthcoming in *Emerson in Context* and *The Oxford Handbook of William Wordsworth.* WILLIAM ELLERY CHANNING

Elaine Roth. Elaine Roth is Associate Professor of Film Studies and Chair of the English Department at Indiana University South Bend. Co-editor of *Motherhood Misconceived: Representing the Maternal in U.S. Films* (SUNY Press, 2009), she has also published articles in *Feminist Media Studies, The Quarterly Review of Film and Video,* and *Genders.* She spent spring 2011 on a Fulbright Senior Lectureship at the Universidad Complutense in Madrid, Spain. MIRANDA JULY

CONTRIBUTORS

John Steen. John Steen is Visiting Assistant Professor of English at Oklahoma State University. His research concerns the relationship between poetic style, psychoanalytic technique, and feeling. An article, "Threshold Poetics: Wallace Stevens and D. W. Winnicott's 'Not-Communicating,'" is forthcoming from *The Wallace Stevens Journal.* TED BERRIGAN

Bette S. Weidman. Bette S. Weidman is Associate Professor of English at Queens College of the City University of New York. She teaches courses in nineteenth-century American literature, Native American literatures, and theory and practice of oral history. Her essay on Charles Frederick Briggs appeared in *American Writers,* Supplement XVIII (2009). Her book publications include *White on Red: Images of the American Indian* (1976) and *Nassau County, Long Island in Early Photographs* (1981). She has published articles on Briggs, Herman Melville, Henry David Thoreau, Willa Cather, and James Welch, as well as on Native American languages in print. MARI SANDOZ

Allen Guy Wilcox. Allen Guy Wilcox was born in Cooperstown, NY, and grew up on his parents' farm in the Mohawk Valley. Educated at Middlebury College, he has lived in Brooklyn, NY since 2005. He is a regular contributor to *The Brooklyn Rail.* JUNOT DÍAZ

AMERICAN WRITERS

PEARL ABRAHAM

(1960—)

Terry Barr

IN HER ESSAY "Divinity School or Trusting the Act of Writing," the novelist Pearl Abraham writes of a formative experience from her early teen years:

> My Aunt Rachel from Israel was visiting. We were in Brooklyn for the day, waiting in the car for my mother and sister, who had stepped out to run an errand. My father was in the driver's seat, reading from Psalms or Mishnah, as was his habit during such stops. Taking my cue from him, I immersed myself in a novel. Aunt Rachel, who must have been bored, tried to engage me in conversation, which I discouraged by keeping my eyes on the page. When my mother returned, Rachel informed her that I was a child who ought to be watched, that I was dangerous. My father was upset that this had been said in front of me, and called it nonsense. I was deeply thrilled because it confirmed for me what I had known all along, though perhaps not so clearly: that I would be someone different, dangerous somehow.
>
> (Rubin, ed., *Who We Are,* p. 228)

Abraham is dangerous, and so are her fictional characters. But the danger, of course, is primarily metaphorical. Offering insights into a closed culture, Abraham takes her readers inside a world many likely know nothing about. In this world she challenges stereotypes of Hasidic Judaism, of Judaism itself, and of individuals who pursue dreams—secular American, religiously messianic, and even legally traitorous. Abraham's vision of America is real, troubling, and provocative, yet this vision unfolds clearly and beautifully through the craft of her evocative prose style.

Pearl Abraham writes about a different America—an America where assimilation is not a dreamed-for reality for most of her fictional characters. These characters strive to maintain their separate world, where they live comfortably within the essence of their most identifying markers. In some cases, these markers are of the Hasidic world that nurtured Abraham herself, but which she left as an adult. In other cases, the markers are of a certain branch of Hasidism that is skeptical, perhaps even fearful, of an even more mystical branch, or of a tight, modern Orthodox adherence to kashrut (keeping kosher) that follows rules without necessarily understanding the spirit from which these rules derived. And then there are markers of political orthodoxy, seen primarily in her non-Jewish characters, the parents of an enlightened liberal orthodoxy who raise children to be free spirits—who place no restrictions on their children nor display any open disapproval about their children's decisions.

In all of her published fiction (four novels and one story as of 2013), her main characters push the boundaries of these markers, this American world they inhabit. Insiders amid their own religious or secular subculture, but outsiders to mainstream American culture, Abraham's central narrative voices attempt to gain a foothold in a world beyond their immediate borders. At first it seems they may be seeking assimilation into something larger, something beyond their families and particular subgroups. Increasingly these characters' journeys become more personal, more internal, and they find themselves caught somewhere between cultures and identities.

For Rachel Benjamin, the narrator and protagonist of Abraham's first novel, *The Romance Reader* (1995), this personal quest is at the center of her young life. If she leaves Hasidism, can she still be a Jew, and if so, what kind of Jew? And can she return to the fold if the outside world is too foreign and not nearly as romantic as she thought? Like her author's other narrative voices, Rachel pushes boundaries. Growing up in the sixties, she wants to read and live the secular romance novels by Victoria Holt that she buys or sometimes steals from drug

stores. She wants to become a lifeguard at a modern Jewish resort and fantasizes that the dashing, married owner of the inn will seduce her away from her restrictive Hasidic culture. She takes chances, scandalizing her parents and their friends by wearing a one-piece bathing suit to the neighborhood pool. And even when her father, the rabbi of his own shul, approves of her lifeguarding, she goes further still. Her younger sister Leah, who both idolizes and fears Rachel, remarks on Rachel's decision to continue wearing beige, seamless stockings to school: "You're crazy.... It's not worth the trouble, not for every day. Swimming will be enough of a fight.... You always go too far" (p. 130).

Leah is right, and not only regarding Rachel, but regarding her narrative descendants in Abraham's three subsequent novels, *Giving Up America* (1998), *The Seventh Beggar* (2004), and *American Taliban* (2010). Desiring independence—clearly a very American quest—these characters push limits and boundaries to such an extent that they sometimes lose sight of what they want. Worse, in her latter two novels, her protagonists go so far inward that they lose themselves and quite literally disappear from their loved ones and from the very pages of the novels themselves. Seeking spiritual enlightenment and an inner world of mystical evolution or submission, they leave us all—their loved ones and we readers—and enter a different world, perhaps even a no-world.

Thus, Abraham might be asking her readers to consider that oldest of American spirit journeys, the one where seeking individualism, where the adventure of the quest to discover one's truest, original American self, is possible, even desirable. But is it possible to find acceptance and self-fulfillment in contemporary America, and if so, what is the cost? And when we find ourselves, what of ourselves do we leave behind for our families and the cultural-religious world that nurtured us? How far inside our culture, the country, or ourselves can we safely travel? To what degree can we ever escape outsider status if we are born into an outsider subculture? These are the questions and themes that Abraham's fiction evokes. The answers and resolutions to these questions and themes, though, will not be simple or easily arrived at. They might even, in the end, be entirely unanswerable, at least in any uniform, orthodox way.

BIOGRAPHY: A TRAVELING SPIRIT

Pearl Abraham was born in Jerusalem, Israel, in 1960, the third of nine children born to Satmar Hasidic parents. Her early life was fluid and kinetic. Before she turned twelve, her father, Hersh Ber Abraham, moved the family between Israel and New York several times. A by-product of this mobility was that Abraham herself grew up speaking Yiddish, Hebrew, and English. Abraham also had to adapt herself continually to the mainly Yiddish- or mainly English-speaking schools she attended. Still, there was a certain privilege in the choice of schools for this Hasidic daughter. As she told Aryeh Lev Stollman:

> I was fortunate, in most ways, to have grown up at a time when my family lived in a community that didn't have Hasidic schools. This meant that I attended an orthodox yeshiva school—we called it *Litvish*, which means it's from the Lithuanian non-Hasidic tradition—that taught girls the texts and commentaries in their original languages. Satmar Hasidic schools don't teach or encourage girls to read and learn biblical Hebrew or Aramaic. When I was in the tenth grade, the school hired a new teacher, a young newly married woman who had graduated from one of the better Hebrew seminaries for women, and she taught us Genesis, complete with the commentaries that discussed and debated various philosophies. This was the first time I was required to consider profound ideas and questions....

Abraham's relationship with her parents and the Satmar branch of Hasidism she was born into has seemingly always straddled fences of belonging. The great-granddaughter of a well-known Jerusalem cabalist, Nuchem Ehrlich, she was raised in a household that forbade "graven images"; in fact, she told Dinitia Smith of the *New York Times,* any doll the children possessed had to have its nose cut off. But while the family was "extremely religious," Abraham maintains that certain stereotypes about the relationship between men and women aren't accurate or fair, especially the one that portrays women as being oppressed

by men. In her view, "Women run the households…. In America, they study in English, whereas boys learn in Yiddish and read and write in ancient Hebrew." Her brothers do not speak fluent English, but "the women's proficiency in English also gives them an advantage in dealing with the outside world" (Smith). This reality, as will be discussed later, provides a thematic tension for her first two novels, particularly, and even influences the third.

As she grew older, however, the tension in her own life built. Eventually she broke from the Hasidic life she was born and raised in, though the exact reasons she did so "remain a mystery" even to her. Perhaps the seeds were planted by her father, whom she described to Smith as "an antinomian, one who goes his own way." Unlike most Hasidic rabbis, her father "is not allied with the teachings of a single rabbi … but embraces the works of many." Thus, at the ultra-Orthodox girls' school in Monsey, New York, she attended in the 1960s, the more secular curriculum allowed her to read not only Jewish authors but also the works of William Shakespeare and Charles Dickens. After obtaining a driver's license, she enrolled in Rockland Community College, unbeknownst to her parents, who thought she was working in a Hasidic bakery. Eventually she transferred to Manhattan's Hunter College, revealing her decision to her parents. But family ties were not irrevocably severed, and her father even traveled to Manhattan regularly "to study sacred texts with her" (Smith).

After completing her degree at Hunter, Abraham obtained her M.F.A. in creative writing from New York University's graduate writing program. Her teaching career has included posts at New York University, Sarah Lawrence College, and the University of Houston. As of 2013 she was on the faculty at Western New England University in Springfield, Massachusetts, teaching creative writing while continuing to write fiction and commentary for many publications including the *Forward*, New York's Jewish newspaper of record. Her first novel, *The Romance Reader*, was a semifinalist for the Discover Award, and her third novel, *The Seventh Beggar*, was one of three finalists for the 2005 Koret Award in Fiction.

Abraham maintains a residence in Manhattan, and has been married once, to a part-Jewish man, a relationship that lasted only seven years and that surely influenced the characters and the main relationship found in her second novel, *Giving Up America*. In that work, a woman leaves her Hasidic family and marries, against her father's dire prophetic warning, a non-Hasidic, Orthodox Jewish man. Her relationship with her family remains strong despite the religious break. Abraham's sister, Sara Jacob, maintains that while their parents felt that they had "failed" when Abraham left, they also recognized that they had to "respect everyone's ways." Abraham visits her family in Monsey often, but she "doesn't cover her head" as Hasidic women are required, when she goes: "Why should I cover it? … I'm not married," she argues (Smith).

Also noting that her parents have never met her boyfriend, a non-Jewish computer engineer, since they "gave [her] other boyfriends such a hard time," Abraham nevertheless says that despite the difficult periods in the past, "Now we are in a good place. They have come to sort of admire me. It's not always perfect…. And they make sure to let me know it's not perfect" (Smith).

Clearly, then, Abraham's life, the inside-outside worlds she has traversed, straddled, and in many ways successfully blended, form the basis for the fictional mirror-world she brings to her readers. In this world there are no easy or perhaps even any clear answers at all; there are only questions that impel her readers to contemplate the various meanings of American life, religion, and the mystical world we inhabit and continue to form.

ESSAY: AMERICA, THE DIVINE, AND THE INDIVIDUAL

Abraham's essay "Divinity School or Trusting the Act of Writing," published in the 2005 collected volume *Who We Are: On Being (and Not Being) a Jewish American Writer*, considers her path as a Hasidic female who was supposed to stay in a closed society, marry a learned man, and raise multiple children as had her mother and

the generations of women before her. This path, though clearly before her, did not appeal to her, nor did she follow it. Happiness for her lay elsewhere, mainly in becoming a writer. For that, she says, her mother "blames" America, and "after years of shrugging my shoulders, I'm beginning to understand that this country did have a great deal to do with who I became" (*Who We Are,* pp. 227–228). Her adopted country's emphasis on individualism—for some, almost a fervent, religious sacrament—and American writers' celebration of individual pursuits, of following one's personal destiny, drew Abraham and caused the "dangerous" label to be attached to her by relatives. Her aunt's remark, she notes, wasn't so much directed at Abraham's reading a novel as it was at her refusal to acknowledge and enter into "conventional social behavior, which any decent Israeli child … understood perfectly. My sin: I had placed personal desire above the needs of the other, thereby rebelling against the familial institution. In other words, I had become an American" (p. 229).

This rebellious, American spirit was encouraged and complemented by two other factors: Abraham came of age in the immediate aftermath of the Woodstock generation, and as she and her family traveled the countryside near that hippie mecca, her father often picked up young hitchhikers. When these alternative Americans saw her bearded father, who acknowledged their peace signs and never judged them, they saw a kindred soul, not understanding that the kinship was with a messianic, Hasidic Jew. Her father, however, understood that in some form, the hippies were seeking "transcendence," and he appreciated their search. Abraham explains that because of her father's "antinomian sensibility," her family lived near other Jewish communities but never in them. And these communities "weren't Hasidic" (p. 230). Clearly, living on the edge of multiple societies impressed Abraham and helped shape her fictional world.

In her essay Abraham relates that the second factor that shaped her independent and rebellious spirit was her immersion in secular American literature, particularly the writings of Ralph Waldo Emerson, the nineteenth-century Transcen-

dentalist who, in his Divinity School address, adopted Jesus Christ's assertion that "I am divine." For Abraham, this assertion attests to the individual's great "potential … to become anything or anyone," a potential deriving perhaps from that individual's "self-created self … [an idea not] distant from the supreme task of the Hasid: to achieve a measure of divinity" (p. 231).

Remarking the similarities between the Emersonian and the Hasidic search, Abraham ties this journey to that of the Hasidic mystic Nachman of Bratslav (1772–1810), who believed in "the divine potential of every individual." She observes, "If the potential to become this mythic figure resides within Everyman, then it is toward the self one must turn to find redemption" (p. 232).

Toward the conclusion of her essay, Abraham returns to her own journey as a writer, likening its solitary practice to the Bratslav belief that one should spend at least an hour a day in silent contemplation. This act, she notes, is ridiculed by other branches of Hasidism. So while she readily acknowledges that

> I have emancipated myself from institutional religion, it's not quite true to say that I live without belief. Writing every day requires trusting the act of writing, a belief in an inner knowledge. As it turns out this belief in inner knowledge or an inner God … is very close to the mystical (Kabbalist) belief that the divine resides within the individual. Since such personal belief isn't dependent on institutionalized religion, it doesn't have the usual constraints. What it does have, strangely enough, is a grounding in Emersonian ideas, which is to say that under the influence of American religion, I returned to an earlier Hasidism. You might say that embracing the New World, becoming anything I wanted to become, in my case a writer, I also became an Old World, antiestablishment Hasid.
>
> (p. 237)

An evolution of which even her mother might be proud.

THE ROMANCE READER

Early in Abraham's first novel, *The Romance Reader,* Rachel Benjamin, teenage daughter of a Brooklyn-based Hasidic rabbi, wants a public

library card. Her teacher promises to issue her a summer reading list when she obtains this privilege, and Rachel can't wait to check out books—secular books. But waiting is too much, and so she and her sister Leah hit the thrift stores, each buying a romance novel: Barbara Cartland's *The Unpredictable Bride* for Leah and a Victoria Holt for Rachel, the cover of which depicts "a woman with long pale hair, wearing a sheer nightgown, run[ning] from a castle" (pp. 24–25). Rachel suggests that they then drop by the library anyway, but Leah admonishes her older sister: "You're crazy.... Half of Monhegan is there on a Friday. Everyone goes to the library before Shabbat." Rachel acknowledges that, indeed, their presence as a rabbi's daughters will be noticed and word will get back to their parents. Disgrace, shame, guilt will certainly be their reward. But these potential hazards don't deter her for long.

This scene gets to the heart of the family conflict—more acutely, the protagonist-narrator Rachel's conflict. How can she remain the dutiful religious daughter in a closed subculture, yet follow her personal dream to the outside world of adventure, romance, and female autonomy? What happens to her family if she pursues this dream—to her own place in the family, and her place as a Hasidic Jew?

Throughout the novel, actually beginning on the very first page, Rachel is mindful of her parents' voices. Just prior to buying their thrift-store novels, Rachel remembers her father's warning after he hears her speaking in English: "The Jews survived in Egypt because of three things. They didn't change their names, they didn't change their clothes, and they didn't change their language. Could we depend on you for our survival?" (p. 24).

In a Yiddish-speaking family where her name is actually "Ruchel," where she must wear modest clothing that covers her blossoming adolescent body, and where she longs for the outer, English-speaking America, Rachel knows that her actions are defiant, rebellious. She understands that pursuing these dreams will hurt her parents and cause tension and harsh feelings within the

family. Yet she cannot *not* follow her romantic heart.

And so scenes like the following erupt. Rachel is seen at the library by family friends; her family is embarrassed, scandalized:

> Father looks down, not saying anything. That doesn't stop Ma. She enjoys making me uncomfortable in front of him, like she's making me pay for my sins. She continues. "... What do you say to someone when unfortunately it's true and you're burning with shame? Your own daughter at the library, reading *trafe* books.... I had to swallow it, and it hurt going down. My eldest daughter ... This is the kind of name she's giving the family.... Look what you're doing to us. Look at your father; his beard is going gray. All because of your sins."
>
> (p. 37)

Later that day, Rachel refuses to sit outside in the company of her mother and the other neighborhood women. She understands that they watch her in "the way you look at a sinner" (p. 39). She longs for the day she will have her own bookcase, as her father does, lined from top to bottom with the books of her choice.

The novel follows the conflicted but loving Benjamin family as it pursues collective and individual dreams. The father's writings and travels to sell his books keep him away for weeks at a time. The mother's care for and nurturing of her seven children sustain her, yet she also longs for Israel and her own aging parents. She threatens to leave for good when she learns that her husband is planning on financing and building yet another house of worship in the community instead of improving their cramped living space. And when they agree that she should take a vacation to Israel, for an unknown length of time, Father departs too on his fund-raising mission, leaving Rachel in charge of the children and the home. This begins her true embrace of autonomy. She and Leah immediately contract for lifeguarding classes so as to secure jobs that summer in the outside world. Without anyone to guard over them, Rachel and Leah do not worry about wearing revealing swimwear or about Rachel's choice of stockings for school dress. And no parental authority can see Rachel reading secular romances in English or hear her speaking

in English to more and more denizens of the forbidden world around her.

Upon her parents' return, Rachel faces the consequences, not all of which are so bad. Father actually admires his daughters for taking jobs that will serve and protect the community. To be a lifeguard, to save lives, is noble in his view. And though he eventually asks the girls to keep themselves covered while doing so, he also buys them real underwater watches to display his pride and confidence in his beloved, responsible daughters.

In other areas, though, compromise is out of the question. Ma finds Rachel's seamless stockings while she is away one day and cuts them to pieces. Father comes home that evening with a brown paper bag. Keeping its contents secret at first, he lectures again:

> "Name, dress, and language. You two call each other by your goyishe names, Rachel instead of Ruchel; you speak a goyishe language, and now you're changing the way you dress. I will not have any of that in this house. This is a Chassidishe home."

> From his bag he dumps out six pairs of seamed beige stockings:

> "If you're old enough to wear beige, you'll wear beige with seams. So everyone will know your legs are covered."

> I will never wear stockings with seams, I say.

Rachel learns then that her father has consulted with her school principal, Reb Berkovitz, in Williamsburg about the stockings: "He went to Williamsburg to talk to a man about girls' stockings. Two men talking about what I should put on my legs. What do they know about girls' legs, about what's comfortable, what looks good?" (pp. 137–138).

Still, no one finds her sacred romance novels, well hidden from parental oversight. A short time later, Rachel, still the unabashed dreamer, considers obtaining another outside world item: a driver's license. "You're crazy," Leah says. "Father will never let a woman drive.... You're dreaming. Where do you get these ideas?" (p. 151).

Where indeed?

Rachel at least continues down some pathways that are familiar and welcome to her parents. Upon completing school, she lands an interview for a job teaching English subjects to second and sixth graders in a Satmar school. Back at home, "Father stokes my cheek the way he did when I was little.... 'Teaching is the most honored, the highest profession in the world,' he says. 'It's the job of every mother. A child learns his first lessons, his first words, even, from his mother' " (pp. 201–202).

But even here, the sword is double-edged because as a maturing young woman, and as the oldest child, Rachel, in her parents' eyes, must get married, and soon. Because until she does, her next-to-eldest sibling, Aaron, cannot get married, and unlike Rachel, whose reputation as a rebel has definitely preceded her, Aaron, a yeshiva boy, will be a highly sought-after match.

Thus, her family pressures Rachel to meet the family of a prospective bridegroom. The boy, Israel, is nothing like Rachel's secular romantic dream-goys. Thin, pale, sickly, and given to nosebleeds, Israel is also shy, gullible, and prone to pleasing not Rachel, but her father, the rabbi. While Rachel resists at first, she soon agrees to a second meeting. Because it might as well be him as another, and because he does have beautiful deep-blue eyes, Rachel agrees to the match. Mazel tovs abound, and soon, after much wedding shopping, Rachel finds herself married, living near her parents, forced to shave her now-matronly head, and experiencing the not-so-romantic dream of a Hasidic Jewish bride.

Israel is intimidated by her, but he longs to make her into the dutiful wife. He wants her to wear seamed stockings, and in exchange, he will buy a radio for her. Rachel refuses all compromise with him and does not try to make life easy. Even in the marriage bed, Israel is unsuccessful, the only bleeding that ever occurs being his habitual nose runs.

Finally, on a separated-by-gender bus one day, Israel falls asleep. At their designated stop, Rachel, without even trying to wake her husband, exits. The bus keeps going, making its appointed rounds with the sleeping Israel still aboard. Rachel, with her marriage bank account intact,

freely walks the Brooklyn streets, checks into a ritzy, secular hotel, and lives as an independent woman for several days, not alerting anyone to her whereabouts. But the next morning, while she is breakfasting in a greasy diner, the smell of frying pig almost chokes her. The outer world, despite her dreams, is not all romantic luster.

After she reemerges from her independent dream life, both families decide that a sanctioned divorce is best for this pair. We never see Israel again, his bus surely depositing him somewhere. Rachel, however, returns to her family's fold, but her place there is forever changed: "I'm home but not at home. I look at Leah, Sarah, Aaron, and Esther. David and Levi are in yeshiva. I can never be one of the children again. I'm a stranger in this house.... I don't belong here" (p. 294).

Coming home seems the least likely ending for Rachel, but we realize that her stay is momentary, that the lure of the outside world is too great. As the critic Nora L. Rubel suggests, Rachel has noticed the "greater freedom" afforded Hasidic males, but knows she can't reach that freedom if she remains in the closed world. Ultimately, "Rachel wants the freedom to ask questions as well as the freedom to disagree with the answers" (Rubel, p. 73). While the bonds of family run deep, leaving, though likely a necessary choice for Rachel, might be harder on her—the one making the journey—than on her family. And with so much freedom in outer America, where should she journey, even when she knows that the journey itself is inevitable? As Abraham says about Rachel, her "move" is "toward more experience … toward self-knowing" (Bolton-Fasman).

GIVING UP AMERICA

While Rachel Benjamin considers her "sacred journey" and remains unsure of where she belongs—no longer an insider in her Hasidic inner culture, but still an outsider in greater America—*Giving Up America*'s central female presence, Deena, has already broken from her Hasidic family at the novel's beginning. Now married to a modern Orthodox Jewish man and living in Brooklyn, she tries to negotiate the outer Manhattan world via a career in advertising. Her husband, Daniel, wants a kosher home and to join the local synagogue. However, Deena wants a complete break from the enclosed world she has left, from any semblance of Judaism. In a marriage not made in heaven and clearly not sanctioned by Deena's Jerusalem-based family, the two must reconsider, or perhaps consider for the first time, their love and passion, as outside forces lure each of them away from their mutual base.

Deena and Daniel meet at Bluth's, a store where Deena is working and where Daniel was formerly employed. She watches the way he moves, likes what she sees even when he exits the store without giving her any sign of goodbye. She likes even more that he returns an hour later and asks for her number. They get engaged soon after, but warnings and ill omens follow. Her father, a Hasidic rabbi with a mystical bent, tells her that, together, the Hebrew letters of both their names add up to 164, the value of the Hebrew word for "pain." And, "if you add the three numbers, you have eleven. One and one are two. Within a mere two years, he concluded, you'll know it was never meant to be. But it will take more than two years to correct your error" (p. 4). While Deena tries to counteract her father's prophecy with her own calculations, the damage is done. Though married six years without incident, in the seventh, the trials begin as they buy their first house and begin its renovations. Numbers might be interpreted freely, but individual will and the influence of outside forces combine to influence destiny.

The two of them pursue individual jobs in Manhattan, and on weekends turn their attention to the house, painting it, expanding its open space. Daniel would like to expand his own experience within Orthodox Judaism, but Deena refuses to join his cause. She questions his desire to join a synagogue, to faithfully adhere to the laws of kashrut, to attend High Holidays services. Are his intentions sincere or merely attempts to follow a prescribed orthodox form? Daniel would like her to accompany him to services, and his mother "expect[s] her daughter-in-law to accompany her" into the women's section. Deena

does go at first, but soon balks at the ritual: "Living at home with my parents I didn't attend services … Hasidic women were never expected to. On regular Saturdays only old grandmothers sit in the synagogue" (p. 37). When she asks Daniel why he insists on attending, his answer is forceful and traditional:

> Some things you just do. … What's wrong with following tradition simply because it exists, because it's what Jews do, and you're one of them? I know one thing: people at work respect my integrity. I follow certain laws and I'm consistent. I always wear my yarmulke and I always eat kosher. On the high holidays, I go to the synagogue, which is better than nothing.
>
> (p. 38)

Deena believes in reflection, in going to one's inner places, but feels that one can do that anywhere on the Sabbath. While she used to enjoy the traditions with her family, now, all she hears is what is forbidden to her on Shabbat. She thinks that "the mechanical way [Daniel] adhered to laws [makes] transgression imaginable" (p. 38). And then she hears her father's voice:

> Orthodoxy without the delight of Hasidism, her father warned, is a very dry thing. The commandment is to serve God with equal parts of love and fear. Orthodox Jews incline toward fear. Hasidim err perhaps on the side of love, which is emotional and therefore more powerful. You were brought up with this love; without it, I fear for your soul. As a child, you were an excellent student only if you loved your teacher; if not, you weren't merely less than excellent, you were miserable.
>
> (pp. 38–39)

From refusing to accompany Daniel to shul in the first year of their marriage, Deena then refuses to observe the Sabbath at all in their second year together.

In Abrahams' interview with Aryeh Lev Stollman, she explains her perspective on these differences between Hasidism and Orthodoxy:

> Quoting from the *Shema*, the prayer derived from verses of the Pentateuch, which directs every Jew to both love and fear God … it has been said that the Hasidim err on one side, they love God, and this, amazingly enough, despite all the terrible things

He's done or allowed to happen, more than they fear Him; the orthodox fear Him more than they love Him. … The two worlds have come closer [over the past twenty years], Hasidic boys are now sent to yeshiva orthodox schools, [but] it probably still doesn't work the other way around; there's even some intermarriage now. … Hasidism also refers back to an older mysticism, and perhaps there is some foundational similarity. The problem is that the mystical life opens one up to a certain solipsism that the yeshiva orthodox finds objectionable. It's an interesting dialectic, though: a religious people, whose faith requires a belief in mystery and miracle, then counters that mystery by remaining as rational as possible in every other respect of their lives, in their scholarship, their interpretation of the law, and so on.

Faith, reason; rationality, emotion; mysticism, skepticism. Love and fear. The dichotomies applied to Hasidism and Orthodoxy also apply to Deena and Daniel. The America they hope to embrace, however, proves even more elusive. At work, each has buddies outside the Jewish world. Daniel, in particular, wants the two of them to socialize with these friends, among them Jill and Ann, who are transplants from the American South. Jill is a Miss America contestant working as a secretary in Daniel's office while pursuing her pageant dream. She's tall, leggy, model-gorgeous. And, she's a shiksa.

Soon, the four are hitting Manhattan dance clubs, and while Daniel still wears his yarmulke, he drinks, dances, and becomes increasingly intoxicated by a world he has never really known. Deena, in the meantime, while enjoying the occasional night out, or even those evenings at home when Jill and Ann come over, nevertheless feels an inner pull, away from partying, away from Orthodoxy. Away from Daniel and the world he is bringing into their lives. As the High Holidays approach in 1987, she begins a new list of resolutions, among which are her "regulars," reading, exercising, doing better at work. Running is her new chosen physical endeavor, and soon she will embrace it beyond reason. But now, as she contemplates the coming new year, she reflects on time and its infinite space:

> She had a house, a job, a husband. She had enough. Then why wasn't she happy? She didn't have enough time to enjoy the things she already had.

She needed more free time, the freedom of time, freedom from the tyranny of work every morning. … She wanted to wake up elsewhere some days, so that just going out in the morning for the paper she'd tread on the cobblestone streets of a strange city; at the corner, she wouldn't know which way to turn, left or right, and it wouldn't matter, there'd be no one expecting her anywhere. … She ought to go somewhere. She ought to call a courier service, leave a note for Daniel, and take off. That was the way to do things, last minute, without much thinking or planning. Just doing. She was always wanting to go. … Daniel would have a fit if she booked a flight, wrote a note, and found herself up above the clouds, flying freely, thinking of nothing and no one. She wouldn't be home to hear his outrage. Was it Daniel who held her back all these years? Somehow marriage didn't go with traveling alone.

(pp. 47–49)

It is a powerful reflection early on in the novel, and it is clearly a foreshadowing. Deena's desire to leave, her inner reflections and her rebellion, give rise to conflict and enable her see that, despite his religious intentions, Daniel is conflicted, too. He's not the man she married, and whether or not her father's prophecy is accurate, it is clear that Daniel's thoughts, at best, have strayed to Jill. And maybe more than just his thoughts.

Deena grows angrier after her fears of the reality of an affair are confirmed, yet does little to impede it. Daniel's late-night phone conversations with Jill are barely veiled, and eventually, Deena leaves for a trial separation at the Manhattan apartment of a friend and coworker. Her daily runs become twice-a-day meditation exercises, and while she certainly fatigues her muscles, she cannot tire or relax her mind.

Daniel pursues her, asking for second chances, fresh dates. But it isn't clear whether he wants to rekindle their marriage or whether he is even more desperate, lost, and lonely than she is.

Deena has moved from Hasidism to an aborted attempt at married Orthodoxy to no religion at all. If anything, running is her religion. Her advertising job suffers, and soon she is seeking out headhunters for new prospects, eventually finding herself on the streets without anything.

Does she "give up America," her life here?

Like Rachel Benjamin, Deena does fly away from marriage, at least, without leaving a word. She lands in Jerusalem, planning to stay an unspecified time back at home with her family. The fit, though, isn't exactly right; she has pains, and these remind her of being a child again:

> When she was eleven, her legs suddenly grew and they hurt. Of all pains, her father said, these are the best kind to have. … Before he could become a great and blessed nation, Abraham had to leave his land, the country of his birth, and his father's house. Go forth for yourself, by yourself, into yourself, God said, addressing all men. … She'd gone forth, and she was coming to know herself, and she would continue this knowing.

(p. 309)

We feel at the novel's close that Deena's relocation in Jerusalem will be only a temporary stop, a time for breathing, greater reflection, and indeed, for coming to know herself. Where she goes from here—back to a different America or a parallel life there—is entirely up to her, up in the clouds of her future.

THE SEVENTH BEGGAR

Abraham's third and most stylistically complex novel, *The Seventh Beggar,* also alters the narrative focus and the inner-outer theme that guided her first two novels. Splitting the work in half with two different male focal points, Abraham develops these protagonists as seekers of an inner truth. This search leads the first, Joel Jakob, eldest son of a Brooklyn Hasidic family and grandson of Berditchev—one of the most respected men of the Brooklyn Hasidim—to a place that frightens and scandalizes his family and the entire community. For the second protagonist, Joel's nephew JakobJoel, the search leads to a secular scientific education and an experiment with artificial intelligence. The reverse symmetry in these men's names becomes a telling narrative arc embodying the nature of family relations and the legacies some former family members leave behind for their beloved ones.

Indeed, Joel Jakob loves his family, respects his father, Reb Moshele, and is especially close

to his sister Ada, who is one year younger. The children are afforded a greater degree of freedom than many Hasidic children receive. Ada creates wardrobes for other Hasidic girls, offering styles that are more modest versions of clothing by contemporary, high-fashion designers. While pursuing religious scholarship that will theoretically lead to a Hasidic son's highest calling—becoming a rabbi—Joel veers slightly off course when he becomes intrigued by the life, philosophy, and tales of Nachman of Bratslav, the nineteenth-century messianic rabbi and mystic who was also the great-grandson of Hasidim's founder, the Baal Shem Tov. Unfortunately, the Bratslav branch of Hasidim is not held in very high esteem by the other branches. Among other reasons, Nachman himself advocated that "it was possible to fulfill the commandments spiritually, with concentrated mind rather than ritualistic activity." This is a "dangerous idea," as even Joel acknowledges (p. 14).

In essence, instead of being lured from his Hasidic inner world to the outside secular world, as Abraham's two previous females protagonists experienced, Joel travels to a more inward place. As befitting the Hasidic male, Joel has access to the mystical and scholarly works of the Jewish sages. First, from a local Hasidic bookstore, Joel surreptitiously buys a copy of Nachman's tales, including the most famous and intentionally unfinished "The Seventh Beggar." While this pursuit isn't exactly forbidden by his own elders, it isn't welcomed, either, as it is dangerous reading for such a young man, only seventeen. When his father discovers Joel's clandestine night reading, he initially tolerates the transgression, wishing only that Joel had asked him about Nachman first so that they could have discussed the dangers and excesses of the Bratslav mystic. Reb Moshele understands that too much of Nachman's mystical world can also lead to scandal in the larger community, perhaps preventing Joel from fulfilling that other duty—living a long and happy married life.

Yet, since he has instilled in his children a sense of independence and freedom—set them on this particular life journey—Reb Moshele wonders what choices and responsibilities he now

has to them and how he should guide his son. Through his branching out, or rather through the thought of branching out, Joel certainly recognizes that the nature of his regimented daily routine of study is making it "impossible to concentrate on any subject long enough to reach a degree of knowledge that could count for something. Which was why, [he] concluded, there was no longer any true greatness in the Hasidic world. To achieve unusual heights in anything, a certain amount of freedom is necessary, even if the result is a failure to fulfill the commandments" (p. 14).

Of course, there's the thematic rub: How is this "certain amount of freedom" determined? And what is the nature of this freedom, especially in such a closed world where everyone, it seems, knows the personal journeys and struggles of everyone else?

From reading about Nachman and from immersing himself in Nachman's tales—almost literally it seems—Joel embarks on a journey with the bookstore proprietor, Reb Yidel, to Uman in the Ukraine, the sacred site of Nachman's grave. Joel undertakes this pilgrimage without his parents' approval or knowledge.

Joel's journey is full of visions, not all of which soothe or enlighten him. Darker, spectral visions invade both his conscious and subconscious mind. He encounters "strange desires" of the flesh upon viewing a scantily clad female demi-spirit. These urges then draw him to an opposite desire to become more machine-like in order to limit his baser desires. If he accomplishes this desire, he might also achieve a

> modern rewrite of the liturgy ... machine terminology would replace the old agricultural linguistics and man would find himself chanting with abilities greater than human, of knowledge deeper and wider than any intelligence, of energies more powerful than the most advanced nuclear fission, of a being who could dispense with binary, Boolean, and bubble searches and solve problems faster than the speed of light.
>
> (pp. 86–87)

Joel's desire foreshadows his nephew's own journey later in the novel. More importantly, as Abraham suggested in her interview with Stoll-

man, Joel's practice of intense meditation is "intended to clear the mind and make room for the sustained concentration necessary for creation."

At the end of his trip, Joel asks himself: "What was the significance of a man's experience in the world? What was the purpose of his journey on earth? And of the journeys within this larger journey?" His answer, derived from the example of Nachman's own journey, is that it is "the journey itself" that is "the point" (p. 88). In other words, living freely means being open to the possibilities of what the journey will bring, of what one may encounter through the journey itself. Not so strangely, perhaps, Abraham argues that "whenever there are confining rules, and usually they're helpful on some level, they're also there to break" (Stollman), perhaps referring also to the novel's complex narrative point of view.

And so Joel, rule-breaker that he is, negotiates with his father a new course of study upon returning from his pilgrimage—a study focused on Bratslav mysticism—and a daily routine that will develop and encourage his desire for inner enlightenment:

> He would open his mind to what was new, to strange experience, even sin. He would encourage it, exhaust it, follow it to the end, until it took him somewhere higher. This, he understood, was the way to greatness: to embrace what was most fearsome. Joel was quite certain now that this was Nachman's great teaching, written one way or another into every one of his tales, most often in the motif of the hero's journey as a personal quest, an exhilarating adventure rather than the traditional joyless exile. … He would reach for a deeper understanding of the world, for a knowledge that was difficult, divine.
>
> (p. 109)

Joel's family tries to offset his inward journey, however, by finding a suitable match for his outer life. But just when they settle an accord with a young Bratslav woman and her family, which is a great compromise for them all, Joel takes another path. Now heavily involved in a mystical chanting based on using "the five primary vowels [of the Hebrew alphabet] in combination with the four letters of the tetragrammaton" (p. 133) that he believes will bring him true enlightenment, he

locates an isolated space—a drainage pipe in a semihidden neighborhood alcove—in which to pursue uninterrupted his hero's quest.

> This … might be as close as he would ever come to experiencing the freedom of the Kabbalists of Safed, who renounced all worldly possessions, left their families behind, traveled far to live in the hills and caves. … He would spend every waking hour in the drainpipe, practically live there. If in these weeks he failed to achieve a level of ecstatic concentration it would prove once and for all that he simply didn't have the capacity for it.
>
> (p. 131)

Unfortunately, neither Joel nor the reader will ever realize his capacity. A torrential rain moves in. Joel is engulfed, and while his body remains missing for several days, it is finally discovered, leaving his family bereft. But what of the world he sought to create?

Freedom and enlightenment are dangerous pursuits. *The Seventh Beggar,* though it might not seem to be doing so, should also remind American readers of all religious denominations that our history is full of noble seekers, heroes, misadventurers, and those whose seemingly pure and individualistic motives have left others emotionally, if not spiritually, devastated. Yet, the American spirit and the American experiment—whether practiced by Hasidic mystics, secular humanists, Christian pilgrims, or Muslim adherents—continue, sometimes inspired by our collective or individual loss, or both.

For we leave our mark. In *The Seventh Beggar,* Joel's sister Ada marries his best friend, Aaron, and their son, JakobJoel, a computer prodigy at MIT, takes up his uncle's pursuits, albeit in a more scientific-objective realm. Hearing the voice of that very uncle—whom of course he never knew—JakobJoel engineers a new design for computer intelligence. He then blends this design with another dream: the possibility of a film script about such intelligence—an attempt to out-Hollywood that most popular of filmmakers, Steven Spielberg. Thus, combining the inherited tales of his uncle; of Nachman's "The Seventh Beggar"; of the Woodstock generation and the Catskill storytelling tradition; and of traditional Hasidic wedding stories, including his

parents' own union, JakobJoel completes Nachman's unfinished tale, though the form of that completion, not easily explainable here, is highly subjective and clearly not for every taste.

And this is Abraham's own achievement: a contemporary tale that weds our desire for completion with an understanding and a reconciling of the past with the present. But Abraham's achievement is also to do so without providing her readers any model for our own experiences because, as Joel learns, our own unique journey is the point. We have stories on which to model our own, but the individual narrative is ours and ours alone. There are no guarantees of our success, of our finding fulfillment, enlightenment, or even knowing that our quest is right or just. We can't even know that giving our children the freedom to pursue their own dream journeys is necessarily the right or best thing to do. Yet we must still make these, and so many other, choices.

Abraham's first three novels, then, show that the American children of Hasidic families take chances no matter the restrictions placed on them. Maybe they take such chances because of these restrictions. This fiction is dangerous, subversive, challenging, and provocative. But isn't that the essence of America itself?

AMERICAN TALIBAN

Pearl Abraham's 2010 novel, *American Taliban,* reads like a suspense novel. The plot moves steadily, enticing the reader into a world where a young and somewhat naive American teenager who is also an avid surfer, John Jude Parish, decides to defer entrance to Brown University in order to find himself while living on the Outer Banks of North Carolina.

As smoothly as Abraham draws this young man's crossroads life, she also draws her readers into disturbing, unsettling questions about parental responsibility and discipline; about freedom and independence; and about the nature of intellectual, emotional, and spiritual inquiry. Finally, her novel considers the allegiances we hold and bear witness to, by imagining what happens when a character's inquiries into his own inner allegiances run afoul of his country's national and international interests.

As in *The Seventh Beggar,* Abraham uses a male protagonist to center these questions and to unfold this inner journey. John Jude Parish will travel deeply within himself, but he will also travel from the Outer Banks to Brooklyn in order to study classical Arabic at a Muslim school. Next, he will decide to travel for a year abroad to Pakistan, immersing himself in the culture, language, religion, and discipline of Islam. Finally, he will be asked by his pan-Islamic center to journey for armed training to the remote northern hills of that country and eventually into Afghanistan, the war zone. At this point the narrative focus shifts from his outer journey to the final inner one experienced by the parents he leaves behind.

Unlike her other three novels, no one in this novel's world is Jewish, much less Hasidic. The novel, then, seems at first to be a departure from the previous three. Yet Abraham still raises similar questions about one person's need to discover truths that might trouble those around him or her. Certainly, John Jude has everything a young man could want: his parents are prosperous, enlightened, and progressive liberals, and they encourage his scholastic and recreational endeavors. They love him intensely; he is their only child. He has a fleet of surfer girls—referred to collectively as "Katie & Co."—with Katie being his lover. He loves philosophy and surfs chat rooms of philosophical inquiry in his downtime. But in none of these activities does he seek, or even seem to know that he should seek, guidance—a focus that will allow him to enter safely into worlds he doesn't even begin to fully comprehend.

The novel opens on John's eighteenth birthday, and though there will be a dinner party that evening, John uses the main part of the day to surf. Heading out to his Saab, he also brings his skateboard, riding from front door to car door, because he "made it a rule not to walk on terra firma. When he wasn't on water, he lived on wheels. He believed in continuous adaptation" (p. 6). While understanding that his mother, Barbara, supports "all [his] ambition," he also

knows that she fears his immersion in the world of wheels and boards because that world is not always controllable and could lead to disaster:

> Remember, she'd say, a hero who's alive benefits from his heroics.
>
> There are worse ways to die, John informed her. Think wu-wei. Live as if you're already dead, unafraid. That's freedom, according to the *Tao*. Also Hegel.
>
> (pp. 6–7)

It's a heady and darkly foreshadowing passage, and in hindsight, the reader wonders at what point we must agree with John and consider him "already dead."

One other moment that informs us about John's life philosophy is seen later that same day as he sets out for the waves. He points out to Katie & Co. that the best waves to surf

> are out there, beyond the fourth breaker. ... They were out here on their own, with no lifeguards, no help for miles, surfing in precisely the kind of conditions they'd promised their parents not to surf. But pushing beyond safe had always gotten them their best rides. ... The punishments, when they came, were also extreme. Each took a turn in raging water, thrashed against sand and rock. One minute John was Moses walking on water and showing off. ... But then the wave turned knifelike and closed out before he could land, and down he went, thrashing, and the force of the next wave came and held him down in the silent dark, the abyss of solitude, a place of no community. Underwater, he was free of communal life, free of Barbara and her social obligations. Here, in the dark, it was silent, and he was alone, with only himself, with only the deep and the dark and the infinite. Which invited his soul to stay and be. Alone. *Alone with the Alone*, one of the titles on his reading list. He should've read that book already. ... To do that, though, he needed air. He had to breathe.
>
> He emerged with the skin on his shoulders raw. He emerged with a prayer on his lips, an invitation to his soul. He would become as he would become.
>
> (p. 11)

This passage encapsulates John Jude's heroic quest, and if we feel a small sense of foreboding and doom, so be it. *American Taliban* too will become what it will become. And John Jude's

pushing beyond limits at this moment surely leads to the novel's main conflicts and its final un-resolution.

An unfortunate skating accident soon leaves John injured, giving him time to read, to study, and to enter more deeply into philosophical chat rooms where he "meets" a young woman named Noor. Soon John relocates to Brooklyn to meet her physically and to study classical Arabic, as he has been intrigued for some time with the language. But he is the only white American and non-Muslim at the school, so he is mistrusted by most of his fellow students. Smitten with Noor, his romance with the Muslim culture also grows. His language skills develop rapidly, and he also buys clothing more suitable to Islamic custom. He adopts the Islamic name "Attar."

Soon his friend Khaled is advocating that Attar join him for a year abroad at Islamia University in Pakistan. But, as Attar learns, Islamia is a Muslim school.

> So, Khaled said nonchalantly. You'll make al shahada. Im'sh'allah. I'll introduce you to the brother in charge at our masjid.
>
> I need to think about it, John said, and realized that he had been thinking about it. To taste is to know, Sufis believed, and he had been looking to know.
>
> (p. 93)

As John/Attar contemplates the shift into this brave new world, he recognizes the break with his parents that is surely required if he is to follow his independent soul:

> No matter what Barbara said, John was convinced that the idea of private prayer as an opportunity to achieve one's highest potential was not a lot of talk about nothing. Still, he would find out for sure, he would learn it and try it and prove for himself whether it was a nothing or a something. He would revisit the masjid and ask the brother to teach him how to perform the salaat. He would know what there is to know. He would find out whether for him, personally, God amounted to an absence or a presence or a nothing. If only he could concentrate all the powers of his heart, as Corbin wrote. If only he could achieve the kind of prayer that serves as an act of creation. He prayed to achieve it.
>
> (p. 114)

These last sentiments link John to *The Seventh Beggar's* Joel Jakob, and like that novel's young

mystic, John Jude Parish will leave his parents and an uncomprehending American society behind. But in order to find what? To create what? Such mysteries are never solved in this novel, perhaps echoing all that we will never know about each other and our private journeys inward.

Abraham told Judy Bolton-Fasman that while she was working on *The Seventh Beggar* in 2001, the news story concerning the American Taliban-ist John Walker Lindh broke, and that she interpreted his experience to be a journey of "spiritual curiosity" that went terribly awry. Clearly, self-discovery and the pursuit of new ideas are at the heart of Abraham's world, both personal and fictional. Such discovery and adventuring often comes at a painful price, but this price, too, is part of the American grain. Though Abraham's major characters suffer, sometimes fail, lose themselves, or start again from a modified home base, they nevertheless make us think and wonder at a spirit—regardless of home life, belief system, or romantic dreams—that goes undaunted into the American landscape and beyond.

"HASIDIC NOIR"

Abraham's short story "Hasidic Noir," which appeared in the volume *Brooklyn Noir* (2004), also pursues her insider-outsider thematic track. The unnamed narrator, a Hasidic private detective, overhears in the Sabbath morning Mikvah that the Dobrover rebbe, nephew of the Grand Rabbi Joel Teitelbaum, has been murdered. This murder may or may not have been precipitated by a long-standing rivalry between the Dobrov and Szebed Hasids. Even the victim's brother-in-law might be involved in the conspiracy. The detective's ears are on alert.

Revealing a bit of his own past, the detective allows the reader to see and feel the weight burdening him:

> I'd had a modicum of experience working homicide, on the fringes really, assisting the New York Police Department on several cases in the nearby Italian and Spanish neighborhoods. The police chief still

calls occasionally with questions about this part of the city that an insider could answer easily. And now, after so many years, it was as an insider that I'd come across this murder, and it was also as an insider that I knew to judge it a politically motivated crime with perpetrators from the top brass. With the Dobrover rebbe out of the way, Szebed could take the Grand Rabbinic throne without a struggle. If I seem to be jumping to conclusions, note that I grew up in this community and continue to live here; I am one of them.

("Hasidic Noir," pp. 37–38)

Also noting that news of the murder appeared in no papers (another sign of the inside nature of this crime, since the closed Hasidic world keeps even its crimes secret), our detective finally reveals that he is the first "Hasidic detective … in the history of Hasidism," and so the case fell to him "for a reason" (p. 38). What that reason is, however, might not ever be revealed.

Like other Abraham protagonists, the narrator is drawn to the life of the mind, admitting that using his brainpower was the lure to his becoming a detective in the first place. Concentrating on the inner world, on the motives out of which people he might know well commit crimes, is a worthwhile yet dangerous undertaking.

In a closed, secretive world, disclosures, such as they are, carry with them even more secrets. The convoluted crime involves deeper family ties, and possibly ends in blank walls, if it even ends that clearly. By the story's conclusion, the detective finds himself on trial in rabbinic court, answering charges that he should have come to the rabbinic elders instead of making public accusations in the *Village Voice* and the *New Yorker.* He is admonished: he never should have gone public at all, for by doing so, the court decrees that he has "besmirched" a good man's name, as well as "the name of God," and done so "in the eyes of other nations." For his deed, he will now have to face "retribution for befouling the name of God." For his punishment, the court will cause him to be "as a limb cut away from a body" (p. 55).

Having the last laugh, though, the detective accuses the entire Szebed court of collaborating to murder the Dobrover rebbe, a crime for which the outer world in which they all live will make

them pay. He then produces the supposed murder victim, a "frail and wraithlike" fifty-three-year-old man, a "Job-like figure that sooner or later every man becomes" (p. 56). Not really murdered but excommunicated—a form of death in the community—the Dobrover appears before them, ready to be "reborn" into the world that tried to dispel him (p. 56). Will he be reaccepted? As the detective says, that will be the court's decision. For he had done his part, giving up himself as the newly dead, replacing one excommunicated shamus/shaman with another. And then, like other Abraham heroes, our narrator exits this world "unseen and unheard" (p. 56).

CONCLUSION

Pearl Abraham continues to be a vibrant American literary voice. Her current events commentaries appear regularly in the *Forward*. She also writes critical essays on occasion that examine other contemporary authors, as in her 2011 piece for the *Michigan Quarterly Review* that challenges the didacticism of Ayaan Hirsi Ali's memoirs *Infidel* and *Nomad*. More fiction certainly appears on the horizon, assuring that readers of all backgrounds will continue to see in Abraham's work a world that disturbs, that challenges us to think and rethink what it means to be inside and outside American culture. By allowing us into a closed world—be that a Hasidic world or one where we see a dawning anti-American consciousness—Abraham encourages us to identify with narrative voices who initially seem starkly unlike us. That is, until we read more closely and come to see that these voices often speak to and for us, which, in the end, can be a troubling and dangerous experience.

Selected Bibliography

WORKS OF PEARL ABRAHAM

NOVELS AND SHORT STORIES
The Romance Reader. New York: Riverhead Books, 1995.
Giving Up America. New York: Riverhead Books, 1998.
"Hasidic Noir." In *Brooklyn Noir.* Edited by Tim McLoughlin. Brooklyn, N.Y.: Akashic Books, 2004.
The Seventh Beggar. New York: Riverhead Books, 2004.
American Taliban. New York: Random House, 2010.

OTHER WORKS
"Divinity School or Trusting the Act of Writing." In *Who We Are: On Being (and Not Being) a Jewish American Writer.* Edited by Derek Rubin. New York: Schocken, 2005.
"The Winged Life of Ayaan Hirsi Ali." *Michigan Quarterly Review* 50, no. 2:299–306 (spring 2011).

CRITICAL STUDIES AND INTERVIEWS
Bolton-Fasman, Judy. "Pearl Abraham Branches Out." *Forward,* May 24, 2010. http://blogs.forward.com/sisterhood -blog/128262/pearl-abraham-branches-out/.
Rubel, Nora L. *Doubting the Devout: The Ultra-Orthodox in the Jewish American Imagination.* New York: Columbia University Press, 2010.
Smith, Dinitia. "An Author's Hasidic Roots Become Her Inspiration." *New York Times,* February 8, 2005. http:// www.nytimes.com/2005/02/08/books/08pear.html.
Stollman, Aryeh Lev. "Pearl Abraham." *BOMB,* spring 2005. http://bombsite.com/issues/91/articles/2728.

GERTRUDE ATHERTON

(1857—1948)

Windy Counsell Petrie

WHILE SHE NOW has been nearly forgotten by literary criticism, Gertrude Atherton, whose literary career spanned more than fifty years and produced almost as many novels, may well have been the most widely read woman writer of her time. An author who topped the best-seller lists and urged the advertisers of her books to pronounce her the greatest American female novelist, Atherton doggedly carved a place for herself in American letters out of an unstable childhood and marriage, early frustrations of her ambition, a purposely peripatetic lifestyle, and an indefatigable quest for new material that would keep her name in print.

Atherton, a Californian by birth, crafted a persona that claimed both the freedoms of the nineteenth century's still-wild West and a highbrow social status she felt was conferred upon her by a distinguished, though then impoverished, bloodline, which purportedly included both Benjamin Franklin and George Sand. Her novels, founded on wide-ranging topics including the history of California, alcoholism, reincarnation, sexual repression and regeneration, World War I, women's suffrage, the Algonquin Circle, the British aristocracy, miners in Montana, the nobility in ancient Greece and Rome, and American statesmen, real and imaginary, all interwoven with romance plots, often created an outcry in the press. Her heroines, ranging from Midwestern clubwomen to suspected murderesses, New York socialites, German opera divas, California chicken farmers, and reincarnated ancient spirits, are no more sensational as characters than Atherton portrayed herself to be in her 1932 autobiography, *Adventures of a Novelist.* Examination of her complicated life, multifarious works, and nearly schizophrenic literary reputation reveals the strains between her three primary, and often

conflicting, desires: gaining personal freedom, pursuing fame and fortune, and acquiring critical acclaim.

EARLY YEARS

Gertrude Franklin Horn was born on October 30, 1857, in "the only place where it was respectable [at that time] in San Francisco—Rincon Hill" (*Adventures of a Novelist,* p. 4). In her autobiography, Atherton carefully traces her ancestry, describing herself as the Californian daughter of a transplanted Southern belle and a Yankee. Yet just as Rincon Hill later became a factory district, so all the other aspects of Atherton's background were tainted. The critic Kevin Starr has worked to debunk the myth of Atherton's aristocratic background, pointing to the shabby but genteel boardinghouses in which Atherton grew up, by emphasizing both her grandfather's and mother's social and financial failures in nineteenth-century San Francisco. As Atherton herself tells it in *Adventures of a Novelist,* her grandfather, Stephen Franklin—whom she revered as a true Southern gentleman—had gone bankrupt and moved his family west from Louisiana to California in the 1850s. Gertrude's father, Thomas Lodowick Horn, was an alcoholic who came to San Francisco from Connecticut to increase his fortune in the shipping business. Her parents separated in 1860, when she was three years old, and there was an enormous scandal when her mother, also named Gertrude, became the first divorcée in San Francisco. A decade later, Atherton's stepfather, John Frederick Ulhorn, an inveterate gambler, tried to commit suicide after being implicated in a forgery. All this she briefly discusses in her autobiography, but with emphasis on how her bloodlines were impressively mixed nonetheless

and how all the tumult of her early years gave her both a wide experience of human nature and an unbreakable determination to make something of herself, despite the odds against her.

Quite a number of Atherton's novels feature child or teenage heroines who hail from San Francisco, face childhood conditions similar to hers, or share her mixed cultural heritage. Lee Tarleton of *American Wives and English Husbands* (1898) grows up in a boardinghouse with her former-Southern-belle mother and is forced into independence early by the death of her alcoholic father and her mother's subsequent invalidism. *The Californians,* also published in 1898, focuses on the friendship of two little girls, Helena Belmont and Magdalena Yorba, two heiresses to millions, one of whom is the issue of a marriage between a Southerner and New Englander, as was Atherton, and the other between a New Englander and a Spaniard. *Patience Sparhawk and Her Times* (1897) opens with the half-Puritan, half-Southern heroine and her best friend, the half-Spanish, half–New Englander Rosita Thrailkill, trying to urge their blind cart horse up a hill. Despite their humble beginnings, their financial crashes, or their parents' alcoholism and abuse (Patience's mother is an alcoholic and Magdalena's father a tyrant, and she and Rosita are both subjected to racial slurs at various points in their youth), all these characters become remarkable women, leaders of society and iconoclasts. Lee Tarleton marries into the English aristocracy, becomes politically astute, and saves her husband's ancestral home. Helena Belmont grows into an international society woman, and she and Magdalena eventually host Henry James on his first trip to San Francisco. Rosita becomes an international opera diva notorious for her love affairs, while Patience rejects religion, marries into a leading East Coast family, leaves to become a newspaperwoman, and is then accused of killing the jealous husband she openly loathed, only to be saved from the electric chair at the last moment.

Atherton may have acquired a taste for scandals from her family and the gossip in 1880s San Francisco, as her first literary effort made a novel out of local scuttlebutt about a mother who had purposely made her daughter into an alcoholic from the cradle. Published in the San Francisco *Argonaut* as "The Randolphs of the Redwoods," in 1882, and then later as *A Daughter of the Vine* in 1899, the book cost its author both friends and family relationships, but Atherton did not care, for, as she later stated, "I had had an immense time and was willing to stand the consequence" ("My Maiden Effort," 1961, p. 11). This may also account for the baffling enjoyment some of her heroines have during their own murder trials and other scandals in her fiction. For instance, Patience Sparhawk knows she may go to the electric chair for a murder she did not commit, but still enjoys being the heroine of a sensation, being center stage in the great drama of the American courtroom, and sits in her jail cell reading article after article about herself.

Like her spirited heroines, Atherton seems to have been in a continual quest for attention and state of rebellion, first against her family and then against her in-laws, for the first twenty-five years of her life. In the memoir, we read that Atherton's grandmother tried to dress her nicely, only to have her roll in the mud; enjoined her to be good for company, only to face a temper tantrum; and reportedly had to tie her to a chair to teach her to learn to sew. As a teenager, she attended two private schools in two years, but returned from the prestigious Sayre Institute in Kentucky when the religious aunt with whom she was staying refused to be responsible for her any longer, reportedly saying, "Gertrude, you're going straight to the devil … but I'll pray for you" (*Adventures,* p. 43). After that, and the business failure and subsequent suicide of William Ralston (the family friend who was financing her education and had also planned to pay for her social debut in a grand Southern style), her education was at an end.

Despite her inconsistent and abruptly cut-off formal education, Atherton decided to be a novelist when she was still a teenager. Her literary aspirations were purportedly awakened on the night her grandfather called her into what was then "the finest private library in California" and declared, "I wish you to become a well-read, intellectual woman. … You will read aloud to me

for two hours every night" (pp. 27, 28). Although she rebelled against reading his "criminally dull" books, she is thankful, she claims, to have been "educated against my will into a taste for serious reading" (p. 29).

However, *Adventures of a Novelist* explains that Atherton's literary tastes budded not only from her grandfather's instruction in the classics but from reading forbidden romance novels from her mother's private stash while hiding in the dirty clothes hamper. Although the autobiography dismisses her mother as a beautiful, spoiled woman with "no sense" (p. 6), Atherton's biographer, Emily Wortis Leider, suggests that young Gertrude experienced childhood emotional abandonment by her mother, who was much more interested in her own social life than in her daughter. Atherton's autobiography recalls that her mother *"sometimes* came into [her] room to say goodnight before leaving" for a party (p. 16, italics added). The dominant impression Atherton provides of her mother is of a stranded Southern belle, a woman who insisted upon being "treated like a queen" and "would have expected to be waited on ... if the wolf were at the door" (pp. 19, 26).

Atherton also assigns her own desire to write to her mother's constant hysteria during her pregnancy with Gertrude, a desire she claims formed a "rotten," but fertile, "spot in her brain" (p. 8). Atherton describes this "rotten spot" in womblike terms, declaring it "took [her] nine months" to write one of her most famous novels and that she had "all the other symptoms" associated with pregnancy as well (p. 225). Atherton also claimed to suffer regularly from "sterile periods" after the completion of a book when the "rotten spot" in her brain seemed "shriveled and dead" (pp. 185, 553). The final indication that she made a literal connection between literary production and female sexuality occurred when, to counteract what she felt was a falling off in her literary productivity in the early 1920s, she underwent the controversial Steinach rejuvenating treatment, a mild stimulation of the ovaries by radiation. Atherton claimed the treatment not only revitalized her ability to write but also was responsible for the fact that from that time

onward she always looked, as Margaret Harriman relates, about twenty-five years younger than she actually was.

Atherton appears to have wanted to be selectively feminine in her public image throughout her career—to appeal to gender stereotypes when it might serve her interests and reject them when they threatened to restrict her. Recounting in her autobiography an early longing to be a greater belle than her mother, Atherton deplores women who neglect their "charm" (p. 469) and does not shy away from revealing the intimacies of a lady's toilet, with discussions of getting facials, penciling her eyebrows, and undergoing anti-aging treatments. She celebrates the "satisfaction ... of knowing [she] was the best-dressed woman on the platform" when she spoke at a rally for Woodrow Wilson (p. 476), and the sensational British novelist Elinor Glyn is the only woman writer treated favorably in Atherton's autobiography, as much for her beauty as for her fiction. Indeed, Atherton even admits envying Glyn her complexion and her sales figures. Atherton molded her image as a self-proclaimed "intellectual siren" all her life. Harriman relates that, living in New York in her mid-sixties, Atherton would sweep into the dining room at the Algonquin Hotel each night with her still-golden hair falling all over her shoulders and claim it had come unpinned in the elevator.

She loved having her picture taken, though she never allowed one to be taken of her at work, and was always amenable to being written up in the newspapers. Even when she was eighty-seven, one interview describes her as an "intellectual siren" who still has "sex appeal" and includes a current photo of her in her ubiquitous off-the-shoulder gown (Anspacher).

In *Adventures of a Novelist,* Atherton emphasizes that her feminine blandishments were simply another tool by which to conquer in the business world, and a means to gather new material. Her response to a suitor's confessed love illustrates her method: "I intend to be a novelist, and I've only been making a study of you ... You've become a bore. I think you'd better go now" (p. 107). According to her memoir, this was a scene she often reprised in her career: her

relationships with each new man gave her a "mental stimulation" to write the next novel and, when the book was done, "he was tactfully or abruptly discarded" (p. 173). Though her contemporaries and biographers speculate that few, or none, of these relationships were ever consummated, Atherton merely says, "I doubt if any artist should marry" (p. 174).

Her own unfortunate experience with matrimony may have been the source of such a declaration. When she was nineteen, Gertrude Horn eloped with George Atherton, one of her mother's boyfriends, and also one of the only eligible young men the nineteen-year-old even knew, since she had never made her social debut. Having fled her frustrating and tumultuous family, Atherton did not find the freedom that she had hoped, perhaps naively, marriage would give her. Descendants of Spanish aristocracy who had migrated from Chile, Atherton's in-laws believed that a woman's place was in the home and that "ladies did not write" (p. 57). Having never been interested in domesticity, Atherton asserts, "The worst trial I had yet been called upon to endure was having a husband continually on my hands" (p. 82), and she reportedly threatened to leave him if he did not get a place in San Francisco for her to live and have a literary salon. Her autobiography casts George Atherton as another example of that type with which Atherton had become so familiar through her mother's exploits: the worthless husband. As if to explain her contempt for him in the memoir, she includes the fact that "he had mismanaged two ranches and failed twice in business" (p. 81).

Perhaps the most startling breach of etiquette in her autobiography is Atherton's expressed wish (p. 112) for her husband's death, so that she could be free to write. George Atherton died in 1877 on a voyage to Chile which was supposed to have restored his failing health, and while Atherton pitied him the indignity of being returned to the United States embalmed in a cask of rum, she clearly did not grieve his loss. She admits later in her memoir that one of her early novels continued her real-life fantasy that her husband would die: "George was my heroine's husband, doomed to extermination by poison" (p. 225). While this is most likely a reference to *Patience Sparhawk and Her Times*, it could also refer to Atherton's *Mrs. Balfame* (1916) or *The Sophisticates* (1931), both of which feature wives who wish their husbands dead, find that some other unknown person has made that wish come true, and then find themselves on trial for their lives, only to be saved at the last moment by a confession or discovery of the real murderer. The refined or intellectual wife who is stifled by a boorish, overbearing husband formed a strong motif in Atherton's literary imagination, and she always frees her heroines at the end of the book to go on to lead lives that they choose for themselves. Like their author, they are not actually murderers but remain unapologetically ruthless nonetheless.

Atherton reveals her own brand of ruthlessness when she relates how she traded her daughter, Muriel (her son Georgie having died from diphtheria at age six), to her mother-in-law in exchange for the money to go to New York and pursue a literary career in 1887. Never apologetic, Atherton dismisses motherhood along with marriage, claiming she lacked a maternal instinct anyway. In one of the very few passages in the autobiography about her daughter, Atherton notes, "I had little to do with her bringing-up, which no doubt was fortunate for her" (p. 114). The only compliment Atherton pays her daughter in her memoir is that Muriel was "a marvelous housekeeper" (p. 539). But Atherton herself, along with all her heroines, absolutely rejected domesticity. As Leider points out, one of the first literary pseudonyms she used was "Asmodeus"—the Hebrew demon and destroyer of domestic happiness. When a chapter on her appeared in *Women Authors of Our Day in Their Homes* in 1903, her interview proudly opens, "I have no home" (Halsey, p. 249). This may have been partly a posture to garner notice and partly a personal conviction, but her antidomestic stance certainly made its way into nearly everything Atherton ever wrote. According to Sybil Weir, Atherton "conceived of herself as leading the fight against the glorification of the domestic heroine" (p. 25). In fact, at the end of her life, in a book of essays titled *Can Women Be Gentlemen?*, Atherton was still decrying the way the

label of "escape literature" had been applied to anything written by a woman as a way of denigrating any work that could not be considered domestic fiction.

ESCAPE FICTIONS

From the earliest point in her career, Atherton linked travel with freedom from domestic responsibilities and associated the ability to write with travel—a connection she expresses repeatedly in her autobiography. Her first venture to the East Coast was made against the wishes of most of her friends and family. To their protests, Atherton reportedly responded: "I want to meet real men of the world, such as you read about in books. I want to live in New York, Paris, London. I want to see the beautiful things in Europe and meet all sorts and kinds of people as different from those out here as possible. I know they would inspire me to write, and I am stagnating" (p. 105). However, the American world of letters, at that time strongly entrenched in New York, was unconvinced that Atherton had any place there at all. *Adventures of a Novelist* tells of Atherton's tramping from publisher to publisher on her first visit to New York, rejected by one and all. The first book she published under her own name, *Hermia Suydam* (1889), is a semiautobiographical account of that experience. In it young Hermia is a daydreamer, poet, and freethinker who, through inheriting a fortune and employing all sorts of beauty specialists, has made herself into an "intellectual siren" whose work is repeatedly rejected by New York publishers for its frankness and emotionality. In the course of conducting a literary salon, Hermia becomes torn between two men, both writers, one who caters to the tame, bourgeois nineteenth-century demands of publishers, and one who does not, preferring to write swashbuckling adventures with historical settings. But just after Hermia chooses the less conventional man, he suddenly drops dead of heart failure, leaving her to fight her literary battles alone. An overwrought book, full of tirades on the conventionality of the literary establishment and verbally (but not physically) torrid love scenes, *Hermia Suydam* is far from Atherton's

best work. But the hurtful reviews of her early work still must have rankled when Atherton wrote her autobiography more than forty years later: in that volume she blames her western origin, her looks, and only incidentally the poor quality of the work for its reception:

> The publishers had left the public in no doubt as to my identity. In advance paragraphs, it had been informed that the young, gifted, and beautiful author was a native of California and descended from one of its pioneer families (which I was not) and had come to make her home in New York and embark upon what no doubt would be a brilliant career. Perhaps this ill-advised "blurb" had something to do with the reception of the book. Perhaps its pages revealed a personality that antagonized the critics. Perhaps it was impertinence for a California writer to invade the sacred precincts, the more particularly as she had not made a reputation in one of the magazines. Perhaps it was merely because I was a woman, and all the critics were men. Whatever the reason, that book had an extraordinary reception. I know now it was not worth the paper it was printed on. Its only merit was that it betrayed a certain originality in conception. It should have been dismissed with a paragraph if noticed at all. But it was greeted with columns of ridicule and even abuse. I was given to understand that I was not wanted, that there was no place for me in any walk of American literature, and the sooner I returned to my native wilds the better.
>
> (p. 143)

Rather than forcing her return to California, these reviews only made her more determined: she instead fled to Europe, where her childhood friend Sybil Sanderson (upon whom she would base more than one of her heroines, including Rosita Thrailkill of *The Californians* and Margarethe Styr in *Tower of Ivory*) had found success in the opera, and "immediately sat down and began another book" (p. 144). Atherton even canceled her New York clipping service in disdain for the injustice she felt she had received there. In 1890s London, she was generally better received, even feted, meeting many literary and artistic figures of renown: James McNeill Whistler, Edwin Austin Abbey, John Singer Sargent, Dante Gabriel Rossetti, Sir Edward Coley Burne-Jones, Sir John Everett Millais, George Frederick Watts, Frederic Leighton, Mrs. Humphry Ward, Violet Hunt, Edmund Gosse, Henry James, Mary

Hunter Austin, Ellen Glasgow, Carl Van Vechten, Sinclair Lewis, Frances Hodgson Burnett, and Amy Lowell.

Atherton's success in 1890s London must be at least partially attributed to the willful, frank, undisciplined heroines who had offended American readers but to the English reading public seemed perfect specimens of the "New Woman" novels of that decade. John Lane and his newly developed Bodley Head imprint were known for publishing "unknowns," "rebels," women authors, and the New Woman novels that had 1890s England all abuzz (Stetz, p. 72), and Atherton fit all four criteria. Not only that, but 1890s England also had embraced what Kevin Starr has noted was an almost "Amazonian" myth of the "spirited independence," physical strength and stature, and "remarkable beauty" of the California girl, which had been popularized by English visitors such as Rudyard Kipling (pp. 357–358). Starr notes that California had "become part of [Atherton's] personal myth" by the 1890s, and she capitalized on it not only on her novels but in articles such as "The Literary Development of California." Her novels and short stories of this period usually feature California settings and examine the mixture of Spanish, Mexican, Southern, and East Coast influences in the development of the state (which Atherton felt perfectly qualified to do because of her own background and the fact that her mother-in-law, Dominga Atherton, was a formidable example of a Spanish lady and matriarch). Even when these works do not function as fictionalized mythical histories of California, their heroes and heroines are stamped with their California origins; in this category, we may place *Los Cerritos* (1890), a novel that focuses on class struggle by depicting a squatters' strike; *The Doomswoman* (1893), in which a young Spanish woman witnesses her lover murdering her brother, his rival for wealth and power; *Before the Gringo Came* (1894), a collection of short stories depicting Spanish American culture of the 1840s; *A Whirl Asunder* (1895), a brief romance set in the gorgeous California redwoods; the previously mentioned *American Wives and English Husbands* (1898) and *The Californians* (1898); *The Valiant Runaways* (1898), which

looks at the conflict between Mexican and American interests in California through the eyes of a group of young boys; the previously mentioned *A Daughter of the Vine* (1899); and *Senator North* (1900), a volume inspired by Atherton's longtime friend James D. Phelan, a U.S. senator from California. *His Fortunate Grace* (1897), a tale of international marriage but of an inferior style and sensitivity to *American Wives and English Husbands,* reuses characters from the earlier California books, such as Helena Belmont, a practice Atherton repeated throughout her career, building on to the mythical Old California she had created in this decade.

In London, Atherton received wonderful reviews of not only the banned-in-America *Patience Sparhawk and Her Times* but also her 1898 novel *American Wives and English Husbands*. When people began to interview her and take her photograph after the success of the latter novel, Atherton felt sufficiently vindicated and established. It had all been part of her plan, she reasoned, for "if I made a reputation in the literary headquarters of the world, America would be forced to acknowledge me" (*Adventures,* p. 227).

Leider's biography speculates that Atherton may have intended to travel in order to enlarge her creative faculties enough to make her an accomplished writer, and this is very likely true, but Atherton herself asserts it as a symbol of her personal freedom, claiming that "it was [her] intention to write every book in a new place, combining travel with work" (*Adventures,* p. 271). Her locations ranged from a French convent to a run-down boardinghouse in Yonkers, an exquisite Munich apartment, and the homes of British nobility. According to Atherton, freedom was "essential to any artist ... and freedom is to be found only through an open mind and a wide and varying horizon" (p. 254). For nearly forty years, she followed that horizon; only when she was well into her seventies did she return to California to stay.

From 1889 to 1902 Atherton's expatriate experiences were centered in England, with trips home to San Francisco and side adventures into Brittany and Rouen, France; Cuba; the New York Adirondacks; and the West Indies. From 1902 to

GERTRUDE ATHERTON

1910 Atherton primarily resided in Munich, Germany, making visits to Hungary, Trieste, London, and back to San Francisco, always using expatriatism as a portal to acceptance in American literary circles and the mythically fierce, willful, Girl-of-the-American-West as a draw for her British readers and critics. In her fiction, as well as in her autobiography, Atherton often affirmed the French cultural critic and novelist Paul Bourget's proclamation that the ultimate religion of America was the worship of the "Individual Will." Atherton dedicated two novels to Bourget and built on his theories, speculating that "the final result [of the religion of the Individual Will] may be a race of harder fibre and larger faculties than any in the history of civilization" (quoted in McClure, p. 56). This willfulness, she felt, was an especial asset to the American woman, who, according to Atherton, was "a composite of all the races of the earth, if not in blood, in points of view … [who has] one dominant and most important attribute—the ability to begin life over again every day in the year, if necessary" ("Divorce in the United Sates," p. 411).

In the first years of the twentieth century Atherton emphasized this radical independence of spirit in her characters by revising the types of naive, presumptuous, willful, or boorish expatriate characters that reflected so poorly on America in other fiction of the time, such as Henry James's Daisy Miller or Edith Wharton's Undine Spragg of *The Custom of the Country*. In *Ancestors*, which was the third-best-selling novel in 1907, Atherton makes a beautiful California-girl-abroad her heroine and appoints an American-born English aristocrat as the girl's intellectual and romantic match. But while the girl defines her true self and discovers her true strength by traveling alone through Europe and then returns to her chicken ranch in California, the man, the novel implies, can only truly test his strength in the anarchy of American society, as represented in the volatile politics of San Francisco. In *Tower of Ivory*—number two on the best-seller list in March 1910—a wealthy American mother and daughter set out to conquer English society with the girl's beauty but find their plans foiled by an American expatriate opera singer who has remade herself from a coal miner's illegitimate child to an international diva in Munich. The character of Margarethe Styr, the older woman and opera singer for whom the young Englishman John Ordham abandons his wife in *Tower of Ivory*, provides an extreme example of the American woman who makes herself over via expatriatism. When she meets Ordham, who is studying for the diplomatic exam in Munich, there are rumors flying that she may be "a runaway—or an abducted princess," though the truth is that her mother was a "steerage immigrant" who may have been Hungarian, and that she never knew who her father was or where he came from (pp. 20–32). Born one Peggy Hill, hailing from a coal-mining town, and not even learning the alphabet until she was fifteen, the self-named Styr came to Germany, she asserts, "with the firm intention of beginning life over again" and becomes internationally renowned for her embodiment of Wagnerian operatic roles (p. 33).

Though Atherton was relatively prolific in her literary production during these years, most of the books of that era seem like overwrought, hasty romances. Among these are *The Travelling Thirds* (1905), wherein an American girl insists on traveling third-class through Spain, to the horror of her extended family, meeting both danger and romance along the way; and *Rezanov* (1906), a story Atherton retold several times in her career about a Russian nobleman who visits California and becomes enchanted with a local Spanish maiden, but dies on a journey to gain the pope's permission to marry the girl. However, her book of short stories titled *The Bell in the Fog and Other Stories* (1905) is well worth noting, and some of them were rereleased in a 2008 collection titled *The Caves of Death*, edited by S. T. Joshi. These years also saw the publication of her notably researched biography of Alexander Hamilton, *The Conqueror* (1902), and the novel *Rulers of Kings* (1904), which explores territory similar to that of *Ancestors*—asking what it takes to be a true leader by having parallel British and American heroes in the book but without the dominant romance plot.

In those first two decades of expatriatism Atherton had also established herself as an

interpreter of American culture in Europe and of European culture for Americans. More significantly, she used her expatriate standing to critique the American establishment that had rejected her, writing articles for English and American magazines titled "Divorce in the United States" (1897), "Literary London" (1899), "The American Husband" (1903), "Why Is American Literature Bourgeois?"(1904), "Some Truths About American Readers" (1904), "The New Aristocracy" (1906), and "Why Have We Not More Great Novelists?" (1908). The last five articles in this list tend to characterize American literature as rather backward, as well as boring, implying that her sensational books were simply more sophisticated than the homey American realism and regionalism promoted and published by William Dean Howells in that era.

In 1911, after a brief American tour with a failed play written at the request of the popular actress Minnie Maddern Fiske, Atherton ventured again to London, this time to study the suffrage movement and write the novel *Julia France and Her Times* (1912). This book also benefited from her earlier research trip to the West Indies, as Atherton has her heroine grow up there in a sheltered, idyllic island existence before she meets her brutal, hard-drinking husband and moves back to England with him. Julia's disillusionment in her marriage leads to her work in the cause of women.

In 1913 Atherton ventured to Italy as well as Montana in search of new material, which resulted in 1914's *Perch of the Devil,* a novel of competition examining not only the ruthlessness of men in the mining business but of women in society and in their pursuit of love. In the book, the two main American female characters, one of working-class stock, the other a spoiled heiress, tour Europe together, where they predictably discover themselves and their potential. The first becomes a leader among the middle-class American women whose self-reliance Atherton so admired while the other, having failed to steal her friend's husband, settles for the social power that will come with her marriage to an Italian nobleman instead.

The onset of World War I and the failure of her daughter Muriel's marriage forced Atherton into more conventional domestic arrangements in her native country. She settled into an apartment with Muriel in New York from 1914 to 1919, doing war work making intermittent trips to Europe that allowed her to write the nonfictional *Life in the War Zone* (1916) and *The Living Present* (1917), a book on French women's response to the war, as well as the novel *The White Morning* (1918), which relied heavily on her experience of the German people while she lived in Munich. *The White Morning* is a fantasy that imagines the women of Germany organizing themselves and rising up to stop the war. The leader of the movement, a stunning, willful beauty as always in an Atherton novel, has to murder her lover to keep him from exposing her and does so without remorse. One of a handful of American female novelists who reported from Europe during World War I, Atherton briefly secured the status of acting as a war correspondent for the *New York Times.* She also finally had the East Coast literary salon of which she had always dreamed, with Muriel to handle all the housekeeping, hospitality, and domestic arrangements for her. When Muriel, deciding that she needed to support herself, moved to take a job at a hospital in the South, the salon literally could not continue without her.

A "NEW GROOVE"

After the war, when an unflattering 1918 piece placed her at the bargain counter with the rest of the popular prewar novelists, Atherton once more felt the need to make herself and her work over, so she moved to Hollywood to find a "new groove" in 1919 (Leider, p. 286). The work Atherton did after World War I and into the 1920s shows her definitely capitalizing not only on Hollywood's possibilities but on the Freudian pop psychology that had become trendy in the postwar years. Almost all these novels deal with the question of repression: sexual, genetic, social, and intellectual. Atherton returned to the familiar ground of Old California in *The Avalanche* (1919), set just after the Great Earthquake of

GERTRUDE ATHERTON

1906. In the book, a prosperous California gentleman marries a beautiful, penniless girl whom he thinks is French, only to find out that her mother and father were actually leaders in the notorious gambling underworld of 1880s San Francisco. At the same time as this truth is uncovered, he finds out that the girl has inherited her family's irrepressible vice and has just gambled away his family's jewels. He retrieves the jewels, pardons the girl's peccadillos, and they presumably live happily ever after. In this book, as in many that she wrote in this phase of her career, Atherton again writes new characters into her already existing fictionalized California, reusing the main character from *Ancestors,* Jack Gwynne, in almost all her novels in the 1920s. After writing a film script titled "Don't Neglect Your Wife," and negotiating a film version of *The Avalanche* (there would eventually be seven films made from her novels), Atherton combined her New York experience with her California background to write *The Sisters-in-Law* (1921), in which the lovely Alexina Groome, a San Franciscan of patrician Southern ancestry, marries a handsome young up-and-coming businessman who becomes so obsessed with the luxury to which her family has been accustomed that he gets himself into debt, gambles in the stock market, and eventually steals the final $40,000 of Alexina's inheritance from her locked bureau. Mortimer Dwight, the worthless husband in this particular novel, has a sister, Gora, whose brilliance has been stunted by her poverty and society's narrow-mindedness until she goes to Europe to do war work. She and Alexina, the sisters-in-law, fall in love with the same Englishman who had visited California when they were younger but who is now a British officer. Alexina, with her irresistible sex appeal, gets the man, and Gora, after nearly giving in to her desire to murder Alexina, redirects her passions into her art.

In *Sleeping Fires* (1922), Atherton casts back to California of the 1860s to tell a tale of the effects of intellectual and sexual repression on a mismated young woman, whose husband has forbidden her even the small escape of reading as an outlet for her imagination. Both she and the man she loves, who smuggles her books until the two are caught and separated, nearly drink themselves to death before they are finally united. Gora Dwight reappears as a monumentally successful author in *Black Oxen* (1923) and *The Sophisticates* (1931), another novel in which a young and lovely wife with every reason to wish her husband dead, but who does not actually kill him herself, is on trial for his murder. The wife in this novel, Melton Abbey, spends extensive time in New York to escape her boorish husband and thus eventually establishes a literary salon in Grand Forks, an exemplary Midwestern town. In this novel, Gora Dwight is associated with the Sophisticates, Atherton's nickname for the authors of the Algonquin Circle, the very visible and outspoken group of New York literati that included Dorothy Parker and always lunched at the Algonquin Hotel, where some of them lived, and where Atherton had also resided when she was in New York.

Neither *The Sophisticates* nor *Black Oxen*, however, are really about Gora Dwight, although her wisdom and perspicacity make her a source of valuable guidance for the other characters in the books. *Black Oxen,* which was also made into a film, is the story of Mary Ogden, now the Countess Zattiany, who has undergone the same Steinach treatment as Atherton herself had and returned to New York from Austria, where her marriage and war work have taken her. However, at first no one recognizes her, since she looks as if she is in her twenties, to the horror of her childhood friends, who are now in their sixties. Ogden/Zattiany nearly marries a highly eligible man thirty years her junior before she decides that, though it was fun to fall in love again, she would rather employ her regained beauty and life experience in the service of Austria, her second home, instead of becoming a mere "Mrs. Clavering" of America. Melanie Dawson, in her new edition of the book, discusses the monumental interest that the book generated in the Steinach treatment, including letters that Atherton received from women asking her questions about getting the treatment for themselves after the book and the film were released. Also noteworthy in *Black Oxen* is Atherton's highly critical portrayal of the youth culture of the 1920s and its symbol, the

flapper. Depicting them as brash, immoral, ill-mannered, and self-destructive, Atherton portrays flappers as greedy children who would be the better for a good spanking and who, while they celebrate their cynical freedom from the myth of "love," are rather weary of having to constantly prove themselves free from sexual repression.

While *Black Oxen* utilized a lot of popular Freudian talk about "complexes" in its depiction of the characters, *The Crystal Cup* (1925) absolutely relies upon them for its plot line and characters. In the novel, the heiress Gita Carteret, who the book implies suffered much sexual harassment, possibly abuse, from her rapscallion father's friends who were always around to drink and gamble with him during her itinerant childhood, is so disgusted by the "hideous lust of men" (p. 24) that she will only agree to an un-consummated, companionate marriage, and she nearly kills her husband when he loses his self-control one night and tries to molest her. At the novel's very end, her repression is released when she agrees to wed a man she truly loves, for whom she will divorce her in-name-only husband, but this resolution seems a bit shallow and hasty. Atherton's fictional world of the 1920s, while still revolving around the basic romance plots her readers could always expect from her, is really a world of "complexes," hormonal balance or imbalance, of functioning or dead ductless glands. In these books, she is as skeptical of love as H. L. Mencken was of the "pseudoscience" (McClure, p. 136) he found in her casual references to Freudian terms.

Despite having been denigrated for her hastiness to pick up on new vocabulary and social trends in her novels, the next phase of Atherton's career, between 1926 and 1932, impressed both readers and critics with its meticulous research. Having gone to Europe to accept the French Legion of Honor for her war work, Atherton met an actress who declared her to be the reincarnation of Aspasia, the morganatic wife of Pericles, a paragon of female beauty, power, and intellect. This inspired her to head for Greece to learn more. In her two novels set in ancient Greece, *The Immortal Marriage* (1927) and *The Jealous Gods* (1928), Atherton shows her mettle for us-

ing travel and research to generate new material: according to William E. Harris, she spent six months wandering in Athens, Sparta, and Asia Minor as well as reading almost two hundred volumes on the era and setting before writing them. These volumes earned the unique academic distinction of being assigned by college professors and added another dimension to Atherton's literary reputation. *Golden Peacock* (1936), which includes a great deal of ancient political intrigue as seen through the eyes of the developing romance of Pomponia, the fictional niece of the great Roman satirist, Horace, and her noble, powerful lover, resulted from research on that same trip as well, as did *Dido, Queen of Hearts* (1929). Biographers speculate that Atherton's interest in these topics was also a reflection of her close relationship to Senator James Phelan and his interest in the ancient past. His beautiful estate at Montalvo always had a suite ready for her to come home to from any of her travels, and his poem about Aspasia formed the frontispiece to *The Immortal Marriage*.

As she aged, Atherton remained more centered in the San Francisco area. Leider relates that in 1941 she moved into her own floor at Muriel's house when poor health made it impossible to keep living on her own. Muriel always remained faithful to her, even having her son pick up his grandmother at her own apartment every night for dinner before she moved in with them. Atherton's faith in the indestructible endurance of women is as strong as ever in her final two novels, *The House of Lee* (1940) and *The Horn of Life* (1942). *The House of Lee* follows a family of three generations of women and their individual responses to the prospect of having to support themselves, their once immense family fortune having been eaten up by the vicissitudes of the twentieth century. Their pluckiness, their mental toughness, originating from the grandmother of the group, who is nicknamed "The General," allows each to find a skill, a way to support herself, sometimes to the surprise and indignation of their friends, who never imagined this would happen. In the end, the book endorses Atherton's own idea that life is never over unless you give up, and a woman can always draw on

her inner resources, remake herself, and begin anew. The women's ingeniousness, as well as the characterization of the family's Chinese retainer Chang, with his wit, power, and knowledge of the San Francisco these "ladies" have never imagined, make this late effort a charming revision and summary of all the generations of women Atherton had ever written about. *The Horn of Life* is similar in conception, depicting a young, now impoverished, woman from an old and distinguished San Francisco family forcing her way into the man's world of business after World War I, with familiar Athertonian obstacles, such as an alcoholic mother and an incorrigible flapper sister, scattered in her path. The book also features the moment that becomes very familiar to the reader of Atherton's fiction: the sudden urge to murder, to take the opportunity to rid oneself of a person standing in the path to fulfillment. In this case, the victim-that-might-have-been is the alcoholic mother of the heroine. *The Horn of Life* was Atherton's last book of fiction. Later in the 1940s she penned two histories of the San Francisco Bay area, *Golden Gate Country* (1945) and *My San Francisco* (1946), adding to the work she had done in *California: An Intimate History* (1914).

FAME AND FORTUNE

Leider shrewdly observes that Atherton "shows an inability to make a distinction between genuine merit and other kinds of ratification: getting published, getting paid, getting noticed" (p. 142). Indeed, Atherton's literary longevity is arguably based in the fact that she was constantly pursuing at least two of these aims at the same time. By continually remodeling her work to meet current market demands, she kept herself almost continually in print and sustained her popularity as a novelist into her eighties. As early as 1904 Atherton reveals her savvy in an article in the *Bookman* titled "Some Truths About American Readers," declaring "the truth is that the population of the United States has so enormously increased in the last thirty years that today there are all sorts of audiences; every author worth his salt will obtain a hearing, and those well above

the average will have the success they deserve" (p. 659). Atherton knew how to acquire new reading publics through travels and generic experimentation—with forays into murder mystery, biography, and historical fiction—but also to retain the public that expected the romance, adventure, iconoclasm, and glamour that attended all her works, no matter what the genre or setting. She often rode the literary current at the time to financial success—for instance, she wrote her first California novel just after Helen Hunt Jackson's wildly popular *Ramona* (1884) came out, and, as she relates in her autobiography, *Patience Sparhawk and Her Times* was born from sensationalistic headlines about a murder trial. Leider notices that Atherton joined the suffrage campaign in 1910 and wrote her suffrage novel *Julia France and Her Times* only when it was the "subject of the hour" (p. 249), while Atherton claims she was "fired with a holy enthusiasm to do something for my downtrodden sex! I had always resented the calm assumption of men that they were the superior sex, and their very real dominance," going on to justify her choices by declaring, "I had succeeded in spite of them" (*Adventures*, p. 453).

Atherton further justifies her market-based means of composition in her memoir by insisting on her status as an innovator. She wrote a novel set in Montana, she says, because "both New York and California were overworked" (*Adventures*, p. 480). Further, though she was inspired to return to California by a magazine query as to why California writers did not write about the history of the state, Atherton claims her own individual right to treat the material, as if she had better staked her claim to it. "Its nuggets were mine," she writes (p. 186). She tells a similar story for almost all the novels she writes: someone asks, in person, or in print, why no one has done this topic, and Atherton goes out and does it. When she sensed readers were growing tired of one vein she had been mining, she simply turned to another.

Perhaps it is better to read her as a successful robber baron of the literary world—eating up narrative territory, mining both new and established claims, and receiving fortune and notoriety

for doing so—than as a failure at maintaining a consistently artistic reputation. Atherton claimed to admire men like J. P. Morgan more than she did literary men like W. D. Howells ("Why Is American Literature Bourgeois?"). When she was more established, she took pleasure in placing her novels with the highest bidder—refusing an agent because she felt she could do better placing the work herself. By the 1920s she had multiple popular and best-selling books. When she signed with Horace Liveright in 1922, she saved the firm from financial disaster. Liveright recalled that Atherton understood the need for publicity and was not above attracting attention to herself by stunts like smoking in public.

"People want to be amused," Atherton declared in 1929, "told a story, not given the detailed description of a single character. Homer, Shakespeare, none of the great writers of all the ages sat down to write exclusively about character. He would have bored us if he had" (Harris, p. 63). In referring to the popularity of Shakespeare and Homer, she legitimates the idea of writing for a popular audience, equating a "give the people what they want" attitude with high art. In fact, Atherton put such great stock in fame as an indirect determinant of literary quality that she tells a parallel story in her autobiography, describing the American soprano Sibyl Sanderson's path to success: according to Atherton, Sanderson opened to terrible reviews but simply packed appreciative audiences long enough that she could no longer be critically denied a reputation. The technique indeed worked for Atherton herself: even in the Depression, an Atherton book was a sound investment; her autobiography had gone into a third edition the year after its initial release.

Money was no trifling matter in Atherton's career, and she did not shy away from saying so. She had been one of Samuel Goldwyn's "Eminent Authors" in the 1920s because of the "generous" financial terms (Adventures, p. 544). Atherton knew that monetary concerns occasionally hindered her literary aspirations. But, as she explains in the memoir with her customary terseness: "dependents induce circumspection" (p. 222). And when she gives brief updates from

time to time on female members of her family throughout her memoir, their husbands—rarely mentioned, never named—are uniform failures. Throughout her life, Atherton found herself having to support her sister, Aleece; to supplement her son-in-law's unstable income for the sake of Muriel; to send her grandchildren to convent schools or private schools like the Isadora Duncan School, first in New York and then in Europe; and to provide for her niece and her aging and beloved nurse, Rose Stoddard, in whose brash humor and indefatigable energy the young girl had found a role model for her own survival. Perhaps in her own way, by listing her many female dependents, Atherton is hinting at the reason she so valued popular interest and financial success. Always on the cutting edge, she kept up with the literary market to the extent of doing a series on the seedier nightspots of San Francisco when she was in her mid-eighties. Damning her with faint praise, the New Yorker pronounced in 1933, "she has enjoyed much popular success and—quite sensibly—asks for nothing more" ("Books, Books, Books," p. 64).

CRITICAL REPUTATION

Atherton wanted it all: not just fame and fortune but literary status. She was devastated when, for the first decade of her career as a novelist, she was labeled a "sensationalist" and her work referred to in sexist terms (Leider, p. 83). The American literary journal the Critic called What Dreams May Come (1888), her first book, published under the pseudonym of "Frank Lin," "literary hysteria" (quoted in Leider, p. 77), and one referred to Hermia Suydam as "Atherton's naked exposure" (p. 82). In her autobiography, Atherton often attributes negative reviews like these to the "sex-jealousy" (Adventures, p. 143) directed at successful women authors by the nineteenth-century male establishment, which critics like Sandra Gilbert and Susan Gubar, along with Elaine Showalter, Judith Fetterley, Nina Baym, and numerous others have documented. However, the label never disappeared entirely: in an anthology published after she was a well-established writer, Frederic Taber Cooper wrote,

GERTRUDE ATHERTON

"Mrs. Atherton, at her worst, lets her pen run riot in a blare of words until the printed paragraph shrills onward and upward into a painful and hysterical shriek" (p. 251). Aspersions on her breeding and manners, or lack thereof, were common: one reviewer labeled her work "the day-dreams of a common shopgirl" (Stevenson, p. 465).

Though she was considered a "renegade" until about 1900, critics began to label Atherton a "preeminent literary novelist" (Leider, p. 290) and compare her to Edith Wharton and Willa Cather in the first decade of the twentieth century. Indeed, by 1904, a reviewer for the *Critic* emphasized her dual social and literary success as an expatriate writer, saying, "no American woman's work has been so popular" (quoted in Leider, p. 239). A further mark of her rising reputation in the first decades of the twentieth century is where she was published and by whom. While her earlier articles of these decades often appeared in magazines such as *Cosmopolitan,* later articles were frequently printed in the *Bookman* and other literary journals. Charlotte McClure notes that Atherton's "twelve separate publications between 1900 and 1910 ... enhanced her reputation," while her 1904 criticism of Howells and his definitions of realism "added a different [academic] dimension" (p. 132) to it. In that same year, a critical volume by W. L. Courtney titled *The Feminine Note in Fiction* provides a mixed evaluation of Atherton's oeuvre thus far, finding her work, while uneven in quality, not only from book to book but within the pages of individual books, worth studying as an "inquiry into the baffling and scintillating paradoxes of the American character" (p. 121).

Throughout her long career, Atherton's literary reputation continued to fluctuate, reaching its apex around 1915 and declining for some years until she wrote her autobiography in 1932. Between 1910 and the onset of World War I, she very briefly earned the approval of Sinclair Lewis when *Perch of the Devil* (1914), and *The White Morning* (1918) showed interest in the middle and working classes. John Curtis Underwood

included analysis of her work in his book *Literature and Insurgency: Ten Studies in Racial Evolution* (1914), claiming that she had drawn the outlines of a "new race of women" (p. 434) in her fiction.

Some of the praise she received was mixed, and denoted mostly the difference between Atherton and other better-known female writers of her era. At the turn of the century, Willa Cather commented upon "dear Mrs. Atherton's ... pretentiou[s attempt to] analyz[e] things that she was once content to admire" and her apparent quest to "produce 'literature' at any cost" ("Four Women Writers," p. 694). In 1911 Henry James Forman wrote that "Mrs. Atherton was no stylist in the sense that Edith Wharton or Willa Cather were stylists. ... She does not, however, lose herself in any sentimental flower garden" (p. 4).

The year 1913 found Atherton contributing an article about "The Woman of Tomorrow" to the *Yale Review* that systematically undermines all common sentimental presumptions about women as the gentler, weaker, more virtuous sex. And in his 1911 anthology Frederic Taber Cooper, for all his criticism of her style, credited her policy of "intellectual anarchy" as a driving force that made her work worth noting (p. 246), and praised her for being "the only woman now writing in English who is able to handle questions of sex with a masculine absence of self-consciousness" (pp. 247–248).

The multiplicity of opinions that critics held—and hold—of Atherton's work can be justified by the vast differences in the topics and quality of her books. Anticipating this issue, Atherton uses her autobiography to insist upon her own standards in answer to the criticisms that she had faced in her career. In one instance, she claims she purposely avoided developing a "flowing style" because "too many had it" (*Adventures,* p. 181). This public rebellion against the dominant aesthetic was a lifelong stance for Atherton: it began as early as 1907 from remarks in an early *New York Times* article titled "Gertrude Atherton Assails 'The Powers,' " and extended until one of her last interviews, at age eighty-seven, in which she calls herself a "literary nonconformist" (Anspacher).

When her outspoken memoir was published in 1932, Mary Ellen Chase of *Commonweal* called it "baffling" in its "egoism and cocksureness" and its "bad taste," remarking that "it reveal[ed] a personality energetic, fearless, adventuresome, but cold and basically selfish" (p. 334). Chase was not alone in her critique. While Arthur Waugh scolded Atherton for her "offenses against good taste," for "there are some tales that good manners refrain from telling" (p. 410), others called the book "unusually frank," "very outspoken" (Field, p. 2), "relentless," and "caustic" (Colton, p. 754). These descriptors of the memoir are indeed warranted. Often Atherton is flippant when common courtesy demands otherwise: for instance, when discussing World War I, she writes, "I missed the thrill of being in Europe when War was declared" (*Adventures,* p. 499). Perhaps Atherton may have known her autobiography might provoke annoyance, for she occasionally attempts to stave off criticism with explanations of her brashness. "I seem to have been born without awe," she writes (p. 170).

Again and again, Atherton shows her awareness of her shortcomings, but she always has an answer for them. She reprints an entire letter from Harold Frederic in her autobiography, in which he warns her to "take the pace a little more slowly, and listen with a more solicitous, reflective ear" to her prose (p. 313). In response, Atherton explains why she did not always heed his words, by saying, "style is a matter of temperament, and unless one is cool and placid and suave by nature ... one cannot preserve a uniform style" (p. 313). She further defends her erratic style by characterizing it as a quality that sets her apart from other writers: "it is easy enough to write well, [but] individuality is inborn" (p. 314). The value she placed on individuality remained a constant in her defenses of her work: she proudly referred to herself, in a 1944 interview, as an "intellectual anarchist" (Anspacher).

As Leider relates, near the end of her career Atherton was seen as a legitimate artist only in limited circles; for example, she founded a San Francisco chapter of PEN, but the New York PEN rejected her application. In 1934 and 1938 she finally and triumphantly had two books—a collection of short stories and a book of social commentary, titled *Can Women Be Gentlemen?*—published by the highly respected firm of Houghton Mifflin, which had turned down her first novel in 1884. The same year, she was elected to the National Institute of Arts and Letters, but not to the American Academy of Arts and Letters as were Ellen Glasgow and Willa Cather. In her eighties, she continued to write and to enjoy the benefits of having become a grand old dame of American letters, with an exhibition of her manuscripts in the Library of Congress in 1943 and a *Life* magazine article celebrating her fifty-sixth book in 1946.

Nearly the only critical attention given to Atherton since her death in 1948 focuses on her from a feminist perspective or as an artifact of California's history. In 1961 Henry James Forman analyzed her persona and fiction in "A Brilliant California Novelist," which overviews her credentials and accomplishments as a "spirited" California native (p. 2) who performed such literary feats as making Alexander Hamilton's "illegitimacy almost a badge of honor" (p. 4). Atherton criticism of the 1970s, largely biographical, focused on her rebellion against the status quo. In this category, we find articles such as "Gertrude Atherton and the New Woman" by Carolyn Forrey, a viewpoint that focuses on heroines who "lacked femininity in traditional terms" but "insisted upon their essential womanliness, especially upon their sexuality" (p. 195), and contrasts Atherton to Mabel Dodge Luhan, another woman born into the middle class who also traveled the world seeking freedom. However, Luhan focused on finding sexual emancipation and fulfillment while Atherton concentrated on being free to develop her career. "The Flappers Were Her Daughters: The Liberated, Literary World of Gertrude Atherton" by Elinor Richey celebrates the way Atherton protected her freedom as a writer and a woman throughout her career and mentions that the last publication from Atherton before her death was a letter to the editor nominating Eleanor Roosevelt for president. Emily Leider's meticulously researched biography, *California's Daughter,* was published in 1991. Since then, Atherton has been hardly

considered in literary criticism, except in the introduction, notes, and appendix to Melanie Dawson's new edition of *Black Oxen.*

Reading Atherton's biography, autobiography, fiction, and criticism, one cannot help feeling a sort of exhausted, reluctant admiration for her determined and endless scrambling, scribbling, and seeking for self-determination and literary status. Despite the tumult of her life and career, she confessed to few regrets, reaffirming in a newspaper interview commemorating her ninetieth birthday: "I've had a good time out of life. And I've learned that if you want something, you've got to go after it" (quoted in Leider, p. 347). Without fail, Gertrude Atherton and her fictional heroines did exactly that.

Selected Bibliography

WORKS OF GERTRUDE ATHERTON

NOVELS

What Dreams May Come. [Frank Lin, pseud.] New York: Belford, 1888.

Hermia Suydam. New York: Current Literature, 1889.

Los Cerritos. New York: John W. Lovell, 1890.

The Doomswoman. New York: J. Selwin Tait, 1893.

Before the Gringo Came. New York: J. Selwin Tait, 1894.

A Whirl Asunder. London: Frederick A. Stokes, 1895.

His Fortunate Grace. New York: D. Appleton, 1897.

Patience Sparhawk and Her Times. London and New York: John Lane/Bodley Head, 1897.

American Wives and English Husbands. New York: Dodd, Mead, 1898.

The Californians. London: John Lane, 1898. Reprint, Ridgewood, N.J.: Gregg Press, 1968.

The Valiant Runaways. New York: Dodd, Mead, 1898.

A Daughter of the Vine. London and New York: John Lane, 1899.

Senator North. London and New York: John Lane/Bodley Head, 1900.

The Aristocrats. London and New York: John Lane, 1901.

Rulers of Kings. London and New York: Harper, 1904.

The Travelling Thirds. London and New York: Harper, 1905.

Rezanov. New York: Authors and Newspapers Association, 1906.

Ancestors. New York: Harper, 1907.

Tower of Ivory. New York: Macmillan, 1910.

Julia France and Her Times. New York: Macmillan, 1912.

Perch of the Devil. New York: Frederick A. Stokes, 1914.

Mrs. Balfame. New York: Frederick A. Stokes, 1916.

The White Morning. New York: Frederick A. Stokes, 1918.

The Avalanche. New York: Frederick A. Stokes, 1919.

Transplanted. New York: Dodd, Mead, 1919.

The Sisters-in-Law. New York: Frederick A. Stokes, 1921.

Sleeping Fires. New York: Frederick A. Stokes, 1922.

Black Oxen. New York: Boni & Liveright, 1923. New ed., edited by Melanie Dawson. Peterborough, Ont., and Buffalo, N.Y.: Broadview Press, 2012.

The Crystal Cup. New York: Boni & Liveright, 1925.

The Immortal Marriage. New York: Boni & Liveright, 1927.

The Jealous Gods. New York: Horace Liveright, 1928.

Dido: Queen of Hearts. New York: Horace Liveright, 1929.

The Sophisticates. New York: Horace Liveright, 1931.

Golden Peacock. Boston: Houghton Mifflin, 1936.

The House of Lee. New York: D. Appleton-Century, 1940.

The Horn of Life. New York: D. Appleton-Century, 1942.

SHORT STORIES

The Bell in the Fog and Other Stories. London and New York: Harper, 1905.

The Foghorn: Stories. Boston: Houghton Mifflin, 1934.

The Caves of Death, and Other Stories. Edited by S. T. Joshi. Tampa, Fla.: University of Tampa Press, 2008.

MEMOIRS

Adventures of a Novelist. New York: Horace Liveright, 1932. (Quotations in the text refer to 3rd ed., New York: Blue Ribbon, 1932.)

"My Maiden Effort." In *My First Publication: Eleven California Authors Describe Their Earliest Appearance in Print.* [San Francisco?]: Book Club of California, 1961.

NONFICTION

"The Literary Development of California." *Cosmopolitan* 10:269–278 (January 1891).

"The Young Person as a Novel Reader." *Critic,* September 11, 1893, pp. 86–87.

"Divorce in the United States." *Contemporary Review* 72:410–415 (September 1897).

"Literary London." *Bookman* 16:65 (June 1899).

The Conqueror. New York: Macmillan, 1902.

"The American Husband." *Fortnightly Review* 74:516–524 (September 1903).

"Some Truths About American Readers." *Bookman* 18:658–660 (February 1904).

"Why Is American Literature Bourgeois?" *North American Review* 178:771–781 (May 1904).

"The New Aristocracy." *Cosmopolitan* 40:621–627 (April 1906).

"Why Have We Not More Great Novelists?" *Current Literature* 44:158–160 (February 1908).

"The Woman of Tomorrow." *Yale Review* 2:412–435 (April 1913).

California: An Intimate History. New York: Harper, 1914. Rev. and enl. eds. New York: Boni & Liveright, 1927; New York: Blue Ribbon Books, 1935.

Life in the War Zone. New York: Systems Printing, 1916.

The Living Present. New York: Frederick Stokes, 1917.

Can Women Be Gentlemen? Boston: Houghton Mifflin, 1938. (Quotes in text refer to the Riverside Press edition, 1938.)

Golden Gate Country. New York: Duell, Sloan, & Pierce, 1945.

My San Francisco. Indianapolis, Ind.: Bobbs-Merrill, 1946.

PAPERS

Collections of Atherton's letters and manuscripts are held at the Bancroft Library of the University of California, Berkeley; the New York Public Library; the Library of Congress; and the California Historical Society in San Francisco.

BIBLIOGRAPHY

McClure, Charlotte S. "A Checklist of the Writings of and About Gertrude Atherton." *American Literary Realism, 1870–1910* 9, no. 2:102–162 (1976).

CRITICAL AND BIOGRAPHICAL STUDIES

Ammons, Elizabeth. *Conflicting Stories: American Women Writers at the Turn into the Twentieth Century.* New York: Oxford University Press, 1991.

Anspacher, Carolyn. "Novelist, Non-Conformist, Intellectual Siren … Gertrude Atherton, at 87, Is in Her Prime." *San Francisco Chronicle,* October 30, 1944.

"Books, Books, Books." *New Yorker,* April 16, 1933, pp. 64–65.

Chase, Mary Ellen. "A Bright Lady." *Commonweal,* July 27, 1932, n.p.

Colton, Arthur. "Mrs. Atherton's Life." *Saturday Review of Literature,* May 28, 1932, p. 754.

Cooper, Frederic Taber. *Some American Story Tellers.* New York: Holt, 1911.

Courtney, W. L. *The Feminine Note in Fiction.* London: Chapman & Hall, 1904.

Field, Louise. "Mrs. Atherton Speaks Her Mind." *New York Times Book Review,* April 10, 1932, p. 2.

Forman, Henry James. "A Brilliant California Novelist, Gertrude Atherton." *California Historical Society Quarterly* 40:1–10 (March 1961).

Forrey, Carolyn. "Gertrude Atherton and the New Woman." *California Historical Society Quarterly* 55:194–209 (fall 1976).

Gilmer, Walker. *Horace Liveright: Publisher of the Twenties.* New York: David Lewis, 1970.

Halsey, Francis W. *Women Authors of Our Day in Their Homes.* New York: J. Pott, 1903.

Harriman, Margaret Case. *The Vicious Circle: The Story of the Algonquin Round Table.* New York: Rinehart, 1951.

Harris, William E. "Contemporary Writers XI—Gertrude Atherton." *Writer* 39:62–64 (1929).

Hart, James D. *The Popular Book: A History of America's Literary Taste.* New York: Oxford University Press, 1950.

Jackson, Joseph Henry. *Gertrude Atherton.* New York: Appleton-Century, 1940.

Leider, Emily Wortis. *California's Daughter: Gertrude Atherton and Her Times.* Stanford, Calif.: Stanford University Press, 1991.

Makowsky, Veronica. "Fear of Feeling and the Turn-of-the-Century Woman of Letters." *American Literary History* 5, no. 2:326–334 (1993).

McClure, Charlotte S. *Gertrude Atherton.* Boston: Twayne, 1979.

Overton, Grant M. *The Women Who Make Our Novels.* New York: Moffat, Yard, 1918. P. 299.

Richey, Eleanor. "The Flappers Were Her Daughters: The Liberated, Literary World of Gertrude Atherton." *American West* 11:4–10, 60–63 (July 1974).

Starr, Kevin. *Americans and the California Dream, 1850–1915.* New York: Oxford University Press, 1973.

Stetz, Margaret Diane. "Sex, Lies, and Printed Cloth: Bookselling at Bodley Head in the Eighteen-Nineties." *Victorian Studies* 35, no. 1:71–86 (autumn 1991).

Stevenson, Lionel. "Atherton Versus Grundy: The Forty Years' War." *Bookman* 69:464–472 (1929).

Underwood, John Curtis. *Literature and Insurgency: Ten Studies in Racial Evolution.* New York: Mitchell Kennerley, 1914.

Van Doren, Dorothy. "Lost Frontier." *Nation,* December 7, 1932, pp. 567–568.

Van Vechten, Carl. "Some Literary Ladies I Have Known." *Yale University Library Gazette* 26, no. 3:97–116 (1952).

Waugh, Arthur. "Autobiographies." *Spectator,* October 1, 1932, p. 410.

Weir, Sybil. "Gertrude Atherton: The Limits of Feminism in the 1890s." *San Jose Studies* 12:24–31 (February 1975).

TED BERRIGAN

(1934—1983)

John Steen

LATE IN HIS life, in a statement for the documentary film *Poetry in Motion,* Ted Berrigan explained that writing poetry was a response to a divine calling: "The gods demand of the system that a certain number of people sing, like the birds do, and it somehow was given to me to be one of those people." Adding that "the major reason I write is because … the whole thing could fall apart," Berrigan, best known for his insouciant wit and immersion in what he called "the level everyday," closed his segment by repeating, "I lift my voice in song. I lift my voice in song" (Padgett, p. 91).

Berrigan's interventions into mid-century U.S. poetry have been often and accurately characterized as sui generis disruptions of highbrow sacred cows by methods so radical that they invoke "terrorist implications" (Watten). Nevertheless these violent "formal break-throughs," as Berrigan termed them (in a recorded reading at New Langton Arts in 1981), ac-company an unparalleled devotion to the art, practice, and potential community of poetry. Despite a relatively short career, Berrigan's prolific writing and publication, coupled with his central position in a New York–based network of collaborators, friends, students, and admirers, left an indelible mark on the practice of poetry and the role of its institutions across the United States.

Although his life and work would come to be intimately associated with New York and its postwar experimental arts scene, Berrigan arrived there in the early 1960s as an outsider in terms of geography as well as education. He had spent the first half of his life in decidedly more provincial locales, which he credited with exert-ing a powerful influence on his temperament and aesthetic proclivities. Even after setting up shop in what he called "the 51st state," Berrigan recalled the South Providence neighborhood of his youth, the stint he served with the U.S. Army in Uijongbu, Korea, and the formative years he spent in Tulsa, Oklahoma, upon returning from military service. References to people and events from these places appear in Berrigan's poetry just as prominently as does New York. Rather than a chronicle of city life, a Berrigan poem shuttles rapidly among multiple physical and mental sites to create a layered portrait of the previously experienced world in contact with present perception and desired future. In a letter to his first wife, a young Berrigan wrote, "I people my poems with nostalgia. They are in part my bright land" (*Dear Sandy,* p. 33).

Berrigan's work most often resembles that of Frank O'Hara, in whom Berrigan found a con-tinual model. As his own work gained attention, he was proud to be associated with the New York School of poetry, which counted among its first generation O'Hara, John Ashbery, Kenneth Koch, and James Schuyler. (Berrigan is regularly known, alongside Ron Padgett, Joe Brainard, and Anne Waldman, as the most prominent member of its "second generation".) Despite this common association, it may be more accurate to regard New York City and the New York School as hubs from which Berrigan's poetic activity, persona, and influence gathered strength to address far-flung poets, poetic schools, and individual readers. While Berrigan's friend and fellow poet Edward Dorn noted that Berrigan's "'failing' was that his subject matter was limited too often to his friends, or circle," it is possible, Dorn hints, to read this very "limitation [as] his greatest strength" (Waldman, ed., *Nice to See You,* p. 178). The narrow focus of Berrigan's poems models inclusivity on a small scale, but simultaneously generates the centripetal force to imagine a more

TED BERRIGAN

complete poetic community in which, as David Shapiro puts it, Berrigan would become "part of a circle whose circumference is everywhere" (*Nice to See You*, p. 227).

Born on November 15, 1934, in Providence, Rhode Island, to Margaret Dugan Berrigan and Edmund Joseph Berrigan, Edmund Joseph "Ted" Berrigan, Jr., was the eldest of four children. His father was an engineer with the Ward Baking Company plant, and his mother worked for the public schools lunch program. Berrigan attended Catholic schools and spent a year at the Dominican-run Providence College before dropping out to join the army, his grades having been quite low. In the sixteen months he spent in Korea in 1954–1955, he heard one gunshot from his tent, but otherwise, he told Ron Padgett, he saw no combat at all. Upon returning to the United States, he settled in Tulsa, Oklahoma.

Tulsa made an unlikely launching point for such a worldly poet but managed to do just that. The city was, like Providence, heavily Catholic, and even more "square" (Padgett, p. 6). And so was Berrigan when he moved there, an army reservist with a car, a job in a music store, and, at one point, a Baptist nurse for a girlfriend. Nevertheless, from a veteran who made his bed every day and rarely drank, Berrigan would start to become, in Tulsa, the inveterate all-night conversationalist, heavy drinker, and pill taker whose image better matched the pace of the downtown New York scene. Much of this transformation Berrigan owed to the friends he made among Tulsa's poets and artists. Three Central High School students—Ron Padgett, Dick Gallup, and Joe Brainard—would usher the older Berrigan into the poetry and art world; when he met them at the age of twenty-four, he had no idea that the friendships—maintained through artistic collaboration, joint publishing ventures, and a lifestyle on the margins of society—would last the rest of his life.

In spite of his young age, Padgett had already made inroads with New York–based poets through his editorship of a small magazine he called the *White Dove Review*. Just after meeting Padgett in a Tulsa bookstore in 1959, Berrigan began publishing in the *Review,* which also printed work by Jack Kerouac, Allen Ginsberg, Paul Blackburn, and LeRoi Jones. Before long, Berrigan began corresponding with these poets and setting his sights on New York. Between the established poets he met there and the tight-knit circle of Midwest transplants, Berrigan's career was nourished from the start by an intimate link between writing and friendship.

Berrigan had spent his years in the Midwest studying at the University of Tulsa on the GI bill, and while he noted the influence of professors there, his friends solidified his desire to be a poet who stood apart from the academic system's "old hierarchy" (Waldman, ed., p. 227). After completing his B.A. degree in 1959, Berrigan wrote an M.A. thesis titled "Bernard Shaw's Treatment of the Individual's Problem of How to Live As Illustrated in Four Plays." This study focused on a theme that would motivate much of Berrigan's poetry: the tensions of being simultaneously in touch with reality and at odds with his environment. In a voice that parodies Frank O'Hara's, Berrigan's "Personal Poem #9" depicts a New York life far beneath his expectations:

I think I was thinking
when I was ahead I'd be somewhere like Perry Street
erudite dazzling slim and badly-loved
contemplating my new book of poetry
to be printed in simple type on old brown paper
feminine marvelous and tough

(*Collected Poems of Ted Berrigan [CP]*, p. 118)

When Tulsa University mailed Berrigan his master's degree in 1962, he was already living in New York City. He returned it with a note abjuring the accolade: "I am master of no art" (*CP*, p. 20). Berrigan's confident proclamation of his novitiate status owed much to a shift he had undergone in Tulsa. In school, Berrigan had discovered George Bernard Shaw and William Shakespeare and would write his most renowned book, *The Sonnets* (1964), in conscious pursuit of the bard's greatness; encouraged by his friends and his own insatiable appetite for reading, Berrigan found inspiration in writers that the

academy ignored, from Thomas Wolfe to Count Korzybski to Jack Kerouac. Moving to New York would mark Berrigan's renewed commitment to self-education under the tutelage of these and other like-minded "masters."

Although his reading list was dominated by men, Berrigan depended heavily on the women in his life, not only as lovers and muses but as collaborators and guides. Like his friend Robert Creeley, Berrigan's literary life was to a certain extent inseparable from his romantic relationships, which he often recalled in the poems. Pat Mitchell, who dated Berrigan in Tulsa and later married Ron Padgett, encouraged Berrigan to enroll in the literature courses where he would discover Shakespeare and Shaw. She introduced him, a completely uninitiated veteran, to the small circle of poets and artists at the university who led him straight to Padgett, Brainard, and Gallup. A young student of Berrigan's at the Madeleine parochial school in Tulsa where Berrigan taught during 1958–1959 became the addressee of the poems of his first book, *A Lily for My Love* (1959). The illicit relationship forced Berrigan to leave Tulsa for several months, and in subsequent years, following William Carlos Williams' example with the 1909 collection *Poems*, Berrigan would destroy as many copies of the sentimental volume as he could. The precedent was set, however: Berrigan's erotic life would spur him to write, and to write about love even when the simplicity of the theme ran counter to his counterparts' edgy aesthetics.

In 1962, already based in New York City, Berrigan traveled to New Orleans and met Sandra Alper. The two were married the same weekend. The drama that ensued—her parents committed her to a mental institution, from which Berrigan "liberated" her and fled to New York—led to an entire volume of letters on subjects personal and aesthetic, and forms the basis of "Personal Poem #9":

I never thought
on the Williamsburg Bridge I'd come so much to
  Brooklyn

just to see lawyers and cops who don't even carry
  guns
taking my wife away and bringing her back

(*CP*, p. 118)

Berrigan wrote most of *The Sonnets* during Sandra's pregnancy with their son, David. "Words for Love," one of his most widely anthologized poems, draws much of its language from letters Berrigan sent to Sandy during her forced hospitalization:

What am I saying?
Only this. My poems do contain
wilde beestes. I write for my Lady
of the Lake. My god is immense, and lonely
but uncowed. I trust my sanity, and I am proud. If
I sometimes grow weary, and seem still, nevertheless
my heart still loves, will break.

(*CP*, p. 116)

Berrigan and Sandy would have one more child, daughter Kate, before separating in 1969, the year he met Alice Notley. He and Notley married in 1972 and had two sons, Anselm and Edmund. Notley wrote that life with Berrigan "consisted of a continuous involvement with poetry … everything we did or said became part of it" (introduction to *Selected Poems,* 1994, p. vii). This "everything" included their rather unconventional family life. Photos from the early 1980s show Berrigan smoking in bed, his wife and their two sons draped over him; Berrigan referred to the boys' bedroom as the "orgy room" in reference to the pornographic murals painted there. Some of Berrigan's best-known poems feature his children. Berrigan composed the last poem of *The Sonnets* on the occasion of David's birth. "In the 51st State," dedicated to his daughter, Kate, bids the children "Au revoir" but adds, "I wouldn't translate that / as 'Goodbye' if I were you." The final lines show Berrigan playing with language even when its content takes on the most serious subjects:

Bon voyage, little ones.
Follow me down
Through the locks. There is no key.

(*CP*, p. 514)

The "master of no art" accepted only one honorific: "They call me, Dad!" (*CP*, p. 573).

Starting out in New York in early 1961, however, Berrigan lived as he had in Tulsa. Impecunious and often lonely, fueled by caffeine and amphetamines, he stayed out nights to read, write, talk, and watch movies with the other Tulsa émigrés. He wrote term papers for Columbia University students to earn money, met the poet Kenneth Koch in his office hours, and started a correspondence with Frank O'Hara. Sheaves of his poems arrived in the mailboxes of small-magazine editors. The pattern would continue the rest of his life: Berrigan voluntarily worked overtime on behalf of the social and literary scene, and in exchange relied on his contacts for sustenance in the form of companionship and small loans. As an economic model, it left Berrigan hovering at the edge of poverty; poetically, the investment bore continual fruit.

Except for a period of time in the late 1960s and early 1970s, when Berrigan taught poetry in U.S. and British universities, New York formed the vibrant backdrop to his prolific writing, consistent publishing, and ceaseless socializing. In Berrigan's posthumously published poem "Insterstices," the rhythms of city life imbue Berrigan's lines with a sense of a human place time-stamped by human measure:

Every day when the sun comes up
I live in the city of New York
Green TIDE behind; pink against blue
Here I am at 8:08 p.m. indefinable ample rhythmic
frame
not asleep, I belong here, I was born, I'm amazed to
be here

(*CP*, p. 612)

While he recounted feeling at first unfit to associate with Ivy League–educated poets and their socialite acquaintances, he rarely shied away from any company. Crashing uptown parties as much for the booze and women as for the luminaries who attended, Berrigan made a name for himself as a personality as well as a poet. Because he devoted himself so seriously to poetry, he endeared himself to the established poets despite what he recognized as his own uncouth, maverick appeal. As Allen Ginsberg put it, he soon became both a "big encourager of Elders and Consul to younger spirits" (*CP*, jacket blurb). In his socializing, teaching, and correspondence, Berrigan would, like O'Hara, gain a reputation as one of the most personally admired and widely loved poets of his time. During a period when divisions among traditions of U.S. poetry often led to fractious personal attacks, Berrigan read and spoke highly of poets as different from each other as Conrad Aiken, Richard Wilbur, Edwin Denby, and Charles Reznikoff. He claimed in an interview, "I like to know all the groups, because that way is the most fun, and the most interesting" (*Talking in Tranquility,* p. 55).

Eschewing other employment, in the late 1960s Berrigan started teaching poetry, first at the St. Mark's Poetry Project (where he taught until 1979) near his home in New York and later during short stints at universities in the United States and England. He held posts at the University of Iowa, University of Michigan, Yale, Northeastern Illinois University, University of Essex, Naropa Institute, Stevens Institute of Technology, and City College of New York. As a teacher, he was "always provocative and serious," one student remembered, and advised students to be students of words that came from the world: "'Most poets are experts in paying infinite attention to their own speech,' he said. 'One must likewise be cognizant and heed the language which reels about everywhere else'" (in Waldman, ed., p. 161). Teaching at the University of Essex in England in 1973–1974, Berrigan helped to publish a small magazine called the *Human Handkerchief* that would gently shift "anti-poetic attitudes on campus" (p. 204). A letter to Tom Clark written during the year wryly sympathized with student life in the provincial town: "It must take lots of pills to go to College here, for certain" (Clark, p. 78).

Wherever he went, Berrigan gained a reputation as an informal teacher, tutor, and mentor. His correspondence and conversation with friends included recommendations for poets to meet and

to read, improvised evaluations of recent poetry, notes on the craft, and advice on publishing.

The story of Berrigan's growing reputation and expanded renown in the late 1960s dovetails with the success of the Poetry Project. Founded in 1966 with grant money from the federal government, and intended to support programming for troubled youth in the city, it quickly became a hub for the downtown poetry scene. With its ongoing reading series held in St. Mark's Church at Second Avenue and Tenth Street, the Project quickly took over the mantle that Lower East Side coffee shops like Les Deux Mégots and Le Metro had held in the early part of the decade. In these "highly social environments," Daniel Kane notes, representatives of "ill-defined and porous poetic 'schools'" had come together to share ideas and take refuge from mainstream culture and its aesthetic ideals (p. 1). Berrigan and Padgett had read often at Le Metro, where they were joined by Allen Ginsberg, Paul Blackburn, Lorenzo Thomas, Diane Wakoski, and Jerome Rothenberg.

Berrigan was a mainstay of the Project from its beginnings. Sunday afternoon readings he hosted at Izzy Young's Folklore Center served as a bridge between the recently ended Le Metro series and the founding of the Project. Just before the Project's official founding, Berrigan introduced John Ashbery, who was reading for the first time in the United States since his return from a decade spent in Paris. Although Berrigan never served as the Project's director, its official leadership often deferred to him as an elder statesman. The workshop in poetry that Berrigan offered in 1966, the Project's first year, marked the start of Berrigan's teaching career and of a series that continues today.

The year 1969 saw several significant changes in Berrigan's life and career. He separated from Sandy Alper; published *Many Happy Returns,* his first trade book following *The Sonnets;* and met Alice Notley, with whom he would spend the rest of his life. During the next five years the two would live all over the country as Ted briefly joined the vibrant poetry community of Bolinas, California (alongside Robert Creeley, Tom Clark, and Joanne Kyger, among others), taught poetry

in positions arranged by friends, and continued to write. Anselm and Edmund were born in Chicago and in England, respectively, before the family returned to New York for good in 1976. By this time, Berrigan had contracted hepatitis, probably owing to his alcoholism, and his poems began to speak more often of illness and of death. Not long after translating Rainer Maria Rilke's famous "Autumn's Day," Berrigan penned his own "Autumn," a short poem of seasonal decline:

Autumn is fun
for these kids
who love me

...

The pills aren't working.

(*CP,* p. 454)

Berrigan's last years were marked increasingly by poor health and by his failure to seek medical help. In her introduction to the 1994 *Selected Poems,* Notley writes that Berrigan had little desire to change his habits—a combination of amphetamines, painkillers, alcohol, and tobacco—or to have his health monitored by doctors, while the couple's financial insecurities gave him an additional excuse for avoiding treatment. Despite the illness, which confined him more and more to his apartment at 101 St. Mark's Place, Berrigan continued to write, to publish, and, most of all, to talk to the visitors and "students" who dropped by. Discoursing liberally on poetry and poetics from his bed, where he lay naked smoking Chesterfields, he resembled a latter-day version of Ezra Pound holding court at St. Elizabeth's hospital some thirty years prior.

An autobiographical poem from the late 1970s ("Look Fred, You're a Doctor, My Problem Is Something Like This") ties his upcoming death to personal development, traced here by means of a geographical progression from Providence to New York. Not unlike Moses surveying the promised land, unable yet to enter into it, the poem presents death as a vista on the horizon that carefully guards its identifying particulars:

Now, there's a new, further
place, whose name I didn't quite catch, and, there-

fore, whose language and rules I can barely
 discern as
up ahead, let alone "what" they might be. It's
1979. I'm 44.

(*CP,* p. 555)

Ted Berrigan died on July 4, 1983, at age forty-eight. The news surprised even those friends who had seen the end coming. Padgett had penned elegiac lines for Berrigan as early as 1971: "Ted, sorry for you / already flying out into what / really is the end of everything." At the same time, however, "no matter how much he punished his body … he seemed to be impervious" (p. 62). Berrigan's strength and persistence made it too easy to take the poet at his word when he claimed, "I will live / To be 110" (*CP,* p. 515).

Speaking at a memorial service held at St. Mark's Church, where Berrigan had read numerous times for the Poetry Project, Stephen Rodefer acknowledged the common view that Berrigan's death could have been prevented, that "he let himself die," and that his later years had seen a decline in his well-known affability (Padgett, p. 62). In response, he suggested that the arc of Berrigan's life integrates these aspects into its edifying project.

Berrigan's last poem compiles overheard voices from the room next to his own, in which Alice watched a Fred Astaire movie. Its closing lines stage a playful argument in which two unidentified voices—do they belong to Berrigan, Notley, or to one of the film's actors?—posture for the poem's closing final words. As the end-stopped punctuation mark on a career of wit, appropriation, and intimate address, it is fitting that Berrigan allows his own voice to be upstaged:

"You're making a big mistake,
writing a poem,
and not watching this."

*

"Shut up. I'm getting the last lines."
"You are not."

(*CP,* p. 650)

Unable to afford a private plot, the family saw Berrigan interred at Calverton National Cemetery on Long Island.

POETRY

Much like Rilke, who penned most of the *Sonnets to Orpheus* in a span of four days, Ted Berrigan composed the bulk of his most famous and lasting contribution to poetry in less than three months. The story of *The Sonnets,* however, like the content of the sequence itself, spans a longer period of time than the frenetic pace of its composition suggests. The individual poems not only draw lines from Berrigan's (and his friends') earlier work; they also narrate a poet's aesthetic development. The legacy of the volume in Berrigan's life and career sometimes overshadowed his subsequent work, but he continued to announce his pride in the accomplishment in the last years of his life. A 1981 reading at New Langton Arts in San Francisco featured the entire sequence, which Berrigan had just edited for a planned republication, and marked one of the major literary events of the decade and a rekindling of interest in the work.

The Sonnets narrates a gradual transition in both geographic and aesthetic terms. The poems feature their immediate environs—the bohemian enclaves of a seething and enticing metropolis—in startling juxtaposition to the places he had called home in his previous twenty-eight years.

Peopled with the names of Berrigan's friends and lovers, *The Sonnets* creates its own audience, often directly addressing individuals as in a letter. Sonnets II, XVIII, XXX, and XVII contain variations on the phrase "Dear Margie, hello. It is 5:15 a.m.," but the final fifteen sonnets substitute "Ron [Padgett]" and "Chris[tine] Murphy" in the phrase, suggesting the various moments in which these addressees became analogous nodal points in the poet's organization of phenomena. Referencing both the erotic and the literary—two of the central conceptual indices for the sequence—these correspondents become witnesses to the poet's late-night need to record the present moment, "It is 5:15 a.m.," as well as its pasts.

The most acclaimed of the poems in the volume, Sonnet XV, derives its lines from Sonnet LIX, which appears after it. Berrigan constructed the second poem by distributing the older poem's

lines so that consecutive lines are placed as far apart as possible in the new poem. The first two lines of the old poem appear as lines 1 and 14 of the new construction, and lines 3 and 4 appear as lines 2 and 13. Despite the regularity of this pattern of rearrangement, Berrigan claimed that he composed it according to "a feeling I was bringing to" Sonnet LIX, which, "I didn't think … was any good" (New Langton Arts).

Like many of the sonnets, XV mentions friends, celebrities, and poets by name and weaves them into a personal environment where exaggerated emotions take shape in outbursts of adjectives. The poem's first line refers to a collage by Joe Brainard and to the recent death of William Carlos Williams, who had proclaimed the sonnet form dead in America. Although *The Sonnets* incorporate lines from previous work, Berrigan wrote them just following Williams' death in early 1963; as a result, they may be read as an oblique elegy for a poet whose short line-ends and emotional intensity had captured Berrigan's interest, if not his utter devotion. As if offering simultaneously an homage and a challenge to Williams' formal legacy, Berrigan retained the number of lines in the poem but jettisoned its rhyme scheme and meter. John Palatella explains: "A Berrigan sonnet can contain abrupt tonal shifts, disjointed syntax and startling enjambments, and the couplet, if there is one, can appear at the poem's end (its traditional spot) or in its middle. If Williams considered the sonnet a Procrustean box, Berrigan turned it into a Rubik's Cube" (p. 26).

To Libby Rifkin, putting together the fragments of a poem like Sonnet XV becomes a way of "compelling the reader to repeat the mournful process of assembling a whole from fragments" and brings the formally experimental poem "closer to the elegiac tradition than might first appear" (p. 648). For his part, Berrigan regarded the poem, in part, as an elegy for himself: "I often think of this book as having the subtitle 'The Sorrows of Young Werther'" (New Langton Arts). At the age of twenty-nine, Berrigan was already capable of writing lines that more explicitly posit the continuing of poems after the death of their speaker. In her introduction to the

Collected Poems, Alice Notley speaks of the role that "the awkward intensity of inexperience" (p. 3) plays in *The Sonnets* as the work of a young man in a new city; at the same time, the poems' frequent return to a consciousness of temporality and finality that belies its author's youth ensures the work's enduring appeal.

In addition to frequent appearances in anthologies, including, as early as 1973, the *Norton Anthology of Modern Poetry,* individual lines from the sonnets became mottoes, titles, and catchphrases for poets and artists within Berrigan's circle. More than its individual lines, however, what Berrigan called the "method" of *The Sonnets* accounts for its long influence on U.S. poetry. Finding the most experimental poets of his generation "already traditionalists" by 1963, and seeking out a "formal breakthrough," Berrigan began generating poems from a host of other poetic sources that included his own and his friends' old (and sometimes discarded) works (New Langton Arts). For the first six poems of the sequence, in which he discovered the process, Berrigan culled lines at random from a chosen group of poems (the sources included his own poems as well as those of Arthur Rimbaud and his friend Dick Gallup). He arranged these into units of fourteen lines, claiming in his journal that he "wrote by ear, and automatically" (*CP,* p. 668). In Padgett's terms, the method of using lines from other writers was "a license granted by Duchamp, Tzara, Arp, and Ernst (and later, Burroughs)" (in Waldman, ed., p. 10). Alice Notley notes that Joe Brainard's artistic work, often done in collaboration with Berrigan—the two made collages—also led Berrigan to the concept of collage that would carry *The Sonnets.*

Later poems further "dismantle" and rearrange Berrigan's own translations of Rimbaud and Rilke as well as quotations from his own letters and conversations. The recurrence of lines from previous sonnets in the later ones creates an insistent, if often dissonant, semantic and sonic echo that Libby Rifkin calls "reverb" (p. 649).

Beginning with its title, *The Sonnets* both disrupts and maintains contact with the form's traditional sources. In a spirit of sidelong grandiosity, he claimed to follow Shakespeare's

model by exploring the social arenas of friendship and conflicted love. Shakespeare's Sonnet LV contrasts the immortality of poetry with the ephemerality of physical existence: "your praise shall still find room / Even in the eyes of all posterity / That wear this world out to the ending doom." Berrigan's first sonnet calls upon the same rhyme, and on the conceit of poetry as a domestic space. In contrast to Shakespeare's enclosed room, however, Berrigan exposes his poem to the elements, where they break apart:

Is there room in the room that you room in?
Upon his structured tomb:

...

We are the sleeping fragments of his sky,
Wind giving presence to fragments.

(*CP*, p. 29)

Like Shakespeare, Berrigan transforms the sonnet form in order to subsume it under his own manipulations. Instead of metrical substitutions in a regular, iambic pentameter meter, the interpolation of extrinsically sourced lines disrupting the single speaker's continuity of thought marks the constitutive formal innovation of *The Sonnets*. Within each poem, line-ends mark otherwise unpunctuated semantic borders. The formal term "sonnet" is retained to call attention to the possibilities latent within a fourteen-line poem for incorporating disparate elements into an albeit provisional unit. As if fourteen lines measured the proper time in which an instantaneous now could register and arrange the marks of the past in advance of an approaching future that would again disperse them, the sonnet form—characterized in both the Italian and Shakespearean forms by its "turn" or "volta"—becomes, in Berrigan's hands, a measure of an individual's capacity to incorporate texts that are temporally and spatially extrinsic to it and then dispense an image of them watermarked by the perceiving and registering body.

The body itself bears a considerable burden both in Berrigan's poetry and in the conditions to which Berrigan submitted his own body while writing it. Infamous for his substance use and for subsisting on a diet of Pepsi and hamburgers, the intense physicality and sexuality of the early

poems does not recede so much as find itself joined by a concern with poor health and death in the later work. Charles Bernstein, taking up this question in the months following Berrigan's death, accounts for the poet's self-harm by referring to the demands of his poetics. "Berrigan's writing poses the startling fact of writing's lethal and consuming importance in requiring the yielding of body and mind to its inexorable priority" (in Waldman, ed., p. 155).

It is no coincidence, then, that Berrigan chooses translations of Arthur Rimbaud as source material for the opening poems of *The Sonnets*. Rimbaud's brief poetic career, followed by years of exile, dissipation, and silence, parallels, in a way, that of Berrigan. Maurice Blanchot writes of Rimbaud that "while still alive, he had poetry cut out of him" (*The Work of Fire*, p. 154); such a process happened for Berrigan, but not all at once. Just as the poems shuttle between disparate times and voices, so Berrigan's life and career alternate rapidly between the silent, anti-poetic disavowals of artistic possibility implicit in his drug and alcohol use and the outspoken, unceasing affirmations of poetic community and efficacy. Returning to the sea, and to a moment when possibility mingles with its demise, in Sonnets LXXVI Berrigan draws on his translation of Rimbaud's "Le bateau ivre" for words to depict his poetic career, in this poem viewed as a ship just beginning its launch. By composing new poems from parts of old ones and continually remaking the poems within the sonnets as versions of their predecessors, Berrigan drastically altered the traditional conception of writing as well as the experience of reading. From the poet's side, this process of "writing the same work into itself" made a body of poems like a self-sustaining "machine," an apparatus that generated its own future at each moment by recombining its own (and extrinsic) pasts (New Langton Arts). Unlike pure automatic writing, Berrigan joined the machinery, operating it by arranging the appropriated fragments according to what Renny Pritikin calls "the mechanics of [his] inspiration" (in Waldman, ed., p. 24).

Berrigan had used his own publishing imprint, *C,* to publish the first edition of *The Son-*

nets in 1964, in an edition of about four hundred copies. Padgett typed the stencils and Brainard designed the cover for the mimeographed and stapled edition. As Berrigan himself gained notoriety in New York's Lower East Side literary and artistic scene, in part because of *C* magazine and in part because of his ceaseless public pursuit of friends and listeners, *The Sonnets*' reputation grew. The 1967 republication by Grove Press increased their audience and garnered Berrigan some critical attention, though no major publication reviewed it. It was not until the year 2000, when Penguin released an edition of *The Sonnets* edited by Alice Notley, that the volume, which *Publishers Weekly* called "a midcentury classic," received the attention many argued it had deserved for more than thirty-five years.

The Sonnets' afterlife in contemporary poetry continues to spark debate and adulation among practitioners of experimental and post-avant poetries in North America. Charles Bernstein notes a struggle between what he sees as *The Sonnets*' "explicit rejection of the psychological 'I' as a locus of the poem's meaning" and a tendency among Berrigan's readers to elevate even the fragmented biographical references in the text to primary significance (in Waldman, ed., p. 154). If anything, he writes, the work's "permutational use of the same phrases in different sequences and its inclusion of external or found language" uses the "broken shards" of a method deriving from confessional poetry in order to "build a structure with altogether different architectural principles" (p. 154).

Even if the sonnets cannot provide the biographical index that some of their lines seem to promise or to seek ("Tell me now, again, who I am"), the book cemented Berrigan's poetic life and style for the following two decades in a way he recognized. Reading the entire sequence in 1981, he admitted a different link between the writing and the life: "It was by writing this ... that I became the person that I am here" (New Langton Arts).

Between the first edition of *The Sonnets* and his next full-fledged book, *Many Happy Returns,* published in 1969, Berrigan wrote in multiple genres and published prolifically in various formats. These included self-published mimeographed works like *Some Things,* a collaboration with Padgett and Brainard, and *Seventeen* (circa 1964), a set of plays he and Padgett wrote in a matter of weeks. For a set of silkscreens titled *10 Things I Do Every Day* (1967), Berrigan's handwriting figured as part of the artwork accompanying images drawn by George Schneeman, who recalls that "Ted didn't feel disadvantaged in working visually" (Fischer, ed., p. 29).

Small magazines continued to play a large part in his career, as they had from the start. He sent his own prolific work and collaborations to Tom Clark, who was poetry editor of the *Paris Review* and also editor of a series of small magazines. Lewis Warsh and Anne Waldman, longtime friends, published Berrigan's poems in *Angel Hair Magazine* and the *World* (which served as the journal for the Poetry Project), and Warsh, with Bernadette Mayer, included his poems often in *United Artists Journal*. During the 1960s, before his work had garnered the attention it would after the *The Sonnets* reached a wider audience with its 1967 republication, small magazines and chapbooks extended Berrigan's reputation to like-minded poets across the country.

After he had accumulated enough material for a book, Berrigan went about the process of constructing it with conscious deliberation. As if in ironic agreement with Wallace Stevens' remark to William Carlos Williams that "a book is a damned serious affair," Berrigan took great pleasure in bringing the individual poems he had penned under the sway of various reading materials, emotions, and events under a single banner. Because the books were published in small editions, often edited by Berrigan's friends, he was able to include drawings or paintings from Joe Brainard, George Schneeman, and Fairfield Porter. Many of the books featured covers especially designed by their publishers in collaboration with Berrigan.

The 1966 volume *Bean Spasms* (republished by Granary Books in late 2012) exemplifies Berrigan's collaborative effort: the poems, inspired by George Schneeman's images, feature work that Berrigan shared and wrote alongside

Ron Padgett and Joe Brainard over a span of several years. Berrigan's portion depicts his wandering and "wondering" through the city, punning salaciously on New York's art galleries as "well hung," and haughtily affirming his own observations with an insistent energy driven in equal parts by mockery and pleasure:

> The rock&roll songs of this earth
> commingling absolute joy AND
> incontrovertible joy of intelligence
> certainly can warm
> can't they? YES!
> and they do.
>
> (*CP*, p. 158)

Aesthetically, the decade, which marked the rising renown of the Lower East Side arts scene more generally, saw Berrigan produce work based on compositional methods like those of *The Sonnets* as well as more strictly lyrical efforts. Many of these poems pioneer a principal of "composition by field" modeled on Charles Olson's work: these poems take up the entirety of the page and use the white space between words and lines as an element of the poem itself. William Burroughs, whose use of the "cut-up" method to compose prose by selecting passages at random from other authors, influenced such poems as "A Boke," in which Berrigan selected lines from a long article James Dickey wrote for the *New Yorker* about a reading tour. Berrigan's version mocks Dickey's colloquial haughtiness:

> The
> applause is long and loud, as if he were
> a Beatle. He reaches a stage,
> mounts, looks at the last of all clocks,
> and leaves. It is 5:15 a.m. It is
> time. He gets up out of bed and stumbles just
> as he steps down from the stage into a
> wave of feathery sweatered girls, a memorable
> thing. No doubt. He gives the best reading of his
> life, one that will shortly thereafter
> have entered a twilight state characterized
> by fantastic energy.
>
> (*CP*, p. 103)

In contrast to the poems of the early 1960s, Berrigan's efforts in the following decade increased his proficiency with the long poem. Aiming to create the rhythms of a mind in active participation with the city life and artistic scene around him, poems like "Train Ride" and "Tambourine Life" continued to address friends and personal concerns by means of allusion, quotation, and conversation, but their meandering continuity permitted Berrigan to loosen *The Sonnets*' constraints on the formal similarity of individual poems. As a result, the poem builds an even more uniform impression from increasingly disparate parts. Kenneth Koch, whom a young Berrigan had met and interviewed in 1961, remembered the poem as an influence on his own work because it managed to be "ahead of everything—absolutely casual, ordinary, and momentary-seeming, without joking, mystery, or false dazzle, and full of buoyancy, sweetness, and high spirits" (in Waldman, ed., p. 125).

For poets already sympathetic to the first generation of New York School poets, Berrigan's work distinguishes itself by an even larger range of content, diction, and method. Jocular asides shade into reverie, conversational diatribes abut lyrical interludes, and aleatory methods of cut-up and appropriation leave room, at times, for lines composed in the contemplative mode. That Berrigan, following his New York School elders, loosened the belt of poetry's high-art status by an additional notch tells only one part of the story. Like O'Hara, he also sought to tighten poetry's hold on the written and writing body as, beset by various obstacles, it avoids or makes contact with others in the physical world. For a poet writing of his provenance and temperament, the word "love" appears frequently in Berrigan's work. The late poem "Cento: A Note on Philosophy," dedicated to Pat Mitchell, borrows a line from O'Hara's early poem "To the Harbormaster" as it puzzles through the conflict between thinking and feeling, past love and its present memory. In so doing, the poem marks the path of love in Berrigan's work as a difficult oscillation between loving people by means of other poems and loving poems at the expense of actual persons:

> Not to mention the chief thing
> We think by feeling. What is there to know?
> Bouncing a red rubber ball in the veins

Though my ship was on the way it got caught in
   some moorings

...

Questions, oh, I hope they do not find you
I go on loving you like water, but
I am in love with poetry. Every way I turn
I think I am bicycling across an Africa of green and
   white fields
Into a symbol.

                         (*CP*, p. 443)

A chief project of Berrigan's last years involved him, once again, in collaboration. Ken and Ann Mikolowski, editors of the Detroit-based Alternative Press, sent Berrigan five hundred blank postcards. The postcard poems he produced in response featured the title on the front and a short poem on the back and were addressed and sent out with the publisher's press packets. During the process, Berrigan decided to consider the poems part of a book. Alice Notley edited them according to his instructions, and the resultant work, *A Certain Slant of Sunlight* (1988), contained one hundred short poems selected from more than two hundred he composed for the postcard series. As before, Berrigan drew on the lines of friends and acquaintances, often soliciting them to write the lines directly on the postcards. Certain poems ("Salutation," "Postcard," and "Ass-face") express anger toward unnamed friends, but, more often than the poems of the previous decade, these poems speak tenderly to people and events in Berrigan's present life. The first stanza of "Anselm" speaks to his ten-year-old son, who would go on to direct the Poetry Project:

it is a well-lit afternoon
across the incredible static of time-space-language
reading a book
"to be born again"
between bouts
through two layers of glass
I call your name.

                         (*CP*, p. 621)

POETIC COMMUNITY

The poetry scene of New York's Lower East Side attracted Berrigan in part because it so seam-lessly and vigorously integrated poetry with social life. More than their American modernist forebears, whose travels and extrapoetic careers kept them geographically and aesthetically distinct, the establishment of New York City as a destination for both U.S. and exiled European avant-garde artists in the 1920s through the 1940s gave midcentury poets access to close friendships and collaborators. Modeled on a tight-knit circle of abstract expressionist painters, and anchored by Frank O'Hara's gregarious personality, poets of the first generation of the New York School wrote, read, and published together. Perhaps more importantly, they also lived, slept, and drank together; in so doing, they coauthored an urban text that incorporated flattery, mockery, gossip, intrigue, and diatribe into the fabric of poems.

Berrigan had discovered the members of the New York School's first generation through Padgett's small magazine, the *White Dove Review*. As a result, by the time he moved to New York, he had already accepted a model of poetic work that would fuel his efforts for more than two decades. Unlike O'Hara, who had written poems from an early age, Berrigan developed as a poet with help from his friends. Reading his poems to friends and sending them to contacts near and far, Berrigan entered his work into the public sphere from the moment of its conception. For Berrigan, poetry as a privileged form of communication "between friends" was more than an expedient function of a social milieu in which poets could safely nourish their outsider status; rather, it laid the groundwork for a serious intervention in prevailing aesthetic norms.

In the spirit of O'Hara's "Personism: A Manifesto," which puts "the poem squarely between the poet and the person," Berrigan takes the occasion of the poem as an opportunity to address, describe, or communicate with a specific person. In "Our Friends," a central section of his long poem "Train Ride," written for Joe Brainard, Berrigan caricatures their mutual acquaintances:

The grotesque John Ashbery of
the bad character
The silly boring Kenneth Koch
The frumpy Jane Freilicher

TED BERRIGAN

The Pain-in-the-Ass Larry
Fagin
The whining Jim Carroll

(CP, p. 274)

Although Ed Dorn would say that this emphasis on his own friends "limited" Berrigan, he would also say that "limitation" itself gave him "humility, possibly his greatest strength" (in Waldman, ed., p. 178). Even a fragment like "Our Friends" demonstrates this humility. Following his mocking invective, Berrigan directs his addressee to respond: "(Now You do some)." Thirteen line-length blanks mark a space within Berrigan's poem for a rejoinder to its characterizations. Although rarely so explicitly as in "Our Friends," many of Berrigan's poems invite participation. Reading his friends' work quite literally gave Berrigan his *materia poetica,* since appropriation of lines originally composed by Padgett, Dick Gallup, and others would stand as one of Berrigan's trademark compositional methods, his own personal challenge to a single-speaker paradigm that leaves lyric open to charges of solipsism and hermetic enclosure.

The New York School gives U.S. poetry its exemplary representative of what Lytle Shaw calls (in the title of his 2006 book on Frank O'Hara) "the poetics of coterie"; Berrigan, whom Libby Rifkin anoints "a producer not only of poetic collages but of poetic coteries" (p. 642), stands as the most ardent guardian of the circle's spirit and integrity. As he came to play a more central role in the Lower East Side poetry scene throughout the 1960s and 1970s, Berrigan followed his elders' example and amplified it: his relentless pursuit of friends, lovers, collaborators, and interlocutors imbued the scene with a new urgency. Rikfin's characterization of Berrigan's elegiac aims in Sonnet XV applies to his poetics more generally. But instead of mourning the fragility of the speaker's voice—the "teeming brain" and "magic hand" that Keats so feared would cease to be—Berrigan laments the fact that death consigns others to an unreliable and inattentive internal witness:

The heart stops briefly when someone dies, one
massive slow stroke as someone passes

from your outside life to your inside,
& then
everything continues
sanely

(CP, pp. 300–301)

Berrigan made use of several different genres to test out the potential for writing to establish close ties. As Rifkin points out, in addition to collaborations in visual art, cartoons, and theater, Berrigan embraced the interview as a means for demonstrating the potential of conversation to achieve the status of art. In addition to giving numerous interviews of his own (often to his own friends, and often while high), he also made a pilgrimage to interview Jack Kerouac for the *Paris Review*. Kerouac's wife tried to keep Berrigan and his cohort of friends from entering the house upon their arrival, afraid that they would tempt the aging author to drink. When Berrigan suggests a revision to a haiku Kerouac has recited during the interview, Kerouac responds, "You got the right idea there, O'Hara!" (p. 89).

Berrigan loved the genre so much that some of the interviews for which he took credit never actually took place. As Tom Clark relates, in the mid-1960s Berrigan took the liberty of fabricating an entire interview with John Cage by interspersing his own jokes with lines cribbed from a published interview given by the Spanish playwright Fernando Arrabal. Not long after it was published in Peter Schjeldahl's *Mother,* the "interview," to Berrigan's great delight, won a $1,000 prize judged by George Plimpton, the famous socialite and then-editor of the *Paris Review*.

Berrigan worried at times that the elite educational backgrounds of his elders in the New York poetry scene would relegate him to the sidelines: O'Hara, Ashbery, and Koch were all Harvard men. At times, Berrigan's famous confidence warred with a painful fear that his dependence on elders revealed his inferiority to them. In response, Berrigan's mentoring of younger poets both shored up his self-regard and revealed a faith in a more democratic poetic camaraderie. As Berrigan made no secret of his reliance on friends for money, he also went out of his way to support them in return, and to find

aid for poets in distress. (He was fond of quoting Damon Runyon's catchphrase "Get the Money!") Berrigan's oeuvre speaks, albeit casually and unsystematically, to the relationship between artistic life and money more frequently than any poet since Wallace Stevens. "Train Dreams" casts money as an obstacle to social harmony: "I like to give people / money.... But it's socially awkward that / some people for almost no reason / have money, & some don't" (*CP*, p. 262). Lines written with Alice Notley give vent to frustration that poetry rarely pays: "You'll do good if you play it like you're / not getting paid. // But you'll do better if the motherfuckers pay you" (*CP*, p. 568). Hovering on the edge of poverty, the couple most often had to settle for doing "good."

In his last years, as Berrigan's life became more and more confined to his apartment and some of his earlier friendships grew strained, younger poets sought him out for assistance, teaching, and mentoring. One of them, Tom Savage, remembers Berrigan arranging for him to move out of an unsafe neighborhood in Brooklyn and then, when the new apartment burned, hosting him for several weeks in his own home. Holding no official post, Berrigan served as an "adviser, father-figure, confidant and fear shrinker" for poets whose rejection of mainstream culture and its opportunities for poets owed much to Berrigan's example (Waldman, ed., p. 159).

Berrigan's care and concern for other poets often manifested as an extension of his own prolific publishing. Reading widely, and often outside the bounds of his experimental scene's accepted tastes, Berrigan doggedly spoke out for poets he discovered and enjoyed. He praised Richard Wilbur and Ogden Nash, two poets far from the Lower East Side's aesthetic. Taking up Ezra Pound's banner, Berrigan championed the work of lesser-known poets like David Schubert, F. T. Prince, and Charles Reznikoff, and worked to see their pieces in print. Shortly after reading all of Edwin Denby's available work, Berrigan devoted a complete issue of *C* to the reclusive poet and dance critic; the issue drew attention to his work and led to the publication of his collected poems a few years later.

LEGACY

As a result of Berrigan's liberal praise and refusal to abide by the bounds of any school's accepted taste, contemporary poetry's debt to his poetics extends beyond any single style. His close friend Anne Waldman described her own poetry as "ponderous" and distant before "Ted Berrigan burst in haranguing, breaking the narratives, taking issue with 'message'" ("Introduction: Angel Hair Feature"). In addition to her own smart, feminist poems and experimental prose, Waldman's direction of Naropa's Jack Kerouac School of Disembodied Poetics in Boulder, Colorado, has given Berrigan's work a steady readership of students in the years since his death.

Eileen Myles, who studied with Berrigan and Notley at the Poetry Project and then went on to be its director, carries the baton of Berrigan's confrontational lexical audacity in her autobiographical, feminist, and political poetics. But even poets too young to have known Berrigan personally find, especially in *The Sonnets,* a style of poetic practice that carries forward elements of traditional lyric and splices them with experimental methods. By repeating phrases at intervals throughout an extended sequence of short poems, Ben Lerner's *Mean Free Path* (2010) creates the "reverb" or echo that gave *The Sonnets* their sonic intensity. His use of enjambment to shift what Berrigan called the line's "thought" without disrupting its syntax marks a strategy for maintaining a poem's continuity without prioritizing a single speaker's meditative agenda.

Perhaps nothing speaks more substantially to Berrigan's role as a generational cornerstone of New York poetry than the fact that his sons Anselm and Edmund also took up careers in poetry. Along with their mother, the two edited Berrigan's *Collected Poems,* whose publication in 2005 brought numerous out-of-print and hard-to-find collections to the attention of American readers. Writing for the *Boston Phoenix,* fellow poet William Corbett notes that the volume's breadth convinces readers that Berrigan's later work, seen for the first time alongside his "extraordinary debut," unites the parts of the oeuvre into a "body in literal presence." If, as Charles Bernstein suggests, Berrigan's work

exemplifies "writing against the body," the *Collected Poems* exhibits the tensions at work in any reading of a self-divided body. In the accepted absence of a self to be fixed in time or place, "Red Shift" (*CP*, p. 516) turns to the substitutive potential of pronouns and the productive possibilities of disguise:

> I'm only pronouns, & I am all of them, & I didn't
> ask for this
>   You did
> I came into your life to change it & it did so & now
> nothing
>   will ever change
> That, and that's that.
> Alone & crowded, unhappy fate, nevertheless
>   I slip softly into the air
> The world's furious song flows through my costume.

Selected Bibliography

WORKS OF TED BERRIGAN

POETRY

A Lily for My Love: 13 Poems. [Providence, R.I.]: [n.p.], 1959.

The Sonnets: New York: Lorenz and Ellen Gude, 1964; New York: Grove Press, 1967; New York: United Artists, 1982; New York: Penguin, 2000.

Many Happy Returns. New York: Corinth Press, 1969.

In the Early Morning Rain. London: Cape Goliard, 1970.

Train Ride (February 18th, 1971): For Joe. New York: Vehicle Editions, 1971.

Clear the Range. New York: Adventures in Poetry/Couch House South, 1977.

So Going Around Cities: New and Selected Poems, 1958–1979. Berkeley, Calif.: Blue Wind Press, 1980.

A Certain Slant of Sunlight. Edited by Alice Notley. Oakland, Calif.: O Books, 1988.

COLLECTIONS

Selected Poems. Edited by Aram Saroyan. New York: Penguin, 1994.

Collected Poems of Ted Berrigan. Edited by Alice Notley with Anselm Berrigan and Edmund Berrigan. Berkeley: University of California Press, 2005.

The Selected Poems of Ted Berrigan. Edited by Alice Notley, Anselm Berrigan, and Edmund Berrigan. Berkeley: University of California Press, 2011.

COLLABORATIONS

Seventeen. With Ron Padgett. New York: Privately published, 1964.

Some Things. With Ron Padgett and Joe Brainard. New York: C, 1964.

Bean Spasms. With Ron Padgett and Joe Brainard. New York: Kulchur Press, 1967; New York: Granary Books, 2012.

Doubletalk. With Anselm Hollo. Iowa City, Iowa: Privately published, 1969.

Memorial Day. With Anne Waldman. New York: Poetry Project, 1971; New York: Funhouse Press, 2005.

Back in Boston Again. With Ron Padgett and Tom Clark. New York: Telegraph Books, 1972.

Yo-Yo's with Money. With Harris Schiff. Henniker, N.H.: United Artists, 1979.

PROSE

"Jack Kerouac, The Art of Fiction No. 41." *Paris Review* 43:60–105 (summer 1968).

"The Business of Writing Poetry." In *Talking Poetics from Naropa Institute* . Vol. 1. Edited by Anne Waldman and Marilyn Webb. Boulder, Colo.: Shambhala, 1978–1979.

Talking in Tranquility: Interviews with Ted Berrigan. Edited by Stephen Ratcliffe and Leslie Scalapino. Bolinas and Oakland, Calif.: Avenue B and O Books, 1991.

Dear Sandy, Hello: Letters from Ted to Sandy Berrigan. Minneapolis, Minn.: Coffee House, 2010.

AUDIO RECORDINGS

"Ted Berrigan." *PennSound*. http://writing.upenn.edu/pennsound/x/Berrigan.php.

"*The Sonnets*: New Langton Arts, San Francisco, June 24, 1981." *PennSound*. http://media.sas.upenn.edu/pennsound/authors/Berrigan/Sonnets-Singles/Berrigan-Ted_The-Sonnets-with-introduction_New-Langton_1981.mp3.

Audio CD accompanying *All Poets Welcome: The Lower East Side Poetry Scene in the 1960s,* by Daniel Kane. Berkeley: University of California Press, 2003. (Includes Berrigan readings of "Memorial Day," Sonnets I–III, and "A Final Sonnet.")

PAPERS

Ted Berrigan Papers, 1961–1975. Rare Book and Manuscript Library, Columbia University.

Ted Berrigan Papers, undated, 1962–1983. Archives and Special Collections, Thomas J. Dodd Research Center, University of Connecticut.

TED BERRIGAN

Ted Berrigan Papers, 1963–1964. Special Collections Research Center, Syracuse University.

Ted Berrigan and Alice Notley Collection, 1954–1983. Manuscript, Archives, and Rare Book Library, Emory University.

CRITICAL AND BIOGRAPHICAL STUDIES

Champion, Miles. "The Poetry Project, 1966–." Poetry Project. http://poetryproject.org/history/insane-podium.

Clark, Tom. *Late Returns: A Memoir of Ted Berrigan.* Bolinas, Calif.: Tombouctou, 1985.

Corbett, William. "Fast and Furious: Ted Berrigan's *Collected Poems.*" *Boston Phoenix,* October 14–20, 2005. http://www.bostonphoenix.com/boston/arts/books/documents/05024263.asp/.

Fischer, Aaron, ed. *Ted Berrigan: An Annotated Checklist.* New York: Granary Books, 1998.

Foster, Edward. *Code of the West: A Memoir of Ted Berrigan.* Boulder, Colo.: Rodent Press, 1994.

Hennessey, Michael S. "Recovering Memorial Day." *Jacket2,* May 28, 2012. http://jacket2.org/commentary/recovering-memorial-day.

Huntsperger, David. *Procedural Form in Postmodern American Poetry: Berrigan, Antin, Silliman, and Hejinian.* New York: Palgrave MacMillan, 2010.

Januzzi, Marisa. "Ted Berrigan." *Talisman* 12:211–215 (spring 1994).

Kane, Daniel. *All Poets Welcome: The Lower East Side Poetry Scene in the 1960s.* Berkeley: University of California Press, 2003.

Notley, Alice. Introduction to *Selected Poems,* by Ted Berrigan. Edited by Aram Saroyan. New York: Penguin, 1994.

Padgett, Ron. *Ted: A Personal Memoir of Ted Berrigan.* Great Barrington, Mass.: Figures, 1993.

Palatella, John. "La Vie de Bohème." *Nation,* January 23, 2006, p. 26.

Poetry in Motion. Directed by Ron Mann. Home Vision Entertainment, 2002. DVD. (Documentary film featuring Berrigan and other poets, originally released in 1982.)

Rifkin, Libbie. *Career Moves: Olson, Creeley, Zukofsky, Berrigan, and the American Avant-Garde.* Madison: University of Wisconsin Press, 2010.

"The Sonnets." *Publishers Weekly.* October 2, 2000. http://www.publishersweekly.com/978-0-14-058927-6.

Thilleman, Tod. "The Berrigan Case." *Talisman* 12:209–210 (spring 1994).

Waldman, Anne. "Introduction: Angel Hair Feature." *Jacket* 16 (March 2002). http://jacketmagazine.com/16/ah1-wald.html.

Waldman, Anne, ed. *Nice to See You: An Homage to Ted Berrigan.* Minneapolis, Minn.: Coffee House, 1991.

Watten, Barrett. "Homage to Lee Crabtree." BarrettWatten.net, February 2, 2010. http://http://barrettwatten.net/texts/entry-08-homage-to-lee-crabtree/2010/02/.

KAY BOYLE

(1902—1992)

Bridget T. Chalk

KAY BOYLE'S LIFE and work spanned the twentieth century. An American expatriate considered a junior member of the Lost Generation, she was an eyewitness to the boiling tensions of the 1930s that led to World War II. After persecution under McCarthyism in the 1950s, she began an academic career and threw herself into the civil rights protests of the following decade in California, intensifying a lifelong interest in contemporary politics that would last until her death in 1992.

A more valuable study than her life, however, is the body of work she produced from her incomparable vantage points. Her formally experimental early novels and stories are penetrating portraits of complex gender dynamics and the range of social pressures on the individual. Her women in particular, though not exclusively, must come to terms with the extent to which their desires are subject to the strictures of convention. In her later poetry and prose, Boyle engages on the deepest levels with the moral implications of world events and maintains a consistent focus on the individual at sea in the turbulent tides of the twentieth century. Boyle's subjects range from women's disempowerment to American and European racism to the obscure motivations behind the rise of Nazism. Evolving from a modernist style invested in innovative forms and narrative techniques to a more realist and popular approach that reached a larger audience, Boyle's eclectic oeuvre demonstrates a lifelong commitment to exploring the relationship between literature and the modern world, and the individual and society.

A TRAVELING LIFE

Kay Boyle was born in St. Paul, Minnesota, on February 19, 1902, to a wealthy family with a complicated dynamic. Her capitalist grandfather, Jesse Peyton Boyle, dominated his ineffectual son Howard, Boyle's father, and carried on a protracted flirtation with her mother, Katherine. Katherine Boyle was a champion of her daughter's talents from a young age, and instilled in her the idea that she would be a great artist. Her grandfather also indulged her ambitions, financing the production of a little magazine published by Boyle and her sister Janet. The family moved to Philadelphia, where Boyle spent most of her childhood, and then, after the loss of their fortune, to Cincinnati, where she spent her teen years and met her first husband, Richard Brault, a French engineering student.

She and Brault moved to New York in 1922, where they married on June 24 and began their professional lives. While he worked as a meter reader and they lived in squalid conditions, Boyle landed a position working as a secretary for the literary magazine *Broom,* Harold Loeb's avant-garde publication under the editorial direction of Lola Ridge. Ridge, after Boyle's mother, became the second major female influence in Boyle's life and would provide emotional and financial support to her for years to come. Boyle facilitated gatherings sponsored by the magazine, at which, among many other up-and-coming literary celebrities, she met such figures as Marianne Moore, William Carlos Williams, Jean Toomer, and Elinor Wylie. Her poetry appeared in *Broom,* and in these years she continued to hone her skills as a poet, novelist, and short story writer. A consummate networker, Boyle made use of the contacts she made in New York throughout the 1920s and 1930s.

In 1923 Boyle and Brault made a trip to Brittany, France, to visit his family, which unexpectedly evolved into Boyle's seventeen-year

expatriation. After living under the stifling conditions of a traditional French bourgeois family with only her writing and correspondence to keep her from despair, Boyle was thought to have developed tuberculosis and went to the South of France to convalesce and to work with the poet and editor Ernest Walsh, who also suffered from the disease. This liberation from a conservative domestic life into the life of a writer set the stage for Boyle's first great love affair. The gravely ill Walsh, remembered by many as a fiery romantic, began a relationship with Boyle that resulted in her pregnancy with a child who would be born after his death in 1926. After the trauma of Walsh's death, with a baby daughter born out of wedlock and an estranged husband, Boyle found herself at a loss for direction.

She eventually secured a job as a ghostwriter for the memoirs of Gladys Palmer—an Englishwoman whose title by marriage was the Dayang Muda of Sarawak—and moved to Paris in the spring of 1928. Boyle had long had her sights set on the city, populated as it was by the best and brightest writers and artists of her day. During her time in Paris she became the acquaintance or friend of some the familiar names of the heady scene of the 1920s, among them Gertrude Stein, James Joyce, Ernest Hemingway, Robert McAlmon, Sylvia Beach, Man Ray, Harry and Caresse Crosby, and Isadora Duncan's brother Raymond Duncan, whose Greek-themed "back to nature" colony Boyle joined for an unhappy six months. She also met the poet and sculptor Laurence Vail, who would become her second husband on April 2, 1932, following her divorce from Brault and his from the socialite and art patron Peggy Guggenheim.

In 1931 Vail and Boyle left Paris to settle down in Nice, where Boyle wrote and produced three more daughters and Vail provided family money, an arrangement that soon wore on both of them. During this period, Boyle became a well-known writer, negotiated publication deals for herself and other writers, and did some of her best work in short fiction. She published her first three novels, many short stories, and several poems in the late twenties and early thirties, and began a long and fruitful relationship with the *New Yorker*. In 1933 the Vails moved to Austria, where Boyle witnessed the economic and political descent of the Austrian people. Living in Tyrol, where Nazi youth were lighting fires in the shape of swastikas, Boyle found her next subject for fiction: the conversion of many young Austrians to Nazism—initially, at least, because of the promise of economic recovery, and seemingly divorced from anti-Semitism as a central creed. In the two years they lived there, Boyle wrote two novels, the collection *365 Days* (1936), and numerous short stories. The family left Austria in 1935 for France and settled in Megève, near Mont Blanc.

Writing industriously during the late 1930s, Boyle fell in love with a well-connected, anti-Fascist Austrian nine years her junior, Baron Joseph von Franckenstein, the romantic male prototype in much of her subsequent fiction. As the Nazi onslaught enveloped all of Europe in the war, Boyle, Vail, and the children fled to the United States in August 1941, and Franckenstein was able to follow shortly thereafter. On returning to New York, Boyle was greeted with great acclaim, having become a household name with her stories in publications ranging from the *New Yorker* to *Ladies' Home Journal*. Living in New York with the extended Vail family, she was dispatched to write about military bases and traveled to Colorado, where Franckenstein, who had become an American citizen, was stationed as a member of the U.S. Army. On February 24, 1943, after her divorce from Vail, Boyle and Franckenstein married; they would have a daughter and a son together.

Franckenstein became a war hero for the Americans by infiltrating the enemy with his knowledge of German. Although the quality of some of Boyle's work declined during this period under the pressure of supporting her large family—she began churning out short stories and producing potboiler novels about the French experience of World War II—she became a foreign correspondent for the *New Yorker* in 1946, writing successful articles and short stories about life in postwar Germany while her husband was posted there with the U.S. State Department. As McCarthyism poisoned the American cultural

climate in the early 1950s, however, Boyle and her Austrian husband came under fire: she for being a suspected Communist, he for being married to one and susceptible to corrupting influence. A long and harrowing ordeal began for the couple, during which Franckenstein was dismissed from his State Department post. The ordeal revealed to Boyle her lack of support in the literary community, particularly from the *New Yorker*. She was unceremoniously let go from the magazine and had to rely on testimony and help from other sources in the long legal battle that ensued. During this period she was blacklisted and had great difficulty placing any of her work, owing to the slander on her name as well as the declining quality of her stories. Finally, after Boyle and her husband had become a cause célèbre for the McCarthy witch hunts, the government declared them cleared of all suspicion in 1957. Franckenstein was reinstated to the State Department five years later, but he died of lung cancer soon thereafter, in 1963.

By this time, Boyle had embarked on a teaching career that had led to a post on the English faculty at San Francisco State University. During the 1960s and 1970s Boyle became heavily involved in domestic politics. She was a staunch supporter of civil rights and joined with students in the historic strike of 1968–1969 at San Francisco State, which sought a new curriculum that would embrace the university's diversity and resulted in the establishment of its College of Ethnic Studies. Interestingly, though an outspoken liberal, critic of the war in Vietnam, and proponent of free speech, she explicitly refused to align herself with the feminist movement, which she saw as "separatist." Joan Mellen posits that Boyle's declining reputation, as well as feminist scholars' slowness to rediscover her early-twentieth-century work, can be attributed partially to her antifeminist commentary.

She continued to write poetry, fiction, and prose into her eighties, and her constant need for money drove her to accept countless speaking engagements, visiting teaching positions, and invitations to appear in public even as her health deteriorated. The 1980s saw the reissue of many of her early works by Virago Modern Classics,

which allowed her to remain in the assisted living community where she spent her last years. After lapsing into a coma, she died on December 27, 1992, at age ninety.

BOYLE'S INTERNATIONAL THEME: PLAGUED BY THE NIGHTINGALE, YEAR BEFORE LAST, *AND* MY NEXT BRIDE

Most of Boyle's early novels, written in the late 1920s and 1930s, are largely autobiographical and concern young American women abroad. Continuing in the vein of Henry James, she explores the confrontation of the new American world with the old European world. The novels are episodic, and refuse traditional plot elements such as self-evident beginnings and endings, continuity, climactic scenes, and explanatory devices. Her style notably follows that of D. H. Lawrence, with elaborate lyrical passages evoking the states of emotion and physical feeling driving her characters.

Her first novel, *Process,* was written in the mid-1920s when she first moved to France, but was lost while she was sending it out to publishers. The scholar and biographer Sandra Spanier located a copy of the manuscript in the New York Public Library and published it in 2001 through the University of Illinois Press. The novel focuses on her life in Cincinnati, after her family lost most of their wealth, and her decision to marry and emigrate to France. It serves as a clear first installment to the group of better-known subsequent novels.

Plagued by the Nightingale (1931) continues to follow Boyle's life, depicting a young American girl, Bridget, who follows her new French husband, Nicolas, to his native Brittany, where they take up residence with his family out of necessity while he attempts, unsuccessfully, to begin his career. Further complicating the couple's ability to begin a life together is an inherited disease in the family that is passed down to male children, signs of which Nicolas is beginning to show. Nevertheless, there is a pervasive compulsion to marry and procreate in the novel. In addition to his family's pressure on Bridget and Nicolas to have a child, Nicolas has

three single sisters who want to marry Luc, a blond doctor friend of their other brother. The three girls display different desires: Annick wants to dedicate her life to God, but her father won't allow it; Marthe melodramatically pines with passion for Luc; and Julie, represented as masculine in appearance, suffers from familial neglect. It is eventually revealed that Luc, though "his charm and his beauty were warm generous things that he gave out in handfuls to them all" (*Plagued,* p. 65), loves the married Bridget.

While Bridget initially considers herself to be "deep in the protective palm of [Nicolas'] family" (p. 7), she quickly realizes that individual choices and desires must be sacrificed to the continuation of the line. The intimacy that provides almost womblike comfort at the beginning of the novel gradually transforms into an insidious web of entrapment and claustrophobia. The politics of marriage represented in the novel change from the freely chosen love of Bridget and Nicolas to protracted negotiations of dowries, dangerous fertility, and severe disillusionment. This compulsion strangles the emotional lives and relationships of the characters, and literally kills the eldest daughter, Charlotte, who, though married to her first cousin and warned against another pregnancy by the doctor, insists on bearing a sixth child. By the end of the novel it is clear that the individual will has almost no place in marriage or procreation. Bridget's potential escape with Luc would betray the family, liberate her from its constraints, and potentially fulfill them both sexually and emotionally. That she chooses to bring Nicolas' child into the world instead, however, suggests that transgression has been harnessed and smothered, and that she will submit to familial and social imperatives.

Bridget chooses to remain in and propagate the family, but it is telling that Boyle herself fled the marriage this novel represents to seek romance and freedom from convention with Ernest Walsh; this affair is depicted in her next novel, *Year Before Last* (1932). When the first segment of *Plagued by the Nightingale* was published in *This Quarter,* it drew praise from William Carlos Williams and Lola Ridge, but, as Mellen notes, the eventual publication of the entire novel in 1931 drew mixed reviews, which focused mostly on her aptitude for the short story form over the novel. Katherine Anne Porter, however, called the novel "superb," "electric," "masterful," and "a magnificent performance" (pp. 35–36).

Year Before Last continues the Boyle biography: an American woman, Hannah, leaves her French husband to become the companion of a poor, dying poet, Martin, who has attempted to extricate himself from an internecine relationship with his older aunt. The novel begins after Hannah's break with her husband, with Martin and Hannah occupying a rented villa recently vacated by Eve, Martin's aunt. Eve is fiercely jealous of Hannah, and exhibits great cruelty and hostility toward the couple throughout the novel. Martin, a spirited Irish American poet dying of tuberculosis, also runs a literary magazine funded by Eve, who withdraws her support when she leaves. This is devastating to Martin who, aside from being a poet, believes deeply in disseminating the work of other poetic geniuses (all figured as male) and locates his value in his role as editor. He says more than once that the magazine is the most important thing to him, and he seems willing to sacrifice Hannah to its cause, though in his weakened condition he backs away from this substitution in act, if not in emotion.

Boyle published the novel to mixed reviews; praise came from writers such as Henry Miller, but many took issue with her mannered style and lack of topicality. And yet *Year Before Last* is significant for its frank representation of the stigma of tuberculosis in early-twentieth-century Europe. The French town of Vence, where D. H. Lawrence died, is part of the novel's geography, and the couple is forced to leave hotel after hotel because of Martin's coughing, a scenario Boyle also dramatizes in the story "On the Run" (1929). Hannah seems immune to the disease, and must adapt to nursing and taking care of all things practical for Martin. Deeply in love with him, she is willing to withstand cruel treatment, subordination, and horrible living conditions just to be with him. The power dynamic between the two, another Lawrentian feature of the novel, vaults Martin to a position of martyred hero and

Hannah to eager slave. She freely chooses to be submissive to a physically weak but emotionally aggressive man, entranced by his love for "the miracle of things spoken out or written" (p. 131), to which he dedicates his life.

In both *Plagued by the Nightingale* and *Year Before Last,* Boyle clearly bases the protagonists on her own experiences, and yet she surprisingly elides any real sense of female creativity. Hannah can "listen, and sew, and cook (Martin's) food for him, but he, as befitted a man, had his mind elsewhere" (p. 111). Indeed, the novel derides the female artist through the character Lady Vanta and Eve's purely financial role in the magazine to which Martin is so passionately dedicated. In the later novel *My Next Bride* (1934), based on her months in Paris with Raymond Duncan's colony, the female protagonist is an artist, but only her early novels with male protagonists focus on aesthetic creation.

My Next Bride again concerns the struggles of a young woman against a harsh European social world, this time as represented in a utopian colony in the middle of Paris. Based on her own horrific experiences with Raymond Duncan, Boyle tells the story of Victoria, a penniless young American painter, who begins to work for Sorrel (the Duncan figure) out of necessity and the hope that she might dedicate her life to something meaningful. The colony is quickly revealed as corrupt and dirty, the residents as miserable, and Sorrel as manipulative, self-centered, and misogynistic. Victoria works in the colony's shop selling scarves and tunics painted by members, and watches over the children of the colony, who are considered children of all, without mothers or fathers. One day Antony, a rich, eccentric young American man, comes into the shop, and Victoria begins going out at night with him, despite the fact that he is married. Ultimately she becomes pregnant after a drunken encounter one night at a party, a fact she must hide from Sorrel. After making herself seriously ill with pills intended to end the pregnancy, she is eventually rescued and taken in by Antony's wife, Fontana. The novel ends dramatically: on their way to a clinic where Victoria will have the abortion, she and Fontana notice a newspaper headline announcing Antony's suicide in New York.

Boyle told her publisher that *My Next Bride* was about relationships between women, a claim that lends importance to the last third of the novel, when, turned out by Sorrel and abandoned by Antony, Fontana comes to her aid. The novel's trajectory suggests that solidarity among women can serve as a bulwark against the parasitic nature of men. This theme is complicated, however, by the situations of minor female characters. In addition to the bickering women of the colony, two exiled Russian aristocrat sisters who live in Victoria's boardinghouse run out of money entirely, and in some of the novel's darkest scenes, fail at securing any kind of employment or support. The redemption found in Fontana's support of Victoria, then, falls short of brightening the sordid world of the novel, ending as it does with the death of Antony and the imminent termination of Victoria's pregnancy. Victoria's resemblance to earlier Boyle characters is clear in her submission, for much of the novel, to men, her psychological struggles and desire for a better life with a more coherent sense of self, and her victimization by social forces, specifically the gendered economy of Paris that offers no clear path to poor women.

BETWEEN MEN: GENTLEMEN I ADDRESS YOU PRIVATELY *AND* MONDAY NIGHT

Two novels from this period center on male relationships and feature characters that exist on the margins of respectable society, struggling to find fulfillment in a hostile world. Both represent rare early work that is not autobiographical; *Gentlemen I Address You Privately* (1934) is an odd, Lawrentian novel about the love between a former priest and an errant sailor that takes place in and around the port city of Le Havre. The plot focuses on the relationship between the protagonist, Munday, and a sailor named Ayton on the run from authorities. Although Ayton moves in with Munday and becomes his companion, the text uses fairly veiled language to represent their evolving relationship. Munday and Ayton eventually take up residence with a squatter, Quespelle,

and his wife, Leonie, an entirely sympathetic character entrapped by her brute husband. Both Munday and Ayton become close to her and she seems to fall in love with Ayton. Though Munday assumes that nothing has happened because of their individual predilections and circumstances, the ending reveals that Leonie is in fact pregnant with Ayton's child.

The book is radical in its representation of both male and female homosexuality. It deconstructs conventional familial and marital relations on many levels, but suggests that those who operate outside of these imperatives will be hounded by the state and society. It is ultimately a dark picture of the non-normative, though one that demonstrates the range of possible relationships to which a man or woman might be drawn. Boyle's tendency to indulge in flights of lyricism that detract from a central force of meaning make the novel difficult to follow. One contemporary reviewer grouped her with other female writers such as Virginia Woolf and Katherine Mansfield as exhibiting a primary note of "sensibility," characterized by "delicacy" and even "withdrawal" from life (Kronenberger, p. 39). Though this declaration about women writers is reductive and misogynist, *Gentlemen* does suffer from a concentration on "ornament" rather than "architecture," or style over substance.

In *Monday Night* (1938), a more successful yet also difficult novel, a writer and a young doctor, thrown together by chance and drink, seek out a famed French toxicologist from a Monday night to Wednesday morning. Wilt, the writer protagonist, gradually constructs a story that the toxicologist, Monsieur Sylvestre, has been serving as a corrupt trial expert, sending innocent men to prison or execution. At the end of the novel Wilt reads an exposé in the newspaper that proves him right but also scoops the story, which he has envisioned as his big break. His ongoing internal lament that he has never written anything successful, and that he cannot, therefore, be considered a writer, is ironically reinforced at the end of the novel: he has the instincts of a great newspaperman, but not the luck or connections to make his way.

Boyle maintains a limited point of view throughout this novel with a radically short time span, and flights of convoluted consciousness mark the text. One reviewer compared the novel to Hemingway's work in subject and style, concerned as it is with "deracinates and casual sojourners in Paris" (Colum, p. 44). Others compare it to works by Edgar Allan Poe and William Faulkner. The atmosphere is one of surreal, drunken consciousness, and follows the broken, long-unsuccessful Wilt from Paris to the suburb of Malmaison and back, bringing along Bernie, who has come from Chicago to meet the famed Sylvestre. The novel dwells on constructing stories and on the authority and truth involved in narrative. Boyle shows that stories also serve as attempts to vindicate the past; Wilt has not made a life as a writer as he thought he would and, out of constructing and telling story after story, seeks to compensate for this. Though the novel was published to a number of negative reviews, others count it among Boyle's best and certainly most evidently modernist work. Dylan Thomas wrote her to tell her it was "a very grand book indeed" (Mellen, p. 218).

THE ENGLISH NOVELLAS: "THE CRAZY HUNTER" AND "THE BRIDEGROOM'S BODY"

In 1940 Boyle published *The Crazy Hunter: Three Short Novels,* which contains two of her best works: the title novella and the long short story "The Bridegroom's Body." The third story was the minor "Big Fiddle," replaced in a 1958 reissue of the work with "Decision," largely ignored by critics. "The Crazy Hunter" and "The Bridegroom's Body" are set in England, a departure from her earlier work set in France or Austria, and engage with the landscape and spirit of the English countryside. The novels attune themselves to the emotional lives of not only characters but also animals—the "crazy" horse of the title and a group of swans, respectively—and the way these provide an approximation of human feelings, relationships, and dynamics, particularly sexual energies. These two novellas deal with the obscure yet powerful feelings of characters, feelings that exist just outside the

level of social discourse, and thus also show a great debt to Lawrence.

An emotionally evocative novella, "The Crazy Hunter" tells the story of Nancy Lombe, a teenage girl who has recently returned to her parents' home from abroad and devotes herself to the care of a horse, given to her by her father, that suddenly goes blind. All those in authority, particularly Nancy's domineering mother, dictate that the horse must be put down, but she refuses to capitulate to this and trains the horse to feel its way through the world night after night: to relearn the world in darkness. Nancy, meanwhile, yearns to leave her parents' home in the English countryside again and experience the more bohemian side of life in Europe. The personal drama among these family members plays out through and with a suffering and helpless, yet dangerous, animal; the plot line of the horse is both literal and stand-alone, serving as an extended symbolic story for the central family romance.

Boyle's complex treatment of gender roles and procreation continues in this novel, as the dominant mother and pathetic father are rendered miserable by the dynamic of their relationship. The story takes place on a stud farm, dedicated to the production of horses, though the gelding of the title is outside the economy of the farm. Nancy is on the brink of sexual awakening, and she deals with the disabled horse's near lack of gender by putting him in with the gentler fillies to run because the colts would be too rough with him. Nancy's sexual and potential reproductive life exists offstage with an Irishman she met in Florence, but she is unsure whether or not she wants to pursue him. Her relationship to the horse is both that of a parent and of a tending daughter, insofar as the horse relates symbolically to her ruined father. In some ways, the poor blinded horse serves as a metaphor for each of the Lombes. The mother almost died as a young woman, and now the delicate, dependent woman with whom her husband fell in love has perished, replaced by a strong woman who grabs the reins of power. The father's potential has been wasted like the horse's, and no one, besides the daughter, has any real use for him any more. Nancy sees the horse's pain and the way in which those in power want to deal with it, and she strains against forces of authority for herself and the horse throughout.

The Crazy Hunter: Three Short Novels cemented Boyle's reputation, prompting one critic to call her "one of the best short-story writers in America" in 1940 (Jack, p. 49). "The Bridegroom's Body," the second story in the collection, shares a setting (an English county estate) and a symbolic method with "The Crazy Hunter." More accurately a long short story, "The Bridegroom's Body" depicts a woman, Lady Glourie, living on a country estate with her husband; she is surrounded by men, defined by men, "as if it were not only the wild cold countryside that drew men to it but as if all life itself and right to life were man's" (p. 149). She is thus excluded from any social activity or role beyond being informed of the status of the swans and sheep on the estate, and rather than appearing more feminine in contrast, her femininity seems eclipsed by the masculine energy surrounding her. So when a nurse must come to take care of the swanherd's ill and pregnant wife, Lady Glourie fantasizes about having womanly companionship again. She recognizes her loneliness among the violence and disease of the animals on the estate, where, in addition to rotfoot spreading through the sheep, two male swans are fighting intermittently: the old cob against the young cob, who is attempting to establish himself with his "wife" on the lake. When the awaited nurse arrives, though, she is a young, reasonably attractive Irish woman, and Lady Glourie must adjust her expectations of solidarity to a dynamic of rivalry, particularly because her husband and the young farmer show their obvious sexual interest in her.

Lady Glourie withdraws from the young nurse, and the story shifts perspectives to show the nurse as disenfranchised, disempowered, and a victim of salacious men rather than a temptress. The story ends with the violent murder of the young cob by the old, a vicious masculine battle over authority and territory that offsets the imagined female conflict of territory over available men. When the murdered swan is discovered,

however, a clear symbol of destructive masculine power, the nurse reveals to Lady Glourie that she has wanted to connect with her but has felt powerless to do so through the barrier of the men surrounding them. Though Miss Cafferty succeeds finally in conveying her love for Mrs. Glourie, the story demonstrates that two women predisposed to join forces and connect deeply can be foiled by a pervasive atmosphere of masculine interests. The death of the young male swan seems to doom any homosocial bond, because of the violent and destructive impulses to which social and sexual relations give rise.

Throughout her fiction, Boyle explores a range of possible relationships among people, not limited to those dictated by social convention. From the homosexual relationship at the center of *Gentlemen* to the emotionally unconsummated female relationship at the heart of "The Bridegroom's Body" to the near-incestuous relationship in the story "Wedding Day" (discussed below), Boyle shows that extrafamilial and extramarital connections exist, though they are often strangled and foiled by normative social forces.

BOYLE AND THE ART OF THE SHORT STORY

Despite her novelistic output, Boyle' reputation rests primarily on her work in the short story. A prolific writer, Boyle produced her most successful work in this genre in the 1930s and 1940s. According to Joan Mellen, Boyle "redefined the short story form, inventing a major version of what came to be known as 'the *New Yorker* story'" (p. 155). Boyle's early stories have an experimental quality to them, with extremely limited perspectives, little to no exposition or plot, and a focus on the machinations of feeling rather than action. As in her novels, Boyle explores the gender dynamics of socially sanctioned relationships in her first few collections. The later stories engage explicitly with the political climate of the mid-twentieth century and are somewhat more action-driven and suspenseful, examining the complexities of life in wartime France and postwar Germany.

Her first commercially published collection, *Wedding Day and Other Stories* (1930), came out at the same time as *Plagued by the Nightingale* and received many positive reviews. Recognizing her for contributions in the late twenties to periodicals like *transition* and *This Quarter,* the literary establishment gave Boyle's new work a good deal of attention.

"Episode in the Life of an Ancestor" is one of the better-known stories in the collection and was a favorite of Boyle's. The story takes place on the Kansas plains and sketches a version of her grandmother. The story is remarkable for its controlled use of perspective, which floats from the grandmother's father to her horse and back again. Like her early novels, the story is preoccupied with gendered expectations: the grandmother's father is bothered by her reputation as "one of the best horsewomen in Kansas" and her lack of interest in domestic pursuits, and feels that it is his duty to generate in his daughter "the streams of gentleness and love that cooled the blood of true women" (*Fifty Stories,* p. 18). When she stays out late one night, the father discovers that the male schoolteacher has been writing her love poetry, and initially becomes furious at his forwardness. The story shifts then to the perspective of the grandmother's horse, a creature moved to ecstasy by her rider's easy domination. The juxtaposition of the father's protective anger with the schoolmaster and the triumphant assertion of dominance the grandmother performs on the horse reveals the strength of the female in the story over the male, and the father becomes ashamed and afraid for the schoolteacher because of the woman's "hard heart" (p. 24).

"Wedding Day," an impressionist and psychological piece that also dramatizes a family's interest in a marriageable daughter, narrates the hours leading up to a young woman's wedding. Her mother treats the day darkly; she is in a "rage," "collapsed," and "deflated," making it clear that she does not support the daughter's "choice" (*Fifty Stories,* pp. 25–26). The dearth of dialogue in the story makes the surrounding circumstances murky; the brother merely repeats "It isn't too late" to the sister as they go for a boat ride. Boyle's descriptive language dwells on the physical similarities in the "blond" beauty of the

siblings, calling them "another race" (p. 27). The natural resemblance of the two suggests that they rightfully belong together, leading some readers to assume the story is about incest, or some unseemly closeness. The lack of exposition, though, suggests that the focus of the story is the parting itself, and the trauma, rather than the joy, which marriage can impart. Boyle frames the wedding as a divisive event, with the description of the brother giving his sister away to the groom rendered tragically: "She turned her face to her brother and suddenly their hearts fled together and sobbed like ringdoves in their bosom. This was the end, the end, the end ..." (p. 29). The story assigns a radically new interpretation to the transition of marriage, from one that, with a union, gestures toward the productive future, to one that, with a rending, marks the past as lost.

Other notable stories in the collection include "Polar Bears and Others" and "Bitte Nehmen Sie Die Blumen," both of which concern the psychological states of people damaged by close emotional relationships and struggling to renew their faith in the interpersonal. Boyle's stylistic method, which some reviewers dismissed as overly mannered, examines seemingly trivial acts—eating lunch, riding a horse—yet plumbs the depths of the people engaged in these acts. In so doing, she reveals the seething sensations and dynamics always active in human emotional life. The way people feel about each other, Boyle suggests through situational irony and rich natural symbolism, cannot be dictated by social arrangement and expectations. Human feeling overruns the compartments we try to place it in, and therefore our interior lives constantly strain against the positions into which we are placed, whether daughter, brother, wife, or father.

Her next two collections, *The First Lover and Other Stories* (1933) and *The White Horses of Vienna and Other Stories* (1936) transition from smaller-scale stories about the emotional lives of individuals, many based on her own experiences or those of people with whom she was close, to stories that engage directly with the political upheavals of the time and their impact on the individual.

"Rest Cure" is based on the last days of D. H. Lawrence, who succumbed to tuberculosis in 1930. Accounts of Lawrence's death clearly struck Boyle deeply, as she had recently watched the father of her child, and her first real love, waste away from the disease. In the story, an ill writer sits anxiously soaking up the last rays of a setting sun, diving mentally into the past, thinking of his coal miner father and a wartime winter spent in Cornwall—biographical snippets of Lawrence. The allegorical setting sun and the protagonist's insistence on his guest recognizing his impending death reinforces the irony of the title—that this "rest" will be a "cure." His wife brings him champagne and a lobster, which he visually connects to his memory of his father. The lobster becomes a vehicle by which the dying writer can confront his father, and at the end of the story, the writer clasps its claw and thinks "in his heart," "Father, help me. Father, Father, he said. I don't want to die" (*Fifty Stories*, p. 38). The odd and almost comical identification of the crustacean with his father, which seems at first to be a dark method of distancing himself from authentic emotion, channels a parent-child bond that seemed permanently lost through life and death. The rich symbolism and psychological movement of the story—the setting sun, the offensively blooming geraniums, the shadow of the healthy publisher fallen on the writer—outweighs the action, of which there is little. And yet the pathos of the primitive, youthful lament from a child to his dead father breaks through the complex association of meaning as a deeply human bond.

Boyle's stories maintain a lyrical style and psychological dramatic focus, particularly on the distortions of the spirit that can occur in flawed or challenged intimate relationships. Her characters demonstrate the ways in which love and the lack of it shapes the people we become, and can instigate tragedy and pathos in ordinary lives. In "Natives Don't Cry," the standoffish governess Miss Henley goes on vacation with a wealthy family and longs for letters from her beau, "Rudolpho," but never gets them. The family, feeling pity for her, ultimately realizes that she has fictionalized Rudolpho, perhaps to the extent that

she herself is convinced of his existence. By the end it becomes clear that the family's perception of Miss Henley's brisk and distant manner misses the emotional pain at her core, which she must cover up with stories of a fictional romance. "Count Lothar's Heart" begins with an Austrian's departure from his family and fiancée to go to war, and then picks up six years later on his return, when he is a changed man. His fiancée tries to recover his old self, and he eventually reveals that he engaged in homosexual acts during his time in a prison camp and that it has hardened his heart. Sharing it with his old friend and lover is cathartic, however, and he and his fiancée put this episode away and make a life together. Whether Boyle writes about the leisured or the military life, she insists on the determinant power that intimate relationships, be they stilted, ruined, or regretted, exercise on the individual life.

"Maiden, Maiden" tells the story of an unhappy couple climbing in the Austrian Alps, who take a guide to help them navigate the mountain passes. Boyle employs imagery of light and dark, heat and cold throughout, and these physical conditions of the setting approximate the emotional lives of the characters. Sarat, the married doctor with whom Willa travels each year to this recreational spot, emerges as distant and unavailable throughout the story, interested only in the thrill of the climb and the escape from his domestic and professional life. This story again owes much to Lawrence, as it echoes in setting and tone the climactic chapters of *Women in Love,* in which Gudrun and Gerald confront their hatred for each other against the backdrop of the frozen, inhuman mountain snow, and Gerald, the cold northern industrialist, dies exposed to the elements. In Boyle's story, though Willa makes up her mind to leave Sarat and start a new life of love with the humble guide, it is not Sarat who dies on the "Maiden" pass, but the guide. The intimacy that Willa and the guide established just the night before is swallowed up by the "utter durability of silent cold" (*Fifty Stories,* p. 146).

The White Horses of Vienna and Other Stories contains some of Boyle's more well-known stories, among them "Astronomer's Wife." This, her most anthologized story, creates a subtle but powerful portrait of a wife gradually realizing her suppression by her lofty intellectual husband. Recollecting Virginia Woolf in tone and theme, the piece begins on an ordinary morning for Mrs. Ames, the wife of an eminent astronomer for whom "the mystery and silence of her husband's mind lay like a chiding finger on her lips" (*Life Being the Best,* p. 28). Though the story concerns the entrapment of women in marriage, it also presents two types of men: the intellectual and condescending husband and the strong, practical plumber who comes to fix a leak. Boyle's imagery of height and depth capture this difference; Mrs. Ames realizes that rather than always looking up to her domineering husband, she might relate levelly to a man like this plumber, who is rough but "comprehensible to her" in his pursuit of material solutions and truths. The story ends with Mrs. Ames following the plumber, literally and figuratively away from her husband, down the drains, "into the heart of the earth" (p. 34). Mrs. Ames travels away from the circumscribed position indicated in the title, away from being merely the great man's wife, and becomes an autonomous woman in touch with her desires as she studies and ultimately pursues the corporeal, accessible world of the plumber away from the cerebral, exclusionary world of her husband.

The collection also features stories set in the United States, such as "White as Snow," "Security," and "Dear Mr. Walrus." Though the stories can be classified by geographic setting, as they are in the later collection *Fifty Stories,* Boyle's main themes, namely suffering, inequality, and failed love, provide a more effective way to group the pieces. Both "Keep Your Pity" and "Dear Mr. Walrus" concern aging people gradually losing the economic means to survive. In the first, the reader meets an aristocratic but virtually destitute English couple living in Nice. A wealthy American tourist resolves to send them some money, charmed by their combination of the "frail and gracious" (*Fifty Stories,* p. 75). Though the couple seems weak and genteel at the beginning of the story, the end reveals them as cunning and aggressive in their suffering. "Dear Mr. Walrus,"

set in Depression-era New York City, is similar in outline to "Keep Your Pity"; three siblings, in their late fifties and sixties but frozen in adolescence, find their fortune lost and must reduce their standard of living drastically to survive. The brother Stuyvesant considers himself a writer, hanging on to a decades-old rejection letter from a publisher that offered him a glimmer of encouragement. Remarkable in the story is the elaborate delusion under which the family exists and which the siblings have maintained for decades. At the end, a family friend finds all three dead by "suicide pact" (*Fifty Stories,* p. 112). Like the Russian sisters in *My Next Bride,* the characters in these two stories find it impossible to transform their ideas of themselves based on economic necessity and drastic changes in lifestyle.

The stories "The Lost," "Black Boy," and "White as Snow" focus on racism in the United States, a social issue Boyle dealt with in her fiction long before the emergence of the civil rights movement. The stories feature children and young adults losing their innocence about the deep-seated prejudices faced by black people in the United States. "Black Boy" and "White as Snow" particularly stage interracial attraction and its policing by others, all of the older generation. In "Black Boy," a young girl befriends the title character on the beach and is eventually rescued by him after being thrown from a horse. As he carries her back to her grandfather, the only reward he gets is a slap across the face. In "The Lost," Boyle combines her themes of war and racism by depicting a young Eastern European orphan who has been promised by a black GI that he can come to live with him after the war. His hopes are dashed when the leader of the orphans' home explains to him that it would be impossible for a white child to live with a black family in the United States. Boyle's penetrating accounts of the realities of race relations demonstrate the stark inhumanity of segregation and prejudice.

Her final story collection, *Nothing Ever Breaks Except the Heart* (1966), includes stories published earlier and a few new stories. The new work focuses mostly on race and class relations

in the United States. "The Ballet of Central Park," for example, is a tragic tale of a wealthy girl who befriends immigrant shoeshine boys in the park, only to be stunned and scarred by the violence seething within their community. Taken together, Boyle's incisive explorations of blows to human dignity, whether set between the wars, in wartime, or in postwar Europe or America, reveal the range of extraordinary external pressures on the individual in the twentieth century and the possible psychological responses to them. Working from the perspective of the individual, moreover, allows Boyle to tap into the often mysterious ways in which people deal with strife.

LITERATURE AND POLITICS: CONFRONTING FASCISM

The O. Henry Prize–winning title story of *White Horses* inaugurates another of Boyle's great subjects: the depiction of the human element in contemporary politics—in this case, burgeoning fascism. "The White Horses of Vienna" takes place in the summer of 1934, just before and after the assassination of the Austrian chancellor Engelbert Dollfuss by Nazi sympathizers. Briefly, a young Jewish doctor comes to help an older doctor who, unbeknownst to the younger Dr. Heine, has hurt himself lighting swastika fires in the mountains. The white horses of the title, which feature in an anecdote Heine tells the family, represent the old, honorable order of royalty in Austria, but more broadly, a kind of shared symbol of a united people, stirred by beauty, majesty, and artistry. Heine gradually realizes the magnitude of the smoldering political tensions in Austria and their implications for his people. The delicacy of the story, however, comes from Boyle's representation of the central characters as both members of races and as individuals who instinctively treat each other gently and respectably despite their racial identities and political affiliations. Indeed, it is in many ways a story about caretaking (all the central characters are in the medical profession, including the older doctor's wife) as a deeply human trait, and the violence which politics and collective beliefs can exert on this trait.

In her descriptions, Boyle focuses on racial differences in her characters' appearances ("the arch of [Heine's] nose"; the doctor's "perfectly white … spotless" appearance [*Fifty Stories,* pp. 153, 152]) that, when viewed as representative of shared beliefs and political positions, should pit the characters against each other. Yet through the ultimate goodness of the characters, seen in Heine's respect for the older doctor and an episode in which the wife saves Heine from catching on fire, the real tragedy of the political turmoil of the 1930s becomes evident. Human connections among individuals must be sacrificed to coarse, broad distinctions of race, creed, and politics. As a harbinger of things to come, the story is a penetrating and revelatory portrait of the forces behind the rise of fascism. "The White Horses of Vienna" depicts a Europe barreling toward great tragedy, in which collective belief and mass movements take precedence over a common humanity and respect for the individual.

Likewise, Boyle based her novel *Death of a Man* (1936) on the time she and her family spent in the Tyrol, during which she gradually realized the severity of the simmering political tensions of 1930s Austria. In the novel, a young American woman, Pendennis, leaves her staid English husband to pursue her love of the rugged Nazi doctor Prochaska, a native of the mountains. Pendennis resembles earlier Boyle heroines (and the young Boyle) in her lack of a secure identity: her marriage proves flimsy, she feels no real connection to her nationality, and she has a troubled family past. This rootlessness leads her to struggle with her feelings for Prochaska, who is passionately dedicated to the Fascist movement, which he feels will bring a better life for all those who have been suffering in his country. In the tragically ironic ending, Prochaska, after having followed Pendennis to Vienna, where she has fled their relationship, speeds away on a train. Pendennis speeds by in the opposite direction on another train, having changed her mind and decided to reunite with Prochaska. Their love cannot survive the political turmoil through which they must survive as individuals.

Boyle was criticized for both "White Horses" and *Death of a Man* for showing sympathy to the Nazi cause. She refuses, ultimately, to villainize the older doctor and his wife in the former, and Prochaska in the latter. It is worth noting, though, that her work of this period shows genuine attempts to probe the human motivations for the Nazi movement, which stem in her Austrian stories from terrible socioeconomic conditions and the lack of a strong democratic political system. During this period Boyle also orchestrated the nonfiction anthology *365 Days,* which sought to represent the year 1934 through vignettes. Boyle solicited clippings from newspapers and short stories related in some way to events recorded in newspapers to provide a story, ranging in topic from American Prohibition to Nazism, for each day of the year. The January 29th story deals with swastika fires in the Tyrol, linked to the newspaper line "Austrian Nazis continue to demonstrate despite warning by pocket Chancellor" (*365 Days,* p. 16). Though not a commercial success, the scope of the ambitious volume underscores Boyle's commitment, seen in her fiction as well, to recording the tumultuous political climate of the day. From her perspective as an American witnessing the rise of fascism in Austria, Boyle provides the reader with invaluable accounts of the individual motivations for embracing this ideology. After the war, she wrote multiple works (including *The Seagull on the Step,* 1955, and *Generation Without Farewell,* 1960) that attempted to warn of the continuing dangers of fascism to Europe and America.

WARTIME AND POSTWAR FICTION

After the outbreak of World War II, Boyle turned her attention to the varied and painful circumstances into which people found themselves thrown during the war. "Defeat" (1941), another O. Henry Prize winner, begins in a France recently defeated by Germany, with French soldiers escaping and retreating from the front lines, profoundly disillusioned by the triumph of the "young, blond-haired" German army (*Fifty Stories,* p. 295). Boyle doesn't focus on the military action of defeat, however, but rather on its spiritual effects and aftermath on the country.

Told as a story within a story, a soldier who has escaped from a prison with a *copain* (pal) tells of their retreat through German-occupied territory to some of his fellow countrymen sitting in a café. The civilians the two men encounter on their voyage range from the overtly hostile, who refuse to offer them food or shelter, to a resolutely patriotic schoolteacher who interrupts her preparations for Bastille Day in an empty schoolhouse to risk her life and get the soldiers clothing and food. The young teacher prompts the narrator to take heart, and to declare that a country isn't defeated "until its women are" (p. 300).

The two men subsequently hide in a garage in a town center, with a view of the square, in which German soldiers have set up an ironic celebration of Bastille Day, after promising Frenchmen coffins and Frenchwomen ball gowns on this national holiday. The men watch the empty square, certain that the women of the town will stay away; eventually, though, they are lured by the food and drink that they have been so long denied. Defeat finally occurs when national pride has been sapped from the women of a country. The story's complicated definition of national identity involves the masculine protection of a female citizenry, who remain loyal to their protectors, come what will. France's loss, then, is not complete until the dedication of the people to their soldiers and, by extension, their country, dissipates. The pain of defeat is psychological and cultural, determined by a moral, not a military, measure.

Many of her wartime stories focus on the displacement of people from their native countries and the complicated and tense relationships among people of different nationalities. "Their Name Is Macaroni," for example, is set in a French resort town, where people show great prejudice to the Italian residents. When Americans arrive with supplies, there is an initial regulation against distributing them to anyone but the French, despite the sizable Italian immigrant population. A French colonel takes a stand to ensure that all children receive rations, and the story ends with an anecdote from just before the Armistice, when two Fascist Italian pilots were buried after trying to bomb the town.

The colonel puts a souvenir flag reading "Venice, 1920" in one of the pilot's coffins, a gesture that signifies the different meaning of nationality that existed before Mussolini and the carnage of the war, which poisoned the idea of Italy for the French and, by extension, the Italians living in France. Stories like "Men," "They Weren't Going to Die," and "This They Took with Them" chronicle the extreme situations faced by people of many nationalities, races, and creeds during the early years of World War II. Austrians on a chain gang in a France at war with Germany, Senegalese imported to serve as cannon fodder for the French, and French and Mexicans fleeing a Nazi-occupied Paris feature in stories about the depths and heights of the human spirit.

Boyle's stories do not only show sympathy for the victims of Germany, however. Her later fiction also included *The Smoking Mountain: Stories of Postwar Germany* (1951), a collection based on her experience living in Allied-occupied Germany. *The Smoking Mountain* includes stories critiquing both the continued cruelty of the German people, like "Cabaret," and the callous American military presence, like "Summer Evening." In the latter, a German butler working an American military cocktail party, after having too many drinks, begs American officers to get him a passport, since he says his mother was from New Jersey. The men cruelly trick him by pretending they can get it, and his tearful display of gratitude empties the evening of mirth and exposes the senseless structure of power and exclusion with which the Americans are operating. The political, Boyle shows over and over, wreaks havoc on the individual. Traditional associations with nationality, like pride, camaraderie, and shared identity, have devolved with the ravages of war into mere reasons for prejudice, cruelty, and a lack of humanity.

POPULAR FICTION: POTBOILERS

Boyle's work of the 1940s signaled a change in her material, but also a shift in her critical reputation, from an innovative stylist with ties to modernism to popular writer of sensational fiction that appeared in wide-circulation magazines.

This stemmed from her desire to make money in this period as well as from a shift to a more overt political consciousness with the outbreak of World War II. She placed many stories in magazines, and the *Saturday Evening Post* serialized two of her novels, *Avalanche* (1944) and *A Frenchman Must Die* (1946). Of the five novels she published in the decade, two, *Primer for Combat* (1942) and *1939* (1948), continue in an experimental and literary vein, and three, the two *Saturday Evening Post* novels and *His Human Majesty* (1949), are often termed "potboilers," filled with improbable situations, crudely sketched characters, and Hollywood-style romance.

Primer for Combat and *1939* both deal with conflicts of loyalty in wartime France, in which Nazi collaboration and a dedication to a seemingly defeated France often appeared the only options, and civilians had ties to both of the nations at war. In the former, written in diary form, a young woman resembling Boyle is living in France with her second husband and young children when she falls in love with an Austrian ski instructor. Loosely following the events of her own romance with Joseph Franckenstein, the novel depicts the heroine's attempts to help the Austrian, who is also married, escape to America. Unlike Franckenstein, however, he takes the moral low ground and ultimately chooses to live in France as a Nazi collaborator. The novel, like many of her wartime short stories, sets the scene of a defeated France that drives individuals to extremes of nationalism or cynicism, and was written to inspire patriotism in an American audience. The novel *1939,* told largely in flashback, concerns the postwar choice that must be made between France and Germany by an individual with ties to both. Both novels stage conflicts faced by people with relationships and loyalties that they are driven by contemporary politics to betray.

Avalanche was a Book of the Month Club selection and the only best seller Boyle ever wrote. Edmund Wilson, however, writing in the *New Yorker,* a magazine Boyle had published in often and with great success, panned the novel, and did great damage to Boyle's literary reputation. The novel, replete with espionage, romance, and moralistic calls to patriotic duty, features a half-American, half-French heroine who travels to France to work for the Resistance movement. The hero is a French ski instructor and Resistance fighter who performs incredible feats of daring, particularly in the climactic rescue of the heroine from the Nazi villain, who has been posing (badly) as a humble village civilian. The hero and heroine marry at the end, at the scene of her rescue, just as they receive news that the Americans are landing in North Africa.

A Frenchman Must Die is similar in tone and pace but takes place after the conclusion of the war and concerns the capture of a Nazi war criminal, whom the hero wants to bring to justice. The love interest in this novel is the Nazi's young secretary, who has been surreptitiously collecting evidence for his conviction. Justice is served by the ending, when the Nazi is killed in a high-speed car chase. *His Human Majesty* (1949), though set in an army camp in Colorado based on the one in which Franckenstein trained during the war, resembles her other wartime novels with its focus on intrigue and shifting loyalties. Written with the demands of serialization in mind, these action-packed potboilers demonstrated new signature traits of romance, adventure, and suspense. *The Seagull on the Step* followed in 1955, another improbable potboiler set in France, and *Generation Without Farewell,* her "German" novel, in 1960. This last novel chronicles a disillusioned German POW's return to his homeland, where he confronts the continued corruption and amorality of his people. Her last novel, the unsuccessful *The Underground Woman* (1975), focuses on the antiwar activities and family struggles of a Boyle-like character in the United States, following closely her own experiences with protest and her daughter's involvement in a shady commune in the late 1960s.

RESUSCITATING THE LOST GENERATION

In the 1960s, though her own creative output slowed somewhat, Boyle dedicated a great deal of time and energy to a volume in which she combined Robert McAlmon's memoirs with

autobiographical vignettes of her own, covering the same period of time. *Being Geniuses Together: 1920–1930* (1968) is a chronicle of expatriate life in France, in the tradition of such famous works as Gertrude Stein's *The Autobiography of Alice B. Toklas* (1933), Hemingway's *A Moveable Feast* (1964), and Malcolm Cowley's *Exile's Return* (1934). Boyle says in the book and elsewhere that the project is a tribute to McAlmon; she revises, shortens, and adds chapters of her own and, in so doing, hopes to "accord to Robert McAlmon his rightful and outstanding place in the history of the literary revolution of the early nineteen-twenties" (*Being Geniuses Together,* p. xi).

Boyle's sections are more personal and reflective than McAlmon's, tracing her experiences and evolving sense of herself as a woman and writer, while McAlmon's largely concern the group of famous writers and artists with whom he worked and socialized. Boyle details her time working in New York on *Broom* with Lola Ridge, and her early attempts at writing, as well as her experiences with Richard Brault's family in Brittany, her affair with Ernest Walsh (Michael), the birth of her daughter, Sharon, working for the Princess of Sarawak in Paris, time with Raymond Duncan as a part of his compound, and meeting with and eventual marriage to Laurence Vail. Many of these experiences had appeared in her novels, and the joint memoir confirms the extent to which her early work was autobiographical.

The memoir also tells of her transition from American to European resident, feeling at first "so totally French … that I scarcely recognized the look of my own features when I happened to catch sight of them in the glass" (pp. 146–147). She reflects on her development as a writer among other women writers, and as a citizen with a political consciousness, moved by the trials of Sacco and Vanzetti and the labor leader Eugene V. Debs. Later in the memoir she details her initiation into the expatriate scene of Paris as a twenty-something, which involved witnessing the decadence, dissolution, and volatility of its most famous members. James Joyce features as a struggling alcoholic and Gertrude Stein as an egotistical authority figure, who, after meeting Boyle once, declined to socialize with her again. Though some criticized her for cashing in on McAlmon's work, her sections of the memoir are much more dynamic and enjoyable to read, and provide a helpful lens into her early work.

POETRY

Though her reputation today rests firmly on her prose, Boyle first appeared in print in Harriet Monroe's *Poetry* in November 1921 with a letter to the editor about modern music, and in December 1922 her poem "Monody to the Sound of Zithers" appeared in the magazine; the poem was anthologized the next year. Boyle considered herself a poet as much as a fiction writer, and throughout the 1920s and 1930s she devoted creative energy to placing poetry in little magazines of modernism. All of her poems, according to the publisher's note, appear in *Collected Poems of Kay Boyle* (1991), a chronologically structured volume that demonstrates her evolving poetic technique.

Her reputation as a writer of poetry won her a Guggenheim Fellowship in 1934 to write a long poem on the history of aviation, a project that was never completed. Critics often cite the influence of William Carlos Williams on her early poetic aesthetic. As in her stories, Boyle uses unexpected phrases and images in her poetic work to jar the reader's sense of the ordinary. In "And Winter" (1926), for example, her use of simile is startling:

Orion fades like the white heel of a runner
and my anguish is as bitter as almond rind
My hands in the underbrush of my sorrow
like children seek the new vines of arbutus
that run in winter like music under the leaves

(*Collected Poems*, p. 22)

This poem to a dead lover relies on layers of simile that shuttle the reader from the mythic world to the natural world to the mysterious tangle of human sorrow. Many of her poems were dedicated explicitly to other writers and artists, like "A Letter to Francis Picabia" (1927), "Angels for Djuna Barnes" (1937), and "Two Twilights for William Carlos Williams" (1959). Reflecting

the shift in her prose career, her later poems largely concern contemporary politics, like "The Lost Dogs of Phnom Penh" (1966) and "A Poem About Black Power" (1966), both pieces urging awareness of human rights. Her free verse, formally experimental poems, though clearly framed at first within the modernist movement, ultimately failed to gain traction as her fiction did.

CRITICAL RECEPTION

Contemporary reviewers responded to Boyle favorably in the early decades of the twentieth century, and more critically when she began to produce popular, commercially driven work. Compared to her modernist forbears and peers like Hemingway, Jean Rhys, and Henry Miller, relatively little critical ink has been spilled about her. Virago Modern Classics reissued several of her books in the late 1980s and early 1990s, corresponding to a spike in interest in her work, but these are not widely available. Indeed, despite the persistent scholarly interest in modernism and the recuperation of previously under-studied women writers, work on Boyle remains relatively rare.

There have been some exceptions to this, however; in 1988, the respected journal *Twentieth-Century Literature* published an entire issue dedicated to Boyle, aiming to resuscitate her reputation. Sandra Spanier edited the volume, having also published a book-length critical-biographical study, *Kay Boyle: Artist and Activist,* in 1986. The first section is a set of essays and reminiscences by friends and colleagues, some produced for the issue, others reprinted, including pieces by William Carlos Williams, Katherine Anne Porter, Studs Terkel, Helga Ensele, Morris Renek, James Laughlin, and Malcolm Cowley. The second section consists of more traditional literary critical essays on a variety of her works.

In 1994 Joan Mellen released her lengthy and detailed biography, titled *Kay Boyle: Author of Herself.* Two collections of critical essays, *Critical Essays on Kay Boyle,* edited by Marilyn Elkins, and *Kay Boyle for the Twenty-First Century,* edited by Thomas Austenfeld, appeared in

1997 and 2008, respectively. Some critics have placed Boyle's work in context with her contemporaries. Donna Hollenberg, for example, compares her representation of abortion with that of H.D., and Craig Monk reads her contributions to *Being Geniuses Together* alongside MacAlmon's as an attempt to mythologize the Lost Generation after the fact. Two essays in Elkins' volume read her as a counterpoint to Edith Wharton, and critics regularly compare her work to that of Hemingway, Faulkner, and Lawrence. Alexa Weik has read Boyle as a "model cosmopolitan," arguing that her early novels depict "development of a cosmopolitan mind" (p. 153) and thereby considering her through the transnational lens prominent in current modernist scholarship.

KAY BOYLE FOR TODAY

Though a handful of books and journal articles have appeared, much work remains to be done on Boyle. Her critical devolution from modernist innovator to commercial fiction writer likely still affects her reputation. Readers introduced to Boyle today, though, will be struck by the breadth of her body of work in terms of genre, subject, and style. Boyle's oeuvre moves from modernism to Hollywood-style drama, from bohemian 1920s Paris to 1970s San Francisco protest rallies, from the injustices of racism to the injustices of fascism and back again. There is perhaps no other writer who represents nearly the whole of the tumultuous twentieth century with such a rich transatlantic perspective. In form and content, Boyle's work offers a great variety of approaches to the relationship between literature and life, and at its most powerful, reminds readers of the individual struggling in the face of social convention, the ravages of war, and political oppression.

Selected Bibliography

WORKS OF KAY BOYLE

NOVELS

Plagued by the Nightingale. London: Jonathan Cape, 1931. Reprint, New York: Penguin, 1990.

Year Before Last. London: Faber, 1932. Reprint, New York: Penguin, 1986.

Gentlemen I Address You Privately. London: Faber, 1934.

My Next Bride. New York: Harcourt, Brace, 1934. Reprint, London: Virago Press, 1986.

Death of a Man. New York: Harcourt, Brace, 1936. Reprint, New York: New Directions, 1989.

Monday Night. London: Faber, 1938.

The Crazy Hunter: Three Short Novels. New York: Harcourt, Brace, 1940. Republished as *Three Short Novels,* Boston: Beacon Press, 1958; New York: New Directions, 1991.

Primer for Combat. New York: Simon & Schuster, 1942.

Avalanche: A Novel of Love and Espionage. New York: Simon & Schuster, 1944.

A Frenchman Must Die. New York: Simon & Schuster, 1946.

1939. New York: Simon & Schuster, 1948.

His Human Majesty. New York: Whittlesey House, McGraw-Hill, 1949.

The Seagull on the Step. New York: Knopf, 1955.

Generation Without Farewell. New York: Knopf, 1960.

The Underground Woman. Garden City, N.Y.: Doubleday, 1975.

Process: A Novel. Edited by Sandra Spanier. Champaign: University of Illinois Press, 2001.

SHORT STORIES

Short Stories. Paris: Black Sun Press, 1929.

Wedding Day and Other Stories. New York: Jonathan Cape and Harrison Smith, 1930.

The First Lover and Other Stories. New York: Harrison Smith and Robert Haas, 1933.

The White Horses of Vienna and Other Stories. New York: Harcourt, Brace, 1936.

Thirty Stories. New York: Simon & Schuster, 1946.

The Smoking Mountain: Stories of Postwar Germany. New York: McGraw-Hill, 1951.

Nothing Ever Breaks Except the Heart. Garden City, N.Y.: Doubleday, 1966.

Life Being the Best & Other Stories. Edited by Sandra Whipple Spanier. New York: New Directions, 1988.

Fifty Stories. Garden City, N.Y.: Doubleday, 1980. Reprint, New York: New Directions, 1992.

POETRY

A Glad Day. Norfolk, Conn.: New Directions, 1938.

American Citizen Naturalized in Leadville, Colorado: A Poem. New York: Simon & Schuster, 1944.

Collected Poems. New York: Knopf, 1962.

Testament for My Students and Other Poems. Garden City, N.Y.: Doubleday, 1970.

This Is Not a Letter and Other Poems. Los Angeles: Sun & Moon Press, 1985.

Collected Poems of Kay Boyle. Port Townsend, Wash.: Copper Canyon Press, 1991.

NONFICTION

Relations & Complications: Being the Recollections of H. H. the Dayang Muda of Sarawak. (Ghostwriter.) London: John Lane, 1929.

365 Days. With Laurence Vail and Nina Conarain. London: Jonathan Cape, 1936.

Breaking the Silence: Why a Mother Tells Her Son About the Nazi Era. New York: Institute of Human Relations Press, 1962.

Being Geniuses Together, 1920–1930. With Robert McAlmon. Garden City, N.Y.: Doubleday, 1968. Reprint, San Francisco: North Point Press, 1984.

The Long Walk at San Francisco State and Other Essays. New York: Grove Press, 1970.

"Report for Lock-up." In *Four Visions of America.* San Francisco: Capra Press, 1977.

Words That Must Somehow Be Said: The Selected Essays of Kay Boyle, 1927–1984. Edited by Elizabeth Bell. London: Chatto and Windus–Hogarth Press, 1985.

CHILDREN'S BOOKS

The Youngest Camel. Boston: Little, Brown, 1939.

Pinky, the Cat Who Liked to Sleep. New York: Crowell-Collier, 1966.

Pinky in Persia. New York: Crowell-Collier, 1968.

PAPERS

Kay Boyle Papers, 1914–1987. Southern Illinois University Special Collections Research Center.

Kay Boyle Papers, 1910-1992. Texas Tech University Southwest Collection/Special Collections Library.

Kay Boyle Papers, 1930–1991. Special Collections, University of Delaware Library.

Kay Boyle Collection, 1945-1990. Harry Ransom Humanities Research Center, University of Texas at Austin.

CRITICAL AND BIOGRAPHICAL STUDIES

Austenfeld, Thomas, ed. *Kay Boyle for the Twenty-First Century.* Trier, Germany: Wissenschaftlicher Verlag Trier, 2008.

Bell, Elizabeth. *Kay Boyle: A Study of the Short Fiction.* New York: Twayne, 1992.

Carpenter, Richard. "Kay Boyle." *College English* 15, no. 2:81–87 (1953).

———. "Kay Boyle: The Figure in the Carpet." *Critique: Studies in Modern Fiction* 7, no. 2:65–78 (1965).

Centing, Richard. "Kay Boyle: The Cincinnati Years." *Ohioana Quarterly* 15:11–13 (1972).

Colum, Mary. "The International vs. the Local Outlook." 1938. In *Critical Essays on Kay Boyle*. Edited by Marilyn Elkins. New York: G. K. Hall, 1997. Pp. 43–45.

Davis, Margo. "Kay Boyle." *Women Writers of the West Coast: Speaking of Their Lives and Careers*. Edited by Marilyn Yalom. Santa Barbara, Calif.: Capra, 1983. Pp. 105–120.

Davis, Phoebe Stein. "The Politics of Modernism in Kay Boyle's *Death of a Man*." In *Challenging Modernism: New Readings in Literature and Culture, 1914–45*. Edited by Stella Deen. Burlington, Vt.: Ashgate, 2002.

Drew, Kathy. "Jails Don't Daunt Protesting Grandmother: Kay Boyle Dedicates Self to Human Dignity." *Lost Generation Quarterly* 4, no. 1:22–23 (1976).

Elkins, Marilyn. "Another Facet of Herself: The Complicated Case of Evelyn Scott and Kay Boyle." In *Evelyn Scott: Recovering a Lost Modernist*. Edited by Dorothy M. Scura and Paul C. Jones. Knoxville: University of Tennessee Press, 2001. Pp. 69–84.

Elkins, Marilyn, ed. *Critical Essays on Kay Boyle*. New York: G. K. Hall, 1997.

Gillette, Meg. "Bedside Manners in Dorothy Parker's 'Lady with a Lamp' and Kay Boyle's *My Next Bride*." *Studies in American Fiction* 35, no. 2:159–179 (2007).

Hollenberg, Donna. "Abortion, Identity Formation, and the Expatriate Woman Writer: H. D. and Kay Boyle in the Twenties." *Twentieth-Century Literature* 40, no. 4:499–517 (1994).

Jack, Peter Monro. "Three Unusual Stories by Kay Boyle." 1940. In *Critical Essays on Kay Boyle*. Edited by Marilyn Elkins. New York: G. K. Hall, 1997. Pp. 48–49.

Kale, Verna. "'A Moveable Feast' or 'A Miserable Time Actually'? Ernest Hemingway, Kay Boyle, and the Modernist Memoir." In *Ernest Hemingway and the Geography of Memory*. Edited by Mark Cirino and Mark P. Ott. Kent, Ohio: Kent State University Press, 2010. Pp. 127–145.

Koch, David V. "Kay Boyle." In *Dictionary of Literary Biography*. Vol. 4, *American Writers in Paris, 1920–1939*. Edited by Karen Lane Rood. Detroit: Gale, 1980. Pp. 46–56.

Kronenberger, Louis. "Kay Boyle's Story of a Moral Crisis." 1933. In *Critical Essays on Kay Boyle*. Edited by Marilyn Elkins. New York: G. K. Hall, 1997.

Lesinska, Zofia P. *Perspectives of Four Women Writers on the Second World War: Gertrude Stein, Janet Flanner, Kay Boyle, and Rebecca West*. New York: Peter Lang, 2002.

Mellen, Joan. *Kay Boyle: Author of Herself*. New York: Farrar, Straus and Giroux, 1994.

Monk, Craig. "Textual Authority and Modern American Autobiography: Robert McAlmon, Kay Boyle, and the Writing of a Lost Generation." *Journal of American Studies* 35, no. 3:485–497 (2001).

Porter, Katherine Anne. "Kay Boyle: Example to the Young." 1931. In *Critical Essays on Kay Boyle*. Edited by Marilyn Elkins. New York: G. K. Hall, 1997. Pp. 33–36.

Spanier, Sandra Whipple. *Kay Boyle: Artist and Activist*. Carbondale: Southern Illinois University Press, 1986.

———. "'Paris Wasn't Like That': Kay Boyle and the Last of the Lost Generation." In *Lives out of Letters: Essays on American Literary Biography and Documentation in Honor of Robert N. Hudspeth*. Edited by Robert D. Habich. Madison, N.J.: Fairleigh Dickinson University Press, 2004. Pp. 169–188.

Spanier, Sandra Whipple, ed. Kay Boyle Issue. *Twentieth-Century Literature* 34, no. 3 (fall 1988).

Tang, Edward. "Occupied Americans: Kay Boyle's Tales of Postwar Germany." *Americana: The Journal of American Popular Culture (1900–Present)* 10, no. 2 (2011). #http://www.americanpopularculture.com/journal/articles/fall_2011/tang.htm..

Weik, Alexa. "The Wandering Woman: The Challenges of Cosmopolitanism in Kay Boyle's Early Novels." In *Kay Boyle for the Twenty-First Century*. Edited by Thomas Austenfeld. Trier, Germany: Wissenschaftlicher Verlag Trier, 2008. Pp. 151–168.

Williams, William Carlos. "The Sonambulists." 1929. In *Critical Essays on Kay Boyle*. Edited by Marilyn Elkins. New York: G. K. Hall, 1997. Pp. 27–30.

WILLIAM ELLERY CHANNING

(1780—1842)

Jacob Risinger

WILLIAM ELLERY CHANNING, the central spokesperson for American Unitarianism in the nineteenth century, had an outsized impact on his age. Ralph Waldo Emerson once claimed that Channing was, while he lived, not only "the star of the American Church" but "a kind of public *Conscience*." In his lecture on "Life and Letters in New England," Emerson described Channing's significance more specifically, arguing that both the sum total *and* the least of his works were integral to the shaping of a young republic's intellectual, religious, and cultural life:

> He was made for the public ... all America would have been impoverished in wanting him. We could not then spare a single word he uttered in public, not so much as the reading a lesson in Scripture, or a hymn, and it is curious that his printed writings are almost a history of the times; as there was no great public interest, political, literary or even economical ... on which he did not leave some printed record of his brave and thoughtful opinion.
>
> (*Complete Works,* vol. 10, pp. 339–340)

Fittingly, then, Channing's own origin corresponded with the volatile emergence of the nation whose cultural life he would help to define.

EARLY LIFE, 1780–1792

At the height of the American Revolution, William Ellery Channing was born on April 7, 1780, in Newport, Rhode Island. Throughout the eighteenth century, Newport's prominent role in the interdependent, or "triangular," trade of slaves, molasses, and rum had ensured its prosperity, but the onset of the Revolution starkly interrupted its fortune. British forces had oc-cupied the city from 1776 to 1779, and the French used Newport as their base in North America from shortly after Channing's birth until the end of the war. Channing grew up in a war-torn Newport, one marked not only by the physical devastation attendant upon a long conflict but by a population that had fallen to less than half of the nine thousand residents who called Newport home at the height of its colonial glory.

If the Revolution and its aftermath stood as a kind of backdrop to Channing's childhood, the prominence of his family ensured that he would remain close to the active political epicenter of the new United States. His father, also William Channing (1751–1793), had attended Princeton with James Madison and Aaron Burr. While he would never achieve more than a modest financial success, he was elected attorney general of Rhode Island in 1777, and he became a federal district attorney for the state in 1790. Channing's mother, Lucy Ellery (1752–1834), was a descendant of Anne Bradstreet; in later years, William would remember her as someone who "had the firmness to see the truth, to speak it, to act upon it" (W. H. Channing, *Life,* p. 10). Channing's maternal grandfather, William Ellery, had represented Rhode Island in the Continental Congress, where he was one of the fifty-six men to sign the Declaration of Independence. With such a family, young William Ellery Channing had a matchless perspective on his times. He sat at the table when George Washington dined at the Channing house in Newport. In the year before his death, he recalled one instance in which his father was particularly willing to share his political passion:

> I recollect, distinctly, the great interest he took in the political questions which agitated the country.

Though but eight or nine years of age, I was present when the Rhode Island Convention adopted the Federal Constitution; and the enthusiasm of that moment I can never forget. My father entered with his whole heart into that unbounded exultation.

(p. 7)

Later, as a senior at Harvard, Channing requited his father's enthusiasm for the Federalist cause by drafting a letter to President John Adams in which he and almost all of his fellow undergraduates pledged their lives to defend "that soil which now affords a peaceful grave to the mouldering bones of our forefathers" (p. 36).

Though the political milieu of Channing's family life is more remarkable, the religious tenor of his childhood was also formative. The Channing family moved back and forth between Newport's First and Second Congregational Churches, between the moderate Calvinism of Ezra Stiles and that of Samuel Hopkins, an abolitionist disciple of Jonathan Edwards who became famous for espousing his willingness "to be damned for the glory of God." Amid these sharp contraries, another outing with his father—described in *Life of William Ellery Channing* (1882; written by his nephew William Henry Channing, and hereafter referred to as *Life*)—stands out as emblematic. Accompanying his father to hear a well-known preacher in a nearby town, Channing was struck not only by the minister's fierce rhetoric but by his assertion that an unavoidable "curse seemed to rest upon the earth" (p. 16). Shocked by the ferocity of the fire-and-brimstone sermon, he imagined that everyone in attendance would immediately give up their worldly pursuits to seek salvation—a thought seemingly confirmed when his father pronounced the sermon to be "Sound doctrine, Sir" (p. 16). On the ride home, Channing cowered in anticipation while his father casually whistled, and upon their return to Newport, his father sat down to read the paper without mentioning the preacher's "alarming intelligence." This blasé continuity of ordinary life amid potentially horrifying circumstances led Channing to question the whole enterprise:

"Could what he had heard be true? No! His father did not believe it; people did not believe it! It was

not true!" He felt that he had been trifled with; that the preacher had deceived him; and from that time he became inclined to distrust everything oratorical, and to measure exactly the meaning of words; he had received a profound lesson on the worth of sincerity.

(p. 16)

If this incident helped kindle his abiding skepticism of the Calvinist worldview, Channing's exposure to a more liberal theology was solidified when he moved to New London, Connecticut, in 1792 to study with his uncle Henry Channing, a clergyman who bucked Calvinist orthodoxy and questioned the divinity of Christ.

HARVARD AND RICHMOND, 1793–1803

The sudden death of Channing's father in 1793 left Lucy Channing and her nine children in a precarious financial position, but since education remained a family priority, Channing diligently continued to prepare for Harvard's entrance exams. He matriculated at Harvard College at the age of fourteen. When he arrived in 1794, Harvard was little more than four brick buildings, three professors, three tutors, and one president. Channing bypassed the austerities and minor humiliations of eighteenth-century undergraduate life by living a half-mile off campus in a sumptuous mansion with his uncle Francis Dana, chief justice of the Commonwealth of Massachusetts. He nevertheless managed to engage with the life of the college, and his conversational and oratorical skills were heightened by the sociability he enjoyed at the Porcellian, the Hasty-Pudding, and other college clubs. Channing was devoted to his studies, and his reading ranged across classic and contemporary history, rhetoric, literature, and philosophy. Over the course of four years, he frequented the college library, borrowing—among other tomes—Longinus, Livy, Cicero, Miguel de Cervantes, Francis Bacon, William Shakespeare, John Locke, Lord Kames, Thomas Reid, Jean-Jacques Rousseau, Hugh Blair, Richard Price, Oliver Goldsmith, and Joseph Priestley.

In 1798 Channing graduated at the top of his class and was consequently chosen to give the closing oration. Though forced by the faculty to

avoid contentious political issues, he spoke on "The Present Age" and criticized the state of post-revolutionary France, a nation he had previously described as "rapacious, lawless, and imperious" (*Life,* p. 36). When Channing reflected back on his college years, he saw the damaging effect of the French Revolution as the prime political and intellectual context of his life at Harvard:

> College was never in a worse state than when I entered it. Society was passing through a most critical stage. The French Revolution had diseased the imagination and unsettled the understanding of men everywhere. The old foundations of social order, loyalty, tradition, habit, reverence for antiquity, were everywhere shaken, if not subverted. The authority of the past was gone. The old forms were outgrown, and new ones had not taken their place. ... The work required men of comprehensive and original minds, able to adapt themselves to the new state of the world.
>
> (p. 30)

The first two decades of Channing's existence were thoroughly grounded in those old forms; he would spend the rest of his post-Harvard life envisioning and explaining the new forms that he imagined were possible. But here, too, the revolution in France helped set a course for his tendency to innovate by leading him to the ministry: as he retrospectively explained his choice of vocation, "the prevalence of infidelity, imported from France, led me to inquire into the evidences of Christianity, and then *I found for what I was made*" (p. 39).

In quest of both financial independence and means to further his studies, Channing agreed to serve as a private tutor for a prominent planter in Richmond, Virginia. His native Federalist assumptions were productively challenged by the prominence of Jeffersonianism in Virginia, and his exposure to the unrestricted converse and warm hospitality enjoyed by Virginians led to his own critique of the typical New England temperament: "I blush for my own people, when I compare the selfish prudence of a Yankee with the generous confidence of a Virginian" (p. 45). At the same time, firsthand acquaintance with the degradations of slavery led to his strong condemnation of that institution. As he put it in one letter, "Language cannot express my detestation of it. ... I should be obliged to show you every vice, heightened by every meanness and added to every misery" (pp. 46–47). As his enthusiasm for Richmond's social life waned, however, Channing devoted himself to an increasingly spartan regime and a rigorous course of study. He stayed up late into the night reading the likes of Adam Ferguson, David Hume, William Godwin, and Mary Wollstonecraft, and when he went to sleep, he forswore the comforts of a bed for the cold severity of the hardwood floor. He kept an abstemious diet, wore threadbare clothes, and went without a much-needed overcoat. Biographers have variously interpreted Channing's asceticism in Richmond as a sustained attempt to overcome effeminacy, suppress the sexual instinct, or ennoble the mind by subverting the body. Andrew Delbanco has aptly noted that his self-denying rituals allowed him to claim for himself the kind of self-mastery that he saw slavery in all its forms as forever impeding; as Channing put it in one of his missives from Virginia, "No empire is so valuable as the empire of one's self" (*Life,* p. 47).

Channing's self-imposed privations irrevocably compromised his health, but in grafting spiritual self-discipline onto his abiding interest in a more secular concept of "disinterested benevolence," they fueled a seriousness of purpose that stayed with him as he left Richmond behind to pursue further theological study. At the same time, Channing's focus on strict self-deprivation foreshadowed the centrality of virtue and moral character in his later articulations of Unitarian thought—a virtue grounded both in the moral perfection of God and the moral capacity of humankind. For the next three years, Channing continued his diligent preparation for the ministry, first at the Redwood Library in Newport, and starting in 1802, as a proctor at Harvard. One of his contemporaries recalled that his "whole soul was engaged in the sacred studies to which he had devoted himself" (p. 85). Whether he was reading the sermons of Joseph Butler, William Law, or any other divine, Channing instinctively turned to writing to clarify his thinking—indeed, in his journals from that period, he urged himself toward greater depths of thought:

WILLIAM ELLERY CHANNING

"It is my misfortune, that I have read much, but have reflected little. Let me reverse this order" (p. 88). In 1802 the Cambridge Association of Ministers granted him a license to preach, and in February 1803, Channing agreed to take over the empty pulpit at the Federal Street Church in Boston—a position he would occupy for the rest of his life.

FEDERAL STREET CHURCH, 1803–1819

Established in Boston with an ample salary, Channing gladly took on the role of paterfamilias, inviting his mother and siblings to abandon Newport in favor of his well-appointed parsonage on Berry Street. Reunited with his family, Channing embraced his new ministerial duties and inaugurated what John Kirkland, a future president of Harvard, described as "a new era in preaching" (*Life,* p. 116). While this essay will consider several of Channing's more famous sermons individually, two ways of gauging the overall effect of his presence in the Federal Street pulpit initially stand out. On a purely quantitative level, Channing's eloquence rapidly increased the size of the once-flagging Federal Street congregation, so much so that the church had to be torn down in 1809 and replaced with a larger edifice. On a qualitative level, comments from Channing's nephew and first biographer elucidate what it was about his sermons that drew so many Bostonians toward Federal Street in the first place:

> He opened to them a large range of thought, presented clear, connected, and complete views of various topics, roused their faculties of discernment by nice discriminations and exact statements, and gratified their taste by the finished simplicity of his style. But the novelty, perhaps, that chiefly stirred his audiences was the directness with which he even then brought his Christian principles to bear upon actual life.
>
> (*Life,* p. 117)

As David Robinson has noted in *The Unitarians and the Universalists,* most accounts of Channing's sermonizing emphasize the interdependence of his "moral earnestness" and "aesthetic appeal" (p. 27). But beyond the substance

and style of his pulpit rhetoric, Channing's broad appeal at this early stage of his career could also be attributed to the moderate position he struck between the liberal bastion of the Congregationalist church and its strictly Calvinist contingent. A short, self-exhorting entry in his journal from the period points toward his deliberate attempt to avoid controversy in favor of a more ecumenical perspective: "Let me promote unity of sentiment, especially on religious and most interesting subjects" (*Life,* p. 112).

The first decade of his ministerial life passed in a relative quiet that was punctured by few significant events. In 1810 his brother Francis fell to consumption, and to the dismay of Channing and many New Englanders, the United States declared war on Britain in 1812. In 1814, with most of his siblings happily settled, Channing gave up his bachelor existence to marry Ruth Gibbs, a cousin, childhood companion, and the daughter of one of Rhode Island's most prosperous tycoons. Ruth's fortune—much of it rooted in rum, real estate, and a vast mercantile concern—would ensure Channing's lifelong financial independence. In 1815 the Channings left the parsonage on Berry Street to take up residence with his mother-in-law on Tremont Street, one of Boston's most opulent enclaves; for the rest of his life, Channing spent long summer vacations at Oakland, the Gibbs family estate in Rhode Island. The Channings had four children, but only two of them survived past infancy.

Theodore Parker once said of Channing that it was "speaking with moderation to say, that no man, of our century, who writes the English tongue, had so much weight with the wise and pious men who speak it" (quoted in *William Ellery Channing: Selected Writings,* p. 3). In just over a decade he had transformed a quiet parish into a focal point of Boston's religious life, but Parker's tribute hinges on Channing's watershed contribution to a theological debate that had been simmering in New England for years. When the Puritans arrived in New England, they brought with them an ardent Calvinism that was quickly incorporated into the American grain. In its most uncompromising form, Calvinism affirmed the "total depravity" of human nature and tied

redemption to "unconditional election," a doctrine that made salvation entirely dependent upon the will of God rather than any human effort. However, the Great Awakening, with its emphasis on personal conviction and morality, swept through the American colonies in the eighteenth century and put orthodox Calvinism under pressure, prompting the established clergy in and around Boston to entertain the possibility of a more liberal theological position. The Enlightenment's investment in reason, tolerance, and human agency also took its toll on the Calvinist worldview. By the turn of the century, divergent opinions on the nature of man and the possibility of his salvation turned into what David Edgell, in *William Ellery Channing: An Intellectual Portrait,* has described as "an ecclesiastical storm" (p. 24).

In 1803 controversy between the liberal-minded and orthodox camps of the Congregationalist church erupted when David Tappan, one of Channing's mentors at Harvard, died and left the Hollis Professorship of Divinity vacant. Orthodox Calvinists, leery of the growing prestige of liberal religion at Harvard, hoped that Jesse Appleton would assume the professorship. Liberals favored the appointment of Henry Ware, who eventually carried the day. While Channing and others attempted to mitigate sectarian spirit, the acrimony that followed in the wake of the "Harvard controversy" resulted in an uncomfortable coexistence within New England Congregationalism as well as an extended war of words and pamphlets. In *Three Prophets of Religious Liberalism,* Conrad Wright has observed that by 1819, the liberals were forced to recognize the distinctiveness of their own theological position and take ownership of the label "Unitarian," a term often deployed by orthodox divines in an attempt to undercut the liberal position. Convinced of its necessity, Channing stepped into the fray, delivering a sermon that Wright has described as both a "party proclamation" and "epoch-making" address (pp. 5–6). In *William Ellery Channing: Selected Writings* (1985), the editor David Robinson has called "Unitarian Christianity" "the single most important sermon in Unitarian his-

tory," but it was also the first of Channing's great works (*Selected Writings,* p. 70).

"UNITARIAN CHRISTIANITY" (1819)

The sermon is a strange genre: simultaneously oral and written, its insignificance in the world of contemporary letters is just a shadow of the high esteem it once enjoyed in the nineteenth century. Like other sermons, "Unitarian Christianity" was the product of a specific time and place, but it also transcended its articulation in print form. In 1819 Channing went to Baltimore to deliver a sermon at the ordination of Jared Sparks, an editor of the *North American Review* who frequently attended the Federal Street Church. The occasion was significant, for it represented Unitarianism's first major foray outside of New England. The hour-and-a-half sermon was quickly printed and even pirated, and it had such a lasting appeal that, as Wright observes, "no pamphlet, save only Tom Paine's *Common Sense,* ever before circulated so widely in this country" (p. 13).

"Unitarian Christianity" is a self-reflexive text; in describing the consanguinity of reason and revelation, Channing attempts to teach as he claims God taught while also modeling the interpretive mode through which he would most like to be understood. In one of the sermon's predominant metaphors, Channing compares God to a wise teacher who avoids perplexing his pupils with unintelligible assertions or "apparent contradictions" (vol. 3, p. 68). In this sense, God surpasses "all other instructors in bringing down truth to our apprehension, and in showing its loveliness and harmony" (p. 69). Channing is actuated by a similar impulse and states at the outset his intention to convey his truth "as clearly as I can" (p. 60). For Channing, there is no irreverence in this godlike aspiration. In the first section of the essay, he articulates a set of principles that Unitarians bring to bear on the interpretation of scripture, all of which are rooted in the "leading principle" that the Bible should be approached just like any other book: "We believe that God, when he speaks to the human race, conforms ... to the established rules of speaking and writing" (p. 61). More specifically, mak-

ing sense of scripture, as of any other text, does not require turning a blind eye to truths derived from observation and experience, the intentions of its authors, or even its historical context. Attempting to come to terms with the new theological possibilities opened up by the "higher criticism" emanating from Germany, Channing looked back to his father's Federalist enthusiasm in describing the affinity of revelation and reason:

> We reason about the Bible as precisely as civilians do about the constitution under which we live; who, you know, are accustomed to limit one provision of that venerable instrument by others, and to fix the precise import of its parts, by inquiring into its general spirit, into the limitations of its authors, and into the prevalent feelings, impressions, and circumstances of the time when it was framed.
>
> (p. 65)

At the same time, Channing cautiously diffused the orthodox allegation that Unitarians elevated reason over and above revelation. Far from being "the antagonist of reason," he held that it worked in alliance with revelation (p. 66). While the use of reason in settling religious questions was fraught with danger, its hazards paled in comparison to the danger of forsaking it.

In the second and longer section of the Baltimore sermon, Channing explains the doctrinal upshots of a rational interpretation of the Bible, emphasizing in particular the beliefs that set Unitarians apart from their orthodox associates. Not surprisingly, he turns first to the tenet responsible for denominating the liberal movement: the rejection of the Trinity in favor of God's essential unity. Appealing to both scripture and the sensibility of his auditors, Channing describes the idea that one God could be made up of three consciousnesses as both "irrational and unscriptural" (p. 71). On a practical level, Channing claims that the Trinity is a potentially idolatrous distraction from God's unity, but he also observes that scripture provides scant evidence for the idea that God comprises "three infinite and equal persons":

> That a doctrine so strange, so liable to misapprehension, so fundamental as this is said to be, and requiring such careful exposition, should be left so undefined and unprotected, to be made out by infer-

ence, and to be hunted through distant and detached parts of Scripture, this is a difficulty, which, we think, no ingenuity can explain.

(p. 72)

The Unitarian rejection of the Trinity gives rise to another point of departure from Christian orthodoxy: in affirming the unity of God, Channing also attests to the distinction and unity of Jesus Christ, dismissing the view that he consists of two souls, "the one divine, the other human; the one weak, the other almighty; the one ignorant, the other omniscient" (p. 76). For Channing, the duality of Christ gives rise to intractable contradictions; either his human suffering belies the infinite and unchangeable nature of God, or his divine nature reduces his humiliation to an empty fiction.

Channing made a thorough case for the unities responsible for the newly adopted name of the liberal Christianity he was endorsing, but, like his fellow Unitarians, he had even larger theological issues in sight. As Wright has observed, Unitarianism's "basic disagreement with orthodoxy was over the nature of man and the doctrines of grace, rather than over the doctrine of the Trinity" (p. 7). The final section of Channing's sermon rejects the Calvinist notion that Jonathan Edwards made famous—the "injurious view" that we are "Sinners in the Hands of an Angry God"—in the course of affirming both God's moral perfection and the correspondent moral potential of humankind (vol. 3, p. 83). Dispensing with divine wrath, Channing dwells on God's parental character and the perfect reconciliation of his justice and mercy; at the same time, he rejects the "unspeakable cruelty" of a God who would make his children's birthright a wholly depraved nature (p. 86). But this realignment of God is matched by an equally compelling realignment of man. In *Channing: The Reluctant Radical,* Jack Mendelsohn makes the crucial observation that the moral perfection of Channing's God "was both understandable and imitable in human terms" (p. 162). As his ascetic regime in Richmond made clear, Channing's religious sensibility had always been linked to a classical conception of virtue. In dealing a blow to the passive position of man in the Calvinist

scheme, Channing makes a case not just for the freedom of the will but for its implication in the justice and happiness of the world:

> We believe that all virtue has its foundation in the moral nature of man, that is, in conscience, or his sense of duty, and in the power of forming his temper and life according to conscience. We believe that these moral faculties are the grounds of responsibility, and the highest distinctions of human nature.
>
> (vol. 3, p. 93)

In highlighting the vast possibility of man's moral nature, Channing aligned himself with the culture of reform that would sweep through Boston in the 1820s and 1830s, but his case for the shared moral nature of both God and man laid the foundation for what, a decade later, would become his most daring spiritual claim—the idea that the "great end" of religion lay in promoting "a growing likeness to the Supreme Being" (p. 228).

"THE MORAL ARGUMENT AGAINST CALVINISM" *(1820)*

In 1820 Channing reprised and refined his argument against Calvinism, this time in the context of a polemical review printed in the *Christian Disciple*, a magazine edited by the Unitarians. As with "Unitarian Christianity," Channing's main ideological argument—that knowledge of God depends upon fully confiding in the faculties that make that knowledge possible—is grounded in an argument about literary style. At the outset of the essay, Channing dismisses a religious rhetoric that had allowed elegance and uncommon turns of phrase to obscure the clarity of divine truth. Aligning his own Unitarian practice with a rejection of "circuitous, measured phraseology" and a return to commonplace speech, Channing suggests that preaching in New England is "becoming more direct, aims more at impression, and seeks the nearest way to men's hearts and consciences" (vol. 1, pp. 220–221). But Channing's delineation of his own style has deeper theological connotations. In his brief account, Calvinism owes its long-standing triumph

to a cultivated fear that circumvents the innate morality and rationality of humankind; the stranglehold of God's wrath ensures that "minds and consciences are subdued by terror" (p. 218). Like bad rhetoric, religious terror appeals to the power of passion rather than reason; for Channing, both kinds of misdirection produce a "soporific" sensibility and concomitant "lethargy" (pp. 221, 219). Channing's essay is essentially a call to conscience, a quiet anticipation of Henry David Thoreau's assertion in *Walden* (1854) that we must "reawaken and keep ourselves awake" (1983 ed., p. 134). Like a direct and plain style, then, rational religion insists on the human capacity to stand in judgment of God and his works. As Channing put it, "We are presumptuous, we are told, in judging of our Creator. But he himself has made this our duty, in giving us a moral faculty; and to decline it, is to violate the primary law of our nature" (vol. 1, p. 232).

Based on that standard of judgment, Channing discloses the thrust of his moral argument: if a doctrine fails to live up to our sense of goodness and justice, it cannot be a true representation of God's character. In forwarding this conclusion, Channing pushed back against a prominent Calvinist counterargument, one that posited a central disconnect between God's incomprehensible infinity and man's finite understanding. To claim, as some Calvinists did, that "the happiness of the universe may require an administration of human affairs which is very offensive to limited understandings" was to negate a cornerstone of emerging Unitarian theology:

> In affirming the existence and perfections of God, we suppose and affirm the existence in ourselves of faculties which correspond to these sublime objects, and which are fitted to discern them. ... Nothing is gained to piety by degrading human nature, for in the competency of this nature to know and judge of God all piety has its foundation.
>
> (pp. 224, 226)

God would always remain incomprehensible, with his powers and purposes exceeding that which could be wholly conceived by the human mind. But for Channing, that incomprehensibility did not equal unintelligibility. In religion, as in

life, complete knowledge was hardly possible, but reason could augment and amplify our partial knowledge of God. Unequivocal about its ability to clarify revelation, the essay concludes on a triumphant note: in celebrating Calvinism's gradual demise, Channing bids farewell to "the theology of the sixteenth century" (p. 240).

THE UNITARIAN MOVEMENT AND TRAVELS ABROAD, 1820–1828

After the Baltimore sermon, Channing became the de facto leader of the new Unitarian movement and was increasingly drawn into the public spotlight. In 1820 he organized the Berry Street Conference, an annual meeting and "bond of union" for liberal ministers that was a direct predecessor of the American Unitarian Association (*Life,* p. 218). That same year, Harvard made him an honorary doctor of divinity. When he returned to Harvard in March 1821 to give the Dudleian Lecture—a vigorous defense of the importance of miracles in Christianity that he titled "The Evidences of Revealed Religion"—a seventeen-year-old Ralph Waldo Emerson was in the audience. In his journal, Emerson later described Channing's lecture as a prime example of the "moral imagination" that he held to be "the highest species of reasoning upon divine subjects" (*Journals,* vol. 2, p. 238).

The combination of his public efforts on behalf of Unitarianism and his regular responsibilities at Federal Street took an increasing toll on his health. A trip to the mountains of New Hampshire and Vermont in 1821 did little to mitigate this deterioration, prompting him to request a year's leave of absence so that he might seek better health in Europe. Sailing from Boston to Liverpool, the Channings spent two months in England before making a Continental tour through France, Switzerland, and Italy. In Switzerland, Channing was thrilled and physically rejuvenated by the rugged sublimity of the Alps. In Florence, he was struck in equal measure by the grandeur of Italian art and what he described as the insensibility of its people to their own masterpieces. Surpassing his pleasure in the scenery and culture of Europe, however, was the satisfaction that Channing derived from meeting several of his favorite British poets. He had extended conversations with William Wordsworth, Robert Southey, and Samuel Taylor Coleridge, but the afternoon that he spent with Wordsworth in Grasmere seems to have made the deepest impression on him:

> Mr. Wordsworth's conversation was free, various, animated. We talked so eagerly as often to interrupt one another. And as I descended into Grassmere [*sic*] near sunset, with the placid lake before me, and Wordsworth talking and reciting poetry with a poet's spirit by my side, I felt that the combination of circumstances was such as my highest hopes could never have anticipated.
>
> (*Life,* p. 342)

Channing rounded out his European adventure by visiting Tintern Abbey, sailing to the Isle of Wight, and communing with leading Unitarians in Bristol, Southampton, and London. By July 1823 he was once again at sea. Beyond improving his spirits and his health, the trip left a lasting mark on Channing after he returned to Boston. In the short term, it helped him recognize that his health and his intellectual aspirations had been held in check by the weight of his increasingly onerous responsibilities. Channing agreed to forgo a quarter of his salary if the Federal Street Society would allow him to hire a junior colleague. In 1824, after preaching fifteen probationary sermons, Ezra Stiles Gannett was selected to fill the vacancy.

In the long term, Channing's intellectual excursion in Europe fueled his desire to make a contribution to the wider world of letters. The space opened up by Gannett's appointment allowed Channing to pursue his literary ambitions, and over the course of the next six years he wrote three ambitious essays for the *Christian Examiner* on John Milton, Napoleon Bonaparte, and François Fénelon. While it would be an understatement to say that these essays are infrequently read in the twenty-first century, Emerson rated Channing's essays on Milton and Napoleon so highly that he described them as "the first specimens in this country of that large criticism which in England had given power and fame to the Edinburgh Review. They were widely read,

and of course immediately fruitful in provoking emulation which lifted the style of Journalism" (*Complete Works,* vol. 10, p. 339). His essays would, in time, cement his reputation abroad, but his sermons were still in high demand at home. In the mid-1820s Elizabeth Palmer Peabody started to make transcriptions of his sermons, and before long, esteemed figures like Daniel Webster were requesting their publication. Though Channing continued to struggle with poor health, his sermon on man's "Likeness to God" suggests that his thoughts were as vital as ever.

"LIKENESS TO GOD" (1828)

In "The Moral Argument Against Calvinism," Channing had savaged the Calvinist conception of God. Describing him as a "heart-withering" figure, he let his depiction of a father who brings totally depraved children into the world only to torture them stand more like a portrait than a caricature (vol. 1, p. 238). Rejecting what he saw as Calvinism's misrepresentation of both divine and human nature, Channing claimed in that essay that it was the correspondence between human and divine faculties that allowed one to make sense of God in the first place. In 1828, when Channing went to Providence to deliver Frederick Farley's ordination sermon, he attempted to deal a final blow to the Calvinist conception of God by explaining this central correspondence with "a calm and pure zeal" (vol. 3, p. 228).

At the outset of his essay "Likeness to God," Channing proposes that the ultimate end of true religion lies in cultivating a "growing likeness to the Supreme Being" (p. 228). This assertion encapsulated many of his deepest theological preoccupations. Rooted in the rational power of the mind, his affirmation of a likeness between the human and the divine entailed not only a recognition of the "intellectual and moral affinity" that humans share with God, but an acknowledgment that the expansion of that affinity would necessitate vigorous moral exertion (p. 229). In other words, "Likeness to God" was not just an inherited condition but an aspiration. As one grows in resemblance to God, faith turns into

vision. Aligned with the mind of the maker, "we are brought into harmony with the creation" and start to see behind the visible fabric of the world "the principles from which the universe sprung" (p. 230).

The radicalism of this view should not be underestimated. For centuries, theologians had emphasized the disparity between the intellect of man and the mind of God. In dramatically overturning this view, Channing's sermon anticipated the Transcendentalists and their fixation on man's innate identity; it is a decisively small step from Channing's emphasis of a "kindred nature" (p. 233) between God and man to Emerson's assertion, in *Nature* (1836), that as "the currents of the Universal Being circulate through me" I become a "part and particle of God" (vol. 1, p. 10). In making such a bold claim, Channing had anticipated orthodox accusations of pantheism, mysticism, and spiritual pride, but he nevertheless saw his own observations as sanctioned by reason, nature, and revelation in equal measure.

Channing called the sermon "Likeness to God," but he could have called it "God's Likeness to Man" just as easily. Most accounts of the sermon's significance place much weight on its emphasis of the potential for humans to approximate the divinity of God. Taken as a whole, however, Channing's reflections on the ability of humans to grow in God's likeness are matched by his contention that all of our ideas about God spring from a distinctly human source:

> Whence do we derive our knowledge of the attributes and perfections which constitute the Supreme Being? I answer, we derive them from our own souls. The divine attributes are first developed in ourselves, and thence transferred to our Creator. The idea of God, sublime and awful as it is, is the idea of our own spiritual nature, purified and enlarged to infinity.
>
> (vol. 3, p. 233)

For Channing, grasping the mind of God requires an act of extrapolation from the "operations and faculties of our own souls"; his intelligence is an extension of ours, refined of all its error and imperfection (p. 233). Similarly, human conscience and the "lawgiver in our own breasts" make it possible to form an idea of God's moral

perfection (p. 234). Countering the view that God's infinite nature places him outside the purview of human conception, Channing goes so far as to argue that the "higher actions" of the soul—the imaginative faculty, for example, or its capacity for disinterestedness—hint at an infinity that becomes our foundation for imagining God's infinity (p. 237).

Infinity aside, however, Channing recognized that man's godlike potential stood in precarious balance with his "animal propensities," and that reason existed in almost constant conflict with passion (p. 251). As Channing put it, "To grow in the likeness of God, we need not cease to be men" (p. 243). But in ordaining a new minister, Channing held out the possibility that religion might appeal to man's better nature, rather than his savage side. In his terms, the right role of a minister was to "speak to men, as to beings liberally gifted, and made for God" (p. 254).

"REMARKS ON NATIONAL LITERATURE" (1830)

Seven years before Emerson claimed that Americans had "listened too long to the courtly muses of Europe" (*Complete Works,* vol. 1, p. 114), Channing framed the same premise as a question: "Shall America be only an echo of what is thought and written under the aristocracies beyond the ocean?" (vol. 1, p. 262). First printed in *The Christian Examiner,* Channing's multifaceted case for the development of a national literature had the immediate effect of solidifying his international reputation. For Channing, literature vastly exceeded the realm of novels and poetry to include writings devoted to the natural sciences and a broad range of works that examined the complexities of human nature and human life. At the beginning of "Remarks on National Literature" (1830), he defines succinctly what he describes at length: "The expression of superior mind in writing, we regard, then, as a nation's literature" (p. 244). The breadth of this definition is important, for it directly informs what he describes as the greatest distinction a country can have. For Channing, a nation's ability to "produce superior men" exceeds all the advantages that it derives from climate, soil, and geography. For example, while acknowledging the genius of Benjamin Franklin and Jonathan Edwards, Channing nevertheless admits that the material prosperity of the United States had noticeably surpassed its contributions to the international republic of letters. As he put it, "We want those lights which make a country conspicuous at a distance" (p. 252).

When Channing starts to enumerate the obstacles that impede the formation of a national literature, the only significant factor that emerges is an American overemphasis on useful knowledge. While Channing owns that Americans had prioritized the cultivation of matter over that of mind, a diplomatic cautiousness tempers his critique of the utilitarian impulse:

> We beg that we may not be misapprehended. We offer these remarks to correct what we deem a disproportioned attention to physical good, and not at all to condemn the expenditure of ingenuity and strength on the outward world. There is a harmony between all our great interests, between inward and outward improvements; and, by establishing among them a wise order, all will be secured.
>
> (pp. 245–246)

Utilitarianism might stand as a threat to the literary enterprise, but Channing also recognizes that it could provide a rationale for its significance. Over the course of the essay, Channing gradually widens his conception of utility. It is not limited to the knowledge that provides necessities of life. In this broad sense, poetry, history, and philosophy are all branches of useful knowledge that minister to "our complex and various nature" (pp. 257). Channing's call for a national literature is not ultimately an appeal for a new and original aesthetic but rather an acknowledgment of the role that intellectual culture plays in national life. It should come as no surprise, then, that Channing also makes his case for a new national literature on religious grounds. Suggesting that the rational exploration of Christianity ought to "take the highest place in a nation's literature," he affirms the compatibility of literary and religious pursuits while also making a bid for his own place in an emergent American canon (p. 251).

While consistently acknowledging the power and importance of British and European literature,

Channing does not hesitate to sound a frequent note of American exceptionalism. He claims, for example, that the democratic structure of the United States would allow its native authors to diffuse their genius throughout a wider range of society. In a similar vein, he holds that Americans occupy a position "from which the great subjects of literature may be viewed more justly than from those which most other nations hold" (p. 267). Providentially placed on a new continent with new institutions and new freedoms, Americans were still looking to the literature of the old world. As Channing pointedly averred, "We boast of our political institutions, and receive our chief teachings, books, impressions, from the school of monarchy" (p. 255). Anticipating a native literature rooted in a "new spirit," Channing's essay was a mile marker on the road to American literary emergence (p. 270). Oliver Wendell Holmes once called Emerson's Phi Beta Kappa address an "intellectual Declaration of Independence," but Emerson's declaration was preceded by Channing's equally independent, though differently inflected, remarks (Edgell, p. 127).

ABOLITION AND LATER YEARS, 1830–1841

In 1819, when Channing pushed back against the Calvinism that had shaped New England from its founding, the scandal in Boston was drowned out by celebration. As his interest in practical reform outstripped his attention to doctrinal affairs over the next two decades, Channing's ability to shake up the establishment earned him as much blame as praise. Consider, for example, how the Brahmins of Beacon Hill would have responded to his claim that a societal overemphasis on wealth would ensure that one day masses of degraded men would discover that "the end and dignity of a human being is to remodel social institutions and manners" (*Life,* p. 515). The height of Channing's fame corresponded with the startlingly rapid urbanization of Boston, and he lent himself to many of the crucial reform projects that such a process made conspicuous: sustainable care for the poor, hospital reform, progressive education, the temperance movement, the elimination of child labor, and the curtailment of debtors' imprisonment. This was a striking range of activism for a man who spent years reading divinity and philosophy late into the night. As Jack Mendelsohn argues, however, what appears to be a reversal was in fact a fulfillment of Channing's own theological positions:

> The clue to the reversal of Channing's usual course of life—he became more involved, more radical, more outspoken, with each of his last twenty years—is that he was an embodiment of his preachments. He believed that religious faith, properly conceived, built constantly stronger, deeper, wider bonds between man and man, between man and his Creator.
>
> (pp. 200–201)

More than any other prompt for reform, however, the antislavery movement exemplified Channing's gradual awakening to both the tangible implications of principles and the social turbulence that would accompany his adherence to them.

Channing's father had owned slaves before the Revolution, and several stayed on as family servants; as a small child, Channing was himself carried to school every day by a former slave. In 1830, however, his wife's arthritis and his own ill health prompted a close encounter with the degradation of slavery that would, in turn, lead him to campaign against it for the rest of his life. Seeking rest in a warmer climate, the Channings spent half a year in St. Croix, where each day Channing would leave his rented rooms to observe and converse with the slaves who toiled at a local plantation. As he described it in his final public oration, "A few steps placed me in the midst of their huts. Here was a volume on slavery opened always before my eyes, and how could I help learning its lessons?" (vol. 6, p. 381). Upon his return to Boston, Channing denounced slavery in moderate terms but remained equally skeptical of extreme rhetoric used by abolitionists like William Lloyd Garrison. In 1835 he published *Slavery,* a short book that cataloged the evils of slavery and decimated the biblical argument in its favor. Critiquing Northerners and Southerners alike, his central objection to an institution that blurred the line between person and property was grounded in the high conception of human nature he had proclaimed in "Unitarian Christianity" and "Likeness to God":

He cannot be property in the sight of God and justice, because he is a Rational, Moral, Immortal Being; because created in God's image, and therefore in the highest sense his child; because created to unfold godlike faculties, and to govern himself by a Divine Law written on his heart, and republished in God's Word. His whole nature forbids that he should be seized as property.

(vol. 2, p. 26)

Slavery was immediately controversial, and in time it became a national best seller. Channing's friend Harriet Martineau claimed that it was "wondered at and sighed over in private houses, rebuked and abused in Congress, and foamed at in the South" (cited in Mendelsohn, p. 253). In casting his fate with the abolitionist cause, Channing had assumed an unsteady position in a deeply divided Boston. While Channing earned admiration from the likes of John Quincy Adams, conservative members of the Federal Street Society snubbed him in passing, and ardent abolitionists like Garrison censured his timidity. Increasingly distraught by the indifference of Bostonians, Channing became more vocal and pointed in his critique. In 1837 he opposed the annexation of Texas in an open letter to Henry Clay, and he helped organize a gathering at Faneuil Hall to protest the lynching of the abolitionist Elijah Lovejoy in Illinois. Progressively disenchanted with his radicalism, the Federal Street congregation prevented Channing from reading announcements for antislavery meetings from the pulpit. In 1840, when his friend and fellow abolitionist Charles Follen was killed in a fire, the standing committee at Federal Street would not let Channing hold a funeral in his own church. Though maintaining a nominal affiliation with the Federal Street Church, Channing relinquished the salary and public functions of the pastorate he had held for almost four decades. He would preach in the pulpit he made famous only one more time before his death.

"SELF-CULTURE" (1838)

In "Likeness to God," Channing had speculated that traces of divinity in the human mind stood as a kind of warrant for the "perpetual unfolding and enlargement" of the powers and faculties that man shared in common with God (vol. 3, p. 241). Often considered to be a precursor to the self-help movement in America, Channing's "Self-Culture" (1838) is a largely secular, realistic, and almost programmatic exploration of what that unfolding and enlargement might look like. Speaking to an audience primarily composed of artisans and laborers, Channing managed to address a favorite topic without indulging in his penchant for theological innovation. His topic was self-culture, "or the care which every man owes to himself, to the unfolding and perfecting of his nature" (vol. 2, p. 354). His structure was equally straightforward: a broad consideration of the central branches of self-culture was followed by a disquisition on the "extensive" means of its promotion. But this taxonomy of personal improvement was predicated on his acknowledgment of each person's "self-searching" and "self-forming" powers (p. 355). In a world that emphasizes externals, self-culture necessitates an inward turn, an exploration of what often looms as "a dark, vague chaos," but for Channing, that exploration stands as prologue to the wondrous work of "determining and forming ourselves" (p. 356). This impetus to reflect and unfold comes across as a natural outgrowth of Channing's stance on man's godlike character, but its religious justification and anti-Calvinist trappings largely drop out of the picture, appearing only in flashes:

Of all the discoveries which men need to make, the most important at the present moment, is that of the self-forming power treasured up in themselves. They little suspect its extent, as little as the savage apprehends the energy which the mind is created to exert on the material world. It transcends in importance all our power over outward nature. There is more of divinity in it, than in the force which impels the outward universe; and yet how little we comprehend it!

(pp. 356–357)

In this representative passage, Channing takes a strange line of approach, for though he attempts to elevate mental self-formation above more outward, material kinds of power, he ends up circling self-consciously around the fact of the outward world. As David Robinson has noted in

his essay on "The Legacy of Channing," critics targeted "Self-Culture" for espousing "a program of self-aggrandizement with disturbingly asocial and egotistical overtones," but for Channing, this work of the self was integrally related to the wider world (p. 228). For example, while Channing points to Christianity as the ultimate means for effecting self-improvement, just below it stands politics, for while the strength of a republic depends upon the education of its citizens, "it is equally true, that a republic is a powerful means of educating the multitude" (p. 386).

But much of the essay strikes a more conventional note. In delineating the branches of self-culture, Channing divides the possibility of improvement into five broad categories: moral, religious, intellectual, social, and practical. There are, of course, interrelations between the categories. In particular, Channing observes that moral, religious, and intellectual self-culture all require disinterestedness: "No part of self-knowledge is more important than to discern clearly these two great principles, the self-seeking and the disinterested; and the most important part of self-culture is to depress the former, and to exalt the latter, or to enthrone the sense of duty within us" (pp. 358–359). Alongside his list of five conventional categories for self-development, Channing includes two often-overlooked branches of self-cultivation: the perception of beauty and the power of utterance. Channing delivered "Self-Culture" just two years after Emerson published *Nature,* and his comments on the connection between the beauty of the world and the sublime attributes of the soul point, once again, to his nascent Transcendentalist leanings. At the same time, his thoughts on the importance of apt speech testify to the social dimension of his self-culture. As he puts it, "A man was not made to shut up his mind in itself; but to give it voice" (p. 367).

As a whole, Channing's discourse turns on the compatibility of self-culture and a life of labor. In the longest section of his address, he outlines the various means for forwarding self-culture that exist in anyone's life. Ranging from the concrete to the abstract, he commends the shaping power of books, religion, occupation, and adverse circumstance, but he also dwells on the necessity of a resolute purpose:

> A vigorous purpose makes much out of life, breathes power into weak instruments, disarms difficulties, and even turns them into assistances. ... A great idea, like this of Self-culture, if seized on clearly and vigorously, burns like a living coal in the soul. He who deliberately adopts a great end, has, by this act, half accomplished it, has scaled the chief barrier to success.
>
> (p. 371)

In a triumph of shrewd rhetoric, Channing effortlessly provides what he commends; in deliberately choosing to listen to his discourse, his auditors had already, in effect, half accomplished their end. But in translating his theological convictions into the idiom of a secular public sphere, Channing also found a way to reconcile the religious and political imperatives that had dramatically shaped his childhood and set the terms for his own self-culture. As Daniel Walker Howe has observed, Channing himself held the lecture in high esteem: when he arranged his collected works for publication, he put "Self-Culture" ahead of everything else.

"AN ADDRESS DELIVERED AT LENOX" (1842) AND BEYOND

In the spring of 1842, Channing and his wife embarked on a trip through rural Pennsylvania, and on their return home they stopped in Lenox, Massachusetts, with hopes that the Berkshires would reinvigorate Channing's health. The mountains agreed with him, and in one letter to Boston he described "finding life a sweeter cup as I approach what are called its dregs, looking round on this fair, glorious creation with a serener love, and finding more to hope for in society at the very time that its evils weigh more on my mind" (*Life,* p. 692).

On August 1, Channing requested the use of the Lenox meetinghouse so that he might mark one source of that hope. In celebrating the fourth anniversary of emancipation in the British West Indies—an event that had resulted in the libera-

tion of 800,000 human beings—Channing recounted his abolitionist awakenings and the singularity of his own position. His tone was mild but earnest: "Do not mix me up with other men, good or bad; but listen to me as a separate witness, standing on my own ground, and desirous to express with all plainness what seems to be the truth" (vol. 6, p. 382). Vivid, full of examples, and charged with empathy, "An Address Delivered at Lenox" invokes one successful emancipation to counter the charge that abolishing slavery in the United States would be a chaotic and lawless affair, a "universal massacre" (p. 400). For Channing, the fear of riots and sundered order implies a severe misunderstanding of human nature. In effect, Channing argues that granting freedom to slaves would prompt them to cultivate the full range of their humanity. It would, in his words, give them not just new courage and dignity, but "a firmer tone, a manlier tread" (p. 393). In treating a man like a beast, slavery makes a mockery of man's innate divinity:

> What is the end and essence of life? It is, to expand all of our faculties and affections. It is, to grow, to gain by exercise new energy, new intellect, new love. It is, to hope, to strive, to bring out what is within us, to press towards what is above us. In other words, it is, to be Free. Slavery is thus at war with the true life of human nature.
>
> (p. 390)

Taking the effects of emancipation in the West Indies as proof, Channing implies—somewhat naively—that the bestowal of freedom will always be accompanied by Christian worship, domestic stability, and economic reconstruction. This is Channing at his most optimistic, the prophet of self-culture who could gladly report of the West Indies that the "emancipated are making progress in intelligence, comforts, purity; and progress is the great good of life" (p. 400). But the view gets even brighter, and Channing cannot help but relish his point: "The spirit of education has sprung up among the people to an extent worthy of admiration" (p. 402).

While Channing was invested in the progressive possibility of the future, his address at Lenox balanced this optimism with a bleak description of the present reality. When pressed, he could still replicate the fire and brimstone aura of the Calvinist church:

> Our own country is, in part, the land of slavery; and slavery becomes more hideous here than anywhere else by its contrast with our free institutions. It is deformity married to beauty. It is as if a flame from hell were to burst forth in the regions of the blessed. No other evil in our country but this should alarm us. Our other difficulties are the mists, dimming our prospects for a moment. This is a dark cloud, scowling over our whole land; and within it the prophetic ear hears the low muttering of the angry thunder.
>
> (p. 413)

The thunder would come, but Channing would be spared its sound. He spent another tranquil month in Lenox and departed for the Green Mountains of Vermont at the beginning of September. He caught typhoid fever on the trip, and after languishing for a month, died in Bennington, Vermont, on October 2, 1842.

Selected Bibliography

WORKS OF WILLIAM ELLERY CHANNING

COLLECTIONS

The Perfect Life in Twelve Discourses. Edited by William Henry Channing. Boston: Roberts Brothers, 1873.

The Works of William Ellery Channing. 6 vols. Boston: American Unitarian Association, 1903. (In this essay, all citations from Channing's work refer to this edition.)

William Ellery Channing: Selected Writings. Edited by David Robinson. New York: Paulist Press, 1985.

OTHER WORKS

The Correspondence of William Ellery Channing, D.D., and Lucy Aikin. Edited by Anna Letitia Le Breton. Boston: Roberts Brothers, 1874.

Dr. Channing's Note-Book. Selected by Grace Ellery Channing. Boston and New York: Houghton, Mifflin, 1887.

PAPERS

William Ellery Channing Papers, 1791–1892. Massachusetts Historical Society, Boston, Mass.

Channing, William Ellery. Papers, 1803–1900; 1803–1980. Andover-Harvard Theological Library, Harvard Divinity School, Cambridge, Mass.

BIOGRAPHICAL STUDIES

Brown, Arthur W. *Always Young for Liberty: A Biography of William Ellery Channing.* Syracuse, N.Y.: Syracuse University Press, 1956.

Chadwick, John White. *William Ellery Channing: Minister of Religion.* Boston: Houghton, Mifflin, 1903.

Channing, William Henry. *The Life of William Ellery Channing, D.D.* Boston: American Unitarian Association, 1882.

Delbanco, Andrew. *William Ellery Channing: An Essay on the Liberal Spirit in America.* Cambridge, Mass.: Harvard University Press, 1981.

Mendelsohn, Jack. *Channing: The Reluctant Radical.* Boston: Little, Brown, 1971.

Peabody, Elizabeth Palmer. *Reminiscences of Rev. Wm. Ellery Channing, D.D.* Boston: Roberts Brothers, 1880.

CRITICAL AND CONTEXTUAL STUDIES

Beer, John. "William Ellery Channing Visits the Lake Poets." *Review of English Studies* 42:212–226 (May 1991).

Edgell, David P. *William Ellery Channing: An Intellectual Portrait.* Boston: Beacon Press, 1955.

Howe, Daniel Walker. *The Unitarian Conscience: Harvard Moral Philosophy, 1805–1861.* Cambridge, Mass.: Harvard University Press, 1970.

Robinson, David. "The Legacy of Channing: Culture as a Religious Category in New England Thought." *Harvard Theological Review* 74:221–239 (April 1981).

———. *The Unitarians and the Universalists.* Westport, Conn., and London: Greenwood Press, 1985.

Spiller, Robert E. "A Case for W. E. Channing." *New England Quarterly* 3:55–81 (January 1930).

Wright, Conrad. *Three Prophets of Religious Liberalism: Channing, Emerson, Parker.* Boston: Beacon Press, 1961.

OTHER SOURCES

Emerson, Ralph Waldo. *The Complete Works of Ralph Waldo Emerson.* 12 vols. Boston and New York: Houghton, Mifflin and Company, 1903.

———. *The Journals and Miscellaneous Notebooks of Ralph Waldo Emerson.* 16 vols. Edited by William Gilman et. al. Cambridge, Mass.: Belknap Press of Harvard University Press, 1960–1982.

Thoreau, Henry David. *Walden and Civil Disobedience.* New York: Penguin, 1983.

JUNOT DÍAZ

(1968—)

Allen Guy Wilcox

JUNOT DÍAZ, ONE of America's most fully developed and imaginative writers at the onset of the twenty-first century, is the author of two volumes of short stories, *Drown* (1996) and *This Is How You Lose Her* (2012), and the Pulitzer Prize–winning novel *The Brief Wondrous Life of Oscar Wao* (2007). A professor of writing at the Massachusetts Institute of Technology, he was the recipient in 2012 of a fellowship from the John D. and Catherine T. MacArthur Foundation.

LIFE

Junot Díaz was born in a clinic in Santo Domingo, the capital of the Dominican Republic, on the very last day of 1968. Only one nurse was present to assist his mother with the birth: it was New Year's Eve, and everyone else who worked in the clinic had left for the night to celebrate.

Santo Domingo, formerly known as Ciudad Trujillo, or Trujillo Town, had only recently begun to emerge from Raphael Trujillo's thirty-year career of despotism and autocracy when Díaz was born. It was a city and a country in many ways blighted by years of isolation from the comity of nations and by politically motivated nepotism, thievery, and murder at home. Trujillo, who was assassinated in 1961, figures heavily in Díaz' writing. A depiction of his killing can be found in lurid, imagistic detail in his novel *The Brief Wondrous Life of Oscar Wao,* published in 2007. In Díaz' writing, and especially in this novel, Trujillo's actual identity becomes transmogrified into an idea: he is the overarching godhead of masculine domineering, desire, and degradation, a theme that runs through all Díaz' work in many instances, large and small. His hubris and disregard for women are special hallmarks of his brutality and exist to lesser degrees in nearly all Díaz' male characters. Simultaneously, Trujillo's spirit becomes conflated in the writing with an ancient Taíno curse, *fukú*, a ruinous kismet that taints families on the scale of a single household as well as on the scale of a nation.

In December 1974 Díaz boarded a Pan Am flight with his family bound for JFK Airport and a new life in the United States. He was about to turn seven. The family had moved from Santo Domingo to join their father in Parlin, New Jersey, an unincorporated hamlet in Middlesex County, south across the Raritan River from Edison. When Junot lived in Parlin, it was best known as the hometown of the rock singer Jon Bon Jovi. At the time of his arrival, he hadn't seen his father in years—this, too, weighs heavily on the paradigm Díaz ascribes to men, especially Dominican men, in his fiction. Absenteeism among fathers is often compensated for with violent mood swings or an overabundance of reprimanding upon their return. Often we encounter scenes of fathers leaving their sons in the car while they jaunt upstairs for an illicit tryst: profligacy and cheating is also a major theme in Díaz' universe.

Once in the United States, Díaz began an edacious, committed relationship with reading in English and in so doing would claim another major portion of his literary inheritance. Though his first language was Spanish, he would not learn to read in that language until he was in his mid-twenties. In this way, a rich relationship with reading in English (a hallmark of every great American writer) and the experience of United States and Western culture, including popular culture, bloomed within Díaz simultaneously during his first years in the States.

Many of the stories he came to treasure in his adolescence were classics of genre fiction and comics culture, reflected in both Oscar and Yunior's appetite for stylized stories of heroes and horrors in *The Brief Wondrous Life of Oscar Wao*. Coming of age during the latent stages of the cold war in the 1980s, Díaz hit his teen years immersed in a culture of atomic fear and nuclear apocalypse, a theme he returns to explicitly again and again. The Iron Curtain was real and seemingly impermeable. Solidarity protests were brutally quashed in Poland, Arnold Schwarzenegger starred as a Soviet narc in *Red Heat*. Television was rife with the anticommunist fear-mongering of President Ronald Reagan's administration and the introduction of "Star Wars" foreign policy.

The move from the Dominican Republic itself Díaz often references as a "sci-fi" event: the DR and New Jersey in the 1970s were separated not only by wildly different levels of development ("third world" to "first world") but, as Díaz suggests, by centuries. So the move to New Jersey, his arrival as an "alien," could readily be understood in terms of science fiction and time travel. End-of-days literature was crammed on bookstore racks, and Díaz, by now set in his rapacious reading habits, couldn't get enough.

Díaz graduated from high school in Old Bridge, New Jersey, in 1987. He entered Kean College in Union, New Jersey, and then transferred to Rutgers University. He worked his way through with a job transporting pool tables, work that would take a serious toll on his back, prompting surgery in 2012 and influencing his writing in *This Is How You Lose Her*, especially the collection's closer, "The Cheater's Guide To Love." He received a B.A. degree in English from Rutgers in 1992 and then entered Cornell University, where he received an M.F.A. in 1995. While at Cornell he wrote a number of the short stories that would be published in his first collection of short stories, *Drown* (1996). In 1997 he began teaching at Syracuse University, and in 2002 joined the faculty of the School of Humanities, Arts, and Social Sciences at the Massachusetts Institute of Technology, where he is the Rudge and Nancy Allen Professor of Writing. Building outward from his fiction writing, Díaz' literary career also includes his work as fiction editor of the *Boston Review*, a position he took up in 2008. In October 2012, following the publication of *This Is How You Lose Her*, it was announced that Díaz was named a MacArthur Foundation fellow and recipient of the "genius" grant, bearing with it a tremendous cash prize of a half-million dollars.

REFIGURING CULTURES

Díaz appears to have lifted himself into the literary world with a similar independence of outside aid as that which brought him into the world on New Year's Eve 1968. His writing possesses a refulgent, overt kind of talent. He is an American writer in the most splendid sense of the word "America." His work, like his person, has made multiple points of contact throughout the Western Hemisphere, from Santo Domingo to Edison, New Jersey; Ithaca, New York; and Cambridge, Massachusetts. Beyond the mere residences and environs of his personal life, Díaz' writing is open to an entire mythology, embracing the literature of the hemisphere, from Derek Walcott to Sandra Cisneros, in one raging swoop. Considered in a taxonomy of contemporary fiction writers, Díaz is a special case: his portraits of Antillean American culture have brought us the addition of a core inscrutable character, Yunior, who thus far has appeared in all of Díaz' books at varying points of inflection to the given narrative.

Díaz' writing style is like an engine that can drop into fifth gear directly from first. Gripping moments of drama follow hard on the heels of passages marked with lyricism and wit. Among his many attributes, wisdom and historical scope included, Díaz can claim a rich intellectual, aesthetic, and moral lineage from sources as diverse as Europe, the Antilles, South America, and the United States, and all this with an authentic ownership of not merely one voice but many voices: Díaz is a ventriloquist of the highest order. He can write women and men, speaking or thinking, in the present moment or deep

into the last century. In his fiction, the points of his dispersive, eclectic literary geography rarely work in isolation: the author's voice careers through each literary locus with the fluency of a polyglot and the effortlessness of a time traveler. There's an old writer's adage, "Write what you know." Immigrants like Díaz, who have deep knowledge of two disparate worlds, shed a light doubly bright in their work.

What is an American writer? A national or geographic designation like "American" could be given to a writer merely for the happy accident of his or her birthplace or residence. Yet a more absorbing and engaging use of the adjective exists, one more figurate. With a strong sense of gumption we might say that an American writer is a writer whose work is emblematic of the United States, and whose literary project in some way embraces core elements of the foundational or literary spirit of the United States—the heroic and the criminal, the brave and the beautiful, the ugly and the exalted. We think of some of the most influential American documents, including the Declaration of Independence, penned by Thomas Jefferson, and *Leaves of Grass*, the major work of the great nineteenth-century poet Walt Whitman. For Díaz, the relationship with the United States is a cultivated, sophisticated, and, crucially, adoptive romance, a love born of reflection, travel, and years of living and working "on the ground," as it were. It's the kind of love one might have for a close family member, at times ornery and exasperated, at times inspired and rejuvenating, but always unconditional.

Díaz' literary oeuvre is obsessed with the lines of American inheritance: the commerce of what we pass onto one another in story and what these stories help us to retain. In his writing, as is common with many great works of American literature, the onion of inheritance peels back continuous layers, and through analysis of style, theme, and explicit annotation of influence, the writing reveals many precursors. These precursors are not limited to recent writers or books, in English or Spanish, but include grander paradigms; even largely forgotten civilizations become the source of metaphor and influence. In *The Brief Wondrous Life of Oscar Wao*, especially,

the reader explores with the narrator what cultural and temperamental gifts the Taíno bequeathed the Antilles, in spirit and in figures like Anacoana, the Golden Flower, an emblem of self-determinism, bravery, beauty, and defiance. This spirit colors the entire novel and presents a model for forms of defiance that mirrors and colors the main characters' experiences. Other issues that play more broadly across the scope of Díaz' fiction include a general inquiry: politically and morally, what does the United States actually have on offer to the world, and what, at the same time, does it wrest from the world? Merging the geopolitical context with a familial one, Díaz' work explores the transaction costs in a family emigrating from the Dominican Republic. What is the fallout for actual Dominican families of U.S. policies backing dictators like Trujillo? Díaz' corpus provides a cost-benefit analysis of that transaction, at once too wise to wax prescriptive and yet too injured to omit an endless stream of collateral damage.

Díaz' vivid, fork-tongued writing style has the distinguishing quality of always saying just enough, and letting the import of his words ring in our afterthoughts. His style has been referred to as a *sofrito* (typically a sauce made for braising, made by slow-cooking carrots, onions, celery) for its precise gathering of elements. These elements, or ingredients, including Island Spanish, Taíno, New Jersey American English, "Ghetto Nerd," and high-flown Victorian English, had been emulsified and served table-ready in his first story collection, *Drown*, published in 1996 by Riverhead Books. As a craftsman Díaz is surefooted, with frequent lyrical flourishes and a number of ribbing, conspiratorial asides, employing his virtuosic capacities in the service of storytelling and rarely, if ever, in spite of it. Never is the reader forced to swallow idle explication or fluff. His words walk the walk—they seem to have faith in themselves—as if the stories he's telling were preordained. The story is, in a sense, already long told. As readers, we are compelled to flip a page more, and another page more. In encountering a Díaz book, we have an experience like finding a torpid, attractive, propulsive family album and irresistibly flipping through.

The coherence of the text makes a reader feel it had to be made that way.

Though Díaz naturally warrants comparison with other major Dominican American or Antillean American writers, the likes of which include Julia Alvarez and Derek Walcott, Díaz' eye and style bring him closer in effect to contemporaries like David Mitchell, the author of the hydra-headed novel *Cloud Atlas.* Less in style, and more in paradigmatic and psychological mode, Díaz picks up on the availability of otherworldliness made present in Gabriel García Márquez, José Donoso, and, separately, in a long list of genre writers, ranging from H. P. Lovecraft, Frank Herbert, and Frank Miller to, perhaps most palpably, J. R. R. Tolkien. In interviews and talks, Díaz hedges an opinion on "great literature" by voicing an abiding concern for what works are privileged by the publishing and critical establishment, and by implication, a supposed tradition of elite circles determining popular tastes by fiat.

In the spring of 2012 a new string of stories began to appear in the *New Yorker,* a publication that has given Díaz' work a home since the mid-1990s. These included, but were not limited to, works collected in Díaz' second book of stories, *This Is How You Lose Her,* notably, the story "Miss Lora." "Miss Lora" reintroduces readers to a continuing leitmotif in Díaz' writing, namely, the sense of otherness driven to deep, almost cosmic suspiciousness between Dominicans and Puerto Ricans.

Another *New Yorker*–published story, the vigorous, lyrical, verbose, and outlandish "Monstro," presaged a possible full-length, all-out science-fiction novel-in-progress, perhaps the next major piece of work on Díaz' publication time line. "Monstro" is the record of a womanizer blown off course—neglecting his health and well being in the face of strange illness and apocalypse—because he is chasing a girl. In many ways, this is a characteristic Díazian paradigm. As he has mentioned in interviews, a fuller measure of Díaz' import as a writer will be taken once his second novel is published.

In the stories and in his first novel, we are carried in the hands of a brother-narrator, Yunior, often one step apart from the major drama but occasionally drawn in to the narrative torrent unavoidably. His pinpointed persona is that of a fiction writer who has seen too much and yet whose tongue-clicking exuberance prevents his silence, or obstructs his silence, and moves him to the reluctant rehashing of an entire epic family story, whether played out across chapters of a novel or stories in a collection, from the beginning, drawing family secrets from the quiet couches and living rooms of immigrants in the Bronx, in New Jersey, in school, on the streets, or at work.

The children in *Drown* are hastily punished for unearthing their parents' local scandals. The moments of moral shock experienced by the children characters are often swallowed and deferred: fiction writing, years after the fact, is among Yunior's methods of coping. As pertinent, the violence inherent in Yunior's family relationships settles into the trope of his pattern of serial cheating. It is the most exact signifier of an inner corruption, a self-sabotaging mechanism that pulls him away from deep commitment.

In a strong sense, though, a disruptive, untrusting family paradigm cannot explain or bear responsibility for all of Yunior's behavior with women. The male wish to test one's mettle by engaging with a potential love match becomes radically amplified in the echo chamber of a writer's imagination. What light is refracted in the prism of his heart might appear unrecognizable when it emerges on the other side. Though outwardly Yunior creates a mantle of masculine effrontery to draw fire from his inner character, his writing bears testament to his deep yearning, his wish to explore, probe, evaluate, and eventually solve the puzzle of his own being. As if this were possible.

We are forced to visit the concept of Díaz as a seer, a painter whose *discours indirect libre*—that is, the unmasked beckoning of voice and perception across a span of paragraphs—is made evident with such lines as "The moon, it has been reported, was full, and the light that rained down cast the leaves of the eucalyptuses into spectral coin" (*Oscar Wao,* p. 146). This sentence belies a painful aggression regarding the subject at hand, masked or deflected by the passive tautology "it

has been reported." Again, in handling Trujillo, Díaz employs a stiff, sarcastic attitude, a sort of "I can barely go into this, you know how bad it gets" comportment. A similar tone emerges in discussing the difficulties for young females in winning the crown prince for themselves with their dark skin and wavy hair.

"Streaky bacon" was Charles Dickens' term for the running together of highbrow and lowbrow styles in the same work, a mixture that might be summed up as sex, gambols, and flights of intellectual insight. It was a mode Dickens pulled off resplendently and terrifyingly, following from that great combiner of character, the creator of personages who overhear themselves and are forever altered, William Shakespeare. Díaz is a contemporary master of that mode, and his language is a steaming cauldron of inheritance and creativity. The self-conscious act of creating a fiction from reality and birthing reality from a contrivance of fictional art in *Oscar Wao* also confirms Miguel de Cervantes' great *Don Quixote* (1605), which many scholars consider the first modern novel, as central to Díaz' literary inheritance.

HISTORY AND MEMORY

An important component in understanding Díaz' writing is an understanding of Taíno culture, a people who, as detailed in Howard Zinn's *A People's History of the United States,* were systematically wiped out of their native environs in Puerto Rico and Hispaniola, the island shared by both Haiti and the Dominican Republic. Visit the Dominican friar Bartolomé de las Casas' seminal tract, *A Short Account of the Destruction of the Indies* (1542), for a contemporary portrait of the travesties. De las Casas, born in Spain, feared God's vengeance against the Spanish for their ravaging of Hispaniola. The Taíno are mentioned on page one of *The Brief Wondrous Life of Oscar Wao,* setting the stage for a profound look, through the years and across cultures, into the curse that weighs down a nation and a family. Implicit in Díaz' book is that what happened to the Taíno people, the theft of their land and their eventual extermination, must

be paid for, at least in the internal mechanism and justice of the fictive realm, and the personal loss experienced, especially by the Cabral family, smacks of the needed, if somewhat arbitrary, recompense.

The displacement of people and culture, the slip-sliding of cultural identity, always has a further rung in Díaz' work: although the main focus of the dislocation is between an oft-American-occupied DR and the throes of an immigrant's existence in New Jersey, the inheritance begins many generations earlier, in the displacement of the Taíno people, which began with the advent of Christopher Columbus and his massacres against indigenous populations.

This spirit of Columbus infuses Díaz' representations of the other important historical touchstone of his fiction, the former Dominican dictator Rafael Trujillo: there is a *fukú,* a curse, at work. Rafael Leonidas Trujillo Molina, known as Trujillo, was dictator and military strongman of the Dominican Republic from 1930 until his assassination in 1961. Throughout Díaz' writing, and especially in *The Brief Wondrous Life of Oscar Wao,* science fiction and fantasy are used to represent the psychological dimensions of complete isolation. Trujillo, also known as El Jefe ("The Boss"), referred to by Yunior as the "Failed Cattle Thief," was the figurehead for a tremendous personality cult. Even the capital, Santo Domingo, was officially named Ciudad Trujillo during his bloody, ruinous tenure.

Secret police thugs were responsible for thousands of political killings, tortures, and imprisonments. No opposition of Trujillo and his regime was tolerated. Even wisecracks about the dictator, made in jest, were met with wild, incommensurate vengeance.

During this period average Dominicans were isolated from the outside world. Díaz implies, as an example, that many Dominicans did not know about World War II until after it had ended. The important consideration here is that Trujillo's reign despoiled and grossly limited the economic, cultural, and personal livelihoods of regular people in the Dominican Republic for more than a generation. His regime engendered a culture of nepotism, betrayal, oppression, and paranoia. The

Servicio de Inteligencia Militar (SIM), known colloquially as the Secret Police, was founded in 1957 and acted as part surveillance operation, part brutalizing force. Thus Díaz conflates Trujillo's regime with the Taíno concept of *fukú*, a deep curse cast upon the island, infecting the country for decades to come.

DROWN

Díaz' first short-story collection, *Drown*, introduces the world to Yunior, and Yunior introduces the world to vibrant interiors, time warps, unfair beatings, island life, and immigrant life in New Jersey, the Bronx, Brooklyn, and the Lower East Side. Typical scenery in these stories includes the adolescent propulsion into jobs and, in many cases, away from high school; irregular commitments to unstable, mystically tinged mothers; a burgeoning teenage libido (emphasis on Dominican male libido, construed here as legendary); the combined dearth and plethora of outlets for that libido; and the cycles of paternal absenteeism, maternal aggression, and paternal denial. The book produced a number of instant classics, such as "Fiesta, 1980" and "How to Date a Browngirl, Blackgirl, Whitegirl, or Halfie."

"How," indeed, is fiction's major concern as a literary genre. To identify the archetypes of human experience, and crucially, to demonstrate and represent, if not to explain, but to portray in literature's mimetic richness, how we move through the changes of life is the central element of what makes fiction fiction. In "How to Date," the convention of a "how-to" guides us into the much deeper and richer issue of how it is to live as Díaz' characters live, and moreover, how it is that those characters' experiences resonate with experiences for a diverse set of humanity.

"How to Date" is the shortest story in *Drown,* yet Díaz is able to smuggle a firestorm of painful, chest-tightening detail about the throes of growing up poor into what is ultimately a street urchin's yarn about how to get one's prospective girlfriend alone long enough to attempt to satisfy each other's budding urges. If the story has a conceit, or a stylistic directive, it is that of a list of instructions: how to make it happen. This "conventional" wisdom, conceived as a "How to," arranged on the page like director's notes to a pornographic film and delivered with the broken pencil-stub cadence of a veteran journalist, is both a note-to-self and free advice for those coming up in the world. Implicit is older brother Rafa's famous career with women. The story, like all of the Yunior stories, comes adorned with a WWRD necklace. What Would Rafa Do?

A major trope in Díaz' world comes to an end, toward the end of *This Is How You Lose Her,* when the reader no longer hears Yunior asking himself that question.

Díaz himself has referenced Herman Melville in interviews as having created a sort of model for a new American writing. Melville's plurality of voice, his inclusion of strangeness, if we consider strangeness especially as a mode of foreignness or otherness, is in its full abundance with the characters on the crew of the *Pequot,* the ship Captain Ahab uses to hunt down the white whale in Melville's masterpiece, *Moby-Dick* (1851).

The stories, or one is tempted to say, "entries," in *Drown* run together in an apt and interlinking succession not because they are chronologically rimed, or geographically—or even psychologically—arranged for narrative parity, but because of the imperative, rounding within each character, to assert one crucial piece more of themselves into the composite of Dominican diaspora in the mid- to late twentieth century. The sequence of the stories creates a kind of anterior understanding, whereby, toward the end of *Drown,* the earlier minor characters, startling passages, revealing images, recurring motifs, serve not only to satisfy the demands of the given stories in which they appear, but to lace up the entire book like a girdle, to bend it back like a palm tree, from which one feels at any instant a prize coconut is about to be launched.

A slice of Island life as represented in "Aguantando," from *Drown:*

We could never get Mami to do anything after work, even cook dinner, if she didn't first sit awhile in her rocking chair. She didn't want to hear nothing about

our problems, the scratches we'd put into our knees, who said what. She'd sit on the back patio with her eyes closed and let the bugs bite mountains onto her arms and legs. Sometimes I climbed the guanábana tree and when she'd open her eyes and catch me smiling down on her, she'd close them again and I would drop twigs onto her until she laughed.

(pp. 73–74)

THE BRIEF WONDROUS LIFE OF OSCAR WAO

At the decade mark from the time *Drown* had been published to such acclaim, resonance, and love in 1996, Díaz had yet to produce and publish its heir apparent. Díaz had been on hiatus, writing constantly, as hindsight informs us, but publishing infrequently. So when Díaz' first novel arrived on the scene in late summer 2007, what could reasonably be called a firestorm took hold of the publishing industry. The *Brief Wondrous Life of Oscar Wao* went on to win, among many accolades, both the National Book Critics Circle Award and, in 2008, the Pulitzer Prize for Fiction.

While the book is told in a lean-in, you-heard-it-hear-first-folks style, the structure is hyper-literary, including hefty footnotes ranging from historical minutiae to cultural arcana. It recounts the history of the Dominican Republic writ large, and the tragic history of the Cabral family within it. It is less a cautionary tale than the tale of a curse, chronicling the stories of those who perished under its pull and those who shouldered the burden of surviving it. In this way, it factors into the Latin American subgenre of the "dictator novels," exemplars of which include Miguel Ángel Asturias' *El Señor Presidente* (1949), Gabriel García Márquez' *The Autumn of the Patriarch* (1975) and *The General in His Labyrinth* (1989), as well as Mario Vargas Llosa's *The Feast of the Goat* (2000), which Díaz repeatedly takes to task for what he considers its blithe, lenient portrayal of Trujillo during his last days. Incidentally, all three of these writers won the Nobel Prize for Literature. The jury is still out on Díaz' ultimate contribution, though it's fair to begin by saying that, while not strictly a "dictator novel," the trope of the dictator's emotional poisoning of the island is a mammoth part of the gorgeous composite that is *The Brief Wondrous Life of Oscar Wao*.

Regarding *Fukú*: "It's perfectly fine if you don't believe in these 'superstitions,'" Yunior writes. "In fact, it's better than fine—it's perfect. Because no matter what you believe, fukú believes in you" (p. 5). There is no better single encapsulation of the Díaz mythos than this. It is the experience of feeling bound by forces greater than oneself, despite an ongoing rational program of extricating oneself from the madness of one's spiritual, emotional, ethnic, and national inheritance.

In Díaz' work, from *Wao* to the uncollected story "Summer Love Overheated," the power of inner lives and family mythologies become self-fulfilling prophecies, destiny, kismet. Indeed, any mantle of thought, embraced and internalized, has an equal and exact fatidical outcome.

The key word in this process is "conviction": a power and attribute maintained almost exclusively in Díaz' work by the female characters. La Inca, Beli's adoptive mother, prays with supreme force and conviction following Beli's beating in the cane fields, a beating nearly as savage, and evocatively as crucial, as the murders of the historical Mirabal sisters—themselves previously represented in Julia Alvarez' novel *In the Time of Butterflies* (1994)—in those same cane fields. In the confines and metaphysics of *The Brief Wondrous Life of Oscar Wao*, La Inca's prayer actually works. It is perhaps Oscar's ultimate distinction from other Dominican male characters in Díaz' fiction that Oscar also carries within him a divine, if destroying, conviction. He is driven not by surface lust but by a deep inner knowledge.

If women are enfranchised by their conviction, men are subject to certain profound inertias. This trope begins in *Drown* and drags through all of Díaz' fiction like a deep-sea fishing net.

Zafa, or counter spell, is the antidote to *fukú* that Yunior intends to foster, writing his account of Oscar's life. *Zafar* in Spanish means undoing or loosening. The attempted *zafa* that is *The Brief Wondrous Life of Oscar Wao* is like the slow loosening of a death grip over years of reflection.

Molded with the unconscious art, in the concretizing, transmogrifying power of human

memory, both at the individual psychic level and scaled upward to include—dare it be said?—cultural memory, things like dragons and curses exist. They color our lives.

It is on this interpretive level that we readers find the primary source of psychic contact with Oscar and his family. But this psychic/linguistic membrane, which helps us distinguish between the slippery realms of imagination, memory, and belief, is punctuated time and again by certain mythic episodes in our protagonist's quest. In those moments of punctuation, the curses—in Oscar's case, the *fukú*—do feel real, and so in a sense become real, while the world in front of him becomes instantly reorganized around this central narrative: *I am accursed, as are my people.*

It should be pointed out that since this suddenly adopted (or continually readopted and discarded) viewpoint exists in that slippery multiverse of imagination and memory, it also slips the constraints of time and causality. One is tempted, in those moments of the mythic punctuation of the membrane of one's living imagination, to review the entirety of one's life history and retroactively apply the curse as an explanation for past misfortunes. Perhaps irrevocably, even as a nonbeliever, or as a person, like Oscar, struggling to exist in U.S. society, where myth is often outsourced to the explicitly fantastic in art, this curse may become a source of meaning, as well as an aesthetic, imaginative filter through which one's self-reflection takes on aspects from the larger culture.

A secondary but indeed no less significant level to which *fukú* is explicitly connected in Díaz' novel is that of those two historic oppressors, "The Admiral" (i.e., Christopher Columbus) and "El Jefe" (Raphael Trujillo). From the opening section of *The Brief, Wondrous Life of Oscar Wao:*

> In Santo Domingo, the Land He Loved Best (what Oscar, at the end, would call the Ground Zero of the New World), the Admiral's very name has become synonymous with both kinds of fukú, little and large; to say his name aloud or even to hear it is to invite calamity on the hearts of you and yours.
>
> (p. 1)

Significant, and a clue to Díaz' finely wrought artistry, is the invocation of Ground Zero. Here Oscar shifts this major center of trauma, which has both a real and a symbolic aspect, identifying it primarily with the capital of the Dominican Republic and only secondarily, through a sort of inevitable inflection, with the United States, the attacks of September 11, 2001, and a larger theme of American nationalism. Crucial are those three short words, "at the end," which build as strong a sense of foreboding and foreshadowing as any reader could wish for from the first page of a novel. Suspense, that is to say, the knowledge or awareness of impending dramatic conflict, functions as both a wellspring of story and, simultaneously, as the context in which characters develop and change.

More than that, those three words, "at the end," imply that by the end of Oscar's journey, he will have turned away from, or will in some sense have been unsuccessful in reconciling, those two aspects of his cultural identity: the island culture of the DR and the street culture of urban New Jersey. Seen in this light, the course of the novel may be seen as a translation of one paradigm (Dominican) into another (Western), employing a pantheon of popular signifiers from both cultures, synthesized in Oscar and the language he employs, his unique voice.

Of Trujillo, the narrator says, succinctly, "He was our Sauron" (p. 2), perfectly distilling both Oscar and Yunior's internal character and love of genre fiction, as well as the sense of omnipotent, evil power inherent in Trujillo's despotic regime. (Sauron, of course, is the evil dictator and titular figure of J. R. R. Tolkien's high-fantasy 1950s masterwork, *The Lord of The Rings.*)

The dichotomy Oscar embodies, and the attempts at reconciliation his life represents, are reflected in two powerful stylistic choices in the fabric of the novel itself. First, we find it in Díaz' effortless, emulsive blending of Victorian (read: bookish) English, street and popular American English, and Dominican Spanish (with special variants that occur when spoken on the island, or in the States.) This stylistic element, Díaz' blending of distinct languages into a new, markedly American whole, marks a continuation and a rich

expanding of a style that was already fully alive when employed in *Drown*.

The second major device is Díaz' use of copious, highly detailed, often darkly humorous footnotes. In one sense, what could be nerdier or stodgier than conjuring up the writings of stuffy Victorian philologists? And yet in another sense, what could be more vital—a more decisive cultural and artistic heist—than deploying a literary convention that satirizes and at the same time expresses key intellectual truths about the author? In a brilliant twist we find a narrator who, instead of cataloging Dominican history as a footnote in American culture and history, tells a Dominican American story as a no-holds-barred reflection of American history itself, and the footnotes represent the resurrection of a history lost on many Americans. Thus the text of *The Brief Wondrous Life of Oscar Wao* is, in a sense, Yunior's *zafa*, his counter curse to undo the family *fukú* that Oscar, Lola, and their mother, Beli, were born into.

Though Yunior's voice and vision bring forth the multiverse that is *The Brief Wondrous Life of Oscar Wao,* and though it is his vision, taste, perspective, and his *zafa* that drives the novel, as a character, he appears for the first time on page 167 of the Faber and Faber paperback edition of the novel—that is to say, not until section 4. Yunior, the watcher; Yunior, the translator. Yunior, the closest approximation of Junot Díaz yet to be found in Díaz' work.

The leitmotif of the mongoose is prominent in *Wao*. Though for many on the island, Díaz suggests, the mongoose is a forgotten member of the animal community, it regains centrality in the *Wao* narrative. Its role is that of trickster and rescuer. It is the power animal or a spirit guide for the Cabral family. In moments when characters begin losing control of their lives, verging into a seemingly prearranged dance with destiny, the mongoose serves as a reminder of a core or innate attitude of defiance; this reawakening of their inner moxie helps pull them back from the brink. The mongoose is the survival instinct, despite the worst odds and the direst of difficulties.

A weight lifter, a *sucio* (read: bad boy) flirt who chases down every *guapa* in sight, Yunior is, behind a mantle of masculinity, a fiction writer, a new American Dominican, who carries in his heart empathy, if not exactly sympathy, for Oscar. What began first was his relationship with Lola, brief, yet born in the aftermath of conflict: Lola nurses Yunior back to health after a brutal street beating. All real relationships in this novel are born in fire. Beli's inheritance included the scalding scars of chicken wire on her back when Trujillo's regime set her parents' house aflame.

A note on the origin of the title of the book itself: it is born out of a mishearing. The perfect mishearing of Oscar Wilde for Oscar Wao, made by Melvin, one of Yunior's close associates, transforms Oscar's character. His adoptive name has both a referential aspect, referring to Wilde, and a strange, new element. This change is a telling distillation not only of Oscar's personal qualities, but of the nature of his personal predicament: torn between generations, countries, and images of himself. Thus the scene in which Melvin mishears Wilde for Wao becomes a representative scene in the book.

Yunior, whose brief, failed "Project Oscar"—an attempt to turn Oscar away from a negative self-image and get him exercising—stands for something profound and touching in Yunior's character. Their arguments elevate from the usual dorm room contretemps into something existential, tinged with an almost teleological understanding that they are splitting ways, finally and, though not yet, forever. Though the attempt to draw Oscar into a positive stream of self-enhancement and self-preservation was finally discarded by Oscar, and that rejection was compounded and sealed in Yunior's angry reaction, the fact of the attempt really stands as a pivotal moment in the evolution of Yunior across all of Díaz' books. Yunior, who must most closely resemble Díaz, who is by turns brash and a cheater, is also, in his way, hyper-literate, hyper-lexical. He is in touch with the nuance and import from Tolkien's work (he often references "the balrog" in people), has more than a soft circumference in heart reserved for the anime film *Akira*

and the like, and understands tenderness, if he is often completely confounded by it.

Oscar's confrontation with his own perceived limits, or with what he'd come to believe as the essence of his own inner nature, precipitated his botched jump—an attempted, calibrated suicide, replete with notes—from the New Brunswick train bridge. It was the jump that brought Lola back, fraught, harried, from her studies in Madrid.

THIS IS HOW YOU LOSE HER

Díaz' second collection of stories, *This Is How You Lose Her,* was released in September 2012, also by Riverhead Books. After three hundred electric pages on Trujillo, the DR, *fukú* and the Cabral family, we get an in-depth look at Yunior and the man he has become. The events in the stories range from his boyhood and the family's first winter in New Jersey, to his adolescence of pot smoking, weight lifting, reading, cutting class, and the death of his brother from cancer. The stories are about his twenties, largely, and his first loves, and span into his early middle-age life, teaching in Boston. If the stories have a common thread it is the dislocation between women and men: between husband and wife, (psychologically, emotionally, and geographically), between boyfriend and girlfriend, and notably, between mother and son.

From the collection's second story, "Nilda," which centers on Yunior's dying brother, Rafa:

> My junior year she started delivering papers so she could make money, and since I was spending a lot of time outside I saw her every now and then. Broke my heart. She wasn't at her lowest yet but she was aiming there and when we passed each other she always smiled and said hi. She was starting to put on weight and she'd cut her hair down to nothing and her moonface was heavy and alone. I always said Wassup and when I had cigarettes I gave them to her. She'd gone to [Rafa's] funeral, along with a couple of his other girls, and what a skirt she'd worn, like maybe she could still convince him of something, and she'd kissed my mother but the vieja hadn't known who she was. I had to tell Mami on the ride home and all she could remember about

her was that she was the one who smelled good. It wasn't until Mami said it that I realized it was true.

(p. 40)

What is the import? It is the women. So many women. As Updike phrased it, "the women who got away." But these women have been memorialized and will never "get away" because they constitute the life of the man: they represent the borderlands of his character; they are his milestones as well as his moral touchstones. They denote where he acted right and where he botched everything. These women are his history, his high school, his inheritance, and the debit he'll use to pay it forward. In Díaz, women provoke the inner dimensions of a man and take the measure of manhood.

"The Cheater's Guide to Love," the closing statement of the collection, is a downright dirge, a breathless plummet into despair and regret. As with many of Díaz' overtly masculine characters, Yunior has a deep relationship with exercise, an almost psychic resonance with lifting weights, running, and doing yoga that reflects cycles of improvement and recovery when they become immersive. Yunior's reclamation of his personal dignity begins to arrive when he wills himself back into exercise. Running is a last-ditch effort, a shot in the dark from someone who has touched bottom; but once the process has begun, it builds like a coral reef, slowly developing an under-the-surface structure strong enough to stop a ship.

The stories are the striations, the wounds, the failed attempts at reparation. Rather than represented directly, the "good times" in Díaz are inflected through the pain of having lost them through cheating. The spotlight might turn on a steamy bedroom scene, or a moment of shared transcendence or passing understanding between characters, but these are fleeting, and the iceberg they reveal is filled with unhappiness, missed opportunity, and loss, loss, loss. Under the cloak of relationship failure, Díaz smuggles in spectacular detail about living in New Jersey as an immigrant, the streets of Perth Amboy and London Terrace and Paterson, about folding linen in hospitals, about dreary days of ennui in front of the television.

JUNOT DÍAZ

In *This Is How You Lose Her,* more than ever before in Díaz' writing, we encounter crisp stories, like fresh linen on the page, which yet take on the shapes of the bodies of the characters who lie there. In the story "Otravida, Otravez," a piece penned originally in the late 1990s, Díaz crafts a perfectly balanced and compelling portrait of all those things which are, often perforce, left behind in the old country. This leaving behind is portrayed as a necessary sort of figurative death, vital in allowing the characters to move forward, without losing their minds, in the new country. In a stylistic departure in the context of the collection, "Otravez" is written from a woman's point of view. In this mode, Díaz is surprisingly strong: Yasmin's character is suffused with the qualities of quiet strength, dignity, and shades of resignation.

Inevitably, a reader finds herself or himself searching the pages and stories of *This Is How You Lose Her* for signs, for evidence, indicating Lola, from *Wao*. In Lola's character, in whom we find so strong and trenchant a spirit, one capable of saying no to even the most powerful temptations and inertias, we see the mirror upon which Yunior's sense of loss takes shape. In *This Is How You Lose Her,* however, the image of Lola is refracted, not reproduced. That she is never explicitly mentioned, and, if ever, is only obliquely alluded to, feels necessary and appropriate. (Could it be her, we ask, the unnamed girlfriend in "The Cheater's Guide to Love"? Although we learn in *Wao* that Lola moves to Florida with her new husband, we are suspicious in *Lose Her* that this woman, for all her vital force and for the supreme loss Yunior feels, might be one and the same, our fictive Lola.) There are different pitches of reality in the two books. In the end, *Wao* had its own impermeable force, like a legend, a mythic tale of doom and destiny. *This Is How You Lose Her* is, by degrees, more austere, cleaner, colder, older, more focused. It picks up where *Drown* leaves off, not merely in form but in tincture, theme, and tone. Yunior is the central persona and Rafa is his elusive brother. Díaz pulls off a miraculous trick turning to *This Is How You Lose Her* (some of whose stories were written and published well before *Wao*). The trick is that he kaleidoscopes Yunior's narrative: using the same colors, Díaz weaves an entirely different portion of the tapestry.

Where *Wao* is exuberant, relentless, vibrant, polyphonic, and infused with a magical, dizzying explanation of human fate, *This Is How You Lose Her* is raw, unadorned, delicate, and singular. In a Wordsworthian sense, it is about opening raw wounds in order to wash them in the antiseptic of confession, allowing them to heal.

THE CENTRALITY OF YUNIOR

If there is a consistent thread in Díaz' three major works to date it is the feeling, time and again, of watching someone close to you fall off a cliff. Díaz, perhaps burdened artistically with what he feels is the cursed weight of Dominican masculinity, is almost exclusively a teller of cautionary tales. No one embodies this burden in a wider range of guises, from hero to zero, than the character Yunior. Who is Yunior? He is both a weight lifter and a writer, both a scalawag womanizer and a fundamentally moral actor who continually betrays his moral center. This self-betrayal is both endemic to manhood, Díaz argues, and the source of the cautionary tales. It is what makes monsters out of men, and Trujillos out of mere monsters.

Present in every book by Díaz, Yunior spins individual yarns and anecdotes into these cautionary tales, and the tales become a web of moral narratives that reflect a nation in diaspora. Yunior is a cheater and a writer. He moves in a wave in from the periphery of Díaz' narratives to the center and back again. The Yunior of *The Brief Wondrous Life of Oscar Wao* is recognizable in *Drown* and *This Is How You Lose Her,* though the events in *Wao* are never alluded to in the story. Perhaps the woman Yunior loses and pines for in "The Cheater's Guide to Love" is the Lola he lost in *Wao,* but while this idea is never denied explicitly, neither is it ever confirmed. For readers of Díaz, these cross-examinations of character arc have been left deliciously underresolved.

Yunior's lengthy, prolonged crisis, insofar as we have had the sharing of it, has the distinction

of not having run him in the way Oscar's brief, wondrous one did him. Yunior was not pulled into the *fukú*. Ultimately, his writing is the unguent that heals his burning.

What is it about Yunior himself, his perspective, that makes a reader buck with delight? As with any story from Ovid to Kafka, great literature demonstrates change, metamorphosis. What claims Yunior and sets him apart from this tradition is the paranoia of curse, of *fukú*, of never quite being able to escape the cycle of self-loathing and self-sabotage. We love reading Yunior's story in part because he is so tough, because he is strong—physically strong, as well as streetwise—and can throw himself into the fight, immersing himself in the narrative and living to tell the tale. We see Yunior as one who, variously, could crush a beer can on his head if he chose; instead he crams his head with voices and contemplation, his heart with unnecessarily damaging *queridas* and a kind of mythic self-sabotage.

It follows that we should ask a more broadly ranging question: What is singular and compelling about a body of literature that features a consistent protagonist—a character who is threaded through every piece of an author's work? What does this say, for example, about the author's literary stance—about his position on what literature is and ought to do? We know that Díaz is capable of high rhetorical denunciation, playful slap-boxing, or an out-and-out brawl. It follows that his mode of social satire—and indeed the author and his narrators have endless torrents of criticism for any and all that would subjugate, oppress, condemn, imprison, pester, or steal, be it Trujillo himself or Yunior's father or winter in northern New Jersey—is wrought not as in Dickens with marionette strings from on high, but by thrusting his personal cognizance onto the stage and, as it were, directly engaging. That he is capable of a panoramic view, as in *Wao,* depends heavily on his seamless ventriloquism.

The centrality of Yunior may mean that Díaz' work writ large makes a strong case for writing as an extension or representation of the multitudes contained within one life and one individual experience of life, especially in story: this is a powerfully American concept, uncovered especially in the poetry of Walt Whitman.

NONFICTION WRITING

In May 2011 Díaz published an essay in the *Boston Review* called "Apocalypse: What Disaster Reveals," a look at the social calculus that calibrates global resources and decision-making and which, Díaz argues, allows for what we would conventionally call "natural disasters" to have such far-flung and devastating consequences. Díaz writes less from a technical standpoint than out of a moral obligation to reset the terms of the conversation surrounding major global tragedies.

In a sense, choosing to write on this subject in a nonfiction forum is of a piece with Díaz' choices as a novelist. The existential fear that had been gathering through Díaz' youth has, with the onset and escalation of the global warming crisis, taken form in more numerous, more painful natural catastrophes. (Though the grim prospect of nuclear holocaust and mutual guaranteed destruction of humanity, such as that which Díaz feared in the 1980s, must evermore be considered a paramount threat to civilization.) Díaz writes about major crises, including the 2010 earthquake in Haiti, arguing that the international response to apocalyptic events reveals the priorities and privileges of those called upon to help. Following John Berger, Díaz defines an apocalypse according to its Greek etymological origins, as "a disruptive event that provokes revelation." What more suitable topic could we conceive for a writer of Díaz' experience and temperament?

> The Asian tsunami of 2004 was a social disaster. The waves were so lethal because the coral reefs that might have protected the vulnerable coasts had been dynamited to facilitate shipping. And the regions that suffered most were those like Nagapattinam, in India, where hotel construction and industrial shrimp farming had already systematically devastated the natural mangrove forests, which are the world's best tsunami-protectors.

Whether in Haiti, Thailand, or India, Díaz outlines the "web of complicity" that has led to

deterioration, ruination, marginalization of vulnerable lands and people. It is a history of imperialism and colonization, abetted by a capitalist infrastructure that ensnared the third world in a "cycle of debt that it never broke free from."

> We are in the age of neoliberal economic integration, of globalization, the magic process that was to deliver the world's poor out of misery and bring untold prosperity to the rest of us. Globalization, of course, did nothing of the sort. Although the Big G was supposed to lift all boats, even a cursory glance at the stats shows that the swell of globalization has had a bad habit of favoring the yachts over rafts by a whole lot.

With an essay like "Apocalypse," Díaz continues to expand his stature as a demotic, democratic American writer, a patriot who criticizes power while enriching the field of discourse. While new information and fresh insight do not always bring delight, they often end their passage in wisdom. Altering Horace's injunction that poetry ought to begin in delight, Díaz' work, whether imaginative or otherwise, most often begins in torment and makes room for the unavoidable delights therein as the narrative progresses. That is to say, Díaz' writing, as evidenced in his essay, has a profound, well-worn relationship with irony and, as well, a moral undercurrent that urges him to sketch the world a better model. What Díaz' writing helps readers cope with, finally, and perhaps more than anything else, is the collapse of our great expectations.

At this writing, Díaz' oeuvre is beginning to deepen and take shape. While gaps of many years have frequently appeared between his books, those gaps appear to be closing. Now that his career has been built upon a sure-footed three-book foundation, we should expect a continually expansive intellectual and creative blossoming, especially in the form of the novel, which is Díaz' opportunity to deal with complex, interlocking, multiscaled, international, and, perhaps, intergalactic crucibles in a searing, sweeping, aesthetically coherent literary vehicle.

Selected Bibliography

WORKS OF JUNOT DÍAZ

NOVELS AND SHORT STORIES

Drown. New York: Riverhead Books, 1996. Quotations in the entry are from the Penguin paperback edition: New York: Penguin, 1997.

The Brief Wondrous Life of Oscar Wao. New York: Riverhead Books, 2007. London: Faber, 2009.

This Is How You Lose Her. New York: Riverhead Books, 2012.

"Monstro." *New Yorker,* June 4, 2012. http://www.newyorker.com/fiction/features/2012/06/04/120604fi_fiction_Díaz.

OTHER WORKS

"Summer Love Overheated." *GQ,* August 2008. Appears as "My Girl in Amsterdam," JunotDíaz.com, http://www.junotDíaz.com/my-girl-in-amsterdam/.

"One Year: Storyteller-in-Chief." *New Yorker,* January 20, 2010. http://www.newyorker.com/online/blogs/newsdesk/2010/01/one-year-storyteller-in-chief.html.

"Apocalypse: What Disaster Reveals." *Boston Review,* May–June, 2011. http://www.bostonreview.net/BR36.3/junot_Díaz_apocalypse_haiti_earthquake.php.

ANDRE DUBUS III

(1959—)

D. Quentin Miller

CHILDREN OF PROMINENT writers who follow the same career path tend to spend much of their careers struggling to emerge from the shadows of their parents. (John Cheever's son Benjamin and daughter Susan are good examples of this phenomenon.) Andre Dubus III is a different case. His father was a prominent member of the school of gritty, realistic fiction writers that includes Richard Yates, Raymond Carver, and Richard Ford. A product of the Iowa Writers' Workshop in the 1970s who wrote almost exclusively in the short story genre, Dubus the elder was well respected critically but never a household name commercially. In contrast, Andre Dubus III has published one collection of short stories but gravitates toward the novel form. His second and most famous novel, *House of Sand and Fog* (1999), was a blockbuster, owing in part to its selection by Oprah Winfrey's televised book club, its selection as a finalist for the National Book Award, and its adaptation into a major motion picture.

Published virtually at the same time as his father's death, *House of Sand and Fog* catapulted Dubus III past his father in terms of public fame and book sales. Both Dubus III and his father were committed to a tough realism with sensitivity to the plights, motivations, and difficulties of their lower-middle-class heroes without resorting to either pity or romanticism. Dubus III spoke of his father's willingness "to hold the fiction writer's magnifying glass to his own soul" (Introduction to *We Don't Live Here Anymore*, p. xiii). The phrase applies equally well to him. And yet, he said in an unpublished personal interview in 2012 that he doesn't see the comparisons between his work and his father's as particularly useful: "We share the same last name, but not the same vision" (Miller). The essential difference between them was his father's unwavering belief in God. Asked which writers he would rather be compared to, he came up with three singer-songwriters: "Bruce Springsteen, Tom Waits, and Lucinda Williams." He added that he would not mind being compared to other fiction writers who are "not postmodern, not hip; [who] don't play with words just to play with words"; who write works in which "characters are the most important part of the story," and that these characters "hopefully ... are written with compassion." He agreed that Russell Banks would make an apt comparison and acknowledged that Ernest Hemingway was a profound influence. Hemingway's characters are much more aloof and more guarded than Dubus' are, though. If Dubus' characters share one common trait, it is this: they hurl themselves into pits of quicksand and immediately begin flailing, causing themselves to sink deeper and eventually drown. Without the element of faith that characterizes his father's writing or the cool stoicism that characterizes Hemingway's, Dubus' work forces us to face humanity's raw wounds, many self-inflicted, and to witness the painful process of healing, or its opposite.

BIOGRAPHY: FROM FIGHTER TO WRITER

Andre Dubus III was born on a U.S. Marine base in Camp Pendleton, California, on September 11, 1959. The second-eldest of four children close together in age, Dubus was raised in difficult circumstances that initially set him on the road to delinquency rather than literary fame. His parents, raised in Louisiana, had lived on a number of marine bases before his father finished his military duties and was accepted into the famous writing workshop at the University of

97

Iowa, where, Andre recalls, such luminaries as Kurt Vonnegut, Jr., would drop by routinely. From there they moved to Haverhill, Massachusetts, where Andre's father had landed a job at now-defunct Bradford College. At that point his parents' marriage quickly soured. As he details in his memoir *Townie* (2011), his father left his mother for a series of younger women he met while teaching. His mother, Patricia Lowe, comes across in the memoir as well meaning and loving but inadequate to the maternal tasks of providing for or protecting her sons and daughters. They moved from one downtrodden mill town in northeastern Massachusetts to another. Patricia struggled to make ends meet, leaving home early in the morning to work in Boston while Andre and his siblings skipped school in favor of experimenting with alcohol, sex, and drugs. Andre's brother Jeb, who battled suicidal depression, impregnated his girlfriend at age seventeen. His sister, while dating a drug addict who drove her into Boston on a late-night binge, was raped multiple times and left for dead. She later married an abusive husband.

Incidents like these encouraged Andre to fulfill what he thought to be the role of a father: to protect himself and his family against a hostile and predatory world. As a teenager he lifted weights intensely, pushing himself to extreme pain in order to strike back against neighborhood bullies and street toughs. He also took up training with a local boxer, but his success as a fighter came not through training or discipline but rather through reckless and decisive first strikes born of uncontrolled rage and adrenaline. *Townie* details Andre's frightening descent from a proud schoolyard scrapper to a menacing barroom enforcer known to local police. A pivotal scene in the memoir details a chilling brawl in a local diner during which Andre and his friends nearly murder a group of thugs who have offended them, using broken coffee mugs and ketchup bottles as weapons as horrified diners cower. Motivated by chivalry in some cases, revenge in others, defense of the underprivileged in others, and terrified vulnerability in all cases, Andre devolved into an angry young man with no sense of his future. After high school he attended nearby Bradford

College, where his father taught, and after receiving his A.A. degree headed for the University of Texas, Austin, where he earned a B.A. degree in sociology in 1981. His experiences in Austin mitigated the provincial ("townie") elements of his personality, but only temporarily: when he returned to northeastern Massachusetts he fell back into his street-fighting ways.

His relationship with his father remained complicated through these years. Although Andre did not hold his father accountable for leaving his family, the memoir contains pointed moments of bewilderment about how little his father provided in terms of money, wisdom, or even companionship during his formative years. At one point his mother accused Andre's father of being afraid to be alone with his children, and there seems to be some truth to that. In a few awkward instances, the young Andre revealed himself to be ignorant of some of the more basic facets of American masculinity, such as the rules of baseball. Yet he was never estranged from his father, and their relationship eventually became one of mutual respect, tempered by the sense that they never knew each other well enough. Andre's father was proud of his son's fighting prowess and even asked him for advice about how to punch a man. The two even considered hiring a professional thug to break the kneecaps of Andre's sister's husband after he beat her. They drank together, and once got into a barroom scrap with a man who was ignoring his wife all night while she sobbed quietly on her bar stool. (Andre learned afterward that his father was carrying a loaded pistol during the fight and had been close to using it.) In order to push beyond this violent milieu and arrive at their mature understanding of one another, they had to find a common middle ground between the poles of real-world toughness and artistic/creative distance.

Ironically, it was not his father who suggested that Andre should write but his mother. He responded, "Who cares about making up stories? I want to do something important for people," and she reacted with horror: "I can't believe you just said that, Andre. I won't tell anyone you just said that" (*Townie*, p. 214). He became inspired to write not because his father did but because

his girlfriend, whom Andre met through one of his father's writing workshops after returning from Austin, was smitten with another writer in the class. Andre found a story that this classmate wrote and was impressed by its power and clarity, inspiring him to try his hand at writing in order to win back his girl.

Writing also became his means of salvation from the violent evils of the world he inhabited, but this salvation did not happen instantly. After his first attempt at writing he left Massachusetts for Madison, Wisconsin, where he had been accepted into the graduate program for an advanced degree in Marxist social science. He quit after four days and returned to Austin, where he fell back into a routine of writing and working out. From there he reunited with his girlfriend in Colorado and took on work as a prison guard and as a private investigator for a bounty hunter. He also published his first story, "Forky," receiving praise from his father, who called to pronounce him "a writer." He recoiled from the word, claiming, "I felt tied only to what gave birth to that word, the *writing,* the sweet labor of it" (*Townie,* p. 292). Part of him continued to resist the profession he was drawn to, born of deep-seated class resentment as well as a reluctance to follow in the path of his father. Yet he continued to approach writing with the same discipline and single-mindedness he had once devoted to weight lifting and boxing. He writes of this transformation in his memoir: "Jabs had become single words, a combination of punches had become sentences, and rounds had become paragraphs. When I was done, whether I had written well or not, something seemed to have left me, those same pent-up forces that would have gone into my fists and feet" (p. 303). He learned the trade of carpentry working alongside his brother, then he found employment in a halfway house, developing empathy for others, which became a key component of his self-imposed training as a writer. He continued to spend time with his father in local bars but claimed that the practice was "beginning to feel old" (p. 304) and that his intellectual curiosity was drawing him to cultural events in and around Boston.

One such cultural event was a modern dance program at Bradford College where one of the performers was Fontaine Dollas, whom he married on June 25, 1989; the couple would have three children. Consciously breaking the pattern of his youth, Andre dedicated himself to fatherhood not in the way his father did, by doing "the best he'd known how to do" (p. 375) despite being what his mother described as "a self-absorbed son of a bitch" (p. 383), but as someone whose parenthood makes him feel "surrounded by love, responsible to it, careful not to hurt it, and so grateful to get it" (p. 373). The memoir, absorbed though it is with his relationship with his father, is dedicated to his children. The family lives in a house he built north of Boston. Having taught part-time at Harvard, Emerson College, and Tufts University, since 2005 he has taught full-time at the University of Massachusetts, Lowell.

CHARACTER STUDIES: THE CAGE KEEPER

Dubus' first book and only collection of stories, published in 1989, can be read as an overture for his novels in terms of its cast of characters and treatment of themes. Characters in these stories tend to fall into one of a few categories: helpless victims; romantic losers who take desperate and self-destructive measures to try to forge their destinies; and would-be heroes whose attempts to help the first two types place them in compromised positions. These stories are violent and confrontational: a knife, a gun, or both figure in virtually all of them. As the narratives expand beyond their dramatic plot points, space is created to examine the meaning of violence, the worth of human relationships (even failed ones), and the possibility for something spiritual that motivates people who live in less-than-ideal circumstances.

A brief bildungsroman can be glimpsed in the story "Wolves in the Marsh," whose protagonist's name (Dean) is nearly an anagram of Andre. The story powerfully evokes the world of a young boy who ventures into nature alone despite his fear of what might lurk there, the "wolves" of the title, which exist only in his imagination. Armed with a BB gun, he sets forth

at dawn to shoot whatever he comes across, but the journey clearly has a deeper purpose. He thinks the marsh looks "dangerous" and admires his own courage: "He liked this picture of himself standing on a hill with his loaded gun, guarding the woods and his family from whatever might try to crawl out of the marsh to get them" (Vintage ed., p. 94). Interspersed with descriptions of Dean's walk into the woods are his memories of his parents' recent divorce. It is clear that Dean's vision of himself as protector and defender is at odds with his inability to heal the wounds of the past. There are no wolves, only a woodpecker that Dean shoots without thinking. The bird's death strikes him immediately as senseless and unrelated to his primary quest to keep the wolves at bay. He feels ashamed that he is afraid to venture into the marsh to make sure it is dead, and blushes to realize that his hero Kit Carson or his father, a retired marine, would have done so. He returns home and mentions the incident to no one, but imagines that he and his brother will return to the scene next spring when the river runs high over the marsh: "Dean would be holding his rifle and Kip would be carrying the BBs, and together they would just stand there, he and his brother, watching the high water as it flowed over the marsh, and carried all the dead things to the sea" (p. 100). What he ultimately hopes for is something greater than a baptism for his sin against nature: a biblical flood that will wash away all the "dead things" that haunt him, not just the woodpecker. He is aware of the sins of his father, having overheard the confession of them in late-night conversations with his mother, but does not explicitly connect his own sin—his senseless act of violence—to his father's sin of abandonment. Yet the story's logic makes the connection clear, and Dean is left with guilt that he believes can only be absolved by a force outside himself.

"Wolves in the Marsh" and "Last Dance," the final story in the collection, dedicated to his grandfather, are the most clearly autobiographical. "Last Dance" is an homage to both his father and grandfather, linked to "Wolves" in terms of its natural setting and the masculine ritual of hunting. In this case, the three generations

cooperate in a turtle hunt. Through great physical effort they eventually capture an enormous loggerhead turtle whose power and perseverance are as formidable as the marsh in the earlier story. The story's central symbol is the turtle's heart that continues to beat long after the animal is apparently dead. Its relentless life drive is also reminiscent of the narrator's awareness of his lost love, "the coolness of the hollow place inside him that still belonged to Mimi" (p. 205). The protagonist is both stoic and brokenhearted, lacking a human outlet for his pain and sublimating it into his relationship with nature and with these men who refuse to express any emotion directly and honestly.

These two stories are somewhat anomalous within the collection. The majority of the stories deal with characters who have experienced trauma and who are having difficulties moving on. Sex, drugs, and alcohol are all failed ways to escape one's pain in these situations. The most devastating story in the collection is "Duckling Girl," about Lorilee, a teenage girl sexually abused by her father and also by two male companions who drag her around town as they drink, snort cocaine, and eventually rob a college-bound young taxi driver named Dave, clearly modeled on the author. Dave heroically insists that Lorilee does not have to go with her companions, suggesting that he will protect her. They stab him and run off, deciding to "leave the bitch" (p. 84). The final perspective is Dave's, watching in perplexed horror as Lorilee laughs hysterically, a "horrible sound" (p. 86) that seems to have no meaning and no end. Redemption seems impossible at the conclusion of this story: Lorilee is so badly damaged that Dave can only focus on the bruise on her cheek.

Both Lorilee and Dave are victims at the mercy of a hostile and indifferent world, and it does not appear that they can do much to change their fates short of escaping or withdrawing. The story is naturalistic in its view of humanity and fate, emphasized by the title "Duckling Girl," a phrase her father uses the first time he sexually assaults her. Both her father and the two male companions who use her note her ugliness. Dave seems to be able to see the beauty in her, "how

prettily the salt-shine of Lorilee's cheek catches the white glow" of overhead lights, but the bruise again occupies his attention (p. 86). Sex in this story is a brutal, self-gratifying act. In "Forky" and "Mountains" sexual intercourse is meant to be a transcendent act, helping an ex-convict and a barmaid in a dead-end relationship, respectively, to escape their circumstances, but both protagonists end up trapped within their battered psyches rather than healing them.

It is clear even in this collection that Dubus yearned to push against the length limitations of the short story. As a character-driven author whose challenge was to translate his fear of a hostile world into faith in human goodness, he would naturally gravitate toward lengthier narrative forms. The two longest stories in the collection are arguably the most compelling. "White Trees, Hammer Moon" is a haunting tale of a character named Rory who has fought a battle to reform himself after causing a car accident that killed a man and that will send him to prison for a year. On the eve of serving his sentence, Rory takes his ex-wife's children camping. The elder, a young teen named Vinnie, sets Rory on edge by calling him by his first name rather than "Dad." The camping trip goes sour right away: the hike to the campsite is longer than Rory had anticipated, and the younger girl, April, shows signs of heat stroke, which actually turns out to be the flu.

The trip goes from mildly unsuccessful to disastrous when Rory decides to indulge in the beer and whiskey he has brought along. He had been sober for a year following the fatal accident, and his furlough depends upon his staying sober. He physically assaults Vinnie and then abandons April as he lurches off after the boy. He smashes his flashlight in the process and drunkenly throws away his lighter, given to him by the children's mother as a token of her love before she left him for another man. Unable to kindle a fire, he never cooks the steaks he has brought for the occasion, and they function as symbols of his good intentions gone rotten. The reader is encouraged both to be sympathetic with Rory, whose life has not gone well, and to be horrified by the way he treats these children despite his love for them, a

motif treated in greater detail in the character of AJ in *The Garden of Last Days* (2008). Knowing that his relapse into alcohol abuse has been a weakness, Rory chastises himself and tries to figure out how to salvage his life. He sets the bar low for himself as he drinks his last beer the morning after his binge, proclaiming that "he's not a ratbastard" (p. 172) because he has resolved not to abandon these children in the woods. He challenges himself to "try leaving a trail of goodness" (p. 173). Yet for all that, we are left with a portrait of a pathetic man. The "hammer moon" of the title refers to carpenters' mistakes: semicircular marks from a hammer that has missed the nail. These moons do not appear when one hits a nail cleanly and purely. Rory remembers how good it feels "when you really get into the groove" (p. 139) of work, and he associates this memory with the best times of his relationship with his ex-wife. But this automatic behavior is also instinctive, which is to say thoughtless. The feeling of freedom and emphasis on good times is a two-edged sword for Rory. He is unable to sort out which elements of his life he can control and which ones he must simply deal with. His indulgence in alcohol at this crucial moment when his responsibility is being tested proves that he is at the mercy of his instincts and unwilling to declare a truce between them and his intellect, a force which is more likely to make him experience guilt, remorse, and thus growth.

"The Cage Keeper" is the longest story in the volume and the one that most thoroughly attempts to reconcile the collection's two opposing viewpoints: one holding that people are hopelessly weak, depraved, or predatory and the other holding that they are capable of redemption. In this story there are two protagonists: the narrator, Al, who is a watchman in a minimum-security prison, and Elroy, who escapes from it. Al is not exactly a hardened warden, but he is positioned between his brother, a rigid tough guy who runs the prison, and Leon, a sympathetic guard popular with the inmates. Al begins the story by revealing his somewhat hardened stance as he justifies his decision for writing up an incarcerated mother. He sees his role as "rule enforcer first, someone to talk to second" (p. 2). He

compares inmates to animals in that they can sense things that he cannot, and he lists a series of stereotypes about inmates, "some definite patterns about these people" (p. 9), that serve to distance himself from them. Going through the escaped Elroy's cell, Al declares his writings "bullshit propaganda" and is ungenerous in his assessment of Elroy's essays published in the house paper, "putting down our president all the time … putting down us and the Department of Corrections. Screw you, Elroy" (p. 13). It is not difficult for the reader to go along with Al's dismissive response to Elroy, especially after we meet him. He has escaped only as far as the parking lot, where he is lurking in Al's car with a bowie knife, drunk and menacing.

Elroy appears to be in complete control despite his intoxication as he commands Al to drive him to Canada. He thoroughly resents the authority of Al and the other "cage keepers" and has developed a rock-solid ideology governing his actions and his rhetoric. He is calculating in the way he forces Al to do his bidding, rigging up an escape-prevention system with a rope. Al initially succumbs without much resistance, but he eventually engages in dialogue with Elroy, whose instability is fueled by alcohol, fatigue, and desperation. Elroy tells Al, "I know that you are looking at a man you have put into a comfortable little pigeonhole: convicted murderer, end of story. But that is not the end of the story, Allen" (p. 40). The story Elroy tells explains his crime, not in such a way to blame it on someone else but in such a way to cause Al to feel empathy. Elroy's son had been killed in the Vietnam War, and he was not told about it until a week after the boy's body had been returned to American soil. When his son's casket was lowered into the back of Elroy's truck indelicately, Elroy took out his rage and frustration on the soldier in charge of the transfer, inadvertently killing him. The relationship between captor and captive immediately changes when Elroy finishes his story, but it is too late: having seized his fate this way, and having determined that he will not finish out his twenty-year sentence, Elroy engages in one final desperate act—robbing a convenience store

for the money they need to cross the Canadian border—and is shot in the process.

Elroy cannot access the change of trajectory he needs to atone for the sins of his past, but Al can benefit from them. He imagines his brother's tough response to Elroy's actions: "We'll put that fucker back behind the walls forever" (p. 50). He simultaneously imagines the convenience store clerk who shot Elroy, how remorseful and shocked she had looked after shooting him. This spectrum between vengeance and empathy is one that Al senses more keenly than he ever has before, aware as he is of Elroy's loss and of the misguided impulses that drive people in desperate circumstances. In his final meditation upon returning home Al is aware of all of the stories he has heard, and of the way he, a cage keeper, has attempted to isolate himself from them. In the ambiguous closing paragraph he deliberately does not lock the door of his car—which would be futile anyway since Elroy had broken in—and when he unlocks the door to the corrections center, the door handle "sticks to [his] fingers like the bottom of an ice cube tray" (p. 54). Al's inability to lock or to unlock a door clearly demonstrates his budding awareness that his story is connected to the stories of others, that his separation from the people in the cages he keeps is an illusion.

THINKING AND FEELING: BLUESMAN

Dubus' first novel, *Bluesman* (1993), continues the author's inquiry into the forces that separate individuals and groups of people. Set in the turbulent 1960s, the novel initially draws attention to stark divisions in American society: blacks and whites, the upper and lower classes, North and South, and men and women. Another division is advanced early in the novel as the young protagonist, Leo Suther, gets his first lesson in how to play the blues. His teacher in this case is his father's best friend, Ryder Stillwell, who says to him, "the way I see it, there are thinkers in this world, and there are feelers. Sometimes there's a little bit of both in one but those fellas don't do much" (Vintage ed., p. 6). He identifies

Leo as a thinker, one clever enough to see right away the falseness of the distinction, but he insists that to be a blues player, "you gotta *feel* something, not think it" (p. 7). Leo is misdiagnosed as a pure thinker because he responds to feelings more readily than to ideas and he has difficulty sorting through intellectual challenges, particularly the one that so divided the United States in those years: the debate over America's war in Vietnam.

This debate, never a simple one, is complicated in *Bluesman* by the introduction of a character who is proud to be a communist, Chick Donovan. Further complicating the situation is that Leo is in love with Chick's daughter, Allie, and that Chick has hired Leo for the summer before his senior year of high school as a construction worker. On the night he first kisses Allie, Leo walks her home and she introduces him to Chick, who points to a portrait on the living room wall of a man he identifies as "one of the great minds of the nineteenth century" (p. 19). It is Karl Marx, though Leo had assumed it was Allie's grandfather. When Chick introduces himself as a communist, Leo thinks he said "columnist" and asks which paper he writes for. He seems out of his depth intellectually with both Allie and her father, but they are both drawn to him and he is more than willing to listen to Chick's lectures on the history of labor revolt as long as they don't interfere with his first love.

The novel could be described as a study in complication, particularly the complicated nature of three subjects: young love, the Vietnam War, and the blues. Of Dubus' three novels, it is the one most clearly drawn from his immediate surroundings, with some characters easily recognizable from his memoir. The protagonist, Leo, like Dubus' brother Jeb, impregnates his teenage girlfriend and forsakes higher education for a career in house construction. Leo's father, Jim, like Dubus' father, is well meaning but an ineffective communicator and an artist who drinks too much. Chick Donovan, like the author himself, is a renovator of old houses who has been drawn to communist thinking and whose willingness to get into fistfights is nearly the death of him. The setting is also familiar.

Although *Bluesman* is set in central Massachusetts rather than in its northeastern corner, the novel takes place in a mill town with a river running through it. The river is a recurrent touchstone and symbol throughout the book. During the summer in which the plot unfolds, the river runs higher than normal, carrying garbage in its flow. The river is where Leo's father goes to communicate with his deceased wife. It represents the inevitable movement of time and the forward motion of Leo's life, which seems at least partially out of his control.

The three main characters and setting are evidently drawn from Dubus' experience, but the plot is of his own invention. Leo is about to turn eighteen when the novel begins and is drifting through his junior year in high school when he and Allie fall hard for one another. Their sexual attraction constitutes most of their relationship: their first kiss comes soon after their first conversation. Even though they are not particularly experienced, they are both well aware of the risks of unprotected sex, and yet they indulge in it frequently. It is not surprising when Allie becomes pregnant, but the plot twists when her mother insists on her having an abortion (not legal in 1967), then Leo talks her out of it, then she goes through with it on her own. When Leo and his father Jim find out about Allie's decision, both of them are upset, confused, and unsure how to respond.

Looming over this central plot thread are two absent figures: Leo's mother, Katie Faye, who died when he was five, and Chick, who, after being attacked by one of his own construction workers, languishes in a coma during the period of his daughter's pregnancy and abortion. Leo discovers his mother's journal, which describes the love between her and Jim as well as Leo's early years before she succumbed to cancer. The tenderness and maturity of his parents' relationship provides a stark contrast to his relationship with Allie, which is little more than teenage lust despite Leo's desire to ascribe deep meaning to it. His mother had been given to excessive feeling, a level of emotion that has been absent from Leo's life since her death. All women, including Allie, become substitute mothers for him: he is

obsessed with their kindness and with their ability to comfort him as well as with the relative size of their breasts.

If Leo's absent mother represents his confusion about how to feel, Chick Donovan represents a cautionary tale about what happens when one allows thinking to dominate one's experience. His militant Marxism is somewhat attractive to Leo even though he doesn't fully understand it. Yet as an ideologue rather than a true thinker, Chick alienates himself from his family and from his workers, leading to the attack that renders him comatose. Leo realizes that "Chick never listened to what anybody said unless it had to do with him or what he thought. And Leo knew why, too: Chick wasn't trying to figure out the world anymore. That man Mr. Marx had done it for him. Now all Chick had to do was find a way to live out what the man had said" (p. 253). While he is recovering, Chick denounces his former self. Leo is supposed to learn a lesson from his mother and Chick together: that a combination of thinking and feeling is desirable in life, if not in the blues.

In some ways, the blues do not make a good teacher for Leo, but they rather act as a metaphor. Ryder calls blues musicians "bridges to Truth City" (p. 8), and the eyes of the legendary bluesman Big Bill Broonzy stare at Leo from a poster on his wall, encouraging him to face the truth rather than to live in the fantasy world he slips into, one in which he and Allie live harmoniously and prosperously with a brood of happy children. The blues are paradoxical, a combination of suffering and joy. Leo is naive in thinking that he can have the latter without the former. The novel's dramatic events—the pregnancy and abortion, Allie's rejection of Leo, and his subsequent impulsive decision to join the army during wartime—constitute the fast-moving river of his life, rushing toward a place he has never imagined. He is a slow learner, impeded by his romanticism. If he learns one lesson by the end of the novel, it is that experience is the only teacher—that suffering through experience is the only way one earns the right to sing the blues (or, in Leo's case, to play them on a harmonica).

Even this lesson is complicated, though. *Bluesman* is characteristic of Dubus' writing insofar as it refuses to accept easy resolutions. The title is ironic in the sense that we are unsure whether Leo ever fully becomes the bluesman he wants to be, or if it is just another of his fantasies: "He looked up at Big Bill's wide-eyed sweating face in the poster. Such a bluesman. What was better than being called that? Nothing, that was it. That was the only way to go" (p. 175). This proclamation comes before a string of catastrophic decisions: Leo dresses up in a suit and gives Allie's mother money for the abortion, then demands half of it back, then uses much of it to buy her an enormous bouquet of flowers, then decides to join a band that no longer has a place for him, and finally (to his father's horror) joins the army, believing the false promise that he will be sent to Europe rather than to Vietnam. He and his father and Ryder give a public blues performance the night before he ships out to boot camp, and although it is successful, Leo fixates on his nervousness and on the mistakes he makes. As in "White Trees, Hammer Moon" and "The Cage Keeper," the focus in *Bluesman* is on the tragic consequences of poor decisions made by well-intentioned, desperate, and romantic characters. We are left with the impression that Leo is neither a bluesman nor someone who will ever become one, but rather a misguided kid whose desire to take control of his destiny will render him a statistic in a futile war.

THE DOOMED AND THE DAMNED: HOUSE OF SAND AND FOG

Dubus' most celebrated work, *House of Sand and Fog*, continues the pattern initiated in *Bluesman*: poor decisions amid challenging circumstances lead to tragic outcomes. His innovation in this novel is to examine what happens when the lives of three such characters collide. Kathy Nicolo is a recovering substance abuser evicted from her house through a combination of a bureaucratic error and her carelessness about rectifying the problem before it is too late. Massoud Behrani is a former Iranian colonel who emigrated with his family to the United States following the deposal

of the Shah of Iran, and who is fed up with his menial jobs to the point that he takes a risk and buys Kathy's house when it is put up for auction. Lester Burdon is the deputy who evicts Kathy from her house but who quickly falls for her and dedicates himself to rectifying the county's wrong by getting her house back, regardless of whether doing so is within his jurisdiction. The action is catalyzed by Behrani's realization that his willingness to buy and resell Kathy's house is legal but unethical, by Kathy's backsliding into drinking, and by Lester's conflicted emotions over leaving his wife and children in order to continue his torrid affair with Kathy. Three characters with such contradictory desires create a perfect storm for tragedy. Dubus encourages his readers to switch allegiances between the three main characters throughout the novel, rooting for one before witnessing his or her fatal decline, then doing the same for the others, and finally looking on in horror as all three plunge into an abyss that the three of them created together.

Before Lester enters the plot in earnest, the novel allows Behrani and Kathy equal narrative space, alternating their stories as the drama escalates. Both tell their story in the first person— Behrani in present tense, Kathy in past. They seem at first a study in opposites. Behrani is obsessed with discipline and criticizes Americans in general for their lack of it, pointing to their indulgences in fast food, alcohol, and sexual licentiousness as evidence. Kathy comes across as one of the many undisciplined Americans, careless in her habits, her appearance, and her decisions. Behrani laments the prosperity of his past, recalling his glory days in Iran before the Islamist revolution in that country. Kathy regards her past as dangerous and out of control, especially when it involved cocaine, which she refers to as "the white snake" responsible for her downfall. She is quick to blame others for her misery, especially her ex-husband who, she believes, used her as part of his own recovery from addiction. She blames the county for the mistake that led to her eviction, and although she is correct, she is also complicit insofar as she did not open or carefully read her mail.

In terms of blaming others and discriminating or prejudging, Behrani is like Kathy in that he blames others, specifically Americans, for not allowing him to get away with his unethical behavior. He acknowledges that flipping houses purchased at auctions is "the legal way to rob" (p. 17). He refers to America as "this terrible country" (p. 22) and criticizes American lifestyles, law, and cultural production even while trying to turn an American-style profit. Though he is hypocritical, there is something appealing about Behrani's business acumen, his ambition, and his understanding of the system. He is also a dedicated family man. The reader is more likely to be wary of Kathy, who seems to have a weak grasp on her past, present, or future life. She is content to clean houses and to stave off her addictive impulses by watching movies, sometimes two or three in a row, an activity that reveals her willingness to live vicariously and passively. Her affair with Lester is built on clutching need rather than genuine love, and the fact that it coincides with her relapse into alcohol abuse makes her seem all the more out of control. Her low self-esteem is evident; she is an adult version of Lorilee from "Duckling Girl," for whom drinking and sex are numbing agents that actually cause pain instead of healing it. She frequently reveals her desire for death and her feelings of insignificance: "I felt like an old magazine somebody finds wedged under a chair cushion, and I knew that's where I wanted to be, under a huge cushion somewhere, curled up cool and private, to sleep a long time" (p. 41). Despite her vulnerability and weaknesses, Kathy has a moral advantage over Behrani in that she would never harm another person just to make a profit for herself. Yet she is at least as guilty as he is of cultural discrimination. Behrani begins the novel by criticizing his coworkers who are immigrants from various nations, insulting their lifestyles and customs and considering himself superior to them. Both Lester and Kathy prejudge the Behranis, criticizing their dress, their language, and their customs. It takes Kathy half the book to get their name right, and she initially doesn't know the difference between Arabic and Farsi. Lester refers to Behrani as an "Arab son of a bitch" (p. 162) amid other slurs.

ANDRE DUBUS III

There is plenty to like and dislike about each of the two primary narrators, and their opposing viewpoints set up an interesting debate between what is legal and what is right. The introduction of Lester Burdon into the narrative, though, destabilizes it radically. Lester is a character who wears the gold star of the law, literally, and yet who is also prepared to abuse it to advance the cause of what he believes to be right. In a masterful scene in a revolving restaurant, the point at which Kathy takes her first drink in three years, Lester admits to planting evidence in order to convict a domestic abuser. Kathy is perversely excited by this admission because it drags Lester down from his superior perch as a law enforcement officer to her level as someone who has broken the law. She also admires his willingness to take fate into his own hands; following his evidence-planting confession she says, with clear admiration, "you just do what you want to, don't you?" (p. 112). Although Lester is a more complex character than just this familiar type—a corrupt cop who is also cheating on his wife and fueling the addictions of a recovering substance abuser—he is clearly not a figure who inspires trust.

In fact, all three main characters lie. Behrani hides the truth of his dubious real estate transaction from his wife and children, and Kathy has not even told her mother that she and her ex-husband are divorced or that she has been evicted. Lester's capacity to lie is clear when he enters Behrani's house under false pretenses, trying to gather information to use against him and lying about his own name in the process. This one lie spirals into a dozen others that catalyze the book's tragic conclusion. In addition to the way the main characters interact with others, it is clear that all three of them lie to themselves. Behrani, for instance, disapproves of his countrymen who physically abuse their wives, yet he does the same; Kathy ridicules the rhetoric of her addiction recovery program, yet she does so as a way of denying her own weakness as she relapses; and Lester styles himself as the chivalrous defender of women, yet he toys with the emotions of his wife and Kathy and is more motivated by self-gratification than by any noble purpose.

The tragic impulses of *House of Sand and Fog* reach a fever pitch during the novel's second half, which adds a third-person narrator with access to Lester's thoughts. After Kathy attempts to commit suicide in what has become the Behranis' house, Lester breaks in and holds the colonel and his family hostage at gunpoint. We learn something of Lester's backstory, yet it is hard to sympathize with him because of the stupidity of the decisions he makes in the present. Sitting down on the Behranis' couch to think through his quandary, he thinks, "the sofa felt too soft, as if he were sinking more deeply into it" (p. 271), clearly a metaphor for his quicksand-like circumstances. He feels more like a cornered animal than like the man he wants to be. He has hurt his wife and failed to understand the depths of his lover's despair, given her relapse into alcohol abuse and her subsequent suicide attempt, both of which are his doing. His feelings of shame convert into masculine aggression, and he sacrifices rational thought in favor of pure instinct; for instance, in threatening Behrani, he feels he has "no choice but to push the square barrel up under the colonel's chin" (p. 271), when of course he has many choices. He refuses to "expose his throat" (p. 278) to his captives, revealing the deep vulnerability that undergirds his aggression. Like Lester, Behrani feels shame for his affiliation with the Shah's regime and in a private moment thinks that he is "finally ... receiving what [he] deserve[s]" (p. 288). In what devolves into a senseless war between these two men over the classic reason for misguided war—property—there are bound to be innocent casualties. In this case, Behrani's son, Esmail, becomes the sacrificial victim as he tries to prevent Lester from forcing his will upon his father. Behrani then murders his wife and commits suicide so that they do not have to deal with the agony of living without their son.

Kathy and Lester are familiar types in Dubus' fiction—the weak woman and the misguided man who takes it upon himself to defend her—but their ignorance sets them apart and makes it seem inevitable that their fate is to end up where they do: in jail, coping with regret. Being photographed upon his booking, Lester feels "that this

computer graphic of his face, this jailhouse mug-shot, was really him, the true Lester" (p. 341). He also admits to himself that the affair with Kathy and the tragic events that ensued made him feel more alive than he had in years. His commitment to his wife and family had been a fiction, or a disguise, like Lester's frequently described crooked mustache. Kathy, in her separate cell, finds herself caught between competing portraits of her by outsiders, a deputy who judges her and a nurse who offers her comfort. She feels she deserves neither: "Neither picture of me was true" (p. 352). Her lawyer encourages her to confess the truth as well, and Kathy says, "The word ['truth'] was like a black bat flittering between us" (p. 354). For Kathy, having lived with addiction and deception her whole life, the truth has become frightening and elusive, but she must now confront it because there is no escape. The novel can be read as a painful stripping away of hypocrisy and discovery of the truth. The cost, however, is high. In the end, two main characters are incarcerated and one is dead, along with the rest of his family. If the novel carries a lesson for the reader, it is to avoid indulging in small lies that feed into larger self-deceptions, and to confront one's past demons with as much strength and honesty as one can muster. The characters within the novel learn this lesson too late, if at all.

IN THE AFTERMATH OF NATIONAL TRAGEDY: THE GARDEN OF LAST DAYS

Cultural and historical commentary is generally in the background of Dubus' fiction. Yet the devastation of the terrorist attacks on September 11, 2001, spurred him to place his usual concerns against a more immediate historical background. Following the lead of the story that some of the 9/11 hijackers had reportedly been drinking at strip clubs in Florida in order to blend into American culture, Dubus situates his third novel in one such club, but his fictional jihadist, Bassam al-Jizani, is just one of a tangle of characters involved in the drama, which is at least as concerned with the abduction of a three-year-old girl as it is with a large-scale terrorist attack.

Placed next to *House of Sand and Fog, The Garden of Last Days* features three familiar character types, with variations, as the three main players on this stage*:* April, a lost and confused single mother whose inability to manage her life leaves her vulnerable; Bassam, an immigrant from the Middle East whose pride, honor, and feelings of inadequacy lead him to turn against Americans; and AJ, a father with an individual code of justice that leads him to desperate and illegal acts. The similarities between these characters and Kathy, Behrani, and Lester from the earlier novel provide some continuity in Dubus' evolution, but the methods and scope of *The Garden of Last Days* are notably different. Other significant characters are also developed in conjunction with the main plot: Lonnie Pike, the principled bouncer at the strip club who longs to save April; Jean, April's landlady, who has assumed the role of surrogate mother to April's neglected daughter, Franny; and Deena and Virginia, AJ's former wife and his mother, respectively, who are powerless to control his reckless behavior. The proliferation of characters within a claustrophobic space and short time frame give Dubus the opportunity to develop his trademark themes of hypocrisy and self-deception while advancing a subtle and meaningful critique of the circumstances leading up to the 9/11 terrorist attacks.

That critique involves America's unwillingness to examine itself with candor and honesty as well as the foreign terrorists' fatal and hypocritical judgment of America's "sins." Television is Dubus' recurrent symbol of America's refusal to look in the mirror. When characters are not indulging in joyless erotic dancing in the Puma Club for Men, they tend to be absorbed in the artificial world of TV. April uses it as an electronic babysitter, mesmerizing her daughter Franny with Disney cartoons and attempting (but failing) to skip over the scarier parts on the night she brings Franny to work, setting off the catastrophic plot that involves the girl's abduction. Bassam's confused judgment of America derives partly from the pornography that can be summoned at will on his hotel's TV screen. AJ's mother, Virginia, finds religion on

the small screen, and his ex-wife Deena seems more interested in it than she is in either her husband or her son. After the terrorist attacks, April describes time passing as "the days and nights of television. The images she wouldn't let Franny see" (p. 521). Contemporary American culture is so mediated that it cannot understand itself, or see itself in an undistorted way.

This is not to suggest that Dubus depicts the United States as a country that brought on 9/11 through its own shortcomings, but rather that it was too distracted to see what was happening, or to place it in context. April, the novel's central figure, does not learn about the attacks until nearly three o'clock that day—almost eight hours after the first hijacking—prompting a bank teller to chide her: "Are you serious? Do you really not know what's just *happened* to us?" (p. 517). The "us" at the end of the sentence links April to her nation for the first time in the novel, near its conclusion. She has been self-absorbed to the point of oblivion, even on the fatal day of the attacks, but especially before. She has compromised her daughter's safety and security by bringing her to a strip club and assuming that her coworkers will be able to look after her while she consorts in a private room with one of the soon-to-be hijackers. Bassam has spent the night insulting April and asking her probing questions about her motivations and her morality. She responds with reticence but is polite enough to him because he keeps throwing hundred-dollar bills her way (when he is not burning them as a way of demonstrating his contempt for what he describes as America's "gods" [p. 176]).

April, who has mastered the ability to mask her emotions with a "nightsmile" that seduces customers at the Puma Club into showering her with money, has fallen victim to a greed that seems characteristically American in the context of this novel. She pretends that the reason she has taken this demeaning job is to provide for her daughter, but she repeatedly says that buying one house would not be enough, that she yearns for two, three, or more. The "last days" of the title indicate an America that has lost sight of its core values, especially those involving family. April, Bassam, and AJ all have in common their estrangement from their true families. While April withdraws into herself and becomes vindictive and neglectful, Bassam unleashes his fury on the nation in general, and AJ—who is no more sympathetic than the others—enacts a fumbling crusade to rescue April's daughter from the den of iniquity where he has spent much of his time and money in recent months while drifting away from his son after abusing his ex-wife. The America that is the backdrop for the novel is self-indulgent, bloated, and consumed by vices that provide no real pleasure.

And yet, the "garden" of the title persists beyond the last days, indicating the possibility for renewal. The garden belongs to Jean, April's landlady, who has struggled to provide Franny with the love and attention that her mother does not give her. Jean is tired, sick, and not very effective throughout the crises of the novel, but she is a solid force of goodness that endures beyond the vice, neglect, terror, violence, and acquisitiveness that have ruined the American garden. Jean sits in her private garden with a glass of wine at the novel's conclusion and tries "not to think of anything. Just to see [her garden]. Its beauty here for as long as she was, as long as she cared for it" (p. 535). A symbol of nature and of the work that goes into cultivating it, the garden represents the authentic American culture that no one else in the novel is able to see. The renewal of American culture depends upon the reader's ability to do so, to see 9/11 as a failed attempt to destroy something that is worth preserving when we look beyond its debased surface and into its honorable core.

CROOKED PATH TO REDEMPTION: TOWNIE

Following his large-scale examination of his nation in the aftermath of 9/11, Dubus returned to his self and his past for his next book. As a memoir, *Townie* functions only partly to provide details of Dubus' life, as described earlier in this essay. It is equally valuable as a meditation on the intersection of violence, masculinity, and social class in contemporary America. Dubus' narrative voice in this work is honest, clear, and unwavering. The descriptions of the many fights

he was involved in may overwhelm or even sicken the reader, but the effect is to transform the trope of violence as exciting or empowering into feelings of revulsion. Since the narrative traces the arc of someone who spirals to a low point before being saved, we have to witness the spiral and feel its effects. The variation on this classic arc is that there are multiple dark nights of the soul and multiple moments of epiphany leading to redemption. *Townie,* in other words, is as ragged and lurching as life itself and thus not as tidy as some contemporary memoirs, but more honest and powerful as a result.

The memoir's power derives from the fact that the author clearly does not admire facets of his former self—his ignorance about the life of the mind, the rashness with which he made decisions, his capacity to intimidate strangers, his unwillingness to listen to others—and yet, he rarely stands in overt judgment of that self. In the same way, he is not judgmental of his father—who comes across as selfish and distant but also warm, likable, and strong—or his mother, who occasionally appears weak and clueless but also caring and dependable. There are relatively few generalized pronouncements in the memoir, but the few it contains are earned. One such pronouncement arrives late in the book, and it is simple wisdom that derives from a lifetime of violent confrontation: "I'd learned this much about physical violence: One hurt demanded another" (p. 336). This revelation provides the key to the memoir's framework. Understanding the nature of violence this way enables its author to break out of the cycle that once entrapped him.

The cycle unquestioningly starts with his parents' separation, which is described in violent terms: "*Separated.* It was a word I'd never thought much about before, but now I pictured them being cut one from the other with a big, sharp knife" (p. 22). The Vietnam War rages on dimly in the background as Andre is confronted with violence all around him, claiming that his brother and his friends "played war" because it was "what we knew from the TV every night" (p. 25). Writing of the painful scene when his father drives away from the house, Andre says

that his brother Jeb "scooped up a handful of gravel and ran down the hill after him, 'You bum! You bum! You bum!' He threw it all at once, the small rocks scattering across the road and into the woods like shrapnel" (p. 24). His father seems unaware that he had declared war. His status as an ex-marine, which manifests itself most evidently in the disciplined way he works and runs on a daily basis, is at odds with his insatiable appetites for alcohol and the sexual attention of younger women. These latter behaviors are the ones he seems unable to control, and they are responsible for his unconscious attack on his family.

One hurt demands another. Each of the family members responds to the end of the marriage differently over the years, but Andre and the two siblings closest to him in age express it most directly. Suzanne, his older sister, becomes involved in relationships that are self-destructive at best, abusive at worst. His younger brother Jeb becomes suicidal, and even years after the divorce, he links his desire to destroy himself to his father's refusal to accept him. In a harrowing scene toward the end of the book, Jeb threatens to kill himself with his father's pistol in front of his girlfriend and Andre. It is clear to Andre that his father has thoroughly rejected Jeb because he did not finish school and because he did not marry the young woman who bore his child. Their father claims that he has rejected his second son "because you don't walk away from *responsibility.* ... I don't like the way he *lives,* Andre. He needs to become a *man*" (p. 308). All of these italicized words are ironic because, of course, Andre's father has done what he has accused Jeb of doing. Perhaps because he develops a close bond to his father over time, Andre only feels "semi-abandoned," but he also links that condition to "hurts" and "bitterness" (p. 332).

In terms of his own method for responding to violence with more violence, Andre takes up bodybuilding and boxing. He characterizes his childhood as a series of encounters with bullies who humiliate him and his family. His early response is to do nothing and to feel inadequate afterward. After a period of indifference toward school coupled with experiments in sex and

drugs, he discovers a bodybuilding magazine and studies "every page." The men in it look like "shaved and massive rage" (p. 80), which becomes the model for his transformation. His father is occasionally summoned back to the house after one of the children is threatened, but Andre grows skeptical that his father is willing to do anything to protect them. In one distressing scene on Thanksgiving, Andre's father arrives well after the appointed time, drunk, with a drunken friend in tow. The friend is suffering from his own separation from his family, and he kisses Andre on the mouth, prompting his father to apologize weakly and explain away the behavior, but Andre is prepared to defend himself violently against the drunken advances of his father's friend if necessary: "it was clear once again that nobody in this world was going to take care of you but *you*" (p. 115).

This declaration of self-sufficiency, however, knows no boundaries. Over the years Andre picks fights not only with those who threaten him but with those who threaten anyone in his general vicinity. His uncontrolled rage is triggered by those who have harmed or even merely insulted his friends and family, but also increasingly by random strangers whose aggression threatens his world order. A racist bumper sticker on a car in Texas is enough to set him off. A man insulting, verbally abusing, or just ogling a woman in a bar is a particular instigation. Late in the memoir, after he is on the crooked path to redemption, he still cannot tamp down this impulse to protect vulnerable women, born undoubtedly of his perception of his mother and sister Suzanne as women who suffered emotional and physical abuse. In an airport, just after publishing his first book in 1989, he beats up two punks who have gotten into a physical confrontation with a woman. In what has become a familiar pattern, he knocks down both of them and is commended by other passengers. Also, not for the first time, the police who arrive on the scene let him go with a wink and even a smile for helping the cause of justice. Nonetheless, at this point in his journey, Andre does not bask in the glow of praise, power, or righteousness: "I stood there feeling depleted and ugly and wrong" (p. 331).

Afterward he converts this feeling into a series of revelations: "*You should've just walked her to the gate, that's it. And don't think you did any of this for her because you didn't. You did it for you. And you need to stop. You need to stop doing this*" (p. 336).

A more complete moment of transformation happens months later, after he gets married and is on a two-week vacation in Europe. It begins with a terrifying dream in which a preacher tells him "You're gonna *die*" (p. 343) as he is surrounded by men in suits and ties, "their hair cut short as Marines" (pp. 340–341), while his wife watches silently. He wakes with existential anxiety, yet doesn't want to share the dream with his wife, and internalizes his fear as he always has. He nearly succumbs to his typical violent reaction to drunken men around him, first in a pub and then on a ferry crossing the Irish Sea. The situation becomes much worse when he finds himself in a railway car containing thirty-five German schoolgirls. The car is invaded by a series of hooligans crossing through to the next car to buy drugs from a dealer, and the young girls are terrified. Andre stands to defend them, preventing anyone from passing through the car so that the girls can sleep and feel safe. Miraculously, he manages to resolve the conflict by talking to a series of street-tough drug users rather than by fighting them. He elicits their stories, and they are persuaded that they are on his side. He writes, "I couldn't remember ever feeling this good. Not just about what I'd somehow done by not doing something else, but about people, the stories inside every one of us, the need for them to be *known*" (p. 355).

This revelation becomes his aesthetic principle. Making known the stories of average, imperfect people is the core of his practice, and although the memoir ends with his father's death and funeral, this is the moment at which the darkness of his past becomes fully converted into an artistic commitment that not only involves restraint—doing something by not doing something else—but by a deep appreciation for and faith in humanity. The conversion from someone who believes that humanity is abusive, vicious, and depraved to someone who believes that

humans can be redeemed if given the chance to tell their stories is complete at this moment, and the trajectory of his career follows accordingly. In the 2012 Miller interview he reacted to another interviewer who suggested that he writes about people with small lives. "There's no such thing as a small life," he insisted. "Every life is huge!"

Selected Bibliography

WORKS OF ANDRE DUBUS III

FICTION AND MEMOIR
The Cage Keeper and Other Stories. New York: Dutton, 1989; New York: Vintage, 2001.

Bluesman. Boston: Faber, 1993; New York: Vintage, 2001.

House of Sand and Fog. New York: Norton, 1999; New York: Vintage, 2000.

The Garden of Last Days. New York: Norton, 2008.

Townie. New York: Norton, 2011, 2012.

Dirty Love. New York: Norton, 2013.

NOVELLAS AND UNCOLLECTED STORIES
"In the Quiet." *Yankee Magazine,* August 1992, p. 50. (Story.)

"The Bartender." Originally published in *Glimmer Train Stories* 30, 1999. Reprinted in *Where Love Is Found: 24 Tales of Connection.* Edited by Susan Burmeister-Brown and Linda B. Swanson-Davies. New York: Washington Square Press, 2006. Pp. 102–141.

"Marla." *Glimmer Train* 54 (spring 2005). Pp. 103–169.

NONFICTION
"Tracks and Ties." In *The Best American Essays 1994.* Edited by Tracy Kidder. Boston: Houghton Mifflin, 1994. (Originally published in *Epoch,* spring 1993.)

New afterword to *The Stories of Breece D'J Pancake.* Boston: Little, Brown, 2002. Pp. 179–186.

Introduction to *We Don't Live Here Anymore: Three Novellas.* By Andre Dubus. New York: Vintage, 2004. Pp. xi–xvii. (Reissue of "We Don't Live Here Anymore," "Adultery," and "Finding a Girl in America.")

"Poetic Justice." *Boston Magazine,* August 2005. http://www.bostonmagazine.com/articles/2006/05/poetic-justice/.

"Home." In *Death by Pad Thai.* Edited by Douglas Bauer. New York: Clarkson Potter, 2006.

"Secret Spaces, Far from Strife." *New York Times,* January 19, 2011. http://www.nytimes.com/2011/01/20/garden/20Domestic.html?_r=1&pagewanted=all.

"In Praise of Strong Women: The Wild One." *More,* May 2011. http://www.more.com/women-men-admire-andre-dubus.

"The Land of No: Love in Class-Riven America." *New Republic,* February 8, 2012. http://www.tnr.com/article/politics/magazine/100520/poverty-manhattan-rent-land-no.

CRITICAL AND BIOGRAPHICAL STUDIES
Abney, Lisa. "Andre Dubus, III." In *Dictionary of Literary Biography.* Vol. 292, *Twenty-First-Century American Novelists.* Edited by Lisa Abney and Suzanne Disheroon Green. Detroit: Gale, 2004. Pp. 74–79.

Dubus, Andre, III. Website. http://andredubus.com/index.html.

Hardin, Michael. "Andre Dubus III's White Whale: *Moby-Dick* and *House of Sand and Fog.*" *Notes on Contemporary Literature* 34, no. 4:15–16 (September 2004).

Newman, Judie. "Blowback: Andre Dubus III's *House of Sand and Fog.*" *Critique: Studies in Contemporary Fiction* 51, no. 4:378–393 (summer 2010).

Sheidley, William. "The Tragedy of Traditional Heroism in Andre Dubus III's *House of Sand and Fog*: A Biocultural Perspective." In *The Image of the Hero II,* edited by Will Wright and Steven Kaplan. Pueblo, Colo.: Society for the Interdisciplinary Study of Social Imagery, 2010. Pp. 155–159.

INTERVIEWS
Birnbaum, Robert. "Interview: Andre Dubus III." *Identity Theory/The Narrative Thread,* October 4, 2000. http://www.identitytheory.com/andre-dubus-iii/.

Formy-Duval, John M. "Interview with Andre Dubus III, Author of *The Garden of Last Days.*" *Contemporary Literature,* June 2008. http://contemporarylit.about.com/od/authorinterviews/a/andreDubusIII.htm.

Gross, Terry. "Writer Andre Dubus III." *Fresh Air.* National Public Radio, June 13, 2003. http://www.npr.org/templates/story/story.php?storyId=1297679.

Macgowan, James. "Oprah Helps a Son Come into His Own." *Ottawa Citizen,* May 13, 2001, p. C12.

McNally, John. "Interview with Andre Dubus III." *Glimmer Train* 50:48–61 (spring 2004).

Miller, D. Quentin. Interview with Andre Dubus III, May 25, 2012.

Wedin, Terrance. "The *Rumpus* Interview with Andre Dubus

III." *Rumpus,* July 20, 2011. http://therumpus.net/2011/07/the-rumpus-interview-with-andre-dubus-iii/.

Weissman, Larry. "A Conversation with Andre Dubus III." *Bold Type.* http://www.randomhouse.com/boldtype/0300/dubus/interview.html.

FILM BASED ON THE WORK OF ANDRE DUBUS III

House of Sand and Fog. Directed by Vadim Perelman; screenplay by Perelman and Shawn Lawrence Otto. Dreamworks, 2003.

CHRISTOPHER DURANG

(1949—)

John M. Clum

THROUGHOUT HIS PLAYWRITING career, which began in the 1970s, Christopher Durang has combined a frightening vision of a chaotic world and satire of cruelly repressive institutions, particularly the Catholic Church, with a gift for madcap comedy. Durang's approach to his work is most aptly described by a phrase from Samuel Beckett that became the source of the title of one of his plays: "Laughing wild amid severest woe." For Durang, the only response to cosmic indifference and human insanity and cruelty is laughter. He wrote of the audience responses to one of his early plays: "Those people who can't laugh at *Nature and Purpose* [*The Nature and Purpose of the Universe*] think that I'm just laughing at suffering. They don't see I'm laughing at how awful it is" (Savran, p. 30). This darkly comic vision is expressed through verbal wit, slapstick, and zany references to popular and high culture. Durang combines elements of traditional farce and absurdist drama with his own unique voice and vision to create comedies that are highly theatrical, even self-referentially metatheatrical.

Durang has described his style as "Absurdist comedy married to real feelings" (*Complete Full-Length Plays,* p. 306). The influence of absurdist playwrights like the Romanian-French Eugène Ionesco (1909–1994) is clear. Much of Ionesco's best work (e.g., *The Bald Soprano, Rhinoceros*) combines a bleak view of an empty, godless world with elements of farce. In Ionesco plays like *The New Tenant* (1955) the inanimate objects that are part of one's environment seem to have a frightening life of their own. Characters seek meaning but experience yields none. One can also recognize in some of Durang's bizarre family dramas the influence of Edward Albee's early absurdist *The American Dream* (1961), as well as the influence of the British farceur Joe Orton

(1933–1967), who was a master of deconstructing conventional domestic drama and rational discourse within the framework of farce. Durang may allude to various dramatic forms and often quotes playwrights he admires, particularly Tennessee Williams, but he eschews conventional linear narrative. Unlike these playwrights, Durang often breaks the fourth wall with direct address to the audience. Because his work avoids the conventions of popular American domestic drama and the pat happy endings of commercial Broadway and television fare, his work has been produced mostly by off-Broadway and regional theaters.

Durang's work falls into two categories: in the first are what he calls "entertainments"—"my parodies and what I might call my 'friendly, silly' plays"—and in the second are his "satiric, dark comedy plays" (*Miss Witherspoon,* p. ix). The entertainments include spoofs of Fyodor Dostoevsky (*The Idiots Karamazov,* written with Albert Innaurato), David Rabe (*The Vietnamization of New Jersey*), Hollywood film genres (*A History of the American Film*), Charles Dickens (*Mrs. Bob Cratchit's Wild Christmas Binge*), and Tennessee Williams (*For Whom the Southern Belle Tolls* and *Desire, Desire, Desire*) as well as cabaret acts like *Das Lusitania Songspiel,* a tour de force based on the idea that Bertolt Brecht was still alive and had written most of what was on Broadway that year (1980), and *Chris Durang and Dawne,* a send-up of a lounge act. These "entertainments," however clever and inventive, are often little more than extended comic sketches. The second, more important category, "satiric, dark comedy plays," often shares elements with the entertainments—a love of parody and witty cultural references and a desire, above all, to make the audience laugh—but these plays

also have an underlying moral outrage at repressive social institutions and a sense of the essential irrationality of human experience.

Writing on Christopher Durang is made both easier and more difficult by the amount of commentary he has provided on his own life and work. In the introductory and explanatory material he has appended to his published work and on his website, www.christopherdurang.com, Durang has generously provided readers with his understanding of the genesis and production history of his work and on how he wants his characters depicted onstage.

One cannot discuss Durang's work without mentioning the importance of his relationship to Catholicism. While most of Durang's contemporaries (e.g., Alfred Uhry, Donald Margulies, Wendy Wasserstein) create worlds that are either secular or Jewish, Durang is unique in his focus on characters who have been damaged by the Catholic Church. His rage at the Church stems in part from its teachings on sexuality. In 2006 he wrote a scathing article titled "Homosexuality: Is It Disgusting, or Is It Delightful?" for the liberal Catholic magazine *Conscience,* in which he rails at the Church's proscriptions against carnal pleasure, from Saint Paul ("that holy mental case") to the present, while never revising its attitude toward birth control or its indifference to war. He ends by saying that he is no longer interested in the Church's opinions on anything. However indifferent he now is toward the Church, much of his best work is informed by his anger at the damaging effects of its teachings. Durang may have lost his faith while he was a student at Harvard, but he was still battling his Catholic education. His most commercially successful play, *Sister Mary Ignatius Explains It All for You* (1979), is his most overtly anti-Catholic, which led to many productions being banned because of Church pressure. Durang is openly gay, but not a "gay playwright" in the sense that his works, unlike those of many gay playwrights writing in the 1980s and 1990s, do not focus on homosexual experience. There are some gay characters in his work (*Sister Mary Ignatius Explains It All for You, Laughing Wild*), but gay politics are only one aspect of his critique of the Church and some

of the basic assumptions of Christianity. Most of his plays focus on rational, well-meaning female protagonists thrust into situations that are totally irrational. Since the late 1970s his response to the madness he sees has moved from pessimism and sometimes bitterness to a conditional optimism. His characters may be misanthropes, but Durang seems to delight in the human eccentricities he presents.

EARLY LIFE AND PLAYS

Christopher Ferdinand Durang was born in suburban Montclair, New Jersey, about fifteen miles west of New York City, on January 2, 1949. His father, Francis Ferdinand Durang, Jr., was an architect; his mother, Patricia Elizabeth, was a secretary. Francis Durang's father and grandfather had been architects, but the family has a connection to the history of American theater: John Durang (1768–1822) was the first well-known professional performer in America; his memoir is an important document in the history of American theater. The Durang family moved a few miles west to Berkeley Heights, New Jersey, where Chris grew up. His parents did not have a happy marriage and young Chris's home life was turbulent. His mother constantly raged against her husband's alcoholism and went through periods of depression caused by her three failed pregnancies (the couple's blood types were incompatible). To add to the stress, there were arguments at gatherings of the extended families. Durang created a version of his family life in *The Marriage of Bette and Boo* (1985). His parents separated when he was thirteen, and his mother later had a second failed marriage to an alcoholic. His family's problems with alcohol were powerful enough to lead him to join a support group for children of alcoholics.

Chris Durang received a Catholic education, first at Our Lady of Peace School in rural New Providence, New Jersey, then at Delbarton School, a highly respected preparatory school run by Benedictine monks outside of Morristown. By the time he graduated from Delbarton, he saw himself as a liberal Catholic who wanted to remain in the Church but knew it needed reform

so that its doctrine could be brought into line with the everyday lives of its parishioners. His religious convictions also led him to oppose the Vietnam War.

Durang's interest in theater started early. His mother took him to Broadway shows, and he had an avid fascination with classic films shown on television, particularly comedies. An uncle was an actor turned stage designer and two of his aunts were musicians. Durang wrote his first script when he was eight years old and had plays produced while he was in junior high school and at Delbarton. Two musicals he cowrote with a friend, Kevin Farrell, were presented by the Summit (New Jersey) Playhouse in summer productions that were directed by his uncle. Though he knew that theater would at least be a strong avocation, he decided to take advantage of a scholarship to Harvard, which did not have an undergraduate theater department.

During his first year at Harvard, where he was a student from 1967 to 1971, he fell into a severe depression that lasted for two years. As he puts it, "on a typical day I might sleep all morning, talk to no one, scrub bathtubs and sinks for two hours [his work-study job], eat alone, then go out to" a film (*Twenty-Seven Short Plays*, p. 230). The depression was a combination of the psychic wounds caused by growing up in an alcoholic family, the loss of faith he experienced during his freshman year at Harvard, anxiety about his homosexuality, and guilt about having testified against his father in his parents' divorce hearing. He told this writer, "My depression was a potent combination of 'nothing works out,' the world is full of pain and death, and there's no God or he doesn't help or answer prayers" (Clum, 2011). That loss of faith and the realization that he was gay (this was pre-Stonewall and gay liberation) created what Durang called "a perfect storm" (Clum, 2011). Fortunately, Durang had the ability to pull himself together enough to pass his courses (except eighteenth-century poetry) and to find a good free psychologist at the Harvard counseling center. During his senior year his depression lifted and along with it his writer's block. He very quickly wrote a full-length play, *The Nature and Purpose of the Uni-verse*, which impressed readers enough to get him accepted into a Harvard playwriting seminar and to win a playwriting competition at Smith College that led to a production.

Though a bit sophomoric, *The Nature and Purpose of the Universe* contains many of the elements of Durang's mature work. The central character is Eleanor, a New Jersey housewife who has an abusive husband and three sons who also mistreat her. The eldest son is a drug dealer, the middle son is a homosexual who brings his transvestite boyfriend home to live with the family, and the youngest son is shunned because he lost his penis in a bizarre accident. As if Eleanor's life is not miserable enough, God sends two agents, Ronald and Elaine, to make it worse. God isn't testing Eleanor as the Old Testament God tested Job: the sadistic deity is simply having fun causing Eleanor to suffer various forms of physical and psychological abuse. Elaine also masquerades as Sister Annie De Maupassant, a radical nun who enlists Eleanor's husband in her plot to assassinate the pope and take his place. By the end of the play the family is forced to move to Iceland, and the beleaguered Eleanor can pray only for a death God will not grant her. The play is suffused with Durang's view of religion: a nasty God and a Catholic Church not only deaf to the suffering of its parishioners but actively cruel toward them.

One's appreciation of *The Nature and Purpose of the Universe* depends on the director and cast finding a way to make the play's extreme cruelty and violence funny. There has to be a cartoon-like quality to the brutal physical and verbal insults Eleanor receives in order to achieve a balance between the madcap stylization and Durang's wish for the audience to feel real sympathy for Eleanor. The balance between violence, farce, and real human emotion is a tricky one, but Durang requires this balance in all of his serious comedies. There are other typical Durang touches, such as direct address to the audience. Ronald, God's agent, acts as a kind of narrator. The dialogue is filled with humorous literary allusions from a myriad of sources, from Tennessee Williams' plays to Peter Weiss's *Marat/Sade* (1964). There is even a camp musi-

cal number sung to the tune of "Tiptoe Through the Tulips."

The Nature and Purpose of the Universe is a daring play in its iconoclasm—Durang has always defined himself as an iconoclast—and its presentation of violent and perverse sexuality. Durang wrote it in the 1960s, when much contemporary drama was daring and confrontational. Experimental works that broke down the actor-audience relationship, such as Richard Schechner's *Dionysus in 69* (1969) and the Living Theatre's 1968 production *Paradise Now,* garnered a great deal of attention for their defiance of bourgeois codes of respectability. Durang was more attached to issues these theatrical revolutionaries would consider irrelevant—the Christian God, the Church, and the nuclear family; but in his own way he was defying the prevailing modes of dramatic representation, particularly the conventions of realistic domestic drama.

The Nature and Purpose of the Universe (a spoof on the title of a Harvard publication, "The Nature and Purpose of the University") was not produced professionally until 1975, but Robert Brustein, dean of the Yale School of Drama, and Howard Stein, head of its playwriting program, were impressed with Durang's unique style and accepted him into the program at Yale. Durang was fortunate enough to be at Yale (1972–1974) with a group of extraordinary students. The actresses Meryl Streep and Sigourney Weaver appeared in productions of his plays during their years at Yale, and Weaver later collaborated with Durang on projects like *Das Lusitania Songspiel.* Fellow playwrights Albert Innaurato and Wendy Wasserstein were both close friends and collaborators. The only major work to come out of his Yale years was his collaboration with Albert Innaurato, *The Idiots Karamazov* (1981), an oddball musical that combines Dostoevsky with Djuna Barnes, Anaïs Nin, Eugene O'Neill, and other literary figures, narrated by Constance Garnett, the celebrated translator of many classic Russian novels. In this spoof, Garnett (originally played by Innaurato wearing a large garden hat, but later by Meryl Streep in witchlike makeup) cannot remember accurately the plots of the

novels she has translated. *The Idiots Karamazov* would be the first of a number of Durang works, most notably *The Actor's Nightmare* (1982), in which a diverse group of plays, novels, and films become conflated into an amusing mélange. The vision of anarchy contained in the lyrics to the final song in *The Idiots Karamazov* could be the epigraph of a number of Durang plays:

> Everything's permitted,
> Everything's allowed,
> And God we have outwitted,
> We're moving with the crowd.
> We see the soul as zero,
> See the soul has fled,
> And no one is our hero,
> And piety is dead.
>
> Everything's permitted,
> All is à la carte.
> And nothing has been fitted,
> All things fall apart. ...

(Complete Full-Length Plays, p. 61)

The Idiots Karamazov was the most important of three Yale collaborations with Innaurato, the others bearing the intriguing titles *I Don't Normally Like Poetry but Have You Read Trees* and *Gyp, The Real-Life Story of Mitzi Gaynor. Idiots* not only got a full production at the Yale Drama School; a few months later it was produced at the professional Yale Repertory Theatre. It was unusual for a student-written work to be given this kind of exposure, but Durang's work gelled with Brustein's aesthetic. During his years at Yale, Durang also honed his skills as an actor through his performances in many productions of his and others' work.

After finishing his degree and a year of odd jobs in the New Haven area, Durang moved to New York in the summer of 1975. Fellow Yale playwrights Albert Innaurato and Wendy Wasserstein were already in the city, so Durang had collegial support. He also had financial support from a CBS playwriting grant Brustein had obtained for him. By this time Durang had also embarked upon a thirteen-year relationship with a young man he met during his second year at the Yale Drama School.

CHRISTOPHER DURANG

THE VIETNAMIZATION OF NEW JERSEY *AND* A HISTORY OF THE AMERICAN FILM

The late 1970s were a crucial time for Durang and his close friends, Innaurato and Wasserstein. Innaurato's comedy about an Italian American family, *Gemini,* first performed in 1976, moved from off Broadway to a successful Broadway run. Innaurato never matched its success and now works primarily in opera. Wasserstein's first hit, *Uncommon Women and Others* (1977), a series of scenes about women's lives during and after attending an elite women's college, led to a thriving career cut short by cancer. Both wrote plays that were closer than Durang's work to the conventional realistic fare that mainstream theater audiences were used to. Nonetheless, Durang had two major productions in the late 1970s: *The Vietnamization of New Jersey,* commissioned by the Yale Drama School and produced there in 1977; and the musical *A History of the American Film* (also 1977), which had productions at major regional theaters in Los Angeles, Hartford, Connecticut, and Washington, D.C., with a short-lived transfer of Washington's Arena Stage production to Broadway in 1978.

The Vietnamization of New Jersey begins as a parody of David Rabe's *Sticks and Bones,* which was produced at the New York Public Theater in 1971 and successfully transferred to Broadway the following year. Rabe's play was something of a parody, set in the world of the popular situation comedy *The Adventures of Ozzie and Harriet,* which began on radio in 1944 and was on television from 1952 to 1966. The show was unique in starring the Nelson family—Ozzie, Harriet, and sons David and Ricky—as themselves. It was the prototype for later wholesome television comedies like *Father Knows Best* and *Leave It to Beaver* that presented an idealized picture of American family life. There was no problem that could not be settled by a loving, if comical, American family in the half-hour of an episode. The world beyond the picket fence of the family's property barely existed. It wasn't even clear what job the fathers held. In *Sticks and Bones* the Nelson family's oldest son, David, comes home from Vietnam blind and haunted by memories of the carnage he saw there. His fam-ily, unwilling to share his experience or any guilt about American involvement in Vietnam, eventually goads him into slashing his wrists so everything can be normal again. The house is haunted by Song, a Vietnamese woman who embodies David's memories. No one can see her but David, but she too has to be exorcised. *Sticks and Bones,* one of four Rabe plays about Vietnam, is heavily ironic and, like his other work, ends with a scene of ritual violence.

Although Durang was against the Vietnam War, which had ended in 1975, he was bound to disagree with the solemnity of Rabe's play. *The Vietnamization of New Jersey,* subtitled *An American Tragedy,* begins as a parody of *Sticks and Bones* but, in a more farcical way, deals with issues of race, gender, and sexuality as well as American imperialism. In this version of *The Adventures of Ozzie and Harriet* the genders are reversed so that Durang's saga can present what he calls his "recurring themes of strong-willed women, overwhelmed men, and the struggles between them" (*Complete Full-Length Plays,* p. 68). Ozzie Ann is another of Durang's beleaguered housewives. Husband Harry loses his job and all his money. Younger son Et is an oversexed idiot. In the first scene, he pours breakfast cereal into his pants and eats it from there. The family has a black live-in maid, Hazel (a TV sitcom about a know-it-all white live-in maid, Hazel, was popular in the early 1960s). As in Rabe's play, older son David returns home from Vietnam blind. He brings with him his new Vietnamese wife, Liat (named after the "Younger than Springtime" Polynesian girl in *South Pacific*), who turns out not to be Vietnamese at all but an Irish American named Maureen O'Hara who seems to be continually having sex with David's younger brother. After losing his job and all the family money, Harry shoots himself. The family and the maid are forced to move outside to a tent until Harry's militaristic, authoritarian brother Larry arrives and takes over the household. At the end, after Ozzie Ann, Larry, Hazel, and Et have performed a patriotic pageant, David sets fire to himself during a fireworks display. Ozzie Ann, mentally and physically exhausted by the carnage in her own home, pours corn flakes all

over the kitchen table while wailing, "It's a mess, it's a mess" (*Complete Full-Length Plays*, p. 112). The bloodbath that ends Rabe's play is replaced in Durang's by a moment of comic futility.

The Vietnamization of New Jersey is filled with quotes from other plays (particularly those of Tennessee Williams), musicals, and television shows. Liat is obsessed with *The King and I*, the Richard Rodgers and Oscar Hammerstein musical about a woman bringing Western values to Asia, while taking the name of a character in the Rodgers and Hammerstein musical about American victory in the South Seas. American imperialism in Asia is celebrated by Durang's characters while the gung-ho militarism personified by Larry is mocked, as is his optimism. At one point Ozzie says, "Larry's language is America's language: 'Stand up straight, stomach in, work hard and you'll survive'" (p. 101), but survival doesn't seem that easy. Ozzie's attempts to voice American optimism falter, most notably after Harry's suicide, when her quotations from plucky fictional characters range from *Gone with the Wind* to the musical *The Unsinkable Molly Brown*:

> It's darkest before the dawn, *not* the cyclone. ... I'm not gonna be licked, I promise you, as God is my witness, I won't be licked. Maureen, do you remember that song in *The Unsinkable Molly Brown?* ...
>
> I'm gonna learn to read and write,
>
> I'm gonna da da da duh duh duh, da,
>
> and if I'm da, da, da, da, da, da, duh, da,
>
> and then I'll da, da, da, duh, duh, duh, duh.
>
> (p. 93)

By the end, with her home reduced to a battle zone, Ozzie Ann's optimism is spent. Of course, as this is a play by Christopher Durang, there is also a visit from a Catholic priest who expounds on the idea that war is God's means of population control.

Full appreciation of this and many of Durang's plays depends on a certain amount of cultural literacy—the more one gets the high culture and pop culture allusions, the more one enjoys the play. At one point, for instance, Ozzie Ann says to Harry, "All you think about is self, self, self" (p. 92), recalling one of Amanda's lines from Tennessee Williams' *Glass Menagerie*, a play Durang would later parody brilliantly in his one-act *For Whom the Southern Belle Tolls*. One could say that Amanda is echoed by many of Durang's garrulous, maddeningly plucky heroines.

The Vietnamization of New Jersey is a highly visual as well as verbal play, filled with oddball sight gags, slapstick, and some frightening violence. Here as elsewhere, Durang constantly surprises his audience with his powers of invention. The play mocks Rabe's solemnity and replaces it with Durang's madcap belief that laughter is the only valid response to the state of the world.

If *The Vietnamization of New Jersey* is both a parody and a "satiric, dark comedy play," *A History of the American Film* (1945), which both celebrates and spoofs the optimism of classic American films of the 1930s and 1940s, could be considered "a friendly, silly play." In this musicalized Hollywood send-up, which had a score by Mel Marvin in its Washington, D.C., and New York productions, the central character is named Loretta, after the famously Catholic film and television star Loretta Young. Loretta is in love with Jimmy (Jimmy Cagney) who never wants to be tied down and who is tempted by the vamp Bette (Davis, obviously). The play takes this trio and a group of supporting characters through a series of film-genre vignettes. In each of these, Loretta is in love with the unattainable Jimmy and falls victim to some disaster. The early vignettes conclude with the characters frozen as a "The End" sign appears, but more misery befalls Loretta when the "The End" sign stops appearing and the action spirals farther downward. Loretta wants only for that sign to appear: "I really don't want to start over again. I want The End sign to come down, and then I can stay frozen behind it forever, and then nothing else can happen to me" (*Complete Full-Length Plays*, p. 196). She always wants to get back to Shantytown, where her story began (an allusion to the

setting of a 1933 Loretta Young film, *Man's Castle*), a place of poverty but also an idealized locus of order and hope. Like most of Durang's heroines, Loretta craves order but gets chaos instead. She is the victim of a variety of misfortunes that rob her of her faith. When a character tells her that God will help her, she responds, "No, he won't. He doesn't like me" (p. 183). The Blessed Mother and Jesus make appearances and we hear the voice of God; none are of any help to our beleaguered heroine. Toward the end, the play speeds quickly through a variety of more contemporary films, but what the characters want is a return to the optimism of films of the past, as they sing in the finale:

Our race will have spiritual values
Like Spencer Tracy in *Boy's Town*.
We'll be idealistic,
Like James Stewart in *Mr. Smith Goes to Washington*.
We'll be for racial tolerance,
Like Gregory Peck in *To Kill a Mockingbird*. ...

(p. 199)

While *A History of American Film* was successful at regional theaters, it was not the kind of fare Broadway audiences wanted. The show worked better with an intimate piano accompaniment than with a full orchestra in a twelve-hundred-seat theater. Durang's great New York success would come off Broadway.

In 1976 Durang's mother, who had previously had breast cancer, was diagnosed with bone cancer. Though he lived only a few miles away from her northern New Jersey home, Durang was under enormous pressure from his extended family to come stay with her and be her full-time caregiver. After all, his mother's three siblings lived with their mother. Her extended family maintained the illusion of a united, supportive unit, but underneath there was constant bickering. Durang's good friend Wendy Wasserstein found a therapist for him who helped him cope with the family demands and feuding. He stayed in New York but spent much of his time with his mother, who died in 1979. Though he claims that his mother's illness and the work associated with the productions of *The Vietnamization of New Jersey* and *A History of the American Film* (four produc-

tions around the country in one year) kept him from his writing, these years were the gestation period for three of his most successful works: *Sister Mary Ignatius Explains It All for You, Baby with the Bathwater,* and *The Marriage of Bette and Boo.*

SISTER MARY IGNATIUS *AND* BEYOND THERAPY

Durang credits the critical and commercial success of *Sister Mary Ignatius Explains It All for You* as the real beginning of his making a living as a writer. The play was first performed in 1979 as part of an evening of one-act plays by various writers. Two years later, Playwrights Horizons produced it on a double bill with a companion piece Durang created for it, *The Actor's Nightmare*. That production transferred a block uptown to the Westside Arts Theatre, where it ran for more than two years. Both one-act plays, separately or together, have been produced by professional, amateur, and university theaters regularly ever since.

Sister Mary Ignatius Explains It All for You is a simpler, more direct play than its predecessors. There are no special effects or musical numbers, and most of the dialogue is direct address to the audience. In this play, Durang comes back to his problems with Catholicism, with its veneer of rationality—there is an explanation for everything—and its indifference to real, lived modern human experience. Basically the play is a lecture on Catholic doctrine delivered by a middle-aged nun whose own life should have taught her that her religion doesn't really work. Sister Mary was one of twenty-six children. Her father was an abusive drunk, her mother a poor drudge trying to keep the family together. Fifteen of the children went into the Church; the other eleven were institutionalized. Clearly none could cope with the complexities and ambiguities of life in the real world. For Mary and her siblings, the comfort and security of Church doctrine is an antidote to an awful past. It gives them a home and a coherent, if unrealistic vision of human experience. What it doesn't provide is compassion. Sister Mary's pet student is a young boy, Thomas, who, like a pet

CHRISTOPHER DURANG

animal, receives a cookie if he can parrot back the correct answers to her doctrinal questions. Durang has said that Thomas is a version of his younger self, the good Catholic boy. Sister Mary laments the fact that Thomas will lose his sweet boyish voice and wishes the church still promoted castrati. The one theological question that provokes Sister Mary's silence is one of the most important: "If God is all powerful, why does He allow evil in the world?" Indeed, much of Mary's version of Catholic doctrine envisions a God indifferent to human needs. "Only God knows the future and He won't tell us," she claims, and when someone asks whether all our prayers are answered, Mary avers that they are, but "sometimes the answer to our prayers is 'no'" (*Twenty-Seven Short Plays*, pp. 388, 390).

All goes well for Sister Mary until four of her former students return to help stage a pageant she wrote that is an unintentional parody of her doctrine: they include Philomena, a single mother; Aloysius, married and with children but an alcoholic; Gary, a homosexual ("You do that thing that makes Jesus puke, don't you?" [p. 402]), and Diane, grieving over her mother's suffering and death from cancer and angry at the abuse she received at the hands of her psychiatrist. For each of them, Sister Mary has an answer but no compassion: "He likes to test us, so that when we choose to love Him, no matter what He does to us, that proves how great and deep our love for Him is" (p. 407). Her response doesn't explain why such a god should be loved. When an enraged Diane pulls a gun, Sister Mary whips out her own gun and kills her. When Gary tells her he made confession that morning, she shoots him: "I have sent him to heaven!" (p. 409).

Sister Mary Ignatius Explains It All for You is, in the hands of the right actress, both hilariously funny and horrifying. The audience has to see her charm and the humor in her violence. "Ta da!" she exclaims when she shoots Diane, as if she has performed a feat of magic. Sister Mary loves to perform and assumes that she and her teachings are going to be loved. She sees herself as a saver of souls, but like many savers of souls, she is merciless. Yet she is a three-dimensional character, not merely a comic persona. Under-

standing her socioeconomic background is important to understanding her character, and understanding the comfort that can come from an unambiguous, simplistic doctrine is important to grasping her motivation. For her and her siblings, it is the clarity of the Church or the madhouse. This is why Diane is her nemesis. Diane's experience—her mother's illness and death, multiple rapes including one by her psychiatrist—has taught her "the utter randomness of things" (p. 406), but rather than accept that principle, which is the basis of much of Durang's comedy, she thinks that the destruction of Sister Mary will somehow bring her peace. Sister Mary is right: "She had no sense of humor" (p. 408). In one sense, Sister Mary's shooting of Diane is yet more proof of randomness.

Sister Mary Ignatius Explains It All for You is built on both verbal and visual wit. The appearance of the four former students in silly pageant costumes—Diane and Gary as Mary and Joseph with Aloysius and Philomena sharing an absurd camel costume—make their entrance into the play absurd, and the final image of young Thomas in Mary's lap reciting his catechism while he has a gun trained on poor Aloysius, who is desperate to get to the bathroom, is both cruel and humorous.

Shortly after the opening of the hit New York production, the play opened around the country. Professional productions featuring such prominent actresses as Lynn Redgrave and Cloris Leachman were extremely successful, even though leaders of the Catholic Church, showing no sense of humor or belief in the First Amendment, sought to ban productions of the play in many cities around the country.

While *Sister Mary Ignatius Explains It All for You* humorously asserts that the doctrines of the Catholic Church do not present convincing or helpful answers to human experience, *Beyond Therapy*, produced on Broadway in 1982, hilariously puts forth the idea that psychoanalysis is equally as irrational and useless. Durang had benefited from psychotherapy, but in *Beyond Therapy*, the doctor is at least as mad as her patients. This work can be included among Durang's "friendly, silly plays," which may have

been one reason for the *New York Times* critic Frank Rich's dislike of the work. There is none of the sense of anger turned into laughter that one finds in works like *Sister Mary Ignatius Explains It All for You.*

The play's heroine, Prudence, is one of those slightly neurotic Durang women who try to be sensible when everyone around her is acting crazy. When the play begins, she is on a not very successful first date with Bruce in a restaurant where service is virtually nonexistent. Prudence has had a series of disastrous relationships including an abusive one with her psychotherapist. Bruce's wife left him after she caught him having sex with the gas man. He is now in a relationship with another man but wants a more socially acceptable heterosexual partner. Prudence, who stayed home and read Dostoevsky instead of attending her high school prom, is attracted to Bruce's sensitivity. He cries at the drop of a hat and offers her the opportunity to "look into the abyss together" (*Complete Full-Length Plays,* p. 228). Bruce is in therapy with Charlotte, who seems mad as a hatter, is emotionally attached to a Snoopy doll, and keeps mixing up words. After a series of bizarre confrontations, Charlotte leaves with Prudence's abusive therapist, Bob goes off with Charlotte's gay sociopath son, and Bruce and Prudence sit at the restaurant table trying to sing "Someone to Watch over Me." If there is any theme in *Beyond Therapy,* it is the one voiced by Bruce: "Life by its very nature is disordered, terrifying. That's when people come together to face the terrors hand in hand" (p. 240).

While *Beyond Therapy* is Durang's most performed play around the country, its Broadway run was cut short by a negative review by Frank Rich that spurred Durang's animus toward the critic and his power in the New York theater. Durang became increasingly frustrated with a system that allowed one man's taste to make or break a production.

BABY WITH THE BATHWATER *AND* THE MARRIAGE OF BETTE AND BOO

Durang's next two plays, *Baby with the Bathwater* and *The Marriage of Bette and Boo,* offer his unique take on domestic drama. The former was produced in 1983 by Durang's Yale mentor, Robert Brustein, at his new artistic home, the American Repertory Theater at Harvard University, while the latter was presented by the New York Shakespeare Festival at the Public Theater in 1985. Both plays are about aspects of the nuclear family and both are about the possibility for humans to learn and change.

Baby with the Bathwater focuses on parenting. The play begins and ends with parents standing over a bassinet that holds their child. At the outset, John and Helen are totally inept parents. In addition to their substance abuse, they are too self-centered to give their baby proper attention. They can't even decide what its gender is or what it should be called—eventually they arbitrarily decide that the male child is female and name him Daisy. A nanny mysteriously appears and proves as poor at child-rearing as John and Helen. She is also a total hedonist who seduces John. Fortunately for the child, Cynthia, a homeless young woman, arrives on the scene. Having lost her own child (a vicious dog ate it), Cynthia becomes attached to the baby. Her choice of bedtime reading may be *Mommie Dearest,* that famous saga of horrific child-rearing, but the baby becomes attached to this unusual but loving young woman. Cynthia decides to rescue the baby from his self-absorbed, ineffectual parents but gets run over by a bus, after which John and Helen vow to be better parents.

Act 2 offers a series of scenes of Daisy growing up. Obviously obsessed with the trauma of Cynthia's death, he either displays depression almost to the point of catatonia or runs toward buses in an effort to reenact Cynthia's death. As a university student he has difficulty beginning term papers, much less ending them, an echo of Durang's Harvard depression. After ten years of therapy, his psychiatrist shouts at him, "PULL YOURSELF TOGETHER!" (*Complete Full-Length Plays,* p. 297), advice the play reinforces. One has to fight the psychic wounds parents can cause. At thirty years old, after over a decade of college spiced with a great deal of promiscuous homo- and heterosexual activity, Daisy decides

to marry his pregnant girlfriend and cut himself off from his parents. In the final scene he and his wife, Susan, are singing a lullaby to their new baby. Durang acknowledges that this is his first "genuinely 'hopeful' ending" (p. 306). Characters can make positive choices that are different from those of their parents. Daisy may not love Susan right away, but unlike his parents he is devoted to raising their son in a loving manner.

In *Baby with the Bathwater,* after more than thirty years of marriage, wife and mother Helen exclaims, "I'm insane because I stayed in a bad marriage and didn't do what I was supposed to do with my life" (p. 298). She dreams of being a novelist but accomplishes nothing. Such futile, repetitive patterns are the subject of Durang's next, most autobiographical and most powerful play, *The Marriage of Bette and Boo,* which tells, as the playwright puts it, "the rather sad story of my parents' marriage and a bit about my place in it" (*Complete Full-Length Plays,* p. 369). Bette and Boo's story is narrated by their son, Matt, the only one of Bette's five children to survive childbirth. Durang played Matt in the New York production of his play, "a head-on way of dealing with the 'author's voice' nature of the part" (p. 372) and reinforcing the playwright-performer's identification with the character. Matt begins, "If one looks hard enough, one can usually see the order that lies beneath the surface" (p. 315). As the play progresses, we learn that what Matt wants to understand is why the people around him don't change, why their repetition of mistakes only ends at the moment of their death. His parents seem caught in an endless cycle. His mother, Bette, has four stillborn babies that place her in a cycle of depression and exacerbates her husband's drinking problem, which leads her to nag him incessantly. When she finally divorces him, she marries another alcoholic. Matt's paternal grandfather also has a drinking problem and is verbally abusive toward his wife and daughter-in-law. His mother has one sister trapped in an unhappy marriage to a constantly absent husband and another so riddled with Catholic guilt that she has nervous breakdowns. Toward the end of the play, Matt asks his paternal grandfather, "Did you all *intend* to live your lives the way you did?" (p. 361). By this time, Matt

has reached a state of Hamlet-like uncertainty: "To sleep. To sleep, perchance to dream, to take the phone off the hook and simply be unreachable. That is less *dramatic* than suicide, but more *reversible.* I can't make sense out of these things anymore" (p. 361).

As Matt narrates the play, he is attempting to write a term paper on Thomas Hardy, but he identifies so strongly with Hardy's pessimism that he conflates his own experience with Hardy's novels: "Perhaps Boo *is* an alcoholic, and Bette is a terrible unending nag in *reaction* to his drinking too much, and also because he isn't 'there' for her, any more than Clym Yeobright is really there for Eustacia Vye in *The Return of the Native,* although admittedly Eustacia Vye is very neurotic, but then so is Bette also" (p. 333). Like Durang, who was for two years incapable of completing his Harvard term papers on time, Matt is unable to see his life or work constructively, nor can he separate his own experience from his studies.

Matt's confusion is also reflected in the play's structure, which is dependent on Durang's/Matt's organization of events. *The Marriage of Bette and Boo* comprises thirty-three short scenes that jump back and forth in time. The first act is basically linear with one intervention, a scene between Matt and his father that takes place twenty years after the events of act 1. Matt's parents have divorced, and Boo says: "I miss your mother, Skip. Nobody should be alone. Do you have any problems, son, you want to talk over? Your old man could help you out" (p. 324). Boo laments the loss of an ideal of marriage, not the reality. The family priest, Father Donnally, lashes out at a retreat for married couples:

> I get so *sick* of these people coming to me after they're married, and they've just gotten to know one another *after* the ceremony, and they've discovered that they have nothing in common and they hate one another. And they want me to come up with a solution. ... What can I do? There is no solution to a problem like that.
>
> (p. 353)

Everything in the play suggests that Bette and Boo were lonely in their marriage, that marriage

does not bring happiness or even companionship. Since we see the entire play through Matt's eyes, we also know that his father's advice or example would be of little use to Matt. This father-son scene is repeated in a more elaborate form, still out of chronological order, in act 2, where it is linked to a more guilt-provoking dinner with his mother: "You know, you're the only one of my children that lived. How long can you stay?" (p. 343). During the second act, Durang repeatedly abandons linear time, and his narrator on occasion begins a scene with "Back into chronology again."

Each act of *The Marriage of Bette and Boo* contains the depiction of a nightmare family holiday. If Thanksgiving and Christmas are supposed to be celebrations of family, Durang's holidays become something quite different. Matt tells the audience that holidays were invented by "a sadistic Englishman" so that "everyone would feel disappointment that their lives had fallen so short of their expectations" (p. 339). For Matt's family, the holidays are more elaborate replays of smaller family hostilities. The Thanksgiving dinner that ends act 1 has Bette screaming at a drunken Boo for trying to vacuum up the gravy that he caused to be spilled as the extended family beat a hasty retreat. The lights dim with Boo unconscious on the floor, Bette obsessing over the gravy, and Matt looking "exhausted and trapped" (p. 337). The Christmas celebration that opens act 2 has Boo's father making cruel jokes about Bette's miscarriages, then pouring his drink in her lap as she screams hysterically.

Bette and Boo are trapped by their spiritual and cultural education. Bette may be one of the two least bright girls in her elementary school class, but she married a good provider whose alcoholism doesn't threaten his position. Bette's mistaken ideas about family come from an odd mix of Catholicism and popular culture. She is obsessed with *Skippy,* one of those sentimental thirties movies with a child star, and wants to name her son after the title character. Some of her pronouncements make no sense at all: "I want a marriage and a family and a home and I'm go-

ing to have them, and if you won't help me, Boo, I'll have them without you" (p. 332).

At Bette and Boo's wedding, Bette's sister Joan was to sing Schubert's "Lachen und Weinen" accompanied by her father and sister, Emily. However, Emily, in a typical moment of panic and confusion, has forgotten the music. "Lachen und Weinen" means "laughing and crying," or, as a character quotes Beckett in Durang's next play, "Laughing wild amid severest woe" (p. 383). In his afterword to *The Marriage of Bette and Boo,* Durang explains that "watching repetitive suffering is very irritating and upsetting, and transforming one's view of it into some combination of sad and funny seems as sensible a thing to do with it as any" (p. 369). "Sensible" seems an odd word to use in the context of this play, which Durang admits some audiences find "too angry." There is always pain in the laughter in his serious comedies. When Boo visits Bette in the hospital after years of separation and they look back on their unhappy marriage, the bizarre disconnection and irony remind one of the couple in Samuel Beckett's *Happy Days:*

BETTE: Do you remember when you tried to vacuum the gravy?

BOO: No.

BETTE: Well, you did. It was very funny. Not at the time, of course. And how you used to keep bottles hidden in the cellar. And all the dead babies.

BOO: *(Smiles, happy.)* Yes, we had some good times.

(p. 366)

Boo, now addled with some neurological disorder, is so eager to see his marriage as the central and best fact of his life that he denies all its unhappiness. Bette now lives totally in the past. Bette's death is a quiet moment of resolution, and Matt's final speech to the audience is a loving, forgiving eulogy that captures the tragedy in Bette's life as well as her silliness: "She is in heaven where she has been reunited with the four dead babies and where she waits for Boo, and for Bonnie Wilson, and Emily, and Pooh Bear and Eeyore, and Kanga and Roo; and for me" (p. 368).

CHRISTOPHER DURANG

LAUGHING WILD

If *The Marriage of Bette and Boo* moves to acceptance and forgiveness, *Laughing Wild* (1987) is an expression of rage. The work is in part Durang's response to the AIDS epidemic that was decimating the gay community in the 1980s and early 1990s. *Laughing Wild*'s characters link disgust with sex with their need for some kind of belief system. The play, which has only two characters, is in three parts: "Laughing Wild," a monologue for a nameless woman; "Seeking Wild," a monologue for a nameless man (originally played by Durang); and "Dreaming Wild," their confrontation. Both the man and the woman are trying with mixed results to contain a generalized rage. The woman has been institutionalized for her anger, which expresses itself as misanthropy—"Have you ever noticed that after you've known someone for just a little while how intolerable you find them?" (p. 384)—and hostility toward anyone who is happy. Her psychotherapy has done little to help her control her rage. The man tries a form of new age spirituality to overcome his lack of control over his life: "Everything in my life works. Except the plumbing, and career and relationships" (p. 394). Both characters have a disgust for sex. Intercourse makes the woman feel suicidal and the man finds sex abhorrent: "terrible viscous discharges erupting in various openings" (p. 396). Much of the man's monologue has to do with institutionalized homophobia as expressed by the government and the Catholic Church. What he finds most outrageous is the idea that God would create AIDS as a means of punishing gay people. Would a just and benevolent God actually think, "I love to connect sex and death, I don't know why I invented sex to begin with, it's a revolting idea, but as long as I have, I want it done *properly* in the *missionary* position with *one* person for life, or I want those who disobey me to die a horrible death from AIDS and syphilis and God knows what else" (p. 399). The man's disgust with sex demonstrates that he has internalized the Church's repressive teachings. He tries New Age spirituality because he craves a sense of joy that might overcome his feeling that life is meaningless.

The man and the woman meet when she accosts him violently in a supermarket for taking too long choosing a can of tuna fish. In the final scene, they share a series of dreams. In one she has killed a famous talk show host and taken over her show, and he appears as the Infant of Prague. Later they meet at a Harmonic Convergence ceremony in Central Park. Finally they dream of reaching empathetic understanding. In this shared fantasy, there is a tentative positive resolution to their anger and anomie.

While the man seems to be a mouthpiece for Durang's attitudes at the time, the woman is a version of the sort of frightening psychologically maimed person one finds in urban settings, the sort of person who screams at strangers in the street. Durang has a gift for creating characters that straddle the line between sanity and insanity as he blurs the boundary between the comic and the serious. The play itself, as the title suggests, is about laughter as a response to deep unhappiness: "Laughing wild amid severest woe."

At the end of his volume of full-length plays, Durang discusses the fallow period he went through after *Laughing Wild*. Some of this was a result of a sense that he was never going to get a fair hearing from *Times* critic Frank Rich. He wrote for film and television and created and appeared in a spoof cabaret act, "Chris Durang and Dawne," that was performed in various theaters and clubs in New York over six years. The concept was that Durang, looking for an easier profession than playwriting, settled on headlining a lounge act that had played Ramada Inns across America. "Dawne" was performed by Sherry Anderson and the actor-writer John Augustine, Durang's partner since 1986. Durang also appeared as an actor in film, on television, and on stage with Julie Andrews in the 1993 Stephen Sondheim retrospective, *Putting It Together*. Since 1994 Durang and Marsha Norman have been co-chairs of the Playwrights Program of the Juilliard School in New York City. Durang and John Augustine share a stone farmhouse in Bucks Country, Pennsylvania, a couple of hours from the city.

CHRISTOPHER DURANG

BETTY'S SUMMER VACATION *AND* MISS WITHERSPOON

Durang's playwriting career resumed with the presentation of his spoof of Tennessee Williams' *The Glass Menagerie, For Whom the Southern Belle Tolls*, first performed off Broadway in 1994 and included in the Manhattan Theatre Club's presentation of six Durang one-act plays of the sort he would categorize as "entertainments," under the title *Durang, Durang*. In 1999 Durang began a new period of theatrical activity, including two full-length musical entertainments, *Adrift in Macao* (premiered in 2002) and *Mrs. Bob Cratchit's Wild Christmas Binge* (premiered in 2005), and two critically acclaimed dark comedies, *Betty's Summer Vacation* (1999) and *Miss Witherspoon* (premiered in 2005). Both full-length plays center on women placed in a world that has lost its moral compass. The plays ask how one can survive psychically intact in such a world. What is left to believe in?

Betty's Summer Vacation, which earned critical accolades even from the *New York Times* and won Obie Awards for playwriting, direction, set design, and acting (Kristine Nielsen), is one of Durang's most inventive and successful plays. It merges violence and farce more brilliantly than ever before, and it successfully balances traditional comic forms, anarchy, and theatrical experimentation. The set, with its eight doors, places the play in the tradition of farce. However, what goes on behind the bedroom doors of this beach resort cottage is so horrifically violent (rape, murder, mutilation, castration) that it evokes laughter. The farce elements in *Betty's Summer Vacation* are linked to elements of the horror film—danger lurking behind doors, screaming women. The targets of Durang's dark satire are not the characters onstage but the audience that has become indifferent to human cruelty through constant exposure to it on television. The satire is underscored by a kind of Greek chorus, which is first heard as a laugh track at certain moments in the play. The laughter from these unseen voices seems indiscriminate and heartless, as when they laugh at news that someone has died in an automobile accident. Eventually they comment on the action and respond to questions from the characters. Nothing bothers the voices more than lack of action to entertain them. They demand constant amusement. During the second act, the voices thunder down from the ceiling and force the characters to perform a mock trial of the perpetrators of the murders enacted in the first act. The verdict is decided not on the basis of justice or law but on entertainment value.

Betty's Summer Vacation depicts a heartless, amoral world. The central character is another relatively sane woman thrust into a mad situation. Betty and her garrulous friend Trudy arrive at a seaside cottage they are planning to share with three other vacationers. One has died in an automobile crash on the way there. The two men who arrive are far from ideal housemates. Buck is single-minded in his pursuit of sex, and celibate Keith is a serial killer who collects the heads of his victims. The house is owned by Mrs. Siezmagraff, Trudy's mother. Durang describes her as Auntie Mame-ish, but like the dowager figure in many classic comedies, Mrs. Siezmagraff is the spokesperson for the skewed values of the world outside. She either denies that her husband sexually abused her daughter or blames Trudy for inciting the abuse. Like Auntie Mame, she wants her life to be a party, and she sees the violence taking place in her cottage as an inconvenience. Her companion is the insane flasher Mr. Vanislaw, who also rapes her daughter. If a seismograph registers earthquakes, Mrs. Siezmagraff is a living measure of the moral deficiencies of her world. She can only perform guilt and remorse as part of a mock television trial. Betty is the only inhabitant of the cottage with any sense of conventional morality, but she cannot stop the chaos and violence that ensues. The police seem ineffectual—one has to go to the station to confess to a crime because they don't seem to make house calls. The voice of society is the voice of television, demanding entertainment and sentiment and making aesthetic, not ethical, judgments. The vacuum the characters inhabit is moral and intellectual. What Durang shows us is narcissism run amok. Murder is justified by childhood trauma. At one point, in

the midst of a game of charades, the serial killer confesses:

> KEITH: I was abused as a child. The memories are starting to come back to me. I think that's why I cut people's heads off. (*No one moves. He gets up and goes to his room. Silence. Everyone is blank-faced.*)
>
> MRS. SIEZMAGRAFF: Well, who's going to do the dishes?
>
> (*Betty's Summer Vacation,* p. 31)

Like the great British farceur Joe Orton, Durang can make the audience laugh but also feel uncomfortable at the extreme cruelty they see—or don't see. What allows us to laugh at *Betty's Summer Vacation* is that the rape, murder, and mutilation take place behind closed doors. We only hear the screams. The flasher has his back to the audience. We laugh at the combination of the violence we know is taking place and the characters' bland responses to it. We can laugh at the characters' discovery of a disembodied penis in the freezer because we haven't seen the mutilated, castrated body. Moreover, a strange sort of justice has been enacted, since the victims of the brutal murders are also malefactors. In the moral schema the characters subscribe to, sex crimes are considered worse than the taking of a life. The play ends with a cataclysm that eliminates all the evildoers. Only Betty survives, but her response seems strangely calm given what she has experienced: "I don't think I could have saved Mrs. Siezmagraff. I don't feel too guilty about it. I mean, they all seemed really terrible. I feel bad for Trudy, sort of ... but well, I don't know what to think" (p. 87). Like many of Durang's characters, Betty realizes that she doesn't care much for other people. Since the play has presented a dark, if hilarious picture of human nature, one can sympathize with Betty's misanthropy. She is only happy at the end when she is alone on the beach hearing the ocean instead of the sound of human voices.

Veronica, the reluctantly reincarnating title character and heroine of *Miss Witherspoon,* is psychically and spiritually more damaged than Betty. In life she suffered from despair—a total lack of hope. She doesn't like people and finds life frightening and painful. After pieces of Skylab fell into her garden, she committed suicide, hoping that death would be literally nothing, but finds instead that she was doomed to a cycle of reincarnation. All she can try to do is sabotage her reincarnations. As a middle-class baby, she goads the family dog into attacking her. As a "trailer trash" child, she overdoses on drugs. Her only happy incarnation is as a dog, but she gets run over. Eventually Jesus comes to her in the guise of a black woman and demands that in her next reincarnation she tell mankind the ways in which they are not following Christ's teachings: "I didn't say Blessed are those who proclaim themselves holier than others and read the Book of Revelation as if it's an instruction booklet" (*Miss Witherspoon,* p. 56). At the end, Miss Witherspoon, returned to the middle-class parents of an earlier incarnation, is in a bassinet preaching world peace.

In *Miss Witherspoon,* Durang uses aspects of Christianity and Eastern religions to offer the thought that only mankind can save the world we seem compelled to destroy. The Catholic Church is no longer a target. Christ's teachings still have validity but have been perverted by various forms of Christianity. Characters are tempted by hopelessness, but the fate of the world is in their hands. *Miss Witherspoon* is not didactic, yet it is a kind of retelling of the Christian myth—a child must save the world. As usual, Durang is inventive and constantly surprising. Jesus works with Gandalf from *The Lord of the Rings.* Purgatory is ruled by an Indian woman. Veronica is a great challenge for a comic actress who must play a variety of roles: middle-aged woman, baby, teenage girl, dog. It was first played by Kristine Nielsen, who has played leading roles in many of Durang's comedies.

WHY TORTURE IS WRONG

In one sense, as the title suggests, *Why Torture Is Wrong, and the People Who Love Them* (premiered in 2009) is Durang's response to the aftermath of 9/11, particularly America's pursuit of the "war on terrorism." It is, however, more a satire on macho behavior and the ways women

cope with it. Felicity is another of Durang's relatively sane women caught up in insane situations. At the beginning of the play, she finds herself in bed with her new husband, Zamir, who the night before drugged her and had them married by the minister-pornographer Reverend Mike. Zamir admits to a fragile male ego: his response to any slight is the threat of violence. Felicity's parents have an equally fraught marriage. Her father, Leonard, is a right-wing extremist who napalms squirrels and has shot Halloween trick-or-treaters for trespassing. When Zamir and Leonard meet, Zamir acts like the terrorist Leonard immediately assumes he is. Leonard is part of a shadow government that has a bizarre set of operatives, one of them a man who only talks in voices of Looney Tunes characters, and another a woman named Hildegarde, who is constantly tripped up by her falling underwear. Felicity's mother Luella's way of coping with her unhappy marriage is to talk endlessly about theater. When Felicity tells her to stop, she responds, "Darling, it's life you should hate, not the theatre" (*Why Torture Is Wrong*, p. 38).

Luella's constant discussions of theater allow Durang to joke about characters committing suicide at plays that are unnecessarily long, like Tom Stoppard's nine-hour trilogy *The Coast of Utopia* (2002), or untheatrical, like Brian Friel's *The Faith Healer* (1979), composed of three long soliloquies. Theatricality, even metatheatricality, is an essential weapon in Durang's arsenal. Here, amid the farce, Durang once again introduces a disembodied narrative voice. Later in the play, the actor playing the Voice appears in a series of supporting roles. Even in satire, Durang wants the audience to remember they are watching theatrical artifice.

Luella foolishly believes that the theater teaches people to act normally, and while Durang's play has hilariously depicted a lot of bizarre behavior, it moves toward a positive, if fantastic, conclusion. When the action spins out of control—Leonard has tortured Zamir and the United States has ordered missile attacks on three Middle Eastern countries—the world is saved by metatheater. Felicity demands that the play go back and start over at the moment when she and

Zamir met: "I want us to have the same characters … but … better ASPECTS of those characters" (p. 62). Zamir will be considerate, Leonard will dance with his wife. At the final curtain, the characters are dancing to "Dancing in the Dark," an apt song for living positively in a chaotic world. Once again, Durang has opted for a tentatively optimistic ending. Felicity tells Zamir, "Oddly, I believe people can change. Just most don't" (p. 68), and Zamir seems sincerely to be trying to change. Lack of empathy and macho responses to perceived threats are the great danger in *Why Torture Is Wrong, and the People Who Love Them*. Durang seems to say that women must find a way to resist the danger of macho behavior. However, only theatrical artifice offers redemption in this play.

VANYA AND SONIA AND MASHA AND SPIKE

The title of Durang's 2011 play *Vanya and Sonia and Masha and Spike*, with its echoes of Anton Chekhov (1860–1904), shows us that we are in the old Durang territory of playful riffs on classic Russian literature. In this play, Durang is both playing with Chekhov and presenting a Chekhovian picture of middle-aged regret. While there are allusions to other Chekhov plays, particularly *The Seagull*, *Uncle Vanya* is in the foreground here. Vanya and his stepsister Sonia, named by eccentric professorial parents, have lived a reclusive life in their country home (set in Bucks County, Pennsylvania, where Durang lives), supported by their movie star sister, Masha. After spending years caring for their now-deceased parents, Vanya and Sonia seem adrift and lonely, but unable to change. Sonia admits at one point, "I can't make decisions. So I do nothing" (2013 performance). Their only regular company is their feisty housekeeper, Cassandra, who, like her namesake, is wont to offer bleak-but-true prophesies. Vanya is gay, but without any romantic life. Enter the self-absorbed Masha, Durang's version of Madame Arkadina from Chekhov's *The Seagull*, with her much younger boyfriend, Spike, an exhibitionistic would-be actor. Unlike Madame Arkadina, Masha acknowledges her negative qualities: "I suppose I'm

monstrous, but lovable monstrous, I hope" (2013 performance). Masha is a flamboyant breath of life, but she, too, realizes the ravages of time when it becomes clear that Spike's real interest is elsewhere. She also threatens Vanya and Sonia's comfortable, though lonely, existence when she announces that she plans to sell the house.

In *Vanya and Sonia and Masha and Spike*, allusions to Chekhov collide with American popular culture, from Walt Disney's *Snow White and the Seven Dwarfs* (1937) to 1950s television to Neil Simon's *Plaza Suite* (1968) and beyond. The title itself is such a collision, echoing not only Chekhov but also the 1969 film *Bob and Carol and Ted and Alice*. Halfway through the first act, Masha arranges for the group to go to a neighbor's costume party and petulantly insists that they all dress in outfits to go with her Snow White costume. As always in a Durang play, events spin out of control but, unlike traditional farce, the action is rooted in well-drawn characters. During the course of the play, every major character is given a hilarious set piece: Masha's explosion of self-absorbed talk, Sonia's impersonation of Maggie Smith in *California Suite* (1978), Spike's reenactment of his audition for a television series, "Entourage 2," and Vanya's climactic explosion of anger and nostalgia after Spike interrupts his attempt to write a play like Konstantin's in *The Seagull*: "I worry about the future. I miss the past" (2013 performance).

Vanya and Sonia and Masha and Spike was a critical and commercial success, transferring from the Lincoln Center Theater to a run on Broadway. In this delightful work, Durang manages to merge the madcap with characters the audience, particularly a middle-aged and older New York audience, can empathize with. There is none of the physical violence of plays like *Betty's Summer Vacation*, though the characters' narcissism can lead to verbal cruelty. To some extent, the play's success in New York was a result of the casting. Durang tailored the play to the talents of two of his long-time colleagues, Sigourney Weaver (Masha) and Kristine Nielsen (Sonia). *Vanya and Sonia and Masha and Spike* shows a kinder and gentler Durang than in many of his other plays,

but it is the work of a comic writer working at the height of his ability.

CONCLUSION

Given Durang's long, distinguished career, it is odd that so little has been written about his work. He receives no more than a mention in the critical studies of contemporary American drama. His peers Nicky Silver and Wendy Wasserstein have received far more attention. Is it that their work fits more comfortably into the American tradition of domestic drama? Perhaps Durang's unique, idiosyncratic work is more difficult to describe or contextualize.

Christopher Durang's career as a writer, teacher, and occasionally, performer continues. After nearly forty years of writing, in the twenty-first centuryhe remained one of the wittiest and most distinctive voices in contemporary American drama, whose best work demands an intelligent, emotionally complex reaction from his audiences. The glib playfulness of some of his "entertainments" cannot take away from the richness of his best work.

Selected Bibliography

WORKS OF CHRISTOPHER DURANG

PLAYS

The Vietnamization of New Jersey. New York: Dramatists Play Service, 1978.

A History of the American Film. New York: Avon Books, 1978.

The Idiots Karamazov. With Albert Innaurato. New York: Dramatists Play Service, 1981.

Beyond Therapy. Garden City, N.Y.: Doubleday, 1981.

Sister Mary Ignatius Explains It All for You and The Actor's Nightmare. New York: Dramatists Play Service, 1982.

Titanic. New York: Dramatists Play Service, 1983. (Includes Durang's notes on producing the play.)

The Marriage of Bette and Boo. New York: Grove Press, 1987.

CHRISTOPHER DURANG

Baby with the Bathwater and Laughing Wild. New York: Grove Press, 1989.

Betty's Summer Vacation. New York: Grove Press, 1999.

Miss Witherspoon, and, Mrs. Bob Cratchit's Wild Christmas Binge. New York: Grove Press, 2006.

Adrift in Macao. New York: Samuel French, 2008.

Why Torture Is Wrong, and the People Who Love Them. New York: Dramatists Play Service, 2011.

Vanya and Sonia and Masha and Spike. Unpublished. Photocopied manuscript, New York, Dramatists Play Service, 2011. (All quotes in essay transcribed from March 13, 2013, performance at the John Golden Theatre, New York, N.Y.)

COLLECTIONS OF PLAYS

Three Short Plays. New York: Dramatists Play Service, 1979. (Contains *The Nature and Purpose of the Universe; Death Comes to Us All, Mary Agnes;* and *'dentity Crisis*.)

Christopher Durang Explains It All for You: Six Plays. New York: Avon Books, 1983. (Contains *The Nature and Purpose of the Universe, 'dentity Crisis, Titanic, The Actor's Nightmare, Sister Mary Ignatius Explains It All for You,* and *Beyond Therapy*.)

Twenty-Seven Short Plays. Lyme, N.H.: Smith and Kraus, 1995. (Contains *Mrs. Sorken; For Whom the Southern Belle Tolls; A Stye of the Eye; Nina in the Morning; Wanda's Visit; Business Lunch at the Russian Tea Room; The Book of Leviticus Show; Naomi in the Living Room; Woman Stand-up; DMV Tyrant; Funeral Parlor; Canker Sores and Other Distractions; The Hardy Boys and the Mystery of Where Babies Come From; 1-900-Desperate; Women in a Playground; Phyllis and Xenobia; Desire, Desire, Desire; Medea* [with Wendy Wasserstein]; *One Minute Play; John and Mary Doe; Diversions; The Nature and Purpose of the Universe; 'dentity Crisis; Death Comes to Us All, Mary Agnes; Titanic; The Actor's Nightmare;* and *Sister Mary Ignatius Explains It All for You*, with extensive commentary by the playwright.)

Durang, Durang. New York: Dramatists Play Service, 1996. (Contains *Mrs. Sorken, For Whom the Southern Belle Tolls, A Stye of the Eye, Nina in the Morning, Wanda's Visit,* and *Business Lunch at the Russian Tea Room*, with extensive advice on production by the *playwright*.)

Complete Full-Length Plays, 1975–1995. Lyme, N.H.: Smith & Kraus, 1997. (Contains *The Idiots Karamazov, The Vietnamization of New Jersey, A History of the American Film, Beyond Therapy, Baby with the Bathwater, The Marriage of Bette and Boo,* and *Laughing Wild*, with extensive commentary by the playwright.)

Naomi in the Living Room & Other Short Plays. New York: Dramatists Play Service, 1998. (Contains *Naomi in the Living Room; Kitty the Waitress; Funeral Parlor; Canker Sores and Other Distractions; Woman Stand-up; DMV Tyrant; Gym Teacher; 1-900-Desperate; One Minute Play; Phyllis and Xenobia; John and Mary Doe; Not My Fault; The Hardy Boys and the Mystery of Where Babies Come From; Medea* [with Wendy Wasserstein]; *Aunt Dan Meets the Madwoman of Chaillot; Desire, Desire, Desire; Cardinal O'Connor; The Book of Leviticus Show; Entertaining Mr. Helms; The Doctor Will See You Now; Under Duress: Words on Fire;* and *An Altar Boy Talks to God*.)

ESSAYS

"Suspending Disbelief." *American Theatre* 16, no. 10:38 (December 1999).

"More Than the 'Right to be Wrong.'" *Conscience* 24, no. 1:32–33 (spring 2003).

"Homosexuality: Is It Disgusting, or Is It Delightful?" *Conscience* 27, no. 1:21–22 (spring 2006).

CRITICAL AND BIOGRAPHICAL STUDIES

Appling, Troy L. "Liturgical Legacies of Arthur Miller: Use of Religion as Ideological (De)Construction in the Plays of Christopher Durang." *Arthur Miller Journal* 4, no. 1:1–7 (spring 2009).

Clum, John M. "'Period of Adjustment'": Marriage in Tennessee Williams and Christopher Durang." In *The Influence of Tennessee Williams: Essays on Fifteen American Playwrights*. Edited by Philip C. Kolin. Jefferson, N.C.: McFarland, 2008. Pp. 162–174.

Dieckman, Susan Burgoyne. "Metatheatre as Antitheatre: Durang's *The Actor's Nightmare*." *American Drama* 1, no. 2:26–41 (spring 1992).

Greene, Alexis. "Joking Aside: A Conversation About Comedy with Christopher Durang, Gina Gionfriddo, Sarah Ruhl, and Wendy Wasserstein." In *Women Writing Plays: Three Decades of the Susan Smith Blackburn Prize*. Edited by Alexis Greene. Austin: University of Texas Press, 2006. Pp. 181–190.

Hirschberg, Stuart. "Who Is George Spelvin in Christopher Durang's *The Actor's Nightmare?*" *Notes on Contemporary Literature* 32, no. 2:11–12 (March 2002).

Humphrey, Lóegaire. *Christopher Durang*. N.p.: Claud Press, 2011. (Compilation of articles, many available online.)

Mae, Christopher H. "Christopher Durang." In *Contemporary Dramatists*, 5th ed. Edited by K. A. Berney. London: St. James, 1993. Pp. 155–156.

Salomon, Julie. *Wendy and the Lost Boys: The Uncommon Life of Wendy Wasserstein*. New York: Penguin, 2011. (This Wasserstein biography contains a good deal of biographical information on Durang.)

INTERVIEWS

Clum, John. Interview with Christopher Durang. October 3, 2011. Unpublished.

Hylton, Kevin. "Christopher Durang." In his *Fine … I'll Talk*

CHRISTOPHER DURANG

with You: Interviews Including Pulitzer, Tony, and Oscar Winning Playwrights and Screenwriters. Seattle: CreateSpace, 2009. Pp, 41–68.

Savran, David. "Christopher Durang." In his *In Their Own Words: Contemporary American Playwrights*. New York: Theatre Communications Group. Pp. 18–34.

JEFFREY EUGENIDES

(1960—)

Joseph Dewey

IT WAS A most curious juxtaposition of high art and pop culture: in June 2007, Jeffrey Eugenides, whose landmark novels had challenged the protocols of post-postmodern fiction writing, appeared on Oprah Winfrey's television show, holding forth on the familiar dais of her iconic afternoon klatch. But, like Thomas Pynchon's quirky cameos on *The Simpsons* or the commercial with Kurt Vonnegut buying a tuxedo using his Discover card or Maya Angelou's line of feel-good greeting cards or Michael Chabon's exotic comic books, Eugenides' appearance on *Oprah* is as initially puzzling as it is ultimately revealing. Unlike Jonathan Franzen and his kerfuffle over being invited on *Oprah* and his concerns over the wholesale appropriation of reading by women, Eugenides was not invited merely as a writer. More than five years after publishing his sprawling Pulitzer Prize–winning family saga *Middlesex,* about a dysfunctional Greek immigrant family in Prohibition-era Detroit, whose central character is a hermaphrodite, raised a girl but who assumes adult life as a man, Eugenides had been invited not only as part of Oprah's much-touted book club but to be part, along with sexologists, psychologists, and a real-life hermaphrodite, of a free-ranging panel discussion on empowering the intersexed, stigmatized by popular culture as near carnival freaks. Eugenides, affable, witty, engaged the audience, made up not of doctoral candidates and publish-or-perish academics but rather old-school readers who, despite postmodernism's concerted efforts to exile works of serious fiction to the university gulag, still relished made-up characters doing made-up things; there was Eugenides genially pretending that Calliope/Cal Stephanides was not a carefully considered, radically innovative narrative construct but rather a real intersexed person, a genetic changeling. It could have been

awkward—imagine Gustav Flaubert guesting on a Dr. Phil show about communication in marriage or J. D. Salinger participating in an ESPN roundtable about funding fencing as part of high school athletics. But Eugenides was in his element—more a storyteller than a writer, with all its fusty academic associations; dangerously hip, yes, but strikingly old school. The dais of *Oprah,* as it turns out, was exactly where he belonged.

Jeffrey Kent Eugenides has emerged to the forefront of the post-Pynchon era, writers born after 1960—among them Michael Chabon, David Eggers, Nathan Englander, Jonathan Safran Foer, Jonathan Franzen, Rick Moody, and Richard Powers—who constitute really the first generation of American writers produced almost entirely by university English departments, specifically creative writing programs, writers who early on traded the easy charm of reading for the intellectual rigors of analysis, studying dense avant-garde theories about narrative construction that questioned the very legitimacy of language. But these writers, alarmed by the dead-end implications of deconstructing books into experimental texts, have sought to restore narrative to a balance, producing serious fictions that maintain both the intellectual reach of formal experimentation and the inviting imperative of storytelling, narratives that perceive the reader not as a shadowy antagonist in some elaborate chess match but as a friend, indeed a necessary element of the writing dynamic. As Eugenides himself argued in an essay marking the one hundredth anniversary of Bloomsday (from James Joyce's *Ulysses* [1922]) the work often cited as commencing the mid-century conversion of novels into texts, "To be different without being confusing, to be radical without promoting a scorched-earth policy, to be intellectual while

remaining emotional and to be emotional without succumbing to sentimentality, to find a new form that is immediately negotiable—these would be the aims I'd shoot for" ("The Father of Modernism").

Eugenides' prominent position among this post-Pynchon generation comes from a slender production, three works each separated by nearly a decade, that at once celebrate and interrogate the coaxing pull of story. His narratives appeal to the lay reader—he has investigated hot-button topics that are flash points on talk shows and radio call-in programs (to date: teen suicide, aberrant sexual identity, bipolar disorder) while anatomizing the dynamic of reading itself, the heroic seduction of storytelling, the bravado of which has appealed to professional readers in academia. His novels are aware they are constructions (no text of serious fiction published after 1960 can pretend otherwise) but without the smarmy self-conscious irony of the writers Eugenides studied who, in the heyday of the avant-garde at midcentury, upended the narrative contract and, in the process, alienated readers who had for centuries gratefully sought the enchanting sanctuary of narrative. After a generation in which serious fiction became synonymous with obscurity, unreadability, aggravated intellectualism, cool sterility, tiresome self-reflexivity, audio-animatronic character premises, and labyrinthine plots, Eugenides wanted readers to enjoy reading. To that end, he reanimated familiar genres—the bildunsgsroman, the family saga, the love triangle. Conscious of his Greek ancestry and of his classical forebears' discovery of the consolation and reach of storytelling, Eugenides tells stories in which readers are aware of the narrative frame, charmed by the all-access intimacy implicit in that confiding imperative. His prose delights, distinguished by pitch-perfect terraced sentences with elegant vocabulary that recall the luxurious sonic appeal of the grand narratives of the nineteenth century. He conjures characters who are approachable, their dilemmas compelling: five beautiful teenage sisters with a gothic death wish; a pretty young girl coming to terms with the reality that she is a he; a woman, an unabashed romantic, facing an impossible choice between two wildly different lovers. And such enthralling story lines further coax with the subtle play of symbols, objects that effortlessly suggest layerings of interpretative possibilities. In short, Eugenides' narratives represent an imperative in American post-postmodernism that is as old as it is new, narratives that are as much stories as they are texts, novels that, like Eugenides' appearance on *Oprah,* bridge (rather than widen) the gap between high art and pop culture.

BIOGRAPHY

Even as a child, Jeffrey Eugenides responded to the dynamic of storytelling—among his earliest recollections is listening to A. A. Milne's classic tales of Winnie-the-Pooh, framed tales that are less about the silly antics of Pooh and his friends in the Hundred Acre Wood and more about the comfort we have always taken in stories told. Born March 8, 1960, Eugenides, the last of three sons, grew up in middle-class comfort in Grosse Pointe, Michigan, a spacious suburb of Detroit. His father, Constantine, a successful mortgage banker born to Greek immigrant parents, prided himself on his assimilation to his new country (he married an Anglo-Irish woman, Eugenides' mother, Wanda, and participated indifferently in the neighborhood Greek Orthodox Church) and worked diligently to give his family a grounding in their adopted culture, which included expensive private prep schooling. Jeffrey attended the prestigious University Liggett School in nearby Grosse Pointe Woods. Not given easily to social interaction, Jeffrey found the sheltering comfort of reading, discovering largely on his own the tragicomic alternate universe of William Faulkner's Yoknapatawpha cycle, the taut psychological bildungsromans of Henry James, the harrowing anti-parables of Fyodor Dostoevsky, the fabulous story cycle of Ovid's *Metamorphoses* (he took Latin for seven years), and the grand historical epics of Leo Tolstoy, each an unironically ambitious exercise in the panoramic reach of story. But it was when his paternal grandmother came to live with the family that Jeffrey discovered his Greek heritage, fascinated

as much by stories of his family's silk farming back in the old country as by his culture's glorious literary past, specifically its invention of storytelling as an expression of community. At sixteen, already an inveterate reader, Eugenides discovered what would become a foundation text for his evolution into a storyteller: Salinger's *Catcher in the Rye* (1951). For the precocious teen, Salinger's tale was less a case study of a sympathetic sociopath tormented by adolescent angst and more a fascinating narrative experiment in voice, like Milne's Pooh stories, less about its subject matter and more about the telling, Salinger at once using first-person narration (the rambling confessions of the darkly charismatic Holden) while questioning its very viability (Holden's distrust of confiding and his penchant for lying). For Eugenides, it was an intriguing study in how to simultaneously tell and not tell a story.

Certain he wanted to study literature, Eugenides attended Brown University in Providence, Rhode Island, working summers back in Detroit, driving cabs and waiting tables. His studies at Brown in the early 1980s coincided with the explosion of interest in bold French narrative theories that deconstructed narrative itself, exposed language as a complex system of signs, and ultimately revealed the fragile nature of any linguistic representation of reality and by extension the vulnerability of narrative itself. Eugenides dutifully investigated the arguments and studied the requisite postmodern game-texts but, now certain he wanted to write, concluded that such radical experiments lacked the humanity of the books he loved and that, ultimately, they were doomed to settle quickly into the tomb dust of university libraries (for Eugenides the exception was Vladimir Nabokov's fiction, which experimented with narrative construction, certainly, but never abandoned character and plot). Eugenides toyed with pursuing theology, moved by his investigation into the meditative philosophy of the Catholic mystic Thomas Merton, whose works encouraged seclusion and rigorous spiritual exploration. Eugenides, after his junior year, backpacked for a year across Europe, a self-styled spiritual pilgrimage that led to a stint volunteer-

ing in the poorest slums of Calcutta to work among the dying under the care of Mother Teresa's Missionaries of Charity. But Eugenides was unprepared for the impoverished conditions, the sheer dimension of the suffering, and the exacting demands of attending to the dying—he stayed there only a week.

Graduating from Brown magna cum laude in 1983, Eugenides was accepted into Stanford University's prestigious M.F.A. program, completing the degree in 1988. He never abandoned his interest in religion—his initial success came with a short story titled "Here Comes Winston, Full of the Holy Spirit," a coming-of-age tale freighted with Pentecostal imagery, which won an inaugural Nicholl Fellowship, a lucrative award from the Academy of Motion Picture Arts and Sciences intended to help promising screenwriters (Eugenides' story is to date the only non–film script to have been awarded a fellowship). After graduating, and a brief time as a staff writer and photographer for *Yachtsman,* a limited-circulation sports magazine in San Francisco, Eugenides relocated to New York City to accept a position as newsletter editor for the American Academy of Poets. The following year he published his first story, "Capricious Gardens," in the *Gettysburg Review,* considered a premier forum for breakthrough fiction and poetry. Set on an Irish farm, the story is an intricate nested narrative-within-narrative of two couples: two men, compelled to handle sudden estrangement from their wives; and two lesbians, American college students hitchhiking across Ireland whom one of the men picks up in capricious Good Samaritan generosity. The man is determined to seduce the prettier of the two girls. The plot centers on the couples' cultivation of artichokes they find growing in one of the farm's neglected gardens, counterpointed by the man's fascination with a faux relic he has purchased in Rome, supposedly the finger bone of St. Augustine, a brooding presence that introduces crucial layerings of morality to the stories the four share about their own damaged relationships. It is both an engrossing story of damaged lives and a complex investigation into contrapuntal narration: splicing Oprah and Pynchon, it asks a cynical, savvy post-

modern reader, too familiar with the shoddy tricks of storytelling and trained to accept only innovation, to indulge the old-school enticements of plot, character, and symbol.

Although Eugenides thrived in the cultural life of Manhattan, he returned to Detroit regularly. There, a chance conversation with his nephew's teenage babysitter about suicide ideations among her friends recalled for Eugenides his own adolescent obsession with the decidedly suicidal Holden Caulfield. It seemed a promising topic for a project far wider than the short story form. Eugenides began to investigate the dark psychology of self-destruction among teenagers, particularly girls. Over the next several years, assisted by fellowships from the National Endowment for the Arts, Eugenides completed his first manuscript, a bleak account of the suicides of five sisters in a Catholic family in the tony suburbs of Detroit in the mid-1970s. The first chapter, which recounts how the eldest Lisbon sister throws herself out of a second-story bedroom window, was published in 1991 in the *Paris Review,* which had long promoted the work of promising new writers; the excerpt won the journal's Aga Khan Prize, which annually recognizes the best work of fiction to appear in its pages.

Anticipation among the literary establishment was keen—the account of the girl's suicide was at once graphic and lyric, a mesmerizing evocation of the understated horror at the core of teen angst too easily ignored in the placid suburbs. When *The Virgin Suicides* was published two years later, the book generated a wide and deep response, catapulting Eugenides into national prominence. It sold more than a million copies worldwide (translated into thirty languages) and was adapted into a brooding atmospheric indie film by first-time director Sofia Coppola. Given its gothic ambience, the novel quickly gained status as an underground must-read among adolescents, a status helped by misgivings of parents and teachers over fears that Eugenides' gauzy narrative might make suicide seem romantic. Eugenides claimed years later that booksellers considered the slender paperback edition of *The Virgin Suicides* the most shoplifted book of the decade.

Now secure financially and positioned among the most promising writers of the post-Pynchon generation, Eugenides cast about for a new project, all the while publishing a steady stream of short stories, mostly in the *New Yorker.* In November 1994 Eugenides' father, a veteran pilot, died in a plane crash while attempting to land near Daytona Beach, Florida. On December 9, 1995, Eugenides married the sculptor and photographer Karen Yamauchi, whom he met while summering at the MacDowell Colony in New Hampshire; after several difficult miscarriages, the couple celebrated the birth of a daughter, Georgia. He made only incremental progress on a second book, despite the clamor of both publishers and readers. In 1999 he moved his family to Berlin; he claimed later that this was to avoid answering questions about a second book. But for nearly a decade (he joked that writing his second novel took longer than the Trojan War), he had been diligently crafting an ambitious narrative that would both investigate his own Greek roots and reflect his fascination with an obscure mid-nineteenth-century memoir of a French schoolteacher named Herculine Barbin, who was raised a girl but who was discovered after puberty to have a penis. The text had been part of his undergraduate study at Brown. Barbin had wrestled with the condition, finding comfort in penning the heartbreaking memoir (destitute, he committed suicide at age thirty). Eugenides was enthralled not only by the humanity of Barbin's story but by the metaphoric premise of such a condition—at last a narrative vehicle that would enable the writer to straddle gender. Eugenides immersed himself in the literature of hermaphroditism and gender definition even as the manuscript underwent sea changes as he struggled to craft the right voice, and the result was 2002's *Middlesex.* Despite its narrative largesse (a score of plotlines that shuttle across nearly eighty years), its sprawling heft (six-hundred-plus pages), its dozens of named characters, its central use of what some would regard as a repugnant genetic condition, and its reanimation of the genre of heroic immigrant literature at a time when America itself struggled with xenophobic questions of immigrant rights, it

became an improbable best seller and the recipient of the 2003 Pulitzer Prize.

Eugenides was now a literary celebrity, distinguished by his Mephistophelean goatee, his balding pate, his poached egg eyes, and his dapper dress. In 2007 he was named professor of creative writing in the University Center for the Creative and Performing Arts at Princeton University. Drawing on his own adolescence among the upscale families in Detroit's suburbs, he began a novel about a late-1970s debutante party, but he found himself increasingly fascinated by the invented family's eldest daughter (perhaps because of his own daughter, now entering adolescence). After two years of drafting, he abandoned the family saga entirely to investigate the woman-child character, specifically questions about her love life. How, why, would she have fallen in love? Perhaps not surprisingly, at the time he was editing a spacious anthology of the world's greatest love stories, *My Mistress's Sparrow Is Dead* (2008). The love story he was working on evolved into a love triangle and drew on his experiences at Brown, his introduction there to literary theory, his fascination with spiritual questing, and even his time among the destitute in Calcutta. *The Marriage Plot* (2011) was praised as an elegant, highly readable work that reanimated the hoary genre of the college love story, using an experimental triptych-narrative voice that re-created the tenor of classic works of nineteenth-century realism to relate the tangled lives of three Brown seniors, who, in the months following their graduation, fall in and out of and then back in love. Although Eugenides, only in his fifties, clearly has more to write, *The Marriage Plot* can serve as a kind of summa text for his vision of narrative as the merger of high artistic seriousness with the broad appeal of old-fashioned storytelling, a post-postmodern narrative as appropriate for Oprah's Book Club as in university classrooms.

OVERVIEW

Eugenides has dared to interrogate the premise of storytelling itself without the snarky self-awareness and narrative gimmickry of canonical postmodern texts. For Eugenides, narrative can do what neither religion nor science (systems he critiques extensively in his fictions) can: narrative can integrate mystery. Early in *Middlesex,* Calliope recalls the ornately decorated interior of a neighborhood Greek Orthodox church where she was baptized, specifically its murals that celebrated two Christs: one was the eye-level Christ depicted on the church walls, the suffering earthbound Christ subjected to the agonies and confusions of the day-to-day, vulnerable to the familiar chaos of expectation and disappointment, suffering, and death; the other was Christ Pantocrator, the formidable, transcendent, all-seeing, heaven-bestriding god figure depicted on the church's massive dome, who, as the author/inspiration of the Gospel texts, rendered the complicated contradictory data of experience into a clear cosmic pattern, constelling the mess of events into a grateful clarity. Like Christ Pantocrator, theology (and science for that matter) hands down meaning, demands that observation yield the reward of understanding and that data validate a system, whether created and sustained by a god or observed and measured by scientists. In contrast, narrative aspires to—rather than attains—understanding. Clerics and scientists distance us from the lives we must lead; for Eugenides, narrative exists in that exhilarating/terrifying tension between planning and improvisation. Storytellers understand what theologians and scientists cannot: that clear sight and insight are never the same. Narrative refuses to redeem the brutal improvisation of raw event into pattern and offers, rather, the complex reward of awareness. That, Eugenides reminds a generation of post-postmodern readers, is why we told stories in the first place, the ancient consolation of narrative.

To re-create that sense of mystery, Eugenides has confronted the greatest liability of the psychological realism he relishes—the pretense of narration itself, the charade of authority that masks the shoddy unreliability of any narrative perspective. After all, someone has to tell a story, whether a character or the author, selecting events, manufacturing some satisfying clarity, and asking the reader to find comfort in that

clarity-enough. But Jeffrey Eugenides' fictions have celebrated—not lamented—the inability of the narrative voice to render what the reader, caught in the vertiginous free fall into the fractal patterns of contingency and terrorized by the hobgoblin of chance, so desperately seeks: understanding. Eugenides' three novels, each a radically different narrative genre, nevertheless form a kind of trilogy that collectively redefines the reach of narration itself and, in the process, foregrounds what few of Oprah's Book Club faithful (indeed few lay readers) ever notice: the heroic presence of the narrator.

THE VIRGIN SUICIDES

The Virgin Suicides does not read like an apprentice work. This story of five ethereal teenage sisters—Cecilia, thirteen; Lux, fourteen; Bonnie, fifteen; Mary, sixteen; and Therese, seventeen, who within months all take their own lives—has none of the tell-tale excesses that traditionally define—and mar—first novels. Eugenides does not clumsily rework semiautobiographical materials (save that the Lisbon family lives in the same Grosse Pointe neighborhoods of his adolescence); nor does he decorate that plot with obvious symbols; nor is his prose line derivative or self-consciously overwrought. Rather, Eugenides revisits a too-familiar genre: narratives that excavate the forbidding logic of why those poised on the promise of adulthood, lonely and hypersensitive teens, would deliberately, irrevocably void that promise. From *The Sorrows of Young Werther* to *The Bell Jar,* these haunting, claustrophobic anti-coming-of-age stories have been used as cautionary tales to scare straight the world's real-life lonely, hypersensitive young adults. However, Eugenides, schooled in narrative design theory, defies the conservative expectations of such an established genre, and not merely from the cumulative pressure of multiple suicides within a single family. Had that story been executed as Oprah's Book Club psychological realism, it would have been prohibitively depressing—after all, there is no suspense, really no plot (the harrowing opening line reveals the sisters' fates).

Rather, we are about the difficult work of trying to assemble some explanation, to dispel the mystery that cloaks the mass suicides.

In an experimental twist on narrative protocol, Eugenides uses a kind of group narrator, a first-person collective "we," a group of neighborhood boys, horny classmates who obsess over the sisters, transfixed by their effortless erotic gravity, watching them from sidewalks, from bedroom windows, across classrooms, and even from a tree house. That intriguing narrative experiment has few literary antecedents—mostly modernist short stories such as Sherwood Anderson's "Death in the Woods" or William Faulkner's "A Rose for Emily." (Debra Shostak argues that when the boys register an unpleasant mushroom-y odor emanating from the Lisbon house, it is Eugenides' sly homage to a similar moment in Faulkner's story.) The boys, now adults but still haunted two decades later by the girls, are determined to gather the abundance of evidence they have secured over the years to fashion a satisfying reading of the suicides. Only a few of the boys/men are named, and we never know how many have been involved in amassing the evidence they have actually cataloged by exhibit number; they never make clear their audience and speak as much to some nameless other as to themselves, trying in understanding the Lisbon girls to make sense of their own adolescence.

They open their memoir with a startling juxtaposition: a suicide during a teenage party. After Cecilia, the youngest Lisbon sister, wearing an antique wedding dress and cradling a laminated picture of the Virgin Mary, had tried to kill herself by slitting her wrists in the bathtub (a pompous hospital psychiatrist assures the distraught parents that the act was a cry for attention and that as remedy they might allow Cecilia to wear makeup), the parents reluctantly agree two weeks after Cecilia is discharged from the hospital to host a party in her honor, a party with boys (some of whom are part of the choral narration), as a way to restore normality. Her scars covered by bracelets that are Scotch-taped to hold them in place, Cecelia is quiet most of the evening. Then, she politely asks her mother's permission to be excused, goes upstairs, and

promptly throws herself out of a bedroom window, impaling herself on a fence spike. The narrators confront for the first time the question why. With mordant humor, they concede, "We didn't understand why Cecilia had killed herself the first time and we understood even less when she did it twice" (p. 29). They admit to reading Cecilia's diary, secreted out by a plumber's assistant, hoping to find some clue; but they find only Magic Marker doodles, a "profusion of colors and curlicues, Candyland ladders and striped shamrocks" (p. 29).

In the aftermath of Cecilia's suicide, we are told, the parents better monitor their daughters' activities—until by late autumn there is an uneasy consensus that Cecilia was a troubled misfit, certainly, but also a "freak of nature" (p. 107), her suicide an isolated event. Indeed what plot there is centers on the attempt of the school lothario, football star Trip Fontaine, to meet Lux, whose smoldering eroticism has enthralled him. He gets Mr. Lisbon to agree reluctantly to his taking Lux to the homecoming dance but only after Trip arranges a group date, finding three friends to escort the other three sisters. Despite wearing homemade dresses that the mother designs to be as loose as choir robes, the girls nevertheless manage to have a normal evening—Lux and Trip are even voted homecoming king and queen. But, after Trip and Lux make love in the end zone of the school's football field, Lux misses her curfew. The parents regret the liberty they had given the girls. They are pulled out of school, kept in "maximum-security isolation" (p. 136), and the father resigns his high school teaching position. The family seldom ventures out and their house falls into casual neglect. Over the winter, the boys never stop watching the house—they can see Lux on the roof in the most inclement weather having sex with boys they don't recognize. Her gyrations mesmerize. She becomes a "carnal angel" (p. 143). Despite the girls' isolation, come spring the boys are sure that the girls are trying to communicate covertly—blinking lamps, leaving cryptic messages in mailboxes, phoning them to play bits of angst-ridden pop songs—but the boys cannot discern any clear message.

One night, however, they receive a clear signal—a mailbox note that tells them to wait for a signal the next evening at midnight. The boys decide they must rescue the Lisbon sisters; they will "borrow" a family car and heroically whisk the imprisoned girls to far-off Florida. They are summoned to the house at midnight by a flashlight. They explain their far-fetched scheme to Lux—she appears interested but says that it would be better to take her mother's much roomier car and tells them she will go sit in the car and that the boys are to wait for the sisters while they pack. The boys wait and wait. They finally venture down into the basement rec room—the party decorations from the night Cecilia died a year earlier are still up—and discover Bonnie hanging from the rafters "like a piñata" (p. 209). In quick order, they find room to room the other sisters: Mary has stuck her head in the gas oven; Therese has taken sleeping pills; and Lux has run the car, the radio playing, in the closed garage. Mary alone survives—but she will take her life weeks later with sleeping pills. Autopsies and newspaper accounts explain only the manner of death—the family, the neighborhood, teachers, doctors, and, most critical for us, the boys years later are all left within a most disquieting mystery.

Thus Eugenides uses the premise of adolescent suicides to investigate not the complex psychological urgencies that make such desperate actions logical (indeed the sisters are kept at a distance) but rather to interrogate the need to assemble that story into coherence. Counselors, doctors, newspaper reporters, neighbors and friends, the family priest—each perspective is unwilling to contend with the forbidding press of uncertainty. They each ask why and without irony shape an answer. We are most aware of the enormous energy of the narrators' inquest, the painstaking effort of those classmates who have spent years gathering evidence: interviews with the parents, testimonials from students, findings from psychologists, eyewitness accounts from anyone who ever visited the Lisbon home from plumbers to florists, even artifacts treated like relics (shoes, half-melted candles, yearbook photos, a jewelry box with a strand of hair, used

makeup)—all to constellate events into a clarifying explanation.

Clearly, in the cool comfort of retrospect, the choral narrator has shaped a Rosetta stone reading of the Lisbon girls, the men's own private myth. For them, the girls were romantic, even erotic damsels in distress, misunderstood by controlling parents and insensitive doctors, trapped in their suburban prison-home, their ritual self-sacrifice a kind of suicide in self-defense, a (melo)dramatic reading that Eugenides cannot endorse. Eugenides undercuts the narrators' conclusions—ironically, multiplying the narrative perceptions does little to magnify the powers of perception. We note how often the boys/men leap toward conclusions, how little they actually know about the Lisbon household—indeed, it does not even occur to them as they wait for the Lisbon sisters to gather their belongings for their supposed flight to Florida that they had been called to the house to witness the mass suicide. The fact is, their effort is finally frustrated—and they apologize for its incompleteness. "In the end we had pieces of the puzzle, but no matter how we put them together, gaps remained, oddly shaped emptinesses mapped by what surrounded them, like countries we couldn't name" (p. 241). Indeed, like the priest, like the doctors, like the journalist camped out at the Lisbon house, the boys struggle against the futility of their enterprise, assuming that evidence must yield explanation, never glimpsing what Eugenides sees so clearly, that certainty, meaning, motivation, are the hobgoblins of little minds terrified over the exhilarating anxieties of life lived.

The Virgin Suicides is thus a contested narrative between the aggressive interrogative imperative of its collective narrator(s) and Eugenides himself. Eugenides embraces the frustration of narration, denies the choral narrator access to wisdom—and we are invited to embrace rather than lament the narrators' imperfect conclusions. It must be enough for us that under the alchemic dazzle of Eugenides' larger author-ity, the suicides of the Lisbon sisters appear to mean something. As readers, we are given an accumulation of objects that under our interactive energy seem to promise the layering of symbols: the annoying fish flies that descend on the neighborhood; the wall clock that hangs precariously off the school wall; the beautiful neighborhood elm trees succumbing to a pestilent invasive beetle; the painting in the Lisbon dining room of Pilgrims plucking a turkey; the two extra canine teeth that each sister has; the fascination Therese has with a ham radio; the mother's observation that fingernails keep growing weeks after death—they, and dozens more, must surely mean something. But they are suggestive, never revelatory. Within the compassionate space of storytelling, for us as readers, the suicides are haunting not because they mean something—that is the foolish, too-earnest obsession of doctors and priests, journalists and teachers, parents and neighbors (and Oprah's audiences)—but rather because they *must* mean something. The modesty of narration embraces the insufficiency of explanation, dismisses the claims to understanding as selfishness and simplification. The pieces of the puzzle are never ours entirely—and that, Eugenides sees, is the special privilege of narrative, post-postmodern or otherwise.

MIDDLESEX

After nearly a decade of anticipation, readers of *The Virgin Suicides* must surely have been puzzled by Eugenides' follow-up work, 2002's *Middlesex*. If *The Virgin Suicides* is spare, intimate, compact, muted, centripetal, even claustrophobic, *Middlesex* is breathtaking in reach, cinematic in execution, in turn heartbreakingly tragic, riotously comic, and joyously bawdy, a tumultuous indulgence of full-throttle narrative, an abundance of engrossing story lines centered on colorful ethnocentric characters across more than eight decades. Yet in this tumultuous multigenerational saga of a Greek American family told through the agency of an adult hermaphrodite, Eugenides is still engaged—as he was in *The Virgin Suicides*—in affirming the wonder of mystery and, simultaneously, upending the traditional conception of narrative voice.

The premise of *Middlesex* may seem at first exploitative, sensational, even gimmicky—the

sexual coming-of-age of a young girl, Calliope Helen Stephanides, a hermaphrodite, a term that despite our culture's careful sensitivity to nontraditional sexual identity still suggests Barnumesque freak shows. That coming-of-age narrative is framed by an adult Cal writing more than twenty years after the events. Now a fortyish cultural attaché for the Foreign Service office in Berlin, Cal is hesitatingly beginning an intimate relationship with a beautiful Asian American photographer, uncertain how to handle his complex sexuality. After all, Cal was raised a girl (the pediatrician, an elderly, half-blind family friend from the old country, noticed nothing unusual) until, in his adolescence, he was diagnosed with 5-alpha-reductase deficiency, a rare genetic condition in which genitalia appear to be female at birth but, owing to a lurking male XY chromosome, in fact transform to male at puberty. In the first two hundred pages Cal relates the genetic history of the condition (his birth, in 1959, does not happen until page 211). We trace the transmission of the abnormal recessive gene for hermaphroditism back to Cal's grandparents, Desdemona and Eleutherios ("Lefty") Stephanides, brother and sister, who in 1922 in their remote mountain village in Asia Minor consummated their attraction for each other amid the mayhem of the Turkish invasion. The two—desperately in love—take advantage of the confusion during the mass evacuations and their emigration to the United States to reinvent themselves: they pretend to meet on board the ship heading to America and are married before the ship docks. After the couple settles with cousins in Detroit, aware of the onus of incest, Desdemona prays not to conceive—when she does, the recessive gene is passed to Cal's father, Milton. After service in the Pacific during World War II and in Korea, Milton marries Tessie, a cousin engaged at the time to the priest at the neighborhood Greek Orthodox parish. Over time, Tessie and Milton realize the American Dream. Using an insurance windfall when his failing bar is burned to the ground during the 1967 Detroit race riots, Milton opens what will become a string of successful hot dog stands and moves the family out to the swanky suburbs of Grosse Pointe, to a beautiful home on Middlesex Boulevard.

Callie grows up quietly in the suburbs—she is considered an exceptionally pretty girl. When at thirteen she is sent to a posh prep school, however, she discovers a powerful attraction for a freckled, red-haired female classmate, whom Cal identifies only as the Obscure Object (a reference taken from the Luis Buñuel film Cal would see years later). More problematically, Callie starts to lose her looks. She does not develop breasts, nor does she menstruate. (Worried, she finally dramatically fakes her first period in church—Cal compares the performance to classic Meryl Streep—and then fakes the monthly return.) Her voice drops, her hair tangles into a rat's nest, and, despite waxing, she sports a thin moustache. Then, on a vacation trip with the Object's family to their summer house in upstate Michigan, Callie watches jealously as the Object makes out with a boy. In retaliation, she endures a most awkward and unsatisfying tryst of her own with the girl's creepy older brother. That night, Callie and the girl end up engaging in a quasi-innocent kissing game; the brother discovers them and loudly accuses them of being lesbians. Panicked, Callie runs off into the night and in the confusion collides with a passing tractor. In the emergency room the doctor notices at last the curious condition of her genitalia.

When Callie's parents consult a specialist in sexual disorders in New York, the doctor recommends continuing to think of Callie as a girl but administering a regimen of hormones and surgically "repairing" her genitalia to stabilize her gender. Callie steals a look at the doctor's file that confirms that she is in fact a male, and when she looks up "hermaphrodite" in the dictionary and discovers a synonym is "monster," she is determined to recover her true self. She runs away and, cutting her hair in a truck stop restroom and donning boy's clothes, hitchhikes across the country, claiming to be on her way to Stanford. S/he ends up in San Francisco where, after a stint among the hippies in Golden Gate Park, s/he is attacked as a freak. Now desperate and homeless, s/he works briefly as a freak attraction in an underground peep show until, after

a raid, s/he must call home to arrange a release and ultimately a return to Detroit. Callie/Cal returns in time to attend her father's funeral: Milton had been killed in a high-speed car chase with a man who had attempted to extort $25,000 in a phony kidnapping scheme (it turns out that the man is the parish priest who long ago had been engaged to his wife). The day of Milton's too-elaborate funeral (an assimilationist, he had had little use for the Orthodox Church), Cal, in a poignant visit with his dying grandmother, is told at last the truth about the long-ago incestuous relationship; and while the rest of the family attends the service, Cal stays behind to fulfill the Greek custom of the son guarding the doorway to ensure the father's ghost does not cross the threshold. The narrative closes with this assertion of Cal's assertion of both his ethnic and gender identities.

Much as Cal/Callie defies boundaries, *Middlesex* has itself eluded definition. It has been approached as a biomedical case study, a docu-text, informed by Eugenides' research into medical literature on gender theory, that explores the condition of the intersexed with sensitivity and candor (Banner; Chu). It has been examined as a political act, an activist text intended to empower the intersexed, to give voice, literally, to those genetic rarities much as in earlier generations forward-reaching texts gave voice to minorities, women, gays, and lesbians (Carroll; Graham). It has been read as an ambitious sociohistorical document, a researched period piece, a sprawling cultural biography that animates the defining mid-decades of the American Century using wide-screen cinematic settings, copious references to historic events and pop culture, and period-accurate detailing from furniture to automobiles to food, using Michigan's Greek American community to investigate the economic, religious, and cultural dimensions of the immigrant migration to the suburbs as an expression of the American Dream (Cohen; Lee; Mallory-Kani). And, despite its old-school feel that recalls the panoramic historic realism of Charles Dickens or Leo Tolstoy, *Middlesex* has been approached as a very postmodern intertext, a dense text-edifice that, like other midcentury ur-intertexts from Wil-

liam Gaddis' *The Recognitions* (1955) to Thomas Pynchon's *Gravity's Rainbow* (1973) is executed by an erudite master-authority using an encyclopedic range of references to other texts that give depth and irony to an already labyrinthine story line. In this reading, *Middlesex* is an intricate bricolage text latticed by allusions to texts from the sciences, classical literature, religion and myth, music, film and television, folk tales, even the dictionary, as well as original texts generated within the narrative (letters, diaries, speeches, doctor's reports, newspaper pieces). As with the master texts of postmodernism, the allusions, scores of them, trigger interpretative speculation for readers willing to track them down: for instance, echoes of T. S. Eliot's *Waste Land* (1922) underscore the brutalities of the evacuation of Smyrna; the evening Desdemona conceives, despite her best intentions, she and Lefty attend a neighborhood theater production based on the Greek legend of the Minotaur, Desdemona aroused by the muscular thighs of the actor playing the monster; Callie plays the blind hermaphrodite seer Tiresias in her prep school production of *Antigone;* the summer home where Callie so disastrously expresses her attraction for the Object is in the same upstate coastal Michigan village where Ernest Hemingway set the coming-of-age stories of Nick Adams, himself conflicted over sexual identity. Eugenides himself has suggested approaching *Middlesex* as an ambitious hybrid narrative that, given its fascination with the engine of genetics and the metaphors of transformation, actually evolves through the three defining eras of narrative history since Homer (Eggers): we begin with the epic (the expansive story of the immigrant family itself, at once ethnic, cultural, religious, political, and economic, moving from the 1922 Greco-Turkish War to the fall of Nixon); that epic tale then evolves into a pitch-perfect modernist Freudian confessional tale of psychological realism, Callie's poignant coming-of-age narrative and her complicated sexual awakening into Cal; and cutting throughout both narratives with appropriately unapologetic intrusiveness is a postmodern self-reflexive arch-text, one that foregrounds its own creation (Cal writing his story years after the fact as

therapy to sort through the implications of his burgeoning relationship with a woman).

Yet *Middlesex* does not have the sterile feel typical of such self-consciously experimental texts. There is an immediacy, a felt dimension to Callie/Cal's coming-of-age narrative that coaxes the reader to engage the character sympathetically despite rather than because of the novel's elaborate formal construction, a generous response that seldom complicates the reading of, say, a Gaddis or Pynchon text. Cal's text is invitatory. We care about Callie/Cal. Like the choral narrator of *The Virgin Suicides,* Cal, in turning to the act of writing, engages a radical act of intimacy with an unnamable reader in an effort to understand his life as part of his movement forward into a new relationship. "I feel you out there, reader. This is the only kind of intimacy I'm comfortable with. Just the two of us, here in the dark" (p. 319). As in *The Virgin Suicides,* that struggle to understand is ultimately a futile endeavor to contain events, a massive exercise in irony that mistakes organization and pattern-shaping for recovering clear purpose. Much as with the doctors and priests and journalists who do more harm than good for the Lisbon family, much like the boys-into-men who simplify the Lisbon sisters into their own erotic myth, Cal struggles for understanding, a protocol Eugenides again undercuts. After all, the history Cal recounts reveals how the hunger for certainty has only led to catastrophe: the barbarities of the Greco-Turkish War; the fiery street riots that embroil Detroit; the Manichaean paranoia of the Nixon White House; the incendiary racist rhetoric, echoing in the Islamic mosque, that Callie's grandmother overhears; the pinheads at Ford Motor Company who fire Callie's grandfather because he associates with "known criminals," in this case a cousin who, desperate for money, bootlegs whiskey from Canada during Prohibition—each the expression of clear-sighted people who reduce the world to Crayola simplifications.

As in *The Virgin Suicides,* Eugenides again indicts the sciences and religion and their pretense at certainty. The opening two hundred pages trace with painstaking care the biological journey of the recessive gene that causes Callie's sexuality—the more we understand its journey, of course, the less we understand it (at its center, recall, is the carnal attraction between a sister and brother). For Eugenides, the defining elements of the human experience—love, violence, family, faith, mortality—sing wide and free of the corralling urgency to understand them. Genes and gods end, ironically, at the same premise—that we cannot tolerate the anxious free fall into contingency. The neighborhood Greek Orthodox Church stays apart from the day-to-day struggles of the neighborhood, sealed off from the street (although the roof leaks), providing an incensed safe house animated by the sterile theatrics of ritual, that too-elegant service the epitome of irony (suggested not only by the carnal appetites of its parishioners but by its popular parish priest, who will die in a high-speed car chase trying to extort money from the Stephanides family). Thematically, then, like *The Virgin Suicides,* *Middlesex* is a contested narrative, a civil war between order and mystery in which the narrator seeks to do what the author rejects—interestingly, Cal actually resembles Eugenides, both forty-something academics living in Berlin, balding, goateed, dapper, socially retarded isolates who gratefully seek the shelter-refuge of writing. Even as the narrator struggles to understand his identity, Eugenides, much as he did in *The Virgin Suicides,* works assiduously to undercut that effort. The story Cal relates is regularly cut by coincidence, the hammer-stroke trauma of the unexpected, the intrusive charm of surprise (both good and bad), implosive events that upend expectations, suggesting that the lived life is a stumbling kind of ad-lib, the wonder and terror of which Eugenides—not Cal—embraces with a Zorba the Greek joyance. Narrative—not science, not religion, not journalism, not history—balances order and mystery, integrates pattern and chaos, embraces design and free will.

That grand theme itself would certainly have made *Middlesex* a landmark post-postmodern text, using the psychological life history of a sexual rarity to unironically extend to a complacent media-saturated age the exhilarating invitation to touch the open energy field of experience. But its genre-busting hybrid form and its sweep-

ing affirmation of the terrifying exhilaration of mystery aside, *Middlesex* engages in a far more radical experiment, one that picks up Eugenides' writerly interest in what he has often termed "impossible" narrative voices, crafting narrative authorities that challenge the reach of traditional storytellers. Cal is a voice. Cal tells us in the memorable opening line that he was born three times—once as a girl, and then thirteen years later in the emergency room as a boy—and "now, at the age of forty-one, I feel another birth coming on" (p. 1)—his "birth" as a storyteller. Like *The Virgin Suicides, Middlesex* is a told story; we hear a voice who talks in the reassuring intimacy of first person nearly two decades after the events, a traditional act of recollection, using the narrative act as diary-therapy to shape events into consequence and clarity, an accepted protocol for narratives since Daniel Defoe's Moll Flanders.

Of course, Eugenides knows the rules, logical and irrefutable—first-person narratives, as readers have come to understand, although immediate and passionate, are bound by what that character knows, sees, hears, understands, giving such narrative authority an inevitable unreliability, its vision shoddy, necessarily tunneled and frustratingly thin. Indeed Eugenides has commented at length over frustrations during the long gestation of *Middlesex* as he attempted to realize the grand story he had conceived within the claustrophobic boundary of traditional first person, trying to capture the panoramic vision appropriate to a family saga and the larger spectacle of American twentieth-century immigrant culture without losing the intimacy, the honest confusions, the bald emotions of his intersexed first person. "So how do you have a first person voice that is also third person?" (Von Moorhem). The answer was to audaciously reinvent first-person limited omniscience into a kind of first-person omniscient, a projector: Cal regularly, unapologetically bursts free of the limits of first person to speculate, to zigzag into characters' heads (male and female with hermaphroditic confidence), to expand beyond the boundaries of his own witness, reenergizing the narrative, gainfully animating long-ago scenes in distant locales, trespassing, invading the private thoughts, the sanctuarial privileged space of others' minds and hearts, to broaden the reach of narrative, to defy its rules. Unreliability is suddenly not a deficiency, not a problem but rather a celebration of the imagination and its grand speculative reach. Indeed we are given riveting you-are-there accounts of events—both historic and familial—that Cal could not have witnessed; we are even given emotional accounts of that tectonic womb moment when the sperm hit the egg and nine months later the moment when Cal is born, his "eyes switched on at last" (p. 215).

With brio, as he did in *The Virgin Suicides,* Eugenides reimagines first person, reenchants staid traditional narrative voice; here, the voice we hear is at once elastic, inventive, and liberated; the voice is a happy paradox, as much wide-lens seer as tortured introspective confessor, as much diligent historian as freewheeling fabulator, as much careful scientist as giddy voyeur. Regularly, without the bemusement of annoyingly self-reflexive narrators of postmodern play-texts who cannot resist mocking their own narrative tricks, Cal reminds the reader that he must now indulge the catapult vision of his imagination to make vivid the events, the people, of his narrative—*Middlesex* is experimental without being intimidating and without distracting from the vivid immediacy and emotions of the story itself. The reconstructed first person is negotiable, accessible, because even with the Panavision reach of his vastly empowered super-first-person narrator, Eugenides refutes the master wisdom voice of the traditional religious texts from which he drew his model for first person–projector. Cal is no Christ Pantocrator. Here, the defining moments of Cal's grand narrative, whether invented or recalled, frustrate even his broad investigatory reach, his high-octane imagination, his boundless curiosity—at critical turns, he concedes the limits of his reach, recognizes the persistence of mystery. Like all of us, Cal is omniscient, and not; transcendent, and not; content, and not; enlightened, and not; confused, and not. Life, as it turns out, both engages and exceeds the grasp of our imagination.

JEFFREY EUGENIDES

THE MARRIAGE PLOT

A love triangle? What could be simpler?

Beautiful, bespectacled Madeleine Hanna, a senior at Brown, a hard-core romantic enchanted by the luxurious excesses of nineteenth-century British novels, has majored in English for the most old-fashioned of reasons—like Oprah's readers, she loves to read, to cozily inter herself among made-up people, happily abandoning the responsibilities of a broader social life. That love is upended when in her senior year she is introduced to chic French narrative theory (it is the early 1980s) that suggests that a book is merely a crafted system of signs, that it can't really be about anything but itself. It is in a seminar in semiotics that, amid the larger confusions of approaching graduation and the proposition at last of making her way out in the real world, Madeleine falls under the spell of the mercurial Leonard Bankhead, a biology major sporting a bandana and chewing a thick wad of tobacco, scruffy, charismatic, antisocial (despite or perhaps because of a hard-earned reputation as a womanizer), an autodidact with a reaching intellect but given to manic depression and suicidal ideations, a misfit who functions most effectively on a regimen of lithium. For her part, Madeleine has been the object of an unrequited obsession since freshman orientation, when she had first met Mitchell Grammaticus, a brilliant Greek American religious studies major from Detroit, a socially awkward isolate gifted with a restless curiosity about Christian Catholic mysticism in an age of unbelief. Before committing to graduate work, he decides to take a kind of spiritual pilgrimage, a backpack tour of Europe (in part to exorcize the ghost of Madeleine), which will come to include a disastrous three-week stint volunteering at Mother Teresa's mission in the ghettos of Calcutta before he returns to New York to confront Madeleine, determined on the very eve of her wedding to demand she not marry Leonard, whose self-destructive egocentrism he sees as toxic.

Gentle reader, who will our comely heroine choose?

For Oprah's readers, the love-triangle dynamic is as reassuringly familiar as it is immensely enthralling; and for academics, given the genre's fall into disfavor (or more often parody) among postwar writers of serious fiction and its devolution into Kindle fodder fit for stranded travelers or bored vacationers, reading *The Marriage Plot* is like running into an old friend. For both audiences, after the epical excess of *Middlesex*'s plotlines and the spongy unreliability and selective amnesia in *The Virgin Suicides,* the narrative here has an attractive day-bright solidity, a clean simplicity in its execution—a tripartite narrative, each chapter dominated by the limited sensibility of one of the three lovers, which collectively, recursively, creates a unified plot.

But not surprisingly Eugenides' love story is not quite so simple. Indeed the love story, the crazy back and forth do-si-do played out among the three crossed lovers, is in the end a marvelous distraction. What interests Eugenides far more is the steady, quiet evolution of Mitchell Grammaticus from frustrated religious studies major, grand opera–sized disappointed lover, and ersatz saint-among-the-wretched into what Eugenides has long (if indirectly) celebrated: the storyteller. *The Marriage Plot,* despite its fascination with the inscrutable logic of love, ends not with a wedding or a kiss, an orgasm or a declaration of love, ironic or otherwise. Rather it ends, as the title suggests, with a plot, the conception of a story line that Mitchell sees with epiphanic suddenness and then shares with Madeleine: an inchoate story idea at once sturdy and fragile, grounded in his own bittersweet experience—his frustrated search for both romantic love and cosmic truth; a story that is part of a centuries-long tradition of love story narratives and yet is strikingly, inexplicably original; in short a story waiting to be told, waiting to be transcribed into the sonic effects of language. As suggested earlier, although it would be absurd to see *The Marriage Plot* as some capstone text (Eugenides, after all, is a robust fifty-something), it does offer satisfying closure to his first three works. After examining (and celebrating) narrative as the sole vehicle sufficient to the mysteries of human experience, it is inevitable now he examine the evolution of the storyteller. As such *The Mar-*

riage Plot succeeds not merely as a love story (although that is riveting) but more as a *Künstlerroman,* the transformation of an unlikely misfit into a writer.

Against Mitchell's heroic emergence, Eugenides plots the far more problematic transformations of Madeleine and Leonard: Madeleine from a reader, rare and passionate, to a dime-a-dozen academic; Leonard from scientist to case study. Despite her brilliance in the classroom, Madeleine is a reader, in love with the soft imprisonment within old-school, big-scale narratives. Her introduction to the philosophy of language and the hip theories of narrative disheartens her—suddenly, she feels guilty about relishing the narratives of John Cheever, John Updike, and her beloved Victorians, narratives of complex characters caught within complex emotional experiences, narratives that have long given texture and urgency to the dilemmas of her own life. Indeed, her dramatic discovery, with Leonard, of the very kind of love her books had so long described coincides with her discovery in semiotics that love itself is a construction of the mind, a sterile social contract; that emotions are complexes of cerebral responses to a mutually agreed upon system of threadbare signs. Madeleine resists the idea—despite Leonard's troubling emotional instability, she recognizes her need, emotionally and physically, as that most mysterious of emotional expressions: love. And after spending a sunny May afternoon in bed with Leonard, Madeleine accepts the vulnerability implicit in any declaration of love (her hoarse voice is edged with a "sense of peril" [p. 66]) only to have a smirking Leonard dismiss the idea—weren't they simply mimicking the hokey dialogue from a Salinger story? They break up.

But, of course, it isn't that easy. Weeks later, Madeleine skips her graduation ceremony entirely to go to the hospital where Leonard has been sent by doctors concerned over his increasing depression. Their relationship rekindled, Madeleine heroically crusades to maintain the integrity of their love and agrees to accompany Leonard on his six-month postgraduate fellowship to Pilgrim Lake, a prestigious Cape Cod research lab. Even as Leonard battles his private

demons and his mood swings, even as he is medicated with lithium that stabilizes his manic depression but quashes his libido and renders him weak and needful, Madeleine bravely assumes the role of nurse (despite misgivings from her mother and her sister), seeing in that dynamic the very essence of heroic love so central to the novels she treasures. But Madeleine herself faces an uncertain future—despite strong grades, she has not found placement in any graduate program. After all, she is a reader, not a student. Given the proximate busyness of so much scientific work (including one of the senior researchers at Pilgrim Lake being awarded a Nobel Prize), Madeleine buys into the theoretical protocols of literary study and studiously revamps an undergraduate thesis on her beloved Jane Austen; with the help of a former professor, she then gets the ramped-up article accepted at a refereed journal, a coup for any fledgling literary scholar. (Eugenides mocks the achievement—the journal clumsily transposes two of the pages.) Indeed Madeleine discovers a cabal of similarly minded reformed readers, all too ready to analyze the Victorian novels they love into chic post-whatever texts. Her acceptance at Columbia even as she and Leonard prepare for their wedding confirms her status now as an academic; she is now a licensed student of literature, too ready to expose the novels she so naively loved to the chill dissection of theoretical analysis. Leonard fares little better. Leonard takes himself off lithium and struggles against the massive commitment of marriage before ingloriously spinning out of control during their honeymoon in Europe. (He ends up in a hospital, injured in a fall in a casino in Monaco.) When they return to New York, Leonard abandons Madeleine, retreating to a cabin back home in Oregon even as Madeleine's parents counsel annulment.

As Madeleine devolves and Leonard fragments, we watch the stealth-emergence of Mitchell Grammaticus. In the end, Mitchell is given the novel's dramatic, if muted, climax. In a novel dealing so frankly with grand emotional displays, Mitchell quietly, unexpectedly cries. Still searching for some reassuring cosmic dimension to experience, Mitchell sits on a back bench at a Quaker meeting house near Princeton, enjoying

the stillness, the exotic quiet of the service. He confronts the devastating emotional miscalculations of his life—foremost his certainty (or, as he sees it now, his dreamy stupidity) that in the end Madeleine would marry him. He has watched Madeleine marry a man he perceives as impossibly wrong for her; he has watched Madeleine abandoned by that same husband, left to gather her shattered confusions; he has shared what turns out to be a disappointing assignation with Madeleine. After all those emotional trials, Mitchell, sitting in the Quaker meeting house, feels the inner-light revelation of the Quaker experience flood him with the certainty not just that he would get over Madeleine (that is the payoff for, say, Oprah's readers) but more, that the long, troubling experience of his emotional catastrophes would make a fetching plot, a story that would justify its own need to be told. Hard-eyed, clear-sighted enough to see the elegant persuasion of mystery, touched by experience but left apart from its coaxing lure, emerging now into a resilient isolation, Mitchell (his elaborate Greek last name means "teacher of language and literature") at last finds that elusive truth for which he has so long searched—not in the safe-haven refuge of books that inter readers within an entirely symbolic landscape where they mistake the easy pitch of sympathy for made-up people for the real thing; not in the texts of classroom analysis that reduce stories to hyper-clever puzzles, sophisticated sign systems, and dense intellectual exercises; not in churches where suffering and agonies, anxieties and fears are contained within the too-satisfying faith in some greater being's providential design; and certainly not in the experience of living an unexamined life, grounded by the evident pointlessness of tiny anticipations and tiny disappointments; but rather in the implosive urgency to tell that story in all its entangling mystery, to tap into that most satisfying dynamic, the near distance of an unnamable but real reader, an intimacy at last his to cherish.

Thus Eugenides defines the post-postmodern storyteller—a compassionate isolate who edges just beyond the magnetic pull of experience; a sentimental pragmatist, a passionate stoic, eyes full of light, who, without irony, without cynicism, stays at once apart and a part, compelled by paradox: a joyful regret, a clear-eyed mysticism, a carnal spiritualism, a hard-eyed romanticism. Mitchell, as fiercely intelligent as he is profoundly emotional, evolves from a frustrated dilettante-cleric and angst-ridden non-lover to be what he never suspects he might be: a storyteller, since Homer the odd man out, the isolate willing to be sequestered in claustrophobic rooms, there to assemble stories into plot, comforted by that still small voice inside him, an expansive and generous selfishness, content not with grandiose cosmic faux-truths of religion or science but rather the modest truths-enough of stories that enlighten as much as they confound.

CONCLUSION

For all his cosmopolitan demeanor and his evident erudition, Jeffrey Eugenides has never forgotten that he is a Detroit native, intrigued by the blue-collar city as emblematic of the energy and reach of America itself, engaged as much by the city's contemporary musical traditions from Motown to the White Stripes as by its gritty working-class heritage, its complex and volatile ethnic and racial mix, and its stupendous rise and precipitous fall as an American industrial hub. But what perhaps is most telling is Eugenides' fascination as a child for a massive mural series at the Detroit Institute of Arts, a fascination that remains "totemic" even as an adult (Foer). Titled simply *Detroit Industry,* the grand-scale frescoes, executed by the Mexican social realist Diego Rivera in the 1930s, use striking religious imagery to capture the breadth and reach of Detroit's techno-industries. The centerpiece of the multi-wall mural is a bold and dramatic re-creation of the assembly line at Ford's River Rouge plant, envisioned here not as soul-crushing and oppressive monotony but as a joyous, even heroic expression of the spirit and vision of the factory workers—black and white, young and old—their muscles straining, their precision movements captured in all their tight choreography. It makes bold and vivid the act of production itself, the sheer vigor of assemblage, hands-on work seldom

appreciated by those who take driving cars for granted. For all his engaging characters, his evident delight in the conjure-act of storytelling, his willingness in the uneasy quietus of the era when postmodern American fiction looked suspiciously on the very viability of narrative itself to use stories to tangle with the foundation experiences of mortality, sexuality, and love, young Jeffrey's infatuation with the Rivera mural foreshadows the larger achievement of the adult Eugenides: redefining the reach of narration. By challenging conventional assumptions about voice, by determining to foreground the unsuspected grandeur, the intricate energy of assemblage itself, Eugenides has elevated (and reanimated) the dynamic of storytelling, constructing stories that enthrall Oprah's audience and texts that intrigue academics.

Selected Bibliography

WORKS OF JEFFREY EUGENIDES

NOVELS

The Virgin Suicides. New York: Farrar, Straus and Giroux, 1993; New York: Warner, 1993.

Middlesex. New York: Farrar, Straus and Giroux, 2002.

The Marriage Plot. New York: Farrar, Straus and Giroux, 2011.

OTHER WORKS

"The Father of Modernism." *Slate,* June 17, 2004. http://www.slate.com/articles/arts/culturebox/features/2004/the_father_of_modernism/the_carnival_of_bloomsday_and_the_death_of_the_western_novel.html.

My Mistress's Sparrow Is Dead. Editor. New York: Harper, 2008.

CRITICAL STUDIES

Banner, Olivia. "'Sing Now, O Muse, of the Recessive Mutation': Interrogating the Genetic Discourse of Sex Variation with Jeffrey Eugenides' *Middlesex*." *Signs* 35, no. 4:843–867 (summer 2010).

Carroll, Rachel. "Retrospective Sex: Rewriting Intersexuality in Jeffrey Eugenides's *Middlesex*." *Journal of American Studies* 44, no. 1:187–201 (2010).

Chu, Patricia E. "D(NA) Coding the Ethnic: Jeffrey Eugenides's *Middlesex*." *Novel* 42, no. 2:278–283 (summer 2009).

Cohen, Samuel. "The Novel in a Time of Terror: *Middlesex*, History, and Contemporary American Fiction." *Twentieth Century Literature* 53, no. 3:371–393 (fall 2007).

Graham, Sarah. "'See Synonyms at MONSTER': En-Freaking Transgender in Jeffrey Eugenides's *Middlesex*." *ARIEL* 40, no. 4:1–18 (October 2009).

Kelly, Adam. "Moments of Decision in Contemporary American Fiction: Roth, Auster, Eugenides." *Critique* 51, no. 4:313–332 (2010).

Lee, Merton. "Why Jeffrey Eugenides' *Middlesex* Is So Inoffensive." *Critique* 51, no. 1:32–46 (2009).

Mallory-Kani, Amy, and Kenneth Womack. "'Why Don't You Just Leave It up to Nature?': An Adaptationist Reading of the Novels of Jeffrey Eugenides." *Mosaic* 40, no. 3:157–174 (September 2007).

Shostak, Debra. "'A Story We Could Live With': Narrative Voice, the Reader, and Jeffrey Eugenides's *The Virgin Suicides*." *Modern Fiction Studies* 55, no. 4:808–832 (winter 2009).

INTERVIEWS

Brown, Mick. "Jeffrey Eugenides: Enduring Love." *Telegraph,* January 5, 2008. http://www.telegraph.co.uk/culture/3670336/Jeffrey-Eugenides-Enduring-love.html.

Eggers, David. "Jeffrey Eugenides Has It Both Ways." *PowellsBooks,* October 10, 2006. http://www.powells.com/blog/interviews/jeffrey-eugenides-has-it-both-ways-by-dave/.

Foer, Jonathan Safran. "Eugenides." *BOMB* 81:74–89 (fall 2002).

Miller, Laura. "Sex, Fate, and Zeus and Hera's Kinkiest Argument." *Salon,* October 8, 2002. http://www.dev10.salon.com/2002/10/08/eugenides_3/.

Von Moorhem, Bram. "The Novel as a Mental Picture of Its Era." *3:A.M.,* 2003. http://www.3ammagazine.com/litarchives/2003/sep/interview_jeffrey_eugenides.html.

FILM BASED ON THE WORK OF JEFFREY EUGENIDES

The Virgin Suicides. Direction and screenplay by Sofia Coppola. American Zoetrope, 1999.

DAVID FERRY

(1924—)

Daniel Bosch

DAVID FERRY IS a respected poet and translator of important poems by ancient and classical poets. His first book of poems, *On the Way to the Island,* was published by the Wesleyan Poetry Series in 1960. Ferry's auspicious publishing debut set a publishing standard from which he has not fallen; his rendering of *Gilgamesh* (1992) and his translations of volumes of Latin verse have been published by Farrar, Straus and Giroux, and his subsequent volumes of poems and translations have been published by the University of Chicago Press.

Ferry's gifts bore most of their fruit after his retirement from teaching, and his laurels—innumerable awards and fellowships—came late in life. For reasons he does not care to discuss in detail, he did not produce a book of his own poems during the period from 1959 until 1983. His participation in the poetry "business" in Boston and Cambridge was consistent (if somewhat recalcitrant), but the brighter light was almost always shining on another. Given that so much of Ferry's work is either a rendering or a translation of a masterwork by a great ancient or modern poet, you might begin to see why his standing as a poet in his own right has been somewhat obscured. Though it is deeply tied to personal experience, Ferry's work derives its energy from the play of sounds in and against the lines he makes, and it is emphatically literary, and therefore less likely to be popular in a half-century when antiliterary movements have held sway. Yet Ferry's superior accomplishment in verse is profoundly obvious, as his work bears out theories of intertextuality, slippery signifiers, and the death of the author that so preoccupied the literary criticism of his day. In the case of David Ferry, for nearly fifty years, a major American poet has been hidden in plain sight.

LIFE

David Russell Ferry was born in Orange, New Jersey, on March 5, 1924, into a prosperous upper-middle-class family. Ferry's paternal great-grandfather and grandfather were Methodist ministers, graduated from Wesleyan, but his uncle and his father were shepherded into business rather than academics or the ministry, and the Ferry brothers dealt in textiles. David was the younger brother to two sisters in the Ferrys' "not un-bookish" home, a place much enlivened by music, as Ferry's father moonlighted as a church organist.

Ferry matriculated at Amherst College in the fall of 1942 and by the end of his freshman year had been drafted for service in World War II. He was stationed in Britain as a member of the Army Air Corps, and he recalls that his "unheroic" wartime service allowed him a great deal of time to read. Following his discharge in 1946, Ferry returned to Amherst to complete his bachelor's degree. In the fall of 1948, Ferry began his studies toward a doctorate in English at Harvard University.

Ferry began to write poems during his graduate studies in Cambridge. Following completion of his coursework in 1952, Ferry was hired to teach at Wellesley College. Ferry's graduate studies culminated in a dissertation that he revised into a book of criticism, *The Limits of Mortality: An Essay on Wordsworth's Major Poems* (1959). On March 22, 1958, he married Anne Elizabeth Davidson (the literary scholar Anne Davidson Ferry, d. 2006); they would have two children, Elizabeth and Stephen. His success as a teacher at Wellesley and the positive reception of this first book led to retention and tenure, and he would remain at the heart of the English Department at Wellesley until his retirement in 1989. It

DAVID FERRY

is only since his retirement, says Ferry, that he has had a "career" as a writer. He continues to write and to translate and to teach (part-time and as a visiting artist) at Boston University and Suffolk University.

THE LIMITS OF MORTALITY: AN ESSAY ON WORDSWORTH'S MAJOR POEMS

Ferry's dissertation develops a case for a conflicted William Wordsworth whose works are "lovingly hostile" to a humanity which has achieved, at great cost, its "successes"— enlightenment, and progress, and industrialization. Thus an explicitly approving portrait of London in the famous sonnet "Upon Westminster Bridge," for example, must be understood to bear witness to Wordsworth's aversion to London as a product of commerce and industry. The speaker of this poem, Ferry argues, can utter the compliments in the poem only when he is looking at a city which for the moment is anything but its smoke-filled, soul-destroying cosmopolitan self. The Wordsworth whom Ferry discovers in his book is aware of the terrors that follow whenever the "mighty heart" of London beats with a strong rhythm; he is also aware that this rhythm is seductive. The stillness that enables London's apparent transformation into a thing of beauty is its death.

After getting tenure at Wellesley, but not necessarily because of his reaching that milestone, Ferry no longer put the balance of his work efforts into scholarship. *The Limits of Mortality* is a powerful reading of Wordsworth, but it is significant chiefly for the ways in which it built a foundation for several of Ferry's lifelong concerns as a poet, especially the sight of death as a prompt for confusion and the articulation of poetic utterance that issues from mixed emotions and internal conflict.

ON THE WAY TO THE ISLAND

Two powerful, nearly contrary impressions of *On the Way to the Island* (1960) are difficult to reconcile. On the one hand, with the exception of

its consistent employment of iambic pentameter, nothing about the book indicates that Ferry will go on to produce the work that characterizes his oeuvre. Each of the poems is well made. The tone overall is rarefied and intellectual, if not academic. Even when the poems are very grave, or very sassy, they are so well-mannered that one forgets about actual speech, especially the sounds of the fragments and sentences people utter when they are full of feeling. Some of *On the Way to the Island* is a bit like Versailles—a "built" environment in which we can't recall raw stones and trees. Though the same could be said of many of the books published by university presses at the time, Ferry's first book is the kind that Beat poets denigrated as stuffy "establishment" poetry, or that Robert Bly and the Deep Image poets would soon be denigrating as a poetry that fails to "leap" or is out of touch with "twofold consciousness." Ferry's work will never again feel this way.

At the same time, all of the most important approaches to poem-making that will prove to be the making of Ferry's life's work are present in *On the Way to the Island* in pure, clear, mature forms. The use of iambic pentameter, especially, is exquisite and already distinctive. The book is dedicated "For A.D.F." (Anne Davidson Ferry), and a strong thread of poems ("Adam's Dream," "To the Fabulous Constellation," "Elegiac," "Descriptive," "Out of That Sea," "On the Way to the Island") develops an eclogue-like Edenic pastoral theme in which the speaker is an Adam and his spouse/partner/helpmeet is an Eve; it is hard to read these poems about how two persons in love constitute a world without feeling their connection to both Ferry's Virgil pastorals and his late poems of loss.

"To the Fabulous Constellation" and "Elegiac" are pendant versions of each other, printed on facing pages so we can't miss their interdependency, and with this gesture Ferry initiates his lifelong investment in working serially, in related poems that generate and share pieces of language and imagery. His so openly and deliberately returning to a bit of fructifying language testifies to an early lack of anxiety on Ferry's part—he

has already cast off any naive notions regarding the originality of individual poems.

On the Way to the Island is carefully crafted to be experienced as a book, rather than merely a collection of poems, and this is emphatically true of all of Ferry's books. That Ferry has translated so many books that are *books,* not miscellanies or collections, has reinforced his aesthetic concern for the structures of whole volumes, but it was there at the start.

The initial poem, "The Embarkation for Cythera," depicts a scene that evokes the title of the book—a group of dandies headed to an island, as rendered by Jean-Antoine Watteau in his painting of that name. This ekphrastic poem establishes Ferry's lifelong commitment to writing in response to works of visual art, a subgenre that verges on translation. From this first instance, Ferry's ekphrastic work is respectful of the reader's own capacity to look at and to grasp the details of the artwork under consideration. His poem is the stronger for the fiction it offers, and our engagement with the speaker, who delights in his departures from the Watteau, is the center of our experience of the poem. Perhaps the speaker is too like one of the cheating lords that he sees in the painting—too confident that he holds the cards he needs and therefore repellent in his eagerness to get laid. Yet, to Ferry's credit, it is not easy to tell if the characterization of this speaker is a deliberate criticism of proto-bourgeois—and thus, bourgeois—entertainments.

All the poems in *On the Way to the Island* might be said to be embarking for Cythera. And reading them, are we not all in the same boat—pursuing, in our ways, the venerable and venereal pleasures we prefer? Questions of empathy, and sympathy, especially for those who are on the skids, homeless, and alcoholic, is a consistent theme in Ferry's oeuvre, and it finds its first of many direct expressions in the poem "At a Low Bar":

While in a bar I bore
Indignity with those
Others whose hearts were sore ...

(p. 40)

When Ferry has republished this poem in later volumes, he has suppressed the "Low" in the title, as if he has come to regret its implication that the speaker of this poem has descended from a higher place to be with the losers in such a dive. Ferry's later poems regarding people who suffer in such ways show a much greater degree of imaginative engagement with and empathetic understanding of their troubles, and the later poems on such people are so passionately spoken that they sidestep any question of condescension.

Whatever the title, this poem participates in a career-long exploration by Ferry of the limits of human knowledge. Over the next sixty years he will consistently create and re-create speakers who move us with the language they use to express how lost they feel, how uncertain they are, how the things they have counted on for their entire lives have slipped or shifted, how little they know except that their humanity is in part constituted by their ignorance. Ferry's exploration of this aspect of the human condition is in part temperamental: "lovingly hostile," even toward his self, he is very apt, in conversation, to remind interviewers that he knows nothing at all, and has read very little.

The most surprising thing about *On the Way to the Island* is that it contains only a single translation, a marvelous poem by the great sixteenth-century French poet Pierre de Ronsard, which is given permanent form in Ferry's English. Neither Ferry nor the reader of *On the Way to the Island* could possibly have imagined that this single translation would be the beginning of a creative life that would be so focused on re-creating great works of the past.

STRANGERS: A BOOK OF POEMS

David Ferry's second book, *Strangers* (1983), broke a twenty-three-year-long poetry silence. The length of time he took to put *Strangers* together is not the only indication that it is carefully made. Prominently printed in large type on the back of the book is a note from Ferry which is worth presenting in full:

The only thing I would want to say to a prospective reader of *Strangers* is this: my ambition has been to complete a book that is really a book, not just a collection of miscellaneous pieces. That is to say, the poems are intended to be highly resonant of one another, more and more so as you read consecutively, and all of them are intended to be responsive to the title and epigraph of the volume. At the same time I have tried for a persisting variety, so that I wouldn't ever seem to have written the same poem twice and so that there would be the least possible wasted motion.

It is an odd notion, a gathering of "strangers." Ferry invites the reader to ask, "Different as they are, what mutual interest(s) do these poems have in common?"

The epigraph referred to by Ferry is from a May 13, 1595, entry in *The Diary of Samuel Ward:* "Think thou how that this is not our home in this world, in which we are strangers, ones not knowing another's speech and language." The poems in *Strangers* can be read as "strangers"; employing Ward's sense of the term, the poems are like Christian souls, displaced—homeless for the human time being, and longing for a coming (millennial) restoration. But it seems more likely that Ferry means for us to hear echoes of an earlier loss, a Babel-like strangeness in the sounds of each of our different tongues. The different poems and sections of poems in *Strangers* are in this way newly estranged languages or sets of language games; for all we know, the condition will be permanent and can be ameliorated only by translation.

The thirty-two poems in *Strangers* develop several of the principal modes in Ferry's first book. The collection contains translations (including, notably, Horace's ode "To Sestius") derived from classical and modern sources; poems that address works of art; poems that cast Ferry and his wife, Anne, as figures in brief pastorals, as if in Eden; brief, quiet poems that address the death of Ferry's sister, Elizabeth; and poems (like "Table Talk" or "Cythera" or, in a reflexive mode, "A Charm") that are concerned with persons who are suffering, or lost. The theme from his first poems that receives a full-throated exploration in *Strangers* is the notion that human knowledge is extremely limited.

The language of *Strangers* is very different from the language of *On the Way to the Island*; both diction and imagery are less ornate, as if Ferry is now intent on evoking contemporary speech. The poem "A Night-Time River Road" opens with the theme of "not knowing," which will from now on undergird all of Ferry's poems:

We were driving down a road.
Where was it we were going?
Where were we going to?
Nobody knew.

(*Strangers*, p. 8)

Ferry has made the poem feel like it is a vision of a late-twentieth-century or early-twenty-first-century American family—each member speaking a language different from the others. (Stoned? Or reading a comic book? Or listening to private skull candy in the back seat?) Here "driver" is enlarged to "d(ark) river," as what is seen fills up the silences inside the car. Later poems in the book refer to data sets that cannot be fully grasped. And on the last page of the book, even poetry is characterized as inscrutable, especially as it is rendered in a schoolroom, where it is the cause of yellow chalk dust: "Looking back, the language scribbles" (p. 48). Perhaps Ferry's growing sense that knowledge is limited encouraged him to root out and banish the speaker of "The Embarkation for Cythera" and his ilk. These poems' confidence does not reside in the notion that any one of us has an advantage. As Horace has it, in Ferry's translation, "Revenant white-faced death is walking not knowing whether / He's going to knock at a rich man's door or a poor man's" (p. 31).

GILGAMESH: A NEW RENDERING IN ENGLISH VERSE

Being a poet, and being attached to the Department of English and American Literature at Harvard University through his wife, Anne, Ferry became close friends with William L. Moran, Harvard's doyen of ancient Akkadian and Sumerian literature and language. Moran gave Ferry the assignment to translate a tablet from the Akkadian epic, and Ferry got hooked.

DAVID FERRY

There was no question of Ferry trying to learn to read the cuneiform; Moran provided a word-for-word "trot" of the tablets he assigned and told Ferry where to look for English translations by earlier scholars and poets. Few translators of Akkadian into English verse have entered into that craft with Ferry's conscientious sense of the powers of verse, and of iambic pentameter in particular, and even fewer translators have started out with such a wealth of circumstantial assistance.

Taking on Moran's "assignment" of *Gilgamesh,* completed and published in 1992, proved to be a turning point in Ferry's writing life; fittingly enough, given the story, it marks a rebirth. Ferry punningly calls his version of the epic a "rendering"—to emphasize how he feels he has reduced the scope and power of the original—and in his rendering he was quite free from any sense of having to try to reproduce visible patterns of language like rhymes and recurrent clausal arrangements. (This would not be the case in a conscientious translation from, say, Latin, or German, or Spanish.) Nor did Ferry feel responsible to re-create in some deliberate and obvious way the alliterative effects that characterize ancient Akkadian verses. Ferry sought a prosody stately yet flexible, and turning to his own English language tradition, he refined his iambic pentameter, adding a higher tolerance for substitution and a particular emphasis on the repetition of phrases within lines and across enjambments without giving up his ability to sound out subtler music or quieter scenes. Ferry also took special care to avoid a prosody that implies that because the *Gilgamesh* epic is ancient it is in any way "primitive."

The prosody in his *Gilgamesh,* so very like linear tile-work, will become Ferry's strongest and most distinctive mode. The brief passage quoted below is not enough evidence to allow one to infer how the prosody structures much more than the individual line, as when the syllable "keep" is laid down twice at the end of the first line. The profounder effects can only be felt over longer passages where lapidary repetition is built into the muscles of the verse. The best way to feel Ferry's accomplishment in *Gilgamesh* and elsewhere is to read the poem aloud:

> Veiled Siduri, a tavern keeper, keeps
> a tavern on the shore of the glittering sea.
>
> They have given a golden mixing-bowl to her
> and an ale-flagon. She gazed along the shore;
>
> she gazed and gazed and saw that there was coming
> along the shore a hairy-bodied man,
>
> a wanderer, who was wearing an animal skin,
> coming toward her tavern along the shore.
>
> (Tablet X, part i, p. 54)

The sonic density achieved by Ferry's placement of particular syllables in lines is distinct from but plays with and against the repetition of names, epithets, and descriptions that are built into the structure of the epic—especially so in those passages where Gilgamesh identifies himself (to Siduri, to Urshànabi, and to Utnapishtim) as a prerequisite for the unfolding of the next episode in the tale. This is not the emphatically alliterative sound of the Akkadian original. It is iambic pentameter, the most common measure of the English verse tradition, but it feels renewed here by its interaction with *Gilgamesh* and with Ferry.

The composer of this *Gilgamesh* is clearly not the same line- and stanza-maker who published *On the Way to the Island* in 1960, but the Akkadian epic gave Ferry opportunities to work on familiar topoi. Grief-stricken Gilgamesh seeks refuge in, and is welcomed to, a tavern, where he might become inebriated, where he might reflect on his own condition and on the condition of humanity, and here we are not so far from "In a Low Bar." And in telling the tale of how "wild" Enkidu is bewildered upon his entrance to urban, cultured Uruk, and then subdued by its king, with whom he is reconciled and conjoined, Ferry expands a career-long meditation on the limits of human understanding. The superhuman figure who emerges from this reconciliation, and whom we might call "Gilgamesh-Enkidu"—one who seems to know what to do when faced with all manner of difficult challenges—is, however, unlike any other figure in Ferry's oeuvre.

DAVID FERRY

DWELLING PLACES: POEMS AND TRANSLATIONS

Dwelling Places (1993) might have made it seem as if Ferry had been studying up on hybridity. The book's mixing of translations and "original" poems ran against the grain of discourse about contemporary poetry in 1993, just as it would today. Such a mixture confuses; for in spite of their graduate school training, many literary journalists and reviewers naively consider translations to be by definition so derivative that little credit for their excellence as poems may be given to the translator, and "original" poems to be by definition wholly original. The critical professions have theorized a pervasive intertextuality but have yet to invent a responsible method for explicating intertextual practices—especially translinguistic practices such as Ferry's.

Dwelling Places is made up of thirty-two poems in four sections followed by a brief envoi. The epigraph, from St. Paul's First Epistle to the Corinthians, is the source of the title and names a central preoccupation of the book: "Even unto this present hour we hunger, and thirst, and are naked, and are buffeted, and have no certain dwelling place." This third book of poems by Ferry might be said to show that his authorial position has "no certain dwelling place," moving as it does back and forth across the waters separating one language and one time from another. It is the mobility exercised by Friedrich Hölderlin in his "Mnemosyne," when his speaker moves from the early nineteenth-century present to a battlefield from the *Iliad,* where, in Ferry's translation, he surveys the corpses of heroes, some "astonished in the bloodsoaked field," and "others, in torment and bewilderment, / by their own hand, compelled by heaven" (p. 44).

In the notes at the end of the volume, Ferry enumerates three distinct modes of translation, but only to say that he has not indicated (and will not indicate) to the reader which of the translations in the book are which. *Dwelling Places* offers "close translations," "freer renderings," and "still freer adaptations" of poems by Poliziano, Hölderlin, Charles Baudelaire (two), Rainer Maria Rilke (two), Samuel Johnson, Johann Wolfgang von Goethe, a Goliardic poet,

Jorge Guillén (a colleague of Ferry's at Wellesley), an anonymous medieval German poet, and from Akkadian (again with assistance from William Moran). His decision to translate a poem by Johnson, a great English precursor who also wrote in Latin, runs almost perversely against the grain: these days Johnson is better remembered as a lexicographer than as a poet, and now that Latin is no longer a nearly universal language of the poetry audience, it may seem that for Johnson to have composed "original" poems in Latin was to hide his light under a bushel basket—a choice not all that different from Ferry's espousal of translation.

Outside of *Gilgamesh, Dwelling Places* contains perhaps Ferry's strongest explorations of speakers who are hungry, thirsty, naked, and buffeted by voices and urges that suggest multiple senses of self. "The Guest Ellen at the Supper for Street People" is a perfect example of the best of Ferry's work in *Dwelling Places* and in this period. It is a sestina, and one in which Ferry has upped the rhetorical ante. The bane of the sestina is gibberish induced by the six repetons. But Ferry's sestina is a portrait of a woman who speaks powerful nonsense, and his deliberate overloading of the form with additional repetition makes her come more clearly into focus. Ellen is as tormented as the language in a sestina, in that she is forever caught in the cycling terms of her own discourses. The stanza sampled below gives a sense of how entranced Ellen is. Note also the simplicity of Ferry's contemporary diction. The poem has become something of a reading piece for Ferry, one that proves the relevance of older forms for modern realities:

> enchanted, still in the old forgotten event
> a prisoner of love, filthy Ellen in her torment,
> guest Ellen in the dining hall in her body,
> hands beating the air in her enchantment,
> sitting alone, gabbling in her garbled voice
> the narrative of the spirits of the unclean.
>
> (p. 7)

"The Guest Ellen ..." is one of the first of Ferry's poems that is recognizably from first line to last a Ferry poem. The lines are taut and draw from a highly charged set of terms that the poem itself

has charged. It participates in the development of several of his principal themes—the speaker is a kind of translator, Ellen is someone whom we cannot "know"—and, along with such poems as "In a (Low) Bar," "Movie Star Peter at the Supper for Street People," "Coffee Lips," and "Song of the Drunkard," is perhaps the most eloquent of his poems on the topos of individual human suffering.

Ferry's aesthetic has always in view the more classical aspect of the tensions that make some "confessional" poetry excellent—the aspect Robert Lowell put into words in his famous injunction that "A poem is an event, not the record of an event," to which Ferry refers, obliquely but unmistakably, in "In the Garden":

The whole plucked stalk is an event in time:
a number of blossoms one above the other,
but some blossoms more fully out than others,
in an intricately regular scale or series.
Of course, since the flower is plucked, it isn't really
an event in time, but only the record of an event.

(p. 36)

Lowell means to remind readers, who are ever-assaulted by and frequently overimpressed by the seeming power of prose declarations about the world, that poetry is distinct from and more powerful than prose. A description in prose—no matter how nicely done—of a sixty-nine-year-old man sitting in his garden to read the poems of Edward Thomas would not *happen* as Ferry's poem does in and through his lines. He has imported (stolen and hybridized) a bit of Lowell's language to remind us, if a pun may be forgiven, that we must not be "impatiens" with verse, because its language is not transparent and its effects must take place over time. The triviality of the narrative of "In the Garden" is part of this subtle exchange with Lowell, and with Virgil of the *Georgics,* who will soon come to be so important for Ferry. The linear furrows of the farmer are conflated here with the verses of the poet. (Thomas makes the same conflation in his gorgeous poem "As the Team's Head-Brass.") A poet minds his garden not to make it as productive of facts and fruit as a Roman farm but to make verses, to turn lines of sound back on each

other so that he listens, or appears to be listening, to "a subtle, brilliant, and a shadowy idea" (p. 37).

THE ODES OF HORACE

Ferry has said that he considers Horace's *Odes* to be the single best book of poetry ever made. And given Horace's place in the history of literature and especially in the history of education in western Europe—for decades in the West, to have been educated meant to have grappled with Horace's ornate syntax and careful diction in Latin translation exercises—Ferry would have expected any expedition into Horace territory to be much criticized.

Ferry's translations in *The Odes of Horace* (1997) draw on the lapidary prosodic strengths developed and refined in his work on the epic of *Gilgamesh.* For those readers who love the book, such as the classical scholars Bernard Knox or Donald Carne-Ross or the poet Mark Rudman, Ferry's translations have made Horace contemporary. Ferry's account of his approach to the *Odes,* from the "Note on the Translations" in the volume, sets his task as a poet in English and anticipates the critics who would want their Horace to be as difficult to understand in translation as he was back in Latin class:

In these translations I have tried, generally speaking, to be as faithful as I could be to Horace's poems. English of course is not Latin and I am most certainly not Horace. Every act of translation is an act of interpretation, and every choice of English word or phrase, every placement of those words or phrases in sentences—made in obedience to the laws and habits of English, not Latin, grammar, syntax, and idioms—and every metrical decision—made in obedience to English, not Latin, metrical laws and habits—reinforces the differences between the interpretation and the original.... There are a few places where I have, however, deliberately gone pretty far away from the Latin poem, by substitution or by omission ... [when] I thought that stricter faithfulness would have made it more difficult to produce a viable English poem. Several times I have provided an anachronistically modern equivalent for something ancient and unfamiliar, for

example, "Ouija board" for "Babylonian numbers."
... But there are not many such places.

(pp. xiv–xv)

Latin scholars tend to agree with Horace (see Ode 3.30) that Horace is capable of monumental success in verse and that his poems are without exception worth reading and, with surprisingly high frequency, superb. Thus the crucial criterion from Ferry's "Note" above is the phrase "viable English poem." A reader of *The Odes of Horace* must ask if each of Ferry's translations is a poem in English, and they must take into account, as they make up their answers to that question, their assessments of how Ferry's prosodic choices (lines, line breaks, sentence syntax, diction, sonic density, etc.) work in English, not Latin, verse.

Twenty-seven of the *Odes* are in Sapphic stanzas, a form that Horace inherited from his Greek precursors. Ferry employs a Sapphic (or pseudo-Sapphic) stanza many times in *The Odes of Horace,* but he also gives himself free rein to borrow, adapt, and invent stanza forms that he feels will help him to create a "viable English poem." A compelling example of such invention is his handling of the shape of the famous Ode 1.14 ("To the Republic") in which Horace compares the state of Rome to a storm-tossed ship at sea. The original Latin poem is in six four-line Sapphic stanzas, but Ferry's translation is in ten widely spaced lines, some of which have three complete clauses per line (e.g., "Your sails are torn! Your masts are shaking! Your oars are gone!" [p. 43]). Such freedoms must be hard won. No doubt the weight of accumulated centuries of translation of this particular poem made it an even more likely candidate for Ferry's exercise of such bold formal innovation.

Ferry's work makes it clear that if we are talking about the creation of truly beautiful verbal objects, the divide between "translator" and "poet" is artificial and cannot logically be maintained. One implication of this claim is that in composing his translations of the *Odes,* Ferry was writing his own poems. How good is Ferry's work on the *Odes* vis-à-vis the work of other contemporary poets working under the constraints of the same *Odes*? Let us compare several brief passages of Ferry's versions of four different

Odes with the same passages handled by very different contemporary translators.

Ode 1.25, "To Lydia," in the translation by Heather McHugh, is literary and fanciful, imagining that the *sound* of horny young men's voices can move not only an aging slattern but, improbably, the shutters on her second-story windows:

How seldom now the shutters rattle
with your lovers' shouts;
how rarely do you lose your sleep
to hot young blood and clamor.
The very door that willingly
indulged their ins and outs
is nowadays of still and stiller
liminals enamored.

(McClatchy, ed., p. 75)

Ferry has found a much more colloquial way to express Lydia's predicament:

It happens less and less often, now, that you
Wake up to hear the sound of gravel thrown

Against your shuttered windows in the night.
It's very seldom, now, that you can't sleep

The whole night through. There used to be a time
The hinges of the door to your house moved ever so

Easily back and forth. Not anymore.

(p. 67)

In a translation of Ode 1.4, "To Sestius," by James Lasdun, several of the lines—especially 1, 3, and 4—alliterate around medial pauses as if influenced by Anglo-Saxon prosody, and this may give readers of English a sense of the age and gravity of Horace:

Winter's melting in the mild west wind;
time to haul the dry-docked boats to the shore.
The farmer has cabin fever; his pent-up flocks
are itching for the meadow, and the meadow's
greening already in its morning thaw.

(McClatchy, ed., p. 27)

Note how odd it seems to have dry docks somewhere other than the shore, and for a farmer to lodge in cabin. Ferry's version, with its single long sentence, also puts hard pressure upon

DAVID FERRY

deliberate caesurae, but there's no hint of Anglo-Saxon epic, and the details of the scene are all in order:

> Now the hard winter is breaking up with the welcome coming
> Of spring and the spring winds; some fishermen,
> Under a sky that looks changed, are hauling their caulked boats
> Down to the water; in the winter stables the cattle
> Are restless; so is the farmer sitting in front of his fire;
> They want to be out of doors in field or pasture;
> The frost is gone from the meadow grass in the early mornings.
>
> (p. 15)

When Richard Howard takes on Ode 4.10, "To Ligurinus," the poem feels libertine, and the erotic charge charges Howard with the urge to take liberties:

> Cocksure and licensed so by Venus' gifts,
> What'll you say to your glass, Ligurinus,
> When "feathers" first poke through unbroken cheeks,
> When a perfect complexion shows … imperfections
> And curls once falling to your shoulders have … fallen?
> That boy can't fathom today's experience;
> Yesterday's flesh can't furbish this strange man.
> "I am," you'll say, "no longer one and the same."
>
> (McClatchy, ed., p. 289)

The forwardness of the play on "cocksure" is delicious in its indelicacy. But for all of Howard's experience in creating plausible voices for historical or literary characters, his translation of the sense at the end of this passage is so aphoristic and artificial as to be nonsensical. Ferry's poem is more accessibly humane, and the confusion of the speaker at the end of the passage is masterfully conveyed in the eye-rhyme and the careful near-echoes of the syllables "know" and "now" and "how":

> Still cruel and still endowed with the power to be so,
> Gifted as you are with the gifts of Venus,
> That moment is coming, when, suddenly, in the glass,
> You see beginning the little signs of change,
> Downy foreshadowing of the beard to come,
> The locks that curl and wanton to the shoulders

> All of a sudden looking a little different,
> The cream-and-rose complexion beyond the beauty
> Of freshest roses now not quite exactly
> The way it had been just yesterday morning.
> Then you will say, Alas for what I was
> When I was younger than I am, Alas
> That then I did not know what I know now;
> Alas, that now I know what I did not know.
>
> (p. 295)

His use of the bawdy register for "endowed" is not nearly so "cocksure" as Howard's choice, but neither does it tip this ode out of balance.

Charles Wright's version of Ode 4.12, "To Virgil," pursues a pseudo-Sapphic stanzaic form, with the fourth line curtailed.

> Already the winds of Thrace, spring's attendant ecstasy,
> Damp down the waves and the sea and swell the sails,
> Meadows shrink back in thaw, rivers quieten their moan,
> Lacking winter's melt.
>
> The swallow comes back and builds her nest again,
> Unfortunate bird, still grieving for luckless Itys,
> Still bearing the endless shame of over-vengefulness
> On her sadistic and lustful king.
>
> (McClatchy, ed., p. 295)

Wright's handling of Horace's images here is not clear—how, for example, do winds "damp down the waves and the sea," instead of increasing turbulence? And his diction choices set the poem into a strange intermediate temporality: "quieten" certainly suggests that he's not trying to make a viable contemporary English poem. Ferry's translation is crystal clear by comparison, and his first six lines set the scene for the poem as they are supposed to do:

> Now the light tempering breezes, agents of Spring,
> Are coming down from the fields of Thrace to fill
> The sails of the little boats, so that at last
>
> They begin to move about on the bay's calm waters.
> The ice has gone from the fields; last week the roar
> Of the rivers swollen with snow began to lessen.
>
> (p. 301)

DAVID FERRY

Ferry's translations of *The Odes of Horace* cemented his reputation as a translator. I have cherry-picked the passages above not only to show that Ferry's versions are clearer and better imagined, but to demonstrate some of the wide variety of approaches Ferry was capable of bringing to the *Odes.* What is admirable in a single dose may wear quite thin in an entire volume. Most self-respecting late-twentieth-century poets are hardly prepared to resist their desires always to go on sounding like themselves.

THE ECLOGUES OF VIRGIL

The ten substantial poems we know as the *Eclogues* were completed and gathered in the mid-thirties BCE under the Latin title *Bucolica,* Virgil's first published book. Along with the poems of Theocritus and with some of the *Epistles* of Horace, they helped to found the pastoral tradition, with the eclogue as a subgenre of pastoral in which country speakers meet in an ideal place (an Arcadia, or an Eden) and discourse rather amiably, sometimes getting cranky, sometimes bursting into song, and often with the explicit objective of denigrating the ways of the city and praising the country life. Frequently, however, an underlying purpose of these speeches is trenchant social or political commentary on contemporary matters of grave importance. Ferry's translation of these works, published in 1999, is his first excursion into the creation of voices for characters whose exchanges change those characters or suggest that the social-emotional world in the poem is altered by the utterances of the poem.

Virgil's *Eclogues* are delightful poems, and the volume is a true book, the fabric of which makes the individual poems more beautiful; the book would be a permanent contribution to literature if Virgil had never written another. Still, since each of Virgil's books is his training ground for the next, it makes sense to see Ferry's translation of the *Eclogues* as the training ground for his eventual complete conquest, in chronological order, of all of Virgil's poems, of his manners of thinking and his styles, a conquest which will be completed with his translation of the *Aeneid,* due in 2016.

One of the ways that Virgil's *Eclogues* differ from Horace's *Odes* is in how the dramatic sites of the poem may be conjured as if in a vacuum. Setting is assumed, speakers are types (or stereotypes), background histories are left unstated. Such a vacuum focuses the reader on the character of the verbal exchanges that Virgil has chosen and created with such particular care. In Virgil's Third Eclogue, which is drawn from Theocritus' first Idyll for example, two country bumpkins, the shepherds Menalcas and Damoetas, all of a sudden appear together in the same pasture. A little verbal sparring leads the two shepherds to pit themselves against each other in a singing contest, and a passerby, Palaemon, who appears out of nowhere and seems to have nothing else to do, agrees to play the role of audience/judge. There is mention of caves and sheep and cattle—*recalled* rather than present caves and sheep and cattle—but the efficiencies of the poem preclude any real attempt to ground it in "reality." The spareness of setting and "props" is crucial to the eclogue, is part of how it insists on the primacy of fictive song. Twelve times the shepherds take their turns singing couplets, responding to the other and egging the other on; in the similarity of their verses Virgil is building a single song, a tense comic duet more than a contest, and part of the fun is the rigidity of Virgil's measures for each shepherd. "Go on, sing to distinguish yourselves, boys," seems to be Virgil's attitude, "but if you make song your individuality will be compromised, for success in poetry is not your own, but the tradition's."

A passage in Ferry's translation illustrates this. The exchange of couplets here recalls the Greek dramatic trope, stichomythia, which typically accelerates the building of tension in a discussion, except that when like characters exchange like-sounding bits of song in the same measures, as here, static builds in the transmissions. The boys give so much advice in such repetitive forms that the advice is almost emptied of content:

DAMOETAS
"You boys gathering flowers and picking strawberries,

DAVID FERRY

Watch out, watch out, there's a cold snake in the
grass."

MENALCAS
"Don't go too near the riverbank, my sheep;
The river's high; the ram has gotten wet."

(pp. 26–27)

The Third Eclogue is particularly trenchant for
Ferry because in it singers sing and are apparently judged but neither one of them emerges the
victor, and because the judge seems to be in possession of a principle that could have foreclosed
the singing contest altogether. The situation is
drastically ambiguous. Was there more—or
less—ambiguity at the sites of judgment of
contemporary American poetry in the 1980s and
1990s? One imagines that David Ferry, living in
Harvard Square and participating in the lively
poetry scene at Harvard, Boston University, Bran-
deis, M.I.T., Tufts, Boston College, and Wellesley, would be acutely aware of the uses and
abuses of judgment whenever the shepherds got
together to sing.

OF NO COUNTRY I KNOW: NEW AND
SELECTED POEMS AND TRANSLATIONS

Just as a painter with thirty or more years of
work under her belt might be the subject of a
major retrospective in a museum large enough to
house most of the canvasses to date in contigu-
ous rooms, Ferry published the nearly three-
hundred-page *Of No Country I Know* with the
University of Chicago Press in 1999. A brief
foreword by the poet, memoirist, and novelist
Alan Shapiro introduces the reader to eight carefully curated "rooms" of Ferry's work. Twenty-
nine "New Poems and Translations"—a selection
as big as a typical single volume of poems—
come first, followed by Ferry's generous selections from *On the Way to the Island, Strangers,*
and *Dwelling Places.*

There are not only new poems but new
sounds in *Of No Country I Know.* Most welcome
is that in this book Ferry's mordant sense of
humor is allowed a generous share of the
spotlight. "The License Plate," for example,
reflects humorously on the text of a "vanity" plate

that reads "GOD HAS." Ferry's speaker responds:
"Has what? / Decided finally what to do about
it? // The answer to the question that you asked? /
... Fucked up? Again?" (p. 21). An exegesis of a
text only six letters long, "The License Plate"
generates an enormous range in just about the
fewest and clearest terms possible. Ferry's soul-
ful wit mocks the text even as it respectfully
acknowledges the constraint imposed on any
automobile owner who would be memorable in
the space provided.

Of No Country I Know was the winner of
several prestigious prizes, and those who know
Ferry's work generally know it through the
volume's expansive breadth. The poems in *Of No
Country I Know* inspired the poet and translator
Rachel Hadas to compose an homage to Ferry,
published in the *New Criterion* in February 2000,
that reads, in part, "The words run clear like
water in these poems. / The fluency feels generous and easy ..." (p. 30). This fluency is like that
referred to in W. B. Yeats's great poem "Adam's
Curse," the fluency which doesn't acknowledge
how much labor went into its achievement. It
also did not directly indicate that it was a fluency
that was only going to get stronger.

THE EPISTLES OF HORACE

Ferry would have gone on to translate *The
Epistles of Horace* (2001) even if his work on
the *Odes* had not been recognized as successful.
The years he spent in hearing and thinking
through, in English, the complex imagination
bodied forth in the *Odes,* and the skills he
advanced as he responded to Horace's Latin diction and prosody, developed in Ferry gifts similar
to yet distinct from those produced by his work
on the *Gilgamesh* tablets, for the impossibility of
his reading the cuneiform original text set for
him sharply different artistic parameters. To have
proceeded in the other direction, to have trained
for the *Epistles* by writing the *Odes,* would have
been a bit like training for fifty-meter sprints by
running half-marathons.

The *Epistles* are personal letters in verse.
Ferry's translations of the *Epistles* aim to capture

157

what he calls the "voice" of Horace the letter writer, but there are twenty-three verse letters in all, and there is little reason to expect that Horace's "voice" be the same when he writes to a good friend as when he writes to the emperor, or that the "voice" he creates in composing a brief note to his patron, Maecenus, should sound identical to that in a letter addressed to one of his books. The different Horaces Ferry allows his *Epistles* to sound contribute to the intense pleasure of reading the book. Two examples must point from here to the full texts where readers might get some sense of the range of these distinct facets of Horace. In a very direct note of nineteen lines written to Horace's pal Vinius Asina, Ferry finds a Horace who is playful, anxious, solicitous, humble by turns, grateful for a favor, but also a condescending and controlling tease:

Just as I've told you over and over, Vinny,
Deliver these books of mine to Augustus only
If you know for sure that he's in good health and
  only
If you know for sure that he's in a good mood and
  only
If it comes about that he asks in person to see it.

(1.13, p. 59)

The letter is a virtuoso performance. Ferry takes thirty-two lines to accomplish his translation of Horace's nineteen lines, and in this ratio we find a sort of a general rule for his work from Latin originals which are so exquisitely concise. Ferry's translation is short enough to preserve the brevity of the poem's "moment": keeping the poem short is part of making it sound just like how a buddy might address a buddy on whom he is relying for help with a particular step in the advancement of his career.

Epistle 2.2, written to Horace's friend Julius Florus, begins with couple of gorgeously phrased thought experiments, brief stories meant to serve as guides for how Julius ought to forgive Horace for having failed to write more often. There is no twentieth-century effort to inform or to be "newsy," so that Horace's use of lines very deliberately and very satisfyingly blurs the line (if there was one, in the first century BCE) between letter writing and poem writing. The theme of 2.2, in the smallest of nutshells, is "how to live, and how hard it is to do that well." The question of writing—or not writing—is the point of embarkation, and writing continues to be the principal reference point. Horace is considerably invested in the notion of self-management, or self-criticism, to the extent that he claims that a person has a personal god "Who dies in a sense when your own breath gives out" (p. 147). This god is both support and critic to a person. And even when Horace is extremely critical of people who "write bad poetry," there is in the letter the sense that everybody who writes any poetry at all writes some "bad poetry," they just don't mistake it for good poetry (or at least they do not do so for very long).

People who write bad poetry are a joke,
But writing makes them happy and it makes them
Happily reverential of themselves.
If they hear no praise from you, what do they care?
Deaf to your silence they'll praise themselves,
  serenely.

(p. 140)

A characteristic bit of David Ferry prosody appears in lines 2 and 3, where his Horace says of bad poets that "writing makes them happy and it makes them." The repetition of the verb and pronoun "makes them" makes the silly bad poets doubly happy, and when the end of that line is enjambed into "Happily reverential of themselves" the effect is doubled again, such that we can feel how all that self-pleasuring is the more emphatically to be avoided. And Ferry's manipulation of the iambic pentameter that undergirds these lines is a fitting recapitulation of the advice Horace offers. Though a measure is relatively strictly enforced in this passage, and though iambs are audible ("... new words in poetry"), perfect ticktock iambics are deferred at every point, until the final line—a line through which Ferry mocks any "oafish" perfection.

THE GEORGICS OF VIRGIL

No less sophisticated a critic than John Dryden called Virgil's *Georgics,* which he translated into English in 1697, "the best poem by the best

poet," and he wasn't responding only to the master's control of prosody, or what he might have called "numbers." The *Georgics'* combination of instruction in country arts and sciences and digression into mythology and politics have influenced the imaginations of Edmund Spenser, William Shakespeare, Ben Jonson, John Milton, George Crabbe, William Blake, James Thomson, John Keats, William Wordsworth, and perhaps most important for David Ferry, Robert Frost. Yet the "numbers" of Virgil's *Georgics* are impressive indeed. A total of 2,188 perfectly modulated hexameters unroll in column after column in the four books. In his *Georgics of Virgil* (2006), it was Ferry's task to try to convey some of the stateliness (derived from strictness) and power (derived from carefully controlled modulation that resists and tempers that strictness) of Virgil's hexameters. Ferry's introduction points out that "in English, a six-foot line comparable to Virgil's … would be … impossible to manage" (p. xix). (The critic Gerald Russello of the *New Criterion* put it this way: dactylic hexameter is "a verse form not readily translatable into English" (p. 89). But even if this weren't so, when Ferry chooses to write the poem in an iambic pentameter with anapestic substitutions, one of our best poets is choosing to bring to "the best poem" his best poetic tools.

The opening sentence of the passage from late in the Fourth Georgic quoted below gives ample evidence for how Ferry's modulation of stresses, caesurae, enjambment, and punctuation in his iambic lines responds faithfully to Virgil's modulation of stresses, enjambment, and caesurae in his dactylic lines:

But if it suddenly happens that the whole
Stock is utterly lost and you don't know how
To go about establishing another,
It's time to disclose the legendary secrets
Of the Arcadian master, by means of which
Bees were engendered from the putrid blood
Of a slaughtered bullock.

(p. 163)

The passage generates breathlessness with a lack of punctuation and the enjambment of five lines out of six. Ferry induces the briefest of pauses in the first lines—after the partially stressed syllable, "But,"—but their measure is irregular (though end-marked, as Virgil would have it, with an iambic foot) and there is no medial pause or caesura until line 5, where it is marked by the comma after "master." Thus his sentence about loss and panic and ignorance about what to do "suddenly" accelerates and then races over the first two precipitous line breaks. The third line, which refers to the possibility of restoration and learning, is a stately, pure iambic line, but with an extra syllable at the end ("-er," which resounds with syllables in crucial terms in the passage: "utterly," "Master," "engendered," and "slaughtered") as if to signal the line's connection to the relative excess of the lines that precede it and follow it. The measure of the final two lines, which introduce the horrifically vivid, alchemical fantasy of *bugonia,* which produces, ultimately, sweetness from rot, is as heavily substituted as that of the first two lines. Yet here again Ferry is careful to mark the ends of lines with iambs, so that the moment that might seem like loss of control is contained by the verse structure that governs the whole.

Readers of these *Georgics* who are familiar with the run of Ferry's work may feel in passages such as this one a subtle yet pervasive tension between the persona of Virgil's speaker, who seems to know so much and to be so sure of so much of what he knows, and Ferry's career-spanning creation and re-creation of speakers who do not "know" anything and are uncertain even of their tools for investigation. It may be compared to a faint afterimage, or an almost inaudible echo, but this tonal complexity makes Ferry's *Georgics* more affecting, and more interesting, rather than less. Virgil revels in his revelation of knowledge long ago disproved, or mythic in its terms and imagery, or anecdotal at second- and third-hand, or in some other way indicating that contemporary readers need to read as skeptics. When we read in the Fourth Georgic that we can restock our apiaries by killing a two-year-old bull in a hut and covering its carcass with herbs, our knowledge that David Ferry has composed the English lines we read ought to shape our experience of the content of Virgil's poem. We know that Ferry puts his faith in

prosody, in the shapes of phrases, lines, stanzas, images, and stories. For, like Virgil, Ferry is not content to make poems that rest upon the supposed correctness of their content.

BEWILDERMENT: NEW POEMS AND TRANSLATIONS

Ferry's 2012 book of new poems confirmed a long and productive career. Structurally, and temperamentally, *Bewilderment* is of a kind with *Dwelling Places* and *Of No Country I Know,* but it even more confidently proceeds to do what most other books of poetry by American poets do not do. This makes sense: Ferry's receipt of the Ruth Lilly Prize from the Poetry Foundation in 2011 may have cemented his already proven resolve to keep on being the stranger, the odd man out who both is and is not the author of some of the best contemporary poems we know. And it may be that the readership for poetry in America has wised up a little. The critic and poet Lloyd Schwartz writes of *Bewilderment,* "In this new book, David Ferry shows us that his magnificent translations are as intimately personal as his own poems are heartbreakingly classical. In his wisdom, his self-awareness, his humor at the ways of the world, he has become our Horace. And even better, in the process he has become even more deeply and indispensably himself" (back cover). In 1990, very few readers of American poetry knew how badly we needed a Horace.

Ferry's *Bewilderment* bewilders a reader of contemporary verse in ways we have come to expect: namely, the complexity of its arrangement into many different sections, this time eight; the presentation of translations and "original" poems as if they are equivalent in their merit or lack of merit, when considered to be works by David Ferry; and a persistent interpenetration of classical motifs and familial themes. In *Bewilderment* we once again explore with Ferry

• the limits of human knowledge (see "One Two Three Four Five," "The Intention of Things," "Coffee Lips," "At a Bar"—recalled for duty here from *On the Way to the Island*—"Ancestral

Lines," "The White Skunk," "In the Reading Room," "Street Scene," and more);

• translation as an opportunity for the creation of a new, contemporary poem, especially, now, a poem with autobiographical import (see "In Despair," "At the Street Corner," "The Departure from Fallen Troy," and more);

• a fascination with the down-and-out and the inebriated, those whose struggle against the world is fundamental, and however intelligent, not intellectual ("Coffee Lips," "At the Street Corner," "Dido in Despair," "Catullus II," "Incubus," and more); and

• the inexhaustible flexibility of iambic pentameter as a medium for different kinds of poems in English, here in even more fluent and vibrant forms, and made more trenchant, perhaps, by several poems in deliberately "experimental" measures ("Untitled," "Found Single-Line Poems," and "Catullus II").

Yet there is radical experimentation in *Bewilderment.* Four new poems addressed to poems by Ferry's longtime friend Arthur Gold develop a project that first surfaced in *Of No Country I Know.* Each of these poems presents the full text of a poem published by Gold, followed by a poem by Ferry that comments upon, elucidates, and responds to it. Here Ferry estranges us from the site of poem-reading, makes it unfamiliar so that we might learn to read again.

Ferry has insisted, as we know, that "every act of translation is an act of interpretation" (*Odes,* p. xiv), and we have sensed his growing confidence in his stance that acts of translation might yield new poems, even in the case of translations of poems by pillars of the literary pantheon which have been translated a thousand times before; yet here Ferry seems to have both raised and twisted the stakes, composing new poems in which a poem by a long-dead (and mainly forgotten) poet and a new poem by Ferry are presented under the same title. Only a poet with a strong respect for the values that inhere in verse well made, and in thoughtful reading, and in how arbitrarily the light of fame can shift, would offer to contemporary readers interpretations in verse of poems that virtually nobody

remembers. In Ferry's selected poems *On This Side of the River* (2012) the "Reading Arthur Gold's ..." poems appear in the same section as the poems regarding outcasts, drunks, wild men, and street people. It remains to be seen if Ferry's poems can lend to Gold's poems some form of permanence they do not appear to have achieved when Gold was publishing and distributing them.

In the "Reading Arthur Gold's ..." poems, Ferry draws upon his experience as an educator who guides less able readers in the explication of poems. Yet here elucidator and maker are co-present and cooperate, and Gold's work is unfolded within the space of the unfolding of a new Ferry poem. Certainly the scholar in Ferry could have written an article in prose to show us how to read his friend's work; yet the poet in Ferry prefers to exemplify rather than to discuss the virtues that make the difference between good readings and poor readings. Ferry's poems, so involved in and attentive to Gold's, *get* the sites of Gold's poems and the import of their central metaphors (e.g., "God on his tracks, / Heading away somewhere ..." [p. 72]). Yet Ferry's speaker is no better than we are, and when Gold's pain suddenly recalls him to his own sister's disease, and pain, and virtue, in the face of imminent death—this is precisely the move that the literary scholar cannot afford to make. The "Reading Arthur Gold's ..." poems are a new kind of poem and they are tours de force.

Many of the poems in *Bewilderment* are shot through with classical allusions and motifs. This interpenetration of worlds is especially powerful when there is a "struggling transaction going on" between words and images composed so that they would be memorable and images and feelings remembered because of the circumstances of our lives. A perfect example of such interpenetration is "Resemblance," when the speaker's surprised ruminations at seeing his dead father having lunch at a restaurant is framed by the myth of Orpheus and Eurydice:

he seemed to be eating, maybe without
Noticing whatever it was he may have been eating;
He seemed to be listening to a conversation
With two or three others—Shades of the Dead come
  back

From where they went to when they went away?—
Or maybe those others weren't speaking at all?
  Maybe
It was a dumbshow? Put on for my benefit?

(p. 108)

"There is a silence that we / Are all of us *forbidden* to cross," Ferry writes a few lines later, and we might only begin to cross it by capacious acts of the imagination such as this one, which sees the speaker as Orpheus, and the speaker's father (in Orange, New Jersey) as Eurydice, and Virgil—of the three, the one who has achieved the greatest degree of immortality—he too is an Orpheus, attempting in his lines to bring the dead "back / From where they went to when they went away." It must be that the resemblance referred to in the title is the likeness of the figure to his father. But it must also be that Ferry's "Resemblance" posits a fundamental likeness between how we read poems and how we read our everyday worlds, so charged is our experience of everything by our impoverished imaginations. One's mind is always "inhibited by its ancestral / Knowledge of the final separation," and always hampered in its navigations of the spaces that separate life and death, 1829 and 2012, Spanish and Mandarin, father and son, lover and lover—or one reader and the text. Yet is there anything more human, or more noble, than to attempt to cross such spaces?

ON THIS SIDE OF THE RIVER

At the heels of the U.S. publication of *Bewilderment*, Waywiser Press in the United Kingdom issued a large selection of Ferry's work called *On This Side of the River* (2012). The eleven sections of the book constitute a claim that when he is not held to a chronological design, Ferry himself sees his own oeuvre as complex and multidimensional. Each section is a single long work or a gathering of poems that share a theme or are concerned with an idea or human situation; most sections juxtapose poems that were composed decades apart, and though one can read the year of composition for each poem in the table of contents, the temporal contexts of many

poems is deliberately blurred in favor of the meanings that are generated by their placements side by side in this volume. As if to emphasize Ferry's growing comfort with the claim that to succeed in a translation *is* to write a poem, many of the thematically coherent sections mix translations with "original" works.

On This Side of the River is stronger because of the interplay of its many sections. The ten poems, mainly about Ferry's family, which make up section 4, for example, make more complex and satisfying reading because they are gathered in one place. (This is true even though section 4 does not constitute the "complete" works of Ferry which mention or address family members or memories of family life.) The family relations of section 4 are wonderfully recast in section 5, which features a long sequence called "Mary in Old Age," with its fictions of life after Christ's death, and then takes up friendship and nonfamilial bonds; and sections 4 and 5 are both answered, in a way, by the single long poem that makes up section 6, a recent translation of an Anglo-Saxon translation of the biblical story of Abraham's willingness to sacrifice Isaac.

The single section that sheds the brightest light on a long-standing strain of Ferry's work is section 8, where he has gathered twenty-two poems that give voice and image to the "wild" men and women, drunks, and outcasts, the walking wounded among us, and to how we who are mainly well either do or do not admit our kinship with them. Section 7 confirms how Ferry has taken up such persons again and again, with ever-greater prosodic power, intellectual and emotional insight, and empathy. Here we meet "The Guest Ellen at the Supper for Street People," "The Proselyte," "At the Street Corner" (from Rilke's "Song of the Dwarf"), our old friend "At a Bar" (from *On the Way to the Island*), an ekphrastic poem called "After Edward Hopper: Somebody in a Bar," "Coffee Lips," "Old People," "Soul" (which likens being an old man to being "the insides of a lobster, / All thought, and indigestion, and pornographic / Inquiry, and getting about, and bewilderment ..." (p. 209), and a relatively free translation of Rilke's "Das Lied des Trinkers," which could not have been com-

posed by any other poet. Rilke's poem is gritty—for a Rilke poem. But Ferry's poem amps up that grittiness and clarifies the imagination of the speaker in ways that only he could have managed. Compared to Ferry's, Rilke's interest in barflies was that of a passing flaneur. Yet, as we have seen, for fifty years Ferry has been scrutinizing himself and society with regard to how it listens to and speaks about the wild man in himself and in society. "Das Lied des Trinkers" is interesting but mediocre Rilke. "Song of the Drunkard" is one of Ferry's small masterpieces.

This selected poems is broad enough to preserve all of the principal strands of Ferry's verse, not the least important of which is his indefatigable investigation of the limits of human knowledge. That those limits are not any less constraining when the subject of inquiry is the self, or one's writing, of course, has not prevented him from constructing an estimable portrait of David Ferry's accomplishment in *On This Side of the River*.

THE AENEID OF VIRGIL

Eighty-eight years old at the time of this writing, Ferry is hard at work on a complete translation of the *Aeneid of Virgil*, which is under contract to be published by Farrar, Straus and Giroux and may be ready for publication as soon as 2016. As of 2013 several portions of Ferry's *Aeneid* have appeared in journals, including the *Paris Review* and *Poetry,* and *Bewilderment* features selections from books 2, 4, and 6, presented as freestanding poems that participate in the development of the themes of the sections in which they appear.

Given his successful translations of the *Eclogues* and the *Georgics,* it is not at all surprising that Ferry would take a stab at Virgil's great epic. What is a bit startling is his claim that he has not yet read the poem all the way through, and that he has taken up each book in turn and is only discovering what happens in the poem as he works to bring it into blank verse. This practice may be seen as consistent with translating individual *Eclogues* and *Georgics* (or *Odes* of Horace) and getting to know them one at a time,

and Ferry likes to say that he is in the same position Virgil was in when he composed his epic poem.

Ferry's prosodic approach to the *Aeneid* is consistent with his approaches to earlier translation projects. He began by determining the measure he would use to convey his version—in this case the measure he knows best, unrhymed iambic pentameter—and then set out to complete the books from first to last. Sometimes, as in the heartrending account (from book 4) of Dido's despair, Ferry's sensibility, so tuned to heartbreaking loss by his own grief, is coincidentally a match for Virgil's. At other times it seems that Ferry's long steeping in Virgil's *Eclogues* and *Georgics* has prepared him especially to take on the epic, and it is his command of prosody that makes Ferry into Virgil's vicar. Though in general his handling of the blank verse line in the Latin epic is quieter, and less repetitive, than it is in his Akkadian epic, there are passages in which powerful echoic effects work beautifully, and a reader who is familiar with Ferry's life's work realizes anew that the sounds that he began to make in his rendering of the *Gilgamesh* are not attributable to an effort to gin up an ancient or "early" music, but represent a breakthrough in Ferry's development as an artist. These breakthrough sounds characterize some but not all of his best verse. In his *Aeneid*, Ferry's management of those sounds has matured and deepened in response to narrative episodes that are longer and more detailed than any he has in the past made himself convey. The passage from book 5 in which Virgil describes the boxing that takes place during the games following Anchises' funeral is a crucial example. There is no better way to close this discussion of Ferry's career than with the final words of Entellus' valedictory address to the awestruck crowd of Trojans who will found Rome. When the scene is read whole, what is abundantly manifest is how Ferry's Virgil expresses the hard-won-ness of Ferry's life, and of his skill, and of his respect for the past and the best ways of the past. When Entellus raises his mighty gauntleted arm to destroy the ox he won by pummeling a man nearly to death,

A single blow between the horns broke into
Its skull and shattered its brains; the steer, its lifeless
Body quivering still, lay stretched on the ground.
He stood above it and poured out from his heart
These words: "Eryx, in place of Dares's death
I offer this better life, and in victory here
I now give up this gauntlet and my art."

(unpublished manuscript)

It is hard not to imagine that Ferry is a particularly apt translator for such a passage, and such a poem. Let us hope that he will reject the example of Entellus, Virgil's master pugilist, and will never decide to retire.

Selected Bibliography

WORKS OF DAVID FERRY

POETRY AND TRANSLATIONS

On the Way to the Island. Middletown, Conn.: Wesleyan University Press, 1960.

A Letter and Some Photographs: A Group of Poems. Seattle: Sea Pen Press & Paper Mill, 1981. (Chapbook.)

Strangers: A Book of Poems. Chicago: University of Chicago Press, 1983.

Gilgamesh: A New Rendering in English Verse. New York: Farrar, Straus and Giroux, 1992.

Dwelling Places: Poems and Translations. Chicago: University of Chicago Press, 1993.

The Odes of Horace: A Translation. New York: Farrar, Straus and Giroux, 1997.

The Eclogues of Virgil: A Translation. New York: Farrar, Straus and Giroux, 1999.

The Epistles of Horace: A Translation. New York: Farrar, Straus and Giroux, 2001.

The Georgics of Virgil: A Translation. Farrar, Straus and Giroux, 2006.

Bewilderment: New Poems and Translations. Chicago: University of Chicago Press, 2012.

The Aeneid of Virgil. New York: Farrar, Straus and Giroux, forthcoming.

SELECTED AND OTHER WORKS

The Limits of Mortality: An Essay on Wordsworth's Major Poems. Middletown, Conn.: Wesleyan University Press, 1959.

DAVID FERRY

Of No Country I Know: New and Selected Poems and Translations. Chicago: University of Chicago Press, 1999.

On This Side of the River: Selected Poems. Oxford: Waywiser Press, 2012.

REVIEWS AND OTHER SOURCES

Bosch, Daniel. "Verse into Verse." *Arts Fuse*, May 6, 2011. http://artsfuse.org/30044/fuse-poetry-commentary-verse-into-verse-poetry-awards-poetry-a-prize/.

Hadas, Rachel. "Reading David Ferry's Poems." *New Criterion* 18:30 (February 2000).

Jenkins, Richard. "Immemorial Elms." *New Republic*, August 30, 1999, pp. 39–42. (Review of *The Eclogues of Virgil*.)

Kinzie, Mary. "2000 Lenore Marshall Prize Citation." *Nation*, October 16, 2000, p. 32.

McClatchy, J. D. *Horace, the Odes: New Translations by Contemporary Poets.* Princeton, N.J.: Princeton University Press, 2002.

Morse, Samuel French. Review of *On the Way to the Island*. *Virginia Quarterly Review* 37:294 (1961).

Russello, Gerald. "Georgics on My Mind." *New Criterion* 23:89–90 (June 2005).

INTERVIEWS

"Interview with David Ferry." In *Talking with Poets*. Edited by Harry Thomas. New York: Handsel Books, 2002.

Kalogeris, George, and Daniel Bosch. "The Art of Poetry: David Ferry." *Paris Review,* forthcoming.

Taylor, Tess. "Always in Disguise." *Poetry Foundation*, May 18, 2011. http://www.poetryfoundation.org/article/242142#article.

TESS GALLAGHER

(1943—)

Cheri Johnson

KNOWN PRIMARILY FOR her intensely personal, emotionally charged free-verse poetry, Tess Gallagher is also a writer of short fiction, essays, and screenplays and has collaborated with other writers and artists on films, plays, and translations. A recipient of an honorary doctorate from Whitman College, her work is regularly published in both literary journals and national magazines (*Atlantic Monthly, New Yorker*), and she has received awards from the National Endowment for the Arts, the New York State Council on the Arts, and the Guggenheim Foundation. Gallagher published her first poem in 1969 in the *Minnesota Review* and has written and published consistently since, in a career that spans over forty years.

LIFE

Tess Gallagher, née Theresa Jeanette Bond, was born in Port Angeles, Washington, a port and logging town on the Olympic Peninsula, on July 21, 1943. The eldest of five children, Gallagher grew up in a working-class household. Her mother, Georgia Morris Bond, and her father, Leslie Bond, were both "gyppo loggers"— independent loggers engaged in small-scale logging operations—and her father also worked on the docks. Her family struggled with the tension and quarrels that went with her father's alcoholism, as well as with other violence and loss. Gallagher's youngest brother was killed in a car accident when Gallagher was twenty, and several years later her uncle Porter Morris, who lived with Gallagher's grandparents on the farm in Windyville, Missouri, where she spent many of her childhood summers, was murdered by three local men over a grudge and forty dollars.

As a child Gallagher studied classical piano and was drawn to painting. In high school she began writing poetry and published articles in the *Port Angeles Daily News*. After graduation she attended the University of Washington, where she was handpicked for Theodore Roethke's last workshop and where she met Larry Gallagher, who would become her first husband in 1964, when she was twenty-one. She left the University of Washington before finishing her degree, but returned to earn her diploma in 1967; her marriage ended two years later. She went on to receive a master's degree at Washington in 1971 and, at the suggestion of Mark Strand, decided to enter the Writers' Workshop at the University of Iowa, where she studied with Donald Justice, Norman Dubie, and Marvin Bell, earning an M.F.A. in poetry in 1974. There she also met her second husband, the poet Michael Burkard; the two were married from 1973 to 1977. At Iowa, Gallagher said in an interview in *Poets & Writers* with Penelope Moffet, her poems, which were concerned with "soulmaking," were not always well-received.

Quickly Gallagher began publishing and receiving accolades for her work. A chapbook of poems, *Stepping Outside,* was published by Penumbra Press in 1974, followed by her first full-length collection in 1976, *Instructions to the Double,* published by Graywolf Press, then based in Port Townsend, Washington. *Instructions to the Double* received an Elliston Book Award.

In the mid-1970s she began teaching at various colleges across the country in one- or two-year stints, beginning as an English instructor at St. Lawrence University in Canton, New York, in 1974. As an assistant professor, a visiting lecturer, and an associate professor of creative writing, she taught at Kirkland College, the University of Montana in Missoula, and the University of Arizona in Tucson. In 1978 Gallagher received a

Guggenheim Fellowship and published two more books of poetry with Graywolf Press, *Under Stars* and a chapbook, *On Your Own*. Much of *Under Stars* was written on a trip to Ireland, a country whose landscapes and culture she has continued to explore in her work. In 1979 she moved in with the short-story writer and recently sober Raymond Carver, who would also become a frequent subject in her work after his death in 1988. In "Raymond Carver: The Kindest Cut," an article on Carver that includes an interview with Gallagher, Gaby Wood reports that Gallagher concerned herself with helping Carver to maintain his sobriety and focus on his work. In the various places the couple lived in together, Gallagher often gave Carver the study and did her own writing in the bathroom or at a park.

In 1980 Gallagher became an associate professor of English and coordinator of the creative writing program at Syracuse University, teaching there, typically only one semester a year, until 1990. She traveled frequently, to Brazil, Argentina, England, France, and Ireland. In 1982 her father died of cancer. Gallagher was prolific in the 1980s, writing plays and publishing several books: two collections of poetry, *Willingly* (1984) and *Amplitude* (1987); her first collection of short fiction, *The Lover of Horses* (1986); her essay collection *A Concert of Tenses* (1986); and, with Raymond Carver, a screenplay about Fyodor Dostoevsky. In June 1988 Gallagher married Carver, who had been diagnosed with lung cancer and a brain tumor. He died later that summer.

In 1990 Gallagher left Syracuse to write full-time in Port Angeles. In 1992 she published *Moon Crossing Bridge,* a collection of poems expressing her deep grief over losing Carver and her struggle to find a way to go on. Three more poetry collections and chapbooks followed in that decade. Gallagher also collaborated with the director Robert Altman on *Short Cuts* (1993), a film based on nine of Raymond Carver's short stories. A grant from the Lyndhurst Foundation allowed her to write *At the Owl Woman Saloon,* which was published in 1997. She taught at Whitman College and Bucknell University and in 1999 won the Maxine Cushing Gray Foundation Award.

In 2000 Gallagher published, with editor Greg Simon, *Soul Barnacles: Ten More Years with Ray,* a collection of diary entries, essays, letters, photographs, and poems about Gallagher and Carver. In August 2002, while caring for her mother—who was suffering from both advancing Alzheimer's and congestive heart failure—Gallagher received her own diagnosis of breast cancer and began treatment. Gallagher's fight with cancer, she said in an interview with Jeff Baker, gave her, as Raymond Carver's literary executor, the courage to pursue something she had been putting off: a fight with Carver's publisher, Knopf, for the publication of original versions of Carver's stories before they were severely edited by Gordon Lish.

Between 1988 and 1997 Gallagher was also involved in controversial legal disputes with Carver's first wife of twenty-seven years, Maryann Carver—who supported Carver financially for some years when they were married so that he could focus on writing—as well as his mother and his children over the proceeds of Carver's estate. Carol Sklenicka, in the epilogue to her biography *Raymond Carver: A Writer's Life* (2009), details the controversy, which includes Gallagher's dispute with Carver's daughter Christine over renewal rights to Carver's work. Gallagher seems to poke fun at the grown child who claims renewal rights to her father's literary work in her story "The Poetry Baron," included in her collection *At the Owl Woman Saloon.*

In the 1990s Gallagher began a relationship with the Irish painter Josie Gray. In 2004 she received a Distinguished Alumnus Award from the University of Washington. She published another collection of poetry with Graywolf Press, *Dear Ghosts*, in 2006, followed by two collaborative works, *Distant Rain* (2006), with Jakuchō Setouchi, and *Barnacle Soup* (2007), with Josie Gray. Gallagher was active in speaking out against the wars in Iraq and Afghanistan instigated by the administration of President George W. Bush. Her mother died in 2009, the same year that Gallagher released a selection from her first two books of short stories in the collection *The Man from Kinvara.*

Gallagher divides her time between Port Angeles and a cottage on Lough Arrow in County Sligo on the west coast of Ireland, next door to her partner Josie Gray. In 2011 she published another collection of new and selected poems, *Midnight Lantern*.

POETRY

In interviews and essays, Gallagher often discusses her poetry in metaphysical, even spiritualistic, terms. In "A Nightshine Beyond Memory: Ten More Years with Ray," included in her essay collection *Soul Barnacles*, Gallagher says that after Carver's death she felt that his presence persisted in her life and that "an osmotic flow of spirit" between the two of them informed her poetry; she calls their writing life together "that all-night diner of soul-making" (p. 226). Critics of her poetry often note her interest in sacredness and spirituality; a common thread in much of the writing about Gallagher's work is the observation that she uses ordinary yet often intimate details of everyday life as a kind of springboard from which to contemplate the grand mysteries of life and death. Shira Richman and Maya Jewell Zeller note that "not unlike Wordsworth, Gallagher manages to enshrine not only the mundane, but the tragic, by seeing the world as her holy place" (p. 85). In her interview with Penelope Moffet, Gallagher mentions the influence of another English lyric poet concerned with the mystery of the soul, John Donne.

Gallagher's early collections received considerable critical attention, and her subsequent work has continued to do so. Some of her early reviews note with surprise a particularly feminine quality in her work. Robert Ross, in his positive review of Gallagher's first chapbook, *Stepping Outside,* is nonetheless openly mystified by the subtlety of Gallagher's images. He predicts that only a few female readers will probably truly understand the book, and compares Gallagher's slyness to that of a skilled stripper. Hayden Carruth, in a review of Gallagher's second full-length collection, *Under Stars,* describes gratefully Gallagher's frank self-reflection and genuine concern, both of which he also associates with a feminine

sensibility. Gallagher, in her interview with Moffet, says that she feels her early poems in particular do speak to the sometimes ridiculous situations women find themselves in, and to the ways women talk about the dangers they feel facing them. She also notes that she likes some "mystery" in a poem and is interested in preserving the "secret" from which it comes.

Caroline McElwee in "Lying Next to the Knife" and Fran Brearton in her review of the collection *Dear Ghosts* take up a theme often addressed in criticism about Gallagher's poetry: the leaps her poems take between various spaces and times, between different phases of a speaker's life or the worlds of the living and the dead. Gallagher speaks to this intentional effect in the essays that make up *A Concert of Tenses* as well as in her introduction to Raymond Carver's *All of Us: The Collected Poems,* in which she mentions that her "feeling that all time—past, present, and future—exists within reach at the moment the poem is being written" was helpful to Carver when he was writing his own poetry (p. xxv).

Referring to the 1976 collection *Instructions to the Double* in her review of *Midnight Lantern* in 2011, Donna Seaman notes the earlier book's deep compassion, a quality often cited by critics and Gallagher's passionate fans. Seaman, in discussing the later work, asserts that Gallagher has not only not lost her emotional concern and sensitivity but enlarged it into a "cosmically affectionate mode" (p. 12). Gallagher often speaks passionately of the world around her, of both the pleasures and challenges of life; in her foreword to the essay anthology *Beyond Forgetting* (2009) she calls taking care of her mother with Alzheimer's a precious act that she values deeply and discusses the kind of poetry she likes best, that which makes her feel and empathize with another person's reality. In her 1997 interview with Katie Bolick, in which she voices her growing uneasiness with the sound-bite quality of much of the information people give and receive in contemporary culture, Gallagher speaks of poetry as a place where the world ought to be engaged in its deepest, fullest way no matter what. Critics often note Gallagher's close atten-

tion to and deep engagement with nature, the landscape of the Pacific Northwest in particular.

Gallagher sometimes feels the critique that her poetry is too dependent on emotion to be taken seriously, as she remarks to Michael Glover when discussing reactions to her poem "The Hug." Some critics, however, like Rochelle Ratner in her review of *Willingly,* describe the techniques Gallagher uses to avoid sentimentality in even very personal poems about members of her family, a common subject—particularly her mother and father, who often become archetypal figures as well—in her work.

Gallagher has reprinted the first poem "Kidnaper," from her first full collection, *Instructions to the Double,* in every selected collection she has put together since the book came out in 1976. Dedicated to Gallagher's sister, the collection speaks to both the dangers and thrills of becoming and being a young woman, in "Kidnaper" almost simultaneously: an image of the first-person speaker rousing interest in a man on the street gives way, over the course of only a few lines, to her body lying in a ravine. Enjambed lines give an excited quality to the gruesome image, which also feels earthy and strangely peaceful, as if the implied violence the speaker has suffered at the hands of this stranger has nonetheless allowed for a close communion with the dirt on which she has been dumped: "I lie / without breath for days among ferns. / Pine needles drift / onto my face and breasts" (p. 11). The effect feels intentionally, provocatively creepy, a kind of sensual reckoning with both the body the speaker has been given and the world in which she must live in that body, a world that offers both natural comforts and the peculiar, grotesque way images of womanly beauty in both contemporary media and folklore are so often associated with their destruction. Like Hansel and Gretel, the speaker, who early in the poem wants to trust the stranger, nonetheless begins leaving a trail of her belongings as soon as she turns away from him. The strange surprises of the poem are not over, as Gallagher quickly makes a move that establishes her poetic interest in leaping between time and space and states of being. The speaker who was alive, then dead, now seems to be alive again, or

in some state that exists between life and death, as she watches and listens to the stranger when he comes back and lifts her out of the leaves.

In "Breasts," another poem in the collection, Gallagher directly addresses her body in an apostrophe, tracing the moment at which being female begins to both expand the possibilities of the future and limit those of the past. Out wrestling with her brothers in the grass, the shirtless speaker is commanded by her mother to put her shirt on, and she notices her developing breasts for the first time. The speaker thinks into a future that is also in the poem's past, in which her growing body leads her to lovers with bloody hands and whiskey breath.

Instructions to the Double is filled with the kind of concrete details, natural and manufactured, human and animal, that are present in much of Gallagher's subsequent poetry, and which build a kind of tableau of working-class life in the small towns and forests of the Pacific Northwest: jagged saws, car lots, bullfrogs, cows, a spar tree ax, wheels rattling over gravel, liquor stores, a mill humming and turning in the water. Members of the speaker's family walk in and out of the tableau, listening to country music, buying ribbons in the dime store. Bits of narrative and information, such as the second stanza in "The Woman Who Raised Goats," in which the speaker explains how her father, and her brothers after him, worked on the docks, are woven into poems that quickly shoot off into disparate or abstract images. The speaker sometimes refers to "my father" or "my mother" but just as often, as in "Instructions to the Double," Gallagher uses the more cryptic and expansive "little mother" and "little father" (p. 67).

In *Under Stars,* Gallagher continues to include poems, like "Four Dancers at an Irish Wedding," that use a grounded physical description of a person or an event from which to leap to references both personal and universal. Watching a father and daughter dance at a wedding, the speaker thinks of her own unidentified partner, from which we jump to the symbiotic image of a magpie on the back of a cow. The section in which this poem appears, "The Ireland Poems," contains many poems like this, and in a poem in

the second section, "The Same Kiss After Many Years," Gallagher again plays with time and space and with figures whose identities feel fluid. As is often the case in *Instructions to the Double*, "The Same Kiss After Many Years" contains unspecified "*we*"s and "*they*"s and "*she*"s and "*he*"s and "*you*"s and "*it*"s that may be the same figures in the past, present, and future, or that may be the figures seeing themselves in different ways, or that may be something else. At times, verbs of several tenses, and several unspecified pronouns, exist within a single thought: "We're / concerned not to have them / missed, so this will happen / painlessly, leaving us all / the better for it" (p. 48).

Gallagher also continues to explore the question, now against the backdrop of a different culture, of what it means to be a woman in this world, as in "Woman Enough." In that poem, set in Ireland, a group of men digging a grave warn the speaker to watch out for the lecherous ghost of the dead man.

Gallagher's narratives begin to expand in poems like "3 A.M. Kitchen: My Father Talking," a persona poem written in her father's voice, addressing Gallagher (the speaker in the poem uses Leslie Bond's nickname for Gallagher, "Threasie"). The poem shows Gallagher's growing interest both in staying in one place and time from beginning to end and in writing in the voice of a character. The speaker narrates his life in terms of the work he has done, from before his marriage to the present, when he spends as much time as he can playing cards because he can't think of anything to work for anymore. "Start Again Somewhere" is also a sustained address, this time to a character named Miguel; the voice that speaks to him is a communal "we" expressing underhanded opinions about the chances he does and doesn't take with women.

After "3 A.M. Kitchen" comes "My Mother Remembers That She Was Beautiful," a detailed portrait of the speaker's mother talking about her youth while seated at a pine table in a restaurant in the wintertime. The speaker considers both her mother's past and identity and her own role in who her mother was and has become. As in the poems about her uncle's murder in *Instructions*

to the Double, Gallagher seems to be expressing a desire to write the lives of those she loves as well as to find her own place in the significant moments, both dramatic and quiet, in her family's history.

In *Willingly,* Gallagher dives even more fully into extended narratives and concrete, full-bodied descriptions, as in the first poem, "Sudden Journey," in which the speaker, remembering a moment she experienced as a child, offers a camera-like portrait of herself: a little girl standing in grass so high her head is only a small brown curve breaking up the yellow. The child lives in the moment before "Breasts," at a time when her bared boyish body can be run over anywhere with rain. The concrete immediacy of the poem, delivered in consistent present tense, is broken by only one metaphor, which occurs in the last line. In this collection Gallagher pays even closer attention to the landscape of the Pacific Northwest, from the rain in "Sudden Journey" to the gray-green mossy light in "Bird-Window-Flying" and "The Shirts."

The narrative in "Boat Ride," a description of a fishing trip with the speaker, her father, and a hungover friend, is so detailed—journalistically so, telling the story as it unfolds from before sunrise to the brightness of the day—that it goes on for seven pages, unlike Gallagher's earlier poems, rarely longer than a page. "Boat Ride," which also brings in family history, bits of dialogue, descriptions of the landscape, and the speaker's musings on language, begins a mode that Gallagher returns to in even greater force in her later collections: a kind of extended riff that leaps from a concrete image, as in her earlier work, but travels more exhaustively through the myriad places in which it finds itself.

Gallagher also becomes more loquacious in another way. Whereas earlier her strange images were often left open-ended and cryptic, here she begins to explain herself. In "Conversation with a Fireman from Brooklyn," a poem that echoes the ideas in "Woman Enough" about the roles of women, Gallagher reports the fireman's sentiments about women firefighters: that he doesn't mind them, except for how sweaty and disgusting they get after fighting a fire. Gallagher

explains the irony clearly at the end of the poem: it's a shame that the women are hated for what they do to prove they are as good as men. In "Crêpes Flambeau," Gallagher is likewise unsatisfied with letting the image—in this case a blushing young waiter getting ready to perform a culinary trick before his audience at a table—stand by itself. Instead the speaker tells us what to make of it: we are given to understand that, because the speaker and the women she is having dinner with are all older and good-looking, the young waiter feels he must try to please them. Contemplating spiritual goodness, the analytical, essayistic, proselike voice in "Linoleum," after expressing the speaker's appreciation for the bug-saving Jains of India, feels anxious, flinching, worried perhaps that she will be misunderstood, seen as silly or naive. She is quick to qualify her admiration by saying that she knows the Jains' behavior makes them bad farmers. If the feel of Gallagher's first two books can be compared to a fantastical production, with playful sleights of hand and rapid visual tricks happening on a darkened stage, perhaps *Willingly* is more like the considered answers in the actors' Q & A after the show is done.

The new poems in *Amplitude,* which includes selections from the first three books, also offer exhaustive considerations of ideas, but here Gallagher returns to tauter lines, even when the poems go on for several pages. Her voice is muscular and athletic in poems in which she continues to give us a speaker who, while going about her day, riffs about subjects summoned up by the details and events of her life, as in "If Poetry Were Not a Morality." The speaker's act of pulling over her car when she first hears Bobby McFerrin scat singing on the radio leads to her musings on Cecil Taylor and to the photo taped up by her typewriter, to cheap welfare coffins and horses, then back to music: Bob Marley and Edith Piaf and Billie Holiday. As in Gallagher's poem "Four Dancers at an Irish Wedding" in *Under Stars,* in which she creates a dancelike feel with repetitions and refrains, Gallagher seems interested here in the effect music can have on the form and sound of her poems. Many of these poems use her usual style of paragraph-like stanzas of irregular length, but in "Bonfire"—a poem that mentions a mazurka and a jig and a speaker who ice skates while holding a violin—she plays with indented lines and scattered spacing that create an airy, improvisatory feel.

Gallagher published several books in the 1990s with presses other than her main publisher, Graywolf. These include *My Black Horse* (1995), a collection of new and previously collected poems published in Britain by Bloodhouse Books; a chapbook, *Owl Spirit Dwelling* (1995), published by Trask House Books in Oregon; and *Portable Kisses: Love Poems,* an expansion of the idea central to a hand-printed limited edition by the same name, inspired by Pablo Neruda's *Twenty Love Poems and a Song of Despair,* that Gallagher had published in 1978 with Sea Pen Press. The second version, published by Capra Press in 1992, is passionate and thorny and clever, filled with whimsical titles like "In the Laboratory of Kisses," "Stubborn Kisses," "Androgynous Kiss," and "Letter to a Kiss That Died for Us."

Published in 1992, four years after Raymond Carver's death, *Moon Crossing Bridge* is perhaps Gallagher's most famous book. In six sections it records Gallagher's grieving process and begins in earnest the creation of a poetic space in which the living and the dead meet, pass one another, converse, and contemplate both the gulfs and the connections between them. In "We're All Pharaohs When We Die," the speaker observes that "Our friends die with us" when we die "because we / used them so well," and is aware not only of her own mortality but of the crushing nearness of the dead to her heart, and the pain of living without them, when she imagines herself with a look of "dead-aliveness" on her face (pp. 55–56). The tone of the book is pressing, somber, grave, and dense. In her review, Margaret K. Powell describes some of the poems as difficult, with language overstretched in an effort to contain Gallagher's grief. The last section of the book, however, with the airiness of poems like *"Un Extraño,"* with its short imagistic lines, feels lighter and at the same time more controlled.

Published fourteen years later, Gallagher's next major collection *Dear Ghosts,* features a

comparatively spare, clear-eyed voice, even in its evocation of the speaker's beloved dead. All of Gallagher's work—her prose as well as her poetry—is filled with an abundance of two reoccurring images: horses and birds. In a few of the collections the images occur literally dozens of times, most often swooping and galloping along; here, the birds and horses are, most tellingly, often dead. In "My Unopened Life," a bird is being chewed up by a cat; the speaker in "Not a Sparrow" finds a dead finch near her bird feeder; in *"Sah Sin,"* she holds a cold hummingbird to her breast in the hopes of trying to revive it. A horse in "The Dogs of Bucharest" is described in the terminology of a morgue. In the face of so much death, including her own—in "The Women of Auschwitz," a woman cuts off her hair in the face of cancer treatments—the voice of the book can't seem to bear the possibility of not saving whatever she can. In "Lie Down with the Lamb," the speaker buys a lamb back from the slaughterhouse, and in "Choices," after seeing a nest in the tree limb she was planning to cut down in order to secure a view, she begins to imagine nests everywhere. Overwhelmed, she can't cut down anything.

Gallagher's 2011 new and selected collection, *Midnight Lantern,* was named a *Publishers Weekly* Top Ten Poetry Book for that year. In her glowing review, Donna Seaman notes the sharpness and coyness of the new poems, included in a section called "Signature." A witty humility that feels freshly considered, or reconsidered—it is reminiscent of the tone in Gallagher's early essay collection *A Concert of Tenses*—combines with what feels like a newfound delight in language. Alliteration and playful repetitions abound in "Barrie Cooke Painting," in which the speaker sits down to have her portrait done. She sees herself with untroubled affection and rollicking, snappy humor:

At our second session he is deciding not
to paint me with hair. He confesses he got up
in the night to try hair, but the fizzog would not
accept fringing. Lucky for him I am intimate
with my pate and prefer it, allowing an unruly
hedge simply to take the scare out of things.

(p. 303)

Discussing the central image of the collection, the handheld light in the poem "Midnight Lantern," Gallagher says in an interview with Rebecca Foresman that it is a symbol of what she tries to achieve in individual poems, moving through what she doesn't know to try to discover something that might help someone else. She does so with a kind of hopeful, humble faith. "The interesting thing about lantern light," she says, "is that it doesn't illuminate very far in front of you."

ESSAYS

Gallagher has written two collections of essays, *A Concert of Tenses: Essays on Poetry* and *Soul Barnacles: Ten More Years with Ray.* Other major essays include the foreword to *Beyond Forgetting: Poetry and Prose About Alzheimer's Disease,* in which Gallagher writes about caring for her mother (Gallagher delivered a different version of the essay as a keynote address at "The Patient: An International Symposium" at Bucknell University in 2006); and "Instead of Dying" (published in *Utne* as "Out of the Drink"), an adaptation of a talk she gave about Raymond Carver's successful struggle for sobriety at the Academi *Intoxication* Conference in Wales, also in 2006.

A Concert of Tenses is made up of both personal essays—including "My Father's Love Letters," in which Gallagher writes about her family, and "Last Class with Roethke," a memoir about her poetry workshop with Theodore Roethke at the University of Washington—and critical pieces that focus on topical literary issues and the work of various poets (Marianne Moore, Laura Jensen, Linda Gregg, and Gallagher's second husband, Michael Burkard). In the personal essays in the collection, as well as in those in *Soul Barnacles,* Gallagher seems driven by an impulse similar to that which underlies much of her poetry: to discover, through examining the important people and events and circumstances of her life, who she is. In the essays, her aim is to analyze specifically who she is as a poet and why. In a straightforward, lucid style, Gallagher describes, in "My Father's Love Let-

ters," how the death of her brother led to her interest in writing about the dead in order to extend their presence beyond memory; in "A Concert of Tenses" and a transcription of her interview with Rachel Berghash, she analyzes her own techniques and poems in detail.

The scholarly essays are interspersed with lively personal details—in "The Poem as Time Machine," Gallagher reveals her burning childhood desire not to have, but to *be* a horse—and feature a smart, youthful voice full of a shimmering intellectual curiosity. Literary matters are addressed in essays like "Poetry in Translation: Literary Imperialism or, Defending the Musk Ox," and "Adding to the Unhappiness: Those Poems You Are Writing," her snappy response to an essay by James Atlas in the *New Republic* in which, according to Gallagher, Atlas moans over the growing number of too many poets with too many resources. Gallagher's passionate and clever analysis gives the impression that although she is perfectly up to the task of taking on the big literary issues of her day, she can't believe her luck that she is getting to do so. She is particularly interested in speaking about the changing roles of women in the world of poetry and in the world at large, and she moves clearly and easily from thoughtful discussions of Jean-Paul Sartre and Ezra Pound to, in "Poetry in Translation," whimsical personifications of clunky translations, such as a figure dripping water on a carpet while wearing a sombrero.

Soul Barnacles, published more than a decade later, features a Gallagher who, though she continues to exhibit her sharp analytical skills, writes with a tone considerably more somber and ponderous. The book includes Gallagher's essays "A Nightshine Beyond Memory" and the forewords she wrote to posthumous collections of Carver's work, as well as various other documents that speak to Carver's last days and the aftermath of his death. Among these are selections from Gallagher's journal of a European trip the couple took in 1987, during which they met with friends and with Carver's European translators and editors; photographs of the trip; a letter of appreciation for Gallagher's poem "Late Fragment" and Carver's *A New Path to the Waterfall* from the film director Jane Campion; transcriptions of interviews Gallagher gave in the years following Carver's death; and a copy of a tribute Gallagher gave to Carver at a memorial for him in London. Also included are letters and essays by Gallagher, Robert Altman, and Robert Coles concerning the film *Short Cuts.* In her letter to Coles, who wrote critically about the film, claiming that its sardonic tone and peripheral treatment of its female characters were untrue to Carver's compassionate spirit, Gallagher defends Altman's choices in a nuanced argument that includes her own reservations about the film and explores the complex issues of translating a work of art into another form.

Overwhelmingly, however, the book feels like a mirror held up to Gallagher's abiding sadness. In "A Nightshine Beyond Memory," Gallagher details the many ways in which she says Carver is very much still with her—she still speaks to him every day, teaches his stories, reads his letters aloud to her students, sees him in many of the people that she meets. She says that she sees no reason to let him go. Gallagher asserts that continuing to live with Carver in these ways gives her great pleasure. The effect of reading about it, though, is bittersweet.

SHORT FICTION

Gallagher's short stories (with the exception of the collaborative stories she wrote with Josie Gray and published in *Barnacle Soup*) have been published in two collections: *The Lover of Horses and Other Stories* (1986) and *At the Owl Woman Saloon* (1997). Gallagher published both of the books with commercial presses, but in 2009 her volume of selected stories, *The Man from Kinvara,* which consists of material from these two collections, was published with Graywolf Press. (All quotations from Gallagher's stories in this section are taken from *The Man from Kinvara.*)

Gallagher's individual stories have been published in both national magazines and literary journals, including the *New Yorker, Glimmer Train Stories, Atlantic Monthly, Five Points, Sycamore Review, Story,* and *ZYZZYVA.*

In interviews and essays Gallagher often credits Carver for inspiring and encouraging her to write *The Lover of Horses,* and she says that she wrote *At the Owl Woman Saloon* because after his death she missed having short stories in the house. For the raw material of the stories themselves, she often credits her mother and other people who tell her stories from their own and others' lives. In her interview with Katie Bolick, Gallagher reports that while she feels equally comfortable in poetry and prose, her approaches to them—the way she wants her work in each form to sound, the material each is best suited to exploring—are very different. If poems are "deep-sea diving," she says, "writing fiction is foraging." Fiction requires an alertness to the world around her, a constant attention to not only what is being said but how: the inflections, rhythms, and phrases distinct to both character and the particular places about which Gallagher writes, most often western Ireland and small struggling towns in the American Pacific Northwest. While the language in poems can be intense and concentrated, Gallagher says, "there are certain blue-gray, incremental areas of experience which can't be conveyed at lyrical pitch.... I like the language of fiction to be very transparent, conventional, even ... so it reaches those gliding, slip-knot sequences of human interaction poetry can't easily get to."

Critics often note this lucid quality in her prose. Reviewed widely in publications big and small—the *New York Times, Publishers Weekly, Kirkus Reviews, Belletrista, Entertainment Weekly*—her fiction has been praised, almost universally so, for the precision of the details, for an elegant simplicity, and for its compassion and empathy and insight into human interactions and relationships. On the question of the depth and scope of the stories, the critics are divided. Caroline McElwee in "Lying Next to the Knife" finds transcendence in the way Gallagher brings ordinary people and acts into the realm of archetype and myth, while Bette Pesetsky, in her review of *The Lover of Horses,* finds many of the stories too predictable and easy. Other writers echo the idea that Gallagher is too heavy-handed with the lessons in her stories, though many note

the uneasy sense of impending danger that follows many of these characters wherever they go, and the resonant psychological, spiritual, and emotional epiphanies on which many of the stories turn, small moments that take on bigger meaning when they provoke characters to reckon with their lives.

Also of note in the body of criticism of Tess Gallagher's fiction is an occasional delicate, even nervous, restraint when it comes to the question of acknowledging Gallagher's relationship with Raymond Carver. At times this delicacy results in patronizing or backhanded praise, as in Charles Cross's review of *The Man from Kinvara.* Cross paints the fact that Gallagher's selected stories were published at roughly the same time as her late husband's as a misfortune, even though it was Gallagher herself who spearheaded the publication of Carver's book. "It would be artistically unfair," writes Cross, "to compare husband and wife. ... The timing of the two books is unfair to her worthy collection."

The twelve stories that make up *The Lover of Horses* are a mix of fable-like metaphorical tales and naturalistic stories concerned with the relationships and struggles of white middle- and working-class small-town Americans. Her prose style in the book is clear and fluid, with subtle humor, an unaffected, natural inflection, and the particular kind of evocative mystery that occurs when we know that characters, even when they are loquacious, even when they are looking us straight in the eye as they speak, are probably not—either because they won't or they can't—telling us everything. In the title story, a young woman narrates in the first person a sweeping generational tale of male forebears—her Irish great-grandfather, her American father—whose rash decisions and charming talents lead the women who love and rely on them to extremes of fascination and despair. After a series of strange and jewel-like surprises—a gray stallion trained to dance the mazurka, a young woman speaking in tongues, Doubt and Death personified—comes the biggest shock, as the narrator, upon the death of her father after ruining his last chance for health at his last epic card game, vows to align herself with him: "to be filled with the

first unsavory desire that would have me. To plunge myself into the heart of my life and be ruthlessly lost forever" (p. 18).

Another fable-like story in the collection, "A Pair of Glasses," works with a similar tone, as the strongly metaphoric image of a small girl who fixates on a pair of dime-store glasses is nonetheless meticulously grounded in the details of her everyday life. These two stories share a quality with some of the poems in Gallagher's first collection, *Instructions to the Double*, particularly "Kidnaper" and "Breasts." Young female narrators, surprised by and passionate about the possibilities of life that have risen all of a sudden before their eyes, are almost immediately also aware of the corresponding dangers. The two stories are written breathlessly, but with a sharp edge. Using the understated tone and the strange and dark but thrilling imagery reminiscent of fairy tales—a girl alone in the wilderness, the ritual cutting of her waist-length hair—Gallagher lays the archetype of the young woman becoming aware of her own powers upon her characters, who are making their first choices about who they will be and what they will do.

"The Lover of Horses" works with several themes and subjects that show up elsewhere in Gallagher's body of fiction: loss and death, alcoholism, and characters who tell their most significant or haunting life stories to others, often strangers, so that they themselves might understand what the stories mean. Speaking to the reader, the narrator in "The Lover of Horses" examines the family debate, giving anecdotes as evidence, of whether her great-grandfather was a gypsy or a drunk or both. Mrs. Herbert, in "Bad Company," finds herself one day in a cemetery talking to a young woman she doesn't know, compelled to tell about the sad end of a man whom she might have married instead of her late husband. In response, the young woman tells the story of her father who, when she was a child, drowned trying to save a drunk man who had swum out into the middle of a river. She didn't understand what was happening when she was a child, the young woman says, and she doesn't understand it now.

Many of the narrators in *The Lover of Horses* are women, and meaning often becomes clear to them only after they have made an unexpected connection with another woman: for Ginny Skoyles in "Turpentine," it's the young Avon Lady with alabaster skin, whose story about going to a psychic Ginny listens to closely, then appropriates as her own, discovering an uneasy, strange power in the mystery of the lie. The narrator in "The Wimp" finds herself confiding in random women in the post office and the supermarket about her feeling that her husband doesn't measure up to her expectations.

Ada in "Girls" wants to connect with her old dear friend Esther, who, despite how close they were as young women striking out on their own, does not remember Ada when they meet years later because she has suffered memory loss after a stroke. In "Girls," Gallagher explores the intricate push and pull of relationships, the ways in which people who love each other both reach out to and reject one another. Ada is having trouble connecting with her grown daughter, Billie; Gallagher often shows women of different generations trying to find common ground. When Ada invites herself along on Billie's business trip to the town where Ada lived next door to her friend Esther for four years, in order to look up Esther and try to see her again, Gallagher builds the sense that this trip holds an importance for Ada beyond having fun reconnecting with an old friend. Ada feels that she needs to see who she was in order to understand, and perhaps bear, who she has become. She yearns to communicate to her daughter the story and structure of her life, as she fears that Billie, preoccupied with her own identity as a businesswoman, has already dismissed this information as unimportant—though perhaps, too, Ada is driven by the suspicion and hope that Billie wants to know but has no idea how to ask for it or how to fit the information into her life as she has decided to live it, a life she knows her mother is not altogether enthusiastic about. "'Why are you telling me about this woman?'" Billie asks Ada on the car ride, "as if she'd suddenly been accused of something" (pp. 96–97). Even as Ada inwardly disapproves of some of Billie's blunt and self-interested behav-

ior, she seems helpless to do much about it. The two women find themselves locked in an awkward seesawing of mother-daughter roles, as Ada defers to her daughter's opinion on what she should wear and makes sandwiches even when Billie doesn't want them, and Billie sometimes asks and sometimes tells her mother what her next move will be.

When Ada discovers that Esther doesn't remember her, she is not so much disappointed as terrified: "She felt as if she had tumbled over a cliff and that there was nothing left now but to fall. How could she have been so insignificant as to have been forgotten?" (p. 100). Oftentimes women in Gallagher's stories live with the fear of being deemed insignificant or not good enough by those they love; they may also be misunderstood, abandoned, or betrayed, like Ginny in "Turpentine," who, when standing in front of the mirror washing paint off her face, can feel behind her her husband's disgust with how she looks. In "Girls," when Esther decides that she likes Ada even though she can't remember her, and invites her to spend the night, Ada watches her daughter rush eagerly off, glad to be rid of her, and she cannot simply enjoy her "new" friendship as Esther can. At one point her sudden bitter disdain for Esther seems spurred by a longing for the pretty young girl she herself was once, the girl to whom Esther is one of the only remaining witnesses: "[Ada] hadn't come here to strike up a friendship with this old scarecrow of a woman" (p. 108). In the middle of the night Ada is frightened, reminded of her own alcoholic husband, when Esther's grown son stumbles into the house drunk. She calls out Esther's name, and Esther comes into her room to comfort her and hold her in her bed. The moment changes something for Ada. The next morning, still sorrowful that Esther has failed to remember her, she nonetheless makes a discovery: that identity can be a secret we keep all on our own, that the most important moments of our lives can define us with no one else's knowledge or approval.

The sixteen stories that make up Gallagher's second collection, *At the Owl Woman Saloon,* have much in common with those in *The Lover of Horses* in terms of subjects and themes. Death and loss, particularly of a spouse, are more often present and deeply felt in the second collection. While in "Girls," Ada has greeted her alcoholic husband's death with some relief, the widower in "A Box of Rocks" does not know what to do with himself after the death of his wife. In *The Lover of Horses,* Gallagher often features powerful connections between women alongside troubled male-female relationships. In *At the Owl Woman Saloon,* we now also have women who are likely to dismiss or disdain other women if doing so will help them bond more closely with their men. The narrator of "My Gun" jokes about writing a book called *"The Men We Love and the Bitches They Left"* (p. 182), and Dotty, in "The Woman Who Prayed," upon discovering evidence of her husband's affair with another woman, focuses in her prayers on her love for her husband but also prays that his mistress will suffer disfigurement. "The Red Ensign," however, harks back to *The Lover of Horses* when the narrator, feeling resentful at the intrusion of men into the local beauty shop, wonders if they have stupidly mistaken the "Owl Woman Salon" for the "Owl Woman Saloon."

Widowers and widows in *At the Owl Woman Saloon* are often dealing not only with the emotional consequences of a partner's death but with the practical and legal ramifications as well. In "My Gun," the female narrator, feeling nervous and unprotected after the death of her husband, considers whether or not to buy a gun and wonders what to do with the unexpected pile of money she finds in her husband's safety-deposit box after his suspicious death. In "Coming and Going," another widow finds herself entangled in her late husband's legal troubles. "Mr. Woodriff's Neckties" features a widow and a widower living next door to one another. Even as the widower helps the widow with yard work and commiserates with her over the fence, it is the dead Mr. Woodriff he thinks of most, a writer with whom he had only a few memorable encounters, but whom the narrator thinks he would have liked growing old next door to. He even dreams that Mr. Woodriff might have written him into one of his stories, "a minor character, walking a dog or passing by just as his main character

needed to clarify something by speaking with a stranger" (p. 187).

In *The Lover of Horses,* a preoccupation with death, and with the question of what will happen to our remains, is treated in "Bad Company," as Mrs. Herbert struggles to bear the fact that she told her husband, before he died, that she would not be buried in the plot next to him as he wished. This subject receives attention in the second collection as well. Tivari in "To Dream of Bears" is fixated on the question and longs to dictate a story of his own death different from the one that he will most likely get. After detailing to the narrator the extensive ways Indian hunters would use every part of a bear's body for meat, medicine, charms, bowstrings, and clothing, he says, "No one will ever use us so well, my friend" (p. 132).

"To Dream of Bears," like Gallagher's earlier stories "The Lover of Horses" and "A Pair of Glasses," features a character whose passion for some creature or act or object becomes the defining obsession of his or her life. The theme of women feeling uneasy about their appearances is also apparent in both collections. In "Creatures," which takes place, like "The Red Ensign," in a beauty parlor, we see another young woman, as in the earlier story "Turpentine," with pale skin that the point-of-view character compares to alabaster. In both stories, the gaze of the older white woman looking at the younger one perhaps touches on the irony, keenly felt by the older woman, of living in a society that makes a political and racial fetish out of young white female skin, even as that type of skin ages so quickly, vulnerable to sun and wind and, like alabaster, showing every spot and crack. In "Creatures," the salon owner Elna believes that "beautifying was nothing more than grabbing Mother Nature by the throat and showing her who was boss" (p. 141). Anguished over the betrayal of her husband and her inability to connect with her grown daughter, she vents her fury on her cat, when the sight of the cat's claws digging into her young client's pale exposed flesh compels her to grab the animal and fling it against a mirror.

More apparent in Gallagher's second collection than in her first is a sense of place, in particular the Pacific Northwest. There are more male characters here, some of them loggers who speak to the decline of the industry, such as the narrator, Billy, of the somber "I Got a Guy Once." In his story of the revenge he takes on a man who cheats him of wages, he offers details about cougars, logging crews, and chainsaws, using the jargon of the industry: "spar trees," "snags," "slash clearing," "gyppo logger." The story includes many details about the changing industry: wild animals clashing with humans as forests are cut down too quickly for them to find anyplace else to go; Japanese companies buying most of the logs, using them as forms for high-rises, then throwing the wood away. Even as Billy cuts down the cheat's spar tree, he is sympathetic to the man's plight, as he knows they are all in the sad mess together.

Some reviewers have noted a significant departure in style and voice from Gallagher's first collection to her second. In *At the Owl Woman Saloon,* Gallagher's voice is more expository than in *The Lover of Horses;* the significance of her characters' feelings and epiphanies does not simmer under the surface of their words and actions but rather is spelled out in an essayistic voice, as in her poetry collection *Willingly.* Billy is aware, in "I Got a Guy Once," of the reasons behind nearly all of his feelings and actions, and he expresses those reasons in an erudite way. When a longshoreman describes to him the fate of their trees in Japan, Billy reports that "it hurt me, hearing about waste I couldn't stop" (p. 117). Here and elsewhere, he expresses a noble sensitivity to both humankind and nature that is similar to the tone in some of the poems in Gallagher's poetry collection *Dear Ghosts.* Billy also understands and explains the ironies and metaphors around him, as when he notes that he and the other loggers take one last look at their camp, "which we hated to leave, maybe for its resemblance to our own stripped-down lives" (p. 120).

Gallagher uses a similar style in most of the other stories in the collection, in particular "Coming and Going," in which she again includes a kind of critical analysis of a character's actions alongside a description of the dramatized event,

in this case a moment in which the point-of-view character, Emily, alone in her house, tries to decide whether or not to let a stranger inside before she finds out what he wants, so that she can get back to an expensive long-distance phone call: "She looked him over again and felt the moment seize her in which women hurriedly judge a man safe with the scantest evidence— that split second in which they lunge past fears into an unreliable security" (p. 163). In this passage, Gallagher not only steps outside the dramatic moment but steps outside of her character completely, as she relates Emily's dilemma and actions to a universal experience. The possibility of physical danger the explanation gestures toward is dissipated when we discover that the man is there only to deliver legal papers.

A departure in many ways in style and subject from both *The Lover of Horses* and the other stories in *At the Owl Woman Saloon* occurs in "The Poetry Baron," a sweetly satiric portrait of a poetry professor at a university who struggles unsuccessfully against a desire to seduce one of his students. Written in many short sections, the richly glorified and wickedly smart language speaks to the professor's delusions of grandeur, also expressed in his growing inability to separate his own daily trials from those of Napoleon. At a meeting with the student he desires, the Poetry Baron "was pleased. He'd performed a kindly act. He had ratified the healing properties of literature. He had also eaten chocolate chip cookies and managed to keep his hands to himself.... Ah, but where was his Caulaincourt to make him swerve off this sweet detour?" (pp. 226–227). Even in the midst of his delusions, the Poetry Baron, like Ada in "Girls" and Elna in "Creatures," cannot get away from a rough relationship with his grown daughter, a welfare mother whose unclear understanding of the financial profits of poetry leads her to press her father about whether or not he has written into his will that she will reap the benefits of his books when he dies, and her subsequent demands that, anyway, she would rather have them now.

As Gallagher has noted in interviews, her story "Rain Flooding Your Campfire" (an earlier version was called "The Harvest") treats the same material as Raymond Carver's story "Cathedral." In her interview with Katie Bolick, Gallagher calls the inspiration for the story—a visit to the couple's house by a friend of hers who is blind— her material. Carver knew she planned to write about the visit, Gallagher says, but he wrote about it anyway, and Gallagher's story, written later, was her own but also speaks to his. "Cathedral" is written in the first-person point of view of a working-class man who is unhappy about the impending visit to his house of his wife's old friend. "Rain Flooding Your Campfire" is narrated by the wife in the story, and Gallagher adds a fourth character, Mr. G., who has already written a "patched-up version" of the events, an account the narrator says in the first sentence of the story that she is "about to set straight" (p. 197).

LITERARY EXECUTOR OF RAYMOND CARVER'S ESTATE

As Raymond Carver's literary executor, Tess Gallagher has been instrumental in promoting Carver's legacy, working on volumes of his collected poems and other writings and ensuring the translation of his work into other languages. Perhaps most famously, she spearheaded the republication of the stories that make up *What We Talk About When We Talk About Love* (1981), the collection that made Carver famous and established his reputation as a minimalist. Carver's editor at Knopf at the time, Gordon Lish, edited the stories heavily, changing titles, rewriting endings, and in some cases cutting stories by more than 50 percent. Gallagher has cited an anguished letter Carver wrote to Lish after he saw the proofs, begging Lish not to publish the edited stories. Lish printed them anyway.

Gallagher successfully had the collection, faithful to Carver's manuscript version, republished under the title *Beginners* in several countries, but Knopf refused permission for a stand-alone American printing. In 2009 Knopf did allow for a Library of America edition of Carver's *Collected Stories* that includes the manuscript version of the book (lightly edited by William L. Stull and Maureen P. Carroll), as well

as the versions of the stories as they were originally published and a copy of Carver's desperate letter to Lish. According to Jeff Baker in "Northwest Writers at Work," Carver's last editor, Gary Fisketjon, believes Carver would not have wanted the stories published in their manuscript version, as Carver, when selecting stories for *Where I'm Calling From: New and Selected Stories,* published shortly before his death, chose to include some of Lish's versions instead of the originals. Gallagher argues that she wants readers to be able to compare the two versions and rethink Carver's development and style as a writer.

COLLABORATIONS

Gallagher has collaborated with other artists on various projects throughout her career, most intensely with Raymond Carver. In interviews and essays she often describes how deeply the two were invested in one another's work, reading nearly everything the other wrote and offering detailed critiques and rewrites. The two also wrote work under both of their names, including two short plays, "The Favor" and "Can I Get You Anything?" The plays, set respectively in a couple's home and in a boutique, are intimate renderings of ordinary yet intense moments in the characters' lives. Carver and Gallagher wrote *Dostoevsky: A Screenplay* (1985) long-distance, sending the script back and forth in the fall of 1982, when he was teaching at Syracuse and she had returned to Port Angeles to care for her dying father. The screenplay features a passionate Dostoevsky who struggles under the often dire political, psychological, and financial restraints on what and how he writes.

Robert Altman's *Short Cuts,* based loosely on nine of Raymond Carver's short stories, released in 1993, offers a mosaic of the lives of several sets of characters, some from Carver's stories, some made up, living not in the Pacific Northwest but in Southern California. In his introduction to the paperback reprinting of the nine stories (also titled *Short Cuts*) that accompanies the film's DVD, Altman writes that he and Gallagher corresponded and met regularly throughout the process of making the film, that she contributed significantly to it, and that she approved of the liberal approach to Carver's material.

Gallagher has also edited and promoted the stories of her partner Josie Gray. The stories were published in *Barnacle Soup and Other Stories of the West of Ireland* in 2008. Gallagher writes in her introduction to the book that she recorded Gray telling the stories and had them transcribed, at which point he made revisions, then gave the manuscripts to Gallagher, who revised further, focusing in particular on reinforcing the rhythms and nuances of Gray's voice in order to more closely replicate the feeling of hearing him tell the stories aloud. The brief yet vivid stories, told in a sly, clever style, weave the details of Gray's life in Ireland—the musicians and priests he knows, a local revolt against fishing licenses, springtime excursions to the bog to cut turf—with tongue-in-cheek renderings of local legends and superstitions, such as, in "Surrounded by Weasels," the image of hypnotized children following a parade of the vengeful beasts.

Distant Rain: A Conversation Between Jakuchō Setouchi & Tess Gallagher, a transcription of a 1990 conversation between Gallagher and the Buddhist nun and novelist Setouchi, is also an art book, printed accordion-style with English and Japanese versions and featuring the work of the painter Keiko Hara. The two women discuss their writing and their grief over lovers who have passed away. When Setouchi remarks that her beloved was married, and for that reason she wasn't allowed to see him before he died, Gallagher discusses her conflicted feelings for Raymond Carver's first wife, Maryann, whom she describes as still angry over the happiness of Gallagher and Carver's relationship. Gallagher regrets not being able to help Maryann get over her anger despite being kind to her.

Most recently Gallagher has championed the fierce, luminous work of the Romanian poet Liliana Ursu. With Ursu and Adam Sorkin, Gallagher has contributed to the translation of two of Ursu's books into English. Early in her relationship with Josie Gray, she encouraged him to begin painting

and now she promotes his work as well, helping to arrange shows for him in the United States.

Selected Bibliography

WORKS OF TESS GALLAGHER

POETRY

Stepping Outside. Lisbon, Iowa: Penumbra Press, 1974. (Hand-printed chapbook.)

Instructions to the Double. Port Townsend, Wash.: Graywolf Press, 1976.

Portable Kisses. Seattle: Sea Pen Press & Paper Mill, 1978. (Hand-printed limited edition.)

On Your Own. Port Townsend, Wash.: Graywolf Press, 1978. (Chapbook.)

Under Stars. Port Townsend, Wash.: Graywolf Press, 1978.

Willingly. Port Townsend, Wash.: Graywolf Press, 1984.

Amplitude: New and Selected Poems. St. Paul, Minn.: Graywolf Press, 1987. (Contains 22 poems from *Instructions to the Double,* 20 from *Under Stars,* 26 from *Willingly,* and 26 new poems.)

Moon Crossing Bridge. St. Paul, Minn.: Graywolf Press, 1992.

Portable Kisses: Love Poems. Santa Barbara, Calif.: Capra Press, 1992. (Contains 4 poems from Seattle, Wash.: Sea Pen Press, 1978, limited edition. Expanded paperback edition published by Capra in 1999.)

My Black Horse: New & Selected Poems. Newcastle upon Tyne, U.K.: Bloodaxe Books, 1995. (Contains an essay, "My Father's Love Letters," from *A Concert of Tenses*; 22 poems from *Instructions to the Double*; 20 from *Under Stars*; 26 from *Willingly*; 26 from *Amplitude*; the entirety [60 poems] of *Moon Crossing Bridge*; and 23 new poems.)

Owl-Spirit Dwelling. Portland, Ore.: Trask House Books, 1995. (Chapbook.)

Dear Ghosts: Poems. St. Paul, Minn.: Graywolf Press, 2006. (Contains single poems from *My Black Horse* and *Portable Kisses.*)

Midnight Lantern: New & Selected Poems. Minneapolis, Minn.: Graywolf Press, 2011. (Contains 14 poems from *Instructions to the Double,* 12 from *Under Stars,* 14 from *Willingly,* 11 from *Amplitude,* 40 from *Moon Crossing Bridge,* 14 from *Portable Kisses,* 12 from *My Black Horse,* and 30 from *Dear Ghosts.* Section of new poems, "Signature," contains 30 poems, including 3 that first appeared in *Dear Ghosts.*)

SHORT FICTION

The Lover of Horses and Other Stories. New York: Harper & Row, 1986.

At the Owl Woman Saloon. New York: Scribner, 1997.

The Man from Kinvara: Selected Stories. Minneapolis, Minn.: Graywolf Press, 2009. (Contains 7 stories from *The Lover of Horses* and 11 from *At the Owl Woman Saloon.*)

ESSAYS

A Concert of Tenses: Essays on Poetry. Ann Arbor: University of Michigan Press, 1986.

Introduction to *A New Path to the Waterfall: Poems,* by Raymond Carver. New York: Atlantic Monthly Press, 1989. Pp. xvii–xxxi.

Introduction to *All of Us: The Collected Poems,* by Raymond Carver. New York: Knopf, 1998. Pp. xxiii–xxx.

Soul Barnacles: Ten More Years with Ray. Edited by Greg Simon. Ann Arbor: University of Michigan Press, 2000. (Also contains diary entries, letters to and from Gallagher, interviews, poetry, and essays by Robert Altman and others.)

Foreword to *Call If You Need Me: The Uncollected Fiction and Other Prose,* by Raymond Carver. Edited by William L. Stull. New York: Vintage Books, 2001. Pp. ix–xv.

"Out of the Drink." *Utne Reader* 141:54–61 (May–June 2007). (Originally published as "Instead of Dying" in *The Sun,* December 2006.)

Foreword to *Beyond Forgetting: Poetry and Prose About Alzheimer's Disease.* Edited by Holly J. Hughes. Kent, Ohio: Kent State University Press, 2009. Pp. xv–xx.

TRANSLATION

With Adam J. Sorkin and Liliana Ursu. *The Sky Behind the Forest: Selected Poems,* by Liliana Ursu. Newcastle upon Tyne, U.K.: Bloodaxe Books, 1997.

With Adam J. Sorkin and Liliana Ursu. *A Path to the Sea,* by Liliana Ursu. New York: Pleasure Boat Studio, 2011.

OTHER WORKS

With Raymond Carver. *Dostoevsky, A Screenplay.* Back-to-Back Series 5. Santa Barbara, Calif.: Capra Press, 1985. (Published in an edition with Ursula K. LeGuin's *King Dog.*)

With Raymond Carver. "The Favor" and "Can I Get You Anything?" One-act plays. In *Tell It All.* Rome: LeConte Books, 2005. (Selections of Raymond Carver's unpublished writings.)

With Jakuchō Setouchi. *Distant Rain: A Conversation Between Jakuchō Setouchi & Tess Gallagher.* Translated from the Japanese edition by Hiromi Hashimoto. Cheney: Eastern Washington University Press, 2006. (Previously published by *Fujinkoron,* a Japanese magazine, in February 1991.)

With Josie Gray. *Barnacle Soup and Other Stories from the West of Ireland.* Cheney: Eastern Washington University Press, 2008. (First published by Blackstaff Press, Belfast, 2007.)

PAPERS

Tess Gallagher Literary Archive, Charvat Collection of American Fiction, Ohio State University.

BIBLIOGRAPHIES

McFarland, Ronald E. *Tess Gallagher.* Boise State University Western Writers Series 120. Boise, Idaho: Boise State University, 1995. (Selected bibliography on pp. 53–56 lists works from 1974 to 1994.)

Stull, William L., and Maureen P. Carroll. "Tess Gallagher." In *American Short-Story Writers Since World War II, Fourth Series.* Edited by Patrick Meanor and Joseph McNicholas. Vol. 244. of *Dictionary of Literary Biography.* Detroit: Gale, 2001. Pp. 127–138. (Bibliography on pp. 127–128 lists works from 1974 to 2000.)

"Tess Gallagher." Poetry Foundation. http://www.poetryfoundation.org/bio/tess-gallagher. (Bibliography at the end of the entry is the most current and complete as of 2012.)

CRITICAL AND BIOGRAPHICAL STUDIES

Altman, Robert. Introduction to *Short Cuts: Selected Stories,* by Raymond Carver. New York: Vintage Books, 1993. Pp. 7–10. (Accompanies DVD edition of Altman's film *Short Cuts,* based on the 9 short stories published in the book.)

Baker, Jeff. "Northwest Writers at Work: Tess Gallagher in Raymond Carver Country." *Oregonian,* September 19, 2009. http://www.oregonlive.com/O/index.ssf/2009/09/northwest_writers_at_work_tess.html.

Derry, Alice. "On Tess Gallagher." *Persimmon Tree: An Online Magazine of the Arts by Women over 60,* issue 6. n.d. http://www.persimmontree.org/articles/Issue6/articles/AliceDerry_OnTessGallagher.pdf.

Glover, Michael. "Tess Gallagher Troubadour Café." *Independent,* June 16, 1995. http://www.independent.co.uk/arts-entertainment/poetry-tess-gallagher-troubadour-cafe-1586641.html.

McElwee, Caroline. "Tess Gallagher: Lying Next to the Knife." *Belletrista,* September–October 2011. http://www.belletrista.com/2011/Issue%2013/features_3.php.

McFarland, Ronald. "American Poets and Blue Collar Work." *Midwest Quarterly* 51, no. 4:323–338 (2010).

Sklenicka, Carol. *Raymond Carver: A Writer's Life.* New York: Scribner, 2009.

"Tess Gallagher, 1943–." *Northwest Schools of Literature:*

Commentary 7. Center for the Study of the Pacific Northwest, University of Washington. http://www.washington.edu/uwired/outreach/cspn/Website/Classroom%20Materials/Reading%20the%20Region/Northwest%20Schools%20of%20Literature/Commentary/7.html.

Wood, Gaby. "Raymond Carver: The Kindest Cut." *Observer,* September 26, 2009. http://www.guardian.co.uk/books/2009/sep/27/raymond-carver-editor-influence.

REVIEWS

Ashley, Renée. "*Dear Ghosts.*" *Literary Review* 50, no. 1:165–168 (fall 2006).

"*At the Owl Woman Saloon.*" *Kirkus Reviews,* July 1, 1997. https://www.kirkusreviews.com/book-reviews/tess-gallagher/at-the-owl-woman-saloon/#review.

"*At the Owl Woman Saloon.*" *Publishers Weekly,* September 1, 1997. http://www.publishersweekly.com/978-0-684-82693-6.

Bailey, Sharon M. "*The Sky Behind the Forest.*" *Slavic and East European Journal* 44, no. 2:331–332 (summer 2000). (Review of Liliana Ursu's *The Sky Behind the Forest.*)

"*Barnacle Soup and Other Stories from the West of Ireland.*" *New York Review of Books* 55, no. 8:39 (2008).

Brearton, Fran. "Letter to My Ghosts." *Guardian,* June 15, 2007. http://www.guardian.co.uk/books/2007/jun/16/featuresreviews.guardianreview23. (Review of *Dear Ghosts.*)

Carruth, Hayden. "Tess Gallagher Critical Essay." *Literature Criticism Series.* Thomson Gale, 2005–2006. (Review of *Under Stars.*)

Cross, Charles. "*The Man from Kinvara* Seattle Times, September 11, 2009. http://seattletimes.com/html/books/2009842473_br11tess.html.

Ferguson, Sarah. "Great Northwest: A Collection of Stories from Tess Gallagher Is Set in Familiar Territory." *New York Times,* October 5, 1997. http://www.nytimes.com/books/97/10/05/reviews/971005.05fergust.html. (Review of *At the Owl Woman Saloon.*)

Friedman, Vanessa V. "*At the Owl Woman Saloon.*" *Entertainment Weekly,* September 26, 1997. http://www.ew.com/ew/article/0,,289537,00.html.

Kakutani, Michiko. "A Sense of Peril." *New York Times,* September 6, 1986. http://www.nytimes.com/1986/09/06/books/books-of-the-times-a-sense-of-peril.html. (Review of *The Lover of Horses.*)

Kirby, David. "Soul Barnacles." *Library Journal,* February 1, 2001, p. 88.

"*The Man from Kinvara: Selected Stories.*" *Publishers Weekly,* July 6, 2009. http://www.publishersweekly.com/978-1-55597-537-1.

Pesetsky, Bette. "Secrets and Surprises in a Durable World." *New York Times,* September 28, 1986. http://www.nytimes.com/1986/09/28/books/secrets-and-surprises-in-a-durable-world.html?pagewanted=all. (Review of *The Lover of Horses.*)

Powell, Margaret K. "*Moon Crossing Bridge.*" *Library Journal*, March 15, 1992, p. 92.

Ratner, Rochelle. "*Willingly/From Dream, from Circumstance.*" *Library Journal*, May 1, 1984, p. 902.

Ross, Robert. "New Poems." *Prairie Schooner* 49, no. 4:364–365 (winter 1975–1976). (Review of *Stepping Outside.*)

Seaman, Donna. "*Dear Ghosts.*" *Booklist,* June 1, 2006, p. 21.

———. "*Midnight Lantern.*" *Booklist,* October 15, 2011, p. 12.

Trueblood, Valerie. "Tess Gallagher, *Instructions to the Double.*" *American Poetry Review* 7:39 (July–August 1978).

INTERVIEWS

Bolick, Katie. "A Conversation with Tess Gallagher." *Atlantic Online,* July 10, 1997. http://www.theatlantic.com/past/docs/unbound/factfict/gallaghe.htm.

Foresman, Rebecca. "Helping People Home: Tess Gallagher on *Midnight Lantern.*" *New Yorker,* November 18, 2011. http://www.newyorker.com/online/blogs/books/2011/11/tess-gallagher-midnight-lantern.html.

Kelley, Rich. "The Library of America Interviews Tess Gallagher, William L. Stull, and Maureen P. Carroll about Raymond Carver." *Library of America e-Newsletter,* August 2009, pp. 1–12. http://www.loa.org/images/pdf/LOA_interview_Gallagher_Stull_Carroll_on_Carver.pdf.

Moffet, Penelope. "An Interview with Tess Gallagher." *Poets & Writers,* July–August 1988. http://www.pw.org/content/an_interview_with_tess_gallagher?cmnt_all=1.

Richman, Shira, and Maya Jewell Zeller. "A Conversation with Tess Gallagher." *Willow Springs* 62:84–99 (fall 2008). http://willowsprings.ewu.edu/interviews/gallagher.pdf.

GAYL JONES

(1949—)

Tracie Church Guzzio

ONE OF THE most controversial and enigmatic of all African American writers, Gayl Jones has garnered as much attention for her personal life as she has for her professional career. Not only does she write blues women stories, she appears to be speaking from experience. Even in her early novels, Jones writes fierce and unrelenting portraits of African American women whose lives and very consciousness illustrate the lasting effects of the traumatic history of slavery in America. Women, as Jones reminds her readers, have suffered from a double bind, as victims in a society as sexist as it is racist. From her first novel, *Corregidora,* to the last, *Mosquito,* Jones portrays race and gender within the larger matrix of transnational histories revealing the global war on people of color and women.

Though most of Jones's acclaim has come through her work as a novelist, she has been a prolific writer in all genres. She is a poet and playwright as well as reviewer and literary critic. She has written on European and Euro-American novelists and poets, often drawing comparisons between the work of her contemporaries to literary classics from all over the world. Her contributions to scholarship on music and orality in African American prose and poetry reflect her own concerns as a writer. Her work, like the work of Langston Hughes, Amiri Baraka, Toni Morrison, and John Edgar Wideman, to name a few, highlights the roots of African American discourse and attempts to keep the oral tradition and its verbal artistry alive in the written word. Of her own work she has admitted that "I used to say that I learned to write by listening to people talk. I still feel that the best of my writing comes from having *heard* rather than having *read*" (Harper, p. 352). She also has argued that the links between African American music and writ-

ing are necessary ones to maintain. Writers still "continue to acknowledge and look to the musician as the artistic vanguard and range finder" (*Liberating Voices*, p. 92). As her writing style developed over time, so did her use of African American musical styles in prose. Her later novels, *The Healing* (1998) and *Mosquito* (1999), resemble jazz compositions. Their digressions, multiple discourse modes, blending of high and "low" cultures, and loosely structured plots imply the polyvocality of jazz. And like jazz, they have found a less receptive audience because of their nonlinear narratives and call-and-response modalities. For Jones, the reader or "the hearer is an equal sharer in the story" (Rushdy, p. 273). Her later novels require an engagement with the text that creates meaning through literary conversations. The open form of these novels invites the reader into a dialogue with the story and its characters.

Her early novels *Corregidora* (1975) and *Eva's Man* (1976) reflect the content of the blues tradition as well. Each of these presents women with limited opportunities for expression or understanding. While Ursa Corregidora and Eva Canada each represent different sides of a blues woman struggling to survive the pain and suffering of her life, neither has really been able to control her life, her body, or her future. To varying degrees of success, these two early characters represent African American womanhood confronting the violence in their lives and their own sexuality, especially within the context of white supremacy and emerging definitions of black nationalist masculinity. Each novel also offers an image of strong black women who respond in pathological ways to racism and abuse. Eva Canada kills a man; the women of *Corregidora* sacrifice their own daughters' individual freedom

in pursuit of symbolic revenge. This image out of the blues tradition is a stereotype that offers African American women "the only means of exercising power" (Dubey, 1994, p. 91) in their lives. Jones's work attempts to deconstruct these images to understand their limitations and even their continuing appeal to African American women living in the twentieth century.

Jones later concluded that these early novels, bound by the restrictions of a more conventional novelistic structure, could not express the themes that she was exploring. Nor were the works mirroring the orality of the traditions that she hoped to bridge with her fiction. She revealed in a 1975 interview with her former professor, the poet Michael Harper, her intentions:

> A lot of connections I made with tradition—with historical and literary things—I started making later. I was writing stories in first person before I made connections with the slave narrative tradition or the tradition of black autobiography, before "oral storytelling" became something you talked about. At first, I just felt that the first person narrative was the most authentic way of telling a story, and I felt that I was using my own voice—telling a story the way that I would talk it.
>
> (Harper, p. 353)

After a novel-writing hiatus, Jones returned to similar themes in her two later works of fiction. Still attempting to mark the connections between oral and written discourse, the two novels have a more pronounced oral (or jazz) quality. Searching for an effective way to deconstruct confining images of African American womanhood, Jones developed multiple and mutable definitions of black women—never choosing the ideal type. Instead Jones's characters confront and critique stereotypes throughout American culture (as well as Americans' stereotyping of other cultures, races, and ethnicities across the globe). Like Delgadina in *Mosquito,* Jones was searching for the "cosmic race," a hybridized and variable identity that crosses racial and gender borders. As she told Charles Rowell in 1982, "right now my work most often contains [voices] generally in the form of oral storytelling monologues—stories within stories" (Rowell, p. 159). It is uncertain whether or not Jones will write another novel, or if she does whether it will continue the trajectory of the two novels from the 1990s or head in a new direction. If Jones does not produce another major work, her contributions to the development of the African American novel will continue to be felt by readers of her fiction and by writers who have responded to her experimentations in language, structure, and voice.

BIOGRAPHY

The foundations for Jones's writing began at home in Lexington, Kentucky. Born on November 23, 1949, to Lucille and Franklin Jones, Jones and her brother grew up in a household that celebrated storytelling. In her interview with Michael Harper, Jones credited her inspiration to write to her days spent listening to her mother and grandmother sharing family stories. Lucille also wrote short stories and read them to her children. Jones recalled this practice as having a special impact on the development of her writing, the best of which, she feels, "comes from having heard rather than read" (Harper, p. 352).

By most accounts, Jones was a shy and very quiet child, especially outside of the home. Jones attended a predominantly white school as a teenager. The experience of being one of the few African American students may have made the already reticent Jones positively silent. Through her imagination and writing, she was able to distinguish herself nonetheless. After graduation, she was accepted to Connecticut College. Leaving the rural South and moving north during the turbulent decade of the 1960s would clearly have been a culture shock to Jones. But in the small, liberal arts college setting, Jones found classmates with similar talents and interests and her writing blossomed.

After receiving a B.A. in English in 1971, Jones began working toward a master's degree in creative writing at Brown University. It was during this time that she began working on the novels that would become *Corregidora* and *Eva's Man.* One of her professors at Brown was Michael Harper, who encouraged the young writer's work and later introduced her to her future editor, Toni Morrison. Jones's confidence

and consciousness developed during her years in the program. Brown, like other prominent universities in the early 1970s, had a meager but vocal population of historically conscious African American students who had come of age during the era of Malcolm X and Martin Luther King, Jr., and the civil rights movement. *Corregidora* and *Eva's Man* reflect the voices of the times as well as Jones's own growing self-awareness as an African American woman. She completed her M.A. degree in 1973—the same year her play, *Chile Woman,* was first produced. By 1975 Jones had also finished her doctoral dissertation (titled "Toward an All-Inclusive Structure") while simultaneously publishing her first novel, *Corregidora.*

Jones's professional life took off with noteworthy speed over the next few years. Following the publication of *Eva's Man* in 1976, Jones began teaching at Wellesley College. She later became an assistant professor of Afro-American and African Studies at the University of Michigan in Ann Arbor. While there she published the short story collection *White Rat* (1977), the long poem *Song for Anninho* (1981), and the poetry collection *The Hermit-Woman* (1983), as well as numerous reviews and other short stories and poems. Jones left the university in 1983 following the legal troubles of her companion, Bob Higgins. The couple lived abroad in Paris for several years before returning in 1988 to help care for Jones's mother, Lucille. Lucille had been ill for some time following the death of Jones's father. By this time, Higgins and Jones had married and Higgins had taken Jones's name as his own. Jones and her husband lived in Kentucky with her mother for several more years, all the time keeping a low profile. Jones published a book of literary criticism, *Liberating Voices: Oral Tradition in African American Literature,* in 1992, but she did not produce a major literary work of her own for six more years.

That work, *The Healing,* published in 1998, earned Jones a National Book Award fiction nomination. But the much-anticipated novel—her first in more than twenty years—was overshadowed by Jones's personal tragedy. Jones's mother had died the year before. Her death had been a

difficult one, and it led to renewed troubles with the legal system and government officials for Jones and her husband. Soon after Jones had appeared in a full-page review in *Newsweek* magazine celebrating her triumphant return to the literary world, police attempted to arrest Jones's husband at their home. Instead of surrendering to police, he committed suicide. Devastated by the turn of events, Jones remained in a hospital for a few months under psychiatric care. After her release, she completed work on the novel *Mosquito,* which was published in 1999. Since that time, Jones has not released another major work of literature. Today, she lives in Lexington, Kentucky. Her literary silence appears to reflect the quiet of her personal life. Her career and private life at this time are an enigma to curious scholars and fans.

CORREGIDORA

Gayl Jones's first novel remains her best known and most often analyzed. It appeared in 1975 during a heightened period of interest in black nationalism. Like its contemporaries, the novel addresses black consciousness within the context of African American slave histories. James Baldwin and Toni Morrison were both vocal advocates of Jones's work and controversial style. Morrison, Jones's editor, was particularly struck by the honesty and brutality of the novel—characteristics that shocked and offended many other readers. Yet the novel and its protagonist are recognizable illustrations of the blues woman stories that have long addressed the pain and suffering of African American women.

Ursa Corregidora is the protagonist and a blues singer. Her singing connects her personal losses with the familial and racial past. Both Ursa and "the novel bear witness to New World history as a history of trauma" (Simon, p. 94). Ursa's great-grandmother was the slave of a Portuguese plantation owner in Brazil named Corregidora. As his slave, Ursa's great-grandmother was raped and prostituted by Corregidora—acts perpetrated against his own slave daughter as well. This generational cycle of abuse and violence is Ursa's legacy. It is a history

known and repeated by all the women of her family. When Ursa is five years old, her great-grandmother passes this history along to her:

> They didn't want to leave no evidence of what they done—so it couldn't be held against them. And I'm leaving evidence. And you got to leave evidence too. And your children got to leave evidence. And when it come time to hold up the evidence, we got to have evidence to hold up. That's why they burned all the papers, so there wouldn't be no evidence to hold up against them.
>
> (*Corregidora*, p. 14)

Ursa, and her mother before her, have been told this family history in order to make certain that the lost records are never forgotten. The women in Ursa's family encourage her to continue this tradition of bearing children as evidence of the horrors of the past that Corregidora attempted to erase. Several critics have pointed out the ironic reversal of the phrase to "bear witness" in this ritual. Ursa's family never demands that she shares these stories with anyone outside of the home to counteract the official record of their past—instead she is merely told she must "bear witnesses."

This commandment explains Ursa's need to sing the blues. As she tells her husband, Mutt, singing "helps me to explain what I can't explain" (p. 56). Ursa carries a tremendous historical weight within her. Yet she has not found the language to adequately express or comprehend its hold on her. Her songs echo the pain of the past, but they cannot offer a remedy. The blues is meant to be a shared experience—a public act of remembrance and catharsis. Despite her great-grandmother's claim that the act of bearing children will address the silences of history, there is no impulse to connect with others to share and manage the grief of the past.

When Ursa experiences her own personal tragedy, the loss is twofold. After Mutt pushes her down the stairs in a fit of jealousy, Ursa loses their unborn child and is later told she will not be able to bear any others. Her identity as a "bearer" of generations of witnesses is denied by nature and by Mutt's actions. Ursa cannot conjure a song to help her express the pain because her blues are disconnected from their inherent power.

She realizes this in the novel when she contemplates the role written for her by her female family members: "Stained with another's past as well as our own. Their past in my blood. I'm a blood. *Are you mine, Ursa, or theirs?*" (p. 45). Her family's demands have enslaved her body and her voice—her identity belongs to the past, not to herself.

Ursa's struggle with the past is a unique one in African American history though it is not unlike the family haunted by the ghost of a dead baby in Morrison's *Beloved* (1987). Ursa's victimization has its roots in the past, but it is recycled by the inability to move beyond the pain suffered by her ancestors. Criticism of the work since the mid-1990s has largely focused on the novel's exploration of trauma. The applications of literary trauma theory have been useful in understanding the relationship between personal and cultural trauma. Within this framework, readers can consider Ursa's actions as a representation of post-traumatic stress disorder. Her family requires her to revisit the site of traumatic memory and thus forces her to relive and reenact the suffering of the past. In this case, it is not even her own personal past that she is encouraged to return to. As with the children of Holocaust survivors, it is the story of trauma handed down "through the blood" that traps Ursa in the suffering of the past. She has also not been taught the tools of survival. No one has taught her how to sing the blues. In fact, her mother criticizes Ursa for performing in public, singing "devil's music."

The past also informs her relationships with others. Both Ursa and her mother have found themselves in situations with men that mimic the sexual violence and emotional isolation suffered by their ancestors. They seemed doomed to repeat the unhealthy cycle of domination and control begun by Corregidora. Mutt and Tadpole attempt to sexually control Ursa, demanding her body and her voice. Ursa has difficulty connecting to either man or to anyone else. Even the prospect of a lesbian relationship does not offer her the intimacy and trust that she needs. Cat's offer is only portrayed as an alternative to the men in Ursa's life. Sexuality is almost always portrayed

in the novel through the framework of domination and ownership. Jones develops the novel and Ursa's growth as a character after the miscarriage. Since Ursa's body has been defined in terms of its breeding functions, once she loses the ability to have children she is ironically able to fight for autonomy from the past. Ursa's lack of her "womb is the genesis for her blues and the source of her creativity. The void left by her womb is filled by the blues, and the blues in turn, become her matrix, her womb, the space where her past and present are accommodated" (Fraile-Marcos, p. 210). Her identity is no longer prescribed by history, but she must first journey into the traumatic memory in order to move beyond its control over her and her subjectivity. Her self-realization of this necessary process involves transforming the blues into a healing song: "They squeezed Corregidora into me, and I sung back in return" (*Corregidora,* p. 103).

Throughout the novel, Jones balances narrative action with memories, dreams, and Ursa's reflections. These sections are italicized to represent the process that Ursa has undertaken to address the past and find her own voice. Some of these spaces are also filled with memories that do not belong to Ursa, existing almost as another layer of her consciousness. Using this structure, Jones reveals Ursa's double consciousness—the conflict between her image of herself and the image that has been given her by others. In this case, Ursa must balance multiple other identities forced upon her—by white society, by African American men, and by her own family. If she is to transform her pain into healing through the blues, she has to negotiate these multiple images, ultimately rejecting them for her own self-fashioned image. This is usually the prerogative of the male in literature, but as a possible blues woman, Ursa's necessary development has antecedents within the tradition. The popular image of the blues woman is a strong, unique, even eccentric, individual. The identity of the blues woman may still be a mask, but it is one of her own creation.

Before Ursa can become her own creation, she must visit her mother to reclaim her autonomy. The journey to see her mother is a symbolic rebirth where Ursa will have the chance to confront the past more directly than in her imagination and memories. She also wants to know, through her consideration of her mother's experiences, whether it is possible to escape the legacy of the women of her family and whether her mother loved her father (hoping that there is a chance for a healthy relationship with a man given the history of sexual violence in her family's past). Ursa needs her mother to share her story, so that they can find mutual understanding and healing. "Despite her initial reluctance to speak," Ursa's mother "offers her story as a gift." This scene has a number of effects including inspiring Ursa to "come to terms with her own story" (Li, p. 136).

The resolution of this visit and of the novel is less clear. Critics have interpreted that the change in Ursa is both a positive affirmation and, conversely, an inability to escape the burden of the past. Ursa returns to Mutt, to the same hotel they once lived in while they were married. This scene could be read as a "traumatic return" implying that Ursa cannot leave the past behind her. Instead she must repeat it. Other readers argue that the scene shows Ursa in a position of control, which is a change in her relationship with Mutt. While Ursa is performing oral sex, she realizes that her great-grandmother was able to leave Corregidora because she had attempted to castrate him with her mouth (a scene that will be repeated in *Eva's Man*). This realization and Mutt's physical passivity in the scene suggests that Ursa is in "sexual control" (Hardack, p. 657). However, even this reading could illustrate that Ursa cannot really be free from the past if the scene is an allusion to her great-grandmother's act. After all, the moment that Ursa's great-grandmother threatens Corregidora and gains her freedom is also the beginning of the plan to bear generations of children to provide evidence of Corregidora's crimes. This decision keeps Ursa and her family bound to Corregidora for decades. Like most blues women, Ursa's story continues to negotiate the thorny intersections of race and gender, revealing that such struggles cannot be resolved, at least in a realistic narrative.

EVA'S MAN

Jones's second novel, *Eva's Man,* was quickly acclaimed as a worthy follow-up to *Corregidora,* but the work was not without its detractors. Several feminist reviewers, including the poet June Jordan in the *New York Times,* criticized the work for its portrayal of the protagonist, Eva Medina Canada. Eva, a longtime victim of sexual intimidation and abuse, sits in a prison cell for killing and then castrating her male partner, Davis Carter. These critics of the work argued that Jones offers Eva as a stereotype—a crazy, angry black woman who kills her lover out of jealousy or in self-defense. Other readers responded to the text primarily on sociological terms, as evidence of the victimization of African American women by men and by the system. In more recent years, scholars of Jones's work have considered the novel and the character of Eva in broader strokes, suggesting to varying degrees that Jones's revision of the African American prison narrative allows for a more complex and liberal reading of the text.

Eva's story begins in a home dominated by a strong male figure. Her father controls Eva and her mother, and when he suspects Eva's mother of adultery he brutally rapes her. Eva quickly learns that women have little or no power, and they are defined by the subjectivity of their body and their sexuality. Eva's growing awareness of women's identity and its inherent powerlessness is further enhanced by her own experiences. As a young woman she is sexually harassed and assaulted. All of these experiences occur at critical junctures in her life. Just at the time she is beginning to feel the beginnings of her own sexual desire, she starts to comprehend that she will have little agency in exerting that desire—instead she will be the recipient of men's will.

There is little in Eva's past or present to contradict the image of female subjugation. She recognizes as a young girl that men misread her mother's intentions—reading in her eyes their own lust and jealousy, as if she were a mirror. But even when men are not present, Eva hears little of her mother's own voice. Instead she often hears her mother listening to her friend, Miss Billie, complain about men and their obsession with sex. These stories do not offer alternatives to Eva—no stories of resistance or female triumph. Nor do the women describe "good men" or healthy relationships. The men in her childhood do not provide Eva with any counterbalance to these stories. Her father is a silent and domineering figure who later rapes her mother. And her mother's friend, Tyrone, makes sexual advances to her when she is twelve. Eva seems to never know a man who does not treat women as sexual prey.

Eva's reaction to men as she grows older seems almost inevitable. Her resistance to the power that men will try to exert over her and her body comes through violence. When Moses attempts to reach between her legs, she stabs his hand. The act is Eva's first "criminal" response to men's sexual domination. And we already know that she is in prison following another. The novel opens in the first-person voice with Eva's brief description of the crime, but since she is already in prison for it, her narrative is hardly styled as a confessional. Nor is it a typical prison narrative. Eva doesn't use her story to indict the system, she does not become a female activist, nor does she find religion. Her tone is matter of fact; she never asks for forgiveness or understanding from the reader. Even when the narrative moves back and forth in time, she does not offer the structure of her storytelling as a matter of evidence for her crime. When she talks to people about the crime (which is very little), she tells us: "they think I'm lying to them, though. I tell them it ain't me lying, it's memory lying. I don't believe that, because the past is still as hard on me as the present, but I tell them that anyway" (*Eva's Man,* p. 5). This is the only time Eva herself suggests that the past has contributed to her present situation.

Eva also tells us that during the police interrogation, the psychiatric evaluation, and the trial she remained silent, but after she went to prison she "started talking" (p. 5). But she never reveals why. Her inability to understand her own motives suggests that Eva lacks a blues voice, through no guilt of her own. It seems she has few examples of it in her life. She hears a woman singing the blues in the bar the night she meets Davis Carter,

but there is no sign she connects to the voice or the song in any meaningful way. She is merely a "blues listener" (Dixon, p. 245). Eva has been cut off from the sustaining traditions of her family, community, and people. Miss Billie tells her, "You got to be true to your ancestors and you got to be true to those that come after you" (*Eva's Man,* pp. 85–86). Despite this advice, Miss Billie never seems to illustrate this herself. Her stories are not ones of women surviving and triumphing. She is interested in the past and in the future in ways that are similar to Ursa's mother in *Corregidora.* Miss Billie's own vision of women is little more than the one she claims that men have of women—as sexual beings, as vessels.

Though Eva inhabits a world where men and women's relationships have been scarred by the wounds of slavery and racism, she has been given no tools to survive that legacy. Nor does she connect with other women in a community of solidarity. This may have been what she was searching for during all of the years of almost consistent movement around the country. No matter where she lived or where she worked, she never settled down and never found a stable community she felt she could be a part of. Even the stories that Eva knows of Medusa and Queen Bee present images of solitary women, not voices of communion. And despite her sexual encounters with her cellmate, Elvira, Eva does not find intimacy or kinship in the relationship. Eva and the world she knows are bereft of any healthy responses to pain, suffering, and isolation.

Even in the prison narrative tradition this is an especially brutal and nihilistic story. Nor does the slave narrative tradition, the progenitor of the African American prison story, offer such a grim portrait of an African American woman's life. Early readers' responses are certainly understandable. Eva is a victim of a racialized society or she is a remorseless, crazy woman. In either of these readings her only power is violence and revenge—she is "an avenging angel" whose "crime is a symbolic liberation from the particular grotesqueness of her society" (Byerman, 1982, p. 452). It is never exactly clear, of course, if Eva sees herself this way, or if readers perceive her as this character. It is also pos-sible that she poisons and later castrates Davis Carter because she knows no other response to men or conceivably to any problem that she may encounter, including anything that may emerge from her own desire. Eva never understands the expressive power that the narrator of the slave or prison narrative or the blues singer discovers in telling her story.

Some critics of the work suggest, however, that Eva's silence may be her act of defiance. As Hershini Bhana Young observes, her "silence could easily be misinterpreted as passivity, as a painful denial of agency and acquiescence to the reality of others' domination" (p. 379). It is conceivable that her silence is a refusal to give people the real story, the real Eva. The silence she offers to policemen, attorneys, and psychologists instead of testimony denies them further control over her identity, her inner self, which "threatens her with imprisonment within monolithic meaning" (Young, p. 387). Her muteness is present when Tyrone attempts to talk to her about his advances and when she is arrested for stabbing Moses, as well as during her murder trial. Nor is she the only female who resists speech for the benefit of others. When Davis' wife comes to the prison to see Eva, the two do not speak to one another, and she offers Eva no reason for the visit. Rather than present a confrontation between wronged women, Jones veers from the stereotypical and even melodramatic expectation of the readers. Even blues songs sometimes offer these types of conflicts between women. Instead, the scene suggests silent understanding between women with common experiences.

Though Eva seems to have no voice in the past, her violent acts against men are suggestive of a woman looking for expression, but she has been taught by others to see the body as the only powerful weapon a woman has (though even this she does not own). There is emphasis on the mouth, Eva's mouth literally or figuratively, in each of these encounters. She warns Moses when he tries to touch her genitals that "her teeth" there may bite him. And her castration of Davis is by her mouth. When she refuses to speak after each of these moments, she controls her mouth. Her mouth (i.e., her voice), unable to find a blues

song, a way to express its longing or pain in a healing manner, loses its human attributes. Eva cannot vocalize her inner thoughts or feelings and therefore responds in more infantile or repressed ways. Unable to locate herself in history or in companionship or community—things she may desperately want as well as need—she is left alone in silence. But whether that silence is a sign of resilience and resistance or of despair is left to the reader's interpretation.

THE HEALING

More than twenty years after *Eva's Man* was published, Jones released the novel *The Healing.* Jones's resurfacing ignited heightened media attention for the work, including a *Newsweek* review. For some time, the praise for the novel was eclipsed by its mere appearance, after such a long time between works, and by Jones's personal tragedies. Despite the publicity, *The Healing* did make the National Book Award short list, and signaled to readers and critics a new development in Jones's writing. Less realistic in style and structure, "*The Healing* constitutes a very conscious and distinct shift in direction with regard to Jones's oeuvre" (Clabough, p. 103). Jones's move toward a more postmodern voice and sensibility—a jazzlike re-creation of narrative—could also be recognized in its characters. The protagonist, Harlan Eagleton, is a faith healer. In a characteristic moment of postmodern self-referentiality, Harlan cures a woman named Sally Canada, a relative of Eva Canada. Jones heals her own literary past through this act, replacing the pain and silence of Eva with Harlan, who is both a storyteller and representative of a mythical conjure woman. The linkage of the two talents reflects Jones's own history as a child and her growth as a writer, and she will continue to develop this change in her work in her later novel, *Mosquito.*

Harlan narrates the novel, but she is also able to read other characters' minds, and at times those thoughts interrupt the work's progression. There is very little plot, and Harlan's description of her past, her grandmother, and her life (and beginnings) as a faith healer violate conventional novelistic structures. The novel's postmodern characteristics are also a reflection of Jones's own theories of the power of orality to shape reality and to resist essentialist notions of black womanhood. While works like *Corregidora* and *Eva's Man* fought against such images, it is not until *The Healing,* through the characters of Harlan and her grandmother, that Jones offers women and narratives that are capable of presenting alternatives.

Interwoven with Harlan's odyssey are the tales of her grandmother, the Turtle Woman. Blending mythology, folk tales, and transformation stories, her turtle tales offer Harlan and the reader a reconstruction of voiceless women into storytellers. The grandmother's transformation of herself from turtle to human, from something silent to "something fully capable of expressing her being" (Stallings, p. 65), recalls African creation stories. Here the creation is not of the natural surroundings but of an individual's expression and subjectivity. The grandmother claims her story, her voice, her very creation, rather than permitting her origins to be cataloged or recorded by an outside observer or a man. In rendering the grandmother this way, Jones "explodes" the "limitations of gender" (Stallings, p. 67). The novel's acceptance of the grandmother's past—or "herstory"—is reminiscent of the magical realism of Latin American writers such as Gabriel García Márquez. Even the carnival imagery of *The Healing* evokes Garcia's "A Very Old Man with Enormous Wings."

The grandmother's tales also offer counternarratives to the types of limited portraits of female identity that are predominant in *Eva's Man* and *Corregidora.* The transformation of silence into expression is what is lacking in Eva's life, and is only barely expressed in Ursa's blues singing in *Corregidora.* The Turtle Woman tales (and the Unicorn Woman stories as well) offer an alternative vision of African American womanhood. As a trickster figure, the turtle must hide itself and its true identity to protect it from predators. The African American literary trope of masking is reconfigured to suggest that African American

women need a tough shell to survive. Jones's fiction is populated by "hard" women, but in *The Healing* this woman forgoes "hardness" in order to experience love with a man who has the ability to see the "real woman" underneath the shell. The gift of transformative powers through the act of love is passed from grandmother to granddaughter. Harlan's ability to heal, to transform pain and suffering to love and understanding, rewrites Jones's former texts of nihilism and isolation. Unlike the legacy of Ursa's grandmother, Harlan's ancestor has bestowed her with an imagination that will free her from the tyranny of others' ideas of who she should be.

Harlan's ancestral past prepares her for the unusual life she is meant to lead. But on the surface, she appears to be a "normal" or "real" woman. There are numerous references in the book to Harlan's image and its various meanings to different characters. Her sister-in-law tells her she does not look like a "nice" woman; the musician, Joan, relishes Harlan's normalcy when they first meet; and when Harlan later becomes a faith healer, people judge her authenticity on their readings of her image and identity. She worries that she needs to look more impressive to be taken seriously by people she meets on the road—but this uncertainty does not keep her from following her calling. She knows that she is also often guilty of labeling people she meets—expecting them to fit her image rather than accept who they are under their shells.

When Harlan first meets Josef Ehelich von Fremd, she judges him by his name, his nationality, his race, and his ethnicity, as well as by her expectations of maleness. The more she tries to fit his identity into a single box, the more ridiculous the "naming" becomes. It is only after they are intimate that she is able to see beyond the associations she brings to his identity. She has similar problems with the guitarist in Joan's band, Jimmy Cuervo. Harlan once again tries to apply labels based on the usual markers, but by this time in the novel, she has become more accepting of hybridization. She uses different languages (and mestiza cultural references, as Jones will in *Mosquito*) to identify Jimmy. She ultimately never resolves "what" Jimmy is; her

acceptance of his multiplicity, much like her belief in the various versions of the Turtle Woman stories her grandmother tells her, connotes her position in the text as a storyteller. Her ability to hear other people's thoughts and stories allows her the mobility and imagination to be their vehicle for expression in the novel.

Harlan's rejection of her middle name—Truth—implies that she is not a universalist or essentialist. Ultimately she is able to accept many "truths" about others. It is notable that she does not abandon the ideals of the historical figure she is named for—Sojourner Truth. Like her counterpart, Harlan wants to use her voice to heal, to change, and to lead her people. Her travels across the country and around the world, visiting "tanks towns" and African villages, prepares her for leadership, but it also allows her to understand connections between people and between the past and the present. Her independence and mobility reflect the blues woman common in Jones's work, but Harlan is not migrant or transient because of loneliness or isolation from community. It is just the reverse. Her journeys eventually even call her to rethink her grandmother's turtle stories. "How come a woman can't follow her ownself to turn human?" she asks (p. 137). Why does her grandmother's transformation depend on a man? Why do most women need a man to find their voice or their purpose? Harlan chooses a life without children or without a stable and committed relationship. She chooses a life usually reserved for men. In doing so, she "embodies a new mode of femininity that breaks free from past restrictive notions" of what it means to be a black female (Venugopal, p. 51).

Unlike Jones's earlier female characters, Harlan claims and controls her own subjectivity. She is not burdened by a traumatic past such as Ursa's, but neither does she need to be bound by the definitions of womanhood that are historically situated. Drawn to other strong and independent women in the book—the Masai healer, Joan the rock star—Harlan realizes she must write her own story. Otherwise, men, and other women, may do it for her. Her grandmother's turtle stories and the transformative power they suggest free her from the past to discover her own "truths."

After Joan stabs her in a jealous fit, Harlan discovers her healing power: "I'm the one who touched my own wound. I'm the one who healed my own self first" (p. 35). Jones's emphasis in the novel on oral storytelling and family stories as the medicine to heal one's self and one's culture confronts the ghosts of other fictional characters from her literary past. She develops these themes and this style in the novel *Mosquito* as well, offering more evidence of the ways that stories address and resist the dominant images of black womanhood in the culture and in Jones's own work.

MOSQUITO

Published in 1999, *Mosquito* is considered by many critics to be one of Jones's best works, as well as her "lightest." That characterization of the novel suggests that it is one of the few that transcends the trauma of the past as well as the conventions of African American novels of the early 1970s that still bore the mark of the politics of the 1960s.

The plot of *Mosquito* develops in a postmodernist style, breaking boundaries, overlapping narratives, languages, and discourses in a reflection of America's growing awareness of its multicultural and transnational identity, or its "salsa style." The novel's voice, its structure, and its protagonist, Sojourner Nadine Jane Nzingha Johnson (or Mosquito), all represent a new development in Jones's writing. Mosquito, with her multiple names and identities, is not Eva Canada, a character silenced by her limited self-perception, or Ursa Corregidora, overly burdened with the weight of history.

But not everyone has been a fan of the work. The noted critic and scholar Henry Louis Gates, Jr., writing in the *New York Times,* was especially critical of the book, including its structure and its experiments with form and narrative. However, as the critic Carrie Tirado Bramen argues, these characteristics of the text are "precisely the point of Jones's novel" (p. 129). The limited varieties of storytelling methods that Gates suggests Jones should abide by are as imprisoning as the narrow definitions of African American female identity.

Mosquito's inability to control her story or the characters within it reflects a desire for fluidity and hybridity rather than stereotyping by gender, race, or ethnicity. The work's style and content "encourages the reader to rethink the conventions of racial representation by radically challenging the conventions of narration" (Bramen, p. 130).

The plot of the novel (despite the book's length) is fairly slim. The majority of the work reads as a series of long digressions by Mosquito. She is the storyteller and story maker and perhaps an echo of Jones's own mother, Lucille. In a blending of fiction and fact (a process that occurs throughout the novel), the epigraph cites Lucille Jones's fictional character, Kate Hickman, as an ancestor of Mosquito. The epigraph is written by Nzingha (one of Mosquito's identities) and belongs to the "Daughters of Nzingha" archives. Like the work of her contemporary John Edgar Wideman, Jones's family stories and fictions cohabit within the same narrative space without any guideposts clarifying what is "real" and what is imaginative. Mosquito informs the reader later in the novel that she is melding fiction and fact and admits to being an unreliable source of information—or at least not the only source there should be for someone else's story: "you can't trust everybody with every story" (p. 384).

Mosquito's inability, or refusal, to see the boundaries between fact and fiction are reinforced in other ways in the novel. Living primarily in Texas City, a fictional border town, she makes her living by driving a truck carrying hazardous chemical detergents. Her movement across borders is fluid and without concern (though she spends most of the time driving alongside the border). She feels as connected to the South as to the North. It is only after others are kept from moving freely between borders that Mosquito becomes more politicized. When she helps an illegal immigrant, she becomes involved in an organization reminiscent of the underground railroad. The Sanctuary movement specifically alludes to the historical practices of the railroad to identify a political and cultural connection between escaped African American slaves and immigrants from south of the border. One of Mosquito's names—Sojourner—further rein-

forces the links between the past and the present and her own role as a leader and orator in the African American tradition. It is Mosquito's orality and its ability to transcend human borders that Jones suggests is the power of story.

Cultural borders are transgressed throughout the novel. Jones highlights the similarities between African Americans and other nonwhites and between North Americans and the rest of the world. By focusing on both "commonalities and distinctiveness [the novel] lays bare the falsity of the perceived oppositions between hemispheric (or universalist) and national (or particular) orientations" (Nwankwo, p. 583). But Jones also draws connections between people of different ethnic and racial backgrounds who share common class distinctions. Many of these connections are drawn by Mosquito in periods of digression when she observes behaviors or sees someone different from herself. As she begins to question her own thought process, critically analyzing assumptions she has about racial differences, the reader is able to trace Jones's arguments about identity. Unlike her rendering of an earlier character such as Eva Canada, Jones allows Mosquito to self-reflect and self-assess.

Mosquito's rambling digressions highlight the deconstruction of fixed identity that Jones is attempting in the novel. This is true whenever she considers her friend, Delgadina, a Chicana bartender. Mosquito wrestles with Delgadina's identity more than her own. She considers Delgadina a true Latina, a representation of North American culture's fascination with passionate, "hot-blooded," sexualized female figures. Mosquito's own attention to Delgadina's looks suggests a "homoerotic charge" (Bramen, p. 136). For a good portion of the novel, Mosquito tries to fix her friend into a received category—committing the same act of appropriation that men attempt of women in *Corregidora* and *Eva's Man*. Mosquito has difficulty locating Delgadina outside of this perceived identity; most often she illustrates the ways that her friend fits the image through her dress, her food, her temper, and her female sexuality. It is Mosquito's attraction to these qualities that harness that image more securely in her mind.

Delgadina experiences these images within her own construction of her identity. Torn between remaining true to herself and to her culture and past, she often feels that she sounds either too European or too Mexican in her writing. Her interest in writing and becoming a detective both suggest a character that is invested in discovery—finding and reading the clues to who she is and translating that exploration into text. A far more politicized character than Mosquito, she uses this self-analysis to address not only her own confusion about her hybrid nature but also to understand the mestiza culture of her people. Delgadina is writing a "border novel" that considers pre-Columbian influences in her culture, the history of the Comanche, life in Texas City—attempts to highlight a balance of preliterate traditions and the historical record. But she is criticized by her fellow writing students:

> A few of 'em said I'm too preoccupied with being a Chicana, you know. And I should write universal stories or some shit. Gringo stories, that's what they mean by universal, or gringa stories, even gringa stories can be universal now. We Chicanos are *la raza cósmica*, the cosmic race. We're already universal.
>
> (p. 487)

If she is going to be honest in her writing, she will have to confront this tension. Yet at times, she is tired of being seen only as a representation of her people—she has to choose one identity over another. Nevertheless, she is, like Mosquito, a Daughter of the Nzingha.

Mosquito's other friend, Monkey Bread, is also a Daughter of the Nzingha. She is known in the novel only by her letters to Mosquito and other textual documents. An actress and assistant to a Hollywood producer, she provides several other borders for Jones to explore: high and low culture, reality and illusion, orality and written literacy, America and the world. Her letters to Mosquito exhibit these borders and their crossings almost simultaneously as she describes the mixing of cultures and religions and races she encounters during her travels. She also discusses movies and Othello, rap music and the blues, *Lord Jim* and LeRoi Jones. Like Delgadina, she inhabits several spaces and identities. Her mobil-

ity across the globe and in time, and therefore in Mosquito's imagination, helps her occupy a less fixed identity in Mosquito's narration. Even Monkey Bread's texts illustrate border crossings. They literally interrupt the pages of the novel—a letter, lines from a film script, poetry, blues lyrics, announcements, newsletters. Many of the texts are part of the material she is collecting as a Daughter of Nzingha.

The goal of the collection is archival—everything produced by the children of the African diaspora needs to be found and catalogued for the sake of memory, history, and "New World African Women." These acts are both literary and historical. They also reflect the necessary relationship between orality and textuality in the novel. Mosquito's storytelling voice (and her letters) are also a part of that tradition that must be collected. As these textual elements appear alongside Mosquito's voice (like her truck that runs alongside the border), they remind us of the privileging of written words over spoken ones—a hierarchy that silenced thousands of stories from the diaspora when the writing of slaves was outlawed by their masters.

The multiple discourses found throughout the novel and within it and the multiple texts collected by the Daughters of the Nzingha reinforce the hybridity and multiplicity of identities that Jones is calling for in the novel and in her later work. Mosquito's circular narrative and digressions that keep the reader moving back and forth in time help illustrate in her developing multicultural, transnational consciousness the connections that lie between us all. Jones's "refusal of beginnings, middles, and ends is the formal manifestation of her vision of race at the end of the century" (McDonald, p. 316). Mosquito realizes these possibilities when she recalls the community of her church:

> Some members of the Perfectability Baptist Church are Negroes, others is colored people, others is blacks (with a small b), others is Blacks (with a big B), others is Afro-Americans, others is African-Americans (hyphenated), others is African Americans (unhyphenated), others is Just Plain Americans, others is New World Africans, others is Descendants of the Victims of the African Diaspora Holocaust, others is Multiracialists, others is Multiethnics, oth-

ers is Sweeter the Juice Multiracial Multiethnics (these are people like myself who have other races and ethnic groups, like Mexicans, Irish, Greeks, and Italians in they ancestry but who resemble pure African gods and goddesses), others are Cosmopolitans Neo-Africans....

(p. 613)

Her enumerations suggest the "cosmic race" that Delgadina calls truly "universal." This image of the multiple possibilities of her own black identity offers a broader resistance to the offensive image she sees on the cover of a satirical magazine, *The Cosmic Pickaninny.* She pronounces: "I know for a fact that the cover photograph ain't me" (p. 56), but it is not until later in the novel that Mosquito's vision is clarified enough to see the alternative African American identities that are possible so that she may embrace her legacy as a Daughter of the Nzingha at the same time she is able to participate in the cosmic race. In the final pages of the novel, Mosquito imagines different identities for herself and family members as well as for her friends—she tells all their stories affirming her place as a transmitter of memory for a chorus of voices.

POETRY

Gayl Jones's poetry has garnered little critical attention in comparison with her novels, which offer multiple interpretations from a variety of critical perspectives; criticism on *Corregidora* alone continues to generate enormous interest, especially among feminist and psychoanalytic theorists. The scholar Casey Clabough suggests that Jones herself may in part be responsible for the lack of criticism on her poetry in that she is often dismissive about "genre boundaries" (p. 102). And at this time, there are only three books of Jones's poetry (though there is a great deal of poetry that has not been collected). *The Hermit-Woman* (1983) offers the broadest range of Jones's poems available in a single publication. Her second collection of short poems, *Xarque and Other Poems,* was published in 1985. Several of the poems, including "Deep Song" and "Jasper Notes," present earlier blues-style poems along with ideas about poetry as a healing art—especially in the tradition of African American women.

Jones's *Song for Anninho* (1981) is a book-length poem concerning the lives of two escaped Brazilian slaves in the sixteenth century. Based on true events, the poem explores the love story between Anninho and Almeyda, two inhabitants of Palmares, a colony started by former slaves in the present-day Brazilian state of Alagoas. In Jones's poem, the colony is a productive and free space in the New World. Because Palmares threatens the global institution of slavery, European traders are continually trying to attack the colony. In 1694 the citizens of the colony were massacred. Anninho is one of the murdered, and Almeyda survives, though she has been brutally scarred by the invaders. As she recovers, through the help of a healer/conjure woman, Almeyda remembers her life with Anninho. The poem is an act of recovery and remembrance as Jones conveys the despair of Almeyda within the larger cultural trauma that the Palmares massacre illustrates about the horrible losses during centuries of slavery.

This little-known event is made more tragic by the awareness of the erasure of these people and their lives through time and through the project of European historiography. Like Corregidora's burning of his plantation's records, Palmares was obscured from the view of the world for centuries. What's more, the massacre is completely justified in the eyes of the soldiers and the government: the slaves had upset the order of civilization.

Like *Mosquito* and *The Healing,* the poem moves back and forth through time. At times Almeyda is recalling a moment with Anninho or her family. Or she "remembers" African ancestors she could never have known or she speaks to Zibatra, the healer who is nursing her back from the brink of death. Zibatra is a "mystic and biblical scholar" who drank "from the vine before the vine / was invented" (p. 7). She is ageless, a mover of time. She seems to set in motion Almeyda's memory. In doing so, her loss is soothed by linking her memories of Anninho to a community of family and ancestors who have gone on before.

Jones originally conceived of the story as a novel titled "Palmares." Though unpublished, it presents the same characters and situations. Jones eventually chose the poetic medium to narrate this history and the traumatic separation of these two lovers. Parts of the *Song for Anninho* also appeared as short poems. Many of the sequences reveal a Edenic period before the invasion when the love between Anninho and Almeyda had a chance to survive in the world. But slavery, colonization, and the inevitability of the end of Palmares robs them of their future. The loss of their love is not the worst suffering; "more devastating than the agony they endure is the (fore)knowledge that none of it will be chronicled" or remembered in history (Clabough, p. 84). Zibatra tells Almeyda that "it is not easy to love / at a time such as this one (p. 46)."

Jones presents Palmares as a mestiza world, a "new world" with new people; in her poem she is able to "render her version of events, a version that highlights African resistance to New World slavery" (King, p. 757). Embedded in Jones's poem is also the myth of the "flying Africans" whose memory of magic words helps them escape slavery. Jones's reimagining of this massacre and of the myth allows the privileging of memory over recorded history. In *Corregidora* this inverted hierarchy deepens the wounds of Ursa and her family. But here Jones equates memory with magic—the kind Zibatra uses to heal Almeyda's heart and body, as well as the ancestors lost to slavery. The "song for Anninho" is a lament and an elegy, as well as a promise to never forget or to stop singing the blues (or recording them in fiction) for those silenced voices of the past.

Selected Bibliography

WORKS OF GAYL JONES

NOVELS AND SHORT STORIES
Corregidora. New York: Random House, 1975.
Eva's Man. New York: Random House, 1976.
White Rat: Short Stories. New York: Random House, 1977.
The Healing. Boston: Beacon, 1998.
Mosquito. Boston: Beacon, 1999.

GAYL JONES

POETRY

Song for Anninho. Detroit: Lotus, 1981.

The Hermit-Woman. Detroit: Lotus, 1983.

Xarque and Other Poems. Detroit: Lotus, 1985.

OTHER WORKS

Chile Woman. Schubert Playbook Series 2, no. 5. New York: Schubert Foundation, 1974. (Play.)

Liberating Voices: Oral Tradition in African American Literature. New York: Penguin, 1992.

PAPERS

Manuscripts and other materials are in the Gayl Jones Collection, Howard Gotlieb Archival Research Center, Boston University.

CRITICAL AND BIOGRAPHICAL STUDIES

Agusti, Clara Escoda. "Strategies of Subversion: The Deconstruction of Madness in *Eva's Man, Corregidora,* and *Beloved*." *Atlantis* 27, no. 1:29–39 (June 2005).

Allen, Donia Elizabeth. "The Role of the Blues in Gayl Jones's *Corregidora*." *Callaloo* 25, no. 1:257–273 (winter 2002).

Basu, Biman. "Public and Private Discourses and the Black Female Subject: Gayl Jones's *Eva's Man*." *Callaloo* 19, no. 1:193–208 (1996).

Bell, Bernard W. "The Liberating Literary and African American Vernacular Voices of Gayl Jones." *Comparative Literature Studies* 36, no. 3:247–258 (summer 1999).

Boutry, Katherine. "Black and Blue: The Female Body of Blues Writing in Jean Toomer, Toni Morrison, and Gayl Jones." In *Black Orpheus: Music in African American Fiction from the Harlem Renaissance to Toni Morrison*. Edited by Saadi A. Simawe. New York: Garland, 2000.

Bramen, Carrie Tirado. "Speaking in Typeface: Characterizing Stereotypes in Gayl Jones's *Mosquito*." *Modern Fiction Studies* 49, no.1:124–154 (spring 2003).

Byerman, Keith. "Black Vortex: The Gothic Structure of *Eva's Man*." *MELUS* 7, no. 4:93–101 (1980).

———. "Intense Behaviors: The Use of the Grotesque in *The Bluest Eye* and *Eva's Man*." *CLA Journal* 25, no. 4:447–457 (June 1982).

Clabough, Casey. *Gayl Jones: The Language of Voice and Freedom in Her Writings*. Jefferson, N.C.: McFarland, 2008.

Collins, Janelle. "'Intimate History': Storyteller and Audience in Gayl Jones's *Corregidora*." *CLA Journal* 47, no. 1:1–31 (2003).

Coser, Stelamaris. "The Dry Wombs of Black Women: Memories of Brazilian Slavery in *Corregidora* and *Song of Anninho*." In her *Bridging the Americas: The Literature of Paule Marshall, Toni Morrison, and Gayl Jones*.

Philadelphia: Temple University Press, 1994. Pp. 120–163.

Davis, Amanda J. "To Build a Nation: Black Women Writers, Black Nationalism, and Violent Reduction of Wholeness." *Frontiers* 26, no. 3:24–53 (2005).

Davison, Carol Margaret. "'Love 'Em and Lynch 'Em': The Castration Motif in Gayl Jones's *Eva's Man*." *African American Review* 29, no. 3:393–410 (autumn 1995).

Dixon, Melvin. "Singing a Deep Song: Language as Evidence in the Novels of Gayl Jones." In *Black Women Writers (1950–1980): A Critical Evaluation*. Edited by Mari Evans. Garden City, N.Y.: Anchor, 1984. Pp. 235–248.

Dubey, Madhu. "Don't You Explain Me." *Black Women Novelists and the Nationalist Aesthetic*. Bloomington: Indiana University Press, 1994. Pp. 89–105.

———. "Gayl Jones and the Matrilineal Metaphor of Tradition." *Signs* 20, no. 2:245–253 (winter 1995).

Fraile-Marcos, Ana. "Lady Sings the Blues: Gayl Jones's *Corregidora*." In *Literature and Music*. Edited by Michael Meyer. Amsterdam: Rodopi, 2002. Pp. 203–227.

Gates, Henry Louis, Jr. "Sanctuary." *New York Times,* November 14, 1999. http://www.nytimes.com/books/99/11/14/reviews/991114.14gatest.html. (Review of *Mosquito*.)

Goldberg, Elizabeth Swanson. "Living the Legacy: Pain, Desire, and Narrative Time in Gayl Jones's *Corregidora*." *Callaloo* 26, no. 2:446–472 (2003).

Gordon, Nickesia. "On the Couch with Dr. Fraud: Insidious Trauma and Distorted Female Community in Gayl Jones's *Eva's Man*." *Obsidian III* 6, no. 1:66–88 (spring–summer 2005).

Gottfried, Amy S. "Angry Arts: Silence, Speech, and Song in Gayl Jones's *Corregidora*." *African American Review* 28, no. 4:559–570 (winter 1994).

Griffiths, Jennifer. "Uncanny Spaces: Trauma, Cultural Memory, and the Female Body in Gayl Jones's *Corregidora* and Maxine Hong Kingston's *The Woman Warrior*." *Studies in the Novel* 38, no. 3:353–371 (fall 2006).

Harb, Sirène. "Memory, History, and Self-Reconstruction in Gayl Jones's *Corregidora*." *Journal of Modern Literature* 31, no. 3:116–136 (spring 2008).

Hardack, Richard. "Making Generations and Bearing Witness: Violence and Orality in Gayl Jones's *Corregidora*." *Prospects* 24:645–661 (October 1999).

Harris, Trudier. "A Spiritual Journey: Gayl Jones's *Song for Anninho*." *Callaloo* 5, no. 3:105–111 (October 1982).

Horvitz, Deborah. "'Sadism Demands a Story': Oedipus, Feminism, and Sexuality in Gayl Jones's *Corregidora* and Dorothy Allison's *Bastard out of Carolina*." *Contemporary Literature* 39, no. 2:238–262 (summer 1998).

Jackson, Richard. "Remembering the 'Disremembered': Modern Black Writers and Latin America." *Callaloo* 13, no. 1:131–144 (winter 1990).

Johnson, Patrick. "Wild Women Don't Get the Blues: A Blues Analysis of Gayl Jones's *Eva's Man*." *Obsidian II* 9, no. 1:26–46 (spring–summer 1994).

Jordan, June. "All About Eva." *New York Times,* May 16, 1976. http://query.nytimes.com/mem/archive/pdf?res=F00F14F83458167493C4A8178ED85F428785F9. (Review of *Eva's Man*.)

King, Lovalerie. "Resistance, Reappropriation, and Reconciliation: The Blues and Flying Africans in Gayl Jones's *Song for Anninho*." *Callaloo* 27, no. 3:755–767 (summer 2004).

LaCroix, David. "Following Her Act: Sequence and Desire in Gayl Jones's *The Healing*." *African American Review* 41, no. 1:115–126 (spring 2007).

Li, Stephanie. "Love and the Trauma of Resistance in Gayl Jones's *Corregidora*." *Callaloo* 29, no. 1:131–151 (winter 2006).

Lionnet, Francois. "Geographies of Pain: Captive Bodies and Violent Acts in the Fictions of Myriam Warner-Vieyra, Gayl Jones, and Bessie Head." *Callaloo* 16, no. 1:132–152 (winter 1993).

McDonald, Joyce Green. "Border Crossings: Women, Race, and Othello in Gayl Jones's *Mosquito*." *Tulsa Studies in Women's Literature* 28, no. 2:315–336 (fall 2009).

Mills, Fiona, and Keith B. Mitchell, eds. *After the Pain: Critical Essays on Gayl Jones*. New York: Peter Lang, 2006.

Nwankwo, Ifeoma C.K. "The Promises and Perils of U.S. African-American Hemispherism: Latin America in Martin Delany's *Blake* and Gayl Jones's *Mosquito*." *American Literary History* 18, no. 3:579–599 (fall 2006).

Passalacqua, Camille. "Witnessing to Heal the Self in Gayl Jones's *Corregidora* and Phyllis Alesia Perry's *Stigmata*." *MELUS* 35, no. 4:139–169 (winter 2010).

Robinson, Sally. "'We're All Consequences of Something': Cultural Mythologies of Gender and Race in the Novels of Gayl Jones." In her *Engendering the Subject: Gender and Self-Representation in Contemporary Women's Fiction*. Albany: SUNY Press, 1991. Pp. 135–187.

Rushdy, Ashraf H. A. "Relate Sexual to Historical: Race, Resistance, and Desire in Gayl Jones's *Corregidora*." *African American Review* 34, no. 2:273–296 (summer 2000).

Sharpe, Christina. "The Costs of Re-Membering: What's at Stake in Gayl Jones's *Corregidora*." In *African American Performance and Theater History: A Critical Reader.* Edited by Harry J. Elam, Jr., and David Krasner. New York: Oxford University Press, 2001. Pp. 306–327.

Simon, Bruce. "Traumatic Repetition: Gayl Jones's *Corregidora*." In *Race Consciousness: African American Studies for the New Century.* Edited by Judith Jackson Fossett and Jeffrey A. Tucker. New York: New York University Press, 1997. Pp. 93–112.

Stallings, L. H. "From Mules to Turtle and Unicorn Women: The Gender-Folk Revolution and the Legacy of Obeah in Gayl Jones's *The Healing*." In *After the Pain: Critical Essays on Gayl Jones*. Edited by Fiona Mills and Keith B. Mitchell. New York: Peter Lang, 2006. Pp. 65–90.

Sweeney, Megan. "Prison Narratives, Narrative Prisons: Incarcerated Women Reading Gayl Jones's *Eva's Man*." *Feminist Studies* 30, no. 2:456–482 (summer 2004).

Tate, Claudia. "*Corregidora*: Ursa's Blues Medley." *Black American Literature Forum* 13, no. 4:139–141 (winter 1979).

Venugopal, Shubha. "Textual Transfigurations and Female Metamorphosis: Reading Gayl Jones's *The Healing*." In *After the Pain: Critical Essays on Gayl Jones*. Edited by Fiona Mills and Keith B. Mitchell. New York: Peter Lang, 2006. Pp. 31–64.

Ward, Jerry, Jr. "Escape from Trublem: The Fiction of Gayl Jones." *Callaloo* 16, no. 3:95–104 (October 1982).

Wilcox, Janelle. "Resistant Silence, Resistant Subject: (Re)Reading Gayl Jones's *Eva's Man*." In *Bodies of Writing, Bodies in Performance*. Edited by Thomas Foster, Carol Siegel, and Ellen E. Berry. New York: New York University Press, 1996. Pp. 72–96.

Young, Hershini Bhana. "Inheriting the Criminalized Black Body: Race, Gender, and Slavery in *Eva's Man*." *African American Review* 39, no. 3:377–394 (fall 2005).

Yukins, Elizabeth. "Bastard Daughters and the Possession of History in *Corregidora* and *Paradise*." *Signs* 28, no. 1:221–249 (autumn 2002).

INTERVIEWS

Harper, Michael. "Gayl Jones: An Interview." In *Chant of Saints: A Gathering of Afro-American Literature, Art, and Scholarship*. Edited by Michael S. Harper and Robert B. Stepto. Urbana: University of Illinois Press, 1979. Pp. 352–375.

Jones, Gayl, and Lucille Jones. "The Storyteller's Art: A Literary Conversation." *Callaloo* 26, no. 3:709–719 (summer 2003).

Rowell, Charles H. "An Interview with Gayl Jones." In *Gayl Jones: The Language of Voice and Freedom in Her Writings,* by Casey Clabough. Jefferson, N.C.: McFarland, 2008. Pp. 157–179.

Tate, Claudia C. "An Interview with Gayl Jones." *Black American Literature Forum* 13, no. 4:142–148 (winter 1979).

MIRANDA JULY

(1974—)

Elaine Roth

THE WRITER, DIRECTOR, performance artist, and actress Miranda July has an extensive Web presence documenting her forays into a wealth of genres. Called a "prolific polymath" and a "hyphenate artist" in a *New York Times Magazine* article that featured her on the cover, she may be best known for her online projects, band recordings, music videos, performance art, art installations, films, and blogs about her films. However, this essay will focus primarily on her work as an author of print texts, where she has also made a sizable contribution.

Miranda July was born Miranda Jennifer Grossinger on February 15, 1974, in Barre, Vermont. Her parents, Richard Grossinger, a writer, and Lindy Hough, a poet, taught at Goddard College. The family moved in 1977 to Berkeley, California, where Grossinger and Hough ran a New Age publishing company, North Atlantic Books, out of their home. Brought up in this literary bohemian milieu, Miranda began writing early; as a teenager she staged plays and performance pieces at the all-ages punk club 924 Gilman in Berkeley. She also assumed the surname of July in her teens and legally changed it in her early twenties. (Curiously, her father's last name, Grossinger, was itself an adopted name, taken on during a case of mistaken paternal identity.) After graduating from the College Preparatory School in Oakland, she attended the University of California–Santa Cruz but dropped out after her sophomore year. She spent most of her twenties in Portland, Oregon, establishing herself as a performance artist and filmmaker, then moved to Los Angeles in 2004. Her debut feature film, *Me and You and Everyone We Know,* premiered in 2005 at the Sundance Festival, where she met her future husband, the independent film director Mike Mills, whose

Thumbsucker was also being screened. (They married in 2009.) In another interesting bit of synchronicity, their second feature films—July's *The Future* and Mills's *Beginners*—were both released in 2011.

As a writer July has published a collection of short stories, *No One Belongs Here More Than You* (2007), which won the Frank O'Connor International Short Story Award. These stories originally appeared in a range of periodicals, from the *New Yorker* to *Harper's* to *McSweeney's,* elite venues for short fiction. Her most recent book, *It Chooses You* (2011), is a photojournalist account of interviews with Los Angeles people who listed items for sale in the local *PennySaver.*

No One Belongs Here More Than You was a best seller and reached a large audience, but July's work also resonates among hipsters in the world of music, art, and literature, from the author Amy Hempel to the music celebrity David Byrne, lead singer for the former band the Talking Heads. The author George Saunders believes her stories contain "a spirit of tenderness and wonder that is wholly unique. They are (let me coin a phrase) *July-esque,* which is to say: infused with wonder at the things of the world" (*No One,* back cover). July's work frequently involves child characters who approach the world with this sense of wide-eyed novelty. July herself, in publicity images, is regularly photographed wide-eyed and unsmiling, in simple, colorful clothing, reflecting this attitude in body and costume. Such insistence on naïveté and simplicity can strike certain audience members, perhaps those who also recognize July's canny skill at managing her career, as inherently disingenuous. It may be in part this sentiment that underwrites the current of resentment that circulates online against this artist, which seems somewhat out of

proportion for a relatively obscure figure. (In fact, most performance artists would probably relish the attention.) The *New York Times Magazine* article was written in part in dialogue with these voices, including the blog *I Hate Miranda July.*

July's work often includes candid internal musings, some jarringly familiar, some laughably ludicrous. Either way, her straightforward approach to the incoherent nature of desire and fantasy, including its darker aspects, is characteristic of her writing, both prose and screenplays. In much of her work, July suggests that the performances that are common and necessary for daily life—at work, at home, as a colleague or a parent—are as much learned acts as any of the odder events she describes in her fiction or undertakes in her performance art. The strangeness of the art piece thus reveals the artificial nature of the type of behavior that has become accepted as normal and natural. Such destabilization of the normal and the natural has historically been the agenda of experimental or avant-garde art.

Much of July's work is fairly ephemeral, appearing online, such as the website *Learning to Love You More,* an online collaboration with other artists, primarily Harrell Fletcher, or in installations such as *Eleven Heavy Things,* interactive sculptures displayed at the Venice Biennale (2009), New York (2010), and Los Angeles (2011). What follows is a description of some of her less ephemeral work: the short story collection, writing that has appeared in the *New Yorker,* and her two films.

NO ONE BELONGS HERE MORE THAN YOU
(SHORT STORIES, 2007)

Miranda July's short story collection was well received and reviewed, garnering positive feedback from well-known writers such as Dave Eggers, an author of books that similarly blend fiction and fact and the founder of the online literary journal *McSweeney's.* July's collection is composed of sixteen short stories, eight of which appeared earlier in other publications, including literary journals such as *Zoetrope: All-Story,* the *Harvard Review,* and the *New Yorker.* A ninth short story, "The Boy from Lam Kien," appeared earlier as a publication in its own right, released by Cloverfield Press. The collection is dedicated to Julia Bryan-Wilson, an art history professor at the University of California–Berkeley and a friend of July's, who has interviewed July and also contributed an essay to the book that grew out of the online project *Learning to Love You More.*

The title of the collection is consistent with July's quirky style: the use of second-person pronouns, the simple words and phrases, the seemingly straightforward yet complicated sentiment (is it a compliment or a put-down?). Many of her other pieces use similar phraseology: *Learning to Love You More; Me and You and Everyone We Know;* or *Things We Don't Understand and Definitely Are Not Going to Talk About,* an early performance piece about relationship crises that grew into the 2011 film *The Future.* The familiar, generally monosyllabic words, the candid emotional register, the multivalent resonance of the words in their disarming simplicity, all recur in July's work.

Although most of the stories use the first-person point of view (a voice that, as Angela Ashman points out, grows out of July's early performance pieces), two employ third person, and two begin in first-person plural, using "we," but resolve back into first-person singular by the end. Most of the narrators are unnamed, and all the stories take place in an unspecified present, a vaguely late-twentieth-, early-twenty-first-century landscape familiar to contemporary readers, though one that is tweaked by July's perspective. The locations are generally unspecified but often populated middle-class areas in the United States, either suburbs or towns, neither rural nor densely urban settings. Although the protagonists are often on their own, there are always other people nearby. Few of the characters have standard day jobs; most exist on the fringes of capitalist culture, in marginal occupations such as peep shows or secretary to a man who may or may not be an accountant. Many are transitory, moving between locations, while others are trapped in one place, immobilized by fear and anxiety.

The first story, "The Shared Patio," describes an encounter between renters who share a patio space. Alienated and lonely, a single woman experiences her married male neighbor's epilepsy attack as an opportunity for intimacy; rather than alerting anyone, she leans against him and fantasizes that he has confessed his devotion to her. Luckily, his wife, a medical professional, shows up and administers first aid. The piece goes back and forth between this brief narrative, printed in standard font, and passages in italics that seem derived from a self-help text, perhaps written by the alienated neighbor herself. She works for a printer that produces the newsletter *Positive,* for HIV-positive readers. The insistently upbeat tone of the newsletter may also inform these italicized passages that reveal the single woman's isolated, angry, even occasionally deranged views.

Although the story has July's typical humorous tone when the woman stubbornly misreads her neighbor's unconscious state in order to steal a moment of physical contact with another human being, the reader also recognizes the genuine danger the neighbor is in, so that the levity of the story is underwritten by this threat of danger. Despite the single woman's skepticism and resistance to the upbeat message of the self-help publications she prints, the story ends with a shift from marginalized alienation to a more cautiously positive approach. An italicized passage departs from the angrier note in the earlier italicized sequences and instead describes a common yoga technique. The passage also sounds genuinely, if tentatively, hopeful: "*Now praise the sky and praise the light within each person under the sky. It's okay to be unsure. But praise, praise, praise*" (p. 11). The narrator's failure to read social signals, comical and dangerous in the story, ultimately opens the collection with a familiar July perspective: a childlike bewilderment with larger social institutions and practices, underscored by a certain amazement at the world, resolving into a gesture toward hope.

"The Swim Team," the second entry, is a brief account, almost a writing exercise, from a young woman to a man who recently broke up with her. It is a framed text, in that it begins with the narrator explaining that she resisted telling her lover this story when they were together, and it ends with their breakup. The story itself follows the young woman during a strange episode in which she decides to conduct swimming lessons for the elderly in her kitchen apartment, with no access to a body of water. Once again, July channels the bossy, knowing tone of a child, combined with a naive sense of possibility—learning to swim on the kitchen floor—in a humorous but poignant way. These unusual "swimming lessons" also recall July's first foray into cinema, the short film *Atlanta* (1996), about a preadolescent swim star and her mother. The story "Swim Team" further touches upon another July theme, that of young people working with the elderly. In the film *Me and You and Everyone We Know,* the protagonist Christine, played by July, not only drives for elderly people but also collaborates with one of her elderly clients, Michael, on an art installation.

The story begins with the fantasies that the narrator's boyfriend imagines about her previous life; his versions involve prostitution and nudity. By contrast, the actual endeavor—teaching swimming without a pool—resembles performance art, in which characters must uphold their allegiance to their assigned roles and their shared enterprise in order for the piece to work. Like much of her fiction, this story teeters between the familiar and the impossible, offering an original vantage on the possibilities of human experience.

The next story, "Majesty," presents a departure in that it specifies a date (October 9, 2002) and gestures toward a place (Sacramento, California). The main character's age is also specific, forty-three, perhaps to create a frisson for the reader when the protagonist begins to have sexual fantasies about the teenage Prince William of England. The story thus raises another theme that emerges frequently in July's stories: sexual desire for adolescents, a taboo subject in a culture with a heightened sense of children in peril from sexual predators. Her frank portrayals of couples with large age gaps is thus noteworthy. Similarly, her forays into childhood sexuality are also unusual. Tolerance for the possibility of mutual desire between people of distant ages

seems fairly challenging in the contemporary moment.

The story contains several examples of unusual desire, from the main character's erotic dream and subsequent fantasies about Prince William to her relationship with her sister, who narrates sexual adventures over the phone for the protagonist's pleasure. The protagonist feels ashamed of her reliance on her sister to provide her with erotic scenarios and resents her for it. This uneasy link between family and sexuality recurs in several July stories, with varying degrees of destructiveness.

"Majesty" also contains another July theme, the significance of pets. The protagonist encounters a woman searching desperately for her dog, Potato, then witnesses Potato on his joyful flight, and finally sees the woman later, grieving, after Potato has been killed. These quick snapshots in the life of the pet are echoed in July's 2011 film *The Future,* which is narrated by a wounded cat, Paw Paw (voiced by July herself). (It's also worth noting that July's husband, Mills, similarly included a talking animal in his film *Beginners*: the male protagonist inherits his father's dog after his father dies, and the son and pet communicate telepathically [the dog's dialogue is conveyed in subtitles]).

"The Man on the Stairs" is a short exploration, once again from an unnamed first-person female voice, of a relationship between a thirty-eight-year-old man and a twenty-five-year-old woman. The age gap is not so significant, except that the woman has desired him for the previous thirteen years, since she was twelve. The bulk of the story takes place during the night as the woman lies in bed, intermittently afraid of a sound on the stairs that she believes is an intruder. Her description of the male intruder begins increasingly to resemble a personification of her unhappiness in her relationship. The story once again uses the language of self-help, or at least self-reflection, as the dissatisfied protagonist muses on how she can improve her life.

In "The Sister," July departs from her earlier protagonists and presents an aging male perspective. The protagonist is a single man in his late sixties, often set up with male friends'

sisters, who unexpectedly becomes involved with one of his own male friends, Victor, a widower. Victor woos the protagonist by pretending that he has a sister he would like to introduce to him. This pretense extends for some time, while the protagonist invents elaborate fantasies about the purported sister. The desire circulating in this story, a mixture of disavowal and mistaken identity, includes the protagonist's fantasies about underage teenage girls, which seemingly underwrite his lack of sexual attraction to adult women. Like the protagonist in "The Shared Patio," glimpses into the protagonist's interior life reveal loneliness and alienation, defensiveness about the weirdness of his desire, and rage at his situation in life. Victor intuits that this evasive range of emotions also includes same-sex desire, and the two embark on a "new life" in the story's conclusion.

"This Person" is a short excursion in the third person, a meditation on the response of a single female, "this person," to a marvelous, magical invitation to a party that resembles a transition to celebrity status, a fantasy scenario of acceptance and admiration from everyone this person has ever known. The brief story, which follows the protagonist's uneasiness with and ultimate rejection of the celebration, can easily be interpreted as an artist's uncertainty about recognition and success, and the lack of credibility generated by praise delivered too readily. At the same time, the protagonist's dissatisfaction, her desire to be alone, and her suspicion of the outpouring of acceptance all compete with her relentless quest for more contact with people: she leaves the party populated by everyone she has ever known to check her mailbox and e-mail, desiring still more communication, even as she evades the abundance provided by the get-together. July, whose work has been praised as well as loathed, surely situates her own work in this short piece.

"It Was Romance" is one of two stories in the collection that uses an unusual storytelling technique that begins with the pronoun "we" but ends with a reduction of that voice to a single person, again a young female voice. The story describes the experience of a group of women gathered for a weekend seminar on romance,

primarily from the group's perspective but occasionally from the point of view of one of the women, who joins another in a shared emotional encounter. The protagonist's interior thoughts reveal her intense loneliness, an emotion she recognizes in a fellow seminar participant, the unmoored Theresa, who sits on the floor by a chair and not in it, from which the protagonist deduces: "This is always a bad sign.... But we have all been there. Chairs are for people, and you're not sure if you are one" (p. 60). This alienation is shared by the protagonist, who has splintered off from the group "we" and the group activities and is standing alone in the hall. At this point, however, she joins Theresa, and the two women sob together. Afterward, they rejoin the final moments of the seminar, and the story returns to the plural voice, in a reassuring suggestion that the women have bonded. If they remain alone in the world, they at least recognize each other's loneliness.

The following piece, "Something That Needs Nothing," is one of the major stories in the collection, a longer contribution that appeared originally in the *New Yorker*. Like the previous entry, it begins by using the plural first person, but it resolves into a solo alienated voice. A grim, seedy story punctuated with moments of levity, it follows two teenage lesbian girls, the protagonist and Pip, her love interest, who does not return her affections, after they graduate from high school and move to Portland, Oregon. Many themes of July's fiction circulate here, such as the candid, unsophisticated voice of youth and the intersection of that voice with the power and danger generated by sexuality and desire. After the girls move into an apartment, they find themselves unable to transition into conventional adult behavior. Instead, fueled by romantic idealism, they reject low-wage employment: "We needed time to consider ourselves, to come up with a theory about who we were and set it to music" (p. 64). The only alternatives they develop to fund this deliberation involve trading on their sexuality: they first place an ad offering themselves to women seeking women, after which the protagonist begins performing in a peep show for men. Pip temporarily abandons her for another

girl, one with more money, but returns and the two girls end up basically squatting in a friend's basement. Although Pip is initially captivated by the costume and persona that accompanies the protagonist's foray into the world of peep show performances, the allure quickly fades for her. The end of the story finds the protagonist alone at work, cut off from Pip, considering quitting her job.

The representation of desperate same-sex, low-income living fueled by employment on the margins of the economy is perhaps informed by July's time in Portland after dropping out of college in the mid-1990s. There she became involved in the flourishing punk rock music scene of the Pacific Northwest, performing and recording with a band called the Need and making music videos for better-known groups like the Seattle band Sleater-Kinney. Several of the bands featured all-female lineups (like Sleater-Kinney) while others were interested in gay and lesbian issues.

A recurring line of dialogue appears in this story. When Pip leaves the protagonist, jobless and unable to pay the rent, the protagonist throws a scene and begs Pip to stay: "I was sobbing and wailing, but not like a cartoon of someone sobbing and wailing—this was really happening" (p. 77). This sense of immediacy also occurs in the story "Majesty," when a woman cries after her dog, Potato, dies: "She had lost someone she loved, she feared for his safety, it was really happening, it was happening now" (p. 27). And in the film *Me and You and Everyone We Know*, July plays an aspiring performance artist who includes a similar line in one of her pieces, this time delivered during a moment of elation.

In July's writing, tension plays out between performance and authenticity, between art and what is claimed as real life; self-conscious characters feel they are playing roles; characters unwittingly inhabit roles; and children, particularly adolescents, try on roles as they face maturity. The line between art and the real is deliberately blurred, with the suggestion that much of human behavior that seems familiar and uncontrived is in fact the result of endless practice; correspondingly the art world, with its careful consideration of the creative process,

trains a lens on the real world and suggests a variety of ways of inhabiting that world. In the midst of this fuzzy distinction between the constructed and the genuine appear moments of intense emotion that July specifically designates as authentically "real," so much so that her characters recognize them when they happen, surprising everyone with their force. Yet the very effort to claim them as real seems excessive, throwing into relief the lack of authenticity underwriting the normal moments that otherwise constitute existence.

The story that follows, "I Kiss a Door," reveals the danger inherent in two themes in July's work: the intersection of family and sexuality; and the desire of older men for younger women. This short meditation, written from the perspective of a woman in the music scene, alights only on erotic moments: feeling a charge from the father of her friend Eleanor as she and the father watch Eleanor perform as the lead singer of her band; sleeping with Eleanor's bandmate and possible love interest, Marshall; and later, running into Marshall and learning that Eleanor had been sexually involved with her father in high school and was now living with him again. It dawns upon the protagonist that the only time Eleanor was free of her father was during her membership in the band, though the protagonist does not seem to recognize that her own seduction of Marshall may have disrupted one of Eleanor's getaway plans. The story explicitly links the female voice, publicly projected in this instance in live performance, with freedom from repressive and threatening male sexuality: the protagonist views the record Eleanor's band produced as "the one amazing piece of evidence of her self. Her very own self, sung in the only voice she had" (p. 97). While the protagonist raises the possibility that the relationship is consensual and Eleanor might actually have chosen to be with her father, the story forecloses on that notion in its closing lines, when it is revealed that Eleanor no longer performs; she maintains no access to a public voice. When Eleanor goes to hear Marshall's band, he asks her if she still sings, to which she laughs and answers, "Still? You flatter me" (p.

97). This end to creative production in the final line of the story, the sacrifice of Eleanor's voice for her father, indicates that July is not attempting to redeem this unusual relationship. Instead, the father's dominance and power silence the daughter. Significantly, however, the world of music and performance functions as an arena for resisting the rule of the father, if only fleetingly.

"The Boy from Lam Kiem" originally appeared as a stand-alone publication. The narrative, about a young woman with agoraphobia who rarely leaves her home, provides an account as she ventures outside, walking toward the Lam Kiem beauty salon next door, and encounters a preadolescent boy from the salon, who follows her home. The boy investigates her belongings and lies in her bed, in another of July's investigations of intergenerational dynamics. The protagonist worries whether she will be judged for letting a child into her house, while the boy asserts his own presexual perspective and suggests that she buy bunk beds so that people can sleep over at her house. When the woman raises the notion that people could sleep in her bed, the boy is surprised; in this account, the adult and child perspectives have trouble communicating. The boy leaves and the woman reclaims the bed, getting in to sleep. Although the two characters have dramatically different viewpoints, the boy's presence and this human exchange have a calming effect on the neurotic woman, and the story ends on a soothed note.

"Making Love in 2003," the next story, is one of the longer and more ambitious—if unwieldy—pieces in the collection. It follows an unstable young female would-be writer who has received advice from a former male professor and brings a draft of her book to his house for him to assess, only to discover that the professor is married to the famous science fiction writer Madeleine L'Engle. The young writer hopes that her former professor, L'Engle's husband, can launch not just her career but also her life. "It was his job to do with me what he would. What would he do? What do the men do with the very talented young women who have finished writing their books? Would he kiss me? Would he invite me to be his daughter or wife or babysitter?

Would he send me and my book to the place where the next thing would happen?" (p. 108). Once again in July's work, the dynamics of power and agency are interlaced with family (the daughter, wife, or babysitter) and sexuality (the kiss).

The professor is not at home when the protagonist arrives, so L'Engle chats politely with her while she waits. The young author, however, fails to connect with the actual author sitting in front of her, condescendingly imagining the older woman as beyond art. "I would normally be writing, she said. I doubted this, but maybe it was true. Maybe she would be writing a letter to her sister or writing the word 'sweaters' on a big box of sweaters before putting it in the attic for the summer" (p. 109). This dismissal amounts to a missed opportunity for this young woman enthralled by an older man; when she finally locates her former professor, he is already involved with another student.

What follows perhaps explains the young woman's fixation on the father figure. The protagonist describes an adolescent experience, detailed in an earlier piece of writing admired by her former professor, an experience of falling in love with a nocturnal apparition, a phenomenon she labels a "dark shape." She has satisfying sex with this dark shape, but later struggles to explain these strange interludes: Was it a metaphor for rape? Was her father the dark shape? While the protagonist resists these explanations, her strange behavior suggests that some odd convergence of power, sexuality, and family governs her relationships with men. After failing to connect with her former professor, the young woman begins working with high school students with special needs and then reverses the terms of her earlier encounters by having a sexual relationship with one of the boys. The affair is short-lived, and the story attempts to end on a positive note as the woman rises from her bed, exhausted by crying, to greet the age-appropriate man next door.

The next story, "Ten True Things," once again begins with a woman obsessed by a man with power over her life, this time her boss, but shifts perspective in several ways. For one, the woman dislikes her boss. She further becomes involved with the man's wife, first by enrolling in the same adult-education sewing class, and then by engaging in a romantic encounter with her. While the protagonist believes she could not be romantically involved with another woman, she seems profoundly emotionally invested in her boss's wife. Meanwhile, the women in the sewing class bond together, including one woman who apparently cannot sew at all. During the final class meeting, in a display for one another, the woman who cannot sew appears before everyone, naked, as the other participants in the class don the kimonos they have made. The classroom has become a space for female intimacy and performance, as the nude woman presents to the other women her creation, which is not a kimono or a covering of any kind. July, whose investment in art extends into arenas that might otherwise be called crafts (one of her online projects involved making clothing), renders the all-woman continuing education classroom as an opportunity for female communication and craftsmanship.

The next item in the collection is a brief, two-page dispatch, "The Moves," about a woman whose dying father presents her with a series of gestures purportedly designed to give women sexual pleasure. The protagonist, who is not lesbian, clings to this borderline obscene advice and imagines sharing it with other women in the future, including her own daughter. The reduction of paternal legacy to the bodily and sexual is both pathetic and ludicrous, though that is not the tone the story adopts. Instead, the perspective of the besotted daughter attempts to claim this exchange as somehow enlightening. An exception because of its upbeat if benighted tone, it nonetheless joins other stories in the collection of powerful male father figures and their perverse sexual relationships to their daughters.

"Mon Plaisir" tells the story of a failing relationship between people of roughly the same age, presumably in their early forties, since they are realizing that they are probably not going to have children. The woman talks about her partner, Carl, their quirky sexual practices, and the rules that govern their lives. Carl is intent on having only authentic experiences and thus can

only take tai chi classes from instructors who use the Chinese words for poses. Yet simultaneously he believes that his practice of transcribing messages from a guru onto a website is a creative and presumably authentic act. The couple's commitment to macrobiotic food, whole grain bread, and meditation is sent up in the story; the diet and practices seem specific not only to northern California but also to the 1970s (today's equivalent would be gluten-free and Pilates).

The story features several moments that recur in July's work. For instance, as the protagonist recounts her problems in her relationship, she makes a list that includes "Important Things That We Don't Understand and Definitely Are Not Going to Talk About," a variation on the title of one of July's earlier performance pieces. When the protagonist comes home and finds Carl meditating, she sits across from him and acts out a scene in which she and Carl converse; she adopts different body poses and modes of speaking to express the two characters, herself and Carl. This performance is quite similar to the art that July's character Christine creates in *Me and You and Everyone We Know,* in which the audience witnesses Christine playing both of the roles of a couple in a photograph. The woman in the short story also buys new shoes as an expression of her desire to live a new life; similarly, in *Me and You,* the protagonist meets her love interest when she buys shoes from him, and the shoe store where he works is one of the primary settings in the film.

Finally, "Mon Plaisir" once again depicts a romantic relationship between people of radically different ages. The couple decides to serve as extras in a film, which turns out to be about a man who falls in love with a child and waits for her to reach adulthood, but dies as she reaches the age of consent. (The ludicrous, creepy premise actually resembles the 2008 film *The Curious Case of Benjamin Button* to some degree.) Seated next to the inappropriate, illegal couple, the woman muses that the actor and young actress were "holding hands and looking into each other's eyes in a way that I, for one, felt uncomfortable with. But it was not my place to judge the love between these two fictional

characters" (p. 163). Instead, in another example of performance shaping life and vice versa, she and her husband begin dramatizing their relationship while playing extras in the background of the film. First they argue and are reprimanded for speaking too loudly. But then, silenced, they pantomime an affection and affinity that they do not in reality share. Delighting in this version of their relationship, they thoroughly enjoy the shoot, are disappointed to go home afterward, and break up that very evening, suddenly aware of their inability to have a meal together in real life, not as extras. The end of the relationship actually serves as the happy ending for the story, in that the reader feels inclined to dislike Carl, given the protagonist's perspective on him. Set free at the end, the protagonist prepares to enjoy her solitude.

"Birthmark" serves as a departure in the collection in that it is told in the third person. In this brief story, the protagonist is a woman who had a birthmark removed in her early twenties but feels haunted by the experience over a decade later. As in the previous story, she is in a precarious, childless relationship, and the reappearance of the birthmark is interpreted by the woman and her boyfriend as a possible rebirth. The perspective of the story shifts from the woman to the man at the end of the story, as he hopes for a new beginning, including having children.

"How to Tell Stories to Children" is the final story in the collection, and one of the strongest. Again, several recurring themes in July's work circulate here: sexuality and the family; relationships between people of dramatically different ages; and children's perspectives. More specific than most of July's other work, this story includes dates (2001) and names (the protagonist is Deb), and covers a swath of time. It begins well after Deb's affair with an older man, when she begins to babysit the infant he and his wife have just had, integrating herself into their dysfunctional household and eventually becoming the primary caregiver for their daughter, Lyon. As Lyon approaches adolescence, the entire group goes to therapy, after which the protagonist begins a sexual relationship with the therapist that is interrupted when Lyon unexpectedly walks in on the

couple in the bedroom, bringing the nascent relationship to an end. Toward the story's close, Lyon goes away to college and herself begins to date the therapist. The final scene finds them all at an uncomfortable Thanksgiving meal in which this uneasy dynamic is revealed. The narrative again revolves around an inappropriate relationship and a childless woman. However, the ending is punctuated with the revelation that Lyon has conceived of Deb as a rival, almost a sibling, rather than a parent. The two women share a love, though filtered through their relationship to men—the therapist and the father. Nonetheless, a same-sex moment of genuine shared emotion rings vividly as the final climax of the story.

ME AND YOU AND EVERYONE WE KNOW
(FILM, 2005)

Childhood and adolescent desire and its relationship to adult sexuality—potentially predatory adult sexuality—recur in July's first film, *Me and You and Everyone We Know*. The film follows several story lines with an ensemble cast. In the main narrative, Christine, played by Miranda July, struggles as a performance artist, provides rides for elderly people for a living, and becomes enamored of a shoe salesman. Meanwhile, the salesman's wife divorces him and he struggles as a newly single father to his two boys, Robbie and Peter. The three live near two teenage girls who flaunt their newly discovered sex appeal in front of the salesman's coworker and also his oldest son, Peter. The film follows each of these characters as they struggle with intimacy and contact in the early twenty-first century.

Me and You enjoyed very positive feedback from critics, winning the Caméra d'Or and three other prizes at the Cannes Film Festival, a special jury prize at the Sundance Film Festival, and the Jury Award for Best Director at the Newport International Film Festival, as well as a number of other significant nominations, such as Best First Screenplay at the Independent Spirit Awards.

One of the story lines follows the two teenage girls with an intermittent sexual interest in the men around them as well as with each other. Heather, the bossier of the two girls, makes demands of Rebecca, her quieter, more sullen companion, although the two join forces to torment Peter, the teenage boy who lives nearby. In one scene, the two girls kiss in order to provoke a grown male neighbor, who responds with pornographic handwritten fantasies about the three of them together. Although the neighbor seems benign enough, he remains a potential threat to the two girls as they attempt to discover how he will respond to various scenarios. Their interactions teeter precariously in terms of who has the upper hand: he is larger and also an adult; but their direct provocations of him demonstrate the charge of their newfound sexuality and the leverage that their allure yields them. At one point the two girls knock on his door, hoping to instigate an encounter. Inside, the neighbor spots them and drops to the floor, hiding like a child, hoping to evade their overtures. The image of a grown man felled by the advances of adolescents reveals the complicated power play in which the three are engaged. Furthermore, the girls don't wait very long for him to answer the door; after a moment, they turn and race away, down the street, in a long slow-motion tracking shot. The girls run toward the camera, suddenly joyful and released, filled with teenage exuberance and free from the potentially dangerous dynamics of adult sexuality, at least for a moment.

While the audience remains uncertain about the girls' safety during their encounters with their adult neighbor, the girls clearly dominate their interactions with Peter, their teenage peer. At one point, stirred by jealousy as well as a latent desire for one another, they propose a joint sexual encounter with Peter, so that he can judge their sexual abilities.

The film is filled with characters considering the roles they perform as part of their everyday lives, as July reveals the performative nature of day-to-day existence. For example, the shoe salesman, in a fit of sudden anxiety, asks his children if he corresponds to the role of a father, to which the children respond with bemusement. The notion of sexuality as a performance is wholly adolescent but reinforced by language, such as the terms sex "acts" and sexual "performance," and also entirely in keeping with July's

interests as a performance artist. In contrast, intimacy plays no role in the girls' interaction with Peter; it seems an entirely unconsidered element. While Peter tolerates and facilitates this encounter (it happens at his house), his emotional response remains uncertain. During this scene, the tables unexpectedly shift between the two girls: Heather, normally the bossy one, finds herself shocked by the experience, despite her dominant demeanor, and momentarily silenced. She is revealed to be more vulnerable than the audience has been led to notice, given her brash and knowing demeanor; she seems suddenly disconcerted and bewildered by the encounter. Meanwhile her friend, Rebecca, the quieter, more submissive of the two, remains entirely unfazed. The sexual behavior is delivered in an almost hilariously matter-of-fact manner, although the audience may feel uneasy witnessing displays of adolescent sexuality. While spectators are surely familiar with performances of teenage love, from *Romeo and Juliet* to *Glee,* the bald, affectless tone of this scene and its mechanical intent (as both survey and practice) provides a striking departure from most representations of adolescent relationships. July's depiction of teenage oscillations between self-assurance and childish timidity make these encounters in her fiction and films unsettling and unpredictable.

In another, potentially more disturbing story line in *Me and You,* Peter's little brother, Robbie, who must be about six or seven years old, embarks on an online relationship with an adult. Robbie first watches Peter engage in dialogue in an adult chat room and then continues the conversation himself, despite his slow computer skills. Robbie's age-appropriate fixation on bodily functions leads him to describe an exchange involving excrement that his unknown but presumably adult interlocutor finds exciting. When this person suggests meeting Robbie, the audience once again fears for the safety of a child haplessly following his own relentless curiosity into the world of adult sexuality—particularly nonnormative sexuality. In the actual encounter, however, the tables once again shift. While Peter and Robbie have been online, the audience has been following the story line of Christine, a

performance artist, and her ambitions to have her work displayed at a local art gallery. Her efforts are seemingly thwarted by the cold demeanor of the art gallery director, Nancy. When Nancy turns out to be the adult engaged online with Robbie, the terms of July's drama seem clear: adults are just as weird as children, and children are uncontained. As a result, the encounter involves unfamiliar, unstable terrain. We first see Nancy sitting on a park bench. As we realize that she is waiting to meet Robbie, her interest in the various adults straying near her becomes comical: the joke is on her, a figure we have been encouraged to dislike, given her chilly reception to Christine's artwork. However, once Robbie shows up and the situation dawns upon Nancy, she becomes more sympathetic. She realizes that her messy, disturbing fantasies have been shared with a child, and she furthermore now has the responsibility of recognizing this child without crushing his childish understanding of their interactions (whatever it may be). She responds by kissing him on the mouth and then walking away. The kiss is unusual: although it is fairly common for adults to kiss children on the mouth, this kiss seems meant both to acknowledge the private exchange they have shared while also rejecting any possibility of extending the communication. As such, this consensual kiss between a grown woman and a grade-school child includes an element of mutual desire—an uneasy representation, again, in the heightened twenty-first-century sensitivity about child sexual exploitation, particularly via the Internet.

Ultimately the film ends on an optimistic note, as Christine's work is accepted into the art gallery, and she and the shoe salesman begin a relationship. The film finally suggests that communication is not only possible in the twenty-first century but perhaps even aided by the technology often denigrated for undermining true human connectedness. The title, for instance, comes from a piece of computer artwork designed by Peter, which he asserts represents the entire network of people he knows. The computer thus facilitates his childish effort to depict human relationships, helping him make the claim that

people are connected. This cautiously upbeat tone characterizes the film and perhaps helped underwrite its success.

THE FUTURE (*FILM, 2011*)

In contrast to her first film, the tone of July's second is determinedly downbeat. It follows the demise of a thirty-something couple as they wait to adopt an ailing cat. Once the adoption occurs, their lives will be dominated by caring for the cat, who requires careful and regular medical attention. Although the animal shelter staff warn that their policy is to euthanize after only a short period of time, the couple manages to delay their return to the shelter long enough for the cat to be put down. In the meantime, the woman in the couple, Sofie, has embarked on an unsatisfying relationship with an older, suburban man. When her boyfriend, Jason, discovers this betrayal, he freezes time in order to forestall their eventual breakup. After this moment of magical realism occurs, however, he realizes that he does not know how to make time resume. As he works to figure this out, days slip by, and he misses the time frame to rescue the cat from the shelter. At the end of the film, Sofie returns to Jason, who grudgingly allows her to stay in their former apartment, but for just one night. The film ends with the couple in the apartment but physically separated from one another, a bleak vantage on what the future holds for the two.

The Future maintains its dispirited tone visually as well. The costumes are primarily earth colors, a departure from the cheerful primary colors featured in *Me and You*. Similarly, the two primary settings for the film, the couple's apartment and the suburban man's home, are chiefly composed of earth tones.

Despite its subdued color palette and depressing subject material, the film does contain moments of levity, as in July's other work. In addition, the film features a performance by one of the subjects in July's book, *It Chooses You*. Joe Putterlik, who was selling his collection of homemade cards to his wife of sixty-two years in the *PennySaver* when July met him, basically plays himself in the film. He gives Jason some advice about relationships and sells him a hair dryer for three dollars. (Sofie goes on to use the hair dryer to tame her hair and appear more suburban during her affair.) Sadly, and somehow in keeping with the spirit of the film, Putterlik died in the fall of 2010, shortly after *The Future* was completed.

July told the *New York Times*'s Katrina Onstad that this film functioned as a way for her to address her transition into marriage. It certainly has a more adult feel than her first film, with fewer child actors and less whimsy. The subject that perhaps provides the most consistently downbeat tone in the film, even more than the death of the cat or the couple's breakup, is Sofie's inability to create. An interpretive dancer, Sofie finds herself stymied despite her best efforts to stay focused; she cuts off Internet service to the couple's apartment, but remains distracted. Perhaps inspired by the writer's block that July herself faced while working on the screenplay, the film follows Sofie's attempts to design a dance, or series of dances, and her ultimate failure to do so. This stasis stands in marked contrast to the prolific energy of the artist in *Me and You*, who seems unable to stop herself from endlessly working on and distributing her pieces. In addition, July herself is no dancer. The dance routines Sofie develops are entertaining, and they also function usefully to literally dramatize the halting, frustrating steps of the creative process. However, they are never particularly accomplished, even comical at times, whereas the art installations that Christine creates in *Me and You*, while low budget and faux naive, nonetheless resonate with a certain intensity entirely lacking in Sofie's dance attempts. The fear of a creative impasse seems to underwrite the ennui of the film, more than fear of a breakup or even of death.

OTHER PRINTED WORK

July has also published material not included in her short story collection, including two short memoirs and a story in the *New Yorker*. One memoir is about making her first movie, *Atlanta,*

a ten-minute video about a preadolescent competitive swimmer. The memoir was written while July was working on her first feature-length film, *Me and You,* and the revelation of the piece is that even *Atlanta,* this seemingly low-stakes production, is in fact all about ambition and drive—the little girl is competing in the Olympics. Meanwhile, the video maker herself goes on to win the Caméra d'Or at the Cannes Film Festival, in a fitting parallel.

The second memoir, "Free Everything," recounts a period of shoplifting, during July's lean years in Portland, in which she is arrested once and fired another time. The narrative begins with a fierceness unlike much of July's other work, invoking Jean Genet's *The Thief's Journal* (*Journal du voleur,* 1949), a manifesto to the interconnected nature of theft, homosexuality, and art. July's story, however, resolves into heterosexuality and more normative behavior, foreclosing on the need or desire to steal or behave excessively.

The short story in the *New Yorker,* "Roy Spivey," is about celebrity, fantasy, and alternate versions of reality. It includes the actual name of a celebrity, much like "Making Love in 2003," which uses Madeleine L'Engle as a character. This story begins by referring to a famous sports figure, but then spends most of its time describing an interaction between an unnamed woman and the famous actor she is seated next to on a plane. The two chat and have a few strangely intimate moments (she unsuccessfully attempts to wash her underarms in the bathroom sink; he sprays her underarms with Febreze; he bites her outstretched arm; he insists that she bite his shoulder). At the end of the flight, they agree upon set of code words they will use to communicate in the airport after the plane has landed, as they meet their respective parties and reenter their actual, non-airbound lives. Once again, in July's work, performance and the real dovetail. The actor gives the woman a phone number and asks her to call, but she instead fetishizes the number, never using it, treasuring it as an emblem of luck conveyed by proximity to celebrity.

Finally, in late 2011, two of July's projects came to fruition simultaneously, in part because her work on these efforts overlapped. While finishing *The Future,* she became stalled. She procrastinated by surfing the Web, as the protagonist in the film does, and by perusing the print ad periodical the *PennySaver,* and she began to respond to ads placed by people selling items. (Similarly, while still in high school, July maintained a correspondence with a pen-pal prisoner, a connection she made based on a magazine ad. Their exchanges became the material for the first play she staged at the club 924 Gilman.) The resulting series of interviews, photographs, and musings on these interactions became another book, *It Chooses You,* published in November 2011. The same month, *The Future* was released on DVD, after a series of limited releases throughout fall 2011. Before the book's release, "The Book Bench" on the *New Yorker* website published five installments from *It Chooses You,* including the initial piece that launched the project. July's interviews include Joe Putterlik, selling the raunchy cards he crafted for his wife; a teenage boy relegated to high school special education who builds ponds in his backyard, where he grows tadpoles and frogs; a Greek immigrant who collects photo albums of other people's travels; and a man going through a sex change and selling a leather jacket. Many of the same concerns that inform her short stories and films—power, sexuality, childhood—reappear in these autobiographical, nonfiction pieces, as life once again imitates art.

In these pieces, while July procrastinated instead of completing her film and followed up on the *PennySaver* ads, she also worried about not being able to have a child (she was thirty-seven in 2011), a concern also voiced by characters in her fiction and films. (She and Mills now have a son, Hopper, born in February 2012.) As July's own life progresses, she will surely continue to bring together reality and creativity in a range of art forms. A relatively young, wildly gifted artist, July clearly has an endless supply of material to deliver to her audiences. Look for more talented work from this prolific, multifaceted writer.

Selected Bibliography

WORKS OF MIRANDA JULY

BOOKS

The Boy from Lam Kien. Los Angeles, Calif.: Cloverfield Press, 2005. (Short story.)

No One Belongs Here More Than You. New York: Scribner, 2007. (Short story collection.)

Learning to Love You More. With Harrell Fletcher. New York: Prestel, 2007. (Art and essays selected from their Web crowdsourcing project.)

It Chooses You. Photographs by Brigitte Sire. San Francisco: McSweeney's, 2011. (Interviews/nonfiction.)

UNCOLLECTED SHORT STORIES

"Jack and Al." New Fiction issue, edited by Rick Moody. *Mississippi Review* 30, no. 3 (fall 2002).

"Roy Spivey." *New Yorker,* June 11, 2007, pp. 90–93.

ANTHOLOGIES

"Birthmark." In *The Paris Review Book of People with Problems.* New York: Picador, 2005. Pp. 261–266.

"Me and You and Everyone We Know." (Screenplay excerpt.) In *The Best American Nonrequired Reading 2006.* Edited by Dave Eggers. New York: Houghton Mifflin, 2006. Pp. 181–192.

"Roy Spivey." In *The Book of Other People.* Edited by Zadie Smith. New York: Penguin, 2008. Pp. 205–216.

"Something That Needs Nothing." In *My Mistress's Sparrow Is Dead.* Edited by Jeffrey Eugenides. New York: Harper, 2008. Pp. 450–470.

NONFICTION

"Atlanta." *New Yorker,* June 11, 2007. http://www.newyorker.com/reporting/2007/06/11/070611fa_fact_july.

"Free Everything." *New Yorker,* October 10, 2011. http://www.newyorker.com/reporting/2011/10/10/111010fa_fact_july.

FEATURE FILMS (WRITER/DIRECTOR)

Me and You and Everyone We Know. IFC Films, FilmFour, 2005.

The Future. Match Factory; Medienboard Berlin-Brandenburg, 2011.

SHORT FILMS

Atlanta, 1996.

The Amateurist, 1998.

Nest of Tens, 2000.

Getting Stronger Every Day, 2001.

Haysha Royko. Animation by Jalal Jemison, 2003.

Are You the Favorite Person of Anyone? Directed by Miguel Arteta, 2005.

AUTHOR'S AND PARTICIPATORY WEBSITES

Miranda July website. http://mirandajuly.com.

Joanie 4 Jackie, 1996. (Video chain letter; archived at Bard College.)

How Will I Know Her? 2002. (Web-based exhibit.)

Learning to Love You More, 2002–2009. www.learningtoloveyoumore.com.

PERFORMANCE ART

Love Diamond, 1998–2000.

The Swan Tool, 2000–2002.

How I Learned to Draw, 2002–2003.

Things We Don't Understand and Are Definitely Not Going to Talk About, 2006–2007.

ART INSTALLATIONS

The Hallway. Yokohama Triennial, 2008.

Eleven Heavy Things. Venice Biennale, 2009; New York, 2010; Los Angeles, 2011.

ARTICLES AND INTERVIEWS

Ashman, Angela. "You and Her and Everything She Knows." *Village Voice Books,* May 1, 2007. http://www.villagevoice.com/2007-05-01/books/you-and-her-and-everything-she-knows/.

Chang, Chris. "Renaissance Riot Grrrl Rising." *Film Comment* 36, no. 4:16 (July 2000).

Durbin, Karen. "Young Filmmaker Tells Hollywood It Can Wait." *New York Times,* June 19, 2005. http://www.nytimes.com/2005/06/19/movies/19durb.html?scp=1&sq=%22hollywood%20can%20wait%22&st=cse.

Onstad, Katrina. "Miranda July Is Totally Not Kidding." *New York Times Magazine,* July 17, 2011, pp. 24–29.

LEONARD KRIEGEL

(1933—)

Sanford Pinsker

LEONARD KRIEGEL IS a polio victim who insists that he be called a "cripple." For him, no euphemism will suffice—not "handicapped," not "disabled," indeed, not any of the well-meaning terms that "normal" people use to console, which is to say, to pity, him. Kriegel is a tough cookie who has earned his voice by forging sentences as steel hard as the braces supporting his deadened legs.

For many years Kriegel proudly described himself as a man on the Left. Given his upbringing in the Bronx, where various immigrant groups learned about democratic America on its rough-and-tumble streets, and given his attraction to the intellectual currents of the 1950s and early 1960s, it is hardly surprising that Kriegel found himself both a liberal and an academic.

At the same time, however, Kriegel was hardly a True Believer, not when he found himself at odds with this or that intellectual fashion but even more so when the Far Left turned its back on Israel and embraced the cause of Palestinian Liberation. "Verbal gymnastics," Kriegel explains in an autumn 2000 article in the *American Scholar,* afford him the opportunity "to speak of lack of faith as the creed of a believing nonbeliever":

> It is the memory of being a believer that tempts old passions. Like a buoy marking the lost lanes of praise and adoration of a God I feared and loved, I yearn for that simplicity.
>
> ("Synagogues," p. 68)

Kriegel (alas?) is destined to live a life of complexity and ambivalence—and this is equally true of his Jewishness. If he neither "observes" the Commandments nor prays in a conventional manner, there is no question that he identifies as a Jew and as a firm supporter of Israel.

What disturbs Kriegel is that liberals of a certain stripe cannot resist rooting for the underdog, and part of the reason is that Jewish liberals of a certain stripe can support nearly any cause so long as it isn't identifiably "Jewish." During the 1970s and 1980s, Manhattan was awash with such types. For a man who had long been a contributor to the *Nation,* a magazine that made no secret of its left-leaning positions, Kriegel found himself betrayed. Identity politics, postmodernist theory, and a general atmosphere of self-righteousness put enormous strains on university life—and City College, where Kriegel worked, was no exception.

Unlike the New York intellectuals more than a decade older than himself (one thinks of such former leftists as Irving Kristol and Sidney Hook), Kriegel probably read these newly minted neoconservatives under the blanket with a flashlight in much the same way that adolescent boys snuck peeks at *Playboy* magazine.

At the very least Kriegel was no doubt shocked to see just how much he was changing politically, and just how much craziness had been unleashed—on campuses, in the streets, and in the halls of government—by the antics of the Hard Left. Every day brought fresh evidence of political correctness gone amock.

The truth of the matter is that Kriegel had stood still while the world moved toward the extremes, both left and right. Small wonder, then, that he found himself uncomfortable both with the Hard Left *and* the Hard Right. He could no longer write about politics for the *Nation,* and at the same time, he never submitted (nor could he ever submit) a piece to the neoconservative *Commentary* magazine. He was a "dangling man," not in the sense that Saul Bellow used the phrase to describe the protagonist of his first novel, but

as a person teetering precariously between two extremes.

Cultural Jewishness of a sort that often happens to those raised in certain boroughs of New York City and that places a lifelong mark on their consciousness is part of what makes Leonard Kriegel Leonard Kriegel. His identification with Jews and Jewsiness only increased over the decades, and when Israel seemed to be threatened, Kriegel could not stand idly by.

The other identifying mark, one that would change him indelibly, was when he met up with the polio virus (or perhaps more correctly, when the polio virus met up with *him*) during the summer of 1944, when he was eleven. Philip Roth's 2010 novella *Nemesis* describes how it was that hot summer in Newark, New Jersey, when polio ran rampant and health officials were in a quandary about what to do. It was much the same story across the river in the Bronx, where Kriegel had lived the ordinary life of a boy enjoying baseball or simply running wherever his will and strong legs would take him.

The polio virus changed everything about Kriegel's former life, and in the process, helped to turn him into a writer. The result is that rather than being a polio victim who happens to be a writer, he is a writer who happens to be a polio victim. The distinction is important because, over a long career, Kriegel has transmogrified his condition into myth, and an "American" myth to boot. Small wonder that his literary specialty is American literature or that he finds himself identifying with students who carry the label "disadvantaged" just as he has lugged around the label of "cripple."

EARY LIFE AND WORK

Leonard Kriegel was born in the Bronx, New York, on May 25, 1933, the son of Fred and Sylvia (Breittholz) Kriegel. Any estimate of his early life must be divided sharply between his life until he was an eleven-year-old and his life after he contracted polio. No doubt hushed discussions about what their afflicted son might do to earn a living dominated the family kitchen-table discussions. The young Kriegel could not help but overhear—and certainly not help but *feel*—the anxiety oozing through their apartment walls.

Decades later he remembered that one possibility was for him to become a jeweler because many "cripples" found work in this vocation. He might also work in assorted craft-related occupations, or perhaps he could develop skills, such as accounting, that could lead to a desk job. One thing was clear: he would not be playing center field for the Brooklyn Dodgers. That dream, as with many others, was gone. Instead, it was replaced by a heightened imagination and, later, the life of a professor and writer. Nobody in his family figured on this.

Kriegel received his B.A. degree from Hunter College (now Hunter College of the City University of New York) in 1955, his M.A. from Columbia University in 1956, and his Ph.D. from New York University in 1960. In 1961 he coedited (with Edith Henrich) a compilation of essays titled *Experiments in Survival,* but it is fair to say that Kriegel launched his writing career with two volumes, both published in 1964, that point to his twin passions as an Americanist and an autobiographical writer. The first, *The Essential Works of the Founding Fathers,* was a paperback anthology. Its items were selected, compiled, and edited in an age so innocent that suspicion about a "political agenda" (unfortunately part of our current cultural landscape) did not surface. Subsequent editing projects would include *Masters of the Short Story* and *Stories of the American Experience* (1971 and 1973, both with Abraham H. Lass), and *The Myth of American Manhood* (1978).

The second volume he published in 1964, *The Long Walk Home,* is of greater importance because it sets into motion Kriegel's painfully candid account of the bone-wracking treatments prescribed for polio patients in the mid-1940s. The opening of his memoir is as unassuming and matter-of-fact as possible: "I was eleven then" (p. 3). The trick is to strike a narrative balance between "then" and now, to make us feel the frights of an eleven-year-old boy and the aesthetic distance of an adult "voice."

Kriegel contracted polio at, of all places, Surprise Lake, a summer camp for Jewish boys from New York City,

> mostly poor boys, the sons of working men, like me, but some were from that nondescript lump, the lower middle class, and there were even a small number of more substantial acolytes of the camper's fellowship, the sons of doctors, lawyers, dentists, and up-and-coming belt manufacturers.
>
> (p. 5)

Kriegel has a keen eye for social distinctions, one formed by his Bronx neighborhood and then fortified by the politics he embraced as an adult. But while these stratifications may have mattered greatly to the young Kriegel, they did not matter a fig to the polio virus that struck down rich and poor alike. The "surprise" that Surprise Lake had in store for Kriegel was one that every parent, rich and poor, feared during the summer of 1944.

Writing about how his polio was discovered and how it was treated can be an invitation to a thousand excesses and a million tears. Kriegel, to his credit, resists every impulse to let sentimentality do the hard work that genuine writing requires. Here, for example, is a rhapsodic display of a sentence that, breath unit by breath unit, is both under control and quintessentially American:

> For under the quilt of night's blackness, I shoulder my way back into that dreary ward, to relive the week that was the dead center of my pain, the real birth of my hate and my fear, my love and my pity, my new man.
>
> (p. 20)

What commingled when he was first diagnosed—hate and fear, love and pity—are the primal building blocks on which the never-ending search for a genuine manhood is formed. It is also clear that some of the cadences here come from William Faulkner, who, in turn, absorbed them from the King James translation of the Bible.

To (become) a man is a long, complicated process for any man but a longer, more complicated process for a "cripple" keenly aware of his physical limitations. As Hayley Mitchell Haugen points out in "The 'Disabled Imagination' and the Masculine Metaphor in the Works of Leonard Kriegel,"

In continuing to write about disability as a lifetime challenge, Kriegel offers a more realistic model that contends that living with chronic illness and disability is a constant battle. With this contention, he provides a counternarrative to the medical model of illness and disability that considers the struggles of the ill and disabled as effectively over once their bodies are rehabilitated and they no longer need immediate medical care.

(p. 102)

Would that it were that easy, or that simple. For Kriegel, living with polio absorbed his consciousness long after he was discharged, as a child, from the rehabilitation center. *The Long Walk Home* ends with a series of full-throated proclamations, including one that links the cost of his legs with the attainment of an authentic self and another that insists the price he had to pay was cheaper than one might have expected.

Fifteen years later, in an essay titled "On Manhood, Disease, and the Authentic Self" (published in *On Men and Manhood*), Kriegel deeply regrets calling his victory "cheap," because, in truth, *every* victory is expensive, fragmentary, and terribly short-lived. What galls Kriegel is that his final flourishes in *The Long Walk Home* are "untruthful," and that, for a writer as discerning and as honest as he is, becomes a nagging burden. But the truth about writing, one even deeper than regrets about sentences past, is that they cannot be unwritten. There is no way Kriegel, or any other writer, can collect every copy of an earlier work and burn them all. They exist, for better or worse, and all Kriegel can do—and, indeed, what he does—is learn from an earlier mistake.

Meanwhile, manhood remains an abiding concern, not only in his first crack at memoir but throughout his career. After enduring (in a cultivated silence) the "tests" of his young manhood—"hot packs, sweat," and then the hot pool—Kriegel faced his suffering firsthand and without flinching.

The New York State Reconstruction Home in West Haverstraw was the official name of the place where these treatments were administered. Kriegel and his young buddies, polio sufferers all, called it "the Rock." The metaphor functioned on a wide variety of levels. As Kriegel explains,

LEONARD KRIEGEL

For two years, [the Rock] served as my sanctuary and my prison. I used to think of it, after I had been home for a few years, as the Alcatraz of my exile. A metaphor for dead legs, I saw myself as Humphrey Bogart then, the Rock looming above me as big as a childhood dream of cruelty on the passive white screen of my soul.

(p. 25)

The passage above is representative because *The Long Walk Home* is simultaneously explanatory and atmospheric. In subsequent essays Kriegel would return to "the Rock" and his first experiences with efforts to manage his polio. It was also the place where he encountered death at first hand (some polio sufferers, confined to iron lungs, simply didn't make it) and where he dealt with what it meant to be a "survivor."

As Richard F. Shepard puts it in the pages of the *New York Times:* "This is not the usual 'How I Licked ...' sort of autobiography. It is written without a trace of false sentimentality or phony revelation." Indeed, it is not the sort of autobiography that Oprah Winfrey would have featured on her talk show. Kriegel's memoir is simply too demanding for conventional daytime TV audiences who are looking for uplift and overcoming obstacles rather than the eye-opening clarity that only first-rate literature can achieve.

By all the usual measures—promotions, tenure, various fellowships—Kriegel has had a successful academic career. He began his journey in academe as an assistant professor at Long Island University (in Brooklyn, N.Y.) in 1960–1961. He married Harriet Bernzweig on August 24, 1957. They had two sons, Mark Benjamin (a sportswriter and author best known for his biography of the football star Joe Namath) and Eric Bruce. Both sons figure prominently in Kriegel's speculations about manhood. In 1961 Kriegel moved to the City College of the City University of New York, where he went through the ranks, eventually becoming a full professor (1972), until his retirement in 1992. He had three Fulbright lectureships at the University of Leiden (1964–1965), University of Groningen (1968–1969), and University of Paris (1981), and was a Guggenheim fellow in 1971–1972 and a Rockefeller fellow in 1976.

EDMUND WILSON

On the face of it, Kriegel's was an academic twice-told tale; but the deeper truth is that he resisted much of the academic fashion that surrounded him. This resistant, sometime even abrasive strain peeked through when he came to write his book-length study of Edmund Wilson, regarded by many as the foremost man of letters in America. Writing about his work would be a daunting task and one that forced Kriegel to realize where he stood in the current world of literary criticism.

In *Edmund Wilson* (1971), after dutifully explaining which of Wilson's works would be explored fully, which rather lightly, and which not at all, Kriegel moves on to make clear what so disturbs him about the New Criticism, as the practice of "deep reading" was then called: "Having become a formal, even institutionalized, aspect of the national culture, it has grown increasingly guilty of taking itself too seriously" (p. 2). So sweeping was its victory over the "old criticism" that had so long prevailed in graduate literary education that the New Criticism was destined to become dryasdust itself. That is the cyclical nature of the world, including the world of literary criticism.

Kriegel was dead right to complain; but what drives his critique is less a quarrel with the niceties of critical theory than it is a deep-seated feeling about the systematic absence of the personal:

All too often, criticism seems a rather sterile intellectual exercise with no more than a peripheral relationship to the world out of which the poet or novelist must create structure, meaning, and vitality. The dilemma of modern literary criticism is that, increasingly, critics write for other critics.

(p. 2)

What Kriegel could not have known in 1971, indeed, what very few of us knew, was that waves of literary theory were about to crash over literary criticism, old and new alike. This makes Kriegel's study of Edmund Wilson seem dated, and it is no doubt true that the name "Edmund Wilson" no longer packs the enormous clout it once did. Still, as Kriegel grapples with Wilson's monumental books, sometimes even daring to

disagree with his eminence, what we see is a Kriegel deeply engaged. There is nothing about the pinheaded, disconnected academic in any of his paragraphs.

In his introduction, Kriegel makes it clear that his book is a "mixed tribute" to Wilson's work and that, much as he admires him, he will not be afraid to utter some unpleasant truths—all in the hope that Wilson himself would approve. In this regard, what Kriegel says about Wilson's *The Wound and the Bow* (1941) is particularly revealing. After giving high praise to the essays on Rudyard Kipling and Charles Dickens, Kriegel finds the title essay, "Philoctetes: The Wound and the Bow," disappointing. Why so? Because

> Wilson's thesis is singularly unconvincing. As an attempt to unify a collection of essays, it leaves the reader wondering whether the disease-creativity metaphorical syndrome was not merely an unwieldy attempt to uncover a substitute for his waning Marxism.
>
> (p. 73)

Worse, Kriegel goes on to charge Wilson with being "so intent on showing us the wound that he is oblivious to the bow" (p. 73). Kriegel may well have a point in his critique of why the "Wound and the Bow" essay fails to bring the other essays of the collection into a satisfactory whole, but there are reasons to suspect that what really upset Kriegel was Wilson's equation of disease and creative power. According to Greek mythology, Philoctetes was a famous archer (he fought in the Trojan War), who was wounded in such a way that he became a pariah. In some versions, snakebite accounts for the wound on his foot, which festers horribly. Other versions are less specific about the cause of the wound, but all agree that Philoctetes found himself alone and increasingly bitter.

The Freudian echoes in Wilson's essay are much more evident than are the Marxist influences because what the wound-and-the-bow thesis comes down to is overcompensation: what the artist loses by enduring a horrible wound is made up for by his creativity. Kriegel, at some level, must have felt that the essay, in some measure, applied to him—and that prompted an understandable denial, even if none of this

"denial" appears in his book on Wilson. What *does* appear, however, is a sense that Wilson doesn't understand what it is to be both a "cripple" and a creative writer.

FALLING INTO LIFE

The fourteen essays collected into *Falling into Life* (1991) are prisms that reflect on Kriegel's maturing sensibility. Without wishing to be, indeed, without being at all comfortable with what is now widely known as the "literature of the disabled," Kriegel is recognized as a writer who surrounds the condition of being a polio victim with the broad expanse of the humanities. The result cannot help but strike many readers as counterintuitive. This is especially true in the collection's title essay. In it, Kriegel argues that learning how to fall, as an eleven-year-old, is what helped him learn how to fall into death: "because I once had to learn how to fall in order to keep that life mine, I now seem to have convinced myself that I must also learn to fall into death" (p. 3).

Kriegel's existential grappling with "falling" blends nearly equal measures of acceptance and triumph. Fear—of falling and all that "falling" implies—is the enemy. Supported by crutches for the first time, Kriegel had to learn the proper technique of falling at exactly the point in his young life when "normals" would imagine exactly the opposite. Shouldn't Lenny learn how to stand upright, and how to protect himself from falling? According to the therapist-healers who know better, what he needs to learn is precisely the opposite.

For Kriegel, "falling into life" was as far from Edmund Wilson's metaphorical equation of wounds and bows; indeed, what Kriegel most wants to insist is that the phrase was not a metaphor at all—it was real, a process learned only through doing, the way a baby learns to crawl, to stand, and then to walk:

> After the steel bands around calves and thighs and pelvis had been covered over by the rich-smelling leather, after the braces had been precisely fitted to

allow my fear-ridden imagination the surety of their holding presence, I was pulled to my feet.

(p. 8)

Lessons in how to fall followed.

Kriegel went over much of this material in *The Long Walk Home,* but in this essay he links early childhood with the onset of middle age: "To create an independent self, a man had to rid himself both of the myths that nurtured him and the myths that held him back" (p. 15). The subsequent essays put meat around these bones by exploring, with both eloquence and depth, the various myths that create and imprison him.

Take his reading of how Jackson's Island affects Tom Sawyer and himself. Kriegel freely admits that, as a writer, he is "a creation of disease" (p. 21). What he learns from following Tom as he "runs" toward Jackson's Island as a sanctuary is that there are no sanctuaries, no entirely safe places. "Run away!" is one of the voices that whisper into the ears of certain American protagonists (Tom is one of them), but as Kriegel discovers,

> when I was ten and ran away from home, I needed laziness. But the models I chose were inadequate. Tom and his friends lacked the balance that would have allowed me to understand that running away did not lead to discovering the authentic self in its day-to-day world. Illness would teach me that I also needed to stand my ground.
>
> (p. 29)

American protagonists tend to divide themselves between those who run away and those who stand their ground. But *serious* American protagonists understand that the latter is a more honorable (if often a more painful) choice. As Eugene Henderson discovers in Saul Bellow's *Henderson the Rain King* (1959), "Truth comes in blows." For Kriegel, the blows came when he was much younger than was Henderson, and they lasted, as well as shaped his life.

At the same time, however, Kriegel was growing increasingly self-conscious about the way polio and his imagination continually intertwined. Some might argue that he had found his niche as a polio sufferer, but that notion galled far more than it gratified: "Ten years ago,

convinced that I had used up whatever literary capital remained in my life, I set out to change direction as a writer. Determined to become more inventive and less autobiographical, I would force myself to shake loose from the obligations of memory" (p. 40).

Easier said than done. In seeking to shake loose from the ties that bind, Kriegel runs into himself around every corner and in virtually every paragraph.

It is the consummate boxer, Barney Ross, who gives Kriegel a chance to ruminate about what power ultimately means. As it turns out, Kriegel met Barney Ross, champion prizefighter, about a month before he met his virus. Kriegel collected baseball cards with, as he puts it, "the greed and avarice of a Chicago commodities broker betting on the future of pork bellies" (p. 48). Barney Ross, the boxer, might have become yet another object of Kriegel's hero worship, but such was not the case. The young Kriegel admired him not because he was a slugger but because he was a mensch, "a man who had performed well within the context of that powerful if self-referential sentimentality of Jewish-American urban life" (p. 48).

An imagination as wide-ranging as Kriegel's has no problem juxtaposing an essay ruminating about Barney Ross with one ruminating about Franz Kafka ("In Kafka's House"); but if the truth be told, Kriegel is always lurking around the edges of his essays. His true subject, deny it as he might, is himself. As he puts it in "Writing the Unlived Life,"

> With each word I wrote [in six books, and more reviews than he cares to count], I was searching for the boy who existed until I was age eleven, when, as I melodramatically phrased it in my first book, *The Long Walk Home,* the knife of virus severed legs from will and I found myself flat on my back, paralyzed with polio.
>
> (p. 85)

Kriegel is certainly not alone in hoping that writing will recapture the past. Marcel Proust's madeleine and the epic quest it presumably inspired is merely one example. But Kriegel's enterprise is tied to the body—the former, pre-

eleven one active and filled with vinegar, and the latter, post-eleven body, passive and forced to make its way on crutches or in a wheelchair. Writing may level the playing field (it can go where the literal body can't), but the reality that he is a cripple marks every essay Kriegel writes, despite his eloquent protestations.

FLYING SOLO

Like *Falling into Life, Flying Solo* (1998) is a collection of fourteen essays that appeared originally in what, for Kriegel, are now "the usual suspects": the *Nation, Virginia Quarterly, Partisan Review, Georgia Review,* and *Sewanee Review.* His abiding subjects remain what they were when he first tried his hand at memoir: being a cripple, becoming a man, and the relationship of pain to both. If his insistence that "pain writes our true memoirs" (p. 163) has a blunt, no-nonsense ring to it, the statement has enough power, and, yes, candor, to convince.

For Kriegel, being a man matters deeply (indeed, he will return to it again and again), and while he realizes full well that the very idea of "manhood" is under wide attack, he cannot *not* comment about it. The year 1979 was at the epicenter of a feminist movement that accused men of a wide range of cultural crimes, both real and imagined. He continues to distinguish between those who want their identities on the cheap and those who know that pain teaches very different, very nuanced lessons.

Recalling a woman who fought a lifelong battle against the body's decay, he says this: "But Judy is dead. I make no claim that the manner of her dying will teach the rest of us some valuable lesson. I do not believe that we learn from the examples of others" (p. 163). So much for what many value as "vicarious experience"—the pain and anguish he shared with Oedipus gouging out his eyes or poor Lear raging on the heath. True, this is not the same pain as, say, getting one's finger actually pricked by a needle, nor are these literary examples the same as a broken heart actually suffered. What Kriegel insists is this: if pain bears the heavy burden of being authentic, it must be immediate, existential, and most of all, attached to an individual.

But with this much insisted upon, Kriegel continues in a rather different, more modulated key:

> Yet in a nation which more and more worships power and wealth and celebrity, I think hers is a better example of human possibility than all the childish rituals urged upon men today. No campfires. No myths. No bonding. Just the refusal to resign the self to its death. And the insistence on the body's struggle, a struggle that teaches us that even when we triumph, it is for the briefest of moments and for the most narrow of choices.
>
> (p. 163)

Kriegel chooses not to mention the poet and essayist Robert Bly by name, but the references to campfires, face painting, and primitive male bonding are surely to his now-embarrassing counsel.

Kriegel's own struggle began when he was "done in"—the descriptive phrase of the day—by polio at the tender age of eleven. Not surprisingly, he repeats this life-altering fact in many of his essays because, in one way or another, most of his ruminations are about the body, and its effects on manhood.

Kriegel not only lost the use of his legs that summer in 1944 but also lost his dreams of becoming a professional athlete and a man. Rage is understandably his reaction to attacks against his body (he pounds at the walls of his apartment when confined to bed with boils until his knuckles bleed), and now, more than fifty years later, one can still feel the anger bubbling up from his diamond-hard prose. The difference, of course, is that illness (which was never, then or now, a metaphor) formed the writer whose twelve meditations on loss give a new meaning to the powers of reflective language.

Kriegel spares very few in *Flying Solo*—not the makers of tepid, politically correct euphemisms such as "physically challenged," not those who find the connections between pain and manhood to be "laughable," and, perhaps, most important of all, not himself. A self-described "personal" writer, Kriegel avoids the traps that sunk so many in an age of confessional poetry

and tell-all afternoon talk shows. At the same time, however, Kriegel freely acknowledges the importance of his younger brother, Abraham:

> Self-portraits are rarely portraits of the self alone. For me, it is my younger brother in whose presence my own mask cracks. In a curiously intimate sense, my brother's life is where my own truest self stands revealed. And if Abe's life is not where I necessarily choose to begin, it is where I so frequently seem to end. Reflections upon the past's meaning, speculation about future possibilities—in the quest to frame a self, to see one's brother is to see oneself anew, alone in the nerve-jangling fun-house of imagination's eye.
>
> (p. 174)

In this sense, Kriegel's unflinching honesty reminds one of Ernest Hemingway, albeit with certain essential differences. Here, from the essay "Wheelchairs," is what he has to say about the swaying rhythms and prideful vanity of a man walking on crutches and that same man confined to a wheelchair:

> The most intimate of embarrassments, it is, as Hemingway said of bravery and courage, probably better not spoken about. But the vanity of walking on braces and crutches offers a man a certain sense of his own durability. A wheelchair is different. It is difficult for any man to feel truly brave in a wheelchair, for it is difficult for him to acknowledge the profound, painful difference between those who sit and those who stand. A crutchwalker knows that he *needs* those braces strapped to his legs and those crutches beneath his shoulders—but they are *his* legs on which he is standing. And he *is* standing.
>
> (p. 41)

Because Kriegel is a man of letters, it is hardly surprising that thoughts about the crippled god Hephaestus and the malformed King Richard would cross his mental screen. In a later piece written for the *Nation,* "Wrestling with Augie March," a hymn of praise to Saul Bellow's *Adventures of Augie March* (1953), Kriegel singles out William Einhorn, the crippled pool-hall philosopher, for special attention.

But books alone hardly constitute the full range of Kriegel's experience. In one essay collected in *Flying Solo* he muses about beaches in winter, in another about the assets and liabilities of the modern supermarket. But no matter where

opportunity takes him, whether it be a visiting professorship in New Mexico or a Fulbright appointment to Holland, Kriegel remains the quintessential New Yorker: smart, flinty, and unfailingly interesting.

The ravages of the body are not a pretty sight, but Kriegel has transmogrified them into a voice utterly his own—and into an art that speaks for the vulnerable humanness we all share. He did not learn how to fly an airplane (one of his serious regrets), but the collection's title essay makes it clear that verbal soaring can be equally hard won and powerful.

Kriegel's essays pack a high quotient of striking, often counterintuitive ideas. Let "A Few Kind Words for Anger" stand as Exhibit A, but it is his images that lodge inside a reader's head long after the final page has been turned. Consider this moment from "Beaches in Winter": Whenever he tried to play on the beaches of Holland with his nearly two-year-old son, he writes,

> my crutches would sink as if I were trying to move on quicksand. The beaches at Noordwijk challenged my fatherhood. It denied my longing to be the American father I wanted to be.
>
> (p. 90)

All too often disparate essays do not a satisfactory collection make, but Kriegel's compilations are a delightful exception to the rule, partly because his now-familiar themes have a way of easily cohering and because he has a savvy sense of how a book-length volume should be constructed.

On one point Elizabeth Hanson would disagree with this assessment. Writing in the pages of the *New York Times* in February 1998 she points out what, to her, is "a puzzling gap"—namely, that "we learn something of his wife, his younger brother, an eccentric uncle, a feisty grandmother and his immigrant father, but almost nothing of his mother."

This is reminiscent of the attacks certain feminist critics hurled at Irving Howe when he titled his magisterial 1976 study of the Lower East Side *World of Our Fathers.* Why not "World of Our Mothers?" they insisted. Howe pointed out there was an entire chapter devoted to the

importance of mothers, but that "World of Our Mothers" is a good title for an essay but not for a book. Howe's critics were not convinced, and one suspects that those who worry about the missing mother in *Flying Solo* won't be convinced either.

By contrast, Ed Peaco offers up a generous serving of well-deserved praise in the *Antioch Review:* "Kriegel makes nimble leaps of thought from the particular to the general and back, as in his tale of determination and revitalization after polio, or his fixation on Wonder Woman, rather than John Wayne or his grandmother, as a model for courage" (pp. 106-107).

Most critics agreed with Peaco's assessment. Kriegel's essays were gaining him the perhaps dubious reputation of being an "essayist's essayist"—meaning fellow essayists, especially if they were also writing for the top-shelf intellectual quarterlies of the day. As Kriegel readily admits, his collections of essays did not become best sellers; he did not become rich or famous. But he *was* known as a skillful, and honest, writer. *Flying Solo* helped this reputation coalesce.

WORKING THROUGH: A TEACHER'S JOURNEY IN THE URBAN UNIVERSITY

James Traub's thoroughly researched, thought-provoking study *City on a Hill: Testing the American Dream at City College* (1994) does not flinch when addressing the passions that erupted at City College during the early 1970s when defenders of high academic standards clashed with those who championed open admissions. The truth of the matter is that City College administrators had little choice: the changing demographics of blacks and Puerto Ricans in New York's boroughs represented both an opportunity to democratize higher education (a mission that many in the City College faculty held sacred) and a way to fill increasingly empty classrooms. The once prototypical City College student was now going to the Ivies and other prestigious colleges. City College had the look of a shabby relative.

For many, the train known as "open admissions" had already left the station, and the only

choice was to support the inevitable with enthusiasm. Besides, who was to say that the new crop of students, with some remedial work on their end and some patience on the faculty's part, wouldn't develop into something akin to the students of City College's glory days?

In retrospect, Kriegel is conflicted about those times, those places, but in the heat of the cultural battle, with passions boiling on both sides, Traub describes Kriegel as an "ardent champion of open admissions and a barn-burning orator in the late 1960s" (p. 78). Kriegel may not have been a household name across America, but in New York City he had "street creds." As a member in good standing of the New York intelligentsia, his essays regularly appeared in the best venues and were widely discussed. For Kriegel, open admissions was a cause that made sense at the time, and his allegiance went easily to the disadvantaged with whom he not so secretly identified. He was, in a word, idealistic, which was hardly the worst crime committed on a college campus during the political turmoil of the 1970s. Traub, who had a chance to interview Kriegel about what he did, and why—and why he now harbors some sobering second thoughts—puts it this way:

> He had eagerly signed up when Mina Shaughnessy asked him to teach Basic Writing, and he dedicated his memoir of the time [*Working Through*] to her. Now Kriegel says, "You wanted so desperately for this to work. The educational Left decided that potential was reality. Never mind that the kid was a functional illiterate; he's really brilliant. Anyone who says that the students I was teaching in 1974 were as good as the students I was teaching in 1964 is either a liar or is perpetrating an out-and-out illusion."
>
> (p. 78)

Kriegel, being Kriegel, was too honest to ignore the evidence before his eyes. Open admissions so lowered the bar that not only were functionally illiterate students able to claim seats in what had once been an intellectual powerhouse but also many in the faculty had no problem praising—and passing—inferior work.

The glaring failures of open admissions must have broken his heart, but a large residue of

LEONARD KRIEGEL

optimism remained. "The previous system was immoral," he told Traub, "and that made open admissions necessary. You knew the standards were changing. You had to have the honesty to admit that, and know that it was worth it" (p. 78).

Curiously enough, one could argue that economic realities drove, say, immigrant Jews to City College, and that in the 1970s it was economic realities that made the concessions of open admissions necessary. In the same vein, one could argue that the post-2008 recession substantially altered the college admissions picture and that the same students who might have chosen more expensive private colleges were once again applying to City College because of its attractive price tag.

Working Through (1972) came into being, Kriegel explains in his preface, because "so much recent writing about higher education in America lacks the felt experience" (p. vii). Enter Mr. Kriegel, who has made the "felt experience" his specialty. Because higher education is filtered through his experiences, it is important that Kriegel put himself "on record" about where he came from and how he sees his chances in America:

> I am, purely by accident, a man representative of a certain time and a certain set of experiences. Born in the thirties, I am a child of the fifties, though I am not part of what has come to be called middle America. Nor was I endowed with the belief that this is the American century, that I could claim its legacy as my own because I was as natural an heir as anyone else.
>
> (p. 3)

Under normal circumstances, one would read Kriegel's words as the testimony of an "outsider," and while there may be this element in his psychic makeup, what he goes on to emphasize is how he, and a generation of college teachers, inherited "the century's liabilities."

Writing in the pages of the *New York Times*, Morris Dickstein praises Kriegel's book for its "plain good sense." Nonetheless, serious quarrels persist about how much, and how fairly, the autobiographical method can be faithful to one's experience and to truth: "the more the writer is determined to be true to his own experience the

less responsible he may become to Truth of a more objective sort."

Dickstein cites Kriegel's account of his graduate school days at Columbia as a particularly telling example: Kriegel remembers in vivid detail just how terrible those years were, but Dickstein is hardly alone in wondering just how accurate, and how fair, Kriegel is being. After all, graduate school was, and for many still is, a draining, stressful time at virtually any university across our land. Columbia hardly deserves the sour rap Kriegel's memory gives it.

Still, Dickstein cannot deny that "what largely sets Kriegel apart from other recent youngish autobiographers is an absence of self-promotion and exhibitionism." Kriegel is not self-effacing, and he is surely not shy when it comes to autobiographical writing; but what shapes Kriegel's restraint is a lifetime of reading the modern voices that meant so much to the New York intellectuals: Edmund Wilson, Alfred Kazin, and Irving Howe. The next generation of autobiographers was more razzle-dazzle, and certainly more inclined to equate getting one's name in the newspapers with importance. Writers learned, first, to "confess" their darkest secrets, be it alcoholism or incest, and then to wallow in their assorted griefs. Kriegel might say that this is not how real literature works, and he even might mention that gushing about one's demons is not "manly" behavior.

One sees an element of Kriegel's fierce independence as he remembers his undergraduate days at Hunter. He clearly admires many of his teachers but prefers to view them from across an invisible boundary. This attitude does not change as the culture posits models of parents as "pals" and teachers as "good friends":

> Despite today's talk about the need for personal relationships between teacher and student, despite the voices angrily declaiming against being mere ciphers on omnipresent I.B.M. cards, I sometimes wonder if whether it is not the student's very individuality that is being distorted by teachers too intent on being his friend. I would never have asked my teachers for personal advice. That was not their function.... Today, however, the line between teacher and student is supposed to disappear. Insofar as this

allows for intellectual equality it is all to the good. However, if it is designed to make the university into a social club, then it serves only to diminish a university's true function. And I prefer the arrangement I had with teachers.

(p. 21)

As Kriegel wraps his mind and heart around academe's thornier problems, it is not uncommon for the word "however" to pop up—to clarify, to add nuance, or simply to demur. Reformer as he may be (there is no reason, after all, for higher education to be as lousy as it was, and still is), Kriegel is uncompromisingly honest about the excesses that often travel under the mantle of radical change. His "however" is a way of saying "Not so fast, buddy" to those who would denigrate values Kriegel, despite his unflagging criticisms, still holds dear. To distinguish between what should be changed and what shouldn't demands more than the slogans and marches that nearly brought higher education to its knees in the late 1960s.

In the decades that followed, opening up the university to a wide spectrum of the disadvantaged has to be a good thing, indeed, the *right* thing, but with certain important caveats: learning requires discipline, an ever-growing love of learning, and most important of all, hard work. Kriegel realized (how could he not?) that ambivalence was outweighing certainty.

Working Through is at least as much Kriegel's odyssey as it is the tale of New York City's educational failures and its occasional successes. Despite his reservations, Dickstein gives the book high marks, especially when he compares Kriegel's work with Alfred Kazin's monumental *Starting Out in the Thirties* (1965). For Dickstein, Kazin's book "may be the best book yet written about how it feels to be an intellectual in contemporary America." By contrast, Kriegel's book is less ambitious, its importance not that of Kazin's work, but *Working Through,* with its wonderful title, is a "success of a far more modest sort, a candid account of daily life at the academic barricades at what may prove to be a turning point in our educational history."

NOTES FOR THE TWO-DOLLAR WINDOW: PORTRAITS FROM AN AMERICAN NEIGHBORHOOD

Kriegel has a feel for evocative places and interesting people. That is what makes him the superb writer he, in fact, is. This collection of portraits, published in 1976, begins with geography, a sense of "place" and the boundaries that define them:

But I always find myself beginning with Jones Avenue. To the east, Lafayette Avenue and the Parkway; west of Jones, 213th Street. On one side, friends; on the other, strangers. A line of demarcation between them. Jones Avenue was my no man's land. Maps are drawn that way between nations, too. And it was Jones Avenue that stood between the block-long apartment house called Dearborn Gardens and the small apartment house on 213th Street to which we moved when I was eight.

(p. 13)

In a lovely, evocative phrase, the southern writer Eudora Welty regarded the landscape of her childhood as "the heart's field." The remark could be applied as well to Kriegel's very different place-of-place. In his Bronx neighborhood, Jews, Irish, and Italian immigrants found themselves teetering uneasily between the Old Worlds they had left and an America they could not entirely understand or entirely trust. "America goniff" (America is a thief), his father would mutter in Yiddish, and the phrase aptly summed up what the new country took from everyone in the neighborhood (Irish, Italian, and Jews alike) and especially from him. As Kriegel puts it,

There were few ways in which my father could define himself. He was neither revolutionary nor gambler; he knew nothing about baseball; he rarely went to the movies because he didn't have time and he did not understand what Hollywood had placed before him; he was not particularly suited to being an American. Man, husband, father, worker, Jew—in his own words, "a horse."

(p. 21)

It is true that immigrant Jews loved baseball and even truer that immigrant Jews created the dream factory known as Hollywood, but Kriegel's father was an example of the counterintuitive immigrant Jew: he was, to his very bones, "a horse," destined to labor ceaselessly in an America that always remained foreign to him.

But America was not foreign to his son, even though he was acutely aware of who hired Jews and who did not, and what was theirs and what was not ours:

> The five-and-ten didn't hire Jews, but I liked the loose chunks of chocolate that were kept in the front stalls and I would take pleasure in stealing as much of it as I could. I was never caught, even though I would sometimes steal the candy under the salesgirl's nose. I stole other things, too—airplane glue, lead soldiers, combs, shoelaces. Sometimes I would throw whatever I had stolen in the trash can outside the bowling alley on Bronx Avenue. The store was *theirs* and I had no guilt about stealing from *them*.
>
> (p. 22)

Kriegel's boasts about his petty thefts are curious: on one hand, he sees the entire enterprise of five-and-tens as unfair. Decades later, what he did as a young shoplifter would take on an all-purpose political dimension and travel under the term "liberation." He *liberated* the chunks of chocolate he so liked, just as he collected unpaid-for sundries. The result is a passage that gives candor a whole new set of meanings.

Kriegel has vivid memories of what it was like to have one's guard always up in a mixed neighborhood such as his was. At the same time, however, there were delicious moments when the sheer love of sports and an individual player's ability mattered more than ethnicity:

> It was the Irish who introduced me to roller hockey. From one end to the other, they scarred the street's asphalt. I was welcomed to the games. We played in an atmosphere that could best be described as absolute. In Dearborn Gardens, ability in sports was important; here it was total. Not even in Harlem schoolyard basketball games have I seen the dedication with which we skated between manhole covers.
>
> (p. 23)

Taken together, Dearborn Gardens taught Kriegel that he was not doomed to be, as his father was, a perpetual stranger in a strange land. America was all around him, and beyond his neighborhood it was as alluring as it was alienating. One suspects that Kriegel's characteristic stance of nuanced ambiguity, of balancing liberal optimism with a clear-eyed allegiance to reality, was born in the youthful energy he describes in *Notes for the Two-Dollar Window*.

ON MEN AND MANHOOD

Kriegel's extended 1979 rumination about manhood, one of his abiding concerns as he aged in the braces and crutches that, as a polio sufferer, allowed him to walk, begins with his crutches sinking into the sand at a beach in Holland as his two-year-old son watches. The painful image on the page is seared in the reader's brain just as the original image is still seared in Kriegel's consciousness. Given this "defeat," how is genuine manhood, genuine fatherhood, possible?

Kriegel answers this question by calling the old certainties into question and by raising new possibilities. In this effort he explores the quint-essentially American autobiographies of Benjamin Franklin, Ulysses S. Grant, and Henry Adams. Franklin sees the unity between the "man of thought" and the "man of action" but also believes that separate-but-equal spheres eventually "split in half." Grant believes in energy while Adams backs off into introspection.

To paraphrase Henry James, it is a complex fate to be an American male—and many would add, he didn't know the half of it. American manhood by the late twentieth century had acquired no end of troubles, ones that James, in an earlier, comfortably patriarchal age, did not have to fret about. But if some of the biographical speculation swirling around him is true, James may well have fretted about the relationship between "manhood" and his own sexual identity.

We can only speculate about such matters, or simply declare them inappropriate for a wide variety of reasons. What we *do* know, however, is that the old verities—*Be strong! Be brave! Be a man!*—have been called into question by blacks, by homosexuals, and most of all, by women.

At a conference in the 1970s titled "The Impact on Men of the Changing Role of Women," Kriegel wonders why "the catalogue of judgment" being leveled on men must necessarily read like a chapter from the Book of Leviticus. As one after another of the conference speakers would have it, manhood is, among other things,

> bourgeois to the core; destructive to bourgeois solidity; individualistic; competitive; timid; tyrannical;

insensitive … Manhood is sexist! Gender is damnation! In biology, we are guilty; in history, the record indicts us on our own testimony.

(p. 196)

How is one to answer such a mélange of contradictory charges? During the turbulent days of the feminist movement, Kriegel was hardly alone in feeling that men were damned if they did and damned if they didn't. This is a case of damned if I do, damned if I don't, and, yes, damned because I'm just, well, damned.

Kriegel begins his response to the "maelstrom" that the conference stirred up in one male speaker (who was abruptly informed that the word must be changed to *"peoplestrom"*) by talking eloquently about his own furies. Once again, he repeats the life-altering tale of how he found himself on a beach in Holland trying to be the manly father his two-year-old son would require of him.

As his crutches sink hopelessly into the sand, Kriegel realizes that his physical limitations have outstripped his will, that he simply cannot be the father one regularly encounters in story and myth. Kriegel never forgot the moment he first described in "Beaches in Winter." However much he willed himself to hold his son and walk along the beach, it was not to be:

> I reach the bottom of the incline. My crutches slice the sand, sink.… The dream evaporates as suddenly as it has seized me. I can barely walk towards my son, the crutches sink deeper and deeper into the sand with each step I take. I will drown in sand before I reach him. I will die of rage unless I can smash it against something. I caricature illusion now. Nonfather, nonrunner, nonhusband, nonman—the vision has popped, I want to scream.

(p. 8)

On Men and Manhood is part inquiry, part meditation. Kriegel looks at American men and sees, cannot help but see, the reflection of a cripple, unable to measure performance when the rules seem always to change. His chronicle of what it means to match the man within to the challenges outside—as husband, as lover, as father—brings the problem into sharp, painful focus.

The glib promises of androgyny miss the point: too much is at stake for the fashionable

talk about definitions, the jingoisms of the women's movement, the buzzwords of pop psychologists. As Vance Bourjaily observes in the pages of the *New York Times,* "Mr. Kriegel is a Socratic teacher, inviting debate, raising questions, offering clarification. He has written a book to be read slowly, in agreement or disagreement, one that provokes a restless urge to amplify."

For Kriegel, manhood on the cheap is at once not earned and not genuine. "The real issues," he insists once again, "still have to do with courage, with the willingness to risk one's substance as a man, with the ability to capture that self one claims" (p. 199).

On Men and Manhood is a brave, ambitious book. Written at a time when loud insistences counted for more than quiet reflections, Kriegel's personal history is only part of the story. His book is also an inquiry into American culture, with its emphasis on sexual performance, on the widening split between mind and body, on power, on success. Much of the discussion about manhood during the 1970s tended to be shrill and, at bottom, sentimental. Kriegel, who writes with icy clarity about rage and anger, knows full well just how counterproductive (however necessary) these extremes can be.

QUITTING TIME

Quitting Time (1982), Kriegel's first novel, is filled with evidence that years of etching distinct characters for his essays had paid off when it came to writing fiction. As with his essays, the novel bristles with ambition and scope, this time focused on the labor movement. *Quitting Time* is at once an account of Barney Kadish's life as a revolutionary and his life in the labor movement to which he pledged his unswerving alliance. The novel's memories begin with 1919, as Barney slips the Truth to Marty Altschuler, his younger disciple and the first narrator/witness entrusted with the telling of Barney's tale:

> Listen … no matter what else, you can depend upon this: a boss is a boss. Sucks your blood, then wipes his ass with your carcass.… It won't be different

until we're all bosses. Which means there will be no bosses.

(p. 4)

Kadish is a Marxist firebrand, a man who lost an eye during an early labor struggle and who is defined by his single-minded, single-visioned purpose ever since. On the garment district's street, Kadish is instantly recognizable as the man with the eye patch and the thundering voice.

Kadish is not a "cripple" in the way that Kriegel defines himself, but he is surely a man whose wound ultimately limited his vision, for *Quitting Time* is the story of Kadish's rise and fall. In this sense, the novel's trajectory reminds one of Robert Penn Warren's *All the King's Men* (1946) and the tragic rhythms of Willie Stark's doomed life. Granted, Kadish is not as memorable as Stark and Kriegel has not written the equal of Warren's masterpiece, but there is much to recommend Kriegel's first novel nonetheless. As Joseph McLellan puts it in the pages of the *Washington Post, Quitting Time* is "an accomplished first novel," with certain key elements that show off Kriegel's use of significant detail. He points to Kadish's omnipresent eye patch:

> Barney Kadish's one eye neatly symbolizes the single-mindedness that was both his strength and his weakness. Through most of his 68 years, Kadish's eye was fixed firmly on revolution—"the revolution that never comes," as his friend and colleague and fellow Communist Gus Constantinou often describes it.

At the tender age of twelve, Barney had memorized entire pages of *The Communist Manifesto,* had read Leo Tolstoy on the peasants, along with works by Anton Chekhov, Sholom Aleichem, Mendele Mocher Sforim, Ivan Turgenev, and I. L. Peretz. He is, in short, every inch the wunderkind, and a character who might well have stepped out of a proletarian novel circa 1933. What saves *Quitting Time,* what makes it so stunningly different, are the prisms of history through which Kadish's revolutionary pronouncements are filtered. As Marty thinks about Barney Kadish and what a life such as his comes to (dead of a heart attack at sixty-eight, in Albuquerque, New Mexico, of all places), he tempers the political rhetoric he remembers with some ruminations of his own:

What could a man like Barney have thought of out there? Everything out in the open, the way each of us learns to proclaim his faith here in America.... Who believes in tomorrow in America? Maybe what Barney Kadish never understood is that America may be beyond the forces of history. No beginning, no end. Nothing. Except now. And that was where Barney Kadish, who believed in the forces of history, died in the arms of his Jewish penitent.

(p. 3)

Quitting Time is built from alternating currents of exactly this sort. Out of Barney Kadish's quarrels with capitalistic bosses, with sweatshop conditions, with grinding poverty, comes rhetoric aimed at building a world more attractive. In him, the messianic urge takes on a decidedly secular twist. This, as it were, is the novel's "prose"; but out of the novel's various narrators, including Marty Altschuler, Gus Constaninou, and his wife, Greta Hedwig Edmundson Kadish, comes the internal struggles that makes for *poetry.* The result is a portrait of Barney's heroism that avoids melodramatic excess and systematic whitewashing.

Something of the novel's richness is incorporated in the multilayered possibilities of "quitting time." On the most obvious level, it refers to that moment when the factory whistle sounds, when the sweatshop's machines turn silent, when the laborers' day is over. But "quitting time" also has a wider application, one that speaks to the grip that Time—and History—has on characters and, conversely, that the characters have on Time. For all the panoramic scenes that merge fiction with fact (Barney Kadish forms the mythical International Pattern Makers, Dyers, and Silk Workers Union at one point and, later, joins John L. Lewis in the CIO strike against General Motors—only to be driven out of union power by the Taft-Hartley Act and the witch hunts of the 1940s and 1950s), *Quitting Time* is a meditation on those times, those places, on what History means in a freewheeling ahistorical America and about the high costs of translating ideological conviction into brutal fact. Heads, and hearts, were broken on both sides of the political spectrum. Kriegel's novel is filled with intricate, complicated responses to the tangled social issues of the day. What makes it remarkable, however, is the way

it portrays human beings rather than cardboard stereotypes.

For an age that has rediscovered the social clashes that once pitted the Left against the Far Left, and those with social vision against those blinded by materialism—in E. L. Doctorow's *Ragtime* (1975), in Warren Beatty's *Reds* (1981)—Leonard Kriegel's novel is a better history, better because it is more, and because it knows the essence of tragedy is that which is, cannot be, and that which cannot be, is.

SUMMING UP

Ironically enough, Kriegel's boyhood neighborhood provided the nuanced texture, the shape and feel, of the streets. Polio and American culture gradually intertwined into a singular vision, and then into a singular "voice." That is the strength of Kriegel's prose and why his personal essays, refracted as they are through the lens of a wider American culture, are so powerful. At its core are the big themes of American literature—the tension between taking flight or standing one's ground; what it means to be a man, and a father; how to be a lover and husband.

Selected Bibliography

WORKS OF LEONARD KRIEGEL

NONFICTION

The Long Walk Home. New York: Appleton-Century, 1964.

Edmund Wilson. Carbondale: Southern Illinois University Press, 1971.

Working Through: A Teacher's Journey in the Urban University. New York: Saturday Review Press, 1972.

Notes for the Two-Dollar Window: Portraits from an American Neighborhood. New York: Saturday Review Press, 1976.

On Men and Manhood. New York: Hawthorn Books, 1979.

Falling into Life: Essays. San Francisco: North Point Press, 1991.

Flying Solo: Reimagining Manhood, Courage, and Loss. Boston: Beacon Press, 1998.

FICTION

Quitting Time: A Novel. New York: Pantheon, 1982.

ANTHOLOGIES

Experiments in Survival. With Edith Henrich. New York: Association for the Aid of Crippled Children, 1961.

Essential Works of the Founding Fathers. New York: Bantam Books, 1964.

Masters of the Short Story. With Abraham H. Lass. New York: New American Library, 1971.

Stories of the American Experience. With Abraham H. Lass. New York: New American, 1973.

The Myth of American Manhood. New York: Dell, 1978.

UNCOLLECTED ESSAYS

"Wanted: A Protestant Novelist." *Commonweal* 83, no. 9:273–278 (1965).

"Dalton Trumbo's *Johnny Got His Gun.*" In *Proletarian Writers of the Thirties.* Edited by David Madden. Carbondale: Southern Illinois University Press, 1968. Pp. 106–113.

"Writers and Ethnicity." *Partisan Review* 54, no. 1:115–120 (winter 1987).

"*Partisan Review* and the New York Intellectuals: A Personal View." *Gettysburg Review* 2, no. 2:227–237 (spring 1989).

"Graffiti: Tunnel Notes of a New Yorker." *American Scholar* 62, no. 3:431–436 (summer 1993).

"Synagogues." *American Scholar* 69, no. 4:61–75 (autumn 2000).

"Wrestling with Augie March." *Nation,* June 23, 2003, pp. 27–32.

CRITICAL STUDIES, REVIEWS, AND INTERVIEWS

Bourjaily, Vance. "It Takes More Than Throwing a Ball; Manhood." *New York Times Book Review,* December 9, 1979. (Review of *On Men and Manhood.*)

Dickstein, Morris. "Torn by Diverse Loyalties." *New York Times Book Review,* November 19, 1972. (Review of *Working Through.*)

Hanson, Elizabeth. Review of *Flying Solo. New York Times Book Review,* February 22, 1998.

Haugen, Hayley Mitchell. "The 'Disabled Imagination' and the Masculine Metaphor in the Works of Leonard Kriegel." In *The Body in Medical Culture.* Edited by Elizabeth Klaver. Albany: SUNY Press, 2009. Pp. 89–109.

McLellan, Joseph. "A Labor of Love & Hate." *Washington Post,* April 3, 1982, p. C5. (Review of *Quitting Time.*)

Peaco, Ed. "*Flying Solo*: Reimagining Manhood, Courage, and Loss." *Antioch Review* 57, no. 1:106–107 (winter 1999).

Shepard, Richard F. "End Papers." *New York Times,* May 7, 1964, p. 35. (Review of *The Long Walk Home*.)

Traub, James. *City on a Hill: Testing the American Dream at City College*. Reading, Mass.: Addison-Wesley, 1994.

Wakefield, Dan. "A Rage to Live: An Interview with Leonard Kriegel." *Sun* 285:4–8 (September 1999).

ANDER MONSON

(1975—)

Amanda Fields

KNOWN FOR A risky and metacognitive approach to his work, Ander Monson has published poetry, fiction, and nonfiction, and he blends these genres as a way of questioning, ruminating upon, and immersing himself and his readers in the structures of writing.

OVERVIEW

Monson was born on April 9, 1975, in Houghton, Michigan, in the Upper Peninsula, and much of his work takes place in and is influenced by this region—from the history and cultural effects of the mining industry to the significant wintry weather. Monson connects this place to the themes of his writing. Characteristics of the place function as metaphors for the ways Monson regards the manipulation of form and content. The action of mining is perhaps an apt analogy for Monson's work, then, as he digs and roots for memories and stories that will compel. The region, too, is characterized by a sense of loneliness influenced by extreme weather conditions and opportunities for work.

Real events and places from the Upper Peninsula and from Monson's life are woven into all of his work. He uses local events from his past as a starting point for more fictional depictions. Because of the blending of nonfiction and fictional elements in his work, it is sometimes difficult to pinpoint the details of Monson's background. In interviews he claims Norwegian, Swedish, and Finnish ancestry. He has one brother, and, while brothers in his writing are often missing an arm, Monson has indicated that his real brother is not armless. For a time when Monson was younger, his family lived in Riyadh, Saudi Arabia, for temporary spans over the course of three years. When prodded to shed some light

on the death of his mother when Monson was a boy, and the resulting appearance of mothers in his text who have died or disappeared, Monson usually politely hedges, though he often writes convincingly about his mother in his nonfiction and poetry. At the same time, he is quite open about other personal matters, such as frequent references to his love for alcohol. Personal artifacts, such as a letter he wrote when he was a boy to his father, can be found on his website, thus filling in some gaps about Monson as a person. In several interviews he has shown a firm commitment to distinguishing between the writing of nonfiction and the writing of autobiography. He does not consider his writing to be autobiographical; in other words, his work plays with, and admits to, the frequent imprecision of memory and narratives of reality.

He received a bachelor's degree in 1997 from Knox College in Galesburg, Illinois, a master's degree in 1999 from Iowa State University, and a master of fine arts degree in 2002 from the University of Alabama. Of his decision to apply to the University of Alabama, he has said in more than one interview that he applied there because he didn't have to choose one genre to apply in, a requirement for most MFA programs in creative writing. After he received his MFA, he taught at Grand Valley State University until 2008, when he joined the faculty at the highly regarded MFA program at the University of Arizona in Tucson, where he is currently an associate professor of nonfiction.

In 1999 he founded the online literary magazine *DIAGRAM*. This journal publishes most genres but frequently focuses on poetry and visual schematics. He is also the editor and publisher of New Michigan Press, also founded in 1999, a small press now located in Tucson,

Arizona, which publishes six to ten chapbooks per year as well as *DIAGRAM* anthologies and broadsides for various reading series. An annual chapbook contest is sponsored by *DIAGRAM* and New Michigan Press.

Monson's work has been published in several literary journals, including *Tin House, Fourth Genre, Indiana Review, Salt Hill, Believer,* and *Fourth River*. His book of essays *Neck Deep and Other Predicaments* earned him a Great Lakes Colleges Association New Writers award, in addition to the Graywolf Press Nonfiction Prize. Monson also runs a website (http://other electricities.com/) that is partly an author website and partly a space for further rumination on the material and structure of his published books. An essay that originally appeared on this website, "Solipsism," was republished by *The Pinch* and subsequently chosen for *The Best American Essays 2008*. "Exteriority," an essay from *Vanishing Point: Not a Memoir* (2010; originally published in *Hotel Amerika*) was a Notable Essay for *The Best American Essays 2009*. Another essay, "Ceremony" (originally published in *The Believer*), was republished in *The Best Creative Nonfiction Volume 2* (2008). In addition to his website and literary journal, Monson maintains a regularly updated Twitter account with over fifteen hundred followers.

Monson has published five books, which are categorized by publishers as two books of poetry (*Vacationland,* 2005; *The Available World,* 2010), one collection of short stories (*Other Electricities,* 2005), and two books of essays (*Neck Deep and Other Predicaments,* 2007; *Vanishing Point: Not a Memoir,* 2010). In addition, Monson collaborated with the artist Kris Ingmundson on a handmade book called *Slow Dancing Through Ether: A Fine Binding Project*. The book makes use of much of the material from *Other Electricities* but in a different form. He has also published chapbooks through New Michigan Press, including *Safety Features* (1999) and *Our Aperture* (2007).

However, such genre categorizations are rather easily refuted when one delves into his works, which cannot often be pinpointed to one conventional genre, and Monson himself does not always accept such categories. For instance, in many interviews, he has conceded to the labeling of *Other Electricities* as a collection of short stories; however, he does not always object to the term "novel" and calls the book a novel at times. As of this writing, Monson continues to publish short pieces and is working on several projects involving both print and electronic media, including fiction and essays.

There are a number of recurring characteristics in Monson's work. First is his constant questioning of form and genre. Second, Monson focuses on questions of memory and truth. Why are we obsessed with the truth of stories, and how do memory and imagination play a role in our reading and understanding of writing and genres? Such questions link with a third characteristic of his writing: considering the public examination of truth in memoir and creative nonfiction. For instance, he questions the hullabaloo over truth and lies in published memoirs, such as James Frey's *A Million Little Pieces*. Fourth, Monson explores the abundance of information and data available in the world, particularly through online and digital media. Fifth, Monson makes explicit the intertextuality of his publications. Every text he writes is connected—not only the printed texts, which often refer to each other, building upon subjects, but also through the extension online of his printed texts. Monson has frequently referred to this intertextuality in a more appealing way than the term itself connotes, calling it a "constellation." Sixth, Monson integrates several signposts in his work that are directed explicitly toward those in the process of reading. For example, he provides a chart of characters with brief plot descriptions in *Other Electricities*. Such moves also reflect an interest in self-awareness as a writer that can demonstrate to readers the reciprocity of the acts of writing and reading. Additionally, Monson often takes on the second-person point of view as a way of implicating the reader but also as a way of distancing himself and others from the parts of his texts that resemble real events or people. Finally, Monson's work shows a focus on arrangement—from visual schematics to meditations on and playfulness with structure. The ar-

rangement connects with his style. He often makes use of the imperative in titles, for instance, as well as anaphora. He repeats the use of particular forms, such as the index, trying out these forms in relationship to different subjects. Frequent themes in his work include loneliness; isolation; early or unexpected deaths and characters with an impulse toward death and danger; grief; popular culture; the possibilities of digital media and older media such as the printed word; music; and the complex narratives and memories of place, including sites of remembrance and sites that have been destroyed or have vanished.

In some ways, Monson is like an autoethnographer, in that he uses his personal experiences to make insightful and, often, humorous observations about the larger social culture he is discussing. The irony (or, more appropriately, the intriguing trait) of Monson's work is that he cloaks some of his memories and personal events even as he inculcates a narrative voice that feels open and trustworthy. He also engages in genre bending, and his work could be a source of study for those scholars interested in genre theory, in which genre is seen as both a situation with a limited set of characteristics but also a space that is flexible, a space where the parameters or characteristics of genre can be changed when questioned and massaged. Bringing the forms of particular genres to the forefront of reflection can cause readers and writers to see form as more than a receptacle for words.

OTHER ELECTRICITIES: STORIES

Other Electricities (2005) is one of Monson's first book-length publications, coming out in the same year as his poetry collection *Vacationland*. Monson often calls *Other Electricities* a novel, although it is published and marketed by Sarabande Books as a collection of stories. Perhaps another way of referring to this book is as a segmented novel, where a thread of stories and themes runs through its entirety, stories that are told from varying viewpoints. Monson has said that the book is a mythology of a real place. While the names of places are real, and there are

recognizable aspects of the region and certain events, the characters, according to Monson, are not real people, though they appear in his other books, including those labeled as nonfiction— sometimes with the same names and sometimes with different names but recognizable traits. The characters are often composites or completely fictional, as he implies in many of his interviews and the published texts themselves.

The book takes place in a small town in the Upper Peninsula of Michigan and centers around a series of characters, all of whom are responding to or are connected in one way or another to deaths that have shaken the community, including a young man who plunges through a frozen waterway on his snowmobile, a young woman who was raped and killed, a young woman who died by drowning, and the mother of the protagonist, referred to as "your protagonist," who either died from cancer when the protagonist was young or left the family to go to Canada. The fate of the mother in the story is deliberately unclear. As a result, "your protagonist" and his brother are left in a house where their father spends his time locked in the attic, listening to shortwave radios and scanners and speaking in his own code across the airwaves.

It is clear that we are meant to think of "your protagonist" as a fictional version of Monson. This character is usually not very far from the action in the book. For instance, he has a crush on the young woman who drowned after a car she was riding in plunged into the lake. We follow his sense of isolation as his mother, his father, and the young woman he liked all vanish in some way. His brother has not only lost these people but has also lost an arm. Both "your protagonist" and his brother are adrift in this place of snowy weather and violent deaths.

Passages are told from the perspectives of numerous characters, from those who were closest to the ones who have died to those who are more anonymous, such as a chapter from the perspective of the diver sent to look for the body of someone who has drowned. Most sequences occur just before or after the deaths, and the chapters are not organized chronologically. The multiple perspectives seem to circle the major

events rather than land directly within them. Chapters taking place closer to the actual events of specific deaths are often told from the perspective of someone who does not have a personal relationship with the deceased, such as the diver. The actual deaths are not detailed. A focus on multiple, incomplete perspectives reflects a sense of the boundaries of narrative as well as the attitudes and limited interpretations of characters, readers, and the writer.

Young people are a driving force in the book, specifically youth of high school age. In particular, there is a clear meditation on the concept of danger as it relates to women, particularly young women. Young women are often discussed in terms of statistics and becoming stories to forewarn others. They are depicted as frequently objectified by the townspeople, even as we come to understand the personal relationships certain characters may have had with these young women. For instance, Carrie Hartfield, who is raped and murdered, is not described as a human being but rather as a desired object. And no part of the text is from her point of view.

There are also many objects in this world that are no longer used for their intended purposes but that are often discovered and reused by young people, and these objects inscribe a reflection upon silence and history. Characters drive old cars around or stumble upon and make use of abandoned vehicles, such as an old bus. In addition, Monson speculates several times upon all of the items that must be at the bottom of the lake, and the historical sensibility offered by this observation is complemented by the motif of quiet as well as discussions about the complexity of the notion of quiet. Items at the bottom of a lake are muffled amid the movement of the water. Similarly, an old abandoned bus, overgrown with weeds, folds in quietly with the noisier surroundings. The notions of quiet and silence are linked to boundaries. As one of the characters notes, "It's like the white space in a frame. It's like milk in a bottle. Bounded. It has to be maintained to keep its shape" (p. 91). These notions are hard to recognize unless bounded by something else. Such a concept might serve as a metaphor for Monson's meditations on form.

Monson also uses inclement weather such as snow and blizzards to indicate the boundaries and solitude that encircle and characterize the town and region. Such silence, influenced by the ice-packed cold of wintry weather, connects with the inability of the townspeople to directly discuss the tragedies that have occurred. Monson often attributes a certain reticence to the habits and culture of the Midwest. In the book, a silence descends and creates a boundary, as in the case of Carrie Hartfield's rape and murder. This event becomes, as Monson writes, "the watershed that divides, that splits, that cleaves the community in half for three years until the act is over and forgotten, buried in the ground like copper and in the papers for future crime historians" (p. 105).

Such quiet is also linked, however, to the desire for danger and, subsequently, to the danger of snow. Therefore, Monson labels this desire, a desire attributed to Carrie Hartfield, as "the white desire—the thing that makes the Finns run from the saunas and jump into the snowbank" (p. 108). Carrie Hartfield, for example, dates a young man who seems delightfully dangerous at first, as someone whom the townspeople view as her complete opposite, and he ends up brutalizing her. The "white desire" affects others, too, such as the young man who simply drives his snowmobile across the lake when he shouldn't, and he plunges through and dies.

The book also contains several visual elements beyond the prose. It opens with "A Table of Contents Provided for Your Convenience," a table of contents unusual in its form in that each section, including the author's acknowledgments page, is listed along with its thematic purpose. Each chapter of the narrative is also labeled with the character's perspective from which it is told.

Next, a character diagram, formatted like a family tree with names and brief descriptions in boxes, follows the acknowledgments page. The boxes of all of the deceased characters are shaded in gray. In some cases, characters are easily recognizable and are present or narrating in multiple chapters; in other cases, the character box describes someone who may have had one line of dialogue or a single moment in the book. Yet all of the characters are described in a way

that shows their relationship to the major events or to the characters closest to the major events. The family tree structure demonstrates the inescapable connections among those who live in towns such as this one.

Following the character diagram is a character guide, which lists several characters and records "their relationship to danger, and an explanation of some symbols commonly found herein" (p. xv). The character list includes recognizable outsiders mentioned only in passing, such as Dwight Yoakam, whose music is mentioned, yet it excludes other characters with entire chapters told from their perspective. The guide also lists the symbolism of certain concepts and themes; however, this is not a neat list of *x* stands for *y*. "The Future," for example, is clarified with the question "is there one or not?" (p. xviii). There is no straightforward answer to what concepts in the book symbolize, and Monson seems to indicate that there should not be.

One potential effect of the character guide is to bring the reader and writer a little closer together in the conspiracy of the narrative, as well as to underscore the characters' (and, perhaps, the writer's) deep connections to the grief in these pages. Even if the events are not inscribed exactly as they may have occurred (or not) in this real place, the grief and the feelings come across as very real, and as very much a part of the writer's life, whether he represents the protagonist or not. The author also converses with the reader, such as when he describes Carrie Hartfield, who is mentioned as the sister of a character named Crisco as well as identified as the character who was raped and murdered. Regarding this description, Monson writes, "Jesus that was awful & I hate to even bring it up, but it won't stay down" (p. xv). In instances such as this, Monson reaches out to the reader, and questions might arise, such as, What parts of a tragic event should one tell, and for what reasons? The question is as much for the reader as for the writer, and the authority to answer such a question is not given exclusively to Monson. Similarly, the short list concerning symbolism is more rumination than imperative.

The flip side of such formats as the character guide is that Monson does not entirely follow the protocol he initiates; if he doesn't list every character, for example, it is not necessarily a "guide" but, rather, another way of viewing the story. Monson traverses back and forth between clarity and confusion, and this can enhance the relationship he develops with readers or it can isolate him, which seems to be the risk of his writing, a risk he gladly and explicitly takes.

Another visual in the book is the series of radio schematics that appear within and between chapters. These schematics are often linked with sentences that are seemingly random, like bits of noise caught as one dials through stations or captures certain frequencies. This graphic could be seen as reflecting the structure and unpredictability of forms, as the schematics reflect a depiction of waves of sound and electricity. The graphic is an imitation but not an exact replica, just like a memory, and just like the narratives we tell ourselves about our lives. The graphic also connects with the image of the protagonist's father in the attic, cut off from his family, listening and speaking over the airwaves. This is both a public and isolated act, connected with loneliness and the damage that the father is doing to his sons even as he reaches out to some other part of the world, other voices and other sounds. The father is absent except over the airwaves. This is a persistent metaphor and concept in the book—that there are always other electricities, other frequencies, vacancies and presences simultaneously inhabiting spaces. Sometimes we recognize these frequencies, but often they go unnoticed.

Finally, Monson inserts an index at the end of the book, which records instances of specific motifs that appear and repeat in the book. Within the index, he also finds ways to integrate more pieces of the narrative. For instance, in the *As*, he alphabetically inserts "an anecdote" that he then narrates, shedding some light on a few of the characters. The index here, like the table of contents, character diagram, and character guide, also serves as a guide for the reader and creates a more explicit relationship between the reader and the writer, which is not a common strategy yet is

related to postmodern perceptions of narrative. Once again, a genre—in this case, the index—is used and expanded by Monson.

Such addendums or supplements to the text expand the notion of boundaries and borders. And these are frequent themes in the chapters, as well. In one chapter, "Constellations," a young man named Timothy marvels at the maps his father has attached to the walls, each map connecting to the next. Monson writes, "It was an incredible thought that the world could be mapped, that there was no spot left on the planet that did not have its shape recorded on paper.... How did experience become translated into these bright colors and borders, topographically defining a common existence?" (p. 140). Readers of Monson's work will come to understand that Timothy's question overlays the analysis and theory that Monson brings to narrative. The world can be structured, shrunken to pleasing patterns, and indeed these are patterns that Monson finds fruitful. At the same time, something is always left out. Like constellations interpreted by groups of people—some interpretations are passed down, while other people may see different patterns and gaps in the stars, and across the world the sky and its stars can be seen.

"Constellations" is an appropriate descriptor not only for the chapter but the segmented book. Monson emphasizes that the motifs in the book act as connectors that support the book's status as a novel and that these motifs create constellations. The motifs circle back on each other, repeat, fold, and connect, and this adds a complexity to the form, structure, and narrative of the book. The book does not ask for a linear reading; rather, a reader invested in the text will become invested in the idea of revolving, returning to, and questioning the narrative as Monson and many of the characters do. And these characters appear elsewhere, such as in monologues in *Vacationland,* the collection of poetry that was published in the same year as *Other Electricities.*

The intertextuality extends to the handmade book Monson collaborated on with Kris Ingmundson, which he references in the final acknowledgments of *Other Electricities.* The project contains three books, which are adapted from passages in *Other Electricities,* along with two more books that are Ingmundson's visual interpretations of the stories in the novel. Monson's website contains photographs of this collaborative project. This project and *Other Electricities* exemplify the call-and-response of Monson's work, its insistence on the consciousness of the book in the world, and the possibilities of various interactions with a book. Monson's first novel shows the value he places on the printed book itself in spite of (or in accordance with) his substantial online presence.

NECK DEEP AND OTHER PREDICAMENTS

Published by Graywolf Press in 2007 and the winner of the Graywolf Press Nonfiction Prize, *Neck Deep and Other Predicaments* is a book of essays that extends Monson's focus on the snowy region of his childhood while he meditates on older and newer forms of media and the influence of specific media on knowledge, memory, and writing. Robert Polito, who judged the Graywolf Press Nonfiction Prize, writes: "Monson is as gaga about gadgets, diagrams, and recondite technical skills as any other modern gearhead. Yet he remains fascinated—and troubled—by all the incidental organizational forms around and inside our knowledge, old and new" (p. xiii). This statement applies to much of Monson's work while aptly reflecting the focus of *Neck Deep.*

As with his other writings, Monson questions form and genre in this book, particularly as these relate to finding meaning in writing. The writing of a personal essay is often touted by writers and teachers of nonfiction as a space where discovery is imminent in the process of writing. In more than one of the essays in this book, Monson explicitly states that he is waiting around in the essay for a discovery or personal epiphany—he is waiting for meaning and significance to emerge. In this text, he places essays in forms that reflect some of the tenets of genre theory. One of the characteristics of genre theory is the emphasis on the simultaneous flexibility and defined boundaries of genres. Those who study Monson's work might note that he works to

define and shift boundaries and that, in his books and in interviews, he questions the tendency to identify genres through labels that are too restrictive.

In "Outline Toward a Theory of the Mine Versus the Mind and the Harvard Outline," Monson structures the essay in the form of the Harvard Outline, a recognizable strategy for high school and first-year composition students that offers the feeling that the essay can be condensed and mapped. Monson laments that this outline is to blame for the numerous essays he gets from students that are formatted in the same way, even as he revels in the pleasure of the code or blueprint it provides and the sense of certainty it engenders. At the same time, although the Harvard Outline may seem to be bounded by specific rules, Monson indicates that perhaps within those parameters there is room for experimentation and change. Monson uses the calculated form of the Harvard Outline to question its capacity for generative thought. It is clear in this essay that Monson's generative thought is at least somewhat inspired by form. Therefore, within the rigid parameters of the Harvard Outline is a shift within the form. This kind of provocative move again calls to mind genre theory, in which the Harvard Outline as a standard form is resisted, manipulated, and transformed. And Monson does not strictly follow the rules of the Harvard Outline, at times allowing the content to determine the movement of the piece rather than the form of the outline. Within the essay he also considers the influence of the mining industry in the Upper Peninsula—its intrigues and failures—on the substance and obsessions of his writing. He tinkers with form, and, as he has pointed out himself in various venues, sometimes he fails, and sometimes he gets it right.

Monson's visual explorations of form continue in the essay "I Have Been Thinking About Snow," in which much of the essay is a series of periods, with groups of sentences clustered at intervals between the periods. The structure reflects both the frustration and intrigue a reader might experience with much of Monson's work, where experimentation with linear patterns challenges the reader to think beyond the narrative to the apparatus of the narrative. The structure also connects deeply with the subject of snow in the essay. A blizzard of periods encircles and packs in each insight, layering, like mounds and drifts of snow. The snow effect also generates a sensation of loneliness, as each insight or anecdote peppered into the essay seems to stand in isolation. Water is often present in the collection, from snow to bathtubs, pools, and boats on a lake.

The setting of Monson's pieces and his analysis of the writing of these pieces often brings together form, place, and content in an effort to meditate upon the significance of such a connection. For example, in "Cranbrook Schools: Adventures in Bourgeois Topologies," Monson writes about the private school he attended and was subsequently expelled from owing to felonious hacking activities that resulted in credit fraud. He returns to the school as an adult, walking its grounds and working to find significance in being in that space. He claims that he has trouble linking the campus he is walking through to his past: "What thesis have I set out to prove? What thesis have I proved? I am trying to find ways to map my experience of the place onto the place itself. How do these two things converge?" (p. 46). He shares his befuddlement with the connections of content and form and purpose with readers; he involves readers in his search.

In this collection, Monson also often writes about seemingly superficial subjects, such as the mechanics and beauty of the automatic car wash (he visits several in an effort to determine which particular business he prefers) or his seriousness about playing disc golf, and he is often quite detailed and sometimes verbose about these subjects. Yet each of these detailed subjects reflects, again, his obsession with memory and form. He writes: "My memories offer up form from formlessness—certainly they are more a mass, morass of things than a toybox of specific childhood forms" (p. 145). In this passage he is discussing the indexing of *Other Electricities* and what this index revealed about the memories he chose to emphasize, the selections he made and makes when crafting a narrative about the past. A focus on the car wash, for instance, not only

gives an appreciative look into the technical workings of this space but also offers a venue for examining the genius of advertising (as in the customer choosing a specific air freshener, described with precision based on its scent) and considering the particular details that the writer, the personal essayist, selects. When Monson reflects upon *Other Electricities,* he notes the predominant themes he writes about, such as armlessness, and he considers what might be behind this preoccupation. Monson shows great interest in what the selection of details reveals about the writer.

This selection of details implies control, but Monson indicates that memory is about both control and a lack of control—a theme discussed across the essay collection. The control (or lack thereof) over a form, a story, or memory is often mentioned and associated with the subject of the essay. For instance, in "Fragments: On Dentistry," the helplessness Monson feels while trapped in a dentist's chair is likened to the helplessness one can feel in the face of writing an essay and searching for its significance through form and content. Both enterprises are about knowledge, craft, and manipulation of a physical form. As Monson writes, "The tooth is a technology. The essay is a technology" (p. 91). Monson's focus on design and aesthetics is present throughout the collection, as are his ruminations about the success or failure of form, as in "Failure: A Meditation." This essay, like the essay about snow, is structured with numerous periods encircling the sentences and seems to be representative of an abundance of information. The periods are representative of a stream of information that is continual even while pausing or stopping. What seems like digressions are not digressions. Such a structure is reminiscent of the stop and start of movements on the Internet (through Web browsing, hyperlinking), with its associative actions. In the snow essay, the periods represent a blizzard, a whiteout that can be connected with this meditation on information. Failure of form is a predominant theme in the collection, but such failures are connected as remnants of the whole; we cannot help but think, for instance, of the snow essay in comparison

with "Failure: A Meditation," and once again our attention is drawn to the functions of form.

As with his other books, Monson is also focused on the readerly obsession with truth when confronted with the genre of nonfiction. He frequently notes that he has probably lied in the book but that, simultaneously, he has been as committed to the truth as he can be. Beyond Monson's perpetual consideration of form and genre, in many ways his waffling between truth and lies can be seen as a response to the cultural moment spawned by the revelation that James Frey's lauded 2003 memoir, *A Million Little Pieces,* was largely a lie. Overall, *Neck Deep and Other Predicaments* immerses both reader and writer not only in the subject of each essay but in the conveyance and craft of form.

VANISHING POINT: NOT A MEMOIR

Vanishing Point: Not a Memoir (2010) is similar to *Neck Deep and Other Predicaments* in that it reads as a collection of loosely connected essays that revolve around themes of truth and memory. The nineteen essays tend to focus on Monson and range in subject from a discussion of the genesis of his name to the history and appeal of Doritos. Monson refines his discussion of memoir and nonfiction in this book with an emphasis on the way that the first-person point of view is shaped and often fails in contemporary nonfiction.

There is an insert at the beginning of the book, with the letter "I" carved out in white space and surrounded by sentences cut off by the "I." Monson seems to be focusing on a particular Americanized "I," such as, for instance, the "I" that focuses on itemizing likes and dislikes and feelings, and how such itemizing creates a sense of the communal that erases the individual. The insert seems to be a confessional for the rest of the book, which often reflects upon the problems of using both "I" and "we." Memoir is seen as problematic in that a simplified and predictable first-person perspective is created; moreover, memoirists are perhaps too concerned about gaining the trust of the reader, too concerned about tidy conclusions, or too convinced that their tales

are worth telling. This is a problem that both troubles and fascinates Monson as he implicates himself in the frequent use of the first person and in the significance of the collective perspective.

Monson delivers a pointed imperative in his choice of title: *Not a Memoir*. The most obvious purpose of this title is to set the book, in its essayistic works, apart from a more linear or conventional memoir with narrative threads reminiscent of a novel. The book moves beyond the personal essay and becomes a theory of literature and writing as well.

Claiming an identity for his work other than memoir opens up the potential for focusing on facets of narrative beyond whether the writing is proven true beyond the shadow of a doubt. In "Voir Dire," Monson links the detailed fact-checking process he underwent for an essay he wrote to his experience as a jury member in a courtroom in which the defendant chose not to speak. In this essay Monson is on jury duty, and he reflects upon the shaping of a story in a courtroom, where "facts" are valued even as pathos runs high; even in the courtroom, the lawyer references the television drama *CSI*, linking fiction to reality. Beyond the courtroom, Monson investigates the truths and confusions with truth in his own memory. For instance, he brings up his experience as an adolescent felon. He admits to believing his mother died from colon cancer, thus encouraging an early colonoscopy on his part, before his brother revealed she died from ovarian cancer. His own confusion about the facts—about such important facts related to major events—can have the unexpected effect of building trust with the reader as Monson presents himself as a fallible narrator with good intentions.

Monson also uses this opportunity to discuss the danger of flatness in the first-person perspective. While he does not object to the idea that everyone can tell his or her story, he is adamant that not everyone can do it well, and that not every story transforms into art. Monson urges readers to reflect upon what "I" means in the context of nonfiction. In some ways, such a reflection is fitting for writers who read other writers; those writers who work on nonfiction are asked to turn inward, to reflect upon the parameters and purposes of their craft. Monson calls attention to the concept of memoir for the reading public as well, a public that has taken up the criticisms of media figures who have shamed those writers of memoir found to be deceiving readers about events in their lives. Readers place trust in nonfiction writers, while they understand fiction writers to be vying for their belief. Yet nonfiction is an opportunity for an understanding of the flawed self. Behind the first-person point of view is a complex human being who selects and crafts a story and cannot always be trusted.

There is another layer to this discussion of story: whose story belongs to whom, and how it is determined to be sincere. Three of the essays are titled "Assembloir," and these are written through bringing together the sentences and memoir passages of other nonfiction writers. This is not explicitly indicated in the pieces themselves; however, a reader can discern through a shift in voice, as well as through an acknowledgment of writers and books in the "Notes" section at the end of the book, that the passages are not Monson's. All of these moments where Monson engages in discussion with truth and storytelling reveal a deep concern with the ability to shape a meaningful story from reality. We are also asked to consider how we can limit language and story, what it is in the process of storytelling that people do or do not own.

As with his other books, Monson continues to shift and manipulate the visual form of the essay. In "How-To," he describes one of the secondary visual features of the book, which is the use of the typographical symbol known as the dagger as a punctuation mark. The daggers next to some of the words in the book are signs that there are more thoughts about these words and concepts that can be found on Monson's website. The book itself is valued but is also connected to possibilities for interaction outside of the text and, in this case, to the associative expansiveness of the Internet. There is a fixity that is both advantageous yet limiting to the written word. Or perhaps Monson means us to read in another way—the associative visuals afforded by the online material to the reader are an imita-

tion of the already associative nature of the mind while reading the printed word. The Web can be a conversation, a distraction, a constellation, or simply another part of the story.

In "Exteriority," Monson structures the essay so that there are no margins, and so part of each word at the beginning and end of each line is struck out—yet we fill in the gap as readers. The structure mimics the action of the essay, wherein he is renovating parts of his house, mostly obsessing with the walls and what is behind them, the layers of remodeling and revision. He meditates upon making things *ours* and the subsequent changes imposed when we leave, the filling up of space, the purpose of walls, which we tend to forget about or only hang our things on even though they stand as structures, hold us up, and protect us in some ways. The bleeding into the margins makes us aware of their function but also their presence: how they serve a particular format rendered invisible to us, a shared language of prose that has been passed down to readers.

Visual elements such as the dagger or the erasure of margins explicitly ask for a different kind of reader interaction than the typical narrative. Readers must determine, for example, if they will interact with the daggers, and why, and when. Should one pause in the midst of reading to look up a daggered word? Should one look them up randomly, or based on which ones seem most intriguing? Should one ignore the daggers completely? As for the margins, a reader must decide whether to plow ahead or not. The words that are cut off at the margins are recognizable enough that one can fill in the gaps, and so readers can simply logically complete the sentences. Or not. All readers make choices about whether to continue, to skim, to give up on a piece of writing, but Monson's work often increases the rate at which such choices need to be made, and challenges why such choices are made.

Additionally, the theme of disappearing or damaged young women emerges in *Vanishing Point,* a theme that characterized *Other Electricities.* Monson discusses those young women with violence done to them, as well as those who have vanished under suspicious circumstances. In

"The Essay Vanishes," he provides a list of young women who have vanished or died. This litany of names both individualizes the young women and objectifies them, as Carrie Hartfield was objectified in *Other Electricities.* Monson seems to be indicating our culture's obsession with the stories of young women and their vulnerability, with the narratives of danger that are conventionally rehearsed to and about young women. We focus on the individual story of one young woman only until it is time for the next story to be publicized, thus perpetuating their objectification.

The motif of vanishing continues. In "Vanishing Point: Former City," for instance, Monson is archiving memories and histories of Grand Rapids, Michigan. "Vanishing Point: Panera" takes place in a Panera Bread bakery-café near Columbus, Ohio. Like the essay about Grand Rapids, this is narrated from a collective "we" perspective, which might lead one to speculate that one of the vanishing points Monson refers to is a moment of collectivity, the moment when the individual might vanish. There is a collectivity and threat of disappearance to the experience in Panera, just as there is one to the stories in "Former City." Panera Bread is an eating place that is multiplied in various spaces, that could easily be moved out or closed, that carries the same smells from bakery to bakery. This sameness can create a sense of safety and comfort for its patrons, but it can also lead to a lack of awareness or consciousness. Like the video game being played in the essay, Panera and Columbus are symptomatic of the contemporary world Monson inhabits, where everything is the same yet empty, and so feels not quite real. Not quite like the truth. Monson, too, has fantasies of vanishing—whether simply disappearing or drinking himself to death.

In "Geas," Monson discusses the death of Dungeons & Dragons founder Gary Gygax, which leads to a detailing of Monson's history with the game as well as his opinions on its newer versions. As with many of his essays, Monson weaves in a particular subject or event with a personal experience—while Monson is thinking about Dungeons & Dragons, he is also

leaving his job teaching in Michigan to join the faculty at the University of Arizona. Monson is feeling sentimental about the place he is leaving, as well as about Gygax's death, but he is also trying to figure out which part of this sentimentality is sincere. He notes that ambiguity about his feelings is one of his weaknesses, since making a decision or a commitment means that the potentiality that was present and active before the decision is now gone.

Monson also reflects on the collective storytelling of Dungeons & Dragons, a type of storytelling that is now a field of study for academics. He emphasizes that his involvement in the game felt quite real. In Greek class as a student, he used an example from fantasy to support a point he was making about a Cyclops, a mythical creature. The example was not accepted by the teacher because it was not "real," and Monson questions how the information gathered from a game or from the imagination is that much different as solid evidence than information collected elsewhere. He laments that newer versions of Dungeons & Dragons require less imagination and provide more of the visuals of the story. In this essay he seems more explicitly to indicate the importance that he finds in readers' interactions with texts and in readers' imaginative roles in stories.

Generally, this book complexly ruminates on the tension between accepting a lack of organization and complete clarity of truth in the world or allowing the falsely contained world to control one's life. Both are tempting paths; both have advantages and pitfalls. As Monson writes, "I want the world interpreted, processed, managed, reduced. And the world comes packaged this way increasingly. Opportunities for intervention, for intercession between it and me, expand" (p. 160). He seems to promote a both/and perspective. In his final essay, "Vanishing Point for Solo Voice," Monson offers a space for both tensions: "I am nowhere now. I am in the air. I am everywhere at once" (p. 184). Monson offers a conceptual view that promotes a feeling that living both ways, simultaneously, is the preferable choice, and these ideas are elaborated in the poetry collection in the following section.

THE AVAILABLE WORLD

In the acknowledgments to his 2010 poetry collection, *The Available World*, Monson notes that some of the poems have been adapted from his 2007 chapbook, *Our Aperture*. *The Available World* is loosely based on the Greek myth of Icarus. Daedalus, Icarus' father, fashioned him wings made of feathers and wax. In spite of his father's warning, Icarus flies too close to the sun. His wings melt, and he drowns in the sea.

The predominant theme in *The Available World* is the abundance of technology and information that characterizes so much of our contemporary awareness, and the speaking voice of most of the poems attempts to navigate this abundance. In the collection, readers are asked to ruminate on the individual and the world via Monson's meditations about new and old media, the digital, the analog, blips, feelings, and the overwhelming loneliness that can come with such copiousness. Such abundance might seem like a tired subject, but this collection feels like another step in Monson's extensive narrative of the collective and the individual, and the narrative expressed in the poems often feels as expansive as a novel. The voice often takes on the semblance of a sly preacher, and indeed the first word in the title of many of these poems is "sermon." Poems also take on the form of the elegy, a response to the (failed) apocalypse, the ode, and the narrative. As with Monson's other work, though, strict adherence to the conventional rules of the genre is not a requirement.

"Sermon, Now Encrypted" (p. 7) depicts the relationship of communication with digital media as "scrambled digit strings." As one who is delivering a sermon, the speaker urges the listener to return home, "clear your Internet Explorer caches." He writes, "We do not need to keep these things close to us; / they are not our names, identities, nor are they addresses / through which light or product might find its way to us." Later he suggests: "What we need here is a tourniquet / to stop the daily flow of information." In the final line of the poem, he writes, "Let us find our way back to what light there is for us remaining." The lines in the poem are in the imperative; however, there is a sense of the collectivity of the mission.

Let us all clear our Internet caches, the speaker suggests, and look for something that possibly used to exist before this, that possibly still remains. The addressed readers are assumed to be panicked or fearful about the threat of the dullest parts of their lives (such as their likes and dislikes for certain things tracked by cookies on the Internet) being exposed. They are less concerned about such identifying details as names and addresses. Such a poem inspires readers to consider the role of digital and social media in the development and understanding of our private selves. The title suggests that the poem is eventually encrypted, and thus made somewhat private; it suggests a future moment when the listener or congregation has encoded, as much as possible, their private lives and many of the mundane choices they have made in exploring the Internet. And a reader may wonder for what purpose certain aspects of identity are seen as too personal for the Internet while others are revealed openly.

Many of the poems that resemble elegies in this collection are part of a thread about family in the book. The armless brother makes another appearance, as well as several pop culture figures that peppered Monson's boyhood. In addition, "Some of Us Have Fewer" (p. 12) is an elegy to Monson's mother, who died when he was a boy. This poem is also an elegy for the functions of memory and the accumulation of memory that one has in regard to various people. As the title says, some of us have fewer memories than others, and his memories of his mother have lessened and were already less substantial than someone who loses their mother as an adult. In the poem, he finds a photograph of his mother with a clipping of hair taped to the back, and he is unsure whether it is his hair or hers. He writes, "Her absence / is pressure like a metal click." There are so many parts of her life that he cannot know. He wonders what he would tell her about his own memories. He itemizes certain images, some of which seem significant and some superfluous. The final line is, "We only have so many bones." The bones in this poem might be seen as the concrete events that Monson refers to, and they are like memories—finite and with a reliance on story.

In "Slow Dance with Icarus," the narrator is at a school dance, dancing with Icarus. The narrator scratches his/her name in the wax on Icarus' shoulder. The narrator and Icarus converse under a cheap disco ball. In this depiction of Icarus, which is figurative, the narrator has a faith in Icarus but also thinks he's a bit nerdy. He represents something archaic and wise while being rather clumsy and uncertain. He is both/and. When the narrator asks Icarus what he thinks about the meaning of a car accident his or her friend was in, Icarus tells the narrator to hush, suggesting that meaning is not his forte. Icarus says, *This is not a lesson, / and I don't know and haven't learned or stayed / in school no more than him or you* (p. 80). This version of Icarus is not the arrogant figure from Greek myth but someone as lost as the narrator.

Like Icarus, Monson takes risks, from the form and formlessness of genre to the danger of technological abundance devolved to mere pixels. We do not, however, know if Monson falls. What we do know is he aims to achieve a balance between what he loves and despises about the world, that he believes the world can be both/and, and that it makes perfect sense that one can simultaneously love and hate copious structures. Ultimately, then, the story of Icarus is not about failure; we are not meant to see Icarus as a straightforward, moralistic myth. Monson draws a more complex figure—a hero both tragic and free, one who revels in beauty, one who fails and succeeds, like most human beings.

AUTHOR WEBSITE AND A CONCLUSION

Ander Monson's website (http://otherelectricities.com) cannot be ignored in any discussion of his work. It is not the usual author website, in which a biography, awards, publications, reviews, interviews, and an author statement make up the majority of the site. These components do exist on his site but in a form most befitting and supplementing his printed work.

Monson uses this website as an extended portal for the ideas in his published books, though of course the site, unlike the printed books, is

subject to changes that Monson might impose at any time, and so it is a fluid artifact representing his collected works. As of this writing, the main page is a radio schematic, and the first link is to information that mainly includes publication news and contact information. There is also a link for events such as readings. The title of each book is a link containing supplemental material, each page formatted and written differently. For example, *Other Electricities* includes extra passages from the book, more information about Ander Monson's personal characteristics, other pieces that have been generated in communication with *Other Electricities,* and information advertising the book, readings, and other events. The link for *The Available World* offers poems, each one of which contains hyperlinks to other poems, as well as a hyperlink to a page to buy the book.

Neck Deep and Other Predicaments is one of the more thorough of Monson's extensions from the printed work to the website. When readers click on the title of this book on the website, they are linked to an image of a card catalog, where each drawer is labeled with a term, such as "Propaganda" or "Reliquary." Monson refers to this card catalog, which he owned in Michigan, in the essay "After Form and Formlessness." When readers click on any of the terms, they are linked to the next page, which offers a card summary in the upper left-hand corner but otherwise varies in its contents. For instance, under "Propaganda," there is a definition of propaganda, which consists of advertisements and explanations of Monson's work. On the page are a brief author biography, links to reviews, a publicity contact, blurbs, and other promotional items. The card summary under "Reliquary" indicates that certain items that might supplement the essays can be found on this page. These include images from Monson's past, such as a book report he wrote that was printed in the *Daily Mining Gazette* (which he elsewhere has admitted to plagiarizing from the back of the book), a letter to his father, and a photo of Monson at age seven.

Under "Sincerity," the title of each piece appearing in *Neck Deep and Other Predicaments* is listed. Next to each title are the categories "Degree of Truthfulness," "Form," and "Type of Failure Risked." The category "Degree of Truthfulness" relates to the predominant theme of this essay collection—how readers' and writers' notions of truth are formed, defined, and reconstituted. Monson seems to be making a point through the structure of "Sincerity" not only about the fuzziness of memory and memoir but also about the futile nature of itemizing what counts as truth, and this speaks to a recent popular obsession on the part of American media with exposing instances of falsity in the works of those authors who have claimed that their books fit squarely in the genre of nonfiction. Monson navigates not only around but through the issue. He treats the issue with playfulness; for instance, he includes the website as a chapter title, and he notes that many of the website "facts" must be true because they appear on a website. In this case, Monson turns a public obsession with truth on its head, as there are far too many instances of the public believing what it reads and sees on the Internet, where anyone can post and create websites, even as the public obsesses about truth on the printed page, where it has less opportunity to be changed or revised. Yet he also converses with the slipperiness of memory while conveying in this page that he is attempting to be truthful (or while being open about not being truthful). This is in evidence through the degrees of truth telling that he assigns to each piece. Monson also uses humor to predict the success of each piece in *Neck Deep and Other Predicaments.* For instance, "Index for X and the Origin of Fires" is not very truthful and the "Type of Failure Risked" in the index is "Confusion."

Vanishing Point: Not a Memoir, too, is thorough in its extension to the website, and it is the book that is most directly linked to its Web page link. The main page is a series of square photographs, some of which link to other pages and many of which don't. The daggers mentioned in the book are also brought up here. A search box offers the opportunity to type in words from the printed book that are punctuated with daggers. Some of the words lead to lengthy passages, while others lead to just a few words. Monson uses the metaphor of a labyrinth on this page,

connecting the labyrinth to the associative actions of the brain. As in a labyrinth, there are paths that go nowhere, and some words are not really discussed; for instance, typing "mother" in the search box takes the reader to a few sentences in which Monson explicitly resists talking about his mother and apologizes, knowing full well, one would guess, that readers would be curious about a mother whose story is not fully told in any of his books. He also suggests the metaphor of a Russian nesting doll, as well as a more familiar metaphor seen in his other books—a constellation. Thus the links to the words that contain daggers in the book give the sensation of the associative. Even as the reader is making an associative move (controlled, somehow, by Monson), Monson is revealing about each word only his associations with it. And these associations link, like so much of Monson's writing, to the partiality of memory and to the idea that our memories and stories are only partially ours and are partially, one could argue, the world's.

The website is useful in that it expands the narrative and form of the texts. It is also an example of overabundance. It suggests that Monson will continue to converse with the reader, and he seems to have an infinite number of ways to do so with the extension of his work to his website, to his journal, and to Twitter. The reader can enter these moments however he or she wishes. Perhaps the website comes first. Perhaps reading every word with a dagger from *Vanishing Point: Not a Memoir* comes before reading the book in a linear fashion. The way the story comes across is partially in the hands of the reader, and partially in the hands of the writer. It is clear that Monson wants it that way.

Selected Bibliography

WORKS OF ANDER MONSON

FICTION AND POETRY

Safety Features. Tucson, Az.: New Michigan Press, 2007.

Other Electricities: Stories. Louisville, Ky.: Sarabande Books, 2005.

Vacationland. North Adams, Mass.: Tupelo Press, 2005.

Our Aperture. Tucson, Az.: New Michigan Press, 2007.

The Available World: Poems. Louisville, Ky.: Sarabande Books, 2010.

NONFICTION

Neck Deep and Other Predicaments: Essays. St. Paul, Minn.: Graywolf Press, 2007.

Vanishing Point: Not a Memoir. St. Paul, Minn.: Graywolf Press, 2010.

CRITICAL STUDIES AND INTERVIEWS

Crist, Meehan. "An Interview with Writer and Editor Ander Monson." *Poets & Writers,* March 31, 2008. http://www.pw.org/content/interview_writer_and_editor_ander_monson?cmnt_all=1.

Pierce, Pamela. Interview with Ander Monson. *Tottenville Review,* n.d. http://www.tottenvillereview.com/ander-monson/.

Ryor, Colleen Marie. Interview with Ander Monson. *Adirondack Review,* spring 2005. http://adirondackreview.homestead.com/interviewmonson.html.

Van Landingham, Corey. "Whatever and It's Yours: Present-Day Vertigo in Ander Monson's *The Available World.*" *Sycamore Review*, October 10, 2010. http://www.sycamorereview.com/2010/10/whatever-and-its-yours-present-day-vertigo-in-ander-monsons-the-available-world/.

MARI SANDOZ

(1896—1966)

Bette S. Weidman

OLD JULES SANDOZ lamented that his firstborn child was a daughter, and so unfit to carry on his work as a locator for European immigrants to the Nebraska High Plains at the turn of the twentieth century. How ironic! The daughter devoted her career as a writer to an intellectual and imaginative re-creation of the plains and its peoples, preserving the story of settlement by Europeans as well as of the lives and struggles of American Indians. Her work is an entirely original approach to the history of her native region, but in its large and generous portrait of people and landscape, it transcends the regionalism to which earlier commentators have assigned it and makes a substantial contribution to American literature. The ultimate irony is that her first book, the biography of her father, *Old Jules* (1935), made the dismissive father an unforgettable character of that time and place.

LIFE

Marie Susette Sandoz (she later adopted the Swiss spelling, "Mari") was born on May 11, 1896, at Mirage Flats, in the Sandhills of Nebraska, the eldest of six children of Jules Ami Sandoz, a Swiss immigrant from a well-to-do family, but a volatile and violent man of some courage and conviction, and his wife Mary Elizabeth Fehr, also Swiss-German, who miraculously withstood her husband's intermittent brutality and the hard physical labor to which she was consigned. While Jules politicked and engaged in local feuds, planned orchards, and envisioned communities, Mary Fehr Sandoz did the planting, cared for the stock, cooked for the endless visitors and new settlers, and handed her young daughter each of her newborn babies at two weeks of age. It is no wonder that Mari Sandoz chose childlessness herself, after a brief early

marriage; she had had plenty of experience of child rearing by the time she was ten or twelve. She writes that at the age of nine she could bake a forty-nine-pound bag of flour into bread with a baby brother suspended on her hip. Education for women was not a priority for Jules; Sandoz was nine before she got any schooling, and she struggled to become a schoolteacher and a writer against her father's will. He mocked and devalued her efforts, including her early prizes and publications.

In spite of his own aborted medical school education, a father who was a respected veterinarian, and a very reputable extended Swiss family, Jules forbade his daughter reading material; she had to hide the novels of Joseph Conrad in the hay in the barn loft, reading in secret. He did provide an education of sorts; as a young girl accompanying her father on an expedition, Mari witnessed his near-death from a rattlesnake bite, which he treated by shooting the poisoned hand. The child was then responsible for driving the bleeding, dying father across an unmarked land behind a frantic team of horses for distant help. On another occasion, Jules sent Mari and a younger brother to live alone in a sod dugout for months, shooting their own game for food, so that he could establish a land claim. Although money was not plentiful, Jules knew how to spend it when it was available, as in his memorable purchase of a record player and phonograph records of classical and popular music. A contradictory character, born of an accidental laming caused by a practical joke and a long-lasting disappointment in love (his Swiss sweetheart had refused to come to America), Jules was a difficult parent but bequeathed three great positive qualities: his intellectual honesty, his visionary commitment to the High Plains, and his appreciation

of the humanity and culture of his Cheyenne and Sioux neighbors. A crackerjack marksman, he earned the respect of his Native American visitors and passed his understanding of them on to the daughter, whose most significant achievement may be her biographies of Crazy Horse and her account of the Cheyenne tragedies that preceded her birth.

Before she could realize her ambition as a writer, however, Sandoz had to escape the blighting influence of her father. She passed an examination to teach school after completing her eighth-grade education. Her first job, in a school in her father's barn, did not take her far, and she married a neighboring rancher, Wray Macumber, in 1914, at the age of eighteen. The marriage lasted only five years. Information about it is scant, as Sandoz always zealously protected her privacy. Perhaps the best glimpse into this period is one represented in fiction; Sandoz's Morissa, a character with whom the writer deeply identifies, endures a short, unsatisfactory marriage entered into impulsively.

After the marriage ended, Mari did not return to her family home. She taught in various country schools, including one in the region in which she later set *Miss Morissa: Doctor of the Gold Trail* (1955); studied in Lincoln at a business college from 1919 to 1921; and worked in a courthouse in Osceola. At this time she was known as "Miss Macumber." Returning to Lincoln, she entered the university as a special student, taking courses in English and history. There she fell under the influence of Professor Melvin Van den Bark, who remained a lifetime friend and literary adviser, and, reading Conrad and Thomas Hardy, developed her ambition to be a writer. She supported herself meagerly by filling capsules for a pharmaceutical company at the rate of twenty-five cents per thousand, and grading themes for the English Department, until she obtained a research position at the Nebraska State Historical Society. Important friendships and some success in publishing her short stories led to her resuming the Sandoz name. Recognition finally came in 1935, when the manuscript of *Old Jules,* then titled "Home on the Running Water," won the *Atlantic Monthly* nonfiction writing contest.

At this point Sandoz quit her job and for the remaining thirty years of her life worked as a full-time writer, except for periods of time as a teacher of creative writing. During these years she lived in Lincoln, in Denver, and finally in New York, where she died of cancer in March 1966.

GENRES

Mari Sandoz's work can be divided into three groups. The first includes the chronological histories of the exploitation and settlement of the plains in her nonfiction series *Beaver Men: Spearheads of Empire, The Buffalo Hunters: The Story of the Hide Men,* and *The Cattlemen from the Rio Grande Across the Far Marias* (a fourth volume on the railroad was never finished); the biography *Old Jules* belongs to the pioneer phase of this history. The second group includes the novels *Slogum House, The Tom-Walker, Son of the Gamblin' Man: The Youth of an Artist, Capital City,* and *Miss Morissa: Doctor of the Gold Trail*; to this body of fiction also belong several volumes of short stories. The finest achievement of her art of fully imagined historical narrative belongs to the last of the three groups: her biography *Crazy Horse: The Strange Man of the Oglalas,* and the exhaustively researched and richly retold story *Cheyenne Autumn.*

The only other writer to whom Sandoz can be compared is her older predecessor, Willa Cather, but Sandoz is a kind of anti-Cather. Where Cather is conservative, Sandoz is radical; where Cather celebrates the European colonization of the West, only minimally regretting the losses to native people and indulging an anti-Mexican bias, Sandoz portrays the full humanity of American Indians; where Cather offers her most memorable portraits to immigrants who ultimately make good economically, Sandoz gives an unsentimental and unsparing portrait of the psychological and economic suffering of people who fought the wars and faced the recurring national and global economic depressions. Reading Cather leaves one feeling reconciled; sacrifices are redeemed. Reading Sandoz leaves one

protesting, angry, unreconciled to the human losses.

The subjects and themes of two younger writers reveal a kinship to the work of Sandoz. These are the novelists Annie Proulx, whose unsparing portrait of contemporary life in Wyoming is justly celebrated, and Louise Erdrich, whose family stories set in North Dakota deliver a Sandoz-like richness of detail and a powerful antiwar theme. Readers of Proulx and Erdrich may find in the earlier work of Mari Sandoz a worthy predecessor.

OLD JULES

Although *Old Jules* (1935) was conceived as the biography of Jules Ami Sandoz, Mari Sandoz wrote to the judges of the Atlantic Non-Fiction Contest that she had "tried in a larger sense to make it the biography of a community, the upper Niobrara country in western Nebraska" (*Old Jules,* p. vii). As she organized and retold her father's stories and the events of her own childhood, she composed an indelible portrait of the homesteader's life, with its exposure to harsh weather, its dependence on the labor of the whole family, its deprivations, sacrifices, social conflicts, and the occasional victory.

The story begins with Jules's confrontation with his Swiss parents, who objected to his choice of a bride in the socially humbler Rosalie. Jules left for America in 1884, situating himself in northeastern Nebraska, but Rosalie would not join him. Marrying in disappointment, he abandoned his first wife, Estelle, who refused to perform the physical labor he exacted. Heading farther west, he came to the town of Valentine, terrorized by vigilante violence, where he equipped himself for a further struggle with the cattlemen who sought to keep settlers from fencing and planting land they wanted for grazing. Finally sighting the Niobrara River, Jules found the land he sought.

One of the most crucial episodes in Jules's life centered on the arrival on the Flats of three immigrants from French Switzerland: Paul Nicolet, Jules Tissot, and Jules Aubert. These young men moved in with Jules Sandoz, renamed him "Old Jules," and helped him with his well-digging project when their high spirits permitted. One day, just as the source of water was about to be struck, they were pulling Sandoz out of the well and decided to have a little fun first. Twirling him to dizziness in the bucket, they failed to notice the fraying rope; Jules fell sixty-five feet to the bottom of the well, crushing his ankle. His friends pulled him out, and then left him to doctor himself with morphine while they went off to file their land claims. Nine days later, his food and medicine run out, his pain unendurable, Jules dragged himself to the trail where he waited to die. Soldiers en route to Fort Robinson found him and took him to the post surgeon, who, amazingly, turned out to be a young, not yet famous Dr. Walter Reed. Reed prepared his patient for amputation, but Jules, barely conscious, sat up to object: "You cut my foot off, doctor, and I shoot you so dead you stink before you hit the ground" (p. 43).

The doctor respected his patient's wish and Jules survived the gangrenous infection, yet he endured a long period of recovery and the leg was permanently lamed and painful. Along with the continued refusal of Rosalie to come to America, the well accident permanently marked Jules's already irascible personality. The penchant for anger and violence that marked his behavior may have served him positively in the war with the cattle interests, but it made him a difficult husband, father, neighbor, and friend.

After his miraculous, if partial, recovery, Jules returned to his dugout on Mirage Flats, where he made friendly connections to the Sioux chiefs White Eye and Young Man Afraid of His Horse. Such connections compensated for worsening relations with ranchers and cowboys. Jules strove to establish local government in order to redirect politics to the support of settlers. The lifelong investment of his time and effort in connecting local politics to national goals was already under way. This commitment attached itself to Jules's vision of a fruitful land. Jules earned his living by selling ammunition, repairing guns, locating and surveying, hunting and trapping, and cultivating his fields. The social life of the region,

anchored by Jules's post office, included dances with fiddling and square dance sets, debates on national politics, even literary gatherings. The European settlers brought music and sociability, but Jules remained desperate for a wife.

After two more failed marriages, his marital problems reached stable ground with the arrival at the locator's door of Mary Fehr, a Swiss woman whose brother had been supposed to meet her in western Nebraska. After realizing her predicament, unable to return and unable to survive the rough country alone, Mary became Jules's fourth wife, the mother of his children, and the labor support his enterprises required. This, of course, is not to say that life went smoothly, but Mary's efficiency, her skills, her cooking, and her hard agricultural labor helped make Jules's vision of a fruitful land a reality.

Political murders, foreclosures, fear of drought, and the failure of crops, barely balanced by the arrival of Mary's widowed mother and sister, accompanied the birth of Jules's first acknowledged child, named Marie, whose first experience of his parenting was a whipping at three months, in retaliation for crying and waking the father. The effects of this whipping lingered long after the summer night in which it was inflicted.

Such was the education of the writer who became Mari Sandoz, absorbing the contradictions in the visionary land settler who corresponded with Teddy Roosevelt, grasped the complexities of local and national politics, and understood the achievement of his old doctor, Walter Reed, in fighting yellow fever, but could not curb his own volatile temperament.

Sandoz's narrative continues, in an even-handed third-person form, through the years of her childhood, focusing on the economic conditions of the settlers, their response to acts of Congress opening up new lands, Jules's struggle with the authorities who wanted him to send his older children to school, and his planting of orchards. The early adulthood of the writer and her siblings coincided with the Great War. Marie escaped the family life into teaching, yet returned from Lincoln, where she was attending the university, when her father fell ill. After a long

decline, Jules died, still envisioning the future of the land.

The completion of the narrative puts to rest in story the long conflict between father and writer, doing full justice to the political and personal complexities of settling a country. Although he was no appreciator of literary or artistic achievement, reckoning gain only in sociopolitical triumph or material reality, Jules would have recognized the unsentimental and unsparing portrait of his life and times. The publication of *Old Jules,* after a long period of rejections and revisions, made Sandoz's career as a writer possible.

THE BEAVER MEN: SPEARHEADS OF EMPIRE

In writing and rewriting *Old Jules* during the thirteen years that she unsuccessfully sought a publisher, Sandoz developed a blend of narration, description, and dialogue that made her writing seem novelistic to readers. This caused confusion in publishing circles, but it made an immediate appeal to readers, who found themselves able to experience life on Jules's homestead on the Niobrara and in the Sandhills. In spite of questions about her choice of genre, Sandoz persisted in this style, re-creating scenes in the plains histories she went on to write, complete with imagined dialogue, dramatized events, and detailed evocation of landscape. These fully imagined scenes hold in place passages of historical narration and analysis of cultural patterns, yet we are never far from the immediacy of the historical moment.

In *The Beaver Men: Spearheads of Empire* (1964), the sounds of life along the St. Lawrence River in the seventeenth century are audible. The author's goal included the representation of the Native American point of view in this period of early interaction, so that we are there at the fur rendezvous at Montreal, among the merchants, the bush lopers, the Frenchmen, and the Indians. Sandoz reserves the last remarks of her first chapter for the shock and surprise of the Indians as they surveyed "the vast mounds of beaver pelts on the piers, great bales and mountains, surely so

many that most of the beaver in the world must be dead" (*Beaver Men,* p. 21).

As she relates the facts about the beaver as an evolving creature, Sandoz provides rich evidence of her love of maps and illustrations and her understanding of the complex interaction of humans and animals. Beaver provided not only food, clothing, and bedding but also medicine: castoreum, dried material from the beaver's rectal glands, was a cure for everything from earache to madness, known as far back as 400 BCE in the writings of Hippocrates. American beaver was a plentiful source for Europeans, whose supplies had vanished, and the market shaped the colonial activities of the French and Dutch, eventually drawing in the English and Spanish.

Woven into the narrative of human interactions is a careful account of the beaver as a builder of dams and lodges, shaper of families and capable underwater swimmer, eater of aspen, cottonwood, and raspberry bushes, invader of Indian corn fields, maker of breather holes or underwater bubbles. In all three of Sandoz's animal-centered histories, there is a fine balance between a healthy knowledge of and respect for the creatures and a shrewd understanding of the economics and politics of the trade based on their capture and sale. A reader can follow both stories, the cyclical one of the animal life and the linear unfolding of human relations.

The Beaver Men: Spearheads of Empire is divided into three multichapter "books," the first largely devoted to the French and Indians of the early period, the second turning to the eighteenth-century shift in commercial power from France to England and the rise of the Hudson's Bay Company, and the third, "Americans to the Western Sea," taking the story into the nineteenth century and the explorations of Meriwether Lewis and William Clark. Exploring the details of political strife between Pawnees, Spanish, Apaches; the complicated alcohol-influenced politics of the Michilimackinac region; the ambitions of the Scottish traders, especially the famous James Mackay; and the transforming influence of the American Revolution, Sandoz never loses sight of the dramatic event, the power of personality, or the underlying struggle of Indians and

Europeans. She tells the story of David Thompson, a Welshman "apprenticed to the Bay Company from a London charity school at fourteen" (p. 174). Where else would a reader meet a youth like this, capable of making himself into a scientist and explorer, traveler among the Mandans in November of 1797?

THE BUFFALO HUNTERS: THE STORY OF THE HIDE MEN

The Buffalo Hunters (1954) gathers into one coherent, richly detailed narrative the conflict of Indian and white civilizations on the Great Plains. On the one side were the varied Indian tribes who lived in small kin groups by hunting the astoundingly prolific buffalo; these people had adapted their foodways, their shelter, their clothing, and their religion to this primary animal of the plains. Sandoz estimates 250,000 Indians in 1492 and 125 million buffalo. On the other side, the increasingly populous whites were interested in individual wealth and building transcontinental railroads; land-hungry settlers struggled within their group with ranchers who sought to supplant the buffalo with huge, individually owned cattle herds grazing on unfenced "free" grass. The Indians could not maintain their way of life without the buffalo and the whites could not transform the plains into settled homesteads and large ranches without destroying the buffalo. Between the end of the Civil War and the end of the nineteenth century, this conflict reached its culminating period.

Sandoz sets the story, an American tragedy, in the context of the geography of the Great Plains, which constitutes half of the United States east of the Mississippi and stretches from Canada to Texas. The land was once home to dinosaurs, mastodons, mammoths, and saber-toothed tigers, but no animal was as well-adapted and numerous as the buffalo, which moved in four-hundred-mile-wide circles around the plains in four large herds. Sandoz follows each of these herds, in the chronological order of their extinction, in the four sections of her work.

Book 1 follows the fate of the Republican herd of Kansas-Nebraska, starting with a day in the life of a white buffalo-hide hunter in 1867. The hunter, having shot and skinned sixty-five buffalo in one day, finds himself surrounded by Sioux. At a dangerous moment he is saved by an old peace chief, Whistler, who is later killed by this same gambler, murderer, and hired gun, Wild Bill Hickok. In Sandoz's account, Hickok is not the stuff of heroic myth. Like Buffalo Bill Cody, who killed buffalo to provide meat for railroad workers, he was a dandy and an egotist, an aficionado of the card tables, who, like the other hunters Sandoz names, cared only for the enormous profits to be reaped by the slaughter of buffalo.

Sandoz describes the buffalo hunt staged for Grand Duke Alexis of Russia, the luxurious tents floored, carpeted, and heated, feasting and participation of Indians with Spotted Tail's untranslated speech complaining of the treatment of his people, and Buffalo Bill Cody as the leader given a large purse of money and a diamond stickpin by the Duke. Along with the royal sightseeing, Sandoz reveals government corruption ineffectively objected to by the rare honest soldier, General Hazen. Hide hunters continue to increase, in spite of disasters like blizzards and an outbreak of rabies carried by skunks, and booming profits lead to the development of trading posts that become semipermanent settlements. In the one called Buffalo City, Sandoz tells of the arrival of gamblers and women:

> They made a fine show as they came up the dusty street that was not quite two blocks long, between buildings that were mostly dugouts or half-and-half. Some of the wagon sheets had been rolled up to show the wares arriving, the barrels and the cases of bottles for the fancy trade, and then the girls of course, all dressed in their best as they sang a gay little song, one of them picking a mandolin very sweetly.... Before the leaves in the brush patches began to yellow two of the new girls were dead, one from galloping consumption, the other from wolf poison she stole out of a hunter's pocket.
>
> (pp. 146–147)

Master of the telling detail, Sandoz follows the Arkansas herd in book 2, assembling a long list of characters dominated by the "ornamental pair,"

Cody and Hickok, including General Philip Sheridan, who recommended killing buffalo to destroy Indians, and General Nelson Miles, who estimated soberly that more than four million buffalo had fallen in the Arkansas region in the three years leading up to 1874. Sandoz reminds us that millions of piles of bones were sold for bone china, carbon, phosphates, and phosphorus and that the killing only increased in spite of Indian attacks, such as the one at Adobe Walls, a hide hunters industrial settlement.

The story of George Armstrong Custer's blundering behavior is woven throughout the book, his opening of the Black Hills in the summer of 1874 a way station on the road to his miscalculation at the Little Bighorn. Sandoz organizes her sources by the section they support, so we can see, in the 1874–1875 period, that she draws much of the detailed information from firsthand memoirs produced by the hide hunters themselves. An example is the richly detailed episodes centered on Johnny Cook's enterprises of 1875, drawn from his 1907 memoir, *The Border and the Buffalo*. Sandoz is drawn to Cook's memoir because he is one of the few hide hunters who was capable of imagining himself in the position of an Indian. In retelling the story of the army strikes on Indians in Palo Duro Canyon in September 1874, she includes details about the aftermath: "They had dragged into the agencies in Indian territory, ragged, starving, the smaller children and the tired old people left behind as they died, although one Kiowa woman carried her dead baby two hundred miles on her back, and fought before she would give it up at the disarming" (p. 237).

Book 3 is devoted to the Texas herd, which dwindled drastically. With the coming of settlers, buffalo hunters turned to cattle ranching, hide rustling, and horse thievery. Tornadoes and hailstones, typhoid for the hunters and starvation for the Indians, led to the defiance of the Southern Cheyenne, trying to return to their old territory with the tragic outcome Sandoz relates in full detail in *Cheyenne Autumn*. The fate of the Cheyenne marks the end of the Texas herd.

Left for the finale is the account in book 4 of the swift demise of the fourth herd, the Northern

buffalo of Montana and Dakota. Hide hunters, unwilling to believe that their livelihood was gone, rode north, joining the Red River Canadian Métis, who had long organized their people for this hunt, selling their meat and robes in the Winnipeg market. Sandoz gives us an unforgettable glimpse of these Métis and their beautiful girls, their music and dance.

Although the Sioux had refused to sell the Black Hills and their hunting grounds, the arrival of the Northern Pacific Railroad made it necessary to move them. Her narrative now reaching her own part of the country, Sandoz draws on stories told in her childhood of the last of the robe hunters. Although whites were legally barred from the land, Indians at the Red Cloud Agency in northwest Nebraska were forced to sign a treaty under threat of starvation of their women and children. Finally, in the late 1880s, the last significant robes and hides of buffalo were sold. The despairing Sioux followed their great chief Sitting Bull, who was arrested and shot while participating in the Ghost Dance, a messiah religion that brought short-lived hope to the native people. A remnant of Sitting Bull's people joined Chief Big Foot (Spotted Elk), who surrendered to the U.S. Army with 106 men and 250 women and children. Soldiers fired their Hotchkiss guns and completed the massacre at Wounded Knee Creek in December 1890. It is here that Mari Sandoz brings her book to a close: "Now the dream of the buffalo, too, was done" (p. 367).

The Buffalo Hunters is the first written of Sandoz's three histories centered on the animals of the plains. It has only a brief bibliography for each section, not as thorough an indication of sources as the later *Cattlemen,* which treats the same subject from the point of view of the white supplanters of buffalo hunters. Surprisingly, this early volume has no index, unlike the other two in the series, but its lucid organization, in sharply etched chapters, makes it extremely readable. Of the three books it tells the most central and important story, sadly a story of waste and failure, for animals and people. It provides a healthy corrective to the mythmaking and heroizing of moral midgets, a necessary look at the development of

the American West—an empire of wealth for a few, suffering and extermination for the native people, and moral and physical degradation for the hunters. The unromantic story of the American West, it should be required reading for every American.

The observation that Sandoz dramatizes scenes and imagines dialogue has been used to discredit her as an academic historian. But Sandoz knew that historians are writers and that their primary task is finding form for their stories. *Old Jules,* more biography than history, follows the chronology of a life, choosing its most characteristic actions as the nodes of its narrative. In the three plains histories, Sandoz is subtler. Within a broadly chronological frame, she finds an appropriate literary shape for each story: the four books of *The Buffalo Hunters* follow the four huge herds and circle with them into the wind of character and event. This is the tragedy of Indian history, and it is deeply appropriate that its form recognizes the sacred number of native cultures.

By contrast, *The Cattlemen* adopts the five-part structure of Shakespearean tragedy to impart the waste and sacrifice unfolding on the plains. In place of a single lamented hero, Sandoz gives us heroic traits dispersed among her many characters, and a full cast of villains, with a satiric edge reserved for those bloated figures of popular culture, Hickok, Cody, Wyatt Earp, and Bat Masterson.

THE CATTLEMEN FROM THE RIO GRANDE ACROSS THE FAR MARIAS

Mari Sandoz's history of the cattle industry in the American West, published in 1958, is characteristically spacious. While it concentrates its greatest detail on the ninety years leading up to its publication, especially on the conflict between ranchers and settlers in the late nineteenth and early twentieth centuries, it begins with a rich perspective on the influence of cattle in human history and prehistory.

Sandoz describes the fossil remains of cattle found in northwestern India, dating from the mid-Pliocene era, and the different forms of the ox passing through the Ice Ages and accompanying

early Neanderthal man. Her narrative pauses at Lascaux Cave in southern France: "Here, in limestone hollowed out by water, is the flowering of the second of the two capital events of man's history—his discovery and proficiency in art" (*Cattlemen,* p. 25). In her description of the famous cave paintings, Sandoz notes the similarity in appearance of the bulls and cows to the early Texas stock. She traces historical references from the Egyptian god Osiris, born of a cow, tomb pictures of King Tutankhamen's cattle, and the Golden Calf of the Jews in the desert of the Old Testament, all the way to the year 982, when Eric the Red brought cattle to Greenland. This long perspective confers a dignity and importance to her subject that lingers to justify the careful detail and respectful attention devoted to every episode of bovine history.

This respectful attention is accorded to the lives of the animals themselves. The book begins with an omniscient witness to the fate of the lead cow of Coronado's 1541 herd, his walking commissary. The landscape of this second season's summer journey of the Spanish conquerors is clearly visualized, with its sickening alkali water holes, red canyons, colorful blooming plants, buffalo that released the wildness in the cattle, and dramatic hailstorms. Sandoz puts us in the scene for a long moment as Coronado sends most of his force back to the Indian pueblos while he persists, with a smaller group, in his search for cities of gold and turquoise. Like the painters of Lascaux, Sandoz memorializes this moment of history with the unforgettable portrait of Coronado's lead cow.

This passage, and a later one witnessing a territorial fight of two bulls, around the year 1800, testify to the writer's feel for the life of the animals—beaver, buffalo, and cattle—whose fates are intertwined with those of humans. Without sentimentality, but with an imaginative energy akin to Walt Whitman's, Sandoz composes the story of North American cattle from the herds bred by the seventeenth-century Spanish missionaries to the increasingly complex spread of the longhorns from Texas to Wyoming. After the chapter following the fate of Coronado's lead cow, we realize that stock raising and the beef industry that followed originated with the progeny of half-wild escapees from the conquistador's Mexican herds. The development of Texas and the states of Kansas, Montana, and Wyoming emerged from the need for unfenced grasslands for the herds that would replace the buffalo.

As readers of *Old Jules,* we know that Sandoz herself was born of immigrant settler stock and particularly of a father who enlisted the help of Teddy Roosevelt to stand up to the violence and intimidation of the cattlemen. But the region of her birth, the Nebraska Sandhills, turned out to be ideal ranching land, and some of her brothers entered that industry. Thus while she offers an unsparing portrait of violence and corruption, she reserves a degree of respect for the cattlemen who operated with honesty, skill, and courage.

The book has a huge cast of characters. Indians, Europeans, men of mixed blood, Northerners, Southerners—Sandoz follows their enterprises, their successes and failures, up the south-to-north trails. "Mavericking," rustling unbranded stock, is reattached to the biography of Samuel Maverick, reputed to own more Texas cattle than anyone else in the 1850s. The reader encounters all those familiar figures from a romanticized western history, Wyatt Earp, Buffalo Bill Cody, Bat Masterson, Wild Bill Hickok, shorn of their latter-day myths and revealed in all their egotism, violence, and corruption. Others, less popularly known, are also followed through the ups and downs of their careers, the very few gifted and reputable ones singled out for thoughtful portraiture. The class-struggle aspect of developing and regulating the cattle industry is clarified in this book, including the contrast between the very wealthy, often foreign, ranch owners and the penniless settlers and cowboys.

The five "books" or acts of this story, worthy of its form of Shakespearean tragedy, come to a climax in the tremendous mayhem associated with the history of Wyoming. The wealthy cattle owners sought to protect the idea of free range; the settlers and smaller ranchers needed to protect their investments in farmland and their domestic stock. The power of capital manipulated the law until finally such horrendous violence broke out that there was public revulsion against the tactics

of lynching, burning, and blacklist. Sandoz gives a clear picture of the final scene of battle between the ranchers, known as the Invaders, and the defenders at the KC Ranch. The Hamlet of the story, Nate Champion, kept a journal during the siege of which he was the final victim. Ultimately the temporary success of the Invaders was ended and they had to be rescued by the National Guard from the wrath of settlers.

Paralleling these events, Sandoz follows the rise and fall of cattle prices closely, yet manages to give a satisfying picture of the ten-day wedding of the daughter of a French-Canadian trapper turned rancher. She brings her narrative back to *Old Jules* in June 1904, when the Kinkaid Act opened up 640 acres to each settler who filed, effectively ending the concept of free range. As the cattle industry modernized and turned toward manufacturing, Sandoz winds up her story with the last of the cattlemen, the rise of Omaha as a meat-packing center, and the role of the railroads. She ends the book with an account of the rodeo, linking her work in theme and spirit closely to that of Annie Proulx, but also returning the rodeo to its roots in Bronze Age bull-grappling in the palace of Minos, in Crete.

SLOGUM HOUSE

Sandoz's first novel, *Slogum House* (1937), begins and ends on the unpeopled overlook from the hogback or ridge of land in northwestern Nebraska to which the house is adjacent. This symbolic scene, from which neighboring fields and distant flats can be seen, focuses the reader's attention on the contested land itself, which stands for the American West and, by extension, all of the United States in the fifty years leading up to the Great Depression of the 1930s. Sandoz has a large story to tell about class privilege, access to land for poor settlers, including immigrants, the rule of law, and economic justice. Nor does she neglect the more traditional novelistic subjects of marriage, love across lines of class and ethnicity, parenting, and the meaning of family.

Between the beginning, when Gulla, the family matriarch, is rising to economic and social power, and the end, when she is dying, defeated by the obesity that symbolizes her greed, the story of the Slogum family emerges as an account of the destructive power of cruelty and selfishness, reined in at last by its own exhaustion. Ironically the family is known by the name of its Swiss-immigrant-descended father, whose intelligence and goodness are undermined by the hired girl, Regula Haber, who seduced him in order to achieve wealth and position. By the time the novel begins, their shotgun marriage has produced two adult sons, Cash and Hab, who carry out their mother's orders to do anything that will increase her landholding, including murder, intimidation, and theft. The oldest daughter, Libby, and the youngest son, Ward, are aligned with their father, Ruedy, whose sensitivity and honorable ways make him contemptible to his wife. Ruedy carries on his real life in a shelter he has built among gardens and ponds as a refuge from his wife and her plans, but he is ineffectual in opposing her. Three other daughters complete the family: Fanny, the beauty sent away to finishing school, who returns at last riddled with venereal disease and tuberculosis; and the twins, Cellie and Annette, whose love affairs are sacrificed to their mother's ambition.

Gulla's ambition, to control the economics and the politics of the county, is achieved by ruthless manipulation. The plot is kept suspenseful by her machinations, worthy of an abortionist's daughter whose sisters were prostitutes and whose brother went to the penitentiary. Gulla conceals murderers, plots thievery and intimidation of settlers in her region, and buys up mortgages so that she can foreclose on her neighbors. On the surface, she reaches for respectability. In the course of forty years, Gulla accumulates land and stock, yet the pain and suffering she bequeaths far outweigh the riches. None of her children marry and produce a next generation. Yet Sandoz's independence can also be seen in the interpretation of her conclusion. Marriage and childbearing are not the necessary happy endings for her; she instead values and

dramatizes emergence into one's real self. Such an end is reserved, in this novel, for Libby, her father, and the locator Leo Platt. On both the realistic and symbolic levels, the novels show how hard won are the victories for decency and cooperation, how much sacrifice and waste are exacted by the thoughtless, the violent, the morally undeveloped.

A persistent question raised by critics is directed at Sandoz's choice of a woman as the embodiment of the greed and cruelty she wishes to indict in the American society of her time. *Slogum House* is hard to bear, filled with the blood of terrible violence: the brutal beating of Ward by Polish farmers who wrongly suspect his love for their girl conceals the elitist desire to ruin her; the emasculation of Fanny's beloved, conspired in by Gulla and her murderous brother; the desperate murder of Link Loder's wife and his suicide following Gulla's foreclosure on a farm they had struggled to keep for forty-five years; the garroting of Hab on his own windmill tower. The best answers to the question of whether Gulla is believable as a character are expressed in Glenda Riley's article "Mari Sandoz's *Slogum House*: Greed as a Woman." Riley quotes Sandoz as writing: "I cannot think of people as divided into sexes so much as into types. To me there are only people, varying a great deal among themselves" (p. 35). Riley goes on to document historical accounts of women who shared Gulla's traits and behaviors, proving that Sandoz's research was as impeccable as her resistance to essentialism.

In *Slogum House,* Sandoz wrote a powerful condemnation of greed. In her next novel, she returned to this subject, placing it in an urban setting, a half-century after the period of *Slogum House*.

CAPITAL CITY

Capital City (1939) is an extraordinary political novel, a bold cautionary tale about the right-wing takeover of state government, abetted by corruption, racism, anti-Semitism, and fascism, enabled by the failing liberalism of a divided elite and fostered by the dire economic conditions of the

Great Depression. It is a novel that surprises the reader at the turn of each page. We achieve some intimacy with a main character who calls himself Hamm Rufe, a man with a love affair and marriage behind him while he is still in vigorous middle life and whose active political life expresses itself in his choice to live in the shantytown section of the capital city of his birth, founded by his liberal visionary grandfather. With its growth, the society of the city has become fragmented; wealth has divided former friends, and a culture of greed, conspicuous consumption, and economic inequality has poisoned the social fabric. This situation has driven Hamm Rufe—his name a pseudonym half-concealing his identity as founder George Rufer's grandson—to grassroots politics, working at the local co-op, writing political analysis of right-wing dangers for the national press, and supporting a liberal farmer as a candidate for the U.S. Senate.

The novel is set in an imaginary state, Kanewa, based on the combined histories of Kansas, Nebraska, and Iowa, with a capital city, Franklin, modeled on Lincoln, where Sandoz was living and working at the Nebraska State Historical Society. The novel begins with the detached overview of an omniscient narrator seeing the city from a height in realistic detail: its busy downtown choked by traffic, its elite hurrying off to a fall festival. Soon the narrator comes down from this remote stance into the shantytown called Herb's Addition, to describe two figures, Hamm Rufe and a man known only as "the Coot," both of whom once belonged to the city's elite but who now, in poverty, are consigned to live at its margins. At first, the reader doesn't identify the derelict-seeming figure of Hamm Rufe as the novel's hero. He and the Coot are a chorus of wise observers of the social and political scene, but halfway through the novel, explaining the sketch of a woman hanging in Rufe's shanty, Sandoz relents to give us background on his meeting with the woman, an activist named Stephani, in Boston twenty years earlier.

With details like this the novel comes closer to having a central character in Hamm Rufe, who rejected his position as a member of one of the

town's leading families. His unacknowledged membership in the town's elite and his activism as an intellectual are Sandoz's symbolic way of complicating her reading of social class. Rufe's objection to the vicious competition and unbridled corruption of the society in which his family is a leading force causes him to pit himself, body and mind, against the capitalists, and by the end of the book, the hero is the sacrifice.

Behind Rufe's struggle to live a politics of inclusion, democracy, and economic justice, the disasters of the novel unfold relentlessly. Two members of the wealthy elite are suicides, revealing the emptiness of their lives. The younger generation is attracted to a fascist youth organization while their elders vitalize the Ku Klux Klan. Innocent children are murdered in gunplay fostered by violence against truckers striking for a decent wage. A poor cripple is burned to death in an arsonist's torching of the shantytown. Young lovers seeking to cross lines of social class are intimidated and beaten. Two refugee children adopted by liberal townspeople are carelessly killed by a hit-and-run driver protected by the authorities.

Thus Hamm Rufe's story is only the scaffolding from which Sandoz suspends many other stories. The novel is structured in the same way as Willa Cather's *Death Comes for the Archbishop,* its multiple stories juxtaposed along the length of a life of a symbolic figure. The central life story structuring these novels embodies the authors' highest values. In *Death Comes for the Archbishop,* Father Latour's life is a triumph, and the novel ends on a note of affirmation. By contrast, in *Capital City,* the death of Hamm Rufe in political street violence and his final recognition by his socialite mother is an ironic negation of the false values of the contemporary United States.

At the novel's publication in 1939, the *Saturday Review of Literature* called the novel "strong meat; not at all for the squeamish." Quoted on the dust jacket of the latest 2007 edition of the book, this judgment seems fair and the weight and relevance of the book greater than ever.

THE TOM-WALKER

The third of Sandoz's novels, begun after the publication of *Crazy Horse* and before *Cheyenne Autumn, The Tom-Walker* (1947) had difficulty achieving publication during World War II. Perhaps its persistent criticism of governmental corruption, accompanied by powerfully imagined social and economic disturbance, seemed too strong for the moment. A family saga of three generations, beginning with Milton Stone's return from the Civil War as an amputee, the novel is divided into three parts.

Book 1, covering the period 1865–1894, begins with the wedding Milton's parents have planned as a surprise, not knowing that their son had a surprise of his own in the lost leg. The young couple makes difficult adjustments and eventually, in the economic downturn of 1873, leaves the Cincinnati home place for northwestern Nebraska. Milton had left for the war as a boy of fourteen, joining William Tecumseh Sherman's army in its march to the sea; now, five years later, his parents have temporarily profited from the war economy, but the good times, based on corruption, don't last. Milton had ambitions to be a doctor but settles for work as a druggist with a traveling patent-medicine wagon. Milton understands the interplay of forces against which he is struggling, but that does not subdue the despair which drives him to drink and infidelity. His wife, Lucinda, faces the loss of her premature twins, the knowledge of her husband's wandering, and the disillusion of an old love, but she recovers her balance, mothers her father-in-law's illegitimate son, and eventually bears a boy of her own. The story of Milton and Lucinda Stone reveals the condition of the country, especially the northwestern plains, in the transforming society of the late nineteenth century.

Book 2 begins with the return of Milton's son, Martin Stone, from his military service in World War I to Sidney, Nebraska, where he expects to find his fiancée faithful. His return has been delayed by a three-year-long hospitalization to recover from being gassed. Of course his Nancy has married, borne two children, and is pregnant with a third. Martin takes out his rage on a friendly dog, showing the temper Sandoz

must have borrowed from Old Jules. Martin's temper continues to haunt him after he marries, exploding at his wife and children and eventually landing him in the hospital for treatment.

He meets his wife, Penny, on a train heading west to Wyoming, her plans also destroyed by the loss of her lover in the war. She takes him home to her parents, who help them get a start as homesteaders. That means dealing not only with problems of irrigation but with the Ku Klux Klan and other lawless elements on the frontier, including the competition between ranchers and settlers. The couple experiences the fellowship of community building, with the neighborly Wheeler P. Scheeler, but also its sorrows, in the tragic death in childbirth of the wife of another neighbor, Plew Tollins.

In the not-too-distant background looms the Teapot Dome scandal, the death of Woodrow Wilson and his League of Nations, and the harsh pro-business policies of Calvin Coolidge. Spring prairie fires, grasshopper devastation, farming accidents, lost babies: all the events of a difficult homesteading life play themselves out against the background of a government that seems to care nothing for its citizens. Martin is interested in plans for government dams and irrigation projects, but he sees no political support and diverts his energies when his former fiancée, Nancy, needs money to get her husband out of jail. For the Stones, Americans who have made large sacrifices for their country and its generous promise, the government seems increasingly unfriendly. The death of a neighbor's two children from diphtheria, followed by Martin's two-year-old daughter Rita running away from his violence, brings the second book to a close. Martin leaves his family, defeated by his anger and the forces arrayed against him. This is the darkest moment in the novel.

Book 3 follows the return from World War II of the second Milton Stone, the older of the two sons of Martin. This is the precocious son, who showed signs of mathematical ability even in childhood. Now he is an engineer, already married, with a child he has never seen. As he returns to Wyoming he recalls his grandfather Milton's arrival to help keep the homestead from foreclo-

sure while Martin was being treated in the veterans' hospital for the psychological breakdown caused by his wartime injury and post-traumatic shock syndrome. The vigor of the old man, iron leg and all, kept them going until Franklin Delano Roosevelt's mortgage moratorium took effect and the government's Turtle Shell irrigation project helped sustain them on their land. Then young Milton was swept off by the war, and by the time of this return to his young family, he has a bullet in his heart that military doctors were unable to remove.

Postwar politics brings him home to the political turmoil of 1948. His wife, Hazel, works for an ambitious senator Milton regards as a fraud. Aware of the pockets of poverty and hunger in postwar society, not just in the United States but across the world he has traveled, Milton experiences fellow-feeling only with his grandfather, since others in the family support the use of the atomic bomb and have adopted a conservative politics out of their new prosperity. The marriage with Hazel fails and his opportunities to know his daughter are very few. As he searches unsuccessfully for a job, the political success of Hazel's senator increases and Milton sees the approaching clashes between a government that protects the rich and a struggling population that is increasingly marginalized.

The novel reaches its climax in Washington, D.C., where Milton finally has the threatening bullet removed. The operation is shadowed by reports of scandal and corruption in the government as the new president, backed by Hazel's senator, takes office. Nightmare imagery emerges: scenes of the overthrow of the government; Milton's thoughts of attempting to take the life of the usurping Senator Potter; and his final ideological separation from Hazel. After a double space on the page, Milton wakes from the anesthetic of his successful surgery, but we are left in doubt, as the narrative concludes, as to whether he is awakening from a nightmare or still in it.

The novel challenges the reader not only with its "it can't happen here" ending but with its relentless confrontation of the costs of war. The three wars, while they represent historical reali-

ties, also symbolize the antihuman violence that leaves mental as well as physical suffering. Although all three of its protagonists go off to war willingly in youth, they return burdened by their exposure to the greed and corruption that undermine military victory. Certainly classifiable as an antiwar novel, *The Tom-Walker* shows that war, in western slang, is the "guyascutus," or monster, loosed on the populace. The costs are not only economic, but social and personal.

The final chapter of book 3 is called "The Guyascutus Loosed," giving this westernism special prominence, and the first chapter in the book,"Skyuglers," also introduces the reader to a word not found in dictionaries. Sandoz fought her eastern editors for the inclusion of these and other such westernisms as *gostratious, honeyfugle, cowalloper*, and *dauncy*, thus marking the novel as a record not only of eighty-three years of American experience but of American language as well. In his volume *American English,* Albert H. Marckwardt reserves a chapter, "Yankee Ingenuity and the Frontier Spirit," for this linguistic phenomenon: "This tendency toward the bizarre creation is a significant feature of American English which can be accounted for in terms of cultural history and linguistic tradition" (p. 102). Marckwardt traces this feature of language to "the Elizabethan tendency toward hyperbole or overstatement." He notes its flourishing on the frontier as a kind of tall talk. "Guyascutus" is on his list of fanciful animals invented by frontiersmen. *The Tom-Walker* itself draws its title from circus slang for a clown on stilts. It serves as a rich image for the clever and difficult survival and mobility of humankind, handicapped by powerful forces. Sandoz's metaphorical use of this inventive language is a mark of her originality. Her vision, in this book, is finally tragicomic, a vision of courageous survival under difficult circumstances.

MISS MORISSA: DOCTOR OF THE GOLD TRAIL

Miss Morissa: Doctor of the Gold Trail (1955) is the sleeper among Sandoz's novels. About a hundred pages shorter than the other four dis-

cussed here, yet filled with event and character, the novel demonstrates the imaginative power with which Sandoz transformed landscape, historical event, documentary sources, and autobiography. The book is dedicated to three frontier women doctors and unnamed others like them, and borrows some aspects of Morissa Kirk's biography from the records they left behind. But what makes the book live—the commitment of Morissa to her work, the endurance and enterprise she shows, her struggle for love and acceptance—comes directly from the character of the author, as dedicated as any medical doctor to her task as a writer practicing cultural healing.

The book draws to it passages in all of Sandoz's work that remember and value the contribution of women to frontier history. In the fiction, these include Libby Slogum, the capable, independent daughter of the wicked, grasping Gulla; Dr. Abigail Allerton, the historian in *Capital City,* who takes heat from the town fathers for revealing unsavory features of Franklin's development; Lucinda and Penny Stone of *The Tom-Walker*; and the unforgettable young schoolteacher of the novella "Winter Thunder," who saves the lives of her students in a blizzard. Behind them, one remembers the portrait of Sandoz's mother and the other women of *Old Jules,* not least of which is the author herself, baking bread, minding babies, and tying tourniquets while still a child herself.

The novel opens with Morissa Kirk's arrival at a pioneer settlement on the Platte River in northwestern Nebraska following her disappointment in love. Her training as a medical doctor had excited the jealousy of her intended sister-in-law, whose genealogical research revealed Morissa's unacknowledged paternity. Ineligible for the upper-class marriage she was about to make, Morissa has traveled west to her stepfather, an engineer building a bridge to gold fields north of the Platte. The district, near the town of Sidney, is one in which Sandoz herself had served as a schoolteacher in her early twenties, after the dissolution of her marriage, and where she was known as "Miss Macumber."

The relationship of marriage and vocation for a woman is the richest subject of the novel, and we are privileged to see it played out against the background of the 1870s and 1880s, those dramatic decades twenty-five years before Sandoz's birth, when ranchers and settlers, Indians and whites, were struggling for the land and its wealth.

The economics, events, and personalities of the period she had carefully described in *The Buffalo Hunters* and *The Cattlemen* are in the background. Morissa's courage, compassion, and skill as a healer enable her to cross barriers between people, and we witness her grief for the Sioux and Cheyenne from her position within the settler/rancher community. The gold rush into the Black Hills, sacred lands to the Sioux, was stimulated by Custer's violation of native treaty rights. The story's immediate historical background, like any rush to extract the riches of a land, symbolizes the destruction of the environment in the name of greed. This is clearly depicted in all of its consequences in crime, disease, vigilante law, and the suffering of children.

At the novel's end, Morissa's hospital, torched by her faithless outlaw husband, is about to be rebuilt by the labor and sacrifice of the settlers, and she herself is anticipating the true marriage she has held off since her arrival on the Platte. In contrast to the conventional novel's end in the fulfillment of marriage, Sandoz concludes with Morissa's recognition by the settlers and her decision to reinvest in her chosen work.

Unlike the epic vision of the plains histories and the native point of view in *Crazy Horse* and *Cheyenne Autumn,* the perspective in *Miss Morissa* is thoroughly grounded in the emerging settler/rancher society. With ample compassion and respect for the suffering and displacement of native peoples, Morissa's story faces toward the future of the land, complete with hospitals, bridges, and irrigation. In this story of the historical process, Sandoz sees clearly what is lost, yet marks with respect what is gained.

The book is probably the best introduction to Sandoz's work, arousing the reader's interest in the more densely factual plains histories, which are shaped by the forces they describe rather than by romantic plot. More direct than the earlier novels, it has fewer plot complications, yet it succeeds in conveying similar themes.

SON OF THE GAMBLIN' MAN: THE YOUTH OF AN ARTIST

This novel, published in 1960, is the most unusual of Sandoz's works, a return at the end of her novel-writing career to the mode of its beginning in *Old Jules.* The novelistic strategies of dramatized scene and dialogue are grafted on to the structure framed by biographical information given to Sandoz by the family of Robert Henry Cozad (1865–1929), who, as Robert Henri, became famous as a painter and leader of the Ashcan School of American art. (The Ashcan School, also known as "The Eight," held a group exhibition in 1908 in New York City; in addition to Henri they included Maurice Prendergast, Arthur B. Davies, George Luks, William J. Glackens, Ernest Lawson, John Sloan, and Everett Shinn.)

Cozad was the younger of two sons of John Jackson Cozad, a community builder in Nebraska whose fortune was based on his success at high stakes gambling. Determined to use his self-made wealth to bring settlers to the West and prominence to his name and family, John Cozad left the Ohio farm on which he was raised and traveled the country and South America as a faro player. Participating in the violence and lawlessness of frontier life, he was an expert in firearms and self-defense but periodically tried, unsuccessfully, to organize communities. He married a Virginian and fathered five children, only two of whom lived through childhood illnesses, and determined at the age of forty-two to establish a new community in the developing West. Walking along the tracks laid by the Union Pacific Railroad Company, not far from the Platte River in Nebraska, he arrived at the Hundredth Meridian sign and chose that place in the Platte Valley for his town center. Sandoz makes this decision the event of the book's first chapter, and in many respects, the book is about "the gamblin' man" and his ambitions.

Like Jules Sandoz, John Jackson Cozad is a contradictory hero. Visionaries and autocrats, these men were fathers not just of their communities but of artist children. Sandoz was an ideal choice to write this account reattaching the internationally known urban artist to his rural western past, because she had traveled his road herself and come to terms, through her art, with a difficult and domineering father.

Just as *Old Jules* ends with the surprising and moving request of the dying Jules that his daughter write his life, Sandoz ends the story of Robert Henri with an epilogue set twenty-one years after the father left his Cozad identity behind. The scene of the last chapter is Robert Henri's New York studio, in which he is completing a portrait of his seventy-two-year-old father. Sandoz dramatizes this as a moment of long-awaited recognition from father to son, a moment she treasured in her own life.

Of course the special value of the book, beyond its vibrant representation of western life at the end of the nineteenth century, is its contribution to art history, its marvelously full description of the contribution to an artist's life of the scenes and characters of his formative years. One would have to look long in the annals of art history to find its equal. It is to be hoped that the book will be reissued one day with plates of its subject's paintings.

CRAZY HORSE: THE STRANGE MAN OF THE OGLALAS

In the foreword to her 1942 biography *Crazy Horse: Strange Man of the Oglalas*, researched in the late 1920s and early 1930s, Sandoz describes her artistic ambition for the book. She chose her words and shaped her syntax to "say some of the things of the Indian for which there are no white-man words" (p. x). She hoped to illuminate the inner life and the sociocultural features of the plains people through the style of her English, evoking weather, landscape, and action with the aid of figures of speech drawn from Native American cultures. Such a project, devoted to the biography of a warrior once regarded as an enemy of the nation, was unprecedented. Only in 1987, with the Native American literary renaissance well under way, did another writer, James Welch, of Blackfoot heritage himself, make a similar effort in his novel *Fools Crow*.

The story of Crazy Horse is understood as the story of his people in their period of crisis, from 1854, when, as a twelve-year-old known as "Curly," he was present during a confrontation with U.S. Army soldiers triggered by the killing of a Mormon settler's cow, to the time of his death in 1877. Sandoz divides her story into three equal parts of six chapters each, with the final part gaining a seventh chapter for the scene of his betrayal and death. This spacious arrangement leaves room for a leisurely narrative of everyday activity as the Lakota try to restore some normalcy among their people after the first crisis of the book. The narrative is written from an omniscient perspective, but one located within the Lakota society. The characters, who are known and named individuals, were drawn from interview and documentary sources. Each chapter is tied to its historical moment with place and date. Thus if Sandoz re-creates the dialogue of a scene known to have occurred, the result is not fiction but fully realized history. At the end of Part 1, young Curly acknowledges his childhood visionary experience and his father, Crazy Horse, recognizes his son's ambition to serve the people with the gift of his own name.

In the second part of the book, young Crazy Horse matures as a warrior during a period of rising difficulty with the whites after the Civil War, including some never-forgiven attacks like the one at Sand Creek in 1864. Disappointed in his love for Black Buffalo Woman, he performs so many heroic acts that he is chosen to participate in a new ceremonial as a "shirt wearer," one who is appointed to lead and protect the people. Constructing her narrative from army records and interviews with Indian elders, Sandoz gives the events their Indian names and interpretations. We read western history from a perspective that is new to the familiar parallel record compiled by the ultimate victors. Painful divisions appear among the Indians, made worse by incursions of

smallpox that take their young and by increasing numbers of white settlers.

There is time in the painstaking account for a history of the long freezing winter of 1866–1867, for the elk hunt, for the performance of the *heyokas* (ceremonial clowns), for the extensions of the railroad and the demotion of Red Cloud even as he signed a peace treaty with the whites. Concluding this period of great danger and tension among the Indian people and between them and the whites, the long disappointment in love between Crazy Horse and Black Buffalo Woman flares into crisis. Leaving her husband and three children, the Lakota woman, niece of Red Cloud, chooses to go with Crazy Horse. The abandoned husband responds by shooting Crazy Horse in the jaw. Sandoz's narrative carefully takes up the cruel aftermath that culminates in stripping Crazy Horse of the honor shirt. He is found unworthy, and indeed he blames himself for a selfish act that divides his people.

Part 3 opens with Crazy Horse's marriage to Black Shawl, begun as a convenience and consolation for the politically influenced loss of Black Buffalo Woman, but ripening into an understanding and supportive relationship. In the eyes of his people, Crazy Horse regains respect by taking revenge on the whites for the death of his brother Little Hawk. The political division between Red Cloud's people, who accept an agency and reservation from the whites, and Crazy Horse's people, who counsel resistance, grows much sharper as the sides divide into "hostiles" and "friendlies." These internal divisions, made deeper by the sales of inferior government goods, lead to the serious loss, in a battle with the Snakes, of Crazy Horse's mentor and friend, Hump, balanced only by the birth of a daughter to Crazy Horse and Black Shawl.

This young life soon flickers out, hastened to its end by white man's disease, and the father's mourning fuels the resistance that accompanies him through his last years. The great victory over the foolhardy Custer gives little relief from the false promises of an agency in the north country and dangerous and deceptive experiences in negotiating with soldier-chiefs and lying and conniving translators. When at last there is no

alternative to save the starving people, Crazy Horse allows himself to be brought to a peace parley. When he realizes he is being taken instead to prison, he resists and is bayoneted while his Indian escort holds his arms.

In its thorough organization and rich detail, Sandoz's account of Crazy Horse's life and death symbolizes the tragedy and waste that marked the Euro-American settlement of this country. One must make special note of the bibliography, which lists all of the interviews Sandoz conducted, as well as the more than fifty interviews she used from the Ricker Collection of the Nebraska State Historical Society. Every episode in the book is tied to a source in documents and letters of the War Department, the Indian Bureau, and manuscripts.

CHEYENNE AUTUMN

Sandoz begins her most arresting book, *Cheyenne Autumn*, published in 1953, with a mise-en-scène, a list of named characters and a precise geographical identification of time and place. A prologue, "Gone Before," offers the events of 1877 and 1878, up to the first chapter of the drama in which 284 Northern Cheyenne slip silently away from the Cheyenne and Arapahoe Agency in the abhorred Indian Territory. The book is an account of the drama of Cheyenne courage and determination, but as a nonfiction history it unfolds this drama against a background of exactness and detail that ties the telling to documentation and makes an indelible record. In her preface, Sandoz hopes that she has not failed her friends in telling the story. Those friends and informants include Old Cheyenne Woman, "who was one of those pulled wounded and bereaved from the Last Hole below Hat Creek bluffs" (p. xiv). In the sixteenth of eighteen chapters we come to Hat Creek. By then we have come to know, in unforgettable specificity, the cruelty, misunderstanding, and waste that shaped western history.

Each of the eighteen chapters marks a step along the route the Northern Cheyenne took when they realized life was no longer viable under U.S. Army supervision in Indian Territory. They had

been promised that they could leave if conditions were inadequate, but like all promises from the U.S. government, this one was abrogated. The courageous leaders, Dull Knife and Little Wolf, and their disciplined people traveled on foot, with few horses or stops for rest, even for a baby's birth or to mourn a child's death.

From the first there is conflict. At the last minute, one extended family decides not to go on the agreed-upon way and their horses are killed as punishment. There is disagreement about the route, which Little Wolf settles after a harangue in which he must display his wounds as a symbol of his authority and sacrifice. As part of her account of unfolding events, Sandoz includes reminders of past history, for "all things that ever happened in a place were always of the today there in the Cheyenne pattern of time" (p. 31). For the Cheyenne, the route is well known; the people always know where they are and what the resources of the place are: water, shelter, defensive positions. After the first confrontation with pursuing soldiers, the Cheyenne surround them, preventing their going for water and forcing their retreat.

Then the first man is killed, out raiding for horses, but the loss is balanced by the arrival of sixteen-year-old Spotted Deer, sent from the agency by his mother to help Old Grandmother. We follow Spotted Deer as the adolescent takes on responsibility and seeks a beloved. As if the political and military problems are not enough, the people are plagued by ordinary ills. The mental problems of Bear Rope are exacerbated by the stress of the escape. In his dementia, he tries to rape his daughter, who kills him in self-defense, an unacceptable but unavoidable act.

Sandoz does not neglect the detail that though the Bear Rope family is ostracized, meat is left behind for them. Children dig lead out of rocks to remake ammunition. Time is allowed for making arrow glue. Social organization and cultural standards remain intact. Two days of respite from running permit description of the features of village life, including joking, lovemaking, and a Cheyenne wedding. Sandoz emphasizes the involvement of all the generations by showing us a grandmother concealed with a newborn, her

daughter in the rifle pits taking the place of a fallen man.

The differences between Dull Knife and Little Wolf reach a crisis when Dull Knife chooses to join Red Cloud at the Sioux agency, while Little Wolf wants to go on to the North. Here the narrative also divides, some chapters following Dull Knife to Red Cloud, alternate chapters describing Little Wolf's band as they hide in Lost Chokecherry Valley. Meanwhile public outrage has filled the newspapers with criticism of the army, which has deployed twenty-four companies of soldiers ineffectively.

When the Dull Knife band reaches Red Cloud, the Sioux leader cannot accept them with his resources barely adequate for his own people. Dull Knife's people are rounded up and imprisoned in barracks, where they are at first treated gently by Lieutenant Chase, a good young officer soon replaced. Surgeon Moseley, a sympathetic white doctor, admires the well-set leg of Sitting Man, but the people are frightened by the search through their bundles, and Little Finger Nail ties his notebook record to his back. (This notebook, marked by bullet holes, is now in the American Museum of Natural History.) Meanwhile, Little Wolf's still-resisting group revalues the old ways in Lost Chokecherry Valley, returning to arrow making, using soapweed, and remembering in their poverty their painted buffalo lodges with beaded linings, long left behind. Little Wolf's people send gifts of meat to the Dull Knife captives, especially after they have success in hunting a great migrating elk herd.

In the army barracks, the people seek to pass on the old knowledge, and since knowledgeable ones are among the Dull Knife people, gifts pass to Little Wolf's band as well. Medicine Woman makes a pouch of "mother's cure" for the hidden ones and shows the girls plants they will need to know. Sandoz gives an account of activities in the barracks: ball games, short hunts, cards and hand games, and tales of a ghost in the guardhouse, associated with Crazy Horse, who died there in 1877.

However, with the appointment of Captain Wessells, conditions grow extreme. Deprived of rations, fuel, and water, the Dull Knife Cheyenne

hold out for a few days, but on January 9, 1879, they break out of the locked barracks through broken windows, in the middle of a freezing night. Pursued, they are rounded up a few at a time near Hat Creek. Forty-eight women and children, a few boys and crippled men, are sent to Red Cloud. The rest are shipped to Kansas to be tried for murder.

Dull Knife escapes and is hidden, eventually returning to Red Cloud. In forty-below-zero January weather, Little Wolf meditates at Bear Butte, where Cheyenne mythology locates the origin of the Chief's Bundle. Finally Little Wolf surrenders to White Hat Clark. To complete the irony, treaty funds are taken from the Cheyenne allotment to pay damages incurred in this lengthy, tragic, mismanaged campaign.

Sandoz ends the story "In the Aftertime." Some interested whites see to the release of those taken to Kansas. Tuberculosis and pneumonia claim some the bullets could not kill. Little Wolf, sunk in despair, gets drunk at Fort Keogh and finally kills Thin Elk, who was always pursuing his wives. After the killing, Little Wolf never again permits himself to smoke the pipe of leadership.

In this book Sandoz has written indispensable American history. For anyone who wants to know of the skill, intellect, imagination, and courage of a native community, *Cheyenne Autumn* cannot be surpassed. The first among American writers to do justice to the tragic story, Sandoz accompanied archival research with mapping and traveling the Cheyenne journey herself. As she moved through the land with the people, in imagination, she rendered their story meticulously, as a sacred trust. This is the most difficult of her books to read, and the most necessary.

Selected Bibliography

WORKS OF MARI SANDOZ

NOVELS

Slogum House. Boston: Little, Brown, 1937; Lincoln: University of Nebraska Press, 1981. (Quotes in essay refer to 1981 edition.)

Capital City. Boston: Little, Brown, 1939; Lincoln: University of Nebraska Press, 1982. (Quotes in essay refer to 1982 edition.)

The Tom-Walker. New York: Dial Press, 1947; Lincoln: University of Nebraska Press, 1984. (Quotes in essay refer to 1984 edition.)

Miss Morissa: Doctor of the Gold Trail. New York: McGraw-Hill, 1955.

The Horsecatcher. Philadelphia: Westminster Press, 1957. (Short historical novel about the Cheyenne in the 1830s.)

Son of the Gamblin' Man: The Youth of an Artist. New York: Clarkson N. Potter, 1960.

The Story Catcher. Philadelphia: Westminster Press, 1963. (Short historical novel about a young Sioux hero who learns to record the history of his people in pictures.)

HISTORIES

Cheyenne Autumn. New York: McGraw-Hill, 1953; Lincoln: University of Nebraska Press, 2005. (Quotes in essay refer to 2005 edition.)

The Buffalo Hunters: The Story of the Hide Men. New York: Hastings House, 1954; Lincoln: University of Nebraska Press, 1978. (Quotes in essay refer to 1978 edition.)

The Cattlemen from the Rio Grande Across the Far Marias. New York: Hastings House, 1958; Lincoln: University of Nebraska Press, 1978. (Quotes in essay refer to 1978 edition.)

Love Song to the Plains. New York: Harper, 1961. (An introduction to the geography and social history of the Great Plains, retelling more compactly the materials of the earlier multivolume plains histories.)

These Were the Sioux. New York: Hastings House, 1961. (Explanation of Sioux culture that describes the work of the Oglala Sioux artist Amos Bad Heart Bull, nine of whose drawings are reproduced in the volume.)

The Beaver Men: Spearheads of Empire. New York: Hastings House, 1964; Lincoln: University of Nebraska Press, 1978. (Quotes in essay refer to 1978 edition.)

The Battle of the Little Bighorn. Philadelphia: Lippincott, 1966. (Expands the chapter treatment of the event in her biography of Crazy Horse to 182 pages of detail; includes an appendix with the names of the enlisted men and a useful bibliography.)

BIOGRAPHIES AND MEMOIR

Old Jules. Boston: Little, Brown, 1935.

Crazy Horse: The Strange Man of the Oglalas. New York: Knopf, 1942.

The Christmas of the Phonograph Records: A Recollection. Lincoln: University of Nebraska Press, 1966. (Includes the autobiographical sketch of the title, retold from *Old Jules,* and nine other autobiographical selections written between 1929 and 1965, along with a Sandoz chronology and a useful checklist of her writings.)

MARI SANDOZ

ANTHOLOGIES

Winter Thunder. Philadelphia: Westminster Press, 1954. (Includes five of Sandoz's stories, including the remarkable "Winter Thunder," based on the true episode in which Sandoz's niece, a young teacher, saved the schoolchildren with whom she was stranded in a nine-day blizzard.)

Hostiles and Friendlies: Selected Short Writings. Lincoln: University of Nebraska Press, 1959. (Anthology divided into three sections, "Recollections," "Indian Studies," and "Short Fiction"; includes a useful autobiographical sketch.)

Old Jules Country: A Selection from Old Jules and Thirty Years of Writing Since the Book Was Published. New York: Hastings House, 1965. (A substantial anthology including two chapters from *The Beaver Men*, four from *Crazy Horse*, four from *Cheyenne Autumn*, three from *The Buffalo Hunters*, four from *The Cattlemen*, three from *Old Jules*, and seven from *These Were the Sioux*; as well as "The Lost Sitting Bull" (also in *Hostiles and Friendlies*); "The Homestead in Perspective," reprinted from *Land Use Policy and Problems in the U.S.* (1963); and two pieces found only here, "Snakes" and "Coyotes and Eagles.")

Sandhill Sundays and Other Recollections. Lincoln: University of Nebraska Press, 1970.

LETTERS

"I Do Not Apologize for the Length of this Letter": The Mari Sandoz Letters on Native American Rights, 1940–1965. Introduced and edited by Kimberli A. Lee. Foreword by John R. Wunder. Lubbock: Texas Tech University Press, 2009.

Letters of Mari Sandoz. Edited by Helen Winter Stauffer. Lincoln: University of Nebraska Press, 1992.

ARCHIVES

Mari Sandoz Collection. Don L. Love Library, University of Nebraska, Lincoln. (See Scott L. Greenwell, *Descriptive Guide to the Mss. Collection*. New Series, No. 63. Lincoln: University of Nebraska Press, 1980.)

Mari Sandoz High Plains Heritage Center. Chadron State College, Chadron, Nebraska.

Nebraska State Historical Society. Lincoln, Nebraska.

Mari Sandoz Collection. Syracuse University, Syracuse, New York.

The Mari Sandoz Heritage Society offers an annual conference and publishes a newsletter four times a year.

BIBLIOGRAPHIES

Complete bibliographies, including individual publication of short stories and articles, are to be found in *Hostiles and Friendlies* and *Sandhill Sundays,* as well as in the biography by Helen Winter Stauffer.

BIOGRAPHICAL STUDIES

Barker, Jane Valentine. *Mari: A Novel*. Boulder: University of Colorado Press, 1997. (Novelized version of Sandoz's stories as recorded in *Old Jules*; rather than fiction, however, this book should be classified as biographical interpretation.)

Stauffer, Helen Winter. *Mari Sandoz: Story Catcher of the Plains*. Lincoln: University of Nebraska Press, 1982. (Indispensable full-length scholarly biography.)

CRITICAL STUDIES

Castille, Philip Dubuisson. "'The Ripening Fascism of the Corn Belt': Lost Democracy in Mari Sandoz's *Capital City*." *Storytelling* 5, no. 2:131–142 (winter 2006).

Dickson, Mary. "*Crazy Horse: The Strange Man of the Oglalas* by Mari Sandoz: Historiography, a Philosophy for Reconstruction." *Great Plains Quarterly* 27, no. 1:39–54 (winter 2007).

Kocks, Dorothea E. *Dream a Little: Land and Social Justice in Modern America*. Berkeley: University of California Press, 2000.

Limbaugh, Elaine E. "A Feminist Reads *Old Jules*." *Platte Valley Review* 17, no. 1:41–50 (winter 1989).

Marckwardt, Albert H. "Yankee Ingenuity and the Frontier Spirit." Chap. 5 of his *American English*. New York: Oxford University Press, 1958. P. 100. (Offers insight into Sandoz's westernisms.)

"Mari Sandoz, Nebraska Sandhills Author: A Centennial Recognition." Special issue. *Great Plains Quarterly* 16, no. 1 (winter 1996). (Published one hundred years after the author's birth, includes a brief introduction by Barbara Rippey and John R. Wunder (pp. 4–7) and four articles: Betsy Downey, "She Does Not Write Like a Historian: Mari Sandoz and the Old and New Western History," pp. 9–28; Lisa R. Lindell, "Recasting Epic Tradition: The Dispossessed as Hero in Sandoz's *Crazy Horse* and *Cheyenne Autumn*," pp. 43–53; Glenda Riley, "Mari Sandoz's *Slogum House*: Greed as Woman," pp. 29–41; and Helen Winter Stauffer, "Mari Sandoz's Portrait of an Artist's Youth: Robert Henri's Nebraska Years," pp. 54–66.)

Nicoll, Bruce. "Mari Sandoz: Nebraska Loner." *American West* 2, no. 2:32–36 (spring 1965).

Stauffer, Helen Winter. "Two Massacres on the Sappa River: Cause and Effect in Mari Sandoz's *Cheyenne Autumn*." *Platte Valley Review* 19, no. 1:25–43 (winter 1991).

Villiger, Laura R. *Mari Sandoz: A Study in Post-Colonial Discourse*. Swiss American Historical Publication 9. New York: Peter Lang, 1994.

NICKY SILVER

(1960—)

Deirdre O'Leary

WHEN NICKY SILVER'S 2011 work *The Lyons* transferred from the Vineyard Theatre to Broadway's Cort Theatre in early 2012, much was made of the fact that this was Mr. Silver's first Broadway production, despite his nearly thirty years of writing plays and a nearly twenty-year career as a celebrated off-Broadway playwright. While the transfer to Broadway undoubtedly gave Silver a larger audience for his works, and increased attention, Nicky Silver has been one of America's most prolifically produced playwrights for decades. Known for his biting dark farces that veer from hilarious to brutal, Silver is a deft creator of alienated, fragmented characters longing for a human connection that eludes them. His plays collectively offer a caustic rebuttal to the nostalgic image of the happy and happily adjusted American family. His fractured stage families are populated by orphaned adult children, alcoholic parents, troubled siblings, WASPS, male prostitutes, misfits, addicts, murderers, scorned lovers, and ardent romantics. The critic David Savran writes that Silver is a dexterous manipulator, "a black farceur in the tradition of Oscar Wilde, Joe Orton and Christopher Durang. Like these playwrights, he delights in pushing the bounds of propriety, in celebrating the inanities that crowd his characters' lives and in dredging up the desires and enmities we are taught to repress" (p. 213). Like the writers Savran mentions, Silver creates worlds that challenge both the characters' and audiences' moral and emotional thresholds, suggesting, as does Edward Albee, that the thin veneer of respectability we cling to barely conceals the despair and alienation we all suffer from and the violence we are all capable of. Yet, to watch a Nicky Silver play is to laugh uproariously, both at the highly farcical antics onstage and at the stinging truths we witness. Perhaps the only thing that took critics by surprise when *The Lyons* opened was that it had taken that long for Nicky Silver to have a play on New York's biggest stage.

The dichotomy of being simultaneously a stage veteran and Broadway novice extends to the surprising lack of academic work done on Silver. He has been the subject of numerous profiles in the *New York Times* and has had his work reviewed consistently by that and other New York papers since the early 1990s. His work is regularly staged in other major theater cities in the United States, including Washington, D.C., Philadelphia, Chicago, and Los Angeles, as well as being a regular staple of regional theater seasons nationwide. Yet he remains not nearly as studied by theater scholars as his contemporaries Christopher Durang, Craig Lucas, or Tony Kushner. This is both challenging and liberating for the writer interested in Silver. The first and only published collection of his plays, *Etiquette and Vitriol: The Food Chain and Other Plays* (1996), includes a fascinating and very funny introduction written by Silver himself. Apart from an extended interview given to David Savran, published in his collection of interviews titled *The Playwright's Voice* (1999), and two essays in the 2008 work *We Will Be Citizens: New Essays on Gay and Lesbian Theatre,* there is a surprising lack of published scholarship on Silver's dramatic work. This essay is intended to go some way toward introducing this playwright to a broader readership, contextualizing his works within contemporary American theater of the late twentieth and early twenty-first centuries, and discussing the pertinent themes and writing strategies that make up his dramaturgy.

EARLY LIFE

Nicholas Silver was born on December 3, 1960, in Philadelphia. In his interview with Savran,

Silver admitted to having "no memory of a moment when I was not interested in theatre" (p. 217). In junior high, he spent summers at the famed Stagedoor Manor performing arts camp, where he performed in as many as ten shows in eight weeks. "We had classes during the day and were in plays at night. And [artistic director Jack Romano] had you doing plays like *Follies* or *The House of Bernarda Alba* when you were ten years old. And this was of course far too sophisticated for us and probably scarred us emotionally but it did alter our aesthetic completely" (Savran, p. 218). The experience appears not to have scarred Silver, and the camp is referenced extensively in his 1999 work *The Eros Trilogy.*

Silver graduated high school a year early and enrolled in the New York University (NYU) Tisch School of the Arts. In his introduction to *Etiquette and Vitriol,* Silver is self-deprecating in his characterization of his undergraduate years as a period of youthful exuberance and growth. However, his arrival in New York coincided with a period of enormous theatrical funding and performance. He commented to Savran on his undergraduate time in New York:

> I came to New York when the New York Shakespeare Festival was at Lincoln Center—there was *Streamers* and *Threepenny Opera* with Raul Julia and *The Cherry Orchard* with Irene Worth and *for colored girls* was on Broadway. I think it was just about that time that Christopher Durang and Wendy Wasserstein were emerging at Playwrights Horizons. This was an incredibly exciting time to be going to the theater in New York City.
>
> (p. 219)

Silver enrolled in the Experimental Theatre Wing (ETW) division, at NYU. The aim of ETW was to expose its students to various aesthetics, traditions, and acting styles in hopes that they would develop their own approach to performance, freed from the expectation that they must follow a prescribed "naturalist" approach. He described the curriculum as follows:

> The idea was that you did a play with [the director] Liz Swados for four weeks, then with [the playwright/actor/director] Charles Ludlam, then with [the noted avant-garde theater company] Mabou Mines, and we were supposed to be picking

an aesthetic that appealed to us. Rather than doing that, I picked from each aesthetic something that I could then manipulate in my own writing to create my own kind of theater.
>
> (p. 219)

This accumulated, intertextual dramaturgy, whether directly the result of his time at NYU or not, has become Silver's signature writing strategy. His plays deliberately, and sometimes confusingly, mix genres and styles, referencing popular culture alongside canonical works by Tennessee Williams and Noël Coward and Oscar Wilde, with wild variations in tone and pacing. To see or read a Silver play is also to hear and see these other dramatic voices and styles. Characters use direct address to the audience, sometimes commenting on the worth of the play itself. While Silver's more recent plays have in some ways moved away from this model, this accumulated dramaturgy is emblematic of his most experimental writing period, his early years in New York.

While Silver did not enroll at NYU with the specific intention of being a writer, at the end of his senior year he wrote his first full-length play. The details of it remain a mystery; in *Etiquette and Vitriol* Silver notes that he was not happy with the result but that the experience did inspire him to commit to a career writing plays.

After graduation, Silver quickly had a few plays produced in New York. *On Fire* was was produced at an off-off-Broadway theater on Forty-Second Street in January of 1982. A year and a half later he produced *Three Short Plays with Long Titles,* which included two one-acts by Silver and one by Leslee Ann. It was produced at the Open Eye on East Eighty-Eighth Street. Neither show is published nor appears to have been reviewed. His next play, *Bridal Hunt* (1982), about a multigenerational Jewish family, was sent to David Copelin, the head of script development at the Phoenix Theatre. Copelin liked the play and organized a staged reading of it with hopes to option a commercial production, but he was unsuccessful. Silver explains, "So here I am fresh out of college and this is really great. But he couldn't raise the money largely because it was about an overtly Jewish family and it was extremely negative and hostile" (Savran, p. 221).

For the next two years, Silver didn't write anything. The nascent AIDS epidemic was devastating the theater community and had taken the life of a close friend. During that period, Silver was approached by someone on the street asking if he had written "a play called *Bridal Hunt* a few years ago?"(*Etiquette*, p. xi). That person explained that he had liked the work and had a small theater company. The company was looking for a play for six actors on a bare stage. While the serendipitous nature of the encounter seems like the plot of a play, this one lacked the requisite happy ending. Silver writes that the eventual play "stunk" (p. xi).

Despite Silver's stinging assessment, the play was produced at the Sanford Meisner Theatre on Eleventh Avenue. According to Silver, no one came. But Robert Coles, who ran the Vortex, a small gay theater that rented space from the Meisner, asked if he would like to submit some works. Silver explains their unique business relationship:

> Here's how it worked: when he couldn't get someone to rent out the theatre he'd call me. I usually had four weeks to write a play, then four weeks to rehearse. I paid for the rehearsal space with money from my day job. I used my friends in the plays whether they were right for their parts or not. ... I directed most of the time, not because I thought I was brilliant or anything, but at that economic bracket the options are slim. We rehearsed for four weeks, in the evenings. ... We built the set [on Sunday], painted it in the morning, rehearsed once, Monday night, to set lights and opened on Tuesday. Usually we'd have eighteen or twenty people in the audience on opening night.
>
> (*Etiquette*, p. xii)

Silver worked that way for approximately five years, working a variety of day jobs (waiter, retail, etc.) and putting on plays at night with very limited resources and support. Yet his output was as prolific as it was varied. Plays produced at the Vortex by Silver include *Artists and Concubines* (1987), about an artist's colony; *Siblings in Paradise (or Moscow when It Sizzles)* (1988); *Fat Men in Skirts* (1988); and *Fetid Itch* (1990), a comedy about an overpowering mother whose son and grandson plot to kill her. *Free Will & Wanton Lust* (1991) is about the complicated relationships of a vain mother, her much younger lover, her pregnant daughter, her estranged son, and her son's fiancée. *Wanking 'Tards* (1990) is about a married woman's sexual fantasy. Silver notes that one of the performances of the play was on the Fourth of July, for an audience of one—the stage manager's mother. *Cats and Dogs* (1991) is a comedy about a man on the verge of suicide and the woman from a crisis center who tries to help him, and *The Nasty Bits* (1991) is a farce set during a dinner party at which a gay playwright, his actress wife, and her actor lover all compete for the attention of a famous producer. Sadly, none of these plays, save *Fat Men in Skirts* and *Free Will & Wanton Lust,* were published, yet *Cats and Dogs* and *The Nasty Bits* were eventually reworked into his later works *The Food Chain* (1994) and *The Agony & the Agony* (2006).

Collectively, Silver's early works reflect the freedom and limitations that the Vortex Theatre arrangement provided for him. The plays have very few characters, few set demands, and minimal props, yet subject matter is purposefully outrageous, with a gleeful disregard for what some would refer to as theatrical propriety and stage realism. The plays test the limits of both an audience's capacity for shock and the theater's ability to contain spectacle and stage violence. While the vast majority of these early works are not published, the provocative, over-the-top *Fat Men in Skirts* perhaps best articulates the spirit of these early days.

FAT MEN IN SKIRTS *(1988)*

Fat Men in Skirts begins with a middle-aged, fashionable Phyllis Hogan blithely informing the audience that she and her son Bishop are the sole survivors of a plane crash. They were en route to Italy, she tells us, to visit her husband, a filmmaker who makes "heartwarming films about lovable extraterrestrials," when their plane went down, stranding them on a deserted island. Bishop, a stuttering eleven-year-old with an obsessive fascination with the films of Katherine Hepburn, is thoroughly terrified by their situation, but Phyllis is resolute and nonplussed, casu-

ally feeding him lipsticks to eat and, when there are none left, calmly hands him a butcher's knife and instructs him to "cut the arm off that nun. Bring it back here and I'll cook it and we'll eat it" (*Etiquette,* p. 229). Phyllis and Bishop will remain on the island for five years, where they will spend their time eating the corpses of the other passengers, engaging in an incestuous relationship, and, particularly in the case of Bishop, degenerating to an obsessive, violent, homicidal animal.

Phyllis and Bishop are eventually rescued, though this only begins another set of troubles, as they are reunited with Howard, Phyllis' husband and Bishop's father. Howard has been having a long-term relationship with Pam, a relationship that began well before Phyllis and Bishop were stranded on the island, and now he finds himself hiding his pregnant lover in various closets and trying to adjust to life with a wife and child he no longer recognizes. Phyllis has deteriorated to such a degree that she cannot leave her room, surrounding herself solely with a growing collection of shoes. Pam, who has been unconvincingly pretending to be the maid, attempts to explain to Phyllis that she and Howard are in love and planning a life together that doesn't include Phyllis or Bishop. Phyllis confesses to Pam that her incestuous relationship with Bishop has in fact continued to the present, and when Pam states that she and Howard will commit Bishop to an institution, Bishop stabs her to death. We learn that Bishop's cannibalism did not end with his being rescued and he has become a cannibalistic serial killer, giving the shoes of his kills to Phyllis. Howard returns home and repeatedly asks where Pam is, until Bishop presents him with her cut-off leg, which he had until recently been snacking on. Howard's shocked realization of his son's depravity is short lived, as Bishop kills him as well, with Phyllis looking on. The mother and son embrace over the corpse of Howard and run off to get salt, for they are both famished.

Act 3 begins one year later, in a hospital where Bishop has been committed. The audience learns that Bishop has also killed his mother and was institutionalized by the courts. The chilling final act involves a Dr. Nestor (played by the same actor who played Howard) trying to get Bishop to admit his crimes and his culpability. Phyllis, whom Bishop initially denies killing, remains onstage, commanding Bishop to deny his crimes. Popo Martin, a hopelessly optimistic paranoid schizophrenic obsessed with making potholders, tries to kiss Bishop. Popo (played by the same actress who played Pam), represents a potential substitute for Bishop's incestuous desire for Phyllis and, though flawed, a possible future as well. At the play's close, Bishop admits his crimes and his culpability:

> I am Bishop Hogan, that is my name, I am not a deacon of the church. I killed my father and his mistress and the next day, my mother, whom I loved. ... It was the judgment of the court that I was mentally ill at the time of these acts. ... And it was my mother's fault. And my father's. And my own. Because I am what I create: And I understand that I must stay awake all the time, because when I sleep, when I shut my eyes, the monkeys come again. And it is no one's fault. It's the nature of the monkeys.
>
> (*Etiquette,* p. 300)

His reference to the monkeys overlaps with Phyllis' dream at the beginning of the play, of her going to the monkey house at the Bronx Zoo and, to her surprise, all she sees are large men swinging around, yelling and throwing food at one another. These fat men are all in skirts, and all have Bishop's face. The dream suggests that our behavior at its most basic level is not of enlightenment but savagery.

After *Fat Men in Skirts* was produced at the Vortex, it was produced by the Woolly Mammoth Theatre in Washington, D.C. In a coincidence no one could have possibly expected, the details of the cannibalistic serial killer Jeffrey Dahmer were made public just as *Fat Men in Skirts* was finishing rehearsals. Reviews were generally positive, though critics expressed some confusion as to the play's message. The *New York Times* critic David Richards wrote: "Exactly what we're to make of this little bit of surrealism, I couldn't say. ... *Fat Men* just wants to put us in an awkward position. Our urge to laugh is constantly battling the notion that we shouldn't be laughing" ("Life's Underside," p. 68). The play was nominated for

the Helen Hayes Award for best new play of 1992, but the award went to *My Children! My Africa!* by Athol Fugard.

FREE WILL & WANTON LUST *(1991)*

The success of *Fat Men in Skirts* prompted Silver to send his next play, *Free Will & Wanton Lust,* to the Woolly Mammoth Theatre following its New York run at the Vortex. It was produced as part of its 1992–1993 season. The play was conceived as a response to Noël Coward's play *The Vortex* (1924), about sexual vanity and drug use among the British upper classes. The play begins with Claire, a character in the tradition of Coward theatrical aristocracy, as she luxuriates in the afterglow of her latest affair with a much younger lover, an affair that has so convincingly restored her youth and beauty that she is awe-struck by her own reflection.

> I am getting younger! It's an absolute fact. Irrefutable. I get younger and younger with every day and every hour. My skin gets firmer and my hair grows thicker ... Should this keep up, I'll soon take to jacks and hoops. And by year's end, I'll be in a crib. I mean, I've always had a spirit for living, but this is really new. ... And I know you're to blame. You're responsible. I was aging, until I met you, and now, it's reversing. My God, I am lucky.
>
> *(Etiquette,* p. 156)

Claire's connubial bliss with her lover Tony is interrupted when her son, Philip, and her pregnant daughter, Amy, arrive. Amy serves as a drunken Greek chorus to the stage antics unfolding around her, which include Philip's fiancée, Vivian, eventually succumbing to Tony's charms. Act 1 ends with Philip interrupting Vivian and Tony. The highly stylized stage performances and arch dialogue do well to enhance the absurdity of the plot, yet buffer the audience from seeing the flawed humanity and internal motivation of the characters. This tragic humanity becomes the focus of act 2, which is made up of extended monologues by Claire and Philip. The monologues are a dramatic shift in tone and style from act 1, with direct address to the audience and little movement. Claire details her mother's emotional breakdown following her miscarriage,

and explains that sex is the only way that she can feel a connection to another human being. Philip tells a haunting and truly frightening story of a love that descended quickly into obsession and possibly to murder. While the monologues appear at first disconnected from the choreographed antics of act 1, they provide the emotional pain that is being desperately masked in the earlier scene.

Act 3 resumes the action of act 1, and Claire learns that Philip kicked Tony out, but not before Amy told him that he was only one of a long list of impressionable young men Claire has taken to her bed. The play ends with Claire racing out to find Tony, and Philip and Amy turning to each other for comfort. They embrace tentatively, then the kiss "becomes mutual and passionate. After a moment, he takes command: they lunge abruptly into a romantic embrace identical to that of Tony and Claire in Act 1" (p. 216).

Silver, in his introduction to the play, describes the work as "odd" and admits that he isn't sure the entire play works. Yet *Free Will* is a very interesting combination of varying theatrical styles, from Coward to Bertolt Brecht to a combination of the two. Lloyd Rose, reviewing the play for the *Washington Post,* agreed with Silver's characterization of the play as somewhat odd, but praised the piece for its haunting use of language:

> *Free Will and Wanton Lust* is strange, a mermaid piece with a satirical upper body and a tragic tail. But no matter what objections you may have to Act 1, Act 2 couldn't work so powerfully without it. And the final image, in which petty, needy reality is swept up into a star-struck, movieland romantic beauty, is breathtaking. However disparate the play's elements, Silver brings them together here with dazzling theatricality, a visual triumph in his own world of words.

Free Will & Wanton Lust won the Helen Hayes Award for best new play for 1993 and was eventually reworked into Silver's 1999 work *The Eros Trilogy,* a collection of three short, thematically related pieces, "Claire," "Philip," and "Roger and Miriam." The three pieces included Claire and Philip's extended monologues from act 2 and new writing, called "Roger and

Miriam," which follows the evolving relationship between a mother and son over twenty-plus years. The same actress plays Claire and Miriam and the same actor plays Philip and Roger. Where the mother-son pairings of Claire/Philip and Phyllis/Bishop Hogan are seemingly doomed from the beginning, marked by emotional abandonment and little communication, Roger and Miriam fare better. The characters sit at two desks facing the audience and read aloud letters they have written to each other. The letters span decades and, more importantly, chart their emotional journey toward each other. What begins as funny letters from a mother to her son in drama camp soon develop into revealing monologues about love, denial, optimism, and resolution. Miriam admits that her decades-plus marriage to Roger's father was based not on love but on mutual disdain. Roger reveals his homosexuality, and asks his mother her thoughts on his various relationships. The play is less concerned with Roger's homosexuality and Miriam's response to it. Rather, it is just one of the aspects of Roger's life that he comes to share openly with Miriam over time. He falls in love, loses a lover to AIDS, and tentatively, yet optimistically, chooses to love again, with Paul, an HIV-positive man. Miriam, we learn, gets divorced, goes to rehab, returns to the workforce, and eventually embarks on an eight-year affair with her boss, Martin. The affair provides her with the emotional intimacy missing from her marriage. As the years pass and the observations, both large and small, are made, Miriam and Roger continue to write each other. They remain seated, their bodies onstage never touching until the end, when Roger crosses the stage and gives his mother a small ceramic elephant, a figurine that had sentimental value to her and was the impetus for their first great fight. The end of the play and the exchange of the gift is a moment of reconciliation and familial growth that has long been denied to most Silver families.

The Eros Trilogy was produced by the Vineyard Theatre in 1999, where it received generally positive, though muted, reviews. Ben Brantley wrote that the play marked a departure from Silver's more generally "slightly sinister" writing style and, with its move toward tenderness and reconciliation, threatens to be conventional. "Hardcore Silver fans will doubtless find things to savor here, but they should expect neither chills nor feverish excitement. This production, unlike most of its author's work, stays fixed at room temperature" ("Giving Mom a Break," p. E1).

By 1992 Silver had tired of working with the Vortex company. He decided to send his next play out to various off-Broadway theaters, with the hopes that someone would produce it. The play, *Pterodactyls,* would become a hit and usher in a period of his greatest critical and commercial success.

PTERODACTYLS *(1993)*

Whereas in his previous plays Nicky Silver meted out punishment and judgment to individuals drunk on their own myopia, *Pterodactyls* takes larger aim, suggesting that all of civilization, represented in the play as the Duncan family, are dinosaurs at the end of their Darwinian cycle. But rather than the Ice Age, it's denial that is killing them.

The play opens with Todd Duncan attempting to deliver a rambling, disjointed lecture on the history of the universe to the audience. Unfortunately, he has forgotten his notes. His lecture becomes a series of disjointed references that reduce the history of civilization down to morsels like, "And amoebas multiplied and became fish—don't ask me how—which evolved into monkeys. And then one day, the monkeys stood up, erect, realized they had opposing thumbs and developed speech. Thus, Mankind was born" (*Pterodactyls,* p. 8). Todd's profound inability to understand either the scope of the history of the universe or man's seemingly miniscule place in it becomes a theme dominant in this work. Todd, we learn, is the prodigal son returned home after many years away to his family, the Duncans, affluent denizens of the Main Line area west of Philadelphia, to whom he reveals that he has AIDS.

Todd's homecoming coincides with his sister, Emma, having just announced her engagement to

Tommy McKorckle. Emma is a hypochondriac with a poor memory, owing to her having, incongruously, swallowed a shoe as a child, and her fiancé is a homeless orphan employed at Salad City. Her mother, Grace Duncan, while initially skeptical of the union, accepts Emma's news and employs Tommy as the family maid, since their previous maid, Flo, has gone missing. Tommy eagerly dons Flo's old uniform and situates himself into the family as the domestic.

When Todd returns home, Emma, with her poor memory, does not remember him. After Todd reveals to his family that he has AIDS, Grace launches manically into party planning mode—simultaneously planning both Emma's wedding and Todd's funeral. Family patriarch Arthur Duncan tries to reunite with his returned son, but he confuses memories of his own childhood with that of his children to such a degree that he is unable to distinguish one from the other. Silver has created a family so wracked with denial that they fail to take the full measure of their existence or acknowledge any fault they may have had in their (and by extension, the human race's) demise. Then Todd, who has incongruously discovered a nearly complete dinosaur skeleton in the backyard, spends much of the rest of the play assembling it, where it hovers over the family, reminding them and the audience of their impending fate.

Todd, whose name, Emma notes, means "death" in German, becomes the agent of death in the play, but also the agent for truth, for his family and himself. He reveals that he got AIDS by knowingly having unprotected sex and dabbled in illicit drug use. He seduces Tommy into having an affair and infects Tommy with the AIDS virus. Tommy, unknowingly, infects Emma and her unborn child with the disease as well, and Todd gives Emma a gun as a wedding present, suggesting that the best way out of this existence is to end her life. Emma, who has also been in denial about her father's molestation for years, commits suicide. She is shown briefly addressing the audience, explaining that she in fact is much happier now that she is dead. Tommy, the audience learns, dies of AIDS, but has been left in the backyard of the Duncan house, owing to the ground being too frozen to dig up for burial. Only Todd and Grace are left in this now empty, cold, emotionless house. Grace, numbed somewhat by her alcohol-induced fog, longs for the release and relief of death, saying that she thinks she died a long time ago. She dies as Todd tells her the story of the dinosaurs, a story he finishes for the audience, explaining that no one really knows why and how the dinosaurs became extinct. "Some people think there was a meteor. Perhaps volcanic ash altered the atmosphere. Some think they overpopulated and the shells of their eggs became too thin. Or they just ran their course, and their end was the order of things. And no tragedy. Or disease. Or God" (p. 74).

Silver, in a conversation with the play's director, David Warren, explained what he felt the play was about:

> Obviously, it's about denial. Denial's just dandy if it gets you through the day, but we're living at a time when, because of AIDS, it carried a terrible price. We have this epidemic because we didn't want to deal with it. Because as a culture we viewed the people who were dying as expendable. And, of course it's a comedy, employing theatrical genre as a shield, or defense, that these characters use to survive.
>
> (*Etiquette*, p. xvi)

Pterodactyls was initially accepted by Playwrights Horizons, where it received a staged reading. By Silver's account, the reading did not go well and, owing to creative differences between Silver and the artistic staff, the play did not premiere there. It was produced in 1993 by the Vineyard Theatre, on East Fifteenth Street in Manhattan, where Silver has chosen subsequently to premiere nearly every one of his plays since. The play was a critical and commercial success, selling out at the Vineyard, where its run was twice extended. It won the Oppenheimer Award, the Kesselring Prize, and was nominated for a Drama Desk Award. The play marked a turning point in Silver's career, with the first line of David Richards' *New York Times* review of the play reading, "Maybe it's time to start taking playwright Nicky Silver seriously" ("Humans Are the Dinosaurs," p. H5). Ben Brantley praised the play as "so nimbly paced and so piercingly

funny that [it] often soars into its own delightful absurdist heaven, with ludicrously mannered swallows" ("Mining Humor," p. C15). There was talk of the production moving to Broadway to the recently vacated Promenade Theater uptown, but the play did not transfer. Edward Albee's Pulitzer Prize–winning *Three Tall Women,* which had also been produced by the Vineyard Theatre, moved there instead.

THE FOOD CHAIN *(1994)*

After the success of *Pterodactyls,* Silver began working on *The Food Chain.* He chose to premiere it at D.C.'s Woolly Mammoth Theatre, largely because that theater had produced some of his earlier work. The production, directed by Silver, was beset by problems, and while it received generally positive reviews, it wasn't a commercial success. However, when it was produced in New York under the direction of Robert Falls, it became Silver's biggest critical and commercial success, with an extended run at the Westside Theatre of 336 performances. The success of *The Food Chain,* coming soon after *Pterodactyls,* established Silver as one of off Broadway's most important theatrical voices.

The Food Chain skewers the emotional food chain we have structured in today's society of instant gratification and obsession with appearances. The play maintains the farcical antics of Silver's earlier work, and while it isn't quite as serious in tone as act 2 of *Pterodactyls,* the play continues Silver's established critique of America's preoccupation with beauty, sex, and material possessions. The play begins with Amanda Dolor, a thirty-year-old high-strung poet, who calls a suicide hotline and is connected to Bea, a caustic, veteran hotline operator. Amanda reveals that her husband of three weeks, Ford, has been missing for the last two, and she launches into a seemingly disjointed yet touching monologue about her downward spiral, which was prompted by a waiter's innocuous question, "Are you alone?" Amanda articulates the desperate need for human connection that many of Silver's characters share, and her barely contained

rage at her romantic failure calls to mind some of the monologues from *Free Will & Wanton Lust.* Amanda's conversation with Bea ends abruptly when Ford returns home, offering no explanation and no words except for a monosyllabic "Well. ..." Amanda fills in the silences, by turn demanding answers as to his whereabouts, confessing her own crippling self-loathing, desperately apologizing for not being attractive enough, and, finally, silently attempting seduction. The act closes as they embrace.

The pairing of Amanda and Ford is contrasted in scene 2 with that of Serge and Otto. Serge is a handsome, thirty-year-old model who had a brief relationship with Otto, an overweight, unemployed bundle of insecurities and clinging tendencies armed with an arsenal of snacks, which he gorges on with reckless abandon. Otto has shown up at Serge's door in the middle of the night, begging him to take him back. Serge is now in love with Ford and makes every attempt to get Otto to leave, with little success. Otto downs Yodels, Fritos, doughnuts, Slim-Fast shakes, and pretzels, receives more than one phone call from his mother, and yet refuses to leave Serge's home. He claims that he cannot move on because, simply, Serge represents the best possible future imagining of his life and he now defines his existence solely in terms of being with him:

> For years now, you've been telling me that. "Get on with your life." ... But you are my life. ... If it's pathetic, it's pathetic. If it's sick or sad or whatever it is—it is the way it is. I love you. And you will love me again. Someday ... or you won't. But I don't intend to give up trying. I see no advantage in surrender.
>
> (*Etiquette,* p. 43)

The final scene reunites all of the characters in Amanda's apartment. Serge shows up looking for Ford; Otto follows Serge and confronts him. Bea turns out to be Otto's mother and provides impromptu counseling to the distressed Amanda, Serge, and Ford. Bea suggests that Ford not choose between Amanda and Serge and that, instead, they should all live together. Otto is then ceremoniously marched out of the apartment by the disappointed Bea, who threatens to put him on a severe diet and strict exercise regime.

The Food Chain is an uproarious work in the tradition of Georges Feydeau, combining the sinister humor of Silver's dramaturgy with the symmetry and pace of farce. Margo Jefferson, in her review in the *New York Times,* noted that "the formal constraints of farce (the fast tempo, the double-dealing plot twists, the artificial symmetries) are good for Mr. Silver, at least for now" ("90's Obsession," p. H4).

RAISED IN CAPTIVITY *(1995)*

Raised in Captivity became the third critical and commercial success in a row for Silver when it premiered at the Vineyard Theatre on February 28, 1995. Almost a response to his *Food Chain* review from the *New York Times,* Silver's *Raised in Captivity* departs significantly from the farcical tone established in his earlier works, to one of restraint and empathy for familiarly damaged characters.

The play begins in a graveyard, after a funeral service for the mother of the fraternal twins Sebastian Bliss and Bernadette Dixon; she was killed by a dislodged shower head. "Odd," remarks Sebastian, who speaks to the audience, "as I knew her to be a person who primarily took baths" (*Raised in Captivity,* p. 1). Sebastian has been in a state of perpetual emotional and professional paralysis since the death of his lover Simon from AIDS, eleven years earlier. His only real contact with another person is in the form of letters he writes to a convicted murderer, Dylan. Sebastian receives little help from his longtime therapist, Hillary, who is down to one client and has completely lost faith in herself, her ability to be loved, and her ability to treat anyone.

Sebastian, in his attempt at forming another relationship, picks up a male prostitute and brings him back to his apartment. His clumsy attempt at intimacy is thwarted violently when the hustler attacks him and cuts his neck. While bleeding, he is visited by his deceased mother, who tells him that he and Bernadette were the result of a violent rape. In order to fully recuperate from his neck wound (and because of his belief in his dead mother's testimony), Sebastian moves in with his

sister and her husband, Kip, who have recently become parents.

Bernadette and Kip are not without their challenges. Kip has left his dental practice and taken up painting, and their apartment is lined with dozens of his white-on-white canvases. Kip is enthusiastically planning on moving the family to Africa, so that they too can start their lives over. As they prepare for their trip, Sebastian receives a letter from Dylan, who tells him not to write him anymore. Dylan hopes that he is setting Sebastian on the path to forging healthy relationships, and his act of liberation is echoed in Bernadette's decision to set her husband free as well. She refuses to go to Africa and frees Kip from any obligation he may feel toward her or their child. Sebastian and Bernadette end the play choosing to raise the baby together, and they name the baby Simon. In the closing moments of the play Sebastian is able to admit that he did truly love Simon, finally weeping for the loss of his lover, his mother, and everyone he misses.

Theater critics embraced the work, noting its deft balance. Ben Brantley wrote, "The roads to alienation, as modern literature can testify, are many and varied. But they have seldom been mapped out with the fearless combination of comic artifice and heart wrenching empathy that Mr. Silver brings to them. *Raised in Captivity* is about guilt, redemption and self-punishment, and against all odds, it is also very funny" ("Alienation," p. C13).

FIT TO BE TIED *(1997)*

The success of *Pterodactyls, The Food Chain,* and *Raised in Captivity* made Nicky Silver one of the most successful playwrights of the 1990s. Written in 1997, *Fit to Be Tied* was produced by Playwrights Horizons. Silver had been chosen as one of ten recipients of $10,000 writing grants from a program sponsored by Amblin Entertainment, Inc., and Playwrights Horizons. *Fit to Be Tied* maintains a number of Silver's standard dramaturgical devices: direct address to the audience, fast-paced, comedic dialogue about

humanity's dysfunction, and intertextual references to other plays, in this case Tony Kushner's *Angels in America*. While it is not Silver's first play to reference AIDS, it is his first AIDS play, even though the audience never learns if the main character does in fact have the disease.

The play begins with Arloc Simpson explaining to the audience that he has done something bad. Arloc is the wealthy son of a deceased industrialist, and the sole inheritor of his father's estate. This has displeased his mother, Nessa, who is unhappily married and wants to leave her husband, Carl. Arloc is longing to open himself up to someone but is paralyzed by the fear that he may be HIV positive. A former lover, Anthony, has died, and Arloc read his obituary's mentioning of "pneumonia" as code for AIDS. Arloc has had a blood test, the results of which he cannot bring himself to read. The envelope sits, unopened in his apartment. Arloc explains that, mostly to escape the envelope, he goes walking in New York City. After hours of walking up and down streets, with no plan or route in mind, he sees the man of his dreams. Arloc has met an angel.

Any angel in a play about AIDS immediately references the epic *Angels in America,* where a young gay man with AIDS is summoned by an angel to be a prophet. Kushner's play won nearly every Tony Award it was nominated for and was almost immediately heralded as the most important AIDS play of the twentieth century. Silver's angel is, by contrast, a bit more lowbrow: a young runaway named Boyd performing in Radio City Music Hall's Christmas Spectacular, a holiday institution in New York City catering mainly to tourists and out-of-town relatives. While Kushner's angel is religious, Silver's is wearing wings covered in spray glitter that may be toxic, for "half the angels have emphysema" (*Fit to Be Tied,* p. 18).

Arloc manages to invite Boyd over to his apartment and, desperate not to lose out on what he thinks is his last chance at happiness, kidnaps him. Boyd is tied to a chair and hauled into the closet minutes before Nessa arrives, drunk with happiness for having finally left Carl. When Arloc steps out to get Nessa's bags, Boyd bursts out of the closet, hurling himself through the door while still bound, gagged, and tied to the chair. Nessa learns that Boyd does not have feelings for Arloc and realizes that he has been kept here against his will. She offers to pay Boyd to continue a relationship with Arloc.

Nessa's plan is partly motivated by her desire to repair her damaged relationship with Arloc. In this way, Nessa and Arloc's dysfunctional relationship is like those of Phyllis and Bishop Hogan, Claire and Philip, Grace and Todd Duncan, and Bea and Otto. Yet Silver gives Nessa and Arloc the reconciliation and hope that the other mother-son relationships lack. Act 2 finds Nessa, Boyd, and Arloc all living in Arloc's apartment. Boyd and Nessa are enthusiastically preparing for Boyd's film project: a solo performance of Arloc as Mary Tyrone in *Long Day's Journey into Night*. Their living arrangement appears to be satisfying to all of them until Carl arrives, begging Nessa to return to him. She refuses and, in a moment overheard by Arloc, expresses her love for Boyd. Arloc confronts Nessa and she denies the feelings, saying that she was just looking for a way to get rid of Carl. While Arloc isn't quite sure that Nessa is telling the truth, the mother and son find that, for the first time in their lives, they have reached a point of mutual respect and understanding. While they may be in love with the same person, jokingly asking Boyd, "Who will you kiss at midnight?," Nessa and Arloc decide that their somewhat triangular relationship with Boyd is worth saving. Armed with the love and support of both Nessa and Boyd, Arloc is now finally ready to read the contents of the envelope. He follows Nessa and Boyd off stage, to a New Year's Eve party, taking the still unopened envelope with him.

Fit to Be Tied did not achieve the critical praise of Silver's other plays from the 1990s, though reviews were generally positive. Ben Brantley wrote, "*Fit to Be Tied* has moments as funny and as poignant as anything from Mr. Silver's *Food Chain* and *Raised in Captivity*" ("Earthbound Angel," p. C13), yet he argued that the play was unable to come together as a fully developed piece.

NICKY SILVER

THE ALTRUISTS (2000)

The Altruists premiered at the Vineyard Theatre on February 20, 2000. The farce revolves around three simultaneous stories in three different apartments, belonging to Ronald, his sister, Sydney, and Cybil. The dialogue cuts quickly from one scene to another, interrupting one conversation to focus on a different one. The play centers on a dedicated, if disorganized and demented, group of young radicals who are quick to march for causes ranging from AIDS research cutbacks to animal testing to the death penalty, yet just as quickly demonstrate their moral bankruptcy when they frame a young man for murder. Sydney, a shallow, anorexic soap-opera actress, has fired a gun three times into the presumed body of her sleeping boyfriend, Ethan. Terrified, she goes to her brother, Ronald, the center of the protest group, for help. Ronald has recently spent the night with Lance, a young runaway prostitute, and has fallen head over heels, though he admits some surprise when Lance reveals his profession. Proclaiming his unaffected devotion, Ronald asks Lance to live with him and offers him sanctuary, support, and love. At the same time that Sydney is confessing to Ronald, a very much alive Ethan enters her apartment and, seeing a gun on the floor and a lifeless lump under the blankets, thinks Sydney is dead. Also at the same time, Cybil, a member of Ronald and Ethan's radical group, is trying to write a letter ending her relationship with her girlfriend, Audrey. When the corpse is revealed to be Audrey and not Sydney or Ethan, the group decides to frame Lance for the murder, despite initial protestations from Ronald. As Lance is set up, the group ironically exits for their planned protest against the unjust conviction of an innocent young man.

The Altruists received mixed reviews after opening. Critics welcomed the frenetic stage energy of the farce, which reminded a number of reviewers of Silver's early work at the Vortex. Yet more than one reviewer opined that Silver was reaching into the same bag of theatrical tricks. After a number of hits in quick succession, critics suggested that what had originally been seen as breathtakingly new was threatening to become perfunctory. The charge of being conventional would not be applied to his next piece, but it would receive the most negative reviews of Silver's career.

BEAUTIFUL CHILD (2004)

Beautiful Child asks the simple yet profound question, "How do we love someone who falls outside our moral code?" In the play, married parents Harry and Nan learn that their son, Isaac, has left his job as an art teacher after it is learned that he began and engaged in a relationship with a student, an eight-year-old boy named Brian. Isaac asks his shocked parents if he might stay with them, as the secret of his affair with Brian is about to be made public. Harry and Nan, whose own marriage has deteriorated into affairs and general contempt for one another, are now forced to decide if they can help and protect their son, and more importantly, how they might see him as their son and not a monster. Isaac had been "a beautiful child," according to Harry, and while they don't pretend that they were perfect parents, Harry and Nan become desperate to figure out some possible reason why Isaac, their beautiful child, may have done this. Harry, who admits to having a strained relationship with Isaac for much of his life, expresses shock and horror at his son's revelation. Nan, conversely, blames herself for Isaac's crime, saying that years ago she suspected he was capable of this and convinced herself that she did not in fact see what she knew she saw. She explains that she had visited him at his new school and observed him teaching his then eight- and nine-year-old students.

> Victor. His name was Victor. And he waited, still sitting, until Isaac came over and looked at his work. Isaac knelt down, next to him, this perfect child, and put his hand, which seemed so huge, on the tiny shoulder. He talked to him, too softly for me to hear, until he smiled, Victor smiled and blushed and looked at his painting, which I couldn't make out from the back of the room. Then Isaac, our son, moved his hand from the shoulder, and placed his hand on the back of his head, the child's head, and then on his cheek, on his mouth, until he lifted his eyes, the child, and looked at our son. … And they didn't speak. They looked at each other, too closely. Like lovers. Heat and fear and so much

sadness in the air between them. And I knew. I knew. I knew what it was. There was nothing else that it could be.

(Beautiful Child, p. 28)

Ultimately Harry and Nan agree to let Isaac live with them, but only on the condition that he be blinded. Such a punishment, they believe, would obviate any potential attraction he might feel for a child in the future, and, as difficult and shocking as it may be, could potentially be the course of action that restores this family. Harry explains his reasoning to Isaac:

> This is not what I want. Not what I wanted. You are mine. My son. I made you and you are a part of me. And I love you and that is my burden, that is my curse. You come here for safety—you come here for help—and you are me! And you are diseased! AND IT MUST STOP! I MUST STOP THIS! I WILL STOP IT AND THERE IS NO OTHER WAY!

(p. 49)

The play ends with Harry returning to the living room after the blinding, and smiling at Nessa. Their union, it would seem, has been strengthened by this ordeal. Critics were quick to point out the biblical references in the play to the story of Abraham and Isaac, yet the sacrifice that is halted in the Bible is enacted in the play, in order to save the nuclear family.

When *Beautiful Child* opened at the Vineyard Theatre, it received some of the worst reviews of any Silver play. Called "smug" and "third rate" by Donald Lyons of the *New York Post,* critics couldn't get past the initial description of pedophilia to fully consider the subject of the play, a parent trying to love their child. Ben Brantley conceded that the premise of the play carried the promise of a crackling evening of theater, and the first act largely worked. But ultimately he called the play "a symbol-laden, poetic exercise that never achieves dramatic weight or credibility" ("A Troubled Marriage," p. E5). Silver wrote of the devastating reception the play received:

> It was a risky play about an unpleasant subject. … As always I went into the process with high hopes. I had a brilliant cast, a wonderful director and every reason to be enthusiastic. It turned out to be the most difficult play of my career. And then came the reviews. … in the spring of 2004 I felt defeated. I don't want to sound silly. I know how lucky I am. I get to earn a living doing something I adore. And I can do it in my bathrobe if I choose to. But that knowledge didn't help at the time. I was depressed. I replaced writing with eating. I replaced eating with sleeping. I replaced sleeping with watching TV. … The point is, I was depressed. Then, one day I decided if I was going to "leave the theatre," I didn't want it to be with a sour taste in my mouth. And so I wrote *The Agony & the Agony.*

(Agony, p. 3)

THE AGONY & THE AGONY (2006)

Very much a return to the farcical humor of Silver's early work, *The Agony & the Agony* most clearly evokes the structure and prose style of *The Food Chain*, though it is based on an unpublished work from his time at the Vortex, *Cats and Dogs.* *The Agony* is about a forty-something gay playwright named Richard who has been rejected by nearly every theatrical agent and producer. However, on this one particular night Richard has had a burst of inspiration and has cranked out fifty pages in a few hours, only to be interrupted when his wife, Lela, comes home and informs him that Anton Knight, a major theatrical producer, is coming to their home that evening. Lela has just met Anton and is hoping that she can wrangle a way into an audition for his revival of *A Streetcar Named Desire.* Richard, it turns out, submitted a script to Anton Knight years ago and was rejected. Though Knight's rejection is one of thousands that Richard has received (and stored in a large accordion binder), he refers to him specifically as the man who ruined his life and immediately begins plotting what he will say to him, now that he has the opportunity for revenge. While Lela tries to get Richard to leave the apartment before Knight arrives, her current lover, Chet, barges in, asking for $5,000. When Chet learns of Knight's imminent arrival, he also refuses to leave, hoping that he will get cast as Nugget the horse in Knight's rumored upcoming revival of *Equus.* Adding to the farce is Anita, Chet's nine-months-pregnant girlfriend, who interrupts the goings-on

in Lela's apartment to see if Chet has indeed gotten the $5,000, and Nathan Leopold, of the murderous pair Leopold and Loeb, who is the subject of Richard's latest play.

Act 1 assembles all of the characters in a frenzied choreographed movement of timed exits, entrances, and exposition. At the end of act 1 the aforementioned Anton Knight arrives, and much to the dismay of everyone (except possibly Richard), Mr. Knight is no longer a successful theatrical producer but has descended into a life of petty larceny and false claims about his theatrical connections, fed to eager wannabe actors who would do anything to get work. He has come to Lela's apartment with no interest in casting her as Blanche but with the hope that she might serve him dinner. He explains his fall from grace as the result of his difficult marriage to a woman who "ruined" him.

Knight's admission is quickly followed by Richard's confronting him for his negative review. Their argument turns physical, and Richard accidentally knocks Knight out cold. While Knight is unconscious, Anita's water breaks, Chet takes her to the hospital, and Lela gets cast as a corpse in an episode of *Law and Order*. As Knight wakes up, Richard ties him to a chair and forces him to listen to his play, the one he wrote in his burst of creativity earlier in the day. The play ends with Richard reading the lines of his play, which are the same as the opening lines of *The Agony & the Agony*. Has this play been Richard's piece of writing all along? Are we to think of the play as a comic *No Exit*, with the action enveloping in on itself, only to begin again? Silver doesn't provide answers to these questions, nor does he appear to dwell on them.

The *Agony & the Agony* was produced as a lab performance by the Vineyard Theatre, meaning that it never opened to the press. It was never formally reviewed, though the playwright's mother, Jill Silver, offered her caustic but funny assessment of the work, which was published on the back cover of the Dramatists Play Service edition: "*The Agony & The Agony* is proof, once and for all, that hard work, grit and determination almost compensate for a total lack of talent."

THREE CHANGES *(2008)*

A few weeks before *Three Changes* opened at Playwrights Horizons, the *New York Times* profiled Nicky Silver on his return to the stage post–*Beautiful Child*. Silver was unapologetically honest about his level of anxiety regarding his new work, and admitted that the negative reviews (of *Beautiful Child* and other works throughout his career) were always going to be nerve-racking for him. He said, "I cannot imagine I will do this long enough for me to have no emotional response to public response. It's very, very painful when writers write mean things about you. That's just the way it is" (Piepenburg, p. AR7). He admitted that he was a very different person and writer from his early days writing *Fat Men in Skirts*. "I'm much less angry that I was at that stage in my life. … I've come to value human beings more than I did. I think I thought art was more important, and I don't. I think people are more important." Interestingly, *Three Changes* is about the destruction of a marriage by a person who ultimately views another person, specifically his brother, as disposable.

Nate and Laurel are a seemingly happy couple living in New York City. Though they have been unable to have a child, they convey enough of a sense of loving familiarity, material comfort, and emotional contentedness to make them believe that everything is fine. All of this changes when Nate's older brother Hal arrives, and he slowly and purposefully pushes Nate out of his own family. While Hal initially appears charming, he eventually becomes an insidious presence in Nate and Laurel's life, taking over Nate's life, wife, and very identity.

This theme of sibling rivalry references Silver's 1998 work *The Maiden's Prayer,* about the fractured relationship between Cynthia, a beautiful and successful young bride, and her hard-drinking sister, Libby. Cynthia has married Taylor, the object of Libby's unrequited love. Libby finds a fellow sufferer in Taylor's childhood friend Paul, who has harbored a secret love for him for years. When Cynthia delivers a stillborn child, her once-ideal marriage disintegrates and she finds support, surprisingly, in the arms of her estranged sister. This quiet, medita-

tive drama, about the nature of love and sacrifice, received mixed reviews from the critics, as did *Three Changes*.

THE LYONS *(2011)*

In the fall of 2011 Nicky Silver's comedy *The Lyons* premiered at his theatrical home, the Vineyard Theatre. The biting comic drama, about the gathering of the Lyons family for the impending death of its patriarch, acknowledges the time-tested tenets of Silver's dramaturgy. The jokes come quickly and are often brutal. As her husband, Ben, lies in a bleak hospital room, Rita Lyons sits in a chair next to his bed, pouring over a decorating magazine and offering up her ideas for her soon-to-be redecorated living room, once her husband isn't alive to argue with her color scheme. This is classic Silver: the caustic, critical mother, the estranged adult children, the displaced father, the ill-fated reunion. In many ways, *The Lyons* stages many of the characters that Silver has created before. And yet, the characters move beyond blaming the parents and bitter self-assessment to argue at the end for the right to personal happiness. Rita Lyons, now widowed, chooses to live out her life in the (possibly temporary) embrace of a younger man, in a tropical paradise, away from her chronically unhappy adult children. Claiming that she has done all that she could for them, she asserts a need to live for herself, to take account of her own happiness, that signals her move toward emotional independence. She is an agent of positive change in ways that earlier Silver mothers, like Phyllis Hogan, Claire, Bea, and Grace Duncan, were not. *The Lyons* ends on a note of rare optimism, with Rita marching confidently toward happiness on a beach, her daughter opening herself to the possibility of happiness, and her son tentatively reaching out for that long-sought human connection.

When *The Lyons* was wrapping up its Broadway run, Silver was asked to document the experience of his first Broadway play for the *New York Times*. He offered up "Bye for Now, Broadway, My New Friend," an assortment of comi-cally self-deprecating anecdotes about his anxieties, such as his suggestion to advertise the play as *The Book of Mormon,* and his admittedly obsessive-compulsive need to attend every performance of the show, telling the actors to "have fun" at every intermission of every performance. Yet he also admitted to retaining the same love of the theater that first brought him to New York in the 1970s, claiming simply that "it's my home." He closed his essay with a story of his trying to get to the famed theater-district restaurant Joe Allen in time to join *Lyons* star Linda Lavin for dinner. He arrived too late and the restaurant was closed, so he headed to Shake Shack, a still hip, though eminently more plebian eating establishment. "It figures," he wrote, casting himself as the perpetual outsider, a lifelong admirer of the theater who is still looking into the private party rooms of celebrity and beautiful people. And yet, this is perhaps another one of his inventions.

Silver's career as playwright, sometime director, and constant worrier continues. After more than three decades of writing plays, his dramas remain some of the funniest, most acerbic farces in the contemporary American canon. He challenges audiences to spend time with characters who are profoundly fractured and isolated, separated from human connection, understanding, and sometimes the world. The community they long for is found in the theater, with the audiences who gather to watch them and listen and be challenged by his words. And to laugh. Always, to laugh.

Selected Bibliography

WORKS OF NICKY SILVER

PLAYS

Pterodactyls (acting edition). New York: Dramatists Play Service, 1994.

Raised in Captivity (acting edition). New York: Dramatists Play Service, 1995.

Etiquette and Vitriol: The Food Chain and Other Plays.

New York: Theatre Communications Group, 1996. (Contains *The Food Chain, Pterodactyls, Free Will & Wanton Lust, Fat Men in Skirts.*)

Fit to Be Tied (acting edition). New York: Dramatists Play Service, 1997.

The Eros Trilogy (acting edition). New York: Dramatists Play Service, 1999.

The Maiden's Prayer (acting edition). New York: Dramatists Play Service, 1999.

The Altruists (acting edition). New York: Dramatists Play Service, 2001.

Beautiful Child (acting edition). New York: Dramatists Play Service, 2004.

The Agony & The Agony (acting edition). New York: Dramatists Play Service, 2008.

Three Changes (acting edition). New York: Dramatists Play Service, 2009.

The Lyons. New York: Theatre Communications Group, 2012.

OTHER WORKS

"Bye for Now, Broadway, My New Friend." *New York Times,* July 8, 2012, p. AR4.

"Theater Talkback: A Seat at the Table." ArtsBeat. *New York Times,* April 26, 2012. http://artsbeat.blogs.nytimes.com/2012/04/26/theater-talkback-a-seat-at-the-table/.

CRITICAL AND BIOGRAPHICAL STUDIES

Piepenburg, Erik. "A New Play and Much Else to Worry About." *New York Times,* August 20, 2008, p. AR 7.

Savran, David. "Nicky Silver." In *The Playwright's Voice: American Dramatists on Memory, Writing, and the Politics of Culture.* New York: Theatre Communications Group, 1999. Pp. 213–236.

Schildcrout, Jordan. "No Tragedy: Queer Evil in the Metaphysical Comedies of Nicky Silver." In *We Will Be Citizens: New Essays on Gay and Lesbian Theatre.* Edited by James Fischer. Jefferson, N.C.: McFarland, 2009. Pp. 90–102.

REVIEWS

Brantley, Ben. "Mining Humor from the Decline of a Class." *New York Times,* October 21, 1993, p. C15. (Review of *Pterodactyls.*)

———. "Alienation, AIDS, and Murder, but Keeping a Sense of Humor." *New York Times,* March 1, 1995, p. C13. (Review of *Raised in Captivity.*)

———. "Earthbound Angel Tangles with Loneliness and Love." *New York Times,* October 21, 1996, p. C13. (Review of *Fit to Be Tied.*)

———. "Thwarted Hearts Tempered by Bons Mots." *New York Times,* February 23, 1998, p. E9. (Review of *The Maiden's Prayer.*)

———. "Giving Mom a Break (Sort of) in a Star Turn." *New York Times,* February 9, 1999, p. E1. (Review of *The Eros Trilogy.*)

———. "But Enough About You: Let's Talk About Me." *New York Times,* March 7, 2000, p. E1. (Review of *The Altruists.*)

———. "A Troubled Marriage and the Trouble with Junior." *New York Times,* February 25, 2004, p. E5. (Review of *Beautiful Child.*)

———. "In a Fragmented World, the Search for Family Cohesion Can Become Scary." *New York Times,* September 17, 2008, p. E5. (Review of *Three Changes.*)

Jefferson, Margo. "90's Obsession Finds a Home in Old Forms." *New York Times,* September 24, 1995, p. H4. (Review of *The Food Chain.*)

Lyons, Donald. "Problem 'Child.'" *New York Post,* February 26, 2004.

Richards, David. "Life's Underside Often Gives You the Woollies." *New York Times,* August 11, 1991, p. 68. (Review of *Fat Men in Skirts.*)

———. "Humans Are the Dinosaurs in *Pterodactyls.*" *New York Times,* October 24, 1993, p. H5. (Review of *Pterodactyls.*)

Rose, Lloyd. "Free Will's Flip Sides; Frenetic Pain and Mirth at Woolly Mammoth." *Washington Post,* January 19, 1993, p. C10. (Review of *Free Will & Wanton Lust.*)

HUNTER S. THOMPSON

(1937—2005)

Jeffrey Bickerstaff

HUNTER S. THOMPSON's work can best be summed up by Frank Mankiewicz' assessment of *Fear and Loathing on the Campaign Trail '72*. Mankiewicz, who served as George McGovern's campaign director, called it "the most accurate and least factual book about the campaign" (quoted in Wenner and Seymour, p. 173). Thompson initially intended to become a novelist, but after failing for years get his fiction published, he wrote freelance newspaper and magazine articles to pay the bills. His artistic breakthrough came when he invented "Gonzo" journalism, a fiction/nonfiction hybrid that transcended New Journalism and relied on Thompson's extraordinary powers of observation and exaggeration. He could recognize and zero in on a particular aspect of a subject, an aspect that captured the essence of a person or event, and magnify it beyond fact to a kind of truth writ large.

Thompson wrote incisively about America, particularly the American Dream, the national character, and the emotional aftermath of the failure of the 1960s countercultural movement. He was a fantastic writer: great rhythm, fascinating verbs, bizarre images, and jarring juxtapositions. And he was funny. He was funny in that scathing way that wounded idealists with a deep moral core often are. His idealism and morality might surprise those familiar only with his image. But beneath the caricature of the madman in the dark aviator shades with the cigarette holder, idealism and morality are there in his work, swirling in a whirlwind of hallucinogenic hyperbole, sustaining Hunter S. Thompson's vision of the American Dream.

LIFE

Hunter Stockton Thompson was born on July 18, 1937, to a modest, middle-class family in Louis-ville, Kentucky. In his 2008 biography of Thompson, *Outlaw Journalist,* William McKeen recounts the ways in which, even during his young boyhood, an odd combination of high-spirited hooliganism and intellectual curiosity was manifest in Hunter's complex personality. On the one hand, he concocted an incendiary device from clothespins and matchsticks that enabled him to ignite piles of autumn leaves from his bicycle. On the other, he frequently led his boisterous companions to the library, where they would sit and read quietly for hours. In the fourth grade, Thompson's house became the meeting place for the staff of the *Southern Star,* a newspaper launched and edited by a friend who had procured a mimeograph machine. Thompson wrote many of the paper's stories, which included detailed accounts of vomiting dogs, dead snakes, and neighborhood scuffles. One particularly newsworthy event occurred the summer before the birth of the *Star,* an event that reflected the other side of the young writer's character. Two FBI agents accused Thompson of destroying a mailbox, which he had in fact demolished by binding it to an intricate network of pulleys and ropes and pulling it in front of an oncoming bus. When told that his accomplices had come clean, Thompson called the agents' bluff, his father took his side, and he got away with his federal crime.

Thompson's father died in the summer of 1952, and Thompson would miss his support when he faced serious legal trouble at the end of high school. Although Hunter was a rowdy boy while his father was living, the elder Thompson wielded authority and provided a moderating influence. With his father gone, the teenage Thompson learned to get alcohol via intimidation of liquor store clerks, bribery of waiters, and outright theft. His booze-fueled mayhem included

robbing the collection box of a local church, getting arrested for vandalizing a gas station, and, on multiple occasions, spending the night in jail for driving drunk. Less than two weeks before his graduation, Thompson's delinquency culminated in the robbery of two couples he and two of his friends discovered making out in a parked car. After one of his accomplices unsuccessfully demanded money, Hunter threatened to rape one of the girls unless they handed over their wallets. The victims wrote down the license plate of the perpetrators' vehicle, and before long Hunter and his friends were in police custody.

Because the other two boys were each sons of prominent attorneys, one received probation and the other a fine of fifty dollars. But the case turned out differently for Thompson, whose family lacked status and wealth. The judge was unmoved by Thompson's pleading mother and the testimony of one of the female victims, who had gotten to know Hunter during visiting hours at the jail and spoke in court on his behalf. In Jann S. Wenner and Corey Seymour's oral history *Gonzo: The Life of Hunter S. Thompson* (2007), a childhood friend underscores the fact that the other boys were released because of the influence of their fathers while Thompson's was dead and gone. The experience jarred Thompson, who seemed to have been a part of that upper-crust world until the very moment it mattered most.

McKeen writes that Thompson's foray into elite Louisville society began when he transferred from Atherton to Male High after he was beaten up by the football team for ridiculing their performance. Male proudly sent graduates to Ivy League schools, and it was the birthplace of the Athenaeum Literary Association, an elite high school club that touted such eminent alumni as Robert Penn Warren. Athenaeum's rituals matched the two sides of Thompson: every Saturday the boys would sit in suits and ties for two or three hours critiquing each other's writing before launching into a night of untrammeled drunken debauchery.

Thompson was developing his literary identity during this time. He began typing out novels by such literary luminaries as F. Scott Fitzgerald,

Ernest Hemingway, John Steinbeck, and William Faulkner to get inside the feel and rhythm of great writing and to cultivate his own style. He published an essay titled "Security" in the Athenaeum yearbook that, with its attack on conformity and differentiation between living and merely existing, suggested a solidifying worldview. One fellow Athenaeum alumnus argues in *Gonzo: The Life* that their youthful rebellion stemmed from an impulse to be more individualistic, which he links to their conception of the American Dream, a concept that would preoccupy Thompson for much of his career. Hunter was also known in high school as "a champion of the underdog," a point of view that would inform his political writing (McKeen, p. 17). So too did his belief that the police lie and that injustice is rampant, two assertions he made in a letter to his mother after being sentenced to sixty days in jail for the robbery incident. He was also voted out of the Athenaeum and forced to miss his graduation. In jail, while thinking about the freedom of his accomplices, Thompson came to believe that the poor are punished for things the rich aren't and that the game is "fixed" (Wenner and Seymour, p. 20).

Thompson joined the air force when he got out of jail. Stationed at the Eglin base near Tallahassee, Florida, he enrolled in night classes at Florida State University. McKeen reports that Eglin's director of education noted Thompson's pursuit of literature courses and, after Thompson lied about editing his high school paper and covering sports for the Louisville *Courier-Journal,* he found himself on the sports staff of the *Command Courier,* the base paper. Thompson had to find a journalism textbook and quickly familiarize himself with such trade phrases as "lede" and "nut graf"; he excelled at writing, though, and he reveled in action verbs and the freedom to coin new words, which had a profound impact on the development of his voice. In his column, "The Spectator," he once incorporated a (fictional) note from the editor, which made it appear as though the piece had been cobbled together in his absence, a device he would notably employ in *Fear and Loathing in Las Vegas* (1989). After six months of diligence,

Thompson fell again into a pattern of carousing and clashes with authority. One bright spot was a notice that he had been reinstated as a member of the Athenaeum's class of 1955. Another was his certainty that he wanted to spend his life expressing his individuality through his type-writer, which he now realized was preferable to having it explode in eruptions of frustrated violence (Thompson, *The Proud Highway,* p. 318).

Thompson conveyed these sentiments toward the end of his air force stint after being deeply impressed by Ayn Rand's *The Fountainhead.* According to McKeen, his literary heroes during this phase of his life included Aldous Huxley, Henry Miller, and H. L. Mencken. Sherwood Anderson's *Winesburg, Ohio* captivated him, and he envisioned his own work exposing the hypoc-risies of America's middle class. He admired Jack Kerouac's *On the Road* and considered it politi-cally important but was unimpressed with the author's other books. He also studied Jean-Paul Sartre, Edmund Wilson, and Thomas Jefferson. His friend the novelist William Kennedy states in *Gonzo: The Life* that Thompson essentially read the Western canon, and he highlights such authors and works as James Joyce's *Ulysses,* J. P. Donleavy's *The Ginger Man,* John Dos Passos' *U.S.A.,* Dylan Thomas, Albert Camus, D. H. Lawrence, *Don Quixote,* Dante's *Inferno, Huckle-berry Finn*, and Norman Mailer. Douglas Brin-kley, the literary executor of Thompson's estate, underscores the influence of Mailer, going so far as to call *Advertisements for Myself* Thompson's "bible" (Wenner and Seymour, p. 435). He also notes that Mailer's coverage of the 1964 Repub-lican Convention in his *Cannibals and Christians* was an important precursor to *Fear and Loathing on the Campaign Trail '72.*

After his honorable discharge from the air force, Thompson took a job as a reporter with the *Jersey Shore Herald* but lasted only a month. He felt the pull of New York and managed to land a position as a copyboy for *Time* magazine. Although *Time* provided tuition assistance and ample time for Thompson to pursue literary style and short-story writing courses at Columbia, his propensity for drinking at work and insulting his superiors ensured the brevity of his tenure. His stint with the *Daily Record* in Middletown, New York, was similarly brief. A reporter colleague recalls in *Gonzo: The Life* that Thompson's bosses disliked him for running around the newsroom barefoot, and they terminated him after he demolished a vending machine to dislodge the candy bar he had paid for.

Thompson was at a crossroads: he could continue with the fantasy of becoming a writer or he could actually commit to it. McKeen writes that he determinedly left his Middletown apart-ment for a cheap, ultra-ascetic cabin in the nearby rural area of Cuddebackville, where he lived hermetically and wrote ceaselessly. He saved his rejection slips and developed a still-unpublished novel titled "Prince Jellyfish." Thompson came to think of himself existentially as a writer dur-ing this time of spartan isolation, and he fostered a feeling of kinship with wordsmiths who preceded him.

The major events in the next long phase of Thompson's professional life made their way into his work. *The Rum Diary* (1998) was inspired by his time in Puerto Rico, which began during the first week of 1960 when he arrived to work for a sports magazine entitled *Sportivo.* Influenced by Henry Miller's descriptions of the area, as well as Miller's combination of fact and fiction, Thompson spent the next year as a caretaker for a large property in Big Sur, California. He wrote an article on the libertine sexual culture of the region that landed him his first national publica-tion and got him evicted. When his grandmother died and left him fifteen thousand dollars, Thompson bought a camera and a ticket to South America, where he successfully established himself as a foreign correspondent. Thompson launched his sojourn just as the *Wall Street Jour-nal* was launching an offshoot called the *National Observer.* Thompson and the *Observer* proved a good fit; his style was too loose for traditional American newspapers and too unpolished for weekly magazines. Upon his return to the United States, the *Observer* offered Thompson a steady job as a features writer, but he opted instead to follow the youth movement to San Francisco. *Observer* editors angered Thompson when they

declared the San Francisco cultural revolution too weird a subject for its audience. Tensions worsened in 1964 when they dismissed the Berkeley Free Speech Movement as an outburst of spoiled rich kids instead of, as Thompson sensed, the initial rumblings of an impending social upheaval.

As his relationship with the *National Observer* frayed, Thompson received a serendipitous letter from Carey McWilliams, editor of the left-leaning liberal journal the *Nation*. The *Nation* published his account of the Free Speech Movement in 1965, and McWilliams himself pitched Thompson the idea of writing about outlaw motorcycle gangs. Thompson's 1965 article on the Hell's Angels led to seven book offers. His *Hell's Angels: A Strange and Terrible Saga,* published in 1967, proved to be an enormous success and catapulted the young author to fame, if not fortune. Thompson used his notoriety to gain access to the 1968 presidential election, which resulted in a disparaging *Pageant* piece on his nemesis Richard Nixon and—after he, along with scores of other journalists, demonstrators, and innocent bystanders were clubbed by Chicago police during the Democratic National Convention—in his increased radicalization and intensified hatred of authority.

After two years of living in Woody Creek, Colorado, during which time he witnessed avaricious developers steadily encroaching into the pristine mountain wilderness, Thompson channeled his righteous rage into local politics when he convinced local hippie attorney Joe Edwards to run for mayor of Aspen on the Freak Power ticket. Thompson himself ran (unsuccessfully) for sheriff of Pitkin County the following year. His first contribution to *Rolling Stone* was his depiction of the Edwards campaign, published during the homestretch of his own run in October 1970. This was the beginning of a relationship that spawned a pair of 1971 articles that evolved into *Fear and Loathing in Las Vegas* and his yearlong coverage of the 1972 presidential election that yielded *Fear and Loathing on the Campaign Trail '72.*

Although Thompson ultimately found the *National Observer* politically stultifying, it played an integral role in the development of his writing. The editor Clifford Ridley recalls in *Gonzo: The Life* that he read the letters Thompson sent with his articles to other editors, who reacted enthusiastically and suggested publishing them. "Chatty Letters During a Journey from Aruba to Rio" signaled the emergence of Thompson's Gonzo style, metajournalism that highlighted the process of journalism, stories that revolved around getting the story. Traipsing across South America, Thompson was unaware that he was part of a loosely defined movement that would come to be known as "New Journalism." Tom Wolfe disliked the term but cataloged the genre in the 1973 anthology *The New Journalism,* which includes Thompson's "The Kentucky Derby Is Decadent and Depraved." Wolfe had become conscious that something was happening in the early sixties when *Esquire* published Gay Talese's feature on the former heavyweight champion Joe Lewis, a piece of factual journalism that employed many techniques of fiction and read like a short story.

Literary devices anchored in factual accuracy, as opposed to what McKeen describes as Thompson's "mixture of fact with fancy" (p. 137), suggests a point where New Journalism crosses into Gonzo territory. James Carville, chief strategist for Bill Clinton's 1992 presidential campaign, marveled that Thompson's "powers of observation were only exceeded by his powers of exaggeration" (Wenner and Seymour, p. 305). Thompson, said Carville, would start with "the slightest grain of something to it and make it into this hilarious thing," and while his articles were entertaining "there were a bunch of insights." William Kennedy argued that Thompson's Las Vegas articles were "hardly journalism." They were rooted in historical fact, but even his notes of the actual events were "a transcript of his performance and his wild and fanciful imagination, the first phase of the novel. What he then wrote was a mutation of the fictional form, which is why his place is secure, because nobody can ever do that again" (pp. 141–142). Kennedy added that the new form Thompson created was "a fictional hybrid with his persona dominant" (p. 331).

Indeed, Thompson's persona, which often went by the name Raoul Duke, was the main character of most of his work from (at least) the time of the Kentucky Derby piece onward. Wolfe and Kennedy noted a change in Thompson after the publication of *Hell Angel's,* when he reveled in his celebrity, put his image at the forefront, and turned his life into a kind of performance art. Kennedy also saw a change in Thompson's writing when his persona "captured" him (pp. 89–90). His former wife Sandy Thompson, to whom he was married from 1963 to 1980, watched her husband transform from a craftsman willing to rewrite a piece multiple times, a person who "wanted to be read and thought of as a serious human being, a serious writer," to the drug- and booze-addled "gonzo person" who "was more about the image. And the way it turned out was absolutely not the life he dreamed" (Wenner and Seymour, pp. 123, 174, 177). The balance between the two sides of Thompson's complex personality had tipped toward the debauched hedonist at the expense of the devoted wordsmith with noble ambitions. He even became a literal cartoon character in 1974 when Garry Trudeau introduced Uncle Duke in *Doonesbury.*

With few exceptions, accounts of the last thirty-plus years of Thompson's life read like a tragic warning against the perils of fame and addiction. He failed to cover the resignation of Richard Nixon, the great political enemy of his adult life. He flew all the way to Zaire to cover the Muhammad Ali–George Foreman fight, but he failed to make it to the stadium and missed seeing Ali—a fellow native of Louisville and countercultural hero—regain the heavyweight title. He blew so many assignments that *Rolling Stone* publisher Jann Wenner eventually gave up on him. He squandered a lucrative public speaking career because his addictions rendered him too unreliable to book. He watched, seemingly helpless, as the changes he supported in the sixties got pushed back by Ronald Reagan and later George W. Bush.

Still, the last phase of his life also had positive periods. Louisville honored its wayward son with Hunter S. Thompson Day in December 1996. In the same year, the prestigious Modern

Library published a twenty-fifth anniversary edition of *Fear and Loathing in Las Vegas,* which was followed by a thirtieth-anniversary edition of *Hell's Angels.* In 1997, the first volume of Thompson's collected correspondence, *The Proud Highway,* was published to outstanding reviews. Thompson was securing his place in American literature by culling his past accomplishments.

But the overall trajectory of his life and work was trending sharply downward. Late-period books were collages of reworked columns and letters; *Better Than Sex* (1994) even contained multiple faxes and photocopies. William Kennedy lamented Thompson's descent into self-parody, while other friends saw him as trapped by the mythological image he created, an image he continued to promote with his weekly ESPN column "Hey Rube" and lackadaisical collections such as *Songs of the Doomed* (1990) and *Kingdom of Fear* (2003). Toward the end, friends would sometimes find him crying alone. Sandy said it was because he was a "tragic figure," tortured by his failure to fulfill his genius (McKeen, p. 349).

Depressed, and with his body breaking down, Hunter S. Thompson committed suicide on February 20, 2005. The press accentuated Thompson's caricature rather than his writing life, and his expensive pyrotechnic memorial certainly didn't help matters. But Tom Wolfe thoughtfully honored the writer more than the image (although there was some indulgence of that side of Hunter, too) in his *Wall Street Journal* remembrance published two days after his death. Wolfe placed Thompson in the tradition of Mark Twain, whose writing was also a concocted mixture of journalism, memoir, and wild invention. He concluded by nominating Thompson as the twentieth century's greatest English-language comic writer.

BATTLING THE GREEDHEADS

Written in the early 1960s but not published until 1998, *The Rum Diary* reads like a novel by a young writer struggling to find his voice and work through questions of what it means to have

integrity and be successful. The protagonist, Paul Kemp, tells his story in the lean, tough-guy language of Ernest Hemingway and Raymond Chandler, replete with sharp verbs, a disdain for phonies, and an inclination toward violence: "The act of selling is repulsive to me. I harbor a secret urge to whack a salesman in the face, crack his teeth and put red bumps around his eyes" (*The Rum Diary,* p. 11). Paul is also upfront with the reader about his own conflicts, which include dueling tendencies toward idealism and a sense of imminent doom, and a hatred for the immorality of profiteering versus a desire to get rich.

Indeed, the means by which Paul could get rich—that is, developing the pristine land on Puerto Rico and the surrounding islands—repulse him as much as salesmen do. Of course in Paul's world salesmen and development are inextricably linked, and after expressing his desire to rough up sellers he disgustedly describes riding on a four-lane highway with housing developments on either side, followed by a sign proclaiming "El Jippo Urbanización," a new subdivision filled with identical houses (p. 12). (*Urbanización* simply means a housing development, while *El Jippo* references the old and culturally dicey term "to gyp," meaning to take by deceit or swindle.) As social criticism, *The Rum Diary* may lack subtlety, but the developers and tourists Thompson lampoons throughout the story probably weren't particularly nuanced, either. Hotels stand between the ocean and old houses that once looked upon the beach. Bars catering to vacationers, decked out in glistening garb, look as though they were brought down intact from Catskills resorts.

As Paul's eye for detail suggests, he's a reporter, and he has just taken a job with the *San Juan Daily News*. He realizes that the paper, founded with the noblest intentions by Ed Lotterman, has been infiltrated and co-opted by moneyed interests after meeting with the recently installed editor Nick Segarra, whom he dismisses as a pimp. Segarra comes from a wealthy and politically connected family; he went to Columbia University and his father was the attorney general of Puerto Rico. Segarra's classmate at Columbia, Hal Sanderson, worked for the *Daily News* for a year before taking a job with the public relations firm Adelante, which hustles to draw investors to Puerto Rico. The simmering tension between authentic journalism and island boosterism erupts when Segarra puts the kibosh on a story written by Paul's friend, Yeamon, detailing why Puerto Ricans emigrate to New York. Paul appreciates the piece for transcending the particulars of Puerto Rico; to him it is about leaving home despite overwhelming odds, and, having left the Midwest for New York, he relates to it. But after meeting with Segarra, Lotterman dismisses the article as a useless collection of people griping and rails against Yeamon for making trouble. Yeamon ultimately takes a stand and loses his job.

Paul's tacit disregard for Segarra gets him ostracized at a time in his life when he feels like he's getting too old to continue making such influential enemies. Sanderson, despite his friendship with Segarra, is decent toward Paul and invites him to his home for dinner. Sanderson bridges the divide between Paul and Segarra and functions as a temptation figure in the narrative. Paul knows he's a phony, but he thinks Sanderson is more or less honest with him. He also respects Sanderson for his work ethic, even if he doesn't have any use for the type of work he does. More importantly, he recognizes the parallels between Sanderson's story, that of a young Midwesterner who moved to New York to reinvent himself, to his own, which implicitly raises the possibility of Paul abandoning journalism for public relations and getting rich. Sanderson nudges Paul toward the dark side when he offers him a thousand-word assignment for the *New York Times* travel section, which, as a puff piece designed to entice New Yorkers to travel to Puerto Rico, inversely mirrors the piece of authentic journalism that cost Yeamon his job. Sanderson also offers Paul a gig writing a brochure for Zimburger, an Adelante client who will use Paul's work to attract investors to the resort, which will include two hotels and a hundred cottages, he is building on Vieques Island. Paul accepts both, and when he jokes that he has to get back to work to finish an exposé, Sanderson tells him not to let his "boy scout ethics" run away with him (p. 105).

Considering the context of the novel's recurring religious metaphors, Sanderson doesn't just tempt Paul, he actually sets out to convert him. In his narration, Paul points to the Hilton Hotel as the cornerstone of what he calls "The Boom," and he states that Conrad Hilton "had come in like Jesus and all the fish had followed" (p. 13). Later he notes that the State Department was using Puerto Rico to demonstrate capitalism's viability in the Caribbean. Those delivering the message, he adds, "saw themselves as heroes and missionaries, bringing the holy message of Free Enterprise to the downtrodden *jibaros*" (p. 69). (Thompson develops this connection between militarism and capitalism in an interesting way, which will be discussed below.) Paul also compares statements from the San Juan Chamber of Commerce to proclamations from Jehovah's Witnesses, and he conjures images of fanatical capitalist crusaders.

Paul, of course, uses these metaphors ironically. Sanderson actually leads him into temptation rather than toward salvation, a point made explicit when, coveting a forty-foot racing sloop, Paul imagines a sign reading "For Sale—One Soul, no less" (p. 149). He thinks it delusional that a person can live a life of material comfort "without hiring himself out as a Judas Goat" (p. 134), an interesting term that references the betrayal of Christ and suggests that he could use his writing not to inform, but to lead the masses—the downtrodden *jibaros*—to a metaphorical slaughter. Finally, he describes the current pushing him to do the right thing as "devilish" because following his conscience would lead him into a life of impoverished insanity (p. 134). According to the logic of the novel, integrity and monetary success simply cannot coexist, and Paul Kemp is a conflicted protagonist who ultimately wants both.

Thompson hints at what fuels Paul's desire for money when he establishes his class position during Sanderson's dinner party. He talks with a New York couple about yachts, which they're familiar with because they come from a world where just about everybody owns one. Paul, by contrast, knows about yachts from having worked on them. Time spent with Sanderson leads Paul to realize he's ready to trade purity for comfort. He is also ready for his own address, a car, and any other large item that would provide him with a stabilizing influence. Soon after procuring a car and place of his own, he considers it merely a good start and sees no reason why he shouldn't have a porch, a garden, or even a beach. Paul's material lust culminates in the scene in which, no longer satisfied with his car and apartment, he finds himself coveting the racing sloop. He even admits to himself that if such a sign asking for his soul had actually been on the bow, he might have struck a deal.

On the other hand, Paul is disgusted by the people, save for Sanderson, who could make him wealthy. He depicts a San Juan cocktail party as an exhibition of "all that was cheap and greedy in human nature" (p. 70). In the same passage he also throws out such terms as "thieves," "hustlers," and "philistines." Later, when he goes to Vieques with Zimburger, he is profoundly moved by the beauty of the land he is about to help befoul. He is snapped out of his reverie by Zimburger's "ugly chattering" about hills on which he planned to plop hotels and houses and line with sewer pipes, swamps he would drain for shopping centers, and clean white beaches already staked for cabanas. Paul had not, he reminds himself, "come here to admire this place, but to write a thing that would sell it" (p. 129). Worse, as he thinks about it later, he is being paid to ruin the only place that had given him a feeling of peace in the last ten years.

Worse still, the money would ultimately come from Zimburger, who personifies all of the despicable traits found in the San Juan cocktail scene and then some. Paul refers to him as a "jackass" and a "greedhead" (pp. 103, 53), the latter epithet being one that Thompson would carry with him into his battle against developers in Aspen. Thompson uses the Zimburger character to represent the overlap of militarism and capitalism, an overlap that can be summed up by the word "empire," which Thompson lambastes as belligerent and greedy. Zimburger had been a captain in the Marine Corps, is a member of the reserves, and often wears his uniform and shouts about his desire to invade Cuba, which had

recently fallen to Fidel Castro during the time in which the novel is set. Thompson also uses the impending development of Vieques to make essentially the same point. Two-thirds of the island was a target range for the marines, who also used the area for maneuvers; now the pristine paradise of the other third was to be mutilated into a resort for American tourists. Later, as he hears explosions in the distance, Paul ruminates on how the U.S. Navy stripped the neighboring island Culebra of its magic when it began using it as an aerial bombing range. Later still, Paul's remembrance of his moment of peace on Vieques is spoiled when he remembers Zimburger and the marines, "the empire builders, setting up frozen food stores and aerial bombing ranges, spreading out like a piss puddle to every corner of the world" (p. 153). In this passage Thompson explicitly puts American consumer capitalism and militarism under the umbrella of empire, which seems intent on reaching every corner of the world. That he likens it to urine leaves little room for misinterpretation.

The last fourth of the novel busily ties up a lot of dramatic loose ends that have to do with the solvency of the newspaper, a lust interest, and legal problems. Allusions to Joseph Conrad are strewn throughout, and Thompson seems to encourage readers to engage *The Rum Diary* with an eye toward *The Heart of Darkness* (1899) and the unfortunately titled *Nigger of the Narcissus* (1897). Paul's conflict is resolved by implication rather than satisfactorily, and Thompson will never be lauded for his development of female or Puerto Rican characters. Still, his criticism of the American empire is barbed, even if the sting was removed by its appearing some thirty-plus years after it was written, and the story indicates that in addition to being concerned with balancing commercial success with personal integrity, Thompson cared deeply about the issue of land development—one might say land exploitation—and despised consumer society's relentless encroachment into nature. *The Rum Diary* thus retroactively provides context for the political stand the author would take in Aspen in 1969 and 1970, when he aligned himself with freaks and dropouts against greedhead land developers.

"The Battle of Aspen" first appeared in *Rolling Stone* magazine in October 1970, and it was republished as "Freak Power in the Rockies" in *The Great Shark Hunt* (1979). The piece opens in a frenzy two hours before the polls were set to close on Election Day 1969, when it appeared that Joe Edwards, a twenty-nine-year-old "head" lawyer who had successfully sued the city of Aspen the year before for harassing hippies, might become the town's new mayor. Thompson put Edwards up to running based on his own Freak Power theory, which basically entailed running a ten-day voter registration campaign aimed at local drug users and dropouts who didn't want to be hassled with politics. Thompson figured that in a three-way race, the Freaks could swing the election, provided they actually showed up to vote.

Thompson's analysis of the difficulty of getting these people to exercise what he calls their "long-dormant vote" provides a snapshot of the ennui gripping what was left of the counterculture in the aftermath of the 1960s. After "the nightmare of failure that gripped America between 1965 and 1970," the "Berkeley-born" idea of defeating the system by fighting it from within via activist politics "gave way to a sort of numb conviction that it made more sense in the long run to Flee, or even to simply hide" (p. 155). Thompson explains that refugees from Haight-Ashbury arrived in Aspen by the hundreds during the late 1960s; many eventually moved on, while many others stayed and took on jobs as carpenters and service sector workers and settled into tiny apartments, shacks on the outskirts of town, and trailers.

From his experience with Bohemian enclaves in San Francisco and Greenwich Village, Thompson understood "the basic futility of seizing turf you can't control" (p. 156). As an astute cultural observer he recognized that the Aspen land grab he was battling matched an unvarying cycle that begins when "a low-rent area suddenly blooms new and loose and human—and then fashionable" (p. 156). This simultaneously attracts media and police attention, which snowballs into even more media, "which then attracts fad-salesmen and hustlers—which means money, and that at-

tracts junkies and jack-rollers." The malevolent action of the latter brings yet more publicity that attracts, "for some perverse reason" Thompson doesn't grasp, "an influx of bored, upward mobile types who dig the menace of 'white ghetto' life" and whose expensive tastes drive the rents up and out of the price range of the original settlers, who move on yet again (p. 156).

The goal of the Freak Power movement was to protect the land and to give leverage to people who valued the area as a place to live rather than as an investment, people who wanted to be able to walk outside and still be able to smile at what they saw. In the context of *The Rum Diary,* one can imagine Thompson working to protect wilderness that had given him the same sense of peace Paul Kemp felt on that Vieques beach. The Zimburgers in this true-life tale were those with the most to lose from an Edwards victory: "the sub-dividers, ski-pimps and city-based land-developers who had come like a plague of poison roaches to buy and sell the whole valley" (pp. 159–160). The Edwards platform promised to prevent the state from building a four-lane highway in town and to go a step farther and ban all downtown automobile traffic. Apartment buildings that would block the view of anybody who might want to look up at the mountains would also be prohibited, as would what Thompson describes as "land-rapes." "Greedheads" would be zoned out of existence to reach the goal of creating "a town where people could live like human beings, instead of slaves to some bogus sense of Progress that is driving us all mad" (p. 160).

Edwards lost by just six votes out of twelve hundred cast, a result close enough for Thompson to try for sheriff the next year. He lost in yet another squeaker, which prevented him, per his own platform, from ripping up the streets and replacing the asphalt with sod, changing the name of the town to "Fat City" to keep the aforementioned greedheads from profiting off the name "Aspen," banning the sale of drugs for profit, ensuring that the sheriff and his deputies never carry firearms in public, and establishing a Research Bureau to provide facts to citizens interested in preventing "land-rapers" from find-

ing loopholes in antiquated laws and setting up such things as tar-vats, scum-drains, and gravel pits.

Despite Edwards' loss and his own impending defeat, "Freak Power in the Rockies" has a tone of optimism that resonates throughout the article. Years after the energy of the youth movement he followed to San Francisco had peaked, Thompson was in the arena, in the Age of Nixon, doing battle against forces he despised and working hard to make his ideals a political reality. This positive energy is missing from "The Kentucky Derby Is Decadent and Depraved" and *Fear and Loathing in Las Vegas.* Nixon's triumph looms large in each work, and each features Thompson as a wounded warrior, bitter and bewildered that the cultural forces he tellingly describes as atavistic have emerged from the upheaval of the sixties unscathed and belligerently un-evolved.

DECADENCE AND DEPRAVITY AND FEAR AND LOATHING

Back home in Louisville to cover the Kentucky Derby roughly fifteen months after Nixon's 1969 inauguration, Thompson is immediately repulsed by a drunken lout from Texas he sizes up as "here once again to make a nineteenth-century ass of himself in the midst of some jaded, atavistic freakout with nothing to recommend it except a very saleable 'tradition'" ("The Kentucky Derby," in *The Great Shark Hunt,* p. 27). To dampen his revelry, Thompson convinces the Texan that the Black Panthers and several busloads of crazy whites are on their way to Louisville to start a riot. This trenchant put-on emanates from a seething resentment Thompson feels toward those so existentially unnerved by the social unrest of the era that they retreat into cynically spectacular carnivals of tradition such as the Derby, a point underscored when the deflated man longingly asks, "Where can you get *away* from it?" and Thompson replies, "Not here" (p. 26).

But it's actually Thompson who can't escape the realities of the counterculture—that is, that Nixon is calling the shots and the conservative backlash continues to gain momentum. Headlines

and radio bulletins heralding the U.S. invasion of Cambodia, the deployment of four thousand troops near Yale University to combat a Black Panther protest, and the National Guard massacring students at Kent State in Ohio hover around the edges of the Derby, haunting the author, tormenting him with news that the movement he embraced is losing in a rout. The Kentucky Derby carousers represent the entrenched caste that has so far survived the revolution, and when Thompson meets up with the English artist Ralph Steadman, who is assigned to illustrate the article, they search out the face that will be the lead drawing, the "mask of the whiskey gentry—a pretentious mix of booze, failed dreams and a terminal identity crisis; the inevitable result of too much inbreeding in a closed and ignorant culture" (p. 31). He adds that the face he sought in Churchill Downs "was a symbol, in my own mind, of the whole doomed atavistic culture that makes the Kentucky Derby what it is" (p. 31).

That the culture that defines the Kentucky Derby is doomed appears, at first glance, to indicate a glimmer of hope. Steadman explains in *Gonzo: The Life* that the story was about the people Thompson hated in Louisville; he was there to get even with the establishment he had been nursing a grudge against for years. After years of living in New York, Puerto Rico, San Francisco, and abroad, it appeared Thompson considered himself beyond Louisville, and even if he couldn't overthrow the gentry that had let him rot in jail, he could write a caustic screed renouncing his hometown and its most sacred ritual. The twist comes the morning after the race, when Thompson and Steadman finally find the quintessentially decadent face they've been looking for, and it turns out to be Thompson's brutally hungover visage in the mirror of his hotel room.

Thompson thus simultaneously railed against and embraced his hometown—he was complicated. More importantly, one phrase describing the face they're looking for, that "pretentious mix of booze, failed dreams and a terminal identity crisis," reads presciently—eerily so—when considered in light of Thompson's final years: his alcoholism, his unrealized literary dreams, and his struggle with his persona. James Silberman, Thompson's editor at Random House, says in reference to *Hell's Angels* that Hunter "was his own subject" (Wenner and Seymour, p. 86); William McKeen, writing about *Prince Jellyfish* in *Outlaw Journalist,* states that regardless of what Thompson "started writing about, he ended up writing about himself" (p. 50). That same idea certainly holds true for "The Kentucky Derby Is Decadent and Depraved," and it also holds true for *Fear and Loathing in Las Vegas.*

There are other similarities between the "Kentucky Derby" and *Las Vegas* pieces. One is the tone of mourning for the decline of the counterculture. Another is the way the author pairs the Thompson/Duke character with a sidekick; in place of Steadman, who did illustrate the book, *Las Vegas* features the protagonist's attorney, Dr. Gonzo. Such a pairing underscores the hero's journey tradition that Thompson embraces, and it prepares the reader for a plunge into the belly of the beast, be it Churchill Downs or the Las Vegas Strip. The call to action occurs in the hallucinogenic *Fear and Loathing in Las Vegas* when a uniformed dwarf delivers a pink telephone to Raoul Duke, who's lounging in the patio section of the Beverly Hills Hotel, expecting the call but not knowing from whom it would come. He hangs up and the quest is set: embark on an excursion into Las Vegas to find the American Dream.

On the literal level the assignment is to cover a motorcycle race called the Mint 400 and, later in part 2, the National District Attorneys Association's Conference on Narcotics and Dangerous Drugs. But the literal level evaporates like ether when the drugs begin to take hold, and the reader is dropped right into the red convertible as it careens along the scorching desert highway toward Vegas. Duke and Gonzo play a tape recorder to counteract the radio, a duality Thompson employs throughout the story. As the radio broadcasts "One Toke over the Line," which name-drops "Sweet Jesus" multiple times, the tape recorder expresses "Sympathy for the Devil" (pp. 4–5).

This reference to the Rolling Stones takes on greater significance when considered in the

context of some of Thompson's other work. Recall that *The Rum Diary*'s Paul Kemp describes the current leading him to do the right thing, his conscience, as "devilish." "Sympathy for the Devil," which alliteratively declares cops criminals and sinners saints, fits perfectly into the Thompson worldview. What's more, in *Fear and Loathing on the Campaign Trail '72,* Thompson compares hearing Bobby Kennedy's voice four years after the senator's assassination to hearing the Stones "cutting through the doldrums of a dull Sunday morning on a plastic FM station." He explains that he feels a "a strange psychic connection between Bobby Kennedy's voice and the sound of the Rolling Stones," a connection rooted in being "part of the same trip, that wild sense of breakthrough in the late Sixties when almost anything seemed possible" (p. 123). Thompson states that the era as a whole peaked on the last day of March 1968 when President Lyndon Johnson announced he wouldn't run for another term. It was a victory against the Old Order, and whether the next president was Gene McCarthy or Bobby Kennedy, the war in Vietnam seemed like it would be over by Christmas.

Of course that triumph was followed by an unrelenting and merciless pushback by the Old Order: Martin Luther King and Bobby Kennedy were assassinated in April and June, the brutal 1968 Democratic National Convention occurred in August, and the choice between Hubert Humphrey—vice president in the Johnson administration—and Richard Nixon was no choice at all. As Thompson puts it, "'The Movement' was finished, except for the trials, and somebody else was dealing" (p. 124). Three years later, "Sympathy for the Devil," a song about revolution that implicates the listener in the death of both Kennedys, functions in a book set in the early days of the Age of Nixon as nostalgia for the energetic high point of the counterculture.

Thompson references other popular songs to signal that the wild sense of breakthrough of his era had degenerated into a controlled step backward. He dismisses John Lennon's rallying cry of "Power to the People—Right On!" as a decade too late, while Dr. Gonzo argues that when "punks" like Lennon try to be serious they

only get in the way (p. 21). In the grand ballroom of the Desert Inn, Debbie Reynolds, a musical comedy star whose heyday was in the fifties, dons a silver Afro wig and dances ridiculously to the trumpeter Harry James's rendition of "Sergeant Pepper." Later in their hotel room, Thompson denounces Three Dog Night's "Joy to the World" as "gibberish" and muses, "First Lennon, now this.… Next we'll have Glenn Campbell screaming 'Where Have All the Flowers Gone?'" (p. 58). Thompson conjures this absurd image of a quintessentially middle-American mainstream star belting out an antiwar song, which isn't much more contradictory than the millionaire former Beatle posing as a man of the people or even more incredible than the Debbie Reynolds ersatz psychedelic spectacle, to suggest that "The Movement's" music had been reduced to bandwagon sloganeering and outright burlesque; it had been co-opted, sanitized, and repackaged for plastic FM stations and soused nightclub audiences. Thompson's immediate juxtaposition of "Joy to the World" with Jefferson Airplane's *Surrealistic Pillow* album, particularly the song "White Rabbit," underscores this distinction between the authentic and parodic.

This isn't to say that "One Toke over the Line" was a hippie ditty scrubbed clean for Middle America (even if it once received an amusingly oblivious performance on *The Lawrence Welk Show*). Vice President Spiro Agnew actually denounced Brewer & Shipley, the folk duo who composed and recorded the song, as subversive to America's youth. Still, the song does act as a counterpoint to "Sympathy for the Devil." In addition to the obvious pitting of Jesus versus Lucifer, "One Toke over the Line" depicts a person sitting in a railway station waiting to go home, an indication that something has ended, which contrasts with the sense that anything was possible at the height of Bobby Kennedy's presidential run. The song actually recurs twice more in the book, each time at the airport amid an ambiance of defeated anxiety. And since "toke" is an obvious reference to marijuana (Agnew got that part right), one could read Thompson's use of the song to suggest that the revolutionary energy of the counterculture was

sapped by rampant drug abuse. Indeed, the excessively stoned Duke and Gonzo can barely even manage to check into a hotel, let alone run a revolution.

In fact, readers who glorify the drug abuse in the book tend to overlook the Samuel Johnson quotation that serves as *Las Vegas'* epigraph: "He who makes a beast of himself gets rid of the pain of being a man." Thompson/Duke is in mourning for The Movement, he's in pain, and he uses drugs to make a beast of himself. A sense of loss abounds: in one particularly noteworthy passage, one of many that suggest that *Fear and Loathing in Las Vegas* is due for an annotated edition, Thompson describes having recently watched Joe Frazier defeat Muhammad Ali, who sought to regain the title he had been stripped of for being a conscientious objector to the Vietnam War. He compares Frazier—however unfairly—to Nixon, and he reads the fight as an appropriate end to the sixties. He also alludes to the conviction and escape of Timothy Leary, the Harvard professor of psychology turned acid advocate who coined the phrase "Turn on, tune in, drop out" in 1967; the domestication of Bob Dylan, who by 1971 was putting out music that strongly suggested he was past his creative peak; the murder of both Kennedys; and the federal prison stint of Owsley Stanley, the sound engineer for the Grateful Dead who set up a private lab and produced over a million hits of LSD.

But perhaps no passage, written by anybody, eulogizes the 1960s as eloquently as Thompson's famous wave rumination. During a "nervous night in Las Vegas," Duke/Thompson recalls San Francisco in the middle sixties being "a very special time and place to be a part of" (pp. 66–67). During that time

> You could strike sparks anywhere. There was a fantastic universal sense that whatever we were doing was *right*, that we were winning....
>
> And that, I think, was the handle—that sense of inevitable victory over the forces of Old and Evil. Not in any mean or military sense; we didn't need that. Our energy would simply *prevail*. There was no point in fighting—on our side or theirs. We had all the momentum; we were riding the crest of a high and beautiful wave....

So now, less than five years later, you can go up on a steep hill in Las Vegas and look West, and with the right kind of eyes you can almost *see* the highwater mark—that place where the wave finally broke and rolled back.

(p. 68)

One of the terrific aspects of *Fear and Loathing in Las Vegas* is how Thompson can switch from the poetic to the analytical. Near the end of the book, he argues that the break in the youth movement came when the Hell's Angels attacked an antiwar march. Thompson pointedly notes that the Angels were acting on their hardhat instincts, which means that the counterculture schism was not just a rift between the Greasers and Longhairs; it was a schism between bikers from the lower or working class versus students from the upper middle class.

This section of *Las Vegas* recalls the extensive reporting Thompson did on the subject in *Hell's Angels*. In that book he establishes the class position of the Hell's Angels early on, stating that the members who do work usually do so either part-time or erratically in warehouses, garages, or on docks. By 1965 the gang had come into fashion among the hipster establishment of the Bay Area as alienated working-class heroes. The publicity the Angels had been getting came after the Berkeley student rebellion, and Thompson writes that those in the radical/liberal intellectual circles interpreted the Angels' notoriety as an indication of a natural alliance. Thompson actually connected the Angels, with whom he'd been riding for a year to research his book, with Ken Kesey and his Merry Pranksters. According to Thompson, they had their best party at Kesey's La Honda property during Labor Day Weekend 1965, when they all bonded over heaping doses of acid.

The honeymoon, as Thompson calls it, came to a spectacular end on October 16 when the Hell's Angels pummeled the participants of a Get Out of Vietnam demonstration at the border of Oakland and Berkeley, a border that itself serves as a class threshold. The Angels who had partied with Berkeley liberals at Kesey's threw fists and epithets at those same liberals: "When push came to shove, the Hell's Angels lined up solidly with

the cops, the Pentagon and the John Birch Society" (*Hell's Angels*, p. 236). This apparently shocked the hipster establishment, but it didn't surprise Thompson, who argues that the Angels' overall outlook has always been fascistic and that "their political views are limited to the same kind of retrograde patriotism that motivates the John Birch Society, the Ku Klux Klan and the American Nazi Party" (pp. 236, 237). The keys to this quotation are Thompson's use of the term "retrograde," which gets us back to "atavistic," and his direct reference to American racism and fascism, which he alludes to in *Fear and Loathing in Las Vegas.*

Thompson refers to Nevada as an atavistic state, and he goes a step further when he refers to Las Vegas as "grossly atavistic" (pp. 71, 173). He suggests that the 1960s, let alone the counterculture, never really took hold in Las Vegas, which he argues is like taking a step back to the 1950s. Vegas is a city without a viable underground newspaper, a city where Frank Sinatra and Dean Martin—two crooners who predate rock and roll—are thought of as "far out," a city filled with middle-American tourists, and a city that welcomes conventions for segregated organizations. In addition to Sinatra, Thompson states that Las Vegas is the turf of Bob Hope and Spiro Agnew; he references the vice president again when he argues that Nixon would have been an ideal mayor, with Attorney General John Mitchell serving as sheriff and Agnew in charge of the sewers. Las Vegas represents the belly of the beast, a kind of interminable Churchill Downs West with lounge singers and slot machines, a terrible place to have to search for the American Dream.

Of course the fact that the American Dream is to be found in such a place goes a long way toward making Thompson's point about what has happened to America. Ironic references to Horatio Alger, who wrote dozens of potboiler rags-to-riches novels extolling the virtues of bootstrap-pulling hard work, abound. In Vegas, however, the gambling masses wish to emerge instantly rich from a chaotic night at the craps and card tables. Worse still, Duke is also horrified to hear "The Battle Hymn of Lieutenant Calley" on the radio when he enters the city, and while covering the motorcycle race he encounters a gang of fascistic rednecks in dune buggies wreaking havoc in the desert. To divert their wrath away from him, Duke points them toward a (presumably nonexistent) big black jeep he says contains the CBS executive who put *The Selling of the Pentagon* on the air. (The "Battle Hymn" was a jingoistic anthem contrived in support of Lieutenant William "Rusty" Calley, who was convicted of the My Lai massacre; the CBS documentary revealed that the Pentagon, in defiance of army regulations, allocated funds to generals doing public relations work for the military. The government responded by subpoenaing CBS files, and when the network refused, a free speech debate raged.) The reactions to My Lai and the Pentagon exposé indicate how deep and wide the nation's militaristic streak runs, and Thompson suggests that such an inclination, combined with the shiny and superficial knee-jerk instant gratification represented by Las Vegas, spells doom for the American Dream.

This doom is realized in a scene, which Thompson constructs, owing to a breakdown suffered by Raoul Duke, as an editor's note introducing a transcription of a conversation that occurs when Duke and Gonzo stop at a taco stand to ask directions to a place called the American Dream. By stripping the scene to the bare basics, just dialogue bookended by a brief note from the "editor," Thompson creates an immediacy that sets up the reader for an image that gives objective form to the book's pervading sense of loss. The proprietors of the taco stand remember the American Dream as the Old Psychiatrist's Club, a discothèque catering not to literal psychiatrists but to the crazies steeped in the drug scene. Here Thompson implies that The Movement, although suffused with drugs and considered crazy, truly believed in the American Dream of reinvention and self-improvement, the dream that a nation could remake itself just as Horatio Alger's plucky protagonists evolved into new and better individuals. The two distinct names for the place indicate two distinct perspectives on the counterculture. That it was located on Paradise Avenue is self-explanatory, as is the fact that

HUNTER S. THOMPSON

Duke and Gonzo discover that it burned down three years ago, which is to say, in 1968. The sojourners find only a slab of charred concrete in a weeded vacant lot.

ON THE CAMPAIGN TRAIL IN 1972

With *Fear and Loathing on the Campaign Trail '72,* which is largely a compilation of the articles he wrote for *Rolling Stone* during the year he spent covering the presidential election, Thompson discovers a glimmer of hope for the American Dream in the form of Senator George McGovern. The book takes the form of a monthly diary of sorts, and save for a few footnotes, each entry represents the perspective of its time; the June articles chronicling McGovern's victory in the California primary, for example, offer no indication of the colossal beating he was in for that November. Although by late summer Thompson recognizes the inevitability of McGovern's defeat, he is still openly disheartened by it and his prose reflects those feelings. Thompson certainly doesn't worry about any breach of journalistic ethics, though. In January he makes it clear that with the exception of sports statistics and Dow Jones reports, "objective journalism" doesn't exist, and the term itself is pompous and contradictory.

He also scorns the boozy camaraderie that develops between politicians and reporters as detrimental to the work that each should be doing. Thompson suggests that because he has no interest in establishing long-term access to those who wield political power, he could write appropriately antagonistic pieces without worrying about torching any bridges. As a result, Thompson's political writing remains trenchant, scathing, and darkly hilarious even after forty years. He describes the personal style of an important McGovern staffer as hovering "somewhere between that of a state trooper and a used-car salesman" (p. 59), and he imagines having a "bastard" from the Ed Muskie campaign "dropped down an elevator shaft" (p. 114). Discussing the imminent demise of Muskie's run, Thompson writes that the candidate "talked like a farmer with terminal cancer trying to borrow money on next year's crop" (p. 127).

Those are rough passages, but nothing compares to the scorn Thompson heaps upon Hubert Humphrey, who was running again for the Democratic nomination. Humphrey, Thompson fumes, "was a swine in '68 and he's worse now," and he rants that the former vice president "should be put in a goddamn bottle and sent out with the Japanese Current" (p. 118). He compares Humphrey's speaking style to "an eighty-year-old woman who just discovered speed" (p. 140); states that even though they don't make them like Hubert anymore, "he should be castrated anyway" (p. 239); and he calls him a "treacherous brain-damaged old vulture" (p. 238). Thompson also renounces the realities of campaign reporting, which makes it difficult for even the best of the objective journalists to write their genuine impressions of a candidate.

Thompson not only relays his genuine impressions, he speculates on the best way for McGovern to forge a winning coalition. In an excerpt that recalls "Freak Power in the Rockies," he states, months before the primaries, that experts dismissing McGovern's chances take it as a given that the politically alienated—a group that includes students, blacks, and dropouts—won't even bother to register to vote. Thompson counters that these groups elevated Bobby Kennedy in 1968, and they're still around. A month later, Thompson optimistically turns his eye toward the roughly twenty-five million people eligible to vote for the first time owing to the baby boom and the Twenty-Sixth Amendment. Combined, these forces constitute what one pollster calls "The Sleeping Giant vote" (p. 57).

In the end, the vaunted youth vote, along with forty-nine states, breaks for Nixon, and Thompson writes a poignant postmortem that delves deep into the national character. Using quotations from Bobby Kennedy, Thompson posits each candidate as representative of one side of the dichotomous American character: McGovern, "the most decent man in the Senate," versus Nixon, who "represents the dark side of the American spirit" (pp. 111, 372). Thompson goes farther, arguing that McGovern is one of only a few twentieth-century presidential candidates "who really understands what a fantastic monu-

ment to all the best instincts of the human race this country might have been, if we could have kept it out of the hands of greedy little hustlers like Richard Nixon" (p. 389). To Thompson, Nixon represents the nation's corrupt and violent side, Mr. Hyde and the Werewolf, the shyster, the bully that most of the world's other countries fear and despise because of America's unhesitating willingness to kill anybody on the planet who threatens its comfort. And he won twice.

Senator McGovern, in an interview with Thompson conducted a month after the election, attributes his loss to the fact that the electorate had grown weary of the activism of the sixties. When Nixon took over, that era receded into the past and things began to quiet down. McGovern posits that his campaign, which looked capable of bringing about fundamental change, scared people leery of falling back into the energetic upheaval of the previous decade. When Thompson pithily suggests that the senator ran "a sixties campaign in the seventies," McGovern agrees (p. 454). Thus, when Thompson, earlier in the book, had recalled Nixon's 1969 inauguration as "a king-hell bummer" with "a stench of bedrock finality to it," he was right (p. 71). Ultimately, the optimism that resonates throughout the early chapters of *Fear and Loathing on the Campaign Trail '72* fades into elegiac tones reminiscent of *Fear and Loathing in Las Vegas*. The Movement was over and it was time to move on, but Thompson's life story suggests that he simply couldn't. And that's a king-hell bummer indeed.

CONCLUSION

Carl Bernstein has said that in spite of Thompson's image as an "outlaw libertine," he was "actually a moralist" (McKeen, p. 293). Thompson's work, a discussion of the national character and the best and worst aspects of it, gives credence to Bernstein's claim. To say that Thompson wrote about the American character by no means contradicts the idea, stated above, that he was his own subject. After Bobby Kennedy's assassination, for example, Thompson couldn't reconcile two aspects of himself, the pacifist and the gun-owning NRA member. He

pitched a story on the gun lobby to *Esquire,* and what was supposed to be a three-thousand-word piece ballooned to over eighty thousand when he delved deep into his own psyche. The conflicting sides of his own character reflected contradictory aspects of America, just as *The Rum Diary* articulates the struggle between integrity and greed, "Freak Power in the Rockies" explores how the drive to participate in activist politics clashes with the desire to drop out, and *Fear and Loathing in Las Vegas* pits sincere idealism against a beastly flippancy. *Esquire* ended up rejecting the story, but Douglas Brinkley sees it as a "fully realized" work from Thompson's brilliant late sixties and early seventies period (McKeen, p. 359). *The Gun Lobby* is one of the books Brinkley plans to release over time to ensure Thompson does not wind up a dismissed figure. These works will undoubtedly, in the same way that the volumes of Thompson's collected letters have, broaden our perspective of both Hunter S. Thompson and what it meant to be an American in the late twentieth century.

Selected Bibliography

WORKS OF HUNTER S. THOMPSON

BOOKS AND ANTHOLOGIES

Hell's Angels: The Strange and Terrible Saga of the Outlaw Motorcycle Gangs. New York: Random House, 1966; New York: Ballantine, 1996; New York: Modern Library, 1999.

Fear and Loathing in Las Vegas: A Savage Journey to the Heart of the American Dream. New York: Random House, 1971; New York: Vintage Books, 1989.

Fear and Loathing on the Campaign Trail '72. San Francisco: Straight Arrow Books, 1973; New York: Grand Central, 1973.

The Great Shark Hunt: Strange Tales from a Strange Time. New York: Summit Books, 1979. (Includes "The Kentucky Derby Is Decadent and Depraved" and "Freak Power in the Rockies.")

The Curse of Lono. New York: Bantam Books, 1983.

Generation of Swine: Tales of Shame and Degradation in the '80s. New York: Summit Books, 1988.

Songs of the Doomed: More Notes on the Death of the American Dream. New York: Simon & Schuster, 1990.

Better Than Sex: Confessions of a Political Junkie. New York: Random House, 1994.

The Rum Diary: A Novel. New York: Simon & Schuster Paperbacks, 1998.

Screw-jack. New York: Simon and Schuster, 2000.

Kingdom of Fear: Loathsome Secrets of a Star-Crossed Child in the Final Days of the American Century. New York: Simon & Schuster, 2003.

Hey Rube: Blood Sport, the Bush Doctrine, and the Downward Spiral of Dumbness: Modern History from the Sports Desk. New York: Simon & Schuster, 2004.

Fear and Loathing at Rolling Stone: The Essential Writing of Hunter S. Thompson. Edited by Jann S. Wenner. New York: Little, Brown, 2008. Republished with an introduction by Paul Scanlon, New York: Simon & Schuster, 2011.

LETTERS

The Proud Highway: Saga of a Desperate Southern Gentleman, 1955–1967. New York: Ballantine, 1997.

Fear and Loathing in America: The Brutal Odyssey of an Outlaw Journalist, 1968–1976. New York: Simon & Schuster, 2000.

CRITICAL AND BIOGRAPHICAL STUDIES

Bingley, Will, and Anthony Hope-Smith. *Gonzo: A Graphic Biography of Hunter S. Thompson.* London: SelfMade-Hero, 2010.

Burns, Jim. "*Hey Rube: Blood Sport, the Bush Doctrine, and the Downward Spiral of Dumbness: Modern History from the Sports Desk* (Book)." *Library Journal* 129, no. 13:89 (2004).

Cleverly, Michael, and Bob Braudis. *The Kitchen Readings: Untold Stories of Hunter S. Thompson.* New York: Harper Perennial, 2008.

Connors, Theresa. "*Fear and Loathing in Las Vegas*: A Savage Journey to the Heart of the American Dream." *Library Journal* 131, no. 12:121 (2006).

Gibney, Alex, director. *Gonzo: The Life and Work of Dr. Hunter S. Thompson: Collector's Edition.* DVD. Magnolia Pictures, 2008.

Hounion, Morris. "*Fear and Loathing in America* (Book Review)." *Library Journal* 125, no. 19:69 (2000).

McKeen, William. *Outlaw Journalist: The Life and Times of Hunter S. Thompson.* New York: Norton, 2008.

Steadman, Ralph. *The Joke's Over: Bruised Memories: Gonzo, Hunter S. Thompson, and Me.* Orlando, Fla.: Harcourt, 2006.

Stephenson, William. *Gonzo Republic: Hunter S. Thompson's America.* New York: Continuum, 2011.

Thompson, Anita. *The Gonzo Way: A Celebration of Dr. Hunter S. Thompson.* Golden, Colo.: Fulcrum, 2007.

Thompson, Anita, ed. *Ancient Gonzo Wisdom: Interviews with Hunter S. Thompson.* Cambridge, Mass.: Da Capo Press, 2009.

Wenner, Jann S., and Corey Seymour. *Gonzo: The Life of Hunter S. Thompson: An Oral Biography.* New York: Little, Brown, 2007.

Wolfe, Tom. "The 20th Century's Greatest Comic Writer in English." *Wall Street Journal,* February 22, 2005. http://online.wsj.com/article/SB110903593760860492.html.

OTHER SOURCES

Perlstein, Rick. *Nixonland: The Rise of a President and the Fracturing of America.* New York: Scribner, 2008.

Pollock, Bruce. "Liner Notes—Tarkio Reissue." BrewerandShipley.com. http://brewerandshipley.com/Bios&Liners/Notes_TarkioReissue.htm.

FILMS BASED ON THE WORKS OF HUNTER S. THOMPSON

Where the Buffalo Roam. (Based on Thompson's "The Banshee Screams for Buffalo Meat.") Directed by Art Linson; screenplay by John Kaye. Universal, 1980.

Fear and Loathing in Las Vegas. Directed by Terry Gilliam; screenplay by Gilliam, Tony Grisoni, Tod Davies, and Alex Cox. Universal, 1998.

The Rum Diary. Directed by Bruce Robinson; screenplay by Robinson. Film District, 2011.

Cumulative Index

All references include volume numbers in boldface roman numerals followed by page numbers within that volume. Subjects of articles are indicated by boldface type.

A

"A" (Zukofsky), **Supp. III Part 2:** 611, 612, 614, 617, 619, 620, 621, 622, 623, 624, 626, 627, 628, 629, 630, 631; **Supp. IV Part 1:** 154; **Supp. XVI:** 287, *287*

Aal, Katharyn Machan, **Supp. IV Part 1:** 332; **Supp. XXIII:** 54

Aaron, Daniel, **IV:** 429; **Supp. I Part 2:** 647, 650

Aaron's Rod (Lawrence), **Supp. I Part 1:** 255

Abacus (Karr), **Supp. XI:** 240–242, 248, 254

Abádi-Nagy, Zoltán, **Supp. IV Part 1:** 280, 289, 291

"Abandoned Farmhouse" (Kooser), **Supp. XIX:** 117, 119

"Abandoned House, The" (L. Michaels), **Supp. XVI:** 214

"Abandoned Newborn, The" (Olds), **Supp. X:** 207

"Abandoned Stone Schoolhouse in the Nebraska Sandhills, An" (Kooser), **Supp. XIX:** 124–125

"Abba Jacob" (Nelson), **Supp. XVIII:** 177

"Abbé François Picquet"(Kenny), **Supp. XXIII:** 153

Abbey, Edward, **Supp. VIII:** 42; **Supp. X:** 24, 29, 30, 31, 36; **Supp. XIII:** 1–18; **Supp. XIV:** 179

Abbey's Road (Abbey), **Supp. XIII:** 12

Abbott, Carl, **Supp. XVIII:** 142

Abbott, Edith, **Supp. I Part 1:** 5

Abbott, Grace, **Supp. I Part 1:** 5

Abbott, Jack Henry, **Retro. Supp. II:** 210

Abbott, Jacob, **Supp. I Part 1:** 38, 39

Abbott, Lyman, **III:** 293

Abbott, Sean, **Retro. Supp. II:** 213

ABC of Color, An: Selections from Over a Half Century of Writings (Du Bois), **Supp. II Part 1:** 186

ABC of Reading (Pound), **III:** 468, 474–475

"Abdication, An" (Merrill), **Supp. III Part 1:** 326

'Abdu'l-Bahá, **Supp. XX: 117, 122**

Abel, Lionel, **Supp. XIII:** 98

Abel, Sam, **Supp. XIII:** 199

Abelard, Peter, **I:** 14, 22

Abeles, Sigmund, **Supp. VIII:** 272

Abeng (Cliff), **Supp. XXII:** 66, 69–71

Abercrombie, Lascelles, **III:** 471; **Retro. Supp. I:** 127, 128

Abernathy, Milton, **Supp. III Part 2:** 616

Abernon, Edgar Vincent, Viscount d', **Supp. XVI:** 191

Aberration of Starlight (Sorrentino), **Supp. XXI:** 234–235

Abhau, Anna. *See* Mencken, Mrs. August (Anna Abhau)

"Abide with Me" (Hoffman), **Supp. XVIII:** 86

Abide with Me (Strout), **Supp. XXIII:** 273, 275, **278–280,** 285

"Ability" (Emerson), **II:** 6

Abingdon, Alexander, **Supp. XVI:** 99

Abish, Walter, **Supp. V:** 44

"Abishag" (Glück), **Supp. V:** 82

"Abnegation, The" (Bronk), **Supp. XXI:** 32

Abney, Lisa, **Supp. XXII:** 9

Abood, Maureen, **Supp. XXII:** 90

"Abortion, The" (Sexton), **Supp. II Part 2:** 682

"Abortions" (Dixon), **Supp. XII:** 153

"About C. D. Wright" (Colburn), **Supp. XV:** 341

"About Effie" (Findley), **Supp. XX: 50**

"About Hospitality" (Jewett), **Retro. Supp. II:** 131

"About Kathryn" (Dubus), **Supp. VII:** 91

"About Language" (Wrigley), **Supp. XVIII:** 300–301

"About Looking Alone at a Place: Arles" (M. F. K. Fisher), **Supp. XVII:** 89, 91

About the House (Auden), **Supp. II Part 1:** 24

About Town: "The New Yorker" and the World It Made (Yagoda), **Supp. VIII:** 151

"About Zhivago and His Poems"(O'Hara), **Supp. XXIII:** 214

"Above Pate Valley" (Snyder), **Supp. VIII:** 293

Above the River (Wright), **Supp. III Part 2:** 589, 606

"Abraham" (Schwartz), **Supp. II Part 2:** 663

Abraham, Nelson Algren. *See* Algren, Nelson

Abraham, Pearl, **Supp. XVII:** 49; **Supp. XX: 177; Supp. XXIV: 1–15**

"Abraham Davenport" (Whittier), **Supp. I Part 2:** 699

"Abraham Lincoln" (Emerson), **II:** 13

Abraham Lincoln: The Prairie Years (Sandburg), **III:** 580, 587–589, 590

Abraham Lincoln: The Prairie Years and the War Years (Sandburg), **III:** 588, 590

Abraham Lincoln: The War Years (Sandburg), **III:** 588, 589–590; **Supp. XVII:** 105

"Abraham Lincoln Walks at Midnight" (Lindsay), **Supp. I Part 2:** 390–391

"Abram Morrison" (Whittier), **Supp. I Part 2:** 699

Abramovich, Alex, **Supp. X:** 302, 309

Abrams, David, **Supp. XXII:** 61

Abrams, M. H., **Supp. XVI:** 19; **Supp. XXIII:** 42

Abridgment of Universal Geography, An: Together with Sketches of History (Rowson), **Supp. XV:** 243

"Absalom" (Rukeyser), **Supp. VI:** 278–279

Absalom, Absalom! (Faulkner), **II:** 64, 65–67, 72, 223; **IV:** 207; **Retro. Supp. I:** 75, 81, 82, 84, 85, 86, 87, 88, 89, 90, 92, 382; **Supp. V:** 261; **Supp. X:** 51; **Supp. XIV:** 12–13

"Absence"(J. Schoolcraft), **Supp. XXIII:** 228, 231

"Absence of Mercy" (Stone), **Supp. V:** 295

"Absentee, The" (Levertov), **Supp. III Part 1:** 284

Absentee Ownership (Veblen), **Supp. I Part 2:** 642

"Absent-Minded Bartender" (X. J. Kennedy), **Supp. XV:** 159

"Absent Thee from Felicity Awhile" (Wylie), **Supp. I Part 2:** 727, 729

"Absolution" (Fitzgerald), **Retro. Supp. I:** 108

"Absolution" (Sobin), **Supp. XVI:** 289

"Abuelita's Ache" (Mora), **Supp. XIII:** 218

Abysmal Brute, The (London), **II:** 467

Abyssinia and the Imperialists (C. L. R. James), **Supp. XXI:** 166

Abyss of Human Illusion, The (Sorrentino), **Supp. XXI:** 225, 227, 237–238

"Academic Story, An" (Simpson), **Supp. IX:** 279–280

"Academic Zoo, The: Theory—in Practice" (Epstein), **Supp. XIV:** 107–108, 109

"A Capella" (Wrigley), **Supp. XVIII:** 300

"Accident" (Minot), **Supp. VI: 208–209**

"Accident, The" (Southern), **Supp. XI:** 295

"Accident, The" (Strand), **Supp. IV Part 2:** 624

Accident/A Day's News (Wolf), **Supp. IV Part 1:** 310

Accidental Tourist, The (Tyler), **Supp. IV Part 2:** 657, 668–669; **Supp. V:** 227

Accordion Crimes (Proulx), **Supp. VII:** 259–261

"Accountability" (Dunbar), **Supp. II Part 1:** 197, 204

"Account of the Method of Drawing Birds" (Audubon), **Supp. XVI:** 12

"Accusation, The" (Wright), **Supp. III Part 2:** 595

"Accusation of the Inward Man, The" (Taylor), **IV:** 156

"Accusing Message from Dead Father" (Karr), **Supp. XI:** 244

Ace, Goodman, **Supp. IV Part 2:** 574

Ache of Appetite, The (Hadas), **Supp. XXIII: 120–121**

Achievement in American Poetry (Bogan), **Supp. III Part 1:** 63–64

Acker, Kathy, **Supp. XII:1–20; Supp. XXI:** 236

Ackerley, J. R., **Supp. XX: 237**

Ackerman, Diane, **Supp. XIII:** 154

"Acknowledgment" (Lanier), **Supp. I Part 1:** 364

Ackroyd, Peter, **Supp. V:** 233; **Supp. XVII:** 180

"Acquaintance in the Heavens, An" (Dillard), **Supp. VI:** 34

"Acquainted with the Night" (Frost), **II:** 155; **Retro. Supp. I:** 137; **Supp. XXI:** 26

Across Spoon River (Masters), **Supp. I Part 2:** 455, 457, 459, 460, 466, 474–475, 476

Across the Layers: Poems Old and New (Goldbarth), **Supp. XII:** 181, **187–189**

Across the River and into the Trees (Hemingway), **I:** 491; **II:** 255–256, 261; **Retro. Supp. I:** 172, **184–185; Supp. XIX:** 248

"Actfive" (MacLeish), **III:** 18–19, 22

Actfive and Other Poems (MacLeish), **III:** 3, 17–19, 21

Action (Shepard), **Supp. III Part 2:** 446

Active Anthology (Pound), **Supp. III Part 2:** 617

Active Service (Crane), **I:** 409

"Act of Creation and Its Artifact, The" (Sorrentino), **Supp. XXI:** 229, 235

Act of Love, An (Wolfert), **Supp. XXI:** 270, **275–277**

Act of Love, An: A Completely Retold Version of the Novel (Wolfert), **Supp. XXI:** 276

Acton, Patricia Nassif, **Supp. X:** 233

Actor's Nightmare, The (Durang), **Supp. XXIV:** 116, 119

Acts and Monuments of These Latter and Perilous Days (Fox), **Supp. XXII:** 36

Acts of Faith (Caputo), **Supp. XIX: 29–30**

"Acts of the Apostles, The" (Bronk), **Supp. XXI:** 28

Actual, The (Bellow), **Retro. Supp. II:** 33

"Actual Experience, Preferred Narratives" (Julier), **Supp. IV Part 1:** 211

Acuff, Roy, **Supp. V:** 335

Ada (Nabokov), **Retro. Supp. I:** 265, 266, 270, 276–277, 278, 279

"Ada" (Stein), **IV:** 43

"Adagia" (Stevens), **IV:** 78, 80, 88, 92

"Adagio" (Hull), **Supp. XXI:** 136–137

"Adam" (Hecht), **Supp. X:** 62

"Adam" (W. C. Williams), **Retro. Supp. I:** 422, 423

"Adam and Eve" (Eugene), **Supp. X:** 204

"Adam and Eve" (Shapiro), **Supp. II Part 2:** 708, 712

"Adamantine Practice of Poetry, The" (Wright), **Supp. XV:** 341–342, 343–344

Adam Bede (G. Eliot), **II:** 181

Adamé, Leonard, **Supp. XIII:** 316

Adam & Eve & the City (W. C. Williams), **Retro. Supp. I:** 423

Adamic, Louis, **Supp. XXIII:** 166

"Adamic Purity as Double Agent" (Whalen-Bridge), **Retro. Supp. II:** 211–212

"Adam Robinson Acquires Grandparents and a Little Sister" (P. E. Jones), **Supp. XXII:** 151

"Adams" (Saunders), **Supp. XIX:** 232

Adams, Althea. *See* Thurber, Mrs. James (Althea Adams)

Adams, Annie. *See* Fields, Annie Adams

Adams, Brooks, **Supp. I Part 2:** 484

Adams, Charles, **Supp. I Part 2:** 644

Adams, Charles Francis, **I:** 1, 4; **Supp. I Part 2:** 484

Adams, Franklin P., **Supp. I Part 2:** 653; **Supp. IX:** 190; **Supp. XV:** 294, 297

Adams, Henry, **I: 1–24,** 111, 243, 258; **II:** 278, 542; **III:** 396, 504; **IV:** 191, 349; **Retro. Supp. I:** 53, 59; **Retro. Supp. II:** 207; **Supp. I Part 1:** 299–300, 301, 314; **Supp. I Part 2:** 417, 492, 543, 644; **Supp. II Part 1:** 93–94, 105; **Supp. III Part 2:** 613; **Supp. IV Part 1:** 31, 208; **Supp. XXIV:** 224

Adams, Mrs. Henry (Marian Hooper), **I:** 1, 5, 10, 17–18

Adams, Henry B., **Supp. I Part 1:** 369

Adams, James Truslow, **Supp. I Part 2:** 481, 484, 486

Adams, J. Donald, **IV:** 438

Adams, John, **I:** 1; **II:** 103, 301; **III:** 17, 473; **Supp. I Part 2:** 483, 506, 507, 509, 510, 511, 517, 518, 520, 524

Adams, John Luther, **Supp. XII:** 209

Adams, John Quincy, **I:** 1, 3, 16–17; **Supp. I Part 2:** 685, 686

Adams, Léonie, **Supp. I Part 2:** 707; **Supp. V:** 79; **Supp. IX:** 229; **Supp. XVII:** 75

Adams, Luella, **Supp. I Part 2:** 652

Adams, Noah, **Supp. XVII:** 218

Adams, Phoebe, **Supp. IV Part 1:** 203; **Supp. VIII:** 124

Adams, Samuel, **Supp. I Part 2:** 516, 525

Adams, Timothy Dow, **Supp. XVI:** 67, 69

Ada; or Ardor (Nabokov), **III:** 247

"Ad Castitatem" (Bogan), **Supp. III Part 1:** 50

Adcock, Betty, **Supp. XVIII:** 181–182, 182

Addams, Jane, **Supp. I Part 1: 1–26; Supp. XI:** 200, 202

Addams, John Huy, **Supp. I Part 1:** 2

"Addendum" (Wright), **Supp. V:** 339

Addiego, John, **Supp. XII:** 182

Adding Machine, The (Rice), **I:** 479

Adding Machine, The: Selected Essays (Burroughs), **Supp. III Part 1:** 93, 97

"Adding to the Unhappiness: Those Poems You Are Writing" (Gallagher), **Supp. XXIV:** 172

Addison, Joseph, **I:** 8, 105, 106–107, 108, 114, 131, 300, 304; **III:** 430

"Address Delivered at Lenox, An" (Channing), **Supp. XXIV: 79–80**

"Addressed to a Political Shrimp, or, Fly upon the Wheel" (Freneau), **Supp. II Part 1:** 267

"Address to My Soul" (Wylie), **Supp. I Part 2:** 729

"Address to the Deist, An" (Wheatley), **Supp. XX: 287**

"Address to the Devil" (Jarman), **Supp. XVII:** 114

Address to the Government of the United States on the Cession of Louisiana to the French, An (Brown), **Supp. I Part 1:** 146

"Address to the Scholars of New England" (Ransom), **III:** 491

"Address with Exclamation Points, A" (Simic), **Supp. VIII:** 283

"Adieu to Norman, Bon Jour to Joan and Jean-Paul"(O'Hara), **Supp. XXIII:** 219

Adisa, Opal Palmer, **Supp. XXII:** 66, 74, 78

"Adjutant Bird, The" (Banks), **Supp. V:** 5

Adkins, Nelson F., **II:** 20

Adler, Alfred, **I:** 248

Adler, Betty, **III:** 103

Adler, George J., **III:** 81

Adler, Renata, **Supp. X:** 171

Admiral of the Ocean Sea: A Life of Christopher Columbus (Morison), **Supp. I Part 2:** 486–488

"Admirals" (Chabon), **Supp. XI:** 72

"Admonition, An" (Brodsky), **Supp. VIII:** 33

"Adolescence" (Bidart), **Supp. XV:** 32

"Adolescence" (Dove), **Supp. IV Part 1:** 245

"Adolescence" (Olds), **Supp. X:** 211

"Adolescence II" (Dove), **Supp. IV Part 1:** 242, 244–245

Adolescent's Christmas, An: 1944 (C. Bly), **Supp. XVI:** 31–32

"Adolf Eichmann" (Carruth), **Supp. XVI:** 47

"Adonais" (Shelley), **II:** 516, 540

Adonai: The Pilgrim of Eternity (Lippard), **Supp. XXIII:** 180, 189, 190

Adorno, Theodor, **Supp. I Part 2:** 645, 650; **Supp. IV Part 1:** 301

"Adrienne Rich: The Poetics of Change" (Gelpi), **Supp. I Part 2:** 554

Adrift in Macao (Durang), **Supp. XXIV:** 125

"Adultery" (Banks), **Supp. V:** 15

"Adultery" (Dubus), **Supp. VII:** 85

Adultery and Other Choices (Dubus), **Supp. VII:** 83–85

Adulthood Rites (O. Butler), **Supp. XIII:** 63, **64–65**

Adult Life of Toulouse Lautrec by Henri Toulouse Lautrec, The (Acker), **Supp. XII:** 5, 6, **8–9**

Adventure (London), **II:** 466

Adventures in Ancient Egypt (Goldbarth), **Supp. XII:** 191

Adventures in Value (Cummings), **I:** 430

"Adventures of a Book Reviewer" (Cowley), **Supp. II Part 1:** 137, 142

Adventures of a Novelist (Atherton), **Supp. XXIV:** 17–18, 19–20, 21

Adventures of Augie March, The (Bellow), **I:** 144, 147, 149, 150, 151, 152–153, 154, 155, 157, 158–159, 164; **Retro. Supp. II:** 19, 20, **22–23**, 24, 30; **Supp. VIII:** 234, 236–237; **Supp. XXIV:** 220

Adventures of a Young Man (Dos Passos), **I:** 488, 489, 492

Adventures of Captain Bonneville (Irving), **II:** 312

Adventures of Harry Franco, The: A Tale of the Great Panic (Briggs), **Supp. XVIII:** 1, 2, 5–8

Adventures of Harry Richmond, The (Meredith), **Supp. XX: 234**

Adventures of Huckleberry Finn, The (Twain), **I:** 307, 506; **II:** 26, 72, 262, 266–268, 290, 418, 430; **III:** 101, 112–113, 357, 554, 558, 577; **IV:** 198, 201–204, 207; **Retro. Supp. I:** 188; **Retro. Supp. II:** 121; **Supp. I Part 1:** 247; **Supp. IV Part 1:** 247, 257; **Supp. IV Part 2:** 502; **Supp. V:** 131; **Supp. VIII:** 198; **Supp. X:** 230; **Supp. XII:** 16; **Supp. XVI:** 222; **Supp. XX: 171; Supp. XXII:** 81

Adventures of Jimmy (Broughton), **Supp. XV:** 146

Adventures of Roderick Random, The (Smollett), **I:** 134

Adventures of the Letter I (Simpson), **Supp. IX:** 266, **273–274**

Adventures of Tom Sawyer, The (Twain), **II:** 26; **III:** 223, 572, 577; **IV:** 199–200, 203, 204; **Supp. I Part 2:** 456, 470; **Supp. XVI:** 66

Adventures While Preaching the Gospel of Beauty (Lindsay), **Supp. I Part 2:** 374, 376, 381, 382–384, 389, 399

Adventures with Ed (Loeffler), **Supp. XIII:** 1

Advertisements for Myself (Mailer), **III:** 27, 35–38, 41–42, 45, 46; **Retro. Supp. II:** 196, 199, 200, 202, 203, 212; **Supp. IV Part 1:** 90, 284; **Supp. XIV:** 157; **Supp. XXIV:** 281

"Advertisements for Myself on the Way Out" (Mailer), **III:** 37

"Advice to a Prophet" (Wilbur), **Supp. III Part 2:** 555–557

Advice to a Prophet and Other Poems (Wilbur), **Supp. III Part 2:** 554–558

"Advice to a Raven in Russia" (Barlow), **Supp. II Part 1:** 65, 74, 80, 83

"Advice to Players" (Bidart), **Supp. XV:** 35

Advice to the Lovelorn (film), **Retro. Supp. II:** 328

Advice to the Privileged Orders, Part I (Barlow), **Supp. II Part 1:** 80

Aegerter, Lindsay Pentolfe, **Supp. XXII:** 69

"Aeneas and Dido" (Brodsky), **Supp. VIII:** 24–25

"Aeneas at Washington" (Tate), **IV:** 129

Aeneid (Virgil), **I:** 396; **II:** 542; **III:** 124; **Supp. XV:** 23; **Supp. XXIV:** 162–163

Aeneus Tacticus, **I:** 136

Aerial View (Barabtarlo), **Retro. Supp. I:** 278

"Aeria the Evanescent" (Sobin), **Supp. XVI:** 292

Aeschylus, **I:** 274, 433; **III:** 398; **IV:** 358, 368, 370; **Retro. Supp. I:** 65; **Supp. I Part 2:** 458, 494

Aesop, **I:** 387; **II:** 154, 169, 302; **III:** 587

Aesthetic (Croce), **III:** 610

"Aesthetics" (Mumford), **Supp. II Part 2:** 476

"Aesthetics of Silence, The" (Sontag), **Supp. III Part 2:** 459

"Aesthetics of the Shah" (Olds), **Supp. X:** 205

"Affair at Coulter's Notch, The" (Bierce), **I:** 202

Affaire de viol, Une (C. Himes). *See Case of Rape, A* (C. Himes)

"Affair of Outposts, An" (Bierce), **I:** 202

Affliction (Banks), **Supp. V:** 15, 16

Affluent Society, The (Galbraith), **Supp. I Part 2:** 648

Afghanistan Picture Show, An: or, How I Saved the World (Vollmann), **Supp. XVII:** 226, **228–229**, 233

"Aficionados, The" (Carver), **Supp. III Part 1:** 137

"Afloat" (Beattie), **Supp. V:** 29

Afloat and Ashore (Cooper), **I:** 351, 355

"Afoot" (P. N. Warren as Kilina), **Supp. XX: 261–262**

Africa, Its Geography, People, and Products (Du Bois), **Supp. II Part 1:** 179

Africa, Its Place in Modern History (Du Bois), **Supp. II Part 1:** 179

"Africa, to My Mother" (D. Diop), **Supp. IV Part 1:** 16

Africana (H. L. Gates, ed.), **Supp. XX: 99**

African American Century, The : How Black Americans Have Shaped Our Country (H. L. Gates), **Supp. XX: 102**

African American Lives (television production), **Supp. XX: 99**

African American Lives 2 (television production), **Supp. XX: 99**

African American National Biography (H. L. Gates, ed.), **Supp. XX: 99**

African American Writers (Smith, ed.), **Supp. XIII:** 115, 127

"African Book" (Hemingway), **II:** 259

"African Chief, The" (Bryant), **Supp. I Part 1:** 168

"African Fragment" (Brooks), **Supp. III Part 1:** 85

African Queen, The (film), **Supp. XI:** 17

"African Roots of War, The" (Du Bois), **Supp. II Part 1:** 174

African Silences (Matthiessen), **Supp. V:** 203

African Treasury, An (Hughes, ed.), **Supp. I Part 1:** 344

"Afrika Revolution" (Baraka), **Supp. II Part 1:** 53

"AFRO-AMERICAN LYRIC" (Baraka), **Supp. II Part 1:** 59

After (Bukiet), **Supp. XVII:** 43, **44–45**

After (Hirshfield), **Supp. XXIII:** 133–135, 139

After All: Last Poems (Matthews), **Supp. IX:** 155, **167–169**

After and Before the Lightning (Ortiz), **Supp. IV Part 2:** 513

"After a Party" (Salinas), **Supp. XIII:** 327

"After Apple-Picking" (Frost), **Retro. Supp. I:** 126, 128

"After Arguing against the Contention That Art Must Come from Discontent" (Stafford), **Supp. XI:** 327

After Confession: Poetry as Autobiography (Harris), **Supp. XIV:** 269

After Confession: Poetry as Autobiography (K. Sontag and D. Graham), **Supp. XV:** 104

"After Cowboy Chicken Came to Town" (Jin), **Supp. XVIII:** 97–98

"After Disappointment" (Jarman), **Supp. XVII:** 118–119

After Disillusion: Poems (Wolf), **Supp. XXII:** 275

"After Edward Hopper: Somebody in a Bar" (Ferry), **Supp. XXIV:** 162

After Experience (Snodgrass), **Supp. VI:** 314–316, 317

"After great pain, a formal feeling comes" (Dickinson), **Retro. Supp. I:** 37

"After Hearing a Waltz by Bartók" (Lowell), **II:** 522

After Henry (Didion), **Supp. IV Part 1:** 195, 196, 199, 207, 208, 211

"After Henry" (Didion), **Supp. IV Part 1:** 211

"After Holbein" (Wharton), **IV:** 325; **Retro. Supp. I:** 382

After Ikkyu and Other Poems (Harrison), **Supp. VIII:** 42

"After-Image" (Bierds), **Supp. XVII:** 31–32

"After-Image" (Caldwell), **I:** 309

After-Images: Autobiographical Sketches (Snodgrass), **Supp. VI:** 314, **319–323**, 324, 326–327

After I's (Zukofsky), **Supp. III Part 2:** 628, 629

Afterlife (Monette), **Supp. X:** 153

Afterlife (Updike), **Retro. Supp. I:** 322

Afterlife, The (Levis), **Supp. XI:** 259, **260–264**

"After Magritte" (McClatchy), **Supp. XII:** 264

"After Making Love" (Dunn), **Supp. XI:** 153

Aftermath (Longfellow), **II:** 490

"Aftermath" (Longfellow), **II:** 498

After New Formalism (A. Finch, ed.), **Supp. XVII:** 74

"Afternoon" (Ellison), **Supp. II Part 1:** 238

"Afternoon at MacDowell" (Kenyon), **Supp. VII:** 159

"Afternoon Miracle, An" (O. Henry), **Supp. II Part 1:** 390

Afternoon of a Faun (Hearon), **Supp. VIII: 63–64**

Afternoon of an Author: A Selection of Uncollected Stories and Essays (Fitzgerald), **II:** 94

"Afternoon of a Playwright" (Thurber), **Supp. I Part 2:** 620

Afternoon of the Unreal (Salinas), **Supp. XIII:** 311, **316–318**

"Afternoon with the Old Man, An" (Dubus), **Supp. VII:** 84

"After Punishment Was Done with Me" (Olds), **Supp. X:** 213

"After Reading *Barely and Widely,*" (Zukofsky), **Supp. III Part 2:** 625, 631

"After Reading 'In the Clearing' for the Author, Robert Frost" (Corso), **Supp. XII:** 130

"After Reading *Mickey in the Night Kitchen* for the Third Time before Bed" (Dove), **Supp. IV Part 1:** 249

"After Reading the Greek Poet"(Kenny), **Supp. XXIII:** 150

"After Reading Tu Fu, I Go Outside to the Dwarf Orchard" (Wright), **Supp. V:** 343

"After Reading Wang Wei, I Go Outside to the Full Moon" (Wright), **Supp. V:** 343

After Shocks, Near Escapes (Dobyns), **Supp. XIII: 80–82**

"After Song, An" (W. C. Williams), **Retro. Supp. I:** 413

After Strange Gods (T. S. Eliot), **I:** 588

After Such Knowledge: Memory, History, and the Legacy of the Holocaust (E. Hoffman), **Supp. XVI:** 152–153, **158–161**

"After the Alphabets" (Merwin), **Supp. III Part 1:** 356

"After the Argument" (Dunn), **Supp. XI:** 149

"After the Baptism" (C. Bly), **Supp. XVI:** 40

"After the Burial" (Lowell), **Supp. I Part 2:** 409

"After the Curfew" (Holmes), **Supp. I Part 1:** 308

"After the Death of John Brown" (Thoreau), **IV:** 185

"After the Denim" (Carver), **Supp. III Part 1:** 144

"After the Dentist" (Swenson), **Supp. IV Part 2:** 645

After the Fall (A. Miller), **III:** 148, 149, 156, 161, 162, 163–165, 166

"After the Fire" (Merrill), **Supp. III Part 1:** 328

"After the Flood" (Sanders), **Supp. XVI:** 274–275

After the Fox (film), **Supp. IV Part 2:** 575

After the Genteel Tradition (Cowley), **Supp. II Part 1:** 143

"After the Heart's Interrogation" (Komunyakaa), **Supp. XIII:** 120

After the Lost Generation: A Critical Study of the Writers of Two Wars (Aldridge), **Supp. IV Part 2:** 680; **Supp. XIX:** 250

"After the Night Office—Gethsemani Abbey" (Merton), **Supp. VIII:** 195–196

After the Others (Weigl), **Supp. XIX:** 282, 283–284

"After the Persian" (Bogan), **Supp. III Part 1:** 64

After the Plague (Boyle), **Supp. XX: 20**

"After the Plague" (Boyle), **Supp. XX: 20**

"After the Pleasure Party" (Melville), **III:** 93

"After the Rain" (Halliday), **Supp. XIX:** 91

"After the Resolution" (Dunn), **Supp. XI:** 151

After the Stroke (Sarton), **Supp. VIII:** 264

"After the Surprising Conversions" (Lowell), **I:** 544, 545; **II:** 550; **Retro. Supp. II:** 187

"After 37 Years My Mother Apologizes for My Childhood" (Olds), **Supp. X:** 208

After This (McDermott), **Supp. XVIII:** 155, **166–167**

Afterthoughts (L. P. Smith), **Supp. XIV:** 339, 345

"Afterthoughts on the Rosenbergs" (Fiedler), **Supp. XIII:** 99

"After Twenty Years" (Rich), **Supp. I Part 2:** 559–560

"Afterwake, The" (Rich), **Supp. I Part 2:** 553

"Afterward" (Wharton), **Retro. Supp. I:** 372

"Afterword"(Hadas), **Supp. XXIII:** 113

"After Working Long" (Kenyon), **Supp. VII:** 170

"After Yitzl" (Goldbarth), **Supp. XII:** 186

"After You, My Dear Alphonse" (Jackson), **Supp. IX:** 119

"After Your Death" (Trethewey), **Supp. XXI:** 255

"After Your Nap" (B. Kelly), **Supp. XVII:** 124

"Again" (Dixon), **Supp. XII:** 157

"Again, Kapowsin" (Hugo), **Supp. VI:** 141

"Again Just Now" (Budbill), **Supp. XIX:** 11

"Against" (Goldbarth), **Supp. XII:** 193

"Against Decoration" (Karr), **Supp. XI:** 248

"Against Epiphanies" (C. Baxter), **Supp. XVII:** 20

Against Interpretation (Sontag), **Supp. III Part 2:** 451, 455; **Supp. XIV:** 15

"Against Interpretation" (Sontag), **Supp. III Part 2:** 456–458, 463

"Against Modernity" (Ozick), **Supp. V:** 272

"Against Nature" (Karr), **Supp. XI:** 243

Against Nature (Updike), **Retro. Supp. I:** 323

Against Our Vanishing: Winter Conversations with Allen Grossman on the Theory and Practice of Poetry (Halliday), **Supp. XIX: 82–84,** 88

"Against Realism" (Halliday), **Supp. XIX:** 93

Against the Cold (Bynner), **Supp. XV:** 51

"Against the Crusades" (Stern), **Supp. IX:** 300

Against the Current: As I Remember F. Scott Fitzgerald (Kroll Ring), **Supp. IX:** 63

Agamben, Giorgio, **Supp. XVI:** 289

Agapida, Fray Antonio (pseudonym). *See* Irving, Washington

"Agassiz" (Lowell), **Supp. I Part 2:** 414, 416

Agassiz, Louis, **II:** 343; **Supp. I Part 1:** 312; **Supp. IX:** 180

Âge cassant, L' (Char; Sobin, trans.), *Supp. XVI:* 282

"Aged Wino's Counsel to a Young Man on the Brink of Marriage, The" (X. J. Kennedy), **Supp. XV:** 156

Agee, Emma, **I:** 26

Agee, James, **I: 25–47,** 293; **IV:** 215; **Supp. IX:** 109; **Supp. XIV:** 92; **Supp. XV:** 143

"Agent, The" (Wilbur), **Supp. III Part 2:** 557–561

Age of Anxiety, The (Auden), **Supp. II Part 1:** 2, 19, 21

"Age of Conformity, The" (Howe), **Supp. VI:** 117

Age of Grief, The: A Novella and Stories (Smiley), **Supp. VI:** 292, **299–301**

Age of Innocence, The (Wharton), **IV:** 320–322, 327–328; **Retro. Supp. I:** 372, 374, **380–381; Supp. IV Part 1:** 23

Age of Longing, The (Koestler), **I:** 258

Age of Reason, The (Paine), **Supp. I Part 2:** 503, 515–517, 520

"Age of Strolling, The" (Stern), **Supp. IX:** 297

"Ages, The" (Bryant), **Supp. I Part 1:** 152, 155, 166, 167

"Ages of the Women, The" (Gibran), **Supp. XX: 115**

"Aggrandizement, The" (Bronk), **Supp. XXI:** 32

"Aging" (Jarrell), **II:** 388

Aging and Gender in Literature (George), **Supp. IV Part 2:** 450

"Agio Neró" (Mora), **Supp. XIII:** 224

"Agitato ma non Troppo" (Ransom), **III:** 493

"Agnes of Iowa" (Moore), **Supp. X:** 165, 178

Agnes of Sorrento (Stowe), **Supp. I Part 2:** 592, 595–596

Agnon, S. Y., **Supp. V:** 266

Agony & the Agony, The (Silver), **Supp. XXIV:** 265, **274–275**

"Agosta the Winged Man and Rasha the Black Dove" (Dove), **Supp. IV Part 1:** 246–247

Agrarian Justice (Paine), **Supp. I Part 2:** 517–518

"Agricultural Show, The" (McKay), **Supp. X:** 139

Agrippa: A Book of the Dead (W. Gibson), **Supp. XVI:** 125

Agua de dos ríos/Water from Two Rivers (Espaillat), **Supp. XXI:** 104, 112–113

Agua Fresca: An Anthology of Raza Poetry (Rodríguez, ed.), **Supp. IV Part 2:** 540

Agua Santa/Holy Water (Mora), **Supp. XIII: 222–225**

Agüero Sisters, The (García), **Supp. XI: 185–190**

Aguiar, Marian, **Supp. XXII:** 68

Aguiar, Sarah Appleton, **Supp. XIII:** 30

Aguilar, Carmen, **Supp. XXIII:** 200

Ah, Wilderness! (O'Neill), **III:** 400–401; **Supp. IV Part 2:** 587

Ah, Wilderness!: The Frontier in American Literature (Humphrey), **Supp. IX:** 104

Ahearn, Barry, **Retro. Supp. I:** 415

Ahearn, Frederick L., Jr., **Supp. XI:** 184

Ahearn, Kerry, **Supp. IV Part 2:** 604

Ahmed Arabi Pasha, **I:** 453

Ahnebrink, Lars, **III:** 328

Ahrens, Sylvia, **Supp. XX: 162**

Ah Sin (Harte), **Supp. II Part 1:** 354–355

"Ah! Sun-flower" (Blake), **III:** 19

Aida (rock musical), **Supp. XXI:** 148

Aidoo, Ama Ato, **Supp. XXII:** 68

AIDS and Its Metaphors (Sontag), **Supp. III Part 2:** 452, 466–468

Aids to Reflection (Coleridge), **II:** 10

Aiieeeee! An Anthology of Asian-American Writers (The Combined Asian Resources Project), **Supp. X:** 292

Aiken, Conrad, **I: 48–70,** 190, 211, 243; **II:** 55, 530, 542; **III:** 458, 460; **Retro. Supp. I:** 55, 56, 57, 58, 60, 62; **Supp. X:** 50, 115; **Supp. XV:** 144, 297, 298, 302, 306, 309; **Supp. XVII:** 135; **Supp. XXIV:** 36

"Aimless Love" (Collins), **Supp. XXI:** 61

"Aim Was Song, The" (Frost), **Retro. Supp. I:** 133

Ainger, Arthur Campbell, **Supp. XX:** 230

Ainsworth, Linda, **Supp. IV Part 1:** 274

Ainsworth, William, **III:** 423

Air-Conditioned Nightmare, The (H. Miller), **III:** 186

Airing Dirty Laundry (Reed), **Supp. X:** 241

"Air Is Full of Little Holes, The" (Brockmeier), **Supp. XXII:** 60

"Airmail from Mother" (Kooser), **Supp. XIX:** 120

"Air Plant, The" (Crane), **I:** 401

Air Raid: A Verse Play for Radio (MacLeish), **III:** 21

"Airs above the Ground" (Sarton), **Supp. VIII:** 261

Air Tight: A Novel of Red Russia. See We the Living (Rand)

Air Up There, The (film, Glaser), **Supp. XVII:** 9

"Airwaves" (Mason), **Supp. VIII:** 146

Airways, Inc. (Dos Passos), **I:** 482

A Is for Anne: Mistress Hutchinson Disturbs the Commonwealth (Schott), **Supp. XXIII:** 240, **246–247**

"A is for Dining Alone" (M. F. K. Fisher), **Supp. XVII:** 86

Aitken, Robert, **Supp. I Part 2:** 504

Aizenberg, Susan, **Supp. XXI:** 131

Akhmadulina, Bella, **Supp. III Part 1:** 268

Akhmatova, Anna, **Supp. III Part 1:** 268, 269; **Supp. VIII:** 20, 21, 25, 27, 30; **Supp. XXI:** 132

Akhmatova Translations, The (Kenyon), **Supp. VII:** 160

"Akhnilo" (Salter), **Supp. IX:** 260

Akins, Zoë, **Supp. XVI:** 187

Aksenev, Vasily P., **Retro. Supp. I:** 278

"Al Aaraaf" (Poe), **III:** 426–427

Al Aaraaf, Tamerlane, and Minor Poems (Poe), **III:** 410

"Alabama Jones" (Mosher), **Supp. XXII:** 204, 211

"Alain Locke and Cultural Pluralism" (Kallen), **Supp. XIV:** 197

"Alain Locke: Bahá'í Philosopher" (Buck), **Supp. XIV:** 199

Alain Locke: Faith and Philosophy (Buck), **Supp. XIV:** 200

Alarçon, **Supp. XVII:** 74

Alarcón, Justo, **Supp. IV Part 2:** 538, 539, 540

Alarcón, Norma, **Supp. XXIII:** 194, 204–205

À la Recherche du Temps Perdu (Proust), **IV:** 428

"Alarm" (X. J. Kennedy), **Supp. XV:** 163

"Alastor" (Shelley), **Supp. I Part 2:** 728

"Alatus" (Wilbur), **Supp. III Part 2:** 563

Alaya (Hirshfield), **Supp. XXIII:** 131

"Alba" (Creeley), **Supp. IV Part 1:** 150

Alba, Richard D., **Supp. XX:** 43

Albee, Edward, **I: 71–96,** 113; **II:** 558, 591; **III:** 281, 387; **IV:** 4, 230; **Retro. Supp. II:** 104; **Supp. VIII:** 331; **Supp. XIII:** 196, 197; **Supp. XXIV:** 113, 263, 270

Albers, Joseph, **Supp. IV Part 2:** 621

Alberti, Rafael, **Supp. XV:** 75

Albright, Margery, **Supp. I Part 2:** 613

"Album, The" (Morris), **III:** 220

Alcestiad, The (Wilder), **IV:** 357, 374

"Alchemist, The" (Bogan), **Supp. III Part 1:** 50

"Alchemist in the City, The" (Hopkins), **Supp. IV Part 2:** 639

Alchymist's Journal, The (Connell), **Supp. XIV:** 80

"Alcmena" (Winters), **Supp. II Part 2:** 801

Alcott, Abba. *See* Alcott, Mrs. Amos Bronson (Abigail May)

Alcott, Amos Bronson, **II:** 7, 225; **IV:** 172, 173, 184; **Retro. Supp. I:** 217; **Supp. I Part 1:** 28, 29–32, 35, 39, 41, 45; **Supp. II Part 1:** 290; **Supp. XVI:** 84, 89

Alcott, Mrs. Amos Bronson (Abigail May), **IV:** 184; **Supp. I Part 1:** 29, 30, 31, 32, 35

Alcott, Anna. *See* Pratt, Anna

Alcott, Louisa May, **IV:** 172; **Supp. I Part 1: 28–46; Supp. IX:** 128; **Supp. XV:** 338; **Supp. XVI:** 84

Alcott, May, **Supp. I Part 1:** 41

Alcuin: A Dialogue (Brown), **Supp. I Part 1:** 126–127, 133

Alden, Hortense. *See* Farrell, Mrs. James T. (Hortense Alden)

Alden, John, **I:** 471; **II:** 502–503

"Alder Fork, The" (Leopold), **Supp. XIV:** 186

Aldington, Perdita, **Supp. I Part 1:** 258

Aldington, Richard, **II:** 517; **III:** 458, 459, 465, 472; **Retro. Supp. I:** 63, 127; **Supp. I Part 1:** 257–262, 270

Aldington, Mrs. Richard. *See* Doolittle, Hilda

Aldo Leopold: His Life and Work (Meine), **Supp. XIV:** 179

"Aldo Leopold's Intellectual Heritage" (Nash), **Supp. XIV:** 191–192

Aldon, Raymond, **Supp. XV:** 297

Aldrich, Thomas Bailey, **II:** 400; **Supp. II Part 1:** 192; **Supp. XIV:** 45; **Supp. XVIII:** 4

Aldrich, Tom, **Supp. I Part 2:** 415

Aldridge, John W., **Supp. I Part 1:** 196; **Supp. IV Part 1:** 286; **Supp. IV Part 2:** 680, 681; **Supp. VIII:** 189; **Supp. XI:** 228; **Supp. XIX:** 250

Aleck Maury Sportsman (Gordon), **II:** 197, 200, 203–204

Alegría, Claribel, **Supp. IV Part 1:** 208

Aleichem, Sholem, **Supp. XXIII:** 4, 7

Aleichem, Sholem, **IV:** 3, 10; **Supp. IV Part 2:** 585

"Alert Lovers, Hidden Sides, and Ice Travelers: Notes on Poetic Form and Energy" (Dunn), **Supp. XI:** 153

"Aleš Debeljak" (Simic), **Supp. VIII:** 279

"Alex" (Oliver), **Supp. VII:** 232

Alexander, Doris, **Supp. XVII:** 99

Alexander, Elizabeth, **Supp. XVIII:** 171, 185, 186; **Supp. XXI:** 246, 257

Alexander, George, **II:** 331

Alexander, Michael, **Retro. Supp. I:** 293

"Alexander Crummell Dead" (Dunbar), **Supp. II Part 1:** 207, 208–209

Alexander's Bridge (Cather), **I:** 313, 314, 316–317, 326; **Retro. Supp. I:** 1, 6, 7, 8

Alexander the Great, **IV:** 322

"Alexandra" (Cather), **Retro. Supp. I:** 7, 9, 17

Alexandrov, V. E., **Retro. Supp. I:** 270

Alexie, Sherman, **Supp. XVIII:** 58

Algic Researches (H. Schoolcraft), **Supp. XXIII:** 227

Algonquin Round Table, **Supp. IX:** 190, 191, 197

Algren, Nelson, **I:** 211; **Supp. V:** 4; **Supp. IX: 1–18; Supp. XII:** 126; **Supp. XIII:** 173; **Supp. XIV:** 3; **Supp. XVII:** 161; **Supp. XXI:** 264; **Supp. XXIII:** 165

Alhambra, The (Irving), **II:** 310–311

Ali, Agha Shahid, **Supp. XVII:** 74

Ali, Ayaan Hirsi, **Supp. XXIV:** 15

Alias Grace (Atwood), **Supp. XIII:** 20, **31–32**

Alice (film; Allen), **Supp. XV:** 2, 11

"Alice Doane's Appeal" (Hawthorne), **II:** 227

"Alice Drops Her Cigarette on the Floor ... " (Findley), **Supp. XX: 50–51**

Alice in Wonderland (Carroll), **Supp. I Part 2:** 622

Alice Ordered Me to Be Made (Notley), **Supp. XXII:** 224, 227, 228

"Alice Ordered Me to Be Made" (Notley), **Supp. XXII:** 227

Alice's Adventures in Wonderland (Carroll), **Supp. XVI:** 261

"Alicia and I Talking on Edna's Steps" (Cisneros), **Supp. VII:** 64

"Alicia Who Sees Mice" (Cisneros), **Supp. VII:** 60

Alien 3 (screenplay, W. Gibson), **Supp. XVI:** 120, 124

"Ali in Havana" (Talese), **Supp. XVII:** 207, 208

Alison, Archibald, **Supp. I Part 1:** 151, 159

Alison's House (Glaspell), **Supp. III Part 1:** 182, 188, 189

Alive (screenplay, Shanley), **Supp. XIV:** 316

Alive and Writing: Interviews with American Authors of the 1980s (McCaffery and Gregory), **Supp. X:** 260

"Alki Beach" (Hugo), **Supp. VI:** 135

Alla Breve Loving (Wright), **Supp. XV:** 339, 340

"Alla Breve Loving" (Wright), **Supp. XV:** 340

"All Around the Town" (Benét), **Supp. XI:** 48, 58

All at Sea (Lardner), **II:** 427

All Aunt Hagar's Children (E. P. Jones), **Supp. XXII:** 140, 143, **150–153**

"All Aunt Hagar's Children" (E. P. Jones), **Supp. XXII:** 151

"All Boy" (Rawlings), **Supp. X:** 222

Allegiances (Stafford), **Supp. XI: 322– 323,** 329

"Allegory of the Cave" (Dunn), **Supp. XI:** 150

"Allegory Unlimited" (Cassill), **Supp. XIX:** 266

Allegro, Johnny (film, Tetzloff), **Supp. XVII:** 62

"Allegro, L' " (Milton), **Supp. XIV:** 8

Allen, Brooke, **Supp. VIII:** 153

Allen, Bruce, **Supp. XXII:** 205, 212; **Supp. XXIII:** 106, 300

Allen, Claudia, **Supp. XXIII:** 79

Allen, Dick, **Supp. IX:** 279

Allen, Donald, **Supp. VIII:** 291; **Supp. XIII:** 112; **Supp. XXIII:** 215, 220

Allen, Frank, **Supp. XI:** 126; **Supp. XII:** 186

Allen, Frederick Lewis, **Supp. I Part 2:** 655

Allen, Gay Wilson, **IV:** 352; **Supp. I Part 2:** 418

Allen, Ivan, **Supp. XXII:** 245

Allen, Paula Gunn. *See* Gunn Allen, Paula

Allen, Robert Moore, **Supp. XX: 164**

Allen, Walter, **I:** 505; **III:** 352; **Supp. IV Part 2:** 685; **Supp. IX:** 231

Allen, Woody, **Supp. I Part 2:** 607, 623; **Supp. IV Part 1:** 205; **Supp. X:** 164; **Supp. XI:** 307; **Supp. XV: 1–18; Supp. XVII:** 48

"Aller et Retour" (Barnes), Supp. III Part 1: 36

Aller Retour New York (H. Miller), **III:** 178, 182, 183

Allerton, Isaac, **Supp. XXII:** 44

Allessandrini, Goffredo, **Supp. IV Part 2:** 520

Alleys of Eden, The (R. O. Butler), **Supp. XII:** 62, **62–64,** 68

All God's Children Need Traveling Shoes (Angelou), **Supp. IV Part 1:** 2, 9–10, 12–13, 17

All God's Chillun Got Wings (O'Neill), **III:** 387, 391, 393–394

All Gone (Dixon), **Supp. XII:** 148, 149

"All Hallows" (Glück), **Supp. V:** 82

"All I Can Remember" (Jackson), **Supp. IX:** 115

"Alligators, The" (Updike), **IV:** 219

Allingham, John Till, **Supp. XV:** 243

All in the Family (Boyce), **Supp. XXI:** 8

"ALL IN THE STREET" (Baraka), **Supp. II Part 1:** 53

Allison, Dorothy, **Supp. XVIII:** 195

"All I Want" (Tapahonso), **Supp. IV Part 2:** 508

"All Little Colored Children Should Play the Harmonica" (Patchett), **Supp. XII:** 309

"All Mountains" (Doolittle), **Supp. I Part 1:** 271

All My Friends Are Going to Be Strangers (McMurtry), **Supp. V:** 224, 228, 229

All My Pretty Ones (Sexton), **Supp. II Part 2:** 678, 679–683

"All My Pretty Ones" (Sexton), **Supp. II Part 2:** 681–682

"All My Sad Captains" (Jewett), **Retro. Supp. II:** 134

All My Sons (A. Miller), **III:** 148, 149, 150, 151–153, 154, 155, 156, 158, 159, 160, 164, 166

All New People (Lamott), **Supp. XX: 135–136**

"All Night, All Night" (Schwartz), **Supp. II Part 2:** 665

All Night Long (Caldwell), **I:** 297

"All-Night Melodies" (Nelson), **Supp. XVIII:** 185

All-Night Visitors (Major), **Supp. XXII: 173–174**

"All of Us" (Major), **Supp. XXII:** 185

All of Us: The Collected Poems (Carver), **Supp. XXIV:** 167

All of What We Loved (Bronk), **Supp. XXI:** 32

"All Our Lost Children: Trauma and Testimony in the Performance of Childhood" (Pace), **Supp. XI:** 245

All Our Yesterdays (Parker), **Supp. XIX: 187–188**

"All Out" (Hecht), **Supp. X:** 72

All Over (Albee), **I:** 91–94

"Allowance" (Minot), **Supp. VI:** 206, 207–208

"Alloy" (Rukeyser), **Supp. VI:** 279

"All Parrots Speak" (Bowles), **Supp. IV Part 1:** 89

Allport, Gordon, **II:** 363–364

All Quiet on the Western Front (Remarque), **Supp. IV Part 1:** 380, 381

"ALL REACTION IS DOOMED-!-!-!" (Baraka), **Supp. II Part 1:** 59

"All Revelation" (Frost), **II:** 160–162

"All Shall Love Me and Despair"(Thompson), **Supp. XXIII:** 295

All Shot Up (C. Himes), **Supp. XVI:** 143, 144

"All Souls" (Gioia), **Supp. XV:** 117

"All Souls" (Wharton), **IV:** 315–316; **Retro. Supp. I:** 382

"All Souls' Night" (Yeats), **Supp. X:** 69

All Souls' Rising (Bell), **Supp. X:** 12, **13– 16,** 17

"All-Star Literary Vaudeville" (Wilson), **IV:** 434–435

Allston, Washington, **II:** 298

All Stories Are True (Wideman), **Supp. X:** 320

"All That Is" (Wilbur), **Supp. III Part 2:** 563

All That Was Possible (Sturgis), **Supp. XX: 227, 232, 235–237**

"All the Bearded Irises of Life: Confessions of a Homospiritual" (Walker), **Supp. III Part 2:** 527

"All the Beautiful Are Blameless" (Wright), **Supp. III Part 2:** 597

ALL: The Collected Poems, 1956–1964 (Zukofsky), **Supp. III Part 2:** 630

ALL: The Collected Short Poems, 1923– 1958 (Zukofsky), **Supp. III Part 2:** 629

All the Conspirators (Isherwood), **Supp. XIV:** 156, 159, 160

All the Dark and Beautiful Warriors (Hansberry), **Supp. IV Part 1:** 360, 374

All the Days and Nights: The Collected Stories (Maxwell), **Supp. VIII:** 151, 158, 169

"All the Dead Dears" (Plath), **Retro. Supp. II:** 246; **Supp. I Part 2:** 537

"All the Dead"(P. Benedict), **Supp. XXIII:** 37

All the Good People I've Left Behind (Oates), **Supp. II Part 2:** 510, 522, 523

"All the Hippos Were Boiled in Their Tanks" (Burroughs and Kerouac), **Supp. III Part 1:** 94

All the King's Men (Warren), **I:** 489; **IV:** 243, 248–249, 252; **Supp. V:** 261; **Supp. VIII:** 126; **Supp. X:** 1; **Supp. XVIII:** 77, 79; **Supp. XXIV:** 226

All the Little Live Things (Stegner), **Supp. IV Part 2:** 599, 604, 605, 606, 609–610, 611, 613

All the Pretty Horses (film), **Supp. VIII:** 175

All the Pretty Horses (McCarthy), **Supp. VIII:** 175, **182–183,** 188

All the Sad Young Men (Fitzgerald), **II:** 94; **Retro. Supp. I:** 108

"All the Time in the World" (Dubus), **Supp. VII:** 91

"All the Way to Flagstaff, Arizona" (Bausch), **Supp. VII:** 47, 49

"All This and More" (Karr), **Supp. XI:** 243

All Tomorrow's Parties (W. Gibson), **Supp. XVI:** 119, 121, 123, 124, **130**

"All Too Real" (Vendler), **Supp. V:** 189

All Trivia: Triva, More Trivia, Afterthoughts, Last Words (L. P. Smith), **Supp. XIV:** 339

All-True Travels and Adventures of Lidie Newton (Smiley), **Supp. VI:** 292, **305–307**

All We Need of Hell (Crews), **Supp. XI:** **114**

Almack, Edward, **Supp. IV Part 2:** 435

al-Maghut, Muhammad, **Supp. XIII:** 278

"Almanac" (Swenson), **Supp. IV Part 2:** 641

Almanac of the Dead (Silko), **Supp. IV Part 2:** 558–559, 560, 561, 570–571

Alma: or, The Dead Women (Notley), **Supp. XXII:** 223, 224, 231, 236

Almon, Bert, **Supp. IX:** 93

"Almost" (Untermeyer), **Supp. XV:** 304

Almost Learning to Live in This World (Schott), **Supp. XXIII:** **247–248**

Almost Revolution, The (Priaulx and Ungar), **Supp. XI:** 228

Alnilam (Dickey), **Supp. IV Part 1:** 176, 186, 188–189

"Alone" (Caputo), **Supp. XIX:** 29

"Alone" (Levine), **Supp. V:** 184, 185, 186

"Alone" (Pickering), **Supp. XXI:** 204

"Alone" (Poe), **Retro. Supp. II:** 266

"Alone" (Singer), **IV:** 15

"Alone" (Winters), **Supp. II Part 2:** 786, 811

"Alone and Lonely" (Budbill), **Supp. XIX:** 10

Aloneness (Brooks), **Supp. III Part 1:** 85, 86

Alone with America (Corso), **Supp. XII:** 131

Alone with America (Howard), **Supp. IX:** 326

"Along America's Edges" (Sobin), **Supp. XVI:** 288

"Along the Color Line" (Du Bois), **Supp. II Part 1:** 173

Along the Illinois (Masters), **Supp. I Part 2:** 472

Alouette, L' (Anouilh), Supp. I Part 1: 286–288

"Alphabet" (Nye), **Supp. XIII:** 283

Alphabet, An (Doty), **Supp. XI:** 120

Alphabet for Gourmets, An (M. F. K. Fisher), **Supp. XVII:** 86, 87, 92

Alphabet of Grace, The (Buechner), **Supp. XII:** 52

"Alphabet of My Dead, An" (Pinsky), **Supp. VI:** 235, 250

"Alphabet of Subjects, An" (Zukofsky), **Supp. III Part 2:** 624

"Alpine Christ, The" (Jeffers), **Supp. II Part 2:** 415, 419

Alpine Christ and Other Poems, The (Jeffers), **Supp. II Part 2:** 419

"Alpine Idyll, An" (Hemingway), **II:** 249; **Retro. Supp. I:** 176

Al Que Quiere! (W. C. Williams), **Retro. Supp. I:** 414, 416, **417,** 428

Alraune (Ewers; Endore, trans.), **Supp. XVII:** 54

Alsop, Joseph, **II:** 579

"Altar, The" (Herbert), **Supp. IV Part 2:** 646

"Altar, The" (MacLeish), **III:** 4

"Altar Boy" (Fante), **Supp. XI:** 160, 164

"Altar of the Dead, The" (James), **Retro. Supp. I:** 229

"Altars in the Street, The" (Levertov), **Supp. III Part 1:** 280

Alter, Robert, **Supp. XII:** 167

Altgeld, John Peter, **Supp. I Part 2:** 382, 455

Althea (Masters), **Supp. I Part 2:** 455, 459

Altick, Richard, **Supp. I Part 2:** 423

Altieri, Charles, **Supp. VIII:** 297, 303; **Supp. XXIII:** 220

Altman, Robert, **Supp. IX:** 143; **Supp. XXIV:** 166, 172

"Alto" (C. Frost), **Supp. XV:** 101

"Altra Ego" (Brodsky), **Supp. VIII:** 31–32

Altruists, The (Silver), **Supp. XXIV:** **273**

A Lume Spento (Pound), **Retro. Supp. I:** 283, 285

"Aluminum House" (F. Barthelme), **Supp. XI:** 26

Alvares, Mosseh, **Supp. V:** 11

Alvarez, A., **Supp. I Part 2:** 526, 527; **Supp. II Part 1:** 99; **Supp. IX:** 248

Alvarez, Joseph A., **Supp. XXII:** 13–14

Alvarez, Julia, **Supp. VII:** **1–21;** **Supp. XI:** 177; **Supp. XVII:** 71, 112; **Supp. XXIV:** 86, 89

"Always a Rose" (L.-Y. Lee), **Supp. XV:** 215, 216

"Always in Good Humor" (Adams), **Supp. XV:** 294

Always Outnumbered, Always Outgunned (Mosley), **Supp. XIII:** 242

"Always the Stories" (Ortiz), **Supp. IV Part 2:** 499, 500, 502, 504, 512

Always the Young Strangers (Sandburg), **III:** 577–578, 579

Always Young and Fair (Richter), **Supp. XVIII:** **215–216**

Amadeus (Shaffer), **Supp. XIV:** 330

"Amahl and the Night Visitors: A Guide to the Tenor of Love" (Moore), **Supp. X:** 167

"Am and Am Not" (Olds), **Supp. X:** 212

"Amanita, The" (Francis), **Supp. IX:** 81

Amaranth (Robinson), **III:** 509, 510, 512, 513, 522, 523

"Amateurs, The" (Swados), **Supp. XIX:** 256

Amazing Adele, The (Barillet and Grédy; Loos, trans.), **Supp. XVI:** 194

Amazing Adventures of Kavalier and Clay, The (Chabon), **Supp. XI:** 68, 76, **77–80; Supp. XXII:** 49

Amazing Adventures of the Escapist, The (Chabon, ed.), **Supp. XIX:** 174

Amazing Science Fiction Stories, **Supp. XVI:** 121

Amazons: An Intimate Memoir by the First Woman to Play in the National Hockey League (DeLillo), **Supp. VI:** 2

Ambassador Morgenthau's Story (Morgenthau), **Supp. XXIII:** 21, 22

Ambassador of Peace, An (Abernon), **Supp. XVI:** 191

Ambassadors, The (H. James), **II:** 320, 333–334, 600; **III:** 517; **IV:** 322; **Retro. Supp. I:** 215, 218, 219, 220, 221, **232–233**

Ambelain, Robert, **Supp. I Part 1:** 260, 273, 274

Ambrose Holt and Family (Glaspell), **Supp. III Part 1:** 175, 181, 184, 187, 188

"Ambrose Seyffert" (Masters), **Supp. I Part 2:** 464

"Ambush" (Komunyakaa), **Supp. XIII:** 122

Amen Corner, The (Baldwin), **Retro. Supp. II:** 5, 7; **Supp. I Part 1:** 48, 51, 54, 55, 56

America (Benét), **Supp. XI:** 46, 47, 51

"America" (Ginsberg), **Supp. II Part 1:** 58–59, 317

"America" (song), **IV:** 410

"America, America!" (poem) (Schwartz), **Supp. II Part 2:** 665

"America, Commerce, and Freedom" (Rowson and Reinagle), **Supp. XV:** 240

"America, Seen Through Photographs, Darkly" (Sontag), **Supp. III Part 2:** 464

"America! America!" (story) (Schwartz), **Supp. II Part 2:** 640, 658–659, 660

America and Americans (Steinbeck), **IV:** 52

"America and the Vidal Chronicles" (Pease), **Supp. IV Part 2:** 687

America as a Civilization (Lerner), **III:** 60

America Behind the Color Line (H. L. Gates), **Supp. XX:** 102, 105

America Beyond the Color Line (television program), **Supp. XX: 99**

America Hispana: A Portrait and a Prospect (W. Frank), **Supp. XX: 76**

"America Independent" (Freneau), **Supp. II Part 1: 261**

America Is Worth Saving (Dreiser), **Retro. Supp. II: 96**

American, The (James), **I:** 226; **II:** 326–327, 328, 331, 334; **IV:** 318; **Retro. Supp. I:** 220, **221,** 228, 376, 381

Americana (DeLillo), **Supp. VI:** 2, **3,** 5, 6, 8, 13, 14

American Adam, The (R. W. B. Lewis), **II:** 457–458; **Supp. XIII:** 93

American Almanac (Leeds), **II:** 110

American Anthem (Doctorow and Suares), **Supp. IV Part 1: 234**

"American Apocalypse" (Gunn Allen), **Supp. IV Part 1: 325**

American Aristocracy (film), **Supp. XVI:** 185–186

American Blood, (Nichols), **Supp. XIII:** 268

American Blues (T. Williams), **IV:** 381, 383

American Buffalo (Mamet), **Supp. XIV:** 239, 241, 242, 244–245, 246, 254, 255

American Caravan: A Yearbook of American Literature (Mumford, ed.), **Supp. II Part 2:** 482

American Cause, The (MacLeish), **III:** 3

American Childhood, An (Dillard), **Supp. VI:** **19–21,** 23, 24, 25, 26, 30, 31

"American Childhood in the Dominican Republic, An" (Alvarez), **Supp. VII:** 2, 5

American Child Supreme, An: The Education of a Liberation Ecologist (Nichols), **Supp. XIII:** 256, 257, 258, 264, 265, 266, 267, 268, 269

American Civilization (C. L. R. James), **Supp. XXI:** 169

American Claimant, The (Twain), **IV:** 194, 198–199

American Crisis I (Paine), **Supp. I Part 2:** 508

American Crisis II (Paine), **Supp. I Part 2:** 508

American Crisis XIII (Paine), **Supp. I Part 2:** 509

"American Critic, The" (J. Spingarn), **I:** 266

American Culture, Canons, and the Case of Elizabeth Stoddard (Smith and Weinauer), **Supp. XV:** 270

American Daughter, An (Wasserstein), **Supp. XV: 330–332,** 333

American Democrat, The (Cooper), **I:** 343, 346, 347, 353

American Desert (Everett), **Supp. XVIII: 62–63**

American Diary (Webb), **Supp. I Part 1:** 5

American Drama since World War II (Weales), **IV:** 385

American Dream, An (Mailer), **III:** 27, 33–34, 35, 39, 41, 43, 44; **Retro. Supp. II:** 203, **204–205**

American Dream, The (Albee), **I:** 74–76, 77, 89, 94; **Supp. XXIV:** 113

"American Dreams" (Simpson), **Supp. IX:** 274

American Earth (Caldwell), **I:** 290, 308

"American Emperors" (Poirier), **Supp. IV Part 2:** 690

American English (Marckwardt), **Supp. XXIV:** 255

American Exodus, An (Lange and Taylor), **I:** 293

American Experience, The (Parkes), **Supp. I Part 2:** 617–618

American Express (Corso), **Supp. XII:** 129

"American Express" (Salter), **Supp. IX:** 260–261

"American Fear of Literature, The" (Lewis), **II:** 451

American Female Patriotism (S. Warner as Wetherell), **Supp. XVIII: 260–261,** 262, 263

American Fictions (Hardwick), **Supp. X:** 171

American Fictions, 1940–1980 (Karl), **Supp. IV Part 1:** 384; **Supp. XXI:** 234

"American Financier, The" (Dreiser), **II:** 428

American Folkways (book series), **I:** 290

American Guerilla in the Philippines (Wolfert), **Supp. XXI:** 267

"American Heart of Darkness: The Moral Vision of Five Novels of the Vietnam War" (Palm), **Supp. XXII:** 103

American Heroine: The Life and Legend of Jane Addams (A. F. Davis), **Supp. I Part 1:** 1

American Historical Novel, The (Leisy), **Supp. II Part 1:** 125

"American Horse" (Erdrich), **Supp. IV Part 1:** 333

American Humor: A Study of the National Character (Rourke), **IV:** 339, 352; **Supp. XIX:** 147

American Hunger (Wright), **Supp. IV Part 1:** 11

"American Husband, The" (Atherton), **Supp. XXIV:** 24

American Indian Anthology, An (Tvedten, ed.), **Supp. IV Part 2:** 505

"American Indian Women: At the Center of Indigenous Resistance in Contemporary North America" (Jaimes and Halsey), **Supp. IV Part 1:** 331

"American in England, An" (Wylie), **Supp. I Part 2:** 707

American Jitters, The: A Year of the Slump (Wilson), **IV:** 427, 428

American Journal (Hayden), **Supp. II Part 1:** 367

American Journey: The Times of Robert F. Kennedy (Plimpton, ed.), **Supp. XVI:** 245

"American Land Ethic, An" (Momaday), **Supp. IV Part 2:** 488

American Landscape, The, **Supp. I Part 1:** 157

American Language, The (Mencken), **II:** 289, 430; **III:** 100, 104, 105, 108, 111, 119–120

American Language, The: Supplement One (Mencken), **III:** 111

American Language, The: Supplement Two (Mencken), **III:** 111

"American Letter" (MacLeish), **III:** 13

"American Liberty" (Freneau), **Supp. II Part 1:** 257

"American Life in Poetry" (column, Kooser), **Supp. XIX:** 116, 127

American Literary History (Harrison), **Supp. VIII:** 37

American Mercury, **Supp. XI:** 163, 164

American Mind, The (Commager), **Supp. I Part 2:** 650

American Moderns: Bohemian New York and the Creation of a New Century (Stansell), **Supp. XVII:** 106

American Moderns: From Rebellion to Conformity (Geismar), **Supp. IX:** 15; **Supp. XI:** 223

"American Names" (Benét), **Supp. XI:** 47

American Nature Writers (Elder, ed.), **Supp. IX:** 25

American Nature Writers (Winter), **Supp. X:** 104

American Negro, The (W. H. Thomas), **Supp. II Part 1:** 168

American Notebooks, The (Hawthorne), **II:** 226

American Novel Since World War II, The (Klein, ed.), **Supp. XI:** 233

Americano, The (film), **Supp. XVI:** 185

"American Original, An: Learning from a Literary Master" (Wilkinson), **Supp. VIII:** 164, 165, 168

American Ornithology (Wilson), **Supp. XVI:** 4, 6

American Pastoral (P. Roth), **Retro. Supp. II:** 279, 289, **292–293; Supp. XI:** 68

American Places (Porter, Stegner and Stegner), **Supp. IV Part 2:** 599

"American Poet" (Shapiro), **Supp. II Part 2:** 702

"American Poetry" (Simpson), **Supp. IX:** 272

American Poetry, 1922: A Miscellany (Untermeyer, ed.), **Supp. XV:** 306

"American Poetry and American Life" (Pinsky), **Supp. VI:** 239–240

American Poetry from the Beginning to Whitman (Untermeyer, ed.), **Supp. XV:** 310

American Poetry since 1900 (Untermeyer, ed.), **Supp. XV:** 306

American Poetry since 1945: A Critical Survey (Stepanchev), **Supp. XI:** 312

American Poetry since 1960 (Mesic), **Supp. IV Part 1:** 175

American Poets since World War II Dictionary of Literary Biography (Gwynn, ed.), **Supp. XV:** 343

American Primer, An (Boorstin), **I:** 253

American Primer, An (Whitman), **IV:** 348

"American Primitive" (W. J. Smith), **Supp. XIII:** 333

American Primitive: Poems (Oliver), **Supp. VII:** 234–237, 238

American Procession, An: The Major American Writers from 1830–1930—the Crucial Century (Kazin), **Supp. VIII:** 105–106, 108

"American Prose Writers" articles (Briggs), **Supp. XVIII:** 11

American Radio Company, The (radio show, Keillor), **Supp. XVI:** 176–177

"American Realist Playwrights, The" (McCarthy), **II:** 562

American Register, or General Repository of History, Politics, and Science, The (Brown, ed.), **Supp. I Part 1:** 146

American Renaissance (Matthiessen), **I:** 259–260; **III:** 310; **Supp. XIII:** 93

"American Rendezvous, An" (Beauvoir), **Supp. IX:** 4

American Scene, The (James), **II:** 336; **III:** 460; **Retro. Supp. I:** 232, 235

American Scenes (Kozlenko, ed.), **IV:** 378

"American Scholar, The" (Emerson), **I:** 239; **II:** 8, 12–13; **Retro. Supp. I:** 62, 74–75, 149, 298; **Retro. Supp. II:** 155; **Supp. I Part 2:** 420; **Supp. IX:** 227, 271; **Supp. XIV:** 104

"American Scholar, The" (Pickering), **Supp. XXI:** 196

Americans in England; or, Lessons for Daughters (Rowson), **Supp. XV:** 240

"American Soldier, The" (Freneau), **Supp. II Part 1:** 269

American Songbag, The (Sandburg), **III:** 583

"American Student in Paris, An" (Farrell), **II:** 45

"American Sublime, The" (Stevens), **IV:** 74

American Taliban (Abraham), **Supp. XXIV:** 2, 12–14

"American Tar, The; or, The Press Gang Defeated" (Rowson and Taylor), **Supp. XV:** 238

"American Temperament, The" (Locke), **Supp. XIV:** 211

American Tragedy, An (Dreiser), **I:** 497, 498, 499, 501, 502, 503, 511–515, 517, 518, 519; **III:** 251; **IV:** 35, 484; **Retro. Supp. II:** 93, 95, 104–108; **Supp. XVII:** 155

"American Triptych" (Kenyon), **Supp. VII:** 165

"American Use for German Ideals" (Bourne), **I:** 228

American Village, The (Freneau), **Supp. II Part 1:** 256, 257

"American Village, The" (Freneau), **Supp. II Part 1:** 256

American Wives and English Husbands (Atherton), **Supp. XXIV:** 18, 22

America's Coming-of-Age (Brooks), **I:** 228, 230, 240, 245, 258; **IV:** 427

America's Humor: From Poor Richard to Doonesbury (Blair and Hill), **Retro. Supp. II:** 286

"America's Part in World Peace" (Locke), **Supp. XIV:** 208

America's Rome (Vance), **Supp. IV Part 2:** 684

America: The Story of a Free People (Commager and Nevins), **I:** 253

America Was Promises (MacLeish), **III:** 16, 17

"Amerika" (Snyder), **Supp. VIII:** 301

Ames, Christopher, **Supp. XVIII:** 242–243

Ames, Fisher, **Supp. I Part 2:** 486

Ames, Lois, **Supp. I Part 2:** 541, 547

Ames, William, **IV:** 158

Ames Stewart, Beatrice, **Supp. IX:** 200

Amichai, Yehuda, **Supp. XI:** 267

Amick, Steve, **Supp. XXII:** 205, 216

Amidon, Stephen, **Supp. XI:** 333

Amiel, Henri F., **I:** 241, 243, 250

Amis, Kingsley, **IV:** 430; **Supp. IV Part 2:** 688; **Supp. VIII:** 167; **Supp. XIII:** 93; **Supp. XV:** 117

Amis, Martin, **Retro. Supp. I:** 278

"Amish, The"(Thompson), **Supp. XXIII:** 295–296

"Amity Hills" (Skloot), **Supp. XX:** 204

Ammons, A. R., **Supp. III Part 2:** 541; **Supp. VII:** 23–38; **Supp. IX:** 41, 42, 46; **Supp. XII:** 121; **Supp. XV:** 115; **Supp. XVII:** 242; **Supp. XIX:** 83

Ammons, Elizabeth, **Retro. Supp. I:** 364, 369; **Retro. Supp. II:** 140

Amnesia Moon (Lethem), **Supp. XVIII:** 136, 138–139

"Among Children" (Levine), **Supp. V:** 192

Among Friends (M. F. K. Fisher), **Supp. XVII:** 89, 90–91, 92

Among My Books (Lowell), **Supp. I Part 2:** 407

"Among School Children" (Yeats), **III:** 249; **Supp. IX:** 52; **Supp. XIV:** 8

"Among the Hills" (Whittier), **Supp. I Part 2:** 703

Among the Isles of Shoals (Thaxter), **Supp. XIII:** 152

"Among Those Present" (Benét), **Supp. XI:** 53

"Amoral Moralist" (White), **Supp. I Part 2:** 648

Amory, Cleveland, **Supp. I Part 1:** 316

Amory, Fred, **Supp. III Part 1:** 2

Amos (biblical book), **II:** 166

Amos and Andy (television program), **Supp. XX:** 103

Amplitude (Gallagher), **Supp. XXIV:** 166, 170

Amran, David, **Supp. XIV:** 150

"Am Strand von Tanger" (Salter), **Supp. IX:** 257

"AMTRAK" (Baraka), **Supp. II Part 1:** 60

"Amulet, The" (Antin), **Supp. XX:** 10

"Amulets" (Hull), **Supp. XXI:** 139

Amy and Isabelle (film), **Supp. XXIII:** 275–276

Amy and Isabelle (Strout), **Supp. X:** 86; **Supp. XXIII:** 273, 274–275, 276–278, 285

"Amy Lowell of Brookline, Mass." (Scott), **II:** 512

Amy Lowell: Portrait of the Poet in Her Time (Gregory), **II:** 512

"Amy Wentworth" (Whittier), **Supp. I Part 2:** 694, 696

Anabase (Perse), **III:** 12

"Anabasis (I)" (Merwin), **Supp. III Part 1:** 342, 346

"Anabasis (II)" (Merwin), **Supp. III Part 1:** 342, 346

Anagrams: A Novel (Moore), **Supp. X:** 163, 164, 167, 169–171, 172

Analects (Confucius), **Supp. IV Part 1:** 14

Analects, The (Pound, trans.), **III:** 472

Analogy (J. Butler), **II:** 8

"Analysis of a Theme" (Stevens), **IV:** 81

Anarchiad, The, A Poem on the Restoration of Chaos and Substantial Night, in Twenty Four Books (Barlow), **Supp. II Part 1:** 70

Anarchist Woman, An (Hapgood), **Supp. XVII:** 102–103; **Supp. XXI:** 5

Anatomy Lesson, and Other Stories, The (Connell), **Supp. XIV:** 84, 87, 89

"Anatomy Lesson, The" (Connell), **Supp. XIV:** 84, 86, 87

Anatomy Lesson, The (P. Roth), **Retro. Supp. II:** 286, 290; **Supp. III Part 2:** 422–423, 425

"Anatomy Lesson of Dr. Nicholaas Tulp, Amsterdam, 1632, The" (Bierds), **Supp. XVII:** 27–28

Anatomy of Criticism (Frye), **Supp. XIII:** 19; **Supp. XIV:** 15

Anatomy of Melancholy (Burton), **III:** 78; **Supp. XVII:** 229

Anatomy of Nonsense, The (Winters), **Supp. II Part 2:** 811, 812

Anaya, Rudolfo A., **Supp. IV Part 2:** 502; **Supp. XIII:** 213, 220; **Supp. XIX:** 97

"Ancestor" (A. Finch), **Supp. XVII:** 72

Ancestors (Atherton), **Supp. XXIV:** 23, 25

Ancestors (Maxwell), **Supp. VIII:** 152, 168

"Ancestors, The" (Tate), **IV:** 128

Ancestral Voice: Conversations with N. Scott Momaday (Woodard), **Supp. IV Part 2:** 484, 485, 486, 489, 493

"Anchorage" (Harjo), **Supp. XII:** 220–221

Ancient Child, The: A Novel (Momaday), **Supp. IV Part 2:** 488, 489–491, 492, 493

"Ancient Egypt/Fannie Goldbarth" (Goldbarth), **Supp. XII:** 191–192

Ancient Evenings (Mailer), **Retro. Supp. II:** 206, 210, 213

Ancient Law, The (Glasgow), **II:** 179–180, 192

Ancient Musics (Goldbarth), **Supp. XII:** 191–192

"Ancient Semitic Rituals for the Dead" (Goldbarth), **Supp. XII:** 191–192

"Ancient World, The" (Doty), **Supp. XI:** 122

& (And) (Cummings), **I:** 429, 431, 432, 437, 445, 446, 448

Andersen, Hans Christian, **I:** 441; **Supp. I Part 2:** 622

Andersen, Hendrik Christian, **Supp. XX: 232**

Anderson, Charles R., **Supp. I Part 1:** 356, 360, 368, 371, 372

Anderson, Frances, **I:** 231

Anderson, Guy, **Supp. X:** 264, 265

Anderson, Henry J., **Supp. I Part 1:** 156

Anderson, Irwin M., **I:** 98–99

Anderson, Mrs. Irwin M., **I:** 98–99

Anderson, Jon, **Supp. V:** 338

Anderson, Judith, **III:** 399

Anderson, Karl, **I:** 99, 103

Anderson, Lorraine, **Supp. XVIII:** 189

Anderson, Margaret, **I:** 103; **III:** 471

Anderson, Margaret Bartlett, **III:** 171

Anderson, Marian, **Supp. XXII:** 283

Anderson, Mary Jane. *See* Lanier, Mrs. Robert Sampson (Mary Jane Anderson)

Anderson, Maxwell, **III:** 159

Anderson, Quentin, **Retro. Supp. I:** 392

Anderson, Robert, **Supp. I Part 1:** 277; **Supp. V:** 108

Anderson, Sally, **Supp. XIII:** 95

Anderson, Sherwood, **I:** 97–120, 211, 374, 375, 384, 405, 423, 445, 480, 487, 495, 506, 518; **II:** 27, 38, 44, 55, 56, 68, 250–251, 263, 271, 289, 451, 456–457; **III:** 220, 224, 382–383, 453, 483, 545, 576, 579; **IV:** 27, 40, 46, 190, 207, 433, 451, 482; **Retro. Supp. I:** 79, 80, 177; **Supp. I Part 2:** 378, 430, 459, 472, 613; **Supp. IV Part 2:** 502; **Supp. V:** 12, 250; **Supp. VIII:** 39, 152; **Supp. IX:** 14, 309; **Supp. XI:** 159, 164; **Supp. XII:** 343; **Supp. XV:** 298; **Supp. XVI:** 17, 20; **Supp. XVII:** 105; **Supp. XX: 69, 75; Supp. XXIII:** 68, 162, 164; **Supp. XXIV:** 136

Anderson, Mrs. Sherwood (Tennessee Mitchell), **I:** 100; **Supp. I Part 2:** 459, 460

Anderson, T. J., **Supp. XIII:** 132

Anderson, Wendy, **Supp. XXI:** 255

Andersson, A., **III:** 252

"And Hickman Arrives" (Ellison), **Retro. Supp. II:** 118, 126; **Supp. II Part 1:** 248

And in the Hanging Gardens (Aiken), **I:** 63

"And It Came to Pass" (Wright), **Supp. XV:** 348

And I Worked at the Writer's Trade (Cowley), **Supp. II Part 1:** 137, 139, 141, 143, 147, 148

"...And Ladies of the Club" (J. W. Miller), **Supp. XX: 161**

And Live Apart (Peacock), **Supp. XIX: 196–197**

Andorra (Cameron), **Supp. XII:** 79, 81, **88–91**

"—and Other Poets" (column; Untermeyer), **Supp. XV:** 294

"*—and Other Poets*" (Untermeyer), *Supp. XV:* 297

Andral, Gabriel, **Supp. I Part 1:** 302

Andre, Michael, **Supp. XII:** 117–118, 129, 132, 133–134

"Andrea Is Changing Her Name" (Brockmeier), **Supp. XXII:** 61

Andre's Mother (McNally), **Supp. XIII:** 206

Andress, Ursula, **Supp. XI:** 307

"Andrew Jackson" (Masters), **Supp. I Part 2:** 472

Andrews, Bruce, **Supp. IV Part 2:** 426

Andrews, Peter, **Supp. XX: 87**

Andrews, Roy Chapman, **Supp. X:** 172

Andrews, Tom, **Supp. XI:** 317

Andrews, Wayne, **IV:** 310

Andrews, William L., **Supp. IV Part 1:** 13; **Supp. XIX:** 72; **Supp. XX: 105**

Andreyev, Leonid Nikolaevich, **I:** 53; **II:** 425

Andria (Terence), **IV:** 363

"Androgynous Kiss" (Gallagher), **Supp. XXIV:** 170

"Andromache" (Dubus), **Supp. VII:** 84

"And Summer Will Not Come Again" (Plath), **Retro. Supp. II:** 242

"And That Night Clifford Died" (Levine), **Supp. V:** 195

And the Band Played On (Shilts), **Supp. X:** 145

"And the Moon Be Still as Bright" (Bradbury), **Supp. IV Part 1:** 106

"And the Sea Shall Give up Its Dead" (Wilder), **IV:** 358

And Things That Go Bump in the Night (McNally), **Supp. XIII: 196–197,** 205, 208

And to Think That I Saw It on Mulberry Street (Geisel), **Supp. XVI:** 100, 101, 104

"And *Ut Pictura Poesis* Is Her Name" (Ashbery), **Supp. III Part 1:** 19

And We Are Millions (Ryan), **Supp. XVIII:** 225

"And Winter" (Boyle), **Supp. XXIV:** 63

"Anecdote and Storyteller" (Howe), **Supp. VI:** 127

"Anecdote of the Jar" (Stevens), **IV:** 83–84

"Anemone" (Rukeyser), **Supp. VI:** 281, 285

"Angel, The" (Buck), **Supp. II Part 1:** 127

"Angel and Unicorn and Butterfly" (Everwine), **Supp. XV:** 76

Angela's Ashes (McCourt), **Supp. XII: 271–279,** 283, 285; **Supp. XXII:** 94

"Angel at the Grave, The" (Wharton), **IV:** 310; **Retro. Supp. I:** 365

"Angel Butcher" (Levine), **Supp. V:** 181

Angel City (Shepard), **Supp. III Part 2:** 432, 445

Angelica (Holding), **Supp. XXII: 120–121**

"Angel Is My Watermark!, The" (H. Miller), **III:** 180

Angell, Carol, **Supp. I Part 2:** 655

Angell, Katharine Sergeant. *See* White, Katharine

Angell, Roger, **Supp. I Part 2:** 655; **Supp. V:** 22; **Supp. VIII:** 139

Angel Landing (Hoffman), **Supp. X: 82–83**

"Angel Levine" (Malamud), **Supp. I Part 2:** 431, 432, 433–434, 437

Angel of Bethesda, The (Mather), **Supp. II Part 2:** 464

"Angel of the Bridge, The" (Cheever), **Supp. I Part 1:** 186–187

"Angel of the Odd, The" (Poe), **III:** 425

Angelo Herndon Jones (Hughes), **Retro. Supp. I:** 203

"Angel on the Porch, An" (Wolfe), **IV:** 451

Angelou, Maya, **Supp. IV Part 1: 1–19; Supp. XI:** 20, 245; **Supp. XIII:** 185; **Supp. XVI:** 259; **Supp. XXI:** 172

"Angel Poem, The" (Stern), **Supp. IX:** 292

Angels and Earthly Creatures (Wylie), **Supp. I Part 2:** 709, 713, 724–730

Angels Flight (Connelly), **Supp. XXI:** 72, **72–73,** 75, 80

"Angels for Djuna Barnes" (Boyle), **Supp. XXIV:** 63

Angels in America: A Gay Fantasia on National Themes (Kushner), **Supp. IX:** 131, 134, **141–146; Supp. XXIV:** 272

"Angels of the Love Affair" (Sexton), **Supp. II Part 2:** 692

"Angel's Trumpet, The"(P. Benedict), **Supp. XXIII:** 48

"Angel Surrounded by Paysans" (Stevens), **IV:** 93

Angel That Troubled the Waters, The (Wilder), **IV:** 356, 357–358

"Anger" (Creeley), **Supp. IV Part 1:** 150–152

Anger (Sarton), **Supp. VIII:** 256

"Anger against Children" (R. Bly), **Supp. IV Part 1:** 73

Angle of Ascent (Hayden), **Supp. II Part 1:** 363, 367, 370

"Angle of Geese" (Momaday), **Supp. IV Part 2:** 485

Angle of Geese and Other Poems (Momaday), **Supp. IV Part 2:** 487, 491

Angle of Repose (Stegner), **Supp. IV Part 2:** 599, 605, 606, 610–611

"*Angle of Repose* and the Writings of Mary Hallock Foote: A Source Study" (Williams-Walsh), **Supp. IV Part 2:** 611

"Anglo-Mongrels and the Rose" (Loy), **Supp. XXII:** 156, 159, 166–167

Anglo-Saxon Century, The (Dos Passos), **I:** 474–475, 483

Angoff, Charles, **III:** 107

"Angola Question Mark" (Hughes), **Supp. I Part 1:** 344

Angry Hills, The (Uris), **Supp. XX: 246, 250**

Angry Wife, The (Sedges), **Supp. II Part 1:** 125

"Angry Women Are Building: Issues and Struggles Facing American Indian Women Today" (Gunn Allen), **Supp. IV Part 1:** 324

"Animal, Vegetable, and Mineral" (Bogan), **Supp. III Part 1:** 66

"Animal Acts" (Simic), **Supp. VIII:** 278

Animal and Vegetable Physiology Considered with Reference to Natural Theol-

ogy (Roget), **Supp. I Part 1:** 312

"Animal Bodies: Corporeality, Class, and Subject Formation in *The Wide, Wide World*" (Mason), **Supp. XVIII:** 263

Animal Dreams (Kingsolver), **Supp. VII:** 199, 204–207

Animal Magnetism (Prose), **Supp. XVI:** 251, 260

"Animals, The" (Merwin), **Supp. III Part 1:** 348

"Animals Are Passing from Our Lives" (Levine), **Supp. V:** 181, 182

Animals in That Country, The (Atwood), **Supp. XIII:** 20, 33

Animals of the Soul: Sacred Animals of the Oglala Sioux (Brown), **Supp. IV Part 2:** 487

"Animals You Eat, The" (X. J. Kennedy), **Supp. XV:** 169

"Animula" (Eliot), **Retro. Supp. I:** 64

Anita Loos Rediscovered (M. A. Loos), **Supp. XVI:** 196

Ankor Wat (Ginsberg), **Supp. II Part 1:** 323

Ann, Leslee, **Supp. XXIV:** 264

"Annabelle" (Komunyakaa), **Supp. XIII:** 117

"Annabel Lee" (Poe), **Retro. Supp. I:** 273; **Retro. Supp. II:** 266

Anna Christie (O'Neill), **III:** 386, 389, 390; **Supp. XXII:** 24

"Anna Grasa" (Weigl), **Supp. XIX:** 278

"Anna in Mourning" (Weigl), **Supp. XIX:** 288

Anna Karenina (Tolstoy), **I:** 10; **II:** 290; **Retro. Supp. I:** 225; **Supp. V:** 323

"Anna Karenina" (Trilling), Supp. III Part 2: 508

Annan, Noel, **Supp. XX: 240**

"Anna's Grace" (Weigl), **Supp. XIX:** 282–283

"Anna Who Was Mad" (Sexton), **Supp. II Part 2:** 692

"Ann Burlak" (Rukeyser), **Supp. VI:** 280

"Anne" (Oliver), **Supp. VII:** 232

"Anne" (R. H. Davis), **Supp. XVI:** 91, 92

"Anne at the Symphony" (Shields), **Supp. VII:** 310

"Anne Bradstreet's Poetic Voices" (Requa), **Supp. I Part 1:** 107

Anne of Geierstein: or, The Maiden of the Mist (Scott), **Supp. XX: 234**

Anne Sexton: The Artist and Her Critics (McClatchy), **Supp. XII:** 253

"Ann from the Street" (Dixon), **Supp. XII:** 146–147

"Ann Garner" (Agee), **I:** 27

"Anniad, The" (Brooks), **Supp. III Part 1:** 77, 78

Annie (musical), **Supp. IV Part 2:** 577

Annie Allen (Brooks), **Supp. III Part 1:** 76–79

Annie Dillard Reader, The (Dillard), **Supp. VI:** 23

Annie Hall (film; Allen), **Supp. IV Part 1:** 205; **Supp. XV:** 1, 2, 4, 5, **6–7,** 14

Annie John (Kincaid), **Supp. VII:** 184–186, 193

Annie Kilburn, a Novel (Howells), **II:** 275, 286, 287

"Annihilation" (X. J. Kennedy), **Supp. XV:** 168

"Annihilation of Matter, The" (Bronk), **Supp. XXI:** 30

Anniversary (Shields), **Supp. VII:** 320, 322, 323, 324

"Annunciation" (Nelson), **Supp. XVIII:** 174

"Annunciation, The" (Le Sueur), **Supp. V:** 130

Ann Vickers (Lewis), **II:** 453

"A No-Account Creole, A" (Chopin), **Retro. Supp. II:** 64

"Anodyne" (Komunyakaa), **Supp. XIII:** 130

Another America/Otra America (Kingsolver), **Supp. VII:** 207–209

"Another Animal" (Swenson), **Supp. IV Part 2:** 639

Another Animal: Poems (Swenson), **Supp. IV Part 2:** 639–641, 649

Another Antigone (Gurney), **Supp. V:** 97, 98, 100, 101, 102, 105

"Another August" (Merrill), **Supp. III Part 1:** 326

"Another Beer" (Matthews), **Supp. IX:** 158

Another Country (Baldwin), **Retro. Supp. II: 9–11,** 14; **Supp. I Part 1:** 51, 52, 56–58, 63, 67, 337; **Supp. II Part 1:** 40; **Supp. VIII:** 349

"Another Language" (Jong), **Supp. V:** 131

Another Mother Tongue: Gay Words, Gay Worlds (Grahn), **Supp. IV Part 1:** 330

"Another Night in the Ruins" (Kinnell), **Supp. III Part 1:** 239, 251

"Another Night with Snow" (W. V. Davis), **Supp. XXI:** 90, 91

"Another Old Woman" (W. C. Williams), **Retro. Supp. I:** 423

Another Part of the Forest (Hellman), **Supp. I Part 1:** 282–283, 297

Another Republic: 17 European and South American Writers (Strand, trans.), **Supp. IV Part 2:** 630

Another Roadside Attraction (Robbins), **Supp. X:** 259, 261, 262, 263, 264, 265–266, **267–269,** 274, 275, 277, 284

Another Side of Bob Dylan (album, Dylan), **Supp. XVIII:** 25

"Another Spring Uncovered" (Swenson), **Supp. IV Part 2:** 644

Another Thin Man (film), **Supp. IV Part 1:** 355

Another Time (Auden), **Supp. II Part 1:** 15

Another Turn of the Crank (Berry), **Supp. X:** 25, 35

"Another upon the Same" (Taylor), **IV:** 161

"Another Voice" (Wilbur), **Supp. III Part 2:** 557

"Another Wife" (Anderson), **I:** 114

"Another Winter Night" (Budbill), **Supp. XIX:** 10

Another Woman (film; Allen), **Supp. XV:** 11

Another You (Beattie), **Supp. V:** 29, 31, 33–34

Anouilh, Jean, **Supp. I Part 1:** 286–288, 297

Ansa, Tina McElroy, **Supp. XVIII:** 195

"Anselm" (Berrigan), **Supp. XXIV:** 43

Ansen, Alan, **Supp. XXIII:** 112, 122, 123

Ansky, S., **IV:** 6

Ansky, Shloime, **Supp. IX:** 131, 138

"Answer, The" (Jeffers), **Supp. III Part 2:** 423

Answered Prayers: The Unfinished Novel (Capote), **Supp. III Part 1:** 113, 125, 131–132; **Supp. XVI:** 245

"Answering the Deer: Genocide and Continuance in the Poetry of American Indian Women" (Gunn Allen), **Supp. IV Part 1:** 322, 325

"Answer of Minerva, The: Pacifism and Resistance in Simone Weil" (Merton), **Supp. VIII:** 204

Antaeus (Wolfe), **IV:** 461

"Ante-Bellum Sermon, An" (Dunbar), **Supp. II Part 1:** 203–204

Antheil, George, **III:** 471, 472; **IV:** 404

Anthem (Rand), **Supp. IV Part 2:** 523

Anthology of Holocaust Literature (Glatstein, Knox, and Margoshes, eds.), **Supp. X:** 70

Anthology of Modern American Poetry (Nelson, ed.), **Supp. XXII:** 271

Anthology of Twentieth-Century Brazilian Poetry, An (Bishop and Brasil, eds.), **Retro. Supp. II:** 50; **Supp. I Part 1:** 94

Anthon, Kate, **I:** 452

Anthony, Adelina, **Supp. XXIII:** 197

Anthony, Andrew, **Supp. XVI:** 235, 245, 246

Anthony, Saint, **III:** 395

Anthony, Susan B., **Supp. XI:** 200

"Anthropologist as Hero, The" (Sontag), **Supp. III Part 2:** 451

"Anthropology of Water, The" (Carson), **Supp. XII: 102–103**

Anthropos: The Future of Art (Cummings), **I:** 430

Antichrist (Nietzsche), **III:** 176

"Anti-Father" (Dove), **Supp. IV Part 1:** 246

"Anti-Feminist Woman, The" (Rich), **Supp. I Part 2:** 550

Antigone (Sophocles), **Supp. I Part 1:** 284; **Supp. X:** 249

"Anti-Memoir"(Dybek), **Supp. XXIII:** 78

Antin, David, **Supp. VIII:** 292; **Supp. XII:** 2, 8

Antin, Mary, **Supp. IX:** 227; **Supp. XVI:** 148, 149; **Supp. XX: 1–16**

Anti-Oedipus: Capitalism and Schizophrenia (Deleuze and Guattari), **Supp. XII:** 4

Antiphon, The (Barnes), **Supp. III Part 1:** 43–44

"Antiquities" (Mather), **Supp. II Part 2:** 452

"Antiquity of Freedom, The" (Bryant), **Supp. I Part 1:** 168

"Antislavery Tocsin, An" (Douglass), **Supp. III Part 1:** 171

Antoine, Andre, **III:** 387

Antonioni, Michelangelo, **Supp. IV Part 1:** 46, 47, 48

Antony and Cleopatra (Shakespeare), **I:** 285

"Antony on Behalf of the Play" (Burke), **I:** 284

"An trentiesme de mon Eage, L" (MacLeish), **III:** 9

Antrim, Donald, **Supp. XX:** 90

"Ants" (R. Bly), **Supp. IV Part 1:** 71

Anxiety of Influence, The (Bloom), **Supp. XIII:** 46

"Any City" (Untermeyer), **Supp. XV:** 296

"Any Object" (Swenson), **Supp. IV Part 2:** 640

Anyplace but Here (Bontemps and Conroy), **Supp. XXII:** 11

"Any Porch" (Parker), **Supp. IX:** 194

Anything Else (film; Allen), **Supp. XV:** 2, 11

"Anywhere Out of This World" (Baudelaire), **II:** 552

Any Woman Can't (Wasserstein), **Supp. XV:** 322

Any Woman's Blues (Jong), **Supp. V:** 115, 123, 126

Anzaldúa, Gloria, **Supp. IV Part 1:** 330; **Supp. XIII:** 223; **Supp. XXIII:** 193, 194, 205

"Apache Tears" (Cliff), **Supp. XXII:** 76

"Aphorisms on Futurism" (Loy), **Supp. XXII:** 159

"Aphorisms on Society" (Stevens), **Retro. Supp. I:** 303

"Apiary IX" (C. Frost), **Supp. XV:** 106

"Apisculptures" (Bierds), **Supp. XVII:** 29

"Apocalypse: What Disaster Reveals" (Díaz), **Supp. XXIV:** 94–95

Apollinaire, Guillaume, **I:** 432; **II:** 529; **III:** 196; **IV:** 80; **Retro. Supp. II:** 326; **Supp. XV:** 182; **Supp. XXIII:** 208

Apologies to the Iroquois (Wilson), **IV:** 429

"Apology" (C. Frost), **Supp. XV:** 103

"Apology, An" (Malamud), **Supp. I Part 2:** 435, 437

"Apology for Bad Dreams" (Jeffers), **Supp. II Part 2:** 427, 438; **Supp. XVII:** 112

"Apology for Crudity, An" (Anderson), **I:** 109

Apology for Poetry (Sidney), **Supp. II Part 1:** 105

Apostle, The (Asch), **Supp. XXIII:** 2, 4, 9, 13–14

"Apostle of the Tules, An" (Harte), **Supp. II Part 1:** 356

"Apostrophe to a Dead Friend" (Kumin), **Supp. IV Part 2:** 442, 451, 452

"Apostrophe to a Pram Rider" (White), **Supp. I Part 2:** 678

"Apostrophe to Man (on reflecting that the world is ready to go to war again)" (Millay), **III:** 127

"Apostrophe to Vincentine, The" (Stevens), **IV:** 90

"Apotheosis" (Kingsolver), **Supp. VII:** 208

"Apotheosis of Martin Luther King, The" (Hardwick), **Supp. III Part 1:** 203–204

Appalachia (Wright), **Supp. V:** 333, 345

Appalachia Inside Out (Miller, Higgs, and Manning, eds.), **Supp. XX:** 166

"Appalachian Book of the Dead III" (Wright), **Supp. V:** 345

"Appalachian Education: A Critique and Suggestions for Reform" (J. W. Miller), **Supp. XX:** 165

"Appalachian Literature: At Home in This World" (J. W. Miller), **Supp. XX:** 165

"Appalachian Values/American Values" (J. W. Miller), **Supp. XX:** 165

Appaloosa (Parker), **Supp. XIX:** 187

"Appeal to H. G. Wells" (Sturgis), **Supp. XX:** 233, 240

"Appeal to Progressives, An" (Wilson), **IV:** 429

Appeal to Reason (Paine), **I:** 490

Appeal to the World, An (Du Bois), **Supp. II Part 1:** 184

Appearance and Reality (Bradley), **I:** 572

"Appendix to 'The Anniad' " (Brooks), **Supp. III Part 1:** 77

"Applause, Applause"(Thompson), **Supp. XXIII:** 289, 291, 301

Apple, Max, **Supp. VIII:** 14; **Supp. XVII:** 1–11, 49–50

Apple, Sam, **Supp. XVII:** 8

"Apple, The" (Kinnell), **Supp. III Part 1:** 250

Applebaum, Anne, **Supp. XVI:** 153

Applebome, Peter, **Supp. XXI:** 38

Applegarth, Mabel, **II:** 465, 478

"Apple-Maggot Fly, The" (Major), **Supp. XXII:** 182

"Apple of Discord, The" (Humphrey), **Supp. IX:** 109

"Apple Peeler" (Francis), **Supp. IX:** 82

"Apple Rind" (C. Frost), **Supp. XV:** 102

"Apples" (Brockmeier), **Supp. XXII:** 51, 53

"Apples, The" (Di Piero), **Supp. XIX:** 46

Appleseed, Johnny (pseudonym). *See* Chapman, John (Johnny Appleseed)

Apple That Astonished Paris, The (Collins), **Supp. XXI:** 53, 57

Appleton, Nathan, **II:** 488

Appleton, Thomas Gold, **Supp. I Part 1:** 306; **Supp. I Part 2:** 415

"Apple Tree, The" (McCarriston), **Supp. XIV:** 263, 268

"Applicant, The" (Plath), **Retro. Supp. II:** 252; **Supp. I Part 2:** 535, 544, 545

"Application, The" (Neugeboren), **Supp. XVI:** 219, 220, 225

"Applications of the Doctrine" (Hass), **Supp. VI:** 100–101

Appointment, The (film), **Supp. IX:** 253

Appointment in Samarra (O'Hara), **III:** 361, 363–364, 365–367, 371, 374, 375, 383

Appreciation of Sarah Orne Jewett (Cary), **Retro. Supp. II:** 132

"Apprentice, The"(Dybek), **Supp. XXIII:** 71

"Approaches, The" (Merwin), **Supp. III Part 1:** 350

"Approaching Artaud" (Sontag), **Supp. III Part 2:** 470–471

"Approaching Prayer" (Dickey), **Supp. IV Part 1:** 175

"Approaching the Mohawk Village: Jogues' Journal"(Kenny), **Supp. XXIII:** 152

Approach to Literature, An: A Collection of Prose and Verse with Analyses and Discussions (Brooks, Warren, and Purser), **Su pp. XIV:**4

"Approach to Thebes, The" (Kunitz), **Supp. III Part 1:** 265–267

Approach to Vedanta, An (Isherwood), **Supp. XIV:** 157, 163, 164

"Appropriation of Cultures, The" (Everett), **Supp. XVIII:** 66

Approximately Paradise (Skloot), **Supp. XX:** 196, 202, 203–204

"Après-midi d'un faune, L' " (Mallarmé), **III:** 8

"April" (Bierds), **Supp. XVII:** 29

"April" (W. C. Williams), **Retro. Supp. I:** 422

"April" (Winters), **Supp. II Part 2:** 788

April, Steve. *See* Lacy, Ed

April Galleons (Ashbery), **Supp. III Part 1:** 26

"April Galleons" (Ashbery), **Supp. III Part 1:** 26

April Hopes (Howells), **II:** 285, 289

"April Lovers" (Ransom), **III:** 489–490

"April Showers" (Wharton), **Retro. Supp. I:** 361

"April Today Main Street" (Olson), **Supp. II Part 2:** 581

April Twilights (Cather), **I:** 313; **Retro. Supp. I:** 5

"Apt Pupil" (King), **Supp. V:** 152

Arabian Nights, **I:** 204; **II:** 8; **Supp. I Part 2:** 584, 599; **Supp. IV Part 1:** 1

"Arabic Coffee" (Nye), **Supp. XIII:** 276

"Araby" (Joyce), **I:** 174; **Supp. VIII:** 15

Aragon, Louis, **I:** 429; **III:** 471; **Retro. Supp. II:** 85, 321

Arana-Ward, Marie, **Supp. VIII:** 84

Ararat (Glück), **Supp. V:** 79, 86–87

Aratani, Mariko, **Supp. XXIII:** 136

Arbre du voyageur, L' (W. J. Smith; Haussmann, trans.), **Supp. XIII:** 347

Arbus, Diane, **Supp. XII:** 188

Arbuthnott, John (pseudonym). *See* Henry, O.

"Arc, The" (Bidart), **Supp. XV:** 25–26, 27

Archaeologist of Morning (Olson), **Supp. II Part 2:** 557

Archaeology of the Circle: New and Selected Poems (Weigl), **Supp. XIX:** 282

"Archaic Maker, The" (Merwin), **Supp. III Part 1:** 357

"Archaic Torso of Apollo" (Rilke), **Supp. XV:** 148

"Archaischer Torso Apollos" (Rilke), **Supp. XVII:** 244

"Archbishop, The" (Gioia), **Supp. XV:** 126, 127

Archer (television show), **Supp. IV Part 2:** 474

Archer, William, **IV:** 131; **Retro. Supp. I:** 228

Archer at Large (Macdonald), **Supp. IV Part 2:** 473

Archer in Hollywood (Macdonald), **Supp. IV Part 2:** 474

"Archetype and Signature: The Relationship of Poet and Poem" (Fiedler), **Supp. XIII:** 101

"Archibald Higbie" (Masters), **Supp. I Part 2:** 461

"Architect, The" (Bourne), **I:** 223

Architect, The (Briggs and Ranlett), **Supp. XVIII:** 3

Arctic Dreams (Lopez), **Supp. V:** 211

Arctic Refuge: A Circle of Testimony (Haines), **Supp. XII:** 205

"Arcturus" (Connell), **Supp. XIV:** 88

À rebours (Huysmans), **Supp. XX:** 239

Arendt, Hannah, **II:** 544; **Retro. Supp. I:** 87; **Retro. Supp. II:** 28, 117; **Supp. I Part 2:** 570; **Supp. IV Part 1:** 386; **Supp. VIII:** 98, 99, 100, 243; **Supp. XII:** 166–167

Arensberg, Louise, **Supp. XXII:** 162

Arensberg, Walter, **IV:** 408; **Retro. Supp. I:** 416; **Supp. XXII:** 162

Aren't You Happy for Me? (Bausch), **Supp. VII:** 42, 51, 54

Areopagitica (Milton), **Supp. I Part 2:** 422

"Are You a Doctor?" (Carver), **Supp. III Part 1:** 139–141

"Are You Mr. William Stafford?" (Stafford), **Supp. XI:** 317

Argall: The True Story of Pocahontas and Captain John Smith (Vollmann), **Supp. XVII:** 225, 226, 231, 232, 233

"Argonauts of 49, California's Golden Age" (Harte), **Supp. II Part 1:** 353, 355

"Arguantando" (Díaz), **Supp. XXIV:** 88–89

"Arguments of Everlasting" (B. Kelly), **Supp. XVII:** 129

"Arguments with the Gestapo Continued: II" (Wright), **Supp. XV:** 344

"Arguments with the Gestapo Continued: Literary Resistance" (Wright), **Supp. XV:** 344

Ari (musical, Uris), **Supp. XX:** 247

Aria da Capo (Millay), **III:** 137–138

Ariadne's Thread: A Collection of Contemporary Women's Journals (Lifshin, ed.), **Supp. XVI:** 37–38

"Arias, 1971" (Hull), **Supp. XXI:** 135

Ariel (Plath), **Retro. Supp. II:** 250–255; **Supp. I Part 2:** 526, 539, 541; **Supp. V:** 79; **Supp. XXI:** 58; **Supp. XXII:** 93

"Ariel" (Plath), **Supp. I Part 2:** 542, 546

"Ariel Poems" (Eliot), **I:** 579

Ariosto, Ludovico, **Supp. XV:** 175

"Ariosto: Critical Notice of His Life and Genius" (Hunt), **Supp. XV:** 175

Arise, Arise (Zukofsky), **Supp. III Part 2:** 619, 629

Aristides. *See* Epstein, Joseph

"Aristocracy" (Emerson), **II:** 6

Aristocracy and Justice (More), **I:** 223

Aristocrat, The (Richter), **Supp. XVIII:** 220

Aristophanes, **I:** 436; **II:** 577; **Supp. I Part 2:** 406

Aristotle, **I:** 58, 265, 280, 527; **II:** 9, 12, 198, 536; **III:** 20, 115, 145, 157, 362, 422, 423; **IV:** 10, 18, 74–75, 89; **Supp. I Part 1:** 104, 296; **Supp. I Part 2:** 423; **Supp. IV Part 1:** 391; **Supp. IV Part 2:** 526, 530; **Supp. X:** 78; **Supp. XI:** 249; **Supp. XII:** 106; **Supp. XIV:** 242–243

Aristotle Contemplating the Bust of Homer (Rembrandt), **Supp. IV Part 1:** 390, 391

"Arkansas Traveller" (Wright), **Supp. V:** 334

Arlen, Harold, **Supp. XXII:** 6

"Arm, The" (X. J. Kennedy), **Supp. XV:** 169

"Armadillo, The" (Bishop), **Supp. I Part 1:** 93

Armadillo in the Grass (Hearon), **Supp. VIII: 58–59**

"Armageddon" (Ransom), **III:** 489, 492

Armageddon (Uris), **Supp. XX: 243, 247, 248, 252–253**

Armah, Aiy Kwei, **Supp. IV Part 1:** 373

Armenian Golgotha: A Memoir of the Armenian Genocide, 1915– 1918 (Grigoris Balakian; trans. Peter Balakian and Sevag), **Supp. XXIII: 28, 29–32**

Armies of the Night, The (Mailer), **III:** 39–40, 41, 42, 44, 45, 46; **Retro. Supp. II:** 205, 206–207, 208; **Supp. IV Part 1:** 207; **Supp. XIV:** 49, 162

"Arm in Arm" (Simpson), **Supp. IX:** 267–268

Arminius, Jacobus, **I:** 557

Armitage, Shelley, **Supp. IV Part 2:** 439

Arm of Flesh, The (Salter), **Supp. IX:** 251

"Armor" (Dickey), **Supp. IV Part 1:** 179

Armored Attack (film), **Supp. I Part 1:** 281

Arms, George W., **Supp. I Part 2:** 416–417

Armstrong, George, **Supp. I Part 2:** 386

Armstrong, Louis, **Retro. Supp. II:** 114

"'Arm the Paper Arm': Kenneth Koch's Postmodern Comedy" (Chinitz), **Supp. XV:** 180, 185

"Army" (Corso), **Supp. XII:** 117, 127

Army Brat (W. J. Smith), **Supp. XIII:** 331, 347

Arna Bontemps Langston Hughes: Letters 1925–1967 (Nichols), **Retro. Supp. I:** 194

"Arna Bontemps Talks About the Renaissance" (Collins), **Supp. XXII:** 7

Arner, Robert D., **Retro. Supp. II:** 62

"Arnie" (Budbill), **Supp. XIX:** 6

Arnold, Edwin T., **Supp. VIII:** 189

Arnold, George W., **Supp. I Part 2:** 411

Arnold, Marilyn, **Supp. IV Part 1:** 220

Arnold, Matthew, **I:** 222, 228, 275; **II:** 20, 110, 338, 541; **III:** 604; **IV:** 349; **Retro. Supp. I:** 56, 325; **Supp. I Part 2:** 416, 417, 419, 529, 552, 602; **Supp. IX:** 298; **Supp. XIV:** 11, 335; **Supp. XIX:** 41; **Supp. XXI:** 90

Arnold, Thurman, **Supp. I Part 2:** 645

Aronson, Steven M. L., **Supp. V:** 4

Around about America (Caldwell), **I:** 290

"Arrangement in Black and White" (Parker), **Supp. IX:** 198

"Arrival at Santos" (Bishop), **Retro. Supp. II:** 46; **Supp. IX:** 45–46

"Arrival of the Bee Box, The" (Plath), **Retro. Supp. II:** 255

Arrivistes, The: Poem 1940–1949 (Simpson), **Supp. IX:** 265, **267–268**

Arrogance (J. Scott), **Supp. XVII: 186– 188,** 189, 191, 192, 194

"Arrow" (Dove), **Supp. IV Part 1:** 250

Arrowsmith (Lewis), **I:** 362; **II:** 445–446, 449

"Arsenal at Springfield, The" (Longfellow), **Retro. Supp. II:** 168

"Arson at Midnight" (Nelson), **Supp. XVIII:** 186

"Arson Plus" (Hammett), **Supp. IV Part 1:** 343; **Supp. XXI:** 68

"Ars Poetica" (Dove), **Supp. IV Part 1:** 250

"Ars Poetica" (Dunn), **Supp. XI:** 154

"Ars Poetica" (MacLeish), **III:** 9–10

"Ars Poetica" (X. J. Kennedy), **Supp. XV:** 154

"Ars Poetica: A Found Poem" (Kumin), **Supp. IV Part 2:** 455

"Ars Poetica; or, Who Lives in the Ivory Tower" (McGrath), **Supp. X:** 117

"Ars Poetica: Some Recent Criticism" (Wright), **Supp. III Part 2:** 603

"Art" (Emerson), **II:** 13

Art (Reza), **Supp. XXI:** 148

"Art and Architecture of the Double Ending, The"(Painter), **Supp. XXIII:** 295

"Art and Neurosis" (Trilling), **Supp. III Part 2:** 502

Art and Technics (Mumford), **Supp. II Part 2:** 483

Art & Ardor: Essays (Ozick), **Supp. V:** 258, 272

Art as Experience (Dewey), **I:** 266

Art by Subtraction (Reid), **IV:** 41

Art Chronicles 1954–1966 (O'Hara), **Supp. XXIII:** 220

Art de toucher le clavecin, L' (Couperin), *III:* 464

Artemis to Actaeon and Other Verse (Wharton), **Retro. Supp. I:** 372

Arte of English Poesie (Puttenham), **Supp. I Part 1:** 113

"Art"(Hadas), **Supp. XXIII:** 115–116

"Art History" (Cliff), **Supp. XXII:** 75–76

Arthur, Anthony, **Supp. IV Part 2:** 606

Arthur Mervyn; or, Memoirs of the Year 1793 (Brown), **Supp. I Part 1:** 137–140, 144

"Article of Faith" (Sobin), **Supp. XVI:** 291

Articles of Light & Elation (Sobin), **Supp. XVI:** 291

Articulation of Sound Forms in Time (Howe), **Supp. IV Part 2:** 419, 431–433

"Artificer" (X. J. Kennedy), **Supp. XV:** 160

"Artificial Nigger, The" (O'Connor), **III:** 343, 351, 356, 358; **Retro. Supp. II:** 229, 232

Artist, The: A Drama without Words (Mencken), **III:** 104

Artist as Revolutionary, The (Buhle), **Supp. XXI:** 172

"Artist of the Beautiful, The" (Hawthorne), **Retro. Supp. I:** 149

Artistry of Grief (Torsney), **Retro. Supp. I:** 224

Artists and Concubines (Silver), **Supp. XXIV:** 265

"Artists' and Models' Ball, The" (Brooks), **Supp. III Part 1:** 72

Art of Detective Fiction, The (Swales), **Supp. XIX:** 183

"Art of Disappearing, The" (Nye), **Supp. XIII:** 287

Art of Drowning, The (Collins), **Supp. XXI:** 54, 60, 64

Art of Eating, The (M. F. K. Fisher), **Supp. XVII:** 87, 90, 91

Art of Fiction, The (Gardner), **Supp. VI:** 73

"Art of Fiction, The" (H. James), **Retro. Supp. I:** 226; **Retro. Supp. II:** 223

Art of Hunger, The (Auster), **Supp. XII:** 22

"Art of Keeping Your Mouth Shut, The" (Heller), **Supp. IV Part 1:** 383

"Art of Literature and Commonsense, The" (Nabokov), **Retro. Supp. I:** 271

Art of Living and Other Stories, The (Gardner), **Supp. VI:** 72

Art of Love, The (Koch), **Supp. XV:** 182

"Art of Love, The" (Koch), **Supp. XV:** 182

Art of Poetry, The (Koch), **Supp. XV:** 175–176, 178, 188

"Art of Poetry, The" (Koch), **Supp. XV:** 182

"Art of Poetry, The" (McClatchy), **Supp. XII:** 262

"Art of Romare Bearden, The" (Ellison), **Retro. Supp. II:** 123

"Art of Storytelling, The" (Simpson), **Supp. IX:** 277

Art of Sylvia Plath, The (Newman), **Supp. I Part 2:** 527

Art of the Moving Picture, The (Lindsay), **Supp. I Part 2:** 376, 391–392, 394; **Supp. XVI:** 185

Art of the Novel (H. James), **Retro. Supp. I:** 227

"Art of Theodore Dreiser, The" (Bourne), **I:** 235

Art of the Personal Essay, The (Lopate, comp.), **Supp. XIII:** 280–281; **Supp. XVI:** 266

Art of the Self, The: Essays a Propos "Steps" (Kosinski), *Supp. VII:* 222

Art of the Wasted Day, The (Hampl), **Supp. XXII:** 85

Arts and Sciences (Goldbarth), **Supp. XII: 184–186**

Arts and Sciences: A Seventies Seduction (Mallon), **Supp. XIX:** 132, 135

"Art's Bread and Butter" (Benét), **Retro. Supp. I:** 108

Artsybashev, Mikhail, **Supp. XXIII:** 1

Arvin, Newton, **I:** 259; **II:** 508; **Retro. Supp. I:** 19, 137

Asali, Muna, **Supp. XIII:** 121, 126

"As a Little Child" (Taggard), **Supp. XXII:** 272

Asbury, Herbert, **Supp. IV Part 1:** 353

Ascent of F6, The (Auden), **Supp. II Part 1:** 11, 13

Ascent to Truth, The (Merton), **Supp. VIII:** 208

Asch, Nathan, **Supp. XV:** 133, 134; **Supp. XXIII:** 4

Asch, Sholem, **IV:** 1, 9, 11, 14; **Retro. Supp. II:** 299; **Supp. XXIII: 1–18**

Ascherson, Neal, **Supp. XII:** 167

Ascher-Walsh, Rebecca, **Supp. XIX:** 54

"As Close as Breathing" (Jarman), **Supp. XVII:** 120

As David Danced (Bronk), **Supp. XXI:** 24

"As David Danced" (Bronk), **Supp. XXI:** 26

As Does New Hampshire and Other Poems (Sarton), **Supp. VIII:** 259

"As Evening Lays Dying" (Salinas), **Supp. XIII:** 319

"As Flowers Are" (Kunitz), **Supp. III Part 1:** 265

"Ash" (Sobin), **Supp. XVI:** 284–285

Ash, Nathan, **Supp. XXII:** 277

Ashbery, John, **Retro. Supp. I:** 313; **Supp. I Part 1:** 96; **Supp. III Part 1: 1–29; Supp. III Part 2:** 541; **Supp. IV Part 2:** 620; **Supp. VIII:** 272; **Supp. IX:** 52; **Supp. XI:** 139; **Supp. XIII:** 85; **Supp. XV:** 176, 177, 178, 188, 250; **Supp. XIX:** 40, 83; **Supp. XXI:** 227; **Supp. XXIII:** 207, 209, 210, 211, 215, 217, 220; **Supp. XXIV:** 33, 37, 44

"Ashes" (Lamott), **Supp. XX: 141**

"Ashes" (Levine), **Supp. V:** 188

"Ashes of the Beacon" (Bierce), **I:** 209

Ashes: Poems Old and New (Levine), **Supp. V:** 178, 188–189

Ashford, Margaret Mary (Daisy), **II:** 426

Ashman, Angela, **Supp. XXIV:** 200

"Ash Wednesday" (Garrett), **Supp. VII:** 109–110

"Ash Wednesday" (Merton), **Supp. VIII:** 199

Ash Wednesday (T. S. Eliot), **I:** 570, 574–575, 578–579, 580, 582, 584, 585; **Retro. Supp. I:** 64

"Ash Wednesday" (T. S. Eliot), **Supp. IV Part 2:** 436

Asian American Authors (Hsu and Palubinskas, eds.), **Supp. X:** 292

Asian American Heritage: An Anthology of Prose and Poetry (Wand), **Supp. X:** 292

Asian Figures (Mervin), **Supp. III Part 1:** 341

Asian Journal of Thomas Merton, The (Merton), **Supp. VIII:** 196, 206, 208

"Asian Peace Offers Rejected without Publication" (R. Bly), **Supp. IV Part 1:** 61

"Asides on the Oboe" (Stevens), **Retro. Supp. I:** 305

"As I Ebb'd with the Ocean of Life" (Whitman), **IV:** 342, 345–346; **Retro. Supp. I:** 404, 405

As I Lay Dying (Faulkner), **II:** 60–61, 69, 73, 74; **IV:** 100; **Retro. Supp. I:** 75, 82, 84, 85, 86, 88, 89, 91, 92; **Supp. IV Part 1:** 47; **Supp. VIII:** 37, 178; **Supp. IX:** 99, 103, 251; **Supp. XIV:** 24

"As I Lay with My Head in Your Lap, Camerado" (Whitman), **IV:** 347

Asimov, Isaac, **Supp. IV Part 1:** 116; **Supp. XVI:** 122

Asinof, Eliot, **II:** 424

As I Remember It (PBS documentary), **Supp. XVIII:** 277

Asirvatham, Sandy, **Supp. XVI:** 249

"As Is the Daughter, So Is Her Mother" (Patchett), **Supp. XII:** 310

"As It Was in the Beginning" (Benét), **Supp. XI:** 56

"As I Walked Out One Evening" (Auden), **Supp. II Part 1:** 13; **Supp. XV:** 126; **Supp. XX: 138**

"As I Went Down by Havre de Grace" (Wylie), **Supp. I Part 2:** 723

Ask a Policeman (Hinojosa), **Supp. XIX: 110–111**

"Ask Me" (Stafford), **Supp. XI:** 326–327

Ask Me Tomorrow (Cozzens), **I:** 365–367, 379

Ask the Dust (Fante), **Supp. XI:** 159, 160, 166, **167–169**, 172, 173, 174

"Ask the Optimist!" (Saunders), **Supp. XIX:** 235

Ask Your Mama (Hughes), **Supp. I Part 1:** 339, 341–342

Ask Your Mama: 12 Moods for Jazz (Hughes), **Retro. Supp. I:** 210, 211

As Little Children (R. P. Smith), **Supp. XIV:** 333

"As One Put Drunk into the Packet Boat" (Ashbery), **Supp. III Part 1:** 18

"Asparagus" (Nelson), **Supp. XVIII:** 178

"Aspects of Robinson" (Kees), **Supp. XV:** 134

Aspects of the Novel (Forster), **Retro. Supp. I:** 232; **Supp. VIII:** 155; **Supp. XXI:** 233

"Aspen and the Stream, The" (Wilbur), **Supp. III Part 2:** 555, 556

Aspern Papers, The (James), **Supp. V:** 101, 102

"Aspern Papers, The" (James), **Retro. Supp. I:** 219, 227, 228

Asphalt Georgics (Carruth), **Supp. XVI:** 54

Asphalt Jungle (film, Huston), **Supp. XIII:** 174

"Asphodel" (Welty), **IV:** 265, 271

"Asphodel, That Greeny Flower" (W. C. Williams), **Retro. Supp. I:** 429

"Aspic and Buttermilk" (Olds), **Supp. X:** 213

Asquith, Herbert Henry, **Retro. Supp. I:** 59

"Ass" (Cisneros), **Supp. VII:** 67

Assante, Armand, **Supp. VIII:** 74

Assassin, The: A Play in Three Acts (Shaw), **Supp. XIX:** 248

Assassins, The (Oates), **Supp. II Part 2:** 512, 517–519

"Assault" (Millay), **III:** 130–131

"Assemblage of Husbands and Wives, An" (Lewis), **II:** 455–456

"Assembloir" (Monson), **Supp. XXIV:** 237

Assembly (O'Hara), **III:** 361

As She Climbed Across the Table (Lethem), **Supp. XVIII: 140–141,** 148

Assignment, Wildlife (LaBastille), **Supp. X:** 99, 104

"Assimiliation in Recent American Jewish Autobiographies" (Krupnick), **Supp. XVI:** 153

Assistant, The (Malamud), **Supp. I Part 2:** 427, 428, 429, 431, 435, 441–445, 451; **Supp. XVI:** 220

Assommoir, L' (Zola), **II:** 291; **III:** 318

Assorted Prose (Updike), **IV:** 215–216, 218; **Retro. Supp. I:** 317, 319, 327

Astaire, Adele, **Supp. XVI:** 187

As They Were (M. F. K. Fisher), **Supp. XVII:** 88, 89, 91

Astor, Mary, **Supp. IV Part 1:** 356; **Supp. XII:** 173

Astoria, or, Anecdotes of an Enterprise beyond the Rocky Mountains (Irving), **II:** 312

"Astounding News by Electric Express via Norfolk! The Atlantic Crossed in Three Days Signal Triumph of Mr. Monck's Flying-Machine . . ." (Poe), **III:** 413, 420

Astraea (Holmes), **III:** 82

Astro, Richard, **Supp. I Part 2:** 429, 445

"Astrological Fricassee" (H. Miller), **III:** 187

"Astronomer's Wife" (Boyle), **Supp. XXIV:** 58

Astrophil and Stella (Sidney), **Supp. XIV:** 128

Asturias, Miguel Ángel, **Supp. XXIV:** 89

"As Weary Pilgrim" (Bradstreet), **Supp. I Part 1:** 103, 109, 122

As We Know (Ashbery), **Supp. III Part 1:** 9, 21–25

"As We Know" (Ashbery), **Supp. III Part 1:** 21–22

Aswell, Edward C., **IV:** 458, 459, 461

"Asylum, The" (Carruth), **Supp. XVI:** 48–49

"As You Like It" (Chopin), **Supp. I Part 1:** 217

As You Like It (Shakespeare), **Supp. I Part 1:** 308

"At a Bar" (Ferry), **Supp. XXIV:** 162

"At a Bar in Charlotte Amalie" (Updike), **IV:** 214

"At a Lecture" (Brodsky), **Supp. VIII:** 33

"At a Low Bar" (Ferry), **Supp. XXIV:** 149

"At a March against the Vietnam War" (R. Bly), **Supp. IV Part 1:** 61

"At a Reading" (McClatchy), **Supp. XII:** 256–257

"Atavism of John Tom Little Bear, The" (O. Henry), **Supp. II Part 1:** 410

"At Chênière Caminada" (Chopin), **Supp. I Part 1:** 220

"At Chinese Checkers" (Berryman), **I:** 182

Atchity, Kenneth John, **Supp. XI:** 227

"At Death's Window" (Lamott), **Supp. XX: 144**

At Eighty-Two (Sarton), **Supp. VIII:** 264

"At Every Gas Station There Are Mechanics" (Dunn), **Supp. XI:** 144

At Fault (Chopin), **Retro. Supp. II:** 57, 60, **62–63; Supp. I Part 1:** 207, 209–211, 220

"At Fifty" (Bronk), **Supp. XXI:** 31

At Heaven's Gate (Warren), **IV:** 243, 247–248, 251

Atheism Refuted: in a Discourse to Prove the Existence of God (Paine), **Supp. I Part 2:** 517

"Athénaïse" (Chopin), **Retro. Supp. II:** 66, 67; **Supp. I Part 1:** 219–220

Atherton, Gertrude, **I:** 199, 207–208; **Supp. XXIV: 17–32**

Athey, Jean L., **Supp. XI:** 184

At Home: Essays, 1982–1988 (Vidal), **Supp. IV Part 2:** 682, 687, 688

"At Home With" (column; Leland), **Supp. XV:** 69

"At Kino Viejo, Mexico" (Ríos), **Supp. IV Part 2:** 541

Atkinson, Brooks, **IV:** 288; **Supp. IV Part 2:** 683; **Supp. XIX:** 244

Atlanta (film, July), **Supp. XXIV:** 201, 209–210

Atlantis (Doty), **Supp. XI:** 121, **126–129**

"Atlantis" (Doty), **Supp. XI:** 127–128

Atlas, James, **Supp. V:** 233; **Supp. XV:** 25; **Supp. XXIV:** 172

Atlas, The (Vollmann), **Supp. XVII:** 226, 227

Atlas Shrugged (Rand), **Supp. IV Part 2:** 517, 521, 523, 524–526, 528, 531

At Liberty (T. Williams), **IV:** 378

"At Melville's Tomb" (H. Crane), **I:** 393; **Retro. Supp. II:** 76, 78, 80, 82

"At Mother Teresa's" (Nye), **Supp. XIII:** 276

"At Nightfall" (Kooser), **Supp. XIX:** 122–123

At Night the Salmon Move (Carver), **Supp. III Part 1:** 142

At Night the States (Notley), **Supp. XXII:** 224, 231–232

"At night the states" (Notley), **Supp. XXII:** 232

"At North Farm" (Ashbery), **Supp. III Part 1:** 1–2

At Paradise Gate (Smiley), **Supp. VI:** 292, **293–294**

"At Paso Rojo" (Bowles), **Supp. IV Part 1:** 87

At Play in the Fields of the Lord (Matthiessen), **Supp. V:** 199, 202, 204–206, 212

"At Play in the Paradise of Bombs" (Sanders), **Supp. XVI:** 272–273, 274, 277

"At Pleasure By" (Pinsky), **Supp. VI:** 245

"A-Train / Ziggurat / Elegy"(Balakian), **Supp. XXIII:** 32

At Risk (Hoffman), **Supp. X:** 87

"At Sea" (Hemingway), **II:** 258

"At Shaft 11" (Dunbar), **Supp. II Part 1:** 212

"At Slim's River" (Haines), **Supp. XII:** 208–209

"At St. Croix" (Dubus), **Supp. VII:** 83, 87

At Sundown (Whittier), **Supp. I Part 2:** 704

"At Sunset" (Simic), **Supp. VIII:** 282

Attaway, William, **Supp. XXI:** 264

Attebery, Brian, **Supp. IV Part 1:** 101

Attendant, The (Bronk), **Supp. XXI:** 24

"Attendant, The" (Bronk), **Supp. XXI:** 26

"Attention"(Hadas), **Supp. XXIII:** 121

"At That Time, or The History of a Joke" (Paley), **Supp. VI:** 229–230

"At the Alhambra"(P. Benedict), **Supp. XXIII:** 40

At the Back of the North Wind (Macdonald), **Supp. XIII:** 75

"At the Birth of an Age" (Jeffers), **Supp. II Part 2:** 432

"At the Bomb Testing Site" (Stafford), **Supp. XI:** 317–318, 321, 323

At the Bottom of the River (Kincaid), **Supp. VII:** 182–184, 185

"At the 'Cadian Ball" (Chopin), **Retro. Supp. II:** 64, 65, 68

"At the Cancer Clinic" (Kooser), **Supp. XIX:** 127

"At the Chelton-Pulver Game" (Auchincloss), **Supp. IV Part 1:** 27

"At the Drugstore" (Taylor), **Supp. V:** 323

At the Edge of the Body (Jong), **Supp. V:** 115, 130

"At the End of the Curse, a Blessing" (Verducci), **Supp. XXII:** 209

At the End of the Open Road (Simpson), **Supp. IX:** 265, 269, **271–273,** 277

At the End of This Summer: Poems 1948– 1954, **Supp. XII:** 211

"At the End of War" (Eberhart), **I:** 522–523

"At the Executed Murderer's Grave" (Wright), **Supp. III Part 2:** 595, 597

"At the Fishhouses" (Bishop), **Retro. Supp. II:** 45; **Supp. I Part 1:** 90, 92

At the Gates of the Animal Kingdom (Hempel), **Supp. XXI:** 115, **122–124**

"At the Grave of My Guardian Angel: St. Louis Cemetery, New Orleans" (Levis), **Supp. XI:** 268–269

"At the Gym" (Doty), **Supp. XI:** 135

"At the Indian Store" (McCarriston), **Supp. XIV:** 271

"At the Lake" (Oliver), **Supp. VII:** 244
"At the Landing" (Welty), **IV:** 265–266; **Retro. Supp. I:** 348
"At the Last" (Bynner), **Supp. XV:** 44
"At the Last Rites for Two Hot Rodders" (X. J. Kennedy), **Supp. XV:** 166
"At the Mountains of Madness" (Lovecraft), **Supp. XXII:** 58
"At the Owl Club, North Gulfport, Mississippi, 1950" (Trethewey), **Supp. XXI:** 249
At the Owl Woman Saloon (Gallagher), **Supp. XXIV:** 166, 172, 173, 174, 175–177
"At the Premiere" (Keillor), **Supp. XVI:** 167
At the Rendezvous of Victory (C. L. R. James), **Supp. XXI:** 172
At the Root of Stars (Barnes), **Supp. III Part 1:** 34
"At the Slackening of the Tide" (Wright), **Supp. III Part 2:** 597
"At the Street Corner" (Ferry), **Supp. XXIV:** 162
"At the Tomb of Walt Whitman" (Kunitz), **Supp. III Part 1:** 262
"At the Tourist Centre in Boston" (Atwood), **Supp. XIII:** 33
"At the Town Dump" (Kenyon), **Supp. VII:** 167
"At the Worcester Museum" (Pinsky), **Supp. VI:** 251
"At the Zoo in Spain" (Major), **Supp. XXII:** 182
"Atticus Finch and the Mad Dog: Harper Lee's *To Kill a Mockingbird*" (Jones), **Supp. VIII:** 128
"Atticus Finch—Right and Wrong" (Freedman), **Supp. VIII:** 127–128
"Attic Which Is Desire, The" (W. C. Williams), **Retro. Supp. I:** 422
"At Tikal" (Bronk), **Supp. XXI:** 28–29
"At Times in Flight: A Parable" (H. Roth), **Supp. IX:** 234
Attitudes toward History (Burke), **I:** 274
Atwan, Robert, **Supp. XVI:** 273, 277
At Weddings and Wakes (McDermott), **Supp. XVIII:** 155, **160–162,** 166
"At White River" (Haines), **Supp. XII:** 208–209
Atwood, Margaret, **Supp. IV Part 1:** 252; **Supp. V:** 119; **Supp. XI:** 317; **Supp. XIII: 19–39,** 291, 306; **Supp. XXI:** 39, 42
"Atwood's Gorgon Touch" (Davey), **Supp. XIII:** 33
"Aubade" (McCarriston), **Supp. XIV:** 271
"Aubade: November" (McCarriston), **Supp. XIV:** 261–262
"Aubade of an Early Homo Sapiens" (C. Frost), **Supp. XV:** 97–98
"Aubade: Opal and Silver" (Doty), **Supp. XI:** 129
"Au Bal Musette" (Van Vechten), **Supp. II Part 2:** 735
Auchincloss, Hugh D., **Supp. IV Part 2:** 679
Auchincloss, Louis, **I:** 375; **III:** 66; **Retro. Supp. I:** 370, 373; **Supp. IV Part 1: 21–38**

"Auction" (Simic), **Supp. VIII:** 278
"Auction, The" (Crane), **I:** 411
"Auction Model 1934" (Z. Fitzgerald), **Supp. IX:** 61
Auden, W. H., **I:** 71, 381, 539; **II:** 367, 368, 371, 376, 586; **III:** 17, 134, 269, 271, 292, 476–477, 504, 527, 530, 542, 615; **IV:** 136, 138, 240, 430; **Retro. Supp. I:** 430; **Retro. Supp. II:** 183, 242, 244, 323; **Supp. I Part 1:** 270; **Supp. I Part 2:** 552, 610; **Supp. II Part 1: 1–28;** **Supp. III Part 1:** 2, 3, 14, 26, 60, 61, 64, 341; **Supp. III Part 2:** 591, 595; **Supp. IV Part 1:** 79, 84, 136, 225, 302, 313; **Supp. IV Part 2:** 440, 465; **Supp. V:** 337; **Supp. VIII:** 19, 21, 22, 23, 30, 32, 155, 190; **Supp. IX:** 94, 287, 288; **Supp. X:** 35, 57, 59, 115–116, 117, 118–119; **Supp. XI:** 243, 244; **Supp. XII:** 253, 264–265, 266, 269–270; **Supp. XIV:** 156, 158, 160, 162, 163; **Supp. XV:** 74, 117–118, 139, 144, 186; **Supp. XIX:** 147, 151; **Supp. XX: 138; Supp. XXI:** 60, 98; **Supp. XXIII:** 117, 207
"Auden's OED" (McClatchy), **Supp. XII:** 264–265
"Audition" (Alvarez), **Supp. VII:** 10
Audubon, John James, **III:** 210; **IV:** 265; **Supp. IX:** 171; **Supp. XVI: 1–14**
Audubon, John Woodhouse, **Supp. XVI:** 10
Audubon, Maria Rebecca, **Supp. XVI:** 11
Audubon, Victor Gifford, **Supp. XVI:** 10
Audubon and His Journals (M. Audubon, ed.), **Supp. XVI:** 11, 12
Audubon Reader, The: The Best Writings of John James Audubon (Sanders, ed.), **Supp. XVI:** 269
Auer, Jane. *See* Bowles, Jane
Auerbach, Eric, **III:** 453
Auerbach, Nina, **Supp. I Part 1:** 40
"August" (Oliver), **Supp. VII:** 235
"August" (Rich), **Supp. I Part 2:** 564
"August 1968" (Auden), **Supp. II Part 1:** 25
"August Darks, The" (Clampitt), **Supp. IX:** 43, **50–51,** 52
Augustine, Saint, **I:** 279, 290; **II:** 537; **III:** 259, 270, 292, 300; **IV:** 69, 126; **Retro. Supp. I:** 247; **Supp. VIII:** 203; **Supp. XI:** 245; **Supp. XIII:** 89; **Supp. XXI:** 83; **Supp. XXII:** 92–93
August Snow (Price), **Supp. VI:** 264
"Au Jardin" (Pound), **III:** 465–466
Aunt Carmen's Book of Practical Saints (Mora), **Supp. XIII: 227–229**
"Aunt Cynthy Dallett" (Jewett), **II:** 393
"Aunt Gladys" (Karr), **Supp. XI:** 241
"Aunt Granny Lith" (Offutt), **Supp. XIX:** 165, 166
"Aunties, The" (Lamott), **Supp. XX: 141**
"Aunt Imogen" (Robinson), **III:** 521
"Aunt Jemima of the Ocean Waves" (Hayden), **Supp. II Part 1:** 368, 379
"Aunt Jennifer's Tigers" (Rich), **Supp. XV:** 252

Aunt Jo's Scrapbooks (Alcott), **Supp. I Part 1:** 43
"Aunt Mary" (Oliver), **Supp. VII:** 232
"Aunt Mary" (Stowe), **Supp. I Part 2:** 587
"Aunt Moon's Young Man" (Hogan), **Supp. IV Part 1:** 400
"Aunt Rectita's Good Friday" (X. J. Kennedy), **Supp. XV:** 166
"Aunt Sarah" (Lowell), **II:** 554
"Aunt Sue's Stories" (Hughes), **Retro. Supp. I:** 197, 199
"Aunt Violet's Canadian Honeymoon/ 1932" (Shields), **Supp. VII:** 311
"Aunt Violet's Things" (Shields), **Supp. VII:** 311–312
"Aurelia: Moon Jellies" (Mora), **Supp. XIII:** 224
"Aurelio" (Di Piero), **Supp. XIX:** 38
Au revoir les enfants (film, Malle), **Supp. XXIII:** 122
Aurora 7 (Mallon), **Supp. XIX:** 132, **135–136**
Aurora Leigh (E. Browning), **Retro. Supp. I:** 33; **Supp. XI:** 197
Aurora Means Dawn (Sanders), **Supp. XVI:** 268
Auroras of Autumn, The (Stevens), **Retro. Supp. I:** 297, 300, **309–312**
"Auroras of Autumn, The" (Stevens), **Retro. Supp. I:** 311, 312; **Supp. III Part 1:** 12
Auschwitz: the Nazis and the "Final Solution" (television documentary), Supp. XVII: 40
Auslander, Joseph, **Supp. XIV:** 120
"Auspex" (Frost), **Retro. Supp. I:** 122
"Auspex" (Lowell), **Supp. I Part 2:** 424
Austen, Jane, **I:** 130, 339, 375, 378; **II:** 272, 278, 287, 568–569, 577; **IV:** 8; **Retro. Supp. I:** 354; **Supp. I Part 1:** 267; **Supp. I Part 2:** 656, 715; **Supp. IV Part 1:** 300; **Supp. VIII:** 125, 167; **Supp. IX:** 128; **Supp. XII:** 310; **Supp. XV:** 338; **Supp. XX: 108; Supp. XXII:** 206
Austenfeld, Thomas, **Supp. XXIV:** 64
Auster, Paul, **Supp. XII: 21–39; Supp. XIV:** 292; **Supp. XXI:** 20
Austerities (Simic), **Supp. VIII: 276–278,** 283
"Austerities" (Simic), **Supp. VIII:** 277
Austin, Mary Hunter, **Retro. Supp. I:** 7; **Supp. IV Part 2:** 503; **Supp. X:** 29; **Supp. XIII:** 154
"Authentic Unconscious, The" (Trilling), **Supp. III Part 2:** 512
Author and Agent: Eudora Welty and Diarmuid Russell (Kreyling), **Retro. Supp. I:** 342, 345, 347, 349–350
"Author at Sixty, The" (Wilson), **IV:** 426
"Author of 'Beltraffio,' The" (James), **Retro. Supp. I:** 227
"Author's Explanation, The" (Larsen), **Supp. XVIII:** 131
"Author's House" (Fitzgerald), **Retro. Supp. I:** 98
"Author's Reflections, An: Willie Loman, Walter Younger, and He Who Must

Live" (Hansberry), **Supp. IV Part 1:** 370

"Author to Her Book, The" (Bradstreet), **Supp. I Part 1:** 119; **Supp. V:** 117–118; **Supp. XV:** 125–126

"Autism Poem #20: The Knot Garden"(Crooker), **Supp. XXIII:** 56–57

"Autobiographical Note" (H. Miller), **III:** 174–175

"Autobiographical Notes" (Baldwin), **Supp. I Part 1:** 54

"Autobiographical Notes" (Holmes), **Supp. I Part 1:** 301

"Autobiographic Chapter, An" (Bourne), **I:** 236

Autobiography (Franklin), **II:** 102, 103, 108, 121–122, 302

Autobiography (James), **I:** 462

"Autobiography" (MacLeish), **III:** 20

Autobiography (Van Buren), **III:** 473

Autobiography (W. C. Williams), **Supp. I Part 1:** 254

Autobiography (Zukofsky), **Supp. III Part 2:** 627

Autobiography by Jesus of Nazareth (Pettis), **Supp. XXIII:** 189

"Autobiography"(Dybek), **Supp. XXIII:** 78

"Autobiography in the Shape of a Book Review" (Bynner), **Supp. XV:** 40

"Autobiography of a Confluence, The" (Gunn Allen), **Supp. IV Part 1:** 321

Autobiography of Alice B. Toklas, The (Stein), **IV:** 26, 30, 35, 43; **Supp. IV Part 1:** 11, 81

Autobiography of an Ex-Colored Man, The (Johnson), **Supp. II Part 1:** 33, 194; **Supp. XVIII:** 127; **Supp. XXII:** 7

Autobiography of a Schizophrenic Girl (Renée), **Supp. XVI:** 64, 66

Autobiography of a Thief, The (Hapgood), **Supp. XVII:** 96, 101–102

Autobiography of Benjamin Franklin (Franklin), **Supp. IV Part 1:** 5

Autobiography of LeRoi Jones, The (Baraka), **Retro. Supp. I:** 411

Autobiography of Malcolm X (Little), **Supp. I Part 1:** 66; **Supp. X:** 27; **Supp. XIII:** 264; **Supp. XXII:** 95

Autobiography of Mark Twain, The (Twain), **IV:** 209

Autobiography of My Mother, The (Kincaid), **Supp. VII:** 182, 188–190, 191, 192, 193

Autobiography of Red: A Novel in Verse (Carson), **Supp. XII:** 97, **106–110**

Autobiography of Upton Sinclair, The (Sinclair), **Supp. V:** 276, 282

Autobiography of W. E. B. Du Bois, The (Du Bois), **Supp. II Part 1:** 159, 186

Autobiography of William Carlos Williams, The (W. C. Williams), **Retro. Supp. I:** 51, 428

Autocrat of the Breakfast-Table, The (Holmes), **Supp. I Part 1:** 306–307

"Automatic Gate, The" (Southern), **Supp. XI:** 294

"Automotive Passacaglia" (H. Miller), **III:** 186

"Autopsy Room, The" (Carver), **Supp. III Part 1:** 137

"Auto Wreck" (Shapiro), **Supp. II Part 2:** 706

"Autre Temps" (Wharton), **IV:** 320, 324

"Autumn" (Berrigan), **Supp. XXIV:** 37

"Autumn, Mist" (Hull), **Supp. XXI:** 133

"Autumn Afternoon" (Farrell), **II:** 45

"Autumnal" (Eberhart), **I:** 540–541

"Autumn Begins in Martins Ferry, Ohio" (Wright), **Supp. III Part 2:** 599

"Autumn Courtship, An" (Caldwell), **I:** 309

"Autumn Equinox" (Skloot), **Supp. XX:** **202**

Autumn Garden, The (Hellman), **Supp. I Part 1:** 285–286, 290

"Autumn Garden, The: Mechanics and Dialectics" (Felheim), **Supp. I Part 1:** 297

"Autumn Holiday, An" (Jewett), **II:** 391; **Retro. Supp. II:** 140–141

"Autumn Musings" (Harte), **Supp. II Part 1:** 336

"Autumn's Day" (Rilke; Berrigan, trans.), **Supp. XXIV:** 37

Autumn Spring (Pickering), **Supp. XXI:** 204–205, 206

"Autumn Within" (Longfellow), **II:** 499

"Autumn Woods" (Bryant), **Supp. I Part 1:** 164

Autum of the Patriarch, The (García Márquez), **Supp. XXIV:** 89

"Au Vieux Jardin" (Aldington), **Supp. I Part 1:** 257

"Aux Imagistes" (W. C. Williams), **Supp. I Part 1:** 266

Available World, The (Monson), **Supp. XXIV:** 230, **239–240,** 241

Avakian, Aram, **Supp. XI:** 294, 295, 309

Avalanche (Boyle), **Supp. XXIV:** 62

Avalanche, The (Atherton), **Supp. XXIV:** 24–25

"Ave Atque Vale" (Bynner), Supp. XV: 49

Avedon, Richard, **Supp. I Part 1:** 58; **Supp. V:** 194; **Supp. X:** 15

Aveling, Edward, **Supp. XVI:** 85

"Avenue" (Pinsky), **Supp. VI:** 248

Avenue Bearing the Initial of Christ into the New World: Poems 1946–1964 (Kinnell), **Supp. III Part 1:** 235, 239–241

"Avenue of the Americas" (Simic), **Supp. VIII:** 278

"Average Torture" (Karr), **Supp. XI:** 243

Avery, George C., **Supp. XX: 84**

Avery, John, **Supp. I Part 1:** 153

"Avey" (Toomer), **Supp. IX:** 317

Avon's Harvest (Robinson), **III:** 510

Awake and Sing! (Odets), **Supp. II Part 2:** 530, 531, 536–538, 550; **Supp. IV Part 2:** 587

"Awake at Midnight"(Schott), **Supp. XXIII:** 246

Awake in Spain (O'Hara), **Supp. XXIII:** 216

Awakening, The (Chopin), **Retro. Supp. I:** 10; **Retro. Supp. II:** 57, 59, 60, 67, 68–71, 73; **Supp. I Part 1:** 200, 201, 202, 211, 220–225; **Supp. V:** 304; **Supp. VIII:** 198; **Supp. XII:** 170

Awakening Land, The (Richter), **Supp. XVIII:** 207, 215

Awful Rowing Toward God, The (Sexton), **Supp. II Part 2:** 694–696

Awiakta, Marilou, **Supp. IV Part 1:** 319, 335

Awkward Age, The (James), **II:** 332; **Retro. Supp. I:** 229, **230–231**

Axe Handles (Snyder), **Supp. VIII: 303–305**

Axel's Castle: A Study in the Imaginative Literature of 1870 to 1930 (Wilson), **I:** 185; **II:** 577; **IV:** 428, 431, 438, 439, 443; **Supp. VIII:** 101

"Ax-Helve, The" (Frost), **Retro. Supp. I:** 133

Azikewe, Nnamdi, **Supp. IV Part 1:** 361

"Aztec Angel" (Salinas), **Supp. XIII:** 314

Aztec Treasure House, The: New and Selected Essays (Connell), **Supp. XIV:** 80, 97

B

Babbitt (Lewis), **II:** 442, 443–445, 446, 447, 449; **III:** 63–64, 394; **IV:** 326

Babbitt, Irving, **I:** 247; **II:** 456; **III:** 315, 461, 613; **IV:** 439; **Retro. Supp. I:** 55; **Supp. I Part 2:** 423

Babcock, Elisha, **Supp. II Part 1:** 69

Babel, Isaac, **IV:** 1; **Supp. IX:** 260; **Supp. XII:** 308–309; **Supp. XVII:** 41; **Supp. XXIII:** 68

Babel, Isaak, **Supp. XIV:** 83, 84

Babel to Byzantium (Dickey), **Supp. IV Part 1:** 177, 185

Baber, Asa, **Supp. XXIII:** 52

Baber, Bob Henry, **Supp. XXIII:** 39

Babeuf, François, **Supp. I Part 2:** 518

"Babies, The" (Strand), **Supp. IV Part 2:** 625

Babouk (Endore), **Supp. XVII: 56–57,** 61, 64

Baby, Come on Inside (Wagoner), **Supp. IX:** 335

Baby, The (Barthelme), **Supp. IV Part 1:** 49

Baby Doll (T. Williams), **IV:** 383, 386, 387, 389, 395

"Baby Face" (Sandburg), **III:** 584

"Babylon Revisited" (Fitzgerald), **II:** 95; **Retro. Supp. I:** 109

"Baby or the Botticelli, The" (Gass), **Supp. VI:** 92

"Baby Pictures of Famous Dictators" (Simic), **Supp. VIII:** 276

"Baby's Breath" (Bambara), **Supp. XI:** 15, 16

"Babysitter, The" (Coover), **Supp. V:** 43–44

"Baby Villon" (Levine), **Supp. V:** 182

Baby with the Bathwater (Durang), **Supp. XXIV: 121–122**

Bacall, Lauren, **Supp. IV Part 1:** 130

"Baccalaureate" (MacLeish), **III:** 4

Bacchae, The (Euripides), **Supp. VIII:** 182

Bach, Johann Sebastian, **Supp. I Part 1:** 363; **Supp. III Part 2:** 611, 612, 619

Bachardy, Don, **Supp. XIV:** 166, 170, 172, 173

Bache, Richard, **Supp. I Part 2:** 504

Bachelard, Gaston, **Supp. XIII:** 225; **Supp. XVI:** 292

"Bachelor Girl, The" (Boyce), **Supp. XXI:** 3

Bachelor Girls (Wasserstein), **Supp. XV:** 327–328, 332

Bachman, John, **Supp. XVI:** 10, 11

Bachmann, Ingeborg, **Supp. IV Part 1:** 310; **Supp. VIII:** 272

Bachofen, J. J., **Supp. I Part 2:** 560, 567

Back Bog Beast Bait (Shepard), **Supp. III Part 2:** 437, 438

Backbone (C. Bly), **Supp. XVI:** 34–36, 37, 40, 41

Back Country, The (Snyder), **Supp. VIII:** 296–299

"Back from the Argentine" (Leopold), **Supp. XIV:** 186

"Background with Revolutionaries" (MacLeish), **III:** 14–15

"Back in the Saddle Again" (Swados), **Supp. XIX:** 259

Back in the World (Wolff), **Supp. VII:** 344, 345

Backis, Charles, **Supp. XXI:** 195

"Backlash Blues, The" (Hughes), **Supp. I Part 1:** 343

"Backlash of Kindness, A" (Nye), **Supp. XIII:** 285, 286

"Backslider, The" (R. Fisher), **Supp. XIX:** 70, 71

"Back Street Guy" (Halliday), **Supp. XIX:** 88

Back to China (Fiedler), **Supp. XIII:** 102–103

Back to Methuselah (Shaw), **IV:** 64

"Backwacking: A Plea to the Senator" (Ellison), **Retro. Supp. II:** 126; **Supp. II Part 1:** 248

Backward Glance, A (Wharton), **Retro. Supp. I:** 360, 363, 366, 378, 380, 382; **Supp. XX:** 229

"Backward Glance o'er Travel'd Roads, A" (Whitman), **IV:** 348

Bacon, Francis, **II:** 1, 8, 11, 15–16, 111; **III:** 284; **Retro. Supp. I:** 247; **Supp. I Part 1:** 310; **Supp. I Part 2:** 388; **Supp. IX:** 104; **Supp. XIV:** 22, 210

Bacon, Helen, **Supp. X:** 57

Bacon, Katie, **Supp. XXII:** 207; **Supp. XXIII:** 275

Bacon, Leonard, **II:** 530; **Supp. XXII:** 273

Bacon, Roger, **IV:** 69

"Bacterial War, The" (Nemerov), **III:** 272

Bad and the Beautiful, The (film), **Supp. XVIII:** 250

Bad Boy Brawly Brown (Mosley), **Supp. XIII:** 237, 239, 240–241

Bad Boys (Cisneros), **Supp. VII:** 58

"Bad Company" (Gallagher), **Supp. XXIV:** 174, 176

"Bad Dream" (Taylor), **Supp. V:** 320

Badè, William Frederic, **Supp. IX:** 178

"Bad Fisherman, The" (Wagoner), **Supp. IX:** 328

Bad for Each Other (film), **Supp. XIII:** 174

"Badger" (Clare), **II:** 387

Badger, A. G., **Supp. I Part 1:** 356

Bad Government and Silly Literature (C. Bly), **Supp. XVI:** 37, 38, 40

Badlands (film; Malick), **Supp. XV:** 351

"Bad Lay" (McCarriston), **Supp. XIV:** 267

Badley, Linda, **Supp. V:** 148

Bad Man, A (Elkin), **Supp. VI:** 47

Bad Man Ballad (Sanders), **Supp. XVI:** 268

Bad Man Blues: A Portable George Garrett (Garrett), **Supp. VII:** 111

"Bad Music, The" (Jarrell), **II:** 369

"Bad People" (Halliday), **Supp. XIX:** 90, 91

"Bad Summer on K2, A" (Krakauer and Child), **Supp. XVIII:** 107, 108

"Bad Woman, A" (Fante), **Supp. XI:** 165

Baeck, Leo, **Supp. V:** 260

Baecker, Diann L., **Supp. VIII:** 128

Baer, William, **Supp. XIII:** 112, 118, 129; **Supp. XXIII:** 124

Baez, Joan, **Supp. IV Part 1:** 200; **Supp. VIII:** 200, 202; **Supp. XVIII:** 24, 25–26, 27

Bag of Bones (King), **Supp. V:** 139, 148, 151

"Bagpipe Music" (MacNeice), **Supp. X:** 117

"Bahá'í Faith: Only Church in World That Does Not Discriminate" (Locke), **Supp. XIV:** 200

Bahá'u'lláh, **Supp. XX:** 117, 121, 122

"Bahá'u'lláh in the Garden of Ridwan" (Hayden), **Supp. II Part 1:** 370, 378

Bahr, David, **Supp. XV:** 66

Bahr, Thomas, **Supp. XXII:** 206, 214

"Bailbondsman, The" (Elkin), **Supp. VI:** 49, 50, 58

Bailey, Gamaliel, **Supp. I Part 2:** 587, 590

Bailey, Peter, **Supp. XVI:** 69

Bailey, William, **Supp. IV Part 2:** 631, 634

Bailey's Café (Naylor), **Supp. VIII:** 226–228

Bailyn, Bernard, **Supp. I Part 2:** 484, 506

Bair, Deirdre, **Supp. X:** 181, 186, 187, 188, 192, 194, 195, 196, 197

Baird, Linnett, **Supp. XII:** 299

Baird, Peggy, **I:** 385, 401

Baiting the Void (Schott), **Supp. XXIII:** 247–248

Bakan, David, **I:** 59

Baker, Carlos, **II:** 259

Baker, Chet, **Supp. XXI:** 131

Baker, David, **Supp. IX:** 298; **Supp. XI:** 121, 142, 153; **Supp. XII:** 175, 191–192; **Supp. XIX:** 115

Baker, George Pierce, **III:** 387; **IV:** 453, 455

Baker, Gladys, **Supp. XIV:** 121

Baker, Houston, **Supp. XXII:** 6

Baker, Houston A., Jr., **Retro. Supp. II:** 121; **Supp. IV Part 1:** 365; **Supp. X:** 324

Baker, Jeff, **Supp. XXIV:** 166, 178

Baker, Katherine, **Supp. XX:** 69

Baker, Kevin, **Supp. XIV:** 96

Baker, Mabel, **Supp. XVIII:** 259, 263, 266–267, 269

Baker, Nicholson, **Supp. XIII:** 41–57

Baker, Robert, **Supp. XVI:** 288, 290

Bakerman, Jane S., **Supp. IV Part 2:** 468

Bakhtin, Mikhail, **Retro. Supp. II:** 273; **Supp. IV Part 1:** 301; **Supp. X:** 120, 239; **Supp. XXII:** 259

Bakst, Léon, **Supp. IX:** 66

Bakunin, Mikhail Aleksandrovich, **IV:** 429

Balaban, John, **Supp. XIX:** 281

Balakian, Anna, **Supp. XXIII:** 20

Balakian, Diran, **Supp. XXIII:** 28

Balakian, Grigoris, **Supp. XXIII:** 28, 29–32

Balakian, Jan, **Supp. XV:** 327

Balakian, Nona, **Supp. XXIII:** 20

Balakian, Peter, **Supp. XXIII:** 19–34

"Balance" (Bierds), **Supp. XVII:** 31

"Balance" (Nelson), **Supp. XVIII:** 174–175

Balbo, Ned, **Supp. XVII:** 120; **Supp. XIX:** 161

Balbuena, Bernado de, **Supp. V:** 11

Balch, Emily Greene, **Supp. I Part 1:** 25

Balcony, The (Genet), **I:** 84

Bald Soprano, The (Ionesco), **I:** 74

Baldwin, David, **Supp. I Part 1:** 47, 48, 49, 50, 51, 54, 65, 66

Baldwin, James, **Retro. Supp. II:** 1–17; **Supp. I Part 1:** 47–71, 337, 341; **Supp. II Part 1:** 40; **Supp. III Part 1:** 125; **Supp. IV Part 1:** 1, 10, 11, 163, 369; **Supp. V:** 201; **Supp. VIII:** 88, 198, 235, 349; **Supp. X:** 136, 324; **Supp. XI:** 288, 294; **Supp. XIII:** 46, 111, 181, 186, 294; **Supp. XIV:** 54, 71, 73, 306; **Supp. XVI:** 135, 141, 143; **Supp. XVIII:** 25; **Supp. XX:** 147; **Supp. XXI:** 245; **Supp. XXIV:** 185

Baldwin, Samuel, **Supp. I Part 1:** 48

Balitas, Vincent D., **Supp. XVI:** 222

Balkian, Nona, **Supp. XI:** 230

Balkun, Mary McAleer, **Supp. XX:** 281

Ball, Gordon, **Supp. XIV:** 148

Ball, John, **Supp. XV:** 202

"Ballad: Between the Box Cars" (Warren), **IV:** 245

"Ballade" (MacLeish), **III:** 4

"Ballade at Thirty-Five" (Parker), **Supp. IX:** 192

"Ballade for the Duke of Orléans" (Wilbur), **Supp. III Part 2:** 556

"Ballade of Broken Flutes, The" (Robinson), **III:** 505

"Ballade of Meaty Inversions" (White), **Supp. I Part 2:** 676

"Ballad of a Thin Man" (song, Dylan), **Supp. XVIII:** 30, 31

"Ballad of Aunt Geneva, The" (Nelson), **Supp. XVIII:** 175

"Ballad of Billie Potts, The" (Warren), **IV**: 241–242, 243, 253

"Ballad of Carmilhan, The" (Longfellow), **II**: 505

"ballad of chocolate Mabbie, the" (Brooks), **Supp. IV Part 1**: 15

"Ballad of Dead Ladies, The" (Villon), **Retro. Supp. I**: 286

Ballad of Dingus Magee, The (Markson), **Supp. XVII**: 139, 141

"Ballad of East and West, The" (Kipling), **Supp. IX**: 246; **Supp. XX**: 23

"Ballad of Jesse Neighbours, The" (Humphrey), **Supp. IX**: 100

"Ballad of Jesus of Nazareth, A" (Masters), **Supp. I Part 2**: 459

"Ballad of John Cable and Three Gentlemen" (Merwin), **Supp. III Part 1**: 342

"Ballad of Larry and Club" (Jarman), **Supp. XVII**: 115

"Ballad of Nat Turner, The" (Hayden), **Supp. II Part 1**: 378

"Ballad of Pearl May Lee, The" (Brooks), **Supp. III Part 1**: 74, 75

Ballad of Remembrance, A (Hayden), **Supp. II Part 1**: 367

"Ballad of Remembrance, A" (Hayden), **Supp. II Part 1**: 368, 372, 373

"Ballad of Ruby, The" (Sarton), **Supp. VIII**: 259–260

"Ballad of San Isidro, The" (Espaillat), **Supp. XXI**: 108

"Ballad of Sue Ellen Westerfield, The" (Hayden), **Supp. II Part 1**: 364

Ballad of the Brown Girl, The (Cullen), **Supp. IV Part 1**: 167, 168, 169–170, 173

"Ballad of the Brown Girl, The" (Cullen), **Supp. IV Part 1**: 168

"Ballad of the Children of the Czar, The" (Schwartz), **Supp. II Part 2**: 649

"Ballad of the Girl Whose Name Is Mud" (Hughes), **Retro. Supp. I**: 205

"Ballad of the Goodly Fere", **III**: 458

"Ballad of the Harp-Weaver" (Millay), **III**: 135

"Ballad of the Sad Cafe, The" (McCullers), **II**: 586, 587, 588, 592, 595, 596–600, 604, 605, 606

"Ballad of the Sixties" (Sarton), **Supp. VIII**: 259

"Ballad of Trees and the Master, A" (Lanier), **Supp. I Part 1**: 370

"Ballad of Typical Lovers" (Taggard), **Supp. XXII**: 277

"Ballad of William Sycamore, The" (Benét), **Supp. XI**: 44, 47

Ballads and Other Poems (Longfellow), **II**: 489; **III**: 412, 422; **Retro. Supp. II**: 157, 168

Ballads for Sale (Lowell), **II**: 527

"Ballads of Lenin" (Hughes), **Supp. I Part 1**: 331

Ballantyne, Sheila, **Supp. V**: 70

Ballard, J. G., **Supp. XVI**: 123, 124; **Supp. XVIII**: 136

Ballard, Josephine. *See* McMurtry, Josephine

"Ballena" (Mora), **Supp. XIII**: 224

"Ballet in Numbers for Mary Ellen, A" (Karr), **Supp. XI**: 241

"Ballet of a Buffoon, The" (Sexton), **Supp. II Part 2**: 693

"Ballet of Central Park, The" (Boyle), **Supp. XXIV**: 59

"Ballet of the Fifth Year, The" (Schwartz), **Supp. II Part 2**: 650

Ball Four (Bouton), **Supp. XX**: **274**

"Ball Game, The" (Creeley), **Supp. IV Part 1**: 140

Ballistics (Collins), **Supp. XXI**: 57, 65

"Ballistics" (Collins), **Supp. XXI**: 65

"Balloon Hoax, The" (Poe), **III**: 413, 420

"Balm of Recognition, The: Rectifying Wrongs through Generations" (E. Hoffman, lecture), **Supp. XVI**: 155

Balo (Toomer), **Supp. III Part 2**: 484

Balsan, Consuelo, **IV**: 313–314

Balthus, **Supp. IV Part 2**: 623

Balthus Poems, The (Dobyns), **Supp. XIII**: 87

Baltimore, Lord, **I**: 132

Balzac, Honoré de, **I**: 103, 123, 339, 376, 474, 485, 499, 509, 518; **II**: 307, 322, 324, 328, 336, 337; **III**: 61, 174, 184, 320, 382; **IV**: 192; **Retro. Supp. I**: 91, 217, 218, 235; **Retro. Supp. II**: 93; **Supp. I Part 2**: 647; **Supp. XVI**: 72

Bambara, Toni Cade, **Supp. XI**: **1–23**

Bam opgrunt (At the abyss) (Asch), **Supp. XXIII**: 6

Banana Bottom (McKay), **Supp. X**: 132, **139–140**

Bananas (film; Allen), **Supp. XV**: 3, 4

Bancal, Jean, **Supp. I Part 2**: 514

Bancroft, George, **I**: 544; **Supp. I Part 2**: 479; **Supp. XXII**: 33

Band, Millen, **Supp. XVIII**: 238

Bandaged Nude, The (Ryan as Finnegan), **Supp. XVIII**: 233, **235–236**

Bandbox (Mallon), **Supp. XIX**: 132, 143

Band of Angels (Warren), **IV**: 245, 254–255

Bandung Files (television series), **Supp. XXI**: 170

Bang the Drum Slowly (Harris), **II**: 424–425

Banjo: A Story without a Plot (McKay), **Supp. X**: 132, **138–139**

"Banjo Song, A" (Dunbar), **Supp. II Part 1**: 197

Bank Director's Son, The: A Real and Intensely Interesting Revelation of City Life (Lippard), **Supp. XXIII**: 184

Bankhead, Tallulah, **IV**: 357; **Supp. IV Part 2**: 574

"Banking Potatoes" (Komunyakaa), **Supp. XIII**: 126

"Bank of England Restriction, The" (Adams), **I**: 4

Banks, Joanne Trautmann, **Supp. XIII**: 297

Banks, Russell, **Supp. V**: **1–19**, 227; **Supp. IX**: 153; **Supp. X**: 85; **Supp. XI**: 178; **Supp. XII**: 295, 309, 343; **Supp. XX**: **90**; **Supp. XXIV**: 97

"Banned Poem" (Nye), **Supp. XIII**: 282

Bannon, Barbara, **Supp. XI**: 228

"Banyan" (Swenson), **Supp. IV Part 2**: 651, 652

"Baptism" (Olsen). *See* "O Yes" (Olsen)

"Baptism" (Trethewey), **Supp. XXI**: 246

Baptism, The (Baraka), **Supp. II Part 1**: 40, 41–42, 43

Baptism of Desire (Erdrich), **Supp. IV Part 1**: 259

Barabtarlo, Gennady, **Retro. Supp. I**: 278

Baraka, Imamu Amiri (LeRoi Jones), **Retro. Supp. I**: 411; **Retro. Supp. II**: 280; **Supp. I Part 1**: 63; **Supp. II Part 1**: **29–63**, 247, 250; **Supp. III Part 1**: 83; **Supp. IV Part 1**: 169, 244, 369; **Supp. VIII**: 295, 329, 330, 332; **Supp. X**: 324, 328; **Supp. XIII**: 94; **Supp. XIV**: 125, 144; **Supp. XXI**: 172, 227, 228; **Supp. XXIII**: 215; **Supp. XXIV**: 34, 183

"Bar at the Andover Inn, The" (Matthews), **Supp. IX**: 168

"Barbados" (Marshall), **Supp. XI**: 281

"Barbara Frietchie" (Whittier), **Supp. I Part 2**: 695–696

Barbarella (film), **Supp. XI**: 293, **307–308**

"Barbarian Status of Women, The" (Veblen), **Supp. I Part 2**: 636–637

Barbarous Coast, The (Macdonald), **Supp. IV Part 2**: 472, 474

Barbary Shore (Mailer), **III**: 27, 28, 30–31, 33, 35, 36, 40, 44; **Retro. Supp. II**: 199–200, 207; **Supp. XIV**: 162

Barber, Charles, **Supp. XXIII**: 125

Barber, David, **Supp. IV Part 2**: 550; **Supp. XII**: 188–189

Barber, Rowland, **Supp. IV Part 2**: 581

Barber, Samuel, **Supp. IV Part 1**: 84

"Barber's Unhappiness, The" (Saunders), **Supp. XIX**: 229

"Barclay of Ury" (Whittier), **Supp. I Part 2**: 693

Barcott, Bruce, **Supp. XVII**: 32

Bard of Savagery, The: Thorstein Veblen and Modern Social Theory (Diggins), **Supp. I Part 2**: 650

"Barefoot Boy, The" (Whittier), **Supp. I Part 2**: 691, 699–700

Barefoot in the Park (Simon), **Supp. IV Part 2**: 575, 578–579, 586, 590

Bare Hills, The (Winters), **Supp. II Part 2**: 786, 788

"Bare Hills, The" (Winters), **Supp. II Part 2**: 790

Barely and Widely (Zukofsky), **Supp. III Part 2**: 627, 628, 635

Barenblat, Rachel, **Supp. XIII**: 274

Barfield, Owen, **III**: 274, 279

"Bargain Lost, The" (Poe), **III**: 411

Barillas, William, **Supp. XIV**: 177

Barillet, Pierre, **Supp. XVI**: 194

Barker, Arthur, **Supp. XIII**: 167

Barker, Clive, **Supp. V**: 142

Barking Dog (Budbill), **Supp. XIX**: 1, 5

"Barking Man" (Bell), **Supp. X**: 9

Barking Man and Other Stories (Bell), **Supp. X**: 9

Barksdale, Richard, **Retro. Supp. I**: 202, 205; **Supp. I Part 1**: 341, 346

Barlow, Joel, **Supp. I Part 1:** 124; **Supp. I Part 2:** 511, 515, 521; **Supp. II Part 1: 65–86,** 268

Barlow, Judith, **Supp. XXI:** 6

Barlow, Ruth Baldwin (Mrs. Joel Barlow), **Supp. II Part 1:** 69

"B.A.R. Man, The" (Yates), **Supp. XI:** 341

Barnaby Rudge (Dickens), **III:** 421

Barnacle Soup and Other Stories of the West of Ireland (Gallagher and Gray), **Supp. XXIV:** 166, 172, 178

Barnard, Frederick, **Supp. I Part 2:** 684

Barnard, Rita, **Retro. Supp. II:** 324

Barn Blind (Smiley), **Supp. VI: 292–293**

"Barn Burning" (Faulkner), **II:** 72, 73; **Supp. IV Part 2:** 682; **Supp. XX: 174**

Barnes, Djuna, **Supp. III Part 1: 31–46; Supp. IV Part 1:** 79, 80; **Supp. XVI:** 282; **Supp. XXII:** 165, 167

Barnes, Kim, **Supp. XVIII:** 293

Barnet, Andrea, **Supp. XXII:** 159, 164

Barnett, Claudia, **Supp. XV:** 323, 330, 334

Barnett, Samuel, **Supp. I Part 1:** 2

Barnhardt, Wilton, **Supp. XXII:** 266

"Barn Owl" (Kooser), **Supp. XIX:** 123

Barnstone, Tony, **Supp. XIII:** 115, 126

Barnstone, Willis, **Supp. I Part 2:** 458

Barnum, P. T., **Supp. I Part 2:** 703

Baroja, Pío, **I:** 478

Baron, Zach, **Supp. XVIII:** 150

"Baroque Comment" (Bogan), **Supp. III Part 1:** 56, 58

"Baroque Sunburst, A" (Clampitt), **Supp. IX:** 49

"Baroque Wall-Fountain in the Villa Sciarra, A" (Wilbur), **Supp. III Part 2:** 553

Barr, Robert, **I:** 409, 424

Barracks Thief, The (Wolff), **Supp. VII:** 344–345

"Barred Owl" (Offutt), **Supp. XIX:** 170

Barren Ground (Glasgow), **II:** 174, 175, 178, 179, 184–185, 186, 187, 188, 189, 191, 192, 193, 194; **Supp. X:** 228

Barrés, Auguste M., **I:** 228

Barresi, Dorothy, **Supp. XV:** 100, 102

Barrett, Amy, **Supp. XVIII:** 136

Barrett, E. B., **Supp. XV:** 309

Barrett, Elizabeth, **Supp. IV Part 2:** 430

Barrett, George, **Supp. IX:** 250

Barrett, Ralph, **Supp. I Part 2:** 462

Barrie, J. M., **Supp. XX: 234**

"Barrie Cooke Painting" (Gallagher), **Supp. XXIV:** 171

Barrier, Rober G., **Supp. XXI:** 48–49

Barrier of a Common Language: An American Looks at Contemporary British Poetry (Gioia), **Supp. XV:** 112, **116–117**

"Barroco: An Essay" (Sobin), **Supp. XVI:** 291

Barron, Jonathan, **Supp. IX:** 299

Barrow, John, **II:** 18

Barrus, Clara, **I:** 220

Barry, Iris, **Supp. XIII:** 170

Barry, Philip, **Retro. Supp. I:** 104; **Supp. IV Part 1:** 83; **Supp. V:** 95

Barstow, Elizabeth Drew. *See* Stoddard, Elizabeth

Bartas, Seigneur du, **IV:** 157

Barth, John, **I: 121–143; Supp. I Part 1:** 100; **Supp. III Part 1:** 217; **Supp. IV Part 1:** 48, 379; **Supp. IX:** 208; **Supp. X:** 263, 301, 302, 307; **Supp. XI:** 309; **Supp. XII:** 29, 289, 316; **Supp. XIII:** 41, 101, 104; **Supp. XVII:** 183; **Supp. XVIII:** 136, 140, 141; **Supp. XX: 21; Supp. XXII:** 259, 261; **Supp. XXIII:** 42

Barth, Karl, **III:** 40, 258, 291, 303, 309; **IV:** 225; **Retro. Supp. I:** 325, 326, 327

Barth, Robert C., **Supp. XV:** 169

Barthé, Richmond, **Retro. Supp. II:** 115

Barthelme, Donald, **Supp. IV Part 1: 39–58,** 227; **Supp. V:** 2, 39, 44; **Supp. VIII:** 75, 138; **Supp. X:** 263; **Supp. XI:** 25; **Supp. XII:** 29; **Supp. XIII:** 41, 46; **Supp. XVI:** 206; **Supp. XIX:** 235

Barthelme, Frederick, **Supp. XI: 25–41; Supp. XXI:** 38

Barthelme, Peter, **Supp. XI:** 25

Barthelme, Steven, **Supp. XI:** 25, 27, 37

Barthes, Roland, **Supp. IV Part 1:** 39, 119, 126; **Supp. XIII:** 83; **Supp. XVI:** 285, 294; **Supp. XVII:** 244

Bartholomew and the Oobleck (Geisel), **Supp. XVI:** 104

"Bar Time" (B. Collins), **Supp. XVII:** 245

"Bartleby, the Scrivener; A Story of Wall-Street" (Melville), **III:** 88–89; **Retro. Supp. I:** 255

Bartleby in Manhattan and Other Essays (Hardwick), **Supp. III Part 1:** 204, 210

"Bartleby the Scrivener" (Melville), **Supp. XVIII:** 4

Bartlet, Phebe, **I:** 562

Bartlett, Lee, **Supp. VIII:** 291

Bartlett, Mary Dougherty, **Supp. IV Part 1:** 335

Barton, Bruce, **III:** 14; **Retro. Supp. I:** 179

Barton, Priscilla. *See* Morison, Mrs. Samuel Eliot (Priscilla Barton)

Barton, Ralph, **Supp. XVI:** 195

Barton, Rev. William E., **Retro. Supp. I:** 179

Bartov, Omer, **Supp. XVI:** 153–154

Bartram, John, **Supp. I Part 1:** 244

Bartram, William, **II:** 313; **Supp. IX:** 171; **Supp. X:** 223

Barzun, Jacques, **Supp. XIV:** 54

"Basement" (Bambara), **Supp. XI:** 5

Basement Tapes, The (album, Dylan), **Supp. XVIII:** 27, 30, 32

"Base of All Metaphysics, The" (Whitman), **IV:** 348

"Base Stealer, The" (Francis), **Supp. IX:** 82

Bashevis, Isaac. *See* Singer, Isaac Bashevis

Bashir, Antonious, **Supp. XX: 116, 120**

Basil Stories, The (Fitzgerald), **Retro. Supp. I:** 109

Basin and Range (McPhee), **Supp. III Part 1:** 309

"Basin of Eggs, A" (Swenson), **Supp. IV Part 2:** 645

"Basket, The" (Lowell), **II:** 522

"Basketball and Beefeaters" (McPhee), **Supp. III Part 1:** 296

"Basketball and Poetry: The Two Richies" (Dunn), **Supp. XI:** 140

"Basketball Player" (L. Michaels), **Supp. XVI:** 209

"Basket of Trips"(Strout), **Supp. XXIII:** 283, 285

Baskin, Leonard, **Supp. X:** 58, 71; **Supp. XV:** 348

Bass, George, **Supp. XXII:** 6

Bass, Rick, **Supp. XIV:** 227; **Supp. XVI: 15–29; Supp. XXI:** 40, 45

Bassard, Katherine Clay, **Supp. XXII:** 148

Basso, Hamilton, **Retro. Supp. I:** 80

Bastard, The (Caldwell), **I:** 291, 292, 308

"Bastille Day" (Lamott), **Supp. XX: 143**

"Bat, The" (Kenyon), **Supp. VII:** 168

Bataille, Georges, **Supp. VIII:** 4; **Supp. XII:** 1

"Batard" (London), **II:** 468–469

Batchelor, John Calvin, **Supp. XIX:** 142

Bate, W. J., **II:** 531

"Bateau ivre, Le" (Rimbaud; Berrigan, trans.), **Supp. XXIV:** 40

Bates, Arlo, **Retro. Supp. I:** 35

Bates, Blanche, **Supp. XVI:** 182

Bates, Kathy, **Supp. XIII:** 207

Bates, Lee, **Retro. Supp. II:** 46

Bates, Milton J., **Supp. XII:** 62

Bates, Sylvia Chatfield, **II:** 586

Bateson, Gregory, **Supp. XV:** 146

"Bath, The" (Carver), **Supp. III Part 1:** 144, 145

"Bath, The" (Snyder), **Supp. VIII:** 302

Bathwater Wine (Coleman), **Supp. XI:** 83, 90, **91**

"Batter my heart, three person'd God" (Donne), **Supp. I Part 2:** 726; **Supp. XVII:** 119

"Battle, The" (Simpson), **Supp. IX:** 268–269

Battle Cry (film), **Supp. XX: 246**

Battle Cry (Uris), **Supp. XX: 243, 246, 248–250, 255, 256**

Battlefield Where the Moon Says I Love You, The (Stanford), **Supp. XV:** 345

Battle for the Solomons (Wolfert), **Supp. XXI:** 267

Battle-Ground, The (Glasgow), **II:** 175, 176, 177, 178, 193

"Battle Hymn of the Republic" (Sandburg), **III:** 585

"Battle Hymn of the Republic, The" (Howe), **III:** 505

"Battle Hymn of the Republic, The" (Updike), **Retro. Supp. I:** 324

Battle of Angels (T. Williams), **IV:** 380, 381, 383, 385, 386, 387

"Battle of Aspen, The" (Thompson), **Supp. XXIV:** 286–287

"Battle of Lovell's Pond, The" (Longfellow), **II:** 493

Battle of the Atlantic, The (Morison), **Supp. I Part 2:** 490

"Battle of the Baltic, The" (Campbell), **Supp. I Part 1:** 309

"Battle of the Bunker, The" (Snodgrass), **Supp. VI:** 319–320

"***Battle of the Century!!!, The***" (Goldbarth), **Supp. XII:** 193

Battle of the Little Big Horn, The (Sandoz), **Supp. XXIII:** 146

Battle-Pieces and Aspects of the War (Melville), **II:** 538–539; **III:** 92; **IV:** 350; **Retro. Supp. I:** 257

"Battler, The" (Hemingway), **II:** 248; **Retro. Supp. I:** 175

"Baubles after Bombs" (Peacock), **Supp. XIX:** 200

"Baudelaire" (Schwartz), **Supp. II Part 2:** 663

Baudelaire, Charles, **I:** 58, 63, 384, 389, 420, 569; **II:** 543, 544–545, 552; **III:** 137, 141–142, 143, 409, 417, 418, 421, 428, 448, 466, 474; **IV:** 74, 79, 80, 87, 211, 286; **Retro. Supp. I:** 56, 90; **Retro. Supp. II:** 261, 262, 322, 326; **Supp. I Part 1:** 271; **Supp. III Part 1:** 4, 6, 105; **Supp. XIII:** 77, 284; **Supp. XV:** 165; **Supp. XXI:** 228; **Supp. XXIV:** 152

Baudrillard, Jean, **Supp. IV Part 1:** 45

Bauer, Dale, **Retro. Supp. I:** 381

Bauer, Douglas, **Supp. XII:** 290

Baum, L. Frank, **Supp. I Part 2:** 621; **Supp. IV Part 1:** 101, 113; **Supp. XII:** 42

Baumann, Walter, **III:** 478

Bausch, Richard, **Supp. VII: 39–56;** **Supp. XVII:** 21

Bawer, Bruce, **Supp. VIII:** 153; **Supp. IX:** 135; **Supp. X:** 187

Baxter, Charles, **Supp. XII:** 22; **Supp. XIV:** 89, 92; **Supp. XVII: 13–24;** **Supp. XXIII:** 289

Baxter, John, **Supp. XI:** 302

Baxter, Richard, **III:** 199; **IV:** 151, 153; **Supp. I Part 2:** 683

"Baxter's Procrustes" (Chesnutt), **Supp. XIV:** 76

"Bay City Blues" (Chandler), **Supp. IV Part 1:** 129

Baylies, William, **Supp. I Part 1:** 153

Baym, Nina, **Supp. IV Part 2:** 463; **Supp. X:** 229; **Supp. XVI:** 92; **Supp. XVIII:** 258, 259; **Supp. XXIV:** 28

"Bayou" (Di Piero), **Supp. XIX:** 37

Bayou Folk (Chopin), **Retro. Supp. II: 64–65,** 73; **Supp. I Part 1:** 200, 216, 218

Baziotes, William, **Supp. XV:** 144

"B.C." (Taggard), **Supp. XXII:** 278

Beach, Anna Hampstead, **Supp. XVII:** 75

Beach, Joseph Warren, **I:** 309, 500; **II:** 27; **III:** 319

Beach, Sylvia, **IV:** 404; **Retro. Supp. I:** 109, 422; **Supp. XXII:** 165

"Beaches in Winter" (Kriegel), **Supp. XXIV:** 220, 225

"Beach Women, The" (Pinsky), **Supp. VI:** 241

"Beaded Pear, The" (Simpson), **Supp. IX:** 276

Beagle, Peter, **Supp. X:** 24

Beam, Jeffrey, **Supp. XII:** 98

Beaman, E. O., **Supp. IV Part 2:** 604

Bean, Michael, **Supp. V:** 203

Bean, Robert Bennett, **Supp. II Part 1:** 170

Bean Eaters, The (Brooks), **Supp. III Part 1:** 79–81

Be Angry at the Sun (Jeffers), **Supp. II Part 2:** 434

Bean Spasms (Berrigan, Padgett, and Brainard), **Supp. XXIV:** 41–42

"Beanstalk Country, The" (T. Williams), **IV:** 383

Bean Trees, The (Kingsolver), **Supp. VII:** 197, 199–201, 202, 207, 209

"Bear" (Hogan), **Supp. IV Part 1:** 412

Bear, The (Faulkner), **Supp. VIII:** 184

"Bear, The" (Faulkner), **II:** 71–72, 73, 228; **IV:** 203; **Supp. IV Part 2:** 434; **Supp. IX:** 95; **Supp. X:** 30; **Supp. XIV:** 32; **Supp. XXI:** 37

"Bear, The" (Kinnell), **Supp. III Part 1:** 244

"Bear, The" (Momaday), **Supp. IV Part 2:** 480, 487

Bear and His Daughter: Stories (Stone), **Supp. V:** 295, 308

Beard, Charles, **I:** 214; **IV:** 429; **Supp. I Part 2:** 481, 490, 492, 632, 640, 643, 647

Beard, James, **I:** 341; **Supp. XVII:** 89, 90

Beard, Mary, **Supp. I Part 2:** 481

"Bearded Oaks" (Warren), **IV:** 240

Bearden, Romare, **Retro. Supp. I:** 209; **Supp. VIII:** 337, 342; **Supp. XXI:** 249

"Beard of Bees, A" (X. J. Kennedy), **Supp. XV:** 171

Beardon, Romare, **Supp. XV:** 144

"Beards, The" (Lethem), **Supp. XVIII:** 148

Beardsley, Aubrey, **II:** 56; **IV:** 77

Beaser, Robert, **Supp. XV:** 259

"Beast" (Swenson), **Supp. IV Part 2:** 639

"Beast & Burden, The: Seven Improvisations" (Komunyakaa), **Supp. XIII:** 120, 121

Beast God Forgot to Invent, The (Harrison), **Supp. VIII:** 37, 46, **51–52**

Beast in Me, The (Thurber), **Supp. I Part 2:** 615

"Beast in the Jungle, The" (James), **I:** 570; **II:** 335; **Retro. Supp. I:** 235; **Supp. V:** 103–104

Beast in View (Rukeyser), **Supp. VI:** 272, 273, 279, 280

Beasts of Bethlehem, The (X. J. Kennedy), **Supp. XV:** 163

"Beat! Beat! Drums!" (Whitman), **III:** 585

Beat Down to Your Soul: What Was the Beat Generation? (Charters, ed.), **Supp. XIV:** 152

"Beatific Effigies" (Bronk), **Supp. XXI:** 31

Beaton, Cecil, **Supp. XVI:** 191

"Beatrice Palmato" (Wharton), **Retro. Supp. I:** 379

Beats, The (Krim, ed.), **Supp. XV:** 338

Beattie, Ann, **Supp. V: 21–37; Supp. XI:** 26; **Supp. XII:** 80, 139, 294; **Supp. XXI:** 118; **Supp. XXIII:** 289

Beattie, L. Elisabeth, **Supp. XX: 164, 165**

Beatty, General Sam, **I:** 193

Beaty, Jerome, **Supp. IV Part 1:** 331

"Beau Monde of Mrs. Bridge, The" (Connell), **Supp. XIV:** 88, 89

Beaumont, Francis, **Supp. I Part 2:** 422

"Beauties of Santa Cruz, The" (Freneau), **Supp. II Part 1:** 260

Beautiful and Damned, The (Fitzgerald), **II:** 88, 89–91, 93, 263; **Retro. Supp. I: 103–105,** 105, 106, 110; **Supp. IX:** 56, 57

Beautiful Changes, The (Wilbur), **Supp. III Part 2:** 544–550

"Beautiful Changes, The" (Wilbur), **Supp. III Part 2:** 549, 550

Beautiful Child (Silver), **Supp. XXIV: 273–274**

"Beautiful Child, A" (Capote), **Supp. III Part 1:** 113, 125

"Beautiful & Cruel" (Cisneros), **Supp. VII:** 63, 67

"Beautiful Wall, Machu Picchu, The" (Bronk), **Supp. XXI:** 31, 32

"Beautiful Woman Who Sings, The" (Gunn Allen), **Supp. IV Part 1:** 326

"Beauty" (Emerson), **II:** 2, 5

"Beauty" (Sanders), **Supp. XVI:** 277

"Beauty" (Wylie), **Supp. I Part 2:** 710

"Beauty and the Beast" (Dove), **Supp. IV Part 1:** 245

"Beauty and the Beast" (fairy tale), **IV:** 266; **Supp. X:** 88

"Beauty and the Shoe Sluts" (Karr), **Supp. XI:** 250

Beauty of the Husband, The: A Fictional Essay in Twenty-Nine Tangos (Carson), **Supp. XII: 113–114**

Beauty Queen, The (P. N. Warren), **Supp. XX: 268–269**

Beauty's Punishment (Rice), **Supp. VII:** 301

Beauty's Release: The Continued Erotic Adventures of Sleeping Beauty (Rice), **Supp. VII:** 301

Beauvoir, Simone de, **IV:** 477; **Supp. I Part 1:** 51; **Supp. III Part 1:** 200–201, 208; **Supp. IV Part 1:** 360; **Supp. IX:** 4

Beaver Men: Spearheads of Empire (Sandoz), **Supp. XXIV:** 244, **246–247**

"Be Careful" (Zach; Everwine, trans.), **Supp. XV:** 86

Be Careful How You Live (Lacy), **Supp. XV:** 203–204

"Because I could not stop for Death—" (Dickinson), **Retro. Supp. I: 38–40,** 41, 43, 44

"Because It Happened" (Goldbarth), **Supp. XII:** 192

"Because of Libraries We Can Say These Things" (Nye), **Supp. XIII:** 283

"Because the Body Is a Flower"(Crooker), **Supp. XXIII:** 55

"Because You Mentioned the Spiritual Life" (Dunn), **Supp. XI:** 154
Bech: A Book (Updike), **IV:** 214; **Retro. Supp. I:** 329, 335
Beck, Dave, **I:** 493
Beck, Ervin, **Supp. XXIII:** 94, 95
Beck, Jack, **Supp. IV Part 2:** 560
Beck, Nicholas, **Supp. XVIII:** 252
Beck, Stefan, **Supp. XXII:** 268
Becker, Carl, **Supp. I Part 2:** 492, 493
Becker, Paula. *See* Modersohn, Mrs. Otto (Paula Becker)
Beckett, Samuel, **I:** 71, 91, 142, 298, 461; **III:** 387; **IV:** 95; **Retro. Supp. I:** 206; **Supp. IV Part 1:** 297, 368–369; **Supp. IV Part 2:** 424; **Supp. V:** 23, 53; **Supp. XI:** 104; **Supp. XII:** 21, 150–151; **Supp. XIII:** 74; **Supp. XIV:** 239; **Supp. XVII:** 185; **Supp. XX:** 17; **Supp. XXI:** 18; **Supp. XXII:** 263
Beckett, Tom, **Supp. IV Part 2:** 419
Beckford, William, **I:** 204
Beckonings (Brooks), **Supp. III Part 1:** 85
"Becky" (Toomer), **Supp. III Part 2:** 481, 483; **Supp. IX:** 312
Becky and Her Friends (Hinojosa), **Supp. XIX:** 108–109
Becoming a Man: Half a Life Story (Monette), **Supp. X:** 146, 147, 149, 151, 152, **155–157**
"Becoming a Meadow" (Doty), **Supp. XI:** 124–125
"Becoming and Breaking: Poet and Poem" (Ríos), **Supp. IV Part 2:** 539
Becoming Canonical in American Poetry (Morris), **Retro. Supp. I:** 40
Becoming Light: New and Selected Poems (Jong), **Supp. V:** 115
Bécquer, Gustavo Adolfo, **Supp. XIII:** 312
"Bed, The" (Dixon), **Supp. XII:** 154
Beddoes, Thomas Lovell, **III:** 469; **Retro. Supp. I:** 285
Bedichek, Roy, **Supp. V:** 225
Bedient, Calvin, **Supp. IX:** 298; **Supp. XII:** 98
"Bed in the Sky, The" (Snyder), **Supp. VIII:** 300
Bednarik, Joseph, **Supp. VIII:** 39
"Bedrock" (Proulx), **Supp. VII:** 253
"Bee, The" (Lanier), **Supp. I Part 1:** 364
Beecher, Catharine, **Supp. I Part 2:** 581, 582–583, 584, 586, 588, 589, 591, 599; **Supp. X:** 103; **Supp. XI:** 193
Beecher, Charles, **Supp. I Part 2:** 588, 589
Beecher, Edward, **Supp. I Part 2:** 581, 582, 583, 584, 588, 591
Beecher, Harriet. *See* Stowe, Harriet Beecher
Beecher, Henry Ward, **II:** 275; **Supp. I Part 2:** 581; **Supp. XI:** 193; **Supp. XVIII:** 4
Beecher, Lyman, **Supp. I Part 2:** 580–581, 582, 583, 587, 588, 599; **Supp. XI:** 193
Beecher, Mrs. Lyman (Roxanna Foote), **Supp. I Part 2:** 580–581, 582, 588, 599

Beeching, Jack, **Supp. X:** 114, 117, 118, 123, 125, 126
"Beehive" (Toomer), **Supp. IX:** 317
"Bee Hunt, The" (Irving), **II:** 313
"Beekeeper's Daughter, The" (Plath), **Retro. Supp. II:** 246–247
"Bee Meeting, The" (Plath), **Retro. Supp. II:** 254–255
Bee Poems (Plath), **Retro. Supp. II:** 254–255
Beer, John, **Supp. XVII:** 239
Beer, Thomas, **I:** 405
Beerbohm, Max, **III:** 472; **IV:** 436; **Supp. I Part 2:** 714
"Beer Bottle" (Kooser), **Supp. XIX:** 117
"Beer in the Sergeant Major's Hat, or The Sun Also Sneezes" (Chandler), **Supp. IV Part 1:** 121
Beers, Henry A., **Supp. XX: 68**
"Bees Bees Bees" (J. Scott), **Supp. XVII:** 188, 190
Beethoven, Ludwig van, **II:** 536; **III:** 118; **IV:** 274, 358; **Supp. I Part 1:** 363; **Supp. VIII:** 103
Beet Queen, The (Erdrich), **Supp. IV Part 1:** 259, 260, 264–265, 266, 273, 274, 275
Befo' de War: Echoes in Negro Dialect (Gordon), **Supp. II Part 1:** 201
"Before" (Goldbarth), **Supp. XII:** 175
"Before" (Snyder), **Supp. VIII:** 301
Before Adam (London), **II:** 466
Before Breakfast (O'Neill), **Supp. XXII:** 22
Before Disaster (Winters), **Supp. II Part 2:** 786, 800
"Before Disaster" (Winters), **Supp. II Part 2:** 801, 815
"Before I Knocked" (D. Thomas), **III:** 534
Beforelife, The (F. Wright), **Supp. XVII:** 240, 245–246
"Before March" (MacLeish), **III:** 15
Before My Life Began (Neugeboren), **Supp. XVI: 224–225**
"Before the Altar" (Lowell), **II:** 516
"Before the Birth of one of her children" (Bradstreet), **Supp. I Part 1:** 118
Before the Gringo Came (Atherton), **Supp. XXIV:** 22
"Before the Sky Darkens" (Dunn), **Supp. XI:** 155
"Begat" (Sexton), **Supp. II Part 2: 693**
Beget, Philippe, **Supp. XXIII:** 74
Beggarman, Thief (Shaw), **Supp. XIX:** 251–252
Beggar on Horseback (Kaufman and Connelly), **III:** 394
"Beggar Said So, The" (Singer), **IV:** 12
Beggars in the House of Plenty (Shanley), **Supp. XIV:** 316, 327–328
Beggar's Opera, The (Gay), **Supp. I Part 2:** 523
Begiebing, Robert, **Retro. Supp. II:** 210
Begin Again (Paley), **Supp. VI:** 221
Beginners (Carver), **Supp. XXIV:** 177
"Beginning and the End, The" (Jeffers), **Supp. II Part 2:** 420–421, 424
"Beginning of Decadence, The" (Jeffers), **Supp. II Part 2:** 420

"Beginning of Enthusiasm, The" (Salinas), **Supp. XIII:** 327–328
Beginning of Wisdom, The (Benét), **I:** 358; **Supp. XI:** 44
"Beginnings of Sorrow, The" (P. Benedict), **Supp. XXIII:** 48
Be Glad You're Neurotic (Bisch), **Supp. I Part 2:** 608
"Begotten of the Spleen" (Simic), **Supp. VIII:** 277
"Behaving Like a Jew" (Stern), **Supp. IX: 290–291,** 294
"Behavior" (Emerson), **II:** 2, 4
Behavior of Titans, The (Merton), **Supp. VIII:** 201
Behind a Mask (Alcott), **Supp. I Part 1:** 36–37, 43–44
"Behind a Wall" (Lowell), **II:** 516
Behind the Movie Camera (radio show), **Supp. XV:** 147
"Behold the Key" (Malamud), **Supp. I Part 2:** 437
Behrendt, Stephen, **Supp. X:** 204
Behrman, S. N., **Supp. V:** 95
Beidler, Peter G., **Supp. IV Part 2:** 557
Beidler, Philip D., **Supp. XII:** 69
Beige Dolorosa (Harrison), **Supp. VIII:** 40, 51
Beiles, Sinclair, **Supp. XII:** 129
Beiliss, Mendel, **Supp. I Part 2:** 427, 446, 447, 448
"Being a Constellation" (A. Finch), **Supp. XVII:** 72
"Being a Lutheran Boy-God in Minnesota" (R. Bly), **Supp. IV Part 1:** 59, 67
Being and Race (Johnson), **Supp. VI:** 193, 199
Being and Time (Heidegger), **Supp. VIII:** 9
Being Busted (Fiedler), **Supp. XIII:** 95, 102, 104
Being Geniuses Together: 1920–1930 (Boyle), **Supp. XXIV:** 63, 64
Being John Malkovich (Kaufman), **Supp. XV:** 16
Being Perfect (Quindlen), **Supp. XVII:** 167, 179
Being There (Kosinski), **Supp. VII:** 215, 216, 222–223
Beiswanger, George, **Retro. Supp. II:** 220
Beka Lamb (Edgell), **Supp. XXIII:** 83, 85, **86–88,** 93–94, 95
Belasco, David, **Supp. XVI:** 182; **Supp. XXI:** 151
Bel Canto (Patchett), **Supp. XII:** 307, 310, **320–322**
Belchamber (Sturgis), **Supp. XX: 227, 233, 238–240**
"Beleaguered City, The" (Longfellow), **II:** 498
Belfry of Bruges, The, and Other Poems (Longfellow), **II:** 489; **Retro. Supp. II:** 157, 168
"Belief" (Levine), **Supp. V:** 186, 190
"Belief in the Self Abandoned, The" (Bronk), **Supp. XXI:** 30
"Beliefs of Writers, The" (Doctorow), **Supp. IV Part 1:** 235–236

Believeniks! (Lethem and Sorrentino), **Supp. XVIII:** 148–149

Believers (C. Baxter), **Supp. XVII:** 20–21, 22

"Believers" (C. Baxter), **Supp. XVII:** 21

"Believers, The/Los Creyentes" (Kingsolver), **Supp. VII:** 208

Belinda (Rice), **Supp. VII:** 301–302

"Belinda's Petition" (Dove), **Supp. IV Part 1:** 245

"Belita" (Ríos), **Supp. IV Part 2:** 541

Belitt, Ben, **Supp. XII:** 260

Bell, Archibald, **Supp. XX: 284, 285**

Bell, Bernard, **Supp. XXII:** 182

Bell, Clive, **IV:** 87

Bell, Daniel, **Supp. I Part 2:** 648

Bell, George Kennedy Allen, **Retro. Supp. I:** 65

Bell, Madison Smartt, **Supp. X: 1–20; Supp. XVII:** 236; **Supp. XIX:** 58–59, 60–61; **Supp. XXI:** 48; **Supp. XXIII:** 43

Bell, Marvin, **Supp. V:** 337, 339; **Supp. IX:** 152; **Supp. XI:** 316; **Supp. XXIV:** 165

Bell, Michael, **Retro. Supp. II:** 139

Bell, Pearl, **Supp. XI:** 233

Bell, Quentin, **Supp. I Part 2:** 636

Bell, Whitfield J., Jr., **II:** 123

Bellafante, Gina, **Supp. VIII:** 85

Bellamy, Edward, **II:** 276; **Supp. I Part 2:** 641; **Supp. XI:** 200, 203

Bellarosa Connection, The (Bellow), **Retro. Supp. II:** 31, 32

"Belle Dollinger" (Masters), **Supp. I Part 2:** 463

Belleforest, François de, **IV:** 370

"Belle Zoraïde, La" (Chopin), **Supp. I Part 1:** 215–216

Bell in the Fog and Other Stories, The (Atherton), **Supp. XXIV:** 23

Bell Jar, The (Plath), **Retro. Supp. II:** 242, **249–250; Supp. I Part 2:** 526, 527, 529, 531–536, 539, 540, 541, 542, 544

Belloc, Hilary, **III:** 176; **IV:** 432

"Bellocq" (Trethewey), **Supp. XXI:** 253

Bellocq, E. J., **Supp. XXI:** 246, 251

Bellocq's Ophelia (Trethewey), **Supp. XXI:** 243, 246, **251–254**

"Bellocq's Ophelia" (Trethewey), **Supp. XXI:** 254

Bellow, Saul, **I:** 113, 138–139, **144–166**, 375, 517; **II:** 579; **III:** 40; **IV:** 3, 19, 217, 340; **Retro. Supp. II: 19–36,** 118, 279, 307, 324; **Supp. I Part 2:** 428, 451; **Supp. II Part 1:** 109; **Supp. IV Part 1:** 30; **Supp. V:** 258; **Supp. VIII:** 98, 176, 234, 236–237, 245; **Supp. IX:** 212, 227; **Supp. XI:** 64, 233; **Supp. XII:** 159, 165, 170, 310; **Supp. XIII:** 106; **Supp. XV:** 143; **Supp. XVI:** 208; **Supp. XVIII:** 90; **Supp. XIX:** 157, 158, 261; **Supp. XX: 244; Supp. XXII:** 268; **Supp. XXIII:** 166

Bellows, George, **Supp. XV:** 295

"Bells, The" (Poe), **III:** 593; **Retro. Supp. II:** 266; **Supp. I Part 2:** 388

"Bells, The" (Sexton), **Supp. II Part 2:** 673

"Bells for John Whiteside's Daughter" (Ransom), **III:** 490

"Bells of Lynn, The" (Longfellow), **II:** 498

"Bells of San Blas, The" (Longfellow), **II:** 490–491, 493, 498

"Bell Tower, The" (Melville), **III:** 91

"Belly, The" (Dobyns), **Supp. XIII:** 87

'Bel of Prairie Eden (Lippard), **Supp. XXIII:** 178, 186

"Belonging" (Pickering), **Supp. XXI:** 202

"Belonging Kind, The" (W. Gibson and J. Shirley), **Supp. XVI:** 123

Beloved (Morrison), **Supp. III Part 1:** 364, 372–379; **Supp. IV Part 1:** 13–14; **Supp. V:** 259; **Supp. VIII:** 343; **Supp. XIII:** 60; **Supp. XXII:** 78, 109; **Supp. XXIV:** 186

Beloved, The (Gibran), **Supp. XX: 125**

"Beloved, The" (Halliday), **Supp. XIX:** 92

Beloved Lady: A History of Jane Addams' Ideas on Reform and Peace (Farrell), **Supp. I Part 1:** 24

Beloved Stranger, The (Bynner), **Supp. XV:** 44, 50

Bemorse, John, **Supp. XX: 62**

Benchley, Robert, **I:** 48, 482; **II:** 435; **III:** 53; **Supp. IX:** 190, 195, 204

Benda, W. T., **Retro. Supp. I:** 13

Bender, Aimee, **Supp. XXII:** 49

Bending of a Twig, The (Coke), **Supp. XX: 235**

Bend Sinister (Nabokov), **III:** 253–254; **Retro. Supp. I:** 265, 266, 270

"Beneath the Sidewalk" (Dunn), **Supp. XI:** 145

"Beneath the Smooth Skin of America" (Sanders), **Supp. XVI:** 275

Benedict, Elizabeth, **Supp. XVIII:** 289

Benedict, Laura, **Supp. XXIII:** 35, 36, 49

Benedict, Pinckney, **Supp. XXIII: 35–50**

Benedict, Ruth, **Supp. IX:** 229

Benefactor, The (Sontag), **Supp. III Part 2:** 451, 455, 468, 469

"Benefit Performance" (Malamud), **Supp. I Part 2:** 431

Benét, Laura, **Supp. XI:** 44

Benét, Rosemary, **Supp. XI:** 44, 51

Benét, Stephen Vincent, **I:** 358; **II:** 177; **III:** 22; **IV:** 129; **Supp. XI: 43–61**

Benét, William Rose, **II:** 530; **Retro. Supp. I:** 108; **Supp. I Part 2:** 709; **Supp. XI:** 43, 44; **Supp. XIV:** 119, 122, 129

Ben Franklin's Wit and Wisdom (Franklin), **II:** 111

Ben-Gurion, David, **Supp. XX: 243**

Ben-Hur (film), **Supp. IV Part 2:** 683

Benigna Machiavelli (Gilman), **Supp. XI:** 201, 208

Benitez, R. Michael, **Retro. Supp. II:** 264

Benito Cereno (Lowell), **II:** 546; **Retro. Supp. II:** 181

"Benito Cereno" (Melville), **III:** 91; **Retro. Supp. I:** 255; **Retro. Supp. II:** 188; **Supp. XVII:** 185

Benito's Dream Bottle (Nye), **Supp. XIII:** 278

"Bênitou's Slave, The" (Chopin), **Retro. Supp. II:** 64

Benjamin, Walter, **Supp. IX:** 133; **Supp. XVI:** 290, 291; **Supp. XXIII:** 28, 29, 30, 31

Benjamin Franklin (Van Doren), **Supp. I Part 2:** 486

"Benjamin Pantier" (Masters), **Supp. I Part 2:** 461

Bennett, Anne Virginia, **II:** 184

Bennett, Arnold, **I:** 103; **II:** 337; **Supp. XVI:** 190

Bennett, Elizabeth, **Supp. VIII:** 58

Bennett, Patrick, **Supp. V:** 225

Bennett, Paula, **Retro. Supp. I:** 29, 33, 42; **Supp. XX: 286**

Bennett, Reginald, **Supp. XXII:** 218

Bennett, William, **Supp. VIII:** 245

Benson, A. C., **Supp. XX: 238**

Benson, Arthur, **Supp. XX: 233**

Benson, E. F., **Supp. XX: 229**

Benson, Heidi, **Supp. XVIII:** 136

Benson, Jackson J., **Supp. IV Part 2:** 613

Benson, Martin, **Supp. XVIII:** 38

Benstock, Shari, **Retro. Supp. I:** 361, 368, 371, 382; **Supp. XX: 240**

Bentham, Jeremy, **I:** 279; **Supp. I Part 2:** 635

Bentley, Anna, **Supp. XXI:** 5

Bentley, Arthur, **Supp. XXI:** 4, 5

Bentley, Eric R., **IV:** 396

Bentley, Nelson, **Supp. IX:** 324

Bentley, Richard, **III:** 79, 86

Benton, Robert, **Supp. IV Part 1:** 236

"Bent Tones" (Wright), **Supp. XV:** 346

Benveniste, Emile, **Supp. XVI:** 292

Benzel, Jan, **Supp. XVI:** 112

Beowulf, **Supp. II Part 1:** 6; **Supp. XVII:** 70, 73

Beran, Carol, **Supp. XIII:** 25

"Berck-Plage" (Plath), **Retro. Supp. II:** 253–254

Bercovitch, Sacvan, **Retro. Supp. I:** 408; **Retro. Supp. II:** 325, 330; **Supp. I Part 1:** 99; **Supp. I Part 2:** 659

Berdyaev, Nikolai, **I:** 494; **III:** 292

"Bereaved Apartments" (Kingsolver), **Supp. VII:** 203

"Bereavement in their death to feel" (Dickinson), **Retro. Supp. I:** 43, 44

"Berenice" (Poe), **III:** 415, 416, 425; **Retro. Supp. II:** 270

Bérénice (Racine), **II:** 573

Berenson, Bernard, **Retro. Supp. I:** 381; **Supp. IV Part 1:** 314; **Supp. XIV:** 335, 336, 337; **Supp. XVII:** 99; **Supp. XXI:** 5

Berenson, Mary Smith, **Supp. XXI:** 4, 5, 6

Berg, James, **Supp. XIV:** 157, 159

Berg, Stephen, **Supp. IV Part 1:** 60

Berger, Alan, **Supp. XVII:** 39

Berger, Charles, **Retro. Supp. I:** 311

Berger, John, **Supp. XVI:** 284; **Supp. XXIII:** 167, 168–169; **Supp. XXIV:** 94

Berger, Roger, **Supp. XIII:** 237

Berger, Thomas, **III:** 258; **Supp. XII:** 171
Berghash, Rachel, **Supp. XXIV:** 172
Bergman, Ingmar, **I:** 291; **Supp. XV:** 7, 8, 12
Bergson, Henri, **I:** 224; **II:** 163, 165, 166, 359; **III:** 8, 9, 488, 619; **IV:** 86, 122, 466, 467; **Retro. Supp. I:** 55, 57, 80; **Supp. IV Part 1:** 42; **Supp. XXII:** 158
Berkeley, Anthony, **Supp. IV Part 1:** 341
Berkeley, George, **II:** 10, 349, 357, 480, 554
Berkman, Alexander, **Supp. XXIII:** 161
Berkman, Leonard, **Supp. XV:** 321
Berkowitz, Gerald, **Supp. IV Part 2:** 590
Berkson, Bill, **Supp. XXIII:** 217, 218
Berlin, Isaiah, **Supp. XXII:** 258
Berlin Alexanderplatz (Döblin), **Supp. XV:** 137
Berlin Stories (Isherwood), **Supp. IV Part 1:** 82; **Supp. XIV:** 155, 156, 161, 162, 164, 165
Berlioz, Hector, **Supp. XV:** 33
Berlyne, Daniel E., **Supp. I Part 2:** 672
Berman, Alexander, **Supp. XVII:** 103
Berman, Carolyn Vellenga, **Supp. XXII:** 147
Bernard Clare (Farrell), **II:** 38, 39
Bernard of Clairvaux, Saint, **I:** 22; **II:** 538
Bernays, Thekla, **Retro. Supp. II:** 65
Berne, Suzanne, **Supp. XII:** 320
Berne, Victoria (pseudonym). *See* Fisher, M. F. K.
Berneis, Peter, **IV:** 383
Bernhard, Brendan, **Supp. XIV:** 163
Bernhard, Thomas, **Supp. XX: 91**
Bernhardt, Sarah, **I:** 484; **Retro. Supp. I:** 377
Bernice (Glaspell), **Supp. III Part 1:** 179
"Bernice Bobs Her Hair" (Fitzgerald), **II:** 88; **Retro. Supp. I:** 103
Bernstein, Aline, **IV:** 455, 456
Bernstein, Andrea, **Supp. IX:** 146
Bernstein, Carl, **Supp. XXIV:** 293
Bernstein, Charles, **Supp. IV Part 2:** 421, 426; **Supp. XXIV:** 40, 41, 45–46
Bernstein, Elizabeth, **Supp. XII:** 318
Bernstein, Leonard, **I:** 28; **Supp. I Part 1:** 288, 289; **Supp. IV Part 1:** 83, 84
Bernstein, Melvin, **Supp. XIV:** 41, 46
Bernstein, Michael André, **Retro. Supp. I:** 427
Bernstein, Richard, **Supp. IX:** 253, 262; **Supp. XII:** 113; **Supp. XIV:** 33; **Supp. XXII:** 261
Berrett, Jesse, **Supp. XIII:** 241, 242
Berrigan, Ted, **Supp. XIV:** 150; **Supp. XXII:** 224, 225, 228, 231; **Supp. XXIII:** 218, 221; **Supp. XXIV: 33–47**
Berroa y Canelo, Quiterio, **Supp. XXI:** 104
"Berry" (Hughes), **Supp. I Part 1:** 329, 330
Berry, Eleanor, **Supp. XXIII:** 246
Berry, Faith, **Retro. Supp. I:** 194, 201
Berry, Walter, **IV:** 313–314, 326
Berry, Wendell, **Supp. VIII:** 304; **Supp. X: 21–39; Supp. XII:** 202; **Supp. XIII:** 1–2; **Supp. XIV:** 179; **Supp.**

XVI: 39, 56; **Supp. XVIII:** 192; **Supp. XXI:** 90
"Berry Feast, A" (Snyder), **Supp. VIII:** 289, 297
Berryman, John, **I: 167–189,** 405, 441–442, 521; **II:** 554; **III:** 273; **IV:** 138, 430; **Retro. Supp. I:** 430; **Retro. Supp. II:** 175, 178; **Supp. I Part 2:** 546; **Supp. II Part 1:** 109; **Supp. III Part 2:** 541, 561, 595, 596, 603; **Supp. IV Part 2:** 620, 639; **Supp. V:** 179–180, 337; **Supp. IX:** 152; **Supp. XI:** 240; **Supp. XV:** 93; **Supp. XVII:** 111; **Supp. XXII:** 83
Berryman, Mrs. John, **I:** 168–169
Berryman's Sonnets (Berryman), **I:** 168, 175–178
"Berry Territory" (Snyder), **Supp. VIII:** 304
Berthoff, Warner, **Supp. I Part 1:** 133
Bertolucci, Bernardo, **Supp. IV Part 1:** 94
"Bertrand Hume" (Masters), **Supp. I Part 2:** 463–464
Besco, Glenn, **Supp. XXIII:** 125
"Best, the Most, The" (Carruth), **Supp. XVI:** 59
Best American Essays 1987, The (G. Talese and R. Atwan, eds.), **Supp. XVI:** 273
Best American Essays 1988, The (Dillard, ed.), **Supp. VIII:** 272
Best American Essays 1989, The (Wolff, ed.), **Supp. XVII:** 208
Best American Essays 1993, The (J. Epstein, ed.), **Supp. XVI:** 275
Best American Essays 1997, The (Frazier, ed.), **Supp. VIII:** 272; **Supp. XVII:** 207
Best American Essays 1999, The (E. Hoagland and R. Atwan, eds.), **Supp. XVI:** 277
Best American Essays 2008, The, **Supp. XXIV:** 230
Best American Essays 2009, The, **Supp. XXIV:** 230
Best American Essays for College Students, The (R. Atwan, ed.), **Supp. XVI:** 273
Best American Fantasy, 2010 (Brockmeier, ed.), **Supp. XXII:** 49–50
Best American New Voices 2001 (C. Baxter, ed.), **Supp. XVII:** 22
Best American Poetry, The: 1988 (Ashbery, ed.), **Supp. III Part 1:** 26
Best American Poetry 2000, The (Dove and Lehman, eds.), **Supp. XXI:** 246
Best American Poetry 2006, The (Collins, ed.), **Supp. XXI:** 54
Best American Short Stories, **I:**174; **II:** 587; **III:** 443; **Supp. IV Part 1:** 102, 315; **Supp. IX:** 114; **Supp. X:** 301
Best American Short Stories, 1915–1050, The, **Supp. IX:** 4
Best American Short Stories 1965, The (Foley, ed.), **Supp. XVI:** 225
Best American Short Stories 1979, The, **Supp. XXIII:** 290
Best American Short Stories 1982, The (Gardner, ed.), **Supp. XVII:** 16

Best American Short Stories 1983, The (A. Tyler, ed.), **Supp. XVI:** 37
Best American Short Stories 1986, The (Carver, ed.), **Supp. XVII:** 17
Best American Short Stories 1988, The (Helprin, ed.), **Supp. XVI:** 16
Best American Short Stories 1989, The (Atwood, ed.), **Supp. XVII:** 18; **Supp. XXI:** 39, 42
Best American Short Stories 1991, The (Adams and Kenison, eds.), **Supp. XVI:** 256
Best American Short Stories 1996, The, **Supp. XXIII:** 295
Best American Short Stories 1997, **Supp. XXII:** 75
Best American Short Stories 2001, The (Kenison and Kingsover, eds.), **Supp. XVI:** 24
Best American Short Stories 2007, The, **Supp. XXIII:** 290
Best American Short Stories of 1942, The, **Supp. V:** 316
Best American Short Stories of 1944, The, **Supp. IX:** 119
Best American Short Stories of the Century (Updike, ed.), **Supp. X:** 163
Best American Short Stories of the Eighties, The (Ravenal, ed.), **Supp. IV Part 1:** 93
Best American Sports Writing of the Century, The (Halberstam, ed.), **Supp. XVII:** 204
"Best China Saucer, The" (Jewett), **Retro. Supp. II:** 145–146
Best Creative Nonfiction Volume 2, The, **Supp. XXIV:** 230
Bester, Alfred, **Supp. XVI:** 123
Best Hour of the Night, The (Simpson), **Supp. IX: 277–279**
Bestiaire, Le (Apollinaire), **IV:** 80
Bestiary, A (Wilbur), **Supp. III Part 2:** 552
"Bestiary for the Fingers of My Right Hand" (Simic), **Supp. VIII:** 274, 275
Best Man, The: A Play About Politics (Vidal), **Supp. IV Part 2:** 683
"Best of Everything, The" (Yates), **Supp. XI:** 341
Best of Pickering, The (Pickering), **Supp. XXI:** 192, 198
Best of Plimpton (Plimpton), **Supp. XVI:** 238, 239, 240
Best Short Plays, The (Mayorga), **IV:** 381
Best Short Stories, The (O'Brien, ed.), **I:** 289
Best Short Stories by Negro Writers, The (Hughes, ed.), **Supp. I Part 1:** 345
Best Short Stories of 1926, The (O'Brien, ed.), **Supp. XVIII:** 279
Best Short Stories of 1934 (O'Brien, ed.), **Supp. XVIII:** 227
Best Short Stories of 1938 (O'Brien, ed.), **Supp. XIX:** 256; **Supp. XX:** 34
Best That Ever Did It, The (Lacy), **Supp. XV:** 201–202
Best Times, The: An Informal Memoir (Dos Passos), **I:** 475, 482
Best Words, Best Order: Essays on Poetry (Dobyns), **Supp. XIII:** 74, **76–78,** 87

Best Years of Our Lives, The (film; Wyler), **Supp. XV:** 195
"BETANCOURT" (Baraka), **Supp. II Part 1:** 33, 34
Bête humaine, La (Zola), **III:** 316, 318
"Bethe" (Hellman), **Supp. I Part 1:** 293
Bethea, David, **Supp. VIII:** 27
Bethel Merriday (Lewis), **II:** 455
Bethke, Bruce, **Supp. XVI:** 121
Bethlehem in Broad Daylight (Doty), **Supp. XI:** 121, **122–123**
Bethune, Mary McLeod, **Retro. Supp. I:** 197; **Supp. I Part 1:** 333
Bethurum, Dorothy, **IV:** 121
"Betrayal" (Lanier), **Supp. I Part 1:** 364
"Betrothed" (Bogan), **Supp. III Part 1:** 49–51
Bettelheim, Bruno, **Supp. I Part 2:** 622; **Supp. X:** 77, 84; **Supp. XIV:** 126; **Supp. XVI:** 33
Better Days (Price), **Supp. VI:** 264
Better Sort, The (James), **II:** 335
Better Than Sex (Thompson), **Supp. XXIV:** 283
"Better Things in Life, The" (Loos), **Supp. XVI:** 194
Betty Leicester (Jewett), **II:** 406
Betty Leicester's Christmas (Jewett), **II:** 406; **Retro. Supp. II:** 145
Betty's Summer Vacation (Durang), **Supp. XXIV: 125–126**
Between Angels (Dunn), **Supp. XI: 149–159**
"Between Angels" (Dunn), **Supp. XI:** 150
Between Fantoine and Agapa (Pinget), **Supp. V:** 39
"Between Memory and History: A Writer's Voice" (Kreisler), **Supp. XVI:** 155
Between Silences: A Voice from China (Jin), **Supp. XVIII:** 91, 92, 93
"Between the Porch and the Altar" (Lowell), **II:** 540–541
"Between the World and Me" (Wright), **Supp. II Part 1:** 228
Between Time and Timbuktu (Vonnegut), **Supp. II Part 2:** 753, 759
Between Two Rivers (Kenny), **Supp. XXIII:** 143
Beuka, Robert A., **Supp. XIX:** 263; **Supp. XXI:** 47
"Be Very Afraid—Of Loss of Liberty at Home" (P. N. Warren), **Supp. XX: 272–273**
Bevis, Howard L., **Supp. I Part 2:** 611
Bevis, John, **Supp. I Part 2:** 503
Bewilderment: New Poems and Translations (Ferry), **Supp. XXIV: 160–161**
"Bewitched" (Wharton), **IV:** 316
Bewley, Marius, **I:** 336
Beyer, Werner, **Supp. XXIII:** 145
Beyle, Marie Henri. *See* Stendhal
Beyond (Goldbarth), **Supp. XII:** 192
Beyond a Boundary (C. L. R. James), **Supp. XXI:** 159, 170–171
Beyond Black Bear Lake (LaBastille), **Supp. X:** 95, **99–102**, 108
"Beyond Charles River to the Acheron" (Lowell), **II:** 541

Beyond Criticism (Shapiro), **Supp. II Part 2:** 703, 711
Beyond Culture (Trilling), **Supp. III Part 2:** 508–512
Beyond Desire (Anderson), **I:** 111
Beyond Document: The Art of Nonfiction Film (Warren, ed.), **Supp. IV Part 2:** 434
Beyond Forgetting (Hughes, ed.; foreword by Gallagher), **Supp. XXIV:** 167, 171
Beyond Good and Evil (Nietzsche), **Supp. IV Part 2:** 519
"Beyond Harm" (Olds), **Supp. X:** 210
Beyond Katrina: A Meditation on the Mississippi Gulf Coast (Trethewey), **Supp. XXI:** 248
"Beyond My Solitude" (Gibran), **Supp. XX: 119**
"Beyond the Alps" (Lowell), **II:** 547, 550
"Beyond the Bayou" (Chopin), **Supp. I Part 1:** 215
Beyond the Boom: New Voices on American Life, Culture and Politics (Teachout), **Supp. XIX:** 137
Beyond the Horizon (O'Neill), **III:** 389; **Supp. XXI:** 13; **Supp. XXII:** 22
Beyond the Hundredth Meridian: John Wesley Powell and the Second Opening of the West (Stegner), **Supp. IV Part 2:** 599, 603–604, 611
"Beyond the Kittery Bridge" (Hatlen), **Supp. V:** 138
Beyond the Law (film) (Mailer), **Retro. Supp. II:** 205
Beyond Therapy (Durang), **Supp. XXIV: 119–120**
"Beyond the Sea (at the sanatorium)" (Salinas), **Supp. XIII:** 325
Beyond the Wall: Essays from the Outside (Abbey), **Supp. XIII:** 13
Beyond the Writers' Workshop: New Ways to Write Creative Nonfiction (C. Bly), **Supp. XVI:** 41
Beyond Tragedy (Niebuhr), **III:** 300–303
Bezner, Kevin, **Supp. XII:** 202
B. F.'s Daughter (Marquand), **III:** 59, 65, 68, 69
Bhagavad Gita, **III:** 566; **IV:** 183
"Biafra: A People Betrayed" (Vonnegut), **Supp. II Part 2:** 760
Bianchi, Martha Dickinson, **I:** 470; **Retro. Supp. I:** 35, 37, 38
Bible, **I:** 191, 280, 414, 421, 490, 506; **II:** 6, 12, 15, 17, 108, 231, 237, 238, 252, 267, 302; **III:** 28, 199, 308–309, 341, 343, 350, 356, 402, 492, 519, 565, 577; **IV:** 11, 13, 42, 57, 60, 67, 152, 153, 154, 155, 164, 165, 296, 337, 341, 367, 369, 370, 371, 438; **Retro. Supp. I:** 91; **Supp. I Part 1:** 4, 6, 63, 101, 104, 105, 113, 193, 369; **Supp. I Part 2:** 388, 433, 494, 515, 516, 517, 583, 584, 587, 589, 653, 689, 690, 691; **Supp. IV Part 1:** 284; **Supp. VIII:** 20; **Supp. IX:** 246; **Supp. XIV:** 225. *See also* names of biblical books; New Testament; Old Testament
Biblia Americana (Mather), **Supp. II Part 2:** 442

Biblical Dialogues between a Father and His Family (Rowson), **Supp. XV:** 245–246
"Bibliography of the King's Book, A, or, Eikon Basilike" (Howe), **Supp. IV Part 2:** 435
Bibliography of the King's Book, A; or, Eikon Basilike (Almack), **Supp. IV Part 2:** 435
Bickel, Freddy. *See* March, Fredric
Bidart, Frank, **Retro. Supp. II:** 48, 50, 52, 182, 183, 184; **Supp. XV: 19–37; Supp. XVIII:** 91,92; **Supp. XIX:** 82
Bid Me to Live (Doolittle), **Supp. I Part 1:** 258, 260, 268, 269, 270
"*Bien* Pretty" (Cisneros), **Supp. VII:** 70
"Bienvenidos" (Mora), **Supp. XIII:** 220
Bierce, Albert, **I:** 191, 209
Bierce, Ambrose, **I: 190–213**, 419; **II:** 74, 264, 271; **IV:** 350; **Retro. Supp. II:** 72
Bierce, Mrs. Ambrose, **I:** 194–195, 199
Bierce, Day, **I:** 195, 199
Bierce, Helen, **I:** 210
Bierce, Leigh, **I:** 195, 198, 208
Bierce, General Lucius Verus, **I:** 191
Bierce, Marcus, **I:** 190, 191
Bierce, Mrs. Marcus, **I:** 190, 191
Bierds, Linda, **Supp. XVII: 25–37**
Biffle, Kent, **Supp. V:** 225
"Bi-Focal" (Stafford), **Supp. XI:** 318, 321
Bigamist's Daughter, A (McDermott), **Supp. XVIII:** 155**,** **156–158**, 160, 166
Big as Life (Doctorow), **Supp. IV Part 1:** 231, 234
Big Bad Love (film, Howard), **Supp. XXI:** 39
Big Bad Love (L. Brown), **Supp. XXI:** 40, 42, **44–45**
"Big Bite" (Mailer), **Retro. Supp. II:** 204
"Big Blonde" (Parker), **Supp. IX:** 189, 192, 193, 195, 196, 203
Big Bozo, The (Glaspell), **Supp. III Part 1:** 182
Bigelow, Gordon, **Supp. X:** 222, 227, 229
Bigelow, Jacob, **Supp. I Part 1:** 302
Bigelow Papers, Second Series, The (Lowell), **Supp. I Part 2:** 406, 415–416
Bigelow Papers, The (Lowell), **Supp. I Part 2:** 406, 407, 408, 410, 411–412, 415, 417, 424
"Big Fiddle" (Boyle), **Supp. XXIV:** 54
Big Fix, The (Lacy), **Supp. XV:** 204–205
Bigfoot Dreams (Prose), **Supp. XVI:** 253–254
Big Funk, The: A Casual Play (Shanley), **Supp. XIV:** 316, **327**
"Big Game" (Boyle), **Supp. XX:** 20
Big Game, The (film), **Supp. XIX:** 244
Big Gold Dream, The (C. Himes), **Supp. XVI:** 143, 144
"Bight, The" (Bishop), **Retro. Supp. II:** 38, 45
Big Hunger: Stories 1932–1959 (Fante), **Supp. XI:** 160
Big Knife, The (Odets), **Supp. II Part 2:** 546, 547, 548

Big Knockover, The (Hammett), **Supp. I Part 1:** 292; **Supp. IV Part 1:** 344, 345, 356

Big Laugh, The (O'Hara), **III:** 362, 373–375

Big Man (Neugeboren), **Supp. XVI:** 219, **220,** 221, 225

Big Money, The (Dos Passos), **I:** 482, 483, 486–487, 489; **Supp. I Part 2:** 646, 647

Big Picture (Everett), **Supp. XVIII:** 54, 66

"Big Picture" (Everett), **Supp. XVIII:** 66

"Big Picture" (Halliday), **Supp. XIX:** 93

"Big Rock Candy Figgy Pudding Pitfall, The" (Didion), **Supp. IV Part 1:** 195

Big Rock Candy Mountain, The (Stegner), **Supp. IV Part 2:** 596, 597, 598, 599, 600, 603, 604, 605, 606–607, 608, 610–611

Bigsby, C. W. E. (Christopher), **Supp. IX:** 137, 140; **Supp. XV:** 332

Big Sea, The (Hughes), **Retro. Supp. I:** 195, 197, 199, 201, 204; **Supp. I Part 1:** 322, 332, 333; **Supp. II Part 1:** 233–234; **Supp. XIX:** 77; **Supp. XXII:** 3

Big Sky, The (Mora), **Supp. XIII:** 221

Big Sleep, The (Chandler), **Supp. IV Part 1:** 122–125, 127, 128, 134

Big Sleep, The (film), **Supp. IV Part 1:** 130; **Supp. XVIII:** 148

Big Strike, The (Ryan as Quin), **Supp. XVIII:** 226,**232–233**

Big Sur (Kerouac), **Supp. III Part 1:** 230

Big Sur and the Oranges of Hieronymous Bosch (H. Miller), **III:** 189–190

Big Town, The (Lardner), **II:** 426, 429

"Big Two-Hearted River" (Hemingway), **II:** 249; **Retro. Supp. I:** 170–171; **Supp. IX:** 106; **Supp. XIV:** 227, 235

"Big Wind" (Roethke), **III:** 531

"Big Winner Rises Late, The" (Dunn), **Supp. XI:** 146

"Bilingual/*Bilingüe*" (essay; Espaillat), *Supp. XXI:* 103

"Bilingual/*Bilingüe*" (poem; Espaillat), *Supp. XXI:* 104

"Bilingual Christmas" (Mora), **Supp. XIII:** 216–217

"Bilingual Sestina" (Alvarez), **Supp. VII:** 10

"Bill" (Winters), **Supp. II Part 2:** 792

"Bill, The" (Malamud), **Supp. I Part 2:** 427, 430, 434

"Bill Collector's Vacation, The" (Hampl), **Supp. XXII:** 83

"Billie Holiday" (Carruth), **Supp. XVI:** 50

Billings, Gladys. *See* Brooks, Mrs. Van Wyck

Billings, Josh, **Supp. XVIII:** 1, 4

Bill of Rites, a Bill of Wrongs, a Bill of Goods, A (Morris), **III:** 237

"Bill's Beans" (Nye), **Supp. XIII:** 283

"Billy" (Gordon), **Supp. IV Part 1:** 306

"Billy" (McCarriston), **Supp. XIV:** 265

Billy Bathgate (Doctorow), **Supp. IV Part 1:** 217, 219, 222, 224, 227, 229–231, 231, 232, 233, 238

Billy Bathgate (film), **Supp. IV Part 1:** 236

Billy Budd, Sailor (Melville), **III:** 40, 93–95; **IV:** 105; **Retro. Supp. I:** 249, **258–260**

Billy Collins Live: A Performance at the Peter Norton Symphony Space April 20, 2005 (CD, Collins), **Supp. XXI:** 51

"Billy Gardner's Ground Out" (Skloot), **Supp. XX: 205, 207**

Billy Phelan's Greatest Game (W. Kennedy), **Supp. VII:** 131, 132, 134, 135, 142–147, 149, 151, 153, 155

Billy Ray's Farm: Essays from a Place Called Tula (L. Brown), **Supp. XXI:** 48, 49

Billy's Boy (P. N. Warren), **Supp. XX: 261, 265–267**

Billy the Kid, **Supp. IV Part 2:** 489, 490, 492

Biloxi Blues (Simon), **Supp. IV Part 2:** 576, 577, 584, 586–587, 590

"Bimini" (Hemingway), **II:** 258

Bingham, Anne, **Supp. XV:** 239

Bingham, Millicent Todd, **I:** 470; **Retro. Supp. I:** 36

Bingham, Remica L., **Supp. XXI:** 256

Bingo Palace, The (Erdrich), **Supp. IV Part 1:** 259, 260, 261, 263–264, 265, 266–267, 268–269, 270, 271–273, 274, 275

"Binsey Poplars" (Hopkins), **Supp. I Part 1:** 94; **Supp. IV Part 2:** 639

Binswanger, Ludwig, **Supp. XV:** 26

Biographia Literaria (Coleridge), **II:** 10; **Retro. Supp. I:** 308

"Biography" (Francis), **Supp. IX:** 77

"Biography" (Pinsky), **Supp. VI:** 235, 236, 239, 241, **243,** 249, 250

Biography and Poetical Remains of the Late Margaret Miller Davidson (Irving), **II:** 314

"Biography in the First Person" (Dunn), **Supp. XI:** 144

"Biography of an Armenian Schoolgirl" (Nye), **Supp. XIII:** 275, 280

"Biography of a Story" (Jackson), **Supp. IX:** 113

Biondi, Joann, **Supp. XI:** 103

"Biopoetics Sketch for *Greenfield Review*" (Harjo), **Supp. XII:** 216

"Biotherm"(O'Hara), **Supp. XXIII:** 208, 218–219

"Birchbrook Mill" (Whittier), **Supp. I Part 2:** 699

"Birches" (Frost), **II:** 154; **Retro. Supp. I:** 132; **Supp. XIII:** 147

Bird, Alan, **Supp. I Part 1:** 260

Bird, Gloria, **Supp. XII:** 216

Bird, Isabella, **Supp. X:** 103

Bird, Robert M., **III:** 423

"Bird, The" (Simpson), **Supp. IX:** 269–270

"Bird, the Bird, the Bird, The" (Creeley), **Supp. IV Part 1:** 149

"Bird, The"(Le Sueur), **Supp. XXIII:** 167

"Bird Banding with the Biologists" (Ray), **Supp. XVIII:** 194

Bird by Bird: Some Instructions on Writing and Life (Lamott), **Supp. XX: 132, 137–138**

"Bird came down the Walk, A" (Dickinson), **Retro. Supp. I:** 37

"Bird Frau, The" (Dove), **Supp. IV Part 1:** 245

"Bird in Hand" (screen story) (West and Ingster), **Retro. Supp. II:** 330

Bird Kingdom of the Mayas (LaBastille), **Supp. X:** 96

Birds and Beasts (W. J. Smith), **Supp. XIII:** 346

"Birds for Christmas, The" (Richard), **Supp. XIX:** 221

Bird's Nest, The (Jackson), **Supp. IX: 124–125**

Birds of America (McCarthy), **II:** 579–583; **Supp. X:** 177

Birds of America (Moore), **Supp. X:** 163, 165, 167, 168, 171, **177–179**

Birds of America, The (Audubon), **Supp. XVI: 5–6,** 7, 9, 10, 12, 13

"Birds of Killingsworth, The" (Longfellow), **Retro. Supp. II:** 164

Birds of North America (Audubon Society), **Supp. X:** 177

"Birds of Vietnam, The" (Carruth), **Supp. XVI:** 55

"Bird-Window-Flying" (Gallagher), **Supp. XXIV:** 169

"Bird-Witted" (Moore), **III:** 214

Birkelo, Cheryl, **Supp. XX: 220–221**

Birkerts, Sven, **Supp. IV Part 2:** 650; **Supp. V:** 212; **Supp. VIII:** 85; **Supp. X:** 311; **Supp. XX:** 92

Birkhead, L. M., **III:** 116

"Birmingham Sunday" (Hughes), **Supp. I Part 1:** 343

Birnbaum, Henry, **Supp. XII:** 128

Birnbaum, Robert, **Supp. X:** 13; **Supp. XVI:** 75; **Supp. XXIII:** 73, 75, 275

Birney, James G., **Supp. I Part 2:** 587, 588

Birstein, Ann, **Supp. VIII:** 100

"Birthday, A" (Untermeyer), **Supp. XV:** 296

Birthday Basket for Tía, A (Mora), **Supp. XIII:** 221

"Birthday Cake" (Carruth), **Supp. XVI:** 59

"Birthday Cake for Lionel, A" (Wylie), **Supp. I Part 2:** 721

"Birthday Girl: 1950" (McCarriston), **Supp. XIV:** 261

"Birthday of Mrs. Pineda, The" (Ríos), **Supp. IV Part 2:** 542, 546

"Birthday Poem, A" (Hecht), **Supp. X:** 64

"Birthday Present, A" (Plath), **Supp. I Part 2:** 531

"Birthmark" (July), **Supp. XXIV:** 206

"Birthmark, The" (Ellison), **Retro. Supp. II:** 116; **Supp. II Part 1:** 237–238

"Birth-mark, The" (Hawthorne), **Retro. Supp. I:** 152

Birth-mark, The: Unsettling the Wilderness in American Literary History (Howe), **Supp. IV Part 2:** 422, 431, 434

Birth of a Nation, The (film), **Supp. I Part 1:** 66

Birth of a World: Bolívar in Terms of His Peoples (W. Frank), **Supp. XX: 80**

Birth of the Poet, The (Gordon), **Supp. XII:** 7

Birth of Tragedy, The (Nietzsche), **Supp. IV Part 1:** 105, 110; **Supp. IV Part 2:** 519; **Supp. VIII:** 182

"Birth of Venus, The" (Botticelli), **IV:** 410

"Birth of Venus, The" (Rukeyser), **Supp. VI:** 281

"Birthplace Revisited" (Corso), **Supp. XII:** 123

"Birthright" (McKay), **Supp. X:** 136

Bisch, Louis E., **Supp. I Part 2:** 608

Bisco, John, **Supp. XVIII:** 11

"B is for Bachelors" (M. F. K. Fisher), **Supp. XVII:** 86

Bishop, Elizabeth, **Retro. Supp. I:** 140, 296, 303; **Retro. Supp. II: 37–56,** 175, 178, 189, 233, 234, 235; **Supp. I Part 1: 72–97,** 239, 320, 326; **Supp. III Part 1:** 6, 7, 10, 18, 64, 239, 320, 326; **Supp. III Part 2:** 541, 561; **Supp. IV Part 1:** 249, 257; **Supp. IV Part 2:** 439, 626, 639, 641, 644, 647, 651, 653; **Supp. V:** 337; **Supp. IX:** 40, 41, 45, 47, 48; **Supp. X:** 58; **Supp. XI:** 123, 136; **Supp. XIII:** 115, 348; **Supp. XV:** 20–21, 100, 101, 112, 119, 249, 251; **Supp. XVII:** 36, 76; **Supp. XXI:** 58, 84, 131; **Supp. XXIII:** 117

Bishop, James, Jr., **Supp. XIII:** 1, 5, 6, 7, 9, 11, 15

Bishop, John Peale, **I:** 432, 440; **II:** 81, 85, 86–87, 91, 209; **IV:** 35, 140, 427; **Retro. Supp. I:** 109; **Supp. I Part 2:** 709

Bishop, John W., **Supp. I Part 1:** 83

Bishop, Judith, **Supp. XVI:** 295

Bishop, Morris, **Supp. I Part 2:** 676

Bishop, William Thomas, **Supp. I Part 1:** 83

"Bishop Orders His Tomb at St. Praxed's Church, The" (R. Browning), **Supp. XV:** 127

"Bishop's Beggar, The" (Benét), **Supp. XI:** 56

"Bismarck" (Chapman), **Supp. XIV:** 52, 53

Bismark, Otto von, **Supp. I Part 2:** 643

Bistro Styx, The (Dove), **Supp. IV Part 1:** 250–251

Bitov, Andrei, **Retro. Supp. I:** 278

Bits of Gossip (R. H. Davis), **Supp. XVI:** 82–83, 84, 85, 89

"Bitte Nehmen Sie Die Blumen" (Boyle), **Supp. XXIV:** 57

"Bitter Drink, The" (Dos Passos), **Supp. I Part 2:** 647

"Bitter Farce, A" (Schwartz), **Supp. II Part 2:** 640, 657–658

"Bitter Pills for the Dark Ladies" (Jong), **Supp. V:** 118

Bitterroot (Burke), **Supp. XIV:** 34, 35

"Bittersweet Nightshade" (Skloot), **Supp. XX: 202**

Bitter Victory (Hardy; Kinnell, trans.), **Supp. III Part 1:** 235

Bittner, William, **Supp. XX: 74,Supp. XX: 77, 76, 78, 80**

Bitzer, G. W. "Billy", **Supp. XVI:** 183

Bixby, Horace, **IV:** 194

Bjerre, Thomas Aervold, **Supp. XXI:** 41, 47

Bjorkman, Frances Maule, **Supp. V:** 285

Bjorkman, Stig, **Supp. XV:** 6

Björnson, Björnstjerne, **II:** 275

Black, Cheryl, **Supp. XXI:** 6

Black 100, The (Salley), **Supp. XIV:** 195

Blackamerican Literature, 1760-Present (R. Miller), **Supp. X:** 324

Black American Literature Forum, **Supp. XI:** 86, 92, 93

Black and Blue (Quindlen), **Supp. XVII:** 166, **176–178**

"Black and Tan" (Bell), **Supp. X:** 9

Black and White (Sorrentino), **Supp. XXI:** 228

Black Armour (Wylie), **Supp. I Part 2:** 708, 709, 712–714, 729

"Black Art" (Baraka), **Supp. II Part 1:** 49, 50–51, 59, 60

"Black Art, The" (Sexton), **Supp. II Part 2:** 682

Black Ball, The (Ellison), **Retro. Supp. II:** 124

Black Bart and the Sacred Hills (Wilson), **Supp. VIII:** 330, 331

Black Beetles in Amber (Bierce), **I:** 204, 209

"Blackberries" (Komunyakaa), **Supp. XIII:** 126

"Blackberry Eating" (Kinnell), **Supp. III Part 1:** 250

"Blackberrying" (D. West), **Supp. XVIII:** 283

Blackberry Winter (Warren), **IV:** 243, 251, 252

Black Betty (Mosley), **Supp. XIII:** 237, **Supp. XIII:** 240, 243

"Black Birch in Winter, A" (Wilbur), **Supp. III Part 2:** 561

"Black Boy" (Boyle), **Supp. XXIV:** 59

Black Boy (Wright), **IV:** 477, 478, 479, 480–482, 488, 489, 494; **Retro. Supp. II:** 117; **Supp. II Part 1:** 235–236; **Supp. IV Part 1:** 11; **Supp. XVIII:** 286

"Black Boys and Native Sons" (Howe), **Retro. Supp. II:** 112

Blackburn, Alex, **Supp. XIII:** 112

Blackburn, Paul, **Supp. XXII:** 164, 169; **Supp. XXIV:** 34, 37

Blackburn, William, **IV:** 100

"Black Buttercups" (Clampitt), **Supp. IX:** 42

Black Cargo, The (Marquand), **III:** 55, 60

Black Cargoes: A History of the Atlantic Slave Trade (Cowley), **Supp. II Part 1:** 140

"Black Cat, The" (Poe), **III:** 413, 414, 415; **Retro. Supp. II:** 264, 267, 269, 270

Black Cherry Blues (Burke), **Supp. XIV:** 30

"Black Christ, The" (Cullen), **Supp. IV Part 1:** 170, 171–172

Black Christ and Other Poems, The (Cullen), **Supp. IV Part 1:** 166, 170

"Black Clay Fish from Oaxaca, A" (Bronk), **Supp. XXI:** 31

"Black Cottage, The" (Frost), **Retro. Supp. I:** 128

"BLACK DADA NIHILISMUS" (Baraka), **Supp. II Part 1:** 39, 41

"Black Death" (Hurston), **Supp. VI:** 153

Black Dog, Red Dog (Dobyns), **Supp. XIII:** 87, **88–89**

"Black Dog, Red Dog" (Dobyns), **Supp. XIII:** 89

Black Dog of Fate: A Memoir (Balakian), **Supp. XXIII:** 19, **20–24,** 24, 25

"Black Earth" (Moore), **III:** 197, 212

Black Echo, The (Connelly), **Supp. XXI:** 67, 68, 75, 80

Black Fire (Jones and Neal, eds.), **Supp. X:** 324, 328

Black Fire: An Anthology of Afro American Writing (Baraka, ed.), **Supp. II Part 1:** 53

Black Flame, The (Du Bois), **Supp. II Part 1:** 159, 185–186

Black Folk, Then and Now: An Essay in the History and Sociology of the Negro Race (Du Bois), **Supp. II Part 1:** 159, 178, 183, 185

Blackford, Holly, **Supp. XXII:** 300

"Black Fox, The" (Whittier), **Supp. I Part 2:** 692

Black Freckles (Levis), **Supp. XI:** 257, 271

"Black Gang", **IV:** 406, 407

Black Genius (Mosley, ed.), **Supp. XIII:** 246

"Black Hood, The" (Francis), **Supp. IX:** 83, 91

Black House, The (Theroux), **Supp. VIII:** 319

Black Humor (Johnson), **Supp. VI:** 187, 199

Black Ice, The (Connelly), **Supp. XXI:** **70,** 75

Black Image in the White Mind, The (Fredrickson), **Supp. I Part 2:** 589

"Black Is My Favorite Color" (Malamud), **Supp. I Part 2:** 437

Black Jacobins, The (C. L. R. James), **Supp. XXI:** 159, 166–167

"Black Jewel, The" (Merwin), **Supp. III Part 1:** 355

Black Lamb and Grey Falcon (R. West), **Supp. XVI:** 152

"Black Laughter" (Taggard), **Supp. XXII:** 274

"Blacklegs" (B. Kelly), **Supp. XVII:** 131

Black Light (Kinnell), **Supp. III Part 1:** 235, 243

"Blacklist and the Cold War, The" (Kramer), **Supp. I Part 1:** 295

Black Literature in America (Baker), **Supp. X:** 324

Black Magic, A Pictorial History of the Negro in American Entertainment (Hughes), **Supp. I Part 1:** 345

Black Magic: Collected Poetry 1961–1967 (Baraka), **Supp. II Part 1:** 45, 49–50

"Blackmailers Don't Shoot" (Chandler), **Supp. IV Part 1:** 121–122

Black Manhattan (Johnson), **Supp. IV Part 1:** 169

Black Mass, A (Baraka), **Supp. II Part 1:** 46, 48–49, 56, 57

"Black Mesa, The" (Merrill), **Supp. III Part 1:** 328

Black Metropolis (Cayton and Drake), **IV:** 475, 486, 488

Black Misery (Hughes), **Supp. I Part 1:** 336

Blackmur, Helen Dickson (Mrs. R. P. Blackmur), **Supp. II Part 1:** 90

Blackmur, Richard P., **I:** 50, 63, 67, 280, 282, 386, 455, 472; **II:** 320, 537; **III:** 194, 208, 462, 478, 497; **Supp. II Part 1: 87–112,** 136; **Supp. II Part 2:** 543, 643; **Supp. XII:** 45

Black Music (Baraka), **Supp. II Part 1:** 47, 51

Black Nativity (Hughes), **Retro. Supp. I:** 196

Black No More (Schuyler), **Supp. XVI:** 142; **Supp. XIX:** 73

Black on Black: "Baby Sister" and Selected Writings (C. Himes), **Supp. XVI:** 145

"Black or White" (Major), **Supp. XXII:** 185

"Blackout" (Hay), **Supp. XIV:** 121

Black Oxen (Atherton), **Supp. XXIV:** 25–26

Black Oxen (Atherton, Dawson, ed.), **Supp. XXIV:** 31

"Black Panther" (Hughes), **Retro. Supp. I:** 211

"Black Petal" (L.-Y. Lee), **Supp. XV:** 224–225

Black Power (Wright), **IV:** 478, 488, 494

"Black Rainbow, A: Modern Afro-American Poetry" (Dove and Waniek), **Supp. IV Part 1:** 244

Black Reconstruction (Du Bois), **Supp. II Part 1:** 159, 162, 171, 182

Black Riders and Other Lines, The (Crane), **I:** 406, 419

Black Riviera, The (Jarman), **Supp. XVII:** 109, 110, **115–116**

Blackrobe: Isaac Jogues (Kenny), **Supp. XXIII:** 143, 147, **151–152,** 153, 154

"Black Rook in Rainy Weather" (Plath), **Supp. I Part 2:** 543, 544; **Supp. XXIII:** 63

Blacks (Brooks), **Supp. III Part 1:** 69, 72, 86, 87

Blacks, The (Genet), **Supp. IV Part 1:** 8

Black Skin, White Masks (Fanon), **Retro. Supp. II:** 118

Black Sleuth, The (J. Bruce), **Supp. XVI:** 143

Black Spear, The (Hayden), **Supp. II Part 1:** 375

Black Spring (H. Miller), **III:** 170, 175, 178, 180–182, 183, 184; **Supp. X:** 187

"Black Stone Lying on a White Stone" (Vallejo), **Supp. XIII:** 324

Black Sun (Abbey), **Supp. XIII:** 4, **8–9,** 17

"Black Swan" (B. Kelly), **Supp. XVII:** 130–131

"Black Swan, The" (Jarrell), **II:** 382

Black Swan, The (Merrill), **Supp. III Part 1:** 319, 320

"Black Tambourine" (Crane), **I:** 387–388; **II:** 371

Black Thunder (Bontemps), **Supp. XXII:** 4, 9

"Black Tuesday" (Swenson), **Supp. IV Part 2:** 646

Black Virgin Mountain (Heinemann), **Supp. XXII:** 103, **114–116**

Black Voices (Chapman), **IV:** 485

"Blackwater Mountain" (Wright), **Supp. V:** 335, 340

"Black Wedding, The" (Singer), **IV:** 12–13

Blackwell, Alice Stone, **Supp. XI:** 195, 197

Blackwell, Elizabeth, **Retro. Supp. II:** 146

Black Woman, The (Bambara, ed.), **Supp. XI:** 1

"Black Workers" (Hughes), **Retro. Supp. I:** 202

"Black Writer and the Southern Experience, The" (Walker), **Supp. III Part 2:** 521

Black Zodiac (Wright), **Supp. V:** 333, 344, 345

Blade Runner (film), **Supp. XI:** 84

Blades, John, **Supp. XX: 87**

"Blades of Steel" (R. Fisher), **Supp. XIX:** 72

Blaine, Anita McCormick, **Supp. I Part 1:** 5

Blaine, Nell, **Supp. XV:** 179; **Supp. XXIII:** 217

Blair, Hugh, **II:** 8, 17; **Supp. I Part 2:** 422

Blair, Robert, **Supp. I Part 1:** 150

Blair, Walter, **II:** 20; **Retro. Supp. II:** 286

Blaisdell, Gus, **Supp. XIV:** 87

Blake, Casey Nelson, **Supp. XX: 69, 70, 78**

Blake, William, **I:** 381, 383, 389, 390, 398, 447, 476, 525, 526, 533; **II:** 321; **III:** 5, 19, 22, 195, 196, 197, 205, 485, 528, 540, 544–545, 567, 572; **IV:** 129; **Retro. Supp. II:** 76, 300; **Supp. I Part 1:** 80; **Supp. I Part 2:** 385, 514, 517, 539, 552, 708; **Supp. V:** 208, 257, 258; **Supp. VIII:** 26, 99, 103; **Supp. X:** 120; **Supp. XII:** 45; **Supp. XIV:** 344; **Supp. XVI:** 282; **Supp. XVII:** 119; **Supp. XX: 115, 116; Supp. XXII:** 225, 257; **Supp. XXIV:** 159

Blakely, Barbara, **Supp. XIII:** 32

Blanc, Marie Thérèse, **Retro. Supp. II:** 135

Blanc-Bentzon, Mme. Thérèse, **II:** 405

Blanchard, Paula, **Retro. Supp. II:** 131, 133–134, 135

Blanche, Jacques-Émile, **Supp. XX: 232**

Blanche of Brandywine (Lippard), **Supp. XXIII:** 178, 185

Blanchot, Maurice, **Supp. XVI:** 288; **Supp. XXIV:** 40

Blancs, Les (Hansberry), **Supp. IV Part 1:** 359, 364, 365, 369, 372–374

Blancs, Les: The Collected Last Plays of Lorraine Hansberry (Nemiroff, ed.), **Supp. IV Part 1:** 365, 368, 374

"'Blandula, Tenulla, Vagula'" (Pound), **III:** 463; **Supp. V:** 336, 337, 345

Blankenship, Tom, **IV:** 193

"Blank Paper" (Peacock), **Supp. XIX:** 198–199

Blank Wall, The (Holding), **Supp. XXII:** 119, 120, 121, 130, **131–133,** 134

Blanshard, Rufus A., **I:** 67

Blassingame, John, **Supp. XX: 106**

Blauvelt, William Satake, **Supp. V:** 171, 173

Blavatsky, Elena Petrovna, **III:** 176

"Blazing in Gold and Quenching in Purple" (Dickinson), **Retro. Supp. I:** 30

Bleak House (Dickens), **II:** 291; **Supp. IV Part 1:** 293

Blechman, Burt, **Supp. I Part 1:** 290

"Bleeder" (Dobyns), **Supp. XIII:** 88

"Bleeding" (Swenson), **Supp. IV Part 2:** 646–647

"Blessed Is the Man" (Moore), **III:** 215

"Blessed Man of Boston, My Grandmother's Thimble, and Fanning Island, The" (Updike), **IV:** 219

"Blessing, A" (Wright), **Supp. III Part 2:** 600, 606

Blessing on the Moon, A (Skibell), **Supp. XVII:** 48

Blessings (Quindlen), **Supp. XVII:** 167, **178–179**

"Blessing the Animals" (Komunyakaa), **Supp. XIII:** 129–130

"Blessing the Children" (Hogan), **Supp. IV Part 1:** 401

Bless Me, Ultima (Anya), **Supp. XIII:** 220

Blew, Mary Clearman, **Supp. XIV:** 227

Bligh, S. M., **I:** 226

"Blight"(Dybek), **Supp. XXIII:** 72

Blind Alleys (film), **Supp. XXI:** 146

Blind Assassin, The (Atwood), **Supp. XIII:** 20, **32**

Blind Bow-Boy, The (Van Vechten), **Supp. II Part 2:** 737, 740–742

"Blind Date" (Halliday), **Supp. XIX:** 85

Blind Date (Kosinski), **Supp. VII:** 215, 224–225

"Blinded by the Light" (Boyle), **Supp. XX: 20**

Blind Lion, The (Gunn Allen), **Supp. IV Part 1:** 324

"Blind Man's Holiday" (O. Henry), **Supp. II Part 1:** 401

Blind Man with a Pistol (C. Himes), **Supp. XVI:** 143, 144

Blindness and Insight (de Man), **Retro. Supp. I:** 67

"Blind Poet, The: Sidney Lanier" (Warren), **Supp. I Part 1:** 371, 373

"Blindsided" (E. P. Jones), **Supp. XXII:** 151–152

"Blind Tom" (R. H. Davis), **Supp. XVI:** 89, 90

Blithedale Romance, The (Hawthorne), **II:** 225, 231, 239, 241–242, 271, 282, 290; **IV:** 194; **Retro. Supp. I:** 63, 149, 152, 156–157, **162–163; Supp. I Part 2:** 579; **Supp. II Part 1:** 280; **Supp. VIII:** 153, 201

Blitzstein, Marc, **Supp. I Part 1:** 277

Blix (Norris), **III:** 314, 322, 327, 328, 333

Blixen, Karen Denisen Baroness. *See* Dinesen, Isak

"Blizzard in Cambridge" (Lowell), **II:** 554

Blizzard Voices, The (Kooser), **Supp. XIX: 123**

Bloch, Ernest, **Supp. XX: 75**

Block, Lawrence, **Supp. XXI:** 67

"Blocks"(O'Hara), **Supp. XXIII:** 214

Blok, Aleksandr Aleksandrovich, **IV:** 443

"Blond" (Trethewey), **Supp. XXI:** 244

Blonde Bait (Lacy), **Supp. XV:** 204

Blonde on Blonde (album, Dylan), **Supp. XVIII:** 20, 27, 30

Blondin, Antoine, **Supp. XVI:** 230

"Blood" (Hoffman), **Supp. XVIII:** 86

"Blood" (Singer), **IV:** 15, 19

Blood, Tin, Straw (Olds), **Supp. X: 212–215**

Blood and Guile (Hoffman), **Supp. XVIII: 83–84**

Blood and Guts in High School (Acker), **Supp. XII:** 5, 6, **11–12**

"Blood Bay, The" (Proulx), **Supp. VII:** 262–263

"Blood-Burning Moon" (Toomer), **Supp. III Part 2:** 483; **Supp. IX:** 314–315

"Bloodchild" (O. Butler), **Supp. XIII:** 61, **69–70**

Bloodchild and Other Stories (O. Butler), **Supp. XIII:** 69

"Blood Donor" (Hay), **Supp. XIV:** 121

Blood for a Stranger (Jarrell), **II:** 367, 368–369, 370–371, 375, 377

Blood Issue (Crews), **Supp. XI:** 103

Bloodlines (Wright), **Supp. V:** 332, 335, 340

Blood Meridian (McCarthy), **Supp. XXIII:** 42

Blood Meridian; or, The Evening Redness in the West (McCarthy), **Supp. VIII:** 175, 177, **180–182,** 188, 190

Blood of My Blood (Gambino), **Supp. XX:** 35

"Blood of the Conquistadores, The" (Alvarez), **Supp. VII:** 7

"Blood of the Lamb, The" (hymn), **Supp. I Part 2:** 385

Blood of the Martyr (Crane), **I:** 422

"Blood of the Martyrs, The" (Benét), **Supp. XI:** 56, 58

Blood of the Prophets, The (Masters), **Supp. I Part 2:** 458, 459, 461

Blood on the Forge (Attaway), **Supp. II Part 1:** 234–235

Blood on the Tracks (album, Dylan), **Supp. XVIII:** 20, 27, 30

"Blood Relatives" (Apple), **Supp. XVII:** 6

"Blood Returns, The" (Kingsolver), **Supp. VII:** 209

"Bloodshed" (C. Ozick), **Supp. XVII:** 43

Bloodshed and Three Novellas (Ozick), **Supp. V:** 259–260, 261, 266–268

"Blood Soup"(Dybek), **Supp. XXIII:** 71

"Blood Stains" (Francis), **Supp. IX:** 86

Blood Work (Connelly), **Supp. XXI: 72**

Blood Work (film, Eastwood), **Supp. XXI:** 74

Bloody Crossroads, The: Where Literature and Politics Meet (Podhoretz), **Supp. VIII: 241–242**

Bloody News from My Friend (Samianto, trans. Balakian), **Supp. XXIII:** 28

Bloom, Alice, **Supp. IV Part 1:** 308

Bloom, Allan, **Retro. Supp. II:** 19, 30, 31, 33–34

Bloom, Claire, **Retro. Supp. II:** 281; **Supp. IX:** 125

Bloom, Harold, **Retro. Supp. I:** 67, 193, 299; **Retro. Supp. II:** 81, 210, 262; **Supp. IV Part 2:** 620, 689; **Supp. V:** 178, 272; **Supp. VIII:** 180; **Supp. IX:** 146, 259; **Supp. XII:** 261; **Supp. XIII:** 46, 47; **Supp. XIV:** 14; **Supp. XV:** 134; **Supp. XVII:** 70, 141; **Supp. XXIII:** 42

Bloom, Larry, **Supp. XIII:** 133

Bloom, Leopold, **I:** 27, 150; **III:** 10

Bloom, Lynn Z., **Supp. IV Part 1:** 6

Bloomfield, Leonard, **I:** 64

Bloomingdale Papers, The (Carruth), **Supp. XVI:** 48–50

"Blossom and Fruit" (Benét), **Supp. XI:** 52–53

Blotner, Joseph, **Retro. Supp. I:** 88

Blouin, Lenora, **Supp. VIII:** 266

"Blouse, The"(Rudman), **Supp. XXIII:** 124

"Blowing Soap Bubbles"(Crooker), **Supp. XXIII:** 56

"Blowin' in the Wind" (song, Dylan), **Supp. XVIII:** 24, 25, 26, 29

Blue Angel (Prose), **Supp. XVI:** 249, 259–260

Blue Angel, The (film), **Supp. XVIII:** 243

Blue Arabesque: A Search for the Sublime (Hampl), **Supp. XXII:** 86, 98–99

"Blue Battalions, The" (Crane), **I:** 419–420

"Blue Bead, The"(Hadas), **Supp. XXIII:** 118, 119

"Bluebeard" (Barthelme), **Supp. IV Part 1:** 47

"Bluebeard" (Millay), **III:** 130

"Blueberries" (Frost), **Retro. Supp. I:** 121, 128

"Blue Boy"(Dybek), **Supp. XXIII:** 76

Blue Calhoun (Price), **Supp. VI:** 265–266

Blue Caterpillar, The (Pickering), **Supp. XXI:** 202–203

Blue City (Macdonald, as Millar), **Supp. IV Part 2:** 466–467

Blue Devils of Nada, The: A Contemporary American Approach to Aesthetics (Murray), **Supp. XIX: 159–160**

Blue Estuaries, The: Poems, 1923–1968 (Bogan), **Supp. III Part 1:** 48, 57, 66

Blue Hammer, The (Macdonald), **Supp. IV Part 2:** 462

"Blue Hotel, The" (Crane), **I:** 34, 415–416, 423

"Blue Hour, The" (Komunyakaa), **Supp. XIII:** 130

Blue in the Face (Auster), **Supp. XII:** 21

Blue Jay's Dance, The: A Birth Year (Erdrich), **Supp. IV Part 1:** 259–260, 265, 270, 272

"Blue Juniata" (Cowley), **Supp. II Part 1:** 144

Blue Juniata: Collected Poems (Cowley), **Supp. II Part 1:** 140

"Blue Lick" (Offutt), **Supp. XIX:** 164, 165

Blue Light (Mosley), **Supp. XIII: 245–247,** 248, 249

"Blue Light Lounge Sutra for the Performance Poets at Harold Park Hotel" (Komunyakaa), **Supp. XIII:** 125

"Blue Meridian" (Toomer), **Supp. III Part 2:** 476, 487; **Supp. IX:** 320

"Blue Moles" (Plath), **Supp. I Part 2:** 539

Blue Mountain Ballads (music) (Bowles), **Supp. IV Part 1:** 84

Blue Movie (Southern), **Supp. XI:** 309

"Blue Notes" (Matthews), **Supp. IX:** 169

Blue Pastoral (Sorrentino), **Supp. XXI:** 226, 235–236

Blue Pastures (Oliver), **Supp. VII:** 229–230, 245

"Blueprint for Negro Writing" (Wright), **Supp. XVIII:** 282–283

"Blueprints" (Kingsolver), **Supp. VII:** 203

Blue Religion, The (Connelly, ed.), **Supp. XXI:** 74–75, 79

Blue Rhine, Black Forest (Untermeyer), **Supp. XV:** 310

"Blue Ribbon at Amesbury, A" (Frost), **Retro. Supp. I:** 138

"Blues Ain't No Mockin Bird" (Bambara), **Supp. XI:** 3

"Blues and the Fable in the Flesh, The" (lecture, Murray), **Supp. XIX:** 153

"Blues Chant Hoodoo Rival" (Komunyakaa), **Supp. XIII:** 117, 118

Blue Screen (Parker), **Supp. XIX:** 186

"Blues for Another Time" (Dunn), **Supp. XI:** 148

"Blues for Jimmy" (McGrath), **Supp. X:** 116

"Blues for John Coltraine, Dead at 41" (Matthews), **Supp. IX:** 157

Blues for Mister Charlie (Baldwin), **Retro. Supp. II:** 8; **Supp. I Part 1:** 48, 61–62, 63

"Blues for Warren" (McGrath), **Supp. X:** 116

Blue Shoe (Lamott), **Supp. XX: 138–140**

Blues If You Want (Matthews), **Supp. IX:** 155, **163–165**

"Blues I'm Playing, The" (Hughes), **Retro. Supp. I:** 204; **Supp. XIX:** 75

"Blue Sky, The" (Snyder), **Supp. VIII:** 306

Bluesman (Dubus III), **Supp. XXIV: 102–104**

"Blues on a Box" (Hughes), **Retro. Supp. I:** 208

"Blues People" (Ellison), **Retro. Supp. II:** 124

Blues People: Negro Music in White America (Baraka), **Retro. Supp. II:** 124; **Supp. II Part 1:** 30, 31, 33–35, 37, 41, 42, 53

"Blue Spruces in Pairs, a Bird Bath Between": (Bronk), **Supp. XXI:** 30

Bluest Eye, The (Morrison), **Supp. III Part 1:** 362, 363–367, 379; **Supp. IV Part 1:** 2, 253; **Supp. VIII:** 213, 214, 227; **Supp. XI:** 4, 91

Bluestone, George, **Supp. IX:** 7, 15

Blue Swallows, The (Nemerov), **III:** 269, 270, 271, 274–275, 278, 284, 286–288

"Blue Tattoo" (Nelson and Espeland), **Supp. XVIII:** 181

Blue Voyage (Aiken), **I:** 53, 56

Bluhm, Norman, **Supp. XXIII:** 217

Blum, Gustav, **Supp. XV:** 194

Blum, Morgan, **I:** 169

Blum, W. C (pseudonym). *See* Watson, James Sibley, Jr.

Blumenthal, Nathaniel. *See* Branden, Nathaniel

Blumenthal, Sidney, **Supp. VIII:** 241

Blunden, Edmund, **Supp. XIX:** 133

Blunt, Wilfrid Scawen, **III:** 459

Bly, Carol, **Supp. XVI: 31–43**

Bly, Robert, **I:** 291; **Supp. III Part 2:** 599; **Supp. IV Part 1: 59–77,** 177; **Supp. IV Part 2:** 623; **Supp. V:** 332; **Supp. VIII:** 279; **Supp. IX:** 152, 155, 265, 271, 290; **Supp. X:** 127; **Supp. XI:** 142; **Supp. XIII:** 284; **Supp. XV:** 74, 176; **Supp. XVI:** 32, 36, 39, 177, 212, 230; **Supp. XVII:** 243, 244; **Supp. XXI:** 83, 84–86, 87, 91, 93, 94, 95; **Supp. XXII:** 83; **Supp. XXIII:** 136; **Supp. XXIV:** 219

"B Negative" (X. J. Kennedy), **Supp. XV: 156–157**

"Boarder, The" (Simpson), **Supp. IX:** 269

Boarding House Blues (Farrell), **II:** 30, 43, 45

Boas, Franz, **I:** 214; **Supp. I Part 2:** 641; **Supp. VIII:** 295; **Supp. IX:** 329; **Supp. XIV:** 199, 209, 210

"Boat, The" (Oliver), **Supp. VII:** 247

"Boat, The" (Sexton), **Supp. II Part 2:** 692

Boating Party, The (Renoir), **Supp. XII:** 188

Boat of Quiet Hours, The (Kenyon), **Supp. VII:** 167–169, 171

"Boat of Quiet Hours, The" (Kenyon), **Supp. VII:** 168

"Boat Ride" (Gallagher), **Supp. XXIV:** 169

"Bob and Spike" (Wolfe), **Supp. III Part 2:** 580

"Bobby Shafter's Gone to Sea" (Swados), **Supp. XIX:** 267

"Bob Dylan's 115th Dream" (song, Dylan), **Supp. XVIII:** 25

Bobrowski, Johannes, **Supp. XV:** 78

Bob the Gambler (F. Barthelme), **Supp. XI:** 30, 31, 32, 34–35, 36–37

Boccaccio, Giovanni, **III:** 283, 411; **IV:** 230

Bocock, Maclin, **Supp. X:** 79

Boddy, Kasia, **Supp. XXII:** 261

Bodelson, Anders, **Supp. XVI:** 33

Bodenheim, Maxwell, **II:** 42, 530; **Retro. Supp. I:** 417; **Supp. I Part 1:** 257

"Bodies" (Oates), **Supp. II Part 2:** 520

"Bodies and Souls: The Haitian Revolution and Madison Smartt Bell's *All Souls' Rising*" (Trouillot), **Supp. X:** 14

Bodies of Water (Cliff), **Supp. XXII:** 66–67, 74–75

Bodies of Work: Essays (Acker), **Supp. XII:** 7

Bodily Harm (Atwood), **Supp. XIII: 25–27**

Bodley Head Jack London (London), **II:** 483

Body (Crews), **Supp. XI: 108–109**

"Body, The" (Heldreth), **Supp. V:** 151

Body and Soul (Conroy), **Supp. XVI:** 63, **72–74,** 77

"Body and Soul: A Meditation" (Kumin), **Supp. IV Part 2:** 442, 452

Body and Soul: Essays on Poetry (Jarman), **Supp. XVII:** 110, **111–112**

"Body and Soul: Parts of a Life" (Jarman), **Supp. XVII:** 112, 113

Body and the Song, The (Bishop), **Retro. Supp. II:** 40

"Body Bright" (Sanders), **Supp. XVI:** 276

Body of Martin Aquilera, The (Everett), **Supp. XVIII:** 57

Body of Poetry, The: Essays on Women, Form, and the Poetic Self (A. Finch), **Supp. XVII:** 69–70, **77–78**

Body of This Death: Poems (Bogan), **Supp. III Part 1:** 47, 49–52, 58

Body of Waking (Rukeyser), **Supp. VI:** 274, 281

"Body of Waking" (Rukeyser), **Supp. VI:** 279

"Body on Fire, the Soul in Flight, The" (Jarman), **Supp. XVII:** 111, 112

Body Rags (Kinnell), **Supp. III Part 1:** 235, 236, 243–245, 250, 253, 254

"Body's Curse, The" (Dobyns), **Supp. XIII:** 87

"Body's Weight" (Espaillat), **Supp. XXI:** 111

"Body's Weight, The" (Dobyns), **Supp. XIII:** 89

Body Traffic (Dobyns), **Supp. XIII:** 87, 89

"'Body with the Lamp Lit Inside, The'" (Mills), **Supp. IV Part 1:** 64

Boehm, David, **Supp. XVII:** 58

Boehme, Jakob, **I:** 10

Bogan, Louise, **I:** 169, 185; **Retro. Supp. I:** 36; **Supp. I Part 2:** 707, 726; **Supp. III Part 1: 47–68; Supp. VIII:** 171, 265; **Supp. IX:** 229; **Supp. X:** 58, 102; **Supp. XIII:** 347; **Supp. XIV:** 129; **Supp. XVII:** 75; **Supp. XXIII:** 145

Bogan, Major Benjamin Lewis, **IV:** 120

Bogart, Humphrey, **Supp. I Part 2:** 623; **Supp. IV Part 1:** 130, 356

Bogdanovich, Peter, **Supp. V:** 226

Bogey Man, The (Plimpton), **Supp. XVI:** 241

Boggs, Francis W., **Supp. XVI:** 182

"Bogs" (Pickering), **Supp. XXI:** 198

"Bohemian, The" (Hapgood), **Supp. XVII:** 103

"Bohemian, The" (Harte), **Supp. II Part 1:** 339

"Bohemian Girl, The" (Cather), **Retro. Supp. I:** 7

"Bohemian Hymn, The" (Emerson), **II:** 19

"Bohemians" (Saunders), **Supp. XIX:** 234

"Boids and Beasties" (Geisel), **Supp. XVI:** 100

Boissevain, Eugen, **III:** 124

Boissière, Ralph de, **Supp. XXI:** 160

Boit, Edward, **Retro. Supp. I:** 366

Bojorquez, Jennifer, **Supp. XII:** 318

"Boke, A" (Berrigan), **Supp. XXIV:** 42

Boker, George, **Supp. XV:** 269

"Bold Words at the Bridge" (Jewett), **II:** 394

Boleslavsky, Richard, **Supp. XIV:** 240, 243

Boleyn, Anne, **Supp. I Part 2:** 461

Bolick, Katie, **Supp. XVI:** 167; **Supp. XXIII:** 135, 137, 138; **Supp. XXIV:** 167, 173, 177

Bolivar, Simon, **Supp. I Part 1:** 283, 284, 285

Bolonik, Kera, **Supp. XVIII:** 60

Bolton, Guy, **Supp. I Part 1:** 281

Bolts of Melody: New Poems of Emily Dickinson (Todd and Bingham, eds.), **I:** 470; **Retro. Supp. I:** 36

"Bomb" (Corso), **Supp. XII:** 117, 124, 125–126, 127

Bombeck, Erma, **Supp. XVII:** 168

Bombs Away (Steinbeck), **IV:** 51–52

"Bona and Paul" (Toomer), **Supp. IX:** 307, 318–319

Bonaparte, Marie, **III:** 418; **Retro. Supp. II:** 264, 266

"Bon-Bon" (Poe), **III:** 425

Bond, The (Boyce), **Supp. XXI:** 5, **11–12**

Bond, The (N. Boyce), **Supp. XVII:** 99, 100

Bondage (Hwang), **Supp. XXI:** 147

Bondsman, The (Massinger), **Supp. XV:** 238

Bondwoman's Narrative, by Hannah Crafts, a Fugitive Slave, Recently Escaped from North Carolina, The, **Supp. XX: 105**

Bone, Martyn, **Supp. XXII:** 247

Bone, Robert, **Supp. IX:** 318–319; **Supp. XI:** 283; **Supp. XVIII:** 285

Bone by Bone (Matthiessen), **Supp. V:** 199, 212, 213, 214

"Bone Deposit" (Ray), **Supp. XVIII:** 194

Boners (Abingdon). *See Schoolboy Howlers* (Abingdon)

"Bones" (Goldbarth), **Supp. XII: 173–174**

"Bones and Jewels" (Monette), **Supp. X:** 159

"Bones and Shells" (Sanders), **Supp. XVI:** 271–272

"Bones of a House" (Cowley). *See* "Blue Juniata"

Bones on Black Spruce Mountain, The (Budbill), **Supp. XIX:** 11–12

Bonetti, Kay, **Supp. VIII:** 47, 152, 159, 160, 165, 168, 170, 223; **Supp. XII:** 61; **Supp. XIV:** 232, 234; **Supp. XXI:** 36

"Bonfire" (Gallagher), **Supp. XXIV:** 170

Bonfire of the Vanities, The (Wolfe), **Supp. III Part 2:** 584–586

Bonheur, Rosa, **Supp. XV:** 276

Bonhoeffer, Dietrich, **Supp. VIII:** 198

Boni, Charles, **Supp. XIV:** 288

Boni and Liveright, **Retro. Supp. I:** 59, 80, 178

Bonicelli, Vittorio, **Supp. XI:** 307

Bonifacius (Mather), **Supp. II Part 2:** 461, 464

Bonnefoy, Yves, **Supp. III Part 1:** 235, 243

Bonner, Robert, **Retro. Supp. I:** 246

Bonneville, Mme. Marguerite, **Supp. I Part 2:** 520, 521

Bonneville, Nicolas de, **Supp. I Part 2:** 511, 518, 519

Bonney, William. *See* Billy the Kid

Bontemps, Arna, **Retro. Supp. I:** 194, 196, 203; **Supp. I Part 1:** 325; **Supp. IV Part 1:** 170; **Supp. IX:** 306, 309; **Supp. XVIII:** 282; **Supp. XXII:** 1–16

Book, A (Barnes), **Supp. III Part 1:** 36, 39, 44

Book about Myself, A (Dreiser), **I:** 515; **Retro. Supp. II:** 104

"Book as a Container of Consciousness, The" (Gass), **Supp. VI:** 92

Booker, Keith, **Supp. XV:** 197

"Bookies, Beware!" (Heller), **Supp. IV Part 1:** 383

"Book Notes and News" (column, Boyce), **Supp. XXI:** 2

Book of American Negro Poetry, The (Johnson), **Supp. IV Part 1:** 165, 166; **Supp. XXII:** 11

Book of Americans, A (Benét), **Supp. XI:** 46, 47, 51

Book of Beb, The (Buechner), **Supp. XII:** 53

Book of Breeething, The (Burroughs), **Supp. III Part 1:** 97, 103

Book of Burlesques, A (Mencken), **III:** 104

Book of Common Prayer, A (Didion), **Supp. IV Part 1:** 196, 198, 203–205, 207, 208

Book of Daniel, The (Doctorow), **Supp. IV Part 1:** 218, 219, 220–222, 227, 231, 237–238, 238; **Supp. V:** 45

Book of Dreams (Kerouac), **Supp. III Part 1:** 225

"Book of Ephraim, The" (Merrill), **Supp. III Part 1:** 330–334

Book of Folly, The (Sexton), **Supp. II Part 2:** 691, 692–694

Book of Gods and Devils, The (Simic), **Supp. VIII: 281**

Book of Guys, The (Keillor), **Supp. XVI:** 177

"Book of Hours of Sister Clotilde, The" (Lowell), **II:** 522

Book of Jamaica, The (Banks), **Supp. V:** 11, 12, 16

"Book of Life" (Bidart), **Supp. XV:** 23

Book of Living Verse, The; English and American Poetry from the Thirteenth Century to the Present Day (Untermeyer, ed.), **Supp. XV:** 310

Book of Love, A (Vildrac; Bynner, trans.), **Supp. XV:** 50

Book of Lyrics (Bynner), **Supp. XV:** 51

Book of Martyrs (Fox). *See Acts and Monuments of These Latter and Perilous Days* (Fox)

Book of Medicines, The (Hogan), **Supp. IV Part 1:** 397, 410, 411–414

"Book of Medicines, The" (Hogan), **Supp. IV Part 1:** 412, 413

"Book of Memory, The" (Auster), **Supp. XII:** 21–22

Book of My Nights (L.-Y. Lee), **Supp. XV:** 215, **223–226**

Book of Negro Folklore, The (Hughes, ed.), **Supp. I Part 1:** 345; **Supp. XXII:** 11–12

Book of Nightmares, The (Kinnell), **Supp. III Part 1:** 235, 236, 243, 244, 246–254

Book of One's Own, A: People and Their Diaries (Mallon), **Supp. XIX:** 134

Book of Prefaces, A (Mencken), **III:** 99–100, 105

Book of Repulsive Women, The (Barnes), **Supp. III Part 1:** 33

Book of Revelation, **Supp. XXIII:** 44

Book of Roses, The (Parkman), **Supp. II Part 2:** 597, 598

Book of the Body, The (Bidart), **Supp. XV:** 21, **25–27**

"Book of the Dead, The" (Rukeyser), **Supp. VI:** 272, 278, 279; **Supp. XV:** 349

"Book of the Grotesque, The" (Anderson), **I:** 106

Book of the Homeless, The (Wharton), **Retro. Supp. I:** 377

Book of the Hopi (Waters), **Supp. X:** 124

Book of Tobit (Bible), **Supp. XII:** 54

Book of Verses, A (Masters), **Supp. I Part 2:** 458

Book of Yaak, The (Bass), **Supp. XVI: 18–19**

"Book of Yolek, The" (Hecht), **Supp. X:** 69, **70–71**

"Books" (Collins), **Supp. XXI:** 55

"Books Considered" (Bloom), **Supp. I Part 1:** 96

"Books I Left Behind, The" (Pickering), **Supp. XXI:** 196

Books in My Life, The (H. Miller), **II:** 176, 189

"Books/P,L,E, The" (Goldbarth), **Supp. XII:** 190

Bookviews, **Supp. XI:** 216

"Book World Live", **Supp. XVIII:** 143–144

"Boolean Algebra: X2=X" (Bronk), **Supp. XXI:** 30

"Boom" (Nemerov), **III:** 278

Boom! (T. Williams), **IV:** 383

Boomer Girls: Poems by Women of the Baby Boom Generation (Gemin and Sergi, eds.), **Supp. XXI:** 246

Boom Town (Wolfe), **IV:** 456

"Boom Town" (Wolfe), **IV:** 469

Boone, Daniel, **II:** 207; **III:** 444; **IV:** 192, 193

Boorstin, Daniel, **I:** 253

Booth, Charles, **Supp. I Part 1:** 13

Booth, John Wilkes, **III:** 588

Booth, Philip, **I:** 522; **Supp. IX:** 269; **Supp. XI:** 141; **Supp. XIII:** 277; **Supp. XV:** 92

Booth, General William, **Supp. I Part 2:** 384, 386

"Booze"(P. Benedict), **Supp. XXIII:** 36

Borah, William, **III:** 475

Borden, Lizzie, **II:** 5

Border and the Buffalo, The (J. Cook), **Supp. XXIV:** 248

Borderlands/La Frontera: The New Mestiza (Anzaldúa), **Supp. XIII:** 223

Border Matters (Saldívar), **Supp. XIX:** 112–113

Borders (Mora), **Supp. XIII:** 213, **215–217**

Border Trilogy (McCarthy), **Supp. VIII:** 175, 182

"Border View, Hot Springs, Texas" (W. V. Davis), **Supp. XXI:** 95

Borel, Pétrus, **III:** 320

Borges, Jorge Luis, **I:** 123, 135, 138, 140, 142; **Supp. III Part 2:** 560; **Supp. IV Part 2:** 623, 626, 630; **Supp. V:** 238; **Supp. VIII:** 15, 348, 349; **Supp. XII:** 21, 147; **Supp. XV:** 34; **Supp. XVI:** 201, 206; **Supp. XVII:** 47; **Supp. XIX:** 131; **Supp. XXIII:** 68

"Borges and I" (Bidart), **Supp. XV:** 34, 35

"Borinken Blues" (Komunyakaa), **Supp. XIII:** 117

"Born, The" (Lamott), **Supp. XX: 143–144**

"Born a Square: The Westerner's Dilemma" (Stegner), **Supp. IV Part 2:** 595; **Supp. V:** 224

"Born Bad" (Cisneros), **Supp. VII:** 62

Born on the Fourth of July (Kovic), **Supp. XIX:** 17

"Borough of Cemeteries" (Shaw), **Supp. XIX:** 246

Borrowed Time: An AIDS Memoir (Monette), **Supp. X:** 145, 146, 147, 152, 154, 155

Bose, Sudip, **Supp. XXII:** 205, 206, 214

Bosmajian, Hamida, **Supp. XXII:** 290

"Bosque del Apache Wildlife Refuge" (Mora), **Supp. XIII:** 218

Boss Dog, The: A Story of Provence (M. F. K. Fisher), **Supp. XVII:** 91

Bost, Suzanne, **Supp. XXII:** 66, 70, 75, 78

"Boston" (Hardwick), **Supp. III Part 1:** 201

Boston (Sinclair), **Supp. V:** 282, 288–289

Boston, B. H., **Supp. XIII:** 312

Boston Adventure (Stafford), **Retro. Supp. II:** 177, 178

"Boston Common" (Berryman), **I:** 172

"Boston Hymn" (Emerson), **II:** 13, 19

Bostonians, The (H. James), **I:** 9; **II:** 282; **IV:** 202; **Retro. Supp. I:** 216, 225

Boston Marriage (Mamet), **Supp. XIV:** 247

"Boston Nativity, The" (Lowell), **II:** 538

Boswell, James, **IV:** 431; **Supp. I Part 2:** 656

Boswell: A Modern Comedy (Elkin), **Supp. VI:** 42, **44–45,** 57

Bosworth, Patricia, **Supp. IV Part 2:** 573, 591

"Bothersome Sex and O'Brien, The" (Ryan as Quin), **Supp. XVIII:** 238

Botticelli (McNally), **Supp. XIII:** 197

Botticelli, Sandro, **IV:** 410; **Retro. Supp. I:** 422

"Botticellian Trees, The" (W. C. Williams), **Retro. Supp. I:** 422

"Bottle of Milk for Mother, A" (Algren), **Supp. IX:** 3

"Bottle of Perrier, A" (Wharton), **IV:** 316

"Bottles" (Kenyon), **Supp. VII:** 171

"Bottom Line, The" (Elkin), **Supp. VI:** 52, **53**

Bottom: On Shakespeare (Zukofsky), **Supp. III Part 2:** 622, 624, 625, 626, 627, 629

Boublil, Alain, **Supp. XXI:** 155

Boucher, Anthony, **Supp. IV Part 2:** 473; **Supp. XV:** 203, 205

Boucicault, Dion, **Supp. XXII:** 70

Boughton, Henrietta Breckenridge. *See* Young, Barbara

Boukreev, Anatoli, **Supp. XVIII:** 112

Boulanger, Nadia, **Supp. IV Part 1:** 81

"Boulot and Boulette" (Chopin), **Supp. I Part 1:** 211

Boulton, Agnes, **III:** 403; **Supp. XXII:** **17–31**

Bound East for Cardiff (O'Neill), **III:** 388

Bound for Glory (Guthrie), **Supp. XVIII:** 23

"Bounty" (Saunders), **Supp. XIX:** 226, 227

"Bounty"(P. Benedict), **Supp. XXIII:** 41

"Bouquet, The" (Stevens), **IV:** 90

"Bouquet of Dark Red Mums, The" (Notley), **Supp. XXII:** 230

"Bouquet of Roses in Sunlight" (Stevens), **IV:** 93

Bourdin, Henri L., **Supp. I Part 1:** 251

Bourgeois, Monique, **Supp. XXII:** 99–100

Bourgeois Poet, The (Shapiro), **Supp. II Part 2:** 701, 703, 704, 713, 714–716

Bourget, James, **IV:** 319

Bourget, Paul, **II:** 325, 338; **IV:** 311, 315; **Retro. Supp. I:** 224, 359, 373; **Supp. XX: 232; Supp. XXIV:** 23

Bourjaily, Vance, **III:** 43; **Supp. IX:** 260; **Supp. XXIV:** 225

Bourke-White, Margaret, **I:** 290, 293, 295, 297

Bourne, Charles Rogers, **I:** 215

Bourne, Mrs. Charles Rogers, **I:** 215

Bourne, Randolph, **I: 214–238,** 243, 245, 246–247, 251, 259; **Supp. I Part 2:** 524; **Supp. XV:** 141, 298, 301

Boursicot, Bernard, **Supp. XXI:** 152, 153, 154

Bouton, Jim "Bulldog", **Supp. XX: 274**

Bouton, John Bell, **Supp. XXIII:** 188, 189

Bowden, Charles, **Supp. XIII:** 17

Bowditch, Nathaniel, **Supp. I Part 2:** 482

Bowen, Barbara, **Supp. IX:** 311

Bowen, Elizabeth, **Retro. Supp. I:** 351; **Supp. IV Part 1:** 299; **Supp. VIII:** 65, 165, 251, 265; **Supp. IX:** 128

Bowen, Francis, **Supp. I Part 2:** 413

Bowen, Henry, **Supp. XVIII:** 4

Bowen, Louise de Koven, **Supp. I Part 1:** 5

Bowen, Michael, **Supp. VIII:** 73

Bowers, John, **Supp. XI:** 217–218

"Bowlers Anonymous" (Dobyns), **Supp. XIII:** 86

Bowles, Emily, **Supp. XVIII:** 200, 202

Bowles, Jane (Jane Auer), **II:** 586; **Supp. IV Part 1:** 89, 92

Bowles, Paul, **I:** 211; **II:** 586; **Supp. II Part 1:** 17; **Supp. IV Part 1: 79–99**

Bowles, Samuel, **I:** 454, 457; **Retro. Supp. I:** 30, 32, 33

"Bowl of Blood, The" (Jeffers), **Supp. II Part 2:** 434

"Bowls" (Moore), **III:** 196

Bowman, James, **I:** 193

"Bows to Drouth" (Snyder), **Supp. VIII:** 303

Box, Edgar (pseudonym). *See* Vidal, Gore

Box and Quotations from Chairman Mao Tse-tung (Albee), **I:** 89–91, 94

Boxer and the Spy, The (Parker), **Supp. XIX:** 190

Box Garden, The (Shields), **Supp. VII:** 314–315, 320

"Box of Pastels, A" (Kooser), **Supp. XIX:** 128

"Box of Rocks, A" (Gallagher), **Supp. XXIV:** 175

"Box Seat" (Toomer), **Supp. III Part 2:** 484; **Supp. IX:** 316, 318

Boy, A (Ashbery), **Supp. III Part 1:** 5

"Boy and Dog" (L. Brown), **Supp. XXI:** 38, 42, **43–44**

Boyce, Horace, **II:** 136

Boyce, Neith, **Supp. XVII:** 96, 97, 98–99, 100, 106; **Supp. XXI: 1–16**

Boyd, Brian, **Retro. Supp. I:** 270, 275

Boyd, Janet L., **Supp. X:** 229

Boyd, Kristen, **Supp. XXIII:** 246

Boyd, Nancy (pseudonym). *See* Millay, Edna St. Vincent

Boyd, Thomas, **I:** 99; **IV:** 427

Boyesen, H. H., **II:** 289

"Boy from Lam Kien, The" (July), **Supp. XXIV:** 200, 204

"Boyhood" (Collins), **Supp. XXI:** 64

"Boyhood" (Farrell), **II:** 28

"Boy in France, A" (Salinger), **III:** 552–553

Boy in the Water (Dobyns), **Supp. XIII:** 75, **84**

Boyle, Kay, **IV:** 404; **Supp. XXIV: 49–66**

Boyle, T. Coraghessan, **Supp. VIII:** 1–17; **Supp. XX: 17–32; Supp. XXI:** 226; **Supp. XXII:** 262

Boyle, Thomas John. *See* Boyle, T. C.

Boynton, H. W., **Supp. IX:** 7

Boynton, Percy Holmes, **Supp. I Part 2:** 415

Boynton, Robert, **Supp. XVII:** 209; **Supp. XVIII:** 105, 107, 116

"Boy on a Train" (Ellison), **Retro. Supp. II:** 124

"Boy Riding Forward Backward" (Francis), **Supp. IX:** 82

"Boys and Girls" (Cisneros), **Supp. VII:** 59–60

Boy's Froissart, The (Lanier), **Supp. I Part 1:** 361

"Boys"(Kenny), **Supp. XXIII:** 149

Boy's King Arthur, The (Lanier), **Supp. I Part 1:** 361

Boy's Mabinogion, The (Lanier), **Supp. I Part 1:** 361

"Boys of '29, The" (Holmes), **Supp. I Part 1:** 308

Boys of '76, The (Coffin), **III:** 577

Boy's Percy, The (Lanier), **Supp. I Part 1:** 361

Boy's Town (Howells), **I:** 418

Boy's Will, A (Frost), **II:** 152, 153, 155–156, 159, 164, 166; **Retro. Supp. I:** 124, 127, 128, 131; **Retro. Supp. II:** 168

"Boy Up a Tree" (Hoffman), **Supp. XVIII:** 86

"Boy Who Wrestled with Angels, The" (Hoffman), **Supp. X:** 90

"Boy with One Shoe, The" (Jewett), **Retro. Supp. II:** 132

"Brace, The" (Bausch), **Supp. VII:** 48

Bracebridge Hall, or, The Humorists (Irving), **I:** 339, 341; **II:** 308–309, 313

Bracher, Frederick, **I:** 378, 380; **Supp. I Part 1:** 185

Brackenridge, Hugh Henry, **Supp. I Part 1:** 124, 127, 145; **Supp. II Part 1:** 65

Brackett, Leigh, **Supp. IV Part 1:** 130

Bradbury, John M., **I:** 288–289; **IV:** 130, 135

Bradbury, Malcolm, **Supp. VIII:** 124; **Supp. XVIII:** 140

Bradbury, Ray, **Supp. I Part 2:** 621–622; **Supp. IV Part 1: 101–118; Supp. XVI:** 122; **Supp. XVII:** 41; **Supp. XXIII:** 290

"Brad Carrigan, American" (Saunders), **Supp. XIX:** 233

Braddon, Mary E., **Supp. I Part 1:** 35, 36

Bradfield, Scott, **Supp. VIII:** 88

Bradford, Gamaliel, **I:** 248, 250

Bradford, Roark, **Retro. Supp. I:** 80

Bradford, William, **Retro. Supp. II:** 161, 162; **Supp. I Part 1:** 110, 112; **Supp. I Part 2:** 486, 494; **Supp. XXII: 33–47**

Bradlee, Ben, **Supp. V:** 201
Bradley, Bill, **Supp. VIII:** 47
Bradley, F. H., **Retro. Supp. I:** 57, 58
Bradley, Francis Herbert, **I:** 59, 567–568, 572, 573
Bradshaw, Barbara, **Supp. XIII:** 313
Bradstreet, Anne, **I:** 178–179, 180, 181, 182, 184; **III:** 505; **Retro. Supp. I:** 40; **Supp. I Part 1: 98–123,** 300; **Supp. I Part 2:** 484, 485, 496, 546, 705; **Supp. V:** 113, 117–118; **Supp. XIII:** 152; **Supp. XIV:** 128; **Supp. XVIII:** 304; **Supp. XXII:** 46
Bradstreet, Elizabeth, **Supp. I Part 1:** 108, 122
Bradstreet, Simon, **I:** 178; **Supp. I Part 1:** 103, 110, 116
Bradstreet, Mrs. Simon. *See* Bradstreet, Anne
Brady, Alice, **III:** 399
Brady, Catherine, **Supp. XXIII:** 301
Brady, Matthew, **Supp. XVIII:** 4
Bragdon, Claude, **Supp. XX: 117**
"Bragdowdy and the Busybody, The" (Thurber), **Supp. I Part 2:** 617
Bragg, Rick, **Supp. XVIII:** 195
"Brahma" (Emerson), **II:** 19, 20
Brahms, Johannes, **III:** 118, 448
"Brahms in Delirium" (Skloot), **Supp. XX:** 203
Braided Creek (Kooser and Harrison), **Supp. XIX:** 126
"Braiding" (L.-Y. Lee), **Supp. XV:** 214
"Brain and the Mind, The" (James), **II:** 346
Brainard, Joe, **Supp. XV:** 33; **Supp. XXIII:** 217; **Supp. XXIV:** 33, 34, 35, 39, 41, 42, 43
"Brain Damage" (Barthelme), **Supp. IV Part 1:** 44
"Braindead Megaphone, The" (Saunders), **Supp. XIX:** 235
Braindead Megaphone, The: Essays (Saunders), **Supp. XIX: 234–236**
"Brain Scan" (Skloot), **Supp. XX: 200**
"Brain to the Heart, The" (Komunyakaa), **Supp. XIII:** 120
Braithwaite, Chris, **Supp. XXII:** 212
Braithwaite, William Stanley, **Retro. Supp. I:** 131; **Supp. IX:** 309; **Supp. XV:** 296–297, 301–302, 305, 306
Brakhage, Stan, **Supp. XII:** 2
Braly, Malcolm, **Supp. XVIII:** 147
"Bramble, The" (Wrigley), **Supp. XVIII:** 301
Brame, Gloria, **Supp. XV:** 113; **Supp. XXIII:** 122
Bramen, Carrie Tirado, **Supp. XXIV:** 192
Bramer, Monte, **Supp. X:** 152
Branch Will Not Break, The (Wright), **Supp. III Part 2:** 596, 598–601; **Supp. IV Part 1:** 60; **Supp. IX:** 159
Brancusi, Constantin, **III:** 201; **Retro. Supp. I:** 292
Brande, Dorothea, **Supp. I Part 2:** 608
Brandel, Marc, **Supp. XXI:** 276
Branden, Nathaniel, **Supp. IV Part 2:** 526, 528
"Branding Cities" (Greenberg), **Supp. XXII:** 244

"Brand-Name Blues" (Kaufmann), **Supp. XI:** 39
Brand New Life, A (Farrell), **II:** 46, 48
Brando, Marlon, **II:** 588; **Supp. IV Part 2:** 560; **Supp. XVIII:** 251
Brandon, Henry, **Supp. I Part 2:** 604, 612, 618
Brandt, Alice, **Supp. I Part 1:** 92
Brandt, Carl, **Supp. XI:** 45
Brant, Sebastian, **III:** 447, 448
Brantley, Ben, **Supp. XXIV:** 268, 269–270, 271, 272, 274
Braque, Georges, **III:** 197; **Supp. IX:** 66
Brashford, Jake, **Supp. X:** 252
Brasil, Emanuel, **Supp. I Part 1:** 94
"Brasília" (Plath), **Supp. I Part 2:** 544, 545
"Brass Buttons" (McCoy), **Supp. XIII:** 161
"Brass Candlestick, The" (Francis), **Supp. IX:** 89
Brass Check, The (Sinclair), **Supp. V:** 276, 281, 282, 284–285
Brass Knuckles (Dybek), **Supp. XXIII: 68–69**
"Brass Ring, The" (Carver), **Supp. III Part 1:** 137
"Brass Spittoons" (Hughes), **Supp. I Part 1:** 326–327
Brass Verdict, The (Connelly), **Supp. XXI: 78–79**
Brats (X. J. Kennedy), **Supp. XV:** 163
Brautigan, Richard, **III:** 174; **Supp. VIII:** 42, 43; **Supp. XII:** 139; **Supp. XVI:** 172; **Supp. XXI:** 53
Brave Cowboy, The (Abbey), **Supp. XIII:** 4–5
Brave Men (Pyle), **Supp. XVII:** 61
Brave New World (Huxley), **II:** 454; **Supp. XIII:** 29; **Supp. XVIII:** 137
"Brave New World" (MacLeish), **III:** 18
Bravery of Earth, A (Eberhart), **I:** 522, 524, 525, 526, 530
"Brave Tailors of Maida, The" (Talese), **Supp. XVII:** 208
"Brave Words for a Startling Occasion" (Ellison), **Retro. Supp. II:** 118
Braving the Elements (Merrill), **Supp. III Part 1:** 320, 323, 325–327, 329
Bravo, The (Cooper), **I:** 345–346, 348
"Bravura" (Francis), **Supp. IX:** 90
Brawley, Benjamin, **Supp. I Part 1:** 327, 332
Brawl in a Tavern, A (Shaw), **Supp. XIX:** 241
Brawne, Fanny, **I:** 284; **II:** 531
Braxton, Joanne, **Supp. IV Part 1:** 12, 15
Brazil (Bishop), **Retro. Supp. II:** 45; **Supp. I Part 1:** 92
"Brazil" (Marshall), **Supp. XI:** 281
Brazil (Updike), **Retro. Supp. I:** 329, 330, 334
"Brazil, January 1, 1502" (Bishop), **Retro. Supp. II:** 47
Braziller, George, **Supp. X:** 24; **Supp. XXIII:** 214
Brazzi, Rossano, **Supp. IV Part 2:** 520
"Bread" (Dickey), **Supp. IV Part 1:** 182
"Bread" (Olds), **Supp. X:** 206

"Bread Alone" (Wylie), **Supp. I Part 2:** 727
Bread in the Wilderness (Merton), **Supp. VIII:** 197, 208
"Bread of Desire, The" (Nelson), **Supp. XVIII:** 177
Bread of Idleness, The (Masters), **Supp. I Part 2:** 460
"Bread of This World, The" (McGrath), **Supp. X:** 119, 127
Bread of Time, The (Levine), **Supp. V:** 180
Bread without Sugar (Stern), **Supp. IX: 297–298**
"Break, The" (Sexton), **Supp. II Part 2:** 689
"Breakaways, The" (Siddons), **Supp. XXII:** 244
Breakfast at Tiffany's (Capote), **Supp. III Part 1:** 113, 117, 119–121, 124, 126
Breakfast of Champions (Vonnegut), **Supp. II Part 2:** 755, 759, 769, 770, 777–778
Breaking and a Death, A (Kees), **Supp. XV:** 145
Breaking and Entering (X. J. Kennedy), **Supp. XV:** 153, **160–162**
Breaking Hard Ground (D. Hunter), **Supp. XVI:** 38
Breaking Ice (McMillan, ed.), **Supp. XIII:** 182–183
Breaking Open (Rukeyser), **Supp. VI:** 274, 281
"Breaking Open" (Rukeyser), **Supp. VI:** 286
Breaking Ranks: A Political Memoir (Podhoretz), **Supp. VIII: 239–241,** 245
"Breaking the Code of Silence: Ideology and Women's Confessional Poetry" (Harris), **Supp. XIV:** 269
"Breaking Up of the Winships, The" (Thurber), **Supp. I Part 2:** 616
Brearton, Fran, **Supp. XXIV:** 167
Breast, The (P. Roth), **Retro. Supp. II:** 287–288; **Supp. III Part 2:** 416, 418
"Breast, The" (Sexton), **Supp. II Part 2:** 687
"Breasts" (Gallagher), **Supp. XXIV:** 168, 174
"Breasts" (Simic), **Supp. VIII:** 275
"Breasts"(Dybek), **Supp. XXIII:** 77
"Breath" (Espaillat), **Supp. XXI:** 109
"Breath" (Levine), **Supp. V:** 185
Breathe No More, My Lady (Lacy), **Supp. XV:** 203
Breathing Lessons (Tyler), **Supp. IV Part 2:** 669–670
Breathing the Water (Levertov), **Supp. III Part 1:** 274, 283, 284
"Breath of Life, The" (C. Baxter), **Supp. XVII:** 23
Breath's Burials (Sobin), **Supp. XVI: 288–289**
Breaux, Zelia, **Retro. Supp. II:** 114
Brecht, Bertolt, **I:** 60, 301; **III:** 161, 162; **IV:** 394; **Supp. I Part 1:** 292; **Supp. II Part 1:** 10, 26, 56; **Supp. IV Part 1:** 359; **Supp. IX:** 131, 133, 140; **Supp. X:** 112; **Supp. XIII:** 206, 286;

Supp. XIV: 162; **Supp. XVIII:** 33; **Supp. XXIV:** 267
Breen, Joseph I., **IV:** 390
Breines, Ron, **Supp. XVIII:** 97
Breit, Harvey, **I:** 433; **III:** 575; **Retro. Supp. II:** 230; **Supp. XVIII:** 254; **Supp. XXI:** 277
Breman, Paul, **Supp. XXII:** 8
Bremer, Anne, **Supp. XXII:** 277
Bremer, Fredrika, **Supp. I Part 1:** 407
Bremer, Richard, **Supp. XXIII:** 236
Brendan: A Novel (Buechner), **Supp. XII:** 53
Brennan, Matthew C., **Supp. XV:** 113, 125; **Supp. XIX:** 121
Brent, David, **Supp. XXII:** 259
Brent, Linda, **Supp. IV Part 1:** 12, 13
Brentano, Franz, **II:** 350; **Supp. XIV:** 198, 199
Brer Rabbit (tales), **Supp. IV Part 1:** 11, 13; **Supp. XIV:** 88
Breslin, James E. B., **Retro. Supp. I:** 430
Breslin, John B., **Supp. IV Part 1:** 308
Breslin, Paul, **Supp. VIII:** 283
Bresson, Robert, **Supp. IV Part 1:** 156
"Bresson's Movies" (Creeley), **Supp. IV Part 1:** 156–157
Breton, André, **III:** 425; **Supp. XIII:** 114; **Supp. XVII:** 244
Brett, George, **II:** 466; **Supp. V:** 286
Brett, Reginald Baliol, **Supp. XX:** 230
Brevoort, Henry, **II:** 298
Brew, Kwesi, **Supp. IV Part 1:** 10, 16
Brewer, Gaylord, **Supp. XV:** 330
"Brewing of Soma, The" (Whittier), **Supp. I Part 2:** 704
Brewsie and Willie (Stein), **IV:** 27
Brewster, Martha, **Supp. I Part 1:** 114
"Brewsterville Croesus, A" (Briggs), **Supp. XVIII:** 16
Brewsterville letters (Briggs), **Supp. XVIII:** 1, 5, 15–16
"Brian Age 7" (Doty), **Supp. XI:** 136
Briand, Paul, **Supp. XVIII:** 155
"Briar Patch, The" (Warren), **IV:** 237
Briar Rose (Coover), **Supp. V:** 52
"Briar Rose (Sleeping Beauty)" (Sexton), **Supp. II Part 2:** 690
Brice, Fanny, **II:** 427
"Brick, The" (Nye), **Supp. XIII:** 276
"Bricklayer in the Snow" (Fante), **Supp. XI:** 164–165
"Brick Layer's Lunch Hour, The" (Ginsberg), **Supp. II Part 1:** 318
Brickman, Marshall, **Supp. XV:** 5
"Bricks, The" (Hogan), **Supp. IV Part 1:** 413
"Bridal Ballad, The" (Poe), **III:** 428
"Bridal Bed, The" (Gibran), **Supp. XX:** 124
Bridal Dinner, The (Gurney), **Supp. V:** 109, 110
Bridal Hunt (Silver), **Supp. XXIV:** 264
"Bride Comes to Yellow Sky, The" (Crane), **I:** 34, 415, 416, 423
Bridegroom, The (Jin), **Supp. XVIII:** 97–98
"Bridegroom, The" (Jin), **Supp. XVIII:** 98

Bridegroom Cometh, The (W. Frank), **Supp. XX:** 77
"Bridegroom's Body, The" (Boyle), **Supp. XXIV:** 54, 55–56
"Bride in the 30's, A" (Auden), **Supp. II Part 1:** 9
Bride of Lammermoor (Scott), **II:** 291
Bride of Samoa (film), **Supp. IV Part 1:** 82
"Bride of the Innisfallen, The" (Welty), **IV:** 278–279; **Retro. Supp. I:** 353
Bride of the Innisfallen, The, and Other Stories (Welty), **IV:** 261, 275–279; **Retro. Supp. I:** 352–353, 355
Brides of the South Wind: Poems 1917–1922 (Jeffers), **Supp. II Part 2:** 419
Bridge, Horatio, **II:** 226
"BRIDGE, THE" (Baraka), **Supp. II Part 1:** 32, 36
Bridge, The (Crane), **Supp. XXIII:** 146
Bridge, The (H. Crane), **I:** 62, 109, 266, 385, 386, 387, 395–399, 400, 402; **IV:** 123, 341, 418, 419, 420; **Retro. Supp. I:** 427; **Retro. Supp. II:** 76, 77, 81, 83, 84–87; **Supp. V:** 342; **Supp. IX:** 306
Bridge, The (Talese), **Supp. XVII:** 202, 203, 208
Bridge at Remagen, The (film), **Supp. XI:** 343
"Bridge Burners, The" (Van Vechten), **Supp. II Part 2:** 733
Bridgehead: The Drama of Israel (W. Frank), **Supp. XX:** 80
Bridge of San Luis Rey, The (Wilder), **I:** 360; **IV:** 356, 357, 360–363, 365, 366
"Bridge of Sighs"(P. Benedict), **Supp. XXIII:** 47–48
Bridge of Years, The (Sarton), **Supp. VIII:** 253
"Bridges" (Kingsolver), **Supp. VII:** 208
Bridges, Harry, **I:** 493; **Supp. XVIII:** 238; **Supp. XIX:** 264
Bridges, Lloyd, **Supp. XV:** 202
Bridges, Robert, **II:** 537; **III:** 527; **Supp. I Part 2:** 721; **Supp. II Part 1:** 21; **Supp. XIV:** 336, 341, 342, 343
"Bridging" (Apple), **Supp. XVII:** 5
Bridgman, P. W., **I:** 278
"Bridle, The" (Carver), **Supp. III Part 1:** 138
"Brief and Blameless Outline of the Ontogeny of Crow, A" (Wright), **Supp. XV:** 347
Brief and Frightening Reign of Phil, The (Saunders), **Supp. XIX:** 230–231, 233
"Brief Début of Tildy, The" (O. Henry), **Supp. II Part 1:** 408
"Brief Encounters on the Inland Waterway" (Vonnegut), **Supp. II Part 2:** 760
Brief History of the Dead, The (Brockmeier), **Supp. XXII:** 57–59, 61
Briefings (Ammons), **Supp. VII:** 29
Brief Interviews with Hideous Men (Wallace), **Supp. X:** 308–310
"Brief Interviews with Hideous Men" (Wallace), **Supp. X:** 309
"Briefly It Enters, and Briefly Speaks" (Kenyon), **Supp. VII:** 174

"Brief Study of the British, A" (Saunders), **Supp. XIX:** 235
Brief Wondrous Life of Oscar Wao, The (Díaz), **Supp. XXIV:** 83, 84, 85, 87, 89–92, 93
Brier, His Book (J. W. Miller), **Supp. XX:** 165, 168, 170
"Brier Grows Wild, The" (J. W. Miller), **Supp. XX:** 170
"Brier Losing Touch with His Traditions, The" (J. W. Miller), **Supp. XX:** 165, 169
Brier Poems, The (J. W. Miller), **Supp. XX:** 168
"Brier Sermon, The—You Must Be Born Again" (J. W. Miller), **Supp. XX:** 165, 169–170
Briffault, Robert, **Supp. I Part 2:** 560, 567
"Brigade de Cuisine" (McPhee), **Supp. III Part 1:** 307–308
Brigadier and the Golf Widow, The (Cheever), **Supp. I Part 1:** 184–185, 192
Briggs, Charles Frederick, **Supp. I Part 2:** 411; **Supp. XVIII:** 1–18
brigham, besmilr, **Supp. XV:** 349
"Bright and Morning Star" (Wright), **IV:** 488
Bright Book of Life: American Novelists and Storytellers from Hemingway to Mailer (Kazin), **Supp. VIII:** 102, 104
Bright Center of Heaven (Maxwell), **Supp. VIII:** 153–155, 164
"Brightness from the North" (B. Kelly), **Supp. XVII:** 131
Brighton Beach Memoirs (Simon), **Supp. IV Part 2:** 576, 577, 584, 586–587, 590
Bright Procession (Sedges), **Supp. II Part 1:** 125
Bright Room Called Day, A (Kushner), **Supp. IX:** 133, 138–141, 142
Brillat-Savarin, Jean Anthelme, **Supp. XVII:** 82, 86, 87
"Brilliance" (Doty), **Supp. XI:** 124, 128
"Brilliant California Novelist, A" (Forman), **Supp. XXIV:** 30
"Brilliant Leaves" (Gordon), **II:** 199
"Brilliant Sad Sun" (W. C. Williams), **Retro. Supp. I:** 422
"Bringing Back the Trumpeter Swan" (Kumin), **Supp. IV Part 2:** 454
Bringing It All Back Home (album, Dylan), **Supp. XVIII:** 20, 25, 26, 30
Bringing It All Back Home (McNally), **Supp. XIII:** 197–198
Bringing the Devil to His Knees (C. Baxter), **Supp. XVII:** 22
"Bringing the Strange Home" (Dunn), **Supp. XI:** 141
"Bring the Day!" (Roethke), **III:** 536
Brinkley, Douglas, **Supp. XIII:** 9; **Supp. XXIV:** 281, 293
Brinkmeyer, Robert H., Jr., **Supp. XI:** 38
Brinnin, John Malcolm, **IV:** 26, 27, 28, 42, 46; **Supp. XV:** 139
Brissot, Jacques Pierre, **Supp. I Part 2:** 511

"Britain's Negro Problem in Sierra Leone" (Du Bois), **Supp. I Part 1:** 176

"British Guiana" (Marshall), **Supp. XI:** 281–282

"British Poets, The" (Holmes), **Supp. I Part 1:** 306

"British Prison Ship, The" (Freneau), **Supp. II Part 1:** 261

Brittan, Gordon G., Jr., **Supp. XIV:** 234

Britten, Benjamin, **II:** 586; **Supp. II Part 1:** 17; **Supp. IV Part 1:** 84

Broadwater, Bowden, **II:** 562

Broadway, Broadway (McNally). *See It's Only a Play* (McNally)

Broadway, J. William, **Supp. V:** 316

Broadway Bound (Simon), **Supp. IV Part 2:** 576, 577, 584, 586–587, 590

Broadway Danny Rose (film; Allen), **Supp. XV:** 9

"Broadway Sights" (Whitman), **IV:** 350

Broccoli, Albert R. "Cubby", **Supp. XI:** 307

Brock

Bröck, Sabine, **Supp. XI:** 275, 277, 278

Brockmeier, Kevin, **Supp. XXII:** 49–63

Brodhead, Richard, **Retro. Supp. II:** 139; **Supp. XIV:** 61

Brodkey, Harold, **Supp. VIII:** 151; **Supp. X:** 160

Brodskii, Iosif Alexsandrovich. *See* Brodsky, Joseph

Brodsky, Joseph, **Supp. VIII:** 19–35; **Supp. X:** 65, 73; **Supp. XV:** 134, 135, 256; **Supp. XXIII:** 122

Brody, Alter, **Supp. XV:** 302, 307

Brodyar, Anatole, **Supp. XIV:** 106

Brokeback Mountain (film), **Supp. XX:** 273

"Brokeback Mountain" (Proulx), **Supp. VII:** 264–265

"Broken Balance, The" (Jeffers), **Supp. II Part 2:** 426

"Broken Field Running" (Bambara), **Supp. XI:** 10, 11

Broken Frieze, The (Everwine), **Supp. XV:** 74, 75, 89

Broken Ground, The (Berry), **Supp. X:** 30

"Broken Home, The" (Merrill), **Supp. III Part 1:** 319, 325

"Broken Oar, The" (Longfellow), **Retro. Supp. II:** 169

"Broken Promise" (MacLeish), **III:** 15

Broken Span, The (W. C. Williams), **IV:** 419; **Retro. Supp. I:** 424

"Broken Tower, The" (H. Crane), **I:** 385, 386, 400, 401–402; **Retro. Supp. II:** 89, 90

Broken Vessels (Dubus), **Supp. VII:** 90–91; **Supp. XI:** 347

"Broken Vessels" (Dubus), **Supp. VII:** 90

Broken Wings, The (al-Ajni&hudot;a al-Mutakassirah) (Gibran), **Supp. XX:** 115, 124, 125

"Broker" (H. Roth), **Supp. IX:** 234

Bromfield, Louis, **IV:** 380

"Brompton Cocktail" (Mamet), **Supp. XIV:** 252

Bromwich, David, **Retro. Supp. I:** 305; **Supp. XII:** 162

"Broncho That Would Not Be Broken, The" (Lindsay), **Supp. I Part 2:** 383

Bronk, William, **Supp. XV:** 115; **Supp. XXI:** 17–34

Brontë, Anne, **Supp. IV Part 2:** 430

Brontë, Branwell, **I:** 462

Brontë, Charlotte, **I:** 458; **II:** 175; **Supp. IV Part 2:** 430; **Supp. IX:** 128; **Supp. XII:** 104, 303; **Supp. XV:** 338; **Supp. XVI:** 158; **Supp. XX:** 108

Brontë, Emily, **I:** 458; **Retro. Supp. I:** 43; **Supp. IV Part 2:** 430; **Supp. IX:** 128; **Supp. X:** 78, 89; **Supp. XV:** 338

"Bronze" (Francis), **Supp. IX:** 76

"Bronze" (Merrill), **Supp. III Part 1:** 336

Bronze Booklets on the History, Problems, and Cultural Contributions of the Negro series, **Supp. XIV:** 202

"Bronze Buckaroo, The" (Baraka), **Supp. II Part 1:** 49

"Bronze Horses, The" (Lowell), **II:** 524

"Bronze Tablets" (Lowell), **II:** 523

Bronzeville Boys and Girls (Brooks), **Supp. III Part 1:** 79

"Bronzeville Mother Loiters in Mississippi, A. Meanwhile, a Mississippi Mother Burns Bacon" (Brooks), **Supp. III Part 1:** 80

"Brooch, The" (Singer), **IV:** 20

Brook, Peter, **Retro. Supp. II:** 182

Brooke, Rupert, **II:** 82; **III:** 3

Brook Evans (Glaspell), **Supp. III Part 1:** 182–185

"Brooking Likeness" (Glück), **Supp. V:** 85

"Brooklyn" (Marshall), **Supp. XI:** 281, 282

"Brooklyn" (Shaw), **Supp. XIX:** 239, 240

Brooklyn Noir (McLoughlin, ed.), **Supp. XXIV:** 14

Brooks, Albert (Al Pew), **Supp. XXI:** 22

Brooks, Cleanth, **I:** 280, 282; **III:** 517; **IV:** 236, 279; **Retro. Supp. I:** 40, 41, 90; **Retro. Supp. II:** 235; **Supp. I Part 2:** 423; **Supp. III Part 2:** 542; **Supp. V:** 316; **Supp. IX:** 153, 155; **Supp. X:** 115, 123; **Supp. XIV:** 1–20; **Supp. XIX:** 246

Brooks, David, **Supp. IV Part 2:** 623, 626, 630; **Supp. VIII:** 232

Brooks, Gwendolyn, **Retro. Supp. I:** 208; **Supp. III Part 1:** 69–90; **Supp. IV Part 1:** 2, 15, 244, 251, 257; **Supp. XI:** 1, 278; **Supp. XIII:** 111, 112, 296; **Supp. XIV:** 73; **Supp. XVIII:** 175, 181, 185; **Supp. XXI:** 230

Brooks, Mel, **Supp. IV Part 1:** 390; **Supp. IV Part 2:** 591

Brooks, Paul, **Supp. IX:** 26, 31, 32

Brooks, Phillips, **II:** 542; **Retro. Supp. II:** 134; **Supp. XIII:** 142

Brooks, Van Wyck, **I:** 106, 117, 215, 222, 228, 230, 231, 233, 236, 239–263, 266, 480; **II:** 30, 271, 285, 309, 337, 482; **III:** 394, 606; **IV:** 171, 312, 427, 433; **Retro. Supp. II:** 46, 137; **Supp. I Part 2:** 423, 424, 650; **Supp. II Part 1:** 137; **Supp. VIII:** 98, 101; **Supp.**

XIV: 11; **Supp. XV:** 298, 301; **Supp. XX:** 68

Brooks, Mrs. Van Wyck (Eleanor Kenyon Stimson), **I:** 240, 245, 250, 252

Brooks, Mrs. Van Wyck (Gladys Billings), **I:** 258

Broom of the System, The (Wallace), **Supp. X:** 301, 302–305, 310

"Brooms" (Simic), **Supp. VIII:** 275

Brosi, George, **Supp. XX:** 166; **Supp. XXIII:** 39

Brosnan, Jim, **II:** 424–425; **Supp. XX:** 195

Brossard, Chandler, **Supp. XXII:** 258

Brother Carl (Sontag), **Supp. III Part 2:** 452

"Brother Death" (Anderson), **I:** 114

Brother Fire (Di Piero), **Supp. XIX:** 35, 38, 45–47

Brotherhood of the Grape, The (Fante), **Supp. XI:** 160, 171–172

Brother in Elysium, The: Ideas of Friendship and Society in the United States (Bronk), **Supp. XXI:** 21, 22, 25, 31

"Brothers" (Anderson), **I:** 114

Brothers, The (F. Barthelme), **Supp. XI:** 25, 28, 29, 30, 32–33

Brothers and Keepers (Wideman), **Supp. X:** 320, 321–322, 323, 325–327, 328, 329–330, 331, 332

Brothers Ashkenazi, The (Singer), **IV:** 2

Brothers Karamazov, The (Dostoevsky), **II:** 60; **III:** 146, 150, 283; **Supp. IX:** 102, 106; **Supp. XI:** 172; **Supp. XII:** 322

Brothers of No Kin (Richter), **Supp. XVIII:** 209

"Brothers of No Kin" (Richter), **Supp. XVIII:** 208

Brother to Dragons: A Tale in Verse and Voices (Warren), **IV:** 243–244, 245, 246, 251, 252, 254, 257

Broughton, James, **Supp. XV:** 146

Broughton, Rhoda, **II:** 174; **IV:** 309, 310; **Supp. XX:** 232

Broun, Heywood, **I:** 478; **II:** 417; **IV:** 432; **Supp. IX:** 190; **Supp. XXII:** 277

Broussais, François, **Supp. I Part 1:** 302

Brouwer, Joel, **Supp. XXII:** 223, 237

Browder, Earl, **I:** 515; **Supp. XX:** 76, 77

Brower, David, **Supp. X:** 29

Brower, Reuben, **Supp. XV:** 20

Brown, Alice, **II:** 523; **Retro. Supp. II:** 136

Brown, Andrew, **Supp. XVI:** 150

Brown, Ashley, **Retro. Supp. II:** 48; **Supp. I Part 1:** 79, 80, 82, 84, 92

Brown, Charles Brockden, **I:** 54, 211, 335; **II:** 74, 267, 298; **III:** 415; **Supp. I Part 1: 124–149; Supp. II Part 1:** 65, 292; **Supp. XXIII:** 178

Brown, Mrs. Charles Brockden (Elizabeth Linn), **Supp. I Part 1:** 145, 146

Brown, Clifford, **Supp. V:** 195

Brown, Deborah, **Supp. XVII:** 75

Brown, Dee, **Supp. IV Part 2:** 504

Brown, Elijah, **Supp. I Part 1:** 125

Brown, Fleda, **Supp. XXIII:** 59

Brown, George Douglas, **III:** 473

Brown, Harry, **Supp. IV Part 2:** 560

Brown, Harvey, **Supp. XIV:** 148

Brown, Himan, **Supp. XIX:** 241, 242

Brown, H. Rap, **Supp. XXI:** 171

Brown, John, **II:** 13; **IV:** 125, 126, 172, 237, 249, 254; **Supp. I Part 1:** 345; **Supp. VIII:** 204

Brown, Joseph Epes, **Supp. IV Part 2:** 487

Brown, Larry, **Supp. XVIII:** 195; **Supp. XXI:** 35–50

Brown, Leonard, **Supp. IX:** 117

Brown, Mary Armitt, **Supp. I Part 1:** 125

Brown, Percy, **II:** 20

Brown, Robert E., **Supp. X:** 12

Brown, Scott, **Supp. XI:** 178

Brown, Slater, **IV:** 123; **Retro. Supp. II:** 79

Brown, Solyman, **Supp. I Part 1:** 156

Brown, Sterling, **Retro. Supp. I:** 198; **Supp. IV Part 1:** 169; **Supp. XIV:** 202; **Supp. XXII:** 1, 8, 12

Brown, Tina, **Supp. XVI:** 176–177

Brown, Wesley, **Supp. V:** 6

Brown, William Wells, **Supp. XXIII:** 184

Brown Decades, The (Mumford), **Supp. II Part 2:** 475, 478, 491–492

Brown Dog (Harrison), **Supp. VIII:** 51

Brown Dog of the Yaak: Essays on Art and Activism (Bass), **Supp. XVI:** 22

"Brown Dwarf of Rügen, The" (Whittier), **Supp. I Part 2:** 696

Browne, Charles Farrar, **II:** 289; **IV:** 193, 196; **Supp. XVIII:** 1, 4

Browne, Roscoe Lee, **Supp. VIII:** 345

Browne, Thomas, **II:** 15–16, 304; **III:** 77, 78, 198, 487; **IV:** 147; **Supp. IX:** 136; **Supp. XII:** 45; **Supp. XVI:** 292

Browne, William, **Supp. I Part 1:** 98

Brownell, W. C., **II:** 14

Brownell, William Crary, **Retro. Supp. I:** 365, 366

Browner, Stephanie P., **Supp. XVIII:** 17

Brown Girl, Brownstones (Marshall), **Supp. XI:** 275, 276, **278–280,** 282

Brownies' Book, The (Hughes), **Supp. I Part 1:** 321

Browning, Elizabeth Barrett, **I:** 458, 459; **Retro. Supp. I:** 33, 43; **Supp. XVIII:** 175–176; **Supp. XX:** 108

Browning, Oscar, **Supp. XX:** 231

Browning, Robert, **I:** 50, 66, 103, 458, 460, 468; **II:** 338, 478, 522; **III:** 5, 8, 467, 469, 484, 511, 521, 524, 606, 609; **IV:** 135, 245, 366, 416; **Retro. Supp. I:** 43, 55, 217; **Retro. Supp. II:** 188, 190; **Supp. I Part 1:** 2, 6, 79, 311; **Supp. I Part 2:** 416, 468, 622; **Supp. III Part 1:** 5, 6; **Supp. IV Part 2:** 430; **Supp. X:** 65; **Supp. XV:** 92, 250, 275

Brownmiller, Susan, **Supp. X:** 252

"Brown River, Smile" (Toomer), **Supp. IV Part 1:** 16

Brownstone Eclogues and Other Poems (Aiken), **I:** 65, 67

Brown: The Last Discovery of America (Rodriguez), **Supp. XIV:** 297, 298, 300, **305–309,** 310, 311–312

Broyard, Anatole, **Supp. IV Part 1:** 39; **Supp. VIII:** 140; **Supp. X:** 186; **Supp.**

XI: 348; **Supp. XVI:** 213

Broyles, Yolanda Julia, **Supp. XIX:** 112

Bruccoli, Matthew, **Retro. Supp. I:** 98, 102, 105, 114, 115, 359; **Supp. IV Part 2:** 468, 470

Bruce, John Edward, **Supp. XVI:** 143

Bruce, Lenny, **Supp. VIII:** 198

Bruce, Virginia, **Supp. XII:** 173

Bruce-Novoa, Juan, **Supp. VIII:** 73, 74

Bruchac, Joseph, **Supp. IV Part 1:** 261, 319, 320, 321, 322, 323, 325, 328, 398, 399, 403, 408, 414; **Supp. IV Part 2:** 502, 506

Brueghel, Pieter, **I:** 174; **Supp. I Part 2:** 475

Brueghel, Pieter, the Elder, **Retro. Supp. I:** 430

Bruell, Edwin, **Supp. VIII:** 126

Brugh, Spangler Arlington. *See* Taylor, Robert

"Bruja: Witch" (Mora), **Supp. XIII:** 214, 220, 221, **Supp. XIII:** 222

Brulé, Claude, **Supp. XI:** 307

Brumer, Andy, **Supp. XIII:** 88

Brummels, J. V., **Supp. XIX:** 119

Brunner, Emil, **III:** 291, 303

"Brush Fire" (J. Wright), **Supp. XVII:** 241

Brustein, Robert, **Supp. VIII:** 331; **Supp. XXIV:** 116

Brutus, **IV:** 373, 374; **Supp. I Part 2:** 471

"Brutus and Antony" (Masters), **Supp. I Part 2:** 472

"Bryan, Bryan, Bryan, Bryan" (Lindsay), **Supp. I Part 2:** 394, 395, 398

Bryan, George, **Retro. Supp. II:** 76

Bryan, Sharon, **Supp. IX:** 154

Bryan, William Jennings, **I:** 483; **IV:** 124; **Supp. I Part 2:** 385, 395–396, 455, 456

Bryant, Austin, **Supp. I Part 1:** 152, 153

Bryant, Frances, **Supp. I Part 1:** 153

Bryant, Louise, **Supp. X:** 136

Bryant, Peter, **Supp. I Part 1:** 150, 151, 152, 153. *See also* George, Peter

Bryant, William Cullen, **I:** 335, 458; **II:** 311; **III:** 81; **IV:** 309; **Retro. Supp. I:** 217; **Retro. Supp. II:** 155; **Supp. I Part 1:** **150–173,** 312, 362; **Supp. I Part 2:** 413, 416, 420; **Supp. IV Part 1:** 165; **Supp. XIII:** 145; **Supp. XIX:** 4

Bryant, Mrs. William Cullen (Frances Fairchild), **Supp. I Part 1:** 153, 169

Bryer, Jackson R., **Supp. IV Part 2:** 575, 583, 585, 586, 589, 591; **Supp. XIII:** 200, **Supp. XIII:** 205

Bryher, Jackson R. (pseudonym). *See* Ellerman, Winifred

Brynner, Witter, **Supp. XXII:** 273

Bubber Goes to Heaven (Bontemps), **Supp. XXII:** 4

"Bubbs Creek Haircut" (Snyder), **Supp. VIII:** 306

Buber, Martin, **II:** 228; **III:** 45, 308, 528; **IV:** 11; **Supp. I Part 1:** 83, 88; **Supp. XVI:** 291

Buccaneers, The (Wharton), **IV:** 327; **Retro. Supp. I:** 382

Buchanan Dying (Updike), **Retro. Supp. I:** 331, 335

Buchbinder, David, **Supp. XIII:** 32

Buchwald, Art, **Supp. XII:** 124–125; **Supp. XVI:** 110–111

Buchwald, Emilie, **Supp. XVI:** 35, 36

Buck, Dudley, **Supp. I Part 1:** 362

Buck, Gene, **II:** 427

Buck, Pearl S., **Supp. II Part 1:** **113–134; Supp. XIV:** 274

Buckdancer's Choice (Dickey), **Supp. IV Part 1:** 176, 177, 178, 180

"Buckdancer's Choice" (Dickey), **Supp. IV Part 1:** 191

Bucke, Richard Maurice, **Retro. Supp. I:** 407

"Buckeyes"(P. Benedict), **Supp. XXIII:** 46

"Buck Fever" (Humphrey), **Supp. IX:** 109

"Buck in the Snow, The" (Millay), **III:** 135

Buckley, Christopher, **Supp. IX:** 169; **Supp. XI:** 257, 329; **Supp. XV:** 76–77, 86

Buckley, James, Jr., **Supp. XVII:** 220

Buckminster, Joseph, **Supp. II Part 1:** 66–67, 69

Bucknell, Katherine, **Supp. XIV:** 170

Bucolics (Auden), **Supp. II Part 1:** 21, 24

Budbill, David, **Supp. XIX:** **1–16**

Budd, Louis J., **IV:** 210

Buddha, **I:** 136; **II:** 1; **III:** 173, 179, 239, 567; **Supp. I Part 1:** 363; **Supp. I Part 2:** 397

Buddha, The: The Story of Siddhartha (film, Grubin), **Supp. XXIII:** 138, 140

"Buddha Boy" (Saunders), **Supp. XIX:** 235

"Buddha's Last Instruction, The" (Oliver), **Supp. VII:** 239

"Buddies"(Kenny), **Supp. XXIII:** 150

Budding Prospects (Boyle), **Supp. VIII:** **8–9; Supp. XX:** 27–28

Buechner, Frederick, **III:** 310; **Supp. XII:** **41–59**

Buell, Lawrence, **Supp. V:** 209; **Supp. IX:** 29; **Supp. XV:** 269, 282

"Buffalo" (Peacock), **Supp. XIX:** 198

"Buffalo, The" (Moore), **III:** 215

"Buffalo Bill". *See* Cody, William

Buffalo Girls (screenplay) (McMurtry), **Supp. V:** 232

Buffalo Girls (McMurtry), **Supp. V:** 229

Buffalo Hunters, The: The Story of the Hide Men (Sandoz), **Supp. XXIV:** 244, **247–249,** 256

Buffett, Jimmy, **Supp. VIII:** 42

Buffon, Comte de, **II:** 101

Buford, Fanny McConnell, **Retro. Supp. II:** 117

Bugeja, Michael, **Supp. X:** 201

Bugged for Murder (Lacy), **Supp. XV:** 205

"Buglesong" (Stegner), **Supp. IV Part 2:** 606

Buhle, Paul, **Supp. XXI:** 172

"Buick" (Shapiro), **Supp. II Part 2:** 705

"Builders" (Yates), **Supp. XI:** **342–343**

Builders, The (Glasgow), **II**: 183–184, 193

"Builders, The" (Hay), **Supp. XIV**: 125

Builders in Sand (W. Frank), **Supp. XX: 68**

Builders of the Bay Colony (Morison), **Supp. I Part 2**: 484–485

"Builders of the Bridge, The" (Mumford), **Supp. II Part 2**: 475

"Building" (Snyder), **Supp. VIII**: 305

"Building, Dwelling, Thinking" (Heidegger), **Retro. Supp. II**: 87

Building a Character (Stanislavsky), **Supp. XIV**: 243

" 'Building' Larry Brown(s) at Algonquin Books of Chapel Hill" (Perry), **Supp. XXI**: 42

"Building of the Ship, The" (Longfellow), **II**: 498; **Retro. Supp. II**: 159, 167, 168

"Build Soil" (Frost), **Retro. Supp. I**: 138, 139

"Build Soil" (Snyder), **Supp. VIII**: 304

Build-Up, The (W. C. Williams), **Retro. Supp. I**: 423

Bukiet, Melvin Jules, **Supp. XVII**: 39–51

Bukowski, Charles, **Supp. III Part 1**: 147; **Supp. XI**: 159, 161, 172, 173; **Supp. XVII**: 245

Bulgakov, Mikhail, **Supp. XIV**: 97

"Bulgarian Poetess, The" (Updike), **IV**: 215, 227; **Retro. Supp. I**: 329

Bull, Ole, **II**: 504

"Bulldozer, The" (Francis), **Supp. IX**: 87

"Bullet in the Brain" (Wolff), **Supp. VII**: 342–343

Bullet Park (Cheever), **Supp. I Part 1**: 185, 187–193, 194, 195

Bullets over Broadway (film; Allen), **Supp. XV**: 12, **12–13**

Bullfight, The (Mailer), **Retro. Supp. II**: 205

Bullins, Ed, **Supp. II Part 1**: 34, 42

Bullock, Sandra, **Supp. X**: 80

"Bull-Roarer, The" (Stern), **Supp. IX**: 297

"Bully, The" (Dubus), **Supp. VII**: 84

"Bulsh" (X. J. Kennedy), **Supp. XV**: 161

Bultmann, Rudolf, **III**: 309

Bulwark, The (Dreiser), **I**: 497, 506, 516–517; **Retro. Supp. II**: 95, 96, 105, 108

Bulwer-Lytton, Edward George, **IV**: 350

"Bums in the Attic" (Cisneros), **Supp. VII**: 62

Bunche, Ralph, **Supp. I Part 1**: 343; **Supp. XIV**: 202; **Supp. XXII**: 12

"Bunchgrass Edge of the World, The" (Proulx), **Supp. VII**: 263

Bunge, Nancy, **Supp. XVII**: 218; **Supp. XXII**: 175, 177, 178, 180, 183

"Bunner Sisters, The" (Wharton), **IV**: 317

Bunting, Basil, **Retro. Supp. I**: 422; **Supp. III Part 2**: 616, 620, 624; **Supp. XIV**: 286

Buntline, Ned, **Supp. XXIII**: 182

Buñuel, Luis, **III**: 184; **Retro. Supp. II**: 337

Bunyan, John, **I**: 445; **II**: 15, 104, 228; **IV**: 80, 84, 156, 437; **Supp. I Part 1**: 32

Bunyan, Paul, **Supp. XXII**: 203

Burana, Lily, **Supp. XI**: 253

Burbank, Luther, **I**: 483

Burbank, Rex, **IV**: 363

Burch, Michael, **Supp. XXI**: 99

Burchfield, Alice, **Supp. I Part 2**: 652, 660

Burden of Proof, The (Turow), **Supp. XVII**: **216–217**, 218

Burden of Southern History, The (Woodward), **Retro. Supp. I**: 75

Burdens of Formality, The (Lea, ed.), **Supp. X**: 58

Burger, Gottfried August, **II**: 306

Burgess, Anthony, **Supp. IV Part 1**: 227; **Supp. IV Part 2**: 685; **Supp. V**: 128; **Supp. XXIII**: 42

Burgh, James, **Supp. I Part 2**: 522

"Burglar of Babylon, The" (Bishop), **Retro. Supp. II**: 47; **Supp. I Part 1**: 93

Burgum, E. B., **IV**: 469, 470

Burham, Philip, **Supp. XX**: **44**

"Burial of Jonathan Brown, The"(Hadas), **Supp. XXIII**: 115

Buried Child (Shepard), **Supp. III Part 2**: 433, 447, 448; **Supp. XIV**: 327

"Buried Lake, The" (Tate), **IV**: 136

Burkard, Michael, **Supp. XXIV**: 165

Burke, Carolyn, **Supp. XXII**: 156, 158, 162, 165, 167, 168

Burke, Edmund, **I**: 9; **III**: 310; **Supp. I Part 2**: 496, 511, 512, 513, 523; **Supp. II Part 1**: 80; **Supp. XVII**: 236

Burke, James Lee, **Supp. XIV**: **21–38**; **Supp. XXI**: 67, 72, 80

Burke, Kenneth, **I**: **264–287**, 291; **III**: 497, 499, 546; **IV**: 123, 408; **Retro. Supp. I**: 297; **Retro. Supp. II**: 117, 120; **Supp. I Part 2**: 630; **Supp. II Part 1**: 136; **Supp. VIII**: 105; **Supp. IX**: 229; **Supp. XIV**: 3; **Supp. XXI**: 89

Burke, William, **Supp. XXI**: 215

"Burl" (Mosher), **Supp. XXII**: 204, 211

Burley, Justin, **Supp. XVI**: 158

"Burly Fading One, The" (Hayden), **Supp. II Part 1**: 366

Burn, Stephen J., **Supp. XX**: **85**; **Supp. XXII**: 266, 268

"Burned" (Levine), **Supp. V**: 186, 192

Burned Diary, The (Olds), **Supp. X**: 215

Burne-Jones, Edward, **Supp. XXII**: 156

Burnett, Allison, **Supp. XVII**: 22

Burnett, David, **Supp. XI**: 299

Burnett, Frances Hodgson, **Supp. I Part 1**: 44

Burnett, Whit, **III**: 551; **Supp. XI**: 294

Burney, Fanny, **Supp. XV**: 232; **Supp. XX**: **108**

Burnham, James, **Supp. I Part 2**: 648

Burnham, John Chynoweth, **I**: 59

"Burning, The" (Welty), **IV**: 277–278; **Retro. Supp. I**: 353

Burning Angel (Burke), **Supp. XIV**: 30, 32

Burning Bright (Steinbeck), **IV**: 51, 61–62

Burning Bright: An Anthology of Sacred Poetry (Hampl, ed.), **Supp. XXII**: 87

"Burning Bush" (Cliff), **Supp. XXII**: 75

Burning Bush (Untermeyer), **Supp. XV: 309**

"Burning Bush" (Untermeyer), **Supp. XV**: 309

Burning Bush, The (Asch), **Supp. XXIII**: 7

Burning Bush, The (H. and G. Herczeg), **Supp. XVII**: 62

Burning Chrome (W. Gibson), **Supp. XVI**: 118, 122, **128**

"Burning Chrome" (W. Gibson), **Supp. XVI**: 117, 120, 123, 124, 128

Burning City (Benét), **Supp. XI**: 46, 58

Burning Daylight (London), **II**: 474, 481

Burning Down the House: Essays on Fiction (C. Baxter), **Supp. XVII**: 13, 20, 21

Burning House, The (Beattie), **Supp. V**: 29

"Burning Ladder, The" (Gioia), **Supp. XV**: 118

Burning Mystery of Anna in 1951, The (Koch), **Supp. XV**: 182–183

"Burning of Paper Instead of Children, The" (Rich), **Supp. I Part 2**: 558

"Burning Shit at An Khe" (Weigl), **Supp. XIX**: 279–280

Burning the Days (Salter), **Supp. XIX**: 252

Burning the Days: Recollections (Salter), **Supp. IX**: 245, 246, 248, 260, **261–262**

"Burning the Small Dead" (Snyder), **Supp. VIII**: 298

Burning Tigris, The: The Armenian Genocide and America's Response (Balakian), **Supp. XXIII**: 19, 21, 22, **25–28**, 30

"Burning Tobacco Beds" (J. W. Miller), **Supp. XX**: **167**

Burns, Carol, **Supp. XVIII**: 162

Burns, David, **III**: 165–166

Burns, Ken, **Supp. XIV**: 14

Burns, Michael, **Supp. XV**: 339

Burns, Robert, **II**: 150, 306; **III**: 592; **IV**: 453; **Supp. I Part 1**: 158; **Supp. I Part 2**: 410, 455, 683, 685, 691, 692; **Supp. IX**: 173; **Supp. XII**: 171; **Supp. XIII**: 3; **Supp. XVIII**: 82

Burnshaw, Stanley, **Retro. Supp. I**: 298, 303; **Supp. III Part 2**: 615

"Burn the Cities" (West), **Retro. Supp. II**: 338

Burnt Mountain (Siddons), **Supp. XXII**: 253

Burnt Norton (T. S. Eliot), **I**: 575, 580–581, 582, 584, 585; **III**: 10

"Burnt Norton" (T. S. Eliot), **Retro. Supp. I**: 66; **Supp. XV**: 216

Burnt-Out Case, A (Greene), **Supp. VIII**: 4

"Burnt-out Spa, The" (Plath), **Retro. Supp. II**: 246

Burn Witch Burn (A. Merritt), **Supp. XVII**: 58

Burr, Aaron, **I**: 7, 549, 550; **II**: 300; **IV**: 264; **Supp. I Part 2**: 461, 483

Burr: A Novel (Vidal), **Supp. IV Part 2:** 677, 682, 684, 685, 687, 688, 689, 691

Burr Oaks (Eberhart), **I:** 533, 535

Burroughs, Edgar Rice, **Supp. IV Part 1:** 101

Burroughs, John, **I:** 220, 236, 506; **IV:** 346; **Supp. IX:** 171

Burroughs, William S., **III:** 45, 174, 258; **Supp. II Part 1:** 320, 328; **Supp. III Part 1: 91–110,** 217, 226; **Supp. IV Part 1:** 79, 87, 90; **Supp. XI:** 297, 308; **Supp. XII:** 1, 3, 118, 121, 124, 129, 131, 136; **Supp. XIV:** 137, 140–141, 143–144, 150; **Supp. XVI:** 123, 135; **Supp. XVII:** 225; **Supp. XVIII:** 137; **Supp. XXIII:** 213; **Supp. XXIV:** 42

Burrow, Trigant, **Supp. II Part 1:** 6

Burrows, Ken, **Supp. V:** 115

Bursey, Jeff, **Supp. XXII:** 257

Burson, Claudia, **Supp. XV:** 343

Burstein, Janet, **Supp. XVII:** 41, 44, 48

"Bursts of Light" (Bronk), **Supp. XXI:** 33

Burt, Stephen, **Supp. XV:** 341, 342, 345, 347, 351; **Supp. XVII:** 18, 246

Burt, Steve, **Supp. V:** 83

Burtis, Thomson, **Supp. XIII:** 163

Burton, Robert, **II:** 535; **III:** 77, 78; **Supp. I Part 1:** 349

Burton, Sue D., **Supp. XIX:** 90

Burton, William Evans, **III:** 412

"Burying Ground by the Ties" (MacLeish), **III:** 14

Bury My Heart at Wounded Knee (Brown), **Supp. IV Part 2:** 504

Bury the Dead (Shaw), **IV:** 381; **Supp. XIX: 242–244,** 249, 252

"Bus Along St. Clair: December, A" (Atwood), **Supp. XIII:** 33

Busch, Frederick, **Supp. X:** 78; **Supp. XII:** 343; **Supp. XVII:** 175

Bush, Barney, **Supp. XII:** 218, 222

Bush, Douglas, **Supp. I Part 1:** 268; **Supp. XIV:** 10

"Busher Comes Back, The" (Lardner), **II:** 422

"Busher's Letters Home, A" (Lardner), **II:** 418–419, 421

Bushrui, Suheil, **Supp. XX: 113, 117, 120, 122, 126–127**

"Business and Poetry" (Gioia), **Supp. XV:** 113, 115

"Business Deal" (West), **IV:** 287

"Business Man, A" (Jewett), **Retro. Supp. II:** 132

Business of Memory, The: The Art of Remembering in an Age of Forgetting (C. Baxter, ed.), **Supp. XVII:** 21

"Business Trip" (Hoffman), **Supp. XVIII:** 86

Buss, Helen M., **Supp. IV Part 1:** 12

Butcher, Margaret Just, **Supp. XIV:** 203

"Butcher, The" (Southern), **Supp. XI:** 294

"Butcher Cock, The"(P. Benedict), **Supp. XXIII:** 46–47

"Butcher Shop" (Simic), **Supp. VIII:** 273

But Gentlemen Marry Brunettes (Loos), **Supp. XVI:** 190–191

"But He Says I Misunderstood" (Notley), **Supp. XXII:** 227

Butler, Benjamin, **I:** 457

Butler, Dorothy. *See* Farrell, Mrs. James T. (Dorothy Butler)

Butler, Elizabeth, **Supp. I Part 1:** 260

Butler, Ethel, **Supp. XIV:** 125

Butler, Hugo, **Supp. XVII:** 63

Butler, James D., **Supp. IX:** 175

Butler, Joseph, **II:** 8, 9

Butler, Judith, **Supp. XII:** 6

Butler, Maud. *See* Falkner, Mrs. Murray C. (Maud Butler)

Butler, Nicholas Murray, **I:** 223; **Supp. I Part 1:** 23; **Supp. III Part 2:** 499

Butler, Octavia, **Supp. XIII: 59–72**

Butler, Robert Olen, **Supp. XII: 61–78,** 319

Butler, Samuel, **II:** 82, 86; **IV:** 121, 440; **Supp. VIII:** 171

Butler-Evans, Elliot, **Retro. Supp. II:** 121

"But Only Mine" (Wright), **Supp. III Part 2:** 595

Butscher, Edward, **Supp. I Part 2:** 526

Butter Battle Book, The (Geisel), **Supp. XVI:** 110

"Buttercups" (Lowell), **Retro. Supp. II:** 187

Butterfield, R. W., **I:** 386

Butterfield, Stephen, **Supp. IV Part 1:** 3, 11

Butterfield 8 (O'Hara), **III:** 361

"Butterflies Under Persimmon" (Jarman), **Supp. XVII:** 120

Butterfly (Harvey), **Supp. XIII:** 184

"Butterfly, The" (Brodksy), **Supp. VIII:** 26

"Butterfly and the Traffic Light, The" (Ozick), **Supp. V:** 263, 265

Butterfly Plague, The (Findley), **Supp. XX:** 50, 52, 53

Butterfly Stories (Vollmann), **Supp. XVII:** 226

"Butterfly-toed Shoes" (Komunyakaa), **Supp. XIII:** 126

Butter Hill and Other Poems (Francis), **Supp. IX:** 88, 89

"Button-Down Builders, The" (Siddons), **Supp. XXII:** 243–244

Buttons, Red, **Supp. IV Part 2:** 574

Buttrick, George, **III:** 301; **Supp. XII:** 47–48

"But What Is the Reader to Make of This?" (Ashbery), **Supp. III Part 1:** 25

Butz, Earl, **Supp. X:** 35

"Buz" (Alcott), **Supp. I Part 1:** 43

Buzinski, Jim, **Supp. XX: 273**

"By an *Objibwa Female* Pen: Invitation to sisters to a walk in the Garden, after a shower"(J. Schoolcraft), **Supp. XXIII:** 230

Byatt, A. S., **Supp. XXI:** 147

By Avon River (Doolittle), **Supp. I Part 1:** 272

"By Blue Ontario's Shore" (Whitman), **Retro. Supp. I:** 399, 400

"By Candlelight" (Major), **Supp. XXII:** 185

"By Disposition of Angels" (Moore), **III:** 214

"By Earth" (Olds), **Supp. X:** 214

"Bye for Now, Broadway, My New Friend" (Silver), **Supp. XXIV:** 276

"By Fire" (Olds), **Supp. X:** 214

Bygones (Untermeyer), **Supp. XV:** 304, **308–309,** 312, 313

By Land, By Sea (Hoffman), **Supp. XVIII:** 86

By Land and by Sea (Morison), **Supp. I Part 2:** 492

Byles, Mather, **Supp. XX: 279, 282**

By-Line: Ernest Hemingway (Hemingway), **II:** 257–258

By Love Possessed (Cozens), **I:** 358, 365, 372–374, 375, 376, 377, 378, 379

"By Morning" (Swenson), **Supp. IV Part 2:** 642

"By Night" (Francis), **Supp. IX:** 76

Bynner, Witter, **II:** 513, 527; **Supp. XIII:** 347; **Supp. XV: 39–54**

Byrd, William, **Supp. IV Part 2:** 425; **Supp. XXI:** 35; **Supp. XXII:** 193

Byrne, Donn, **IV:** 67

Byron, George Gordon, Lord, **I:** 343, 568, 577; **II:** 135, 193, 296, 301, 303, 310, 315, 331, 566; **III:** 82, 137, 170, 409, 410, 412, 469; **IV:** 245, 435; **Supp. I Part 1:** 150, 312, 349; **Supp. I Part 2:** 580, 591, 683, 685, 719; **Supp. XIII:** 139; **Supp. XVI:** 188, 203, 206, 210

"Byron's Cain" (L. Michaels), **Supp. XVI:** 203

"Bystanders" (Matthews), **Supp. IX:** 160

By the Bias of Sound (Sobin), **Supp. XVI:** 281

By the North Gate (Oates), **Supp. II Part 2:** 504

"By the People" (Stratton-Porter), **Supp. XX: 221**

By the Shores of Silver Lake (L. I. Wilder), **Supp. XXII:** 294, 295, 299

"By the Waters of Babylon" (Benét), **Supp. XI:** 56, 58

By the Waters of Manhattan (Reznikoff), **Supp. XIV:** 288, 293, 294

By the Waters of Manhattan: An Annual (Reznikoff), **Supp. XIV:** 277, 280, 289

By the Waters of Manhattan: Selected Verse (Reznikoff), **Supp. XIV:** 281, 291

By the Well of Living and Seeing and the Fifth Book of the Maccabees (Reznikoff), **Supp. XIV:** 281

By the Well of Living and Seeing: New and Selected Poems 1918–1973 (Reznikoff), **Supp. XIV:** 281, 287–288, 295

By Way of Orbit (O'Neill), **III:** 405

Byzantine Parables (Notley), **Supp. XXII:** 235, 237

C

"C 33" (H. Crane), **I:** 384; **Retro. Supp. II:** 76

Cabala, The (Wilder), **IV:** 356, 358–360, 369, 374

"Cabaret" (Boyle), **Supp. XXIV:** 61

Cabaret (film), **Supp. XIV:** 155, 162

Cabaret (play), **Supp. XIV:** 162; **Supp. XVII:** 45

Cabbages and Kings (O. Henry), **Supp. II Part 1:** 394, 409

Cabell, James Branch, **II:** 42; **III:** 394; **IV:** 67, 359, 360; **Retro. Supp. I:** 80; **Supp. I Part 2:** 613, 714, 718, 721; **Supp. X:** 223

"Cabin, The" (Carver), **Supp. III Part 1:** 137, 146

Cabin, The: Reminiscence and Diversions (Mamet), **Supp. XIV:** 240

Cabinet of Dr. Caligari, The (film), **Retro. Supp. I:** 268

Cable, George Washington, **II:** 289; **Retro. Supp. II:** 65; **Supp. I Part 1:** 200; **Supp. II Part 1:** 198; **Supp. XIV:** 63

Cables to the Ace; or, Familiar Liturgies of Misunderstanding (Merton), **Supp. VIII:** 208

Cabot, James, **II:** 14; **IV:** 173

Cabot, John, **Supp. I Part 2:** 496, 497

Cachoeira Tales and Other Poems, The (Nelson), **Supp. XVIII: 178–179**

"Cachoiera Tales, The" (Nelson), **Supp. XVIII:** 179

Cactus Flower (Barillet and Grédy), **Supp. XVI:** 194

"Caddy's Diary, A" (Lardner), **II:** 421–422

"Cadence" (Dubus), **Supp. VII:** 84–85

Cadieux, Isabelle, **Supp. XIII:** 127

"Cadillac Flambé" (Ellison), **Retro. Supp. II:** 119, 126; **Supp. II Part 1:** 248

Cadillac Jack (McMurtry), **Supp. V:** 225

Cadillac Jukebox (Burke), **Supp. XIV:** 32

Cadle, Dean, **Supp. I Part 2:** 429

Cady, Edwin H., **II:** 272

"Caedmon" (Garrett), **Supp. VII:** 96–97

Caesar, Julius, **II:** 12, 502, 561–562; **IV:** 372, 373

Caesar, Sid, **Supp. IV Part 2:** 574, 591

"Cafeteria, The" (Singer), **Retro. Supp. II:** 316

Cage, John, **Supp. IV Part 1:** 84; **Supp. V:** 337, 341; **Supp. XXIII:** 211

"Cage and the Prairie: Two Notes on Symbolism, The" (Bewley), **Supp. I Part 1:** 251

Cage Keeper, The (Dubus III), **Supp. XXIV: 99–102**

"Cage Keeper, The" (Dubus III), **Supp. XXIV:** 101–102, 104

Cage of Age, The (Bronk), **Supp. XXI:** 32

Cage of Spines, A (Swenson), **Supp. IV Part 2:** 641–642, 647

"Cage of the Body, The"(Schott), **Supp. XXIII:** 243–244

Cagney, James, **Supp. IV Part 1:** 236; **Supp. XIII:** 174

Cagney, William, **Supp. XIII:** 174

Cahalan, James, **Supp. XIII:** 1, 2, 3, 4, 12

Cahan, Abraham, **Supp. IX:** 227; **Supp. XIII:** 106; **Supp. XXI:** 3, 14; **Supp. XXIII:** 1, 2, 9, 16

Cahill, Tim, **Supp. XIII:** 13

Cain, James M., **III:** 99; **Supp. IV Part 1:** 130; **Supp. XI:** 160; **Supp. XIII:** 159, 165

Cain, Kathleen Shine, **Supp. XX: 247, 248**

Caird, G. B., **Supp. XXI:** 91–92

Cairns, Huntington, **III:** 103, 108, 114, 119

Cairo! Shanghai! Bombay! (Williams and Shapiro), **IV:** 380

Cake (Bynner), **Supp. XV:** 50

Cakes and Ale (Maugham), **III:** 64

Calabria, Frank, **Supp. XIII:** 164

Calamity Jane (Martha Jane Canary), **Supp. V:** 229–230; **Supp. X:** 103

"Calamus" (Whitman), **IV:** 342–343; **Retro. Supp. I:** 52, 403, 404, 407

Calasso, Roberto, **Supp. IV Part 1:** 301

Calder, William M., III, **Supp. XXIII:** 112

Calderón, Hector, **Supp. IV Part 2:** 544

Caldwell, Christopher, **Supp. IV Part 1:** 211

Caldwell, Erskine, **I:** 97, 211, **288–311;** **IV:** 286; **Supp. IV Part 2:** 601; **Supp. XXI:** 35; **Supp. XXII:** 196

Caldwell, Mrs. Erskine (Helen Lannegan), **I:** 289

Caldwell, Mrs. Erskine (Margaret Bourke-White), **I:** 290, 293–295, 297

Caldwell, Mrs. Erskine (Virginia Fletcher), **I:** 290

Caldwell, Reverend Ira Sylvester, **I:** 289, 305

Caldwell, Zoe, **Supp. XIII:** 207

Caleb Williams (Godwin), **III:** 415

"Calendar" (Creeley), **Supp. IV Part 1:** 158

Calendar of Saints for Unbelievers, A (Wescott), **Supp. XIV:** 342

Calendars (A. Finch), **Supp. XVII: 76–77**

Calhoun, John C., **I:** 8; **III:** 309

"Caliban in the Coal Mines" (Untermeyer), **Supp. XV:** 296

"California" (Carruth), **Supp. XVI:** 56

"California" (Didion), **Supp. IV Part 1:** 195

"California, This Is Minnesota Speaking" (Dunn), **Supp. XI:** 146

California and Oregon Trail, The (Parkman), **Supp. I Part 2:** 486

California: An Intimate History (Atherton), **Supp. XXIV:** 27

California Daughter (Leider), **Supp. XXIV:** 30

"California Hills in August" (Gioia), **Supp. XV:** 118–119

Californians (Jeffers), **Supp. II Part 2:** 415, 418, 420

Californians, The (Atherton), **Supp. XXIV:** 18, 21, 22

"California Oaks, The" (Winters), **Supp. II Part 2:** 798

"California Plush" (Bidart), **Supp. XV:** 23

"California Republic" (Didion), **Supp. IV Part 1:** 205

"California Requiem, A" (Gioia), **Supp. XV:** 126

California Suite (film), **Supp. IV Part 2:** 589

California Suite (Simon), **Supp. IV Part 2:** 581, 582

"Caligula" (Lowell), **II:** 554

Callahan, John F., **Retro. Supp. II:** 119, 126, 127

"Call at Corazón" (Bowles), **Supp. IV Part 1:** 82, 87

Calle, Sophia, **Supp. XII:** 22

"Called Back" (Kazin), **Supp. VIII:** 104

Calley, Captain William, **II:** 579

Calley, John, **Supp. XI:** 305

Callicott, J. Baird, **Supp. XIV:** 184

Calligrammes (Apollinaire), **I:** 432

"Calling Jesus" (Toomer), **Supp. III Part 2:** 484

Calling Myself Home (Hogan), **Supp. IV Part 1:** 397, 399, 400, 401, 413

Calling the Wind: Twentieth Century African-American Short Stories (Major, ed.), **Supp. XXII:** 172

Calling Western Union (Taggard), **Supp. XXII:** 271–272, **281–283**

Call It Experience (Caldwell), **I:** 290–291, 297

"Call It Fear" (Harjo), **Supp. XII:** 220

Call It Sleep (H. Roth), **Supp. VIII:** 233; **Supp. IX:** 227, 228, **229–231; Supp. XIII:** 106

"Call Letters: Mrs. V. B." (Angelou), **Supp. IV Part 1:** 15

Call Me Ishmael (Olson), **Supp. II Part 2:** 556; **Supp. XXI:** 21

Call Me Shakespeare (Endore), **Supp. XVII:** 65

Call of the Gospel, The (Mather), **Supp. II Part 2:** 448

Call of the Wild, The (London), **II:** 466, 470–471, 472, 481

"Call of the Wild, The" (Snyder), **Supp. VIII:** 301

"Calloway's Code" (O. Henry), **Supp. II Part 1:** 404

"Call to Arms" (Mumford), **Supp. II Part 2:** 479

Call to Arms, The (film), **Retro. Supp. I:** 325

Calmer, Ned, **Supp. XI:** 219

Calvert, George H., **Supp. I Part 1:** 361

Calverton, V. F., **Supp. VIII:** 96

Calvin, John, **II:** 342; **IV:** 160, 490

Calvino, Italo, **Supp. IV Part 2:** 623, 678; **Supp. XIX:** 34; **Supp. XXI:** 225; **Supp. XXII:** 263

Cambridge Companion to Native American Literature, The (Porter and Roemer, eds.), **Supp. XX:** 270

Cambridge Edition of the Works of F. Scott Fitzgerald, The (Bruccoli, ed.), **Retro. Supp. I:** 115

Cambridge Film Handbook for On the Waterfront (Rapf), **Supp. XVIII:** 251

"Cambridge"(O'Hara), **Supp. XXIII:** 219

"Cambridge Thirty Years Ago" (Lowell), **Supp. I Part 2:** 419

Cambridge University Press, **Retro. Supp. I:** 115

"Camellia Sabina" (Moore), **III:** 208, 215

"Cameo" (Trethewey), **Supp. XXI:** 250

"Cameo Appearance" (Simic), **Supp. VIII:** 283

"Camera Notes" (column, Stratton-Porter), **Supp. XX: 217**

Camera Obscura (Nabokov), **III:** 255

Cameron, Angus, **Supp. XXI:** 268, 269, 275, 278

Cameron, Elizabeth, **I:** 10, 17

Cameron, Kenneth W., **II:** 16

Cameron, Peter, **Supp. XII: 79–95**

Cameron, Sharon, **Retro. Supp. I:** 43; **Retro. Supp. II:** 40

Camerson, Don, **I:** 10, 17

Camino, Léon Felipe, **Retro. Supp. II:** 89

Camino Real (T. Williams), **IV:** 382, 385, 386, 387, 388, 391, 392, 395, 398

Camões, Luiz Vaz de, **II:** 133; **Supp. I Part 1:** 94

"Camouflaging the Chimera" (Komunyakaa), **Supp. XIII: 122–123**

Camp, James, **Supp. XV:** 165

Camp, Walter, **II:** 423

Campana, Dino, **Supp. V:** 337

Campbell, Alan, **Supp. IV Part 1:** 353; **Supp. IX:** 196, 198, 201

Campbell, Alexander, **Supp. I Part 2:** 381, 395

Campbell, Donna, **Retro. Supp. II:** 139

Campbell, E. Simms, **Supp. XXII:** 12

Campbell, Helen, **Supp. XI:** 200, 206

Campbell, James, **Supp. XII:** 127

Campbell, James Edwin, **Supp. II Part 1:** 202

Campbell, Joanna (pseudonym). *See* Bly, Carol

Campbell, Joseph, **I:** 135; **IV:** 369, 370; **Supp. IX:** 245

Campbell, Lewis, **III:** 476

Campbell, Thomas, **II:** 8, 303, 314; **III:** 410; **Supp. I Part 1:** 309, 310

Campbell, Virginia, **Supp. XIII:** 114

Campbell, Will D., **Supp. XXI:** 247

Campbell (Hale), Janet, **Supp. IV Part 2:** 503

"Campers Leaving: Summer 1981" (Kenyon), **Supp. VII:** 169

"Camp Evergreen" (Kenyon), **Supp. VII:** 168

"Camping in Madera Canyon" (Swenson), **Supp. IV Part 2:** 649

Campion, Jane, **Supp. XXIV:** 172

Campion, Thomas, **I:** 439; **Supp. VIII:** 272

Campo, Rafael, **Supp. XVII:** 112

Camus, Albert, **I:** 53, 61, 292, 294, 494; **II:** 57, 244; **III:** 292, 306, 453; **IV:** 6, 211, 236, 442, 487; **Retro. Supp. I:** 73; **Retro. Supp. II:** 20; **Supp. I Part 2:** 621; **Supp. VIII:** 11, 195, 241; **Supp. XI:** 96; **Supp. XIII:** 74, 165, 233, 247; **Supp. XVII:** 137

Camuto, Christopher, **Supp. V:** 212–213

"Canada" (Di Piero), **Supp. XIX:** 39

Canada Fragrant with Resin, **Supp. XVI:** 149

Canadé, Eugene, **Supp. XXI:** 22, 23

"Canadian Mosaic, The" (Beran), **Supp. XIII:** 25

"Canadians and Pottawatomies" (Sandburg), **III:** 592–593

"Can a Good Wife Be a Good Sport?" (T. Williams), **IV:** 380

"Canal, The: A Poem on the Application of Physical Science to Political Economy" (Barlow), **Supp. II Part 1:** 73

Canary, Martha Jane. *See* Calamity Jane (Martha Jane Canary)

"Canary for One, A" (Hemingway), **Retro. Supp. I:** 170, 189

Canary in a Cat House (Vonnegut), **Supp. II Part 2:** 758

"Canary in Bloom" (Dove), **Supp. IV Part 1:** 248

Canby, Henry Seidel, **IV:** 65, 363

"Cancer" (McClatchy), **Supp. XII:** 266

"Cancer Match, The" (Dickey), **Supp. IV Part 1:** 182

"Canción y Glosa" (Merwin), **Supp. III Part 1:** 342

Candide (Hellman), **I:** 28; **Supp. I Part 1:** 288–289, 292

Candide (Voltaire), **Supp. I Part 1:** 288–289; **Supp. XI:** 297; **Supp. XVI:** 189

Candide (Voltaire; Wilbur, trans.), **Supp. III Part 2:** 560

"Candle Hat" (Collins), **Supp. XXI:** 60

Candle in the Cabin, The (Lindsay), **Supp. I Part 2:** 398, 400

"Candles" (Plath), **Retro. Supp. II:** 248, 257

Candles in Babylon (Levertov), **Supp. III Part 1:** 283

Candles in the Sun (T. Williams), **IV:** 381

Candles of Your Eyes, The (Purdy), **Supp. VII:** 278

Candy (Southern), **Supp. XI:** 297, **298–299,** 305

"Candy-Man Beechum" (Caldwell), **I:** 309

Cane (Toomer), **Supp. III Part 2:** 475, 481–486, 488; **Supp. IV Part 1:** 164, 168; **Supp. IX:** 305, 306, 307, **308–320; Supp. XIX:** 73; **Supp. XX:** 73

"Cane in the Corridor, The" (Thurber), **Supp. I Part 2:** 616

Canfield, Cass, **Supp. I Part 2:** 668

Canfield, Dorothy, **Retro. Supp. I:** 4, 11, 14, 18; **Supp. XX: 39.** *See also* Fisher, Dorothy Canfield

Can Grande's Castle (Lowell), **II:** 518, 524

"Canicula di Anna" (Carson), **Supp. XII: 101–102**

"Can I Get You Anything?" (Carver and Gallagher), **Supp. XXIV:** 178

"Canis Major" (Frost), **Retro. Supp. I:** 137

"Canned Stuff" (Pickering), **Supp. XXI:** 198

Cannery Row (Steinbeck), **IV:** 50, 51, 64–65, 66, 68

Cannibal Galaxy, The (Ozick), **Supp. V:** 270

Cannibals and Christians (Mailer), **III:** 38–39, 40, 42; **Retro. Supp. II:** 203, 204, 205; **Supp. XXIV:** 281

Canning, George, **I:** 7, 8

Canning, Richard, **Supp. X:** 147

Cannon, Jimmy, **II:** 424

Cannon, Steve, **Retro. Supp. II:** 111

Cannon between My Knees, A (Gunn Allen), **Supp. IV Part 1:** 324

Canolle, Jean, **Supp. XVI:** 194

"Canonization, The" (Donne), **Supp. XIV:** 8

"Can Poetry Matter?" (Gioia), **Supp. XV:** 113, 114

Can Poetry Matter?: Essays on Poetry and American Culture (Gioia), **Supp. XV:** 112, **113–115**

"Canso" (Merwin), **Supp. III Part 1:** 344

Can Such Things Be? (Bierce), **I:** 203, 204, 205, 209

Canterbury Tales (Chaucer), **II:** 504; **III:** 411; **IV:** 65

Canterbury Tales, The (Chaucer), **Supp. XIX:** 4

"Canticle of Her Coming and Going" (Espaillat), **Supp. XXI:** 106

"Canto Amor" (Berryman), **I:** 173

Canto I (Pound), **III:** 469, 470; **Retro. Supp. I:** 286

Canto II (Pound), **III:** 470

Canto III (Pound), **III:** 470

Canto IV (Pound), **III:** 470

Canto VIII (Pound), **III:** 472

Canto IX (Pound), **III:** 472

Canto X (Pound), **III:** 472

Canto XIII (Pound), **III:** 472

Canto XXXIX (Pound), **III:** 468

Canto LXV (Pound), **Retro. Supp. I:** 292

Canto LXXXI (Pound), **III:** 459; **Retro. Supp. I:** 293

Cantor, Lois, **Supp. IV Part 1:** 285

Cantos (Pound), **I:** 482; **III:** 13–14, 17, 457, 462, 463, 466, 467, 469–470, 472–473, 474, 475, 476, 492; **Retro. Supp. I:** 284, 292, **292–293,** 293, 427; **Supp. I Part 1:** 272; **Supp. II Part 1:** 5; **Supp. II Part 2:** 420, 557, 564, 644; **Supp. IV Part 1:** 153; **Supp. V:** 343, 345; **Supp. VIII:** 305; **Supp. XIV:** 55, 96; **Supp. XV:** 349

"Cantus Planis" (Pound), **III:** 466

Cantwell, Robert, **Retro. Supp. I:** 85; **Supp. VIII:** 96; **Supp. XIII:** 292

Can Women Be Gentlemen? (Atherton), **Supp. XXIV:** 20–21, 30

"Canyon de Chelly, Return, 1978"(Kenny), **Supp. XXIII:** 155

"Can You Carry Me" (O'Hara), **III:** 369

Can You See Me Yet? (Findley), **Supp. XX: 52–53**

Canzoneri, Robert, **IV:** 114, 116

Canzoni (Pound), **Retro. Supp. I:** 286, 288, 413

"Cap" (Shaw), **Supp. IV Part 1:** 345

"Cape Breton" (Bishop), **Supp. I Part 1:** 92; **Supp. IX:** 45

Cape Cod (Thoreau), **II:** 540

"Cape Cod, Rome, and Jerusalem" (Chapman), **Supp. XIV:** 55

Capital City (Sandoz), **Supp. XXIV:** 244, **252–253,** 255
Capitalism: The Unknown Ideal (Rand), **Supp. IV Part 2:** 518, 527, 531, 532
Caponi, Gena Dagel, **Supp. IV Part 1:** 95
Capote, Truman, **Supp. I Part 1:** 291, 292; **Supp. III Part 1: 111–133; Supp. III Part 2:** 574; **Supp. IV Part 1:** 198, 220; **Supp. VIII:** 105; **Supp. XII:** 43, 249; **Supp. XV:** 146; **Supp. XVI:** 245–246; **Supp. XVII:** 236
Capouya, Emile, **Supp. I Part 1:** 50
Cappetti, Carla, **Supp. IX:** 4, 8
Capra, Frank, **Supp. XVI:** 102
Capra, Fritjof, **Supp. X:** 261
"Capricious Gardens" (Eugenides), **Supp. XXIV:** 133–134
Capron, Marion, **Supp. IX:** 193
"Capsule History of Conservation, A" (Stegner), **Supp. IV Part 2:** 600
"Captain Carpenter" (Ransom), **III:** 491
Captain Craig (Robinson), **III:** 508, 523; **Supp. II Part 1:** 192
"Captain Jim's Friend" (Harte), **Supp. II Part 1:** 337
"Captain Jones's Invitation" (Freneau), **Supp. II Part 1:** 261
"Captain's Son, The" (Taylor), **Supp. V:** 314, 325, 327
"Captain's Wife, The" (Salter), **Supp. IX:** 261
"Capt Christopher Levett (of York)" (Olson), **Supp. II Part 2:** 576, 577
Captive Israel (Reznikoff), **Supp. XIV:** 283
"Captivity and Restoration of Mrs. Mary Rowlandson, The" (Howe), **Supp. IV Part 2:** 419, 431, 434
"Captivity of the Fly" (MacLeish), **III:** 19
"Captured Goddess, The" (Lowell), **II:** 520
Caputi, Jane, **Supp. IV Part 1:** 334, 335
Caputo, Philip, **Supp. XI:** 234; **Supp. XIX: 17–31; Supp. XXII:** 104
Capuzzo, Michael, **Supp. XIII:** 254
Car (Crews), **Supp. XI: 110–111**
Carabi, Angels, **Supp. VIII:** 223; **Supp. XII:** 215
"Caramels" (Zinberg), **Supp. XV:** 195
"Caravaggio: Swirl & Vortex" (Levis), **Supp. XI:** 258, 269
Caravan (Bynner), **Supp. XV:** 50
Carby, Hazel B., **Supp. IV Part 1:** 13; **Supp. XXI:** 171
"Carcassonne" (Faulkner), **Retro. Supp. I:** 81
Card, Antha E., **Supp. I Part 2:** 496
Cárdenas, Lupe, **Supp. IV Part 2:** 538, 539, 540
Cardinale, Anthony, **Supp. XVII:** 239
Cardinale, Ernesto, **Supp. XII:** 225
"Cardinal Ideograms" (Swenson), **Supp. IV Part 2:** 645
"Cards" (Beattie), **Supp. V:** 31
"Career Woman" (Hay), **Supp. XIV:** 131
Carefree (film, Sandrich), **Supp. XVII:** 59
"Careful" (Carver), **Supp. III Part 1:** 138

Careful and Strict Enquiry into the Modern Prevailing Notions of That Freedom of Will, Which Is Supposed to be Essential to Moral Agency, Vertue and Vice, Reward and Punishment, Praise and Blame, A (Edwards), **I:** 549, 557, 558, 562
Carel: A Poem and Pilgrimage in the Holy Land (Melville), **III:** 92–93
Careless Love and Its Apostrophes (Bronk), **Supp. XXI:** 32
"Carentan O Carentan" (Simpson), **Supp. IX:** 267
Carew, Thomas, **IV:** 453
Carey, Gary, **Supp. XVI:** 186
Carey, Lynn, **Supp. XXIII:** 273
Carey, Mathew, **Supp. XV:** 238
"Car Games" (Conroy), **Supp. XVI:** 72
Cargill, Oscar, **Supp. II Part 1:** 117
Caribbean as Columbus Saw It (Morison and Obregon), **Supp. I Part 2:** 488
"Caribou Kitchen" (A. Finch), **Supp. XVII:** 76–77
Caribou Rising: Defending the Porcupine Herd, Gwich-'in Culture, and the Arctic National Wildlife Refuge (Bass), **Supp. XVI:** 27–28, 28
"Caring for the World"(Schott), **Supp. XXIII:** 249–250
Carl, K. A., **III:** 475
Carleton, George W., **Supp. XVIII:** 4
Carlin, George, **Supp. XXI:** 51
Carlin, Terry, **Supp. XXI:** 4, 5, 14
Carlisle, Harry, **Supp. XVIII:** 223, 233
Carl Krinken: His Christmas Stocking (S. and A. Warner), **Supp. XVIII:** 264
"Carlos Who Died, and Left Only This, The" (Ríos), **Supp. IV Part 2:** 547
Carlotta (empress of Mexico), **Supp. I Part 2:** 457
Carl Sandburg (Golden), **III:** 579
Carlson, Susan L., **Supp. XV:** 323
Carlyle, Thomas, **I:** 103, 279; **II:** 5, 7, 11, 15–16, 17, 20, 145, 315; **III:** 82, 84, 85, 87; **IV:** 169, 182, 338, 350; **Retro. Supp. I:** 360, 408; **Supp. I Part 1:** 2, 349; **Supp. I Part 2:** 410, 422, 482, 485, 552
"Carma" (Toomer), **Supp. III Part 2:** 481–483; **Supp. IX:** 312–313
"Carmen de Boheme" (Crane), **I:** 384
Carmen Jones (film), **Supp. I Part 1:** 66
Carmina Burana, **Supp. X:** 63
Carmon, Walt, **Supp. XXII:** 277
Carnegie, Andrew, **I:** 483; **IV:** 192; **Supp. I Part 2:** 639, 644; **Supp. V:** 285
Carnegie, Dale, **Supp. I Part 2:** 608
"Carnegie Hall: Rescued" (Moore), **III:** 215
Carne-Ross, Donald S., **Supp. I Part 1:** 268, 269; **Supp. XXIV:** 153
Carnes, Mark C., **Supp. X:** 14
"Carnets" poems (Sobin), **Supp. XVI:** 286–287
Carnovsky, Morris, **III:** 154
"Carol for Carolyn, A" (A. Finch), **Supp. XVII:** 74, 75
Caroling Dusk: An Anthology of Verse by Negro Poets (Cullen), **Supp. IV Part 1:** 166, 169

"Carol of Occupations" (Whitman), **I:** 486
"Carolyn Kizer and the Chain of Women" (A. Finch), **Supp. XVII:** 74–75
Carolyn Kizer: Perspectives on Her Life and Work (A. Finch), **Supp. XVII: 74–75**
"Carpe Diem" (Frost), **Supp. XII:** 303
"Carpe Noctem, if You Can" (Thurber), **Supp. I Part 2:** 620
Carpenter, Dan, **Supp. V:** 250
Carpenter, David, **Supp. VIII:** 297
Carpenter, Edward, **Supp. XX: 230**
Carpenter, Frederic I., **II:** 20
"Carpenter Bee" (Trethewey), **Supp. XXI:** 250
Carpentered Hen and Other Tame Creatures, The (Updike), **IV:** 214; **Retro. Supp. I:** 320
Carpenter's Gothic (Gaddis), **Supp. IV Part 1:** 288, 289–291, 293, 294
Carr, Dennis W., **Supp. IV Part 2:** 560
Carr, Elias, **Supp. XIV:** 57
Carr, Rosemary. *See* Benét, Rosemary
Carrall, Aaron, **Supp. IV Part 2:** 499
Carrel, Alexis, **IV:** 240
"Carrell/Klee/and Cosmos's Groom" (Goldbarth), **Supp. XII:** 183
"Carriage from Sweden, A" (Moore), **III:** 212
Carrie (King), **Supp. V:** 137
Carried Away (Harrison), **Supp. VIII:** 39
Carrier of Ladders (Merwin), **Supp. III Part 1:** 339, 346, 350–352, 356, 357
"Carriers of the Dream Wheel" (Momaday), **Supp. IV Part 2:** 481
Carriers of the Dream Wheel: Contemporary Native American Poetry (Niatum, ed.), **Supp. IV Part 2:** 484, 505
Carrington, Carroll, **I:** 199
"Carrion Spring" (Stegner), **Supp. IV Part 2:** 604
Carroll, Charles, **Supp. I Part 2:** 525
Carroll, Lewis, **I:** 432; **II:** 431; **III:** 181; **Supp. I Part 1:** 44; **Supp. I Part 2:** 622, 656; **Supp. XVI:** 103
Carroll, Maureen P., **Supp. XXIV:** 177
"Carrots, Noses, Snow, Rose, Roses" (Gass), **Supp. VI:** 87
Carrouges, Michel, **Supp. IV Part 1:** 104
"Carrousel, The" (Rilke), **III:** 558
Carruth, Hayden, **Supp. IV Part 1:** 66; **Supp. VIII:** 39; **Supp. IX:** 291; **Supp. XIII:** 112; **Supp. XXII:** 273–274; **Supp. XVI: 45–61; Supp. XIX:** 1; **Supp. XXI:** 31; **Supp. XXIV:** 167
Carruth, Joe-Anne McLaughlin, **Supp. XVI:** 47
"Carry" (Hogan), **Supp. IV Part 1:** 412
"Carrying On" (Dunn), **Supp. XI:** 145
Cars of Cuba (García), **Supp. XI:** 190
Carson, Anne, **Supp. XII: 97–116; Supp. XV:** 252
Carson, Johnny, **Supp. IV Part 2:** 526
Carson, Rachel, **Supp. V:** 202; **Supp. IX: 19–36; Supp. X:** 99; **Supp. XVI:** 36
Carson, Tom, **Supp. XI:** 227
Cart, Michael, **Supp. X:** 12
Carter, Elliott, **Supp. III Part 1:** 21
Carter, Hodding, **Supp. XIV:** 2

Carter, Jared, **Supp. XVII:** 110

Carter, Jimmy, **Supp. I Part 2:** 638; **Supp. XIV:** 107

Carter, Marcia, **Supp. V:** 223

Carter, Mary, **Supp. IV Part 2:** 444

Carter, Paul, **Supp. XX: 77, 78**

Carter, Peter, **Supp. XVIII:** 267

Carter, Stephen, **Supp. XI:** 220

Cartesian Sonata and Other Novellas (Gass), **Supp. VI: 92–93**

Cartier, Jacques, **Supp. I Part 2:** 496, 497

Cartier-Bresson, Henri, **Supp. VIII:** 98

"Cartographies of Silence" (Rich), **Supp. I Part 2:** 571–572

"Cartography" (Espaillat), **Supp. XXI:** 107

Cartwright, Louis, **Supp. XIV:** 147, 149, 151

Carver, Raymond, **Supp. III Part 1: 135–151; Supp. IV Part 1:** 342; **Supp. V:** 22, 23, 220, 326; **Supp. VIII:** 15; **Supp. X:** 85, 167; **Supp. XI:** 26, 65, 116, 153; **Supp. XII:** 79, 139, 289, 294; **Supp. XIX:** 209; **Supp. XXI:** 36, 115, 116, 118, 119; **Supp. XXIII:** 289, 296; **Supp. XXIV:** 97, 166, 167, 173, 177–178

Carver: A Life in Poems (Nelson), **Supp. XVIII:** 171, 172, **181–182,** 183

Carville, James, **Supp. XXIV:** 282

Carving Hawk (Kenny), **Supp. XXIII:** 143, 150

Cary, Alice, **Retro. Supp. II:** 145; **Supp. XV:** 273; **Supp. XXII:** 206

Cary, Phoebe, **Supp. XV:** 273

Cary, Richard, **Retro. Supp. II:** 132, 137

"Casabianca" (Bishop), **Retro. Supp. II:** 42; **Supp. I Part 1:** 86

Casablanca (film), **Supp. VIII:** 61; **Supp. XV:** 14

Casanova: His Known and Unknown Life (Endore), **Supp. XVII:** 54

"Casa solariega, La" ("The Family Mansion") (Espaillat), **Supp. XXI:** 107

"Case Against Mist, The" (Halliday), **Supp. XIX:** 91

Case for West-Indian Self-Government, The (C. L. R. James), **Supp. XXI:** 159, 161

Case of Rape, A (C. Himes), **Supp. XVI:** 143

Case of the Crushed Petunias, The (T. Williams), **IV:** 381

Case of the Officers of Excise (Paine), **Supp. I Part 2:** 503–504

Casey, Helen Marie, **Supp. XXIII:** 246

Casey, John, **Supp. X:** 164

Cash, Arthur, **Supp. IV Part 1:** 299

Cashman, Nellie, **Supp. X:** 103

Casiero, Robert, **Supp. XIV:** 167

Casino Royale (film), **Supp. XI: 306–307**

Caskey, William, **Supp. XIV:** 166

"Cask of Amontillado, The" (Poe), **II:** 475; **III:** 413; **Retro. Supp. II:** 268, 269, 270, 273

Caso, Frank, **Supp. XVIII:** 95

Caspary, Vera, **Supp. XIX:** 78

Casper, Robert N., **Supp. XV:** 339, 347

Casper and His Friends (S. and A. Warner), **Supp. XVIII:** 264

Cassada (Salter), **Supp. IX: 251–252**

Cassada, Jackie, **Supp. XXIII:** 291

Cassady, Carolyn, **Supp. XIV:** 150

Cassady, Neal, **Supp. II Part 1:** 309, 311; **Supp. XIV:** 137, 144

"Cassandra Southwick" (Whittier), **Supp. I Part 2:** 693

Cassell, Verlin, **Supp. XI:** 315

Cassill, Ronald Verlin, **Supp. V:** 323; **Supp. XVIII:** 72; **Supp. XIX:** 266

Cassirer, Ernst, **I:** 265; **IV:** 87, 89

Cass Timberlane (Lewis), **II:** 455–456

Cast a Cold Eye (McCarthy), **II:** 566

Castaway (Cozzens), **I:** 363, 370, 374, 375, 379

"Caste in America" (Du Bois), **Supp. II Part 1:** 169

Castiglione, Baldassare, **I:** 279; **III:** 282

"Castilian" (Wylie), **Supp. I Part 2:** 714

Castillo, Ana, **Supp. XI:** 177; **Supp. XXIII:** 194

"Castle in Lynn, A" (McCarriston), **Supp. XIV:** 265, 268

"Castles and Distances" (Wilbur), **Supp. III Part 2:** 550

Castle Sinister (Marquand), **III:** 58

Cast of Thousands (Loos), **Supp. XVI:** 192, 193, 195

Castro, Fidel, **II:** 261, 434; **Supp. XX: 80**

Cast the First Stone (C. Himes), **Supp. XVI:** 135, 137–138

"Casual Incident, A" (Hemingway), **II:** 44

"Casualty Report" (Halliday), **Supp. XIX:** 85

Caswell, Michelle, **Supp. XXII:** 262

"Cat, The" (Matthews), **Supp. IX: 157–158**

Cat, You Better Come Home (Keillor), **Supp. XVI:** 177

"Catbird Seat, The" (Thurber), **Supp. I Part 2:** 623

"Catch" (Francis), **Supp. IX:** 82

Catch-22 (Heller), **III:** 558; **Supp. IV Part 1:** 379, 380, 381–382, 383, 384–386, 387, 390, 391, 392, 393, 394; **Supp. V:** 244, 248; **Supp. XII:** 167–168; **Supp. XXIII:** 100

Catcher in the Rye, The (Salinger), **I:** 493; **III:** 551, 552, 553–558, 567, 571; **Retro. Supp. I:** 102; **Retro. Supp. II:** 222, 249; **Supp. I Part 2:** 535; **Supp. V:** 119; **Supp. VIII:** 242; **Supp. XI:** 65; **Supp. XVII:** 2; **Supp. XXIII:** 100; **Supp. XXIV:** 133

"Catching Frogs" (Kenyon), **Supp. VII:** 170

Catching the Mermother (A. Finch), **Supp. XVII:** 72

catechism of d neoamerican hoodoo church (Reed), **Supp. X:** 240, 241

Catered Affair, The (film), **Supp. IV Part 2:** 683

"Cathay" (Goldbarth), **Supp. XII:** 185, 186

Cathay (Pound), **II:** 527; **Retro. Supp. I:** 289

Cathedral (Carver), **Supp. III Part 1:** 144–146; **Supp. XII:** 139

"Cathedral" (Carver), **Supp. III Part 1:** 144–145; **Supp. XXIV:** 177

Cathedral, The (Lowell), **Supp. I Part 2:** 407, 416–417

Cather, Willa, **I: 312–334,** 405; **II:** 51, 96, 177, 404, 412; **III:** 453; **IV:** 190; **Retro. Supp. I: 1–23,** 355, 382; **Retro. Supp. II:** 71, 136; **Supp. I Part 2:** 609, 719; **Supp. IV Part 1:** 31; **Supp. VIII:** 101, 102, 263; **Supp. X:** 103; **Supp. XIII:** 253; **Supp. XIV:** 112; **Supp. XV:** 40, 51; **Supp. XVI:** 226; **Supp. XVIII:** 207; **Supp. XIX:** 131; **Supp. XXIII:** 290; **Supp. XXIV:** 29, 30, 244

Catherine, Saint, **II:** 211

Catherine II, **Supp. I Part 2:** 433

Catholic Art and Culture (Watkin), **Retro. Supp. II:** 187

"Catholic Novelist in the Protestant South, The" (O'Connor), **Retro. Supp. II:** 223, 224

"Cathy Queen of Cats" (Cisneros), **Supp. VII:** 59

Cat Inside, The (Burroughs), **Supp. III Part 1:** 105

Cat in the Hat, The (Geisel), **Supp. XVI:** 106–107, 112

Cat in the Hat Come Back, The (Geisel), **Supp. XVI:** 107

"Cat in the Hat for President, The" (Coover), **Supp. V:** 44, 46–47

Cat in The Hat Songbook, The (Geisel), **Supp. XVI:** 104

Cato, **II:** 114, 117

Cat on a Hot Tin Roof (T. Williams), **II:** 190; **IV:** 380, 382, 383, 386, 387, 389, 390, 391, 394, 395, 397–398

"Cat People: What Dr. Seuss Really Taught Us" (Menand), **Supp. XVI:** 106

Cats and Dogs (Silver), **Supp. XXIV:** 265, 274

Cat's Cradle (Vonnegut), **Supp. II Part 2:** 758, 759, 767–768, 770, 771, 772; **Supp. V:** 1

Cat's Eye (Atwood), **Supp. XIII: 29–30**

Catskill Eagle, A (Parker), **Supp. XIX:** 185

"Cat's Meow, A" (Brodsky), **Supp. VIII:** 31

Cat's Quizzer, The (Geisel), **Supp. XVI:** 111

"Catterskill Falls" (Bryant), **Supp. I Part 1:** 160

"Cattle Car Complex" (T. Rosenbaum), **Supp. XVII:** 48

Cattlemen from the Rio Grande Across the Far Marias (Sandoz), **Supp. XXIV:** 244, **249–251,** 256

Catullus, **Supp. XII:** 2, 13, **112; Supp. XV:** 23, 27, 35, 36

Catullus, Gaius Valerius, **I:** 381; **Supp. I Part 1:** 261; **Supp. I Part 2:** 728

Catullus (Gai Catulli Veronensis Liber) (Zukofsky), **Supp. III Part 2:** 625,

627, 628, 629

"Catullus: *Carmina*" (Carson), **Supp. XII: 112**

"Catullus: Excrucior" (Bidart), *Supp. XV:* 32, 35

"Cat Walked Through the Casserole, The" (Nelson and Espeland), **Supp. XVIII: 181**

Cat Walked Through the Casserole and Other Poems for Children (Nelson and Espeland), **Supp. XVIII:** 181

"Cat Who Aspired to Higher Things, The" (X. J. Kennedy), **Supp. XV:** 163

"Caucasian Storms Harlem, The" (R. Fisher), **Supp. XIX:** 78

Caudwell, Christopher, **Supp. X:** 112; **Supp. XXII:** 284

"Caul, The" (Banks), **Supp. V:** 10–11

Cause for Wonder (Morris), **III:** 232–233

"Causerie" (Tate), **IV:** 129

Causes and Consequences (Chapman), **Supp. XIV:** 41, 49, 51

"Causes of American Discontents before 1768, The" (Franklin), **II:** 120

Causley, Charles, **Supp. XV:** 117

Cavafy, Constantine P., **Supp. IX:** 275; **Supp. XI:** 119, 123; **Supp. XXI:** 131; **Supp. XXIII:** 150

Cavalcade of America, The (radio program), **III:** 146

Cavalcanti (Pound, opera), **Retro. Supp. I:** 287

Cavalcanti, Guido, **I:** 579; **III:** 467; **Supp. III Part 2:** 620, 621, 622, 623

Cavalieri, Grace, **Supp. IV Part 2:** 630, 631

"Cavalry Crossing the Ford" (Whitman), **IV:** 347

"Cave, The" (Bass), **Supp. XVI:** 23

Cave, The (Warren), **IV:** 255–256

Cavelieri, Grace, **Supp. XXIII:** 135

Cavell, Stanley, **Retro. Supp. I:** 306–307, 309

Cavender's House (Robinson), **III:** 510

Caver, Christine, **Supp. XXI:** 215

Caves of Death, The (Atherton; Joshi, ed.), **Supp. XXIV:** 23

"Caviar" (Boyle), **Supp. XX: 19**

Caviare at the Funeral (Simpson), **Supp. IX:** 266, **276–277**

"Cawdor" (Jeffers), **Supp. II Part 2:** 431

Caxton, William, **III:** 486

Cayton, Horace, **IV:** 475, 488

Cazamian, Louis, **II:** 529

"Ceiling, The" (Brockmeier), **Supp. XXII:** 52–53

Celan, Paul, **Supp. X:** 149; **Supp. XII:** 21, 110–111; **Supp. XVI:** 284–285, 288; **Supp. XVII:** 241

"Celebrated Jumping Frog of Calaveras County, The" (Twain), **IV:** 196

Celebrated Jumping Frog of Calaveras County, The, and Other Sketches (Twain), **IV:** 197

Celebration (Crews), **Supp. XI:** 103, **108**

Celebration (Swados), **Supp. XIX:** 269–270

Celebration at Dark (W. J. Smith), **Supp. XIII:** 332

"Celebration for June 24th" (McGrath), **Supp. X:** 116

Celebration of the Sound Through (Sobin), **Supp. XVI:** 284–285

Celebrations after the Death of John Brennan (X. J. Kennedy), **Supp. XV:** 165

Celebrity (film; Allen), **Supp. XV:** 11

"Celebrity" (Pickering), **Supp. XXI:** 198

"Celery" (Stein), **IV:** 43

"Celestial Games" (Conroy), **Supp. XVI:** 72

"Celestial Globe" (Nemerov), **III:** 288

Celestial Navigation (Tyler), **Supp. IV Part 2:** 662–663, 671

"Celestial Railroad, The" (Hawthorne), **Retro. Supp. I:** 152; **Supp. I Part 1:** 188

Celibate Season, A (Shields), **Supp. VII:** 323, 324

Cellini (Shanley), **Supp. XIV:** 316, **329–330**

"Cemetery at Academy, California" (Levine), **Supp. V:** 182

Cemetery Nights (Dobyns), **Supp. XIII:** 85, 87, 89

"Censors As Critics: *To Kill a Mockingbird* As a Case Study" (May), **Supp. VIII:** 126

"Census-Taker, The" (Frost), **Retro. Supp. I:** 129

"Centaur, The" (Swenson), **Supp. IV Part 2:** 641

Centaur, The (Updike), **IV:** 214, 216, 217, 218, 219–221, 222; **Retro. Supp. I:** 318, 322, 324, 331, 336

"Centennial Meditation of Columbia, The" (Lanier), **Supp. I Part 1:** 362

Centeno, Agusto, **IV:** 375

"Centipede" (Dove), **Supp. IV Part 1:** 246

"Cento: A Note on Philosophy" (Berrigan), **Supp. XXIV:** 42–43

"Central Man, The" (Bloom), **Supp. IV Part 2:** 689

"Central Park" (Lowell), **II:** 552

Central Park (Wasserstein and Drattel), **Supp. XV:** 333

Central Park West (Allen), **Supp. XV:** 13

Century of Dishonor, A (Jackson), **Retro. Supp. I:** 31

"Cerebral Snapshot, The" (Theroux), **Supp. VIII:** 313

"Ceremonies" (Rukeyser), **Supp. VI:** 279

"Ceremony" (Monson), **Supp. XXIV:** 230

Ceremony (Silko), **Supp. IV Part 1:** 274, 333; **Supp. IV Part 2:** 557–558, 558–559, 559, 561–566, 570; **Supp. XVIII:** 59

Ceremony (Wilbur), **Supp. III Part 2:** 550–551

"Ceremony, The" (Harjo), **Supp. XII:** 230

"Ceremony, The—Anatomy of a Massacre" (E. Hoffman, play), **Supp. XVI:** 160

Ceremony in Lone Tree (Morris), **III:** 229–230, 232, 238, 558

Ceremony of Brotherhood, A (Anaya and Ortiz, eds.), **Supp. IV Part 2:** 502

Cerf, Bennett, **III:** 405; **IV:** 288; **Retro. Supp. II:** 330; **Supp. XIII:** 172; **Supp. XIX:** 244

"Certain Attention to the World, A" (Haines), **Supp. XII:** 201

"Certain Beasts, Like Cats" (Bronk), **Supp. XXI:** 30

Certain Distance, A (Francis), **Supp. IX:** 85

"Certain Music, A" (Rukeyser), **Supp. VI:** 273

Certain Noble Plays of Japan (Pound), **III:** 458

Certain People (Wharton), **Retro. Supp. I:** 382

"Certain Poets" (MacLeish), **III:** 4

Certain Slant of Sunlight, A (Berrigan), **Supp. XXIV:** 43

"Certain Testimony" (Bausch), **Supp. VII:** 48

Certificate, The (Singer), **IV:** 1; **Retro. Supp. II: 314–315**

"Cerulean" (Everett), **Supp. XVIII:** 66

Cervantes, Lorna Dee, **Supp. IV Part 2:** 545

Cervantes, Miguel de, **I:** 130, 134; **II:** 8, 272, 273, 276, 289, 302, 310, 315; **III:** 113, 614; **IV:** 367; **Retro. Supp. I:** 91; **Supp. I Part 2:** 406; **Supp. V:** 277; **Supp. XIII:** 17; **Supp. XXIII:** 4

Césaire, Aimé, **Supp. X:** 132, 139; **Supp. XIII:** 114

"Cesarean" (Kenyon), **Supp. VII:** 173

Cézanne, Paul, **II:** 576; **III:** 210; **IV:** 26, 31, 407; **Supp. V:** 333, 341–342; **Supp. XIX:** 36

Chabon, Michael, **Supp. XI: 63–81;** **Supp. XVI:** 259; **Supp. XIX:** 135, 138, 174, 223; **Supp. XX: 177;** **Supp. XXII:** 49; **Supp. XXIV:** 131

Chaboseau, Jean, **Supp. I Part 1:** 260

Chace, Bill, **Supp. XXI:** 256

Chagall, Marc, **Supp. XXIII:** 6

Chaikin, Joseph, **Supp. III Part 2:** 433, 436–437

"Chain, The" (Kumin), **Supp. IV Part 2:** 452

Chainbearer, The (Cooper), **I:** 351, 352–353

"Chain of Love, A" (Price), **Supp. VI: 258–259,** 260

Chain Saw Dance, The (Budbill), **Supp. XIX: 5–6**

Chains of Dew (Glaspell), **Supp. III Part 1:** 181

Chalk Face (W. Frank), **Supp. XX: 73–74**

Challacombe, Robert Hamilton, **III:** 176

Challenge (Untermeyer), **Supp. XV:** 296, 303

"Challenge" (Untermeyer), **Supp. XV:** 296

Chalmers, George, **Supp. I Part 2:** 514, 521

"Chambered Nautilus, The" (Holmes), **Supp. I Part 1:** 254, 307, 312–313, 314

Chamberlain, John, **Supp. I Part 2:** 647; **Supp. IV Part 2:** 525

Chamberlain, Neville, **II:** 589; **Supp. I Part 2:** 664

Chamber Music (Joyce), **III:** 16

Chambers, Richard, **Supp. III Part 2:** 610, 611, 612

Chambers, Whittaker, **Supp. III Part 2:** 610; **Supp. IV Part 2:** 526; **Supp. XV:** 143

Chameleon (C. Baxter), **Supp. XVII:** 14–15

"Champ, The" (Zinberg), **Supp. XV:** 193

"Champagne Regions" (Ríos), **Supp. IV Part 2:** 553

"Champion" (Lardner), **II:** 420–421, 428, 430

Champion, Laurie, **Supp. VIII:** 128

Champollion-Figeac, Jean Jacques, **IV:** 426

"Chance" (Doolittle), **Supp. I Part 1:** 271

Chance, Frank, **II:** 418

Chance Acquaintance, A (Howells), **II:** 278

"Chance Encounter, A" (Swados), **Supp. XIX:** 261, 262

"Chanclas" (Cisneros), **Supp. VII:** 61

Chandler, Raymond, **Supp. III Part 1:** 91; **Supp. IV Part 1: 119–138,** 341, 344, 345; **Supp. IV Part 2:** 461, 464, 469, 470, 471, 472, 473; **Supp. XI:** 160, 228; **Supp. XII:** 307; **Supp. XIII:** 159, 233; **Supp. XIV:** 21; **Supp. XV:** 119; **Supp. XVI:** 122; **Supp. XVII:** 137; **Supp. XVIII:** 136,137, 137–138; **Supp. XIX:** 178, 189; **Supp. XXI:** 67; **Supp. XXII:** 119; **Supp. XXIV:** 284

Chandler, Sherry, **Supp. XXIII:** 247

Chaney, "Professor" W. H., **II:** 463–464

Chang, Leslie C., **Supp. IV Part 1:** 72

"Change, The: Kyoto-Tokyo Express" (Ginsberg), **Supp. II Part 1:** 313, 329

Changed Man, A (Prose), **Supp. XVI:** 261–262

"Changeling" (Espaillat), **Supp. XXI:** 100

Changeling (Middleton), **Retro. Supp. I:** 62

"Changeling, The" (Lowell), **Supp. I Part 2:** 409

"Changeling, The" (Whittier), **Supp. I Part 2:** 697

Change of World, A (Rich), **Supp. I Part 2:** 551, 552

"Changes of Mind" (Baker), **Supp. XIII:** 52

"Changes of the Soul" (Taggard), **Supp. XXII:** 280

"Change the Joke and Slip the Yoke" (Ellison), **Retro. Supp. II:** 118

Change Your Bedding! (O'Hara), **Supp. XXIII:** 210

Changing Light at Sandover, The (Merrill), **Supp. III Part 1:** 318, 319, 323, 327, 332, 335–336; **Supp. XII:** 269–270; **Supp. XV:** 264

"Changing Same, The" (Baraka), **Supp. II Part 1:** 47, 51, 53

Changing the Bully Who Rules the World: Reading and Thinking about Ethics (C. Bly), **Supp. XVI:** 32, **39–40,** 41

Chanler, Mrs. Winthrop, **I:** 22; **IV:** 325

Channing, Carol, **IV:** 357

Channing, Edward, **Supp. I Part 2:** 479–480

Channing, Edward Tyrrel, **Supp. I Part 1:** 155; **Supp. I Part 2:** 422

Channing, William Ellery, **I:** 336; **II:** 224, 495; **IV:** 172, 173, 176, 177; **Retro. Supp. I:** 54; **Supp. I Part 1:** 103; **Supp. I Part 2:** 589; **Supp. XXIV: 67–81**

Channing, William Henry, **IV:** 178; **Supp. II Part 1:** 280, 285; **Supp. XXIV:** 68

Channing: The Reluctant Radical (Mendelsohn), **Supp. XXIV:** 72

Chanson de Roland, La, **I:** 13

"Chanson un Peu Naïve" (Bogan), **Supp. III Part 1:** 50–51

"Chanteuse" (Doty), **Supp. XI:** 119

"Chant for May Day" (Hughes), **Supp. I Part 1:** 331

Chants (Mora), **Supp. XIII: 214–215**

Chaos (Dove), **Supp. IV Part 1:** 243

"Chaperone, The" (Van Vechten), **Supp. II Part 2:** 728

Chaplin, Charles Spencer "Charlie," **I:** 27, 32, 43, 386, 447; **III:** 403; **Supp. I Part 2:** 607; **Supp. IV Part 1:** 146; **Supp. IV Part 2:** 574; **Supp. XX:** 75; **Supp. XXI:** 170; **Supp. XXII:** 25, 26

"Chaplinesque" (H. Crane), **Retro. Supp. II:** 79

"Chapman" (Rukeyser), **Supp. VI:** 273

Chapman, Abraham, **IV:** 485

Chapman, George, **Supp. I Part 2:** 422

Chapman, John (Johnny Appleseed), **Supp. I Part 2:** 397

Chapman, John Jay, **IV:** 436; **Supp. XIV: 39–56**

Chapman, Stephen, **Supp. XIII:** 12

Chappell, Fred, **Supp. IV Part 1:** 69; **Supp. XI:** 317; **Supp. XVIII:** 87

Chapters in a Mythology: The Poetry of Sylvia Plath (Kroll), **Supp. I Part 2:** 541–543

Chapters on Erie (Adams and Adams), **Supp. I Part 2:** 644

Chapter Two (Simon), **Supp. IV Part 2:** 575, 586

"Chapter VI" (Hemingway), **II:** 252

Char, René, **Supp. XVI:** 282; **Supp. XVII:** 244

"Character" (Emerson), **II:** 6

"Character of Aboriginal Historical Tradition"(J. Schoolcraft), **Supp. XXIII:** 228–229

"Character of Presidents, The" (Doctorow), **Supp. IV Part 1:** 224

"Character of Socrates, The" (Emerson), **II:** 8–9

Character of the Poet, The (Simpson), **Supp. IX:** 273, 275, 278

"Characters in Fiction" (McCarthy), **II:** 562

"Charades" (Moore), **Supp. X:** 178

"Charge It" (Fante), **Supp. XI:** 164–165

Chariot in the Sky: A Story of the Jubilee Singers (Bontemps), **Supp. XXII:** 6, 13

"Charity" (Peacock), **Supp. XIX:** 221–222

Charity (Richard), **Supp. XIX: 220–222**

Charlatan, The (Singer), **IV:** 1

"Charles" (Jackson), **Supp. IX:** 125

Charles, Larry, **Supp. XVIII:** 21

"Charles Baxter, August Kleinzahler, Adrienne Rich: Contemporary Stevensians and the Problem of 'Other Lives' " (S. Burt), **Supp. XVII:** 18–19

Charles Goodnight: Cowman and Plainsman (Haley), **Supp. V:** 226

Charles Simic: Essays on the Poetry (Weigl), **Supp. VIII:** 269

Charles the Bold, Duke of Burgundy, **III:** 487

Charleville, Victoria Verdon, **Supp. I Part 1:** 200–201, 205, 206, 210

Charley's Aunt (B. Thomas), **II:** 138

Charlie Chan Is Dead: An Anthology of Contemporary Asian American Fiction (Hagedorn), **Supp. X:** 292

"Charlie Christian Story, The" (Ellison), **Retro. Supp. II:** 121

"Charlie Howard's Descent" (Doty), **Supp. XI:** 122

Charlotte: A Tale of Truth (Rowson), **Supp. I Part 1:** 128; **Supp. XV: 234–235,** 238. *See also Charlotte Temple* (Rowson)

Charlotte's Daughter; or, The Three Orphans (Rowson), **Supp. XV: 246**

Charlotte's Web (White), **Supp. I Part 2:** 655, 656, 658, 667, 670

Charlotte Temple (Rowson), **Supp. XV:** 229, **238–239.** *See also Charlotte: A Tale of Truth* (Rowson)

Charm, The (Creeley), **Supp. IV Part 1:** 139, 141, 144, 149–150

Charmed Life, A (McCarthy), **II:** 571–574

Charming Billy (McDermott), **Supp. XVIII:** 155, **162–164,** 166

Charms for the Easy Life (Gibbons), **Supp. X:** 45, **47–48**

Charnel Rose, The (Aiken), **I:** 50, 57, 62

Charney, Samuel, **Supp. XXIII:** 6

Charon's Cosmology (Simic), **Supp. VIII: 276–278**

Charterhouse, The (Percy), **Supp. III Part 1:** 388

Chart for Rough Water (W. Frank), **Supp. XX: 78**

Charvat, William, **II:** 244

Charyn, Jerome, **Supp. XVII:** 5

Chase, Mary Ellen, **Retro. Supp. II:** 243, 245; **Supp. XXIV:** 30

Chase, Richard, **IV:** 202, 443; **Retro. Supp. I:** 40, 395

Chase, Salmon P., **Supp. I Part 2:** 584

Chase, Stuart, **Supp. I Part 2:** 609

Chase, The (Foote), **Supp. I Part 1:** 281

Chasing the Dime (Connelly), **Supp. XXI:** 74

"Chaste Land, The" (Tate), **IV:** 122

Château, The (Maxwell), **Supp. VIII:** 152, 160, **165–167,** 168, 169

Chatham, Russell, **Supp. VIII:** 40

"Chattanooga Nights" (L. Brown), **Supp. XXI:** 39

Chatterdon, The Black Death, and Meri-wether Lewis (Reznikoff), **Supp. XIV:** 288

Chatterton, Thomas, **Supp. I Part 1:** 349; **Supp. I Part 2:** 410, 716

Chatterton, Wayne, **Supp. IX:** 2, 4, 11–12

"Chatty Letters During a Journey from Aruba to Rio" (Thompson), **Supp. XXIV:** 282

Chatwin, Bruce, **Supp. VIII:** 322

Chaucer, Geoffrey, **I:** 131; **II:** 11, 504, 516, 542, 543; **III:** 283, 411, 473, 492, 521; **Retro. Supp. I:** 135, 426; **Supp. I Part 1:** 356, 363; **Supp. I Part 2:** 422, 617; **Supp. V:** 259; **Supp. XII:** 197; **Supp. XVII:** 70; **Supp. XIX:** 4

Chauncy, Charles, **I:** 546–547; **IV:** 147

Chavez, César, **Supp. V:** 199

Chávez, Denise, **Supp. IV Part 2:** 544; **Supp. XI:** 316

Chavez, Lydia, **Supp. VIII:** 75

Chavkin, Allan, **Supp. IV Part 1:** 259

Chavkin, Nancy Feyl, **Supp. IV Part 1:** 259

Chawla, Louise, **Supp. XXI:** 24

Chayefsky, Paddy, **Supp. XI:** 306

Cheang, Shu Lea, **Supp. XI:** 20

"Cheater's Guide To Love, The" (Díaz), **Supp. XXIV:** 84, 92, 93

"Cheat Takes Over" (Leopold), **Supp. XIV:** 189

"Cheers" (Carver), **Supp. III Part 1:** 138

Cheetham, James, **Supp. I Part 2:** 521

Cheever, Benjamin Hale, **Supp. I Part 1:** 175; **Supp. XXIV:** 97

Cheever, David W., **Supp. I Part 1:** 304

Cheever, Ezekiel, **Supp. I Part 1:** 174, 193

Cheever, Federico, **Supp. I Part 1:** 175

Cheever, Fred, **Supp. I Part 1:** 174

Cheever, Frederick L., **Supp. I Part 1:** 174

Cheever, John, **Retro. Supp. I:** 116, 333, 335; **Supp. I Part 1:** 174–199; **Supp. V:** 23, 95; **Supp. VIII:** 151; **Supp. IX:** 114, 208; **Supp. XI:** 65, 66, 99; **Supp. XII:** 140; **Supp. XIV:** 93; **Supp. XV:** 119, 142; **Supp. XXIII:** 104, 109, 275

Cheever, Mrs. John (Mary Winternitz), **Supp. I Part 1:** 175

Cheever, Mary Liley, **Supp. I Part 1:** 174

Cheever, Susan. *See* Cowley, Susan Cheever (Susan Cheever)

Cheever Evening, A (Gurney), **Supp. V:** 95

Chekhov, Anton, **I:** 52, 90; **II:** 27, 38, 44, 49, 198, 542; **III:** 362, 467; **IV:** 17, 53, 359, 446; **Retro. Supp. I:** 5, 355; **Retro. Supp. II:** 299; **Supp. I Part 1:** 196; **Supp. II Part 1:** 6; **Supp. IV Part 2:** 585; **Supp. V:** 265; **Supp. VIII:** 153, 332; **Supp. IX:** 260, 265, 274; **Supp. XI:** 66; **Supp. XII:** 94, 307; **Supp. XIII:** 79; **Supp. XIV:** 87, 242; **Supp. XV:** 320, 329; **Supp. XVIII:** 102; **Supp. XIX:** 172, 241; **Supp. XXII:** 60; **Supp. XXIII:** 162, 290

"Chekhov's Sense of Writing as Seen Through His Letters" (Dobyns), **Supp.**

XIII: 77–78

"Chemin de Fer" (Bishop), **Retro. Supp. II:** 41; **Supp. I Part 1:** 80, 85, 86

Cheney, Brainard, **Retro. Supp. II:** 229

Cheney, Matthew, **Supp. XXII:** 50

Chenzira, Ayoka, **Supp. XI:** 19

Chéri (Colette; stage adaptation, Loos), **Supp. XVI:** 194

Cherkovski, Neeli, **Supp. XII:** 118, 132, 134

Chernyshevski, Nikolai, **III:** 261, 262, 263; **Retro. Supp. I:** 269

Cherokee Lottery, The: A Sequence of Poems (W. J. Smith), **Supp. XIII:** 340–344

"Cherríe Moraga's Radical Revision of *Death of a Salesman*"(Wiley), **Supp. XXIII:** 199

Cherry (Karr), **Supp. XI:** 239, **251–254**

"Cherrylog Road" (Dickey), **Supp. XVIII:** 191

Cherry Orchard, The (Chekhov), **IV:** 359, 426; **Supp. VIII:** 153

Cheslock, Louis, **III:** 99, 118, 119

Chesnutt, Charles Waddell, **Supp. II Part 1:** 174, 193, 211; **Supp. IV Part 1:** 257; **Supp. XIV: 57–78**

"Chess House, The" (Dixon), **Supp. XII:** 139

Chessman, Caryl, **Supp. I Part 2:** 446

Chester, Alfred, **Retro. Supp. II:** 111, 112; **Supp. X:** 192

Chesterfield, Lord, **II:** 36

Chesterton, Gilbert Keith, **I:** 226; **IV:** 432

Cheuse, Alan, **Supp. IV Part 2:** 570

Chevigny, Bell Gale, **Supp. XI:** 283

Cheyenne Autumn (Sandoz), **Supp. XXIII:** 146; **Supp. XXIV:** 244, 248, 256, **258–260**

"Chicago" (Sandburg), **III:** 581, 592, 596; **Supp. III Part 1:** 71

Chicago (Shepard), **Supp. III Part 2:** 439

Chicago: City on the Make (Algren), **Supp. IX:** 1, 3

"*Chicago Defender* Sends a Man to Little Rock, The" (Brooks), **Supp. III Part 1:** 80–81

"Chicago Hamlet, A" (Anderson), **I:** 112

Chicago Loop (Theroux), **Supp. VIII:** 324

"Chicago Picasso, The" (Brooks), **Supp. III Part 1:** 70–71, 84

Chicago Poems (Sandburg), **III:** 579, 581–583, 586

"Chicano/Borderlands Literature and Poetry" (Ríos), **Supp. IV Part 2:** 537, 538, 542, 545

Chick, Nancy, **Supp. IV Part 1:** 1

"Chickamauga" (Bierce), **I:** 201

"Chickamauga" (Wolfe), **IV:** 460

Chickamauga (Wright), **Supp. V:** 333, 343–344

"Chickamauga" (Wright), **Supp. V:** 334

"Chicken Market" (Skloot), **Supp. XX: 198, 200**

"Chiefly about War Matters" (Hawthorne), **II:** 227; **Retro. Supp. I:** 165

"Chiffon" (Hull), **Supp. XXI:** 138

"Child" (Plath), **Supp. I Part 2:** 544

Child, Greg, **Supp. XVIII:** 107

Child, Julia, **Supp. XVII:** 89, 90

Child, Lydia Maria, **Supp. XIII:** 141; **Supp. XVIII:** 11

"Child, The" (Ríos), **Supp. IV Part 2:** 543

"Child by Tiger, The" (Wolfe), **IV:** 451

"Childhood" (Wright), **Supp. V:** 341

Childhood, A: The Biography of a Place (Crews), **Supp. XI:** 102–103, 245

"Childhood, When You Are in It . . ." (Kenyon), **Supp. VII:** 160, 170

Childhood and Other Neighborhoods (Dybek), **Supp. XXIII:** 68, **69–70**

"Childhood Sketch" (Wright), **Supp. III Part 2:** 589

"Child Is Born, A" (Benét), **Supp. XI:** 46

"Child Is the Meaning of This Life, The" (Schwartz), **Supp. II Part 2:** 659–660

"Childlessness" (Merrill), **Supp. III Part 1:** 323

"Childless Woman" (Plath), **Supp. I Part 2:** 544

Child-Life (Whittier and Larcom, eds.), **Supp. XIII:** 142

Child-Life in Prose (Whittier and Larcom, eds.), **Supp. XIII:** 142

Childlike Life of the Black Tarantula, The (Acker), **Supp. XII:** 4, 6, **7–8**

"Child Margaret" (Sandburg), **III:** 584

"Child of Courts, The" (Jarrell), **II:** 378, 379, 381

Child of God (McCarthy), **Supp. VIII: 177–178**

Child of My Heart (McDermott), **Supp. XVIII:** 155, **164–166**

"CHILD OF THE THIRTIES" (Baraka), **Supp. II Part 1:** 60

"Child on Top of a Greenhouse" (Roethke), **III:** 531

Children (Gurney), **Supp. V:** 95, 96

"Children" (Stowe), **Supp. I Part 2:** 587

"Children, The" (Jarman), **Supp. XVII:** 116

Children, The (Wharton), **IV:** 321, 326; **Retro. Supp. I:** 381

"Children, the Sandbar, That Summer" (Rukeyser), **Supp. VI:** 274

Children and Others (Cozzens), **I:** 374

Children Is All (Purdy), **Supp. VII:** 277, 278, 282

"Children of Adam" (Whitman), **IV:** 342; **Retro. Supp. I:** 403, 405

Children of Job, The: American Second-Generation Witnesses to the Holocaust (A. Berger), **Supp. XVII:** 39

Children of Light (Stone), **Supp. V:** 304–306

Children of Light and the Children of Darkness, The (Niebuhr), **III:** 292, 306, 310

Children of the Frost (London), **II:** 469, 483

Children of the Holocaust (H. Epstein), **Supp. XVII:** 48; **Supp. XXII:** 95

"Children of the Lord's Supper, The" (Tegnér), **Retro. Supp. II:** 155, 157

Children of the Market Place (Masters), **Supp. I Part 2:** 471

"Children on Their Birthdays" (Capote), **Supp. III Part 1:** 114, 115

Children Playing Before a Statue of Hercules (Sedaris, ed.), **Supp. XXIII:** 289

"Children Selecting Books in a Library" (Jarrell), **II:** 371

Children's Hour, The (Hellman), **Supp. I Part 1:** 276–277, 281, 286, 297

"Children's Rhymes" (Hughes), **Supp. I Part 1:** 340

Childress, Mark, **Supp. X:** 89

Child's Garden of Verses, A (Stevenson), **Supp. IV Part 1:** 298, 314; **Supp. XIII:** 75

"Child's Nature, A" (Jin), **Supp. XVIII:** 93

"Child's Reminiscence, A" (Whitman), **IV:** 344

Childwold (Oates), **Supp. II Part 2:** 519–520

Chile Woman (G. Jones), **Supp. XXIV:** 185

Chill, The (Macdonald), **Supp. IV Part 2:** 473

Chills and Fever (Ransom), **III:** 490, 491–492, 493

Chilly Scenes of Winter (Beattie), **Supp. V:** 21, 22, 23, 24, 26, 27

Chime of Words, A: The Letters of Logan Pearsall Smith (Tribble, ed.), **Supp. XIV:** 348–349

Chimera (C. Frost), **Supp. XV:** 94, 95, 100

"Chimes for Yahya" (Merrill), **Supp. III Part 1:** 329

Chin, Frank, **Supp. V:** 164, 172

Chin, Mei, **Supp. XVIII:** 95

"China" (Johnson), **Supp. VI: 193–194**

Chinaberry Tree, The (Fauset), **Supp. XIX:** 73

"Chinaman's Hat" (Kingston), **Supp. V:** 169

China Men (Kingston), **Supp. V:** 157, 158, 159, 160, 161, 164–169; **Supp. X:** 292; **Supp. XV:** 220

"China Poet, The" (Sturgis), **Supp. XX: 233, 240**

China Trace (Wright), **Supp. V:** 332, 340, 341, 342

"Chinese Apples" (Di Piero), **Supp. XIX:** 40

Chinese Apples: New and Selected Poems (Di Piero), **Supp. XIX:** 33, 36, 37, 38, 39, 40, 44, 45, 46, 47–48

Chinese Classics (Legge), **III:** 472

Chinese Materia Medica (P. Smith), **III:** 572

"Chinese New Year" (Hull), **Supp. XXI:** 135

"Chinese Nightingale, The" (Lindsay), **Supp. I Part 2:** 392–393, 394

Chinese Nightingale and Other Poems, The (Lindsay), **Supp. I Part 2:** 392

Chinese Siamese Cat, The (Tan), **Supp. X:** 289

Chinese Translations, The (Bynner), **Supp. XV:** 47, 52

Chinitz, David, **Supp. XV:** 180, 185

"Chinoiseries" (Lowell), **II:** 524–525

Chip (Untermeyer), **Supp. XV:** 310

Chirico, Giorgio de, **Supp. III Part 1:** 14

Chirico, Miriam M., **Supp. XV:** 323

"Chiron" (Winters), **Supp. II Part 2:** 801

"Chitlins at the Waldorf" (Crouch), **Supp. XIX:** 158

"Chloroform Jags" (J. Scott), **Supp. XVII:** 189

Chodorov, Jerome, **IV:** 274

"Choice, The" (Karr), **Supp. XI:** 251

"Choice of Accommodations, A" (Lahiri), **Supp. XXI:** 183

"Choice of Profession, A" (Malamud), **Supp. I Part 2:** 437

Choice of Wars, A (Shaw), **Supp. XIX:** 245

"Choices" (Gallagher), **Supp. XXIV:** 171

Chomei, Kamo No, **IV:** 170, 171, 184

Chomsky, Noam, **Supp. IV Part 2:** 679

Choosing not Choosing (Cameron), **Retro. Supp. I:** 43

Chopin, Felix, **Supp. I Part 1:** 202

Chopin, Frédéric, **Supp. I Part 1:** 363

Chopin, Jean, **Supp. I Part 1:** 206

Chopin, Kate, **II:** 276; **Retro. Supp. I:** 10, 215; **Retro. Supp. II: 57–74;** **Supp. I Part 1: 200–226; Supp. V:** 304; **Supp. X:** 227; **Supp. XVIII:** 194

"Chopin in Winter"(Dybek), **Supp. XXIII:** 72

"Choral: The Pink Church" (W. C. Williams), **Retro. Supp. I:** 428

"Chord" (Merwin), **Supp. III Part 1:** 356

"Chord"(Dybek), **Supp. XXIII:** 78

"Chords and Dischords" (column; Untermeyer), **Supp. XV:** 294

"Chorus, The"(Hadas), **Supp. XXIII:** 119–120

Choruses from Iphigenia in Aulis (Doolittle, trans.), **Supp. I Part 1:** 257, 268, 269

"Chosen Blindness" (Karr), **Supp. XI:** 251

Chosen Country (Dos Passos), **I:** 475, 490–491

Chosen Place, The Timeless People, The (Marshall), **Supp. XI:** 275, 276, **282–284**

Chosŏn (Lowell), **II:** 513

Choukri, Mohamed, **Supp. IV Part 1:** 92

Chovteau, Mane Thérèse, **Supp. I Part 1:** 205

Chris Durang and Dawne (Durang), **Supp. XXIV:** 113, 124

"ChrisEaster" (Peacock), **Supp. XIX:** 198, 199

Chrisman, Robert, **Supp. IV Part 1:** 1

Christabel (Coleridge), **Supp. IV Part 2:** 465

"Christ for Sale" (Lowell), **II:** 538

Christian, Graham, **Supp. XII:** 193

Christian Dictionary, A (Wilson), **IV:** 153

"Christian in World Crisis, The" (Merton), **Supp. VIII:** 203

Christianity and Power Politics (Niebuhr), **III:** 292, 303

"Christianity and the Survival of Creation" (Berry), **Supp. X:** 30

Christianity of Sholem Asch, The: An Appraisal from the Jewish Viewpoint (Lieberman), **Supp. XXIII:** 3, 7

"Christian Minister, The" (Emerson), **II:** 10

Christian Philosopher, The (Mather), **Supp. II Part 2:** 463–464

Christian Realism and Practical Problems (Niebuhr), **III:** 292, 308

"Christian Roommates, The" (Updike), **IV:** 226–227; **Retro. Supp. I:** 319, 323

Christiansen, Carrie, **I:** 210

Christian's Secret of a Happy Life, The (H. W. Smith), **Supp. XIV:** 333–334

Christie, Agatha, **Supp. IV Part 1:** 341; **Supp. IV Part 2:** 469

Christ in Concrete (di Donato), **Supp. XX: 33, 34–40, 42, 43, 46**

"Christ in Concrete" (di Donato), **Supp. XX:** 34

Christine (King), **Supp. V:** 139, 148

"Christ Light, The" (Chopin), **Retro. Supp. II:** 61

"Christmas" (Saunders), **Supp. XIX:** 232

"Christmas, or the Good Fairy" (Stowe), **Supp. I Part 2:** 586

"Christmas 1944" (Levertov), **Supp. III Part 1:** 274

"Christmas Banquet, The" (Hawthorne), **II:** 227

Christmas Card, A (Theroux), **Supp. VIII:** 322

Christmas Carol, A (Dickens), **Retro. Supp. I:** 196; **Supp. I Part 2:** 409–410; **Supp. X:** 252, 253

"Christmas Eve at Johnson's Drugs N Goods" (Bambara), **Supp. XI:** 11–12

"Christmas Eve in the Time of War: A Capitalist Meditates by a Civil War Monument" (Lowell), **II:** 538

"Christmas Eve under Hooker's Statue" (Lowell), **II:** 539–540

"Christmas Gift" (Warren), **IV:** 252–253

"Christmas Greeting, A" (Wright), **Supp. III Part 2:** 601

"Christmas Hymn, A" (Wilbur), **Supp. III Part 2:** 557

Christmas Memory, A (Capote), **Supp. III Part 1:** 118, 119, 129

"Christmass Poem" (West), **Retro. Supp. II:** 338

Christmas Story (Mencken), **III:** 111

"Christmas to Me" (Lee), **Supp. VIII:** 113

Christographia (Taylor), **IV:** 164–165

Christ on a Clothesline (Loy), **Supp. XXII:** 168

"*Christ on the Cross*/Nuestro Señor Crucificado" (Mora), **Supp. XIII:** 229

Christopher, Mary (pseudonym). See West, Dorothy

Christopher and His Kind: 1929–1939 (Isherwood), **Supp. XIV:** 157, 163, 164, 171

"Christopher Cat" (Cullen), **Supp. IV Part 1:** 173

Christopher Columbus, Mariner (Morison), **Supp. I Part 2:** 488

Christopher Isherwood: A Critical Biography (Finney), **Supp. XIV:** 158

Christophersen, Bill, **Supp. IX:** 159, 167; **Supp. XI:** 155; **Supp. XIII:** 87; **Supp. XXI:** 103

"Christ's Passion" (Karr), **Supp. XI:** 251
Christus: A Mystery (Longfellow), **II:** 490, 493, 495, 505–507; **Retro. Supp. II:** 161, 165, 166
Chroma (F. Barthelme), **Supp. XI:** 30, 33, 34
"Chroma" (F. Barthelme), **Supp. XI:** 31
"Chronicle of Race Relations, A" (Du Bois), **Supp. II Part 1:** 182
Chronicle of the Conquest of Granada (Irving), **II:** 310
Chronicles: Volume One (Dylan), **Supp. XVIII:** 20, 21, 23, 24, 28, **32–33**
"Chronologues" (Goldbarth), **Supp. XII:** 183, 184
"Chrysanthemums, The" (Steinbeck), **IV:** 53
"Chrysaor" (Longfellow), **II:** 498
Chu, Louis, **Supp. X:** 291
Chuang, Hua, **Supp. X:** 291
Chuang-Tzu, **Supp. VIII:** 206
"Chunk of Amethyst, A" (R. Bly), **Supp. IV Part 1:** 72
Church, Margaret, **IV:** 466
"Church and the Fiction Writer, The" (O'Connor), **Retro. Supp. II:** 223, 233; **Supp. XVIII:** 161
"Church Going" (Larkin), **Supp. XXI:** 93
"Churchgoing" (Nelson), **Supp. XVIII:** 173
Churchill, Charles, **Supp. XV:** 232
Churchill, Winston, **I:** 9, 490; **Supp. I Part 2:** 491
Church of Dead Girls, The (Dobyns), **Supp. XIII:** 75, **83–84**
"Church of Omnivorous Light, The" (Wrigley), **Supp. XVIII:** 306–307
"Church of the Latter Day Saints, The" (Mosher), **Supp. XXII:** 208
"Church Porch, The" (Herbert), **IV:** 153
Church Psalmody, Selected from Dr. Watts and Other Authors (Mason and Greene, ed.), **I:** 458
Ciannic, Saint, **II:** 215
Ciano, Edda, **IV:** 249
Ciardi, John, **I:** 169, 179, 535; **III:** 268; **Supp. IV Part 1:** 243; **Supp. IV Part 2:** 639; **Supp. IX:** 269, 324; **Supp. XII:** 119
Cicada (Haines), **Supp. XII: 206–207**
"Cicadas" (Wilbur), **Supp. III Part 2:** 549
Cicero, **I:** 279; **II:** 8, 14–15; **III:** 23; **Supp. I Part 2:** 405
Cider House Rules, The (Irving), **Supp. VI:** 164, **173–175**
"Cigales" (Wilbur), **Supp. III Part 2:** 549
"Cigarette" (L. Michaels), **Supp. XVI:** 214
Cimarron, Rose (Burke), **Supp. XIV:** 22, 35
"Cimetière Marin, Le" (Valéry), **IV:** 91–92
Cimino, Michael, **Supp. X:** 126
Cincinnati Kid, The (film), **Supp. XI: 306**
"Cinderella" (Jarrell), **II:** 386
"Cinderella" (Perrault), **IV:** 266, 267

"Cinderella" (Sexton), **Supp. II Part 2:** 691
"Cinema, The" (Salter), **Supp. IX:** 257
Cinema of Tony Richardson, The: Essays and Interviews (Phillips), **Supp. XI:** 306
Cinthio, **IV:** 370
Ciolkowski, Laura, **Supp. XVI:** 24
CIOPW (Cummings), **I:** 429
"Circe" (Welty), **Retro. Supp. I:** 353
Circle Game, The (Atwood), **Supp. XIII:** 20, 33
Circle in the Dirt (Moraga), **Supp. XXIII:** 195, 202
"Circle in the Fire, A" (O'Connor), **III:** 344–345, 349–350, 351, 353, 354; **Retro. Supp. II:** 229, 232
"Circle of Breath" (Stafford), **Supp. XI:** 318, 322
Circle of Hanh, The (Weigl), **Supp. XIX:** 273, 275, 282, **284–286**
"Circles" (Emerson), **I:** 455, 460
"Circles" (Lowell), **II:** 554
Circumference: Varieties of Metaphysical Verse 1456–1928 (Taggard, ed.), **Supp. XXII:** 279
"Circus, The" (Porter), **III:** 443, 445
"Circus Animals' Desertion" (Yeats), **I:** 389
"Circus in the Attic" (Warren), **IV:** 253
Circus in the Attic, The (Warren), **IV:** 243, 251–253
"Circus in Three Rings" (Plath), **Retro. Supp. II:** 243; **Supp. I Part 2:** 536
Circus of Needs, A (Dunn), **Supp. XI: 147–148**
"Cirque d'Hiver" (Bishop), **Supp. I Part 1:** 85
Cisneros, Sandra, **Supp. IV Part 2:** 544; **Supp. VII: 57–73; Supp. XI:** 177; **Supp. XVII:** 71; **Supp. XXII:** 177
Cities of the Interior (Nin), **Supp. X:** 182
Cities of the Plain (McCarthy), **Supp. VIII:** 175, **186–187**
Cities of the Red Night (Burroughs), **Supp. III Part 1:** 106
"Citizen Cain" (Baraka), **Supp. II Part 1:** 49
Citizen Kane (film), **Retro. Supp. I:** 115; **Supp. V:** 251; **Supp. XI:** 169
"Citizen of the World" (Goldsmith), **II:** 299
Citro, Joseph, **Supp. XXII:** 208, 218
"City" (Francis), **Supp. IX:** 87
"City and Country"(Hadas), **Supp. XXIII:** 115, 116
City and the Pillar, The (Vidal), **Supp. IV Part 2:** 677, 680–681; **Supp. XIV:** 170
"*City and the Pillar, The,* as Gay Fiction" (Summers), **Supp. IV Part 2:** 680–681
"City Articles" series (Briggs), **Supp. XVIII:** 12
City Block (W. Frank), **Supp. XX: 71, 72, 76**
City Boy (L. Michaels), **Supp. XVI:** 212
"City Boy" (L. Michaels), **Supp. XVI:** 203–204

City Boy (Thompson), **Supp. XXIII:** 294, **298–299**
City Dog (Di Piero), **Supp. XIX:** 33–34, 35, 38, 46, 48
"City Dog" (Di Piero), **Supp. XIX:** 47
City in History, The (Mumford), **Supp. II Part 2:** 495
"City in the Sea, The" (Poe), **III:** 411; **Retro. Supp. II:** 274
City in Which I Love You, The (L.-Y. Lee), **Supp. XV:** 212, **215–220**
"City in Which I Love You, The" (L.-Y. Lee), **Supp. XV:** 215, **217–218**
City Life (Barthelme), **Supp. IV Part 1:** 44, 47
City of Bones (Connelly), **Supp. XXI: 74–75,** 77
"City of Change, A" (Bynner), **Supp. XV:** 45
City of Dreadful Night (Siegel), **Supp. XXII:** 258
City of Glass (Auster), **Supp. XII:** 22, **24–26**
City of God, The (St. Augustine), **IV:** 126
City of Names (Brockmeier), **Supp. XXII:** 55–56, 57
"City of Refuge, The" (R. Fisher), **Supp. XIX:** 65, 66, **67–68**
City of Refuge, The: The Collected Stories of Rudolph Fisher (McCluskey, ed.), **Supp. XIX:** 68–69
City of the Living and Other Stories, The (Stegner), **Supp. IV Part 2:** 599, 609, 613
City of Words: American Fiction 1950-1970 (T. Tanner), **Supp. XVI:** 69
City of Your Final Destination, The (Cameron), **Supp. XII:** 79, 82, **91–94**
"City on a Hill" (Lowell), **II: 552**
City on a Hill: Testing the American Dream at City College (Traub), **Supp. XXIV:** 221
"City Person Encountering Nature, A" (Kingston), **Supp. V:** 170
"City Planners, The" (Atwood), **Supp. XIII:** 33
"City Winter, A"(O'Hara), **Supp. XXIII:** 210
City Winter and Other Poems, A (O'Hara), **Supp. XXIII:** 210, 214
City Without Men (film), **Supp. XVIII:** 247
City Without Walls (Auden), **Supp. II Part 1:** 24
Civil Disobedience (Thoreau), **IV:** 185; **Supp. I Part 2:** 507
Civilization in the United States (Stearns), **I:** 245
"Civil Rights" (Lanier), **Supp. I Part 1:** 357
CivilWarLand in Bad Decline (Saunders), **Supp. XIX: 224–227**
"CivilWarLand in Bad Decline" (Saunders), **Supp. XIX:** 224–225, 227
Civitatis Anthology of African American Slave Narratives, The (H. L. Gates and Andrews, eds.), **Supp. XX: 105**
Cixous, Hélène, **Supp. X:** 102; **Supp. XIII:** 297; **Supp. XV:** 347
Clabough, Casey, **Supp. XXIV:** 194

Claiborne, Craig, **Supp. XVII:** 89

Claiborne, William, **I:** 132

"Claim, The"(Balakian), **Supp. XXIII:** 20

Claiming an Identity They Taught Me to Despise (Cliff), **Supp. XXII:** 66, 67–68, 70

Claiming of Sleeping Beauty, The (Rice), **Supp. VII:** 301

Clampitt, Amy, **Supp. IX: 37–54; Supp. X:** 120; **Supp. XI:** 249; **Supp. XV:** 251, 256

Clancy's Wake, At (Crane), **I:** 422

"Clandeboye" (Leopold), **Supp. XIV:** 189

Clara Howard; or, The Enthusiasm of Love (Brown), **Supp. I Part 1:** 145

Clara's Ole Man (Bullins), **Supp. II Part 1:** 42

Clare, John, **II:** 387; **III:** 528; **Supp. XVI:** 295

Clarel: A Poem and Pilgrimage in the Holy Land (Melville), **Retro. Supp. I:** 257

Clarence Major and His Art (Bell), **Supp. XXII:** 182

Clarissa (Richardson), **II:** 111; **Supp. I Part 2:** 714; **Supp. V:** 127; **Supp. XV:** 231; **Supp. XX: 236**

Clark, Alex, **Supp. XII:** 307

Clark, Charles, **I:** 470

Clark, Eleanor. *See* Warren, Mrs. Robert Penn (Eleanor Clark)

Clark, Francis Edward, **II:** 9

Clark, Geoffrey, **Supp. XI:** 342

Clark, Harry Hayden, **Supp. I Part 2:** 423

Clark, John Bates, **Supp. I Part 2:** 633

Clark, Kenneth, **Supp. XIV:** 342, 348; **Supp. XIX:** 151

Clark, Lewis Gaylord, **Supp. XVIII:** 4, 7, 8

Clark, Shirley, **Supp. XXI:** 22

Clark, Thomas, **Supp. III Part 2:** 629; **Supp. IV Part 1:** 140, 145, 147

Clark, Tom, **Supp. XXIV:** 36, 37, 41, 44

Clark, Walter, **Supp. XI:** 315

Clark, William, **III:** 14; **IV:** 179, 283

Clark, Willis Gaylord, **Supp. I Part 2:** 684

Clarke, Brock, **Supp. XXIII:** 109

Clarke, James Freeman, **Supp. II Part 1:** 280

Clarke, John, **Supp. IV Part 1:** 8

Clarke, John J., **III:** 356

Clarke, Samuel, **II:** 108

Clark Lectures, **Retro. Supp. I:** 65

Claros varones de Belken (Hinojosa). *See Fair Gentlemen of Belken County* (Hinojosa)

Clash by Night (Odets), **Supp. II Part 2:** 531, 538, 544–546, 550, 551

Classical Tradition, The (Highet), **Supp. I Part 1:** 268

Classic Ballroom Dances (Simic), **Supp. VIII:** 271, **276–278,** 283

Classics (Hadas), **Supp. XXIII: 124**

Classics and Commercials: A Literary Chronicle of the Forties (Wilson), **IV:** 433

"Classics"(Hadas), **Supp. XXIII:** 124

"CLASS STRUGGLE" (Baraka), **Supp. III Part 1:** 55

"Claude Glass, The: 1890" (Bierds), **Supp. XVII:** 27

Claudel, Paul, **I:** 60

Claudelle Inglish (Caldwell), **I:** 304

Clavel, Marcel, **I:** 343

"CLAY" (Baraka), **Supp. II Part 1:** 54

Clay, Henry, **I:** 8; **Supp. I Part 2:** 684, 686

Clay's Ark (O. Butler), **Supp. XIII:** 63

Clayton, John J., **Supp. IV Part 1:** 238

"Clean, Well Lighted Place, A" (Hemingway), **Retro. Supp. I:** 181

"Clear, with Light Variable Winds" (Lowell), **II:** 522

"Clear Days" (White), **Supp. I Part 2:** 664, 665

Clearing (Berry), **Supp. X:** 22

"Clearing, A" (Simpson), **Supp. IX:** 280

"Clearing, The" (Kenyon), **Supp. VII:** 174

"Clearing the Title" (Merrill), **Supp. III Part 1:** 336

"Clearing Up the Question of Stesichoros' Blinding by Helen" (Carson), **Supp. XII:** 107–108

"Clear Morning" (Glück), **Supp. V:** 88

"Clearness" (Wilbur), **Supp. III Part 2:** 544, 550

"Clear Night" (Wright), **Supp. V:** 341

Clear Pictures: First Loves, First Guides (Price), **Supp. VI:** 253, 254, 255, 256, 265

Clear Springs (Mason), **Supp. VIII:** 134–136, 137–138, 139, 147

Cleary, Rebecca Lauck, **Supp. XVIII:** 195

Cleaver, Eldridge, **Retro. Supp. II:** 12; **Supp. IV Part 1:** 206; **Supp. X:** 249

"Cleaving, The" (L.-Y. Lee), **Supp. XV:** 215, **218–220**

Cleland, John, **Supp. V:** 48, 127

Clemenceau, Georges, **I:** 490

"Clemency" (Wrigley), **Supp. XVIII:** 307–308

Clemens, Jane, **I:** 247

Clemens, Orion, **IV:** 193, 195

Clemens, Samuel Langhorne. *See* Twain, Mark

Clemens, Mrs. Samuel Langhorne (Olivia Langdon), **I:** 197, 208, 247; **Supp. I Part 2:** 457

Clemens, Susie, **IV:** 208

Clementine Recognitions (novel), **Supp. IV Part 1:** 280

Clements, Colin Campbell, **Supp. XVI:** 190

Clemons, Walter, **Supp. IV Part 1:** 305, 307

Cleopatra, **III:** 44; **IV:** 373; **Supp. I Part 1:** 114

"Clepsydra" (Ashbery), **Supp. III Part 1:** 10–15

"Clerks, The" (Robinson), **III:** 517–518

"Cleveland" (Halliday), **Supp. XIX:** 90

Cleveland, Carol, **Supp. IX:** 120, 125

Cleveland, Ceil, **Supp. V:** 222

Cleveland, Grover, **II:** 126, 128, 129, 130, 137, 138; **Supp. I Part 2:** 486

"Clever Magician Carrying My Heart, A" (Salinas), **Supp. XIII:** 323

Cliff, Michelle, **Supp. XXII: 65–80**

"Cliff, The" (C. Baxter), **Supp. XVII:** 16–17

Clifford, Craig, **Supp. IX:** 99

Clift, Montgomery, **III:** 161

Clifton, Lucille, **Supp. XVIII:** 177

Climate of Monastic Prayer, The (Merton), **Supp. VIII:** 205, 207

Climb, The (Boukreev), **Supp. XVIII:** 112

"Climber, The" (Mason), **Supp. VIII:** 140–141

Climbing High: A Woman's Account of Surviving the Everest Tragedy (Gammelgaard), **Supp. XVIII:** 112

"Climbing the Tower" (Crews), **Supp. XI:** 102

Clinton, De Witt, **I:** 338

"Clipped Wings" (H. Miller), **III:** 176–177

Clippinger, David, **Supp. XXI:** 24

Clive, Robert, **Supp. I Part 2:** 505

Clock Winder, The (Tyler), **Supp. IV Part 2:** 661–662, 670

Clock Without Hands (McCullers), **II:** 587–588, 604–606

Clockwork Orange, A (Burgess), **Supp. XIII:** 29

Clorindy (Cook), **Supp. II Part 1:** 199

"Close, The" (Jarman), **Supp. XVII:** 113

"Close Calls" (Wolff), **Supp. VII:** 332–333

"Closed Book, A" (Mosley), **Supp. XIII:** 237

Close Quarters (Heinemann), **Supp. XXII:** 103, **104–109,** 111, 115

Close Range: Wyoming Stories (Proulx), **Supp. VII:** 261–265

"Close Reading: Windows"(Hirshfield), **Supp. XXIII:** 131

Closers, The (Connelly), **Supp. XXI: 76–77**

Closest Possible Union, The (J. Scott), **Supp. XVII: 185–186,** 188, 191

Close the Book (Glaspell), **Supp. III Part 1:** 179

"Close the Book" (Lowell), **II:** 554

Close to Me & Closer ... (The Language of Heaven) and Désamère (Notley), **Supp. XXII:** 234

Close to Shore: A True Story of Terror in an Age of Innocence (Capuzzo), **Supp. XIII:** 254

Closet Writing & Gay Reading: The Case of Melville's Pierre (Creech), **Retro. Supp. I:** 254

Closing Circle, The (Commoner), **Supp. XIII:** 264

Closing of the American Mind, The (Bloom), **Retro. Supp. II:** 19, 30, 31

"Closing of the Rodeo, The" (W. J. Smith), **Supp. XIII:** 332

Closing Time (Heller), **Supp. IV Part 1:** 382, 386, 391–394

Closset, Marie, **Supp. VIII:** 251, 265

Clotel (Brown), **Supp. XXIII:** 184

"Cloud, The" (Shelley), **Supp. I Part 2:** 720

"Cloud and Fame" (Berryman), **I**: 173
Cloud Atlas (D. Mitchell), **Supp. XXIV:** 86
Cloud Forest, The: A Chronicle of the South American Wilderness (Matthiessen), **Supp. V:** 202, 204
"Cloud on the Way, The" (Bryant), **Supp. I Part 1:** 171
"Cloud River" (Wright), **Supp. V:** 341
"Clouds" (Levine), **Supp. V:** 184
Cloudsplitter (Banks), **Supp. V:** 16
"Clover" (Lanier), **Supp. I Part 1:** 362–364
Clover and Other Poems (Lanier), **Supp. I Part 1:** 362
"Clown" (Corso), **Supp. XII:** 127
Clown in the Belfry, The: Writings on Faith and Fiction (Buechner), **Supp. XII:** 53
Cluck, Julia, **Supp. I Part 2:** 728
Clum, John M., **Supp. XIII: 200,** 201, 209
Cluny, Hugo, **IV:** 290
Clurman, Harold, **I:** 93; **IV:** 381, 385
Clytus, Radiclani, **Supp. XIII:** 128, **Supp. XIII:** 129, 132
"C.O." (Wrigley), **Supp. XVIII:** 298
"Coal: Beginning and End" (Winters), **Supp. II Part 2:** 791
Coale, Howard, **Supp. XIII:** 15
"Coals" (Hoffman), **Supp. XVIII:** 86
"Coast, The" (column), **Supp. IV Part 1:** 198
"Coast Guard's Cottage, The" (Wylie), **Supp. I Part 2:** 723
Coast of Chicago, The (Dybek), **Supp. XXIII: 72–74,** 75
Coast of Trees, A (Ammons), **Supp. VII:** 24, 34
"Coast-Range Christ, The" (Jeffers), **Supp. II Part 2:** 414, 419
"Coast-Road, The" (Jeffers), **Supp. II Part 2:** 425
"Coat, The" (Everwine), **Supp. XV:** 80
Coates, Joseph, **Supp. VIII:** 80; **Supp. XXII:** 205
Coates, Robert, **I:** 54; **IV:** 298
"Coatlicue's Rules: Advice from an Aztec Goddess" (Mora), **Supp. XIII:** 223
"Coats" (Kenyon), **Supp. VII:** 172
Cobb, Lee J., **III:** 153
Cobb, Ty, **III:** 227, 229
Cobbett, William, **Supp. I Part 2:** 517; **Supp. XV:** 237
"Cobbler Keezar's Vision" (Whittier), **Supp. I Part 2:** 699
"Cobweb, The" (Carver), **Supp. III Part 1:** 148
Cobwebs From an Empty Skull (Bierce), **I:** 195
Coccimiglio, Vic, **Supp. XIII:** 114
"Cock-a-Doodle-Doo!" (Melville), **III:** 89
"Cockayne" (Emerson), **II:** 6
"Cock-Crow" (Gordon), **II:** 219
Cock Pit (Cozzens), **I:** 359, 378, 379
Cockpit (Kosinski), **Supp. XII:** 21
Cockpit: A Novel (Kosinski), **Supp. VII:** 215, 223–224, 225

"Cock Robin Takes Refuge in the Storm House" (Snodgrass), **Supp. VI:** 319
Cocktail Hour, The (Gurney), **Supp. V:** 95, 96, 100, 101, 103, 105, 108
Cocktail Hour and Two Other Plays: Another Antigone and *The Perfect Party* (Gurney), **Supp. V:** 100
Cocktail Party, The (Eliot), **I:** 571, 582–583; **III:** 21; **Retro. Supp. I:** 65; **Supp. V:** 101, 103
Cocteau, Jean, **III:** 471; **Retro. Supp. I:** 82, 378; **Supp. IV Part 1:** 82; **Supp. XVI:** 135; **Supp. XX: 236**
"Coda: Wilderness Letter" (Stegner), **Supp. IV Part 2:** 595
"Code, The" (Frost), **Retro. Supp. I:** 121, 128
Codman, Florence, **Supp. II Part 1:** 92, 93
Codman, Ogden, Jr., **Retro. Supp. I:** 362, 363
Codrescu, Andrei, **Supp. XXII:** 155
Cody, William ("Buffalo Bill"), **I:** 440; **III:** 584; **Supp. V:** 230
"Coffee Lips" (Ferry), **Supp. XXIV:** 153, 162
Coffey, Michael, **Supp. V:** 243; **Supp. XV:** 65; **Supp. XX: 88**
Coffey, Warren, **III:** 358
Coffin, Charles, **III:** 577
Cogan, David J., **Supp. IV Part 1:** 362
Cogan, Joshua, **Supp. XXI:** 247
Coghill, Nevill, **Supp. II Part 1:** 4; **Supp. XIV:** 13
Cohan, George M., **II:** 427; **III:** 401
Cohen, Edward M., **Supp. XVI:** 212
Cohen, Esther, **Supp. XV:** 323
Cohen, Hettie, **Supp. II Part 1:** 30
Cohen, Joshua, **Supp. XXII:** 268
Cohen, Marty, **Supp. X:** 112
Cohen, Norman J., **Supp. IX:** 132, 143
Cohen, Rosetta, **Supp. XV:** 257
Cohen, Sarah Blacher, **Supp. V:** 273
Cohen, Victor, **Supp. XVIII:** 235, 236
"Coherent Decentering: Towards a New Model of the Poetic Self" (A. Finch), **Supp. XVII:** 76
"Coin" (Goldbarth), **Supp. XII:** 187
Coindreau, Maurice, **III:** 339
Coiner, Constance, **Supp. XIII:** 297, 302
Coit, Lille Hitchcock, **Supp. X:** 103
"Coitus" (Pound), **III:** 466
Coke, Desmond, **Supp. XX: 235**
Colburn, Nadia Herman, **Supp. XV:** 339, 341, 347
"Cold, The" (Kenyon), **Supp. VII:** 164
"Cold, The" (Winters), **Supp. II Part 2:** 790–791, 809, 811
"Cold-blooded Creatures" (Wylie), **Supp. I Part 2:** 729
Colden, Cadwallader, **Supp. I Part 1:** 250
"Colder the Air, The" (Bishop), **Supp. I Part 1:** 86
Cold Feet (Harrison), **Supp. VIII:** 39
Cold Frame (C. Frost), **Supp. XV:** 93, 96
Cold Ground Was My Bed Last Night (Garrett), **Supp. VII:** 98

"Cold Ground Was My Bed Last Night" (Garrett), **Supp. VII:** 100
"Cold Hill Side, The"(Hadas), **Supp. XXIII:** 121
"Cold Night, The" (W. C. Williams), **Retro. Supp. I:** 418
"Cold Plunge into Skin Diving, A" (Knowles), **Supp. XII:** 241
Cold Spring, A (Bishop), **Retro. Supp. II:** 45
Cold Springs Harbor (Yates), **Supp. XI:** 348
Cold War American Poetry, **Supp. V:** 182
Cold War and the Income Tax, The (Wilson), **IV:** 430
Cole, Bruce, **Supp. XX: 106**
Cole, Goody, **Supp. I Part 2:** 696–697
Cole, Lester, **Retro. Supp. II:** 329
Cole, Nat King, **Retro. Supp. I:** 334; **Supp. X:** 255
Cole, Thomas, **Supp. I Part 1:** 156, 158, 171
Cole, William, **Supp. XIX:** 120
"Coleman" (Karr), **Supp. XI:** 244
Coleman, Wanda, **Supp. XI: 83–98**
Coleridge, Samuel Taylor, **I:** 283, 284, 447, 522; **II:** 7, 10, 11, 19, 71, 169, 273, 301, 502, 516, 549; **III:** 77, 83–84, 424, 461, 488, 523; **IV:** 74, 173, 250, 349, 453; **Retro. Supp. I:** 65, 308; **Supp. I Part 1:** 31, 311, 349; **Supp. I Part 2:** 376, 393, 422; **Supp. IV Part 2:** 422, 465; **Supp. V:** 258; **Supp. IX:** 38, 50; **Supp. XIII:** 139; **Supp. XIV:** 21–22; **Supp. XV:** 250; **Supp. XXI:** 52, 55; **Supp. XXIII:** 231; **Supp. XXIV:** 74
Coles, Katharine, **Supp. IV Part 2:** 630
Coles, Robert, **Supp. XXIV:** 172, 265
Colette, Sidonie-Gabrielle, **Supp. VIII:** 40, 171; **Supp. XVI:** 193–194
"Coliseum, The" (Poe), **III:** 411
Collage of Dreams (Spencer), **Supp. X:** 196
"Collapse of Tomorrow, The" (Mumford), **Supp. II Part 2:** 482
"Collected by a Valetudinarian" (E. Stoddard), **Supp. XV:** 286–287
Collected Earlier Poems (Hecht), **Supp. X:** 58, 59
Collected Earlier Poems (W. C. Williams), **Retro. Supp. I:** 414, 428
Collected Earlier Poems 1940–1960 (Levertov), **Supp. III Part 1:** 273, 275
Collected Essays (Tate), **IV:** 133–134
Collected Essays of Ralph Ellison, The (Ellison), **Retro. Supp. II:** 119
Collected Essays of Robert Creeley, The (Creeley), **Supp. IV Part 1:** 153, 154
Collected Later Poems (W. C. Williams), **Retro. Supp. I:** 428
Collected Plays (A. Miller), **III:** 158
Collected Plays, 1974–1983 (Gurney), **Supp. V:** 99
Collected Poems (Aiken), **I:** 50
Collected Poems (Berrigan), **Supp. XXIV:** 39, 45, 46
Collected Poems (Burke), **I:** 269
Collected Poems (Cummings), **I:** 430, 439, 441

Collected Poems (Doolittle), **Supp. I Part 1:** 264–267, 269

Collected Poems (Frost), **Retro. Supp. I:** 136

Collected Poems (Hull), **Supp. XXI:** 141

Collected Poems (Kees; Justice, ed.), **Supp. XV:** 134

Collected Poems (Lindsay), **Supp. I Part 2:** 380, 387, 392, 396–397, 400

Collected Poems (Lowell), **Supp. XV:** 20

Collected Poems (Markson), **Supp. XVII:** 143

Collected Poems (Moore), **III:** 194, 215

Collected Poems (O'Hara), **Supp. XXIII:** 207, 211, 220

Collected Poems (Price), **Supp. VI:** 267

Collected Poems (Simpson), **Supp. IX:** 279

Collected Poems (W. C. Williams), **IV:** 415; **Retro. Supp. I:** 430

Collected Poems (Winters), **Supp. II Part 2:** 791, 810

Collected Poems (Wright), **Supp. III Part 2:** 602

Collected Poems (Yeats), **Supp. XV:** 152

Collected Poems, 1918–1938 (Taggard), **Supp. XXII:** 283

Collected Poems, 1923–1953 (Bogan), **Supp. III Part 1:** 64

Collected Poems, 1936–1976 (Francis), **Supp. IX:** 77, 80, **87**

Collected Poems, The (Stevens), **III:** 273; **IV:** 75, 76, 87, 93; **Retro. Supp. I:** 296, 309

Collected Poems 1909–1935 (Eliot), **I:** 580; **Retro. Supp. I:** 66

Collected Poems 1909–1962 (Eliot), **I:** 583

Collected Poems 1917–1952 (MacLeish), **III:** 3, 4, 19

Collected Poems 1921–1931 (W. C. Williams), **Retro. Supp. I:** 422; **Supp. XIV:** 285

Collected Poems 1930–1960 (Eberhart), **I:** 522, 525–526, 540, 541

Collected Poems: 1939–1989 (W. J. Smith), **Supp. XIII:** 332, 340, 343, 345

Collected Poems: 1940–1978 (Shapiro), **Supp. II Part 2:** 703, 717

Collected Poems: 1951–1971 (Ammons), **Supp. VII:** 24, 26–29, 32, 33

Collected Poems: 1956–1976 (Wagoner), **Supp. IX:** 323, **328–329**

Collected Poems of Amy Clampitt, The (Clampitt), **Supp. IX:** 37, 44, 53

Collected Poems of George Garrett (Garrett), **Supp. VII:** 109

Collected Poems of Hart Crane, The (Crane), **I:** 399–402

Collected Poems of James Agee, The (Fitzgerald, ed.), **I:** 27–28

Collected Poems of James T. Farrell, The (Farrell), **II:** 45

Collected Poems of Kay Boyle (Boyle), **Supp. XXIV:** 63

Collected Poems of Langston Hughes, The (Rampersad and Roessel, ed.), **Retro. Supp. I:** 194, 196, 212

Collected Poems of Muriel Rukeyser, The (Rukeyser), **Supp. VI:** 274

Collected Poems of Thomas Merton, The, **Supp. VIII:** 207, 208

Collected Poetry (Auden), **Supp. II Part 1:** 18

Collected Prose (Wright), **Supp. III Part 2:** 596

Collected Prose, The (Bishop), **Retro. Supp. II:** 51

Collected Recordings (W. C. Williams), **Retro. Supp. I:** 431

Collected Shorter Poems, 1946-1991 (Carruth), **Supp. XVI:** 47

Collected Short Stories, The (Wharton), **Retro. Supp. I:** 362, 363, 366

Collected Sonnets (Millay), **III:** 136–137

Collected Stories (Carver), **Supp. XXIV:** 177

Collected Stories, 1939–1976 (Bowles), **Supp. IV Part 1:** 92

Collected Stories, The (Paley), **Supp. VI:** 218

Collected Stories, The (Price), **Supp. VI:** 266

Collected Stories, The (Theroux), **Supp. VIII:** 318

Collected Stories, The (Wharton), **Retro. Supp. I:** 361

Collected Stories of Amy Hempel, The (Hempel), **Supp. XXI:** 115, 117

Collected Stories of Eudora Welty, The (Welty), **Retro. Supp. I:** 355

Collected Stories of Isaac Bashevis Singer (Singer), **Retro. Supp. II: 307–308**

Collected Stories of Katherine Anne Porter (Porter), **III:** 454

Collected Stories of Peter Taylor (Taylor), **Supp. V:** 314, 320, 323–324, 325, 326

Collected Stories of Richard Yates, The, **Supp. XI:** 349

Collected Stories of Wallace Stegner (Stegner), **Supp. IV Part 2:** 599, 605

Collected Stories of William Faulkner (Faulkner), **II:** 72; **Retro. Supp. I:** 75

Collected Stories of William Humphrey, The (Humphrey), **Supp. IX:** 106

Collected Works (Bierce), **I:** 204, 208–210

Collected Works of Buck Rogers in the 25th Century, The (Bradbury), **Supp. IV Part 1:** 101

Collected Writings, The (Z. Fitzgerald; Bruccoli, ed.), **Supp. IX:** 65, 68

Collecting the Animals (Everwine), **Supp. XV:** 73, 75, **78–81**, 85, 88

Collection of Epigrams, **II:** 111

Collection of Poems, on American Affairs, and a Variety of Other Subjects . . . (Freneau), **Supp. II Part 1:** 274

Collection of Select Aphorisms and Maxims (Palmer), **II:** 111

"Collectors" (Carver), **Supp. III Part 1:** 141–142

Collette, **Supp. XVII:** 86

Collier, John, **Supp. XXI:** 8

Collier, Lucy Wood, **Supp. XXI:** 8

Collier, Michael, **Supp. XVII:** 23, 110

Collingwood, R. G., **I:** 278

Collins, Billy, **Supp. XI:** 143; **Supp. XIV:** 123; **Supp. XVII:** 245; **Supp. XXI: 51–66; Supp. XXIII:** 138

Collins, Doug, **Supp. V:** 5

Collins, Eddie, **II:** 416

Collins, L. M., **Supp. XXII:** 7

Collins, Richard, **Supp. XI:** 171

Collins, Ronald, **Supp. XXI:** 24

Collins, Wilkie, **Supp. I Part 1:** 35, 36; **Supp. IV Part 1:** 341; **Supp. XX: 236**

Collins, William, **Supp. I Part 2:** 714

Collinson, Peter , **II:** 114

Collinson, Peter (pseudonym). *See* Hammett, Dashiell

Colloff, Pamela, **Supp. XIII:** 281

Colloque Sentimental (ballet), **Supp. IV Part 1:** 83

"Colloquy" (Kees), **Supp. XV:** 133

"Colloquy in Black Rock" (Lowell), **II:** 535; **Retro. Supp. II:** 178

"Colloquy of Monos and Una, The" (Poe), **III:** 412

"Colloquy on a Bed" (Bronk), **Supp. XXI:** 31

Colonel's Dream, The (Chesnutt), **Supp. XIV:** 63, 75–76

Colônia, Regina, **Retro. Supp. II:** 53

Colony (Siddons), **Supp. XXII:** 239

Color (Cullen), **Supp. IV Part 1:** 164, 166, 167, 168

"Colorado" (Beattie), **Supp. V:** 27

Color and Democracy: Colonies and Peace (Du Bois), **Supp. II Part 1:** 184, 185

"Color-Blind Raspberry Picker, The"(Hadas), **Supp. XXIII:** 113

Color Curtain, The (Wright), **IV:** 478, 488

"Colored Americans" (Dunbar), **Supp. II Part 1:** 197

Colored People (H. L. Gates), **Supp. XX: 101, 103, 104–105, 109, 111**

"Color Line, The" (Douglass), **Supp. III Part 1:** 163–165

Color Line, The (W. B. Smith), **Supp. II Part 1:** 168

Color of a Great City, The (Dreiser), **Retro. Supp. II:** 104

Color of Darkness (Purdy), **Supp. VII:** 271

Color Purple, The (Walker), **Supp. III Part 2:** 517, 518, 520, 525–529, 532–537; **Supp. VIII:** 141; **Supp. X:** 252, 330; **Supp. XX: 107**

Color Schemes (Cheang; film), **Supp. XI:** 20

"Colors of Night, The" (Momaday), **Supp. IV Part 2:** 490

"Colors without Objects" (Swenson), **Supp. IV Part 2:** 645

"Color: The Unfinished Business of Democracy" (Locke), **Supp. XIV:** 202, 207

Colossus, The (Plath), **Retro. Supp. II: 245–247; Supp. I Part 2:** 529, 531, 536, 538, 540; **Supp. V:** 79; **Supp. XI:** 317

"Colossus, The" (Plath), **Retro. Supp. II:** 250; **Supp. XXIII:** 113

Colossus of Maroussi, The (H. Miller), **III:** 178, 185–186

"Colt, The" (Stegner), **Supp. IV Part 2:** 600

Coltelli, Laura, **Supp. IV Part 1:** 323, 330, 335, 409; **Supp. IV Part 2:** 493, 497, 559

Colter: The True Story of the Best Dog I Ever Had (Bass), **Supp. XVI:** 23

Coltrane, John, **Supp. VIII:** 197; **Supp. XXII:** 172

Colum, Mary, **I:** 246, 252, 256; **Supp. I Part 2:** 708, 709

"Columba" (Cliff), **Supp. XXII:** 74, 76

Columbiad, The (Barlow), **Supp. II Part 1:** 67, 72, 73, 74, 75–77, 79

Columbia History of the American Novel, **Supp. XV:** 270

Columbia Literary History of the United States, **Supp. XV:** 270

"Columbian Ode" (Dunbar), **Supp. II Part 1:** 199

"Columbia U Poesy Reading—1975" (Corso), **Supp. XII:** 134

Columbus, Christopher, **I:** 253; **II:** 6, 310; **III:** 8; **Supp. I Part 2:** 397, 479, 480, 483, 486–488, 491, 495, 497, 498

"Columbus to Ferdinand" (Freneau), **Supp. II Part 1:** 255

Comanche Moon (McMurtry), **Supp. V:** 232

"Come, Break With Time" (Bogan), **Supp. III Part 1:** 52

Come, Thief (Hirshfield), **Supp. XXIII:** 134, 138

Come Along with Me (Jackson), **Supp. IX:** 117, 118, 122

Come Back, Charleston Blue (film), **Supp. XVI:** 144

Comeback, The (Gurney), **Supp. V:** 97

"Come Back to the Raft Ag'in, Huck Honey!" (Fiedler), **Supp. XIII:** 93, **96–97,** 101

Come Blow Your Horn (Simon), **Supp. IV Part 2:** 574, 575, 577, 578, 586, 587, 591

Come By Here (Major), **Supp. XXII:** 171, 182

"Come Dance with Me in Ireland" (Jackson), **Supp. IX:** 119

"Comedian as the Letter C, The" (Stevens), **IV:** 84–85, 88; **Retro. Supp. I:** 297, 301, 302

"Comedy Cop" (Farrell), **II:** 45

Comedy of a Country House (J. Sturgis), **Supp. XX: 238**

"Comedy's Greatest Era" (Agee), **I:** 31

"Come In" (Frost), **Retro. Supp. I:** 139

"Come On, Baby" (Zinberg), **Supp. XV:** 195

"Come on Back" (Gardner), **Supp. VI:** 73

"Come Out into the Sun" (Francis), **Supp. IX:** 82

Come Out into the Sun: Poems New and Selected (Francis), **Supp. IX: 82–83**

"Come out the Wilderness" (Baldwin), **Supp. I Part 1:** 63

Comer, Anjanette, **Supp. XI:** 305

Comer, Cornelia, **I:** 214

"Come Rain or Come Shine" (song), **Supp. XXII:** 6

"Come Shining: The Spiritual South" (exhibition; Luster), **Supp. XV:** 350

Come with Me: Poems for a Journey (Nye), **Supp. XIII:** 279

"Comforts of Home, The" (O'Connor), **III:** 349, 351, 355; **Retro. Supp. II:** 237

Comic Artist, The (Glaspell and Matson), **Supp. III Part 1:** 182

"Comic Imagination of the Young Dickens, The" (Wright), **Supp. III Part 2:** 591

"Comic Textures and Female Communities 1937 and 1977: Clare Boothe and Wendy Wasserstein" (Carlson), **Supp. XV:** 323

Comic Tragedies (Alcott), **Supp. I Part 1:** 33

Coming After (Notley), **Supp. XXII:** 223, 227, 230, 232, 236

"Coming and Going" (Gallagher), **Supp. XXIV:** 175, 176–177

"Coming Close" (Levine), **Supp. V:** 192

Coming Forth by Day of Osiris Jones, The (Aiken), **I:** 59

"Coming Home" (Gordon), **Supp. IV Part 1:** 309

"Coming Home to Vermont" (McCarriston), **Supp. XIV:** 269

"Coming in From the Cold" (Walker), **Supp. III Part 2:** 526

Coming into Eighty (Sarton), **Supp. VIII:** 262

"Coming into Eighty" (Sarton), **Supp. VIII:** 262

Coming into the Country (McPhee), **Supp. III Part 1:** 298, 301–306, 309, 310

Coming Into Writing (Cixous), **Supp. X:** 102

Coming of Age in Mississippi (Moody), **Supp. IV Part 1:** 11

Comings Back (Goldbarth), **Supp. XII:** 180

"Coming to Canada--Age Twenty Two" (Shields), **Supp. VII:** 311

Coming to Canada: Poems (Shields), **Supp. VII:** 311–312

"Coming to Memoir as a Journalist" (Epstein), **Supp. XXII:** 95

"Coming to the Morning" (Merwin), **Supp. III Part 1:** 356

"Coming to This" (Strand), **Supp. IV Part 2:** 627

Comiskey, Charles, **II:** 422

Commager, Henry Steele, **I:** 253; **Supp. I Part 1:** 372; **Supp. I Part 2:** 484, 647, 650

Command the Morning (Buck), **Supp. II Part 1:** 125

"CommComm" (Saunders), **Supp. XIX:** 234

"Commencement Address, A" (Brodsky), **Supp. VIII:** 31

"Commencement Day Address, The" (Schwartz), **Supp. II Part 2:** 660

Commentaries (Caesar), **II:** 502, 561

"Commentary" (Auden), **Supp. II Part 1:** 13

"Comment on Curb" (Hughes), **Supp. I Part 1:** 340

"Comments/Questions" (Nelson), **Supp. XVIII:** 172

"Commerce" (Nye), **Supp. XIII:** 281

Commins, Saxe, **Retro. Supp. I:** 73; **Retro. Supp. II:** 337

Commodity of Dreams & Other Stories, A (Nemerov), **III:** 268–269, 285

Common Carnage (Dobyns), **Supp. XIII:** 87

"Common Ground, A" (Levertov), **Supp. III Part 1:** 277

"Common Life, The" (Auden), **Supp. IV Part 1:** 302, 313

"Common Meter" (R. Fisher), **Supp. XIX:** 71

Common Room, A: Essays 1954–1987 (Price), **Supp. VI:** 264–265, 267

Commons, John, **Supp. I Part 2:** 645

Common Sense (Paine), **II:** 117; **Supp. I Part 1:** 231; **Supp. I Part 2:** 505, 506–508, 509, 513, 516, 517, 521

Communal Cot (Loy), **Supp. XXII:** 168

"Communication" (Dobyns), **Supp. XIII:** 91

"Communion" (Dubus), **Supp. VII:** 91

Communion (Mora), **Supp. XIII: 217–219**

Communist Manifesto, The (Marx and Engels), **II:** 463; **Supp. XXI:** 162–163

"Community Life" (Moore), **Supp. X:** 178

"Community of Glaciers, The" (Bass), **Supp. XVI:** 23

Comnes, Gregory, **Supp. IV Part 1:** 283, 284, 291

"Companions, The" (Nemerov), **III:** 269, 278, 287

Company of Poets, A (Simpson), **Supp. IX:** 265, 275

Company of Women, The (Gordon), **Supp. IV Part 1:** 302–304, 304, 306, 313

Company She Keeps, The (McCarthy), **II:** 562, 563–566

"Comparisons of Wonder" (Jarman), **Supp. XVII:** 114

Compass Flower, The (Merwin), **Supp. III Part 1:** 353, 357

"Compassionate Friendship" (Doolittle), **Supp. I Part 1:** 257, 258, 259, 260, 271

"Compatibility" (C. Frost), **Supp. XV:** 103

"Compendium" (Dove), **Supp. IV Part 1:** 248

"Complaint" (W. C. Williams), **Retro. Supp. I:** 418

"Complete Birth of the Cool, The" (Wright), **Supp. XV:** 343, 344

Complete Collected Poems of William Carlos Williams, 1906–1938, The (W. C. Williams), **Retro. Supp. I:** 424

"Complete Destruction" (W. C. Williams), **IV:** 413

"Complete Life of John Hopkins, The" (O. Henry), **Supp. II Part 1:** 405

Complete Poems (Frost), **II:** 155, 164

Complete Poems (Reznikoff), **Supp. XIV:** 281

Complete Poems (Sandburg), **III:** 590–592, 594, 596

Complete Poems, The (Bishop), **Retro. Supp. II:** 49; **Supp. I Part 1:** 72, 82, 94

Complete Poems, The (Bradbury), **Supp. IV Part 1:** 105

Complete Poems, The: 1927–1979 (Bishop), **Retro. Supp. II:** 51

Complete Poems of Emily Dickinson, The (Bianchi and Hampson, eds.), **Retro. Supp. I:** 35

Complete Poems of Emily Dickinson, The (Johnson, ed.), **I:** 470

Complete Poems of Frederick Goddard Tuckerman, The (Momaday), **Supp. IV Part 2:** 480

Complete Poems of Hart Crane, The, **Retro. Supp. II:** 81

Complete Poems to Solve, The (Swenson), **Supp. IV Part 2:** 652

Complete Poetical Works (Hulme), **III:** 464

Complete Poetical Works (Longfellow), **Retro. Supp. II:** 154

Complete Poetical Works (Lowell), **II:** 512, 516–517

Complete Poetical Works of Amy Lowell, The, **Supp. XV:** 295–296

Complete Stories (O'Connor), **Supp. X:** 1

Complete Tragedies, The: Euripedes II, **Supp. XV:** 50

"Complete with Starry Night and Bourbon Shots" (Goldbarth), **Supp. XII:** 192–193

Complete Works of Kate Chopin, The (Seyersted, ed.), **Supp. I Part 1:** 212, 225

Complete Works of the Gawain-Poet (Gardner), **Supp. VI:** 64, 65

"Complex Histories, Contested Memories: Some Reflections on Remembering Difficult Pasts" (E. Hoffman, lecture), **Supp. XVI:** 155

"Complicated Thoughts About a Small Son" (White), **Supp. I Part 2:** 678

"Compliments of the Season" (O. Henry), **Supp. II Part 1:** 392, 399

"Compline" (Auden), **Supp. II Part 1:** 23

"Composing a Life" (Pickering), **Supp. XXI:** 191, 196

Composition as Explanation (Stein), **IV:** 32, 33, 38

"Composition as Explanation" (Stein), **IV:** 27, 28

"Compounding *of* Consciousness" (James), **II:** 358–359

Comprehensive Bibliography (Hanneman), **II:** 259

Compton-Burnett, Ivy, **I:** 93; **II:** 580; **Supp. XXIII:** 209

"Comrade Laski, C.P.U.S.A. \[M.L.\]" (Didion), **Supp. IV Part 1:** 200

Comstock, Anthony, **Retro. Supp. II:** 95

Comus (Milton), **II:** 12; **Supp. I Part 2:** 622

Conan Doyle, Arthur. *See* Doyle, Arthur Conan

Conceptions of Reality in Modern American Poetry (Dembo), **Supp. I Part 1:** 272

"Concept of Character in Fiction, The" (Gass), **Supp. VI:** 85, **86**

Concept of Dread, The (Kierkegaard), **III:** 305

Concerning Children (Gilman), **Supp. XI:** 206

"Concerning Mold upon the Skin, Etc." (J. Scott), **Supp. XVII:** 188

"Concerning Necessity" (Carruth), **Supp. XVI:** 57

"Concerning Some Recent Criticism of His Work" (Doty), **Supp. XI:** 131

Concerning the End for Which God Created the World (Edwards), **I:** 549, 557, 559

"Concerning Things That Can Be Doubled"(Crooker), **Supp. XXIII:** 64

Concerto for Two Pianos, Winds, and Percussion (Bowles), **Supp. IV Part 1:** 83

"Concert of Tenses, A" (Gallagher), **Supp. XXIV:** 172

Concert of Tenses, A: Essays on Poetry (Gallagher), **Supp. XXIV:** 166, 167, 171–172

Conchologist's First Book, The (Poe), **III:** 412

Conclusive Evidence (Nabokov), **III:** 247–250, 252

"Concord Hymn" (Emerson), **II:** 19

Concrete Blonde, The (Connelly), **Supp. XXI:** **70–71**, 78, 80

"Concrete Universal, The: Observations on the Understanding of Poetry" (Ransom), **III:** 480

Concurring Beasts (Dobyns), **Supp. XIII:** 76

Condé, Maryse, **Supp. XXIII:** 94

Condensed Novels and Other Papers (Harte), **Supp. II Part 1:** 342

"Condition, The" (Karmi; Everwine, trans.), **Supp. XV:** 78

Condition of Man, The (Mumford), **Supp. II Part 2:** 483, 484, 486, 495–496, 498

"Condolence" (Parker), **Supp. IX:** 191

"Condominium, The" (Elkin), **Supp. VI:** 49, **50–51**, 55, 56

Condon, Charles R., **Supp. XIII:** 163

Condor and the Cows, The: A South American Travel Diary (Isherwood and Caskey), **Supp. XIV:** 166

"Condor and the Guests, The" (Connell), **Supp. XIV:** 86

Condorcet, Marquis de, **Supp. I Part 2:** 511

Conduct of Life, The (Emerson), **II:** 1–5, 8

Conduct of Life, The (Mumford), **Supp. II Part 2:** 485, 496–497

"Conductor of Nothing, The" (Levine), **Supp. V:** 189

Coney Island of the Mind, A (Ferlinghetti), **Supp. XIX:** 4; **Supp. XXI:** 53

"Conference Male, The" (Mora), **Supp. XIII:** 218

"Confession" (Peacock), **Supp. XIX:** 206

"Confessional" (Bidart), **Supp. XV:** 29–30, 31

"Confessional Poem" (Nelson), **Supp. XVIII:** 174

Confession de Claude, La (Zola), **I:** 411

"Confession of a House-Breaker, The" (Jewett), **Retro. Supp. II:** 146–147

Confession of Jereboam O. Beauchamp, The (pamphlet), **IV:** 253

Confessions (Augustine), **I:** 279; **Supp. XVI:** 288; **Supp. XXII:** 93

Confessions (Rousseau), **I:** 226

Confessions of a Barbarian: Selections from the Journals of Edward Abbey, 1951–1989 (Abbey; Petersen, ed.), **Supp. XIII:** 2, 4

"Confessions of a Latina Author" (Mora), **Supp. XIII:** 221

"Confessions of a Wannabe Negro" (McKnight), **Supp. XX: 152–153, 158**

Confessions of Nat Turner, The (Styron), **IV:** 98, 99, 105, 113–117; **Supp. X:** 16, 250

Confetti (Mora), **Supp. XIII:** 221

Confidence (James), **II:** 327, 328

Confidence-Man, The (Melville), **III:** 91; **Retro. Supp. I:** 255–256, 257; **Retro. Supp. II:** 121; **Supp. XIV:** 49

Confidence Man, The (Van Vechten), **Supp. II Part 2:** 737

Confidential Clerk, The (Eliot), **I:** 570, 571–572, 583, 584; **Retro. Supp. I:** 65

Confident Years, 1885–1915, The (Brooks), **I:** 257, 259; **Supp. I Part 2:** 650

"Configurations" (Ammons), **Supp. VII:** 28

Configurations: New and Selected Poems, 1958–1998 (Major), **Supp. XXII: 182**

Confronting the Horror: The Novels of Nelson Algren (Giles), **Supp. IX:** 11, 15

Confucius, **II:** 1; **III:** 456, 475; **Supp. IV Part 1:** 14

Confusion (Cozzens), **I:** 358, 359, 377, 378

"Confusion of Planes We Must Wander in Sleep, The" (Weigl), **Supp. XIX:** 283

Congdon, Don, **Supp. XXII:** 204

Congo (film), **Supp. IV Part 1:** 83

Congo (screenplay, Shanley), **Supp. XIV:** 316

"Congo, The" (Lindsay), **Supp. I Part 2:** 388–389, 392, 395

Congo and Other Poems, The (Lindsay), **Supp. I Part 2:** 379, 382, 389, 390, 391

"Congregation" (Trethewey), **Supp. XXI:** 245, 247

"Congregation of Grackles, A"(Crooker), **Supp. XXIII:** 63

"Congress of the Insomniacs, The" (Simic), **Supp. VIII:** 281–282
Congreve, William, **III:** 195; **Supp. V:** 101; **Supp. XVIII:** 12
Coningsby (Disraeli), **II:** 127
"Conjectural Reading" (Bronk), **Supp. XXI:** 31
Conjectures of a Guilty Bystander (Merton), **Supp. VIII:** 197, 206, 207
Conjugal Bliss: A Comedy of Marital Arts (Nichols), **Supp. XIII:** 269
"Conjugation of the Paramecium, The" (Rukeyser), **Supp. VI:** 271
Conjugations and Reiterations (Murray), **Supp. XIX:** 161
"Conjuration" (Wilbur), **Supp. III Part 2:** 551
Conjure (recording), **Supp. X:** 241
Conjure (Reed), **Supp. X:** 240, 242
Conjure-Man Dies, The: A Mystery Tale of Dark Harlem (R. Fisher), **Supp. XVI:** 143; **Supp. XIX:** 65, 71, **77–78**
Conjure Woman, The (Chesnutt), **Supp. II Part 1:** 193; **Supp. XIV:** 57, **58–61**, 62, 63
Conklin, Grof, **Supp. I Part 2:** 672
Conklin, Peggy, **Supp. XXII:** 27
Conkling, Hilda, **II:** 530
Conkling, Roscoe, **III:** 506
Conley, Robert J., **Supp. V:** 232
Conley, Susan, **Supp. XIII:** 111, 112
Connaroe, Joel, **Supp. IV Part 2:** 690
"Connecticut Lad, A" (White), **Supp. I Part 2:** 677
"Connecticut Valley" (Cowley), **Supp. II Part 1:** 141–142
Connecticut Yankee in King Arthur's Court, A (Twain), **I:** 209; **II:** 276; **IV:** 205
Connell, Evan S., **Supp. XIV: 79–100; Supp. XXIII:** 302
Connell, Norreys (pseudonym). *See* O'Riordan, Conal Holmes O'Connell
Connelly, Marc, **III:** 394; **Supp. I Part 2:** 679; **Supp. IX:** 190
Connelly, Michael, **Supp. XXI: 67–82**
Conner, Dan, **Supp. XXIII:** 125
Connery, Thomas B., **Supp. XVII:** 106
Connoisseur, The (Connell), **Supp. XIV:** 87
"Connoisseur of Chaos" (Stevens), **IV:** 89; **Retro. Supp. I:** 306
Connolly, Cyril, **Supp. XIV:** 158, 343, 348
Connors, Elizabeth. *See* Lindsay, Mrs. Vachel (Elizabeth Connors)
Connotations (Kenny), **Supp. XXIII:** 143, 144, 146, 150, 155
Conover, Roger, **Supp. I Part 1:** 95
Conover, Roger L., **Supp. XXII:** 155, 162
Conquering Horse (Manfred), **Supp. X:** 126
Conqueror, The (Atherton), **Supp. XXIV:** 23
"Conqueror Worm, The" (Poe), **Retro. Supp. II:** 261
Conquest of Canaan (Dwight), **Supp. I Part 1:** 124
Conquistador (MacLeish), **III:** 2, 3, 13–14, 15

Conrad, Alfred, **Retro. Supp. II:** 245
Conrad, Alfred H., **Supp. I Part 2:** 552
Conrad, C. A., **Supp. XXII:** 155
Conrad, David, **Supp. I Part 2:** 552
Conrad, Jacob, **Supp. I Part 2:** 552
Conrad, Joseph, **I:** 123, 343, 394, 405, 409, 415, 421, 485, 506, 575–576, 578; **II:** 58, 73, 74, 91, 92, 144, 263, 320, 338, 595; **III:** 28, 102, 106, 328, 464, 467, 491, 512; **IV:** 476; **Retro. Supp. I:** 80, 91, 106, 108, 231, 274, 377; **Retro. Supp. II:** 222; **Supp. I Part 1:** 292; **Supp. I Part 2:** 621, 622; **Supp. IV Part 1:** 197, 341; **Supp. IV Part 2:** 680; **Supp. V:** 249, 251, 262, 298, 307, 311; **Supp. VIII:** 4, 310; **Supp. XIV:** 112; **Supp. XVI:** 158, 212; **Supp. XVIII:** 98, 102; **Supp. XIX:** 27; **Supp. XX: 195; Supp. XXIV:** 286
Conrad, Paul, **Supp. I Part 2:** 552
Conrad, Peter, **Supp. IV Part 2:** 688
"Conrad Aiken: From Savannah to Emerson" (Cowley), **Supp. II Part 1:** 43
Conrad Richter's Ohio Trilogy (Edwards), **Supp. XVIII:** 220
Conroy, Frank, **Supp. VIII:** 145; **Supp. XI:** 245; **Supp. XVI: 63–78; Supp. XXII:** 50
Conroy, Jack, **Supp. XXII:** 1, 5, 10
Conroy, Pat, **Supp. XVIII:** 193; **Supp. XXII:** 239
Cons, Scams, and Grifts (Gores), **Supp. XXI:** 70
Conscience with the Power and Cases thereof (Ames), **IV:** 158
"Conscientious Objector, The" (Shapiro), **Supp. II Part 2:** 710
"Consciousness and Dining" (Harrison), **Supp. VIII:** 46
"Conscription Camp" (Shapiro), **Supp. II Part 2:** 705
"Consejos de Nuestra Señora de Guadalupe: Counsel from the Brown Virgin" (Mora), **Supp. XIII:** 224
"Conservation Esthetic" (Leopold), **Supp. XIV:** 179, 181, 186, 189–190
"Conserving Natural and Cultural Diversity: The Prose and Poetry of Pat Mora" (Murphy), **Supp. XIII:** 214
Considerable Town, A (M. F. K. Fisher), **Supp. XVII:** 90
"Considerations by the Way" (Emerson), **II:** 2, 5
Consider the Oyster (M. F. K. Fisher), **Supp. XVII:** 84, 87
Considine, Bob, **II:** 424
"Consolation" (Bausch), **Supp. VII:** 48
"Consolations" (Stafford), **Supp. XI:** 329
"Conspiracy of History, The: E. L. Doctorow's *The Book of Daniel*" (Levine), **Supp. IV Part 1:** 221
Conspiracy of Kings, The (Barlow), **Supp. II Part 1:** 80
Conspiracy of Pontiac, The (Parkman), **Supp. II Part 2:** 590, 595, 596, 599–600
Constab Ballads (McKay), **Supp. X:** 131, 133

Constance (Kenyon), **Supp. VII:** 170–172
Constancy (Boyce), **Supp. XVII:** 100; **Supp. XXI:** 6, 7, 12
"Constellation Orion, The" (Kooser), **Supp. XIX:** 120
Construction of Boston, The (Koch), **Supp. XV:** 187
"Constructive Work" (Du Bois), **Supp. II Part 1:** 172
"Consumer's Report" (X. J. Kennedy), **Supp. XV:** 161–162
"Consumption" (Bryant), **Supp. I Part 1:** 169–170
Contact Collection of Contemporary Writers (McAlmon), **Supp. XXII:** 166
"Contagiousness of Puerperal Fever, The" (Holmes), **Supp. I Part 1:** 303–304
"Contemplation in a World of Action" (Merton), **Supp. VIII:** 204
"Contemplation of Poussin" (Sarton), **Supp. VIII:** 261
"Contemplations" (Bradstreet), **Supp. I Part 1:** 112, 113, 119–122
Contemporaries (Kazin), **Supp. VIII:** 102, **103–104**
Contemporary American Playwrights (Bigsby), **Supp. XV:** 332
Contemporary American Poetry (Poulin, ed.), **Supp. IX:** 272; **Supp. XI:** 259
Contemporary Authors Autobiography, **Supp. XXII:** 225
Contending Forces (Hopkins), **Supp. XVIII:** 284
"Contentment" (Holmes), **Supp. I Part 1:** 307
"Contents" (Halliday), **Supp. XIX:** 92
"Contest, The" (Paley), **Supp. VI:** 223, 230, 231
"Contest for Aaron Gold, The" (P. Roth), **Supp. III Part 2:** 403
Continental Drift (Banks), **Supp. V:** 13–14, 16, 227
Continental Op, The (Hammett), **Supp. IV Part 1:** 344
Continent's End: An Anthology of Contemporary California Poets (Taggard, Sterling, and Rorty, eds.), **Supp. XXII:** 276
Continuing Education, A (Pickering), **Supp. XXI:** 194, 195–196
Continuity of American Poetry, The (Pearce), **Supp. I Part 1:** 111; **Supp. I Part 2:** 475
Continuous Harmony, A: Essays Cultural and Agricultural (Berry), **Supp. X:** 33
Continuous Life, The (Strand), **Supp. IV Part 2:** 630, 631–633
Contoski, Victor, **Supp. XII:** 181
"Contract" (Lardner), **II:** 432
"Contraption, The" (Swenson), **Supp. IV Part 2:** 643
"Contrariness of the Mad Farmer, The" (Berry), **Supp. X:** 35
"Contrast, a Spenetic Effusion, The" (J. Schoolcraft), **Supp. XXIII:** 231–232
"Contrition" (Dubus), **Supp. VII:** 84
"Control Burn" (Snyder), **Supp. VIII:** 301

"Control Is the Mainspring" (Komunyakaa), **Supp. XIII:** 122, 124

"Controlling the 'Sloppiness of Things' in Frank Conroy's *Stop-Time*" (Strychacz), **Supp. XVI:** 69–70

Control of Nature, The (McPhee), **Supp. III Part 1:** 310–313

Controversial Sholem Asch, The (Siegel), **Supp. XXIII:** 3

"Conventional Wisdom, The" (Elkin), **Supp. VI: 52–53**

"Convergence" (Ammons), **Supp. VII:** 28

"Convergence of the Twain, The" (Hardy), **Supp. VIII:** 31, 32

Conversation (Aiken), **I:** 54

Conversation at Midnight (Millay), **III:** 138

"Conversation of Eiros and Charmion, The" (Poe), **III:** 412

"Conversation on Conversation" (Stowe), **Supp. I Part 2:** 587

"Conversations in Moscow" (Levertov), **Supp. III Part 1:** 282

Conversations on Some of the Old Poets (Lowell), **Supp. I Part 2:** 405

Conversations with Albert Murray (Maguire, ed.), **Supp. XIX:** 160–161

Conversations with Byron (Blessington), **Retro. Supp. II:** 58

Conversations with Eudora Welty (Prenshaw, ed.), **Retro. Supp. I:** 339, 340, 341, 342, 343, 352, 354

"Conversations with Helmholtz" (Allen), **Supp. XV:** 15

Conversations with Ishmael Reed (Dick and Singh, eds.), **Supp. X:** 244

Conversations with James Baldwin (Standley and Pratt, eds.), **Retro. Supp. II:** 6

Conversations with Richard Wilbur (Wilbur), **Supp. III Part 2:** 542–543

"Conversation with a Fireman from Brooklyn" (Gallagher), **Supp. XXIV:** 169–170

"Conversation with My Father, A" (Paley), **Supp. VI:** 220

"Conversion of the Jews, The" (P. Roth), **Retro. Supp. II:** 281; **Supp. III Part 2:** 404, 406

Convict, The: Stories (Burke), **Supp. XIV:** 25

"Convicta et Combusta" (J. Scott), **Supp. XVII:** 189

"Convolvulus" (Schott), **Supp. XXIII:** 248

"Convoy" (Weigl), **Supp. XIX:** 278

Conway, Jill, **Supp. I Part 1:** 19

Coode, John, **I:** 132

Cook, Bruce, **Supp. XII:** 130, 131, 133–134

Cook, Captain James, **I:** 2

Cook, Eleanor, **Retro. Supp. I:** 311

Cook, Elisha, **Supp. IV Part 1:** 356

Cook, Elizabeth Christine, **II:** 106

Cook, George Cram "Jig", **Supp. XXI:** 5, 6

Cook, Johnny, **Supp. XXIV:** 248

Cook, Mercer, **Supp. IV Part 1:** 368

Cook, Richard, **Supp. XXII:** 158

Cooke, Alistair, **III:** 113, 119, 120

Cooke, Delmar G., **II:** 271

Cooke, Grace MacGowan, **Supp. V:** 285

Cooke, Philip Pendleton, **III:** 420

Cooke, Rose Terry, **II:** 401; **Retro. Supp. II:** 51, 136, 138; **Supp. XIII:** 152

"Cookie" (Taylor), **Supp. V:** 320

"Cookies, The" (Nye), **Supp. XIII:** 281

Cooking of Provincial France, The (M. F. K. Fisher), **Supp. XVII:** 89

Cook-Lynn, Elizabeth, **Supp. IV Part 1:** 325

Coolbrith, Ina, **I:** 193, 196

"Coole Park" (Yeats), **Supp. VIII:** 155, 159

"Coole Park and Ballylee" (Yeats), **Supp. VIII:** 156

Cooler by the Lake (Heinemann), **Supp. XXII:** 103, **114**

Cooley, John, **Supp. V:** 214

Cooley, Peter, **Supp. XIII:** 76

Coolidge, Calvin, **I:** 498; **II:** 95; **Supp. I Part 2:** 647

Cooling Time: An American Poetry Vigil (Wright), **Supp. XV:** 353

"Cool Million, A" (screen story) (West and Ingster), **Retro. Supp. II:** 330

Cool Million, A (West), **III:** 425; **IV:** 287, 288, 297–299, 300; **Retro. Supp. II:** 321, 322–323, 328, **335–337**

"Cool Tombs" (Sandburg), **III:** 554

Coon, Ross, **IV:** 196

Cooney, Seamus, **Supp. XIV:** 289

"Coon Hunt" (White), **Supp. I Part 2:** 669

Co-op (Sinclair), **Supp. V:** 290

Cooper, Bernard, **Supp. XI:** 129

Cooper, Frederic Taber, **Supp. XX: 219–220; Supp. XXIV:** 28–29

Cooper, Gary, **Supp. IV Part 2:** 524

Cooper, James Fenimore, **I:** 211, 257, **335–357; II:** 74, 277, 295–296, 302, 306, 309, 313, 314; **III:** 51; **IV:** 205, 333; **Retro. Supp. I:** 246; **Retro. Supp. II:** 160; **Supp. I Part 1:** 141, 155, 156, 158, 171, 372; **Supp. I Part 2:** 413, 495, 579, 585, 652, 660; **Supp. IV Part 1:** 80; **Supp. IV Part 2:** 463, 469; **Supp. V:** 209–210; **Supp. VIII:** 189; **Supp. XIV:** 227; **Supp. XVIII:** 4; **Supp. XXIII:** 178

Cooper, Mrs. James Fenimore (Susan A. De Lancey), **I:** 338, 351, 354

Cooper, Jane, **Supp. XV:** 259

Cooper, Rand Richards, **Supp. XVI:** 74

Cooper, Susan Fenimore, **I:** 337, 354

Cooper, William, **I:** 337–338, 351

Cooper, Mrs. William, **I:** 337

Cooperman, Robert, **Supp. XXIII:** 247

Coover, Robert, **Supp. IV Part 1:** 388; **Supp. V: 39–55; Supp. XII:** 152; **Supp. XIV:** 96; **Supp. XVII:** 6; **Supp. XXI:** 236; **Supp. XXII:** 259

Copacetic (Komunyakaa), **Supp. XIII: 116–118,** 126

Cope, Wendy, **Supp. XV:** 117

Copelin, David, **Supp. XXIV:** 264

Copland, Aaron, **II:** 586; **Supp. I Part 1:** 281; **Supp. III Part 2:** 619; **Supp. IV Part 1:** 79, 80–81, 84; **Supp. XXII:** 283

Coplas de Don Jorge Manrique (Longfellow, trans.), **II:** 488, 492

Coppée, François Edouard Joachim, **II:** 325

Copperhead, The (Frederic), **II:** 134–135

Copperhead Cane (J. W. Miller), **Supp. XX: 163, 164, 166–167**

Copper Sun (Cullen), **Supp. IV Part 1:** 167, 168

Coppola, Francis Ford, **Supp. XI:** 171, 172; **Supp. XII:** 75

Coprolites (Goldbarth), **Supp. XII: 177–178,** 180, 183

Coral and Captive Israel (Reznikoff), **Supp. XIV:** 288

"Coral Ring, The" (Stowe), **Supp. I Part 2:** 586

"Cora Unashamed" (Hughes), **Supp. I Part 1:** 329, 330

"Corazón del Corrido" (Mora), **Supp. XIII:** 225

Corban Ephphata (Li Lin Lee), **Supp. XV:** 225

Corbett, Gentlemen Jim, **II:** 416

Corbett, William, **Supp. XI:** 248; **Supp. XVI:** 286, 295; **Supp. XXIV:** 45

Corbière, Jean Antoine, **II:** 354–355, 528

Cordiall Water, A: A garland of Odd & Old Receipts to Assuage the Ills of Man and Beast (M. F. K. Fisher), **Supp. XVII:** 88, 90

Cording, Robert, **Supp. IX:** 328; **Supp. XII:** 184

Core, George, **Supp. XVIII:** 86; **Supp. XXI:** 193

Corelli, Marie, **III:** 579

Corey, Lewis, **Supp. I Part 2:** 645

"Corinna's Going a-Maying" (Herrick), **Supp. XIV:** 8, 9

"Coriolan" (Eliot), **I:** 580

"Coriolanus and His Mother" (Schwartz), **Supp. II Part 2:** 643, 644–645

"Corkscrew" (Hammett), **Supp. IV Part 1:** 345, 347

Corkum, Gerald, **I:** 37

Corky's Brother (Neugeboren), **Supp. XVI:** 225

"Corky's Brother" (Neugeboren), **Supp. XVI:** 225

Corliss, Richard, **Supp. VIII:** 73

Corman, Cid, **Supp. III Part 2:** 624, 625, 626, 627, 628; **Supp. IV Part 1:** 144; **Supp. VIII:** 292; **Supp. XV:** 74, 153; **Supp. XXI:** 23, 27

"Corn" (Lanier), **Supp. I Part 1:** 352, 353, 354, 356–361, 364, 366

Corn, Alfred, **Supp. IX:** 156; **Supp. XV:** 250

Corneille, Pierre, **Supp. I Part 2:** 716; **Supp. IX:** 131

Cornell, Esther, **I:** 231

Cornell, Joseph, **Supp. XXI:** 131; **Supp. XXII:** 167, 168

Cornell, Katherine, **IV:** 356

Cornell, Valerie, **Supp. XX: 94–95**

"Corners" (Dunn), **Supp. XI:** 148

Cornhuskers (Sandburg), **III:** 583–585

"Corn-Planting, The" (Anderson), **I:** 114

"Corn story (or the origin of corn)"(J. Schoolcraft), **Supp. XXIII:** 234–235

Cornucopia: New and Selected Poems, 1975–2002 (Peacock), **Supp. XIX: 203–204**

Corn Village (Le Sueur), **Supp. XXIII:** 167

Coronation Murder-Mystery, The (O'Hara, Ashbery, and Koch), **Supp. XXIII:** 217

"Coroner's Report" (Wrigley), **Supp. XVIII:** 295

"Corporal of Artillery" (Dubus), **Supp. VII:** 84, 85

"Corpse Plant, The" (Rich), **Supp. I Part 2:** 555

Corpus Christi (McNally), **Supp. XIII: 205–206,** 209

Corradi, Juan, **Supp. IV Part 1:** 208

Corrections, The (Franzen), **Supp. XIX:** 54; **Supp. XX: 83, 84, 85, 90, 91, 91–93, 95**

Corregidora (G. Jones), **Supp. XXIV:** 183–184, **185–187,** 190, 193, 194, 195

"Correspondences" (Baudelaire), **I:** 63

"Corrido de Gregorio Cortez" (Mora), **Supp. XIII:** 225

"Corrigenda" (Komunyakaa), **Supp. XIII:** 115, 116

Corrosive Sublimate (Sorrentino), **Supp. XXI:** 226, 228

Corruption City (McCoy), **Supp. XIII:** 175

Corso, Gregory, **Supp. II Part 1:** 30; **Supp. IV Part 1:** 90; **Supp. XII: 117–138; Supp. XIV:** 150; **Supp. XVI:** 135; **Supp. XXI:** 53; **Supp. XXIII:** 215

Corsons Inlet (Ammons), **Supp. VII:** 25–26, 28–29, 36

"Corsons Inlet" (Ammons), **Supp. VII:** 25–26

Cortázar, Julio, **Retro. Supp. I:** 278; **Supp. XXII:** 265

"Cortège for Rosenbloom" (Stevens), **IV:** 81

Cortez, Hernando, **III:** 2

" 'Coruscating Glamour': Lynda Hull and the Movies" (Goldstein), **Supp. XXI:** 134

Cory, William Johnson, **Supp. XX: 230, 231**

Coser, Lewis, **Supp. I Part 2:** 650

Cosgrave, Patrick, **Retro. Supp. II:** 185

Cosmic Optimism: A Study of the Interpretation of Evolution by American Poets from Emerson to Robinson (Conner), **Supp. I Part 1:** 73

Cosmological Eye, The (H. Miller), **III:** 174, 184

"Cosmological Eye, The" (H. Miller), **III:** 183

"Cosmos" (Beattie), **Supp. V:** 35

"Cost, The" (Hecht), **Supp. X:** 62–63

Costello, Bonnie, **Retro. Supp. II:** 40

Costello, Mark, **Supp. XXIII:** 290

Costner, Kevin, **Supp. VIII:** 45

"Cost of Living, The" (Malamud), **Supp. I Part 2:** 429, 437

"Costume as Metaphor" (Bronk), **Supp. XXI:** 26

Cott, Jonathan, **Supp. XVI:** 104, 106

"Cottagers' Corner" column (D. West), **Supp. XVIII:** 286

"Cottage Street, 1953" (Wilbur), **Supp. III Part 2:** 543, 561

"Cottagette, The" (Gilman), **Supp. XI:** 207

Cotten, Joseph, **Supp. IV Part 2:** 524

Cotter, James Finn, **Supp. X:** 202

Cotton, John, **Supp. I Part 1:** 98, 101, 110, 111, 116

Cotton, Joseph, **Supp. XII:** 160

Cotton, Seaborn, **Supp. I Part 1:** 101

Cotton Club, The (Major), **Supp. XXII:** 174

"Cotton Club Classics" (Halliday), **Supp. XIX:** 92, 93

Cotton Comes to Harlem (C. Himes), **Supp. XVI:** 143, 144

Cotton Comes to Harlem (film, O. Davis), **Supp. XVI:** 144

"Cotton Song" (Toomer), **Supp. IX:** 312

Couch, W. T., **Supp. X:** 46

Coughlin, Ruth Pollack, **Supp. VIII:** 45

Coulette, Henri, **Supp. V:** 180; **Supp. XIII:** 312; **Supp. XV:** 74, 75

Coultrap-McQuin, Susan, **Supp. XVI:** 85, 92

"Council of State, A" (Dunbar), **Supp. II Part 1:** 211, 213

"Count Dracula" (Allen), **Supp. XV:** 15

"Countee Cullen at 'The Heights' " (Tuttleton), **Supp. IV Part 1:** 166

Counterfeiters, The (Gide), **Supp. IV Part 1:** 80; **Supp. IV Part 2:** 681

"Countering" (Ammons), **Supp. VII:** 28

Counterlife, The (P. Roth), **Retro. Supp. II:** 279, 280, 291; **Supp. III Part 2:** 424–426

Counter-Statement (Burke), **I:** 270–272; **IV:** 431

"Countess, The" (Whittier), **Supp. I Part 2:** 691, 694

Count Frontenac and New France Under Louis XIV (Parkman), **Supp. II Part 2:** 607, 609–610

"Counting Small-Boned Bodies" (R. Bly), **Supp. IV Part 1:** 62

"Counting the Body"(Schott), **Supp. XXIII:** 251–252

"Counting the Children" (Gioia), **Supp. XV: 122–123**

"Counting the Mad" (Justice), **Supp. VII:** 117

"Count Lothar's Heart" (Boyle), **Supp. XXIV:** 58

Count of Monte Cristo, The (Dumas), **III:** 386, 396; **Supp. XVII:** 64, 216

"Countries We Live In, The" (Zach; Everwine, trans.), **Supp. XV:** 87

"Country Boy in Boston, The" (Howells), **II:** 255

Country By-Ways (Jewett), **II:** 402

Country Doctor, A (Jewett), **II:** 391, 392, 396, 404–405; **Retro. Supp. II:** 131, 141, 146

"Country Full of Swedes" (Caldwell), **I:** 297, 309

Country Girl, The (Odets), **Supp. II Part 2:** 546, 547, 548–549

"Country House" (Kumin), **Supp. IV Part 2:** 446

"Country Husband, The" (Cheever), **Supp. I Part 1:** 184, 189

"Country Life" (Pickering), **Supp. XXI:** 197

"Country Marriage" (C. Frost), **Supp. XV:** 99

Countrymen of Bones (R. O. Butler), **Supp. XII:** 62, **65–66**

"Country Mouse, The" (Bishop), **Retro. Supp. II:** 37, 38, 51

Country Music: Selected Early Poems (Wright), **Supp. V:** 332, 335, 338, 342

Country of a Thousand Years of Peace, The (Merrill), **Supp. III Part 1:** 321, 322, 331

"Country of Elusion, The" (O. Henry), **Supp. II Part 1:** 407

Country Of Language, The (Sanders), **Supp. XVI:** 277

Country of Marriage, The (Berry), **Supp. X:** 33

Country of Strangers, A (Richter), **Supp. XVIII:** 217

Country of Survivors (Di Piero), **Supp. XIX:** 36

Country of the Pointed Firs, The (Jewett), **II:** 392, 399, 405, 409–411; **Retro. Supp. I:** 6; **Retro. Supp. II:** 134, 136, 139, 140, 141, 145, 146, 147; **Supp. VIII:** 126; **Supp. XIII:** 152; **Supp. XXIII:** 275, 278

"Country Printer, The" (Freneau), **Supp. II Part 1:** 269

"Country Wife, The" (Gioia), **Supp. XV:** 120

Count Your Bullets (film), **Supp. XVII:** 141

Count Zero (W. Gibson), **Supp. XVI:** 19, **126–127,** 129

Coup, The (Updike), **Retro. Supp. I:** 331, 334, 335

"Coup de Grâce, The" (Bierce), **I:** 202

Couperin, François, **III:** 464

"Couple, The" (Olds), **Supp. X:** 206

"Couple of Hamburgers, A" (Thurber), **Supp. I Part 2:** 616

"Couple of Nuts, A" (Z. Fitzgerald), **Supp. IX:** 58, 71, 72

"Couples" (Halliday), **Supp. XIX:** 89

Couples (Updike), **IV:** 214, 215, 216, 217, 227, 229–230; **Retro. Supp. I:** 320, 327, 330; **Supp. XII:** 296

Cournos, John, **III:** 465; **Supp. I Part 1:** 258

"Course in Creative Writing, A" (Stafford), **Supp. XI:** 327

"Course of a Particular, The" (Stevens), **Retro. Supp. I:** 312

"Coursier de Jeanne d'Arc, Le" (McCarriston), **Supp. XIV:** 267–268

Courtier, The (Castiglione), **III:** 282

" 'Courtin,' The" (Lowell), **Supp. I Part 2:** 415

"Courting of Sister Wisby, The" (Jewett), **Retro. Supp. II:** 134, 135, 146

"Courting the Famous Figures at the Grotto of Improbable Thought" (B. Kelly), **Supp. XVII:** 127–128

Courtney, W. L., **Supp. XXIV:** 29

"Courtship" (Dove), **Supp. IV Part 1:** 248

"Courtship, A"(Thompson), **Supp. XXIII:** 293

"Courtship, Diligence" (Dove), **Supp. IV Part 1:** 248

Courtship of Miles Standish, The (Longfellow), **II:** 489, 502–503; **Retro. Supp. II:** 155, **161–162,** 163, 166, 168

"Cousin Aubrey" (Taylor), **Supp. V:** 328

Cousine Bette (Balzac), **Retro. Supp. II:** 98

Couturier, Maurice, **Supp. IV Part 1:** 44

Covarrubias, Miguel, **Supp. XVI:** 187

"Covered Bridges" (Kingsolver), **Supp. VII:** 203

"Cover Photograph" (Nelson), **Supp. XVIII:** 173

"Cover Stories" (Skloot), **Supp. XX: 195, 207**

"Cover Versions" (Halliday), **Supp. XIX:** 84

Cowan, Lester, **III:** 148

Cowan, Louise, **IV:** 120, 125

Coward, Noel, **Retro. Supp. I:** 65; **Supp. I Part 1:** 332; **Supp. V:** 101; **Supp. XV:** 329; **Supp. XXIV:** 267

"Cowardice" (Theroux), **Supp. VIII:** 313

Cowboy Mouth (Shepard), **Supp. III Part 2:** 441–442

"Cowboys" (Salter). *See* "Dirt" (Salter)

Cowboys (Shepard), **Supp. III Part 2:** 432

Cowboys #2 (Shepard), **Supp. III Part 2:** 437, 438

Cowell, Henry, **Supp. IV Part 1:** 80, 82

Cowen, Philip, **Supp. XX:** 2

Cowen, Wilson Walker, **Supp. IV Part 2:** 435

Cowie, Alexander, **IV:** 70

"Cow in Apple Time, The" (Frost), **II:** 154; **Retro. Supp. I:** 131

Cowl, Jane, **IV:** 357

Cowley, Abraham, **III:** 508; **IV:** 158; **Supp. I Part 1:** 357

Cowley, Malcolm, **I:** 246, 253, 254, 255, 256, 257, 283, 385; **II:** 26, 57, 94, 456; **III:** 606; **IV:** 123; **Retro. Supp. I:** 73, 91, 97; **Retro. Supp. II:** 77, 83, 89, 221, 330; **Supp. I Part 1:** 174; **Supp. I Part 2:** 609, 610, 620, 647, 654, 678; **Supp. II Part 1:** 103, **135–156; Supp. VIII:** 96; **Supp. XV:** 142; **Supp. XX:** 76

Cowley, Marguerite Frances Baird (Mrs. Malcolm Cowley), **Supp. I Part 2:** 615; **Supp. II Part 1:** 138, 139

Cowley, Muriel Maurer (Mrs. Malcolm Cowley), **Supp. II Part 1:** 139

Cowley, Susan Cheever (Susan Cheever), **Supp. I Part 1:** 175; **Supp. IX:** 133; **Supp. XXIV:** 97

Cowper, William, **II:** 17, 304; **III:** 508, 511; **Supp. I Part 1:** 150, 151, 152; **Supp. I Part 2:** 539

"Cow Wandering in the Bare Field, The" (Jarrell), **II:** 371, 388

Cox, Martha Heasley, **Supp. IX:** 2, 4, 11–12

Cox, Sidney, **Retro. Supp. I:** 131; **Supp. XXI:** 19, 21

Cox, Stephen, **Supp. IV Part 2:** 523, 524

Cox, Steve, **Supp. XIX:** 116, 128

Coxey, Jacob, **II:** 464

"Coxon Fund, The" (James), **Retro. Supp. I:** 228

"Coy Mistress" (A. Finch), **Supp. XVII:** 72

Coyne, Patricia, **Supp. V:** 123

"Coyote Ortiz: *Canis latrans latrans* in the Poetry of Simon Ortiz" (P. C. Smith), **Supp. IV Part 2:** 509

Coyote's Daylight Trip (Gunn Allen), **Supp. IV Part 1:** 320, 324

Coyote Was Here (Ortiz), **Supp. IV Part 2:** 499

Cozzens, James Gould, **I:** 358–380; **II:** 459

Crabbe, George, **II:** 304; **III:** 469, 508, 511, 521; **Supp. XXIV:** 159

"Crab-Boil" (Dove), **Supp. IV Part 1:** 249

"Cracked Looking-Glass, The" (Porter), **III:** 434, 435, 446

"Cracker Chidlings" (Rawlings), **Supp. X:** 224, 228

Cracks (Purdy), **Supp. VII:** 277–278

Crack-Up, The (Fitzgerald), **II:** 80; **III:** 35, 45; **Retro. Supp. I:** 113, 115; **Supp. V:** 276; **Supp. IX:** 61

"Crack-Up, The" (Fitzgerald), **I:** 509; **Retro. Supp. I:** 113, 114

"Crack-up of American Optimism, The: Vachel Lindsay, the Dante of the Fundamentalists" (Viereck), **Supp. I Part 2:** 403

"Cradle and the Bookcase, The"(Hadas), **Supp. XXIII:** 122

Cradle Will Rock, The (Blitzstein), **Supp. I Part 1:** 277, 278

Craft of Fiction, The (Lubbock), **I:** 504; **Supp. VIII:** 165

Craft of Peter Taylor, The (McAlexander, ed.), **Supp. V:** 314

Craig, David M., **Supp. XXII:** 187, 191, 192

Craig, Gordon, **III:** 394; **Supp. XXI:** 6

Crain, Jane Larkin, **Supp. V:** 123; **Supp. XII:** 167, 168

Crais, Robert, **Supp. XXI:** 70

Cram, Ralph Adams, **I:** 19

Cramer, Steven, **Supp. XI:** 139; **Supp. XV:** 26

"Cranbrook Schools: Adventures in Bourgeois Topologies" (Monson), **Supp. XXIV:** 235

Crandall, Reuben, **Supp. I Part 2:** 686

Crane, Agnes, **I:** 406

Crane, Edmund, **I:** 407

Crane, Hart, **I:** 61, 62, 97, 109, 116, 266, **381–404; II:** 133, 215, 306, 368, 371, 536, 542; **III:** 260, 276, 453, 485, 521; **IV:** 122, 123–124, 127, 128, 129, 135, 139, 140, 141, 341, 380, 418, 419; **Retro. Supp. I:** 427; **Retro. Supp. II:**

75–91; **Supp. I Part 1:** 86; **Supp. II Part 1:** 89, 152; **Supp. III Part 1:** 20, 63, 350; **Supp. V:** 342; **Supp. VIII:** 39; **Supp. IX:** 38, 229, 320; **Supp. X:** 115, 116, 120; **Supp. XI:** 123, 131; **Supp. XII:** 198; **Supp. XV:** 138; **Supp. XIX:** 35; **Supp. XX: 80; Supp. XXI:** 131, 132, 136, 230; **Supp. XXII:** 274; **Supp. XXIII:** 146, 174, 207

Crane, Jonathan, Jr., **I:** 407

Crane, Jonathan Townley, **I:** 406

Crane, Mrs. Jonathan Townley, **I:** 406

Crane, Luther, **I:** 406

Crane, Milton, **Supp. XV:** 144

Crane, Nellie, **I:** 407

Crane, R. S., **Supp. I Part 2:** 423

Crane, Stephen, **I:** 34, 169–170, 201, 207, 211, **405–427,** 477, 506, 519; **II:** 58, 144, 198, 262, 263, 264, 276, 289, 290, 291; **III:** 314, 317, 334, 335, 454, 505, 585; **IV:** 207, 208, 256, 350, 475; **Retro. Supp. I:** 231, 325; **Retro. Supp. II:** 97, 123; **Supp. I Part 1:** 314; **Supp. III Part 2:** 412; **Supp. IV Part 1:** 350, 380; **Supp. IV Part 2:** 680, 689, 692; **Supp. VIII:** 98, 105; **Supp. IX:** 1, 14; **Supp. X:** 223; **Supp. XI:** 95; **Supp. XII:** 50; **Supp. XIV:** 21, 50, 51, 227; **Supp. XVII:** 71, 228; **Supp. XVIII:** 74, 75; **Supp. XXIII:** 26

Crane, William, **I:** 407

Cranford (Gaskell), **Supp. IX:** 79

Crashaw, William, **IV:** 145, 150, 151, 165

"Crash Report" (McGrath), **Supp. X:** 116

Crater, The (Cooper), **I:** 354, 355

Cratylus (Plato), **II:** 10

Cravan, Arthur, **Supp. XXII:** 164, 169

"Craven Street Gazette" (Franklin), **II:** 119

"Crawdad, The" (F. Wright), **Supp. XVII:** 244

Crawdad Creek (Sanders), **Supp. XVI:** 269

Crawford, Brad, **Supp. XI:** 133

Crawford, Eva, **I:** 199

Crawford, F. Marion, **III:** 320

Crawford, Joan, **Supp. I Part 1:** 67

Crawford, John E., **Supp. XXIII:** 165

Crawford, Kathleen, **I:** 289

"Crayon House" (Rukeyser), **Supp. VI:** 273

Crayon Miscellany, The (Irving), **II:** 312–313

Crazed, The (Jin), **Supp. XVIII: 99–100**

"Crazy about her Shrimp" (Simic), **Supp. VIII:** 282

"Crazy Cock" (H. Miller), **III:** 177

Crazy Gypsy (Salinas), **Supp. XIII:** 311, **313–315,** 316

"Crazy Gypsy" (Salinas), **Supp. XIII:** 313–314

Crazy Horse, **Supp. IV Part 2:** 488, 489

Crazy Horse (McMurtry), **Supp. V:** 233

Crazy Horse in Stillness (Heyen), **Supp. XIII:** 344

Crazy Horse: The Strange Man of the Oglaglas (Sandoz), **Supp. XXIV:** 244, 256, **257–258**

"Crazy Hunter, The" (Boyle), **Supp. XXIV: 54–55**

Crazy Hunter, The: Three Short Novels (Boyle), **Supp. XXIV: 54–56**

"Crazy in the Stir" (C. Himes), **Supp. XVI:** 137

Crazy Kill, The (C. Himes), **Supp. XVI:** 143

Creating a Role (Stanislavsky), **Supp. XIV:** 243

"Creation, According to Coyote, The" (Ortiz), **Supp. IV Part 2:** 505

Creation: A Novel (Vidal), **Supp. IV Part 2:** 677, 685, 688

"Creation of Anguish" (Nemerov), **III:** 269

"Creation Story" (Gunn Allen), **Supp. IV Part 1:** 325

"Creative and Cultural Lag" (Ellison), **Retro. Supp. II:** 116; **Supp. II Part 1:** 229; **Supp. XVIII:** 283

Creative Criticism (Spingarn), **I:** 266

"Creative Democracy" (Locke), **Supp. XIV:** 208

Creative Present, The (Balkian and Simmons, eds.), **Supp. XI:** 230

"Creatures" (Gallagher), **Supp. XXIV:** 176, 177

Creatures in an Alphabet (illus. Barnes), **Supp. III Part 1:** 43

"Credences of Summer" (Stevens), **IV:** 93–94

"Credentials" (Halliday), **Supp. XIX:** 90

"Credo" (Bynner), **Supp. XV:** 50

"Credo" (Du Bois), **Supp. II Part 1:** 169

"Credo" (Jeffers), **Supp. II Part 2:** 424

"Credos and Curios" (Thurber), **Supp. I Part 2:** 606, 613

Creech, James, **Retro. Supp. I:** 254

"Creed for Americans, A" (Benét), **Supp. XI:** 52

"Creed of a Beggar, The" (Lindsay), **Supp. I Part 2:** 379

Creegan, Andy, **Supp. XIX:** 205

Creekmore, Hubert, **II:** 586

Creeley, Robert, **Retro. Supp. I:** 411; **Supp. II Part 1:** 30; **Supp. III Part 1:** 2; **Supp. III Part 2:** 622, 626, 629; **Supp. IV Part 1: 139–161,** 322, 325; **Supp. XI:** 317; **Supp. XIII:** 104, 112; **Supp. XIV:** 150; **Supp. XVI:** 283; **Supp. XXI:** 23, 27, 227, 230; **Supp. XXII:** 227; **Supp. XXIV:** 35, 37

Creelman, James Ashmore, **Supp. XVI:** 186–187

"Cremona Violin, The" (Lowell), **II:** 523

"Crêpe de Chine" (Doty), **Supp. XI:** 128

"Crêpes Flambeau" (Gallagher), **Supp. XXIV:** 170

"Cressy" (Harte), **Supp. II Part 1:** 354, 356

"Cretan Woman, The" (Jeffers), **Supp. II Part 2:** 435

Crèvecoeur, Michel-Guillaume Jean de, **I:** 229; **Supp. I Part 1: 227–252**

Crèvecoeur's Eighteenth-Century Travels in Pennsylvania and New York (Adams), **Supp. I Part 1:** 251

Crevel, René, **Supp. XIV:** 343

Crewe-Jones, Florence, **Supp. XVII:** 58

Crewe Train (Macaulay), **Supp. XII:** 88

Crews, Harry, **Supp. X:** 11, 12; **Supp. XI: 99–117,** 245; **Supp. XVIII:** 195; **Supp. XXI:** 35, 38, 40, 44

Crews, James, **Supp. XXIII:** 134–135

Crichton, Michael, **Supp. XIV:** 316

Crick, Philip, **Supp. XVI:** 289

Cricket (C. L. R. James; Grimshaw, ed.), **Supp. XXI:** 172

"Cricket" (C. Miller), **Supp. XXII:** 199

"Crickets" (R. O. Butler), **Supp. XII:** 71

Criers and Kibitzers, Kibitzers and Criers (Elkin), **Supp. VI: 45–46,** 57

Crime and Punishment (Dostoevsky), **II:** 60, 130; **IV:** 484; **Supp. IV Part 2:** 525; **Supp. VIII:** 282; **Supp. XII:** 281; **Supp. XVII:** 155; **Supp. XVIII:** 278; **Supp. XIX:** 276

Crime at Scottsboro, The (Endore), **Supp. XVII:** 59

Crime Beat (Connelly), **Supp. XXI:** 67, 79

Crimes and Misdemeanors (film; Allen), **Supp. XV:** 1, 2, **11,** 12

"Criminal"(Strout), **Supp. XXIII:** 283, 285

Crisis papers (Paine), **Supp. I Part 2:** 508–509, 510

"Criteria of Negro Art" (Du Bois), **Supp. II Part 1:** 181; **Supp. XIX:** 66–67

"Critiad, The" (Winters), **Supp. II Part 2:** 794, 799

Critical Anthology A (Untermeyer), **Supp. XV:** 310

Critical Essays on Charlotte Perkins Gilman (Karpinski, ed.), **Supp. XI:** 201

Critical Essays on Kay Boyle (Elkins, ed.), **Supp. XXIV:** 64

Critical Essays on Peter Taylor (McAlexander), **Supp. V:** 319, 320, 323–324

Critical Essays on Robert Bly (W. V. Davis), **Supp. IV Part 1:** 64, 69

Critical Essays on Wallace Stegner (Arthur), **Supp. IV Part 2:** 606

Critical Fable, A (Lowell), **II:** 511–512, 527, 529–530

Critical Guide to Leaves of Grass, A (J. Miller), **IV:** 352

Critical Response to Joan Didion, The (Felton), **Supp. IV Part 1:** 210

Critical Temper of Alain Locke, The: A Selection of His Essays on Art and Culture (Stewart, ed.), **Supp. XIV: 196, 210–211,** 213

"Critic as Artist, The" (Wilde), **Supp. X:** 189

Criticism and Fiction (Howells), **II:** 288

Criticism and Ideology (Eagleton), **Retro. Supp. I:** 67

Criticism in the Borderlands (Calderón and Saldívar, eds.), **Supp. IV Part 2:** 544

"Critics, The" (Jong), **Supp. V:** 119

"Critics and Connoisseurs" (Moore), **III:** 209

Critic's Notebook, A (Howe), **Supp. VI:** 126–128

"Critic's Task, The" (Kazin), **Supp. VIII:** 103

"Critic Who Does Not Exist, The" (Wilson), **IV:** 431

"Critique de la Vie Quotidienne" (Barthelme), **Supp. IV Part 1:** 50

Critique of Pure Reason (Kant), **Supp. XVI:** 184

Croce, Benedetto, **I:** 58, 255, 265, 273, 281; **III:** 610

Crockett, Davy, **II:** 307; **III:** 227; **IV:** 266; **Supp. I Part 2:** 411

"Crocodilopolis" (Cliff), **Supp. XXII:** 76

Crofter and the Laird, The (McPhee), **Supp. III Part 1:** 301–302, 307

Croly, Herbert, **I:** 229, 231, 235; **IV:** 436

Cromwell, Oliver, **IV:** 145, 146, 156; **Supp. I Part 1:** 111

Cronenberg, David, **Supp. XXI:** 152, 154

Cronin, A. J., **Supp. XVII:** 59

Cronin, Dr. Archibald, **III:** 578

Cronin, Justin, **Supp. X:** 10

Crooke, Dr. Helkiah, **Supp. I Part 1:** 98, 104

Crooked Little Heart (Lamott), **Supp. XX: 138**

Crooker, Barbara, **Supp. XXIII: 51–66,** 245, **246,** 251

Crooks, Alan, **Supp. V:** 226

Crooks, Robert, **Supp. XIII:** 237

"Crop, The" (O'Connor), **Retro. Supp. II:** 223–225

Crosby, Caresse, **I:** 385; **III:** 473; **Retro. Supp. II:** 85; **Supp. XII:** 198

Crosby, Harry, **I:** 385; **Retro. Supp. II:** 85

"Cross" (Hughes), **Supp. I Part 1:** 325; **Supp. XVIII:** 124

Cross, Charles, **Supp. XXIV:** 173

Crossan, John Dominic, **Supp. V:** 251

"Cross Country Snow" (Hemingway), **II:** 249

Cross Creek (Rawlings), **Supp. X:** 223, 226, 228, **231–232,** 233, 234, 235

Cross Creek Cookery (Rawlings), **Supp. X:** 233

Crossing, The (McCarthy), **Supp. VIII:** 175, **184–186**

"Crossing, The" (Swenson), **Supp. IV Part 2:** 644

"Crossing Brooklyn Ferry" (Whitman), **IV:** 333, 340, 341; **Retro. Supp. I:** 389, 396, 397, 400–401; **Supp. XXIII:** 109

"Crossing into Poland" (Babel), **Supp. XIV:** 84

Crossings (Chuang), **Supp. X:** 291

"Crossings" (Hogan), **Supp. IV Part 1:** 412

Crossing the Water (Plath), **Retro. Supp. II:** 248; **Supp. I Part 2:** 526, 538

Crossing to Safety (Stegner), **Supp. IV Part 2:** 599, 606, 612, 613–614

"Cross of Snow, The" (Longfellow), **II:** 490; **Retro. Supp. II:** 169–170

"Crossover" (O. Butler), **Supp. XIII:** 61

"Cross-Roads, The" (Lowell), **II:** 523

"Crossroads of the World Etc." (Merwin), **Supp. III Part 1:** 347, 348

Cross-Section (Seaver), **IV:** 485

Cross the Border, Close the Gap (Fiedler), **Supp. XIII:** 104

Cross Ties (X. J. Kennedy), **Supp. XV:** 165, **166–167**

"Cross Ties" (X. J. Kennedy), **Supp. XV:** 158

Crouch, Stanley, **Supp. XIX:** 158

"Croup" (Karr), **Supp. XI:** 243

Crouse, Russel, **III:** 284

"Crow" (Hogan), **Supp. IV Part 1:** 405

Crow (Hughes), **Supp. XV:** 347, 348

"Crow, The" (Creeley), **Supp. IV Part 1:** 148–149

Crow and the Heart,The (Carruth), **Supp. XVI:** 47–48

"Crowded Street, The" (Bryant), **Supp. I Part 1:** 168

Crowder, A. B., **Supp. XI:** 107

"Crow Jane" (Baraka), **Supp. II Part 1:** 38

Crow Mercies (Schott), **Supp. XXIII:** **252–254**

"Crow Mercies" (Schott), **Supp. XXIII:** 253

Crowninshield, Frank, **III:** 123; **Supp. IX:** 201

Crown of Columbus (Erdrich and Dorris), **Supp. IV Part 1:** 260

"Crows, The" (Bogan), **Supp. III Part 1:** 50, 51

Crucial Instances (Wharton), **Retro. Supp. I:** 365, 367

Crucible, The (A. Miller), **III:** 147, 148, 155, 156–158, 159, 166; **Supp. XIII:** 206

"Crucified" (Gibran), **Supp. XX:** **119**

"Crucifix in the Filing Cabinet" (Shapiro), **Supp. II Part 2:** 712

"Crude Foyer" (Stevens), **Retro. Supp. I:** 310

"Cruel and Barbarous Treatment" (McCarthy), **II:** 562, 563

"Cruel Mother, The" (B. Kelly), **Supp. XVII:** 126

Cruise of the Dazzler, The (London), **II:** 465

Cruise of the Snark, The (London), **II:** 476–477

"Cruising with the Beach Boys" (Gioia), **Supp. XV:** 118

" 'Crumbling Idols' by Hamlin Garland" (Chopin), **Supp. I Part 1:** 217

"Crusade of the Excelsior, The" (Harte), **Supp. II Part 1:** 336, 354

"Crusoe in England" (Bishop), **Retro. Supp. II:** 50; **Supp. I Part 1:** 93, 95, 96; **Supp. III Part 1:** 10, 18

Cruz-Hacker, Alba, **Supp. XXI:** 107

Cry, the Beloved Country (Paton), **Supp. VIII:** 126

Cryer, Dan, **Supp. VIII:** 86, 88; **Supp. XII:** 164

Crying of Lot 49, The (Pynchon), **Supp. II Part 2:** 618, 619, 621, 630–633

"Crying Sisters, The" (Rand), **Supp. IV Part 2:** 524

"Crying Wolf" (C. Frost), **Supp. XV:** 101

"Cry of the Graves, The" (Gibran), **Supp. XX:** **124**

Cryptogram, The (Mamet), **Supp. XIV:** 240, 247, 255

"Crystal, The" (Aiken), **I:** 60

"Crystal, The" (Lanier), **Supp. I Part 1:** 364, 370

"Crystal Cage, The" (Kunitz), **Supp. III Part 1:** 258

Crystal Cup, The (Atherton), **Supp. XXIV:** 26

Crystal Vision (Sorrentino), **Supp. XXI:** 235, 236

"Crytal" (Sobin), **Supp. XVI:** 283

Cry to Heaven (Rice), **Supp. VII:** 300–301

"Cuba" (Hemingway), **II:** 258

"Cuba Libre" (Baraka), **Supp. II Part 1:** 33

Cuba: Prophetic Island (W. Frank), **Supp. XX:** **80, 81**

"Cubism, Barcelona" (Hull), **Supp. XXI:** 137

Cudjoe, Selwyn, **Supp. IV Part 1:** 6

"Cudjo's Own Story of the Last American Slaver" (Hurston), **Supp. VI:** 153

Cudlipp, Thelma, **I:** 501

Cudworth, Ralph, **II:** 9, 10

"Cuentista" (Mora), **Supp. XIII:** 224

"Cuento de agua santa, Un" (Mora), **Supp. XIII:** 224

Cujo (King), **Supp. V:** 138–139, 143, 149, 152

Cukor, George, **Supp. XVI:** 192

Cullen, Countee, **Retro. Supp. I:** 207; **Retro. Supp. II:** 114; **Supp. I Part 1:** 49, 325; **Supp. III Part 1:** 73, 75, 76; **Supp. IV Part 1: 163–174; Supp. IX:** 306, 309; **Supp. X:** 136, 140; **Supp. XIII:** 186; **Supp. XVIII:** 122,131, 185, 279, 280, 282, 284; **Supp. XIX:** 78; **Supp. XXII:** 3, 6, 7, 8

"Cultivation of Christmas Trees, The" (Eliot), **I:** 579

"Cult of Personality in American Letters, The" (Swados), **Supp. XIX:** 265

"Cult of the Best, The" (Arnold), **I:** 223

"Cultural Exchange" (Hughes), **Supp. I Part 1:** 341

"Cultural Pluralism: A New Americanism" (Locke), **Supp. XIV:** 195

"Cultural Relativism and Ideological Peace" (Locke), **Supp. XIV:** 202, 212

"Culture" (Emerson), **III:** 2, 4

"Culture, Self, and Style" (Gass), **Supp. VI:** 88

"Culture and Religion" (Olds), **Supp. X:** 214

Culture of Cities, The (Mumford), **Supp. II Part 2:** 492, 494–495

Cummings, E. E., **I:** 44, 48, 64, 105, 176, **428–450,** 475, 477, 482, 526; **III:** 20, 196, 476; **IV:** 384, 402, 415, 427, 433; **Retro. Supp. II:** 178, 328; **Supp. I Part 2:** 622, 678; **Supp. III Part 1:** 73; **Supp. IV Part 2:** 637, 641; **Supp. IX:** 20; **Supp. XV:** 312, 338

Cummings, Robert, **Supp. IV Part 2:** 524

Cummins, Ann, **Supp. XXIII:** 280

Cummins, James, **Supp. XVII:** 74

Cunard, Lady, **III:** 459

Cunningham, J. V., **Supp. XV:** 169

Cunningham, Merce, **Supp. IV Part 1:** 83; **Supp. XV:** 187

Cunningham, Michael, **Supp. XII:** 80; **Supp. XV: 55–71**

Cunningham, Rodger, **Supp. XXIII:** 38–39

Cup of Gold (Steinbeck), **IV:** 51, 53, 61–64, 67

"Cupola, The" (Bogan), **Supp. III Part 1:** 53

"Curandera" (Mora), **Supp. XIII:** 214, 222

Curé de Tours, Le (Balzac), **I:** 509

Cure for Dreams, A: A Novel (Gibbons), **Supp. X: 45–47,** 48, 50

Curie, Marie, **IV:** 420, 421; **Supp. I Part 2:** 569

Curie, Pierre, **IV:** 420

Curiosa Americana (Mather), **Supp. II Part 2:** 463

Curiosities (Matthews), **Supp. IX:** 151, 152

"Curious Case of Sidd Finch, The" (Plimpton), **Supp. XVI:** 244

"Curious Shifts of the Poor" (Dreiser), **Retro. Supp. II:** 97

"Current" (Espaillat), **Supp. XXI:** 106

"Currents and Counter-Currents in Medical Science" (Holmes), **Supp. I Part 1:** 305

"Curried Cow" (Bierce), **I:** 200

Curry, Professor W. C., **IV:** 122

Curse of the Jade Scorpion, The (film; Allen), **Supp. XV:** 11

Curse of the Starving Class (Shepard), **Supp. III Part 2:** 433, 447–448

Curse of the Werewolf, The (film), **Supp. XVII:** 56

"Curse on a Thief, A" (X. J. Kennedy), **Supp. XV:** 171

"Curtain, The" (Chandler), **Supp. IV Part 1:** 122

Curtain Calls: British and American Women and the Theater, 1660–1820 (Saar), **Supp. XV:** 237

Curtain of Green, A (Welty), **IV:** 261–264, 268, 283

"Curtain of Green, A" (Welty), **IV:** 263–264

Curtain of Green and Other Stories, A (Welty), **Retro. Supp. I:** 343, 344, 345, 346, 347, 355

Curtain of Trees (opera), **Supp. IV Part 2:** 552

"Curtain Raiser, A" (Stein), **IV:** 43, 44

"Curtains" (Cisneros), **Supp. VII:** 66

Curtin, John, **Supp. IX:** 184

Curtis, George William, **Supp. I Part 1:** 307; **Supp. XVIII:** 3, 14

Curve (Goldbarth), **Supp. XII:** 181

Curve of Binding Energy, The (McPhee), **Supp. III Part 1:** 301

Curzon, Mary, **III:** 52

Cushing, Caleb, **Supp. I Part 2:** 684, 686

Cushman, Howard, **Supp. I Part 2:** 652

Cushman, Stephen, **Retro. Supp. I:** 430

"Custard Heart, The" (Parker), **Supp. IX:** 201

Custer, General George, **I:** 489, 491

Custer Died for Your Sins (Deloria), **Supp. IV Part 1:** 323; **Supp. IV Part 2:** 504

"Custody"(Schott), **Supp. XXIII:** 241
"Custom House, The" (Hawthorne), **II:** 223; **Retro. Supp. I:** 147–148, 157; **Supp. XXI:** 181
Custom of the Country, The (Wharton), **IV:** 318; **Retro. Supp. I:** 374, **375– 376; Supp. XXIV:** 23
"Cut" (Plath), **Retro. Supp. II:** 253
"Cut-Glass Bowl, The" (Fitzgerald), **II:** 88
Cutting, Bronson, **III:** 600
Cutting Lisa (Everett), **Supp. XVIII: 56**
"Cuttings, *later*" (Roethke), **III:** 532
"Cyberpunk" (Bethke), **Supp. XVI:** 121
Cyberspace trilogy (W. Gibson). *See* Sprawl trilogy (W. Gibson)
"Cycles, The" (Pinsky), **Supp. VI:** 250– 252
Cynic's Word Book, The (Bierce), **I:** 197, 205, 208, 209, 210
Cynthia Ozick (Lowin), **Supp. V:** 273
Cynthia Ozick's Comic Art (Cohen), **Supp. V:** 273
Cynthia Ozick's Fiction (Kauvar), **Supp. V:** 273
"Czeslaw Milosz and Memory" (Hampl), **Supp. XXII:** 92

D

Da Capo: Best Music Writing 2002 (Lethem, ed.), **Supp. XVIII:** 148
Dacey, Philip, **Supp. IV Part 1:** 70
Dacier, André, **II:** 10
"Dad" (Cullen), **Supp. IV Part 1:** 167
"Daddy" (Plath), **Retro. Supp. II:** 250– 251; **Supp. I Part 2:** 529, 542, 545, 546; **Supp. II Part 2:** 688; **Supp. XXII:** 30; **Supp. XXIII:** 112, 113
"Daddy"(Hadas), **Supp. XXIII:** 112, 113
Daddy's Little Boy (Collins), **Supp. XXI:** 54
"Daemon, The" (Bogan), **Supp. III Part 1:** 58, 61
"Daemon Lover, The" (Jackson), **Supp. IX:** 116–117
"Daffodils" (Nelson and Espeland), **Supp. XVIII:** 181
"Daffodils" (Wordsworth), **Supp. XIII:** 284
"Daffy Duck in Hollywood" (Ashbery), **Supp. III Part 1:** 18
D'Agata, John, **Supp. XII:** 97, 98
Dago Red (Fante), **Supp. XI:** 160, 169
Dahl, Roald, **Supp. IX:** 114
Dahlberg, Edward, **I:** 231; **Retro. Supp. I:** 426; **Supp. III Part 2:** 624; **Supp. XIV:** 148; **Supp. XVIII:** 148; **Supp. XXII:** 257
Dahlberg, R'lene, **Supp. XIV:** 148
Daiches, David, **Retro. Supp. II:** 243; **Supp. I Part 2:** 536
Daily Horoscope (Gioia), **Supp. XV:** 112, **118–121,** 126
"Daily Horoscope" (Gioia), **Supp. XV:** 119
Daily Modernism (Podnieks), **Supp. X:** 189
Dain Curse, The (Hammett), **Supp. IV Part 1:** 348

"Daisies" (Glück), **Supp. V:** 88
"Daisy" (Oates), **Supp. II Part 2:** 523
Daisy (S. and A. Warner), **Supp. XVIII:** 268
Daisy-Head Mayzie (Geisel), **Supp. XVI:** 112
Daisy Miller (H. James), **Retro. Supp. I:** 216, 220, 222, 223, 228, 231; **Supp. XVIII:** 165; **Supp. XXIV:** 23
"Daisy Miller" (H. James), **II:** 325, 326, 327, 329; **IV:** 316
Dale, Charlie, **Supp. IV Part 2:** 584
Daley, Yvonne, **Supp. XXII:** 216
Dali, Salvador, **II:** 586; **Supp. IV Part 1:** 83; **Supp. XIII:** 317
Dalibard, Thomas-François, **II:** 117
"Dallas-Fort Worth: Redband and Mistletoe" (Clampitt), **Supp. IX:** 45
"Dalliance of Eagles, The" (Whitman), **IV:** 348
Dalva (Harrison), **Supp. VIII:** 37, 45, 46, **48–49**
Daly, Carroll John, **Supp. IV Part 1:** 343, 345
Daly, John, **II:** 25, 26
Daly, Julia Brown, **II:** 25, 26
"Dalyrimple Goes Wrong" (Fitzgerald), **II:** 88
"Dam, The" (Rukeyser), **Supp. VI:** 283
Damas, Leon, **Supp. X:** 139
Damascus Gate (Stone), **Supp. V:** 308– 311
Damballah (Wideman), **Supp. X:** 319, 320, 321, 322, 323, 326, 327, 331, 333–334
Dameshek, Brandon, **Supp. XIX:** 273, 277, 287
Damnation of Theron Ware, The (Frederic), **II:** 140–143, 144, 146, 147; **Retro. Supp. I:** 325
Damned If I Do (Everett), **Supp. XVIII:** 66
"Damned Thing, The" (Bierce), **I:** 206
Damon, Matt, **Supp. VIII:** 175
Damon, S. Foster, **I:** 26; **II:** 512, 514, 515
"Damon and Vandalia" (Dove), **Supp. IV Part 1:** 252
Dana, H. W. L., **I:** 225
Dana, Richard Henry, **I:** 339, 351; **Supp. I Part 1:** 103, 154, 155; **Supp. I Part 2:** 414, 420
Dana, Richard Henry, Jr., **III:** 81; **Supp. XX: 227**
Dana, Robert, **Supp. V:** 178, 180
"Dana Gioia and Fine Press Printing" (Peich), **Supp. XV:** 117
"Dance" (Kenny), **Supp. XXIII:** 148
"Dance, The" (Crane), **I:** 109
"Dance, The" (Roethke), **III:** 541
"Dance, The" (W. C. Williams), **Supp. XVII:** 113
Dance and the Railroad, The (Hwang), **Supp. XXI:** 145, 146
Dance of Death, The (Auden), **Supp. II Part 1:** 10
Dance of Death, The (Bierce and Harcourt), **I:** 196
Dance of Life, The (Ellis), **Supp. XX: 117**

Dance of the Sleepwalkers (Calabria), **Supp. XIII:** 164
"Dance of the Solids, The" (Updike), **Retro. Supp. I:** 323
"Dancer" (Hoffman), **Supp. XVIII:** 86
"Dancer, The" (Swados), **Supp. XIX:** 261, 263–264
"Dancers Work by Forgetting" (Espaillat), **Supp. XXI:** 102
"Dances of Madness" (Schott), **Supp. XXIII:** 245
Dances with Wolves (film), **Supp. X:** 124
Dance to the Music of Time, A (Powell), **Supp. XVIII:** 146
Dancing After Hours (Dubus), **Supp. VII:** 91
Dancing Back Strong the Nation (Kenny), **Supp. XXIII:** 144, **148**
Dancing Bears, The (Merwin), **Supp. III Part 1:** 343–344
Dancing on the Stones (Nichols), **Supp. XIII:** 256, 257, 259, 267, 269
"Dancing the Jig" (Sexton), **Supp. II Part 2:** 692
Dandelion Wine (Bradbury), **Supp. IV Part 1:** 101, 109–110
Dandurand, Karen, **Retro. Supp. I:** 30
"Dandy Frightening the Squatters, The" (Twain), **IV:** 193–194
Dangel, Mary Jo, **Supp. XVIII:** 156
Dangerous Crossroads (film), **Supp. XIII:** 163
Dangerous Moonlight (Purdy), **Supp. VII:** 278
"Dangerous Road Before Martin Luther King" (Baldwin), **Supp. I Part 1:** 52
"Dangerous Summer, The" (Hemingway), **II:** 261
Dangerous Thoughts (Ryan as Quin), **Supp. XVIII:** 226
"Dangers of Authorship, The" (Blackmur), **Supp. II Part 1:** 147
Dangling Man (Bellow), **I:** 144, 145, 147, 148, 150–151, 153–154, 158, 160, 161, 162, 163; **Retro. Supp. II:** 19, 20–21, 22, 23; **Supp. VIII:** 234; **Supp. XIX:** 157
"Dang Little Squirt" (Bontemps), **Supp. XXII:** 4
Daniel (biblical book), **Supp. I Part 1:** 105
Daniel (film), **Supp. IV Part 1:** 236
Daniel, Arnaut, **III:** 467
Daniel, Robert W., **III:** 76
Daniel, Samuel, **Supp. I Part 1:** 369
Daniel Deronda (G. Eliot), **I:** 458
Daniels, Frank, **Supp. XXII:** 196
Daniels, Kate, **Supp. XVII:** 112
Danielson, Linda, **Supp. IV Part 2:** 569
D'Annunzio, Gabriele, **II:** 515
Danny and the Deep Blue Sea: An Apache Dance (Shanley), **Supp. XIV:** 315, **318–319,** 320, 321, 323, 324
Danny O'Neill pentalogy (Farrell), **II:** 35–41
Danse Macabre (King), **Supp. IV Part 1:** 102; **Supp. V:** 144
"Danse Russe" (W. C. Williams), **IV:** 412–413
"Dans le Restaurant" (Eliot), **I:** 554, 578

Dans l'ombre des cathédrales (Ambelain), **Supp. I Part 1:** 273

Dante Alighieri, **I:** 103, 136, 138, 250, 384, 433, 445; **II:** 8, 274, 278, 289, 490, 492, 493, 494, 495, 504, 508, 524, 552; **III:** 13, 77, 124, 182, 259, 278, 448, 453, 467, 533, 607, 609, 610–612, 613; **IV:** 50, 134, 137, 138, 139, 247, 437, 438; **Retro. Supp. I:** 62, 63, 64, 66, 360; **Retro. Supp. II:** 330; **Supp. I Part 1:** 256, 363; **Supp. I Part 2:** 422, 454; **Supp. III Part 2:** 611, 618, 621; **Supp. IV Part 2:** 634; **Supp. V:** 277, 283, 331, 338, 345; **Supp. VIII:** 27, 219–221; **Supp. X:** 120, 121, 125; **Supp. XII:** 98; **Supp. XV:** 254; **Supp. XVII:** 227, 241

Danvis Tales: Selected Stories (Robinson; Budbill, ed.), **Supp. XIX:** 6

Danziger, Adolphe, **I:** 199–200

Danziger, Jeff, **Supp. XXII:** 208

Dar (Nabokov), **III:** 246, 255

D'Arcy, Randall, **Supp. XVII:** 76

Dardis, Tom, **Supp. XVIII:** 249

"Dare's Gift" (Glasgow), **II:** 190

Dark and Feeling, The: Black American Writers and Their Work (Major), **Supp. XXII:** 180

Dark Angel, The (Bolton), **Supp. I Part 1:** 281

"Dark Angel Travels With Us to Canada and Blesses Our Vacation, The" (Dunn), **Supp. XI:** 146

Dark Carnival (Bradbury), **Supp. IV Part 1:** 102

Darker (Strand), **Supp. IV Part 2:** 619, 626–628

Darker Face of the Earth, The (Dove), **Supp. IV Part 1:** 255–257

"Dark Fire" (Hadas), **Supp. XXIII:** 126

Dark Green, Bright Red (Vidal), **Supp. IV Part 2:** 677

Dark Half, The (King), **Supp. V:** 141

Dark Harbor: A Poem (Strand), **Supp. IV Part 2:** 633–634

"Dark Hills, The" (Robinson), **III:** 523

Dark Horses (X. J. Kennedy), **Supp. XV:** 167–170

Dark Hours, The (W. V. Davis), **Supp. XXI:** 91–92, 93

Dark Laughter (Anderson), **I:** 111, 116; **II:** 250–251

"Darkling Alphabet, A" (Snodgrass), **Supp. VI:** 323

Darkling Child (Merwin and Milroy), **Supp. III Part 1:** 346

"Darkling Summer, Ominous Dusk, Rumorous Rain" (Schwartz), **Supp. II Part 2:** 661

"Darkling Thrush" (Hardy), **Supp. IX:** 40

"Dark Men, The" (Dubus), **Supp. VII:** 86

Dark Mirrors (Sobin), **Supp. XVI:** 295

Dark Mother, The (W. Frank), **Supp. XX:** 70–71

Dark Mountains, The (Hoffman), **Supp. XVIII:** 76–77

Darkness and the Light, The (Hecht), **Supp. X:** 58

Darkness at Noon (Koestler), **Supp. XXIII:** 1

Darkness More Than Night, A (Connelly), **Supp. XXI:** 73–74, 80

"Darkness on the Edge of Town" (O'Brien), **Supp. V:** 246

Darkness Surrounding Us, The (Sorrentino), **Supp. XXI:** 227, 228

Darkness under the Trees/Walking behind the Spanish (Salinas), **Supp. XIII:** 311, 319–324

"Dark Night" (St. John of the Cross), **Supp. XV:** 30

Dark Night of the Soul, The (St. John of the Cross), **I:** 1, 585

"Dark Ones" (Dickey), **Supp. IV Part 1:** 182

Dark Power (Holding), **Supp. XXII:** 122–123, 124

Dark Princess: A Romance (Du Bois), **Supp. II Part 1:** 179, 181–182

Dark Room, The (T. Williams), **IV:** 381

Dark Sacred Night (CD), **Supp. XXI:** 75

Dark Shadows (television show), **Supp. XIX:** 57

"Dark Summer" (Bogan), **Supp. III Part 1:** 51, 53

Dark Summer: Poems (Bogan), **Supp. III Part 1:** 52–53, 57

"Dark Tower, The" (column), **Supp. IV Part 1:** 168, 170

Dark Tower, The: The Gunslinger (King), **Supp. V:** 152

Dark Tower IV, The: Wizard and Glass (King), **Supp. V:** 139

Dark Tunnel, The (Macdonald as Millar), **Supp. IV Part 2:** 465, 466

"Dark TV Screen" (Simic), **Supp. VIII:** 282

"Dark Voyage, The" (McLay), **Supp. XIII:** 21

"Dark Walk, The" (Taylor), **Supp. V:** 320–321, 322, 326

Darkwater: Voices from Within the Veil (Du Bois), **Supp. II Part 1:** 178, 180, 183

Dark Waves and Light Matter (Goldbarth), **Supp. XII:** 176, 193

Dark World (Carruth), **Supp. XVI:** 55

"Darling" (Nye), **Supp. XIII:** 283–284

"Darling, The" (Chekhov), **Supp. IX:** 202

Darling-Darling (Barillet and Grédy; Loos, trans.), **Supp. XVI:** 194

Darnell, Linda, **Supp. XII:** 173

Darragh, Tina, **Supp. IV Part 2:** 427

Darreu, Robert Donaldson, **Supp. II Part 1:** 89, 98, 102

Darrow, Clarence, **Supp. I Part 1:** 5; **Supp. I Part 2:** 455

Dartmouth, Earl of, **Supp. XX:** 284

Darwin, Charles, **I:** 457; **II:** 323, 462, 481; **III:** 226, 231; **IV:** 69, 304; **Retro. Supp. I:** 254; **Retro. Supp. II:** 60, 65; **Supp. I Part 1:** 368; **Supp. IX:** 180; **Supp. XI:** 203; **Supp. XVI:** 13; **Supp. XX:** 18

"Darwin in 1881" (Schnackenberg), **Supp. XV:** 253, 254, 258

Daryush, Elizabeth, **Supp. V:** 180

Dasburg, Andrew, **Supp. XXI:** 6

Dash, Julie, **Supp. XI:** 17, 18, 20

Dashell, Alfred, **Supp. X:** 224

"DAS KAPITAL" (Baraka), **Supp. II Part 1:** 55

Datlow, Ellen, **Supp. XVI:** 123

"Datum Centurio" (Wallace), **Supp. X:** 309

Daudet, Alphonse, **II:** 325, 338

"Daughter" (Caldwell), **I:** 309

"Daughter in the House" (X. J. Kennedy), **Supp. XV:** 160

Daughter of Earth (Smedly), **Supp. XIII:** 295

Daughter of the Land, A (Stratton-Porter), **Supp. XX:** 222

Daughter of the Snows, A (London), **II:** 465, 469–470

Daughter of the Vine, A (Atherton), **Supp. XXIV:** 18, 22

"Daughters" (Anderson), **I:** 114

Daughters (Marshall), **Supp. XI:** 275, 276, 277, 286–288, 289, 290

"Daughters, 1900" (Nelson), **Supp. XVIII:** 175

Daughters, I Love You (Hogan), **Supp. IV Part 1:** 397, 399, 401

"Daughters of Invention" (Alvarez), **Supp. VII:** 9

Daughters of the Dust (Dash; film), **Supp. XI:** 17, 18; **Supp. XX:** 154

Daumier, Honoré, **IV:** 412

Dave, R. A., **Supp. VIII:** 126

Davenport, Abraham, **Supp. I Part 2:** 699

Davenport, Gary, **Supp. IX:** 98

Davenport, Guy, **Supp. XIV:** 96; **Supp. XXI:** 235

Davenport, Herbert J., **Supp. I Part 2:** 642

Davenport, James, **I:** 546

Daves, E. G., **Supp. I Part 1:** 369

Davey, Frank, **Supp. XIII:** 33

"David" (Garrett), **Supp. VII:** 109–110

"David" (Gordon), **Supp. IV Part 1:** 298–299

David, Gray, **Supp. XX:** 260

"David and Agnes, a Romance" (Keillor), **Supp. XVI:** 175

David Blaize (Benson), **Supp. XX:** 234

David Copperfield (Dickens), **I:** 458; **II:** 290; **Retro. Supp. I:** 33; **Supp. XVI:** 65, 72; **Supp. XX:** 234

"David Crockett's Other Life" (Nye), **Supp. XIII:** 282

Davideis (Cowley), **IV:** 158

David Harum (Westcott), **I:** 216

"David Lynch Keeps His Head" (Wallace), **Supp. X:** 314

David Show, The (Gurney), **Supp. V:** 97

Davidson, Cathy, **Supp. XV:** 238

Davidson, Donald, **I:** 294; **III:** 495, 496; **IV:** 121, 122, 124, 125, 236; **Supp. II Part 1:** 139; **Supp. XIV:** 2; **Supp. XX:** 164

Davidson, James West, **Supp. XXII:** 218

Davidson, Jo, **Supp. XXI:** 7

Davidson, John, **Retro. Supp. I:** 55

Davidson, Michael, **Supp. VIII:** 290, 293, 294, 302–303

Davidson, Phebe, **Supp. XXIII:** 252

Davidson, Sara, **Supp. IV Part 1:** 196, 198, 203

Davidson, Sue, **Supp. XIX:** 260

Davidsz de Heem, Jan, **Supp. XI:** 133

Davie, Donald, **III:** 478; **Supp. IV Part 2:** 474; **Supp. V:** 331; **Supp. X:** 55, 59; **Supp. XVII:** 111, 112, 121

Davies, Arthur, **III:** 273

Davies, Sir John, **III:** 541

Davies, Marion, **Supp. XVI:** 186

Da Vinci, Leonardo, **I:** 274; **II:** 536; **III:** 210

Davis, Allen F., **Supp. I Part 1:** 1, 7

Davis, Allison, **Supp. I Part 1:** 327

Davis, Angela, **Supp. I Part 1:** 66; **Supp. X:** 249

Davis, Arthur B., **Supp. XVIII:** 119

Davis, Bette, **I:** 78; **Supp. I Part 1:** 67

Davis, Bill, **Supp. XIII:** 267

Davis, Christina, **Supp. XV:** 264

Davis, Cynthia, **Supp. XVIII:** 281, 286

Davis, Donald, **Supp. XIII:** 93

Davis, Elizabeth Gould, **Supp. I Part 2:** 567

Davis, George, **II:** 586

Davis, Glover, **Supp. V:** 180, 182, 186

Davis, Jefferson, **II:** 206; **IV:** 122, 125, 126

Davis, Jordan, **Supp. XV:** 178, 181, 186, 188

Davis, Katie, **Supp. VIII:** 83

Davis, L. J., **Supp. XI:** 234

Davis, Lydia, **Supp. XII:** 24; **Supp. XVII:** 21

Davis, Marcia, **Supp. XVIII:** 91, 100

Davis, Mary H., **Supp. XVIII:** 77

Davis, Miles, **Supp. XV:** 346; **Supp. XXII:** 172

Davis, Ossie, Jr., **Supp. IV Part 1:** 362; **Supp. XVI:** 144

Davis, Rebecca Harding, **Supp. I Part 1:** 45; **Supp. XIII:** 292, 295, 305; **Supp. XVI: 79–96**

Davis, Richard Harding, **III:** 328; **Supp. II Part 1:** 393; **Supp. XVI:** 85

Davis, Robert Gorham, **II:** 51; **IV:** 108

Davis, Stuart, **IV:** 409; **Supp. XV:** 295; **Supp. XXI:** 6

Davis, Thadious, **Supp. XVIII:** 120, 121, 123, 127, 129

Davis, Thulani, **Supp. XI:** 179; **Supp. XIII:** 233, 234, 239

Davis, William Virgil, **Supp. IV Part 1:** 63, 64, 68, 69, 70; **Supp. XXI: 83–96**

Davison, Peter, **Supp. XXI:** 91

Davy's Lake (M. Finch), **Supp. XVII:** 69

Dawn (Dreiser), **I:** 498, 499, 503, 509, 515, 519

Dawn (O. Butler), **Supp. XIII:** 63, **64**

"Dawnbreaker" (Hayden), **Supp. II Part 1:** 370

Dawn in Russia (W. Frank), **Supp. XX: 76**

Dawn Patrol, The (film), **Supp. XIV:** 81

"Dawn Patrol: A Review of the Literature of the Negro for 1948" (Locke), **Supp. XIV:** 211

Dawson, Edward, **IV:** 151

Dawson, Emma, **I:** 199

Dawson, Melanie, **Supp. XXIV:** 25, 31

Dawson, Ruth, **Supp. XI:** 120

Day, Dorothy, **II:** 215; **Supp. I Part 2:** 524; **Supp. X:** 142

Day, Fred Holland, **Supp. XX: 114, 115**

Day, Georgiana, **Supp. I Part 2:** 585

Day, Richard, **Supp. XVIII:** 251

Dayan, Joan, **Retro. Supp. II:** 270

"Day Book" (Notley), **Supp. XXII:** 230

Day Book, A (Creeley), **Supp. IV Part 1:** 155

"Daybreak" (Kinnell), **Supp. III Part 1:** 250

"Daybreak Blues" (Kees), **Supp. XV:** 133

"Day-Breakers, The" (Bontemps), **Supp. XXII:** 8

"Daybreak in Alabama" (Hughes), **Retro. Supp. I:** 211; **Supp. I Part 1:** 344

Day by Day (Lowell), **Retro. Supp. II:** 184, 186, 191

"Day-Care Field Trip: Aquarium" (Karr), **Supp. XI:** 243

"Day-Dream, A" (Bryant), **Supp. I Part 1:** 160

"Day-Dream of a Grocer, The" (Twain), **Supp. XVIII:** 9

"Day for Poetry and Song, A" (Douglass), **Supp. III Part 1:** 172

"Day in the Life of Half of Rumpel-stiltskin, A" (Brockmeier), **Supp. XXII:** 50, 52, 53

"Day Lady Died, The" (O'Hara), **Supp. XIX:** 85; **Supp. XXIII:** 216, 219

Day Late and a Dollar Short, A (McMillan), **Supp. XIII:** 184, **Supp. XIII:** 185, **191–192**

"Day longs for the evening, The" (Levertov), **Supp. III Part 1:** 274

Daynard, Jodi, **Supp. XVIII:** 97

Day of a Stranger (Merton), **Supp. VIII:** 203

"Day of Days, A" (James), **II:** 322

Day of Doom (Wigglesworth), **IV:** 147, 155, 156

Day of the Body (C. Frost), **Supp. XV:** 93, **98–100,** 106

Day of the Locust, The (West), **I:** 298; **IV:** 288, 299–306; **Retro. Supp. II:** 321, 323, 324, 329, **337–338; Supp. II Part 2:** 626; **Supp. XI:** 296; **Supp. XII:** 173; **Supp. XIII:** 170; **Supp. XIV:** 328; **Supp. XVIII:** 246

"Day on the Big Branch, A" (Nemerov), **III:** 275–276

"Day on the Connecticut River, A" (Merrill), **Supp. III Part 1:** 336

Day Room, The (DeLillo), **Supp. VI:** 4

"Days" (Emerson), **II:** 19, 20

"Days and Nights" (Koch), **Supp. XV:** 179, 180

"Days and Nights: A Journal" (Price), **Supp. VI:** 265

Days Before, The (Porter), **III:** 433, 453

Days in the Yellow Leaf (Hoffman), **Supp. XVIII:** 75

"Days of 1935" (Merrill), **Supp. III Part 1:** 325, 328

"Days of 1941 and '44" (Merrill), **Supp. III Part 1:** 336

"Days of 1964" (Merrill), **Supp. III Part 1:** 328, 352

"Days of 1971" (Merrill), **Supp. III Part 1:** 328

"Days of 1981" (Doty), **Supp. XI:** 123

"Days of Awe: The Birth of Lucy Jane" (Wasserstein), **Supp. XV:** 332

"Days of Edward Hopper" (Haines), **Supp. XII:** 210

"Days of Heaven" (Bass), **Supp. XVI:** 20

Days of Obligation: An Argument with My Mexican Father (Rodriguez), **Supp. XIV:** 298, 300, **302–305,** 307, 310

Days of Our Lives (soap opera), **Supp. XI:** 83

Days of Our Lives Lie in Fragments: New and Old Poems (Garrett), **Supp. VII:** 109–110, 111

Days of the Phoenix (Brooks), **I:** 266

Days of Wine and Roses (J. P. Miller), **Supp. XIII:** 262

Days: Tangier Journal, 1987–1989 (Bowles), **Supp. IV Part 1:** 94

Days to Come (Hellman), **Supp. I Part 1:** 276, 277–278

Days without End (O'Neill), **III:** 385, 391, 397

"Day's Work, A" (Capote), **Supp. III Part 1:** 120

"Day's Work, A" (Porter), **III:** 443, 446

"Day the Presidential Candidate Came to Ciudad Tamaulipas, The" (Caldwell), **I:** 309

"Day the Singer Fell, The" (Swados), **Supp. XIX:** 258

Day the World ended, The (Coover), **Supp. V:** 1

"Day with Conrad Green, A" (Lardner), **II:** 428–429, 430

"Deacon's Masterpiece, The" (Holmes), **Supp. I Part 1:** 302, 307

"Dead, The" (Collins), **Supp. XXI:** 64

"Dead, The" (Joyce), **I:** 285; **III:** 343; **Supp. XXIII:** 71

Dead and the Living, The (Olds), **Supp. X:** 201, **204–206,** 207

"Dead Body, The" (Olds), **Supp. X:** 210

"Dead by the Side of the Road, The" (Snyder), **Supp. VIII:** 301

"Dead Doe" (B. Kelly), **Supp. XVII:** 128–129

Dead End (Kingsley), **Supp. I Part 1:** 277, 281

Dead Father, The (Barthelme), **Supp. IV Part 1:** 43, 47, 50–51

"Dead Fiddler, The" (Singer), **IV:** 20

Dead Fingers Talk (Burroughs), **Supp. III Part 1:** 103

"Dead Hand" series (Sinclair), **Supp. V:** 276, 277, 281

"Dead Languages, The" (Humphrey), **Supp. IX:** 109

Dead Lecturer, The (Baraka), **Supp. II Part 1:** 31, 33, 35–37, 49

Dead Letters Sent (Kenny), **Supp. XXIII:** 143, 145

"Dead Letters Sent (By the Ontario Shores)"(Kenny), **Supp. XXIII:** 145

Deadline at Dawn (Odets), **Supp. II Part 2:** 546

"Dead-Lock and Its Key, A" (E. Stoddard), **Supp. XV:** 286

"Dead Loon, The" (Bynner), **Supp. XV: 44–45**

Deadly Affair, A (Lacy), **Supp. XV:** 205–206

Deadly is the Female (film), **Supp. XVII:** 62

Dead Man's Walk (McMurtry), **Supp. V:** 231, 232

Dead Man's Walk (screenplay; McMurtry and Ossana), **Supp. V:** 231

Dead Man Walking (opera libretto, McNally), **Supp. XIII:** 207

Dead Poets Society (film), **Supp. XXI:** 192, 193, 194, 199

"Dead Reckoning" (Jarman), **Supp. XVII:** 113

"Dead Soldier's Talk, The" (Jin), **Supp. XVIII:** 92

Dead Souls (Gogol), **I:** 296

"Dead Souls on Campus" (Kosinski), **Supp. VII:** 222

"Dead Wingman, The" (Jarrell), **II:** 374

"Dead Wood, Green Wood" (Hadas), **Supp. XXIII:** 120

"Dead Yellow Women" (Hammett), **Supp. IV Part 1:** 345

Dead Zone, The (King), **Supp. V:** 139, 143, 144, 148, 152

Dean, James, **I:** 493

Dean, Man Mountain, **II:** 589

Deane, Silas, **Supp. I Part 2:** 509, 524

"Dean of Men" (Taylor), **Supp. V:** 314, 323

Dean's December, The (Bellow), **Retro. Supp. II:** 30–31

"Dear Adolph" (Benét), **Supp. XI:** 46

"Dear America" (Ortiz), **Supp. IV Part 2:** 503

"Dear Dark Continent" (Notley), **Supp. XXII:** 223

"Dearest M—" (Carruth), **Supp. XVI:** 59

Dear Ghosts (Gallagher), **Supp. XXIV:** 166, 167, 170–171, 176

"Dear Judas" (Jeffers), **Supp. II Part 2:** 431–432, 433

Dear Juliette (Sarton), **Supp. VIII:** 265

Dear Lovely Death (Hughes), **Retro. Supp. I:** 203; **Supp. I Part 1:** 328

"Dear Mr. Walrus" (Boyle), **Supp. XXIV:** 58–59

Dear Rafe (Hinojosa), **Supp. XIX:** 98, **105–106**

"Dear Villon" (Corso), **Supp. XII:** 135

"Dear World" (Gunn Allen), **Supp. IV Part 1:** 321

Deasy, Philip, **Supp. XX: 42**

Death (Allen), **Supp. XV:** 3

"Death" (Corso), **Supp. XII:** 127

"Death" (Lowell), **II:** 536

"Death" (Mailer), **III:** 38

"Death" (W. C. Williams), **Retro. Supp. I:** 422

"Death" (West), **IV:** 286

"Death and Absence" (Glück), **Supp. V:** 82

Death and Birth of David Markand, The (W. Frank), **Supp. XX: 76–77**

Death and Taxes (Parker), **Supp. IX:** 192

"Death and the Child" (Crane), **I:** 414

"Death as a Society Lady" (Hecht), **Supp. X:** 71–72

Death before Bedtime (Vidal as Box), **Supp. IV Part 2:** 682

"Death Be Not Proud" (Donne), **Supp. XVI:** 158

"Death by Water" (Eliot), **I:** 395, 578

Death Comes for the Archbishop (Cather), **I:** 314, 327, 328–330; **Retro. Supp. I:** 16–18, 21; **Supp. XIII:** 253; **Supp. XXIV:** 253

Death in Paradise (Parker), **Supp. XIX:** 186

Death in the Afternoon (Hemingway), **II:** 253; **IV:** 35; **Retro. Supp. I:** 182; **Supp. VIII:** 182; **Supp. XVI:** 205; **Supp. XIX:** 246; **Supp. XX: 76**

"Death in the Country, A" (Benét), **Supp. XI:** 53–54

Death in the Family, A (Agee), **I:** 25, 29, 42, 45

Death in the Fifth Position (Vidal as Box), **Supp. IV Part 2:** 682

"Death in the Woods" (Anderson), **I:** 114, 115; **Supp. XXIV:** 136

Death in the Woods and Other Stories (Anderson), **I:** 112, 114, 115

Death in Venice (Mann), **III:** 231; **Supp. IV Part 1:** 392; **Supp. V:** 51

"Death in Viet Nam" (Salinas), **Supp. XIII:** 315

"Death in Winter" (C. Frost), **Supp. XV:** 98

Death Is a Lonely Business (Bradbury), **Supp. IV Part 1:** 102, 103, 111–112, 115

"Death Is Not the End" (Wallace), **Supp. X:** 309

Death Is the Place (Bronk), **Supp. XXI:** 32

Death Kit (Sontag), **Supp. III Part 2:** 451, 468–469

Death Likes It Hot (Vidal as Box), **Supp. IV Part 2:** 682

"*Death*/Muerta" (Mora), **Supp. XIII:** 228

Death Notebooks, The (Sexton), **Supp. II Part 2:** 691, 694, 695

"Death of a Columnist" (Siddons), **Supp. XXII:** 241–242

Death of Adam, The: Essays on Modern Thought (Robinson), **Supp. XXI:** 212

"Death of a Jazz Musician" (W. J. Smith), **Supp. XIII:** 334

Death of a Kinsman, The (Taylor), **Supp. V:** 324, 326

Death of a Man (Boyle), **Supp. XXIV:** 60

"Death of an Old Seaman" (Hughes), **Retro. Supp. I:** 199

"Death of a Pig" (White), **Supp. I Part 2:** 665–668

Death of a Salesman (A. Miller), **I:** 81; **III:** 148, 149, 150, 153–154, 156, 157, 158, 159, 160, 163, 164, 166; **IV:** 389; **Supp. IV Part 1:** 359; **Supp. XIV:** 102, 239, 254, 255; **Supp. XV:** 205; **Supp. XX: 27; Supp. XXIII:** 199

"Death of a Soldier, The" (Stevens), **Retro. Supp. I:** 299, 312. *see also* "Lettres d'un Soldat" (Stevens)

"Death of a Soldier, The" (Wilson), **IV:** 427, 445

"Death of a Toad" (Wilbur), **Supp. III Part 2:** 550

"Death of a Traveling Salesman" (Welty), **IV:** 261; **Retro. Supp. I:** 344

"Death of a Young Son by Drowning" (Atwood), **Supp. XIII:** 33

Death of Bessie Smith, The (Albee), **I:** 76–77, 92

Death of Billy the Kid, The (Vidal), **Supp. IV Part 2:** 683

Death of Cock Robin, The (Snodgrass), **Supp. VI:** 315, **317–319,** 324

Death of Dreams, A (Hoffman), **Supp. XVIII:** 79

"Death of General Wolfe, The" (Paine), **Supp. I Part 2:** 504

"Death of Halpin Frayser, The" (Bierce), **I:** 205

"Death of Justina, The" (Cheever), **Supp. I Part 1:** 184–185

Death of Life, The (Barnes), **Supp. III Part 1:** 34

Death of Malcolm X, The (Baraka), **Supp. II Part 1:** 47

"Death of Marilyn Monroe, The" (Olds), **Supp. X:** 205

"Death of Me, The" (Malamud), **Supp. I Part 2:** 437

"Death of Slavery, The" (Bryant), **Supp. I Part 1:** 168–169

"Death of St. Narcissus, The" (Eliot), **Retro. Supp. I:** 291

"Death of the Ball Turret Gunner, The" (Jarrell), **II:** 369–370, 372, 374, 375, 376, 378

"Death of the Fathers, The" (Sexton), **Supp. II Part 2:** 692

"Death of the Flowers, The" (Bryant), **Supp. I Part 1:** 170

Death of the Fox (Garrett), **Supp. VII:** 99, 101–104, 108

"Death of the Hat, The" (Collins), **Supp. XXI:** 59

"Death of the Hired Man, The" (Frost), **III:** 523; **Retro. Supp. I:** 121, 128; **Supp. IX:** 261

Death of the Kapowsin Tavern (Hugo), **Supp. VI:** 133–135

"Death of the Kapowsin Tavern" (Hugo), **Supp. VI:** 137, 141

"Death of the Lyric, The: The Achievement of Louis Simpson" (Jarman and McDowell), **Supp. IX:** 266, 270, 276

"Death of Venus, The" (Creeley), **Supp. IV Part 1:** 143, 144–145

"Death on All Fronts" (Ginsberg), **Supp. II Part 1:** 326

"Deaths" (Dunn), **Supp. XI:** 147

"Death Sauntering About" (Hecht), **Supp. X:** 72

Deaths for the Ladies (and Other Disasters) (Mailer), **Retro. Supp. II:** 203

Death's Jest-Book (Beddoes), **Retro. Supp. I:** 285

Death Song (McGrath), **Supp. X:** 127

"Death the Carnival Barker" (Hecht), **Supp. X:** 72

"Death the Film Director" (Hecht), **Supp. X:** 72

"Death the Judge" (Hecht), **Supp. X:** 72

"Death the Mexican Revolutionary" (Hecht), **Supp. X:** 72

"Death the Oxford Don" (Hecht), **Supp. X:** 72

"Death the Painter" (Hecht), **Supp. X:** 72

Death the Proud Brother (Wolfe), **IV:** 456

"Death to Van Gogh's Ear!" (Ginsberg), **Supp. II Part 1:** 320, 322, 323

"Death Warmed Over!" (Bradbury), **Supp. IV Part 1:** 104–105, 112

Death Wish, The (Holding), **Supp. XXII:** 120, **123,** 134, 135

Débâcle, La (Zola), **III:** 316

"Debate with the Rabbi" (Nemerov), **III:** 272

Debeljak, Aleš, **Supp. VIII:** 272

De Bellis, Jack, **Supp. I Part 1:** 366, 368, 372

Debo, Annette, **Supp. XXI:** 254

DeBoer-Langworthy, Carol, **Supp. XVII:** 98, 99, 100

De Bosis, Lauro, **IV:** 372

"Debriefing" (Sontag), **Supp. III Part 2:** 468–470

Debs, Eugene, **I:** 483, 493; **III:** 580, 581; **Supp. I Part 2:** 524; **Supp. IX:** 1, 15; **Supp. XXIII:** 161, 162

Debt to Pleasure, The (Lanchester), **Retro. Supp. I:** 278

Debussy, Claude, **Retro. Supp. II:** 266; **Supp. XIII:** 44

"Decades" (Sorrentino), **Supp. XXI:** 229

Decameron (Boccaccio), **III:** 283, 411; **Supp. IX:** 215

"Deceased" (Hughes), **Retro. Supp. I:** 208

"December" (Oliver), **Supp. VII:** 245

"December 1, 1994" (Stern), **Supp. IX:** 299

December 7 (film, Ford), **Supp. XVIII:** 247

"December 24" (Di Piero), **Supp. XIX:** 39

"December 28: Returning to Chicago" (Di Piero), **Supp. XIX:** 39

"December Dawn" (Skloot), **Supp. XX:** **202**

"December Eclogue" (Winters), **Supp. II Part 2:** 794

"Decent Woman, A" (Boulton), **Supp. XXII:** 22–23

De Cenzo, Giorgia, **Supp. XXI:** 256

Deception (P. Roth), **Retro. Supp. II:** 291; **Supp. III Part 2:** 426–427

"Deceptions" (Dobyns), **Supp. XIII:** 77

De Chiara, Ann. *See* Malamud, Mrs. Bernard (Ann de Chiara)

De Chirico, Giorgio, **Supp. XIII:** 317

"Decided Loss, A" (Poe), **II:** 411

"Decision" (Boyle), **Supp. XXIV:** 54

"Decisions to Disappear" (Dunn), **Supp. XI:** 144

"Decisive Moment, The" (Auster), **Supp. XIV:** 292

Decker, James A., **Supp. III Part 2:** 621

Declaration of Gentlemen and Merchants and Inhabitants of Boston, and the Country Adjacent, A (Mather), **Supp. II Part 2:** 450

"Declaration of Paris, The" (Adams), **I:** 4

Declaration of the Rights of Man and the Citizen, **Supp. I Part 2:** 513, 519

Declaration of Universal Peace and Liberty (Paine), **Supp. I Part 2:** 512

Declension in the Village of Chung Luong (Weigl), **Supp. XIX:** 287, 288

Decline and Fall (Waugh), **Supp. I Part 2:** 607; **Supp. XV:** 182

Decline and Fall of the English System of Finance, The (Paine), **Supp. I Part 2:** 518

Decline and Fall of the Roman Empire, The (Gibbons), **Supp. III Part 2:** 629

"Decline of Book Reviewing, The" (Hardwick), **Supp. III Part 1:** 201–202

Decline of the West, The (Spengler), **I:** 270; **IV:** 125

"Decolonizing the Tongue: Reading Speech and Aphasia in the Work of Michelle Cliff" (Aguiar), **Supp. XXII:** 68

Deconstructing Harry (film; Allen), **Supp. XV:** 12, **13**

"Décor" (X. J. Kennedy), **Supp. XV:** 171

"Decoration Day" (Jewett), **II:** 412; **Retro. Supp. II:** 138

Decoration of Houses, The (Wharton and Codman), **IV:** 308; **Retro. Supp. I:** 362, 363–364, 366

"Decoy" (Ashbery), **Supp. III Part 1:** 13–14

Decter, Midge, **Supp. XX: 248**

Dedalus, Stephen, **Supp. XIX:** 47

"De Daumier-Smith's Blue Period" (Salinger), **III:** 560–561

"Dedication" (Nelson), **Supp. XVIII:** 173, 180

"Dedication and Household Map" (Erdrich), **Supp. IV Part 1:** 272

"Dedication Day" (Agee), **I:** 34

"Dedication for a Book" (Hay), **Supp. XIV:** 125

"Dedication for a Book of Criticism" (Winters), **Supp. II Part 2:** 801

"Dedication in Postscript, A" (Winters), **Supp. II Part 2:** 801

Dedications and Other Darkhorses (Komunyakaa), **Supp. XIII:** 112, **113–114**

"Dedication to Hunger" (Glück), **Supp. V:** 83

"Dedication to My Wife, A" (Eliot), **I:** 583

Dee, Jonathan, **Supp. XXIII:** 302

Dee, Ruby, **Supp. IV Part 1:** 362

Deeds of Utmost Kindness (Gander), **Supp. XV:** 340

Deegan, Thomas, **Supp. XXIII:** 100, 107–108

"Deep Breath at Dawn, A" (Hecht), **Supp. X:** 58

Deep End, The (film), **Supp. XXII:** 120, 131, 133

Deeper into Movies: The Essential Kael Collection from '69 to '72 (Kael), **Supp. IX:** 253

"Deeper Wisdom, The" (Hay), **Supp. XIV:** 129

Deep Green Sea (R. O. Butler), **Supp. XII:** 62, **74**

Deephaven (Jewett), **II:** 398–399, 400, 401, 410, 411; **Retro. Supp. II:** 133, 134, 135, 136, 137, 138, 140, 141, 143, 144

"Deep Sight and Rescue Missions" (Bambara), **Supp. XI:** 18–19

Deep Sightings and Rescue Missions: Fiction, Essays, and Conversations (Bambara), **Supp. XI:** 1, 3, **14–20**

Deep Sleep, The (Morris), **III:** 224–225

"Deep Song" (G. Jones), **Supp. XXIV:** 194

Deep South (Caldwell), **I:** 305, 309, 310

Deepstep Come Shining (Wright), **Supp. XV:** 337, 341, 344, **349–350,** 351, 353

"Deep Water" (Marquand), **III:** 56

"Deep Woods" (Nemerov), **III:** 272–273, 275

"Deer at Providencia, The" (Dillard), **Supp. VI:** 28, 32

Deer Camp: Last Light in the Northeast Kingdom (Ostrum, ed.), **Supp. XXII:** 218

"Deer Dancer" (Harjo), **Supp. XII:** 224–225

"Deer Ghost" (Harjo), **Supp. XII:** 225

Deer Park, The (Mailer), **I:** 292; **III:** 27, 31–33, 35–36, 37, 39, 40, 42, 43, 44; **Retro. Supp. II: 200–202,** 205, 207, 211

Deer Park, The: A Play (Mailer), **Retro. Supp. II:** 205

Deer Pasture, The (Bass), **Supp. XVI:** 15, 16, 23

Deerslayer, The (Cooper), **I:** 341, 349, 350, 355; **Supp. I Part 1:** 251

"Defeat" (Boyle), **Supp. XXIV: 60–61**

Defence, The (Nabokov), **Supp. XXII:** 263

"Defence of Poesie, The" (Bronk), **Supp. XXI:** 32

"Defence of Poesy, The" (Sidney), **Supp. V:** 250

"Defence of Poetry" (Longfellow), **II:** 493–494

"Defender of the Faith" (P. Roth), **Retro. Supp. II:** 281; **Supp. III Part 2:** 404, 407, 420

"Defending *The Searchers* (Scenes in the Life of an Obsession)" *(Lethem), Supp. XVIII:* 136,141

"Defenestration in Prague" (Matthews), **Supp. IX:** 168

Defenestration of Prague (Howe), **Supp. IV Part 2:** 419, 426, 429–430

Defense, The (Nabokov), **III:** 251–252; **Retro. Supp. I:** 266, 268, **270–272**

"Defense of Poetry" (Francis), **Supp. IX:** 83–84

DeFeo, Ronald, **Supp. XXIII:** 106

Defiant Ones, The (film), **Supp. I Part 1:** 67

"Defining the Age" (W. V. Davis), **Supp. IV Part 1:** 64

"Definition" (Ammons), **Supp. VII:** 28

Defoe, Daniel, **I:** 204; **II:** 104, 105, 159, 304–305; **III:** 113, 423; **IV:** 180; **Supp. I Part 2:** 523; **Supp. V:** 127

De Forest, John William, **II:** 275, 280, 288, 289; **IV:** 350

DeFrees, Madeline, **Supp. XVIII:** 293

"Deganawidah: The Peacemaker"(Kenny), **Supp. XXIII:** 151

Degas, Brian, **Supp. XI:** 307

Degler, Carl, **Supp. I Part 2:** 496

"Degrees of Fidelity" (Dunn), **Supp. XI:** 148, 156

Deguy, Michel, **Supp. XV:** 178

De Haven, Tom, **Supp. XI:** 39; **Supp. XII:** 338–339

Deitch, Joseph, **Supp. VIII:** 125

"Dejection" (Coleridge), **II:** 97

DeJong, Constance, **Supp. XII:** 4

DeJong, David Cornel, **I:** 35

Dekker,Thomas, **Supp. XVII:** 232

de Kooning, Elaine de, **Supp. XXIII:** 210, 217

de Kooning, Willem, **Supp. XII:** 198; **Supp. XV:** 177, 178

de Kooning, Willem de, **Supp. XXIII:** 208, 210, 211, 217, 220

Delacroix, Henri, **I:** 227

De La Mare, Walter, **III:** 429; **Supp. II Part 1:** 4; **Supp. XVII:** 69

Delamotte, Eugenia C., **Supp. XI:** 279

De Lancey, James, **I:** 338

De Lancey, Mrs. James (Anne Heathcote), **I:** 338

De Lancey, Susan A. *See* Cooper, Mrs. James Fenimore

De Lancey, William Heathcote, **I:** 338, 353

Delano, Amasa, **III:** 90

Delattre, Roland A., **I:** 558

De Laurentiis, Dino, **Supp. XI:** 170, 307

De la Valdéne, Guy, **Supp. VIII:** 40, 42

Delbanco, Andrew, **Supp. XXIV:** 69

Delbanco, Nicholas, **Supp. XXII:** 204

Del Cabral, Manuel, **Supp. XXI:** 104

DelCorso's Gallery (Caputo), **Supp. XIX:** 22–23

Delectorskaya, Lydia, **Supp. XXII:** 99

De l'éducation d'un homme sauvage (Itard), **Supp. I Part 2:** 564

"Delft" (Goldbarth), **Supp. XII:** 189

Delft: An Essay-Poem (Goldbarth), **Supp. XII:** 187

Delicate Balance, A (Albee), **I:** 86–89, 91, 93, 94

Delicate Balance, The (Hay), **Supp. XIV:** 121, 122, 124, 129, 133–134

"Delicate Balance, The" (Hay), **Supp. XIV:** 122

"Delicate Prey, The" (Bowles), **Supp. IV Part 1:** 86

Delicate Prey and Other Stories, The (Bowles), **Supp. IV Part 1:** 86–87

Délie (Scève), **Supp. III Part 1:** 11

Delights & Shadows (Kooser), **Supp. XIX:** 115, 116, 117, 121, **127–128**

DeLillo, Don, **Retro. Supp. I:** 278; **Retro. Supp. II:** 279; **Supp. VI:** 1–18; **Supp. IX:** 212; **Supp. XI:** 68; **Supp. XII:** 21, 152; **Supp. XVII:** 183; **Supp. XVIII:** 136, 140; **Supp. XIX:** 54; **Supp. XX:** 83, 87, 91; **Supp. XXIII:** 109

De Lint, Charles, **Supp. XXII:** 59

DeLisle, Anne, **Supp. VIII:** 175

Deliverance (Dickey), **Supp. IV Part 1:** 176, 186–188, 190; **Supp. X:** 30; **Supp. XX: 173–174; Supp. XXIII:** 43, 50

Deliverance, The (Glasgow), **II:** 175, 176, 177–178, 181

"Delivering" (Dubus), **Supp. VII:** 87

Dell, Floyd, **I:** 103, 105; **Supp. I Part 2:** 379; **Supp. XV:** 295; **Supp. XVII:** 96; **Supp. XXI:** 6; **Supp. XXII:** 275

Della Francesca, Piero, **Supp. XV:** 262

"Della Primavera Trasportata al Morale" (W. C. Williams), **Retro. Supp. I:** 419, 422

DeLoria, Philip J., **Supp. XIV:** 306

Deloria, Vine, Jr., **Supp. IV Part 1:** 323; **Supp. IV Part 2:** 504

"Delta Autumn" (Faulkner), **II:** 71

"Delta Factor, The" (Percy), **Supp. III Part 1:** 386

Delta of Venus: Erotica (Nin), **Supp. X:** 192, 195

Delta Wedding (Welty), **IV:** 261, 268–271, 273, 281; **Retro. Supp. I:** 349–350, 351

Delusions (Berryman), **I:** 170

De Man, Paul, **Retro. Supp. I:** 67; **Supp. XVII:** 70

DeMarinis, Rick, **Supp. XIV:** 22

DeMars, James, **Supp. IV Part 2:** 552

Dembo, L. S., **I:** 386, 391, 396, 397, 398, 402; **III:** 478; **Supp. I Part 1:** 272; **Supp. XIV:** 277, 282, 288, 290

"Dementia Translucida" (Bierds), **Supp. XVII:** 33

"Demeter"(Crooker), **Supp. XXIII:** 61

"Demeters"(Hadas), **Supp. XXIII:** 113

Demetrakopoulous, Stephanie A., **Supp. IV Part 1:** 12

DeMille, Cecil B., **Supp. IV Part 2:** 520; **Supp. XV:** 42

Demme, Jonathan, **Supp. V:** 14

Democracy (Adams), **I:** 9–10, 20; **Supp. IV Part 1:** 208; **Supp. XIX:** 139

Democracy (Didion), **Supp. IV Part 1:** 198, 208–210

"Democracy" (Lowell), **Supp. I Part 2:** 419

Democracy and Education (Dewey), **I:** 232

Democracy and Other Addresses (Lowell), **Supp. I Part 2:** 407

Democracy and Social Ethics (Addams), **Supp. I Part 1:** 8–11

Democracy in America (Tocqueville), **Retro. Supp. I:** 235; **Supp. XIV:** 306

Democratic Vistas (Whitman), **IV:** 333, 336, 348–349, 351, 469; **Retro. Supp. I:** 408; **Supp. I Part 2:** 456

Democritus, **I:** 480–481; **II:** 157; **III:** 606; **Retro. Supp. I:** 247

"Demon Lover, The" (Rich), **Supp. I Part 2:** 556

"Demonstrators, The" (Welty), **IV:** 280; **Retro. Supp. I:** 355

DeMott, Benjamin, **Supp. IV Part 1:** 35; **Supp. V:** 123; **Supp. XIII:** 95; **Supp. XIV:** 106

DeMott, Robert, **Supp. VIII:** 40, 41

Demuth, Charles, **IV:** 404; **Retro. Supp. I:** 412, 430; **Supp. XXI:** 6

"Demystified Zone" (Paley), **Supp. VI:** 227

Denby, Edwin, **Supp. XXIV:** 36, 45

Denmark Vesey (opera) (Bowles), **Supp. IV Part 1:** 83

Dennett, Daniel, **Supp. XXII:** 265

Denney, Joseph Villiers, **Supp. I Part 2:** 605

Denney, Reuel, **Supp. XII:** 121; **Supp. XXI:** 19

Dennie, Joseph, **II:** 298; **Supp. I Part 1:** 125

Denniston, Dorothy Hamer, **Supp. XI:** 276, 277

"Den of Lions" (Plath), **Retro. Supp. II:** 242

"Dental Assistant, The" (Simpson), **Supp. IX:** 280

Den Uyl, Douglas, **Supp. IV Part 2:** 528, 530

"Deodand, The" (Hecht), **Supp. X:** 65

"Departing" (Cameron), **Supp. XII:** 81

"Departure" (Glück), **Supp. V:** 89

"Departure" (Plath), **Supp. I Part 2:** 537

"Departure, The" (Freneau), **Supp. II Part 1:** 264

"Departure from Hydra, The" (Koch), **Supp. XV:** 180–181

Departures (Justice), **Supp. VII:** 124–127

Departures and Arrivals (Shields), **Supp. VII:** 320, 322

"Depressed by a Book of Bad Poetry, I Walk Toward an Unused Pasture and Invite the Insects to Join Me" (Wright), **Supp. III Part 2:** 600

"Depressed Person, The" (Wallace), **Supp. X:** 309

"Depression Days" (Mora), **Supp. XIII:** 224–225

"Deprived of Unhappiness" (Pickering), **Supp. XXI:** 203

De Puy, John, **Supp. XIII:** 12

D'Erasmo, Stacey, **Supp. IX:** 121

Derby, J. C., **Supp. XVIII:** 4

De Reilhe, Catherine, **Supp. I Part 1:** 202

De Rerum Natura (Lucretius), **II:** 162

"De Rerum Virtute" (Jeffers), **Supp. II Part 2:** 424

De Rioja, Francisco, **Supp. I Part 1:** 166

"Derivative Sport in Tornado Alley" (Wallace), **Supp. X:** 314

Derleth, August, **Supp. I Part 2:** 465, 472

Deronda, Daniel, **II:** 179

Derricotte, Toi, **Supp. XVIII:** 177

Derrida, Jacques, **Supp. IV Part 1:** 45; **Supp. XV:** 215, 224; **Supp. XVI:** 285, 288

Deruddere, Dominique, **Supp. XI:** 173
Der Wilde Jäger (Bürger), **II:** 306
Derzhavin, Gavrila Romanovich, **Supp. VIII:** 27
Desai, Anita, **Supp. XVI:** 156, 157, 158
Désamère (Notley), **Supp. XXII:** 226
De Santis, Christopher, **Retro. Supp. I:** 194
Descartes, René, **I:** 255; **III:** 618–619; **IV:** 133
"Descendant of Solomon and the Queen of Sheba" (Major), **Supp. XXII:** 182
Descendents, The (Glasgow), **II:** 173, 174–175, 176
Descending Figure (Glück), **Supp. V:** 83–84
"Descending Theology: Christ Human" (Karr), **Supp. XI:** 251
"Descending Theology: The Garden" (Karr), **Supp. XI:** 251
"Descent, The" (W. C. Williams), **Retro. Supp. I:** 428, 429
"Descent from the Cross" (Eliot), **Retro. Supp. I:** 57, 58
"Descent in the Maelström, A" (Poe), **Retro. Supp. II:** 274
"Descent into Proselito" (Knowles), **Supp. XII:** 237
"Descent into the Maelström, A" (Poe), **III:** 411, 414, 416, 424
Descent of Alette, The (Notley), **Supp. XXII:** 223, 224, 226, 227, 233–234
Descent of Man (Boyle), **Supp. VIII:** 1, 12–13; **Supp. XX: 17, 18,** 20
"Descent of Man" (Boyle), **Supp. VIII:** 14; **Supp. XX:** 18
Descent of Man, The (Darwin), **Supp. XIV:** 192
Descent of Man, The (Wharton), **IV:** 311; **Retro. Supp. I:** 367
Descent of Man and Other Stories, The (Wharton), **Retro. Supp. I:** 367
Descent of Winter, The (W. C. Williams), **Retro. Supp. I:** 419, 428
De Schloezer, Doris, **III:** 474
"Describers" (Halliday), **Supp. XIX:** 85
"Description" (Doty), **Supp. XI:** 126
"Description of the great Bones dug up at Clavarack on the Banks of Hudsons River A.D. 1705, The" (Taylor), **IV:** 163, 164
"Description without Place" (Stevens), **Retro. Supp. I:** 422
"Desert" (Hughes), **Retro. Supp. I:** 207
"Deserted Cabin" (Haines), **Supp. XII:** 203
Deserted Village, The (Goldsmith), **II:** 304
Desert Is My Mother, The/El desierto es mi madre (Mora), **Supp. XIII:** 214, 221
Desert Music, The (W. C. Williams), **IV:** 422; **Retro. Supp. I:** 428, 429
"Desert Music, The" (W. C. Williams), **Retro. Supp. I:** 428, 429
"Desert Places" (Frost), **II:** 159; **Retro. Supp. I:** 121, 123, 129, 138, 299; **Supp. XIV:** 229
Desert Rose, The (McMurtry), **Supp. V:** 225, 231

Desert Solitaire (Abbey), **Supp. X:** 30; **Supp. XIII: 7–8,** 12; **Supp. XIV:** 177, 179
"Design" (Frost), **II:** 158, 163; **Retro. Supp. I:** 121, 126, 138, 139; **Supp. IX:** 81; **Supp. XVII:** 132; **Supp. XVIII:** 298
"Designated National Park, A" (Ortiz), **Supp. IV Part 2:** 509
"Designs on a Point of View" (Everwine), **Supp. XV:** 76
DeSilva, Bruce, **Supp. XXII:** 205, 206, 217
Des Imagistes (Pound), **II:** 513; **Supp. I Part 1:** 257, 261, 262
Desire (album, Dylan), **Supp. XVIII:** 28
"Desire" (Beattie), **Supp. V:** 29
Desire (Bidart), **Supp. XV: 32–34,** 35
"Desire" (Everwine), **Supp. XV:** 85
Desire, Desire, Desire (Durang), **Supp. XXIV:** 113
"Desire and Denial" (Bronk), **Supp. XXI:** 26
"Désirée's Baby" (Chopin), **Retro. Supp. II:** 64, 65; **Supp. I Part 1:** 213–215
"Desire"(Hadas), **Supp. XXIII:** 117
Desire under the Elms (O'Neill), **III:** 387, 390
"Desolate Field, The" (W. C. Williams), **Retro. Supp. I:** 418
"Desolation, A" (Ginsberg), **Supp. II Part 1:** 313
Desolation Angels (Kerouac), **Supp. III Part 1:** 218, 225, 230
"Desolation Is a Delicate Thing" (Wylie), **Supp. I Part 2:** 729
"Desolation Row" (song, Dylan), **Supp. XVIII:** 30
Despair (Nabokov), **Retro. Supp. I:** 270, 274
Desperate Characters (Fox), **Supp. XX: 91**
"Despisals" (Rukeyser), **Supp. VI:** 282
Des Pres, Terrence, **Supp. X:** 113, 120, 124
"Destiny and the Lieutenant" (McCoy), **Supp. XIII:** 171
"Destruction of Kreshev, The" (Singer), **IV:** 13; **Retro. Supp. II:** 307
Destruction of the European Jews, The (Hilberg), **Supp. V:** 267
"Destruction of the Goetheanum, The" (Salter), **Supp. IX:** 257
"Destruction of the Long Branch, The" (Pinsky), **Supp. VI:** 239, 240, 243–244, 245, 247, 250
Destructive Element, The (Spender), **Retro. Supp. I:** 216
"Detail & Parody for the poem 'Paterson' " (W. C. Williams), **Retro. Supp. I:** 424
Detmold, John, **Supp. I Part 2:** 670
De Tolnay, Charles, **Supp. XXII:** 255
Detour at Night (Endore), **Supp. XVII:** 64
Deuce, The (R. O. Butler), **Supp. XII:** 62, **69–70,** 72
Deus Lo Volt! (Connell), **Supp. XIV:** 80, 81, 95
Deuteronomy (biblical book), **II:** 166

Deutsch, Andre, **Supp. XI:** 297, 301
Deutsch, Babette, **Supp. I Part 1:** 328, 341; **Supp. XV:** 305
Deutsch, Michel, **Supp. IV Part 1:** 104
"Devaluation Blues: Ruminations on Black Families in Crisis" (Coleman), **Supp. XI:** 87
Devane, William, **Supp. XI:** 234
Devasahayam, Madona, **Supp. XXII:** 260
"Development of My Mind and Character, The" (Notley), **Supp. XXII:** 227
"Development of the Literary West" (Chopin), **Retro. Supp. II:** 72
"Development of the Modern English Novel, The" (Lanier), **Supp. I Part 1:** 370–371
DeVeriante (Herbert of Cherbury), **II:** 108
"Devil and Daniel Webster, The" (Benét), **III:** 22; **Supp. XI:** 45–46, 47, 50–51, 52
Devil and Daniel Webster and Other Writings, The (Benét), **Supp. XI:** 48
"Devil and Tom Walker, The" (Irving), **II:** 309–310
Devil At Large, The: Erica Jong on Henry Miller (Jong), **Supp. V:** 115, 131
Devil-Doll, The (film, Browning), **Supp. XVII:** 58–59
Devil Finds Work, The (Baldwin), **Retro. Supp. II:** 14; **Supp. I Part 1:** 48, 52, 66–67
Devil in a Blue Dress (Mosley), **Supp. XIII:** 237, 239
"Devil in Manuscript, The" (Hawthorne), **II:** 226; **Retro. Supp. I:** 150–151
Devil in Paradise, A (H. Miller), **III:** 190
"Devil in the Belfry, The" (Poe), **III:** 425; **Retro. Supp. II:** 273
"Devil Is a Busy Man, The" (Wallace), **Supp. X:** 309
Devil's Dictionary, The (Bierce), **I:** 196, 197, 205, 208, 209, 210
Devil's Stocking, The (Algren), **Supp. IX:** 5, 16
"Devil's Thumb, The" (Krakauer), **Supp. XVIII:** 107
Devil's Tour, The (Karr), **Supp. XI:** 240, **242–244**
Devil Tree, The (Kosinski), **Supp. VII:** 215, 222, 223
"Devising" (Ammons), **Supp. VII:** 28
Devlin, Paul, **Supp. XIX:** 159
De Voto, Bernard, **I:** 247, 248; **II:** 446; **Supp. IV Part 2:** 599, 601
"Devout Meditation in Memory of Adolph Eichmann, A" (Merton), **Supp. VIII:** 198, 203
De Vries, Peter, **Supp. I Part 2:** 604
Dewberry, Elizabeth, **Supp. XII:** 62, 72
Dewey, John, **I:** 214, 224, 228, 232, 233, 266, 267; **II:** 20, 27, 34, 229, 361; **III:** 112, 294–295, 296, 303, 309–310, 599, 605; **IV:** 27, 429; **Supp. I Part 1:** 3, 5, 7, 10, 11, 12, 24; **Supp. I Part 2:** 493, 641, 647, 677; **Supp. V:** 290; **Supp. IX:** 179; **Supp. XIV:** 3; **Supp. XV:** 41
Dewey, Joseph, **Supp. IX:** 210
Dewey, Thomas, **IV:** 161

Dewey Defeats Truman (Mallon), **Supp. XIX:** 132, 137, **138**

Dexter, Peter, **Supp. XIV:** 221

De Young, Charles, **I:** 194

Dhairyam, Sagari, **Supp. IV Part 1:** 329, 330

Dharma Bums, The (Kerouac), **Supp. III Part 1:** 230, 231; **Supp. VIII:** 289, 305

"D. H. Lawrence" (Bynner), **Supp. XV:** 46

D. H. Lawrence: An Unprofessional Study (Nin), **Supp. X:** 182–183

D. H. Lawrence: The World of the Major Novels (Sanders), **Supp. XVI:** 267

D'Houdetot, Madame, **Supp. I Part 1:** 250

"Diabetes" (Dickey), **Supp. IV Part 1:** 182

Diaghilev, Sergei, **Supp. I Part 1:** 257

Dial (publication), **I:** 58, 109, 115, 116, 215, 231, 233, 245, 261, 384, 429; **II:** 8, 430; **III:** 194, 470, 471, 485; **IV:** 122, 171, 427; **Retro. Supp. I:** 58; **Retro. Supp. II:** 78; **Supp. I Part 2:** 642, 643, 647; **Supp. II Part 1:** 168, 279, 291; **Supp. II Part 2:** 474; **Supp. III Part 2:** 611

"Dialectical Materialism" (Weigl), **Supp. XIX:** 281

Dialectical Materialism and the Fate of Humanity (C. L. R. James), **Supp. XXI:** 169

"Dialectics of Love, The" (McGrath), **Supp. X:** 116

"Dialogue" (Rich), **Supp. I Part 2:** 560

Dialogue, A (Baldwin and Giovanni), **Supp. I Part 1:** 66

"Dialogue Between Franklin and the Gout" (Franklin), **II:** 121

"Dialogue Between General Wolfe and General Gage in a Wood near Boston, A" (Paine), **Supp. I Part 2:** 504

"Dialogue between Old England and New" (Bradstreet), **Supp. I Part 1:** 105–106, 110–111, 116

"Dialogue between the Writer and a Maypole Dresser, A" (Taylor), **IV:** 155

Dialogues (Bush, ed.), **III:** 4

Dialogues in Limbo (Santayana), **III:** 606

"Dialogue: William Harvey; Joan of Arc" (Goldbarth), **Supp. XII:** 178

Dialogue with a Dead Man (J. W. Miller), **Supp. XX: 163, 164, 167**

"Diamond as Big as the Ritz, The" (Fitzgerald), **II:** 88–89

Diamond Cutters and Other Poems, The (Rich), **Supp. I Part 2:** 551, 552, 553

"Diamond Guitar, A" (Capote), **Supp. III Part 1:** 124

Diamond Necklace, A (Notley), **Supp. XXII:** 228

"Diana and Persis" (Alcott), **Supp. I Part 1:** 32, 41

"Diaper Brigade, The" (Ryan as Quin), **Supp. XVIII:** 230

Diaries of Charlotte Perkins Gilman (Knight, ed.), **Supp. XI:** 201

"Diary–1903" (Boyce), **Supp. XXI:** 8

Diary of a Chambermaid, The (film; Renoir), **Supp. XVI:** 193

Diary of Anaïs Nin, The (1931–1974), **Supp. X:** 181, 185–189, 191, 192, 193, 195

Diary of Anne Frank, The, **Supp. XXI:** 245

Diary of a Rapist, The: A Novel (Connell), **Supp. XIV:** 80, 82, 94

Diary of a Yuppie (Auchincloss), **Supp. IV Part 1:** 31, 32–33

Diary of "Helena Morley", The (Bishop, trans.), **Retro. Supp. II:** 45, 51; **Supp. I Part 1:** 92

Dias, Robert Vas, **Supp. XXII:** 164, 169

Díaz, Junot, **Supp. XXIV: 83–95**

Díaz del Castillo, Bernál, **III:** 13, 14

Dick, Philip K., **Supp. XVI:** 123; **Supp. XVIII:** 136, 137, 138, 139, 142; **Supp. XXII:** 49

Dickens, Charles, **I:** 152, 198, 505; **II:** 98, 179, 186, 192, 271, 273–274, 288, 290, 297, 301, 307, 316, 322, 559, 561, 563, 577, 582; **III:** 146, 247, 325, 368, 411, 421, 426, 572, 577, 613–614, 616; **IV:** 21, 192, 194, 211, 429; **Retro. Supp. I:** 33, 91, 218; **Retro. Supp. II:** 204; **Supp. I Part 1:** 13, 34, 35, 36, 41, 49; **Supp. I Part 2:** 409, 523, 579, 590, 622, 675; **Supp. IV Part 1:** 293, 300, 341; **Supp. IV Part 2:** 464; **Supp. VIII:** 180; **Supp. IX:** 246; **Supp. XI:** 277; **Supp. XII:** 335, 337; **Supp. XIII:** 233; **Supp. XV:** 62; **Supp. XVI:** 63, 65–66, 72–73, 202; **Supp. XVIII:** 7, 136, 146; **Supp. XX: 21, 87, 195; Supp. XXII:** 206; **Supp. XXIII:** 4, 85, 290; **Supp. XXIV:** 87

Dickey, James, **I:** 29, 535; **III:** 268; **Retro. Supp. II:** 233; **Supp. III Part 1:** 354; **Supp. III Part 2:** 541, 597; **Supp. IV Part 1: 175–194; Supp. V:** 333; **Supp. X:** 30; **Supp. XI:** 312, 317; **Supp. XV:** 115, 348; **Supp. XVIII:** 191, 299; **Supp. XIX:** 282; **Supp. XXI:** 35; **Supp. XXIII:** 43, 50; **Supp. XXIV:** 42

Dick Gibson Show, The (Elkin), **Supp. VI:** 42, **48–49**

Dickie, Margaret, **Retro. Supp. II:** 53, 84

Dickinson, Donald, **Retro. Supp. I:** 206, 212

Dickinson, Edward, **I:** 451–452, 453

Dickinson, Mrs. Edward, **I:** 451, 453

Dickinson, Emily, **I:** 384, 419, 433, **451–473; II:** 272, 276, 277, 530; **III:** 19, 194, 196, 214, 493, 505, 508, 556, 572, 576; **IV:** 134, 135, 331, 444; **Retro. Supp. I: 25–50; Retro. Supp. II:** 39, 40, 43, 45, 50, 76, 134, 155, 170; **Supp. I Part 1:** 29, 79, 188, 372; **Supp. I Part 2:** 375, 546, 609, 682, 691; **Supp. II Part 1:** 4; **Supp. III Part 1:** 63; **Supp. III Part 2:** 600, 622; **Supp. IV Part 1:** 31, 257; **Supp. IV Part 2:** 434, 637, 641, 643; **Supp. V:** 79, 140, 332, 335; **Supp. VIII:** 95, 104, 106, 108, 198, 205, 272; **Supp.** **IX:** 37, 38, 53, 87, 90; **Supp. XII:** 226; **Supp. XIII:** 153, 339; **Supp. XIV:** 45, 127–128, 133, 261, 284; **Supp. XV:** 287, 303, 309; **Supp. XVI:** 288; **Supp. XVII:** 71, 73, 74, 75, 132; **Supp. XVIII:** 301; **Supp. XIX:** 86; **Supp. XX: 106, 108; Supp. XXI:** 52, 61, 64, 132, 214; **Supp. XXII:** 81, 82, 225, 277–278; **Supp. XXIII:** 19, 165

Dickinson, Gilbert, **I:** 469

Dickinson, Goldsworthy Lowes, **Supp. XIV:** 336

Dickinson, Lavinia Norcross, **I:** 451, 453, 462, 470

Dickinson, Stephanie, **Supp. XXIII:** 250

Dickinson, Mrs. William A. (Susan Gilbert), **I:** 452, 453, 456, 469, 470

Dickinson, William Austin, **I:** 451, 453, 469

Dickinson and the Strategies of Reticence (Dobson), **Retro. Supp. I:** 29, 42

Dickson, Helen. *See* Blackmur, Helen Dickson

Dickstein, Morris, **Supp. XIII:** 106; **Supp. XXIV:** 222, 223

"Dick Whittington and His Cat", **Supp. I Part 2:** 656

"DICTATORSHIP OF THE PROLETARIAT, THE" (Baraka), **Supp. II Part 1:** 54

Dictionary of Afro-American Slang (Major), **Supp. XXII:** 172, 174, 180

Dictionary of Literary Biography (Barron and Meyer, eds.), **Supp. XVIII:** 173; **Supp. XIX:** 195

Dictionary of Literary Biography (Gwynn, ed.), **Supp. XVIII:** 173; **Supp. XIX:** 121

Dictionary of Literary Biography (Kibler, ed.), **Supp. IX:** 94, 109; **Supp. XI:** 297

Dictionary of Literary Biography (Knight, ed.), **Supp. XIV:** 144

Dictionary of Literary Biography (Martine, ed.), **Supp. XXII:** 187

Dictionary of Literary Biography (Sicher, ed.), **Supp. XVII:** 41

Dictionary of Literary Biography (*Twentieth-Century American Nature Poets,* Bryson and Thompson, eds.), **Supp. XXIII:** 129

Dictionary of Modern English Usage, A (Fowler), **Supp. I Part 2:** 660

"Dictum: For a Masque of Deluge" (Merwin), **Supp. III Part 1:** 342–343

"Didactic Poem" (Levertov), **Supp. III Part 1:** 280

Diderot, Denis, **II:** 535; **IV:** 440; **Supp. XVI:** 293; **Supp. XVII:** 145

Did I Ever Tell You How Lucky You Are? (Geisel), **Supp. XVI:** 109

Didion, Joan, **Retro. Supp. I:** 116; **Retro. Supp. II:** 209; **Supp. I Part 1:** 196, 197; **Supp. III Part 1:** 302; **Supp. IV Part 1: 195–216; Supp. XI:** 221; **Supp. XII:** 307

Dido, **I:** 81

Dido, Queen of Hearts (Atherton), **Supp. XXIV:** 26

Di Donato, Peter, **Supp. XX: 34**

Di Donato, Pietro, **Supp. XX: 33–47**

"Did 'Paco's Story' Deserve Its Award" (Kakutani), **Supp. XXII:** 109

"Did You Ever Dream Lucky?" (Ellison), **Supp. II Part 1:** 246

Dieckmann, Katherine, **Supp. XXIII:** 295, 296

"Die-Hard, The" (Benét), **Supp. XI:** 54–55, 56

Diehl, Digby, **Supp. IV Part 1:** 204

Dien Cai Dau (Komunyakaa), **Supp. XIII:** 121, **122–124,** 125, 131, 132

Dies, Martin, **Supp. XVIII:** 229

"Dies Irae" (Lowell), **II:** 553

Die Zeit Ohne Beispiel, (Goebbels), **III:** 560

Difference Engine, The (W. Gibson and B. Sterling), **Supp. XVI:** 121, 124, **128–129**

Different Drummer, A (Larkin; film), **Supp. XI:** 20

Different Fleshes (Goldbarth), **Supp. XII:** 181–182, 188

Different Hours (Dunn), **Supp. XI:** 139, 142, 143, 155

"Different Road, A" (Strout), **Supp. XXIII:** 282–283

Different Seasons (King), **Supp. V:** 148, 152

Different Ways to Pray (Nye), **Supp. XIII:** 274, 275, 277, 285, 287

"Different Ways to Pray" (Nye), **Supp. XIII:** 275

"Difficulties of a Statesman" (Eliot), **I:** 580

"Difficulties of Modernism and the Modernism of Difficulty" (Poirier), **Supp. II Part 1:** 136

Diff'rent (O'Neill), **III:** 389; **Supp. XXII:** 22

Di Filippo, Paul, **Supp. XXII:** 260, 261

DiGaetani, John L., **Supp. XIII:** 200

Digges, Deborah, **Supp. XXIII:** 57

"Digging" (Sanders), **Supp. XVI:** 272

"Digging in the Garden of Age I Uncover a Live Root" (Swenson), **Supp. IV Part 2:** 649

Digging Up the Dirt (Moraga), **Supp. XXIII:** 197

Diggins, John P., **Supp. I Part 2:** 650

"Dignity of Life, The" (C. Bly), **Supp. XVI:** 34, 36–37

Digregorio, Charles, **Supp. XI:** 326

"Digression on *Number 1,* 1948" (O'Hara), **Supp. XXIII:** 214

"Dilemma" (Budbill), **Supp. XIX:** 2

"Dilemma of Determinism, The" (James), **II:** 347–348, 352

"Dilemma of the Negro Writer, The" (speech, C. Himes), **Supp. XVI:** 140

"Dilettante, The" (Wharton), **IV:** 311, 313

"Dilettante, The: A Modern Type" (Dunbar), **Supp. II Part 1:** 199

Dillard, Annie, **Supp. VI: 19–39; Supp. VIII:** 272; **Supp. X:** 31; **Supp. XIII:** 154

Dillard, R. H. W., **Supp. XII:** 16

Dillman, Bradford, **III:** 403; **Supp. XII:** 241

Dillon, Brian, **Supp. X:** 209

Dillon, George, **III:** 141; **Supp. III Part 2:** 621

Dillon, Millicent, **Supp. IV Part 1:** 95

Dilsaver, Paul, **Supp. XIII:** 112

Dilthey, Wilhelm, **I:** 58

Dime-Store Alchemy: The Art of Joseph Cornell, **Supp. VIII:** 272

"Diminuendo" (Dunn), **Supp. XI:** 152–153

"Dimout in Harlem" (Hughes), **Supp. I Part 1:** 333

"Dinah's Lament" (Nelson), **Supp. XVIII:** 183

Dinesen, Isak, **IV:** 279; **Supp. VIII:** 171; **Supp. XVI:** 250

Dining Room, The (Gurney), **Supp. V:** 105–106

"Dinner at ------, A" (O. Henry), **Supp. II Part 1:** 402

"Dinner at Sir Nigel's" (Bowles), **Supp. IV Part 1:** 94

Dinner at the Homesick Restaurant (Tyler), **Supp. IV Part 2:** 657, 667–668

"Dinner at Uncle Borris's" (Simic), **Supp. VIII:** 272

Dinner Bridge (Lardner), **II:** 435

Dinosaur Tales (Bradbury), **Supp. IV Part 1:** 103

"Diogenes Invents a Game" (Karr), **Supp. XI:** 240–241

"Diogenes Tries to Forget" (Karr), **Supp. XI:** 241

Diomede, Matthew, **Supp. XX: 46**

Dionysis in Doubt (Robinson), **III:** 510

Dionysus in 69 (Schechner), **Supp. XXIV:** 116

Diop, Birago, **Supp. IV Part 1:** 16

Diop, David, **Supp. IV Part 1:** 16

Di Piero, W. S., **Supp. XVII:** 241; **Supp. XIX:** 33–48

Di Prima, Diane, **Supp. III Part 1:** 30; **Supp. XIV:** 125, 144, 148, 150

Dirda, Michael, **Supp. XXI:** 233

Direction of Poetry, The: An Anthology of Rhymed and Metered Verse Written in the English Language since 1975 (Richman, ed.), **Supp. XV:** 250, 251

Direction of Poetry, The: Rhymed and Metered Verse Written in the English Language since 1975 (Richman), **Supp. XI:** 249

"Directive" (Bishop), **Retro. Supp. II:** 42

"Directive" (Frost), **III:** 287; **Retro. Supp. I:** 140; **Supp. VIII:** 32, 33

"Dire Cure" (Matthews), **Supp. IX:** 168

"Dirge" (Dunbar), **Supp. II Part 1:** 199

"Dirge without Music" (Millay), **III:** 126

"Dirt" (Salter), **Supp. IX:** 257, 260, 261

"Dirt and Desire: Essay on the Phenomenology of Female Pollution in Antiquity" (Carson), **Supp. XII: 111**

Dirty Bird Blues (Major), **Supp. XXII: 180–181**

Dirty Dingus Magee (film), **Supp. XVII:** 139

"Dirty English Potatoes" (X. J. Kennedy), **Supp. XV:** 165

"Dirty Memories" (Olds), **Supp. X:** 211

Dirty Story (Shanley), **Supp. XIV:** 316, 331

"Dirty Word, The" (Shapiro), **Supp. II Part 2:** 710

Dirty Work (L. Brown), **Supp. XXI:** 37, 39, 40, 42, **45**

"'Disabled Imagination' and the Masculine Metaphor in the Works of Leonard Kriegel, The" (Haugen), **Supp. XXIV:** 215

Disappearance of the Jews, The (Mamet), **Supp. XIV:** 249–250, 250–251, 252, 254

Disappearances (Auster), **Supp. XII:** 23

"Disappearances" (Hogan), **Supp. IV Part 1:** 401

Disappearances (Mosher), **Supp. XXII:** 204, 205, 206, 207, 208, 209, **210**

"Disappeared, The " (C. Baxter), **Supp. XVII:** 19

Disappearing Acts (McMillan), **Supp. XIII:** 182, 183, **188–189,** 192

Disappearing Ink: Poetry at the End of Print Culture (Gioia), **Supp. XV:** 112

"Disappointment, The" (Creeley), **Supp. IV Part 1:** 143

"Disappointment and Desire" (R. Bly), **Supp. IV Part 1:** 71

Disappointment Artist, The (Lethem), **Supp. XVIII:** 135, 141, **148**

"Discards" (Baker), **Supp. XIII:** 53, 55–56

Discerning the Signs of the Times (Niebuhr), **III:** 300–301, 307–308

Disch, Thomas M., **Supp. XIX:** 1

"Disciple of Bacon, The" (Epstein), **Supp. XII:** 163–164

"Discipline" (L. Brown), **Supp. XXI:** 44

Discomfort, Zone, The: A Personal History (Franzen), **Supp. XX: 83, 84, 95**

"Discordants" (Aiken), **I:** 65

Discourse on Method (Descartes), **I:** 255

"Discourtesies" (Kirsch), **Supp. XV:** 341

"Discovering Theme and Structure in the Novel" (Schuster), **Supp. VIII:** 126

"Discovery" (Freneau), **Supp. II Part 1:** 258

"Discovery of the Madeiras, The" (Frost), **Retro. Supp. I:** 139

"Discovery of What It Means to Be an American, The" (Baldwin), **Supp. I Part 1:** 54–55

Discovery! The Search for Arabian Oil (Stegner), **Supp. IV Part 2:** 599

"Discrete Series" (Zukofsky), **Supp. III Part 2:** 616

"Discretions of Alcibiades" (Pinsky), **Supp. VI:** 241

"Disease, The" (Rukeyser), **Supp. VI:** 279

Disenchanted, The (play, Schulberg and Breit), **Supp. XVIII:** 254

Disenchanted, The (Schulberg), **II:** 98; **Retro. Supp. I:** 113; **Supp. XVIII: 247–250,** 253

Disenchantments: An Anthology of Modern Fairy Tale Poetry (Mieder), **Supp. XIV:** 126

"Dish of Green Pears, A" (Ríos), **Supp. IV Part 2:** 552

"Disillusion and Dogma" (Untermeyer), **Supp. XV:** 306

Dismantling the Silence (Simic), **Supp. VIII: 273–274,** 275, 276

Disney, Walt, **III:** 275, 426

"Disney of My Mind" (Chabon), **Supp. XI:** 63

Disobedience (Notley), **Supp. XXII:** 235, 236

Dispatches (Herr), **Supp. XI:** 245; **Supp. XIX:** 17

"Displaced Person, The" (O'Connor), **III:** 343–344, 350, 352, 356; **Retro. Supp. II:** 229, 232, 236

"Disposal" (Snodgrass), **Supp. VI:** 314

Dispossessed, The (Berryman), **I:** 170, 172, 173, 174, 175, 176, 178

"Disquieting Muses, The" (Plath), **Supp. I Part 2:** 538

Disraeli, Benjamin, **II:** 127

Dissent (Didion), **Supp. IV Part 1:** 208

"Dissent in Ashcroft's America" (P. N. Warren), **Supp. XX: 273**

"Dissenting Opinion on Kafka, A" (Wilson), **IV:** 437–438

Dissent in Three American Wars (Morison, Merk, and Freidel), **Supp. I Part 2:** 495

Dissertation on Liberty and Necessity, Pleasure and Pain, A (Franklin), **II:** 108

Dissertations on Government; the Affairs of the Bank: and Paper Money (Paine), **Supp. I Part 2:** 510

"Distance" (Carver), **Supp. III Part 1:** 146

"Distance" (Everwine), **Supp. XV:** 85

"Distance" (Paley), **Supp. VI:** 222

"Distance, The" (Karr), **Supp. XI:** 241

"Distance from the Sea, A" (Kees), **Supp. XV:** 147

"Distance Nowhere" (Hughes), **Retro. Supp. I:** 207

"Distance Up Close, The" (Peacock), **Supp. XIX:** 196–197, 198

"Distant Episode, A" (Bowles), **Supp. IV Part 1:** 84–85, 86, 90

Distant Episode, A: The Selected Stories (Bowles), **Supp. IV Part 1:** 79

Distant Rain: A Conversation Between Jakuchō Setouchi & Tess Gallagher (Setouchi and Gallagher), **Supp. XXIV:** 166, 178

Distinguished Guest, The (Miller), **Supp. XII: 299–301**

Distortions (Beattie), **Supp. V:** 21, 23, 24, 25, 27

"Distrest Shepherdess, The" (Freneau), **Supp. II Part 1:** 258

District of Columbia (Dos Passos), **I:** 478, 489–490, 492

Disturber of the Peace (Manchester), **III:** 103

Disturbing the Peace (Yates), **Supp. XI:** 345, 346

"Diver, The" (Hayden), **Supp. II Part 1:** 368, 372, 373

"Divided Life of Jean Toomer, The" (Toomer), **Supp. III Part 2:** 488

Divided Self, The (Laing), **Supp. XX: 95**

Divina Commedia (Longfellow, trans.), **II:** 490, 492, 493

"Divina Pastora, La" (C. L. R. James), **Supp. XXI:** 160

"Divine, The" (Di Piero), **Supp. XIX:** 41

"Divine Collaborator" (Simic), **Supp. VIII:** 282

Divine Comedies (Merrill), **Supp. III Part 1:** 324, 329–332

Divine Comedy (Dante), **I:** 137, 265, 400, 446; **II:** 215, 335, 490, 492, 493; **III:** 13, 448, 453; **Supp. V:** 283, 331, 338, 345; **Supp. X:** 253; **Supp. XIV:** 6; **Supp. XIX:** 36, 39

"Divine Image, The" (Blake), **Supp. V:** 257

Divine Pilgrim, The (Aiken), **I:** 50, 55

Divine Right's Trip (Norman), **Supp. XXIII:** 42

Divine Tragedy, The (Longfellow), **II:** 490, 500, 505, 506, 507; **Retro. Supp. II:** 165, 166

Divine Weekes and Workes (Sylvester, trans.), **Supp. I Part 1:** 104

Divine Weeks (Du Bartas), **IV:** 157–158

Diving into the Wreck: Poems 1971–1972 (Rich), **Supp. I Part 2:** 550, 559–565, 569; **Supp. XV:** 252

"Diving Past African Violets" (A. Finch), **Supp. XVII:** 72

Diving Rock on the Hudson, A (H. Roth), **Supp. IX:** 236, **237–238**

"Divinity in Its Fraying Fact, A" (Levis), **Supp. XI:** 271

"Divinity School Address" (Emerson), **II:** 12–13

"Divinity School or Trusting the Act of Writing" (Abraham), **Supp. XXIV:** 1, 3–4

"Divisions upon a Ground" (Hecht), **Supp. X:** 58

"Divorce" (Karr), **Supp. XI:** 244

"Divorced Fathers and Pizza Crusts" (Halliday), **Supp. XIX:** 93

Divorced in America: Marriage in an Age of Possibility (Epstein), **Supp. XIV:** 113

"Divorce Dream" (Halliday), **Supp. XIX:** 90

"Divorce in the United States" (Atherton), **Supp. XXIV:** 24

Dix, Douglas Shields, **Supp. XII:** 14

Dixie City Jam (Burke), **Supp. XIV:** 32

Dixon, Ivan, **Supp. IV Part 1:** 362

Dixon, Stephen, **Supp. XII: 139–158**

Dixon, Terrell F., **Supp. XVI:** 21

Dixon, Thomas, Jr., **Supp. II Part 1:** 169, 171, 177

Djinn (Robbe-Grillet), **Supp. V:** 48

D'Lugoff, Burt, **Supp. IV Part 1:** 362, 370

Dmytryk, Edward, **Supp. XX: 41**

Do, Lord, Remember Me (Garrett), **Supp. VII:** 98–100, 110

"Doaksology, The" (Wolfe), **IV:** 459

Do Androids Dream of Electric Sheep? (Dick), **Supp. XVIII:** 137

Dobie, J. Frank, **Supp. V:** 225; **Supp. XIII:** 227

Döblin, Alfred, **Supp. XV:** 137

Dobriansky, Lev, **Supp. I Part 2:** 648, 650

Dobrin, Sidney I., **Supp. XVIII:** 192, 195

Dobson, Joanne, **Retro. Supp. I:** 29, 31, 42; **Supp. XVIII:** 259

Dobyns, Stephen, **Supp. XIII: 73–92**

"Docking at Palermo" (Hugo), **Supp. VI:** 137–138

"Dock Rats" (Moore), **III:** 213

"Dock-Witch, The" (Ozick), **Supp. V:** 262, 264

"Doc Mellhorn and the Pearly Gates" (Benét), **Supp. XI:** 55

"Doctor, The" (Dubus), **Supp. VII:** 80–81

"Doctor and the Doctor's Wife, The" (Hemingway), **II:** 248; **Retro. Supp. I:** 174, 175

Doctor Breen's Practice, a Novel (Howells), **I:** 282

Doctor Faustus (Mann), **III:** 283

Doctor Jazz (Carruth), **Supp. XVI:** 47, 59

"Doctor Jekyll" (Sontag), **Supp. III Part 2:** 469

"Doctor Leavis and the Moral Tradition" (Trilling), **Supp. III Part 2:** 512–513

Doctor Martino and Other Stories (Faulkner), **II:** 72; **Retro. Supp. I:** 84

"Doctor of the Heart, The" (Sexton), **Supp. II Part 2:** 692

Doctorow, E. L., **Retro. Supp. I:** 97; **Supp. III Part 2:** 590, 591; **Supp. IV Part 1: 217–240; Supp. V:** 45; **Supp. XVI:** 73; **Supp. XVII:** 183; **Supp. XX: 84, 90; Supp. XXI:** 18–19; **Supp. XXII:** 268

Doctor Sax (Kerouac), **Supp. III Part 1:** 220–222, 224–227

Doctor Sleep (Bell), **Supp. X: 9–11**

"Doctors' Row" (Aiken), **I:** 67

Doctor's Son and Other Stories, The (O'Hara), **III:** 361

Doctor Stories, The (W. C. Williams), **Retro. Supp. I:** 424

"Doctor's Wife, The" (Ozick), **Supp. V:** 262, 265

Doctor Zhivago (Pasternak), **IV:** 434, 438, 443

"Documentary" (Simic), **Supp. VIII:** 282

Dodd, Elizabeth, **Supp. V:** 77

Dodd, Wayne, **Supp. IV Part 2:** 625

Dodge, Mabel, **Supp. XX: 69; Supp. XXI:** 5, 6, 8, 12; **Supp. XXII:** 158, 161. *See also* Luhan, Mabel Dodge

Dodson, Owen, **Supp. I Part 1:** 54

Dodsworth (Lewis), **II:** 442, 449–450, 453, 456

Doenitz, Karl, **Supp. I Part 2:** 491

Does Civilization Need Religion? (Niebuhr), **III:** 293–294

"Does 'Consciousness' Exist?" (James), **II:** 356

"Does Education Pay?" (Du Bois), **Supp. II Part 1:** 159

"Dog" (B. Kelly), **Supp. XVII:** 126

Dog (Shepard), **Supp. III Part 2:** 434

"Dog Act, The" (Komunyakaa), **Supp. XIII:** 114–115

"Dog and the Playlet, The" (O. Henry), **Supp. II Part 1:** 399

Dog Beneath the Skin, The (Auden), **Supp. II Part 1:** 10
"Dog Creek Mainline" (Wright), **Supp. V:** 340
"Dogfight" (W. Gibson and Swanwick), **Supp. XVI:** 128
Dog in the Manger, The (Vega; Merwin, trans.), **Supp. III Part 1:** 341, 347
Dog of the Marriage, The (Hempel), **Supp. XXI:** 115, 116, 117, 118, **126–127**
"Dog"(P. Benedict), **Supp. XXIII:** 36–37, 39
Dogs Bark, but the Caravan Rolls On (Conroy), **Supp. XVI:** 63, 70, 74, **75–76**
Dogs Bark, The: Public People and Private Places (Capote), **Supp. III Part 1:** 120, 132
"Dog's Eye" (J. W. Miller), **Supp. XX:** 167
"Dogs of Bucharest, The" (Gallagher), **Supp. XXIV:** 171
Dogs of God (Benedict), **Supp. XXIII:** 35, **41–45,** 49–50
Dog Soldiers (Stone), **Supp. V:** 298, 299–301
Dog Star, The (Di Piero), **Supp. XIX:** 38, **40–41,** 43
"Dog Stories" (Prose), **Supp. XVI:** 256
Dog & the Fever, The (Quevedo), **Retro. Supp. I:** 423
"Dogtown Letters, The" (Jarman and R. McDowell), **Supp. XVII:** 111
"Dogwood, The" (Levertov), **Supp. III Part 1:** 276
"Dogwood Tree, The: A Boyhood" (Updike), **IV:** 218; **Retro. Supp. I:** 318, 319
Doig, Ivan, **Supp. XIV:** 227
"Doing Battle with the Wolf" (Coleman), **Supp. XI:** 87–88
"Doing Jigsaw Puzzles" (Crooker), **Supp. XXIII:** 56
Doing Literary Business: American Women Writers in the Nineteenth Century (Coultrap-McQuin), **Supp. XVI:** 85
Doings and Undoings (Podhoretz), **Supp. VIII: 236–237**
"Do-It-Yourself" (C. Baxter), **Supp. XVII:** 14–15
Dolan, Jill, **Supp. XV:** 327
Dolben, Digby Mackworth, **Supp. XX: 230**
"Dolce Far' Niente" (Humphrey), **Supp. IX:** 106
Dolci, Carlo, **III:** 474–475
Dollars and Cents (A. Warner), **Supp. XVIII:** 264
"Dollhouse, The" (Haines), **Supp. XII:** 204
Dollmaker's Ghost, The (Levis), **Supp. XI:** 259, 260, **264–268**
Doll's House, A (Ibsen), **III:** 523; **IV:** 357; **Supp. XVI:** 182
Dolmetsch, Arnold, **III:** 464
Dolores Claiborne (King), **Supp. V:** 138, 141, 147, 148, 149–150, 152
"Dolph Heyliger" (Irving), **II:** 309

Dolphin, The (Lowell), **Retro. Supp. II:** 183, 186, 188, **190–191; Supp. XII:** 253–254
"Dolphins" (Francis), **Supp. IX:** 83
Dome of Many-Coloured Class, A (Lowell), **II:** 515, 516–517
Domesday Book (Masters), **Supp. I Part 2:** 465, 466–469, 471, 473, 476
"Domestic Economy" (Gilman), **Supp. XI:** 206
"Domestic Manners" (Hardwick), **Supp. III Part 1:** 211
Domestic Work (Trethewey), **Supp. XXI:** 243, 244, **248–251,** 254
"Domestic Work, 1937" (Trethewey), **Supp. XXI:** 248
"Dominant White, The" (McKay), **Supp. X:** 134
Dominguez, Robert, **Supp. VIII:** 83
Domini, John, **Supp. XIX:** 45; **Supp. XXI:** 235
Dominique, Jean. *See* Closset, Marie
Donahoe, Edward, **Supp. XVIII:** 132
Donahue, Phil, **Supp. IV Part 2:** 526; **Supp. X:** 311
Donaldson, Susan, **Supp. XXII:** 148
Doña Perfecta (Galdós), **II:** 290
Dong, Stella, **Supp. XVI:** 222
Don Juan (Byron), **Supp. XV:** 259
"DON JUAN IN HELL" (Baraka), **Supp. II Part 1:** 33
Donkey of God, The (Untermeyer), **Supp. XV:** 310
"Donna mi Prega" (Cavalcanti), **Supp. III Part 2:** 620, 621, 622
Donn-Byrne, Brian Oswald. *See* Byrne, Donn
Donne, John, **I:** 358–359, 384, 389, 522, 586; **II:** 254; **III:** 493; **IV:** 83, 88, 135, 141, 144, 145, 151, 156, 165, 331, 333; **Retro. Supp. II:** 76; **Supp. I Part 1:** 80, 364, 367; **Supp. I Part 2:** 421, 424, 467, 725, 726; **Supp. III Part 2:** 614, 619; **Supp. VIII:** 26, 33, 164; **Supp. IX:** 44; **Supp. XII:** 45, 159; **Supp. XIII:** 94, 130; **Supp. XIV:** 122; **Supp. XV:** 92, 251; **Supp. XVI:** 158, 204; **Supp. XVIII:** 35, 39, 50–51, 307; **Supp. XXIV:** 167
Donne's Sermons: Selected Passages (L. P. Smith, ed.), **Supp. XIV:** 342
Donoghue, Denis, **I:** 537; **Supp. IV Part 1:** 39; **Supp. VIII:** 105, 189
Donohue, H. E. F., **Supp. IX:** 2, 3, 15, 16
Donoso, José, **Supp. XXIV:** 86
Do Not Deny Me (Thompson), **Supp. XXIII: 300–301**
"Do Not Weep Maiden, For War Is Kind" (Crane), **Supp. XVIII:** 75
Donovan, Josephine, **Retro. Supp. II:** 138, 139, 147
Don Quixote (Cervantes), **I:** 134; **II:** 291, 434; **III:** 113, 614; **Supp. I Part 2:** 422; **Supp. IX:** 94; **Supp. XXIV:** 87
Don Quixote: Which Was a Dream (Acker), **Supp. XII:** 5, **12–14**
Don't Ask (Levine), **Supp. V:** 178
Don't Ask Questions (Marquand), **III:** 58

Don't Bet on the Prince: Contemporary Feminist Fairy Tales in North America and England (Zipes), **Supp. XIV:** 126
Don't Drink the Water (Allen), **Supp. XV:** 3, **14**
Don't Look Back (film, Pennebaker), **Supp. XVIII:** 19
"Don't Neglect Your Wife" (script, Atherton), **Supp. XXIV:** 25
"Don't Shoot the Warthog" (Corso), **Supp. XII:** 123
"Don't Tell Mother" (Wasserstein), **Supp. XV:** 319
"Don't Think Twice, It's All Right" (song, Dylan), **Supp. XVIII:** 24
Don't Worry About the Kids (Neugeboren), **Supp. XVI:** 226
"Don't Worry About the Kids" (Neugeboren), **Supp. XVI:** 226
Don't You Want to Be Free? (Hughes), **Retro. Supp. I:** 203; **Supp. I Part 1:** 339
"Doodler, The" (Merrill), **Supp. III Part 1:** 321
Doolan, Moira, **Retro. Supp. II:** 247
Doolittle, Hilda (H. D.), **II:** 517, 520–521; **III:** 194, 195–196, 457, 465; **IV:** 404, 406; **Retro. Supp. I:** 288, 412, 413, 414, 415, 417; **Supp. I Part 1:** **253–275; Supp. I Part 2:** 707; **Supp. III Part 1:** 48; **Supp. III Part 2:** 610; **Supp. IV Part 1:** 257; **Supp. V:** 79; **Supp. XV:** 43, 249, 301, 302; **Supp. XVII:** 77; **Supp. XXII:** 88; **Supp. XXIV:** 64
Doolittle, Thomas, **IV:** 150
"Doomed by Our Blood to Care" (Orfalea), **Supp. XIII:** 278
"Doomsday" (Plath), **Retro. Supp. II:** 242
Doomsters, The (Macdonald), **Supp. IV Part 2:** 462, 463, 472, 473
Doomswoman, The (Atherton), **Supp. XXIV:** 22
Doonesbury (Trudeau), **Supp. XXIV:** 283
"Door, The" (Creeley), **Supp. IV Part 1:** 145, 146, 156–157
"Door, The" (White), **Supp. I Part 2:** 651, 675–676
"Door in the Dark, The" (Frost), **II:** 156
Door in the Hive, A (Levertov), **Supp. III Part 1:** 283, 284
"Door of the Trap, The" (Anderson), **I:** 112
"Doors" (Dybek), **Supp. XXIII:** 69
Doors (Hoffman), **Supp. XVIII:** 86–87
"Doors" (Hoffman), **Supp. XVIII:** 86–87
"Doors, Doors, Doors" (Sexton), **Supp. II Part 2:** 681
Doors, The, **Supp. X:** 186
"Doorways into the Depths" (Sanders), **Supp. XVI:** 272
Doreski, William, **Retro. Supp. II:** 185
Dorfman, Ariel, **Supp. IX:** 131, 138
Dorfman, Joseph, **Supp. I Part 2:** 631, 647, 650
Dorman, Jen, **Supp. XI:** 240
Dorn, Edward, **Supp. IV Part 1:** 154; **Supp. XXIV:** 33, 44
Dorn, Sarah, **Supp. XXI:** 243

"Dorothea Dix, Samaritan" (J. Scott), **Supp. XVII:** 189

Dorr, Julia, **Supp. XV:** 286

Dorris, Michael, **Supp. IV Part 1:** 260, 272

Dos Passos, John, **I:** 99, 288, 374, 379, **474–496**, 517, 519; **II:** 74, 77, 89, 98; **III:** 2, 28, 29, 70, 172, 382–383; **IV:** 340, 427, 433; **Retro. Supp. I:** 105, 113, 187; **Retro. Supp. II:** 95, 196; **Supp. I Part 2:** 646; **Supp. III Part 1:** 104, 105; **Supp. V:** 277; **Supp. VIII:** 101, 105; **Supp. XIV:** 24; **Supp. XV:** 135, 137, 182; **Supp. XVII:** 105, 107; **Supp. XXI:** 8; **Supp. XXIII:** 68

"Dos Passos: Poet Against the World" (Cowley), **Supp. II Part 1:** 143, 145

Dostoevsky: A Screenplay (Carver and Gallagher), **Supp. XXIV:** 178

Dostoevsky, Fyodor, **I:** 53, 103, 211, 468; **II:** 60, 130, 275, 320, 587; **III:** 37, 61, 155, 174, 176, 188, 189, 267, 272, 283, 286, 354, 357, 358, 359, 467, 571, 572; **IV:** 1, 7, 8, 17, 21, 50, 59, 106, 110, 128, 134, 285, 289, 476, 485, 491; **Retro. Supp. II:** 20, 204, 299; **Supp. I Part 1:** 49; **Supp. I Part 2:** 445, 466; **Supp. IV Part 2:** 519, 525; **Supp. VIII:** 175; **Supp. X:** 4–5; **Supp. XI:** 161; **Supp. XII:** 322; **Supp. XVI:** 63; **Supp. XVII:** 225; **Supp. XVIII:** 278, 280; **Supp. XX:** 45; **Supp. XXIII:** 4; **Supp. XXIV:** 132

Doty, Mark, **Supp. IX:** 42, 300; **Supp. XI: 119–138; Supp. XXI:** 129, 130, 131, 139, 141; **Supp. XXIII:** 126, 221

Doty, M. R. *See* Dawson, Ruth; Doty, Mark

Double, The (Dostoevsky), **Supp. IX:** 105

"Double, The" (Levis), **Supp. XI:** 260, **261–263**

Double, The (Rank), **Supp. IX:** 105

Double Agent, The (Blackmur), **Supp. II Part 1:** 90, 108, 146

Double Axe, The (Jeffers), **Supp. II Part 2:** 416, 434

"Double Blind" (Skloot), **Supp. XX: 194, 208**

Doubleday, Frank, **I:** 500, 502, 515, 517; **III:** 327

Doubleday, Mrs. Frank, **I:** 500

Double Deuce (Parker), **Supp. XIX:** 183

Double Down (F. and S. Barthelme), **Supp. XI:** 27, 34, 35, 36–38

Double Dream of Spring, The (Ashbery), **Supp. III Part 1:** 11–13

Double Fold: Libraries and the Assault on Paper (Baker), **Supp. XIII:** 52, 56

Double Game (Calle), **Supp. XII:** 22

"Double Gap, The" (Auchincloss), **Supp. IV Part 1:** 33

"Double-Headed Snake of Newbury, The" (Whittier), **Supp. I Part 2:** 698

Double Honeymoon (Connell), **Supp. XIV:** 80, 87

Double Image, The (Levertov), **Supp. III Part 1:** 274, 276

"Double Image, The" (Sexton), **Supp. II Part 2:** 671, 677–678

Double Indemnity (film), **Supp. IV Part 1:** 130

Double Legacy: Reflections on a Pair of Deaths (Hadas), **Supp. XXIII:** 123, **126–127**

"Double Limbo" (Komunyakaa), **Supp. XIII:** 132

Double Man, The (Auden), **Supp. III Part 1:** 16; **Supp. X:** 118

"Double Ode" (Rukeyser), **Supp. VI:** 282–283, 286

Double Persephone (Atwood), **Supp. XIII:** 19

Double Play (Parker), **Supp. XIX: 189–190**

Doubles in Literary Psychology (Tymms), **Supp. IX:** 105

Double Vision: American Thoughts Abroad (Knowles), **Supp. XII:** 249

"Doubt on the Great Divide" (Stafford), **Supp. XI:** 322

Dougherty, Robin, **Supp. XXII:** 205

Dougherty, Steve, **Supp. X:** 262

Douglas, Aaron, **Supp. I Part 1:** 326

Douglas, Alfred, **Supp. X:** 151

Douglas, Ann, **Supp. XII:** 136; **Supp. XVIII:** 258; **Supp. XX: 69**

Douglas, Claire, **III:** 552

Douglas, Ellen, **Supp. XXI:** 38

Douglas, George (pseudonym). *See* Brown, George Douglas

Douglas, Kirk, **Supp. XIII:** 5–6

Douglas, Lloyd, **IV:** 434

Douglas, Marjory Stoneman, **Supp. XVIII:** 195

Douglas, Melvyn, **Supp. V:** 223

Douglas, Michael, **Supp. XI:** 67

Douglas, Paul, **III:** 294

Douglas, Stephen A., **III:** 577, 588–589; **Supp. I Part 2:** 456, 471

Douglas, William O., **III:** 581

Douglass, Frederick, **Supp. I Part 1:** 51, 345; **Supp. I Part 2:** 591; **Supp. II Part 1:** 157, 195, 196, 292, 378; **Supp. III Part 1: 153–174; Supp. IV Part 1:** 1, 2, 13, 15, 256; **Supp. VIII:** 202; **Supp. XVIII:** 16; **Supp. XX: 109, 281; Supp. XXIII:** 167

Douglass, Thomas E., **Supp. XXIII:** 36

Douglass Pilot, The (Baldwin, ed.), **Supp. I Part 1:** 49

Dove, Belle, **I:** 451

Dove, Rita, **Supp. IV Part 1: 241–258; Supp. XVII:** 71, 110; **Supp. XVIII:** 172, 174; **Supp. XXI:** 243, 246, 247, 249, 251

"Dover Beach" (Arnold), **Retro. Supp. I:** 325; **Supp. XIX:** 41

Dow, Lorenzo, **IV:** 265

Dowd, Douglas, **Supp. I Part 2:** 645, 650

"Do We Understand Each Other?" (Ginsberg), **Supp. II Part 1:** 311

Dowie, William, **Supp. V:** 199

Do with Me What You Will (Oates), **Supp. II Part 2:** 506, 515–517

Dowling, Eddie, **IV:** 394

Down and Out (Shanley), **Supp. XIV:** 317

"Down at City Hall" (Didion), **Supp. IV Part 1:** 211

"Down at the Cross" (Baldwin), **Retro. Supp. II:** 1, 2, 7, 12, 13, 15; **Supp. I Part 1:** 60, 61

"Down at the Dinghy" (Salinger), **III:** 559, 563

"Down by the Station, Early in the Morning" (Ashbery), **Supp. III Part 1:** 25

Downey, Sharon D., **Supp. XX: 244**

Downhill Racer (film), **Supp. IX:** 253

"Down Home" (J. W. Miller), **Supp. XX: 169**

"Down in Alabam" (Bierce), **I:** 193

Downing, Ben, **Supp. XII:** 175, 189, 190–191

Downing, Major Jack (pseudonym). *See* Smith, Seba

Down in My Heart (Stafford), **Supp. XI:** 313, 315

Down Mailer's Way (Solotaroff), **Retro. Supp. II:** 203

"Down the Highway" (song, Dylan), **Supp. XVIII:** 24

Down the Rabbit Hole: Adventures and Misadventures in the Realm of Children's Literature (Lanes), **Supp. XVI:** 104

Down There on a Visit (Isherwood), **Supp. XIV:** 159, 161, 164, **168–169**, 170, 171

Down the River (Abbey), **Supp. XIII:** 12–13

"Down the River with Henry Thoreau" (Abbey), **Supp. XIII:** 12–13

Down These Mean Streets (P. Thomas), **Supp. XIII:** 264

Down the Starry River (Purdy), **Supp. VII:** 278

Down to the River: Portraits of Iowa Musicians (Dyas), **Supp. XIX:** 174

Downtown (Siddons), **Supp. XXII:** 239, 240, 242, **247–249, 251–252,** 253

"Downtrodden Mary's Failed Campaign of Terror" (Saunders), **Supp. XIX:** 226

"Downward Path to Wisdom, The" (Porter), **III:** 442, 443, 446

"Down Where I Am" (Hughes), **Supp. I Part 1:** 344

Down with Starvation Wages in Southeast Missouri (C. L. R. James), **Supp. XXI:** 169

"Dowsing for Joy" (Skloot), **Supp. XX: 203**

Dowson, Ernest C., **I:** 384

Doyle, Arthur Conan, **Retro. Supp. I:** 270; **Supp. IV Part 1:** 128, 341; **Supp. IV Part 2:** 464, 469; **Supp. XI:** 63

Doyle, C. W., **I:** 199

"Draba" (Leopold), **Supp. XIV:** 186

Drabble, Margaret, **Supp. IV Part 1:** 297, 299, 305

Drabelle, Dennis, **Supp. XIII:** 13

Drach, Ivan, **Supp. III Part 1:** 268

Dracula (film), **Supp. IV Part 1:** 104; **Supp. XVII:** 57

"Draft Horse, The" (Frost), **Retro. Supp. I:** 141

"Draft Lyrics for *Candide*" (Agee), **I:** 28

Draft of XVI Cantos, A (Pound), **III:** 472; **Retro. Supp. I:** 292

Draft of XXX Cantos, A (Pound), **III:** 196; **Retro. Supp. I:** 292

Drafts &Fragments (Pound), **Retro. Supp. I:** 293

Dragon Country (T. Williams), **IV:** 383

Dragone, Nichole, **Supp. XXIII:** 157

Dragon Seed (Buck), **Supp. II Part 1:** 124

Drake, Benjamin, **Supp. I Part 2:** 584

Drake, Daniel, **Supp. I Part 2:** 584

Drake, Sir Francis, **Supp. I Part 2:** 497

Drake, Robert, **Supp. XX:** 274

Drake, St. Clair, **IV:** 475

Drake, Sylvia, **Supp. XXI:** 155

Drake, William, **Supp. XV:** 295

Dramatic Duologues (Masters), **Supp. I Part 2:** 461

"Drapery Factory, Gulfport. Mississippi, 1956" (Trethewey), **Supp. XXI:** 246

Drattel, Deborah, **Supp. XV:** 333

Drat These Brats (X. J. Kennedy), **Supp. XV:** 163

"Draught" (Cowley), **Supp. II Part 1:** 141, 142

Drayton, Michael, **IV:** 135; **Retro. Supp. II:** 76

"Dr. Bergen's Belief" (Schwartz), **Supp. II Part 2:** 650

Dr. Bloodmoney (Dick), **Supp. XVIII:** 138

"Dreadful Has Already Happened, The" (Strand), **Supp. IV Part 2:** 627

Dread Road, The (Le Sueur), **Supp. XXIII:** 168, 169, **169–170,** 173

"Dream, A" (Ginsberg), **Supp. II Part 1:** 312

"Dream, A" (Tate), **IV:** 129

"Dream, The" (Hayden), **Supp. II Part 1:** 368, 377

Dream at the End of the World, The: Paul Bowles and the Literary Renegades in Tangier (Green), **Supp. IV Part 1:** 95

"Dream Avenue" (Simic), **Supp. VIII:** 282

"Dream Boogie" (Hughes), **Retro. Supp. I:** 208; **Supp. I Part 1:** 339–340

"Dreambook Bestiary" (Komunyakaa), **Supp. XIII:** 120

Dreamer (Johnson), **Supp. VI:** 186, **196–199**

dreamer examines his pillow, the (Shanley), **Supp. XIV:** 315, **327**

"Dreamer in a Dead Language" (Paley), **Supp. VI:** 217

Dreaming in Cuban (García), **Supp. XI:** 178, **179–185,** 190

"Dreaming of Hair" (L.-Y. Lee), **Supp. XV:** 214

"Dreaming the Breasts" (Sexton), **Supp. II Part 2:** 692

"Dreaming Water" (Espaillat), **Supp. XXI:** 102

"Dream Interpretation" (Hadas), **Supp. XXIII:** 113, 121

"Dream Interpreted, The" (Paine), **Supp. I Part 2:** 505

Dream Jumbo (Longo), **Supp. XVI:** 124

Dream Keeper, The (Hughes), **Supp. I Part 1:** 328, 332, 333, 334

Dream Keeper and Other Poems, The (Hughes), **Retro. Supp. I:** 201, 202

Dreamland (Baker), **Supp. XIV:** 96

"Dream-Land" (Poe), **Retro. Supp. II:** 274

Dream Life of Balso Snell, The (West), **IV:** 286, 287, 288–290, 291, 297; **Retro. Supp. II:** 321, 322, 327, 328, **330–332**

"Dream Machine, The" (Hadas), **Supp. XXIII:** 122–123

Dream Me Home Safely: Writers on Growing up in America (Shreve, ed.), **Supp. XXIII:** 284

Dream of a Common Language, The: Poems, 1974–1977 (Rich), **Supp. I Part 2:** 551, 554, 569–576

Dream of Arcadia: American Writers and Artists in Italy (Brooks), **I:** 254

Dream of Governors, A (Simpson), **Supp. IX:** 265, **269–270**

"Dream of Italy, A" (Masters), **Supp. I Part 2:** 458

"Dream of Mourning, The" (Glück), **Supp. V:** 84

"Dream of the Blacksmith's Room, A" (R. Bly), **Supp. IV Part 1:** 73

"Dream of the Cardboard Lover" (Haines), **Supp. XII:** 204

Dream of the Golden Mountains, The (Cowley), **Supp. II Part 1:** 139, 141, 142, 144

"Dream Pang, A" (Frost), **II:** 153

"Dreams About Clothes" (Merrill), **Supp. III Part 1:** 328–329

"Dreams"(Dybek), **Supp. XXIII:** 73

Dreams from Bunker Hill (Fante), **Supp. XI:** 160, 166, **172–173**

"Dreams"(Kenny), **Supp. XXIII:** 153

"Dreams of Adulthood" (Ashbery), **Supp. III Part 1:** 26

"Dreams of Glory on the Mound" (Plimpton), **Supp. XVI:** 238–239

"Dreams of Math" (Kenyon), **Supp. VII:** 160–161

"Dreams of the Animals" (Atwood), **Supp. XIII:** 33

"Dream Variations" (Hughes), **Retro. Supp. I:** 198; **Supp. I Part 1:** 323

"Dream Vision" (Olsen), **Supp. XIII:** 295–296

Dream Work (Oliver), **Supp. VII:** 234–235, 236–238, 240

Dred: A Tale of the Great Dismal Swamp (Stowe), **Supp. I Part 2:** 592

Dreiser, Theodore, **I:** 59, 97, 109, 116, 355, 374, 375, 475, 482, **497–520; II:** 26, 27, 29, 34, 38, 44, 74, 89, 93, 180, 276, 283, 428, 444, 451, 456–457, 467–468; **III:** 40, 103, 106, 251, 314, 319, 327, 335, 453, 576, 582; **IV:** 29, 35, 40, 135, 208, 237, 475, 482, 484; **Retro. Supp. I:** 325, 376; **Retro. Supp. II:** **93–110,** 114, 322; **Supp. I Part 1:** 320; **Supp. I Part 2:** 461, 468; **Supp. III Part 2:** 412; **Supp. IV Part 1:** 31, 236, 350; **Supp. IV Part 2:** 689; **Supp. V:** 113, 120; **Supp. VIII:** 98, 101, 102; **Supp. IX:** 1, 14, 15, 308; **Supp. XI:** 207; **Supp. XIV:** 111;

Supp. XVII: 95, 96–97, 105, 155; **Supp. XVIII:** 1, 6, 76, 226; **Supp. XXI:** 275; **Supp. XXIII:** 161, 164

"Drenched in Light" (Hurston), **Supp. VI:** 150–151

Drennen, Eileen M., **Supp. XXII:** 241, 243

Dresser, Paul, **Retro. Supp. II:** 94, 103

Dress Gray (teleplay), **Supp. IV Part 2:** 683

Dress Gray (Truscott), **Supp. IV Part 2:** 683

"Dressing for Dinner" (Ríos), **Supp. IV Part 2:** 548

Dressing Up for the Carnival (Shields), **Supp. VII:** 328

"Dress Rehearsal" (Skloot), **Supp. XX:** **204**

Drew, Bettina, **Supp. IX:** 2, 4

Drew, Elizabeth, **Retro. Supp. II:** 242, 243

Drexler, Eric, **Supp. XVI:** 121

Dreyfus, Alfred, **Supp. I Part 2:** 446

"Dr. Hanray's Second Chance" (Richter), **Supp. XVIII:** 218

Drift and Mastery (Lippmann), **I:** 222–223

"Driftwood" (C. Frost), **Supp. XV:** 106–107

"Drinker, The" (Lowell), **II:** 535, 550

"Drinking Cold Water" (Everwine), **Supp. XV:** 80–81

"Drinking from a Helmet" (Dickey), **Supp. IV Part 1:** 180

Drinking Gourd, The (Hansberry), **Supp. IV Part 1:** 359, 365–367, 374

Drinks before Dinner (Doctorow), **Supp. IV Part 1:** 231, 234–235

Driscoll, David, **Supp. XIX:** 241, 242

Driskill, Qwo-Li, **Supp. XXIII:** 147, 148, 149

Drive, He Said (Larner), **Supp. XVI:** 220

"Drive Home, The" (Banks), **Supp. V:** 7

"Driver" (Merrill), **Supp. III Part 1:** 331

"Driving Alone in Winter" (W. V. Davis), **Supp. XXI:** 89, 90, 94

"Driving Through Minnesota During the Hanoi Bombings" (R. Bly), **Supp. IV Part 1:** 61; **Supp. XVII:** 243

"Driving through Oregon" (Haines), **Supp. XII:** 207

"Driving to Oregon"(Thompson), **Supp. XXIII:** 291

"Driving toward the Lac Qui Parle River" (R. Bly), **Supp. IV Part 1:** 61

"Dr. Jack-o'-Lantern" (Yates), **Supp. XI:** 340–341

Dr. Jekyll and Mr. Hyde (film), **Supp. XVII:** 57

"Drone" (Coleman), **Supp. XI:** 85–86

Drop City (Boyle), **Supp. XX:** **30–31**

Drown (Díaz), **Supp. XXIV:** 83, 84, 85, 86, **88–89,** 90, 93

"Drowned Man, The: Death between Two Rivers" (McGrath), **Supp. X:** 116

"Drowning" (Boyle), **Supp. XX:** **18**

"Drowning 1954" (Keillor), **Supp. XVI:** 172

Drowning Pool, The (film), **Supp. IV Part 2:** 474

Drowning Pool, The (Macdonald), **Supp. IV Part 2:** 470, 471

Drowning Season, The (Hoffman), **Supp. X:** 82

Drowning with Others (Dickey), **Supp. IV Part 1:** 176, 178, 179

"Drowsy Day, A" (Dunbar), **Supp. II Part 1:** 198

Dr. Seuss. *See* Geisel, Theodor Seuss (Dr. Seuss)

Dr. Seuss and Mr. Geisel (J. and N. Morgan), **Supp. XVI:** 103

Dr. Seuss Goes to War: The World War II Editorial Cartoons of Theodor Seuss Geisel (Minear), **Supp. XVI:** 101

Dr. Seuss's ABC (Geisel), **Supp. XVI:** 99

Dr. Strangelove; or, How I Learned to Stop Worrying and Love the Bomb (film), **Supp. XI:** 293, **301–305**

Drugiye Berega (Nabokov), **III:** 247–250, 252

"Drug Shop, The, or Endymion in Edmonstoun" (Benét), **Supp. XI:** 43

"Drug Store" (Shapiro), **Supp. II Part 2:** 705

"Drugstore in Winter, A" (Ozick), **Supp. V:** 272

Drukman, Steven, **Supp. XIII:** 195, 197, 202

"Drum" (Hogan), **Supp. IV Part 1:** 413

"Drum, The" (Alvarez), **Supp. VII:** 7

"Drumlin Woodchuck, A" (Frost), **II:** 159–160; **Retro. Supp. I:** 138

Drummond, William, **Supp. I Part 1:** 369

Drummond de Andrade, Carlos, **Supp. IV Part 2:** 626, 629, 630

Drums at Dusk (Bontemps), **Supp. XXII:** 5, 9–10

Drum-Taps (Whitman), **IV:** 346, 347, 444; **Retro. Supp. I:** 406

"Drunken Fisherman, The" (Lowell), **II:** 534, 550

"Drunken Sisters, The" (Wilder), **IV:** 374

Drunk in the Furnace, The (Merwin), **Supp. III Part 1:** 345–346

"Drunk in the Furnace, The" (Merwin), **Supp. III Part 1:** 346

Druten, John van, **Supp. XIV:** 162

"Dr. Williams' Position" (Pound), **Supp. XVII:** 226–227

Dryden, John, **II:** 111, 542, 556; **III:** 15; **IV:** 145; **Retro. Supp. I:** 56; **Supp. I Part 1:** 150; **Supp. I Part 2:** 422; **Supp. IX:** 68; **Supp. XIV:** 5; **Supp. XV:** 258; **Supp. XX:** 280; **Supp. XXIV:** 158

Drye, Captain Frank, **Retro. Supp. II:** 115

Dry Salvages, The (Eliot), **I:** 581

"Dry Salvages, The" (Eliot), **Retro. Supp. I:** 66

"Dry September" (Faulkner), **II:** 72, 73

"Dry Spring"(Thompson), **Supp. XXIII:** 291

Dry Sun, Dry Wind (Wagoner), **Supp. IX:** 323, 324

D'Souza, Dinesh, **Supp. X:** 255

"Dual" (Goldbarth), **Supp. XII:** 188

"Dual Curriculum" (Ozick), **Supp. V:** 270

"Dualism" (Reed), **Supp. X:** 242

Duane's Depressed (McMurtry), **Supp. V:** 233

Du Bartas, Guillaume, **Supp. I Part 1:** 98, 104, 111, 118, 119

Duberman, Martin, **Supp. I Part 2:** 408, 409

Dubie, Norman, **Supp. XXIV:** 165

"Dubin's Lives" (Malamud), **Supp. I Part 2:** 451

Dubious Honors (M. F. K. Fisher), **Supp. XVII:** 91

"Dubliners" (J. Joyce), **Supp. XVI:** 41

Dubliners (Joyce), **I:** 130, 480; **III:** 471; **Supp. VIII:** 146

Dublin's Lives (Malamud), **Supp. XIX:** 142

Du Bois, Nina Gomer (Mrs. W. E. B. Du Bois), **Supp. II Part 1:** 158; **Supp. XIV:** 200

Du Bois, Shirley Graham, **Supp. II Part 1:** 186; **Supp. XXI:** 171. *See also* Graham, Shirley

Du Bois, W. E. B., **I:** 260; **Supp. I Part 1:** 5, 345; **Supp. II Part 1:** 33, 56, 61, **157–189**, 195; **Supp. IV Part 1:** 9, 164, 170, 362; **Supp. X:** 133, 134, 137, 139, 242; **Supp. XIII:** 186, 233, 238, 243, 244, 247; **Supp. XIV:** 54, 69, 72, 201, 202; **Supp. XVI:** 135; **Supp. XVIII:** 119, 122, 126, 130; **Supp. XIX:** 67, 69, 77; **Supp. XX: 102, 105, 106; Supp. XXI:** 166, 277; **Supp. XXII:** 3

Dubreuil, Jean, **Supp. IV Part 2:** 425

Dubus, Andre, **Supp. VII: 75–93; Supp. XI:** 347,**Supp. XI:** 349; **Supp. XIV:** 21; **Supp. XXIV:** 97

Dubus, Andre, III, **Supp. XXIV: 97–112**

Duchamp, Marcel, **IV:** 408; **Retro. Supp. I:** 416, 417, 418, 430; **Supp. IV Part 2:** 423, 424; **Supp. XII:** 124; **Supp. XV:** 157; **Supp. XXII:** 162, 163, 168

"Duchess at Prayer, The" (Wharton), **Retro. Supp. I:** 365

Duchess of Malfi, The (Webster), **IV:** 131

"Duckling Girl" (Dubus III), **Supp. XXIV:** 100–101, 105

Duck Soup (film), **Supp. IV Part 1:** 384

Duck Variations, The (Mamet), **Supp. XIV:** 239, 240, 249

Ducornet, Rikki, **Supp. XXII:** 261

Dudley, Anne. *See* Bradstreet, Anne

Dudley, Joseph, **III:** 52

Dudley, Thomas, **III:** 52; **Supp. I Part 1:** 98, 99, 110, 116

"Duenna"(Schott), **Supp. XXIII:** 249

"Duet, With Muffled Brake Drums" (Updike), **Retro. Supp. I:** 319

Duet for Cannibals (Sontag), **Supp. III Part 2:** 452, 456

Duffey, Bernard, **Supp. I Part 2:** 458, 471

Duffield, Pitts, **Supp. XXI:** 3

Duffus, R. L., **Supp. I Part 2:** 650

Duffy, Martha, **Supp. IV Part 1:** 207; **Supp. XX: 244**

Duffy, William, **Supp. XVI:** 32

Du Fu (Tu Fu), **Supp. XV:** 217

Dufy, Raoul, **I:** 115; **IV:** 80

Dugan, Alan, **Supp. XIII:** 76

Dugan, James, **Supp. XV:** 197

"Dugout"(Kenny), **Supp. XXIII:** 155

Duhamel, Marcel, **Supp. XVI:** 135, 143

Dujardin, Edouard, **I:** 53

"Duke de l'Omelette, The" (Poe), **III:** 411, 425

"Duke in His Domain, The" (Capote), **Supp. III Part 1:** 113, 126

Duke of Deception, The (G. Wolff), **Supp. II Part 1:** 97; **Supp. XI:** 246

"Duke's Child, The" (Maxwell), **Supp. VIII:** 172

"Dulce et Decorum Est" (Owen), **Supp. XVIII:** 92

"Dulham Ladies, The" (Jewett), **II:** 407, 408; **Retro. Supp. II:** 143

Duluth (Vidal), **Supp. IV Part 2:** 677, 685, 689, 691–692

Dumas, Alexandre, **III:** 386; **Supp. XVII:** 64

"Dumb Ox, The" (Lewis), **Retro. Supp. I:** 170

"Dummy, The" (Sontag), **Supp. III Part 2:** 469

"Dump Ground, The" (Stegner), **Supp. IV Part 2:** 601

Dunant, Sarah, **Supp. XIX:** 186

Dunayevskaya, Raya, **Supp. XXI:** 169

Dunbar, Alice Moore (Mrs. Paul Laurence Dunbar), **Supp. II Part 1:** 195, 200, 217

Dunbar, Paul Laurence, **Supp. I Part 1:** 320; **Supp. II Part 1:** 174, **191–219; Supp. III Part 1:** 73; **Supp. IV Part 1:** 15, 165, 170; **Supp. X:** 136; **Supp. XI:** 277; **Supp. XIII:** 111; **Supp. XXII:** 11

Duncan, Harry, **Supp. XV:** 75

Duncan, Isadora, **I:** 483; **Supp. XV:** 42, 50

Duncan, Robert, **Retro. Supp. II:** 49; **Supp. III Part 2:** 625, 626, 630, 631; **Supp. VIII:** 304; **Supp. XVI:** 282–283; **Supp. XXIII:** 213

Dunciad, The (Pope), **I:** 204

Dunford, Judith, **Supp. VIII:** 107

Dunlap, William, **Supp. I Part 1:** 126, 130, 137, 141, 145

Dunn, Stephen, **Supp. XI: 139–158; Supp. XIX:** 85

Dunne, Finley Peter, **II:** 432

Dunne, John Gregory, **Supp. IV Part 1:** 197, 198, 201, 203, 207

"Dunnet Shepherdess, A" (Jewett), **II:** 392–393; **Retro. Supp. II:** 139

Dunning, Stephen, **Supp. XIV:** 126

Dunning, William Archibald, **Supp. II Part 1:** 170; **Supp. XIV:** 48

Dunnock, Mildred, **III:** 153

Dunster, Henry, **Supp. I Part 2:** 485

"Duo Tried Killing Man with Bacon" (Goldbarth), **Supp. XII:** 176

Dupee, F. W., **I:** 254; **II:** 548; **Supp. VIII:** 231; **Supp. IX:** 93, 96

DuPlessis, Rachel Blau, **Supp. IV Part 2:** 421, 426, 432; **Supp. XVI:** 284

Duplicate Keys (Smiley), **Supp. VI:** 292, **294–296**

Duplications, The (Koch), **Supp. XV:** 181, 183, 186

Durable Fire, A (Sarton), **Supp. VIII:** 260

Durand, Asher, B., **Supp. I Part 1:** 156, 157

Durand, Régis, **Supp. IV Part 1:** 44

Durang, Christopher, **Supp. XXIV: 113–130,** 263

"Durango Suite" (Gunn Allen), **Supp. IV Part 1:** 326

Durant, Kenneth, **Supp. XXII:** 278, 281

"Durations" (Matthews), **Supp. IX:** 152–153, 154

Dürer, Albrecht, **III:** 212; **Supp. XII:** 44

Durham, David Anthony, **Supp. XVIII:** 100

"During Fever" (Lowell), **II:** 547

Durkheim, Émile, **I:** 227; **Retro. Supp. I:** 55, 57; **Supp. I Part 2:** 637, 638

Durrell, Lawrence, **III:** 184, 190; **IV:** 430; **Supp. X:** 108, 187; **Supp. XVI:** 294

Dürrenmatt, Friedrich, **Supp. IV Part 2:** 683

Duse, Eleonora, **II:** 515, 528

Dusk and Other Stories (Salter), **Supp. IX: 260–261**

Dusk of Dawn: An Essay Toward an Autobiography of a Race Concept (Du Bois), **Supp. II Part 1:** 159, 183, 186

"Dust" (R. Fisher), **Supp. XIX:** 71

"Dusting" (Alvarez), **Supp. VII:** 4

"Dusting" (Dove), **Supp. IV Part 1:** 247, 248

"Dusting" (Schnackenberg), **Supp. XV:** 256

"Dust of Snow" (Frost), **II:** 154

Dust Tracks on a Road (Hurston), **Supp. IV Part 1:** 5, 11; **Supp. VI:** 149, 151, 158–159

"Dusty Braces" (Snyder), **Supp. VIII:** 302

Dutchman (Baraka), **Supp. II Part 1:** 38, 40, 42–44, 54, 55

"Dutch Nick Massacre, The" (Twain), **IV:** 195

"Dutch Picture, A" (Longfellow), **Retro. Supp. II:** 171

Dutton, Charles S., **Supp. VIII:** 332, 342

Dutton, Clarence Earl, **Supp. IV Part 2:** 598

Duvall, Robert, **Supp. V:** 227

"Duwamish" (Hugo), **Supp. VI:** 136

"Duwamish, Skagit, Hoh" (Hugo), **Supp. VI:** 136–137

"Duwamish No. 2" (Hugo), **Supp. VI:** 137

Duyckinck, Evert, **III:** 77, 81, 83, 85; **Retro. Supp. I:** 155, 247, 248; **Supp. I Part 1:** 122, 317

Duyckinck, George, **Supp. I Part 1:** 122

"Dvonya" (Simpson), **Supp. IX:** 274

Dwelling Places: Poems and Translations (Ferry), **Supp. XXIV: 152–153**

Dwellings: A Spiritual History of the Living World (Hogan), **Supp. IV Part 1:** 397, 410, 415–416, 417

Dwight, Sereno E., **I:** 547

Dwight, Timothy, **Supp. I Part 1:** 124; **Supp. I Part 2:** 516, 580; **Supp. II Part 1:** 65, 69

Dworkin, Andrea, **Supp. XII:** 6

Dwyer, Jim, **Supp. XVI:** 16, 19

Dyas, Sandra, **Supp. XIX:** 174

Dybbuk, A, or Between Two Worlds: Dramatic Legend in Four Acts (Kushner), **Supp. IX:** 138

Dybbuk, The (Ansky), **IV:** 6

Dybek, Stuart, **Supp. XXIII: 67–81**

Dybuk, The (Ansky), **Supp. XXIII:** 8

Dyer, Geoff, **Supp. X:** 169

Dyer, Joyce, **Supp. XX: 166**

Dyer, R. C., **Supp. XIII:** 162

Dyer, Richard, **Supp. XXII:** 261

Dyer's Thistle (Balakian), **Supp. XXIII:** 25

Dying Animal, The (P. Roth), **Retro. Supp. II:** 288

"Dying Elm, The" (Freneau), **Supp. II Part 1:** 258

"Dying Indian, The" (Freneau), **Supp. II Part 1:** 262

"Dying Man, The" (Roethke), **III:** 540, 542, 543–545

Dykeman, Wilma, **Supp. XX: 163**

Dylan, Bob, **Supp. VIII:** 202; **Supp. XIII:** 114, 119; **Supp. XV:** 349, 350; **Supp. XVIII: 19–34; Supp. XXII:** 83

Dylan's Visions of Sin (Ricks), **Supp. XVIII:** 20

"Dynamics of Heroic Action, The" (lecture, Murray), **Supp. XIX:** 153

Dynamo (O'Neill), **III:** 396

"Dynasties" (Gibran), **Supp. XX: 118**

"Dysfunctional Narratives: Or, 'Mistakes Were Made' " (C. Baxter), **Supp. XVII:** 20

"Dysfunctional Nation" (Karr), **Supp. XI:** 245

Dyson, A. E., **Retro. Supp. II:** 247

Dyson, Freeman, **Supp. XVII:** 42

E

"Each and All" (Emerson), **II:** 19

Each Happiness Ringer by Lions (Hirshfield), **Supp. XXIII:** 135

Each in His Season (Snodgrass), **Supp. VI:** 324, 327

"Each Like a Leaf" (Swenson), **Supp. IV Part 2:** 644

Eads, Martha Greene, **Supp. XVIII:** 49

Eady, Cornelius, **Supp. XXI:** 246

Eager, Allen, **Supp. XI:** 294

"Eagle, The" (Tate), **IV:** 128

"Eagle and the Mole, The" (Wylie), **Supp. I Part 2:** 710, 711, 713, 714, 729

"Eagle and the Skylark, The" (Gibran), **Supp. XX: 124**

Eagle as Wide as the World, The (X. J. Kennedy), **Supp. XV:** 162, 164

"Eagle Poem" (Harjo), **Supp. XII:** 224, 226

"Eagles" (Dickey), **Supp. IV Part 1:** 186

Eagle's Mile, The (Dickey), **Supp. IV Part 1:** 178, 185–186

"Eagle That Is Forgotten, The" (Lindsay), **Supp. I Part 2:** 382, 387

Eagleton, Terry, **Retro. Supp. I:** 67

Eakin, Paul John, **Supp. VIII:** 167, 168; **Supp. XIII:** 225; **Supp. XVI:** 70

Eakins, Thomas, **Supp. XIV:** 338; **Supp. XXII:** 18–19

Eames, Emma, **Supp. XX: 232, 240**

Eames, Roscoe, **II:** 476

"Earl: My Life with a Louse" (Keillor), **Supp. XVI:** 176

"Earl Painter" (Banks), **Supp. V:** 14–15

"Early Adventures of Ralph Ringwood, The" (Irving), **II:** 314

Early Americana (Richter), **Supp. XVIII:** 208, 210, 211, 220

Early Autumn (Parker), **Supp. XIX:** 184–185

Early Ayn Rand, The: A Selection of Her Unpublished Fiction (Rand), **Supp. IV Part 2:** 520

Early Dark (Price), **Supp. VI:** 262

Early Diary of Anaïs Nin, The, **Supp. X:** 184, 192

Early Elkin (Elkin), **Supp. VI: 42–43,** 45

"Early Evenin' Blues" (Hughes), **Retro. Supp. I:** 205

"Early Evening, Frankfort, Kentucky" (Trethewey), **Supp. XXI:** 243, 250

"Early History of a Seamstress" (Reznikoff), **Supp. XIV:** 277, 289

Early History of a Sewing-Machine Operator (Reznikoff), **Supp. XIV:** 289

"Early History of a Sewing-Machine Operator" (Reznikoff), **Supp. XIV:** 277

"Early History of a Writer" (Reznikoff), **Supp. XIV:** 278, 290

"Early in the Morning" (L.-Y. Lee), **Supp. XV:** 214

Early Lectures of Ralph Waldo Emerson, The (Emerson), **II:** 11

Early Light (Di Piero), **Supp. XIX:** 38, **38–40**

Early Lives of Melville, The (Sealts), **Retro. Supp. I:** 257

"Early Marriage" (Richter), **Supp. XVIII:** 209

Early Martyr and Other Poems, An (W. C. Williams), **Retro. Supp. I:** 423

"Early Morning: Cape Cod" (Swenson), **Supp. IV Part 2:** 641

"Early Rooms" (Hirshfield), **Supp. XXIII:** 130

"Early Spring between Madison and Bellingham" (R. Bly), **Supp. IV Part 1:** 71

Early Writing (O'Hara), **Supp. XXIII:** 220

Earnhardt, Dale, **Supp. XII:** 310

Earnshaw, Doris, **Supp. IV Part 1:** 310

"Earth" (Bryant), **Supp. I Part 1:** 157, 164, 167

"Earth, The" (Sexton), **Supp. II Part 2:** 696

Earth Abides (Stewart), **Supp. XVIII:** 138

"Earth and Fire" (Berry), **Supp. X:** 27

Earth as Air, The: An Ars Poetica (Sobin), **Supp. XVI: 285–286**

"Earth Being" (Toomer), **Supp. IX:** 320

Earth Goat (online), **Supp. XXII:** 61

Earth Gods, The (Gibran), **Supp. XX: 116, 123**

"Earthly Care a Heavenly Discipline" (Stowe), **Supp. I Part 2:** 586

"Earthly City of the Jews, The" (Kazin), **Retro. Supp. II:** 286

Earthly Meditations (Wrigley), **Supp. XVIII:** 304–305

"Earthly Meditations" (Wrigley), **Supp. XVIII:** 304–306

Earthly Possessions (Tyler), **Supp. IV Part 2:** 665–666, 671

Earth Power Coming (Ortiz, ed.), **Supp. IV Part 2:** 502

"Earth's Holocaust" (Hawthorne), **II:** 226, 231, 232, 242; **III:** 82; **Retro. Supp. I:** 152

Earth Without You, The (F. Wright), **Supp. XVII:** 243

Eason, Laura, **Supp. XXIII:** 79

East Coker (Eliot), **I:** 580, 581, 582, 585, 587

"East Coker" (Eliot), **Retro. Supp. I:** 66; **Supp. VIII:** 195, 196

"Easter" (Toomer), **Supp. III Part 2:** 486

"Easter, an Ode" (Lowell), **II:** 536

"Easter 1916" (Yeats), **Supp. XXI:** 61

"Easter Morning" (Ammons), **Supp. VII:** 34

"Easter Morning" (Clampitt), **Supp. IX:** 45

"Easter Ode, An" (Dunbar), **Supp. II Part 1:** 196

"Easter"(O'Hara), **Supp. XXIII:** 211

Easter Parade, The (Yates), **Supp. XI:** 346, 349

"Easter Sermon, 1866" (Nelson), **Supp. XVIII:** 177

"Easter Service" (Di Piero), **Supp. XIX:** 39–40

"Easter Sunday: Recollection" (Gunn Allen), **Supp. IV Part 1:** 322

"Easter Wings" (Herbert), **Supp. IV Part 2:** 646

"East European Cooking" (Simic), **Supp. VIII:** 277

East Is East (Boyle), **Supp. VIII:** 1–3; **Supp. XX: 23–24, 25, 28**

Eastlake, William, **Supp. XIII:** 12

East Lynne (Wood), **Supp. I Part 1:** 35, 36; **Supp. I Part 2:** 459, 462; **Supp. XVI:** 182

Eastman, Elaine Goodale, **Supp. X:** 103

Eastman, Max, **Supp. III Part 2:** 620; **Supp. X:** 131, 134, 135, 137; **Supp. XV:** 295; **Supp. XVI:** 185; **Supp. XVII:** 96; **Supp. XXI:** 6; **Supp. XXII:** 274, 275, 277

East of Eden (Steinbeck), **IV:** 51, 56–57, 59

"East of the Sun and West of the Moon" (Merwin), **Supp. III Part 1:** 344

Easton, Alison, **Retro. Supp. II:** 143, 144, 145

Easton, Bret Ellis, **Supp. XI:** 65

Easton, Nina J., **Supp. XIX:** 137

Easton, Robert, **Supp. IV Part 2:** 461, 474

East River (Asch), **Supp. XXIII:** 1, 3, 7, **14–15**

East Wind (Lowell), **II:** 527

East Wind: West Wind (Buck), **Supp. II Part 1:** 114–115

Easy Rawlins mysteries, **Supp. XIII:** 236, **237–241,** 242

Easy Rider (film), **Supp. XI:** 293, **308,** 309

Eat a Bowl of Tea (Chu), **Supp. X:** 291

"Eating " (Bass), **Supp. XVI:** 23–24

"Eating Alone" (L.-Y. Lee), **Supp. XV:** 214

"Eating Barley Sugar and Waiting to Be Ninety"(Hadas), **Supp. XXIII:** 120–121

Eating Naked (Dobyns), **Supp. XIII: 78–79**

"Eating Out" (L. Michaels), **Supp. XVI:** 209

"Eating Poetry" (Strand), **Supp. IV Part 2:** 626

"Eating the Whole" (C. Frost), **Supp. XV:** 101

"Eating Together" (L.-Y. Lee), **Supp. XV:** 214

"Eating with My Fingers" (C. Frost), **Supp. XV:** 97

Eaton, Edith, **Supp. X:** 291

Eaton, Mark A., **Supp. XXIII:** 129, 130, 136

Eaton, Peggy, **Supp. I Part 2:** 461

Eaton, Winnifred, **Supp. X:** 291

"Eatonville Anthology, The" (Hurston), **Supp. VI:** 152

Eat Pray Love (Gilbert), **Supp. XXII:** 83, 90

Eat the Document (film, Pennebaker), **Supp. XVIII:** 19, 26, 27, 28

"Ebb and Flow, The" (Taylor), **IV:** 161

"Ebenezer Marsh, 1725" (Schnackenberg), **Supp. XV:** 256

Eben Holden (Bacheller), **I:** 216

Eberhardt, Isabelle, **Supp. IV Part 1:** 92

Eberhart, Mrs., **I:** 521–522, 530

Eberhart, Richard, **I: 521–543; II:** 535–536; **III:** 527; **IV:** 416; **Retro. Supp. II:** 176, 178; **Supp. I Part 1:** 83; **Supp. XII:** 119

Eble, Kenneth E., **Supp. I Part 1:** 201

"Ecce Homo" (Cliff), **Supp. XXII:** 76

Eccentricities of a Nightingale (T. Williams), **IV:** 382, 385, 397, 398

Ecclesiastica Historia Integram Ecclesiae (Taylor), **IV:** 163

"Echart" (Sobin), **Supp. XVI:** 289

"Echo, The" (Bowles), **Supp. IV Part 1:** 84, 86, 87

Echoes inside the Labyrinth (McGrath), **Supp. X:** 127

Echo Park (Connelly), **Supp. XXI: 77–78**

Eckehart, Meister, **Supp. XV:** 225

Eckhart, Maria, **Supp. V:** 212

Eclipse (Hogan), **Supp. IV Part 1:** 397, 400, 402

Eclipse, a Nightmare (Montalembert), **Supp. XV:** 349

"Eclipse"(Schott), **Supp. XXIII:** 252

Eclogues (Virgil), **Supp. VIII:** 31; **Supp. XXIV:** 156

Eclogues of Virgil, The (Ferry, trans.), **Supp. XXIV: 156–157**

"Ecologue" (Ginsberg), **Supp. II Part 1:** 326

"Ecologues of These States 1969–1971" (Ginsberg), **Supp. II Part 1:** 325

Ecology of a Cracker Childhood (Ray), **Supp. XVIII:** 189, 191, 192, 193, **195–199,** 201, 202, 204

"Economics of Negro Emancipation in the United States, The" (Du Bois), **Supp. II Part 1:** 174

"Economics of the Cracker Landscape: Poverty as an Environmental Issue in Larry Brown's *Joe*" (Watson), **Supp. XXI:** 46

"Economic Theory of Women's Dress, The" (Veblen), **Supp. I Part 2:** 636

Economy of the Unlost: Reading Simonides of Keos with Paul Celan (Carson), **Supp. XII:** 110–111

Ecotactics: The Sierra Club Handbook for Environmental Activists (Mitchell and Stallings, eds.), **Supp. IV Part 2:** 488

"Ecstasy" (Bierds), **Supp. XVII:** 34

"Ecstasy" (Olds), **Supp. X:** 206

"Ecstasy of Influence, The" (Lethem), **Supp. XVIII:** 150

"Ecstatic" (Komunyakaa), **Supp. XIII:** 131

Edda, **Supp. X:** 114

Eddy, Mary Baker, **I:** 583; **III:** 506

Edel, Leon, **I:** 20; **II:** 338–339; **Retro. Supp. I:** 218, 224, 231

Edelberg, Cynthia, **Supp. IV Part 1:** 155

"Eden and My Generation" (Levis), **Supp. XI:** 270

Edenbaum, Robert, **Supp. IV Part 1:** 352

Eden Tree (Bynner), **Supp. XV:** 42, 51

Edenville Owls (Parker), **Supp. XIX:** 190

Eder, Richard, **Supp. XII:** 189; **Supp. XV:** 62, 187, 259, 261

Edgar Huntly; or, Memoirs of a Sleep-Walker (Brown), **Supp. I Part 1:** 140–144, 145

"Edge" (Plath), **Retro. Supp. II:** 256; **Supp. I Part 2:** 527, 547

Edge, Mary E., **II:** 316

Edgell, David, **Supp. XXIV:** 71

Edgell, Zee, **Supp. XXIII: 83–96**

"Edge of Possibility, The: Susan Warner and the World of Sunday School Fiction" (S. Gates), **Supp. XVIII:** 267

"Edge of the Great Rift, The" (Theroux), **Supp. VIII:** 325

Edge of the Sea, The (Carson), **Supp. IX:** 19, **25–31,** 32

Edgers, Geoff, **Supp. XV:** 113

Edgeworth, Maria, **II:** 8; **Supp. XV:** 231; **Supp. XX: 108**

Edible Woman, The (Atwood), **Supp. XIII:** 19, 20, **20–21**

"Edict by the King of Prussia, An" (Franklin), **II:** 120

Edie: An American Biography (Stein), **Supp. XVI:** 245

Edinburgh Days: or, Doing What I Want to Do (Pickering), **Supp. XXI:** 200–201

Edison, Thomas A., **I:** 483; **Supp. I Part 2:** 392

Edith Wharton (Joslin), **Retro. Supp. I:** 376

Edith Wharton: A Biography (Lewis), **Retro. Supp. I:** 362

Edith Wharton: A Woman in Her Time (Auchincloss), **Retro. Supp. I:**

Edith Wharton: Matters of Mind and Spirit (Singley), **Retro. Supp. I:** 373

Edith Wharton's Argument with America (Ammons), **Retro. Supp. I:** 364

Edith Wharton's Brave New Politics (Bauer), **Retro. Supp. I:** 381

Edith Wharton's Letters from the Underworld (Waid), **Retro. Supp. I:** 360

Edith Wharton: Traveller in the Land of Letters (Goodwyn), **Retro. Supp. I:** 370

"Editing and Glosses" (Reznikoff), **Supp. XIV:** 283

Editing of Emily Dickinson, The (Franklin), **Retro. Supp. I:** 41

"Editor and the Schoolma'am, The" (Frederic), **II:** 130

"Editor's Easy Chair" (Howells), **II:** 276

"Editor's Study, The" (Howells), **II:** 275, 276, 285

"Editor Whedon" (Masters), **Supp. I Part 2:** 463

Edlin, Mari, **Supp. X:** 266

Edman, Irwin, **III:** 605

Edmond (Mamet), **Supp. XIV:** 241, 248, 249, 250

Edmonds, Dale, **Supp. XXIII:** 291

Edmondson, Belinda, **Supp. XXII:** 70

Edmundson, Mark, **Retro. Supp. II:** 262

Edmund Wilson (Kriegel), **Supp. XXIV: 216–217**

Edsel (Shapiro), **Supp. II Part 2:** 703, 704, 717–719

Edson, Margaret, **Supp. XVIII: 35–52**

Edson, Russell, **Supp. VIII:** 279

"Educated American Woman, An" (Cheever), **Supp. I Part 1:** 194

"Education, An" (Ozick), **Supp. V:** 267

Education and Living (Bourne), **I:** 252

"Education by Poetry" (Frost), **Supp. XV:** 215

"Education of a Storyteller, The" (Bambara), **Supp. XI:** 20

Education of Black People, The (Du Bois), **Supp. II Part 1:** 186

Education of Harriet Hatfield, The (Sarton), **Supp. VIII: 257–258**

Education of Henry Adams, The (Adams), **I:** 1, 5, 6, 11, 14, 15–18, 19, 20–21, 111; **II:** 276; **III:** 504; **Retro. Supp. I:** 53, 59; **Supp. IX:** 19; **Supp. XIV:** 299

*Education of H*y*m*a*n K*a*p*l*a*n, The* (Rosten), **Supp. XVII:** 9

"Education of Mingo, The" (Johnson), **Supp. VI:** 193, 194

"Education of Norman Podhoretz, The" (Goldberg), **Supp. VIII:** 238

Education of Oscar Fairfax, The (Auchincloss), **Supp. IV Part 1:** 25, 36

"Education of the Poet" (Glück), **Supp. V:** 78, 80

Education sentimentale (Flaubert), **III:** 315

"Education the Imagination" (Koch), **Supp. XV:** 175–176, 177

Edwards, Clifford, **Supp. XVIII:** 220

Edwards, Eli. *See* McKay, Claude

Edwards, Esther, **I:** 545

Edwards, Harry Stillwell, **Supp. XXII:** 193

Edwards, John, **I:** 478

Edwards, Jonathan, **I: 544–566; II:** 432; **Retro. Supp. II:** 187; **Supp. I Part 1:** 301, 302; **Supp. I Part 2:** 552, 594, 700; **Supp. IV Part 2:** 430; **Supp. VIII:** 205; **Supp. XXIV:** 72

Edwards, Sarah, **I:** 545

Edwards, Thomas, **Supp. XV:** 20

Edwards, Thomas R., **Supp. XVI:** 207

Edwards, Timothy, **I:** 545

Edwards-Yearwood, Grace, **Supp. VIII:** 81; **Supp. XXII:** 213

"Edwin Arlington Robinson" (Cowley), **Supp. II Part 1:** 144

Edwin Arlington Robinson (Winters), **Supp. II Part 2:** 812

Edwin Booth (play), **Supp. IV Part 1:** 89

E. E. Cummings (Marks), **I:** 438

E. E. Cummings: A Miscellany (Cummings), **I:** 429, 441

E. E. Cummings: A Miscellany, Revised (Cummings), **I:** 429

"Effects of Analogy" (Stevens), **Retro. Supp. I:** 297

Effluences from the Sacred Caves; More Selected Essays and Reviews (Carruth), **Supp. XVI:** 46

"Effort at Speech between Two People" (Rukeyser), **Supp. VI:** 276, 284

"Efforts of Affection" (Moore), **III:** 214

"Efforts of Affection: A Memoir of Marianne Moore" (Bishop), **Retro. Supp. II:** 52

Egan, Jennifer, **Supp. XIX: 49–63; Supp. XXIII:** 299, 300

Egan, Leona, **Supp. XXI:** 6

"Egg, The" (Anderson), **I:** 113, 114

"Egg, The" (Snyder), **Supp. VIII:** 302

Eggers, David, **Supp. XXIV:** 131, 200

Eggleston, George Cary, **Supp. XVIII:** 15

"Eggplant Epithalamion, The" (Jong), **Supp. V:** 119

"Eggs" (Olds), **Supp. X:** 206

"Eggshell" (Stern), **Supp. IX:** 299

Egoist, The (Meredith), **II:** 186

Egorova, Lubov, **Supp. IX:** 58

"Egotism, or the Bosom Sergent" (Hawthorne), **II:** 227, 239

"Egyptian Pulled Glass Bottle in the Shape of a Fish, An" (Moore), **III:** 195, 213

Ehrenfels, Christian von, **Supp. XIV:** 198

Ehrenpreis, Irvin, **Supp. XII:** 128

Ehrenreich, Barbara, **Supp. XVII:** 210

Ehrhart, W. D., **Supp. XIX:** 281

Ehrlich, Gretel, **Supp. XIV:** 227; **Supp. XVIII:** 189

Eichmann, Adolf, **Supp. XII:** 166

Eichmann in Jerusalem (Arendt), **Retro. Supp. II:** 28; **Supp. VIII:** 243; **Supp. XII:** 166

"Eichmann in New York: The New York Intellectuals and the Hannah Arendt Controversy" (Rabinbach), **Supp. XII:** 166

"Eidolon" (Warren), **IV:** 239

"Eiger Dreams" (Krakauer), **Supp. XVIII:** 107

Eiger Dreams: Ventures Among Men and Mountains (Krakauer), **Supp. XVIII:** 105, 106, 107

Eight Cousins (Alcott), **Supp. I Part 1:** 29, 38, 42, 43

18 Poems from the Quechua (Strand, trans.), **Supp. IV Part 2:** 630

"18 West 11th Street" (Merrill), **Supp. III Part 1:** 323, 328

1876: A Novel (Vidal), **Supp. IV Part 2:** 677, 684, 688, 689, 691, 692; **Supp. XIX:** 141

"18,000 CDs" (Halliday), **Supp. XIX:** 92

"Eighth Air Force" (Jarrell), **II:** 373–374, 377

Eight Harvard Poets, **I:** 429, 475

"Eighth Avenue Incident" (Halliday), **Supp. XIX:** 89–90

"Eighth Day, The" (Apple), **Supp. XVII:** 6, 50

"Eighth Ditch, The" (Baraka), **Supp. II Part 1:** 40

"'80s Pastoral: Frederick Barthelme's *Moon Deluxe* Ten Years On" (Peters), **Supp. XI:** 39

Eight Men (Wright), **IV:** 478, 488, 494

80 Flowers (Zukofsky), **Supp. III Part 2:** 631

Eikon Basilike, The, **Supp. IV Part 2:** 435

Eileen (Masters), **Supp. I Part 2:** 460

Eimi (Cummings), **I:** 429, 433, 434, 439–440

"Einstein" (MacLeish), **III:** 5, 8, 10–11, 18–19

Einstein, Albert, **I:** 493; **III:** 8, 10, 21, 161; **IV:** 69, 375, 410, 411, 421; **Retro. Supp. I:** 63; **Supp. I Part 2:** 609, 643; **Supp. III Part 2:** 621; **Supp. V:** 290; **Supp. XII:** 45

Eiseley, Loren, **III:** 227–228

Eisenberg, Deborah, **Supp. XXIII:** 290

Eisenhower, Dwight D., **I:** 136, 376; **II:** 548; **III:** 215; **IV:** 75; **Supp. I Part 1:** 291; **Supp. III Part 2:** 624; **Supp. V:** 45

Eisenstadt, Jill, **Supp. XVIII:** 135

Eisenstein, Sergei, **I:** 481; **Supp. XXI:** 170

Eisinger, Chester E., **I:** 302; **II:** 604; **Supp. IX:** 15

Eisner, Douglas, **Supp. X:** 155

Elam, Angela, **Supp. XI:** 290

El Bernardo (Balbuena), **Supp. V:** 11

Elbert, Sarah, **Supp. I Part 1:** 34, 41

Elder, Donald, **II:** 417, 426, 435, 437; **Supp. XV:** 137

Elder, John, **Supp. IX:** 25

Elder, Lonne, III, **Supp. IV Part 1:** 362

Elder, Richard, **Supp. XII:** 172

"Elder Sister, The" (Olds), **Supp. X:** 205–206

Elder Statesman, The (Eliot), **I:** 572, 573, 583; **Retro. Supp. I:** 53, 65

E. L. Doctorow (Harter and Thompson), **Supp. IV Part 1:** 217

Eldredge, Kay, **Supp. IX:** 254, 259

Eldridge, Florence, **III:** 154, 403; **IV:** 357

Eleanor of Aquitaine, **III:** 470

Eleanor of Guienne, **I:** 14

Eleanor: or, Slave Catching in the Quaker City (Lippard), **Supp. XXIII:** 180, 185

"Elect, The" (Taylor), **Supp. V:** 323

"Elections, Nicaragua, 1984" (Kingsolver), **Supp. VII:** 208

Elective Affinities (Goethe; Bogan and Mayer, trans.), **Supp. III Part 1:** 63

Electra (Euripides), **III:** 398

Electra (Sophocles), **III:** 398; **IV:** 370; **Supp. IX:** 102

"Electra on Azalea Path" (Plath), **Supp. I Part 2:** 538

"Electrical Storm" (Bishop), **Supp. I Part 1:** 93

"Electrical Storm" (Hayden), **Supp. II Part 1:** 370

"Electric Arrows" (Proulx), **Supp. VII:** 256

"Electric Girl, The"(P. Benedict), **Supp. XXIII:** 40

"Electricity Saviour" (Olds), **Supp. X:** 215

Electric Kool-Aid Acid Test, The (Wolfe), **Supp. III Part 2:** 575–577, 582–584; **Supp. XI:** 239

Electric Lady, The (film), **Supp. XI:** 309

Electronic Book Review, **Supp. XXII:** 256, 257, 261

Elegant Extracts (Knox), **II:** 8

"Elegant Tom Dillar" (Briggs), **Supp. XVIII:** 17

"Elegiac" (Ferry), **Supp. XXIV:** 148–149

Elegiac Feelings American (Corso), **Supp. XII: 131–134**

"Elegiac Fragments" (Everwine), **Supp. XV:** 89

Elegies (Rukeyser), **Supp. VI:** 273

"Elegies" (Rukeyser), **Supp. VI:** 272

"Elegies for Paradise Valley" (Hayden), **Supp. II Part 1:** 363

"Elegy" (Bidart), **Supp. XV:** 25, 29

Elegy (Levis), **Supp. XI:** 257, 259, 261, **271–272**

"Elegy" (Merwin), **Supp. III Part 1:** 351

"Elegy" (Stafford), **Supp. XI:** 322

"Elegy" (Tate), **IV:** 128

"Elegy, for the U.S.N. Dirigible, Macon, An" (Winters), **Supp. II Part 2:** 810

"Elegy Ending in the Sound of a Skipping Rope" (Levis), **Supp. XI:** 271–272

"Elegy for 41 Whales Beached in Florence, Oregon, June 1979" (Bierds), **Supp. XVII:** 27

"Elegy for D. H. Lawrence, An" (W. C. Williams), **Retro. Supp. I:** 421

"Elegy for My Father" (Strand), **Supp. IV Part 2:** 628

"Elegy for My Mother" (Wagoner), **Supp. IX:** 330

"Elegy for Redondo Beach" (Jarman), **Supp. XVII:** 112, 113

Elegy for September, An (Nichols), **Supp. XIII:** 268

"Elegy for Thelonious" (Komunyakaa), **Supp. XIII:** 118

"Elegy for the Lost Umbrella"(Stallings), **Supp. XXIII:** 124

"Elegy for the Native Guards" (Trethewey), **Supp. XXI:** 255

"Elegy for the U.S.N. Dirigible, Macon, A" (Winters), **Supp. II Part 2:** 810

"Elegy in Dialogue" (Taggard), **Supp. XXII:** 276

"Elegy"(J. Schoolcraft), **Supp. XXIII:** 231

"Elegy of Last Resort" (Nemerov), **III:** 271

"Elegy with a Thimbleful of Water in the Cage" (Levis), **Supp. XI:** 272

Elegy Written in a Country Churchyard (Gray), **I:** 68

"Elegy Written in a Country Churchyard" (Gray), **Supp. XIV:** 8

"Elementary Scene, The" (Jarrell), **II:** 387, 388, 389

"Elements" (M. Frank), **Supp. X:** 213

Elements of Style, The (Strunk), **Supp. I Part 2:** 670

"Elenita, Cards, Palm, Water" (Cisneros), **Supp. VII:** 64

"Eleonora" (Poe), **III:** 412

Eleothriambos (Lee), **IV:** 158

"Elephant & Ocean" (Notley), **Supp. XXII:** 230

"Elephants" (Moore), **III:** 203

"Elephant's Dance, The" (D. West), **Supp. XVIII:** 281

"Elevator, The" (Dixon), **Supp. XII:** 154

"Elevator Boy" (Hughes), **Retro. Supp. I:** 200; **Supp. I Part 1:** 326

"Eleven" (Cisneros), **Supp. VII:** 69

Eleven Essays in the European Novel (Blackmur), **Supp. II Part 1:** 91, 111

Eleven Heavy Things (installation, July), **Supp. XXIV:** 200

Eleven Kinds of Loneliness (Yates), **Supp. XI:** 340–343, 349

Eleven Poems on the Same Theme (Warren), **IV:** 239–241

"Eleven Times a Poem" (Corso), **Supp. XII:** 132, 133

El Greco (Doménikos Theotokópoulos), **I:** 387; **III:** 212

El-Hage, George N., **Supp. XX: 116**

"El-Hajj Malik El-Shabazz" (Hayden), **Supp. II Part 1:** 379

"Eli, the Fanatic" (P. Roth), **Supp. III Part 2:** 407–408

Elia, Nada, **Supp. XXII:** 73

Eliade, Mircea, **Supp. XVI:** 292

Elie, Paul, **Supp. XXII:** 91–92

Eliot, Charles William, **I:** 5; **II:** 345; **Retro. Supp. I:** 55; **Supp. I Part 2:** 479; **Supp. IX:** 94

Eliot, George, **I:** 375, 458, 459, 461, 467; **II:** 179, 181, 191–192, 275, 319, 324, 338, 577; **IV:** 311, 322; **Retro. Supp. I:** 218, 220, 225; **Supp. I Part 1:** 370; **Supp. I Part 2:** 559, 579; **Supp. IV Part 1:** 31, 297; **Supp. IV Part 2:** 677; **Supp. V:** 258; **Supp. IX:** 38, 43, 51; **Supp. XI:** 68; **Supp. XII:** 335; **Supp. XIV:** 344; **Supp. XX:** 108

Eliot, T. S., **I:** 48, 49, 52, 59, 60, 64, 66, 68, 105, 107, 215–216, 236, 243, 256, 259, 261, 266, 384, 386, 395, 396, 399, 403, 430, 433, 441, 446, 475, 478, 479, 482, 521, 522, 527, **567–591; II:** 65, 96, 158, 168, 316, 371, 376, 386, 529, 530, 532, 537, 542, 545; **III:** 1, 4, 5, 6, 7–8, 9, 10, 11, 14, 17, 20, 21, 23, 26, 34, 174, 194, 195–196, 205–206, 220, 236, 239, 269, 270–271, 277–278, 301, 409, 428, 435, 436, 453, 456–457, 459–460, 461–462, 464, 466, 471, 476, 478, 485, 488, 492, 493, 498, 504, 509, 511, 517, 524, 527, 539, 572, 575, 586, 591, 594, 600, 613; **IV:** 27, 74, 82, 83, 95, 122, 123, 127, 129, 134, 138, 140, 141, 191, 201, 237, 331, 379, 402, 403, 418, 419, 420, 430, 431, 439, 442, 491; **Retro. Supp. I: 51–71,** 74, 80, 89, 91, 171, 198, 210, 283, 289, 290, 292, 296, 298, 299, 311, 324, 359, 411, 413, 414, 416, 417, 420, 428; **Retro. Supp. II:** 79, 178, 189, 262, 326; **Supp. I Part 1:** 257, 264, 268, 270, 274, 299; **Supp. I Part 2:** 387, 423, 455, 536, 554, 624, 659, 721; **Supp. II Part 1:** 1, 4, 8, 20, 30, 91, 98, 103, 136, 314; **Supp. III Part 1:** 9, 10, 26, 31, 37, 41, 43, 44, 48, 62–64, 73, 91, 99–100, 105–106, 273; **Supp. III Part 2:** 541, 611, 612, 617, 624; **Supp. IV Part 1:** 40, 47, 284, 380, 404; **Supp. IV Part 2:** 436; **Supp. V:** 79, 97, 101, 338, 343, 344; **Supp. VIII:** 19, 21, 93, 102, 105, 182, 195, 205, 290, 292; **Supp. IX:** 158–159, 229; **Supp. X:** 59, 115, 119, 124, 187, 324; **Supp. XI:** 242; **Supp. XII:** 45, 159, 198, 308; **Supp. XIII:** 77, 104, 115, 332, 341–342, 344, 346; **Supp. XIV:** 5, 13, 107, 287, 290, 306, 347; **Supp. XV:** 20, 51, 139, 177, 181, 186, 216, 218, 250, 251, 258, 298, 302, 303, 306, 307; **Supp. XVI:** 158–159, 204, 207, 282; **Supp. XVII:** 36, 71, 75, 111, 240; **Supp. XVIII:** 136; **Supp. XIX: 12; Supp. XX: 86, 108, 199; Supp. XXIII:** 25, 60, 166

Eliot's Early Years (Gordon), **Retro. Supp. I:** 55

"Elizabeth" (Longfellow), **I:** 502

"Elizabeth, 1905" (Schnackenberg), **Supp. XV:** 253, 256

Elizabeth Appleton (O'Hara), **III:** 362, 364, 375–377

"Elizabeth Bishop (1911–1979)" (Merrill), **Retro. Supp. II:** 53

"Elizabeth Bishop in Brazil" (Brown), **Supp. I Part 1:** 96

"Elizabeth Bishop's *North & South*" (Lowell), **Retro. Supp. II:** 40–41

"Elizabeth Gone" (Sexton), **Supp. II Part 2:** 674, 681

Elizabeth Rex (Findley), **Supp. XX: 62–63**

Elizabeth Stoddard and the Boundaries of Bourgeois Culture (Mahoney), **Supp. XV:** 270
Elk Heads on the Wall (Ríos), **Supp. IV Part 2:** 540
Elkin, Stanley, **Supp. VI:** 41–59
Elkins, Andrew, **Supp. XXIII:** 131, 135
Elkins, Marilyn, **Supp. XXIV:** 64
"Elk Song" (Hogan), **Supp. IV Part 1:** 406
Ella in Bloom (Hearon), **Supp. VIII:** 70–71
Elledge, Jim, **Supp. XIII:** 88
Ellen Foster: A Novel (Gibbons), **Supp. X:** 41, **42–44,** 46, 47, 49, 50
Ellen Montgomery's Bookshelf (S. and A. Warner), **Supp. XVIII:** 264
Ellen Rogers (Farrell), **II:** 42–43
"Ellen's Dream" (Gioia), **Supp. XV:** 128
"Ellen West" (Bidart), **Supp. XV: 26–27**
Eller, Ernest, **Supp. I Part 2:** 497
Ellerman, Winifred, **Supp. I Part 1:** 258–259. *See also* McAlmon, Mrs. Robert (Winifred Ellerman)
"*El libro de la sexualidad*" (Simic), *Supp. VIII:* 283
Ellington, Duke, **Retro. Supp. II:** 115; **Supp. IV Part 1:** 360; **Supp. IX:** 164
Elliot, Charles, **Supp. V:** 161
Elliot, George P., **Supp. XV:** 92
Elliott, George B., **III:** 478
Ellipse, The: Selected Poems of Leonardo Sinisgalli (Di Piero, trans.), **Supp. XIX:** 34
"Ellipsis" (C. Frost), **Supp. XV:** 107
Ellis, Albert, **Supp. IV Part 2:** 527
Ellis, Anne, **Supp. XVI:** 38
Ellis, Bret Easton, **Supp. XII:** 81; **Supp. XVIII:** 135
Ellis, Brett Easton, **Supp. X:** 7
Ellis, Charles, **Supp. I Part 1:** 99
Ellis, Havelock, **II:** 276; **Supp. XX: 117, 235; Supp. XXII:** 198
Ellis, John Harvard, **Supp. I Part 1:** 103
Ellis, Katherine, **IV:** 114
Ellis, Kelly, **Supp. XXI:** 249
Ellis, Ron, **Supp. XXII:** 209
Ellis, Thomas Sayers, **Supp. XXI:** 246
Ellison, Harlan, **Supp. XIII:** 61
Ellison, Ralph, **IV:** 250, 493; **Retro. Supp. II:** 3, **111–130; Supp. II Part 1:** 33, **221–252; Supp. IV, Part 1:** 374; **Supp. VIII:** 105, 245; **Supp. IX:** 114, 316; **Supp. X:** 324; **Supp. XI:** 18, 92, 275; **Supp. XIII:** 186, 233, 305; **Supp. XIV:** 306; **Supp. XV:** 194; **Supp. XVI:** 135, 139; **Supp. XVIII:** 59, 61, 62, 277, 283; **Supp. XIX:** 148, 149, 155
Ellmann, Maud, **Supp. IV Part 1:** 302
Ellmann, Richard, **Supp. VIII:** 105; **Supp. XV:** 74
Ellroy, James, **Supp. XIV:** 26; **Supp. XXI:** 71
Elman, Richard, **Supp. V:** 40
"Elmer" (Faulkner), **Retro. Supp. I:** 79, 80
Elmer Gantry (Lewis), **I:** 26, 364; **II:** 447–449, 450, 455
Elmer the Great (Lardner), **II:** 427

"Elms" (Glück), **Supp. V:** 85
"Elms Dying, The—And My Friend, Lew Stillwell, Dead" (Bronk), **Supp. XXI:** 31
Eloges (Perse), **Supp. XIII:** 344
"Eloquence of Grief, An" (Crane), **I:** 411
"El Paso Del Norte"(Kenny), **Supp. XXIII:** 150
"El Río Grande" (Mora), **Supp. XIII:** 224
"*El* Round up" (Alvarez), **Supp. VII:** 11
"El Salvador: Requiem and Invocation" (Levertov), **Supp. III Part 1:** 284
Elsasser, Henry, **I:** 226
"Elsa Wertman" (Masters), **Supp. I Part 2:** 462–463
Elsie John and Joey Martinez: Two Stories (Huncke), **Supp. XIV:** 148
Elsie Venner (Holmes), **Supp. I Part 1:** 243, 315–316
Elton, Charles, **Supp. XIV:** 192
Éluard, Paul, **III:** 528; **Supp. IV Part 1:** 80; **Supp. XVII:** 244
Elvins, Kells, **Supp. III Part 1:** 93, 101
Ely, Richard T., **Supp. I Part 1:** 5; **Supp. I Part 2:** 640, 645
"Emancipation. A Life Fable" (Chopin), **Retro. Supp. II:** 59; **Supp. I Part 1:** 207–208
"Emancipation in the British West Indies" (Emerson), **II:** 13
"Emancipation Proclamation, The" (Emerson), **II:** 13
Emanuel, James, **Supp. I Part 1:** 346
Embargo, The (Bryant), **Supp. I Part 1:** 152–153
"Embarkation for Cythera, The" (Ferry), **Supp. XXIV:** 149
Embarrassments (James), **Retro. Supp. I:** 229
Embezzler, The (Auchincloss), **Supp. IV Part 1:** 24, 30–31
"Embroidery, The" (C. Frost), **Supp. XV:** 97
"Emerald" (Doty), **Supp. XI:** 131
"Emerald, The" (Merrill), **Supp. III Part 1:** 328
Emerald City (Egan), **Supp. XIX:** 49, **52–53**
"Emerald City" (Egan), **Supp. XIX:** 52
"Emergence of Flight from Aristotle's Mud, The" (Goldbarth), **Supp. XII:** 190
Emergency Exit (Major), **Supp. XXII:** 174, **175,** 182
"Emergency Haying" (Carruth), **Supp. XVI:** 55
"Emergency Room" (Mora), **Supp. XIII:** 218
"Emerging Voices: The Teaching of Writing" (Mora), **Supp. XIII:** 220
Emerson, and Other Essays (Chapman), **Supp. XIV:** 41–44
Emerson, Ellen, **Supp. I Part 1:** 33
Emerson, John, **Supp. XVI:** 185, 186, 190, 192
Emerson, Ralph Waldo, **I:** 98, 217, 220, 222, 224, 228, 239, 246, 251, 252, 253, 257, 260, 261, 283, 386, 397, 402, 424, 433, 444, 447, 455, 458, 460–461, 463, 464, 485, 561; **II: 1–24,**
49, 92, 127–128, 169, 170, 226, 233, 237, 273–274, 275, 278, 289, 295, 301, 313, 315, 336, 338, 344, 402, 491, 503; **III:** 53, 82, 171, 174, 260, 277, 409, 424, 428, 453, 454, 507, 576–577, 606, 614; **IV:** 60, 167, 169, 170, 171, 172, 173–174, 176, 178, 183, 186, 187, 192, 201, 202, 211, 335, 338, 340, 342, 350; **Retro. Supp. I:** 34, 53, 54, 57, 62, 74–75, 76, 125, 148–149, 152–153, 159, 217, 250, 298, 392, 400, 403; **Retro. Supp. II:** 96, 113, 135, 142, 155, 207, 262; **Supp. I Part 1:** 2, 28–29, 31, 33, 188, 299, 308–309, 317, 358, 365, 366, 368; **Supp. I Part 2:** 374, 383, 393, 407, 413, 416, 420, 422, 474, 482, 580, 582, 602, 659, 679; **Supp. II Part 1:** 280, 288; **Supp. III Part 1:** 387; **Supp. IV Part 2:** 439, 597, 619; **Supp. V:** 118; **Supp. VIII:** 42, 105, 106, 108, 198, 201, 204, 205, 292; **Supp. IX:** 38, 90, 175, 176, 181; **Supp. X:** 42, 45, 121, 223; **Supp. XI:** 203; **Supp. XIII:** 141, 145, 233, 246, **Supp. XIII:** 247; **Supp. XIV:** 41–44, 46, 54, 104, 177; **Supp. XV:** 219, 224; **Supp. XVI:** 84; **Supp. XVII:** 42, 236; **Supp. XX: 115, 116; Supp. XXI:** 217; **Supp. XXIII:** 161, 190; **Supp. XXIV:** 4, 67, 74, 77
"Emerson and the Essay" (Gass), **Supp. VI:** 88
"Emerson the Lecturer" (Lowell), **Supp. I Part 2:** 420, 422
Emerson-Thoreau Award, **Retro. Supp. I:** 67
Emery, Clark, **III:** 478
Emery, Mary Lou, **Supp. XXII:** 73
E. M. Forster (Trilling), **Supp. III Part 2:** 496, 501, 504
"Emigre in Autumn, An" (Gioia), **Supp. XV:** 120
"Emily Dickinson and Class" (Erkkila), **Retro. Supp. I:** 42–43
Emily Dickinson Editorial Collective, **Retro. Supp. I:** 47
Emily Dickinson in Southern California (X. J. Kennedy), **Supp. XV: 164–165**
"Emily Dickinson's Defunct" (Nelson), **Supp. XVIII:** 173
Emily Dickinson: Woman Poet (Bennett), **Retro. Supp. I:** 42
Eminent Victorians (Strachey), **Supp. I Part 2:** 485
Emma (Austen), **Supp. XVIII:** 149
"Emma and Eginhard" (Longfellow), **III:** 505
"Emma Enters a Sentence of Elizabeth Bishop's" (Gass), **Supp. VI:** 93
Emmanuel Appodocca: or, A Blighted Life (Philip), **Supp. XXI:** 160
"Emmaus" (Di Piero), **Supp. XIX:** 42, 43
Emperor Jones, The (O'Neill), **II:** 278; **III:** 391, 392
Emperor of Haiti (Hughes), **Supp. I Part 1:** 339
"Emperor of Ice Cream, The" (Stevens), **IV:** 76, 80–81

"Emperors" (Dunn), **Supp. XI:** 155

"Emperor's New Clothes, The" (Anderson), **I:** 441

"Empire" (Ford), **Supp. V:** 69

Empire: A Novel (Vidal), **Supp. IV Part 2:** 677, 684, 686, 690; **Supp. XIX:** 132

"Empire Builders" (MacLeish), **III:** 14

Empire City, The: or, New York by Night and Day (Lippard), **Supp. XXIII:** 178, 180, 183, 184, 185

Empire Falls (Russo), **Supp. XII: 339–343**

Empire of Summer, The (Doty), **Supp. XI:** 120

Empire of the Senseless (Acker), **Supp. XII:** 5, **6**, **14–16**

"Empires" (Simic), **Supp. VIII:** 282

"Emporium" (Shapiro), **Supp. II Part 2:** 705

Empress of the Splendid Season (Hijuelos), **Supp. VIII: 86–89**

Empson, William, **I:** 522, 533; **II:** 536; **III:** 286, 497, 498, 499; **IV:** 136, 431; **Retro. Supp. I:** 263; **Retro. Supp. II:** 253; **Supp. XVI:** 190

Empty Bed, The (Hadas), **Supp. XXIII:** 117–118

Empty Hands, The (Bronk), **Supp. XXI:** 31

"Empty Hills, The" (Winters), **Supp. II Part 2:** 792, 793, 796

Empty Mirror, Early Poems (Ginsberg), **Supp. II Part 1:** 308, 311, 313–314, 319, 329

"Empty Room" (Hughes), **Supp. I Part 1:** 337

"Empty Threat, An" (Frost), **II:** 159

Emshwiller, Ed, **Supp. XVIII:** 145

"Encantadas, The" (Melville), **III:** 89; **Supp. XVIII:** 4

Enchanter, The (Nabokov), **Retro. Supp. I:** 266

"Enclosed Dreams, Highways and Labyrinths: Jonathan Lethem's *Amnesia Moon*" (Rossi), *Supp. XVIII:* 139

"Encomium Twenty Years Later" (Tate), **I:** 381

"Encounter" (Espaillat), **Supp. XXI:** 107

"Encounter, The" (Pound), **III:** 466

Encounter in April (Sarton), **Supp. VIII:** 259

"Encounter in April" (Sarton), **Supp. VIII:** 259

"Encountering the Sublime" (McClatchy), **Supp. XII:** 261

"Encounter in Vindija Cave, Present-Day Croatia: Late October"(Schott), **Supp. XXIII:** 254

"Encounter on the Seine: Black Meets Brown" (Baldwin), **Retro. Supp. II:** 2

Encounters with Chinese Writers (Dillard), **Supp. VI:** 19, 23, 31

Encounters with the Archdruid (McPhee), **Supp. III Part 1:** 292–294, 301; **Supp. X:** 30

Encyclopedia of Arkansas History and Culture, The (online), **Supp. XXII:** 50

Encyclopedia of Scotland, The (A. Finch), **Supp. XVII: 70–71**

Encyclopedia of World Biography, The, **Supp. XXI:** 74

"End, The" (Olds), **Supp. X:** 205

"Endangered Species" (Mora), **Supp. XIII:** 219–220

Endecott and the Red Cross (Lowell), **II:** 545

Endgame (Beckett), **Supp. XIII:** 196; **Supp. XXII:** 263

"Endgame" (Tan), **Supp. X:** 290

"Endicott and the Red Cross" (Hawthorne), **Retro. Supp. II:** 181, 187–188

"End of Books, The" (Coover), **Supp. V:** 53

End of Books, The (Coover), **Supp. XXII:** 259

End of Dreams, The (Skloot), **Supp. XX: 196, 202–203**

End of Education, The (Postman), **Supp. XI:** 275

"End of FIRPO in the World, The" (Saunders), **Supp. XIX:** 229

"End of Season" (Warren), **IV:** 239–240

"End of Something, The" (Hemingway), **II:** 248

End of the Affair, The (Greene), **Supp. XI:** 99

End of the Age of Innocence, The (Price), **Retro. Supp. I:** 377

"End of the Line, The" (Jarrell), **III:** 527

"End of the Rainbow, The" (Jarrell), **II:** 386

End of the Road (film), **Supp. XI:** 309

End of the Road, The (Barth), **I:** 121, 122, 126–131; **Supp. XI:** 309; **Supp. XVIII:** 140, 141

"End of the World, The" (Gioia), **Supp. XV:** 126

"End of the World, The" (MacLeish), **III:** 8

Endor (Nemerov), **III:** 269, 270, 279

Endore, Guy, **Supp. XVII: 53–67**

"Ends" (Dixon), **Supp. XII:** 153

End to Innocence, An: Essays on Culture and Politics (Fiedler), **Supp. XIII: 98–99**

Endure: The Diaries of Charles Walter Stetson (Stetson), **Supp. XI:** 196

"Enduring Chill, The" (O'Connor), **III:** 349, 351, 357; **Retro. Supp. II:** 236

Enduring Vision of Norman Mailer, The (Leeds), **Retro. Supp. II:** 204

Endymion (Keats), **IV:** 405; **Retro. Supp. I:** 412

End Zone (DeLillo), **Supp. VI:** 2, 3, 4, 10, 11, 12

Enemies (Boyce and Hapgood), **Supp. XVII:** 100; **Supp. XXI:** 7, 13

Enemies: A Love Story (Singer), **IV:** 1; **Retro. Supp. II: 310–311**

Enemy, The: Time (T. Williams), **IV:** 391

Enemy of the People, An (adapt. Miller), **III:** 154–156

"Energy Vampire" (Ginsberg), **Supp. II Part 1:** 326

"Enforcement of the Slave Trade Laws, The" (Du Bois), **Supp. II Part 1:** 161

"Engaging the Past" (Bell), **Supp. X:** 17

Engel, Bernard F., **I:** 532

Engels, Friedrich, **IV:** 429, 443–444; **Supp. I Part 1:** 13; **Supp. XXI:** 162

Engineer of Beasts, The (Sanders), **Supp. XVI:** 270

Engineer of Moonlight (DeLillo), **Supp. VI:** 4

Engineers and the Price System, The (Veblen), **I:** 475–476; **Supp. I Part 2:** 638, 642, 648

Engines of Creation: the Coming Era of Nanotechnology (Drexler), **Supp. XVI:** 121

"England" (Moore), **III:** 203, 207, 214

Englander, Nathan, **Supp. XX: 177, 179;** **Supp. XXIV:** 131

Engle, Paul, **III:** 542; **Retro. Supp. II:** 220, 221; **Supp. V:** 337; **Supp. XI:** 315; **Supp. XIII:** 76; **Supp. XVIII:** 72

English, Zoë, **Supp. XVI:** 293

English Elegy, The: Studies in the Genre from Spenser to Yeats (Sacks), **Supp. IV Part 2:** 450

English Hours (James), **II:** 337; **Retro. Supp. I:** 235

English Language, The (L. P. Smith), **Supp. XIV:** 341

English-Latin Gradus or Verse Dictionary, An (Ainger), **Supp. XX: 230**

"English Lesson"(Strout), **Supp. XXIII:** 273–274, 284

Englishmen of Letters (James), **II:** 327

English Notebooks, The (Hawthorne), **II:** 226, 227–228

English Novel, The (Lanier), **Supp. I Part 1:** 371

English Poets, The: Lessing, Rousseau (Lowell), **Supp. I Part 2:** 407

English Prosody and Modern Poetry (Shapiro), **Supp. II Part 2:** 710

English Traits (Emerson), **II:** 1, 5, 6–7, 8

"English Writers on America" (Irving), **II:** 308

Engstrand, Stuart, **Supp. I Part 1:** 51

"Enigma Variations" (Nelson), **Supp. XVIII:** 177

"Enoch and the Gorilla" (O'Connor), **Retro. Supp. II:** 225

Enormous Changes at the Last Minute (Paley), **Supp. VI:** 218

"Enormous Changes at the Last Minute" (Paley), **Supp. VI:** 226, 232

"Enormous Radio, The" (Cheever), **Supp. I Part 1:** 175–177, 195

Enormous Radio and Other Stories, The (Cheever), **Supp. I Part 1:** 175–177

Enormous Room, The (Cummings), **I:** 429, 434, 440, 445, 477; **Supp. XXI:** 277

"Enough for a Lifetime" (Buck), **Supp. II Part 1:** 127

Enough Rope (Parker), **Supp. IX:** 189, 192

Enquiry Concerning Political Justice (Godwin), **Supp. I Part 1:** 126, 146

"En Route" (Boulton), **Supp. XXII:** 25

Entered From the Sun (Garrett), **Supp. VII:** 105–106, 107–109

"Entering the Building" (Notley), **Supp. XXII:** 237

"Entering the Kingdom" (Oliver), **Supp. VII:** 234

Entertaining Strangers (Gurney), **Supp. V:** 98, 99

Enter without Desire (Lacy), **Supp. XV:** 201

Entranced, The (Lippard), **Supp. XXIII:** 178, 180, 190

Entrance: Four Chicano Poets, **Supp. XIII:** 316

Entrance to Porlock, The (Buechner), **Supp. XII:** 52

Entries (Berry), **Supp. X:** 23

"Entropy" (Pynchon), **Supp. II Part 2:** 619, 621

Entry in an Unknown Hand (F. Wright), **Supp. XVII:** 240, 244, 245

Environmental Imagination, The (Buell), **Supp. V:** 209; **Supp. IX:** 29

"Envoy" (Collins), **Supp. XXI:** 57

"Envoys, The" (Merrill), **Supp. III Part 1:** 326

"Envy; or, Yiddish in America" (Ozick), **Supp. V:** 263, 265–266

"Eolian Harp, The" (Coleridge), **I:** 284

"Eolian Harp, The"(Coleridge), **Supp. XXIII:** 231

"Eototo" (Sobin), **Supp. XVI:** 283–284

"Ephemera, The" (Franklin), **II:** 121

Ephesians (biblical book), **Supp. I Part 1:** 117

Epictetus, **III:** 566

"Epicurean, The" (Auchincloss), **Supp. IV Part 1:** 25

Epicurus, **I:** 59

Epidemic of Genius, An (Wolfert), **Supp. XXI:** 278

"Epigram" (Lowell), **II:** 550

"Epilogue" (Lowell), **Retro. Supp. II:** 191

"Epimanes" (Poe), **III:** 411

"Epimetheus" (Longfellow), **II:** 494

"Epiphany" (X. J. Kennedy), **Supp. XV:** 166, 167

"Epipsychidion" (Shelley), **Supp. I Part 2:** 718

Episode in Palmetto (Caldwell), **I:** 297, 307

"Episode in the Life of an Ancestor" (Boyle), **Supp. XXIV:** 56

"Epistle" (L.-Y. Lee), **Supp. XV:** 212

Epistles (Horace), **Supp. XXIV:** 156

Epistles of Horace, The (Ferry, trans.), **Supp. XXIV: 157–158**

Epistle to a Godson (Auden), **Supp. II Part 1:** 24

"Epistle to Be Left in the Earth" (MacLeish), **III:** 13

"Epistle to George William Curtis" (Lowell), **Supp. I Part 2:** 416

"Epistle to Léon-Paul Fargue" (MacLeish), **III:** 15

"Epitaph Ending in And, The" (Stafford), **Supp. XI:** 321–322

Epitaph for a Dead Beat (Markson), **Supp. XVII: 136–138,** 141; 139

Epitaph for a Desert Anarchist (Bishop), **Supp. XIII:** 1

Epitaph for a Tramp (Markson), **Supp. XVII:** 136, 137, 139 142

"Epitaph for Fire and Flower" (Plath), **Supp. I Part 2:** 537

"Epitaph for the Race of Man" (Millay), **III:** 127–128

"Epithalamium" (Auden), **Supp. II Part 1:** 15

"Epstein" (P. Roth), **Retro. Supp. II:** 281; **Supp. III Part 2:** 404, 406–407, 412, 422

Epstein, Barbara, **Supp. XIX:** 268

Epstein, Helen, **Supp. XVII:** 47; **Supp. XXII:** 95

Epstein, Jacob, **Supp. XXIII:** 6

Epstein, Jason, **Supp. VIII:** 233

Epstein, Joseph, **Supp. IV Part 2:** 692; **Supp. VIII:** 236, 238; **Supp. XIV: 101–117; Supp. XVI:** 230, 275

Epstein, Leslie, **Supp. XII: 159–174; Supp. XVIII:** 92, 99

Epstein, Philip, **Supp. XII:** 159

"Equal in Paris" (Baldwin), **Retro. Supp. II:** 3; **Supp. I Part 1:** 52

"Equals" (Untermeyer), **Supp. XV:** 304

Equation for Evil (Caputo), **Supp. XIX:** 25–26

"Equations of the Light" (Gioia), **Supp. XV:** 125

"Equilibrists, The" (Ransom), **III:** 490, 494

"Equinox"(Crooker), **Supp. XXIII:** 55

"Equipment for Pennies" (H. Roth), **Supp. IX:** 233

Erasmus, Desiderius, **Supp. XV:** 258

Erasure (Everett), **Supp. XVIII:** 54, 60, **61–62**

"Erat Hora" (Pound), **III:** 463; **Retro. Supp. I:** 413

Erdrich, Louise, **Supp. IV Part 1: 259–278,** 333, 404; **Supp. X:** 290; **Supp. XVIII:** 189; **Supp. XXIV:** 245

"Erectus" (Karr), **Supp. XI:** 243

"Ere Sleep Comes Down to Soothe the Weary Eyes" (Dunbar), **Supp. II Part 1:** 199, 207–208

"Ergo Non Sum. Est." (Bronk), **Supp. XXI:** 31

"Ergotism"(Schott), **Supp. XXIII:** 245

Erikson, Erik, **I:** 58, 214, 218

Erisman, Fred, **Supp. VIII:** 126

Erkkila, Betsy, **Retro. Supp. I:** 42; **Supp. XX: 281, 287, 287–288**

Ernest, John, **Supp. XXI:** 24

"Ernest: or Parent for a Day" (Bourne), **I:** 232

Ernst, Max, **Retro. Supp. II:** 321

"Eros" (Komunyakaa), **Supp. XIII:** 130

"Eros and Anteros" (E. Stoddard), **Supp. XV:** 283

Eros and Civilization (Marcuse), **Supp. XII:** 2

"Eros at Temple Stream" (Levertov), **Supp. III Part 1:** 278–279

Eros the Bittersweet (Carson), **Supp. XII:** 97, **98–99**

Eros Trilogy, The (Silver), **Supp. XXIV:** 264, 267

"Eros Turannos" (Robinson), **III:** 510, 512, 513–516, 517, 518

"Eroticism in Women" (Nin), **Supp. X:** 195

"Errand" (Carver), **Supp. III Part 1:** 149

Erskine, Albert, **IV:** 261; **Retro. Supp. II:** 117

Erskine, John, **I:** 223; **Supp. X:** 183; **Supp. XIV:** 120

Erstein, Hap, **Supp. IV Part 2:** 589, 590

"Escape" (MacLeish), **III:** 4

Escape Artist, The (Wagoner), **Supp. IX:** 324, **334–335**

"Escape"(Thompson), **Supp. XXIII:** 301

Escher, M. C., **Supp. XII:** 26; **Supp. XVI:** 102

"Escudilla" (Leopold), **Supp. XIV:** 188

Eshleman, Clayton, **Supp. XVI:** 284

"Eskimo Love" (Apple), **Supp. XVII:** 5

Espaillat, Rhina P., **Supp. XXI: 97–114**

Esparza, Laura, **Supp. XXIII:** 197

Espeland, Pamela, **Supp. XVIII:** 180, 181

Espen, Hal, **Supp. X:** 15

Espey, John, **III:** 463, 468, 478

Esposito, Michael, **Supp. XX: 34, 40**

Esposito, Scott, **Supp. XVII:** 234

Esquibel, Catrióna Rueda, **Supp. XXIII:** 202

Essais (Renouvier), **II:** 344–345

Essay Concerning Human Understanding, An (Locke), **I:** 554; **II:** 8, 348–349

Essay on American Poetry (Brown), **Supp. I Part 1:** 156

"Essay on Aristocracy" (Paine), **Supp. I Part 2:** 515

"Essay on Friendship, An" (McClatchy), **Supp. XII:** 258–259

"Essay on Love" (Carruth), **Supp. XVI:** 56

Essay on Man (Pope), **II:** 111; **Supp. I Part 2:** 516

"Essay on Marriage" (Carruth), **Supp. XVI:** 48

Essay on Our Changing Order (Veblen), **Supp. I Part 2:** 629, 642

"Essay on Poetics" (Ammons), **Supp. VII:** 29–31

Essay on Projects (Defoe), **II:** 104

"Essay on Psychiatrists" (Pinsky), **Supp. VI:** 237, 238, 241, 242, 249, 250

Essay on Rime (Shapiro), **I:** 430; **Supp. II Part 2:** 702, 703, 708–711

"Essay on Sanity" (Dunn), **Supp. XI:** 147

"Essay on the Character of Robespierre" (Paine), **Supp. I Part 2:** 515

Essay on the Chinese Written Character (Fenollosa), **III:** 474

"Essay on What I Think About Most" (Carson), **Supp. XII: 111–112**

Essays (Emerson), **II:** 1, 7, 8, 12–13, 15, 21

Essays, Speeches, and Public Letters by William Faulkner (Meriweather, ed.), **Retro. Supp. I:** 77

Essays in Anglo-Saxon Law (Adams), **I:** 5

Essays in London (James), **II:** 336

Essays in Radical Empiricism (James), **II:** 355, 356–357

Essays on Norman Mailer (Lucid), **Retro. Supp. II:** 195

Essays on the Nature and Principles of Taste (Alison), **Supp. I Part 1:** 151

Essays to Do Good (Mather), **II:** 104; **Supp. II Part 2:** 461, 467

"Essay: The Love of Old Houses" (Doty), **Supp. XI:** 136

"Essay Toward a Point of View, An" (Brooks), **I:** 244

"Essay Vanishes, The" (Monson), **Supp. XXIV:** 238

"Essence, Absence, and Sobin's *Venus Blue*" (English), **Supp. XVI:** 293

Essential Haiku, The (Hass), **Supp. VI:** 102

Essential Keats (Levine, ed.), **Supp. V:** 179

"Essential Oils—are wrung" (Dickinson), **I:** 471; **Retro. Supp. I:** 43, 46

"Essentials" (Toomer), **Supp. III Part 2:** 486

Essentials: A Philosophy of Life in Three Hundred Definitions and Aphorisms (Toomer), **Supp. III Part 2:** 486

Essentials: Definitions and Aphorisms (Toomer), **Supp. IX:** 320

"Essentials of Spontaneous Prose" (Kerouac), **Supp. III Part 1:** 227–228

Essential Works of the Founding Fathers, The (Kriegel, ed.), **Supp. XXIV:** 214

Estampas del valle y otras obras (Hinojosa). *See Valley, The* (Hinojosa)

Esta puente, mi espalda: Voces de mujeres tercermundistas en los Estados Unidos (Moraga, Castillo, and Alarcón, eds.), **Supp. XXIII:** 194

"Estate Sale" (Nye), **Supp. XIII:** 283

Estess, Sybil, **Supp. IV Part 2:** 449, 452

Esther (Adams), **I:** 9–10, 20

"Esther" (Toomer), **Supp. IX:** 313–314

"Esther Kahn" (Symons), **Supp. XX: 239**

"Esthétique du Mal" (Stevens), **IV:** 79; **Retro. Supp. I:** 300, 311, 312

"Estoy-eh-muut and the Kunideeyahs (Arrowboy and the Destroyers)" (film), **Supp. IV Part 2:** 560

Estrada, Genaro, **Retro. Supp. II:** 89

Estray, The (Longfellow, ed.), **Retro. Supp. II:** 155

Esty, William, **III:** 358

"Etching, An" (Masters), **Supp. I Part 2:** 458

"Eternal Goodness, The" (Whittier), **Supp. I Part 2:** 704

Eternal Spring, The (Boyce), **Supp. XVII:** 100; **Supp. XXI:** 4, 5, 11

"Eternity, An" (W. C. Williams), **Retro. Supp. I:** 423

"Eternity Is Now" (Roethke), **III:** 544–545

"Ethan Brand" (Hawthorne), **II:** 227

Ethan Frome (Wharton), **IV:** 316–317, 327; **Retro. Supp. I:** 372–373; **Supp. IX:** 108; **Supp. XVIII:** 216; **Supp. XXIII:** 275, 281

"Ethical Turn in Postcolonial Theory and Narrative, The: Michelle Cliff's *No Telephone to Heaven*" (Moynagh), **Supp. XXII:** 73

Ethics (Spinoza), **IV:** 12; **Retro. Supp. II:** 300

"Ethics of Culture, The" (Locke), **Supp. XIV:** 211

"Ethnics of Frank Costello, The" (Talese), **Supp. XVII:** 202

Etiquette and Vitriol: The Food Chain and Other Plays (Silver), **Supp. XXIV:** 263, 264

"Étiquettes Jaunes, Les"(O'Hara), **Supp. XXIII:** 214

"Etude" (Kooser), **Supp. XIX:** 115

Etulain, Richard, **Supp. IV Part 2:** 597, 601, 604, 606, 607, 608, 610, 611

"Etymology" (Nelson), **Supp. XVIII:** 185

Euclid, **III:** 6, 620

"Euclid Alone Has Looked on Beauty Bare" (Millay), **III:** 133

"Euclidean Spaces: Linear Time" (Bronk), **Supp. XXI:** 31

Eugene, Frank, **Supp. X:** 204

Eugene Onegin (Pushkin), **III:** 246, 263

Eugene Onegin (Pushkin; Nabokov, trans.), **Retro. Supp. I:** 266, 267, 272

Eugenides, Jeffrey, **Supp. XIX:** 138; **Supp. XXI:** 229; **Supp. XXIV: 131–146**

Eugénie, Empress, **IV:** 309

Eugénie Grandet (Balzac), **II:** 328

"Eugénie Grandet" (Barthelme), **Supp. IV Part 1:** 47

"Eulogy for Richard Hugo (1923–1982)" (Wagoner), **Supp. IX:** 330–331

"Eulogy on the Flapper" (Z. Fitzgerald), **Supp. IX:** 71

Eumenides (Aeschylus), **Retro. Supp. I:** 65

"E Unibus Pluram: Television and U.S. Fiction" (Wallace), **Supp. X:** 315–316

"Euphemisms" (Matthews), **Supp. IX: 167–168**

Eureka (Poe), **III:** 409, 424, 428–429

Eurekas (Goldbarth), **Supp. XII:** 181

Euripides, **I:** 325; **II:** 8, 282, 543; **III:** 22, 145, 398; **IV:** 370; **Supp. I Part 1:** 268, 269, 270; **Supp. I Part 2:** 482; **Supp. V:** 277

"Euripides and Professor Murray" (Eliot), **Supp. I Part 1:** 268

"Euripides—A Playwright" (West), **IV:** 286; **Retro. Supp. II:** 326

"Europe" (Ashbery), **Supp. III Part 1:** 7–10, 13, 18

European Discovery of America, The: The Northern Voyages (Morison), **Supp. I Part 2:** 496–497

Europeans, The (H. James), **I:** 452; **II:** 327, 328; **Retro. Supp. I:** 216, 220

Europe Central (Vollmann), **Supp. XVII:** 225, 226, 227, 229, 231, **233–235,** 236

"Europe! Europe!" (Ginsberg), **Supp. II Part 1:** 320, 322

Europe of Trusts, The: Selected Poems (Howe), **Supp. IV Part 2:** 420, 422, 426

Europe without Baedeker (Wilson), **IV:** 429

Eurydice in the Underworld (Acker), **Supp. XII:** 7

Eustace, Saint, **II:** 215

Eustace Chisholm and the Works (Purdy), **Supp. VII:** 273–274, 279–280

"Euthanasia" (Tate), **IV:** 122

"Evaluation" (Bronk), **Supp. XXI:** 32

Eva-Mary (McCarriston), **Supp. XIV:** 259, 260, **263–268**

"Evangeline" (Dixon), **Supp. XII:** 153

Evangeline (Longfellow), **II:** 489, 501–502; **Retro. Supp. II:** 155, **156–159,** 162, 164; **Supp. I Part 2:** 586

Evanier, David, **Supp. XVI:** 212

Evans, Alice, **Supp. XVII:** 71, 72

Evans, Mary Ann. *See* Eliot, George

Evans, Oliver, **Supp. IV Part 1:** 85, 91

Evans, Sandy, **Supp. XIII:** 129

Evans, Walker, **I:** 36, 38, 293; **Retro. Supp. II:** 85

Eva's Man (G. Jones), **Supp. XXIV:** 183, 184, 185, **188–190,** 193

Eve (A. Finch), **Supp. XVII: 72–74**

"Eve" (W. C. Williams), **Retro. Supp. I:** 423

Even Cowgirls Get the Blues (Robbins), **Supp. X:** 259, 260, 261, 262–263, 264, 266, **269–271,** 272, 274, 277, 284; **Supp. XIII:** 11

"Evening" (Carver), **Supp. III Part 1:** 148

Evening (Minot), **Supp. VI:** 204–205, 208, **213–215**

"Evening at a Country Inn" (Kenyon), **Supp. VII:** 167

"Evening in Advent, An" (W. V. Davis), **Supp. XXI:** 92

"Evening in a Lumber Yard"(Le Sueur), **Supp. XXIII:** 165

"Evening in a Sugar Orchard" (Frost), **Retro. Supp. I:** 133

"Evening in Nuevo Leon, An" (Caldwell), **I:** 309

"Evening in the Sanitarium" (Bogan), **Supp. III Part 1:** 61

Evening Light, The (Skloot), **Supp. XX: 196, 201–202**

"Evening Love-of-Self" (Taggard), **Supp. XXII:** 280–281

"Evening of the 4th of July, The" (Kees), **Supp. XV:** 140, 142

"Evening on the Cote d'Azur" (Yates), **Supp. XI:** 349

Evening Performance, An: New and Selected Short Stories (Garrett), **Supp. VII:** 109

"Evenings at Home" (Hardwick), **Supp. III Part 1:** 195–196

"Evening's at Seven, The" (Thurber), **Supp. I Part 2:** 616

"Evening Star" (Bogan), **Supp. III Part 1:** 56

Evening Star, The (McMurtry), **Supp. V:** 230

Evening Star, The (screenplay, McMurtry), **Supp. V:** 232

"Evening Sun" (Kenyon), **Supp. VII:** 168

Evening Sun Turned Crimson, The (Huncke), **Supp. XIV:** 140, 149–150

"Evening Sun Turned Crimson, The" (Huncke), **Supp. XIV:** 137–138, 139

"Evening Wind, The" (Bryant), **Supp. I Part 1:** 164

"Evening without Angels" (Stevens), **Retro. Supp. I:** 302

Evening with Richard Nixon, An (Vidal), **Supp. IV Part 2:** 683

"Even Sea, The" (Swenson), **Supp. IV Part 2:** 641

Even Stephen (Perelman and West), **Retro. Supp. II:** 328

"Event, An" (Wilbur), **Supp. III Part 2:** 547, 554

"Event, The" (Dove), **Supp. IV Part 1:** 242, 247–248

"Even the Vanishing Housed"(Hirshfield), **Supp. XXIII:** 132

"Eventide" (Brooks), **Supp. III Part 1:** 73

"Eventide" (Purdy), **Supp. VII:** 270

"Event Itself, The" (Carruth), **Supp. XVI:** 47

Eve of Saint Agnes, The (Keats), **II:** 82, 531

"Eve of St. Agnes, The" (Clampitt), **Supp. IX:** 40

"Ever a Bridegroom: Reflections on the Failure of Texas Literature" (McMurtry), **Supp. V:** 225

Everett, Alexander Hill, **Supp. I Part 1:** 152

Everett, Percival, **Supp. XVIII:** 53–67

Everlasting Story of Nory, The (Baker), **Supp. XIII:** 52, **Supp. XIII:** 53–55

"Everly Brothers, The" (Skloot), **Supp. XX:** 199

Ever-Present Past, The (Hamilton), **Supp. XVI:** 196

Evers, Medgar, **IV:** 280; **Retro. Supp. II:** 13; **Supp. I Part 1:** 52, 65

Everson, William, **Supp. XXII:** 276

Everwine, Peter, **Supp. V:** 180; **Supp. XIII:** 312; **Supp. XV:** 73–90

"Everybody's Protest Novel" (Baldwin), **Retro. Supp. II:** 4; **Supp. I Part 1:** 50, 51

"Everybody's Reading Li Po' Silk-screened on a Purple T-Shirt" (Komunyakaa), **Supp. XIII:** 120

Everybody's Story: Writing by Older Minnesotans (C. Bly, ed.), **Supp. XVI:** 38

"Everybody Was Very Nice" (Benét), **Supp. XI:** 53

"Everyday Alchemy" (Taggard), **Supp. XXII:** 274–275, 276, 279

"Every-Day Girl, A" (Jewett), **Retro. Supp. II:** 132

"Everyday Use" (Walker), **Supp. III Part 2:** 534

"Every-Day Work" (Jewett), **Retro. Supp. II:** 132

Everyman (Ashbery), **Supp. XXIII:** 210

Everyone Says I Love You (film; Allen), **Supp. XV:** 11

Every Pleasure (Goldbarth), **Supp. XII:** 181

Every Soul Is a Circus (Lindsay), **Supp. I Part 2:** 384, 394, 399

"Everything Is a Human Being" (Walker), **Supp. III Part 2:** 527

Everything Is Illuminated (Foer), **Supp. XII:** 169

Everything Is Now (Cliff), **Supp. XXII:** 67, 74, 76

"Everything Stuck to Him" (Carver), **Supp. III Part 1:** 143

Everything That Moves (Schulberg), **Supp. XVIII:** 254

Everything That Rises Must Converge (O'Connor), **III:** 339, 348–349, 350–351; **Retro. Supp. II:** 235, 236–237

"Everything That Rises Must Converge" (O'Connor), **III:** 349, 352, 357; **Retro. Supp. II:** 236

Everything You Always Wanted to Know about Sex (film; Allen), **Supp. XV:** 4–5, 13

Eve's Diary (Twain), **IV:** 208–209

"Eve Speaks" (Untermeyer), **Supp. XV:** 300

"Eve the Fox" (Gunn Allen), **Supp. IV Part 1:** 331

"Evidence" (Harjo), **Supp. XII:** 219

"Evidence-cum-Witness: Subaltern History, Violence, and the (De)formation of a Nation in Michelle Cliff's *No Telephone to Heaven*" (Sethuraman), **Supp. XXII:** 73

Evidence of the Senses, The (Kelley), **Supp. IV Part 2:** 529

Evidence of Things Not Seen, The (Baldwin), **Retro. Supp. II:** 15

"Evidences of Revealed Religion, The" (Channing), **Supp. XXIV:** 74

"Evil Seekers, The" (Sexton), **Supp. II Part 2:** 696

"Evolution" (Swenson), **Supp. IV Part 2:** 639

Evolving the Idol: The Poetry of Gustaf Sobin (Crick), **Supp. XVI:** 289

Ewing, Jon, **Supp. X:** 253

Ewings, The (O'Hara), **III:** 383

"Examination at the Womb Door" (Hughes), **Supp. XV:** 347

"Examination of the Hero in a Time of War" (Stevens), **Retro. Supp. I:** 305–306, 308

"Excavation of Troy" (MacLeish), **III:** 18

Excellent Becomes the Permanent, The (Addams), **Supp. I Part 1:** 25

"Excelsior" (Longfellow), **Retro. Supp. II:** 169

"Excerpts from Swan Lake" (Cameron), **Supp. XII:** 80, 84

"Excerpts from the Epistemology Workshops" (Rand), **Supp. IV Part 2:** 529

"Excess of Charity" (Wylie), **Supp. I Part 2:** 720

"Exchange, The" (Swenson), **Supp. IV Part 2:** 644

"Excitement, The " (Jarman), **Supp. XVII:** 120–121

"Exclusive" (Olds), **Supp. X:** 206

"Excrement Poem, The" (Kumin), **Supp. IV Part 2:** 448

"Excursion" (Garrett), **Supp. VII:** 100

Excursions (Thoreau), **IV:** 188

"Excursion to Canada, An" (Thoreau), **Supp. XVIII:** 4

"Excursus of Reassurance in Begonia Time, An" (Carruth), **Supp. XVI:** 58

Executioner (Weigl), **Supp. XIX:** 277

Executioner's Song, The (Mailer), **Retro. Supp. II:** 108, 209

Exekiel, **Supp. XXI:** 91

"Exercise and Abstinence" (Swados), **Supp. XIX:** 265

Exercises in History, Chronology, and Biography, in Question and Answer (Rowson), **Supp. XV:** 245

Ex-Friends: Falling Out with Allen Ginsberg, Lionel and Diana Trilling, Lillian Hellman, Hannah Arendt, and Norman Mailer (Podhoretz), **Supp. VIII:** 239, 242–244

"Exhausted Bug, The" (R. Bly), **Supp. IV Part 1:** 73

"Exhortation" (Bogan), **Supp. III Part 1:** 58

"Exhortation" (McKay), **Supp. X:** 135

"Ex-husband"(Schott), **Supp. XXIII:** 249

"Exile" (Gass), **Supp. VI:** 92

"Exile" (Oates), **Supp. II Part 2:** 523

Exile, The (Buck), **Supp. II Part 1:** 119, 131

"Exiles, The" (Bradbury), **Supp. IV Part 1:** 113

"Exiles, The" (Whittier), **Supp. I Part 2:** 692–693

Exiles and Fabrications (Scott), **II:** 512

Exile's Daughter, The (Spencer), **Supp. II Part 1:** 121

"Exile's Departure, The" (Whittier), **Supp. I Part 2:** 683

Exiles from Paradise: Zelda and Scott Fitzgerald (Mayfield), **Supp. IX:** 65

"Exile's Letter" (Karr), **Supp. XI:** 241

Exile's Return (Cowley), **Supp. III Part 1:** 136, 138, 140, 141, 144, 147, 148

"Exile's Return, The" (Lowell), **II:** 539; **Retro. Supp. II:** 187

Exiles: Three Short Novels (Caputo), **Supp. XIX:** 25, 26–27

"Existences" (Stafford), **Supp. XI:** 324

Existentialism from Dostoevsky to Sartre (W. Kaufmann), **Supp. XVII:** 137

Exit into History (Hoffman), **Supp. XVI:** 148, 150, 151–153

Exit to Eden (Rampling), **Supp. VII:** 301–302

Exley (Clarke), **Supp. XXIII:** 109

Exley, Frederick, **Supp. XVI:** 69; **Supp. XVII:** 135; **Supp. XXIII:** 78, 97–110

Exodus (biblical book), **IV:** 300

Exodus (film), **Supp. XX:** 246

Exodus (Uris), **Supp. IV Part 1:** 379; **Supp. XX:** 243–244, 244, 245, 247, 248, 250–251, 257

Exodus Revisited (Uris), **Supp. XX:** 247

"Exorcism" (Snodgrass), **Supp. VI:** 314

"Exorcism, An" (Malamud), **Supp. I Part 2:** 435

Exorcist, The (film), **Supp. I Part 1:** 66

"Expanded Composition, The" (Major), **Supp. XXII:** 174

"Expanding Rooms" (Notley), **Supp. XXII:** 229

"Expanses" (Dickey), **Supp. IV Part 1:** 186

"Ex Parte" (Lardner), **II:** 432

"Expatiation on the Combining of Weathers at Thirty-seventh and Indiana

Where the Southern More or Less Crosses the Dog, The" (Carruth), **Supp. XVI:**51–52

"Expectant Father Compares His Wife to a Rabbit, An" (White), **Supp. I Part 2:** 678

"Expedition to the Pole, An" (Dillard), **Supp. VI:** 32, 34

"Expelled" (Cheever), **Supp. I Part 1:** 174, 186

Expense of Greatness, The (Blackmur), **Supp. II Part 1:** 90, 107

Expense of Vision, The (Holland), **Retro. Supp. I:** 216

"Expensive Gifts" (Miller), **Supp. XII:** 294

"Expensive Moment, The" (Paley), **Supp. VI:** 222, **227–228,** 230

Expensive People (Oates), **Supp. II Part 2:** 509, 510–511

"Experience" (Emerson), **Supp. XIV:** 42

"Experience and Fiction" (Jackson), **Supp. IX:** 121

"Experience and the Objects of Knowledge in the Philosophy of F. H. Bradley" (Eliot), **I:** 572; **Retro. Supp. I:** 59

Experience of Literature, The (Trilling), **Supp. III Part 2:** 493

"Experiences and Principles of an Historian" (Morison), **Supp. I Part 2:** 492

Experimental Death Unit # 1 (Baraka), **Supp. II Part 1:** 46

"Experimental Life, The" (Bourne), **I:** 217, 220

"Experiment in Misery, An" (S. Crane), **I:** 411; **Retro. Supp. II:** 97

Experiments and Observations on Electricity (Franklin), **II:** 102, 114–115

Experiments in Survival (Kriegel and Henrich, eds.), **Supp. XXIV:** 214

"Expiation" (Hoffman), **Supp. XVIII:** 86

"Expiation" (Wharton), **Retro. Supp. I:** 367

"Explaining Evil" (Gordon), **Supp. IV Part 1:** 310

"Explaining Ted Kooser" (Gioia), **Supp. XIX:** 121

"Explanation" (Stevens), **IV:** 79

Explanation of America, An (Pinsky), **Supp. VI:** 237, **241–243**

Exploding Gravy (X. J. Kennedy), **Supp. XV:** 163

"Exploit" (Wharton), **IV:** 324

"Exploration in the Great Tuolumne Cañon" (Muir), **Supp. IX:** 181

"Explorer, The" (Brooks), **Supp. III Part 1:** 79–80

"Exploring the Magalloway" (Parkman), **Supp. II Part 2:** 591

Expositor's Bible, The (G. A. Smith), **III:** 199

Expressions of Sea Level (Ammons), **Supp. VII:** 24, 28, 36

"Exteriority" (Monson), **Supp. XXIV:** 230, 238

Extract from Captain Stormfeld's Visit to Heaven (Twain), **IV:** 209–210

Extracts from Adam's Diary (Twain), **IV:** 208–209

"*Extraño, Un*" *(Gallagher), Supp. XXIV:* 170

"Exulting, The" (Roethke), **III:** 544

"Eye, The" (Bowles), **Supp. IV Part 1:** 93

Eye, The (Nabokov), **III:** 251

Eye-Beaters, Blood, Victory, Madness, Buckhead and Mercy, The (Dickey), **Supp. IV Part 1:** 178, 182–183

"Eye for an Eye, An" (Humphrey), **Supp. IX:** 108

"Eye in the Rock, The" (Haines), **Supp. XII:** 208, 209

Eye in the Sky (Dick), **Supp. XVIII:** 138

"Eye-Mote, The" (Plath), **Retro. Supp. II:** 246, 247

"Eye of Paris, The" (H. Miller), **III:** 183–184

Eye of the Poet, The: Six Views of the Art and Craft of Poetry (Citino, ed.), **Supp. XIII:** 115; **Supp. XXI:** 54

"Eye of the Rock, The" (Haines), **Supp. XII:** 208

"Eye of the Story, The" (Porter), **IV:** 279

Eye of the Story, The: Selected Essays and Reviews (Welty), **Retro. Supp. I:** 339, 342, 344, 345, 346, 351, 354, 355, 356

"Eyes, The" (Wharton), **IV:** 315

"Eyes like They Say the Devil Has" (Ríos), **Supp. IV Part 2:** 543, 544

Eyes of the Dragon, The (King), **Supp. V:** 139, 152

Eyes of the Heart: A Memoir of the Lost and Found (Buechner), **Supp. XII:** 53

"Eyes of Zapata" (Cisneros), **Supp. VII:** 70

"Eyes to See" (Cozzens), **I:** 374

Eye-to-Eye (Nye), **Supp. XIII:** 274

Eysturoy, Annie O., **Supp. IV Part 1:** 321, 322, 323, 328

Ezekiel (biblical book), **II:** 541

"Ezekiel" (R. Fisher), **Supp. XIX:** 71

Ezekiel, Mordecai, **Supp. I Part 2:** 645

"Ezekiel Learns" (R. Fisher), **Supp. XIX:** 71

"Ezra Pound" (Bynner), **Supp. XV:** 49

"Ezra Pound: His Cantos" (Zukofsky), **Supp. III Part 2:** 612, 619, 622

Ezra Pound's Mauberley (Espey), **III:** 463

"Ezra Pound's Very Useful Labors" (Schwartz), **Supp. II Part 2:** 644

F

Faas, Ekbert, **Supp. VIII:** 292

"Fabbri Tape, The" (Auchincloss), **Supp. IV Part 1:** 21–22

Faber, Geoffrey, **Retro. Supp. I:** 63

Faber Book of Movie Verse, The (French and Wlaschin, eds.), **Supp. XVI:** 294

"Fable" (Merwin), **Supp. III Part 1:** 343

"Fable" (Wylie), **Supp. I Part 2:** 714

Fable, A (Faulkner), **II:** 55, 73; **Retro. Supp. I:** 74

"Fable, A" (Glück), **Supp. V:** 86

"Fable, The" (Winters), **Supp. II Part 2:** 792, 793, 796

"Fable Containing a Reflection the Size of a Match Head in Its Pupil, A" (Brockmeier), **Supp. XXII:** 59

"Fable Ending in the Sound of a Thousand Parakeets, A" (Brockmeier), **Supp. XXII:** 59

Fable for Critics, A (Lowell), **Supp. I Part 2:** 406, 407–408, 409, 412–413, 416, 420, 422

"Fable for Critics, A" (Lowell), **Supp. XVIII:** 3, 8

"Fable of the War, A" (Nemerov), **III:** 272

Fables (Gay), **II:** 111

Fables and Distances: New and Selected Essays (Haines), **Supp. XII:** 197, 199, 207–208, 211

Fables for Our Time (Thurber), **Supp. I Part 2:** 610

Fables of Identity: Studies in Poetic Mythology (Frye), **Supp. X:** 80

Fables of La Fontaine, The (Moore), **III:** 194, 215

"Fables of Representation: Poetry of the New York School" (Hoover), **Supp. XV:** 179

"Fables of the Fallen Guy" (Rosaldo), **Supp. IV Part 2:** 544

"Fables of the Moscow Subway" (Nemerov), **III:** 271

"Fable with a Photograph of a Glass Mobile on the Wall, A" (Brockmeier), **Supp. XXII:** 59

"Fable with Slips of White Paper Spilling from the Pockets, A" (Brockmeier), **Supp. XXII:** 59

Fabulators, The (Scholes), **Supp. V:** 40

Fabulous Small Jews (Epstein), **Supp. XIV:** 112

Face against the Glass, The (Francis), **Supp. IX:** 80–81

Face in the Crowd, A (film, Kazan), **Supp. XVIII:** 252–253

Face of Time, The (Farrell), **II:** 28, 34, 35, 39

Faces of Jesus, The (Buechner), **Supp. XII:** 53

Face to the Wind (film), **Supp. XVII:** 141

Face Value (Hwang), **Supp. XXI:** 148, 154, 155

Fachinger, Petra, **Supp. XVI:** 153

"Facing It" (Komunyakaa), **Supp. XIII:** 117, 124, 125

Facing Shadows (Jin), **Supp. XVIII:** 92, **93**

Facing the Music (L. Brown), **Supp. XXI:** 39, 42, **42–44**

"Facing the Music" (L. Brown), **Supp. XXI:** 38–39, 41, 42, 43

"Facing the Music: What's Wrong with All Those Happy Endings" (Neal), **Supp. XXI:** 41

"Facing West from California's Shores" (Jeffers), **Supp. II Part 2:** 437–438

Fact, Fiction, and Representation: Four Novels by Gilbert Sorrentino (Mackey), **Supp. XXI:** 236

"Fact in Fiction, The" (McCarthy), **II:** 562

"Fact of Blackness, The" (Fanon), **Supp. XX:** 152
"Facts" (Franzen), **Supp. XX:** 85
"Facts" (Levine), **Supp. V:** 193
"Facts" (Oliver), **Supp. VII:** 231–232
"Facts" (Snyder), **Supp. VIII:** 301
"Facts, The" (Lardner), **II:** 431
Facts, The: A Novelist's Autobiography (P. Roth), **Retro. Supp. II:** 280, 291; **Supp. III Part 2:** 401, 405, 417, 426
"Facts and Traditions Respecting the Existence of Indigenous Intermittent Fever in New England" (Holmes), **Supp. I Part 1:** 303
"Facts in the Case of M. Valdemar, The" (Poe), **III:** 416
Faderman, Lillian, **Retro. Supp. II:** 135; **Supp. XIII:** 313
Fadiman, Clifton, **II:** 430, 431, 443, 591–592; **Supp. IX:** 8; **Supp. XVI:** 100, 106; **Supp. XVII:** 87, 90; **Supp. XXIII:** 2
Fading, My Parmacheene Belle (J. Scott), **Supp. XVII:** 184–185, 188
"Fado" (McClatchy), **Supp. XII:** 265–266
Faerie Queene, The (Spenser), **III:** 487; **IV:** 253; **Supp. XIV:** 6; **Supp. XV:** 181
Faery, Rebecca Blevins, **Retro. Supp. I:** 374
Fagan, Kathy, **Supp. V:** 180; **Supp. XV:** 73
Fagan, Louise, **Supp. XIX:** 204, 205
Fahrenheit 451 (Bradbury), **Supp. IV Part 1:** 101, 102, 104, 107–109, 110, 113; **Supp. XIII:** 29
"Failure" (Gioia), **Supp. XV:** 125
"Failure" (Zach; Everwine, trans.), **Supp. XV:** 86
"Failure: A Meditation" (Monson), **Supp. XXIV:** 236
"Failure of David Barry, The" (Jewett), **Retro. Supp. II:** 132
Fainlight, Ruth, **Supp. XV:** 261, 264
Faint Perfume (Gale), **Supp. I Part 2:** 613
Fair, Bryan K., **Supp. VIII:** 128
Fairbanks, Douglas, **Supp. XVI:** 185, 186
Fairchild, Frances. *See* Bryant, Mrs. William Cullen (Frances Fairchild)
Fairchild, Hoxie, **Supp. XIV:** 120
Fairfield, Flora (pseudonym). *See* Alcott, Louisa May
Fair Gentlemen of Belken County (Hinojosa), **Supp. XIX:** 105
Fairly Conventional Woman, A (Shields), **Supp. VII:** 312, 316, 318
"Fairly Sad Tale, A" (Parker), **Supp. IX:** 192
Fair Warning (R. O. Butler), **Supp. XII:** 62, 75–76
Faith (Goldbarth), **Supp. XII:** 181, 182–183
Faith and History (Niebuhr), **III:** 308
Faith and the Good Thing (Johnson), **Supp. VI:** 187, 188–190, 191, 193, 194, 196
Faith for Living (Mumford), **Supp. II Part 2:** 479–480

Faithful Narrative of the Surprising Works of God in the Conversion of Many Hundred Souls in Northampton, and the Neighboring Towns and Villages of New-Hampshire in New-England, A (Edwards), **I:** 545, 562
"Faith Healer" (Komunyakaa), **Supp. XIII:** 117
"Faith in a Tree" (Paley), **Supp. VI:** 217–218, 224, 230
"Faith in Search of Understanding" (Updike), **Retro. Supp. I:** 327
"Faith of an Historian" (Morison), **Supp. I Part 2:** 492
"Faith of Fishermen, The" (J. W. Miller), **Supp. XX:** 170
Faker's Dozen, A (Bukiet), **Supp. XVII:** 47
Falcoff, Mark, **Supp. VIII:** 88
Falcon (Hammett), **Supp. IV Part 1:** 351
Falconer (Cheever), **Supp. I Part 1:** 176, 193–195, 196
Falconer, A. F., **Supp. XIV:** 2
"Falcon of Ser Federigo, The" (Longfellow), **II:** 505
Falcon: Poems on Soviet Themes (Taggard), **Supp. XXII:** 284
Falk, Peter, **Supp. XI:** 174
Falkner, Dean, **II:** 55
Falkner, John, **II:** 55
Falkner, Murray, **II:** 55
Falkner, Murray C., **II:** 55
Falkner, Mrs. Murray C. (Maud Butler), **II:** 55
Falkner, William C., **II:** 55
"Fall" (Francis), **Supp. IX:** 76
"Fall, The" (Bass), **Supp. XVI:** 25
"Fall 1961" (Lowell), **II:** 550
"Fallen Western Star: The Decline of San Francisco as a Literary Region" (Gioia), **Supp. XV:** 112, 115–116
"Fallen Western Star" Wars, The: A Debate about Literary California (Foley, ed.), **Supp. XV:** 112, 116
"Fall in Corrales" (Wilbur), **Supp. III Part 2:** 556
Falling (Dickey), **Supp. IV Part 1:** 178, 181–182
"Falling" (Dickey), **Supp. IV Part 1:** 182
"Falling Asleep over the Aeneid" (Lowell), **II:** 542; **Retro. Supp. II:** 188
Falling in Place (Beattie), **Supp. V:** 28–29
"Falling into Holes in Our Sentences" (R. Bly), **Supp. IV Part 1:** 71
Falling into Life (Kriegel), **Supp. XXIV:** 217–219
"Fall Journey" (Stafford), **Supp. XI:** 322
Fall of America, The: 1965–1971 (Ginsberg), **Supp. II Part 1:** 323, 325, 327; **Supp. XV:** 264
Fall of Eve, The (Loos), **Supp. XVI:** 187
Fall of the City, The: A Verse Play for Radio (MacLeish), **III:** 20
"Fall of the House of Usher, The" (Poe), **III:** 412, 414, 415, 419; **Retro. Supp. II:** 270
Fall of the Magicians, The (Kees), **Supp. XV:** 144

Fall of the Year, The (Mosher), **Supp. XXII:** 205, 206, 208, 209, 214
"Fall of Troy, Teh"(Hadas), **Supp. XXIII:** 113
Fallows, James, **Supp. VIII:** 241
Fall Quarter (Kees), **Supp. XV:** 141
Fall & Rise (Dixon), **Supp. XII:** 147–148, 148, 153, 157
Falls, Robert, **Supp. XXI:** 148; **Supp. XXIV:** 270
"Falls, The" (Olds), **Supp. X:** 215
"Falls, The" (Saunders), **Supp. XIX:** 229
"Falls Fight, The" (Howe), **Supp. IV Part 2:** 431–432
Falon, Janet Ruth, **Supp. IV Part 2:** 422
False Coin (Swados), **Supp. XIX:** 260–261, 263
"False Dawn" (Wharton), **Retro. Supp. I:** 381
"False Documents" (Doctorow), **Supp. IV Part 1:** 220, 236
"False Leads" (Komunyakaa), **Supp. XIII:** 116
Falwell, Jerry, **Supp. XX:** 273
Fame and Obscurity: Portraits by Gay Talese (Talese), **Supp. XVII:** 202, 203, 204
Fame & Folly: Essays (Ozick), **Supp. V:** 272
"Familiar Epistle to a Friend, A" (Lowell), **Supp. I Part 2:** 416
Familiar Territory: Observations on American Life (Epstein), **Supp. XIV:** 106
"Familiar Things" (Pickering), **Supp. XXI:** 204
"Family" (Sanders), **Supp. XVI:** 276
"Family" (Wilson), **IV:** 426
Family, Kinship, and Sympanthy in Nineteenth-Century America (Weinstein), **Supp. XVIII:** 261
"Family, The" (Taggard), **Supp. XXII:** 284
"Family Affair, A" (Chopin), **Retro. Supp. II:** 71
"Family and Socialism, The" (Ryan as Quin), **Supp. XVIII:** 238
Family Arsenal, The (Theroux), **Supp. VIII:** 322
"Family Barcus, The"(Thompson), **Supp. XXIII:** 299
Family Chronicle: An Odyssey from Russia to America (Reznikoff), **Supp. XIV:** 277, 288, 289
Family Devotions (Hwang), **Supp. XXI:** 145, 146
"Family History" (Mora), **Supp. XIII:** 217
"Family History, A" (R. H. Davis), **Supp. XVI:** 82
Family Honor (Parker), **Supp. XIX:** 186
Family Life (Banks), **Supp. V:** 7
"Family Matters" (Alvarez), **Supp. VII:** 10
Family Moskat, The (Singer), **IV:** 1, 17, 20, 46; **Retro. Supp. II:** 304
"Family of Little Feet, The" (Cisneros), **Supp. VII:** 61
Family Party, A (O'Hara), **III:** 362

Family Pictures (Brooks), **Supp. III Part 1:** 69, 85, 86

Family Pictures (Miller), **Supp. XII:** 291, **295–297,** 299

"Family Portrait" (Trethewey), **Supp. XXI:** 250

"Family Reunion" (J. W. Miller), **Supp. XX: 167**

"Family Reunion" (X. J. Kennedy), **Supp. XV:** 169

Family Reunion, The (Eliot), **I:** 570–571, 572, 581, 584, 588; **Retro. Supp. I:** 62, 65

"Family Secrets" (Kingsolver), **Supp. VII:** 208

"Family Sideshow, The" (Karr), **Supp. XI:** 245

"Family Story, The" (Skloot), **Supp. XX: 195**

"Family Ties" (Mora), **Supp. XIII:** 215

"Family Tree" (Komunyakaa), **Supp. XIII:** 117–118, 126

"Family Wasserstein, The" (Hoban), **Supp. XV:** 319, 325

Famous American Negroes (Hughes), **Supp. I Part 1:** 345

"Famous Gilson Bequest, The" (Bierce), **I:** 204

Famous Last Words (Findley), **Supp. XX: 49, 55–56**

Famous Negro Athletes (Bontemps), **Supp. XXII:** 6

Famous Negro Music Makers (Hughes), **Supp. I Part 1:** 345

"Famous New York Trials" (Ellison), **Supp. II Part 1:** 230

Fanatics, The (Dunbar), **Supp. II Part 1:** 213–214

Fancher, Edwin, **Retro. Supp. II:** 202

Fancher, Lou, **Supp. XVI:** 177

"Fancy and Imagination" (Poe), **III:** 421

Fancy Dancer, The (P. N. Warren), **Supp. XX: 267–268**

"Fancy Flights" (Beattie), **Supp. V:** 25

"Fancy's Show Box" (Hawthorne), **II:** 238

"Fancy Woman, The" (Taylor), **Supp. V:** 316–317, 319, 323

"Fang" (Goldbarth), **Supp. XII:** 190

Fanny: Being the True History of the Adventures of Fanny Hackabout-Jones (Jong), **Supp. V:** 115, 127

Fanny Hill (Cleland), **Supp. V:** 48, 127

Fan of Swords, The (al-Maghut), **Supp. XIII:** 278

Fanon, Frantz, **Retro. Supp. II:** 118; **Supp. X:** 131, 141; **Supp. XX:** 152

"Fan's Further Notes, A"(Exley), **Supp. XXIII:** 108

Fanshawe (Hawthorne), **II:** 223–224; **Retro. Supp. I:** 149, 151

Fan's Notes, A: A Fictional Memoir (Exley), **Supp. XVI:** 69; **Supp. XXIII:** 78, 97, 98, **99–103,** 106, 109

"Fantasia on 'The Nut-Brown Maid'" (Ashbery), **Supp. III Part 1:** 19

"Fantasia on the Relations between Poetry and Photography" (Strand), **Supp. IV Part 2:** 631

"Fantastic Fables" (Bierce), **I:** 209

"Fantasy"(O'Hara), **Supp. XXIII:** 220

Fante, John, **Supp. XI: 159–176**

Faraday, Michael, **I:** 480–481

Far and Away (Jarman), **Supp. XVII:** 110, 115

"Far and Away" (Jarman), **Supp. XVII:** 115

"Farewell" (Emerson), **II:** 13

"Farewell" (Ryan as Quin), **Supp. XVIII:** 229

Farewell, My Lovely (Chandler), **Supp. IV Part 1:** 122, 125–126, 127, 128, 130

"Farewell, My Lovely!" (White), **Supp. I Part 2:** 661–663, 665

Farewell, The (Gibran), **Supp. XX: 121**

"Farewell Performance" (Merrill), **Supp. III Part 1:** 336–337

Farewell-Sermon Preached at the First Precinct in Northampton, after the People's Publick Rejection of their Minister, A (Edwards), **I:** 548, 562

"Farewell Sweet Dust" (Wylie), **Supp. I Part 2:** 727–728

"Farewell to America, A" (Wheatley), **Supp. XX: 283**

Farewell to Arms, A (Hemingway), **I:** 212, 421, 476, 477; **II:** 68–69, 248–249, 252–253, 254, 255, 262, 265; **Retro. Supp. I:** 171, 178, **180–182,** 187, 189; **Retro. Supp. II:** 108; **Supp. IV Part 1:** 380–381, 381; **Supp. VIII:** 179; **Supp. XII:** 241–242; **Supp. XXI:** 277

"Farewell to Miles" (Berryman), **I:** 173

"Farewell to My Union Brothers" (Ryan as Quin), **Supp. XVIII:** 238

Farewell to Reform (Chamberlain), **Supp. I Part 2:** 647

Farewell to Sport (Gallico), **Supp. XVI:** 238

"Farewell to the Middle Class" (Updike), **Retro. Supp. I:** 321

Far Field, The (Roethke), **III:** 528, 529, 539, 545, 547–548

"Far Field, The" (Roethke), **III:** 537, 540

Far-Flung (Cameron), **Supp. XII:** 81

Far from the Madding Crowd (Hardy), **II:** 291

Faríd, 'Umar ibn al-, **Supp. XX: 117**

Faris, Athénaíse Charleville, **Supp. I Part 1:** 204

Farley, Abbie, **I:** 458

Farley, Harriet, **Supp. XIII:** 140

"Farm, The" (Creeley), **Supp. IV Part 1:** 155

Farmer (Harrison), **Supp. VIII:** 39, **44–45**

Farmer, Frances, **Supp. XV:** 196–197

Farmer, Richard, **Supp. XIV:** 2

"Farmer and the Fox, The" (Leopold), **Supp. XIV:** 188

Farmer Boy (L. I. Wilder), **Supp. XXII:** 294, 297, 299

"Farmers' Daughters, The" (W. C. Williams), **Retro. Supp. I:** 423

Farmers Hotel, The (O'Hara), **III:** 361

"Farmer's Sorrow, A" (Jewett), **Retro. Supp. II:** 132

"Farmer's Wife, The" (Sexton), **Supp. II Part 2:** 676

"Farm Garden" (Nelson), **Supp. XVIII:** 186

"Farm Implements and Rutabagas in a Landscape" (Ashbery), **Supp. III Part 1:** 13

Farming: A Hand Book (Berry), **Supp. X:** 31, 35

"Farmlights in Iowa" (Kooser), **Supp. XIX:** 120

"Farm on the Great Plains, The" (Stafford), **Supp. XI:** 322

Farnol, Jeffrey, **Supp. I Part 2:** 653

Far North (Shepard), **Supp. III Part 2:** 433, 435

"Far Northern Birch, The" (Francis), **Supp. IX:** 90

Farnsworth, Elizabeth, **Supp. XI:** 139

"Farrago" (Kees), **Supp. XV:** 145

Farrand, Max, **II:** 122

Farrar, Geraldine, **Retro. Supp. I:** 10

Farrar, John, **II:** 191; **Supp. XI:** 47

Farrell, Barry, **Supp. XIV:** 142

Farrell, James Francis, **II:** 25, 26

Farrell, James T., **I:** 97, 288, 475, 508, 517, 519; **II: 25–53,** 416, 424; **III:** 28, 114, 116, 118, 119, 317, 382; **IV:** 211, 286; **Retro. Supp. II:** 196, 327; **Supp. I Part 2:** 679; **Supp. VIII:** 96, 97; **Supp. XIV:** 3; **Supp. XV:** 141

Farrell, Mrs. James T. (Dorothy Butler), **II:** 26

Farrell, Mrs. James T. (Hortense Alden), **II:** 26, 27, 45, 48

Farrell, John, **II:** 26

Farrell, John C., **Supp. I Part 1:** 24

Farrell, Kate, **Supp. XV:** 187–188,**Supp. XV:** 190

Farrell, Kevin, **II:** 26

Farrell, Mary, **II:** 25

"Far Rockaway" (Schwartz), **Supp. II Part 2:** 649

Farrow, Mia, **Supp. XV:** 8, 10

Far Side of the Dollar, The (Macdonald), **Supp. IV Part 2:** 473

Farther Off from Heaven (Humphrey), **Supp. IX:** 93, 96, 101, **103–104,** 105, 109

Far Tortuga (Matthiessen), **Supp. V:** 201, 206–207

"Fascinating Fascism" (Sontag), **Supp. III Part 2:** 465

"Fascination of Cities, The" (Hughes), **Supp. I Part 1:** 325

Fashion, Power, Guilt and the Charity of Families (Shields), **Supp. VII:** 323

Fasman, Jonathan, **Supp. V:** 253

Fast, Howard, **Supp. I Part 1:** 295; **Supp. XXI:** 277; **Supp. XXIII:** 165

Fast, Jonathan, **Supp. V:** 115

Fast and Loose (Wharton), **Retro. Supp. I:** 361

"Faster than Light" (Nelson), **Supp. XVIII:** 178–179

"Fastest Runner on Sixty-first Street, The" (Farrell), **II:** 45

Fast Lane on a Dirt Road (Sherman), **Supp. XXII:** 205

Fast Sooner Hound, The (Bontemps and Conroy), **Supp. XXII:** 5, 10–11

"Fat" (Carver), **Supp. III Part 1:** 141

Fatal Interview (Millay), **III:** 128–129, 130

"Fatality" (Bausch), **Supp. VII:** 54

Fatal Lady (film), **Supp. XIII:** 166

"Fate" (Emerson), **II:** 2–3, 4, 16; **Supp. XIV:** 42

"Fate" (Koch), **Supp. XV:** 183

"Fate" (Mailer), **Retro. Supp. II:** 207

"Fate of Pleasure, The" (Trilling), **Supp. III Part 2:** 510

Fate of the Jury, The (Masters), **Supp. I Part 2:** 466, 468, 469

"Fat Girl, The" (Dubus), **Supp. VII:** 84, 85

"Father" (Kooser), **Supp. XIX:** 117, 127

"Father" (Levine), **Supp. V:** 188

"Father" (Sanders), **Supp. XVI:** 277

"Father" (Trethewey), **Supp. XXI:** 253

"Father" (Walker), **Supp. III Part 2:** 522

"Father, The" (Carver), **Supp. III Part 1:** 137, 140

Father, The (Olds), **Supp. X: 209–211**

"Father Abraham" (Faulkner), **Retro. Supp. I:** 81, 82

Fatheralong: A Meditation on Fathers and Sons, Race and Society (Wideman), **Supp. X:** 320, 332–333, 334, 335

"Father and Daughter" (Eberhart), **I:** 539

Father and Glorious Descendant (Lowe), **Supp. X:** 291

"Father and Son" (Eberhart), **I:** 539

Father and Son (Farrell), **II:** 34, 35, 290, 291

Father and Son (Gosse), **Supp. VIII:** 157

"Father and Son" (Hughes), **Retro. Supp. I:** 204; **Supp. I Part 1:** 329, 339

"Father and Son" (Kunitz), **Supp. III Part 1:** 262

Father and Son (L. Brown), **Supp. XXI:** 36, 40, 41, **46–47**

"Father and Son" (Schwartz), **Supp. II Part 2:** 650

Father Bombo's Pilgrimage to Mecca (Freneau), **Supp. II Part 1:** 254

Father Fisheye (Balakian), **Supp. XXIII:** 19

"Father Fisheye"(Balakian), **Supp. XXIII:** 19

"Father Fitzgerald" (Nelson and Espeland), **Supp. XVIII:** 181

"Father Guzman" (Stern), **Supp. IX: 293,** 296

"Father John Melby and the Ghost of Amy Elizabeth" (Brockmeier), **Supp. XXII:** 60

Father of the Blues (Bontemps as Handy), **Supp. XXII:** 5

"Father out Walking on the Lawn, A" (Dove), **Supp. IV Part 1:** 246

"Fathers" (Creeley), **Supp. IV Part 1:** 157–158

Fathers, The (Tate), **IV:** 120, 127, 130, 131–133, 134, 141; **Supp. X:** 52

Fathers and Crows (Vollmann), **Supp. XVII:** 226, 231–232

"Fathers and Daughters, Mothers and Sons"(Hadas), **Supp. XXIII:** 119

"Fathers and Sons" (Hemingway), **II:** 249, 265–266; **Retro. Supp. I:** 175

"Father's Body, The" (Dickey), **Supp. IV Part 1:** 176

"Father's Day" (Connelly), **Supp. XXI:** 79–80

"Father's Story, A" (Dubus), **Supp. VII:** 88

"Father's Voice" (Stafford), **Supp. XI:** 322

"Fat Lady, The" (Carruth), **Supp. XVI:** 48

"Fat Man, Floating" (Dunn), **Supp. XI:** 144

Fat Men in Skirts (Silver), **Supp. XXIV: 265–267,** 275

"Fat Tuesday"(P. Benedict), **Supp. XXIII:** 38

Faulkner, Barry, **Supp. XV:** 41

Faulkner, William, **I:** 54, 97, 99, 105, 106, 115, 117, 118, 123, 190, 204–205, 211, 288, 289, 291, 292, 297, 305, 324, 374, 378, 423, 480, 517; **II:** 28, 51, **54–76,** 131, 174, 194, 217, 223, 228, 230, 259, 301, 306, 431, 458–459, 542, 594, 606; **III:** 45, 70, 108, 164, 218, 220, 222, 236–237, 244, 292, 334, 350, 382, 418, 453, 454, 482, 483; **IV:** 2, 4, 33, 49, 97, 98, 100, 101, 120, 131, 203, 207, 211, 217, 237, 257, 260, 261, 279, 280, 352, 461, 463; **Retro. Supp. I: 73–95,** 215, 339, 347, 356, 379, 382; **Retro. Supp. II:** 19, 221, 326; **Supp. I Part 1:** 196, 197, 242, 372; **Supp. I Part 2:** 450, 621; **Supp. III Part 1:** 384–385, 396; **Supp. IV Part 1:** 47, 130, 257, 342; **Supp. IV Part 2:** 434, 463, 468, 502, 677, 682; **Supp. V:** 58, 59, 138, 210, 226, 237, 261, 262, 334–336; **Supp. VIII:** 37, 39, 40, 104, 105, 108, 175, 176, 180, 181, 183, 184, 188, 189, 215; **Supp. IX:** 20, 95; **Supp. X:** 44, 228; **Supp. XI:** 92, 247; **Supp. XII:** 16, 289, 310, 313; **Supp. XIII:** 100, 169; **Supp. XIV:** 1, 12–13, 21, 24, 93, 306; **Supp. XV:** 92, 135, 338; **Supp. XVI:** 148, 189; **Supp. XVII:** 225; **Supp. XVIII:** 76, 84, 90, 148, 249; **Supp. XIX:** 97, 154, 166; **Supp. XX: 137, 162, 185, 195; Supp. XXI:** 36, 38, 256; **Supp. XXII:** 193, 203, 205; **Supp. XXIII:** 166; **Supp. XXIV:** 54, 64, 132, 136, 215

Faulkner: A Collection of Critical Essays (Warren), **Retro. Supp. I:** 73

Faulkner at Nagano (Jelliffe, ed.), **I:** 289; **II:** 63, 65

Faulkner-Cowley File, The: Letters and Memories 1944–1962 (Cowley, ed.), **Retro. Supp. I:** 73, 92; **Supp. II Part 1:** 140, 141

"Faultlines"(Hadas), **Supp. XXIII:** 117–118

"Faun" (Plath), **Supp. I Part 2:** 537

"Fauna" (Jeffers), **Supp. II Part 2:** 415

Fauset, Arthur Huff, **Supp. XVIII:** 126

Fauset, Jessie, **Supp. I Part 1:** 321, 325; **Supp. IV Part 1:** 164

Fauset, Jessie Redmon, **Supp. XVIII:** 122,127; **Supp. XIX:** 69, 78

Faust (Goethe), **I:** 396; **II:** 489; **III:** 395; **Supp. II Part 1:** 16; **Supp. IX:** 141

Faust, Beatrix Hapgood, **Supp. XXI:** 8

Faust, Clarence H., **II:** 20

Faute de l'Abbé Mouret, La (Zola), **III:** 322

"Favor, The" (Carver and Gallagher), **Supp. XXIV:** 178

Favor Island (Merwin), **Supp. III Part 1:** 346, 347

"Favor of Love, A" (Peacock), **Supp. XIX:** 203

"Favrile" (Doty), **Supp. XI:** 131

"Fawn, with a Bit of Green" (Swados), **Supp. XIX:** 258

Fay (L. Brown), **Supp. XXI:** 40, 41, 47

Fay, Bernard, **IV:** 41

"Fear, The" (Frost), **Retro. Supp. I:** 128

Fear and Loathing in Las Vegas (Thompson), **Supp. XXIV:** 280, 282, 283, 287, **288–292,** 293

Fear and Loathing on the Campaign Trail '72 (Thompson), **Supp. XXIV:** 279, 281, 282, 289, **292–293**

Fear and Trembling (Kierkegaard), **Supp. XX: 132**

"Fear & Fame" (Levine), **Supp. V:** 192

Fearful Child, The (C. Frost), **Supp. XV:** 96, 97, 106

"Fearful Child, The" (C. Frost), **Supp. XV:** 96

Fearing, Kenneth, **Supp. XV:** 138

"Fearless" (Mosley), **Supp. XIII:** 241

Fearless Jones (Mosley), **Supp. XIII: 241–242**

"Fear of Concrete" (Halliday), **Supp. XIX:** 91

Fear of Fifty: A Midlife Memoir (Jong), **Supp. V:** 114, 115, 116, 131

Fear of Flying (Jong), **Supp. V:** 113, 115, 116, 119–123, 124, 129

"Feast, The" (Kinnell), **Supp. III Part 1:** 239, 250

Feast of All Saints, The (Rice), **Supp. VII:** 299–301

Feast of Love, The (C. Baxter), **Supp. XVII:** 13, 21–22

Feast of Love, The (film, R. Benton), **Supp. XVII:** 22

Feast of Snakes, A (Crews), **Supp. XI:** 102, **107–108; Supp. XXI:** 40

"Feast of Stephen, The" (Hecht), **Supp. X:** 63–64

Feast of the Goat, The (Llosa), **Supp. XXIV:** 89

"Featherbed for Critics, A" (Blackmur), **Supp. II Part 1:** 93, 151

Feather Crowns (Mason), **Supp. VIII: 146–147**

"Feathers" (Carver), **Supp. III Part 1:** 145

Feathers (Van Vechten), **Supp. II Part 2:** 736, 749

"Feathers, The" (Hogan), **Supp. IV Part 1:** 416

"February" (Ellison), **Supp. II Part 1:** 229

"February 14th" (Levine), **Supp. V:** 194

February in Sydney (Komunyakaa), **Supp. XIII: 124–125,** 129

"February in Sydney" (Komunyakaa), **Supp. XIII:** 125

"February: Thinking of Flowers" (Kenyon), **Supp. VII:** 171

"Feces" (McClatchy), **Supp. XII:** 266, 267–268

Fechner, Gustav, **II:** 344, 355, 358, 359, 363

Feder, Lillian, **IV:** 136; **Supp. XVI:** 49, 50

Federal Arts Project, **Supp. III Part 2:** 618

Federigo, or, The Power of Love (Nemerov), **III:** 268, 276, 282, 283–284, 285

"Fedge, The" (Halliday), **Supp. XIX:** 93

"Fedora" (Chopin), **Supp. I Part 1:** 220

Fedorko, Kathy A., **Retro. Supp. I:** 361, 374

"Feeling and Precision" (Moore), **III:** 206

Feeling Italian: The Art of Ethnicity in America (Ferraro), **Supp. XX:** 43

"Feeling of Effort, The" (James), **II:** 349

Feeling Very Strange: The Slipstream Anthology (Kelly and Kessel, eds.), **Supp. XIX:** 231

"Feel Like a Bird" (Swenson), **Supp. IV Part 2:** 639

"Feel Me" (Swenson), **Supp. IV Part 2:** 647

Feeney, Mary, **Supp. IX:** 152, 154

Feinsilver, Pamela, **Supp. XX: 135**

Feinstein, Herbert, **Supp. XIX:** 260

Feinstein, Sascha, **Supp. XIII:** 125

Feldman, Charles K., **Supp. XI:** 307

Feldman, Morton, **Supp. XXIII:** 211

Fellini, Federico, **Supp. XII:** 172; **Supp. XV:** 8

"Fellini the Cat" (Peacock), **Supp. XIX:** 206

"Fellow Citizens" (Sandburg), **III:** 553

Fellows, John, **Supp. I Part 2:** 520

Fellow Travelers (Mallon), **Supp. XIX:** 132**, 143–144**

"Felo de Se" (Wylie), **Supp. I Part 2:** 727, 729

Felton, Sharon, **Supp. IV Part 1:** 210

"Female Author" (Plath), **Retro. Supp. II:** 243

"Female Frailty" (Freneau), **Supp. II Part 1:** 258

"Female Laughter and Comic Possibilities: *Uncommon Women and Others*" (Chirico), **Supp. XV:** 323

Female Patriot, The; or, Nature's Rights (Rowson), **Supp. XV:** 237–238

Female Prose Writers of America (Hart), **Supp. XVIII:** 257, 264

"Female Voice in *To Kill a Mockingbird,* The: Narrative Strategies in Film and Novel" (Shakelford), **Supp. VIII:** 129

" 'Feminine' Epic, The" (Notley), **Supp. XXII:** 232, 234, 236

"Feminine Landscape of Leslie Marmon Silko's *Ceremony,* The" (Gunn Allen),

Supp. IV Part 1: 324

Feminine Note in Fiction, The (Courtney), **Supp. XXIV:** 29

Feminism and the Politics of Literary Reputation: The Example of Erica Jong (Templin), **Supp. V:** 116

"Feminismo" (Robbins), **Supp. X:** 272

"Feminist Criticism in the Wilderness" (Showalter), **Supp. X:** 97

"Feminist Manifesto" (Loy), **Supp. XXII:** 160

Feminization of American Culture, The (Douglas), **Supp. XVIII:** 258

"Fence, The" (Oliver), **Supp. VII:** 232

"Fence Posts" (Snyder), **Supp. VIII:** 304

Fences (Wilson), **Supp. VIII:** 329, 330, 331, **334–337,** 350

Fenick, Elizabeth, **Retro. Supp. II:** 221

"Fenimore Cooper's Literary Offenses" (Twain), **IV:** 204–205

Fennell, Frank L., **Supp. XVII:** 177–178

Fenollosa, Ernest, **III:** 458, 465, 466, 474, 475, 477; **Retro. Supp. I:** 289; **Supp. IV Part 1:** 154

Fenollosa, Mrs. Ernest, **III:** 458

"Fenstad's Mother" (C. Baxter), **Supp. XVII:** 18

Fenton, Charles, **Supp. XI:** 43

Fenton, James, **Supp. XV:** 117

Ferdinand: Including "It Was" (Zukofsky), **Supp. III Part 2:** 630

"Fergus" (Bourne), **I:** 229

Ferguson, James, **Supp. I Part 2:** 503

Ferguson, Otis, **Supp. IX:** 7

Ferguson, William, **Supp. XII:** 189

Ferguson Affair, The (Macdonald), **Supp. IV Part 2:** 473

Fergusson, Francis, **I:** 265, 440; **Supp. XV:** 20

Ferlinghetti, Lawrence, **Supp. IV Part 1:** 90; **Supp. VIII:** 290, 292; **Supp. XII:** 121, 125; **Supp. XIII:** 275; **Supp. XIX:** 4; **Supp. XXI:** 53; **Supp. XXIII:** 219

Fermata, The (Baker), **Supp. XIII: 49–52,** 54

"Fern" (Toomer), **Supp. III Part 2:** 481; **Supp. IX:** 313

Fern, Fanny, **Retro. Supp. I:** 246; **Supp. V:** 122

Fernández, Enrique, **Supp. VIII:** 73

Fernandez, Ramon, **Retro. Supp. I:** 302, 303; **Supp. XVI:** 214

"Fern-Beds in Hampshire Country" (Wilbur), **Supp. III Part 2:** 558

"Fern Hill" (D. Thomas), **IV:** 93; **Supp. XX: 204**

"Fern-Life" (Larcom), **Supp. XIII:** 143

Ferragammo, Salvatore, **Supp. XVI:** 192

Ferraro, Thomas J., **Supp. XX: 34, 43**

Ferreo, Guglielmo, **Supp. I Part 2:** 481

Ferris, Anthony, **Supp. XX:** 124

Ferry, David, **Supp. XXIV: 147–164**

"Ferry, The" (Cliff), **Supp. XXII:** 74

Fessenden, Thomas Green, **II:** 300

Fessier, Michael, **Supp. XIII:** 164

"Festival Aspect, The" (Olson), **Supp. II Part 2:** 585

"Festival of Regrets, The" (Wasserstein), **Supp. XV:** 333

Festival of San Joaquin, The (Edgell), **Supp. XXIII:** 84, 85, **90–91,** 94

Fetching the Dead (Sanders), **Supp. XVI:** 269

Fêtes galantes (Verlaine), **IV:** 79

Fetid Itch (Silver), **Supp. XXIV:** 265

"Fetish" (McClatchy), **Supp. XII:** 256

Fetterley, Judith, **Retro. Supp. II:** 139; **Supp. XXIV:** 28

"Feud" (Zinberg), **Supp. XV:** 195

"Fever" (Carver), **Supp. III Part 1:** 145

"Fever 103'" (Plath), **Supp. I Part 2:** 541

Fever Pitch (Hornby), **Supp. XII:** 286; **Supp. XXIII:** 109

Fever: Twelve Stories (Wideman), **Supp. X:** 320

"Few Don'ts by an Imagiste, A" (Pound), **III:** 465; **Retro. Supp. I:** 288; **Supp. I Part 1:** 261–262

"Few Kind Words for Anger, A" (Kriegel), **Supp. XXIV:** 220

"Few Stray Comments on the Cultivation of the Lyric, A" (Sobin), **Supp. XVI:** 285

"Few Words of Introduction, A" (McNally), **Supp. XIII:** 198–199

Feydeau, Georges, **Supp. XXIV:** 271

Fiamengo, Janice, **Supp. XIII:** 35

Fiber (Bass), **Supp. XVI:** 22

"Fiber: A Post-Pastoral Georgic" (Gifford), **Supp. XVI:** 22

Ficke, Arthur Davison, **Supp. XIII:** 347; **Supp. XV:** 40, 42, 43, 46, 48, 49

"Fiction" (Stafford), **Supp. XI:** 327

"Fiction: A Lens on Life" (Stegner), **Supp. IV Part 2:** 595, 596, 600

Fictional World of William Hoffman, The (Frank, ed.), **Supp. XVIII:** 74, 79, 80, 87

Fiction and the Figures of Life (Gass), **Supp. VI:** 85

Fiction of Joseph Heller, The (Seed), **Supp. IV Part 1:** 391

Fiction of Paule Marshall, The (Denniston), **Supp. XI:** 276

Fiction of the Forties (Eisinger), **I:** 302; **II:** 604

Fictions in Autobiography: Studies in the Art of Self-Invention (Eakin), **Supp. XVI:** 70

"Fiction Writer and His Country, The" (O'Connor), **III:** 342; **Retro. Supp. II:** 223, 225; **Supp. II Part 1:** 148

Fiddler's Trance, The (Skloot), **Supp. XX: 196, 202**

Fidelity (Glaspell), **Supp. III Part 1:** 177

Fiedler, Leslie A., **II:** 27; **III:** 218; **Retro. Supp. II:** 280, 324; **Supp. II Part 1:** 87; **Supp. IV Part 1:** 42, 86; **Supp. IX:** 3, 227; **Supp. X:** 80; **Supp. XIII: 93–110; Supp. XIV:** 11; **Supp. XVIII:** 146; **Supp. XIX:** 251; **Supp. XXIII:** 42

Fiedler on the Roof: Essays on Literature and Jewish Identity (Fiedler), **Supp. XIII:** 106–107

"Fie! Fie! Fi-Fi!" (Fitzgerald), **Retro. Supp. I:** 100

Field, Eugene, **Supp. II Part 1:** 197

Field, John, **IV:** 179

"Field Events" (Bass), **Supp. XVI:** 19
"Field Full of Black Cats, A" (C. Frost), **Supp. XV:** 101
Field Guide, (Hass), **Supp. VI:** 97–98, **99–101,** 102, 103, 106
Field Guide to Contemporary Poetry and Poetics (Friebert and Young, eds.), **Supp. XI:** 270
"Field Guide to the Western Birds" (Stegner), **Supp. IV Part 2:** 609
Fielding, Henry, **I:** 134; **II:** 302, 304–305; **III:** 61; **Supp. I Part 2:** 421, 422, 656; **Supp. IV Part 2:** 688; **Supp. V:** 127; **Supp. IX:** 128; **Supp. XI:** 277; **Supp. XVIII:** 2, 7
Fielding, Richard, **Supp. XV:** 232
"Field-larks and Blackbirds" (Lanier), **Supp. I Part 1:** 355
Field of Honor (Hay), **Supp. XIV:** 120–121, 125, 130
"Field of Honor" (Hay), **Supp. XIV:** 120–121, 129–130
Field of Vision, The (Morris), **III:** 226–228, 229, 232, 233, 238
"Field Report" (Corso), **Supp. XII:** 124, **136**
"Fields" (Wright), **Supp. XV:** 342
Fields, Annie Adams, **II:** 401, 402, 403–404, 406, 412; **IV:** 177; **Retro. Supp. II:** 134, 135, 142; **Supp. I Part 1:** 317; **Supp. XVI:** 84, 88
Fields, James T., **II:** 274, 279, 402–403; **Retro. Supp. II:** 135; **Supp. I Part 1:** 317; **Supp. XIII:** 150; **Supp. XVI:** 84, 88
Fields, Mrs. James T., **Supp. XIV:** 44, 46. *See* Fields, Annie Adams
Fields, Joseph, **IV:** 274
Fields, The (Richter), **Supp. XVIII: 213–214,** 220
Fields, W. C., **II:** 427; **IV:** 335
"Fields at Dusk, The" (Salter), **Supp. IX:** 260
Fields of Fire (Webb), **Supp. XXII:** 115
Fields of Praise, The (Nelson), **Supp. XVIII:** 171, 173, **177–178**
Fields of Wonder (Hughes), **Retro. Supp. I:** 206, 207; **Supp. I Part 1:** 333–334
Fierce Invalids Home from Hot Climates (Robbins), **Supp. X:** 267, 276–277, **282–285**
Fiery, Marion, **Supp. XXII:** 293
Fiery Chariot, The (Hurston), **Supp. VI:** 155–156
"Fiesta, 1980" (Díaz), **Supp. XXIV:** 88
15 Poems (Banks), **Supp. V:** 5
"Fifteenth Farewell" (Bogan), **Supp. III Part 1:** 51, 58
"Fifth Avenue, Uptown" (Baldwin), **Supp. I Part 1:** 52
"Fifth Avenue—Spring Afternoon" (Untermeyer), **Supp. XV:** 296
Fifth Book of Peace, The (Kingston), **Supp. V:** 173
Fifth Chinese Daughter (Wong), **Supp. X:** 291
Fifth Column, The (Hemingway), **II:** 254, 258; **Retro. Supp. I:** 184
"Fifth Column of the Fencerow" (Leopold), **Supp. XIV:** 185

Fifth Decad of Cantos, The (Pound), **Retro. Supp. I:** 292
"Fifth Movement: *Autobiography*" (Zukofsky), **Supp. III Part 2:** 611
Fifth Sunday (Dove), **Supp. IV Part 1:** 251, 252–253
"Fifth Sunday" (Dove), **Supp. IV Part 1:** 252
50 Poems (Cummings), **I:** 430, 440, 442–443, 444–445, 446
Fifty Best American Short Stories (O'Brien), **III:** 56
"Fifty Dollars" (Elkin), **Supp. VI: 43–44**
"55 Miles to the Gas Pump" (Proulx), **Supp. VII:** 264
55 Poems (Zukofsky), **Supp. III Part 2:** 611, 621
"Fifty Grand" (Hemingway), **II:** 250, 424; **Retro. Supp. I:** 177
Fifty Stories (Boyle), **Supp. XXIV:** 58
"Fifty Suggestions" (Poe), **Retro. Supp. II:** 266
"52 Oswald Street" (Kinnell), **Supp. III Part 1:** 251
Fifty Years Among Authors, Editors, and Publishers (Derby), **Supp. XVIII:** 4
"Fifty Years Among the Black Folk" (Du Bois), **Supp. II Part 1:** 169
"Fifty Years of American Poetry" (Jarrell), **Retro. Supp. I:** 52
Fig Connection, The (Franzen and Siebert), **Supp. XX:** 84
Fight, The (Mailer), **Retro. Supp. II:** 207, 208
Fight Back: For the Sake of the People, For the Sake of the Land (Ortiz), **Supp. IV Part 2:** 497, 498, 499, 503, 510–512, 514
"Fighters, The" (Zinberg), **Supp. XV:** 193
Fight for Freedom (Hughes), **Supp. I Part 1:** 345
Fighting Angel (Buck), **Supp. II Part 1:** 119, 131
Fighting France; From Dunkerque to Belfort (Wharton), **Retro. Supp. I:** 377, 378
Fightin': New and Collected Stories (Ortiz), **Supp. IV Part 2:** 513
"Figlia che Piange, La" (Eliot), **I:** 570, 584; **III:** 9
Figliola, Samantha, **Supp. V:** 143
"Figure a Poem Makes, The" (Frost), **Retro. Supp. I:** 139
"Figured Wheel, The" (Pinsky), **Supp. VI:** 243, 244, 245, 246
Figured Wheel, The: New and Collected Poems (Pinsky), **Supp. VI:** 247–248
"Figure in the Carpet, The" (James), **Retro. Supp. I:** 228, 229
"Figure in the Doorway, The" (Frost), **Retro. Supp. I:** 138
Figure of Fulfillment, The (Lerperger; Miller, trans.), **Supp. XX:** 165, 167–**168**
Figures from the Double World (McGrath), **Supp. X: 118–119**
Figures in Black: Words, Signs, and the "Racial" Self (H. L. Gates), **Supp. XX: 99, 100, 106, 107**

"Figures in the Clock, The" (McCarthy), **II:** 561–562
Figures Made Visible in the Sadness of Time (Everwine), **Supp. XV:** 75, 88
Figures of Time (Hayden), **Supp. II Part 1:** 367
Filbin, Thomas, **Supp. XXIII:** 299
"Filling Out a Blank" (Wagoner), **Supp. IX:** 324
Fillmore, Millard, **III:** 101
Film Flam: Essays on Hollywood (McMurtry), **Supp. V:** 228
Films of Ayn Rand, The (Cox), **Supp. IV Part 2:** 524
Filo, John, **Supp. XII:** 211
Filreis, Alan, **Supp. XXI:** 262, 267, 268, 269, 271, 273, 275, 277, 278
Filson, John, **Retro. Supp. I:** 421
Final Beast, The (Buechner), **Supp. XII: 49–51**
"Finale" (Longfellow), **II:** 505, 506–507
"Final Fear" (Hughes), **Supp. I Part 1:** 338
Final Harvest: Emily Dickinson's Poems (Johnson, ed.), **I:** 470, 471
"Finally Harriet" (Wolfert), **Supp. XXI: 265–267**
Final Payments (Gordon), **Supp. IV Part 1:** 297, 299, 300–302, 304, 306, 314
"Final Report, A" (Maxwell), **Supp. VIII:** 169
"Final Soliloquy of the Interior Paramour" (Stevens), **Retro. Supp. I:** 312
Final Solution, The (Reitlinger), **Supp. XII:** 161
Financier, The (Dreiser), **I:** 497, 501, 507, 509; **Retro. Supp. II:** 94, 101–102, 105; **Supp. XVIII:** 246
Finch, Annie, **Supp. XVII: 69–79**
Finch, Henry Leroy, **Supp. XVII:** 69
Finch, Margaret Rockwell, **Supp. XVII:** 69
Finch, Robert, **Supp. XIV:** 186–187
"Finches, Little Pats of Butter on the Wing" (Crooker), **Supp. XXIII:** 62
Find a Victim (Macdonald), **Supp. IV Part 2:** 467, 472, 473
Fin de Chéri, La (Colette; stage adaptation, Loos), **Supp. XVI:** 194
Finder, Henry, **Supp. XX:** 90
"Fin de Saison Palm Beach" (White), **Supp. I Part 2:** 673
"Finding a Bible in an Abandoned Cabin" (Wrigley), **Supp. XVIII: 293–294,** 296, 297, 300, 301, 303
Finding a Form (Gass), **Supp. VI:** 91–92, 93
Finding a Girl in America (Dubus), **Supp. VII:** 85–88
"Finding a Girl in America" (Dubus), **Supp. VII:** 87
"Finding Beads" (Hogan), **Supp. IV Part 1:** 400
Finding Losses (Bronk), **Supp. XXI:** 31, 32
"Finding of Zach, The" (Dunbar), **Supp. II Part 1:** 212
Findings and Keepings: Analects for an Autobiography (Mumford), **Supp. II Part 2:** 483

Finding the Center: Narrative Poetry of the Zuni Indians (Tedlock), **Supp. IV Part 2:** 509

Finding the Islands (Merwin), **Supp. III Part 1:** 353, 357

"Finding the Place: A Migrant Childhood" (Stegner), **Supp. IV Part 2:** 597

Findley, Timothy, **Supp. XX:** 49–65

"Find the Woman" (Macdonald, as Millar), **Supp. IV Part 2:** 466

Fine, David, **Supp. XI:** 160

Fine, Richard, **Supp. XVIII:** 248

Fine Clothes to the Jew (Hughes), **Retro. Supp. I:** 200, 201, 203, 205; **Supp. I Part 1:** 326–328

"Fine Old Firm, A" (Jackson), **Supp. IX:** 120

Fine Preserving (Plagemann), **Supp. XVII:** 91

Fine Preserving: M. F. K. Fisher's Annotated Edition of Catherine Plagemann's Cookbook (Plagemann; M. F. K. Fisher, ed.), **Supp. XVII:** 91

Finer Grain, The (James), **II:** 335

Fine Writing (L. P. Smith), **Supp. XIV:** 347

"Finis" (X. J. Kennedy), **Supp. XV:** 169

"Finished Basement" (Di Piero), **Supp. XIX:** 47

Finished Man, The (Garrett), **Supp. VII:** 96, 97–98

Fink, Jonathan, **Supp. XXI:** 244, 245, 248, 255, 256

Fink, Mike, **IV:** 266

Finkelstein, Norman, **Supp. XXI:** 24, 33

Finkle, David, **Supp. XXI:** 47

Finley, John H., **II:** 418

Finn, David, **Supp. VIII:** 106–107

Finnegan, Robert (pseudonym). *See* Ryan, Paul William

Finnegans Wake (Joyce), **III:** 7, 12, 14, 261; **IV:** 182, 369–370, 418, 421; **Supp. I Part 2:** 620; **Supp. II Part 1:** 2; **Supp. XIII:** 191; **Supp. XVIII:** 32

Finney, Brian, **Supp. XIV:** 158, 160, 161, 165, 166, 167, 169

"Finnish Rhapsody" (Ashbery), **Supp. III Part 1:** 26

Finster, Howard, **Supp. XV:** 349

Firbank, Ronald, **IV:** 77, 436; **Supp. XXIII:** 209

"Fire" (Hughes), **Supp. I Part 1:** 327

"Fire and Cloud" (Wright), **IV:** 488

"Fire and Ice" (Frost), **II:** 154; **Retro. Supp. I:** 133; **Supp. XIX:** 122

Fire and Ice (Stegner), **Supp. IV Part 2:** 598, 607–608

"Fire and the Cloud, The" (Hurston), **Supp. VI:** 158

"Fire and the Hearth, The" (Faulkner), **II:** 71

Firebird (Doty), **Supp. XI:** 119–120, 121, **132–133,** 134

"Firebombing, The" (Dickey), **Supp. IV Part 1:** 180–181, 187, 189–190

"Fireborn Are at Home in Fire, The" (Sandburg), **III:** 591

"Fire by Night" (R. Fisher), **Supp. XIX:** 70–71

"Fire Chaconne" (Francis), **Supp. IX:** 87

Firecrackers (Van Vechten), **Supp. II Part 2:** 740, 742–744, 749

"Fire Dreams"(Thompson), **Supp. XXIII:** 296

Fire: From "A Journal of Love," the Unexpurgated Diary of Anaïs Nin, 1934–1937, **Supp. X:** 184, 185, 189, 194, 195

"Fireman, The " (Bass), **Supp. XVI:** 24

Fireman's Wife and Other Stories, The (Bausch), **Supp. VII:** 48, 54

Fire Next Time, The (Baldwin), **Retro. Supp. II:** 5, 8, 9; **Supp. I Part 1:** 48, 49, 52, 60–61

"Fire Next Time, The" (Baldwin). *See* "Down at the Cross" (Baldwin)

"Fire of Driftwood, The" (Longfellow), **II:** 499; **Retro. Supp. II:** 159, 168

"Fire of Life" (McCullers), **II:** 585

Fire on the Mountain (Abbey), **Supp. XIII:** 6

"Fire Poem" (Merrill), **Supp. III Part 1:** 321

"Fires" (Bass), **Supp. XVI:** 20

"Fires" (Carver), **Supp. III Part 1:** 136–139, 147

Fire Screen, The (Merrill), **Supp. III Part 1:** 319, 325–329

"Fire Season" (Didion), **Supp. IV Part 1:** 199

"Fire Sequence" (Winters), **Supp. II Part 2:** 791, 796, 800

Fire Sermon (Morris), **III:** 238–239

"Fire Sermon, The" (Eliot), **Retro. Supp. I:** 60–61

Fires: Essays, Poems, Stories (Carver), **Supp. III Part 1:** 136, 140, 142, 146–147

Fireside Travels (Lowell), **Supp. I Part 2:** 407, 419–420

Firestarter (King), **Supp. V:** 140, 141, 144; **Supp. IX:** 114

"fire the bastards" (Green), **Supp. IV Part 1:** 285

"Fire-Truck, A" (Wilbur), **Supp. III Part 2:** 556

"Fireweed" (Clampitt), **Supp. IX: 44–45**

"Firewood" (Banks), **Supp. V:** 15

"Fireworks" (Ford), **Supp. V:** 69

"Fireworks" (Shapiro), **Supp. II Part 2:** 707

Fireworks: A History and Celebration (Plimpton), **Supp. XVI:** 245

Fir-Flower Tablets (Lowell), **II:** 512, 526–527

Firger, Jessica, **Supp. XIX:** 51, 58, 59, 62

Firkins, Oscar W., **II:** 271; **Supp. XV:** 297, 309

"Firmament, The" (Bryant), **Supp. I Part 1:** 162

Firmat, Gustavo Pérez, **Supp. VIII:** 76, 77, 79; **Supp. XI:** 184

"First American, The" (Toomer), **Supp. III Part 2:** 480, 487

"First Birth" (Olds), **Supp. X:** 212

First Book of Africa, The (Hughes), **Supp. I Part 1:** 344–345

First Book of Jazz, The (Hughes), **Supp. I Part 1:** 345

First Book of Negroes, The (Hughes), **Supp. I Part 1:** 345

First Book of Rhythms, The (Hughes), **Supp. I Part 1:** 345

First Book of the West Indies, The (Hughes), **Supp. I Part 1:** 345

Firstborn (Glück), **Supp. V:** 80, 81, 82, 84

"Firstborn" (Wright), **Supp. V:** 340

"First Chaldaic Oracle" (Carson), **Supp. XII: 111**

"First Communion" (Fante), **Supp. XI:** 160

"First Confession" (X. J. Kennedy), **Supp. XV: 154–155**

"First Day of School, The" (Gibbons), **Supp. X:** 41, 42

"First Death in Nova Scotia" (Bishop), **Supp. I Part 1:** 73

"First Formal" (Olds), **Supp. X:** 212

First Four Books of Poems, The (Glück), **Supp. V:** 81, 83

First Four Years, The (L. I. Wilder), **Supp. XXII:** 296, 298, 299–300

"First Grade" (Stafford), **Supp. XI:** 328

First Hand (Bierds), **Supp. XVII:** 32, 34–36

"First Hawaiian Bank" (Nye), **Supp. XIII:** 278

"First Heat" (Taylor), **Supp. V:** 323

First Hour, The (Di Piero), **Supp. XIX:** 36–37, 40

"First Hour of the Night, The" (Bidart), **Supp. XV: 30–32**

"First Hunters and the Last, The" (Sobin), **Supp. XVI:** 292

"First Job, The" (Cisneros), **Supp. VII:** 62

"1st Letter on Georges" (Olson), **Supp. II Part 2:** 578

First Light (C. Baxter), **Supp. XVII:** 15, **17–18,** 19, 22

First Light (Preston), **Supp. XVII:** 18

First Light (Wagoner), **Supp. IX:** 330

"First Love" (Welty), **IV:** 264; **Retro. Supp. I:** 347

First Love: A Lyric Sequence (Untermeyer), **Supp. XV:** 295

First Lover and Other Stories, The (Boyle), **Supp. XXIV: 57–58**

First Man, The (O'Neill), **III:** 390

First Manifesto (McGrath), **Supp. X:** 115

"First Meditation" (Roethke), **III:** 545–546

"First Noni Daylight, The" (Harjo), **Supp. XII:** 219

"First Passover" (Longfellow), **II:** 500–501

"First Person Female" (Harrison), **Supp. VIII:** 40, 41, 48

"First Place, The" (Wagoner), **Supp. IX:** 328

First Poems (Buechner), **Supp. XII:** 45

First Poems (Merrill), **Supp. III Part 1:** 318–321, 323

First Poems 1946–1954 (Kinnell), **Supp. III Part 1:** 235, 238–239

"First Praise" (W. C. Williams), **Retro. Supp. I:** 413

First Principles (Spencer), **Supp. I Part 1:** 368

"First Reader" (Collins), **Supp. XXI:** 55–56

"First Ride and First Walk" (Goldbarth), **Supp. XII:** 182–183

"First Seeing the St. Lawrence River"(Kenny), **Supp. XXIII:** 152

"First Seven Years, The" (Malamud), **Supp. I Part 2:** 431

"First Sex" (Olds), **Supp. X:** 208

"First Snow" (Mosher), **Supp. XXII:** 211

"First Snow in Alsace" (Wilbur), **Supp. III Part 2:** 545, 546, 559

"First Song" (Kinnell), **Supp. III Part 1:** 239

"First Spade in the West, The" (Fiedler), **Supp. XIII:** 103

"First Steps" (McClatchy), **Supp. XII:** 256

First There Is the Need (Reznikoff), **Supp. XIV:** 291

"First Things First" (Auden), **Supp. II Part 1:** 13

"First Thought, Best Thought" (Ginsberg), **Supp. II Part 1:** 327

"First Time I Saw Paris, The" (Fante), **Supp. XI:** 174

"First Travels of Max" (Ransom), **III:** 490–491

"First Tycoon of Teen, The" (Wolfe), **Supp. III Part 2:** 572

"First Views of the Enemy" (Oates), **Supp. II Part 2:** 508

"First Wife, The" (Buck), **Supp. II Part 1:** 127

First Words before Spring (Untermeyer), **Supp. XV:** 310

"First World War" (White), **Supp. I Part 2:** 665

"Fish" (F. Barthelme), **Supp. XI:** 26

"Fish" (Levis), **Supp. XI:** 259–260

Fish, Stanley, **Supp. IV Part 1:** 48; **Supp. XIV:** 14, 15

"Fish, The" (Bishop), **Supp. XV:** 100, 102

"Fish, The" (Moore), **III:** 195, 197, 209, 211, 213–214; **Supp. XXI:** 26

"Fish, The" (Oliver), **Supp. VII:** 236

"Fish, The/Lago Chapala" (Everwine), **Supp. XV:** 82–83

"Fish and Shadow" (Pound), **III:** 466

"Fishboy" (Richard), **Supp. XIX:** 212–213

Fishboy: A Ghost's Story (Richard), **Supp. XIX:** 209, 213–220, 221

Fishburne, Laurence, **Supp. VIII:** 345

"Fish Cannery" (Fante), **Supp. XI:** 167

Fisher, Alexander Metcalf, **Supp. I Part 2:** 582

Fisher, Alfred, **Retro. Supp. II:** 243

Fisher, Barbara, **Supp. XXII:** 206

Fisher, Craig, **Supp. V:** 125

Fisher, Dorothy Canfield, **Retro. Supp. I:** 21, 133; **Supp. II Part 1:** 117. *See also* Canfield, Dorothy

Fisher, Mary, **Supp. I Part 2:** 455

Fisher, M. F. K., **Supp. XVII:** 81–93

Fisher, Phillip, **Retro. Supp. I:** 39

Fisher, Rudolph, **Retro. Supp. I:** 200; **Supp. I Part 1:** 325; **Supp. X:** 139; **Supp. XVI:** 143; **Supp. XIX:** 65–80

Fisher, Vardis, **Supp. IV Part 2:** 598

Fisher King, The (Marshall), **Supp. XI:** 275–276, **288–290**

"Fisherman, The" (Merwin), **Supp. II Part 1:** 346

"Fisherman and His Wife, The" (Welty), **IV:** 266

"Fisherman from Chihuahua, The" (Connell), **Supp. XIV:** 86

"Fishing" (Harjo), **Supp. XII:** 227–228

"Fishing Idyll, A" (Mosher), **Supp. XXII:** 209

"Fish in the Stone, The" (Dove), **Supp. IV Part 1:** 245, 257

"Fish in the unruffled lakes" (Auden), **Supp. II Part 1:** 8–9

"Fish R Us" (Doty), **Supp. XI:** 135

Fisk, James, I: 4, 474

Fiske, John, **Supp. I Part 1:** 314; **Supp. I Part 2:** 493

Fisketjon, Gary, **Supp. XXIV:** 178

"Fit Against the Country, A" (Wright), **Supp. III Part 2:** 591–592, 601

Fitch, Clyde, **Supp. IV Part 2:** 573

Fitch, Elizabeth. *See* Taylor, Mrs. Edward (Elizabeth Fitch)

Fitch, James, **IV:** 147

Fitch, Noël Riley, **Supp. X:** 186, 187

"Fitting, The" (Hull), **Supp. XXI:** 134, 135

Fit to Be Tied (Silver), **Supp. XXIV: 271–272**

Fitts, Dudley, **I:** 169, 173; **Supp. I Part 1:** 342, 345; **Supp. XIII:** 346; **Supp. XXII:** 281

FitzGerald, Edward, **Supp. I Part 2:** 416; **Supp. III Part 2:** 610

Fitzgerald, Ella, **Supp. XIII:** 132

Fitzgerald, F. Scott, **I:** 107, 117, 118, 123, 188, 221, 288, 289, 358, 367, 374–375, 382, 423, 476, 482, 487, 495, 509, 511; **II: 77–100**, 257, 263, 272, 283, 415, 416, 417–418, 420, 425, 427, 430, 431, 432, 433, 434, 436, 437, 450, 458–459, 482, 560; **III:** 2, 26, 35, 36, 37, 40, 44, 45, 69, 106, 244, 284, 334, 350–351, 453, 454, 471, 551, 552, 572; **IV:** 27, 49, 97, 101, 126, 140, 191, 222, 223, 287, 297, 427, 471; **Retro. Supp. I:** 1, 74, **97–120**, 178, 180, 186, 215, 359, 381; **Retro. Supp. II:** 257, 321, 326, 328; **Supp. I Part 1:** 196, 197; **Supp. I Part 2:** 622; **Supp. III Part 2:** 409, 411, 585; **Supp. IV Part 1:** 123, 197, 200, 203, 341; **Supp. IV Part 2:** 463, 468, 607, 689; **Supp. V:** 23, 95, 226, 251, 262, 276, 313; **Supp. VIII:** 101, 103, 106, 137; **Supp. IX:** 15, 20, 55, 57–63, 199; **Supp. X:** 225; **Supp. XI:** 65, 221, 334; **Supp. XII:** 42, 173, 295; **Supp. XIII:** 170, 263; **Supp. XV:** 135; **Supp. XVI:** 64, 75, 191, 192, 294; **Supp. XVIII:** 148, 246, 248, 251, 254; **Supp. XX: 74; Supp. XXI:** 262; **Supp. XXII:** 82, 92; **Supp. XXIII:** 68, 101, 174

Fitzgerald, Robert, **I:** 27–28; **III:** 338, 348; **Retro. Supp. II:** 179, 221, 222, 223, 228, 229; **Supp. IV Part 2:** 631; **Supp. XV:** 112, 249; **Supp. XXII:** 281; **Supp. XXIII:** 112

Fitzgerald, Zelda (Zelda Sayre), **I:** 482; **II:** 77, 79, 82–85, 88, 90–91, 93, 95; **Supp. IV Part 1:** 310; **Supp. IX:** 55–73; **Supp. X:** 172. *See also* Sayre, Zelda

"Fitzgerald's Tragic Sense" (Schorer), **Retro. Supp. I:** 115

"Fitzgerald: The Romance of Money" (Cowley), **Supp. II Part 1:** 143

5 Detroits (Levine), **Supp. V:** 178

Five Came Back (West), **IV:** 287

Five Corners (screenplay, Shanley), **Supp. XIV:** 316

"Five-Dollar Bill, The" (D. West as Mary Christopher), **Supp. XVIII:** 282

"Five Dollar Guy, The" (W. C. Williams), **Retro. Supp. I:** 423

Five Easy Pieces (film), **Supp. V:** 26

"Five Elephants" (Dove), **Supp. IV Part 1:** 244–245

"Five Fucks" (Lethem), **Supp. XVIII:** 139

Five Groups of Verse (Reznikoff), **Supp. XIV:** 279, 282

Five Hundred Hats of Bartholomew Cubbins, The (Geisel), **Supp. XVI:** 100

Five Hundred Scorpions (Hearon), **Supp. VIII:** 57, 65, **66**

Five Indiscretions (Ríos), **Supp. IV Part 2:** 545–547

Five Men and Pompey (Benét), **Supp. XI:** 43, 44

Five Plays (Hughes), **Retro. Supp. I:** 197, 209

"Five Psalms" (Jarman), **Supp. XVII:** 120

Five Temperaments (Kalstone), **Retro. Supp. II:** 40

5,000 Fingers of Dr. T, The (film), **Supp. XVI:** 103

Five Young American Poets, **I:** 170; **II:** 367

Fixer, The (Malamud), **Supp. I Part 2:** 428, 435, 445, 446–448, 450, 451

"Fixin' Road" (Boulton), **Supp. XXII:** 23

"Fix It (Winter)"(Hadas), **Supp. XXIII:** 115

Fjellestad, Danuta Zadworna, **Supp. XVI:** 150

Flaccus, Kimball, **Retro. Supp. I:** 136

Flacius, Matthias, **IV:** 163

"Flagellant's Song" (X. J. Kennedy), **Supp. XV:** 165

Flag for Sunrise, A (Stone), **Supp. V:** 301–304

Flagg, Fannie, **Supp. XXII:** 213–214

Flag of Childhood, The: Poems from the Middle East (Nye, ed.), **Supp. XIII:** 280

"Flag of Summer" (Swenson), **Supp. IV Part 2:** 645

Flagons and Apples (Jeffers), **Supp. II Part 2:** 413, 414, 417–418

Flags in the Dust (Faulkner), **Retro. Supp. I:** 81, 82, 83, 86, 88

Flamel, Nicolas, **Supp. XII:** 178

Flaming Corsage, The (W. Kennedy), **Supp. VII:** 133, 153–156

Flammarion, Camille, **Supp. I Part 1:** 260

Flanagan, John T., **Supp. I Part 2:** 464, 465, 468

Flanner, Janet, **Supp. XVI:** 195

"Flannery O'Connor: Poet to the Outcast" (Sister Rose Alice), **III:** 348

Flappers and Philosophers (Fitzgerald), **II:** 88; **Retro. Supp. I:** 103; **Supp. IX:** 56

"Flappers Were Her Daughters, The: The Liberated, Literary World of Gertrude Atherton" (Richey), **Supp. XXIV:** 30

Flash and Filigree (Southern), **Supp. XI:** 295, **296–297**

"Flashcards" (Dove), **Supp. IV Part 1:** 250

Flash Fiction: Seventy-two Very Short Stories (J. Thomas, ed.), **Supp. XVI:** 268

"Flash in the Pan" (Shaw), **Supp. XIX:** 245

"Flat Sky of Summer"(Balakian), **Supp. XXIII:** 25

Flatt, Lester, **Supp. V:** 335

Flaubert, Gustave, **I:** 66, 123, 130, 272, 312, 314, 315, 477, 504, 506, 513, 514; **II:** 182, 185, 194, 198–199, 205, 209, 230, 289, 311, 316, 319, 325, 337, 392, 401, 577, 594; **III:** 196, 207, 251, 315, 461, 467, 511, 564; **IV:** 4, 29, 31, 37, 40, 134, 285, 428; **Retro. Supp. I:** 5, 215, 218, 222, 225, 235, 287; **Supp. III Part 2:** 411, 412; **Supp. XI:** 334; **Supp. XIV:** 87, 336; **Supp. XXIII:** 254

"Flavia and Her Artists" (Cather), **Retro. Supp. I:** 5

Flavoring of New England, The (Brooks), **I:** 253, 256

Flavor of Man, The (Toomer), **Supp. III Part 2:** 487

"Flaw, The" (Peacock), **Supp. XIX:** 206

Flaxman, Josiah, **Supp. I Part 2:** 716

"Flea, The" (Donne), **Supp. XVIII:** 307

"Flèche d'Or" (Merrill), **Supp. III Part 1:** 328

Flecker, James Elroy, **Supp. I Part 1:** 257

"Flee on Your Donkey" (Sexton), **Supp. II Part 2:** 683, 685

Fleming, Ian, **Supp. XI:** 307; **Supp. XX: 195**

Fleming, Rene, **Supp. XII:** 321

Fleming, Robert E., **Supp. XVII:** 155; **Supp. XXII:** 184

Flesch, Rudolf, **Supp. XVI:** 105, 106

Flesh and Blood (Cunningham), **Supp. XV: 63–65**

Flesh and Blood (play; Cunnigham and Gaitens), **Supp. XV:** 65

"Fleshbody" (Ammons), **Supp. VII:** 27

Fletcher, H. D., **II:** 517, 529

Fletcher, John, **Supp. IV Part 2:** 621

Fletcher, John Gould, **I:** 243; **II:** 517, 529; **III:** 458; **Supp. I Part 1:** 263; **Supp. I Part 2:** 422; **Supp. XV:** 298, 302, 306, 307, 308

Fletcher, Phineas, **Supp. I Part 1:** 369

Fletcher, Virginia. *See* Caldwell, Mrs. Erskine (Virginia Fletcher)

Fleurs du mal, Les (Beaudelaire; Millay and Dillon, trans.), **III:** 141–142

"Flight" (Bierds), **Supp. XVII:** 36

"Flight" (Updike), **IV:** 218, 222, 224; **Retro. Supp. I:** 318

Flight (White), **Supp. XVIII:** 127

"Flight, The" (Haines), **Supp. XII:** 204–205

"Flight, The" (Roethke), **III:** 537–538

Flight 115; or, Pas de Fumer sur la Piste (O'Hara and Berkson), **Supp. XXIII:** 217, 218

Flight among the Tombs (Hecht), **Supp. X:** 58, **71–74**

"Flight for Freedom" (McCoy), **Supp. XIII:** 170

"Flight from Byzantium" (Brodsky), **Supp. VIII:** 30–31

"Flight of Besey Lane, The" (Jewett), **Retro. Supp. II:** 139

Flight of the Rocket, The (Fitzgerald), **II:** 89

Flights of the Harvest-Mare (Bierds), **Supp. XVII:** 26–27

Flight to Canada (Reed), **Supp. X:** 240, **249–252**

Flinn, Mary, **Supp. XVII:** 110

Flint, F. S., **II:** 517; **III:** 459, 464, 465; **Retro. Supp. I:** 127; **Supp. I Part 1:** 261, 262

Flint, Helen, **Supp. XXII:** 278

Flint, R. W., **Supp. XVI:** 47, 49, 57

"Flitting Flies" (X. J. Kennedy), **Supp. XV:** 166, **167**

Flivver King, The (Sinclair), **Supp. V:** 290

Floating House, The (Sanders), **Supp. XVI:** 269

Floating Light Bulb, The (Allen), **Supp. XV:** 2, 3, 13

Floating Opera, The (Barth), **I:** 121, 122–126, 127, 129, 130, 131

"Floating Poem, Unnumbered, The" (Rich), **Supp. I Part 2:** 572–573

"Floating Trees" (Wright), **Supp. XV:** 348

Flood (Matthews), **Supp. IX:** 154, **160–161**

Flood (Warren), **IV:** 252, 256–257

"Flood of Years, The" (Bryant), **Supp. I Part 1:** 159, 170, 171; **Supp. I Part 2:** 416

"Floor and the Ceiling, The" (W. J. Smith), **Supp. XIII:** 345, 346

"Floor Plans" (Komunyakaa), **Supp. XIII:** 114

"Floral Conversation" (Peacock), **Supp. XIX:** 200

"Floral Decorations for Bananas" (Stevens), **IV:** 8

Florida (Acker), **Supp. XII:** 5

"Florida" (Bishop), **Retro. Supp. II:** 43

"Florida Road Workers" (Hughes), **Retro. Supp. I:** 203

"Florida Sunday, A" (Lanier), **Supp. I Part 1:** 364, 366

Florist's Daughter, The (Hampl), **Supp. XXII:** 84, 85, 94, **95–98**

"Flossie Cabanis" (Masters), **Supp. I Part 2:** 461–462

"Flounder" (Trethewey), **Supp. XXI:** 244, 245, 246, 251

Flow Chart (Ashbery), **Supp. VIII:** 275

"Flowchart" (Ashbery), **Supp. III Part 1:** 26

Flower, Dean, **Supp. XXII:** 205, 212

Flower, Fruit, and Thorn Pieces (Richter), **Supp. XVI:** 182

Flower-de-Luce (Longfellow), **II:** 490

Flower Drum Song (Rodgers and Hammerstein), **Supp. XXI:** 148

Flower Drum Song, The (Lee), **Supp. XXI:** 148

Flower Fables (Alcott), **Supp. I Part 1:** 33

"Flower-Fed Buffaloes, The" (Lindsay), **Supp. I Part 2:** 398

"Flower Garden" (Jackson), **Supp. IX:** 119

"Flower-gathering" (Frost), **II:** 153

Flower Herding on Mount Monadnock (Kinnell), **Supp. III Part 1:** 235, 239, 241–244

"Flower Herding on Mount Monadnock" (Kinnell), **Supp. III Part 1:** 242

"Flowering Death" (Ashbery), **Supp. III Part 1:** 22

"Flowering Dream, The" (McCullers), **II:** 591

"Flowering Judas" (Porter), **III:** 434, 435–436, 438, 441, 445, 446, 450–451

Flowering Judas and Other Stories (Porter), **III:** 433, 434

Flowering of New England, The (Brooks), **IV:** 171–172; **Supp. VIII:** 101

Flowering of the Rod (Doolittle), **Supp. I Part 1:** 272

Flowering Peach, The (Odets), **Supp. II Part 2:** 533, 547, 549–550

"Flowering Plum" (Glück), **Supp. V:** 82

"Flowers for Marjorie" (Welty), **IV:** 262

"Flowers of the Fallow" (Larcom), **Supp. XIII:** 143, 145–146

"Flowers Well if anybody" (Dickinson), **Retro. Supp. I:** 30

"Fluff and Mr. Ripley" (D. West), **Supp. XVIII:** 284

"Fly, The" (Kinnell), **Supp. III Part 1:** 249

"Fly, The" (Shapiro), **Supp. II Part 2:** 705

"Fly, The" (Simic), **Supp. VIII:** 278

Flye, Father James Harold, **I:** 25, 26, 35–36, 37, 42, 46; **IV:** 215

"Fly in Buttermilk, A" (Baldwin), **Retro. Supp. II:** 8

Flying at Night: Poems 1965–1985 (Kooser), **Supp. XIX:** 128

"Flying High" (Levertov), **Supp. III Part 1:** 284

"Flying Home" (Ellison), **Retro. Supp. II:** 117, **125–126**; **Supp. II Part 1:**

235, 238–239

"Flying Home" (Kinnell), **Supp. III Part 1:** 250

"Flying Home" and Other Stories (Ellison), **Retro. Supp. II:** 119, 124

"Flying Home from Utah" (Swenson), **Supp. IV Part 2:** 645

"Flying over Clouds" (Gioia), **Supp. XV:** 118

Flying Solo (Kriegel), **Supp. XXIV: 219–221**

"Flying to Hanoi" (Rukeyser), **Supp. VI:** 279

Flynn, Elizabeth Gurley, **Supp. XVIII:** 225

Flynn, Richard, **Supp. XVII:** 115; **Supp. XVIII:** 183

Fly-Truffler, The (Sobin), **Supp. XVI: 294–295,** 296

Foata, Anne, **Supp. XI:** 104

FOB (Hwang), **Supp. XXI:** 143, 144, 145, 146, **148–150**

Focillon, Henri, **IV:** 90

Focus (A. Miller), **III:** 150–151, 156

Foer, Jonathan Safran, **Supp. XII:** 169; **Supp. XX: 177; Supp. XXIV:** 131

Foerster, Norman, **I:** 222; **Supp. I Part 2:** 423, 424; **Supp. IV Part 2:** 598

"Fog" (Sandburg), **III:** 586

"Fog Galleon" (Komunyakaa), **Supp. XIII:** 127

"Foggy and dripping" (Kooser), **Supp. XIX:** 125

"Foggy Lane, The" (Simpson), **Supp. IX:** 274

"Fog Man, The" (Boyle), **Supp. XX:** 20

Folded Leaf, The (Maxwell), **Supp. III Part 1:** 62; **Supp. VIII: 159–162**

Folding Star, The (Hollinghurst), **Supp. XIII:** 52

Foley, Jack, **Supp. X:** 125; **Supp. XV:** 112, 116; **Supp. XVII:** 77

Foley, Martha, **II:** 587; **Supp. XVI:** 225

Folk-Lore in the Old Testament (Frazer), **Supp. XX: 116–117**

Folks from Dixie (Dunbar), **Supp. II Part 1:** 211–212

Folkways (Sumner), **III:** 102

Follain, Jean, **Supp. IX:** 152, 154

Follett, Wilson, **I:** 405; **Supp. XIII:** 173

Follower of Dusk (Salinas), **Supp. XIII:** 326

"Following the Bones" (W. V. Davis), **Supp. XXI:** 96

Following the Equator (Twain), **II:** 434; **IV:** 208

Follow Me Home (Hoffman), **Supp. XVIII:** 86

Folly (Minot), **Supp. VI:** 205, 208, **210–213**

Folly of Others, The (Boyce), **Supp. XVII:** 100; **Supp. XXI:** 10

Folsom, Charles, **Supp. I Part 1:** 156

Folsom, Ed, **Retro. Supp. I:** 392

Folson, Marcia McClintock, **Retro. Supp. II:** 139

Fonda, Henry, **Supp. I Part 1:** 67; **Supp. IV Part 1:** 236

Fonda, Jane, **III:** 284; **Supp. XI:** 307

Fonda, Peter, **Supp. VIII:** 42; **Supp. XI:** 293, 308

"Fondled Memories" (Molesworth), **Supp. XIX:** 121–122

"Fond Memories of a Black Childhood" (D. West), **Supp. XVIII:** 289

Foner, Eric, **Supp. I Part 2:** 523

Fong and the Indians (Theroux), **Supp. VIII:** 314, 315, **316–317**

Fontanne, Lynn, **III:** 397

Food and Drink (Untermeyer), **Supp. XV:** 310

Food Chain, The (Silver), **Supp. XXIV:** 265, **270–271,** 274

Fool for Love (Shepard), **Supp. III Part 2:** 433, 447, 448

Fooling with Words (PBS special, Moyers), **Supp. XXIII:** 139

"Foolishness" (Pickering), **Supp. XXI:** 197

Fools (Simon), **Supp. IV Part 2:** 584–585

Fools Crow (Welch), **Supp. XXIV:** 257

Fool's Progress, The: An Honest Novel (Abbey), **Supp. XIII:** 4, **13–15**

Foot Book, The (Geisel), **Supp. XVI:** 108

Foote, Horton, **Supp. I Part 1:** 281; **Supp. VIII:** 128, 129

Foote, Mary Hallock, **Retro. Supp. II:** 72; **Supp. IV Part 2:** 611

Foote, Roxanna. *See* Beecher, Mrs. Lyman (Roxanna Foote)

Foote, Samuel, **Supp. I Part 2:** 584

Foote, Stephanie, **Retro. Supp. II:** 139

"Foot Fault" (pseudonym). *See* Thurber, James

Footing on This Earth, A (Hay), **Supp. XIV:** 125, 126, 130

"Footing up a Total" (Lowell), **II:** 528

"Footnote to Howl" (Ginsberg), **Supp. II Part 1:** 316–317

"Footnote to Weather Forecasts, A" (Brodsky), **Supp. VIII:** 32

Footprints (Hearon), **Supp. VIII: 69–70**

Footprints (Levertov), **Supp. III Part 1:** 272, 281

"Footsteps of Angels" (Longfellow), **II:** 496

"For A, at Fourteen" (Weigl), **Supp. XIX:** 287

For a Bitter Season: New and Selected Poems (Garrett), **Supp. VII:** 99–100

"For a Dead Kitten" (Hay), **Supp. XIV:** 119–120

"For a Dead Lady" (Robinson), **III:** 508, 513, 517

"For a Ghost Who Once Placed Bets in the Park" (Levis), **Supp. XI:** 265

"For a Lamb" (Eberhart), **I:** 523, 530, 531

"For All" (Snyder), **Supp. VIII:** 304

"For All Tuesday Travelers" (Cisneros), **Supp. VII:** 67–68

"For a Lost Child" (Stafford), **Supp. XI:** 329

"For a Marriage" (Bogan), **Supp. III Part 1:** 52

"For an Emigrant" (Jarrell), **II:** 371

"For Anna Akmatova" (Lowell), **II:** 544

"For Anna Mae Pictou Aquash, Whose Spirit Is Present Here and in the Dappled Stars" (Harjo), **Supp. XII:** 225

"For Anne, at a Little Distance" (Haines), **Supp. XII:** 207

"For Annie" (Poe), **III:** 427; **Retro. Supp. II:** 263

"For an Old Friend Encountered Unexpectedly" (Espaillat), **Supp. XXI:** 111–112

"For a Southern Man" (Cisneros), **Supp. VII:** 67

"For Bailey" (Angelou), **Supp. IV Part 1:** 15

Forbes, Malcolm, **Supp. IV Part 1:** 94

"Forbidden, The" (Glück), **Supp. XIV:** 269

"For Bill Nestrick (1940–96)" (Bidart), **Supp. XV:** 35

For Bread Alone (Choukri), **Supp. IV Part 1:** 92

"Force" (Di Piero), **Supp. XIX:** 35–36, 42, 44

Force of Desire, The (Bronk), **Supp. XXI:** 31, 32

Force of Evil (film, Polonsky), **Supp. XXI:** 261, 272, 275

Force of Spirit, The (Sanders), **Supp. XVI:** 277–278

Forché, Carolyn, **Supp. IV Part 1:** 208; **Supp. XIX:** 193

Ford, Arthur, **Supp. IV Part 1:** 140

Ford, Ford Madox, **I:** 288, 405, 409, 417, 421, 423; **II:** 58, 144, 198, 257, 263, 265, 517, 536; **III:** 458, 464–465, 470–471, 472, 476; **IV:** 27, 126, 261; **Retro. Supp. I:** 127, 177, 178, 186, 231, 286–287, 418; **Supp. II Part 1:** 107; **Supp. III Part 2:** 617; **Supp. VIII:** 107; **Supp. XIV:** 3

Ford, Harrison, **Supp. VIII:** 323

Ford, Harry, **Supp. V:** 179; **Supp. XIII:** 76

Ford, Henry, **I:** 295, 480–481; **III:** 292, 293; **Supp. I Part 1:** 21; **Supp. I Part 2:** 644; **Supp. III Part 2:** 612, 613; **Supp. IV Part 1:** 223; **Supp. V:** 290

Ford, John, **Supp. I Part 2:** 422; **Supp. III Part 2:** 619; **Supp. XVIII:** 247

Ford, Mark, **Supp. XXIII:** 220

Ford, Mary K., **Supp. XX: 239**

Ford, Richard, **Supp. IV Part 1:** 342; **Supp. V:** 22, **57–75; Supp. XXIV:** 97

Ford, Webster (pseudonym). *See* Masters, Edgar Lee

"Fording and Dread" (Harrison), **Supp. VIII:** 41

"Ford Madox Ford" (Lowell), **II:** 547; **Retro. Supp. II:** 188

"For Dudley" (Wilbur), **Supp. III Part 2:** 558

Fordyce, David, **II:** 113

For Eager Lovers (Taggard), **Supp. XXII: 274–275**

Foregone Conclusion, A (Howells), **II:** 278–279, 282

"Foreign Affairs" (Kunitz), **Supp. III Part 1:** 265

"Foreigner, A" (Bynner), **Supp. XV:** 46

"Foreigner, The" (Jewett), **II:** 409–410; **Retro. Supp. II:** 133, 142

"Foreigners" (Jarman), **Supp. XVII:** 113

"Foreign Language, The" (Franzen), **Supp. XX: 84**

"Foreign Shores" (Salter), **Supp. IX:** 260

Forensic and the Navigators (Shepard), **Supp. III Part 2:** 439

Forerunner, The (Boyce), **Supp. XXI:** 2, 4, **10–11**

Forerunner, The: His Parables and Poems (Gibran), **Supp. XX: 115, 118–119, 119**

Foreseeable Future, The (Price), **Supp. VI:** 265

Foreseeable Futures (Matthews), **Supp. IX:** 155, **163,** 169

Foresman, Rebecca, **Supp. XXIV:** 171

"For Esmé with Love and Squalor" (Salinger), **III:** 560

"Forest" (Simic), **Supp. VIII:** 273

Forest, Jean-Claude, **Supp. XI:** 307

Forester's Letters (Paine), **Supp. I Part 2:** 508

"Forest Hymn, A" (Bryant), **Supp. I Part 1:** 156, 162, 163, 164, 165, 170

"Forest in the Seeds, The" (Kingsolver), **Supp. VII:** 203

Forest of the South, The (Gordon), **II:** 197

"Forest of the South, The" (Gordon), **II:** 199, 201

Forest without Leaves (Adams and Haines), **Supp. XII:** 209

"Forever, Said the Duck" (Lethem), **Supp. XVIII:** 139

"Forever and the Earth" (Bradbury), **Supp. IV Part 1:** 102

"Forever in That Year" (Carruth), **Supp. XVI:** 51

"Forever"(Thompson), **Supp. XXIII:** 296

"Forever Young" (Jarman and R. McDowell), **Supp. XVII:** 111

"For Fathers of Girls" (Dunn), **Supp. XI:** 146

For Frank O'Hara's Birthday (Notley), **Supp. XXII:** 224, 227

"For/From Lew" (Snyder), **Supp. VIII:** 303

"For Garrison Keillor, Fantasy Is a Lot More Fun then Reality" (Letofsky), **Supp. XVI:** 167

"For George Santayana" (Lowell), **II:** 547

"Forgetfulness" (Collins), **Supp. XXI:** 58

"Forgiveness" (Peacock), **Supp. XIX:** 200

Forgotten Helper, The: A Story for Children (Moore), **Supp. X:** 175

"Forgotten in an Old Notebook" (F. Wright), **Supp. XVII:** 244

Forgotten Village, The (Steinbeck), **IV:** 51

"For Grace, After a party"(O'Hara), **Supp. XXIII:** 214

"For Grizzel McNaught (1709–1792)" (A. Finch), **Supp. XVII:** 72

Forgue, Guy J., **III:** 118, 119

For Her Dark Skin (Everett), **Supp. XVIII:** 56, 60

"FOR HETTIE" (Baraka), **Supp. II Part 1:** 32

"FOR HETTIE IN HER FIFTH MONTH" (Baraka), **Supp. II Part 1:** 32, 38

"For Homer" (Corso), **Supp. XII:** 135

"For I'm the Boy" (Barthelme), **Supp. IV Part 1:** 47

"For James Dean"(O'Hara), **Supp. XXIII:** 214

"For Janice and Kenneth to Voyage"(O'Hara), **Supp. XXIII:** 214

"For Jeff" (Kooser), **Supp. XIX:** 125

"For Jessica, My Daughter" (Strand), **Supp. IV Part 2:** 629

"For John, Who Begs Me not to Enquire Further" (Sexton), **Supp. II Part 2:** 676

"For Johnny Pole on the Forgotten Beach" (Sexton), **Supp. II Part 2:** 675

"For Joy to Leave Upon" (Ortiz), **Supp. IV Part 2:** 508

"For Judy, Whose Husband Is Undergoing Surgery"(Crooker), **Supp. XXIII:** 61

"Fork" (Simic), **Supp. VIII:** 275

"For Karl Shapiro, Having Gone Back to the Sonnet" (Kooser), **Supp. XIX:** 118

"Forky" (Dubus III), **Supp. XXIV:** 99, 101

For Lancelot Andrewes (Eliot), **Retro. Supp. I:** 64

For Lizzie and Harriet (Lowell), **Retro. Supp. II:** 183, 186, 190

"Forlorn Hope of Sidney Lanier, The" (Leary), **Supp. I Part 1:** 373

For Love (Creeley), **Supp. IV Part 1:** 139, 140, 142–145, 147–149, 150, 154

"For Love" (Creeley), **Supp. IV Part 1:** 145

For Love (Miller), **Supp. XII: 297–299,** 299

For Love of Imabelle (C. Himes), **Supp. XVI:** 135, 143, 144

Form, Cycle, Infinity: Landscape Imagery in the Poetry of Robert Frost and George Seferis (Hadas), **Supp. XXIII: 121–122**

"Formal Elegy" (Berryman), **I:** 170

Formal Feeling Comes, A (A. Finch, ed.), **Supp. XVII: 71–72**

"Formalist Criticism: Its Principles and Limits" (Burke), **I:** 282

Forman, Henry James, **Supp. XXIV:** 29, 30

Forman, Milos, **Supp. IV Part 1:** 236

"Form and Function of the Novel, The" (Goldbarth), **Supp. XII:** 183

"For Marse Chouchoute" (Chopin), **Retro. Supp. II:** 60

"For Mary Ann Youngren" (Bidart), **Supp. XV:** 29

"Format and Form" (A. Rich), **Supp. XVII:** 74

"Formation of a Separatist, I" (Howe), **Supp. IV Part 2:** 427

"Form Is Emptiness" (Baraka), **Supp. II Part 1:** 51

"For Mr. Death Who Stands with His Door Open" (Sexton), **Supp. II Part 2:** 695

Forms of Discovery (Winters), **Supp. II Part 2:** 812, 813

Forms of Fiction, The (Gardner and Dunlap), **Supp. VI:** 64

"For My Children" (Karr), **Supp. XI:** 254

"For My Daughter" (Kees), **Supp. XV:** 141, 147

"For My Daughter" (Olds), **Supp. X:** 206

"For My Former Wife, Watching TV, in the Past" (Kooser), **Supp. XIX:** 120

"For My Lover, Returning to His Wife" (Sexton), **Supp. II Part 2:** 688

Fornés, Maria Irene, **Supp. XXI:** 144; **Supp. XXIII:** 194, 200

"For Night to Come" (Stern), **Supp. IX:** 292

"For Once, Then, Something" (Frost), **II:** 156–157; **Retro. Supp. I:** 126, 133, 134

"For Peg: A Remnant of Song Still Distantly Sounding" (Carruth), **Supp. XVI:** 54

"For Pot-Boiling" (Hay), **Supp. XIV:** 128

"For Radicals" (Bourne), **I:** 221

"For Rainer Gerhardt" (Creeley), **Supp. IV Part 1:** 142–143, 147

Forrestal, James, **I:** 491; **Supp. I Part 2:** 489

Forrester, Fanny, **Supp. XVIII:** 13

Forrey, Carolyn, **Supp. XXIV:** 30

"For Richard After All" (Kingsolver), **Supp. VII:** 208

"For Sacco and Vanzetti" (Kingsolver), **Supp. VII:** 208

"Forsaken Brother, The"(J. Schoolcraft), **Supp. XXIII:** 235

"Forsaken Merman" (Arnold), **Supp. I Part 2:** 529

"For S.F.S. 1875–1962" (J. W. Miller), **Supp. XX: 166**

For Spacious Skies (Buck), **Supp. II Part 1:** 131

Forster, E. M., **I:** 292; **IV:** 201; **Retro. Supp. I:** 59, 232; **Supp. III Part 2:** 503; **Supp. V:** 258; **Supp. VIII:** 155, 171; **Supp. IX:** 128; **Supp. XII:** 79, 81; **Supp. XIV:** 159, 160, 163; **Supp. XV:** 62; **Supp. XVI:** 236; **Supp. XVIII:** 143; **Supp. XX: 229, 235, 239, 240; Supp. XXI:** 233

Forster, John, **II:** 315

Fort, Paul, **II:** 518, 528, 529; **Retro. Supp. I:** 55

"For the Ahkoond" (Bierce), **I:** 209

For the Body (Nelson), **Supp. XVIII:** 173

For the Century's End: Poems 1990–1999 (Haines), **Supp. XII: 211–213**

"For the Chinese New Year and Bill Berkson"(O'Hara), **Supp. XXIII:** 218

"For the Dedication of the New City Library, Boston" (Holmes), **Supp. I Part 1:** 308

"For the Fallen" (Levine), **Supp. V:** 188

For the Health of the Land: Previously Unpublished Essays and Other Writings (Leopold), **Supp. XIV:** 183

"For the Lady in the Black Raincoat Who Slept Through an Entire Poetry Reading" (Espaillat), **Supp. XXI:** 108

"For the Last Wolverine" (Dickey), **Supp. IV Part 1:** 182

"For the Lovers of the Absolute" (Simic), **Supp. VIII:** 278–279

"For the Man Cutting the Grass" (Oliver), **Supp. VII:** 235

"For the Marriage of Faustus and Helen" (H. Crane), **I:** 395–396, 399, 402; **Retro. Supp. II:** 78–79, 82

"For the Meeting of the National Sanitary Association, 1860" (Holmes), **Supp. I Part 1:** 307

For the New Intellectual (Rand), **Supp. IV Part 2:** 521, 526–527, 527, 532

"For the New Railway Station in Rome" (Wilbur), **Supp. III Part 2:** 554

"For the Night" (Kenyon), **Supp. VII:** 163

"For Theodore Roethke: 1908–1963" (Lowell), **II:** 554

"For the Poem *Patterson*" (W. C. Williams), **Retro. Supp. I:** 424

"For the Poets of Chile" (Levine), **Supp. V:** 188

"FOR THE REVOLUTIONARY OUTBURST BY BLACK PEOPLE" (Baraka), **Supp. II Part 1:** 55

"For the Sleepless" (Dunn), **Supp. XI:** 145

For the Time Being (Auden), **Supp. II Part 1:** 2, 17, 18

For the Time Being (Dillard), **Supp. VI:** 23, 27, 29, 32, **34–35**

"For the Twentieth Century" (Bidart), **Supp. XV:** 35

For the Union Dead (Lowell), **II:** 543, 550–551, 554, 555; **Retro. Supp. II:** 181, 182, 186, 189; **Supp. X:** 53

"For the Union Dead" (Lowell), **II:** 551; **Retro. Supp. II:** 189

"For the Walking Dead" (Komunyakaa), **Supp. XIII:** 121

"For the West" (Snyder), **Supp. VIII:** 299

"For the Word Is Flesh" (Kunitz), **Supp. III Part 1:** 262–264

"Fortress, The" (Glück), **Supp. V:** 82

"Fortress, The" (Sexton), **Supp. II Part 2:** 682

Fortress of Solitude, The (Lethem), **Supp. XVIII:** 135, 136, **145–148,** 150

"Fort Robinson" (Kooser), **Supp. XIX:** 120

"Fortunate Traveler" (Hull), **Supp. XXI:** 140

Fortune, T. Thomas, **Supp. II Part 1:** 159

Fortune's Bones: The Manumission Requiem (Nelson), **Supp. XVIII:** 171, 172–173, 182–183

Fortune's Daughter (Hoffman), **Supp. X:** 77, 85

"Fortune Spill, The" (Nelson), **Supp. XVIII:** 175

45 Mercy Street (Sexton), **Supp. II Part 2:** 694, 695, 697

Forty Poems Touching on Recent American History (Bly, ed.), **Supp. IV Part 1:** 61

42nd Parallel, The (Dos Passos), **I:** 482, 484–485

Forty Stories (Barthelme), **Supp. IV Part 1:** 47, 49, 53, 54

For Whom the Bell Tolls (Hemingway), **II:** 249, 254–255, 261; **III:** 18, 363; **Retro. Supp. I:** 115, 176–177, 178, **184,** 187; **Supp. XVII:** 229

For Whom the Southern Belle Tolls (Durang), **Supp. XXIV:** 113, 118, 125

Foscolo, Ugo, **II:** 543

Foss, Sam Walter, **Supp. II Part 1:** 197

"Fossils, The" (Kinnell), **Supp. III Part 1:** 244

Foster, Edward, **Supp. IV Part 2:** 431, 434; **Supp. XVI:** 281, 293; **Supp. XXI:** 33

Foster, Edward Halsey, **Supp. XII:** 120, 129, 130, 135; **Supp. XVIII:** 265, 268

Foster, Emily, **II:** 309

Foster, Frances Smith, **Supp. XX: 287**

Foster, Hannah, **Supp. XV:** 234

Foster, John Wilson, **Supp. XIII:** 32–33

Foster, Phil, **Supp. IV Part 2:** 574

Foster, Richard, **Supp. XV:** 269

Foster, Stephen, **Supp. I Part 1:** 100–101; **Supp. I Part 2:** 699

Foucault, Michel, **Supp. VIII:** 5; **Supp. XII:** 98; **Supp. XV:** 344; **Supp. XVI:** 285

"Founder, The" (Stern), **Supp. IX:** 297

Founding of Harvard College, The (Morison), **Supp. I Part 2:** 485

"Fountain, The" (Bryant), **Supp. I Part 1:** 157, 165, 166, 168

Fountain, The (O'Neill), **III:** 391

Fountain and Other Poems, The (Bryant), **Supp. I Part 1:** 157

Fountainhead, The (film), **Supp. IV Part 2:** 524

Fountainhead, The (Rand), **Supp. IV Part 2:** 517, 521–523, 525, 531; **Supp. XXIV:** 281

Fountainhead, The: A Fiftieth Anniversary Celebration (Cox), **Supp. IV Part 2:** 523

"Fountain Piece" (Swenson), **Supp. IV Part 2:** 641

4-H Club (Shepard), **Supp. III Part 2:** 439

"Four Ages of Man, The" (Bradstreet), **Supp. I Part 1:** 111, 115

Four American Indian Literary Masters (Velie), **Supp. IV Part 2:** 486

"Four Angers"(Hadas), **Supp. XXIII:** 115

"Four Beasts in One; the Homo Cameleopard" (Poe), **III:** 425

Four Black Revolutionary Plays (Baraka), **Supp. II Part 1:** 45; **Supp. VIII:** 330

"Four Brothers" (Di Piero), **Supp. XIX:** 37

"Four Brothers, The" (Sandburg), **III:** 585

"Four Dancers at an Irish Wedding" (Gallagher), **Supp. XXIV:** 168, 170

Four Days (screenplay, P. Benedict), **Supp. XXIII:** 35

Four Dogs and a Bone and the Wild Goose (Shanley), **Supp. XIV:** 316, **328–329**

"Four Evangelists, The" (Komunyakaa), **Supp. XIII:** 131

"Four for Sir John Davies" (Roethke), **III:** 540, 541

"Four Girls, The" (Alvarez), **Supp. VII:** 7

"Four Horse Songs" (Harjo), **Supp. XII:** 220

"400-Meter Free Style" (Kumin), **Supp. IV Part 2:** 442

"400-Pound CEO, The" (Saunders), **Supp. XIX:** 225

Fourier, Charles, **II:** 342

"Four in a Family" (Rukeyser), **Supp. VI:** 272

Four in Hand: A Quartet of Novels (Warner), **Supp. VIII:** 164

"Four Lakes' Days" (Eberhart), **I:** 525

"Four Mad Studies" (Di Piero), **Supp. XIX:** 37

"Four Meetings" (James), **II:** 327

Four Million, The (O. Henry), **Supp. II Part 1:** 394, 408

"Four Monarchyes" (Bradstreet), **Supp. I Part 1:** 105, 106, 116

"Four Mountain Wolves" (Silko), **Supp. IV Part 2:** 561

Four of a Kind (Marquand), **III:** 54, 55

"Four of the Horsemen (Hypertense and Stroke, Coronary Occlusion and Cerebral Insult)" (Karr), **Supp. XI:** 250

"Four Poems" (Bishop), **Supp. I Part 1:** 92

"Four Poems at the End of Summer"(Hadas), **Supp. XXIII:** 117

"Four Preludes on Playthings of the Wind" (Sandburg), **III:** 586

Four Quartets (T. S. Eliot), **I:** 570, 576, 580–582, 585, 587; **II:** 537; **III:** 539; **Retro. Supp. I:** 66, 67; **Supp. II Part 1:** 1; **Supp. IV Part 1:** 284; **Supp. V:** 343, 344; **Supp. VIII:** 182, 195; **Supp. XIII:** 344; **Supp. XIV:** 167; **Supp. XV:** 216, 260, 266

Four Saints in Three Acts (Stein), **IV:** 30, 31, 33, 43, 44–45

"Four Seasons" (Bradstreet), **Supp. I Part 1:** 112–113

Four Seasons of Success, The (Schulberg), **Supp. XVIII:** 254

"Four Sides of One Story" (Updike), **Retro. Supp. I:** 328

"Four Skinny Trees" (Cisneros), **Supp. VII:** 64

"14: In A Dark Wood: Wood Thrushes" (Oliver), **Supp. VII:** 244

"14 Men Stage Head Winter 1624/ 25" (Olson), **Supp. II Part 2:** 574

14 Stories (Dixon), **Supp. XII:** 141, **145–147**

Fourteen Hundred Thousand (Shepard), **Supp. III Part 2:** 439

Fourteen Sisters of Emilio Montez O'Brien, The (Hijuelos), **Supp. VIII: 82–85**

Fourteen Stories (Buck), **Supp. II Part 1:** 126

"Fourteenth Ward, The" (H. Miller), **III:** 175

Fourth Book of Peace, The (Kingston), **Supp. V:** 173

"Fourth Down" (Marquand), **III:** 56

Fourth Group of Verse, A (Reznikoff), **Supp. XIV:** 282, 284

"Fourth of July in Maine" (Lowell), **II:** 535, 552–553

Fourth Wall, The (Gurney), **Supp. V:** 109–110

Fowler, Douglas, **Supp. IV Part 1:** 226, 227

Fowler, Gene, **Supp. VIII:** 290

Fowler, Henry Watson, **Supp. I Part 2:** 660

Fowler, Karen Joy, **Supp. XXII:** 49

Fowler, Singrid, **Supp. VIII:** 249, 258

Fowler, Virginia C., **Supp. VIII:** 224

Fox, Alan, **Supp. XIII:** 120

Fox, Dixon Ryan, **I:** 337

Fox, Joe, **Supp. IX:** 259, 261

Fox, John, **Supp. XIII:** 166; **Supp. XXII:** 36

Fox, Linda C., **Supp. XIII:** 217–218

Fox, Paula, **Supp. XX: 91**

Fox, Ruth, **Supp. I Part 2:** 619

"Fox, The" (Levine), **Supp. V:** 181, 189

Fox-Genovese, Elizabeth, **Supp. IV Part 1:** 286; **Supp. XXII:** 190, 192, 200

Fox in Socks (Geisel), **Supp. XVI:** 108, 112

"Fox Night" (Jarman), **Supp. XVII:** 120

Fox of Peapack, The (White), **Supp. I Part 2:** 676, 677–678

"Fox of Peapack, The" (White), **Supp. I Part 2:** 677

"Fox Point Health Clinic, 1974" (Halliday), **Supp. XIX:** 89, 93

Fox's Earth (Siddons), **Supp. XXII:** 239

Foye, Raymond, **Supp. XIV:** 150

Fradkin, Lori, **Supp. XIX:** 52

Fraenkel, Michael, **III:** 178, 183

"Fragging" (Komunyakaa), **Supp. XIII:** 123

Fragile Beauty, A: John Nichols' Milagro Country: Text and Photographs from His Life and Work (Nichols), **Supp. XIII:** 268

"Fragility" (Shields), **Supp. VII:** 318

"Fragment" (Ashbery), **Supp. III Part 1:** 11, 13, 14, 19, 20

"Fragment" (Lowell), **II:** 516

"Fragment" (Ortiz), **Supp. IV Part 2:** 507

"Fragment of a Meditation" (Tate), **IV:** 129

"Fragment of an Agon" (Eliot), **I:** 579–580

"Fragment of a Prologue" (Eliot), **I:** 579–580

"Fragment of New York, 1929" (Eberhart), **I:** 536–537

"Fragments" (Emerson), **II:** 19

"Fragments for Fall" (Salinas), **Supp. XIII:** 320–321

"Fragments of a Hologram Rose" (W. Gibson), **Supp. XVI:** 122, 123, 128

"Fragments of a Liquidation" (Howe), **Supp. IV Part 2:** 426

"Fragments: On Dentistry" (Monson), **Supp. XXIV:** 236

Fragonard, Jean Honoré, **III:** 275; **IV:** 79

Fraiman, Susan, **Supp. IV Part 1:** 324

"Frame for Poetry, A" (W. J. Smith), **Supp. XIII:** 333

France, Anatole, **IV:** 444; **Supp. I Part 2:** 631; **Supp. XIV:** 79

France and England in North America (Parkman), **Supp. II Part 2:** 596, 600–605, 607, 613–614

Franchere, Hoyt C., **II:** 131

Franchiser, The (Elkin), **Supp. VI:** 51–52, 58

Franciosi, Robert, **Supp. XIV:** 283

Francis, Lee, **Supp. IV Part 2:** 499

Francis, Richard, **Supp. XV:** 121

Francis, Robert, **Supp. IX:** 75–92

Francis of Assisi, Saint, **III:** 543; **IV:** 69, 375, 410; **Supp. I Part 2:** 394, 397, 441, 442, 443

Franco, Francisco, **II:** 261

Franco, Harry (pseudonym). *See* Briggs, Charles Frederick

Franconia (Fraser), **Retro. Supp. I:** 136

"Franconia" tales (Abbott), **Supp. I Part 1:** 38

Frank, Anne, **Supp. X:** 149; **Supp. XVII:** 39

Frank, Frederick S., **Retro. Supp. II:** 273

Frank, James M., **Supp. XIV:** 1

Frank, Jerome, **Supp. I Part 2:** 645

Frank, Joseph, **II:** 587

Frank, Mary, **Supp. X:** 213

Frank, Robert, **Supp. XI:** 295; **Supp. XII:** 127; **Supp. XIV:** 150

Frank, Sheldon, **Supp. XXII:** 210

Frank, Waldo, **I:** 106, 109, 117, 229, 236, 245, 259, 400; **Retro. Supp. II:** 77, 79, 83; **Supp. IX:** 308, 309, 311, 320; **Supp. XV:** 298; **Supp. XX:** 67–82

Frank, W. L., Jr., **Supp. XVIII:** 77

Frankel, Charles, **III:** 291

Frankel, Haskel, **Supp. I Part 2:** 448

Frankenberg, Lloyd, **I:** 436, 437, 445, 446; **III:** 194

Frankenheimer, John, **Supp. XI:** 343

Frankenstein (film), **Supp. IV Part 1:** 104; **Supp. XVII:** 57

Frankenstein (Gardner), **Supp. VI:** 72

Frankenstein (Shelley), **Supp. XII:** 79

Frankfurter, Felix, **I:** 489

"Frankie" (Keillor), **Supp. XVI:** 167

Frankie and Johnny (film), **Supp. XIII:** 206

Frankie and Johnny in the Clair de Lune (McNally), **Supp. XIII: 200,** 201

Franklin, Benjamin, **II:** 6, 8, 92, **101–125,** 127, 295, 296, 302, 306; **III:** 74, 90; **IV:** 73, 193; **Supp. I Part 1:** 306; **Supp. I Part 2:** 411, 503, 504, 506, 507, 510, 516, 518, 522, 524, 579, 639; **Supp. VIII:** 202, 205; **Supp. XIII:** 150; **Supp. XIV:** 306; **Supp. XVIII:** 12; **Supp. XX: 284; Supp. XXIV:** 224

Franklin, Cynthia, **Supp. IV Part 1:** 332

Franklin, Ruth, **Supp. XVI:** 160

Franklin, R. W., **Retro. Supp. I:** 29, 41, 43, 47

Franklin, Sarah, **II:** 122

Franklin, Temple, **II:** 122

Franklin, Walt, **Supp. XXIII:** 54

Franklin, Wayne, **Supp. XXII:** 205

Franklin, William, **II:** 122; **Supp. I Part 2:** 504

Franklin Evans (Whitman), **Retro. Supp. I:** 393

"Frank O'Connor and *The New Yorker*" (Maxwell), **Supp. VIII:** 172

Frank O'Hara: Poet Among Painters (Perloff), **Supp. XXIII:** 210

Franks, Lucinda, **Supp. XIII:** 12

"Frank Sinatra Has a Cold" (Talese), **Supp. XVII:** 203

"Frank Stanford of the Mulberry Family: An Arkansas Epilogue" (Wright), **Supp. XV:** 339–340

"Franny" (Salinger), **III:** 564, 565–566

Franny and Zooey (Salinger), **III:** 552, 564–567; **IV:** 216; **Supp. XIII:** 263

Franscell, Ron, **Supp. XXII:** 206, 216

Franzen, Jonathan, **Retro. Supp. II:** 279; **Supp. XIX:** 54; **Supp. XX: 83–97; Supp. XXII:** 255; **Supp. XXIV:** 131

Fraser, G. S., **Supp. XII:** 128; **Supp. XIV:** 162

Fraser, Joe, **III:** 46

Fraser, Marjorie Frost, **Retro. Supp. I:** 136

Frayn, Michael, **Supp. IV Part 2:** 582

Frazee, E. S., **Supp. I Part 2:** 381

Frazee, Esther Catherine. *See* Lindsay, Mrs. Vachel Thomas (Esther Catherine Frazee)

Frazer, Sir James G., **I:** 135; **II:** 204; **III:** 6–7; **IV:** 70; **Retro. Supp. I:** 80; **Supp. I Part 1:** 18; **Supp. I Part 2:** 541; **Supp. XX:** 117

Frazier, Ian, **Supp. VIII:** 272

Frazier, Kathleen, **Supp. XXI:** 22

"Freak Power in the Rockies" (Thompson), **Supp. XXIV:** 286–287, 292, 293

"Freak Show, The" (Sexton), **Supp. II Part 2:** 695

Freaks: Myths and Images of the Secret Self (Fiedler), **Supp. XIII:** 106, 107

Freckles (film), **Supp. XX:** 223

Freckles (Stratton-Porter), **Supp. XX: 211, 218, 218–219, 222**

Freddy's Book (Gardner), **Supp. VI:** 72

Frederic, Harold, **I:** 409; **II: 126–149,** 175, 276, 289; **Retro. Supp. I:** 325; **Supp. XXIV:** 30

"Frederick Douglass" (Dunbar), **Supp. II Part 1:** 197, 199

"Frederick Douglass" (Hayden), **Supp. II Part 1:** 363

Frederick Douglass: Slave, Fighter, Freeman (Bontemps), **Supp. XXII:** 13

Frederick the Great, **II:** 103; **Supp. I Part 2:** 433

Fredrickson, George M., **Supp. I Part 2:** 589

"Free" (O'Hara), **III:** 369

Free, and Other Stories (Dreiser), **Retro. Supp. II:** 104

Free Agents (Apple), **Supp. XVII:** 5–6

Free Air (Lewis), **II:** 441

Freedman, Monroe H., **Supp. VIII:** 127

Freedman, Richard, **Supp. V:** 244

Freedom (Franzen), **Supp. XXII:** 255

"Freedom" (Larsen), **Supp. XVIII:** 124

"Freedom" (White), **Supp. I Part 2:** 659

"Freedom, New Hampshire" (Kinnell), **Supp. III Part 1:** 238, 239, 251

"Freedom and Discipline" (Carruth), **Supp. XVI:** 50

Freedom Business, The (Nelson), **Supp. XVIII: 186**

Freedom Is the Right to Choose: An Inquiry into the Battle for the American Future (MacLeish), **III:** 3

"Freedom's a Hard-Bought Thing" (Benét), **Supp. XI:** 47, 48

"Freedom's Plow" (Hughes), **Supp. I Part 1:** 346

Free Enterprise (Cliff), **Supp. XXII:** 66–67, **77–78**

"Free Everything" (July), **Supp. XXIV:** 210

"Free Fantasia: Tiger Flowers" (Hayden), **Supp. II Part 1:** 363, 366

Freeing of the Dust, The (Levertov), **Supp. III Part 1:** 281–282

"Free Lance, The" (Mencken), **III:** 104, 105

Free-Lance Pallbearers, The (Reed), **Supp. X:** 240, **242–243,** 244

Freeland (Lane), **Supp. XXII:** 297

Free Life, A (Jin), **Supp. XVIII: 101–102**

Freeloaders, The (Lacy), **Supp. XV:** 204

"Free Man" (Hughes), **Supp. I Part 1:** 333

Freeman, Chris, **Supp. XIV:** 157, 159

Freeman, Douglas Southall, **Supp. I Part 2:** 486, 493

Freeman, John, **Supp. XVIII:** 90

Freeman, Joseph, **II:** 26; **Supp. I Part 2:** 610; **Supp. XXII:** 274, 277

Freeman, Mary E. Wilkins, **II:** 401; **Retro. Supp. II:** 51, 136, 138; **Supp. IX:** 79

Freeman, Morgan, **Supp. XII:** 317

Freeman, Suzanne, **Supp. X:** 83

Free Man, The (Richter), **Supp. XVIII:** 215

"Free Man's Worship, A" (Russell), **Supp. I Part 2:** 522

Freewheelin' Bob Dylan, The (album, Dylan), **Supp. XVIII:** 20, 24, 29

Free Will & Wanton Lust (Silver), **Supp. XXIV:** 265, **267–268,** 270

Freilicher, Jane, **Supp. XV:** 178; **Supp. XXIII:** 209, 210, 212, 217

Freinman, Dorothy, **Supp. IX:** 94

Frémont, John Charles, **Supp. I Part 2:** 486

Fremont-Smith, Eliot, **Supp. XIII:** 263

Fremstad, Olive, **I:** 319; **Retro. Supp. I:** 10

French, Warren, **Supp. XII:** 118–119

French Chef, The (television program), **Supp. XVII:** 89

French Connection, The (film), **Supp. V:** 226

"French Informal Report, The"(Kenny), **Supp. XXIII:** 152

French Leave (X. J. Kennedy), **Supp. XV:** 165

Frenchman Must Die, A (Boyle), **Supp. XXIV:** 62

French Poets and Novelists (James), **II:** 336; **Retro. Supp. I:** 220

"French Scarecrow, The" (Maxwell), **Supp. VIII:** 169, 170

French Ways and Their Meaning (Wharton), **IV:** 319; **Retro. Supp. I:** 378

Freneau, Eleanor Forman (Mrs. Philip Freneau), **Supp. II Part 1:** 266

Freneau, Philip M., **I:** 335; **II:** 295; **Supp. I Part 1:** 124, 125, 127, 145; **Supp. II Part 1:** 65, **253–277**

Frenzy (Everett), **Supp. XVIII: 59–60**

Frescoes for Mr. Rockefeller's City (MacLeish), **III:** 14–15

"Fresh Air" (Koch), **Supp. XV:** 181, 185

Fresh Air Fiend: Travel Writings, 1985–2000 (Theroux), **Supp. VIII:** 325

Fresh Brats (X. J. Kennedy), **Supp. XV:** 163

"Freshman" (Sanders), **Supp. XVI:** 277

Freud, Sigmund, **I:** 55, 58, 59, 66, 67, 135, 241, 242, 244, 247, 248, 283; **II:** 27, 370, 546–547; **III:** 134, 390, 400, 418, 488; **IV:** 7, 70, 138, 295; **Retro. Supp. I:** 80, 176, 253; **Retro. Supp. II:** 104; **Supp. I Part 1:** 13, 43, 253, 254, 259, 260, 265, 270, 315; **Supp. I Part 2:** 493, 527, 616, 643, 647, 649; **Supp. IV Part 2:** 450; **Supp. VIII:** 103, 196; **Supp. IX:** 102, 155, 161, 308; **Supp. X:** 193, 194; **Supp. XII:** 14–15; **Supp. XIII:** 75; **Supp. XIV:** 83; **Supp. XV:** 219; **Supp. XVI:** 157–158, 161, 292; **Supp. XXII:** 165, 198

"Freud and Literature" (Trilling), **Supp. III Part 2:** 502–503

Freudian Psychology and Veblen's Social Theory, The (Schneider), **Supp. I Part 2:** 650

Freudian Wish and Its Place in Ethics, The (Holt), **I:** 59

"Freud's Room" (Ozick), **Supp. V:** 268

Freud: The Mind of the Moralist (Sontag and Rieff), **Supp. III Part 2:** 455

"Freud: Within and Beyond Culture" (Trilling), **Supp. III Part 2:** 508

Frey, Charles, **Supp. XXII:** 301

Frey, Hillary, **Supp. XIX:** 55; **Supp. XXII:** 53

Frey, James, **Supp. XXII:** 95; **Supp. XXIII:** 109; **Supp. XXIV:** 230, 236

"Friday Morning Trial of Mrs. Solano, The" (Ríos), **Supp. IV Part 2:** 538, 548

Friebert, Stuart, **Supp. XIX:** 276

Frieburger, William, **Supp. XIII:** 239

Friede, Donald, **Supp. XVII:** 85, 86, 87, 90

Friedenberg, Edgar Z., **Supp. VIII:** 240

Friedman, Bruce Jay, **I:** 161; **Supp. IV Part 1:** 379

Friedman, Lawrence S., **Supp. V:** 273

Friedman, Milton, **Supp. I Part 2:** 648

Friedman, Norman, **I:** 431–432, 435, 439

Friedman, Stan, **Supp. XII:** 186

Friedmann, Georges, **Supp. I Part 2:** 645

"Fried Sausage" (Simic), **Supp. VIII:** 270

Friend, Julius, **Retro. Supp. I:** 80

Friend, The (Coleridge), **II:** 10

"Friend Husband's Latest" (Sayre), **Retro. Supp. I:** 104

"Friendly Debate between a Conformist and a Non-Conformist, A" (Wild), **IV:** 155

"Friendly Neighbor" (Keillor), **Supp. XVI:** 172

Friend of the Earth, A (Boyle), **Supp. VIII:** 12, 16; **Supp. XX:** 29–30

"Friend of the Fourth Decade, The" (Merrill), **Supp. III Part 1:** 327

"Friends" (Beattie), **Supp. V:** 23, 27

"Friends" (Paley), **Supp. VI:** 219, 226

"Friends" (Sexton), **Supp. II Part 2:** 693

Friend's Delight, The (Bierce), **I:** 195

"Friends from Philadelphia" (Updike), **Retro. Supp. I:** 319

"Friendship" (Emerson), **Supp. II Part 1:** 290

Friends: More Will and Magna Stories (Dixon), **Supp. XII:** 148, 149

"Friends of Heraclitus, The" (Simic), **Supp. VIII:** 284

"Friends of Kafka, The" (Singer), **Retro. Supp. II:** 308

"Friends of the Family, The" (McCarthy), **II:** 566

"Friend to Alexander, A" (Thurber), **Supp. I Part 2:** 616

"Frigate Pelican, The" (Moore), **III:** 208, 210–211, 215

"Frill, The" (Buck), **Supp. XIV:** 274

"Fringe, The" (Bass), **Supp. XVI:** 19

Frobenius, Leo, **III:** 475; **Supp. III Part 2:** 620

Froebel, Friedrich, **Supp. XIV:** 52–53

Frog (Dixon), **Supp. XII:** 151

"Frog Dances" (Dixon), **Supp. XII:** 151

"Frog Pond, The" (Kinnell), **Supp. III Part 1:** 254

"Frogs" (Nelson), **Supp. XVIII:** 176

"Frog Takes a Swim" (Dixon), **Supp. XII:** 152

Frohock, W. M., **I:** 34, 42

Frolic of His Own, A (Gaddis), **Supp. IV Part 1:** 279, 291, 292–294; **Supp. XX:** 91

"From a Mournful Village" (Jewett), **Retro. Supp. II:** 146

"From an Alabama Farm" (Nelson), **Supp. XVIII:** 182

"From an Old House in America" (Rich), **Supp. I Part 2:** 551, 565–567

From Another World (Untermeyer), **Supp. XV:** 293, 303, 310–311, 313

"From a Roadside Motel" (F. Wright), **Supp. XVII:** 245

"From a Survivor" (Rich), **Supp. I Part 2:** 563

From A to Z (musical review; Allen), **Supp. XV:** 3, 13

From a Work in Progress (Notley), **Supp. XXII:** 232

"From a Work in Progress" (Notley), **Supp. XXII:** 232

From a Writer's Notebook (Brooks), **I:** 254

From Bauhaus to Our House (Wolfe), **Supp. III Part 2:** 580, 581, 584

From Bondage (H. Roth), **Supp. IX:** 236, **238–240**

"From *Chants* to *Borders* to *Communion*" *(Fox), Supp. XIII:* 217, 217–218

"From Chicago" (Anderson), **I:** 108–109

From Colony to Nation: Women Activists and the Gendering of Politics in Belize, 1912–1982 (Macpherson), **Supp. XXIII:** 84

From Death to Morning (Wolfe), **IV:** 450, 456, 458

"From Dick to Lethem: The Dickian Legacy, Postmodernism, and Avant-Pop in Jonathan Lethem's *Amnesia Moon*" *(Rossi), Supp. XVIII:* 137, 138–139

"From Discord, a Wife Makes a Nice New Life—Too Nice" (Linfield), **Supp. XVII:** 177

From Down to the Village (Budbill), **Supp. XIX: 6–7**

"From Feathers to Iron" (Kunitz), **Supp. III Part 1:** 261

"From Fifth Avenue Up" (Barnes), **Supp. III Part 1:** 33, 44

"From Gorbunov and Gorchakov" (Brodsky), **Supp. VIII:** 26

"From Grand Canyon to Burbank" (H. Miller), **III:** 186

"From Hell to Breakfast", **Supp. IX:** 326–327

From Here to Eternity (film), **Supp. XI:** 221

From Here to Eternity (J. Jones), **I:** 477; **Supp. XI:** 215, 216, 217, 218, **219–221**, 223, 224, 226, 229, 230, 231, 232, 234; **Supp. XIX:** 248; **Supp. XX:** 248; **Supp. XXII:** 140

From Here to Eternity (miniseries), **Supp. XI:** 234

From Jordan's Delight (Blackmur), **Supp. II Part 1:** 91

"From Lumaghi Mine" (Wrigley), **Supp. XVIII:** 295

Fromm, Erich, **I:** 58; **Supp. VIII:** 196

From Morn to Midnight (Kaiser), **I:** 479

"From Native Son to Invisible Man" (Locke), **Supp. IX:** 306

"From Pico, the Women: A Life" (Creeley), **Supp. IV Part 1:** 149

From Plotzk to Boston (Antin), **Supp. XX:** 2

From Ritual to Romance (Weston), **II:** 540; **III:** 12; **Supp. I Part 2:** 439

From Room to Room (Kenyon), **Supp. VII:** 163–165, 166, 167

"From Room to Room" (Kenyon), **Supp. VII:** 159, 163–165

From Sand Creek: Rising in this Heart Which Is Our America (Ortiz), **Supp. IV Part 2:** 512–513

"From Sea Cliff, March" (Swenson), **Supp. IV Part 2:** 649

From Stone Orchard: A Collection of Memories (Findley), **Supp. XX:** 57

"From the Antigone" (Yeats), **III:** 459

From the Ashes: Voices of Watts (Schulberg, ed.), **Supp. XVIII:** 254

From the Barrio: A Chicano Anthology (Salinas and Faderman, eds.), **Supp. XIII:** 313

From the Beginning (Notley), **Supp. XXII:** 226, 235–236

From the Briarpatch File: On Context, Procedure, and American Identity (Murray), **Supp. XIX:** 161

"From the Childhood of Jesus" (Pinsky), **Supp. VI:** 244–245, 247

"From the Corpse Woodpiles, From the Ashes" (Hayden), **Supp. II Part 1:** 370

"From the Country to the City" (Bishop), **Supp. I Part 1:** 85, 86

"From the Cupola" (Merrill), **Supp. III Part 1:** 324–325, 331

"From the Dark Side of the Earth" (Oates), **Supp. II Part 2:** 510

"From the Diary of a New York Lady" (Parker), **Supp. IX:** 201

"From the Diary of One Not Born" (Singer), **IV:** 9

"From the Dreams" (Notley), **Supp. XXII:** 224

"From the East, Light" (Carver), **Supp. III Part 1:** 138

From the First Nine: Poems 1946–1976 (Merrill), **Supp. III Part 1:** 336

"From the Flats" (Lanier), **Supp. I Part 1:** 364

From the Flower Courtyard (Everwine), **Supp. XV:** 75

From the Heart of Europe (Matthiessen), **III:** 310

From the Meadow: Selected and New Poems (Everwine), **Supp. XV:** 75, **88–89**

"From the Memoirs of a Private Detective" (Hammett), **Supp. IV Part 1:** 343

"From the Nursery" (Kenyon), **Supp. VII:** 171

"From the Poets in the Kitchen" (Marshall), **Supp. XI:** 277

From the Terrace (O'Hara), **III:** 362

"From the Thirties: Tillie Olsen and the Radical Tradition" (Rosenfelt), **Supp. XIII:** 296, 304

"From Trollope's Journal" (Bishop), **Retro. Supp. II:** 47

"Front, A" (Jarrell), **II:** 374

Front, The (film), **Supp. I Part 1:** 295

"Front and the Back Parts of the House, The" (Maxwell), **Supp. VIII:** 169

Frontier Eden (Bigelow), **Supp. X:** 227

"Frontiers of Culture" (Locke), **Supp. XIV:** 213

"Front Lines" (Snyder), **Supp. VIII:** 301

Front Runner, The (P. N. Warren), **Supp. XX: 259, 262–264**

Frost, A. B., **Retro. Supp. II:** 72

Frost, Carol, **Supp. XV: 91–109**

Frost, Isabelle Moodie, **II:** 150, 151

Frost, Jeanie, **II:** 151

Frost, Richard, **Supp. XV:** 92

Frost, Robert, **I:** 26, 27, 60, 63, 64, 171, 229, 303, 326, 418; **II:** 55, 58, **150–172**, 276, 289, 388, 391, 471, 523, 527, 529, 535; **III:** 5, 23, 67, 269, 271, 272, 275, 287, 453, 510, 523, 536, 575, 581, 591; **IV:** 140, 190, 415; **Retro. Supp. I:** 67, **121–144**, 276, 287, 292, 298, 299, 311, 413; **Retro. Supp. II:** 40, 47, 50, 146, 178, 181; **Supp. I Part 1:** 80, 242, 263, 264; **Supp. I Part 2:** 387, 461, 699; **Supp. II Part 1:** 4, 19, 26, 103; **Supp. III Part 1:** 63, 74–75, 239, 253; **Supp. III Part 2:** 546, 592, 593; **Supp. IV Part 1:** 15; **Supp. IV Part 2:** 439, 445, 447, 448, 599, 601; **Supp. VIII:** 20, 30, 32, 98, 100, 104, 259, 292; **Supp. IX:** 41, 42, 75, 76, 80, 87, 90, 266, 308; **Supp. X:** 64, 65, 66, 74, 120, 172; **Supp. XI:** 43, 123, 150, 153, 312; **Supp. XII:** 130, 241, 303, 307; **Supp. XIII:** 143, 147, 334–335; **Supp. XIV:** 42, 122, 222, 229; **Supp. XV:** 21, 51, 65, 96, 212, 215, 250, 256, 293, 296, 299, 301, 302, 306, 348; **Supp. XVII:** 36, 110, 115–116; **Supp. XVIII:** 298, 300; **Supp. XIX:** 1, 123; **Supp. XX: 69, 199; Supp. XXI:** 19, 28, 51, 99, 104, 107, 205; **Supp. XXII:** 206; **Supp. XXIII:** 79, 145; **Supp. XXIV:** 159

Frost, William Prescott, **II:** 150–151

"Frost: A Dissenting Opinion" (Cowley), **Supp. II Part 1:** 143

Frost: A Time to Talk (Francis), **Supp. IX:** 76, **85–86**

"Frost at Midnight" (Coleridge), **Supp. X:** 71

"Frost Flowers" (Kenyon), **Supp. VII:** 168

"Frost: He Is Sometimes a Poet and Sometimes a Stump-Speaker" (News-Week), **Retro. Supp. I:** 137

Frothingham, Nathaniel, **I:** 3

Frothingham, Octavius B., **IV:** 173

"Frozen City, The" (Nemerov), **III:** 270

"Frozen Fields, The" (Bowles), **Supp. IV Part 1:** 80

"Fructifying a Cycle: Homage to Alan Ansen"(Hadas), **Supp. XXIII:** 123

"Fruit Garden Path, The" (Lowell), **II:** 516

"Fruit of the Flower" (Cullen), **Supp. IV Part 1:** 167

Fruit of the Tree, The (Wharton), **IV:** 314–315; **Retro. Supp. I:** 367, **370–371**, 373

"Fruit of Travel Long Ago" (Melville), **III:** 93

Fruits and Vegetables (Jong), **Supp. V:** 113, 115, 117, 118, 119

"Fruits of the Sea, The" (Di Piero), **Supp. XIX:** 47

Frumkes, Lewis Burke, **Supp. XII:** 335–336

Fry, Christopher, **Supp. I Part 1:** 270

Fry, Roger, **Supp. XIV:** 336

Fry, Stephen M., **Supp. XIX:** 159

Frye, Joanne, **Supp. XIII:** 292, 296, 298, 302

Frye, Northrop, **Supp. I Part 2:** 530; **Supp. II Part 1:** 101; **Supp. X:** 80; **Supp. XIII:** 19; **Supp. XIV:** 11, 15; **Supp. XVI:** 149, 156; **Supp. XX: 50;**

Supp. XXIII: 42
Fryer, Judith, **Retro. Supp. I:** 379
F. Scott Fitzgerald: A Critical Portrait (Piper), **Supp. IX:** 65
"F. S. F., 1896–1996, R.I.P." (Doctorow), **Retro. Supp. I:** 97
Fuchs, Daniel, **Supp. XIII:** 106
Fuchs, Miriam, **Supp. IV Part 1:** 284
Fuehrer Bunker, The (Snodgrass), **Supp. VI:** 314, 315–317, 319–321
Fuel (Nye), **Supp. XIII:** 277, **282–284**
"Fuel" (Nye), **Supp. XIII:** 283
Fuertes, Gloria, **Supp. V:** 178
Fugard, Athol, **Supp. VIII:** 330; **Supp. XIII:** 205
Fugitive Group, The (Cowan), **IV:** 120
Fugitive Kind, The (T. Williams), **IV:** 381, 383
Fugitives, The (the group), **IV:** 122, 124, 125, 131, 237, 238
Fugitives, The: A Critical Account (Bradbury), **IV:** 130
"Fugitive Slave Law, The" (Emerson), **II:** 13
Fugitive's Return (Glaspell), **Supp. III Part 1:** 182–184
Fuller, B. A. G., **III:** 605
Fuller, Edmund, **Supp. XXII:** 211, 212
Fuller, Hiram, **Supp. XVIII:** 12,14
Fuller, Jesse "Lonecat", **Supp. XV:** 147
Fuller, Margaret, **I:** 261; **II:** 7, 276; **IV:** 172; **Retro. Supp. I:** 155–156, 163; **Retro. Supp. II:** 46; **Supp. I Part 2:** 524; **Supp. II Part 1:** 279–306; **Supp. IX:** 37; **Supp. XVIII:** 3, 11, 12, 16
Fuller, Thomas, **II:** 111, 112
Fullerton, Morton, **Supp. XX:** 231
Fullerton Street (Wilson), **Supp. VIII:** 331
"Full Fathom Five" (Plath), **Supp. I Part 2:** 538
Full Measure: Modern Short Stories on Aging (D. Sennett, ed.), **Supp. XVI:** 37
Full Monty, The (musical, McNally), **Supp. XIII:** 207
"Full Moon" (Hayden), **Supp. II Part 1:** 370
Full Moon and Other Plays (Price), **Supp. VI:** 266
"Full Moon and You're Not Here" (Cisneros), **Supp. VII:** 71–72
"Full Moon: New Guinea" (Shapiro), **Supp. II Part 2:** 707
"Fullness of Life, The" (Wharton), **Retro. Supp. I:** 363
Full of Life (Fante), **Supp. XI:** 160
Full of Life (film), **Supp. XI:** 170
Full of Lust and Good Usage (Dunn), **Supp. XI:** 145–147
"Full Summer" (Olds), **Supp. X:** 212
Fulton, Ben, **Supp. XXII:** 207
Fulton, Robert, **Supp. I Part 2:** 519; **Supp. II Part 1:** 73
Fun and Games (Major), **Supp. XXII:** 180
"Functional Poem" (Halliday), **Supp. XIX:** 85
Function of Criticism, The (Winters), **Supp. II Part 2:** 812, 813

"Fundamentalism" (Tate), **IV:** 125
"Fundamental Project of Technology, The" (Kinnell), **Supp. III Part 1:** 253
"Funeral of Bobò, The" (Brodsky), **Supp. VIII:** 27, 28
"Funnel" (Sexton), **Supp. II Part 2:** 675
"Furious Seasons, The" (Carver), **Supp. III Part 1:** 137
Furious Seasons and Other Stories (Carver), **Supp. III Part 1:** 142, 143, 146
"Furious Versions" (L.-Y. Lee), **Supp. XV:** 215–217, 218, 220
"Furnished Room, The" (Hayden), **Supp. II Part 1:** 386–387, 394, 397, 399, 406, 408
"Furor Scribendi" (O. Butler), **Supp. XIII:** 70
Furors Die (Hoffman), **Supp. XVIII:** 80–81
Fur Person, The (Sarton), **Supp. VIII:** 264–265
Further Adventures with You (Wright), **Supp. XV:** 339, 342, 343–345
Further Fables for Our Time (Thurber), **Supp. I Part 2:** 612
"Further in Summer than the Birds" (Dickinson), **I:** 471
Further Poems of Emily Dickinson (Bianchi and Hampson, ed.), **Retro. Supp. I:** 35
Further Range, A (Frost), **II:** 155; **Retro. Supp. I:** 132, 136, 137, 138, 139
"Fury, The" (Skloot), **Supp. XX: 197**
"Fury of Aerial Bombardment, The" (Eberhart), **I:** 535–536
"Fury of Flowers and Worms, The" (Sexton), **Supp. II Part 2:** 694
"Fury of Rain Storms, The" (Sexton), **Supp. II Part 2:** 695
Fury of the Jungle (film), **Supp. XIII:** 163
Fussell, Paul, **Supp. V:** 241
"Future, if Any, of Comedy, The" (Thurber), **Supp. I Part 2:** 620
Future, The (film, July), **Supp. XXIV:** 199, 200, 202, **209,** 210
Future in the Present, The (C. L. R. James), **Supp. XXI:** 172
Future is Ours, Comrade, The: Conversations with the Russians (Kosinski), **Supp. VII:** 215
Futureland: Nine Stories of an Imminent World (Mosley), **Supp. XIII: 247–249**
"Future Life, The" (Bryant), **Supp. I Part 1:** 170
Future of Southern Letters, The (J. W. Miller), **Supp. XX: 161**
Future of the Race, The (H. L. Gates), **Supp. XX: 101, 104, 111**
Future Punishment of the Wicked, The (Edwards), **I:** 546

G

"Gabriel" (Rich), **Supp. I Part 2:** 557
Gabriel, Ralph H., **Supp. I Part 1:** 251
Gabriel, Trip, **Supp. V:** 212
Gabriel Conroy (Harte), **Supp. II Part 1:** 354

"Gabriel's Truth" (Kenyon), **Supp. VII:** 166
Gaddis, William, **Supp. IV Part 1: 279–296; Supp. IV Part 2:** 484; **Supp. V:** 52; **Supp. IX:** 208; **Supp. X:** 301, 302; **Supp. XX: 83, 91; Supp. XXI:** 226; **Supp. XXIII:** 107
Gadiot, Pud, **Supp. XI:** 295
Gain (Powers), **Supp. IX:** 212, **220–221**
Gaines, Ernest J., **Supp. X:** 24, 250
Gaines, James R., **Supp. IX:** 190
Gainor, J. Ellen, **Supp. XXI:** 6
Gaitens, Peter, **Supp. XV:** 65
Galamain, Ivan, **Supp. III Part 2:** 624
Galassi, Jonathan, **Supp. XVIII:** 92; **Supp. XIX:** 34; **Supp. XXII:** 177
Galatea 2.2 (Powers), **Supp. IX:** 212, **219–220**
"Galatea Encore" (Brodsky), **Supp. VIII:** 31
Galbraith, John Kenneth, **Supp. I Part 2:** 645, 650
Galdós, Benito Pérez. *See* Pérez Galdós, Benito
Gale, Zona, **Supp. I Part 2:** 613; **Supp. VIII:** 155
Galehouse, Maggie, **Supp. XXI:** 215
"Gale in April" (Jeffers), **Supp. II Part 2:** 423
Galignani, Giovanni Antonio, **II:** 315
Galileo Galilei, **I:** 480–481; **Supp. XII:** 180; **Supp. XIII:** 75
Gallagher, Tess, **Supp. XVI:** 36; **Supp. XVII:** 110; **Supp. XXI:** 246; **Supp. XXIV: 165–181**
Gallant, Mavis, **Supp. VIII:** 151
Gallatin, Albert, **I:** 5
"Gallery" (Goldbarth), **Supp. XII:** 188
"Gallery of Real Creatures, A" (Thurber), **Supp. I Part 2:** 619
Gallico, Paul, **Supp. XVI:** 238
Gallows Songs (Snodgrass), **Supp. VI:** 317
Gallup, Dick, **Supp. XXIV:** 34, 35, 39, 44
Gallup, Donald, **III:** 404, 478
Galsworthy, John, **III:** 70, 153, 382
Galton Case, The (Macdonald), **Supp. IV Part 2:** 463, 473, 474
Galvin, Frances, **Supp. XXI:** 5
"Gal Young 'Un" (Rawlings), **Supp. X:** 228
Gambino, Richard, **Supp. XX: 35**
"Gambler, the Nun, and the Radio, The" (Hemingway), **II:** 250
"Gambler's Wife, The" (Dunbar), **Supp. II Part 1:** 196
Gambone, Philip, **Supp. XII:** 81
"Gambrel Roof, A" (Larcom), **Supp. XIII:** 144
"Game at Salzburg, A" (Jarrell), **II:** 384, 389
Game Management (Leopold), **Supp. XIV:** 182
"Game of Catch, A" (Wilbur), **Supp. III Part 2:** 552
Game Players of Titan, The (Dick), **Supp. XVIII:** 138
"Games in Frank Conroy's *Stop-Time*" (T. Adams), **Supp. XVI:** 67

"Games Two" (Wilbur), **Supp. III Part 2:** 550

Gammelgaard, Lene, **Supp. XVIII:** 112

"Gamut, The" (Angelou), **Supp. IV Part 1:** 15

Gander, Forrest, **Supp. XV:** 339, 340, 342

Gandhi, Indira, **Supp. X:** 108

Gandhi, Mahatma, **III:** 179, 296–297; **IV:** 170, 185, 367; **Supp. VIII:** 203, 204; **Supp. X:** 27

Gandhi on Non-Violence (Merton, ed.), **Supp. VIII:** 204–205

Gang of Five: Leaders at the Center of the Conservative Crusade (Easton), **Supp. XIX:** 137

"Gang of Mirrors, The" (Simic), **Supp. VIII:** 283

Gannett, Ezra Stiles, **Supp. XXIV:** 74

Gansevoort, Guert, **III:** 94

Gansevoort, Peter, **III:** 92

"Gap" (Bierds), **Supp. XVII:** 35–36

Garabedian, Michael, **Supp. XIII:** 115

Garbage (Ammons), **Supp. VII:** 24, 35–36

Garbage (Dixon), **Supp. XII:** 147, 148

Garbage Man, The (Dos Passos), **I:** 478, 479, 481, 493

Garber, Frederick, **Supp. IX:** 294–295

Garbo, Greta, **Supp. I Part 2:** 616

García, Cristina, **Supp. VIII:** 74; **Supp. XI:** 177–192

García Lorca, Federico. *See* Lorca, Federico García

"García Lorca: A Photograph of the Granada Cemetery, 1966" (Levis), **Supp. XI:** 264

García Márquez, Gabriel, **Supp. V:** 244; **Supp. VIII:** 81, 82, 84, 85; **Supp. XII:** 147, 310, 316, 322; **Supp. XIII:** 226; **Supp. XVII:** 45; **Supp. XXIV:** 86, 89, 190

Gard, Claire, **Supp. XXIII:** 94

Gardaphe, Fred, **Supp. XX: 38, 41**

"Garden" (Marvell), **IV:** 161; **Supp. XVI:** 204

"Garden, The" (Glück), **Supp. V:** 83

"Garden, The" (Strand), **Supp. IV Part 2:** 629

"Garden Among Tombs" (B. Kelly), **Supp. XVII:** 126

"Garden by Moonlight, The" (Lowell), **II:** 524

"Gardener Delivers a Fawn, The" (C. Frost), **Supp. XV:** 99

Gardener's Son, The (McCarthy), **Supp. VIII:** 187

Garden God, The: A Tale of Two Boys (Reid), **Supp. XX: 235**

"Gardenias" (Doty), **Supp. XI:** 122

"Gardenias" (Monette), **Supp. X:** 159

"Garden Lodge, The" (Cather), **I:** 316, 317

Garden of Adonis, The (Gordon), **II:** 196, 204–205, 209

Garden of Earthly Delights, A (Oates), **Supp. II Part 2:** 504, 507–509

Garden of Earthly Delights, The (Bosch), **Supp. XXII:** 255, 261

"Garden of Eden" (Hemingway), **II:** 259

Garden of Eden, The (Hemingway), **Retro. Supp. I:** 186, **187–188**

"Garden of Flesh, Garden of Stone" (B. Kelly), **Supp. XVII:** 128

Garden of Last Days, The (Dubus III), **Supp. XXIV:** 101, **107–108**

"Garden of the Moon, The" (Doty), **Supp. XI:** 122

Garden of the Prophet, The (Gibran), **Supp. XX: 119, 122**

"Garden of the Trumpet Tree, The" (B. Kelly), **Supp. XVII:** 131

"Gardens, The" (Oliver), **Supp. VII:** 236

"Gardens of Mont-Saint-Michel, The" (Maxwell), **Supp. VIII:** 169

"Gardens of the Villa D'Este, The" (Hecht), **Supp. X:** 59

"Gardens of Zuñi, The" (Merwin), **Supp. III Part 1:** 351

Garden Thieves, The: Twentieth Century African-American Poetry (Major, ed.), **Supp. XXII:** 172

Gardiner, Judith Kegan, **Supp. IV Part 1:** 205

Gardner, Erle Stanley, **Supp. IV Part 1:** 121, 345

Gardner, Isabella, **IV:** 127

Gardner, John, **Supp. I Part 1:** 193, 195, 196; **Supp. III Part 1:** 136, 142, 146; **Supp. VI: 61–76**

Gardner, Thomas, **Supp. XXI:** 214

Gardons, S. S. *See* Snodgrass, W. D.

"Gare de Lyon" (M. F. K. Fisher), **Supp. XVII:** 91

Garfield, John, **Supp. XII:** 160

Garibaldi, Giuseppe, **I:** 4; **II:** 284

Garibay, Angel M., **Supp. XV:** 77

Garland, Hamlin, **I:** 407; **II:** 276, 289; **III:** 576; **Retro. Supp. I:** 133; **Retro. Supp. II:** 72; **Supp. I Part 1:** 217; **Supp. IV Part 2:** 502; **Supp. XVIII:** 6

Garland Companion, The (Zverev), **Retro. Supp. I:** 278

"Garments" (Gibran), **Supp. XX: 124**

Garments the Living Wear (Purdy), **Supp. VII:** 278–279, 280–281

Garner, Dwight, **Supp. X:** 202; **Supp. XVIII:** 89

Garnett, Edward, **I:** 405, 409, 417; **III:** 27

Garrett, George P., **Supp. I Part 1:** 196; **Supp. VII: 95–113; Supp. X:** 3, 7; **Supp. XI:** 218; **Supp. XVIII:** 74, 75

Garrigue, Jean, **Supp. XII:** 260

Garrison, Deborah, **Supp. IX:** 299

Garrison, Fielding, **III:** 105

Garrison, William Lloyd, **Supp. I Part 2:** 524, 588, 683, 685, 686, 687; **Supp. XIV:** 54; **Supp. XXIV:** 77

"Garrison of Cape Ann, The" (Whittier), **Supp. I Part 2:** 691, 694

Garry Moore Show (television show), **Supp. IV Part 2:** 575

"Garter Motif" (White), **Supp. I Part 2:** 673

Gartner, Zsuzsi, **Supp. X:** 276

Garvey, Marcus, **Supp. III Part 1:** 175, 180; **Supp. IV Part 1:** 168; **Supp. X:** 135, 136; **Supp. XXI:** 166, 168; **Supp. XXII:** 7

Gas (Kaiser), **I:** 479

Gas-House McGinty (Farrell), **II:** 41–42

Gaskell, Elizabeth, A., **Supp. I Part 2:** 580

Gasoline (Corso), **Supp. XII:** 118, **121–123,** 134

Gasoline Wars, The (Thompson), **Supp. XXIII:** 290

"Gasoline Wars, The"(Thompson), **Supp. XXIII:** 291

Gass, William H., **Supp. V:** 44, 52, 238; **Supp. VI: 77–96; Supp. IX:** 208; **Supp. XII:** 152; **Supp. XIV:** 305; **Supp. XVII:** 183

Gassner, John, **IV:** 381; **Supp. I Part 1:** 284, 292

"Gas Stations" (Apple), **Supp. XVII:** 4

Gastronomical Me, The (M. F. K. Fisher), **Supp. XVII:** 84, 85, 87, 91, 92

Gates, David, **Supp. V:** 24; **Supp. XIII:** 93; **Supp. XVI:** 73, 74; **Supp. XX: 92**

Gates, Elmer, **I:** 515–516

Gates, Henry Louis, Jr., **Retro. Supp. I:** 194, 195, 203; **Supp. X:** 242, 243, 245, 247; **Supp. XVIII:** 287; **Supp. XIX:** 147, 149; **Supp. XX: 99–112, 279, 286; Supp. XXIV:** 192

Gates, Lewis E., **III:** 315, 330

Gates, Sondra Smith, **Supp. XVIII:** 267, 269

Gates, The (Rukeyser), **Supp. VI:** 271, 274, 281

"Gates, The" (Rukeyser), **Supp. VI:** 286

Gates, Tudor, **Supp. XI:** 307

Gates of Ivory, the Gates of Horn, The (McGrath), **Supp. X:** 118

Gates of Wrath, The; Rhymed Poems (Ginsberg), **Supp. II Part 1:** 311, 319

"Gathering" (Trethewey), **Supp. XXI:** 249

Gathering Forces, The (C. L. R. James), **Supp. XXI:** 171

"Gathering of Dissidents, A" (Applebaum), **Supp. XVI:** 153

Gathering of Fugitives, A (Trilling), **Supp. III Part 2:** 506, 512

Gathering of Zion, The: The Story of the Mormon Trail (Stegner), **Supp. IV Part 2:** 599, 602–603

Gather Together in My Name (Angelou), **Supp. IV Part 1:** 2, 3, 4–6, 11

Gathorne-Hardy, Robert, **Supp. XIV:** 344, 347, 348, 349

Gaudier-Brzeska, Henri, **III:** 459, 464, 465, 477

Gaughran, Richard, **Supp. XXI:** 47–48

Gauguin, Paul, **I:** 34; **IV:** 290; **Supp. IV Part 1:** 81; **Supp. XII:** 128

"Gauguin in Oregon" (Skloot), **Supp. XX: 203**

"Gauley Bridge" (Rukeyser), **Supp. VI:** 278

Gauss, Christian, **II:** 82; **IV:** 427, 439–440, 444

Gauthier, Jacquie, **Supp. XIX:** 204

Gautier, Théophile, **II:** 543; **III:** 466, 467; **Supp. I Part 1:** 277

Gay, John, **II:** 111; **Supp. I Part 2:** 523; **Supp. XIV:** 337
Gay, Peter, **I:** 560
Gay, Sydney Howard, **Supp. I Part 1:** 158; **Supp. XVIII:** 3
Gay, Walter, **IV:** 317
Gayatri Prayer, The, **III:** 572
Gay Canon, The (Drake), **Supp. XX:** 274
"Gay Chaps at the Bar" (Brooks), **Supp. III Part 1:** 74, 75
" 'Gay Culture': Still of the Wild Frontier" (P. N. Warren), **Supp. XX:** 272
Gaylord, Winfield R., **III:** 579–580
Gay Talese Reader, The: Portraits & Encounters (Talese), **Supp. XVII:** 202, 208
"Gaze, The"(Hadas), **Supp. XXIII:** 120
"Gazebo" (Carver), **Supp. III Part 1:** 138, 144, 145
Gazer's Spirit, The (Hollander), **Supp. XIX:** 121
Gazer Within, The, and Other Essays by Larry Levis, **Supp. XI:** 270
Gazzara, Ben, **Supp. VIII:** 319
Gazzo, Michael V., **III:** 155
"Geas" (Monson), **Supp. XXIV:** 238–239
"Geese Flying over Hamilton, New York"(Balakian), **Supp. XXIII:** 24
"Geese Gone Beyond" (Snyder), **Supp. VIII:** 304
Geffen, David, **Supp. XXI:** 154
"Gegenwart" (Goethe), **Supp. II Part 1:** 26
Geisel, Theodor Seuss (Dr. Seuss), **Supp. X:** 56; **Supp. XVI:** 97–115
Geismar, Maxwell, **II:** 178, 431; **III:** 71; **Supp. IX:** 15; **Supp. XI:** 223
Geist, Bill, **Supp. XXIII:** 298
Gelb, Arthur, **IV:** 380; **Supp. XXI:** 12
Gelb, Barbara, **Supp. XXI:** 12
Gelbart, Larry, **Supp. IV Part 2:** 591
Gelder, Robert Van, **Supp. XIII:** 166
Gelfant, Blanche H., **II:** 27, 41; **Supp. XVII:** 161
Gelfman, Jean, **Supp. X:** 3
Gellert, Hugo, **Supp. XXII:** 277
Gellhorn, Martha. *See* Hemingway, Mrs. Ernest (Martha Gellhorn)
Gelpi, Albert, **Supp. I Part 2:** 552, 554, 560
Gelpi, Barbara, **Supp. I Part 2:** 560
Gemin, Pamela, **Supp. XXI:** 246
Gemini (Innaurato), **Supp. XXIV:** 117
Gemini: an extended autobiographical statement on my first twenty-five years of being a black poet (Giovanni), **Supp. IV Part 1:** 11
"Gen" (Snyder), **Supp. VIII:** 302
"Gender Norms" (Radinovsky), **Supp. XV:** 285
"Gender of Sound, The" (Carson), **Supp. XII:** 106
"Genealogies"(Hadas), **Supp. XXIII:** 116
"Genealogy" (Komunyakaa), **Supp. XIII:** 129
"General Aims and Theories" (Crane), **I:** 389
General Died at Dawn, The (Odets), **Supp. II Part 2:** 546

"General Gage's Confession" (Freneau), **Supp. II Part 1:** 257
"General Gage's Soliloquy" (Freneau), **Supp. II Part 1:** 257
General History of the Robberies and Murders of the Most Notorious Pyrates from Their First Rise and Settlement in the Island of New Providence to the Present Year, A (Johnson), **Supp. V:** 128
General in His Labyrinth, The (García Márquez), **Supp. XXIV:** 89
"General Returns from One Place to Another, The"(O'Hara), **Supp. XXIII:** 216–217
"General William Booth Enters into Heaven" (Lindsay), **Supp. I Part 2:** 374, 382, 384, 385–388, 389, 392, 399
General William Booth Enters into Heaven and Other Poems (Lindsay), **Supp. I Part 2:** 379, 381, 382, 387–388, 391
"Generation of the Dispossessed" (P. N. Warren), **Supp. XX:** 272
"Generations"(Kenny), **Supp. XXIII:** 154
"Generations of Men, The" (Frost), **Retro. Supp. I:** 128; **Supp. XIII:** 147
Generation Without Farewell (Boyle), **Supp. XXIV:** 60, 62
Generous Man, A (Price), **Supp. VI:** 259, 260, 261
Genesis (biblical book), **I:** 279; **II:** 540; **Retro. Supp. I:** 250, 256; **Supp. XII:** 54
"Genesis" (Stegner), **Supp. IV Part 2:** 604
Genesis: Book One (Schwartz), **Supp. II Part 2:** 640, 651–655
Gene Stratton-Porter (Richards), **Supp. XX:** 217–218
Gene Stratton-Porter, Naturalist and Novelist (Long), **Supp. XX:** 212
"Gene Stratton-Porter: Women's Advocate" (Obuchowski), **Supp. XX:** 222
Genet, Jean, **I:** 71, 82, 83, 84; **Supp. IV Part 1:** 8; **Supp. XI:** 308; **Supp. XII:** 1; **Supp. XIII:** 74; **Supp. XVII:** 95; **Supp. XXIII:** 213; **Supp. XXIV:** 210
"Genetic Coding" (Sorrentino), **Supp. XXI:** 227
"Genetic Expedition" (Dove), **Supp. IV Part 1:** 249, 257
"Genetics of Justice" (Alvarez), **Supp. VII:** 19
"Genial Host, The" (McCarthy), **II:** 564
"Genie in the Bottle, The" (Wilbur), **Supp. III Part 2:** 542
"Genius, The" (MacLeish), **III:** 19
Genius and Lust: A Journey through the Major Writings of Henry Miller (Mailer), **Retro. Supp. II:** 208
"Genius Child" (Hughes), **Retro. Supp. I:** 203
"Genius," The (Dreiser), **I:** 497, 501, 509–511, 519; **Retro. Supp. II:** 94–95, **102–103,** 104, 105
Genova, Lisa, **Supp. XXIII:** 127

"Genteel Tradition in American Philosophy, The" (Santayana), **I:** 222
"Gentle Communion" (Mora), **Supp. XIII:** 218–219
Gentle Crafter, The (O. Henry), **Supp. II Part 1:** 410
"Gentle Lena, The" (Stein), **IV:** 37, 40
Gentleman Caller, The (T. Williams), **IV:** 383
"Gentleman from Cracow, The" (Singer), **IV:** 9
"Gentleman of Bayou Têche, A" (Chopin), **Supp. I Part 1:** 211–212
"Gentleman of Shalott, The" (Bishop), **Supp. I Part 1:** 85, 86
Gentleman's Agreement (Hobson), **III:** 151
"Gentleman's Agreement" (Richard), **Supp. XIX:** 220–221
Gentlemen I Address You Privately (Boyle), **Supp. XXIV:** 53–54
Gentlemen Prefer Blondes (Loos; musical adaptation), **Supp. XVI:** 193
Gentlemen Prefer Blondes: The Illuminating Diary of a Professional Lady (Loos), **Supp. XVI:** 181, 183, 186, **188–189**
Gentlemen Prefer "Books" (J. Yeats), **Supp. XVI:** 190
Gentle People, The: A Brooklyn Fable (Shaw), **Supp. XIX:** 244–245, 249
Gentry, Marshall Bruce, **Supp. IV Part 1:** 236
"Genuine Man, The" (Emerson), **II:** 10
"Genus Narcissus" (Trethewey), **Supp. XXI:** 256
Geo-Bestiary (Harrison), **Supp. VIII:** 53
"Geode" (Frost), **II:** 161
Geographical History of America, The (Stein), **IV:** 31, 45; **Supp. XVIII:** 148
Geography and Plays (Stein), **IV:** 29–30, 32, 43, 44
Geography III (Bishop), **Retro. Supp. II:** 50; **Supp. I Part 1:** 72, 73, 76, 82, 93, 94, 95
Geography of a Horse Dreamer (Shepard), **Supp. III Part 2:** 432
Geography of Home, The: California's Poetry of Place (Bluckey and Young, eds.), **Supp. XIII:** 313
Geography of Lograire, The (Merton), **Supp. VIII:** 208
Geography of the Heart (Johnson), **Supp. XI:** 129
"Geometric Poem, The" (Corso), **Supp. XII:** 132, 133–134
George, Diana Hume, **Supp. IV Part 2:** 447, 449, 450
George, Henry, **II:** 276; **Supp. I Part 2:** 518
George, Jan, **Supp. IV Part 1:** 268
George, Lynell, **Supp. XIII:** 234–235, 237, 249
George, Peter, **Supp. XI:** 302, 303, 304
George and the Dragon (Shanley), **Supp. XIV:** 315
George Bernard Shaw: His Plays (Mencken), **III:** 102
George Mills (Elkin), **Supp. VI:** 53–54**

George Palmer Putnam: Representative American Publisher (Greenspan), **Supp. XVIII:** 257

"George Robinson: Blues" (Rukeyser), **Supp. VI:** 279

George's Mother (Crane), **I:** 408

"George Thurston" (Bierce), **I:** 202

George Washington Crossing the Delaware (Koch), **Supp. XV:** 186

"George Washington"(Kenny), **Supp. XXIII:** 154

Georgia Boy (Caldwell), **I:** 288, 305–306, 308, 309, 310

"Georgia Dusk" (Toomer), **Supp. IX:** 309

"Georgia: Invisible Empire State" (Du Bois), **Supp. II Part 1:** 179

"Georgia Night" (Toomer), **Supp. III Part 2:** 481

Georgia Scenes (Longstreet), **II:** 70, 313; **Supp. I Part 1:** 352

Georgics (Virgil), **Retro. Supp. I:** 135; **Supp. XVI:** 22; **Supp. XXIV:** 153

Georgics of Virgil, The (Ferry. trans.), **Supp. XXIV: 158–160**

Georgoudaki, Ekaterini, **Supp. IV Part 1:** 12

Gerald McBoing-Boing (film), **Supp. XVI:** 102

"Geraldo No Last Name" (Cisneros), **Supp. VII:** 60–61

Gerald's Game (King), **Supp. V:** 141, 148–150, 151, 152

Gerald's Party (Coover), **Supp. V:** 49–50, 51, 52

Gérando, Joseph Marie de, **II:** 10

"Geranium" (O'Connor), **Retro. Supp. II:** 221, 236

Gerard, Jeremy, **Supp. XXI:** 147

Gerber, Dan, **Supp. VIII:** 39

Gerhardt, Rainer, **Supp. IV Part 1:** 142

"German Girls! The German Girls!, The" (MacLeish), **III:** 16

"German Refugee, The" (Malamud), **Supp. I Part 2:** 436, 437

"Germany's Reichswehr" (Agee), **I:** 35

Germinal (Zola), **III:** 318, 322

Gernsback, Hugo, **Supp. IV Part 1:** 101

"Gernsback Continuum, The" (W. Gibson), **Supp. XVI:** 123, 128

"Gerontion" (Eliot), **I:** 569, 574, 577, 578, 585, 588; **III:** 9, 435, 436; **Retro. Supp. I:** 290; **Supp. XV:** 341; **Supp. XVI:** 158–159

Gerry, Elbridge, **Supp. I Part 2:** 486

"Gerry's Jazz" (Komunyakaa), **Supp. XIII:** 125

Gershwin, Ira, **Supp. I Part 1:** 281

"Gert" (Monette), **Supp. X:** 158

"Gertrude Atherton and the New Woman" (Forrey), **Supp. XXIV:** 30

Gertrude of Stony Island Avenue (Purdy), **Supp. VII:** 281–282

Gertrude Stein (Sprigge), **IV:** 31

Gertrude Stein: A Biography of Her Work (Sutherland), **IV:** 38

"Gertrude Stein and the Geography of the Sentence" (Gass), **Supp. VI:** 87

Gesell, Silvio, **III:** 473

"Gestalt at Sixty" (Sarton), **Supp. VIII:** 260

"Gesture of a Woman-in-Process" (Trethewey), **Supp. XXI:** 249–250

"Gesture toward an Unfound Renaissance, A" (Stafford), **Supp. XI:** 323

"Get It Again" (Halliday), **Supp. XIX:** 85

Getlin, Josh, **Supp. V:** 22; **Supp. VIII:** 75, 76, 78, 79

"Getting Along" (Larcom), **Supp. XIII:** 144

"Getting Along with Nature" (Berry), **Supp. X:** 31–32

"Getting Away from Already Pretty Much Being Away from It All" (Wallace), **Supp. X:** 314–315

"Getting Born" (Shields), **Supp. VII:** 311

Getting Even (Allen), **Supp. XV:** 3, 14, 15

"Getting Lucky" (L. Michaels), **Supp. XVI:** 205, 209

"Getting Out of Jail on Monday" (Wagoner), **Supp. IX:** 327

"Getting Over Arnette"(P. Benedict), **Supp. XXIII:** 39

"Getting There" (Plath), **Supp. I Part 2:** 539, 542

"Getting to the Poem" (Corso), **Supp. XII:** 135

Getty, J. Paul, **Supp. X:** 108

Getty, Norris, **Supp. XV:** 136–137, 138, 139, 142, 143, 145, 146

Gettysburg, Manila, Acoma (Masters), **Supp. I Part 2:** 471

"Gettysburg: July 1, 1863" (Kenyon), **Supp. VII:** 172

Gevers, Nick, **Supp. XXII:** 59

Geyer, Bernadette, **Supp. XXIII:** 251

Ghachem, Malick, **Supp. X:** 17

Ghazálí, al-, **Supp. XX: 117**

"Ghazals: Homage to Ghalib" (Rich), **Supp. I Part 2:** 557

Ghost, The (Crane), **I:** 409, 421

"Ghost, The" (Peacock), **Supp. XIX:** 199

"Ghost Cat" (Peacock), **Supp. XIX:** 206

"Ghost Chant, et alii" (Komunyakaa), **Supp. XIII:** 114

Ghost in the Music, A (Nichols), **Supp. XIII:** 267

"Ghost Jam"(Hadas), **Supp. XXIII:** 119

"Ghostlier Demarcations, Keener Sounds" (Vendler), **Supp. I Part 2:** 565

"Ghostly Father, I Confess" (McCarthy), **II:** 565–566

Ghostly Lover, The (Hardwick), **Supp. III Part 1:** 194–196, 208, 209

Ghost Money (Hull), **Supp. XXI:** 129, **132–135,** 136

Ghost of Meter, The (A. Finch), **Supp. XVII:** 71, 73

"Ghost of the Buffaloes, The" (Lindsay), **Supp. I Part 2:** 393

Ghost of Tradition, The (Walzer), **Supp. XVIII:** 174

Ghosts (Auster), **Supp. XII:** 22, **24,26–27**

Ghosts (Ibsen), **III:** 152

Ghosts (Wharton), **IV:** 316, 327

Ghosts of Tsavo: Stalking the Mystery Lions of East Africa (Caputo), **Supp. XIX:** 28

Ghost Town (Coover), **Supp. V:** 52–53

Ghost Trio, The (Bierds), **Supp. XVII:** 29, **30**

Ghost Writer, The (P. Roth), **Retro. Supp. II:** 22, 290, 291; **Supp. III Part 2:** 420–421; **Supp. XVII:** 43

Giachetti, Fosco, **Supp. IV Part 2:** 520

"Giacometti" (Wilbur), **Supp. III Part 2:** 551

Giacometti, Alberto, **Supp. VIII:** 168, 169

Giacomo, Padre, **II:** 278–279

Giant's House, The: A Romance (McCracken), **Supp. X:** 86

"Giant Snail" (Bishop), **Retro. Supp. II:** 49

Giant Weapon, The (Winters), **Supp. II Part 2:** 810

"Giant Woman, The" (Oates), **Supp. II Part 2:** 523

Gibbon, Edward, **I:** 4, 378; **IV:** 126; **Supp. I Part 2:** 503; **Supp. III Part 2:** 629; **Supp. XIII:** 75; **Supp. XIV:** 97

Gibbons, James, **Supp. XVII:** 228

Gibbons, Kaye, **Supp. X: 41–54;** **Supp. XII:** 311

Gibbons, Reginald, **Supp. X:** 113, 124, 127; **Supp. XV:** 105; **Supp. XIX:** 40, 41–42, 281

Gibbons, Richard, **Supp. I Part 1:** 107

"Gibbs" (Rukeyser), **Supp. VI:** 273

Gibbs, Barbara, **Supp. IV Part 2:** 644

Gibbs, Wolcott, **Supp. I Part 2:** 604, 618; **Supp. VIII:** 151

Gibran, Kahlil, **Supp. XX: 69, 113–129**

"GIBSON" (Baraka), **Supp. II Part 1:** 54

Gibson, Charles Dana, **Supp. X:** 184

Gibson, Graeme, **Supp. XIII:** 20

Gibson, Wilfrid W., **Retro. Supp. I:** 128

Gibson, William, **Supp. XVI: 117–133;** **Supp. XXII:** 49

Giddins, Gary, **Supp. XIII:** 245

Gide, André, **I:** 271, 290; **II:** 581; **III:** 210; **IV:** 53, 289; **Supp. I Part 1:** 51; **Supp. IV Part 1:** 80, 284, 347; **Supp. IV Part 2:** 681, 682; **Supp. VIII:** 40; **Supp. X:** 187; **Supp. XIV:** 24, 348; **Supp. XVII:** 242

Gideon Planish (Lewis), **II:** 455

Gielgud, John, **I:** 82; **Supp. XI:** 305

Gierow, Dr. Karl Ragnar, **III:** 404

Gifford, Bill, **Supp. XI:** 38

Gifford, Terry, **Supp. XVI:** 22

"Gift, The" (Creeley), **Supp. IV Part 1:** 153

"Gift, The" (Doolittle), **Supp. I Part 1:** 267

Gift, The (Hyde), **Supp. XVIII:** 150

"Gift, The" (Jarman), **Supp. XVII:** 116

"Gift, The" (L.-Y. Lee), **Supp. XV:** 213, 214

Gift, The (Nabokov), **III:** 246, 255, 261–263; **Retro. Supp. I:** 264, 266, **268–270,** 273, 274–275, 278

"Gift from the City, A" (Updike), **Retro. Supp. I:** 320

"Gift of God, The" (Robinson), **III:** 512, 517, 518–521, 524

Gift of the Black Folk, The: The Negroes in the Making of America (Du Bois), **Supp. II Part 1:** 179
"Gift of the Magi, The" (O. Henry), **Supp. II Part 1:** 394, 406, 408
"Gift of the Osuo, The" (Johnson), **Supp. VI:** 194
"Gift of the Prodigal, The" (Taylor), **Supp. V:** 314, 326
"Gift Outright, The" (Frost), **II:** 152; **Supp. IV Part 1:** 15
Gigi (Colette; stage adaptation, Loos), **Supp. XVI:** 193
"Gigolo" (Plath), **Retro. Supp. II:** 257
"G.I. Graves in Tuscany" (Hugo), **Supp. VI:** 138
"Gila Bend" (Dickey), **Supp. IV Part 1:** 185–186
Gilbert, Elizabeth, **Supp. XXII:** 83, 90
Gilbert, Jack, **Supp. IX:** 287
Gilbert, Peter, **Supp. IX:** 291, 300
Gilbert, Roger, **Supp. XI:** 124
Gilbert, Sandra M., **Retro. Supp. I:** 42; **Retro. Supp. II:** 324; **Supp. IX:** 66; **Supp. XV:** 270; **Supp. XXIV:** 28
Gilbert, Susan. *See* Dickinson, Mrs. William A.
Gilbert and Sullivan, **Supp. IV Part 1:** 389
"Gilbert Stuart Portrait of Washington, The" (Kooser), **Supp. XIX:** 124
Gil Blas (Le Sage), **II:** 290
Gilded Age, The (Twain), **III:** 504; **IV:** 198
Gilded Lapse of Time, A (Schnackenberg), **Supp. XV:** 258, **260–263**
"Gilded Lapse of Time, A" (Schnackenberg), **Supp. XV:** 257
"Gilded Six-Bits, The" (Hurston), **Supp. VI:** 154–155
Gilder, R. W., **Retro. Supp. II:** 66; **Supp. I Part 2:** 418
Gildersleeve, Basil, **Supp. I Part 1:** 369
Gilead (Robinson), **Supp. XXI:** 212, **216–220,** 223
Giles, H. A., **Retro. Supp. I:** 289
Giles, James R., **Supp. IX:** 11, 15; **Supp. XI:** 219, 223–224, 228, 234
"Giles Corey of the Salem Farms" (Longfellow), **II:** 505, 506; **Retro. Supp. II:** 166, 167
Giles Goat-Boy (Barth), **I:** 121, 122–123, 129, 130, 134, 135–138; **Supp. V:** 39
Gilgamesh: A New Rendering in English Verse (Ferry), **Supp. XXIV:** 147, **150–151**
Gill, Brendan, **Supp. I Part 2:** 659, 660
Gillespie, Nick, **Supp. XIV:** 298, 311
Gillette, Chester, **I:** 512
Gillian, Maria Mazziotti, **Supp. XXIII:** 248
Gilligan, Carol, **Supp. XIII:** 216; **Supp. XXII:** 18
Gillis, Jim, **IV:** 196
Gillis, Steve, **IV:** 195
Gilman, Charlotte Perkins, **Supp. I Part 2:** 637; **Supp. V:** 121, 284, 285; **Supp. XI: 193–211; Supp. XIII:** 295, 306; **Supp. XVI:** 84; **Supp. XXIII:** 26

Gilman, Daniel Coit, **Supp. I Part 1:** 361, 368, 370
Gilman, Richard, **IV:** 115; **Supp. IV Part 2:** 577; **Supp. XIII:** 100; **Supp. XIX:** 251
Gilmore, Eddy, **Supp. I Part 2:** 618
Gilmore, Lyman, **Supp. XXI:** 20, 22, 24
Gilmore, Mikal, **Supp. XVI:** 123, 124
Gilpin, Charles, **III:** 392
Gilpin, Dewitt, **Supp. XV:** 197
Gilpin, Laura, **Retro. Supp. I:** 7
Gilpin, Sam, **Supp. V:** 213
Gilpin, William, **Supp. IV Part 2:** 603
"Gil's Furniture Bought & Sold" (Cisneros), **Supp. VII:** 61–62, 64
Gilyard, Keith, **Supp. XXI:** 246
"Gimcrackery" articles (Briggs), **Supp. XVIII:** 8–9
"Gimpel the Fool" (Singer), **IV:** 14; **Retro. Supp. II:** 22, 307
Gimpel the Fool and Other Stories (Singer), **IV:** 1, 7–9, 10, 12
"Gin" (Levine), **Supp. V:** 193
"Gingerbread House, The" (Coover), **Supp. V:** 42–43
Gingerbread Lady, The (Simon), **Supp. IV Part 2:** 580, 583–584, 588
Gingerich, Willard, **Supp. IV Part 2:** 510
Gingertown (McKay), **Supp. X:** 132, 139
Gingold, Hermione, **Supp. XV:** 13
Gingrich, Arnold, **Retro. Supp. I:** 113; **Supp. XVII:** 88; **Supp. XX: 34**
Ginna, Robert, **Supp. IX:** 259
Ginsberg, Allen, **I:** 183; **Retro. Supp. I:** 411, 426, 427; **Retro. Supp. II:** 280; **Supp. II Part 1:** 30, 32, 58, **307–333; Supp. III Part 1:** 2, 91, 96, 98, 100, 222, 226; **Supp. III Part 2:** 541, 627; **Supp. IV Part 1:** 79, 90, 322; **Supp. IV Part 2:** 502; **Supp. V:** 168, 336; **Supp. VIII:** 239, 242–243, 289; **Supp. IX:** 299; **Supp. X:** 120, 204; **Supp. XI:** 135, 297; **Supp. XII:** 118–119, 121–122, 124, 126, 130–131, 136, 182; **Supp. XIV:** 15, 53, 54, 125, 137, 141, 142, 143–144, 148, 150, 269, 280, 283; **Supp. XV:** 134, 177, 263; **Supp. XVI:** 123, 135; **Supp. XVII:** 138, 243; **Supp. XVIII:** 20, 27, 29, 30; **Supp. XXI:** 53; **Supp. XXII:** 172, 225; **Supp. XXIII:** 211, 213, 215; **Supp. XXIV:** 34, 36, 37
Gioia, Dana, **Supp. IX:** 279; **Supp. XII:** 209; **Supp. XIII:** 337; **Supp. XV:** 111–131, 251; **Supp. XVII:** 69, 72, 112; **Supp. XIX:** 117, 144; **Supp. XXI:** 99; **Supp. XXIII:** 112
Giono, Jean, **Supp. XVI:** 135
Giordano, Tony J., **Supp. XXIII:** 125
Giotto di Bondone, **Supp. I Part 2:** 438; **Supp. XI:** 126
Giovani, Regula, **Supp. XV:** 270
Giovanni, Nikki, **Supp. I Part 1:** 66; **Supp. II Part 1:** 54; **Supp. IV Part 1:** 11; **Supp. VIII:** 214; **Supp. XXII:** 11
Giovanni's Room (Baldwin), **Retro. Supp. II:** 5, 6, **6–7,** 8, 10; **Supp. I Part 1:** 51, 52, 55–56, 57, 60, 63, 67; **Supp. III Part 1:** 125

Giovannitti, Arturo, **I:** 476; **Supp. XV:** 299, 301, 302, 307
"Giraffe" (Swenson), **Supp. IV Part 2:** 651
Giraldi, Giovanni Battista. *See* Cinthio
"Girl" (Kincaid), **Supp. VII:** 182–183
Girl, The (Le Sueur), **Supp. XXIII: 172–174**
"Girl, The" (Olds), **Supp. X:** 207
"Girl Friend Poems" (Wright), **Supp. XV:** 349
"Girl from Lynn Bathes Horse!!" (McCarriston), **Supp. XIV:** 266
"Girl from Red Lion, P.A., A" (Mencken), **III:** 111
Girl in Glass, The: Love Poems (W. J. Smith), **Supp. XIII:** 335
Girl in Landscape (Lethem), **Supp. XVIII:** 136, **141–143**
"Girl in the Grave, The" (McCoy), **Supp. XIII:** 170
Girl Like I, A (Loos), **Supp. XVI:** 181, 183, 184, 187, 194, 196
"Girl of the Golden West" (Didion), **Supp. IV Part 1:** 195, 208, 211
Girl of the Golden West, The (Puccini), **III:** 139
Girl of the Limberlost (film), **Supp. XX: 223**
Girl of the Limberlost (Stratton-Porter), **Supp. XX: 211, 221–222**
"Girl on a Scaffold" (C. Frost), **Supp. XV:** 98
"Girl on the Baggage Truck, The" (O'Hara), **III:** 371–372
"Girls" (Gallagher), **Supp. XXIV:** 174–175, 177
Girls at Play (Theroux), **Supp. VIII:** 314, 315, 316, **317**
"Girls at the Sphinx, The" (Farrell), **II:** 45
"Girls in Their Summer Dresses, The" (Shaw), **Supp. XIX:** 246
Girl Sleuth, The: A Feminist Guide (Mason), **Supp. VIII:** 133, 135, **139,** 142
"Girl's Story, A" (Bambara), **Supp. XI:** 10–11
"Girl the Prince Liked, The" (Z. Fitzgerald), **Supp. IX:** 71
Girl Who Had to Die, The (Holding), **Supp. XXII: 126–127**
Girl Who Loved Tom Gordon, The (King), **Supp. V:** 138, 152
"Girl Who Raised Pigeons, The" (E. P. Jones), **Supp. XXII:** 143
Girl with Curious Hair (Wallace), **Supp. X:** 301, **305–308**
"Girl with Curious Hair" (Wallace), **Supp. X:** 306
"Girl with Silver Eyes, The" (Hammett), **Supp. IV Part 1:** 344, 345
"Girl with Talent, The" (Z. Fitzgerald), **Supp. IX:** 71
Girodias, Maurice, **III:** 171; **Supp. XI:** 297
Giroux, Robert, **Retro. Supp. II:** 177, 229, 235; **Supp. IV Part 1:** 280; **Supp. VIII:** 195; **Supp. XV:** 146
Gish, Dorothy, **Retro. Supp. I:** 103

Gish, Lillian, **Supp. XVI:** 184

Gissing, George, **II:** 138, 144

Gitagovinda, **Supp. XXII:** 258

Gita-govínda: Love Songs of Radha and Krishna (Jayadeva; Siegel, trans.), **Supp. XXII:** 258

Gittings, Robert, **II:** 531

"Given" (C. Frost), **Supp. XV:** 96

Given Sugar, Given Salt (Hirshfield), **Supp. XXIII:** 133

"Give Us Back Our Country" (Masters), **Supp. I Part 2:** 472

Give Us This Day (film, Dmytryk), **Supp. XX:** 40–41

"Give Way, Ye Gates" (Roethke), **III:** 536

"Give Your Heart to the Hawks" (Jeffers), **Supp. II Part 2:** 433

"Giving Blood" (Updike), **IV:** 226; **Retro. Supp. I:** 332

Giving Good Weight (McPhee), **Supp. III Part 1:** 307

"Giving in to You" (X. J. Kennedy), **Supp. XV:** 160

"Giving Myself Up" (Strand), **Supp. IV Part 2:** 627

Giving Up America (Abraham), **Supp. XXIV:** 2, 3, 7–9

Giving Up the Ghost (Moraga), **Supp. XXIII:** 197–199

G. K. the DJ (Keillor), **Supp. XVI:** 171

Glackens, William, **Retro. Supp. II:** 103

Gladden, Washington, **III:** 293; **Supp. I Part 1:** 5

Gladstone, William Ewart, **Supp. I Part 2:** 419

"Gladys Poem, The" (Alvarez), **Supp. VII:** 10

"Glance at German 'Kultur,' A" (Bourne), **I:** 228

Glance Away, A (Wideman), **Supp. X:** 320

"Glance from the Bridge, A" (Wilbur), **Supp. III Part 2:** 551

"Glance in the Mirror, A" (Swados), **Supp. XIX:** 261–262

Glance toward Shakespeare, A (Chapman), **Supp. XIV:** 44

Glancy, Diane, **Supp. XXI:** 246

Glanville-Hicks, Peggy, **Supp. IV Part 1:** 84

Glare (Ammons), **Supp. VII:** 35–36

Glasgow, Cary, **II:** 173, 182

Glasgow, Ellen, **II:** 173–195; **IV:** 328; **Supp. X:** 228, 234; **Supp. XXIV:** 30

Glasmon, Kubec, **Supp. XIII:** 166

Glaspell, Susan, **Supp. III Part 1:** 175–191; **Supp. X:** 46; **Supp. XVII:** 99; **Supp. XXI:** 5

"Glass" (Francis), **Supp. IX:** 80

Glass, Irony, and God (Carson), **Supp. XII:** 97, 104–106

Glass, Philip, **Supp. XXI:** 146, 147

"Glass Ark, The" (Komunyakaa), **Supp. XIII:** 129

Glass Bees, The (Jünger; Bogan and Mayer, trans.), **Supp. III Part 1:** 63

"Glass Blower of Venice" (Malamud), **Supp. I Part 2:** 450

"Glass Essay, The" (Carson), **Supp. XII:** 104–105

"Glass Face in the Rain, A: New Poems" (Stafford), **Supp. XI:** 327–328

Glass Key, The (Hammett), **Supp. IV Part 1:** 351–353

"Glass Meadows" (Bausch), **Supp. VII:** 53–54

Glass Menagerie, The (T. Williams), **I:** 81; **IV:** 378, 379, 380, 382, 383, 385, 386, 387, 388, 389, 390, 391, 392, 393–394, 395, 398; **Supp. IV Part 1:** 84

"Glass Mountain, The" (Barthelme), **Supp. IV Part 1:** 47

"Glass Tent, The" (Everwine), **Supp. XV:** 76

Glatstein, Jacob, **Supp. X:** 70

Glazer, Nathan, **Supp. VIII:** 93, 243

"Gleaners, The" (Merwin), **Supp. III Part 1:** 346

Gleanings in Europe (Cooper), **I:** 346

Gleason, Ralph J., **Supp. IX:** 16

Glenday, Michael, **Retro. Supp. II:** 210

Glengarry Glen Ross (film), **Supp. XIV:** 242

Glengarry Glen Ross (Mamet), **Supp. XIV:** 239, 240, 242, 245, 246, 250, 254, 255

Glimcher, Arne, **Supp. VIII:** 73

"Glimpses" (Jones), **Supp. XI:** 218

Glimpses of the Moon, The (Wharton), **II:** 189–190; **IV:** 322–323; **Retro. Supp. I:** 381

"Glimpses of Vietnamese Life" (Levertov), **Supp. III Part 1:** 282

Glisson, J. T., **Supp. X:** 234

Gloria Mundi (Frederic), **II:** 144–145

Gloria Naylor (Fowler), **Supp. VIII:** 224

"Glorious Fourth, The" (Ryan as Quin), **Supp. XVIII:** 229

Glorious Ones, The (Prose), **Supp. XVI:** 251

Glory of Hera, The (Gordon), **II:** 196–197, 198, 199, 217–220

Glory of the Conquered, The (Glaspell), **Supp. III Part 1:** 176

Gloss, Molly, **Supp. XXIII:** 280

Glossary of Literary Terms (Abrams), **Supp. XVI:** 19

Glotfelty, Cheryll, **Supp. IX:** 25

Glover, Joyce Lee, **Supp. XIX:** 112

Glover, Michael, **Supp. XXIV:** 168

Glow, The (Wrigley), **Supp. XVIII:** 295

"Glow, The" (Wrigley), **Supp. XVIII:** 296–297, 307

Gluck, Christoph Willibald, **II:** 210, 211

Glück, Louise, **Supp. V:** 77–94; **Supp. VIII:** 272; **Supp. X:** 209; **Supp. XIV:** 269; **Supp. XV:** 19, 252; **Supp. XVII:** 241

"Glutton, The" (Shapiro), **Supp. II Part 2:** 705

"Glutton for Punishment, A" (Yates), **Supp. XI:** 341

Glyph (Everett), **Supp. XVIII:** 60–61

Gnädiges Fräulein, The (T. Williams), **IV:** 382, 395, 398

Gnomes and Occasions (Nemerov), **III:** 269

Gnomologia (Fuller), **II:** 111

"Gnothis Seauton" (Emerson), **II:** 11, 18–19

Go (Holmes), **Supp. XIV:** 144

"Go Ahead; Goodbye; Good Luck; and Watch Out" (Bronk), **Supp. XXI:** 31

"Goal of Intellectual Men, The" (Eberhart), **I:** 529–530

Go-Between, The (Hartley), **Supp. I Part 1:** 293

Gobineau, Joseph Arthur de, **Supp. XIV:** 209

God (Allen), **Supp. XV:** 3

God and the American Writer (Kazin), **Supp. VIII:** 108–109

Godard, Jean-Luc, **Supp. I Part 2:** 558

Godbey (Masters), **Supp. I Part 2:** 472

God Bless You, Mr. Rosewater (Vonnegut), **Supp. II Part 2:** 758, 767, 768–769, 771, 772

Goddess Abides, The (Buck), **Supp. II Part 1:** 129, 131–132

Gödel, Kurt, **Supp. IV Part 1:** 43

Godfather (Puzo), **Supp. IV Part 1:** 390

Godfires (Hoffman), **Supp. XVIII:** 81–82

God in Ruins, A (Uris), **Supp. XX:** 247, 256

"God in the Doorway" (Dillard), **Supp. VI:** 28

"God is a distant-stately Lover" (Dickinson), **I:** 471

Godkin, E. L., **II:** 274

God Knows (Heller), **Supp. IV Part 1:** 386, 388–389

God Made Alaska for the Indians (Reed), **Supp. X:** 241

God of His Fathers, The (London), **II:** 469

God of Vengeance, The (Asch), **IV:** 11; **Supp. XXIII:** 5, 8–9

Go Down, Moses (Faulkner), **Retro. Supp. I:** 75, 82, 85, 86, 88, 89, 90, 92; **Supp. XVIII:** 203

"Go Down, Moses" (Faulkner), **II:** 71–72

Go Down, Moses (Hayden), **Supp. II Part 1:** 365

Go Down, Moses and Other Stories (Faulkner), **II:** 71; **Supp. X:** 52

"Go Down Death A Funeral Sermon" (Johnson), **Supp. IV Part 1:** 7

"God Rest Ye Merry, Gentlemen" (Hemingway), **IV:** 122

Godric (Buechner), **Supp. XII:** 53

Gods, The (Goldbarth), **Supp. XII:** 189, 190

Gods Arrive, The (Wharton), **IV:** 326–327; **Retro. Supp. I:** 382

God Save the Child (Parker), **Supp. XIX:** 183–184

"God Save the Rights of Man" (Freneau), **Supp. II Part 1:** 268

"Gods|Children" (Swenson), **Supp. IV Part 2:** 645

"God's Christ Theory" (Carson), **Supp. XII:** 106

God's Country (Everett), **Supp. XVIII:** 57–58, 64, 65

God's Country and My People (Morris), **III:** 238

Gods Determinations touching his Elect: and the Elects Combat in their Con-

version, and Coming up to God in Christ together with the Comfortable Effects thereof (Taylor), **IV:** 155–160, 165

God-Seeker, The (Lewis), **II:** 456

God Sends Sunday (Bontemps), **Supp. XXII:** 2, 3, 9

God's Favorite (Simon), **Supp. IV Part 2:** 575, 586, 588, 590

"God's Fool" (Gibran), **Supp. XX:** 118

God's Little Acre (Caldwell), **I:** 288, 289, 290, 297, 298–302, 305–306, 309, 310; **Supp. XXII:** 196

God's Man: A Novel in Wood Cuts (Ward), **I:** 31

Gods of Winter, The (Gioia), **Supp. XV:** 112, **121–125**

"Gods of Winter, The" (Gioia), **Supp. XV:** 117

"God's Peace in November" (Jeffers), **Supp. II Part 2:** 420

God's Silence (F. Wright), **Supp. XVII:** 240, 246–247

"God Stiff" (Carson), **Supp. XII:** 106

God's Trombones (Johnson), **Supp. II Part 1:** 201

"God's Youth" (Untermeyer), **Supp. XV:** 296

"God the Father and the Empty House" (McCarriston), **Supp. XIV:** 273

Godwin, William, **II:** 304; **III:** 415; **Supp. I Part 1:** 126, 146; **Supp. I Part 2:** 512, 513–514, 522, 709, 719

God without Thunder (Ransom), **III:** 495–496, 499

Godwulf Manuscript, The (Parker), **Supp. XIX:** **178–182**

Goebbels, Josef, **III:** 560

Goebel, Irma, **Supp. X:** 95

Goen, C. C., **I:** 560

Goethe, Johann Wolfgang von, **I:** 181, 396, 587–588; **II:** 5, 6, 320, 344, 488, 489, 492, 502, 556; **III:** 395, 453, 607, 612, 616; **IV:** 50, 64, 173, 326; **Retro. Supp. I:** 360; **Retro. Supp. II:** 94; **Supp. I Part 2:** 423, 457; **Supp. II Part 1:** 26; **Supp. III Part 1:** 63; **Supp. IX:** 131, 308; **Supp. X:** 60; **Supp. XI:** 169; **Supp. XVIII:** 278; **Supp. XX:** 84; **Supp. XXIV:** 152

Go for the Body (Lacy), **Supp. XV:** 201, 204

Gogan, Robert, **Supp. XXI:** 24

Gogol, Nikolai, **I:** 296; **IV:** 1, 4; **Retro. Supp. I:** 266, 269; **Supp. VIII:** 14; **Supp. XVII:** 45; **Supp. XVIII:** 102; **Supp. XXII:** 59

Goia, Dana, **Supp. XIX:** 121

Goines, Donald, **Supp. XXIII:** 174

"Going, Going, Gone" (Skloot), **Supp. XX:** 207

Going, William T., **Supp. VIII:** 126

Going After Cacciato (O'Brien), **Supp. V:** 237, 238, 239, 244–246, 248, 249

Going All the Way (Wakefield), **Supp. VIII:** 43

"Going Critical" (Bambara), **Supp. XI:** 14

Going Down (Markson), **Supp. XVII:** 136, 138, **139–140**, 141, 142–143, 144, 145

Going for the Rain (Ortiz), **Supp. IV Part 2:** 499, 505–508, 509, 514

"Going Home by Last Night" (Kinnell), **Supp. III Part 1:** 244

"Going Home in America" (Hardwick), **Supp. III Part 1:** 205

"Going Home"(Kenny), **Supp. XXIII:** 144, 148

"Going North" (Salinas), **Supp. XIII:** 316

Going Places (L. Michaels), **Supp. XVI:** 201, **203–206**

"Going Places" (L. Michaels), **Supp. XVI:** 203

"Going South" (J. W. Miller), **Supp. XX:** **169**

Going South (Lardner and Buck), **II:** 427

Going To and Fro and Walking Up and Down (Reznikoff), **Supp. XIV:** 280, 282, 284, 285

Going to Meet the Man (Baldwin), **Supp. I Part 1:** 60, 62–63; **Supp. XX:** **147**

"Going to Meet the Man" (Baldwin), **Retro. Supp. II:** 8, 9; **Supp. I Part 1:** 62–63

"Going to Naples" (Welty), **IV:** 278; **Retro. Supp. I:** 352, 353

"Going to Shrewsbury" (Jewett), **II:** 393

"Going to the Bakery" (Bishop), **Supp. I Part 1:** 93

Going-to-the-Stars (Lindsay), **Supp. I Part 2:** 398

Going-to-the-Sun (Lindsay), **Supp. I Part 2:** 397–398

Going to the Territory (Ellison), **Retro. Supp. II:** 119, 123–124

"Going towards Pojoaque, A December Full Moon/72" (Harjo), **Supp. XII:** 218

"Going Under" (Dubus), **Supp. VII:** 83

"Gold" (Francis), **Supp. IX:** 82

Gold (O'Neill), **III:** 391

Gold, Arthur, **Supp. XXIV:** 160, 161

Gold, Don, **Supp. XXII:** 258

Gold, Michael, **II:** 26; **IV:** 363, 364, 365; **Retro. Supp. II:** 323; **Supp. I Part 1:** 331; **Supp. I Part 2:** 609; **Supp. XIV:** 288; **Supp. XXII:** 277

Goldbarth, Albert, **Supp. XII:** **175–195**

Goldbarth's Book of Occult Phenomena (Goldbarth), **Supp. XII:** 181

Goldberg, Carole, **Supp. XXII:** 207

Goldberg, Michael, **Supp. XXIII:** 210, 216, 217

Goldberg, S. L., **Supp. VIII:** 238

"Gold Bug, The" (Poe), **III:** 410, 413, 419, 420

Gold Bug Variations, The (Powers), **Supp. IX:** 210, 212, **216–217**, 219

Gold Cell, The (Olds), **Supp. X:** **206–209**

Gold Diggers, The (Monette), **Supp. X:** 153

Golde, Miss (Mencken's Secretary), **III:** 104, 107

Golden, Harry, **III:** 579, 581; **Supp. VIII:** 244

Golden, Mike, **Supp. XI:** 294, 295, 297, 299, 303

Golden Age, The (Gurney), **Supp. V:** 101–103

Golden Apples (Rawlings), **Supp. X:** **228–229**, 230, 234

Golden Apples, The (Welty), **IV:** 261, 271–274, 281, 293; **Retro. Supp. I:** 341, 342, 343, **350–351**, 352, 355

Golden Apples of the Sun, The (Bradbury), **Supp. IV Part 1:** 102, 103

Golden Book of Springfield, The (Lindsay), **Supp. I Part 2:** 376, 379, 395, 396

Golden Bough, The (Frazer), **II:** 204, 549; **III:** 6–7; **Supp. I Part 1:** 18; **Supp. IX:** 123; **Supp. X:** 124

Golden Bowl, The (James), **II:** 320, 333, 335; **Retro. Supp. I:** 215, 216, 218–219, 232, **234–235**, 374

Golden Boy (Odets), **Supp. II Part 2:** 538, 539, 540–541, 546, 551

Golden Calves, The (Auchincloss), **Supp. IV Part 1:** 35

Golden Child (Hwang), **Supp. XXI:** 147–148

Golden Day, The (Mumford), **Supp. II Part 2:** 471, 475, 477, 483, 484, 488–489, 493

Golden Fleece, The (Gurney), **Supp. V:** 97

Golden Gate (film, Madden), **Supp. XXI:** 147

Golden Gate, The (Seth), **Supp. XVII:** 117

Golden Gate Country (Atherton), **Supp. XXIV:** 27

Golden Grove, The: Selected Passages from the Sermons and Writings of Jeremy Taylor (L. P. Smith), **Supp. XIV:** 345

"Golden Heifer, The" (Wylie), **Supp. I Part 2:** 707

"Golden Honeymoon, The" (Lardner), **II:** 429–430, 431

Golden Journey, The (W. J. Smith and Bogan, comps.), **Supp. XIII:** 347

Golden Ladder series (S. and A. Warner), **Supp. XVIII:** 267

"Golden Lads" (Marquand), **III:** 56

Golden Legend, The (Longfellow), **II:** 489, 490, 495, 505, 506, 507; **Retro. Supp. II:** 159, 165, 166

Golden Mean and Other Poems, The (Tate and Wills), **IV:** 122

Golden Peacock (Atherton), **Supp. XXIV:** 26

"Golden Retrievals" (Doty), **Supp. XI:** 132

Golden Shakespeare, The: An Anthology (L. P. Smith), **Supp. XIV:** 349

Golden Slippers: An Anthology of Negro Poetry for Young Readers (Bontemps, ed.), **Supp. XXII:** 5, 11

Goldensohn, Lorrie, **Retro. Supp. II:** 51

Golden State (Bidart), **Supp. XV:** 21, **23–25**

"Golden State" (Bidart), **Supp. XV:** 23, 24, 25

Golden States (Cunningham), **Supp. XV:** 55, **56–59,** 63

Golden Treasury of Best Songs and Lyrical Poems in the English Language (Palgrave), **Retro. Supp. I:** 124

Golden Treasury of the Best Songs and Lyrical Poems in the English Language (Palgrave), **Supp. XIV:** 340

Golden Whales of California and Other Rhymes in the American Language, The (Lindsay), **Supp. I Part 2:** 394–395, 396

"Goldfish Bowl, The" (Francis), **Supp. IX:** 78

Gold Fools (Sorrentino), **Supp. XXI:** 237

Goldin Boys, The (Epstein), **Supp. XIV:** 112

Golding, Arthur, **III:** 467, 468

Golding, William, **Supp. IV Part 1:** 297

Goldini, Carlo, **II:** 274

Goldkorn Tales (Epstein), **Supp. XII:** **163–164**

Goldman, Albert, **Supp. XI:** 299

Goldman, Arnold, **Supp. XXI:** 13

Goldman, Emma, **III:** 176, 177; **Supp. I Part 2:** 524; **Supp. XVII:** 96, 103, 104; **Supp. XXIII:** 162

Goldman, William, **Supp. IV Part 2:** 474

"Gold Mountain Stories" project (Kingston), **Supp. V:** 164

Gold of Chickaree, The (S. and A. Warner), **Supp. XVIII:** 267, 268, 269

Goldring, Douglas, **III:** 458

Goldsmith, Oliver, **II:** 273, 282, 299, 304, 308, 314, 315, 514; **Retro. Supp. I:** 335; **Supp. I Part 1:** 310; **Supp. I Part 2:** 503, 714, 716; **Supp. XVIII:** 12

Gold Standard and the Logic of Naturalism, The (W. B. Michaels), **Retro. Supp. I:** 369

Goldstein, Laurence, **Supp. XXI:** 134

Goldstein, Rebecca, **Supp. XVII:** 44

Goldwater, Barry, **I:** 376; **III:** 38

Goldwyn, Samuel, **Retro. Supp. II:** 199; **Supp. I Part 1:** 281; **Supp. XXIV:** 28

Golem, The (Leivick), **IV:** 6; **Supp. XXIII:** 8

"Golgotha Is a Mountain" (Bontemps), **Supp. XXII:** 3, 8

"Goliardic Song" (Hecht), **Supp. X:** 63

"Go Like This" (Moore), **Supp. X:** 165

Goll, Ivan, **Supp. III Part 1:** 235, 243–244; **Supp. III Part 2:** 621

Gomes, Albert, **Supp. XXI:** 160

Goncharova, Natalya, **Supp. IX:** 66

Goncourt, Edmond de, **II:** 325, 328; **III:** 315, 317–318, 321; **Retro. Supp. I:** 226

Goncourt, Jules de, **II:** 328; **III:** 315, 317–318, 321

Gone Fishin' (Mosley), **Supp. XIII:** **235–236,** 240

"Gone to War" (E. Stoddard), **Supp. XV:** 282

"Gone West" (Rodriguez), **Supp. XIV:** 308

Gone with the Wind (film), **Retro. Supp. I:** 113

Gone with the Wind (Mitchell), **II:** 177; **Retro. Supp. I:** 340; **Supp. XX: 243; Supp. XXII:** 190, 195

Gongora y Argote, Luis de, **II:** 552

Gonzalez, David, **Supp. VIII:** 85

González, Jovita, **Supp. XIX:** 99

Gonzo: The Life of Hunter S. Thompson (Wenner and Seymour), **Supp. XXIV:** 280, 281, 282, 288

Gooch, Brad, **Supp. XII:** 121; **Supp. XXIII:** 218, 220

Good, George, **Supp. XI:** 306

"Good, the Plaid, and the Ugly, The" (Wasserstein), **Supp. XV:** 327

"Good and Not So Good, The" (Dunn), **Supp. XI:** 141

"Good Anna, The" (Stein), **IV:** 37, 40, 43

Good As Gold (Heller), **Supp. IV Part 1:** 386, 388, 394

Good as I Been to You (album, Dylan), **Supp. XVIII:** 28

Good Boys and Dead Girls and Other Essays (Gordon), **Supp. IV Part 1:** 309–310

Good Brother, The (Offutt), **Supp. XIX:** 163, **168–169**

"Good-by and Keep Cold" (Frost), **Retro. Supp. I:** 135

"Good-bye" (Emerson), **II:** 19

"Goodbye, Christ" (Hughes), **Retro. Supp. I:** 202, 203

Goodbye, Columbus (P. Roth), **Retro. Supp. II:** 280, 281, 290; **Supp. III Part 2:** 403–406; **Supp. XIV:** 112; **Supp. XX: 177**

"Goodbye, Columbus" (P. Roth), **Supp. III Part 2:** 401, 404, 408–409, 411

Goodbye, Columbus and Five Short Stories (P. Roth), **Retro. Supp. II:** 279

"Goodbye, Goldeneye" (Swenson), **Supp. IV Part 2:** 651

"Goodbye, Mr. Chipstein" (Epstein), **Supp. XIV:** 103, 108

"Goodbye, My Brother" (Cheever), **Supp. I Part 1:** 175, 177, 193

"Goodbye and Good Luck" (Paley), **Supp. VI:** 219, 223

Goodbye Girl, The (film), **Supp. IV Part 2:** 589

Goodbye Girl, The (musical), **Supp. IV Part 2:** 576, 588

Goodbye Girl, The (Simon), **Supp. IV Part 2:** 575

Goodbye Look, The (Macdonald), **Supp. IV Part 2:** 473, 474

"Good-Bye My Fancy" (Whitman), **IV:** 348

"Goodbye to All That" (Didion), **Supp. IV Part 1:** 197

Goodbye to All That (Graves), **I:** 477

Goodbye to Berlin (Isherwood), **Supp. XIV:** 159, 161, 162, 169

"Good-Bye to the Mezzogiorno" (Auden), **Supp. II Part 1:** 19

"Goodbye to the Poetry of Calcium" (Wright), **Supp. III Part 2:** 599

"Good Company" (Matthews), **Supp. IX:** 160

"Good Country People" (O'Connor), **III:** 343, 350, 351, 352, 358; **Retro. Supp.**

II: 229, 232

Good Day to Die, A (Harrison), **Supp. VIII: 42–44,** 45, 47

Good Doctor, The (Simon), **Supp. IV Part 2:** 575, 585

Good Earth, The (Buck), **Supp. I Part 1:** 49; **Supp. II Part 1:** 115–175, 118, 125, 132

Good European, The (Blackmur), **Supp. II Part 1:** 91

Good Evening Mr. & Mrs. America, and All the Ships at Sea (Bausch), **Supp. VII:** 41, 47, 52

"Good Friday" (Jarman), **Supp. XVII:** 116

"Good Girl" (Peacock), **Supp. XIX:** 199

Good Gray Poet, The (O'Connor), **Retro. Supp. I:** 407

Good Health and How We Won It (Sinclair), **Supp. V:** 285–286

Good Hearts (Price), **Supp. VI:** 259, 265

"Good Job Gone, A" (Hughes), **Retro. Supp. I:** 204

Good Journey, A (Ortiz), **Supp. IV Part 2:** 497, 499, 503, 505, 509–510, 514

Good Luck in Cracked Italian (Hugo), **Supp. VI:** 133, 137–138

Goodman, Allegra, **Supp. XII:** 159; **Supp. XVI:** 205; **Supp. XX: 177**

Goodman, Ellen, **Supp. XVI:** 103

Goodman, Jack, **Supp. XXI:** 277

Goodman, Jenny, **Supp. XV:** 343, 344

Goodman, Paul, **I:** 218, 261; **III:** 39; **Supp. I Part 2:** 524; **Supp. VIII:** 239–240

Goodman, Philip, **III:** 105, 108

Goodman, Walter, **Supp. IV Part 2:** 532

Good Man Is Hard to Find, A (O'Connor), **III:** 339, 343–345

"Good Man Is Hard to Find, A" (O'Connor), **III:** 339, 344, 353; **Retro. Supp. II:** 230–231

Good Man Is Hard to Find and Other Stories, A (O'Connor), **Retro. Supp. II:** 229, **230–232**

Good Morning, America (Sandburg), **III:** 592–593

"Good Morning, Major" (Marquand), **III:** 56

Good Morning, Midnight (Rhys), **Supp. III Part 1:** 43

"Good Morning, Revolution" (Hughes), **Retro. Supp. I:** 201, 203

Good Morning Blues: The Autobiography of Count Basie (Murray), **Supp. XIX:** 159

Good Morning Revolution: Uncollected Writings of Social Protest (Hughes), **Retro. Supp. I:** 194, 201, 202, 209

Good Mother, The (Miller), **Supp. XII:** 289, **290–294,** 299, 301

Good News (Abbey), **Supp. XIII: 11–12**

"Good News from New-England" (Johnson), **Supp. I Part 1:** 115

Good News of Death and Other Poems (Simpson), **Supp. IX:** 265, **268–269**

"Goodnight, Saigon" (lecture, Caputo), **Supp. XIX:** 17, 30

Good Night, Willie Lee, I'll See You in the Morning (Walker), **Supp. III Part**

2: 520, 531

"Good Oak" (Leopold), **Supp. XIV:** 185, 187, 191

"Good Old Times, The: New York Fifty Years Ago" (Briggs), **Supp. XVIII:** 15

"Good Pine, A" (Offutt), **Supp. XIX:** 174

Goodrich, Chris, **Supp. XXII:** 206, 214

Goodrich, Samuel G., **Supp. I Part 1:** 38

Good Scent from a Strange Mountain, A (R. O. Butler), **Supp. XII:** 62, **70–72**

Good School, A (Yates), **Supp. XI:** 334, **346–347,** 348, 349

"*Good Shepherdess, The*/La Buena Pastora" (Mora), **Supp. XIII:** 228–229

Good Will (Smiley), **Supp. VI:** 292, **299–300**

Goodwin, K. L., **III:** 478

Goodwin, Stephen, **Supp. V:** 314, 316, 322, 323, 325

"Good Word for Winter, A" (Lowell), **Supp. I Part 2:** 420

Goodwyn, Janet, **Retro. Supp. I:** 370

Goody, Alex, **Supp. XXII:** 160

"Goophered Grapevine, The" (Chesnutt), **Supp. XIV:** 57, **58–61**

"Goose Fish, The" (Nemerov), **III:** 272, 284

"Goose Pond" (Kunitz), **Supp. III Part 1:** 262

Goose-Step, The (Sinclair), **Supp. V:** 276

Gordimer, Nadine, **Supp. XV:** 251

Gordon, Ambrose, **Supp. XV:** 144

Gordon, A. R., **III:** 199

Gordon, Caroline, **II:** **196–222,** 536, 537; **III:** 454, 482; **IV:** 123, 126–127, 139, 282; **Retro. Supp. II:** 177, 222, 229, 233, 235; **Supp. II Part 1:** 139

Gordon, Charles G., **I:** 454

Gordon, Don, **Supp. X:** 119

Gordon, Eugene, **Supp. II Part 1:** 170; **Supp. XVIII:** 280

Gordon, Fran, **Supp. XIII:** 111

Gordon, James Morris, **II:** 197

Gordon, Lois, **Supp. IV Part 1:** 48; **Supp. V:** 46

Gordon, Lyndall, **Retro. Supp. I:** 55

Gordon, Mary, **Supp. IV Part 1: 297–317**

Gordon, Neil, **Supp. XVI:** 156

Gordon, Peter, **Supp. XII:** 3–4, 4–5, 8

Gordon, Ruth, **IV:** 357; **Supp. XX: 50**

Gore, Thomas Pryor, **Supp. IV Part 2:** 679

Gores, Joe, **Supp. XXI:** 70

Gorey, Edward, **IV:** 430, 436; **Supp. XXIII:** 209

Gorilla, My Love (Bambara), **Supp. XI:** 1, **2–7**

"Gorilla, My Love" (Bambara), **Supp. XI:** 2, 3–4

Gorki, Maxim, **I:** 478; **II:** 49; **III:** 402; **IV:** 299; **Supp. I Part 1:** 5, 51; **Supp. XIX:** 241

Gorky, Maxim, **Supp. XXIII:** 1, 4

Gorney, Cynthia, **Supp. XVI:** 112

Gorra, Michael, **Supp. V:** 71

Goslings, The (Sinclair), **Supp. V:** 276, 281

Go South to Sorrow (Rowan), **Supp. XIV:** 306

Gospel According to Joe, The (Gurney), **Supp. V:** 99

"Gospel According to Saint Mark, The" (Gordon), **Supp. IV Part 1:** 310

Gospel according to the Son (Mailer), **Retro. Supp. II:** 213

"Gospel for the Twentieth Century, The" (Locke), **Supp. XIV:** 206

"Gospel of Beauty, The" (Lindsay), **Supp. I Part 2:** 380, 382, 384, 385, 391, 396

Gospels, The (di Donato), **Supp. XX: 45–46**

Gospel Singer, The (Crews), **Supp. XI:** 102, **109**

Gosse, Edmund, **II:** 538; **IV:** 350; **Supp. VIII:** 157

"Gossip" (Conroy), **Supp. XVI:** 71–72

Gossips, Gorgons, and Crones: The Fates of the Earth (Caputi), **Supp. IV Part 1:** 335

Go Tell It on the Mountain (Baldwin), **Retro. Supp. II:** 1, 2, 3, **4–5,** 7, 14; **Supp. I Part 1:** 48, 49, 50, 51, 52, 53–54, 55, 56, 57, 59, 61, 63, 64, 67; **Supp. II Part 1:** 170

Gotera, Vince, **Supp. XIII:** 115, 116, 119, 121, 127

Gothic Revival, The: An Essay on the History of Taste (Clark), **Supp. XIV:** 348

Gothic Writers (Thomson, Voller, and Frank, eds.), **Retro. Supp. II:** 273

"Go to the Devil and Shake Yourself" (song), **Supp. I Part 2:** 580

"Go to the Shine That's on a Tree" (Eberhart), **I:** 523

Go to the Widow-Maker (Jones), **Supp. XI:** 214, **225–226,** 227, 229, 233

"Gots Is What You Got" (Di Piero), **Supp. XIX:** 35, 36, 38, 41, 42, 45–46

Gottfried, Alex, **Supp. XIX:** 260

Gottfried, Martin, **Supp. IV Part 2:** 584

Gotthelf, Allan, **Supp. IV Part 2:** 528

Gottlieb, Adolph, **Supp. XV:** 144

Gottlieb, Edward, **Supp. XX: 250**

Gottlieb, Leopold, **Supp. XXIII:** 6

Gottlieb, Morton, **Supp. XVI:** 196

Gottlieb, Robert, **Supp. IV Part 2:** 474

Gottschalk and the Grande Tarantelle (Brooks), **Supp. III Part 1:** 86

"Gottschalk and the Grande Tarantelle" (Brooks), **Supp. III Part 1:** 86–87

Gould (Dixon), **Supp. XII:** 152, **153**

Gould, Edward Sherman, **I:** 346

Gould, Janice, **Supp. IV Part 1:** 322, 327; **Supp. XII:** 229

Gould, Jay, **I:** 4

Gould, Joe, **Supp. XV:** 143

Gourd Dancer, The (Momaday), **Supp. IV Part 2:** 481, 487, 491, 493

Gourmont, Remy de, **I:** 270, 272; **II:** 528, 529; **III:** 457, 467–468, 477; **Retro. Supp. I:** 55

Gouverneurs de la Rosée (Roumain), **Supp. IV Part 1:** 360, 367

Government Girl (film, Nichols), **Supp. XVIII:** 247

"Governors of Wyoming, The" (Proulx), **Supp. VII:** 264

"Gowane"(Kenny), **Supp. XXIII:** 147–148

Goyen, William, **Supp. V:** 220

Grabhorn, Janet, **Supp. XV:** 142

"Grace" (Budbill), **Supp. XIX:** 2

"Grace" (Dubus), **Supp. VII:** 91

"Grace" (Harjo), **Supp. XII:** 224

Grace Notes (Dove), **Supp. IV Part 1:** 248–250, 252

Grace (Eventually): Thoughts on Faith (Lamott), **Supp. XX: 143–145**

Grade, Chaim, **Supp. XVII:** 41

"Graduation" (Dubus), **Supp. VII:** 84

Grady, Henry W., **Supp. I Part 1:** 370

Graeber, Laurel, **Supp. V:** 15

Graham, Billy, **I:** 308

Graham, David, **Supp. XV:** 104; **Supp. XIX:** 81

Graham, Don, **Supp. XI:** 252, 254

Graham, Jorie, **Supp. IX:** 38, 52; **Supp. X:** 73; **Supp. XII:** 209; **Supp. XIII:** 85; **Supp. XVII:** 110, 111, 133, 240, 241, 242

Graham, Martha, **Supp. XI:** 152

Graham, Maryemma, **Retro. Supp. I:** 201, 204

Graham, Nan, **Supp. XII:** 272

Graham, Sheilah, **II:** 94; **Retro. Supp. I:** 97, 113–114, 115; **Supp. IX:** 63

Graham, Shirley, **Supp. I Part 1:** 51; **Supp. XXI:** 277. *See also* Du Bois, Shirley Graham

Graham, Stephen, **Supp. I Part 2:** 397

Graham, Tom (pseudonym). *See* Lewis, Sinclair

"Graham House, April '76"(Balakian), **Supp. XXIII:** 24

Grahn, Judy, **Supp. IV Part 1:** 325, 330; **Supp. XXIII:** 195

"Grain Field" (Crapsey), **Supp. XVII:** 77

Grainger, Percy, **Supp. I Part 2:** 386

Grain of Mustard Seed, A (Sarton), **Supp. VIII: 259–260,** 263

Gramar (Lowth), **II:** 8

Grammar of Motives, A (Burke), **I:** 272, 275, 276–278, 283, 284

Gramsci, Antonio, **Supp. XX: 35–36**

Granados, Gabriel Bernal, **Supp. XV:** 350

Granath, Jack, **Supp. XVIII:** 93

Granberry, Edwin, **I:** 288

Grand Canyon, Inc. (Everett), **Supp. XVIII:** 66

Grand Design, The (Dos Passos), **I:** 489–490

"Grande Malade, The" (Barnes), **Supp. III Part 1:** 36

"Grandfather" (Dunn), **Supp. XI:** 147

"Grandfather and Grandson" (Singer), **Retro. Supp. II:** 307

Grandfathers, The (Richter), **Supp. XVIII: 219–220**

"Grandfather's Blessing" (Alvarez), **Supp. VII:** 2

"Grand Forks" (Bierds), **Supp. XVII:** 34

"Grand Forks" (Simpson), **Supp. IX:** 280–281

"Grand Inquisitor" (Dostoevsky), **IV:** 106

Grandissimes (Cable), **II:** 291

"Grand-Master Nabokov" (Updike), **Retro. Supp. I:** 317

"Grand Miracle, The" (Karr), **Supp. XI:** 251

"Grandmother" (Gunn Allen), **Supp. IV Part 1:** 320, 325

"Grandmother in Heaven" (Levine), **Supp. V:** 186

"Grandmother of the Sun: Ritual Gynocracy in Native America" (Gunn Allen), **Supp. IV Part 1:** 328

Grandmothers of the Light: A Medicine Woman's Sourcebook (Gunn Allen, ed.), **Supp. IV Part 1:** 332, 333–334

"Grandmother Songs, The" (Hogan), **Supp. IV Part 1:** 413

"Grandpa and the Statue" (A. Miller), **III:** 147

"Grandparents" (Lowell), **II:** 550

"Grandsire Bells, The" (Bierds), **Supp. XVII:** 28–29

"Grandstand Complex, The" (McCoy), **Supp. XIII:** 166

Grange, Red, **II:** 416

Granger's Index to Poetry (anthology), **Retro. Supp. I:** 37, 39

Granite & Cedar (Miller), **Supp. XXII:** 214

Grant, Gavin, **Supp. XIX:** 175

Grant, Lee, **Supp. XIII:** 295

Grant, Madison, **Supp. II Part 1:** 170

Grant, Richard, **Supp. X:** 282

Grant, Ulysses S., **I:** 4, 15; **II:** 542; **III:** 506, 584; **IV:** 348, 446; **Supp. I Part 2:** 418; **Supp. XXIV:** 224

Grantwood, **Retro. Supp. I:** 416, 417

"Grapes, The" (Hecht), **Supp. X:** 65–66

"Grape Sherbet" (Dove), **Supp. IV Part 1:** 246

Grapes of Wrath, The (Steinbeck), **I:** 301; **III:** 589; **IV:** 51, 53–55, 59, 63, 65, 67, 68, 69; **Supp. V:** 290; **Supp. XI:** 169; **Supp. XIV:** 181; **Supp. XV:** 351; **Supp. XX: 28**

"Grapevine, The" (Ashbery), **Supp. III Part 1:** 4

"Grass" (Sandburg), **III:** 584

Grass, Günter, **Supp. VIII:** 40

Grass County (Kooser), **Supp. XIX:** 119

"Grasse: The Olive Trees" (Wilbur), **Supp. III Part 2:** 550

Grass Harp, The (Capote), **Supp. III Part 1:** 114–117, 123

Grass Still Grows, The (A. Miller), **III:** 146

"Grating Parmesan"(Crooker), **Supp. XXIII:** 56

Gratitude to Old Teachers (R. Bly), **Supp. IV Part 1:** 73

Grattan, Bill, **Supp. XXIII:** 273, 274, 275, 276, 279, 280

Graupner, Gottlieb, **Supp. XV:** 240, 244

"Grave, A" (Moore), **III:** 195, 202, 208, 213

Grave, The (Blair), **Supp. I Part 1:** 150

"Grave, The" (Porter), **III:** 433, 443, 445–446

"Grave, The" (Winters), **Supp. II Part 2:** 795, 796

"Graven Image" (O'Hara), **III:** 320

Grave of Light: New and Selected Poems, 1970–2005 (Notley), **Supp. XXII:** 226, 235, 236

Grave of the Right Hand, The (Wright), **Supp. V:** 332, 338, 339

"Grave Piece" (Eberhart), **I:** 533

Graves, Billy, **Supp. I Part 2:** 607

Graves, John, **Supp. V:** 220

Graves, Morris, **Supp. X:** 264

Graves, Peter, **Supp. IV Part 2:** 474

Graves, Rean, **Supp. I Part 1:** 326

Graves, Robert, **I:** 437, 477, 523; **Supp. I Part 2:** 541; **Supp. IV Part 1:** 280, 348; **Supp. IV Part 2:** 685

"Graveyard Blues" (Trethewey), **Supp. XXI:** 245, 255, 256

Graveyard for Lunatics, A (Bradbury), **Supp. IV Part 1:** 102, 114–116

Gravity's Rainbow (Pynchon), **Supp. II Part 2:** 617, 618–619, 621–625, 627, 630, 633–636; **Supp. IV Part 1:** 279; **Supp. V:** 44; **Supp. XIV:** 49; **Supp. XVII:** 236; **Supp. XXII:** 255; **Supp. XXIV:** 140

Gray, Cecil, **Supp. I Part 1:** 258

Gray, Francine Du Plessix, **Supp. V:** 169

Gray, James, **III:** 207; **Supp. I Part 2:** 410

Gray, Jeffrey, **Supp. XV:** 27

Gray, Josie, **Supp. XXIV:** 166, 167, 172, 178

Gray, Paul, **Supp. IV Part 1:** 305; **Supp. IV Part 2:** 639; **Supp. XVI:** 74; **Supp. XVIII:** 94

Gray, Thomas, **I:** 68; **Supp. I Part 1:** 150; **Supp. I Part 2:** 422, 716

Gray, Thomas A., **Supp. I Part 2:** 710

"Gray Heron, The" (Kinnell), **Supp. III Part 1:** 250

"Gray Mills of Farley, The" (Jewett), **Retro. Supp. II:** 132, 144

"Gray Poem" (Everwine), **Supp. XV:** 81

Grayson, Charles, **Supp. XIII:** 171

"Gray Squirrel" (Francis), **Supp. IX:** 90

"Gray Wolf's H 'ant, The" (Chesnutt), **Supp. XIV:** 60

Grealy, Lucy, **Supp. XII:** 310

Greasy Lake (Boyle), **Supp. VIII:** 14–15

"Greasy Lake" (Boyle), **Supp. VIII:** 15; **Supp. XX: 18–19**

Greasy Lake & Other Stories (Boyle), **Supp. XX:** 17, 18–19

"Great Adventure of Max Breuck, The" (Lowell), **II:** 522

Great American Novel, The (P. Roth), **Retro. Supp. II:** 283, 288–289; **Supp. III Part 2:** 414–416

Great American Short Novels (Phillips, ed.), **Supp. VIII:** 156

Great Battles of the World (Crane), **I:** 415

"Great Carousel, The" (Untermeyer), **Supp. XV:** 296

Great Christian Doctrine of Original Sin Defended, The . . . (Edwards), **I:** 549, 557, 559

Great Circle (Aiken), **I:** 53, 55, 57

"Great Class-Reunion Bazaar, The" (Theroux), **Supp. VIII:** 312

Great Day, The (Hurston), **Supp. VI:** 154

Great Days (Barthelme), **Supp. IV Part 1:** 39

Great Days, The (Dos Passos), **I:** 491

Great Digest (Pound, trans.), **III:** 472

"Great Divider, The" (Saunders), **Supp. XIX:** 235

"Great Elegy for John Donne" (Brodsky), **Supp. VIII:** 21, 23

"Greater Good, A" (Di Piero), **Supp. XIX:** 39

Greater Inclination, The (Wharton), **Retro. Supp. I:** 363, **364–365,** 366

Greater Sea, The (Gibran), **Supp. XX: 118**

"Greater Self, The" (Gibran), **Supp. XX: 118**

"Greater Torment, The" (Blackmur), **Supp. II Part 1:** 92

Greatest Hits 1969–1996 (Salinas), **Supp. XIII:** 311

"Greatest of These, The" (C. Miller), **Supp. XXII:** 188, 196

"Greatest Thing in the World, The" (Mailer), **Retro. Supp. II:** 196

Great Expectations (Acker), **Supp. XII:** 5, **9–11**

Great Expectations (Dickens), **III:** 247; **Supp. I Part 1:** 35; **Supp. XVI:** 73; **Supp. XVIII:** 146

"Great Expectations, No Satisfaction" (D. Gates), **Supp. XVI:** 73

"Great Figure, The" (W. C. Williams), **IV:** 414

"Great Fillmore Street Buffalo Drive, The" (Momaday), **Supp. IV Part 2:** 493

Great Gatsby, The (Fitzgerald) (Modern Library), **Retro. Supp. I:** 113

Great Gatsby, The (Fitzgerald), **I:** 107, 375, 514; **II:** 77, 79, 83, 84, 85, 87, 91–93, 94, 96, 98; **III:** 244, 260, 372, 572; **IV:** 124, 297; **Retro. Supp. I:** 98, 105, **105–108,** 110, 114, 115, 335, 359; **Retro. Supp. II:** 107, 201; **Supp. II Part 2:** 626; **Supp. III Part 2:** 585; **Supp. IV Part 2:** 468, 475; **Supp. IX:** 57, 58; **Supp. X:** 175; **Supp. XI:** 65, 69, 334; **Supp. XVI:** 64, 75; **Supp. XVIII:** 76, 148, 165; **Supp. XX: 59, 60, 61, 72; Supp. XXII:** 81, 82, 88; **Supp. XXIII:** 101

Great God Brown, The (O'Neill), **III:** 165, 391, 394–395

Great Goodness of Life: A Coon Show (Baraka), **Supp. II Part 1:** 47

Great Heart: The History of a Labrador Adventure (Davidson and Rugge), **Supp. XXII:** 218

Great Inclination, The (Wharton), **IV:** 310

"Great Infirmities" (Simic), **Supp. VIII:** 277

Great Jones Street (DeLillo), **Supp. VI:** 2, 3, 8–9, 11, 12

"Great Lawsuit, The: Man *versus* Men: Woman *versus* Women" (Fuller), **Retro. Supp. I:** 156; **Supp. II Part 1:** 292

"Great Men and Their Environment" (James), **II:** 347

"Great Mississippi Bubble, The" (Irving), **II:** 314

Great Railway Bazaar, The: By Train through Asia (Theroux), **Supp. VIII:** 318, 319, **320–321,** 322

"Great Scott" (Conroy), **Supp. XVI:** 75, 77

Great Shark Hunt, The (Thompson), **Supp. XXIV:** 286

"Great Sleigh-Ride of Brewsterville, The" (Briggs), **Supp. XVIII:** 16

Great Stories of Suspense (Millar, ed.), **Supp. IV Part 2:** 474

Great Topics of the World (Goldbarth), **Supp. XII:** 187, 189, 191

Great Valley, The (Masters), **Supp. I Part 2:** 465

Great World and Timothy Colt, The (Auchincloss), **Supp. IV Part 1:** 25, 31, 32

Grédy, Jean-Pierre, **Supp. XVI:** 194

"Greek Boy, The" (Bryant), **Supp. I Part 1:** 168

Greek Mind/Jewish Soul: The Conflicted Art of Cynthia Ozick (Strandberg), **Supp. V:** 273

"Greek Partisan, The" (Bryant), **Supp. I Part 1:** 168

"Greeks, The" (McCarriston), **Supp. XIV:** 271

"Greeks, the Chines, or Say the Mayans, The" (Bronk), **Supp. XXI:** 31

Greeley, Horace, **II:** 7; **IV:** 197, 286–287

Green, Ashbel, **Supp. IV Part 2:** 474

Green, Henry, **IV:** 279; **Retro. Supp. I:** 354; **Supp. III Part 1:** 3; **Supp. XI:** 294–295, 296, 297; **Supp. XII:** 315

Green, Jack, **Supp. IV Part 1:** 284–285

Green, Martin, **Supp. I Part 1:** 299

Green, Michelle, **Supp. IV Part 1:** 95

Green, Rose Basile, **Supp. XX:** 33, 41

"Green Automobile, The" (Ginsberg), **Supp. II Part 1:** 322

Greenberg, Clement, **Supp. XV:** 141, 143, 144, 145

Greenberg, Eliezer, **Supp. I Part 2:** 432; **Supp. XXIII:** 7

Greenberg, Hayim, **Supp. XXIII:** 3

Greenberg, Jonathan, **Supp. XII:** 285

Greenberg, Miriam, **Supp. XXII:** 244

Greenberg, Samuel, **I:** 393

Green Bough, A (Faulkner), **Retro. Supp. I:** 84

"Green Canoe" (Halliday), **Supp. XIX:** 88

Green Centuries (Gordon), **II:** 196, 197–207, 209

"Green Crab's Shell, A" (Doty), **Supp. XI:** 126

"Green Door, The" (O. Henry), **Supp. II Part 1:** 395

Greene, A. C., **Supp. V:** 223, 225

Greene, Graham, **I:** 480; **II:** 62, 320; **III:** 57, 556; **Retro. Supp. I:** 215; **Supp. I Part 1:** 280; **Supp. IV Part 1:** 341; **Supp. V:** 298; **Supp. IX:** 261; **Supp. XI:** 99,**Supp. XI:** 104; **Supp. XIII:** 233; **Supp. XVIII:** 79; **Supp. XIX:** 29–30

Greene, Helga, **Supp. IV Part 1:** 134, 135

Greene, J. Lee, **Retro. Supp. II:** 121

Greene, Nathanael, **Supp. I Part 2:** 508

Greene, Richard Tobias, **III:** 76

Greene, Robert, **Supp. XVII:** 232

Green Eggs and Ham (Geisel), **Supp. XVI:** 108, 109

"Greene-ing of the Portables, The" (Cowley), **Supp. II Part 1:** 140

"Greenest Continent, The" (Stevens), **Retro. Supp. I:** 304

Greenfeld, Josh, **III:** 364

Greenfield, Josh, **Supp. XIX:** 269

"Green Hell" (Boyle), **Supp. XX:** 18

Green Hills of Africa (Hemingway), **II:** 253; **Retro. Supp. I:** 182, 186

Greening of America, The (C. Reich), **Supp. XVII:** 3

"Green Lagoons, The" (Leopold), **Supp. XIV:** 188

"Green Lampshade" (Simic), **Supp. VIII:** 283

Greenlanders, The (Smiley), **Supp. VI:** 292, **296–298,** 299, 305, 307

Greenlaw, Edwin A., **IV:** 453

"Greenleaf" (O'Connor), **III:** 350, 351; **Retro. Supp. II:** 233, 237

Greenman, Walter F., **I:** 217, 222

Green Memories (Mumford), **Supp. II Part 2:** 474, 475, 479, 480–481

Green Mountain Ghosts, Ghouls, and Unsolved Mysteries (Citro), **Supp. XXII:** 208, 218

"Green Pasture, The" (Leopold), **Supp. XIV:** 184

Green Pastures, The (Connelly), **Supp. II Part 1:** 223

"Green Red Brown and White" (Swenson), **Supp. IV Part 2:** 639

"Green River" (Bryant), **Supp. I Part 1:** 155, 164

Green Shadows, White Whale (Bradbury), **Supp. IV Part 1:** 102, 103, 116

"Green Shirt, The" (Olds), **Supp. X:** 209

"Greensleeves" (Jarman), **Supp. XVII:** 113

"Greensleeves" (Notley), **Supp. XXII:** 228

Greenslet, Ferris, **I:** 19; **Retro. Supp. I:** 9, 10, 11, 13; **Retro. Supp. II:** 41

Greenspan, Alan, **Supp. IV Part 2:** 526

Greenspan, Ezra, **Supp. XVIII:** 257

Greenstreet, Sydney, **Supp. IV Part 1:** 356

"Green Thought, A" (L. Michaels), **Supp. XVI:** 204

"Green-Thumb Boy" (Nelson), **Supp. XVIII:** 182

Greenwald, Ted, **Supp. IV Part 2:** 423

Green Wall, The (Wright), **Supp. III Part 2:** 591, 593, 595

Green Wave, The (Rukeyser), **Supp. VI:** 273, 280

"Green Ways" (Kunitz), **Supp. III Part 1:** 265

Green with Beasts (Merwin), **Supp. III Part 1:** 340, 344–346

Greenwood, Grace, **Supp. XIII:** 141

"Greeting Card Verse" (Peacock), **Supp. XIX:** 200

Gregerson, Linda, **Supp. IV Part 2:** 651; **Supp. X:** 204–205; **Supp. XI:** 142

"Gregorio Valdes" (Bishop), **Retro. Supp. II:** 51

Gregory, Alyse, **I:** 221, 226, 227, 231

Gregory, Horace, **II:** 512; **Supp. III Part 2:** 614, 615; **Supp. IX:** 229; **Supp. XV:** 143

Gregory, Lady Isabella Augusta, **III:** 458

Gregory, Sinda, **Supp. X:** 260, 268

Grendel (Gardner), **Supp. VI:** 63, **67,** 68, 74

Grenstone Poems (Bynner), **Supp. XV:** 44

"Gretel in Darkness" (Glück), **Supp. V:** 82

Gretta (Caldwell), **I:** 301, 302

Greuze, Jean Baptiste, **Supp. I Part 2:** 714

Grey, Zane, **Supp. XIII:** 5

Greyhounding This America (Kenny), **Supp. XXIII: 155**

Gridley Firing (Hayford), **Supp. XXII:** 204

"Grief Has Stamped" (Pedersen; Nelson, trans.), **Supp. XVIII:** 180

Grieg, Michael, **Supp. XV:** 133, 148

Griffin, Bartholomew, **Supp. I Part 1:** 369

Griffin, John Howard, **Supp. VIII:** 208; **Supp. XXI:** 74

Griffin, Merv, **Supp. IV Part 2:** 526

Griffith, Albert J., **Supp. V:** 325

Griffith, D. W., **I:** 31, 481–482; **Retro. Supp. I:** 103, 325; **Supp. XI:** 45; **Supp. XVI:** 183, 184; **Supp. XXI:** 170

Griffith, Paul, **Supp. XVIII:** 173, 175

Griffiths, Clyde, **I:** 511

Grile, Dod (pseudonym). *See* Bierce, Ambrose

Grimm, Herman, **II:** 17

Grimm brothers, **II:** 378; **III:** 101, 491, 492; **IV:** 266; **Supp. I Part 2:** 596, 622; **Supp. X:** 78, 84, 86

Grimshaw, Anna, **Supp. XXI:** 172

Grinnell, George Bird, **Supp. XVI:** 13

Gris, Juan, **I:** 442; **Retro. Supp. I:** 430

Griswold, Rufus Wilmot, **III:** 409, 429; **Retro. Supp. II:** 261, 262; **Supp. XV:** 277, 278; **Supp. XVI:** 8, 10–11

Grogg, Sam, Jr., **Supp. IV Part 2:** 468, 471

Gromer, Crystal, **Supp. XII:** 297

Gronlund, Laurence, **II:** 276

Grooms, Red, **Supp. XV:** 178

Grooves: A Kind of Mystery (Brockmeier), **Supp. XXII:** 55, 56, 59

"Groping for Trouts" (Gass), **Supp. VI:** 87

Grosholz, Emily, **Supp. XII:** 185; **Supp. XIX:** 37–38, 278

Grosman un zun (Grosman and Son) (Asch), **Supp. XXIII:** 7

Gross, Robert A., **Supp. XIX:** 151

Gross, Terry, **Supp. XVI:** 167; **Supp. XXI:** 247, 255

"Grosse Fuge" (Doty), **Supp. XI:** 126–127

Grossman, Allen, **Retro. Supp. II:** 83; **Supp. XVIII:** 91; **Supp. XIX:** 82, 86, 94

Grosz, George, **III:** 172; **IV:** 438; **Retro. Supp. II:** 321; **Supp. X:** 137

"Grotesque in Modern Fiction, The" (E. Hoffman, Ph.D. dissertation), **Supp. XVI:** 147

"Groundhog, The" (Eberhart), **I:** 523, 530–532, 533

"Ground on Which I Stand, The" (Wilson), **Supp. VIII:** 331

"Ground Swell" (Jarman), **Supp. XVII:** 118

Group, The (McCarthy), **II:** 570, 574–578

"Group of Two, A" (Jarrell), **II:** 368

Group Therapy (Hearon), **Supp. VIII:** **64–65**

"Grove" (Goldbarth), **Supp. XII:** 176

Groves of Academe, The (McCarthy), **II:** 568–571

Growing into Love (X. J. Kennedy), **Supp. XV:** 153, **158–160**

Growing Pains (J. S. Untermeyer), **Supp. XV:** 303

"Growing Season, The" (Caldwell), **I:** 309

Growing Up Gay: A Literary Anthology (Singer, ed.), **Supp. IV Part 1:** 330

"Growing Up Good in Maycomb" (Shaffer), **Supp. VIII:** 128

"Grown-Up" (Jewett), **Retro. Supp. II:** 134

"Growth" (Lowell), **II:** 554

"Growth and Decay in Recent Verse" (Untermeyer), **Supp. XV:** 299

Growth of the American Republic, The (Morison and Commager), **Supp. I Part 2:** 484

"Growtown Buggle, The" (Jewett), **Retro. Supp. II:** 132

Grubin, David, **Supp. XXIII:** 138

Gruenberg, Louis, **III:** 392

Grumbach, Doris, **II:** 560

"Gryphon" (C. Baxter), **Supp. XVII:** 14, 17

"Guacamaja" (Leopold), **Supp. XIV:** 188–189

Guardian Angel, The (Holmes), **Supp. I Part 1:** 315–316

"Guardian of the Law" (R. Fisher), **Supp. XIX:** 71

Guard of Honor (Cozzens), **I:** 370–372, 375, 376–377, 378, 379

Guardsman, The (Molnar), **Supp. XVI:** 187

Guare, John, **Supp. XIII:** 196, 207

Gubar, Susan, **Retro. Supp. I:** 42; **Retro. Supp. II:** 324; **Supp. XVI:** 66; **Supp. XV:** 270; **Supp. XXIV:** 28

Guerard, Albert, Jr., **Supp. X:** 79; **Supp. XIII:** 172

Guérin, Maurice de, **I:** 241

"Guerrilla Handbook, A" (Baraka), **Supp. II Part 1:** 36

Guess and Spell Coloring Book, The (Swenson), **Supp. IV Part 2:** 648

Guess Who's Coming to Dinner (film), **Supp. I Part 1:** 67

Guest, Barbara, **Supp. XXIII:** 215

Guest, Judith, **Supp. XVI:** 36

Guest, Val, **Supp. XI:** 307

Guest Book (Bynner), **Supp. XV:** 51

"Guest Ellen at the Supper for Street People, The" (Ferry), **Supp. XXIV:** 152–153, 162

"Guests of Mrs. Timms, The" (Jewett), **II:** 408; **Retro. Supp. II:** 135

Guevara, Martha, **Supp. VIII:** 74

Guevara, Fray Miguel de, **Supp. XXI:** 104

"Guevara . . .Guevara" (Salinas), **Supp. XIII:** 312–313, 315

Guggenheim, Peggy, **Supp. XXII:** 165

Guided Tours of Hell (Prose), **Supp. XVI:** 257, 261

"Guided Tours of Hell" (Prose), **Supp. XVI:** 257

Guide for the Perplexed (Maimonides), **Supp. XVII:** 46

Guide in the Wilderness, A (Cooper), **I:** 337

"Guidelines" (Espaillat), **Supp. XXI:** 99

"Guide to Dungeness Spit, A" (Wagoner), **Supp. IX:** 325–326, 329

Guide to Ezra Pound's Selected Cantos' (Kearns), **Retro. Supp. I:** 292

Guide to Kulchur (Pound), **III:** 475

Guide to the Ruins (Nemerov), **III:** 269, 270–271, 272

Guillén, Jorge, **Supp. XXIV:** 152

Guillén, Nicolás, **Retro. Supp. I:** 202; **Supp. I Part 1:** 345

Guillevic, Eugene, **Supp. III Part 1:** 283

"Guilt, The" (Peacock), **Supp. XIX:** 200

"Guilty Man, The" (Kunitz), **Supp. II Part 1:** 263

Guilty of Everything: The Autobiography of Herbert Huncke (Huncke), **Supp. XIV:** 138, 140, 141, 150

Guilty Pleasures (Barthelme), **Supp. IV Part 1:** 44, 45, 53

Guimond, James, **Supp. XXI:** 228

Guinness, Alec, **Retro. Supp. I:** 65; **Supp. XX: 50**

Gulag Archipelago, The (Solzhenitsyn), **Supp. XVII:** 229

"Gulf, The" (Dunn), **Supp. XI:** 149

Gulistan (Saadi), **II:** 19

Gullible's Travels (Lardner), **II:** 426, 427

Gulliver, Adelaide Cromwell, **Supp. XVIII:** 286

"Gulliver Found" (Bronk), **Supp. XXI:** 33

Gulliver's Travels (Swift), **I:** 209, 348, 366; **II:** 301; **Supp. I Part 2:** 656; **Supp. XI:** 209; **Supp. XVI:** 110

"Gulls" (Hayden), **Supp. II Part 1:** 367

"Gulls, The" (Nemerov), **III:** 272

"Gulls on Dumps" (Di Piero), **Supp. XIX:** 41

"Gun, The" (Dobyns), **Supp. XIII:** 88

Gun, with Occasional Music (Lethem), **Supp. XVIII: 137–138**

Günderode: A Translation from the German (Fuller), **Supp. II Part 1:** 293

Gundy, Jeff, **Supp. XI:** 315; **Supp. XVI:** 46, 265, 275

Gunfight at the O.K. Corral (film), **Supp. XX: 246**

Gunman's Rhapsody (Parker), **Supp. XIX:** 187

Gunn, Robin Wright, **Supp. XXI:** 243, 244

Gunn, Thom, **Supp. IX:** 269

Gunn, Thomas, **Supp. V:** 178

Gunn Allen, Paula, **Supp. IV Part 1:** **319–340,** 404; **Supp. IV Part 2:** 499, 502, 557, 568; **Supp. XII:** 218

"Gunnar's Sword" (C. Bly), **Supp. XVI:** 34, 35, 37, 42

"Guns as Keys; and the Great Gate Swings" (Lowell), **II:** 524

Gurdjieff, Georges, **Supp. V:** 199; **Supp. IX:** 320

Gurganus, Allan, **Supp. XII:** 308–309, 310

Gurko, Leo, **III:** 62

Gurney, A. R., **Supp. V: 95–112; Supp. IX:** 261

Gurney, Mary (Molly) Goodyear, **Supp. V:** 95

Gussow, Mel, **Supp. IX:** 93; **Supp. XII:** 325, 328, 341

Gustavus Vassa, the African (Vassa), **Supp. IV Part 1:** 11

Gusto, Thy Name Was Mrs. Hopkins: A Prose Rhapsody (Francis), **Supp. IX:** 89

Guston, Philip, **Supp. XXIII:** 210

Gute Mensch von Sezuan, Der (Brecht), **Supp. IX:** 138

Gutenberg, Johann, **Supp. I Part 2:** 392

Guthrie, A. B., **Supp. X:** 103

Guthrie, Woody, **Supp. XVIII:** 23

Gutman, Herbert, **Supp. I Part 1:** 47

Guttenplan, D. D., **Supp. XI:** 38

"Gutting of Couffignal, The" (Hammett), **Supp. IV Part 1:** 345

Guy Domville (James), **II:** 331; **Retro. Supp. I:** 228

"Gwendolyn" (Bishop), **Retro. Supp. II:** 51

Gwynn, R. S., **Supp. XVIII:** 184

Gypsy Ballads (Hughes, trans.), **Supp. I Part 1:** 345

Gypsy's Curse, The (Crews), **Supp. XI:** **110**

"Gyroscope, The" (Rukeyser), **Supp. VI:** 271

Gysin, Brion, **Supp. XII:** 129

H

Haardt, Sara. *See* Mencken, Mrs. H. L. (Sara Haardt)

Haas, Robert, **Supp. XXII:** 177

Habakkuk (biblical book), **III:** 200, 347

Habibi (Nye), **Supp. XIII:** 273, **279**

"Habit" (James), **II:** 351

Habitations of the Word (Gass), **Supp. VI:** 88

"Hack, The" (Swados), **Supp. XIX:** 267

"Hackberry"(P. Benedict), **Supp. XXIII:** 37–38, 39

Hacker, Marilyn, **Supp. XV:** 250; **Supp. XVII:** 71, 76, 112; **Supp. XVIII:** 177, 178

Hackett, David, **Supp. XII:** 236

Hadas, Rachel, **Supp. XXIII: 111–128; Supp. XXIV:** 157

Hadda, Janet, **Retro. Supp. II:** 317

Haddád, 'Abd al-Masíh, **Supp. XX:** 116

Haeckel, Ernst Heinrich, **II:** 480

Haegert, John, **Supp. XVI:** 69

Hafif, Marcia, **Supp. IV Part 2:** 423

Hagar's Daughter (P. Hopkins), **Supp. XVI:** 143

Hagedorn, Jessica, **Supp. X:** 292

Hagen, Beulah, **Supp. I Part 2:** 679

Hager, Kelly, **Supp. XVIII:** 183

Haggard, Rider, **III:** 189

Hagoromo (play), **III:** 466

Hagstrum, Jean, **Supp. XV:** 74

"Hail Mary" (Fante), **Supp. XI:** 160, 164

Haines, George, IV, **I:** 444

Haines, John, **Supp. XII: 197–214**

"Hair" (Corso), **Supp. XII:** 117, 126, 127

"Hair, The" (Carver), **Supp. III Part 1:** 137

"Haircut" (Lardner), **II:** 430, 436

"Hair Dressing" (Untermeyer), **Supp. XV:** 304, 305

Hairpiece: A Film for Nappy-Headed People (Chenzira; film), **Supp. XI:** 19–20

"Hairs" (Cisneros), **Supp. VII:** 59

Hairs/Pelitos (Cisneros), **Supp. VII:** 58

Hairy Ape, The (O'Neill), **III:** 391, 392, 393

"Haïta the Shepherd" (Bierce), **I:** 203

Haj, The (Uris), **Supp. XX: 244, 245, 247, 255–256**

Haldeman, Anna, **Supp. I Part 1:** 2

Hale, Edward Everett, **Supp. I Part 2:** 584; **Supp. XI:** 193, 200

Hale, John Parker, **Supp. I Part 2:** 685

Hale, Nancy, **Supp. VIII:** 151, 171

Haley, Alex, **Supp. I Part 1:** 47, 66

Haley, J. Evetts, **Supp. V:** 226

"Half a Century Gone" (Lowell), **II:** 554

Half-a-Hundred: Tales by Great American Writers (Grayson, ed.), **Supp. XIII:** 171

Half Asleep in Frog Pajamas (Robbins), **Supp. X:** 259, **279–282**

Half Breed, The (film), **Supp. XVI:** 185

Half-Century of Conflict, A (Parkman), **Supp. II Part 2:** 600, 607, 610

"Half Deity" (Moore), **III:** 210, 214, 215

"Half Hour of August" (Ríos), **Supp. IV Part 2:** 552

Half-Lives (Jong), **Supp. V:** 115, 119

Half Moon Street: Two Short Novels (Theroux), **Supp. VIII:** 322, 323

Half of Paradise (Burke), **Supp. XIV:** 22, 24

Half-Past Nation Time (Johnson), **Supp. VI:** 187

"Half-Skinned Steer, The" (Proulx), **Supp. VII:** 261–262

"Half Sonnets" (Jarman), **Supp. XVII:** 115

Half Sun Half Sleep (Swenson), **Supp. IV Part 2:** 645–646

Halfway (Kumin), **Supp. IV Part 2:** 441–442

"Halfway" (Rich), **Supp. I Part 2:** 553

Halfway Down the Hall: New and Selected Poems (Hadas), **Supp. XXIII: 118–119**

Halfway Home (Monette), **Supp. X:** 154

Halfway to Silence (Sarton), **Supp. VIII:** 261

Half You Don't Know, The: Selected Stories (Cameron), **Supp. XII:** 79, 80, 81

Haliburton, Thomas Chandler, **II:** 301; **IV:** 193; **Supp. I Part 2:** 411

Halifax, Lord, **II:** 111

Hall, Daniel, **Supp. XII:** 258

Hall, Donald, **I:** 567; **III:** 194; **Supp. IV Part 1:** 63, 72; **Supp. IV Part 2:** 621; **Supp. IX:** 269; **Supp. XIV:** 82, 126; **Supp. XV:** 21, 153, 176; **Supp. XVI:** 39, 230, 235; **Supp. XX: 194; Supp. XXI:** 86; **Supp. XXIII:** 209

Hall, Hazel, **Supp. XXII:** 275

Hall, James, **II:** 313; **Supp. I Part 2:** 584, 585

Hall, James Baker, **Supp. X:** 24

Hall, Rachel, **Supp. XXIII:** 301

Hall, Timothy L., **Supp. VIII:** 127, 128

Halleck, Fitz-Greene, **Supp. I Part 1:** 156, 158

"Hallelujah: A Sestina" (Francis), **Supp. IX:** 82

"Hallelujah on the Bum" (Abbey), **Supp. XIII:** 2

"Haller's Second Home" (Maxwell), **Supp. VIII:** 169

Halliday, Mark, **Supp. XV:** 19, 20, 21, 23, 25, 27, 30; **Supp. XIX: 81–95**

Hallock, Rev. Moses, **Supp. I Part 1:** 153

Hall of Mirrors, A (Stone), **Supp. V:** 295, 296–299, 300, 301

"Hallowe'en" (Huncke), **Supp. XIV:** 145

"Halloween Party, The" (Chabon), **Supp. XI:** 72

Halloween Tree, The (Bradbury), **Supp. IV Part 1:** 102, 112–113

"Halls, The" (Halliday), **Supp. XIX:** 90

Hallwas, John E., **Supp. I Part 2:** 454

Halpern, Daniel, **Supp. IV Part 1:** 94–95, 95

Halsey, Theresa, **Supp. IV Part 1:** 330, 331

"Halt in the Desert, A" (Brodsky), **Supp. VIII:** 24

"Halves" (Dunn), **Supp. XI:** 149

Hamburg, Victoria, **Supp. XVI:** 126

Hamerik, Asger, **Supp. I Part 1:** 356

Hamill, Pete, **Supp. XX: 244, 255**

Hamill, Sam, **Supp. X:** 112, 125, 126, 127

Hamilton, Alexander, **I:** 485; **Supp. I Part 2:** 456, 483, 509

Hamilton, Alice, **Supp. I Part 1:** 5

Hamilton, David, **Supp. IX:** 296

Hamilton, Edith, **Supp. XVI:** 196

Hamilton, Lady Emma, **II:** 524

Hamilton, Hamish, **Supp. I Part 2:** 617

Hamilton, Walton, **Supp. I Part 2:** 632

Hamilton Stark (Banks), **Supp. V:** 8, 9–10, 11

"Hamlen Brook" (Wilbur), **Supp. III Part 2:** 564

"Hamlet" (Laforgue), **I:** 573; **III:** 11

Hamlet (Miller and Fraenkel), **III:** 178, 183

Hamlet (Shakespeare), **I:** 53, 183, 205, 377, 586–587; **II:** 158, 531; **III:** 7, 11, 12, 183; **IV:** 116, 131, 227; **Supp. I Part 1:** 369; **Supp. I Part 2:** 422, 457, 471; **Supp. IV Part 2:** 612; **Supp. IX:** 14

Hamlet, The (Faulkner), **II:** 69–71, 73, 74; **IV:** 131; **Retro. Supp. I:** 82, 91, 92; **Supp. VIII:** 178; **Supp. IX:** 103; **Supp. XI:** 247

"Hamlet and His Problems" (Eliot), **I:** 586–587

Hamlet of A. MacLeish, The (MacLeish), **III:** 11–12, 14, 15, 18

Hamlin, Eva, **Retro. Supp. II:** 115

"Hammer" (Bidart), **Supp. XV:** 35

Hammer, Adam, **Supp. XIII:** 112

Hammer, Langdon, **Retro. Supp. II:** 45, 53; **Supp. X:** 65

"Hammer Man, The" (Bambara), **Supp. XI:** 4–5

Hammett, Dashiell, **IV:** 286; **Retro. Supp. II:** 327; **Supp. I Part 1:** 286, 289, 291, 292, 293, 294, 295; **Supp. III Part 1:** 91; **Supp. IV Part 1:** 120, 121, **341–357; Supp. IV Part 2:** 461, 464, 468, 469, 472, 473; **Supp. IX:** 200; **Supp. XI:** 228; **Supp. XIII:** 159; **Supp. XIV:** 21; **Supp. XVII:** 137; **Supp. XIX:** 178; **Supp. XXI:** 68

Hammon, Jupiter, **Supp. XXII:** 11

Hammond, John, **Supp. XVIII:** 24

Hammond, Karla, **Supp. IV Part 2:** 439, 442, 448, 637, 640, 644, 648

Hampl, Patricia, **Supp. IX:** 291; **Supp. XI:** 126; **Supp. XVII:** 21; **Supp. XXII: 81–101**

Hampson, Alfred Leete, **Retro. Supp. I:** 35–36, 38

"Hamrick's Polar Bear" (Caldwell), **I:** 309–310

Hamsun, Knut, **Supp. VIII:** 40; **Supp. XI:** 161, 167; **Supp. XII:** 21, 128

Hancock, John, **Supp. I Part 2:** 524; **Supp. XX:** 282

Hancock, Wade, **Supp. XVI:** 34

Handbook of North American Indians (Sando), **Supp. IV Part 2:** 510

Handcarved Coffins: A Nonfiction Account of an American Crime (Capote), **Supp. III Part 1:** 131

Handel, Georg Friedrich, **III:** 210; **IV:** 369

"Handfasting" (Wright), **Supp. XV:** 343

"Handfuls" (Sandburg), **III:** 584

"Handle with Care" (Fitzgerald), **Retro. Supp. I:** 114

Handley, William R., **Supp. XVIII:** 58

Handmaid's Tale, The (Atwood), **Supp. XIII:** 19, 20, **27–29**

"Hand of Casino, 1954, A" (Skloot), **Supp. XX: 194, 202**

"Hand of Emmagene, The" (Taylor), **Supp. V:** 314, 325–326

Hand of the Potter, The: A Tragedy in Four Acts (Dreiser), **Retro. Supp. II:** 104; **Supp. XVII:** 96
"Hands" (Anderson), **I:** 106, 107
"Hands" (Mora), **Supp. XIII:** 215
Hands of Orlac, The (M. Renard; Crewe-Jones, trans.), **Supp. XVII:** 58
Hand to Mouth (Auster), **Supp. XII:** 21
"Hand to Mouth" (Auster), **Supp. XII:** 31
Handy, Lowney, **Supp. XI:** 217, 220, 221, 225
Handy, W. C., **Supp. VIII:** 337
Handy Guide for Beggars, A (Lindsay), **Supp. I Part 2:** 376–378, 380, 382, 399
Haney, David, **Supp. XXI:** 253
"Hanged Man, A" (Cliff), **Supp. XXII:** 74
"Hanging Burley" (J. W. Miller), **Supp. XX:** 167
Hanging Garden, The (Wagoner), **Supp. IX:** 338–339
"Hanging Gardens of Tyburn, The" (Hecht), **Supp. X:** 58
"Hanging of the Crane, The" (Longfellow), **Retro. Supp. II:** 169, 171
Hanging On (Conroy), **Supp. XVI:** 69
"Hanging Pictures in Nanny's Room" (Kenyon), **Supp. VII:** 164
"Hanging the Wash" (Alvarez), **Supp. VII:** 4
"Hangman, The" (Sexton), **Supp. II Part 2:** 680, 691
Hangover Mass (X. J. Kennedy), **Supp. XV:** 165
Hangsaman (Jackson), **Supp. IX:** 116, 123, **124**
Hanh, Thich Nhat, **Supp. V:** 199
Hanks, Lucy, **III:** 587
Hanks, Nancy. *See* Lincoln, Mrs. Thomas (Nancy Hanks)
Hanley, Lynne T., **Supp. IV Part 1:** 208
"Hanlon Mountain in Mist" (J. W. Miller), **Supp. XX: 164, 166–167**
Hanna, Mark, **Supp. I Part 2:** 395
Hannah, Barry, **Supp. X:** 285; **Supp. XIX:** 209; **Supp. XXI:** 38, 118
Hannah and Her Sisters (film; Allen), **Supp. XV: 9, 10–11**
"Hannah Armstrong" (Masters), **Supp. I Part 2:** 461
"Hannah Binding Shoes" (Larcom), **Supp. XIII:** 141, 143
"Hannah Byde" (D. West), **Supp. XVIII:** 280
Hannah's House (Hearon), **Supp. VIII:** 58, **60–61**
Hanneman, Audre, **II:** 259
Hannibal Lecter, My Father (Acker), **Supp. XII:** 6
Hanoi (McCarthy), **II:** 579
"Hanoi Drifting, January 2003" (Weigl), **Supp. XIX:** 288
Hansberry, Lorraine, **Supp. IV Part 1: 359–377; Supp. VIII:** 329
Hanscom, Leslie, **Supp. XI:** 229
"Hansel and Gretel" (Prose), **Supp. XVI:** 256, 258

Hansen, Erik, **Supp. V:** 241
Hansen, Harry, **IV:** 366; **Supp. XXII:** 194, 277
Han-shan, **Supp. VIII:** 292
Hanson, Curtis, **Supp. XI:** 67
Hanson, Elizabeth, **Supp. XXIV:** 220
Han Suyin, **Supp. X:** 291
Hanzlicek, C. G., **Supp. XV:** 73
Hapgood, Charles H., II, **Supp. XXI:** 6
Hapgood, Hutchins, **Supp. XVII: 95–108; Supp. XXI:** 1, 3, 9, 10
Hapgood, Norman, **Supp. XXI:** 2
Hapgoods, The: Three Earnest Brothers (Marcaccio), **Supp. XVII:** 106
"Happenings: An Art of Radical Juxtaposition" (Sontag), **Supp. III Part 2:** 456
"Happenstance" (Komunyakaa), **Supp. XIII:** 130
Happenstance (Shields), **Supp. VII:** 315–318, 320, 323, 324, 326
Happersberger, Lucien, **Supp. I Part 1:** 51
"Happiest I've Been, The" (Updike), **IV:** 219
Happily Ever After (Quindlen), **Supp. XVII:** 167
"Happiness" (Oliver), **Supp. VII:** 236
"Happiness" (Sandburg), **III:** 582–583
"Happiness"(Hadas), **Supp. XXIII:** 117
Happiness of Getting It Down Right, The (Steinman, ed.), **Supp. VIII:** 172
"Happiness of the Garden Variety" (Richard), **Supp. XIX:** 212
"Happy Birthday" (Bambara), **Supp. XI:** 4
Happy Birthday (Loos), **Supp. XVI:** 193
Happy Birthday, Wanda June (Vonnegut), **Supp. II Part 2:** 759, 776–777
Happy Birthday of Death, The (Corso), **Supp. XII: 127–129**
Happy Childhood, A (Matthews), **Supp. IX:** 155, 160, **161–163**
Happy Days (Beckett), **Retro. Supp. I:** 206; **Supp. XXIV:** 123
Happy Days, 1880–1892 (Mencken), **III:** 100, 111, 120
"Happy End" (Simic), **Supp. VIII:** 276–277
"Happy Failure, The" (Melville), **III:** 90
Happy Families Are All Alike (Taylor), **Supp. V:** 322–323, 325
Happy Isles of Oceania, The: Paddling the Pacific (Theroux), **Supp. VIII:** 324
"Happy Journey to Trenton and Camden, The" (Wilder), **IV:** 366
"Happy Man, The" (Lethem), **Supp. XVIII:** 139
"Happy Marriage, The" (MacLeish), **III:** 15–16
Happy Marriage and Other Poems, The (MacLeish), **III:** 4
Happy to Be Here (Keillor), **Supp. XVI:** 165, 171
"Happy To Be Here" (Keillor), **Supp. XVI:** 168
"Hapworth 16, 1924" (Salinger), **III:** 552, 571–572
Haram, Karen, **Supp. XXIII:** 276
"Harbor Dawn, The" (H. Crane), **Supp. XXI:** 132, 136

"Harbor Lights" (Doty), **Supp. XI:** 122
Harcourt, Alfred, **II:** 191, 451–452; **III:** 587; **Retro. Supp. I:** 131; **Supp. XV:** 308
Harcourt, Lewis, **Supp. XX: 232–233**
Harcourt, T. A., **I:** 196
Hard Candy, a Book of Stories (T. Williams), **IV:** 383
"Hardcastle Crags" (Plath), **Supp. I Part 2:** 537
"Hard Daddy" (Hughes), **Retro. Supp. I:** 200
"Hardened Criminals, The" (Lethem), **Supp. XVIII:** 139
Harder They Fall, The (Schulberg), **Supp. XV:** 194, 201
Hard Facts (Baraka), **Supp. II Part 1:** 54, 55, 58
Hard Freight (Wright), **Supp. V:** 332, 339–340
Hard Hours, The (Hecht), **Supp. X:** 57, **59–62,** 63, 64
Hardie, Kier, **Supp. I Part 1:** 5
Harding, Walter, **IV:** 177, 178
Harding, Warren G., **I:** 486; **II:** 253, 433; **Supp. I Part 1:** 24
"Hard Kind of Courage, The" (Baldwin), **Supp. I Part 1:** 52
Hard Laughter (Lamott), **Supp. XX: 132–133**
Hard Maple (S. and A. Warner), **Supp. XVIII:** 264
"Hard Rain's A-Gonna Fall, A" (song, Dylan), **Supp. XVIII:** 26, 29
"Hard Time Keeping Up, A" (Ellison), **Retro. Supp. II:** 124
Hard Times (Dickens), **Supp. I Part 2:** 675
"Hard Times in Elfland, The" (Lanier), **Supp. I Part 1:** 365
"Hard Traveling: *Fay*'s Deep South Landscape of Violence" (Beuka), **Supp. XXI:** 47
Hardwick, Elizabeth, **II:** 543, 554, 566; **Retro. Supp. II:** 179, 180, 183, 184, 190, 221, 228–229, 245; **Supp. I Part 1:** 196; **Supp. III Part 1: 193–215; Supp. IV Part 1:** 299; **Supp. V,** 319; **Supp. X,** 171; **Supp. XII:** 209; **Supp. XIV:** 89
"Hard Work 1956" (Dunn), **Supp. XI:** 147
Hardy, Barbara, **Supp. I Part 2:** 527
Hardy, Oliver, **Supp. I Part 2:** 607; **Supp. IV Part 2:** 574
Hardy, René, **Supp. III Part 1:** 235
Hardy, Thomas, **I:** 59, 103, 292, 317, 377; **II:** 181, 184–185, 186, 191–192, 271, 275, 372, 523, 542; **III:** 32, 453, 485, 508, 524; **IV:** 83, 135, 136; **Retro. Supp. I:** 141, 377–378; **Supp. I Part 1:** 217; **Supp. I Part 2:** 429, 512; **Supp. II Part 1:** 4, 26; **Supp. VIII:** 32; **Supp. IX:** 40, 78, 85, 108, 211; **Supp. X:** 228; **Supp. XI:** 311; **Supp. XIII:** 294, **Supp. XIII:** 130; **Supp. XIV:** 24; **Supp. XV:** 170; **Supp. XVIII:** 74; **Supp. XIX:** 86, 87; **Supp. XX: 195; Supp. XXI:** 109

Hardy and the Poetry of Truth-Seeking (Halliday), **Supp. XIX:** 82
Harjo, Joy, **Supp. IV Part 1:** 325, 404; **Supp. IV Part 2:** 499, 507; **Supp. XII: 215–234; Supp. XVIII:** 189
Harlan's Race (P. N. Warren), **Supp. XX: 264–265**
"Harlem" (Hughes), **Retro. Supp. I:** 194, 204; **Supp. I Part 1:** 340; **Supp. VIII:** 213
Harlem, Mecca of the New Negro (Locke), **Supp. XIV:** 201
"Harlem Dancer, The" (McKay), **Supp. X:** 134
Harlem Gallery (Tolson), **Retro. Supp. I:** 208, 209, 210
Harlem Glory: A Fragment of Aframerican Life (McKay), **Supp. X:** 132, **141–142**
Harlem: Negro Metropolis (McKay), **Supp. X:** 132, 141, 142
Harlem Renaissance Remembered, The (Bontemps, ed.), **Supp. XXII:** 7
"Harlem Runs Wild" (McKay), **Supp. X:** 140
Harlem Shadows (McKay), **Supp. X:** 131–132, 136
Harlem Underground (Lacy), **Supp. XV:** 206
"Harlequin of Dreams, The" (Lanier), **Supp. I Part 1:** 365
Harlot's Ghost (Mailer), **Retro. Supp. II:** 211–212
Harlow, Jean, **IV:** 256; **Retro. Supp. I:** 110
"Harm" (C. Frost), **Supp. XV:** 101
Harmon, William, **Retro. Supp. I:** 37; **Supp. XI:** 248
"Harmonic" (F. Barthelme), **Supp. XI:** 26
Harmonium (Stevens), **III:** 196; **IV:** 76, 77, 78, 82, 87, 89, 92; **Retro. Supp. I:** 296, 297, 299, **300–302,** 301, 302
"Harmony of the Gospels" (Taylor), **IV:** 149
Harmony of the World (C. Baxter), **Supp. XVII:** 16–17
"Harmony of the World" (C. Baxter), **Supp. XVII:** 16
Harnett, Vincent, **Supp. XV:** 198
"Harp, The" (Weigl), **Supp. XIX:** 278
Harper (film), **Supp. IV Part 2:** 473
Harper, Donna, **Retro. Supp. I:** 194, 195, 209
Harper, Frances E. Watkins, **Supp. II Part 1:** 201–202; **Supp. XVIII:** 284; **Supp. XXII:** 11
Harper, Gordon Lloyd, **Retro. Supp. II:** 23
Harper, Michael S., **Retro. Supp. II:** 116, 123; **Supp. XV:** 74; **Supp. XXIV:** 184
Harper, William Rainey, **Supp. I Part 2:** 631
Harper's Anthology of 20th Century Native American Poetry (Niatum, ed.), **Supp. IV Part 1:** 331
"Harriet" (Lowell), **II:** 554
Harrigan, Edward, **II:** 276; **III:** 14
Harriman, Margaret, **Supp. XXIV:** 19
Harrington, Michael, **I:** 306

Harrington, Ollie, **Supp. XVI:** 142–143
Harris, Celia, **Retro. Supp. I:** 9
Harris, Corra, **Supp. XXII:** 190, 193, 196
Harris, George, **II:** 70
Harris, George Washington, **Supp. XXII:** 193
Harris, Joel Chandler, **III:** 338; **Supp. I Part 1:** 352; **Supp. II Part 1:** 192, 201; **Supp. XIV:** 61; **Supp. XX: 103**
Harris, Judith, **Supp. XIV:** 269
Harris, Julie, **II:** 587, 601; **Supp. IX:** 125
Harris, Leonard, **Supp. XIV:** 196, 211–212
Harris, MacDonald, **Supp. XI:** 65
Harris, Marie, **Supp. IX:** 153
Harris, Peter, **Supp. X:** 206, 207
Harris, Susan K., **Supp. XV:** 269
Harris, Thomas, **Supp. XIV:** 26; **Supp. XXI:** 67, 78
Harris, Victoria Frenkel, **Supp. IV Part 1:** 68, 69
Harris, Violet J., **Supp. XXII:** 10, 13
Harris, William E., **Supp. XXIV:** 26
Harris, Wilson, **Supp. XXI:** 170
Harrison, Colin, **Supp. XIV:** 26
Harrison, Hazel, **Retro. Supp. II:** 115
Harrison, Jim, **Supp. VIII: 37–56; Supp. XIX:** 125, 126
Harrison, Judy, **Supp. XXIII:** 278
Harrison, Kathryn, **Supp. X:** 191
Harrison, Ken, **Supp. IX:** 101
Harrison, Oliver (pseudonym). *See* Smith, Harrison
Harrod, Lois Marie, **Supp. XXIII:** 131–132
Harry: A Portrait (Boyce), **Supp. XVII:** 104; **Supp. XXI:** 7, **13–14**
Harryhausen, Ray, **Supp. IV Part 1:** 115
Harryman, Carla, **Supp. XV:** 344
"Harry of Nothingham" (Hugo), **Supp. VI:** 146–147
"Harry's Death" (Carver), **Supp. III Part 1:** 146
"Harsh Judgment, The" (Kunitz), **Supp. III Part 1:** 264
Hart, Albert Bushnell, **Supp. I Part 2:** 479, 480, 481
Hart, Bernard, **I:** 241, 242, 248–250, 256
Hart, Henry, **Retro. Supp. II:** 187; **Supp. XIV:** 97
Hart, James D., **Supp. XVIII:** 257
Hart, John Seely, **Supp. XVIII:** 257, 258, 264
Hart, Lorenz, **III:** 361
Hart, Moss, **Supp. IV Part 2:** 574; **Supp. XV:** 329
Hart, Pearl, **Supp. X:** 103
"Hart Crane" (Tate), **I:** 381
"Hart Crane and Poetry: A Consideration of Crane's Intense Poetics with Reference to 'The Return' " (Grossman), **Retro. Supp. II:** 83
Harte, Anna Griswold, **Supp. II Part 1:** 341
Harte, Bret, **I:** 193, 195, 203; **II:** 289; **IV:** 196; **Retro. Supp. II:** 72; **Supp. II Part 1: 335–359,** 399; **Supp. XV:** 115
Harte, Walter Blackburn, **I:** 199
Harter, Carol C., **Supp. IV Part 1:** 217

Hartigan, Grace, **Supp. XXIII:** 210, 212, 217
Hartley, David, **III:** 77
Hartley, Lois, **Supp. I Part 2:** 459, 464–465
Hartley, L. P., **Supp. I Part 1:** 293
Hartley, Marsden, **IV:** 409, 413; **Retro. Supp. I:** 430; **Supp. X:** 137; **Supp. XV:** 298
Hartman, Geoffrey, **Supp. IV Part 1:** 119; **Supp. XII:** 130, 253
Hartman, Saidiya, **Supp. XX: 154**
Harum, David, **II:** 102
"Harvard" (Lowell), **II:** 554
Harvard College in the Seventeenth Century (Morison), **Supp. I Part 2:** 485
"Harvest" (E. P. Jones), **Supp. XXII:** 141
"Harvest, The" (Hempel), **Supp. XXI:** 115, **122–123**
Harvester, The (Stratton-Porter), **Supp. XX: 211, 212, 218, 221**
"*Harvester, The:* The Natural Bounty of Gene Stratton-Porter" (Birkelo), **Supp. XX: 220–221**
"Harvesters of Night and Water" (Hogan), **Supp. IV Part 1:** 412
"Harvest Song" (Toomer), **Supp. III Part 2:** 483
Harvill Book of 20th Century Poetry in English, **Supp. X:** 55
Harvin, Emily, **Supp. XXIII:** 174
"Harv Is Plowing Now" (Updike), **Retro. Supp. I:** 318
Haselden, Elizabeth Lee, **Supp. VIII:** 125
"Hasidic Noir" (Abraham), **Supp. XXIV: 14–15**
Haskell, Mary, **Supp. XX: 115, 117**
Hass, Robert, **Supp. VI: 97–111; Supp. VIII:** 24, 28; **Supp. XI:** 142, 270; **Supp. XIV:** 83, 84; **Supp. XXI:** 60
Hassam, Childe, **Retro. Supp. II:** 136
Hassan, Ihab, **IV:** 99–100, 115; **Supp. XI:** 221
Hasse, Henry, **Supp. IV Part 1:** 102
Hasty-Pudding, The (Barlow), **Supp. II Part 1:** 74, 77–80
"Hater of Mediocrity, The" (Boulton), **Supp. XXII:** 23
Hate That Hate Produced, The (CBS documentary), **Supp. XX: 102**
Hatful of Rain, A (Gazzo), **III:** 155
Hatlen, Burton, **Supp. V:** 138, 139–140; **Supp. XXI:** 24
"Hatred"(O'Hara), **Supp. XXIII:** 212
"Hattie Bloom" (Oliver), **Supp. VII:** 232
Haugen, Hayley Mitchell, **Supp. XXIV:** 215
Haunch, Paunch, and Jowl (Ornitz), **Supp. IX:** 227
"Haunted Landscape" (Ashbery), **Supp. III Part 1:** 22
Haunted Merchant, The (Briggs), **Supp. XVIII:** 2, 8
"Haunted Mind" (Simic), **Supp. VIII:** 282
"Haunted Mind, The" (Hawthorne), **II:** 230–231
"Haunted Oak, The" (Dunbar), **Supp. II Part 1:** 207, 208
"Haunted Palace, The" (Poe), **III:** 421

"Haunted Valley, The" (Bierce), **I:** 200

Haunting, The (film), **Supp. IX:** 125

Haunting of Hill House, The (Jackson), **Supp. IX:** 117, 121, 126

Hauptmann, Gerhart, **III:** 472

Haussmann, Sonja, **Supp. XIII:** 331, **Supp. XIII:** 347

"Havanna vanities come to dust in Miami" (Didion), **Supp. IV Part 1:** 210

Havel, Hippolyte, **Supp. XXI:** 4, 6

Haven, Cynthia, **Supp. XV:** 252, 264; **Supp. XXIII:** 134, 138, 139

Haven's End (Marquand), **III:** 55, 56, 63, 68

"Have You Ever Faked an Orgasm" (Peacock), **Supp. XIX:** 199

"Have You Ever Tried to Enter the Long Black Branches" (Oliver), **Supp. VII:** 247

"Having a Coke with You"(O'Hara), **Supp. XXIII:** 219

"Having Been Interstellar" (Ammons), **Supp. VII:** 25

"Having It Out With Melancholy" (Kenyon), **Supp. VII:** 171

"Having Lost My Sons, I Confront the Wreckage of the Moon: Christmas, 1960" (Wright), **Supp. III Part 2:** 600

"Having Snow" (Schwartz), **Supp. II Part 2:** 652

"Having Words"(Thompson), **Supp. XXIII:** 293–294

"Hawaii, Washington, Vermont: A Frame for the Verse" (Taggard), **Supp. XXII:** 281–282

Hawaiian Hilltop (Taggard), **Supp. XXII:** 275

Hawai'i One Summer (Kingston), **Supp. V:** 157, 160, 166, 169–170

Haweis, Stephen, **Supp. XXII:** 157, 158, 159, 161, 163, 165

"Hawk, The" (Francis), **Supp. IX:** 81

Hawke, David Freeman, **Supp. I Part 2:** 511, 516

Hawkes, John, **I:** 113; **Retro. Supp. II:** 234; **Supp. III Part 1:** 2; **Supp. V:** 40; **Supp. IX:** 212; **Supp. XVII:** 183; **Supp. XXI:** 210

Hawkins, Gary, **Supp. XXI:** 35, 39

Hawkins, William, **II:** 587

Hawk in the Rain, The (Hughes), **Retro. Supp. II:** 244; **Supp. I Part 2:** 537, 540

Hawk Is Dying, The (Crews), **Supp. XI:** 111

Hawk Moon (Shepard), **Supp. III Part 2:** 445

Hawks, Howard, **Supp. IV Part 1:** 130; **Supp. XVIII:** 148

"Hawk's Cry in Autumn, The" (Brodsky), **Supp. VIII:** 29

"Hawk's Shadow" (Glück), **Supp. V:** 85

Hawk's Well, The (Yeats), **III:** 459–460

Hawley, Adelaide, **Supp. XIV:** 207

Hawley, Joseph, **I:** 546

Hawthorne (James), **II:** 372–378; **Retro. Supp. I:** 220, **223–224**

"Hawthorne" (Longfellow), **Retro. Supp. II:** 169

"Hawthorne" (Lowell), **II:** 550

Hawthorne, Julian, **II:** 225; **Supp. I Part 1:** 38; **Supp. XV:** 274

Hawthorne, Nathaniel, **I:** 106, 204, 211, 340, 355, 363, 384, 413, 458, 561–562; **II:** 7, 8, 40, 60, 63, 74, 89, 127–128, 138, 142, 198, **223–246,** 255, 259, 264, 267, 272, 274, 277, 281, 282, 295, 307, 309, 311, 313, 322, 324, 326, 402, 408, 446, 501, 545; **III:** 51, 81–82, 83, 84, 85, 87, 88, 91, 92, 113, 316, 359, 412, 415, 421, 438, 453, 454, 507, 565, 572; **IV:** 2, 4, 167, 172, 179, 194, 333, 345, 453; **Retro. Supp. I:** 1, 53, 59, 62, 63, 91, **145–167,** 215, 218, 220, 223, 248–249, 252, 257, 258, 330, 331, 365; **Retro. Supp. II:** 136, 142, 153, 156–157, 158, 159, 187, 221; **Supp. I Part 1:** 38, 188, 197, 317, 372; **Supp. I Part 2:** 420, 421, 545, 579, 580, 582, 587, 595, 596; **Supp. III Part 2:** 501; **Supp. IV Part 1:** 80, 127, 297; **Supp. IV Part 2:** 463, 596; **Supp. V:** 152; **Supp. VIII:** 103, 105, 108, 153, 201; **Supp. IX:** 114; **Supp. X:** 78; **Supp. XI:** 51, 78; **Supp. XII:** 26; **Supp. XIII:** 102; **Supp. XIV:** 48; **Supp. XV:** 269, 272, 282; **Supp. XVI:** 83, 84, 157; **Supp. XVII:** 42; **Supp. XVIII:** 258, 260; **Supp. XXI:** 201; **Supp. XXIII:** 161, 190, 290

Hawthorne, Mrs. Nathaniel (Sophia Peabody), **II:** 224, 244; **III:** 75, 86

Hawthorne, Rose, **II:** 225

Hawthorne, Una, **II:** 225

"Hawthorne and His Mosses" (Melville), **Retro. Supp. I:** 254; **Supp. XIV:** 48

"Hawthorne Aspect \[of Henry James\], The" (Eliot), **Retro. Supp. I:** 63

"Hawthorne in Solitude" (Cowley), **Supp. II Part 1:** 143

Hay, John, **I:** 1, 10, 12, 14–15; **Supp. I Part 1:** 352

Hay, Mrs. John, **I:** 14

Hay, Sara Henderson, **Supp. XIV: 119–135**

Hayakawa, S. I., **I:** 448; **Supp. I Part 1:** 315; **Supp. XV:** 176

Hayden, Robert, **Supp. II Part 1: 361–383;** **Supp. IV Part 1:** 169; **Supp. XIII:** 115, 127; **Supp. XIV:** 119, 123

Hayden, Sterling, **Supp. XI:** 304

Haydn, Hiram, **IV:** 100, 358

Hayduke Lives! (Abbey), **Supp. XIII: 16**

Hayek, Friedrich A. von, **Supp. IV Part 2:** 524

Hayes, Helen, **Supp. XVI:** 193, 195

Hayes, Ira, **Supp. IV Part 1:** 326

Hayes, Richard, **Supp. V:** 320

Hayes, Rutherford B., **Supp. I Part 2:** 419

Hayford, James, **Supp. XXII:** 204, 218

Haygood, Wil, **Supp. VIII:** 79

"Haying While the Sun Shines" (L. I. Wilder), **Supp. XXII:** 290

Hayne, Paul Hamilton, **Supp. I Part 1:** 352, 354, 355, 360, 372

Haynes, Todd, **Supp. XVIII:** 23

Haynes-Smith, William, **Supp. XX: 231, 232, 233**

Hayward, Florence, **Retro. Supp. II:** 65

Hayward, John, **Retro. Supp. I:** 67

Hayward, Leland, **Supp. XIX:** 250

Haywood, "Big" Bill, **I:** 483; **Supp. V:** 286; **Supp. XXIII:** 162

Hazan, Joe, **Supp. XXIII:** 212

Hazard, Grace, **II:** 530

Hazard of Fortunes, A (Howells), **Retro. Supp. II:** 288

Hazard of New Fortunes, A (Howells), **II:** 275, 276, 286–297, 290

Hazel, Robert, **Supp. VIII:** 137, 138

Hazen, General W. B., **I:** 192, 193

Hazlitt, Henry, **Supp. IV Part 2:** 524

Hazlitt, William, **I:** 58, 378; **II:** 315; **Supp. XXI:** 205

Hazmat (McClatchy), **Supp. XII: 265–270**

Hazo, Samuel, **I:** 386; **Supp. XIV:** 123, 124

Hazzard, Shirley, **Supp. VIII:** 151

H.D. *See* Doolittle, Hilda

"He" (Porter), **III:** 434, 435

"Head and Shoulders" (Fitzgerald), **Retro. Supp. I:** 101

Headhunter (Findley), **Supp. XX: 57–59, 60, 61**

"Head-Hunter, The" (O. Henry), **Supp. II Part 1:** 403

"Headless Hawk, The" (Capote), **Supp. III Part 1:** 124

Headlines (T. Williams), **IV:** 381

Headlong Hall (Peacock), **Supp. I Part 1:** 307

Headmaster, The (McPhee), **Supp. III Part 1:** 291, 294, 298

"Head of Joaquín Murrieta, The" (Rodriguez), **Supp. XIV:** 303

Headsman, The (Cooper), **I:** 345–346

Heads of Grain (al-Sanábil) (Gibran), **Supp. XX: 124**

"Headwaters" (Momaday), **Supp. IV Part 2:** 486

"Head Wound" (Halliday), **Supp. XIX:** 92

Healing, The (G. Jones), **Supp. XXIV:** 183, 185, **190–192,** 195

Healy, Eloise Klein, **Supp. XI:** 121, 124, 126, 127, 129, 137

Healy, Tim, **II:** 129, 137

Heaney, Sally, **Supp. XVII:** 241

Heaney, Seamus, **Retro. Supp. II:** 245; **Supp. IX:** 41, 42; **Supp. X:** 67, 122; **Supp. XII:** 249; **Supp. XV:** 256; **Supp. XXI:** 54, 243

"Heard through the Walls of the Race-track Glen Motel" (X. J. Kennedy), **Supp. XV:** 170

Hearn, Lafcadio, **I:** 211; **II:** 311

Hearon, Shelby, **Supp. VIII: 57–72**

Hearst, Patty, **Supp. IV Part 1:** 195

Hearst, William Randolph, **I:** 198, 207, 208; **IV:** 298

Heart and Perimeter (Bierds), **Supp. XVII: 28–29**

"Heart and the Lyre, The" (Bogan), **Supp. III Part 1:** 65

"Heart as Origami, The (Hirshfield), **Supp. XXIII:** 132

"Heartbeat" (Harjo), **Supp. XII:** 221–222

Heartbreak Hotel (Siddons), **Supp. XXII:** 239, 241, 242

Heartbreak Kid, The (film), **Supp. IV Part 2:** 575, 589

"Heart Failure"(Schott), **Supp. XXIII:** 252

Heart for the Gods of Mexico, A (Aiken), **I:** 54

"Hear the Nightingale Sing" (Gordon), **II:** 200

Hear the Wind Blow (Sanders), **Supp. XVI:** 268

Heart is a Lonely Hunter, The (McCullers), **II:** 586, 588–593, 604, 605

Heart of a Woman, The (Angelou), **Supp. IV Part 1:** 2, 5, 7–9, 9, 14, 17

Heart of Darkness (Conrad), **Retro. Supp. II:** 292; **Supp. V:** 249, 311; **Supp. VIII:** 4, 316; **Supp. XIX:** 28; **Supp. XX:** 18, 57–58; **Supp. XXIV:** 286

"Heart of Darkness" (Conrad), **I:** 575, 578; **II:** 595; **Supp. XVI:** 212

Heart of Darkness (Didion), **Supp. IV Part 1:** 207

Heart of Dixie (film), **Supp. XXII:** 239, 241

Heart of Haiku, The (Hirshfield), **Supp. XXIII:** 137–138

Heart of Happy Hollow, The (Dunbar), **Supp. II Part 1:** 214

Heart of Knowledge, The: American Indians on the Bomb (Gunn Allen and Caputi, eds.), **Supp. IV Part 1:** 334–335

"Heart of Knowledge, The: Nuclear Themes in Native American Thought and Literature" (Caputi), **Supp. IV Part 1:** 335

Heart of the Earth (Moraga), **Supp. XXIII:** 196

"Heart of the Park, The " (O'Connor), **Retro. Supp. II:** 225

Heart of the West (O. Henry), **Supp. II Part 1:** 410

"Hearts, The" (Pinsky), **Supp. VI:** 245–247, 248

"'Hearts and Flowers' " (MacLeish), **III:** 8

"Hearts and Heads" (Ransom), **Supp. I Part 1:** 373

"Heart's Graveyard Shift, The" (Komunyakaa), **Supp. XIII:** 120

Heart-Shape in the Dust (Hayden), **Supp. II Part 1:** 365, 366

Heart's Needle (Snodgrass), **I:** 400

"Heart's Needle" (Snodgrass), **Supp. VI:** 311–313, 320

"Hearts of Oak" (Rowson), **Supp. XV:** 243

"Heart Songs" (Proulx), **Supp. VII:** 254

Heart Songs and Other Stories (Proulx), **Supp. VII:** 252–256, 261

Heart to Artemis, The (Bryher), **Supp. I Part 1:** 259

Heartwood (Burke), **Supp. XIV:** 35

Heath, Shirley, **Supp. XX: 90**

Heath Anthology of American Literature, The, **Supp. IX:** 4; **Supp. XV:** 270, 313

Heathcote, Anne. *See* De Lancey, Mrs. James

"Heathen Chinee, The" (Harte), **Supp. II Part 1:** 350–351, 352

Heathen Days, 1890–1936 (Mencken), **III:** 100, 111

Heath-Stubbs, John, **Supp. XV:** 153

Heat's On, The (C. Himes), **Supp. XVI:** 143, 144

"Heaven" (Dunn), **Supp. XI:** 154

"Heaven" (Levine), **Supp. V:** 182

"Heaven" (Patchett), **Supp. XII:** 309

Heaven and Earth: A Cosmology (Goldbarth), **Supp. XII:** 187

"Heaven and Earth in Jest" (Dillard), **Supp. VI:** 24, 28

"Heaven as Anus" (Kumin), **Supp. IV Part 2:** 448

Heavenly Conversation, The (Mather), **Supp. II Part 2:** 460

"Heavenly Feast, The" (Schnackenberg), **Supp. XV:** 257, 259

Heavens (Untermeyer), **Supp. XV:** 306

Heavens and Earth (Benét), **Supp. XI:** 44

Heaven's Coast (Doty), **Supp. XI:** 119, 121, 129–130, 134; **Supp. XXIII:** 126

Heaven's Prisoners (Burke), **Supp. XIV:** 23, 29

"Heavy Angel, The" (Everwine), **Supp. XV:** 80

"Heavy Bear Who Goes with Me, The" (Schwartz), **Supp. II Part 2:** 646

"Heavy Trash" (Halliday), **Supp. XIX:** 92, 93

Hebert, Ernest, **Supp. XXII:** 207

"He Came Also Still" (Zukofsky), **Supp. III Part 2:** 612

Hecht, Anthony, **IV:** 138; **Supp. III Part 2:** 541, 561; **Supp. X: 55–75; Supp. XII:** 269–270; **Supp. XV:** 251, 256

Hecht, Ben, **I:** 103; **II:** 42; **Supp. I Part 2:** 646; **Supp. XI:** 307; **Supp. XIII:** 106

Hecht, S. Theodore, **Supp. III Part 2:** 614

Heckewelder, John, **II:** 503

"Hedge Island" (Lowell), **II:** 524

Hedges, William I., **II:** 311–312

"He 'Digesteth Harde Yron' " (Moore), **Supp. IV Part 2:** 454

Hedin, Robert, **Supp. XII:** 200, 202

Hedylus (Doolittle), **Supp. I Part 1:** 259, 270

"Heel & Toe To the End" (W. C. Williams), **Retro. Supp. I:** 430

Heffernan, Michael, **Supp. XII:** 177

"HEGEL" (Baraka), **Supp. II Part 1:** 53

Hegel, Georg Wilhelm Friedrich, **I:** 265; **II:** 358; **III:** 262, 308–309, 480, 481, 487, 607; **IV:** 86, 333, 453; **Supp. I Part 2:** 633, 635, 640, 645; **Supp. XVI:** 289

"Hegemony of Race, The" (Du Bois), **Supp. II Part 1:** 181

Hegger, Grace Livingston. *See* Lewis, Mrs. Sinclair (Grace Livingston Hegger)

"He Had Spent His Youth Dreaming" (Dobyns), **Supp. XIII:** 90

Heidegger, Martin, **II:** 362, 363; **III:** 292; **IV:** 491; **Retro. Supp. II:** 87; **Supp. V:** 267; **Supp. VIII:** 9; **Supp. XVI:** 283, 288

Heidenmauer, The (Cooper), **I:** 345–346

Heidi Chronicles, The (Wasserstein), **Supp. IV Part 1:** 309; **Supp. XV:** 319, 325–327

"Height of the Ridiculous, The" (Holmes), **Supp. I Part 1:** 302

Heilbroner, Robert, **Supp. I Part 2:** 644, 648, 650

Heilbrun, Carolyn G., **Supp. IX:** 66; **Supp. XI:** 208; **Supp. XIV:** 161, 163; **Supp. XX: 108**

Heilman, Robert Bechtold, **Supp. XIV:** 11, 12

Heilpern, John, **Supp. XIV:** 242

Heim, Michael, **Supp. V:** 209

Heine, Heinrich, **II:** 272, 273, 277, 281, 282, 387, 544; **IV:** 5; **Supp. XV:** 293, 299; **Supp. XVI:** 188

Heineman, Frank, **Supp. III Part 2:** 619

Heinemann, Larry, **Supp. XXII: 103–117**

Heinlein, Robert, **Supp. IV Part 1:** 102; **Supp. XVI:** 122; **Supp. XVIII:** 149

Heinz, Helen. *See* Tate, Mrs. Allen (Helen Heinz)

Heiress, The (film), **Retro. Supp. I:** 222

"Heirs" (Nye), **Supp. XIII:** 284

"He Is Not Worth the Trouble" (Rowson), **Supp. XV:** 240

"He Knew" (C. Himes), **Supp. XVI:** 137

"Helas" (Creeley), **Supp. IV Part 1:** 150, 158

Helburn, Theresa, **IV:** 381

Heldreth, Leonard, **Supp. V:** 151

"Helen" (Lowell), **II:** 544

"Helen, Thy Beauty Is to Me" (Fante), **Supp. XI:** 169

"Helen: A Courtship" (Faulkner), **Retro. Supp. I:** 81

"Helen I Love You" (Farrell), **II:** 28, 45

Helen in Egypt (Doolittle), **Supp. I Part 1:** 260, 272, 273, 274; **Supp. XV:** 264

Helen Keller: Sketch for a Portrait (Brooks), **I:** 254

"Helen of Tyre" (Longfellow), **II:** 496

Heliodora (Doolittle), **Supp. I Part 1:** 266

"He Lives On the Landing" (Espaillat), **Supp. XXI:** 108

"Helix" (Sobin), **Supp. XVI:** 283

Hellbox (O'Hara), **III:** 361

Helle, Anita, **Supp. XXIII:** 117

Heller, Joseph, **III:** 2, 258; **IV:** 98; **Retro. Supp. II:** 324; **Supp. I Part 1:** 196; **Supp. IV Part 1: 379–396; Supp. V:** 244; **Supp. VIII:** 245; **Supp. XI:** 307; **Supp. XII:** 167–168; **Supp. XV:** 322; **Supp. XVII:** 139; **Supp. XXIII:** 100

"Hell-Heaven" (Lahiri), **Supp. XXI: 181–183,** 183, 184–186, 188

Hellman, Lillian, **I:** 28; **III:** 28; **Supp. I Part 1: 276–298; Supp. IV Part 1:** 1, 12, 83, 353, 355, 356; **Supp. VIII:** 243; **Supp. IX:** 196, 198, 200–201, 204

Hellmann, Lillian, **Retro. Supp. II:** 327

Hello (Creeley), **Supp. IV Part 1:** 155, 157

"Hello, Hello Henry" (Kumin), **Supp. IV Part 2:** 446

"Hello, Stranger" (Capote), **Supp. III Part 1:** 120

Hello Dolly! (musical play), **IV:** 357

Hell's Angels: A Strange and Terrible Saga (Thompson), **Supp. XXIV:** 282, 283, 288, 290–291

Hellyer, John, **Supp. I Part 2:** 468

Helm, Bob, **Supp. XV:** 147

Helm, Levon, **Supp. XVIII:** 26

Helmets (Dickey), **Supp. IV Part 1:** 175, 178, 180

"Helmsman, The" (Doolittle), **Supp. I Part 1:** 266

"Help" (Barth), **I:** 139

"Help Her to Believe" (Olsen). *See* "I Stand There Ironing" (Olsen)

Helprin, Mark, **Supp. XIX:** 142

"Helsinki Window" (Creeley), **Supp. IV Part 1:** 158

"Hema and Kaushik" (Lahiri), **Supp. XXI:** 183, 188

Hemenway, Robert E., **Supp. IV Part 1:** 6

Hemingway, Dr. Clarence Edwards, **II:** 248, 259

Hemingway, Ernest, **I:** 28, 64, 97, 99, 105, 107, 117, 150, 162, 190, 211, 221, 288, 289, 295, 367, 374, 378, 421, 423, 445, 476, 477, 478, 482, 484–485, 487, 488, 489, 491, 495, 504, 517; **II:** 27, 44, 51, 58, 68–69, 78, 90, 97, 127, 206, **247–270,** 289, 424, 431, 456, 457, 458–459, 482, 560, 600; **III:** 2, 18, 20, 35, 36, 37, 40, 61, 108, 220, 334, 363, 364, 382, 453, 454, 471–472, 476, 551, 575, 576, 584; **IV:** 27, 28, 33, 34, 35, 42, 49, 97, 108, 122, 126, 138, 190, 191, 201, 216, 217, 257, 297, 363, 404, 427, 433, 451; **Retro. Supp. I:** 74, 98, 108, 111, 112, 113, 115, **169–191,** 215, 292, 359, 418; **Retro. Supp. II:** 19, 24, 30, 68, 115, 123; **Supp. I Part 2:** 621, 658, 678; **Supp. II Part 1:** 221; **Supp. III Part 1:** 146; **Supp. III Part 2:** 617; **Supp. IV Part 1:** 48, 102, 123, 197, 236, 342, 343, 344, 348, 350, 352, 380–381, 383; **Supp. IV Part 2:** 463, 468, 502, 607, 679, 680, 681, 689, 692; **Supp. V:** 237, 240, 244, 250, 336; **Supp. VIII:** 40, 101, 105, 179, 182, 183, 188, 189, 196; **Supp. IX:** 16, 57, 58, 94, 106, 260, 262; **Supp. X:** 137, 167, 223, 225; **Supp. XI:** 214, 221; **Supp. XIII:** 96, 255, 270; **Supp. XIV:** 24, 83; **Supp. XV:** 69, 135; **Supp. XVI:** 203, 205–206, 208, 210, 233, 236–237, 281–282; **Supp. XVII:** 4, 105, 107, 137, 228, 229; **Supp. XVIII:** 74, 90, 102; **Supp. XIX:** 131, 154, 157, 246; **Supp. XX: 45, 74, 76; Supp. XXI:** 7, 8, 36, 262; **Supp. XXIII:** 4, 68, 166, 174, 275, 299; **Supp. XXIV:** 54, 64, 97, 284

Hemingway, Mrs. Ernest (Hadley Richardson), **II:** 257, 260, 263

Hemingway, Mrs. Ernest (Martha Gellhorn), **II:** 260

Hemingway, Mrs. Ernest (Mary Welsh), **II:** 257, 260

Hemingway, Mrs. Ernest (Pauline Pfeiffer), **II:** 260

"Hemingway in Paris" (Cowley), **Supp. II Part 1:** 144

"Hemingway Story, A" (Dubus), **Supp. VII:** 91

"Hemingway: The Old Lion" (Cowley), **Supp. II Part 1:** 143

"Hemp, The" (Benét), **Supp. XI:** 44

Hempel, Amy, **Supp. XIX:** 209; **Supp. XXI: 115–128**

"Henchman, The" (Whittier), **Supp. I Part 2:** 696

Henderson, Alice Corbin, **Supp. I Part 2:** 387; **Supp. XV:** 302–303

Henderson, Darwin L., **Supp. XIII:** 213, 221–222

Henderson, Jane, **Supp. VIII:** 87; **Supp. XX: 84**

Henderson, Katherine, **Supp. IV Part 1:** 203, 207

Henderson, Linda. *See* Hogan, Linda

Henderson, Robert W., **Supp. VIII:** 124

Henderson, Stephen, **Supp. IV Part 1:** 365

Henderson, the Rain King (Bellow), **I:** 144, 147, 148, 152, 153, 154, 155, 158, 160, 161, 162–163; **Retro. Supp. II:** 19, **24–25,** 30

"Hen Flower, The" (Kinnell), **Supp. III Part 1:** 247–248

Henie, Sonja, **Supp. XII:** 165

Henkin, Joshua, **Supp. XXII:** 216

Henle, James, **II:** 26, 30, 38, 41; **Supp. IX:** 2

Henley, Beth, **Supp. XXI:** 145

Hennesy, Dale, **Supp. XV:** 5

Henninger, Katherine, **Supp. XXI:** 253

Henri, Robert, **IV:** 411; **Supp. I Part 2:** 376

Henrich, Edith, **Supp. XXIV:** 214

Henry, Arthur, **I:** 515; **Retro. Supp. II:** 97

Henry, DeWitt, **Supp. XI:** 342

Henry, O., **I:** 201; **III:** 5; **Supp. I Part 2:** 390, 462; **Supp. II Part 1: 385–412; Supp. XV:** 40

Henry, Robert, **Retro. Supp. II:** 103

Henry, William A., III, **Supp. IV Part 2:** 574

Henry and Clara (Mallon), **Supp. XIX:** 132, **136–137,** 139, 141

Henry and June (film), **Supp. X:** 186

Henry and June: From the Unexpurgated Diary of Anaïs Nin, **Supp. X:** 184, 185, 187, 194

Henry Holt and Company, **Retro. Supp. I:** 121, 131, 133, 136

Henry IV (Shakespeare), **III:** 166; **Supp. VIII:** 164

"Henry James, Jr." (Howells), **II:** 289; **Retro. Supp. I:** 220

"Henry James and the Art of Teaching" (Rowe), **Retro. Supp. I:** 216

"Henry Manley, Living Alone, Keeps Time" (Kumin), **Supp. IV Part 2:** 451

"Henry Manley Looks Back" (Kumin), **Supp. IV Part 2:** 451

"Henry Manley" poems (Kumin), **Supp. IV Part 2:** 446

Henry Miller Reader, The (Durrell, ed.), **III:** 175, 190

"Henry's Confession" (Berryman), **I:** 186

Henry VIII (Shakespeare), **Supp. IX:** 235

Henslee, **Supp. IV Part 1:** 217

Henson, Josiah, **Supp. I Part 2:** 589

Hentoff, Margot, **Supp. IV Part 1:** 205

Hentz, Caroline Lee, **Supp. I Part 2:** 584

Henze, Hans Werner, **Supp. II Part 1:** 24

"He of the Assembly" (Bowles), **Supp. IV Part 1:** 90

Hepburn, Katharine, **Supp. IX:** 189; **Supp. XI:** 17

Heraclitus, **II:** 1, 163; **IV:** 86

Herakles: A Play in Verse (MacLeish), **III:** 21, 22

Herald of the Autochthonic Spirit (Corso), **Supp. XII:** 134–136

He Ran All the Way (film), **Supp. XVII:** 63

Herberg, Will, **III:** 291

Herbert, Edward, **II:** 11

Herbert, Francis (pseudonym). *See* Bryant, William Cullen

Herbert, George, **II:** 12; **IV:** 141, 145, 146, 151, 153, 156, 165; **Retro. Supp. II:** 40; **Supp. I Part 1:** 80, 107, 108, 122; **Supp. IV Part 2:** 646; **Supp. XV:** 92, 212, 251; **Supp. XXI:** 109

Herbert, Zbigniew, **Supp. VIII:** 20

Herbert Huncke Reader, The (Schafer, ed.), **Supp. XIV:** 137, 138, 139, 140, 145, 147, 150, 151–152

Herbert of Cherbury, Lord, **II:** 108

"Herbert White" (Bidart), **Supp. XV:** 24, 27

Herbst, Josephine, **Retro. Supp. II:** 325, 328; **Supp. XIII:** 295

"Her Choice" (Larcom), **Supp. XIII:** 144

"Her Dead Brother" (Lowell), **Retro. Supp. II:** 188

"Her Dream Is of the Sea" (Ríos), **Supp. IV Part 2:** 546

"Here" (Kenyon), **Supp. VII:** 164

Here and Beyond (Wharton), **Retro. Supp. I:** 382

Here and Now (Levertov), **Supp. III Part 1:** 275, 276

"Here and There" (Wallace), **Supp. X:** 305–306

Here Comes the Mystery Man (Sanders), **Supp. XVI:** 269

"Here Comes Winston, Full of the Holy Spirit" (Eugenides), **Supp. XXIV:** 133

Heredia, Juanita, **Supp. XI:** 185, 190

Heredity and Variation (Lock), **Retro. Supp. I:** 375

Heredity: A Psychological Study of Its Phenomena, Laws, Causes, and Consequences (Ribot), **Supp. XX: 238**

"Here Inside My Forehead" (Rasmussen; Nelson and Espeland, trans.), **Supp. XVIII:** 180

Here is Your War (Pyle), **Supp. XVII:** 61
Here Let Us Feast (M. F. K. Fisher), **Supp. XVII:** 86, 87
Here Lies (Parker), **Supp. IX:** 192
Herendeen, Anne, **Supp. XXII:** 275
Here on Earth (Hoffman), **Supp. X:** 77, 89
Heresy and the Ideal: On Contemporary Poetry (Baker), **Supp. XI:** 142
"Here to Learn" (Bowles), **Supp. IV Part 1:** 93
"Here to Yonder" (Hughes), **Retro. Supp. I:** 205
"Her Father's Letters" (Milburn), **Supp. XI:** 242
"Her Favorite Story" (Richard), **Supp. XIX:** 211, 212
Herford, Reverend Brooke, **I:** 471
Herford, Will, **Supp. XXII:** 275
"Her Game" (Skloot), **Supp. XX: 196, 202**
Hergesheimer, Joseph, **Supp. I Part 2:** 620; **Supp. XVI:** 187
"Heritage" (Cullen), **Supp. IV Part 1:** 164–165, 168, 170, 171
"Heritage" (Hogan), **Supp. IV Part 1:** 413
"Her Kind" (Sexton), **Supp. II Part 2:** 687
Herland (Gilman), **Supp. XI:** 208–209
Herman, Florence. *See* Williams, Mrs. William Carlos (Florence Herman)
Herman, Jan, **Supp. XIV:** 150–151
Herman, William (pseudonym). *See* Bierce, Ambrose
"Her Management" (Swenson), **Supp. IV Part 2:** 642
"Herman Melville" (Auden), **Supp. II Part 1:** 14
Herman Melville (Mumford), **Supp. II Part 2:** 471, 476, 489–491
"Hermes of the Ways" (Doolittle), **Supp. I Part 1:** 266
"Hermes: Port Authority: His Song" (Di Piero), **Supp. XIX:** 47
Hermetic Definition (Doolittle), **Supp. I Part 1:** 271, 272, 273, 274
Hermia Suydam (Atherton), **Supp. XXIV:** 21, 28
"Hermitage, The" (Haines), **Supp. XII:** 205–206
Hermit and the Wild Woman, The (Wharton), **IV:** 315; **Retro. Supp. I:** 371
"Hermit and the Wild Woman, The" (Wharton), **Retro. Supp. I:** 372
"Hermit Meets the Skunk, The" (Kumin), **Supp. IV Part 2:** 447
Hermit of 69th Street, The: The Working Papers or Norbert Kosky (Kosinski), **Supp. VII:** 215, 216, 223, 226–227
"Hermit of Saba, The" (Freneau), **Supp. II Part 1:** 259
"Hermit Picks Berries, The" (Kumin), **Supp. IV Part 2:** 447
Hermit's Story, The (Bass), **Supp. XVI:** 23–24
"Hermit Thrush, A" (Clampitt), **Supp. IX:** 40

Hermit-Woman, The (G. Jones), **Supp. XXIV:** 185, 194
Hernández, Miguel, **Supp. V:** 194; **Supp. XIII:** 315, 323; **Supp. XXI:** 104
Herne, James A., **II:** 276; **Supp. II Part 1:** 198
Hernton, Calvin, **Supp. X:** 240
"Hero, The" (Moore), **III:** 200, 211, 212
Hero, The: A Study in Tradition, Myth, and Drama (Raglan), **I:** 135; **Supp. XIX:** 147
Hero and the Blues, The (Murray), **Supp. XIX:** 153, 154
Hérodiade (Mallarmé), **I:** 66
Herodotus, **Supp. I Part 2:** 405
Heroes, The (Ashbery), **Supp. III Part 1:** 3
Heroes and Saints (Moraga), **Supp. XXIII:** 195, 196, 197, **203–204**
Heroes and Saints and Other Plays (Moraga), **Supp. XXIII:** 197
Hero in America, The (Van Doren), **II:** 103
"Heroines of Nature: Four Women Respond to the American Landscape" (Norwood), **Supp. IX:** 24
"Heron, The" (Roethke), **III:** 540–541
"Her One Bad Eye" (Karr), **Supp. XI:** 244
"Her Own People" (Warren), **IV:** 253
Her Place in These Designs (Espaillat), **Supp. XXI:** 99, 104
"Her Quaint Honour" (Gordon), **II:** 196, 199, 200
Herr, Michael, **Supp. XI:** 245; **Supp. XIX:** 17
Herreshoff, David, **Supp. XIX:** 265
Herrick, Robert, **II:** 11, 18, 444; **III:** 463, 592; **IV:** 453; **Retro. Supp. I:** 319; **Retro. Supp. II:** 101; **Supp. I Part 2:** 646; **Supp. XIII:** 334; **Supp. XIV:** 8, 9; **Supp. XV:** 155; **Supp. XXI:** 14
Herrmann, John, **Retro. Supp. II:** 328; **Supp. XXII:** 277
"Hers" (column, Prose), **Supp. XVI:** 254
Herschdorfer, Helen, **Supp. XXI:** 262
Herschel, Sir John, **Supp. I Part 1:** 314
"Her Sense of Timing" (Elkin), **Supp. VI:** 56, 58
Hersey, John, **IV:** 4; **Supp. I Part 1:** 196; **Supp. XVI:** 105–106; **Supp. XX:** 251
"Her Sweet turn to leave the Homestead" (Dickinson), **Retro. Supp. I:** 44
"Her Untold Story"(Thompson), **Supp. XXIII:** 301
Herzog (Bellow), **I:** 144, 147, 149, 150, 152, 153, 154, 155, 156, 157, 158, 159–160; **Retro. Supp. II:** 19, **26–27**; **Supp. IV Part 1:** 30; **Supp. XIX:** 157
Herzog, Tobey C., **Supp. XXII:** 116
Heschel, Abraham, **Supp. XXI:** 110, 112
Hesford, Walter A., **Supp. XV:** 215, 217, 218
"He/She" (Dunn), **Supp. XI:** 149
"Hesitation Blues" (Hughes), **Retro. Supp. I:** 211
He Sleeps (McKnight), **Supp. XX:** 151, **152–155, 158**

"He Sleeps" (McKnight), **Supp. XX: 152, 155**
Hesse, Hermann, **Supp. V:** 208
Hester, Carolyn, **Supp. XVIII:** 24
"Hetch Hetchy Valley" (Muir), **Supp. IX:** 185
He Who Gets Slapped (Andreyev), **II:** 425
"He Who Spits at the Sky" (Stegner), **Supp. IV Part 2:** 605
"He Will Not Leave a Note" (Ríos), **Supp. IV Part 2:** 548
Hewitt, James, **Supp. XV:** 240
Hewlett, Maurice, **I:** 359
Heyen, William, **Supp. XIII:** 285, 344; **Supp. XV:** 212
"Hey! Hey!" (Hughes), **Supp. I Part 1:** 327–328
Hey Rub-a-Dub-Dub (Dreiser), **I:** 515; **II:** 26; **Retro. Supp. II:** 104, 105, 108
"Hey Sailor, What Ship?" (Olsen), **Supp. XIII:** 293, 294, 298, **299**
Heyward, DuBose, **Supp. XVIII:** 281; **Supp. XIX:** 78
Hiawatha (Longfellow), **Supp. I Part 1:** 79; **Supp. III Part 2:** 609, 610; **Supp. XXI:** 53
"Hibernaculum" (Ammons), **Supp. VII:** 26–27
Hichborn, Philip, **Supp. I Part 2:** 707, 708
Hichborn, Mrs. Philip. *See* Wylie, Elinor
"Hic Jacet" (W. C. Williams), **Retro. Supp. I:** 414
Hickok, Guy, **Supp. XXI:** 7
Hickok, James Butler ("Wild Bill"), **Supp. V:** 229, 230
Hicks, Granville, **I:** 254, 259, 374; **II:** 26; **III:** 342, 355, 452; **Supp. I Part 1:** 361; **Supp. I Part 2:** 609; **Supp. IV Part 1:** 22; **Supp. IV Part 2:** 526; **Supp. VIII:** 96, 124; **Supp. XII:** 250; **Supp. XIII:** 263; **Supp. XXI:** 276; **Supp. XXII:** 279
Hicks, Sally, **Supp. XXI:** 255
Hicok, Bethany, **Retro. Supp. II:** 39
"Hidden" (Nye), **Supp. XIII:** 283
"Hidden Gardens" (Capote), **Supp. III Part 1:** 125
Hidden Law, The (Hecht), **Supp. X:** 58
"Hidden Name and Complex Fate" (Ellison), **Supp. II Part 1:** 245
Hiddenness, Uncertainty, Surprise: Three Generative Energies of Poetry (Hirshfield), **Supp. XXIII:** 137
Hidden Wound, The (Berry), **Supp. X:** 23, 25, 26–27, 29, 34, 35
"Hide-and-Seek" (Francis), **Supp. IX:** 81
"Hiding" (Minot), **Supp. VI:** 203, 206
Hiding Place (Wideman), **Supp. X:** 320, 321, 327, 329, 331–332, 333
"Hidin' Out in Honky Heaven: On Race Relations in Vermont" (Budbill), **Supp. XIX:** 5
Hienger, Jorg, **Supp. IV Part 1:** 106
Hieronymus Bosch (De Tolnay), **Supp. XXII:** 255
Higgins, George, **Supp. IV Part 1:** 356
Higginson, Thomas Wentworth, **I:** 451–452, 453, 454, 456, 458, 459, 463,

464, 465, 470; **Retro. Supp. I:** 26, 31, 33, 35, 39, 40; **Supp. I Part 1:** 307, 371; **Supp. IV Part 2:** 430

Higgs, Robert, **Supp. XX: 166**

"High Bridge above the Tagus River at Toledo, The" (W. C. Williams), **Retro. Supp. I:** 429

"High Dive: A Variant" (Kumin), **Supp. IV Part 2:** 442

"High Diver" (Francis), **Supp. IX:** 82

"Higher Keys, The" (Merrill), **Supp. III Part 1:** 335–336

Higher Learning in America, The (Veblen), **Supp. I Part 2:** 630, 631, 641, 642

Highet, Gilbert, **Supp. I Part 1:** 268

"High Heav'd my breast"(J. Schoolcraft), **Supp. XXIII:** 235

High Noon (film), **Supp. V:** 46

"High on Sadness" (Komunyakaa), **Supp. XIII:** 114

"High School Senior" (Olds), **Supp. X:** 212

Highsmith, Patricia, **Supp. IV Part 1:** 79, 94, 132; **Supp. XXII:** 136

"High Tide" (Marquand), **III:** 56

High Tide in Tucson: Essays from Now or Never (Kingsolver), **Supp. VII:** 198, 201, 209

"High-Toned Old Christian Woman, A" (Stevens), **Retro. Supp. I:** 301

"High Water" (Mosher), **Supp. XXII:** 205, 211

"Highway, The" (Merwin), **Supp. III Part 1:** 346

Highway 61 Revisited (album, Dylan), **Supp. XVIII:** 20, 27, 30, 32

"Highway 61 Revisited" (song, Dylan), **Supp. XVIII:** 30

"Highway 99E from Chico" (Carver), **Supp. III Part 1:** 136

"Highway Apple Trees" (Espaillat), **Supp. XXI: 100–102**

High Window, The (Chandler), **Supp. IV Part 1:** 127–129, 130, 131

"High Yaller" (R. Fisher), **Supp. XIX:** 72

Hijuelos, Oscar, **Supp. IV Part 1:** 54; **Supp. VIII: 73–91**

Hike and the Aeroplane (Lewis), **II:** 440–441

Hilberg, Raul, **Supp. V:** 267

Hildebrand, Al, **III:** 118

Hiler, Hilaire, **Retro. Supp. II:** 327; **Supp. III Part 2:** 617

"Hill, A" (Hecht), **Supp. X:** 59–60, 63

Hill, Abram, **Supp. XV:** 194

Hill, Anita, **Supp. XX: 110**

Hill, Hamlin, **Retro. Supp. II:** 286

Hill, James J., **Supp. I Part 2:** 644

Hill, Joe, **I:** 493; **Supp. XVIII:** 224; **Supp. XXIII:** 162

Hill, Lee, **Supp. XI:** 293, 294, 297, 299, 301, 305, 307

Hill, Pamela Smith, **Supp. XXII:** 295

Hill, Patti, **I:** 289

Hill, Peggy, **Supp. XIII:** 163

"Hill, The" (Strand), **Supp. IV Part 2:** 627

"Hill, The" (Toomer), **Supp. III Part 2:** 486

Hill, Vernon, **Supp. I Part 2:** 397

"Hillcrest" (Robinson), **III:** 504

Hill-Lubin, Mildred A., **Supp. IV Part 1:** 13

Hillman, Sidney, **Supp. I Part 1:** 5

Hillringhouse, Mark, **Supp. IX:** 286, 288, 299

Hills Beyond, The (Wolfe), **IV:** 450, 451, 460, 461

"Hills Beyond, The" (Wolfe), **IV:** 460

Hillside and Seaside in Poetry (Larcom, ed.), **Supp. XIII:** 142

"Hillside Thaw, A" (Frost), **Retro. Supp. I:** 133

"Hills Like White Elephants" (Hemingway), **Retro. Supp. I:** 170

Hills of the Shatemuc, The (S. Warner), **Supp. XVIII:** 266

"Hill-Top View, A" (Jeffers), **Supp. II Part 2:** 417

Hill Towns (Siddons), **Supp. XXII:** 239, 253

"Hill Wife, The" (Frost), **II:** 154; **Retro. Supp. I:** 131

Hillyer, Catherine, **Supp. XV:** 244

Hillyer, Robert, **I:** 475; **Supp. IX:** 75; **Supp. XIV:** 11

Hilton, James, **Supp. XIII:** 166

"Hiltons' Holiday, The" (Jewett), **II:** 391; **Retro. Supp. II:** 134

Him (Cummings), **I:** 429, 434–435

Himes, Chester Bomar, **Retro. Supp. II:** 117; **Supp. I Part 1:** 51, 325; **Supp. XIII:** 233; **Supp. XVI: 135–146**

Himes, Norman, **Supp. V:** 128

"Him on a Bicycle" (Weigl), **Supp. XIX:** 276

"Him with His Foot in His Mouth" (Bellow), **Retro. Supp. II:** 34

Him with His Foot in His Mouth and Other Stories (Bellow), **Retro. Supp. II:** 31

Hinchman, Sandra K., **Supp. IV Part 1:** 210

Hinckley, David, **Supp. XXII:** 215

Hindemith, Paul, **IV:** 357; **Supp. IV Part 1:** 81

Hindsell, Oliver, **Supp. XIII:** 162

Hindus, Milton, **Supp. XIV:** 288, 291, 292, 293; **Supp. XXIII:** 16

Hines, Suzanne, **Supp. XIV:** 151

Hinge Picture (Howe), **Supp. IV Part 2:** 423–424

Hinojosa, Rolando, **Supp. XIX: 97–114**

"Hinterlands" (W. Gibson), **Supp. XVI:** 123, 128

"Hippies: Slouching towards Bethlehem" (Didion), **Supp. IV Part 1:** 200

Hippolytus (Euripides), **II:** 543; **Supp. I Part 1:** 270

Hippolytus Temporizes (Doolittle), **Supp. I Part 1:** 270

"Hips" (Cisneros), **Supp. VII:** 61, 62

"Hipster's Hipster" (Ginsberg), **Supp. XIV:** 141

Hirsch, Edward D., **Supp. V:** 177; **Supp. IX:** 262; **Supp. XIV:** 15; **Supp. XV:** 78, 225; **Supp. XVII:** 23; **Supp. XIX:** 202; **Supp. XXIII:** 124

Hirsch, Sidney, **Supp. XIV:** 1. *See* Mttron-Hirsch, Sidney

Hirschfeld, Jane, **Supp. XVII:** 241

Hirschorn, Clive, **Supp. IV Part 2:** 577, 579

Hirshfield, Jane, **Supp. XXIII: 129–141**

Hirson, Roger, **Supp. XI:** 343

"His Bride of the Tomb" (Dunbar), **Supp. II Part 1:** 196

"His Chest of Drawers" (Anderson), **I:** 113, 114

"His Daily Journal"(Kenny), **Supp. XXIII:** 153

"His Father's Whistle" (Wrigley), **Supp. XVIII:** 299

His First, Best Country (J. W. Miller), **Supp. XX: 163, 166, 172–175**

His Fortunate Grace (Atherton), **Supp. XXIV:** 22

His Human Majesty (Boyle), **Supp. XXIV:** 62

"His Last Day" (C. Himes), **Supp. XVI:** 137

"His Lover" (Dubus), **Supp. VII:** 86

"His Music" (Dunn), **Supp. XI:** 149

"His Own Key" (Ríos), **Supp. IV Part 2:** 543

His Picture in the Papers (film; Emerson), **Supp. XVI:** 185

His Religion and Hers (Gilman), **Supp. XI:** 209

Hiss, Alger, **Supp. XV:** 143

"Hiss, Chambers, and the Age of Innocence" (Fiedler), **Supp. XIII:** 99

"His Shield" (Moore), **III:** 211

"His Story" (Cisneros), **Supp. VII:** 67

His Thought Made Pockets & the Plane Buckt (Berryman), **I:** 170

"His Three Women" (Gioia), **Supp. XV:** 119–120

Histoire comparée des systèmes de philosophie (Gérando), **II:** 10

Histoire de la brume, L' (Dybek; trans. Beget), **Supp. XXIII:** 74

Historical and Moral View of the Origin and Progress of the French Revolution (Wollstonecraft), **Supp. I Part 1:** 126

"Historical Conceptualization" (Huizinga), **I:** 255

Historical Evidence and the Reading of Seventeenth-Century Poetry (Brooks), **Supp. XIV:** 11

"Historical Interpretation of Literature, The" (Wilson), **IV:** 431, 433, 445

Historical Jesus, The: The Life of a Mediterranean Jewish Peasant (Crossan), **Supp. V:** 251

Historical Life of Jesus, The (Pettis), **Supp. XXIII:** 189

"Historical Value of Crèvecoeur's *Voyage . . .,*" (Adams), **Supp. I Part 1:** 251

"History" (Emerson), **II:** 13, 15

"History" (Hughes), **Supp. I Part 1:** 344

History (Lowell), **Retro. Supp. II:** 183, 190

"History" (Simic), **Supp. VIII:** 279

"History, Myth, and the Western Writer" (Stegner), **Supp. IV Part 2:** 596, 601

"History among the Rocks" (Warren), **IV:** 252

History as a Literary Art (Morison), **Supp. I Part 2:** 493

"History as Fate in E. L. Doctorow's Tale of a Western Town" (Arnold), **Supp. IV Part 1:** 220

"History Is the Memory of Time" (Olson), **Supp. II Part 2:** 574

"History Lesson" (Trethewey), **Supp. XXI:** 248, 249

"History Lessons" (Komunyakaa), **Supp. XIII:** 126

History Man, The (Bradbury), **Supp. XVIII:** 140

"History of a Literary Movement" (Nemerov), **III:** 270

"History of a Literary Radical, The" (Bourne), **I:** 215, 235, 236

History of a Radical: Essays by Randolph Bourne (Brooks), **I:** 245

"History of Armenia, The"(Balakian), **Supp. XXIII:** 23, 24

"History of Buttons, The" (Goldbarth), **Supp. XII:** 187

History of English Literature (Taine), **III:** 323

History of English Prosody (Saintsbury), **Supp. XV:** 181

History of Fortus, The (Emerson), **II:** 8

History of Henry Esmond, The (Thackeray), **II:** 91, 130

History of Modern Poetry, A (Perkins), **Supp. I Part 2:** 475; **Supp. XV:** 185

History of My Heart (Pinsky), **Supp. VI:** 243, 244, 245

History of New York, from the Beginning of the World to the End of the Dutch Dynasty, A (Irving), **II:** 300–303, 304, 310

History of Pendennis, The (Thackeray), **II:** 291

"History of Red, The" (Hogan), **Supp. IV Part 1:** 411

"History of Rodney, The" (Bass), **Supp. XVI:** 20

History of Roxbury Town (Ellis), **Supp. I Part 1:** 99

History of Southern Literature, The (Rubin), **Supp. XX: 161**

History of the African-American People (Proposed) by Strom Thurmond, The (Everett and Kincaid), **Supp. XVIII:** 62, **63–64**

History of the American Film, A (Durang), **Supp. XXIV:** 113, 117, **118–119**

History of the Conquest of Mexico (Prescott), **Retro. Supp. I:** 123

History of the Conquest of Peru (Morison, ed.), **Supp. I Part 2:** 494

History of the Dividing Line betwixt Virginia and North Carolina (Byrd), **Supp. IV Part 2:** 425

History of the Life and Voyages of Christopher Columbus, A (Irving), **II:** 310, 314

History of the Navy of the United States of America (Cooper), **I:** 347

History of the Rise and Fall of the Slave-power in America (Wilson), **Supp. XIV:** 48, 49

History of the Russian Revolution, A (Trotsky), **Supp. XXI:** 161

History of the United States (Bancroft), **Supp. XXII:** 33

History of the United States of America during the Administrations of Thomas Jefferson and James Madison (Adams), **I:** 6–9, 10, 20, 21

History of the Work of Redemption, A (Edwards), **I:** 560

History of United States Naval Operations in World War II (Morison), **Supp. I Part 2:** 490–492

History of Womankind in Western Europe, The, **Supp. XI:** 197

"History Teacher, The" (Collins), **Supp. XXI:** 57

"History Through a Beard" (Morison), **Supp. I Part 2:** 490

His Toy, His Dream, His Rest (Berryman), **I:** 169, 170, 183, 184–186

"His Words" (Roethke), **III:** 544

Hitchcock, Ada. *See* MacLeish, Mrs. Archibald (Ada Hitchcock)

Hitchcock, Alfred, **IV:** 357; **Supp. IV Part 1:** 132; **Supp. VIII:** 177; **Supp. XX: 253**; **Supp. XXII:** 119

Hitchcock, George, **Supp. X:** 127; **Supp. XVII:** 110

"Hitch Haiku" (Snyder), **Supp. VIII:** 297

"Hitch-Hikers, The" (Welty), **IV:** 262

"Hitchhiking Is Illegal in Nevada" (Lethem), **Supp. XVIII:** 136

Hitchins, Christopher, **Supp. VIII:** 241

Hitler, Adolf, **I:** 261, 290, 492; **II:** 146, 454, 561, 565, 592; **III:** 2, 3, 110, 115, 140, 156, 246, 298, 446; **IV:** 5, 17, 18, 298, 372; **Supp. I Part 2:** 431, 436, 446, 664; **Supp. V:** 290

Hitler, Wendy, **III:** 404

Hitler Lives ? (film), **Supp. XVI:** 102

Hix, H. L., **Supp. XV:** 114

H. L. Mencken, a Portrait from Memory (Angoff), **III:** 107

"H. L. Mencken Meets a Poet in the West Side Y.M.C.A." (White), **Supp. I Part 2:** 677

H. L. Mencken: The American Scene (Cairns), **III:** 119

H. M. Pulham, Esquire (Marquand), **II:** 482–483; **III:** 58, 59, 65, 68–69

Hnizdovsky, Jacques, **Supp. XIII:** 346

"Hoadley's Test Case in Indiana" (Neugeboren), **Supp. XVI:** 219

Hoagland, Edward, **Supp. XIV:** 80; **Supp. XVI:** 277; **Supp. XXII:** 204, 206

Hoagland, Tony, **Supp. XIX:** 81, 89

"Hoarder, The" (Sexton), **Supp. II Part 2:** 692

"Hoarfrost" (C. Baxter), **Supp. XVII:** 15

Hoban, Phoebe, **Supp. XV:** 319, 325

Hoban, Russell, **Supp. XXIII:** 42

Hobb, Gormley, **I:** 203

Hobbes, Thomas, **I:** 277; **II:** 9, 10, 540; **III:** 306; **IV:** 88; **Supp. XII:** 33; **Supp. XIV:** 5, 7

Hobson, Geary, **Supp. IV Part 1:** 321; **Supp. IV Part 2:** 502

Hobson, J. A., **I:** 232

Hobson, John A., **Supp. I Part 2:** 650

Hobson, Laura Z., **III:** 151

Hocking, Agnes, **Supp. VIII:** 251

Hocking, William Ernest, **III:** 303

Hodge, Merle, **Supp. XXIII:** 94

Hodges, Campbell B., **Supp. XIV:** 8

Hodgson, Captain Joseph, **III:** 328

Hoffa, Jimmy, **I:** 493

Hoffenberg, Mason, **Supp. XI:** 294, 297, 299, 305

Hoffer, Eric, **Supp. VIII:** 188; **Supp. XIX:** 264

Hoffman, Abbie, **Supp. XIV:** 150

Hoffman, Alice, **Supp. X: 77–94; Supp. XIII:** 13

Hoffman, Allen, **Supp. XVII:** 42, 44

Hoffman, Daniel, **Retro. Supp. II:** 265

Hoffman, Daniel G., **I:** 405; **II:** 307; **Supp. XI:** 152

Hoffman, Dustin, **Supp. IV Part 1:** 236

Hoffman, E. T. A., **Supp. XVI:** 157

Hoffman, Eva, **Supp. XVI: 147–164**

Hoffman, Frederick J., **I:** 60, 67; **II:** 443; **IV:** 113

Hoffman, Josiah Ogden, **II:** 297, 300

Hoffman, Matilda, **II:** 300, 314

Hoffman, Paul, **Supp. XV:** 141–142

Hoffman, Roy, **Supp. XX: 177**

Hoffman, Todd, **Supp. XVIII:** 101

Hoffman, William, **Supp. XVIII: 69–88**

Hoffman, William M., **Supp. X:** 153

Hoffmann, E. T. A., **III:** 415

Hofmann, Hans, **Supp. XV:** 144

Hofmeister, Tim, **Supp. XIX:** 115

Ho for a Hat (W. J. Smith), **Supp. XIII:** 346

Hofstadter, Richard, **Supp. VIII:** 98, 99, 108

Hogan, Linda, **Supp. IV Part 1:** 324, 325, **397–418; Supp. XVIII:** 189

Hogan, Randolph, **Supp. XVI:** 252–253

Hogan, Ron, **Supp. XVIII:** 138, 139

Hogarth, William, **Supp. XII:** 44

Hogg, James, **I:** 53; **Supp. I Part 1:** 349; **Supp. IX:** 275

Hoggart, Richard, **Supp. XIV:** 299

"Hog-Nosed Snake, The" (Kooser), **Supp. XIX:** 128

Hogue, W. Lawrence, **Supp. XXII:** 175–176

Hohne, Karen, **Supp. V:** 147

Hojoki (Chomei), **IV:** 170

Holbrook, David, **Supp. I Part 2:** 526–527, 546

Holcroft, Thomas, **Supp. I Part 2:** 514

Holden, Jonathan, **Supp. XI:** 143

Holden, Raymond, **Supp. XIV:** 121–122

Holden, William, **Supp. XI:** 307

Hölderlin, Friedrich, **Supp. XVI:** 48; **Supp. XXIV:** 152

Holding, Elisabeth Sanxay, **Supp. XXII: 119–137**

"Holding On" (Levine), **Supp. V:** 184

Holding the Line: Women in the Great Arizona Mine Strike of 1983 (Kingsolver), **Supp. VII:** 197, 201–202, 204

"Holding the Mirror Up to Nature" (Nemerov), **III:** 275, 276

"Hold Me" (Levine), **Supp. V:** 186

Hold the Press (film), **Supp. XIII:** 163

Hold with the Hares (Zinberg), **Supp. XV:** 197–198,**Supp. XV:** 203

"Hole in the Floor, A" (Wilbur), **Supp. III Part 2:** 556–557

Holiday (Barry), **Retro. Supp. I:** 104

"Holiday" (Porter), **III:** 454

Holiday (W. Frank), **Supp. XX: 72–73**

Holiday, Billie, **Supp. I Part 1:** 80; **Supp. IV Part 1:** 2, 7; **Supp. XIX:** 147

Holiday Song for Four-Part Chorus of Mixed Voices with Piano Accompaniment (Taggard and Schuman), **Supp. XXII:** 283

Holinshed, Raphael, **IV:** 370

Holladay, Polly, **Supp. XXI:** 6

Holland, Josiah, **Supp. I Part 2:** 420

Holland, Laurence Bedwell, **Retro. Supp. I:** 216

Holland, Theodore, **I:** 453

Holland, Mrs. Theodore, **I:** 453, 455, 465

Holland, William, **IV:** 381

Hollander, John, **Supp. III Part 2:** 541; **Supp. IV Part 2:** 642; **Supp. IX:** 50, 153, 155; **Supp. XII:** 254, 255, 260; **Supp. XV:** 256; **Supp. XVII:** 112; **Supp. XIX:** 121; **Supp. XXIII:** 112

Hollenberg, Donna, **Supp. XXIV:** 64

Holley, Marietta, **Supp. XIII:** 152

Holliday, Billie, **Supp. XXI:** 131

Hollinghurst, Alan, **Supp. XIII:** 52

Hollins Critic (Nelson), **Supp. XIX:** 3

Hollis, Thomas Brand, **Supp. I Part 2:** 514

Hollow Men, The (T. S. Eliot), **I:** 574, 575, 578–579, 580, 585; **III:** 586; **Retro. Supp. I:** 63, 64

"Hollow Tree, A" (R. Bly), **Supp. IV Part 1:** 64, 66

Hollyberrys at the Shore, The, **Supp. X:** 42

"Hollywood!" (Vidal), **Supp. IV Part 2:** 688

Hollywood: American Movie-City (Rand, unauthorized), **Supp. IV Part 2:** 519

Hollywood: A Novel of America in the 1920s (Vidal), **Supp. IV Part 2:** 677, 684, 686, 688, 690, 691

Hollywood Ending (film; Allen), **Supp. XV:** 11

Hollywood on Trial (film), **Supp. I Part 1:** 295

Holmes, Abiel, **Supp. I Part 1:** 300, 301, 302, 310

Holmes, Mrs. Abiel (Sarah Wendell), **Supp. I Part 1:** 300

Holmes, John, **I:** 169; **Supp. II Part 1:** 87; **Supp. IV Part 2:** 440–441; **Supp. XIV:** 119

Holmes, John Clellon, **Supp. XII:** 118; **Supp. XIV:** 144, 150

Holmes, Martha Stoddard, **Supp. XX: 205, 207**

Holmes, Oliver Wendell, **I:** 487; **II:** 225, 273–274, 402, 403; **III:** 81–82, 590, 591–592; **IV:** 429, 436; **Retro. Supp. II:** 155; **Supp. I Part 1:** 103, 243, 254, **299–319; Supp. I Part 2:** 405, 414, 415, 420, 593, 704, 705; **Supp. XI:** 194; **Supp. XXIV:** 77

Holmes, Oliver Wendell, Jr., **I:** 3, 19; **Supp. IV Part 2:** 422

Holmes, Mrs. Oliver Wendell (Amelia Jackson), **Supp. I Part 1:** 303

Holmes, Steven J., **Supp. IX:** 172, 177

Holmes, Ted, **Supp. V:** 180

Holmes, William Henry, **Supp. IV Part 2:** 603–604

Holocaust (Reznikoff), **Supp. XIV:** 281, **291–293**

Holocaust in American Life, The (Novick), **Supp. XVI:** 154

Holt, Edwin E., **I:** 59

Holt, Felix, **II:** 179

Holt, Henry, **II:** 348; **III:** 587

Holt, Patricia, **Supp. XIV:** 89

Holtby, Winifred, **Supp. I Part 2:** 720

Holy Ghostly, The (Shepard), **Supp. III Part 2:** 437–438, 447

"Holy Innocents, The" (Lowell), **II:** 539

Holy Sonnets (Donne), **IV:** 145; **Supp. I Part 1:** 367; **Supp. III Part 2:** 619; **Supp. XIII:** 130–131; **Supp. XVIII:** 50–51

"Holy Terror, A" (Bierce), **I:** 203

"Holy Terror, The" (Maxwell), **Supp. VIII:** 169

Holy the Firm (Dillard), **Supp. VI:** 23, **29**, 30, 31, 32

Holy War, The (Bunyan), **IV:** 156

"Holy Week"(Thompson), **Supp. XXIII:** 300

"Homage to Arthur Rimbaud" (Wright), **Supp. V:** 339

Homage to Baudelaire (Duncan, ed.), **Supp. XV:** 75

Homage to Catalonia (Orwell), **Supp. XVII:** 229

"Homage to Che Guevara" (Banks), **Supp. V:** 5

Homage to Clio (Auden), **Supp. II Part 1:** 24

"Homage to Elizabeth Bishop" (Ivask, ed.), **Supp. I Part 1:** 96

"Homage to Ezra Pound" (Wright), **Supp. V:** 339

Homage to Frank O'Hara (Ashbery), **Supp. III Part 1:** 2–3

"Homage to Franz Joseph Haydn" (Hecht), **Supp. X:** 69

"Homage to Hemingway" (Bishop), **IV:** 35

Homage to Mistress Bradstreet (Berryman), **I:** 168, 169, 170–171, 172, 174, 175, 178–183, 184, 186

"Homage to Paul Cézanne" (Wright), **Supp. V:** 341–342

Homage to Sextus Propertius (Pound), **Retro. Supp. I:** 290

"Homage to Sextus Propertius" (Pound), **III:** 462, 476; **Supp. III Part 2:** 622

"Homage to Shakespeare" (Cheever), **Supp. I Part 1:** 180

"Homage to the Empress of the Blues" (Hayden), **Supp. II Part 1:** 379

"Homage to the Memory of Wallace Stevens" (Justice), **Supp. VII:** 126

Homage to Theodore Dreiser (Warren), **I:** 517

Homans, Margaret, **Supp. X:** 229

"Home" (Hughes), **Supp. I Part 1:** 329, 330

"Home" (Mora), **Supp. XIII:** 217

Home (Robinson), **Supp. XXI:** 212, **220–223**

Home (Updike), **Retro. Supp. I:** 320

"Home" (Weigl), **Supp. XIX:** 287

"Home, Home on the Strange" (J. D. Reed), **Supp. XVI:** 174

"Home, Sweet Home" (Fante), **Supp. XI:** 164, 165

Home, The (Gilman), **Supp. XI: 206–207**

"Home, The" (Jarman), **Supp. XVII:** 116

"Home Address" (Bronk), **Supp. XXI:** 27

"Home after Three Months Away" (Lowell), **II:** 547

Home and Colonial Library (Murray), **Retro. Supp. I:** 246

"Home and the Open Road: The Nonfiction of Larry Brown" (Barrier), **Supp. XXI:** 48–49

Home as Found (Cooper), **I:** 348, 349, 350, 351

Home at the End of the World, A (Cunningham), **Supp. XV: 59–62,** 63

"Home Away from Home, A" (Humphrey), **Supp. IX:** 101

Home Book of Shakespeare Quotations (Stevenson), **Supp. XIV:** 120

"Home Burial" (Frost), **Retro. Supp. I:** 124, 125, 128, **129–130; Supp. VIII:** 31; **Supp. XV:** 159; **Supp. XIX:** 9

Homecoming (Alvarez), **Supp. VII:** 1, 3–5, 9

"Homecoming" (Carruth), **Supp. XVI:** 55

"Homecoming" (McGrath), **Supp. X:** 116

"Homecoming, The" (Gioia), **Supp. XV:** 123, 124

Homecoming, The (Wilson), **Supp. VIII:** 330

Homecoming Game, The (Nemerov), **III:** 268, 282, 284–285

"Home during a Tropical Snowstorm I Feed My Father Lunch" (Karr), **Supp. XI:** 241–242, 248

Home Economics (Berry), **Supp. X:** 28, 31–32, 35, 36, 37

"Home Economics for Halfbacks" (Skloot), **Supp. XX: 195, 207**

Home from the Hill (film), **Supp. IX:** 95

Home from the Hill (Humphrey), **Supp. IX:** 93, 95, **96–98,** 104, 106, 109

"Home Grown" (Vital), **Supp. XVI:** 160

"Homeland" (Merwin), **Supp. III Part 1:** 351

Homeland and Other Stories (Kingsolver), **Supp. VII:** 199, 202–204, 207

Home on the Range (Baraka), **Supp. II Part 1:** 47

Homeplace (Siddons), **Supp. XXII:** 253

Home Place, The (Morris), **III:** 221, 222, 232

Homeplace, The (Nelson), **Supp. XVIII: 174–175**

Homer, **I:** 312, 433; **II:** 6, 8, 133, 302, 543, 544, 552; **III:** 14, 21, 278, 453, 457, 473, 567; **IV:** 54, 371; **Retro. Supp. I:** 59; **Supp. I Part 1:** 158, 283; **Supp. I Part 2:** 494; **Supp. X:** 36, 120, 122; **Supp. XIV:** 21; **Supp. XVII:** 70, 227

Homer, Louise, **Retro. Supp. I:** 10

Homer, Winslow, **Supp. XXI:** 243

"Home Range" (Leopold), **Supp. XIV:** 184, 185

"Home Repairs" (Skloot), **Supp. XX: 204**

Homer's Art (Notley), **Supp. XXII:** 232

"Homer's Art" (Notley), **Supp. XXII:** 232–233

"Homesick Blues" (Hughes), **Supp. I Part 1:** 327

Home: Social Essays (Baraka), **Supp. II Part 1:** 45, 61

"Homesteading on the Extraterrestrial Frontier" (Abbott), **Supp. XVIII:** 142

Home to Harlem (McKay), **Supp. X:** 132, 137–138, **138–139; Supp. XVIII:** 127

"Home Videos" (Brockmeier), **Supp. XXII:** 60

Homeward Bound (Cooper), **I:** 348

"Homeward Star, The" (Palmer), **Supp. XV:** 81–82

Homewood trilogy (Wideman), **Supp. X:** 319

"Homework" (Cameron), **Supp. XII:** 80, **83,** 84

"Homily" (Tate), **IV:** 121–122

Homing with the Birds (Stratton-Porter), **Supp. XX: 212, 216, 222**

"Homme Moyen Sensuel, L' " (Pound), **III:** 462

Homme révolté, L' (Camus), III: 306

"Homoeopathy and Its Kindred Delusions" (Holmes), **Supp. I Part 1:** 303–304, 305

Homo Ludens (Huizinga), **II:** 416–417, 425

"Homosexuality: Is It Disgusting, or Is It Delightful?" (Durang), **Supp. XXIV:** 114

"Homosexuality"(O'Hara), **Supp. XXIII:** 212

"Homosexual Villain, The" (Mailer), **III:** 36

"Homo Will Not Inherit" (Doty), **Supp. XI:** 128

"Homunculus, The: A Novel in One Chapter" (McKnight), **Supp. XX: 152**

Hone and Strong Diaries of Old Manhattan, The (Auchincloss, ed.), **Supp. IV Part 1:** 23

"Honey" (Beattie), **Supp. V:** 33

"Honey" (Wright), **Supp. III Part 2:** 589

"Honey, We'll Be Brave" (Farrell), **II:** 45

Honey and Salt (Sandburg), **III:** 594–596

"Honey and Salt" (Sandburg), **III:** 594

"Honey Babe" (Hughes), **Supp. I Part 1:** 334

"Honey Tree, The" (Oliver), **Supp. VII:** 236

Hong, Maxine. *See* Kingston, Maxine Hong

Hongo, Garrett, **Supp. X:** 292; **Supp. XIII:** 114; **Supp. XVII:** 112

"Honkytonk" (Shapiro), **Supp. II Part 2:** 705

"Honky Tonk in Cleveland, Ohio" (Sandburg), **III:** 585

Honorable Men (Auchincloss), **Supp. IV Part 1:** 23

Honor Thy Father (Talese), **Supp. XVII:** 204–205, 210

Hood, Tom, **I:** 195

"Hoodoo in America" (Hurston), **Supp. VI:** 153–154

"Hook" (Wright), **Supp. III Part 2:** 604

Hook, Sidney, **I:** 265; **Supp. IV Part 2:** 527; **Supp. VIII:** 96, 100; **Supp. XIV:** 3

Hooker, Adelaide. *See* Marquand, Mrs. John P. (Adelaide Hooker)

Hooker, Isabella Beecher, **Supp. XI:** 193

Hooker, Samuel, **IV:** 162, 165

Hooker, Thomas, **II:** 15–16; **IV:** 162

Hooper, Marian. *See* Adams, Mrs. Henry (Marian Hooper)

Hoosier Holiday, A (Dreiser), **Retro. Supp. II:** 104

Hoover, Herbert, **Supp. I Part 2:** 638

Hoover, J. Edgar, **Supp. XIII:** 170

Hoover, Paul, **Supp. XV:** 179

"Hope" (Bontemps), **Supp. XXII:** 2

"Hope" (Jarrell), **II:** 389

"Hope" (Matthews), **Supp. IX:** 163

Hope, A. D., **Supp. XIII:** 347

Hope, Lynn, **Supp. II Part 1:** 38

"Hope Atherton's Wanderings" (Howe), **Supp. IV Part 2:** 432

"Hopeless Kill, The"(Kenny), **Supp. XXIII:** 145

Hope of Heaven (O'Hara), **III:** 361

"Hopes Rise" (Boyle), **Supp. XX:** 20

"Hop-Frog" (Poe), **Retro. Supp. II:** 264, 268, 269

Hopkin, Pauline, **Supp. XVI:** 143

Hopkins, Anne Yale, **Supp. I Part 1:** 100, 102, 113

Hopkins, Gerard Manley, **I:** 171, 179, 397, 401, 522, 525, 533; **II:** 537; **III:** 197, 209, 523; **IV:** 129, 135, 141, 421; **Retro. Supp. II:** 40; **Supp. I Part 1:** 79, 81, 94; **Supp. III Part 2:** 551; **Supp. IV Part 1:** 178; **Supp. IV Part 2:** 637, 638, 639, 641, 643; **Supp. V:** 337; **Supp. IX:** 39, 42; **Supp. X:** 61, 115; **Supp. XIII:** 294; **Supp. XIV:** 83; **Supp. XV:** 250, 347; **Supp. XVI:** 282; **Supp. XVII:** 241; **Supp. XVIII:** 78, 79; **Supp. XX:** 230; **Supp. XXIII:** 121

Hopkins, Gerard Walter Sturgis, **Supp. XX: 229, 233, 240**

Hopkins, L. A., **I:** 502

Hopkins, Lemuel, **Supp. II Part 1:** 70

Hopkins, Miriam, **IV:** 381; **Supp. I Part 1:** 281

Hopkins, Pauline, **Supp. XVIII:** 284

Hopkins, Samuel, **I:** 547, 549; **Supp. XXIV:** 68

Hopkins, Vivian, **II:** 20

Hopkinson, Francis, **Supp. I Part 2:** 504

Hopler, Jay, **Supp. XXIII:** 132

Hopper (Strand), **Supp. IV Part 2:** 632

Hopper, Dennis, **Supp. XI:** 293, 308

Hopper, Edward, **IV:** 411, 413; **Supp. IV Part 2:** 619, 623, 631, 634; **Supp. XIX:** 117

Hopwood, Avery, **Supp. IV Part 2:** 573

Horace, **II:** 8, 154, 169, 543, 552, 568; **III:** 15; **IV:** 89; **Supp. I Part 2:** 423; **Supp. IX:** 152; **Supp. X:** 65; **Supp. XII:** 258, 260, 262

Horae Canonicae (Auden), **Supp. II Part 1:** 21

"Horatian Ode" (Marvell), **IV:** 135

"Horatian Ode upon Cromwell's Return from Ireland" (Marvell), **Supp. XIV:** 10

Horgan, Paul, **Supp. XV:** 46, 49, 52

Horkheimer, Max, **Supp. I Part 2:** 645; **Supp. IV Part 1:** 301

Horn, Dara, **Supp. XVII:** 50; **Supp. XX: 177**

Horn, Mother, **Supp. I Part 1:** 49, 54

Hornby, Nick, **Supp. XII:** 286; **Supp. XXIII:** 109

Horn of Africa (Caputo), **Supp. XIX:** 21–23

Horn of Life, The (Atherton), **Supp. XXIV:** 26, 27

"Horn of Plenty" (Hughes), **Retro. Supp. I:** 210; **Supp. I Part 1:** 342

Horovitz, Israel, **Supp. XV:** 321

Horowitz, James. *See* Salter, James

Horowitz, Mark, **Supp. V:** 219, 231

"Horrible" (Halliday), **Supp. XIX:** 91

"Horse, The" (Levine), **Supp. V:** 182

"Horse, The" (Wright), **Supp. III Part 2:** 592, 601

"Horse, The"(Le Sueur), **Supp. XXIII:** 168

Horse Eats Hay (play), **Supp. IV Part 1:** 82

Horse Feathers (film), **Supp. IV Part 1:** 384

"Horseflies" (Wrigley), **Supp. XVIII:** 307

Horse Has Six Legs, The (Simic), **Supp. VIII:** 272

"Horselaugh on Dibber Lannon" (Fante), **Supp. XI:** 164

Horseman, Pass By (McMurtry), **Supp. V:** 220–221, 224

"Horses" (Doty), **Supp. XI:** 122

Horses and Men (Anderson), **I:** 112–113, 114

"Horses and Men in Rain" (Sandburg), **III:** 584

"Horse Show, The" (W. C. Williams), **Retro. Supp. I:** 423

Horses Make a Landscape More Beautiful (Walker), **Supp. III Part 2:** 521, 533

"Horse Thief" (Caldwell), **I:** 310

"Horseweed" (Offutt), **Supp. XIX:** 166, 167

Horse With a Green Vinyl Mane (P. N. Warren), **Supp. XX: 261**

"Horsie" (Parker), **Supp. IX:** 193

Horton, George Moses, **Supp. XXII:** 11

Horton, Philip, **I:** 383, 386, 387, 393, 441; **Supp. XV:** 138

Horton Hatches the Egg (Geisel), **Supp. XVI:** 100, 112

Horton Hears a Who! (Geisel), **Supp. XVI:** 102

"Horton's Ape"(P. Benedict), **Supp. XXIII:** 41

Horwitz, Tony, **Supp. XVIII:** 195–196

Hosea (biblical book), **II:** 166

Hospers, John, **Supp. IV Part 2:** 528

"Hospice" (Hull), **Supp. XXI:** 138

Hospital, Janette Turner, **Supp. IV Part 1:** 311–302

Hospital Sketches (Alcott), **Supp. I Part 1:** 34, 35

Hostages to Fortune (Humphrey), **Supp. IX:** 96, **104–106,** 109

Hostess to Murder (Holding), **Supp. XXII:** 126, **127**

"Hot Combs" (Trethewey), **Supp. XXI:** 249

"Hot Cross Bum" (Loy), **Supp. XXII:** 168

"Hot Dog" (Stern), **Supp. IX: 298–299**

"Hotel, The"(Hadas), **Supp. XXIII:** 121

"Hotel Bar" (McClatchy), **Supp. XII:** 269

Hotel Dwellers, The (Lacy), **Supp. XV:** 205

Hotel Insomnia (Simic), **Supp. VIII:** 280, **281–282**

Hotel Lambosa and Other Stories (Koch), **Supp. XV:** 186

Hotel New Hampshire, The (Irving), **Supp. VI:** 163, 164, **172–173,** 177, 179; **Supp. XIX:** 164

"Hot-Foot Hannibal" (Chesnutt), **Supp. XIV:** 60

"Hot Ice"(Dybek), **Supp. XXIII:** 72–73

"Hot Night on Water Street" (Simpson), **Supp. IX:** 269, 270

"Hot Time, A" (Gunn Allen), **Supp. IV Part 1:** 333

Houdini, Harry, **IV:** 437

"Hound of Heaven" (Thompson), **Retro. Supp. I:** 55

"Hourglass, The" (Kees), **Supp. XV:** 147

"Hour in Chartres, An" (Bourne), **I:** 228

"Hour of Peonies, The"(Crooker), **Supp. XXIII:** 58

Hours, The (Cunningham), **Supp. XII:** 80; **Supp. XV: 65–68**

"Hours before Eternity" (Caldwell), **I:** 291

House, Bridge, Fountain, Gate (Kumin), **Supp. IV Part 2:** 448, 449, 451, 454

House, Edward, **Supp. I Part 2:** 643

"House, The" (Merrill), **Supp. III Part 1:** 323

House at Pooh Corner, The (Milne), **Supp. IX:** 189

"House at the End of the World, The" (Brockmeier), **Supp. XXII:** 52, 53

House Behind the Cedars, The (Chesnutt), **Supp. XIV: 69–71**

Houseboat Days (Ashbery), **Supp. III Part 1:** 18–20

Housebreaker of Shady Hill and Other Stories, The (Cheever), **Supp. I Part 1:** 184

"House by the Sea, The" (E. Stoddard), **Supp. XV:** 277

House by the Sea, The (Sarton), **Supp. VIII:** 264

House Divided, A (Buck), **Supp. II Part 1:** 118

"House Divided, The/La Casa Divida" (Kingsolver), **Supp. VII:** 207

"House Guest" (Bishop), **Retro. Supp. II:** 49; **Supp. I Part 1:** 93

Household Saints (film), **Supp. XVI:** 256

Household Saints (Prose), **Supp. XVI:** 252–253, 254, 261

"House in Athens, The" (Merrill), **Supp. III Part 1:** 323

House in the Uplands, A (Caldwell), **I:** 297, 301, 306

"House in Turk Street, The" (Hammett), **Supp. IV Part 1:** 344

"House in Winter, The" (Sarton), **Supp. VIII:** 259

"House in Winter, The"(Hirshfield), **Supp. XXIII:** 132

"Housekeeping" (Alvarez), **Supp. VII:** 3–5, 10

Housekeeping (Robinson), **Supp. XXI:** 210–211, **212–216,** 218, 223

"Housekeeping" (Trethewey), **Supp. XXI:** 249

"Housekeeping for Men" (Bourne), **I:** 231

House Made of Dawn (Momaday), **Supp. IV Part 1:** 274, 323, 326; **Supp. IV Part 2:** 479, 480, 481–484, 485, 486, 504, 562

Houseman, John, **Supp. IV Part 1:** 173

House Next Door, The (Siddons), **Supp. XXII:** 239

House Next Door, The (television movie), **Supp. XXII:** 239

House of Dust, The: A Symphony (Aiken), **I:** 50

House of Earth trilogy (Buck), **Supp. II Part 1:** 118, 123

House of Five Talents, The (Auchincloss), **Supp. IV Part 1:** 21, 25–27

"House of Flowers" (Capote), **Supp. III Part 1:** 123

House of Games (Mamet), **Supp. XIV:** 243

House of Houses (Mora), **Supp. XIII:** 213, 215, 218, 219, 223–224, **225–227,** 228, 229

House of Incest (Nin), **Supp. III Part 1:** 43; **Supp. X:** 187, 190, 193

House of Lee, The (Atherton), **Supp. XXIV:** 26–27

House of Life, The: Rachel Carson at Work (Brooks), **Supp. IX:** 26

House of Light (Oliver), **Supp. VII:** 238–240

House of Mirth, The (Wharton), **II:** 180, 193; **IV:** 311–313, 314, 316, 318, 323, 327; **Retro. Supp. I:** 360, 366, 367, **367–370,** 373, 380; **Supp. XX: 239, 240**

"House of Mist, The" (Rand), **Supp. IV Part 2:** 524

"House of My Own, A" (Cisneros), **Supp. VII:** 64

"House of Night, The" (Freneau), **Supp. II Part 1:** 259, 260

"House of Representatives and Me, The" (Conroy), **Supp. XVI:** 75

House of Sand and Fog (Dubus III), **Supp. XXIV:** 97, **104–107**

House of Sleeping Beauties, The (Hwang), **Supp. XXI:** 146

House of the Far and Lost, The (Wolfe), **IV:** 456

"House of the Injured, The" (Haines), **Supp. XII:** 203

"House of the One Father" (Antin), **Supp. XX: 3, 13**

House of the Prophet, The (Auchincloss), **Supp. IV Part 1:** 31

House of the Seven Gables (Hawthorne), **I:** 106; **II:** 60, 224, 225, 231, 237, 239, 240–241, 243, 244; **Retro. Supp. I:** 63, 149, **160–162,** 163, 164; **Supp. I Part 2:** 579

House of the Solitary Maggot, The (Purdy), **Supp. VII:** 274–275

"House on 15th S.W., The" (Hugo), **Supp. VI:** 140

"House on Main Street, The" (B. Kelly), **Supp. XVII:** 127

House on Mango Street, The (Cisneros), **Supp. VII:** 58, 59–64, 65, 66, 67, 68, 72

"House on Mango Street, The" (Cisneros), **Supp. VII:** 59

House on Marshland, The (Glück), **Supp. V:** 81–83, 84

"House on Moscow Street, The" (Nelson), **Supp. XVIII:** 174

"House on the Heights, A" (Capote), **Supp. III Part 1:** 120

"House on the Hill, The" (Robinson), **III:** 505, 524

"House Raising" (Offutt), **Supp. XIX:** 166

"Houses" (Hogan), **Supp. IV Part 1:** 402

"Houses, The" (Merwin), **Supp. III Part 1:** 354

"Houses of the Spirit" (Karr), **Supp. XI:** 250

"House Sparrows" (Hecht), **Supp. X: 68**

"House That Doesn't House, The" (Bronk), **Supp. XXI:** 34

House That Tai Maing Built, The (Lee), **Supp. X:** 291

"House Unroofed by the Gale" (Tu Fu), **II:** 526

"House Where Mark Twain Was Born, The" (Masters), **Supp. I Part 2:** 472

"Housewife" (Hempel), **Supp. XXI:** 124

"Housewife" (Sexton), **Supp. II Part 2:** 682

" 'Housing the Deliberations': New York, War, and Frank O'Hara"(Ward), **Supp. XXIII:** 218

Housman, A. E., **III:** 15, 136, 606; **Supp. II Part 1:** 4; **Supp. IV Part 1:** 165; **Supp. XV:** 40–41

Houston Trilogy (McMurtry), **Supp. V:** 223–225

How" (Ginsberg), **Supp. XIV:** 142, 143

"How" (Moore), **Supp. X:** 167

"How About This?" (Carver), **Supp. III Part 1:** 141

"How America Came to the Mountains" (J. W. Miller), **Supp. XX: 169**

"How Annandale Went Out" (Robinson), **III:** 513

Howard, Arliss, **Supp. XXI:** 39

Howard, Ben, **Supp. XVI:** 54

Howard, Gerald, **Supp. XII:** 21

Howard, Jane, **Retro. Supp. I:** 334

Howard, June, **Retro. Supp. II:** 139

Howard, Leon, **Supp. I Part 2:** 408, 422, 423

Howard, Maureen, **Supp. XII:** 285; **Supp. XVII:** 183

Howard, Richard, **Retro. Supp. II:** 43; **Supp. IV Part 2:** 624, 626, 640; **Supp. VIII:** 273; **Supp. IX:** 324, 326; **Supp. X:** 152; **Supp. XI:** 317; **Supp. XII:** 254; **Supp. XIII:** 76; **Supp. XV:** 23, 24; **Supp. XXIV:** 155

Howard, Vilma, **Retro. Supp. II:** 111, 112

Howards, J. Z., **Supp. VIII:** 178

Howards End (Forster), **Supp. XII:** 87

Howarth, Cora, **I:** 408, 409

Howbah Indians (Ortiz), **Supp. IV Part 2:** 513

"How Black Sees Green and Red" (McKay), **Supp. X:** 136

How Britain Rules Africa (Padmore), **Supp. XXI:** 166

"How David Did Not Care" (R. Bly), **Supp. IV Part 1:** 73

"How Did I Love Him?" (Nelson), **Supp. XVIII:** 176

"How Do I Love Thee?" (Browning), **Supp. XVIII:** 176

Howe, Daniel Walker, **Supp. XXIV:** 79

Howe, Darcus, **Supp. XXI:** 170

Howe, E.W., **I:** 106

Howe, Florence, **Supp. XIII:** 295, 306

Howe, Harriet, **Supp. XI:** 200, 201

Howe, Irving, **IV:** 10; **Retro. Supp. I:** 369; **Retro. Supp. II:** 112, 286; **Supp. I Part 2:** 432; **Supp. II Part 1:** 99; **Supp. VI: 113–129; Supp. VIII:** 93, 232; **Supp. IX:** 227; **Supp. X:** 203, 245; **Supp. XII:** 160; **Supp. XIII:** 98; **Supp. XIV:** 103–104, 104; **Supp. XVII:** 50; **Supp. XIX:** 257, 265; **Supp. XXIII:** 3, 7; **Supp. XXIV:** 220–221, 222

Howe, James Wong, **Supp. I Part 1:** 281; **Supp. V:** 223

Howe, Julia Ward, **III:** 505; **Retro. Supp. II:** 135

Howe, M. A. DeWolfe, **I:** 258; **II:** 406; **Supp. XIV:** 54

Howe, Mary Manning, **Supp. IV Part 2:** 422

Howe, Samuel, **Supp. I Part 1:** 153

Howe, Susan, **Retro. Supp. I:** 33, 43; **Supp. IV Part 2: 419–438; Supp. XVI:** 284

Howell, Chris, **Supp. XIII:** 112

Howell, James, **II:** 111

Howells, Margaret, **II:** 271

Howells, William C., **II:** 273

Howells, William Dean, **I:** 109, 192, 204, 210, 211, 254, 355, 407, 411, 418, 459, 469; **II:** 127–128, 130, 131, 136, 137, 138, 140, **271–294,** 322, 331–332, 338, 397–398, 400, 415, 444, 451, 556; **III:** 51, 118, 314, 327–328, 461, 576, 607; **IV:** 192, 202, 342, 349; **Retro. Supp. I:** 220, 334, 362, 378; **Retro. Supp. II:** 93, 101, 135, 288; **Supp. I Part 1:** 306, 318, 357, 360, 368; **Supp. I Part 2:** 414, 420, 645–646; **Supp. II Part 1:** 198, 352; **Supp. IV Part 2:** 678; **Supp. VIII:** 98, 101, 102; **Supp. XI:** 198, 200; **Supp. XIV:** 45–46; **Supp. XV:** 269, 274, 285, 287; **Supp. XVIII:** 6; **Supp. XXIV:** 24

Howells, Mrs. William Dean (Elinor Mead), **II:** 273

Howells, Winifred, **II:** 271

"Howells as Anti-Novelist" (Updike), **Retro. Supp. I:** 334

Howells: His Life and World (Brooks), **I:** 254

Hower, Edward, **Supp. XII:** 330, 343

Howes, Barbara, **Supp. XIII:** 331

How Good Is David Mamet, Anyway? (Heilpern), **Supp. XIV:** 242

"How I Became a Shadow" (Purdy), **Supp. VII:** 269

"How I Came to Vedanta" (Isherwood), **Supp. XIV:** 164

"How I Come to You" (Peacock), **Supp. XIX:** 198

"How I Learned to Sweep" (Alvarez), **Supp. VII:** 4

"How I Spent My Forties" (Wasserstein), **Supp. XV:** 325, 330, 332

"How It Began" (Stafford), **Supp. XI:** 327

"How It Feels to Be Colored Me" (Hurston), **Supp. VI:** 152

"How It Is" (Budbill), **Supp. XIX:** 10

"How It Is" (Everwine), **Supp. XV:** 79, 86

"How I Told My Child About Race" (Brooks), **Supp. III Part 1:** 78

"How I Went to the Mines" (Harte), **Supp. II Part 1:** 336

"How I Write" (Franzen), **Supp. XX: 84**

"How I Write" (Welty), **IV:** 279, 280

"How I Wrote *The Promised Land*" (Antin), **Supp. XX:** 3

"How Jonah Did Not Care" (R. Bly), **Supp. IV Part 1:** 73

Howl (Ginsberg), **Retro. Supp. I:** 426; **Supp. III Part 1:** 92; **Supp. IV Part 1:** 90; **Supp. V:** 336; **Supp. VIII:** 290; **Supp. XIV:** 15, 126, 157; **Supp. XVIII:** 20, 29

"How Laddie and the Princess Spelled Down at the Christmas Bee" (Stratton-Porter), **Supp. XX: 216**

Howl and Other Poems (Ginsberg), **Supp. II Part 1:** 308, 317–318, 319; **Supp. X:** 123

Howlett, William, **Retro. Supp. I:** 17

Howl: Original Draft Facsimile, Transcript and Variant Versions (Gimsberg), **Supp. XIV:** 142

"How Many Midnights" (Bowles), **Supp. IV Part 1:** 86–87

"How Many Nights" (Kinnell), **Supp. III Part 1:** 245–246

How Much? (Blechman), **Supp. I Part 1:** 290

"How Much Are You Worth" (Salinas), **Supp. XIII:** 325–326

"How Much Earth" (Levine), **Supp. V:** 184

How Much Earth: The Fresno Poets (Buckley, Oliveira, and Williams, eds.), **Supp. XIII:** 313

"How Not to Forget" (Bartov), **Supp. XVI:** 153–154

"How Poetry Comes to Me" (Corso), **Supp. XII:** 122

"How Poetry Comes to Me" (Snyder), **Supp. VIII:** 305

How Reading Changed My Life (Quindlen), **Supp. XVII:** 167, 179–180

"How She Came By Her Name: An Interview with Louis Massiah" (Bambara), **Supp. XI:** 20

"How Soon Hath Time" (Ransom), **IV:** 123

How Spring Comes (Notley), **Supp. XXII:** 226, 229

How Stella Got Her Groove Back (McMillan), **Supp. XIII:** 185, **190–191**

How the Alligator Missed Breakfast (Kinney), **Supp. III Part 1:** 235, 253

"How the Devil Came Down Division Street" (Algren), **Supp. IX:** 3

How the García Girls Lost Their Accents (Alvarez), **Supp. VII:** 3, 5–9, 11, 15, 17, 18

How the Grinch Stole Christmas! (Geisel), **Supp. XVI:** 102

How the Other Half Lives (Riis), **I:** 293

"How the Saint Did Not Care" (R. Bly), **Supp. IV Part 1:** 73

"How the Women Went from Dover" (Whittier), **Supp. I Part 2:** 694, 696, 697

"How To" (Carruth), **Supp. XVI:** 51

"How-To" (Monson), **Supp. XXIV:** 237

How To Be Alone: Essays (Franzen), **Supp. XX: 83, 90, 93–94**

"How to Be an Other Woman" (Moore), **Supp. X:** 165, 167, 168

"How to Become a Writer" (Moore), **Supp. X:** 167, 168

"How to Be Happy: Another Memo to Myself" (Dunn), **Supp. XI:** 145

How To Cook a Wolf (M. F. K. Fisher), **Supp. XVII:** 84–85, 87

"How to Date a Browngirl, Blackgirl, Whitegirl, or Halfie" (Díaz), **Supp. XXIV:** 88

How to Develop Your Personality (Shellow), **Supp. I Part 2:** 608

How to Know God: The Yoga Aphorisms of Patanjali (Isherwood and Prabhavananda)), **Supp. XIV:** 164

"How To Like It" (Dobyns), **Supp. XIII: 85–86**

"How to Live on $36,000 a Year" (Fitzgerald), **Retro. Supp. I:** 105

"How to Live. What to Do" (Stevens), **Retro. Supp. I:** 302

"How Tom is Doin' " (Kees), **Supp. XV:** 143

How to Read (Pound), **Supp. VIII:** 291

How to Read a Novel (Gordon), **II:** 198

How to Read a Poem and Fall in Love with Poetry (Hirsch), **Supp. XIX:** 202

How to Read a Poem: And Fall in Love with Poetry (Hirsch), **Supp. XXIII:** 124

How to Read a Poem . . . and Start a Poetry Circle (Peacock), **Supp. XIX:** 194, 202–203, 205

How to Save Your Own Life (Jong), **Supp. V:** 115, 123–125, 130

"How to Study Poetry" (Pound), **III:** 474

"How to Talk to Your Mother" (Moore), **Supp. X:** 167, 172

"How to Tell Stories to Children" (July), **Supp. XXIV:** 206–207

How to Win Friends and Influence People (Carnegie), **Supp. I Part 2:** 608

How to Worry Successfully (Seabury), **Supp. I Part 2:** 608

How to Write (Stein), **IV:** 32, 34, 35

"How to Write a Blackwood Article" (Poe), **III:** 425; **Retro. Supp. II:** 273

"How to Write a Memoir Like This" (Oates), **Supp. III Part 2:** 509

"How to Write Like Somebody Else" (Roethke), **III:** 540

How to Write Short Stories (Lardner), **II:** 430, 431

"How Vincentine Did Not Care" (R. Bly), **Supp. IV Part 1:** 73

How We Became Human: New and Selected Poems (Harjo), **Supp. XII:** **230–232**

"How We Danced" (Sexton), **Supp. II Part 2:** 692

How We Got Insipid (Lethem), **Supp. XVIII:** 149

"How We Got in Town and Out Again" (Lethem), **Supp. XVIII:** 149

"How You Sound??" (Baraka), **Supp. II Part 1:** 30

Hoy, Philip, **Supp. X:** 56, 58

Hoyer, Linda Grace (pseudonym). *See* Updike, Mrs. Wesley

Hoyt, Constance, **Supp. I Part 2:** 707

Hoyt, Elinor Morton. *See* Wylie, Elinor

Hoyt, Helen, **Supp. XXII:** 275

Hoyt, Henry (father), **Supp. I Part 2:** 707

Hoyt, Henry (son), **Supp. I Part 2:** 708

Hoyt, Henry Martyn, **Supp. I Part 2:** 707

Hsu, Kai-yu, **Supp. X:** 292

Hsu, Ruth Y., **Supp. XV:** 212

Hubba City (Reed), **Supp. X:** 241

Hubbard, Elbert, **I:** 98, 383

Hubbell, Jay B., **Supp. I Part 1:** 372

"Hubbub, The" (Ammons), **Supp. VII:** 35

Huber, François, **II:** 6

Huckins, Olga, **Supp. IX:** 32

Huckleberry Finn (Twain). *See Adventures of Huckleberry Finn, The* (Twain)

Hud (film), **Supp. V:** 223, 226

Hudgins, Andrew, **Supp. X:** 206; **Supp. XVII:** 111, 112; **Supp. XVIII:** 176

Hudson, Henry, **I:** 230

"Hudsonian Curlew, The" (Snyder), **Supp. VIII:** 302

Hudson River Bracketed (Wharton), **IV:** 326–327; **Retro. Supp. I:** 382

Huebsch, B. W., **III:** 110

Hueffer, Ford Madox, **Supp. I Part 1:** 257, 262. *See also* Ford, Ford Madox

Huene-Greenberg, Dorothee von, **Supp. XX: 46**

Huff (television series), **Supp. XIX:** 222

"Hug, The" (Gallagher), **Supp. XXIV:** 168

Hug Dancing (Hearon), **Supp. VIII:** 67–68

Huge Season, The (Morris), **III:** 225–226, 227, 230, 232, 233, 238

Hugging the Jukebox (Nye), **Supp. XIII: 275–276,** 277

"Hugging the Jukebox" (Nye), **Supp. XIII:** 276

Hughes, Brigid, **Supp. XVI:** 247

Hughes, Carolyn, **Supp. XII:** 272, 285

Hughes, Frieda, **Supp. I Part 2:** 540, 541

Hughes, Glenn, **Supp. I Part 1:** 255

Hughes, H. Stuart, **Supp. VIII:** 240

Hughes, James Nathaniel, **Supp. I Part 1:** 321, 332

Hughes, Ken, **Supp. XI:** 307

Hughes, Langston, **Retro. Supp. I: 193–214; Retro. Supp. II:** 114, 115, 117, 120; **Supp. I Part 1: 320–348; Supp. II Part 1:** 31, 33, 61, 170, 173, 181, 227, 228, 233, 361; **Supp. III Part 1:** 72–77; **Supp. IV Part 1:** 15, 16, 164, 168, 169, 173, 243, 368; **Supp. VIII:** 213; **Supp. IX:** 306, 316; **Supp. X:** 131, 136, 139, 324; **Supp. XI:** 1; **Supp. XIII:** 75, 111, 132, 233; **Supp. XVI:** 135, 138; **Supp. XVIII:** 90, 277, 279, 280, 281, 282; **Supp. XIX:** 72, 75, 77; **Supp. XXI:** 243; **Supp. XXII:** 3, 4, 5, 6, 8, 13–14; **Supp. XXIV:** 183

Hughes, Nicholas, **Supp. I Part 2:** 541

Hughes, Robert, **Supp. X:** 73

Hughes, Ted, **IV:** 3; **Retro. Supp. II:** 244, 245, 247, 257; **Supp. I Part 2:** 536, 537, 538, 539, 540, 541; **Supp. XV:** 117, 347, 348; **Supp. XXII:** 30

Hughes, Thomas, **Supp. I Part 2:** 406

"Hugh Harper" (Bowles), **Supp. IV Part 1:** 94

Hughie (O'Neill), **III:** 385, 401, 405

Hugh Selwyn Mauberley (Pound), **I:** 66, 476; **III:** 9, 462–463, 465, 468; **Retro. Supp. I: 289–290,** 291, 299; **Supp. XIV:** 272

Hugo, Richard, **Supp. VI: 131–148; Supp. IX:** 296, 323, 324, 330; **Supp. XI:** 315, 317; **Supp. XII:** 178; **Supp. XIII:** 112, 113, 133; **Supp. XVIII:** 293, 299; **Supp. XXI:** 243

Hugo, Victor, **II:** 290, 490, 543; **Supp. IV Part 2:** 518; **Supp. IX:** 308

Hui-neng, **III:** 567

Huis Clos (Sartre), **Supp. IV Part 1:** 84

Huizinga, Johan, **I:** 225; **II:** 416–417, 418, 425

Hulbert, Ann, **Supp. XI:** 38–39

Hull, Lynda, **Supp. XI:** 131; **Supp. XXI: 129–142**

Hulme, Thomas E., **I:** 68, 69, 475; **III:** 196, 209, 463–464, 465; **IV:** 122; **Supp. I Part 1:** 261, 262; **Supp. XV:** 43

Human, All Too Human (Nietzsche), **Supp. X:** 48

"Human Culture" (Emerson), **II:** 11–12

Human Factor, The (Greene), **Supp. V:** 298

"Human Figures" (Doty), **Supp. XI:** 123–124

"Human Fly, The" (Boyle), **Supp. XX: 19**

"Human Geography" (Jarman), **Supp. XVII:** 116

"Human Immortality" (James), **II:** 353–354

"Human Life" (Emerson), **II:** 11–12

"Human Pig" (Jin), **Supp. XVIII:** 99

Human Rights, Human Wrongs: The Oxford Amnesty Lectures, 2001, **Supp. XVI:** 155

"Human Soul as a Rube Goldberg Device, The: A Choose-Your-Own-Adventure-Story" (Brockmeier), **Supp. XXII:** 60–61

Human Stain, The (P. Roth), **Retro. Supp. II:** 279, 289, 294–295

"Human Things" (Nemerov), **III:** 279

Human Universe (Olson), **Supp. II Part 2:** 571

"Human Universe" (Olson), **Supp. II Part 2:** 565, 567

Human Vibration (Richter), **Supp. XVIII:** 209

Human Wishes (Hass), **Supp. VI:** 105–106, 107

Human Work (Gilman), **Supp. XI:** 206

Humbert, Humbert, **Supp. X:** 283

Humble Inquiry into the Rules of the Word of God, An, Concerning the Qualifications Requisite to a Complete Standing and Full Communion in the Visible Christian Church (Edwards), **I:** 548

Humboldt, Alexander von, **III:** 428

Humboldt's Gift (Bellow), **Retro. Supp. II:** 19, 28–29, 34; **Supp. XIII:** 320

Hume, David, **I:** 125; **II:** 349, 357, 480; **III:** 618

Humes, Harold, **Supp. V:** 201; **Supp. XIV:** 82

Humes, Harry, **Supp. XIX:** 281; **Supp. XXIII:** 54

Humes, H. L. "Doc", **Supp. XI:** 294

"Humility" (Hoffman), **Supp. XVIII:** 86

Hummer, T. R., **Supp. XIX:** 278; **Supp. XXI:** 91

"Hummingbirds, The" (Welty), **IV:** 273

Humors and/or Not So Humorous (Kenny), **Supp. XXIII:** 155

Humphrey, William, **Supp. IX: 93–112; Supp. XV:** 353

Humphreys, Christmas, **Supp. V:** 267

Humphreys, David, **Supp. II Part 1:** 65, 69, 70, 268

Humphreys, Josephine, **Supp. XII:** 311

Humphries, Rolfe, **III:** 124; **Retro. Supp. I:** 137

Hunchback of Notre Dame, The (film), **Supp. IV Part 1:** 101

Hunches in Bunches (Geisel), **Supp. XVI:** 111

Huncke, Herbert, **Supp. XII:** 118; **Supp. XIV: 137–153**

Huncke's Journal (Huncke), **Supp. XIV:** 139, 144, 145, 146

Hundred Camels in the Courtyard, A (Bowles), **Supp. IV Part 1:** 90

"Hundred Collars, A" (Frost), **Retro. Supp. I:** 128; **Supp. XIII:** 147

Hundred Secret Senses, The (Tan), **Supp. X:** 289, 293, 295, 297, 298, 299

Hundreds of Hens and Other Poems for Children by Halfdan Rasmussen (Nelson and Espeland, trans.), **Supp. XVIII:** 180

Hundred White Daffodils, A: Essays, Interviews, Newspaper Columns, and One Poem (Kenyon), **Supp. VII:** 160–162, 165, 166, 167, 174

Huneker, James, **III:** 102

Hunger (Hamsun), **Supp. XI:** 167

"Hunger" (Hogan), **Supp. IV Part 1:** 411

"Hunger . . ." (Rich), **Supp. I Part 2:** 571

"Hungerfield" (Jeffers), **Supp. II Part 2:** 416–417, 436

Hungerfield and Other Poems (Jeffers), **Supp. II Part 2:** 422

Hunger of Memory: The Education of Richard Rodriguez (Rodriguez), **Supp. XIV:** 297, 298, **298–302,** 310

Hungry Ghosts, The (Oates), **Supp. II Part 2:** 504, 510

Hungry Hearts (Prose), **Supp. XVI:** 253

"Hungry Intellectual, A"(Le Sueur), **Supp. XXIII:** 164

Hungry Woman, The: A Mexican Medea (Moraga), **Supp. XXIII:** 196

Hunnewell, Susannah, **Supp. VIII:** 83

Hunt, Harriot K., **Retro. Supp. II:** 146

Hunt, Leigh, **II:** 515–516; **Supp. XV:** 175

Hunt, Richard Morris, **IV:** 312

Hunt, Robert, **Supp. XV:** 42, 49, 52

Hunt, William, **II:** 343

"Hunter" (Bierds), **Supp. XVII:** 30

Hunter, Dianna, **Supp. XVI:** 38

Hunter, Dr. Joseph, **II:** 217

Hunter, J. Paul, **Supp. IV Part 1:** 332

Hunter, Kim, **Supp. I Part 1:** 286

"Hunter of Doves" (Herbst), **Retro. Supp. II:** 325

"Hunter of the West, The" (Bryant), **Supp. I Part 1:** 155

Hunters, The (film), **Supp. IX:** 250

Hunters, The (Salter), **Supp. IX:** 246, **249–250**

Hunters and Gatherers (Prose), **Supp. XVI:** 257

"Hunters in the Snow" (Brueghel), **I:** 174; **Retro. Supp. I:** 430

"Hunters in the Snow" (Wolff), **Supp. VII:** 339–340

"Hunter's Moon—Eating the Bear" (Oliver), **Supp. VII:** 234

"Hunter's Vision, The" (Bryant), **Supp. I Part 1:** 160

Hunting for Hope: A Father's Journey (Sanders), **Supp. XVI:** 276–277, 278

"Hunting Is Not Those Heads on the Wall" (Baraka), **Supp. II Part 1:** 45

Huntington, Collis P., **I:** 198, 207

"Hunt in the Black Forest, The" (Jarrell), **II:** 379–380

Huntley, Jobe, **Supp. I Part 1:** 339

"Hurrah, Hurrah" (Nelson), **Supp. XVIII:** 175

Hurray Home (Wideman), **Supp. X:** 320

Hurricane (radio play, Boyce), **Supp. XXI:** 13

"Hurricane, The" (Crane), **I:** 401

"Hurricane, The" (Freneau), **Supp. II Part 1:** 262

"Hurricane Belle" (Notley), **Supp. XXII:** 228

"Hurry Kane" (Lardner), **II:** 425, 426, 427

"Hurry up Please It's Time" (Sexton), **Supp. II Part 2:** 694, 695

Hurst, Fannie, **Supp. XVIII:** 278, 279

Hurston, Zora Neale, **Retro. Supp. I:** 194, 198, 200, 201, 203; **Supp. I Part 1:** 325, 326, 332; **Supp. II Part 1:** 33; **Supp. IV Part 1:** 5, 11, 12, 164, 257; **Supp. VI: 149–161; Supp. VIII:** 214; **Supp. X:** 131, 139, 232, 242; **Supp. XI:** 85; **Supp. XIII:** 185, 233, 236, 295, 306; **Supp. XVIII:** 122, 279, 280, 282; **Supp. XIX:** 72, 75; **Supp. XX: 107; Supp. XXII:** 12

Hurt, John, **Supp. XIII:** 132

"Hurt Hawks"(Jeffers), **Supp. XXIII:** 145

Hurwitt, Robert, **Supp. XXIII:** 281

Husbands and Wives (film; Allen), **Supp. XV: 12**

"Husband's Song, The" (Di Piero), **Supp. XIX:** 39

Husband's Story, The (Shields), **Supp. VII:** 316. *See also* "Happenstance" (Shields)

Husserl, Edmund, **II:** 362, 363; **IV:** 491; **Supp. IV Part 1:** 42, 43

Hussey, Jo Ella, **Supp. XII:** 201

Hustler, The (film), **Supp. XI:** 306

Huston, John, **I:** 30, 31, 33, 35; **II:** 588; **III:** 161; **Supp. IV Part 1:** 102, 116, 355; **Supp. XI:** 307; **Supp. XIII:** 174

"Huswifery" (Taylor), **IV:** 161; **Supp. I Part 2:** 386

"Hut, The" (Sobin), **Supp. XVI:** 284–285

Hutchens, John K., **Supp. IX:** 276

Hutcheson, Francis, **I:** 559

Hutchins, Patricia, **III:** 478

Hutchinson, Abigail, **I:** 562

Hutchinson, Anne, **Supp. I Part 1:** 100, 101, 113; **Supp. IV Part 2:** 434; **Supp. VIII:** 202, 205

Hutchinson, George, **Supp. XVIII:** 119–120, 121, 132

Hutchinson, Thomas, **Supp. XX: 282**

Hutton, James, **Supp. IX:** 180

Huwayyik, Yusuf, **Supp. XX: 115**

Huxley, Aldous, **II:** 454; **III:** 281, 428, 429–430; **IV:** 77, 435; **Supp. I Part 2:** 714; **Supp. XIV:** 3, 164; **Supp. XVI:** 189, 192; **Supp. XVIII:** 137;

Supp. XXIII: 85–86; **Supp. XXIV:** 281

Huxley, Julian, **Supp. VIII:** 251; **Supp. X:** 108

Huxley, Juliette, **Supp. VIII:** 251, 265

Huxley, Thomas, **III:** 102, 108, 113, 281; **Retro. Supp. II:** 60, 65, 93

Huxley, Thomas Henry, **Supp. I Part 1:** 368

Huysmans, Joris Karl (Charles Marie Georges), **I:** 66; **III:** 315; **IV:** 286; **Retro. Supp. II:** 326; **Supp. XX: 239**

"*Hwame, Koshkalaka,* and the Rest: Lesbians in American Indian Cultures" (Gunn Allen), **Supp. IV Part 1:** 330

Hwang, David Henry, **Supp. X:** 292; **Supp. XXI: 143–157**

"Hyacinth Drift" (Rawlings), **Supp. X: 226–227**

Hyde, Lewis, **Supp. XVIII:** 150

"Hydrangeas" (C. Frost), **Supp. XV:** 106

"Hydras, The" (Merwin), **Supp. III Part 1:** 349

Hydriotaphia, The; or, Death of Dr. Browne: An Epic Farce about Death and Primitive Capital Accumulation (Kushner), **Supp. IX:** 133, **136–138**

"Hydriotaphia; or, Urne-Buriall" (Browne), **Supp. IX:** 136–137

Hyman, Stanley Edgar, **I:** 129, 264, 363, 377, 379; **Retro. Supp. II:** 118; **Supp. IX:** 113, 114, 117, 118, 121, 122, 128

Hymen (Doolittle), **Supp. I Part 1:** 266

"Hymie's Bull" (Ellison), **Retro. Supp. II:** 124; **Supp. II Part 1:** 229

"Hymn Books" (Emerson), **II:** 10

"HYMN FOR LANIE POO" (Baraka), **Supp. II Part 1:** 31, 37

"Hymn from a Watermelon Pavilion" (Stevens), **IV:** 81

"Hymn of the Sea, A" (Bryant), **Supp. I Part 1:** 157, 163, 165

Hymns of St. Bridget and Other Writings (O'Hara and Berkson), **Supp. XXIII:** 220

"Hymns of St. Bridget"(O'Hara and Berkson), **Supp. XXIII:** 218

"Hymns of the Marshes" (Lanier), **Supp. I Part 1:** 364

"Hymn to Death" (Bryant), **Supp. I Part 1:** 169, 170

"Hymn to Earth" (Wylie), **Supp. I Part 2:** 727–729

"Hymn to the Night" (Longfellow), **Supp. I Part 2:** 409

Hynes, Jennifer, **Supp. XV:** 207

Hynes, Samuel, **Supp. XIV:** 159

Hyperion (Longfellow), **II:** 488, 489, 491–492, 496; **Retro. Supp. II:** 58, 155–156

"Hypocrite Auteur" (MacLeish), **III:** 19

"Hypocrite Swift" (Bogan), **Supp. III Part 1:** 55

"Hysteria" (Eliot), **I:** 570

I

I (Dixon), **Supp. XII:** 141, 155, **156–157**

I, etcetera (Sontag), **Supp. III Part 2:** 451–452, 469

"If I Could Write This in Fire, I Would Write This in Fire" (Cliff), **Supp. XXII:** 65–66, 68–69

If I Die in a Combat Zone (O'Brien), **Supp. V:** 238, 239, 240, 245

"If I Had My Way" (Creeley), **Supp. IV Part 1:** 157

"If I Might Be" (Chopin), Retro. Supp. II: 61

"I Find the Real American Tragedy" (Dreiser), **Retro. Supp. II:** 105

If I Ran the Circus (Geisel), **Supp. XVI:** 105

If I Ran the Zoo (Geisel), **Supp. XVI:** 104–105

If It Die (Gide), **I:** 290

"If It Were Not for You" (Carruth), **Supp. XVI:** 57

"If I Were a Man" (Gilman), **Supp. XI:** 207

"If I Were the Wind" (Leopold), **Supp. XIV:** 184

If Morning Ever Comes (Tyler), **Supp. IV Part 2:** 658–659

If Mountains Die: A New Mexico Memoir (Nichols), **Supp. XIII:** 255, 257, 267

I Forgot to Go to Spain (Harrison), **Supp. VIII:** 39, **52–53**

"If Poetry Were Not a Morality" (Gallagher), **Supp. XXIV:** 170

If the River Was Whiskey (Boyle), **Supp. VIII:** 15–16; **Supp. XX:** 17, 19

"If They Knew Yvonne" (Dubus), **Supp. VII:** 81

"If We Had Bacon" (H. Roth), **Supp. IX:** 232, 234

"If We Had Known" (Francis), **Supp. IX:** 78

"If We Must Die" (McKay), **Supp. IV Part 1:** 3; **Supp. X:** 132, 134

"If We Take All Gold" (Bogan), **Supp. III Part 1:** 52

If You Call This a Cry Song (Carruth), **Supp. XVI:** 56

If You Want to Write (Ueland), **Supp. XVII:** 13

I Gaspiri (Lardner), **II:** 435

"I Gather the Limbs of Osiris" (Pound), **Retro. Supp. I:** 287

I Get on the Bus (McKnight), **Supp. XX: 148–150, 152**

"I Give You Back" (Harjo), **Supp. XII:** 223

Ignatius of Loyola, **IV:** 151; **Supp. XI:** 162

Ignatow, David, **Supp. XIII:** 275

"Ignis Fatuus" (Tate), **IV:** 128

"Ignorant Lust after Knowledge, The" (Bronk), **Supp. XXI:** 31

"I Go Back to May 1937" (Olds), **Supp. X:** 207

I Go Dreaming Serenades (Salinas), **Supp. XIII:** 316

"I Got a Guy Once" (Gallagher), **Supp. XXIV:** 176

I Got the Blues (Odets), **Supp. II Part 2:** 530

Iguana Killer, The (Ríos), **Supp. IV Part 2:** 542–544

"I Had Eight Birds Hatcht in One Nest" (Bradstreet), **Supp. I Part 1:** 102, 115, 117, 119

"I had no time to Hate" (Dickinson), **Retro. Supp. I:** 44–45, 46

I Had Trouble in Getting to Solla Sollew (Geisel), **Supp. XVI:** 108, 109

I Hate Miranda July (blog), **Supp. XXIV:** 200

"I Have a Rendezvous with Life" (Cullen), **Supp. IV Part 1:** 168

"I Have Been Thinking About Snow" (Monson), **Supp. XXIV:** 235

"I Have Increased Power" (Ginsberg), **Supp. II Part 1:** 313

"I Have Moved West" (Taggard), **Supp. XXII:** 274

"I Have Seen Black Hands" (Wright), **Supp. II Part 1:** 228

"I Hear an Army" (Joyce), **Supp. I Part 1:** 262

"I heard a Fly buzz when I died" (Dickinson), **Retro. Supp. I:** 38

"I Heard Immanuel Singing" (Lindsay), **Supp. I Part 2:** 379

I Heard It Through the Grapevine (Turner), **Supp. XX: 110**

"I Hear It Was Charged against Me" (Whitman), **IV:** 343

I Hear Men Talking (Le Sueur), **Supp. XXIII:** 162, 167, **171–172**

"I Held a Shelley Manuscript" (Corso), **Supp. XII:** 128

"I Held His Name" (Ríos), **Supp. IV Part 2:** 547

"Ike and Nina" (Boyle), **Supp. XX: 19**

"I Kiss a Door" (July), **Supp. XXIV:** 204

I Knew a Phoenix (Sarton), **Supp. VIII:** 249, 251–252

"I Know a Man" (Creeley), **Supp. IV Part 1:** 147–148, 149

I Know Some Things: Stories about Childhood by Contemporary Writers (Moore, ed.), **Supp. X:** 175

"I Know Why the Caged Bird Cannot Read" (Prose), **Supp. XVI:** 259

I Know Why the Caged Bird Sings (Angelou), **Supp. IV Part 1:** 2–4, 5, 7, 11, 12, 13, 14, 15, 17; **Supp. XVI:** 259

"Ikon: The Harrowing of Hell" (Levertov), **Supp. III Part 1:** 284

Ile (O'Neill), **III:** 388

"I Led Three Lives" (television program), **Supp. XX: 195**

"I Let Him Take Me" (Cisneros), **Supp. VII:** 71

Iliad (Bryant, trans.), **Supp. I Part 1:** 158

Iliad (Homer), **II:** 470; **Supp. IV Part 2:** 631; **Supp. IX:** 211; **Supp. X:** 114; **Supp. XVII:** 117; **Supp. XXI:** 36

Iliad (Pope, trans.), **Supp. I Part 1:** 152

"I like to see it lap the Miles" (Dickinson), **Retro. Supp. I:** 37

"I Live Up Here" (Merwin), **Supp. III Part 1:** 349

"I'll Be Doing More of Same" (Franzen), **Supp. XX: 89**

"Illegal Alien" (Mora), **Supp. XIII:** 215

"Illegal Days, The" (Paley), **Supp. VI:** 222

"Illegibility" (F. Wright), **Supp. XVII:** 244

Illig, Joyce, **Retro. Supp. II:** 20

"Illinois" (Masters), **Supp. I Part 2:** 458

"Illinois Bus Ride" (Leopold), **Supp. XIV:** 189

Illinois Poems (Masters), **Supp. I Part 2:** 472

"Illinois Village, The" (Lindsay), **Supp. I Part 2:** 381

"Ill-Lit" (F. Wright), **Supp. XVII:** 245

Ill-Lit: Selected & New Poems (F. Wright), **Supp. XVII:** 245

Illness as Metaphor (Sontag), **Supp. III Part 2:** 452, 461, 466

I'll Take My Stand ("Twelve Southerners"), **II:** 196; **III:** 496; **IV:** 125, 237; **Supp. X:** 25, 52–53; **Supp. XIV:** 3

"I'll Take You to Tennessee" (Connell), **Supp. XIV:** 82

Illumination (Frederic), **II:** 141

Illumination, The (Brockmeier), **Supp. XXII:** 61

Illumination Night (Hoffman), **Supp. X:** 85, **86,** 88, 89

Illuminations (Rimbaud), **Supp. XXI:** 233

Illusion and Reality (Caudwell), **Supp. XXII:** 284

Illusion comique, L' (Corneille), **Supp. IX:** 138

"Illusion of Eternity, The" (Eberhart), **I:** 541

"Illusion of Fiction in Frank Conroy's *Stop-Time,* The" (R. Ramsey), **Supp. XVI:** 69

Illusions (Dash; film), **Supp. XI:** 20

"Illusions" (Emerson), **II:** 2, 5, 14, 16

Illustrated Man, The (Bradbury), **Supp. IV Part 1:** 102, 103, 113

Illustrations of China and Its People (Thompson), **Supp. XXI:** 151

Illustrations of Political Economy (Martineau), **Supp. II Part 1:** 288

"I Look at My Hand" (Swenson), **Supp. IV Part 2:** 638, 647

I Love Gootie: My Grandmother's Story (Apple), **Supp. XVII: 9–10**

I Love Myself When I Am Laughing . . . : A Zora Neale Hurston Reader (Walker), **Supp. III Part 2:** 531, 532

"I Love the Way It Goes"(O'Hara), **Supp. XXIII:** 220

"I'm a Fool" (Anderson), **I:** 113, 114, 116; **Supp. I Part 2:** 430

Image and Idea (Rahv), **Supp. II Part 1:** 146

Image and the Law, The (Nemerov), **III:** 268, 269–271, 272

"Image in the Mirror, The" (Swados), **Supp. XIX:** 265

"Images" (Hass), **Supp. VI:** 103

"Images and 'Images' " (Simic), **Supp. VIII:** 274

"Images for Godard" (Rich), **Supp. I Part 2:** 558

"Images of Walt Whitman" (Fiedler), **IV:** 352

"Imaginary Dialogue, An" (Espaillat), **Supp. XXI:** 103

"Imaginary Friendships of Tom McGrath, The" (Cohen), **Supp. X:** 112

"Imaginary Iceberg, The" (Bishop), **Retro. Supp. II:** 42; **Supp. I Part 1:** 86, 88

"Imaginary Jew, The" (Berryman), **I:** 174–175

Imaginary Letters (Pound), **III:** 473–474

Imaginary Paintings (C. Baxter), **Supp. XVII:** 18–19

"Imaginary Prisons" (Schnackenberg), **Supp. XV:** 257, 258

Imagination and Fancy; or, Selections from the English Poets, illustrative of those first requisites of their art; with markings of the best passages, critical notices of the writers, and an essay in answer to the question 'What is Poetry?' (Hunt), **II:** 515–516

"Imagination as Value" (Stevens), **Retro. Supp. I:** 298

"Imagination of Disaster, The" (Gordon), **Supp. IV Part 1:** 306

Imaginative Qualities of Actual Things (Sorrentino), **Supp. XXI:** 226, 230, 231–232, 234

"Imagine a Day at the End of Your Life" (Beattie), **Supp. V:** 33

Imagined London: A Tour of the World's Greatest Fictional City (Quindlen), **Supp. XVII:** 167, 180

Imagineering Atlanta (Rutheiser), **Supp. XXII:** 244

"Imagine Kissing Pete" (O'Hara), **III:** 372; **Supp. VIII:** 156

Imaging Robert: My Brother, Madness, and Survival (Neugeboren), **Supp. XVI:** 225, **226–229**

"Imagining How It Would Be to Be Dead" (Eberhart), **I:** 533

Imagining Los Angeles: A City in Fiction (Fine), **Supp. XI:** 160

"Imagining Their Own Hymns" (B. Kelly), **Supp. XVII:** 126–127

"Imagining the Midwest" (Sanders), **Supp. XVI:** 275–276

Imagining the Worst: Stephen King and the Representations of Women (Lant and Thompson), **Supp. V:** 141

"Imagisme" (Pound), **Retro. Supp. I:** 288

Imagistes, Des: An Anthology of the Imagists (Pound, ed.), **III:** 465, 471; **Retro. Supp. I:** 288

Imago (O. Butler), **Supp. XIII:** 63, **65–66**

"Imago" (Stevens), **IV:** 74, 89

Imagoes (Coleman), **Supp. XI:** 89–90

I Married a Communist (P. Roth), **Retro. Supp. II:** 289, 293–294

I Married an Angel (film), **Supp. XVI:** 193

"I May, I Might, I Must" (Moore), **III:** 215

Imbusch, Kevin, **Supp. XXIII:** 125

"I'm Crazy" (Salinger), **III:** 553

"I'm Here" (Roethke), **III:** 547

Imitations (Lowell), **II:** 543, 544–545, 550, 555; **Retro. Supp. II:** 181, 187

"Imitations of Drowning" (Sexton), **Supp. II Part 2:** 684, 686

"Immaculate Man" (Gordon), **Supp. IV Part 1:** 311

"Immanence of Dostoevsky, The" (Bourne), **I:** 235

"Immigrants" (Mora), **Supp. XIII:** 216

Immigrant Saint: The Life of Mother Cabrini (di Donato), **Supp. XX: 44**

"Immigrant Story, The" (Paley), **Supp. VI:** 230

Immobile Wind, The (Winters), **Supp. II Part 2:** 786

"Immobile Wind, The" (Winters), **Supp. II Part 2:** 788, 811

"Immolatus" (Komunyakaa), **Supp. XIII:** 126

"Immoral Proposition, The" (Creeley), **Supp. IV Part 1:** 144

"Immortal Autumn" (MacLeish), **III:** 13

"Immortality Ode" (Nemerov), **III:** 87

Immortality Ode (Wordsworth), **II:** 17; **Supp. I Part 2:** 673

Immortal Marriage, The (Atherton), **Supp. XXIV:** 26

"Immortal Woman, The" (Tate), **IV:** 130, 131, 137

"I'm Not Ready to Die Yet" (Harjo), **Supp. XII:** 231

I'm Not There (film, Haynes), **Supp. XVIII:** 23

"I'm on My Way" (Salinas), **Supp. XIII:** 320

"Impasse" (Hughes), **Supp. I Part 1:** 343

"Impatient Mary" (Taggard), **Supp. XXII:** 278

Imperative Duty, An, a Novel (Howells), **II:** 286

Imperial Eyes: Travel Writing and Transculturation (Pratt), **Retro. Supp. II:** 48

Imperial Germany and the Industrial Revolution (Veblen), **Supp. I Part 2:** 642, 643

Imperial Way, The: By Rail from Peshawar to Chittagong (Theroux), **Supp. VIII:** 323

"Implosions" (Rich), **Supp. I Part 2:** 556

"Imp of the Perverse, The" (Poe), **III:** 414–415; **Retro. Supp. II:** 267

Impolite Interviews, **Supp. XI:** 293

"Importance of Artists' Biographies, The" (Goldbarth), **Supp. XII:** 183, 184, 191

Importance of Being Earnest, The (Wilde), **Supp. XIV:** 324, 339

"Important Houses, The" (Gordon), **Supp. IV Part 1:** 315

"Impossible Indispensability of the Ars Poetica, The" (Carruth), **Supp. XVI:** 57

"Impossible to Tell" (Pinsky), **Supp. VI:** 247, 248

"Imposter, The" (West), **Retro. Supp. II:** 322, 327

"Impressionism and Symbolism in *Heart of Darkness*" (Watt), **Supp. VIII:** 4

"Impressionism"(Crooker), **Supp. XXIII:** 57

"Impressions of a European Tour" (Bourne), **I:** 225

"Impressions of a Plumber" (H. Roth), **Supp. IX:** 228, 234

"Impressions of Europe, 1913–1914" (Bourne), **I:** 225

"I Must Have Called and So He Comes" (Notley), **Supp. XXII:** 224

"I'm Walking behind the Spanish" (Salinas), **Supp. XIII:** 323–324

"I/Myself" (Shields), **Supp. VII:** 311

"In a (Low) Bar" (Ferry), **Supp. XXIV:** 153

"In Absence" (Lanier), **Supp. I Part 1:** 364

"In Absentia" (Bowles), **Supp. IV Part 1:** 94

"In a Cab" (Untermeyer), **Supp. XV:** 296

"In a Country Cemetery" (Kooser), **Supp. XIX:** 120

"In a Dark Room, Furniture" (Nye), **Supp. XIII:** 274

"In a Dark Time" (Roethke), **III:** 539, 547, 548

In a Different Voice (Gilligan), **Supp. XXII:** 18

"In a Disused Graveyard" (Frost), **Retro. Supp. I:** 126, 133

In a Dusty Light (Haines), **Supp. XII:** 207

"In a Garden" (Lowell), **II:** 513

"In a Hard Intellectual Light" (Eberhart), **I:** 523

"In a Hollow of the Hills" (Harte), **Supp. II Part 1:** 354

In America (Sontag), **Supp. XIV:** 95–96

"In Amicitia" (Ransom), **IV:** 141

In a Narrow Grave: Essays on Texas (McMurtry), **Supp. V:** 220, 223

"Inanna" (A. Finch), **Supp. XVII:** 72

"In Another Country" (Hemingway), **I:** 484–485; **II:** 249

In April Once (Percy), **Retro. Supp. I:** 341

"In a Prominent Bar in Secaucus One Day" (X. J. Kennedy), **Supp. XV:** 154, 155–156

"In Armenia, 1987"(Balakian), **Supp. XXIII:** 25

In A Shallow Grave (Purdy), **Supp. VII:** 272

In a shlekhter tsayt (In a bad time) (Asch), **Supp. XXIII:** 4

"In a Station of the Metro" (Pound), **Retro. Supp. I:** 288; **Supp. I Part 1:** 265; **Supp. XIV:** 284–285

"In a Strange Town" (Anderson), **I:** 114, 115

"In Athens Once" (Rodriguez), **Supp. XIV:** 303

"In a Tub" (Hempel), **Supp. XXI:** 119

In Battle for Peace: The Story of My 83rd Birthday (Du Bois), **Supp. II Part 1:** 185

In Bed One Night & Other Brief Encounters (Coover), **Supp. V:** 49, 50

"In Bertram's Garden" (Justice), **Supp. VII:** 117

"In Blackwater Woods" (Oliver), **Supp. VII:** 244, 246

In Black & Whitey (Lacy), **Supp. XV:** 206–207

"In Broad Daylight" (Jin), **Supp. XVIII:** 94

In Broken Country (Wagoner), **Supp. IX:** 330

"In California" (Simpson), **Supp. IX:** 271

"In Camp" (Stafford), **Supp. XI:** 329

"Incant against Suicide" (Karr), **Supp. XI:** 249

"In Celebration of My Uterus" (Sexton), **Supp. II Part 2:** 689

"Incendiary, The" (Rowson), **Supp. XV:** 234

"In Certain Places and Certain Times There Can Be More of You" (Dunn), **Supp. XI:** 144

Incest: From "A Journal of Love," the Unexpurgated Diary of Anaïs Nin, 1932–1934 (Nin), **Supp. X:** 182, 184, 185, 187, 191

"In Chandler Country" (Gioia), **Supp. XV:** 119

Inchbald, Elizabeth, **II:** 8

"In Cheever Country" (Gioia), **Supp. XV:** 119

Inchiquin, the Jesuit's Letters (Ingersoll), **I:** 344

"Incident" (Cullen), **Supp. IV Part 1:** 165, 166

Incidental Numbers (Wylie), **Supp. I Part 2:** 708

Incidentals (Sandburg), **III:** 579

Incidentals in the Day World (Notley), **Supp. XXII:** 223, 226, 227

Incident at Vichy (A. Miller), **III:** 165, 166

Incidents in the Life of a Slave Girl (Brent), **Supp. IV Part 1:** 13

Incidents in the Life of a Slavegirl (Jacobs), **Supp. XVI:** 85

"Incipience" (Rich), **Supp. I Part 2:** 559

"In Clare" (McCarriston), **Supp. XIV:** 270–271

Including Horace (Untermeyer), **Supp. XV:** 301, 303–304

In Cold Blood: A True Account of a Multiple Murder and Its Consequences (Capote), **Retro. Supp. II:** 107–108; **Supp. I Part 1:** 292; **Supp. III Part 1:** 111, 117, 119, 122, 123, 125–131; **Supp. III Part 2:** 574; **Supp. IV Part 1:** 220; **Supp. XIV:** 162

In Cold Hell, in Thicket (Olson), **Supp. II Part 2:** 571

"In Cold Hell, in Thicket" (Olson), **Supp. II Part 2:** 558, 563–564, 566, 572, 580

"Incoming Tide"(Strout), **Supp. XXIII:** 282, 285

"Incomparable Light, The" (Eberhart), **I:** 541

Incorporative Consciousness of Robert Bly, The (Harris), **Supp. IV Part 1:** 68

In Country (Mason), **Supp. VIII:** 133, **142–143,** 146

"In Country of Conscience" (J. W. Miller), **Supp. XX: 165**

"Incredible Survival of Coyote, The" (Snyder), **Supp. VIII:** 297

"Increment" (Ammons), **Supp. VII:** 28

In Defense of Ignorance (Shapiro), **Supp. II Part 2:** 703, 704, 713–714

In Defense of Reason (Winters), **Supp. I Part 1:** 268

In Defense of Women (Mencken), **III:** 109

Indelible (Hadas), **Supp. XXIII: 119**

Independence Day (film), **Supp. X:** 80

Independence Day (Ford), **Supp. V:** 57, 62–63, 67–68

"Independent Candidate, The, a Story of Today" (Howells), **II:** 277

"Indestructible Mr. Gore, The" (Vidal), **Supp. IV Part 2:** 679

Index of American Design, **Supp. III Part 2:** 618

"India" (Rodriguez), **Supp. XIV:** 302

"Indian at the Burial-Place of His Fathers, An" (Bryant), **Supp. I Part 1:** 155–156, 167–168

"Indian Burying Ground, The" (Freneau), **Supp. II Part 1:** 264, 266

"Indian Camp" (Hemingway), **II:** 247–248, 263; **Retro. Supp. I:** 174–175, 176, 177, 181; **Supp. XVI:** 208

Indian Country (Caputo), **Supp. XIX:** 22–25

Indian Country (Matthiessen), **Supp. V:** 211

"Indian Country" (McCarriston), **Supp. XIV:** 271

"Indian Country" (Simpson), **Supp. IX:** 274

Indian Earth (Bynner), **Supp. XV:** 46

"Indian Girls" (McCarriston), **Supp. XIV:** 272–273

"Indian Manifesto" (Deloria), **Supp. IV Part 1:** 323

"Indian Names" (Sigourney), **Retro. Supp. II:** 47

"Indian Student, The" (Freneau), **Supp. II Part 1:** 264

"Indian Student, The" (Simpson), **Supp. IX:** 280

Indian Summer (Howells), **II:** 275, 279–281, 282

Indian Summer (Knowles), **Supp. XII:** 249, 250

Indian Summer: Musings on the Gift of Life (Pickering), **Supp. XXI:** 204

"Indian Uprising, The" (Barthelme), **Supp. IV Part 1:** 44

"Indian Wooing" (C. Miller), **Supp. XXII:** 197–198

Indifferent Children, The (Auchincloss), **Supp. IV Part 1:** 25

Indirections (Cox), **Supp. XXI:** 21

Indiscretions (Pound), **Retro. Supp. I:** 284

"Indispensability of the Eyes, The" (Olds), **Supp. X:** 202

"In Distrust of Merits" (Moore), **III:** 201, 214

"Individual and the State, The" (Emerson), **II:** 10

Individualism, Old and New (Dewey), **Supp. I Part 2:** 677

"Indolence" (Pickering), **Supp. XXI:** 203

In Dreams Begin Responsibilities (Schwartz), **Supp. II Part 2:** 642, 645–650

"In Dreams Begin Responsibilities" (Schwartz), **Supp. II Part 2:** 641, 649, 654

In Dubious Battle (Steinbeck), **IV:** 51, 55–56, 59, 63

"In Durance" (Pound), **Retro. Supp. I:** 285

"Industry of Hard Kissing, The" (Ríos), **Supp. IV Part 2:** 547

"In Duty Bound" (Gilman), **Supp. XI:** 196–197

"I Need, I Need" (Roethke), **III:** 535–536

"I Need Help" (Stern), **Supp. IX:** 290

"Ineffectual Marriage" (Loy), **Supp. XXII:** 165

"Inés in the Kitchen" (García), **Supp. XI:** 190

"I never saw a Moor" (Dickinson), **Retro. Supp. I:** 37

I Never Told Anybody: Teaching Poetry Writing in a Nursing Home (Koch), **Supp. XV:** 190

"I Never Will Be Married, I'd Rather Be Excus'd" (Rowson), **Supp. XV:** 240

Inevitable Exiles (Kielsky), **Supp. V:** 273

"Inevitable Trial, The" (Holmes), **Supp. I Part 1:** 318

"Inexhaustible Hat, The" (Wagoner), **Supp. IX:** 327

"In Extremis" (Berry), **Supp. X:** 23

Inez, Colette, **Supp. XXIII:** 54, 245

"Infancy" (Wilder), **IV:** 375

"Infant Boy at Midcentury" (Warren), **IV:** 244–245, 252

Infante, Guillermo Cabrera, **Retro. Supp. I:** 278

"Infant Sea Turtles" (F. Wright), **Supp. XVII:** 245

Infants of the Spring (Thurman), **Supp. XVIII:** 281; **Supp. XIX:** 73

Inferno (Dante), **IV:** 139; **Supp. V:** 338; **Supp. VIII:** 219–221

Inferno of Dante, The (Pinsky), **Supp. VI:** 235, 248

Infidel (Ali), **Supp. XXIV:** 15

"Infidelity" (Komunyakaa), **Supp. XIII:** 130

Infidels (album, Dylan), **Supp. XVIII:** 28

"Infiltration of the Universe" (MacLeish), **III:** 19

Infinite Jest: A Novel (Wallace), **Supp. X:** 301, **310–314; Supp. XX: 91**

"Infinite Reason, The" (MacLeish), **III:** 19

"Infirmity" (Lowell), **II:** 554

"Infirmity" (Roethke), **III:** 548

In Five Years Time (Haines), **Supp. XII:** 206

"In Flower" (Snodgrass), **Supp. VI:** 325

"Influence of Landscape upon the Poet, The" (Eliot), **Retro. Supp. I:** 67

"In Football Season" (Updike), **IV:** 219

Informer, The (film), **Supp. III Part 2:** 619

Ingersoll, Charles J., **I:** 344

Ingersoll, Robert Green, **Supp. II Part 1:** 198

Ingmundson, Kris, **Supp. XXIV:** 230, 234

Ingraham, Lloyd, **Supp. XVI:** 184

Ingster, Boris, **Retro. Supp. II:** 330

Inhabitants, The (Morris), **III:** 221–222

"Inheritance and Invention in Li-Young Lee's Poetry" (Xiaojing), **Supp. XV:** 214

"Inheritance"(Kenny), **Supp. XXIII:** 154

"Inheritance of Tools, The" (Sanders), **Supp. XVI:** 273

Inheritors (Glaspell), **Supp. III Part 1:** 175, 179–181, 186, 189

"In Hollywood with the Zuni God of War" (Major), **Supp. XXII:** 180

"In Honor of David Anderson Brooks, My Father" (Brooks), **Supp. III Part 1:** 79

"Inhumanist, The" (Jeffers), **Supp. II Part 2:** 423, 426

"In Illo Tempore" (Karr), **Supp. XI:** 242

"In Interims: Outlyer" (Harrison), **Supp. VIII:** 38

"Initial" (F. Wright), **Supp. XVII:** 243

"Injudicious Gardening" (Moore), **III:** 198

"Injustice" (Paley), **Supp. VI:** 220

Injustice Collectors, The (Auchincloss), **Supp. IV Part 1:** 25

Ink, Blood, Semen (Goldbarth), **Supp. XII:** 181, 183

Ink Dark Moon, The: Love Poems by Ono no Komachi and Izumi Shikibu (Aratani and Hirshfield, trans.), **Supp. XXIII:** 136

Ink Truck, The (W. Kennedy), **Supp. VII:** 132, 133–138, 140, 141, 149, 152

In Life Sentences: Literary Essays (Epstein), **Supp. XIV:** 112

"In Limbo" (Wilbur), **Supp. III Part 2:** 544, 561

In Limestone Country (Sanders), **Supp. XVI:** 272

"In Line" (Major), **Supp. XXII:** 185

In Love and Trouble: Stories of Black Women (Walker), **Supp. III Part 2:** 520, 521, 530, 531, 532

In Mad Love and War (Harjo), **Supp. XII:** **224–226**

"In Memoriam" (Emerson), **II:** 13

"In Memoriam" (Hay), **Supp. XIV:** 122, 127

"In Memoriam" (Tennyson), **Retro. Supp. I:** 325; **Supp. I Part 2:** 416

In Memoriam: 1933 (Reznikoff), **Supp. XIV:** 280, 285

In Memoriam to Identity (Acker), **Supp. XII:** 5, **16–18**

"In Memory of Arthur Winslow" (Lowell), **II:** 541, 547, 550; **Retro. Supp. II:** 187

"In Memory of Congresswoman Barbara Jordan" (Pinsky), **Supp. VI:** 250

"In Memory of Joe Brainard" (Bidart), **Supp. XV:** 33

"In Memory of My Feelings" (O'Hara), **Supp. XV:** 215–216

In Memory of My Feelings (O'Hara; Berkson, ed.), **Supp. XXIII:** 220

"In Memory of My Feelings"(O'Hara), **Supp. XXIII:** 208, 215–216

"In Memory of W. B. Yeats" (Auden), **Supp. VIII:** 19, 30; **Supp. XI:** 243, 244; **Supp. XIX:** 85

"In Memory of W. H. Auden" (Stern), **Supp. IX:** 288

"In Memory"(Schott), **Supp. XXIII:** 254

"In Mercy on Broadway" (Doty), **Supp. XI:** 132

In Morocco (Wharton), **Retro. Supp. I:** 380; **Supp. IV Part 1:** 81

Inmost Leaf, The: A Selection of Essays (Kazin), **Supp. VIII:** 102, 103

In Motley (Bierce), **I:** 209

In My Father's Court (Singer), **IV:** 16–17; **Retro. Supp. II:** **301–302**

"In My Life" (Dubus), **Supp. VII:** 81

Innaurato, Albert, **Supp. XXIV:** 113, 116, 117

"In Navaho Country" (Bronk), **Supp. XXI:** 30

Inner Circle, The (Boyle), **Supp. XX:** 24, 26

Inner Landscape (Sarton), **Supp. VIII:** 259

Inner Room, The (Merrill), **Supp. III Part 1:** 336

"In Nine Sleep Valley" (Merrill), **Supp. III Part 1:** 328

Innocent Mrs. Duff, The (Holding), **Supp. XXII:** 119, 120, 123, **130–131**, 135, 136

Innocents, The: A Story for Lovers (Lewis), **II:** 441

Innocents Abroad, The; or, The New Pilgrim's Progress (Twain), **II:** 275, 434; **IV:** 191, 196, 197–198

Innocents at Cedro, The: A Memoir of Thorstein Veblen and Some Others (Duffus), **Supp. I Part 2:** 650

"In Off the Cliffs of Moher" (McCarriston), **Supp. XIV:** 270

In Old Plantation Days (Dunbar), **Supp. II Part 1:** 214

In Ole Virginia (Page), **Supp. II Part 1:** 201

In Orbit (Morris), **III:** 236

In Other Words (Swenson), **Supp. IV Part 2:** 650–652

In Other Words: Literature by Latinas of the United States (Fernandez, ed.), **Supp. XXI:** 104

In Our Terribleness (Some elements and meaning in black style) (Baraka), **Supp. II Part 1:** 52, 53

In Our Time (Hemingway), **I:** 117; **II:** 68, 247, 252, 263; **IV:** 42; **Retro. Supp. I:** 170, 173, 174, 178, 180; **Supp. IX:** 106

"In Our Time" (Wolfe), **Supp. III Part 2:** 584

"Inpatient" (Kenyon), **Supp. VII:** 169

In Persuasion Nation (Saunders), **Supp. XIX:** **231–234**

"In Persuasion Nation" (Saunders), **Supp. XIX:** 233–234

In Pharaoh's Army: Memories of the Lost War (Wolff), **Supp. VII:** 331–334, 335, 338

"In Plaster" (Plath), **Supp. I Part 2:** 540

"In Prague, in Montmartre" (Bierds), **Supp. XVII:** 27

"In Praise of Johnny Appleseed" (Lindsay), **Supp. I Part 2:** 397

"In Praise of Limestone" (Auden), **Supp. II Part 1:** 20–21; **Supp. VIII:** 23

In Pursuit of a Vanishing Star (Sobin), **Supp. XVI:** **294**

In Quest of the Ordinary (Cavell), **Retro. Supp. I:** 307

Inquiry into the Moral and Religious Character of the American Government, An (H. Warner), **Supp. XVIII:** 259

Inquiry into the Nature of Peace, An (Veblen), **Supp. I Part 2:** 642

Inquisitor, The (Rowson), **Supp. XV: 232,** 238

In Radical Pursuit (Snodgrass), **Supp. VI:** 312, 316, 318

In Reckless Ecstasy (Sandburg), **III:** 579

In Recognition of William Gaddis (Kuehl and Moore), **Supp. IV Part 1:** 279

"In Retirement" (Malamud), **Supp. I Part 2:** 437

"In Retrospect" (Angelou), **Supp. IV Part 1:** 15

"In Right" (Wolfert), **Supp. XXI:** 263, 264, 272

"Inroads of Time, The" (D. West), **Supp. XVIII:** 286–287

In Russia (A. Miller), **III:** 165

"In Sabine" (Chopin), **Supp. I Part 1:** 213

"In School-Days" (Whittier), **Supp. I Part 2:** 699–700

"Inscription for the Entrance to a Wood" (Bryant), **Supp. I Part 1:** 154, 155, 161–162

Inscriptions, 1944–1956 (Reznikoff), **Supp. XIV:** 281

In Search of America: The Image of the United States in Travel Writing of the 1980s and 1990s (Rutkowska), **Supp. XXII:** 208

"In Search of a Motif for Expressive Female Figuration" (Major), **Supp. XXII:** 184

In Search of Bisco (Caldwell), **I:** 296

In Search of Nella Larsen: A Biography of the Color Line (Hutchinson), **Supp. XVIII:** 120

"In Search of Our Mothers' Gardens" (Walker), **Supp. III Part 2:** 520–532, 524, 525, 527, 529, 532–533, 535, 536; **Supp. IX:** 306; **Supp. XVIII:** 200, 283

"In Search of Thomas Merton" (Griffin), **Supp. VIII:** 208

"In Search of Yage" (Burroughs), **Supp. III Part 1:** 98

"Insect Life in Florida" (Hull), **Supp. XXI:** 133

Insel (Loy), **Supp. XXII:** 167

"Insertion of Self into a Space of Border-less Possibilities, The" (Fjellestad), **Supp. XVI:** 150

"In Shadow" (Crane), **I:** 386

"In Sickness and in Health" (Auden), **Supp. II Part 1:** 15

"In Sickness and in Health" (Humphrey), **Supp. IX:** 94

Inside Diameter: The France Poems (Major), **Supp. XXII:** 182

Inside His Mind (A. Miller), **III:** 154

Inside Memory (Findley), **Supp. XX: 51, 63**

"Inside Norman Mailer" (Apple), **Supp. XVII:** 3, 4

"Insider Baseball" (Didion), **Supp. IV Part 1:** 211

Inside Sports magazine, **Supp. V:** 58, 61

"Insipid Profession of Jonathan Horne-boom, The" (Lethem), **Supp. XVIII:** 149

"In So Many Dark Rooms" (Hogan), **Supp. IV Part 1:** 400

"Insomnia" (Bishop), **Supp. I Part 1:** 92

"Insomniac" (Plath), **Supp. I Part 2:** 539

"In Spain, Throwing Carnations" (P. N. Warren), **Supp. XX: 272**

"Inspiration for Greatness" (Caldwell), **I:** 291

"Instability of Race Types, The" (Boas), **Supp. XIV:** 209

"Installation #6" (Beattie), **Supp. V:** 33

"Instead of Dying" (Gallagher), **Supp. XXIV:** 171

"Intersties" (Berrigan), **Supp. XXIV:** 36

Instinct of Workmanship and the State of the Industrial Arts, The (Veblen), **Supp. I Part 2:** 642

Instincts of the Herd in Peace and War, The (Trotter), **I:** 249

Institute (Calvin), **IV:** 158, 160

"Instruction Manual, The" (Ashbery), **Supp. III Part 1:** 6–7, 10, 12

Instructions, The (Levin), **Supp. XXII:** 268

"Instructions for the Afternoon" (Gioia), **Supp. XV:** 120

Instructions to the Double (Gallagher), **Supp. XXIV:** 165, 167, 168, 169, 174

"Instructions to the Double" (Gallagher), **Supp. XXIV:** 168

"Instruction to Myself" (Brooks), **Supp. III Part 1:** 87

Instrument, The (O'Hara), **III:** 362, 364

"In Such Times, Ties Must Bind" (Nye), **Supp. XIII:** 286

"Insurance and Social Change" (Stevens), **Retro. Supp. I:** 297

Insurgent Mexico (Reed), **I:** 476

In Suspect Terrain (McPhee), **Supp. III Part 1:** 309, 310

"In Tall Grass" (Sandburg), **III:** 585

"Integer Vitae" (Horace), **Supp. XV:** 304

Intellectual History, An (Senghor), **Supp. X:** 139

"Intellectual Pre-Eminence of Jews in Modern Europe, The" (Veblen), **Supp. I Part 2:** 643–644

Intellectual Things (Kunitz), **Supp. III Part 1:** 260, 262–264

Intellectual versus the City, The (White), **I:** 258

"In Temporary Pain" (Bynner), **Supp. XV:** 41–42

Intentions (Wilde), **Retro. Supp. I:** 56

"Interest in Life, An" (Paley), **Supp. VI:** 222, 224–225

Interest of Great Britain Considered, with Regard to Her Colonies and the Acqui-sition of Canada and Guadeloupe, The (Franklin), **II:** 119

Interior Landscapes (Vizenor), **Supp. IV Part 1:** 262

Interiors (film; Allen), **Supp. IV Part 1:** 205; **Supp. XV:** 1, 7, 10

Interlocking Lives (Koch), **Supp. XV:** 185

"Interlude" (A. Lowell), **Retro. Supp. II:** 46

Interlunar (Atwood), **Supp. XIII:** 35

"Intermezzo" (Schnackenberg), **Supp. XV:** 254

"In Terms of the Toenail: Fiction and the Figures of Life" (Gass), **Supp. VI:** 85

"International Episode, An" (James), **II:** 327

International Workers Order, **Retro. Supp. I:** 202

Interpretation of Christian Ethics, An (Niebuhr), **III:** 298–300, 301, 302

"Interpretation of Dreams, The" (Matthews), **Supp. IX:** 162–163

Interpretation of Music of the XVIIth and XVIIIth Centuries, The (Dolmetsch), **III:** 464

Interpretations and Forecasts: 1922–1972 (Mumford), **Supp. II Part 2:** 481

Interpretations of Poetry and Religion (Santayana), **III:** 611

Interpreter of Maladies (Lahiri), **Supp. XXI:** 175–176, **177–180**, 183

"Interpreter of Maladies" (Lahiri), **Supp. XXI:** 183, 184

Interpreters and Interpretations (Van Vechten), **Supp. II Part 2:** 729, 733–734

"Interrogate the Stones" (MacLeish), **III:** 9

Interrogations at Noon (Gioia), **Supp. XV:** 112, **125–127**, 128, 129

"Interrupted Conversation, An" (Van Vechten), **Supp. II Part 2:** 735

"Interrupted Elegy" (Peacock), **Supp. XIX:** 200

Intersect: Poems (Shields), **Supp. VII:** 310–311

Intersexes, The (Prime-Stevenson as Mayne), **Supp. XX: 235**

Interstate (Dixon), **Supp. XII:** 140, 152–153, 153, 156

"Interview" (Hay), **Supp. XIV:** 132

"Interview, The" (Thurber), **Supp. I Part 2:** 616

"Interview With a Lemming" (Thurber), **Supp. I Part 2:** 603

"Interview with Larry Rivers, An"(O'Hara), **Supp. XXIII:** 214

"Interview with Peter Everwine, An" (Veinberg and Buckley), **Supp. XV:** 76–77

"Interview with the Crab" (Lethem), **Supp. XVIII:** 148

Interview with the Vampire (Rice), **Supp. VII:** 287, 288–291, 297–298, 303

"Interview with the Vampire" (Rice), **Supp. VII:** 288

Interzone (Burroughs), **Supp. IV Part 1:** 90

"In the Absence of Bliss" (Kumin), **Supp. IV Part 2:** 453

"In the Afternoon" (Dunn), **Supp. XI:** 146

"In the Alley" (Elkin), **Supp. VI: 46–47**

In the American Grain (W. C. Williams), **Retro. Supp. I:** 420–421

In the American Jungle (W. Frank), **Supp. XX: 76**

In the American Tree (Silliman), **Supp. IV Part 2:** 426

In the Bank of Beautiful Sins (Wrigley), **Supp. XVIII: 300–302**

In the Bar of a Tokyo Hotel (T. Williams), **IV:** 382, 386, 387, 391, 393

In the Beauty of the Lilies (Updike), **Retro. Supp. I:** 322, 325, 326, 327, 333

"In the Beeyard" (Bierds), **Supp. XVII:** 29

"In the Beginning" (Quindlen), **Supp. XVII:** 166

"In the Beginning . . ." (Simic), **Supp. VIII:** 270, 271

In the Belly of the Beast: Letters from Prison (Abbott), **Retro. Supp. II:** 210

"In the Black Morning" (Wolfert), **Supp. XXI:** 265

"In the Black Museum" (Nemerov), **III:** 275

"In the Blink of God's Eye" (E. P. Jones), **Supp. XXII:** 150

"In the Bodies of Words" (Swenson), **Supp. IV Part 2:** 651

"In the Box"(Kenny), **Supp. XXIII:** 155

"In the Cage" (Gass), **Supp. VI:** 85

In the Cage (James), **Retro. Supp. I:** 229

"In the Cage" (James), **II:** 332; **Retro. Supp. I:** 231

"In the Cage" (Lowell), **Retro. Supp. II:** 187

"In the Cave at Lone Tree Meadow" (Haines), **Supp. XII:** 212

"In the Cemetery Where Al Jolson Is Buried" (Hempel), **Supp. XXI:** 115, **121–122**

"In the City Ringed with Giants" (Kingsolver), **Supp. VII:** 209

"In the Clearing" (Brodsky), **Supp. VIII:** 32

In the Clearing (Frost), **II:** 153, 155, 164; **Retro. Supp. I:** 121, 122, 141

"In the Closet of the Soul" (Walker), **Supp. III Part 2:** 526

"In the Cold Air Register" (W. V. Davis), **Supp. XXI:** 94

"In the Confidence of a Story-Writer" (Chopin), **Retro. Supp. II:** 66–67; **Supp. I Part 1:** 217

In the Country of Last Things (Auster), **Supp. XII:** 23, **29–30,** 31, 32

"In the Courtyard of the Isleta Missions" (R. Bly), **Supp. IV Part 1:** 71

"In the Dark" (Levine), **Supp. V:** 194

"In the Dark New England Days" (Jewett), **Retro. Supp. II:** 139

"In the Days of Prismatic Colour" (Moore), **III:** 205, 213

In the Days of the Comet (Wells), **Supp. XX: 233, 240**

In the Electric Mist with Confederate Dead (Burke), **Supp. XIV:** 30, 31–32

"In the Field" (Wilbur), **Supp. III Part 2:** 558

"In the 51st State" (Berrigan), **Supp. XXIV:** 35

"In the First Stanza" (C. Kizer), **Supp. XVII:** 75

"In the Fleeting Hand of Time" (Corso), **Supp. XII:** 122–123

"In the Footsteps of Gutenberg" (Mencken), **III:** 101

"In the Forest" (Simpson), **Supp. IX:** 270

"In the Forest of the Laughing Elephant" (Caputo), **Supp. XIX:** 27

"In the Forties" (Lowell), **II:** 554

"In the Garden" (Ferry), **Supp. XXIV:** 153

In the Garden of the North American Martyrs (Wolff), **Supp. VII:** 341–342

In the Garret (Van Vechten), **Supp. II Part 2:** 735

"In the Grove: The Poet at Ten" (Kenyon), **Supp. VII:** 160

"In the Hall of Mirrors" (Merrill), **Supp. III Part 1:** 322

In the Harbor (Longfellow), **II:** 491

In the Heart of the Heart of the Country (Gass), **Supp. VI: 82–83,** 84, 85, 93

In the Heat of the Night (Ball), **Supp. XV:** 202

In the Heat of the Night (film), **Supp. I Part 1:** 67

In the Hollow of His Hand (Purdy), **Supp. VII:** 278–280

In the House of Light (Everwine, trans.), **Supp. XV:** 73, 75, **76–78,** 82

"In the Laboratory of Kisses" (Gallagher), **Supp. XXIV:** 170

In the Lake of the Woods (O'Brien), **Supp. V:** 240, 243, 250–252

In the Land of the White Death: A Epic Story of Survival in the Siberian Arctic (Albanov), **Supp. XVIII:** 114

"In the Last Days" (Everwine), **Supp. XV:** 88, 89

"In the Late Summer Garden"(Crooker), **Supp. XXIII:** 55

In the Loyal Mountains (Bass), **Supp. XVI: 19–20**

"In the Loyal Mountains" (Bass), **Supp. XVI:** 20

In the Mecca (Brooks), **Supp. III Part 1:** 74

"In the Mecca" (Brooks), **Supp. III Part 1:** 70, 83–84

In the Midst of Life (Bierce), **I:** 200–203, 204, 206, 208, 212

"In the Miro District" (Taylor), **Supp. V:** 323

In the Miro District and Other Stories (Taylor), **Supp. V:** 325–326

In the Money (W. C. Williams), **Retro. Supp. I:** 423

"In the Motel" (X. J. Kennedy), **Supp. XV:** 163

"In the Naked Bed, in Plato's Cave" (Schwartz), **Supp. II Part 2:** 646–649

In the Name of the Neither (Sobin), **Supp. XVI:** 291

"In the Night" (Kincaid), **Supp. VII:** 183

In the Night Season: A Novel (Bausch), **Supp. VII:** 52–53

"In the Old Neighborhood" (Dove), **Supp. IV Part 1:** 241, 257

"In the Old World" (Oates), **Supp. II Part 2:** 503, 504

"In the Park" (Huncke), **Supp. XIV:** 139

In the Pines (Notley), **Supp. XXII:** 236–237

"In the Pit" (Proulx), **Supp. VII:** 255, 261

In the Pond (Jin), **Supp. XVIII: 95–96**

In the Presence of the Sun (Momaday), **Supp. IV Part 2:** 489, 490, 491–493, 493

"In the Quiet Night" (Li Po), **Supp. XV:** 47

"In the Realm of the Fisher King" (Didion), **Supp. IV Part 1:** 211

"In the Red Room" (Bowles), **Supp. IV Part 1:** 93

"In the Region of Ice" (Oates), **Supp. II Part 2:** 520

In the Room We Share (Simpson), **Supp. IX:** 279

"In These Dissenting Times" (Walker), **Supp. III Part 2:** 522

"In the Shadow of Gabriel, A.D.1550" (Frederic), **II:** 139

In the Shadow of Memory (Skloot), **Supp. XX: 193, 196, 205, 205–206**

"In the Shadow of Memory" (Skloot), **Supp. XX: 206**

In the Shadow of the Morning: Essays on Wild Lands, Wild Waters, and a Few Untamed People (Caputo), **Supp. XIX:** 28–29

In the Spirit of Crazy Horse (Matthiessen), **Supp. V:** 211

"In the Subway" (Untermeyer), **Supp. XV:** 296

In the Summer House (Jane Bowles), **Supp. IV Part 1:** 83, 89

In the Tennessee Country (Taylor), **Supp. V:** 328

"In the Thick of Darkness" (Salinas), **Supp. XIII:** 325

In the Time of Butterflies (Alvarez), **Supp. XXIV:** 89

"In the Time of the Blossoms" (Mervin), **Supp. III Part 1:** 352

In the Time of the Butterflies (Alvarez), **Supp. VII:** 1, 12–15, 18

In the Time of the Present (Kenny), **Supp. XXIII:** 146, **156**

"In the Tube" (Jarman), **Supp. XVII:** 121

"In the Tunnel Bone of Cambridge" (Corso), **Supp. XII:** 120–121

"In the Upper Pastures" (Kumin), **Supp. IV Part 2:** 453

In the Valley (Frederic), **II:** 133–134, 136, 137

"In the Village" (Bishop), **Retro. Supp. II:** 38; **Supp. I Part 1:** 73, 74–75, 76, 77, 78, 88

"In the Waiting Room" (Bishop), **Retro. Supp. II:** 50; **Supp. I Part 1:** 81, 94, 95; **Supp. IV Part 1:** 249

"In the Ward: The Sacred Wood" (Jarrell), **II:** 376, 377

In the Western Night: Collected Poems 1965–90 (Bidart), **Supp. XV:** 19, **30–32**

"In the White Night" (Beattie), **Supp. V:** 30–31

"In the Wind My Rescue Is" (Ammons), **Supp. VII:** 25

"In the Winter Dark" (Peacock), **Supp. XIX:** 206

In the Winter of Cities (T. Williams), **IV:** 383

"In the X-Ray of the Sarcophagus of Tapero" (Goldbarth), **Supp. XII:** 191

"In the Yard" (Swenson), **Supp. IV Part 2:** 647

In the Zone (O'Neill), **III:** 388

In This, Our Life (film), **Supp. I Part 1:** 67

"In This Country, but in Another Language, My Aunt Refuses to Marry the Men Everyone Wants Her To" (Paley), **Supp. VI:** 225

"In This Dream" (J. W. Miller), **Supp. XX: 170**

In This Hung-up Age (Corso), **Supp. XII: 119–120,** 129

In This Our Life (Glasgow), **II:** 175, 178, 189

In This Our World (Gilman), **Supp. XI:** 196, 200, 202

"In Those Days" (Jarrell), **II:** 387–388

"Intimately Connected to the Zeitgeist" (Franzen), **Supp. XX: 94**

"In Time of War" (Auden), **Supp. II Part 1:** 8, 13

In Times Like These (Edgell), **Supp. XXIII:** 84, **89–90,** 94

"Into Egypt" (Benét), **Supp. XI:** 56, 57–58

Intolerance (film; Griffith), **Supp. XVI:** 184

"Into My Own" (Frost), **II:** 153; **Retro. Supp. I:** 127

"Into Night" (McKnight), **Supp. XX: 151–152**

Into the Interior (Cliff), **Supp. XXII:** 67, 78–79

"Into the Night Life . . ." (H. Miller), **III:** 180, 184

"Into the Nowhere" (Rawlings), **Supp. X:** 220

Into the Stone (Dickey), **Supp. IV Part 1:** 178

"Into the Stone" (Dickey), **Supp. IV Part 1:** 179

Into the Stone and Other Poems (Dickey), **Supp. IV Part 1:** 176

Into the Wild (Krakauer), **Supp. XVIII:** 106, **107–108,** 116, 117

Into Thin Air: A Personal Account of the Mount Everest Disaster (Krakauer), **Supp. XVII:** 210; **Supp. XVIII:** 105, **109–113,** 117

In Touch: The Letters of Paul Bowles (J. Miller, ed.), **Supp. IV Part 1:** 95

"Intoxicated, The" (Jackson), **Supp. IX:** 116

"Intrigue" (Crane), **I:** 419

"Introducing the Fathers" (Kumin), **Supp. IV Part 2:** 452

Introductio ad Prudentiam (Fuller), **II:** 111

"Introduction" (Strout; *Ploughshares* spring 2010), **Supp. XXIII:** 284

"Introduction to a Haggadah" (Paley), **Supp. VI:** 219

Introduction to Objectivist Epistemology (Rand), **Supp. IV Part 2:** 527, 528–529

Introduction to Objectivist Epistemology 2nd ed. (Rand), **Supp. IV Part 2:** 529

"Introduction to Poetry" (Collins), **Supp. XXI:** 57

Introduction to Poetry, An (Gioia and X. J. Kennedy), **Supp. XV:** 113, 153

"Introduction to Some Poems, An" (Stafford), **Supp. XI:** 311, 324

Introduction to the Geography of Iowa, The (Doty), **Supp. XI:** 120

"Introduction to the Hoh" (Hugo), **Supp. VI:** 136–137

"Introduction to *The New Writing in the USA*" (Creeley), **Supp. IV Part 1:** 153–154

"Introduction to William Blake, An" (Kazin), **Supp. VIII:** 103

Introitus (Longfellow), **II:** 505, 506–507

"Intruder, The" (Dubus), **Supp. VII:** 76–78, 91

Intruder, The (Maeterlinck), **I:** 91

Intruder in the Dust (Faulkner), **II:** 71, 72; **Supp. XVI:** 148

"Invaders, The" (Haines), **Supp. XII:** 205

Invaders, The (W. Frank), **Supp. XX:** **79–80**

Invasion of Privacy: The Cross Creek Trial of Marjorie Kinnan Rawlings (Acton), **Supp. X:** 233

Inventing Memory: A Novel of Mothers and Daughters (Jong), **Supp. V:** 115, 129

Inventing the Abbotts (Miller), **Supp. XII: 294–295**

"Invention of Autobiography. The" (Hampl), **Supp. XXII:** 93–94

"Invention of God in a Mouthful of Milk, The" (Karr), **Supp. XI:** 250

Invention of Solitude, The (Auster), **Supp. XII:** 21–22

Inventions of the March Hare (Eliot), **Retro. Supp. I:** 55–56, 58

"Inventions of the March Hare" (Eliot), **Retro. Supp. I:** 55

"Inventory" (Parker), **Supp. IX:** 192

"Inverted Forest, The" (Salinger), **III:** 552, 572

"Investigation" (Ryan as Quin), **Supp. XVIII:** 227–228

"Investigations of a Dog" (Kafka), **IV:** 438

"Investiture, The" (Banks), **Supp. V:** 7

"Investiture at Cecconi's" (Merrill), **Supp. III Part 1:** 336

"Invicibility" (O'Hara), **Supp. XXIII:** 214

"Invisible" (Pickering), **Supp. XXI:** 201

Invisible Circus, The (Egan), **Supp. XIX:** 49, **50–52**

Invisible Company, The (Sanders), **Supp. XVI:** 270–271

Invisible Man (Ellison), **IV:** 493; **Retro. Supp. II:** 3, 12, 111, 112, 113, 117, 119, **120–123,** 125; **Supp. II Part 1:** 40, 170, 221, 224, 226, 227, 230, 231–232, 235, 236, 241–245; **Supp. IX:** 306; **Supp. X:** 242; **Supp. XI:** 18, 92; **Supp. XVIII:** 59; **Supp. XIX:** 154, 155

Invisible: Poems (Nye), **Supp. XIII:** 277

Invisible Spectator, An (Sawyer-Lauçanno), **Supp. IV Part 1:** 95

Invisible Swords (Farrell), **II:** 27, 46, 48–49

Invisible Worm, The (Millar), **Supp. IV Part 2:** 465

Invitation to a Beheading (Nabokov), **III:** 252–253, 254, 257–258; **Retro. Supp. I:** 265, 270, 273

"Invitation to the Country, An" (Bryant), **Supp. I Part 1:** 160

"Invocation" (McKay), **Supp. X:** 134

"Invocation" (Untermeyer), **Supp. XV:** 296

"Invocation to Kali" (Sarton), **Supp. VIII:** 260

"Invocation: *To my Maternal Grandfather on hearing his descent from Chippewa ancestors misrepresented*" (J. Schoolcraft), **Supp. XXIII:** 232

"Invocation to the Social Muse" (MacLeish), **III:** 15

"In Weather" (Hass), **Supp. VI: 102–103**

"In Your Fugitive Dream" (Hugo), **Supp. VI:** 143

"In Your Good Dream" (Hugo), **Supp. VI:** 143–144

"Iola, Kansas" (Clampitt), **Supp. IX:** 45–46

Iola Leroy (Harper), **Supp. XVIII:** 284

Ion (Doolittle, trans.), **Supp. I Part 1:** 269, 274

Ion (Plato), **I:** 523

"Ione" (Dunbar), **Supp. II Part 1:** 199

Ionesco, Eugène, **I:** 71, 74, 75, 84, 295; **II:** 435; **Supp. VIII:** 201; **Supp. XIX:** 131; **Supp. XXIV:** 113

Ionica (Cory), **Supp. XX:** 230

Ionica II (Cory), **Supp. XX:** 230

"I Only Am Escaped Alone to Tell Thee" (Nemerov), **III:** 272, 273–274

"I Opened All the Portals Wide" (Chopin), **Retro. Supp. II:** 71

I Ought to Be in Pictures (Simon), **Supp. IV Part 2:** 584

Iphigenia (Notley), **Supp. XXII:** 226, 235

Iphigenia in Tauris (Euripedes), **Supp. XV:** 42, 50

I Promessi Sposi (Manzoni), **II:** 291

"I Put My Hand on My Son's Head" (Kooser), **Supp. XIX:** 120

Iram, Dhát al-'Imád (Gibran), **Supp. XX:** 116

"Iraq Drifting, July 2003" (Weigl), **Supp. XIX:** 288

"Irascibles, The" (Kees), **Supp. XV:** 145–146

Ireland: A Terrible Beauty (Uris), **Supp. XX: 244, 245–246, 246, 254**

"I Remember" (Sexton), **Supp. II Part 2:** 680

"Irenicon" (Shapiro), **Supp. II Part 2:** 704

Irigaray, Luce, **Supp. XII:** 6

Iris (Jarman), **Supp. XVII:** 110, **116–117**

"Iris by Night" (Frost), **Retro. Supp. I:** 132

"Irises" (L.-Y. Lee), **Supp. XV:** 214–215

Irish in America, The (Coffey, ed.), **Supp. XIX:** 133

Irish Stories of Sarah Orne Jewett, The (Jewett), **Retro. Supp. II:** 142

Irish Triangle, An (Barnes), **Supp. III Part 1:** 34

"Iron Characters, The" (Nemerov), **III:** 279, 282

"Iron Hans" (Sexton), **Supp. II Part 2:** 691

Iron Heel, The (London), **II:** 466, 480

Iron John: A Book about Men (R. Bly), **Supp. IV Part 1:** 59, 67; **Supp. XVI:** 177

"Iron Table, The" (Jane Bowles), **Supp. IV Part 1:** 82–83

"Iron Throat, The" (Olsen), **Supp. XIII:** 292, 297, 299

Ironweed (W. Kennedy), **Supp. VII:** 132, 133, 134, 135, 142, 144, 145–147, 148, 150, 153

"Irony as Art: The Short Fiction of William Humphrey" (Tebeaux), **Supp. IX:** 109

"Irony Is Not Enough: Essay on My Life as Catherine Deneuve" (Carson), **Supp. XII: 112–113**

Irony of American History, The (Niebuhr), **III:** 292, 306–307, 308

"Irrational Element in Poetry, The" (Stevens), **Retro. Supp. I:** 298, 301

"Irrevocable Diameter, An" (Paley), **Supp. VI:** 231–232

Irvine, Lorna, **Supp. XIII:** 26

Irving, Ebenezer, **II:** 296

Irving, Sir Henry, **IV:** 350

Irving, John, **Supp. VI: 163–183; Supp. X:** 77, 85

Irving, John Treat, **II:** 296

Irving, Peter, **II:** 296, 297, 298, 299, 300, 303

Irving, Washington, **I:** 211, 335, 336, 339, 343; **II: 295–318,** 488, 495; **III:** 113; **IV:** 309; **Retro. Supp. I:** 246; **Supp. I Part 1:** 155, 157, 158, 317; **Supp. I Part 2:** 377, 487, 585; **Supp. II Part 1:** 335; **Supp. IV Part 1:** 380; **Supp.**

XVIII: 12; **Supp. XXIII:** 178

Irving, William, **II:** 296

Irving, William, Jr., **II:** 296, 297, 298, 299, 303

Irwin, Mark, **Supp. XII:** 21, 22, 24, 29

Irwin, Robert, **Supp. XX:** 120

Irwin, William Henry, **Supp. II Part 1:** 192

Is 5 (Cummings), **I:** 429, 430, 434, 435, 440, 445, 446, 447

"Isaac and Abraham" (Brodsky), **Supp. VIII:** 21

"Isaac and Archibald" (Robinson), **III:** 511, 521, 523

Isaacs, Neil D., **Supp. XIX:** 255

"Isabelle" (Saunders), **Supp. XIX:** 225

"Isabel Sparrow" (Oliver), **Supp. VII:** 232

Isaiah (biblical book), **Supp. I Part 1:** 236; **Supp. I Part 2:** 516; **Supp. XXI:** 107

"Isaiah Beethoven" (Masters), **Supp. I Part 2:** 461

I Sailed with Magellan (Dybek), **Supp. XXIII:** 75–78, 79

"I Saw in Louisiana a Live-Oak Growing" (Whitman), **I:** 220

"I Shall Be Released" (Dylan), **Supp. XV:** 349

I Shall Spit on Your Graves (film), **Supp. I Part 1:** 67

Isháq, Adib, **Supp. XX:** 117

Isherwood, Christopher, **II:** 586; **Supp. II Part 1:** 10, 11, 13; **Supp. IV Part 1:** 79, 82, 102; **Supp. XI:** 305; **Supp. XIV:** 155–175; **Supp. XVI:** 194

Isherwood Century, The (Berg and Freeman), **Supp. XIV:** 157, 159

Isherwood's Fiction (Schwerdt), **Supp. XIV:** 155

Ishiguro, Kazuo, **Supp. VIII:** 15

Ishi Means Man (Merton), **Supp. VIII:** 208

"Ishmael's Dream" (Stern), **Supp. IX:** 287

I Should Have Stayed Home (McCoy), **Supp. XIII:** 167, **168–170,** 171

"I Should Worry" (Kees), **Supp. XV:** 140

"I Sigh in the Afternoon" (Salinas), **Supp. XIII:** 318

"I Sing the Body Electric" (Whitman), **Retro. Supp. I:** 394, 395

"Isis: Dorothy Eady, 1924" (Doty), **Supp. XI:** 122

"Is It O.K. to Be a Luddite?" (Pynchon), **Supp. XVI:** 128

"Is It True?" (Hughes), **Supp. I Part 1:** 342

I: Six Nonlectures (Cummings), **I:** 430, 433, 434

"Island" (Hughes), **Supp. I Part 1:** 340

Island Garden, An (Thaxter), **Retro. Supp. II:** 136; **Supp. XIII:** 152

Island Holiday, An (Henry), **I:** 515

Island in the Atlantic (W. Frank), **Supp. XX:** 79

"Island of the Fay, The" (Poe), **III:** 412, 417

Islands (Siddons), **Supp. XXII:** 239

"Islands, The" (Hayden), **Supp. II Part 1:** 373

"Island Sheaf, An" (Doty), **Supp. XI:** 136

Islands in the Stream (Hemingway), **II:** 258; **Retro. Supp. I:** 186

Isn't It Romantic (Wasserstein), **Supp. XV:** 323–325, 327

Is Objectivism a Religion? (Ellis), **Supp. IV Part 2:** 527

"Isolation of Modern Poetry, The" (Schwartz), **Supp. II Part 2:** 644

"Israel" (Reznikoff), **Supp. XIV:** 283

Israel Potter, or Fifty Years of Exile (Melville), **III:** 90; **Supp. XVIII:** 4

"Israfel" (Poe), **III:** 411

Is Sex Necessary? (Thurber and White), **Supp. I Part 2:** 607, 612, 614, 653

"Issues, The" (Olds), **Supp. X:** 205

"Istanbul" (Collins), **Supp. XXI:** 60

"I Stand Here Ironing" (Olsen), **Supp. XIII:** 292, 294, 296, 298, 300, 305

I Stole a Million (West), **IV:** 287

"Is Verse a Dying Technique?" (Wilson), **IV:** 431

It (Creeley), **Supp. IV Part 1:** 157, 158

IT (King), **Supp. V:** 139, 140, 141, 146–147, 151, 152

"It" (Olds), **Supp. X:** 208

Italian American Reconciliation: A Folktale (Shanley), **Supp. XIV:** 315, **324–326,** 328, 330

Italian Backgrounds (Wharton), **Retro. Supp. I:** 370

Italian Hours (James), **I:** 12; **II:** 337; **Retro. Supp. I:** 235

Italian Journeys (Howells), **II:** 274

"Italian Morning" (Bogan), **Supp. III Part 1:** 58

Italian Villas and Their Gardens (Wharton), **IV:** 308; **Retro. Supp. I:** 361, 367

Italie, Hillel, **Supp. XV:** 128

It All Adds Up: From the Dim Past to the Uncertain Future (Bellow), **Retro. Supp. II:** 32

"It Always Breaks Out" (Ellison), **Retro. Supp. II:** 126; **Supp. II Part 1:** 248

Itard, Jean-Marc Gaspard, **Supp. I Part 2:** 564

"I taste a liquor never brewed" (Dickinson), **Retro. Supp. I:** 30, 37

It Came from Outer Space (film), **Supp. IV Part 1:** 102

It Can't Happen Here (Lewis), **II:** 454

It Chooses You (July), **Supp. XXIV:** 199, 209, 210

"It Don't Mean a Thing If It Ain't Got That Swing" (Matthews), **Supp. IX:** **164–165**

I Tell You Now (Ortiz), **Supp. IV Part 2:** 500

"Ithaca" (Glück), **Supp. V:** 89

It Happened One Night (Capra), **Supp. XV:** 197

It Has Come to Pass (Farrell), **II:** 26

"I think to live May be a Bliss" (Dickinson), **Retro. Supp. I:** 44

"I Thought It Was Harry" (Bronk), **Supp. XXI:** 31

I Thought of Daisy (Wilson), **IV:** 428, 434, 435

"Itinerary of an Obsession" (Kumin), **Supp. IV Part 2:** 450

"It Is a Strange Country" (Ellison), **Supp. II Part 1:** 238

"It Is Dangerous to Read Newspapers" (Atwood), **Supp. XIII:** 33

"It Must Be Abstract" (Stevens), **IV:** 95; **Retro. Supp. I:** 307

"It Must Change" (Stevens), **Retro. Supp. I:** 300, 307, 308

"It Must Give Pleasure" (Stevens), **Retro. Supp. I:** 307, 308, 309

"'It Out-Herods Herod. Pray You, Avoid It'" (Hecht), **Supp. X:** 62, 64

"It's All Over Now, Baby Blue" (song, Dylan), **Supp. XVIII:** 30

It's Loaded, Mr. Bauer (Marquand), **III:** 59

It's Nation Time (Baraka), **Supp. II Part 1:** 52, 53

"It's Nation Time" (Baraka), **Supp. II Part 1:** 53

It's Only a Play (McNally), **Supp. XIII:** 198

It Was (Zukofsky), **Supp. III Part 2:** 630

"It Was Romance" (July), **Supp. XXIV:** 202–203

It Was the Nightingale (Ford), **III:** 470–471

"It Was When" (Snyder), **Supp. VIII:** 300

Ivanhoe (Scott), **I:** 216; **Supp. I Part 2:** 410

Ivens, Bryna, **Supp. XV:** 311, 312

Ivens, Joris, **I:** 488; **Retro. Supp. I:** 184

"Iverson Boy, The" (Simpson), **Supp. IX:** 280

"Ives" (Rukeyser), **Supp. VI:** 273, 283

Ives, George H., **Supp. I Part 1:** 153

Ivory Grin, The (Macdonald), **Supp. IV Part 2:** 471, 472

"Ivory Novel, The" (Halliday), **Supp. XIX:** 90

Ivory Tower, The (James), **II:** 337–338

"Ivory Tower, The: Louis Untermeyer as Critic" (Aiken), **Supp. XV:** 298

Ivry, Sara, **Supp. XX:** 179

"Ivy Winding" (Ammons), **Supp. VII:** 33

Iwamatsu, Mako, **Supp. XXI:** 150

"I Wandered Lonely as a Cloud" (Wordsworth), **Retro. Supp. I:** 121–122; **Supp. X:** 73; **Supp. XIV:** 184

"I want, I want" (Plath), **Retro. Supp. II:** 246

"I Wanted to Be There When My Father Died" (Olds), **Supp. X:** 210

"I Want to Be a Father Like the Men" (Cisneros), **Supp. VII:** 71

"I Want to Be Miss America" (Alvarez), **Supp. VII:** 18

"I Want to Know Why" (Anderson), **I:** 114, 115, 116; **II:** 263

"I Want You Women Up North To Know" (Olsen), **Supp. XIII:** 292, 297

"I Was Born in Lucerne" (Levine), **Supp. V:** 181, 189

"I Was Marching" (Le Sueur), **Supp. XXIII:** 167

"I Was Really Very Hungry" (M. F. K. Fisher), **Supp. XVII:** 91

"I Went into the Maverick Bar" (Snyder), **Supp. VIII:** 301

"I Will Lie Down" (Swenson), **Supp. IV Part 2:** 640

I Will Say Beauty (C. Frost), **Supp. XV:** 96, **105–107**

I Wonder As I Wander (Hughes), **Retro. Supp. I:** 196, 203; **Supp. I Part 1:** 329, 332–333

I Would Have Saved Them If I Could (L. Michaels), **Supp. XVI:** 203, 205, **206–210**

"Iyani: It goes this Way" (Gunn Allen), **Supp. IV Part 1:** 321

"I years had been from home" (Dickinson), **I:** 471

Iyer, Pico, **Supp. V:** 215

Izzo, David Garrett, **Supp. XIV:** 155, 156, 159, 160, 161, 163, 169, 171

J

Jab (Halliday), **Supp. XIX: 91–94**

"Jachid and Jechidah" (Singer), **IV:** 15

Jack and Jill (Alcott), **Supp. I Part 1:** 42

"Jack and the Beanstalk" (Hay), **Supp. XIV:** 124

"Jack in the Pot" (D. West), **Supp. XVIII:** 283

Jack Kelso (Masters), **Supp. I Part 2:** 456, 471–472

Jacklight (Erdrich), **Supp. IV Part 1:** 259, 270

Jack London, Hemingway, and the Constitution (Doctorow), **Supp. IV Part 1:** 220, 222, 224, 232, 235

Jackman, Harold, **Supp. XVIII:** 131

Jackpot (Caldwell), **I:** 304

"Jack Schmidt, Arts Administrator" (Keillor), **Supp. XVI:** 171

"Jack Schmidt on the Burning Sands" (Keillor), **Supp. XVI:** 171

Jackson, Amelia. *See* Holmes, Mrs. Oliver Wendell (Amelia Jackson)

Jackson, Andrew, **I:** 7, 20; **III:** 473; **IV:** 192, 248, 298, 334, 348; **Supp. I Part 2:** 456, 461, 473, 474, 493, 695

Jackson, Blyden, **Supp. I Part 1:** 337

Jackson, Charles, **Supp. I Part 1:** 303

Jackson, George, **Supp. I Part 1:** 66

Jackson, Helen Hunt, **I:** 459, 470; **Retro. Supp. I:** 26, 27, 30–31, 32, 33

Jackson, James, **Supp. I Part 1:** 302, 303

Jackson, J. O., **III:** 213

Jackson, Joe, **Supp. I Part 2:** 441

Jackson, Katherine Gauss, **Supp. VIII:** 124

Jackson, Lawrence, **Retro. Supp. II:** 113, 115

Jackson, Lawrence P., **Supp. XXII:** 140

Jackson, Melanie, **Supp. X:** 166

Jackson, Michael, **Supp. VIII:** 146

Jackson, Richard, **II:** 119; **Supp. IX:** 165

Jackson, Shelley, **Supp. XVIII:** 136

Jackson, Shirley, **Supp. IX: 113–130**

Jackson, Thomas J. ("Stonewall"), **IV:** 125, 126

"Jackson Hotel" (Hull), **Supp. XXI:** 134, 135

Jackson Pollock (O'Hara), **Supp. XXIII:** 214–215

"Jackson Square" (Levertov), **Supp. III Part 1:** 276

Jackstraws (Simic), **Supp. VIII:** 280, 282–283

"Jackstraws" (Simic), **Supp. VIII: 283**

Jack Tier (Cooper), **I:** 354, 355

"Jacob" (Garrett), **Supp. VII:** 109–110

"Jacob" (Schwartz), **Supp. II Part 2:** 663

Jacob, Max, **Supp. XV:** 178, 182

"Jacob and the Indians" (Benét), **Supp. XI:** 47–48

Jacobs, Catherine Haydon, **Supp. XXI:** 98

Jacobs, Harriet, **Supp. XVI:** 85

Jacobs, Jill Suzanne, **Supp. XX: 178, 186**

Jacobs, Rita D., **Supp. XII:** 339

Jacobsen, Josephine, **Supp. XIII:** 346; **Supp. XIV:** 260

"Jacob's Ladder" (Rawlings), **Supp. X:** 224, 228

Jacob's Ladder, The (Levertov), **Supp. III Part 1:** 272, 276–278, 281

"Jacob's Ladder, The" (Levertov), **Supp. III Part 1:** 278

Jacobson, Dale, **Supp. X:** 112

Jacobson, Kristin, **Supp. XVIII:** 113

Jacobson, Leslie, **Supp. XV:** 323

Jacoby, Russell, **Supp. IV Part 2:** 692

"Jacquerie, The" (Lanier), **Supp. I Part 1:** 355, 356, 360, 364, 370

Jacques le fataliste (D. Diderot), **Supp. XVII:** 145

Jade Mountain, The: A Chinese Anthology, Being Three Hundred Poems of the T'ang Dynasty (Bynner, trans.), **II:** 527; **Supp. XV:** 46, 47, 48

Jafsie and John Henry: Essays on Hollywood, Bad Boys, and Six Hours of Perfect Poker (Mamet), **Supp. XIV:** 252

Jaguar Totem (LaBastille), **Supp. X:** 99, 106, **107–109**

Jailbird (Vonnegut), **Supp. II Part 2:** 760, 779–780

Jaimes, M. Annette, **Supp. IV Part 1:** 330, 331

Jain, Manju, **Retro. Supp. I:** 53, 58

"Jake Flower, The" (Major), **Supp. XXII:** 182

Jake's Women (Simon), **Supp. IV Part 2:** 576, 588

"Jakie's Mother" (Fante), **Supp. XI:** 164

Jakobson, Roman, **Supp. IV Part 1:** 155

"Jamaica Kincaid's New York" (Kincaid), **Supp. VII:** 181

James, Alice, **I:** 454; **Retro. Supp. I:** 228, 235

James, A. Lloyd, **Supp. XIV:** 343

James, Caryn, **Supp. X:** 302, 303

James, C. L. R. (Cyril Lionel Robert), **Supp. XXI: 159–173**

James, Etta, **Supp. X:** 242

James, Henry, **I:** 4, 5, 9, 10, 12, 15, 16, 20, 52, 93, 109, 211, 226, 228, 244, 246, 251, 255, 258, 259, 336, 363, 374, 375, 379, 384, 409, 429, 436, 439, 452, 454, 459, 461–462, 463, 464, 485, 500, 504, 513, 514, 517–518, 571; **II:** 38, 58, 60, 73, 74, 95, 138, 140, 144, 147, 196, 198, 199, 228, 230, 234, 243, 259, 267, 271, 272, 275, 276, 278, 281, 282, 283, 284, 285, 286, 287, 288, 290, 306, 309, 316, **319–341,** 398, 404, 410, 415, 427, 444, 542, 544, 547–548, 556, 600; **III:** 44, 51, 136, 194–195, 199, 206, 208, 218, 228–229, 237, 281, 319, 325, 326, 334, 409, 453, 454, 457, 460, 461, 464, 511, 522, 576, 607; **IV:** 8, 27, 34, 37, 40, 53, 58, 73, 74, 134, 168, 172, 182, 198, 202, 285, 308, 309, 310, 311, 314, 316, 317, 318, 319, 321, 322, 323, 324, 328, 347, 352, 359, 433, 439, 476; **Retro. Supp. I:** 1, 8, 53, 56, 59, 108, 112, **215–242,** 272, 283, 284, 362, 366, 367, 368, 371, 373, 374, 375, 376, 377, 378, 379; **Retro. Supp. II:** 93, 135, 136, 203, 223; **Supp. I Part 1:** 35, 38, 43; **Supp. I Part 2:** 414, 454, 608, 609, 612–613, 618, 620, 646; **Supp. II Part 1:** 94–95; **Supp. III Part 1:** 14, 200; **Supp. III Part 2:** 410, 412; **Supp. IV Part 1:** 31, 35, 80, 127, 197, 349, 353; **Supp. IV Part 2:** 613, 677, 678, 682, 689, 693; **Supp. V:** 97, 101, 103, 258, 261, 263, 313; **Supp. VIII:** 98, 102, 156, 166, 168; **Supp. IX:** 121; **Supp. XI:** 153; **Supp. XIII:** 102; **Supp. XIV:** 40, 110, 112, 335, 336, 348, 349; **Supp. XV:** 41; **Supp. XVII:** 5, 47; **Supp. XVIII:** 160, 258; **Supp. XX: 227, 228, 232, 233, 238, 240; Supp. XXI:** 225; **Supp. XXII:** 89; **Supp. XXIV:** 132, 224

James, Henry (father), **II:** 7, 275, 321, 337, 342–344, 364; **IV:** 174; **Supp. I Part 1:** 300

James, Henry (nephew), **II:** 360

James, Horace, **Supp. XIV:** 57

James, P. D., **Supp. XIX:** 131

James, William, **I:** 104, 220, 224, 227, 228, 255, 454; **II:** 20, 27, 165, 166, 276, 321, 337, **342–366,** 411; **III:** 303, 309, 509, 599, 600, 605, 606, 612; **IV:** 26, 27, 28–29, 31, 32, 34, 36, 37, 43, 46, 291, 486; **Retro. Supp. I:** 57, 216, 227, 228, 235, 295, 300, 306; **Supp. I Part 1:** 3, 7, 11, 20; **Supp. XIV:** 40, 50, 197, 199, 212, 335; **Supp. XVII:** 97

James, William (grandfather), **II:** 342

James Baldwin: The Legacy (Troupe, ed.), **Retro. Supp. II:** 15

James Baldwin—The Price of the Ticket (film), **Retro. Supp. II:** 2

James Dickey and the Politics of Canon (Suarez), **Supp. IV Part 1:** 175

"James Dickey on Yeats: An Interview" (Dickey), **Supp. IV Part 1:** 177

James Hogg: A Critical Study (Simpson), **Supp. IX:** 269, 276

"James Is a Girl" (Egan), **Supp. XIX:** 61

James Jones: A Friendship (Morris), **Supp. XI:** 234

James Jones: An American Literary Orientalist Master (Carter), **Supp. XI:** 220

"James Jones and Jack Kerouac: Novelists of Disjunction" (Stevenson), **Supp. XI:** 230

James Jones: Reveille to Taps (television documentary), **Supp. XI:** 234

Jameson, Anna Brownell, **Supp. XXIII:** 225, 226, 232, 235

Jameson, F. R., **Supp. IV Part 1:** 119

Jameson, Sir Leander Starr, **III:** 327

James Shore's Daughter (Benét), **Supp. XI:** 48

"James Thurber" (Pollard), **Supp. I Part 2:** 468

"James Whitcomb Riley (From a Westerner's Point of View)" (Dunbar), **Supp. II Part 1:** 198

Jammes, Francis, **II:** 528; **Retro. Supp. I:** 55

"Jan, the Son of Thomas" (Sandburg), **III:** 593–594

Jan. 31 (Goldbarth), **Supp. XII:** 177, **178–179,** 180

"Jane Awake"(O'Hara), **Supp. XXIII:** 210

Janeczko, Paul, **Supp. XIII:** 280

Jane Eyre (Brontë), **Supp. XVI:** 158; **Supp. XXII:** 120

Janet, Pierre, **I:** 248, 249, 252; **Retro. Supp. I:** 55, 57

Jane Talbot: A Novel (Brown), **Supp. I Part 1:** 145–146

"Janet Waking" (Ransom), **III:** 490, 491

"Janice" (Jackson), **Supp. IX:** 117

Janowitz, Tama, **Supp. X:** 7

Jantz, Harold S., **Supp. I Part 1:** 112

"January" (Barthelme), **Supp. IV Part 1:** 54

"January" (W. V. Davis), **Supp. XXI:** 89, 90

January Man, The (screenplay, Shanley), **Supp. XIV:** 316

"January Thaw" (Leopold), **Supp. XIV:** 183–184

"Janus" (Beattie), **Supp. V:** 31

Janzen, Jean, **Supp. V:** 180

"Japan" (Collins), **Supp. XXI:** 56

Japanese Americans: The Formation and Transformations of an Ethnic Group (Spickard), **Supp. XXI:** 149

"Japanese Beetles" (X. J. Kennedy), **Supp. XV:** 161, 165

Japanese by Spring (Reed), **Supp. X:** 241, **253–255**

Japanese Cooking: A Simple Art (Tsuji), **Supp. XVII:** 90

"Japan's Young Dreams" (Geisel), **Supp. XVI:** 102

Jara, Victor, **Supp. IV Part 2:** 549

Jarecki, Dave, **Supp. XXIII:** 239

Jarman, Mark, **Supp. IV Part 1:** 68; **Supp. IX:** 266, 270, 276; **Supp. XII:** 209; **Supp. XV:** 251; **Supp. XVIII:** 178

Jarmon, Mark, **Supp. XVII: 109–122**

Jarrell, Randall, **I:** 167, 169, 173, 180; **II: 367–390,** 539–540; **III:** 134, 194, 213, 268, 527; **IV:** 352, 411, 422;

Retro. Supp. I: 52, 121, 135, 140; **Retro. Supp. II:** 44, 177, 178, 182; **Supp. I Part 1:** 89; **Supp. I Part 2:** 552; **Supp. II Part 1:** 109, 135; **Supp. III Part 1:** 64; **Supp. III Part 2:** 541, 550; **Supp. IV Part 2:** 440; **Supp. V:** 315, 318, 323; **Supp. VIII:** 31, 100, 271; **Supp. IX:** 94, 268; **Supp. XI:** 311, 315; **Supp. XII:** 121, 260, 297; **Supp. XV:** 93, 153; **Supp. XVII:** 111

Jarrell, Mrs. Randall (Mary von Schrader), **II:** 368, 385

Jarry, Alfred, **Retro. Supp. II:** 326; **Supp. XV:** 177–178, 182, 188

Jarvis, John Wesley, **Supp. I Part 2:** 501, 520

Jaskoski, Helen, **Supp. IV Part 1:** 325; **Supp. XXII:** 166

"Jasmine" (Komunyakaa), **Supp. XIII:** 132

"Jason" (Hecht), **Supp. X:** 62

"Jason" (MacLeish), **III:** 4

Jason and Medeia (Gardner), **Supp. VI:** 63, **68–69**

"Jasper Notes" (G. Jones), **Supp. XXIV:** 194

Jaspers, Karl, **III:** 292; **IV:** 491

Jauss, David, **Supp. XXI:** 129, 132, 133, 134, 139

Jay, William, **I:** 338

Jayber Crow (Berry), **Supp. X:** 28, 34

"Jaz Fantasia" (Sandburg), **III:** 585

"Jazz Age Clerk, A" (Farrell), **II:** 45

Jazz Country: Ralph Ellison in America (Porter), **Retro. Supp. II:** 127

"Jazzonia" (Hughes), **Supp. I Part 1:** 324

Jazz Poetry Anthology, The (Komunyakaa and Feinstein, eds.), **Supp. XIII:** 125

"Jazztet Muted" (Hughes), **Supp. I Part 1:** 342

J. B.: A Play in Verse (MacLeish), **II:** 163, 228; **III:** 3, 21–22, 23; **Supp. IV Part 2:** 586

"Jealous" (Ford), **Supp. V:** 71

Jealous Gods, The (Atherton), **Supp. XXIV:** 26

Jealousies, The: A Faery Tale, by Lucy Vaughan Lloyd of China Walk, Lambeth (Keats), **Supp. XII:** 113

Jean-Christophe (Rolland), **Supp. XX:** 70

"Jean Harlow's Wedding Night" (Wasserstein), **Supp. XV:** 328

Jean Huguenot (Benét), **Supp. XI:** 44

"Jeff Briggs's Love Story" (Harte), **Supp. II Part 1:** 355

Jeffers, Robinson, **I:** 66; **III:** 134; **Retro. Supp. I:** 202; **Supp. II Part 2: 413–440;** **Supp. VIII:** 33, 292; **Supp. IX:** 77; **Supp. X:** 112; **Supp. XI:** 312; **Supp. XV:** 113, 114, 115; **Supp. XVII:** 111, 112, 117; **Supp. XXI:** 87; **Supp. XXIII:** 145

Jeffers, Una Call Kuster (Mrs. Robinson Jeffers), **Supp. II Part 2:** 414

Jefferson, Blind Lemon, **Supp. VIII:** 349

Jefferson, Margo, **Supp. XX: 87; Supp. XXIV:** 271

Jefferson, Thomas, **I:** 1, 2, 5, 6–8, 14, 485; **II:** 5, 6, 34, 217, 300, 301, 437;

III: 3, 17, 18, 294–295, 306, 310, 473, 608; **IV:** 133, 243, 249, 334, 348; **Supp. I Part 1:** 146, 152, 153, 229, 230, 234, 235; **Supp. I Part 2:** 389, 399, 456, 474, 475, 482, 507, 509, 510, 511, 516, 518–519, 520, 522; **Supp. X:** 26; **Supp. XIV:** 191; **Supp. XX: 285; Supp. XXIV:** 85, 281

Jefferson and/or Mussolini (Pound), **Retro. Supp. I:** 292

"Jefferson Davis as a Representative American" (Du Bois), **Supp. II Part 1:** 161

J-E-L-L-O (Baraka), **Supp. II Part 1:** 47

"Jelly-Bean, The" (Fitzgerald), **II:** 88

"Jellyfish, A" (Moore), **III:** 215

Jemie, Onwuchekwa, **Supp. I Part 1:** 343

Jenkins, J. L., **I:** 456

Jenkins, Joe, **Supp. XX: 117, 120, 122**

Jenkins, Kathleen, **III:** 403

Jenkins, Susan, **IV:** 123

Jenks, Deneen, **Supp. IV Part 2:** 550, 554

Jenks, Tom, **Supp. XIX:** 51

Jennie Gerhardt (Dreiser), **I:** 497, 499, 500, 501, 504–505, 506, 507, 519; **Retro. Supp. II:** 94, **99–101**

"Jennie M'Grew" (Masters), **Supp. I Part 2:** 468

Jennifer Lorn (Wylie), **Supp. I Part 2:** 709, 714–717, 718, 721, 724

Jennison, Peter S., **Supp. XIX:** 268

"Jenny Garrow's Lover" (Jewett), **II:** 397

"Jerboa, The" (Moore), **III:** 203, 207, 209, 211–212

Jeremiah, **Supp. X:** 35

Jeremy's Version (Purdy), **Supp. VII:** 274

"Je Reviens"(Dybek), **Supp. XXIII:** 78

"Jericho" (Lowell), **II:** 536

Jerome, Judson, **Supp. XXIII:** 54

"Jerry's Garage" (Budbill), **Supp. XIX:** 7

"Jersey City Gendarmerie, Je T'aime" (Lardner), **II:** 433

Jersey Rain (Pinsky), **Supp. VI:** 235, **247–250**

"Jerusalem" (Nye), **Supp. XIII:** 287

Jerusalem: Song of Songs (Uris), **Supp. XX: 244–245, 246, 255**

Jerusalem the Golden (Reznikoff), **Supp. XIV:** 280, 285, 286

Jessup, Richard, **Supp. XI:** 306

"Je Suis Perdu" (Taylor), **Supp. V:** 314, 321–322

Jesuits in North America in the Seventeenth Century, The (Parkman), **Supp. II Part 2:** 597, 603–605

Jesus, **I:** 27, 34, 68, 89, 136, 552, 560; **II:** 1, 16, 197, 198, 214, 215, 216, 218, 219, 239, 373, 377, 379, 537, 538, 539, 549, 569, 585, 591, 592; **III:** 39, 173, 179, 270, 291, 296–297, 300, 303, 305, 307, 311, 339, 340, 341, 342, 344, 345, 346, 347, 348, 352, 353, 354, 355, 436, 451, 489, 534, 564, 566, 567, 582; **IV:** 51, 69, 86, 107, 109, 117, 137, 138, 141, 144, 147, 149, 150, 151, 152, 155, 156, 157, 158, 159, 163, 164, 232, 241, 289, 293, 294, 296, 331, 364, 392, 396, 418, 430; **Supp. I Part 1:** 2, 54,

104, 107, 108, 109, 121, 267, 371; **Supp. I Part 2:** 379, 386, 458, 515, 580, 582, 583, 587, 588, 683; **Supp. V:** 280

Jesus, the Son of Man (Gibran), **Supp. XX:** 115–116, 117, 122–123

"Jesus Asleep" (Sexton), **Supp. II Part 2:** 693

"Jesus of Nazareth, Then and Now" (Price), **Supp. VI:** 268

"Jesus Papers, The" (Sexton), **Supp. II Part 2:** 693

"Jesus Raises Up the Harlot" (Sexton), **Supp. II Part 2:** 693

"Jesus Stories, The" (Brockmeier), **Supp. XXII:** 52

Jetée, La (film), **Supp. IV Part 2:** 436

"Jeune Parque, La" (Valéry), **IV:** 92

"Jew as Writer/The Writer as Jew, The: Reflections on Literature and Identity" (Apple), **Supp. XVII:** 1, 9

"Jewbird, The" (Malamud), **Supp. I Part 2:** 435

"Jewboy, The" (P. Roth), **Supp. III Part 2:** 412

Jewett, Caroline, **II:** 396

Jewett, Katharine, **Retro. Supp. II:** 46

Jewett, Mary, **II:** 396, 403

Jewett, Rutger, **Retro. Supp. I:** 381

Jewett, Sarah Orne, **I:** 313; **II:** 391–414; **Retro. Supp. I:** 6, 7, 19; **Retro. Supp. II:** 51, 52, 131–151, 156; **Supp. I Part 2:** 495; **Supp. VIII:** 126; **Supp. IX:** 79; **Supp. XIII:** 153; **Supp. XXIII:** 275, 278

Jewett, Theodore Furber, **II:** 395

Jewett, Dr. Theodore Herman, **II:** 396–397, 402

"Jew for Export, The" (Mamet), **Supp. XIV:** 251–252

Jew in Our Day, The (W. Frank), **Supp. XX:** 79

Jew in the American Novel, The (Fiedler), **Supp. XIII:** 106

"Jewish Graveyards, Italy" (Levine), **Supp. V:** 190

"Jewish Hunter, The" (Moore), **Supp. X:** 163, 165, **174**

Jewison, Norman, **Supp. XI:** 306; **Supp. XIV:** 316

Jews of Shklov (Schneour), **IV:** 11

Jews without Money (Gold), **Supp. XIV:** 288–289

JFK (film), **Supp. XIV:** 48

Jig of Forslin, The: A Symphony (Aiken), **I:** 50, 51, 57, 62, 66

"Jig Tune: Not for Love" (McGrath), **Supp. X:** 116

"Jihad" (McClatchy), **Supp. XII:** 266

"Jilting of Granny Weatherall, The" (Porter), **III:** 434, 435, 438

Jim Crow's Last Stand (Hughes), **Retro. Supp. I:** 205

Jiménez, Juan Ramón, **Supp. XIII:** 315, 323

Jimmie Higgins (Sinclair), **Supp. V:** 288

"Jimmy Harlow" (X. J. Kennedy), **Supp. XV:** 170

Jimmy's Blues (Baldwin), **Retro. Supp. II:** 8, 9, 15

Jim's Book: A Collection of Poems and Short Stories (Merrill), **Supp. III Part 1:** 319

Jin, Ha, **Supp. XVIII: 89–104**

Jitney (Wilson), **Supp. VIII:** 330, 331, 351

Jitterbug Perfume (Robbins), **Supp. X:** 273, **274–276,** 279

Joachim, Harold, **Retro. Supp. I:** 58

Joan, Pope, **IV:** 165

Joanna and Ulysses (Sarton), **Supp. VIII: 254–255**

Joan of Arc, **IV:** 241; **Supp. I Part 1:** 286–288; **Supp. I Part 2:** 469

Joans, Ted, **Supp. IV Part 1:** 169

Job (biblical book), **II:** 165, 166–167, 168; **III:** 21, 199, 512; **IV:** 13, 158; **Supp. I Part 1:** 125

Job, The (Burroughs and Odier), **Supp. III Part 1:** 97, 103

Job, The: An American Novel (Lewis), **II:** 441

"Job History" (Proulx), **Supp. VII:** 262

Jobim, Antonio Carlos, **Supp. IV Part 2:** 549

Jobim, Antônio Carlos, **Supp. XXI:** 100

"Job of the Plains, A" (Humphrey), **Supp. IX:** 101

"Jody Rolled the Bones" (Yates), **Supp. XI:** 335, 341

"Joe" (Alvarez), **Supp. VII:** 7–8

Joe (Brown), **Supp. XVIII:** 195

Joe (L. Brown), **Supp. XXI:** 41, **45–46,** 47

"Joe, the Vanishing American" (Swados), **Supp. XIX:** 258–259

Joe Hill: A Biographical Novel (Stegner), **Supp. IV Part 2:** 599

Joe Jones (Lamott), **Supp. XX: 134–135**

"Joe Louis: The King as a Middle-Aged Man" (Talese), **Supp. XVII:** 202

"Joe Messenger Is Dreaming"(P. Benedict), **Supp. XXIII:** 47

"Joe's Jitters" (Bronk), **Supp. XXI:** 27

Joe Turner's Come and Gone (Wilson), **Supp. VIII:** 334, **337–342,** 345

Joe versus the Volcano (screenplay, Shanley), **Supp. XIV:** 316

"Joey Martiney" (Huncke), **Supp. XIV:** 149

Johannes in Eremo (Mather), **Supp. II Part 2:** 453

John XXIII, Pope, **Supp. I Part 2:** 492

John (biblical book), **I:** 68; **Supp. XV:** 222, 224

"John" (Shields), **Supp. VII:** 310–311

John, Augustus, **Supp. XXII:** 157

John, Elton, **Supp. XXI:** 148

"John, John Chinaman" (Buck), **Supp. II Part 1:** 128

John Addington Symonds: A Biographical Study (Brooks), **I:** 240, 241

John-a Dreams: A Tale (J. Sturgis), **Supp. XX:** 233

"John Archer's Nose" (R. Fisher), **Supp. XIX:** 71–72, 78

John Barleycorn (London), **II:** 467, 481

John Brown (Du Bois), **Supp. II Part 1:** 171–172

"John Brown" (Emerson), **II:** 13

"John Brown" (Lindsay), **Supp. I Part 2:** 393

John Brown's Body (Benét), **II:** 177; **Supp. XI:** 45, 46, 47, **56–57**

John Brown: The Making of a Martyr (Warren), **IV:** 236

John Bull in America; or, The New Munchausen (Paulding), **I:** 344

"John Burke" (Olson), **Supp. II Part 2:** 579, 580

"John Burns of Gettysburg" (Harte), **Supp. II Part 1:** 343

"John Carter" (Agee), **I:** 27

John Chancellor Makes Me Cry (Siddons), **Supp. XXII:** 245

"John Coltrane: Where Does Art Come From?" (Baraka), **Supp. II Part 1:** 60

John Deth: A Metaphysical Legend and Other Poems (Aiken), **I:** 61

"John Endicott" (Longfellow), **II:** 505, 506; **Retro. Supp. II:** 165–166, 167

"John Evereldown" (Robinson), **III:** 524

John Fante Reader, The (Cooper, ed.), **Supp. XI:** 174

John Fante: Selected Letters, 1932–1981 (Cooney, ed.), **Supp. XI:** 170

"John Gardner: The Writer As Teacher" (Carver), **Supp. III Part 1:** 136, 146–147

John Gaunt (R. H. Davis), **Supp. XVI:** 89

John Jay Chapman and His Letters (Howe), **Supp. XIV:** 54

John Keats (Lowell), **II:** 530–531

"John Kinsella's Lament for Mrs. Mary Moore" (Yeats), **Supp. XVII:** 144

"John Lamar" (R. H. Davis), **Supp. XVI:** 89–90

John Lane, **Retro. Supp. I:** 59

"John L. Sullivan" (Lindsay), **Supp. I Part 2:** 394, 395

"John Marr" (Melville), **III:** 93

John Marr and Other Sailors (Melville), **III:** 93; **Retro. Supp. I:** 257

John Muir: A Reading Bibliography (Kimes and Kimes), **Supp. IX:** 178

Johnny Appleseed and Other Poems (Lindsay), **Supp. I Part 2:** 397

"Johnny Bear" (Steinbeck), **IV:** 67

Johnny Got His Gun (Trumbo), **Supp. XXI:** 45

"Johnny Mnemonic" (W. Gibson), **Supp. XVI:** 122, 123–125, 128, 131

"Johnny Panic and the Bible of Dreams" (Plath), **Retro. Supp. II:** 245

"Johnny Ray" (Ríos), **Supp. IV Part 2:** 543

Johnny Tremain (Forbes), **Supp. XIX:** 235

John of the Cross (Saint), **I:** 585; **Supp. IV Part 1:** 284; **Supp. XV:** 223; **Supp. XVII:** 112

John Paul Jones: A Sailor's Biography (Morison), **Supp. I Part 2:** 494–495

"John Redding Goes to Sea" (Hurston), **Supp. VI:** 150

Johns, George Sibley, **Retro. Supp. II:** 65

Johns, Jasper, **Supp. XXIII:** 217

Johns, Orrick, **Retro. Supp. II:** 71

John Sloan: A Painter's Life (Brooks), **I:** 254

"John Smith Liberator" (Bierce), **I:** 209

Johnson, Alexandra, **Supp. X:** 86

Johnson, Alvin, **I:** 236; **Supp. XV:** 304

Johnson, Ben, **Retro. Supp. I:** 56

Johnson, Buffie, **Supp. IV Part 1:** 94

Johnson, Caitlin, **Supp. XXIII:** 281

Johnson, Carol Siri, **Supp. XXIII:** 257, 258, 264, 269

Johnson, Charles, **Supp. I Part 1:** 325; **Supp. V:** 128; **Supp. VI: 185–201; Supp. X:** 239; **Supp. XIII:** 182; **Supp. XIX:** 160

Johnson, Charles S., **Supp. IX:** 309; **Supp. XXII:** 6, 7

Johnson, Claudia Durst, **Supp. VIII:** 126–127

Johnson, Clifton, **Supp. XXI:** 248, 250

Johnson, Denis, **Supp. XXI:** 118, 131

Johnson, Dennis, **Supp. XIX:** 209

Johnson, Diane, **Supp. XIII:** 127

Johnson, Dianne, **Retro. Supp. I:** 196

Johnson, Eastman, **IV:** 321

Johnson, Edward, **IV:** 157; **Supp. I Part 1:** 110, 115

Johnson, Fenton, **Supp. XI:** 129

Johnson, Georgia Douglas, **Supp. IV Part 1:** 164

Johnson, Helene, **Supp. XVIII:** 282

Johnson, James Weldon, **Retro. Supp. II:** 114; **Supp. I Part 1:** 324, 325; **Supp. II Part 1:** 33, 194, 200, 202–203, 206–207; **Supp. III Part 1:** 73; **Supp. IV Part 1:** 7, 11, 15, 16, 164, 165, 166, 169; **Supp. X:** 42, 136, **246; Supp. XVIII:** 122, 127, 282; **Supp. XIX:** 73

Johnson, Joyce, **Supp. XIV:** 150

Johnson, Kent, **Supp. XV:** 347

Johnson, Lady Bird, **Supp. IV Part 1:** 22

Johnson, Lyndon B., **I:** 254; **II:** 553, 582; **Retro. Supp. II:** 27

Johnson, Marguerite. *See* Angelou, Maya

Johnson, Maurice, **Supp. XV:** 136, 137, 138

Johnson, Michael K., **Supp. XVIII:** 59, 64

Johnson, Mordecai, **Supp. XIV:** 202

Johnson, Nunnally, **Supp. IV Part 1:** 355

Johnson, Pamela Hansford, **IV:** 469

Johnson, Rafer, **Supp. I Part 1:** 271

Johnson, Reed, **Supp. IV Part 2:** 589

Johnson, Richard, **Supp. XIII:** 132

Johnson, Robert, **Supp. IV Part 1:** 146; **Supp. VIII:** 15, 134

Johnson, Robert K., **Supp. IV Part 2:** 573, 584

Johnson, Robert Underwood, **Supp. IX:** 182, 184, 185

Johnson, Samuel, **II:** 295; **III:** 491, 503; **IV:** 452; **Retro. Supp. I:** 56, 65; **Supp. I Part 1:** 33; **Supp. I Part 2:** 422, 498, 503, 523, 656; **Supp. IV Part 1:** 34, 124; **Supp. XI:** 209; **Supp. XII:** 159; **Supp. XIII:** 55, 347; **Supp. XVI:** 204; **Supp. XVII:** 1; **Supp. XXIV:** 152

Johnson, Sarah Anne, **Supp. XVIII:** 145; **Supp. XIX:** 49, 50, 52, 54, 55, 56, 58, 59, 60, 61

Johnson, Steve, **Supp. XVI:** 177

Johnson, Thomas H., **I:** 470–471; **IV:** 144, 158; **Retro. Supp. I:** 26, 28, 36, 39, 40, 41, 43

Johnson, Walter, **II:** 422

Johnson, Willard "Spud", **Supp. XV:** 42, 46

"Johnson Girls, The" (Bambara), **Supp. XI:** 7

Johnsrud, Harold, **II:** 562

Johnston, Basil, **Supp. IV Part 1:** 269

Johnston, Mary, **II:** 194

Johnston, Robert M., **Supp. I Part 1:** 369

"John Sutter" (Winters), **Supp. II Part 2:** 810

John's Wife (Coover), **Supp. V:** 51–52

John the Baptist, **I:** 389; **II:** 537, 591

John Wesley Harding (album, Dylan), **Supp. XVIII:** 27

Jolas, Eugène, **Retro. Supp. II:** 85, 328; **Supp. IV Part 1:** 80

Jolie Blon's Bounce (Burke), **Supp. XIV:** 26, 33–34

Jolly (Mamet), **Supp. XIV:** 240, 254

"Jolly Corner, The" (James), **I:** 571; **Retro. Supp. I:** 235

"Jon" (Saunders), **Supp. XIX:** 232, 234

"Jonah" (Lowell), **II:** 536

Jonah's Gourd Vine (Hurston), **Supp. VI:** 149, 155

"Jonathan Edwards" (Holmes), **Supp. I Part 1:** 302, 315

"Jonathan Edwards in Western Massachusetts" (Lowell), **II:** 550

Jonathan Franzen at the End of Postmodernism (Burns), **Supp. XX: 85**

Jonathan Troy (Abbey), **Supp. XIII:** 4, 13

Jones, Anne, **Supp. X:** 8

Jones, Anne Goodwyn, **Supp. XXII:** 252

Jones, Carolyn M., **Supp. VIII:** 128; **Supp. XIX:** 160

Jones, Chuck, **Supp. XVI:** 102

Jones, David, **Supp. XVII:** 241

Jones, Dennis, **Supp. XXIII:** 228, 233

Jones, Derek Anson, **Supp. XVIII:** 38, 39

Jones, Edith Newbold. *See* Wharton, Edith

Jones, Edward P., **Supp. XXI:** 247; **Supp. XXII: 139–153**

Jones, E. Stanley, **III:** 297

Jones, Everett LeRoi. *See* Baraka, Imamu Amiri

Jones, Gayl, **Supp. XXIV: 183–197**

Jones, George Frederic, **IV:** 309

Jones, Grover, **Supp. XIII:** 166

Jones, Harry, **Supp. I Part 1:** 337

Jones, Howard Mumford, **I:** 353; **Supp. IV Part 2:** 606; **Supp. XIV:** 11

Jones, James, **III:** 40; **IV:** 98; **Supp. XI: 213–237; Supp. XIX:** 248, 252; **Supp. XX: 248**

Jones, James Earl, **Supp. VIII:** 334; **Supp. XI:** 309

Jones, Jennifer, **Supp. IV Part 2:** 524

Jones, John Paul, **II:** 405–406; **Supp. I Part 2:** 479, 480, 494–495

Jones, Kirkland C., **Supp. XVIII:** 173, 174, 175; **Supp. XXII:** 9

Jones, LeRoi. *See* Baraka, Imamu Amiri

Jones, Louis B., **Supp. XVI:** 41

Jones, Loyal, **Supp. XX: 170**

Jones, Lucretia Stevens Rhinelander, **IV:** 309

Jones, Madison, **Retro. Supp. II:** 235; **Supp. X:** 1

Jones, Major (pseudonym). *See* Thompson, William T.

Jones, Malcolm, **Supp. V:** 219; **Supp. XX: 93, 138**

Jones, Mildred, **Supp. XVIII:** 281

Jones, Robert Edmond, **III:** 387, 391, 394, 399; **Supp. XXI:** 6, 12

Jones, Sharon L., **Supp. XVIII:** 280, 285, 286

Jones, Tommy Lee, **Supp. V:** 227

"Jones's Private Argyment" (Lanier), **Supp. I Part 1:** 352

"Jones's *The Thin Red Line:* The End of Innocence" (Michel-Michot), **Supp. XI:** 224–225

Jong, Allan, **Supp. V:** 115

Jong, Erica, **Supp. V: 113–135**

Jong-Fast, Molly Miranda, **Supp. V:** 115

Jonson, Ben, **I:** 58, 358; **II:** 11, 16, 17, 18, 436, 556; **III:** 3, 463, 575–576; **IV:** 395, 453; **Retro. Supp. II:** 76; **Supp. I Part 2:** 423; **Supp. IV Part 2:** 585; **Supp. XX: 197; Supp. XXIV:** 159

Jonsson, Thorsten, **Retro. Supp. I:** 73

Joplin, Janis, **Supp. IV Part 1:** 206; **Supp. XI:** 239

Joplin, Scott, **Supp. IV Part 1:** 223

Jordan, A. Van, **Supp. XVIII:** 172

Jordan, Barbara, **Supp. VIII:** 63; **Supp. XI:** 249

Jordan, David, **Supp. XIX:** 141

Jordan, June, **Supp. XII:** 217; **Supp. XXII:** 172; **Supp. XXIV:** 188

Jordan, Marie, **Supp. XV:** 224

Jo's Boys (Alcott), **Supp. I Part 1:** 32, 35, 40–41, 42

Joseph Heller (Ruderman), **Supp. IV Part 1:** 380

"Josephine Has Her Day" (Thurber), **Supp. I Part 2:** 606

Josephine Stories, The (Fitzgerald), **Retro. Supp. I:** 109

"Joseph Martinez" (Huncke), **Supp. XIV:** 149

"Joseph Pockets" (Stern), **Supp. IX:** 292

Josephson, Matthew, **I:** 259

"José's Country" (Winters), **Supp. II Part 2:** 789, 790

Joshi, S. T., **Supp. XXIV:** 23

Joshua (biblical book), **Supp. I Part 2:** 515

"Joshua Clark"(Kenny), **Supp. XXIII:** 154

Joslin, Katherine, **Retro. Supp. I:** 376

Journal (Emerson), **Supp. I Part 1:** 309

"Journal" (L. Michaels), **Supp. XVI:** 213

Journal (Thoreau), **IV:** 175

Journal (Woolman), **Supp. VIII:** 202

"Journal for My Daughter" (Kunitz), **Supp. III Part 1:** 268

"Journal of an Airman" (Auden), **Supp. XIX:** 151

Journal of Arthur Stirling, The (Sinclair), **Supp. V:** 280

"Journal of a Solitary Man, The" (Hawthorne), **II:** 226

Journal of a Solitude (Sarton), **Supp. VIII:** 256, 262–263

Journal of My Other Self (Rilke), **Retro. Supp. II:** 20

Journal of the Fictive Life (Nemerov), **III:** 267, 268, 269, 272, 273, 274, 280–281, 284–285, 286, 287

Journal of the Plague Year, A (Defoe), **III:** 423

"Journal of the Year of the Ox, A" (Wright), **Supp. V:** 343

Journals (Thoreau), **Supp. I Part 1:** 299

Journals and Other Documents on the Life and Voyages of Christopher Columbus (Morison, ed.), **Supp. I Part 2:** 494

Journals of Ralph Waldo Emerson, The (Emerson), **II:** 8, 17, 21

Journals of Susanna Moodie, The: Poems (Atwood), **Supp. XIII:** 33

"Journey, A" (Wharton), **Retro. Supp. I:** 364

"Journey, The" (Winters), **Supp. II Part 2:** 795

"Journey, The" (Wright), **Supp. III Part 2:** 605–606

"Journey, the Arrival and the Dream, The" (Gioia), **Supp. XV:** 120

"Journey, The: For Jane at Thirteen" (Kumin), **Supp. IV Part 2:** 442

Journey and Other Poems, The (Winters), **Supp. II Part 2:** 786, 794, 795, 796, 799, 800, 801

Journey Around My Room: The Autobiography of Louise Bogan—A Mosaic (Bogan), **Supp. III Part 1:** 47, 48, 52, 53

Journey Down, The (Bernstein), **IV:** 455

Journey Home, The (Abbey), **Supp. XIII:** 2, 12

"Journey into Speech, A" (Cliff), **Supp. XXII:** 69

Journeyman (Caldwell), **I:** 297, 302–304, 307, 309

Journeyman: Travels of a Writer (Findley), **Supp. XX: 50**

Journey of Tai-me, The (Momaday), **Supp. IV Part 2:** 485

"Journey of the Magi" (Eliot), **Retro. Supp. I:** 64

Journey to a War (Auden and Isherwood), **Supp. II Part 1:** 13; **Supp. XIV:** 156, 158, 162

Journey to Love (W. C. Williams), **IV:** 422; **Retro. Supp. I:** 429

Journey to My Father; Isaac Bashevis Singer (Zamir), **Retro. Supp. II:** 317

"Journey to Nine Miles" (Walker), **Supp. III Part 2:** 527

"Journey to the Interior" (W. J. Smith), **Supp. XIII:** 339, 340

Journey with Genius: Recollections and Reflections Concerning the D. H. Lawrences (Bynner), **Supp. XV:** 46

Jowett, Benjamin, **Supp. XIV:** 335

"Joy" (Moore), **Supp. X:** 174

"Joy" (Singer), **IV:** 9; **Retro. Supp. II:** 307

Joyce, Cynthia, **Supp. X:** 194, 195, 196

Joyce, James, **I:** 53, 105, 108, 130, 174, 256, 285, 377, 395, 475–476, 478, 480, 483, 576; **II:** 27, 42, 58, 73, 74, 198, 209, 264, 320, 569; **III:** 7, 16, 26–27, 45, 174, 181, 184, 261, 273, 277, 343, 396, 398, 465, 471, 474; **IV:** 32, 73, 85, 95, 103, 171, 182, 211, 286, 370, 412, 418, 419, 428, 434, 456; **Retro. Supp. I:** 59, 63, 75, 80, 89, 91, 108, 109, 127, 287, 290, 292, 334, 335, 420; **Retro. Supp. II:** 221, 326; **Supp. I Part 1:** 257, 262, 270; **Supp. I Part 2:** 437, 546, 613, 620; **Supp. II Part 1:** 136; **Supp. III Part 1:** 35, 36, 65, 225, 229; **Supp. III Part 2:** 611, 617, 618; **Supp. IV Part 1:** 40, 47, 80, 227, 300, 310; **Supp. IV Part 2:** 424, 677; **Supp. V:** 261, 331; **Supp. VIII:** 14, 40, 103; **Supp. IX:** 211, 229, 235, 308; **Supp. X:** 115, 137, 194, 324; **Supp. XI:** 66; **Supp. XII:** 139, 151, 165, 191, 289; **Supp. XIV:** 83; **Supp. XVI:** 41, 189, 282; **Supp. XVII:** 44; **Supp. XIX:** 151, 172; **Supp. XXI:** 7; **Supp. XXII:** 141, 143–144; **Supp. XXIII:** 162

Joy Comes in the Morning (J. Rosen), **Supp. XVII:** 50

Joy in the Morning (B. Smith), **Supp. XXIII:** 257, 258, **269–270**

Joy Luck Club, The (Tan), **Supp. X:** 289, 291, 293, 294, 296, 297, 298, 299

"Joy of Sales Resistance, The" (Berry), **Supp. X:** 36

J R (Gaddis), **Supp. IV Part 1:** 279, 280, 285–289, 291, 294; **Supp. IV Part 2:** 484; **Supp. XXI:** 226

Juana Inés de la Cruz, Sor, **Supp. XXI:** 94, 104

Juan de la Cruz (John of the Cross), **Supp. XXI:** 99, 104

"Juan's Song" (Bogan), **Supp. III Part 1:** 50

Juba to Jive: A Dictionary of African-American Slang (Major), **Supp. XXII:** 172, 180

Jubilate Agno (Smart), **Supp. IV Part 2:** 626

Judah, Hettie, **Supp. XIII:** 246

Judah the Pious (Prose), **Supp. XVI:** 249, 250, 262

"Judas Maccabaeus" (Longfellow), **II:** 506; **Retro. Supp. II:** 165, 167

Judd, Sylvester, **II:** 290; **Supp. I Part 2:** 420

Judd Rankin's Daughter (Glaspell), **Supp. III Part 1:** 186–188

Jude the Obscure (Hardy), **Supp. I Part 1:** 217

Judevine (Budbill), **Supp. XIX:** 4, **8–9,** 12

Judevine: A Play in Three Acts/Two Acts (Budbill), **Supp. XIX: 12–13**

Judge, Jane, **Supp. XXII:** 191

"Judgement Day" (O'Connor), **III:** 349, 350; **Retro. Supp. II:** 236

Judgment Day (Farrell), **II:** 29, 31, 32, 34, 39

"Judgment of Paris, The" (Merwin), **Supp. III Part 1:** 350

Judgment of Paris, The (Vidal), **Supp. IV Part 2:** 680, 682

"Judgment of the Sage, The" (Crane), **I:** 420

Judith (Farrell), **II:** 46, 48

"Judith" (Garrett), **Supp. VII:** 109–110

"Juggernaut" (Bass), **Supp. XVI:** 16–17

"Jug of Sirup, A" (Bierce), **I:** 206

"Jugurtha" (Longfellow), **II:** 499

"Juice or Gravy" (P. Roth), **Retro. Supp. II:** 279

"Juke Box Love Song" (Hughes), **Retro. Supp. I:** 209

"Julia" (Hellman), **Supp. I Part 1:** 280, 293

Julia France and Her Times (Atherton), **Supp. XXIV:** 24, 27

"Julia Miller" (Masters), **Supp. I Part 2:** 461

Julian (Vidal), **Supp. IV Part 2:** 677, 684–685, 685, 689

Julian the Apostate, **Retro. Supp. I:** 247

"Julian Vreden" (Bowles), **Supp. IV Part 1:** 94

Julie and Romeo (Ray), **Supp. XII:** 308, 310

Julien, Isaac, **Supp. XI:** 19

Julie; ou, La nouvelle Héloïse (Rousseau), **Supp. XVI:** 184

Julier, Laura, **Supp. IV Part 1:** 211

Julip (Harrison), **Supp. VIII: 51**

Julius Caesar (Shakespeare), **I:** 284

July, Miranda, **Supp. XXIV: 199–211**

"July Midnight" (Lowell), **II:** 521

Jumel, Madame, **Supp. I Part 2:** 461

Jumping Out of Bed (R. Bly), **Supp. IV Part 1:** 71

"Jump-Up Day" (Kingsolver), **Supp. VII:** 203

"Junctions" (Lamott), **Supp. XX: 143**

"June 1940" (Kees), **Supp. XV:** 141

"June Light" (Wilbur), **Supp. III Part 2:** 545

June Moon (Lardner and Kaufman), **II:** 427

"June Recital" (Welty), **IV:** 272–273

Juneteenth (Ellison), **Retro. Supp. II:** 119, 124, **126–128**

"Juneteenth" (Ellison), **Retro. Supp. II:** 119, 126; **Supp. II Part 1:** 248

"June the Third" (Gander), **Supp. XV:** 340

June-Tree: New and Selected Poems, 1974–2000 (Balakian), **Supp. XXIII:** 19, **24–25,** 32

Jung, Carl, **I:** 58, 135, 241, 248, 252, 402; **III:** 400, 534, 543; **Supp. I Part 2:** 439; **Supp. IV Part 1:** 68, 69; **Supp. VIII:** 45; **Supp. X:** 193; **Supp. XV:** 214; **Supp. XX: 63, 117**

Junger, Ernst, **Supp. III Part 1:** 63

Jungle, The (Sinclair), **III:** 580; **Supp. V:** 281–284, 285, 289

Jungle Lovers (Theroux), **Supp. VIII:** 314, 315, 316, **317**

"Junior Addict" (Hughes), **Supp. I Part 1:** 343

"Juniper" (Francis), **Supp. IX:** 79

"Junk" (Wilbur), **Supp. III Part 2:** 556

Junker, Howard, **Supp. XV:** 116

Junkie: Confessions of an Unredeemed Drug Addict (Burroughs), **Supp. III Part 1:** 92, 94–96, 101

Junky (Burroughs), **Supp. XIV:** 143

Juno and the Paycock (O'Casey), **Supp. IV Part 1:** 361

"Jupiter Doke, Brigadier General" (Bierce), **I:** 204

Jupiter Laughs (A. Cronin), **Supp. XVII:** 59

Jurgen (Cabell), **III:** 394; **IV:** 286; **Retro. Supp. I:** 80; **Supp. I Part 2:** 718

Jury of Her Peers, A: American Women Writers from Anne Bradstreet to Annie Proulx (Showalter), **Supp. XX:** **274**

Jusserand, Jules, **II:** 338

Just above My Head (Baldwin), **Retro. Supp. II:** 14–15

"Just a Little One" (Parker), **Supp. IX:** 191

Just and the Unjust, The (Cozzens), **I:** 367–370, 372, 375, 377, 378, 379

Just an Ordinary Day (Jackson), **Supp. IX:** 120

Just Before Dark: Collected Nonfiction (Harrison), **Supp. VIII:** 41, 45, 46, 53

"Just Before the War with the Eskimos" (Salinger), **III:** 559

"Just Boys" (Farrell), **II:** 45

"Just for the Thrill: An Essay on the Difference Between Women and Men" (Carson), **Supp. XII:** **103–104**

"Justice" (Hughes), **Supp. I Part 1:** 331

"Justice, A" (Faulkner), **Retro. Supp. I:** 83

Justice, Donald, **Retro. Supp. I:** 313; **Supp. III Part 2:** 541; **Supp. V:** 180, 337, 338, 341; **Supp. VII:** **115–130**; **Supp. XI:** 141, 315; **Supp. XIII:** 76, 312; **Supp. XV:** 74, 93, 118, 119, 134; **Supp. XVII:** 110, 120, 246; **Supp. XX:** 199; **Supp. XXIV:** 165

Justice and Expediency (Whittier), **Supp. I Part 2:** 686

"Justice Denied in Massachusetts" (Millay), **III:** 140

Justice for Salcido (Endore), **Supp. XVII:** 63

Justice of Gold in the Damnation of Sinners, The (Edwards), **I:** 559

"Justice to Feminism" (Ozick), **Supp. V:** 272

"Just Introduced" (Taggard), **Supp. XXII:** 274

Just Kids (Smith), **Supp. XXII:** 94

"Just Like a Woman" (Dylan), **Supp. XV:** 350

"Just Like Job" (Angelou), **Supp. IV Part 1:** 15

"Just One of the Boys" (Swados), **Supp. XIX:** 259

Just Whistle: A Valentine (Wright), **Supp. XV:** **346–348**

Just Wild About Harry (H. Miller), **III:** 190

Juvenal, **II:** 8, 169, 552

K

"K, The" (Olson), **Supp. II Part 2:** 558, 563, 569

Kabir, **Supp. IV Part 1:** 74

"Kabnis" (Toomer), **Supp. III Part 2:** 481, 484; **Supp. IX:** 309, 310, **319–320**

Kachel, Elsie. *See* Stevens, Mrs. Wallace (Elsie Kachel)

"Kaddish" (Ginsberg), **Supp. II Part 1:** 319, 327

Kaddish and Other Poems, 1958–1960 (Ginsberg), **Supp. II Part 1:** 309, 319–320; **Supp. XIV:** 269

Kael, Pauline, **Supp. IX:** 253; **Supp. XV:** 147, 148

Kafka, Franz, **II:** 244, 565, 569; **III:** 51, 253, 418, 566, 572; **IV:** 2, 113, 218, 437–439, 442; **Retro. Supp. II:** 20, 221, 282; **Supp. I Part 1:** 197; **Supp. III Part 1:** 105; **Supp. III Part 2:** 413; **Supp. IV Part 1:** 379; **Supp. IV Part 2:** 623; **Supp. VIII:** 14, 15, 103; **Supp. XII:** 21, 37, 98, 168; **Supp. XIII:** 305; **Supp. XVI:** 17, 201, 206, 209; **Supp. XVII:** 244; **Supp. XX:** **18, 21, 85, 87**; **Supp. XXII:** 89, 90, 94; **Supp. XXIII:** 68

Kafka Americana (Lethem and Scholtz), **Supp. XVIII:** 144–145

Kaganoff, Penny, **Supp. XI:** 122

Kagan's Superfecta (A. Hoffman), **Supp. XVII:** 42

Kahane, Jack, **III:** 171, 178

Kahn, Otto, **I:** 385; **IV:** 123; **Retro. Supp. II:** 81, 84, 85; **Supp. XX:** 75

Kahn, R. T., **Supp. XI:** 216

"Kai, Today" (Snyder), **Supp. VIII:** 300

Kaiser, Georg, **I:** 479

Kaiser, Henry, **Supp. I Part 2:** 644

Kakutani, Michiko, **Supp. IV Part 1:** 196, 201, 205, 211, 212; **Supp. V:** 63; **Supp. VIII:** 81, 84, 86, 88, 141; **Supp. X:** 171, 301, 302, 310, 314; **Supp. XI:** 38, 179; **Supp. XII:** 165, 171, 172, 299; **Supp. XVI:** 71; **Supp. XVII:** 6; **Supp. XIX:** 142; **Supp. XX:** **92, 94**; **Supp. XXII:** 109

Kalem, T. E., **Supp. IV Part 2:** 585

Kalevala (Finnish epic), **II:** 503, 504; **Retro. Supp. II:** 155

Kalevala (Lönnrot), **Retro. Supp. II:** 159, 160

Kalfus, Ken, **Supp. XVII:** 50

Kalki: A Novel (Vidal), **Supp. IV Part 2:** 677, 682, 685, 691, 692

Kallan, Richard A., **Supp. XX:** **244**

Kallen, Horace, **I:** 229; **Supp. I Part 2:** 643; **Supp. XIV:** 195, 197, 198

Kallman, Chester, **II:** 586; **Supp. II Part 1:** 15, 17, 24, 26

"Kallundborg Church" (Whittier), **Supp. I Part 2:** 696

Kalstone, David, **Retro. Supp. II:** 40

Kamel, Rose, **Supp. XIII:** 306

Kamenev, Lev, **Supp. XXI:** 167

Kamera Obskura (Nabokov), **III:** 255

Kamhi, Michelle Moarder, **Supp. IV Part 2:** 529, 530

Kaminsky, Wally, **Supp. XVIII:** 72

Kamp, David, **Supp. XVIII:** 150

Kandy-Kolored Tangerine-Flake Streamline Baby, The (Wolfe), **Supp. III Part 2:** 569, 573–576, 580, 581

Kane, Daniel, **Supp. XXIV:** 37

Kane, Julie, **Supp. XVII:** 78

Kane, Lesley, **Supp. XIV:** 250

Kanellos, Nicolás, **Supp. VIII:** 82; **Supp. XIII:** 213

Kanin, Garson, **Supp. IV Part 2:** 574

"Kansas City Coyote" (Harjo), **Supp. XII:** 219, 222

"Kansas Emigrants, The" (Whittier), **Supp. I Part 2:** 687

Kant, Immanuel, **I:** 61, 277, 278; **II:** 10–11, 362, 480, 580–581, 582, 583; **III:** 300, 480, 481, 488, 612; **IV:** 90; **Supp. I Part 2:** 640; **Supp. IV Part 2:** 527; **Supp. XIV:** 198, 199; **Supp. XVI:** 184

Kanter, Hal, **IV:** 383

Kapital, Das (Marx), **III:** 580; **Supp. XXI:** 161, 162, 163

Kaplan, Abraham, **I:** 277

Kaplan, Justin, **I:** 247–248; **Retro. Supp. I:** 392

Kaplan, Mary Jo, **Supp. XIX:** 266

Kaplan, Steven, **Supp. V:** 238, 241, 243, 248

Karate Is a Thing of the Spirit (Crews), **Supp. XI:** **112–113**

Karbo, Karen, **Supp. X:** 259, 262

"Karintha" (Toomer), **Supp. IX:** 311

Karl, Frederick R., **Supp. IV Part 1:** 384; **Supp. XXI:** 234

"Karloff and the Rock" (Di Piero), **Supp. XIX:** 44

Karl Shapiro's America (film), **Supp. II Part 2:** 703

Karmi, T., **Supp. XV:** 78, 88

Karr, Mary, **Supp. XI:** **239–256**; **Supp. XIII:** 285; **Supp. XV:** 223; **Supp. XVI:** 63, 70, 77; **Supp. XVII:** 242

Karyotakis, Konstantine, **Supp. XXIII:** 125

Kasabian, Linda, **Supp. IV Part 1:** 206

Kasper, Catherine, **Supp. XVI:** 294–295

Kate Chopin (Toth), **Retro. Supp. II:** 71

Kate Chopin: A Critical Biography (Seyersted), **Retro. Supp. II:** 65; **Supp. I Part 1:** 225

Kate Chopin and Edith Wharton: An Annotated Bibliographical Guide to Secondary Sources (Springer), **Supp. I Part 1:** 225

Kate Chopin and Her Creole Stories (Rankin), **Retro. Supp. II:** 57; **Supp. I Part 1:** 200, 225

"Kate Chopin's *The Awakening* in the Perspective of Her Literary Career" (Arms), **Supp. I Part 1:** 225

Kate Vaiden (Price), **Supp. VI:** 264, 265

"Käthe Kollwitz" (Rukeyser), **Supp. VI:** 283, 284

Katherine and Jean (Rice), **Supp. VII:** 288

"Kathleen" (Whittier), **Supp. I Part 2:** 693

Kathleen and Frank: The Autobiography of a Family (Isherwood), **Supp. XIV:** 158, 171

Kathy Goes to Haiti (Acker), **Supp. XII:** 5

Katz, Alan, **Supp. XXII:** 177

Katz, Alex, **Supp. XV:** 185

Katz, Jonathan, **Supp. XII:** 179

Katz, Steve, **Supp. V:** 44

Katz, Steven T., **Supp. XVI:** 154

Katzenberg, Jffrey, **Supp. XXI:** 154

Kauffman, Carol, **Supp. XI:** 295

Kauffmann, Stanley, **III:** 452; **Supp. I Part 2:** 391; **Supp. XVI:** 74

Kaufman, Boris, **Supp. XVIII:** 251

Kaufman, Charlie, **Supp. XV:** 16

Kaufman, Ellen, **Supp. XXIII:** 132, 133

Kaufman, George S., **II:** 427, 435, 437; **III:** 62, 71–72, 394; **Retro. Supp. II:** 327; **Supp. IV Part 2:** 574; **Supp. IX:** 190; **Supp. XV:** 329

Kaufmann, James, **Supp. XI:** 39

Kaufmann, Walter, **Supp. XVII:** 137

Kauvar, Elaine M., **Supp. V:** 273

Kavanaugh (Longfellow), **I:** 458; **II:** 489, 491; **Retro. Supp. II:** 156; **Supp. I Part 2:** 420

Kaveney, Roz, **Supp. XI:** 39

Kawabata, Yasunari, **Supp. XV:** 186; **Supp. XXI:** 146

Kay Boyle: Artist and Activist (Spanier), **Supp. XXIV:** 64

Kay Boyle: Author of Herself (Mellen), **Supp. XXIV:** 64

Kay Boyle for the Twenty-First Century (Austenfeld, ed.), **Supp. XXIV:** 64

Kaye-Smith, Sheila, **Supp. XVIII:** 130–131

Kazan, Elia, **III:** 153, 163; **IV:** 383; **Supp. I Part 1:** 66, 295; **Supp. XVI:** 193; **Supp. XVIII:** 250–251, 252

Kazin, Alfred, **I:** 248, 417, 419, 517; **II:** 177, 459; **IV:** 236; **Retro. Supp. II:** 206, 243, 246, 286; **Supp. I Part 1:** 195, 196, 294, 295, 296; **Supp. I Part 2:** 536, 631, 647, 650, 678, 679, 719; **Supp. II Part 1:** 143; **Supp. IV Part 1:** 200, 382; **Supp. V:** 122; **Supp. VIII:** 93–111; **Supp. IX:** 3, 227; **Supp. XIII:** 98, 106; **Supp. XIV:** 11; **Supp. XV:** 142; **Supp. XXIII:** 2, 106; **Supp. XXIV:** 222

Keach, Stacey, **Supp. XI:** 309

Kean, Danuta, **Supp. XXI:** 80

Keane, Sarah, **Supp. I Part 1:** 100

Kearns, Cleo McNelly, **Retro. Supp. I:** 57

Kearns, George, **Retro. Supp. I:** 292

Keating, AnnLouise, **Supp. IV Part 1:** 330

Keaton, Buster, **I:** 31; **Supp. I Part 2:** 607; **Supp. IV Part 2:** 574

Keaton, Diane, **Supp. XV:** 5

Keats, John, **I:** 34, 103, 284, 314, 317–318, 385, 401, 448; **II:** 82, 88, 97, 214, 368, 512, 516, 530–531, 540, 593; **III:** 4, 10, 45, 122, 133–134, 179, 214, 237, 272, 275, 469, 485, 523; **IV:** 360, 405, 416; **Retro. Supp. I:** 91, 301, 313, 360, 395, 412; **Supp. I Part 1:** 82, 183, 266, 267, 312, 349, 362, 363, 365; **Supp. I Part 2:** 410, 422, 424, 539, 552, 675, 719, 720; **Supp. III Part 1:** 73; **Supp. IV Part 1:** 123, 168, 325; **Supp. IV Part 2:** 455; **Supp. VIII:** 41, 273; **Supp. IX:** 38, 39, 45; **Supp. XI:** 43, 320; **Supp. XII:** 9, 113, 255; **Supp. XIII:** 131, 281; **Supp. XIV:** 274; **Supp. XV:** 92; **Supp. XVII:** 76, 112; **Supp. XIX:** 33, 276; **Supp. XX:** 115, 116; **Supp. XXI:** 131; **Supp. XXIV:** 159

Keats, John (other), **Supp. IX:** 190, 195, 200

Keegan, Abigail, **Supp. XXIII:** 129, 130, 136

"Keela, the Outcast Indian Maiden" (Welty), **IV:** 263

Keeley, Mary Paxton, **Supp. XV:** 136

"Keen Scalpel on Racial Ills" (Bruell), **Supp. VIII:** 126

Keep, The (Egan), **Supp. XIX:** 49, **56–61**

"Keep A-Inchin' Along" (Van Vechten), **Supp. III Part 2:** 744

Keeping (Goldbarth), **Supp. XII:** 179–180, 180

"Keeping Informed in D.C." (Nemerov), **III:** 287

Keeping Slug Woman Alive: A Holistic Approach to American Indian Texts (Sarris), **Supp. IV Part 1:** 329

'"Keeping Their World Large' " (Moore), **III:** 201–202

Keeping the Night (Everwine), **Supp. XV:** 75, **81–85,** 86

"Keeping Things Whole" (Strand), **Supp. IV Part 2:** 624

Keep It Simple: A Defense of the Earth (Nichols), **Supp. XIII:** 268

"Keep the Saving Habit" (L. I. Wilder), **Supp. XXII:** 290

"Keep Your Pity" (Boyle), **Supp. XXIV:** 58, 59

Kees, Weldon, **Supp. X:** 118; **Supp. XII:** 198; **Supp. XV:** 113, 114, 115, **133–149**

Keillor, Garrison, **Supp. XII:** 343; **Supp. XIII:** 274; **Supp. XVI:** **165–179;** **Supp. XXI:** 53, 62; **Supp. XXII:** 83; **Supp. XXIII:** 57, 58, 138

Keillor, Gary Edward. *See* Keiller, Garrison

Keith, Brian, **Supp. IV Part 2:** 474

Keith, Minor C., **I:** 483

Kelleghan, Fiona, **Supp. XVIII:** 136, 139, 140

Keller, A. G., **III:** 108

Keller, Christopher J., **Supp. XVIII:** 192, 195

Keller, Helen, **I:** 254, 258; **Supp. XXIII:** 161

Keller, Lynn, **Supp. IV Part 2:** 423; **Supp. V:** 78, 80

Kelley, David, **Supp. IV Part 2:** 528, 529

Kelley, Florence, **Supp. I Part 1:** 5, 7

Kelley, Mary, **Supp. XVIII:** 257, 260

Kelley, Robin, **Supp. XVIII:** 231

Kellogg, Reverend Edwin H., **III:** 200

Kellogg, Paul U., **Supp. I Part 1:** 5, 7, 12

Kelly, **II:** 464

Kelly, Brigit Pegeen, **Supp. XVII: 123–134; Supp. XXIII:** 54

Kelly, Emmett, **Supp. XI:** 99, 106

Kelly, Gene, **Supp. XXI:** 148

Kelly, James Patrick, **Supp. XVIII:** 145; **Supp. XIX:** 231

Kelly, Walt, **Supp. XI:** 105

Kelly, William, **Supp. XV:** 75, 88

Kelsey, Penelope Myrtle, **Supp. XXIII:** 143, 153–164

Kelsh, Nick, **Supp. XVII:** 167, 179

Kemble, Fanny, **Retro. Supp. I:** 228

Kemble, Gouverneur, **II:** 298

Kemble, Peter, **II:** 298

Kempton, Murray, **Supp. VIII:** 104

Kempton-Wace Letters, The (London and Strunsky), **II:** 465

Kennan, George F., **Supp. VIII:** 241

Kennedy, Albert J., **Supp. I Part 1:** 19

Kennedy, Arthur, **III:** 153

Kennedy, Burt, **Supp. IV Part 1:** 236

Kennedy, Jeffery, **Supp. XXI:** 6

Kennedy, J. Gerald, **Retro. Supp. II:** 271

Kennedy, John F., **I:** 136, 170; **II:** 49, 152–153; **III:** 38, 41, 42, 234, 411, 415, 581; **IV:** 229; **Supp. I Part 1:** 291; **Supp. I Part 2:** 496; **Supp. VIII:** 98, 104, 203; **Supp. XII:** 132

Kennedy, Mrs. John F., **I:** 136

Kennedy, John Pendleton, **II:** 313; **Supp. XXII:** 193

Kennedy, Robert, **Supp. V:** 291

Kennedy, Robert F., **I:** 294; **Supp. I Part 1:** 52; **Supp. XI:** 343

Kennedy, Sarah, **Supp. XVIII:** 293, 299, 301

Kennedy, William, **Supp. VII: 131–157; Supp. XVII:** 135; **Supp. XIX:** 141; **Supp. XX: 90; Supp. XXIV:** 281, 282, 283

Kennedy, X. J., **Supp. V:** 178, 182; **Supp. XV:** 113, **151–173**

Kenner, Hugh, **III:** 475, 478; **IV:** 412; **Supp. I Part 1:** 255; **Supp. IV Part 2:** 474; **Supp. XV:** 147; **Supp. XXI:** 235

Kenneth Koch, a Tragedy (O'Hara and Rivers), **Supp. XXIII:** 217

"Kenneth Koch's 'Serious Moment' " (Spurr), **Supp. XV:** 183

Kenneth Millar/Ross Macdonald: A Checklist (Bruccoli), **Supp. IV Part 2:** 464, 469, 471

Kenney, Michael, **Supp. XIX:** 51, 52–53

Kenney, Susan, **Supp. XVIII:** 288, 289

Kenny, Maurice, **Supp. IV Part 2:** 502; **Supp. XXIII: 143–159**

Kent, George, **Supp. IV Part 1:** 11

Kent, Rockwell, **Supp. XV:** 41; **Supp. XXII:** 281

Kenton, Edna, **Supp. XXI:** 6

Kenton, Maxwell. *See* Burnett, David; Hoffenberg, Mason; Southern, Terry

"Kent State, May 1970" (Haines), **Supp. XII:** 211

"Kentucky Derby Is Decadent and Depraved, The" (Thompson), **Supp.**

XXIV: 282, **287–288**

Kentucky Straight (Offutt), **Supp. XIX: 163–167,** 171, 172

Kenya, the Land of Conflict (Kenyatta), **Supp. XXI:** 166

Kenyatta, Jomo, **Supp. X:** 135; **Supp. XXI:** 166

Kenyon, Jane, **Supp. VII: 159–177; Supp. VIII:** 272

Keogh, Tom, **Supp. XVI:** 230

Kepler, Johannes, **III:** 484; **IV:** 18

Keplinger, David, **Supp. XIX:** 273

Keppel, Frederick P., **I:** 214

"Kéramos" (Longfellow), **II:** 494; **Retro. Supp. II:** 167, 169

Kéramos and Other Poems (Longfellow), **II:** 490

Kercheval, Jesse Lee, **Supp. XIX:** 51

Kerim, Ussin, **Supp. IX:** 152

Kermode, Frank, **IV:** 133; **Retro. Supp. I:** 301

Kern, Jerome, **II:** 427

Kerouac, Jack, **III:** 174; **Retro. Supp. I:** 102; **Supp. II Part 1:** 31, 307, 309, 318, 328; **Supp. III Part 1:** 91–94, 96, 100, **217–234; Supp. IV Part 1:** 90, 146; **Supp. V:** 336; **Supp. VIII:** 42, 138, 289, 305; **Supp. IX:** 246; **Supp. XII:** 118, 121, 122, 123, 126, 131, 132; **Supp. XIII:** 275, 284; **Supp. XIV:** 137, 138, 141, 142, 143–144; **Supp. XV:** 134, 221; **Supp. XVI:** 123; **Supp. XVII:** 135, 138; **Supp. XX:** 17; **Supp. XXIII:** 100, 213; **Supp. XXIV:** 34, 44

Kerr, Deborah, **Supp. XI:** 307

Kerr, Orpheus C. (pseudonym). *See* Newell, Henry

Kerr, Walter, **Supp. IV Part 2:** 575, 579

Kerridge, Richard, **Supp. XVI:** 26

Kesey, Ken, **III:** 558; **Supp. III Part 1:** 217; **Supp. V:** 220, 295; **Supp. X:** 24, 265; **Supp. XI:** 104; **Supp. XXIII:** 100

Kessel, John, **Supp. XVIII:** 145; **Supp. XIX:** 231

Kessler, Milton, **Supp. XIX:** 195

Kesten, Stephen, **Supp. XI:** 309

Ketchum, Liza, **Supp. XIX:** 266

Ketchup (Shanley), **Supp. XIV:** 315

Kevane, Bridget, **Supp. XI:** 185, 190

"Key, The" (Welty), **IV:** 262

"Keys" (Nye), **Supp. XIII:** 281

"Key to the Highway" (Halliday), **Supp. XIX:** 84

Key to Uncle Tom's Cabin, A (Stowe), **Supp. I Part 2:** 580

Key West (H. Crane), **Retro. Supp. II:** 84

"Key West" (H. Crane), **I:** 400

Key West: An Island Sheaf (Crane), **I:** 385, 399–402

"Khalil the Heretic" (Gibran), **Supp. XX: 124**

Khrushchev, Nikita, **I:** 136

Kiang Kang-hu, **Supp. XV:** 45, 47

Kick for a Bite, A (Cobbett), **Supp. XV:** 237

"Kicking the Candles Out" (Jarman), **Supp. XVII:** 113

Kid, The (Aiken), **I:** 61

Kid, The (Chaplin), **I:** 386

Kidder, Tracy, **Supp. III Part 1:** 302; **Supp. XVIII:** 106, 114

Kiddush Ha-Shem: An Epic of 1648 (Asch), **Supp. XXIII:** 3, 6, **10,** 11, 12, 16

Kidesh ha-Shem (Sanctification of the name) (Asch), **Supp. XXIII:** 6

Kidman, Nicole, **Supp. X:** 80

"Kidnaper" (Gallagher), **Supp. XXIV:** 168, 174

"Kidnapping in the Family, A" (Fante), **Supp. XI:** 164

"Kid's Guide to Divorce, The" (Moore), **Supp. X:** 167, 172

Kidwell, Clara Sue, **Supp. IV Part 1:** 333

Kielsky, Vera Emuma, **Supp. V:** 273

Kiely, Brendan, **Supp. XVII:** 75

Kieran, John, **II:** 417

Kierkegaard, Søren Aabye, **II:** 229; **III:** 292, 305, 309, 572; **IV:** 438, 491; **Retro. Supp. I:** 326; **Retro. Supp. II:** 222; **Supp. V:** 9; **Supp. VIII:** 7–8; **Supp. XX: 132**

Kiernan, Robert F., **Supp. IV Part 2:** 684

Kieseritsky, L., **III:** 252

Kilgo, Jim, **Supp. XVIII:** 192

"Kilim" (McClatchy), **Supp. XII:** 258

Kilina, Patricia (pseudonym). *See* Warren, Patricia Nell

"Killed at Resaca" (Bierce), **I:** 202

"Killed at the Ford" (Longfellow), **Retro. Supp. II:** 170–171

Killens, John Oliver, **Supp. IV Part 1:** 8, 369

"Killer in the Rain" (Chandler), **Supp. IV Part 1:** 122

"Killers, The" (Hemingway), **II:** 249; **Retro. Supp. I:** 188, 189

Killers, The: A Narrative of Real Life in Philadelphia (Lippard), **Supp. XXIII:** 178, 184

Killing Mister Watson (Matthiessen), **Supp. V:** 212, 214

"Killing of a State Cop, The" (Ortiz), **Supp. IV Part 2:** 499

Killing of Sister George, The (Marcus), **Supp. I Part 1:** 277

"Killings" (Dubus), **Supp. VII:** 85–86

"Killing the Ghost of Ripton" (Carruth), **Supp. XIX:** 1

"Killing the Plants" (Kenyon), **Supp. VII:** 167, 168

Kilmer, Joyce, **Supp. I Part 2:** 387; **Supp. XV:** 294

Kilpatrick, James K., **Supp. X:** 145

Kilvert, Francis, **Supp. VIII:** 172

Kim (Kipling), **Supp. X:** 230

Kim, Alfred, **Supp. XI:** 140

Kim, Sharon, **Supp. XVIII:** 267

Kimball, Frederic, **Supp. XXI:** 146

Kimball, J. Golden, **Supp. IV Part 2:** 602

Kimbrough, Mary Craig. *See* Sinclair, Mary Craig (Mary Craig Kimbrough)

Kimes, Maymie B., **Supp. IX:** 178

Kimes, William F., **Supp. IX:** 178

Kimmelman, Bert, **Supp. XXI:** 24

"Kin" (Welty), **IV:** 277; **Retro. Supp. I:** 353

Kinard, Agnes Dodds, **Supp. XIV:** 122, 123, 127

Kincaid, Jamaica, **Supp. VII: 179–196**

Kincaid, James, **Supp. XVIII:** 62, 63

"Kindness" (Dunn), **Supp. XI:** 149, 150

"Kindness" (Nye), **Supp. XIII:** 285

"Kindness" (Plath), **Retro. Supp. II:** 256

Kind of Light that Shines on Texas, The (McKnight), **Supp. XX: 151–152**

"Kind of Light that Shines on Texas, The" (McKnight), **Supp. XX: 151**

Kind of Order, A Kind of Folly, A: Essays and Conversations (Kunitz), **Supp. III Part 1:** 262, 268

Kindred (O. Butler), **Supp. XIII: 59–60,** 69

"Kind Sir: These Woods" (Sexton), **Supp. II Part 2:** 673

Kinds of Love (Sarton), **Supp. VIII: 253– 254,** 256

Kinfolk (Buck), **Supp. II Part 1:** 126

King, Alexander, **IV:** 287

King, Carole, **Supp. XII:** 308

King, Clarence, **I:** 1

King, Ernest, **Supp. I Part 2:** 491

King, Fisher, **II:** 425

King, Francis, **Supp. XIV:** 155, 156, 166, 169

King, Grace, **Retro. Supp. II:** 136

King, Martin Luther, Jr., **Retro. Supp. II:** 12, 13; **Supp. XVIII:** 24; **Supp. XX: 281**

King, Michael, **Supp. XII:** 182

King, Queen, Knave (Nabokov), **III:** 251; **Retro. Supp. I:** 270

King, Starr, **Supp. II Part 1:** 341, 342

King, Stephen, **Supp. IV Part 1:** 102, 104; **Supp. IV Part 2:** 467; **Supp. V: 137–155; Supp. IX:** 114; **Supp. XIII:** 53; **Supp. XXIII:** 290

King, Tabitha (Mrs. Stephen King), **Supp. V:** 137

King, The (Barthelme), **Supp. IV Part 1:** 47, 52

"King, The" (Gibran), **Supp. XX: 123– 124**

King Coffin (Aiken), **I:** 53–54, 57

"King David" (Benét), **Supp. XI:** 44

"King David" (Reznikoff), **Supp. XIV:** 283

Kingdom and the Power, The (Talese), **Supp. XVII:** 202, 203, 204, 210

Kingdom by the Sea, The: A Journey around Great Britain (Theroux), **Supp. VIII:** 323

"Kingdom County Come" (Mosher), **Supp. XXII:** 211–212

Kingdom of Earth (T. Williams), **IV:** 382, 386, 387, 388, 391, 393, 398

"Kingdom of Earth, The" (T. Williams), **IV:** 384

Kingdom of Fear (Thompson), **Supp. XXIV:** 283

Kingfisher, The (Clampitt), **Supp. IX:** 38

"Kingfishers, The" (Olson), **Supp. II Part 2:** 557, 558–563, 582

King Jasper (Robinson), **III:** 523

King Kong (film), **Supp. IV Part 1:** 104; **Supp. XVII:** 58

King Lear (Shakespeare), **I:** 538; **II:** 540, 551; **Retro. Supp. I:** 248; **Supp. IV Part 1:** 31, 36; **Supp. IX:** 14; **Supp. XI:** 172; **Supp. XV:** 349

King Leopold's Soliloquy (Twain), **IV:** 208

King My Father's Wreck, The (Simpson), **Supp. IX:** 266, 267, 270, 275, 276

King of Babylon Shall Not Come Against You, The (Garrett), **Supp. VII:** 110–111; **Supp. X:** 3

"King of Beasts" (P. N. Warren), **Supp. XX:** 272

"King of Folly Island, The" (Jewett), **II:** 394; **Retro. Supp. II:** 132, 133

King of Kings (film), **Supp. IV Part 2:** 520

King of Paris (Endore), **Supp. XVII:** 64

"King of the Bingo Game" (Ellison), **Retro. Supp. II:** 117, 125; **Supp. II Part 1:** 235, 238, 240–241

"King of the Cats, The" (Benét), **Supp. XI:** 49–50

"King of the Clock Tower" (Yeats), **III:** 473

"King of the Desert, The" (O'Hara), **III:** 369

King of the Fields, The (Singer), **Retro. Supp. II:** 317

King of the Jews (Epstein), **Supp. XII:** 161, **166–170,** 172

King of the Mountain (Garrett), **Supp. VII:** 96, 97

"King of the River" (Kunitz), **Supp. III Part 1:** 263, 267–268

"King of the Sea" (Marquand), **III:** 60

"King over the Water" (Blackmur), **Supp. II Part 1:** 107

"King Pandar" (Blackmur), **Supp. II Part 1:** 92, 102

"King Pest" (Poe), **Retro. Supp. II:** 273

Kingsblood Royal (Lewis), **II:** 456

Kingsbury, John, **Supp. I Part 1:** 8

"King's Daughters, Home for Unwed Mothers, 1948" (Stanford), **Supp. XV:** 345

King's Henchman, The (Millay), **III:** 138–139

Kingsley, Sidney, **Supp. I Part 1:** 277, 281

King's Mare, The (Canolle; Loos, trans.), **Supp. XVI:** 194

"King's Missive, The" (Whittier), **Supp. I Part 2:** 694

Kingsolver, Barbara, **Supp. VII:** 197–214; **Supp. XIII:** 16; **Supp. XVIII:** 189

King's Stilts, The (Geisel), **Supp. XVI:** 100, 104

Kingston, Earll, **Supp. V:** 160

Kingston, Maxine Hong, **Supp. IV Part 1:** 1, 12; **Supp. V:** **157–175,** 250; **Supp. X:** 291–292; **Supp. XI:** 18, 245; **Supp. XV:** 220, 223

"King Volmer and Elsie" (Whittier), **Supp. I Part 2:** 696

Kinkaid, Jamaica, **Supp. XXII:** 65

Kinmont, Alexander, **Supp. I Part 2:** 588–589

Kinnaird, John, **Retro. Supp. I:** 399

Kinnell, Galway, **Supp. III Part 1: 235–256; Supp. III Part 2:** 541; **Supp. IV Part 2:** 623; **Supp. V:** 332; **Supp. VIII:** 39; **Supp. XI:** 139; **Supp. XII:** 241; **Supp. XV:** 212; **Supp. XVI:** 53; **Supp. XXII:** 83

Kinsella, Thomas, **Supp. XX: 195–196, 197, 207**

Kinsey, Alfred, **IV:** 230; **Supp. XIV:** 140

Kinzie, Mary, **Supp. XII:** 181; **Supp. XXIII:** 124

"Kipling" (Trilling), **Supp. III Part 2:** 495

Kipling, Rudyard, **I:** 421, 587–588; **II:** 271, 338, 404, 439; **III:** 55, 328, 508, 511, 521, 524, 579; **IV:** 429; **Supp. IV Part 2:** 603; **Supp. X:** 255; **Supp. XX:** 23

Kirby, David, **Supp. XIII:** 89; **Supp. XIX:** 81

Kirkland, Caroline, **Supp. XVIII:** 258

Kirkland, David, **Supp. XVI:** 186

Kirkland, Jack, **I:** 297

Kirkland, John, **Supp. XXIV:** 70

Kirkpatrick, Jeane, **Supp. VIII:** 241

Kirkus, Virginia, **Supp. XV:** 198

Kirkwood, Cynthia A., **Supp. XI:** 177, 178, 179

Kirp, David L., **Supp. XI:** 129

Kirsch, Adam, **Supp. XV:** 251, 260, 264, 266, 341, 347, 350–351

Kirstein, Lincoln, **Supp. II Part 1:** 90, 97; **Supp. IV Part 1:** 82, 83; **Supp. XXII:** 281

Kishef-makherin fun Kastilye, Di (The witch of Castle) (Asch), **Supp. XXIII:** 6

"Kiss, The" (Di Piero), **Supp. XIX:** 45, 47

Kiss, The (Harrison), **Supp. X:** 191

"Kiss, The" (Sexton), **Supp. II Part 2:** 687

"Kiss Away" (C. Baxter), **Supp. XVII:** 20

Kissel, Howard, **Supp. IV Part 2:** 580

Kiss Hollywood Good-by (Loos), **Supp. XVI:** 190, 195

Kissinger, Henry, **Supp. IV Part 1:** 388; **Supp. XII:** 9, 14

Kiss of the Spider Woman, the Musical (McNally), **Supp. XIII:** 207, **Supp. XIII:** 208

Kiss Tomorrow Good-bye (McCoy), **Supp. XIII:** 170, **172–173,** 174

"Kit and Caboodle" (Komunyakaa), **Supp. XIII:** 115

Kit Brandon: A Portrait (Anderson), **I:** 111

Kitchen, Judith, **Supp. IV Part 1:** 242, 245, 252; **Supp. IX:** 163; **Supp. XI:** 312, 313, 315, 317, 319, 320, 326, 329; **Supp. XV:** 215, 219

"Kitchenette" (Brooks), **Retro. Supp. I:** 208

Kitchen God's Wife, The (Tan), **Supp. X:** 289, 292, 293, 294–295, 296–297, 298–299

"Kitchen Terrarium: 1983" (McCarriston), **Supp. XIV:** 270

Kit O'Brien (Masters), **Supp. I Part 2:** 471

Kittel, Frederick August. *See* Wilson, August

Kittredge, Charmian. *See* London, Mrs. Jack (Charmian Kittredge)

Kittredge, William, **Supp. VIII:** 39; **Supp. XI:** 316; **Supp. XII:** 209; **Supp. XIII:** 16

"Kitty Hawk" (Frost), **II:** 164; **Retro. Supp. I:** 124, 141

Kizer, Carolyn, **Supp. XVII:** 71, 72, 73, 74

Klaidman, Stephen, **Supp. XIX:** 269

Klail City (Hinojosa), **Supp. XIX:** 97, **101–103**

Klail City Death Trip (Hinojosa). *See Ask a Policeman* (Hinojosa); *Becky and Her Friends* (Hinojosa); *Dear Rafe* (Hinojosa); *Fair Gentlemen of Belken County* (Hinojosa); *Klail City* (Hinojosa); *Korean Love Songs from Klail City Death Trip* (Hinojosa); *Partners in Crime: A Rafe Buenrostro Mystery* (Hinojosa); *Rites and Witnesses: A Comedy* (Hinojosa); *Useless Servants, The* (Hinojosa); *Valley, The* (Hinojosa)

Klein, Joe, **Supp. XII:** 67–68

Klein, Marcus, **Supp. I Part 2:** 432; **Supp. XI:** 233

Kleist, Heinrich von, **Supp. IV Part 1:** 224

Kline, Franz, **Supp. XII:** 198; **Supp. XXIII:** 210, 211, 217

Kline, George, **Supp. VIII:** 22, 28

Klinghoffer, David, **Supp. XVI:** 74

Klinkowitz, Jerome, **Supp. IV Part 1:** 40; **Supp. X:** 263; **Supp. XI:** 347; **Supp. XXI:** 233

Klise, James, **Supp. XXII:** 53

Kloefkorn, Bill, **Supp. XIX:** 119

Knapp, Adeline, **Supp. XI:** 200

Knapp, Friedrich, **III:** 100

Knapp, Samuel, **I:** 336

Knapp, Samuel Lorenzo, **Supp. XV:** 246

"Kneeling Down to Look into a Culvert" (R. Bly), **Supp. XXI:** 88

Kneel to the Rising Sun (Caldwell), **I:** 304, 309

"Knees/Dura-Europos" (Goldbarth), **Supp. XII:** 185

"Knife" (Simic), **Supp. VIII:** 275

Knight, Arthur, **Supp. XIV:** 144

Knight, Etheridge, **Supp. XI:** 239; **Supp. XXIII:** 174

Knight, Lania, **Supp. XXIII:** 273, 274, 275, 276, 279, 280

"Knight in Disguise, The" (Lindsay), **Supp. I Part 2:** 390

Knightly Quest, The (T. Williams), **IV:** 383

Knight's Gambit (Faulkner), **II:** 72

Knish, Anne. *See* Ficke, Arthur Davison

"Knit One, Purl Two" (K. Snodgrass), **Supp. XVI:** 42

"Knock" (Dickey), **Supp. IV Part 1:** 182

Knocked Out Loaded (album, Dylan), **Supp. XVIII:** 28

"Knocking Around" (Ashbery), **Supp. III Part 1:** 22

"Knocking on Heaven's Door" (Lamott), **Supp. XX: 140–141**

"Knocking on Three, Winston" (Epstein), **Supp. XIV:** 109

Knock on Any Door (film, Ray), **Supp. XVII:** 150

Knock on Any Door (W. Motley), **Supp. XVII: 150–155,** 159, 160; 158

Knockout Artist, The (Crews), **Supp. XI: 113–114**

Knoll, Robert E., **Supp. XV:** 118

Knopf, Alfred A., **III:** 99, 105, 106, 107; **Retro. Supp. I:** 13, 19, 317; **Supp. I Part 1:** 324, 325, 327; **Supp. IV Part 1:** 125, 354; **Supp. XIII:** 172

Knopf, Blanche, **Supp. I Part 1:** 324, 325, 327, 328, 332, 341; **Supp. IV Part 1:** 128, 346, 348; **Supp. XIII:** 169

"Knot, The" (Rich), **Supp. I Part 2:** 555

Knotts, Kristina, **Supp. XIII:** 238

"Knowing, The" (Olds), **Supp. X:** 215

"Knowledge Forwards and Backwards" (Stern), **Supp. IX:** 296

"Knowledge of Plates" (Bronk), **Supp. XXI:** 33

Knowles, John, **Supp. IV Part 2:** 679; **Supp. XII: 235–250; Supp. XX: 84**

Known World, The (E. P. Jones), **Supp. XXII:** 139, 140, 142, **146–150,** 150

Knox, Bernard, **Supp. XXIV:** 153

Knox, Frank, **Supp. I Part 2:** 488, 489

Knox, Israel, **Supp. X:** 70

Knox, Vicesimus, **II:** 8

Knoxville: Summer of 1915 (Agee), **I:** 42–46

Knudson, R. Rozanne, **Supp. IV Part 2:** 648

Kober, Arthur, **Supp. I Part 1:** 292

Koch, Frederick, **IV:** 453

Koch, John, **Supp. VIII:** 88

Koch, Kenneth, **Supp. XV: 175–192; Supp. XIX:** 81; **Supp. XXIII:** 124, 207, 209, 210, 211, 215, 217, 220; **Supp. XXIV:** 33, 36, 42, 44

Koch, Vivienne, **III:** 194; **IV:** 136, 140; **Retro. Supp. I:** 428, 430

"Kochinnenako in Academe: Three Approaches to Interpreting a Keres Indian Tale" (Gunn Allen), **Supp. IV Part 1:** 329

"Kodachromes of the Island" (Hayden), **Supp. II Part 1:** 367, 380

Koestler, Arthur, **I:** 258; **Supp. I Part 2:** 671; **Supp. XXIII:** 1

Kokkinen, Eila, **Supp. XIV:** 146, 148

"Kola Street"(Asch), **Supp. XXIII:** 7

Kolba, Ellen D., **Supp. XVIII:** 257

Kolbenheyer, Dr. Frederick, **Supp. I Part 1:** 207

Kolodny, Annette, **Supp. X:** 97, 103, 229

Komisarjevsky, W. P., **Supp. XXIII:** 5

"Komodo" (C. Frost), **Supp. XV:** 95

Komunyakaa, Yusef, **Supp. XIII: 111– 136; Supp. XXI:** 129, 139; **Supp. XXIII:** 254

Konigsberg, Allan Stewart. *See* Allen, Woody

Kon-Tiki (Heyerdahl), **II:** 477

Koopman, Harry Lyman, **Retro. Supp. I:** 40

Ko; or, A Season on Earth (Koch), **Supp. XV:** 175, 180, 181, 183, 186

Kooser, Ted, **Supp. XV:** 113, 115; **Supp. XIX: 115–130; Supp. XXI:** 243

Kootz, Samuel, **Supp. XV:** 144

Kora and Ka (Doolittle), **Supp. I Part 1:** 270

Kora in Hell (W. C. Williams), **Retro. Supp. I:** 416, **417–418,** 419, 430, 431; **Supp. XXI:** 232

Korb, Rena, **Supp. XI:** 2

Korczak, Janosz, **Supp. X:** 70

Korean Love Songs from Klail City Death Trip (Hinojosa), **Supp. XIX:** 98, **103– 104**

Kornblatt, Joyce Reiser, **Supp. XV:** 62

Kornfield, Jack, **Supp. XX: 142; Supp. XXIII:** 138

Korrektur (Bernhard), **Supp. XX: 91**

Kort, Amy, **Supp. XIII:** 148

Korwin, Yala, **Supp. XXI:** 99

Kosinski, Jerzy, **Supp. VII: 215–228; Supp. XII:** 21

"Kostas Tympakianakis" (Merrill), **Supp. III Part 1:** 326

Koteliansky, S. S., **Supp. VIII:** 251, 265

Kouidis, Virginia M., **Supp. XXII:** 161, 162, 166, 167, 169

Kovic, Ron, **Supp. XIX:** 17; **Supp. XXII:** 104

Kowloon Tong (Theroux), **Supp. VIII:** 325

Kozlenko, William, **IV:** 378, 381

Krabbenhoft, Ken, **Supp. XVII:** 112

Kraft, James, **Supp. XV:** 40, 41, 42, 43, 52

Krakauer, Jon, **Supp. XVII:** 210; **Supp. XVIII: 105–118**

Kramer, Dale, **Supp. I Part 2:** 669

Kramer, Glenn Philip, **Supp. XXIII:** 125

Kramer, Hilton, **III:** 537; **Supp. I Part 1:** 295, 296; **Supp. VIII:** 239; **Supp. XV:** 113; **Supp. XIX:** 269

Kramer, Lawrence, **Supp. IV Part 1:** 61, 65, 66; **Supp. IX:** 291

Kramer, Peter D., **Supp. XVI:** 229

Kramer, Stanley, **II:** 421, 587

Krapp's Last Tape (Beckett), **I:** 71; **III:** 387; **Retro. Supp. I:** 206

Krassner, Paul, **Supp. IV Part 1:** 385; **Supp. XI:** 293

Kraus, Karl, **Supp. XX: 84**

Krauth, Leland, **Supp. XVIII:** 58

Kreisler, Harry, **Supp. XVI:** 155

Kreitman, Esther, **IV:** 2

"Kremlin of Smoke" (Schnackenberg), **Supp. XV:** 257–258

Kreymborg, Alfred, **II:** 530; **III:** 465; **IV:** 76; **Retro. Supp. I:** 417; **Supp. XV:** 301, 306; **Supp. XXII:** 161–162

Kriegel, Leonard, **Supp. XXIV: 213–228**

Krim, Seymour, **Supp. XV:** 338; **Supp. XVI:** 217; **Supp. XVIII:** 285

Krisak, Len, **Supp. XXI:** 99, 104

Kristeva, Julia, **Supp. XII:** 6

Kristofferson, Kris, **Supp. XIII:** 119

Kristol, Irving, **Supp. VIII:** 93, 244; **Supp. XIII:** 98

Krivak, Andrew, **Supp. XVII:** 242

Kroll, Jack, **Supp. IV Part 2:** 590; **Supp. XXIII:** 103

Kroll, Judith, **Supp. I Part 2:** 541–543, 544, 546

Kroll Ring, Frances. *See* Ring, Frances Kroll

Krondorfer, Björn, **Supp. XVI:** 160

Kronenberger, Louis, **Supp. XXII:** 191, 192

Krook, Dorothea, **Retro. Supp. II:** 243

Kropotkin, Peter, **I:** 493; **Supp. I Part 1:** 5; **Supp. IV Part 2:** 521

Kruif, Paul de, **II:** 446

Krupat, Arnold, **Supp. IV Part 2:** 500

Krupnick, Mark, **Supp. XVI:** 153

Krutch, Joseph Wood, **II:** 459; **III:** 425; **IV:** 70, 175

Krutikov, Mikhail, **Supp. XXIII:** 11

Kublai Khan, **III:** 395

"Kubla Khan" (Coleridge), **Supp. XIII:** 131, 283

Kubrick, Stanley, **Supp. IV Part 1:** 392; **Supp. XI:** 293,**Supp. XI:** 301, 302– 303

"Kubuku Rides (This Is It) " (L. Brown), **Supp. XXI:** 39, 42–43

Kuehl, John, **Supp. IV Part 1:** 279, 284, 285, 287

Kuehl, Linda, **Supp. IV Part 1:** 199

"Kugelmass Episode, The" (Allen), **Supp. XV:** 15, 16

Kukachin, Princess, **III:** 395

"Ku Klux" (Hughes), **Retro. Supp. I:** 205

Kulshrestha, Chirantan, **Retro. Supp. II:** 21

Kumin, Maxine, **Supp. IV Part 2: 439– 457; Supp. XIII:** 294; **Supp. XVII:** 71, 75–76; **Supp. XX: 164**

Kundera, Milan, **Supp. VIII:** 241

Kunerth, Jeff, **Supp. XXI:** 47

Kunitz, Stanley, **I:** 179, 180, 181, 182, 521; **II:** 545; **Supp. III Part 1: 257– 270; Supp. V:** 79; **Supp. XI:** 259; **Supp. XIII:** 341

Kuo, Helena, **Supp. X:** 291

Kuropatkin, General Aleksei Nikolaevich, **III:** 247–248

Kurth, Peter, **Supp. XVIII:** 145

Kurzy of the Sea (Barnes), **Supp. III Part 1:** 34

Kushner, Tony, **Supp. IX: 131–149; Supp. XX: 177; Supp. XXI:** 145; **Supp. XXIV:** 263

Kussy, Bella, **IV:** 468

Kutnik, Jerzy, **Supp. XXII:** 177

Kuttner, Henry, **Supp. IV Part 1:** 102

Kuzma, Greg, **Supp. XV:** 118

Kyger, Joanne, **Supp. XXIV:** 37

L

LaBastille, Anne, **Supp. X: 95–110**

"Labor's Cultural Degradation" (Swados), **Supp. XIX:** 264–265

"Labours of Hercules, The" (Moore), **III:** 201

La Bruyère, Jean de, **I:** 58
La Bufera e Altro (Montale), **Supp. V:** 337
LaBute, Neil, **Supp. XXI:** 147
Labyrinth of Love (Untermeyer), **Supp. XV:** 312
Labyrinth of Solitude, The (Paz), **Supp. XIII:** 223
Lacan, Jacques, **Supp. IV Part 1:** 45; **Supp. VIII:** 5; **Supp. XII:** 98
La Casa en Mango Street (Cisneros), **Supp. VII:** 58–59
Lachaise, Gaston, **I:** 434
"Lackawanna" (Merwin), **Supp. III Part 1:** 350
Lackawanna Elegy (Goll; Kinnell, trans.), **Supp. III Part 1:** 235, 243–244
Laclède, Pierre, **Supp. I Part 1:** 205
"Lacquer Prints" (Lowell), **II:** 524–525
Lacy, Ed, **Supp. XV:** 193–210
Ladder, The (Rasmussen; Nelson, trans.), **Supp. XVIII:** 180–181
Ladder of Years (Tyler), **Supp. IV Part 2:** 657, 671–672
Ladders to Fire (Nin), **Supp. X:** 185
Laddie (Stratton-Porter), **Supp. XX: 211, 213**
"Laddie, the Princess and the Pie" (Stratton-Porter), **Supp. XX: 216**
"Ladies" (Coleman), **Supp. XI:** 93
Ladies Almanack (Barnes), **Supp. III Part 1:** 37–39, 42; **Supp. XXII:** 167
Ladies Auxiliary, The (Mirvis), **Supp. XX: 177, 179–185**
"Ladies in Spring" (Welty), **IV:** 276–277; **Retro. Supp. I:** 353
Lady, The (Richter), **Supp. XVIII: 211–212,** 220
Lady Audley's Secret (Braddon), **Supp. I Part 1:** 35, 36
"Lady Barberina" (James), **Retro. Supp. I:** 227
"Lady Bates" (Jarrell), **II:** 380–381
Lady Chatterley's Lover (Lawrence), **III:** 170; **IV:** 434; **Supp. XVI:** 267
Ladye Annabel (Lippard), **Supp. XXIII:** 178
Lady from Louisiana (film, Vorhaus), **Supp. XVII:** 59
"Lady from Redhorse, A" (Bierce), **I:** 203
Lady in Kicking Horse Reservoir, The (Hugo), **Supp. VI:** 134, **138–139**
Lady in the Lake, The (Chandler), **Supp. IV Part 1:** 127, 129–130
"Lady in the Lake, The" (Chandler), **Supp. IV Part 1:** 129
Lady in the Lake, The (film), **Supp. IV Part 1:** 130
"Lady in the Pink Mustang, The" (Erdrich), **Supp. IV Part 1:** 270
"Lady Is Civilized, The" (Taylor), **Supp. V:** 315
Lady Is Cold, The (White), **Supp. I Part 2:** 653
Lady Killer (Holding), **Supp. XXII:** 126, **127,** 130
"Lady Lazarus" (Plath), **Retro. Supp. II:** 250, 251, 255; **Supp. I Part 2:** 529, 535, 542, 545
Lady of Aroostook, The (Howells), **II:** 280

"Lady of Bayou St. John, A" (Chopin), **Retro. Supp. II:** 58
"Lady of the Lake, The" (Malamud), **Supp. I Part 2:** 437
Lady Oracle (Atwood), **Supp. XIII:** 21, **23–24**
"Lady Poverty" (Notley), **Supp. XXII:** 234–235
Lady Sings the Blues (film), **Supp. I Part 1:** 67
"Lady's Maid's Bell, The" (Wharton), **IV:** 316
"Lady Wentworth" (Longfellow), **II:** 505
"Lady with a Lamp" (Parker), **Supp. IX:** 193
"Lady with the Heron, The" (Merwin), **Supp. III Part 1:** 343
"Lady with the Pet Dog, The" (Chekov), **Supp. XXII:** 60
"Lady with the Pet Tribble, The" (Brockmeier), **Supp. XXII:** 60
La Farge, John, **I:** 1, 2, 20; **II:** 322, 338; **Retro. Supp. I:** 217
La Farge, Oliver, **Supp. IV Part 2:** 503
Lafayette, Marquis de, **I:** 344, 345; **II:** 405–406; **Supp. I Part 2:** 510, 511, 683
"La Figlia che Piange" (Eliot), **Retro. Supp. I:** 63
La Follette, Robert, **I:** 483, 485, 492; **III:** 580
La Fontaine, Jean de, **II:** 154; **III:** 194; **IV:** 80
Laforgue, Jules, **I:** 386, 569, 570, 572–573, 575, 576; **II:** 528; **III:** 8, 11, 466; **IV:** 37, 79, 80, 122; **Retro. Supp. I:** 55, 56; **Supp. XIII:** 332, 335, 346; **Supp. XV:** 165
La Gallienne, Eva, **Supp. VIII:** 251
"Lager Beer" (Dunbar), **Supp. II Part 1:** 193
"La Gringuita: On Losing a Native Language" (Alvarez), **Supp. VII:** 18
Laguna Woman (Silko), **Supp. IV Part 2:** 557, 560–561
Lahiri, Jhumpa, **Supp. XXI: 175–189; Supp. XXIII:** 289
Lahr, John, **Supp. XXI:** 18
Laing, R. D., **Supp. I Part 2:** 527; **Supp. XX:** 94
La kabbale pratique (Ambelain), **Supp. I Part 1:** 273
"Lake, The" (Bradbury), **Supp. IV Part 1:** 101
Lake, The (play), **Supp. IX:** 189
Lakeboat (Mamet), **Supp. XIV:** 240–241
"Lake Chelan" (Stafford), **Supp. XI:** 321
Lake Effect Country (Ammons), **Supp. VII:** 34, 35
"Lake Isle of Innisfree, The" (Yeats), **Retro. Supp. I:** 413; **Supp. XIX:** 92
"Lake Return" (Wright), **Supp. XV:** 345
Lake Wobegon Days (Keillor), **Supp. XVI:** 165, 166, **173–174**
Lake Wobegon Summer 1956 (Keillor), **Supp. XVI:** 178
Lalic, Ivan V., **Supp. VIII:** 272
Lamantia, Philip, **Supp. VIII:** 289
Lamb, Brian, **Supp. XIX:** 156; **Supp. XX: 101**

Lamb, Charles, **III:** 111, 207; **Supp. VIII:** 125
Lamb, Wendy, **Supp. IV Part 2:** 658
Lambardi, Marilyn May, **Retro. Supp. II:** 45–46
Lamb in His Bosom (C. Miller), **Supp. XXII:** 187, **189–191,** 193–194, 195, 197, 198, 199, 200
"Lame Feet of Salvation, The" (W. V. Davis), **Supp. XXI:** 87–88
"Lament" (Wilbur), **Supp. III Part 2:** 550
Lament and Chastisement (O'Hara), **Supp. XXIII:** 209
"Lamentation in Winter"(Schott), **Supp. XXIII:** 243
"Lamentations" (Glück), **Supp. V:** 83, 84
"Lament for Dark Peoples" (Hughes), **Retro. Supp. I:** 199
"Lament for Saul and Jonathan" (Bradstreet), **Supp. I Part 1:** 111
"Lament-Heaven" (Doty), **Supp. XI:** 125
"Lament of a New England Mother, The" (Eberhart), **I:** 539
Laments for the Living (Parker), **Supp. IX:** 192
"Lame Shall Enter First, The" (O'Connor), **III:** 348, 351, 352, 355, 356–357, 358; **Retro. Supp. II:** 237
Lamia (Keats), **II:** 512; **III:** 523
Lamming, George, **Supp. XXI:** 170
Lamott, Anne, **Supp. XX: 131–146**
La Motte-Fouqué, Friedrich Heinrich Karl, **III:** 77, 78
L'Amour, Louis, **Supp. XIII:** 5
Lamp for Nightfall, A (Caldwell), **I:** 297
Lamplit Answer, The (Schnackenberg), **Supp. XV:** 251, 254, **256–260**
"Lana Turner Has Collapsed!"(O'Hara), **Supp. XXIII:** 220
"Lance" (Nabokov), **Retro. Supp. I:** 266
Lancelot (Percy), **Supp. III Part 1:** 384, 395–396
Lancelot (Robinson), **III:** 513, 522
Lanchester, John, **Retro. Supp. I:** 278
"Land" (Emerson), **II:** 6
"Land Aesthetic, The" (Callicott), **Supp. XIV:** 184
Land and Freedom (film, Loach), **Supp. XXIII:** 163
"Land and Language" (J. W. Miller), **Supp. XX: 170**
Landau, Deborah, **Supp. XI:** 122, 123
"Land beyond the Blow, The" (Bierce), **I:** 209
"Land Ethic, The" (Leopold), **Supp. XIV:** 179, 180, 183, 191, 192
Landfall (Wagoner), **Supp. IX:** 330
"Landing in Luck" (Faulkner), **Retro. Supp. I:** 85
"Landing on the Moon" (Swenson), **Supp. IV Part 2:** 643
"Landings" (Hoffman), **Supp. XVIII:** 86
"Landing Under Water, I See Roots" (A. Finch), **Supp. XVII:** 76
"Land"(Kenny), **Supp. XXIII:** 147
Landlord at Lion's Head, The (Howells), **II:** 276, 287–288
Landmarks of Healing: A Study of House Made of Dawn (Scarberry-García),

Supp. IV Part 2: 486

Land of Little Rain, The (Dillard), **Supp. VI:** 27–28

Land of Look Behind, The (Cliff), **Supp. XXII:** 65–66, 68–69

Land of the Free U.S.A. (MacLeish), **I:** 293; **III:** 16–17

Land of Unlikeness (Lowell), **II:** 537–538, 539, 547; **Retro. Supp. II:** 177, 178, **184–185**

Landor, Walter Savage, **III:** 15, 469; **Supp. I Part 2:** 422

"Landscape" (Sarton), **Supp. VIII:** 259

"Landscape #11" (Halliday), **Supp. XIX:** 93

Landscape and Journey (W. V. Davis), **Supp. XXI:** 83, 88, 90, **92–93**, 95

"Landscape as a Nude" (MacLeish), **III:** 14

Landscape at the End of the Century (Dunn), **Supp. XI:** 139, 143, **150–151**

"Landscape Chamber, The" (Jewett), **II:** 408–409

"Landscape for the Disappeared" (Komunyakaa), **Supp. XIII:** 120, 126

Landscape in American Poetry (Larcom), **Supp. XIII:** 142

"Landscape Painter, A" (James), **II:** 322; **Retro. Supp. I:** 219

"Landscape Symbolism in Kate Chopin's *At Fault*" (Arner), **Retro. Supp. II:** 62

"Landscape: The Eastern Shore" (Barth), **I:** 122

"Landscape with Boat" (Stevens), **Retro. Supp. I:** 306

"Landscape with Bottles"(Schott), **Supp. XXIII:** 242

"Landscape with the Fall of Icarus" (Brueghel), **Retro. Supp. I:** 430

Land's End: A Walk through Provincetown (Cunningham), **Supp. XV:** 69

Land That Drank the Rain, The (Hoffman), **Supp. XVIII:** 76, 80, 81, 82

"Land Where There Is No Death, The" (Benét), **Supp. XI:** 56

Lane, Ann, **Supp. XI:** 195, 208

Lane, Cornelia. *See* Anderson, Mrs. Sherwood

Lane, Homer, **Supp. II Part 1:** 6; **Supp. XIV:** 160

Lane, John, **Supp. XXIV:** 22

Lane, Nathan, **Supp. XIII:** 207

Lane, Rose Wilder, **Supp. IV Part 2:** 524; **Supp. XXII:** 293–294, 295, 296, 297, 301

Lanes, Selma G., **Supp. XVI:** 104, 107

Lang, Andrew, **Retro. Supp. I:** 127

Lang, Violet, **Supp. XII:** 119

Lang, V. R. "Bunny", **Supp. XXIII:** 209

Langdon, Olivia. *See* Clemens, Mrs. Samuel Langhorne (Olivia Langdon)

Lange, Carl Georg, **II:** 350

Lange, Dorothea, **I:** 293; **Supp. XIV:** 181

Langland, Joseph, **III:** 542

Langston Hughes, American Poet (Walker), **Supp. III Part 2:** 530–531

Langston Hughes and the "Chicago Defender": Essays on Race, Politics,

and Culture (De Santis, ed.), **Retro. Supp. I:** 194

Langston Hughes: Modern Critical Views (Bloom, ed.), **Retro. Supp. I:** 193

Langston Hughes Reader, The (Hughes), **Retro. Supp. I:** 202; **Supp. I Part 1:** 345

Langston Hughes: The Poet and His Critics (Barksdale), **Retro. Supp. I:** 202

"Language, Visualization and the Inner Library" (Shepard), **Supp. III Part 2:** 436, 438, 449

Language and Imagery of the Bible, The (Caird), **Supp. XXI:** 91–92

"Language and the Writer" (Bambara), **Supp. XI:** 18

Language As Gesture (Blackmur), **Supp. II Part 1:** 108

Language as Symbolic Action (Burke), **I:** 275, 282, 285

Language Book, The (Andrews and Bernstein), **Supp. IV Part 2:** 426

"Language Divine!"(J. Schoolcraft), **Supp. XXIII:** 225

Language in Thought and Action (Hayakawa), **I:** 448

"Language of Being and Dying, The" (Gass), **Supp. VI:** 91

"Language of Home, The" (Wideman), **Supp. X:** 320, 323–324

Language of Life, The (Moyers, television series), **Supp. XIII:** 274, 276

Language of the American South, The (Brooks), **Supp. XIV:** 14

"Language of the Brag, The" (Olds), **Supp. X:** 204

"Language We Know, The" (Ortiz), **Supp. IV Part 2:** 500

Lanier, Clifford, **Supp. I Part 1:** 349, 350, 353, 355, 356, 371

Lanier, James F. D., **Supp. I Part 1:** 350

Lanier, Lyle H., **Supp. X:** 25

Lanier, Robert Sampson, **Supp. I Part 1:** 349, 351, 355, 356, 361

Lanier, Mrs. Robert Sampson (Mary Jane Anderson), **Supp. I Part 1:** 349

Lanier, Sidney, **IV:** 444; **Supp. I Part 1:** **349–373**; **Supp. I Part 2:** 416; **Supp. IV Part 1:** 165

Lanier, Mrs. Sidney (Mary Day), **Supp. I Part 1:** 351, 355, 357, 361, 362, 364, 370, 371

"Lanier as Poet" (Parks), **Supp. I Part 1:** 373

"Lanier's Reading" (P. Graham), **Supp. I Part 1:** 373

"Lanier's Use of Science for Poetic Imagery" (Beaver), **Supp. I Part 1:** 373

Lankes, J. J., **Supp. XXII:** 275

Lannegan, Helen. *See* Caldwell, Mrs. Erskine

Lannin, Paul, **II:** 427

Lanny Budd novels (Sinclair), **Supp. V:** 290

Lant, Kathleen Margaret, **Supp. V:** 141

Lanterns on the Levee (Percy), **Supp. XXII:** 193

Lanthenas, François, **Supp. I Part 2:** 515

"Lanyard, The" (Collins), **Supp. XXI:** 56, **62–64**

Laotzu, **III:** 173, 189, 567; **Supp. XV:** 39, 46, 48

Lapine, James, **Supp. XXI:** 147–148

"Lapis Lazuli" (Yeats), **I:** 532; **III:** 40

Laplace, Pierre Simon de, **III:** 428

Lapouge, M. G., **Supp. I Part 2:** 633

Lappa, Katherine, **Supp. XV:** 176

Lapsing to Grace (Espaillat), **Supp. XXI:** 99, 100

Lapsley, Gaillard, **Supp. XX:** 231

Laqueur, Thomas, **Supp. XVI:** 154

Larbaud, Valery, **IV:** 404; **Supp. XIII:** 332; **Supp. XIV:** 338

Larcom, Lucy, **Retro. Supp. II:** 145; **Supp. XIII:** **137–157**

Larcom's Poetical Works (Larcom), **Supp. XIII:** 142

Lardner, John, **II:** 437

Lardner, Ring, **I:** 487; **II:** 44, 91, 259, 263, **415–438**; **III:** 566, 572; **IV:** 433; **Retro. Supp. I:** 105; **Retro. Supp. II:** 222; **Supp. I Part 2:** 609; **Supp. IX:** 200; **Supp. XVI:** 189

Lardner, Ring, Jr., **Supp. XI:** 306

"Lardner, Shakespeare and Chekhov" (Matthews), **II:** 430

"Large Bad Picture" (Bishop), **Retro. Supp. II:** 43; **Supp. I Part 1:** 73, 80–82, 85, 86, 89, 90

"Large Coffee" (Lardner), **II:** 437

Large Glass, or The Bride Stripped Bare by Her Bachelors, Even (Duchamp), **Supp. IV Part 2:** 423, 424

Largo (Handel), **IV:** 369

"Lark" (Taggard), **Supp. XXII:** 280

Lark, The (Hellman), **Supp. I Part 1:** 286–288, 297

Lark: Four-Part Chorus for Mixed Voices (A Capella) with Baritone Solo (Taggard and Copland), **Supp. XXII:** 283

Larkin, Philip, **Supp. I Part 2:** 536; **Supp. XI:** 243, 249; **Supp. XIII:** 76, 85; **Supp. XV:** 117, 251; **Supp. XVII:** 110; **Supp. XVIII:** 173; **Supp. XX:** 199; **Supp. XXI:** 84, 93

Larkin, Sharon Alile, **Supp. XI:** 20

Larmore, Phoebe, **Supp. X:** 266

Larner, Jeremy, **Supp. XVI:** 220

La Rochefoucauld, François de, **I:** 279; **II:** 111; **Supp. XIV:** 130

"La Rose des Vents" (Wilbur), **Supp. III Part 2:** 550

"Larry Brown's *Dirty Work*: A Study of Man's Responsibility for Suffering" (Prevost), **Supp. XXI:** 45

"Larry"(O'Hara), **Supp. XXIII:** 212

Larry's Party (Shields), **Supp. VII:** 324, 326–327

Larsen, Nella, **Supp. I Part 1:** 325, 326; **Supp. IV Part 1:** 164; **Supp. XVIII:** **119–134**

Larson, Charles, **Supp. IV Part 1:** 331

Larson, Clinton, **Supp. XI:** 328

Larson, Kelli, **Supp. XVIII:** 131

LaRue, Dorie, **Supp. XXI:** 43

"Larval Stage of a Bookworm" (Mencken), **III:** 101

La Salle and the Discovery of the Great West (Parkman), **Supp. II Part 2:** 595, 598, 605–607; **Supp. XVIII:** 114

Las Casas, Bartolomé de, **Supp. XXIV:** 87

Lasch, Christopher, **I:** 259

Lasdun, James, **Supp. XXIV:** 154

Lasher (Rice), **Supp. VII:** 299–300

Lask, Thomas, **III:** 576; **Supp. XVI:** 250

Laski, Harold, **Supp. I Part 2:** 632, 643

Lass, Abraham H., **Supp. XXIV:** 214

Lassalle, Ferdinand, **IV:** 429

Lasser, Louise, **Supp. XV:** 4

"Last Acts" (Olds), **Supp. X:** 210

Last Adam, The (Cozzens), **I:** 362–363, 364, 368, 375, 377, 378, 379

Last Analysis, The (Bellow), **I:** 152, 160, 161; **Retro. Supp. II:** 26

Last and Lost Poems of Delmore Schwartz (Phillips, ed.), **Supp. II Part 2:** 661, 665

Last Avant-Garde, The: The Making of the New York School of Poets (Lehman), **Supp. XV:** 178–179, 187

Last Beautiful Days of Autumn, The (Nichols), **Supp. XIII:** 254, 255, 267, 269

Last Blue (Stern), **Supp. IX: 299–300**

Last Book, The (Pickering), **Supp. XXI:** 203–204

Last Carousel, The (Algren), **Supp. IX:** 16

Last Centennial, The (P. N. Warren as Kilina), **Supp. XX: 261–262**

"Last Child" (X. J. Kennedy), **Supp. XV:** 162, 165

"Last Class with Roethke" (Gallagher), **Supp. XXIV:** 171

Last Clean Shirt, The (film, Leslie and O'Hara), **Supp. XXIII:** 217

Last Coyote, The (Connelly), **Supp. XXI: 71**

"Last Dance" (Dubus III), **Supp. XXIV:** 100

"Last Day in the Field, The" (Gordon), **II:** 200

"Last Day of the Last Furlough" (Salinger), **III:** 552–553

"Last Days of Alice" (Tate), **IV:** 129

"Last Days of August, The" (Nye), **Supp. XIII:** 284

"Last Days of John Brown, The" (Thoreau), **IV:** 185

Last Days of Louisiana Red, The (Reed), **Supp. X:** 240, **248–249**

Last Decade, The (Trilling), **Supp. III Part 2:** 493, 499

"Last Demon, The" (Singer), **IV:** 15, 21

Last Detective, The (Crais), **Supp. XXI:** 70

Last Exit to Brooklyn (Selby), **Supp. III Part 1:** 125; **Supp. XXI:** 227, 231

Last Flower, The (Thurber), **Supp. I Part 2:** 610

"Last Frontier" (McCarriston), **Supp. XIV:** 272

Last Generation, The (Moraga), **Supp. XXIII:** 201

Last Gentleman, The (Percy), **Supp. III Part 1:** 383–388, 392–393

"Last Good Country, The" (Hemingway), **II:** 258–259

Last Good Time, The (Bausch), **Supp. VII:** 45–46

"Last Great Saloon, The" (Exley), **Supp. XXIII:** 103

"Last Hiding Places of Snow, The" (Kinnell), **Supp. III Part 1:** 252

"Last Hours, The" (Dunn), **Supp. XI:** 141

Last House: Reflections, Dreams, and Observations, 1943–1991 (M. F. K. Fisher), **Supp. XVII:** 92

Last Husband and Other Stories, The (Humphrey), **Supp. IX:** 94

Last Jew in America, The (Fiedler), **Supp. XIII:** 103

"Last Jew in America, The" (Fiedler), **Supp. XIII:** 103

Last Laugh, Mr. Moto (Marquand), **III:** 57

"Last Leaf, The" (Holmes), **Supp. I Part 1:** 302, 309

"Last Leaf, The" (Porter), **III:** 444

"Last Lie, The" (Weigl), **Supp. XIX:** 279

"Last Light" (Major), **Supp. XXII:** 185

"Last Look at the Lilacs" (Stevens), **IV:** 74

Last Man, The (Kees), **Supp. XV:** 142, 143, 145

"Last May" (Dixon), **Supp. XII: 143**

"Last Mermother, The" (A. Finch), **Supp. XVII:** 72

"Last Mohican, The" (Malamud), **Supp. I Part 2:** 437–438, 450, 451

"Lastness" (Kinnell), **Supp. III Part 1:** 248–249

"Last Night" (Olds), **Supp. X:** 212

"Last Night at Tía's" (Alvarez), **Supp. VII:** 5

Last Night of Summer, The (Caldwell), **I:** 292–293

Last Notes from Home (Exley), **Supp. XXIII:** 97, 98, **106–108**

Last of Mr. Norris, The (Isherwood), **Supp. XIV:** 161

"Last of the Brooding Miserables, The" (Karr), **Supp. XI:** 250

"Last of the Caddoes, The" (Humphrey), **Supp. IX:** 101

Last of the Crazy People, The (Findley), **Supp. XX: 51–52**

"Last of the Gold Star Mothers, The" (C. Bly), **Supp. XVI:** 34, 35, 36

"Last of the Legions, The" (Benét), **Supp. XI:** 56, 57

Last of the Mohicans, The (Cooper), **I:** 341, 342, 349

Last of the Red Hot Lovers (Simon), **Supp. IV Part 2:** 575, 583, 589

"Last of the Valerii, The" (James), **II:** 327; **Retro. Supp. I:** 218

"Last One, The" (Merwin), **Supp. III Part 1:** 355

Last Picture Show, The (film), **Supp. V:** 223, 226

Last Picture Show, The (McMurtry), **Supp. V:** 220, 222–223, 233

Last Place on Earth, The: Scott and Amundsen's Race to the South Pole (Huntford), **Supp. XVIII:** 114

Last Puritan, The (Santayana), **III:** 64, 600, 604, 607, 612, 615–617

"Last Ride Together, The" (Browning), **I:** 468

"Last River, The" (Kinnell), **Supp. III Part 1:** 236

Last Song, The (Harjo), **Supp. XII:** 218

"Last Song for the Mend-It Shop" (Nye), **Supp. XIII:** 283

"Last Tango in Fresno" (Salinas), **Supp. XIII:** 318

"Last Trip to Greece" (Hadas), **Supp. XXIII:** 118–119

Last Tycoon, The: An Unfinished Novel (Fitzgerald), **II:** 84, 98; **Retro. Supp. I:** 109, 114, **114–115; Retro. Supp. II:** 337; **Supp. IV Part 1:** 203; **Supp. IX:** 63; **Supp. XII:** 173; **Supp. XIII:** 170; **Supp. XVIII:** 248, 250

"Last WASP in the World, The" (Fiedler), **Supp. XIII:** 103

"Last Watch, The" (Gibran), **Supp. XX: 119**

Last Watch of the Night: Essays Too Personal and Otherwise (Monette), **Supp. X:** 147, 148, 153, **157–159**

"Last Word, The" (column, Quindlen), **Supp. XVII:** 165, 167, 170

Last Word, The: Letters between Marcia Nardi and William Carlos Williams (O'Neil, ed.), **Retro. Supp. I:** 427

"Last Words" (Levine), **Supp. V:** 190

"Last Words" (Olds), **Supp. X:** 210

Last Worthless Evening, The (Dubus), **Supp. VII:** 87–88

"Las Vegas (What?) Las Vegas (Can't Hear You! Too Noisy) Las Vegas! ! ! !" (Wolfe), **Supp. III Part 2:** 572

"Late" (Bogan), **Supp. III Part 1:** 53

"Late Air" (Bishop), **Supp. I Part 1:** 89

"Late Autumn" (Sarton), **Supp. VIII:** 261

"Late Bronze, Early Iron: A Journey Book" (Sobin), **Supp. XVI:** 290

Late Child, The (McMurtry), **Supp. V:** 231

"Late Conversation" (Doty), **Supp. XI:** 122

"Late Elegy for John Berryman, A" (W. V. Davis), **Supp. XXI:** 91

"Late Encounter with the Enemy, A" (O'Connor), **III:** 345; **Retro. Supp. II:** 232

Late Fire, Late Snow (Francis), **Supp. IX: 89–90**

"Late Fragment" (Gallagher), **Supp. XXIV:** 172

Late George Apley, The (Marquand), **II:** 482–483; **III:** 50, 51, 52, 56–57, 58, 62–64, 65, 66

Late George Apley, The (Marquand and Kaufman), **III:** 62

"Late Hour" (Everwine), **Supp. XV:** 85

Late Hour, The (Strand), **Supp. IV Part 2:** 620, 629–630

"Lately, at Night" (Kumin), **Supp. IV Part 2:** 442

"Late Moon" (Levine), **Supp. V:** 186

"Late Night Ode" (McClatchy), **Supp. XII:** 262–263

Later (Creeley), **Supp. IV Part 1:** 153, 156, 157

Later Life (Gurney), **Supp. V:** 103, 105

La Terre (Zola), **III:** 316, 322

Later the Same Day (Paley), **Supp. VI:** 218

"Late September in Nebraska" (Kooser), **Supp. XIX:** 120

Late Settings (Merrill), **Supp. III Part 1:** 336

"Late Sidney Lanier, The" (Stedman), **Supp. I Part 1:** 373

"Late Snow & Lumber Strike of the Summer of Fifty-Four, The" (Snyder), **Supp. VIII:** 294

"Late Start, A" (L. Brown), **Supp. XXI:** 40–41

"Latest Freed Man, The" (Stevens), **Retro. Supp. I:** 306

"Latest Injury, The" (Olds), **Supp. X:** 209

Latest Literary Essays and Addresses (Lowell), **Supp. I Part 2:** 407

"Late Subterfuge" (Warren), **IV:** 257

"Late Summer Lilies" (Weigl), **Supp. XIX:** 288

"Late Supper, A" (Jewett), **Retro. Supp. II:** 137

"Late Victorians" (Rodriguez), **Supp. XIV:** 303–304

"Late Walk, A" (Frost), **II:** 153; **Retro. Supp. I:** 127

Latham, Edyth, **I:** 289

Lathrop, George Parsons, **Supp. I Part 1:** 365

Lathrop, H. B., **Supp. III Part 2:** 612

Lathrop, Julia, **Supp. I Part 1:** 5

Latière de Trianon, La (Wekerlin), **II:** 515

"La Tigresse" (Van Vechten), **Supp. II Part 2:** 735, 738

Latimer, Hugh, **II:** 15

Latimer, Margery, **Supp. IX:** 320

La Traviata (Verdi), **III:** 139

"Latter-Day Warnings" (Holmes), **Supp. I Part 1:** 307

La Turista (Shepard), **Supp. III Part 2:** 440

Lauber, John, **Supp. XIII:** 21

Laud, Archbishop, **II:** 158

"Lauds" (Auden), **Supp. II Part 1:** 23

"Laughing Man, The" (Salinger), **III:** 559

Laughing Matters (Siegel), **Supp. XXII:** 260

Laughing to Keep From Crying (Hughes), **Supp. I Part 1:** 329–330

Laughing Wild (Durang), **Supp. XXIV:** 114, **124**

"Laughing with One Eye" (Schnackenberg), **Supp. XV:** 253

Laughlin, James, **III:** 171; **Retro. Supp. I:** 423, 424, 428, 430, 431; **Supp. VIII:** 195; **Supp. XV:** 140; **Supp. XVI:** 284; **Supp. XXI:** 29

Laughlin, Jay, **Supp. II Part 1:** 94

Laughlin, J. Laurence, **Supp. I Part 2:** 641

Laughter in the Dark (Nabokov), **III:** 255–258; **Retro. Supp. I:** 270

Laughter on the 23rd Floor (Simon), **Supp. IV Part 2:** 575, 576, 588, 591–592

"Launcelot" (Lewis), **II:** 439–440

"Laura Dailey's Story" (Bogan), **Supp. III Part 1:** 52

Laurel, Stan, **Supp. I Part 2:** 607; **Supp. IV Part 2:** 574

Laurel and Hardy Go to Heaven (Auster), **Supp. XII:** 21

Laurence, Alexander, **Supp. XVIII:** 138

Laurence, Dan H., **II:** 338–339

Laurens, John, **Supp. I Part 2:** 509

Lauter, Paul, **Supp. XV:** 313

Lautréamont, Comte de, **III:** 174

Lavender Locker Room, The (P. N. Warren), **Supp. XX: 261, 273–274**

Law, John, **Supp. XI:** 307

Law and Order (television), **Supp. XVII:** 153

Law and the Testimony, The (S. and A. Warner), **Supp. XVIII:** 264

Lawd Today (Wright), **IV:** 478, 492

Law for the Lion, A (Auchincloss), **Supp. IV Part 1:** 25

"Law Lane" (Jewett), **II:** 407

"Lawns of June, The" (Peacock), **Supp. XIX:** 196

"Law of Nature and the Dream of Man, The: Ruminations of the Art of Fiction" (Stegner), **Supp. IV Part 2:** 604

Lawrence, D. H., **I:** 291, 336, 377, 522, 523; **II:** 78, 84, 98, 102, 264, 517, 523, 532, 594, 595; **III:** 27, 33, 40, 44, 46, 172, 173, 174, 178, 184, 229, 261, 423, 429, 458, 546–547; **IV:** 138, 339, 342, 351, 380; **Retro. Supp. I:** 7, 18, 203, 204, 421; **Retro. Supp. II:** 68; **Supp. I Part 1:** 227, 230, 243, 255, 257, 258, 263, 329; **Supp. I Part 2:** 546, 613, 728; **Supp. II Part 1:** 1, 9, 20, 89; **Supp. IV Part 1:** 81; **Supp. VIII:** 237; **Supp. X:** 137, 193, 194; **Supp. XII:** 172; **Supp. XIV:** 310; **Supp. XV:** 45, 46, 158, 254; **Supp. XVI:** 267; **Supp. XX: 69; Supp. XXII:** 198; **Supp. XXIII:** 166, 275; **Supp. XXIV:** 51, 52, 57, 58, 64

Lawrence, Elizabeth, **Supp. XXIII:** 259, 264

Lawrence, Frieda, **Supp. XV:** 46

Lawrence, Rhoda, **Supp. I Part 1:** 45

Lawrence, Seymour, **Supp. IX:** 107; **Supp. XI:** 335, 346, 348

Lawrence, T. E., **Supp. XIV:** 159

Lawrence of Arabia (Aldington), **Supp. I Part 1:** 259

Lawrence of Arabia (film), **Supp. I Part 1:** 67

Laws (Hadas), **Supp. XXIII: 119–120,** 124

Laws (Plato), **Supp. IV Part 1:** 391

Laws of Ice, The (Price), **Supp. VI:** 264

Laws of Our Fathers, The (Turow), **Supp. XVII: 218–219**

Lawson, John Howard, **I:** 479, 482

Lawton Girl, The (Frederic), **II:** 132–133, 144

Layachi, Larbi (Driss ben Hamed Charhadi), **Supp. IV Part 1:** 92, 93

Layard, John, **Supp. XIV:** 160

Lay Down My Sword and Shield (Burke), **Supp. XIV:** 22, 25, 34

"Layers, The" (Kunitz), **Supp. III Part 1:** 260, 266–267

"Layers, The: Some Notes on 'The Abduction' " (Kunitz), **Supp. III Part 1:** 266

"Lay-mans Lamentation, The" (Taylor), **IV:** 162–163

Lay of the Land, The: Metaphor as Experience and History in American Life and Letters (Kolodny), **Supp. X:** 97

"Layover" (Hass), **Supp. VI:** 109

"Lay Preacher" (Dennie), **Supp. I Part 1:** 125

Layton, Irving, **Supp. XII:** 121

Lazar, Irving "Swifty", **Supp. XIX:** 250

Lazarillo de Tormes (Mendoza), **III:** 182

Lazar Malkin Enters Heaven (S. Stern), **Supp. XVII:** 42; **Supp. XX: 178**

Lazarus Laughed (O'Neill), **III:** 391, 395–396

Lazer, Hank, **Supp. IX:** 265

Lea, Luke, **IV:** 248

Leachman, Cloris, **Supp. XXI:** 146

Leacock, Stephen, **Supp. IV Part 2:** 464

"LEADBELLY GIVES AN AUTOGRAPH" (Baraka), **Supp. II Part 1:** 49

Leaflets: Poems, 1965–1968 (Rich), **Supp. I Part 2:** 551, 556–557

"League of American Writers, The: Communist Organizational Activity among American Writers 1929–1942" (Wolfe), **Supp. III Part 2:** 568

League of Brightened Philistines and Other Papers, The (Farrell), **II:** 49

Leahy, Anna, **Supp. XXI:** 246

"Leakage" (Skloot), **Supp. XX: 202**

Leal, Luis, **Supp. XIX:** 98, 112

"Leaning" (Webb), **Supp. XX: 56**

Leaning Forward (Paley), **Supp. VI:** 221

"Leaning Tower, The" (Porter), **III:** 442, 443, 446–447

Leaning Tower and Other Stories, The (Porter), **III:** 433, 442, 443–447

"Leap, The" (Dickey), **Supp. IV Part 1:** 182

"Leaping Up into Political Poetry" (R. Bly), **Supp. IV Part 1:** 61, 63

Leap Year (Cameron), **Supp. XII:** 79–80, 81, **85–86,** 88

Lear, Edward, **III:** 428, 536; **Supp. XVI:** 103

Lear, Linda, **Supp. IX:** 19, 22, 25, 26

Learned Ladies, The (Molière; Wilbur, trans.), **Supp. III Part 2:** 560

"Learning a Dead Language" (Merwin), **Supp. III Part 1:** 345

Learning a Trade: A Craftsman's Notebooks, 1955–1997 (Price), **Supp. VI:** 254, 255, 267

"Learning Bones" (Espaillat), **Supp. XXI:** 107

Learning to Live in This World (Schott), **Supp. XXIII:** 248

Learning to Love: Exploring Solitude and Freedom (Merton), **Supp. VIII:** 200

Learning to Love You More (website), **Supp. XXIV:** 200

"Learning to Read" (Harper), **Supp. II Part 1:** 201–202

"Learning to Speak" (Everwine), **Supp. XV:** 79

"Learning to Work Together" (L. I. Wilder), **Supp. XXII:** 290

Learning Tree, The (Park), **Supp. XIX:** 154

Leary, Lewis, **III:** 478

Leary, Paris, **Supp. IV Part 1:** 176

Leary, Timothy, **Supp. X:** 265; **Supp. XIV:** 150

Lease, Joseph, **Supp. XXI:** 246

Least Heat Moon, William, **Supp. V:** 169

Leather-Stocking Tales, The (Cooper), **I:** 335

Leatherwood God, The (Howells), **II:** 276, 277, 288

Leave It to Beaver (television show), **Supp. XX:** 103

"Leave Me Alone a Little" (Taggard), **Supp. XXII:** 274

"Leaves" (Updike), **Retro. Supp. I:** 323, 329, 335

Leaves and Ashes (Haines), **Supp. XII:** 206

Leaves from the Notebook of a Tamed Cynic (Niebuhr), **III:** 293

Leaves of Grass (1856) (Whitman), **Retro. Supp. I:** 399–402

Leaves of Grass (1860) (Whitman), **Retro. Supp. I:** 402–405

Leaves of Grass (Whitman), **II:** 8; **IV:** 331, 332, 333, 334, 335, 336, 340, 341–342, 348, 350, 405, 464; **Retro. Supp. I:** 387, 388, 389, 390, **392–395,** 406, 407, 408; **Retro. Supp. II:** 93; **Supp. I Part 1:** 365; **Supp. I Part 2:** 416, 579; **Supp. III Part 1:** 156; **Supp. V:** 170; **Supp. VIII:** 275; **Supp. IX:** 265; **Supp. X:** 120; **Supp. XIV:** 334; **Supp. XV:** 218; **Supp. XVIII:** 4; **Supp. XIX:** 276; **Supp. XXI:** 205; **Supp. XXII:** 92; **Supp. XXIII:** 165; **Supp. XXIV:** 85

"Leaves of Grass" (Whitman), **IV:** 463

Leaves of the Tree, The (Masters), **Supp. I Part 2:** 460

"Leaving" (Hogan), **Supp. IV Part 1:** 400

"Leaving" (Wilbur), **Supp. III Part 2:** 563

"Leaving, The" (B. Kelly), **Supp. XVII:** 127, 132

Leaving a Doll's House: A Memoir (C. Bloom), **Retro. Supp. II:** 281

Leaving Another Kingdom: Selected Poems (Stern), **Supp. IX:** 296

"Leaving Bartram's Garden in Southwest Philadelphia" (Di Piero), **Supp. XIX:** 46

"Leaving Brooklyn" (Neugeboren), **Supp. XVI:** 226

Leaving Cheyenne (McMurtry), **Supp. V:** 220, 221–222, 224, 229

Leaving Home (Keillor), **Supp. XVI:** 175

"Leaving One, The" (Offutt), **Supp. XIX:** 165–166

"Leaving the Island" (Olds), **Supp. X:** 214

"Leaving the Yellow House" (Bellow), **Retro. Supp. II:** 27, 32

"Leaving Town" (Kenyon), **Supp. VII:** 163

Leavis, F. R., **I:** 522; **III:** 462–463, 475, 478; **Retro. Supp. I:** 67; **Retro. Supp. II:** 243; **Supp. I Part 2:** 536; **Supp. VIII:** 234, 236, 245

Leavis, Queenie, **Supp. XX: 232**

"Leavis-Snow Controversy, The" (Trilling), **Supp. III Part 2:** 512

Leavitt, Caroline, **Supp. XX: 186**

Leavitt, David, **Supp. VIII:** 88

Lebanon (C. Miller), **Supp. XXII:** 198–199

Le Braz, Anatole, **Supp. XIII:** 253

Le Carre, John, **Supp. XX: 195**

Lecker, Robert, **Supp. XIII:** 21

LeClair, Thomas (Tom), **Supp. IV Part 1:** 286; **Supp. V:** 53; **Supp. XII:** 152; **Supp. XX: 93; Supp. XXII:** 206, 210, 261, 264

Le Conte, Joseph, **II:** 479; **III:** 227–228

"Lecture, The" (Singer), **IV:** 21

"LECTURE PAST DEAD CATS" (Baraka), **Supp. II Part 1:** 52

Lectures in America (Stein), **IV:** 27, 32, 33, 35, 36, 41, 42

"Lectures on Poetry" (Bryant), **Supp. I Part 1:** 159, 161

Lectures on Rhetoric (Blair), **II:** 8

"Leda and the Swan" (Yeats), **III:** 347; **Supp. IX:** 52

Ledger (Fitzgerald), **Retro. Supp. I:** 109, 110

Lee (Masters), **Supp. I Part 2:** 471

Lee, Baayork, **Supp. XXI:** 148

Lee, C. Y., **Supp. XXI:** 148

Lee, Don, **Supp. XII:** 295; **Supp. XVII:** 13, 14, 15, 16

Lee, Don L. *See* Madhubuti, Haki R.

Lee, Gypsy Rose, **II:** 586; **III:** 161; **Supp. IV Part 1:** 84

Lee, Harper, **Supp. VIII: 113–131**

Lee, Harriett, **Supp. XV:** 230

Lee, James Kyun-Jin, **Supp. XV:** 213

Lee, James W., **Supp. IX:** 94, 97, 109

Lee, James Ward, **Supp. VIII:** 57

Lee, Li Lin, **Supp. XV:** 211, 212

Lee, Li-Young, **Supp. XV: 211–228; Supp. XVII:** 241

Lee, Richard E., **Supp. XIX:** 226, 227

Lee, Robert E., **II:** 150, 206; **IV:** 126; **Supp. I Part 2:** 471, 486

Lee, Samuel, **IV:** 158

Lee, Spike, **Retro. Supp. II:** 12; **Supp. XI:** 19; **Supp. XIII:** 179, 186; **Supp. XVI:** 144; **Supp. XX: 110**

Lee, Virginia Chin-lan, **Supp. X:** 291

Leeds, Barry, **Retro. Supp. II:** 204

Leeds, Daniel, **II:** 110

Leeds, Titan, **II:** 110, 111

Leeming, David, **Retro. Supp. II:** 4, 10

"Lees of Happiness, The" (Fitzgerald), **II:** 88

"Le Filme" (Weigl), **Supp. XIX:** 288

Left Out in the Rain: New Poems 1947–1985 (Snyder), **Supp. VIII:** 305

"Legacy" (Dunn), **Supp. XI:** 148

"Legacy" (Komunyakaa), **Supp. XIII:** 132

"Legacy" (W. V. Davis), **Supp. XXI:** 93–94

"Legacy of Aldo Leopold, The" (Stegner), **Supp. XIV:** 193

"Legacy of Channing, The" (Robinson), **Supp. XXIV:** 79

Legacy of Fear, A (Farrell), **II:** 39

"Legacy of the Ancestral Arts, The" (Locke), **Supp. XIV:** 201

Legacy of the Civil War, The: Meditations on the Centennial (Warren), **IV:** 236

"Legal Alien" (Mora), **Supp. XIII:** 215

"Legal Tender Act, The" (Adams), **I:** 5

Légende de la mort, La (Le Braz), **Supp. XIII:** 253

"Legend of Duluoz, The" (Kerouac), **Supp. III Part 1:** 218, 226, 227, 229

"Legend of Lillian Hellman, The" (Kazin), **Supp. I Part 1:** 297

"Legend of Monte del Diablo, The" (Harte), **Supp. II Part 1:** 339

"Legend of Paper Plates, The" (Haines), **Supp. XII:** 204

"Legend of Sammtstadt, A" (Harte), **Supp. II Part 1:** 355

"Legend of Sleepy Hollow, The" (Irving), **II:** 306–308

Legends (Lowell), **II:** 525–526

Legends and Dreams (P. N. Warren), **Supp. XX: 261**

Legends of Mexico (Lippard), **Supp. XXIII:** 178, 186

Legends of New England (Whittier), **Supp. I Part 2:** 684, 692

Legends of the Fall (Harrison), **Supp. VIII:** 38, 39, **45–46,** 48

"Legends of the Revolution"(series, Lippard), **Supp. XXIII:** 178

Legends of the West (Hall), **II:** 313

Léger, Fernand, **Retro. Supp. I:** 292

Legge, James, **III:** 472

Leggett, William, **Supp. I Part 1:** 157

"Legion, The" (Karr), **Supp. XI:** 243

"Legs" (Halliday), **Supp. XIX:** 90

Legs (W. Kennedy), **Supp. VII:** 133, 134, 138–142, 143, 151

Le Guin, Ursula K., **Supp. IV Part 1:** 333; **Supp. XXII:** 49

Lehan, Richard, **Retro. Supp. II:** 104

Lehman, David, **Supp. IX:** 161; **Supp. XIII:** 130; **Supp. XV:** 178–179, 180, 187, 190; **Supp. XXI:** 246

Lehmann, John, **Retro. Supp. II:** 243; **Supp. XIV:** 158, 159

Lehmann, Paul, **III:** 311

Lehmann-Haupt, Christopher, **Retro. Supp. II:** 291; **Supp. IV Part 1:** 205, 209, 306; **Supp. IX:** 95, 103; **Supp. XVI:** 73, 210, 294, 295; **Supp. XXII:** 205, 213; **Supp. XXIII:** 103

Lehrer, Jim, **Supp. XVIII:** 39

Leiber, Fritz, **Supp. XVI:** 123

Leibling, A. J., **Supp. XIV:** 112

Leibniz, Gottfried Wilhelm von, **II:** 103; **III:** 428

Leibowitz, Herbert A., **I:** 386; **Supp. XV:** 78

Leich, Roland, **Supp. XIV:** 123
Leichum, Laura, **Supp. XIX:** 197
Leider, Emily Wortis, **Supp. XXIV:** 19, 20, 22, 26, 27, 30
Leighton, Betty, **Supp. XXI:** 42
Leimbach, Laura, **Supp. XXIII:** 54
Leithauser, Brad, **Retro. Supp. I:** 133; **Supp. XV:** 250; **Supp. XVII:** 112; **Supp. XXII:** 207
Leitz, Robert, **Supp. XIV:** 62
Leivick, H., **IV:** 6
Lekachman, Robert, **Supp. I Part 2:** 648
Leland, Charles, **Supp. II Part 1:** 193
Leland, Charles Godfrey, **I:** 257
Leland, John, **Supp. XV:** 69; **Supp. XIX:** 157
Lem, Stanislaw, **Supp. IV Part 1:** 103
"Le marais du cygne" (Whittier), **Supp. I Part 2:** 687
Lemay, Harding, **Supp. VIII:** 125; **Supp. IX:** 98
Lemercier, Eugène, **Retro. Supp. I:** 299
Lemkin, Raphael, **Supp. XXIII:** 31
"Lemorne *versus* Huell" (E. Stoddard), **Supp. XV:** 270, 273, 283
Le Morte D'Arthur Notes (Gardner), **Supp. VI:** 65, 66
Lenin, V. I., **I:** 366, 439, 440; **III:** 14–15, 262, 475; **IV:** 429, 436, 443–444; **Supp. I Part 2:** 647; **Supp. XXI:** 164
"Lenny Dying, Pacific Standard Time"(Thompson), **Supp. XXIII:** 294
"Lenore" (Poe), **III:** 411
"Lenox Avenue: Midnight" (Hughes), **Retro. Supp. I:** 198
"Lens of Poetry, The" (Bronk). *See Attendant, The* (Bronk)
Leonard, Elmore, **Supp. IV Part 1:** 356; **Supp. X:** 5; **Supp. XIV:** 26
Leonard, John, **Supp. IV Part 1:** 24; **Supp. IV Part 2:** 474; **Supp. V:** 164, 223–224; **Supp. XI:** 13; **Supp. XVIII:** 147, 148; **Supp. XIX:** 269; **Supp. XXI:** 233, 239
Leonardo da Vinci, **Supp. XII:** 44; **Supp. XXII:** 171
León-Portilla, Miguel, **Supp. XV:** 77
Leontiev, Constantine, **Supp. XIV:** 98
Leopard, The (Lampedusa), **Supp. XII:** 13–14
Leopardi, Giacomo, **II:** 543; **Supp. XIX:** 33, 43
"Leopard Man's Story, The" (London), **II:** 475
Leopard's Mouth Is Dry and Cold Inside, The (Levis), **Supp. XI:** 258
Leopold, Aldo, **Supp. V:** 202; **Supp. X:** 108; **Supp. XIV:** 177–194; **Supp. XXI:** 203
"Leper's Bell, the" (Komunyakaa), **Supp. XIII:** 118
Lerman, Leo, **Supp. X:** 188; **Supp. XVI:** 194
Lerner, Ben, **Supp. XXIV:** 45
Lerner, Max, **III:** 60; **Supp. I Part 2:** 629, 630, 631, 647, 650, 654
Lerperger, Emil, **Supp. XX: 165, 167**
"Lesbos" (Plath), **Retro. Supp. II:** 254
Lesesne, Teri, **Supp. XIII:** 277

LeSieg, Theo (pseudonym). *See* Geisel, Theodor Seuss (Dr. Seuss)
Leskov, Nikolai, **IV:** 299
Leslie, Alfred, **Supp. XII:** 127; **Supp. XXIII:** 217
"Less and Less Human, O Savage Spirit" (W. Stevens), **Supp. XVI:** 64
Lesser, Wendy, **Supp. IV Part 2:** 453; **Supp. XII:** 297; **Supp. XVI:** 201
Lessing, Gotthold, **Supp. I Part 2:** 422
"Lesson, The" (Bambara), **Supp. XI:** 5–6
"Lesson, The" (Dunbar), **Supp. II Part 1:** 199
"Lesson, The" (Olsen), **Supp. XIII:** 297
"Lesson, The"(Schott), **Supp. XXIII:** 254
"Lesson for the Ill Clothed and Ill Fed, A" (Ryan as Quin), **Supp. XVIII:** 230–231
Lesson of the Master, The (James), **Supp. XVIII:** 248
"Lesson of the Master, The" (James), **Retro. Supp. I:** 227
Lesson of the Masters: An Anthology of the Novel from Cervantes to Hemingway (Cowley-Hugo, ed.), **Supp. II Part 1:** 140
"Lesson on Concealment, A" (Brown), **Supp. I Part 1:** 133
"Lessons" (Epstein), **Supp. XII:** 163
"Lessons from an Older Man"(Thompson), **Supp. XXIII:** 293
"Lessons of the Body" (Simpson), **Supp. IX:** 267
Less than One (Brodsky), **Supp. VIII:** 22, 29–31
Lester, Jerry, **Supp. IV Part 2:** 574
Lester, Ketty, **Supp. XV:** 133, 147
Le Style Apollinaire (Zukofsky), **Supp. III Part 2:** 616
Le Sueur, Arthur, **Supp. XXIII:** 161, 162
LeSueur, Joe, **Supp. XXIII:** 212, 216, 218, 220
Le Sueur, Meridel, **Supp. V:** 113, 130; **Supp. XII:** 217; **Supp. XXIII: 161– 176**
"Let America Be America Again" (Hughes), **Retro. Supp. I:** 202; **Supp. I Part 1:** 331
Let Evening Come (Kenyon), **Supp. VII:** 160, 169–171
Lethem, Jonathan, **Supp. IX:** 122; **Supp. XVIII: 135–153; Supp. XXII:** 49
Let It Come Down (Bowles), **Supp. IV Part 1:** 87
Let It Ride (Pickering), **Supp. XXI:** 198– 199
"Let Me Be" (Levine), **Supp. V:** 181, 189
"Let Me Begin Again" (Levine), **Supp. V:** 181, 189
"Let No Charitable Hope" (Wylie), **Supp. I Part 2:** 713–714, 729
Let No Man Write My Epitaph (film, Leacock), **Supp. XVII:** 150, 158
Let No Man Write My Epitaph (W. Motley), **Supp. XVII:** 150, **158–160**
Let Noon Be Fair (W. Motley), **Supp. XVII:** 161
Letofsky, Irv, **Supp. XVI:** 167
"Let one Eye his watches keep/While the Other Eye doth sleep" (Fletcher),

Supp. IV Part 2: 621
Let's Balance the Books (radio show; Untermeyer), **Supp. XV:** 311
"Letter . . ." (Whittier), **Supp. I Part 2:** 687
"Letter, A" (Bogan), **Supp. III Part 1:** 54
"Letter, May 2, 1959" (Olson), **Supp. II Part 2:** 579, 580
"Letter, Much Too Late" (Stegner), **Supp. IV Part 2:** 613
"Letter, The" (Boulton), **Supp. XXII:** 22
"Letter, The" (Gioia), **Supp. XV:** 120
"Letter, The" (Malamud), **Supp. I Part 2:** 435–436
"Letter about Money, Love, or Other Comfort, If Any, The" (Warren), **IV:** 245
Letter Addressed to the People of Piedmont, on the Advantages of the French Revolution, and the Necessity of Adopting Its Principles in Italy, A (Barlow), **Supp. II Part 1:** 80, 81
"Letter for Marion, A" (McGrath), **Supp. X:** 116
"Letter from Aldermaston" (Merwin), **Supp. III Part 1:** 347
"Letter from a London Attic" (Pickering), **Supp. XXI:** 194
"Letter from a Region in My Mind" (Baldwin). *See* "Down at the Cross"
"Letter from Aunt Belle, A" (Kooser), **Supp. XIX:** 117
Letter from Li Po, A (Aiken), **I:** 68
"Letter from 'Manhattan' " (Didion), **Supp. IV Part 1:** 205
"Letter from the Country" (column, C. Bly), **Supp. XVI:** 33
Letter from the End of the Twentieth Century (Harjo), **Supp. XII:** 223
"Letter from the End of the Twentieth Century" (Harjo), **Supp. XII:** 227
"Letter Home" (Trethewey), **Supp. XXI:** 254
"Letter on Céline" (Kerouac), **Supp. III Part 1:** 232
Letters (Cato), **II:** 114
Letters (Landor), **Supp. I Part 2:** 422
Letters (White), **Supp. I Part 2:** 651, 653, 675, 680
Letters (Wolfe), **IV:** 462
"Letters, The" (Swados), **Supp. XIX:** 261, 262
Letters and Leadership (Brooks), **I:** 228, 240, 245, 246
"Letters for the Dead" (Levine), **Supp. V:** 186
Letters from an American Farmer (Crèvecoeur), **Supp. I Part 1:** 227–251
Letters from Maine (Sarton), **Supp. VIII: 261**
"Letters from Maine" (Sarton), **Supp. VIII:** 261
"Letters from My Father" (R. O. Butler), **Supp. XII:** 71
Letters from the Country (C. Bly), **Supp. XVI: 33–34,** 35, 37
Letters from the Earth (Twain), **IV:** 209

Letters from the East (Bryant), **Supp. I Part 1:** 158

"Letters from the Ming Dynasty" (Brodsky), **Supp. VIII:** 28

Letters of Angelicus and Fidelio Fobb (O'Hara and Berkson), **Supp. XXIII:** 218

Letters of a Traveller (Bryant), **Supp. I Part 1:** 158

Letters of a Traveller, Second Series (Bryant), **Supp. I Part 1:** 158

Letters of Emily Dickinson, The (Johnson and Ward, eds.), **I:** 470; **Retro. Supp. I:** 28

Letters of William James (Henry James, ed.), **II:** 362

Letters on Various Interesting and Important Subjects . . . (Freneau), **Supp. II Part 1:** 272

Letters to a Niece (Adams), **I:** 22

Letters to a Teacher (Pickering), **Supp. XXI:** 195, 201–202

Letters to a Young Poet (Rilke), **Supp. XIII:** 74; **Supp. XV:** 93

"Letters to Dead Imagists" (Sandburg), **I:** 421

"Letters Written on a Ferry While Crossing Long Island Sound" (Sexton), **Supp. II Part 2:** 683

"Letter to Abbé Raynal" (Paine), **Supp. I Part 2:** 510

"Letter to a Kiss That Died for Us" (Gallagher), **Supp. XXIV:** 170

Letter to a Man in the Fire: Does God Exist or Does He Care? (Price), **Supp. VI:** 267–268

"Letter to American Teachers of History, A" (Adams), **I:** 19

Letter to an Imaginary Friend (McGrath), **Supp. X:** 111, 112–113, 116, **119–125**

"Letter to a Reader" (Sanders), **Supp. XVI:** 266, 267, 268, 269, 275

"Letter to a Young Author" (P. N. Warren), **Supp. XX: 272**

"Letter to a Young Contributor" (Higginson), **Retro. Supp. I:** 31

"Letter to a Young Writer" (Price), **Supp. VI:** 267

"Letter to Bell from Missoula" (Hugo), **Supp. VI:** 142–143

"Letter to E. Franklin Frazier" (Baraka), **Supp. II Part 1:** 49

"Letter to Elaine Feinstein" (Olson), **Supp. II Part 2:** 561

"Letter to Francis Picabia, A" (Boyle), **Supp. XXIV:** 63

"Letter to Freddy" (music) (Bowles), **Supp. IV Part 1:** 82

"Letter to Garber from Skye" (Hugo), **Supp. VI:** 146

"Letter to George Washington" (Paine), **Supp. I Part 2:** 517

"Letter to His Brother" (Berryman), **I:** 172, 173

Letter to His Countrymen, A (Cooper), **I:** 346, 347, 349

"Letter to Kizer from Seattle" (Hugo), **Supp. VI:** 142

Letter to Lord Byron (Auden), **Supp. II Part 1:** 11

"Letter to Lord Byron" (Mumford), **Supp. II Part 2:** 494

"Letter to Matthews from Barton Street Flats" (Hugo), **Supp. VI:** 133

"Letter to Minnesota" (Dunn), **Supp. XI:** 146

"Letter to Mr." (Poe), **III:** 411

"Letter Too Late to Vallejo" (Salinas), **Supp. XIII:** 313, 324

"Letter to Sister Madeline from Iowa City" (Hugo), **Supp. VI:** 142–143

"Letter to Soto" (Salinas), **Supp. XIII:** 325

"Letter to the Lady of the House" (Bausch), **Supp. VII:** 48

"Letter to the Rising Generation, A" (Comer), **I:** 214

"Letter to Walt Whitman" (Doty), **Supp. XI:** 135–136

"Letter to Wendell Berry, A" (Stegner), **Supp. IV Part 2:** 600

"Letter Writer, The" (Singer), **IV:** 20–21

"Let the Air Circulate" (Clampitt), **Supp. IX:** 45

Let the Hurricane Roar (Lane), **Supp. XXII:** 297

"Letting Down of the Hair, The" (Sexton), **Supp. II Part 2:** 692

Letting Go (P. Roth), **Retro. Supp. II:** 282, 283; **Supp. III Part 2:** 403, 404, 409–412

"Letting the Puma Go" (Dunn), **Supp. XI:** 149

"Lettres d'un Soldat" (Stevens), **Retro. Supp. I:** 299

Let Us Go into the Starry Night (Shanley), **Supp. XIV:** 317

Let Us Highly Resolve (Stratton-Porter), **Supp. XX: 223**

Let Us Now Praise Famous Men (Agee and Evans), **I:** 25, 27, 35, 36–39, 42, 45, 293

Let Your Mind Alone! (Thurber), **Supp. I Part 2:** 608

Leutze, Emanuel, **Supp. X:** 307

Levels of the Game (McPhee), **Supp. III Part 1:** 292, 294, 301

Levertov, Denise, **Retro. Supp. I:** 411; **Supp. III Part 1: 271–287; Supp. III Part 2:** 541; **Supp. IV Part 1:** 325; **Supp. VIII:** 38, 39; **Supp. XVI:** 39, 40; **Supp. XIX:** 282; **Supp. XXI:** 228; **Supp. XXII:** 83, 168, 177

Levi, Primo, **Supp. X:** 149; **Supp. XVII:** 48

Leviathan (Auster), **Supp. XII:** 27, **33–34**

"Leviathan" (Lowell), **II:** 537, 538

"Leviathan" (Merwin), **Supp. III Part 1:** 345

Levin, Adam, **Supp. XXII:** 268

Levin, Harry, **Supp. I Part 2:** 647

Levin, Jennifer, **Supp. X:** 305

Levin, Meyer, **Supp. XX: 34**

Lévinas, Emmanuel, **Supp. XVI:** 290, 291

Levine, Ellen, **Supp. V:** 4; **Supp. XI:** 178

Levine, Paul, **Supp. IV Part 1:** 221, 224

Levine, Philip, **Supp. III Part 2:** 541; **Supp. V: 177–197,** 337; **Supp. IX:** 293; **Supp. XI:** 123, 257, 259, 267, 271, 315; **Supp. XIII:** 312; **Supp. XV:** 73, 74, 212; **Supp. XIX:** 45

Levine, Rosalind, **Supp. XII:** 123

Levine, Sherry, **Supp. XII:** 4

Levis, Larry, **Supp. V:** 180; **Supp. IX:** 299; **Supp. XI: 257–274; Supp. XIII:** 312; **Supp. XV:** 73; **Supp. XVII:** 110

Lévi-Strauss, Claude, **Supp. I Part 2:** 636; **Supp. IV Part 1:** 45; **Supp. IV Part 2:** 490; **Supp. XVIII:** 190

Levitation: Five Fictions (Ozick), **Supp. V:** 268–270

"Levitation with Baby" (Nelson), **Supp. XVIII:** 173

Levitt, Saul, **Supp. XV:** 197

Levy, Alan, **Supp. IV Part 2:** 574, 589

Levy, D. A., **Supp. XXIII:** 174

Levy, G. Rachel, **Supp. I Part 2:** 567

Levy, Julien, **Supp. XXII:** 167, 168

Lévy-Bruhl, Lucien, **Retro. Supp. I:** 57

Levy Mayer and the New Industrial Era (Masters), **Supp. I Part 2:** 473

Lewes, George Henry, **II:** 569

Lewin, Albert, **Supp. XIV:** 279, 293

Lewis, C. Day, **III:** 527

Lewis, Dr. Claude, **II:** 442

Lewis, David Levering, **Supp. XVIII:** 127; **Supp. XIX:** 74, 75; **Supp. XXII:** 13

Lewis, Edith, **I:** 313; **Retro. Supp. I:** 19, 21, 22

Lewis, Edwin, J., **II:** 439, 442

Lewis, Jerry, **Supp. IV Part 2:** 575; **Supp. X:** 172

Lewis, John L., **I:** 493

Lewis, Lilburn, **IV:** 243

Lewis, Lorene, **Supp. IV Part 2:** 596, 597

Lewis, Lucy, **IV:** 243

Lewis, Maggie, **Supp. V:** 23

Lewis, Meriwether, **II:** 217; **III:** 14; **IV:** 179, 243, 283

Lewis, Merrill, **Supp. IV Part 2:** 596, 597

Lewis, Michael, **II:** 451, 452; **Supp. XVII:** 210

Lewis, Robert Q., **Supp. IV Part 2:** 574

Lewis, R. W. B., **I:** 386, 561; **II:** 457–458; **Retro. Supp. I:** 362, 367; **Supp. I Part 1:** 233; **Supp. XIII:** 93; **Supp. XXIII:** 42

Lewis, Sinclair, **I:** 116, 212, 348, 355, 362, 374, 378, 487, 495; **II:** 27, 34, 74, 79, 271, 277, 306, **439–461,** 474; **III:** 28, 40, 51, 60, 61, 63–64, 66, 70, 71, 106, 394, 462, 572, 606; **IV:** 53, 326, 366, 455, 468, 475, 482; **Retro. Supp. I:** 332; **Retro. Supp. II:** 95, 108, 197, 322; **Supp. I Part 2:** 378, 613, 709; **Supp. IV Part 2:** 678; **Supp. V:** 278; **Supp. IX:** 308; **Supp. X:** 137; **Supp. XVII:** 41; **Supp. XVIII:** 278; **Supp. XXII:** 190; **Supp. XXIII:** 165, 166; **Supp. XXIV:** 29

Lewis, Mrs. Sinclair (Dorothy Thompson), **II:** 449–450, 451, 453

Lewis, Mrs. Sinclair (Grace Livingston Hegger), **II:** 441

Lewis, Wyndham, **III:** 458, 462, 465, 470; **Retro. Supp. I:** 59, 170, 292;

Supp. III Part 2: 617
Lewisohn, Ludwig, **Supp. XXIII:** 1
Lexicon Tetraglotton (Howell), **II:** 111
"Lexington Avenue Musedog" (Peacock), **Supp. XIX:** 204
"Leyenda" (Mora), **Supp. XIII:** 214
Leyner, Mark, **Supp. XIX:** 223
Leyte (Morison), **Supp. I Part 2:** 491
"Liar, The" (Baraka), **Supp. II Part 1:** 36
"Liars, The" (Sandburg), **III:** 586
Liars' Club, The: A Memoir (Karr), **Supp. XI:** 239, 240, 241, 242, **244–248,** 252, 254; **Supp. XVI:** 70
Liar's Dice (C. Frost), **Supp. XV:** 93, 96
"Liar's Dice" (C. Frost), **Supp. XV:** 94, 107
Liars in Love (Yates), **Supp. XI:** 348, 349
Libation Bearers, The (Aeschylus), **III:** 398; **Supp. IX:** 103
Li Bay. *See* Li Po
Libby, Anthony, **Supp. XIII:** 87
Libera, Padre, **II:** 278
Liberal Imagination, The (Trilling), **III:** 308; **Retro. Supp. I:** 97, 216; **Supp. II Part 1:** 146; **Supp. III Part 2:** 495, 498, 501–504
Liberating Voices: Oral Tradition in African American Literature (G. Jones), **Supp. XXIV:** 185
Liberation (J. Scott), **Supp. XVII:** 192, **194–196**
"Liberation" (Winters), **Supp. II Part 2:** 791
Liber Brunenesis (yearbook), **IV:** 286
Liberties, The (Howe), **Supp. IV Part 2:** 426–428, 430, 432
Liberties of America, The (H. Warner), **Supp. XVIII:** 259
Liberty Jones (play), **Supp. IV Part 1:** 83
"Liberty Tree" (Paine), **Supp. I Part 2:** 505
Libra (DeLillo), **Supp. VI:** 2, **4, 5,** 6, **7,** 9, 10, 12, 13, 14, 16
Library for Juana, A (Mora), **Supp. XIII:** 218
Library of America, **Retro. Supp. I:** 2
"Library of Babel, The" (J. Borges), **Supp. XVII:** 47
"Library of Law, A" (MacLeish), **III:** 4
"Library of Moloch, The" (Bukiet), **Supp. XVII:** 47, 49
"Librettos for Eros" (Gander), **Supp. XV:** 340
Lice, The (Merwin), **Supp. III Part 1:** 339, 341–342, 346, 348, 349, 355
"License Plate, The" (Ferry), **Supp. XXIV:** 157
Lichtenberg, Georg Christoph, **Supp. XIV:** 339
Lichtenstein, Roy, **Supp. I Part 2:** 665; **Supp. XV:** 186
"Liddy's Orange" (Olds), **Supp. X:** 209
"Lie, The" (Antin), **Supp. XX:** 7, **9–10**
Lieberman, Herman (Chaim), **Supp. XXIII:** 3, 7
Lieberman, Laurence, **Supp. XI:** 323–324

Liebestod (Wagner), **I:** 284, 395
Liebling, A. J., **IV:** 290; **Supp. VIII:** 151; **Supp. XVI:** 167
Lie Down in Darkness (Styron), **IV:** 98, 99, 100–104, 105, 111; **Supp. XI:** 343
"Lie Down with the Lamb" (Gallagher), **Supp. XXIV:** 171
Lie of the Mind, A (Shepard), **Supp. III Part 2:** 433, 435, 441, 447–449
"Lies" (Haines), **Supp. XII:** 204
Lies (Hoffman), **Supp. XVIII: 78–79**
"Lies and Consequences" (Pickering), **Supp. XXI:** 204
Lies Like Truth (Clurman), **IV:** 385
Lieutenant, The (Dubus), **Supp. VII:** 78
"Life" (Wharton), **Retro. Supp. I:** 372
Life along the Passaic River (W. C. Williams), **Retro. Supp. I:** 423
Life Among the Savages (Jackson), **Supp. IX:** 115, **125**
Life and Adventures of Charles Anderson Chester, The (Lippard), **Supp. XXIII:** 184
"Life and Death Kisses, The" (Grossman), **Supp. XIX:** 87
Life and Gabriella (Glasgow), **II:** 175, 176, 182–183, 184, 189
"Life and I" (Wharton), **Retro. Supp. I:** 360, 361, 362
"Life and Letters" (Epstein), **Supp. XIV:** 104–105
"Life and Letters in New England" (Emerson), **Supp. XXIV:** 67
Life and Letters of Harrison Gray Otis, Federalist, 1765–1848, The (Morison), **Supp. I Part 2:** 480–481
Life and Letters of Sir Henry Wotton (L. P. Smith), **Supp. XIV:** 340–341
Life and Mind of Emily Dickinson, The (Taggard), **Supp. XXII:** 279
Life and Times of Frederick Douglass, Written by Himself, The (Douglass), **Supp. III Part 1:** 155, 159–163
Life and Writings of Horace McCoy, The (Wolfson), **Supp. XIII:** 172, 174
"Life as a Visionary Spirit" (Eberhart), **I:** 540, 541
"Life at Angelo's, A" (Benét), **Supp. XI:** 53
Life at Happy Knoll (Marquand), **III:** 50, 61
Life Before Man (Atwood), **Supp. XIII: 24–25**
"Life Cycle of Common Man" (Nemerov), **III:** 278
"Lifecycle Stairmaster" (Karr), **Supp. XI:** 250
Life Estates (Hearon), **Supp. VIII: 68–69**
Life for Life's Sake (Aldington), **Supp. I Part 1:** 256
Life Full of Holes, A (Layachi), **Supp. IV Part 1:** 92
"Lifeguard" (Updike), **IV:** 226; **Retro. Supp. I:** 325
"Lifeguard, The" (Dickey), **Supp. IV Part 1:** 179–180
"Life in the 30s" (column, Quindlen), **Supp. XVII:** 165, 167–169
Life in the Clearings (Shields), **Supp. VII:** 313

"Life in the Country: A City Friend Asks, 'Is It Boring?' " (Paley), **Supp. VI:** 231
Life in the Forest (Levertov), **Supp. III Part 1:** 282–283
Life in the Iron Mills (R. H. Davis), **Supp. XIII:** 292, 295, 299, 305; **Supp. XVI:** 79–82, **85–88,** 91
Life in the Iron Mills and Other Stories (T. Olson, ed.), **Supp. XVI:** 83
Life in the Theatre, A (Mamet), **Supp. XIV:** 241, 255
Life in the War Zone (Atherton), **Supp. XXIV:** 24
Life Is a Miracle: An Essay Against Modern Superstition (Berry), **Supp. X:** 35
"Life Is Fine" (Hughes), **Supp. I Part 1:** 334, 338
"Life Is Motion" (Stevens), **IV:** 74
Life & Letters of Gene Stratton-Porter (Meehan), **Supp. XX: 213**
Life of Albert Gallatin, The (Adams), **I:** 6, 14
"Life of a Man of the World, The"(Lippard), **Supp. XXIII:** 189
Life of an Ordinary Woman, The: Anne Ellis (A. Ellis), **Supp. XVI:** 38
Life of Captain Cipriani, The: An Account of British Government in the West Indies (C. L. R. James), **Supp. XXI:** 161
Life of Dryden (Johnson), **Retro. Supp. II:** 223
Life of Emily Dickinson, The (Sewall), **Retro. Supp. I:** 25
Life of Forms, The (Focillon), **IV:** 90
Life of Franklin Pierce (Hawthorne), **Retro. Supp. I:** 163
Life of George Cabot Lodge, The (Adams), **I:** 21
Life of George Washington (Irving), **II:** 314, 315–316
Life of Henry James (Edel), **Retro. Supp. I:** 224
"Life of Irony, The" (Bourne), **I:** 219
Life of Jesus (Renan), **Supp. XX: 122**
"Life of Lincoln West, The" (Brooks), **Supp. III Part 1:** 86
Life of Mary, The (Rilke; F. Wright, trans.), **Supp. XVII:** 244
Life of Michelangelo (Grimm), **II:** 17
"Life of Nancy, The" (Jewett), **Retro. Supp. II:** 133, 144
Life of Oliver Goldsmith, The, with Selections from His Writings (Irving), **II:** 315
Life of Phips (Mather), **Supp. II Part 2:** 451, 452, 459
Life of Poetry, The (Rukeyser), **Supp. VI:** 271, 273, 275–276, 282, 283, 286
Life of Samuel Johnson (Boswell), **Supp. I Part 2:** 656
Life of Savage (Johnson), **Supp. I Part 2:** 523
Life of the Drama, The (Bentley), **IV:** 396
"Life of the Mind, The" (Kees), **Supp. XV:** 140
Life of the Right Reverend Joseph P. Machebeuf, The (Howlett), **Retro. Supp. I:** 17

Life of Thomas Paine, author of Rights of Men, With a Defence of his Writings (Chalmers), **Supp. I Part 2:** 514

Life of Thomas Paine, The (Cobbett), **Supp. I Part 2:** 517

"Life of Towne, The" (Carson), **Supp. XII: 102**

Life of William Ellery Channing (W. H. Channing), **Supp. XXIV:** 68

"Life on Beekman Place, A" (Naylor), **Supp. VIII:** 214

"Life on the Black List" (Endore), **Supp. XVII:** 63

Life on the Hyphen: The Cuban-American Way (Firmat), **Supp. VIII:** 76; **Supp. XI:** 184

Life on the Mississippi (Twain), **I:** 209; **IV:** 198, 199; **Supp. I Part 2:** 440

"Life on the Rocks: The Galápagos" (Dillard), **Supp. VI:** 32

"Life Stories, East and West" (E. Hoffman), **Supp. XVI:** 157

Life Story (Baker), **II:** 259

Life Studies (Lowell), **I:** 400; **II:** 384, 386, 543, 546–550, 551, 555; **Retro. Supp. II:** 180, 185, 186, 188, 189, 191; **Supp. I Part 2:** 543; **Supp. XI:** 240, 244, 250, 317; **Supp. XII:** 255; **Supp. XIV:** 15; **Supp. XV:** 252

"Life Studies" (Lowell), **Retro. Supp. II:** 188

"Life Styles in the Golden Land" (Didion), **Supp. IV Part 1:** 200

Life Supports: New and Collected Poems (Bronk), **Supp. XXI:** 19, 31, 32

"Life That Is, The" (Bryant), **Supp. I Part 1:** 169

"Life Work" (Stafford), **Supp. XI:** 329–330

"Life You Save May Be Your Own, The" (O'Connor), **III:** 344, 350, 354; **Retro. Supp. II:** 229, 230, 233

Lifshin, Lyn, **Supp. XVI:** 37

"Lifting, The" (Olds), **Supp. X:** 210

"Ligeia" (Poe), **III:** 412, 414; **Retro. Supp. II:** 261, 270, 271, 275

Liggett, Walter W., **Supp. XIII:** 168

Light, James F., **IV:** 290; **Retro. Supp. II:** 325

Light, Kate, **Supp. XVII:** 109

Light and Dark (Bronk), **Supp. XXI: 27–29,** 31

"Light and the Sufferer" (Lethem), **Supp. XVIII:** 139–140

Light around the Body, The (R. Bly), **Supp. IV Part 1:** 61–62, 62; **Supp. XVII:** 243; **Supp. XXI:** 84–85

"Light Comes Brighter, The" (Roethke), **III:** 529–530

"Light from Above" (Eberhart), **I:** 541

Light in August (Faulkner), **II:** 63–64, 65, 74; **IV:** 207; **Retro. Supp. I:** 82, 84, 85, 86, 89, 92; **Supp. XIV:** 12

Light in the Forest, The (Richter), **Supp. XVIII: 216–217**

Light in the Morning (Baker), **Supp. XVIII:** 263, 269

"Light Man, A" (James), **II:** 322; **Retro. Supp. I:** 219

"Lightning" (Barthelme), **Supp. IV Part 1:** 53

"Lightning" (Bynner), **Supp. XV:** 44

"Lightning" (Oliver), **Supp. VII:** 235

"Lightning, The" (Swenson), **Supp. IV Part 2:** 645

"Lightning Flash, The" (Gibran), **Supp. XX:** 123

"Lightning Rod Man, The" (Melville), **III:** 90; **Supp. XVIII:** 4

"Light of the World, The" (Hemingway), **II:** 249

"Lights"(Dybek), **Supp. XXIII:** 72

"Lights in the Windows" (Nye), **Supp. XIII:** 280

"Lights Must Never Go Out, The"(Hadas), **Supp. XXIII:** 125

"Light Through the Window, The" (Brockmeier), **Supp. XXII:** 52, 59

Light Verse and Satires (Bynner), **Supp. XV:** 52

Light Years (Salter), **Supp. IX: 257–259**

"LIKE, THIS IS WHAT I MEANT!" (Baraka), **Supp. II Part 1:** 59

"Like All the Other Nations" (Paley), **Supp. VI:** 220

"Like a Rolling Stone" (song, Dylan), **Supp. XVIII:** 20, 30

"Like Decorations in a Nigger Cemetery" (Stevens), **IV:** 74, 79; **Retro. Supp. I:** 305

Like Ghosts of Eagles (Francis), **Supp. IX:** 86

"Like Life" (Moore), **Supp. X:** 163, 165, **172–173**

Like Life: Stories (Moore), **Supp. X:** 163, **171–175,** 177, 178

"Likeness to God" (Channing), **Supp. XXIV: 75–76,** 77, 78

"Like Talk" (Mills), **Supp. XI:** 311

"Like the New Moon I Will Live My Life" (R. Bly), **Supp. IV Part 1:** 71

Li'l Abner (Capp), **IV:** 198

"Lilacs" (Lowell), **II:** 527

"Lilacs, The" (Wilbur), **Supp. III Part 2:** 557–558

"Lilacs for Ginsberg" (Stern), **Supp. IX:** 299

Liliom (Molnar), **Supp. XVI:** 187

Lilith's Brood (O. Butler), **Supp. XIII:** 63

Lillabulero Press, **Supp. V:** 4, 5

Lillian Hellman (Adler), **Supp. I Part 1:** 297

Lillian Hellman (Falk), **Supp. I Part 1:** 297

Lillian Hellman: Playwright (Moody), **Supp. I Part 1:** 280

Lillo, George, **II:** 111, 112

"Lily Daw and the Three Ladies" (Welty), **IV:** 262

Lily for My Love, A (Berrigan), **Supp. XXIV:** 35

Lima, Agnes de, **I:** 231, 232

Lima, Frank, **Supp. XXIII:** 217, 221

Lima, Maria Helena, **Supp. XXII:** 73

Lima Beans (Kreymborg), **Supp. XXII:** 163

"Limbo: Altered States" (Karr), **Supp. XI:** 249–250

"Limen" (Trethewey), **Supp. XXI:** 250

Lime Orchard Woman, The (Ríos), **Supp. IV Part 2:** 538, 547–550, 553

"Lime Orchard Woman, The" (Ríos), **Supp. IV Part 2:** 548

Limitations (Turow), **Supp. XVII: 222–223**

"Limits" (Emerson), **II:** 19

Limits of Mortality, The: An Essay on Wordsworth's Major Poems (Ferry), **Supp. XXIV:** 147, 148

Lincoln, Abraham, **I:** 1, 4, 30; **II:** 8, 13, 135, 273, 555, 576; **III:** 576, 577, 580, 584, 587–590, 591; **IV:** 192, 195, 298, 347, 350, 444; **Supp. I Part 1:** 2, 8, 26, 309, 321; **Supp. I Part 2:** 379, 380, 382, 385, 390, 397, 399, 418, 424, 454, 456, 471, 472, 473, 474, 483, 579, 687; **Supp. VIII:** 108; **Supp. IX:** 15; **Supp. XIV:** 73

Lincoln, Kenneth, **Supp. IV Part 1:** 329; **Supp. IV Part 2:** 507

Lincoln, Thomas, **III:** 587

Lincoln, Mrs. Thomas (Nancy Hanks), **III:** 587

Lincoln: A Novel (Vidal), **Supp. IV Part 2:** 677, 684, 685, 688, 689–690, 691, 692

Lincoln Lawyer, The (Connelly), **Supp. XXI: 77,** 78

Lincoln on Race and Slavery (H. L. Gates), **Supp. XX: 108–109**

"Lincoln Relics, The" (Kunitz), **Supp. III Part 1:** 269

Lincoln: The Man (Masters), **Supp. I Part 2:** 471, 473–474

Lindbergh, Charles A., **I:** 482

"Linden Branch, The" (MacLeish), **III:** 19, 20

Linden Hills (Naylor), **Supp. VIII:** 214, 218, **219–223**

Linderman, Lawrence, **Supp. IV Part 2:** 579, 583, 585, 589

Lindner, April, **Supp. XV:** 111, 119

Lindsay, Howard, **III:** 284

Lindsay, John, **Supp. I Part 2:** 374

Lindsay, Olive, **Supp. I Part 2:** 374, 375, 392

Lindsay, Vachel, **I:** 384; **II:** 263, 276, 530; **III:** 5, 505; **Retro. Supp. I:** 133; **Supp. I Part 1:** 324; **Supp. I Part 2: 374–403,** 454, 473, 474; **Supp. III Part 1:** 63, 71; **Supp. XV:** 293, 297, 299, 301, 306; **Supp. XVI:** 184–185

Lindsay, Mrs. Vachel (Elizabeth Connors), **Supp. I Part 2:** 398, 399, 473

Lindsay, Vachel Thomas, **Supp. I Part 2:** 374, 375

Lindsay, Mrs. Vachel Thomas (Esther Catherine Frazee), **Supp. I Part 2:** 374, 375, 384–385, 398

Lindsey, David, **Supp. XIV:** 26

"Line, The" (Olds), **Supp. X:** 206

Lineage of Ragpickers, Songpluckers, Elegiasts, and Jewelers, A (Goldbarth), **Supp. XII:** 191

"Line"(Crooker), **Supp. XXIII:** 58

Line Dance (Crooker), **Supp. XXIII:** 56, **58–60**

"Line Dance"(Crooker), **Supp. XXIII:** 59

"Line of Least Resistance, The" (Wharton), **Retro. Supp. I:** 366

Line Out for a Walk, A: Familiar Essays (Epstein), **Supp. XIV:** 107

"Liner Notes for the Poetically Unhep" (Hughes), **Retro. Supp. I:** 210

"Lines After Rereading T. S. Eliot" (Wright), **Supp. V:** 343

"Lines Composed a Few Miles Above Tintern Abbey" (Wordsworth), **Supp. III Part 1:** 12

"Lines Composed Over Three Thousand Miles from Tintern Abbey" (Collins), **Supp. XXI:** 57–58

"Lines for an Interment" (MacLeish), **III:** 15

"Lines for My Father" (Cullen), **Supp. IV Part 1:** 167

"Lines from Israel" (Lowell), **II:** 554

"Lines from Pietro Longhi" (Sobin), **Supp. XVI:** 289

"Lines on Revisiting the Country" (Bryant), **Supp. I Part 1:** 164

"Lines Suggested by a Tennessee Song" (Agee), **I:** 28

"Lines to a Friend Asleep"(J. Schoolcraft), **Supp. XXIII:** 228, 230

"Line-Storm Song, A" (Frost), **Retro. Supp. I:** 127

"Lines written at Castle Island, Lake Superior"(J. Schoolcraft), **Supp. XXIII:** 229, 232, 233

"Lines Written at Port Royal" (Freneau), **Supp. II Part 1:** 264

"Lines Written in an Asylum" (Carruth), **Supp. XVI:** 48

"Lines Written in Manassas", **Supp. XV:** 99–100

Lineup, The (Connelly), **Supp. XXI:** 67, 68–69

"Line Written in the Dark Illegible Next Day" (F. Wright), **Supp. XVII:** 242

Linfield, Susie, **Supp. XVII:** 169, 177

Lingeman, Richard, **Supp. X:** 82; **Supp. XXII:** 104

Linn, Elizabeth. *See* Brown, Mrs. Charles Brockden (Elizabeth Linn)

Linn, John Blair, **Supp. I Part 1:** 145

Linnaeus, Carolus, **II:** 6; **Supp. I Part 1:** 245

"Linnets" (Levis), **Supp. XI:** 260, 261

"Linoleum" (Gallagher), **Supp. XXIV:** 170

"Linoleum Roses" (Cisneros), **Supp. VII:** 63, 66

Linotte: 1914–1920 (Nin), **Supp. X:** 193, 196, 197

Linschoten, Hans, **II:** 362, 363, 364

"Lion" (B. Kelly), **Supp. XVII:** 133

"Lion and Honeycomb" (Nemerov), **III:** 275, 278, 280

Lion and the Archer, The (Hayden), **Supp. II Part 1:** 366, 367

Lion and the Honeycomb, The (Blackmur), **Supp. II Part 1:** 91

Lion Country (Buechner), **Supp. XII:** 52, 53

Lionel Lincoln (Cooper), **I:** 339, 342

"Lion for Real, The" (Ginsberg), **Supp. II Part 1:** 320

Lionhearted, The: A Story about the Jews of Medieval England (Reznikoff), **Supp. XIV:** 280, 289

Lion in the Garden (Meriweather and Millgate), **Retro. Supp. I:** 91

"Lionizing" (Poe), **III:** 411, 425

"Lions, Harts, and Leaping Does" (Powers), **III:** 356

Lions and Shadows: An Education in the Twenties (Isherwood), **Supp. XIV:** 158, 159, 160, 162

"Lions in Sweden" (Stevens), **IV:** 79–80

Lipman, William R., **Supp. XIII:** 170

Li Po, **Supp. XI:** 241; **Supp. XII:** 218; **Supp. XV:** 47, 217

Lippard, George, **Supp. XXIII: 177–192**

Lippmann, Walter, **I:** 48, 222–223, 225; **III:** 291, 600; **IV:** 429; **Supp. I Part 2:** 609, 643; **Supp. VIII:** 104

Lipschitz, Moryce, **Supp. XXIII:** 6

Lips Together, Teeth Apart (McNally), **Supp. XIII: 201–202,** 208, 209

Lipsyte, Robert, **Supp. XVI:** 220

Lipton, James, **Supp. IV Part 2:** 576, 577, 579, 583, 586, 588

Lipton, Lawrence, **Supp. IX:** 3

Lisbon Traviata, The (McNally), **Supp. XIII:** 198, **199–200,** 201, 204, 208

Lish, Gordon, **Supp. XIX:** 209; **Supp. XXI:** 115, 121; **Supp. XXIII:** 274; **Supp. XXIV:** 166, 177

Lisicky,Paul, **Supp. XI:** 120, 131, 135

Lisk, Thomas, **Supp. XXI:** 24

"Lisp, The" (Olds), **Supp. X:** 211

Listen, Ruben Fontanez (Neugeboren), **Supp. XVI: 220–221**

"Listeners, The" (de la Mare), **Supp. XVII:** 69

"Listeners and Readers: The Unforgetting of Vachel Lindsay" (Trombly), **Supp. I Part 2:** 403

"Listening" (J. W. Miller), **Supp. XX: 167**

"Listening" (Paley), **Supp. VI:** 218, 231, 232

"Listening" (Stafford), **Supp. XI:** 321, 322

Listening to Prozac (P. Kramer), **Supp. XVI:** 229

"Listening to the Desert" (Henderson), **Supp. XIII:** 221–222

"Listening to the Mockingbird" (Woodard), **Supp. VIII:** 128

Listening to Your Life: Daily Meditations with Frederick Buechner (Buechner), **Supp. XII:** 53

Listen to the Desert/Oye al desierto (Mora), **Supp. XIII:** 221

"Listen to the People" (Benét), **Supp. XI:** 51–52

Liston, Sonny, **III:** 38, 42

Li T'ai-po, **II:** 526

"Litany" (Ashbery), **Supp. III Part 1:** 21–22, 25, 26

"Litany" (Collins), **Supp. XXI:** 56–57

"Litany" (Sandburg), **III:** 593

"Litany, The" (Gioia), **Supp. XV:** 125, 126

"Litany for Dictatorships" (Benét), **Supp. XI:** 46, 58

"Litany for Survival, A" (Lorde), **Supp. XII:** 220

"Litany of the Dark People, The" (Cullen), **Supp. IV Part 1:** 170, 171

"Litany of the Heroes" (Lindsay), **Supp. I Part 2:** 397

"Litany of Washington Street, The" (Lindsay), **Supp. I Part 2:** 376, 398–399

Literary Anthropology (Trumpener and Nyce), **Retro. Supp. I:** 380

Literary Art and Activism of Rick Bass, The (Weltzien), **Supp. XVI:** 20–21

"Literary Blacks and Jews" (Ozick), **Supp. V:** 272

"Literary Career of Elizabeth Barstow Stoddard, The" (Matlack), **Supp. XV:** 269

Literary Criticism: A Short History (Brooks and Wimsatt), **Supp. XIV:** 12

"Literary Criticism of Georg Lukács, The" (Sontag), **Supp. III Part 2:** 453

"Literary Development or California, The" (Atherton), **Supp. XXIV:** 22

Literary Disruptions (Klinkowitz), **Supp. XXI:** 233

Literary Essays of Thomas Merton, The, **Supp. VIII:** 207

"Literary Folk As They Came and Went with Ourselves" (E. Stoddard), **Supp. XV:** 274

Literary Friends and Acquaintance (Howells), **Supp. I Part 1:** 318; **Supp. XV:** 287

"Literary Heritage of Tennyson, The" (Locke), **Supp. XIV:** 197

Literary History of the United States (Spiller et al., ed.), **Supp. I Part 1:** 104; **Supp. II Part 1:** 95

"Literary Importation" (Freneau), **Supp. II Part 1:** 264

"Literary Life of America, The" (Brooks), **I:** 245

"Literary London" (Atherton), **Supp. XXIV:** 24

Literary Outlaw: The Life and Times of William S. Burroughs (Morgan), **Supp. XIV:** 141

Literary Situation, The (Cowley), **Supp. II Part 1:** 135, 140, 144, 146, 147, 148

"Literary Worker's Polonius, The" (Wilson), **IV:** 431, 432

"Literature" (Emerson), **II:** 6

Literature (X. J. Kennedy), **Supp. XV:** 153

Literature and American Life (Boynton), **Supp. I Part 2:** 415

Literature and Insurgency: Ten Studies in Racial Evolution (Underwood), **Supp. XXIV:** 29

Literature and Life (Howells), **Supp. XIV:** 45–46

Literature and Morality (Farrell), **II:** 49

"Literature and Place: Varieties of Regional Experience" (Erisman), **Supp. VIII:** 126

"Literature as a Symptom" (Warren), **IV:** 237

"Literature in Low Life" (Hapgood), **Supp. XVII:** 103

"Literature of Exhaustion, The" (Barth), **Supp. IV Part 1:** 48

"Lithuanian Nocturne" (Brodsky), **Supp. VIII:** 29

"Lit Instructor" (Stafford), **Supp. XI:** 321

Littauer, Kenneth, **Retro. Supp. I:** 114

Little Acts of Kindness (Budbill), **Supp. XIX:** 3, **14–15**

"Little Bernhardt" (Shaw), **Supp. XIX:** 246

Little Big Man (Berger), **Supp. XII:** 171

Little Big Man (film), **Supp. X:** 124

Littlebird, Harold, **Supp. IV Part 2:** 499

Littlebird, Larry, **Supp. IV Part 2:** 499, 505

Little Birds: Erotica (Nin), **Supp. X:** 192, 195

"Little Brown Baby" (Dunbar), **Supp. II Part 1:** 206

"Little Brown Jug" (Baraka), **Supp. II Part 1:** 51

"Little Burst, A"(Strout), **Supp. XXIII:** 282

"Little by Little"(Hadas), **Supp. XXIII:** 115

Little Casino (Sorrentino), **Supp. XXI:** 237, 238

"Little Clown, My Heart" (Cisneros), **Supp. VII:** 71

"Little Cosmic Dust Poem" (Haines), **Supp. XII:** 209–210

"Little Country Girl, A" (Chopin), **Retro. Supp. II:** 71

"Little Curtis" (Parker), **Supp. IX:** 193

Little Disturbances of Man, The (Paley), **Supp. VI:** 218

"Little Dog" (Hughes), **Supp. I Part 1:** 329

Little Dorrit (Dickens), **Supp. I Part 1:** 35

"Little Edward" (Stowe), **Supp. I Part 2:** 587

"Little Elegy" (X. J. Kennedy), **Supp. XV:** 155

"Little Elegy for Antonio Machado"(O'Hara), **Supp. XXIII:** 220

Little Essays Drawn from the Writings of George Santayana (L. P. Smith), **Supp. XIV:** 342

"Little Expressionless Animals" (Wallace), **Supp. X:** 305

"Little Fable" (Hay), **Supp. XIV:** 131

Little Face and Other Stories (Thompson), **Supp. XXIII:** 293–294

"Little Face"(Thompson), **Supp. XXIII:** 293

Littlefield, Catherine, **Supp. IX:** 58

Little Fling, A (Pickering), **Supp. XXI:** 203

Little Foxes, The (Hellman), **Supp. I Part 1:** 276, 278–279, 281, 283, 297

"Little Fred, the Canal Boy" (Stowe), **Supp. I Part 2:** 587

"Little French Mary" (Jewett), **II:** 400

Little Friend, Little Friend (Jarrell), **II:** 367, 372, 375–376

"Little Gidding" (Eliot), **I:** 582, 588; **II:** 539; **Retro. Supp. I:** 66

"Little Girl, My Stringbean, My Lovely Woman" (Sexton), **Supp. II Part 2:** 686

"Little Girl, The" (Paley), **Supp. VI:** 222, **228–229**

"Little Girl Tells a Story to a Lady, A" (Barnes), **Supp. III Part 1:** 36

"Little Goose Girl, The" (Grimm), **IV:** 266

Little Ham (Hughes), **Retro. Supp. I:** 203; **Supp. I Part 1:** 328, 339

Little House in the Big Woods (L. I. Wilder), **Supp. XXII:** 294, 295, 296, 297, 298–299, 300

Little House on the Prairie (L. I. Wilder), **Supp. XXII:** 294, 295–296, 297, 299, 301

Little House on the Prairie (television series), **Supp. XXII:** 289

"Little House" series (L. A. Wilder), **Supp. XXII:** 289

Little House Traveler, A (L. I. Wilder), **Supp. XXII:** 301

Little Ignorance, A (Schott), **Supp. XXIII:** 239, 241

Little King, The (Bynner), **Supp. XV:** 42, 50

Little Lady of the Big House, The (London), **II:** 481–482

Little Liar, The (film; Ingraham), **Supp. XVI:** 184–185

"Little Lion Face" (Swenson), **Supp. IV Part 2:** 651

"Little Lobelia's Song" (Bogan), **Supp. III Part 1:** 66

"Little Local Color, A" (Henry), **Supp. II Part 1:** 399

Little Lord Fauntleroy (Burnett), **Retro. Supp. I:** 188; **Supp. XVI:** 182

"Little Lyric" (Hughes), **Supp. I Part 1:** 334

Little Man, Little Man (Baldwin), **Supp. I Part 1:** 67

"Little Man at Chehaw Station, The" (Ellison), **Retro. Supp. II:** 123

Little Me (musical), **Supp. IV Part 2:** 575

Little Men (Alcott), **Supp. I Part 1:** 32, 39, 40

"Little Morning Music, A" (Schwartz), **Supp. II Part 2:** 662–663

Little Ocean (Shepard), **Supp. III Part 2:** 447

"Little Old Girl, A" (Larcom), **Supp. XIII:** 144

"Little Old Spy" (Hughes), **Supp. I Part 1:** 329

Little Orphan Annie (film), **Supp. XVIII:** 244

"Little Owl Who Lives in the Orchard" (Oliver), **Supp. VII:** 239

"Little Peasant, The" (Sexton), **Supp. II Part 2:** 690

"Little People"(Kenny), **Supp. XXIII:** 151

"Little Rapids, The" (Swenson), **Supp. IV Part 2:** 645

Little Red Song Book (Hill), **Supp. XVIII:** 224

Little Regiment and Other Episodes of the American Civil War, The (Crane), **I:** 408

Little River: New and Selected Poems (McCarriston), **Supp. XIV:** 269–272

"Little Road not made of Man , A" (Dickinson), **Retro. Supp. I:** 44

Little Sister, The (Chandler), **Supp. IV Part 1:** 122, 130, 131–132

"Little Sleep's-Head Sprouting Hair in the Moonlight" (Kinnell), **Supp. III Part 1:** 247

"Little Snow White" (Grimm), **IV:** 266

"Little Spirit, or Boy-Man, The: An Odjibwa Tale"(J. Schoolcraft), **Supp. XXIII:** 234

Little Star (Halliday), **Supp. XIX:** 82, **84–85,** 87

"Little Star" (Halliday), **Supp. XIX:** 83, 84, 93

"Little Testament of Bernard Martin, Aet. 30" (Mumford), **Supp. II Part 2:** 472, 473, 474

"Little Things" (Olds), **Supp. X:** 208

Little Tour in France (James), **II:** 337

Little Town, The (Asch), **Supp. XXIII:** 4, 5, **7–8**

"Little Travel Diary, A"(O'Hara), **Supp. XXIII:** 220

Little Women (Alcott), **Supp. I Part 1:** 28, 29, 32, 35, 37, 38, 39–40, 41, 43, 44; **Supp. IX:** 128

Little Yellow Dog, A (Mosley), **Supp. XIII:** 237, 241

"Liturgy and Spiritual Personalism" (Merton), **Supp. VIII:** 199

Litz, A. Walton, **Retro. Supp. I:** 306

"Liu Ch'e" (Pound), **III:** 466

"Live" (Sexton), **Supp. II Part 2:** 684, 686

Live from Baghdad (screenplay, Shanley), **Supp. XIV:** 316

Live from Golgotha (Vidal), **Supp. IV Part 2:** 677, 682, 691, 692

Live Now and Pay Later (Garrett), **Supp. VII:** 111

"Live-Oak with Moss" (Whitman), **Retro. Supp. I:** 403

Live or Die (Sexton), **Supp. II Part 2:** 670, 683–687

Liveright, Horace, **Retro. Supp. I:** 80, 81, 83; **Supp. I Part 2:** 464; **Supp. XX: 71, 75; Supp. XXII:** 25; **Supp. XXIV:** 28

Livermore, Elizabeth, **Supp. XXII:** 70

Lives (Plutarch), **II:** 5, 104

Lives of a Cell, The (L. Thomas), **Retro. Supp. I:** 322, 323

Lives of Distinguished American Naval Officers (Cooper), **I:** 347

"Lives of Gulls and Children, The" (Nemerov), **III:** 271, 272

Lives of the Animals (Wrigley), **Supp. XVIII: 306–308**

Lives of the Artists (Vasari), **Supp. I Part 2:** 450

"Lives of the Bohemians" (Lethem), **Supp. XVIII:** 135

Lives of the Heart, The (Hirshfield), **Supp. XXIII:** 132–133, 135

Lives of the Muses, The: Nine Women and the Artists They Inspired (Prose), **Supp. XVI:** 250, 260

"Lives of the Philosophers, The" (Brockmeier), **Supp. XXII:** 59, 61

Lives of the Poets (Doctorow), **Supp. IV Part 1:** 234

"Lives of the Poets" (Doctorow), **Supp. IV Part 1:** 234

"Lives of the—Wha'?, The" (Goldbarth), **Supp. XII:** 191

"Living" (Wright), **Supp. XV:** 345

Living, The (Dillard), **Supp. VI:** 23

"Living at Home" (Gordon), **Supp. IV Part 1:** 311

Living by Fiction (Dillard), **Supp. VI:** 23, 31, **32,** 33

Living by the Word (Walker), **Supp. III Part 2:** 521, 522, 526, 527, 535

Living End, The (Elkin), **Supp. VI: 54,** 58

Living Instead (Bronk), **Supp. XXI:** 32

"Living in the Flatlands" (Carruth), **Supp. XVI:** 54

Living in Time (Hadas), **Supp. XXIII:** 120**, 122–123**

Living Is Easy, The (D. West), **Supp. XVIII:** 277, 280, **284–286,** 287

"Living Like Weasels" (Dillard), **Supp. VI:** 26, 33

Living Novel, The (Hicks), **III:** 342

Living of Charlotte Perkins Gilman, The (Gilman), **Supp. XI:** 193, 209

Living off the Country: Essays on Poetry and Place (Haines), **Supp. XII:** 199, 203, 207

"Living on a Giant" (X. J. Kennedy), **Supp. XV:** 163

Living Out Loud (Quindlen), **Supp. XVII:** 166, **167–169**

Living Present, The (Atherton), **Supp. XXIV:** 24

Living Reed, The (Buck), **Supp. II Part 1:** 129–130

Livingston, Myra Cohn, **Supp. XV:** 153, 162

Living Theater, **Retro. Supp. I:** 424

"Living There" (Dickey), **Supp. IV Part 1:** 182–183

Living the Spirit: A Gay American Indian Anthology (Roscoe, ed.), **Supp. IV Part 1:** 330

Living to Prowl (Pickering), **Supp. XXI:** 203

"Living with a Peacock" (O'Connor), **III:** 350

"Livvie" (Welty), **IV:** 265; **Retro. Supp. I:** 348–349

"Livvie Is Back" (Welty), **Retro. Supp. I:** 351

Livy, **II:** 8

Lizzie (film), **Supp. IX:** 125

"Llantos de La Llorona: Warnings from the Wailer" (Mora), **Supp. XIII:** 217, 224

"L'Lapse" (Barthelme), **Supp. IV Part 1:** 45–47, 48

Llosa, Mario Vargas, **Supp. XIX:** 131; **Supp. XXIV:** 89

Lloyd, Fabien. *See* Cravan, Arthur

Lloyd, Henry Demarest, **Supp. I Part 1:** 5

Lloyd George, Harold, **I:** 490

"LMFBR" (Snyder), **Supp. VIII:** 302

Loach, Ken, **Supp. XXIII:** 163

"Loaded Inflections" (Halliday), **Supp. XIX:** 90, 91

"Loam" (Sandburg), **III:** 584–585

"Loan, The" (Malamud), **Supp. I Part 2:** 427, 428, 431, 437

Loberer, Eric, **Supp. XV:** 339

"Local" (McCarriston), **Supp. XIV:** 270

Local Color (Capote), **Supp. III Part 1:** 120

"Local Color" (London), **II:** 475

"Local Family Keeps Son Happy" (Keillor), **Supp. XVI:** 168, 169

Local Girls (Hoffman), **Supp. X:** 77, **90–91,** 92

"Local Girls" (Hoffman), **Supp. X:** 90

Local Habitation & A Name, A (Kooser), **Supp. XIX:** 116, 118, **119–120**

Local Men (Whitehead), **Supp. XV:** 339

Local Time (Dunn), **Supp. XI:** 143, **148–149**

Local Wonders: Seasons in the Bohemian Alps (Kooser), **Supp. XIX:** 115, **126**

"Location" (Halliday), **Supp. XIX:** 87

Lock, Helen, **Supp. XIII:** 233, 237–238

Lock, Robert H., **IV:** 319; **Retro. Supp. I:** 375

Locke, Alain, **Retro. Supp. II:** 115; **Supp. I Part 1:** 323, 325, 341; **Supp. II Part 1:** 53, 176, 182, 228, 247; **Supp. IV Part 1:** 170; **Supp. IX:** 306, 309; **Supp. X:** 134, 137, 139; **Supp. XIV: 195–219; Supp. XVIII:** 122; **Supp. XIX:** 69, 75; **Supp. XXII:** 7, 13

Locke, Duane, **Supp. IX:** 273

Locke, John, **I:** 554–555, 557; **II:** 15–16, 113–114, 348–349, 480; **III:** 294–295; **IV:** 149; **Supp. I Part 1:** 130, 229, 230; **Supp. I Part 2:** 523

Locke, Sondra, **II:** 588

"Locked House, A" (Snodgrass), **Supp. VI:** 323

Locked Room, The (Auster), **Supp. XII:** 22, 24, **27–28**

Locket, The (Masters), **Supp. I Part 2:** 460

Lockridge, Ross, Jr., **Supp. XIX:** 263

"Locksley Hall" (Tennyson), **Supp. IX:** 19

Lockwood Concern, The (O'Hara), **III:** 362, 364, 377–382

"Locus" (Ammons), **Supp. VII:** 28

"Locus" (Hayden), **Supp. II Part 1:** 361–362, 381

"Locusts, the Plaza, the Room, The" (Kees), **Supp. XV:** 141

Loden, Barbara, **III:** 163

Lodge, Henry Cabot, **I:** 11–12, 21

Lodge, Mrs. Henry Cabot, **I:** 11–12, 19

Lodge, Thomas, **IV:** 370

Loeb, Gerald, **Supp. IV Part 2:** 523

Loeb, Harold, **Supp. XXIV:** 49

Loeb, Jacques, **I:** 513; **Retro. Supp. II:** 104; **Supp. I Part 2:** 641

Loeffler, Jack, **Supp. XIII:** 1, 3, 12, 14, 16

Loftus, Mary J., **Supp. XXI:** 245

Lofty Dogmas (A. Finch, M. Kumin and D. Brown, eds.), **Supp. XVII:** 75–76

"Log" (Merrlll), **Supp. III Part 1:** 328

Logan, Rayford W., **Supp. II Part 1:** 171, 194; **Supp. XIV:** 73

Logan, William, **Supp. X:** 201, 213; **Supp. XI:** 131, 132; **Supp. XII:** 98, 107, 113, 184; **Supp. XV:** 212, 226, 251, 257, 260–261, 262,**Supp. XV:** 263, 266

Log Book of "The Loved One," The, **Supp. XI:** 306

Logenbach, James, **Supp. XVII:** 183

"Logging and Pimping and 'Your Pal, Jim' " (Maclean), **Supp. XIV:** 229

Logue, Christopher, **Supp. XIV:** 82

Lohengrin (Wagner), **I:** 216

Lohrfinck, Rosalind, **III:** 107, 117

Lolita (Nabokov), **III:** 246, 247, 255, 258–261; **Retro. Supp. I:** 263, 264, 265, 266, 269, 270, **272–274,** 275; **Supp. V:** 127, 252; **Supp. VIII:** 133; **Supp. XVI:** 294; **Supp. XXII:** 260

"Lolita" (Parker), **Supp. IX:** 193

Lolly Dinks' Doings (E. Stoddard), **Supp. XV:** 273,**Supp. XV:** 286

Lombardi, Marilyn May, **Retro. Supp. II:** 40

London, Eliza, **II:** 465

London, Jack, **I:** 209; **II:** 264, 440, 444, 451, **462–485; III:** 314, 580; **Supp. IV Part 1:** 236; **Supp. V:** 281; **Supp. IX:** 1, 14; **Supp. XIII:** 312; **Supp. XIV:** 227; **Supp. XV:** 115; **Supp. XVI:** 181; **Supp. XVIII:** 90; **Supp. XXII:** 203

London, Mrs. Jack (Bessie Maddern), **II:** 465, 466, 473, 478

London, Mrs. Jack (Charmian Kittredge), **II:** 466, 468, 473, 476, 478, 481

London, John, **II:** 464, 465

London, Scott, **Supp. XIV:** 301, 307, 311

London Embassy, The (Theroux), **Supp. VIII:** 323

London Fields (Amis), **Retro. Supp. I:** 278

"London Letter" (column; Eliot), **Supp. XV:** 306

London Magazine (Plath), **Supp. I Part 2:** 541

London Snow: A Christmas Story (Theroux), **Supp. VIII:** 322

London Suite (Simon), **Supp. IV Part 2:** 576, 581, 582, 588

London: The Biography (Ackroyd), **Supp. XVII:** 180

Loneliness of the Long Distance Runner, The (Sillitoe), **Supp. XX: 195**

Lonely Are the Brave (film), **Supp. XIII:** 6

"Lonely Coast, A" (Proulx), **Supp. VII:** 264

Lonely Crusade (C. Himes), **Supp. XVI:** 135, 139–140

Lonely for the Future (Farrell), **II:** 46, 47

"Lonely Gay Teen Seeking Same" (Egan), **Supp. XIX:** 61
Lonely Impulse of Delight, A (Shanley), **Supp. XIV:** 317–318
"Lonely Street, The" (W. C. Williams), **IV:** 413
"Lonely Worker, A" (Jewett), **Retro. Supp. II:** 132
Lonergan, Wayne, **Supp. I Part 1:** 51
Lonesome Boy (Bontemps), **Supp. XXII:** 6, 13–14
Lonesome Dove (McMurtry), **Supp. V:** 226–228, 231, 232, 233
Lonesome Traveler (Kerouac), **Supp. III Part 1:** 219, 225
"Lonesome Whistle Blowing" (Skow), **Supp. XVI:** 174
"Lone Striker, A" (Frost), **Retro. Supp. I:** 136, 137
Long, Ada, **Supp. V:** 178
Long, Haniel, **Supp. XV:** 46, 49
Long, Huey, **I:** 489; **II:** 454; **IV:** 249; **Supp. IV Part 2:** 679; **Supp. XIV:** 14
Long, John Luther, **Supp. XXI:** 150
Long, Judith Reick, **Supp. XX:** 212, 215, 217, 223
Long, Ray, **II:** 430; **III:** 54
Long after Midnight (Bradbury), **Supp. IV Part 1:** 102
Long Ago in France: The Years in Dijon (M. F. K. Fisher), **Supp. XVII:** 91
Long and Happy Life, A (Price), **Supp. VI:** 258, **259–260,** 262, 264, 265
Long Approach, The (Kumin), **Supp. IV Part 2:** 452–453, 453
Longbottom, Robert, **Supp. XXI:** 148
Long Christmas Dinner, The (Wilder), **IV:** 357, 365; **Supp. V:** 105
Long Christmas Dinner and Other Plays (Wilder), **IV:** 365–366
Long Day's Dying, A (Buechner), **Supp. XII:** 45–47
Long Day's Journey into Night (O'Neill), **III:** 385, 401, 403–404; **Supp. IV Part 1:** 359; **Supp. XIV:** 327; **Supp. XXI:** 13; **Supp. XXII:** 27, 29, 30
Long Desire, A (Connell), **Supp. XIV:** 79, 80, 97
"Long Distance" (Stafford), **Supp. XI:** 329
"Long-Distance Runner, The" (Paley), **Supp. VI:** 221–222, 228, 230
Long Dream, The (Wright), **IV:** 478, 488, 494
"Long Embrace, The" (Levine), **Supp. V:** 187
"Long Enough" (Rukeyser), **Supp. VI:** 274
"Longest Night of My Life, The " (Nichols), **Supp. XIII:** 269
Longfellow, Henry Wadsworth, **I:** 458, 471; **II:** 274, 277, 295–296, 310, 313, 402, **486–510; III:** 269, 412, 421, 422, 577; **IV:** 309, 371; **Retro. Supp. I:** 54, 123, 150, 155, 362; **Retro. Supp. II: 153–174; Supp. I Part 1:** 158, 299, 306, 317, 362, 368; **Supp. I Part 2:** 405, 406, 408, 409, 414, 416, 420, 586, 587, 602, 699, 704; **Supp. II Part 1:** 291, 353; **Supp. III Part 2:**

609; **Supp. IV Part 1:** 165; **Supp. IV Part 2:** 503; **Supp. XII:** 260; **Supp. XIII:** 141; **Supp. XIV:** 120; **Supp. XVIII:** 4; **Supp. XXI:** 51; **Supp. XXIII:** 223
"Long Feud" (Untermeyer), **Supp. XV:** 309
Long Feud: Selected Poems (Untermeyer), **Supp. XV:** 312
"Long Fourth, A" (Taylor), **Supp. V:** 313
Long Fourth and Other Stories, A (Taylor), **Supp. V:** 318–319
Long Gay Book, A (Stein), **IV:** 42
Long Goodbye, The (Chandler), **Supp. IV Part 1:** 120, 122, 132–134, 135
Long Goodbye, The (T. Williams), **IV:** 381
"Long Hair" (Snyder), **Supp. VIII:** 300
Longing for Home, The: Recollections and Reflections (Buechner), **Supp. XII:** 53
Longinus, Dionysius Cassius, **I:** 279
"Long-Legged House, The" (Berry), **Supp. X:** 21, 24–25, 27, 31
Long Live Man (Corso), **Supp. XII:** 129–130, 132
Long Love, The (Sedges), **Supp. II Part 1:** 125
Long Made Short (Dixon), **Supp. XII:** 152
Long March, The (Styron), **IV:** 97, 99, 104–107, 111, 113, 117
"Long Night, The" (Bambara), **Supp. XI:** 9
"Long Novel, A" (Ashbery), **Supp. III Part 1:** 6
Longo, Robert, **Supp. XVI:** 124
Long Patrol, The (Mailer), **III:** 46
"Long Point Light" (Doty), **Supp. XI:** 127
Long Road of Woman's Memory, The (Addams), **Supp. I Part 1:** 17–18
"Long Run, The" (Wharton), **IV:** 314
Long Season, The (Brosnan), **II:** 424, 425; **Supp. XX: 195**
"Long Shadow of Lincoln, The: A Litany" (Sandburg), **III:** 591, 593
Longshot O'Leary (McGrath), **Supp. X:** 117
"Long Shower, The" (Francis), **Supp. IX:** 90
"Long Stemmed Roses" (Jarman), **Supp. XVII:** 115
Longstreet, Augustus B., **II:** 70, 313; **Supp. I Part 1:** 352; **Supp. V:** 44; **Supp. X:** 227
"Long Summer" (Lowell), **II:** 553–554
"Long Term" (Dunn), **Supp. XI:** 149
"Long Thoughts, The"(Dybek), **Supp. XXIII:** 71
Longtime Companion (film), **Supp. X:** 146, 152
Long Valley, The (Steinbeck), **IV:** 51
Long View (Taggard), **Supp. XXII: 283–284**
Long Voyage Home, The (O'Neill), **III:** 388
"Long Wail, A" (Crews), **Supp. XI:** 101
"Long Walk, The" (Bogan), **Supp. III Part 1:** 61

Long Walk Home, The (Kriegel), **Supp. XXIV:** 214–216
Long Walks and Intimate Talks (Paley), **Supp. VI:** 221
Long Way from Home, A (McKay), **Supp. X:** 132, 140
Long Winter, The (L. I. Wilder), **Supp. XXII:** 291, 294, 295
Lönnrot, Elias, **Retro. Supp. II:** 159
Looby, Christopher, **Supp. XIII:** 96
Look, Stranger! (Auden), **Supp. II Part 1:** 11
"Look, The" (Olds), **Supp. X:** 210
Look at Me (Egan), **Supp. XIX:** 49, **53–56,** 60, 61
Look at the Harlequins (Nabokov), **Retro. Supp. I:** 266, 270
"Look for My White Self" (Ammons), **Supp. VII:** 25
"Look Fred, You're a Doctor, My Problem Is Something Like This" (Berrigan), **Supp. XXIV:** 37
Look Homeward, Angel (Wolfe), **II:** 457; **IV:** 450, 452, 453, 454, 455–456, 461, 462, 463, 464, 468, 471; **Supp. XI:** 216
"Looking" (Sanders), **Supp. XVI:** 277
"Looking a Mad Dog Dead in the Eyes" (Komunyakaa), **Supp. XIII:** 114
"Looking at Each Other" (Rukeyser), **Supp. VI:** 280, 285–286
"Looking at Kafka" (P. Roth), **Supp. III Part 2:** 402
"Looking at Women" (Sanders), **Supp. XVI:** 274
"Looking Back" (Harjo), **Supp. XII:** 218
"Looking Back" (Merwin), **Supp. III Part 1:** 352
"Looking Back at Girlhood" (Jewett), **Retro. Supp. II:** 131, 133
Looking Backward (Bellamy), **II:** 276; **Supp. I Part 2:** 641; **Supp. XI:** 200
"Looking for a Ship" (McPhee), **Supp. III Part 1:** 312–313
"Looking for Dragon Smoke" (R. Bly), **Supp. IV Part 1:** 60
Looking for Holes in the Ceiling (Dunn), **Supp. XI:** 139, **143–145**
Looking for Langston (Julien; film), **Supp. XI:** 19, 20
Looking for Lincoln (television production), **Supp. XX: 99**
Looking for Luck (Kumin), **Supp. IV Part 2:** 453, 454–455
"Looking for Mr. Green" (Bellow), **Retro. Supp. II:** 27
"Looking for the Buckhead Boys" (Dickey), **Supp. IV Part 1:** 182, 183
"Looking Forward to Age" (Harrison), **Supp. VIII:** 49
"Looking from Inside My Body" (R. Bly), **Supp. IV Part 1:** 71
"Looking Glass, The" (Wharton), **Retro. Supp. I:** 382
"Lookout's Journal" (Snyder), **Supp. VIII:** 291
"Looks Like They'll Never Learn" (McCoy), **Supp. XIII:** 166
"Look to the Woods" (P. N. Warren), **Supp. XX: 272**

"Look to Thy Heart . . ." (Hay), **Supp. XIV:** 130

Loon, Hendrik Willem van, **Supp. XVI:** 185

Loon Lake (Doctorow), **Supp. IV Part 1:** 219, 222, 224–227, 230, 231, 232, 233

"Loon Point" (O'Brien), **Supp. V:** 237

Loos, Adolf, **Supp. XVI:** 187

Loos, Anita, **Supp. XVI: 181–199**

Loos, Mary Anita, **Supp. XVI:** 196

Loose Canons (H. L. Gates), **Supp. XX: 101, 108, 109–110, 111**

Loosestrife (Dunn), **Supp. XI: 152–154**

"Loosestrife" (Dunn), **Supp. XI:** 154

"Loose Woman" (X. J. Kennedy), **Supp. XV:** 159

Loose Woman: Poems (Cisneros), **Supp. VII:** 58, 71–72

Lopate, Edward, **Supp. XVI:** 266

Lopate, Philip, **Supp. XII:** 184; **Supp. XIII:** 280–281; **Supp. XVI:** 230

Lopatnikoff, Nikolai, **Supp. XIV:** 123

Lopez, Barry, **Supp. IV Part 1:** 416; **Supp. V:** 211; **Supp. X:** 29, 31; **Supp. XIII:** 16; **Supp. XIV:** 227

Lopez, Rafael, **Supp. IV Part 2:** 602

Lorax, The (Geisel), **Supp. XVI:** 109–110

Lorca, Federico García, **IV:** 380; **Supp. I Part 1:** 345; **Supp. IV Part 1:** 83; **Supp. VIII:** 38, 39; **Supp. XIII:** 315, 323, 324; **Supp. XV:** 186; **Supp. XXI:** 100

Lord, Judge Otis P., **I:** 454, 457, 458, 470

Lorde, Audre, **Supp. I Part 2:** 550, 571; **Supp. IV Part 1:** 325; **Supp. XI:** 20; **Supp. XII:** 217, 220; **Supp. XIII:** 295; **Supp. XVII:** 71; **Supp. XXIII:** 194

Lord Jim (Conrad), **I:** 422; **II:** 26; **Retro. Supp. II:** 292; **Supp. I Part 2:** 623; **Supp. IV Part 2:** 680; **Supp. V:** 251

"Lord of Hosts" (Pinsky), **Supp. VI:** 244

Lord of the Flies (W. Golding), **Supp. XVI:** 65

Lord of the Rings (Tolkien), **Supp. V:** 140

Lords of Misrule, The (X. J. Kennedy), **Supp. XV:** 154, **170–171**

Lords of the Housetops (Van Vechten), **Supp. II Part 2:** 736

Lord's Prayer, **I:** 579

Lord Timothy Dexter of Newburyport, Mass. (Marquand), **III:** 55

Lord Weary's Castle (Lowell), **II:** 538, 542–551; **Retro. Supp. II:** 178, **186–187,** 188; **Supp. XV:** 252

"Lorelei" (Plath), **Retro. Supp. II:** 246; **Supp. I Part 2:** 538

"Lorenzo" (Bynner), **Supp. XV:** 46, 50

Lorimer, George Horace, **II:** 430; **Retro. Supp. I:** 101, 113

Lorre, Peter, **Supp. IV Part 1:** 356

"Los Alamos" (Momaday), **Supp. IV Part 2:** 482

Los Amigos de Becky (Hinojosa). *See Becky and Her Friends* (Hinojosa)

"Los Angeles, 1980" (Gunn Allen), **Supp. IV Part 1:** 325

"Los Angeles Days" (Didion), **Supp. IV Part 1:** 211

Los Cerritos (Atherton), **Supp. XXIV:** 22

"Lo! School in Poetry, The" (Taggard), **Supp. XXII:** 276

"Loser, The" (Talese), **Supp. XVII:** 202, 208

Loser and Still Champion: Muhammad Ali (Schulberg), **Supp. XVIII:** 254

Losey, Joseph, **IV:** 383

Lose Your Mother: A Journey Along the Atlantic Slave Route (Hartman), **Supp. XX: 154**

"Losing a Language" (Merwin), **Supp. III Part 1:** 356

Losing Battles (Welty), **IV:** 261, 281–282; **Retro. Supp. I:** 341, 352, **353–354**

"Losing the Marbles" (Merrill), **Supp. III Part 1:** 337

"Losing Track of Language" (Clampitt), **Supp. IX:** 38, 40

Losses (Jarrell), **II:** 367, 372, 373–375, 376, 377, 380–381

"Losses" (Jarrell), **II:** 375–376

Lossky, N. O., **Supp. IV Part 2:** 519

"Loss of Breath" (Poe), **III:** 425–426

"Loss of My Arms and Legs, The" (Kingsolver), **Supp. VII:** 208

"Loss of the Creature, The" (Percy), **Supp. III Part 1:** 387

"Lost" (Wagoner), **Supp. IX:** 328

"Lost, The" (Boyle), **Supp. XXIV:** 59

"Lost, The/Los Perdidos" (Kingsolver), **Supp. VII:** 208

"Lost and Found" (Levine), **Supp. V:** 188

"Lost and Found" (Nelson), **Supp. XVIII:** 176

"Lost Bodies" (Wright), **Supp. V:** 342

"Lost Boy, The" (Wolfe), **IV:** 451, 460, 466–467

"Lost Children, The" (Crooker), **Supp. XXIII:** 54

"Lost Decade, The" (Fitzgerald), **II:** 98

"Lost Dogs of Phnom Penh, The" (Boyle), **Supp. XXIV:** 64

"Lost Fugue for Chet" (Hull), **Supp. XXI:** 137–138, 141

Lost Galleon and Other Tales, The (Harte), **Supp. II Part 1:** 344

Lost Get-Back Boogie, The (Burke), **Supp. XIV:** 22, 25

"Lost Girls, The" (Hogan), **Supp. IV Part 1:** 406–407

Lost Grizzlies, The: A Search for Survivors in the Wilderness of Colorado (Bass), **Supp. XVI:** 25, 26

Lost Highway (film), **Supp. X:** 314

Lost Illusions (Balzac), **I:** 500

"Lost in Nostalgia: The Autobiographies of Eva Hoffman and Richard Rodriguez" (Fachinger), **Supp. XVI:** 153

Lost in the Bonewheel Factory (Komunyakaa), **Supp. XIII: 114–115,** 116

Lost in the City (E. P. Jones), **Supp. XXII:** 140, 142, **143–146,** 148, 149

Lost in the Cosmos: The Last Self-Help Book (Percy), **Supp. III Part 1:** 397

Lost in the Funhouse (Barth), **I:** 122, 135, 139; **Supp. X:** 307

"Lost in the Whichy Thicket" (Wolfe), **Supp. III Part 2:** 573, 574

Lost in Translation (E. Hoffman), **Supp. XVI:** 147, **148–151,** 153, 154, 159

"Lost in Translation" (Hass), **Supp. VIII:** 28

"Lost in Translation" (Merrill), **Supp. III Part 1:** 324, 329–330

Lost in Yonkers (film), **Supp. IV Part 2:** 588

Lost in Yonkers (Simon), **Supp. IV Part 2:** 576, 577, 584, 587–588, 590–591

"Lost Jerusalem" (Untermeyer), **Supp. XV:** 307

Lost Lady, A (Cather), **I:** 323–325, 327; **Retro. Supp. I:** **15–16,** 20, 21, 382

Lost Light (Connelly), **Supp. XXI:** 72, **75–76**

"Lost Lives" (Sorrentino), **Supp. XXI:** 226

"Lost Lover, A" (Jewett), **II:** 400–401, 402; **Retro. Supp. II:** 137

"Lost Loves" (Kinnell), **Supp. III Part 1:** 237, 245

Lost Man's River (Matthiessen), **Supp. V:** 212, 213, 214, 215

"Lost on September Trail, 1967" (Ríos), **Supp. IV Part 2:** 540

Lost Puritan (Mariani), **Retro. Supp. II:** 189

Lost Roads Project, The: A Walk-In Book of Arkansas (exhibition; Wright and Luster), **Supp. XV:** 337, 348

"Lost Sailor, The" (Freneau), **Supp. II Part 1:** 264

Lost Son, The (Roethke), **III:** 529, 530–532, 533

"Lost Son, The" (Roethke), **III:** 536, 537–539, 542

"Lost Sons" (Salter), **Supp. IX:** 260

Lost Souls (Singer). *See Meshugah* (Singer)

"Lost" (Thompson), **Supp. XXIII:** 299, 300

Lost Weekend, The (Jackson), **Supp. XIII:** 262

"Lost World, A" (Ashbery), **Supp. III Part 1:** 9

"Lost World, The" (Chabon), **Supp. XI:** 72–73

Lost World, The (Jarrell), **II:** 367, 368, 371, 379–380, 386, 387

"Lost World, The" cycle (Chabon), **Supp. XI: 71–73**

"Lost World of Richard Yates, The: How the Great Writer of the Age of Anxiety Disappeared from Print" (O'Nan), **Supp. XI:** 348

"Lost Young Intellectual, The" (Howe), **Supp. VI:** 113, **115–116**

Lost Zoo, The: (A Rhyme for the Young, But Not Too Young) (Cullen), **Supp. IV Part 1:** 173

Loti, Pierre, **II:** 311, 325; **Supp. IV Part 1:** 81

"Lot of People Bathing in a Stream, A" (Stevens), **IV:** 93

Lotringer, Sylvère, **Supp. XII:** 4

"Lot's Wife" (Nemerov), **III:** 270

"Lottery, The" (Jackson), **Supp. IX:** 113, 114, 118, 120, **122–123**

Lottery, The; or, The Adventures of James Harris (Jackson), **Supp. IX:** 113, 115, 116, 124, 125

Lotze, Hermann, **III:** 600

Loud and Clear (Quindlen), **Supp. XVII:** 167, **170–172**

Louganis, Greg, **Supp. XX: 264**

"Louie, His Cousin & His Other Cousin" (Cisneros), **Supp. VII:** 60

Louis, Joe, **II:** 589; **Supp. IV Part 1:** 360

Louis, Pierre Charles Alexandre, **Supp. I Part 1:** 302, 303

"Louisa, Please Come Home" (Jackson), **Supp. IX:** 122

Louis Lambert (Balzac), **I:** 499

"Louis Simpson and Walt Whitman: Destroying the Teacher" (Lazer), **Supp. IX:** 265

"Louis Zukofsky: *All: The Collected Short Poems, 1923–1958*" (Creeley), **Supp. IV Part 1:** 154

"Lounge" (Francis), **Supp. IX:** 83

Lounsberry, Barbara, **Supp. XVII:** 208

Lounsbury, Thomas R., **I:** 335

Louter, Jan, **Supp. XI:** 173

"Love" (Collins), **Supp. XXI:** 61

"Love," (Gibran), **Supp. XX: 119**

"Love" (Olson), **Supp. II Part 2:** 571

"Love" (Paley), **Supp. VI:** 219, 222, 230

Love, Deborah, **Supp. V:** 208, 210

Love Alone: 18 Elegies for Rog (Monette), **Supp. X:** 146, 154

Love Always (Beattie), **Supp. V:** 29, 30, 35

Love among the Cannibals (Morris), **III:** 228, 230–231

"Love Among the Ruins" (Mosley), **Supp. XIII:** 247

Love and Death (film; Allen), **Supp. XV:** 2, **5–6,** 7, 11

Love and Death in the American Novel (Fiedler), **Supp. XIII:** 93, 96, **99–101,** 104

Love and Exile (Singer), **Retro. Supp. II: 302–304,** 315

Love and Fame (Berryman), **I:** 170

Love and Friendship (Bloom), **Retro. Supp. II:** 31, 33–34

Love and Glory (Parker), **Supp. XIX:** 189

"Love and How to Cure It" (Wilder), **IV:** 365

Love and Other Games of Chance (Siegel), **Supp. XXII:** 255, 256, **261–265,** 266, 267

Love and Scorn: New and Selected Poems (C. Frost), **Supp. XV:** 95, 96, 100, 103–105, 106

Love and Theft (album, Dylan), **Supp. XVIII:** 28, 31

"Love and the Hate, The" (Jeffers), **Supp. II Part 2:** 434–435

Love and the Incredibly Old Man (Siegel), **Supp. XXII: 267–268**

Love and Will (Dixon), **Supp. XII:** 148, 149

Love and Work (Price), **Supp. VI:** 261

"Love as a Great Power" (Bronk), **Supp. XXI:** 31

"Love Calls Us to the Things of This World" (Wilbur), **Supp. III Part 2:** 544, 552–553

Love Course, The (Gurney), **Supp. V:** 98

Lovecraft, H. P., **Supp. XXII:** 49

Loved One, The (film), **Supp. XI: 305–306,** 307

Loved One, The (Waugh), **Supp. XI:** 305

Love Expert, The (film; Kirkland), **Supp. XVI:** 186

Love Feast (Buechner), **Supp. XII:** 52

Love for Love (Congreve), **Supp. XVIII:** 12

"Love Fossil" (Olds), **Supp. X:** 203

"Love"(Hadas), **Supp. XXIII:** 117

Love in a Dead Language (Siegel), **Supp. XXII:** 255, **258–261,** 265–266, 267

Love in Buffalo (Gurney), **Supp. V:** 96

"Love—In Other Words" (Lee), **Supp. VIII:** 113

"Love in the Air" (Jin), **Supp. XVIII:** 93–94

"Love in the Morning" (Dubus), **Supp. VII:** 91

Love in the Ruins: The Adventures of a Bad Catholic at a Time near the End of the World (Percy), **Supp. III Part 1:** 385, 387, 393–394, 397–398

Love in the Western World (de Rougemont), **Retro. Supp. I:** 328

"Love Is a Deep and a Dark and a Lonely" (Sandburg), **III:** 595

Lovejoy, Elijah P., **Supp. I Part 2:** 588; **Supp. XXIV:** 28

Lovejoy, Owen R., **Supp. I Part 1:** 8

Lovejoy, Thomas, **Supp. X:** 108

Lovelace, Richard, **II:** 590

"Love Letter (Schnackenberg), **Supp. XV:** 258–259

Love Letters (film), **Supp. IV Part 2:** 524

Love Letters (Gurney), **Supp. V:** 105, 108–109

Love Letters, The (Massie), **Supp. IV Part 2:** 524

Love Letters and Two Other Plays: The Golden Age and *What I Did Last Summer* (Gurney), **Supp. V:** 100

"Love Lies Sleeping" (Bishop), **Retro. Supp. II:** 42

Love Life (Mason), **Supp. VIII:** 145–146

"Love Life" (Mason), **Supp. VIII: 145–146**

Lovell, Julia, **Supp. XVIII:** 101

Lovely Bones, The (Sebold), **Supp. XXII:** 55

Lovely Lady, The (Lawrence), **Retro. Supp. I:** 203

"Lovely Lady, The" (Lawrence), **Supp. I Part 1:** 329

Love Me (Keillor), **Supp. XVI:** 178

Love Medicine (expanded version) (Erdrich), **Supp. IV Part 1:** 263, 273, 274, 275

Love Medicine (Erdrich), **Supp. IV Part 1:** 259, 260, 261, 263, 265, 266, 267–268, 270, 271, 274–275; **Supp. X:** 290

"Love Minus Zero/No Limit" (song, Dylan), **Supp. XVIII:** 31

"Love Nest, The" (Lardner), **II:** 427, 429

Love Nest, The, and Other Stories (Lardner), **II:** 430–431, 436

Lovenheim, Barbara, **Supp. X:** 169

"Love of Annunziata, The" (di Donato), **Supp. XX: 40**

"Love of Elsie Barton: A Chronicle, The" (Warren), **IV:** 253

Love of Landry, The (Dunbar), **Supp. II Part 1:** 212

"Love of Morning, The" (Levertov), **Supp. III Part 1:** 284

Love of the Last Tycoon, The: A Western. See *Last Tycoon, The*

"Love on the Bon Dieu" (Chopin), **Supp. I Part 1:** 213

Love on the Hoof (O'Hara and Lima), **Supp. XXIII:** 217

Love Poems (Sexton), **Supp. II Part 2:** 687–689

Love Poems (Tentative Title) (O'Hara), **Supp. XXIII:** 219

Love Poems of May Swenson, The (Swenson), **Supp. IV Part 2:** 652, 653

"Love Poet" (Agee), **I:** 28

"Lover" (Hoffman), **Supp. XVIII:** 87

"Love Ritual" (Mora), **Supp. XIII:** 215

Lover of Horses, The (Gallagher), **Supp. XXIV:** 166, 172, 173–174, 176

"Lover of Horses, The" (Gallagher), **Supp. XXIV:** 173–174, 176

Loveroot (Jong), **Supp. V:** 115, 130

"Lovers, The" (Berryman), **I:** 174

"Lovers, The" (Buck), **Supp. II Part 1:** 128

"Lover's Garden, A" (Ginsberg), **Supp. II Part 1:** 311

"Lovers of the Poor, The" (Brooks), **Supp. III Part 1:** 81, 85

Lovers Should Marry (Martin), **Supp. IV Part 1:** 351

"Lover's Song" (Yeats), **Supp. I Part 1:** 80

"Love Rushes By" (Salinas), **Supp. XIII:** 326–327

"Love's Ghost" (Nelson), **Supp. XVIII:** 176

Lovesick (Stern), **Supp. IX: 295–296**

Love's Labour's Lost (Shakespeare), **III:** 263

Love's Old Sweet Song (Saroyan), **Supp. IV Part 1:** 83

"Love Song During Riot with Many Voices" (Hull), **Supp. XXI:** 136

"Love Song of J. Alfred Prufrock, The" (T. S. Eliot), **I:** 52, 66, 569–570; **III:** 460; **Retro. Supp. I:** 55, 56, 57, 60; **Supp. II Part 1:** 5; **Supp. XIII:** 346; **Supp. XVI:** 150

"Love Song of St. Sebastian" (Eliot), **Retro. Supp. I:** 57

"Love Songs" (Loy), **Supp. XXII:** 161

"Love Songs to Joannes" (Loy), **Supp. XXII:** 161, 163

Love's Pilgrimage (Sinclair), **Supp. V:** 286

"Love the Wild Swan" (Jeffers), **Supp. VIII:** 33

Love to Mamá: A Tribute to Mothers (Mora, ed.), **Supp. XIII:** 221

Lovett, Robert Morss, **II:** 43

"Love-Unknown" (Herbert), **Supp. I Part 1:** 80

Love! Valor! Compassion! (film), **Supp. XIII:** 206

Love! Valour! Compassion! (McNally), **Supp. XIII:** 199, **203–204,** 208, 209

"Love *versus* Law" (Stowe), **Supp. I Part 2:** 585–586

"Love Wall" (Peacock), **Supp. XIX:** 200

Love with a Few Hairs (Mrabet), **Supp. IV Part 1:** 92

Loving a Woman in Two Worlds (R. Bly), **Supp. IV Part 1:** 66, 67, 68–69, 71, 72

Loving in the War Years: Lo que nunca pasó por sus labios (Moraga), **Supp. XXIII:** 194, 195

"Loving on Borrowed Time" (J. W. Miller), **Supp. XX: 164**

"Loving Shepherdess, The" (Jeffers), **Supp. II Part 2:** 432

"Loving the Killer" (Sexton), **Supp. II Part 2:** 688

"Loving Wife" (C. Miller), **Supp. XXII:** 196–197, 199

Lovin' Molly (film), **Supp. V:** 223, 226

Low Country (Siddons), **Supp. XXII:** 239

Lowe, John, **Supp. XIII:** 238

Lowe, Pardee, **Supp. X:** 291

Lowell, Abbott Lawrence, **I:** 487; **II:** 513; **Supp. I Part 2:** 483

Lowell, Amy, **I:** 231, 384, 405, 475, 487; **II:** 174, **511–533,** 534; **III:** 465, 581, 586; **Retro. Supp. I:** 131, 133, 288; **Retro. Supp. II:** 46, 175; **Supp. I Part 1:** 257–259, 261–263, 265, 266; **Supp. I Part 2:** 465, 466, 707, 714, 729; **Supp. XIV:** 128; **Supp. XV:** 43, 293, 295, 297, 298, 299, 300, 301, 303, 306; **Supp. XX: 69; Supp. XXII:** 161

Lowell, Blanche, **Supp. I Part 2:** 409

Lowell, Harriet, **II:** 553, 554

Lowell, James Russell, **I:** 216, 458; **II:** 273, 274, 289, 302, 320, 402, 529, 530, 532, 534, 551; **III:** 409; **IV:** 129, 171, 175, 180, 182–183, 186; **Retro. Supp. I:** 228; **Retro. Supp. II:** 155, 175, 326; **Supp. I Part 1:** 168, 299, 300, 303, 306, 311, 312, 317, 318, 362; **Supp. I Part 2: 404–426; Supp. II Part 1:** 197, 291, 352; **Supp. XV:** 278, 279; **Supp. XVI:** 84; **Supp. XVIII:** 2–3, 4, 8, 12

Lowell, Mrs. James Russell (Maria White), **Supp. I Part 2:** 405, 406, 414, 424

Lowell, Percival, **II:** 513, 525, 534

Lowell, Robert, **I:** 172, 381, 382, 400, 442, 521, 544–545, 550; **II:** 371, 376, 377, 384, 386–387, 532, **534–557; III:** 39, 44, 142, 508, 527, 528–529, 606; **IV:** 120, 138, 402, 430; **Retro. Supp. I:** 67, 140, 411; **Retro. Supp. II:** 27, 40, 44, 46, 48, 50, **175–193,** 221, 228–229, 235, 245; **Supp. I Part 1:** 89; **Supp. I Part 2:** 538, 543, 554; **Supp. III Part 1:** 6, 64, 84, 138, 147, 193, 194, 197–202, 205–208; **Supp. III**

Part 2: 541, 543, 555, 561, 599; **Supp. IV Part 2:** 439, 620, 637; **Supp. V:** 81, 179, 180, 315–316, 337, 344; **Supp. VIII:** 27, 100, 271; **Supp. IX:** 325; **Supp. X:** 53, 58; **Supp. XI:** 146, 240, 244, 250, 317; **Supp. XII:** 253–254, 255; **Supp. XIII:** 76; **Supp. XIV:** 15, 126, 269; **Supp. XV:** 20, 22, 93, 184, 249, 251, 253, 340; **Supp. XVII:** 239; **Supp. XIX:** 197; **Supp. XX: 199, 203; Supp. XXI:** 131; **Supp. XXIII:** 211, 220; **Supp. XXIV:** 153

Lowell, Rose, **Supp. I Part 2:** 409

"Lowell in the Classroom" (Vendler), **Retro. Supp. II:** 191

Lowenthal, Michael, **Supp. XII:** 82

Lower Depths, The (Gorki), **III:** 402

"Lower the Standard" (Shapiro), **Supp. II Part 2:** 715

Lowes, John Livingston, **II:** 512, 516, 532; **IV:** 453, 455

Lowin, Joseph, **Supp. V:** 273

"Low-Lands" (Pynchon), **Supp. II Part 2:** 620, 624

Lowle, Percival, **Supp. I Part 2:** 404

Lownsbrough, John, **Supp. IV Part 1:** 209, 211

Lowry, Beverly, **Supp. XXI:** 48

Lowry, Malcolm, **Supp. XVII:** 135, 136

Lowth, Richard, **II:** 8

Loy, Mina, **III:** 194; **Supp. XXII: 155–170**

Loy, Myrna, **Supp. IV Part 1:** 355

"Loyal Woman's No, A" (Larcom), **Supp. XIII:** 142, 143–144

"Luani of the Jungle" (Hughes), **Supp. I Part 1:** 328

Lubbock, Percy, **I:** 504; **II:** 337; **IV:** 308, 314, 319, 322; **Retro. Supp. I:** 366, 367, 373; **Supp. VIII:** 165; **Supp. XX: 231**

Lubin, Isidor, **Supp. I Part 2:** 632

Lubow, Arthur, **Supp. VIII:** 310

Lucas, Craig, **Supp. XXIV:** 263

Lucas, Victoria (pseudonym). *See* Plath, Sylvia

Luce, Dianne C., **Supp. VIII:** 189

Lucid, Robert F., **Retro. Supp. II:** 195, 204

"Lucid Eye in Silver Town, The" (Updike), **IV:** 218

"Lucid Walking" (A. Finch), **Supp. XVII:** 72

"Lucinda Matlock" (Masters), **Supp. I Part 2:** 461, 465

"Luck" (Dunn), **Supp. XI:** 149

Luck of Barry Lyndon, The (Thackeray), **II:** 290

"Luck of Roaring Camp, The" (Harte), **Supp. II Part 1:** 335, 344, 345–347

"Luck of the Bogans, The" (Jewett), **Retro. Supp. II:** 142

Lucky Life (Stern), **Supp. IX: 290–291**

"Lucky Lucy's Daily Dream Book" (Di Piero), **Supp. XIX:** 38–39

Lucretius, **I:** 59; **II:** 162, 163; **III:** 600, 610–611, 612; **Supp. I Part 1:** 363

Lucy (Kincaid), **Supp. VII:** 180, 185, 186, 187–188, 194

Lucy, Saint, **II:** 211

Lucy Crown (Shaw), **Supp. XIX:** 251

Lucy Gayheart (Cather), **I:** 331; **Retro. Supp. I:** 19

"Lucy Tavish's Journey" (E. Stoddard), **Supp. XV:** 286

Lucy Temple (Rowson). *See Charlotte's Daughter; or, The Three Orphans*

Ludlow, Andrea, **Supp. XVIII:** 90

Ludvigson, Susan, **Supp. IV Part 2:** 442, 446, 447, 448, 451

Lueders, Edward, **Supp. XVI:** 265

"Luggage" (Bidart), **Supp. XV:** 35

Luhan, Mabel Dodge, **Retro. Supp. I:** 7; **Supp. XV:** 46, 50; **Supp. XXIV:** 30. *See also* Dodge, Mabel

Lu Ji, **Supp. VIII:** 303

Luke (biblical book), **III:** 606

"Luke Havergal" (E. A. Robinson), **Supp. XVII:** 69

"Luke Havergal" (Robinson), **III:** 524

Lukeman, Gary, **Supp. XV:** 221

Luks, George, **IV:** 411; **Retro. Supp. II:** 103

"Lullaby" (Auden), **Supp. II Part 1:** 9

"Lullaby" (Bishop), **Supp. I Part 1:** 85

"Lullaby" (Everwine), **Supp. XV:** 89

"Lullaby" (Silko), **Supp. IV Part 2:** 560, 568–569

"Lullaby for Amy" (Jarman), **Supp. XVII:** 113, 121

"Lullaby of Cape Cod" (Brodsky), **Supp. VIII:** 27–28

Lullaby Raft (Nye), **Supp. XIII:** 278

Lullaby Raft (Nye, album), **Supp. XIII:** 274

Lullaby: The Comforting of Cock Robin (Snodgrass), **Supp. VI:** 324

"Lulls" (Walker), **Supp. III Part 2:** 525

"Lulu" (Wedekind), **Supp. XII:** 14

Lulu on the Bridge (film), **Supp. XII:** 21

Lulu's Library (Alcott), **Supp. I Part 1:** 43

"Lumber" (Baker), **Supp. XIII:** 55, 56

"Lumens, The" (Olds), **Supp. X:** 209

Lume Spento, A (Pound), **III:** 470

Lumet, Sidney, **Supp. IV Part 1:** 236; **Supp. IX:** 253

Luminous Debris: Reflecting on Vestige in Provence and Languedoc (Sobin), **Supp. XVI: 291–293,** 293–294

"Lumumba's Grave" (Hughes), **Supp. I Part 1:** 344

"Luna, Luna" (Mora), **Supp. XIII:** 217

Lunar Baedecker (Loy), **Supp. XXII:** 165, **Supp. XXII:** 167, 166, 168

Lunar Baedecker and Time-Tables (Loy), **Supp. XXII:** 168

Lunar Follies (Sorrentino), **Supp. XXI:** 226, 237, 238–239

Lunch Poems (O'Hara), **Supp. XXIII:** 219–220, 220

Lunsford, Bascom Lamar, **Supp. XX: 163**

Lupercal (Hughes), **Retro. Supp. II:** 245; **Supp. I Part 2:** 540

Lupton, Mary Jane, **Supp. IV Part 1:** 7

Lure of the Labrador Wild, The (Wallace), **Supp. XXII:** 218

Luria, Isaac, **IV:** 7

Lurie, Alison, **Supp. X:** 166; **Supp. XVI:** 103, 111–112

Lusitania Songspiel, Das (Durang), **Supp. XXIV:** 113, 116
Lust and Other Stories (Minot), **Supp. VI:** 205
Luster, Deborah, **Supp. XV:** 337,**Supp. XV:** 353, 348, 349, 350
Lustgarten, Edith, **III:** 107
Lustra (Pound), **Retro. Supp. I:** 289, 290
Luther, Martin, **II:** 11–12, 506; **III:** 306, 607; **IV:** 490
"Luther on Sweet Auburn" (Bambara), **Supp. XI:** 16–17
Lux, Thomas, **Supp. XI:** 270; **Supp. XIX:** 276
Luxury Girl, The (McCoy), **Supp. XIII:** 163
Lyall, Sarah, **Supp. XIII:** 247
Lycidas (Milton), **II:** 540; **IV:** 347; **Retro. Supp. I:** 60; **Retro. Supp. II:** 186; **Supp. I Part 1:** 370; **Supp. IX:** 41
Lycographia (Paullini), **Supp. XVII:** 55
"Lydia and Marian" (Rowson), **Supp. XV:** 234
Lydon, Susan, **Supp. XII:** 170
Lyell, Charles, **Supp. IX:** 180
Lyell, Frank H., **Supp. VIII:** 125
Lyford, Harry, **Supp. I Part 2:** 679
"Lying" (Wilbur), **Supp. III Part 2:** 547, 562
"Lying and Looking" (Swenson), **Supp. IV Part 2:** 652
"Lying in a Hammock at William Duffy's Farm in Pine Island, Minnesota" (Wright), **Supp. III Part 2:** 589, 599, 600
"Lying in the Pollen and Water" (C. Frost), **Supp. XV:** 96
Lying Ladies, The (Ryan as Finnegan), **Supp. XVIII: 233–235,** 237
"Lying Next to the Knife" (McElwee), **Supp. XXIV:** 167, 173
Lyles, Lois F., **Supp. XI:** 7, 8
Lyly, John, **III:** 536; **Supp. I Part 1:** 369
Lynch, Anne, **Supp. XV:** 273
Lynch, Doris, **Supp. XVI:** 294
Lynchburg (Gander), **Supp. XV:** 340
"Lynched Man, The" (Karr), **Supp. XI:** 241
Lynchers, The (Wideman), **Supp. X:** 320
"Lynching, The" (McKay), **Supp. I Part 1:** 63
"Lynching of Jube Benson, The" (Dunbar), **Supp. II Part 1:** 214
"Lynching Song" (Hughes), **Supp. I Part 1:** 331
Lynd, Staughton, **Supp. VIII:** 240
Lynda Hull: Collected Poems (Hull), **Supp. XXI:** 129
Lynn, Kenneth, **Supp. XIII:** 96–97
Lynn, Kenneth S., **Supp. XIV:** 103
Lynn, Vera, **Supp. X:** 304
Lyon, George Ella, **Supp. XX: 161–162**
Lyon, Kate, **I:** 409; **II:** 138, 143, 144
Lyon, Thomas, **Supp. IX:** 175
"Lyonnesse" (Plath), **Supp. I Part 2:** 541
Lyons, Bonnie, **Supp. V:** 58; **Supp. VIII:** 138
Lyons, Donald, **Supp. XXIV:** 274
Lyons, The (Silver), **Supp. XXIV:** 263, **276**

Lyotard, Jean-François, **Supp. IV Part 1:** 54
Lyrical Ballads (Wordsworth), **III:** 583; **IV:** 120; **Supp. IX:** 274; **Supp. XI:** 243; **Supp. XV:** 21; **Supp. XIX:** 1
Lyrics of Love and Laughter (Dunbar), **Supp. II Part 1:** 207
Lyrics of Lowly Life (Dunbar), **Supp. II Part 1:** 197, 199, 200, 207
Lyrics of the Hearthside (Dunbar), **Supp. II Part 1:** 206
Lytal, Tammy, **Supp. XI:** 102
Lytle, Andrew, **IV:** 125; **Retro. Supp. II:** 220, 221, 235; **Supp. II Part 1:** 139; **Supp. X:** 1, 25; **Supp. XI:** 101
Lyttelton, Alfred, **Supp. XX: 230**
Lytton of Knebworth. *See* Bulwer-Lytton, Edward George

M

Mabie, Hamilton W., **Supp. XVIII:** 257
MCabe, Susan, **Supp. XXII:** 234
McAlexander, Hubert H., **Supp. V:** 314, 319, 320, 323
McAlmon, Robert, **IV:** 404; **Retro. Supp. I:** 418, 419, 420; **Retro. Supp. II:** 328; **Supp. I Part 1:** 259; **Supp. III Part 2:** 614; **Supp. XXII:** 166, 215; **Supp. XXIV:** 62, 63
McAlmon, Mrs. Robert (Winifred Ellerman), **III:** 194. *See also* Ellerman, Winifred
McAninch, Jerry, **Supp. XI:** 297, 298
Macaulay, Catherine, **Supp. I Part 2:** 522
Macaulay, Rose, **Supp. XII:** 88; **Supp. XIV:** 348
Macaulay, Thomas, **II:** 15–16; **III:** 113, 591–592
Macauley, Robie, **Retro. Supp. II:** 228; **Supp. X:** 56
Macbeth (Shakespeare), **I:** 271; **IV:** 227; **Retro. Supp. I:** 131; **Supp. I Part 1:** 67; **Supp. I Part 2:** 457; **Supp. IV Part 1:** 87; **Supp. XIV:** 8
Macbeth (silent film), **Supp. XVI:** 184
MacBeth, George, **Retro. Supp. II:** 250
MacBride, Roger, **Supp. XXII:** 297, 301
McCafferty, Larry, **Supp. XVII:** 227
McCaffery, Larry, **Supp. IV Part 1:** 217, 227, 234; **Supp. V:** 53, 238; **Supp. VIII:** 13, 14; **Supp. X:** 260, 268, 301, 303, 307; **Supp. XVI:** 117; **Supp. XXII:** 177
McCann, Janet, **Supp. XXIII:** 51, 53, 54, 64
McCann, Jannet, **Supp. XXI:** 92
McCarriston, Linda, **Supp. X:** 204; **Supp. XIV: 259–275**
McCarthy, Charles Joseph, Jr. *See* McCarthy, Cormac
McCarthy, Cormac, **Supp. VIII: 175–192; Supp. XII:** 310; **Supp. XVII:** 185; **Supp. XXI:** 38, 40; **Supp. XXII:** 49; **Supp. XXIII:** 42, 44
McCarthy, Eugene, **Retro. Supp. II:** 182
McCarthy, Joseph, **I:** 31, 492; **II:** 562, 568; **Supp. I Part 1:** 294, 295; **Supp. I Part 2:** 444, 611, 612, 620; **Supp. XV:** 198, 311–312; **Supp. XXIII:** 7

McCarthy, Mary, **II:** 558–584; **Supp. I Part 1:** 84; **Supp. IV Part 1:** 209, 297, 310; **Supp. VIII:** 96, 99, 100; **Supp. X:** 177; **Supp. XI:** 246; **Supp. XIV:** 3; **Supp. XV:** 142; **Supp. XVI:** 64, 70; **Supp. XVII:** 43
McCay, Maura, **Supp. XII:** 271, 276
McClanahan, Ed, **Supp. X:** 24
McClanahan, Thomas, **Supp. XII:** 125–126
McClatchy, J. D., **Supp. XII: 253–270; Supp. XV:** 185, 257, 258
McClaurin, Irma, **Supp. XXIII:** 84, 86, 93, 94
McClellan, John L., **I:** 493
McClung, Isabelle, **Retro. Supp. I:** 5
McClure, Charlotte, **Supp. XXIV:** 29
McClure, John, **Retro. Supp. I:** 80
McClure, Michael, **Supp. II Part 1:** 32; **Supp. VIII:** 289; **Supp. XVI:** 283
McClure, S. S., **I:** 313; **II:** 465; **III:** 327; **Retro. Supp. I:** 5, 6, 9; **Supp. XV:** 40
McCluskey, John, Jr., **Supp. XIX:** 65, 68, 71, 72, 78
McCombs, Judith, **Supp. XIII:** 33
McConagha, Alan, **Supp. XVI:** 166
McConnell, Frank, **Supp. X:** 260, 274
McCorkle, Jill, **Supp. X:** 6; **Supp. XVIII:** 195
McCourt, Frank, **Supp. XII: 271–287**
McCoy, Horace, **Supp. XIII: 159–177**
McCracken, Elizabeth, **Supp. X:** 86; **Supp. XII:** 310, 315–316, 321
McCrae, Fiona, **Supp. XVIII:** 60, 62
McCullers, Carson, **I:** 113, 190, 211; **II:** 585–608; **IV:** 282, 384, 385, 386; **Retro. Supp. II:** 324; **Supp. II Part 1:** 17; **Supp. IV Part 1:** 31, 84; **Supp. IV Part 2:** 502; **Supp. VIII:** 124; **Supp. XII:** 309; **Supp. XIV:** 120; **Supp. X:** 338
McCullers, Reeves, **III:** 585, 586, 587
McDavid, Raven I., **III:** 120; **Supp. XIV:** 14
McDermott, Alice, **Supp. XII:** 311; **Supp. XVIII: 155–169**
McDermott, John J., **II:** 364
MacDiarmid, Hugh, **Supp. X:** 112
Macdonald, C. G., **Supp. XVII:** 73–74
Macdonald, Dwight, **I:** 233, 372, 379; **III:** 39; **Supp. V:** 265; **Supp. XIV:** 340; **Supp. XV:** 140
McDonald, E. J., **Supp. I Part 2:** 670
Macdonald, George, **Supp. XIII:** 75
MacDonald, Jeanette, **II:** 589
Macdonald, Ross, **Supp. IV Part 1:** 116, 136; **Supp. IV Part 2: 459–477; Supp. XIII:** 233; **Supp. XVIII:** 137,136; **Supp. XXI:** 67
MacDonald, Ruth K., **Supp. XVI:** 102
McDonnell, Thomas P., **Supp. XX: 45**
MacDougall, Ruth Doan, **Supp. XV:** 58; **Supp. XVI:** 174
MacDowell, Edward, **I:** 228; **III:** 504, 508, 524
McDowell, Frederick P. W., **II:** 194
McDowell, Mary, **Supp. I Part 1:** 5
McDowell, Robert, **Supp. IX:** 266, 270, 276, 279
MacDowell, Robert, **Supp. XI:** 249

McDowell, Robert, **Supp. XVII:** 109, 110, 111

McDowell. Deborah, **Supp. XVIII:** 125, 129

McElderry, Margaret K., **Supp. XV:** 162

McElligot's Pool (Geisel), **Supp. XVI:** 104

McElrath, Joseph, **Supp. XIV:** 62

McElroy, Joseph, **Supp. IV Part 1:** 279, 285

McElwee, Caroline, **Supp. XXIV:** 167, 173

McEuen, Kathryn, **II:** 20

McEwen, Arthur, **I:** 206

McFarland, Ron, **Supp. IX:** 323, 327, 328, 333

McGann, Jerome, **Retro. Supp. I:** 47

McGill, Meredith, **Supp. XVIII:** 17

McGillis, Ian, **Supp. XVIII:** 150

MacGillivray, William, **Supp. XVI:** 8

McGinity, Keren, **Supp. XX:** 9

McGovern, Edythe M., **Supp. IV Part 2:** 573, 582, 585

McGovern, George, **III:** 46

MacGowan, Christopher, **Retro. Supp. I:** 430

MacGowan, Kenneth, **III:** 387, 391

McGrath, Douglas, **Supp. XV:** 12

McGrath, Joseph, **Supp. XI:** 307, 309

McGrath, Patrick, **Supp. IX:** 113; **Supp. XXII:** 58

McGrath, Thomas, **Supp. X: 111–130**

"McGrath on McGrath" (McGrath), **Supp. X:** 119, 120

McGuane, Thomas, **Supp. V:** 53, 220; **Supp. VIII:** 39, 40, 42, 43

MacGuffin, The (Elkin), **Supp. VI: 55–56**

McGuiness, Daniel, **Supp. XV:** 261

Machado y Ruiz, Antonio, **Supp. XIII:** 315, 323

Machan, Tibor, **Supp. IV Part 2:** 528

McHaney, Pearl, **Supp. XXI:** 244, 255, 256, 257

McHaney, Thomas, **Supp. XVIII:** 199, 203

Machen, Arthur, **IV:** 286

Machiavelli, Niccolò, **I:** 485; **Supp. XIX:** 34

"Machine-Gun, The" (Jarrell), **II:** 371

"Machine Song" (Anderson), **I:** 114

McHugh, Heather, **Supp. XIX:** 84; **Supp. XXIV:** 154

McHugh, Vincent, **Supp. XV:** 147

McInerney, Jay, **Supp. X:** 7, 166; **Supp. XI:** 65; **Supp. XII:** 81; **Supp. XVIII:** 148

"Mac in Love" (Dixon), **Supp. XII: 142**

McIntire, Holly, **Supp. V:** 338

McIntosh, Maria, **Retro. Supp. I:** 246

Mack, Maynard, **Supp. XIV:** 12

Mackail, John William, **Supp. I Part 1:** 268; **Supp. I Part 2:** 461

McKay, Claude, **Supp. I Part 1:** 63; **Supp. III Part 1:** 75, 76; **Supp. IV Part 1:** 3, 79, 164; **Supp. IX:** 306; **Supp. X: 131–144; Supp. XI:** 91; **Supp. XVII:** 74; **Supp. XVIII:** 122, 127, 280, 282; **Supp. XIX:** 73; **Supp. XX: 69; Supp. XXII:** 275

McKay, Donald, **Supp. I Part 2:** 482

McKay, Nellie Y., **Supp. XX: 105**

McKee, Elizabeth, **Retro. Supp. II:** 221, 222

McKee, Ellen, **Retro. Supp. II:** 67

McKeen, William, **Supp. XXIV:** 279, 280, 281, 282, 288

McKenney, Eileen, **IV:** 288; **Retro. Supp. II:** 321, 330

McKenney, Ruth, **IV:** 288; **Retro. Supp. II:** 321; **Supp. XVIII:** 238

MacKenzie, Agnes, **I:** 199

Mackenzie, Captain Alexander, **III:** 94

Mackenzie, Compton, **II:** 82; **Retro. Supp. I:** 100, 102

McKenzie, Geraldine, **Supp. XII:** 107

MacKenzie, Margaret, **I:** 199

Mackey, Louis, **Supp. XXI:** 236, 237

McKibben, Bill, **Supp. XVIII:** 192

McKinley, William, **I:** 474; **III:** 506; **Supp. I Part 2:** 395–396, 707

MacKinnon, Catharine, **Supp. XII:** 6

McKnight, Reginald, **Supp. XX: 147–159**

MacLachlan, Suzanne L., **Supp. XII:** 300, Supp. XII: 299

McLaverty, Michael, **Supp. X:** 67

McLay, Catherine, **Supp. XIII:** 21

Maclean, Alasdair, **Supp. V:** 244

McLean, Carolyn (pseudonym). *See* Bly, Carol

Maclean, Norman, **Supp. XIV: 221–237; Supp. XVI:** 98

MacLeish, Archibald, **I:** 283, 293, 429; **II:** 165, 228; **III: 1–25,** 427; **Supp. I Part 1:** 261; **Supp. I Part 2:** 654; **Supp. IV Part 1:** 359; **Supp. IV Part 2:** 586; **Supp. X:** 120; **Supp. XIV:** 11

MacLeish, Mrs. Archibald (Ada Hitchcock), **III:** 1

MacLeish, Kenneth, **III:** 1

McLellan, Joseph, **Supp. XXIV:** 226

McLennan, Gordon Lawson, **Supp. IX:** 89

McLeod, A. W., **Supp. I Part 1:** 257

McLuhan, Marshall, **Supp. IV Part 2:** 474

McLure, Michael, **Supp. XIV:** 150

Macmahon, Arthur, **I:** 226

McMahon, Helen, **Supp. IV Part 2:** 579

McMichael, Barbara Lloyd, **Supp. XXII:** 206, 207, 215, 216

McMichael, George, **Supp. VIII:** 124

McMichael, Morton, **Supp. I Part 2:** 707

McMichaels, James, **Supp. XIII:** 114

McMillan, James B., **Supp. VIII:** 124

McMillan, Terry, **Supp. XIII: 179–193**

McMullan, Jim, **Supp. XIV:** 124

McMurtry, Josephine, **Supp. V:** 220

McMurtry, Larry, **Supp. V: 219–235; Supp. X:** 24; **Supp. XI:** 172

McNally, Terrence, **Supp. XIII: 195–211**

McNally, T. M., **Supp. XX: 92**

McNamee, Thomas, **Supp. XXII:** 218

McNamer, Deirdre, **Supp. XI:** 190

McNeese, Gretchen, **Supp. V:** 123

MacNeice, Louis, **II:** 586; **III:** 527; **Supp. II Part 1:** 17, 24; **Supp. IV Part 2:** 440; **Supp. X:** 116; **Supp. XIII:** 347

McNeil, Claudia, **Supp. IV Part 1:** 360, 362

M-a-c-n-o-l-i-a (Jordan), **Supp. XVIII:** 172

McPhee, John, **Supp. III Part 1: 289–316; Supp. X:** 29, 30; **Supp. XVIII:** 106–107, 114

MacPherson, Aimee Semple, **Supp. V:** 278

Macpherson, Anne, **Supp. XXIII:** 84

McPherson, Dolly, **Supp. IV Part 1:** 2, 3, 4, 6, 8, 11, 12

McPherson, James Alan, **Supp. XXII:** 141

McPherson, James Allen, **Retro. Supp. II:** 126

Macpherson, Jay, **Supp. XIII:** 19

MacPherson, Jennifer, **Supp. XXIII:** 248

MacPherson, Kenneth, **Supp. I Part 1:** 259

McPherson, Sandra, **Supp. XXIII:** 57

McPhillips, Robert, **Supp. XV:** 119, 250, 251, 252, 264, 266; **Supp. XXIII:** 111, 112, 114, 127

McQuade, Molly, **Supp. VIII:** 277, 281; **Supp. IX:** 151, 163; **Supp. XX: 90**

McQueen, Steve, **Supp. XI:** 306

Macrae, John, **I:** 252–253

McRobbie, Angela, **Supp. IV Part 2:** 691

MacShane, Frank, **Supp. IV Part 2:** 557; **Supp. XI:** 214, 216

"MacSwiggen" (Freneau), **Supp. II Part 1:** 259

McTaggart, John, **I:** 59

McTeague (Norris), **III:** 314, 315, 316–320, 322, 325, 327–328, 330, 331, 333, 335; **Retro. Supp. II:** 96; **Supp. IX:** 332

McWhorter, Dianne, **Supp. XXIII:** 38

McWilliams, Carey, **Supp. XI:** 169; **Supp. XXIV:** 282

Madama Butterfly (opera, Puccini), **III:** 139; **Supp. XXI:** 150, 155

"Madam and the Minister" (Hughes), **Supp. I Part 1:** 335

"Madam and the Wrong Visitor" (Hughes), **Supp. I Part 1:** 335

"Madame and Ahmad" (Bowles), **Supp. IV Part 1:** 93

"Madame Bai and the Taking of Stone Mountain" (Bambara), **Supp. XI:** 14–15

Madame Bovary (Flaubert), **II:** 185; **Retro. Supp. I:** 225; **Retro. Supp. II:** 70; **Supp. XI:** 334; **Supp. XX: 58**

"Madame Célestin's Divorce" (Chopin), **Supp. I Part 1:** 213

Madame Curie (film), **Retro. Supp. I:** 113

"Madame de Mauves" (James), **II:** 327; **Retro. Supp. I:** 218, 220

Madame de Treymes (Wharton), **IV:** 314, 323; **Retro. Supp. I:** 376

"Madame Rose Hanie" (Gibran), **Supp. XX: 124**

"Madame Swann at Home"(Hadas), **Supp. XXIII:** 113

"Madam's Calling Cards" (Hughes), **Retro. Supp. I:** 206

Madden, David, **Supp. IV Part 1:** 285

Maddern, Bessie. *See* London, Mrs. Jack (Bessie Maddern)
Mad Dog Black Lady (Coleman), **Supp. XI:** 85–89, 90
Mad Dog Blues (Shepard), **Supp. III Part 2:** 437, 438, 441
Maddox, Lucy, **Supp. IV Part 1:** 323, 325
Mad Ducks and Bears: Football Revisited (Plimpton), **Supp. XVI:** 243
Mademoiselle Coeur-Brisé (Sibon, trans.), **IV:** 288
Mademoiselle de Maupin (Gautier), **Supp. I Part 1:** 277
"Mad Farmer, Flying the Flag of Rough Branch, Secedes from the Union, The" (Berry), **Supp. X:** 35
"Mad Farmer Manifesto, The: The First Amendment" (Berry), **Supp. X:** 35
"Mad Farmer's Love Song, The" (Berry), **Supp. X:** 35
Madheart (Baraka), **Supp. II Part 1:** 47
Madhouse, The (Farrell), **II:** 41
Madhubuti, Haki R. (Don L. Lee), **Supp. II Part 1:** 34, 247; **Supp. IV Part 1:** 244
Madison, Charles, **Supp. XXIII:** 6, 13
Madison, Dolley, **II:** 303
Madison, James, **I:** 1, 2, 6–9; **II:** 301; **Supp. I Part 2:** 509, 524
"Madison Smartt Bell: *The Year of Silence*" (Garrett), **Supp. X:** 7
Mad Love (film, Freund), **Supp. XVII:** 58
"Madman, A" (Updike), **Retro. Supp. I:** 320
Madman, The: His Parables and Poems (Gibran), **Supp. XX:** 115, 118, 125
"Madman's Song" (Wylie), **Supp. I Part 2:** 711, 729
Madonick, Michael, **Supp. XVII:** 123
"Madonna" (Lowell), **II:** 535–536
"Madonna of the Evening Flowers" (Lowell), **II:** 524
"Madonna of the Future, The" (James), **Retro. Supp. I:** 219
"Mad Song" (Gioia), **Supp. XV:** 128
Madwoman in the Attic, The (Gilbert and Gubar), **Retro. Supp. I:** 42; **Supp. IX:** 66
"Maelzel's Chess-Player" (Poe), **III:** 419, 420
"Maestria" (Nemerov), **III:** 275, 278–279
Maeterlinck, Maurice, **I:** 91, 220; **Supp. XX:** 115, 116
"Magazine-Writing Peter Snook" (Poe), **III:** 421
Magdeburg Centuries (Flacius), **IV:** 163
Magellan, Ferdinand, **Supp. I Part 2:** 497
Maggie: A Girl of the Streets (S. Crane), **I:** 407, 408, 410–411, 416; **IV:** 208; **Retro. Supp. II:** 97, 107; **Supp. XVII:** 228; **Supp. XXIII:** 165
Maggie Cassidy (Kerouac), **Supp. III Part 1:** 220–221, 225, 227, 229, 232
Maggie-Now (B. Smith), **Supp. XXIII:** 258, 267–269
"Maggie of the Green Bottles" (Bambara), **Supp. XI:** 2–3

"Maggie's Farm" (song, Dylan), **Supp. XVIII:** 25, 26
"Magi" (Plath), **Supp. I Part 2:** 544–545
"Magi, The" (Garrett), **Supp. VII:** 97
"Magic" (Pickering), **Supp. XXI:** 202
"Magic" (Porter), **III:** 434, 435
"Magical Thinking" (Hull), **Supp. XXI:** 137, 139
Magic Barrel, The (Malamud), **Supp. I Part 2:** 427, 428, 430–434
"Magic Barrel, The" (Malamud), **Supp. I Part 2:** 427, 428, 431, 432–433
Magic Christian, The (film), **Supp. XI:** 309
Magic Christian, The (Southern), **Supp. XI:** 297, 299–301, 309
Magic City (Komunyakaa), **Supp. XIII:** 125–127, 128, 131
"Magic Flute, The" (Epstein), **Supp. XII:** 165
Magic Flute, The (Mozart), **III:** 164
Magician of Lublin, The (Singer), **IV:** 6, 9–10; **Retro. Supp. II:** 308–309
Magician's Assistant, The (Patchett), **Supp. XII:** 307, 310, 317–320, 322
"Magician's Wife, The" (Gordon), **Supp. IV Part 1:** 306
Magic Journey, The (Nichols), **Supp. XIII:** 266–267
Magic Keys, The (Murray), **Supp. XIX:** 157–158
Magic Kingdom, The (Elkin), **Supp. VI:** 42, 54–55, 56, 58
"Magic Mirror, The: A Study of the Double in Two of Doestoevsky's Novels" (Plath), **Supp. I Part 2:** 536
Magic Mountain, The (Mann), **III:** 281–282; **Supp. IV Part 2:** 522; **Supp. XII:** 321; **Supp. XVII:** 137
Magic Tower, The (Willams), **IV:** 380
Magnaghi, Ambrogio, **Supp. XVI:** 286
Magnalia Christi Americana (Mather), **II:** 302; **Supp. I Part 1:** 102; **Supp. I Part 2:** 584; **Supp. II Part 2:** 441, 442, 452–455, 460, 467, 468; **Supp. IV Part 2:** 434
Magnes, Judah, **Supp. XXIII:** 6
Magnificat (Nelson), **Supp. XVIII:** 176–177
"Magnificent Little Gift" (Salinas), **Supp. XIII:** 318
"Magnifying Mirror" (Karr), **Supp. XI:** 240
Magpie, The (Baldwin, ed.), **Supp. I Part 1:** 49
"Magpie Exhorts"(Schott), **Supp. XXIII:** 250
Magpie's Shadow, The (Winters), **Supp. II Part 2:** 786, 788
"Magpie's Song" (Snyder), **Supp. VIII:** 302
Magritte, René, **Supp. IV Part 2:** 623
Maguire, Roberta S., **Supp. XIX:** 160–161
Magus, The (Fowles), **Supp. XIX:** 58
Mahan, Albert Thayer, **Supp. I Part 2:** 491
Mahan, David C., **Supp. XXI:** 86
"Mahatma Joe" (Bass), **Supp. XVI:** 19
Mahlis, Kristen, **Supp. XXIII:** 90, 94

"Mahogany Tree, The" (M. F. K. Fisher), **Supp. XVII:** 88
Mahomet and His Successors (Irving), **II:** 314
Mahoney, Jeremiah, **IV:** 285
Mahoney, Lynn, **Supp. XV:** 270
"Maiden, Maiden" (Boyle), **Supp. XXIV:** 58
"Maiden in a Tower" (Stegner), **Supp. IV Part 2:** 613
Maiden's Prayer, The (Silver), **Supp. XXIV:** 275–276
"Maiden Without Hands" (Sexton), **Supp. II Part 2:** 691
"Maid of St. Philippe, The" (Chopin), **Retro. Supp. II:** 63
"Maid's Shoes, The" (Malamud), **Supp. I Part 2:** 437
Mailer, Fanny, **III:** 28
Mailer, Isaac, **III:** 28
Mailer, Norman, **I:** 261, 292, 477; **III:** 26–49, 174; **IV:** 98, 216; **Retro. Supp. II:** 182, 195–217, 279; **Supp. I Part 1:** 291, 294; **Supp. III Part 1:** 302; **Supp. IV Part 1:** 90, 198, 207, 236, 284, 381; **Supp. IV Part 2:** 689; **Supp. VIII:** 236; **Supp. XI:** 104, 218, 222, 229; **Supp. XIV:** 49, 53, 54, 111, 162; **Supp. XVII:** 225, 228, 236; **Supp. XVIII:** 19–20; **Supp. XX:** 90; **Supp. XXIII:** 105, 106; **Supp. XXIV:** 281
"Maimed Man, The" (Tate), **IV:** 136
Maimonides, Moses, **Supp. XVII:** 46–47
Main Currents in American Thought: The Colonial Mind, 1625–1800 (Parrington), **I:** 517; **Supp. I Part 2:** 484
"Maine Roustabout, A" (Eberhart), **I:** 539
"Maine Speech" (White), **Supp. I Part 2:** 669–670
Maine Woods, The (Thoreau), **IV:** 188
Mains d'Orlac, Les (M. Renard), **Supp. XVII:** 58
Main Street (Lewis), **I:** 362; **II:** 271, 440, 441–442, 447, 449, 453; **III:** 394; **Supp. XIX:** 142; **Supp. XXII:** 282
"Maintenance" (Pickering), **Supp. XXI:** 204
Maitland, Margaret Todd, **Supp. XVI:** 292
Majdoubeh, Ahmad, **Supp. XX:** 116
"Majesty" (July), **Supp. XXIV:** 201–202, 203
Major, Clarence, **Supp. XXII:** 171–186
"Majorat, Das" (Hoffman), **III:** 415
Major Barbara (Shaw), **III:** 69
"Major Chord, The" (Bourne), **I:** 221
Majors and Minors (Dunbar), **Supp. II Part 1:** 197, 198
"Major's Tale, The" (Bierce), **I:** 205
Make Believe (J. Scott), **Supp. XVII:** 191–192, 193, 194, 195
Make-Believe Town: Essays and Remembrances (Mamet), **Supp. XIV:** 240, 251
Make It New (Pound), **III:** 470
Makers and Finders (Brooks), **I:** 253, 254, 255, 257, 258

Makers of the Modern World (Untermeyer), **Supp. XV:** 312

"Making a Change" (Gilman), **Supp. XI:** 207

"Making a Living" (Sexton), **Supp. II Part 2:** 695

"Making Changes" (L. Michaels), **Supp. XVI:** 204

"Making Do" (Hogan), **Supp. IV Part 1:** 406

Making Face, Making Soul: Haciendo Caras, Creative and Critical Perspectives by Feminists of Color (Anzaldúa, ed.), **Supp. IV Part 1:** 330

Making It (Podhoretz), **Supp. VIII:** 231, 232, 233, **237–238,** 239, 244

"Making Light of Auntie" (X. J. Kennedy), **Supp. XV:** 163

"Making Love in 2003" (July), **Supp. XXIV:** 204–205, 210

"Making of a Marginal Farm, The" (Berry), **Supp. X:** 22

Making of Americans, The (Stein), **IV:** 35, 37, 40–42, 45, 46; **Supp. III Part 1:** 37

"Making of Ashenden, The" (Elkin), **Supp. VI:** 49, 50

"Making of a Soldier USA, The" (Simpson), **Supp. IX:** 270

"Making of Garrison Keillor, The" (McConagha), **Supp. XVI:** 166"

Making of Modern Atlanta, The (documentary), **Supp. XXII:** 251

"Making of Paths, The" (Stegner), **Supp. IV Part 2:** 614

"Making of Poems, The" (W. J. Smith), **Supp. XIII:** 348

Making of the Modern Mind (Randall), **III:** 605

Making the Light Come: The Poetry of Gerald Stern (Somerville), **Supp. IX:** 296–297

"Making Up Stories" (Didion), **Supp. IV Part 1:** 196, 203, 205

Making Your Own Days: The Pleasures of Reading and Writing Poetry (Koch), **Supp. XV:** 188; **Supp. XXIII:** 124

Maladies de la volonté, Les (Ribot), **Supp. XX:** 238

Malady of the Ideal, The: Oberman, Maurice de Guérin, and Amiel (Brooks), **I:** 240, 241, 242

Malamud, Bernard, **I:** 144, 375; **II:** 424, 425; **III:** 40, 272; **IV:** 216; **Retro. Supp. II:** 22, 279, 281; **Supp. I Part 2:** 427–453; **Supp. IV Part 1:** 297, 382; **Supp. V:** 257, 266; **Supp. IX:** 114, 227; **Supp. XIII:** 106, 264, 265, 294; **Supp. XVI:** 220

Malamud, Mrs. Bernard (Ann de Chiara), **Supp. I Part 2:** 451

Malanga, Gerard, **Supp. III Part 2:** 629; **Supp. XXIII:** 221

Malaquais, Jean, **Retro. Supp. II:** 199

Malatesta, Sigismondo de, **III:** 472, 473

Malcolm (Purdy), **Supp. VII:** 270–273, 277

"Malcolm Cowley and the American Writer" (Simpson), **Supp. II Part 1:** 147

Malcolm Lowry's "Volcano": Myth Symbol Meaning (Markson), **Supp. XVII:** 142, 144

"MALCOLM REMEMBERED (FEB. 77)" (Baraka), **Supp. II Part 1:** 60

Malcolm X, **Retro. Supp. II:** 12, 13; **Supp. I Part 1:** 52, 63, 65, 66; **Supp. IV Part 1:** 2, 10; **Supp. VIII:** 330, 345; **Supp. X:** 240; **Supp. XIV:** 306

Malcolm X (film), **Retro. Supp. II:** 12

"Maldrove" (Jeffers), **Supp. II Part 2:** 418

Male, Roy, **II:** 239

Male Animal, The (Thurber), **Supp. I Part 2:** 605, 606, 610–611

"Malediction upon Myself" (Wylie), **Supp. I Part 2:** 722

Malefactors, The (Gordon), **II:** 186, 199, 213–216; **IV:** 139

"Malest Cornifici Tuo Catullo" (Ginsberg), **Supp. II Part 1:** 315

Malick, Terrence, **Supp. XI:** 234; **Supp. XV:** 351

Malin, Irving, **I:** 147; **Supp. XVI:** 71–72

"Malinche's Tips: Pique from Mexico's Mother" (Mora), **Supp. XIII:** 223

"Malinke's Atonement" (Antin), **Supp. XX:** 10

"Mallard" (C. Frost), **Supp. XV:** 98, 99

Mallarmé, Stéphane, **I:** 66, 569; **II:** 529, 543; **III:** 8, 409, 428; **IV:** 80, 86; **Retro. Supp. I:** 56; **Supp. I Part 1:** 261; **Supp. II Part 1:** 1; **Supp. III Part 1:** 319–320; **Supp. III Part 2:** 630; **Supp. XIII:** 114; **Supp. XV:** 158; **Supp. XVI:** 282, 285

Malle, Louis, **Supp. XXIII:** 122

Mallia, Joseph, **Supp. XII:** 26, 29, 37

Mallon, Anne-Marie, **Supp. XXI:** 215

Mallon, Thomas, **Supp. IV Part 1:** 200, 209; **Supp. XIX:** 131–145

Maloff, Saul, **Supp. VIII:** 238

Malory, Thomas, **II:** 302; **III:** 486; **IV:** 50, 61; **Supp. IV Part 1:** 47

"Mal Paso Bridge" (Jeffers), **Supp. II Part 2:** 415, 420

Malraux, André, **I:** 33–34, 127, 509; **II:** 57, 376; **III:** 35, 310; **IV:** 236, 247, 434; **Retro. Supp. I:** 73; **Retro. Supp. II:** 115–116, 119; **Supp. II Part 1:** 221, 232; **Supp. XIX:** 157

Maltese Falcon, The (film), **Supp. IV Part 1:** 342, 353, 355

Maltese Falcon, The (Hammett), **IV:** 286; **Supp. IV Part 1:** 345, 348–351

Mama (McMillan), **Supp. XIII:** 182, 187–188

"Mama and Daughter" (Hughes), **Supp. I Part 1:** 334

Mama Day (Naylor), **Supp. VIII:** 223–226, 230

"Mama I Remember" (Nelson), **Supp. XVIII:** 173

Mama Poc: An Ecologist's Account of the Extinction of a Species (LaBastille), **Supp. X:** 99, **104–105,** 106

Mama Poems, The (Kenny), **Supp. XXIII:** 143, **154**

Mama's Bank Account (K. Forbes), **Supp. XVII:** 9

Mama's Promises (Nelson), **Supp. XVIII:** 173–174

"Mama Still Loves You" (Naylor), **Supp. VIII:** 214

Mambo Hips and Make Believe (Coleman), **Supp. XI:** **94–96**

Mambo Kings, The (film), **Supp. VIII:** 73, 74

Mambo Kings Play Songs of Love, The (Hijuelos), **Supp. VIII:** 73–74, **79–82**

"Ma'me Pélagie" (Chopin), **Retro. Supp. II:** 64

Mamet, David, **Supp. XIV:** 239–258, 315

"Mamie" (Sandburg), **III:** 582

Mammedaty, Novarro Scott. *See* Momaday, N. Scott

"Mammon and the Archer" (O. Henry), **Supp. II Part 1:** 394, 408

Mammonart (Sinclair), **Supp. V:** 276–277

"Mammy" (D. West), **Supp. XVIII:** 283

"Mamouche" (Chopin), **Retro. Supp. II:** 66

Mamoulian, Rouben, **Supp. XVIII:** 281

"Man" (Corso), **Supp. XII:** 130

"Man" (Herbert), **II:** 12

"Man Against the Sky, The" (Robinson), **III:** 509, 523

"Man and a Woman Sit Near Each Other, A" (R. Bly), **Supp. IV Part 1:** 71

Man and Boy (Morris), **III:** 223, 224, 225

"Man and the Snake, The" (Bierce), **I:** 203

"Man and Woman" (Caldwell), **I:** 310

Manassas (Sinclair), **Supp. V:** 280, 281, 285

"Man Bring This Up Road" (T. Williams), **IV:** 383–384

"Man Carrying Thing" (Stevens), **IV:** 90

Manchester, William, **III:** 103

"Man Child, The" (Baldwin), **Supp. I Part 1:** 63

Man Could Stand Up, A (Ford), **I:** 423

"Mandarin's Jade" (Chandler), **Supp. IV Part 1:** 125

Mandel, Charlotte, **Supp. XVI:** 57

Mandelbaum, Maurice, **I:** 61

Mandelstam, Osip, **Retro. Supp. I:** 278; **Supp. III Part 1:** 268; **Supp. VIII:** 21, 22, 23, 27; **Supp. XIII:** 77; **Supp. XV:** 254, 261, 263

"Mandelstam: The Poem as Event" (Dobyns), **Supp. XIII:** 78

"Mandolin" (Dove), **Supp. IV Part 1:** 247

"Mandoline" (Verlaine), **IV:** 79

"Man Eating" (Kenyon), **Supp. VII:** 173

"Manet in Late Summer" (Skloot), **Supp. XX: 201**

"Man Feeding Pigeons" (Clampitt), **Supp. IX: 49–50,** 52

Manfred, Frederick, **Supp. X:** 126

Man from Kinvara, The (Gallagher), **Supp. XXIV:** 166, 172, 173

Man From Limbo, The (Endore), **Supp. XVII:** 55

Man fun natseres, Der (Asch), **Supp. XXIII:** 6

"Mango Says Goodbye Sometimes" (Cisneros), **Supp. VII:** 64

Manhattan (film; Allen), **Supp. IV Part 1:** 205; **Supp. XV:** 5, **7–8**, 13

"Manhattan Dawn" (Justice), **Supp. VII:** 117

"Manhattan: Luminism" (Doty), **Supp. XI:** 135

Manhattan Murder Mystery (film; Allen), **Supp. XV:** 5, 11

Manhattan Transfer (Dos Passos), **I:** 26, 475, 478, 479, 480, 481, 482–484, 487; **II:** 286; **Supp. I Part 1:** 57

"Mania" (Lowell), **II:** 554

"Manic in the Moon, The" (Thurber), **Supp. I Part 2:** 620

Manifest; and Furthermore (Bronk), **Supp. XXI:** 32

"Manifesto: A Press Release from PRKA" (Saunders), **Supp. XIX:** 235

Manikin, The (J. Scott), **Supp. XVII:** 189–191, 192, 194

"Man in Black" (Plath), **Supp. I Part 2:** 538

Man in Prehistory (Chard), **Supp. XII:** 177–178

Man in the Black Coat Turns, The (R. Bly), **Supp. IV Part 1:** 66–68, 71, 73

"Man in the Brooks Brothers Shirt, The" (McCarthy), **II:** 563–564

"Man in the Drawer, The" (Malamud), **Supp. I Part 2:** 437

Man in the Flying Lawn Chair and Other Excursions and Observations, The (Plimpton), **Supp. XVI:** 234

Man in the Gray Flannel Suit, The (Wilson), **Supp. IV Part 1:** 387

Man in the High Castle, The (Dick), **Supp. XVIII:** 138

Man in the Middle, The (Wagoner), **Supp. IX:** 324, **332–333**

"Man in the Rain, The" (Ryan as Quin), **Supp. XVIII:** 226

"Man in the Toolhouse, The" (Swados), **Supp. XIX:** 263

Mankiewicz, Frank, **Supp. XXIV:** 279

Mankiewicz, Herman, **Supp. XVI:** 189

Mankiewicz, Joseph, **Retro. Supp. I:** 113

Mankowitz, Wolf, **Supp. XI:** 307

"Man Made of Words, The" (Momaday), **Supp. IV Part 2:** 481, 484–485, 486, 487, 488

Man-Made World, The (Gilman), **Supp. XI:** 207

"Man-Moth, The" (Bishop), **Retro. Supp. II:** 42; **Supp. I Part 1:** 85–87, 88

Mann, Charles, **Retro. Supp. II:** 40

Mann, Erika, **Supp. II Part 1:** 11

Mann, Seymour (Samuel Weisman), **Supp. V:** 113

Mann, Thomas, **I:** 271, 490; **II:** 42, 539; **III:** 231, 281–282, 283; **IV:** 70, 73, 85; **Supp. IV Part 1:** 392; **Supp. IV Part 2:** 522; **Supp. V:** 51; **Supp. IX:** 21; **Supp. XI:** 275; **Supp. XII:** 173, 310, 321; **Supp. XIV:** 87; **Supp. XVII:** 137; **Supp. XIX:** 147, 151, 157; **Supp. XX:** 85; **Supp. XXIII:** 4

Mannequins' Demise: A Play in Eight Scenes (Budbill), **Supp. XIX:** 12

Mannerhouse (Wolfe), **IV:** 460

Manner Music, The (Reznikoff), **Supp. XIV:** 293–295

"Manners" (Bishop), **Supp. I Part 1:** 73

"Manners" (Emerson), **II:** 4, 6

"Manners, Morals, and the Novel" (Trilling), **Supp. III Part 2:** 502, 503

Mannheim, Karl, **I:** 279; **Supp. I Part 2:** 644

Manning, Ambrose, **Supp. XX:** **166**

Manning, Frederic, **III:** 459

Manning, Robert, **Supp. IX:** 236

Mannix, Daniel P., **Supp. II Part 1:** 140

Man Nobody Knows, The (B. Barton), **Retro. Supp. I:** 179

Mano, D. Keith, **Supp. XVI:** 250

Mano, Guy Levis, **Supp. XVI:** 282

"Man of Indeterminate Age on a Subway Grate, A" (DI Piero), **Supp. XIX:** 47

"Man of Letters" (Pickering), **Supp. XXI:** 192, 195–196

"Man of Letters as a Man of Business, The" (Howells), **Supp. XIV:** 45–46

"Man of No Account, The" (Harte), **Supp. II Part 1:** 339

"Man of the Crowd, The" (Poe), **III:** 412, 417; **Retro. Supp. I:** 154

Man on Spikes (Asinof), **II:** 424

Man on Stage (Dixon), **Supp. XII:** 141, **154–155**

"Man on the Dump, The" (Stevens), **IV:** 74; **Retro. Supp. I:** 306

"Man on the Stairs, The" (July), **Supp. XXIV:** 202

"Man on the Train, The" (Percy), **Supp. III Part 1:** 387

Manor, The (Singer), **IV:** 6, 17–19

Manrique, Jorge, **Retro. Supp. II:** 154

Mansart Builds a School (Du Bois), **Supp. II Part 1:** 185–186

Man's Fate (Malraux), **I:** 127; **Retro. Supp. II:** 121

"Man's Fate A Film Treatment of the Malraux Novel" (Agee), **I:** 33–34

Mansfield, June, **Supp. X:** 183, 194

Mansfield, Katherine, **III:** 362, 453

Mansfield, Stephanie, **Supp. IV Part 1:** 227

Man's Hope (Malraux), **IV:** 247

Mansion, The (Faulkner), **II:** 73; **Retro. Supp. I:** 74, 82

Man's Nature and His Communities (Niebuhr), **III:** 308

Manson, Charles, **Supp. IV Part 1:** 205

"Man Splitting Wood in the Daybreak, The" (Kinnell), **Supp. III Part 1:** 254

"Man's Pride" (Jeffers), **Supp. II Part 2:** 417

"Man's Story, The" (Anderson), **I:** 114

Man's Woman, A (Norris), **III:** 314, 322, 328, 329, 330, 332, 333

Man That Corrupted Hadleyburg, The (Twain), **I:** 204; **IV:** 208

"Man That Was Used Up, The" (Poe), **III:** 412, 425

"Mantis" (Zukofsky), **Supp. III Part 2:** 617

"'Mantis': An Interpretation" (Zukofsky), **Supp. III Part 2:** 617–618

"Man to Know in the Restaurants, The" (Siddons), **Supp. XXII:** 244

Man to Send Rain Clouds, The (Rosen, ed.), **Supp. IV Part 2:** 499, 505, 513

"Man to Send Rain Clouds, The" (Silko), **Supp. IV Part 2:** 559

Mantrap (Lewis), **II:** 447

Manuductio Ad Ministerium (Mather), **Supp. II Part 2:** 465–467

"Manuelzinho" (Bishop), **Retro. Supp. II:** 47–48

Manuscript Books of Emily Dickinson, The (Franklin, ed.), **Retro. Supp. I:** 29, 41

"Man Waiting for It to Stop, A" (Dunn), **Supp. XI:** 144

"Man Who Became a Woman, The" (Anderson), **I:** 114

"Man Who Carries the Desert Around Inside Himself, The: For Wally" (Komunyakaa), **Supp. XIII:** 125

"Man Who Closed Shop, The" (Dunn), **Supp. XI:** 149

Man Who Gave Up His Name, The (Harrison), **Supp. VIII:** 45, 52

Man Who Had All the Luck, The (A. Miller), **III:** 148, 149, 164, 166

"Man Who Knew Belle Star, The" (Bausch), **Supp. VII:** 46

"Man Who Knew Coolidge, The" (Lewis), **II:** 449

Man Who Knew Coolidge, The: Being the Soul of Lowell Schmaltz, Constructive and Nordic Citizen (Lewis), **II:** 450

Man Who Lived Underground, The (Wright), **Supp. II Part 1:** 40

"Man Who Lived Underground, The" (Wright), **IV:** 479, 485–487, 492; **Retro. Supp. II:** 121

"Man Who Made Me Love Him, The" (Weigl), **Supp. XIX:** 278

"Man Who Makes Brooms, The" (Nye), **Supp. XIII:** 276

"Man Who Studied Yoga, The" (Mailer), **III:** 35–36; **Retro. Supp. II:** 200

"Man Who Wanted to Win, The" (McCoy), **Supp. XIII:** 161

Man Who Was There, The (Morris), **III:** 220–221

"Man Who Writes Ants, The" (Merwin), **Supp. III Part 1:** 348

"Man with a Family" (Humphrey), **Supp. IX:** 94

Man without a Country, The (Hale), **I:** 488

"Man with the Blue Guitar, The" (Stevens), **I:** 266; **IV:** 85–87; **Retro. Supp. I:** **303–305**, 306, 307, 309

Man with the Blue Guitar and Other Poems, The (Stevens), **IV:** 76; **Retro. Supp. I:** 303, 422

Man with the Golden Arm, The (Algren), **Supp. V:** 4; **Supp. IX:** 1, 3, **9–11**, 14, 15

Man with the Golden Arm, The (film), **Supp. IX:** 3

"Man with the Golden Beef, The" (Podhoretz), **Supp. IX:** 3

"Man with the Hoe, The" (Markham), **Supp. XV:** 115

Man with the Mask, The (Lippard), **Supp. XXIII:** 178, 183–184, 188

Many a Monster (Ryan as Finnegan), **Supp. XVIII:** 233, **236–238**

Manyan Letters (Olson), **Supp. II Part 2:** 571

Many Circles (Goldbarth), **Supp. XII:** 193

"Many Handles" (Sandburg), **III:** 594

"Many Happy Returns" (Auden), **Supp. II Part 1:** 15

Many Happy Returns (Berrigan), **Supp. XXII:** 224; **Supp. XXIV:** 37, 41

Many Loves (W. C. Williams), **Retro. Supp. I:** 424

"Many Mansions" (H. Roth), **Supp. IX:** 233, 234

Many Marriages (Anderson), **I:** 104, 111, 113

"Many of Our Waters: Variations on a Poem by a Black Child" (Wright), **Supp. III Part 2:** 602

"Many Swans" (Lowell), **II:** 526

"Many Thousands Gone" (Baldwin), **Retro. Supp. II:** 4; **Supp. I Part 1:** 51

"Many Wagons Ago" (Ashbery), **Supp. III Part 1:** 22

Many-Windowed House, A (Cowley), **Supp. II Part 1:** 141, 143

"Many-Windowed House, A" (Cowley), **Supp. II Part 1:** 137

Mao II (DeLillo), **Supp. VI:** 2, 4, **5**, 6, **7**, 8, 9, 14, 16

"Map, The" (Bishop), **Retro. Supp. II:** 41; **Supp. I Part 1:** 72, 82, 85–88, 93

"Map, The" (Strand), **Supp. IV Part 2:** 623–624

"Maple Leaf, The" (Joplin), **Supp. IV Part 1:** 223

"Maple Tree, The" (D. West), **Supp. XVIII:** 284

Map of Another Town: A Memoir of Provence (M. F. K. Fisher), **Supp. XVII:** 88, 89, 92

"Map of Montana in Italy, A" (Hugo), **Supp. VI:** 139

Mapp and Lucia (Benson), **Supp. XX:** **229**

Mapping American Culture (Franklin and Steiner), **Supp. XXII:** 205

"Maps" (Hass), **Supp. VI:** 103–104

Mapson, Jo-Ann, **Supp. IV Part 2:** 440, 454

Map to the Next World, A: Poems and Tales (Harjo), **Supp. XII: 228–230**

"Maquillage" (Hull), **Supp. XXI:** 133

"Mara" (Jeffers), **Supp. II Part 2:** 434

Ma Rainey's Black Bottom (Wilson), **Supp. VIII:** 331, **332–334**, 346, 349, 350

Maranen (Asch), **Supp. XXIII:** 10

Marat, Jean Paul, **IV:** 117; **Supp. I Part 2:** 514, 515, 521

"Marathon" (Glück), **Supp. V:** 85

Marble Faun, The (Faulkner), **II:** 55, 56; **Retro. Supp. I:** 79

Marble Faun, The; or, The Romance of Monte Beni (Hawthorne), **II:** 225, 239, 242–243, 290, 324; **IV:** 167; **Retro. Supp. I:** 63, 149, 163, **164–165; Supp. I Part 1:** 38; **Supp. I Part 2:** 421,

596; **Supp. XIII:** 102

Marbles (Brodsky), **Supp. VIII:** 26–27

Marburg, Anita, **Supp. XXII:** 281

Marcaccio, Michael, **Supp. XVII:** 97, 106

"March" (W. C. Williams), **Retro. Supp. I:** 418

March, Alan, **Supp. XVI:** 242

March, Fredric, **III:** 154, 403; **IV:** 357; **Supp. X:** 220

"March, March on Down the Field" (Shaw), **Supp. XIX:** 246

Marchalonis, Shirley, **Supp. XIII:** 138, 140, 141, 143, 147–148

"Marché aux Oiseaux" (Wilbur), **Supp. III Part 2:** 550

"Märchen, The" (Jarrell), **II:** 378–379

March Hares (Frederic), **II:** 143–144

Marching Men (Anderson), **I:** 99, 101, 103–105, 111

"Marching Music" (Simic), **Supp. VIII:** 281

"Marcia" (R. H. Davis), **Supp. XVI:** 91–92

Marcks, Greg, **Supp. XVIII:** 150

Marckwardt, Albert H., **Supp. XXIV:** 255

Marco Millions (O'Neill), **III:** 391, 395

Marcosson, Isaac, **III:** 322

Marcus, Greil, **Supp. XVIII:** 30, 53

Marcus, Steven, **Retro. Supp. II:** 196, 200

Marcus Aurelius, **II:** 1; **III:** 566; **Supp. XVIII:** 304

Marcuse, Herbert, **Supp. I Part 2:** 645; **Supp. VIII:** 196; **Supp. XII:** 2

Mardi and a Voyage Thither (Melville), **I:** 384; **II:** 281; **III:** 77–79, 84, 87, 89; **Retro. Supp. I:** 247, 254, 256

Margaret (Judd), **II:** 290

Margaret & Dusty (Notley), **Supp. XXII:** 231

"Margaret Fuller, 1847" (Clampitt), **Supp. IX:** 43

"Marginalia" (Wilbur), **Supp. III Part 2:** 544

Margin of Hope, A: An Intellectual Autobiography (Howe), **Supp. VI:** 113–114, 117, 125, 128

"Margins of Maycomb, The: A Rereading of *To Kill a Mockingbird*" (Phelps), **Supp. VIII:** 128

Margoshes, Samuel, **Supp. X:** 70

"Margrave" (Jeffers), **Supp. II Part 2:** 426

Margret Howth (R. H. Davis), **Supp. XVI:** 81, 83, 84, **88–89**

Margret Howth: A Story of Today (J. Yellin, ed.), **Supp. XVI:** 88

Margulies, Donald, **Supp. XXI:** 145

"Maria Concepción" (Porter), **III:** 434–435, 451

Mariani, Paul L., **Retro. Supp. I:** 412, 419; **Retro. Supp. II:** 189

Marianne Moore Reader, (Moore), **III:** 199

Marie Antoinette (film), **Retro. Supp. I:** 113

Marie Blythe (Mosher), **Supp. XXII:** 206, 209, **212**

Marie Laveau (Prose), **Supp. XVI:** 251

Mariella Gable, Sister, **III:** 339, 355

"Marijuana and a Pistol" (C. Himes), **Supp. XVI:** 137

"Marijuana Notation" (Ginsberg), **Supp. II Part 1:** 313

Maril, Herman, **Supp. XXI:** 22, 23

Marilyn: A Biography (Mailer), **Retro. Supp. II:** 208

"Marin" (Cisneros), **Supp. VII:** 60, 61

Marin, Jay, **Retro. Supp. II:** 325

"Marina" (Eliot), **I:** 584, 585; **Retro. Supp. I:** 64

Mariners, Renegades, and Castaways (C. L. R. James), **Supp. XXI:** 159, 169–170

"Marine Surface, Low Overcast" (Clampitt), **Supp. IX: 47–48**

Marinetti, F. T., **Supp. XXII:** 159, 160, 161, 163

Marinetti, Tommaso, **Retro. Supp. I:** 59

Marionettes, The (Faulkner), **Retro. Supp. I:** 79

"Mari Sandoz's *Slogum House:* Greed as a Woman" (Riley), **Supp. XXIV:** 252

Maritain, Jacques, **I:** 402

Maritime Compact (Paine), **Supp. I Part 2:** 519

Maritime History of Massachusetts, 1783–1860, The (Morison), **Supp. I Part 2:** 481–483

Marjolin, Jean-Nicolas, **Supp. I Part 1:** 302

Marjorie Kinnan Rawlings: Sojourner at Cross Creek (Silverthorne), **Supp. X:** 220, 234

"Mark, The" (Bogan), **Supp. III Part 1:** 52

Marker, Chris, **Supp. IV Part 2:** 434, 436

"Market" (Hayden), **Supp. II Part 1:** 368, 369

Marketplace, The (Frederic), **II:** 145–146

Markham, Edwin, **I:** 199, 207; **Supp. XV:** 115

Markings (Hammarskjold), **Supp. II Part 1:** 26

Mark of the Vampire (film, Browning), **Supp. XVII:** 58

Markopoulos, Gregory, **Supp. XII:** 2

Markowick-Olczakova, Hanna, **Supp. X:** 70

Marks, Alison, **Supp. I Part 2:** 660

Marks, Barry A., **I:** 435, 438, 442, 446

Markson, David, **Supp. XVII: 135–147**

Mark Twain in Eruption (Twain), **IV:** 209

Mark Twain's America (De Voto), **I:** 248

Mark Twain's Autobiography (Twain), **IV:** 209

Marley, Bob, **Supp. IX:** 152

Marlowe, Christopher, **I:** 68, 368, 384; **II:** 590; **III:** 259, 491; **Retro. Supp. I:** 127; **Retro. Supp. II:** 76; **Supp. I Part 2:** 422; **Supp. XXI:** 227

Marlowe, Kimberly B., **Supp. XXII:** 214

"Marlowe Takes on the Syndicate" (Chandler), **Supp. IV Part 1:** 135

Marne, The (Wharton), **IV:** 319, 320; **Retro. Supp. I:** 378

Marquand, John, **Supp. XI:** 301

Marquand, Mrs. John P. (Adelaide Hooker), **III:** 57, 61

Marquand, Mrs. John P. (Christina Sedgwick), **III:** 54, 57
Marquand, J. P., **I:** 362, 375; **II:** 459, 482–483; **III: 50–73,** 383; **Supp. I Part 1:** 196; **Supp. IV Part 1:** 31; **Supp. V:** 95
Marquand, Philip, **III:** 52
Marquis, Don, **Supp. I Part 2:** 668
Marrásh, Francis al-, **Supp. XX:** 117
"Marriage" (Corso), **Supp. XII:** 117, 124, **127–128**
Marriage (Moore), **III:** 194
"Marriage" (Moore), **III:** 198–199, 213
"Marriage, A" (Untermeyer), **Supp. XV:** 305
Marriage A-la-Mode (Dryden), **Supp. IX:** 68
Marriage and Other Science Fiction (Goldbarth), **Supp. XII:** 189, 190
"Marriage in the Sixties, A" (Rich), **Supp. I Part 2:** 554
Marriage of Bette and Boo, The (Durang), **Supp. XXIV:** 114, 121, **122–123**
Marriage of Heaven and Hell (Blake), **Supp. XXII:** 257
"Marriage of Heaven and Hell, The" (Blake), **III:** 544–545; **Supp. VIII:** 99
"Marriage of Phaedra, The" (Cather), **Retro. Supp. I:** 5
Marriage Plot, The (Eugenides), **Supp. XXIV:** 135, **143–145**
"Marriage Rhapsody"(Hadas), **Supp. XXIII:** 114
Married (Strindberg), **Supp. XXII:** 23
"Married" (Taggard), **Supp. XXII:** 274
Married Men (Wolfert), **Supp. XXI:** 277
Marrow of Tradition, The (Chesnutt), **Supp. XIV:** 63, **71–75,** 76
Marryat, Captain Frederick, **III:** 423
"Marrying Absurd" (Didion), **Supp. IV Part 1:** 200
"Marrying Iseult?" (Updike), **Retro. Supp. I:** 329
Marrying Man (Simon), **Supp. IV Part 2:** 588
"Marrying the Hangman" (Atwood), **Supp. XIII:** 34
Marry Me: A Romance (Updike), **Retro. Supp. I:** 329, 330, 332
"Mars and Hymen" (Freneau), **Supp. II Part 1:** 258
Marsden, Dora, **III:** 471; **Retro. Supp. I:** 416
Marsena (Frederic), **II:** 135, 136–137
Marsh, Edward, **Supp. I Part 1:** 257, 263
Marsh, Frederick T., **Supp. XX: 39, 46**
Marsh, Fred T., **Supp. IX:** 232
Marsh, John R., **Supp. XIX:** 187
Marsh, Mae, **Supp. I Part 2:** 391
Marshall, George, **III:** 3
Marshall, John, **Supp. I Part 2:** 455; **Supp. XVI:** 117; **Supp. XIX:** 62; **Supp. XXIII:** 275, 276
Marshall, Paule, **Supp. IV Part 1:** 8, 14, 369; **Supp. XI:** 18, **275–292; Supp. XIII:** 295; **Supp. XX: 154**
Marshall, Tod, **Supp. XV:** 224; **Supp. XVII:** 25, 26, 29, 32
"Marshall Carpenter" (Masters), **Supp. I Part 2:** 463

"Marshes of Glynn, The" (Lanier), **Supp. I Part 1:** 364, 365–368, 370, 373
"'Marshes of Glynn, The': A Study in Symbolic Obscurity" (Ross), **Supp. I Part 1:** 373
Marsh Island, A (Jewett), **II:** 405; **Retro. Supp. II:** 134
"Marshland Elegy" (Leopold), **Supp. XIV:** 187, 189
"Mars Is Heaven!" (Bradbury), **Supp. IV Part 1:** 103, 106
Mars-Jones, Adam, **Supp. XXI:** 116
Marsman, Henrik, **Supp. IV Part 1:** 183
Marston, Ed, **Supp. IV Part 2:** 492
Marston, Elsa, **Supp. XXIII:** 241
Marta y Maria (Valdes), **II:** 290
"Martha's Lady" (Jewett), **Retro. Supp. II:** 140, 143
Marthe, Saint, **II:** 213
Martial, **II:** 1, 169; **Supp. IX:** 152
Martian Chronicles, The (Bradbury), **Supp. IV Part 1:** 102, 103, 106–107
Martian Time-Slip (Dick), **Supp. XVIII:** 142
Martin, Benjamin, **Supp. I Part 2:** 503
Martin, Charles, **Supp. XVII:** 112
Martin, Dick, **Supp. XII:** 44
Martin, Jay, **I:** 55, 58, 60, 61, 67; **III:** 307; **Retro. Supp. II:** 326, 327, 329; **Supp. XI:** 162
Martin, John, **Supp. XI:** 172
Martin, Judith, **Supp. V:** 128
Martin, Nell, **Supp. IV Part 1:** 351, 353
Martin, Reginald, **Supp. X:** 247, 249
Martin, Robert, **Supp. XX:** 165
Martin, Stephen-Paul, **Supp. IV Part 2:** 430
Martin, Tom, **Supp. X:** 79
Martin du Gard, Roger, **Supp. I Part 1:** 51
Martineau, Harriet, **Supp. II Part 1:** 282, 288, 294; **Supp. XVIII:** 7; **Supp. XXIV:** 78
Martin Eden (London), **II:** 466, 477–481
Martinelli, Sheri, **Supp. IV Part 1:** 280
Martínez, Guillermo, **Supp. XIII:** 313
Martinez-Avila, Raul, **Supp. XXIII:** 125
Martini, Adrienne, **Supp. XVIII:** 35
Mart'nez, Rafael, **Retro. Supp. I:** 423
Marty (Chayefsky), **Supp. XV:** 205
"Martyr, The" (Porter), **III:** 454
Martz, Louis L., **IV:** 151, 156, 165; **Supp. I Part 1:** 107; **Supp. XIV:** 12; **Supp. XXI:** 85
Marvell, Andrew, **IV:** 135, 151, 156, 161, 253; **Retro. Supp. I:** 62, 127; **Retro. Supp. II:** 186, 189; **Supp. I Part 1:** 80; **Supp. XII:** 159; **Supp. XIV:** 10; **Supp. XXI:** 204; **Supp. XXI:** 227; **Supp. XXIII:** 62
"Marvella, for Borrowing" (Ríos), **Supp. IV Part 2:** 551
"Marvelous Sauce, The", **Supp. XVII:** 189
Marvels and Masterpieces (al-Badá'i' wa'l-Tará'if) (Gibran), **Supp. XX: 116, 124**
Marx, Eleanor, **Supp. XVI:** 85

Marx, Karl, **I:** 60, 267, 279, 283, 588; **II:** 376, 462, 463, 483, 577; **IV:** 429, 436, 443–444, 469; **Retro. Supp. I:** 254; **Supp. I Part 2:** 518, 628, 632, 633, 634, 635, 639, 643, 645, 646; **Supp. III Part 2:** 619; **Supp. IV Part 1:** 355; **Supp. VIII:** 196; **Supp. IX:** 133; **Supp. X:** 119, 134; **Supp. XIII:** 75; **Supp. XXI:** 162, 263
Marx, Leo, **Supp. I Part 1:** 233
"Marxism and Monastic Perpectives" (Merton), **Supp. VIII:** 196
Mary (Asch), **Supp. XXIII:** 2, 7, **14**
Mary (Nabokov), **Retro. Supp. I: 267– 268,** 270, 277
"Mary" (Trethewey), **Supp. XXI:** 246
"Mary in Old Age" (Ferry), **Supp. XXIV:** 162
"Mary Karr, Mary Karr, Mary Karr, Mary Karr" (Harmon), **Supp. XI:** 248
Maryles, Daisy, **Supp. XII:** 271
Mary Magdalene, **I:** 303
Mary; or, The Test of Honour (Rowson), **Supp. XV: 233,** 236
"Mary O'Reilly" (Anderson), **II:** 44
"Mary Osaka , I Love You" (Fante), **Supp. XI:** 169
"Mary Snorak the Cook, Skermo the Gardener, and Jack the Parts Man Provide Dinner for a Wandering Stranger" (Grossman), **Supp. XIX:** 87
"Mary's Song" (Plath), **Supp. I Part 2:** 541
"Mary Winslow" (Lowell), **Retro. Supp. II:** 187
Marzynski, Marian, **Supp. XVI:** 153
Masefield, John, **II:** 552; **III:** 523
Masked and Anonymous (film, Dylan and Charles), **Supp. XVIII:** 21, 28
Mask for Janus, A (Merwin), **Supp. III Part 1:** 339, 341, 342
Maslin, Janet, **Supp. XVI:** 213; **Supp. XXI:** 79
Maslow, Abraham, **Supp. I Part 2:** 540
Maso, Carole, **Supp. XXII:** 261
Mason, Bobbie Ann, **Supp. VIII: 133– 149; Supp. XI:** 26; **Supp. XII:** 294, 298, 311; **Supp. XX:** 162
Mason, Charlotte, **Supp. XIV:** 201
Mason, David, **Supp. V:** 344; **Supp. XV:** 116, 251; **Supp. XVII:** 109, 110, 112, 121; **Supp. XVIII:** 182, 183
Mason, Jennifer, **Supp. XVIII:** 263
Mason, Lowell, **I:** 458
Mason, Margaret, **Supp. XXIII:** 209
Mason, Marsha, **Supp. IV Part 2:** 575, 586
Mason, Otis Tufton, **Supp. I Part 1:** 18
Mason, Walt, **Supp. XV:** 298
Mason & Dixon (Pynchon), **Supp. XVII:** 232
"Mason Jars by the Window" (Ríos), **Supp. IV Part 2:** 548
"Masque in Green and Black"(Hadas), **Supp. XXIII:** 121
Masque of Mercy, A (Frost), **II:** 155, 165, 167–168; **Retro. Supp. I:** 131, 140
"Masque of Mummers, The" (MacLeish), **III:** 18

"Masque of Pandora, The" (Longfellow), **Retro. Supp. II:** 167

Masque of Pandora, The, and Other Poems (Longfellow), **II:** 490, 494, 506; **Retro. Supp. II:** 169

Masque of Poets, A (Lathrop, ed.), **Retro. Supp. I:** 31; **Supp. I Part 1:** 365, 368

Masque of Reason, A (Frost), **II:** 155, 162, 165–167; **Retro. Supp. I:** 131, 140; **Retro. Supp. II:** 42

"Masque of the Red Death, The" (Poe), **III:** 412, 419, 424; **Retro. Supp. II:** 262, 268–269

"Masquerade" (Banks), **Supp. V:** 7

Massachusetts, Its Historians and Its History (Adams), **Supp. I Part 2:** 484

"Massachusetts 1932" (Bowles), **Supp. IV Part 1:** 94

"Massachusetts to Virginia" (Whittier), **Supp. I Part 2:** 688–689

"Massacre and the Mastermind, The" (Bausch), **Supp. VII:** 49

"Massacre at Scio, The" (Bryant), **Supp. I Part 1:** 168

"Massacre of the Innocents, The" (Simic), **Supp. VIII:** 282

Masses and Man (Toller), **I:** 479

"Masseur de Ma Soeur, Le" (Hecht), **Supp. X:** 58

Massey, Raymond, **Supp. IV Part 2:** 524

"Mass Eye and Ear: The Ward" (Karr), **Supp. XI:** 244

"Mass for the Day of St. Thomas Didymus" (Levertov), **Supp. III Part 1:** 283

Massie, Chris, **Supp. IV Part 2:** 524

Massing, Michael, **Supp. IV Part 1:** 208

Massinger, Philip, **Supp. I Part 2:** 422; **Supp. XV:** 238

Master Builder, The (Ibsen), **Supp. IV Part 2:** 522

Master Class (McNally), **Supp. XIII:** 204–205, 208

"Masterful" (Matthews), **Supp. IX:** 161–162

Mastering the Art of French Cooking (Child), **Supp. XVII:** 89

"Master Misery" (Capote), **Supp. III Part 1:** 117

Master of Dreams: A Memoir of Isaac Bashevis Singer (Telushkin), **Retro. Supp. II:** 317

"Master of Secret Revenges, The" (Gass), **Supp. VI:** 93

Master of the Crossroads (Bell), **Supp. X:** 16–17

"'Masterpiece of Filth, A': Portrait of Knoxville Forgets to Be Fair" (Howards), **Supp. VIII:** 178

Masterpieces of American Fiction, **Supp. XI:** 198

"Master Player, The" (Dunbar), **Supp. II Part 1:** 200

Masters, Edgar Lee, **I:** 106, 384, 475, 480, 518; **II:** 276, 529; **III:** 505, 576, 579; **IV:** 352; **Retro. Supp. I:** 131; **Supp. I Part 2:** 378, 386, 387, **454–478; Supp. III Part 1:** 63, 71, 73, 75; **Supp. IV Part 2:** 502; **Supp. IX:** 308; **Supp. XIV:** 282–283; **Supp. XV:** 256,

293, 297, 301, 306

Masters, Hardin W., **Supp. I Part 2:** 468

Masters, Hilary, **Supp. IX:** 96

Masters of Sociological Thought (Coser), **Supp. I Part 2:** 650

Masters of the Dew (Roumain), **Supp. IV Part 1:** 367

Masters of the Short Story (Kriegel and Lass, eds.), **Supp. XXIV:** 214

"Masters of War" (song, Dylan), **Supp. XVIII:** 24

"Master's Pieces, The" (H. L. Gates), **Supp. XX:** 109

Matchmaker, The (Wilder), **IV:** 357, 369, 370, 374; **Supp. XX:** 50

Mate of the Daylight, The, and Friends Ashore (Jewett), **II:** 404; **Retro. Supp. II:** 146–147

Materassi, Mario, **Supp. IX:** 233

Mather, Cotton, **II:** 10, 104, 302, 506, 536; **III:** 442; **IV:** 144, 152–153, 157; **Supp. I Part 1:** 102, 117, 174, 271; **Supp. I Part 2:** 584, 599, 698; **Supp. II Part 2:** 441–470; **Supp. IV Part 2:** 430, 434

Mather, Increase, **II:** 10; **IV:** 147, 157; **Supp. I Part 1:** 100

Mathews, Cornelius, **III:** 81; **Supp. I Part 1:** 317

Mathews, Shailer, **III:** 293

"Matinees" (Merrill), **Supp. III Part 1:** 319, 327

"Matins" (C. Frost), **Supp. XV:** 105

"Matins" (Glück), **Supp. V:** 88

"Matins" (Nelson), **Supp. XVIII:** 177

Matisse, Henri, **III:** 180; **IV:** 90, 407; **Supp. I Part 2:** 619; **Supp. VIII:** 168; **Supp. IX:** 66; **Supp. X:** 73, 74; **Supp. XXII:** 98, 99

"Matisse: Blue Interior with Two Girls–1947" (Hecht), **Supp. X:** 73–74

"Matisse: The Red Studio" (Snodgrass), **Supp. VI:** 316–317

Matlack, James, **Supp. XV:** 269, 271, 286

Matlock, Lucinda, **Supp. I Part 2:** 462

Matos, Juan, **Supp. XXI:** 104

Matrimaniac, The (film), **Supp. XVI:** 185, 186

Matrix Trilogy, The (film), **Supp. XVI:** 271

Matson, Harold, **Supp. XIII:** 164, 166, 167, 169, 172

Matson, Peter, **Supp. IV Part 1:** 299

Matson, Suzanne, **Supp. VIII:** 281

Matters of Fact and Fiction: Essays 1973–1976 (Vidal), **Supp. IV Part 2:** 687

Matters of Life and Death: New American Stories (Wolff, ed.), **Supp. XXIII:** 289

Matthew (biblical book), **IV:** 164; **Supp. XV:** 222

Matthew Arnold (Trilling), **Supp. III Part 2:** 500–501

Matthews, Jackson, **Supp. XVI:** 282

Matthews, T. S., **II:** 430; **Supp. XV:** 142

Matthews, William, **Supp. V:** 4, 5; **Supp. IX:** 151–170; **Supp. XIII:** 112; **Supp. XXI:** 87

Matthiessen, F. O., **I:** 254, 259–260, 517; **II:** 41, 554; **III:** 310, 453; **IV:** 181;

Retro. Supp. I: 40, 217; **Retro. Supp. II:** 137; **Supp. IV Part 2:** 422; **Supp. XIII:** 93; **Supp. XIV:** 3; **Supp. XXI:** 277

Matthiessen, Peter, **Supp. V:** 199–217, 332; **Supp. XI:** 231, 294; **Supp. XIV:** 82; **Supp. XIX:** 230; **Supp. XXIV:** 268

Mattingly, Garrett, **Supp. IV Part 2:** 601

Mattos, Anita, **Supp. XXIII:** 197

Mattu, Ravi, **Supp. XVI:** 124

"Maud Island" (Caldwell), **I:** 310

Maud Martha (Brooks), **Supp. III Part 1:** 74, 78–79, 87; **Supp. XI:** 278

"Maud Muller" (Whittier), **Supp. I Part 2:** 698

Maugham, W. Somerset, **III:** 57, 64; **Supp. IV Part 1:** 209; **Supp. X:** 58; **Supp. XIV:** 161

Maule's Curse: Seven Studies in the History of American Obscurantism (Winters), **Supp. II Part 2:** 807–808, 812

"Mau-mauing the Flak Catchers" (Wolfe), **Supp. III Part 2:** 577

Maupassant, Guy de, **I:** 309, 421; **II:** 191–192, 291, 325, 591; **IV:** 17; **Retro. Supp. II:** 65, 66, 67, 299; **Supp. I Part 1:** 207, 217, 223, 320; **Supp. XIV:** 336

"Maurice Barrès and the Youth of France" (Bourne), **I:** 228

Maurice Kenny: Celebrations of a Mohawk Writer (Kelsey, ed.), **Supp. XXIII:** 143

Maurier, George du, **II:** 338

Maurras, Charles, **Retro. Supp. I:** 55

Maus II: And Here My Troubles Began (A. Speigelman), **Supp. XVII:** 48

Mauve Gloves & Madmen, Clutter & Vine (Wolfe), **Supp. III Part 2:** 581

Maverick, Augustus, **Supp. XVIII:** 4

Maverick in Mauve (Auchincloss), **Supp. IV Part 1:** 26

"Mavericks, The" (play) (Auchincloss), **Supp. IV Part 1:** 34

"Mavericks, The" (story) (Auchincloss), **Supp. IV Part 1:** 32

"Max" (H. Miller), **III:** 183

Max, D. T., **Supp. XXI:** 117

Max and the White Phagocytes (H. Miller), **III:** 178, 183–184

Maximilian (emperor of Mexico), **Supp. I Part 2:** 457–458

Maximilian: A Play in Five Acts (Masters), **Supp. I Part 2:** 456, 457–458

"Maximus, to Gloucester" (Olson), **Supp. II Part 2:** 574

"Maximus, to himself" (Olson), **Supp. II Part 2:** 565, 566, 567, 569, 570, 572

Maximus Poems, The (Olson), **Retro. Supp. I:** 209; **Supp. II Part 2:** 555, 556, 563, 564–580, 584; **Supp. VIII:** 305; **Supp. XV:** 170, 264, 349; **Supp. XVI:** 287

Maximus Poems 1–10, The (Olson), **Supp. II Part 2:** 571

Maximus Poems IV, V, VI (Olson), **Supp. II Part 2:** 555, 580, 582–584

Maximus Poems Volume Three, The (Olson), **Supp. II Part 2:** 555, 582, 584–585

"Maximus to Gloucester, Letter 19 (A Pastoral Letter)" (Olson), **Supp. II Part 2:** 567

"Maximus to Gloucester, Sunday July 19" (Olson), **Supp. II Part 2:** 580

"Maximus to himself June 1964" (Olson), **Supp. II Part 2:** 584

Maxwell, Glyn, **Supp. XV:** 252, 253, 260, 261, 263, 264

Maxwell, William, **Supp. I Part 1:** 175; **Supp. III Part 1:** 62; **Supp. VIII:** 151–174; **Supp. XVII:** 23

May, Abigail (Abba). *See* Alcott, Mrs. Amos Bronson (Abigail May)

May, Elaine Tyler, **Supp. XXII:** 81, 95

May, Jill, **Supp. VIII:** 126

"May 24, 1980" (Brodsky), **Supp. VIII:** 28

"May 1968" (Olds), **Supp. X:** 211–212

Mayakovsky, Vladimir, **Supp. XXIII:** 207

"Mayakovsky"(O'Hara), **Supp. XXIII:** 212, 214

"Mayan Glyphs Unread, The" (Bronk), **Supp. XXI:** 31

"Mayan Warning" (Mora), **Supp. XIII:** 214

Maybe (Hellman), **Supp. IV Part 1:** 12

"Maybe" (Oliver), **Supp. VII:** 239

"Maybe, Someday" (Ritsos), **Supp. XIII:** 78

May Blossom (Belasco), **Supp. XVI:** 182

"Mayday" (Faulkner), **Retro. Supp. I:** 80

"May Day" (Fitzgerald), **II:** 88–89; **Retro. Supp. I:** 103

"May Day Dancing, The" (Nemerov), **III:** 275

May Days (Pickering), **Supp. XXI:** 197–198

May Days: An Anthology of Verse from Masses-Liberator (Taggard, ed.), **Supp. XXII:** 275–276

"May Day Sermon to the Women of Gilmer County, Georgia, by a Woman Preacher Leaving the Baptist Church" (Dickey), **Supp. IV Part 1:** 182

Mayer, Bernadette, **Supp. XXIV:** 41

Mayer, Elizabeth, **Supp. II Part 1:** 16; **Supp. III Part 1:** 63

Mayer, John, **Retro. Supp. I:** 58

Mayer, Louis B., **Supp. XII:** 160; **Supp. XVIII:** 250

Mayes, Wendell, **Supp. IX:** 250

Mayfield, Sara, **Supp. IX:** 65

Mayflower, The (Stowe), **Supp. I Part 2:** 585, 586

Mayle, Peter, **Supp. XVI:** 295

Maynard, Joyce, **Supp. V:** 23

Maynard, Tony, **Supp. I Part 1:** 65

Mayne, Xavier. *See* Prime-Stevenson, Edward Irenaeus

Mayo, Robert, **III:** 478

Mayor (Allen), **Supp. XXII:** 245

Mayorga, Margaret, **IV:** 381

"May-Pole of Merry Mount, The" (Hawthorne), **Supp. XXII:** 44

"Maypole of Merrymount, The" (Hawthorne), **II:** 229

"May Queen" (Di Piero), **Supp. XIX:** 41

May Sarton: Selected Letters 1916–1954, **Supp. VIII:** 265

"May Sun Sheds an Amber Light, The" (Bryant), **Supp. I Part 1:** 170

"May Swenson: The Art of Perceiving" (Stanford), **Supp. IV Part 2:** 637

May the Generations Die in the Right Order (Schott), **Supp. XXIII:** 248–250

"Maze" (Eberhart), **I:** 523, 525–526, 527

Mazel (R. Goldstein), **Supp. XVII:** 44

Mazower, David, **Supp. XXIII:** 4, 5

Mazur, Gail, **Supp. XVIII:** 92

Mazurkiewicz, Margaret, **Supp. XI:** 2

Mazzini, Giuseppe, **Supp. I Part 1:** 2, 8; **Supp. II Part 1:** 299

M. Butterfly (Hwang), **Supp. X:** 292; **Supp. XXI:** 143, 147, **150–154**

Mc. Names starting with Mc are alphabetized as if spelled Mac.

"M. Degas Teaches Art & Science at Durfee Intermediate School, Detroit, 1942" (Levine), **Supp. V:** 181, 193

"Me, Boy Scout" (Lardner), **II:** 433

Me, Vashya! (T. Williams), **IV:** 381

Mead, Elinor. *See* Howells, Mrs. William Dean (Elinor Mead)

Mead, George Herbert, **II:** 27, 34; **Supp. I Part 1:** 5; **Supp. I Part 2:** 641

Mead, Margaret, **Supp. I Part 1:** 49, 52, 66; **Supp. IX:** 229

Mead, Taylor, **Supp. XV:** 187

Meade, Frank, **Retro. Supp. II:** 114

Meade, Marion, **Supp. IX:** 191, 193, 194, 195

Meadow, Lynne, **Supp. XIII:** 198

"Meadow House" (Carruth), **Supp. XVI:** 48

Meadowlands (Glück), **Supp. V:** 88–90

"Mean, Mrs." (Gass), **Supp. VI:** 83

"Me and the Mule" (Hughes), **Supp. I Part 1:** 334

Me and You and Everyone We Know (film, July), **Supp. XXIV:** 199, 200, 201, 203, 206, **207–209**

Mean Free Path (Lerner), **Supp. XXIV:** 45

"Meaningless Institution, A" (Ginsberg), **Supp. II Part 1:** 313

"Meaning of a Literary Idea, The" (Trilling), **Supp. III Part 2:** 498

"Meaning of Birds, The" (C. Smith), **Supp. X:** 177

"Meaning of Death, The, An After Dinner Speech" (Tate), **IV:** 128, 129

"Meaning of Life, The" (Tate), **IV:** 137

"Meaning of Simplicity, The" (Ritsos), **Supp. XIII:** 78

Means of Escape (Caputo), **Supp. XIX:** 18, 21, 25

Mean Spirit (Hogan), **Supp. IV Part 1:** 397, 404, 407–410, 415, 416–417

Meantime, The (Bronk), **Supp. XXI:** 31

Mearns, Hughes, **III:** 220

"Measure" (Hass), **Supp. VI: 99–100,** 101

"Measuring My Blood" (Vizenor), **Supp. IV Part 1:** 262

Meatyard, Gene, **Supp. X:** 30

Me: By Jimmy (Big Boy) Valente (Keillor), **Supp. XVI:** 177

Mechan, Dennis B., **Supp. XVI:** 267–268

Mechanic, The (Bynner and DeMille), **Supp. XV:** 42, 50

"Mechanism" (Ammons), **Supp. VII:** 28

"Mechanism in Thought and Morals" (Holmes), **Supp. I Part 1:** 314

Mecom, Mrs. Jane, **II:** 122

"Meddlesome Jack" (Caldwell), **I:** 309

Medea (Jeffers), **Supp. II Part 2:** 435

Medea and Some Poems, The (Cullen), **Supp. IV Part 1:** 169, 173

"Me Decade and the Third Great Awakening, The" (Wolfe), **Supp. III Part 2:** 581

"Médecin Malgré Lui, Le" (W. C. Williams), **IV:** 407–408

"Medfield" (Bryant), **Supp. I Part 1:** 157

Medical History of Contraception, A (Himes), **Supp. V:** 128

"Medicine Song" (Gunn Allen), **Supp. IV Part 1:** 326

Médicis, Marie de, **II:** 548

Medina (McCarthy), **II:** 579

"Meditation, A" (Eberhart), **I:** 533–535

"Meditation 1.6" (Taylor), **IV:** 165

"Meditation 1.20" (Taylor), **IV:** 165

"Meditation 2.68A" (Taylor), **IV:** 165

"Meditation 2.102" (Taylor), **IV:** 150

"Meditation 2.112" (Taylor), **IV:** 165

"Meditation 20" (Taylor), **IV:** 154–155

"Meditation 40" (Second Series) (Taylor), **IV:** 147

"Meditation at Lagunitas" (Hass), **Supp. VI:** 104–105; **Supp. XXI:** 60

"Meditation at Oyster River" (Roethke), **III:** 537, 549

Meditations (Descartes), **III:** 618

Meditations (Marcus Aurelius), **Supp. XVIII:** 304

"Meditations for a Savage Child" (Rich), **Supp. I Part 2:** 564–565

Meditations from a Movable Chair (Dubus), **Supp. VII:** 91

Meditations in an Emergency (O'Hara), **Supp. XXIII: 213–214,** 219, 220

"Meditations in an Emergency"(O'Hara), **Supp. XXIII:** 212, 214

"Meditations in a Swine Yard" (Komunyakaa), **Supp. XIII:** 131

"Meditations of an Old Woman" (Roethke), **III:** 529, 540, 542, 543, 545–547, 548

"Meditations on Grass"(Crooker), **Supp. XXIII:** 55

Meditations on the Insatiable Soul (R. Bly), **Supp. IV Part 1:** 72–73

Meditative Poems, The (Martz), **IV:** 151

"Mediterranean, The" (Tate), **IV:** 129

"Medium of Fiction, The" (Gass), **Supp. VI:** 85–86

"Medley" (Bambara), **Supp. XI:** 9

"Medusa" (Bogan), **Supp. III Part 1:** 50, 51

Meehan, Jeannette Porter, **Supp. XX: 213, 214, 217, 220, 224**

Meehan, Thomas, **Supp. IV Part 2:** 577–578, 586, 590

Meek, Martha, **Supp. IV Part 2:** 439, 440, 441, 442, 445, 447, 448

Meeker, Richard K., **II:** 190

Meese, Elizabeth, **Supp. XIII:** 297

"Meeting" (J. W. Miller), **Supp. XX: 167**

"Meeting, The" (F. Wright), **Supp. XVII:** 245

"Meeting and Greeting Area, The" (Cameron), **Supp. XII: 84–85**

Meeting by the River, A (Isherwood), **Supp. XIV:** 164, **170–171,** 172

"Meeting-House Hill" (Lowell), **II:** 522, 527

"Meeting in the Kitchen, The" (Schnackenberg), **Supp. XV:** 256

"Meeting South, A" (Anderson), **I:** 115

"Meeting the Mountains" (Snyder), **Supp. VIII:** 300

Meeting Trees (Sanders), **Supp. XVI:** 269

Meet Me at the Morgue (Macdonald), **Supp. IV Part 2:** 472

Mehta, Sonny, **Supp. XI:** 178

Mehta, Ved, **Supp. XX: 87**

Meine, Curt, **Supp. XIV:** 179

Meiners, R. K., **IV:** 136, 137, 138, 140

Meinong, Alexius, **Supp. XIV:** 198, 199

Meisner, Sanford, **Supp. XIV:** 240, 242

Meister, Charles W., **II:** 112

Mejia, Jaime, **Supp. XIX:** 97

"Melancholia" (Dunbar), **Supp. II Part 1:** 194

Melancholy Baby (Parker), **Supp. XIX:** 186

"Melanctha" (Stein), **IV:** 30, 34, 35, 37, 38–40, 45

"Melancthon" (Moore), **III:** 212, 215

Melbourne House (S. and A. Warner), **Supp. XVIII:** 268

Meliboeus Hipponax (Lowell). *See Bigelow Papers, The* (Lowell)

Melinda and Melinda (Allen), **Supp. XV:** 16

Mellaart, James, **Supp. I Part 2:** 567

Mellard, James, **Supp. IV Part 1:** 387

Mellen, Joan, **Supp. XXIV:** 51, 52, 56, 64

Mellon, Andrew, **III:** 14

Mellor, W. M., **Supp. XX: 56**

Melnick, Jeffrey, **Supp. X:** 252

Melnyczuk, Askold, **Supp. IV Part 1:** 70

Melodrama Play (Shepard), **Supp. III Part 2:** 440–441, 443, 445

Melodramatists, The (Nemerov), **III:** 268, 281–283, 284

Melopoeia (Espaillat and Tavano), **Supp. XXI:** 99–100

Melting-Pot, The (Zangwill), **I:** 229

"Melungeons" (Offutt), **Supp. XIX:** 171

Melville, Allan, **III:** 74, 77

Melville, Gansevoort, **III:** 76

Melville, Herman, **I:** 104, 106, 211, 288, 340, 343, 348, 354, 355, 561–562; **II:** 27, 74, 224–225, 228, 230, 232, 236, 255, 259, 271, 272, 277, 281, 295, 307, 311, 319, 320, 321, 418, 477, 497, 539–540, 545; **III:** 29, 45, 70, **74–98,** 359, 438, 453, 454, 507, 562–563, 572, 576; **IV:** 57, 105, 194, 199, 202, 250, 309, 333, 345, 350, 380, 444, 453; **Retro. Supp. I:** 54, 91, 160, 215, 220, **243–262; Retro. Supp. II:** 76; **Supp. I Part 1:** 147, 238, 242, 249, 309, 317, 372; **Supp. I Part 2:** 383, 495, 579, 580, 582, 602; **Supp. IV Part 2:** 463, 613; **Supp. V:** 279, 281, 298, 308; **Supp. VIII:** 48, 103, 104, 105, 106, 108, 156, 175, 181, 188; **Supp. XI:** 83; **Supp. XII:** 282; **Supp. XIII:** 294, 305; **Supp. XIV:** 48, 227; **Supp. XV:** 287; **Supp. XVII:** 42, 185; **Supp. XVIII:** 1, 4, 6, 7, 9; **Supp. XXI:** 169; **Supp. XXII:** 174, 262; **Supp. XXIII:** 164, 165, 174, 190; **Supp. XXIV:** 88

Melville, Mrs. Herman (Elizabeth Shaw), **III:** 77, 91, 92

Melville, Maria Gansevoort, **III:** 74, 77, 85

Melville, Thomas, **III:** 77, 79, 92; **Supp. I Part 1:** 309

Melville, Whyte, **IV:** 309

Melville Goodwin, USA (Marquand), **III:** 60, 65–66

Melville's Marginalia (Cowen), **Supp. IV Part 2:** 435

"Melville's Marginalia" (Howe), **Supp. IV Part 2:** 435

Member of the Wedding, The (McCullers), **II:** 587, 592, 600–604, 605, 606; **Supp. VIII:** 124

"Meme Ortiz" (Cisneros), **Supp. VII:** 60

Memmon (song cycle) (Bowles), **Supp. IV Part 1:** 82

Memnoch the Devil (Rice), **Supp. VII:** 289, 290, 294, 296–299

"Memoir" (Hempel), **Supp. XXI:** 118

"Memoir" (Untermeyer), **II:** 516–517

"Memoir, A" (Koch), **Supp. XV:** 184

"Memoirist's Apology, A" (Karr), **Supp. XI:** 245, 246

Memoir of Mary Ann, A (O'Connor), **III:** 357

Memoir of Thomas McGrath, A (Beeching), **Supp. X:** 114, 118

Memoirs (W. Frank), **Supp. XX: 67, 69, 70, 81**

Memoirs of a Preacher, a Revelation of the Church and the Home, The (Lippard), **Supp. XXIII:** 178, 183–184, 188, 190

Memoirs of Arii Taimai (Adams), **I:** 2–3

"Memoirs of Carwin, the Biloquist" (Brown), **Supp. I Part 1:** 132

Memoirs of Hecate County (Wilson), **IV:** 429

Memoirs of Margaret Fuller Ossoli (Fuller), **Supp. II Part 1:** 280, 283, 285

"Memoirs of Stephen Calvert" (Brown), **Supp. I Part 1:** 133, 144

Memorabilia (Xenophon), **II:** 105

Memorable Providences (Mather), **Supp. II Part 2:** 458

Memorial, The: Portrait of a Family (Isherwood), **Supp. XIV:** 156, 159, 160–161

"Memorial Day" (Cameron), **Supp. XII:** 80, **82–83**

"Memorial for the City" (Auden), **Supp. II Part 1:** 20

"Memorial Rain" (MacLeish), **III:** 15

"Memorial to Ed Bland" (Brooks), **Supp. III Part 1:** 77

"Memorial Tribute" (Wilbur), **Supp. IV Part 2:** 642

"Memories" (Whittier), **Supp. I Part 2:** 699

Memories of a Catholic Girlhood (McCarthy), **II:** 560–561, 566; **Supp. XI:** 246; **Supp. XVI:** 64, 70

"Memories of East Texas" (Karr), **Supp. XI:** 239

"Memories of Uncle Neddy" (Bishop), **Retro. Supp. II:** 38; **Supp. I Part 1:** 73, 93

"Memories of West Street and Lepke" (Lowell), **II:** 550

"Memory" (Epstein), **Supp. XII:** 163

"Memory" (Everwine), **Supp. XV:** 82

"Memory, A" (Welty), **IV:** 261–262; **Retro. Supp. I:** 344–345

"Memory, Narrative, and the Discourses of Identity in *Abeng* and *No Telephone to Heaven*" (Smith), **Supp. XXII:** 70

"Memory, The" (Gioia), **Supp. XV:** 119

Memory and Enthusiasm: Essays, 1975–1985 (Di Piero), **Supp. XIX:** 34, 41, 42

"Memory and Imagination" (Hampl), **Supp. XXII:** 94

Memory Gardens (Creeley), **Supp. IV Part 1:** 141, 157

"Memory Harbor" (Skloot), **Supp. XX: 201**

Memory of Murder, A (Bradbury), **Supp. IV Part 1:** 103

Memory of Old Jack, The (Berry), **Supp. X:** 34

Memory of Two Mondays, A (A. Miller), **III:** 153, 156, 158–159, 160, 166

"Memo to Non-White Peoples" (Hughes), **Retro. Supp. I:** 209

"Men" (Boyle), **Supp. XXIV:** 61

Men, Women and Ghosts (Lowell), **II:** 523–524

Menaker, Charlotte, **Supp. XIX:** 266

Menaker, Daniel, **Supp. VIII:** 151; **Supp. XXIII:** 276

Menand, Louis, **Supp. XIV:** 40, 197; **Supp. XVI:** 106, 107; **Supp. XXIII:** 104–105

Men and Angels (Gordon), **Supp. IV Part 1:** 304–305, 306, 308

Men and Brethen (Cozzens), **I:** 363–365, 368, 375, 378, 379

Men and Cartoons (Lethem), **Supp. XVIII:** 145, **148**

"Men and Women" (R. Bly), **Supp. IV Part 1:** 72

"Men at Forty" (Justice), **Supp. VII:** 126–127

Mencius (Meng-tzu), **IV:** 183

Mencken, August, **III:** 100, 108

Mencken, August, Jr., **III:** 99, 109, 118–119

Mencken, Mrs. August (Anna Abhau), **III:** 100, 109
Mencken, Burkhardt, **III:** 100, 108
Mencken, Charles, **III:** 99
Mencken, Gertrude, **III:** 99
Mencken, H. L., **I:** 199, 210, 212, 235, 245, 261, 405, 514, 515, 517; **II:** 25, 27, 42, 89, 90, 91, 271, 289, 430, 443, 449; **III:** **99–121**, 394, 482; **IV:** 76, 432, 440, 475, 482; **Retro. Supp. I:** 1, 101; **Retro. Supp. II:** 97, 98, 102, 265; **Supp. I Part 2:** 484, 629–630, 631, 647, 651, 653, 659, 673; **Supp. II Part 1:** 136; **Supp. IV Part 1:** 201, 314, 343; **Supp. IV Part 2:** 521, 692, 693; **Supp. XI:** 163–164, 166; **Supp. XIII:** 161; **Supp. XIV:** 111; **Supp. XV:** 297, 301, 303; **Supp. XVI:** 187–188, 189; **Supp. XVII:** 106; **Supp. XXII:** 23, 187, 277; **Supp. XXIV:** 26, 281
Mencken, Mrs. H. L. (Sara Haardt), **III:** 109, 111
"Men Deified Because of Their Cruelty" (Simic), **Supp. VIII:** 282
Mendelbaum, Paul, **Supp. V:** 159
Mendele, **IV:** 3, 10
Mendelief, Dmitri Ivanovich, **IV:** 421
Mendelsohn, Daniel, **Supp. X:** 153, 154; **Supp. XV:** 257, 258, 261, 266
Mendelsohn, Jack, **Supp. XXIV:** 72, 77
Mendelssohn, Moses, **Supp. XXIII:** 4
Mendes, Alfred, **Supp. XXI:** 160
"Mending Wall" (Frost), **II:** 153–154; **Retro. Supp. I:** 128, 130; **Supp. X:** 64
Men from the Boys, The (Lacy), **Supp. XV:** 202, 205
Men in the Off Hours (Carson), **Supp. XII:** **111–113**
"Men in the Storm, The" (Crane), **I:** 411
"Men Loved Wholly Beyond Wisdom" (Bogan), **Supp. III Part 1:** 50
"Men Made Out of Words" (Stevens), **IV:** 88
Men Must Act (Mumford), **Supp. II Part 2:** 479
Mennes, John, **II:** 111
Mennoti, Gian Carlo, **Supp. IV Part 1:** 84
Men of Brewster Place, The (Naylor), **Supp. VIII:** 213, **228–230**
"Men of Color, to Arms!" (Douglass), **Supp. III Part 1:** 171
Men of Good Hope: A Story of American Progressives (Aaron), **Supp. I Part 2:** 650
Mens' Club, The (film), **Supp. XVI:** 212–213
Men's Club, The (L. Michaels), **Supp. XVI:** 206, **210–212**
"Menstruation at Forty" (Sexton), **Supp. II Part 2:** 686
"Mental Hospital Garden, The" (W. C. Williams), **Retro. Supp. I:** 428
Mental Radio (Sinclair), **Supp. V:** 289
Mentoria; or, The Young Lady's Friend (Rowson), **Supp. XV:** **233–234**, 238
"Men We Carry in Our Minds, The" (Sanders), **Supp. XVI:** 273

Men Who Made the Nation, The (Dos Passos), **I:** 485
Men Without Women (Hemingway), **II:** 249; **Retro. Supp. I:** 170, 176; **Supp. IX:** 202
"Merced" (Rich), **Supp. I Part 2:** 563
"Mercedes" (E. Stoddard), **Supp. XV:** 278
"Mercedes Hospital" (Bishop), **Retro. Supp. II:** 51
"Mercenary, A" (Ozick), **Supp. V:** 267
Mercer, Johnny, **Supp. XXII:** 6
Merchandising (Hwang), **Supp. XXI:** 147
Merchant of Venice, The (Shakespeare), **IV:** 227; **Supp. XIV:** 325
Mercury Theatre, **Retro. Supp. I:** 65
Mercy, Pity, Peace, and Love (Ozick), **Supp. V:** 257, 258
Mercy, The (Levine), **Supp. V:** 194–195
Mercy of a Rude Stream (H. Roth), **Supp. IX:** 231, 234, **235–242**
"Mercy" (P. Benedict), **Supp. XXIII:** 49
Mercy Philbrick's Choice (Jackson), **Retro. Supp. I:** 26, 27, 33
Mercy Street (Sexton), **Supp. II Part 2:** 683, 689
"Mercy" (Thompson), **Supp. XXIII:** 295, 296
Meredith, George, **II:** 175, 186; **Supp. IV Part 1:** 300
Meredith, Mary. *See* Webb, Mary
Meredith, William, **II:** 545; **Retro. Supp. II:** 181
"Merely by Wilderness" (Peacock), **Supp. XIX:** 199
"Merely to Know" (Rich), **Supp. I Part 2:** 554
"Mère Pochette" (Jewett), **II:** 400
"Merger II, The" (Auchincloss), **Supp. IV Part 1:** 34
Meri (Asch), **Supp. XXIII:** 5, 11
"Mericans" (Cisneros), **Supp. VII:** 69
"Merida, 1969" (Matthews), **Supp. IX:** 151
"Meridian" (Clampitt), **Supp. IX:** **48–49**
Meridian (Walker), **Supp. III Part 2:** 520, 524, 527, 528, 531–537
Mérimée, Prosper, **II:** 322
Meriwether, James B., **Retro Supp. I:** 77, 91
"Meriwether Connection, The" (Cowley), **Supp. II Part 1:** 142
Merker, Kim K., **Supp. XI:** 261; **Supp. XV:** 75, 77
"Merlin" (Emerson), **II:** 19, 20
Merlin (Robinson), **III:** 522
"Merlin Enthralled" (Wilbur), **Supp. III Part 2:** 544, 554
"Mermother" (A. Finch), **Supp. XVII:** 72
Merril, Judith, **Supp. XVI:** 123
Merrill, Cavafy, Poems, and Dreams (Hadas), **Supp. XXIII:** **123–124**
Merrill, Christopher, **Supp. XI:** 329
Merrill, James, **Retro. Supp. I:** 296; **Retro. Supp. II:** 53; **Supp. III Part 1:** **317–338**; **Supp. III Part 2:** 541, 561; **Supp. IX:** 40, 42, 48, 52; **Supp. X:** 73; **Supp. XI:** 123, 131, 249; **Supp. XII:** 44, 254, 255, 256, 261–262, 269–

270; **Supp. XIII:** 76, 85; **Supp. XV:** 249, 250, 253; **Supp. XVII:** 123; **Supp. XXIII:** 112, 122, 123
Merrill, Mark (pseudonym). *See* Markson, David
Merrill, Robert, **Retro. Supp. II:** 201
Merrill, Ronald, **Supp. IV Part 2:** 521
Merritt, Abraham, **Supp. XVII:** 58
Merritt, Theresa, **Supp. VIII:** 332
Merritt, Vernon, **Supp. XXII:** 245
"Merry-Go-Round" (Hughes), **Retro. Supp. I:** 194, 205; **Supp. I Part 1:** 333
Merry-Go-Round, The (Van Vechten), **Supp. II Part 2:** 734, 735
Merry Month of May, The (Jones), **Supp. XI:** **227–228**
Merry Widow, The (Lehar), **III:** 183
Merton, Thomas, **III:** 357; **Supp. VIII:** **193–212**; **Supp. XXII:** 83, 90; **Supp. XXIV:** 133
Merwin, W. S., **Supp. III Part 1:** **339–360**; **Supp. III Part 2:** 541; **Supp. IV Part 2:** 620, 623, 626; **Supp. V:** 332; **Supp. IX:** 152, 155, 290; **Supp. XIII:** 274, 277; **Supp. XV:** 222, 342; **Supp. XIX:** 82; **Supp. XXI:** 95
Meryman, Richard, **Supp. IV Part 2:** 579, 583
Meshiekhs tsaytn (Times of the Messiah) (Asch), **Supp. XXIII:** 5
Meshugah (Singer), **Retro. Supp. II:** **315–316**
Mesic, Michael, **Supp. IV Part 1:** 175
Mesic, Penelope, **Supp. X:** 15
Message in the Bottle, The (Percy), **Supp. III Part 1:** 387–388, 393, 397
"Message in the Bottle, The" (Percy), **Supp. III Part 1:** 388
"Message of Flowers and Fire and Flowers, The" (Brooks), **Supp. III Part 1:** 69
Messengers Will Come No More, The (Fiedler), **Supp. XIII:** 103
Messerli, Douglas, **Supp. XVI:** 293
Messiah (Vidal), **Supp. IV Part 2:** 677, 680, 681–682, 685, 691, 692
"Messiah, The" (Wasserstein), **Supp. XV:** 328
Messiah of Stockholm, The (Ozick), **Supp. V:** 270–271; **Supp. XVII:** 42
Messud, Claire, **Supp. XVIII:** 98
Metamorphic Tradition in Modern Poetry (Quinn), **IV:** 421
Metamorphoses (Ovid), **II:** 542–543; **III:** 467, 468; **Supp. XV:** 33; **Supp. XVI:** 20; **Supp. XX: 280; Supp. XXIV:** 132
Metamorphoses (Pound, trans.), **III:** 468–469
Metamorphosis (Kafka), **Supp. XXI:** 89
Metamorphosis, The (Kafka), **IV:** 438; **Retro. Supp. II:** 287–288; **Supp. VIII:** 3
"Metamorphosis and Survival" (Woodcock), **Supp. XIII:** 33
"Metaphor as Mistake" (Percy), **Supp. III Part 1:** 387–388
Metaphor & Memory: Essays (Ozick), **Supp. V:** 272

Metaphor of Trees and Last Poems (Bronk), **Supp. XXI:** 32

"Metaphors of a Magnifico" (Stevens), **IV:** 92

Metaphysical Club, The (Menand), **Supp. XIV:** 40, 197

"Metaphysical Poets, The" (Eliot), **I:** 527, 586

"Metaphysics" (Ginsberg), **Supp. II Part 1:** 313

Metcalf, Paul, **Supp. XIV:** 96; **Supp. XXIII:** 163, 174

"Meteor, The" (Bradbury), **Supp. IV Part 1:** 102

Methinks the Lady...(Endore), **Supp. XVII:** 61–62

"Metonymy as an Approach to the Real World" (Bronk), **Supp. XXI:** 30

Metress, Christopher P., **Supp. V:** 314

Metrical History of Christianity, The (Taylor), **IV:** 163

Metropolis, The (Sinclair), **Supp. V:** 285

"Metterling Lists, The" (Allen), **Supp. XV:** 15

"Metzengerstein" (Poe), **III:** 411, 417

Mew, Charlotte, **Retro. Supp. II:** 247

Mewshaw, Michael, **Supp. V:** 57; **Supp. X:** 82

"Mexican Hands" (Ryan as Quin), **Supp. XVIII:** 227

"Mexico" (Lowell), **II:** 553, 554

"Mexico, Age Four" (Salinas), **Supp. XIII:** 315

Mexico City Blues (Kerouac), **Supp. III Part 1:** 225, 229

"Mexico Is a Foreign Country: Five Studies in Naturalism" (Warren), **IV:** 241, 252

"Mexico's Children" (Rodriguez), **Supp. XIV:** 302

Meyer, Carolyn, **Supp. XIX:** 194–195, 197

Meyer, Donald B., **III:** 298

Meyer, Ellen Hope, **Supp. V:** 123

Meyer, Robert, **Supp. XXI:** 23

Meyers, Jeffrey, **Retro. Supp. I:** 124, 138; **Retro. Supp. II:** 191

Meynell, Alice, **Supp. I Part 1:** 220

Mezey, Robert, **Supp. IV Part 1:** 60; **Supp. V:** 180; **Supp. XIII:** 312; **Supp. XV:** 74

Mezzanine, The (Baker), **Supp. XIII:** 41–43, 44, 45, 48, 55

"Mezzo Cammin" (Longfellow), **II:** 490

"Mi Abuelo" (Ríos), **Supp. IV Part 2:** 541

Miami (Didion), **Supp. IV Part 1:** 199, 210

Miami and the Siege of Chicago (Mailer), **Retro. Supp. II:** 206

Miasma (Holding), **Supp. XXII:** 121–122

"Michael" (Wordsworth), **III:** 523

Michael, Magali Cornier, **Supp. XIII:** 32

"Michael Angelo: A Fragment" (Longfellow), **II:** 490, 494, 495, 506; **Retro. Supp. II:** 167

"Michael Egerton" (Price), **Supp. VI:** 257–258, 260

Michael Kohlhaas (Kleist), **Supp. IV Part 1:** 224

Michael O'Halloran (Stratton-Porter), **Supp. XX: 222**

Michaels, Leonard, **Supp. XVI: 201–215**

Michaels, Walter Benn, **Retro. Supp. I:** 115, 369, 379

Michael Scarlett (Cozens), **I:** 358–359, 378

"Michael's Veterans Remember" (Espaillat), **Supp. XXI:** 110

Michaux, Henri, **Supp. XVI:** 288

Michelangelo, **I:** 18; **II:** 11–12; **III:** 124; **Supp. I Part 1:** 363; **Supp. XVII:** 112

Michel-Michot, Paulette, **Supp. XI:** 224–225

Michelson, Albert, **IV:** 27

Mickelsson's Ghosts (Gardner), **Supp. VI:** 63, **73–74**

Mickiewicz, Adam, **Supp. II Part 1:** 299

"Microscope" (Trethewey), **Supp. XXI:** 251

Midair (Conroy), **Supp. XVI:** 63, **71–72**

"Mid-Air" (Conroy), **Supp. XVI:** 69, 71

Mid-American Chants (Anderson), **I:** 109, 114

"Midas" (Winters), **Supp. II Part 2:** 801

"Mid-August at Sourdough Mountain Lookout" (Snyder), **Supp. VIII:** 292–293

Midcentury (Dos Passos), **I:** 474, 475, 478, 490, 492–494; **Supp. I Part 2:** 646

Mid-Century American Poets, **III:** 532

"Mid-Day" (Doolittle), **Supp. I Part 1:** 266–267

"Middle Age" (Lowell), **II:** 550

"Middle-Aged, Middle-Class Woman at Midnight, A" (Taggard), **Supp. XXII:** 282–283

"Middleaged Man, The" (Simpson), **Supp. IX:** 274–275

Middle Ages, The (Gurney), **Supp. V:** 96, 105, 108

Middlebrook, Diane Wood, **Supp. IV Part 2:** 444, 451

"Middle Daughter, The" (Kingsolver), **Supp. VII:** 209

Middlemarch (G. Eliot), **I:** 457, 459; **II:** 290, 291; **Retro. Supp. I:** 225; **Supp. I Part 1:** 174; **Supp. IX:** 43; **Supp. XI:** 68; **Supp. XII:** 335

Middle of My Tether, The: Familiar Essays (Epstein), **Supp. XIV: 106–107**

"Middle of Nowhere, The" (Wagoner), **Supp. IX:** 327–328

Middle of the Journey, The (Trilling), **Supp. III Part 2:** 495, 504–506

"Middle of the Way" (Kinnell), **Supp. III Part 1:** 242

"Middle Passage" (Hayden), **Supp. II Part 1:** 363, 375–376

Middle Passage (Johnson), **Supp. VI: 194–196**, 198, 199; **Supp. XIII:** 182

Middlesex (Eugenides), **Supp. XXIV:** 131, 134–135, **138–142**

"Middle Toe of the Right Foot, The" (Bierce), **I:** 203

Middleton, Thomas, **Retro. Supp. I:** 62

"Middle Way, The"(Hadas), **Supp. XXIII:** 121

Middle Years, The (James), **II:** 337–338; **Retro. Supp. I:** 235

"Middle Years, The" (James), **Retro. Supp. I:** 228, 272

"Midnight" (Dunn), **Supp. XI:** 147

"Midnight Consultations, The" (Freneau), **Supp. II Part 1:** 257

Midnight Cry, A (Mather), **Supp. II Part 2:** 460

"Midnight Gladness" (Levertov), **Supp. III Part 1:** 284–285

Midnight Lantern (Gallagher), **Supp. XXIV:** 167, 171

"Midnight Lantern" (Gallagher), **Supp. XXIV:** 171

"Midnight Magic" (Mason), **Supp. VIII:** 146

Midnight Magic: Selected Stories of Bobbie Ann Mason (Mason), **Supp. VIII:** 148

Midnight Mass (Bowles), **Supp. IV Part 1:** 93

"Midnight Postscript" (F. Wright), **Supp. XVII:** 245, 246

Midnight Queen, The (Lippard), **Supp. XXIII:** 180

"Midnight Show" (Shapiro), **Supp. II Part 2:** 705

"Midpoint" (Updike), **Retro. Supp. I:** 321, 323, 327, 330, 335

Midpoint and Other Poems (Updike), **IV:** 214

"Midrash on Happiness" (Paley), **Supp. VI:** 217

"Midsummer" (Bronk), **Supp. XXI:** 30

"Midsummer in the Blueberry Barrens" (Clampitt), **Supp. IX:** 40–41

"Midsummer Letter" (Carruth), **Supp. XVI:** 47

Midsummer Night's Dream, A (Shakespeare), **Supp. I Part 1:** 369–370; **Supp. X:** 69

Midsummer Night's Sex Comedy, A (film; Allen), **Supp. XV:** 8

"Midwest" (Stafford), **Supp. XI:** 317

"Midwest Poetics" (C. Baxter), **Supp. XVII:** 18

Mieder, Wolfgang, **Supp. XIV:** 126

Mies van der Rohe, Ludwig, **Supp. IV Part 1:** 40

Mighty Aphrodite (film; Allen), **Supp. XV:** 11

"Mighty Fortress, A" (Leopold), **Supp. XIV:** 185

"Mighty Lord, The (Rowson), **Supp. XV:** 243

"Migration, The" (Tate), **IV:** 130

Mihailovitch, Bata, **Supp. VIII:** 272

Mikado, The (Gilbert and Sullivan), **Supp. XXI:** 151

Miklitsch, Robert, **Supp. IV Part 2:** 628, 629

Mikolowski, Ken and Ann, **Supp. XXIV:** 43

Mila 18 (Uris), **Supp. IV Part 1:** 379; **Supp. XX: 244, 247, 248, 251–252, 253**

Milagro Beanfield War, The (film), **Supp. XIII:** 267
Milagro Beanfield War, The (Nichols), **Supp. XIII:** 253, **265–266**
Milburn, Michael, **Supp. XI:** 239, 242
Milch, David, **Supp. XI:** 348
Mild Day, The (Bronk), **Supp. XXI:** 32
Miles, Barry, **Supp. XII:** 123
Miles, Jack, **Supp. VIII:** 86
Miles, Josephine, **Supp. XIII:** 275
Miles, Julie, **I:** 199
Miles, Kitty, **I:** 199
"Miles of Night, The" (Halliday), **Supp. XIX:** 91
Milestone, Lewis, **Supp. I Part 1:** 281
Miles Wallingford (Cooper). *See Afloat and Ashore* (Cooper)
Milford, Kate, **Supp. XVIII:** 150
Milford, Nancy, **II:** 83; **Supp. IX:** 60
Milhaud, Darius, **Supp. IV Part 1:** 81
Miligate, Michael, **IV:** 123, 130, 132
"Militant Nudes" (Hardwick), **Supp. III Part 1:** 210–211
Milk (film), **Supp. XX: 269**
"Milk Bottles" (Anderson), **I:** 114
"Milk Prose" (Weigl), **Supp. XIX:** 278
Milk Train Doesn't Stop Here Anymore, The (T. Williams), **IV:** 382, 383, 384, 386, 390, 391, 392, 393, 394, 395, 398
Mill, James, **II:** 357
Mill, John Stuart, **III:** 294–295; **Supp. XI:** 196; **Supp. XIV:** 22
Millar, Kenneth. *See* Macdonald, Ross
Millar, Margaret (Margaret Sturm), **Supp. IV Part 2:** 464, 465
Millay, Cora, **III:** 123, 133–134, 135–136
Millay, Edna St. Vincent, **I:** 482; **II:** 530; **III: 122–144; IV:** 433, 436; **Retro. Supp. II:** 48; **Supp. I Part 2:** 707, 714, 726; **Supp. IV Part 1:** 168; **Supp. IV Part 2:** 607; **Supp. V:** 113; **Supp. IX:** 20; **Supp. XIV:** 120, 121, 122, 127; **Supp. XV:** 42, 46, 51, 250, 293, 307; **Supp. XVII:** 69, 75, 96; **Supp. XXII:** 273; **Supp. XXIII:** 164
Millennium Approaches (Kushner), **Supp. IX:** 141, 142, 145
Miller, Arthur, **I:** 81, 94; **III: 145–169; Supp. IV Part 1:** 359; **Supp. IV Part 2:** 574; **Supp. VIII:** 334; **Supp. XIII:** 127; **Supp. XIV:** 102, 239; **Supp. XVI:** 194
Miller, Mrs. Arthur (Ingeborg Morath), **III:** 162–163
Miller, Mrs. Arthur (Marilyn Monroe), **III:** 161, 162–163
Miller, Mrs. Arthur (Mary Grace Slattery), **III:** 146, 161
Miller, Brown, **Supp. IV Part 1:** 67
Miller, Carol, **Supp. IV Part 1:** 400, 405, 409, 410, 411
Miller, Caroline, **Supp. XXII: 187–201**
Miller, Henry, **I:** 97, 157; **III:** 40, **170–192; IV:** 138; **Retro. Supp. II:** 327; **Supp. I Part 2:** 546; **Supp. V:** 119, 131; **Supp. X:** 183, 185, 187, 194, 195; **Supp. XIII:** 1, 17; **Supp. XXII:** 88, 256, 257, 258; **Supp. XXIII:** 100; **Supp. XXIV:** 52, 281

Miller, Henry (actor), **Supp. XVI:** 182
Miller, Herman, **Supp. I Part 2:** 614, 617
Miller, James E., Jr., **IV:** 352
Miller, Jean Baker, **Supp. XXII:** 18
Miller, Jeffrey, **Supp. IV Part 1:** 95
Miller, J. Hillis, **Supp. IV Part 1:** 387
Miller, Jim Wayne, **Supp. XX: 161–176; Supp. XXIII:** 39
Miller, Joaquin, **I:** 193, 195, 459; **Supp. II Part 1:** 351
Miller, John Duncan, **Supp. I Part 2:** 604
Miller, John E., **Supp. XXII:** 295
Miller, John M., **Supp. XXII:** 214, 218
Miller, Jonathan, **Retro. Supp. II:** 181
Miller, Laura, **Supp. XIII:** 48; **Supp. XIX:** 53, 54, 56; **Supp. XXII:** 239
Miller, Marilyn, **Supp. XVI:** 187
Miller, Matt, **Supp. XV:** 211
Miller, Matthew, **Supp. XVI:** 47, 51
Miller, Orilla, **Supp. I Part 1:** 48
Miller, Perry, **I:** 546, 547, 549, 550, 560; **IV:** 186; **Supp. I Part 1:** 31, 104; **Supp. I Part 2:** 484; **Supp. IV Part 2:** 422; **Supp. VIII:** 101
Miller, R. Baxter, **Retro. Supp. I:** 195, 207
Miller, Robert Ellis, **II:** 588
Miller, Ruth, **Supp. X:** 324
Miller, Stuart, **Supp. XVI:** 242
Miller, Sue, **Supp. X:** 77, 85; **Supp. XI:** 190; **Supp. XII: 289–305**
Miller of Old Church, The (Glasgow), **II:** 175, 181
"Miller's Tale" (Chaucer), **III:** 283
Miller Williams and the Poetry of the Particular (Burns), **Supp. XV:** 339
Millett, Kate, **Supp. X:** 193, 196
Millgate, Michael, **Retro. Supp. I:** 91
Mill Hand's Lunch Bucket (Bearden), **Supp. VIII:** 337
Millhauser, Steven, **Supp. XXII:** 49
Millier, Brett C., **Retro. Supp. II:** 39
Milligan, Bryce, **Supp. XIII:** 274, 275, 277
Million Little Pieces, A (Frey), **Supp. XXII:** 95; **Supp. XXIII:** 109; **Supp. XXIV:** 230, 236
Millions of Strange Shadows (Hecht), **Supp. X:** 57, **62–65**
"Million Young Workmen, 1915, A" (Sandburg), **III:** 585
Millroy the Magician (Theroux), **Supp. VIII:** 325
Mills, Alice, **Supp. XIII:** 233
Mills, Benjamin Fay, **III:** 176
Mills, C. Wright, **Supp. I Part 2:** 648, 650
Mills, Florence, **Supp. I Part 1:** 322
Mills, Ralph J., Jr., **III:** 530; **Supp. IV Part 1:** 64; **Supp. XI:** 311
Mills, Tedi López, **Supp. XVI:** 281
Mills of the Kavanaughs, The (Lowell), **II:** 542–543, 546, 550; **III:** 508; **Retro. Supp. II:** 178, 179, 188; **Supp. XXIII:** 211
"Mills of the Kavanaughs, The" (Lowell), **II:** 542–543
Milne, A. A., **Supp. IX:** 189; **Supp. XXIV:** 132, 133
Milne, A. J. M., **I:** 278

Milosz, Czeslaw, **Supp. III Part 2:** 630; **Supp. VIII:** 20, 22; **Supp. XI:** 267, 312; **Supp. XVII:** 241; **Supp. XX: 165; Supp. XXI:** 132; **Supp. XXII:** 92; **Supp. XXIII:** 134, 140
Miltner, Robert, **Supp. XI:** 142
Milton, Edith, **Supp. VIII:** 79; **Supp. X:** 82
Milton, John, **I:** 6, 138, 273, 587–588; **II:** 11, 15, 113, 130, 411, 540, 542; **III:** 40, 124, 201, 225, 274, 468, 471, 486, 487, 503, 511; **IV:** 50, 82, 126, 137, 155, 157, 241, 279, 347, 422, 461, 494; **Retro. Supp. I:** 60, 67, 127, 360; **Retro. Supp. II:** 161, 295; **Supp. I Part 1:** 124, 150, 370; **Supp. I Part 2:** 412, 422, 491, 501, 522, 622, 722, 724; **Supp. IV Part 2:** 430, 634; **Supp. VIII:** 294; **Supp. X:** 22, 23, 36; **Supp. XII:** 180; **Supp. XIV:** 5, 7; **Supp. XX: 108; Supp. XXIII:** 122; **Supp. XXIV:** 159
Milton, John R., **Supp. IV Part 2:** 503
Milton and His Modern Critics (L. P. Smith), **Supp. XIV:** 347
"Milton by Firelight" (Snyder), **Supp. II Part 1:** 314; **Supp. VIII:** 294
"Miltonic Sonnet, A" (Wilbur), **Supp. III Part 2:** 558
Mimesis (Auerbach), **III:** 453
"Mimnermos and the Motions of Hedonism" (Carson), **Supp. XII: 99–100**
"Mimnermos Interviews, The" (Carson), **Supp. XII: 100–101**
Mims, Edwin, **Supp. I Part 1:** 362, 364, 365, 371
"Mind" (Wilbur), **Supp. III Part 2:** 554
"Mind, The" (Kinnell), **Supp. III Part 1:** 245
Mind Breaths: Poems 1972–1977 (Ginsberg), **Supp. II Part 1:** 326
Mindfield: New and Selected Poems (Corso), **Supp. XII: 136**
"Mind in the Modern World" (Trilling), **Supp. III Part 2:** 512
"Mind Is Shapely, Art Is Shapely" (Ginsberg), **Supp. II Part 1:** 327
Mindlin, Henrique, **Supp. I Part 1:** 92
Mind of My Mind (O. Butler), **Supp. XIII:** 62, 63
Mind of Primitive Man, The (Boas), **Supp. XIV:** 209
Mind-Reader, The (Wilbur), **Supp. III Part 2:** 560–562
"Mind-Reader, The" (Wilbur), **Supp. III Part 2:** 561–562
"Mind's Landscape on an Early Winter Day, The" (Bronk), **Supp. XXI:** 28
Mindwheel (Pinsky), **Supp. VI:** 235
Minear, Richard H., **Supp. XVI:** 101, 102
"Mined Country" (Wilbur), **Supp. III Part 2:** 546–548
"Minefields" (Espaillat), **Supp. XXI:** 106
"Mine Own John Berryman" (Levine), **Supp. V:** 179–180
Miner, Bob, **Supp. V:** 23
Miner, Earl, **III:** 466, 479
Miner, Madonne, **Supp. XIII:** 29
Miner, Valerie, **Supp. XXIII:** 295, 296

"Minerva Writes Poems" (Cisneros), **Supp. VII:** 63–64, 66

Mingus, Charles, **Supp. IX:** 152

"Mingus in Diaspora" (Matthews), **Supp. IX:** 166

"Mingus in Shadow" (Matthews), **Supp. IX:** 168–169

Ming Yellow (Marquand), **III:** 56

"Minimal, The" (Roethke), **III:** 531–532

Minimus Poems, The (X. J. Kennedy), **Supp. XV:** 169–170

"Mini-novela: *Rosa y sus espinas*" (Mora), *Supp. XIII:* 218

"Minions of Midas, The" (London), **II:** 474–475

Minister's Charge, The, or The Apprenticeship of Lemuel Barber (Howells), **II:** 285–286, 287

Minister's Wooing, The (Stowe), **II:** 541

"Minister's Wooing, The" (Stowe), **Supp. I Part 2:** 592–595

"Ministration of Our Departed Friends, The" (Stowe), **Supp. I Part 2:** 586–587

"Minneapolis Poem, The" (Wright), **Supp. III Part 2:** 601–602

Minnesota Grain Show, The (radio, Keillor), **Supp. XVI:** 170

"Minnesota Transcendentalist" (Peseroff), **Supp. IV Part 1:** 71

Minnie, Temple, **II:** 344

Minority Report: H. L. Mencken's Notebooks (Mencken), **III:** 112

Minor Pleasures of Life, The (Macaulay), **Supp. XIV:** 348

"Minor Poems" (Eliot), **I:** 579

"Minor Poet" (Hay), **Supp. XIV:** 127

"Minor Topics" (Howells), **II:** 274

Minot, Stephen, **Supp. XXIII:** 290

Minot, Susan, **Supp. VI: 203–215**

"Minotaur Loves His Labyrinth, The" (Simic), **Supp. VIII:** 270, 279, 281

"Minstrel Man" (Hughes), **Supp. I Part 1:** 325

Mint (Nye), **Supp. XIII:** 277

"Minting Time" (Sarton), **Supp. VIII:** 259

Mint Snowball (Nye), **Supp. XIII:** 277–278, **284–285**

"Mint Snowball" (Nye), **Supp. XIII:** 278, 284

"Mint Snowball II" (Nye), **Supp. XIII:** 284, 285

Minty Alley (C. L. R. James), **Supp. XXI:** 159, 161

Mintzlaff, Dorothy, **Supp. XV:** 153

Minus, Marian, **Supp. XVIII:** 282

Minutes to Go (Corso, Gysin, Beiles and Burroughs), **Supp. XII:** 129

Mi querido Rafa (Hinojosa). See *Dear Rafe* (Hinojosa)

Mirabai: Ecstatic Poems (Hirshfield and Bly, trans.), **Supp. XXIII:** 136

Mirabell: Books of Number (Merrill), **Supp. III Part 1:** 332–334

"Miracle" (Carver), **Supp. III Part 1:** 139–140

Miracle at Verdun (Chlumberg), **Supp. XIX:** 242

Miracle Boy and Other Stories (P. Benedict), **Supp. XXIII:** 35, **45–50**

"Miracle Boy"(P. Benedict), **Supp. XXIII:** 45–46, 50

"Miracle for Breakfast, A" (Bishop), **Retro. Supp. II:** 43

Miracle of Catfish, A (L. Brown), **Supp. XXI:** 39–40, 47, **48**

"Miracle of Lava Canyon, The" (Henry), **Supp. II Part 1:** 389, 390

Miracle of Mindfulness, The: A Manual on Meditation (Thich Nhat Hanh), **Supp. V:** 199–200

Mirage (Masters), **Supp. I Part 2:** 459, 470, 471

"Mirages, The" (Hayden), **Supp. II Part 1:** 373

"Miranda" (Buck), **Supp. II Part 1:** 128

Miranda, Carmen, **Supp. XII:** 165

Miranda, Francisco de, **Supp. I Part 2:** 522

"Miranda Over the Valley" (Dubus), **Supp. VII:** 81–83

"Miriam" (Capote), **Supp. III Part 1:** 117, 120, 122

"Miriam" (Whittier), **Supp. I Part 2:** 691, 703

"Miriam Tazewell" (Ransom), **Supp. X:** 58

"Mirror" (Merrill), **Supp. III Part 1:** 322

"Mirror" (Plath), **Retro. Supp. II:** 248–249, 257

"Mirror, The" (Glück), **Supp. V:** 83

"Mirror, The"(Hadas), **Supp. XXIII:** 116

"Mirroring Evil: Nazi Images/Recent Art" (Epstein), **Supp. XII:** 166

"Mirror of Leopold Leopoldovitch Siegelevsky, The" (Siegel), **Supp. XXII:** 257–258

Mirrors (Creeley), **Supp. IV Part 1:** 156

Mirrors and Windows (Nemerov), **III:** 269, 275–277

Mirrors of Astonishment (Hadas), **Supp. XXIII: 115–116**

"Mirrors of Chartres Street" (Faulkner), **II:** 56

Mirsky, Norman, **Supp. XX: 244**

Mirvis, Tova, **Supp. XX: 177–191**

Misanthrope, The (Molière; Wilbur, trans.), **Supp. III Part 2:** 552, 560

Miscellaneous Poems (Rowson), **Supp. XV:** 243

Miscellaneous Works of Mr. Philip Freneau, Containing His Essays and Additional Poems (Freneau), **Supp. II Part 1:** 263, 264, 266

Miscellany of American Poetry, A (Untermeyer, ed.), **Supp. XV:** 305, 310

Misérables, Les (Hugo), **II:** 179; **Supp. I Part 1:** 280

Misery (King), **Supp. V:** 140, 141, 142, 147–148, 151, 152

Mises, Ludwig von, **Supp. IV Part 2:** 524

Misfits, The (A. Miller), **III:** 147, 149, 156, 161–162, 163

Misfit: The Strange Life of Frederick Exley (Yardley), **Supp. XXIII:** 97

"Mishösha, or the Magician and his daughters: A Chippewa Tale"(J. Schoolcraft), **Supp. XXIII:** 234, 235

"Misogamist, The" (Dubus), **Supp. VII:** 86–87

Misread City, The: New Literary Los Angeles (Gioia and Timberg, eds.), **Supp. XV:** 116

Misrepresentations Corrected, and Truth Vindicated, in a Reply to the Rev. Mr. Solomon Williams's Book (Edwards), **I:** 549

Miss Crandall's School for Young Ladies & Little Misses of Color (Nelson and Alexander), **Supp. XVIII:** 171, 175, 181, **185–186**

"Miss Cynthie" (R. Fisher), **Supp. XIX:** 65, 69

Miss Doll, Go Home (Markson), **Supp. XVII:** 138

"Miss Ella" (Z. Fitzgerald), **Supp. IX:** 57, 59, **71–72**

"Miss Emily and the Bibliographer" (Tate), **Supp. II Part 1:** 103

"Miss Furr and Miss Skeene" (Stein), **IV:** 29–30

"Missing Child" (Simic), **Supp. VIII:** 282

"Missing in Action" (Komunyakaa), **Supp. XIII:** 123, 124

Missing/Kissing: Missing Marisa, Kissing Christine (Shanley), **Supp. XIV:** 316

Missing Link (X. J. Kennedy), **Supp. XV:** 165

"Missing Poem, The" (Halliday), **Supp. XIX:** 93–94

"Mission of Jane, The" (Wharton), **Retro. Supp. I:** 367

"Missions, The" (Rodriguez), **Supp. XIV:** 303

Mission to Moscow (film), **Supp. I Part 1:** 281

"Mississippi" (Bass), **Supp. XVI:** 17

"Mississippi" (Faulkner), **Retro. Supp. I:** 77

"Mississippi" (Simpson), **Supp. IX:** 271

"Miss Kate in H-1" (Twain), **IV:** 193

Miss Kelly (Holding), **Supp. XXII: 133–134**

Miss Leonora When Last Seen (Taylor), **Supp. V:** 323

Miss Lonelyhearts (West), **I:** 107; **II:** 436; **III:** 357; **IV:** 287, 288, 290–297, 300, 301, 305, 306; **Retro. Supp. II:** 321, 322, 325, 328, **332–335**

"Miss Lora" (Díaz), **Supp. XXIV:** 86

Miss Mamma Aimee (Caldwell), **I:** 308, 309, 310

"Miss Mary Pask" (Wharton), **IV:** 316; **Retro. Supp. I:** 382

"Miss McEnders" (Chopin), **Retro. Supp. II:** 67

Miss Morissa: Doctor of the Gold Trail (Sandoz), **Supp. XXIV:** 244, **255–256**

"Missoula Softball Tournament" (Hugo), **Supp. VI:** 132

Miss Ravenel's Conversion from Secession to Loyalty (De Forest), **IV:** 350

Miss Saigon (musical), **Supp. XXI:** 155

"Miss Tempy's Watchers" (Jewett), **II:** 401; **Retro. Supp. II:** 139

"Miss Terriberry to Wed in Suburbs" (Updike), **Retro. Supp. I:** 335
"Miss Urquhart's Tiara" (Jarman), **Supp. XVII:** 116
Miss Witherspoon (Durang), **Supp. XXIV:** 113, **126**
"Mist, The" (King), **Supp. V:** 144
"Mistaken Charity, A" (Freeman), **Retro. Supp. II:** 138
"Mister Brother" (Cunningham), **Supp. XV:** 68
Misterioso (Sorrentino), **Supp. XXI:** 236, 237
"Mister Toussan" (Ellison), **Retro. Supp. II:** 124–125; **Supp. II Part 1:** 238
"Mistress of Sydenham Plantation, The" (Jewett), **Retro. Supp. II:** 141
Mitcham, Matthew, **Supp. XX: 264**
Mitchell, Burroughs, **Supp. XI:** 218, 222, 227
Mitchell, David, **Supp. XXIV:** 86
Mitchell, Don, **Supp. XXII:** 207, 211, 212
Mitchell, Joan, **Supp. XXIII:** 210
Mitchell, Margaret, **II:** 177; **Supp. XX: 243; Supp. XXII:** 195
Mitchell, Pat, **Supp. XXIV:** 35, 42
Mitchell, Roger, **Supp. IV Part 1:** 70; **Supp. XV:** 213, 215
Mitchell, Dr. S. Weir, **IV:** 310
Mitchell, Tennessee. *See* Anderson, Mrs. Sherwood (Tennessee Mitchell)
Mitchell, Verner, **Supp. XVIII:** 281, 286
Mitchell, Wesley C., **Supp. I Part 2:** 632, 643
"Mitchie-Gawa" (Taggard), **Supp. XXII:** 272
Mitch Miller (Masters), **Supp. I Part 2:** 456, 466, 469–471, 474, 475, 476
Mitchum, Robert, **Supp. IX:** 95, 250
Mitgang, Herbert, **Supp. IV Part 1:** 220, 226, 307; **Supp. VIII:** 124; **Supp. XIX:** 251; **Supp. XX: 243**
Mitla Pass (Uris), **Supp. XX: 244, 247, 248, 256**
Mixed Company: Collected Short Stories (Shaw), **Supp. XIX:** 251
"Mixed Sequence" (Roethke), **III:** 547
Miyazawa Kenji, **Supp. VIII:** 292
Mizener, Arthur, **II:** 77, 81, 84, 94; **IV:** 132; **Supp. XVIII:** 249
Mizner, Addison, **Supp. XVI:** 191
Mizner, Wilson, **Supp. XVI:** 191, 195
Mladenoff, Nancy, **Supp. X:** 176
"M'liss: An Idyl of Red Mountain" (Harte), **Supp. II Part 1:** 339
"Mnemonic Devices" (Goldbarth), **Supp. XII:** 183
"Mnemosyne" (Hölderlin), **Supp. XXIV:** 152
"Mobile in Back of the Smithsonian, The" (Swenson), **Supp. IV Part 2:** 646
Mobilio, Albert, **Supp. VIII:** 3; **Supp. XVIII:** 144; **Supp. XIX:** 45
Moby Dick (film), **Supp. IV Part 1:** 102, 116
Moby Dick; or, The Whale (Melville), **I:** 106, 354; **II:** 33, 224–225, 236, 539–540; **III:** 28–29, 74, 75, 77, 81, 82, 83–86, 87, 89, 90, 91, 93, 94, 95, 359, 453, 556; **IV:** 57, 199, 201, 202; **Retro. Supp. I:** 160, 220, 243, 244, 248, **249–253,** 254, 256, 257, 335; **Retro. Supp. II:** 121, 186, 275; **Supp. I Part 1:** 249; **Supp. I Part 2:** 579; **Supp. IV Part 2:** 613; **Supp. V:** 281; **Supp. VIII:** 106, 188, 198; **Supp. XXI:** 159; **Supp. XXII:** 81, 268; **Supp. XXIV:** 88
Mock, John, **Supp. XIII:** 174
"Mocking-Bird, The" (Bierce), **I:** 202
"Mock Orange" (Glück), **Supp. V:** 84–85
Modarressi, Mitra, **Supp. IV Part 2:** 657
Models of Misrepresentation: On the Fiction of E. L. Doctorow (Morris), **Supp. IV Part 1:** 231
Model World and Other Stories, A (Chabon), **Supp. XI:** 66
Modern American and British Poetry (Untermeyer, ed.), **Supp. XV:** 306
Modern American Poetry (Untermeyer, ed.), **Supp. XV:** 293, 303, 306, 312
Modern American Verse (Untermeyer, ed.), **Supp. XV:** 301
Modern Brazilian Architecture (Bishop, trans.), **Supp. I Part 1:** 92
Modern British Poetry (Untermeyer, ed.), **Supp. XV:** 305, 308, 312
Modern Fiction Studies, **Supp. V:** 238
Modern Fiction Studies (Haegert), **Supp. XVI:** 69
Modern Instance a Novel, A (Howells), **II:** 275, 279, 282–283, 285
Modern Library, The, **Retro. Supp. I:** 112, 113
Modern Mephistopheles, A (Alcott), **Supp. I Part 1:** 37–38
Modern Poetic Sequence, The (Rosenthal), **Supp. V:** 333
"Modern Poetry" (Crane), **I:** 390
Modern Poetry and the Tradition (Brooks), **Supp. XIV:** 5–7
"Modern Race Creeds and Their Fallacies" (Locke), **Supp. XIV:** 210
Modern Rhetoric, with Readings (Brooks and Warren), **Supp. XIV:** 11
"Modern Sorcery" (Simic), **Supp. VIII:** 283
Modern Times (album, Dylan), **Supp. XVIII:** 28, 31, 33
"Modern Times" (Zukofsky), **Supp. III Part 2:** 624
Modern Writer, The (Anderson), **I:** 117
Modersohn, Otto, **Supp. I Part 2:** 573
Modersohn, Mrs. Otto (Paula Becker), **Supp. I Part 2:** 573–574
"Modes of Being" (Levertov), **Supp. III Part 1:** 282
Modest Enquiry into the Nature and Necessity of a Paper-Currency, A (Franklin), **II:** 108–109
"Modest Proposal, A" (Swift), **I:** 295; **Retro. Supp. II:** 287
"Modest Proposal with Feline Feeling, A" (Neugeboren), **Supp. XVI:** 219
"Modest Self-Tribute, A" (Wilson), **IV:** 431, 432
Moeller, Philip, **III:** 398, 399
"Moench von Berchtesgaden, Der" (Voss), **I:** 199–200
Moers, Ellen, **Retro. Supp. II:** 99
Moe's Villa and Other Stories (Purdy), **Supp. VII:** 270, 280
Moffat, Juan, **Supp. XX: 52**
Moffet, Penelope, **Supp. XXIV:** 165, 167
Mogen, David, **Supp. IV Part 1:** 106
Mohammed, **I:** 480; **II:** 1
Mohawk (Russo), **Supp. XII: 326–328**
Moir, William Wilmerding, **Supp. V:** 279
Mojo Hand (Phillips), **Supp. XXIII:** 174
Moldaw, Carol, **Supp. XV:** 264; **Supp. XVII:** 127, 130
"Moles" (Oliver), **Supp. VII:** 235
Molesworth, Charles, **Supp. IV Part 1:** 39; **Supp. VIII:** 292, 306; **Supp. XIX:** 121–122
Molière (Jean-Baptiste Poquelin), **III:** 113; **Supp. I Part 2:** 406; **Supp. III Part 2:** 552, 560; **Supp. IV Part 2:** 585; **Supp. V:** 101
"Molino Rojo, El" (Ríos), **Supp. IV Part 2:** 544
Moll Flanders (Defoe), **Supp. V:** 127; **Supp. XIII:** 43
"Molloch in State Street" (Whittier), **Supp. I Part 2:** 687
"Moll Pitcher" (Whittier), **Supp. I Part 2:** 684
"Molly Brant, Iroquois Matron" (Gunn Allen), **Supp. IV Part 1:** 331
"Molly Brant to Willie"(Kenny), **Supp. XXIII:** 153
Molnar, Ferenc, **Supp. XVI:** 187
"Moloch" (H. Miller), **III:** 177
Momaday, N. Scott, **Supp. IV Part 1:** 274, 323, 324, 404; **Supp. IV Part 2: 479–496,** 504, 557, 562; **Supp. XII:** 209; **Supp. XVIII:** 58
" 'Momentary Stay against Confusion,' A: Frank Conroy's *Stop-Time*" (T. Adams), **Supp. XVI:** 69
Moment of Untruth (Lacy), **Supp. XV:** 206, 207
Moments of the Italian Summer (Wright), **Supp. III Part 2:** 602
Moment to Moment: Poems of a Mountain Recluse (Budbill), **Supp. XIX:** 2, 7, **9–10**
"Momus" (Robinson), **III:** 508
Monaghan, Charles, **Supp. XIX:** 155
Monaghan, Pat, **Supp. XI:** 121
Monaghan, Patricia, **Supp. XVII:** 76, 123, 127, 129
Mona Lisa Overdrive (W. Gibson), **Supp. XVI:** 119, 120, **127–128**
"Mon Ami" (Bourne), **I:** 227
Monday Night (Boyle), **Supp. XXIV:** 54
Monet, Claude, **Retro. Supp. I:** 378
"Monet's 'Waterlilies' " (Hayden), **Supp. II Part 1:** 361–362
Monette, Paul, **Supp. X: 145–161**
Money (Amis), **Retro. Supp. I:** 278
"Money" (Matthews), **Supp. IX:** 166
"Money" (Nemerov), **III:** 287
Money, Money, Money (Wagoner), **Supp. IX:** 324, **333–334**
Moneyball: The Art of Winning an Unfair Game (M. Lewis), **Supp. XVII:** 210

Moneychangers, The (Sinclair), **Supp. V:** 285

Money Writes! (Sinclair), **Supp. V:** 277

Monica, Saint, **IV:** 140

Monikins, The (Cooper), **I:** 348, 354

Monk, Craig, **Supp. XXIV:** 64

Monk, Thelonious, **Supp. XVIII:** 62

Monk and the Hangman's Daughter, The (Bierce), **I:** 199–200, 209

"Monkey" (Weigl), **Supp. XIX:** 278

"Monkey Garden, The" (Cisneros), **Supp. VII:** 63

"Monkey Puzzle, The" (Moore), **III:** 194, 207, 211

Monkeys (Minot), **Supp. VI:** 203–205, **206–210**

"Monkeys, The" (Moore), **III:** 201, 202

Monkey Wars, The (Weigl), **Supp. XIX:** 276, 278–280

Monkey Wrench Gang, The (Abbey), **Supp. VIII:** 42; **Supp. XIII: 9–11,** 16

"Monk of Casal-Maggiore, The" (Longfellow), **II:** 505

"Monocle de Mon Oncle, Le" (Stevens), **IV:** 78, 84; **Retro. Supp. I:** 301; **Supp. III Part 1:** 20; **Supp. X:** 58

"Monody to the Sound of Zithers" (Boyle), **Supp. XXIV:** 63

"Monolog from a Mattress" (Untermeyer), **Supp. XV:** 307

"Monologue for Mothers" (Taggard), **Supp. XXII:** 279

"Mon Plaisir" (July), **Supp. XXIV:** 205–206

Monro, Harold, **III:** 465; **Retro. Supp. I:** 127; **Supp. XV:** 296

Monroe, Harriet, **I:** 235, 384, 390, 393; **III:** 458, 581, 586; **IV:** 74; **Retro. Supp. I:** 58, 131; **Retro. Supp. II:** 82, 83; **Supp. I Part 1:** 256, 257, 258, 262, 263, 267; **Supp. I Part 2:** 374, 387, 388, 464, 610, 611, 613, 614, 615, 616; **Supp. XIV:** 286; **Supp. XV:** 43, 299, 302

Monroe, James, **Supp. I Part 2:** 515, 517

Monroe, Lucy, **Retro. Supp. II:** 70

Monroe, Marilyn, **III:** 161, 162–163

Monroe's Embassy; or, the Conduct of the Government in Relation to Our Claims to the Navigation of the Mississippi (Brown), **Supp. I Part 1:** 146

Monson, Ander, **Supp. XXIV: 229–242**

"Monsoon Season" (Komunyakaa), **Supp. XIII:** 122

Monsour, Leslie, **Supp. XV:** 125

"Monster, The" (Crane), **I:** 418

Monster, The, and Other Stories (Crane), **I:** 409

"Monstro" (Díaz), **Supp. XXIV:** 86

Montage of a Dream Deferred (Hughes), **Retro. Supp. I:** 194, **208–209; Supp. I Part 1:** 333, 339–341

Montagu, Ashley, **Supp. I Part 1:** 314

"Montaigne" (Emerson), **II:** 6

Montaigne, Michel de, **II:** 1, 5, 6, 8, 14–15, 16, 535; **III:** 600; **Retro. Supp. I:** 247; **Supp. XIV:** 105; **Supp. XXI:** 111, 205

Montale, Eugenio, **Supp. III Part 1:** 320; **Supp. V:** 337–338; **Supp. VIII:** 30;

Supp. XV: 112

Montalembert, Hughes de, **Supp. XV:** 349

"Montana Memory" (Maclean), **Supp. XIV:** 221

"Montana; or the End of Jean-Jacques Rousseau" (Fiedler), **Supp. XIII: 97–98**

"Montana Ranch Abandoned" (Hugo), **Supp. VI:** 139

"Mont Blanc" (Shelley), **Supp. IX:** 52

Montcalm, Louis Joseph de, **Supp. I Part 2:** 498

Montcalm and Wolfe (Parkman), **Supp. II Part 2:** 596, 609, 610, 611–613

Montemarano, Nicholas, **Supp. XVI:** 227

Montgomery, Benilde, **Supp. XIII:** 202

Montgomery, George, **Supp. XXIII:** 209

Montgomery, Robert, **Supp. I Part 2:** 611; **Supp. IV Part 1:** 130

Month of Sundays, A (Updike), **Retro. Supp. I:** 325, 327, 329, 330, 331, 333, 335

Monti, Luigi, **II:** 504

Montoya, José, **Supp. IV Part 2:** 545

"Montrachet-le-Jardin" (Stevens), **IV:** 82

Mont-Saint-Michel and Chartres (Adams), **I:** 1, 9, 12–14, 18, 19, 21; **Supp. I Part 2:** 417

Montserrat (Hellman), **Supp. I Part 1:** 283–285

Montserrat (Robles), **Supp. I Part 1:** 283–285

"Monument, The" (Bishop), **Supp. I Part 1:** 89

Monument, The (Strand), **Supp. IV Part 2:** 629, 630

"Monument in Utopia, A" (Schnackenberg), **Supp. XV:** 261, 263

"Monument Mountain" (Bryant), **Supp. I Part 1:** 156, 162

"Monument to After-Thought Unveiled, A" (Frost), **Retro. Supp. I:** 124

Moo (Smiley), **Supp. VI:** 292, **303–305**

Moods (Alcott), **Supp. I Part 1:** 33, 34–35, 43

Moody, Anne, **Supp. IV Part 1:** 11

Moody, Richard, **Supp. I Part 1:** 280

Moody, Rick, **Supp. XXI:** 117; **Supp. XXIV:** 131

Moody, Ron, **Supp. XXII:** 49

Moody, William Vaughn, **III:** 507; **IV:** 26

Moody, Mrs. William Vaughn, **I:** 384; **Supp. I Part 2:** 394

Moody-Freeman, Julie, **Supp. XXIII:** 91, 94, 95

"Moon" (A. Finch), **Supp. XVII:** 77

Moon, Henry Lee, **Supp. XVIII:** 281, 285

"Moon and the Night and the Men, The" (Berryman), **I:** 172

Moon Crossing Bridge (Gallagher), **Supp. XXIV:** 166, 170

"Moon Deluxe" (F. Barthelme), **Supp. XI:** 26, 27, 33, 36

Mooney, Tom, **I:** 505

"Moon-Face" (London), **II:** 475

Moon-Face and Other Stories (London), **II:** 483

"Moon Flock" (Dickey), **Supp. IV Part 1:** 186

Moon for the Misbegotten, A (O'Neill), **III:** 385, 401, 403, 404

Moon in a Mason Jar (Wrigley), **Supp. XVIII: 295–298**

Moon in Its Flight, The (Sorrentino), **Supp. XXI:** 226

"Moon in Its Flight, The" (Sorrentino), **Supp. XXI:** 229

Moon Is a Gong, The (Dos Passos). *See Garbage Man, The* (Dos Passos)

Moon Is Down, The (Steinbeck), **IV:** 51

Moon Lady, The (Tan), **Supp. X:** 289

"Moonlight Alert" (Winters), **Supp. II Part 2:** 801, 811, 815

"Moonlight: Chickens on a Road" (Wrigley), **Supp. XVIII:** 295–296, 297

"Moonlit Night" (Reznikoff), **Supp. XIV:** 285–286

Moon of the Caribbees, The (O'Neill), **III:** 388

Moon Palace (Auster), **Supp. XII:** 22, 27, **30–32**

"Moonshine" (Komunyakaa), **Supp. XIII:** 127, 128

"Moon Solo" (Laforgue), **Supp. XIII:** 346

Moonstone, The (Collins), **Supp. XX: 236**

Moonstruck (screenplay, Shanley), **Supp. XIV:** 315, 316, **321–324**

"Moon upon her fluent Route, The" (Dickinson), **I:** 471

Moony's Kid Don't Cry (T. Williams), **IV:** 381

Moore, Arthur, **Supp. I Part 1:** 49

Moore, Deborah Dash, **Supp. XX: 246**

Moore, George, **I:** 103

Moore, Hannah, **Supp. XV:** 231

Moore, John Milton, **III:** 193

Moore, Julie L., **Supp. XXIII:** 252

Moore, Lorrie, **Supp. VIII:** 145; **Supp. X: 163–180**

Moore, Marianne, **I:** 58, 285, 401, 428; **III: 193–217,** 514, 592–593; **IV:** 74, 75, 76, 91, 402; **Retro. Supp. I:** 416, 417; **Retro. Supp. II:** 39, 44, 48, 50, 82, 178, 179, 243, 244; **Supp. I Part 1:** 84, 89, 255, 257; **Supp. I Part 2:** 707; **Supp. II Part 1:** 21; **Supp. III Part 1:** 58, 60, 63; **Supp. III Part 2:** 612, 626, 627; **Supp. IV Part 1:** 242, 246, 257; **Supp. IV Part 2:** 454, 640, 641; **Supp. XIV:** 124, 130; **Supp. XV:** 306, 307; **Supp. XVII:** 131; **Supp. XXI:** 98; **Supp. XXII:** 273–274

Moore, Marie Lorena. *See* Moore, Lorrie

Moore, Mary Tyler, **Supp. V:** 107

Moore, Mary Warner, **III:** 193

Moore, Dr. Merrill, **III:** 506

Moore, Steven, **Supp. IV Part 1:** 279, 283, 284, 285, 287; **Supp. XII:** 151; **Supp. XVII:** 230, 231, 232; **Supp. XXII:** 261, 265

Moore, Sturge, **III:** 459

Moore, Thomas, **II:** 296, 299, 303; **Supp. IX:** 104; **Supp. X:** 114; **Supp. XXIII:** 138

Moore, Virginia, **Supp. XV:** 308

Moorehead, Caroline, **Supp. XIV:** 337
Moorepack, Howard, **Supp. XV:** 199
"Moorings" (Hoffman), **Supp. XVIII:** 87
Moos, Malcolm, **III:** 116, 119
"Moose, The" (Bishop), **Retro. Supp. II:** 50; **Supp. I Part 1:** 73, 93, 94, 95; **Supp. IX:** 45, 46
"Moose Wallow, The" (Hayden), **Supp. II Part 1:** 367
"Moowis, The Indian Coquette"(J. Schoolcraft), **Supp. XXIII:** 234
"Moquihuitzin's Answer" (Everwine), **Supp. XV:** 78
Mora, Pat, **Supp. XIII:** 213–232
Moraga, Cherríe, **Supp. XXIII:** 193–206
"Moral Argument Against Calvinism, The" (Channing), **Supp. XXIV:** 73–74, 75
"Moral Bully, The" (Holmes), **Supp. I Part 1:** 302
"Moral Character, the Practice of Law, and Legal Education" (Hall), **Supp. VIII:** 127
"Moral Equivalent for Military Service, A" (Bourne), **I:** 230
"Moral Equivalent of War, The" (James), **II:** 361; **Supp. I Part 1:** 20
"Moral Imperatives for World Order" (Locke), **Supp. XIV:** 207, 213
Moralités Légendaires (Laforgue), **I:** 573
"Morality and Mercy in Vienna" (Pynchon), **Supp. II Part 2:** 620, 624
"Morality of Indian Hating, The" (Momaday), **Supp. IV Part 2:** 484
"Morality of Poetry, The" (Wright), **Supp. III Part 2:** 596–597, 599
Moral Man and Immoral Society (Niebuhr), **III:** 292, 295–297
"Morals Is Her Middle Name" (Hughes), **Supp. I Part 1:** 338
"Morals of Chess, The" (Franklin), **II:** 121
"Moral Substitute for War, A" (Addams), **Supp. I Part 1:** 20
"Moral Theology of Atticus Finch, The" (Shaffer), **Supp. VIII:** 127
"Moral Thought, A" (Freneau), **Supp. II Part 1:** 262
Moran, Thomas, **Supp. IV Part 2:** 603–604
Moran, William L., **Supp. XXIV:** 150–151, 152
Moran of the Lady Letty (Norris), **II:** 264; **III:** 314, 322, 327, 328, 329, 330, 331, 332, 333
Morath, Ingeborg. *See* Miller, Mrs. Arthur (Ingeborg Morath)
Moravec, Paul, **Supp. XIX:** 123
Moravia, Alberto, **I:** 301
More (Crooker), **Supp. XXIII:** 60–62
Moré, Gonzalo, **Supp. X:** 185
More, Henry, **I:** 132
More, Paul Elmer, **I:** 223–224, 247; **Supp. I Part 2:** 423
Moreau, Gustave, **I:** 66
"More Blues and the Abstract Truth" (Wright), **Supp. XV:** 345
More Boners (Abingdon), **Supp. XVI:** 99

More Conversations with Eudora Welty (Prenshaw, ed.), **Retro. Supp. I:** 340, 341, 342, 343, 344, 352, 353, 354
More Dangerous Thoughts (Ryan as Quin), **Supp. XVIII:** 226, **229–230,** 231, 238
More Die of Heartbreak (Bellow), **Retro. Supp. II:** 31, 33, 34
"More Girl Than Boy" (Komunyakaa), **Supp. XIII:** 117
"More Light! More Light!" (Hecht), **Supp. X:** 60
"More Like an Extension of the Spirit: Clothing in Lyric Poems"(Hadas), **Supp. XXIII:** 124
"Morella" (Poe), **III:** 412; **Retro. Supp. II:** 270
"More Love in the Western World" (Updike), **Retro. Supp. I:** 327–328, 329
"Morels" (W. J. Smith), **Supp. XIII:** 336–339
Moreno, Gary, **Supp. XV:** 5
"More Observations Now" (Conroy), **Supp. XVI:** 75
"More of a Corpse Than a Woman" (Rukeyser), **Supp. VI:** 280
"More Pleasant Adventures" (Ashbery), **Supp. III Part 1:** 1
More Poems to Solve (Swenson), **Supp. IV Part 2:** 640, 642, 648
More Stately Mansions (O'Neill), **III:** 385, 401, 404–405
"More Than Human" (Chabon), **Supp. XI:** 71–72
More Things Change The More They Stay the Same, The (J. W. Miller), **Supp. XX:** 164
More Triva (L. P. Smith), **Supp. XIV:** 339
Morgan, Edmund S., **IV:** 149; **Supp. I Part 1:** 101, 102; **Supp. I Part 2:** 484
Morgan, Edwin, **Supp. IV Part 2:** 688
Morgan, Emanuel. *See* Bynner, Witter
Morgan, Henry, **II:** 432; **IV:** 63
Morgan, Jack, **Retro. Supp. II:** 142
Morgan, J. P., **I:** 494; **III:** 14, 15
Morgan, Judith, **Supp. XVI:** 103
Morgan, Neil, **Supp. XVI:** 103
Morgan, Robert, **Supp. V:** 5; **Supp. XX:** 161, 162
Morgan, Robin, **Supp. I Part 2:** 569
Morgan, Ted, **Supp. XIV:** 141
Morgan's Passing (Tyler), **Supp. IV Part 2:** 666–667, 668, 669
Morgenstern, Dan, **Supp. XIX:** 159
Morgenthau, Hans, **III:** 291, 309
Morgenthau, Henry, Sr., **Supp. XXIII:** 21, 22, 26, 30
Morgesons, The (E. Stoddard), **Supp. XV:** 270, 273, 274, 278, **279–282,** 283
Morgesons and Other Writings, Published and Unpublished, The (Buell and Zagarell), **Supp. XV:** 269
Moricand, Conrad, **III:** 190
Morison, Samuel Eliot, **Supp. I Part 2:** 479–500; **Supp. XXII:** 35
Morison, Mrs. Samuel Eliot (Elizabeth Shaw Greene), **Supp. I Part 2:** 483

Morison, Mrs. Samuel Eliot (Priscilla Barton), **Supp. I Part 2:** 493, 496, 497
Morita, Pat, **Supp. XXI:** 146
"Morituri Salutamus" (Longfellow), **II:** 499, 500; **Retro. Supp. II:** 169; **Supp. I Part 2:** 416
"Moriturus" (Millay), **III:** 126, 131–132
Morley, Christopher, **III:** 481, 483, 484; **Supp. I Part 2:** 653; **Supp. IX:** 124
Morley, Edward, **IV:** 27
Morley, Lord John, **I:** 7
Mormon Country (Stegner), **Supp. IV Part 2:** 598, 601–602
"Morning, The" (Updike), **Retro. Supp. I:** 329
"Morning after My Death, The" (Levis), **Supp. XI:** 260, 263–264
"Morning Arrives" (F. Wright), **Supp. XVII:** 244
Morning Face (Stratton-Porter), **Supp. XX:** 223
Morning for Flamingos, A (Burke), **Supp. XIV:** 30, 31, 32
"Morning Glory" (Merrill), **Supp. III Part 1:** 337
Morning Glory, The (R. Bly), **Supp. IV Part 1:** 63–65, 66, 71
"Morning Imagination of Russia, A" (W. C. Williams), **Retro. Supp. I:** 428
Morning in Antibes (Knowles), **Supp. XII:** 249
Morning in the Burned House (Atwood), **Supp. XIII:** 20, 35
Morning Is Near Us, The (Glaspell), **Supp. III Part 1:** 184–185
Morning Noon and Night (Cozzens), **I:** 374, 375, 376, 377, 379, 380
"Morning of the Day They Did It, The" (White), **Supp. I Part 2:** 663
"Morning Prayers" (Harjo), **Supp. XII:** 231
"Morning Roll Call" (Anderson), **I:** 116
"Morning Roundup" (Sorrentino), **Supp. XXI:** 228
"Morning Shadows" (Skloot), **Supp. XX:** 199
"Mornings in a New House" (Merrill), **Supp. III Part 1:** 327
"Mornings in Ormos"(Hadas), **Supp. XXIII:** 112, 113, 123
Mornings Like This (Dillard), **Supp. VI:** 23, 34
"Morning Song" (Plath), **Retro. Supp. II:** 252; **Supp. XXIII:** 115
Morning Watch, The (Agee), **I:** 25, 39–42
"Morning with Broken Window" (Hogan), **Supp. IV Part 1:** 405
Morrell, Ottoline, **Retro. Supp. I:** 60
Morris, Bernard E., **Supp. XV:** 154, 169
Morris, Christopher D., **Supp. IV Part 1:** 231, 236
Morris, Gary, **Supp. XXII:** 262
Morris, George Sylvester, **Supp. I Part 2:** 640
Morris, Gouverneur, **Supp. I Part 2:** 512, 517, 518
Morris, Lloyd, **III:** 458
Morris, Robert, **Supp. I Part 2:** 510
Morris, Timothy, **Retro. Supp. I:** 40

Morris, William, **II:** 323, 338, 523; **IV:** 349; **Supp. I Part 1:** 260, 356; **Supp. XI:** 202

Morris, Willie, **Supp. XI:** 216, 231, 234; **Supp. XIX:** 151, 252

Morris, Wright, **I:** 305; **III: 218–243,** 558, 572; **IV:** 211

Morrison, Charles Clayton, **III:** 297

Morrison, Jim, **Supp. IV Part 1:** 206

Morrison, Toni, **Retro. Supp. II:** 15, 118; **Supp. III Part 1: 361–381; Supp. IV Part 1:** 2, 13, 14, 250, 253, 257; **Supp. V:** 169, 259; **Supp. VIII:** 213, 214; **Supp. X:** 85, 239, 250, 325; **Supp. XI:** 4, 14, 20, 91; **Supp. XII:** 289, 310; **Supp. XIII:** 60, 185; **Supp. XVI:** 143; **Supp. XVII:** 183; **Supp. XX: 108; Supp. XXI:** 172, 243; **Supp. XXII:** 65, 78; **Supp. XXIV:** 183, 184, 185

"Morro Bay" (Jeffers), **Supp. II Part 2:** 422

Morrow, W. C., **I:** 199

Morse, Jedidiah, **Supp. XV:** 243

Morse, Robert, **Supp. XI:** 305

Morse, Samuel F. B., **Supp. I Part 1:** 156

Morse, Samuel French, **Supp. XXI:** 17, 19, 23, 27

Mortal Acts, Mortal Words (Kinnell), **Supp. III Part 1:** 235, 236, 237, 249–254

Mortal Antipathy, A (Holmes), **Supp. I Part 1:** 315–316

"Mortal Enemies" (Humphrey), **Supp. IX:** 109

"Mortal Eternal" (Olds), **Supp. X:** 214

Mortal No, The (Hoffman), **IV:** 113

Mortal Stakes (Parker), **Supp. XIX:** 183–184

Morte D'Arthur, Le (Malory), **Supp. IV Part 1:** 47

Mortmere Stories, The (Isherwood and Upward), **Supp. XIV:** 159

Morton, David, **Supp. IX:** 76

Morton, Jelly Roll, **Supp. X:** 242

Morton, Thomas, **Supp. XXII:** 44, 45, 46

"Mosaic of the Nativity: Serbia, Winter 1993" (Kenyon), **Supp. VII:** 173

Mosby's Memoirs and Other Stories (Bellow), **Retro. Supp. II:** 27

"Moscow, Idaho" (Offutt), **Supp. XIX:** 170

Moscow under Fire (Caldwell), **I:** 296

Moser, Barry, **Supp. XIV:** 223

Moses (Asch), **Supp. XXIII:** 7

Moses (Untermeyer), **Supp. XV: 309**

Moses, Man of the Mountain (Hurston), **Supp. VI:** 149, 158, 160

"Moses on Sinai" (Untermeyer), **Supp. XV:** 300

Mosher, Howard Frank, **Supp. XXII: 203–221**

Moskowitz, Alfred, **Supp. XXI:** 98, 106

Mosle, Sara, **Supp. XI:** 254

Mosley, Walter, **Supp. XIII: 233–252; Supp. XVI:** 143

Mosquito (G. Jones), **Supp. XXIV:** 183, 184, 185, 190, **192–194,** 195

Mosquito Coast, The (film), **Supp. VIII:** 323

Mosquito Coast, The (Theroux), **Supp. VIII:** 321, **322–323**

Mosquitos (Faulkner), **II:** 56; **Retro. Supp. I:** 79, 81

Moss, Howard, **III:** 452; **Supp. IV Part 2:** 642; **Supp. IX:** 39; **Supp. XIII:** 114; **Supp. XV:** 143, 152

Moss, Stanley, **Supp. XI:** 321

Moss, Thylias, **Supp. XI:** 248

Mosses from an Old Manse (Hawthorne), **I:** 562; **II:** 224; **III:** 82, 83; **Retro. Supp. I:** 157, 248

"Moss of His Skin" (Sexton), **Supp. II Part 2:** 676

Most, Doug, **Supp. XVIII:** 101

"Most Extraordinary Case, A" (James), **II:** 322; **Retro. Supp. I:** 218

"Most Girl Part of You, The" (Hempel), **Supp. XXI:** 116

Most Likely to Succeed (Dos Passos), **I:** 491

"Most of It, The" (Frost), **Retro. Supp. I:** 121, 125, 129, 139; **Supp. XVIII:** 300

"Most Popular Novels in America, The" (Mabie), **Supp. XVIII:** 257

Motel Chronicles (Shepard), **Supp. III Part 2:** 445

"Mother" (Kooser), **Supp. XIX:** 117, 126, 127

"Mother" (Paley), **Supp. VI: 222–223**

Mother (Schjeldahl), **Supp. XXIV:** 44

"Mother" (Snyder), **Supp. VIII:** 298

Mother (Whistler), **IV:** 369

Mother, The (Buck), **Supp. II Part 1:** 118–119

"Mother and Jack and the Rain" (Sexton), **Supp. II Part 2:** 686

"Mother and Son" (Tate), **IV:** 128, 137–138

Mother Country: Britain, the Welfare State and Nuclear Pollution (Robinson), **Supp. XXI:** 211

Mother Courage and Her Children (Brecht), **III:** 160; **Supp. IX:** 140; **Supp. XII:** 249

"Mother Earth: Her Whales" (Snyder), **Supp. VIII:** 302

"Motherhood" (Swenson), **Supp. IV Part 2:** 645

Mother Hubbard (Reed), **Supp. X:** 241

Motherless Brooklyn (Lethem), **Supp. XXII:** 49

Motherless in Brooklyn (Lethem), **Supp. XVIII:** 135, **143–144**

Mother Love (Dove), **Supp. IV Part 1:** 250–251, 254

"Mother Marie Therese" (Lowell), **Retro. Supp. II:** 188

Mother Night (Vonnegut), **Supp. II Part 2:** 757, 758, 767, 770, 771

"Mother Rosarine" (Kumin), **Supp. IV Part 2:** 442

"Mothers and Daughters in the Fiction of the New Republic" (Davidson), **Supp. XV:** 238

"Mother's lament for the absence of a child, A"(J. Schoolcraft), **Supp.**

XXIII: 236

Mother's Recompense, The (Wharton), **IV:** 321, 324; **Retro. Supp. I:** 382

"Mother's Tale, A" (Agee), **I:** 29–30

"Mother's Things" (Creeley), **Supp. IV Part 1:** 141

"Mother Suite, The"(Crooker), **Supp. XXIII:** 61

"Mother's Voice" (Creeley), **Supp. IV Part 1:** 156

Mother to Daughter, Daughter to Mother (Olsen, ed.), **Supp. XIII:** 295

"Mother Tongue" (Simic), **Supp. VIII:** 283

"Mother to Son" (Hughes), **Retro. Supp. I:** 199, 203; **Supp. I Part 1:** 321–322, 323

Motherwell, Robert, **Supp. XV:** 145; **Supp. XXI:** 125

"Mother Writes to the Murderer, The: A Letter" (Nye), **Supp. XIII:** 276

Moths of the Limberlost (Stratton-Porter), **Supp. XX: 218**

"Motion, The" (Olson), **Supp. II Part 2:** 571

Motion of History, The (Baraka), **Supp. II Part 1:** 55, 56

"Motive for Metaphor, The" (Stevens), **IV:** 89; **Retro. Supp. I:** 310

Motiveless Malignity (Auchincloss), **Supp. IV Part 1:** 31

Motke ganef (Asch), **Supp. XXIII:** 5

Motley, John Lothrop, **Supp. I Part 1:** 299; **Supp. I Part 2:** 479; **Supp. XX: 228, 231**

Motley, Willard, **Supp. XVII: 149–163; Supp. XXIII:** 145

"Motor Car, The" (White), **Supp. I Part 2:** 661

Motor-Flight Through France (Wharton), **I:** 12; **Retro. Supp. I:** 372

Mott, Michael, **Supp. VIII:** 204, 208

Motta, Gustavo, **Supp. XXIII:** 125

Mottetti: Poems of Love: The Motets of Eugenio Montale (Montale; Gioia, trans.), **Supp. XV:** 112, **127–128**

Mottke, the Thief (Asch), **Supp. XXIII: 9,** 12

Mottke, the Thief (Asch; tr. Willa and Edwin Muir), **Supp. XXIII:** 5

Mouawad, Nelly, **Supp. XX: 126**

"Mountain, The" (Frost), **Retro. Supp. I:** 121

"Mountain Hermitage, The: Pages from a Japanese Notebook" (Passin), **Supp. XIII:** 337

Mountain Interval (Frost), **II:** 154; **Retro. Supp. I:** 131, 132, 133

"Mountain Lion" (Hogan), **Supp. IV Part 1:** 412

"Mountain Music" essays (Sanders), **Supp. XVI:** 276–277

Mountain on the Desert, The (Richter), **Supp. XVIII:** 216, 219

Mountainous Journey, A (Tuqan), **Supp. XIII:** 278

"Mountains" (Dubus III), **Supp. XXIV:** 101

Mountains, The (Wolfe), **IV:** 461

Mountains and Rivers without End (Snyder), **Supp. VIII:** 295, **305–306**

"Mountains grow unnoticed, The" (Dickinson), **Retro. Supp. I:** 46

Mountains Have Come Closer, The (J. W. Miller), **Supp. XX:** 165, 168, 169–**170**

Mountains Look Down, The: A History of Chichester, a Company Town in the Catskills (Bennett), **Supp. XXII:** 218

Mountains of California, The (Muir), **Supp. IX:** 183

"Mountain Whippoorwill, The" (Benét), **Supp. XI:** 44–45, 46, 47

"Mount-Joy: or Some Passages Out of the Life of a Castle-Builder" (Irving), **II:** 314

"Mount Venus" (Wright), **Supp. XV:** 346

"Mourners" (Kooser), **Supp. XIX:** 127

"Mourners, The" (Malamud), **Supp. I Part 2:** 431, 435, 436–437

Mourners Below (Purdy), **Supp. VII:** 274, 280

"Mourning and Melancholia" (Freud), **Supp. IV Part 2:** 450; **Supp. XVI:** 161

Mourning Becomes Electra (O'Neill), **III:** 391, 394, 398–400

"Mourning Doves" (Pedersen; Nelson, trans.), **Supp. XVIII:** 180

"Mourning Poem for the Queen of Sunday" (Hayden), **Supp. II Part 1:** 379–380

"Mouse Elegy" (Olds), **Supp. X:** 209

Mouse Is Born, A (Loos), **Supp. XVI:** 193

"Mouse Roulette Wheel, The" (C. Bly), **Supp. XVI:** 34

Moustapha's Eclipse (McKnight), **Supp. XX:** 147, 150

"Mouth of Brass" (Humphrey), **Supp. IX:** 101

Moveable Feast, A (Hemingway), **II:** 257; **Retro. Supp. I:** 108, 171, **186–187**

Movement, The: Documentary of a Struggle for Equality (Student Nonviolent Coordinating Committee), **Supp. IV Part 1:** 369

"Move over Macho, Here Comes Feminismo" (Robbins), **Supp. X:** 272

Movers and Shakers (Sochen), **Supp. XXI:** 1

"Moves, The" (July), **Supp. XXIV:** 205

"Move to California, The" (Stafford), **Supp. XI:** 318, 321

"Movie" (Shapiro), **Supp. II Part 2:** 707

Movie at the End of the World, The (McGrath), **Supp. X:** 127

Moviegoer, The (Percy), **Supp. III Part 1:** 383–385, 387, 389–392, 394, 397

"Movie Magazine, The: A Low 'Slick' " (Percy), **Supp. III Part 1:** 385

Movies (Dixon), **Supp. XII:** 147

Movies About the Movies (Ames), **Supp. XVIII:** 242–243

"Movie Star Peter at the Supper for Street People" (Ferry), **Supp. XXIV:** 153

"Moving Around" (Matthews), **Supp. IX:** 155

"Moving Finger, The" (Wharton), **Retro. Supp. I:** 365

"Moving Inward at Last" (Bly), **Supp. XXI:** 84–85

Moving On (McMurtry), **Supp. V:** 223–224

"Moving On" (Pickering), **Supp. XXI:** 197

Moving Pictures: Memoirs of a Hollywood Prince (Schulberg), **Supp. XVIII:** 242, 243, 254

Moving Target, The (Macdonald), **Supp. IV Part 2:** 462, 463, 467, 470, 471, 473, 474

Moving Target, The (Merwin), **Supp. III Part 1:** 346, 347–348, 352, 357

"Mowbray Family, The" (Farrell and Alden), **II:** 45

"Mowing" (Frost), **II:** 169–170; **Retro. Supp. I:** 127, 128

"Moxan's Master" (Bierce), **I:** 206

Moxley, Jennifer, **Supp. XVII:** 70

Moyers, Bill, **Supp. IV Part 1:** 267; **Supp. VIII:** 331; **Supp. XI:** 126, 132; **Supp. XII:** 217; **Supp. XIII:** 274, 276; **Supp. XV:** 212; **Supp. XXIII:** 129, 130, 131, 139

Moynagh, Maureen, **Supp. XXII:** 73

Moynihan, Daniel Patrick, **Retro. Supp. II:** 123; **Supp. VIII:** 241; **Supp. XIX:** 150–151

"Moyshele"(Asch), **Supp. XXIII:** 4

"Mozart" (C. Frost), **Supp. XV:** 94

Mozart, Wolfgang Amadeus, **I:** 479, 588; **IV:** 74, 358; **Supp. IV Part 1:** 284

"Mozart and the Gray Steward" (Wilder), **IV:** 358

Mrabet, Mohammed, **Supp. IV Part 1:** 92, 93

Mr. and Mrs. Baby and Other Stories (Strand), **Supp. IV Part 2:** 631

"Mr. and Mrs. Fix-It" (Lardner), **II:** 431

Mr. Arcularis (Aiken), **I:** 54, 56

"Mr. Big" (Allen), **Supp. XV:** 15

Mr. Bridge (Connell), **Supp. XIV:** 80, 82, 93; **Supp. XXIII:** 302

Mr. Brown Can Moo! Can You? (Geisel), **Supp. XVI:** 104

"Mr. Bruce" (Jewett), **II:** 397; **Retro. Supp. II:** 134, 143

"Mr. Burnshaw and the Statue" (Stevens), **Retro. Supp. I:** 298, 303

"Mr. Carson Death on His Nights Out" (McGrath), **Supp. X:** 118

Mr. Clemens and Mark Twain (Kaplan), **I:** 247–248

"Mr. Coffee and Mr. Fixit" (Carver), **Supp. III Part 1:** 145

"Mr. Cornelius Johnson, Office-Seeker" (Dunbar), **Supp. II Part 1:** 211, 213

"Mr. Costyve Duditch" (Toomer), **Supp. III Part 2:** 486

"Mr. Dajani, Calling from Jericho" (Nye), **Supp. XIII:** 286–287

"Mr. Edwards and the Spider" (Lowell), **I:** 544; **II:** 550; **Retro. Supp. II:** 187

Mr. Field's Daughter (Bausch), **Supp. VII:** 47–48, 51–52

"Mr. Flood's Party" (Robinson), **III:** 512

"Mr. Forster's Pageant" (Maxwell), **Supp. VIII:** 172

"Mr. Frost's Chickens" (Oliver), **Supp. VII:** 232–233

Mr. Hodge and Mr. Hazard (Wylie), **Supp. I Part 2:** 708, 709, 714, 721–724

"Mr. Hueffer and the Prose Tradition" (Pound), **III:** 465

Mr. Ives' Christmas (Hijuelos), **Supp. VIII:** 85–86

Mr. Kelso's Lion (Bontemps), **Supp. XXII:** 7

"Mr. Longfellow and His Boy" (Sandburg), **III:** 591

"Mr. Luna and History" (Ríos), **Supp. IV Part 2:** 551

"Mr. Mitochondria" (Stollman), **Supp. XVII:** 50

Mr. Moto Is So Sorry (Marquand), **III:** 57, 58

Mr. Norris Changes Trains (Isherwood), **Supp. XIV:** 161

"Mr. Preble Gets Rid of His Wife" (Thurber), **Supp. I Part 2:** 615

"Mr. Rat"(Thompson), **Supp. XXIII:** 301–302

"Mr. Rolfe" (Wilson), **IV:** 436

Mr. Rutherford's Children (S. and A. Warner), **Supp. XVIII:** 264

"Mrs. Adis" (Kaye-Smith), **Supp. XVIII:** 130–131

Mrs. Albert Grundy: Observations in Philistia (Frederic), **II:** 138–139

Mr. Sammler's Planet (Bellow), **I:** 144, 147, 150, 151, 152, 158; **Retro. Supp. II:** 19, 28, 30

"Mrs. Balfame" (Atherton), **Supp. XXIV:** 20

"Mrs. Bilingsby's Wine" (Taylor), **Supp. V:** 323

Mrs. Bob Cratchit's Wild Christmas Binge (Durang), **Supp. XXIV:** 113, 125

Mrs. Bridge: A Novel (Connell), **Supp. XIV:** 79, 80, 81, 82, **89–94**, 95; **Supp. XXIII:** 302

"Mrs. Cassidy's Last Year" (Gordon), **Supp. IV Part 1:** 306

Mrs. Dalloway (Woolf), **Supp. IV Part 1:** 299; **Supp. VIII:** 5; **Supp. XV:** 55, 65–66

"Mr. Shelley Speaking" (Wylie), **Supp. I Part 2:** 719

"Mrs. Jellison" (Hay), **Supp. XIV:** 123

"Mrs. Krikorian" (Olds), **Supp. X:** 211

"Mrs. Maecenas" (Burke), **I:** 271

"Mrs. Mandrill" (Nemerov), **III:** 278

"Mrs. Manstey's View" (Wharton), **Retro. Supp. I:** 362, 363

"Mrs. Mobry's Reason" (Chopin), **Retro. Supp. II:** 61

Mr. Spaceman (R. O. Butler), **Supp. XII:** 62, **74–75**

Mrs. Reynolds (Stein), **IV:** 43

"Mrs. Sen's" (Lahiri), **Supp. XXI:** 177–**178**, 180–181

Mrs. Stevens Hears the Mermaids Singing (Sarton), **Supp. VIII:** 252–253, **256–257**

Mrs. Ted Bliss (Elkin), **Supp. VI:** 56, 58

"Mrs. Turner Cutting the Grass" (Shields), **Supp. VII:** 319–320

"Mrs. Walpurga" (Rukeyser), **Supp. VI:** 273

"Mr. Thompson's Prodigal" (Harte), **Supp. II Part 1:** 354

"Mr. Trumm's Eyes"(Schott), **Supp. XXIII:** 243

Mr. Vertigo (Auster), **Supp. XII: 34–35,** 36

"Mr. Vonnegut in Sumatra" (Saunders), **Supp. XIX:** 235

"Mr. Whittier" (Scott), **Supp. I Part 2:** 705

Mr. Wilson's War (Dos Passos), **I:** 485

"Mr. Woodriff's Neckties" (Gallagher), **Supp. XXIV:** 175–176

"MS. Found in a Bottle" (Poe), **III:** 411, 416; **Retro. Supp. II:** 274

"Ms. Lot" (Rukeyser), **Supp. VI:** 281

Ms. Magazine, **Supp. V:** 259

Mttron-Hirsch, Sidney, **III:** 484–485

"Muchas Gracias Por Todo" (Nye), **Supp. XIII:** 282–283

"Much Madness is divinest Sense" (Dickinson), **Retro. Supp. I:** 37–38

"Muck-A-Muck" (Harte), **Supp. II Part 1:** 342

"Mud Below, The" (Proulx), **Supp. VII:** 262

Mudge, Alden, **Supp. XIV:** 35

"Mudman"(P. Benedict), **Supp. XXIII:** 47

Mudrick, Marvin, **Retro. Supp. II:** 289

"Mud Season" (Kenyon), **Supp. VII:** 167–168

Mueller, Lisel, **Supp. I Part 1:** 83, 88; **Supp. XIV:** 268

Muggli, Mark, **Supp. IV Part 1:** 207

Muhammad, Elijah, **Supp. I Part 1:** 60

Muir, Edwin, **I:** 527; **II:** 368; **III:** 20; **Supp. XXII:** 166; **Supp. XXIII:** 1

Muir, John, **Supp. VIII:** 296; **Supp. IX:** 33, **171–188; Supp. X:** 29; **Supp. XIV:** 177, 178, 181

Muir, Willa, **Supp. XXIII:** 1

Muirhead, Deborah, **Supp. XVIII:** 186

Mujica, Barbara, **Supp. VIII:** 89

Mulas, Franco, **Supp. XX: 38**

Mulatto (Hughes), **Retro. Supp. I:** 197, 203; **Supp. I Part 1:** 328, 339

Mulching of America, The (Crews), **Supp. XI:** 107

Muldoon, William, **I:** 500–501

Mule Bone (Hughes and Hurston), **Retro. Supp. I:** 194, 203; **Supp. VI:** 154

Mules and Men (Hurston), **Supp. VI:** 149, 153, 154, 160

Mulford, Prentice, **I:** 193

Mullennix, Joel, **Supp. XXIII:** 281

Mulligan, Robert, **Supp. VIII:** 128, 129

Mulligan Stew (Sorrentino), **Supp. XII:** 139; **Supp. XXI:** 233

Mullins, Eustace, **III:** 479

Mullins, Priscilla, **II:** 502–503

"Multiplication of Wool, The" (Sanders), **Supp. XVI:** 268

Multitudes, Multitudes (Clampitt), **Supp. IX:** 39

Mumbo Jumbo (Reed), **Supp. X:** 240, 242, **245–248,** 251

Mumford, Lewis, **I:** 245, 250, 251, 252, 259, 261; **II:** 271, 473–474; **Supp. I Part 2:** 632, 638; **Supp. II Part 2: 471–501**

Mumford, Sophia Wittenberg (Mrs. Lewis Mumford), **Supp. II Part 2:** 474, 475

"Mummers, The" (Di Piero), **Supp. XIX:** 44

Mummy, The (film), **Supp. IV Part 1:** 104; **Supp. XVII:** 57

Mundo y Palabra (Espaillat), **Supp. XXI:** 104

"Mundus et Infans" (Auden), **Supp. II Part 1:** 15

"Munich, 1938" (Lowell), **II:** 554

"Munich Mannequins, The" (Plath), **Retro. Supp. II:** 256

"Municipal Report, A" (Henry), **Supp. II Part 1:** 406–407

Munro, Alice, **Supp. IX:** 212; **Supp. X:** 290; **Supp. XII:** 289–290, 310; **Supp. XXIII:** 289, 296

Munsey, Frank, **I:** 501

Munson, Gorham, **I:** 252, 388, 432; **Retro. Supp. II:** 77, 78, 79, 82, 83; **Supp. I Part 2:** 454; **Supp. XX: 70, 74**

Münsterberg, Hugo, **Supp. XIV:** 197

Murakami, Haruki, **Supp. XVI:** 124

"Murano" (Doty), **Supp. XI:** 131

Murasaki, Lady, **II:** 577

Muratori, Fred, **Supp. XVI:** 281

Muray, Nicholas, **Supp. I Part 2:** 708

Murder, My Sweet (film), **Supp. IV Part 1:** 130

"Murderer Guest, The" (Gordon), **Supp. IV Part 1:** 306

"Murderers" (L. Michaels), **Supp. XVI:** 207–208

Murder in Mount Holly (Theroux), **Supp. VIII:** 315–316

Murder in the Cathedral (T. S. Eliot), **I:** 571, 573, 580, 581; **II:** 20; **Retro. Supp. I:** 65; **Retro. Supp. II:** 222

Murder of Lidice, The (Millay), **III:** 140

"Murders in the Rue Morgue, The" (Poe), **III:** 412, 416, 419–420; **Retro. Supp. II:** 271, 272; **Supp. XIX:** 77

Murdoch, Iris, **Supp. VIII:** 167; **Supp. XVIII:** 136,149

Murnau, F. W., **Supp. XV:** 128

Murphy, Brenda, **Supp. XXI:** 6

Murphy, Jacqueline Shea, **Retro. Supp. II:** 143

Murphy, Patrick, **Supp. XIII:** 214

Murphy, Richard, **Retro. Supp. II:** 250; **Supp. XXIII:** 75

Murray, Albert, **Retro. Supp. II:** 119, 120; **Supp. XIX: 147–162**

Murray, Bill, **Supp. XXI:** 51

Murray, Edward, **I:** 229

Murray, G. E., **Supp. X:** 201; **Supp. XI:** 143, 155

Murray, Gilbert, **III:** 468–469

Murray, Jan, **Supp. IV Part 2:** 574

Murray, John, **II:** 304; **III:** 76, 79; **Retro. Supp. I:** 246

Murray, Judith Sargent, **Supp. XV:** 236–237

Murray, Les, **Supp. XIX:** 131

Murray, Margaret A., **Supp. V:** 128

Murrell, John A., **IV:** 265

Mursell, James L., **Supp. I Part 2:** 608

"Muse" (Ammons), **Supp. VII:** 29

"Muse, Postmodern and Homeless, The" (Ozick), **Supp. V:** 272

"Musée des Beaux Arts" (Auden), **Retro. Supp. I:** 430; **Supp. II Part 1:** 14

"Musée des Beaux Arts Revisited" (Collins), **Supp. XXI:** 60

"Muse of Aboutness, The" (Baker), **Supp. XVI:** 288

Muses Are Heard, The (Capote), **Supp. III Part 1:** 126

"Muses of Terrence McNally, The" (Zinman), **Supp. XIII:** 207–208

"Muse's Tragedy, The" (Wharton), **Retro. Supp. I:** 364

Museum (Dove), **Supp. IV Part 1:** 245–247, 248

"Museum" (Hass), **Supp. VI:** 107

Museums and Women (Updike), **Retro. Supp. I:** 321

"Museum Vase" (Francis), **Supp. IX:** 83

"Mushrooms" (Plath), **Retro. Supp. II:** 246; **Supp. I Part 2:** 539

"Music" (Oliver), **Supp. VII:** 236

Music (al-Músíqá) (Gibran), **Supp. XX: 115, 124**

Music After the Great War (Van Vechten), **Supp. II Part 2:** 732

Music and Bad Manners (Van Vechten), **Supp. II Part 2:** 733

Music Appreciation (Skloot), **Supp. XX: 196, 197–201**

"Music for a Farce" (Bowles), **Supp. IV Part 1:** 83

Music for Chameleons (Capote), **Supp. III Part 1:** 120, 125–127, 131, 132

"Music for Museums?" (Van Vechten), **Supp. II Part 2:** 732

"Music for the Movies" (Van Vechten), **Supp. II Part 2:** 733

"Music from Spain" (Welty), **IV:** 272

Music Like Dirt (Bidart), **Supp. XV:** 35

"Music Like Dirt" (Bidart), **Supp. XV:** 35

Music of Chance, The (Auster), **Supp. XII:** 21, 23, **32–33**

"Music of My Own Kind Too, The" (Budbill), **Supp. XIX:** 10

"Music of Prose, The" (Gass), **Supp. VI:** 92

Music of Spain, The (Van Vechten), **Supp. II Part 2:** 734, 735

"Music of the Spheres" (Epstein), **Supp. XII:** 165

"Music School" (B. Kelly), **Supp. XVII:** 124

Music School, The (Updike), **IV:** 214, 215, 219, 226, 227; **Retro. Supp. I:** 320, 328, 329, 330

"Music School, The" (Updike), **Retro. Supp. I:** 326, 329, 335

"Music Swims Back to Me" (Sexton), **Supp. II Part 2:** 673

Muske, Carol, **Supp. IV Part 2:** 453–454

"Mussel Hunter at Rock Harbor" (Plath), **Supp. I Part 2:** 529, 537

Musset, Alfred de, **I:** 474; **II:** 543

Mussolini, Benito, **III:** 115, 473, 608; **IV:** 372, 373; **Supp. I Part 1:** 281, 282; **Supp. I Part 2:** 618; **Supp. V:** 290; **Supp. XVI:** 191

"Mustafa Ferrari" (X. J. Kennedy), **Supp. XV:** 170–171

Mustich, James, **Supp. XXI:** 52

"Must the Novelist Crusade?" (Welty), **IV:** 280

"Mutability of Literature, The" (Irving), **II:** 308

"Mutation of the Spirit" (Corso), **Supp. XII:** 132, 133

Mute, The (McCullers), **II:** 586

Mutilated, The (T. Williams), **IV:** 382, 386, 393

Mutiny of the Elsinore, The (London), **II:** 467

"Muttsy" (Hurston), **Supp. XVIII:** 279

Muyumba, Walton, **Supp. XIX:** 158

"My Adventures as a Social Poet" (Hughes), **Retro. Supp. I:** 194, 207

"My Alba" (Ginsberg), **Supp. II Part 1:** 320, 321

My Alexandria (Doty), **Supp. XI:** 119, 120, 121, **123–125,** 130

"My Amendment" (Saunders), **Supp. XIX:** 232

My Amputations (Major), **Supp. XXII:** 174, **175–176**

My Ántonia (Cather), **I:** 321–322; **Retro. Supp. I:** 1, 3, 4, **11–13,** 14, 17, 18, 22; **Supp. IV Part 2:** 608; **Supp. XVI:** 226

"My Appearance" (Wallace), **Supp. X:** 306–307

My Argument with the Gestapo: A Macaronic Journal (Merton), **Supp. VIII:** 207; **Supp. XV:** 344

"My Arkansas" (Angelou), **Supp. IV Part 1:** 15

"My Aunt" (Holmes), **Supp. I Part 1:** 302, 310

"My Beginnings" (Simpson), **Supp. IX:** 273

"My Bird Problem" (Franzen), **Supp. XX: 94**

My Black Horse (Gallagher), **Supp. XXIV:** 170

"My Bodyguard" (Notley), **Supp. XXII:** 230

My Bondage and My Freedom (Douglass), **Supp. III Part 1:** 155, 173

My Brother (Kincaid), **Supp. VII:** 191–193

"My Brother Paul" (Dreiser), **Retro. Supp. II:** 94

"My Brothers the Silent" (Merwin), **Supp. III Part 1:** 349–350

"My Brother's Work" (Dunn), **Supp. XI:** 147

"My Brother Takes a Hammer to the Mirror" (F. Wright), **Supp. XVII:** 244

"My Butterfly" (Frost), **II:** 151; **Retro. Supp. I:** 124

"My Children, and a Prayer for Us" (Ortiz), **Supp. IV Part 2:** 507

My Children! My Africa! (Fugard), **Supp. XXIV:** 267

"My College Sex Group" (Peacock), **Supp. XIX:** 199

"My Coney Island Uncle" (Swados), **Supp. XIX:** 267–268

"My Confession" (McCarthy), **II:** 562

"My Confessional Sestina" (Gioia), **Supp. XV:** 123

"My Corner" (Major), **Supp. XXII:** 184

My Country and My People (Yutang), **Supp. X:** 291

"My Country 'Tis of Thee" (Reznikoff), **Supp. III Part 2:** 616

"My Daughter Considers Her Body" (Skloot), **Supp. XX: 197–198, 200**

My Days of Anger (Farrell), **II:** 34, 35–36, 43

"My Dear Niece" (Boyce), **Supp. XXI:** 10

"My Dear Republican Mother" (C. Bly), **Supp. XVI:** 31–32

My Death My Life by Pier Paolo Pasolini (Acker), **Supp. XII:** 7

My Dog Stupid (Fante), **Supp. XI:** 160, **170–171**

My Dog Tulip (Ackerley), **Supp. XX:** 237

"My Ear-Rings"(J. Schoolcraft), **Supp. XXIII:** 226

My Emily Dickinson (Howe), **Retro. Supp. I:** 33, 43; **Supp. IV Part 2:** 430–431

"My English" (Alvarez), **Supp. VII:** 2

Myers, John Bernard, **Supp. XXIII:** 210, 219

Myers, Linda A., **Supp. IV Part 1:** 10

"My Extended Family" (Theroux), **Supp. VIII:** 311

"My Father" (Budbill), **Supp. XIX:** 5

"My Father" (L. Michaels), **Supp. XVI:** 214

"My Father" (Sterne), **IV:** 466

"My Father at Eighty-Five" (R. Bly), **Supp. IV Part 1:** 73

"My Father Is a Simple Man" (Salinas), **Supp. XIII:** 324

"My Father Is with Me" (Budbill), **Supp. XIX:** 15

"My Father: October 1942" (Stafford), **Supp. XI:** 323

My Father Photographed with Friends (Bronk), **Supp. XXI:** 26–27,**Supp. XXI:** 31

"My Father Photographed with Friends" (Bronk), **Supp. XXI:** 23, 27

"My Fathers Came From Kentucky" (Lindsay), **Supp. I Part 2:** 395

"My Father's Employment"(Schott), **Supp. XXIII:** 247

"My Father's Friends" (Maxwell), **Supp. VIII:** 171

"My Father's Ghost" (Wagoner), **Supp. IX:** 330

"My Father's God" (Fante), **Supp. XI:** 160, 174

"My Father's House" (L.-Y. Lee), **Supp. XV:** 225

"My Father's Love Letters" (Gallagher), **Supp. XXIV:** 171–172

"My Father's Love Letters" (Komunyakaa), **Supp. XIII:** 127

"My Father Speaks to me from the Dead" (Olds), **Supp. X:** 210

"My Father's Telescope" (Dove), **Supp. IV Part 1:** 246, 248

"My Father with Cigarette Twelve Years Before the Nazis Could Break His Heart" (Levine), **Supp. V:** 194

"My Favorite Murder" (Bierce), **I:** 205

My Favorite Plant: Writers and Gardeners on the Plants They Love (Kincaid), **Supp. VII:** 193–194

My Favorites in Suspense (Hitchcock, ed.), **Supp. XXII:** 119

"My Fifty-Plus Years Celebrate Spring" (Salinas), **Supp. XIII:** 327

"My First Book" (Harte), **Supp. II Part 1:** 343

My First Summer in the Sierra (Muir), **Supp. IX:** 172, 173, **178–181,** 183, 185; **Supp. XIV:** 177

"My Flamboyant Grandson" (Saunders), **Supp. XIX:** 231–232

"My Fountain Pen" (McClatchy), **Supp. XII:** 254, 260

My Friend, Henry Miller (Perlès), **III:** 189

My Friend, Julia Lathrop (Addams), **Supp. I Part 1:** 25

"My Friend, Walt Whitman" (Oliver), **Supp. VII:** 245

"My Garden Acquaintance" (Lowell), **Supp. I Part 2:** 420

My Garden \[Book\]: (Kincaid), **Supp. VII:** 193–194

"My Good-bye" (Weigl), **Supp. XIX:** 288

"My Grandfather" (Lowell), **II:** 554

"My Grandmother's Love Letters" (H. Crane), **Retro. Supp. II:** 78

My Grandparents Were Married for Sixty-five Years (Schott), **Supp. XXIII:** 240–241

"My Grandson, Home at Last" (Angelou), **Supp. IV Part 1:** 13

My Green Hills of Jamaica (McKay), **Supp. X:** 132, 142

"My Gun" (Gallagher), **Supp. XXIV:** 175

My Guru and His Disciple (Isherwood), **Supp. XIV:** 157, 164, 172

"My Heart" (Collins), **Supp. XXI:** 58

My Heart's in the Highlands (Saroyan), **Supp. IV Part 1:** 83

"My High School Reunion" (Kingston), **Supp. V:** 169

"My House New-Painted" (Bronk), **Supp. XXI:** 30

"My Ideal Home" (Stratton-Porter), **Supp. XX:** 222

"My Indigo" (L.-Y. Lee), **Supp. XV:** 214

"My Kinsman, Major Molineux" (Hawthorne), **II:** 228, 229, 237–239, 243; **Retro. Supp. I:** 153–154, 158, 160, 161; **Retro. Supp. II:** 181, 187; **Supp. XVI:** 157

My Kinsman, Major Molineux (Lowell), **II:** 545–546

"My Last Afternoon with Uncle Devereux Winslow" (Lowell), **II:** 547–548; **Retro. Supp. II:** 189

"My Last Drive" (Hardy), **Supp. VIII:** 32

"My Last Duchess" (Browning), **Supp. XV:** 121

Myles, Eileen, **Supp. XXIV:** 45

"My Life" (Strand), **Supp. IV Part 2:** 627

My Life, Starring Dara Falcon (Beattie), **Supp. V:** 31, 34–35

My Life a Loaded Gun: Dickinson, Plath, Rich, and Female Creativity (Bennett), **Retro. Supp. I:** 29

My Life and Hard Times (Thurber), **Supp. I Part 2:** 607, 609

My Life as a Man (P. Roth), **Retro. Supp. II:** 281, 286, 289; **Supp. III Part 2:** 401, 404, 405, 417–418

"My Life as a P.I.G., or the True Adventures of Smokey the Cop" (Abbey), **Supp. XIII:** 3

"My life closed twice before its close" (Dickinson), **Retro. Supp. I:** 38

"My Life had stood a Loaded Gun" (Dickinson), **Retro. Supp. I:** 42, 43, 45, 46; **Supp. IV Part 2:** 430

My Life of Absurdity (C. Himes), **Supp. XVI:** 145

"My Life with Medicine" (Nye), **Supp. XIII:** 282

"My Life with *Playboy*" (Plimpton), **Supp. XVI:** 246

"My Life with R. H. Macy" (Jackson), **Supp. IX:** 118

"My Little Utopia" (Simic), **Supp. VIII:** 283

My Lives and How I Lost Them (Cullen), **Supp. IV Part 1:** 173

"My Lord Bag of Rice" (C. Bly), **Supp. XVI:** 40

My Lord Bag of Rice: New and Selected Stories (C. Bly), **Supp. XVI:** 41

"My Lost City" (Fitzgerald), **Retro. Supp. I:** 102

"My Lost Youth" (Longfellow), **II:** 487, 499; **Retro. Supp. II:** 168

My Love Affair with America: The Cautionary Tale of a Cheerful Conservative (Podhoretz), **Supp. VIII:** 232, 233, 237, **244–246**

"My Lover Has Dirty Fingernails" (Updike), **Retro. Supp. I:** 332, 333

"My lover is tall and handsome" (J. Schoolcraft), **Supp. XXIII:** 235

"My Lucy Friend Who Smells Like Corn" (Cisneros), **Supp. VII:** 68–69

"My Mammogram" (McClatchy), **Supp. XII:** 263–264

"My Man Bovanne" (Bambara), **Supp. XI:** 2

"My Mariner" (Larcom), **Supp. XIII:** 147

My Mark Twain (Howells), **II:** 276

"My Metamorphosis" (Harte), **Supp. II Part 1:** 339

My Mistress's Sparrow Is Dead (Eugenides, ed.), **Supp. XXIV:** 135

"My Moby Dick" (Humphrey), **Supp. IX:** 95

"My Monkey" (Nelson), **Supp. XVIII:** 178

"My Moral Life" (Halliday), **Supp. XIX:** 89

My Mortal Enemy (Cather), **I:** 327–328; **Retro. Supp. I:** 16–17; **Supp. I Part 2:** 719

My Mother, My Father and Me (Hellman), **Supp. I Part 1:** 290–291

"My Mother and My Sisters" (Ortiz), **Supp. IV Part 2:** 499

My Mother: Demonology (Acker), **Supp. XII:** 6

"My Mother Is Speaking from the Desert" (Gordon), **Supp. IV Part 1:** 309, 314

"My Mother Remembers That She Was Beautiful" (Gallagher), **Supp. XXIV:** 169

"My Mother's Goofy Song" (Fante), **Supp. XI:** 164

"My Mother's Memoirs, My Father's Lie, and Other True Stories" (Banks), **Supp. V:** 15

"My Mother's Nipples" (Hass), **Supp. VI:** 109

"My Mother's Story" (Kunitz), **Supp. III Part 1:** 259

"My Mother"(Taylor), **Supp. XXIII:** 231

"My Mother Then and Now" (Wasserstein), **Supp. XV:** 327

"My Mother with Purse the Summer They Murdered the Spanish Poet" (Levine), **Supp. V:** 194

My Movie Business: A Memoir (Irving), **Supp. VI:** 164

"My Name" (Cisneros), **Supp. VII:** 60

"My Negro Problem—And Ours" (Podhoretz), **Supp. VIII: 234–236**

"My Neighborhood"(Dybek), **Supp. XXIII:** 69

"My New Diet" (Karr), **Supp. XI:** 241

My Next Bride (Boyle), **Supp. XXIV: 53, 59**

"My Number" (Collins), **Supp. XXI:** 64

"My Old Man" (Hemingway), **II:** 263

My Other Life (Theroux), **Supp. VIII:** 310, 324

"My Own Story" (E. Stoddard), **Supp. XV:** 273, 279, 283

My Own True Name: New and Selected Poems for Young Adults, 1984–1999 (Mora), **Supp. XIII:** 222

"My Parents Have Come Home Laughing" (Jarman), **Supp. XVII:** 113

"My Passion for Ferries" (Whitman), **IV:** 350

"My People" (Hughes), **Retro. Supp. I:** 197; **Supp. I Part 1:** 321–322, 323

"My Philosophy" (Allen), **Supp. XV:** 15

"My Playmate" (Whittier), **Supp. I Part 2:** 699–700

"My Priests" (Monette), **Supp. X:** 159

Myra Breckinridge (Vidal), **Supp. IV Part 2:** 677, 685–686, 689, 691

"My Raptor" (A. Finch), **Supp. XVII:** 72

"My Recollections of S. B. Fairchild" (Jackson), **Supp. IX:** 118–119

"My Religion" (Carson), **Supp. XII: 105–106**

"My Road to Hell Was Paved" (Patchett), **Supp. XII:** 310–311

Myron (Vidal), **Supp. IV Part 2:** 677, 685, 686, 691

"My Roomy" (Lardner), **II:** 420, 421, 428, 430

"My Sad Self" (Ginsberg), **Supp. II Part 1:** 320

My San Francisco (Atherton), **Supp. XXIV:** 27

My Secret History (Theroux), **Supp. VIII:** 310, 324

"Myself" (Audubon), **Supp. XVI:** 1–2, 5, 12

Myself Painting (Major), **Supp. XXII: 184–185**

"My Shoes" (Simic), **Supp. VIII:** 275

"My Side of the Matter" (Capote), **Supp. III Part 1:** 114, 115

My Silk Purse and Yours: The Publishing Scene and American Literary Art (Garrett), **Supp. VII:** 111; **Supp. X:** 7

My Sister Eileen (McKenney), **IV:** 288; **Retro. Supp. II:** 321

My Sister's Hand in Mine: The Collected Works of Jane Bowles, **Supp. IV Part 1:** 82–83

"My Son" (Strand), **Supp. IV Part 2:** 629

My Son, John (film), **Supp. I Part 1:** 67

"My Son, the Murderer" (Malamud), **Supp. I Part 2:** 437

"My Son the Man" (Olds), **Supp. X:** 212

"My Speech to the Graduates" (Allen), **Supp. XV:** 16

"Mysteries of Caesar, The" (Hecht), **Supp. X:** 73

"Mysteries of Eleusis, The" (Hardwick), **Supp. III Part 1:** 195

Mysteries of Paris, The (Sue), **Supp. XXIII:** 182

Mysteries of Pittsburgh, The (Chabon), **Supp. XI:** 65, 68, **69–71**; **Supp. XIX:** 135

Mysteries of Small Houses (Notley), **Supp. XXII:** 223, 224, 226, 234–235

"Mysterious Case of R, The" (Conroy), **Supp. XVI:** 72

Mysterious Stranger, The (Twain), **IV:** 190–191, 210

Mystery, A (Shields). *See Swann* (Shields)

"Mystery, The" (Dunbar), **Supp. II Part 1:** 199, 210

"Mystery, The" (Glück), **Supp. V:** 91

Mystery and Manners (O'Connor), **Retro. Supp. II:** 230

"'Mystery Boy' Looks for Kin in Nashville" (Hayden), **Supp. II Part 1:** 366, 372

"Mystery of Coincidence, The" (Conroy), **Supp. XVI:** 74

"Mystery of Heroism, A" (Crane), **I:** 414

"Mystery of Marie Rogêt, The" (Poe), **III:** 413, 419; **Retro. Supp. II:** 271

"Mystic" (Plath), **Retro. Supp. II:** 257; **Supp. I Part 2:** 539, 541

"Mystical Poet, A" (Bogan), **Retro. Supp. I:** 36

"Mystic of Sex, The—A First Look at D. H. Lawrence" (Nin), **Supp. X:** 188

"Mystic Vision in 'The Marshes of Glynn' " (Warfel), **Supp. I Part 1:** 366, 373

"Mystification" (Poe), **III:** 425

"My Strange New Poetry" (Halliday), **Supp. XIX:** 88, 94

My Study Windows (Lowell), **Supp. I Part 2:** 407

"My Teacher" (Conroy), **Supp. XVI:** 75

"Myth" (Rukeyser), **Supp. VI:** 281–282

"Myth" (Trethewey), **Supp. XXI:** 245, 255, 256

"Myth"(Hadas), **Supp. XXIII:** 119

"Mythmaker" (Trethewey), **Supp. XXI:** 243

Myth of American Manhood, The (Kriegel, ed.), **Supp. XXIV:** 214

Myth of Sisyphus, The (Camus), **I:** 294; **Supp. XIII:** 165

"Myth of the Happy Worker, The" (Swados), **Supp. XIX:** 265

"Myth of the Isolated Artist, The" (Oates), **Supp. II Part 2:** 520

Myth of the Machine, The (Mumford), **Supp. II Part 2:** 476, 478, 482, 483, 493, 497

"Myth of the Powerful Worker, The" (Swados), **Supp. XIX:** 265

Mythology and the Romantic Tradition in English Poetry (Bush), **Supp. I Part 1:** 268

Myths and Texts (Snyder), **Supp. VIII:** 295–296

"Myths of Bears, The" (Bass), **Supp. XVI:** 19, 20

"My *Tocaya*" (Cisneros), **Supp. VII:** 69

My Uncle Dudley (Morris), **I:** 305; **III:** 219–220

"My Uncle's Favorite Coffee Shop" (Nye), **Supp. XIII:** 283

"My Unopened Life" (Gallagher), **Supp. XXIV:** 171

"My Weariness of Epic Proportions" (Simic), **Supp. VIII:** 276

My Wicked Wicked Ways (Cisneros), **Supp. VII:** 58, 64–68, 71

"My Wicked Wicked Ways" (Cisneros), **Supp. VII:** 58, 64–66

My Wisdom (Thompson), **Supp. XXIII:** 291–293

"My Word-house" (Mora), **Supp. XIII:** 219, 225

My Works and Days (Mumford), **Supp. II Part 2:** 475, 477, 481

"My World and My Critics" (Stratton-Porter), **Supp. XX:** 220

My World and Welcome to It (Thurber), **Supp. I Part 2:** 610

N

Nabokov, Peter, **Supp. IV Part 2:** 490

Nabokov, Véra, **Retro. Supp. I:** 266, 270

Nabokov, Vladimir, **I:** 135; **III:** 244–266, 283, 286; **Retro. Supp. I:** 263–281, 317, 335; **Supp. I Part 1:** 196; **Supp. II Part 1:** 2; **Supp. IV Part 1:** 135; **Supp. V:** 127, 237, 251, 252, 253; **Supp. VIII:** 105, 133, 138; **Supp. IX:** 152, 212, 261; **Supp. X:** 283; **Supp.** **XI:** 66; **Supp. XII:** 310; **Supp. XIII:** 46, 52; **Supp. XVI:** 148, 294; **Supp. XVIII:** 98, 102; **Supp. XXII:** 263; **Supp. XXIV:** 133

Nabokov's Dozen (Nabokov), **Retro. Supp. I:** 266

Nabokov's Garden: A Guide to Ada (Mason), **Supp. VIII:** 138

Naca, Kristin, **Supp. XIII:** 133

Nadeau, Robert, **Supp. X:** 261, 270

Nadel, Alan, **Supp. IV Part 1:** 209

Naimy, Mikhail, **Supp. XX: 116, 119, 120**

Naipaul, V. S., **Supp. IV Part 1:** 297; **Supp. VIII:** 314; **Supp. X:** 131; **Supp. XIV:** 111; **Supp. XX: 87; Supp. XXI:** 170; **Supp. XXII:** 240, 241, 242, 246, 253

Naison, Mark, **Supp. XVIII:** 231

Naked and the Dead, The (Mailer), **I:** 477; **III:** 26, 27, 28–30, 31, 33, 35, 36, 44; **Retro. Supp. II: 197–199; Supp. IV Part 1:** 381; **Supp. XI:** 218; **Supp. XIX:** 248; **Supp. XX: 248; Supp. XXI:** 277

Naked Author (di Donato), **Supp. XX: 45**

Naked Babies (Quindlen and Kelsh), **Supp. XVII:** 167, 179

Naked in Garden Hills (Crews), **Supp. XI:** 102, **110**

Naked Lunch (Burroughs), **Supp. III Part 1:** 92–95, 97–105; **Supp. IV Part 1:** 90

"Naked Nude" (Malamud), **Supp. I Part 2:** 450

Naked Poetry (Berg and Mezey, eds.), **Supp. IV Part 1:** 60

Naked Poetry (Levine), **Supp. V:** 180

Naked Revenge (film), **Supp. XVII:** 141

Nall, Gus, **Supp. XXII:** 172, 184

Namedropping: Mostly Literary Memoirs (Coover), **Supp. V:** 40

"Name in the Papers" (Hughes), **Supp. I Part 1:** 330

Name Is Archer, The (Macdonald, under Millar), **Supp. IV Part 2:** 466

"Name Is Burroughs, The" (Burroughs), **Supp. III Part 1:** 93

Name Is Fogarty, The: Private Papers on Public Matters (Farrell), **II:** 49

"Names" (Carruth), **Supp. XVI:** 54, 56

"Names, The" (Collins), **Supp. XXI:** 54, 61–62

Names, The (DeLillo), **Supp. VI:** 3, 10, 13, 14

Names, The (Momaday), **Supp. IV Part 2:** 479, 480, 483, 486, 487, 488, 489

Namesake, The (Lahiri), **Supp. XXI:** 176, 184, **186–188**

Names and Faces of Heroes, The (Price), **Supp. VI:** 258, 260

Names of the Lost, The (Levine), **Supp. V:** 177–178, 179, 187–188

"Naming for Love" (Carruth), **Supp. XVI:** 48

"Naming Myself" (Kingsolver), **Supp. VII:** 208

"Naming of Names, The" (Sanders), **Supp. XVI:** 268

Naming of the Beasts, The (Stern). *See Rejoicings: Selected Poems, 1966–* *1972* (Stern)

Naming the Unseen (Ray), **Supp. XVIII:** 192, **193–195**

"Naming the Unseen" (Ray), **Supp. XVIII:** 203

Nana (Zola), **III:** 321

"Nancy Culpepper" (Mason), **Supp. VIII:** 141

Nancy Drew stories, **Supp. VIII:** 133, 135, 137, 142

"Nancy Knapp" (Masters), **Supp. I Part 2:** 461

"Naola Beauty Academy, New Orleans, 1943" (Trethewey), **Supp. XXI:** 246

"Naomi Counting Time"(Thompson), **Supp. XXIII:** 293

"Naomi Shihab Nye: U.S. Mideast-History a Harbinger of 9-11?" (Nye), **Supp. XIII:** 286

"Naomi Trimmer" (X. J. Kennedy), **Supp. XV:** 170

"Nap, The" (Banks), **Supp. V:** 7

"Napoleon" (Emerson), **II:** 6

Napoleon I, **I:** 6, 7, 8, 474; **II:** 5, 309, 315, 321, 523; **Supp. I Part 1:** 153; **Supp. I Part 2:** 518, 519

Napolitano, Louise, **Supp. XX: 35, 45, 46–47**

Narcissa and Other Fables (Auchincloss), **Supp. IV Part 1:** 21, 34

"Narcissus as Narcissus" (Tate), **IV:** 124

"Narcissus Leaves the Pool" (Epstein), **Supp. XIV:** 110

Narcissus Leaves the Pool: Familiar Essays (Epstein), **Supp. XIV:** 110

Nardal, Paulette, **Supp. X:** 139

Nardi, Marcia, **Retro. Supp. I:** 426, 427

"Narragansett Boulevard" (Halliday), **Supp. XIX:** 91

Narration (Stein), **IV:** 27, 30, 32, 33, 36

Narrative of a Four Months' Residence among the Natives of a Valley of the Marquesas Islands (Melville), **III:** 76

Narrative of Arthur Gordon Pym, The (Poe), **III:** 412, 416; **Retro. Supp. II:** 265, **273–275; Supp. XI:** 293

"Narrative of Arthur Gordon Pym, The" (Poe), **Supp. XXII:** 58

Narrative of the Life of Frederick Douglass, an American Slave, Written by Himself (Douglass), **Supp. III Part 1:** 154–159, 162, 165; **Supp. IV Part 1:** 13; **Supp. VIII:** 202

"Narrativity Scenes" (Wright), **Supp. XV:** 345

Narrenschiff, Das (Brant), **III:** 447

"Narrow Fellow in the Grass, A" (Dickinson), **Retro. Supp. I:** 30, 37

Narrow Heart, A: Portrait of a Woman (Gordon), **II:** 197, 217

Narrow Rooms (Purdy), **Supp. VII:** 274

Narrows, The (Connelly), **Supp. XXI:** 71, **76**

Nasby, Petroleum, **Supp. XVIII:** 1

Nash, Noreen, **Supp. XXII:** 256

Nash, Ogden, **Supp. XXI:** 51; **Supp. XXIV:** 45

Nash, Roderick, **Supp. IX:** 185; **Supp. XIV:** 191–192

Nash, Susan Smith, **Supp. XVI:** 274

Nash, Thomas, **Supp. III Part 1:** 387–388

Nashe, Thomas, **I:** 358; **Supp. XVII:** 232

Nashville (film), **Supp. IX:** 143

"Nashville Gone to Ashes" (Hempel), **Supp. XXI:** 115, 118, **120–121**

Nashville Skyline (album, Dylan), **Supp. XVIII:** 27

Nason, Elias, **Supp. XV:** 242

Nasser, Gamal Abdel, **IV:** 490

Nasty Bits (Silver), **Supp. XXIV:** 265

Natalie Mann (Toomer), **Supp. III Part 2:** 484–486

Nathan, George Jean, **II:** 91; **III:** 103, 104, 106, 107; **IV:** 432; **Supp. IV Part 1:** 343; **Supp. IX:** 56–57; **Supp. XIII:** 161; **Supp. XXII:** 23

"Nathanael West" (Herbst), **Retro. Supp. II:** 325

Nathanael West: The Art of His Life (Martin), **Retro. Supp. II:** 325

Nathan Coulter (Berry), **Supp. X:** 24, 33

National Dream, The: Building the Impossible Railway (Findley and Whitehead), **Supp. XX:** 51

"Nationalist, The" (Anderson), **I:** 115

"Nation Is Like Ourselves, The" (Baraka), **Supp. II Part 1:** 53

"Native, The" (Olds), **Supp. X:** 215

"Native American Attitudes to the Environment" (Momaday), **Supp. IV Part 2:** 481, 491

Native American Renaissance (Lincoln), **Supp. IV Part 2:** 507

Native American Testimony (Nabokov, ed.), **Supp. IV Part 2:** 490

"Native Blessing" (Ray), **Supp. XVIII:** 202

Native Guard (Trethewey), **Supp. XXI:** 243, 244, 247, **254–257**

"Native Guard" (Trethewey), **Supp. XXI:** 256

"Native Hill, A" (Berry), **Supp. X:** 21

Native in a Strange Land: Trials & Tremors (Coleman), **Supp. XI:** 84–85, 87

Native of Winby and Other Tales, A (Jewett), **II:** 396; **Retro. Supp. II:** 138

"Natives Don't Cry" (Boyle), **Supp. XXIV:** 57–58

Native Son (Wright), **IV:** 476, 477, 478, 479, 481, 482–484, 485, 487, 488, 491, 495; **Retro. Supp. II:** 107, 116; **Supp. I Part 1:** 51, 64, 67, 337; **Supp. II Part 1:** 170, 235–236; **Supp. IX:** 306; **Supp. XIV:** 73; **Supp. XVII:** 155; **Supp. XVIII:** 283, 286; **Supp. XXI:** 169

"Native Trees" (Merwin), **Supp. III Part 1:** 355

Natorp, Paul, **Supp. XIV:** 198

Natural, The (Malamud), **II:** 424, 425; **Retro. Supp. II:** 288; **Supp. I Part 2:** 438–441, 443

"*Natural, The:* Malamud's World Ceres" (Wasserman), **Supp. I Part 2:** 439

"Natural History" (Olds), **Supp. X:** 210

"Natural History Note" (Hay), **Supp. XIV:** 124, 130

"Natural History of Some Poems, A" (Harrison), **Supp. VIII:** 53

"Natural History of the Dead" (Hemingway), **II:** 206; **Retro. Supp. I:** 176

"Naturally Superior School, A" (Knowles), **Supp. XII:** 235, 240–241

"Natural Method of Mental Philosophy" (Emerson), **II:** 14

"Natural Resources" (Rich), **Supp. I Part 2:** 575

Natural Selection (F. Barthelme), **Supp. XI:** 2, 28, 32, 33

Nature (Emerson), **I:** 463; **II:** 1, 8, 12, 16; **IV:** 171, 172–173; **Supp. XXIV:** 75, 79

"Nature" (Emerson), **Retro. Supp. I:** 250; **Supp. I Part 2:** 383; **Supp. III Part 1:** 387; **Supp. IX:** 178

"Nature, Inc." (Lewis), **II:** 441

Nature and Destiny of Man, The (Niebuhr), **III:** 292, 303–306, 310

"Nature and Life" (Emerson), **II:** 19

"Nature and New America Painting"(O'Hara), **Supp. XXIII:** 212

"Nature and Nurture: When It Comes to Twins, Sometimes It's Hard to Tell the Two Apart" (Bausch), **Supp. VII:** 40

Nature and Purpose of the Universe, The (Durang), **Supp. XXIV:** **115–116**

"Nature-Metaphors" (Lanier), **Supp. I Part 1:** 352

Nature Morte (Brodsky), **Supp. VIII:** 25

Nature of Evil, The (James), **II:** 343

Nature of Peace, The (Veblen), **Supp. I Part 2:** 642

Nature of Things, The (television show), **Supp. XX:** 51

Nature of True Virtue, The (Edwards), **I:** 549, 557–558, 559

Nature: Poems Old and New (Swenson), **Supp. IV Part 2:** 652

Nature's Economy: A History of Ecological Ideas (Worster), **Supp. IX:** 19

Naumburg, Margaret, **Supp. XX:** **68, 74–75**

Nausea (Sartre), **Supp. VIII:** 7

"Navajo Blanket, A" (Swenson), **Supp. IV Part 2:** 649

Navarette, Don Martín de, **II:** 310

Navarro, Ramon, **Supp. IV Part 1:** 206

Navigator, The (film), **I:** 31

Navratilova, Martina, **Supp. XX:** **264**

Naylor, Gloria, **Supp. VIII:** **213–230;** **Supp. XX:** **108**

Naylor, Paul Kenneth, **Supp. IV Part 2:** 420

Nazarene, The (Asch), **Supp. XXIII:** 2, 3, 4, 6, 9, **12–13,** 14, 15, 16

Nazarene, The: or, The Last of the Washingtons (Lippard), **Supp. XXIII:** 183, 184, 187, 190

Nazimova, **III:** 399

Neal, Darlin', **Supp. XXI:** 41

Neal, Larry, **Retro. Supp. II:** 112, 128; **Supp. X:** 324, 328

Neal, Lawrence P., **Supp. II Part 1:** 53

Neal, Patricia, **Supp. I Part 1:** 286; **Supp. IV Part 2:** 524; **Supp. V:** 223

Neale, Walter, **I:** 192, 208

"Near Damascus" (Di Piero), **Supp. XIX:** 43

Nearer the Moon: From "A Journal of Love," the Unexpurgated Diary of Anaïs Nin, 1937–1939, **Supp. X:** 184, 185

Near-Johannesburg Boy and Other Poems, The (Brooks), **Supp. III Part 1:** 86

Near Klamath (Carver), **Supp. III Part 1:** 137

"Near Perigord" (Pound), **Retro. Supp. I:** 289, 290

"Near Spring" (Pickering), **Supp. XXI:** 198

Near the Ocean (Lowell), **II:** 543, 550, 551–553, 554, 555; **Retro. Supp. II:** 182, 186, 189–190

"Near View of the High Sierra, A" (Muir), **Supp. IX:** 183

Nebeker, Helen, **Supp. IX:** 122

"Nebraska Blizzard" (F. Wright), **Supp. XVII:** 247

Necessary Angel, The (Stevens), **IV:** 76, 79, 89, 90

Necessities of Life: Poems, 1962–1965 (Rich), **Supp. I Part 2:** 553, 555

"Necessity of Lemons, The"(Schott), **Supp. XXIII:** 247, 248

Nechayev, Sergey, **Supp. XXI:** 164

Neck Deep and Other Predicaments (Monson), **Supp. XXIV:** 230, **234–236,** 241

"Necrological" (Ransom), **III:** 486–489, 490, 492

Ned Christie's War (Conley), **Supp. V:** 232

"Need for a Cultural Base to Civil Rites & Bpower Mooments, The" (Baraka), **Supp. II Part 1:** 48

"Need for Christian Preaching, The" (Buechner), **Supp. XII:** 49

Needful Things (King), **Supp. V:** 139, 146

"Needle" (Simic), **Supp. VIII:** 275

"Needle Trade" (Reznikoff), **Supp. XIV:** 277, 289

"Need of Being Versed in Country Things, The" (Frost), **II:** 154; **Retro. Supp. I:** 133, 135

"Need to Say It, The" (Hampl), **Supp. XXII:** 94

Neel, Philippe, **Supp. XIV:** 338

Neelakantappa, Tara, **Supp. XV:** 104–105

Neeley, Barbara, **Supp. XVI:** 143

"Negative Capability" (Komunyakaa), **Supp. XIII:** 131

Negligible Tales (Bierce), **I:** 209

"Negotiating the Darkness, Fortified by Poets' Strength" (Karr), **Supp. XI:** 254; **Supp. XIII:** 285

Negotiating with the Dead (Atwood), **Supp. XIII:** 20, 35

Negritude movement, **Supp. X:** 131, 139

"Negro" (Hughes), **Supp. I Part 1:** 321–322

Negro, The (Du Bois), **Supp. II Part 1:** 178, 179, 185

Negro, The: The Southerner's Problem (Page), **Supp. II Part 1:** 168

Negro and His Music, The (Locke), **Supp. XIV:** 202

"Negro Artisan, The" (Du Bois), **Supp. II Part 1:** 166

"Negro Artist and the Racial Mountain, The" (Hughes), **Retro. Supp. I:** 200, 207; **Supp. I Part 1:** 323, 325; **Supp. IV Part 1:** 169

Negro Art: Past and Present (Locke), **Supp. XIV:** 202

"Negro Assays the Negro Mood, A" (Baldwin), **Supp. I Part 1:** 52

"Negro Citizen, The" (Du Bois), **Supp. II Part 1:** 179

"Negro Dancers" (Hughes), **Retro. Supp. I:** 199; **Supp. I Part 1:** 324

Negroes in America, The (McKay), **Supp. X:** 132, 136

"Negroes of Farmville, Virginia, The: A Social Study" (Du Bois), **Supp. II Part 1:** 166

Negro Family, The: The Case for National Action (Moynihan), **Retro. Supp. II:** 123

"Negro Farmer, The" (Du Bois), **Supp. II Part 1:** 167

"Negro Fight, The" (column, C. L. R. James), **Supp. XXI:** 169

"Negro Ghetto" (Hughes), **Supp. I Part 1:** 331

Negro in America, The (Locke), **Supp. XIV:** 208

Negro in American Civilization, The (Du Bois), **Supp. II Part 1:** 179

Negro in American Culture, The (Locke and Butcher), **Supp. XIV:** 202–203

Negro in Art, The: A Pictorial Record of the Negro Artist and of the Negro Theme in Art (Locke), **Supp. XIV:** 202

"Negro in Large Cities, The" (Du Bois), **Supp. II Part 1:** 169

"Negro in Literature and Art, The" (Du Bois), **Supp. II Part 1:** 174

Negro in New York, The (Ellison), **Supp. II Part 1:** 230

"Negro in the Black Belt, The: Some Social Sketches" (Du Bois), **Supp. II Part 1:** 166

Negro in the Caribbean, The (Williams), **Supp. XXI:** 166

"Negro in the Three Americas, The" (Locke), **Supp. XIV:** 211

"Negro in the Well, The" (Caldwell), **I:** 309

"Negro Love Song, A" (Dunbar), **Supp. II Part 1:** 204

"Negro Martyrs Are Needed" (C. Himes), **Supp. XVI:** 138

Negro Mother, The (Hughes), **Supp. I Part 1:** 328

Negro Mother and Other Dramatic Recitations, The (Hughes), **Retro. Supp. I:** 203

Negro Novel in America, The (Bone), **Supp. IX:** 318–319; **Supp. XVIII:** 285

Negro Publication Society of America, **Retro. Supp. I:** 205

"Negro Renaissance, The: Jean Toomer and the Harlem of the 1920s" (Bontemps), **Supp. IX:** 306

"Negro Schoolmaster in the New South, A" (Du Bois), **Supp. II Part 1:** 168

"Negro's Contribution to American Culture, The" (Locke), **Supp. XIV:** 210, 211

"Negro Sermon, A: Simon Legree" (Lindsay), **Supp. I Part 1:** 393

"Negro Sings of Rivers, The" (Hughes), **Supp. IV Part 1:** 16

"Negro Speaks of Rivers, The" (Hughes), **Retro. Supp. I:** 199; **Supp. I Part 1:** 321

"Negro Spirituals, The (Locke), **Supp. XIV:** 201

"Negro Takes Stock, The" (Du Bois), **Supp. II Part 1:** 180

"Negro Theatre, The" (Van Vechten), **Supp. II Part 2:** 735

"Negro Voter Sizes Up Taft, A" (Hurston), **Supp. VI:** 160

"Negro Writer and His Roots, The: Toward a New Romanticism" (Hansberry), **Supp. IV Part 1:** 364

"Negro Youth Speaks" (Locke), **Supp. XIV:** 201

"Nehemias Americanus" (Mather), **Supp. II Part 2:** 453

Nehru, Jawaharlal, **IV:** 490

"Neighbor" (Hugo), **Supp. VI:** 135–136

"Neighborhood Drunk"(Dybek), **Supp. XXIII:** 71

"Neighbors" (Carver), **Supp. III Part 1:** 135, 139, 141; **Supp. XI:** 153

"Neighbors" (Hogan), **Supp. IV Part 1:** 405

"Neighbors, The" (Hay), **Supp. XIV:** 126

"Neighbour Rosicky" (Cather), **I:** 331–332

Neil Simon (Johnson), **Supp. IV Part 2:** 573

"Neil Simon's Jewish-Style Comedies" (Walden), **Supp. IV Part 2:** 584, 591

"Neil Simon: Toward Act III?" (Walden), **Supp. IV Part 2:** 591

Neilson, Heather, **Supp. IV Part 2:** 681

Neiman, Gilbert, **Supp. XV:** 140

"Neither Out Far Nor In Deep" (Frost), **I:** 303; **Retro. Supp. I:** 121, 138

"Nellie Clark" (Masters), **Supp. I Part 2:** 461

Nelson, Alice Dunbar, **Supp. XVII:** 75

Nelson, Cary, **Supp. XVIII:** 226, 227, 230, 231; **Supp. XXII:** 271

Nelson, Ernest, **I:** 388

Nelson, Howard, **Supp. IV Part 1:** 66, 68; **Supp. XIX:** 3; **Supp. XXI:** 95

Nelson, Lord Horatio, **II:** 524

Nelson, Lynn (pseudonym). *See* Nelson, Marilyn

Nelson, Marilyn, **Supp. XVII:** 74, 112; **Supp. XVIII: 171–188**

Nelson, Shirley, **Supp. XII:** 293

Nelson, Steve, **Supp. XVIII:** 226

Nelson Algren (Cox and Chatterton), **Supp. IX:** 11–12

Nelson Algren: A Life on the Wild Side (Drew), **Supp. IX:** 2

Nemerov, David, **II:** 268

Nemerov, Howard, **III: 267–289; IV:** 137, 140; **Supp. III Part 2:** 541;

Supp. IV Part 2: 455, 650; **Supp. IX:** 114

Nemesis (P. Roth), **Supp. XXIV:** 214

Nemiroff, Robert Barron, **Supp. IV Part 1:** 360, 361, 365, 369, 370, 374

Neoconservative Criticism: Norman Podhoretz, Kenneth S. Lynn, and Joseph Epstein (Winchell), **Supp. VIII:** 241; **Supp. XIV:** 103

"Neo-Formalism: A Dangerous Nostalgia" (Sadoff), **Supp. XXI:** 100

"Neo-Hoodoo Manifesto, The" (Reed), **Supp. X:** 242

Neon Rain, The (Burke), **Supp. XIV:** 22, 24, 26–27, 28–29, 30

Neon Vernacular (Komunyakaa), **Supp. XIII:** 121, **127–128,** 131

Neon Wilderness, The (Algren), **Supp. IX:** 3, 4

Neo-Slave Narratives (Rushdy), **Supp. X:** 250

Nepantla: Essays from the Land in the Middle (Mora), **Supp. XIII:** 213, **219–221,** 227

Nephew, The (Purdy), **Supp. VII:** 271, 273, 282

"Nereids of Seriphos, The" (Clampitt), **Supp. IX:** 41

Nericcio, William, **Supp. XIV:** 304–305

Neruda, Pablo, **Supp. I Part 1:** 89; **Supp. IV Part 2:** 537; **Supp. V:** 332; **Supp. VIII:** 272, 274; **Supp. IX:** 157, 271; **Supp. X:** 112; **Supp. XI:** 191; **Supp. XII:** 217; **Supp. XIII:** 114, 315, 323; **Supp. XXI:** 61, 100; **Supp. XXIV:** 170

Nesbit, Edith, **Supp. VIII:** 171

Nesbit, Lynn, **Supp. XXIII:** 100

Nesbitt, Robin, **Supp. VIII:** 89

Nessmuk (George Washington Sears), **Supp. XIX:** 10

Nesting Ground, The (Wagoner), **Supp. IX:** 324, **325–326**

Nest of Ninnies, A (Ashbery and Schuyler), **Supp. III Part 1:** 3; **Supp. XV:** 178

"Nests"(Le Sueur), **Supp. XXIII:** 165

Net of Cobwebs (Holding), **Supp. XXII:** 126, **129–130,** 134

Net of Magic: Wonders and Deceptions in India (Siegel), **Supp. XXII:** 262

Nets to Catch the Wind (Wylie), **Supp. I Part 2:** 709, 710–712, 714

Nettleton, Asahel, **I:** 458

"Net to Snare the Moonlight, A" (Lindsay), **Supp. I Part 2:** 387

Neubauer, Carol E., **Supp. IV Part 1:** 9

Neugeboren, Jacob Mordecai. *See* Neugeboren, Jay

Neugeboren, Jay, **Supp. XVI: 217–231**

Neugroschel, Joachim, **Supp. IX:** 138

Neuhaus, Richard John, **Supp. VIII:** 245; **Supp. XIX:** 144

Neumann, Erich, **Supp. I Part 2:** 567; **Supp. IV Part 1:** 68, 69

Neuromancer (W. Gibson), **Supp. XII:** 15; **Supp. XVI:** 117, 119–120, 122, 124, **125–126,** 127, 129, 131

Neurotica: Jewish Writers on Sex (Bukiet, ed.), **Supp. XVII:** 48

"Neurotic America and the Sex Impulse" (Dreiser), **Retro. Supp. II:** 105

Neutra, Richard, **Supp. XVI:** 192

"Never Bet the Devil Your Head" (Poe), **III:** 425; **Retro. Supp. II:** 273

Never Come Morning (Algren), **Supp. IX:** 3, **7–9**

Never in a Hurry: Essays on People and Places (Nye), **Supp. XIII:** 273, **280–282,** 286

"Never Marry a Mexican" (Cisneros), **Supp. VII:** 70

"Never Room with a Couple" (Hughes), **Supp. I Part 1:** 330

"Nevertheless" (Moore), **III:** 214

Nevins, Allan, **I:** 253; **Supp. I Part 2:** 486, 493

"Nevsky Prospekt" (Olds), **Supp. X:** 205

New Adam, The (Untermeyer), **Supp. XV:** 304, 305

New Addresses (Koch), **Supp. XV:** 177, 184

"New Age of the Rhetoricians, The" (Cowley), **Supp. II Part 1:** 135

New American Cyclopedia, **Supp. XVIII:** 4

New American Literature, The (Pattee), **II:** 456

New American Novel of Manners, The (Klinkowitz), **Supp. XI:** 347

"New American Ode, The" (Wright), **Supp. XV:** 346

New American Poetry, 1945–1960, The (Allen, ed.), **Supp. VIII:** 291, 292; **Supp. XIII:** 112; **Supp. XXIII:** 215–216

"New American Writer, A" (W. C. Williams), **Retro. Supp. II:** 335

New and Collected Poems (Reed), **Supp. X:** 241

New and Collected Poems (Wilbur), **Supp. III Part 2:** 562–564

New and Selected Poems (Nemerov), **III:** 269, 275, 277–279

New and Selected Poems (Oliver), **Supp. VII:** 240–241, 245

New and Selected Poems (W. J. Smith), **Supp. XIII:** 332

New and Selected Poems (Wagoner), **Supp. IX: 326–327**

New and Selected Poems, 1958–1998 (Sorrentino), **Supp. XXI:** 229

New and Selected Poems: 1974–1994 (Dunn), **Supp. XI: 151–152**

New and Selected Things Taking Place (Swenson), **Supp. IV Part 2:** 648–650, 651

"New Aristocracy, The" (Atherton), **Supp. XXIV:** 24

"New Art Gallery Society, The" (Wolfe), **Supp. III Part 2:** 580

Newberger, Julee, **Supp. XVIII:** 168

New Black Poetry, The (Major, ed.), **Supp. XXII:** 172, 174, 176, 180

"New Capitalist Tool, The" (Wasserstein), **Supp. XV:** 328

Newcomb, Ralph, **Supp. XIII:** 12

Newcomb, Robert, **II:** 111

New Conscience and an Ancient Evil, A (Addams), **Supp. I Part 1:** 14–15, 16

"New Conservatism in American Poetry, The" (Wakoski), **Supp. XVII:** 112

"New Conservatives, The: Intellectuals in Retreat" (Epstein), **Supp. XIV:** 103

New Criticism, The (Ransom), **III:** 497–498, 499, 501

"New Day, A" (Levine), **Supp. V:** 182

Newdick, Robert Spangler, **Retro. Supp. I:** 138

Newdick's Season of Frost (Newdick), **Retro. Supp. I:** 138

New Dictionary of Quotations, A (Mencken), **III:** 111

New Directions Anthology in Prose and Poetry (Laughlin, ed.), **Supp. XVI:** 284

"New Directions in Poetry" (D. Locke), **Supp. IX:** 273

"New Dog, The: Variations on a Text by Jules Laforgue" (C. Frost), **Supp. XV:** 98

Newell, Henry, **IV:** 193

"New England" (Lowell), **II:** 536

"New England" (Robinson), **III:** 510, 524

"New England Bachelor, A" (Eberhart), **I:** 539

"New Englander, The" (Anderson), **I:** 114

New England Girlhood, A (Larcom), **Supp. XIII:** 137, 142, 143, 144, **147–154**

New England Gothic Literature (Ringel), **Supp. XXII:** 205

New England: Indian Summer (Brooks), **I:** 253, 256

New England Local Color Literature (Donovan), **Retro. Supp. II:** 138

"New England Sabbath-Day Chace, The" (Freneau), **Supp. II Part 1:** 273

New-England Tale, A (Sedgwick), **I:** 341

New England Tragedies, The (Longfellow), **II:** 490, 505, 506; **Retro. Supp. II:** 165, 167

New English Canaan (Morton), **Supp. XXII:** 45

New Era in American Poetry, The (Untermeyer, ed.), **Supp. XV:** 301, 303, 306

Newer Ideals of Peace (Addams), **Supp. I Part 1:** 11–12, 15, 16–17, 19, 20–21

"New Experience in Millinery, A" (Stratton-Porter), **Supp. XX: 216**

New Feminist Criticism, The: Essays on Women, Literature, and Theory (Showalter), **Supp. X:** 97

New Fire: To Put Things Right Again (Moraga), **Supp. XXIII:** 197

"New Folsom Prison" (Matthews), **Supp. IX:** 165

New Formalism, The: A Critical Introduction (McPhillips), **Supp. XV:** 250, 251, 252, 264

Newfound (J. W. Miller), **Supp. XX: 163, 166, 170–172**

New Found Land: Fourteen Poems (MacLeish), **III:** 12–13

"New Hampshire, February" (Eberhart), **I:** 536

New Hampshire: A Poem with Notes and Grace Notes (Frost), **II:** 154–155; **Retro. Supp. I:** 132, 133, 135

New Hard-Boiled Writers (Panek), **Supp. XIV:** 27

"New Home" (Richter), **Supp. XVIII:** 209

New Industrial State, The (Galbraith), **Supp. I Part 2:** 648

"New Journalism, The" (Wolfe), **Supp. III Part 2:** 571

New Journalism, The (Wolfe and Johnson, eds.), **Supp. III Part 2:** 570, 579–581, 583, 586; **Supp. XXIV:** 282

New Left, The: The Anti-Industrial Revolution (Rand), **Supp. IV Part 2:** 527

"New Letters from Thomas Jefferson" (Stafford), **Supp. XI:** 324

New Letters on the Air: Contemporary Writers on Radio, **Supp. X:** 165, 169, 173

"New Life" (Glück), **Supp. V:** 90

New Life, A (Malamud), **Supp. I Part 2:** 429–466

"New Life, The" (Bynner), **Supp. XV:** 44

"New Life, The"(Schott), **Supp. XXIII:** 242

"New Life at Kyerefaso" (Sutherland), **Supp. IV Part 1:** 9

"New Light on Veblen" (Dorfman), **Supp. I Part 2:** 650

"New Man, A" (E. P. Jones), **Supp. XXII:** 144

Newman, Charles, **Supp. I Part 2:** 527, 546–548

Newman, Edwin, **Supp. IV Part 2:** 526

Newman, Frances, **Supp. XXII:** 198

Newman, Judie, **Supp. IV Part 1:** 304, 305

Newman, Paul, **Supp. IV Part 2:** 473, 474

New Man, The (Merton), **Supp. VIII:** 208

"New Mecca, The" (Saunders), **Supp. XIX:** 235, 236

"New Medea, The" (Howells), **II:** 282

New Mexico trilogy (Nichols), **Supp. XIII:** 269

New Morning (album, Dylan), **Supp. XVIII:** 27, 33

"New Mother" (Olds), **Supp. X:** 206

"New Mothers, The" (Shields), **Supp. VII:** 310

New Music (Price), **Supp. VI:** 264, 265

"New Mutants, The" (Fiedler), **Supp. XIII:** 104

"New Name for Some Old Ways of Thinking, A" (James), **II:** 353

New Native American Novel, The: Works in Progress (Bartlett), **Supp. IV Part 1:** 335

"New Natural History, A" (Thurber), **Supp. I Part 2:** 619

New Negro, The (Locke), **Supp. XIX:** 69

"New Negro, The" (Locke), **Supp. XIV:** 201

New Negro, The (Locke, ed.), **Supp. II Part 1:** 176; **Supp. IX:** 309; **Supp. X:** 137; **Supp. XXII:** 8

New Negro, The: An Interpretation (Locke, ed.), **Retro. Supp. I:** 199; **Supp. IV Part 1:** 170; **Supp. XIV:** 195, 201–202

New Negro for a New Century, A (Washington, Wood, and Williams), **Supp. XIV:** 201

New New Journalism, The (R. Boynton), **Supp. XVII:** 209

"New Nomads, The" (E. Hoffman), **Supp. XVI:** 161

"New Orleans" (Carruth), **Supp. XVI:** 50

New Orleans Sketches (Faulkner), **Retro. Supp. I:** 80

New Path to the Waterfall, A (Carver), **Supp. III Part 1:** 138–140, 147, 149; **Supp. XXIV:** 172

"New Poem, The" (Wright), **Supp. V:** 339, 340

"New Poems" (MacLeish), **III:** 19

"New Poems" (Oliver), **Supp. VII:** 240

New Poems 1960 (Bynner), **Supp. XV:** 51

New Poems: 1980–88 (Haines), **Supp. XII:** 209–210

New Poetry, The (Monroe and Henderson, eds.), **Supp. I Part 2:** 387

"New Poetry Handbook, The" (Strand), **Supp. IV Part 2:** 626

New Poetry of Mexico (Strand, trans.), **Supp. IV Part 2:** 630

New Poets of England and America (Hall, Pack, and Simpson, eds.), **Supp. IV Part 2:** 621

"Newport of Anchuria" (Henry), **Supp. II Part 1:** 409

New Princeton Encyclopedia of Poetry and Poetics (Preminger and Brogan, eds.), **Supp. XV:** 250

"*New Republic* Moves Uptown, The" (Cowley), **Supp. II Part 1:** 142

"New Rose Hotel" (W. Gibson), **Supp. XVI:** 120, 122, 124

"News, The" (McClatchy), **Supp. XII:** 269

"New Season" (Levine), **Supp. V:** 188

New Seeds of Contemplation (Merton), **Supp. VIII:** 200, 208

News from the Glacier: Selected Poems 1960–1980 (Haines), **Supp. XII:** 207, 208–209

"News Item" (Parker), **Supp. IX:** 190

New Song, A (Hughes), **Retro. Supp. I:** 202; **Supp. I Part 1:** 328, 331–332

"New Song"(Kenny), **Supp. XXIII:** 156

Newson-Horst, Adele, **Supp. XXIII:** 95

"New South, The" (Lanier), **Supp. I Part 1:** 352, 354, 370

New Southern Girl, The: Female Adolescence in the Works of 12 Women Authors (Town), **Supp. XVIII:** 195

Newspaper Days, 1899–1906 (Mencken), **III:** 100, 102, 120

"New Spirit, The" (Ashbery), **Supp. III Part 1:** 14, 15

New Spoon River, The (Masters), **Supp. I Part 2:** 461–465, 473

New Star Chamber and Other Essays, The (Masters), **Supp. I Part 2:** 455–456, 459

New Tales of the Vampires (Rice), **Supp. VII:** 290

New Tenant, The (Ionesco), **Supp. XXIV:** 113

New Testament, **I:** 303, 457, 458; **II:** 167; **III:** 305; **IV:** 114, 134, 152; **Retro. Supp. I:** 58, 140, 360; **Supp. I Part 1:** 104, 106; **Supp. I Part 2:** 516; **Supp. XVII:** 155; **Supp. XXIII:** 13. *See also* names of New Testament books

New Testament, A (Anderson), **I:** 101, 114

"New Theory of Thorstein Veblen, A" (Galbraith), **Supp. I Part 2:** 650

Newton, Benjamin Franklin, **I:** 454

Newton, Huey P., **Supp. I Part 1:** 66; **Supp. IV Part 1:** 206

Newton, Isaac, **I:** 132, 557; **II:** 6, 103, 348–349; **III:** 428; **IV:** 18, 149

Newton, Maud, **Supp. XXIII:** 290

Newton, Sarah Emily, **Supp. XV:** 234

"New-Wave Format, A" (Mason), **Supp. VIII:** 141, 143, 147

New West of Edward Abbey, The (Ronald), **Supp. XIII:** 4

"New Wife" (Halliday), **Supp. XIX:** 89

New Wolves, The: The Return of the Mexican Wolf to the American Southwest (Bass), **Supp. XVI:** 26–27

New Woman's Survival Sourcebook, The (Rennie and Grimstead, eds.), **Supp. I Part 2:** 569

New World, The (Bronk), **Supp. XXI:** 25–26, 31

New World, The (Bynner), **Supp. XV:** 41, 42

New World, The: Tales (Banks), **Supp. V:** 8, 9, 10

New World Naked, A (Mariani), **Retro. Supp. I:** 419

New Worlds of Literature (Beaty and Hunter, eds.), **Supp. IV Part 1:** 331

New World Writing (Updike), **IV:** 217

New Year Letter (Auden), **Supp. II Part 1:** 14, 16

"New Year's Day" (Wharton), **Retro. Supp. I:** 381

"New Year's Eve" (Schwartz), **Supp. II Part 2:** 640, 656–657

New Year's Eve/1929 (Farrell), **II:** 43

"New Year's Eve 1968" (Lowell), **II:** 554

New Year's Eve: A Play (W. Frank), **Supp. XX:** 75

"New Year's Gift, The" (Stowe), **Supp. I Part 2:** 587

"New Year Two Thousand, The" (Weigl), **Supp. XIX:** 287–288

"New York" (Capote), **Supp. III Part 1:** 122

"New York" (Moore), **III:** 196, 198, 202, 206

"New York 1965" (Bowles), **Supp. IV Part 1:** 94

New York: A Serendipiter's Journey (Talese), **Supp. XVII:** 202, 203

"New York Breeze" (Halliday), **Supp. XIX:** 85

New York City Arts Project, **Supp. III Part 2:** 618

"New York City in 1979"(Acker), **Supp. XII:** 5

New York Edition, **Retro. Supp. I:** 235

"New York Edition" (James), **II:** 336, 337

"New York Gold Conspiracy, The" (Adams), **I:** 4

New York Hat, The (film; Griffith), **Supp. XVI:** 183

New York Intellectuals, **Supp. VIII:** 93

"New York Intellectuals, The" (Howe), **Supp. VI:** 120

"New York Is a City of Things Unnoticed" (Talese), **Supp. XVII:** 202, 209

New York: Its Upper Ten and Lower Million (Lippard), **Supp. XXIII:** 180, 183, 184

New York Jew (Kazin), **Supp. VIII:** 95, **97–100**

"New York Theater: Isn't It Romantic" (Wasserstein), **Supp. XV:** 320

New York Trilogy, The (Auster), **Supp. XII:** 21, **24–28**

Next (McNally), **Supp. XIII:** 197

"Next in Line, The" (Bradbury), **Supp. IV Part 1:** 102

Next Room of the Dream, The (Nemerov), **III:** 269, 275, 278, 279–280, 284

"Next Time I Crossed the Line into Oklahoma, The" (Wright), **Supp. XV:** 345

Next-to-Last Things: New Poems and Essays (Kunitz), **Supp. III Part 1:** 257–259, 261, 262, 265, 266, 268

"'Next to Reading Matter' " (Henry), **Supp. II Part 1:** 399

Nexus (H. Miller), **III:** 170, 187, 188, 189

Niatum, Duane, **Supp. IV Part 1:** 331; **Supp. IV Part 2:** 505

Nice and Noir (Schwartz), **Supp. XIV:** 23

"Nice Girl" (Nelson), **Supp. XVIII:** 178

Nice Jewish Boy, The (P. Roth), **Supp. III Part 2:** 412

Nicholas II, Tsar, **Supp. I Part 2:** 447

"Nicholas in the Park" (Halliday), **Supp. XIX:** 88

Nicholls, Peter, **Supp. XIX:** 232

Nichols, Charles, **Retro. Supp. I:** 194

Nichols, Dudley, **Supp. XVIII:** 247

Nichols, John Treadwell, **Supp. XIII:** **253–272**

Nichols, Luther, **Supp. X:** 265

Nichols, Mike, **Supp. IV Part 1:** 234; **Supp. IV Part 2:** 577

Nicholson, Colin, **Supp. VIII:** 129

Nicholson, Harold, **Supp. XIV:** 163

Nicholson, Jack, **Supp. V:** 26; **Supp. VIII:** 45; **Supp. XI:** 308

Nicholson, John, **Supp. XVI:** 293

Nick Adams Stories, The (Hemingway), **II:** 258; **Retro. Supp. I:** 174

"Nick and the Candlestick" (Plath), **Supp. I Part 2:** 544

Nickel and Dimed: On (Not) Getting By in America (Ehrenreich), **Supp. XVII:** 210

Nickel Mountain: A Pastoral Novel (Gardner), **Supp. VI:** 63, 64, 68, **69**

"Nicodemus" (Keillor), **Supp. XVI:** 167

Nicoll, Allardyce, **III:** 400

Nicoloff, Philip, **II:** 7

Niebuhr, Gustav, **III:** 292

Niebuhr, H. Richard, **I:** 494

Niebuhr, Lydia, **III:** 292

Niebuhr, Reinhold, **III: 290–313; Supp. I Part 2:** 654; **Supp. XX:** 79

Niedecker, Lorine, **Supp. III Part 2:** 616, 623; **Supp. XIV:** 287; **Supp. XXIII:** 174

Nielsen, Ed, **Supp. IX:** 254

Nielson, Dorothy, **Supp. I Part 2:** 659

Nietzsche, Friedrich Wilhelm, **I:** 227, 283, 383, 389, 396, 397, 402, 509; **II:** 7, 20, 27, 42, 90, 145, 262, 462, 463, 577, 583, 585; **III:** 102–103, 113, 156, 176; **IV:** 286, 491; **Supp. I Part 1:** 254, 299, 320; **Supp. I Part 2:** 646; **Supp. IV Part 1:** 104, 105–106, 107, 110, 284; **Supp. IV Part 2:** 519; **Supp. V:** 277, 280; **Supp. VIII:** 11, 181, 189; **Supp. X:** 48; **Supp. XII:** 98; **Supp. XIV:** 339; **Supp. XX:** 117

Nieves, Felipe, **Supp. XVIII:** 90

Niflis, N. Michael, **Supp. IV Part 1:** 175

Niger, S. *See* Charney, Samuel

Nigger Heaven (Van Vechten), **Supp. II Part 2:** 739, 744–746; **Supp. XVIII:** 123, 127; **Supp. XIX:** 76

"Nigger Jeff" (Dreiser), **Retro. Supp. II:** 97

Nigger of the "Narcissus," The (Conrad), **II:** 91; **Retro. Supp. I:** 106; **Supp. XVIII:** 224; **Supp. XXIV:** 286

"NIGGY THE HO" (Baraka), **Supp. II Part 1:** 54

"Night, Death, Mississippi" (Hayden), **Supp. II Part 1:** 369

'*Night, Mother* (Norman), **Supp. VIII:** 141

"Night above the Avenue" (Merwin), **Supp. III Part 1:** 355

"Night among the Horses, A" (Barnes), **Supp. III Part 1:** 33–34, 39, 44

"Night and the Madman" (Gibran), **Supp. XX:** 118

Night at the Movies, A, or, You Must Remember This: Fictions (Coover), **Supp. V:** 50–51

"Night at the Opera, A" (Matthews), **Supp. IX:** 167

"Night before the Sentence Is Carried Out, The" (Wright), **Supp. XV:** 341

"Nightbird" (Komunyakaa), **Supp. XIII:** 132

Night-Blooming Cereus, The (Hayden), **Supp. II Part 1:** 367, 373

"Night-Blooming Cereus, The" (Hayden), **Supp. II Part 1:** 367

Night-Born, The (London), **II:** 467

"Nightbreak" (Rich), **Supp. I Part 2:** 556

"Nightclub" (Collins), **Supp. XXI:** 60

Night Dance (Price), **Supp. VI:** 264

"Night Dances, The" (Plath), **Supp. I Part 2:** 544

"Night Dream, The" (MacLeish), **III:** 15

"Night Ferry" (Doty), **Supp. XI:** 124

"Nightfishing" (Schnackenberg), **Supp. XV:** 254

"Nighthawks"(Dybek), **Supp. XXIII:** 73, 74

"Night I Met Little Floyd, The" (Wright), **Supp. XV:** 345–346

Night in Acadie, A (Chopin), **Retro. Supp. II: 66–67,** 73; **Supp. I Part 1:** 200, 219, 220, 224

"Night in Acadie, A" (Chopin), **Retro. Supp. II:** 66

"Night in June, A" (W. C. Williams), **Retro. Supp. I:** 424

"Night in New Arabia, A" (Henry), **Supp. II Part 1:** 402

Night in Question, The: Stories (Wolff), **Supp. VII:** 342–344

"Night Journey" (Roethke), **Supp. III Part 1:** 260

"Night Letter to the Reader" (Collins), **Supp. XXI:** 55

Night Light (Justice), **Supp. VII:** 126–127

"Nightmare" (Kumin), **Supp. IV Part 2:** 442

Nightmare Factory, The (Kumin), **Supp. IV Part 2:** 444–447, 451

"Nightmare Factory, The" (Kumin), **Supp. IV Part 2:** 445, 453

Nightmare on Main Street (Poe), **Retro. Supp. II:** 262

"Nightmare" poems (Benét), **Supp. XI:** 46, 58

"Night Mirror" (L.-Y. Lee), **Supp. XV:** 225

Night Music (Odets), **Supp. II Part 2:** 541, 543, 544

"Night of First Snow" (R. Bly), **Supp. IV Part 1:** 71

Night of January 16th (Rand), **Supp. IV Part 2:** 527

Night of the Iguana, The (T. Williams), **IV:** 382, 383, 384, 385, 386, 387, 388, 391, 392, 393, 394, 395, 397, 398

"Night of the Iguana, The" (T. Williams), **IV:** 384

"Night of the Living Beanfield: How an Unsuccessful Cult Novel Became an Unsuccessful Cult Film in Only Fourteen Years, Eleven Nervous Breakdowns, and $20 Million" (Nichols), **Supp. XIII:** 267

Night Passage (Parker), **Supp. XIX:** 185–186

Night Rider (Warren), **IV:** 243, 246–247

Nights (Doolittle), **Supp. I Part 1:** 270, 271

Nights and Days (Merrill), **Supp. III Part 1:** 319, 320, 322–325

"Nights and Days" (Rich), **Supp. I Part 2:** 574

"Night's for Cryin,' The" (C. Himes), **Supp. XVI:** 137

"Night Shift" (Plath), **Supp. I Part 2:** 538

"Nightshine Beyond Memory, A: Ten More Years with Ray" (Gallagher), **Supp. XXIV:** 167, 172

Night-Side (Oates), **Supp. II Part 2:** 522

"Night-Side" (Oates), **Supp. II Part 2:** 523

Night-Side, The (Skloot), **Supp. XX: 193, 196, 205, 208**

Nights in the Gardens of Brooklyn (Swados), **Supp. XIX: 261–264**

"Nights in the Gardens of Brooklyn" (Swados), **Supp. XIX:** 261

"Night Sketches: Beneath an Umbrella" (Hawthorne), **II:** 235–237, 238, 239, 242; **Supp. XXI:** 201

"Night Sport" (Hoffman), **Supp. XVIII:** 86, 87

"Night-Sweat" (Lowell), **II:** 554

"Night-Talk" (Ellison), **Retro. Supp. II:** 126; **Supp. II Part 1:** 248

Night Thoughts (Young), **III:** 415

"Night-Time River Road, A" (Ferry), **Supp. XXIV:** 150

Night Traveler, The (Oliver), **Supp. VII:** 233

"Night Watch" (Gioia), **Supp. XV:** 117

"Night Watch, The" (Wright), **Supp. V:** 339

"Night We All Had Grippe, The" (Jackson), **Supp. IX:** 118

Nightwood (Barnes), **Supp. III Part 1:** 31, 32, 35–37, 39–43

Night World and the Word Night, The (F. Wright), **Supp. XVII:** 240, 244–245

"Nihilist as Hero, The" (Lowell), **II:** 554; **Retro. Supp. II:** 190

Nijinsky, Vaslav, **Supp. XV:** 28–29

Nikolai Gogol (Nabokov), **Retro. Supp. I:** 266

"Nilda" (Díaz), **Supp. XXIV:** 92

Niles, Thomas, **Retro. Supp. I:** 35

Niles, Thomas, Jr., **Supp. I Part 1:** 39

Nilsson, Christine, **Supp. I Part 1:** 355

Nilsson, Harry, **Supp. XI:** 309

Nilsson, Jenny Lind, **Supp. XVI:** 177

Nimitz, Chester, **Supp. I Part 2:** 491

"Nimram" (Gardner), **Supp. VI:** 73

Nims, John Frederick, **III:** 527; **Supp. XVII:** 112

Nin, Anaïs, **III:** 182, 184, 190; **Supp. III Part 1:** 43; **Supp. IV Part 2:** 680; **Supp. X: 181–200; Supp. XIX:** 134

"9" (Oliver), **Supp. VII:** 244

"9 Failures of the Imagination" (Lethem), **Supp. XVIII:** 148

"Nine-Ball" (Offutt), **Supp. XIX:** 166, 167

Nine Dragons (Connelly), **Supp. XXI:** 74, **79–80**

"Nine from Eight" (Lanier), **Supp. I Part 1:** 352–354

Nine Gates: Entering the Mind of Poetry (Hirshfield), **Supp. XXIII:** 136, 137

Nine Headed Dragon River: Zen Journals 1969–1982 (Matthiessen), **Supp. V:** 199

Nine Horses (Collins), **Supp. XXI:** 55, 60, 61, 62, 65

"Nine Horses" (Collins), **Supp. XXI:** 61

Ninemile Wolves,The (Bass), **Supp. XVI:** 24–25, 26

"Nine Nectarines" (Moore), **III:** 203, 209, 215

Nine Plays (Reznikoff), **Supp. XIV:** 288

"Nine Poems for the Unborn Child" (Rukeyser), **Supp. VI:** 280–281, 284

Nine Stories (Nabokov), **Retro. Supp. I:** 266

Nine Stories (Salinger), **III:** 552, 558–564

"19 Hadley Street" (Schnackenberg), **Supp. XV:** 253

19 Necromancers from Now (Reed), **Supp. X:** 240

19 Varieties of Gazelle (Nye), **Supp. XIII:** 275, **286–288**

"19 Varieties of Gazelle" (Nye), **Supp. XIII:** 286

1984 (Orwell), **Supp. XIII:** 29; **Supp. XVIII:** 137, 138

"1940" (Stafford), **Supp. XI:** 328–329

"1945–1985: Poem for the Anniversary" (Oliver), **Supp. VII:** 237

1919 (Dos Passos), **I:** 482, 485–486, 487, 489, 490, 492

"1975" (Wright), **Supp. V:** 341

"1973"(Hirshfield), **Supp. XXIII:** 130

"1910" (Mora), **Supp. XIII:** 215

"1938" (Komunyakaa), **Supp. XIII:** 114

1939 (Boyle), **Supp. XXIV:** 62

"1939" (Taylor), **Supp. V:** 316

1933 (Levine), **Supp. V:** 185–187

"1933" (Levine), **Supp. V:** 188

"Nineteenth New York, The" (Doctorow), **Supp. IV Part 1:** 232

"1929" (Auden), **Supp. II Part 1:** 6

"1926" (Kees), **Supp. XV:** 135

"93990" (Saunders), **Supp. XIX:** 233

"90 North" (Jarrell), **II:** 370, 371

90 Trees (Zukofsky), **Supp. III Part 2:** 631

95 Poems (Cummings), **I:** 430, 433, 435, 439, 446, 447

"91 Revere Street" (Lowell), **II:** 547; **Retro. Supp. II:** 188; **Supp. XI:** 240

Ninety Percent of Everything (Lethem, Kelly and Kessel), **Supp. XVIII:** 145

"92 Days" (L. Brown), **Supp. XXI:** 44–45

"Nine Years Later" (Brodsky), **Supp. VIII:** 32

"Nirvana" (Lanier), **Supp. I Part 1:** 352

Nirvana Blues, The (Nichols), **Supp. XIII:** 266, 267

Nishikigi (play), **III:** 466

Niven, David, **Supp. XI:** 307

Nixon (film), **Supp. XIV:** 48

Nixon, Richard M., **I:** 376; **III:** 38, 46; **Supp. I Part 1:** 294, 295; **Supp. V:** 45, 46, 51; **Supp. XII:** 14; **Supp. XIV:** 306

"NJ Transit" (Komunyakaa), **Supp. XIII:** 132

Nketia, J. H., **Supp. IV Part 1:** 10

Nketsia, Nana, **Supp. IV Part 1:** 2, 10

Nkize, Julius, **Supp. IV Part 1:** 361

Nkrumah, Kwame, **I:** 490, 494; **Supp. IV Part 1:** 361; **Supp. X:** 135

Nkrumah and the Ghana Revolution (C. L. R. James), **Supp. XXI:** 159, 171–172

NO (Major), **Supp. XXII:** 174

Noailles, Anna de, **IV:** 328

Noa Noa (Gauguin), **I:** 34

Nobel Lecture (Singer), **Retro. Supp. II:** 300

"No Better Than a 'Withered Daffodil'" (Moore), **III:** 216

Noble, David W., **Supp. I Part 2:** 650

Noble, Marianne, **Supp. XVIII:** 267

"Noble Rider and the Sound of Words, The" (Stevens), **Retro. Supp. I:** 299

Noble Savage, The (Coover), **Supp. V:** 40

"No Bobolink reverse His Singing" (Dickinson), **Retro. Supp. I:** 45

Nobodaddy (MacLeish), **III:** 5–6, 8, 10, 11, 18, 19, 20

"Nobodaddy" (W. Blake), **Supp. XVII:** 245

"Nobody in Hollywood" (Bausch), **Supp. VII:** 54

Nobody Knows My Name (Baldwin), **Supp. XIII:** 111

"Nobody Knows My Name" (Baldwin), **Retro. Supp. II:** 8; **Supp. I Part 1:** 52

Nobody Knows My Name: More Notes of a Native Son (Baldwin), **Retro. Supp. II:** 6, 8; **Supp. I Part 1:** 47, 52, 55

"Nobody knows this little Rose" (Dickinson), **Retro. Supp. I:** 30

"Nobody Said Anything" (Carver), **Supp. III Part 1:** 141

"Nobody's Business" (Lahiri), **Supp. XXI:** 183

Nobody's Fool (Russo), **Supp. XII:** 326, **331–335**, 340

"No Change of Place" (Auden), **Supp. II Part 1:** 5

"Noche Triste, La" (Frost), **Retro. Supp. I:** 123

Nock, Albert Jay, **I:** 245; **Supp. IV Part 2:** 521, 524

"No Coward Soul Is Mine" (Brontë), **I:** 458

"No Crime in the Mountains" (Chandler), **Supp. IV Part 1:** 129

"Nocturne" (Komunyakaa), **Supp. XIII:** 126

"Nocturne" (MacLeish), **III:** 8

"Nocturne at Bethesda" (Bontemps), **Supp. XXII:** 3, 8

"Nocturne in a Deserted Brickyard" (Sandburg), **III:** 586

Nocturne of Remembered Spring (Aiken), **I:** 50

No Direction Home (documentary film, Scorsese), **Supp. XVIII:** 22, 23, 29

No Direction Home (Shelton), **Supp. XVIII:** 21

No Door (Wolfe), **IV:** 451–452, 456

"No Door" (Wolfe), **IV:** 456

"No Epitaph" (Carson), **Supp. XII:** 111

No Exit (Sartre), **I:** 82, 130; **Supp. XIV:** 320

No Exit (Sartre; Bowles, trans.), **Supp. IV Part 1:** 84

No Gifts from Chance (Benstock), **Retro. Supp. I:** 361

"No-Good Blues" (Komunyakaa), **Supp. XIII:** 130

No Hero (Marquand), **III:** 57

No Heroes: A Memoir of Coming Home (Offutt), **Supp. XIX:** 163, **172–174**, 175

No! In Thunder (Fiedler), **Supp. XIII:** 101

"Noiseless Patient Spider" (Whitman), **III:** 555; **IV:** 348; **Supp. IV Part 1:** 325

Noises Off (Frayn), **Supp. IV Part 2:** 582

Noi vivi. See We the Living (film)

"No Jury Would Convict" (Shaw), **Supp. XIX:** 245

"No Lamp Has Ever Shown Us Where to Look" (MacLeish), **III:** 9

Nolan, Sidney, **Retro. Supp. II:** 189

No Laughing Matter (Heller and Vogel), **Supp. IV Part 1:** 384, 389

No Love Lost, a Romance of Travel (Howells), **II:** 277

Nomad (Ali), **Supp. XXIV:** 15

No Man Is an Island (Merton), **Supp. VIII:** 207

"No More This Home" (Taggard), **Supp. XXII:** 277, 280

No Mother to Guide Her (Loos), **Supp. XVI:** 194

No Name in the Street (Baldwin), **Retro. Supp. II:** 13, 14; **Supp. I Part 1:** 47, 48, 52, 65–66, 67

No Nature: New and Selected Poems (Snyder), **Supp. VIII: 305**

Nonconformist's Memorial, The (Howe), **Supp. IV Part 2:** 434, 435–436

Nonconformity (Algren), **Supp. IX:** 15

None but the Lonely Heart (film), **Supp. II Part 2:** 546

Nones (Auden), **Supp. II Part 1:** 21

"Nones" (Auden), **Supp. II Part 1:** 22–23

None Shall Look Back (Gordon), **II:** 205–207, 208

"No No, Bad Daddy" (Nelson), **Supp. XVIII:** 177, 178

"Non-Tenured" (Halliday), **Supp. XIX:** 90, 91

Nonverbal Communication: Notes on the Visual Perception of Human Relations (Kees and Ruesch), **Supp. XV:** 147

"Noon" (Bryant), **Supp. I Part 1:** 157

No One Belongs Here More Than You (July), **Supp. XXIV:** 199, **200–207**

"No One Remembers" (Levine), **Supp. V:** 187

"Noon Walk on the Asylum Lawn" (Sexton), **Supp. II Part 2:** 673

"Noon Wine" (Porter), **III:** 436, 437–438, 442, 446

"No Pain Whatsoever" (Yates), **Supp. XI:** 341

"No Place for You, My Love" (Welty), **IV:** 278, 279; **Retro. Supp. I:** 353

No Plays of Japan, The (Waley), **III:** 466

No Pockets in a Shroud (McCoy), **Supp. XIII:** 166–168, 171, 172, 173, 174

"No Poem So Fine" (Francis), **Supp. IX:** 83

Norcross, Frances, **I:** 456, 462

Norcross, Louise, **I:** 456, 462

Nordfeldt, B. J. O., **Supp. XXI:** 6

Nordfeldt, Margaret, **Supp. XXI:** 6

Nordyke, Lewis, **Supp. XIII:** 5

No Relief (Dixon), **Supp. XII:** 139, **142–143**

No Resting Place (Humphrey), **Supp. IX:** 94, **106–108**

Norfolk Poems, The (Carruth), **Supp. XVI:** 47, 48

Norma (Bellini), **IV:** 309

Norma Ashe (Glaspell), **Supp. III Part 1:** 175, 186–187

"Normal Life, A"(Thompson), **Supp. XXIII:** 300

"Normal Motor Adjustments" (Stein and Solomons), **IV:** 26

Norman, Charles, **III:** 479

Norman, Gurney, **Supp. X:** 24; **Supp. XXIII:** 42

Norman, Jessye, **Supp. XX:** 110

Norman, Marsha, **Supp. VIII:** 141; **Supp. XXI:** 145; **Supp. XXIV:** 124

Norman Mailer (Poirier), **Retro. Supp. II:** 207–208

Norman Mailer: Modern Critical Views (Bloom), **Retro. Supp. II:** 205

Norman Mailer Revisited (Merrill), **Retro. Supp. II:** 201

Norna; or, The Witch's Curse (Alcott), **Supp. I Part 1:** 33

Norris, Charles, **III:** 320; **Retro. Supp. I:** 100; **Supp. XVIII:** 226

Norris, Frank, **I:** 211, 355, 500, 506, 517, 518, 519; **II:** 89, 264, 276, 289, 307; **III:** 227, **314–336,** 596; **IV:** 29; **Retro. Supp. I:** 100, 325; **Retro. Supp. II:** 96, 101; **Supp. III Part 2:** 412; **Supp. VIII:** 101, 102; **Supp. IX:** 14, 15; **Supp. XV:** 115

"North" (Budbill), **Supp. XIX:** 7–8

"North" (Hugo), **Supp. VI:** 135

North, Milou (pseudonym), **Supp. IV Part 1:** 260. See also Dorris, Michael; Erdrich, Louise

North, Sir Thomas, **IV:** 370

"North American Sequence" (Roethke), **I:** 171–172, 183; **III:** 529, 545, 547, 548

"North Beach" (Snyder), **Supp. VIII:** 289

North Country: A Personal Journey Through the Borderland (Mosher), **Supp. XXII:** 203–204, 206, 212, **217–218**

"North Country Sketches" (McClatchy), **Supp. XII:** 256

"Northeast Playground" (Paley), **Supp. VI:** 226–227, 229

Northern Borders (Mosher), **Supp. XXII:** 203, 204, 206, 207, 208, 209, **213–214**

Northern Lights (O'Brien), **Supp. V:** 237, 239, 241–244, 250

"Northern Motive" (Levine), **Supp. V:** 195

Northfield Poems (Ammons), **Supp. VII:** 29

"Northhanger Ridge" (Wright), **Supp. V:** 335, 340

"North Haven" (Bishop), **Retro. Supp. II:** 50

"North Labrador" (Crane), **I:** 386

North of Boston (Frost), **II:** 152, 153–154, 527; **Retro. Supp. I:** 121, 125, 127, **128–130,** 131; **Supp. I Part 1:** 263; **Supp. XIII:** 146

North of Jamaica (Simpson), **Supp. IV Part 2:** 448; **Supp. IX:** 275, 276

North of the Danube (Caldwell), **I:** 288, 290, 293, 294, 309, 310

North: Poems of Home (Kenny), **Supp. XXIII:** 147–148

Northrup, Cyrus, **Supp. I Part 1:** 350

North Sea (Jarman), **Supp. XVII:** 110, 113

"North Sea Undertaker's Complaint, The" (Lowell), **II:** 550

North & South (Bishop), **Retro. Supp. II: 41–43; Supp. I Part 1:** 72, 84, 85, 89

North Star, The (Hellman), **Supp. I Part 1:** 281

Northup, Solomon, **Supp. XIV:** 32

"Northwest Writers at Work" (Baker), **Supp. XXIV:** 178

"North Winter" (Carruth), **Supp. XVI:** 53

Norton, Charles Eliot, **I:** 223, 568; **II:** 279, 322–323, 338; **Retro. Supp. I:** 371; **Retro. Supp. II:** 135; **Supp. I Part 1:** 103; **Supp. I Part 2:** 406, 479

Norton, Jody, **Supp. VIII:** 297

Norton, John, **Supp. I Part 1:** 99, 110, 112, 114

Norton Anthology of African American Literature, The (H. L. Gates and McKay, eds.), **Supp. X:** 325; **Supp. XX: 105**

Norton Anthology of American Literature, **Supp. X:** 325; **Supp. XV:** 270

Norton Anthology of Literature by Women (Gilbert and Gubar, eds.), **Supp. XV:** 270

Norton Anthology of Modern Poetry, The, **Supp. XI:** 259; **Supp. XV:** 258; **Supp. XXIV:** 35, 39

Norton Anthology of Poetry, The, **Supp. XVIII:** 20

Norton Anthology of Short Fiction, The, **Supp. IX:** 4

Norton Book of Personal Essays, The, **Supp. XIV:** 105

Norton Lectures, **Retro. Supp. I:** 65

Norwood, Vera, **Supp. IX:** 24

No Safe Harbour (Porter), **III:** 447

Nosferatu: An Opera Libretto (Gioia), **Supp. XV:** 112, **128**

"Nosferatu's Serenade" (Gioia), **Supp. XV:** 128

No Siege Is Absolute (Char; version of F. Wright), **Supp. XVII:** 244

"No Snake" (A. Finch), **Supp. XVII:** 72

"No Speak English" (Cisneros), **Supp. VII:** 63

"Nostalgia" (Collins), **Supp. XXI:** 57

"Nostalgia" (Saunders), **Supp. XIX:** 235

Nostalgia for 70 (J. W. Miller), **Supp. XX: 165**

"Nostalgia of the Lakefronts" (Justice), **Supp. VII:** 118, 119, 120

"Nostalgic Mood" (Farrell), **II:** 45

No Star Is Lost (Farrell), **II:** 34, 35, 44

Nostrandt, Jeanne, **Supp. XVIII:** 80–81

Nostromo (Conrad), **II:** 600; **IV:** 245

"Nosty Fright, A" (Swenson), **Supp. IV Part 2:** 651

Not about Nightingales (T. Williams), **IV:** 381

"Not a Sparrow" (Gallagher), **Supp. XXIV:** 171

"Not a Womb in the House" (Quindlen), **Supp. XVII:** 166, 171

Not Coming to Be Barked At (Kooser), **Supp. XIX:** 116, **120**

Not Dancing (Dunn), **Supp. XI:** 143, **148**

"Note about *Iconographs,* A" (Swenson), **Supp. IV Part 2:** 646

Notebook (Lowell), **Retro. Supp. II:** 186, 190; **Supp. V:** 343

Notebook 1967–68 (Lowell), **II:** 553–555; **Retro. Supp. II:** 182, 186, 190

Notebook of Malte Laurids Brigge, The (Rilke), **III:** 571

Notebooks (Fitzgerald), **Retro. Supp. I:** 110

Notebooks of Captain George, The (Renoir), **Supp. XXII:** 257

No Telephone to Heaven (Cliff), **Supp. XXII:** 66, 69, 71–72

"Note on Abraham Lincoln" (Vidal), **Supp. IV Part 2:** 688

"Note on Commercial Theatre" (Hughes), **Retro. Supp. I:** 207

"Note on Ezra Pound, A" (Eliot), **Retro. Supp. I:** 290

"Note on Lanier's Music, A" (P. Graham), **Supp. I Part 1:** 373

Note on Literary Criticism, A (Farrell), **II:** 26, 49

"Note on Poetry, A" (Doolittle), **Supp. I Part 1:** 254, 267–268

"Note on Realism, A" (Anderson), **I:** 110

"Note on the Limits of 'History' and the Limits of 'Criticism,' A" (Brooks), **Supp. XIV:** 11

"Note on the Poetry of Love, A" (Untermeyer), **Supp. XV:** 304

"Note on the Truth of the Tales, A" (Vollmann), **Supp. XVII:** 230

"Notes" (Dove), **Supp. IV Part 1:** 246

"Notes for a Moving Picture: The House" (Agee), **I:** 33, 34

"Notes for an Autobiography" (Van Vechten), **Supp. II Part 2:** 749

"Notes for a Novel About the End of the World" (Percy), **Supp. III Part 1:** 393

"Notes for a Preface" (Sandburg), **III:** 591, 596–597

"NOTES FOR A SPEECH" (Baraka), **Supp. II Part 1:** 33

Notes for the Green Box (Duchamp), **Supp. IV Part 2:** 423

Notes for the Two-Dollar Window: Portraits from an American Neighborhood (Kriegel), **Supp. XXIV: 223–224**

Notes from a Bottle Found on the Beach at Carmel (Connell), **Supp. XIV:** 80, 87, 96, 97

Notes from a Sea Diary: Hemingway All the Way (Algren), **Supp. IX:** 16

"Notes from the Childhood and Girlhood" (Brooks), **Supp. III Part 1:** 77

"Notes from the River" (Stern), **Supp. IX:** 285, 287, 294, 295

Notes from Underground (Dostoevsky), **III:** 571; **IV:** 485; **Retro. Supp. II:** 121

Notes Left Behind: Last and Selected Poems (Hayford), **Supp. XXII:** 218

"Notes of a Faculty Wife" (Jackson), **Supp. IX:** 126

"Notes of a Native Daughter" (Didion), **Supp. IV Part 1:** 196, 197, 200, 201

Notes of a Native Son (Baldwin), **Retro. Supp. II:** 1, 2, 3, 5, 6; **Supp. I Part 1:** 50, 52, 54; **Supp. IV Part 1:** 163

"Notes of a Native Son" (Baldwin), **Supp. I Part 1:** 50, 54

Notes of a Son and Brother (James), **II:** 337; **Retro. Supp. I:** 235

"Notes on a Departure" (Trilling), **Supp. III Part 2:** 498

"Notes on Babbitt and More" (Wilson), **IV:** 435

"Notes on 'Camp' " (Sontag), **Supp. III Part 2:** 455–456; **Supp. XIV:** 167

Notes on Democracy (Mencken), **III:** 104, 107–108, 109, 116, 119

Notes on Dialectics (C. L. R. James), **Supp. XXI:** 169

"Notes on Free Verse" (Dobyns), **Supp. XIII:** 77

"Notes on 'Layover' " (Hass), **Supp. VI:** 109

"Notes on Memory and Enthusiasm" (Di Piero), **Supp. XIX:** 42

Notes on Novelists (James), **II:** 336, 337; **Retro. Supp. I:** 235

"Notes on Nukes, Nookie, and Neo-Romanticism" (Robbins), **Supp. X:** 272

"Notes on Poetry" (Eberhart), **I:** 524, 527–528, 529

"Notes on Teaching"(Hadas), **Supp. XXIII:** 122

"Notes on the Craft of Poetry" (Strand), **Supp. IV Part 2:** 626

"Notes on the Decline of Outrage" (Dickey), **Supp. IV Part 1:** 181

"Notes on the New Formalism" (Gioia), **Supp. XV:** 113, 114–115

"Notes on the Novel-as-Autobiography" (P. Bailey), **Supp. XVI:** 69

"Notes on 'The Poetry of Everday Life' " (Notley), **Supp. XXII:** 232

Notes on the State of Virginia (1781–1782) (Jefferson), **Supp. XIV:** 191

"Notes to Be Left in a Cornerstone" (Benét), **Supp. XI:** 46, 58

"Notes toward a Supreme Fiction" (Stevens), **IV:** 87–89; **Retro. Supp. I:** 300, 306, **306–309,** 311; **Supp. I Part 1:** 80

"Notes towards a Poem That Can Never Be Written" (Atwood), **Supp. XIII:** 34–35

"Not Exactly for Talia" (Halliday), **Supp. XIX:** 94

No Thanks (Cummings), **I:** 430, 431, 432, 436, 437, 441, 443, 446

Not Heaven: A Novel in the Form of Prelude, Variations, and Theme (W. Frank), **Supp. XX: 80**

"Nothing" (C. Frost), **Supp. XV:** 94

"Nothing Big" (Komunyakaa), **Supp. XIII:** 121

Nothing Ever Breaks Except the Heart (Boyle), **Supp. XXIV:** 59

Nothing for Tigers (Carruth), **Supp. XVI:** 47, 48, 50

"Nothing Gold Can Stay" (Frost), **Retro. Supp. I:** 133

"Nothing in Heaven Functions as It Ought" (X. J. Kennedy), **Supp. XV:** 158–159

Nothing Makes You Free: Writings by Descendants of Jewish Holocaust Survivors (Bukiet, ed.), **Supp. XVII: 39–40,** 48–49

"Nothing Missing" (O'Hara), **III:** 369

Nothing Personal (Baldwin), **Supp. I Part 1:** 58, 60

Nothing Sacred (film), **Supp. XVIII:** 243

"Nothing Song, The" (Snodgrass), **Supp. VI:** 326

"Nothing Stays Put" (Clampitt), **Supp. IX:** 42

"Nothing Will Yield" (Nemerov), **III:** 279

No Third Path (Kosinski), **Supp. VII:** 215

"Not Ideas About the Thing but the Thing Itself" (Stevens), **IV:** 87

"No Time" (Collins), **Supp. XXI:** 61

Notions of the Americans: Picked up by a Travelling Bachelor (Cooper), **I:** 343–345, 346

"Not-Knowing" (Barthelme), **Supp. IV Part 1:** 48

"Not Leaving the House" (Snyder), **Supp. VIII:** 300

Notley, Alice, **Supp. XXII: 223–238; Supp. XXIII:** 221; **Supp. XXIV:** 35, 37, 39, 41, 43, 45

"'Not Marble nor the Gilded Monument' " (MacLeish), **III:** 12

Not Mine to Finish: Poems, 1928–1934 (Taggard), **Supp. XXII:** 280

"Not My Bones" (Nelson), **Supp. XVIII:** 183

Not Now But Now (M. F. K. Fisher), **Supp. XVII:** 86, 90

"Not Quite Social" (Frost), **II:** 156

"Not Sappho, Sacco" (Rukeyser), **Supp. VI:** 277

"Not Sixteen" (Anderson), **I:** 114

"Not Slightly" (Stein), **IV:** 44

Not So Deep as a Well (Parker), **Supp. IX:** 192

"Not Somewhere Else, but Here" (Rich), **Supp. I Part 2:** 552, 573

Not-So-Simple Neil Simon (McGovern), **Supp. IV Part 2:** 573

Not So Simple: The "Simple" Stories by Langston Hughes (Harper), **Retro. Supp. I:** 194, 209

"Not the Point" (Cameron), **Supp. XII:** 83

"Not They Who Soar" (Dunbar), **Supp. II Part 1:** 199

Not This Pig (Levine), **Supp. V:** 178, 181, 182–183

"Not to Be Satan nor to Deal with Him" (Bronk), **Supp. XXI:** 32

Not to Eat; Not for Love (Weller), **III:** 322

Not Wanted on the Voyage (Findley), **Supp. XX: 50, 56–57,** 59

Not Without Laughter (Hughes), **Retro. Supp. I:** 197, 198, 201; **Supp. I Part 1:** 328, 332; **Supp. XIX:** 73, 154

Nouvelle Héloïse, La (Rousseau), **Supp. XV:** 232

Nova Express (Burroughs), **Supp. III Part 1:** 93, 103, 104; **Supp. XVIII:** 137

Novel, The (Bulwer), **Retro. Supp. II:** 58

Novel, The: An Alternative History (Moore), **Supp. XXII:** 261

"Novel as a Function of American Democracy, The" (Ellison), **Retro. Supp. II:** 124

"Novel Démeublé, The" (Cather), **Retro. Supp. I:** 15

Novel History: Historians and Novelists Confront America's Past (and Each Other) (Carnes), **Supp. X:** 14

"Novelists of 2007" (Halliday), **Supp. XIX:** 90

Novella (Goethe; Bogan and Mayer, trans.), **Supp. III Part 1:** 63

Novellas and Other Writings (Wharton), **Retro. Supp. I:** 360

"Novel of the Thirties, A" (Trilling), **Supp. III Part 2:** 499

Novels and Other Writings (Bercovitch), **Retro. Supp. II:** 325

Novels and Tales of Henry James, The (James), **Retro. Supp. I:** 232

"Novel-Writing and Novel-Reading" (Howells), **II:** 276, 290

"November" (Larcom), **Supp. XIII:** 143

"November Cotton Flower" (Toomer), **Supp. IX:** 312

November Twenty Six Nineteen Sixty Three (Berry), **Supp. X:** 24

"Novices" (Moore), **III:** 200–201, 202, 213

Novick, Peter, **Supp. XVI:** 154–155

"Novogodnee" ("New Year's Greetings") (Tsvetayeva), **Supp. VIII:** 30

"Novotny's Pain" (P. Roth), **Supp. III Part 2:** 403

"No Voyage" (Oliver), **Supp. VII:** 231

No Voyage and Other Poems (Oliver), **Supp. VII:** 230–231, 232

Now and Another Time (Hearon), **Supp. VIII:** 58, **61–62**

Now and Then (Buechner), **Supp. XII:** 49, 53

"Now and Then, America" (Mora), **Supp. XIII:** 217

"Nowhere" (J. Scott), **Supp. XVII:** 189

Nowhere Is a Place: Travels in Patagonia (Theroux and Chatwin), **Supp. VIII:** 322

"Now I Am Married" (Gordon), **Supp. IV Part 1:** 299

"Now I Lay Me" (Hemingway), **II:** 249; **Retro. Supp. I:** 175

"Now I Lay Me" (Olds), **Supp. X:** 208

"Now Is the Air Made of Chiming Balls" (Eberhart), **I:** 523

"No Word" (Kunitz), **Supp. III Part 1:** 263

"No Worst" (Nelson), **Supp. XVIII:** 177, 178

Now Sheba Sings the Song (Angelou), **Supp. IV Part 1:** 16

"Now That We Live" (Kenyon), **Supp. VII:** 165

"Now the Servant's Name Was Malchus" (Wilder), **IV:** 358

"Now We Know" (O'Hara), **III:** 368–369

NOW with Bill Moyers (television), **Supp. XIII:** 286

Noyes, Alfred, **IV:** 434

Nuamah, Grace, **Supp. IV Part 1:** 10

"Nuances of a Theme by Williams" (Stevens), **Retro. Supp. I:** 422

Nuclear Age, The (O'Brien), **Supp. V:** 238, 243, 244, 246–248, 249, 251

"Nuclear Arms and Morality" (Sanders), **Supp. XVI:** 266

"Nude at a Dressing Table" (Peacock), **Supp. XIX:** 204

Nude Croquet (Fiedler), **Supp. XIII:** 103

"Nude Descendig a Staircase" (X. J. Kennedy), **Supp. XV:** 168

Nude Descending a Staircase (Duchamp), **IV:** 408; **Retro. Supp. I:** 416; **Supp. XXII:** 162

Nude Descending a Staircase (X. J. Kennedy), **Supp. XV:** 153, **154–157**

Nugent, Bruce, **Retro. Supp. I:** 200

Nugent, Elliot, **Supp. I Part 2:** 606, 611, 613

Nuggets and Dust (Bierce), **I:** 195

"Nullipara" (Olds), **Supp. X:** 209

Number One (Dos Passos), **I:** 489

"Numbers" (Skloot), **Supp. XX: 196, 207**

"Numbers, Letters" (Baraka), **Supp. II Part 1:** 50

Nunc Dimittis (Brodsky), **Supp. VIII:** 25–26, 28

"Nun No More, A" (Fante), **Supp. XI:** 160

"Nun's Priest's Tale" (Chaucer), **III:** 492

Nunzio, Nanzia, **IV:** 89

Nuptial Flight, The (Masters), **Supp. I Part 2:** 460, 471

"Nuptials" (Tate), **IV:** 122

"Nurse Whitman" (Olds), **Supp. X:** 203

Nurture (Kumin), **Supp. IV Part 2:** 453–454, 455

Nussbaum, Emily, **Supp. XI:** 143

Nussbaum, Felicity A., **Supp. X:** 189

Nutcracker, The (Tchaikovsky), **Retro. Supp. I:** 196

"Nux Postcoenatica" (Holmes), **Supp. I Part 1:** 303

Nyce, James M., **Retro. Supp. I:** 380

Nye, Naomi Shihab, **Supp. XI:** 316; **Supp. XIII: 273–290; Supp. XXIII:** 253

Nyerere, Julius, **Supp. X:** 135

"Nympholepsy" (Faulkner), **Retro. Supp. I:** 81

Nymphs of the Valley ('Ará'is al-Murúj) (Gibran), **Supp. XX: 115, 124, 125**

O

"Ö" (Dove), **Supp. IV Part 1:** 245

Oak and Ivy (Dunbar), **Supp. II Part 1:** 98

"Oak Bluffs" column (D. West), **Supp. XVIII:** 286

Oak Openings, The (Cooper), **I:** 354, 355

Oandasan, Bill, **Supp. IV Part 2:** 499

Oasis, The (McCarthy), **II:** 566–568

Oates, Joyce Carol, **Supp. II Part 2: 503–527; Supp. IV Part 1:** 205; **Supp. IV Part 2:** 447, 689; **Supp. V:** 323; **Supp. XI:** 239; **Supp. XII:** 343; **Supp. XIII:** 306; **Supp. XIV:** 26, 109; **Supp. XXIII:** 35

"Oath, The" (Tate), **IV:** 127

Obbligati (Hecht), **Supp. X:** 57

Ober, Harold, **Retro. Supp. I:** 101, 103, 105, 110, 113

Oberndorf, Clarence P., **Supp. I Part 1:** 315

Obey, André, **IV:** 356, 375

"Obit" (Lowell), **II:** 554

"Obituaries" (Collins), **Supp. XXI:** 65

"Objective Value of a Social Settlement, The" (Addams), **Supp. I Part 1:** 4

"Objective Woman, The" (Jong), **Supp. V:** 119

Objectivist Anthology, An, **Supp. XIV:** 287

"Objectivist Ethics, The" (Rand), **Supp. IV Part 2:** 530–532

"Objectivists" Anthology, An (Zukofsky), **Supp. III Part 2:** 613, 615

Object Lessons (Quindlen), **Supp. XVII: 173–174**

"Objects" (Wilbur), **Supp. III Part 2:** 545–547

Oblique Prayers (Levertov), **Supp. III Part 1:** 283

"Oblivion" (Justice), **Supp. VII:** 121

Oblivion Seekers, The (Eberhardt), **Supp. IV Part 1:** 92

"Oblong Box, The" (Poe), **III:** 416

"Obnoxious Truth, The" (Notley), **Supp. XXII:** 234

Obregon, Maurice, **Supp. I Part 2:** 488

O'Briant, Don, **Supp. X:** 8

O'Brien, Edward, **Supp. XV:** 140

O'Brien, Edward J., **I:** 289; **III:** 56; **Supp. XVIII:** 227; **Supp. XIX:** 256; **Supp. XX: 34**

O'Brien, Edwin, **Supp. XVIII:** 208

O'Brien, Fitzjames, **I:** 211

O'Brien, Geoffrey, **Supp. IV Part 2:** 471, 473

O'Brien, Joe, **Supp. XXI:** 5, 6

O'Brien, John, **Supp. V:** 48, 49; **Supp. X:** 239, 244; **Supp. XXI:** 228, 229, 233

O'Brien, Tim, **Supp. V: 237–255; Supp. XI:** 234; **Supp. XVII:** 14; **Supp. XXI:** 122

"Obscene Poem, An" (Creeley), **Supp. IV Part 1:** 150

Obscure Destinies (Cather), **I:** 331–332; **Retro. Supp. I:** 19

"Observation Relative to the Intentions of the Original Founders of the Academy in Philadelphia" (Franklin), **II:** 114

"Observations" (Dillard), **Supp. VI:** 34

Observations (Moore), **III:** 194, 195–196, 197, 199, 203, 205, 215

"Observations Now" (Conroy), **Supp. XVI:** 75

Observations: Photographs by Richard Avedon: Comments by Truman Capote, **Supp. III Part 1:** 125–126

Obuchowski, Mary DeJong, **Supp. XX: 222**

O Canada: An American's Notes on Canadian Culture (Wilson), **IV:** 429–430

"O Carib Isle!" (Crane), **I:** 400–401

O'Casey, Sean, **III:** 145; **Supp. IV Part 1:** 359, 361, 364

"Occidentals" (Ford), **Supp. V:** 71–72

Occom, Samuel, **Supp. XX: 288**

"Occultation of Orion, The" (Longfellow), **Retro. Supp. II:** 168

"Occurrence at Owl Creek Bridge, An" (Bierce), **I:** 200–201; **II:** 264

"Ocean 1212-W" (Plath), **Supp. I Part 2:** 528

"Ocean of Words" (Jin), **Supp. XVIII:** 94

Ocean of Words: Army Stories (Jin), **Supp. XVIII:** 89, 92, **93–94**

O'Connell, Nicholas, **Supp. IX:** 323, 325, 334

O'Connell, Shaun, **Supp. XXI:** 231

O'Connor, Edward F., Jr., **III:** 337

O'Connor, Flannery, **I:** 113, 190, 211, 298; **II:** 606; **III: 337–360; IV:** 4, 217, 282; **Retro. Supp. II:** 179, **219–239,** 272, 324; **Supp. I Part 1:** 290; **Supp. III Part 1:** 146; **Supp. V:** 59, 337; **Supp. VIII:** 13, 14, 158; **Supp. X:** 1, 26, 69, 228, 290; **Supp. XI:** 104; **Supp. XIII:** 294; **Supp. XIV:** 93; **Supp. XV:** 338; **Supp. XVI:** 219; **Supp. XVII:** 43, 114; **Supp. XVIII:** 156, 161, 194; **Supp. XIX:** 166, 209, 223; **Supp. XXI:** 197; **Supp. XXIII:** 289

O'Connor, Frank, **III:** 158; **Retro. Supp. II:** 242; **Supp. I Part 2:** 531; **Supp. VIII:** 151, 157, 165, 167, 171; **Supp. XV:** 74

O'Connor, Philip F., **Supp. XXIII:** 290

O'Connor, Richard, **II:** 467

O'Connor, T. P., **II:** 129

O'Connor, William, **IV:** 346; **Retro. Supp. I:** 392, 407

O'Connor, William Van, **III:** 479; **Supp. I Part 1:** 195

"Octascope" (Beattie), **Supp. V:** 27, 28

"Octaves" (Robinson), **Supp. III Part 2:** 593

"Octet" (Wallace), **Supp. X:** 309

October (Isherwood), **Supp. XIV:** 157, 164

"October" (Oliver), **Supp. VII:** 241

"October" (Swenson), **Supp. IV Part 2:** 649

"October, 1866" (Bryant), **Supp. I Part 1:** 169

"October 1913" (McCarriston), **Supp. XIV:** 266

"October and November" (Lowell), **II:** 554

"October in the Railroad Earth" (Kerouac), **Supp. III Part 1:** 225, 227, 229

October Light (Gardner), **Supp. VI:** 63, **69–71,** 72

"October Maples, Portland" (Wilbur), **Supp. III Part 2:** 556

October Palace, The (Hirshfield), **Supp. XXIII:** 131

"October: With Rain" (W. V. Davis), **Supp. XXI:** 94

"Octopus, An" (Moore), **III:** 202, 207–208, 214

"Octopus, The" (Merrill), **Supp. III Part 1:** 321

Octopus, The (Norris), **I:** 518; **III:** 314, 316, 322–326, 327, 331–333, 334, 335

"O Daedalus, Fly Away Home" (Hayden), **Supp. II Part 1:** 377–378

"OD and Hepatitis Railroad or Bust, The" (Boyle), **Supp. VIII:** 1

Odd Couple, The (1985 version, Simon), **Supp. IV Part 2:** 580

Odd Couple, The (film), **Supp. IV Part 2:** 589

Odd Couple, The (Simon), **Supp. IV Part 2:** 575, 579–580, 585, 586; **Supp. XVII:** 8

Odd Jobs (Updike), **Retro. Supp. I:** 334

Odd Mercy (Stern), **Supp. IX: 298–299**

Odd Number (Sorrentino), **Supp. XXI:** 236

"Odds, The" (Hecht), **Supp. X:** 64–65

"Odds, The" (Salinas), **Supp. XIII:** 321

"Ode" (Emerson), **II:** 13

"Ode" (Sobin), **Supp. XVI:** 284–285

"Ode" (X. J. Kennedy), **Supp. XV:** 160

"Ode (Intimations of Immortality)" (Matthews), **Supp. IX:** 162

"Ode for Memorial Day" (Dunbar), **Supp. II Part 1:** 199

"Ode for the American Dead in Asia" (McGrath), **Supp. X:** 119

"Ode: For the Budding of Islands" (Sobin), **Supp. XVI:** 287

"Ode Inscribed to W. H. Channing" (Emerson), **Supp. XIV:** 46

"Ode: Intimations of Immortality" (Wordsworth), **Supp. I Part 2:** 729; **Supp. III Part 1:** 12; **Supp. XIV:** 8

"Ode in Time of Crisis" (Taggard), **Supp. XXII:** 271

Odell, Margeretta Matilda, **Supp. XX: 278, 284, 288**

"Ode: My 24th Year" (Ginsberg), **Supp. II Part 1:** 312

"Ode on a Grecian Urn" (Keats), **I:** 284; **III:** 472; **Supp. XII:** 113; **Supp. XIV:** 8, 9–10; **Supp. XV:** 100; **Supp. XXI:** 64

"Ode on Human Destinies" (Jeffers), **Supp. II Part 2:** 419

"Ode on Indolence" (Keats), **Supp. XII:** 113

"Ode on Melancholy" (Keats), **Retro. Supp. I:** 301

Ode Recited at the Harvard Commemoration (Lowell), **Supp. I Part 2:** 416–418, 424

"Ode Recited at the Harvard Commemoration" (Lowell), **II:** 551

Odes (Horace), **Supp. XXIV:** 153

Odes (O'Hara), **Supp. XXIII:** 216

"Ode: Salute to the French Negro Poets"(O'Hara), **Supp. XXIII:** 216

"Ode Secrète" (Valéry), **III:** 609

"Odes of Estrangement" (Sobin), **Supp. XVI:** 289

Odes of Horace, The (Ferry, trans.), **Supp. XXIV: 153–156**

"Odes to Natural Processes" (Updike), **Retro. Supp. I:** 323

"Ode: The Capris" (Halliday), **Supp. XIX:** 88

"Ode to a Nightingale" (Keats), **II:** 368; **Retro. Supp. II:** 261; **Supp. IX:** 52

"Ode to Autumn" (Masters), **Supp. I Part 2:** 458

"Ode to Cervantes" (Salinas), **Supp. XIII:** 324

"Ode to Coit Tower" (Corso), **Supp. XII:** 122

"Ode to Ethiopia" (Dunbar), **Supp. II Part 1:** 199, 207, 208, 209

"Ode to Fear" (Tate), **IV:** 128

Ode to Harvard and Other Poems, An (Bynner), **Supp. XV:** 41, 44

"Ode to Joy"(O'Hara), **Supp. XXIII:** 208, 216

"Ode to Meaning" (Pinsky), **Supp. VI: 249–250,** 251

"Ode to Michael Goldberg ('s Birth and Other Births)"(O'Hara), **Supp. XXIII:** 209, 216, 218

"Ode to Night" (Masters), **Supp. I Part 2:** 458

"Ode to Our Young Pro-Consuls of the Air" (Tate), **IV:** 135

"Ode to the Austrian Socialists" (Benét), **Supp. XI:** 46, 58

"Ode to the Confederate Dead" (Tate), **II:** 551; **IV:** 124, 133, 137; **Supp. X:** 52

"Ode to the Johns Hopkins University" (Lanier), **Supp. I Part 1:** 370

"Ode to the Maggot" (Komunyakaa), **Supp. XIII:** 130

"Ode to the Mexican Experience" (Salinas), **Supp. XIII:** 316–317

"Ode to the Virginian Voyage" (Drayton), **IV:** 135

"Ode to the West Wind" (Shelley), **Retro. Supp. I:** 308; **Supp. I Part 2:** 728; **Supp. IX:** 52; **Supp. XII:** 117; **Supp. XIV:** 271–272; **Supp. XV:** 221

"Ode to Walt Whitman" (Benét), **Supp. XI:** 52

"Ode to Willem de Kooning"(O'Hara), **Supp. XXIII:** 208, 216

Odets, Clifford, **Supp. I Part 1:** 277, 295; **Supp. I Part 2:** 679; **Supp. II Part 2: 529–554; Supp. IV Part 2:** 587; **Supp. V:** 109; **Supp. VIII:** 96; **Supp. XVIII:** 238; **Supp. XX: 34**

Odier, Daniel, **Supp. III Part 1:** 97

"Odi et Amo" (Catullus), **Supp. XV:** 27, 32, 35

"Odom"(P. Benedict), **Supp. XXIII:** 41

O'Donnell, George Marion, **II:** 67

O'Donnell, Mary King, **Supp. XVIII:** 232

O'Donnell, Thomas F., **II:** 131

"Odor of Verbena" (Faulkner), **II:** 66

O'Doul, Lefty, **II:** 425

"Odysseus to Telemachus" (Brodsky), **Supp. VIII:** 25

Odyssey (Bryant, trans.), **Supp. I Part 1:** 158

Odyssey (Homer), **III:** 14, 470; **Retro. Supp. I:** 286, 290; **Retro. Supp. II:** 121; **Supp. I Part 1:** 185; **Supp. IV Part 2:** 631; **Supp. IX:** 211; **Supp. X:** 114; **Supp. XIV:** 191; **Supp. XVII:** 117; **Supp. XXI:** 36

"Odyssey of a Wop, The" (Fante), **Supp. XI:** 164, 165

Oedipus Rex (Sophocles), **I:** 137; **III:** 145, 151, 152, 332; **Supp. I Part 2:** 428

Oedipus Tyrannus (Sophocles), **II:** 203; **Supp. XV:** 265

Oehlschlaeger, Fritz, **Supp. IX:** 123

Oelze, Richard, **Supp. XXII:** 167

"Of Alexander Crummell" (Du Bois), **Supp. II Part 1:** 170

O'Faoláin, Seán, **Supp. II Part 1:** 101

Of a World That Is No More (Singer), **IV:** 16

"Of Booker T. Washington and Others" (Du Bois), **Supp. II Part 1:** 168

"Of Bright & Blue Birds & the Gala Sun" (Stevens), **IV:** 93

"Of Christian Heroism" (Ozick), **Supp. V:** 272

"Of Dying Beauty" (Zukofsky), **Supp. III Part 2:** 610

"Of Epiphanies and Poets" (Phillips), **Supp. XX: 221**

"Of 'Father and Son' " (Kunitz), **Supp. III Part 1:** 262

Offenbach, Jacques, **II:** 427

"Offering for Mr. Bluehart, An" (Wright), **Supp. III Part 2:** 596, 601

"Offerings" (Mason), **Supp. VIII:** 141

"Offertory" (Hempel), **Supp. XXI: 126–127**

Official Entry Blank (Kooser), **Supp. XIX:** 116, **117–118**

"Official Entry Form" (Kooser), **Supp. XIX:** 117

"Official Piety" (Whittier), **Supp. I Part 2:** 687

"Offloading for Mrs. Schwartz" (Saunders), **Supp. XIX:** 225–226

"Of Freemasons, Kings, and Constitutions" (P. N. Warren), **Supp. XX: 273**

"Off-Shore Pirates, The" (Fitzgerald), **II:** 88

Off the Beaten Path (Proulx), **Supp. VII:** 261

Off the Beaten Path: Stories of Place, **Supp. XVI:** 22

"Off the Cuff" (Simpson), **Supp. IX:** 278

"Off the Highway" (Wolfert), **Supp. XXI:** 265

Off the Map (Levine), **Supp. V:** 178

Offut, Chris, **Supp. XIX: 163–176**

Of Gravity and Angels (Hirshfield), **Supp. XXIII:** 131

O'Flaherty, George, **Supp. I Part 1:** 202, 205–206

O'Flaherty, Kate. *See* Chopin, Kate

O'Flaherty, Thomas, **Supp. I Part 1:** 202, 203–204, 205

O'Flaherty, Thomas, Jr., **Supp. I Part 1:** 202

"Of Maids and Other Muses" (Alvarez), **Supp. VII:** 11

"Of Margaret" (Ransom), **III:** 491

Of Mice and Men (Steinbeck), **IV:** 51, 57–58

"Of Modern Poetry" (Stevens), **IV:** 92

Of No Country I Know: New and Selected Poems and Translations (Ferry), **Supp. XXIV: 157**

Of Plymouth Plantation (Bradford), **Retro. Supp. II:** 161, 162; **Supp. XXII:** 33, **35–47**

Of Plymouth Plantation (Morison, ed.), **Supp. I Part 2:** 494

"Ofrenda for Lobo" (Mora), **Supp. XIII:** 224

"Often" (Kenyon), **Supp. VII:** 171

"Often, in Dreams, He Moved through a City" (Dobyns), **Supp. XIII:** 90

"Of the Coming of John" (Du Bois), **Supp. II Part 1:** 170

"Of the Culture of White Folk" (Du Bois), **Supp. II Part 1:** 175

Of the Farm (Updike), **IV:** 214, 217, 223–225, 233; **Retro. Supp. I:** 318, 329, 332

"Of the Four-Winged Cherubim as Signature" (Sobin), **Supp. XVI:** 287

"Of 'The Frill' " (McCarriston), **Supp. XIV:** 274

"Of the Passing of the First-Born" (Du Bois), **Supp. II Part 1:** 170

"Of the Sorrow Songs" (Du Bois), **Supp. II Part 1:** 170

"Of the Wings of Atlanta" (Du Bois), **Supp. II Part 1:** 170

Of This Time, Of This Place (Trilling), **Supp. III Part 2:** 498, 504

Of Time and the River (Wolfe), **IV:** 450, 451, 452, 455, 456, 457, 458, 459, 462, 464–465, 467, 468, 469

Of Woman Born: Motherhood as Experience and Institution (Rich), **Supp. I Part 2:** 554, 567–569

Of Women and Their Elegance (Mailer), **Retro. Supp. II:** 209

Ogden, Archie, **Supp. XIII:** 174

Ogden, Henry, **II:** 298

Ogden, Uzal, **Supp. I Part 2:** 516

Ogle, Connie, **Supp. XXIII:** 300, 301

"Oh, Atonement" (Weigl), **Supp. XIX:** 287

"Oh, Fairest of the Rural Maids" (Bryant), **Supp. I Part 1:** 169

"Oh, Immobility, Death's Vast Associate" (Dobyns), **Supp. XIII:** 89

"Oh, Joseph, I'm So Tired" (Yates), **Supp. XI:** 348

Oh, the Places You'll Go! (Geisel), **Supp. XVI:** 111

Oh, the Thinks You can Think! (Geisel), **Supp. XVI:** 111

"O'Halloran's Luck" (Benét), **Supp. XI:** 47

O'Hara, Frank, **Supp. XII:** 121; **Supp. XV:** 93, 176, 177, 178, 179–180, 182, 186, 187, 215–216; **Supp. XIX:** 81, 85; **Supp. XXII:** 226, 236; **Supp. XXIII: 207–222; Supp. XXIV:** 33, 34, 36, 42, 43, 44

O'Hara, J. D., **Supp. IV Part 1:** 43; **Supp. V:** 22; **Supp. XVI:** 221; **Supp. XXI:** 228

O'Hara, John, **I:** 375, 495; **II:** 444, 459; **III:** 66, **361–384; IV:** 59; **Retro. Supp. I:** 99, 112; **Supp. I Part 1:** 196; **Supp. II Part 1:** 109; **Supp. IV Part 1:** 31, 383; **Supp. IV Part 2:** 678; **Supp. V:** 95; **Supp. VIII:** 151, 156; **Supp. IX:** 208; **Supp. XIX:** 209

O'Hara's Choice (Uris), **Supp. XX: 247, 256–257**

O'Hehir, Andrew, **Supp. XII:** 280

O. Henry Biography (C. A. Smith), **Supp. II Part 1:** 395

"Ohio Pagan, An" (Anderson), **I:** 112, 113

Ohio trilogy (Richter), **Supp. XVIII:** 212–215

Oh Mercy (album, Dylan), **Supp. XVIII:** 28, 33

Oh Say Can You Say? (Geisel), **Supp. XVI:** 111

Oil! (Sinclair), **Supp. V:** 276, 277–279, 282, 288, 289

Oil Notes (Bass), **Supp. XVI:** 17

"Oil Painting of the Artist as the Artist" (MacLeish), **III:** 14

"O-jib-way Maid, The"(J. Schoolcraft), **Supp. XXIII:** 235

O'Keeffe, Georgia, **Supp. IX:** 62, 66; **Supp. XX: 75**

"Oklahoma" (Levis), **Supp. XI:** 267

Oktenberg, Adrian, **Supp. XVII:** 76; **Supp. XXI:** 253; **Supp. XXIII:** 133

"Old, Old, Old, Old Andrew Jackson" (Lindsay), **Supp. I Part 2:** 398

"Old Amusement Park, An" (Moore), **III:** 216

"Old Angel Midnight" (Kerouac), **Supp. III Part 1:** 229–230

"Old Apple Dealer, The" (Hawthorne), **II:** 227, 233–235, 237, 238

"Old Apple-Tree, The" (Dunbar), **Supp. II Part 1:** 198

"Old Army Game, The" (Garrett), **Supp. VII:** 100–101

"Old Aunt Peggy" (Chopin), **Retro. Supp. II:** 64

"Old Barn at the Bottom of the Fogs, The" (Frost), **Retro. Supp. I:** 138

Old Battle-Ax, The (Holding), **Supp. XXII: 128–129**

Old Beauty and Others, The (Cather), **I:** 331

"Old Boys, Old Girls" (E. P. Jones), **Supp. XXII:** 151

Old Bruin: Commodore Matthew C. Perry, 1794–1858 (Morison), **Supp. I Part 2:** 494–495

"Old Cracked Tune, An" (Kunitz), **Supp. III Part 1:** 264

Old Curiosity Shop, The (Dickens), **I:** 458; **Supp. I Part 2:** 409

Oldest Killed Lake in North America, The (Carruth), **Supp. XVI:** 51

"Oldest Man, The" (M. F. K. Fisher), **Supp. XVII:** 91

"Old Farmer, The" (Jeffers), **Supp. II Part 2:** 418

Old-Fashioned Girl, An (Alcott), **Supp. I Part 1:** 29, 41, 42

"Old Father Morris" (Stowe), **Supp. I Part 2:** 586

"Old Flame, The" (Lowell), **II:** 550

"Old Florist" (Roethke), **III:** 531

"Old Folsom Prison" (Matthews), **Supp. IX:** 165

Old Forest, The (Taylor), **Supp. V:** 320, 321, 326, 327

"Old Forest, The" (Taylor), **Supp. V:** 313, 321, 323, 326

Old Forest and Other Stories (Taylor), **Supp. V:** 326

Old Friends and New (Jewett), **II:** 402; **Retro. Supp. II:** 137, 140

Old Glory, The (Lowell), **II:** 543, 545–546, 555; **Retro. Supp. II:** 188

Old Helmet, The (S. and A. Warner), **Supp. XVIII:** 267

"Old Homestead, The" (Dunbar), **Supp. II Part 1:** 198

"Old House" (Espaillat), **Supp. XXI:** 112, 113

"Old Iron" (Nye), **Supp. XIII:** 276

"Old Ironsides" (Holmes), **Supp. I Part 1:** 302

Old Jules (Sandoz), **Supp. XXIV:** 243, 244, **245–246,** 249, 251, 255, 257

"Old Lady We Saw, An" (Shields), **Supp. VII:** 310–311

"Old Love" (Singer), **Retro. Supp. II:** 307

"Old McGrath Place, The" (McGrath), **Supp. X:** 114

"Old Maid, The" (Wharton), **Retro. Supp. I:** 381, 382

"Old Man" (Faulkner), **II:** 68, 69

Old Man and the Sea, The (Hemingway), **II:** 250, 256–257, 258, 265; **III:** 40; **Retro. Supp. I:** 180, **185,** 186

"Old Man Drunk" (Wright), **Supp. III Part 2:** 595

"Old Man Feeding Hens" (Francis), **Supp. IX:** 78

"Old Man on the Hospital Porch" (Ríos), **Supp. IV Part 2:** 546–547

Old Man Rubbing His Eyes (R. Bly), **Supp. IV Part 1:** 65

"Old Manse, The" (Hawthorne), **II:** 224

"Old Man's Winter Night, An" (Frost), **Retro. Supp. I:** 126, 131

Old Man Who Love Cheese, The (Keillor), **Supp. XVI:** 177

"Old Man with a Dog" (Wright), **Supp. XV:** 346

Old Marriage and New (Kooser), **Supp. XIX: 120–121**

"Old Meeting House, The" (Stowe), **Supp. I Part 2:** 586

"Old Memory, An" (Dunbar), **Supp. II Part 1:** 198

"Old Men, Old Horses" (P. N. Warren as Kilina), **Supp. XX: 262**

"Old Men, The" (McCarthy), **II:** 566

"Old Men Pitching Horseshoes" (X. J. Kennedy), **Supp. XV:** 166

Old Money (Wasserstein), **Supp. XV: 333–334**

"Old Morgue, The" (Prose), **Supp. XVI:** 250

Old Morning Program, The (radio show, Keillor). *See Prairie Home Companion, A* (radio show, Keillor)

"Old Mortality" (Porter), **III:** 436, 438–441, 442, 445, 446

"Old Mrs. Harris" (Cather), **I:** 332; **Retro. Supp. I:** 19

Old Neighborhood, The (Mamet), **Supp. XIV:** 240, 241, 242, 249–250, 251, 252, 254

Old New York (Wharton), **IV:** 322; **Retro. Supp. I:** 381

"Ol' Doc Hyar" (Campbell), **Supp. II Part 1:** 202

"Old of the Moon" (Offutt), **Supp. XIX:** 165, 166

Old One-Two, The (Gurney), **Supp. V:** 98

"Old Order, The" (Porter), **III:** 443, 444–445, 451

"Old Osawatomie" (Sandburg), **III:** 584

Old Patagonia Express, The: By Train through the Americas (Theroux), **Supp. VIII:** 322

"Old People" (Ferry), **Supp. XXIV:** 162

"Old People, The" (Faulkner), **II:** 71–72

"Old Photograph, An" (Kooser), **Supp. XIX:** 121

"Old Poet Moves to a New Apartment 14 Times, The" (Zukofsky), **Supp. III Part 2:** 628

Old Possum's Book of Practical Cats (T. S. Eliot), **Supp. XIII:** 228, 344

"Old Red" (Gordon), **II:** 199, 200, 203

Old Red and Other Stories (Gordon), **II:** 157

Old Régime in Canada, The (Parkman), **Supp. II Part 2:** 600, 607, 608–609, 612

Old Religion, The (Mamet), **Supp. XIV:** 253

Olds, Sharon, **Supp. X: 201–217; Supp. XI:** 139, 142, 244; **Supp. XII:** 229; **Supp. XIV:** 265; **Supp. XVII:** 114, 240; **Supp. XXI:** 249

"Old Saws" (Garrett), **Supp. VII:** 96–97

Old South, The: "A Summer Tragedy" and Other Stories (Bontemps), **Supp. XXII:** 7

"Old Stories" (Skloot), **Supp. XX: 200**

Old Testament, **I:** 109, 181, 300, 328, 401, 410, 419, 431, 457, 458; **II:** 166, 167, 219; **III:** 270, 272, 348, 390, 396; **IV:** 41, 114, 152, 309; **Retro. Supp. I:** 122, 140, 249, 311, 360; **Retro. Supp. II:** 299; **Supp. I Part 1:** 60, 104, 106, 151; **Supp. I Part 2:** 427, 515, 516; **Supp. IX:** 14. *See also* names of Old Testament books

"Old Things, The" (James), **Retro. Supp. I:** 229

"Old Times on the Mississippi" (Twain), **IV:** 199

Oldtown Folks (Stowe), **Supp. I Part 2:** 587, 596–598

"Old Town of Berwick, The" (Jewett), **Retro. Supp. II:** 132

"Old Trails" (Robinson), **III:** 513, 517

"Old Tyrannies" (Bourne), **I:** 233

"Old West" (Bausch), **Supp. VII:** 48

"Old Whorehouse, An" (Oliver), **Supp. VII:** 235

"Old Woman" (Pinsky), **Supp. VI:** 238

"Old Woman of Beare, The" (X. J. Kennedy), **Supp. XV:** 156

"Old Word, The" (Simic), **Supp. VIII:** 282

"Old-World Landowners" (Gogol), **Supp. XV:** 262

Oldys, Francis. *See* Chalmers, George

Oleanna (Mamet), **Supp. XIV:** 239, 241, 245, 248, 250

Olendorf, Donna, **Supp. IV Part 1:** 196

"Olga Poems, The" (Levertov), **Supp. III Part 1:** 279–281

"Olive Groves of Thasos, The" (Clampitt), **Supp. IX: 51–52**

Olive Kitteridge (Strout), **Supp. XXIII:** 273, 275, **280–284,** 285

Oliver, Bill, **Supp. VIII:** 138

Oliver, Douglas, **Supp. XXII:** 225, 226, 233, 235

Oliver, Mary, **Supp. VII: 229–248; Supp. X:** 31; **Supp. XVI:** 39; **Supp. XVII:** 111, 240; **Supp. XXIII:** 51

Oliver, Sydney, **I:** 409

Oliver Goldsmith: A Biography (Irving), **II:** 315

Oliver Twist (Dickens), **I:** 354; **Supp. IV Part 2:** 464

"Olivia" (Salinas), **Supp. XIII:** 316

"Olivier Bergmann" (Halliday), **Supp. XIX:** 93–94

Olivieri, David (pseudonym), **Retro. Supp. I:** 361. *See also* Wharton, Edith

Ollive, Samuel, **Supp. I Part 2:** 503

Olmsted, Frederick Law, **Supp. I Part 1:** 355

Olor de la memoria, El/The Scent of Memory (Espaillat), **Supp. XXI:** 104

Olsen, Lance, **Supp. IV Part 1:** 54; **Supp. IV Part 2:** 623

Olsen, Tillie, **Supp. V:** 114, 220; **Supp. XIII: 291–309; Supp. XVI:** 83, 90

Olshan, Joseph, **Supp. XIX:** 52

Olson, Charles, **Retro. Supp. I:** 209; **Supp. II Part 1:** 30, 328; **Supp. II Part 2: 555–587; Supp. III Part 1:** 9, 271; **Supp. III Part 2:** 542, 624; **Supp. IV Part 1:** 139, 144, 146, 153, 154, 322; **Supp. IV Part 2:** 420, 421, 423, 426; **Supp. VIII:** 290, 291; **Supp. XII:** 2, 198; **Supp. XIII:** 104; **Supp. XIV:** 96; **Supp. XV:** 177; **Supp. XXI:** 19, 21, 23; **Supp. XXIV:** 42

Olson, Clarence, **Supp. XX: 84, 85, 86**

Olson, Ray, **Supp. XVII:** 111, 112, 119

"Ol' Tunes, The" (Dunbar), **Supp. II Part 1:** 197

"O Lull Me, Lull Me" (Roethke), **III:** 536–537

O'Malley, Anne, **Supp. XXII:** 56

Omar Khayyam, **Supp. I Part 1:** 363

O'Meally, Robert, **Retro. Supp. II:** 112

Omega the Unknown (comic book series), **Supp. XVIII:** 149

"Omen" (Komunyakaa), **Supp. XIII:** 126, 127

Omensetter's Luck (Gass), **Supp. VI: 80–82,** 87

Omeros (Walcott), **Supp. XV:** 264

"Ominous Baby, An" (Crane), **I:** 411

Ommateum, with Doxology (Ammons), **Supp. VII:** 24–26, 27, 28, 36

Omni-Americans, The: New Perspectives on Black Experience and American Culture (Murray), **Supp. XIX:** 147, **149–151,** 154

"Omnibus Jaunts and Drivers" (Whitman), **IV:** 350

Omoo: A Narrative of Adventures in the South Seas (Melville), **III:** 76–77, 79, 84; **Retro. Supp. I:** 247

O My Land, My Friends (H. Crane), **Retro. Supp. II:** 76

"On Abrigador Hill" (Nelson), **Supp. XVIII:** 183

"On a Certain Condescension in Foreigners" (Lowell), **Supp. I Part 2:** 419

"On a Certain Engagement South of Seoul" (Carruth), **Supp. XVI:** 47

"On a Child Who Lived One Minute" (X. J. Kennedy), **Supp. XV:** 152, 155

"On Acquiring Riches" (Banks), **Supp. V:** 5

On a Darkling Plain (Stegner), **Supp. IV Part 2:** 598, 607

On a Fire on the Moon (Mailer), **Retro. Supp. II:** 206

"On a Hill Far Away" (Dillard), **Supp. VI:** 28

"On a Honey Bee, Drinking from a Glass and Drowned Therein" (Freneau), **Supp. II Part 1:** 273

"On a Monument to a Pigeon" (Leopold), **Supp. XIV:** 187–188

"On a Mountainside" (Wagoner), **Supp. IX:** 332

O'Nan, Stewart, **Supp. XI:** 348

"On an Old Photograph of My Son" (Carver), **Supp. III Part 1:** 140

"Onan's Soliloquy" (X. J. Kennedy), **Supp. XV:** 165

"On a Proposed Trip South" (W. C. Williams), **Retro. Supp. I:** 413

Onassis, Jacqueline Kennedy, **Supp. XVIII:** 287

"On a Tree Fallen across the Road" (Frost), **Retro. Supp. I:** 134

"On a View of Pasadena from the Hills" (Winters), **Supp. II Part 2:** 795, 796–799, 814

"On a Visit to a Halfway House after a Long Absence" (Salinas), **Supp. XIII:** 325

"On a Windy Night" (Dixon), **Supp. XII:** 155

On Becoming a Novelist (Gardner), **Supp. VI:** 64

"On Being an American" (Toomer), **Supp. III Part 2:** 479

"On Being Asked to Write a Poem against the War in Vietnam" (Carruth), **Supp. XVI:** 55–56

"On Being a Woman" (Parker), **Supp. IX:** 201

On Being Blue (Gass), **Supp. VI:** 77, 78, 86, 94; **Supp. XIV:** 305

"On Being Brought from Africa to America" (Wheatley), **Supp. XX: 280–281, 286–287**

"On Being Too Inhibited" (Hay), **Supp. XIV:** 130

"On Being Unable to Read" (Cornell), **Supp. XX: 94–95**

On Beyond Zebra! (Geisel), **Supp. XVI:** 105

"On Burroughs' Work" (Ginsberg), **Supp. II Part 1:** 320

Once (Walker), **Supp. III Part 2:** 519, 522, 530

Once at Antietam (Gaddis), **Supp. IV Part 1:** 285

"Once by the Pacific" (Frost), **II:** 155; **Retro. Supp. I:** 122, 137

"Once More, the Round" (Roethke), **III:** 529

Once More around the Block: Familiar Essays (Epstein), **Supp. XIV: 107**

"Once More to the Lake" (White), **Supp. I Part 2:** 658, 668, 673–675

"On Certain Political Measures Proposed to Their Consideration" (Barlow), **Supp. II Part 1:** 82

"Once There Was Light" (Kenyon), **Supp. VII:** 171–172

"On *Credo Ut Intelligam*" (Bronk), **Supp. XXI:** 31

Ondaatje, Michael, **Supp. IV Part 1:** 252

"On Dining Alone" (M. F. K. Fisher), **Supp. XVII:** 83

On Distant Ground (R. O. Butler), **Supp. XII:** 62, **66–68,** 69, 74

"On Divers Geometries" (Bronk), **Supp. XXI:** 31

"On Dreams"(Hadas), **Supp. XXIII:** 117

"One, The" (Weigl), **Supp. XIX:** 282–283

"1 January 1965" (Brodsky), **Supp. VIII:** 23–24

O'Neale, Sondra, **Supp. IV Part 1:** 2

"One A.M. with Voices" (X. J. Kennedy), **Supp. XV:** 157

"One Arm" (T. Williams), **IV:** 383

One Arm, and Other Stories (T. Williams), **IV:** 383

"One Art" (Bell), **Supp. X:** 2

One Art (Bishop), **Retro. Supp. II:** 51

"One Art" (Bishop), **Retro. Supp. II:** 50; **Supp. I Part 1:** 72, 73, 82, 93, 94–95, 96; **Supp. XV:** 126; **Supp. XXI:** 58; **Supp. XXIII:** 117

"One Art: The Poetry of Elizabeth Bishop, 1971–1976" (Schwartz), **Supp. I Part 1:** 81

One Big Self: Prisoners of Louisiana (Wright and Luster), **Supp. XV:** 337, 344, 350, **351–353**

"One Blessing had I than the rest" (Dickinson), **Retro. Supp. I:** 45

"One Body" (Hass), **Supp. VI:** 106

One Boy's Boston, 1887–1901 (Morison), **Supp. I Part 2:** 494

"One Coat of Paint" (Ashbery), **Supp. III Part 1:** 26

"One Dash-Horses" (Crane), **I:** 416

One Day (Morris), **III:** 233–236

One Day, When I Was Lost (Baldwin), **Retro. Supp. II:** 13; **Supp. I Part 1:** 48, 66, 67

"One Dead Friend" (Kumin), **Supp. IV Part 2:** 441

One Destiny: An Epistle to the Christians (Asch), **Supp. XXIII:** 2, 7

One Fish Two Fish Red Fish Blue Fish (Geisel), **Supp. XVI:** 108

One Flesh (Major), **Supp. XXII: 183–184**

One Flew Over the Cuckoo's Nest (Kesey), **III:** 558

One Flew Over the Cuckoo's Nest (Kesey), **Supp. XXIII:** 100

"One for the Road" (Swados), **Supp. XIX:** 259

One for the Rose (Levine), **Supp. V:** 178, 179, 181, 187, 189–191

"One for the Rose" (Levine), **Supp. V:** 181, 190

"One Friday Morning" (Hughes), **Supp. I Part 1:** 330

"One Holy Night" (Cisneros), **Supp. VII:** 69–70

"One Home" (Stafford), **Supp. XI:** 321

100 Faces of Death, The, Part IV (Boyle), **Supp. VIII:** 16

100 Great Poets of the English Language (Gioia, ed.), **Supp. XXI:** 99

100 Years of Negro Freedom (Bontemps), **Supp. XXII:** 6

$106,000 Blood Money (Hammett), **Supp. IV Part 1:** 345

"$106,000 Blood Money" (Hammett), **Supp. IV Part 1:** 345, 346

One Hundred Days in Europe (Holmes), **Supp. I Part 1:** 317

180 More: Extraordinary Poems for Every Day (Collins, ed.), **Supp. XXI:** 54

158-Pound Marriage, The (Irving), **Supp. VI:** 163, 164, **167–170**

O'Neil, Elizabeth Murrie, **Retro. Supp. I:** 427

O'Neill, Brendan, **Supp. XII:** 286

O'Neill, Eugene, **I:** 66, 71, 81, 94, 393, 445; **II:** 278, 391, 427, 585; **III:** 151, 165, **385–408; IV:** 61, 383; **Retro. Supp. II:** 82, 104; **Supp. III Part 1:** 177–180, 189; **Supp. IV Part 1:** 359; **Supp. IV Part 2:** 587, 607; **Supp. V:** 277; **Supp. VIII:** 332, 334; **Supp. XIV:** 239, 320, 328; **Supp. XVI:** 193; **Supp. XVII:** 96, 99–100, 103, 105, 107; **Supp. XX: 69; Supp. XXI:** 6, 13; **Supp. XXII:** 17, 18, 22, 28

O'Neill, Oona, **Supp. XXII:** 25, 26

"One Is a Wanderer" (Thurber), **Supp. I Part 2:** 616

One Is the Sun (P. N. Warren), **Supp. XX: 269–270**

One L (Turow), **Supp. XVII: 214,** 215, 217

"One Last Look at the Adige: Verona in the Rain" (Wright), **Supp. III Part 2:** 603

One Life (Rukeyser), **Supp. VI:** 273, 281, 283

One Life at a Time, Please (Abbey), **Supp. XIII:** 13

One Man in His Time (Glasgow), **II:** 178, 184

"One Man's Fortunes" (Dunbar), **Supp. II Part 1:** 211, 212–213

One Man's Initiation (Dos Passos), **I:** 476–477, 479, 488

One Man's Meat (White), **Supp. I Part 2:** 654, 669, 676

"One Man's Meat" (White), **Supp. I Part 2:** 655

One Matchless Time: A Life of William Faulkner (Parini), **Supp. XXII:** 205

"One Moment on Top of the Earth" (Nye), **Supp. XIII:** 282

One More July: A Football Dialogue with Bill Curry (Plimpton), **Supp. XVI:** 243

"One More"(Kenny), **Supp. XXIII:** 156

"One More Song" (Lindsay), **Supp. I Part 2:** 400–401

"One More Thing" (Carver), **Supp. III Part 1:** 138, 144

"One More Time" (Gordon), **II:** 200

One Nation (Stegner), **Supp. IV Part 2:** 599, 608

"One-Night Homecoming" (X. J. Kennedy), **Supp. XV:** 167

"ONE NIGHT STAND" (Baraka), **Supp. II Part 1:** 32

"One of Our Conquerors" (Bourne), **I:** 223

One of Ours (Cather), **I:** 322–323; **Retro. Supp. I:** 1, 3, **13–15,** 20

"One of the Missing" (Bierce), **I:** 201–202

"One of the Rooming Houses of Heaven" (Doty), **Supp. XI:** 131

"One of the Smallest" (Stern), **Supp. IX:** 299–300

"One of Us" (Fante), **Supp. XI:** 165

Oneóta: or, The Red Race of America (H. Schoolcraft), **Supp. XXIII:** 232

"One Out of Twelve: Writers Who Are Women in Our Century" (Olsen), **Supp. XIII:** 294

"One Part Humor, 2 Parts Whining" (Kakutani), **Supp. XI:** 38

"One Person" (Wylie), **Supp. I Part 2:** 709, 724–727

"One Sister have I in our house" (Dickinson), **Retro. Supp. I:** 34

165 Meeting House Lane (Notley), **Supp. XXII:** 224, 225, 226

"One Song, The" (Strand), **Supp. IV Part 2:** 619

"One Summer in Spain" (Coover), **Supp. V:** 40

One That Got Away, The (Everett), **Supp. XVIII:** 54

1000 Airplanes on the Roof (Glass, Hwang, and Sirlin), **Supp. XXI:** 147

One Thousand Avant-Garde Plays (Koch), **Supp. XV:** 187

"One Thousandth, The" (Weigl), **Supp. XIX:** 288

One Time, One Place: Mississippi in the Depression, a Snapshot Album (Welty), **Retro. Supp. I:** 339, 343, 344

1 x 1 (One Times One) (Cummings), **I:** 430, 436, 438–439, 441, 446, 447, 448

"One Touch of Nature" (McCarthy), **II:** 580

One Train (Koch), **Supp. XV:** 177, 184

"One Trip Abroad" (Fitzgerald), **II:** 95

One True Thing (film), **Supp. XVII:** 176

One True Thing (Quindlen), **Supp. XVII:** 166, **174–176**

"One Way" (Creeley), **Supp. IV Part 1:** 150–151

One Way or Another (Cameron), **Supp. XII:** 81

One-Way Ticket (Hughes), **Retro. Supp. I:** 206, 207, 208; **Supp. I Part 1:** 333–334

One Way to Heaven (Cullen), **Supp. IV Part 1:** 170, 172

One Way to Reconstruct the Scene (W. V. Davis), **Supp. XXI:** 83, **88–91**

"One Way to Reconstruct the Scene" (W. V. Davis), **Supp. XXI: 88–89,** 90, 91, 92, **93**

One Way to Spell Man (Stegner), **Supp. IV Part 2:** 595, 598, 601, 609

"One Way to Spell Man" (Stegner), **Supp. IV Part 2:** 601

One Whose Eyes Open When You Close Your Eyes, The (F. Wright), **Supp. XVII:** 240, 243

"One Who Skins Cats, The" (Gunn Allen), **Supp. IV Part 1:** 331

"One Who Went Forth to Feel Fear" (Grimms), **Supp. X:** 86

"One Winter I Devise a Plan of My Own" (Ríos), **Supp. IV Part 2:** 549

One Winter Night in August (X. J. Kennedy), **Supp. XV:** 154, 162

One World at a Time (Kooser), **Supp. XIX:** 116, **122–123**

One Writer's Beginnings (Welty), **Retro. Supp. I:** 339, 340, 341, 343, 344, 355–356

"One Year" (Olds), **Supp. X:** 210

On Fire (L. Brown), **Supp. XXI:** 41, **48–49**

On Fire (Silver), **Supp. XXIV:** 264

"On First Looking Into Chapman's Homer" (Keats), **Supp. XXI:** 64

"On First Looking Out through Juan de la Cosa's Eyes" (Olson), **Supp. II Part 2:** 565, 566, 570, 579

"On First Opening *The Lyric Year*" (W. C. Williams), **Retro. Supp. I:** 414

"On Freedom's Ground" (Wilbur), **Supp. III Part 2:** 562

On Glory's Course (Purdy), **Supp. VII:** 275–276, 279, 280

On Grief and Reason (Brodsky), **Supp. VIII: 31–32**

"On Hearing a Symphony of Beethoven" (Millay), **III:** 132–133

"On Hearing the Airlines Will Use a Psychological Profile to Catch Poten-

tial Skyjackers" (Dunn), **Supp. XI:** 144–145

On Human Finery (Bell), **Supp. I Part 2:** 636

"On *Imagerie:* Esther Williams, 1944" (Sobin), **Supp. XVI:** 294

"On Imagination" (Wheatley), **Supp. XX: 281**

"On Imminence: An Essay" (Sobin), **Supp. XVI:** 291

On Kingdom Mountain (Mosher), **Supp. XXII:** 203, 205, 206, 207, 208, 209, 212, 214, **216**

Onkl Mozes (Uncle Moses) (Asch), **Supp. XXIII:** 5

"On leaving my children John and Jane at School, in the Atlantic states, and preparing to return to the interior"(J. Schoolcraft), **Supp. XXIII:** 227, 228, 232, 233, 235, 236

On Liberty (Mill), **Supp. XI:** 196

"On Looking Alone at a Place" (M. F. K. Fisher), **Supp. XVII:** 91

"On Looking at a Copy of Alice Meynell's Poems, Given Me, Years Ago, by a Friend" (Lowell), **II:** 527–528

"On Lookout Mountain" (Hayden), **Supp. II Part 1:** 380

Only a Few of Us Left (Marquand), **III:** 55

"Only Animal, The" (F. Wright), **Supp. XVII:** 245

"Only a Pawn in Their Game" (song, Dylan), **Supp. XVIII:** 24

Only as Far as Brooklyn (Kenny), **Supp. XXIII: 148–151,** 152

"Only Bar in Dixon, The" (Hugo), **Supp. VI:** 140, 141

Only Dangerous Thing, The (Di Piero), **Supp. XIX: 37–38**

Only Dark Spot in the Sky, The (Dove), **Supp. IV Part 1:** 244

"Only Good Indian, The" (Humphrey), **Supp. IX:** 101

"Only Goodness" (Lahiri), **Supp. XXI:** 186, 188

Only in America (Golden), **Supp. VIII:** 244

"Only in the Dream" (Eberhart), **I:** 523

"Only Path to Tomorrow, The" (Rand), **Supp. IV Part 2:** 524

"Only Rose, The" (Jewett), **II:** 408

"Only Son of the Doctor, The" (Gordon), **Supp. IV Part 1:** 305, 306

"Only the Cat Escapes", **Supp. XII:** 150–151

"Only the Dead Know Brooklyn" (Wolfe), **IV:** 451

"Only When I Am Quiet and Do Not Speak"(Hirshfield), **Supp. XXIII:** 133

Only When I Laugh (Simon), **Supp. IV Part 2:** 575

Only World, The (Hull), **Supp. XXI:** 129, **138–141**

On Man and Manhood (Kriegel), **Supp. XXIV: 224–225**

"On Manhood, Disease, and the Authentic Self" (Kriegel), **Supp. XXIV:** 215

"On Meditation"(J. Schoolcraft), **Supp. XXIII:** 229

"On Messrs. Hussey and Coffin" (Wheatley), **Supp. XX: 280**

On Moral Fiction (Gardner), **Supp. VI:** 61, **71,** 72, 73

"On Morality" (Didion), **Supp. IV Part 1:** 196

"On Mt. Philo in November" (Di Piero), **Supp. XIX:** 37, 39

"On My Own" (Levine), **Supp. V:** 181, 189–190

"On My Own Work" (Wilbur), **Supp. III Part 2:** 541–542

On Native Grounds: An Interpretation of Modern American Prose Literature (Kazin), **I:** 517; **Supp. I Part 2:** 650; **Supp. VIII:** 93, 96–97, 98, **100–102**

"On Not Being a Dove" (Updike), **Retro. Supp. I:** 323

"On Open Form" (Merwin), **Supp. III Part 1:** 347–348, 353

On Photography (Sontag), **Supp. III Part 2:** 451, 458, 462–465

"On Poetry"(Hadas), **Supp. XXIII:** 115, 116

"On Political Poetry" (R. Bly), **Supp. IV Part 1:** 61

On Politics: A Carnival of Buncombe (Moos, ed.), **III:** 116

"On Pretentiousness" (Kushner), **Supp. IX:** 131–132

"On Quitting a Little College" (Stafford), **Supp. XI:** 321

"On Reading Eckerman's Conversations with Goethe" (Masters), **Supp. I Part 2:** 458

On Reading Shakespeare (L. P. Smith), **Supp. XIV:** 345–346

"On Reading to Oneself" (Gass), **Supp. VI:** 88, 89

"On Recollection" (Wheatley), **Supp. XX: 287**

On Revolution (Arendt), **Retro. Supp. I:** 87

On Second Thought (Kenny), **Supp. XXIII:** 144

"On Seeing Larry Rivers's *Washington Crossing the Delaware* at the Museum of Modern Art" (O'Hara), **Supp. XV:** 186; **Supp. XXIII:** 208, 214

"On Seeing Red" (Walker), **Supp. III Part 2:** 527

"On Social Plays" (A. Miller), **III:** 147, 148, 159

Onstad, Katrina, **Supp. XXIV:** 209

"On Steinbeck's Story 'Flight' " (Stegner), **Supp. IV Part 2:** 596

"On Style" (Sontag), **Supp. III Part 2:** 456–459, 465–466

"On Suicide" (Hay), **Supp. XIV:** 130, 132

"On Teaching the Young Laurel to Shoot" (Bynner), **Supp. XV:** 50

"On the Antler" (Proulx), **Supp. VII:** 252–253

"On the Avenue" (Espaillat), **Supp. XXI:** 112

On the Banks of Plum Creek (L. I. Wilder), **Supp. XXII:** 294, 299

"On the Banks of the Wabash" (Paul Dresser), **Retro. Supp. II:** 94

"On the Beach, at Night" (Whitman), **IV:** 348

"On the Bosom of This Grave and Wasted Land I Will Lay My Head" (Ray), **Supp. XVIII:** 189

On the Boundary (Tillich), **Retro. Supp. I:** 326

"On the Building of Springfield" (Lindsay), **Supp. I Part 2:** 381

"On the Coast of Maine" (Hayden), **Supp. II Part 1:** 381

On the Contrary: Articles of Belief (McCarthy), **II:** 559, 562

"On the Death of a Friend's Child" (Lowell), **Supp. I Part 2:** 409

"On the Death of Cardinal Tisserant" (Bronk), **Supp. XXI:** 32

"On the Death of General Wooster" (Wheatley), **Supp. XX: 287**

"On the Death of Rev. Mr. George Whitefield—1770" (Wheatley), **Supp. XX: 280,Supp. XX: 282–283**

"On the Death of Senator Thomas J. Walsh" (Winters), **Supp. II Part 2:** 802, 806

"On the Death of Yeats" (Bogan), **Supp. III Part 1:** 59

"On the Death of Zhukov" (Brodsky), **Supp. VIII:** 27

"On the Disadvantages of Central Heating" (Clampitt), **Supp. IX:** 41, 47, 52

"On the Doric Rock, Lake Superior"(J. Schoolcraft), **Supp. XXIII:** 232

On the Drumhead: A Selection from the Writing of Mike Quin (Carlisle, ed.), **Supp. XVIII:** 223, 226

"On the Edge" (Levine), **Supp. V:** 181–182

On the Edge and Over (Levine), **Supp. V:** 178, 180–182, 186

On the Edge of the Great Rift: Three Novels of Africa (Theroux), **Supp. VIII:** 316

"On the Edge of Visible Light"(Schott), **Supp. XXIII:** 242

"On the Eve of the Feast of the Immaculate Conception, 1942" (Lowell), **II:** 538; **Retro. Supp. II:** 185

"On the Eyes of an SS Officer" (Wilbur), **Supp. III Part 2:** 548

"On the Failure of Meaning in the Absence of Objective Analogs" (Bronk), **Supp. XXI:** 31

"On the Fall of General Earl Cornwallis" (Freneau), **Supp. II Part 1:** 261

"On the Folly of Writing Poetry" (Freneau), **Supp. II Part 1:** 263

On the Frontier (Auden and Isherwood), **Supp. II Part 1:** 13; **Supp. XIV:** 163

On the Great Atlantic Rainway: Selected Poems, 1950–1988 (Koch), **Supp. XV:** 177

"On the History of Poetry" (Halliday), **Supp. XIX:** 88, 89

"On the Hysterical Playground" (Watman), **Supp. XX: 93**

"On the Island" (Stern), **Supp. IX:** 290

"On the Late Eclipse" (Bryant), **Supp. I Part 1:** 152

On the Laws of the Poetic Art (Hecht), **Supp. X:** 58

On the Line (Swados), **Supp. XIX: 258–260**

"On the Line" (Swados), **Supp. XIX:** 259

"On the Marginal Way" (Wilbur), **Supp. III Part 2:** 558, 559

On the Mesa (Nichols), **Supp. XIII:** 268

"On the Moon and Matriarchal Consciousness" (Neumann), **Supp. IV Part 1:** 68

"On the Morning after the Sixties" (Didion), **Supp. IV Part 1:** 205, 206

On the Motion and Immobility of Douve (Bonnefoy; Kinnell, trans.), **Supp. III Part 1:** 235

"On the Mullica"(Schott), **Supp. XXIII:** 253

"On the Murder of Lieutenant José del Castillo by the Falangist Bravo Martinez, July 12, 1936" (Levine), **Supp. V:** 187

"On the Night of a Friend's Wedding" (Robinson), **III:** 524

"On the Occasion of a Poem: Richard Hugo" (Wright), **Supp. III Part 2:** 596

On the Occasion of My Last Afternoon (Gibbons), **Supp. X:** 46, **50–53**

On the Origin of Species (Darwin), **Supp. XIV:** 192

"On the Parapet" (Tanner), **Retro. Supp. II:** 205

"On the Platform" (Nemerov), **III:** 287

On the Poetry of Philip Levine: Stranger to Nothing (Levis), **Supp. XI:** 257

"On the Pottlecombe Cornice" (Sturgis), **Supp. XX: 233, 240**

"On the Powers of the Human Understanding" (Freneau), **Supp. II Part 1:** 274

On the Prejudices, Predilections, and Firm Beliefs of William Faulkner (Brooks), **Supp. XIV:** 13

"On the Pulse of Morning" (Angelou), **Supp. IV Part 1:** 15–17

"On the Railway Platform" (Jarrell), **II:** 370

"On the Rainy River" (O'Brien), **Supp. V:** 250

On the Rebound: A Story and Nine Poems (Purdy), **Supp. VII:** 276–277

"On the Religion of Nature" (Freneau), **Supp. II Part 1:** 275

"On the River" (Dunbar), **Supp. II Part 1:** 193

"On the River" (Levine), **Supp. V:** 193

On the River Styx and Other Stories (Matthiessen), **Supp. V:** 212

On the Road (Kerouac), **Retro. Supp. I:** 102; **Supp. III Part 1:** 92, 218, 222–224, 226, 230–231; **Supp. V:** 336; **Supp. X:** 269; **Supp. XIII:** 275; **Supp. XIV:** 138, 150; **Supp. XV:** 221; **Supp. XVIII:** 20, 138; **Supp. XXI:** 53; **Supp. XXIV:** 281

"On the Road Home" (Stevens), **Retro. Supp. I:** 306

On the Road with the Archangel (Buechner), **Supp. XII:** 54

"On the Rope" (Richard), **Supp. XIX:** 211–212

"On the Run" (Boyle), **Supp. XXIV:** 52

On These I Stand: An Anthology of the Best Poems of Countee Cullen (Cullen), **Supp. IV Part 1:** 173

"On the Skeleton of a Hound" (Wright), **Supp. III Part 2:** 593

"On the Staten Island Ferry"(Kenny), **Supp. XXIII:** 154

"On the Street" (Peacock), **Supp. XIX:** 199

"On the Street: Monument" (Gunn Allen), **Supp. IV Part 1:** 326

"On the Subway" (Olds), **Supp. X:** 207

"On the System of Policy Hitherto Pursued by Their Government" (Barlow), **Supp. II Part 1:** 82

"On the Teaching of Modern Literature" (Trilling), **Supp. III Part 2:** 509–510

"On the Uniformity and Perfection of Nature" (Freneau), **Supp. II Part 1:** 275

"On the Universality and Other Attributes of the God of Nature" (Freneau), **Supp. II Part 1:** 275

"On the Use of Trisyllabic Feet in Iambic Verse" (Bryant), **Supp. I Part 1:** 156

On the Verge: Emerging Poets (Ellis and Lease, eds.), **Supp. XXI:** 246

On the Waterfront (film, Kazan), **Supp. XVIII: 250–251,** 252, **253**

"On the Way Home" (L. I. Wilder), **Supp. XXII:** 292

On the Way to the Island (Ferry), **Supp. XXIV:** 147, **148–149,** 150

"On the Way to the San Remo"(O'Hara), **Supp. XXIII:** 212, 219

On the Way toward a Phenomenological Psychology: The Psychology of William James (Linschoten), **II:** 362

"On the Way to Work" (Dunn), **Supp. XI:** 149–150

"On the Wide Heath" (Millay), **III:** 130

"On the Writing of Novels" (Buck), **Supp. II Part 1:** 121

On the Yard (Braly), **Supp. XVIII:** 147

On This Island (Auden), **Supp. II Part 1:** 11

On This Side of the River (Ferry), **Supp. XXIV: 161–162**

"On Time" (O'Hara), **III:** 369–370

"Ontological Episode of the Asylum" (Carruth), **Supp. XVI:** 48, 50

"Ontology of the Sentence, The" (Gass), **Supp. VI:** 77

"On Top" (Leopold), **Supp. XIV:** 188

"On Top" (Snyder), **Supp. VIII:** 304

"On Translating Akhmatova" (Kunitz), **Supp. III Part 1:** 268

"On Turning Ten" (Collins), **Supp. XXI:** 64

"On Waking to Old Debts" (Keillor), **Supp. XVI:** 167

On William Stafford: The Worth of Local Things (Andrews, ed.), **Supp. XI:** 311, 312, 317, 321, 324, 326

"On Writing" (Carver), **Supp. III Part 1:** 142–143

"On Writing" (Nin), **Supp. X:** 182

On Your Own (Gallagher), **Supp. XXIV:** 166

Opatoshu, Joseph, **IV:** 9

"Open Boat, The" (Crane), **I:** 408, 415, 416–417, 423; **Retro. Supp. I:** 325; **Supp. XIV:** 51

Open Boat and Other Stories (Crane), **I:** 408

Open Door, The (Skloot), **Supp. XX:** 194, 196, 208

Open Heart: A Patient's Story of Life-Saving Medicine and Life-Giving Friendship (Neugeboren), **Supp. XVI:** 217, **229–230**

Open House (Roethke), **III:** 529–530, 540

"Open House" (Roethke), **III:** 529

"Opening, An" (Swenson), **Supp. IV Part 2:** 639

Opening of the Field, The (Duncan), **Supp. III Part 2:** 625

Opening the Hand (Merwin), **Supp. III Part 1:** 341, 353, 355

"Open Letter" (Roethke), **III:** 532, 534

"Open Letter to Surrealists Everywhere, An" (H. Miller), **III:** 184

Open Meeting, The (Gurney), **Supp. V:** 98

Open Net (Plimpton), **Supp. XVI:** 241

"Open Road, The" (Dreiser), **II:** 44

Open Sea, The (Masters), **Supp. I Part 2:** 471

Open Season: Sporting Adventures (Humphrey), **Supp. IX:** 95

"Open Secret" (Nelson), **Supp. XVIII:** 185

"Open the Gates" (Kunitz), **Supp. III Part 1:** 264–265, 267

"Opera Company, The" (Merrill), **Supp. III Part 1:** 326

Operating Instructions: A Journal of My Son's First Year (Lamott), **Supp. XX:** 136–137, 142

"Operation, The" (Sanders), **Supp. XVI:** 266

"Operation, The" (Sexton), **Supp. II Part 2:** 675, 679

Operation Shylock: A Confession (P. Roth), **Retro. Supp. II:** 279, 280, 291

Operation Sidewinder (Shepard), **Supp. III Part 2:** 434–435, 439, 446–447

Operations in North African Waters (Morison), **Supp. I Part 2:** 490

Operation Wandering Soul (Powers), **Supp. IX:** 212, **217–219**

Opffer, Emil, **Retro. Supp. II:** 80

"Opinion" (Du Bois), **Supp. II Part 1:** 173

Opinionator, The (Bierce), **I:** 209

Opinions of Oliver Allston (Brooks), **I:** 254, 255, 256

O Pioneers! (Cather), **I:** 314, 317–319, 320; **Retro. Supp. I:** 1, 5, 6, **7–9**, 10, 13, 20; **Retro. Supp. II:** 136

Oppen, George, **IV:** 415; **Supp. III Part 2:** 614, 615, 616, 626, 628; **Supp. XIV:** 285, 286, 287; **Supp. XVI:** 282, 283; **Supp. XVII:** 243; **Supp. XXI:**

19, **Supp. XXI:** 29, 23; **Supp. XXIII:** 165–166, 168

Oppenheim, James, **I:** 106, 109, 239, 245; **Supp. XV:** 294, 296, 298, 299, 301, 302, 307, 313; **Supp. XX: 68**

Oppenheimer, J. Robert, **I:** 137, 492

Oppenheimer, Judy, **Supp. IX:** 115, 116, 118, 120, 126

"Opportunity for American Fiction, An" (Howells), **Supp. I Part 2:** 645–646

Opposing Self, The (Trilling), **Supp. III Part 2:** 506–507

"Opposition" (Lanier), **Supp. I Part 1:** 368, 373

Oprah's Roots: An African American Lives Special (television production), **Supp. XX:** 99

Opticks: A Poem in Seven Sections (Goldbarth), **Supp. XII:** 177, **178**

Optimist's Daughter, The (Welty), **IV:** 261, 280; **Retro. Supp. I:** 339, 355

"Optimist's Daughter, The" (Welty), **IV:** 280–281

Options (O. Henry), **Supp. II Part 1:** 410

Opus Posthumous (Stevens), **IV:** 76, 78

Opus Posthumous (W. Stevens), **Supp. XVII:** 241

Oracle at Stoneleigh Court, The (Taylor), **Supp. V:** 328

Orage, Alfred, **III:** 473

"O/Rain-in-the-Face"(Kenny), **Supp. XXIII:** 156

Orange, Max (pseudonym). *See* Heller, Joseph

Orange Fish, The (Shields), **Supp. VII:** 318, 320, 323, 328

Orangery, The (Sorrentino), **Supp. XXI:** 228

Oranges (exhibition, Hartigan), **Supp. XXIII:** 210

Oranges (McPhee), **Supp. III Part 1:** 298–299, 301, 309

Oranges: 12 Pastorals (O'Hara), **Supp. XXIII:** 210

"Oranging of America, The" (Apple), **Supp. XVII:** 3–4, 6

Oranging of America and Other Short Stories, The (Apple), **Supp. XVII:** 1–2, **3–4**, 7, 8

Oration Delivered at Washington, July Fourth, 1809 (Barlow), **Supp. II Part 1:** 80, 83

Orations and Addresses (Bryant), **Supp. I Part 1:** 158

Orators, The (Auden), **Supp. II Part 1:** 6, 7, 11, 18–19

Orbach, Jerry, **Supp. XXIII:** 103

Orb Weaver, The (Francis), **Supp. IX:** 81–82

"Orchard" (Doolittle), **Supp. I Part 1:** 263–264, 265, 266

"Orchard" (Eberhart), **I:** 539

Orchard, The (B. Kelly), **Supp. XVII:** 123, 127, **130–133**

"Orchard, The" (B. Kelly), **Supp. XVII:** 133

Orchard Keeper, The (McCarthy), **Supp. VIII:** 175–176

Orchestra (Davies), **III:** 541

"Orchids" (Roethke), **III:** 530–531

"Or Consider Prometheus" (Clampitt), **Supp. IX:** 44

Ordeal of Mansart, The (Du Bois), **Supp. II Part 1:** 185–186

Ordeal of Mark Twain, The (Brooks), **I:** 240, 247, 248; **II:** 482

Ordering the Façade: Photography and Contemporary Southern Women's Writing (Henninger), **Supp. XXI:** 253

"Order of Insects" (Gass), **Supp. VI:** 83

Order Out of Chaos (McPherson), **Supp. IV Part 1:** 2, 12

"Ordinary Afternoon in Charlottesville, An" (Wright), **Supp. V:** 344

"Ordinary Days" (Dunn), **Supp. XI:** 151

"Ordinary Evening in New Haven, An" (Stevens), **IV:** 91–92; **Retro. Supp. I:** 297, 300, 311, 312

Ordinary Heroes (Turow), **Supp. XVII:** 221–222, 223

Ordinary Life (Crooker), **Supp. XXIII:** 56

Ordinary Love (Smiley), **Supp. VI:** 292, **299–300**

Ordinary Love; and Good Will: Two Novellas (Smiley), **Supp. VI:** 292, **299–300**

Ordinary Miracles (Jong), **Supp. V:** 115, 130–131

"Ordinary Time: Virginia Woolf and Thucydides on War" (Carson), **Supp. XII:** 111

"Ordinary Women, The" (Stevens), **IV:** 81

Ordways, The (Humphrey), **Supp. IX:** 95, **98–100**, 109; **Supp. XV:** 353

"Oread" (Doolittle), **II:** 520–521; **Supp. I Part 1:** 265–266

Oregon Message, An (Stafford), **Supp. XI:** 328–329

Oregon Trail, The (Parkman), **II:** 312; **Supp. II Part 2:** 592, 595–596, 598, 606

Oresteia (Aeschylus), **Supp. IX:** 103

"Orestes at Tauris" (Jarrell), **II:** 376, 377

Orfalea, Gregory, **Supp. XIII:** 278

Orfeo ed Euridice (Gluck), **II:** 210, 211

Orff, Carl, **Supp. X:** 63

"Organizer's Wife, The" (Bambara), **Supp. XI:** 8–9

"Organmeister: Hasse After Marien-kirche" (Bierds), **Supp. XVII:** 34

"Orgy" (Rukeyser), **Supp. VI:** 280

Orgy, The (Rukeyser), **Supp. VI:** 274, 283

"Orgy of Southerness, An" (Pickering), **Supp. XXI:** 203

"Oriental Rug"(Balakian), **Supp. XXIII:** 23, 24–25

"Orientation of Hope, The" (Locke), **Supp. XIV:** 212–213

Orient Express (Dos Passos), **I:** 480

"Orient Express, The" (Jarrell), **II:** 382, 383–384

Origen, Adamantius, **IV:** 153

"Origin" (Harjo), **Supp. XII:** 219

Original Child Bomb: Points for Meditation to Be Scratched on the Walls of a Cave (Merton), **Supp. VIII:** 203

Original Essays on the Poetry of Anne Sexton (George), **Supp. IV Part 2:** 450

"Original Follies Girl, The" (Z. Fitzgerald), **Supp. IX:** 71

Original Light (Goldbarth), **Supp. XII:** 181, **183–184,** 188

Original Love (Peacock), **Supp. XIX: 199–201,** 206

Original of Laura, The (Nabokov), **Retro. Supp. I:** 266

"Original Sin" (Jeffers), **Supp. II Part 2:** 426

"Original Sin" (Warren), **IV:** 245

Origin: Hawaii (Taggard), **Supp. XXII:** 272, 284

"Origin of Extermination in the Imagination, The" (Gass), **Supp. VI:** 89

Origin of Species, The (Darwin), **II:** 173, 462; **Supp. XVI:** 13

Origin of the Brunists, The (Coover), **Supp. V:** 39, 41, 52

"Origin of the Miscodeed, or the Maid of Taquimenon"(J. Schoolcraft), **Supp. XXIII:** 235

"Origin of the Robin, The"(J. Schoolcraft), **Supp. XXIII:** 234, 235

"Origins and History of Consciousness" (Rich), **Supp. I Part 2:** 570

"Origins of a Nonfiction Writer" (Talese), **Supp. XVII:** 208

"Origins of a Poem" (Levertov), **Supp. III Part 1:** 273

"Origins of the Beat Generation, The" (Kerouac), **Supp. III Part 1:** 231

Origo, Iris, **IV:** 328

"O'Riley's Late-Bloomed Little Son" (X. J. Kennedy), **Supp. XV:** 159

"Orion" (Rich), **Supp. I Part 2:** 557

O'Riordan, Conal Holmes O'Connell, **III:** 465

Orlacs Hände (film, Weine), **Supp. XVII:** 58

Orlando (V. Woolf), **Supp. XVII:** 86

Orlando (Woolf), **Supp. I Part 2:** 718; **Supp. VIII:** 263; **Supp. XII:** 9

Orlando Furioso (Ariosto), **Supp. XV:** 175

Orlik, Emil, **Supp. XXIII:** 6

Orloff, Chana, **Supp. XXIII:** 6

Orlovsky, Peter, **Supp. XII:** 121, 126; **Supp. XIV:** 150; **Supp. XVIII:** 27

Ormonde, Czenzi, **Supp. IV Part 1:** 132

Ormond; or, The Secret Witness (Brown), **Supp. I Part 1:** 133–137

Ornament and Crime (Loos), **Supp. XVI:** 187

Orne, Sarah. *See* Jewett, Sarah Orne

Ornithological Biography; or, An Account of the Habits of the Birds of the United States of America, and Interspersed with Delineations of American Scenery and Manners (Audubon), **Supp. XVI:**13; **7–10**

"Ornithology" (Hull), **Supp. XXI:** 138–139

Ornitz, Samuel, **Supp. IX:** 227; **Supp. XIII:** 166

Ornstein, Leo, **Supp. XX: 75**

O'Rourke, William, **Supp. XXII:** 213

Orphan Angel, The (Wylie), **Supp. I Part 2:** 707, 709, 714, 717, 719–721, 722, 724

Orphan's Tale, An (Neugeboren), **Supp. XVI:** 222, 223

Orpheus (Rukeyser), **Supp. VI:** 273

"Orpheus" (Winters), **Supp. II Part 2:** 801

"Orpheus, Eurydice, Hermes" (Rilke), **Supp. VIII:** 31, 32

"Orpheus (1)" (Atwood), **Supp. XIII:** 35

"Orpheus (2)" (Atwood), **Supp. XIII:** 35

"Orpheus Alone" (Strand), **Supp. IV Part 2:** 632

Orpheus Descending (T. Williams), **IV:** 380, 381, 382, 385, 386, 387, 389, 391–392, 395, 396, 398

Orr, David, **Supp. XXI:** 62

Orr, Peter, **Supp. I Part 2:** 538, 540, 543

Orse, Brian, **Supp. XX: 264**

Ortega y Gasset, José, **I:** 218, 222; **Supp. IV Part 2:** 521; **Supp. XXIII:** 165

Ortiz, Simon J., **Supp. IV Part 1:** 319, 404; **Supp. IV Part 2: 497–515,** 557; **Supp. XII:** 217, 218

"Ortlieb's Uptown Taproom" (Di Piero), **Supp. XIX:** 46, 47

Orton, Joe, **Supp. XXIV:** 113, 126, 263

O'Ruddy, The (Crane), **I:** 409, 424

Orwell, George, **I:** 489; **II:** 454, 580; **Supp. I Part 2:** 523, 620; **Supp. II Part 1:** 143; **Supp. IV Part 1:** 236; **Supp. V:** 250; **Supp. VIII:** 241; **Supp. XIV:** 112, 158; **Supp. XVII:** 228, 229; **Supp. XVIII:** 137, 138; **Supp. XX: 86**

Osborn, Dwight, **III:** 218–219, 223

"Osborn Look, The" (Morris), **III:** 221

Osgood, Frances, **Supp. XVII:** 75

Osgood, J. R., **II:** 283

O'Shea, Kitty, **II:** 137

O'Shea, Milo, **Supp. XI:** 308

"Oshkikwe's Baby" (traditional Chippewa story), **Supp. IV Part 1:** 333

Oshogay, Delia, **Supp. IV Part 1:** 333

Ossana, Diana, **Supp. V:** 230–231, 232

Ossian, **Supp. I Part 2:** 491

Ossip, Kathleen, **Supp. X:** 201

"Osso Bucco" (Collins), **Supp. XXI:** 60

Ostanovka v Pustyne (A halt in the wilderness) (Brodsky), **Supp. VIII:** 21

Oster, Judith, **Supp. XVI:** 151

Ostriker, Alicia, **Supp. I Part 2:** 540; **Supp. IV Part 2:** 439, 447, 449; **Supp. X:** 207, 208; **Supp. XI:** 143; **Supp. XV:** 251

Ostrom, Hans, **Retro. Supp. I:** 195

Oswald, Lee Harvey, **III:** 234, 235

Oswald II (DeLillo), **Supp. VI:** 16

Oswald's Tale (Mailer), **Retro. Supp. II:** 212–213

"Otagamiad, The"(J. Schoolcraft), **Supp. XXIII:** 223

O Taste and See (Levertov), **Supp. III Part 1:** 278–279, 281

Othello (Shakespeare), **I:** 284–285

"Other, The" (Sexton), **Supp. II Part 2:** 692

Other America, The (Harrington), **I:** 306

"Other American Renaissance, The" (Tompkins), **Supp. XVIII:** 258

Other Destinies: Understanding the American Indian Novel (Owens), **Supp. IV Part 1:** 404

otherelectricities.com, **Supp. XXIV:** 240–241

Other Electricities: Stories (Monson), **Supp. XXIV:** 230, **231–234,** 235–236, 238, 241

"Other Frost, The" (Jarrell), **Retro. Supp. I:** 121

Other Gods: An American Legend (Buck), **Supp. II Part 1:** 123, 130–131

Other House, The (James), **Retro. Supp. I:** 229

"Other League of Nations, The" (Ríos), **Supp. IV Part 2:** 552

"Other Margaret, The" (Trilling), **Supp. III Part 2:** 504–505

"Other Miller, The" (Wolff), **Supp. VII:** 343–344

"Other Mothers" (Paley), **Supp. VI:** 225

"Other Night at Columbia, The" (Trilling), **Supp. XII:** 126

"Other People's Secrets" (Hampl), **Supp. XXII:** 94

"Other Robert Frost, The" (Jarrell), **Retro. Supp. I:** 135

Others (Shields), **Supp. VII:** 310

Other Side, The (Gordon), **Supp. IV Part 1:** 299, 306, 307–309, 310–311

Other Side, The/El Otro Lado (Alvarez), **Supp. VII:** 9–12

"Other Side, The"(Hadas), **Supp. XXIII:** 120

Other Side of the River, The (Wright), **Supp. V:** 332–333, 342

"Other Side of the River, The" (Wright), **Supp. V:** 335

"Other Tradition, The" (Ashbery), **Supp. III Part 1:** 15, 18

"Other Two, The" (Wharton), **Retro. Supp. I:** 367

Other Voices, Other Rooms (Capote), **Supp. III Part 1:** 113–118, 121, 123–124

"Other Wanderer, The" (Gibran), **Supp. XX: 124**

"Other War, The" (Cowley), **Supp. II Part 1:** 144

"Otherwise" (Kenyon), **Supp. VII:** 172, 174

Otherwise: New and Selected Poems (Kenyon), **Supp. VII:** 167, 172–174

Otherwise Than Being; or, Beyond Essence (Lévinas), **Supp. XVI:** 290, 291

"Other Woman, The" (Anderson), **I:** 114

"Other World, The" (Wrigley), **Supp. XVIII:** 307

Other Worlds Than This (Hadas), **Supp. XXIII:** 118, **124–125**

Otho the Great: A Tragedy in Five Acts (Keats), **Supp. XII:** 113

Otis, Harrison Gray, **Supp. I Part 2:** 479–481, 483, 486, 488

Otis, James, **III:** 577; **Supp. I Part 2:** 486; **Supp. XV:** 229

O to Be a Dragon (Moore), **III:** 215

"Otravida, Otravez" (Díaz), **Supp. XXIV:** 93

Otto, Rudolf, **Supp. XVII:** 243

"Ouija" (McClatchy), **Supp. XII:** 269–270

Oupensky, Peter, **Supp. XIV:** 188

Our America (Michaels), **Retro. Supp. I:** 379

Our America (W. Frank), **I:** 229; **Supp. IX:** 308; **Supp. XX:** 69–70, 75

Our Aperture (Monson), **Supp. XXIV:** 230, 239

"Our Assistant's Column" (Twain), **IV:** 193

"Our Bourgeois Literature" (Sinclair), **Supp. V:** 281

Our Brains and What Ails Them (Gilman), **Supp. XI:** 207

Our Century (Wilder), **IV:** 374

"Our Christmas Party" (E. Stoddard), **Supp. XV:** 273, 278

Our Country (Strong), **Supp. XIV:** 64

"Our Countrymen in Chains!" (Whittier), **Supp. I Part 2:** 688

"Our Cultural Humility" (Bourne), **I:** 223, 228

Our Depleted Society (Seymour), **Supp. XIII:** 264

"Our Dust" (Wright), **Supp. XV:** 345, 346

"Our Father Who Drowns the Birds" (Kingsolver), **Supp. VII:** 208–209

"Our First House" (Kingston), **Supp. V:** 169

Our Gang (P. Roth), **Retro. Supp. II:** 287; **Supp. III Part 2:** 414; **Supp. IV Part 1:** 388

"Our Good Day" (Cisneros), **Supp. VII:** 60

Our Ground Time Here Will Be Brief (Kumin), **Supp. IV Part 2:** 450–452

Our House in the Last World (Hijuelos), **Supp. VIII:** 73, 76–79, 87, 88

"Our Lady" (A. Finch), **Supp. XVII:** 77

"*Our Lady of the Annunciation*/Nuestra Señora de Anunciación" (Mora), **Supp. XIII:** 217, 224, 228

"Our Lady of Troy" (MacLeish), **III:** 3, 20

"Our Limitations" (Holmes), **Supp. I Part 1:** 314

"Our Martyred Soldiers" (Dunbar), **Supp. II Part 1:** 193

"Our Master" (Whittier), **Supp. I Part 2:** 704

"Our Mother Pocahontas" (Lindsay), **Supp. I Part 2:** 393

Our Mr. Wrenn: The Romantic Adventures of a Gentle Man (Lewis), **II:** 441

Our National Parks (Muir), **Supp. IX:** 181, 184

Our New York: A Personal Vision in Words and Photographs (Kazin), **Supp. VIII:** 106–107

Our Nig (Wilson), **Supp. XX:** 105

"Our Old Aunt Who Is Now in a Retirement Home" (Shields), **Supp. VII:** 310

Our Old Home: A Series of English Sketches (Hawthorne), **II:** 225; **Retro. Supp. I:** 163

"Our Own Movie Queen" (Z. Fitzgerald), **Supp. IX:** 71

"Our River Now" (L.-Y. Lee), **Supp. XV:** 224, 225

Our Selves (Bronk), **Supp. XXI:** 32

Ourselves to Know (O'Hara), **III:** 362, 365

Our Sister Killjoy: or, Reflections from a Black-Eyed Squint (Aidoo), **Supp. XXII:** 68

"Our Story Begins" (Wolff), **Supp. VII:** 345

"Our Sweating Selves" (Di Piero), **Supp. XIX:** 36

Our Town (Wilder), **IV:** 357, 364, 365, 366, 368–369

"Our Unplanned Cities" (Bourne), **I:** 229, 230

Our Wonder World, **Retro. Supp. I:** 341

Ouspensky, P. D., **I:** 383; **Supp. XX:** 116

"Out" (Harjo), **Supp. XII:** 219

"'Out, Out'" (Frost), **Retro. Supp. I:** 131

"Outcast" (McKay), **Supp. X:** 135

"Outcasts of Poker Flats, The" (Harte), **Supp. II Part 1:** 345, 347–348

Outcroppings (Harte), **Supp. II Part 1:** 343

Out Cry (T. Williams), **IV:** 383, 393

"Outcry, The" (James), **Retro. Supp. I:** 235

"Outdoor Shower" (Olds), **Supp. X:** 214

Outer Banks (Siddons), **Supp. XXII:** 239

Outerbridge Reach (Stone), **Supp. V:** 306–308

Outer Dark (McCarthy), **Supp. VIII:** 176–177

Outermost Dream, The: Essays and Reviews (Maxwell), **Supp. VIII:** 171–172

"Outing, The" (Baldwin), **Supp. I Part 1:** 63

Outlaw Journalist (McKeen), **Supp. XXIV:** 279, 288

"Out Like a Lamb" (Dubus), **Supp. VII:** 91

"Outline of an Autobiography" (Toomer), **Supp. III Part 2:** 478

"Outline Toward a Theory of the Mine Versus the Mind and the Harvard Outline" (Monson), **Supp. XXIV:** 235

Outlyer and Ghazals (Harrison), **Supp. VIII:** 41

"Out of Business" (Mora), **Supp. XIII:** 217

Out of Eden: Essays on Modern Art (Di Piero), **Supp. XIX:** 41, 42

"Out of My Deeper Heart" (Gibran), **Supp. XX:** 118

Out of My League (Plimpton), **Supp. XVI:** 233, 239

"Out of Nowhere into Nothing" (Anderson), **I:** 113

"Out of Season" (Hemingway), **II:** 263

"Out of the Cradle Endlessly Rocking" (Whitman), **IV:** 342, 343–345, 346, 351; **Retro. Supp. I:** 404, 406

"Out of the Deeps" (E. Stoddard), **Supp. XV:** 286

"Out of the Hospital and Under the Bar" (Ellison), **Retro. Supp. II:** 118–119; **Supp. II Part 1:** 246

"Out of the Rainbow End" (Sandburg), **III:** 594–595

"Out of the Sea, Early" (Swenson), **Supp. IV Part 2:** 645

"Out of the Snow" (Dubus), **Supp. VII:** 91

Out of the Stars (Purdy), **Supp. VII:** 281–282

"Out of the Woods" (Offutt), **Supp. XIX:** 169–170

Out of the Woods: Stories (Offutt), **Supp. XIX:** 163, 167, **169–172,** 175

"Out of Your Nakedness, Out of My Nakedness"(Hadas), **Supp. XXIII:** 125

"Outrageous" (Pickering), **Supp. XXI:** 202

Outre-Mer: A Pilgrimage beyond the Sea (Longfellow), **II:** 313, 491; **Retro. Supp. II:** 155, 165

"Outside" (Stafford), **Supp. XI:** 318

Outside, The (Glaspell), **Supp. III Part 1:** 179, 187

"Outside In" (Pickering), **Supp. XXI:** 197

Outsider, The (Wright), **IV:** 478, 481, 488, 491–494, 495

Outside World, The (Mirvis), **Supp. XX: 177, 178, 185–190**

Out Went the Candle (Swados), **Supp. XIX:** 257

Out West (Shanley), **Supp. XIV:** 317

"Out with the Old" (Yates), **Supp. XI:** 342

"Ouzo for Robin" (Merrill), **Supp. III Part 1:** 326

"Oval Portrait, The" (Poe), **III:** 412, 415; **Retro. Supp. II:** 270

"Oven Bird, The" (Frost), **Retro. Supp. I:** 131; **Supp. XI:** 153; **Supp. XIX:** 15

"Over 2,000 Illustrations and a Complete Concordance" (Bishop), **Retro. Supp. II:** 45; **Supp. I Part 1:** 90–91

"Over by the River" (Maxwell), **Supp. VIII:** 169, 170

"Overcoat, The" (Gogol), **Supp. XXII:** 59

"Overgrown Pasture, The" (Lowell), **II:** 523

"Overheard through the Walls of the Invisible City" (Bidart), **Supp. XV:** 32

"Over Kansas" (Ginsberg), **Supp. II Part 1:** 320

Overland to the Islands (Levertov), **Supp. III Part 1:** 275, 276

Overlook, The (Connelly), **Supp. XXI: 78**

"Overlooking Lake Champlain" (Di Piero), **Supp. XIX:** 47

"Overnight Pass" (X. J. Kennedy), **Supp. XV:** 168

Overreachers, The (Talese), **Supp. XVII:** 202

"Over-Soul, The" (Emerson), **II:** 7

Over the Blue Mountain (Richter), **Supp. XVIII:** 220

"Over the Edge"(Hadas), **Supp. XXIII:** 115

"Over the Hill" (Dubus), **Supp. VII:** 76, 79–80

Overtime (Gurney), **Supp. V:** 104

"Overwhelming Question, An" (Taylor), **Supp. V:** 323

Ovid, **I:** 62; **II:** 542–543; **III:** 457, 467, 468, 470; **Retro. Supp. I:** 63; **Supp. IV Part 2:** 634; **Supp. XII:** 264

"Ovid in Exile" (Di Piero), **Supp. XIX:** 44

"Ovid's Farewell" (McClatchy), **Supp. XII:** 257–258

Owen, David, **II:** 34

Owen, Maureen, **Supp. IV Part 2:** 423

Owen, Wilfred, **II:** 367, 372; **III:** 524; **Supp. X:** 146; **Supp. XVII:** 245; **Supp. XVIII:** 92; **Supp. XIX:** 17

Owens, Hamilton, **III:** 99, 109

Owens, Louis, **Supp. IV Part 1:** 404

"O Where Are You Going?" (Auden), **Supp. X:** 116

"Owl, The" (Wrigley), **Supp. XVIII:** 297–298, 301

Owl in the Attic, The (Thurber), **Supp. I Part 2:** 614

Owl in the Mask of the Dreamer, The: Collected Poems (Haines), **Supp. XII:** 211

"Owl in the Sarcophagus, The" (Stevens), **Retro. Supp. I:** 300

Owl's Clover (Stevens), **Retro. Supp. I:** 298, **303–304**

"Owl's Clover" (Stevens), **IV:** 75

Owl's Insomnia, Poems by Rafael Alberti, The (Strand, trans.), **Supp. IV Part 2:** 630

Owl Spirit Dwelling (Gallagher), **Supp. XXIV:** 170

Owlstone Crown, The (X. J. Kennedy), **Supp. XV:** 162, **164**

"Owl Who Was God, The" (Thurber), **Supp. I Part 2:** 610

Owning Jolene (Hearon), **Supp. VIII:** **66–67**

"Owning the Masters" (Nelson), **Supp. XVIII:** 171

Oxford Anthology of American Literature, The, **III:** 197; **Supp. I Part 1:** 254

Oxford Book of American Verse (Matthiessen, ed.), **Retro. Supp. I:** 40

Oxford Book of Children's Verse in America, The (Hall, ed.), **Supp. XIV:** 126

Oxford Companion to Twentieth-Century Poetry (Hamilton, ed.), **Supp. XVII:** 243

Oxford History of the American People, The (Morison), **Supp. I Part 2:** 495–496

Oxford History of the United States, 1783–1917, The (Morison), **Supp. I Part 2:** 483–484

"Oxford Town" (song, Dylan), **Supp. XVIII:** 24

Oxherding Tale (Johnson), **Supp. VI:** **190–192,** 193, 194, 196

Oxley, William, **Supp. XV:** 125

"O Yes" (Olsen), **Supp. XIII:** 294, 298, **299–300,** 301

"O Youth and Beauty!" (Cheever), **Retro. Supp. I:** 335

"Oysters" (Sexton), **Supp. II Part 2:** 692

"Ozark Odes" (Wright), **Supp. XV:** 346

Ozick, Cynthia, **Supp. V:** **257–274;** **Supp. VIII:** 141; **Supp. X:** 192; **Supp. XVII:** 42, 43, 49, 50

O-Zone (Theroux), **Supp. VIII:** 323–324

P

Pace, Patricia, **Supp. XI:** 245

Pacernik, Gary, **Supp. IX:** 287, 291

"Pacific Distances" (Didion), **Supp. IV Part 1:** 211

"Pacific Village" (M. F. K. Fisher), **Supp. XVII:** 83

Pack, Robert, **Supp. IV Part 2:** 621

"Packed Dirt, Churchgoing, a Dying Cat, a Traded Cat" (Updike), **IV:** 219

Packer, Nancy Huddleston, **Supp. XXIII:** 290

"Packing Mother's Things" (C. Frost), **Supp. XV:** 97

Pack of Lies (Sorrentino), **Supp. XXI:** 236, 237

Paco's Story (Heinemann), **Supp. XXII:** 103, **109–114,** 115

Paddock, Joe, **Supp. XVI:** 36

Paddock, Nancy, **Supp. XVI:** 36

Padel, Ruth, **Supp. XII:** 107

Padgett, Ron, **Supp. XV:** 190; **Supp. XXIII:** 218, 221; **Supp. XXIV:** 33, 34, 35, 37, 38, 39, 41, 42, 43, 44

Padmore, Dorothy, **Supp. XXI:** 166

Padmore, George, **Supp. XXI:** 166

"Paesano with a Trowel" *(Time),* **Supp. XX:** **46**

Pafko at the Wall (DeLillo), **Supp. VI:** 4

"Paganini and the Powers of Darkness" (Skloot), **Supp. XX:** **201**

"Pagan Prayer" (Cullen), **Supp. IV Part 1:** 170

Pagan Rabbi, The (Ozick), **Supp. V:** 262, 264, 265; **Supp. XVII:** 43

Pagan Rabbi and Other Stories, The (Ozick), **Supp. V:** 260, 261, 263–265

Pagan Spain (Wright), **IV:** 478, 488, 495

Page, Geraldine, **Supp. XV:** 7

Page, Kirby, **III:** 297

Page, Myra, **Supp. XXIII:** 166

Page, Thomas Nelson, **II:** 174, 176, 194; **Supp. XIV:** 61; **Supp. XXII:** 193

Page, Walter Hines, **II:** 174, 175; **Supp. I Part 1:** 370

Page, William, **Supp. XVIII:** 2, 11

Pages from a Cold Island (Exley), **Supp. XXIII:** 97, **103–106,** 108

"Pages from Cold Point" (Bowles), **Supp. IV Part 1:** 85, 86, 87

Paid on Both Sides: A Charade (Auden), **Supp. II Part 1:** 6, 18–19

Paige, Satchel, **Supp. I Part 1:** 234

Paige, T. D. D., **III:** 475

"Pail, The" (R. Bly), **Supp. XXI:** 85

Pain, Joseph, **Supp. I Part 2:** 502

Paine, Albert Bigelow, **I:** 249

Paine, Thomas, **I:** 490; **II:** 117, 302; **III:** 17, 148, 219; **Retro. Supp. I:** 390; **Supp. I Part 1:** 231; **Supp. I Part 2:** 501–525; **Supp. XI:** 55

"Pain has an Element of Blank" (Dickinson), **Retro. Supp. I:** 44

"Painstaking Historian, The" (Skloot), **Supp. XX:** **205–206**

"Paint and Powder" (Z. Fitzgerald), **Supp. IX:** 71

Painted Bird, The (Kosinski), **Supp. VII:** 215–217, 219–221, 222, 227

Painted Desert (F. Barthelme), **Supp. XI:** 28–29, 32

Painted Dresses (Hearon), **Supp. VIII:** 63

"Painted Head" (Ransom), **III:** 491, 494; **Supp. II Part 1:** 103, 314

Painted Turtle: Woman with Guitar (Major), **Supp. XXII:** **178–180,** 182

Painted Word, The (Wolfe), **Supp. III Part 2:** 580–581, 584; **Supp. XV:** 143

Painter, Pamela, **Supp. XXIII:** 295

"Painter, The" (Ashbery), **Supp. III Part 1:** 5–6, 13

Painter Dreaming in the Scholar's House, The (Nemerov), **III:** 269

"Painters" (Rukeyser), **Supp. VI:** 281

"Painting a Mountain Stream" (Nemerov), **III:** 275

"Pair a Spurs" (Proulx), **Supp. VII:** 263–264

"Pair of Bright Blue Eyes, A" (Taylor), **Supp. V:** 321

"Pair of Glasses, A" (Gallagher), **Supp. XXIV:** 174, 176

"Pajamas" (Olds), **Supp. X:** 206

Pakula, Alan, **Supp. XIII:** 264

Palace at 4 A.M. (Giacometti), **Supp. VIII:** 169

Palahniuk, Chuck, **Supp. XXI:** 116

"Palantine, The" (Whittier), **Supp. I Part 2:** 694, 696

Palatella, John, **Retro. Supp. II:** 48; **Supp. XXIV:** 39

"Palatski Man, The"(Dybek), **Supp. XXIII:** 70

Pale Fire (Nabokov), **III:** 244, 246, 252, 263–265; **Retro. Supp. I:** 264, 265, 266, 270, 271, 272, 276, 278, 335; **Supp. V:** 251, 253; **Supp. XXII:** 260

"Pale Horse, Pale Rider" (Porter), **III:** 436, 437, 441–442, 445, 446, 449

Pale Horse, Pale Rider: Three Short Novels (Porter), **III:** 433, 436–442; **Supp. VIII:** 157

"Pale Pink Roast, The" (Paley), **Supp. VI:** 217

"Pale Rider" (B. Kelly), **Supp. XVII:** 132–133

Paley, Grace, **Supp. VI:** **217–233;** **Supp. IX:** 212; **Supp. X:** 79, 164; **Supp. XII:** 309; **Supp. XXI:** 118; **Supp. XXII:** 172

Paley, William, **II:** 9

Palgrave, Francis Turner, **Retro. Supp. I:** 124; **Supp. XIV:** 340

Palgrave's Golden Treasury (Palgrave), **IV:** 405

Palimpsest (Doolittle), **Supp. I Part 1:** 259, 268, 269, 270–271

Palimpsest (Vidal), **Supp. X:** 186

"Palingenesis" (Longfellow), **II:** 498

Pal Joey (O'Hara), **III:** 361, 367–368
"Pal Joey" stories (O'Hara), **III:** 361
Pallbearers Envying the One Who Rides (Dobyns), **Supp. XIII:** 89
Palm, Edward Frederick, **Supp. XXII:** 103
"Palm, The" (Merwin), **Supp. III Part 1:** 355
Palmer, Charles, **II:** 111
Palmer, Elihu, **Supp. I Part 2:** 520
Palmer, George Herbert, **Supp. XIV:** 197
Palmer, Michael, **Supp. IV Part 2:** 421; **Supp. XVI:** 284; **Supp. XVII:** 240
Palmer, Samuel, **Supp. XV:** 81
Palmerston, Lord, **I:** 15
Palm-of-the-Hand-Stories (Kawabata), **Supp. XV:** 186
"Palm Wine" (McKnight), **Supp. XX:** **155**
"Palo Alto: The Marshes" (Hass), **Supp. VI:** 100
Palpable God, A: Thirty Stories Translated from the Bible with an Essay on the Origins and Life of Narrative (Price), **Supp. VI:** 262, 267
Palubinskas, Helen, **Supp. X:** 292
Pamela (Richardson), **Supp. V:** 127; **Supp. XX: 236; Supp. XXII:** 120
Pamela's First Musical (Wasserstein), **Supp. XV:** 333
Panache de bouquets (Komunyakaa; Cadieux, trans.), **Supp. XIII:** 127
Pan-African movement, **Supp. II Part 1:** 172, 175
Pancake, Breece D'J, **Supp. XXIII:** 35
Pandaemonium (Epstein), **Supp. XII:** 161, **172–173**
"Pandora" (Adams), **I:** 5
Pandora: New Tales of Vampires (Rice), **Supp. VII:** 295
Panek, LeRoy, **Supp. XIV:** 27
"Pangolin, The" (Moore), **III:** 210
Panic: A Play in Verse (MacLeish), **III:** 2, 20
Panic in Needle Park (film), **Supp. IV Part 1:** 198
Pankey, Eric, **Supp. XIX:** 44
Pantagruel (Rabelais), **II:** 112
"Pantaloon in Black" (Faulkner), **II:** 71
"Panther, The: A Bedtime Story"(P. Benedict), **Supp. XXIII:** 40
Panther and the Lash, The (Hughes), **Retro. Supp. I:** 204, 211; **Supp. I Part 1:** 342–344, 345–346
"Panthers, The" (Southern), **Supp. XI:** 295
"Panties and the Buddha" (Peacock), **Supp. XIX:** 199
"Pan *versus* Moses" (Ozick), **Supp. V:** 262
"Paolo Castelnuovo" (Everwine), **Supp. XV:** 83–84
"Papa and Mama Dance, The" (Sexton), **Supp. II Part 2:** 688
"Papago II"(Kenny), **Supp. XXIII:** 149–150
"Papago I"(Kenny), **Supp. XXIII:** 149–150
"Papa Who Wakes Up Tired in the Dark" (Cisneros), **Supp. VII:** 62

Pape, Greg, **Supp. V:** 180; **Supp. XIII:** 312; **Supp. XV:** 73
"Paper Covers Rock"(Thompson), **Supp. XXIII:** 291
Paper Doll (Parker), **Supp. XIX:** 184
"Paper Dolls Cut Out of a Newspaper" (Simic), **Supp. VIII:** 282
"Paper House, The" (Mailer), **III:** 42–43
Paper Lion (film, March), **Supp. XVI:** 242
Paper Lion: Confessions of a Last-String Quarterback (Plimpton), **Supp. XVI:** **242–243**
Papernick, Jon, **Supp. XVII:** 50
Papers on Literature and Art (Fuller), **Supp. II Part 1:** 292, 299
Papini, Giovanni, **Supp. XVI:** 195; **Supp. XXII:** 159, 161, 163
Papp, Joseph, **Supp. IV Part 1:** 234; **Supp. XXI:** 145
"Paprika Johnson" (Barnes), **Supp. III Part 1:** 33
"Par" (Bausch), **Supp. VII:** 54
"Parable from a Christian" (Notley), **Supp. XXII:** 235
"Parable in the Later Novels of Henry James" (Ozick), **Supp. V:** 257
"Parable of the Gift" (Glück), **Supp. V:** 89
"Parable of the Hostages" (Glück), **Supp. V:** 89
"Parable of the King" (Glück), **Supp. V:** 89
Parable of the Sower (O. Butler), **Supp. XIII: 66–67,** 69
Parable of the Talents (O. Butler), **Supp. XIII:** 61,**Supp. XIII:** 66, **67–69**
"Parable of the Trellis" (Glück), **Supp. V:** 89
Parachutes & Kisses (Jong), **Supp. V:** 115, 123, 125–126, 129
"Paradelle for Susan" (Collins), **Supp. XXI:** 58
"Parade of Painters" (Swenson), **Supp. IV Part 2:** 645
"Paradigm, The" (Tate), **IV:** 128
Paradise (Barthelme), **Supp. IV Part 1:** 52
"Paradise" (Caputo), **Supp. XIX:** 26–27
"Paradise" (Doty), **Supp. XI:** 123
Paradise, Piece by Piece (Peacock), **Supp. XIX:** 193, 194–195, 195–196, **201–202**
Paradise Lost (Milton), **I:** 137; **II:** 168, 549; **IV:** 126; **Supp. XII:** 173, 297; **Supp. XV:** 181; **Supp. XX: 280**
Paradise Lost (Odets), **Supp. II Part 2:** 530, 531, 538–539, 550
Paradise Now (Living Theater), **Supp. XXIV:** 116
"Paradise of Bachelors and the Tartarus of Maids, The" (Melville), **III:** 91
Paradise of Bombs, The (Sanders), **Supp. XVI:** 265, 272–273
Paradise Poems (Stern), **Supp. IX: 293–294,** 295
Paradiso (Dante), **Supp. IX:** 50
"Paradoxes and Oxymorons" (Ashbery), **Supp. III Part 1:** 23–24

Paradox of Progressive Thought, The (Noble), **Supp. I Part 2:** 650
Paragon, The (Knowles), **Supp. XII:** 249
"Paragraphs" (Carruth), **Supp. XVI:** 52–53
"Parameters" (Dunn), **Supp. XI:** 154
"Para Mi Tataranieto El Astropionero" (Espaillat), **Supp. XXI:** 104
"Paraphrase" (Crane), **I:** 391–392, 393
"Pardon, The" (Wilbur), **Supp. III Part 2:** 544, 550
Paredes, Américo, **Supp. XIII:** 225; **Supp. XIX:** 97, 98, 100
Paredes, Raymund A., **Supp. XIII:** 320, 321
"Parentage" (Stafford), **Supp. XI:** 321, 322
Parentheses: An Autobiographical Journey (Neugeboren), **Supp. XVI:** 217, 218, 219, 221, 226
"Parents" (F. Barthelme), **Supp. XI:** 34
"Parents Taking Shape" (Karr), **Supp. XI:** 243
"Parents' Weekend: Camp Kenwood" (Kenyon), **Supp. VII:** 169
Pareto, Vilfredo, **II:** 577
Paretsky, Sara, **Supp. IV Part 2:** 462; **Supp. XIV:** 26
Parini, Jay, **Supp. X:** 17; **Supp. XIX:** 120, 129; **Supp. XX: 243; Supp. XXI:** 192; **Supp. XXII:** 205
"Paris" (Collins), **Supp. XXI:** 60
"Paris" (Stern), **Supp. IX:** 300
"Paris, 7 A.M." (Bishop), **Retro. Supp. II:** 41, 42; **Supp. I Part 1:** 85, 89
Paris, Bob, **Supp. XX: 264**
Paris, Paris (Shaw), **Supp. XIX:** 240
Paris France (Stein), **IV:** 45
Park, Ed, **Supp. XXII:** 255
Park, Robert, **IV:** 475
"Park Bench" (Hughes), **Supp. I Part 1:** 331–332
Park City (Beattie), **Supp. V:** 24, 35–36
"Park City" (Beattie), **Supp. V:** 35
Parker, Charlie, **Supp. I Part 1:** 59; **Supp. X:** 240, 242, 246; **Supp. XIII:** 129
Parker, Dorothy, **Retro. Supp. II:** 327; **Supp. IV Part 1:** 353; **Supp. IX:** 62, 114, **189–206; Supp. X:** 164; **Supp. XI:** 28; **Supp. XVIII:** 242, 246, 252
Parker, Emily, **Supp. XVIII:** 102
Parker, Idella, **Supp. X:** 232, 234–235
Parker, Joan, **Supp. XIX:** 187
Parker, Lonnae O'Neal, **Supp. XXIII:** 276
Parker, Muriel, **Supp. IX:** 232
Parker, Patricia, **Supp. XV:** 242
Parker, Robert B., **Supp. IV Part 1:** 135, 136; **Supp. XIX: 177–192**
Parker, Robert Dale, **Supp. XXIII:** 223, 228, 229
Parker, Theodore, **Supp. I Part 1:** 38; **Supp. I Part 2:** 518; **Supp. XXIV:** 70
Parker, Thomas, **Supp. I Part 1:** 102
"Parker's Back" (O'Connor), **III:** 348, 352, 358
"Parkersburg" (Halliday), **Supp. XIX:** 92
Parkes, Henry Bamford, **Supp. I Part 2:** 617

Park-Fuller, Linda, **Supp. XIII:** 297
Parkman, Francis, **II:** 278, 310, 312; **IV:** 179, 309; **Supp. I Part 2:** 420, 479, 481–482, 486, 487, 493, 498; **Supp. II Part 2: 589–616**
Parkman Reader, The (Morison, ed.), **Supp. I Part 2:** 494
Parks, Gordon, Sr., **Supp. XI:** 17
Parks, Larry, **Supp. I Part 1:** 295
Parks, Rosa, **Supp. I Part 1:** 342
"Park Street Cemetery, The" (Lowell), **II:** 537, 538
Par le Détroit (cantata) (Bowles), **Supp. IV Part 1:** 82
Parliament of Fowls, The (Chaucer), **III:** 492
Parmenides (Plato), **II:** 10
Parnassus (Emerson), **II:** 8, 18
Parnell, Charles Stewart, **II:** 129, 137
Parole (film), **Supp. XIII:** 166
Parole Fixer (film), **Supp. XIII:** 170
Parrington, Vernon Louis, **I:** 254, 517, 561; **III:** 335, 606; **IV:** 173; **Supp. I Part 2:** 484, 640
Parrish, Dillwyn, **Supp. XVII:** 83–84, 90
Parrish, Robert, **Supp. XI:** 307
"Parrot, The" (Merrill), **Supp. III Part 1:** 320
"Parsley" (Dove), **Supp. IV Part 1:** 245, 246
Parson, Annie, **Supp. I Part 2:** 655
Parsons, Elsie Clews, **I:** 231, 235
Parsons, Ian, **Supp. IX:** 95
Parsons, Louella, **Supp. XII:** 173
Parsons, Talcott, **Supp. I Part 2:** 648
Parsons, Theophilus, **II:** 396, 504; **Retro. Supp. II:** 134; **Supp. I Part 1:** 155
"Parthian Shot, The" (Hammett), **Supp. IV Part 1:** 343
Partial Glossary, A (Bronk), **Supp. XXI:** 26
Partial Payments: Essays on Writers and Their Lives (Epstein), **Supp. XIV:** 111
Partial Portraits (James), **II:** 336
"Partial Relief" (Halliday), **Supp. XIX:** 91
Partial Truth (Nelson), **Supp. XVIII: 175–176,** 178
"Particulars" (Pickering), **Supp. XXI:** 197
Parties (Van Vechten), **Supp. II Part 2:** 739, 747–749
"Parting" (Kunitz), **Supp. III Part 1:** 263
"Parting Gift" (Wylie), **Supp. I Part 2:** 714
"Parting Glass, The" (Freneau), **Supp. II Part 1:** 273
"Partings" (Hogan), **Supp. IV Part 1:** 413
Partington, Blanche, **I:** 199
Partisans (Matthiessen), **Supp. V:** 201
"Partner, The" (Roethke), **III:** 541–542
Partners, The (Auchincloss), **Supp. IV Part 1:** 31, 34
Partners in Crime: A Rafe Buenrostro Mystery (Hinojosa), **Supp. XIX: 107–108**
"Part of a Letter" (Wilbur), **Supp. III Part 2:** 551

Part of a Long Story: Eugene O'Neill as a Young Man in Love (Boulton), **Supp. XXII:** 18, 21, 27–30
Part of Speech, A (Brodsky), **Supp. VIII:** 22
"Part of the Bee's Body Embedded in the Flesh, The" (C. Frost), **Supp. XV:** 105, 107
"Part of the Story" (Dobyns), **Supp. XIII:** 79
Part of Vermont, A (Taggard), **Supp. XXII:** 284
Parton, Sara, **Retro. Supp. I:** 246
Partridge, Jeffrey F., **Supp. XV:** 219
Partridge, John, **II:** 110, 111
"Parts of a Journal" (Gordon), **Supp. IV Part 1:** 310
Parts of a World (Stevens), **Retro. Supp. I: 305–306,** 307, 309, 313
"Parturition" (Loy), **Supp. XXII:** 159, 160–161
"Party, The" (Dunbar), **Supp. II Part 1:** 198, 205–206
"Party, The" (Taylor), **Supp. V:** 315
Party at Jack's, The (Wolfe), **IV:** 451–452, 469
"Party Down at the Square, A" (Ellison), **Retro. Supp. II:** 124
Party of Five (television series), **Supp. XIX:** 222
Pascal, Blaise, **II:** 8, 159; **III:** 292, 301, 304, 428; **Retro. Supp. I:** 326, 330
"Paskudnyak" (Pilcer), **Supp. XVII:** 50
"Pass, The" (Neugeboren), **Supp. XVI:** 225
"Passage" (Crane), **I:** 391
"Passage in the Life of Mr. John Oakhurst, A" (Harte), **Supp. II Part 1:** 353–354
Passage in the Night, A (Asch), **Supp. XXIII:** 7
"Passages" (Duncan), **Supp. XVI:** 287
"Passages from a Relinquished Work" (Hawthorne), **Retro. Supp. I:** 150
Passages toward the Dark (McGrath), **Supp. X:** 126, 127
"Passage to India" (Whitman), **IV:** 348
Passage to India, A (Forster), **II:** 600; **Supp. XVIII:** 143
Passaro, Vince, **Supp. X:** 167, 302, 309, 310
"Passenger, The" (Brockmeier), **Supp. XXII:** 52
"Passenger Pigeons" (Jeffers), **Supp. II Part 2:** 437
Passin, Herbert, **Supp. XIII:** 337
Passing (Larsen), **Supp. XVIII:** 119, 123, **127–130**
"Passing Beauty" (C. Frost), **Supp. XV:** 97
"Passing of Grandison, The" (Chesnutt), **Supp. XIV:** 62, **66–69**
"Passing of Sister Barsett, The" (Jewett), **Retro. Supp. II:** 138–139, 143
"Passing Show, The" (Bierce), **I:** 208
"Passing Through" (Kunitz), **Supp. III Part 1:** 265
"Passion, The" (Barnes), **Supp. III Part 1:** 36

"Passion, The" (Merwin), **Supp. III Part 1:** 343
Passionate, Accurate Story, The: Making Your Heart's Truth into Literature (C. Bly), **Supp. XVI: 41–42**
Passionate Pilgrim, A (James), **II:** 324; **Retro. Supp. I:** 219
"Passionate Pilgrim, A" (James), **II:** 322, 323–324; **Retro. Supp. I:** 218
Passion Play (Kosinski), **Supp. VII:** 215, 225–226
Passions of Uxport, The (Kumin), **Supp. IV Part 2:** 444
Pass It On (Hadas), **Supp. XXIII: 115,** 123
"Pass It On, I"(Hadas), **Supp. XXIII:** 115
"Pass It On, II"(Hadas), **Supp. XXIII:** 115
"Passive Resistance" (McKay), **Supp. X:** 133
Passport to the War (Kunitz), **Supp. III Part 1:** 261–264
Passwords (Stafford), **Supp. XI: 329–330**
"Past, The" (Bryant), **Supp. I Part 1:** 157, 170
Past, The (Kinnell), **Supp. III Part 1:** 235, 253–254
"Past, The" (Kinnell), **Supp. III Part 1:** 254
Past and Present (Carlyle), **Supp. I Part 2:** 410
Pasternak, Boris, **II:** 544; **Supp. XXIII:** 209
"Pastiches et Pistaches" (Van Vechten), **Supp. II Part 2:** 732
"Past Is the Present, The" (Moore), **III:** 199–200
"Pastoral" (Carver), **Supp. III Part 1:** 137, 146
"Pastoral" (Dove), **Supp. IV Part 1:** 249
"Pastoral" (Trethewey), **Supp. XXI:** 257
"Pastoral Hat, A" (Stevens), **IV:** 91
Pastoralia (Saunders), **Supp. XIX: 227–229**
"Pastoralia" (Saunders), **Supp. XIX:** 227, 229
"Pastor Dowe at Tacaté" (Bowles), **Supp. IV Part 1:** 87
Pastorela (ballet) (Kirstein), **Supp. IV Part 1:** 83
Pastorius, Francis Daniel, **Supp. I Part 2:** 700
"Pasture Poems" (Kumin), **Supp. IV Part 2:** 446
Pastures of Heaven, The (Steinbeck), **IV:** 51
Patch, Jerry, **Supp. XVIII:** 38
Patchen, Kenneth, **Supp. III Part 2:** 625
Patchett, Ann, **Supp. XII: 307–324**
Patchwork Planet (Lethem), **Supp. XVIII:** 150
Pater, Walter, **I:** 51, 272, 476; **II:** 27, 338; **III:** 604; **IV:** 74; **Retro. Supp. I:** 56, 79; **Retro. Supp. II:** 326; **Supp. I Part 2:** 552; **Supp. IX:** 66
Paterna (Mather), **Supp. II Part 2:** 451
"Paterson" (Ginsberg), **Supp. II Part 1:** 314–315, 321, 329
Paterson (W. C. Williams), **I:** 62, 446; **IV:** 418–423; **Retro. Supp. I:** 209,

284, 413, 419, 421, **424–428,** 428, 429, 430; **Retro. Supp. II:** 321, 328; **Supp. II Part 2:** 557, 564, 625; **Supp. VIII:** 275, 305; **Supp. XIV:** 96; **Supp. XV:** 264, 349

Paterson, Book Five (W. C. Williams), **IV:** 422–423

Paterson, Book One (W. C. Williams), **IV:** 421–422

Paterson, Isabel, **Supp. IV Part 2:** 524

Paterson, Part Three (W. C. Williams), **IV:** 420–421

Pat Garrett and Billy the Kid (film, Peckinpah), **Supp. XVIII:** 27

"Path, The" (Bryant), **Supp. I Part 1:** 169

Pathfinder, The (Cooper), **I:** 349, 350, 355

Pat Hobby Stories, The (Fitzgerald), **Retro. Supp. I:** 114

"Pathos of Low Life, The" (Hapgood), **Supp. XVII:** 103

"Patience of a Saint, The" (Humphrey), **Supp. IX:** 106

Patience Sparhawk and Her Times (Atherton), **Supp. XXIV:** 18, 20, 22, 27

Patient 002 (Skloot), **Supp. XX: 194, 208**

Patinkin, Mandy, **Supp. IV Part 1:** 236

Paton, Alan, **Supp. VIII:** 126

Patria Mia (Pound), **III:** 460–461; **Retro. Supp. I:** 284

"Patria Mia" (Pound), **Retro. Supp. I:** 284

"Patriarch, The" (Alvares), **Supp. V:** 11

"Patrick Kavanagh at First Light" (Skloot), **Supp. XX: 204**

Patrimony: A True Story (P. Roth), **Retro. Supp. II:** 279, 280, 291; **Supp. III Part 2:** 427

Patriot, The (Buck), **Supp. II Part 1:** 122–123

Patriot, The (Connell), **Supp. XIV:** 94–95

Patriotic Gore: Studies in the Literature of the American Civil War (Wilson), **III:** 588; **IV:** 430, 438, 443, 445–445, 446; **Supp. VIII:** 100

"Patriotic Thing, The" (Ryan as Quin), **Supp. XVIII:** 229

"Patriots, The/Los Patriotas" (Kingsolver), **Supp. VII:** 209

Patron Saint of Liars, The (Patchett), **Supp. XII:** 307, 310, **311–314,** 317

Pattee, Fred L., **II:** 456

Patten, Gilbert, **II:** 423

Patten, Simon, **Supp. I Part 2:** 640

Patternmaster (O. Butler), **Supp. XIII:** 61, 62, 63

Patternmaster Series (O. Butler), **Supp. XIII: 62–63**

Pattern Recognition (W. Gibson), **Supp. XVI:** 124, **130–131**

"Patterns" (Lowell), **II:** 524

Patterson, Floyd, **III:** 38

Patterson, Margot, **Supp. XXII:** 85

Patterson, William M., **Supp. I Part 1:** 265

Patton, General George, **III:** 575; **Supp. I Part 2:** 664

"Patty-Cake, Patty-Cake...A Memoir" (Apple), **Supp. XVII:** 7

Paul, Saint, **I:** 365; **II:** 15, 494; **IV:** 122, 154, 164, 335; **Retro. Supp. I:** 247; **Supp. I Part 1:** 188

Paul, Sherman, **I:** 244; **IV:** 179

"Paula Becker to Clara Westhoff" (Rich), **Supp. I Part 2:** 573–574

"Paula Gunn Allen" (Ruppert), **Supp. IV Part 1:** 321

Paul Ardenheim, the Monk of Wissahikon (Lippard), **Supp. XXIII:** 178, 186, 187, 189, 190

Paul Bowles: Romantic Savage (Caponi), **Supp. IV Part 1:** 95

Paulding, James Kirke, **I:** 344; **II:** 298, 299, 303; **Supp. I Part 1:** 157

Pauley, Jane, **Supp. XXI:** 39

Paul Jones (Hapgood), **Supp. XVII:** 100–101

Paul Marchand, F.M.C. (Chesnutt), **Supp. XIV:** 76

"Paul Monette: The Brink of Summer's End" (film), **Supp. X:** 152

"Paul Revere" (Longfellow), **II:** 489, 501

"Paul Revere's Ride" (Longfellow), **Retro. Supp. II:** 163

"Paul's Case" (Cather), **I:** 314–315; **Retro. Supp. I:** 3, 5

Paulsen, Friedrich, **III:** 600

"Pauper Witch of Grafton, The" (Frost), **Retro. Supp. II:** 42

"Pause by the Water, A" (Merwin), **Supp. III Part 1:** 354

"Pavane for the Nursery, A" (W. J. Smith), **Supp. XIII:** 335

"Pavement, The" (Olson), **Supp. II Part 2:** 571

Pavese, Cesare, **Supp. XXI:** 132

Pavic, Milorad, **Supp. XXII:** 265

Pavilion of Women (Buck), **Supp. II Part 1:** 125–126

"Pawnbroker, The" (Kumin), **Supp. IV Part 2:** 442, 443–444, 451

Pawnbroker, The (Wallant), **Supp. XVI:** 220

"Paying Dues" (Bass), **Supp. XVI:** 16

Payne, Daniel, **Supp. V:** 202

Payne, John Howard, **II:** 309

Payne Tom, **Supp. XXII:** 266

Paz, Octavio, **Supp. III Part 2:** 630; **Supp. VIII:** 272; **Supp. XI:** 191; **Supp. XIII:** 223

P. D. Kimerakov (Epstein), **Supp. XII:** 160, **162**

Peabody, Elizabeth, **Retro. Supp. I:** 155–156, 225

Peabody, Elizabeth Palmer, **Supp. XXIV:** 75

Peabody, Francis G., **III:** 293; **Supp. I Part 1:** 5

Peabody, Josephine Preston, **III:** 507; **Supp. XX:** 115

Peaceable Kingdom, The (Prose), **Supp. XVI:** 256–257

Peace and Bread in Time of War (Addams), **Supp. I Part 1:** 21, 22–23

"Peace Between Black and White in the United States" (Locke), **Supp. XIV:** 205

Peace Breaks Out (Knowles), **Supp. XII:** 249

"Peacemaker"(Kenny), **Supp. XXIII:** 151

"Peace March, The" (Simpson), **Supp. IX:** 279

"Peace of Cities, The" (Wilbur), **Supp. III Part 2:** 545

"Peace of Mind" (Boyle), **Supp. XX: 19**

"Peaches—Six in a Tin Box, Sarajevo" (Cisneros), **Supp. VII:** 67

Peachtree Road (Siddons), **Supp. XXII:** 239, 240, 242, **246–247, 248–251,** 252

Peaco, Ed, **Supp. XXIV:** 221

Peacock, Doug, **Supp. VIII:** 38; **Supp. XIII:** 12

Peacock, Gibson, **Supp. I Part 1:** 360

Peacock, Molly, **Supp. XVII:** 74; **Supp. XIX: 193–207**

"Peacock, The" (Merrill), **Supp. III Part 1:** 320

"Peacock, The" (Mosher), **Supp. XXII:** 211

Peacock, Thomas Love, **Supp. I Part 1:** 307; **Supp. VIII:** 125

"Peacock Room, The" (Hayden), **Supp. II Part 1:** 374–375

"Peacocks of Avignon, The" (Swados), **Supp. XIX:** 263

Pearce, Richard, **Supp. IX:** 254

Pearce, Roy Harvey, **II:** 244; **Supp. I Part 1:** 111, 114; **Supp. I Part 2:** 475

"Pearl" (Kooser), **Supp. XIX:** 127–128

Pearl, The (Steinbeck), **IV:** 51, 62–63

Pearlman, Daniel, **III:** 479

Pearlman, Mickey, **Supp. XIII:** 293, 306

Pearl of Orr's Island, The (Stowe), **Supp. I Part 2:** 592–593, 595

"Pearls" (A. Finch), **Supp. XVII:** 72

Pears, Peter, **II:** 586; **Supp. IV Part 1:** 84

Pearson, Drew, **Supp. XIV:** 126

Pearson, Norman Holmes, **Supp. I Part 1:** 259, 260, 273

"Pear Tree" (C. Frost), **Supp. XV:** 105

"Peasants' Way O' Thinkin' " (McKay), **Supp. X:** 133

Pease, Donald E., **Supp. IV Part 2:** 687

"Peboan and Seegwun (Winter and Spring): A Chippewa Allegory"(J. Schoolcraft), **Supp. XXIII:** 235

Peck, Gregory, **Supp. VIII:** 128, 129; **Supp. XII:** 160, 173

Peckinpah, Sam, **Supp. XI:** 306; **Supp. XVIII:** 27

"Peck of Gold, A" (Frost), **II:** 155

Peculiar Treasures: A Biblical Who's Who (Buechner), **Supp. XII:** 53

"Pedal Point" (Francis), **Supp. IX:** 87

Pedersen, Inge, **Supp. XVIII:** 179

"Pedersen Kid, The" (Gass), **Supp. VI:** 83

"Pedigree, The" (Creeley), **Supp. IV Part 1:** 150

Peebles, Melvin Van, **Supp. XI:** 17; **Supp. XVI:** 144

"Peed Onk" (Moore). *See* "People Like That Are the Only People Here: Canonical Babbling in Peed Onk" (Moore)

"Peeler, The" (O'Connor), **Retro. Supp. II:** 225

Peich, Michael, **Supp. XV:** 113, 117

Peikoff, Leonard, **Supp. IV Part 2:** 520, 526, 529

Peirce, Charles Sanders, **II:** 20, 352–353; **III:** 599; **Supp. I Part 2:** 640; **Supp. III Part 2:** 626

Pelagius, **III:** 295

"Pelican, The" (Merrill), **Supp. III Part 1:** 320

"Pelican, The" (Wharton), **IV:** 310; **Retro. Supp. I:** 364

Pellacchia, Michael, **Supp. XIII:** 16

Pelley, Denise, **Supp. XIX:** 205

Pelonero, Michael, **Supp. XXIII:** 125

Peltier, Leonard, **Supp. V:** 212

"Penance"(Dybek), **Supp. XXIII:** 69

"Pen and Paper and a Breath of Air" (Oliver), **Supp. VII:** 245

Pence, Amy, **Supp. XV:** 211, 223

"Pencil, The" (Chandler), **Supp. IV Part 1:** 135

Pencillings by the Way (Willis), **II:** 313; **Supp. XVIII:** 12

"Pencils" (Sandburg), **III:** 592

Pendleton, Devon, **Supp. XVIII:** 151

"Pendulum" (Bradbury and Hasse), **Supp. IV Part 1:** 102

"Penelope's Song" (Glück), **Supp. V:** 89

Penelope: The Story of the Half-Scalped Woman (Schott), **Supp. XXIII:** 240, **244–245**

Penhally (Gordon), **II:** 197, 199, 201–203, 204

"Penis" (McClatchy), **Supp. XII:** 266–267

Penitent, The (di Donato), **Supp. XX: 44, 45**

Penitent, The (Singer), **Retro. Supp. II:** 309–310, 313

Penland, Nell Bates, **Supp. XXII:** 188

Penn, Robert, **I:** 489

Penn, Sean, **Supp. XI:** 107

Penn, Thomas, **II:** 118

Penn, William, **Supp. I Part 2:** 683

Penna, Sandro, **Supp. XIX:** 34

Pennebaker, D. A., **Supp. XVIII:** 19, 26

"Pennsylvania Pilgrim, The" (Whittier), **Supp. I Part 2:** 700

"Pennsylvania Planter, The" (Freneau), **Supp. II Part 1:** 268

Penny, Rob, **Supp. VIII:** 330

"Penny, The" (D. West), **Supp. XVIII:** 283–284

Penrod (Tarkington), **III:** 223

"Penseroso, Il" (Milton), **Supp. XIV:** 8

Pensieri (Leopardi; Di Piero, trans.), **Supp. XIX:** 34

"Pensive Hours"(J. Schoolcraft), **Supp. XXIII:** 230–231

Pentagon of Power, The (Mumford), **Supp. II Part 2:** 498

Pentimento (Hellman), **Supp. I Part 1:** 280, 292–294, 296; **Supp. IV Part 1:** 12; **Supp. VIII:** 243

"Peonies at Dusk" (Kenyon), **Supp. VII:** 171

People, The (Glaspell), **Supp. III Part 1:** 179

People, Yes, The (Sandburg), **III:** 575, 589, 590, 591

"PEOPLE BURNING, THE" (Baraka), **Supp. II Part 1:** 49

"People in Hell Just Want a Drink of Water" (Proulx), **Supp. VII:** 263

"People Like That Are the Only People Here: Canonical Babbling in Peed Onk" (Moore), **Supp. X:** 168, **178–179**

People Live Here: Selected Poems 1949–1983 (Simpson), **Supp. IX:** 269, 277

"People Next Door, The" (Simpson), **Supp. IX:** 279

People of the Abyss, The (London), **II:** 465–466

"People on the Roller Coaster, The" (Hardwick), **Supp. III Part 1:** 196

People Shall Continue, The (Ortiz), **Supp. IV Part 2:** 510

People's History of the United States, A (Zinn), **Supp. XXIV:** 87

"People's Surroundings" (Moore), **III:** 201, 202, 203

"People v. Abe Lathan, Colored, The" (Caldwell), **I:** 309

"Peppermint Lounge Revisited, The" (Wolfe), **Supp. III Part 2:** 571

Peppis, Paul, **Supp. XXII:** 160

Pepys, Samuel, **Supp. I Part 2:** 653

"Perchance to Dream" (Franzen), **Supp. XX: 90, 93**

Perchance to Dream: Robert B. Parker's Sequel to Raymond Chandler's "Big Sleep" (Parker), **Supp. XIX:** 189

"Perch'io non spero di tornar giammai" (Cavalcanti), **Supp. III Part 2:** 623

Perch of the Devil (Atherton), **Supp. XXIV:** 24, 29

Percy, Thomas, **Supp. XIV:** 2

Percy, Walker, **Supp. III Part 1: 383–400; Supp. IV Part 1:** 297; **Supp. V:** 334; **Supp. X:** 42; **Supp. XIV:** 21; **Supp. XIX:** 209

Percy, William, **Supp. V:** 334

Percy, William Alexander, **Retro. Supp. I:** 341; **Supp. XXII:** 193

Peregrin, Tony, **Supp. XV:** 69

"Peregrine" (Wylie), **Supp. I Part 2:** 712–713, 714

Perelman, Bob, **Supp. XII:** 23

Perelman, S. J., **IV:** 286; **Retro. Supp. I:** 342; **Retro. Supp. II:** 321, 322, 325, 326, 327, 336; **Supp. IV Part 1:** 353; **Supp. XI:** 66

Perestroika (Kushner), **Supp. IX:** 141, 142, 145

Péret, Benjamin, **Supp. VIII:** 272

Peretz, Isaac Leib, **IV:** 1, 3; **Retro. Supp. II:** 299; **Supp. XXIII:** 4, 7, 8–9

Pérez Galdós, Benito, **II:** 275

Perfect Analysis Given by a Parrot, A (T. Williams), **IV:** 395

"Perfect Couple, The" (Nelson), **Supp. XVIII:** 173

"Perfect Day for Bananafish, A" (Salinger), **III:** 563–564, 571

Perfect Fiction, The (Sorrentino), **Supp. XXI:** 228

Perfect Ganesh, A (McNally), **Supp. XIII: 202–203,** 208, 209

"Perfect Gerbil, The: Reading Barthelme's 'The School' " (Saunders), **Supp. XIX:** 235

"Perfect Knight, The" (Chandler), **Supp. IV Part 1:** 120

Perfect Mother, The (Schott), **Supp. XXIII: 241–242**

Perfect Party, The (Gurney), **Supp. V:** 100, 105, 106–107

"Perfect Things" (F. Barthelme), **Supp. XI:** 30, 33–34

"Performance, The" (Dickey), **Supp. IV Part 1:** 178–179, 181

"Perfume" (Mora), **Supp. XIII:** 218

"Perhaps the World Ends Here" (Harjo), **Supp. XII:** 228, 231

Perhaps Women (Anderson), **I:** 114

Pericles (Shakespeare), **I:** 585; **Supp. III Part 2:** 624, 627, 629

"Period Metaphor" (Bronk), **Supp. XXI:** 33

Period of Adjustment (T. Williams), **IV:** 382, 386, 387, 388, 389, 390, 392, 393, 394, 397

"Period Pieces from the Mid-Thirties" (Agee), **I:** 28

"Periphery" (Ammons), **Supp. VII:** 28

Perkins, David, **Supp. I Part 2:** 459, 475; **Supp. XV:** 185

Perkins, Maxwell, **I:** 252, 289, 290; **II:** 87, 93, 95, 252; **IV:** 452, 455, 457, 458, 461, 462, 463, 469; **Retro. Supp. I:** 101, 105, 108, 109, 110, 113, 114, 178; **Supp. IX:** 57, 58, 60, 232; **Supp. X:** 219, 224, 225, 229, 230, 233; **Supp. XI:** 218, 227

Perlès, Alfred, **III:** 177, 183, 187, 189

Perloff, Marjorie, **Supp. I Part 2:** 539, 542; **Supp. IV Part 1:** 68; **Supp. IV Part 2:** 420, 424, 432; **Supp. XXII:** 161, 271; **Supp. XXIII:** 210, 220

Permanence and Change (Burke), **I:** 274

Permanent Errors (Price), **Supp. VI:** 261

"Permanent Traits of the English National Genius" (Emerson), **II:** 18

Permit Me Voyage (Agee), **I:** 25, 27

"Perosa Canavese" (Everwine), **Supp. XV:** 84

Perrault, Charles, **IV:** 266; **Supp. I Part 2:** 622

Perrin, Noel, **Supp. XVI:** 34; **Supp. XXII:** 205, 207, 211, 218

Perrins, Carol. *See* Frost, Carol

Perry, Anne, **Supp. V:** 335

Perry, Bliss, **I:** 243

Perry, Donna, **Supp. IV Part 1:** 322, 327, 335

Perry, Edgar A., **III:** 410

Perry, Keith Ronald, **Supp. XXI:** 42

Perry, Lincoln, **Supp. V:** 24, 33

Perry, Matthew C., **Supp. I Part 2:** 494–495

Perry, Patsy Brewington, **Supp. I Part 1:** 66

Perry, Phyllis Alesia, **Supp. XVIII:** 96

Perry, Ralph Barton, **I:** 224; **II:** 356, 362, 364; **Supp. XIV:** 197

Perry, Dr. William, **II:** 395, 396

Perse, St.-John, **III:** 12, 13, 14, 17; **Supp. III Part 1:** 14; **Supp. IV Part 1:** 82;

Supp. XIII: 344; **Supp. XV:** 178
"Persephone in Hell" (Dove), **Supp. IV Part 1:** 250, 251
"Persephone"(Le Sueur), **Supp. XXIII:** 162, 165, **170–171**
"Persimmons" (L.-Y. Lee), **Supp. XV:** 211, 213
"Persistence of Desire, The" (Updike), **IV:** 222–223, 228
"Persistence of Poetry, The" (Bynner), **Supp. XV:** 49
"Persistences" (Hecht), **Supp. X: 68–69**
Person, Place, and Thing (Shapiro), **Supp. II Part 2:** 702, 705
Personae of Ezra Pound (Pound), **III:** 458
Personae: The Collected Poems (Pound), **Retro. Supp. I:** 285, 286; **Supp. I Part 1:** 255; **Supp. XVII:** 32
"Personal" (Stern), **Supp. IX:** 299
"Personal and Occasional Pieces" (Welty), **Retro. Supp. I:** 355
"Personal and the Individual, The" (L. Michaels), **Supp. XVI:** 201
Personal Injuries (Turow), **Supp. XVII:** **219–220,** 221, 223
"Personalities" (column, Briggs), **Supp. XVIII:** 15
Personal Narrative (Edwards), **I:** 545, 552, 553, 561, 562; **Supp. I Part 2:** 700
"Personal Poem #9" (Berrigan), **Supp. XXIV:** 34, 35
"Personal Poem"(O'Hara), **Supp. XXIII:** 219
Personal Recollection of Joan of Arc (Twain), **IV:** 208
Personals (Bontemps), **Supp. XXII:** 7, 8
"Personals" (Didion), **Supp. IV Part 1:** 200
"Personism" (O'Hara), **Supp. XV:** 181
"Personism: A Manifesto" (O'Hara), **Supp. XXIII:** 212, 215; **Supp. XXIV:** 43
Persons and Places (Santayana), **III:** 615
Persons in Hiding (film), **Supp. XIII:** 170
Persons in Hiding (Hoover), **Supp. XIII:** 170
Person Sitting in Darkness, A (Twain), **IV:** 208
"Perspective" (Francis), **Supp. IX:** 78
"Perspective: Anniversary D-Day" (Karr), **Supp. XI:** 241
Perspectives by Incongruity (Burke), **I:** 284–285
"Perspectives: Is It Out of Control?" (Gleason), **Supp. IX:** 16
Perspectives on Cormac McCarthy (Arnold and Luce, eds.), **Supp. VIII:** 189
Persse, Dudley Jocelyn, **Supp. XX: 232**
Pertes et Fracas (McCoy), **Supp. XIII:** 175
"Peruvian Child" (Mora), **Supp. XIII:** 218
Peseroff, Joyce, **Supp. IV Part 1:** 71
Pesetsky, Bette, **Supp. XXIV:** 173
"Pestilence" (Nelson), **Supp. XVIII:** 186

Pest Maiden, The (Schott), **Supp. XXIII:** **245–246**
"Peter" (Cather), **Retro. Supp. I:** 4
"Peter" (Moore), **III:** 210, 212
Peter, Saint, **III:** 341, 346; **IV:** 86, 294
Peterkin, Julia, **Supp. I Part 1:** 328; **Supp. XXII:** 12, 189
"Peter Klaus" (German tale), **II:** 306
Peter Pan (Barrie), **Supp. XV:** 319
"Peter Parley" works (Goodrich), **Supp. I Part 1:** 38
"Peter Pendulum" (Poe), **III:** 425
"Peter Quince at the Clavier" (Stevens), **IV:** 81, 82
Peter Rabbit tales, **Retro. Supp. I:** 335
Peters, Cora, **Supp. I Part 2:** 468
Peters, Jacqueline, **Supp. XII:** 225
Peters, Margot, **Supp. VIII:** 252
Peters, Robert, **Supp. XIII:** 114
Peters, S. H. (pseudonym). *See* Henry, O.
Peters, Timothy, **Supp. XI:** 39
"Peter's Avocado" (Rodriguez), **Supp. XIV:** 308–309
Petersen, David, **Supp. XIII:** 2
Petersen, Donald, **Supp. V:** 180; **Supp. XV:** 74, 92
Peterson, Dorothy, **Supp. XVIII:** 131, 132
Peterson, George, **Supp. XXII:** 250
Peterson, Houston, **I:** 60
Peterson, Roger Tory, **Supp. V:** 202
Peterson, Virgilia, **Supp. IV Part 1:** 30
Peter Whiffle: His Life and Works (Van Vechten), **Supp. II Part 2:** 728–729, 731, 735, 738–741, 749
"Petey and Yotsee and Mario" (H. Roth), **Supp. IX:** 234
"Petition, A" (Winters), **Supp. II Part 2:** 785
"Pet Milk"(Dybek), **Supp. XXIII:** 74
"'Pet Negro' System, The" (Hurston), **Supp. VI:** 159
"Petra and Its Surroundings" (Frost), **Retro. Supp. I:** 124
Petrarch, **I:** 176; **II:** 590; **III:** 4
"Petrarch, Shakespeare, and the Blues" (C. Frost), **Supp. XV:** 92, 104, 105
"Petrified Man" (Welty), **IV:** 262; **Retro. Supp. I:** 345, 351
"Petrified Man, The" (Twain), **IV:** 195
"Petrified Woman, The" (Gordon), **II:** 199
Petronius, **III:** 174, 179
Petry, Ann, **Supp. VIII:** 214; **Supp. XI:** 6, 85; **Supp. XVIII:** 286
Pet Sematary (King), **Supp. V:** 138, 143, 152
Pettengill, Richard, **Supp. VIII:** 341, 345, 348
Pettingell, Phoebe, **Supp. XV:** 251, 256–257, 262
Pettis, Joyce, **Supp. XI:** 276, 277, 278, 281
Pettis, Olive G., **Supp. XXIII:** 189
Petty, Jill, **Supp. XXI:** 244, 248, 249, 250
Pfaelzer, Jean, **Supp. XVI:** 88, 90
Pfaff, Timothy, **Supp. V:** 166
Pfeil, Fred, **Supp. XIV:** 36
Pfister, Karin, **IV:** 467, 475
Phaedo (Plato), **II:** 10

Phaedra (Lowell and Barzun, trans.), **II:** 543–544
"Phantasia for Elvira Shatayev" (Rich), **Supp. I Part 2:** 570
Phantasms of War (Lowell), **II:** 512
"Phantom of the Movie Palace, The" (Coover), **Supp. V:** 50–51
Phantom Ship, The (Marryat), **Supp. XVII:** 55
"Pharaoh, The" (Kenyon), **Supp. VII:** 172
"Pharmacy"(Strout), **Supp. XXIII:** 281
Pharr, Mary, **Supp. V:** 147
"Phases" (E. Stoddard), **Supp. XV:** 273
"Phases" (Stevens), **Retro. Supp. I:** 299
Phases of an Inferior Planet (Glasgow), **II:** 174–175
"Pheasant, The" (Carver), **Supp. III Part 1:** 146
Phelan, Alice, **Supp. XXII:** 193
Pheloung, Grant, **Supp. XI:** 39
Phelps, Donald, **Supp. XXIII:** 174
Phelps, Elizabeth Stuart, **Retro. Supp. II:** 146; **Supp. XIII:** 141; **Supp. XVI:** 80
Phelps, Teresa Godwin, **Supp. VIII:** 128
Phelps, William Lyon "Billy", **Supp. XX: 68, 75, 220**
"Phenomena and Laws of Race Contacts, The" (Locke), **Supp. XIV:** 210
"Phenomenology of Anger, The" (Rich), **Supp. I Part 2:** 562–563, 571
Phenomenology of Moral Experience, The (Mandelbaum), **I:** 61
"Phenomenology of *On Moral Fiction*" (Johnson), **Supp. VI:** 188
Phidias, **Supp. I Part 2:** 482
Philadelphia Fire (Wideman), **Supp. X:** 320, 334
Philadelphia Negro, The (Du Bois), **Supp. II Part 1:** 158, 163–164, 166
Philbrick, Thomas, **I:** 343
"Philemon and Baucis"(Hadas), **Supp. XXIII:** 114
"Phil in the Marketplace" (Lethem), **Supp. XVIII:** 148
Philip, Jim, **Supp. XII:** 136
Philip, Maxwell, **Supp. XXI:** 160
Philip, Prince, **Supp. X:** 108
"Philip of Pokanoket" (Irving), **II:** 303
Philippians (biblical book), **IV:** 154
"Philippine Conquest, The" (Masters), **Supp. I Part 2:** 456
"Philip Roth Reconsidered" (Howe), **Retro. Supp. II:** 286
"Philistinism and the Negro Writer" (Baraka), **Supp. II Part 1:** 39, 44
Phillips, Adam, **Supp. XII:** 97–98
Phillips, Anne K., **Supp. XX: 221**
Phillips, Carl, **Supp. XXI:** 246
Phillips, David Graham, **II:** 444; **Retro. Supp. II:** 101
Phillips, Gene D., **Supp. XI:** 306
Phillips, Jayne Anne, **Supp. XIV:** 21
Phillips, J. J., **Supp. XXIII:** 174
Phillips, J. O. C., **Supp. I Part 1:** 19
Phillips, Robert, **Supp. XIII:** 335, 344
Phillips, Wendell, **Supp. I Part 1:** 103; **Supp. I Part 2:** 524

Phillips, Willard, **Supp. I Part 1:** 154, 155

Phillips, William, **Supp. VIII:** 156

Phillips, William L., **I:** 106

"Philly Babylon" (Di Piero), **Supp. XIX:** 46

"Philoctetes"(Hadas), **Supp. XXIII:** 115

"Philoctetes: The Wound and the Bow" (Wilson), **Supp. XXIV:** 217

"Philosopher, The" (Farrell), **II:** 45

Philosopher of the Forest (pseudonym). *See* Freneau, Philip

Philosophes classiques, Les (Taine), **III:** 323

"Philosophical Cobbler, The" (Sanders), **Supp. XVI:** 268

"Philosophical Concepts and Practical Results" (James), **II:** 352

"Philosophical Investigation of Metaphor, A" (Gass), **Supp. VI:** 79

Philosophical Transactions (Watson), **II:** 114

"Philosophy, Or Something Like That" (P. Roth), **Supp. III Part 2:** 403

"Philosophy and Its Critics" (James), **II:** 360

"Philosophy and the Form of Fiction" (Gass), **Supp. VI:** 85

"Philosophy for People" (Emerson), **II:** 14

"Philosophy in Warm Weather" (Kenyon), **Supp. VII:** 168

"Philosophy Lesson" (Levine), **Supp. V:** 195

Philosophy of Alain Locke, The: Harlem Renaissance and Beyond (Harris, ed.), **Supp. XIV:** 196, 211–212

"Philosophy of Composition, The" (Poe), **III:** 416, 421; **Retro. Supp. II:** 266, 267, 271

Philosophy of Friedrich Nietzsche, The (Mencken), **III:** 102–103

"Philosophy of Handicap, A" (Bourne), **I:** 216, 218

"Philosophy of History" (Emerson), **II:** 11–12

Philosophy of Literary Form, The (Burke), **I:** 275, 281, 283, 291

Philosophy of the Human Mind, The (Stewart), **II:** 8

Philosophy: Who Needs It (Rand), **Supp. IV Part 2:** 517, 518, 527, 533

Philoxenes, **Supp. VIII:** 201

"Phineas" (Knowles), **Supp. XII:** 238–240

Phineas: Six Stories (Knowles), **Supp. XII:** 249

"Phocion" (Lowell), **II:** 536

Phoebe Light (Notley), **Supp. XXII:** 227

Phoenix and the Turtle, The (Shakespeare), **I:** 284

"Phoenix Lyrics" (Schwartz), **Supp. II Part 2:** 665

"Phone Booths, The" (Jarman), **Supp. XVII:** 112–113

"Phony War Films" (Jones), **Supp. XI:** 217, 232

"Photograph: Carlisle Indian School (1879–1918)"(Kenny), **Supp. XXIII:** 156

"Photograph: Migrant Worker, Parlier, California, 1967" (Levis), **Supp. XI:** 272

"Photograph of a Bawd Drinking Raleigh Rye" (Trethewey), **Supp. XXI:** 254

"Photograph of a Child on a Vermont Hillside" (Kenyon), **Supp. VII:** 168

"Photograph of My Mother as a Young Girl" (Gioia), **Supp. XV:** 119

"Photograph of the Girl" (Olds), **Supp. X:** 205

"Photograph of the Unmade Bed" (Rich), **Supp. I Part 2:** 558

Photographs (Welty), **Retro. Supp. I:** 343

"Photographs, The" (Barthelme), **Supp. IV Part 1:** 53

"Photography" (Levine), **Supp. V:** 194

Phyrrho, **Retro. Supp. I:** 247

"Physical Universe" (Simpson), **Supp. IX:** 278

"Physicist We Know, A" (Shields), **Supp. VII:** 310

"Physics and Cosmology in the Fiction of Tom Robbins" (Nadeau), **Supp. X:** 270

Physiologie du goût (Brillat-Savarin), **Supp. XVII:** 82, 86

Physiology of Taste, The; or, Meditations on Transcendent Gastronomy (Brillat-Savarin; M. F. K. Fisher, trans.), **Supp. XVII:** 86, 87, 91

"Physiology of Versification, The: Harmonies of Organic and Animal Life" (Holmes), **Supp. I Part 1:** 311

Physique de l'Amour (Gourmont), **III:** 467–468

Piaf, Edith, **Supp. IV Part 2:** 549

Piaget, Jean, **Supp. XIII:** 75

"Piano" (Lawrence), **Supp. XV:** 254

"Piano Fingers" (Mason), **Supp. VIII:** 146

Piano Lesson, The (Bearden), **Supp. VIII:** 342

Piano Lesson, The (Wilson), **Supp. VIII:** 342–345

Piano Man's Daughter, The (Findley), **Supp. XX: 59–61**

"Piano Player, The"(Strout), **Supp. XXIII:** 283, 285

Piatt, James, **Supp. I Part 2:** 420

Piatt, John J., **II:** 273

Piazza, Ben, **Supp. XIII:** 163

Piazza, Paul, **Supp. XIV:** 157, 160, 171

"Piazza de Spagna, Early Morning" (Wilbur), **Supp. III Part 2:** 553

Piazza Tales (Melville), **III:** 91

Picabia, Francis, **Retro. Supp. I:** 416; **Retro. Supp. II:** 331; **Supp. XXII:** 162

Picasso (Stein), **IV:** 28, 32, 45

Picasso, Pablo, **I:** 429, 432, 440, 442, 445; **II:** 602; **III:** 197, 201, 470; **IV:** 26, 31, 32, 46, 87, 407, 436; **Retro. Supp. I:** 55, 63; **Supp. IV Part 1:** 81; **Supp. IX:** 66

Piccione, Anthony, **Supp. XV:** 212

"Piccola Comedia" (Wilbur), **Supp. III Part 2:** 561

Pickard, Samuel T., **Supp. I Part 2:** 682

Picked-Up Pieces (Updike), **Retro. Supp. I:** 320, 322, 323, 335

Picker, Lauren, **Supp. VIII:** 78, 83

Picker, Tobias, **Supp. XII:** 253

Pickering, Sam, **Supp. XXI: 191–207**

Pickford, Mary, **Retro. Supp. I:** 325; **Supp. I Part 2:** 391

"Picking and Choosing" (Moore), **III:** 205

"Picnic" (Peacock), **Supp. XIX:** 206

Picnic, Lightning (Collins), **Supp. XXI:** 54, 60

"Picnic, Lightning" (Collins), **Supp. XXI:** 64–65

Picnic Cantata (music) (Bowles), **Supp. IV Part 1:** 89

"Picnic Remembered" (Warren), **IV:** 240

Pictorial History of the Negro in America, A (Hughes), **Supp. I Part 1:** 345

"Picture, The" (Olson), **Supp. II Part 2:** 574

Picture Bride (Son), **Supp. X:** 292

"Picture I Want, The" (Olds), **Supp. X:** 209

Picture of Dorian Gray, The (Wilde), **Supp. IX:** 105

"Picture of Little J. A. in a Prospect of Flowers, A" (Ashbery), **Supp. III Part 1:** 3

Picture Palace (Theroux), **Supp. VIII:** 322

"Pictures" (Pickering), **Supp. XXI:** 197

"Pictures at an Extermination" (Epstein), **Supp. XII:** 161

"Pictures from an Expedition" (Duffy), **Supp. IV Part 1:** 207

Pictures from an Institution (Jarrell), **II:** 367, 385

Pictures from Brueghel (W. C. Williams), **Retro. Supp. I:** 429–431

"Pictures from Brueghel" (W. C. Williams), **Retro. Supp. I:** 419

"Pictures of Columbus, the Genoese, The" (Freneau), **Supp. II Part 1:** 258

Pictures of Fidelman: An Exhibition (Malamud), **Supp. I Part 2:** 450–451

"Pictures of the Artist" (Malamud), **Supp. I Part 2:** 450

Pictures of the Floating World (Lowell), **II:** 521, 524–525

Pictures of Travel (Heine), **II:** 281

Picturesque America; or, the Land We Live In (Bryant, ed.), **Supp. I Part 1:** 158

"Picturesque Ghetto, The" (Hapgood), **Supp. XVII:** 101

"Picturesque: San Cristóbal de las Casas" (Mora), **Supp. XIII:** 218

Picture This (Heller), **Supp. IV Part 1:** 386, 388, 390–391

Picturing Will (Beattie), **Supp. V:** 29, 31–32, 34

"Pie" (X. J. Kennedy), **Supp. XV:** 170

"Piece, A" (Creeley), **Supp. IV Part 1:** 155, 156

"Piece of Moon, A" (Hogan), **Supp. IV Part 1:** 407

Piece of My Heart, A (Ford), **Supp. V:** 57, 58–61, 62

Piece of My Mind, A: Reflections at Sixty (Wilson), **IV:** 426, 430, 438, 441
"Piece of News, A" (Welty), **IV:** 263; **Retro. Supp. I:** 345, 346
Pieces (Creeley), **Supp. IV Part 1:** 155
Pieces and Pontifications (Mailer), **Retro. Supp. II:** 209–210
Pieces of the Frame (McPhee), **Supp. III Part 1:** 293
"Pie of the Month"(Thompson), **Supp. XXIII:** 300
Pierce, Franklin, **II:** 225, 226, 227; **III:** 88; **Retro. Supp. I:** 150, 163, 164, 165
Pierce, Frederick, **Retro. Supp. I:** 136
Piercy, Josephine K., **Supp. I Part 1:** 103
"Pierian Handsprings" (column, Untermeyer), **Supp. XV:** 294
Pierpont, Claudia Roth, **Supp. X:** 192, 193, 196
Pierre et Jean (Maupassant), **I:** 421
Pierre: or The Ambiguities (Melville), **III:** 86–88, 89; **IV:** 194; **Retro. Supp. I:** 249, 253–254, 256; **Supp. I Part 2:** 579
Pierrepont, Sarah. *See* Edwards, Sarah
Pierrot qui pleure et Pierrot qui rit (Rostand), **II:** 515
Pierson, George W, **Supp. XXII:** 289
Pig Cookies (Ríos), **Supp. IV Part 2:** 537, 550, 552–554
Pigeon Feathers (Updike), **IV:** 214, 218, 219, 221–223, 226
"Pigeon Feathers" (Updike), **Retro. Supp. I:** 318, 322, 323
"Pigeons" (Rilke), **II:** 544
"Pigeons, The" (Espaillat), **Supp. XXI:** 98
"Pigeon Woman" (Swenson), **Supp. IV Part 2:** 644
"Pig Helmet and the Wall of Life"(P. Benedict), **Supp. XXIII:** 48–49
Pigs in Heaven (Kingsolver), **Supp. VII:** 197, 199, 209–210
Pike County Ballads, The (Hay), **Supp. I Part 1:** 352
Piket, Vincent, **Supp. IV Part 1:** 24
Pilar San-Mallafre, Maria del, **Supp. V:** 40
Pilcer, Sonya, **Supp. XVII:** 50
Pilgrim (Findley), **Supp. XX: 61–62**
"Pilgrim" (Freneau), **Supp. I Part 1:** 125
"Pilgrimage" (Ray), **Supp. XVIII:** 193
"Pilgrimage" (Sontag), **Supp. III Part 2:** 454–455
"Pilgrimage" (Trethewey), **Supp. XXI:** 255
"Pilgrimage, The" (Maxwell), **Supp. VIII:** 169, 171
Pilgrimage of Festus, The (Aiken), **I:** 50, 55, 57
Pilgrimage of Henry James, The (Brooks), **I:** 240, 248, 250; **IV:** 433
Pilgrim at Tinker Creek (Dillard), **Supp. VI:** 22, **23–26,** 28, 29, **30–31,** 34; **Supp. XVIII:** 189
"Pilgrim Makers" (Lowell), **II:** 541
Pilgrim's Harbor (Skloot), **Supp. XX: 196, 207**
Pilgrim's Progress (Bunyan), **I:** 92; **II:** 15, 168, 572; **Supp. I Part 1:** 32, 38;

Supp. I Part 2: 599
Pili's Wall (Levine), **Supp. V:** 178, 183–184
"Pillar of Fire" (Bradbury), **Supp. IV Part 1:** 113–114
Pillars of Hercules, The: A Grand Tour of the Mediterranean (Theroux), **Supp. VIII:** 325
"Pillow" (L.-Y. Lee), **Supp. XV:** 224
Pilot, The (Cooper), **I:** 335, 337, 339, 342–343, 350
"Pilot from the Carrier, A" (Jarrell), **II:** 374
"Pilots, Man Your Planes" (Jarrell), **II:** 374–375
"Pilots, The" (Levertov), **Supp. III Part 1:** 282
Pilsudski, Joseph, **Supp. XXIII:** 6
"Pimp's Revenge, A" (Malamud), **Supp. I Part 2:** 435, 450, 451
Pinball (Kosinski), **Supp. VII:** 215, 226
Pinchot, Gifford, **Supp. IX:** 184; **Supp. XIV:** 178
Pindar, **I:** 381; **II:** 543; **III:** 610
"Pine" (Dickey), **Supp. IV Part 1:** 183
Pine Barrens, The (McPhee), **Supp. III Part 1:** 298–301, 309
"Pineys, The" (Stern), **Supp. IX:** 288, 296
Pinget, Robert, **Supp. V:** 39
Pinhook: Finding Wholeness in a Fragmented Land (Ray), **Supp. XVIII:** 189, 192, 202–204
"Pink Dog" (Bishop), **Retro. Supp. II:** 48
"Pink Dress, The" (Boulton), **Supp. XXII:** 19
Pinker, James B., **I:** 409; **Retro. Supp. I:** 231
Pinkerton, Jan, **Supp. V:** 323–324
"Pink Moon—The Pond" (Oliver), **Supp. VII:** 234
Pinktoes (C. Himes), **Supp. XVI: 142**
Pinocchio in Venice (Coover), **Supp. V:** 40, 51
Pinsker, Sanford, **Retro. Supp. II:** 23; **Supp. V:** 272; **Supp. IX:** 293, 327; **Supp. XI:** 251, 254, 317
Pinsky, Robert, **Retro. Supp. II:** 50; **Supp. VI: 235–251; Supp. IX:** 155, 158; **Supp. XIII:** 277, 285; **Supp. XXI:** 243; **Supp. XXIII:** 111, 124
Pinter, Harold, **I:** 71; **Supp. XIII:** 20, 196; **Supp. XIV:** 239; **Supp. XVI:** 207
Pinto, Ferdinand Mendes (pseudonym). *See* Briggs, Charles Frederick
Pinto and Sons (Epstein), **Supp. XII:** 170, **171–172**
Pinto letters (Briggs), **Supp. XVIII:** 3, **12–13**
"Pinup" (Collins), **Supp. XXI:** 59
"Pioneer Girl" (L. I. Wilder), **Supp. XXII:** 290, 293, 294, 295
Pioneers, The (Cooper), **I:** 336, 337, 339, 340–341, 342, 348; **II:** 313
Pioneers of France in the New World (Parkman), **Supp. III Part 2:** 599, 602
"Pioneers! O Pioneers!" (Whitman), **Retro. Supp. I:** 8

"Pioneer's Vision, The" (Larcom), **Supp. XIII:** 140
Pious and Secular America (Niebuhr), **III:** 308
Pipe Night (O'Hara), **III:** 361, 368
Piper, Dan, **Supp. IX:** 65
Pipers at the Gates of Dawn: The Wisdom of Children's Literature (Cott), **Supp. XVI:** 104
"Piper's Rocks" (Olson), **Supp. IV Part 1:** 153
"Pipistrelles" (B. Kelly), **Supp. XVII:** 129–130
Pipkin, Charles W., **Supp. XIV:** 3
Pippa Passes (Browning), **IV:** 128
Piquion, René, **Supp. I Part 1:** 346
Pirandello, Luigi, **Supp. IV Part 2:** 576, 588
Piranesi, Giovanni Battista, **Supp. XV:** 258
Pirate, The (Robbins), **Supp. XII:** 6
Pirate, The (Scott), **I:** 339
Pirates of Penzance, The (Gilbert and Sullivan), **IV:** 386
Pisan Cantos, The (Pound), **III:** 476; **Retro. Supp. I:** 140, 283, 285, 293; **Supp. III Part 1:** 63; **Supp. V:** 331, 337; **Supp. XIV:** 11; **Supp. XV:** 351
Pisarev, Dimitri, **Supp. XXI:** 164
Piscator, Erwin, **IV:** 394
"Pissaro: Tropical Impressions"(Kenny), **Supp. XXIII:** 146
Pissarro, Camille, **I:** 478
"Pissing off the Back of the Boat into the Nevernais Canal" (Matthews), **Supp. IX:** 160–161
Pistol, The (Jones), **Supp. XI:** 219, **223–224,** 227, 234
Pit, The (Norris), **III:** 314, 322, 326–327, 333, 334
"Pit, The" (Roethke), **III:** 538
"Pit and the Pendulum, The" (Poe), **III:** 413, 416; **Retro. Supp. II:** 264, 269–270, 273
"Pitcher" (Francis), **Supp. IX:** 82
"Pitcher, The" (Dubus), **Supp. VII:** 87
Pitchford, Nicola, **Supp. XII:** 13
"Pits, The" (D. Graham), **Supp. XI:** 252, 254
Pitt, William, **Supp. I Part 2:** 510, 518
Pitts, Rebecca, **Supp. XXII:** 280, 281
"Pittsburgh" (Carruth), **Supp. XVI:** 58
"Pity Me" (Wylie), **Supp. I Part 2:** 729
Pity the Monsters (Williamson), **Retro. Supp. II:** 185
Pius II, Pope, **III:** 472
Pius IX, Pope, **II:** 79
"Piute Creek" (Snyder), **Supp. VIII:** 293
Pixley, Frank, **I:** 196
Pizer, Donald, **III:** 321; **Retro. Supp. II:** 100, 199
"Place" (Hoffman), **Supp. XVIII:** 86
"Place at the Outskirts" (Simic), **Supp. VIII:** 282
Place Called Estherville, A (Caldwell), **I:** 297, 307
Place Called Freedom, A (Sanders), **Supp. XVI:** 269
Place for My Head, A (Hoffman), **Supp. XVIII:** 76

"Place in Fiction" (Welty), **IV:** 260, 279

Place of Dead Roads, The (Burroughs), **Supp. III Part 1:** 196

Place of Love, The (Shapiro), **Supp. II Part 2:** 702, 706

"Place of Poetry, The" (Stevens), **Retro. Supp. I:** 304

Place of Science in Modern Civilization and Other Essays, The (Veblen), **Supp. I Part 2:** 629, 642

"Place of Trumpets, The" (B. Kelly), **Supp. XVII:** 127

Place on Earth, A (Berry), **Supp. X:** 33–34, 36

Places Left Unfinished at the Time of Creation (Santos), **Supp. XIII:** 274

"Places to Look for Your Mind" (Moore), **Supp. X:** 174–175

"Place They'd Never Seen, A: The Theater" (Wasserstein), **Supp. XV:** 332

"Place to Live, A" (Levertov), **Supp. III Part 1:** 281

"Place to Stand, A" (Price), **Supp. VI:** 258

Place to Stand, A (Wagoner), **Supp. IX:** 324

"Place (Any Place) to Transcend All Places, A" (W. C. Williams), **Retro. Supp. I:** 422

"Place Where My Poems Are Coming From, The"(Crooker), **Supp. XXIII:** 64

Placi, Carlo, **IV:** 328

Plagemann, Catherine, **Supp. XVII:** 91

"Plagiarist, The" (Singer), **IV:** 19

Plagued by the Nightingale (Boyle), **Supp. XXIV:** 51–52, 53, 56

Plague of Dreamers, A (Stern), **Supp. XX: 178**

Plainest Narrative, The (Bronk), **Supp. XXI:** 31

"Plain Language from Truthful James" (Harte). *See* "Heathen Chinee, The"

"Plain Sense of Things, The" (Stevens), **Retro. Supp. I:** 298, 299, 307, 312

"Plain Song" (Carruth), **Supp. XVI:** 54

Plain Song (Harrison), **Supp. VIII: 38–39**

"Plain Song" (Kooser), **Supp. XIX:** 120

"Plain Song for Comadre, A" (Wilbur), **Supp. III Part 2:** 554

"Plain Talk". *See Common Sense* (Paine)

Plaint of a Rose, The (Sandburg), **III:** 579

Plain Truth: Or, Serious Considerations on the Present State of the City of Philadelphia, and Province of Pennsylvania (Franklin), **II:** 117–119

Plainwater: Essays and Poetry (Carson), **Supp. XII:** 97, **99–104**

Plan B (C. Himes), **Supp. XVI:** 143, 144

Plan B: Further Thoughts on Faith (Lamott), **Supp. XX: 142–143**

"Planchette" (London), **II:** 475–476

"Planetarium" (Rich), **Supp. I Part 2:** 557

Planet News: 1961–1967 (Ginsberg), **Supp. II Part 1:** 321

Planet Waves (album, Dylan), **Supp. XVIII:** 27

"Plantation a beginning, a" (Olson), **Supp. II Part 2:** 573

Plant Dreaming Deep (Sarton), **Supp. VIII:** 250, 263

Plante, David, **Supp. IV Part 1:** 310

Planting a Sequoia (Gioia), **Supp. XV:** 117

"Planting a Sequoia" (Gioia), **Supp. XV:** 111, 112, 117, **121–122**

"Plants Fed On By Fawns" (B. Kelly), **Supp. XVII:** 133

Plarr, Victor, **III:** 459, 477

Plath, James, **Retro. Supp. I:** 334; **Supp. XXIII:** 73, 74, 80

Plath, Sylvia, **Retro. Supp. II:** 181, **241–260; Supp. I Part 2: 526–549,** 554, 571; **Supp. III Part 2:** 543, 561; **Supp. IV Part 2:** 439; **Supp. V:** 79, 81, 113, 117, 118, 119, 344; **Supp. X:** 201, 202, **203,** 215; **Supp. XI:** 146, 240, 241, 317; **Supp. XII:** 217, 308; **Supp. XIII:** 35, 76, 312; **Supp. XIV:** 269; **Supp. XV:** 123, 148, 184, 252, 253, 340; **Supp. XVII:** 239; **Supp. XXI:** 58; **Supp. XXII:** 30, 92, 93; **Supp. XXIII:** 63, 64, 112, 113, 254

Plath, Warren, **Supp. I Part 2:** 528

Plato, **I:** 224, 279, 383, 389, 485, 523; **II:** 5, 8, 10, 15, 233, 346, 391–392, 591; **III:** 115, 480, 600, 606, 609, 619–620; **IV:** 74, 140, 333, 363, 364; **Retro. Supp. I:** 247; **Retro. Supp. II:** 31; **Supp. I Part 2:** 595, 631; **Supp. IV Part 1:** 391; **Supp. IV Part 2:** 526; **Supp. X:** 78

"Plato" (Emerson), **II:** 6

"Platonic Relationship, A" (Beattie), **Supp. V:** 22

Platonic Scripts (Justice), **Supp. VII:** 115

Platonov, Dmitri, **Supp. VIII:** 30

Platt, Anthony M., **Supp. I Part 1:** 13–14

Platt, Edward, **Supp. XXIII:** 97

Platte River (Bass), **Supp. XVI:** 19

"Platte River" (Bass), **Supp. XVI:** 20

Plausible Prejudices: Essays on American Writing (Epstein), **Supp. XIV:** 111

Plautus, Titus Maccius, **IV:** 155; **Supp. III Part 2:** 630

Play and Other Stories, The (Dixon), **Supp. XII:** 148, 149

Playback (script) (Chandler), **Supp. IV Part 1:** 131

Playback (Chandler), **Supp. IV Part 1:** 134–135; **Supp. XVIII:** 138

"Play Ball!" (Francis), **Supp. IX:** 89

Playboy of the Western World, The (Synge), **Supp. III Part 1:** 34

Play Days (Jewett), **Retro. Supp. II:** 135

Play Days: A Book of Stories for Children (Jewett), **II:** 401–402

Player Piano (Vonnegut), **Supp. II Part 2:** 756, 757, 760–765

Players (DeLillo), **Supp. VI:** 3, 6, 8, 14

"Players, The" (W. J. Smith), **Supp. XIII:** 340, 343

"Playground, The" (Bradbury), **Supp. IV Part 1:** 104

Playing at Stillness (Espaillat), **Supp. XXI:** 112

Playing in the Dark (Morrison), **Retro. Supp. II:** 118; **Supp. XIII:** 185–186

"Playing the Bawd at Twenty" (Skloot), **Supp. XX: 204–205**

Play in Poetry (Untermeyer), **Supp. XV:** 310

"Playin with Punjab" (Bambara), **Supp. XI:** 6

Play It Again Sam (Allen), **Supp. XV:** 2, 3, 14

Play It as It Lays (Didion), **Supp. IV Part 1:** 198, 201–203, 203, 211

Play It as It Lays (film), **Supp. IV Part 1:** 198

"Plays and Operas Too" (Whitman), **IV:** 350

Plays of Negro Life: A Source-Book of Native American Drama (Locke and Gregory), **Supp. XIV:** 202

Plays: Winesburg and Others (Anderson), **I:** 113

"Playthings" (Komunyakaa), **Supp. XIII:** 126

"Playtime: Danish Fun" (Larsen), **Supp. XVIII:** 120, 122–123

"Playtime: Three Scandinavian Stories" (Larsen), **Supp. XVIII:** 122–123

Playwright's Voice, The (Savran), **Supp. XIII:** 209; **Supp. XV:** 321; **Supp. XXIV:** 263

Plaza Suite (Simon), **Supp. IV Part 2:** 575, 581–582, 583, 589

Pleading Guilty (Turow), **Supp. XVII: 218,** 219

"Plea for Captain Brown, A" (Thoreau), **IV:** 185

"Please" (Komunyakaa), **Supp. XIII:** 122

"Please Don't Kill Anything" (A. Miller), **III:** 161

"Please Don't Take My Sunshine Away" (Conroy), **Supp. XVI:** 69

Pleasure Dome (Frankenberg), **I:** 436

Pleasure Dome (Komunyakaa), **Supp. XIII:** 113, 121, **131–133**

Pleasure of Hope, The (Emerson), **II:** 8

"Pleasure of Ruins, The" (McClatchy), **Supp. XII:** 256

"Pleasures of Formal Poetry, The" (Bogan), **Supp. III Part 1:** 51

"Pleasures of Peace, The" (Koch), **Supp. XV:** 180

"Plea to the Protestant Churches, A" (Brooks), **Supp. XIV:** 4

Plimpton, George, **Supp. IV Part 1:** 386; **Supp. V:** 201; **Supp. VIII:** 82, 157; **Supp. IX:** 256; **Supp. XI:** 294; **Supp. XIV:** 82; **Supp. XVI: 233–248**

Pliny the Elder, **Supp. XVI:** 292

Pliny the Younger, **II:** 113

"Ploesti Isn't Long Island" (Zinberg), **Supp. XV:** 195

"Plot against the Giant, The" (Stevens), **IV:** 81

Plotinus, **Supp. XV:** 33; **Supp. XVI:** 291

Plough and the Stars, The (O'Casey), **III:** 159

"Ploughing on Sunday" (Stevens), **IV:** 74

Plowing the Dark (Powers), **Supp. IX:** 212–213, **221–224**

Plum Bun (Fauset), **Supp. XVIII:** 127; **Supp. XIX:** 73

Plumed Serpent, The (Lawrence), **Supp. XV:** 46

"Plumet Basilisk, The" (Moore), **III:** 203, 208, 215

Plumly, Stanley, **Supp. IV Part 2:** 625

Plummer, Amanda, **Supp. IV Part 1:** 236

Plunder (serial movie), **Supp. IV Part 2:** 464

Plunket, Robert, **Supp. XV:** 68

"Plunkville Patriot" (O'Henry), **Supp. II Part 1:** 389

"Pluralism and Ideological Peace" (Locke), **Supp. XIV:** 202, 212

"Pluralism and Intellectual Democracy" (Locke), **Supp. XIV:** 202, 208, 212

Pluralistic Universe, A (James), **II:** 342, 348, 357–358

Plutarch, **II:** 5, 8, 16, 555; **Retro. Supp. I:** 360; **Supp. XVI:** 292

Plymell, Charles, **Supp. XIV:** 149

Plymell, Pam, **Supp. XIV:** 149

Pnin (Nabokov), **III:** 246; **Retro. Supp. I:** 263, 265, 266, 275, 335

"Po' Boy Blues" (Hughes), **Supp. I Part 1:** 327

Pocahontas, **I:** 4; **II:** 296; **III:** 584

"Pocahontas to Her English Husband, John Rolfe" (Gunn Allen), **Supp. IV Part 1:** 331

"Pocketbook and Sauerkraut" (Di Piero), **Supp. XIX:** 35, 36, 41, 42, 45

"Pocket Poem" (Kooser), **Supp. XIX:** 128

Podhoretz, Norman, **IV:** 441; **Retro. Supp. II:** 323; **Supp. IV Part 1:** 382; **Supp. VIII:** 93, **231–247; Supp. IX:** 3; **Supp. XIV:** 103

Podnieks, Elizabeth, **Supp. X:** 189, 190, 191, 192

"Pod of the Milkweed" (Frost), **Retro. Supp. I:** 141

Poe, Edgar Allan, **I:** 48, 53, 103, 190, 194, 200, 210, 211, 261, 340, 459; **II:** 74, 77, 194, 255, 273, 295, 308, 311, 313, 421, 475, 482, 530, 595; **III:** 259, **409–432,** 485, 507, 593; **IV:** 123, 129, 133, 141, 187, 261, 345, 350, 432, 438, 439, 453; **Retro. Supp. I:** 41, 273, 365, 421; **Retro. Supp. II:** 102, 104, 160, 164, 220, **261–277,** 322; **Supp. I Part 1:** 36, 309; **Supp. I Part 2:** 376, 384, 385, 388, 393, 405, 413, 421, 474, 682; **Supp. II Part 1:** 385, 410; **Supp. III Part 2:** 544, 549–550; **Supp. IV Part 1:** 80, 81, 101, 128, 341, 349; **Supp. IV Part 2:** 464, 469; **Supp. VIII:** 105; **Supp. IX:** 115; **Supp. X:** 42, 78; **Supp. XI:** 85, 293; **Supp. XIII:** 100, 111; **Supp. XVI:** 294; **Supp. XVIII:** 3, 11; **Supp. XX: 74; Supp. XXIII:** 161, 164, 169, 177, 178; **Supp. XXIV:** 54

Poe, Edgar Allen, **Supp. XV:** 275; **Supp. XXI:** 51

Poe Abroad: Influence, Reputation, Affinities (Vines), **Retro. Supp. II:** 261

"Poem" (Bishop), **Retro. Supp. II:** 40; **Supp. I Part 1:** 73, 76–79, 82, 95

"Poem" (Harrison), **Supp. VIII:** 38

"Poem" (Justice), **Supp. VII:** 125

"Poem" (Kunitz), **Supp. III Part 1:** 263

"Poem" (Notley), **Supp. XXII:** 228–229

"Poem" (O'Hara), **Supp. XIX:** 85

"Poem" (Wright), **Supp. III Part 2:** 590

"Poem About Black Power, A" (Boyle), **Supp. XXIV:** 64

"Poem About George Doty in the Death House, A" (Wright), **Supp. III Part 2:** 594–595, 597–598

"Poem about People" (Pinsky), **Supp. VI: 240–241,** 244, 248

"Poem as Mask, The" (Rukeyser), **Supp. VI:** 281, 285

"Poem as Time Machine, The" (Gallagher), **Supp. XXIV:** 172

"Poem Beginning 'The' " (Zukofsky), **Supp. III Part 2:** 610, 611, 614

"Poem Catching Up with an Idea" (Carruth), **Supp. XVI:** 56

"Poem for a Birthday" (Plath), **Supp. I Part 2:** 539

"POEM FOR ANNA RUSS AND FANNY JONES, A" (Baraka), **Supp. II Part 1:** 58

"Poem for Black Hearts, A" (Baraka), **Supp. II Part 1:** 50

"POEM FOR DEEP THINKERS, A" (Baraka), **Supp. II Part 1:** 55

"Poem for D. H. Lawrence" (Creeley), **Supp. IV Part 1:** 141

"Poem for Dorothy, A" (Merwin), **Supp. III Part 1:** 342

"Poem for Hemingway and W. C. Williams" (Carver), **Supp. III Part 1:** 147

"Poem for my Son" (Kumin), **Supp. IV Part 2:** 442

"Poem for People Who Are Understandably Too Busy to Read Poetry" (Dunn), **Supp. XI:** 147

"Poem for Someone Killed in Spain, A" (Jarrell), **II:** 371

"Poem for the Blue Heron, A" (Oliver), **Supp. VII:** 235–236

"Poem for Two Voices" (Everwine), **Supp. XV:** 89

"Poem For Willie Best, A" (Baraka), **Supp. II Part 1:** 36

"Poem in Prose" (Bogan), **Supp. III Part 1:** 58

"Poem in Which I Refuse Contemplation" (Dove), **Supp. IV Part 1:** 249

"Poem Is a Walk, A" (Ammons), **Supp. VII:** 36

"Poem Like a Grenade, A" (Haines), **Supp. XII:** 204

"Poem of Flight, The" (Levine), **Supp. V:** 189

"Poem of Liberation, The" (Stern), **Supp. IX:** 292

Poem of the Cid (Merwin, trans.), **Supp. III Part 1:** 347

"Poem of the Forgotten" (Haines), **Supp. XII:** 202–203

"Poem (V (F) W)"(O'Hara), **Supp. XXIII:** 219

"Poem on a Line by Anne Sexton, 'We Are All Writing God's Poem' "(Crooker), **Supp. XXIII:** 59

"Poem on the Memorable Victory Obtained by the Gallant Captain Paul Jones" (Freneau), **Supp. II Part 1:** 261

"Poem out of Childhood" (Rukeyser), **Supp. VI:** 272, 277

Poem-Paintings (O'Hara and Bluhm), **Supp. XXIII:** 217

"Poem Read at the Dinner Given to the Author by the Medical Profession" (Holmes), **Supp. I Part 1:** 310–311

Poems (Auden), **Supp. II Part 1:** 6

Poems (Berryman), **I:** 170

Poems (Bryant), **II:** 311; **Supp. I Part 1:** 155, 157

Poems (Cummings), **I:** 430, 447

Poems (E. Stoddard), **Supp. XV:** 274

Poems (Eliot), **I:** 580, 588; **IV:** 122; **Retro. Supp. I:** 59, 291

Poems (Emerson), **II:** 7, 8, 12–13, 17

Poems (Holmes), **Supp. I Part 1:** 303

Poems (Koch), **Supp. XV:** 179

Poems (Lowell), **Supp. I Part 2:** 405

Poems (Moore), **III:** 194, 205, 215

Poems (Poe), **III:** 411

Poems (Reznikoff), **Supp. XIV:** 282, 283, 284, 285

Poems (Tate), **IV:** 121

Poems (W. C. Williams), **Retro. Supp. I:** 412–413, 416, 424

Poems (W. J. Smith), **Supp. XIII:** 332

Poems (Williams), **Supp. XXIV:** 35

Poems (Winters), **Supp. II Part 2:** 809, 810

Poems (Wordsworth), **I:** 468

Poems, 1909–1925 (Eliot), **Retro. Supp. I:** 64

Poems, 1924–1933 (MacLeish), **III:** 7, 15

Poems, 1943–1956 (Wilbur), **Supp. III Part 2:** 554

Poems, The (Freneau), **Supp. II Part 1:** 263

Poems 1918–1975 : The Complete Poems of Charles Reznikoff (Cooney, ed.), **Supp. XIV:** 289

Poems 1940–1953 (Shapiro), **Supp. II Part 2:** 703, 711

Poems 1947–1954 (Kees), **Supp. XV:** 147

Poems: 1947–1957 (W. J. Smith), **Supp. XIII:** 333

Poems 1957–1967 (Dickey), **Supp. IV Part 1:** 178, 181

Poems about God (Ransom), **III:** 484, 486, 491; **IV:** 121

"Poems about Painting" (Snodgrass), **Supp. VI:** 316

Poems and Essays (Ransom), **III:** 486, 490, 492

Poems and New Poems (Bogan), **Supp. III Part 1:** 60–62

"Poems and Places" (Haines), **Supp. XII:** 203

Poems and Poetry of Europe, The (Longfellow, ed.), **Retro. Supp. II:** 155

Poems by Emily Dickinson (Todd and Higginson, eds.), **I:** 469, 470; **Retro. Supp. I:** 35, 39

Poems by Emily Dickinson, Second Series (Todd and Higginson, eds.), **I:** 454; **Retro. Supp. I:** 35

Poems by Emily Dickinson, The (Bianchi and Hampson, eds.), **Retro. Supp. I:** 35

Poems by Emily Dickinson, Third Series (Todd, ed.), **Retro. Supp. I:** 35

Poems by James Russell Lowell, Second Series (Lowell), **Supp. I Part 2:** 406, 409

Poems by Sidney Lanier, (Lanier), **Supp. I Part 1:** 364

Poems from Black Africa (Hughes, ed.), **Supp. I Part 1:** 344

"Poems I Have Lost, The" (Ortiz), **Supp. IV Part 2:** 507

Poems: North & South–A Cold Spring, (Bishop), **Supp. I Part 1:** 83, 89

Poems of a Jew (Shapiro), **Supp. II Part 2:** 703, 712–713

"Poems of a Mountain Recluse" (Budbill), **Supp. XIX:** 9, 10

Poems of Anna Akhmatova, The (Kunitz and Hayward, trans.), **Supp. III Part 1:** 269

Poems of Emily Dickinson, The (Bianchi and Hampson, eds.), **Retro. Supp. I:** 35

Poems of Emily Dickinson, The (Johnson, ed.), **I:** 470

Poems of François Villon (Kinnell, trans.), **Supp. III Part 1:** 235, 243, 249

"Poems of Our Climate, The" (Stevens), **Retro. Supp. I:** 313

Poems of Philip Freneau, Written Chiefly during the Late War (Freneau), **Supp. II Part 1:** 261

Poems of Places (Longfellow, ed.), **II:** 490; **Retro. Supp. II:** 155; **Supp. I Part 1:** 368

Poems of Stanley Kunitz, The (Kunitz), **Supp. III Part 1:** 258, 263, 264, 266, 268

"Poems of These States" (Ginsberg), **Supp. II Part 1:** 323, 325

Poems of Two Friends (Howells and Piatt), **II:** 273, 277

"POEM SOME PEOPLE WILL HAVE TO UNDERSTAND, A" (Baraka), **Supp. II Part 1:** 49

Poems on Slavery (Longfellow), **II:** 489; **Retro. Supp. II:** 157, 168; **Supp. I Part 2:** 406

Poems on Various Subjects (Rowson), **Supp. XV:** 232

Poems on Various Subjects, Religious and Moral (Wheatley), **Supp. XX: 277, 282, 284, 285, 289**

Poem Spoken at the Public Commencement at Yale College, in New Haven; September 1, 1781, A (Barlow), **Supp. II Part 1:** 67–68, 74, 75

Poems Retrieved (O'Hara), **Supp. XXIII:** 220

Poems to Solve (Swenson), **Supp. IV Part 2:** 642

Poems Written and Published during the American Revolutionary War (Freneau), **Supp. II Part 1:** 273, 274

Poems Written between the Years 1768 and 1794 (Freneau), **Supp. II Part 1:** 269

"Poem That Took the Place of a Mountain" (Olson), **Supp. II Part 2:** 582

"Poem to My First Lover" (Olds), **Supp. X:** 206

"Poem to the Reader" (Olds), **Supp. X:** 213

"Poem with No Ending, A" (Levine), **Supp. V:** 186, 190

"Poem You Asked For, The" (Levis), **Supp. XI:** 259–260

Poe Poe Poe Poe Poe Poe Poe (Hoffman), **Retro. Supp. II:** 265

Poesía Náhuatl, **Supp. XV:** 77

Poésies 1917–1920 (Cocteau), **Retro. Supp. I:** 82

"Poesis: A Conceit" (Sobin), **Supp. XVI:** 288

"Poet" (Taggard), **Supp. XXII:** 284

Poet, The (Connelly), **Supp. XXI: 71, 78**

"Poet, The" (Dunbar), **Supp. II Part 1:** 207, 209–210

"Poet, The" (Emerson), **II:** 13, 19, 20, 170

"Poet, The" (Ortiz), **Supp. IV Part 2:** 505

"Poet and His Book, The" (Millay), **III:** 126, 138

"Poet and His Public, The" (Jarrell), **Supp. I Part 1:** 96

"Poet and His Song, The" (Dunbar), **Supp. II Part 1:** 199

"Poet and the Person, The" (Kinard), **Supp. XIV:** 127

"Poet and the Queen, The" (Shaw), **Supp. XIX:** 241

"Poet and the World, The" (Cowley), **Supp. II Part 1:** 145

"Poet as Anti-Specialist, The" (Swenson), **Supp. IV Part 2:** 638, 643

"Poet as *Curandera*" (Mora), **Supp. XIII:** 214, 220

"Poet as Hero, The: Keats in His Letters" (Trilling), **Supp. III Part 2:** 506–507

"Poet as Religious Moralist, The" (Larson), **Supp. XI:** 328

"Poet at Seven, The" (Rimbaud), **II:** 545

Poet at the Breakfast-Table, The (Holmes), **Supp. I Part 1:** 313–314

"Poète contumace, Le" (Corbiere), **II:** 384–385

"Poet for President, A" (Mora), **Supp. XIII:** 220–221

Poetic Achievement of Ezra Pound, The (Alexander), **Retro. Supp. I:** 293

Poetic Diction: A Study in Meaning (Barfield), **III:** 274, 279

"Poetic Principle, The" (Poe), **III:** 421, 426; **Retro. Supp. II:** 266

"Poetics" (Ammons), **Supp. VII:** 29–30

Poetics (Aristotle), **III:** 422; **Supp. XI:** 249; **Supp. XIII:** 75; **Supp. XIV:** 243; **Supp. XV:** 265

Poetics of Space, The (Bachelard), **Supp. XIII:** 225; **Supp. XVI:** 292

"Poetics of the Periphery: Literary Experimentalism in Kathy Acker's *In Memoriam to Identity*" (Acker), Supp. *XII:* 17

"Poetics of the Physical World, The" (Kinnell), **Supp. III Part 1:** 239

"Poetics of Tourette Syndrome, The: Language, Neurobiology, and Poetry" (Schleifer), **Supp. XVIII:** 144

Poet in the World, The (Levertov), **Supp. III Part 1:** 271, 273, 278, 282

"Poet or the Growth of a Lit'ry Figure" (White), **Supp. I Part 2:** 676

Poetry (Barber), **Supp. IV Part 2:** 550

"Poetry" (Moore), **III:** 204–205, 215

"Poetry" (Nye), **Supp. XIII:** 282

"Poetry" (Wrigley), **Supp. XVIII:** 301–302

"Poetry, Community and Climax" (Snyder), **Supp. VIII:** 290

"Poetry, Pleasure, and the Hedonist Reader" (Collins), **Supp. XXI:** 54

"Poetry: A Metrical Essay" (Holmes), **Supp. I Part 1:** 310

"Poetry and Belief in Thomas Hardy" (Schwartz), **Supp. II Part 2:** 666

Poetry and Criticism (Nemerov, ed.), **III:** 269

"Poetry and Drama" (Eliot), **I:** 588

Poetry and Fiction: Essays (Nemerov), **III:** 269, 281

"Poetry and Place" (Berry), **Supp. X:** 22, 28, 31, 32

Poetry and Poets (Lowell), **II:** 512

"Poetry and Religion" (Jarman), **Supp. XVII:** 111

Poetry and the Age (Jarrell), **IV:** 352; **Retro. Supp. I:** 121; **Supp. II Part 1:** 135

"Poetry and the Primitive: Notes on Poetry as an Ecological Survival Technique" (Snyder), **Supp. VIII:** 291, 292, 299, 300

"Poetry and the Public World" (MacLeish), **III:** 11

Poetry and the World (Pinsky), **Supp. VI:** 236, 239, 244, 247

Poetry and Truth (Olson), **Supp. II Part 2:** 583

"Poetry and Uncertainty"(Hirshfield), **Supp. XXIII:** 137

"Poetry As a Way of Life" (Bishop interview), **Retro. Supp. II:** 53

"Poetry as Survival" (Harrison), **Supp. VIII:** 45

"Poetry Baron, The" (Gallagher), **Supp. XXIV:** 166, 177

"Poetry Failure" (Halliday), **Supp. XIX:** 92

Poetry for Students (Taibl), **Supp. XV:** 255

"Poetry for the Advanced" (Baraka), **Supp. II Part 1:** 58

"Poetry Friendship on Earth" (Halliday), **Supp. XIX:** 90, 91

Poetry Handbook, A (Oliver), **Supp. VII:** 229, 245

Poetry Home Repair Manual, The (Kooser), **Supp. XIX:** 116, 128

Poetry in Motion (film), **Supp. XXIV:** 33

Poetry in Motion: 100 Poems from the Subways and Buses (Peacock, ed.),

Supp. XIX: 195

"Poetry in Translation: Literary Imperialism or, Defending the Musk Ox" (Gallagher), **Supp. XXIV:** 172

"Poetry of Barbarism, The" (Santayana), **IV:** 353

Poetry of Chaucer, The (Gardner), **Supp. VI: 63**

Poetry of Meditation, The (Martz), **IV:** 151; **Supp. I Part 1:** 107

Poetry of Mourning: The Modern Elegy from Hardy to Heaney (Ramazani), **Supp. IV Part 2:** 450

Poetry of Stephen Crane, The (Hoffman), **I:** 405

Poetry of the Negro, 1746–1949, The (Hughes and Bontemps), **Supp. I Part 1:** 345; **Supp. XXII:** 11

Poetry 180: A Turning Back to Poetry (Collins, ed.), **Supp. XXI:** 54

Poetry Reading against the Vietnam War, A (Bly and Ray, eds.), **Supp. IV Part 1:** 61, 63

"Poetry Workshop, The" (column, Kumin), **Supp. XX: 164**

"Poetry Wreck, The" (Shapiro), **Supp. II Part 2:** 717

Poetry Wreck, The: Selected Essays (Shapiro), **Supp. II Part 2:** 703, 704, 717

"Poets" (X. J. Kennedy), **Supp. XV:** 158

Poet's Alphabet, A: Reflections on the Literary Art and Vocation (Bogan), **Supp. III Part 1:** 55, 64

Poets and Poetry of America (Griswold), **Supp. XV:** 277

Poet's Choice (Engle and Langland, eds.), **III:** 277, 542

Poet's Guide to Poetry, A (Kinzie), **Supp. XXIII:** 124

"Poet's Husband Engages in Gourmet Cooking, The" (Espaillat), **Supp. XXI:** 99

Poets of the Old Testament, The (Gordon), **III:** 199

Poets of Today (Wheelock, ed.), **Supp. IV Part 2:** 639

Poets on Poetry (Nemerov, ed.), **III:** 269

"Poet's Tact, and a Necessary Tactlessness, The" (C. Frost), **Supp. XV:** 94–95

"Poet's View, A" (Levertov), **Supp. III Part 1:** 284

"Poet's Voice, The" (Oliver), **Supp. VII:** 245

"Poets with History and Poets Without History"(Tsvetaeva), **Supp. XXIII:** 168

"Poet Turns on Himself, The" (Dickey), **Supp. IV Part 1:** 177, 181, 185

Poganuc People (Stowe), **Supp. I Part 2:** 581, 596, 599–600

Pogo (comic strip), **Supp. XI:** 105

Pohrt, Tom, **Supp. XIX:** 123

Poincaré, Raymond, **IV:** 320

"Point, The" (Hayden), **Supp. II Part 1:** 373

"Point at Issue!, A" (Chopin), **Retro. Supp. II:** 61; **Supp. I Part 1:** 208

"Point of Age, A" (Berryman), **I:** 173

Point of No Return (Marquand), **III:** 56, 59–60, 65, 67, 69

Point Reyes Poems (R. Bly), **Supp. IV Part 1:** 71

"Points" (Hoffman), **Supp. XVIII:** 86

Points for a Compass Rose (Connell), **Supp. XIV:** 79, 80, 96

"Point Shirley" (Plath), **Supp. I Part 2:** 529, 538

Points in Time (Bowles), **Supp. IV Part 1:** 93

"Points West" (column), **Supp. IV Part 1:** 198

Poirier, Richard, **I:** 136, 239; **III:** 34; **Retro. Supp. I:** 134; **Retro. Supp. II:** 207–208; **Supp. I Part 2:** 660, 665; **Supp. IV Part 2:** 690

Poison Pen (Garrett), **Supp. VII:** 111

Poisonwood Bible, The (Kingsolver), **Supp. VII:** 197–198, 202, 210–213

Poitier, Sidney, **Supp. IV Part 1:** 360, 362

Pokerface (Collins), **Supp. XXI:** 53

"Polack Reverie" (Halliday), **Supp. XIX:** 88

Polanco, Richard, **Supp. XX: 260**

"Polar Bear" (Heller), **Supp. IV Part 1:** 383

"Polar Bears and Others" (Boyle), **Supp. XXIV:** 57

"Polar Seas and Sir John Franklin, The" (Briggs), **Supp. XVIII:** 14

Pole, Rupert, **Supp. X:** 185

"Pole Star" (MacLeish), **III:** 16

Po Li, **Supp. I Part 1:** 262

Police (Baraka), **Supp. II Part 1:** 47

"Police" (Corso), **Supp. XII:** 117, 127

"Police Court Saturday Morning" (X. J. Kennedy), **Supp. XV:** 170

"Police Dreams" (Bausch), **Supp. VII:** 47

Politian (Poe), **III:** 412

"Political and Practical Conceptions of Race, The" (Locke), **Supp. XIV:** 209–210

Political Essays (Lowell), **Supp. I Part 2:** 407

Political Fable, A (Coover), **Supp. V:** 44, 46, 47, 49, 51

"Political Fables" (Mather), **Supp. II Part 2:** 450

"Political Interests" (Stevens), **Retro. Supp. I:** 295

"Political Litany, A" (Freneau), **Supp. II Part 1:** 257

"Political Migrations: A Family Story" (Mallon), **Supp. XIX:** 141–142

"Political Pastoral" (Frost), **Retro. Supp. I:** 139

"Political Poem" (Baraka), **Supp. II Part 1:** 36

Politics (Acker), **Supp. XII:** 3, 4

Politics (Macdonald), **I:** 233–234

"Politics" (Paley), **Supp. VI:** 217

"Politics, Structure, and Poetic Development" (McCombs), **Supp. XIII:** 33

"Politics and the English Language" (Orwell), **Retro. Supp. II:** 287; **Supp. I Part 2:** 620

Politics and the Novel (Howe), **Supp. VI:** 113

"Politics and the Personal Lyric in the Poetry of Joy Harjo and C. D. Wright" (Goodman), **Supp. XV:** 344

"Politics of Ethnic Authorship, The: Li-Young Lee, Emerson, and Whitman at the Banquet Table" (Partridge), **Supp. XV:** 219

"Politics of Silence, The" (Monette), **Supp. X:** 148

Polito, Robert, **Supp. XVIII:** 33; **Supp. XXIV:** 234

Politt, Katha, **Supp. XII:** 159

Poliziano (Angelo Ambrogini), **Supp. XXIV:** 152

Polk, James, **Supp. XIII:** 20

Polk, James K., **I:** 17; **II:** 433–434

Pollack, Sydney, **Supp. XIII:** 159

"Pollen" (Nye), **Supp. XIII:** 284

Pollitt, Katha, **Supp. X:** 186, 191, 193; **Supp. XVI:** 39

Pollock, Jackson, **IV:** 411, 420; **Supp. XV:** 145, 177, 178; **Supp. XIX:** 33; **Supp. XXIII:** 208, 210, 211

"Polly" (Chopin), **Retro. Supp. II:** 72

Polo, Marco, **III:** 395

Polonsky, Abraham, **Supp. XXI:** 261, 275

Polybius, **Supp. I Part 2:** 491

"Polydore" (Chopin), **Retro. Supp. II:** 66

"Pomegranate" (Glück), **Supp. V:** 82

"Pomegranate Seed" (Wharton), **IV:** 316; **Retro. Supp. I:** 382

Ponce de Leon, Luis, **III:** 391

"Pond, The" (Nemerov), **III:** 272

"Pond at Dusk, The" (Kenyon), **Supp. VII:** 168

Ponder Heart, The (Welty), **IV:** 261, 274–275, 281; **Retro. Supp. I:** 351–352

"Ponderosa Pine" (Huncke), **Supp. XIV:** 146

Ponsot, Margaret, **Supp. XVII:** 241

"Pony" (Sanders), **Supp. XVI:** 277

"Pony Car"(P. Benedict), **Supp. XXIII:** 47

Poodle Springs (Parker and Chandler), **Supp. IV Part 1:** 135; **Supp. XIX:** 189

Poodle Springs Story, The (Chandler), **Supp. IV Part 1:** 135

"Pool, The" (Doolittle), **Supp. I Part 1:** 264–265

Poole, Ernest, **II:** 444

"Pool Lights" (F. Barthelme), **Supp. XI:** 25, 26–27, 36

"Pool Room in the Lions Club" (Merwin), **Supp. III Part 1:** 346

"Poolside" (Skloot), **Supp. XX: 202–203**

"Poor Black Fellow" (Hughes), **Retro. Supp. I:** 204

"Poor Bustard, The" (Corso), **Supp. XII:** 134

"Poor but Happy" (Mamet), **Supp. XIV:** 252, 253

"Poor Dead Feet of My First Husband, The"(Schott), **Supp. XXIII:** 241

Poore, Charles, **III:** 364; **Supp. XIX:** 257, 264; **Supp. XX: 38**

Poor Fool (Caldwell), **I:** 291, 292, 308
Poorhouse Fair, The (Updike), **IV:** 214, 228–229, 232; **Retro. Supp. I:** 317, 320
"Poor Joanna" (Jewett), **II:** 394
"Poor Man's Pudding and Rich Man's Crumbs" (Melville), **III:** 89–90
"Poor Richard" (James), **II:** 322
Poor Richard's Almanac (undated) (Franklin), **II:** 112
Poor Richard's Almanac for 1733 (Franklin), **II:** 108, 110
Poor Richard's Almanac for 1739 (Franklin), **II:** 112
Poor Richard's Almanac for 1758 (Franklin), **II:** 101
Poor White (Anderson), **I:** 110–111
"Poor Working Girl" (Z. Fitzgerald), **Supp. IX:** 71
Popa, Vasko, **Supp. VIII:** 272
Pope, Alexander, **I:** 198, 204; **II:** 17, 114; **III:** 263, 267, 288, 517; **IV:** 145; **Retro. Supp. I:** 335; **Supp. I Part 1:** 150, 152, 310; **Supp. I Part 2:** 407, 422, 516, 714; **Supp. II Part 1:** 70, 71; **Supp. X:** 32, 36; **Supp. XII:** 260; **Supp. XV:** 258; **Supp. XX:** 280
Pope, James, **Supp. XXII:** 196
Pope-Hennessy, James, **Supp. XIV:** 348
"Pope's Penis, The" (Olds), **Supp. X:** 207
"Poplar, Sycamore" (Wilbur), **Supp. III Part 2:** 549
Popo and Fifina: Children of Haiti (Hughes and Bontemps), **Retro. Supp. I:** 203; **Supp. XXII:** 4, 10, 12
"Poppies" (Oliver), **Supp. VII:** 240
"Poppies in July" (Plath), **Supp. I Part 2:** 544
"Poppies in July"(Crooker), **Supp. XXIII:** 61
"Poppies in October" (Plath), **Supp. I Part 2:** 544
"Poppycock" (Francis), **Supp. IX:** 87
"Poppy Juice" (Taggard), **Supp. XXII:** 276
"Poppy Seed" (Lowell), **II:** 523
"Popular Art and the Cultural Tradition" (C. L. R. James), **Supp. XXI:** 170
Popular Book, The: A History of America's Literary Taste (Hart), **Supp. XVIII:** 257, 258
Popular Culture (Goldbarth), **Supp. XII:** 186
Popular History of the United States (Gay), **Supp. I Part 1:** 158
"Popular Songs" (Ashbery), **Supp. III Part 1:** 6
"Populist Manifesto" (Ferlinghetti), **Supp. VIII:** 290
"Porcelain Bowl" (Glück), **Supp. V:** 83
Porcher, Frances, **Retro. Supp. II:** 71
Porco, Mike, **Supp. XVIII:** 24
"Porcupine, The" (Kinnell), **Supp. III Part 1:** 244
Porcupine's Kiss, The (Dobyns), **Supp. XIII:** 89–90
"Por esas coases que pasan" (Hinojosa), **Supp. XIX:** 101
Porgy and Bess (film), **Supp. I Part 1:** 66

Porgy and Bess (play), **Supp. IV Part 1:** 6
"Porn Bought my Football" (Offutt), **Supp. XIX:** 163
"Porphyria's Lover" (Browning), **II:** 522
Portable Beat Reader, The (Charters, ed.), **Supp. XIV:** 152
Portable Blake, The (Kazin, ed.), **Supp. VIII:** 103
Portable Faulkner, The (Cowley, ed.), **II:** 57, 59; **Retro. Supp. I:** 73
Portable Kisses: Love Poems (Gallagher), **Supp. XXIV:** 170
Portable Paul and Jane Bowles, The (Dillon), **Supp. IV Part 1:** 95
Portable Veblen, The (Veblen), **Supp. I Part 2:** 630, 650
"Porte-Cochere" (Taylor), **Supp. V:** 320
"Porter" (Hughes), **Supp. I Part 1:** 327
"Porter" (Nelson), **Supp. XVIII:** 175
Porter, Bern, **III:** 171
Porter, Cole, **Supp. IX:** 189
Porter, Eliot, **Supp. IV Part 2:** 599
Porter, Fairfield, **Supp. XV:** 178; **Supp. XXIII:** 209, 211, 212; **Supp. XXIV:** 41
Porter, Herman W., **Supp. I Part 1:** 49
Porter, Horace, **Retro. Supp. II:** 4, 127
Porter, Jacob, **Supp. I Part 1:** 153
Porter, Katherine Anne, **I:** 97, 385; **II:** 194, 606; **III:** 433–455, 482; **IV:** 26, 138, 246, 261, 279, 280, 282; **Retro. Supp. I:** 354; **Retro. Supp. II:** 233, 235; **Supp. IV Part 1:** 31, 310; **Supp. V:** 225; **Supp. VIII:** 156, 157; **Supp. IX:** 93, 94, 95, 98, 128; **Supp. X:** 50; **Supp. XIII:** 294; **Supp. XIV:** 3; **Supp. XV:** 338; **Supp. XXIV:** 52
Porter, Noah, **Supp. I Part 2:** 640
Porter, William Sydney. *See* Henry, O.
"Porter Paints a Picture"(O'Hara), **Supp. XXIII:** 212
Porteus, Beilby, **Supp. I Part 1:** 150
"Portland Going Out, The" (Merwin), **Supp. III Part 1:** 345
Portnoy's Complaint (P. Roth), **Retro. Supp. II:** 282–286, 291; **Supp. III Part 2:** 401, 404, 405, 407, 412–414, 426; **Supp. V:** 119, 122; **Supp. XI:** 140; **Supp. XVII:** 8, 43; **Supp. XX:** 177
Port of Saints (Burroughs), **Supp. III Part 1:** 106
"Portrait" (Dixon), **Supp. XII:** 154
"Portrait, A" (Parker), **Supp. IX:** 192–193
"Portrait, The" (Kunitz), **Supp. III Part 1:** 263
"Portrait, The" (Wharton), **Retro. Supp. I:** 364
"Portrait d'une Femme" (Pound), **Retro. Supp. I:** 288
Portrait in Brownstone (Auchincloss), **Supp. IV Part 1:** 21, 23, 27, 31
"Portrait in Georgia" (Toomer), **Supp. IX:** 314
"Portrait in Greys, A" (W. C. Williams), **Retro. Supp. I:** 416
"Portrait of a Girl in Glass" (T. Williams), **IV:** 383

"Portrait of a Jewelry Drummer" (Untermeyer), **Supp. XV:** 299–300
"Portrait of a Lady" (Eliot), **I:** 569, 570, 571, 584; **III:** 4; **Retro. Supp. I:** 55, 56, 62
Portrait of a Lady, The (James), **I:** 10, 258, 461–462, 464; **II:** 323, 325, 327, 328–329, 334; **Retro. Supp. I:** 215, 216, 217, 219, 220, 223, **224–225,** 232, 233, 381
"Portrait of an Artist" (P. Roth), **Supp. III Part 2:** 412
Portrait of an Eye: Three Novels (Acker), **Supp. XII:** 6, **7–9**
"Portrait of an Invisible Man" (Auster), **Supp. XII:** 21
"Portrait of a Supreme Court Judge" (Untermeyer), **Supp. XV:** 299
Portrait of Bascom Hawkes, A (Wolfe), **IV:** 451–452, 456
Portrait of Edith Wharton (Lubbock), **Retro. Supp. I:** 366
Portrait of Logan Pearsall Smith, Drawn from His Letters and Diaries, A (Russell, ed.), **Supp. XIV:** 349
Portrait of Picasso as a Young Man (Mailer), **Retro. Supp. II:** 213
"Portrait of the Artist as an Old Man, A" (Humphrey), **Supp. IX:** 109
Portrait of the Artist as a Young Man, A (Joyce), **I:** 475–476; **III:** 471, 561; **Retro. Supp. I:** 127; **Retro. Supp. II:** 4, 331; **Supp. IX:** 236; **Supp. XIII:** 53, 95
"Portrait of the Artist with Hart Crane" (Wright), **Supp. V:** 342
"Portrait of the Great White Hunter Fox-hunting in the Absence of Big Game" (Major), **Supp. XXII:** 183
"Portrait of the Intellectual as a Yale Man" (McCarthy), **II:** 563, 564–565
"Portrait of the Reader with a Bowl of Cereal, A" (Collins), **Supp. XXI:** 55
"Portrait of the Self . . . , A" (Sobin), **Supp. XVI:** 288
Portraits and Elegies (Schnackenberg), **Supp. XV:** 249, **253–256**
"Portraits of Grief" *(New York Times),* **Supp. XIX:** 142
"Port Town" (Hughes), **Retro. Supp. I:** 199
Portuguese Voyages to America in the Fifteenth Century (Morison), **Supp. I Part 2:** 488
"Po' Sandy" (Chesnutt), **Supp. XIV:** 60
Poseidon Adventure, The (film), **Supp. XII:** 321
Poseidon Adventure, The (Gallico), **Supp. XVI:** 238
"Poseidon and Company" (Carver), **Supp. III Part 1:** 137
"Positive Obsession" (O. Butler), **Supp. XIII:** 70
Poss, Stanley, **Supp. XIV:** 166
Possession (Byatt), **Supp. XXI:** 147
"Possessions" (H. Crane), **I:** 392–393; **Retro. Supp. II:** 78
Possible World, A (Koch), **Supp. XV:** 184
Postal Inspector (film), **Supp. XIII:** 166

Postcards (Proulx), **Supp. VII:** 249, 256–258, 262

"Postcard to Send to Sumer, A" (Bronk), **Supp. XXI:** 31

"Postcolonialism and Autobiography" (Skinner and Waller), **Supp. XXII:** 78

"Postcolonial Tale, A" (Harjo), **Supp. XII:** 227

"Posthumous Letter to Gilbert White" (Auden), **Supp. II Part 1:** 26

"Post-Larkin Triste" (Karr), **Supp. XI:** 242–243

Postlethwaite, Diana, **Supp. XII:** 317–318; **Supp. XVI:** 176

"Postlude" (W. C. Williams), **Retro. Supp. I:** 415

Postman, Neil, **Supp. XI:** 275

Postman Always Rings Twice, The (Cain), **Supp. XIII:** 165–166

Postman Always Rings Twice, The (film), **Supp. XIV:** 241

"Postmaster and the Clerk, The" (Budbill), **Supp. XIX:** 9

"Postmortem Guide, A" (Dunn), **Supp. XI:** 155

Postrel, Virginia, **Supp. XIV:** 298, 311

"Postscript" (Du Bois), **Supp. II Part 1:** 173

"Postscript" (Nye), **Supp. XIII:** 287

Postsouthern Sense of Place, The (Bone), **Supp. XXII:** 247

"Potato" (Wilbur), **Supp. III Part 2:** 545

"Potatoes' Dance, The" (Lindsay), **Supp. I Part 2:** 394

Pot of Earth, The (MacLeish), **III:** 5, 6–8, 10, 12, 18

"Pot Roast" (Strand), **Supp. IV Part 2:** 629

Potshot (Parker), **Supp. XIX:** 185

Pot Shots at Poetry (Francis), **Supp. IX:** 83–84

Potter, Beatrix, **Supp. I Part 2:** 656; **Supp. XVI:** 100

Potter, Stephen, **IV:** 430

Potter's House, The (Stegner), **Supp. IV Part 2:** 598, 606

Poulenc, Francis, **Supp. IV Part 1:** 81

Poulin, Al, Jr., **Supp. IX:** 272; **Supp. XI:** 259

Pound, Ezra, **I:** 49, 58, 60, 66, 68, 69, 105, 236, 243, 256, 384, 403, 428, 429, 475, 476, 482, 487, 521, 578; **II:** 26, 55, 168, 263, 316, 371, 376, 513, 517, 520, 526, 528, 529, 530; **III:** 2, 5, 8, 9, 13–14, 17, 174, 194, 196, 278, 430, 453, **456–479,** 492, 504, 511, 523, 524, 527, 575–576, 586, 590; **IV:** 27, 28, 407, 415, 416, 433, 446; **Retro. Supp. I:** 51, 52, 55, 58, 59, 63, 82, 89, 127, 140, 171, 177, 178, 198, 216, **283–294,** 298, 299, 359, 411, 412, 413, 414, 417, 418, 419, 420, 423, 426, 427, 430, 431; **Retro. Supp. II:** 178, 183, 189, 326; **Supp. I Part 1:** 253, 255–258, 261–268, 272, 274; **Supp. I Part 2:** 387, 721; **Supp. II Part 1:** 1, 8, 20, 30, 91, 136; **Supp. III Part 1:** 48, 63, 64, 73, 105, 146, 225, 271; **Supp. III Part 2:** 542, **609–617,** 619, 620, 622, 625, 626, 628, 631; **Supp. IV Part 1:** 153, 314; **Supp. V:** 331, 338, 340, 343, 345; **Supp. VIII:** 39, 105, 195, 205, 271, 290, 291, 292, 303; **Supp. IX:** 291; **Supp. X:** 24, 36, 112, 120, 122; **Supp. XII:** 97; **Supp. XIV:** 11, 55, 83, 272, 284, 286, 287, 347; **Supp. XV:** 20, 42, 43, 51, 93, 161, 181, 297, 298, 299, 301, 302, 306; **Supp. XVI:** 47, 282; **Supp. XVII:** 111, 226–227; **Supp. XIX:** 42; **Supp. XXI:** 33; **Supp. XXII:** 165; **Supp. XXIII:** 26, 166, 174; **Supp. XXIV:** 37

Pound, Louise, **Retro. Supp. I:** 4; **Supp. XV:** 137

Pound, T. S., **I:** 428

"Pound Reweighed" (Cowley), **Supp. II Part 1:** 143

Powell, Anthony, **Supp. XVIII:** 136, 146; **Supp. XIX:** 131

Powell, Betty, **Retro. Supp. II:** 140

Powell, D. A., **Supp. XXIII:** 221

Powell, Dawn, **Supp. IV Part 2:** 678, 682; **Supp. XIX:** 143

Powell, Dick, **Supp. IX:** 250

Powell, John Wesley, **Supp. IV Part 2:** 598, 604, 611

Powell, Lawrence Clark, **III:** 189

Powell, Margaret K., **Supp. XXIV:** 170

Powell, William, **Supp. IV Part 1:** 355

"Power" (Corso), **Supp. XII:** 117, 126, 127, **128**

"Power" (Emerson), **II:** 2, 3

"Power" (Rich), **Supp. I Part 2:** 569

Power, Samantha, **Supp. XXIII:** 25, 26, 27

"Power and Light" (Dickey), **Supp. IV Part 1:** 182

Power and the Glory, The (Greene), **III:** 556

"Powerhouse" (Welty), **Retro. Supp. I:** 343, 346

"Power Never Dominion" (Rukeyser), **Supp. VI:** 281

"Power of Fancy, The" (Freneau), **Supp. II Part 1:** 255

Power of Myth, The (Campbell), **Supp. IX:** 245

"Power of Prayer, The" (Lanier), **Supp. I Part 1:** 357

"Power of Stories, The" (Sanders), **Supp. XVI:** 278

"Power of Suggestion" (Auchincloss), **Supp. IV Part 1:** 33

Power of Sympathy, The (Brown), **Supp. II Part 1:** 74

Power Politics (Atwood), **Supp. XIII:** 20, 33–34, 35

Powers, Catherine A., **Supp. XXII:** 217

Powers, J. F., **Supp. V:** 319; **Supp. XVII:** 43

Powers, Kim, **Supp. VIII:** 329, 340

Powers, Richard, **Supp. IX: 207–225; Supp. XVII:** 183; **Supp. XX: 93; Supp. XXII:** 49; **Supp. XXIV:** 131

Powers of Attorney (Auchincloss), **Supp. IV Part 1:** 31, 32, 33

"Powers of Darkness" (Wharton), **Retro. Supp. I:** 379

Powys, John Cowper, **Supp. I Part 2:** 454, 476; **Supp. IX:** 135

Poynton, Jerome, **Supp. XIV:** 147, 150

Pozorski, Aimee L., **Supp. XXII:** 160, 166

Practical Agitation (Chapman), **Supp. XIV:** 41

Practical Criticism: A Study of Literary Judgment (Richards), **Supp. XIV:** 3, 16

Practical Magic (film), **Supp. X:** 80

Practical Magic (Hoffman), **Supp. X:** 78, 82, **88–89**

"Practical Methods of Meditation, The" (Dawson), **IV:** 151

Practical Navigator, The (Bowditch), **Supp. I Part 2:** 482

Practice of Perspective, The (Dubreuil), **Supp. IV Part 2:** 425

Practice of Reading, The (Donoghue), **Supp. VIII:** 189

Pragmatism: A New Name for Some Old Ways of Thinking (James), **II:** 352

"Pragmatism's Conception of Truth" (James), **Supp. XIV:** 40

Prague Orgy, The (P. Roth), **Retro. Supp. II:** 280

"Praire, The" (Clampitt), **Supp. IX:** 42

"Prairie" (Sandburg), **III:** 583, 584

Prairie, The (Cooper), **I:** 339, 342

"Prairie Birthday" (Leopold), **Supp. XIV:** 185

Prairie Home Companion, A (Keillor, radio program), **Supp. XIII:** 274; **Supp. XVI:** 169–171, 173–178

Prairie Home Morning Show, A (Keillor, radio program), **Supp. XVI:** 171

"Prairie Life, A Citizen Speaks" (Dunn), **Supp. XI:** 145

"Prairies, The" (Bryant), **Supp. I Part 1:** 157, 162, 163, 166

Praise (Hass), **Supp. VI:** 104–105, 106

"Praise for an Urn" (Crane), **I:** 388

"Praise for Sick Women" (Snyder), **Supp. VIII:** 294

"Praise in Summer" (Wilbur), **Supp. III Part 2:** 546–548, 560, 562

"Praise of a Palmtree" (Levertov), **Supp. III Part 1:** 284

"Praise of the Committee" (Rukeyser), **Supp. VI:** 278

"Praises, The" (Goldbarth), **Supp. XII:** 185

"Praises, The" (Olson), **Supp. II Part 2:** 558, 560, 563, 564

Praises and Dispraises (Des Pres), **Supp. X:** 120

Praisesong for the Widow (Marshall), **Supp. IV Part 1:** 14; **Supp. XI:** 18, 276, 278, **284–286,** 287; **Supp. XX: 154**

"Praise to the End!" (Roethke), **III:** 529, 532, 539

Prajadhipok, King of Siam, **I:** 522

Prater Violet (Isherwood), **Supp. XIV: 164–166,** 169–170, 171

Pratt, Anna (Anna Alcott), **Supp. I Part 1:** 33

Pratt, Louis H., **Retro. Supp. II:** 6

Pratt, Mary Louise, **Retro. Supp. II:** 48

Pratt, Parley, **Supp. IV Part 2:** 603
"Prattler" (newspaper column), **I:** 207
"Prattler, The" (Bierce), **I:** 196
"Prayer" (Gioia), **Supp. XV:** 117
"Prayer" (Olds), **Supp. X:** 204
"Prayer" (Peacock), **Supp. XIX:** 198, 199, 200
"Prayer" (Toomer), **Supp. IX:** 318
"Prayer, A" (Kushner), **Supp. IX: 134**
"Prayer for Columbus" (Whitman), **IV:** 348
"Prayer for My Daughter" (Yeats), **II:** 598
"Prayer for My Grandfather to Our Lady, A" (Lowell), **II:** 541–542
"Prayer for my Son" (C. Frost), **Supp. XV:** 98–99
"Prayer for Our Daughters" (Jarman), **Supp. XVII:** 120
Prayer for Owen Meany, A (Irving), **Supp. VI:** 164, 165, 166, **175–176**
"PRAYER FOR SAVING" (Baraka), **Supp. II Part 1:** 52–53
"Prayer in Spring, A" (Frost), **II:** 153, 164
"Prayer Meeting" (Di Piero), **Supp. XIX:** 46, 47
"Prayer on All Saint's Day" (Cowley), **Supp. II Part 1:** 138, 153
Prayers for Dark People (Du Bois), **Supp. II Part 1:** 186
"Prayer to Hermes" (Creeley), **Supp. IV Part 1:** 156, 157
"Prayer to Masks" (Senghor), **Supp. IV Part 1:** 16
"Prayer to the Child of Prague" (Salinas), **Supp. XIII:** 327
"Prayer to the Good Poet" (Wright), **Supp. III Part 2:** 603
"Prayer to the Pacific" (Silko), **Supp. IV Part 2:** 560
"Pray without Ceasing" (Emerson), **II:** 9–10
Praz, Mario, **IV:** 430
"Preacher, The" (Whittier), **Supp. I Part 2:** 698–699
Preacher and the Slave, The (Stegner), **Supp. IV Part 2:** 599, 608, 609
Precaution (Cooper), **I:** 337, 339
"Precautions"(Karyotakis, trans. Hadas), **Supp. XXIII:** 125
"Preconceptions of Economic Science, The" (Veblen), **Supp. I Part 2:** 634
Predecessors, Et Cetera (Clampitt), **Supp. IX:** 37
"Predicament, A" (Poe), **Retro. Supp. II:** 273
Predilections (Moore), **III:** 194
Prefaces and Prejudices (Mencken), **III:** 99, 104, 106, 119
Preface to a Twenty Volume Suicide Note. . . . (Baraka), **Supp. II Part 1:** 31, 33–34, 51, 61
"Preference" (Wylie), **Supp. I Part 2:** 713
"Prejudice against the Past, The" (Moore), **IV:** 91
Prejudices (Mencken), **Supp. I Part 2:** 630

Prejudices: A Selection (Farrell, ed.), **III:** 116
Prejudices: First Series (Mencken), **III:** 105
"Preliminary Remarks on the Poetry in the First Person" (Wright), **Supp. XV:** 339
Prelude, A: Landscapes, Characters and Conversations from the Earlier Years of My Life (Wilson), **IV:** 426, 427, 430, 434, 445
Prelude, The (Wordsworth), **III:** 528; **IV:** 331, 343; **Supp. I Part 2:** 416, 676; **Supp. XI:** 248
Prelude and Liebestod (McNally), **Supp. XIII:** 201
"Preludes" (Eliot), **I:** 573, 576, 577; **Retro. Supp. I:** 55; **Supp. IV Part 2:** 436
Preludes for Memnon (Aiken), **I:** 59, 65
Preludes from Memnon (Aiken), **Supp. X:** 50
"Prelude to an Evening" (Ransom), **III:** 491, 492–493
Prelude to Darkness (Salinas), **Supp. XIII:** 311, **318–319,** 320
"Prelude to the Present" (Mumford), **Supp. II Part 2:** 471
"Premature Burial, The" (Poe), **III:** 415, 416, 418; **Retro. Supp. II:** 270
"Premeditations"(Schott), **Supp. XXIII:** 247
Preminger, Otto, **Supp. IX:** 3, 9; **Supp. XX: 246–247**
"Premonition" (Hay), **Supp. XIV:** 122
"Premonitions of the Bread Line" (Komunyakaa), **Supp. XIII:** 114, 115
Prenshaw, Peggy Whitman, **Supp. X:** 229
"Preparations" (Silko), **Supp. IV Part 2:** 560
Preparatory Meditations (Taylor), **IV:** 145, 148, 149, 150, 152, 153, 154–155, 164, 165
"Prepare" (Carruth), **Supp. XVI:** 59
Prepositions: The Collected Critical Essays of Louis Zukofsky (Zukofsky), **Supp. III Part 2:** 630
Prescott, Anne, **Supp. IV Part 1:** 299
Prescott, Orville, **Supp. IV Part 2:** 680; **Supp. XI:** 340; **Supp. XXIII:** 13
Prescott, Peter, **Supp. X:** 83
Prescott, Peter S., **Supp. XVI:** 212
Prescott, William, **Retro. Supp. I:** 123
Prescott, William Hickling, **II:** 9, 310, 313–314; **IV:** 309; **Supp. I Part 2:** 414, 479, 493, 494
"Prescription of Painful Ends" (Jeffers), **Supp. II Part 2:** 424
"Presence, The" (Gordon), **II:** 199, 200
"Presence, The" (Kumin), **Supp. IV Part 2:** 445, 455
Presence and Desire: Essays on Gender, Sexuality, Performance (Dolan), **Supp. XV:** 327
"Presence of Others, The" (Kenyon), **Supp. VII:** 164
Presences (Taylor), **Supp. V:** 325
"Present Age, The" (Emerson), **II:** 11–12
Present Danger, The: Do We Have the Will to Reverse the Decline of Ameri-

can Power? (Podhoretz), **Supp. VIII:** 241
"Present for the Boy, A" (Swados), **Supp. XIX:** 259
Present for Young Ladies, A (Rowson), **Supp. XV:** 245
"Present Hour" (Sandburg), **III:** 593–594
Present Philosophical Tendencies (Perry), **I:** 224
"Present State of Ethical Philosophy, The" (Emerson), **II:** 9
"Present State of Poetry, The" (Schwartz), **Supp. II Part 2:** 666
"Preservation of Innocence" (Baldwin), **Supp. I Part 1:** 51
"Preserving Wildness" (Berry), **Supp. X:** 28, 29, 32
"President and Other Intellectuals, The" (Kazin), **Supp. VIII:** 104
Presidential Papers, The (Mailer), **III:** 35, 37–38, 42, 45; **Retro. Supp. II:** 203, 204, 206
"Presidents" (Merwin), **Supp. III Part 1:** 351
Presnell, Robert, Sr., **Supp. XIII:** 166
Pressley, Nelson, **Supp. XVIII:** 37–38
"PRES SPOKE IN A LANGUAGE" (Baraka), **Supp. II Part 1:** 60
Presumed Innocent (Turow), **Supp. XVII:** 214–216, 223; 217
"Pretext, The" (Wharton), **Retro. Supp. I:** 371
Pretty Baby (film), **Supp. XXI:** 252
Pretty Boy Floyd (McMurtry), **Supp. V:** 231
"Pretty Girl, The" (Dubus), **Supp. VII:** 87–88
"Pretty Mouth and Green My Eyes" (Salinger), **III:** 560
"Previous Condition" (Baldwin), **Supp. I Part 1:** 51, 55, 63
"Previous Tenant, The" (Simpson), **Supp. IX:** 278–279
Prevost, Verbie Lovorn, **Supp. XXI:** 45
Priaulx, Allan, **Supp. XI:** 228
Price, Alan, **Retro. Supp. I:** 377
Price, Reynolds, **Supp. VI: 253–270; Supp. IX:** 256, 257
Price, Richard, **II:** 9; **Supp. I Part 2:** 522; **Supp. XX: 85**
Price, The (A. Miller), **III:** 165–166
"Price Is Right, The" (Skloot), **Supp. XX: 198–199**
"Price of the Harness, The" (Crane), **I:** 414
Pricksongs & Descants; Fictions (Coover), **Supp. V:** 39, 42, 43, 49, 50
"Pride" (Hughes), **Supp. I Part 1:** 331
Pride and Prejudice (Austen), **II:** 290
Prideaux, Tom, **Supp. IV Part 2:** 574, 590
"Priesthood, The" (Winters), **Supp. II Part 2:** 786
Priestly, Joseph, **Supp. I Part 2:** 522
Primary Colors, The (A. Theroux), **Supp. VIII:** 312
"Primary Ground, A" (Rich), **Supp. I Part 2:** 563
"Prime" (Auden), **Supp. II Part 1:** 22

"Primer Class" (Bishop), **Retro. Supp. II:** 38, 51

Primer for Blacks (Brooks), **Supp. III Part 1:** 85

Primer for Combat (Boyle), **Supp. XXIV:** 62

"Primer for the Nuclear Age" (Dove), **Supp. IV Part 1:** 246

Primer mensaje a la América Hispana (W. Frank), **Supp. XX: 76**

Primer of Ignorance, A (Blackmur), **Supp. II Part 1:** 91

Prime-Stevenson, Edward Irenaeus, **Supp. XX: 235**

Primitive, The (C. Himes), **Supp. XVI:** 139, **141–142**

"Primitive Black Man, The" (Du Bois), **Supp. II Part 1:** 176

"Primitive Like an Orb, A" (Stevens), **IV:** 89; **Retro. Supp. I:** 309

Primitive People (Prose), **Supp. XVI:** 255, 256, 257

"Primitive Singing" (Lindsay), **Supp. I Part 2:** 389–390

Primitivism and Decadence (Winters), **Supp. II Part 2:** 786, 803–807, 812

Primrose, Archibald Philip, **Supp. XX: 230**

Prince, F. T., **Supp. XXIV:** 45

Prince, Richard, **Supp. XII:** 4

"Prince, The" (Jarrell), **II:** 379

"Prince, The" (Winters), **Supp. II Part 2:** 802

Prince and the Pauper, The (Twain), **IV:** 200–201, 206

Prince Hagen (Sinclair), **Supp. V:** 280

Prince of a Fellow, A (Hearon), **Supp. VIII:** 58, **62–63**

Princess, The (Tennyson), **Supp. I Part 2:** 410

Princess and the Goblins, The (Macdonald), **Supp. XIII:** 75

Princess Casamassima, The (James), **II:** 276, 291; **IV:** 202; **Retro. Supp. I:** 216, 221, 222, 225, **226–227**

"Princess Casamassima, The" (Trilling), **Supp. III Part 2:** 502, 503

Princess of Arcady, A (Henry), **Retro. Supp. II:** 97

"Principles" (Du Bois), **Supp. II Part 1:** 172

Principles of Literary Criticism (Richards), **I:** 274; **Supp. I Part 1:** 264; **Supp. XIV:** 3

Principles of Psychology, The (James), **II:** 321, 350–352, 353, 354, 357, 362, 363–364; **IV:** 28, 29, 32, 37

Principles of Psychology, The (W. James), **Supp. XVII:** 97

Principles of Zoölogy (Agassiz), **Supp. I Part 1:** 312

Prior, Sir James, **II:** 315

Prior, Matthew, **II:** 111; **III:** 521

"Prison, The" (Malamud), **Supp. I Part 2:** 431, 437

"Prisoned Love" (Boyce), **Supp. XXI:** 9

"Prisoner of Ours, The" (Weigl), **Supp. XIX:** 288

Prisoner of Second Avenue, The (Simon), **Supp. IV Part 2:** 583, 584

Prisoner of Sex, The (Mailer), **III:** 46; **Retro. Supp. II:** 206

Prisoner of Zenda, The (film), **Supp. I Part 2:** 615

Prisoner's Dilemma (Powers), **Supp. IX:** 212, **214–216,** 221

Prison Memoirs of an Anarchist (A. Berkman), **Supp. XVII:** 103–104

Pritchard, William, **Supp. XVI:** 71

Pritchard, William H., **Retro. Supp. I:** 131, 141; **Supp. IV Part 1:** 285; **Supp. IV Part 2:** 642; **Supp. XI:** 326

Pritchett, V. S., **II:** 587; **Supp. II Part 1:** 143; **Supp. VIII:** 171; **Supp. XIII:** 168

Pritikin, Renny, **Supp. XXIV:** 40

"Privatation and Publication" (Cowley), **Supp. II Part 1:** 149

Private Contentment (Price), **Supp. VI:** 263

"Private History of a Campaign That Failed" (Twain), **IV:** 195

Private I, The: Privacy in a Public World (Peacock, ed.), **Supp. XIX:** 193, 203

Private Life of Axie Reed, The (Knowles), **Supp. XII:** 249

Private Line (Major), **Supp. XXII:** 174

"Private Man Confronts His Vulgarities at Dawn, A" (Dunn), **Supp. XI:** 146

Private Memoirs and Confessions of a Justified Sinner, The (Hogg), **Supp. IX:** 276

"Private Property and the Common Wealth" (Berry), **Supp. X:** 25

Private Snafu series (Geisel), **Supp. XVI:** 102

"Private Theatricals" (Howells), **II:** 280

Private Women, Public Stage: Literary Domesticity in Nineteenth-Century America (Kelley), **Supp. XVIII:** 257

Privilege, The (Kumin), **Supp. IV Part 2:** 442–444, 451

Prize Stories 1918 : The O. Henry Awards, **Supp. XVI:** 16

"Probe" (Ryan as Quin), **Supp. XVIII:** 229

"Probing the Dark" (Komunyakaa), **Supp. XIII:** 131

"Problem from Hell, A": America and the Age of Genocide (Power), **Supp. XXIII:** 25, 27–28

"Problem from Milton, A" (Wilbur), **Supp. III Part 2:** 550

"Problem of Anxiety, The" (Koch), **Supp. XV:** 183

"Problem of Being, The" (James), **II:** 360

Problem of Classification in the Theory of Value, The (Locke), **Supp. XIV:** 199

"Problem of Evil into Cocoon" (Taggard), **Supp. XXII:** 284

"Problem of Housing the Negro, The" (Du Bois), **Supp. II Part 1:** 168

"Problem of the Religious Novel, The" (Isherwood), **Supp. XIV:** 172

Problems and Other Stories (Updike), **Retro. Supp. I:** 322, 329

Problems of Dostoevsky's Poetics (Bakhtin), **Supp. XXII:** 259

"Problem Solving" (Goldbarth), **Supp. XII:** 185

Procedures for Underground (Atwood), **Supp. XIII:** 33

"Procedures for Underground" (Atwood), **Supp. XIII:** 33

Process (Boyle), **Supp. XXIV:** 51

Procession, The (al-Mawákib) (Gibran), **Supp. XX: 116, 124**

Processional (Lawson), **I:** 479

"Procession at Candlemas, A" (Clampitt), **Supp. IX:** 41

"Proclamation" (Saunders), **Supp. XIX:** 235

Proclus, **Retro. Supp. I:** 247

"Prodigal" (Ammons), **Supp. VII:** 29

"Prodigal" (Hoffman), **Supp. XVIII:** 86

"Prodigal, The" (Bishop), **Supp. I Part 1:** 90, 92

Prodigal Parents, The (Lewis), **II:** 454–455

"Prodigy" (Simic), **Supp. VIII:** 278

Producers, The (film, M. Brooks), **Supp. XVII:** 45

"Proem" (Crane), **I:** 397

"Proem, The: By the Carpenter" (O. Henry), **Supp. II Part 1:** 409

"Professions for Women" (Woolf), **Supp. XIII:** 305

"Professor" (Hughes), **Supp. I Part 1:** 330

"Professor, The" (Bourne), **I:** 223

Professor at the Breakfast Table, The (Holmes), **Supp. I Part 1:** 313, 316

"Professor Clark's Economics" (Veblen), **Supp. I Part 2:** 634

Professor of Desire, The (P. Roth), **Retro. Supp. II:** 288; **Supp. III Part 2:** 403, 418–420

Professor's House, The (Cather), **I:** 325–336; **Retro. Supp. I:** 16

"Professor Veblen" (Mencken), **Supp. I Part 2:** 630

Proffer, Carl R., **Supp. VIII:** 22

Profile Makers, The (Bierds), **Supp. XVII:** 29, **30–32,** 33

"Profile of the Tenderloin Street Prostitute, A" (Vollmann), **Supp. XVII:** 230

Profits of Religion, The (Sinclair), **Supp. V:** 276

"Prognosis" (Warren), **IV:** 245

"Progress" (F. Wright), **Supp. XVII:** 247

"Progress Report" (Simic), **Supp. VIII:** 278

"Project for a Trip to China" (Sontag), **Supp. II Part 2:** 454, 469

"Project for *The Ambassadors*" (James), **Retro. Supp. I:** 229

"Projection" (Nemerov), **III:** 275

"Projective Verse" (Olson), **Supp. III Part 1:** 30; **Supp. III Part 2:** 555, 556, 557, 624; **Supp. IV Part 1:** 139, 153; **Supp. VIII:** 290

"Projector, The" (Baker), **Supp. XIII:** 53, 55

Prokofiev, Sergey Sergeyevich, **Supp. IV Part 1:** 81

"Prolegomena, Section 1" (Pound), **Supp. III Part 2:** 615–616

"Prolegomena, Section 2" (Pound), **Supp. III Part 2:** 616

"Prolegomenon to a Biography of Mailer" (Lucid), **Retro. Supp. II:** 195

Proletarian Literature in the United States (Hicks), **Supp. I Part 2: 609– 610**

"Prologue" (MacLeish), **III:** 8, 14

Prologue, for Full Chorus of Mixed Voices and Orchestra (Taggard and Schuman), **Supp. XXII:** 283

"Prologue to a Life" (D. West), **Supp. XVIII:** 280

"Prologue to Our Time" (Mumford), **Supp. III Part 2:** 473

"Prometheus" (Longfellow), **II:** 494

Prometheus Bound (Lowell), **II:** 543, 544, 545, 555

Promise, The (Buck), **Supp. II Part 1:** 124

"Promise, The" (Olds), **Supp. X:** 213

"Promise and Fulfillment" (D. West), **Supp. XVIII:** 278

Promised Land (Parker), **Supp. XIX:** 183, 184, 190

Promised Land, The (M. Antin), **Supp. IX:** 227; **Supp. XVI:** 148, 149; **Supp. XX:** 1, 2, 3, **4–9,** 11

Promised Land, The (Porter), **III:** 447

"Promised Land, The" (R. Fisher), **Supp. XIX:** 72

Promised Lands (Sontag), **Supp. III Part 2:** 452

Promise of American Life, The (Croly), **I:** 229

"Promise of Blue Horses, The" (Harjo), **Supp. XII:** 228

Promise of Rest, The (Price), **Supp. VI:** 262, 266

Promises (Warren), **Supp. XIV:** 15

Promises, Promises (musical), **Supp. IV Part 2:** 575

Promises: Poems 1954–1956 (Warren), **IV:** 244–245, 249, 252

"Promise This When You Be Dying" (Dickinson), **Retro. Supp. I:** 44, 46

"Pronoun Variations"(Hadas), **Supp. XXIII:** 120

Proof, The (Winters), **Supp. II Part 2:** 786, 791, 792–794

Proofs and Theories: Essays on Poetry (Glück), **Supp. V:** 77, 79, 92; **Supp. XIV:** 269

"Propaganda of History, The" (Du Bois), **Supp. II Part 1:** 182

Propertius, Sextus, **III:** 467; **Retro. Supp. II:** 187; **Supp. XII:** 2

Property Of: A Novel (Hoffman), **Supp. X:** 77, 79, **80–82**

"Property of Loss" (W. V. Davis), **Supp. XXI:** 95

"Prophecy of Samuel Sewall, The" (Whittier), **Supp. I Part 2:** 699

Prophet, The (Asch), **Supp. XXIII:** 7

Prophet, The (Gibran), **Supp. XX: 113, 115, 119–121, 126**

"Prophet, The" (Notley), **Supp. XXII:** 229

"Prophet and the Child, The" (Gibran), **Supp. XX: 123**

Propheteers, The (Apple), **Supp. XVII: 6–7**

"Prophetic Pictures, The" (Hawthorne), **II:** 227

"Proportion" (Lowell), **II:** 525

"Proposal" (Carver), **Supp. III Part 1:** 149

Proposals Relating to the Education of Youth in Pensilvania (Franklin), **II:** 113

"Proposed New Version of the Bible" (Franklin), **II:** 110

Prose, Francine, **Supp. XII:** 333; **Supp. XVI: 249–264; Supp. XIX:** 209; **Supp. XXIII:** 300

"Prose for Departure" (Merrill), **Supp. III Part 1:** 336

Prose Pieces (Bynner), **Supp. XV:** 52

"Prose Poem as an Evolving Form, The" (R. Bly), **Supp. IV Part 1:** 64

"Proserpina and the Devil" (Wilder), **IV:** 358

"Prosody" (Espaillat), **Supp. XXI:** 102

"Prosody" (Shapiro), **Supp. II Part 2:** 710

Prospect before Us, The (Dos Passos), **I:** 491

"Prospective Immigrants Please Note" (Rich), **Supp. I Part 2:** 555

Prospect of Peace, The (Barlow), **Supp. II Part 1:** 67, 68, 75

Prospects of Literature, The (L. P. Smith), **Supp. XIV:** 343

Prospects on the Rubicon (Paine), **Supp. I Part 2:** 510–511

Prospectus of a National Institution, to Be Established in the United States (Barlow), **Supp. II Part 1:** 80, 82

Prospice (Browning), **IV:** 366

"Protestant Easter" (Sexton), **Supp. II Part 2:** 684

"Prothalamion" (Schwartz), **Supp. II Part 2:** 649, 652

"Prothalamion" (Spenser), **Retro. Supp. I:** 62

Proud, Robert, **Supp. I Part 1:** 125

"Proud Farmer, The" (Lindsay), **Supp. I Part 2:** 381

Proud Flesh (Humphrey), **Supp. IX:** 94, 95, 96, **102–103,** 104, 105, 109

"Proud Flesh" (Warren), **IV:** 243

Proud Highway, The (Thompson), **Supp. XXIV:** 283

Proud Lady (Boyce), **Supp. XXI:** 7, 12

"Proud Lady" (Wylie), **Supp. I Part 2:** 711–712

Proulx, Annie, **Supp. VII: 249–267; Supp. XXIV:** 245, 251

Proust, Marcel, **I:** 89, 319, 327, 377, 461; **II:** 377, 514, 606; **III:** 174, 181, 184, 244–245, 259, 471; **IV:** 32, 201, 237, 301, 312, 328, 359, 428, 431, 434, 439, 443, 466, 467; **Retro. Supp. I:** 75, 89, 169, 335; **Supp. III Part 1:** 10, 12, 14, 15; **Supp. IV Part 2:** 600; **Supp. VIII:** 103; **Supp. IX:** 211; **Supp. X:** 193, 194; **Supp. XII:** 289; **Supp. XIV:** 24, 83, 95; **Supp. XVI:** 295; **Supp. XXI:** 231; **Supp. XXIII:** 122

Proverbs, **Supp. X:** 45

"Proverbs" (Jarman), **Supp. XVII:** 118

"Providence" (Komunyakaa), **Supp. XIII:** 132

"Provident Woman, A" (Boyce), **Supp. XXI:** 10

"Provincetown Postcards" (F. Wright), **Supp. XVII:** 244

"Provincia deserta" (Pound), **Retro. Supp. I:** 289

"Provisional Remarks on Being / A Poet / of Arkansas" (Wright), **Supp. XV:** 337

Pruette, Lorine, **Supp. IV Part 2:** 522

Prufrock and Other Observations (Eliot), **I:** 569–570, 571, 573, 574, 576–577, 583, 584, 585; **Retro. Supp. I:** 59, 62

"Prufrock's Perivigilium" (T. S. Eliot), **Retro. Supp. I:** 57

Pryor, Richard, **Supp. XIII:** 343

Pryse, Marjorie, **Retro. Supp. II:** 139, 146

"Psalm" (Ginsberg), **Supp. II Part 1:** 312

"Psalm" (Simic), **Supp. VIII:** 282

"Psalm, A, or Supplication for mercy, and confession of Sin, addressed to the Author of Life, in the Odjibway-Alqonquin tongue"(J. Schoolcraft), **Supp. XXIII:** 232

"Psalm and Lament" (Justice), **Supp. VII:** 116, 117–118, 120–122, 124

"Psalm for Pinhook" (Ray), **Supp. XVIII:** 202

"Psalm Jew, The"(Asch). *See Salvation* (Asch)

"Psalm of Life, A" (Longfellow), **II:** 489, 496; **Retro. Supp. II:** 164, 168, 169; **Supp. I Part 2:** 409

"Psalm of the West" (Lanier), **Supp. I Part 1:** 362, 364

"Psalm: Our Fathers" (Merwin), **Supp. III Part 1:** 350

Psalms (biblical book), **I:** 83; **II:** 168, 232; **Retro. Supp. I:** 62; **Supp. I Part 1:** 125

Psalms, Hymns, and Spiritual Songs of the Rev. Isaac Watts, The (Worcester, ed.), **I:** 458

Psychiatric Novels of Oliver Wendell Holmes, The (Oberndorf), **Supp. I Part 1:** 315

"Psychology and Form" (Burke), **I:** 270

Psychology: Briefer Course (James), **II:** 351–352

Psychology of Art (Malraux), **IV:** 434

Psychology of Insanity, The (Hart), **I:** 241–242, 248–250

Psychopathia Sexualis (Shanley), **Supp. XIV:** 316, **329**

Psychophysiks (Fechner), **II:** 358

Pterodactyls (Silver), **Supp. XXIV: 268– 270**

"Pu-239" (Kalfus), **Supp. XVII:** 50

"Publication is the Auction" (Dickinson), **Retro. Supp. I:** 31

"Public Bath, The" (Snyder), **Supp. VIII:** 298

Public Burning, The (Coover), **Supp. IV Part 1:** 388; **Supp. V:** 44, 45, 46–47, 48, 51, 52; **Supp. XVII:** 6

"Public Burning of Julius and Ethel Rosenberg, The: An Historical Romance" (Coover), **Supp. V:** 44

"Public Figure" (Hay), **Supp. XIV:** 124
"Public Garden, The" (Lowell), **II:** 550
Public Good (Paine), **Supp. I Part 2:** 509–510
Public Poetry of Robert Lowell, The (Cosgrave), **Retro. Supp. II:** 185
"Public & Private" (column, Quindlen), **Supp. XVII:** 165, 167, 169–170
Public Speech: Poems (MacLeish), **III:** 15–16
Public Spirit (Savage), **II:** 111
"Public Woman, A" (Cliff), **Supp. XXII:** 76
Puccini, Giacomo, **Supp. XXI:** 150, 151
"Puck" (Monette), **Supp. X:** 157–158
Pudd'nhead Wilson (Twain), **I:** 197
"Pudd'nhead Wilson's Calendar" (Twain), **I:** 197
"Pueblo Revolt, The" (Sando), **Supp. IV Part 2:** 510
Puella (Dickey), **Supp. IV Part 1:** 178, 185
Pulitzer, Alfred, **Retro. Supp. I:** 257
Pull Down Vanity (Fiedler), **Supp. XIII:** 103
Pullman, George, **Supp. I Part 1:** 9
"Pullman Car Hiawatha" (Wilder), **IV:** 365–366
Pull My Daisy (film), **Supp. XII:** 126–127
"Pulp Cutters' Nativity, A" (Budbill), **Supp. XIX:** 9
"Pulpit and the Pew, The" (Holmes), **Supp. I Part 1:** 302
"Pulse-Beats and Pen-Strokes" (Sandburg), **III:** 579
"Pump, The" (Humphrey), **Supp. IX:** 101
Pump House Gang, The (Wolfe), **Supp. III Part 2:** 575, 578, 580, 581
Punch, Brothers, Punch and Other Sketches (Twain), **IV:** 200
Punch: The Immortal Liar, Documents in His History (Aiken), **I:** 57, 61
Punishment Without Vengeance (Vega; Merwin, trans.), **Supp. III Part 1:** 341, 347
"Pupil" (F. Barthelme), **Supp. XI:** 26
"Pupil, The" (H. James), **Supp. XX:** 233
"Pupil, The" (James), **II:** 331; **Retro. Supp. I:** 217, 219, 228
"Purchase" (Banks), **Supp. V:** 6
"Purchase of Some Golf Clubs, A" (O'Hara), **III:** 369
"Purdah" (Plath), **Supp. I Part 2:** 602
Purdy, Charles, **Supp. VIII:** 330
Purdy, James, **Supp. VII: 269–285**
Purdy, Theodore, **Supp. VIII:** 153
Pure (C. Frost), **Supp. XV:** 93, **101–102,** 104, 106
"Pure" (C. Frost), **Supp. XV:** 101–102
"Pure and the Good, The: On Baseball and Backpaking" (Maclean), **Supp. XIV:** 222
"Pure Good of Theory, The" (Stevens), **Retro. Supp. I:** 310
Purgatorio (Dante), **III:** 182
"Purim Parade" (Espaillat), **Supp. XXI:** 108
Puritan Family (Morgan), **Supp. I Part 1:** 101

"Puritanical Pleasures" (Hardwick), **Supp. III Part 1:** 213–214
Puritan Origins of the American Self, The (Bercovitch), **Supp. I Part 1:** 99
Puritan Pronaos, The: Studies in the Intellectual Life of New England in the Seventeenth Century (Morison), **Supp. I Part 2:** 485
"Puritan Realism: *The Wide, Wide World* and *Robinson Crusoe*" (Kim), **Supp. XVIII:** 267
Puritans, The (P. Miller), **Supp. VIII:** 101
"Puritan's Ballad, The" (Wylie), **Supp. I Part 2:** 723
"Purloined Letter, The" (Poe), **Retro. Supp. II:** 271, 272
Purple Cane Road (Burke), **Supp. XIV:** 32, 33
Purple Decades, The (Wolfe), **Supp. III Part 2:** 584
"Purple Hat, The" (Welty), **IV:** 264
Purple Rose of Cairo, The (film; Allen), **Supp. XV:** 1, **9–10,** 12, 14
Purser, John T., **Supp. XIV:** 4
"Pursuit of Happiness" (Simpson), **Supp. IX:** 279
"Pursuit of Happiness, The" (Ashbery), **Supp. III Part 1:** 23
Pursuit of the Prodigal, The (Auchincloss), **Supp. IV Part 1:** 25
Pushcart at the Curb, A (Dos Passos), **I:** 478, 479
"Pushcart Man" (Hughes), **Supp. I Part 1:** 330
Pushcart Prize, XIII, The (Ford), **Supp. V:** 58
Pushcart Prize VII, The (Hendeson, ed.), **Supp. XVII:** 16
Pushcart Prize XIV, The (Henderson, ed.), **Supp. XVII:** 18
Pushcart Prize XX, The (Henderson, ed.), **Supp. XVII:** 20
"Pushing 100" (Mora), **Supp. XIII:** 215
Pushkin, Aleksander, **III:** 246, 261, 262; **Retro. Supp. I:** 266, 269; **Supp. XVI:** 188
Pussy, King of the Pirates (Acker), **Supp. XII:** 6–7
"Pussycat and the Expert Plumber Who Was a Man, The" (A. Miller), **III:** 146–147
Pussycat Fever (Acker), **Supp. XII:** 6
Putnam, George Haven, **Supp. XVIII:** 257, 260
Putnam, George P., **II:** 314; **Supp. XVIII:** 3–4, 14, 260
Putnam, Phelps, **I:** 288
Putnam, Samuel, **II:** 26; **III:** 479; **Supp. III Part 2:** 615
"Put Off the Wedding Five Times and Nobody Comes to It" (Sandburg), **III:** 586–587
Puttenham, George, **Supp. I Part 1:** 113
Puttermesser Papers, The (Ozick), **Supp. V:** 269
"Putting a Burden Down" (Peacock), **Supp. XIX:** 199
Putting It Together (Sondheim), **Supp. XXIV:** 124

"Putting on *Visit to a Small Planet*" (Vidal), **Supp. IV Part 2:** 683
Put Yourself in My Shoes (Carver), **Supp. III Part 1:** 139
"Put Yourself in My Shoes" (Carver), **Supp. III Part 1:** 139, 141
Putzi, Jennifer, **Supp. XV:** 284
Puzo, Mario, **Supp. IV Part 1:** 390
"Puzzle of Modern Society, The" (Kazin), **Supp. VIII:** 103
Pygmalion (Shaw), **Supp. XII:** 14
Pyle, Ernie, **III:** 148; **Supp. V:** 240; **Supp. XVII:** 61
Pylon (Faulkner), **II:** 64–65, 73; **Retro. Supp. I:** 84, 85
Pynchon, Thomas, **III:** 258; **Retro. Supp. I:** 278; **Retro. Supp. II:** 279, 324; **Supp. II Part 2:** 557, **617–638; Supp. III Part 1:** 217; **Supp. IV Part 1:** 53, 279; **Supp. IV Part 2:** 570; **Supp. V:** 40, 44, 52; **Supp. VIII:** 14; **Supp. IX:** 207, 208, 212; **Supp. X:** 260, 301, 302; **Supp. XI:** 103; **Supp. XII:** 289; **Supp. XIV:** 49, 53, 54, 96; **Supp. XVI:** 123, 128; **Supp. XVII:** 183, 225, 232, 236; **Supp. XIX:** 223; **Supp. XX:** 21, 83, 87; **Supp. XXIII:** 42, 101
Pyne, John, **Supp. XXI:** 7
Pyne, Mary, **Supp. XXI:** 7
Pyrah, Gill, **Supp. V:** 126
"Pyramid Club, The" (Doctorow), **Supp. IV Part 1:** 234
"Pyrography" (Ashbery), **Supp. III Part 1:** 18
Pythagoras, **I:** 332
Pythagorean Silence (Howe), **Supp. IV Part 2:** 426, 428–429

Q

QBVII (television movie), **Supp. XX: 247**
QBVII (Uris), **Supp. XX: 244, 247, 248, 251, 253–254**
"Qebehseneuf" (Goldbarth), **Supp. XII:** 186
"Quadroons, The" (Child), **Supp. XVIII:** 124
"Quai d'Orléans" (Bishop), **Supp. I Part 1:** 89
"Quail for Mr. Forester" (Humphrey), **Supp. IX:** 94
"Quail in Autumn" (W. J. Smith), **Supp. XIII:** 334–335, 339
Quaker City, The: or, The Monks of Monk Hall (Lippard), **Supp. XXIII:** 177, 178–179, **180–183,** 184, 187, 188–189, 190
"Quaker Graveyard in Nantucket, The" (Lowell), **II:** 54, 550; **Retro. Supp. II:** 178, 186–187
"Quake Theory" (Olds), **Supp. X:** 203
Qualey, Carlton C., **Supp. I Part 2:** 650
Quality of Hurt, The (C. Himes), **Supp. XVI:** 137, 145
"Quality of Wine" (Carruth), **Supp. XVI:** 59
"Quality Time" (Kingsolver), **Supp. VII:** 203
"Quandary" (F. Wright), **Supp. XVII:** 244

Quang-Ngau-chè, **III:** 473

Quarles, Francis, **I:** 178, 179

"Quarrel" (Taggard), **Supp. XXII:** 276

Quarry, The (Chesnutt), **Supp. XIV:** 76

"Quarry, The" (Nemerov), **III:** 272

Quarry, The: New Poems (Eberhart), **I:** 532, 539

Quartermain, Peter, **Supp. IV Part 2:** 423, 434

Quatermain, Peter, **Supp. XXII:** 163

"Quaternions, The" (Bradstreet), **Supp. I Part 1:** 104–106, 114, 122

"Quatrains for Ishi" (Komunyakaa), **Supp. XIII:** 129

Queechy (S. Warner as Wetherell), **Supp. XVIII:** 257, **264–266**

"Queen Elizabeth and the Blind Girl or Music for the Dead Children" (B. Kelly), **Supp. XVII:** 124, 125

"Queen of the Blues" (Brooks), **Supp. III Part 1:** 75

Queen of the Damned, The (Rice), **Supp. VII:** 290, 292–293, 297, 299

Queen of the Mob (film), **Supp. XIII:** 170

"Queens of France" (Wilder), **IV:** 365

"Queen's Twin, The" (Jewett), **Retro. Supp. II:** 138

Queen's Twin, The, and Other Stories (Jewett), **Retro. Supp. II:** 140

Queen Victoria (Strachey), **Supp. I Part 2:** 485, 494; **Supp. XIV:** 342

Queer (Burroughs), **Supp. III Part 1:** 93–102

"Queer Aztlán"(Moraga), **Supp. XXIII:** 201

"Queer Beer" (Hansberry), **Supp. IV Part 1:** 374

"Quelques considérations sur la méthode subjective" (James), **II:** 345–346

"Quest, The" (Gibran), **Supp. XX: 124**

"Question" (Swenson), **Supp. IV Part 2:** 640

"Question and Answer" (Hughes), **Retro. Supp. I:** 211

"Questioning Faces" (Frost), **Retro. Supp. I:** 141

"Question Mark in the Circle, The" (Stegner), **Supp. IV Part 2:** 597

"Questionnaire, The" (Snodgrass), **Supp. VI:** 318

"Question of Fidelity, A" (Beauvoir), **Supp. IX:** 4

"Question of Loneliness, A" (Swados), **Supp. XIX:** 262

"Question of Our Speech, The" (Ozick), **Supp. V:** 272

"Question of Simone de Beauvoir, The" (Algren), **Supp. IX:** 4

Questions About Angels (Collins), **Supp. XXI:** 54, 58, 59, 60, 64

Questions for Ecclesiastes (Jarman), **Supp. XVII:** 109, 110, **118–119**

"Questions of Geography" (Hollander), **Supp. I Part 1:** 96

Questions of Travel (Bishop), **Retro. Supp. II:** **46–48; Supp. I Part 1:** 72, 83, 92, 94

"Questions of Travel" (Bishop), **Retro. Supp. II:** 47

"Questions to Tourists Stopped by a Pineapple Field" (Merwin), **Supp. III Part 1:** 355

"Questions without Answers" (T. Williams), **IV:** 384

"Quest of the Purple-Fringed, The" (Frost), **Retro. Supp. I:** 139

Quest of the Silver Fleece, The (Du Bois), **Supp. II Part 1:** 176–178

Quevedo y Villegas, Francisco Gómez, **Retro. Supp. I:** 423

Quickly: A Column for Slow Readers (Mailer), **Retro. Supp. II:** 202

Quicksand (Larsen), **Supp. XVIII:** 119, 121, 122, **124–127**

Quicksand and Passing (Larsen; McDowell, ed.), **Supp. XVIII:** 125

"Quies," (Pound), **Retro. Supp. I:** 413

Quiet American, The (Greene), **Supp. XIX:** 29

"Quiet and clear" (Kooser), **Supp. XIX:** 125

Quiet City (Shaw), **Supp. XIX:** 244

Quiet Days in Clichy (H. Miller), **III:** 170, 178, 183–184, 187

"Quiet Desperation" (Simpson), **Supp. IX:** 277–278

"Quiet Light, A" (Skloot), **Supp. XX: 203**

"Quiet of the Mind" (Nye), **Supp. XIII:** 284

"Quiet Woman, The" (Taggard), **Supp. XXII:** 274

"QUILLA" (Trethewey), **Supp. XXI:** 246

"Quilting" (D. West), **Supp. XVIII:** 283

Quin, Mike (pseudonym). *See* Ryan, Paul William

Quincy, Edmund, **Supp. XVIII:** 4

Quindlen, Anna, **Supp. XVI:** 108; **Supp. XVII: 165–181**

Quinlan, Kathleen, **Supp. X:** 80

Quinn, Anthony, **Supp. XXI:** 46

Quinn, John, **III:** 471

Quinn, Paul, **Supp. V:** 71

Quinn, Sister M. Bernetta, **III:** 479; **IV:** 421

Quinn, Vincent, **I:** 386, 401, 402; **Supp. I Part 1:** 270

"Quinnapoxet" (Kunitz), **Supp. III Part 1:** 263

Quinn's Book (W. Kennedy), **Supp. VII:** 133, 148–150, 153

Quintero, José, **III:** 403

Quintilian, **IV:** 123

Quinzaine for This Yule, A (Pound), **Retro. Supp. I:** 285

Quite Contrary: The Mary and Newt Story (Dixon), **Supp. XII: 144,** 153

Quitting Time (Kriegel), **Supp. XXIV: 225–227**

Quod Erat Demonstrandum (Stein), **IV:** 34

Quo Vadis? (Sienkiewicz), **Supp. IV Part 2:** 518; **Supp. XVI:** 182

R

Raab, Max, **Supp. XI:** 309

"Rabbi, The" (Hayden), **Supp. II Part 1:** 363, 369

Rabbit, Run (Updike), **IV:** 214, 223, 230–234; **Retro. Supp. I:** 320, 325, 326, 327, 331, 333, 335; **Supp. XI:** 140; **Supp. XII:** 298; **Supp. XVI:** 220

"Rabbit, The" (Barnes), **Supp. III Part 1:** 34

Rabbit at Rest (Updike), **Retro. Supp. I:** 334

Rabbit Factory, The (L. Brown), **Supp. XXI:** 40, **47–48**

"Rabbit Factory, The: Escaping the Isolation of the Cage" (Gaughran), **Supp. XXI:** 47–48

Rabbit Is Rich (Updike), **Retro. Supp. I:** 334

Rabbit novels (Updike), **Supp. V:** 269

Rabbit Redux (Updike), **IV:** 214; **Retro. Supp. I:** 332, 333

Rabbit's Umbrella, The (Plimpton), **Supp. XVI:** 244

"Rabbits Who Caused All the Trouble, The" (Thurber), **Supp. I Part 2:** 610

Rabe, David, **Supp. XXIV:** 117

Rabelais, and His World (Bakhtin), **Retro. Supp. II:** 273

Rabelais, François, **I:** 130; **II:** 111, 112, 302, 535; **III:** 77, 78, 174, 182; **IV:** 68; **Supp. I Part 2:** 461

Rabelais and His World (Bakhtin), **Supp. X:** 120

Rabinbach, Anson, **Supp. XII:** 166

Rabinowitz, Paula, **Supp. V:** 161

"Race" (Emerson), **II:** 6

"Race, Privilege, and the Politics of (Re)Writing History: An Analysis of the Novels of Michelle Cliff" (Edmondson), **Supp. XXII:** 70

"Race Contacts and Inter-Racial Relations" (Locke), **Supp. XIV:** 211

"Race Contacts and Inter-Racial Relations: A Study in the Theory and Practice of Race" (lectures, Locke), **Supp. XIV:** 199, 209

Race Contacts and Interracial Relations: Lectures on the Theory and Practice of Race (Locke, Stewart, ed.), **Supp. XIV:** 196, **209–210**

"'RACE LINE' IS A PRODUCT OF CAPITALISM, THE" (Baraka), **Supp. II Part 1:** 61

"Race of Life, The" (Thurber), **Supp. I Part 2:** 614

"Race Problems and Modern Society" (Toomer), **Supp. III Part 2:** 486

Race Questions, Provincialism, and Other American Problems (Royce), **Supp. XIV:** 199

"Race Riot, Tulsa, 1921" (Olds), **Supp. X:** 205

Race Rock (Matthiessen), **Supp. V:** 201

"Races, The" (Lowell), **II:** 554

"Rachel" (D. West), **Supp. XVIII:** 289

Rachel Carson: Witness for Nature (Lear), **Supp. IX:** 19

Rachel River (film, Smolan), **Supp. XVI:** 36

"Racial Progress and Race Adjustment" (Locke), **Supp. XIV:** 210

Racine, Jean Baptiste, **II:** 543, 573; **III:** 145, 151, 152, 160; **IV:** 317, 368, 370;

Supp. I Part 2: 716
Radcliffe, Ann, **Supp. XX: 108**
Radiance (Crooker), **Supp. XXIII:** 57–58
"Radical" (Moore), **III:** 211
"Radical Chic" (Wolfe), **Supp. III Part 2:** 577–578, 584, 585
Radical Chic & Mau-mauing the Flak Catchers (Wolfe), **Supp. III Part 2:** 577–578
Radical Empiricism of William James, The (Wild), **II:** 362, 363–364
Radicalism in America, The (Lasch), **I:** 259
"Radical Jewish Humanism: The Vision of E. L. Doctorow" (Clayton), **Supp. IV Part 1:** 238
"Radically Condensed History of Postindustrial Life, A" (Wallace), **Supp. X:** 309
Radical's America, A (Swados), **Supp. XIX: 264–265**
Radinovsky, Lisa, **Supp. XV:** 284, 285
"Radio" (O'Hara), **III:** 369
Radio Days (film; Allen), **Supp. XV:** 9
"Radio Pope" (Goldbarth), **Supp. XII:** 188, 192
Raditzer (Matthiessen), **Supp. V:** 201
Radkin, Paul, **Supp. I Part 2:** 539
"Rafaela Who Drinks Coconut & Papaya Juice on Tuesdays" (Cisneros), **Supp. VII:** 63
Rafelson, Bob, **Supp. XIV:** 241
Raffalovich, Marc-André, **Supp. XIV:** 335
Rafferty, Terence, **Supp. XX: 87, 92**
"Raft, The" (Lindsay), **Supp. I Part 2:** 393
Rag and Bone Shop of the Heart, The: Poems for Men (Bly, Hillman, and Meade, eds.), **Supp. IV Part 1:** 67
Rage in Harlem (C. Himes). *See For Love of Imabelle* (C. Himes)
Rage to Live, A (O'Hara), **III:** 361
Raglan, Lord, **I:** 135
Rago, Henry, **Supp. III Part 2:** 624, 628, 629
"Rag Rug"(Hadas), **Supp. XXIII:** 118
Ragtime (Doctorow), **Retro. Supp. II:** 108; **Supp. IV Part 1:** 217, 222–224, 231, 232, 233, 234, 237, 238; **Supp. V:** 45; **Supp. XXIV:** 227
"Ragtime" (Doctorow), **Supp. IV Part 1:** 234
Ragtime (film), **Supp. IV Part 1:** 236
Ragtime (musical, McNally), **Supp. XIII:** 207
Rahab (W. Frank), **Supp. XX: 71–72, 76**
Rahaim, Liz, **Supp. XVII:** 2
Rahv, Philip, **Retro. Supp. I:** 112; **Supp. II Part 1:** 136; **Supp. VIII:** 96; **Supp. IX:** 8; **Supp. XIV:** 3; **Supp. XV:** 140
"Raid" (Hughes), **Retro. Supp. I:** 208
Raids on the Unspeakable (Merton), **Supp. VIII:** 201, 208
Raikin, Judith, **Supp. XXII:** 66
Rail, DeWayne, **Supp. XIII:** 312
Rain and Other Fictions (Kenny), **Supp. XXIII:** 157
"Rain and the Rhinoceros" (Merton), **Supp. VIII:** 201

Rainbow, The (Lawrence), **III:** 27
"Rainbows" (Marquand), **III:** 56
Rainbow Stories, The (Vollmann), **Supp. XVII:** 226, 227, 230, 231, 233
Rainbow Tulip, The (Mora), **Supp. XIII:** 221
"Rain Country" (Haines), **Supp. XII:** 210
"Rain-Dream, A" (Bryant), **Supp. I Part 1:** 164
Raine, Kathleen, **I:** 522, 527
"Rain Falling Now, The" (Dunn), **Supp. XI:** 147
"Rain Flooding Your Campfire" (Gallagher), **Supp. XXIV:** 177
"Rain in the Heart" (Taylor), **Supp. V:** 317, 319
Rain in the Trees, The (Merwin), **Supp. III Part 1:** 340, 342, 345, 349, 354–356
"Rainmaker, The" (Humphrey), **Supp. IX:** 101
Raintree County (Lockridge), **Supp. XIX:** 263
Rainwater, Catherine, **Supp. V:** 272
"Rainy Day" (Longfellow), **II:** 498
"Rainy Day, The" (Buck), **Supp. II Part 1:** 127
"Rainy Mountain Cemetery" (Momaday), **Supp. IV Part 2:** 486
Rainy Mountain Christmas Doll (painting) (Momaday), **Supp. IV Part 2:** 493
"Rainy Season: Sub-Tropics" (Bishop), **Supp. I Part 1:** 93
"Rainy Sunday" (Espaillat), **Supp. XXI:** 106
Raised in Captivity (Silver), **Supp. XXIV: 271**
"Raise High the Roof Beam, Carpenters" (Salinger), **III:** 567–569, 571
Raise High the Roof Beam, Carpenters; and Seymour: An Introduction (Salinger), **III:** 552, 567–571, 572
Raise Race Rays Raze: Essays Since 1965 (Baraka), **Supp. II Part 1:** 47, 52, 55
Raisin (musical), **Supp. IV Part 1:** 374
Raising Demons (Jackson), **Supp. IX: 125–126**
Raisin in the Sun, A (unproduced screenplay) (Hansberry), **Supp. IV Part 1:** 360
Raisin in the Sun, A (film: Columbia Pictures), **Supp. IV Part 1:** 360, 367
Raisin in the Sun, A (Hansberry), **Supp. IV Part 1:** 359, 360, 361, 362–364; **Supp. VIII:** 343
Raisin in the Sun, A (television film: American Playhouse), **Supp. IV Part 1:** 367, 374
Rajan, R., **I:** 390
"Rake, The" (Mamet), **Supp. XIV:** 240
Rake's Progress, The (opera), **Supp. II Part 1:** 24
Rakosi, Carl, **Supp. III Part 2:** 614, 615, 616, 617, 618, 621, 629; **Supp. XIV:** 286, 287
Ralegh, Sir Walter, **Supp. I Part 1:** 98
Raleigh, John Henry, **IV:** 366
Ralph, Brett, **Supp. XVII:** 245
Ramakrishna, Sri, **III:** 567

Ramakrishna and His Disciples (Isherwood), **Supp. XIV:** 164
Ramazani, Jahan, **Supp. IV Part 2:** 450
"Ramble of Aphasia, A" (O. Henry), **Supp. II Part 1:** 410
Ramey, Phillip, **Supp. IV Part 1:** 94
Ramírez, Juan, **Supp. XXIII:** 203
Ramona (Jackson), **Supp. XXIV:** 27
Rampersad, Arnold, **Retro. Supp. I:** 196, 200, 201, 204; **Supp. IV Part 1:** 244, 250
Rampling, Anne, **Supp. VII:** 201. *See also* Rice, Anne
Rampling, Charlotte, **Supp. IX:** 253
Ramsey, Priscilla R., **Supp. IV Part 1:** 15
Ramsey, Roger, **Supp. XVI:** 69
Ramsey, William, **Supp. XVIII:** 66
Ramus, Petrus, **Supp. I Part 1:** 104
Rand, Ayn, **Supp. I Part 1:** 294; **Supp. IV Part 2: 517–535**
Randall, Jarrell, 1914–1965 (Lowell, Taylor, and Warren, eds.), **II:** 368, 385
Randall, John H., **III:** 605
Randolph, John, **I:** 5–6
Randolph, Ladette, **Supp. XXIII:** 274
"Randolphs of the Redwoods, The" (Atherton), **Supp. XXIV:** 18
"Range-Finding" (Frost), **Retro. Supp. I:** 131
Range of the Possible (T. Marshall), **Supp. XVII:** 36
Rangoon (F. Barthelme), **Supp. XI:** 25
Rangus, Eric, **Supp. XXI:** 244, 254
Rank, Otto, **I:** 135; **Supp. IX:** 105; **Supp. X:** 183, 185, 193
Ranke, Leopold von, **Supp. I Part 2:** 492
Rankin, Daniel, **Retro. Supp. II:** 57, 72; **Supp. I Part 1:** 200, 203, 225
Rankin, Tom, **Supp. XXI:** 36
Rankine, Annette, **Supp. XX: 69**
Ranlett, William H., **Supp. XVIII:** 3
Ransohoff, Martin, **Supp. XI:** 305, 306
Ransom, John Crowe, **I:** 265, 301; **II:** 34, 367, 385, 389, 536–537, 542; **III:** 454, **480–502,** 549; **IV:** 121, 122, 123, 124, 125, 127, 134, 140, 141, 236, 237, 433; **Retro. Supp. I:** 90; **Retro. Supp. II:** 176, 177, 178, 183, 220, 228, 246; **Supp. I Part 1:** 80, 361; **Supp. I Part 2:** 423; **Supp. II Part 1:** 90, 91, 136, 137, 139, 318; **Supp. II Part 2:** 639; **Supp. III Part 1:** 318; **Supp. III Part 2:** 542, 591; **Supp. IV Part 1:** 217; **Supp. V:** 315, 331, 337; **Supp. X:** 25, 56, 58; **Supp. XIV:** 1; **Supp. XIX:** 123; **Supp. XXIII:** 145
"Rape" (Coleman), **Supp. XI:** 89–90
"Rape, The" (Baraka), **Supp. II Part 1:** 40
Rape of Bunny Stuntz, The (Gurney), **Supp. V:** 109
"Rape of Philomel, The" (Shapiro), **Supp. II Part 2:** 720
"Rape of the Lock, The" (Pope), **Supp. XIV:** 8
Rapf, Joanna, **Supp. XVIII:** 251
Raphael, **I:** 15; **III:** 505, 521, 524; **Supp. I Part 1:** 363
"Rapist" (Dunn), **Supp. XI:** 144

Rap on Race, A (Baldwin and Mead), **Supp. I Part 1:** 66

"Rappaccini's Daughter" (Hawthorne), **II:** 229

"Rapture of the Deep" (Hempel), **Supp. XXI: 123**

"Rapunzel" (Sexton), **Supp. II Part 2:** 691

Rare & Endangered Species: A Novella & Short Stories (Bausch), **Supp. VII:** 51, 54

"Raree Show" (MacLeish), **III:** 9

Rascoe, Burton, **III:** 106, 115

Raskin, Jonah, **Supp. XV:** 116

Raskin, Saul, **Supp. XXIII:** 6

"Raskolnikov" (Simic), **Supp. VIII:** 282

Rasmussen, Douglas, **Supp. IV Part 2:** 528, 530

Rasmussen, Halfdan, **Supp. XVIII:** 180

Rasselas (Johnson), **Supp. XI:** 209

Rathmann, Andrew, **Supp. XV:** 34

Ratiner, Steven, **Supp. XXIII:** 134

"Rat in the Engine" (Espaillat), **Supp. XXI:** 106

"Ration" (Baraka), **Supp. II Part 1:** 50

"Rationale of Verse, The" (Poe), **III:** 427–428; **Retro. Supp. II:** 266

Ratner, Rochelle, **Supp. XV:** 105; **Supp. XXIV:** 168

Ratner's Star (DeLillo), **Supp. VI:** 1, 2, 3, 4, 10, 12, 14; **Supp. XVIII:** 140

"Rat of Faith, The" (Levine), **Supp. V:** 192

Rattigan, Terence, **III:** 152

Raugh, Joseph, **Supp. I Part 1:** 286

Rauh, Ida, **Supp. XXI:** 6

Rauschenberg, Robert, **Supp. XV:** 187

Rauschenbusch, Walter, **III:** 293; **Supp. I Part 1:** 7

Ravelstein (Bellow), **Retro. Supp. II:** 19, **33–34**

Raven, Simon, **Supp. XII:** 241

Raven, The (film, Friedlander), **Supp. XVII:** 58

"Raven, The" (Poe), **III:** 413, 421–422, 426; **Retro. Supp. II:** 265, 266–267; **Supp. XVII:** 58

Raven, The, and Other Poems (Poe), **III:** 413

Ravenal, Shannon, **Supp. IV Part 1:** 93

"Raven Days, The" (Lanier), **Supp. I Part 1:** 351

Ravenel, Shannon, **Supp. XXI:** 39

Ravenna, Michael. *See* Welty, Eudora

"Ravens at Deer Creek" (Wrigley), **Supp. XVIII:** 299–300, 306

Raven's Road (Gunn Allen), **Supp. IV Part 1:** 330, 335

Raver, Anne, **Supp. XVIII:** 191

"Ravine, The" (Carruth), **Supp. XVI:** 53

Ravits, Martha, **Supp. XXI:** 215

Raw Heaven (Peacock), **Supp. XIX: 196–197**

Rawlings, Marjorie Kinnan, **Supp. X: 219–237; Supp. XVIII:** 194–195

Rawlins, C. L., **Supp. XVII:** 72, 73

Ray, David, **Supp. IV Part 1:** 61

Ray, Janisse, **Supp. XVIII: 189–206**

Ray, Jeanne Wilkinson, **Supp. XII:** 308, 310

Ray, John, **II:** 111, 112

Ray, Man, **IV:** 404; **Retro. Supp. I:** 416; **Supp. XII:** 124; **Supp. XXIII:** 6

Ray, Nicholas, **Supp. XVIII:** 253

Ray Bradbury Theatre, The (television show), **Supp. IV Part 1:** 103

Raymond, Henry J., **Supp. XVIII:** 4

"Raymond and Ann" (Budbill), **Supp. XIX:** 9

Raymond Carver: A Writer's Life (Sklenicka), **Supp. XXIV:** 166

"Raymond Carver: The Kindest Cut" (Wood), **Supp. XXIV:** 166

"Razor's Edge, The" (Wasserstein), **Supp. XV:** 328

Reactionary Essays on Poetry and Ideas (Tate), **Supp. II Part 1:** 106, 146

Read, Deborah, **II:** 122

Read, Forrest, **III:** 478

Read, Herbert, **I:** 523; **II:** 372–373, 377–378; **Retro. Supp. I:** 54; **Supp. III Part 1:** 273; **Supp. III Part 2:** 624, 626

Read, William A., **Supp. XIV:** 4

Reade, Charles, **Supp. I Part 2:** 580

Reader, Constant. *See* Parker, Dorothy

Reader, Dennis J., **Supp. I Part 2:** 454

"Reader, The" (F. Wright), **Supp. XVII:** 246

Reader's Block (Markson), **Supp. XVII: 143–145,** 146

Reader's Encyclopedia, The: An Encyclopedia of World Literature and the Arts (W. Benét), **Supp. XI:** 44

Reader's Guide to William Gaddis's The Recognitions, A (Moore), **Supp. IV Part 1:** 283

Reader's Map of Arkansas (Wright), **Supp. XV:** 348

"Reader's Tale, A" (Doty), **Supp. XI:** 119, 120, 128, 129

"Reading" (Auden), **Supp. VIII:** 155

"Reading, The" (Di Piero), **Supp. XIX:** 41

"Reading, Writing, Region" (J. W. Miller), **Supp. XX: 165**

"Reading an Anthology of Chinese Poems of the Sung Dynasty, I Pause to Admire the Length and Clarity of Their Titles" (Collins), **Supp. XXI:** 56

"Reading at Forty" (Pickering), **Supp. XXI:** 196

"Reading Group Guide", **Supp. XI:** 244–245

"Reading Lao Tzu Again in the New Year" (Wright), **Supp. V:** 343

"Reading Late of the Death of Keats" (Kenyon), **Supp. VII:** 169

"Reading Myself" (Lowell), **II:** 555

Reading Myself and Others (P. Roth), **Retro. Supp. II:** 282; **Supp. V:** 45

"Reading *Ode to the West Wind* 25 Years Later" (McCarriston), **Supp. XIV:** 271–272

"Reading of the Psalm, The" (Francis), **Supp. IX:** 79

"Reading Ovid" (Di Piero), **Supp. XIX:** 44

"Reading Philosophy at Night" (Simic), **Supp. VIII:** 272

Reading Rilke: Reflections on the Problems of Translation (Gass), **Supp. VI:** 92, **93–94**

"Reading Rorty and Paul Celan One Morning in Early June" (Wright), **Supp. V:** 343

"Reading Sarcophagi: An Essay" (Sobin), **Supp. XVI:** 290

"Readings of History" (Rich), **Supp. I Part 2:** 554

"Reading the Signs, Empowering the Eye" (Bambara), **Supp. XI:** 17–18

Reading the Spirit (Eberhart), **I:** 525, 527, 530

Ready, Richard M., **Supp. XIX:** 154

"Ready Or Not" (Baraka), **Supp. II Part 1:** 50

Reagan, Ronald, **Supp. IV Part 1:** 224–225

"Real Bowery, The" (Hapgood), **Supp. XVII:** 103

"Real Class" (Vidal), **Supp. IV Part 1:** 35

Real Cool Killers, The (C. Himes), **Supp. XVI:** 143

Real Dope, The (Lardner), **II:** 422–423

"Real Estate" (Moore), **Supp. X:** 178

"Real Gone Guy, A" (McGrath), **Supp. X:** 117

"Real Horatio Alger Story, The" (Cowley), **Supp. II Part 1:** 143

"Realities" (MacLeish), **III:** 4

"Reality in America" (Trilling), **Supp. III Part 2:** 495, 502

"Reality! Reality! What Is It?" (Eberhart), **I:** 536

Reality Sandwiches, 1953–60 (Ginsberg), **Supp. II Part 1:** 315, 320

"Reality U.S.A." (Halliday), **Supp. XIX:** 89

Real Life of Sebastian Knight, The (Nabokov), **III:** 246; **Retro. Supp. I:** 266, 269, 270, 274

"Really Good Jazz Piano, A" (Yates), **Supp. XI:** 342

"Real Movie, with Stars, The" (Hull), **Supp. XXI:** 136

Real Presence: A Novel (Bausch), **Supp. VII:** 42–43, 50

"Real Revolution Is Love, The" (Harjo), **Supp. XII:** 224, 225–226

"Real Surrounding, The: On Canaletto's Venice" (Bronk), **Supp. XXI:** 32

"Real Thing, The" (H. James), **Retro. Supp. I:** 228; **Retro. Supp. II:** 223

"Real Two-Party System" (Vidal), **Supp. IV Part 2:** 679

Real West Marginal Way, The (Hugo), **Supp. VI:** 132, 134; **Supp. XVIII:** 299

"Real World around Us, The" (Carson), **Supp. IX:** 21

Reaper Essays, The (Jarman and McDowell), **Supp. IX:** 270; **Supp. XVII:** 110–111

"*Reaper* Interviews Jean Doh and Sean Dough, The" (Jarman and McDowell), **Supp. XVII:** 110

"Reapers" (Toomer), **Supp. III Part 2:** 481; **Supp. IX:** 312

Reason and Other Women (Notley), **Supp. XXII:** 224, 227, 235, 236, 237

"Reason and Race: A Review of the Literature of the Negro for 1946" (Locke), **Supp. XIV:** 206

"Reason for Moving, A" (Strand), **Supp. IV Part 2:** 624

"Reason for Stories, The: Toward a Moral Fiction" (Stone), **Supp. V:** 298, 300

Reasons for Moving (Strand), **Supp. IV Part 2:** 624–626, 626

"Reasons for Music" (MacLeish), **III:** 19

"Reasons of the Body" (Sanders), **Supp. XVI:** 274

Reasons to Live (Hempel), **Supp. XXI:** 115, 117, 118, **119–122**

Rebecca (du Maurier), **Supp. XIX:** 57–58; **Supp. XXII:** 120

Rebecca, or, The Fille de Chambre (Rowson), **Supp. XV:** 229, **235–236,** 238

Rebecca Harding Davis Reader, A (Pfaelzer, ed.), **Supp. XVI:** 88, 90

Rebel Angels: Twenty-five Poets of the New Formalism (Jarman and Mason, eds.), **Supp. XV:** 251; **Supp. XVII:** 109, 110, 112, 121

"Rebellion" (Lowell), **Retro. Supp. II:** 187

Rebel Powers (Bausch), **Supp. VII:** 41, 45–46, 49–51

Rebel without a Cause (film), **Supp. XII:** 9

"Rebirth" (McKnight), **Supp. XX: 147, 157**

"Rebirth of God and the Death of Man, The " (Fiedler), **Supp. XIII:** 108

Rebolledo, Tey Diana, **Supp. XIII:** 214

Reb Shloyme nogid: A poeme fun yidishn leben (Shloyme the wealthy: A poem of Jewish life)(Asch), **Supp. XXIII:** 4, 5

Recapitulation (Stegner), **Supp. IV Part 2:** 598, 600, 612–613

"Recapitulation, The" (Eberhart), **I:** 522

"Recapitulations" (Shapiro), **Supp. II Part 2:** 701, 702, 708, 710–711

"Receding Horizons" (Lethem and Scholtz), **Supp. XVIII:** 145

"Recencies in Poetry" (Zukofsky), **Supp. III Part 2:** 615

Recent Killing, A (Baraka), **Supp. II Part 1:** 55

"Recent Negro Fiction" (Ellison), **Supp. II Part 1:** 233, 235

"Recessional" (A. Finch), **Supp. XVII:** 70–71

"Recital, The" (Ashbery), **Supp. III Part 1:** 14

"Recitative" (H. Crane), **I:** 390; **Retro. Supp. II:** 78

Reckless Eyeballing (Reed), **Supp. X:** 241

Reckless Moment, The (film), **Supp. XXII:** 120, 131, 132

Recognitions, The (Gaddis), **Supp. IV Part 1:** 279, 280–285, 286, 287, 288, 289, 291, 292, 294; **Supp. XX: 91; Supp. XXIV:** 140

"Recollection and Perhaps a Tribute, A" (Espaillat), **Supp. XXI:** 103–104

Recollections (R. H. Stoddard), **Supp. XV:** 271

Recollections of Logan Pearsall Smith: The Story of a Friendship (Gathorne-Hardy), **Supp. XIV:** 344

"Reconciliation" (Whitman), **IV:** 347

"Reconstructed but Unregenerate" (Ransom), **III:** 496

"Reconstruction and Its Benefits" (Du Bois), **Supp. II Part 1:** 171

Recovering (Sarton), **Supp. VIII:** 264

Recovering the U.S. Hispanic Literary Heritage (Paredes), **Supp. XIII:** 320

"Recovery" (Dove), **Supp. IV Part 1:** 248

Rector of Justin, The (Auchincloss), **Supp. IV Part 1:** 21, 23, 27–30, 36

"Recurrent Dream" (Nelson), **Supp. XVIII:** 176

"RED AUTUMN" (Baraka), **Supp. II Part 1:** 55

Red Badge of Courage, The (S. Crane), **I:** 201, 207, 212, 405, 406, 407, 408, 412–416, 419, 421, 422, 423, 477, 506; **II:** 264; **III:** 317; **IV:** 350; **Retro. Supp. II:** 108; **Supp. IV Part 1:** 380; **Supp. XIV:** 51; **Supp. XVII:** 228; **Supp. XVIII:** 75; **Supp. XXI:** 277

"Redbirds" (C. Frost), **Supp. XV:** 99

"Red Bow, The" (Saunders), **Supp. XIX:** 232–233, 234

"Redbreast in Tampa" (Lanier), **Supp. I Part 1:** 364

"Red Brocade" (Nye), **Supp. XIII:** 288

Redburn: His First Voyage (Melville), **III:** 79–80, 84; **Retro. Supp. I:** 245, 247–248, 249; **Supp. XVIII:** 6

Red Calico (Miller and Bowden), **Supp. XXII:** 188

"Red Carpet for Shelley, A" (Wylie), **Supp. I Part 2:** 724

Red Channels (Harnett), **Supp. XV:** 198

"Red Clowns" (Cisneros), **Supp. VII:** 63

Red Coal, The (Stern), **Supp. IX: 291–292**

Red Coat, The (Shanley), **Supp. XIV:** 316–317

"Red Cords" (Lamott), **Supp. XX: 142**

"Red"(Crooker), **Supp. XXIII:** 63

"Red Cross" (Hughes), **Retro. Supp. I:** 205

Red Cross (Shepard), **Supp. III Part 2:** 440, 446

Red Death, A (Mosley), **Supp. XIII:** 237, 239, 240

"Red Deer" (C. Frost), **Supp. XV:** 101

Redding, Josephine, **Supp. XXI:** 2

Redding, Saunders, **Supp. I Part 1:** 332, 333

Reddings, J. Saunders, **Supp. IV Part 1:** 164

Red Dust (Levine), **Supp. V:** 178, 183–184, 188

"Red Dust" (Levine), **Supp. V:** 184

"Redemption" (Gardner), **Supp. VI:** 72

Redemption (Uris), **Supp. XX: 244, 246, 247, 248, 254, 255**

"Red Ensign, The" (Gallagher), **Supp. XXIV:** 175, 176

"Redeployment" (Nemerov), **III:** 267, 272

Redfield, Robert, **IV:** 475

Redford, Robert, **Supp. IX:** 253, 259; **Supp. XIII:** 267; **Supp. XIV:** 223

Redgrave, Lynn, **Supp. V:** 107

Red Harvest (Hammett), **Supp. IV Part 1:** 346–348, 348; **Supp. IV Part 2:** 468; **Supp. XXI:** 272

"Red Hat, The"(Hadas), **Supp. XXIII:** 111, 113, 118, 119, 124, 128

Red-Headed Woman (film), **Retro. Supp. I:** 110; **Supp. XVI:** 191

"Red Horse Wind over Albuquerque" (Harjo), **Supp. XII:** 219

Red Hot Vacuum, The (Solotaroff), **Retro. Supp. II:** 281

Rediscovery of America, The (W. Frank), **Supp. XX: 75**

Rediscovery of Man, The (W. Frank), **Supp. XX: 67–68, 80**

"Red Leaves" (Faulkner), **II:** 72

"Red Meat: What Difference Did Stesichoros Make?" (Carson), **Supp. XII:** 107

"Red Pawn" (Rand), **Supp. IV Part 2:** 520

Red Pony, The (Steinbeck), **IV:** 50, 51, 58, 70

Redrawing the Boundaries (Fisher), **Retro. Supp. I:** 39

Red Robins, The (Koch), **Supp. XV:** 185–186, 187

Red Roses for Bronze (Doolittle), **Supp. I Part 1:** 253, 268, 271

Red Rover, The (Cooper), **I:** 342–343, 355

Reds (Beatty), **Supp. XXIV:** 227

"Red Shift" (Berrigan), **Supp. XXIV:** 46

"Red Silk Stockings" (Hughes), **Retro. Supp. I:** 200

Redskins, The (Cooper), **I:** 351, 353

"Red Sox Nation, North" (Mosher), **Supp. XXII:** 209

"Red Star, Winter Orbit" (W. Gibson and B. Sterling), **Supp. XVI:** 123

Red Suitcase (Nye), **Supp. XIII:** 277, 278, 287

Red the Fiend (Sorrentino), **Supp. XXI:** 227, 231, 237

Red Wallflower, A (S. Warner), **Supp. XVIII:** 260

"Red Wheelbarrow, The" (W. C. Williams), **IV:** 411–412; **Retro. Supp. I:** 419, 430

"Red Wind" (Chandler), **Supp. IV Part 1:** 122

"Red Wing Church, The" (Kooser), **Supp. XIX:** 119

"Redwings" (Wright), **Supp. III Part 2:** 603

Reed, Edward Bliss, **Supp. XV:** 297, 298, 300

Reed, Ishmael, **Retro. Supp. II:** 111, 324–325; **Supp. II Part 1:** 34; **Supp. X: 239–257,** 331; **Supp. XIII:** 181, 182; **Supp. XVI:** 143; **Supp. XX: 107; Supp. XXII:** 172

Reed, J. D., **Supp. XVI:** 174

Reed, John, **I:** 48, 476, 483; **Supp. X:** 136; **Supp. XV:** 295, 299; **Supp. XVII:** 96, 99, 100; **Supp. XVIII:** 225; **Supp. XXI:** 6, 12; **Supp. XXII:** 274, 275; **Supp. XXIII:** 161, 162

Reed, Lou, **Retro. Supp. II:** 266

"Reedbeds of the Hackensack, The" (Clampitt), **Supp. IX:** 41

"Reed of Pan, A" (McCullers), **II:** 585

Reedy, Billy, **Retro. Supp. II:** 65, 67, 71, 73

Reedy, William Marion, **Supp. I Part 2:** 456, 461, 465

Reef, The (Wharton), **IV:** 317–318, 322; **Retro. Supp. I:** 372, **373–374**

Reena and Other Stories (Marshall), **Supp. XI:** 275, 277, 278

"Reese in Evening Shadow" (Skloot), **Supp. XX: 204**

Reeve, F. D., **Supp. XV:** 344, 349

Reeve's Tale (Chaucer), **I:** 131

"Refiguring the Postcolonial Imagination: Tropes of Visuality in Writing by Rhys, Kincaid, and Cliff" (Emery), **Supp. XXII:** 73

"Reflection from Anita Loos" (Empson), **Supp. XVI:** 190

"Reflections" (Carruth), **Supp. XVI:** 54

"Reflections" (Komunyakaa), **Supp. XIII:** 117

Reflections at Fifty and Other Essays (Farrell), **II:** 49

"Reflections by a Fire" (Sarton), **Supp. VIII:** 259

Reflections in a Golden Eye (McCullers), **II:** 586, 588, 593–596, 604; **IV:** 384, 396

Reflections of a Jacobite (Auchincloss), **Supp. IV Part 1:** 31

Reflections on a Gift of Watermelon Pickle (Dunning), **Supp. XIV:** 126

Reflections on Poetry and Poetics (Nemerov), **III:** 269

"Reflections on the Constitution of Nature" (Freneau), **Supp. II Part 1:** 274

"Reflections on the Death of the Reader" (Morris), **III:** 237

Reflections on the End of an Era (Niebuhr), **III:** 297–298

"Reflections on the Life and Death of Lord Clive" (Paine), **Supp. I Part 2:** 505

Reflections on the Revolution in France (Burke), **Supp. I Part 2:** 511, 512

Reflections: Thinking Part I (Arendt), **Supp. I Part 2:** 570

"Reflex Action and Theism" (James), **II:** 345, 363

Reflex and Bone Structure (Major), **Supp. XXII: 174–175**

"Refrains/Remains/Reminders" (Goldbarth), **Supp. XII:** 180–181, 181

"Refuge" (Kingsolver), **Supp. VII:** 208

"Refuge, A" (Goldbarth), **Supp. XII:** 190

Refugee Children: Theory, Research, and Services (Ahearn and Athey, eds.), **Supp. XI:** 184

"Refugees, The" (Jarrell), **II:** 371

"Refusal" (C. Frost), **Supp. XV:** 102

"Refusal to Publish Fifth Book" (Halliday), **Supp. XIX:** 94

Regarding Wave (Snyder), **Supp. VIII: 299–300**

Regina (Epstein), **Supp. XII: 170–171**

"Regional Literature of the South" (Rawlings), **Supp. X:** 228

"Regional Writer, The" (O'Connor), **Retro. Supp. II:** 223, 225

Régnier, Henri de, **II:** 528–529

Regulators, The (King), **Supp. V:** 141

Rehder, Robert, **Supp. IV Part 1:** 69

Rehearsing Absence (Espaillat), **Supp. XXI:** 99

Reich, Tova, **Supp. XVI:** 158

Reichel, Hans, **III:** 183

Reichl, Ruth, **Supp. X:** 79, 85

Reid, B. L., **II:** 41, 47

Reid, Forrest, **Supp. XX:** 235

Reid, Thomas, **II:** 9; **Supp. I Part 1:** 151

Reign of Snakes (Wrigley), **Supp. XVIII:** 293, **302–306**

"Reign of Snakes" (Wrigley), **Supp. XVIII:** 302–304

Reign of Wonder, The (Tanner), **I:** 260

Rein, Yevgeny, **Supp. VIII:** 22

Reinagle, Alexander, **Supp. XV:** 238, 240

"Reincarnation" (Dickey), **Supp. IV Part 1:** 181–182

Reine des pommes, La (C. Himes). *See For Love of Imabelle* (C. Himes)

Reiner, Carl, **Supp. IV Part 2:** 591

Reinfeld, Linda, **Supp. IV Part 2:** 421

Reinhardt, Max, **Supp. XV:** 307

Reinventing the Enemy's Language: Contemporary Native Women's Writing of North America (Bird and Harjo, eds.), **Supp. XII:** 216, 217

Reisman, Jerry, **Supp. III Part 2:** 618

Reiter, Amy, **Supp. XIX:** 54, 56

Reitlinger, Gerald, **Supp. XII:** 161

Reivers, The: A Reminiscence (Faulkner), **I:** 305; **II:** 57, 73; **Retro. Supp. I:** 74, 82, 91

"Rejoicings" (Stern), **Supp. IX:** 289–290

Rejoicings: Selected Poems, 1966–1972 (Stern), **Supp. IX: 289–290**

Relation of My Imprisonment, The (Banks), **Supp. V:** 8, 12–13

"Relations between Poetry and Painting, The" (Stevens), **Retro. Supp. I:** 312

Relations of the Alabama-Georgia Dialect to the Provincial Dialects of Great Britain, The (Brooks), **Supp. XIV:** 3

Relative Stranger, A (C. Baxter), **Supp. XVII:** 19, 22

"Relativity of Beauty, The" (Rawlings), **Supp. X:** 226

Relearning the Alphabet (Levertov), **Supp. III Part 1:** 280, 281

"Release" (C. Baxter), **Supp. XVII:** 15

"Release, The" (MacLeish), **III:** 16

Reles, Abe ("Kid Twist"), **Supp. IV Part 1:** 382

"Relevance of an Impossible Ethical Ideal, The" (Niebuhr), **III:** 298

"Religion" (Dunbar), **Supp. II Part 1:** 199

"Religion" (Emerson), **II:** 6

Religion of Nature Delineated, The (Wollaston), **II:** 108

"Religious Instruction" (Peacock), **Supp. XIX:** 200, 201

Religious Rebel, A: The Letters of "H. W. S." (Mrs. Pearsall Smith) (L. P. Smith), **Supp. XIV:** 349

"Reluctance" (Frost), **II:** 153

Reluctantly: Autobiographical Essays (Carruth), **Supp. XVI:** 45–46, 50

Remains (Snodgrass), **Supp. VI:** 311, **313–314**

"Remains, The" (Strand), **Supp. IV Part 2:** 627

"Remarks on Color" (Wright), **Supp. XV:** 346

"Remarks on National Literature" (Channing), **Supp. XXIV: 76–77**

"Remarks on Spencer's *Definition of Mind as Correspondence*" (James), **II:** 345

Remarque, Erich Maria, **Retro. Supp. I:** 113; **Supp. IV Part 1:** 380

Rembrandt, **II:** 536; **IV:** 310; **Supp. IV Part 1:** 390, 391

"Rembrandt, The" (Wharton), **IV:** 310

"Rembrandt's Hat" (Malamud), **Supp. I Part 2:** 435, 437

Rembrandt Takes a Walk (Strand), **Supp. IV Part 2:** 631

"Rembrandt to Rembrandt" (Robinson), **III:** 521–522

Remembered Earth, The: An Anthology of Contemporary Native American Literature (Hobson, ed.), **Supp. IV Part 1:** 321

Remembered Yesterdays (Johnson), **Supp. IX:** 184

"Remembering" (Angelou), **Supp. IV Part 1:** 15

"Remembering Allen Tate" (Cowley), **Supp. II Part 1:** 153

"Remembering Barthes" (Sontag), **Supp. III Part 2:** 451, 471

"Remembering Guston" (Kunitz), **Supp. III Part 1:** 257

"Remembering James Laughlin" (Karr), **Supp. XI:** 242

Remembering Laughter (Stegner), **Supp. IV Part 2:** 598, 606, 607, 608, 611, 614

"Remembering Lobo" (Mora), **Supp. XIII:** 220, 227

"Remembering My Father" (Berry), **Supp. X:** 23

"Remembering My Parents Remembering the Books They Read" (Espaillat), **Supp. XXI:** 107

"Remembering that Island" (McGrath), **Supp. X:** 116

"Remembering the Children of Auschwitz" (McGrath), **Supp. X:** 127

"Remembering the Lost World" (Jarrell), **II:** 388

"Remembering the Sixties" (Simpson), **Supp. IX:** 279

Remember Me to Tom (T. Williams), **IV:** 379–380

"Remember the Moon Survives" (Kingsolver), **Supp. VII:** 209

Remember to Remember (H. Miller), **III:** 186

"Remembrance, A" (Gioia), **Supp. XV:** 112

Remembrance of Things Past (Proust), **Supp. IV Part 2:** 600; **Supp. XII:** 9; **Supp. XIII:** 44

Remembrance Rock (Sandburg), **III:** 590

Reminiscence, A (Ashbery), **Supp. III Part 1:** 2

Remnick, David, **Supp. XVI:** 246

"Remora" (Merrill), **Supp. III Part 1:** 326

"Removal" (White), **Supp. I Part 2:** 664–665

"Removal, The" (Merwin), **Supp. III Part 1:** 350, 351

"Removal Service Request" (Halliday), **Supp. XIX:** 90

Removed from Time (Matthews and Feeney), **Supp. IX:** 154

Remsen, Ira, **Supp. I Part 1:** 369

"Rémy de Gourmont, A Distinction" (Pound), **III:** 467

"Renaissance" (Carruth), **Supp. XVI:** 56

Renaissance in the South (Bradbury), **I:** 288–289

Renaldo and Clara (film, Dylan and Shepard), **Supp. XVIII:** 21, 28, 31

"Renaming the Kings" (Levine), **Supp. V:** 184

Renan, Ernest, **Supp. XX: 122**

Renan, Joseph Ernest, **II:** 86; **IV:** 440, 444

Renard, Jules, **IV:** 79

"Renascence" (Millay), **III:** 123, 125–126, 128; **Supp. XV:** 42

Renault, Mary, **Supp. IV Part 2:** 685

"Rendezvous, The" (Kumin), **Supp. IV Part 2:** 455

René, Norman, **Supp. X:** 146, 152

Renée (anonymous author), **Supp. XVI:** 64, 66

"Renegade, The" (Jackson), **Supp. IX:** 120

Renewal of Life series (Mumford), **Supp. II Part 2:** 476, 479, 481, 482, 485, 495, 497

"Reno Hill ... Little Bighorn"(Kenny), **Supp. XXIII:** 155

Renoir, Jean, **Supp. XII:** 259; **Supp. XXII:** 256

Renouvrier, Charles, **II:** 344–345, 346

"Renunciation" (Banks), **Supp. V:** 10

Renza, Louis A., **Retro. Supp. II:** 142

"Repair" (Peacock), **Supp. XIX:** 204

"Repeating Dream" (Gander), **Supp. XV:** 340

Repent in Haste (Marquand), **III:** 59

Reperusals and Re-Collections (L. P. Smith), **Supp. XIV:** 346–347

"Repetitive Heart, The: Eleven Poems in Imitation of the Fugue Form" (Schwartz), **Supp. II Part 2:** 645–646

"Replacing Regionalism" (Murphy), **Retro. Supp. II:** 143

Replansky, Naomi, **Supp. X:** 119

"Reply to Mr. Wordsworth" (MacLeish), **III:** 19

"Report, A" (Jin), **Supp. XVIII:** 93

"Report from a Forest Logged by the Weyhaeuser Company" (Wagoner), **Supp. IX:** 328

"Report from North Vietnam" (Paley), **Supp. VI:** 227

Report from Part One (Brooks), **Supp. III Part 1:** 70, 72, 80, 82–85

Report from Part Two (Brooks), **Supp. III Part 1:** 87

Report on a Game Survey of the North Central States (Leopold), **Supp. XIV:** 182

"Report on the Barnhouse Effect" (Vonnegut), **Supp. II Part 2:** 756

"Report to an Academy, A" (Kafka), **Supp. XX:** 18

"Report to Crazy Horse" (Stafford), **Supp. XI: 324–325**

"Repose of Rivers" (H. Crane), **I:** 393; **Retro. Supp. II:** 78, 81

"Repossession of a Heritage, The" (Zagarell), **Supp. XV:** 270, 281

Repp, John, **Supp. XXIII:** 302

"Representation and the War for Reality" (Gass), **Supp. VI:** 88

Representative Men (Emerson), **II:** 1, 5–6, 8

"Representing Far Places" (Stafford), **Supp. XI:** 321

Repression and Recovery (Nelson), **Supp. XVIII:** 226

"REPRISE OF ONE OF A. G.'S BEST POEMS" (Baraka), **Supp. II Part 1:** 59

"Reproducing Ourselves Is All Very Well" (E. Hoffman), **Supp. XVI:** 155

Republic (Plato), **I:** 485

"Republican Manifesto, A" (Paine), **Supp. I Part 2:** 511

Republic of Love, The (Shields), **Supp. VII:** 323–324, 326, 327

"Requa" (Olsen), **Supp. XIII:** 294, **302–303,** 304

Requa, Kenneth A., **Supp. I Part 1:** 107

"Requa I" (Olsen). *See* "Requa" (Olsen)

"Request for Offering" (Eberhart), **I:** 526

"Requiem" (Akhmatova), **Supp. VIII:** 20

"Requiem" (LaBastille), **Supp. X:** 105

Requiem for a Nun (Faulkner), **II:** 57, 72–73

Requiem for Harlem (H. Roth), **Supp. IX:** 235, 236, **240–242**

"Rescue, The" (Updike), **IV:** 214

Rescued Year, The (Stafford), **Supp. XI: 321–322**

"Rescued Year, The" (Stafford), **Supp. XI:** 322, 323

"Rescue with Yul Brynner" (Moore), **III:** 215

"Rescuing Moon"(P. Benedict), **Supp. XXIII:** 40

"Resemblance" (Bishop), **Supp. I Part 1:** 86

"Resemblance" (Ferry), **Supp. XXIV:** 161

"Resemblance between a Violin Case and a Coffin, A" (T. Williams), **IV:** 378–379

"Reservations" (Taylor), **Supp. V:** 323

"Reserved Memorials" (Mather), **Supp. II Part 2:** 446, 449

"Resignación" (Espaillat), **Supp. XXI:** 104

"Resignation"(J. Schoolcraft), **Supp. XXIII:** 228, 229–230

"Resistance to Civil Government" (Thoreau), **Supp. X:** 27, 28

Resist Much, Obey Little (Berry), **Supp. XIII:** 2

Resolution (Parker), **Supp. XIX:** 187

"Resolution and Independence" (Wordsworth), **Supp. XV:** 346

"Resort" (Hampl), **Supp. XXII:** 86–87

Resort and Other Poems (Hampl), **Supp. XXII:** 83, 86–87

Resources of Hope (R. Williams), **Supp. IX:** 146

"Respectable Place, A" (O'Hara), **III:** 369

"Respectable Woman, A" (Chopin), **Retro. Supp. II:** 66

"Respite" (Pedersen; Nelson, trans.), **Supp. XVIII:** 180

Responses (Wilbur), **Supp. III Part 2:** 541

"Response to a Rumor that the Oldest Whorehouse in Wheeling, West Virginia, Has Been Condemned" (Wright), **Supp. III Part 2:** 602

"Rest Cure" (Boyle), **Supp. XXIV:** 57

Restif de La Bretonne, Nicolas, **III:** 175

"Rest of Life, The" (Gordon), **Supp. IV Part 1:** 311

Rest of Life, The: Three Novellas (Gordon), **Supp. IV Part 1:** 310–312

Rest of the Way, The (McClatchy), **Supp. XII:** 255, **258–259**

Restoration comedy, **Supp. I Part 2:** 617

Restorers, The (Di Piero), **Supp. XIX:** 42–43, 44

"Restorers, The" (Di Piero), **Supp. XIX:** 43

"Restraint" (F. Barthelme), **Supp. XI:** 26

"Result" (Emerson), **II:** 6

"Résumé" (Parker), **Supp. IX:** 189

"Resurrecting Methuselah" (E. P. Jones), **Supp. XXII:** 151

Resurrection (Della Francesca), **Supp. XV:** 262

"Resurrection" (Harjo), **Supp. XII:** 224

"Resurrection" (Jin), **Supp. XVIII:** 94–95

Resurrection, The (Gardner), **Supp. VI:** 61, 63, **64–65,** 68, 69, 73, 74

"Retort" (Hay), **Supp. XIV:** 133

Retour amont (Char; Sobin, trans.), **Supp. XVI:** 282

Retrieval System, The (Kumin), **Supp. IV Part 2:** 449, 451, 452

"Retrievers in Translation" (Doty), **Supp. XI:** 132

"Retroduction to American History" (Tate), **IV:** 129

"Retrospects and Prospects" (Lanier), **Supp. I Part 1:** 352

"Return" (Corso), **Supp. XII:** 135

"Return" (Creeley), **Supp. IV Part 1:** 141, 145

"Return" (MacLeish), **III:** 12

"Return, The" (Bidart), **Supp. XV:** 32–33

"Return, The" (Bontemps), **Supp. XXII:** 3, 8

"Return, The" (Pound), **Retro. Supp. I:** 288

"Return, The" (Ray), **Supp. XVIII:** 194

"Return, The" (Roethke), **III:** 533

"Return, The: Orihuela, 1965" (Levine), **Supp. V:** 194

"Return: An Elegy, The" (Warren), **IV:** 239

"Return: Buffalo" (Hogan), **Supp. IV Part 1:** 411

"Returning" (Komunyakaa), **Supp. XIII:** 122

"Returning a Lost Child" (Glück), **Supp. V:** 81

"Returning from the Enemy" (Harjo), **Supp. XII:** 229–230

"Returning the Borrowed Road" (Komunyakaa), **Supp. XIII:** 113, 133

"Return of Alcibiade, The" (Chopin), **Retro. Supp. II:** 58, 64

Return of Ansel Gibbs, The (Buechner), **III:** 310; **Supp. XII: 48**

"Return of Eros to Academe, The" (Bukiet), **Supp. XVII:** 47

"Return of Spring" (Winters), **Supp. II Part 2:** 791

Return of the Native, The (Hardy), **II:** 184–185, 186

Return of the Vanishing American, The (Fiedler), **Supp. XIII:** 103

Return to a Place Lit by a Glass of Milk (Simic), **Supp. VIII:** 274, 276, 283

"Return to Lavinia" (Caldwell), **I:** 310

"Return to Thin Air: The Everest Disaster Ten Years Later" *(Outside)*, **Supp. XVIII:** 113

Return to Zion, The (Asch), **Supp. XXIII:** 5

Reuben (Wideman), **Supp. X:** 320

Reuben and Rachel; or, Tales of Old Times (Rowson), **Supp. XV: 240–241**

Reunion (Mamet), **Supp. XIV:** 240, 247, 254

"Reunion in Brooklyn" (H. Miller), **III:** 175, 184

Reuther brothers, **I:** 493

"Reveille" (Kingsolver), **Supp. VII:** 208

"Reveille" (Untermeyer), **Supp. XV:** 300

"Reveille, The" (Harte), **Supp. II Part 1:** 342–343

Revelation (biblical book), **II:** 541; **IV:** 104, 153, 154; **Supp. I Part 1:** 105, 273

"Revelation" (O'Connor), **III:** 349, 353–354; **Retro. Supp. II:** 237

"Revelation" (Warren), **III:** 490

Revenge (Harrison), **Supp. VIII:** 39, 45

"Revenge of Hamish, The" (Lanier), **Supp. I Part 1:** 365

"Revenge of Hannah Kemhuff, The" (Walker), **Supp. III Part 2:** 521

"Revenge of Rain-in-the-Face, The" (Longfellow), **Retro. Supp. II:** 170

"Reverberation"(Kenny), **Supp. XXIII:** 155

Reverberator, The (James), **Retro. Supp. I:** 227

"Reverdure" (Berry), **Supp. X:** 22

Reverdy, Pierre, **Supp. XV:** 178, 182; **Supp. XXIII:** 208

"Reverend Father Gilhooley" (Farrell), **II:** 45

Reverse Transcription (Kushner), **Supp. IX:** 138

Reversible Errors (Turow), **Supp. XVII: 220–221**

"Rev. Freemont Deadman" (Masters), **Supp. I Part 2:** 463

Reviewer's ABC, A (Aiken), **I:** 58

Review of Contemporary Fiction, 1990 (Tabbi, ed.), **Supp. XVII:** 143

"Revolt, against the Crepuscular Spirit in Modern Poetry" (Pound), **Retro. Supp. I:** 286

"Revolution" (C. L. R. James), **Supp. XXI:** 160

"Revolution" (Taggard), **Supp. XXII:** 275

"Revolutionary Answer to the Negro Problem in the USA, The" (statement, C. L. R. James), **Supp. XXI:** 169

Revolutionary Petunias (Walker), **Supp. III Part 2:** 520, 522, 530

Revolutionary Road (Yates), **Supp. XI:** 334, **335–340**

"Revolutionary Symbolism in America" (Burke), **I:** 272

"Revolutionary Theatre, The" (Baraka), **Supp. II Part 1:** 42

Revolution in Taste, A: Studies of Dylan Thomas, Allen Ginsberg, Sylvia Plath, and Robert Lowell (Simpson), **Supp. IX:** 276

"Revolution in the Revolution in the Revolution" (Snyder), **Supp. VIII:** 300

Revon, Marcel, **II:** 525

"Rewaking, The" (W. C. Williams), **Retro. Supp. I:** 430

"Rewrite" (Dunn), **Supp. XI:** 147

Rexroth, Kenneth, **II:** 526; **Supp. II Part 1:** 307; **Supp. II Part 2:** 436; **Supp. III Part 2:** 625, 626; **Supp. IV Part 1:** 145–146; **Supp. VIII:** 289; **Supp. XIII:** 75; **Supp. XIV:** 287; **Supp. XV:** 140, 141, 146; **Supp. XXII:** 168

Reynolds, Ann (pseudonym). *See* Bly, Carol

Reynolds, Clay, **Supp. XI:** 254

Reynolds, David, **Supp. XV:** 269; **Supp. XXIII:** 187

Reynolds, Sir Joshua, **Supp. I Part 2:** 716

Reynolds, Quentin, **IV:** 286

Reza, Yasmina, **Supp. XXI:** 148

Rezanov (Atherton), **Supp. XXIV:** 23

Reznikoff, Charles, **IV:** 415; **Retro. Supp. I:** 422; **Supp. III Part 2:** 615, 616, 617, 628; **Supp. XIV: 277–296;** **Supp. XXIII:** 174; **Supp. XXIV:** 36, 45

"Rhapsodist, The" (Brown), **Supp. I Part 1:** 125–126

"Rhapsody on a Windy Night" (Eliot), **Retro. Supp. I:** 55

Rhetoric of Motives, A (Burke), **I:** 272, 275, 278, 279

Rhetoric of Religion, The (Burke), **I:** 275, 279

"Rhobert" (Toomer), **Supp. IX:** 316–317

"Rhode Show" (Mallon), **Supp. XIX:** 137–138

"Rhododendrons" (Levis), **Supp. XI:** 260, 263

Rhubarb Show, The (radio, Keillor), **Supp. XVI:** 178

"Rhyme of Sir Christopher, The" (Longfellow), **II:** 501

Rhymes to Be Traded for Bread (Lindsay), **Supp. I Part 2:** 380, 381–382

Rhys, Ernest, **III:** 458

Rhys, Jean, **Supp. III Part 1:** 42, 43; **Supp. XVIII:** 131

"Rhythm & Blues" (Baraka), **Supp. II Part 1:** 37–38

Rhythms (Reznikoff), **Supp. XIV:** 279, 282, 283

Rhythms II (Reznikoff), **Supp. XIV:** 282, 283, 284

Ribalow, Harold, **Supp. IX:** 236

Ribbentrop, Joachim von, **IV:** 249

Ribicoff, Abraham, **Supp. IX:** 33

Ribot, Théodule Armand, **Supp. XX: 238**

Ricardo, David, **Supp. I Part 2:** 628, 634

Rice, Allen Thorndike, **Retro. Supp. I:** 362

Rice, Anne, **Supp. VII: 287–306**

Rice, Elmer, **I:** 479; **III:** 145, 160–161

Rice, Mrs. Grantland, **II:** 435

Rice, Philip Blair, **IV:** 141

Rice, Stan, **Supp. XII:** 2

Rice, Tim, **Supp. XXI:** 148

Rice, Tom, **Supp. XIV:** 125

Rich, Adrienne, **Retro. Supp. I:** 8, 36, 42, 47, 404; **Retro. Supp. II:** 43, 191, 245; **Supp. I Part 2:** 546–547, **550–578; Supp. III Part 1:** 84, 354; **Supp. III Part 2:** 541, 599; **Supp. IV Part 1:** 257, 325; **Supp. V:** 82; **Supp. VIII:** 272; **Supp. XII:** 217, 229, 255; **Supp. XIII:** 294; **Supp. XIV:** 126, 129; **Supp. XV:** 176, 252; **Supp. XVII:** 32, 74; **Supp. XIX:** 83, 193; **Supp. XXII:** 65, 66

Rich, Arnold, **Supp. I Part 2:** 552

Rich, Frank, **Supp. IV Part 2:** 585, 586; **Supp. V:** 106; **Supp. XXI:** 146; **Supp. XXIV:** 121, 124

Richard, Mark, **Supp. XIX: 209–222**

Richard Cory (Gurney), **Supp. V:** 99–100, 105

"Richard Hunt's 'Arachne' " (Hayden), **Supp. II Part 1:** 374

Richard II (Shakespeare), **Supp. XVII:** 244

Richard III (Shakespeare), **Supp. I Part 2:** 422

Richards, Bertrand F., **Supp. XX: 217–218**

Richards, Constance S., **Supp. XXII:** 73

Richards, David, **Supp. IV Part 2:** 576; **Supp. XXIV:** 266, 269

Richards, Grant, **I:** 515

Richards, I. A., **I:** 26, 273–274, 279, 522; **III:** 498; **IV:** 92; **Supp. I Part 1:** 264, 265; **Supp. I Part 2:** 647

Richards, Ivor Armonstrong, **Supp. XIV:** 2–3, 16

Richards, Laura E., **II:** 396; **III:** 505–506, 507

Richards, Leonard, **Supp. XIV:** 48

Richards, Lloyd, **Supp. IV Part 1:** 362; **Supp. VIII:** 331

Richards, Rosalind, **III:** 506

Richards, Tad, **Supp. XVII:** 77

Richardson, Alan, **III:** 295

Richardson, Charles, **Supp. XVIII:** 14, 15

Richardson, Dorothy, **I:** 53; **II:** 320; **Supp. III Part 1:** 65

Richardson, Helen Patges, **Retro. Supp. II:** 95

Richardson, Henry Hobson, **I:** 3, 10

Richardson, Maurice, **Supp. XII:** 241

Richardson, Samuel, **I:** 134; **II:** 104, 111, 322; **Supp. V:** 127; **Supp. IX:** 128; **Supp. XV:** 232; **Supp. XX: 236**

Richardson, Tony, **Supp. XI:** 305, 306

"Richard Wright and Recent Negro Fiction" (Ellison), **Retro. Supp. II:** 116

"Richard Wright's Blues" (Ellison), **Retro. Supp. II:** 117, 124

"Richard Yates: A Requiem" (Lawrence), **Supp. XI:** 335

"Rich Boy, The" (Fitzgerald), **II:** 94; **Retro. Supp. I:** 98, 108

Richer, the Poorer, The: Sketches and Reminiscences (D. West), **Supp. XVIII:** 277, 289

"Riches" (Bausch), **Supp. VII:** 54

Richey, Elinor, **Supp. XXIV:** 30

Richler, Mordecai, **Supp. XI:** 294, 297

Rich Man, Poor Man (miniseries), **Supp. XIX:** 252

Rich Man, Poor Man (Shaw), **Supp. XIX:** 251–252

Richman, Robert, **Supp. XI:** 249; **Supp. XV:** 120–121, 251

Richman, Shira, **Supp. XXIV:** 167

Richmond (Masters), **Supp. I Part 2:** 471

Richmond, M. A., **Supp. XX: 277, 279, 282, 286, 289, 290**

Rich Relations (Hwang), **Supp. XXI:** 146–147

Richter, Conrad, **Supp. X:** 103; **Supp. XVIII: 207–222**

Richter, Jean Paul, **II:** 489, 492; **Supp. XVI:** 182

Rick Bass (Weltzien), **Supp. XVI:** 20

Rickman, Clio, **Supp. I Part 2:** 519

Ricks, Christopher, **Retro. Supp. I:** 56; **Supp. XVIII:** 20, 30, 32

Riddel, Joseph N., **IV:** 95

"Riddle, The" (Hay), **Supp. XIV:** 130

"Ride in an Omnibus, A" (Briggs), **Supp. XVIII:** 9, 16

"Riders to the Blood-Red Wrath" (Brooks), **Supp. III Part 1:** 82–83

Riders to the Sea (Synge), **III:** 157

Ridge, Lola, **Supp. IX:** 308; **Supp. XV:** 307; **Supp. XXIV:** 49, 52

Riding, Alan, **Supp. XVI:** 294

Riding, Laura, **I:** 437

"Riding Out at Evening" (McCarriston), **Supp. XIV:** 262–263

Riding the Iron Rooster: By Train through China (Theroux), **Supp. VIII:** 324

Ridley, Clifford, **Supp. XXIV:** 282

Riesenberg, Felix, **I:** 360, 361

Riesman, David, **Supp. I Part 2:** 649, 650

"Rif, to Music, The" (Bowles), **Supp. IV Part 1:** 89

Riffs & Reciprocities (Dunn), **Supp. XI: 154–155**

Rifkin, Libby, **Supp. XXIV:** 39, 44

Rifles, The (Vollmann), **Supp. XVII:** 226, 233

Riggs, Marlon, **Supp. XI:** 19

Right Distance, The (Pickering), **Supp. XXI:** 196–197

Right Madness on Skye, The (Hugo), **Supp. VI:** 145–147

Rights of Man (Paine), **Supp. I Part 2:** 508, 511, 512–514, 516, 519, 523

"Rights of Woman" (Rowson), **Supp. XV:** 243

"Rights of Women, The" (Brown). *See Alcuin: A Dialogue* (Brown)

Right Stuff, The (Wolfe), **Supp. III Part 2:** 581–584

Right Thoughts in Sad Hours (Mather), **IV:** 144

Rigney, Barbara Hill, **Supp. VIII:** 215

"Rigorists" (Moore), **III:** 198

Rihani, Ameen, **Supp. XX: 115**

Rihoku, **Supp. XXII:** 228

Riis, Jacob A., **I:** 293; **Supp. I Part 1:** 13; **Supp. XVII:** 101, 106

Riley, Glenda, **Supp. XXIV:** 252

Riley, James Whitcomb, **I:** 205; **Supp. II Part 1:** 192, 193, 196, 197

Rilke, Rainer Maria, **I:** 445, 523; **II:** 367, 381, 382–383, 389, 543, 544; **III:** 552, 558, 563, 571, 572; **IV:** 380, 443; **Retro. Supp. II:** 20, 187; **Supp. I Part 1:** 264; **Supp. I Part 2:** 573; **Supp. III Part 1:** 239, 242, 246, 283, 319–320; **Supp. IV Part 1:** 284; **Supp. V:** 208, 343; **Supp. VIII:** 30, 40; **Supp. X:** 164; **Supp. XI:** 126; **Supp. XIII:** 74, 88; **Supp. XV:** 93, 212, 222, Supp. XV: 223, 225; **Supp. XVI:** 292; **Supp. XVII:** 244; **Supp. XXII:** 89, 90, 94; **Supp. XXIII:** 207; **Supp. XXIV:** 37, 38, 152, 162

Rilke on Love and Other Difficulties (Rilke), **Supp. X:** 164

"Rilke's Growth as a Poet" (Dobyns), **Supp. XIII:** 77

"Rimbaud" (Kerouac), **Supp. III Part 1:** 232

Rimbaud, Arthur, **I:** 381, 383, 389, 391, 526; **II:** 528, 543, 545; **III:** 23, 174, 189; **IV:** 286, 380, 443; **Retro. Supp. I:** 56; **Retro. Supp. II:** 187, 326; **Supp. III Part 1:** 14, 195; **Supp. IV Part 2:** 624; **Supp. VIII:** 39, 40; **Supp. XII:** 1, 16, 128, 255; **Supp. XIII:** 284; **Supp. XIV:** 338; **Supp. XVIII:** 23, 33; **Supp. XXI:** 225, 233; **Supp. XXIII:** 207; **Supp. XXIV:** 39, 40

Rindge, Debora, **Supp. XXI:** 246

Rinehart, Stanley, **III:** 36

Ring, Frances Kroll, **Supp. IX:** 63, 64

Ring and the Book, The (Browning), **Supp. I Part 2:** 416, 468

Ring cycle (Wagner), **Supp. IV Part 1:** 392

Ringe, Donald, **I:** 339, 343; **Retro. Supp. II:** 270

Ringel, Faye, **Supp. XXII:** 205, 207

"Ringing" (Bierds), **Supp. XVII:** 28

"Ringing the Bells" (Sexton), **Supp. II Part 2:** 672, 687

Ringle, Ken, **Supp. X:** 15

Ring of Heaven: Poems (Hongo), **Supp. X:** 292

Rink, The (musical, McNally), **Supp. XIII:** 207

Rio Lobo (film), **Supp. XVI:** 246

Ríos, Alberto Alvaro, **Supp. IV Part 2: 537–556**

"Riot" (Brooks), **Supp. III Part 1:** 71, 84–85

Ripening (Le Sueur), **Supp. XXIII:** 165

Ripley, Ezra, **II:** 8; **IV:** 172

Rip-off Red, Girl Detective (Acker), **Supp. XII:** 3–4

Ripostes (Pound), **Retro. Supp. I:** 287–288, 413

Ripostes of Ezra Pound, The, Whereunto Are Appended the Complete Poetical Works of T. E. Hulme, with Prefatory Note (Pound), **III:** 458, 464, 465

Riprap (Snyder), **Supp. VIII: 292–294,** 295

"Riprap" (Snyder), **Supp. VIII:** 293–294

"Rip Van Winkle" (Irving), **II:** 304–306; **Supp. I Part 1:** 185

Rischin, Moses, **Supp. XVII:** 101, 103, 106

Risco-Lozado, Eliezar, **Supp. XIII:** 313

Rise and Shine (Quindlen), **Supp. XVII:** 179

Rise of David Levinsky, The (Cahan), **Supp. IX:** 227; **Supp. XIII:** 106

Rise of Silas Lapham, The (Howells), **II:** 275, 279, 283–285; **IV:** 202; **Retro. Supp. II:** 93, 101

"Rise of the Middle Class" (Banks), **Supp. V:** 10

Rising and Falling (Matthews), **Supp. IX:** 154, **160**

"Rising Daughter, The" (Olds), **Supp. X:** 204

Rising from the Plains (McPhee), **Supp. III Part 1:** 309–310

Rising Glory of America, The (Brackenridge and Freneau), **Supp. I Part 1:** 124; **Supp. II Part 1:** 67, 253, 256, 263

"Rising of the Storm, The" (Dunbar), **Supp. II Part 1:** 199

Rising Sun in the Pacific, The (Morison), **Supp. I Part 2:** 490

Rising Up and Rising Down (Vollmann), **Supp. XVII:** 225, 226, **229–230,** 232, 233, 235–236

Risk Pool, The (Russo), **Supp. XII: 328–331**

Ristovic, Aleksandar, **Supp. VIII:** 272

"Rita Dove: Identity Markers" (Vendler), **Supp. IV Part 1:** 247, 257

Ritchey, John, **Supp. XIV:** 122
Ritchie, Anne Thackeray, **Supp. XX:** 231, **233**
"Rite of Passage" (Olds), **Supp. X:** 206
"Rites and Ceremonies" (Hecht), **Supp. X:** 61
Rites and Witnesses: A Comedy (Hinojosa), **Supp. XIX: 106–107**
"Rites of Spring, The" (Morris), **III:** 223
Ritivoi, Andreea Deciu, **Supp. XVI:** 148
Ritschl, Albrecht, **III:** 309, 604
Ritsos, Yannis, **Supp. X:** 112
"Ritsos and the Metaphysical Moment" (Dobyns), **Supp. XIII:** 78
Rittenhouse, David, **Supp. I Part 2:** 507
Rittenhouse, Jessie, **Supp. XV:** 295
"Ritual, The" (Jarman), **Supp. XVII:** 114
"Ritual and Renewal: Keres Traditions in the Short Fiction of Leslie Silko" (Ruoff), **Supp. IV Part 2:** 559
Ritz, The (film), **Supp. XIII:** 206
Ritz, The (McNally), **Supp. XIII:** 198
"Rival, The" (Plath), **Retro. Supp. II:** 254
Riven Rock (Boyle), **Supp. VIII:** 5–6; **Supp. XX: 25–26**
"River" (Ammons), **Supp. VII:** 28
"River, The" (O'Connor), **III:** 344, 352, 353, 354, 356; **Retro. Supp. II:** 229, 231–232
Rivera, Tomás, **Supp. XIII:** 216, 221; **Supp. XIX:** 97, 102
Riverbed (Wagoner), **Supp. IX: 327–328**
"River Driftwood" (Jewett), **Retro. Supp. II:** 132, 133, 147
"River Jordan, The" (DeLillo), **Supp. VI:** 3, 4
River King, The (Hoffman), **Supp. X:** 78, 85, 90, **91–92**
"River Merchant's Wife: A Letter, The" (Pound), **III:** 463
"River Now, The" (Hugo), **Supp. VI:** 144
River of Forgetfulness, The (Hadas), **Supp. XXIII: 120**
"River of Rivers in Connecticut, The" (Stevens), **Retro. Supp. I:** 313
River of the Mother of God and Other Essays by Aldo Leopold, The (Leopold), **Supp. XIV:** 180
"River"(O'Hara), **Supp. XXIII:** 212
"River Profile" (Auden), **Supp. II Part 1:** 26
"River Road" (Kunitz), **Supp. III Part 1:** 260
"River Runs Through It, A" (Maclean), **Supp. XIV:** 222–223, **223–229,** 233, 234, 235; **Supp. XVI:** 98
River Runs Through It and Other Stories, A (Maclean), **Supp. XIV:** 221, 223
Rivers, Allison, **Supp. XXIII:** 51
Rivers, Larry, **Supp. III Part 1:** 3; **Supp. XV:** 177, 178, 186; **Supp. XXIII:** 209, 210, 211, 212, 215, 216, 217, 220
Rivers and Mountains (Ashbery), **Supp. III Part 1:** 10, 26
Riverside Drive (Simpson), **Supp. IX: 275–276**
Riverside Poetry (Auden, Moore, and Shapiro, eds.), **Supp. XXI:** 98

Rivers to the Sea (Teasdale), **Supp. XV:** 295
"River"(Strout), **Supp. XXIII:** 283
River Styx, Ohio, and Other Poems, The (Oliver), **Supp. VII:** 231, 232
"River That Is East, The" (Kinnell), **Supp. III Part 1:** 241–242
"River"(theater performance, Strout), **Supp. XXIII:** 281
"River Towns" (Masters), **Supp. I Part 2:** 473
Rives, Amélie, **II:** 194
Rivière, Jacques, **Retro. Supp. I:** 63
"Rivington's Last Will and Testament" (Freneau), **Supp. II Part 1:** 261
"Rivulet, The" (Bryant), **Supp. I Part 1:** 155, 162
Rix, Alice, **I:** 199
RL's Dream (Mosley), **Supp. XIII:** 234, **244–245,** 249
Roach, Max, **Supp. X:** 239
"Road, Roadsides, and the Disparate Frames of a Sequence" (Sobin), **Supp. XVI:** 288
Road, The (McCarthy), **Supp. XXII:** 49
Road Between, The (Farrell), **II:** 29, 38, 39–40
"Road Between Here and There, The" (Kinnell), **Supp. III Part 1:** 254
"Road Home, The" (Hammett), **Supp. IV Part 1:** 343
Road Home, The (Harrison), **Supp. VIII:** 37, 45, 48, **49–50,** 53
Road Is Before Us, The (Boulton), **Supp. XXII:** 17, 25–26
Roadless Yaak, The: Reflections and Observations about One of Our Last Great Wild Places (Bass, ed.), **Supp. XVI:** 23
"Road Not Taken, The" (R. Frost), **II:** 154; **Retro. Supp. I:** 131; **Supp. XI:** 150; **Supp. XV:** 127
"Roadside Flowers" (Collins), **Supp. XXI:** 61
Roadside Poems for Summer Travellers (Larcom, ed.), **Supp. XIII:** 142
"Roadside Resurrection, A" (L. Brown), **Supp. XXI:** 40, 42
Roads of Destiny (O. Henry), **Supp. II Part 1:** 410
Road through the Wall, The (Jackson), **Supp. IX:** 115, 118, 120, 123–124
"Road to Avignon, The" (Lowell), **II:** 516
"Road to Hell, The" (Fante), **Supp. XI:** 160
Road to Los Angeles, The (Fante), **Supp. XI:** 160, 166, 167, **168,** 172
Road to Many a Wonder, The (Wagoner), **Supp. IX:** 327, **336**
Road to the Temple, The (Glaspell), **Supp. III Part 1:** 175, 182, 186; **Supp. XXI:** 6
Road to Wellville, The (Boyle), **Supp. VIII:** 6–8; **Supp. XX: 24–25, 26, 28**
Road to Xanadu, The (Lowes), **IV:** 453
"Road Warrior" (Pickering), **Supp. XXI:** 204
"Roan Stallion" (Jeffers), **Supp. II Part 2:** 428–429
"Roast-beef" (Stein), **IV:** 43

Roast Leviatham (Untermeyer), **Supp. XV:** 307
"Roast Possum" (Dove), **Supp. IV Part 1:** 247, 248
Robards, Jason, Jr., **III:** 163, 403
Robb, Christina, **Supp. XV:** 251
Robbe-Grillet, Alain, **I:** 123; **IV:** 95; **Supp. IV Part 1:** 42; **Supp. V:** 47, 48; **Supp. XXIII:** 213
Robber Bride, The (Atwood), **Supp. XIII: 30–31**
Robber Bridegroom, The (Welty), **IV:** 261, 266–268, 271, 274; **Retro. Supp. I:** 347
Robbins, Harold, **Supp. XII:** 6
Robbins, Henry, **Supp. IV Part 1:** 198, 201, 210, 211
Robbins, Katherine Robinson, **Supp. X:** 264
Robbins, Thomas, **Supp. XV:** 271
Robbins, Tom, **Supp. IV Part 1:** 227; **Supp. VIII:** 14; **Supp. X: 259–288; Supp. XIII:** 11
"Robe, The" (Douglas), **IV:** 434
Robert Bly (Sugg), **Supp. IV Part 1:** 68
"Robert Bly" (W. V. Davis), **Supp. IV Part 1:** 70
"Robert Bly and the Trouble with America" (Mitchell), **Supp. IV Part 1:** 70
Robert Bly: An Introduction to the Poetry (Nelson), **Supp. IV Part 1:** 66
Robert Bly: The Poet and His Critics (W. V. Davis), **Supp. IV Part 1:** 63; **Supp. XXI:** 84, **85–86,** 87, 95
Robert Coover: The Universal Fiction-making Process (Gordon), **Supp. V:** 46
Robert Creeley (Ford), **Supp. IV Part 1:** 140
Robert Creeley and the Genius of the American Common Place (Clark), **Supp. IV Part 1:** 140
Robert Creeley's Poetry: A Critical Introduction (Edelberg), **Supp. IV Part 1:** 155
Robert Frost (Meyers), **Retro. Supp. I:** 138
Robert Lowell (Meyers), **Retro. Supp. II:** 191
Robert Lowell and the Sublime (Hart), **Retro. Supp. II:** 187
Robert Lowell's Shifting Colors (Doreski), **Retro. Supp. II:** 185
Robert Lowell: The First Twenty years (Staples), **Retro. Supp. II:** 187
Roberts, Carol, **Supp. XX: 53**
Roberts, David, **Supp. XVIII:** 106
Roberts, Diane, **Supp. X:** 15
Roberts, J. M., **IV:** 454
Roberts, Leo, **II:** 449
Roberts, Margaret, **II:** 449; **IV:** 453, 454
Roberts, Matthew, **Retro. Supp. II:** 324
Roberts, Meade, **IV:** 383
Roberts, Michael, **I:** 527, 536
Roberts, Richard, **III:** 297
Roberts, Victoria, **Supp. XIX:** 205
Roberts, Wally, **Supp. XI:** 119, 120, 126
Roberts, William, **Supp. XI:** 343
Roberts Brothers, **Retro. Supp. I:** 31, 35

Robertson, David, **Supp. VIII:** 305
Robertson, D. B., **III:** 311
Robertson, Lisa, **Supp. XXII:** 155
Robertson, Nan, **Supp. IV Part 1:** 300
Robertson, William, **II:** 8
Robert the Devil (Merwin, trans.), **Supp. III Part 1:** 341, 346
Robeson, Paul, **III:** 392; **Supp. IV Part 1:** 360, 361; **Supp. X:** 137; **Supp. XIX:** 66; **Supp. XXI:** 167
Robeson, Susan L., **Supp. XVIII:** 268
Robespierre, Maximilien, **Supp. I Part 2:** 514, 515, 517
"Robinson" (Kees), **Supp. XV:** 143–144
Robinson, Christopher L., **Supp. XII:** 13, 14
Robinson, David, **Supp. XXIV:** 70, 71, 78–79
Robinson, Dean, **III:** 506
Robinson, Edward, **III:** 505
Robinson, Edward G., **Supp. XI:** 306
Robinson, Edwin Arlington, **I:** 480; **II:** 388, 391, 529, 542; **III:** 5, **503–526,** 576; **Supp. I Part 2:** 699; **Supp. II Part 1:** 191; **Supp. III Part 1:** 63, 75; **Supp. III Part 2:** 592, 593; **Supp. IX:** 77, 266, 276, 308; **Supp. XV:** 256, 299, 300, 301, 306; **Supp. XVII:** 69; **Supp. XIX:** 123
Robinson, Forrest G., **Supp. IV Part 2:** 597, 601, 604
Robinson, Herman, **III:** 506–507
Robinson, H. M., **IV:** 369, 370
Robinson, Jackie, **Supp. I Part 1:** 338
Robinson, James Harvey, **I:** 214; **Supp. I Part 2:** 492
Robinson, James K., **Supp. IX:** 328
Robinson, Margaret G., **Supp. IV Part 2:** 597, 601, 604
Robinson, Marilynne, **Supp. XXI: 209–224; Supp. XXII:** 50
Robinson, Mary, **Supp. XI:** 26
Robinson, Rowland E., **Supp. XIX:** 6
Robinson, Sugar Ray, **Supp. IV Part 1:** 167
Robinson, Ted, **Supp. XIII:** 166
Robinson Crusoe (Defoe), **II:** 159; **III:** 113, 423; **IV:** 369; **Retro. Supp. II:** 274; **Supp. I Part 2:** 714; **Supp. IV Part 2:** 502
Robison, Mary, **Supp. V:** 22; **Supp. XXI:** 115, 116, 118
Roblès, Emmanuel, **Supp. I Part 1:** 283
"Robstown" (Salinas), **Supp. XIII:** 315
Rochefort, Christina, **Supp. XVI:** 143
Rochefoucauld, Louis Alexandre, **Supp. I Part 2:** 510
"Rock" (Nye), **Supp. XIII:** 287
Rock (Wagoner), **Supp. IX:** 324, **334,** 335
Rock, Catherine, **Supp. XII:** 17
Rock, The (Eliot), **Retro. Supp. I:** 65
Rock, The (Stevens), **Retro. Supp. I:** 309, 312
"Rock, The" (Stevens), **Retro. Supp. I:** 312
Rockaway (Shanley), **Supp. XIV:** 315
"Rock Climbers, The" (Francis), **Supp. IX:** 82
Rock-Drill (Pound), **Retro. Supp. I:** 293

Rockefeller, John D., **I:** 273; **III:** 580; **Supp. I Part 2:** 486; **Supp. V:** 286; **Supp. XXIII:** 26
Rockefeller, Nelson, **III:** 14, 15
Rockets and Rodeos and Other American Spectacles (Mallon), **Supp. XIX:** 137
Rocket to the Moon (Odets), **Supp. II Part 2:** 541–543, 544
Rock Garden, The (Shepard), **Supp. III Part 2:** 432, 447
"Rocking Horse Winner, The" (Lawrence), **Supp. I Part 1:** 329
Rocking the Boat (Vidal), **Supp. IV Part 2:** 683
"Rockpile, The" (Baldwin), **Supp. I Part 1:** 63
Rock Springs (Ford), **Supp. V:** 57, 58–59, 68–69
Rocky Mountains, The: or, Scenes, Incidents, and Adventures in the Far West; Digested from the Journal of Captain E. L. E Bonneville, of the Army of the United States, and Illustrated from Various Other Sources (Irving), **II:** 312
Rodden, John, **Supp. XVI:** 63, 69, 72
Roddenberry, Gene, **Supp. XXII:** 60
Rodefer, Stephen, **Supp. XXIV:** 38
Roderick, David, **Supp. XV:** 223
Roderick Hudson (James), **II:** 284, 290, 324, 326, 328; **Retro. Supp. I:** 219, **220–221,** 221, 226; **Supp. IX:** 142
Rodgers, Richard, **III:** 361
Rodgers, Ronald, **Supp. IV Part 2:** 503
Rodker, John, **III:** 470
Rodman, Selden, **Supp. I Part 1:** 83; **Supp. X:** 115
Rodney, Walter, **Supp. XXI:** 171
"Rodrigo Returns to the Land and Linen Celebrates" (Cisneros), **Supp. VII:** 68
Rodríguez, Diane, **Supp. XXIII:** 203
Rodriguez, Randy A., **Supp. XIV:** 312
Rodriguez, Richard, **Supp. XIV: 297–313**
Roethke, Charles, **III:** 531
Roethke, Theodore, **I:** 167, 171–172, 183, 254, 285, 521; **III:** 273, **527–550; IV:** 138, 402; **Retro. Supp. II:** 178, 181, 246; **Supp. I Part 2:** 539; **Supp. III Part 1:** 47, 54, 56, 239, 253, 260–261, 350; **Supp. IV Part 2:** 626; **Supp. IX:** 323; **Supp. XV:** 140, 145, 212; **Supp. XVIII:** 90; **Supp. XX: 199; Supp. XXIII:** 19; **Supp. XXIV:** 165, 171
"Roger Malvin's Burial" (Hawthorne), **II:** 243; **Retro. Supp. I:** 153
Rogers, Michael, **Supp. X:** 265, 266
Rogers, Pattiann, **Supp. XVIII:** 189
Rogers, Samuel, **II:** 303; **Supp. I Part 1:** 157
Rogers, Will, **I:** 261; **IV:** 388
Roger's Version (Updike), **Retro. Supp. I:** 325, 327, 330
Roget, Peter Mark, **Supp. I Part 1:** 312
"Rogue River Jet-Board Trip, Gold Beach, Oregon, July 4, 1977" (Carver), **Supp. III Part 1:** 140
"Rogue's Gallery" (McCarthy), **II:** 563
Rohr, Richard, **Supp. XX: 143**
Roland de La Platière, Jean Marie, **II:** 554

Rolando Hinojosa and the American Dream (Glover), **Supp. XIX:** 112
Rolando Hinojosa: A Reader's Guide (Zilles), **Supp. XIX:** 112
Rolando Hinojosa Reader, The (Saldívar, ed.), **Supp. XIX:** 112
Rôle du Nègre dans la culture des Amériques, La (Locke), **Supp. XIV:** 202
"Role of a Lifetime, The" (Skloot), **Supp. XX: 203**
"Role of Society in the Artist, The" (Ammons), **Supp. VII:** 34
Rolfe, Alfred, **IV:** 427
Rolfe, Frederick, **Supp. XX: 235**
"Roll, Jordan, Roll" (spiritual), **Supp. IV Part 1:** 16
Rolland, Romain, **Supp. XX: 70**
"Roll Call" (Hoffman), **Supp. XVIII:** 86
"Roll Call" (Komunyakaa), **Supp. XIII:** 123
Rolle, Esther, **Supp. IV Part 1:** 367
Rollin, Charles, **II:** 113
Rolling Stones (O. Henry), **Supp. II Part 1:** 410
Rolling Thunder Logbook (Shepard), **Supp. III Part 2:** 433
Rolling Thunder Logbook, The (Shepard), **Supp. XVIII:** 31
"Rolling Up" (Simpson), **Supp. IX:** 265, 274, 280
Rollins, Howard E., Jr., **Supp. IV Part 1:** 236
Rollins, Hyder E., **Supp. IV Part 1:** 168
Rollins, Sonny, **Supp. V:** 195
"Rollo" tales (Abbott), **Supp. I Part 1:** 38
"Roma I" (Wright), **Supp. V:** 338
"Roma II" (Wright), **Supp. V:** 338
Romains, Jules, **I:** 227
Román, David, **Supp. XIII:** 208
Romance, A (Weigl), **Supp. XIX: 277–278**
"Romance, A" (Weigl), **Supp. XIX:** 278
"Romance and a Reading List" (Fitzgerald), **Retro. Supp. I:** 101
Romance of a Plain Man, The (Glasgow), **II:** 175, 180–181
"Romance of Certain Old Clothes, The" (James), **II:** 322; **Retro. Supp. I:** 218
Romance Reader, The (Abraham), **Supp. XXIV:** 1–2, 3, **4–7**
"Roman Elegies" (Brodsky), **Supp. VIII:** 29
"Roman Fever" (Wharton), **Retro. Supp. I:** 382
"Roman Fountain" (Bogan), **Supp. III Part 1:** 56
"Romanitas of Gore Vidal, The" (Tatum), **Supp. IV Part 2:** 684
Romaniuk, Zbigniew, **Supp. XVI:** 154
Romano, John, **Supp. XV:** 253
"Roman Sarcophagus, A" (Lowell), **II:** 544
Roman Spring of Mrs. Stone, The (T. Williams), **IV:** 383, 385
"Romantic, The" (Bogan), **Supp. III Part 1:** 50
Romantic Comedians, The (Glasgow), **II:** 175, 186, 190, 194

Romantic Education, A (Hampl), **Supp. XXII:** 82, 83, **87–90,** 91
Romantic Egoists, The (Auchincloss), **Supp. IV Part 1:** 25
Romantic Egotist, The (Fitzgerald), **II:** 82
"Romantic Egotist, The" (Fitzgerald), **Retro. Supp. I:** 100
"Romanticism and Classicism" (Hulme), **III:** 196
"Romanticism Comes Home" (Shapiro), **Supp. II Part 2:** 713
Romantic Manifesto, The: A Philosophy of Literature (Rand), **Supp. IV Part 2:** 521, 523, 527, 529–530
"Romantic Regionalism of Harper Lee, The" (Erisman), **Supp. VIII:** 126
"Rome" (W. C. Williams), **Retro. Supp. I:** 420
Rome Brothers, **Retro. Supp. I:** 393
Romeo and Juliet (Shakespeare), **Supp. V:** 252; **Supp. VIII:** 223
Romola (G. Eliot), **II:** 291; **IV:** 311
Romulus: A New Comedy (Vidal), **Supp. IV Part 2:** 683
Romulus der Grosse (Dürrenmatt), **Supp. IV Part 2:** 683
Ronald, Ann, **Supp. XIII:** 4, 5, 6, 7, 9, 11
"Rondel for a September Day" (White), **Supp. I Part 2:** 676
"Ron Narrative Reconstructions, The" (Coleman), **Supp. XI:** 83
"Ron Padgett's Visual Imagination" (Notley), **Supp. XXII:** 224
Ronsard, Pierre de, **Supp. X:** 65; **Supp. XV:** 165
Rood, John, **IV:** 261
"Roof, the Steeple, and the People, The" (Ellison), **Retro. Supp. II:** 118, 126; **Supp. II Part 1:** 248
"Room" (Levertov), **Supp. III Part 1:** 282
Roomates (film, P. Yates), **Supp. XVII:** 8, 9
Roomates: My Grandfather's Story (Apple), **Supp. XVII:** 2, **7–9**
"Room at the Heart of Things, A" (Merrill), **Supp. III Part 1:** 337
Room Called Remember, A: Uncollected Pieces (Buechner), **Supp. XII:** 53
"Roomful of Hovings, A" (McPhee), **Supp. III Part 1:** 291, 294
Room of One's Own, A (Woolf), **Supp. V:** 127; **Supp. IX:** 19; **Supp. XIII:** 305
Room Rented by a Single Woman (Wright), **Supp. XV:** 340–341
"Rooms" (Collins), **Supp. XXI:** 61
Room Temperature (Baker), **Supp. XIII:** 41, **43–45,** 48, 50
Room to Swing (Lacy), **Supp. XV:** 202, 203, 205, 207
"Room Upstairs, The" (Gioia), **Supp. XV:** 120–121, 124
Roosevelt, Eleanor, **IV:** 371; **Supp. IV Part 2:** 679
Roosevelt, Franklin, **Supp. V:** 290
Roosevelt, Franklin Delano, **I:** 482, 485, 490; **II:** 553, 575; **III:** 2, 18, 69, 110, 297, 321, 376, 476, 580, 581; **Supp. I**

Part 2: 488, 489, 490, 491, 645, 654, 655
Roosevelt, Kermit, **III:** 508
Roosevelt, Theodore, **I:** 14, 62; **II:** 130; **III:** 508; **IV:** 321; **Retro. Supp. I:** 377; **Supp. I Part 1:** 1, 21; **Supp. I Part 2:** 455, 456, 502, 707; **Supp. V:** 280, 282; **Supp. IX:** 184; **Supp. XIX:** 29; **Supp. XX:** 221; **Supp. XXIII:** 26
Roosevelt After Inauguration And Other Atrocities (Burroughs), **Supp. III Part 1:** 98
"Roosevelt Chair, The" (Skloot), **Supp. XX:** 205
"Roosters" (Bishop), **Retro. Supp. II:** 39, 43, 250; **Supp. I Part 1:** 89
Root, Abiah, **I:** 456
Root, Elihu, **Supp. IV Part 1:** 33
Root, Simeon, **I:** 548
Root, Timothy, **I:** 548
Rootabaga Stories (Sandburg), **III:** 583, 587
"Rootedness: The Ancestor as Foundation" (Morrison), **Supp. III Part 1:** 361
"Roots" (Halliday), **Supp. XIX:** 88
Roots in the Soil (film), **Supp. IV Part 1:** 83
"Rope" (Porter), **III:** 451
Rope, The (O'Neill), **III:** 388
Ropemakers of Plymouth, The (Morison), **Supp. I Part 2:** 494
"Ropes" (Nye), **Supp. XIII:** 276
"Rope's End, The" (Nemerov), **III:** 282
Roquelaure, A. N., **Supp. VII:** 301. *See also* Rice, Anne
Rorem, Ned, **Supp. IV Part 1:** 79, 84; **Supp. XXIII:** 217
Rorschach Test (F. Wright), **Supp. XVII:** 240, 245
Rorty, James, **Supp. XXII:** 276, 277
"Rosa" (Ozick), **Supp. V:** 271
Rosa, Rodrigo Rey, **Supp. IV Part 1:** 92
Rosaldo, Renato, **Supp. IV Part 2:** 544
"Rosalia" (Simic), **Supp. VIII:** 278
Roscoe, Will, **Supp. IV Part 1:** 330
"Roscoe in Hell" (McKnight), **Supp. XX:** 151
"Rose" (Dubus), **Supp. VII:** 88
Rose (L.-Y. Lee), **Supp. XV:** 211, **212–215,** 218
Rose, Alice, Sister, **III:** 348
Rose, Charlie, **Supp. XIX:** 26, 30
Rose, Lloyd, **Supp. XXIV:** 267
Rose, Mickey, **Supp. XV:** 3
Rose, Philip, **Supp. IV Part 1:** 362
"Rose, The" (Roethke), **III:** 537
"Rose, The" (W. C. Williams), **Retro. Supp. I:** 419
Rose, Where Did You Get That Red?: Teaching Great Poetry to Children (Koch), **Supp. XV:** 189
"Rose for Emily, A" (Faulkner), **II:** 72; **Supp. IX:** 96; **Supp. XX:** 179; **Supp. XXIV:** 136
Rose-Hued Cities (P. N. Warren), **Supp. XX:** 261
Rose in Bloom (Alcott), **Supp. I Part 1:** 42

"Rose-Johnny" (Kingsolver), **Supp. VII:** 203
Rose Madder (King), **Supp. V:** 141, 148, 150, 152
"Rose-Morals" (Lanier), **Supp. I Part 1:** 364
Rosen, Jonathan, **Supp. XVII:** 50; **Supp. XX:** 179
Rosen, Kenneth, **Supp. IV Part 2:** 499, 505, 513
Rosen, Norma, **Supp. XVII:** 49, 50
Rosenbaum, Alissa Zinovievna. *See* Rand, Ayn
Rosenbaum, Thane, **Supp. XVII:** 48
Rosenberg, Bernard, **Supp. I Part 2:** 650
Rosenberg, Harold, **Supp. XV:** 143; **Supp. XIX:** 159; **Supp. XXIII:** 211
Rosenberg, Julia, **Supp. XVIII:** 136
Rosenberg, Julius and Ethel, **Supp. I Part 1:** 295; **Supp. I Part 2:** 532; **Supp. V:** 45
Rosenberg, Liz, **Supp. XV:** 251
Rosenberg, Shlomo, **Supp. XXIII:** 6
Rosenbloom, Joel, **Supp. IV Part 2:** 527
Rosenfeld, Alvin H., **Supp. I Part 1:** 120
Rosenfeld, Isaac, **Supp. XII:** 160
Rosenfeld, Paul, **I:** 116, 117, 231, 245
Rosenfelt, Deborah, **Supp. XIII:** 296, 304
Rosenfield, Isaac, **IV:** 3
Rosengarten, Theodore, **Supp. XVIII:** 183
Rosenthal, Ira, **Supp. XIV:** 146–147
Rosenthal, Lois, **Supp. VIII:** 258
Rosenthal, M. L., **II:** 550; **III:** 276, 479; **Supp. V:** 333
Rosenthal, Peggy, **Supp. XVII:** 119
Rose of Wissahikon, The (Lippard), **Supp. XXIII:** 178
"Rose Pogonias" (Frost), **Retro. Supp. I:** 127
"Rose Red and Snow White" (Grimms), **Supp. X:** 82
"Rose Room" (Sorrentino), **Supp. XXI:** 228
"Roses" (Conroy), **Supp. XVI:** 72
"Roses" (Dove), **Supp. IV Part 1:** 246
"Roses and Skulls" (Goldbarth), **Supp. XII:** 192
"Roses for Lubbock" (Nye), **Supp. XIII:** 281
"Roses Only" (Moore), **III:** 195, 198, 200, 202, 215
Rose Tattoo, The (T. Williams), **IV:** 382, 383, 387, 388, 389, 392–393, 394, 397, 398
Rose Theatre (Sorrentino), **Supp. XXI:** 236
"Rosewood, Ohio" (Matthews), **Supp. IX:** 160
Rosie (Lamott), **Supp. XX: 133–134**
Rosinante to the Road Again (Dos Passos), **I:** 478
Roskies, David, **Supp. XVII:** 39, 44, 49–50
Roskolenko, Harry, **Supp. XV:** 179
Rosmersholm (Ibsen), **III:** 152
Rosmond, Babette, **II:** 432
Ross, Eleanor. *See* Taylor, Eleanor Ross
Ross, Harold, **Supp. I Part 1:** 174; **Supp. I Part 2:** 607, 617, 653, 654, 655,

660; **Supp. VIII:** 151, 170; **Supp. IX:** 190

Ross, Herbert, **Supp. XV:** 2

Ross, Jean, **Supp. XXI:** 144, 146

Ross, John F., **II:** 110

Ross, Lillian, **Retro. Supp. II:** 198

Ross, Mary, **Supp. XXII:** 195

Ross, Mitchell S., **Supp. IV Part 2:** 692; **Supp. X:** 260

Ross, Robert, **Supp. XXIV:** 167

Rossen, Robert, **Supp. XI:** 306

Rosset, Barney, **III:** 171

Rossetti, Christina, **Supp. XIV:** 128

Rossetti, Dante Gabriel, **I:** 433; **II:** 323; **Retro. Supp. I:** 128, 286; **Supp. I Part 2:** 552; **Supp. XXII:** 156

Rossetti, William Michael, **Retro. Supp. I:** 407

Rossi, Umberto, **Supp. XVIII:** 137, 138–139

Rossini, Clare, **Supp. XVII:** 111

Rosskam, Edwin, **IV:** 477

Ross Macdonald (Bruccoli), **Supp. IV Part 2:** 468, 470

Rostand, Edmond, **II:** 515; **Supp. IV Part 2:** 518

Rosten, Leo, **Supp. XVII:** 9

Rosy Crucifixion, The (H. Miller), **III:** 170, 187, 188–189, 190

Rote Walker, The (Jarman), **Supp. XVII:** 110, **113–115**

Roth, Henry, **Supp. IV Part 1:** 314; **Supp. VIII:** 233; **Supp. IX: 227–243; Supp. XIII:** 106

Roth, Philip, **I:** 144, 161; **II:** 591; **Retro. Supp. II:** 22, **279–297; Supp. I Part 1:** 186, 192; **Supp. I Part 2:** 431, 441, 443; **Supp. II Part 1:** 99; **Supp. III Part 2: 401–429; Supp. IV Part 1:** 236, 379, 388; **Supp. V:** 45, 119, 122, 257, 258; **Supp. VIII:** 88, 236, 245; **Supp. IX:** 227; **Supp. XI:** 64, 68, 99, 140; **Supp. XII:** 190, 310; **Supp. XIV:** 79, 93, 111, 112; **Supp. XVI:** 206; **Supp. XVII:** 43, 48, 183; **Supp. XVIII:** 89; **Supp. XXI:** 234; **Supp. XXII:** 268

Roth, Rita, **Supp. XVI:** 112

Roth, William, **Supp. XV:** 142

Rothenberg, Jerome, **Supp. VIII:** 292; **Supp. XII:** 3; **Supp. XXIV:** 37

Rothermere, Lady Mary, **Retro. Supp. I:** 63

Rothko, Mark, **Supp. XV:** 144

Rothstein, Mervyn, **Supp. VIII:** 142

"Rouen, France"(Kenny), **Supp. XXIII:** 152

"Rouge High" (Hughes), **Supp. I Part 1:** 330

Rougemont, Denis de, **II:** 586; **IV:** 216; **Retro. Supp. I:** 328, 329, 330, 331

Rough Edges (Skloot), **Supp. XX: 196**

Roughing It (Twain), **II:** 312; **IV:** 195, 197, 198

Roughing It in the Bush (Shields), **Supp. VII:** 313

"Rough Outline" (Simic), **Supp. VIII:** 276

"Rough-Skinned Newt, The"(Schott), **Supp. XXIII:** 253–254

Rough South of Larry Brown, The (film, Hawkins), **Supp. XXI:** 39

Rougon-Macquart, Les (Zola), **II:** 175–176

Roumain, Jacques, **Retro. Supp. I:** 202; **Supp. IV Part 1:** 360, 367

"Round, The" (Kunitz), **Supp. III Part 1:** 268

"Roundelay Between Two Shepherdesses, A" (Notley), **Supp. XXII:** 229

"Round Trip" (Dunn), **Supp. XI:** 148–149

Round Up (Lardner), **II:** 426, 430, 431

Rourke, Constance, **I:** 258; **IV:** 339, 352

Rourke, Milton, **Retro. Supp. II:** 89

Rousseau, Jean-Jacques, **I:** 226; **II:** 8, 343; **III:** 170, 178, 259; **IV:** 80, 173, 440; **Supp. I Part 1:** 126; **Supp. I Part 2:** 637, 659; **Supp. IV Part 1:** 171; **Supp. XI:** 245; **Supp. XVI:** 292; **Supp. XXI:** 83

Roussel, Raymond, **Supp. III Part 1:** 6, 7, 10, 15, 16, 21; **Supp. XV:** 182

"Route 302" (Halliday), **Supp. XIX:** 93

"Routes" (Everwine), **Supp. XV:** 82

"Route Six" (Kunitz), **Supp. III Part 1:** 258

Route Two (Erdrich and Dorris), **Supp. IV Part 1:** 260

"Routine Things Around the House, The" (Dunn), **Supp. XI:** 148

Rover Boys (Winfield), **III:** 146

Rovit, Earl, **IV:** 102

Rowan, Carl T., **Supp. XIV:** 306

Rowe, Anne I., **Supp. X:** 223

Rowe, John Carlos, **Retro. Supp. I:** 216

Rowe, Kenneth Thorpe, **Supp. XXIII:** 258

Rowell, Charles, **Supp. XXI:** 250, 254, 255; **Supp. XXIV:** 184

"Rowing" (Sexton), **Supp. II Part 2:** 696

"Rowing Endeth, The" (Sexton), **Supp. II Part 2:** 696

Rowlandson, Mary, **Supp. IV Part 2:** 430, 431

"Rows of Cold Trees, The" (Winters), **Supp. II Part 2:** 790–791, 800

Rowson, Susanna, **Supp. I Part 1:** 128; **Supp. XV: 229–248**

Roxanna Slade (Price), **Supp. VI:** 267

Roxie Hart (Watkins), **Supp. XVI:** 188

Royal Family, The (Vollmann), **Supp. XVII:** 226, 230, 233

"Royal Palm" (Crane), **I:** 401

Royce, Josiah, **I:** 443; **III:** 303, 600; **IV:** 26; **Retro. Supp. I:** 57; **Supp. XIV:** 197, 199; **Supp. XVII:** 97

"Roy McInnes" (Budbill), **Supp. XIX:** 6–7

"Roy Spivey" (July), **Supp. XXIV:** 210

Royster, Sarah Elmira, **III:** 410, 429

Royte, Elizabeth, **Supp. XV:** 59

Rózewicz, Tadeusz, **Supp. X:** 60

R. S. Thomas: Poetry and Theology (W. V. Davis), **Supp. XXI: 86–87**

Ruas, Charles, **Supp. IV Part 1:** 383

Ruback, Max, **Supp. XXIII:** 290

Rubáiyát (Khayyám), **I:** 568

Rubáiyát of Omar Khayyam (Fitzgerald), **Supp. I Part 2:** 416; **Supp. III Part 2:** 610; **Supp. XV:** 156

"Rubber Life" (Prose), **Supp. XVI:** 256

Rubel, Nora L., **Supp. XXIV:** 7

Rub from Snub, A (Swanwick), **Supp. XV:** 237

"Rubicon" (Cliff), **Supp. XXII:** 76

Rubin, Louis, **Supp. I Part 2:** 672, 673, 679; **Supp. X:** 42

Rubin, Louis D., Jr., **IV:** 116, 462–463

Rubin, Stan, **Supp. XIV:** 307, 310

Rubin, Stan Sanvel, **Supp. IV Part 1:** 242, 245, 252

Rubins, Josh, **Supp. XX: 89**

"Ruby Brown" (Hughes), **Supp. I Part 1:** 327

"Ruby Daggett" (Eberhart), **I:** 539

Rucker, Rudy, **Supp. X:** 302

Rudd, Hughes, **Supp. XII:** 141

"Rude Awakening, A" (Chopin), **Retro. Supp. II:** 64

Rudens (Plautus), **Supp. III Part 2:** 630

Ruderman, Judith, **Supp. IV Part 1:** 380

Rudge, Olga, **Supp. V:** 338

Rudikoff, Sonya, **Supp. XIV:** 113

Rudman, Mark, **Supp. XXIII:** 124; **Supp. XXIV:** 153

Rueckert, William, **I:** 264

Ruesch, Jurgen, **Supp. XV:** 147

Rugby Chapel (Arnold), **Supp. I Part 2:** 416

"Rugby Road" (Garrett), **Supp. VII:** 100

Rugge, John, **Supp. XXII:** 218

Ruining the New Road (Matthews), **Supp. IX:** 154, **155–157**

"Ruins of Italica, The" (Bryant, trans.), **Supp. I Part 1:** 166

Rukeyser, Muriel, **Retro. Supp. II:** 48; **Supp. VI: 271–289; Supp. XV:** 349; **Supp. XVII:** 74

"Rule of Phase Applied to History, The" (Adams), **I:** 19

Rule of the Bone (Banks), **Supp. V:** 16

Rulers of Kings (Atherton), **Supp. XXIV:** 23

"Rules by Which a Great Empire May Be Reduced to a Small One" (Franklin), **II:** 120

Rules For the Dance: A Handbook for Reading and Writing Metrical Verse (Oliver), **Supp. VII:** 229, 247

Rules of the Game, The (film), **Supp. XII:** 259

Rulfo, Juan, **Supp. IV Part 2:** 549

Rumba (film, Gering), **Supp. XVII:** 57

Rumbaut, Rubén, **Supp. XII:** 184

Rum Diary, The (Thompson), **Supp. XXIV:** 281, **283–286**, 293

Rümelin-Oesterlen, Natalie, **Supp. XX: 235**

Rumens, Carol, **Supp. XI:** 14; **Supp. XVI:** 212

Rumi, **Supp. XX: 117**

"Rumination of Rivers, The" (Bronk), **Supp. XXI:** 32

Rumkowski, Chaim, **Supp. XII:** 168

Rummel, Mary Kay, **Supp. XIII:** 280

"Rumor and a Ladder" (Bowles), **Supp. IV Part 1:** 93

Rumor of War, A (Caputo), **Supp. XIX: 17–21**, 25, **30**

Rumors (Simon), **Supp. IV Part 2:** 582–583, 591

Rumpelstiltskin (Gardner), **Supp. VI:** 72

"Rumpelstiltskin" (Grimm), **IV:** 266

"Rumpelstiltskin" (Sexton), **Supp. II Part 2:** 690

"Runagate Runagate" (Hayden), **Supp. II Part 1:** 377

"Runes" (Nemerov), **III:** 267, 277–278

Run Man Run (C. Himes), **Supp. XVI:** 142, 143

"Runner, The" (Grossman), **Supp. XIX:** 83

"Running" (Wilbur), **Supp. III Part 2:** 558–559

"RUNNING-AWAY" (Strout), **Supp. XXIII:** 274

Running Dog (DeLillo), **Supp. VI:** 3, 6, 8, 14

"Running in Church" (A. Finch), **Supp. XVII:** 72

"Running the Table" Conroy), **Supp. XVI:** 75

"Run of Bad Luck, A" (Proulx), **Supp. VII:** 253–254

Run of Jacks, A (Hugo), **Supp. VI:** 131, 133, 134, 135, 136

Run River (Didion), **Supp. IV Part 1:** 197, 199–200, 201

Ruoff, A. LaVonne Brown, **Supp. IV Part 1:** 324, 327; **Supp. IV Part 2:** 559

Rupert, Jim, **Supp. XII:** 215

Ruppert, James, **Supp. IV Part 1:** 321

Rural Hours (Cooper), **Supp. XIII:** 152

"Rural Route" (Wright), **Supp. V:** 340

"Rural South, The" (Du Bois), **Supp. II Part 1:** 174

Rush, Benjamin, **Supp. I Part 2:** 505, 507

Rushdie, Salman, **Supp. IV Part 1:** 234, 297

Rushdy, Ashraf, **Supp. X:** 250

Rushing, Jimmy, **Retro. Supp. II:** 113

Rusk, Dean, **II:** 579

Ruskin, John, **II:** 323, 338; **IV:** 349; **Retro. Supp. I:** 56, 360; **Supp. I Part 1:** 2, 10, 87, 349; **Supp. I Part 2:** 410

Rusnak, Karl, **Supp. XVIII:** 149

Russell, Ada Dwyer, **II:** 513, 527

Russell, Bertrand, **II:** 27; **III:** 605, 606; **Retro. Supp. I:** 57, 58, 59, 60; **Supp. I Part 2:** 522; **Supp. V:** 290; **Supp. XII:** 45; **Supp. XIV:** 337

Russell, Diarmuid, **Retro. Supp. I:** 342, 345, 346–347, 349–350

Russell, George, **Retro. Supp. I:** 342

Russell, Herb, **Supp. I Part 2:** 465–466

Russell, John, **Supp. XIV:** 344, 347, 348

Russell, Peter, **III:** 479

Russell, Richard, **Supp. XI:** 102

Russell, Robert, **Supp. XX:** 195

Russell, Sue, **Supp. IV Part 2:** 653

Russello, Gerald, **Supp. XXIV:** 159

Russert, Margaret, **Supp. XVIII:** 62

Russert, Tim, **Supp. XII:** 272

Russia at War (Caldwell), **I:** 296

"Russia Between Myth and Reality: From *Meri* to *Three Cities*" (Krutikov), *Supp. XXIII:* 11

Russian Journal, A (Steinbeck), **IV:** 52, 63

Russo, Richard, **Supp. XI:** 349; **Supp. XII: 325–344; Supp. XXIII:** 302

"Rusty Autumn" (Swenson), **Supp. IV Part 2:** 640

Rutabaga-Roo: I've Got a Song and It's for You (Nye, album), **Supp. XIII:** 274

Ruth (biblical book), **Supp. I Part 2:** 516

Ruth, George Herman ("Babe"), **II:** 423; **Supp. I Part 2:** 438, 440

Rutheiser, Charles, **Supp. XXII:** 244

Ruth Hall (Fern), **Supp. V:** 122

Ruthven, K. K., **Supp. XXII:** 261

Rutkowska, Malgorzata, **Supp. XXII:** 208

Rutledge, Ann, **III:** 588; **Supp. I Part 2:** 471

Ruwe, Donelle R., **Supp. XII:** 215

Ryan, Katy, **Supp. XXI:** 215

Ryan, Kay, **Supp. XXI:** 20

Ryan, Maureen, **Supp. XXI:** 215

Ryan, Paul William, **Supp. XVIII: 223–239**

Ryan, Paul William (Mike Quin), **Supp. XXI:** 264–265

Ryder (Barnes), **Supp. III Part 1:** 31, 36–38, 42, 43

"Ryder" (Rukeyser), **Supp. VI:** 273, 283

Ryle, Herbert Edward, **Supp. XX: 230**

Rymer, Thomas, **IV:** 122

"Ryōkan Says" (Budbill), **Supp. XIX:** 11

S

S. (Updike), **Retro. Supp. I:** 330, 331, 332, 333

S-1 (Baraka), **Supp. II Part 1:** 55, 57

Saadi, **II:** 19

Saar, Doreen Alvarez, **Supp. XV:** 237

Sabbatai Zevi (Asch), **Supp. XXIII:** 12

"Sabbath, The" (Stowe), **Supp. I Part 2:** 587

"Sabbath Mom" (White), **Supp. I Part 2:** 671–672

Sabbaths (Berry), **Supp. X:** 31

Sabbath's Theater (P. Roth), **Retro. Supp. II:** 279, 288

"Sabbioneta to Parma" (Di Piero), **Supp. XIX:** 36–37

Sabines, Jaime, **Supp. V:** 178

"Sabotage" (Baraka), **Supp. II Part 1:** 49, 53

"Saboteur" (Jin), **Supp. XVIII:** 97

Sacco, Nicola, **I:** 482, 486, 490, 494; **II:** 38–39, 426; **III:** 139–140; **Supp. I Part 2:** 446; **Supp. V:** 288–289; **Supp. IX:** 199; **Supp. XXII:** 277

Sachs, Hanns, **Supp. I Part 1:** 259; **Supp. X:** 186

Sack Full of Old Quarrels, A (Weigl), **Supp. XIX:** 277

"Sacks" (Carver), **Supp. III Part 1:** 143–144

Sacks, Oliver, **Supp. XVIII:** 143

Sacks, Peter, **Supp. IV Part 2:** 450

Sackville-West, Vita, **Supp. VIII:** 263

"Sacrament of Divorce, The" (Patchett), **Supp. XII:** 309

"Sacrament of Self: Catholic Roots of Contemporary Memoir" (lecture, Hampl), **Supp. XXII:** 81

"Sacraments" (Dubus), **Supp. VII:** 91

Sacred and Profane Memories (Van Vechten), **Supp. II Part 2:** 735, 749

"Sacred Chant for the Return of Black Spirit and Power" (Baraka), **Supp. II Part 1:** 51

"Sacred Factory, The" (Toomer), **Supp. IX:** 320

Sacred Fount, The (James), **II:** 332–333; **Retro. Supp. I:** 219, 228, 232

"Sacred Heart" (Egan), **Supp. XIX:** 52

"Sacred Hoop, The: A Contemporary Perspective" (Gunn Allen), **Supp. IV Part 1:** 324

Sacred Hoop, The: Recovering the Feminine in American Indian Traditions (Gunn Allen), **Supp. IV Part 1:** 319, 320, 322, 324, 325, 328–330, 331, 333, 334

Sacred Journey, The (Buechner), **Supp. XII:** 42, 53

"Sacred Thing, The" (Ryan as Quin), **Supp. XVIII:** 227

Sacred Wood, The (Eliot), **IV:** 431; **Retro. Supp. I:** 59, 60; **Supp. I Part 1:** 268; **Supp. II Part 1:** 136, 146

Sacrifice, The (Bidart), **Supp. XV:** 22, **27–30,** 35

"Sacrifice, The" (Bidart), **Supp. XV:** 29

"Sacrifice, The" (Oates), **Supp. II Part 2:** 523

Sacrilege of Alan Kent, The (Caldwell), **I:** 291–292

"Sad Brazil" (Hardwick), **Supp. III Part 1:** 210

Sad Days of Light (Balakian), **Supp. XXIII:** 20

"Sad Dust Glories" (Ginsberg), **Supp. II Part 1:** 376

Sad Dust Glories: Poems Written Work Summer in Sierra Woods (Ginsberg), **Supp. II Part 1:** 326

Sade, Marquis de, **III:** 259; **IV:** 437, 442; **Supp. XII:** 1, 14–15

Sad-Faced Boy (Bontemps), **Supp. XXII:** 5, 12

Sad Flower in the Sand, A (film), **Supp. XI:** 173

Sad Heart at the Supermarket, A (Jarrell), **II:** 386

"Sadie" (Matthiessen), **Supp. V:** 201

"Sadie and Maud" (Brooks), **Supp. XVIII:** 175

Sadness and Happiness (Pinsky), **Supp. VI:** 235, **237–241**

"Sadness of Brothers, The" (Kinnell), **Supp. III Part 1:** 237, 251

"Sadness of Days, The" (Salinas), **Supp. XIII:** 325

Sadness of Days, The: Selected and New Poems (Salinas), **Supp. XIII:** 311, **324–326**

"Sadness of Lemons, The" (Levine), **Supp. V:** 184

Sadoff, Ira, **Supp. XVII:** 241; **Supp. XXI:** 100

"Sad Rite" (Karr), **Supp. XI:** 243

"Sad Strains of a Gay Waltz" (Stevens), **Retro. Supp. I:** 302

"Safe" (Gordon), **Supp. IV Part 1:** 299, 306

"Safe in their Alabaster Chambers" (Dickinson), **Retro. Supp. I:** 30

Safer, Morley, **Supp. XIX:** 25

"Safe Subjects" (Komunyakaa), **Supp. XIII:** 118

Safety Features (Monson), **Supp. XXIV:** 230

"Safeway" (F. Barthelme), **Supp. XI:** 26, 27, 36

Saffin, John, **Supp. I Part 1:** 115

Saffy, Edna, **Supp. X:** 227

Sagan, Miriam, **Supp. XXIII:** 133

"Saga of an American Ranch" (P. N. Warren), **Supp. XX: 261**

"Saga of Arturo Bandini" (Fante), **Supp. XI:** 159, **166–169**

"Saga of King Olaf, The" (Longfellow), **II:** 489, 505; **Retro. Supp. II:** 154, 155, 164

"Sage of Stupidity and Wonder, The" (Goldbarth), **Supp. XII:** 191

Sahl, Mort, **II:** 435–436

"Sah Sin" (Gallagher), *Supp. XXIV:* 171

"Said" (Dixon), **Supp. XII:** 149–150

Said, Edward, **Supp. XXI:** 153

"Sailing after Lunch" (Stevens), **IV:** 73

Sailing Alone Around the Room: New and Selected Poems (Collins), **Supp. XXI:** 54, 56, 62

"Sailing Home from Rapallo" (Lowell), **Retro. Supp. II:** 189

Sailing through China (Theroux), **Supp. VIII:** 323

"Sailing to Byzantium" (Yeats), **III:** 263; **Supp. VIII:** 30; **Supp. X:** 74; **Supp. XI:** 281

"Sail Made of Rags, The" (Nye), **Supp. XIII:** 277

"Sailor off the Bremen" (Shaw), **Supp. XIX:** 247

"Sailors Lost at Sea" (Shields), **Supp. VII:** 318

"St Anne/Santa Ana" (Mora), **Supp. XIII:** 229

"Saint Anthony of Padua/San Antonio de Padua" (Mora), **Supp. XIII:** 228

"St. Augustine and the Bullfights" (Porter), **III:** 454

Sainte-Beuve, Charles Augustin, **IV:** 432

St. Elmo (Wilson), **Retro. Supp. I:** 351–352

"Saint Emmanuel the Good, Martyr" (Unamuno; Everwine, trans.), **Supp. XV:** 79

Sainte Vierge, La (Picabia), **Retro. Supp. II:** 331

Saint-Exupéry, Antoine de, **Supp. IX:** 247

"St. Francis Einstein of the Daffodils" (W. C. Williams), **IV:** 409–411

Saint-Gaudens, Augustus, **I:** 18, 228; **II:** 551

Saint-Gaudens, Homer, **Supp. XV:** 41

"St. George, the Dragon, and the Virgin" (R. Bly), **Supp. IV Part 1:** 73

St. George and the Godfather (Mailer), **III:** 46; **Retro. Supp. II:** 206, 208

Saint Jack (Theroux), **Supp. VIII:** 319

St. John, David, **Supp. V:** 180; **Supp. XI:** 270, 272; **Supp. XIII:** 312

St. John, Edward B., **Supp. IV Part 2:** 490

St. John, James Hector. *See* Crèvecoeur, Michel-Guillaume Jean de

"Saint John and the Back-Ache" (Stevens), **Retro. Supp. I:** 310

Saint Judas (Wright), **Supp. III Part 2: 595–599**

"Saint Judas" (Wright), **Supp. III Part 2:** 598–599

St. Louis Woman (Bontemps and Cullen), **Supp. IV Part 1:** 170

St. Mawr (Lawrence), **II:** 595

Saint Maybe (Tyler), **Supp. IV Part 2:** 670–671

"Saint Nicholas" (Moore), **III:** 215

"Saint"(O'Hara), **Supp. XXIII:** 219

St. Petersburg (Biely), **Supp. XII:** 13

Saint-Phalle, Niki de, **Supp. XV:** 187

"St. Roach" (Rukeyser), **Supp. VI:** 286

"Saint Robert" (Dacey), **Supp. IV Part 1:** 70

Saintsbury, George, **IV:** 440; **Supp. XV:** 181

Saints' Everlasting Rest, The (Baxter), **III:** 199; **IV:** 151, 153

Saint-Simon, Claude Henri, **Supp. I Part 2:** 648

"St. Thomas Aquinas" (Simic), **Supp. VIII:** 281

Saks, Gene, **Supp. IV Part 2:** 577, 588

Salamun, Tomaz, **Supp. VIII:** 272

Salazar, Dixie, **Supp. V:** 180; **Supp. XV:** 73

Saldívar, José David, **Supp. IV Part 2:** 544, 545; **Supp. XIX:** 110, 112–113

Sale, Richard, **Supp. IV Part 1:** 379

Sale, Roger, **Supp. V:** 244

Saleh, Dennis, **Supp. V:** 182, 186

"Salem" (Lowell), **II:** 550

Salemi, Joseph, **Supp. IV Part 1:** 284

Salem's Lot (King), **Supp. V:** 139, 144, 146, 151

"Sale of the Hessians, The" (Franklin), **II:** 120

Salick, Roydan, **Supp. XXIII:** 93, 94

Salinas, Luis Omar, **Supp. IV Part 2:** 545; **Supp. V:** 180; **Supp. XIII: 311–330; Supp. XV:** 73

"Salinas Is on His Way" (Salinas), **Supp. XIII:** 317

"Salinas Sends Messengers to the Stars" (Salinas), **Supp. XIII:** 317

"Salinas Summering at the Caspian and Thinking of Hamlet" (Salinas), **Supp. XIII:** 320

"Salinas Wakes Early and Goes to the Park to Lecture Sparrows" (Salinas), **Supp. XIII:** 320

Salinger, Doris, **III:** 551

Salinger, J. D., **II:** 255; **III: 551–574; IV:** 190, 216, 217; **Retro. Supp. I:** 102, 116, 335; **Supp. IV Part 2:** 502; **Supp. V:** 23, 119; **Supp. VIII:** 151; **Supp. XI:** 2, 66; **Supp. XIV:** 93; **Supp. XXIII:** 100

Salisbury, Harrison, **Supp. I Part 2:** 664

Salle, David, **Supp. XII:** 4

Salley, Columbus, **Supp. XIV:** 195

"Sally" (Cisneros), **Supp. VII:** 63

"Sally's Choice" (E. Stoddard), **Supp. XV:** 282

Salmagundi; or, The Whim-Whams and Opinions of Launcelot Langstaff Esq., and Others (Irving), **II:** 299, 300, 304

Salmon, Edward G., **Supp. XVIII:** 258

Salome (Strauss), **IV:** 316

Salon (online magazine), **Supp. VIII:** 310; **Supp. X:** 202

"Salt"(Crooker), **Supp. XXIII:** 62

Salt Eaters, The (Bambara), **Supp. XI:** 1, **12–14**

Salt Ecstasies, The (White), **Supp. XI:** 123

Salter, James, **Supp. IX: 245–263; Supp. XVI:** 237, 247; **Supp. XIX:** 252

Salter, Mary Jo, **Supp. IV Part 2:** 653; **Supp. IX:** 37, 292; **Supp. XV:** 251, 253; **Supp. XVII:** 112; **Supp. XXIII:** 112

Salt Garden, The (Nemerov), **III:** 269, 272–275, 277

"Salt Garden, The" (Nemerov), **III:** 267–268

Salting the Ocean (Nye, ed.), **Supp. XIII:** 280

"Salt Lesson, The" (C. Frost), **Supp. XV:** 92, 96

"Salt Lesson, The" (C. Frost), **Supp. XV:** 99

"Salts and Oils" (Levine), **Supp. V:** 190

Salt to the Devil (film, Dmytryk), **Supp. XX:** 41

Saltzman, Arthur, **Supp. XIII:** 48

Saltzman, Harry, **Supp. XI:** 307

"Salut au Monde!" (Whitman), **Retro. Supp. I:** 387, 396, 400

"Salute" (MacLeish), **III:** 13

Salute (Shaw), **Supp. XIX:** 244

"Salute to Mister Yates, A" (Dubus), **Supp. XI:** 347, 349

Salute to Spring (Le Sueur), **Supp. XXIII:** 164, 165, 166, 172

Salvador (Didion), **Supp. IV Part 1:** 198, 207–208, 210

"Salvage" (Clampitt), **Supp. IX:** 41

Salvation (Asch), **Supp. XXIII:** 3, 4, **12, 13, 15**

Salvos: An Informal Book About Books and Plays (W. Frank), **Supp. XX: 75**

Samain, Albert, **II:** 528

Same Door, The (Updike), **IV:** 214, 219, 226; **Retro. Supp. I:** 320

"Same in Blues" (Hughes), **Retro. Supp. I:** 208

"Same Kiss After Many Years, The" (Gallagher), **Supp. XXIV:** 169

Same River Twice, The (Offutt), **Supp. XIX:** 163, 164, **167–168,** 175

"Samhain" (A. Finch), **Supp. XVII:** 72

Sam Lawson's Oldtown Fireside Stories (Stowe), **Supp. I Part 2:** 587, 596, 598–599

Sam Patch, the High, Wide & Handsome Jumper (Bontemps and Conroy), **Supp. XXII:** 5, 11

"Sa'm Pèdi" (Bell), **Supp. X:** 17

"Sampler, A" (MacLeish), **III:** 4

Sampoli, Maria, **Supp. V:** 338

Sampson, Edward, **Supp. I Part 2:** 664, 673

Sampson, Martin, **Supp. I Part 2:** 652

"Sam's Dad" (Lamott), **Supp. XX:** 142–143

Sam's Legacy (Neugeboren), **Supp. XVI:** 221, 222

Samson Agonistes (Milton), **III:** 274

"Samson and Delilah" (Masters), **Supp. I Part 2:** 459

Samuel, Maurice, **Supp. XXIII:** 1, 7

Samuel de Champlain: Father of New France (Morison), **Supp. I Part 2:** 496–497

Samuels, Charles Thomas, **Retro. Supp. I:** 334

"Samuel Sewall" (Hecht), **Supp. X:** 58

"Samwheel" (Lamott), **Supp. XX:** 144–145

Sanborn, Franklin B., **IV:** 171, 172, 178

Sanborn, Kate, **Supp. XIII:** 152

Sanborn, Sara, **Supp. XIV:** 113

Sanchez, Carol Anne, **Supp. IV Part 1:** 335

Sanchez, Carol Lee, **Supp. IV Part 2:** 499, 557

Sanchez, Sonia, **Supp. II Part 1:** 34

Sánchez Beras, César, **Supp. XXI:** 100, 104

Sanctified Church, The (Hurston), **Supp. VI:** 150

"Sanction of the Victims, The" (Rand), **Supp. IV Part 2:** 528

Sanctuary (Faulkner), **II:** 57, 61–63, 72, 73, 74, 174; **Retro. Supp. I:** 73, 84, 86–87, 87; **Supp. I Part 2:** 614; **Supp. XII:** 16

"Sanctuary" (Larsen), **Supp. XVIII:** 119, 130–131

Sanctuary (Wharton), **IV:** 311

"Sanctuary" (Wylie), **Supp. I Part 2:** 711

"Sanctuary, The" (Nemerov), **III:** 272, 274

Sanctuary V (Schulberg), **Supp. XVIII:** 254

"Sanctus" (Nelson), **Supp. XVIII:** 183

Sand, George, **II:** 322; **Retro. Supp. I:** 235, 372; **Supp. XV:** 275

"Sandalphon" (Longfellow), **II:** 498

Sand and Foam: A Book of Aphorisms (Gibran), **Supp. XX:** 115, 121–122

Sandbox, The (Albee), **I:** 74–75, 89

Sandburg, Carl, **I:** 103, 109, 384, 421; **II:** 529; **III:** 3, 20, 575–598; **Retro. Supp. I:** 133, 194; **Supp. I Part 1:** 257, 320; **Supp. I Part 2:** 387, 389, 454, 461, 653; **Supp. III Part 1:** 63, 71, 73, 75; **Supp. IV Part 1:** 169; **Supp. IV Part 2:** 502; **Supp. IX:** 1, 15, 308; **Supp. XIII:** 274, 277; **Supp. XV:** 293, 299, 300, 301, 302, 306; **Supp. XXII:** 275; **Supp. XXIII:** 161, 165

Sandburg, Mrs. Carl (Lillian Steichen), **III:** 580

Sandburg, Helga, **III:** 583

Sandburg, Janet, **III:** 583, 584

Sandburg, Margaret, **III:** 583, 584

Sand County Almanac and Sketches Here and There, A (Leopold), **Supp. XIV:** 177, 178, 182–192

"Sand Creek, Colorado"(Kenny), **Supp. XXIII:** 155

"Sand Dabs" (Oliver), **Supp. VII:** 245

"Sand Dunes" (Frost), **Retro. Supp. I:** 137; **Retro. Supp. II:** 41

Sander, August, **Supp. IX:** 211

Sanders, Mark, **Supp. XIX:** 119, 121

Sanders, Scott Russell, **Supp. XVI:** 265–280

Sandlin, Tim, **Supp. XXII:** 114

"Sandman, The" (Barthelme), **Supp. IV Part 1:** 47

Sandman's Dust (Bukiet), **Supp. XVII:** 40, 41

Sando, Joe S., **Supp. IV Part 2:** 510

Sandoe, James, **Supp. IV Part 1:** 131; **Supp. IV Part 2:** 470

Sandoval, Chela, **Supp. XXIII:** 204

Sandoz, Mari, **Supp. XV:** 141; **Supp. XXIII:** 146; **Supp. XXIV:** 243–261

Sandperl, Ira, **Supp. VIII:** 200

"Sand-Quarry and Moving Figures" (Rukeyser), **Supp. VI:** 271, 278

Sand Rivers (Matthiessen), **Supp. V:** 203

"Sand Roses, The" (Hogan), **Supp. IV Part 1:** 401

Sands, Diana, **Supp. IV Part 1:** 362

Sands, Robert, **Supp. I Part 1:** 156, 157

"Sands at Seventy" (Whitman), **IV:** 348

"Sandstone Farmhouse, A" (Updike), **Retro. Supp. I:** 318

Sandy Bottom Orchestra,The (Keillor and Nilsson), **Supp. XVI:** 177

Sanford, John, **IV:** 286, 287

San Francisco (film), **Supp. XVI:** 181, 192

"San Francisco" (Hempel), **Supp. XXI:** 118

"San Francisco Blues" (Kerouac), **Supp. III Part 1:** 225

Sangamon County Peace Advocate, The (Lindsay), **Supp. I Part 2:** 379

Sanger, Margaret, **Supp. I Part 1:** 19; **Supp. XXI:** 6; **Supp. XXIII:** 161

Sankofa (film), **Supp. XX:** 154

Sansom, William, **IV:** 279

Sans Soleil (film), **Supp. IV Part 2:** 436

"Santa" (Sexton), **Supp. II Part 2:** 693

Santa Claus: A Morality (Cummings), **I:** 430, 441

"Santa Fe, New Mexico"(Kenny), **Supp. XXIII:** 150

"Santa Fé Trail, The" (Lindsay), **Supp. I Part 2:** 389

"Santa Lucia" (Hass), **Supp. VI:** 105–106

"Santa Lucia II" (Hass), **Supp. VI:** 105–106

Santayana, George, **I:** 222, 224, 236, 243, 253, 460; **II:** 20, 542; **III:** 64, 599–622; **IV:** 26, 339, 351, 353, 441; **Retro. Supp. I:** 55, 57, 67, 295; **Retro. Supp. II:** 179; **Supp. I Part 2:** 428; **Supp. II Part 1:** 107; **Supp. X:** 58; **Supp. XIV:** 199, 335, 340, 342; **Supp. XVI:** 189; **Supp. XVII:** 97, 106; **Supp. XX:** 228, 229, 231

Santiago, Esmeralda, **Supp. XI:** 177

"Santorini: Stopping the Leak" (Merrill), **Supp. III Part 1:** 336

Santos, John Phillip, **Supp. XIII:** 274

Santos, Sherod, **Supp. VIII:** 270

Sapir, Edward, **Supp. VIII:** 295; **Supp. XVI:** 283

"Sapphics for Patience" (A. Finch), **Supp. XVII:** 72

Sapphira and the Slave Girl (Cather), **I:** 331; **Retro. Supp. I:** 2, 19–20

Sappho, **II:** 544; **III:** 142; **Supp. I Part 1:** 261, 269; **Supp. I Part 2:** 458; **Supp. XII:** 98, 99; **Supp. XVII:** 74

"Sappho" (Wright), **Supp. III Part 2:** 595, 604

"Sappho, Keats"(Hadas), **Supp. XXIII:** 113

"Sara" (song, Dylan), **Supp. XVIII:** 28

"Sarah" (Schwartz), **Supp. II Part 2:** 663

Sarah; or, The Exemplary Wife (Rowson), **Supp. XV:** 242

"Saratoga" mysteries (Dobyns), **Supp. XIII:** 79–80

Sargent, John Singer, **II:** 337, 338; **Supp. XX:** 231

Sarlós, Robert K., **Supp. XXI:** 7, 12, 13

Saroyan, Aram, **Supp. XV:** 182

Saroyan, William, **III:** 146–147; **IV:** 393; **Supp. I Part 2:** 679; **Supp. IV Part 1:** 83; **Supp. IV Part 2:** 502; **Supp. XIII:** 280; **Supp. XXIII:** 20

Sarris, Greg, **Supp. IV Part 1:** 329, 330

Sarton, George, **Supp. VIII:** 249

Sarton, May, **Supp. III Part 1:** 62, 63; **Supp. VIII:** 249–268; **Supp. XIII:** 296; **Supp. XVII:** 71

Sartoris (Faulkner), **II:** 55, 56–57, 58, 62; **Retro. Supp. I:** 77, 81, 82, 83, 88

Sartor Resartus (Carlyle), **II:** 26; **III:** 82

Sartre, Jean-Paul, **I:** 82, 494; **II:** 57, 244; **III:** 51, 204, 292, 453, 619; **IV:** 6, 223, 236, 477, 487, 493; **Retro. Supp. I:** 73; **Supp. I Part 1:** 51; **Supp. IV Part 1:** 42, 84; **Supp. VIII:** 11; **Supp. IX:** 4; **Supp. XIII:** 74, 171; **Supp. XIV:** 24; **Supp. XVII:** 137; **Supp. XXIV:** 281

Sassone, Ralph, **Supp. X:** 171

Sassoon, Siegfried, **II:** 367; **Supp. XV:** 308; **Supp. XIX:** 18

Satan in Goray (Singer), **IV:** 1, 6–7, 12; **Retro. Supp. II:** 303, 304–305

Satan Says (Olds), **Supp. X:** 201, 202, 202–204, 215

"Satan Says" (Olds), **Supp. X:** 202; **Supp. XVII:** 114

Satanstoe (Cooper), **I:** 351–352, 355

"Sather Gate Illumination" (Ginsberg), **Supp. II Part 1:** 329

"Satire as a Way of Seeing" (Dos Passos), **III:** 172

Satires of Persius, The (Merwin, trans.), **Supp. III Part 1:** 347

Satirical Rogue on Poetry, The (Francis). *See Pot Shots at Poetry* (Francis)

Satori in Paris (Kerouac), **Supp. III Part 1:** 231

"Saturday" (Salinas), **Supp. XIII:** 315

"Saturday Matinee" (Trethewey), **Supp. XXI:** 251

Saturday Night at the War (Shanley), **Supp. XIV:** 315

"Saturday Rain" (Kees), **Supp. XV:** 136

"Saturday Route, The" (Wolfe), **Supp. III Part 2:** 580

Satyagraha (Gandhi), **IV:** 185

"Satyr's Heart, The" (B. Kelly), **Supp. XVII:** 132

Saucedo, José Guadalupe, **Supp. XXIII:** 197

Saul and Patsy (C. Baxter), **Supp. XVII:** 22–23

"Saul and Patsy" (C. Baxter), **Supp. XVII:** 17

"Saul and Patsy Are Getting Comfortable in Michigan" (C. Baxter), **Supp. XVII:** 22

"Saul and Patsy Are in Labor" (C. Baxter), **Supp. XVII:** 20, 22

"Saul and Patsy Are Pregnant" (C. Baxter), **Supp. XVII:** 22

Saunders, George, **Supp. XIX:** 223–237; **Supp. XXII:** 49; **Supp. XXIV:** 199

Saunders, Richard, **II:** 110

Savage, Augusta, **Retro. Supp. II:** 115

Savage, James, **II:** 111

Savage, Tom, **Supp. XXIV:** 45

Savage Holiday (Wright), **IV:** 478, 488

Savage in Limbo: A Concert Play (Shanley), **Supp. XIV:** 315, 319–321, 323, 324

Savage Love (Shepard and Chaikin), **Supp. III Part 2:** 433

Savage Place, A (Parker), **Supp. XIX:** 185

Savage Wilds (Reed), **Supp. X:** 241

Save Me, Joe Louis (Bell), **Supp. X:** 7, 10, **11–12**

Save Me the Waltz (Z. Fitzgerald), **II:** 95; **Retro. Supp. I:** 110; **Supp. IX:** 58, 59, 65, **66–68**

Savers, Michael, **Supp. XI:** 307

Saving Lives (Goldbarth), **Supp. XII:** 192

Saving Private Ryan (film), **Supp. V:** 249; **Supp. XI:** 234

Savings (Hogan), **Supp. IV Part 1:** 397, 404, 405, 406, 410

Saving Sebastian (Taylor), **Supp. XXIII:** 57

Savo, Jimmy, **I:** 440

Savran, David, **Supp. IX:** 145; **Supp. XIII:** 209; **Supp. XV:** 321; **Supp. XXIV:** 263, 264

"Sawdust" (Offutt), **Supp. XIX:** 164

Sawyer-Lauçanno, Christopher, **Supp. IV Part 1:** 95

Saxon, Lyle, **Retro. Supp. I:** 80

"Saxophone" (Di Piero), **Supp. XIX:** 38

"Sax's and Selves" (Halliday), **Supp. XIX:** 88

"Say All" (Ray), **Supp. XVIII:** 193

Say and Seal (S. and A. Warner), **Supp. XVIII:** 258, 266

Saye and Sele, Lord, **Supp. I Part 1:** 98

Sayer, Mandy, **Supp. XIII:** 118

Sayers, Dorothy, **Supp. IV Part 1:** 341; **Supp. IV Part 2:** 464

Sayers, Valerie, **Supp. XI:** 253; **Supp. XVIII:** 99

"Say Good-bye" (Weigl), **Supp. XIX:** 288

"Sayings/For Luck" (Goldbarth), **Supp. XII:** 176

"Saying What Needs To Be Said" (Skloot), **Supp. XX: 201**

Say! Is This the U.S.A.? (Caldwell), **I:** 293, 294–295, 304, 309, 310

Saylor, Bruce, **Supp. XII:** 253

Sayre, Joel, **Supp. XIII:** 166

Sayre, Nora, **Supp. XII:** 119

Sayre, Zelda, **Retro. Supp. I:** 101, 102–103, 104, 105, 108, 109, 110, 113, 114. *See also* Fitzgerald, Zelda (Zelda Sayre)

"Say Yes" (Wolff), **Supp. VII:** 344

"Say You Love Me" (Peacock), **Supp. XIX:** 198

Scafe, Suzanne, **Supp. XXIII:** 94, 95

"Scale" (Halliday), **Supp. XIX:** 92

"Scales of the Eyes, The" (Nemerov), **III:** 272, 273, 277

Scalpel (McCoy), **Supp. XIII: 174–175**

Scalpel (screen treatment, McCoy), **Supp. XIII:** 174

Scandalabra (Zelda Fitzgerald), **Supp. IX:** 60, 61, 65, 67, **68–70**

"Scandal Detectives, The" (Fitzgerald), **II:** 80–81; **Retro. Supp. I:** 99

Scarberry-García, Susan, **Supp. IV Part 2:** 486

Scarborough, Dorothy, **Supp. XVIII:** 279–280

Scarecrow, The (Connelly), **Supp. XXI:** 71, 74, 78, **79**

"Scarecrow, The" (Farrell), **II:** 45

"Scarf, A" (Shields), **Supp. VII:** 328

Scarlet Cabinet, The (Notley), **Supp. XXII:** 233

Scarlet Letter, The (Hawthorne), **II:** 63, 223, 224, 231, 233, 239–240, 241, 243, 244, 255, 264, 286, 290, 291, 550; **Retro. Supp. I:** 63, 145, 147, 152, **157–159**, 160, 163, 165, 220, 248, 330, 335; **Retro. Supp. II:** 100; **Supp. I Part 1:** 38; **Supp. II Part 1:** 386; **Supp. VIII:** 108, 198; **Supp. XII:** 11; **Supp. XVII:** 143; **Supp. XX: 178, 183; Supp. XXII:** 147

"Scarlet Letter Aleph, The" (Mirvis), **Supp. XX: 183**

Scarlet Plague, The (London), **II:** 467

Scarlet Sister Mary (Peterkin), **Supp. XXII:** 189

Scar Lover (Crews), **Supp. XI:** 103, 107, **114–115**

"Scarred Girl, The" (Dickey), **Supp. IV Part 1:** 180

Scates, Maxine, **Supp. XIV:** 264, 265, 274

"Scenario" (H. Miller), **III:** 184

"Scene" (Howells), **II:** 274

"Scene in Jerusalem, A" (Stowe), **Supp. I Part 2:** 587

"Scenes" (Shields), **Supp. VII:** 318

Scènes d'Anabase (chamber music) (Bowles), **Supp. IV Part 1:** 82

"Scenes from a Documentary History of Mississippi" (Trethewey), **Supp. XXI:** 255–256

Scenes from American Life (Gurney), **Supp. V:** 95, 96, 105, 108

Scenes from Another Life (McClatchy), **Supp. XII: 255–256**

"Scenes from Childhood" (W. V. Davis), **Supp. XXI:** 95

"Scenes of Childhood" (Merrill), **Supp. III Part 1:** 322, 323, 327

"Scented Herbage of My Breast" (Whitman), **IV:** 342–343

"Scent of a Woman's Ink" (Prose), **Supp. XVI:** 259

"Scent of Unbought Flowers, The" (Ríos), **Supp. IV Part 2:** 547

Scepticisms (Aiken), **I:** 58

Scève, Maurice, **Supp. III Part 1:** 11

Schad, Christian, **Supp. IV Part 1:** 247

Schafer, Benjamin G., **Supp. XIV:** 144

Schafer, William, **Supp. XIX:** 164, 172

Schaller, George, **Supp. V:** 208, 210–211

Schapiro, Meyer, **II:** 30

Scharmann, Hermann Balthazar, **Supp. XII:** 41

Scharper, Alice, **Supp. XXII:** 175

Scharper, Diane, **Supp. XXIII:** 134

Schary, Dore, **Supp. IV Part 1:** 365; **Supp. XIII:** 163

Schatz, Tom, **Supp. XVIII:** 242

Schaum, Melita, **Supp. XXII:** 166

Schaumbergh, Count de, **II:** 120

Schechner, Richard, **Supp. XXIV:** 116

Scheele, Roy, **Supp. XVI:** 54; **Supp. XXI:** 103

Scheeman, George, **Supp. XXII:** 230

Scheffauer, G. H., **I:** 199

"Scheherazade" (Ashbery), **Supp. III Part 1:** 18

Scheick, William, **Supp. V:** 272

Schelberg, Budd, **Supp. XVIII: 241–256**

Scheler, Max, **I:** 58

Schelling, Friedrich, **Supp. I Part 2:** 422

Schenck, Joseph, **Supp. XVI:** 186

Schenk, Margaret, **I:** 199

Scheponik, Peter, **Supp. X:** 210

Scherer, Loline, **Supp. XIII:** 161

"Scherzo"(Hadas), **Supp. XXIII:** 113

Schevill, James, **I:** 116

Schickel, Richard, **Supp. XV:** 1

Schifano, Mario, **Supp. XXIII:** 217

Schifano, Paul, **Supp. I Part 2:** 622

Schildkraut, Rudolph, **Supp. XXIII:** 8

Schiller, Andrew, **II:** 20

Schiller, Frederick, **Supp. V:** 290

Schiller, Johann Christoph Friedrich von, **I:** 224; **Supp. IV Part 2:** 519; **Supp. XVI:** 292

Schiller, Lawrence, **Retro. Supp. II:** 208, 212, 214

Schimmel, Harold, **Supp. V:** 336

"Schizoid Nature of the Implied Author in Twentieth-Century American Ethnic Novels, The" (Nelson), **Supp. XVIII:** 172

Schjeldahl, Peter, **Supp. XXIV:** 44

Schlegel, Augustus Wilhelm, **III:** 422, 424

Schlegell, David von, **Supp. IV Part 2:** 423

Schleiermacher, Friedrich, **III:** 290–291, 309

Schleifer, Ronald, **Supp. XVIII:** 144

Schlepping Through the Alps (S. Apple), **Supp. XVII:** 8

Schlesinger, Arthur, Jr., **III:** 291, 297–298, 309

Schleuning, Neala, **Supp. XXIII:** 165

Schmidt, Jon Zlotnik, **Supp. IV Part 1:** 2

Schmidt, Kaspar. *See* Stirner, Max

Schmidt, Michael, **Supp. X:** 55

Schmitt, Carl, **I:** 386–387

Schmitz, Neil, **Supp. X:** 243

Schnackenberg, Gjertrud, **Supp. XV: 249–268**

Schneeman, George, **Supp. XXIV:** 41

Schneider, Alan, **I:** 87

Schneider, Louis, **Supp. I Part 2:** 650

Schneider, Romy, **Supp. IV Part 2:** 549

Schneider, Steven, **Supp. IX:** 271, 274

Schnellock, Emil, **III:** 177

Schneour, Zalman, **IV:** 11

"Schnetzer Day" (Halliday), **Supp. XIX:** 93

Schnitzler, Arthur, **Supp. XV:** 307; **Supp. XVI:** 187

Schoerke, Meg, **Supp. XVII:** 110

"Scholar Gypsy, The" (Arnold), **II:** 541

"Scholastic and Bedside Teaching" (Holmes), **Supp. I Part 1:** 305

Schöler, Bo, **Supp. IV Part 1:** 399, 400, 403, 407, 409; **Supp. IV Part 2:** 499

Scholes, Robert, **Supp. V:** 40, 42

Scholtz, Carter, **Supp. XVIII:** 144

Schomburg, Arthur, **Supp. X:** 134; **Supp. XXII:** 6

Schomburg Library of Nineteenth-Century Black Women Writers (H. L. Gates, ed.), **Supp. XX: 105**

Schönberg, Claude-Michel, **Supp. XXI:** 155

Schoolboy Howlers (Abingdon), **Supp. XVI:** 99

Schoolcraft, Henry Rowe, **II:** 503; **Retro. Supp. II:** 160; **Supp. XXIII:** 223, 227, 228, 232, 233–234

Schoolcraft, Jane Johnston (Bamewawagezhikaquay), **Supp. XXIII: 223–238**

"School Daze" (Bambara), **Supp. XI:** 19

School Daze (film), **Supp. XI:** 19, 20

"Schoolhouse" (Levis), **Supp. XI:** 258

"School of Giorgione, The" (Pater), **I:** 51

"School Play, The" (Merrill), **Supp. III Part 1:** 336

"Schooner Fairchild's Class" (Benét), **Supp. XI:** 55

Schopenhauer, Arthur, **III:** 600, 604; **IV:** 7; **Retro. Supp. I:** 256; **Retro. Supp. II:** 94; **Supp. I Part 1:** 320; **Supp. I Part 2:** 457; **Supp. X:** 187; **Supp. XVI:** 184

Schorer, Mark, **II:** 28; **III:** 71; **Retro. Supp. I:** 115; **Supp. IV Part 1:** 197, 203, 211; **Supp. XVI:** 206

Schott, Penelope Scambly, **Supp. XXIII: 239–256**

Schott, Webster, **Supp. IX:** 257

Schotts, Jeffrey, **Supp. XII:** 193

Schrader, Mary von. *See* Jarrell, Mrs. Randall (Mary von Schrader)

Schreiber, Jan, **Supp. XXI:** 105, 111

Schreiner, Olive, **I:** 419; **Supp. XI:** 203

Schroeder, Eric James, **Supp. V:** 238, 244

Schubert, Bernard L., **Supp. XVII:** 58

Schubert, David, **Supp. XXIV:** 45

Schubert, Franz Peter, **Supp. I Part 1:** 363

Schubnell, Matthias, **Supp. IV Part 2:** 486

Schudel, Matt, **Supp. XXII:** 205, 214

Schulberg, Budd, **II:** 98; **Retro. Supp. I:** 113; **Supp. XIII:** 170; **Supp. XV:** 194

Schulberg, Stuart, **Supp. XVIII:** 254

Schulman, Grace, **Supp. XXIII:** 58

Schulman, Tom, **Supp. XXI:** 193, 194

Schulz, Bruno, **Supp. IV Part 2:** 623; **Supp. XVII:** 41

Schuman, William, **Supp. XII:** 253; **Supp. XXII:** 283

Schumann, Dr. Alanson Tucker, **III:** 505

Schuster, Edgar H., **Supp. VIII:** 126

Schuyler, George S., **III:** 110; **Supp. XVI:** 142; **Supp. XIX:** 78

Schuyler, James, **Supp. XV:** 177, 178; **Supp. XXIII:** 207, 212, 215, 217; **Supp. XXIV:** 33

Schuyler, William, **Supp. I Part 1:** 211

"Schuylkill, The" (Halliday), **Supp. XIX:** 92

Schwartz, Delmore, **I:** 67, 168, 188, 288; **IV:** 128, 129, 437; **Retro. Supp. II:** 29, 178; **Supp. II Part 1:** 102, 109; **Supp. II Part 2: 639–668; Supp. VIII:** 98; **Supp. IX:** 299; **Supp. XIII:** 320; **Supp. XIV:** 3; **Supp. XV:** 184; **Supp. XIX:** 257

Schwartz, Leonard, **Supp. XVI:** 289

Schwartz, Lloyd, **Supp. I Part 1:** 81; **Supp. XXIV:** 160

Schwartz, Marilyn, **Supp. XII:** 126, 128, 130, 132

Schwartz, Meryl F., **Supp. XXII:** 65, 66

Schwartz, Richard B., **Supp. XIV:** 23, 27

Schwarz, A. B. Christa, **Supp. XIX:** 77, 79

Schwed, Peter, **Supp. XXII:** 119

Schweitzer, Albert, **Supp. IV Part 1:** 373

Schweitzer, Harold, **Supp. X:** 210

Schwerdt, Lisa M., **Supp. XIV:** 155, 171

Schwitters, Kurt, **III:** 197; **Retro. Supp. II:** 322, 331, 336; **Supp. IV Part 1:** 79

"Science" (Jeffers), **Supp. II Part 2:** 426

Science and Health with Key to the Scriptures (Eddy), **I:** 383

"Science Favorable to Virtue" (Freneau), **Supp. II Part 1:** 274

Science of English Verse, The (Lanier), **Supp. I Part 1:** 368, 369

"Science of the Night, The" (Kunitz), **Supp. III Part 1:** 258, 265

"Sci-Fi Floater Genius" (Halliday), **Supp. XIX:** 91

Sciolino, Martina, **Supp. XII:** 9

"Scissors" (C. Baxter), **Supp. XVII:** 19

Scofield, Sandra, **Supp. XXI:** 119

Scooter tetralogy (Murray). *See Magic Keys, The* (Murray); *Seven League Boots, The* (Murray); *Spyglass Tree, The* (Murray); *Train Whistle Guitar* (Murray)

Scopes, John T., **III:** 105, 495

"Scorched Face, The" (Hammett), **Supp. IV Part 1:** 344

"Scorn" (C. Frost), **Supp. XV:** 105

"Scorpion, The" (Bowles), **Supp. IV Part 1:** 84, 86

Scorsese, Martin, **Supp. IV Part 1:** 356; **Supp. XVIII:** 22

Scott, Anne Firor, **Supp. I Part 1:** 19

Scott, A. O., **Supp. X:** 301, 302; **Supp. XII:** 343

Scott, Evelyn, **Retro. Supp. I:** 73; **Supp. XXII:** 198

Scott, Gavin, **Supp. XXII:** 218

Scott, George C., **III:** 165–166; **Supp. XI:** 304

Scott, George Lewis, **Supp. I Part 2:** 503, 504

Scott, Hazel, **Supp. XXII:** 12

Scott, Herbert, **Supp. V:** 180

Scott, Howard, **Supp. I Part 2:** 645

Scott, Joanna, **Supp. XVII: 183–197**

Scott, Lizabeth, **Supp. IV Part 2:** 524

Scott, Lynn Orilla, **Retro. Supp. II:** 12

Scott, Mark, **Retro. Supp. I:** 127

Scott, Nathan A., Jr., **II:** 27

Scott, Paul, **Supp. IV Part 2:** 690

Scott, Ridley, **Supp. XIII:** 268

Scott, Walter, **Supp. XVI:** 7, 13

Scott, Sir Walter, **I:** 204, 339, 341, 343, 354; **II:** 8, 17, 18, 217, 296, 301, 303, 304, 308; **III:** 415, 482; **IV:** 204, 453; **Retro. Supp. I:** 99; **Supp. I Part 2:** 579, 580, 685, 692; **Supp. IV Part 2:** 690; **Supp. IX:** 175; **Supp. X:** 51, 114

Scott, Winfield Townley, **II:** 512; **Supp. I Part 2:** 705; **Supp. XV:** 51

Scottsboro boys, **I:** 505; **Supp. I Part 1:** 330

Scottsboro Limited (Hughes), **Retro. Supp. I:** 203; **Supp. I Part 1:** 328, 330–331, 332

Scoundrel Time (Hellman), **Supp. I Part 1:** 294–297; **Supp. IV Part 1:** 12; **Supp. VIII:** 243

Scrambled Eggs Super! (Geisel), **Supp. XVI:** 105

Scrambled Eggs & Whiskey: Poems, 1991–1995 (Carruth), **Supp. XVI:** 47

Scratch (MacLeish), **III:** 22–23

"Scratch Music" (Wright), **Supp. XV:** 343

"Scream, The" (Lowell), **II:** 550

"Screamer, The" (Coleman), **Supp. XI: 92–93**

"Screamers, The" (Baraka), **Supp. II Part 1:** 38

"Screen Guide for Americans" (Rand), **Supp. IV Part 2:** 524

"Screen Memory" (Cliff), **Supp. XXII:** 75

"Screeno" (Schwartz), **Supp. II Part 2:** 660

Screens, The (Genet), **Supp. XII:** 12

Screen Sirens Scream! (Parla and Mitchell), **Supp. XXII:** 256

Scribblers on the Roof: Contemporary American Jewish Fiction (Bukiet and Roskies, eds.), **Supp. XVII:** 39, 49–50

Scripts for the Pageant (Merrill), **Supp. III Part 1:** 332, 333, 335

Scrolls from the Dead Sea, The (Wilson), **IV:** 429

Scruggs, Earl, **Supp. V:** 335

Scudder, Horace Elisha, **II:** 400, 401; **Retro. Supp. II:** 67; **Supp. I Part 1:** 220; **Supp. I Part 2:** 410, 414

Scully, James, **Supp. XII:** 131

"Sculpting the Whistle" (Ríos), **Supp. IV Part 2:** 549

"Sculptor" (Plath), **Supp. I Part 2:** 538

"Sculptor's Funeral, The" (Cather), **I:** 315–316; **Retro. Supp. I:** 5, 6; **Supp. XV:** 40

Scum (Singer), **Retro. Supp. II:** 316–317

Scupoli, Lorenzo, **IV:** 156

"Scythe Song" (Lang), **Retro. Supp. I:** 128

Sea and the Mirror, The: A Commentary on Shakespeare's "The Tempest" (Auden), *Supp. II Part 1:* 2, 18

Sea around Us, The (Carson), **Supp. IX:** 19, **23–25**

Sea around Us, The (film), **Supp. IX:** 25

Sea Birds Are Still Alive, The (Bambara), **Supp. XI:** 1, 4, **7–12**

"Sea Birds Are Still Alive, The" (Bambara), **Supp. XI:** 8

"Sea-Blue and Blood-Red" (Lowell), **II:** 524

Seabrook, John, **Supp. VIII:** 157

"Sea Burial from the Cruiser Reve" (Eberhart), **I:** 532–533

Seabury, David, **Supp. I Part 2:** 608

"Sea Calm" (Hughes), **Retro. Supp. I:** 199

"Sea Chanty" (Corso), **Supp. XII:** 118

"Sea Dream, A" (Whitter), **Supp. I Part 2:** 699

"Seafarer, The" (Pound, trans.), **Retro. Supp. I:** 287

Seagall, Harry, **Supp. XIII:** 166

Sea Garden (Doolittle), **Supp. I Part 1:** 257, 259, 266, 269, 272

Seager, Allan, **IV:** 305

Seagull on the Step, The (Boyle), **Supp. XXIV:** 60, 62

"Seagulls and Children" (C. Frost), **Supp. XV:** 95

Sea Lady, The (Boyce), **Supp. XXI:** 8, 13

"Sea Lily" (Doolittle), **Supp. I Part 1:** 266

Sea Lions, The (Cooper), **I:** 354, 355

Sealts, Merton M., Jr., **Retro. Supp. I:** 257

Seaman, Benjamin, **Supp. XXIII:** 69–70, 72

Seaman, Donna, **Supp. VIII:** 86; **Supp. X:** 1, 4, 12, 16, 213; **Supp. XV:** 65; **Supp. XVIII:** 102; **Supp. XIX:** 53, 55, 57, 58, 59, 60, 61; **Supp. XXI:** 236; **Supp. XXII:** 266; **Supp. XXIII:** 71, 74, 134, 135, 298; **Supp. XXIV:** 167, 171

"Seamy Side, The"(Hadas), **Supp. XXIII:** 119

"Séance, The" (Singer), **IV:** 20

Séance and Other Stories, The (Singer), **IV:** 19–21

"Sea Oak" (Saunders), **Supp. XIX:** 228, 229, 231

Sea of Cortez (Steinbeck), **IV:** 52, 54, 62, 69

Sea of Grass, The (film), **Supp. XVIII:** 211

Sea of Grass, The (Richter), **Supp. XVIII:** **210–211,** 215–216, 217, 220

"Sea Pieces" (Melville), **III:** 93

Searchers, The (film, Ford), **Supp. XVIII:** 57, 58, 135–136, 141

Searches and Seizures (Elkin), **Supp. VI: 49**

"Search for Southern Identity, The" (Woodward), **Retro. Supp. I:** 75; **Supp. XXII:** 194

Search for the King, A: A Twelfth-Century Legend (Vidal), **Supp. IV Part 2:** 681

Searching for Caleb (Tyler), **Supp. IV Part 2:** 663–665, 671

"Searching for Poetry: Real *vs.* Fake" (B. Miller), **Supp. IV Part 1:** 67

Searching for Survivors (Banks), **Supp. V:** 7

"Searching for Survivors (I)" (Banks), **Supp. V:** 8

"Searching for Survivors (II)" (Banks), **Supp. V:** 7, 8

Searching for the Ox (Simpson), **Supp. IX:** 266, **274–275**

"Searching for the Ox" (Simpson), **Supp. IX:** 275, 280

"Searching in the Britannia Tavern" (Wagoner), **Supp. IX:** 327

Searching Wing, The, (Hellman), **Supp. I Part 1:** 277, 278, 281–282, 283, 292, 297

Search-Light. *See* Frank, Waldo

"Search Party, The" (Matthews), **Supp. IX: 156**

Searle, Ronald, **Supp. I Part 2:** 604, 605

Sea Road to the Indies (Hart), **Supp. XIV:** 97

"Seascape" (Bishop), **Retro. Supp. II:** 42–43

"Sea's Green Sameness, The" (Updike), **IV:** 217

Seaside and the Fireside, The (Longfellow), **II:** 489; **Retro. Supp. II:** 159, 168

Season in Hell, A (Rimbaud), **III:** 189

Seasons, The (Thomson), **II:** 304; **Supp. I Part 1:** 151

Seasons' Difference, The (Buechner), **Supp. XII:** 47

Seasons of Celebration (Merton), **Supp. VIII:** 199, 208

Seasons of the Heart: In Quest of Faith (Kinard, comp.), **Supp. XIV:** 127

"Seasons of the Soul" (Tate), **IV:** 136–140

Seasons on Earth (Koch), **Supp. XV: 183–184**

"Sea Surface Full of Clouds" (Stevens), **IV:** 82

"Sea Tides" (Hoffman), **Supp. XVIII:** 87

"Sea Treader" (Hoffman), **Supp. XVIII:** 87

"Sea Unicorns and Land Unicorns" (Moore), **III:** 202–203

Seaver, Richard, **Supp. XI:** 301

"Seaweed" (Longfellow), **II:** 498

Sea-Wolf, The (London), **II:** 264, 466, 472–473

Sebald, W. G., **Supp. XIV:** 96; **Supp. XXI:** 92

Sebold, Alice, **Supp. XXII:** 55

Seckler, David, **Supp. I Part 2:** 650

"2nd Air Force" (Jarrell), **II:** 375

Second American Revolution and Other Essays (1976–1982), The (Vidal), **Supp. IV Part 2:** 679, 687, 688

Secondary Colors, The (A. Theroux), **Supp. VIII:** 312

Second Avenue (O'Hara), **Supp. XXIII:** 216

"Second Avenue"(O'Hara), **Supp. XXIII:** 208, 211, 218

Second Blush, The (Peacock), **Supp. XIX:** 197, **205–206**

Second Chance (Auchincloss), **Supp. IV Part 1:** 33

"Second Chances" (Hugo), **Supp. VI:** 144, 145

Second Coming, The (Percy), **Supp. III Part 1:** 383, 384, 387, 388, 396–397

"Second Coming, The" (Yeats), **III:** 294; **Retro. Supp. I:** 290, 311; **Supp. VIII:** 24; **Supp. XVI:** 159; **Supp. XIX:** 85

Second Decade, The. See Stephen King, The Second Decade: "Danse Macabre" to "The Dark Half" (Magistrale)

Second Dune, The (Hearon), **Supp. VIII:** 58, **59–60**

Second Flowering, A: Works and Days of the Lost Generation (Cowley), **Retro. Supp. II:** 77; **Supp. II Part 1:** 135, 141, 143, 144, 147, 149

Second Growth (Stegner), **Supp. IV Part 2:** 599, 608

"Second Hour of the Night, The" (Bidart), **Supp. XV:** 32, **33–34**

Second Marriage (F. Barthelme), **Supp. XI:** 32, 33

"Second Marriage" (McCarriston), **Supp. XIV:** 262

"Second Mortgage" (Shaw), **Supp. XIX:** 245–246

Second Nature (Hoffman), **Supp. X:** 88, 89

Seconds, The (Bierds), **Supp. XVII: 33–34**

Second Set, The (Komunyakaa and Feinstein, eds.), **Supp. XIII:** 125

Second Sex, The (Beauvoir), **Supp. IV Part 1:** 360

"Second Sight" (Mosher), **Supp. XXII:** 214

Second Stone, The (Fiedler), **Supp. XIII:** 102

"Second Swimming, The" (Boyle), **Supp. VIII:** 13, 14

Second Tree from the Corner (White), **Supp. I Part 2:** 654

"Second Tree from the Corner" (White), **Supp. I Part 2:** 651

Second Twenty Years at Hull-House, The: September 1909 to September 1929, with a Record of a Growing World Consciousness (Addams), **Supp. I Part 1:** 24–25

Second Voyage of Columbus, The (Morison), **Supp. I Part 2:** 488

Second Words, (Atwood), **Supp. XIII:** 35

Second World, The (Blackmur), **Supp. II Part 1:** 91

Secret, The (E. Hoffman), **Supp. XVI:** 151, **155–158,** 161

"Secret, The" (Levine), **Supp. V:** 195

Secret Agent, The (Conrad), **Supp. IV Part 1:** 341

Secret Agent X-9 (Hammett), **Supp. IV Part 1:** 355

"Secret Courts of Men's Hearts, The: Code and Law in Harper Lee's *To Kill a Mockingbird*" (Johnson), **Supp. VIII:** 126

"Secret Dog, The" (Cameron), **Supp. XII: 83–84**

Secret Garden, The (Burnett), **Supp. I Part 1:** 44

"Secret Garden, The" (Hoffman), **Supp. XVIII:** 86

"Secret Gladness, A" (C. Frost), **Supp. XV:** 91

Secret Historie (J. Smith), **I:** 131

Secret History of the Dividing Line (Howe), **Supp. IV Part 2:** 424, 425–426

"Secret Integration, The" (Pynchon), **Supp. II Part 2:** 624

"Secret Life of Musical Instruments, The" (Wright), **Supp. XV:** 343

"Secret Life of Walter Mitty, The" (Thurber), **Supp. I Part 2:** 623; **Supp. XVI:** 233

"Secret Lion, The" (Ríos), **Supp. IV Part 2:** 543, 544

"Secret Nature of the Mechanical Rabbit, The"(P. Benedict), **Supp. XXIII:** 49

"Secret Ocean, The" (Jarman), **Supp. XVII:** 120

Secret of Poetry, The: Essays (Jarman), **Supp. XVII:** 110, 111, 120

"Secret of the Russian Ballet, The" (Van Vechten), **Supp. II Part 2:** 732

"Secret Prune" (Ríos), **Supp. IV Part 2:** 549

Secret River, The (Rawlings), **Supp. X:** 233

Secrets and Surprises (Beattie), **Supp. V:** 23, 27, 29

Secrets from the Center of the World (Harjo), **Supp. XII: 223–224**

"Secret Sharer, The" (Conrad), **Supp. IX:** 105

"Secret Sharer, The" (J. Conrad), **Supp. XVI:** 158

"Secret Society, A" (Nemerov), **III:** 282

Secrets of the Heart (Gibran), **Supp. XX: 116**

Secrets of the Universe: Scenes from the Journey Home (Sanders), **Supp. XVI:** 273–274

"Secular" (Trethewey), **Supp. XXI:** 249

Secular Journal of Thomas Merton, The, **Supp. VIII:** 206

"Security" (Boyle), **Supp. XXIV:** 58

"Security" (Stafford), **Supp. XI:** 329

"Security"(Strout), **Supp. XXIII:** 283

Sedaris, David, **Supp. XXIII:** 289

Sedges, John (pseudonym). *See* Buck, Pearl S.

Sedgwick, Catherine Maria, **I:** 341; **Supp. I Part 1:** 155, 157

Sedgwick, Christina. *See* Marquand, Mrs. John P. (Christina Sedgwick)

Sedgwick, Ellery, **I:** 217, 229, 231; **III:** 54–55

Sedgwick, Eve, **Supp. XX: 267**

Sedgwick, Henry, **Supp. I Part 1:** 156

Sedgwick, Robert, **Supp. I Part 1:** 156

Sedore, Timothy, **Supp. XIV:** 312

"Seduction and Betrayal" (Hardwick), **Supp. III Part 1:** 207

Seduction and Betrayal: Women and Literature (Hardwick), **Supp. III Part 1:** 194, 204, 206–208, 212, 213; **Supp. XIV:** 89

See, Carolyn, **Supp. XXII:** 206, 217

Seed, David, **Supp. IV Part 1:** 391

"Seed Eaters, The" (Francis), **Supp. IX:** 82

"Seed Leaves" (Wilbur), **Supp. III Part 2:** 558

"Seeds" (Anderson), **I:** 106, 114

Seeds of Contemplation (Merton), **Supp. VIII:** 199, 200, 207, 208

Seeds of Destruction (Merton), **Supp. VIII:** 202, 203, 204, 208

"Seeing Red" (column, Ryan as Quin), **Supp. XVIII:** 226

"See(k)ing the Self: Mirrors and Mirroring in Bicultural Texts" (Oster), **Supp. XVI:** 151

Seeing through the Sun (Hogan), **Supp. IV Part 1:** 397, 400, 401–402, 402, 413

"See in the Midst of Fair Leaves" (Moore), **III:** 215

"Seekers, The" (McGrath), **Supp. X:** 117

"Seeking a Vision of Truth, Guided by a Higher Power" (Burke), **Supp. XIV:** 21, 23

"Seele im Raum" (Jarrell), **II:** 382–383

"Seele im Raum" (Rilke), **II:** 382–383

"See Naples and Die" (Hecht), **Supp. X:** 69, 70

"Seen from the 'L' " (Barnes), **Supp. III Part 1:** 33

"See the Moon?" (Barthelme), **Supp. IV Part 1:** 42, 49–50, 50

Sefarim, Mendele Mokher, **Supp. XXIII:** 4

Segal, D. (pseudonym). *See* Singer, Isaac Bashevis

Segal, George, **Supp. XI:** 343

Segal, Lore, **Supp. XVI:** 203

Segregation: The Inner Conflict in the South (Warren), **IV:** 237, 238, 246, 252

"*Se:* Hegel's Absolute and Heidegger's *Ereignis*" (Agamben), **Supp. XVI:** 289

Seidel, Frederick, **I:** 185

Seidman, Hugh, **Supp. XXI:** 228

Seize the Day (Bellow), **I:** 144, 147, 148, 150, 151, 152, 153, 155, 158, 162; **Retro. Supp. II:** 19, **23–24,** 27, 32, 34; **Supp. I Part 2:** 428

Selby, Hubert, **Supp. III Part 1:** 125

Selby, Hubert, Jr., **Supp. XXI:** 227

Selby, John, **Retro. Supp. II:** 221, 222

Selden, John, **Supp. XIV:** 344

Seldes, Gilbert, **II:** 437, 445; **Retro. Supp. I:** 108

Selected Criticism: Prose, Poetry (Bogan), **Supp. III Part 1:** 64

Selected Essays (Eliot), **I:** 572

Selected Essays and Reviews (Carruth), **Supp. XVI:** 46

Selected Journals and Other Writings (Audubon), **Supp. XVI:** 10, 12, 13

Selected Letters (Bynner), **Supp. XV:** 52

Selected Letters (W. C. Williams), **Retro. Supp. I:** 430

Selected Letters, 1940–1956 (Kerouac), **Supp. XIV:** 137, 144

Selected Letters of Robert Frost (Thompson, ed.), **Retro. Supp. I:** 125

Selected Levis, The (Levis), **Supp. XI:** 257, 272

Selected Plays (O'Hara), **Supp. XXIII:** 216

Selected Poems (Aiken), **I:** 69

Selected Poems (Ashbery), **Supp. III Part 1:** 25–26

Selected Poems (Berrigan), **Supp. XXIV:** 37

Selected Poems (Brodsky), **Supp. VIII:** 22

Selected Poems (Brooks), **Supp. III Part 1:** 82–83

Selected Poems (Bynner), **Supp. XV:** 51, 52

Selected Poems (Corso), **Supp. XII:** 129

Selected Poems (Dove), **Supp. IV Part 1:** 241, 243, 250

Selected Poems (Frost), **Retro. Supp. I:** 133, 136

Selected Poems (Guillevic; Levertov, trans.), **Supp. III Part 1:** 283

Selected Poems (Hayden), **Supp. II Part 1:** 363, 364, 367

Selected Poems (Hughes), **Retro. Supp. I:** 202; **Supp. I Part 1:** 341, 345, 346

Selected Poems (Hugo), **Supp. VI:** 143

Selected Poems (Jarrell), **II:** 367, 370, 371, 374, 377, 379, 380, 381, 382, 384

Selected Poems (Justice), **Supp. VII:** 115

Selected Poems (Kinnell), **Supp. III Part 1:** 235, 253

Selected Poems (Levine, 1984), **Supp. V:** 178, 179

Selected Poems (Lowell), **II:** 512, 516; **Retro. Supp. II:** 184, 186, 188, 190

Selected Poems (Merton), **Supp. VIII:** 207, 208

Selected Poems (Moore), **III:** 193, 194, 205–206, 208, 215

Selected Poems (Notley), **Supp. XXII:** 234

Selected Poems (O'Hara; Allen, ed.), **Supp. XXIII:** 220

Selected Poems (O'Hara; Ford, ed.), **Supp. XXIII:** 220

Selected Poems (Pound), **Retro. Supp. I:** 289, 291

Selected Poems (R. Bly), **Supp. IV Part 1:** 60, 62, 65, 66, 68, 69–71

Selected Poems (Ransom), **III:** 490, 492

Selected Poems (Reznikoff), **Supp. XIV:** 288

Selected Poems (Rukeyser), **Supp. VI:** 274

Selected Poems (Sexton), **Supp. IV Part 2:** 449

Selected Poems (Sorrentino), **Supp. XXI:** 226

Selected Poems (Strand), **Supp. IV Part 2:** 630

Selected Poems, 1923–1943 (Warren), **IV:** 241–242, 243

Selected Poems, 1928–1958 (Kunitz), **Supp. III Part 1:** 261, 263–265

Selected Poems, 1938–1988 (McGrath), **Supp. X:** 127

Selected Poems, 1958–1980 (Sorrentino), **Supp. XXI:** 228

Selected Poems, 1963–1983 (Simic), **Supp. VIII:** 275

Selected Poems 1936–1965 (Eberhart), **I:** 541

Selected Poems: 1957–1987 (Snodgrass), **Supp. VI:** 314–315, 323, 324

Selected Poems 1965–1975 (Atwood), **Supp. XIII:** 32–34

Selected Poems: 1975–2005 (Skloot), **Supp. XX:** 196

Selected Poems II: Poems Selected and New, 1976–1986 (Atwood), **Supp. XIII:** 20, 34–35

Selected Poems of Ezra Pound (Pound), **Supp. V:** 336

Selected Poems of Gabriela Mistral (Hughes, trans.), **Supp. I Part 1:** 345

Selected Poetry of Amiri Baraka/LeRoi Jones (Baraka), **Supp. II Part 1:** 58

Selected Poetry of Hayden Carruth, The (Carruth), **Supp. XVI:** 53

Selected Stories (Dubus), **Supp. VII:** 88–89

Selected Stories of Richard Bausch, The (Bausch), **Supp. VII:** 42

Selected Translations (Snodgrass), **Supp. VI:** 318, 324, **325–326**

Selected Verse of Margaret Haskins Durber, The (Keillor), **Supp. XVI:** 171

Selected Witter Bynner, The, **Supp. XV:** 52

Selected Works of Djuna Barnes, The (Barnes), **Supp. III Part 1:** 44

Selected Writings 1950–1990 (Howe), **Supp. VI:** 116–117, 118, 120

Selected Writings of John Jay Chapman, The (Barzun), **Supp. XIV:** 54

Select Epigrams from the Greek Anthology (Mackail), **Supp. I Part 2:** 461

"Selecting a Reader" (Kooser), **Supp. XIX:** 119–120

"Selene Afterwards" (MacLeish), **III:** 8

"Self" (James), **II:** 351

Self, William, **Supp. XXII:** 172

Self and the Dramas of History, The (Niebuhr), **III:** 308

Self-Consciousness (Updike), **Retro. Supp. I:** 318, 319, 320, 322, 323, 324

"Self-Culture" (Channing), **Supp. XXIV:** **78–79**

"Self-Exposed, The" (X. J. Kennedy), **Supp. XV:** 159

Self-Help: Stories (Moore), **Supp. X:** 163, 166, **167–169,** 174, 175

"Self-Importance" (Halliday), **Supp. XIX:** 90

Self-Interviews (Dickey), **Supp. IV Part 1:** 179

"Self-Made Man, A" (Crane), **I:** 420

"Self Pity" (C. Frost), **Supp. XV:** 93, 94, 101, 102, 104

Self Portrait (album, Dylan), **Supp. XVIII:** 27

"Self-Portrait" (Creeley), **Supp. IV Part 1:** 156

"Self-Portrait" (Mumford), **Supp. II Part 2:** 471

"(Self) Portrait" (Trethewey), **Supp. XXI:** 253

"Self-Portrait" (Wylie), **Supp. I Part 2:** 729

"Self Portrait at Fifty-three" (Weigl), **Supp. XIX:** 288

Self-Portrait: Ceaselessly into the Past (Millar, ed. Sipper), **Supp. IV Part 2:** 464, 469, 472, 475

"Self-Portrait in a Convex Mirror" (Ashbery), **Supp. III Part 1:** 5, 7, 9, 16–19, 22, 24, 26

"Self-Portrait with 1911 NY Yankees Cap" (Skloot), **Supp. XX:** 202

"Self-Reliance" (Emerson), **II:** 7, 15, 17; **Retro. Supp. I:** 159; **Retro. Supp. II:** 155; **Supp. X:** 42, 45

Selfwolf (Halliday), **Supp. XIX:** 81, **89–91,** 93

Sélincourt, Ernest de, **Supp. I Part 2:** 676

Selinger, Eric, **Supp. XVI:** 47

Selinger, Eric Murphy, **Supp. XI:** 248

Sell, Henry, **Supp. XVI:** 188

Sellers, Isaiah, **IV:** 194–195

Sellers, Peter, **Supp. XI:** 301, 304, 306, 307, 309

Sellers, William, **IV:** 208

Seltzer, Mark, **Retro. Supp. I:** 227

Selznick, David O., **Retro. Supp. I:** 105, 113; **Supp. IV Part 1:** 353; **Supp. XVIII:** 242; **Supp. XXII:** 195

Semi, Allen (pseudonym). *See* Larsen, Nella

"Semi-Lunatics of Kilmuir, The" (Hugo), **Supp. VI:** 145

"Semiotics/The Doctor's Doll" (Goldbarth), **Supp. XII:** 183–184

Semmelweiss, Ignaz, **Supp. I Part 1:** 304

Senancour, Étienne Divert de, **I:** 241

Senator North (Atherton), **Supp. XXIV:** 22

Sendak, Maurice, **Supp. IX:** 207, 208, 213, 214; **Supp. XVI:** 110

Seneca, **II:** 14–15; **III:** 77

Senghor, Leopold Sédar, **Supp. IV Part 1:** 16; **Supp. X:** 132, 139

Senier, Siobhan, **Supp. IV Part 1:** 330

"Senility" (Anderson), **I:** 114

Senior, Olive, **Supp. XXIII:** 94

"Senior Partner's Ethics, The" (Auchincloss), **Supp. IV Part 1:** 33

Senlin: A Biography (Aiken), **I:** 48, 49, 50, 52, 56, 57, 64

Sennett, Dorothy, **Supp. XVI:** 43

Sennett, Mack, **III:** 442

"Señora X No More" (Mora), **Supp. XIII:** 218

"Señor Ong and Señor Ha" (Bowles), **Supp. IV Part 1:** 87

Señor Presidente, El (Asturias), **Supp. XXIV:** 89

Sensational Designs: The Cultural Work of American Fiction, 1790–1860 (Tompkins), **Supp. XVIII:** 258–259

Sense of Beauty, The (Santayana), **III:** 600

Sense of Life in the Modern Novel, The (Mizener), **IV:** 132

"Sense of Shelter, A" (Updike), **Retro. Supp. I:** 318

"Sense of the Meeting, The" (Conroy), **Supp. XVI:** 72

Sense of the Past, The (James), **II:** 337–338

"Sense of the Past, The" (Trilling), **Supp. III Part 2:** 503

"Sense of the Present, The" (Hardwick), **Supp. III Part 1:** 210

"Sense of the Sleight-of-Hand Man, The" (Stevens), **IV:** 93

"Sense of Where You Are, A" (McPhee), **Supp. III Part 1:** 291, 296–298

"Sensibility! O La!" (Roethke), **III:** 536

"Sensible Emptiness, A" (Kramer), **Supp. IV Part 1:** 61, 66

"Sensuality Plunging Barefoot Into Thorns" (Cisneros), **Supp. VII:** 68

"Sentence" (Barthelme), **Supp. IV Part 1:** 47

Sent for You Yesterday (Wideman), **Supp. X:** 320, 321

"Sentimental Education, A" (Banks), **Supp. V:** 10

"Sentimental Journey" (Oates), **Supp. II Part 2:** 522, 523

"Sentimental Journey, A" (Anderson), **I:** 114

Sentimental Journey, A (Sterne), **Supp. I Part 2:** 714

"Sentimental Journeys" (Didion), **Supp. IV Part 1:** 211

Sentimental Journey through France and Italy, A (Sterne), **Supp. XV:** 232

"Sentiment of Rationality, The" (James), **II:** 346–347

"Separated Father" (Halliday), **Supp. XIX:** 92, 93

Separate Flights (Dubus), **Supp. VII:** 78–83

"Separate Flights" (Dubus), **Supp. VII:** 83

Separate Peace, A (Knowles), **Supp. IV Part 2:** 679; **Supp. XII:** **241–249**

Separate Way (Reznikoff), **Supp. XIV:** 280

"Separating" (Updike), **Retro. Supp. I:** 321

"Separation, The" (Kunitz), **Supp. III Part 1:** 263

"Sepia High Stepper" (Hayden), **Supp. II Part 1:** 379

September (film; Allen), **Supp. XV:** 11

"September" (Komunyakaa), **Supp. XIII:** 130

"September" (Pickering), **Supp. XXI:** 198

"September 1, 1939" (Auden), **Supp. II Part 1:** 13; **Supp. IV Part 1:** 225; **Supp. VIII:** 30, 32; **Supp. XV:** 117–118

September 11, 2001: American Writers Respond (Heyen), **Supp. XIII:** 285

"September's Book" (Notley), **Supp. XXII:** 229

September Song (Humphrey), **Supp. IX:** 101, 102, **108–109**

"September Twelfth, 2001" (X. J. Kennedy), **Supp. XV:** 171

"Sept Vieillards, Les" (Millay, trans.), **III:** 142

Sequel to Drum-Taps (Whitman), **Retro. Supp. I:** 406

"Sequence, Sometimes Metaphysical" (Roethke), **III:** 547, 548

Sequence of Seven Plays with a Drawing by Ron Slaughter, A (Nemerov), **III:** 269

Sequoya, Jana, **Supp. IV Part 1:** 334

Seraglio, The (Merrill), **Supp. III Part 1:** 331

Seraphita (Balzac), **I:** 499

Seraph on the Suwanee (Hurston), **Supp. VI:** 149, 159–160

Serenissima: A Novel of Venice (Jong). *See Shylock's Daughter: A Novel of Love in Venice (Serenissima)* (Jong)

Sergeant, Elizabeth Shepley, **I:** 231, 236, 312, 319, 323, 328

Sergeant Bilko (television show), **Supp. IV Part 2:** 575

Sergi, Paula, **Supp. XXI:** 246

"Serious Talk, A" (Carver), **Supp. III Part 1:** 138, 144

Serly, Tibor, **Supp. III Part 2:** 617, 619

"Sermon, Now Encrypted" (Monson), **Supp. XXIV:** 239–240

"Sermon by Doctor Pep" (Bellow), **I:** 151

Sermones (Horace), **II:** 154

"Sermon for Our Maturity" (Baraka), **Supp. II Part 1:** 53

"Sermon in the Cotton Field" (Nelson), **Supp. XVIII:** 177

Sermons and Soda Water (O'Hara), **III:** 362, 364, 371–373, 382

"Sermons on the Warpland" (Brooks), **Supp. III Part 1:** 84

"Serpent in the Wilderness, The" (Masters), **Supp. I Part 2:** 458

Servant of the Bones (Rice), **Supp. VII:** 298, 302

"Servant to Servants, A" (Frost), **Retro. Supp. I:** 125, 128; **Supp. X:** 66

Serve It Forth (M. F. K. Fisher), **Supp. XVII:** 83, 86, 87, 89, 92

Service, Robert W., **Supp. XXI:** 51; **Supp. XXII:** 203

Seshachari, Neila, **Supp. V:** 22

"Session, The" (Adams), **I:** 5

"Sestina" (Bishop), **Supp. I Part 1:** 73, 88

Set-angya, **Supp. IV Part 2:** 493

Seth, Vikram, **Supp. XVII:** 117

Seth's Brother's Wife (Frederic), **II:** 131–132, 137, 144

Sethuraman, Ramchandran, **Supp. XXII:** 73

Setouchi, Jakuchō, **Supp. XXIV:** 166

Set This House on Fire (Styron), **IV:** 98, 99, 105, 107–113, 114, 115, 117

Setting Free the Bears (Irving), **Supp. VI:** 163, **166–167,** 169–170

Setting the Tone (Rorem), **Supp. IV Part 1:** 79

Settle, Mary Lee, **Supp. IX:** 96

Settlement Horizon, The: A National Estimate (Woods and Kennedy), **Supp. I Part 1:** 19

"Settling the Colonel's Hash" (McCarthy), **II:** 559, 562

Setzer, Helen, **Supp. IV Part 1:** 217

"Seurat's Sunday Afternoon along the Seine" (Schwartz), **Supp. II Part 2:** 663–665

Sevag, Aris, **Supp. XXIII:** 28, 29

7 Years from Somehwere (Levine), **Supp. V:** 178, 181, 188–189

Seven against Thebes (Aeschylus; Bacon and Hecht, trans.), **Supp. X:** 57

Seven Ages of Man, The (Wilder), **IV:** 357, 374–375

Seven Deadly Sins, The (Wilder), **IV:** 357, 374–375

Seven Descents of Myrtle, The (T. Williams), **IV:** 382

"Seven Fat Brides, The" (P. Abraham), **Supp. XVII:** 50

Seven Guitars (Wilson), **Supp. VIII:** 331, **348–351**

Seven Lady Godivas, The (Geisel), **Supp. XVI:** 100, 103

Seven League Boots, The (Murray), **Supp. XIX: 156–157**

Seven-League Crutches, The (Jarrell), **II:** 367, 372, 381, 382, 383–384, 389

Seven Mountains of Thomas Merton, The (Mott), **Supp. VIII:** 208

Seven-Ounce Man, The (Harrison), **Supp. VIII:** 51

"Seven Places of the Mind" (Didion), **Supp. IV Part 1:** 200, 210

Seven Plays (Shepard), **Supp. III Part 2:** 434

"Seven Selves, The" (Gibran), **Supp. XX: 118**

"Seven Sentences" (Dybek), **Supp. XXIII:** 74

"Seven Stanzas at Easter" (Updike), **IV:** 215

Seven Storey Mountain, The (Merton), **Supp. VIII:** 193, 195, 198, 200, 207, 208

Seventeen (Berrigan and Padgett), **Supp. XXIV:** 41

Seventh Beggar, The (Abraham), **Supp. XXIV:** 2, 3, **9–12,** 13, 14

Seventh Heaven (Hoffman), **Supp. X:** 87, 89

"Seventh of March" (Webster), **Supp. I Part 2:** 687

"7000 Romaine, Los Angeles 38" (Didion), **Supp. IV Part 1:** 200

"Seventh Street" (Toomer), **Supp. IX:** 316

Seven Types of Ambiguity (Empson), **II:** 536; **IV:** 431

77 Dream Songs (Berryman), **I:** 168, 169, 170, 171, 174, 175, 183–188

73 Poems (Cummings), **I:** 430, 431, 446, 447, 448

Seven Valleys and the Four Valleys, The (Bahá'u'lláh), **Supp. XX: 121**

"Several Short Questions About Crumbs" (Schott), **Supp. XXIII:** 249

Sevier, Jack, **IV:** 378

Sévigné, Madame de, **IV:** 361

Sewall, Richard, **Retro. Supp. I:** 25

Sewall, Samuel, **IV:** 145, 146, 147, 149, 154, 164; **Supp. I Part 1:** 100, 110

Sewell, Elizabeth, **Supp. XIII:** 344

"Sex" (Carruth), **Supp. XVI:** 58

Sex, Economy, Freedom and Community (Berry), **Supp. X:** 30, 36

"Sex Camp" (Mamet), **Supp. XIV:** 240

Sex Castle, The (Lacy), **Supp. XV:** 206

Sex & Character (Weininger), **Retro. Supp. I:** 416

"Sext" (Auden), **Supp. II Part 1:** 22

Sexton, Anne, **Retro. Supp. II:** 245; **Supp. I Part 2:** 538, 543, 546; **Supp. II Part 2: 669–700; Supp. III Part 2:** 599; **Supp. IV Part 1:** 245; **Supp. IV Part 2:** 439, 440–441, 442, 444, 447, 449, 451, 620; **Supp. V:** 113, 118, 124; **Supp. X:** 201, 202, 213; **Supp. XI:** 146, 240, 317; **Supp. XII:** 217, 253, 254, 256, 260, 261; **Supp. XIII:** 35, 76, 294, 312; **Supp. XIV:** 125, 126, 132, 269; **Supp. XV:** 123, 252, 340; **Supp. XVII:** 239; **Supp. XIX:** 82, 203; **Supp. XX:** 199

Sexual Behavior in the American Male (Kinsey), **Supp. XIII:** 96–97

Sexual Perversity in Chicago (Mamet), **Supp. XIV:** 239, 240, 246–247, 249

"Sexual Revolution, The" (Dunn), **Supp. XI:** 142

Sexus (H. Miller), **III:** 170, 171, 184, 187, 188

"Sex Without Love" (Olds), **Supp. X:** 206

"Sexy" (Lahiri), **Supp. XXI:** 183–184

Seyersted, Per E., **Retro. Supp. II:** 65; **Supp. I Part 1:** 201, 204, 211, 216, 225; **Supp. IV Part 2:** 558

Seyfried, Robin, **Supp. IX:** 324

Seymour, Corey, **Supp. XXIV:** 280

Seymour, Miranda, **Supp. VIII:** 167

"Seymour: An Introduction" (Salinger), **III:** 569–571, 572

"Shack" (L. Brown), **Supp. XXI:** 49

Shacochis, Bob, **Supp. VIII:** 80

"Shadow" (Creeley), **Supp. IV Part 1:** 158

"Shadow, The" (Lowell), **II:** 522

Shadow and Act (Ellison), **Retro. Supp. II:** 119; **Supp. II Part 1:** 245–246

"Shadow and Shade" (Tate), **IV:** 128

"Shadow and the Flesh, The" (London), **II:** 475

"Shadow A Parable" (Poe), **III:** 417–418

Shadow Country (Gunn Allen), **Supp. IV Part 1:** 322, 324, 325–326

Shadow Man, The (Gordon), **Supp. IV Part 1:** 297, 298, 299, 312–314, 315

Shadow of a Dream, The, a Story (Howells), **II:** 285, 286, 290

Shadow of a Man (Moraga), **Supp. XXIII:** 195, 197, **199–203**

"Shadow of the Crime, The: A Word from the Author" (Mailer), **Retro. Supp. II:** 214

Shadow on the Dial, The (Bierce), **I:** 208, 209

"Shadow Passing" (Merwin), **Supp. III Part 1:** 355

Shadowplay (C. Baxter), **Supp. XVII:** 15, 19–20

Shadows (Gardner), **Supp. VI:** 74

Shadows and Fog (film; Allen), **Supp. XV:** 11

Shadows Burning (Di Piero), **Supp. XIX:** 42, 43–44

Shadows by the Hudson (Singer), **IV:** 1

Shadows of Africa (Matthiessen), **Supp. V:** 203

Shadows on the Hudson (Singer), **Retro. Supp. II:** **311–313**

Shadows on the Rock (Cather), **I:** 314, 330–331, 332; **Retro. Supp. I:** 18

Shadow Train (Ashbery), **Supp. III Part 1:** 23–24, 26

"Shad-Time" (Wilbur), **Supp. III Part 2:** 563

Shaffer, Thomas L., **Supp. VIII:** 127, 128

Shaft (Parks; film), **Supp. XI:** 17

Shaftesbury, Earl of, **I:** 559

Shahid, Irfan, **Supp. XX: 113, 127**

Shahn, Ben, **Supp. X:** 24

Shakedown for Murder (Lacy), **Supp. XV:** 203

Shakelford, Dean, **Supp. VIII:** 129

Shaker, Why Don't You Sing? (Angelou), **Supp. IV Part 1:** 16

Shakespear, Mrs. Olivia, **III:** 457; **Supp. I Part 1:** 257

"Shakespeare" (Emerson), **II:** 6

Shakespeare, William, **I:** 103, 271, 272, 284–285, 358, 378, 433, 441, 458, 461, 573, 585, 586; **II:** 5, 8, 11, 18, 72, 273, 297, 302, 309, 320, 411, 494, 577, 590; **III:** 3, 11, 12, 82, 83, 91, 124, 130, 134, 145, 153, 159, 183, 210, 263, 286, 468, 473, 492, 503, 511, 567, 575–576, 577, 610, 612, 613, 615; **IV:** 11, 50, 66, 127, 132, 156, 309, 313, 362, 368, 370, 373, 453; **Retro. Supp. I:** 43, 64, 91, 248; **Retro. Supp. II:** 114, 299; **Supp. I Part 1:** 79, 150, 262, 310, 356, 363, 365, 368, 369, 370; **Supp. I Part 2:** 397, 421, 422, 470, 494, 622, 716, 720; **Supp. II Part 2:** 624, 626; **Supp. IV Part 1:** 31, 83, 87, 243; **Supp. IV Part 2:** 430, 463, 519, 688; **Supp. V:** 252, 280, 303; **Supp. VIII:** 160, 164; **Supp. IX:** 14, 133; **Supp. X:** 42, 62, 65, 78; **Supp. XII:** 54–57, 277, 281;

Supp. XIII: 111, 115, 233; **Supp. XIV:** 97, 120, 225, 245, 306; **Supp. XV:** 92; **Supp. XVIII:** 278; **Supp. XXII:** 206; **Supp. XXIV:** 33, 34, 40, 87, 159

Shakespeare and His Forerunners (Lanier), **Supp. I Part 1:** 369

Shakespeare in Harlem (Hughes), **Retro. Supp. I:** 194, 202, 205, 206, 207, 208; **Supp. I Part 1:** 333, 334, 345

Shalit, Gene, **Supp. VIII:** 73

Shalit, Wendy, **Supp. XX: 179, 182, 186**

Shall We Gather at the River (Wright), **Supp. III Part 2:** 601–602; **Supp. XVII:** 241

"Shame" (Oates), **Supp. II Part 2:** 520

"Shame" (Wilbur), **Supp. III Part 2:** 556

"Shame and Forgetting in the Information Age" (C. Baxter), **Supp. XVII:** 21

"Shameful Affair, A" (Chopin), **Retro. Supp. II:** 61

Shamela (Fielding), **Supp. V:** 127

"Shampoo, The" (Bishop), **Retro. Supp. II:** 46; **Supp. I Part 1:** 92

Shange, Ntozake, **Supp. VIII:** 214; **Supp. XVII:** 70; **Supp. XVIII:** 172; **Supp. XXI:** 172

Shank, Randy, **Supp. X:** 252

Shankaracharya, **III:** 567

Shanley, John Patrick, **Supp. XIV: 315–332**

Shannon, Sandra, **Supp. VIII:** 333, 348

"Shape of Flesh and Bone, The" (MacLeish), **III:** 18–19

Shape of Me and Other Stuff, The (Geisel), **Supp. XVI:** 111

Shape of the Journey, The (Harrison), **Supp. VIII:** 53

Shapes of Clay (Bierce), **I:** 208, 209

Shaping Joy, A: Studies in the Writer's Craft (Brooks), **Supp. XIV:** 13

Shapiro, Alan, **Supp. XXIV:** 157

Shapiro, Charles, **Supp. XIX:** 257, 259–260

Shapiro, David, **Supp. XII:** 175, 185; **Supp. XXIV:** 34

Shapiro, Dorothy, **IV:** 380

Shapiro, Karl, **I:** 430, 521; **II:** 350; **III:** 527; **Supp. II Part 2: 701–724; Supp. III Part 2:** 623; **Supp. IV Part 2:** 645; **Supp. X:** 116; **Supp. XI:** 315; **Supp. XIX:** 117, 118, 119; **Supp. XXI:** 98

Shapiro, Laura, **Supp. IX:** 120; **Supp. XX: 87, 89**

"Shared Patio, The" (July), **Supp. XXIV:** 201, 202

Sharif, Omar, **Supp. IX:** 253

"Shark Meat" (Snyder), **Supp. VIII:** 300

Shatayev, Elvira, **Supp. I Part 2:** 570

Shaviro, Steven, **Supp. VIII:** 189

Shaw, Chris, **Supp. XXIII:** 155–156

Shaw, Colonel Robert Gould, **II:** 551

Shaw, Elizabeth. *See* Melville, Mrs. Herman (Elizabeth Shaw)

Shaw, George Bernard, **I:** 226; **II:** 82, 271, 276, 581; **III:** 69, 102, 113, 145, 155, 161, 162, 163, 373, 409; **IV:** 27, 64, 397, 432, 440; **Retro. Supp. I:**

100, 228; **Supp. IV Part 1:** 36; **Supp. IV Part 2:** 585, 683; **Supp. V:** 243–244, 290; **Supp. IX:** 68, 308; **Supp. XI:** 202; **Supp. XII:** 94; **Supp. XIV:** 343; **Supp. XVII:** 100; **Supp. XXIV:** 33, 34

Shaw, Irwin, **IV:** 381; **Supp. IV Part 1:** 383; **Supp. IX:** 251; **Supp. XI:** 221, 229, 231; **Supp. XIX: 239–254**

Shaw, Joseph Thompson ("Cap"), **Supp. IV Part 1:** 121, 345, 351; **Supp. XIII:** 161

Shaw, Judge Lemuel, **III:** 77, 88, 91

Shaw, Lytle, **Supp. XXIII:** 208; **Supp. XXIV:** 44

Shaw, Peter, **Supp. XVI:** 70

Shaw, Robert B., **Supp. XXIII:** 112

Shaw, Sarah Bryant, **Supp. I Part 1:** 169

Shaw, Wilbur, Jr., **Supp. XIII:** 162

Shawl, The (Mamet), **Supp. XIV:** 245

Shawl, The (Ozick), **Supp. V:** 257, 260, 271

"Shawl, The" (Ozick), **Supp. V:** 271–272

Shawl and Prarie du Chien, The: Two Plays (Mamet), **Supp. XIV:** 243–244

Shawn, William, **Supp. VIII:** 151, 170

"Shawshank Redemption, The" (King), **Supp. V:** 148

She (Haggard), **III:** 189

Shea, Renee, **Supp. XXIII:** 85, 86, 90, 95

Sheaffer, Louis, **Supp. XXI:** 6

Shearer, Flora, **I:** 199

"Sheaves, The" (Robinson), **III:** 510, 524

"She Came and Went" (Lowell), **Supp. I Part 2:** 409

"She-Devil" (Nelson), **Supp. XVIII:** 178

She-Devil Circus (Nelson), **Supp. XVIII:** 176, **178**

Sheed, Wilfrid, **IV:** 230; **Supp. XI:** 233; **Supp. XXI:** 233

Sheeler, Charles, **IV:** 409; **Retro. Supp. I:** 430

"Sheep Child" (B. Kelly), **Supp. XVII:** 131–132

"Sheep Child, The" (Dickey), **Supp. XVII:** 131–132

Sheeper (Rosenthal), **Supp. XIV:** 147

Sheffer, Jonathan, **Supp. IV Part 1:** 95

She Had Some Horses (Harjo), **Supp. XII: 220–223,** 231

"She Had Some Horses" (Harjo), **Supp. XII:** 215, 222

"Shell, The" (Humphrey), **Supp. IX:** 94

Shelley, Mary, **Supp. XX: 108**

Shelley, Percy Bysshe, **I:** 18, 68, 381, 476, 522, 577; **II:** 331, 516, 535, 540; **III:** 412, 426, 469; **IV:** 139; **Retro. Supp. I:** 308, 360; **Supp. I Part 1:** 79, 311, 349; **Supp. I Part 2:** 709, 718, 719, 720, 721, 722, 724, 728; **Supp. IV Part 1:** 235; **Supp. V:** 258, 280; **Supp. IX:** 51; **Supp. XII:** 117, 132, 136–137, 263; **Supp. XIV:** 271–272; **Supp. XV:** 92, 175, 182; **Supp. XX: 115; Supp. XXI:** 131

Shellow, Sadie Myers, **Supp. I Part 2:** 608

"Shelter" (C. Baxter), **Supp. XVII:** 19

"Shelter" (Doty), **Supp. XI:** 132

Sheltered Life, The (Glasgow), **II**: 174, 175, 179, 186, 187–188

Sheltering Sky, The (Bowles), **Supp. IV Part 1**: 82, 84, 85–86, 87

Sheltering Sky, The (film), **Supp. IV Part 1**: 94, 95

Shelton, Frank, **Supp. IV Part 2**: 658

Shelton, Richard, **Supp. XI**: 133; **Supp. XIII**: 7

Shelton, Robert, **Supp. XVIII**: 20, 21, 22, 23, 24, 25, 26

Shelton, Mrs. Sarah. *See* Royster, Sarah Elmira

Shenandoah (Schwartz), **Supp. II Part 2**: 640, 651–652

"Shenandoah" (Shapiro), **Supp. II Part 2**: 704

Shepard, Alice, **IV**: 287

Shepard, Gregory, **Supp. XXII**: 119

Shepard, Harvey, **Supp. XVII**: 240

Shepard, Jim, **Supp. XXI**: 115

Shepard, Odell, **II**: 508; **Supp. I Part 2**: 418

Shepard, Richard F., **Supp. XXIV**: 216

Shepard, Sam, **Supp. III Part 2: 431–450**; **Supp. XVIII**: 21, 28, 31; **Supp. XXI**: 144, 145

Shepard, Thomas, **I**: 554; **IV**: 158

"Shepherd of Resumed Desire, The" (Wright), **Supp. XV**: 349

Sheppard Lee (Bird), **III**: 423

"She Remembers the Future" (Harjo), **Supp. XII**: 222

Sheridan, Richard Brinsley, **Retro. Supp. I**: 127

Sherlock, William, **IV**: 152

Sherman, Joe, **Supp. XXII**: 205

Sherman, Sarah Way, **Retro. Supp. II**: 145

Sherman, Stuart Pratt, **I**: 222, 246–247; **Supp. I Part 2**: 423

Sherman, Susan, **Supp. VIII**: 265

Sherman, Tom, **IV**: 446

Sherman, William T., **IV**: 445, 446

Sherry, Denver William, **Supp. XXII**: 190

Sherwood, Robert, **II**: 435; **Supp. IX**: 190

Sherwood Anderson & Other Famous Creoles (Faulkner), **I**: 117; **II**: 56

Sherwood Anderson Reader, The (Anderson), **I**: 114, 116

Sherwood Anderson's Memoirs (Anderson), **I**: 98, 101, 102, 103, 108, 112, 116

Sherwood Anderson's Notebook (Anderson), **I**: 108, 115, 117

"She Sings" (Taggard), **Supp. XXII**: 272

She Stoops to Conquer (Goldsmith), **II**: 514

Shestov, Lev, **Supp. VIII**: 20, 24

Shetley, Vernon, **Supp. IX**: 292; **Supp. XI**: 123

"She Wept, She Railed" (Kunitz), **Supp. III Part 1**: 265

"Shiddah and Kuziba" (Singer), **IV**: 13, 15

Shidyak, Paris al-, **Supp. XX: 117**

Shield of Achilles, The (Auden), **Supp. II Part 1**: 21

"Shield of Achilles, The" (Auden), **Supp. II Part 1**: 21, 25

Shields, Carol, **Supp. VII: 307–330**

Shields, John C., **Supp. XX: 279, 280, 281, 286**

Shifting Landscape: A Composite, 1925–1987 (H. Roth), **Supp. IX: 233–235**

Shifts of Being (Eberhart), **I**: 525

Shigematsu, Soiko, **Supp. III Part 1**: 353

Shihab, Aziz, **Supp. XIII**: 273

Shih-hsiang Chen, **Supp. VIII**: 303

Shiksa Goddess; or, How I Spent My Forties (Wasserstein), **Supp. XV**: 319, 320, 325, 332, 333

"Shiloh" (Mason), **Supp. VIII**: 140

Shiloh and Other Stories (Mason), **Supp. VIII**: 133, **139–141**, 143, 145

Shilts, Randy, **Supp. X**: 145

Shimmering Verge, The (one-woman show, Peacock), **Supp. XIX**: 194, **204–205**

Shining, The (King), **Supp. V**: 139, 140, 141, 143–144, 146, 149, 151, 152

"Shining Ones, The" (P. N. Warren), **Supp. XX: 272**

Shining Victory (film, Rapper), **Supp. XVII**: 60

Shinn, Everett, **Retro. Supp. II**: 103

Shi Pei Pu, **Supp. XXI**: 152, 153, 154

"Ship in a Bottle"(Strout), **Supp. XXIII**: 283

"Ship of Death" (Lawrence), **Supp. I Part 2**: 728

Ship of Fools (Porter), **III**: 433, 447, 453, 454; **IV**: 138

Shipping News, The (Proulx), **Supp. VII**: 249, 258–259

"Ships" (O. Henry), **Supp. II Part 1**: 409

Ships Going into the Blue: Essays and Notes on Poetry (Simpson), **Supp. IX**: 275

Ship to America, A (Singer), **IV**: 1

"Shipwreck, The" (Merwin), **Supp. III Part 1**: 346

Shirley, John, **Supp. XVI**: 123, 128

"Shirt" (Pinsky), **Supp. VI: 236–237**, 239, 240, 241, 245, 247

"Shirt Poem, The" (Stern), **Supp. IX**: 292

"Shirts, The" (Gallagher), **Supp. XXIV**: 169

"Shirts of a Single Color" (Ryan), **Supp. XVIII**: 227

"Shiva and Parvati Hiding in the Rain" (Pinsky), **Supp. VI**: 244

Shively, Charley, **Retro. Supp. I**: 391; **Supp. XII**: 181, 182

Shnayerson, Michael, **Supp. XIX**: 248

"Shock of Good Poetry, The"(Hirshfield), **Supp. XXIII**: 136

Shock of Recognition, The (Wilson), **II**: 530

Shock of the New, The (Hughes), **Supp. X**: 73

Shoe Bird, The (Welty), **IV**: 261; **Retro. Supp. I**: 353

Shoemaker of Dreams (Ferragammo), **Supp. XVI**: 192

"Shoes" (O. Henry), **Supp. II Part 1**: 409

"Shoes of Wandering, The" (Kinnell), **Supp. III Part 1**: 248

Sholem Asch: Zayn levn un zayne verk (Sholem Asch: His life and his work), **Supp. XXIII**: 6

Sholl, Betsy, **Supp. XXI**: 129, 131

"Shooters, Inc." (Didion), **Supp. IV Part 1**: 207, 211

"Shooting, The" (Dubus), **Supp. VII**: 84, 85

"Shooting Niagara; and After?" (Carlyle), **Retro. Supp. I**: 408

"Shooting Script" (Rich), **Supp. I Part 2**: 558; **Supp. IV Part 1**: 257

Shooting Star, A (Stegner), **Supp. IV Part 2**: 599, 608–609

"Shooting the Works" (Di Piero), **Supp. XIX**: 41–42

Shooting the Works: On Poetry and Pictures (Di Piero), **Supp. XIX: 41–42**

"Shooting Whales" (Strand), **Supp. IV Part 2**: 630

"Shopgirls" (F. Barthelme), **Supp. XI**: 26, 27, 33, 36

Shopping for Joe (O'Hara and Steven Rivers), **Supp. XXIII**: 217

"Shopping with Bob Berwick" (Halliday), **Supp. XIX**: 88

Shop Talk (P. Roth), **Retro. Supp. II**: 282

Shoptaw, John, **Supp. IV Part 1**: 247

Shore Acres (Herne), **Supp. II Part 1**: 198

Shorebirds of North America, The (Matthiessen), **Supp. V**: 204

Shore House, The (Jewett), **II**: 397

Shore Leave (Wakeman), **Supp. IX**: 247

"Shoreline Horses" (Ríos), **Supp. IV Part 2**: 553

"Shoreline Life" (Skloot), **Supp. XX: 201**

Shores of Light, The: A Literary Chronicle of the Twenties and Thirties (Wilson), **IV**: 432, 433

Shorey, Paul, **III**: 606

Short Account of the Destruction of the Indies, A (Las Casas), **Supp. XXIV**: 87

Short and the Long of It, The (Kenny), **Supp. XXIII**: 155–156

Short Cuts (film, Altman), **Supp. IX**: 143; **Supp. XXIV**: 166, 172, 178

"Short End, The" (Hecht), **Supp. X**: 65

"Shorter View, The" (X. J. Kennedy), **Supp. XV**: 160, 168

Short Fiction of Norman Mailer, The (Mailer), **Retro. Supp. II**: 205

Short Friday and Other Stories (Singer), **IV**: 14–16

Short Guide to a Happy Life, A (Quindlen), **Supp. XVII**: 167, 179

"Short Happy Life of Francis Macomber, The" (Hemingway), **II**: 250, 263–264; **Retro. Supp. I**: 182; **Supp. IV Part 1**: 48; **Supp. IX**: 106

Short Night, The (Turner), **Supp. XV**: 201

Short Novels of Thomas Wolfe, The (Wolfe), **IV**: 456

Short Poems (Berryman), **I**: 170

"SHORT SPEECH TO MY FRIENDS" (Baraka), **Supp. II Part 1**: 35

Short Stories (Rawlings), **Supp. X**: 224

Short Stories: Five Decades (Shaw), **Supp. XIX:** 252–253
"Short Story, The" (Welty), **IV:** 279
Short Story Masterpieces, **Supp. IX:** 4
Short Studies of American Authors (Higginson), **I:** 455
"Short-timer's Calendar" (Komunyakaa), **Supp. XIII:** 125
Shosha (Singer), **Retro. Supp. II:** 313–314
Shostak, Debra, **Supp. XXIV:** 136
Shostakovich, Dimitri, **IV:** 75; **Supp. VIII:** 21
Shot of Love (album, Dylan), **Supp. XVIII:** 28
"Shots" (Ozick), **Supp. V:** 268
Shotts, Jeffrey, **Supp. XV:** 103, 104
"Should Wizard Hit Mommy?" (Updike), **IV:** 221, 222, 224; **Retro. Supp. I:** 335
Shoup, Barbara, **Supp. XV:** 55, 59, 62, 69
"Shoveling Snow with Buddha" (Collins), **Supp. XXI:** 60
"Shovel Man, The" (Sandburg), **III:** 553
Showalter, Elaine, **Retro. Supp. I:** 368; **Supp. IV Part 2:** 440, 441, 444; **Supp. X:** 97; **Supp. XVI:** 80, 92; **Supp. XX:** 274; **Supp. XXIV:** 28
"Shower of Gold" (Welty), **IV:** 271–272
Shribman, David M., **Supp. XXII:** 205, 218
"Shrike and the Chipmunks, The" (Thurber), **Supp. I Part 2:** 617
Shrimp Girl (Hogarth), **Supp. XII:** 44
"Shrine and the Burning Wheel, The" (Jarman), **Supp. XVII:** 116
"Shrine with Flowers" (Di Piero), **Supp. XIX:** 43, 44
"Shriveled Meditation" (X. J. Kennedy), **Supp. XV:** 170
Shropshire Lad, A (Housman), **Supp. XV:** 41
"Shrouded Stranger, The" (Ginsberg), **Supp. II Part 1:** 312
"Shroud of Color, The" (Cullen), **Supp. IV Part 1:** 166, 168, 170, 171
Shrunken Head of Pancho Villa, The (Valdez), **Supp. XXIII:** 203
Shtetl (film; Marzynski), **Supp. XVI:** 153
Shtetl: The Life and Death of a Small Town and the World of Polish Jews (E. Hoffman), **Supp. XVI:** 152, 153–155
Shue, Elizabeth, **Supp. XXIII:** 276
Shuffle (L. Michaels), **Supp. XVI:** 202, 203, 213
Shuffle Along (musical), **Supp. I Part 1:** 322; **Supp. X:** 136
Shultz, George, **Supp. IV Part 1:** 234
Shurr, William, **Retro. Supp. I:** 43
Shuster, Joel, **Supp. XI:** 67
Shusterman, Richard, **Retro. Supp. I:** 53
"Shut a Final Door" (Capote), **Supp. III Part 1:** 117, 120, 124
Shut Up, He Explained (Lardner), **II:** 432
Shylock's Daughter: A Novel of Love in Venice (Serenissima) (Jong), **Supp. V:** 115, 127, 128–129

Siamanto (Atom Yarjanian), **Supp. XXIII:** 28
"Siasconset: How It Arose and What It Is" (Briggs), **Supp. XVIII:** 9
Siberian Village, The (Dove), **Supp. IV Part 1:** 255, 256
Sibley, Celestine, **Supp. XXII:** 194, 199
Sibley, Mulford Q., **Supp. I Part 2:** 524
"Sibling Mysteries" (Rich), **Supp. I Part 2:** 574
Siblings (Quindlen and Kelsh), **Supp. XVII:** 167, 179
Siblings in Paradise (or Moscow when It Sizzles) (Silver), **Supp. XXIV:** 265
Sibon, Marcelle, **IV:** 288
"Sicilian Emigrant's Song" (W. C. Williams), **Retro. Supp. I:** 413
Sicilian Miniatures (Sobin), **Supp. XVI:** 288
"Sick Wife, The" (Kenyon), **Supp. VII:** 173, 174
"'Sic transit gloria mundi' " (Dickinson), **Retro. Supp. I:** 30
Sid Caesar Show (television show), **Supp. IV Part 2:** 575
Siddons, Anne Rivers, **Supp. XXII:** 239–254
Siddons, Sarah, **II:** 298
Side Effects (Allen), **Supp. XV:** 3, 14, 15–16
Side of Paradise, This (Fitgerald), **Supp. IX:** 56
Sidnee Poet Heroical, The (Baraka), **Supp. II Part 1:** 55
Sidney, Algernon, **II:** 114
Sidney, Mary, **Supp. I Part 1:** 98
Sidney, Philip, **II:** 470; **Supp. I Part 1:** 98, 111, 117–118, 122; **Supp. I Part 2:** 658; **Supp. II Part 1:** 104–105; **Supp. V:** 250; **Supp. XII:** 264; **Supp. XIV:** 128
Sidney, Sylvia, **Supp. I Part 1:** 67
Sidney Lanier: A Bibliographical and Critical Study (Starke), **Supp. I Part 1:** 371
Sidney Lanier: A Biographical and Critical Study (Starke), **Supp. I Part 1:** 371
Siebert, Kathy, **Supp. XX:** 84
Siege (Shaw), **Supp. XIX:** 244
Siegel, Barry, **Supp. XIV:** 82
Siegel, Ben, **Supp. XXIII:** 3, 4, 10, 11, 12, 14, 16
Siegel, Catherine, **Supp. XII:** 126
Siegel, Jerry, **Supp. XI:** 67
Siegel, Lee, **Supp. XXII:** 255–269
"Siege of London, The" (James), **Retro. Supp. I:** 227
Siegle, Robert, **Supp. XII:** 8
Sienkiewicz, Henryk, **Supp. IV Part 2:** 518; **Supp. XVI:** 182
"Sierra Kid" (Levine), **Supp. V:** 180–181
Sigal, Clancy, **Supp. XXI:** 44; **Supp. XXIII:** 166
Sigg, Eric, **Retro. Supp. I:** 53
"Sight" (Merwin), **Supp. III Part 1:** 356
Sighted Singer, The (Halliday), **Supp. XIX:** 82, 86–87
"Sight in Camp in the Daybreak Gray and Dim, A" (Whitman), **II:** 373

Sights and Spectacles (McCarthy), **II:** 562
"Sights from a Steeple" (Hawthorne), **Retro. Supp. I:** 62; **Supp. XXI:** 201
Sights Unseen (Gibbons), **Supp. X:** 49–50
"Signals" (Carver), **Supp. III Part 1:** 143
"Signature for Tempo" (MacLeish), **III:** 8–9
"Signed Confession of Crimes against the State" (Merton), **Supp. VIII:** 201
Signifying Monkey, The (Hughes), **Retro. Supp. I:** 195
Signifying Monkey, The: A Theory of Afro-American Literary Criticism (H. L. Gates), **Supp. X:** 243; **Supp. XX:** 99, 106–107
"Signing, The" (Dixon), **Supp. XII:** 146
Sign in Sidney Brustein's Window, The (Hansberry), **Supp. IV Part 1:** 359, 365, 369, 370–372
Sign of Jonas, The (Merton), **Supp. VIII:** 194–195, 195, 197, 200, 206, 207
"Sign of Saturn, The" (Olds), **Supp. X:** 206
"Signs, Oakvale, Mississippi, 1941" (Trethewey), **Supp. XXI:** 248–249
Signs and Wonders (Bukiet), **Supp. XVII:** 45–46
Sigourney, Lydia, **Supp. I Part 2:** 684
Sikora, Malgorzata, **Retro. Supp. II:** 324
Silas Marner (G. Eliot), **II:** 26
Silberg, Richard, **Supp. XV:** 116
Silberman, James, **Supp. XXIV:** 288
"Silence" (Moore), **III:** 212
"Silence" (Poe), **III:** 416
"Silence" (Sanders), **Supp. XVI:** 278
"Silence, A" (Clampitt), **Supp. IX:** 53
"Silence—A Fable" (Poe), **III:** 416
Silence and Metaphor (Bronk), **Supp. XXI:** 31, 32
"Silence Before Harvest, The" (Merwin), **Supp. III Part 1:** 352
Silence Dogood Papers, The (Franklin), **II:** 106–107
Silence in the Snowy Fields (R. Bly), **Supp. IV Part 1:** 60–61, 62, 63, 65, 66, 72; **Supp. XXI:** 84, 85
Silence of History, The (Farrell), **II:** 46–47
Silence of the Lambs, The (T. Harris), **Supp. XXI:** 78
Silence Opens, A (Clampitt), **Supp. IX:** 53
Silences (Olsen), **Supp. XIII:** 293, 294, 295, 296, 304–306
"Silences: When Writers Don't Write" (Olsen), **Supp. XIII:** 294
Silencing the Past: Power and the Production of History (Trouillot), **Supp. X:** 14
"Silent in America" (Levine), **Supp. V:** 183
Silent Life, The (Merton), **Supp. VIII:** 208
Silent Partner, The (Odets), **Supp. II Part 2:** 539
"Silent Poem" (Francis), **Supp. IX:** 86
"Silent Season of a Hero, The" (Talese), **Supp. XVII:** 203–204
"Silent Slain, The" (MacLeish), **III:** 9

"Silent Snow, Secret Snow" (Aiken), **I:** 52

Silent Spring (Carson), **Supp. V:** 202; **Supp. IX:** 19, 24, **31–34; Supp. XIV:** 177; **Supp. XVI:** 36; **Supp. XVIII:** 189

Silhouettes of American Life (R. H. Davis), **Supp. XVI:** 85

"Silken Tent, The" (Frost), **Retro. Supp. I:** 138–139; **Supp. IV Part 2:** 448

Silko, Leslie Marmon, **Supp. IV Part 1:** 274, 319, 325, 333–334, 335, 404; **Supp. IV Part 2:** 499, 505, **557–572; Supp. V:** 169; **Supp. XI:** 18; **Supp. XII:** 217; **Supp. XVIII:** 58

Silliman, Ron, **Supp. IV Part 2:** 426; **Supp. XV:** 344; **Supp. XVII:** 70, 77

Silliman's Blog (R. Silliman), **Supp. XVII:** 70

Silman, Roberta, **Supp. X:** 6

Silver, Nicky, **Supp. XXIV:** 128, **263–277**

Silverblatt, Michael, **Supp. XV:** 224

"Silver Crown, The" (Malamud), **Supp. I Part 2:** 434–435, 437; **Supp. V:** 266

"Silver Dish, The" (Bellow), **Retro. Supp. II:** 30

"Silver Filigree" (Wylie), **Supp. I Part 2:** 707

"Silver Lake" (B. Kelly), **Supp. XVII:** 130

Silverman, Joseph, **Supp. XXIII:** 8

Silvers, Phil, **Supp. IV Part 2:** 574

Silverthorne, Elizabeth, **Supp. X:** 220, 221, 222, 226, 234

"Silver To Have and to Hurl" (Didion), **Supp. IV Part 1:** 197

Simic, Charles, **Supp. V:** 5, 332; **Supp. VIII:** 39, **269–287; Supp. XI:** 317; **Supp. XV:** 179, 185; **Supp. XIX:** 277, 282

"Similar Cases" (Gilman), **Supp. XI:** 200, 202

Similitudes, from the Ocean and Prairie (Larcom), **Supp. XIII:** 141

Simmel, Georg, **Supp. I Part 2:** 644; **Supp. XVII:** 98

Simmons, Charles, **Supp. XI:** 230

Simmons, Maggie, **Retro. Supp. II:** 21

Simms, Michael, **Supp. XII:** 184

Simms, William Gilmore, **I:** 211

Simon, Greg, **Supp. XXIV:** 166

Simon, John, **Supp. IV Part 2:** 691

Simon, Neil, **Supp. IV Part 2: 573–594; Supp. VIII:** 8

Simone, Nina, **Supp. XXI:** 243

"Simon Gerty" (Wylie), **Supp. I Part 2:** 713

Simonides, **Supp. XII:** 110–111

"Simon Ortiz" (Gingerich), **Supp. IV Part 2:** 510

Simon Ortiz (Wiget), **Supp. IV Part 2:** 509

"Simple" (Peacock), **Supp. XIX:** 200

"Simple Art of Murder, The" (Chandler), **Supp. IV Part 1:** 121, 341

"Simple Autumnal" (Bogan), **Supp. III Part 1:** 52–53

Simple Heart (Flaubert), **I:** 504

Simple Honorable Man, A (Richter), **Supp. XVIII:** 208, 218, **219,** 220

"Simple Purchase, A" (Peacock), **Supp. XIX:** 199

Simple Speaks his Mind (Hughes), **Retro. Supp. I:** 209; **Supp. I Part 1:** 337

Simple Stakes a Claim (Hughes), **Retro. Supp. I:** 209; **Supp. I Part 1:** 337

Simple's Uncle Sam (Hughes), **Retro. Supp. I:** 209; **Supp. I Part 1:** 337

Simple Takes a Wife (Hughes), **Retro. Supp. I:** 209; **Supp. I Part 1:** 337

Simple Truth, The (Hardwick), **Supp. III Part 1:** 199, 200, 208

Simple Truth, The (Levine), **Supp. V:** 178, 179, 193–194

"Simple Widsom, The" (Skloot), **Supp. XX: 207**

"Simplicity" (Sanders), **Supp. XVI:** 276

Simply Heavenly (Hughes), **Retro. Supp. I:** 209; **Supp. I Part 1:** 338, 339

Simpson, Louis, **Supp. III Part 2:** 541; **Supp. IV Part 2:** 448, 621; **Supp. VIII:** 39, 279; **Supp. IX: 265–283,** 290; **Supp. XI:** 317; **Supp. XII:** 130; **Supp. XIII:** 337

Simpson, Mona, **Supp. XVI:** 206

"Sin" (C. Frost), **Supp. XV:** 96

Sinatra, Frank, **Supp. IX:** 3; **Supp. X:** 119; **Supp. XI:** 213

Sincere Convert, The (Shepard), **IV:** 158

Sincerely, Willis Wayde (Marquand), **III:** 61, 63, 66, 67–68, 69

Sincerity (Rowson), **Supp. XV:** 242

Sincerity and Authenticity (Trilling), **Supp. III Part 2:** 510–512

"Sincerity and Objectification: With Special Reference to the Work of Charles Reznikoff" (Zukofsky), **Supp. XIV:** 286

Sinclair, Mary Craig (Mary Craig Kimbrough), **Supp. V:** 275, 286, 287

Sinclair, Upton, **II:** 34, 440, 444, 451; **III:** 580; **Retro. Supp. II:** 95; **Supp. V: 275–293; Supp. VIII:** 11

Sinclair Lewis: An American Life (Schorer), **II:** 459

"Singapore" (Oliver), **Supp. VII:** 239, 240

Singer, Bennett L., **Supp. IV Part 1:** 330

Singer, Beth, **Supp. XIV:** 203

Singer, Isaac Bashevis, **I:** 144; **IV: 1–24; Retro. Supp. II:** 22, **299–320; Supp. IX:** 114; **Supp. XVIII:** 215, 220; **Supp. XXI:** 106; **Supp. XXII:** 258

Singer, Israel Joshua, **IV:** 2, 16, 17; **Retro. Supp. II:** 302; **Supp. XVII:** 41

Singer, Joshua, **IV:** 4

Singer, Rabbi Pinchos Menachem, **IV:** 16

Singin' and Swingin' and Gettin' Merry Like Christmas (Angelou), **Supp. IV Part 1:** 2, 5, 6–7, 9, 13, 14

"Singing & Doubling Together" (Ammons), **Supp. VII:** 34–35

Singing Jailbirds (Sinclair), **Supp. V:** 277

"Singing the Black Mother" (Lupton), **Supp. IV Part 1:** 7

Single Hound, The (Sarton), **Supp. VIII:** 251, 265

Single Hound, The: Poems of a Lifetime (Dickinson; Bianchi, ed.), **Retro. Supp. I:** 35

Single Man, A (Isherwood), **Supp. XIV:** 157, 164, **169–170,** 171

"Single Sonnet" (Bogan), **Supp. III Part 1:** 56–58

Singley, Carol, **Retro. Supp. I:** 373

Singular Family, A: Rosacoke and Her Kin (Price), **Supp. VI: 258–259,** 260

"Singular First Person, The" (Sanders), **Supp. XVI:** 274

Singularities (Howe), **Supp. IV Part 2:** 431

Sin in Their Blood (Lacy), **Supp. XV:** 200

"Sinister Adolescents, The" (Dos Passos), **I:** 493

Sinister Street (Mackenzie), **II:** 82

Sinking of Clay City, The (Wrigley), **Supp. XVIII: 294–295**

Sinners in the Hands of an Angry God (Edwards), **I:** 546, 552–553, 559, 562; **Supp. XXIV:** 72

Sinning with Annie, and Other Stories (Theroux), **Supp. VIII:** 318

"Sins of Kalamazoo, The" (Sandburg), **III:** 586

Sintram and His Companions (La Motte-Fouqué), **III:** 78

"Siope" (Poe), **III:** 411

"Sipapu: A Cultural Perspective" (Gunn Allen), **Supp. IV Part 1:** 323

Sipchen, Bob, **Supp. X:** 145

Sipper, Ralph B., **Supp. IV Part 2:** 475

"Sire" (Cisneros), **Supp. VII:** 62–63, 64

"Siren and Signal" (Zukofsky), **Supp. III Part 2:** 611, 612

Sirens of Titan, The (Vonnegut), **Supp. II Part 2:** 757, 758, 760, 765–767

"Sir Galahad" (Tennyson), **Supp. I Part 2:** 410

Sirin, V. (pseudonym), **Retro. Supp. I:** 266. *See also* Nabokov, Vladimir

Sirlin, Jerome, **Supp. XXI:** 147

Sir Vadia's Shadow: A Friendship across Five Continents (Theroux), **Supp. VIII:** 309, 314, 321, 325

"Sir William's Reply to Molly"(Kenny), **Supp. XXIII:** 153

"Sis" (F. Barthelme), **Supp. XI:** 26

"S is for Sad" (M. F. K. Fisher), **Supp. XVII:** 86

Sisley, Alfred, **I:** 478

Sissman, L. E., **Supp. X:** 69

"Sister" (Hughes), **Retro. Supp. I:** 208

"Sister" (Lamott), **Supp. XX: 142**

"Sister, The" (July), **Supp. XXIV:** 202

Sister Age (M. F. K. Fisher), **Supp. XVII:** 88, 91

Sister Carrie (Dreiser), **I:** 482, 497, 499, 500, 501–502, 503–504, 505, 506, 515, 519; **III:** 327; **IV:** 208; **Retro. Supp. I:** 376; **Retro. Supp. II:** 93, **96–99; Supp. XVIII:** 76, 243; **Supp. XXIII:** 165

Sister Mary Ignatius Explains It All for You (Durang), **Supp. XXIV:** 114, **119–120**

"Sister of the Minotaur" (Stevens), **IV:** 89; **Supp. IX:** 332

"Sisters" (Boulton), **Supp. XXII:** 20

"Sisters" (Nelson), **Supp. XVIII:** 176

"Sisters, The" (Whittier), **Supp. I Part 2:** 696

Sister's Choice (Showalter), **Retro. Supp. I:** 368

Sisters-in-Law, The (Atherton), **Supp. XXIV:** 25

Sisters of the Earth: Women's Prose and Poetry About Nature (Anderson, ed.), **Supp. XVIII:** 189

Sisters Rosensweig, The (Wasserstein), **Supp. XV:** 320, **328–330**

"Sisyphus" (Kumin), **Supp. IV Part 2:** 443, 444, 451

"Sitalkas" (Doolittle), **Supp. I Part 1:** 266

"Sites of Memory" (Cliff), **Supp. XXII:** 69, 74

Sitney, P. Adams, **Supp. XII:** 2

Sitting Bull, **Supp. IV Part 2:** 492

"Sitting in a Rocking Chair Going Blind" (Komunyakaa), **Supp. XIII:** 114

Sitting In: Selected Writings on Jazz, Blues, and Related Topics (Carruth), **Supp. XVI:** 46

"Sitting Up Late with My Father, 1977" (F. Wright), **Supp. XVII:** 247

Sitti's Secrets (Nye), **Supp. XIII:** 278

Situation Normal (A. Miller), **III:** 148, 149, 156, 164

Situation of Poetry, The: Contemporary Poetry and Its Traditions (Pinsky), **Supp. VI:** 237–238, 239, 241, 242

Sitwell, Edith, **IV:** 77; **Supp. I Part 1:** 271

"Six Brothers" (Cisneros), **Supp. VII:** 67

Six Characters in Search of an Author (Pirandello), **Supp. IV Part 2:** 576

"Six Days: Some Rememberings" (Paley), **Supp. VI:** 226

"65290" (Leopold), **Supp. XIV:** 184–185

Six French Poets (Lowell), **II:** 528–529

"Six in All" (Bierds), **Supp. XVII:** 31

Six Lips (Schott), **Supp. XXIII: 251–252**

"Six Persons" (Baraka), **Supp. II Part 1:** 53

Six Sections from Mountains and Rivers without End (Snyder), **Supp. VIII:** 305

"Sixteen Months" (Sandburg), **III:** 584

1601, or Conversation as It Was by the Fireside in the Time of the Tudors (Twain), **IV:** 201

"Sixth-Month Song in the Foothills" (Snyder), **Supp. VIII:** 297

Sixties, The (magazine) (R. Bly), **Supp. IV Part 1:** 60; **Supp. IX:** 271

"Sixty" (Dunn), **Supp. XI:** 155

"Sixty Acres" (Carver), **Supp. III Part 1:** 141

"64 Elmgrove" (Halliday), **Supp. XIX:** 88

"69 Hidebound Opinions, Propositions, and Several Asides from a Manila Folder concerning the Stuff of Poetry" (Wright), **Supp. XV:** 344–345

Sixty Stories (Barthelme), **Supp. IV Part 1:** 41, 42, 44, 47, 49, 50

63: Dream Palace (Purdy), **Supp. VII:** 270–271

"Six Variations" (Levertov), **Supp. III Part 1:** 277–278

"Six-Year-Old Boy" (Olds), **Supp. X:** 206

"Six Years Later" (Brodsky), **Supp. VIII:** 26, 28

"Size and Sheer Will" (Olds), **Supp. X:** 206

Size of Thoughts, The: Essays and Other Lumber (Baker), **Supp. XIII: 52–53,** 55, 56

Sizwe Bansi Is Dead (Fugard), **Supp. VIII:** 330

Sjöwall, Maj, **Supp. XX:** 87

"Skagway" (Haines), **Supp. XII:** 206

"Skaters, The" (Ashbery), **Supp. III Part 1:** 10, 12, 13, 18, 25

"Skaters, The" (Jarrell), **II:** 368–369

Skau, Michael, **Supp. XII:** 129, 130, 132, 134

Skeeters Kirby (Masters), **Supp. I Part 2:** 459, 470, 471

Skeleton Crew (King), **Supp. V:** 144

"Skeleton in Armor, The" (Longfellow), **Retro. Supp. II:** 168

"Skeleton's Cave, The" (Bryant), **Supp. I Part 1:** 157

Skelton, John, **III:** 521

Skepticisms (Aiken), **Supp. XV:** 298, 302

Sketch Book of Geoffrey Crayon, Gent., The (Irving), **II:** 295, 303, 304–308, 309, 311, 491; **Supp. I Part 1:** 155

Sketches of Art (Jameson), **Retro. Supp. II:** 58

Sketches of Eighteenth Century America (Crèvecoeur), **Supp. I Part 1:** 233, 240–241, 250, 251

"Sketches of Female Biography" (Rowson), **Supp. XV:** 245

Sketches of Switzerland (Cooper), **I:** 346

Sketches Old and New (Twain), **IV:** 198

"Sketch for a Job-Application Blank" (Harrison), **Supp. VIII:** 38

"Sketch"(Kenny), **Supp. XXIII:** 155

Sketch of Old England, by a New England Man (Paulding), **I:** 344

Skibell, Joseph, **Supp. XVII:** 48

"Skier and the Mountain, The" (Eberhart), **I:** 528–529

"Skin-Boats: 1830, The" (Bierds), **Supp. XVII:** 28

Skinker, Mary Scott, **Supp. IX:** 20

Skinner, Ewart, **Supp. XXII:** 78

Skinny Island (Auchincloss), **Supp. IV Part 1:** 33

Skinny Legs and All (Robbins), **Supp. X:** 267, 273, **276–279**

Skin of Our Teeth, The (Wilder), **IV:** 357, 358, 369–372; **Supp. IV Part 2:** 586; **Supp. XX:** 50

"Skins" (Wright), **Supp. V:** 340

Skins and Bones: Poems 1979–1987 (Gunn Allen), **Supp. IV Part 1:** 321, 331

"Skipper Ireson's Ride" (Whittier), **Supp. I Part 2:** 691, 693–694

"Skirmish at Sartoris" (Faulkner), **II:** 67

"Skirt" (Halliday), **Supp. XIX:** 90

Skirts and Slacks (Di Piero), **Supp. XIX:** 35, 36, 38, 45–47

Sklenicka, Carol, **Supp. XXIV:** 166

Skloot, Floyd, **Supp. XX: 193–209**

Skotheim, Robert Allen, **Supp. XVII:** 104

Skow, John, **Supp. V:** 213; **Supp. XVI:** 174

Skube, Michael, **Supp. XVIII:** 96

"Skunk Cabbage" (Bronk), **Supp. XXI:** 31

"Skunk Cabbage" (Oliver), **Supp. VII:** 235, 236

"Skunk Hour" (Lowell), **II:** 548–550; **Retro. Supp. II:** 188, 189; **Supp. XIV:** 269; **Supp. XX: 203**

Sky, The Stars, The Wilderness, The (Bass), **Supp. XVI:** 19, 20

Sky Changes, The (Sorrentino), **Supp. XXI:** 228, 230, 231

"Sky Dance" (Leopold), **Supp. XIV:** 186

"Sky Line" (Taylor), **Supp. V:** 316

"Sky Line, The" (Mumford), **Supp. II Part 2:** 475

"Skyscraper" (Sandburg), **III:** 581–582

Sky's the Limit, The: A Defense of the Earth (Nichols), **Supp. XIII:** 268

"Sky Valley Rider" (Wright), **Supp. V:** 335, 340

Sky-Walk; or the Man Unknown to Himself (Brown), **Supp. I Part 1:** 127–128

"Slang in America" (Whitman), **IV:** 348

Slappy Hooper, the Wonderful Sign Painter (Bontemps and Conroy), **Supp. XXII:** 5, 11

Slapstick (Vonnegut), **Supp. II Part 2:** 753, 754, 778

Slapstick Tragedy (T. Williams), **IV:** 382, 393

Slate, Lane, **Supp. IX:** 251, 253

Slattery, Mary Grace. *See* Miller, Mrs. Arthur (Mary Grace Slattery)

"Slaughterer, The" (Singer), **IV:** 19

Slaughterhouse-Five (Vonnegut), **Supp. II Part 2:** 755, 758–759, 760, 770, 772–776; **Supp. V:** 41, 244; **Supp. XIX:** 235

Slaughter Rule, The (film; Alex and Andrew Smith), **Supp. XIX:** 174

Slave, The (Baraka), **Supp. II Part 1:** 42, 44, 56

Slave, The: A Novel (Singer), **IV:** 13; **Retro. Supp. II: 305–307**

"Slave Canal" (Ray), **Supp. XVIII:** 193

"Slave Coffle" (Angelou), **Supp. IV Part 1:** 16

Slave of the Sky (P. N. Warren), **Supp. XX: 261**

"Slave on the Block" (Hughes), **Supp. I Part 1:** 329

Slave Power, The: The Free North and Southern Domination, 1780–1860 (Richards), **Supp. XIV:** 48

"Slave Quarters" (Dickey), **Supp. IV Part 1:** 181

Slavery (Channing), **Supp. XXIV:** 77–78

"Slave's Dream, The" (Longfellow), **Supp. I Part 2:** 409

Slave Ship: A Historical Pageant (Baraka), **Supp. II Part 1:** 47–49, 53, 56–57

"Slave-Ships, The" (Whittier), **Supp. I Part 2:** 687–688

Slaves in Algiers; or, A Struggle for Freedom (Rowson), **Supp. XV:** 236–237

"Slave Trade, The: View from the Middle Passage" (Major), **Supp. XXII:** 182

Slavs! Thinking about the Longstanding Problems of Virtue and Happiness (Kushner), **Supp. IX:** 146

Sledge, Eugene, **Supp. V:** 250

Sleek for the Long Flight (Matthews), **Supp. IX:** 154, 155, **157–158**

Sleep (Dixon), **Supp. XII:** 154

"Sleep, The" (Strand), **Supp. IV Part 2:** 627

Sleeper (film; Allen), **Supp. XV:** 5

"Sleeper, The" (Poe), **III:** 411

"Sleeper 1, The" (Hay), **Supp. XIV:** 132–133

"Sleeper 2, The" (Hay), **Supp. XIV:** 132–133

"Sleepers, The" (Whitman), **IV:** 336

"Sleepers in Jaipur" (Kenyon), **Supp. VII:** 172

Sleepers in Moon-Crowned Valleys (Purdy), **Supp. VII:** 274, 275

Sleepers Joining Hands (R. Bly), **Supp. XXI:** 85

"Sleepers Joining Hands" (R. Bly), **Supp. IV Part 1:** 63, 73

Sleeping Beauty (Macdonald), **Supp. IV Part 2:** 474, 475

Sleeping Beauty, The (Carruth), **Supp. XVI:** 53, 57–58

"Sleeping Beauty Syndrome, The: The New Agony of Single Men" (Wasserstein), **Supp. XV:** 328

Sleeping Fires (Atherton), **Supp. XXIV:** 25

"Sleeping Fury, The" (Bogan), **Supp. III Part 1:** 58

Sleeping Fury, The: Poems (Bogan), **Supp. III Part 1:** 55–58

Sleeping Gypsy and Other Poems, The (Garrett), **Supp. VII:** 96–98

Sleeping in the Forest (Oliver), **Supp. VII:** 233

"Sleeping in the Forest" (Oliver), **Supp. VII:** 233–234

Sleeping in the Woods (Wagoner), **Supp. IX:** 328

Sleeping on Fists (Ríos), **Supp. IV Part 2:** 540

Sleeping on the Wing: An Anthology of Modern Poetry (Koch and Farrell, eds.), **Supp. XV:** 187–188

"Sleeping on the Wing" (O'Hara), **Supp. XXIII:** 214

"Sleeping Standing Up" (Bishop), **Supp. I Part 1:** 85, 89, 93

"Sleeping with Animals" (Kumin), **Supp. IV Part 2:** 454

Sleeping with One Eye Open (Strand), **Supp. IV Part 2:** 621–624, 623, 628

Sleep in Thunder (Lacy), **Supp. XV:** 206

"Sleepless, The" (L.-Y. Lee), **Supp. XV:** 224

"Sleepless at Crown Point" (Wilbur), **Supp. III Part 2:** 561

Sleepless Nights (Hardwick), **Supp. III Part 1:** 193, 208–211

"Sleepless Nights" (Nelson), **Supp. XVIII:** 174

"Sleep-Walkers, The" (Gibran), **Supp. XX:** 118

Sleepy Lagoon Mystery, The (Endore), **Supp. XVII:** 60

"Sleepy People" (Lethem), **Supp. XVIII:** 140

Sleigh, Tom, **Supp. XIX:** 38, 40

Sleight, Ken, **Supp. XIII:** 12

Slick, Sam (pseudonym). *See* Haliburton, Thomas Chandler

"Slick Gonna Learn" (Ellison), **Retro. Supp. II:** 116; **Supp. II Part 1:** 237–238

"Slight Rebellion off Madison" (Salinger), **III:** 553

"Slight Sound at Evening, A" (White), **Supp. I Part 2:** 672

"Slim Graves Show, The" (Keillor), **Supp. XVI:** 172

"Slim Greer" series (Hayden), **Supp. II Part 1:** 369

"Slim in Hell" (Hayden), **Supp. II Part 1:** 369

"Slim Man Canyon" (Silko), **Supp. IV Part 2:** 560

"Slip, Shift, and Speed Up: The Influence of Robinson Jeffers's Narrative Syntax" (Jarman), **Supp. XVII:** 111, 112

"Slippery Fingers" (Hammett), **Supp. IV Part 1:** 343

Slipping-Down Life, A (Tyler), **Supp. IV Part 2:** 660–661

Sloan, Jacob, **IV:** 3, 6

Sloan, John, **I:** 254; **IV:** 411; **Retro. Supp. II:** 103; **Supp. XXII:** 277

Sloane, John, **Supp. XV:** 295

"Slob" (Farrell), **II:** 25, 28, 31

Slocum, Joshua, **Supp. I Part 2:** 497

Slogum House (Sandoz), **Supp. XXIV:** 244, **251–252,** 255

Slonim, Véra. *See* Nabokov, Véra

Slopen, Beverly, **Supp. XX:** 59

Slouching towards Bethlehem (Didion), **Supp. IV Part 1:** 196, 197, 200–201, 202, 206, 210

Slovic, Scott, **Supp. XVI:** 277

"Slow Child with a Book of Birds" (Levis), **Supp. XI:** 268

"Slow Dance with Icarus" (Monson), **Supp. XXIV:** 240

Slow Dancing Through Ether: A Fine Binding Project (Monson and Ingmundson), **Supp. XXIV:** 230, 234

"Slow Down for Poetry" (Strand), **Supp. IV Part 2:** 620

Slow Music (Taggard), **Supp. XXII:** 284

"Slow Pacific Swell, The" (Winters), **Supp. II Part 2:** 790, 793, 795, 796, 799

Slow Parade (Kees), **Supp. XV:** 137

Slow Train Coming (album, Dylan), **Supp. XVIII:** 28

Slow Transparency (Hadas), **Supp. XXIII: 113–114**

"Slum Church" (Espaillat), **Supp. XXI:** 110–111

"Slumgullions" (Olsen), **Supp. IV Part 1:** 54

Slumgullion Stew: An Edward Abbey Reader (Abbey), **Supp. XIII:** 4

Slung, Michelle, **Supp. XX:** 87

"S & M" (Komunyakaa), **Supp. XIII:** 114

"Small" (C. Frost), **Supp. XV:** 102

Small, Albion, **Supp. I Part 1:** 5

"Small, Good Thing, A" (Carver), **Supp. III Part 1:** 145, 147

Small, Miriam Rossiter, **Supp. I Part 1:** 319

Small Boy and Others, A (James), **II:** 337, 547; **Retro. Supp. I:** 235

"Small but Urgent Request to the Unknowable" (Karr), **Supp. XI:** 243

Small Ceremonies (Shields), **Supp. VII:** 312–315, 320

Small Craft Warnings (T. Williams), **IV:** 382, 383, 384, 385, 386, 387, 392, 393, 396, 398

"Small Degrees" (Brockmeier), **Supp. XXII:** 52, 59

"Small Fry" (Peacock), **Supp. XIX:** 206

Small Place, A (Kincaid), **Supp. VII:** 186–187, 188, 191

"Small Rain, The" (Pynchon), **Supp. II Part 2:** 620

Small Room, The (Sarton), **Supp. VIII:** 252, **255–256**

Smalls, Bob, **II:** 128

"Small Song for Andrew" (Weigl), **Supp. XIX:** 280

Small Time Crooks (film; Allen), **Supp. XV:** 11

Small Town, A (Hearon), **Supp. VIII: 65–66**

"Small Vases from Hebron, The" (Nye), **Supp. XIII:** 283

"Small Vision, The" (Goldbarth), **Supp. XII:** 180

"Small Voice from the Wings" (Everwine), **Supp. XV:** 76

"Small Wire" (Sexton), **Supp. II Part 2:** 696

Small Worlds (A. Hoffman), **Supp. XVII:** 44

Smardz, Zofia, **Supp. XVI:** 155

Smart, Christopher, **III:** 534; **Supp. I Part 2:** 539; **Supp. IV Part 2:** 626

Smart, Joyce H., **Supp. XI:** 169

"Smart Cookie, A" (Cisneros), **Supp. VII:** 64

"Smash" (Thompson), **Supp. XXIII:** 301, 302

"Smashup" (Thurber), **Supp. I Part 2:** 616

Smedly, Agnes, **Supp. XIII:** 295

"Smell of a God, The" (Peacock), **Supp. XIX:** 199

"Smelt Fishing" (Hayden), **Supp. II Part 1:** 367

"Smile of the Bathers, The" (Kees), **Supp. XV:** 145

"Smile on the Face of a Kouros, The" (Bronk), **Supp. XXI:** 31

"Smiles" (Dunn), **Supp. XI:** 151

Smiles, Samuel, **Supp. X:** 167

Smiley, Jane, **Supp. VI: 291–309; Supp. XII:** 73, 297; **Supp. XIII:** 127; **Supp. XIX:** 54

Smith, Adam, **II:** 9; **Supp. I Part 2:** 633, 634, 639; **Supp. XVII:** 235

Smith, Annick, **Supp. XIV:** 223

Smith, Barbara, **Supp. XXIII:** 194

Smith, Benjamin, **IV:** 148

Smith, Bernard, **I:** 260

Smith, Bessie, **Retro. Supp. I:** 343; **Supp. VIII:** 330; **Supp. XIX:** 147

Smith, Betty, **Supp. XXIII: 257–271**

Smith, Charlie, **Supp. X:** 177

Smith, Dale, **Supp. XV:** 136, 138, 139

Smith, Dave, **Supp. V:** 333; **Supp. XI:** 152; **Supp. XII:** 178, 198; **Supp. XIX:** 277, 282

Smith, David, **Supp. XIII:** 246, 247

Smith, David Nichol, **Supp. XIV:** 2

Smith, Dinitia, **Supp. VIII:** 74, 82, 83; **Supp. XVIII:** 162; **Supp. XXIV:** 2–3

Smith, Elihu Hubbard, **Supp. I Part 1:** 126, 127, 130

Smith, Ernest J., **Supp. XXIII:** 111, 113, 117

Smith, George Adam, **III:** 199

Smith, Hannah Whitall, **Supp. XIV:** 333, 334, 338

Smith, Harrison, **II:** 61

Smith, Henry Nash, **IV:** 210; **Supp. I Part 1:** 233

Smith, Herbert F., **Supp. I Part 2:** 423

Smith, Iain Crichton, **Supp. XVIII:** 196

Smith, James, **II:** 111

Smith, Jedediah Strong, **Supp. IV Part 2:** 602

Smith, Jerome, **Supp. IV Part 1:** 369

Smith, Joe, **Supp. IV Part 2:** 584

Smith, John, **I:** 4, 131; **II:** 296

Smith, John Allyn, **I:** 168

Smith, Johnston (pseudonym). *See* Crane, Stephen

Smith, Katherine Capshaw, **Supp. XXII:** 10, 13–14

Smith, Kellogg, **Supp. I Part 2:** 660

Smith, Lamar, **II:** 585

Smith, Mrs. Lamar (Marguerite Walters), **II:** 585, 587

Smith, Lane, **Supp. XIX:** 231

Smith, Larry David, **Supp. XVIII:** 22

Smith, Lee, **Supp. XII:** 311; **Supp. XVIII:** 195; **Supp. XXII:** 206, 213

Smith, Lillian, **Supp. XXII:** 67

Smith, Logan Pearsall, **Supp. XIV: 333– 351**

Smith, Lula Carson. *See* McCullers, Carson

Smith, Mark, **Supp. XVIII:** 155

Smith, Martha Nell, **Retro. Supp. I:** 33, 43, 46, 47

Smith, Mary Rozet, **Supp. I Part 1:** 5, 22

Smith, Oliver, **II:** 586

Smith, Patricia Clark, **Supp. IV Part 1:** 397, 398, 402, 406, 408, 410; **Supp. IV Part 2:** 509; **Supp. XII:** 218

Smith, Patrick, **Supp. VIII:** 40, 41

Smith, Patti, **Supp. XII:** 136; **Supp. XIV:** 151

Smith, Porter, **III:** 572

Smith, Red, **II:** 417, 424

Smith, Robert McClure, **Supp. XV:** 270

Smith, Robert Pearsall, **Supp. XIV:** 333

Smith, Sarah A., **Supp. XVIII:** 99

Smith, Seba, **Supp. I Part 2:** 411

Smith, Sidonie, **Supp. IV Part 1:** 11; **Supp. XXII:** 70

Smith, Stevie, **Supp. V:** 84

Smith, Sydney, **II:** 295; **Supp. XIV:** 112

Smith, Thorne, **Supp. IX:** 194

Smith, Valerie, **Supp. XXII:** 146

Smith, Wendy, **Supp. XII:** 330, 335; **Supp. XVIII:** 89, 92

Smith, Wilford Bascom "Pitchfork", **Supp. XIII:** 168

Smith, William, **II:** 114

Smith, William Gardner, **Supp. XVI:** 142–143

Smith, William Jay, **Supp. XIII: 331– 350**

"Smoke" (Di Piero), **Supp. XIX:** 38

Smoke (film), **Supp. XII:** 21

Smoke and Steel (Sandburg), **III:** 585– 587, 592

"Smokehouse" (Offutt), **Supp. XIX:** 166, 167

"Smokers" (Wolff), **Supp. VII:** 340–341

Smokey Bites the Dust (film, C. Griffith), **Supp. XVII:** 9

Smoking Mountain, The: Stories of Postwar Germany (Boyle), **Supp. XXIV:** 61

"Smoking My Prayers" (Ortiz), **Supp. IV Part 2:** 503

"Smoking Room, The" (Jackson), **Supp. IX:** 116

"Smoky Gold" (Leopold), **Supp. XIV:** 186

Smolan, Sandy, **Supp. XVI:** 36

Smollett, Tobias G., **I:** 134, 339, 343; **II:** 304–305; **III:** 61; **Supp. XVIII:** 7

Smooding, Robert, **Supp. XXIII:** 294

Smuggler's Bible, A (McElroy), **Supp. IV Part 1:** 285

Smuggler's Handbook, The (Goldbarth), **Supp. XII:** 181, 183

Smugglers of Lost Soul's Rock, The (Gardner), **Supp. VI: 70**

Smyth, Albert Henry, **II:** 123

Smyth, Jacqui, **Supp. XXI:** 215

"Snack Firm Maps New Chip Push" (Keillor), **Supp. XVI:** 168, 169

"Snail, The" (Hay), **Supp. XIV:** 124

"Snake, The" (Berry), **Supp. X:** 31

"Snake, The" (Crane), **I:** 420

"Snakecharmer" (Plath), **Supp. I Part 2:** 538

"Snakes, Mongooses" (Moore), **III:** 207

"Snakeskin" (Kooser), **Supp. XIX:** 123

"Snakes of September, The" (Kunitz), **Supp. III Part 1:** 258

"Snapshot of 15th S.W., A" (Hugo), **Supp. VI:** 141

"Snapshot Rediscovered, A" (X. J. Kennedy), **Supp. XV:** 170

"Snapshots in an Album" (Espaillat), **Supp. XXI:** 111

"Snapshots of a Daughter-in-Law" (Rich), **Supp. I Part 2:** 553–554

Snapshots of a Daughter-in-Law: Poems, 1954–1962 (Rich), **Supp. I Part 2:** 550–551, 553–554; **Supp. XII:** 255

Snaring the Flightless Birds (Bierds), **Supp. XVII:** 26

Sneetches and Other Stories, The (Geisel), **Supp. XVI:** 109

"Sneeze, The" (Chekhov), **Supp. IV Part 2:** 585

Snell, Ebenezer, **Supp. I Part 1:** 151

Snell, Thomas, **Supp. I Part 1:** 153

"Snob, The" (Boulton), **Supp. XXII:** 23

"Snob, The" (Shapiro), **Supp. II Part 2:** 705

Snobbery: The America Version (Epstein), **Supp. XIV:** 102, 114–115

Snodgrass, Kathleen, **Supp. XVI:** 42

Snodgrass, W. D., **I:** 400; **Retro. Supp. II:** 179; **Supp. III Part 2:** 541; **Supp. V:** 337; **Supp. VI: 311–328; Supp. XI:** 141, 315; **Supp. XIII:** 312; **Supp. XV:** 92, 153; **Supp. XVII:** 239

"Snow" (C. Baxter), **Supp. XVII:** 19

"Snow" (Frost), **Retro. Supp. I:** 133

"Snow" (Haines), **Supp. XII:** 212

"Snow" (Sexton), **Supp. II Part 2:** 696

"Snow" (W. V. Davis), **Supp. XXI:** 89, 90, 93

Snow, C. P., **Supp. I Part 2:** 536

Snow, Hank, **Supp. V:** 335

Snow Ball, The (Gurney), **Supp. V:** 99

"Snow-Bound" (Whittier), **Supp. I Part 2:** 700–703

"Snow Bound at Eagle's" (Harte), **Supp. II Part 1:** 356

"Snowflakes" (Longfellow), **II:** 498

"Snow Goose, The" (Gallico), **Supp. XVI:** 238

Snow-Image and Other Twice Told Tales, The (Hawthorne), **II:** 237; **Retro. Supp. I:** 160

"Snowing in Greenwich Village" (Updike), **IV:** 226; **Retro. Supp. I:** 321

"Snow in New York" (Swenson), **Supp. IV Part 2:** 644

Snow Leopard, The (Matthiessen), **Supp. V:** 199, 207–211

"Snow Man, The" (Stevens), **IV:** 82–83; **Retro. Supp. I:** 299, 300, 302, 306, 307, 312; **Supp. XXI:** 60

"Snowmass Cycle, The" (Dunn), **Supp. XI:** 152

Snow: Meditations of a Cautious Man in Winter (Banks), **Supp. V:** 6

Snow Poems, The (Ammons), **Supp. VII:** 32–34

Snowshoe Trek to Otter River (Budbill), **Supp. XIX:** 11

Snow's Music, The (Skloot), **Supp. XX: 196, 204–205**

"Snows of Kilimanjaro, The" (Hemingway), **II:** 78, 257, 263, 264; **Retro. Supp. I:** 98, 182; **Supp. XII:** 249

"Snows of Studiofiftyfour, The" (Plimpton), **Supp. XVI:** 245

"Snow Songs" (Snodgrass), **Supp. VI:** 324

"Snowstorm, The" (Oates), **Supp. II Part 2:** 523

"Snowstorm as It Affects the American Farmer, A" (Crèvecoeur), **Supp. I Part 1:** 251

Snow White (Barthelme), **Supp. IV Part 1:** 40, 47, 48–49, 50, 52; **Supp. V:** 39

"Snowy Egret" (Weigl), **Supp. XIX:** 280–281

"Snowy Mountain Song, A" (Ortiz), **Supp. IV Part 2:** 506

Snyder, Gary, **Supp. III Part 1:** 350; **Supp. IV Part 2:** 502; **Supp. V:** 168–169; **Supp. VIII:** 39, **289–307; Supp. XVI:** 283; **Supp. XXII:** 276

Snyder, Mike, **Supp. XIV:** 36

"So-and-So Reclining on Her Couch" (Stevens), **IV:** 90

"Soapland" (Thurber), **Supp. I Part 2:** 619

Soares, Lota de Macedo, **Retro. Supp. II:** 44; **Supp. I Part 1:** 89, 94

"Sobbin' Women, The" (Benét), **Supp. XI:** 47

Sobin, Gustaf, **Supp. XVI: 281–298**

Sochen, June, **Supp. XXI:** 1

Social Ethics (Gilman), **Supp. XI:** 207

"Social Function of the Story Teller, The" (lecture, Murray), **Supp. XIX:** 153

"Socialism and the Negro" (McKay), **Supp. X:** 135

"Socialism of the Skin, A (Liberation, Honey!)" (Kushner), **Supp. IX:** 135

Social Thought in America: The Revolt against Formalism (White), **Supp. I Part 2:** 648, 650

"Society, Morality, and the Novel" (Ellison), **Retro. Supp. II:** 118, 123–124

"Sociological Habit Patterns in Linguistic Transmogrification" (Cowley), **Supp. II Part 1:** 143

"Sociological Poet, A" (Bourne), **I:** 228

Socrates, **I:** 136, 265; **II:** 8–9, 105, 106; **III:** 281, 419, 606; **Supp. I Part 2:** 458; **Supp. XII:** 98

Socrates Fortlow stories (Mosley), **Supp. XIII: 242–243**

So Forth (Brodsky), **Supp. VIII:** 32–33

"So Forth" (Brodsky), **Supp. VIII:** 33

"Soft Flame" (Skloot), **Supp. XX: 203**

Soft Machine, The (Burroughs), **Supp. III Part 1:** 93, 103, 104

"Soft Mask" (Karr), **Supp. XI:** 243

Soft Side, The (James), **II:** 335; **Retro. Supp. I:** 229

"Soft Spring Night in Shillington, A" (Updike), **Retro. Supp. I:** 318, 319

"Soft Wood" (Lowell), **II:** 550–551

"So Help Me" (Algren), **Supp. IX:** 2

Soil and Survival: Land Stewardship and the Future of American Agriculture (C. Bly, J. Paddock and N. Paddock), **Supp. XVI:** 36–37

"Soirée in Hollywood" (H. Miller), **III:** 186

Sojourner, The (Rawlings), **Supp. X:** 233–234

"Sojourn in a Whale" (Moore), **III:** 211, 213

"Sojourns" (Didion), **Supp. IV Part 1:** 205

Sokolow, Jayme, **Supp. XIX:** 134

Solanus, Jane, **Supp. XVI:** 293

Solar Lottery (Dick), **Supp. XVIII:** 138

Solar Storms (Hogan), **Supp. IV Part 1:** 397, 410, 414–415

"Soldier, The" (Frost), **II:** 155

"Soldier Asleep at the Tomb" (Schnackenberg), **Supp. XV:** 262–263

Soldier Blue (film), **Supp. X:** 124

"Soldier of Fortune" (Wright), **Supp. XV:** 341

"Soldier's Home" (Hemingway), **Retro. Supp. I:** 189

Soldier's Joy (Bell), **Supp. X:** 7, **7–8,** 10, 11; **Supp. XXIII:** 43

Soldiers of the Storm (film), **Supp. XIII:** 163

Soldiers' Pay (Faulkner), **I:** 117; **II:** 56, 68; **Retro. Supp. I:** 80, 81

"Soldier's Testament, The" (Mumford), **Supp. II Part 2:** 473

"Soliloquy: Man Talking to a Mirror" (Komunyakaa), **Supp. XIII:** 116–117

"Solipsism" (Monson), **Supp. XXIV:** 230

"Solitary Confinement" (X. J. Kennedy), **Supp. XV:** 157

"Solitary Pond, The" (Updike), **Retro. Supp. I:** 323

So Little Time (Marquand), **III:** 55, 59, 65, 67, 69

"Solitude" (Maupassant), **Supp. I Part 1:** 223

Solo Faces (Salter), **Supp. IX: 259–260**

Solomon, Andy, **Supp. X:** 11

Solomon, Carl, **Supp. XIV:** 143, 150

Solomon, Charles, **Supp. VIII:** 82

Solomon, Deborah, **Supp. XXI:** 245

Solomon, Henry, Jr., **Supp. I Part 2:** 490

Solomons, Leon, **IV:** 26

So Long, See You Tomorrow (Maxwell), **Supp. VIII:** 156, 160, 162, **167–169; Supp. XVII:** 23

"So Long Ago" (Bausch), **Supp. VII:** 41–42

Solotaroff, Robert, **Retro. Supp. II:** 203

Solotaroff, Theodore, **III:** 452–453; **Retro. Supp. II:** 281; **Supp. I Part 2:** 440, 445; **Supp. X:** 79; **Supp. XI:** 340; **Supp. XII:** 291; **Supp. XIX:** 268

Solstice (Di Piero), **Supp. XIX:** 36

"Solstice" (Jeffers), **Supp. II Part 2:** 433, 435

"Solstice, The" (Merwin), **Supp. III Part 1:** 356

"Solus Rex" (Nabokov), **Retro. Supp. I:** 274

"Solutions" (McCarthy), **II:** 578

"Solving the Puzzle" (Dunn), **Supp. XI:** 152

Solzhenitsyn, Alexandr, **Retro. Supp. I:** 278; **Supp. VIII:** 241

"Some Afternoon" (Creeley), **Supp. IV Part 1:** 150–151

Some American People (Caldwell), **I:** 292, 294, 295, 296, 304, 309

"Some Ashes Drifting above Piedra, California" (Levis), **Supp. XI:** 264–265

"Some Aspects of the Grotesque in Southern Fiction" (O'Connor), **Retro. Supp. II:** 223, 224

"Some Birds on a Dun Field" (Bronk), **Supp. XXI:** 27

"Somebody Always Grabs the Purple" (H. Roth), **Supp. IX:** 234

Somebody in Boots (Algren), **Supp. IX:** 3, **5–7,** 12

Somebody's Darling (McMurtry), **Supp. V:** 225

Some Came Running (film), **Supp. XI:** 213

Some Came Running (Jones), **Supp. XI:** 214, 215, 220, **222–223,** 226, 227, 232

Some Can Whistle (McMurtry), **Supp. V:** 229

"Some Children of the Goddess" (Mailer), **Retro. Supp. II:** 204

Someday, Maybe (Stafford), **Supp. XI: 323–325; Supp. XIII:** 281

"Some Dreamers of the Golden Dream" (Didion), **Supp. IV Part 1:** 200

Some Faces in the Crowd (Schulberg), **Supp. XVIII:** 252

"Some Foreign Letters" (Sexton), **Supp. II Part 2:** 674

"Some General Instructions" (Koch), **Supp. XV:** 182

"Some Good News" (Olson), **Supp. II Part 2:** 575, 576, 577

"Some Grass along a Ditch Bank" (Levis), **Supp. XI:** 266

"Some Greek Writings" (Corso), **Supp. XII:** 130

Some Honorable Men: Political Conventions, 1960–1972 (Mailer), **Retro. Supp. II:** 208

Some Imagist Poets (Lowell), **III:** 511, 518, 520; **Supp. I Part 1:** 257, 261

"Some keep the Sabbath going to Church" (Dickinson), **Retro. Supp. I:** 30; **Supp. XVIII:** 301

"Some Laughed" (L. Michaels), **Supp. XVI:** 207

"Some Like Indians Endure" (Gunn Allen), **Supp. IV Part 1:** 330

"Some Like Them Cold" (Lardner), **II:** 427–428, 430, 431; **Supp. IX:** 202

"Some Lines from Whitman" (Jarrell), **IV:** 352

"Some Matters Concerning the Occupant" (Keillor), **Supp. XVI:** 167

"Some Musicians Play Chamber Music for Us" (Bronk), **Supp. XXI:** 27–28

"Some Negatives: X. at the Chateau" (Merrill), **Supp. III Part 1:** 322

"Some Neglected Points in the Theory of Socialism" (Veblen), **Supp. I Part 2:** 635

"Some Notes for an Autobiographical Lecture" (Trilling), **Supp. III Part 2:** 493, 497, 500

"Some Notes on French Poetry" (R. Bly), **Supp. IV Part 1:** 61

"Some Notes on Miss L." (West), **IV:** 290–291, 295; **Retro. Supp. II:** 322

"Some Notes on Organic Form" (Levertov), **Supp. III Part 1:** 272, 279

"Some Notes on Teaching: Probably Spoken" (Paley), **Supp. VI:** 225

"Some Notes on the Gazer Within" (Levis), **Supp. XI:** 270

"Some Notes on Violence" (West), **IV:** 304; **Retro. Supp. II:** 322, 323

"Some Observations Now" (Conroy), **Supp. XVI:** 75

Some Observations of a Stranger at Zuni in the Later Part of the Century (Major), **Supp. XXII:** 179–180

"Some Observations of a Stranger at Zuni in the Later Part of the Century" (Major), **Supp. XXII:** 179

Some of the Dharma (Kerouac), **Supp. III Part 1:** 225

"Some of Us Have Fewer" (Monson), **Supp. XXIV:** 240

"Someone Is Buried" (Salinas), **Supp. XIII:** 324

"Someone Puts a Pineapple Together" (Stevens), **IV:** 90–91

"Someone's Blood" (Dove), **Supp. IV Part 1:** 245

"Someone Talking" (Harjo), **Supp. XII:** 219–220

"Someone Talking to Himself" (Wilbur), **Supp. III Part 2:** 557

"Someone to Watch Over Me" (Stern), **Supp. IX:** 300

Someone to Watch Over Me: Stories (Bausch), **Supp. VII:** 53

Some People, Places, & Things That Will Not Appear in My Next Novel (Cheever), **Supp. I Part 1:** 184–185

"Some Poets' Criticism and the Age" (Yenser), **Supp. XV:** 113–114

Some Problems of Philosophy: A Beginning of an Introduction to Philosophy (James), **II:** 360–361

"Some Questions You Might Ask" (Oliver), **Supp. VII:** 238–239

"Some Remarks on Humor" (White), **Supp. I Part 2:** 672

"Some Remarks on Rhythm" (Roethke), **III:** 548–549

Somers, Fred, **I:** 196

Somerville, Jane, **Supp. IX:** 289, 296–297

"Some Secrets" (Stern), **Supp. IX:** 286, 287, 288, 289, 295

Some Sort of Epic Grandeur (Bruccoli), **Retro. Supp. I:** 115, 359

"Something" (Oliver), **Supp. VII:** 236

Something Happened (Heller), **Supp. IV Part 1:** 383, 386–388, 389, 392

"*Something Happened:* The Imaginary, the Symbolic, and the Discourse of the Family" (Mellard), **Supp. IV Part 1:** 387

Something in Common (Hughes), **Supp. I Part 1:** 329–330

Something Inside: Conversations with Gay Fiction Writers (Gambone), **Supp. XII:** 81

"Something Matters but We Don't " (Bronk), **Supp. XXI:** 32

"Something Might Be Gaining" (Mosher), **Supp. XXII:** 209

"Something New" (Stern), **Supp. IX:** 290

Some Things (Berrigan, Padgett, and Brainard), **Supp. XXIV:** 41

Something Said (Sorrentino), **Supp. XXI:** 226, 227, 229, 235

"Something's Going to Happen" (Zinberg), **Supp. XV:** 196

"Something Spurious from the Mindinao Deep" (Stegner), **Supp. IV Part 2:** 605

"Something That Needs Nothing" (July), **Supp. XXIV:** 203

"Something to Believe In" (Pitts), **Supp. XXII:** 280

Something to Declare (Alvarez), **Supp. VII:** 1, 2, 11, 17–19

Something to Remember Me By (Bellow), **Retro. Supp. II:** 32

"Something to Remember Me By" (Bellow), **Retro. Supp. II:** 32

Something Wicked This Way Comes (Bradbury), **Supp. IV Part 1:** 101, 110–111

"Something Wild . . ." (T. Williams), **IV:** 381

"Some Thoughts" (McNally), **Supp. XIII:** 207

"Some Thoughts on the Line" (Oliver), **Supp. VII:** 238

"Sometimes, Reading" (Stafford), **Supp. XI:** 314

"Sometimes It Just Happens That Way, That's All" (Hinojosa), **Supp. XIX:** 101

"Sometimes I Wonder" (Hughes), **Supp. I Part 1:** 337

Sometimes Mysteriously (Salinas), **Supp. XIII:** 311, **326–328**

"Sometimes Mysteriously" (Salinas), **Supp. XIII:** 328

Some Trees (Ashbery), **Supp. III Part 1:** 3–7, 12

"Some Trees" (Ashbery), **Supp. III Part 1:** 2

"Some Truths About American Readers" (Atherton), **Supp. XXIV:** 24, 27

"Some Views on the Reading and Writing of Short Stories" (Welty), **Retro. Supp. I:** 351

"Somewhere" (Nemerov), **III:** 279–280

"Somewhere Else" (Paley), **Supp. VI:** 227

"Somewhere in Africa" (Sexton), **Supp. II Part 2:** 684–685

"Somewhere Is Such a Kingdom" (Ransom), **III:** 492

"Somewhere near Phu Bai: (Komunyakaa), **Supp. XIII:** 123–124

Some Words (Bronk), **Supp. XXI:** 32

"Some Words with a Mummy" (Poe), **III:** 425

"Some Yips and Barks in the Dark" (Snyder), **Supp. VIII:** 291

Sommers, Michael, **Supp. IV Part 2:** 581

Sommers, William, **I:** 387, 388

"Somnambulisma" (Stevens), **Retro. Supp. I:** 310

"So Much Summer" (Dickinson), **Retro. Supp. I:** 26, 44, 45

"So Much the Worse for Boston" (Lindsay), **Supp. I Part 2:** 398

"So Much Water So Close to Home" (Carver), **Supp. III Part 1:** 143, 146

Son, Cathy, **Supp. X:** 292

"Son, The" (Dove), **Supp. IV Part 1:** 245

"Son and Father" (Pickering), **Supp. XXI:** 197

"Sonata" (Schnackenberg), **Supp. XV:** 259

"Sonata for the Invisible" (Harjo), **Supp. XII:** 228

Sonata for Two Pianos (Bowles), **Supp. IV Part 1:** 83

Son at the Front, A (Wharton), **II:** 183; **IV:** 320; **Retro. Supp. I:** 378

Sondheim, Stephen, **Supp. XII:** 260; **Supp. XVI:** 194

Son Excellence Eugène Rougon (Zola), **III:** 322

Son from Sleep, A (Hadas), **Supp. XXIII:** **114–115**

Song (B. Kelly), **Supp. XVII:** 123, **127–130**

"Song" (B. Kelly), **Supp. XVII:** 127

"Song" (Bogan), **Supp. III Part 1:** 57

"Song" (Bryant). *See* "Hunter of the West, The"

"Song" (Dunbar), **Supp. II Part 1:** 199

"Song" (Espaillat), **Supp. XXI:** 106–107

"Song" (Ginsberg), **Supp. II Part 1:** 317

"Song" (Kenyon), **Supp. VII:** 169

"Song" (Rich), **Supp. I Part 2:** 560

"Song" (Wylie), **Supp. I Part 2:** 729

"Song, A" (Creeley), **Supp. IV Part 1:** 145

"Song, The" (Gioia), **Supp. XV:** 117

Song and Idea (Eberhart), **I:** 526, 529, 533, 539

"Song: Enlightenment" (X. J. Kennedy), **Supp. XV:** 169

"Song for a Lover Killed in Battle"(J. Schoolcraft), **Supp. XXIII:** 235

Song for Anninho (G. Jones), **Supp. XXIV:** 185, 195

Song for My Father, A: A Play in Two Acts (Budbill), **Supp. XIX:** 3, **15–16**

"Song for Myself and the Deer to Return On" (Harjo), **Supp. XII:** 225

"Song for My Sixtieth Year" (Carruth), **Supp. XVI:** 54

"Song for Occupations, A" (Whitman), **Retro. Supp. I:** 394

"Song for Simeon, A" (Eliot), **Retro. Supp. I:** 64

"Song for the Coming of Smallpox" (Wagoner), **Supp. IX:** 329, 330

"Song for the End of Time" (Gioia), **Supp. XV:** 126–127

"Song for the First People" (Wagoner), **Supp. IX:** 328

"Song for the Last Act" (Bogan), **Supp. III Part 1:** 64

"Song for the Middle of the Night, A" (Wright), **Supp. III Part 2:** 594

"Song for the Rainy Season" (Bishop), **Supp. I Part 1:** 93–94, 96

"Song for the Romeos, A" (Stern), **Supp. IX:** 296

"Song for Woody" (song, Dylan), **Supp. XVIII:** 24

"Song from a Courtyard Window" (Gioia), **Supp. XV:** 119

"Song III" (Taggard), **Supp. XXII:** 284

"Song in the Front Yard, A" (Brooks), **Supp. XVIII:** 181

"Songline of Dawn" (Harjo), **Supp. XII:** 229

"Song: Love in Whose Rich Honor" (Rukeyser), **Supp. VI:** 285

"Song: Now That She Is Here" (Carruth), **Supp. XVI:** 59

"Song of Advent, A" (Winters), **Supp. II Part 2:** 789

"Song of a Man Who Rushed at the Enemy" (Wagoner), **Supp. IX:** 329, 330

"Song of Courage, A" (Masters), **Supp. I Part 2:** 458

Song of God, The: Bhagavad-Gita (Isherwood and Prabhavananda, trans.), **Supp. XIV:** 156, 157, 164

Song of Hiawatha, The (Longfellow), **II:** 501, 503–504; **Retro. Supp. II:** 155, **159–161**, 162, 163; **Supp. XXIII:** 223, 234–235

"Song of Innocence, A" (Ellison), **Retro. Supp. II:** 126; **Supp. II Part 1:** 248

"Song of My Fiftieth Birthday, The" (Lindsay), **Supp. I Part 2:** 399

"Song of Myself" (Whitman), **II:** 544; **III:** 572, 584, 595; **IV:** 333, 334, 337–339, 340, 341, 342, 344, 348, 349, 351, 405; **Retro. Supp. I:** 388, 389, 395–399, 400; **Supp. V:** 122; **Supp. IX:** 131, 136, 143, 328, 331; **Supp. XIV:** 139; **Supp. XVIII:** 194, 304; **Supp. XXII:** 81

Song of Napalm (Weigl), **Supp. XIX:** 278–282

"Song of Napalm" (Weigl), **Supp. XIX:** 276–277

Song of Russia (film), **Supp. I Part 1:** 281, 294; **Supp. XVII:** 60–61

"Song of Self" (Huncke), **Supp. XIV:** 138–139, 145

Song of Solomon (biblical book), **III:** 118; **IV:** 150

Song of Solomon (Morrison), **Supp. III Part 1:** 364, 368, 369, 372, 379; **Supp. XVIII:** 55

Song of Songs (biblical book), **II:** 538; **IV:** 153–154; **Supp. XV:** 221

"Song of the Answerer" (Whitman), **Retro. Supp. I:** 393, 399

Song of the Cardinal, The (Stratton-Porter), **Supp. XX: 217, 218, 219**

"Song of the Chattahoochee, The" (Lanier), **Supp. I Part 1:** 365, 368

"Song of the Degrees, A" (Pound), **III:** 466

"Song of the Drunkard" (Ferry), **Supp. XXIV:** 153, 162

"Song of the Dryads" (Taggard), **Supp. XXII:** 272

"Song of the Exposition" (Whitman), **IV:** 332

"Song of the Gavilan" (Leopold), **Supp. XIV:** 189

"Song of the Gourd" (Wright), **Supp. XV:** 348–349

"Song of the Greek Amazon" (Bryant), **Supp. I Part 1:** 168

Song of the Lark, The (Cather), **I:** 312, 319–321, 323; **Retro. Supp. I:** 1, 3, 7, **9–11**, 13, 19, 20

"Song of the Okogis, or Frog in Spring"(J. Schoolcraft), **Supp. XXIII:** 232, 233, 235

"Song of the Open Road" (McGrath), **Supp. X:** 127

"Song of the Open Road" (Whitman), **IV:** 340–341; **Retro. Supp. I:** 400; **Supp. IX:** 265

"Song of the Redwood Tree" (Whitman), **IV:** 348

"Song of the Scullery" (McCarriston), **Supp. XIV:** 272

"Song of the Sky Loom" (traditional Tewa poem), **Supp. IV Part 1:** 325

"Song of the Son" (Toomer), **Supp. III Part 2:** 482–483; **Supp. IX:** 313

"Song of the Sower, The" (Bryant), **Supp. I Part 1:** 169

"Song of the Stars" (Bryant), **Supp. I Part 1:** 163

"Song of the Swamp-Robin, The" (Frederic), **II:** 138

"Song of the Vermonters, The" (Whittier), **Supp. I Part 2:** 692

"Song of Three Smiles" (Merwin), **Supp. III Part 1:** 344

"Song of Wandering Aengus, The" (Yeats), **IV:** 271; **Retro. Supp. I:** 342, 350

"Song of Welcome" (Brodsky), **Supp. VIII:** 32

"Song on Captain Barney's Victory" (Freneau), **Supp. II Part 1:** 261

"Song/Poetry and Language-Expression and Perception" (Ortiz), **Supp. IV Part 2:** 500, 508

"Song: 'Rough Winds Do Shake the Darling Buds of May' " (Simpson), **Supp. IX:** 268

Songs (Boyce), **Supp. XXI:** 9

Songs and Satires (Masters), **Supp. I Part 2:** 465–466

Songs and Sonnets (L. P. Smith), **Supp. XIV:** 341

Songs and Sonnets (Masters), **Supp. I Part 2:** 455, 459, 461, 466

"Songs for a Colored Singer" (Bishop), **Supp. I Part 1:** 80, 85

Songs for a Summer's Day (A Sonnet Cycle) (MacLeish), **III:** 3

Songs for Eve (MacLeish), **III:** 3, 19

"Songs for Eve" (MacLeish), **III:** 19

"Songs for My Father" (Komunyakaa), **Supp. XIII:** 128

Songs for the Unborn Second Baby (Notley), **Supp. XXII:** 228

"Songs for Two Seasons" (C. Frost), **Supp. XV:** 95–96

Songs from This Earth on Turtle's Back: Contemporary American Indian Poetry (Bruchac, ed.), **Supp. IV Part 1:** 320, 328

"Songs of a Housewife" (Rawlings), **Supp. X:** 221–222

"Songs of Billy Bathgate, The" (Doctorow), **Supp. IV Part 1:** 230

Songs of Innocence (Blake), **Supp. I Part 2:** 708

Songs of Jamaica (McKay), **Supp. X:** 131, 133

"Songs of Maximus, The" (Olson), **Supp. II Part 2:** 567

"Songs of Parting" (Whitman), **IV:** 348

Songs of the Doomed (Thompson), **Supp. XXIV:** 283

Songs of the North: A Sigurd Olson Reader (Mosher, ed.), **Supp. XXII:** 218

Songs of the Sierras (J. Miller), **I:** 459

Songs of Three Centuries (Whittier and Larcom, eds.), **Supp. XIII:** 142

"Song to David" (Smart), **III:** 534

"Song to No Music, A" (Brodsky), **Supp. VIII:** 26

"Song V" (Taggard), **Supp. XXII:** 284

Soniat, Katherine, **Supp. XXI:** 245

Sonneschein, Rosa, **Retro. Supp. II:** 65

"Sonnet" (Rukeyser), **Supp. VI:** 284

"Sonnet Crown for Two Voices" (Bierds), **Supp. XVII:** 35

"Sonnet"(J. Schoolcraft), **Supp. XXIII:** 229

"Sonnets" (Carruth), **Supp. XVI:** 56

Sonnets, The (Berrigan), **Supp. XXII:** 224; **Supp. XXIV:** 33, 34, 35, 37, 38–41, 45

"Sonnets at Christmas" (Tate), **IV:** 135

Sonnets to Orpheus (Rilke), **Supp. XV:** 222; **Supp. XXIV:** 38

"Sonnet-To Zante" (Poe), **III:** 421

"Sonnet XV" (Berrigan), **Supp. XXIV:** 38–39, 44

"Sonny's Blues" (Baldwin), **Retro. Supp. II:** 7, 8, 10, 14; **Supp. I Part 1:** 58–59, 63, 67; **Supp. XI:** 288

Son of Laughter, The: A Novel (Buechner), **Supp. XII:** 54

Son of Perdition, The (Cozzens), **I:** 359–360, 377, 378, 379

Son of the Circus, A (Irving), **Supp. VI:** 165, 166, **176–179**

Son of the Gamblin' Man: The Youth of an Artist (Sandoz), **Supp. XXIV:** 244, **256–257**

"Son of the Gods, A" (Bierce), **I:** 202

Son of the Morning (Oates), **Supp. II Part 2:** 518, 519, 520–522

Son of the Morning Star: Custer and the Little Bighorn (Connell), **Supp. XIV:** 80, 82, 97

"Son of the Romanovs, A" (Simpson), **Supp. IX:** 273–274

Son of the Wolf, The (London), **II:** 465, 469

"Son of the Wolfman" (Chabon), **Supp. XI:** 76

"Sonrisas" (Mora), **Supp. XIII:** 216, 219

Sons (Buck), **Supp. II Part 1:** 117–118

Sons and Lovers (Lawrence), **III:** 27

Sontag, Kate, **Supp. XV:** 104

Sontag, Susan, **IV:** 13, 14; **Retro. Supp. II:** 279; **Supp. I Part 2:** 423; **Supp. III Part 2:** 451–473; **Supp. VIII:** 75; **Supp. XIV:** 14, 15, 95–96, 167; **Supp.**

XVI: 201, 204, 206; **Supp. XX: 205; Supp. XXI:** 243

"Soonest Mended" (Ashbery), **Supp. III Part 1:** 1, 13

"Sootfall and Fallout" (White), **Supp. I Part 2:** 671

Sophisticates, The (Atherton), **Supp. XXIV:** 20, 25

Sophocles, **I:** 274; **II:** 291, 385, 577; **III:** 145, 151, 152, 153, 159, 398, 476, 478, 609, 613; **IV:** 291, 363, 368, 370; **Supp. I Part 1:** 153, 284; **Supp. I Part 2:** 491; **Supp. V:** 97; **Supp. VIII:** 332; **Supp. XV:** 265, 266

"Sophronsiba" (Bourne), **I:** 221

Sorayam, Aram, **Supp. XXII:** 25

Sorby, Angela, **Supp. XXIII:** 132

Sorcerer's Apprentice, The: Tales and Conjurations (Johnson), **Supp. VI:** 192–193, 194

"Sorcerer's Eye, The" (Nemerov), **III:** 283

Sordello (Browning), **III:** 467, 469, 470

"Sordid? Good God!" (Williams), **Retro. Supp. II:** 334

So Red the Rose (Young), **Supp. XXII:** 190, 193

"Sorghum" (Mason), **Supp. VIII:** 146

Sorkin, Adam, **Supp. XXIV:** 178

Sorokin, Pitirim, **Supp. I Part 2:** 679

Sorrentino, Christopher, **Supp. XVIII:** 148

Sorrentino, Gilbert, **Retro. Supp. I:** 426; **Supp. IV Part 1:** 286; **Supp. XII:** 139; **Supp. XXI:** 225–241; **Supp. XXII:** 261

Sorrento (Notley), **Supp. XXII:** 231

"Sorrow" (Komunyakaa), **Supp. XIII:** 119

Sorrow Dance, The (Levertov), **Supp. III Part 1:** 279–280, 283

"Sorrowful Guest, A" (Jewett), **Retro. Supp. II:** 137

Sorrows of Fat City, The: A Selection of Literary Essays and Reviews (Garrett), **Supp. VII:** 111

Sorrows of Young Werther, The (Goethe), **Supp. XI:** 169; **Supp. XX: 234, 236**

Sorrows of Young Werther, The (Goethe; Bogan and Mayer, trans.), **Supp. III Part 1:** 63

"Sorry Fugu" (Boyle), **Supp. XX: 19**

"Sorting Facts; or, Nineteen Ways of Looking at Marker" (Howe), **Supp. IV Part 2:** 434, 436

"Sort of Song, A" (W. C. Williams), **Supp. XVII:** 243

"S O S" (Baraka), **Supp. II Part 1:** 50

"So Sassafras" (Olson), **Supp. II Part 2:** 574

"So There" (Creeley), **Supp. IV Part 1:** 157

"So This Is Nebraska" (Kooser), **Supp. XIX:** 120

Sotirov, Vasil, **Supp. IX:** 152

Soto, Gary, **Supp. IV Part 2:** 545; **Supp. V:** 180; **Supp. XI:** 270; **Supp. XIII:** 313, 315, 316, 320, 323; **Supp. XV:** 73

"Soto Thinking of the Ocean" (Salinas), **Supp. XIII:** 321

"Sotto Voce" (Kunitz), **Supp. III Part 1:** 265

Sot-Weed Factor, The (Barth), **I:** 122, 123, 125, 129, 130, 131–134, 135; **Supp. XXII:** 259

"Soul" (Ferry), **Supp. XXIV:** 162

Soul, The (Brooks), **I:** 244

Soul and Body of John Brown, The (Rukeyser), **Supp. VI:** 273

Soul Barnacles: Ten More Years with Ray (Gallagher; Simon, ed.), **Supp. XXIV:** 166, 167, 171, 172

Soul Clap Hands and Sing (Marshall), **Supp. XI:** 276, 278, **280–282**

Soul Expeditions (Singer). *See* Shosha (Singer)

Soul Gone Home (Hughes), **Retro. Supp. I:** 203; **Supp. I Part 1:** 328

"Soul inside the Sentence, The" (Gass), **Supp. VI:** 88

Soul Is Here for Its Own Joy, The (Bly, ed.), **Supp. IV Part 1:** 74

Soul of Man under Socialism, The (Wilde), **Supp. IX:** 134–135

"Soul of Spain, The \[In the manner of Gertrude Stein\]" (Hemingway), **Supp. XX: 74**

Soul of the Far East, The (Lowell), **II:** 513

"Soul on Bench" (Halliday), **Supp. XIX:** 91

Soul on Ice (Cleaver), **Retro. Supp. II:** 12, 13

"Souls Belated" (Wharton), **Retro. Supp. I:** 364

"Soul selects her own Society, The" (Dickinson), **Retro. Supp. I:** 37

Souls of Black Folk, The (Du Bois), **Supp. II Part 1:** 33, 40, 160, 168–170, 176, 183; **Supp. IV Part 1:** 164; **Supp. IX:** 305, 306; **Supp. X:** 133; **Supp. XIII:** 185, 238, 243

Souls of Black Folk. The (Du Bois), **Supp. XX: 102**

"Sound, The" (Olds), **Supp. X:** 214

Sound and Beauty (Hwang), **Supp. XXI:** 146

"Sound and Fury" (O. Henry), **Supp. II Part 1:** 402

Sound and the Fury, The (Faulkner), **I:** 480; **II:** 55, 57, 58–60, 73; **III:** 237; **IV:** 100, 101, 104; **Retro. Supp. I:** 73, 75, 77, 82, **83–84,** 86, 88, 89, 90, 91, 92; **Supp. VIII:** 215; **Supp. IX:** 103; **Supp. X:** 44; **Supp. XII:** 33; **Supp. XIV:** 12; **Supp. XVII:** 138; **Supp. XVIII:** 84

"Sound Bites" (Alvarez), **Supp. VII:** 11

Sound I Listened For, The (Francis), **Supp. IX:** 78–79, 87

"Soundless Trumpet, The" (Antin), **Supp. XX: 12**

"Sound Mind, Sound Body" (Lowell), **II:** 554

Sound of a Voice, The (Hwang), **Supp. XXI:** 146

"Sound of Distant Thunder, A" (Elkin), **Supp. VI:** 42–43, 44

"Sound of Light, The" (Merwin), **Supp. III Part 1:** 356

Sound of Mountain Water, The (Stegner), **Supp. IV Part 2:** 595, 596, 598, 600, 608

"Sound of Talking" (Purdy), **Supp. VII:** 270

Sounds of Poetry (television special, Moyers), **Supp. XXIII:** 139

Sounds of Poetry, The (Pinsky), **Supp. VI:** 236, 247, 248; **Supp. XXIII:** 124

Sound the Stars Make Rushing Through the Sky, The: The Writings of Jane Johnston Schoolcraft (Parker, ed.), **Supp. XXIII:** 223–224, 227, 228

Soupault, Philippe, **IV:** 288, 404; **Retro. Supp. II:** 85, 321, 324

Source (Doty), **Supp. XI:** 121, **134–137**

"Source" (Doty), **Supp. XI:** 136

"Source, The" (Olds), **Supp. X:** 211

"Source, The" (Porter), **III:** 443

Source of Light, The (Price), **Supp. VI: 262,** 266

"Sources of Soviet Conduct, The" (Kennan), **Supp. VIII:** 241

Sour Grapes (W. C. Williams), **Retro. Supp. I:** 418

"Sour Grapes"(Moraga), **Supp. XXIII:** 202

"Sourwood Nocturne" (Skloot), **Supp. XX: 202**

"South" (Levis), **Supp. XI:** 266

"South" (Trethewey), **Supp. XXI:** 247, 256

"South, The" (Hughes), **Supp. I Part 1:** 321

South American Journey (W. Frank), **Supp. XX: 79**

"Southampton Variations"(O'Hara), **Supp. XXIII:** 212

"Southbound on the Freeway" (Swenson), **Supp. IV Part 2:** 643

South Dakota Guidebook, The (C. Baxter), **Supp. XVII:** 15

Southern, Terry, **Supp. IV Part 1:** 379; **Supp. V:** 40, 201; **Supp. XI: 293–310; Supp. XVI:** 230

Southern Cross, The (Wright), **Supp. V:** 332, 342

"Southern Cross, The" (Wright), **Supp. V:** 338

"Southerner's Problem, The" (Du Bois), **Supp. II Part 1:** 168

"Southern Girl" (Zelda Fitzgerald), **Supp. IX:** 71

"Southern Gothic" (Trethewey), **Supp. XXI:** 256

"Southern History" (Trethewey), **Supp. XXI:** 256, 257

"Southern Mode of the Imagination, A" (Tate), **IV:** 120

"Southern Romantic, A" (Tate), **Supp. I Part 1:** 373

"Southern Sojourn, A" (Hoffman), **Supp. XVIII:** 87

Southern Terry, **Supp. XIV:** 82

Southey, Robert, **II:** 304, 502; **Supp. I Part 1:** 154; **Supp. XXIV:** 74

"South Lingers On, The" (R. Fisher), **Supp. XIX:** 69–70

South Moon Under (Rawlings), **Supp. X:** **225–226,** 229, 233

South Pacific Affair (Lacy), **Supp. XV:** 206

Southpaw, The (Harris), **II:** 424–425

"South Sangamon" (Cisneros), **Supp. VII:** 66

South to a Very Old Place (Murray), **Supp. XIX: 151–153**

Southwell, Robert, **IV:** 151

Southwick, Marcia, **Supp. XI:** 259

Southworth, E. D. E. N, **Retro. Supp. I:** 246

Souvenir of the Ancient World, Selected Poems of Carlos Drummond de Andrade (Strand, trans.), **Supp. IV Part 2:** 630

"Sow" (Plath), **Supp. I Part 2:** 537

"Sowing and Reaping in *Furors Die*" (Nostrandt), **Supp. XVIII:** 80–81

Soyinka, Wole, **Supp. XX:** 100

"Space" (Brockmeier), **Supp. XXII:** 51

Space between Our Footsteps, The: Poems and Paintings from the Middle East (Nye, ed.), **Supp. XIII:** 280

"Space Quale, The" (James), **II:** 349

"Spaces Between, The" (Kingsolver), **Supp. VII:** 209

"Space Where Sex Should Be, The: Toward a Definition of the Black Literary Tradition" (Nelson), **Supp. XVIII:** 172

Spackman, Peter, **Supp. XVI:** 221

Spacks, Patricia, **Supp. XVI:** 251

"Spain" (Auden), **Supp. II Part 1:** 12–13, 14

"Spain in Fifty-Ninth Street" (White), **Supp. I Part 2:** 677

Spanier, Sandra, **Supp. XXIV:** 51, 64

"Spanish-American War Play" (Crane), **I:** 422

Spanish Ballads (Merwin, trans.), **Supp. III Part 1:** 347

Spanish Bayonet (Benét), **Supp. XI:** 45, 47

Spanish Earth, The (film), **Retro. Supp. I:** 184

Spanish Papers and Other Miscellanies (Irving), **II:** 314

"Spanish Revolution, The" (Bryant), **Supp. I Part 1:** 153, 168

Spanish Student, The (Longfellow), **II:** 489, 506; **Retro. Supp. II:** 165

"Spanish Winter" (Egan), **Supp. XIX:** 52

Spanking the Maid (Coover), **Supp. V:** 47, 48, 49, 52

Spare Change (Parker), **Supp. XIX:** 186–187

Spargo, John, **Supp. I Part 1:** 13

"Spark, The" (Wharton), **Retro. Supp. I:** 381

"Sparkles from the Wheel" (Whitman), **IV:** 348

Sparks, Debra, **Supp. X:** 177

Sparks, Jared, **Supp. I Part 1:** 156; **Supp. XXIV:** 71

"Sparrow" (Berry), **Supp. X:** 31

Sparrow, Henry, **III:** 587

Sparrow, Mrs. Henry, **III:** 587

"Sparrow's Gate, The" (B. Kelly), **Supp. XVII:** 133

Spaulding, William, **Supp. XVI:** 106

"Spawning Run, The" (Humphrey), **Supp. IX:** 95

"Speak, Gay Memory" (Kirp), **Supp. XI:** 129

"Speak, Hoyt-Schermerhorn" (Lethem), **Supp. XVIII:** 148

Speak, Memory (Nabokov), **III:** 247–250, 252; **Retro. Supp. I:** 264, 265, 266, 267, 268, 277; **Supp. XVI:** 148

Speak, Memory (V. Nabakov), **Supp. XVII:** 47

Speaking and Language (Shapiro), **Supp. II Part 2:** 721

Speaking for Nature: How Literary Naturalists from Henry Thoreau to Rachel Carson Have Shaped America (Brooks), **Supp. IX:** 31

Speaking for Ourselves: American Ethnic Writing (Faderman and Bradshaw, eds.), **Supp. XIII:** 313

Speaking of Accidents (Everwine), **Supp. XV:** 75, 88

"Speaking of Accidents" (Everwine), **Supp. XV:** 88–89

"Speaking of Counterweights" (White), **Supp. I Part 2:** 669

Speaking of Literature and Society (Trilling), **Supp. III Part 2:** 494, 496, 499

"Speaking of Love" (Gioia), **Supp. XV:** 124–125

Speaking of Race, Speaking of Sex: Hate Speech, Civil Rights, and Civil Liberties (H. L. Gates, Griffin, Lively, and Strossen), **Supp. XX: 111**

Speaking on Stage (Kolin and Kullman, eds.), **Supp. IX:** 145

Speaking on Stage: Interviews with Contemporary American Playwrights (Balakian), **Supp. XV:** 327

"Speaking Passions" (Kitchen), **Supp. XV:** 215

Speak of the Devil (Holding), **Supp. XXII: 127**

Speak What We Feel (Not What We Ought to Say): Reflections on Literature and Faith (Buechner), **Supp. XII:** 57

Spear, Roberta, **Supp. V:** 180; **Supp. XV:** 73

"Special Kind of Fantasy, A: James Dickey on the Razor's Edge" (Niflis), **Supp. IV Part 1:** 175

"Special Pleading" (Lanier), **Supp. I Part 1:** 364

"Special Problems in Teaching Leslie Marmon Silko's *Ceremony*" (Gunn Allen), **Supp. IV Part 1:** 333

Special Providence, A (Yates), **Supp. XI:** 342, **344–345**

"Special Time, a Special School, A" (Knowles), **Supp. XII:** 236

Special View of History, The (Olson), **Supp. II Part 2:** 566, 569, 572

Specimen Days (Whitman), **IV:** 338, 347, 348, 350; **Retro. Supp. I:** 408

Specimens of the American Poets, **Supp. I Part 1:** 155

"Spectacles, The" (Poe), **III:** 425

Spectator Bird, The (Stegner), **Supp. IV Part 2:** 599, 604, 606, 611–612

Spector, Robert, **Supp. XIII:** 87

Spectra: A Book of Poetic Experiments (Bynner and Ficke), **Supp. XV:** 43

"Spectre Bridegroom, The" (Irving), **II:** 304

"Spectre Pig, The" (Holmes), **Supp. I Part 1:** 302

"Speculating Woman" (X. J. Kennedy), **Supp. XV:** 168

"Speech Sounds" (O. Butler), **Supp. XIII:** 61, **70**

"Speech to a Crowd" (MacLeish), **III:** 16

"Speech to the Detractors" (MacLeish), **III:** 16

"Speech to the Young" (Brooks), **Supp. III Part 1:** 79, 86

"Speech to Those Who Say Comrade" (MacLeish), **III:** 16

Speedboat (Adler), **Supp. X:** 171

Speed of Darkness, The (Rukeyser), **Supp. VI:** 274, 281

Speed-the-Plow (Mamet), **Supp. XIV:** 241, 246, 249, 250, 251

"Speedy Gonzales Was the Fastest Mouse in Mexico" (P. N. Warren as Kilina), **Supp. XX: 262**

Speilberg, Steven, **Supp. XI:** 234

Speirs, Logan, **Supp. XIX:** 282

"Spell" (Francis), **Supp. IX:** 87

"Spell, The" (Peacock), **Supp. XIX:** 198, 200

"Spell for the Manufacture & Use of a Magic Carpet" (Hull), **Supp. XXI:** 132–133, 139, 141

Spelling Dictionary, A (Rowson), **Supp. XV:** 244

Spence, Thomas, **Supp. I Part 2:** 518

Spence + Lila (Mason), **Supp. VIII:** 133, **143–145**

Spencer, Edward, **Supp. I Part 1:** 357, 360

Spencer, Herbert, **I:** 515; **II:** 345, 462–463, 480, 483, 536; **III:** 102, 315; **IV:** 135; **Retro. Supp. II:** 60, 65, 93, 98; **Supp. I Part 1:** 368; **Supp. I Part 2:** 635

Spencer, Sharon, **Supp. X:** 185, 186, 195, 196

Spencer, Theodore, **I:** 433; **Supp. III Part 1:** 2

Spender, Natasha, **Supp. IV Part 1:** 119, 127, 134

Spender, Stephen, **II:** 371; **III:** 504, 527; **Retro. Supp. I:** 216; **Retro. Supp. II:** 243, 244; **Supp. I Part 2:** 536; **Supp. II Part 1:** 11; **Supp. IV Part 1:** 82, 134; **Supp. IV Part 2:** 440; **Supp. X:** 116

Spengler, Oswald, **I:** 255, 270; **II:** 7, 577; **III:** 172, 176; **Retro. Supp. II:** 324; **Supp. I Part 2:** 647

Spens, Sir Patrick, **Supp. I Part 2:** 404

Spenser, Edmund, **I:** 62; **III:** 77, 78, 89; **IV:** 155, 453; **Retro. Supp. I:** 62; **Supp. I Part 1:** 98, 152, 369; **Supp. I Part 2:** 422, 719; **Supp. XXIV:** 159

"Spenser's Ireland" (Moore), **III:** 211, 212

"Spermaceti Papers"(Lippard), **Supp. XXIII:** 178

Sperry, Margaret, **Supp. IV Part 1:** 169

Spheres of Existence (C. L. R. James), **Supp. XXI:** 172

Sphere: The Form of a Motion (Ammons), **Supp. VII:** 24, 32, 33, 35, 36

"Sphinx" (Hayden), **Supp. II Part 1:** 373

"Spiced Plums" (Ríos), **Supp. IV Part 2:** 553

Spickard, Paul, **Supp. XXI:** 149

"Spider and the Ghost of the Fly, The" (Lindsay), **Supp. I Part 2:** 375

Spider Bay (Van Vechten), **Supp. II Part 2:** 746

"Spider Heart, The" (Peacock), **Supp. XIX:** 200

"Spiders" (Schwartz), **Supp. II Part 2:** 665

Spider's House, The (Bowles), **Supp. IV Part 1:** 87–89, 90, 91

Spider Woman's Granddaughters: Traditional Tales and Contemporary Writing by Native American Women (Gunn Allen, ed.), **Supp. IV Part 1:** 320, 326, 332–333; **Supp. IV Part 2:** 567

Spiegel, Sam, **Supp. XVIII:** 251, 252

Spiegelman, Art, **Supp. XVII:** 48

Spiegelman, Willard, **Supp. XI:** 126

Spielberg, Steven, **Supp. XXI:** 154

Spillane, Mickey, **Supp. IV Part 2:** 469, 472; **Supp. XV:** 200; **Supp. XVIII:** 236, 237

Spiller, Robert E., **I:** 241; **Supp. I Part 1:** 104

Spillers, Hortense, **Supp. XX: 109**

"Spillikins: Gregor Mendel at the Table" (Bierds), **Supp. XVII:** 34–35

Spillville (Hampl), **Supp. XXII:** 98

Spillway (Barnes), **Supp. III Part 1:** 44

Spingarn, Amy, **Supp. I Part 1:** 325, 326

Spingarn, Joel, **I:** 266; **Supp. I Part 1:** 325

Spinoza, Baruch, **I:** 493; **II:** 590, 593; **III:** 600; **IV:** 5, 7, 11, 12, 17; **Retro. Supp. II:** 300; **Supp. I Part 1:** 274; **Supp. I Part 2:** 643; **Supp. XVI:** 184

"Spinoza of Market Street, The" (Singer), **IV:** 12–13; **Retro. Supp. II:** 307

"Spinster" (Plath), **Supp. I Part 2:** 536

"Spinster's Tale, A" (Taylor), **Supp. V:** 314–315, 316–317, 319, 323

Spiral of Memory, The: Interviews (Coltelli, ed.), **Supp. XII:** 215

Spires, Elizabeth, **Supp. X:** 8

"Spire Song" (Bowles), **Supp. IV Part 1:** 80

Spirit and Flame: An Anthology of African American Poetry (Gilyard, ed.), **Supp. XXI:** 246

Spirit and the Flesh, The: Sexual Diversity in American Indian Culture (W. L. Williams), **Supp. IV Part 1:** 330

"Spirit Birth" (Cullen), **Supp. IV Part 1:** 168

Spirit Brides (Gibran). *See Nymphs in the Valley*

Spirit in Man, The (Jung), **Supp. IV Part 1:** 68

"Spirit in Me, The" (Hoffman), **Supp. XVIII:** 87

"Spirit Made Visible" (art exhibit), **Supp. XXII:** 180

Spirit of Culver (West), **IV:** 287

Spirit of Labor, The (Hapgood), **Supp. XVII:** 96, 99, 101–102; **Supp. XXI:** 4

Spirit of Romance, The (Pound), **III:** 470; **Retro. Supp. I:** 286

Spirit of the Ghetto, The: Studies of the Jewish Quarter of New York (Hapgood), **Supp. XVII:** 96, 101, 103, 106

Spirit of Youth and the City Streets, The (Addams), **Supp. I Part 1:** 6–7, 12–13, 16, 17, 19

"Spirits" (Bausch), **Supp. VII:** 46–47

Spirits, and Other Stories (Bausch), **Supp. VII:** 46–47, 54

"Spirit Says, You Are Nothing, The" (Levis), **Supp. XI:** 265–266

Spirits Rebellious (al-Arwá&hudot; al-Mutamarrida) (Gibran), **Supp. XX: 115, 124, 125**

Spiritual Adventures (Symons), **Supp. XX:** 239

Spiritual Conflict, The (Scupoli), **IV:** 156

Spiritual Exercises, The (Loyola), **IV:** 151; **Supp. XI:** 162

"Spiritual Manifestation, A" (Whittier), **Supp. I Part 2:** 699

"Spirituals and Neo-Spirituals" (Hurston), **Supp. VI:** 152–153

Spits, Ellen Handler, **Supp. XII:** 166

"Spitzbergen Tales" (Crane), **I:** 409, 415, 423

Spitzer, Philip, **Supp. XIV:** 21

"Spleen" (Eliot), **I:** 569, 573–574

Spleen de Paris, Le (Baudelaire), **Supp. XIV:** 337

Splendid Drunken Twenties, The (Van Vechten), **Supp. II Part 2:** 739–744

Splendide-Hôtel (Sorrentino), **Supp. XXI:** 233

Splendid Table, The (radio show), **Supp. XXIII:** 138

"Splinters" (Bukiet), **Supp. XVII:** 47

"Split Infinitive" (Pickering), **Supp. XXI:** 204

"Splitting an Order" (Kooser), **Supp. XIX:** 128–129

"Splittings" (Rich), **Supp. I Part 2:** 570–571

"Splitting Wood at Six Above" (Kumin), **Supp. IV Part 2:** 449

Spofford, Harriet Prescott, **Supp. XIII:** 143

Spoils of Poynton, The (James), **I:** 463; **Retro. Supp. I:** 229–230

Spoken Page, The (Nye), **Supp. XIII:** 274

"Spokes" (Auster), **Supp. XII:** 23

Spokesmen (Whipple), **II:** 456

Spook Sonata, The (Strindberg), **III:** 387, 392

Spooky Art, The: A Book about Writing (Mailer), **Retro. Supp. II:** 214

"Spoon, The" (Simic), **Supp. VIII:** 275

Spoon River Anthology (Masters), **I:** 106; **III:** 579; **Supp. I Part 2:** 454, 455, 456, 460–465, 466, 467, 471, 472, 473, 476; **Supp. IX:** 306; **Supp. XIV:** 282–283; **Supp. XIX:** 121; **Supp. XXII:** 282

Sport and a Pastime, A (Salter), **Supp. IX: 254–257; Supp. XVI:** 237

Sporting Club, The (McGuane), **Supp. VIII:** 43

Sport of the Gods, The (Dunbar), **Supp. II Part 1:** 193, 200, 207, 214–217

Sports Illustrated Training with Weights (Parker and Marsh), **Supp. XIX:** 187

"Sportsman Born and Bred, A" (Plimpton), **Supp. XVI:** 241

Sportsman's Sketches, A (Turgenev), **I:** 106; **IV:** 277

Sportswriter, The (Ford), **Supp. V:** 57, 58, 62–67

"Spotted Horses" (Faulkner), **IV:** 260

Sprague, Morteza, **Retro. Supp. II:** 115

Spratling, William, **II:** 56; **Retro. Supp. I:** 80

Sprawl trilogy (W. Gibson), **Supp. XVI:** 117, 122, 124

"Spray, The" (Lethem), **Supp. XVIII:** 148

"Spray Paint King, The" (Dove), **Supp. IV Part 1:** 252–253

Spreading Fires (Knowles), **Supp. XII:** 249

Sprigge, Elizabeth, **IV:** 31

"Spring" (Kooser), **Supp. XIX:** 126

"Spring" (Millay), **III:** 126

"Spring" (Mora), **Supp. XIII:** 217

"Spring 1967" (Carruth), **Supp. XVI:** 55

Spring and All (W. C. Williams), **Retro. Supp. I:** 412, 418, **418–420,** 427, 430, 431

"Spring and All" (W. C. Williams), **Retro. Supp. I:** 419

Spring Awakening (Wedeking, trans. Franzen), **Supp. XX: 85**

"Spring Break-Up" (Carruth), **Supp. XVI:** 56

"Spring Bulletin" (Allen), **Supp. XV:** 15

Springer's Progress (Markson), **Supp. XVII: 141–142,** 143, 146

"Spring Evening" (Farrell), **II:** 45

"Spring Evening" (Kenyon), **Supp. VII:** 173

"Springfield Magical" (Lindsay), **Supp. I Part 2:** 379

Spring in New Hampshire and Other Poems (McKay), **Supp. X:** 131, 135

"Spring Notes from Robin Hill" (Carruth), **Supp. XVI:** 48

"Spring Pastoral" (Wylie), **Supp. I Part 2:** 707

"Spring Pools" (Frost), **II:** 155; **Retro. Supp. I:** 137

"Spring Snow" (Matthews), **Supp. IX:** 160

"SPRING SONG" (Baraka), **Supp. II Part 1:** 60

Springsteen, Bruce, **Supp. VIII:** 143

"Spring Strains" (W. C. Williams), **Retro. Supp. I:** 416

Spring Tides (Morison), **Supp. I Part 2:** 494

Springtime and Harvest (Sinclair), **Supp. V:** 280

"Springtime for You" (Halliday), **Supp. XIX:** 87

Spruance, Raymond, **Supp. I Part 2:** 479, 491

"Spruce Has No Taproot, The" (Clampitt), **Supp. IX:** 41–42

"Spunk" (Hurston), **Supp. VI:** 150, 151–152

Spunk: The Selected Stories (Hurston), **Supp. VI:** 150

Spurr, David, **Supp. XV:** 183

Spy, The (Cooper), **I:** 335, 336, 337, 339, 340; **Supp. I Part 1:** 155

"Spy, The" (Francis), **Supp. IX:** 81

Spy, The (Freneau), **Supp. II Part 1:** 260

Spyglass Tree, The (Murray), **Supp. XIX:** **155–156**

Spy in the House of Love, A (Nin), **Supp. X:** 186

Squanto, **Supp. I Part 2:** 486

"Square Business" (Baraka), **Supp. II Part 1:** 49

Square Root of Wonderful, The (McCullers), **II:** 587–588

"Squash in Blossom" (Francis), **Supp. IX:** 81

"Squatter on Company Land, The" (Hugo), **Supp. VI:** 133

"Squatter's Children" (Bishop), **Retro. Supp. II:** 47

"Squeak, Memory" (Bukiet), **Supp. XVII:** 47

Squeeze Play (Auster), **Supp. XII:** 21

Squires, Radcliffe, **IV:** 127; **Supp. XV:** 118

Squirrels (Mamet), **Supp. XIV:** 240

S.S. Gliencairn (O'Neill), **III:** 387, 388, 405

S.S. San Pedro (Cozzens), **I:** 360–362, 370, 378, 379

"Ssshh" (Olds), **Supp. X:** 215

"Stacking the Straw" (Clampitt), **Supp. IX:** 41

Stade, George, **Supp. IV Part 1:** 286

Staël, Madame de, **II:** 298

"Staff of Life, The" (H. Miller), **III:** 187

Stafford, Jean, **II:** 537; **Retro. Supp. II:** 177; **Supp. V:** 316

Stafford, William, **Supp. IV Part 1:** 72; **Supp. IV Part 2:** 642; **Supp. IX:** 273; **Supp. XI:** **311–332; Supp. XIII:** 76, 274, 276, 277, 281, 283; **Supp. XIV:** 119, 123; **Supp. XX: 161; Supp. XXI:** 246

"Stage All Blood, The" (MacLeish), **III:** 18

"Staggerlee Wonders" (Baldwin), **Retro. Supp. II:** 15

Stained White Radiance, A (Burke), **Supp. XIV:** 28, 31

Stalin, Joseph, **I:** 261, 490; **II:** 39, 40, 49, 564; **III:** 30, 298; **IV:** 372; **Supp. V:** 290; **Supp. XXI:** 164, 165, 167

"Stalking" (J. W. Miller), **Supp. XX: 167**

"Stalking the Billion-Footed Beast: A Literary Manifesto for the New Social

Novel" (Wolfe), **Supp. III Part 2:** 586

Stallings, A. E., **Supp. XXIII:** 111, 124

Stallings, H. A., **Supp. XXII:** 194

Stallman, R. W., **I:** 405

Stamberg, Susan, **Supp. IV Part 1:** 201; **Supp. XII:** 193

Stamford, Anne Marie, **Supp. XII:** 162

Stanard, Mrs. Jane, **III:** 410, 413

Stand, The (King), **Supp. V:** 139, 140–141, 144–146, 148, 152

"Standard of Liberty, The" (Rowson), **Supp. XV:** 243

"Standard of Living, The" (Parker), **Supp. IX:** **198–199**

Stander, Lionel, **Supp. I Part 1:** 289

"Standing and the Waiting, The" (M. F. K. Fisher), **Supp. XVII:** 83

Standing by Words (Berry), **Supp. X:** 22, 27, 28, 31, 32, 33, 35

Standing Fast (Swados), **Supp. XIX:** **268–269**

"Standing Halfway Home" (Wagoner), **Supp. IX:** 324

"Standing In" (Caputo), **Supp. XIX:** 26

Standing Still and Walking in New York (O'Hara), **Supp. XXIII:** 220

Stand in the Mountains, A (Taylor), **Supp. V:** 324

Standish, Burt L. (pseudonym). *See* Patten, Gilbert

Standish, Miles, **I:** 471; **II:** 502–503

Standley, Fred L., **Retro. Supp. II:** 6

Stand Still Like the Hummingbird (H. Miller), **III:** 184

"Stand Up" (Salinas), **Supp. XIII:** 315

Stand with Me Here (Francis), **Supp. IX:** 76

Stanford, Ann, **Retro. Supp. I:** 41; **Supp. I Part 1:** 99, 100, 102, 103, 106, 108, 109, 113, 117; **Supp. IV Part 2:** 637

Stanford, Charles Villiers, **Supp. XX: 228**

Stanford, Donald E., **II:** 217

Stanford, Frank, **Supp. XV:** 338, 339, 341, 342–343, 343, 345, 348, 350

Stanford, Ginny (Crouch), **Supp. XV:** 339

Stanford, Leland, **I:** 196, 198

Stanislavsky, Konstantin, **Supp. XIV:** 240, 243

Stanley, Jodee, **Supp. XIX:** 52

"Stanley Kunitz" (Oliver), **Supp. VII:** 237

Stansell, Christine, **Supp. XVII:** 106; **Supp. XXI:** 4

Stanton, Frank L., **Supp. II Part 1:** 192

Stanton, Robert J., **Supp. IV Part 2:** 681

"Stanzas, Written in 1815 before going to hear my Father read religious services" (J. Schoolcraft), **Supp. XXIII:** 229

"Stanzas from the Grande Chartreuse" (Arnold), **Supp. I Part 2:** 417

Stanzas in Meditation (Stein), **Supp. III Part 1:** 13

Staples, Hugh, **Retro. Supp. II:** 187

Star, Alexander, **Supp. X:** 310

Starbuck, George, **Retro. Supp. II:** 53, 245; **Supp. I Part 2:** 538; **Supp. IV Part 2:** 440; **Supp. XIII:** 76

Star Child (Gunn Allen), **Supp. IV Part 1:** 324

"Star Dust" (Wrigley), **Supp. XVIII:** 296

Stardust Lounge, The (Digges), **Supp. XXIII:** 57

Stardust Memories (film; Allen), **Supp. XV:** 1, 4, **8,** 9, 13

"Stare, The" (Updike), **Retro. Supp. I:** 329

"Starfish, The" (R. Bly), **Supp. IV Part 1:** 72

"Staring at the Sea on the Day of the Death of Another" (Swenson), **Supp. IV Part 2:** 652

Star Is Born, A (film), **Supp. IV Part 1:** 198; **Supp. IX:** 198; **Supp. XVIII:** 242, 243

Stark, David, **Supp. XII:** 202

Stark, Heidi, **Supp. XXIII:** 228, 233

"Stark Boughs on the Family Tree" (Oliver), **Supp. VII:** 232

Starke, Aubrey Harrison, **Supp. I Part 1:** 350, 352, 356, 360, 362, 365, 370, 371

Starkey, David, **Supp. XII:** 180, 181

Star Ledger (Hull), **Supp. XXI:** 129, **136–138**

"Star Ledger" (Hull), **Supp. XXI:** 136

"Starlight" (Levine), **Supp. V:** 188

"Starlight Scope Myopia" (Komunyakaa), **Supp. XIII:** 123, 124

Starnino, Carmine, **Supp. XVII:** 74

"Star of the Nativity" (Brodsky), **Supp. VIII:** 33

Starr, Ellen Gates, **Supp. I Part 1:** 4, 5, 11

Starr, Jean. *See* Untermeyer, Jean Starr

Starr, Kevin, **Supp. XXIV:** 17, 22

Starr, Ringo, **Supp. XI:** 309

Star Rover, The (London), **II:** 467

"Starry Night, The" (Sexton), **Supp. II Part 2:** 681

"Stars" (Frost), **II:** 153

Stars, the Snow, the Fire, The: Twenty-five Years in the Northern Wilderness (Haines), **Supp. XII: 199–201,** 206, 209

Star Shines over Mt. Morris Park, A (H. Roth), **Supp. IX:** 227, 236, **236–237**

"Stars of the Summer Night" (Longfellow), **II:** 493

"Stars over Harlem" (Hughes), **Retro. Supp. I:** 207

"Star-Spangled" (García), **Supp. XI:** 177, 178

Star-Spangled Girl, The (Simon), **Supp. IV Part 2:** 579

"Star-Splitter, The" (Frost), **Retro. Supp. I:** 123, 133

Stars Principal (McClatchy), **Supp. XII:** **256–258**

"Start Again Somewhere" (Gallagher), **Supp. XXIV:** 169

"Star That Would Not Shine, The" (C. L. R. James), **Supp. XXI:** 160

"Starting from Paumanok" (Whitman), **IV:** 333

Starting from Troy (Hadas), **Supp. XXIII:** **113**

Starting Out in the Thirties (Kazin), **Supp. VIII: 95–97; Supp. XXIV:** 223

Star Trek television series, **Supp. XXII:** 60

"Starved Lovers" (MacLeish), **III:** 19

Starved Rock (Masters), **Supp. I Part 2:** 465

"Starving Again" (Moore), **Supp. X:** 163, 172, 175

"Starving"(Strout), **Supp. XXIII:** 283, 285

"State, The" (Bourne), **I:** 233

State and Main (Mamet), **Supp. XIV:** 241

"Statement of Principles" (Ransom), **III:** 496

"Statement: Phillipa Allen" (Rukeyser), **Supp. VI:** 283–284

"Statements on Poetics" (Snyder), **Supp. VIII:** 291, 292

"Statement with Rhymes" (Kees), **Supp. XV:** 139

"State of the Art, The" (Elkin), **Supp. VI:** 52

"State of the Arts, The" (Wasserstein), **Supp. XV:** 332

State of the Nation (Dos Passos), **I:** 489

"State of the Union" (Vidal), **Supp. IV Part 2:** 678

Static Element, The: Selected Poems of Natan Zach (Everwine, trans.), **Supp. XV:** 73, 75, **85–88**

"Statue, The" (Berryman), **I:** 173

"Statue and Birds" (Bogan), **Supp. III Part 1:** 50

"Statue of an Unkown Soldier, The" (Kooser), **Supp. XIX:** 124

"Statues, The" (Schwartz), **Supp. II Part 2:** 654, 659

"Status Rerum" (Pound), **Supp. I Part 1:** 257

Stavans, Ilan, **Supp. XI:** 190

"Stave Church" (W. V. Davis), **Supp. XXI:** 93, 94

"Staying Afloat"(Strout), **Supp. XXIII:** 274

"Staying Alive" (Levertov), **Supp. III Part 1:** 281

Staying Alive (Wagoner), **Supp. IX:** 324, **326**

"Staying at Ed's Place" (Swenson), **Supp. IV Part 2:** 648

Staying Put : Making a Home in a Rest-less World (Sanders), **Supp. XVI:** 274–275

Stay Me, Oh Comfort Me: Journals and Stories, 1933–1941 (M. F. K. Fisher), **Supp. XVII:** 92

Stayton, Richard, **Supp. IX:** 133

Steadman, Goodman, **IV:** 147

Steadman, Ralph, **Supp. XXIV:** 288

"Steak" (Snyder), **Supp. VIII:** 301

Steal Away: Selected and New Poems (Wright), **Supp. XV:** 337, 340, 348, 350–351

Stealing Beauty (Minot), **Supp. VI:** 205

Stealing Glimpses (McQuade), **Supp. IX:** 151

Stealing the Language: The Emergence of Women's Poetry in America (Ostriker), **Supp. XV:** 251

"Stealing the Thunder: Future Visions for American Indian Women, Tribes, and Literary Studies" (Gunn Allen), **Supp. IV Part 1:** 331

"Steam Shovel Cut" (Masters), **Supp. I Part 2:** 468

Stearns, Harold, **I:** 245; **Supp. XVII:** 106

Stedman, Edmund Clarence, **Supp. I Part 1:** 372; **Supp. II Part 1:** 192; **Supp. XV:** 115, 269, 273, 274, 282, 286

Steel, Sharon, **Supp. XIX:** 61

Steele, Margaret, **Supp. XXI:** 5

Steele, Max, **Supp. XIV:** 82

Steele, Sir Richard, **I:** 378; **II:** 105, 107, 300; **III:** 430

Steele, Timothy, **Supp. XV:** 251; **Supp. XVII:** 112; **Supp. XXIII:** 111

Steele, Wilbur Daniel, **Supp. XXI:** 5

Steelwork (Sorrentino), **Supp. XXI:** 227, 230, 231, 232

Steenburgen, Mary, **Supp. IV Part 1:** 236

Steeple Bush (Frost), **II:** 155; **Retro. Supp. I:** 140; **Retro. Supp. II:** 42

"Steeple-Jack, The" (Moore), **III:** 212, 213, 215

"Steerage" (Goldbarth), **Supp. XII:** 187

Steers, Nina, **Retro. Supp. II:** 25

Stefans, Brian Kim, **Supp. XXII:** 226

Steffens, Lincoln, **II:** 577; **III:** 580; **Retro. Supp. I:** 202; **Retro. Supp. II:** 101; **Supp. I Part 1:** 7; **Supp. XVII:** 98, 101, 106–107; **Supp. XXI:** 2, 3, 5, 7, 10; **Supp. XXIII:** 162

Stegner, Page, **IV:** 114, 116; **Supp. IV Part 2:** 599

Stegner, Wallace, **Supp. IV Part 2: 595–618; Supp. V:** 220, 224, 296; **Supp. X:** 23, 24; **Supp. XIV:** 82, 193, 230, 233; **Supp. XVIII:** 192; **Supp. XXII:** 204, 205, 208

"Stegner's Short Fiction" (Ahearn), **Supp. IV Part 2:** 604

Steichen, Edward, **III:** 580, 594–595

Steichen, Lillian. *See* Sandburg, Mrs. Carl (Lillian Steichen)

Steiger, Rod, **Supp. VIII:** 269; **Supp. XI:** 305

Stein, Edith, **Supp. XXII:** 92–93, 167

Stein, Gertrude, **I:** 103, 105, 476; **II:** 56, 251, 252, 257, 260, 262–263, 264, 289; **III:** 71, 454, 471–472, 600; **IV: 24–48,** 368, 375, 404, 415, 443, 477; **Retro. Supp. I:** 108, 170, 176, 177, 186, 418, 422; **Retro. Supp. II:** 85, 207, 326, 331; **Supp. I Part 1:** 292; **Supp. III Part 1:** 13, 37, 225, 226; **Supp. III Part 2:** 626; **Supp. IV Part 1:** 11, 79, 80, 81, 322; **Supp. IV Part 2:** 468; **Supp. V:** 53; **Supp. IX:** 55, 57, 62, 66; **Supp. XII:** 1, 139; **Supp. XIV:** 336; **Supp. XVI:** 187; **Supp. XVII:** 98, 105, 107; **Supp. XVIII:** 148; **Supp. XXI:** 7, 33; **Supp. XXII:** 158, 159; **Supp. XXIII:** 166, 207

Stein, Howard, **Supp. XXIV:** 116

Stein, Jean, **Supp. XVI:** 245

Stein, Karen F., **Supp. XIII:** 29, 30

Stein, Leo, **IV:** 26; **Supp. XIV:** 336; **Supp. XV:** 298

Stein, Lorin, **Supp. XII:** 254; **Supp. XVIII:** 137, 139

Steinbeck, John, **I:** 107, 288, 301, 378, 495, 519; **II:** 272; **III:** 382, 453, 454, 589; **IV: 49–72; Retro. Supp. II:** 19, 196; **Supp. IV Part 1:** 102, 225; **Supp. IV Part 2:** 502; **Supp. V:** 290, 291; **Supp. VIII:** 10; **Supp. IX:** 33, 171; **Supp. XI:** 169; **Supp. XIII:** 1, 17; **Supp. XIV:** 21, 181; **Supp. XVII:** 228; **Supp. XVIII:** 90, 102, 254; **Supp. XIX:** 3

Steinbeck, Olive Hamilton, **IV:** 51

Steinberg, Saul, **Supp. VIII:** 272

Steinberg, Sybil, **Supp. XVII:** 165, 166; **Supp. XXIII:** 241

Steinem, Gloria, **Supp. IV Part 1:** 203; **Supp. XXIII:** 104, 105, 106

Steiner, George, **Retro. Supp. I:** 327; **Supp. IV Part 1:** 286; **Supp. XVI:** 230

Steiner, Michael, **Supp. XXII:** 205

Steiner, Nancy, **Supp. I Part 2:** 529

Steiner, Stan, **Supp. IV Part 2:** 505

Steinfels, Margaret, **Supp. XVII:** 170

Steinhoff, Eirik, **Supp. XVI:** 290

Steinman, Michael, **Supp. VIII:** 172

Steinmetz, Charles P., **Supp. XXIII:** 161

Steinmetz, Charles Proteus, **I:** 483

Steinway Quintet Plus Four, The (Epstein), **Supp. XII:** 159, **162–166**

Stekel, Wilhelm, **III:** 554

Stella (Goethe), **Supp. IX:** 133, 138

Stella (Kushner), **Supp. IX:** 133

Stella, Joseph, **I:** 387

"Stellaria" (Francis), **Supp. IX:** 83

Stelligery and Other Essays (Wendell), **Supp. I Part 2:** 414

St. Elmo (Evans), **Supp. XXII:** 120

Stendhal, **I:** 316; **III:** 465, 467; **Supp. I Part 1:** 293; **Supp. I Part 2:** 445

Stepanchev, Stephen, **Supp. XI:** 312

Stephen, Leslie, **IV:** 440

Stephen, Sir Leslie, **IV:** 440; **Supp. I Part 1:** 306

Stephen, Saint, **II:** 539; **IV:** 228

Stephen Crane (Berryman), **I:** 169–170, 405

Stephen King, The Second Decade: "Danse Macabre" to "The Dark Half" (Magistrale), *Supp. V:* 138, 146, 151

Stephen King: The Art of Darkness (Winter), **Supp. V:** 144

Stephens, Jack, **Supp. X:** 11, 14, 15, 17

Stephens, James, **Supp. XIX:** 204

Stephens, Uriah, **Supp. XXIII:** 187

Stephenson, Gregory, **Supp. XII:** 120, 123

Stephenson, Neal, **Supp. XXII:** 49

"Stepping Out" (Dunn), **Supp. XI:** 140, 141

Stepping Outside (Gallagher), **Supp. XXIV:** 165, 167

Steps (Kosinski), **Supp. VII:** 215, 221–222, 225

"Steps" (Nye), **Supp. XIII:** 288

Steps to the Temple (Crashaw), **IV:** 145

"Steps Toward Poverty and Death" (R. Bly), **Supp. IV Part 1:** 60

Stepto, Robert B., **Retro. Supp. II:** 116, 120, 123

Sterile Cuckoo, The (Nichols), **Supp. XIII:** 258, **259–263,** 264

Sterling, Bruce, **Supp. XVI:** 118, 121, 123, 124, 128–129

Sterling, George, **I:** 199, 207, 208, 209; **II:** 440; **Supp. V:** 286; **Supp. XXII:** 276, 277

Sterling, Phillip, **Supp. XXIII:** 102

Stern, Bernhard J., **Supp. XIV:** 202, 213

Stern, Daniel, **Supp. VIII:** 238

Stern, Frederick C., **Supp. X:** 114, 115, 117

Stern, Gerald, **Supp. IX: 285–303; Supp. XI:** 139, 267; **Supp. XV:** 211, 212

Stern, Madeleine B., **Supp. I Part 1:** 35

Stern, Maurice, **IV:** 285

Stern, Philip Van Doren, **Supp. XIII:** 164

Stern, Richard, **Retro. Supp. II:** 291

Stern, Richard G., **Retro. Supp. II:** 204

Stern, Steven, **Supp. XVII:** 42, 48, 49; **Supp. XX: 178**

"Sterne" (Schwartz), **Supp. II Part 2:** 663

Sterne, Laurence, **II:** 302, 304–305, 308; **III:** 454; **IV:** 68, 211, 465; **Supp. I Part 2:** 714; **Supp. IV Part 1:** 299; **Supp. V:** 127; **Supp. X:** 324; **Supp. XV:** 232

Sterritt, David, **Supp. IV Part 2:** 574

Stetson, Caleb, **IV:** 178

Stetson, Charles Walter, **Supp. XI:** 195, 196, 197, 202, 204, 209

Steve Nelson, American Radical (Nelson), **Supp. XVIII:** 226

Stevens, Frances Simpson, **Supp. XXII:** 159, 162

Stevens, James, **Supp. XXIII:** 152

Stevens, Wallace, **I:** 60, 61, 266, 273, 462, 521, 528, 540–541; **II:** 56, 57, 530, 552, 556; **III:** 19, 23, 194, 216, 270–271, 272, 278, 279, 281, 453, 463, 493, 509, 521, 523, 600, 605, 613, 614; **IV: 73–96,** 140, 141, 332, 402, 415; **Retro. Supp. I:** 67, 89, 193, 284, 288, **295–315,** 335, 403, 411, 416, 417, 422; **Retro. Supp. II:** 40, 44, 326; **Supp. I Part 1:** 80, 82, 257; **Supp. II Part 1:** 9, 18; **Supp. III Part 1:** 2, 3, 12, 20, 48, 239, 318, 319, 344; **Supp. III Part 2:** 611; **Supp. IV Part 1:** 72, 393; **Supp. IV Part 2:** 619, 620, 621, 634; **Supp. V:** 337; **Supp. VIII:** 21, 102, 195, 271, 292; **Supp. IX:** 41; **Supp. X:** 58; **Supp. XI:** 123, 191, 312; **Supp. XIII:** 44, 45; **Supp. XV:** 39, 41, 92, 115, 250, 261, 298, 302, 306, 307; **Supp. XVI:** 64, 158, 202, 210, 288; **Supp. XVII:** 36, 42, 110, 129, 130, 240, 241; **Supp. XIX:** 7, 40, 86, 87; **Supp. XXI:** 19, 28, 60, 133; **Supp. XXII:** 162; **Supp. XXIII:** 53, 57, 65; **Supp. XXIV:** 41, 45

Stevens, Mrs. Wallace (Elsie Kachel), **IV:** 75

"Stevens and the Idea of the Hero" (Bromwich), **Retro. Supp. I:** 305

Stevens and the Interpersonal (Halliday), **Supp. XIX: 85–86**

Stevenson, Adlai, **II:** 49; **III:** 581

Stevenson, Anne, **Supp. XV:** 121; **Supp. XVII:** 74

Stevenson, Burton E., **Supp. XIV:** 120

Stevenson, David, **Supp. XI:** 230

Stevenson, Robert Louis, **I:** 2, 53; **II:** 283, 290, 311, 338; **III:** 328; **IV:** 183–184, 186, 187; **Retro. Supp. I:** 224, 228; **Supp. I Part 1:** 49; **Supp. II Part 1:** 404–405; **Supp. IV Part 1:** 298, 314; **Supp. VIII:** 125; **Supp. XIII:** 75; **Supp. XIV:** 40; **Supp. XVII:** 69; **Supp. XXI:** 204

Stevick, Robert D., **III:** 509

Stewart, Dugald, **II:** 8, 9; **Supp. I Part 1:** 151, 159; **Supp. I Part 2:** 422

Stewart, George, **Supp. XVIII:** 138

Stewart, Jeffrey C., **Supp. XIV:** 196, 209, 210

Stewart, Randall, **II:** 244; **Supp. XX: 164**

Stewart, Robert E., **Supp. XI:** 216

"St. Francis of Assisi" (Di Piero), **Supp. XIX:** 43

Stickeen (Muir), **Supp. IX:** 182

Sticks and Bones (Rabe), **Supp. XXIV:** 117

"Sticks and Stones" (L. Michaels), **Supp. XVI:** 205

Sticks and Stones (Mumford), **Supp. II Part 2:** 475, 483, 487–488

Sticks & Stones (Matthews), **Supp. IX:** 154, 155, 157, 158

Stieglitz, Alfred, **Retro. Supp. I:** 416; **Retro. Supp. II:** 103; **Supp. VIII:** 98; **Supp. XVII:** 96; **Supp. XX: 74, 75**

"Stigmata" (Oates), **Supp. II Part 2:** 520

Stiles, Ezra, **II:** 108, 122; **IV:** 144, 146, 148; **Supp. XXIV:** 68

Still, James, **Supp. XX: 163**

Still, William Grant, **Retro. Supp. I:** 203

Still Alice (Genova), **Supp. XXIII:** 127

"Stillborn" (Plath), **Supp. I Part 2:** 544

"Still Here" (Hughes), **Retro. Supp. I:** 211

"Still Just Writing" (Tyler), **Supp. IV Part 2:** 658

"Still Life" (Hecht), **Supp. X:** 68

"Still Life" (Malamud), **Supp. I Part 2:** 450

Still Life (Pickering), **Supp. XXI:** 198

"Still Life" (Pickering), **Supp. XXI:** 198

"Still Life" (Sandburg), **III:** 584

"Still Life: Moonlight Striking up on a Chess-Board" (Lowell), **II:** 528

"Still Life Or" (Creeley), **Supp. IV Part 1:** 141, 150, 158

Still Life with Oysters and Lemon (Doty), **Supp. XI:** 119, 121, **133–134**

Still Life with Woodpecker (Robbins), **Supp. X:** 260, **271–274,** 282

"Still Moment, A" (Welty), **IV:** 265; **Retro. Supp. I:** 347

Stillness (Gardner), **Supp. VI:** 74

"Stillness in the Air" (Dickinson), **Supp. XV:** 261

Stillness of Dancing, The (Bierds), **Supp. XVII:** 27–28

"Still Small Voices, The" (Fante), **Supp. XI:** 164

Still Such (Salter), **Supp. IX:** 246

"Still the Place Where Creation Does Some Work on Itself" (W. V. Davis), **Supp. IV Part 1:** 68

Stimpson, Catharine R., **Supp. IV Part 2:** 686

Stimson, Eleanor Kenyon. *See* Brooks, Mrs. Van Wyck

"Stimulants, Poultices, Goads" (Wright), **Supp. XV:** 349

"Stings" (Plath), **Retro. Supp. II:** 255; **Supp. I Part 2:** 541

"Stirling Street September" (Baraka), **Supp. II Part 1:** 51

Stirner, Max, **II:** 27

"Stirrup-Cup, The" (Lanier), **Supp. I Part 1:** 364

Stitt, Peter, **Supp. IV Part 1:** 68; **Supp. IV Part 2:** 628; **Supp. IX:** 152, 163, 291, 299; **Supp. XI:** 311, 317; **Supp. XIII:** 87; **Supp. XV:** 98, 99; **Supp. XIX:** 121

Stivers, Valerie, **Supp. X:** 311

St. John, David, **Supp. XV:** 73, 253

St. Louis Woman (Bontemps and Cullen), **Supp. XXII:** 6

St. Mark, Tyler, **Supp. XX: 260**

Stock, Noel, **III:** 479

Stockton, Frank R., **I:** 201

Stoddard, Charles Warren, **I:** 193, 195, 196; **Supp. II Part 1:** 192, 341, 351

Stoddard, Elizabeth, **II:** 275; **Supp. XV: 269–291**

Stoddard, Richard, **Supp. I Part 1:** 372

Stoddard, Richard Henry, **Supp. XV:** 269, 271, 272, 273, 274, 278, 279, 286

Stoddard, Solomon, **I:** 545, 548; **IV:** 145, 148

Stoffman, Judy, **Supp. XVIII:** 97

Stoic, The (Dreiser), **I:** 497, 502, 508, 516; **Retro. Supp. II:** 95, 96, 101, 108

Stokes, Geoffrey, **Supp. XV:** 256

Stokes, Olivia Egleston Phelps, **Supp. XVIII:** 261

"Stolen Calf, The" (Dunbar), **Supp. II Part 1:** 196

Stolen Jew, The (Neugeboren), **Supp. XVI: 222–224,** 225

Stolen Past, A (Knowles), **Supp. XII:** 249

Stolen Words: Forays into the Origins and Ravages of Plagiarism (Mallon), **Supp. XIX: 134–135**

Stollman, Aryeh Lev, **Supp. XVII:** 49; **Supp. XXIV:** 2, 8, 10–11

Stolmar, Thomas, **Supp. XVIII:** 138

Stomping the Blues (Murray), **Supp. XIX: 158–159**

"Stone" (Ozick), **Supp. XVII:** 50

Stone, Edward, **III:** 479

Stone, Herbert S., **Supp. XXI:** 2

Stone, I. F., **Supp. XIV:** 3

Stone, Irving, **II:** 463, 466, 467

Stone, Oliver, **Supp. XIV:** 48, 316

Stone, Phil, **II:** 55

Stone, Richard, **Supp. XIV:** 54

Stone, Robert, **Supp. V: 295–312; Supp. X:** 1; **Supp. XIX:** 54

Stone, Rosetta (pseudonym). *See* Geisel, Theodor Seuss (Dr. Seuss)

Stone, Wilmer, **Supp. I Part 1:** 49

Stone and the Shell, The (Hay), **Supp. XIV:** 122, 123, 127, 130

"Stone Bear, The" (Haines), **Supp. XII:** 206–207, 212

"Stone City" (Proulx), **Supp. VII:** 251–253

Stone Country (Sanders), **Supp. XVI:** 271–272

Stone Diaries, The (Shields), **Supp. VII:** 307, 315, 324–326, 327

"Stone Dreams" (Kingsolver), **Supp. VII:** 203

Stone Harp, The (Haines), **Supp. XII: 204,** 205, 206, 207

Stonemason, The (McCarthy), **Supp. VIII:** 175, 187

"Stones" (Hoffman), **Supp. XVIII:** 86

"Stones" (Kumin), **Supp. IV Part 2:** 447

Stones (lithograph series, O'Hara and Rivers), **Supp. XXIII:** 217

"Stones, The" (Plath), **Supp. I Part 2:** 535, 539

"Stones in My Passway, Hellhounds on My Trail" (Boyle), **Supp. VIII:** 15

Stones of Florence, The (McCarthy), **II:** 562

"Stone Walls" (Sarton), **Supp. VIII:** 259

"Stop" (Wilbur), **Supp. III Part 2:** 556

Stop-Loss (screenplay, Richard), **Supp. XIX:** 222

"Stop Me If You've Heard This One" (Lardner), **II:** 433

Stopover: Tokyo (Marquand), **III:** 53, 57, 61, 70

Stoppard, Tom, **Retro. Supp. I:** 189

"Stopping by Woods" (Frost), **II:** 154

"Stopping by Woods on a Snowy Evening" (Frost), **Retro. Supp. I:** 129, 133, 134, 135, 139

Stopping Westward (Richards), **II:** 396

"Stop Player. Joke No. 4" (Gaddis), **Supp. IV Part 1:** 280

Stop-Time (Conroy), **Supp. XVI: 63–71,** 72, 75, 76–77

"Store, The" (E. P. Jones), **Supp. XXII:** 144–145

Store, The (Stribling), **Supp. VIII:** 126; **Supp. XXII:** 195

"*Store* and *Mockingbird:* Two Pulitzer Novels about Alabama" (Going), **Supp. VIII:** 126

Store of a Million Items, The (Cliff), **Supp. XXII:** 67, 74, 75

"Store of a Million Items, The" (Cliff), **Supp. XXII:** 75

Storer, Edward, **Supp. I Part 1:** 261, 262

Stories, Fables and Other Diversions (Nemerov), **III:** 268–269, 285

Stories: Elizabeth Stoddard, **Supp. XV:** 270

"Stories for Sale" (Kolba), **Supp. XVIII:** 257

Stories for the Sixties (Yates, ed.), **Supp. XI:** 343

Stories from Our Living Past (Prose), **Supp. XVI:** 251

Stories from the Italian Poets (Hunt), **Supp. XV:** 175

Stories from the Old Testament Retold (L. P. Smith), **Supp. XIV:** 342

Stories from World Literature, **Supp. IX:** 4

"Stories in the Snow" (Leopold), **Supp. XIV:** 183

Stories of an Imaginary Childhood (Bukiet), **Supp. XVII: 41–44,** 45

Stories of F. Scott Fitzgerald, The (Cowley, ed.), **Retro. Supp. I:** 115

Stories of F. Scott Fitzgerald, The (Fitzgerald), **II:** 94

Stories of Modern America, **Supp. IX:** 4

Stories of Stephen Dixon, The (Dixon), **Supp. XII:** 152

Stories of the American Experience (Kriegel and Lass, eds.), **Supp. XXIV:** 214

Stories of the Spanish Civil War (Hemingway), **II:** 258

Stories Revived (James), **II:** 322

Stories that Could Be True (Stafford), **Supp. XI:** 325–327

Stories Toto Told Me (Rolfe), **Supp. XX:** 235

Storm, The (Buechner), **Supp. XII: 54–57**

"Storm, The" (Chopin), **Retro. Supp. II:** 60, 68; **Supp. I Part 1:** 218, 224

Storm, The (al-'Awásif) (Gibran), **Supp. XX: 116, 124, 125**

"Storm Fear" (Frost), **II:** 153; **Retro. Supp. I:** 127

"Storm Ship, The" (Irving), **II:** 309

"Storm Warnings" (Kingsolver), **Supp. VII:** 207–208

"Stormy Weather" (Ellison), **Supp. II Part 1:** 233

"Story" (Everwine), **Supp. XV:** 89

"Story, A" (Jarrell), **II:** 371

Story, Julian, **Supp. XX: 232**

Story, Richard David, **Supp. IV Part 2:** 575, 588

Story, William Wetmore, **Supp. XX: 228**

"Story about Chicken Soup, A" (Simpson), **Supp. IX: 272–273**

"Story about the Anteater, The" (Benét), **Supp. XI:** 53

"Story About the Body, A" (Hass), **Supp. VI: 107–108**

"Story for Teddy, A" (Swados), **Supp. XIX:** 266–267

Story for Teddy, A—and Others (Swados), **Supp. XIX: 266–268**

"Story Hearer, The" (Paley), **Supp. VI:** 230, 231

"Story Hour" (Hay), **Supp. XIV:** 124

"Story Hour" (Jarman), **Supp. XVII:** 116

Story Hour: A Second Look at Cinderella, Bluebeard, and Company (Hay), **Supp. XIV:** 119, 124, 125, 132, 133

Story of a Country Town, The (Howe), **I:** 106

Story of a Lover, The (Hapgood), **Supp. XVII:** 99, 100, 104; **Supp. XXI:** 3, 5, 7

Story of an American Family, The: Letters of the Hapgood Family, 1648–1917 (Boyce), **Supp. XVII:** 97; **Supp. XXI:** 9, 14

"Story of an Hour, The" (Chopin), **Retro. Supp. II:** 72; **Supp. I Part 1:** 212–213, 216

Story of a Novel, The (Wolfe), **IV:** 456, 458

"Story of a Proverb, The" (Lanier), **Supp. I Part 1:** 365

"Story of a Proverb, The: A Fairy Tale for Grown People" (Lanier), **Supp. I Part 1:** 365

Story of a Story and Other Stories, The: A Novel (Dixon), **Supp. XII:** 155

Story of a Wonder Man, The (Lardner), **II:** 433–434

"Story of a Year, The" (James), **Retro. Supp. I:** 218

Story of George Washington Carver, The (Bontemps), **Supp. XXII:** 13

Story of G.I. Joe, The (film, Wellman), **Supp. XVII:** 61, 62

"Story of Gus, The" (A. Miller), **III:** 147–148

"Story of How a Wall Stands, A" (Ortiz), **Supp. IV Part 2:** 499, 507

Story of Mist, The (Dybek), **Supp. XXIII: 74–75,** 78

"Story of Mist, The"(Dybek), **Supp. XXIII:** 74–75

Story of Mount Desert Island, Maine, The (Morison), **Supp. I Part 2:** 494

Story of My Boyhood and Youth, The (Muir), **Supp. IX: 172–174,** 176

Story of My Father, The: A Memoir (Miller), **Supp. XII:** 301

Story of O, The (Réage), **Supp. XII:** 9, 10

Story of Our Lives, The (Strand), **Supp. IV Part 2:** 620, 628–629, 629

"Story of Poppy Van Buster, The" (Briggs), **Supp. XVIII:** 8

Story of the Negro (Bontemps), **Supp. XXII:** 6, 12–13

Story of the Normans, The, Told Chiefly in Relation to Their Conquest of England (Jewett), **II:** 406

Story of the Telegraph, The (Briggs, and Maverick), **Supp. XVIII:** 4

"Story of Toby, The" (Melville), **III:** 76

"Story of To-day, A" (Davis). *See also Margret Howth*

"Story of To-day, A" (R. H. Davis), **Supp. XVI:** 88, 89

Story of Utopias, The (Mumford), **Supp. II Part 2:** 475, 483–486, 495

Story of Wine in California, The (M. F. K. Fisher), **Supp. XVII:** 88

Story on Page One, The (Odets), **Supp. II Part 2:** 546

Storyteller (Silko), **Supp. IV Part 2:** 558, 559, 560, 561, **566–570**

"Storyteller" (Silko), **Supp. IV Part 2:** 569

"*Storyteller:* Grandmother Spider's Web" (Danielson), **Supp. IV Part 2:** 569

"Storyteller's Notebook, A" (Carver), **Supp. III Part 1:** 142–143

Story Teller's Story, A: The Tale of an American Writer's Journey through His Own Imaginative World and through the World of Facts . . . (Anderson), **I:** 98, 101, 114, 117

"Story That Could Be True, A" (Stafford), **Supp. XI:** 326

"Stout Gentleman, The" (Irving), **II:** 309

Stover at Yale (Johnson), **III:** 321

Stowe, Calvin, **IV:** 445; **Supp. I Part 2:** 587, 588, 590, 596, 597

Stowe, Charles, **Supp. I Part 2:** 581, 582

Stowe, Eliza, **Supp. I Part 2:** 587

Stowe, Harriet Beecher, **II:** 274, 399, 403, 541; **Retro. Supp. I:** 34, 246; **Retro. Supp. II:** 4, 138, 156; **Supp. I Part 1:** 30, 206, 301; **Supp. I Part 2:** 579–601; **Supp. III Part 1:** 154, 168, 171; **Supp. IX:** 33; **Supp. X:** 223, 246, 249, 250; **Supp. XI:** 193; **Supp. XIII:** 141, 295; **Supp. XV:** 278; **Supp. XVI:** 82, 85

Stowe, Samuel Charles, **Supp. I Part 2:** 587

Stowe, William, **Supp. IV Part 1:** 129

Strachey, Lytton, **I:** 5; **IV:** 436; **Retro. Supp. I:** 59; **Supp. I Part 2:** 485, 494; **Supp. XIV:** 342; **Supp. XVI:** 191

"Stradivari" (Bierds), **Supp. XVII:** 28

Straight Cut (Bell), **Supp. X:** 5, **6–7,** 10

Straight Man (Russo), **Supp. XII:** 335–339, 340

Straits: Poems (Koch), **Supp. XV:** 184

Strand, Mark, **Supp. IV Part 2: 619–636; Supp. V:** 92, 332, 337, 338, 343; **Supp. IX:** 155; **Supp. XI:** 139, 145; **Supp. XII:** 254; **Supp. XIII:** 76; **Supp. XV:** 74; **Supp. XXIV:** 165

Strand, Paul, **Supp. VIII:** 272

Strandberg, Victor, **Supp. V:** 273

Strange, Sharan, **Supp. XXI:** 246

"Strange Beautiful Woman, A" (Nelson), **Supp. XVIII:** 173

Strange Bedfellows (Woods), **Supp. XXI:** 70

Strange Case of Dr. Jekyll and Mr. Hyde, The (Stevenson), **II:** 290

Strange Children, The (Gordon), **II:** 196, 197, 199, 211–213

Strange Commonplace, A (Sorrentino), **Supp. XXI:** 232, 237, 238

Strange Crime in Bermuda, The (Holding), **Supp. XXII: 124–125,** 127, 129

Strange Fire (Bukiet), **Supp. XVII: 46**

"Strange Fruit" (Harjo), **Supp. XII:** 224, 225

"Strange Fruit" (song), **Supp. I Part 1:** 80; **Supp. XVIII:** 228

Strange Interlude (O'Neill), **III:** 391, 397–398; **IV:** 61; **Supp. XXII:** 24

Stranger, The (Camus), **I:** 53, 292; **Supp. VIII:** 11; **Supp. XV:** 352

"Stranger, The" (Rich), **Supp. I Part 2:** 555, 560

"Stranger, The" (Salinger), **III:** 552–553

Strange Relation (Hadas), **Supp. XXIII:** 111, 113, 120, **127**

"Stranger in My Own Life, A: Alienation in American Indian Poetry and Prose" (Gunn Allen), **Supp. IV Part 1:** 322

Stranger in the Kingdom, A (Mosher), **Supp. XXII:** 204, 205, 206, 207, 208, 209, **212–213**

"Stranger in the Village" (Baldwin), **Retro. Supp. II:** 3; **Supp. I Part 1:** 54; **Supp. IV Part 1:** 10

"Stranger in Town" (Hughes), **Supp. I Part 1:** 334

"Strangers" (Howe), **Supp. VI:** 120

Strangers: A Book of Poems (Ferry), **Supp. XXIV: 149–150**

Strangers and Wayfarers (Jewett), **Retro. Supp. II:** 138

"Strangers from the Horizon" (Merwin), **Supp. III Part 1:** 356

Strangers on a Train (Highsmith), **Supp. IV Part 1:** 132

"Strange Story, A" (Taylor), **Supp. V:** 323

"Strange Story, A" (Wylie), **Supp. I Part 2:** 723

Strange Things (Atwood), **Supp. XIII:** 35

"Strato in Plaster" (Merrill), **Supp. III Part 1:** 328

Stratton-Porter, Gene, **Supp. XX: 211–225**

Straus, Ralph, **Supp. XIII:** 168

Straus, Roger, **Supp. VIII:** 82; **Supp. XV:** 59

Strauss, Harold, **Supp. XV:** 137

Strauss, Helen, **Supp. XXIII:** 258

Strauss, Johann, **I:** 66

Strauss, Richard, **IV:** 316

Strauss, Robert, **Supp. XI:** 141, 142

Stravinsky (De Schloezer), **III:** 474

Stravinsky, Igor, **Retro. Supp. I:** 378; **Supp. IV Part 1:** 81; **Supp. XI:** 133; **Supp. XV:** 265

"Stravinsky's Three Pieces 'Grotesques,' for String Quartet" (Lowell), **II:** 523

Straw, The (O'Neill), **III:** 390

"Strawberry Milkshake" (Halliday), **Supp. XIX:** 92, 94

"Stray Document, A" (Pound), **II:** 517

"Strays" (Richard), **Supp. XIX:** 210–211, 220

Streaks of the Tulip, The: Selected Criticism (W. J. Smith), **Supp. XIII:** 333, 334, 344, **347–348**

Streamline Your Mind (Mursell), **Supp. I Part 2:** 608

Strecker, Trey, **Supp. XXI:** 238

"Street, Cloud" (Ríos), **Supp. IV Part 2:** 549

Street, The (Petry), **Supp. XVIII:** 286

Streetcar Named Desire, A (T. Williams), **IV:** 382, 383, 385, 386, 387, 389–390, 395, 398; **Supp. IV Part 1:** 359

Street in Bronzeville, A (Brooks), **Retro. Supp. I:** 208; **Supp. III Part 1:** 74–78

"Street Moths" (X. J. Kennedy), **Supp. XV:** 170

"Street Musicians" (Ashbery), **Supp. III Part 1:** 18

"Street of Crocodiles" (Hull), **Supp. XXI:** 130

"Street off Sunset, A" (Jarrell), **II:** 387

"Streets" (Dixon), **Supp. XII: 145–146**

Streets in Their Own Ink (Dybek), **Supp. XXIII:** 78

Streets in the Moon (MacLeish), **III:** 5, 8–11, 15, 19

"Streets of Laredo" (screenplay) (McMurtry and Ossana), **Supp. V:** 226, 230

Streets of Laredo (McMurtry), **Supp. V:** 230

Streets of Night (Dos Passos), **I:** 478, 479–480, 481, 488

Streitfield, David, **Supp. XIII:** 234; **Supp. XVI:** 63

Strength of Fields, The (Dickey), **Supp. IV Part 1:** 178

"Strength of Fields, The" (Dickey), **Supp. IV Part 1:** 176, 184–185

"Strength of Gideon, The" (Dunbar), **Supp. II Part 1:** 212

Strength of Gideon and Other Stories, The (Dunbar), **Supp. II Part 1:** 211, 212

"Strenuous Artistry" (Zagarell), **Supp. XV:** 281

Strether, Lambert, **II:** 313

Stribling, T. S., **Supp. VIII:** 126

Strickland, Barbara, **Supp. XIX:** 102

Strickland, Joe (pseudonym). *See* Arnold, George W.

"Strictly Bucolic" (Simic), **Supp. VIII:** 278

Strictly Business (O. Henry), **Supp. II Part 1:** 410

"Strike, The" (Olsen), **Supp. XIII:** 292, 297

Strike at Shane's, The (Skloot), **Supp. XX: 216**

"Strikers" (Untermeyer), **Supp. XV:** 296

Strindberg, August, **I:** 78; **III:** 145, 165, 387, 390, 391, 392, 393; **IV:** 17; **Supp. XVII:** 100; **Supp. XXII:** 23

"String, The" (Dickey), **Supp. IV Part 1:** 179

String Light (Wright), **Supp. XV: 345–346**

"String Quartet, The" (Weigl), **Supp. XIX:** 278

"Strivings of the Negro People" (Du Bois), **Supp. II Part 1:** 167

Stroby, W. C., **Supp. XIV:** 26

Strohbach, Hermann, **Supp. XI:** 242

"Stroke of Good Fortune, A" (O'Connor), **III:** 344; **Retro. Supp. II:** 229, 232

Strom, Stephen, **Supp. XII:** 223

Strong, Anna Louise, **Supp. XVIII:** 238; **Supp. XXIII:** 166

Strong, George Templeton, **IV:** 321

Strong, Josiah, **Supp. XIV:** 64

"Strong Draughts of Their Refreshing Minds" (Dickinson), **Retro. Supp. I:** 46

Strong Motion (Franzen), **Supp. XX: 85, 88–89, 92, 95**

Strong Opinions (Nabokov), **Retro. Supp. I:** 263, 266, 270, 276

"Strong Room of the House, The" (Bronk), **Supp. XXI:** 32

"Strong Women" (Dorman), **Supp. XI:** 240

Strout, Elizabeth, **Supp. X:** 86; **Supp. XXIII: 273–287**

Structure of Nations and Empires, The (Niebuhr), **III:** 292, 308

"Structure of Rime, The" (Duncan), **Supp. XVI:** 287

Structuring the Void (Klinkowitz), **Supp. XXI:** 233

Struggle, The (film; Griffith), **Supp. XVI:** 191

"Strumpet Song" (Plath), **Retro. Supp. II:** 246; **Supp. I Part 2:** 536

Strunk, William, **Supp. I Part 2:** 652, 662, 670, 671, 672

Strunsky, Anna, **II:** 465

"Strut for Roethke, A" (Berryman), **I:** 188

Strychacz, Thomas F., **Supp. XVI:** 69–70

Stuart, Dabney, **Supp. XVIII:** 79

Stuart, Gilbert, **I:** 16

Stuart, J. E. B., **III:** 56

Stuart, Jesse, **Supp. XX: 162–163, 165**

Stuart, Michael, **Supp. XV:** 140

Stuart Little (White), **Supp. I Part 2:** 655–658

"Stubborn Kisses" (Gallagher), **Supp. XXIV:** 170

Stuckey, W. J., **Supp. XXII:** 191–192

"Student, The" (Moore), **III:** 212, 215

"Student of Clouds" (Collins), **Supp. XXI:** 60

"Student of Salmanaca, The" (Irving), **II:** 309

"Student's Wife, The" (Carver), **Supp. III Part 1:** 141

Studies in American Indian Literature: Critical Essays and Course Designs (Gunn Allen), **Supp. IV Part 1:** 324, 333

Studies in Classic American Literature (Lawrence), **II:** 102; **III:** 33; **IV:** 333; **Retro. Supp. I:** 421

Studies in Short Fiction (Edmonds), **Supp. XXIII:** 291

Studies in Short Fiction (Malin), **Supp. XVI:** 71

Studies in the Psychology of Sex (Ellis), **Supp. XX: 235**

"Studs" (Farrell), **II:** 25, 28, 31

Studs Lonigan: A Trilogy (Farrell), **II:** 25, 26, 27, 31–34, 37, 38, 41–42

"Study in Orange and White" (Collins), **Supp. XXI:** 60

"Study of Images" (Stevens), **IV:** 79

"Study of Lanier's Poems, A" (Kent), **Supp. I Part 1:** 373

Study of Milton's Prosody (Bridges), **II:** 537

"Study of the Negro Problems, The" (Du Bois), **Supp. II Part 1:** 165

Stuewe, Paul, **Supp. IV Part 1:** 68

Stuhlmann, Gunther, **Supp. X:** 182, 184, 185, 187

Stull, William L., **Supp. XXIV:** 177

Stultifera Navis (Brant), **III:** 447

Sturak, John Thomas, **Supp. XIII:** 162, 163, 165, 168

Sturgeon, Theodore, **Supp. XVIII:** 145

Sturgis, George, **III:** 600

Sturgis, Howard, **IV:** 319; **Retro. Supp. I:** 367, 373

Sturgis, Howard Overing, **Supp. XX: 227–242**

Sturgis, Julian Russell, **Supp. XX: 228, 233, 238**

Sturgis, Susan, **III:** 600

Sturm, Margaret. *See* Millar, Margaret

Stuttaford, Genevieve, **Supp. IX:** 279

Stuyvesant, Peter, **II:** 301

"Style" (Nemerov), **III:** 275

Styles of Radical Will (Sontag), **Supp. III Part 2:** 451, 459, 460–463

"Stylist, The" (Egan), **Supp. XIX:** 51, 52

Styne, Jule, **Supp. XVI:** 193

Styron, William, **III:** 40; **IV:** 4, **97–119,** 216; **Supp. V:** 201; **Supp. IX:** 208; **Supp. X:** 15–16, 250; **Supp. XI:** 229, 231, 343; **Supp. XIV:** 82; **Supp. XVI:** 235–236; **Supp. XXIII:** 107, 109

Suares, J. C., **Supp. IV Part 1:** 234

Suarez, Ernest, **Supp. IV Part 1:** 175; **Supp. V:** 180

Suarez, Ray, **Supp. XXI:** 243

"Sub, The" (Dixon), **Supp. XII:** 146

Subjection of Women, The (Mill), **Supp. XI:** 196, 203

"Subjective Necessity for Social Settlements" (Addams), **Supp. I Part 1:** 4

"Subject of Childhood, A" (Paley), **Supp. VI:** 221; **Supp. XXI:** 118

"Submarginalia" (Howe), **Supp. IV Part 2:** 422

Substance and Shadow (James), **II:** 344

"Subterranean Homesick Blues" (song, Dylan), **Supp. XVIII:** 25

Subterraneans, The (Kerouac), **Supp. III Part 1:** 225, 227–231

"Subtitle" (Kees), **Supp. XV:** 139

Subtreasury of American Humor, A (White and White), **Supp. I Part 2:** 668

"Suburban Culture, Imaginative Wonder: The Fiction of Frederick Barthelme" (Brinkmeyer), **Supp. XI:** 38

Suburban Sketches (Howells), **II:** 274, 277

"Subversive Element, The" (Ryan as Quin), **Supp. XVIII:** 230

"Subverted Flower, The" (Frost), **Retro. Supp. I:** 139

"Subway, The" (Tate), **IV:** 128

"Subway Singer, The" (Clampitt), **Supp. IX:** 45

"Success" (Mora), **Supp. XIII:** 217

Successful Love and Other Stories (Schwartz), **Supp. II Part 2:** 661, 665

Succession, The: A Novel of Elizabeth and James (Garrett), **Supp. VII:** 104–107, 108

"Success is counted sweetest" (Dickinson), **Retro. Supp. I:** 30, 31–32, 38; **Supp. XV:** 126

Success Stories (Banks), **Supp. V:** 14–15

"Success Story" (Banks), **Supp. V:** 15

"Such Counsels You Gave to Me" (Jeffers), **Supp. II Part 2:** 433

Such Silence (Milburn), **Supp. XI:** 242

"Such Things Happen Only in Books" (Wilder), **IV:** 365

Such Was the Season (Major), **Supp. XXII: 177–178,** 179, 182

"Sudden Journey" (Gallagher), **Supp. XXIV:** 169

Suddenly, Last Summer (film) (Vidal), **Supp. IV Part 2:** 683

Suddenly Last Summer (T. Williams), **I:** 73; **IV:** 382, 383, 385, 386, 387, 389, 390, 391, 392, 395–396, 397, 398

Suder (Everett), **Supp. XVIII: 54–55**

Sudermann, Hermann, **I:** 66

Sue, Eugène, **Supp. XXIII:** 182

Sugg, Richard P., **Supp. IV Part 1:** 68

"Suggestion from a Friend" (Kenyon), **Supp. VII:** 171

"Suicide" (Barnes), **Supp. III Part 1:** 33

"Suicide off Egg Rock" (Plath), **Supp. I Part 2:** 529, 538

Suicides and Jazzers (Carruth), **Supp. XVI:** 46

"Suicide's Note" (Hughes), **Retro. Supp. I:** 199

"Suitable Surroundings, The" (Bierce), **I:** 203

"Suitcase, The" (Ozick), **Supp. V:** 262, 264

"Suite for Augustus, A" (Dove), **Supp. IV Part 1:** 245

"Suite for Emily" (Hull), **Supp. XXI:** 139–140

"Suite for Lord Timothy Dexter" (Rukeyser), **Supp. VI:** 283, 285

"Suite from the Firebird" (Stravinsky), **Supp. XI:** 133

"Suitor, The" (Kenyon), **Supp. VII:** 164–165

Sukarno, **IV:** 490

Sukenick, Ronald, **Supp. V:** 39, 44, 46; **Supp. XII:** 139

Sula (Morrison), **Supp. III Part 1:** 362, 364, 367, 368, 379; **Supp. VIII:** 219

Sullivan, Andrew, **Supp. IX:** 135

Sullivan, Arthur, **Supp. XX: 228**

Sullivan, Frank, **Supp. IX:** 201

Sullivan, Harry Stack, **I:** 59

Sullivan, Jack, **Supp. X:** 86; **Supp. XII:** 331

Sullivan, Noel, **Retro. Supp. I:** 202; **Supp. I Part 1:** 329, 333

Sullivan, Richard, **Supp. VIII:** 124

Sullivan, Walter, **Supp. VIII:** 168

"Sullivan County Sketches" (Crane), **I:** 407, 421

"Sumach and Goldenrod: An American Idyll" (Mumford), **Supp. II Part 2:** 475

Suma Genji (Play), **III:** 466

Sumerian Vistas (Ammons), **Supp. VII:** 34, 35

"Summa Lyrica" (Grossman), **Supp. XIX:** 86

"Summer" (Emerson), **II:** 10

Summer (Gioia), **Supp. XV:** 117

"Summer" (Lowell), **II:** 554

Summer (Wharton), **IV:** 317; **Retro. Supp. I:** 360, 367, 374, **378–379,** 382; **Supp. XXIII:** 275, 281

Summer, Bob, **Supp. X:** 1, 5, 6, 42

Summer and Smoke (T. Williams), **IV:** 382, 384, 385, 386, 387, 395, 397, 398; **Supp. IV Part 1:** 84

Summer Anniversaries, The (Justice), **Supp. VII:** 115, 117

Summer Blue (Skloot), **Supp. XX: 196, 207–208**

"Summer Commentary, A" (Winters), **Supp. II Part 2:** 808

"Summer Day" (O'Hara), **III:** 369

"Summer Days, The" (Oliver), **Supp. VII:** 239

"Summer Evening" (Boyle), **Supp. XXIV:** 61

"Summer Love Overheated" (Díaz), **Supp. XXIV:** 89

Summer Never Ends (W. Frank), **Supp. XX:** 78

"Summer Night" (Hughes), **Supp. I Part 1:** 325

"Summer Night, A" (Auden), **Supp. II Part 1:** 8

"Summer Night—Broadway" (Untermeyer), **Supp. XV:** 296

"Summer Noon: 1941" (Winters), **Supp. II Part 2:** 811

"Summer of '82" (Merwin), **Supp. III Part 1:** 355–356

Summer on the Lakes in 1843 (Fuller), **Supp. II Part 1:** 279, 295–296

"Summer People" (Hemingway), **II:** 258–259

"Summer People, The" (Jackson), **Supp. IX:** 120

"Summer People, The" (Merrill), **Supp. III Part 1:** 325–326

"Summer Perdu" (Halliday), **Supp. XIX:** 89

"Summer Planning" (Halliday), **Supp. XIX:** 92

"Summer Ramble, A" (Bryant), **Supp. I Part 1:** 162, 164

Summers, Claude J., **Supp. IV Part 2:** 680–681; **Supp. XIV:** 161, 169

Summers, Robert, **Supp. IX:** 289

"Summer Solstice, New York City" (Olds), **Supp. X:** 207

"Summer's Reading, A" (Malamud), **Supp. I Part 2:** 430–431, 442

"Summer Storm" (Gioia), **Supp. XV:** 127

"Summer Storm" (Simpson), **Supp. IX:** 268

"'Summertime and the Living . . .'" (Hayden), **Supp. II Part 1:** 363, 366

Summertime Island (Caldwell), **I:** 307–308

"Summer Tragedy" (Bontemps), **Supp. XXII:** 9

"Summer: West Side" (Updike), **Retro. Supp. I:** 320

"Summer with Tu Fu, A" (Carruth), **Supp. XVI:** 55, 58

"Summit Beach, 1921" (Dove), **Supp. IV Part 1:** 249

Summoning of Stones, A (Hecht), **Supp. X:** 57, 58, **58–59**

"Summons" (Untermeyer), **Supp. XV:** 296

Summons to Memphis, A (Taylor), **Supp. V:** 313, 314, 327

Summons to the Free, A (Benét), **Supp. XI:** 47

Sumner, Charles, **I:** 3, 15; **Supp. I Part 2:** 685, 687

Sumner, John, **Retro. Supp. II:** 95

Sumner, John B., **I:** 511

Sumner, William Graham, **III:** 102, 108; **Supp. I Part 2:** 640

"Sumptuous Destination" (Wilbur), **Supp. III Part 2:** 553

"Sun" (Moore), **III:** 215

"Sun" (Swenson), **Supp. IV Part 2:** 640

"Sun, Sea, and Sand" (Marquand), **III:** 60

Sun Also Rises, The (Hemingway), **I:** 107; **II:** 68, 90, 249, 251–252, 260, 600; **III:** 36; **IV:** 35, 297; **Retro. Supp. I:** 171, **177–180**, 181, 189; **Supp. I Part 2:** 614; **Supp. XIII:** 263; **Supp. XVIII:** 74

"Sun and Moon" (Kenyon), **Supp. VII:** 168

"Sun and the Still-born Stars, The" (Southern), **Supp. XI:** 295

Sun at Midnight (Soseki; Merwin and Shigematsu, trans.), **Supp. III Part 1:** 353

"Sun Crosses Heaven from West to East Bringing Samson Back to the Womb, The" (R. Bly), **Supp. IV Part 1:** 73

"Sun Dance Shield" (Momaday), **Supp. IV Part 2:** 491

Sunday, Billy, **II:** 449

"Sunday Afternoons" (Komunyakaa), **Supp. XIII:** 127

Sunday after the War (H. Miller), **III:** 184

"Sunday at Home" (Hawthorne), **II:** 231–232

"Sunday Following Mother's Day, The" (E. P. Jones), **Supp. XXII:** 145

"Sunday Morning" (Stevens), **II:** 552; **III:** 278, 463, 509; **IV:** 92–93; **Retro. Supp. I:** 296, 300, 301, 304, 307, 313; **Supp. XV:** 120; **Supp. XVI:** 210; **Supp. XVII:** 42; **Supp. XIX:** 40; **Supp. XXI:** 28, 133; **Supp. XXIII:** 57

"Sunday Morning Apples" (Crane), **I:** 387

"Sunday Morning Prophecy" (Hughes), **Supp. I Part 1:** 334

"Sunday Morning with the Sensational Nightingales" (Collins), **Supp. XXI:** 60

"Sundays" (B. Kelly), **Supp. XVII:** 124–125

"Sundays" (Salter), **Supp. IX:** 257

"Sundays, They Sleep Late" (Rukeyser), **Supp. VI:** 278

"Sundays of Satin-Legs Smith, The" (Brooks), **Supp. III Part 1:** 74, 75

"Sundays Visiting" (Ríos), **Supp. IV Part 2:** 541

Sundial, The (Jackson), **Supp. IX: 126–127**

Sundog (Harrison), **Supp. VIII: 46–48**

Sun Dogs (R. O. Butler), **Supp. XII: 64–65**

Sun Do Move, The (Hughes), **Supp. I Part 1:** 339

Sundquist, Eric, **Supp. XIV:** 66, 71

"Sunfish" (C. Frost), **Supp. XV:** 100–101, 102

"Sunflower Sutra" (Ginsberg), **Supp. II Part 1:** 317, 321; **Supp. XV:** 215

Sunlight Dialogues, The (Gardner), **Supp. VI:** 63, **68,** 69, 70

"Sunlight Is Imagination" (Wilbur), **Supp. III Part 2:** 549

"Sunny Ridge, The" (Halliday), **Supp. XIX:** 92

Sun Out: Selected Poems, 1952–1954 (Koch), **Supp. XV:** 179

"Sunrise" (Lanier), **Supp. I Part 1:** 370

"Sunrise and the Bomb" (Halliday), **Supp. XIX:** 84, 85, 92

"Sunrise runs for Both, The" (Dickinson), **Retro. Supp. I:** 45

Sunrise with Seamonsters: Travels and Discoveries, 1964–1984 (Theroux), **Supp. VIII:** 311, 313, 323, 325

"Sun Rising" (Donne), **Supp. VIII:** 164

"Sunset" (Ransom), **III:** 484

"Sunset from Omaha Hotel Window" (Sandburg), **III:** 584

Sunset Gun (Parker), **Supp. IX:** 192

Sunset Limited (Burke), **Supp. XIV:** 32, 33

Sunset Limited (Harrison), **Supp. VIII:** 51

"Sunset Maker, The" (Justice), **Supp. VII:** 123

Sunset Maker, The: Poems, Stories, a Memoir (Justice), **Supp. VII:** 116, 118, 119, 123–124

Sunshine Boys, The (film), **Supp. IV Part 2:** 589

Sunshine Boys, The (Simon), **Supp. IV Part 2:** 575, 584–585

"Sunthin' in the Pastoral Line" (Lowell), **Supp. I Part 2:** 415–416

Sun to Sun (Hurston), **Supp. VI:** 154

Sun Tracks (Ortiz), **Supp. IV Part 2:** 499, 500

Sun Under Wood (Hass), **Supp. VI:** 103, 108–109

"Superb Lily, The" (Pinsky), **Supp. VI:** 250

"Super Goat Man" (Lethem), **Supp. XVIII:** 148

"Superman Comes to the Supermarket" (Mailer), **Retro. Supp. II:** 204

"Supermarket in California, A" (Ginsberg), **Supp. XI:** 135

"Supernatural Love" (Schnackenberg), **Supp. XV:** 257, 259–260

Supernatural Love: Poems 1976–1992 (Schnackenberg), **Supp. XV:** 253, 256, 260, 263

Suplee, Curt, **Supp. XVI:** 202

"Supper After the Last, The" (Kinnell), **Supp. III Part 1:** 239

"Supposedly Fun Thing I'll Never Do Again, A" (Wallace), **Supp. X:** 315

Supposedly Fun Thing I'll Never Do Again, A: Essays and Arguments (Wallace), **Supp. X: 314–316**

Suppressed Desires (Glaspell and Cook), **Supp. III Part 1:** 178; **Supp. XXI:** 6

Suppression of the African Slave Trade to the United States of America, 1638–1870 (Du Bois), **Supp. II Part 1:** 157, 162

Supreme Fiction, The (Stevens), **Supp. XVI:** 158

"Supremes, The" (Jarman), **Supp. XVII:** 115

Sure Hand of God, The (Caldwell), **I:** 297, 302

Sure Signs: New and Selected Poems (Kooser), **Supp. XIX:** 116, 117, **121–122**

"Surety and Fidelity Claims" (Stevens), **Retro. Supp. I:** 296, 309

Surface of Earth, The (Price), **Supp. VI:** 261–262

"Surfaces" (Ammons), **Supp. VII:** 36

Surfaces and Masks (Major), **Supp. XXII:** 180

Surfacing (Atwood), **Supp. XIII:** 20, 21, **22–23,** 24, 33, 35

"Surgeon at 2 A.M." (Plath), **Supp. I Part 2:** 545

Summer Knowledge (Schwartz), **Supp. II Part 2:** 662, 665

"Surprise" (Kenyon), **Supp. VII:** 173

Surprised by Sin: The Reader in Paradise Lost (Fish), **Supp. XIV:** 15

Surreal South (eds. P. Benedict and L. Benedict), **Supp. XXIII:** 35

"Surround, The Imagining Herself as the Environment,/She Speaks to James Wright at Sundow" (Dickey), **Supp. IV Part 1:** 185

"Surrounded by Weasels" (Gray and Gallagher), **Supp. XXIV:** 178

"Survey of Literature" (Ransom), **III:** 480

"Survey of the Literature, A" (Saunders), **Supp. XIX:** 235

"Surveyor, The" (H. Roth), **Supp. IX:** 233, 234

Survival (Atwood), **Supp. XIII:** 20, 22, 35

"Survival as Tao, Beginning at 5:00 A.M." (Carruth), **Supp. XVI:** 56

Survival of the Bark Canoe, The (McPhee), **Supp. III Part 1:** 301, 302, 308, 313

Survival This Way: Interviews with American Indian Poets (Bruchac), **Supp. IV Part 2:** 506

"Surviving Love" (Berryman), **I:** 173

Survivor (O. Butler), **Supp. XIII:** 62, 63

Susan and Anna Warner (Foster), **Supp. XVIII:** 265

Susan and God (film; Cukor), **Supp. XVI:** 192

Susanna Moodie: Voice and Vision (Shields), **Supp. VII:** 313

Susan Warner ("Elizabeth Wetherell") (A. Warner), **Supp. XVIII:** 259, 260

Suspect in Poetry, The (Dickey), **Supp. IV Part 1:** 177

"Sustained by Fiction" (Hoffman), **Supp. X:** 90, 92

"Susto" (Ríos), **Supp. IV Part 2:** 553

Sutherland, Donald, **IV:** 38, 44; **Supp. IX:** 254

Sutherland, Efua, **Supp. IV Part 1:** 9, 16

Sutherland-Smith, James, **Supp. X:** 211, 212

Sut Lovingood (Harris), **II:** 70; **Supp. XXII:** 193

Sutton, Roger, **Supp. X:** 266

Sutton, Walter, **III:** 479

"Sutton Pie Safe, The"(P. Benedict), **Supp. XXIII:** 36

Suttree (McCarthy), **Supp. VIII: 178– 180,** 189

Suvero, Mark di, **Supp. IX:** 251

Svevo, Italo, **Supp. XIV:** 112

Swados, Harvey, **Supp. XI:** 222; **Supp. XIX: 255–271**

Swales, Martin, **Supp. XIX:** 183

Swallow, Alan, **Supp. X:** 112, 115, 116, 120, 123

Swallow Barn (J. P. Kennedy), **II:** 313

Swallow Barn (Kennedy), **Supp. XXII:** 193

Swallow the Lake (Major), **Supp. XXII:** 174

"Swamp Boy" (Bass), **Supp. XVI:** 20

Swan, Barbara, **Supp. IV Part 2:** 447

Swan, Jon, **Supp. IV Part 1:** 176

Swan Lake (Tchaikovsky), **Supp. IX:** 51

"Swan Legs" (Stern), **Supp. IX:** 299

Swann (Shields), **Supp. VII:** 315, 318– 323, 326

Swann, Brian, **Supp. IV Part 2:** 500

Swanson, Gloria, **II:** 429

Swanson, Stevenson, **Supp. XIV:** 111

Swanton, John Reed, **Supp. VIII:** 295

Swan Watch (Schulberg), **Supp. XVIII:** 254

Swanwick, John, **Supp. XV:** 237

Swanwick, Michael, **Supp. XVI:** 128

"Swarm, The" (Plath), **Retro. Supp. II:** 255

"Sway" (Simpson), **Supp. IX:** 276

Sweat (Hurston), **Supp. VI:** 152

Swedenborg, Emanuel, **II:** 5, 10, 321, 342, 343–344, 396

Sweeney Agonistes (Eliot), **I:** 580; **Retro. Supp. I:** 64, 65; **Retro. Supp. II:** 247

"Sweeney Among the Nightingales" (Eliot), **III:** 4

"Sweeper, The" (Kooser), **Supp. XIX:** 125

Sweet, Blanche, **Supp. I Part 2:** 391

Sweet, Timothy, **Supp. IV Part 1:** 330

Sweet and Lowdown (film; Allen), **Supp. XV:** 11

Sweet and Sour (O'Hara), **III:** 361

"Sweet Armageddon" (Hoffman), **Supp. XVIII:** 85, 86

Sweet Bird of Youth (T. Williams), **IV:** 382, 383, 385, 386, 387, 388, 389, 390, 391, 392, 395, 396, 398; **Supp. IV Part 1:** 84, 89

Sweet Charity (musical), **Supp. IV Part 2:** 575

Sweet Flypaper of Life, The (Hughes), **Supp. I Part 1:** 335–336

"Sweetgrass"(Kenny), **Supp. XXIII:** 148

"Sweetheart" (Notley), **Supp. XXII:** 231

"Sweetheart of the Song Tra Bong, The" (O'Brien), **Supp. V:** 243, 249

"Sweethearts" (Ford), **Supp. V:** 69

Sweet Hereafter, The (Banks), **Supp. V:** 15–16

Sweet Lorain (Weigl), **Supp. XIX:** 282

Sweet Machine (Doty), **Supp. XI:** 121, **131–132,** 135

Sweet Sue (Gurney), **Supp. V:** 105, 107– 108

Sweet Sweetback's Baadasss Song (Peebles; film), **Supp. XI:** 17

Sweet Thursday (Steinbeck), **IV:** 50, 52, 64–65

Sweet Will (Levine), **Supp. V:** 178, 187, 189, 190

"Sweet Will" (Levine), **Supp. V:** 190

"Sweet Willy"(J. Schoolcraft), **Supp. XXIII:** 226, 231

"Sweet Words on Race" (Hughes), **Retro. Supp. I:** 211

Sweezy, Paul, **Supp. I Part 2:** 645

"Swell-Looking Girl, A" (Caldwell), **I:** 310

Swenson, May, **Retro. Supp. II:** 44; **Supp. IV Part 2: 637–655; Supp. XIX:** 123

Swetman, Glenn R., **Supp. XXI:** 91

"Swift" (Schwartz), **Supp. II Part 2:** 663

Swift, Jonathan, **I:** 125, 194, 209, 441; **II:** 110, 302, 304–305, 577; **III:** 113; **IV:** 68; **Retro. Supp. I:** 66; **Supp. I Part 2:** 406, 523, 603, 656, 665, 708, 714; **Supp. IV Part 1:** 51; **Supp. IV Part 2:** 692; **Supp. XI:** 105, 209; **Supp. XII:** 276; **Supp. XV:** 258; **Supp. XVI:** 110; **Supp. XVIII:** 2, 12

"Swimmer" (Francis), **Supp. IX:** 82

"Swimmer" (Skloot), **Supp. XX: 199, 200**

"Swimmer, The" (Cheever), **Supp. I Part 1:** 185, 187

"Swimmer, The" (Glück), **Supp. V:** 82

"Swimmers" (Untermeyer), **Supp. XV:** 300

"Swimmers, The" (Fitzgerald), **Retro. Supp. I:** 110, 111

"Swimmers, The" (Tate), **IV:** 136

"Swimming" (Harjo), **Supp. XII:** 218

"Swimming Pool, The"(Strout), **Supp. XXIII:** 284

"Swim Team, The" (July), **Supp. XXIV:** 201

Swinburne, Algernon C., **I:** 50, 384, 568; **II:** 3, 4, 129, 400, 524; **IV:** 135; **Retro. Supp. I:** 100; **Supp. I Part 1:** 79; **Supp. I Part 2:** 422, 552; **Supp. XIV:** 120, 344

"Swinburne as Poet" (Eliot), **I:** 576

Swinger of Birches, A: A Portrait of Robert Frost (Cox), **Retro. Supp. I:** 132

"Swinging an Arc Before Him As He Goes" (Espaillat), **Supp. XXI:** 108

"Swinging on a Birch-Tree" (Larcom), **Supp. XIII:** 147

Swiss, Tom, **Supp. XIX:** 40

Switch, The (Dixon), **Supp. XII:** 141

Swope, D. B., **Supp. IX:** 95

Sword Blades and Poppy Seed (Lowell), **II:** 518, 520, 522, 532

Sword of God, The: Jeanne D'Arc (Endore), **Supp. XVII:** 55

Sybil (Auchincloss), **Supp. IV Part 1:** 25

Sybil and Chryssa (S. and A. Warner), **Supp. XVIII:** 264

"Sycamore" (Stern), **Supp. IX:** 294

"Sycamore, The" (Moore), **III:** 216

"Sycamores, The" (Whittier), **Supp. I Part 2:** 699

Sylvester, Johnny, **Supp. I Part 2:** 438

Sylvester, Joshua, **I:** 178, 179; **II:** 18; **III:** 157; **Supp. I Part 1:** 98, 104, 114, 116

Sylvia (Gurney), **Supp. V:** 105

"Sylvia" (L. Michaels), **Supp. XVI:** 202, 213

"Sylvia" (Larcom), **Supp. XIII:** 144

"Sylvia" (Stern), **Supp. IX:** 297

Sylvia: A Fictional Memoir (L. Michaels), **Supp. XVI:** 202, 213
Sylvia Plath: Method and Madness (Butscher), **Supp. I Part 2:** 526
Sylvia Plath: Poetry and Existence (Holbrook), **Supp. I Part 2:** 526–527
"Sylvia's Death" (Sexton), **Supp. II Part 2:** 671, 684, 685
"Symbol and Image in the Shorter Poems of Herman Melville" (Dickey), **Supp. IV Part 1:** 176
Symbolist Movement in Literature, The (Symons), **I:** 50, 569; **Retro. Supp. I:** 55
Symonds, John Addington, **I:** 241, 242, 251, 259; **IV:** 334; **Supp. XIV:** 329, 335; **Supp. XX: 230**
Symons, Arthur, **I:** 50, 569; **Retro. Supp. I:** 55; **Supp. XX: 239**
Symons, Julian, **Supp. IV Part 1:** 343, 351
"Sympathy" (Dunbar), **Supp. IV Part 1:** 15
Sympathy of Souls, A (Goldbarth), **Supp. XII:** 175, 176, **186–187**
"Symphony, The" (Lanier), **Supp. I Part 1:** 352, 360–361, 364; **Supp. I Part 2:** 416
Symposium (Plato), **Retro. Supp. II:** 31; **Supp. IV Part 1:** 391
Symposium: To Kill a Mockingbird (Alabama Law Review), **Supp. VIII:** 127, 128
Symptoms and Madness (Major), **Supp. XXII:** 174
Symptoms of Being 35 (Lardner), **II:** 434
Synanon (Endore), **Supp. XVII:** 65
Synanon (film, Quine), **Supp. XVII:** 65
Synanon City (Endore), **Supp. XVII:** 65
Syncopated Cakewalk, The (Major), **Supp. XXII:** 174
Synge, John Millington, **I:** 434; **III:** 591–592; **Supp. III Part 1:** 34; **Supp. VIII:** 155
Synthetic Philosophy (Spencer), **II:** 462–463
"Syringa" (Ashbery), **Supp. III Part 1:** 19–21, 25
"Syrinx" (Clampitt), **Supp. IX:** 53
"Syrinx" (Merrill), **Supp. III Part 1:** 328
Syrkin, Marie, **Supp. XIV:** 279, 288, 291
"System, The" (Ashbery), **Supp. III Part 1:** 14, 15, 18, 21–22
System of Dante's Hell, The (Baraka), **Supp. II Part 1:** 39–41, 55
"System of Dante's Inferno, The" (Baraka), **Supp. II Part 1:** 40
"System of Doctor Tarr and Professor Fether, The" (Poe), **III:** 419, 425
System of General Geography, A (Brown), **Supp. I Part 1:** 146
Szaylay, Michael, **Supp. XXI:** 267
Sze, Mai-mai, **Supp. X:** 291
Szentgyorgyi, Tom, **Supp. IX:** 135, 136, 140, 141–142
Szulc, Tad, **Supp. XVI:** 154
Szymborka, Wislawa, **Supp. XI:** 267
Szymborska, Wislawa, **Supp. XVIII:** 29

"T-2 Tanker Blues" (Snyder), **Supp. VIII:** 294
Tabios, Eileen, **Supp. XV:** 214, 225, 226
"Table of Delectable Contents, The" (Simic), **Supp. VIII:** 276
Tabloid Dreams (R. O. Butler), **Supp. XII: 70–72,** 74
Tacey Cromwell (Richter), **Supp. XVIII: 211,** 215, 217
Tacitus, Cornelius, **I:** 485; **II:** 113
Tadic, Novica, **Supp. VIII:** 272
Taft (Patchett), **Supp. XII:** 307, 312, **314–317**
"Tag" (Hughes), **Supp. I Part 1:** 341
Taggard, Genevieve, **IV:** 436; **Supp. XXII: 271–287**
Taggart, John, **Supp. IV Part 2:** 421
Tagore, Rabindranath, **I:** 383; **Supp. XX: 117**
"Taibele and Her Demon" (Singer), **Retro. Supp. II:** 307
Taibl, Erika, **Supp. XV:** 255
"Tailor Shop, The" (H. Miller), **III:** 175
"Tails" (Dixon), **Supp. XII:** 154
Taine, Hippolyte, **I:** 503; **II:** 271; **III:** 323; **IV:** 440, 444
"Tain't So" (Hughes), **Supp. I Part 1:** 330
"Taipei Tangle" (Halliday), **Supp. XIX:** 91
Takasago (play), **III:** 466
Takazauckas, Albert, **Supp. XXIII:** 203
Take Away the Darkness (Bynner), **Supp. XV:** 51
Take Heart (Peacock), **Supp. XIX: 197–199,** 206
Take Me Back: A Novel (Bausch), **Supp. VII:** 41, 43–45, 46, 49
"Take My Saddle from the Wall: A Valediction" (McMurtry), **Supp. V:** 219
"'Take No for an Answer'" (Didion), **Supp. IV Part 1:** 203
"Take Pity" (Malamud), **Supp. I Part 2:** 427, 428, 435, 436, 437
"Takers, The" (Olds), **Supp. X:** 205
"Take the I Out" (Olds), **Supp. X:** 213
Take the Money and Run (film; Allen), **Supp. XV: 3–4,** 6
"Taking Away the Name of a Nephew" (Ríos), **Supp. IV Part 2:** 545–546
Taking Care of Mrs. Carroll (Monette), **Supp. X:** 153
"Taking of Captain Ball, The" (Jewett), **Retro. Supp. II:** 134
"Taking Off Emily Dickinson's Clothes" (Collins), **Supp. XXI:** 59, 60
"Taking Out the Lawn Chairs" (Karr), **Supp. XI:** 241
"Taking the Bypass" (J. Epstein), **Supp. XIV:** 110; **Supp. XVI:** 230
"Taking the Forest" (Howe), **Supp. IV Part 2:** 433
"Taking the Lambs to Market" (Kumin), **Supp. IV Part 2:** 455
Talbot, Daniel, **Supp. XIX:** 264
"Tale, A" (Bogan), **Supp. III Part 1:** 50, 51
Taleb-Khyar, Mohamed, **Supp. IV Part 1:** 242, 243, 244, 247, 257

Talented Mr. Ripley, The (Highsmith), **Supp. XXII:** 119
"Tale of Jerusalem, A" (Poe), **III:** 411
Tale of Possessors Self-Dispossessed, A (O'Neill), **III:** 404
Tale of the Body Thief, The (Rice), **Supp. VII:** 290, 293–294, 297
Tale of Two Cities, A (film), **Supp. I Part 1:** 67
"Tale of Two Liars, A" (Singer), **IV:** 12
Tales (Baraka), **Supp. II Part 1:** 39, 55
Tales (Poe), **III:** 413
Tales and Stories for Black Folks (Bambara, ed.), **Supp. XI:** 1
Tales before Midnight (Benét), **Supp. XI:** 46, 53, 57
Talese, Gay, **Supp. XVI:** 273; **Supp. XVII: 199–211; Supp. XXIV:** 282
Tales of a Traveller (Irving), **II:** 309–310
Tales of a Wayside Inn (Longfellow), **II:** 489, 490, 501, 502, 504–505; **Retro. Supp. II:** 154, **162–165**
Tales of Glauber-Spa (Bryant, ed.), **Supp. I Part 1:** 157
Tales of Manhattan (Auchincloss), **Supp. IV Part 1:** 23
Tales of Men and Ghosts (Wharton), **IV:** 315; **Retro. Supp. I:** 372
Tales of My People (Asch), **Supp. XXIII:** 7
Tales of Rhoda, The (Rice), **Supp. VII:** 288
Tales of Soldiers and Civilians (Bierce), **I:** 200–203, 204, 206, 208, 212
Tales of the Argonauts (Harte), **Supp. II Part 1:** 337, 348, 351
Tales of the Fish Patrol (London), **II:** 465
Tales of the Grotesque and Arabesque (Poe), **II:** 273; **III:** 412, 415; **Retro. Supp. II:** 270
Tales of the Jazz Age (Fitzgerald), **II:** 88; **Retro. Supp. I:** 105; **Supp. IX:** 57
Tales You Won't Believe (Stratton-Porter), **Supp. XX: 217**
Taliaferro, Frances, **Supp. XXII:** 210
"Talisman, A" (Moore), **III:** 195–196
Talisman, The (King), **Supp. V:** 140, 144, 152
"Talkin Bout Sonny" (Bambara), **Supp. XI:** 6–7
"Talking" (Merwin), **Supp. III Part 1:** 354
Talking All Morning (R. Bly), **Supp. IV Part 1:** 59, 60, 61, 62, 64, 65
Talking Dirty to the Gods (Komunyakaa), **Supp. XIII: 130–131**
Talking History (television program), **Supp. XXI:** 172
"Talking Horse" (Malamud), **Supp. I Part 2:** 435
Talking Soft Dutch (McCarriston), **Supp. XIV: 260–263,** 266, 270, 271
"Talking to Barr Creek" (Wagoner), **Supp. IX:** 328
"Talking to Sheep" (Sexton), **Supp. II Part 2:** 695
Talking to the Sun: An Illustrated Anthology of Poems for Young People (Koch and Farrell, eds.), **Supp. XV:** 188

T

"Talking Water" (Taggard), **Supp. XXII:** 276

"Talk of Heroes" (C. Bly), **Supp. XVI:** 34

"Talk of the Town" (*The New Yorker* column), **IV:** 215; **Supp. IV Part 1:** 53, 54

"Talk on Guadalcanal" (Wolfert), **Supp. XXI:** 264

Talk Talk (Boyle), **Supp. XX: 24**

"Talk with the Yellow Kid, A" (Bellow), **I:** 151

Tallent, Elizabeth, **Supp. IV Part 2:** 570

Tallman, Warren, **Supp. IV Part 1:** 154

TallMountain, Mary, **Supp. IV Part 1:** 324–325

Talma, Louise, **IV:** 357

Talmadge, Constance, **Supp. XVI:** 186, 187, 196

Talmadge, Norma, **Supp. XVI:** 186, 187, 196

Talmadge Girls, The (Loos), **Supp. XVI:** 186, 196

Talmey, Allene, **Supp. IV Part 1:** 197; **Supp. XIII:** 172

Talmud, **IV:** 8, 17

Taltos: Lives of the Mayfair Witches (Rice), **Supp. VII:** 299–300

"Tamar" (Jeffers), **Supp. II Part 2:** 427–428, 436

Tamar and Other Poems (Jeffers), **Supp. II Part 2:** 416, 419

"Tambourine Life" (Berrigan), **Supp. XXIV:** 42

Tambourines to Glory (Hughes), **Supp. I Part 1:** 338–339

"Tame Indians" (Jewett), **Retro. Supp. II:** 141

"Tamerlane" (Poe), **III:** 426

Tamerlane and Other Poems (Poe), **III:** 410

"Tammany Man, The" (Hapgood), **Supp. XVII:** 103

"Tam O'Shanter" (Burns), **II:** 306

Tamsen Donner: A Woman's Journey (Whitman), **Supp. XXI:** 246

Tan, Amy, **Supp. X: 289–300**

Tangential Views (Bierce), **I:** 209

"Tangier 1975" (Bowles), **Supp. IV Part 1:** 94

Tanguay, Pablo, **Supp. XXIII:** 299

"Tankas" (McClatchy), **Supp. XII:** 266

Tanner, Laura E., **Supp. X:** 209; **Supp. XXI:** 217

Tanner, Obour, **Supp. XX: 281, 288**

Tanner, Tony, **I:** 260, 261; **Retro. Supp. II:** 205; **Supp. IV Part 1:** 285; **Supp. XVI:** 65, 69

Tannhäuser (Wagner), **I:** 315

"Tan Ta Ra, Cries Mars....," (Wagoner), **Supp. IX:** 325

Tao of Physics, The (Capra), **Supp. X:** 261

Tao Teh Ching (Bynner, trans.), **Supp. XV:** 46, 47

Tapahonso, Luci, **Supp. IV Part 1:** 404; **Supp. IV Part 2:** 499, 508

Tape for the Turn of the Year (Ammons), **Supp. VII:** 31–33, 35

"Tapestry" (Ashbery), **Supp. III Part 1:** 22–23

"Tapestry" (E. P. Jones), **Supp. XXII:** 152

"Tapiama" (Bowles), **Supp. IV Part 1:** 89–90

"Tapiola" (W. C. Williams), **Retro. Supp. I:** 429

Tappan, Arthur, **Supp. I Part 2:** 588

Tapping the White Cane of Solitude (F. Wright), **Supp. XVII:** 243

Taps at Reveille (Fitzgerald), **II:** 94, 96; **Retro. Supp. I:** 113

Tar: A Midwest Childhood (Anderson), **I:** 98, 115; **II:** 27

Tarantino, Quentin, **Supp. IV Part 1:** 356

Tarantula (Dylan), **Supp. XVIII:** 21, 29, **31–32**

Tar Baby (Morrison), **Supp. III Part 1:** 364, 369–372, 379; **Supp. IV Part 1:** 13

Tarbell, Ida, **III:** 322, 580; **Retro. Supp. II:** 101

"Target Practice" (Offutt), **Supp. XIX:** 171

"Target Study" (Baraka), **Supp. II Part 1:** 49–50, 54

Tarkington, Booth, **II:** 444; **III:** 70; **Retro. Supp. I:** 100; **Supp. XV:** 41

Tarnawsky, Yuriy (George) Orest, **Supp. XX: 259**

Tarpon (film), **Supp. VIII:** 42

Tarr, Rodger L., **Supp. X:** 222, 224, 226

Tárrega, Francisco, **Supp. XXI:** 100

Tartt, Donna, **Supp. XVIII:** 135

Tartuffe (Molière; Wilbur, trans.), **Supp. III Part 2:** 560

Tarumba, Selected Poems of Jaime Sabines (Levine and Trejo, trans.), **Supp. V:** 178

Tarzan Finds a Son (film, Weismuller), **Supp. XX: 18**

"Tarzan Is an Expatriate" (Theroux), **Supp. VIII:** 313

Tasis, Juan de, **Supp. XXI:** 104

Task, The (Cowper), **II:** 304

Tasker Street (Halliday), **Supp. XIX:** 82, **87–89**

Tasso, Torquato, **I:** 276

Taste of Palestine, A: Menus and Memories (Shihab), **Supp. XIII:** 273

Tate, Alan, **Supp. XV:** 141

Tate, Allen, **I:** 48, 49, 50, 67, 69, 381, 382, 386, 390, 396, 397, 399, 402, 441, 468; **II:** 197–198, 367, 536, 537, 542, 551, 554; **III:** 424, 428, 454, 482, 483, 485, 493, 495, 496, 497, 499, 500, 517; **IV: 120–143**, 236, 237, 433; **Retro. Supp. I:** 37, 41, 90; **Retro. Supp. II:** 77, 79, 82, 83, 89, 176, 178, 179; **Supp. I Part 1:** 364, 371; **Supp. I Part 2:** 423; **Supp. II Part 1:** 90–91, 96, 98, 103–104, 136, 139, 144, 150, 151, 318; **Supp. II Part 2:** 643; **Supp. III Part 2:** 542; **Supp. V:** 315, 331; **Supp. X:** 1, 52; **Supp. XIV:** 2; **Supp. XXI:** 256; **Supp. XXII:** 277

Tate, Mrs. Allen (Caroline Gordon). *See* Gordon, Caroline

Tate, Mrs. Allen (Helen Heinz), **IV:** 127

Tate, Mrs. Allen (Isabella Gardner), **IV:** 127

Tate, Benjamin Lewis Bogan, **IV:** 127

Tate, Greg, **Supp. XIII:** 233, 237

Tate, James, **Supp. V:** 92, 338; **Supp. VIII:** 39, 279; **Supp. XV:** 250; **Supp. XVII:** 242

Tate, John Allen, **IV:** 127

Tate, Michael Paul, **IV:** 127

Tate, Nancy, **II:** 197

Tatonetti, Lisa, **Supp. XXIII:** 149–150

Tattooed Countess, The (Van Vechten), **I:** 295; **Supp. II Part 2:** 726–728, 738, 742

Tattooed Feet (Nye), **Supp. XIII:** 274

"Tattoos" (McClatchy), **Supp. XII:** 266–267, 268

"Tattoos" (Wright), **Supp. V:** 335, 340

Tatum, Anna, **I:** 516

Tatum, James, **Supp. IV Part 2:** 684

Taupin, René, **II:** 528, 529; **Supp. III Part 2:** 614, 615, 617, 621

Tavano, John, **Supp. XXI:** 99

Tawney, Richard Henry, **Supp. I Part 2:** 481

Taylor, Ann, **Supp. XXIII:** 231

Taylor, Bayard, **II:** 275; **Supp. I Part 1:** 350, 361, 362, 365, 366, 372; **Supp. XV:** 269

Taylor, Chuck, **Supp. XXIII:** 57

Taylor, Cora. *See* Howarth, Cora

Taylor, Deems, **III:** 138

Taylor, Edward, **III:** 493; **IV: 144–166; Supp. I Part 1:** 98; **Supp. I Part 2:** 375, 386, 546

Taylor, Mrs. Edward (Elizabeth Fitch), **IV:** 147, 165

Taylor, Mrs. Edward (Ruth Wyllys), **IV:** 148

Taylor, Eleanor Ross, **Supp. V:** 317, 318

Taylor, Elizabeth, **II:** 588

Taylor, Frank, **III:** 81

Taylor, Frederick Winslow, **Supp. I Part 2:** 644

Taylor, Graham, **Supp. I Part 1:** 5

Taylor, Henry, **Retro. Supp. I:** 212; **Supp. XI:** 317; **Supp. XIII:** 333

Taylor, Henry W., **IV:** 144

Taylor, Jeremy, **II:** 11; **III:** 487; **Supp. I Part 1:** 349; **Supp. XII:** 45; **Supp. XIV:** 344, 345

Taylor, John, **IV:** 149

Taylor, Katherine, **Supp. VIII:** 251

Taylor, Kezia, **IV:** 148

Taylor, Nathaniel W., **Supp. I Part 2:** 580

Taylor, Paul, **I:** 293

Taylor, Peter, **Retro. Supp. II:** 179; **Supp. V: 313–329; Supp. XIV:** 3

Taylor, Raynor, **Supp. XV:** 238

Taylor, Richard, **IV:** 146

Taylor, Robert, **Supp. I Part 1:** 294; **Supp. XV:** 135, 138; **Supp. XVI:** 277

Taylor, Samuel A., **Supp. XX: 253**

Taylor, Stephan, **Supp. XVI:** 203

Taylor, Thomas, **II:** 10

Taylor, William, **IV:** 145–146

Taylor, Zachary, **I:** 3; **II:** 433–434

Tchelitchew, Peter, **II:** 586

Tea and Sympathy (Anderson), **Supp. I Part 1:** 277; **Supp. V:** 108

"Tea at the Palaz of Hoon" (Stevens), **Retro. Supp. I:** 300, 302, 306

"Teacher's Pet" (Thurber), **Supp. I Part 2:** 605–606

"Teaching and Story Telling" (Maclean), **Supp. XIV:** 234

Teaching a Stone to Talk: Expeditions and Encounters (Dillard), **Supp. VI:** 23, 26, 28, 32, 33, 34–35

"Teaching Emily Dickenson"(Hadas), **Supp. XXIII:** 115

"Teaching Hanh the Blues" (Weigl), **Supp. XIX:** 287

Teachings of Don B., The (Barthelme), **Supp. IV Part 1:** 53

Teachout, Terry, **Supp. XIX:** 137

Teale, Edwin Way, **Supp. XIII:** 7

Teall, Dorothy, **I:** 221

Team Team Team (film), **Supp. IX:** 251

"Tea on the Mountain" (Bowles), **Supp. IV Part 1:** 90

"Tea Party, The" (MacLeish), **III:** 11

Tear and a Smile, A (Dam'a wa Ibtisáma) (Gibran), **Supp. XX: 116, 118, 124**

Teare, Brian, **Supp. XXII:** 236

"Tears, Idle Tears" (Lord Tennyson), **Supp. XIV:** 8

"Tears of the Pilgrims, The" (McClatchy), **Supp. XII:** 256

Teasdale, Sara, **Retro. Supp. I:** 133; **Supp. I Part 2:** 393, 707; **Supp. XIV:** 127; **Supp. XV:** 295, 297, 301, 305, 307, 308; **Supp. XVII:** 69, 75

"Tease" (Swados), **Supp. XIX:** 267

Tebeaux, Elizabeth, **Supp. IX:** 109

"Technical Manifesto of Futurist Literature" (Marinetti), **Supp. XXII:** 161

Technics and Civilization (Mumford), **Supp. I Part 2:** 638; **Supp. II Part 2:** 479, 493, 497

Technics and Human Development (Mumford), **Supp. I Part 2:** 638; **Supp. II Part 2:** 497

"Technology, The" (Egan), **Supp. XIX:** 61

"Teddy" (Salinger), **III:** 561–563, 571

"Te Deum" (Reznikoff), **Supp. XIV:** 281

Tedlock, Dennis, **Supp. IV Part 2:** 509

"Teeth Mother Naked at Last, The" (R. Bly), **Supp. IV Part 1:** 63, 68, 73

Teggart, Richard, **Supp. I Part 2:** 650

Tegnér, Esaias, **Retro. Supp. II:** 155

Teilhard de Chardin, Pierre, **Supp. I Part 1:** 314

Tekonwatonti/Molly Brant (Kenny), **Supp. XXIII:** 143, 147, 151, **152–153,** 154

Telephone, The (film), **Supp. XI:** 309

"Telephone Call, A" (Parker), **Supp. IX: 202–203**

"Telephone Number of the Muse, The" (Justice), **Supp. VII:** 124–125

Telephone Poles and Other Poems (Updike), **IV:** 214, 215

"Television" (Beattie), **Supp. V:** 33

Teller, Edward, **I:** 137

"Telling" (Ortiz), **Supp. IV Part 2:** 509

"Telling It in Black and White: The Importance of the Africanist Presence in *To Kill a Mockingbird*" (Baecker), **Supp. VIII:** 128

Telling Secrets (Buechner), **Supp. XII:** 53–54

Telling Stories (Didion), **Supp. IV Part 1:** 197

"Telling Stories" (Didion), **Supp. IV Part 1:** 197

"Telling the Bees" (Whittier), **Supp. I Part 2:** 694–695

Telling the Little Secrets (J. Burstein), **Supp. XVII:** 44

Telling the Truth: The Gospel as Tragedy, Comedy, and Fairy Tale (Buechner), **Supp. XII:** 53

"Tell Me" (Hughes), **Supp. VIII:** 213

"Tell Me, Sir, ... What Is 'Black' Literature?" (H. L. Gates), **Supp. XX: 108**

Tell Me, Tell Me (Moore), **III:** 215

Tell Me Again (Notley), **Supp. XXII:** 224, 230–231

Tell Me Again How the White Heron Rises and Flies across the Nacreous River at Twilight toward the Distant Islands (Carruth), **Supp. XVI:**56

Tell Me a Riddle (film), **Supp. XIII:** 295

Tell Me a Riddle (Olsen), **Supp. XIII:** 294, 296, **298–302,** 303, 305

"Tell Me a Riddle" (Olsen), **Supp. XIII:** 294, 297, 298, **300–302,** 305

"Tell Me a Story" (McDermott), **Supp. XVIII:** 177

Tell Me How Long the Train's Been Gone (Baldwin), **Retro. Supp. II:** 9, **11–12,** 14; **Supp. I Part 1:** 48, 52, 63–65, 67

"Tell Me My Fortune" (Epstein), **Supp. XII:** 163

Tell Me True: Memoir, History, and Writing a Life (Hampl and May, eds.), **Supp. XXII:** 81–82, 84, **94–95**

Tell Me Your Answer True (Sexton), **Supp. II Part 2:** 683

Tell My Horse (Hurston), **Supp. VI:** 149, 156, 158

"Tell-Tale Heart, The" (Poe), **III:** 413, 414–415, 416; **Retro. Supp. II:** 267, 269, 270

"Tell the Women We're Going" (Carver), **Supp. III Part 1:** 138, 144

"Telluride Blues—A Hatchet Job" (Abbey), **Supp. XIII:** 10

Telushkin, Dvorah, **Retro. Supp. II:** 317

Temblor (Howe), **Supp. IV Part 2:** 431

Tempering of Eugene O'Neill, The (D. Alexander), **Supp. XVII:** 99

"Temper of Steel, The" (Jones), **Supp. XI:** 218

Tempers, The (W. C. Williams), **Retro. Supp. I: 413–414,** 415, 416, 424

Tempest, The (Shakespeare), **I:** 394; **II:** 12; **III:** 40, 61, 263; **Retro. Supp. I:** 61; **Supp. IV Part 2:** 463; **Supp. V:** 302–303; **Supp. XII:** 54–57; **Supp. XV:** 255, 256

Temple, Minnie, **II:** 323

Temple, The (Herbert), **IV:** 145, 153

Temple, William, **III:** 303

Temple House (E. Stoddard), **Supp. XV:** 273, **284–286**

Temple of My Familiar, The (Walker), **Supp. III Part 2:** 521, 527, 529, 535, 537; **Supp. IV Part 1:** 14

"Temple of the Holy Ghost, A" (O'Connor), **III:** 344, 352; **Retro. Supp. II:** 232

Templin, Charlotte, **Supp. V:** 116

Temporary Shelter (Gordon), **Supp. IV Part 1:** 299, 305–307

"Temporary Shelter" (Gordon), **Supp. IV Part 1:** 306

Temptation Game, The (Gardner), **Supp. VI:** 72

"Temptation of St. Anthony, The" (Barthelme), **Supp. IV Part 1:** 47

Temptations, The, **Supp. X:** 242

"10 Best Weathers of 1983, The" (Notley), **Supp. XXII:** 224

"10 Things I Do Every Day" (Berrigan), **Supp. XXII:** 224; **Supp. XXIV:** 41

"Tenancy, A" (Merrill), **Supp. III Part 1:** 322, 323

"Tenant" (Hoffman), **Supp. XVIII:** 86

Tenants, The (Malamud), **Supp. I Part 2:** 448–450

"Ten Best Issues of Comic Books, The" (Notley), **Supp. XXII:** 224

Ten Commandments (McClatchy), **Supp. XII: 262–265**

Ten Days That Shook the World (Reed), **II:** 577; **Supp. X:** 136; **Supp. XVIII:** 225

Tendencies in Modern American Poetry (Lowell), **II:** 529

"Tender, Hilarious Reminiscences of Life in Mythical Lake Wobegon" (MacDougall), **Supp. XVI:** 174

Tender Buttons (G. Stein), **I:** 103, 105; **IV:** 27, 42–43; **Retro. Supp. II:** 331; **Supp. XV:** 347

"Tenderfoot" (Haines), **Supp. XII:** 209

Tender Is the Night (Fitzgerald), **I:** 375; **II:** 79, 84, 91, 95–96, 97, 98, 420; **Retro. Supp. I:** 105, 108, 109, **110–112,** 114; **Supp. IX:** 59, 60, 61; **Supp. XV:** 197; **Supp. XXI:** 11

"Tenderloin" (Crane), **I:** 408

"Tenderly" (Dobyns), **Supp. XIII:** 86–87

"Tender Man, A" (Bambara), **Supp. XI:** 9–10

"Tenderness" (Dunn), **Supp. XI:** 149, 150

"Tender Offer, The" (Auchincloss), **Supp. IV Part 1:** 34

"Tender Organizations, The" (C. Bly), **Supp. XVI:** 40, 42

"Tenebrae" (Komunyakaa), **Supp. XIII:** 132

Tenenbaum, Joseph, **Supp. XX: 253**

"Ten Forty-Four" (Kingsolver), **Supp. VII:** 208

Ten Indians (Bell), **Supp. X:** 7, **12**

Ten Introductions: A Collection of Modern Verse (Taggard and Fitts, ed.), **Supp. XXII:** 281

Tennant, Agnieszka, **Supp. XX: 140**

"Ten Neglected American Writers Who Deserve to Be Better Known" (Cantor), **Supp. IV Part 1:** 285

Tennent, Gilbert, **I:** 546

Tennessee Day in St. Louis (Taylor), **Supp. V:** 324

"Tennessee's Partner" (Harte), **Supp. II Part 1:** 345, 348–350

"Tennis" (Pinsky), **Supp. VI:** 241, 242

Tennis Court Oath, The (Ashbery), **Supp. III Part 1:** 7, 9, 12, 14, 26

Ten North Frederick (O'Hara), **III:** 361

Tennyson, Alfred, Lord, **I:** 587–588; **II:** 18, 82, 273, 338, 404, 439, 604; **III:** 5, 409, 469, 485, 511, 521, 523; **Retro. Supp. I:** 100, 325; **Retro. Supp. II:** 135; **Supp. I Part 1:** 349, 356; **Supp. I Part 2:** 410, 416, 552; **Supp. IX:** 19; **Supp. X:** 157; **Supp. XIII:** 111; **Supp. XIV:** 40, 120; **Supp. XV:** 275; **Supp. XVIII:** 78

"Tenochtitlan" (Bronk), **Supp. XXI:** 31

"Ten O'Clock News" (Ortiz), **Supp. IV Part 2:** 503–504

"Te-Non-An-At-Che"(Kenny), **Supp. XXIII:** 151

Ten Poems (Dove), **Supp. IV Part 1:** 244

Ten Poems of Francis Ponge Translated by Robert Bly and Ten Poems of Robert Bly Inspired by the Poems by Francis Ponge (R. Bly), **Supp. IV Part 1:** 71

"Tension in Poetry" (Tate), **IV:** 128, 129, 135

Tenth Muse, The (Bradstreet), **Supp. I Part 1:** 102, 103, 114

10,000 Days of Thunder: A History of the Vietnam War (Caputo), **Supp. XIX:** 29

"Tent on the Beach, The" (Whittier), **Supp. I Part 2:** 703

"Ten True Things" (July), **Supp. XXIV:** 205

"Teodoro Luna Confesses after Years to His Brother, Anselmo the Priest, Who Is Required to Understand, But Who Understands Anyway, More Than People Think" (Ríos), **Supp. IV Part 2:** 552

Teodoro Luna's Two Kisses (Ríos), **Supp. IV Part 2:** 550–552, 553

"Tepeyac" (Cisneros), **Supp. VII:** 69

"Terce" (Auden), **Supp. II Part 1:** 22

Terence, **IV:** 155, 363; **Supp. I Part 2:** 405

Terkel, Studs, **Supp. IV Part 1:** 364

"Term" (Merwin), **Supp. III Part 1:** 356–357

"Terminal Days at Beverly Farms" (Lowell), **Retro. Supp. II:** 189

Terminating, or Sonnet LXXV, or "Lass Meine Schmerzen nicht verloren sein, or Ambivalence" (Kushner), Supp. IX: 132

Terminations (James), **Retro. Supp. I:** 229

"Terminus" (Emerson), **II:** 13, 19

"Terminus" (Wharton), **Retro. Supp. I:** 371

"Terms in Which I Think of Reality, The" (Ginsberg), **Supp. II Part 1:** 311

Terms of Endearment (film), **Supp. V:** 226

Terms of Endearment (McMurtry), **Supp. V:** 224–225

"Terrace, The" (Wilbur), **Supp. III Part 2:** 550

Terrarium (Sanders), **Supp. XVI:** 270

"Terrence McNally" (Bryer), **Supp. XIII:** 200

"Terrence McNally" (Di Gaetani), **Supp. XIII:** 200

Terrence McNally: A Casebook (Zinman), **Supp. XIII:** 209

"Terrestrial Cuckoo"(O'Hara), **Supp. XXIII:** 210

"Terrible Peacock, The" (Barnes), **Supp. III Part 1:** 33

Terrible Threes, The (Reed), **Supp. X:** 241, 253

Terrible Twos, The (Reed), **Supp. X:** 241, **252–253**

"Terrific Mother" (Moore), **Supp. X:** 178

Territory Ahead, The (Morris), **III:** 228–229, 236

Terrorism (Wright), **Supp. XV:** 341, 342

"Terrorism" (Wright), **Supp. XV:** 341

Terry, Edward A., **II:** 128, 129

Terry, Rose, **Supp. I Part 2:** 420

Tertium Organum (Ouspensky), **I:** 383; **Supp. XX:** 116

Tess of the d'Urbervilles (Hardy), **II:** 181; **Retro. Supp. II:** 100

"Testament" (Berry), **Supp. X:** 36

"Testament" (Carruth), **Supp. XVI:** 59

"Testament (Or, Homage to Walt Whitman)" (Jong), **Supp. V:** 130

"Testament of Flood" (Warren), **IV:** 253

Testament of François Villon, The (Pound, opera), **Retro. Supp. I:** 287

"Testament: Vermeer in December" (Bierds), **Supp. XVII:** 33

"Testimonia on the Question of Stesichoros' Blinding by Helen" (Carson), **Supp. XII:** 107

"Testimonies of a Roasted Chicken" (Jarman), **Supp. XVII:** 120

"Testimony" (Komunyakaa), **Supp. XIII:** 129

"Testimony of James Apthorp, The" (Kees), **Supp. XV:** 146

Testimony: The United States (1885–1890): Recitative (Reznikoff), **Supp. XIV:** 279, 280, 281, 285, **289–291**

Testimony: The United States (1891–1900): Recitative (Reznikoff), **Supp. XIV:** 291

Testing-Tree, The (Kunitz), **Supp. III Part 1:** 260, 263, 264, 267, 268

"Testing-Tree, The" (Kunitz), **Supp. III Part 1:** 269

Test of Poetry, A (Zukofsky), **Supp. III Part 2:** 618, 622

"Teutonic Scholar" (X. J. Kennedy), **Supp. XV:** 161

"Texas Moon, and Elsewhere, The" (McMurtry), **Supp. V:** 225

Texas Poets in Concert: A Quartet (Gwynn, ed.), **Supp. XIII:** 277

Texas Summer (Southern), **Supp. XI:** 309

Texasville (McMurtry), **Supp. V:** 228, 233

Thacher, Molly Day, **IV:** 381

Thackeray, William Makepeace, **I:** 194, 354; **II:** 182, 271, 282, 288, 316, 321, 322; **III:** 64, 70; **IV:** 326; **Retro. Supp. I:** 218; **Supp. I Part 1:** 307; **Supp. I Part 2:** 421, 495, 579; **Supp. IV Part 1:** 297; **Supp. IX:** 200; **Supp. XI:** 277; **Supp. XIV:** 306; **Supp. XX:** **228**

Thaddeus, Janice Farrar, **Supp. IV Part 1:** 299

"Thailand" (Barthelme), **Supp. IV Part 1:** 41

Thalberg, Irving, **Retro. Supp. I:** 109, 110, 114; **Supp. XVI:** 191, 192

Thales, **I:** 480–481

Thalia Trilogy (McMurtry), **Supp. V:** 220–223, 234

Tham, Claire, **Supp. VIII:** 79

"Thanatopsis" (Bryant), **Supp. I Part 1:** 150, 154, 155, 170

Thanatos Syndrome, The (Percy), **Supp. III Part 1:** 385, 397–399

"Thanks Can Be Named to Death" (Peacock), **Supp. XIX:** 199

"Thanksgiving" (Glück), **Supp. V:** 83

"Thanksgiving, A" (Auden), **Supp. II Part 1:** 26

"Thanksgiving for a Habitat" (Auden), **Supp. II Part 1:** 24

Thanksgivings (Traherne), **Supp. XVI:** 288

"Thanksgiving Spirit" (Farrell), **II:** 45

Thanksgiving Visitor, The (Capote), **Supp. III Part 1:** 116, 118, 119

"Thank You, Esther Forbes" (Saunders), **Supp. XIX:** 235

Thank You, Fog (Auden), **Supp. II Part 1:** 24

"Thank You, Lord" (Angelou), **Supp. IV Part 1:** 15

Thank You, Mr. Moto (Marquand), **III:** 57, 58

Thank You and Other Poems (Koch), **Supp. XV:** 180–181

"Thank You in Arabic" (Nye), **Supp. XIII:** 273, 281

"Thar's More in the Man Than Thar Is in the Land" (Lanier), **Supp. I Part 1:** 352–353, 359–360

"That Evening Sun" (Faulkner), **II:** 72; **Retro. Supp. I:** 75, 83

That Horse (Hogan), **Supp. IV Part 1:** 397, 404, 405

"That House, This Room" (W. V. Davis), **Supp. XXI:** 90

"That I Had the Wings" (Ellison), **Supp. II Part 1:** 238

That Night (McDermott), **Supp. XVIII:** 155, **158–160,** 162, 163, 166

"That's the Place Indians Talk About" (Ortiz), **Supp. IV Part 2:** 511

That Tantalus (Bronk), **Supp. XXI:** 31

"That the Soul May Wax Plump" (Swenson), **Supp. IV Part 2:** 650

"That the Universe Is Chrysalid" (Sobin), **Supp. XVI:** 284

"That Tree" (Porter), **III:** 434–435, 446, 451

That Was the Week That Was (television program), **Supp. XIV:** 125

"That Year" (Olds), **Supp. X:** 203

"Thaw" (C. Frost), **Supp. XV:** 93, 104, 105

Thaxter, Celia, **Retro. Supp. II:** 136, 147; **Supp. XIII:** 143, 153

Thayer, Abbott, **I:** 231

Thayer, Scofield, **I:** 231; **Retro. Supp. I:** 58

Thayer and Eldridge, **Retro. Supp. I:** 403

"Theater" (Toomer), **Supp. IX:** 309, 317–318

"Theater Chronicle" (McCarthy), **II:** 562

"Theater Problems? Call Dr. Chekhov" (Wasserstein), **Supp. XV:** 320

Theatricals (James), **Retro. Supp. I:** 228

The Blacker the Berry: A Novel of Negro Life (Thurman), **Supp. XVIII:** 281; **Supp. XIX:** 73

"Theft" (Porter), **III:** 434, 435

Theft, A (Bellow), **Retro. Supp. II:** 31–32, 34

The Harder They Fall (Schulberg), **Supp. XVIII:** 247, 253

The Harder They Fall: Celebrities Tell Their Real-Life Stories of Addiction and Recovery (F. Wright), **Supp. XVII:** 240

Their Eyes Were Watching God (Hurston), **Supp. VI:** 149, 152, 156–157; **Supp. XX: 107**

Their Heads Are Green and Their Hands Are Blue: Scenes from the Non-Christian World (Bowles), **Supp. IV Part 1:** 89

"Their Losses" (Taylor), **Supp. V:** 320

"Their Name is Macaroni" (Boyle), **Supp. XXIV:** 61

"Their Sleep" (W. V. Davis), **Supp. XXI:** 93

Their Wedding Journey (Howells), **II:** 277–278; **Retro. Supp. I:** 334

them (Oates), **Supp. II Part 2:** 503, 511–514

Theme Is Freedom, The (Dos Passos), **I:** 488–489, 492, 494

Theme Time Radio Hour (radio show, Dylan), **Supp. XVIII:** 28

"Theme with Variations" (Agee), **I:** 27

"Then" (Barthelme), **Supp. IV Part 1:** 48

"Then as Now" (Cliff), **Supp. XXII:** 76

"The Night Rhonda Ferguson Was Killed" (E. P. Jones), **Supp. XXII:** 144

"Then It All Came Down" (Capote), **Supp. III Part 1:** 125, 131

Theocritus, **II:** 169; **Retro. Supp. I:** 286; **Supp. XXIV:** 156

Theodore Roethke's Far Fields: The Evolution of His Poetry (Balakian), **Supp. XXIII:** 19

"Theodore the Poet" (Masters), **Supp. I Part 2:** 461

Theological Position, A (Coover), **Supp. V:** 44

Theophrastus, **I:** 58

"Theoretical and Scientific Conceptions of Race, The" (Locke), **Supp. XIV:** 209

"Theoretical Subject(s) of *This Bridge Called My Back,* The"(Alarcón), **Supp. XXIII:** 204–205

"Theories of Time and Space" (Trethewey), **Supp. XXI:** 255

Theory and Practice of Rivers and Other Poems, The (Harrison), **Supp. VIII:** 47, 49

Theory of Business Enterprise, The (Veblen), **Supp. I Part 2:** 638, 641, 644

Theory of Flight (Rukeyser), **Supp. VI:** 272, 275, **277–278,** 284

"Theory of Flight" (Rukeyser), **Supp. VI:** 277–278

Theory of Moral Sentiments, The (A. Smith), **Supp. I Part 2:** 634

Theory of the Leisure Class, The (Veblen), **I:** 475–476; **Supp. I Part 2:** 629, 633, 641, 645; **Supp. IV Part 1:** 22

"There" (Taylor), **Supp. V:** 323

"There Are No Such Trees in Alpine California" (Haines), **Supp. XII:** 207

"There Goes (Varoom! Varoom!) That Kandy-Kolored Tangerine-Flake Streamline Baby" (Wolfe), **Supp. III Part 2:** 569–571

"There Have Been Changes" (Pickering), **Supp. XXI:** 202–203

"There Is a Lesson" (Olsen), **Supp. XIII:** 292, 297

"There is a Man" (Espaillat), **Supp. XXI:** 108–109

"There Is Only One of Everything" (Atwood), **Supp. XIII:** 34

There Is Something Out There (McNally). *See And Things That Go Bump in the Night* (McNally)

"There Must Be" (Peacock), **Supp. XIX:** 199

"There's a certain Slant of light" (Dickinson), **Retro. Supp. I:** 38

There's a Wocket in My Pocket! (Geisel), **Supp. XVI:** 111

Thérèse de Lisieux, Saint, **Supp. VIII:** 195

"There She Is She Is Taking Her Bath" (Anderson), **I:** 113, 114

"There Was a Child Went Forth" (Whitman), **IV:** 348

"There Was a Man, There Was a Woman" (Cisneros), **Supp. VII:** 70

"There Was an Old Woman She Had So Many Children She Didn't Know What to Do" (Cisneros), **Supp. VII:** 60

"There Was a Youth Whose Name Was Thomas Granger" (Olson), **Supp. II Part 2:** 558, 560, 563

There Were Giants in the Land (Benét), **Supp. XI:** 50

There You Are (Simpson), **Supp. IX:** 279–280

"There You Are" (Simpson), **Supp. IX:** 279

"Thermopylae" (Clampitt), **Supp. IX:** 43

Theroux, Alexander, **Supp. VIII:** 312

Theroux, Marcel, **Supp. VIII:** 325

Theroux, Paul, **Supp. V:** 122; **Supp. VIII: 309–327**

"These Are My People" (Hayden), **Supp. II Part 1:** 365

These Are My Same Hands (Schott), **Supp. XXIII:** 241, 242

"These are the days when Birds come back" (Dickinson), **Retro. Supp. I:** 30

"These Days" (Olds), **Supp. X:** 215

"These Flames and Generosities of the Heart: Emily Dickinson and the Illogic of Sumptuary Values" (Howe), **Supp. IV Part 2:** 431

"These Hands" (Brockmeier), **Supp. XXII:** 51, 52, 53

These Happy Golden Years (L. I. Wilder), **Supp. XXII:** 294, 297, 299

These Low Grounds (Turpin), **Supp. XVIII:** 283

"These saw Visions" (Dickinson), **Retro. Supp. I:** 46

These Thirteen (Faulkner), **II:** 72

These Three (film), **Supp. I Part 1:** 281

These Times (Untermeyer), **Supp. XV: 299–300,** 303

"These Times" (Untermeyer), **Supp. XV:** 300

"Thessalonica: A Roman Story" (Brown), **Supp. I Part 1:** 133

Thévenaz, Paul, **Supp. XV:** 42

Thew, Harvey, **Supp. XIII:** 166

"They Ain't the Men They Used To Be" (Farrell), **II:** 45

"They Burned the Books" (Benét), **Supp. XI:** 46

They Came Like Swallows (Maxwell), **Supp. VIII: 155–159,** 168, 169

"They Can't Turn Back" (Baldwin), **Supp. I Part 1:** 52

They Do Not: The Letters of a Non-Professional Lady Arranged for Public Consumption (Clements), **Supp. XVI:** 190

They Feed They Lion (Levine), **Supp. V:** 178, 179, 181, 184–185, 186

"They Feed They Lion" (Levine), **Supp. V:** 188

"They Lion Grow" (Levine), **Supp. V:** 184–185

"They're Not Your Husband" (Carver), **Supp. III Part 1:** 141, 143

They're Playing Our Song (musical), **Supp. IV Part 2:** 589

They Seek a City (Bontemps and Conroy), **Supp. XXII:** 5, 11

They Shall Inherit the Laughter (Jones), **Supp. XI:** 217, 218, 232

"They Shall Not Die" (Ryan as Quin), **Supp. XVIII:** 228–229

They Shoot Horses (film), **Supp. XIII:** 159

They Shoot Horses, Don't They? (McCoy), **Supp. XIII:** 159, **164–166,** 168, 171, 172, 174

"They Sing, They Sing" (Roethke), **III:** 544

They Stooped to Folly (Glasgow), **II:** 175, 186–187

They Were Expendable (film), **Supp. XVIII:** 247

"They Weren't Going to Die" (Boyle), **Supp. XXIV:** 61

They Whisper (R. O. Butler), **Supp. XII: 72–73**

They Who Knock at Our Gates: A Complete Gospel of Immigration (Antin), **Supp. XX: 2–3, 10–11, 12**

"Thick and Thin"(Hadas), **Supp. XXIII:** 119

Thidwick the Big-Hearted Moose (Geisel), **Supp. XVI:** 104

Thief's Journal, The (Genet), **Supp. XXIV:** 210

"Thief's Philosophy of Life, The" (Hapgood), **Supp. XVII:** 103

"Thief's Wife, The" (B. Kelly), **Supp. XVII:** 125–126

"Thieves" (Yates), **Supp. XI:** 349

Thieves of Paradise (Komunyakaa), **Supp. XIII:** 113, **128–130,** 132

"Thimble, The" (Kenyon), **Supp. VII:** 164

"Thing and Its Relations, The" (James), **II:** 357

"Things" (Haines), **Supp. XII:** 207

"Things" (Kenyon), **Supp. VII:** 169

"Things, The" (Kinnell), **Supp. III Part 1:** 246

Things As They Are (Stein), **IV:** 34, 37, 40

"Things Can Be Named to Death" (Peacock), **Supp. XIX:** 199

"Things Don't Stop" (Nye), **Supp. XIII:** 287

Things Gone and Things Still Here (Bowles), **Supp. IV Part 1:** 91

"Things of August" (Stevens), **Retro. Supp. I:** 309

Things of This World (Wilbur), **Supp. III Part 2:** 552–555

Things That Fall from the Sky (Brockmeier), **Supp. XXII: 50–53**

"Things That Fall from the Sky" (Brockmeier), **Supp. XXII:** 51, 53

Things Themselves: Essays and Scenes (Price), **Supp. VI:** 261

Things They Carried, The (T. O'Brien), **Supp. V:** 238, 239, 240, 243, 248–250; **Supp. XVII:** 14; **Supp. XXI:** 122

"Things to Do in New York City" (Berrigan), **Supp. XXII:** 224

Things We Don't Understand and Definitely Are Not Going to Talk About (performance piece, July), **Supp. XXIV:** 200

"Thing That Killed My Father Off, The" (Carver), **Supp. III Part 1:** 143

Thingy World!: or, How We Got to Where We Are: A Satire in One Act (Budbill), **Supp. XIX: 13–14**

"Think about It" (Conroy), **Supp. XVI:** 75

Think Back on Us . . . (Cowley), **Supp. II Part 1:** 139, 140, 142

Think Fast, Mr. Moto (Marquand), **III:** 57, 58

"Thinking about Barbara Deming" (Paley), **Supp. VI:** 227

"Thinking about Being Called Simple by a Critic" (Stafford), **Supp. XI:** 328

Thinking about the Longstanding Problems of Virtue and Happiness: Essays, a Play, Two Poems, and a Prayer (Kushner), **Supp. IX:** 131, 134, 135

"Thinking about the Past" (Justice), **Supp. VII:** 123–124

"Thinking about Western Thinking" (Didion), **Supp. IV Part 1:** 204, 206

"'Thinking against Oneself': Reflections on Cioran" (Sontag), **Supp. III Part 2:** 459–460

"Thinking Back Through Our Mothers: Traditions in Canadian Women's Writing" (Shields), **Supp. VII:** 307–308

"Thinking for Berky" (Stafford), **Supp. XI:** 320

"Thinking like a Mountain" (Leopold), **Supp. XIV:** 188, 189

"Thinking of the Lost World" (Jarrell), **II:** 338–389

Thinking Out Loud (Quindlen), **Supp. XVII: 167, 169–170**

Thin Man, The (film), **Supp. IV Part 1:** 342, 355

Thin Man, The (Hammett), **Supp. IV Part 1:** 354–355

"Thinnest Shadow, The" (Ashbery), **Supp. III Part 1:** 5

"Thin People, The" (Plath), **Supp. I Part 2:** 538, 547

Thin Red Line, The (film; Malick), **Supp. V:** 249; **Supp. XV:** 351

Thin Red Line, The (Jones), **Supp. XI:** 219, **224–225,** 229, 231, 232, 233, 234

"Thin Strips" (Sandburg), **III:** 587

"Third and Final Continent, The" (Lahiri), **Supp. XXI: 178–180**

"Third Avenue in Sunlight" (Hecht), **Supp. X:** 61

"Third Body, A" (R. Bly), **Supp. IV Part 1:** 71

Third Circle, The (Norris), **III:** 327

"Third Expedition, The" (Bradbury), **Supp. IV Part 1:** 103, 106

Third Generation, The (C. Himes), **Supp. XVI:** 135, **140–141**

Third Life of Grange Copeland, The (Walker), **Supp. III Part 2:** 520, 527–536

Third Mind, The (Burroughs), **Supp. XII:** 3

Third Rose, The (Brinnin), **IV:** 26

"Third Sermon on the Warpland, The" (Brooks), **Supp. III Part 1:** 85

"Third Thing That Killed My Father Off, The" (Carver), **Supp. III Part 1:** 144

Third Violet, The (Crane), **I:** 408, 417–418

Thirlwall, John C., **Retro. Supp. I:** 430

"Thirst: Introduction to Kinds of Water" (Carson), **Supp. XII:** 103

"13, 1977, 21" (Lethem), **Supp. XVIII:** 148

13 by Shanley (Shanley), **Supp. XIV:** 316

13 Seconds: A Look Back at the Kent State Shootings (Caputo), **Supp. XIX:** 29

Thirteen Hands: A Play in Two Acts (Shields), **Supp. VII:** 322–323

Thirteen O'Clock (Benét), **Supp. XI:** 46

Thirteen Other Stories (Purdy), **Supp. VII:** 278

Thirteen Stories and Thirteen Epitaphs (Vollmann), **Supp. XVII:** 226

"Thirteenth and Pennsylvania" (Stafford), **Supp. XI:** 324

Thirteenth Month, The (Pedersen; Nelson, trans.), **Supp. XVIII:** 179–180

"Thirteen Ways of Looking at a Blackbird" (Stevens), **IV:** 94; **Supp. IX:** 47; **Supp. XVII:** 130; **Supp. XXIII:** 253

"Thirteen Ways of Looking at a Blackbird" (W. Stevens), **Supp. XX:** 110

Thirteen Ways of Looking at a Black Man (H. L. Gates), **Supp. XX: 102, 110**

30/6 (poetry chapbook), **Supp. V:** 5, 6

"30. Meditation. 2. Cor. 5.17. He Is a New Creature" (Taylor), **IV:** 144

30: Pieces of a Novel (Dixon), **Supp. XII: 152, 153–154**

"Thirty Bob a Week" (Davidson), **Retro. Supp. I:** 55

"Thirty Delft Tiles" (Doty), **Supp. XI:** 131

"35/10" (Olds), **Supp. X:** 206

"35,000 Feet—The Lanterns" (Goldbarth), **Supp. XII:** 182

31 Letters and 13 Dreams (Hugo), **Supp. VI:** 141–144

Thirty Poems (Bryant), **Supp. I Part 1:** 157, 158

Thirty-Six Poems (Warren), **IV:** 236, 239, 240

"33" (Alvarez), **Supp. VII:** 4

"3275" (Monette), **Supp. X:** 148, 159

Thirty Years (Marquand), **III:** 56, 60–61

Thirty Years of Treason (Bentley), **Supp. I Part 2:** 297

This, My Letter (Hay), **Supp. XIV:** 121, 122, 129, 131

"This, That & the Other" (Nemerov), **III:** 269

This Body Is Made of Camphor and Gopherwood (R. Bly), **Supp. IV Part 1:** 63–65, 66, 71; **Supp. XXI:** 85

This Boy's Life: A Memoir (T. Wolff), **Supp. VII:** 334–339, 340, 343; **Supp. XI:** 246, 247

This Bridge Called My Back: Writings by Radical Women of Color (Moraga and Anzaldúa, eds.), **Supp. XXIII:** 193, 194, 196, **204–205**

"This Bright Dream" (Benét), **Supp. XI:** 55

This Coffin Has No Handles (McGrath), **Supp. X:** 117

"This Configuration" (Ashbery), **Supp. III Part 1:** 22

"This Corruptible" (Wylie), **Supp. I Part 2:** 727, 729

"This Crazy Wickedness, Little Nests of Light" (Notley), **Supp. XXII:** 228

"This Crutch That I Love" (Nye), **Supp. XIII:** 288

"This Gentile World" (H. Miller), **III:** 177

"This Hand" (Wylie), **Supp. I Part 2:** 713

"This Hour" (Olds), **Supp. X:** 212

"This House I Cannot Leave" (Kingsolver), **Supp. VII:** 208

This Hunger (Nin), **Supp. X:** 185

"This Is a Photograph of Me" (Atwood), **Supp. XIII:** 33

"This Is a Poem, Good Afternoon" (Keillor), **Supp. XVI:** 167

This Is How You Lose Her (Díaz), **Supp. XXIV:** 83, 84, 86, 88, **92–93**

"This Is It" (Stern), **Supp. IX:** 290

"This Is Just to Say" (W. C. Williams), **Supp. XI:** 328

"This Is My Heart" (Harjo), **Supp. XII:** 230

This Is Not a Novel (Markson), **Supp. XVII:** 145–146

"This Is Not Who We Are" (Nye), **Supp. XIII:** 285, 286

This Is Our Time: Secular Cantata No. 1, Mixed Voice Chorus and Orchestra (Taggard, Schuman and Weissleder), **Supp. XXII:** 283

"This Is Us, Excellent" (Richard), **Supp. XIX:** 212

"This Is What I Said" (Salinas), **Supp. XIII:** 322

This Journey (Wright), **Supp. III Part 2:** 605–606

"This Lime-Tree Bower My Prison" (Coleridge), **Supp. XXI:** 52, 55

This Man and This Woman (Farrell), **II:** 42

"This Monkey, My Back" (Boyle), **Supp. XX:** 17

"This Morning" (Kenyon), **Supp. VII:** 164

"This Morning, This Evening, So Soon" (Baldwin), **Supp. I Part 1:** 63

"This Morning Again It Was in the Dusty Pines" (Oliver), **Supp. VII:** 240

This Music Crept by Me upon the Waters (MacLeish), **III:** 21

"This New England: Newport, Vermont" (Mosher), **Supp. XXII:** 209

This People Israel: The Meaning of Jewish Existence (Baeck), **Supp. V:** 260

"This Person" (July), **Supp. XXIV:** 202

"This Personal Maze Is Not the Prize" (Selinger), **Supp. XI:** 248

"This Place in the Ways" (Rukeyser), **Supp. VI:** 273–274

This Property Is Condemned (T. Williams), **IV:** 378

This Proud Heart (Buck), **Supp. II Part 1:** 119–120

This Same Sky: A Collection of Poems from around the World (Nye, ed.), **Supp. XIII:** 280

"This Sandwich Has No Mayonnaise" (Salinger), **III:** 552–553

This Shape We're In (Lethem), **Supp. XVIII:** 145

"This Shape We're In" (Lethem), **Supp. XVIII:** 148

This Side of Paradise (Fitzgerald), **I:** 358; **II:** 77, 80, 81, 82–83, 84, 85–87, 88; **Retro. Supp. I:** 99–100, **101–102,** 103, 105, 106, 110, 111; **Supp. XVIII:** 248

This Singing World: An Anthology of Modern Poetry for Young People (Untermeyer, ed.), **Supp. XV:** 306

This Strange Joy: Selected Poems of San-dro Penna (Di Perio, trans.), **Supp. XIX:** 34

This Stubborn Self: Texas Autobiographies (Almon), **Supp. XIII:** 288

"This They Took with Them" (Boyle), **Supp. XXIV:** 61

This Thing Don't Lead to Heaven (Crews), **Supp. XI:** 112

This Time: New and Selected Poems (Stern), **Supp. IX:** 290–291, **299**

"Thistle Seed in the Wind" (Francis), **Supp. IX:** 81

"Thistles in Sweden, The" (Maxwell), **Supp. VIII:** 169

"This Tokyo" (Snyder), **Supp. VIII:** 298

This Tree Will Be Here for a Thousand Years (revised edition) (R. Bly), **Supp. IV Part 1:** 66

This Tree Will Be Here for a Thousand Years (R. Bly), **Supp. IV Part 1:** 65–66, 71, 72

This Very Earth (Caldwell), **I:** 297, 302

This Wheel's on Fire: Levon Helm and the Story of the Band (Helm), **Supp. XVIII:** 26

This Woman (di Donato), **Supp. XX:** 33, **41–42, 46**

Thoens, Karen, **Supp. V:** 147

Thomas, Brandon, **II:** 138

Thomas, Debra, **Supp. XIII:** 114

Thomas, D. M., **Supp. VIII:** 5

Thomas, Dylan, **I:** 49, 64, 382, 432, 526, 533; **III:** 21, 521, 528, 532, 534; **IV:** 89, 93, 136; **Supp. I Part 1:** 263; **Supp. III Part 1:** 42, 47; **Supp. V:** 344; **Supp. VIII:** 21; **Supp. IX:** 114; **Supp. X:** 115; **Supp. XV:** 74; **Supp. XVII:** 135; **Supp. XX:** 199, 204; **Supp. XXIV:** 54

Thomas, Edna Lewis, **Supp. XVIII:** 281

Thomas, Edward, **II:** 154; **Retro. Supp. I:** 127, 131, 132; **Supp. I Part 1:** 263; **Supp. II Part 1:** 4

Thomas, James, **Supp. XVI:** 268

Thomas, Joseph, **Supp. XVIII:** 183

Thomas, J. Parnell, **Supp. I Part 1:** 286; **Supp. XV:** 198

Thomas, Lewis, **Retro. Supp. I:** 323

Thomas, Lorenzo, **Supp. XXIV:** 37

Thomas, Louisa, **Supp. XXIII:** 280, 283

Thomas, Rob, **Supp. XVIII:** 100, 101

Thomas, R. S., **Supp. XXI:** 83, 86–87, 93, 95, 96

Thomas, William I., **Supp. I Part 2:** 641

Thomas-a-Kempis, **Retro. Supp. I:** 247

Thomas and Beulah (Dove), **Supp. IV Part 1:** 242, 247–248, 249; **Supp. XVIII:** 174; **Supp. XXI:** 249

Thomas Aquinas (Saint), **I:** 13, 14, 265, 267; **III:** 270; **Retro. Supp. II:** 222; **Supp. IV Part 2:** 526

"Thomas at the Wheel" (Dove), **Supp. IV Part 1:** 248

"Thomas Eakins and the Photograph of a Man in Motion" (Major), **Supp. XXII:** 183

"Thomas Eakins' Delaware River Paintings" (Major), **Supp. XXII:** 183

"Thomas McGrath: Words for a Vanished Age" (Vinz), **Supp. X:** 117

Thomas Merton on Peace, **Supp. VIII:** 208

Thomas Merton Studies Center, The, **Supp. VIII:** 208

Thompson, Barbara, **Supp. V:** 322

Thompson, Caroline, **Supp. XXIII:** 291

Thompson, Cy, **I:** 538

Thompson, Daniel, **Supp. XXIII:** 174

Thompson, Dorothy, **II:** 449–450, 451, 453; **Supp. XV:** 307

Thompson, Edward, **Supp. XXI:** 172

Thompson, E. P., **Supp. X:** 112, 117

Thompson, Francis, **Retro. Supp. I:** 55

Thompson, Frank, **II:** 20

Thompson, George, **Supp. I Part 2:** 686; **Supp. XXIII:** 182

Thompson, Hunter S., **Supp. VIII:** 42; **Supp. XI:** 105; **Supp. XIII:** 1, 17; **Supp. XVII:** 95, 102, 228; **Supp. XXIV:** 279–294

Thompson, James R., **Supp. IV Part 1:** 217

Thompson, Jean, **Supp. XXIII:** 289–305

Thompson, John, **Supp. V:** 323; **Supp. XXI:** 151

Thompson, Juliet, **Supp. XX:** 117

Thompson, Lawrance, **II:** 508

Thompson, Lawrance Roger, **Retro. Supp. I:** 138, 141

Thompson, Lisa B., **Supp. XXIII:** 202

Thompson, Morton, **Supp. XIII:** 170

Thompson, Theresa, **Supp. V:** 141

Thompson, William T., **Supp. I Part 2:** 411

Thomson, James, **II:** 304; **Supp. I Part 1:** 150, 151; **Supp. XXIV:** 159

Thomson, Virgil, **IV:** 45; **Supp. IV Part 1:** 81, 83, 84, 173; **Supp. XVI:** 195

"Thoreau" (Lowell), **Supp. I Part 2:** 420, 422

Thoreau, Henry David, **I:** 98, 104, 228, 236, 257, 258, 261, 305, 433; **II:** 7, 8, 13, 17, 101, 159, 224, 273–274, 295, 312–313, 321, 457–458, 540, 546–547; **III:** 171, 174, 186–187, 189, 208, 214–215, 453, 454, 507, 577; **IV:** 167–189, 191, 341; **Retro. Supp. I:** 51, 62, 122; **Retro. Supp. II:** 13, 96, 142, 158; **Supp. I Part 1:** 29, 34, 116, 188, 299, 358; **Supp. I Part 2:** 383, 400, 420, 421, 507, 540, 579, 580, 655, 659, 660, 664, 678; **Supp. III Part 1:** 340, 353; **Supp. IV Part 1:** 236, 392, 416; **Supp. IV Part 2:** 420, 430, 433, 439, 447; **Supp. V:** 200, 208; **Supp. VIII:** 40, 42, 103, 105, 198, 201, 204, 205, 292, 303; **Supp. IX:** 25, 90, 171; **Supp. X:** 21, 27, 28–29, 101, 102; **Supp. XI:** 155; **Supp. XIII:** 1, 17; **Supp. XIV:** 40, 54, 106, 177, 181; **Supp. XVIII:** 4; **Supp. XX:** 116, 221; **Supp. XXI:** 203, 217; **Supp. XXII:** 206; **Supp. XXIII:** 174

Thoreau, John, **IV:** 171, 182

Thoreau, Mrs. John, **IV:** 172

"Thoreau's Hound: On Hiddenness" (Hirshfield), **Supp. XXIII:** 137

"Thorn, The" (Gordon), **Supp. IV Part 1:** 314

Thorne, Francis, **Supp. XII:** 253

"Thorn Merchant, The" (Komunyakaa), **Supp. XIII:** 119–120

Thornton, Billy Bob, **Supp. VIII:** 175

Thornton, Lionel, **III:** 291

"Thorofare" (Minot), **Supp. VI: 209–210**

"Thorow" (Howe), **Supp. IV Part 2:** 419, 420, 421, 431, 433–434

Thorp, Willard, **Supp. XIII:** 101

Thorslev, Peter L., Jr., **I:** 524

Thorstein Veblen (Dowd), **Supp. I Part 2:** 650

Thorstein Veblen (Qualey, ed.), **Supp. I Part 2:** 650

Thorstein Veblen: A Chapter in American Economic Thought (Teggart), **Supp. I Part 2:** 650

Thorstein Veblen: A Critical Interpretation (Riesman), **Supp. I Part 2:** 649, 650

Thorstein Veblen: A Critical Reappraisal (Dowd, ed.), **Supp. I Part 2:** 650

Thorstein Veblen and His America (Dorfman), **Supp. I Part 2:** 631, 650

Thorstein Veblen and the Institutionalists: A Study in the Social Philosophy of Economics (Seckler), **Supp. I Part 2:** 650

"Those before Us" (Lowell), **II:** 550

"Those Being Eaten by America" (R. Bly), **Supp. IV Part 1:** 62

Those Bones Are Not My Child (Bambara), **Supp. XI:** 1, 14, **20–22**

Those Extraordinary Twins (Twain), **IV:** 205–206

"Those Graves in Rome" (Levis), **Supp. XI:** 266

"Those of Us Who Think We Know" (Dunn), **Supp. XI:** 146

Those That Be in Bondage (Webber), **Supp. XXI:** 160

"Those Times . . ." (Sexton), **Supp. II Part 2:** 670, 684

"Those Various Scalpels" (Moore), **III:** 202

"Those Were the Days" (Levine), **Supp. V:** 190

"Those Who Don't" (Cisneros), **Supp. VII:** 60

"Those Who Thunder" (Hogan), **Supp. IV Part 1:** 406

"Thought, A" (Sarton), **Supp. VIII:** 262

Thought and Character of William James (Perry), **II:** 362

Thoughtbook of Francis Scott Key Fitzgerald (Fitzgerald), **Retro. Supp. I:** 99

"Thought Experiment" (Saunders), **Supp. XIX:** 235

"Thoughtful Roisterer Declines the Gambit, The" (Hecht), **Supp. X:** 63

"Thought of Heaven, The" (Stern), **Supp. IX:** 297

"Thoughts after Lambeth" (Eliot), **I:** 587; **Retro. Supp. I:** 324

Thoughts and Reflections (Lord Halifax), **II:** 111

Thoughts in Solitude (Merton), **Supp. VIII:** 207

"Thoughts on Being Bibliographed" (Wilson), **IV:** 435

"Thoughts on the Establishment of a Mint in the United States" (Paine), **Supp. I Part 2:** 512

"Thoughts on the Gifts of Art" (Kenyon), **Supp. VII:** 167

Thousand Acres, A (Smiley), **Supp. VI:** 292, **301–303**

"Thousand and Second Night, The" (Merrill), **Supp. III Part 1:** 324

"Thousand Dollar Vagrant, The" (Olsen), **Supp. XIII:** 292, 297

"Thousand Faces of Danny Torrance, The" (Figliola), **Supp. V:** 143

"Thousand Genuflections, A" (McCarriston), **Supp. XIV:** 266

Thousand-Mile Walk to the Gulf, A (Muir), **Supp. IX: 177–178**

"Thou Shalt Not Steal" (McClatchy), **Supp. XII:** 264

"Thread, The" (Merwin), **Supp. III Part 1:** 351

Three (film), **Supp. IX:** 253

3-3-8 (Marquand), **III:** 58

"3 A.M. Kitchen: My Father Talking" (Gallagher), **Supp. XXIV:** 169

"Three Academic Pieces" (Stevens), **IV:** 90

"Three Agee Wards, The" (Morris), **III:** 220–221

"Three American Singers" (Cather), **Retro. Supp. I:** 10

"Three Around the Old Gentleman" (Berryman), **I:** 188

"Three Avilas, The" (Jeffers), **Supp. II Part 2:** 418

"Three Black Women Writers" (C. L. R. James), **Supp. XXI:** 172

Three Books of Song (Longfellow), **II:** 490

"Three Bushes" (Yeats), **Supp. I Part 1:** 80

Three Cantos (Pound), **Retro. Supp. I:** 290

Three Centuries of Harvard (Morison), **Supp. I Part 2:** 485

Three Changes (Silver), **Supp. XXIV:** 275

Three Circles of Light (di Donato), **Supp. XX: 33, 42–43, 44, 46**

Three Cities: A Trilogy (Asch), **Supp. XXIII:** 1, 5, **10–12**

Three Comrades (Remarque), **Retro. Supp. I:** 113

"Three Corollaries of Cultural Relativism" (Locke), **Supp. XIV:** 202

"Three-Day Blow, The" (Hemingway), **II:** 248

Three Essays on America (Brooks), **I:** 246

Three Farmers on Their Way to a Dance (Powers), **Supp. IX:** 211–212, **213–214**, 222

"Three Fates, The" (Benét), **Supp. XI:** 48–49, 50

"Three Generations of Secrets" (A. Finch), **Supp. XVII:** 73

"Three Gifts, The" (Gibran), **Supp. XX: 124**

Three Gospels (Price), **Supp. VI:** 267

365 Days (Boyle), **Supp. XXIV:** 50, 60

"Three Kings, The: Hemingway, Faulkner, and Fitzgerald" (Ford), **Supp. V:** 59

Three Lives (Auchincloss), **Supp. IV Part 1:** 25

Three Lives (Stein), **I:** 103; **IV:** 26, 27, 31, 35, 37–41, 42, 45, 46; **Supp. IX:** 306; **Supp. XXIII:** 166

"THREE MOVEMENTS AND A CODA" (Baraka), **Supp. II Part 1:** 50

Three One Act Plays (Riverside Drive, Old Saybrook, and *Central Park West)* (Allen), **Supp. XV:** 3

Three on the Tower: The Lives and Works of Ezra Pound, T. S. Eliot, and William Carlos Williams (Simpson), **Supp. IX:** 276

Three Papers on Fiction (Welty), **IV:** 261

Three-Penny Opera (Brecht), **I:** 301; **Supp. XIV:** 162

"Three Percent Own All the Wealth" (Ryan as Quin), **Supp. XVIII:** 231–232

Three Philosophical Poets (Santayana), **III:** 610–612

"Three Pigs in Five Days" (Prose), **Supp. XVI:** 257, 258

"Three Players of a Summer Game" (T. Williams), **IV:** 383

Three Poems (Ashbery), **Supp. III Part 1:** 2, 3, 14, 15, 18, 24–26

"Three Poems for my Daughter" (Di Piero), **Supp. XIX:** 40

"Three Pokes of a Thistle" (Nye), **Supp. XIII:** 281

Three Prophets of Religious Liberalism (Wright), **Supp. XXIV:** 71

Three Roads, The (Macdonald, under Millar), **Supp. IV Part 2:** 466, 467

Three Short Plays with Long Titles (Silver and Ann), **Supp. XXIV:** 264

"Three Silences of Molinos, The" (Longfellow), **Retro. Supp. II:** 169

Three Sisters, The (Chekhov), **Supp. XV:** 323

"Three Sisters, The" (Cisneros), **Supp. VII:** 64

Three Soldiers (Dos Passos), **I:** 477–478, 480, 482, 488, 493–494; **Supp. XXI:** 277

"Three Songs at the End of Summer" (Kenyon), **Supp. VII:** 169–170

"Three Steps to the Graveyard" (Wright), **Supp. III Part 2:** 593, 596

Three Stories and Ten Poems (Hemingway), **II:** 68, 263; **Supp. XVII:** 105

Three Tall Women (Albee), **Supp. XXIV:** 270

Three Taverns, The (Robinson), **III:** 510

"Three Taverns, The" (Robinson), **III:** 521, 522

Three Tenant Families (Agee), **I:** 37–38

Three Tenors, One Vehicle: A Book of Songs (X. J. Kennedy, Camp, and Waldrop), **Supp. XV:** 165

"Three Types of Poetry" (Tate), **IV:** 131

"Three Vagabonds of Trinidad" (Harte), **Supp. II Part 1:** 338

"Three Waterfalls, The" (Lanier), **Supp. I Part 1:** 350

"Three-Way Mirror" (Brooks), **Supp. III Part 1:** 69–70

Three Weeks in Spring (Parker and Parker), **Supp. XIX:** 187

"Three Women" (Plath), **Supp. I Part 2:** 539, 541, 544, 545, 546

Three Young Poets (Swallow, ed.), **Supp. X:** 116

Threnody (Emerson), **Supp. I Part 2:** 416

"Threnody" (Emerson), **II:** 7

"Threnody for a Brown Girl" (Cullen), **Supp. IV Part 1:** 166

"Threshing-Floor, The" (Baldwin), **Supp. I Part 1:** 50

Threshold (film), **Supp. IX:** 254

"Threshold" (Goldbarth), **Supp. XII:** 175

Threshold (Jackson), **Supp. IX:** 117

"Throat" (Goldbarth), **Supp. XII:** 177–178

Throne of Labdacus, The (Schnackenberg), **Supp. XV:** 260, 263–266

Thrones (Pound), **Retro. Supp. I:** 293

Through Dooms of Love (Kumin), **Supp. IV Part 2:** 444

"Through the Black Curtain" (Kingston), **Supp. V:** 169

Through the Forest: New and Selected Poems, 1977–1987 (Wagoner), **Supp. IX:** 330–331

"Through the Hills of Spain" (Salinas), **Supp. XIII:** 315

"Through the Hole in the Mundane Millstone" (West), **Retro. Supp. II:** 321, 322

Through the Ivory Gate (Dove), **Supp. IV Part 1:** 242, 243, 251, 252, 253–254, 254

"Through the Kitchen Window, Chiapas" (Nye), **Supp. XIII:** 277

Through the Safety Net (C. Baxter), **Supp. XVII:** 17, 22

"Through the Smoke Hole" (Snyder), **Supp. VIII:** 299

Throw Like a Girl (Thompson), **Supp. XXIII: 299–300**

"Throw Like a Girl"(Thompson), **Supp. XXIII:** 299, 300

"Thrush Relinquished, The" (Grossman), **Supp. XIX:** 83

Thucydides, **II:** 418; **IV:** 50; **Supp. I Part 2:** 488, 489, 492; **Supp. IV Part 1:** 391; **Supp. XIII:** 233

Thunderbolt and Lightfoot (film), **Supp. X:** 126

"Thunder from a Cloudless Sky" (Mosher), **Supp. XXII:** 209

"Thunderhead" (MacLeish), **III:** 19

Thurber, James, **I:** 487; **II:** 432; **IV:** 396; **Supp. I Part 2: 602–627,** 653, 654, 668, 672, 673, 679; **Supp. II Part 1:** 143; **Supp. IV Part 1:** 349; **Supp. IX:** 118; **Supp. XIV:** 104; **Supp. XVI:** 167; **Supp. XVII:** 4

Thurber, Mrs. James (Althea Adams), **Supp. I Part 2:** 613, 615, 617

Thurber, Mrs. James (Helen Muriel Wismer), **Supp. I Part 2:** 613, 617, 618

Thurber, Robert, **Supp. I Part 2:** 613, 617

Thurber, Rosemary, **Supp. I Part 2:** 616

Thurber, William, **Supp. I Part 2:** 602

Thurber Album, The (Thurber), **Supp. I Part 2:** 611, 619

Thurber Carnival, The (Thurber), **Supp. I Part 2:** 620; **Supp. XIV:** 104

Thurman, Judith, **Supp. IV Part 1:** 309

Thurman, Wallace, **Retro. Supp. I:** 200; **Supp. I Part 1:** 325, 326, 328, 332; **Supp. IV Part 1:** 164; **Supp. X:** 136, 139; **Supp. XVI:** 135; **Supp. XVIII:** 279, 281; **Supp. XIX:** 78; **Supp. XXII:** 2

"Thursday" (Millay), **III:** 129

"Thurso's Landing" (Jeffers), **Supp. II Part 2:** 433

"Thus Do I Refute Gioia" (Junker), **Supp. XV:** 116

"Thus Far by Faith" (Nelson), **Supp. XVIII:** 177

Thus Spake Zarathustra (Nietzsche), **II:** 463; **Supp. IV Part 1:** 110; **Supp. IV Part 2:** 519

Thwaite, Lady Alicia. *See* Rawlings, Marjorie Kinnan

Thy Neighbor's Wife (Talese), **Supp. XVII:** 204, 205–206, 207, 208, 210

"Tiara" (Doty), **Supp. XI:** 122

"Tibetan Time" (Prose), **Supp. XVI:** 255

Ticket for a Seamstitch, A (Harris), **II:** 424–425

Tickets for a Prayer Wheel (Dillard), **Supp. VI:** 22, 34

Ticket That Exploded, The (Burroughs), **Supp. III Part 1:** 93, 103, 104

Tickless Time (Glaspell), **Supp. III Part 1:** 179

Ticknor, George, **II:** 488; **Supp. I Part 1:** 313

Ticknor, William, **Supp. XVIII:** 258

"Ti Démon" (Chopin), **Supp. I Part 1:** 225

Tide of Time, The (Masters), **Supp. I Part 2:** 471

"Tide of Voices" (Hull), **Supp. XXI:** 132, 133–134, 136

"Tide Rises, the Tide Falls, The" (Longfellow), **I:** 498

"Tides" (Hoffman), **Supp. XVIII:** 86

Tidewater Blood (Hoffman), **Supp. XVIII: 82–83**

Tidyman, Ernest, **Supp. V:** 226

Tietjens, Eunice, **Supp. XV:** 47, 297

"Tiger" (Blake), **Supp. I Part 1:** 80; **Supp. VIII:** 26

Tiger (Bynner), **Supp. XV:** 42, 50

"Tiger, The" (Buechner), **Supp. XII:** 48

Tiger in the House, The (Van Vechten), **Supp. II Part 2:** 736

Tiger Joy (Benét), **Supp. XI:** 45

Tiger-Lilies (Lanier), **Supp. I Part 1:** 350–351, 357, 360, 371

Tiger Who Wore White Gloves, The: or, What You Are, You Are (Brooks), **Supp. III Part 1:** 86

Till, Emmett, **Supp. I Part 1:** 61

Till, Eric, **Supp. XXIII:** 103

Tillich, Paul, **II:** 244; **III:** 291, 292, 303, 309; **IV:** 226; **Retro. Supp. I:** 325, 326, 327; **Supp. V:** 267; **Supp. XIII:** 74, 91

Tillie Olsen: A Study of the Short Fiction (Frye), **Supp. XIII:** 292, 296, 298, 299, 302

Tillman, Lynne, **Supp. XII:** 4

Tillotson, John, **II:** 114

Tillotson, Kristen, **Supp. XVII:** 23

Tillstrom, Burr, **Supp. XIV:** 125

Till the Day I Die (Odets), **Supp. II Part 2:** 530, 533–536, 552

Tilton, Eleanor, **Supp. I Part 1:** 317

Tilton, Theodore, **Supp. XVIII:** 4

Timaeus (Plato), **II:** 10; **III:** 609

Tim: A Story of School Life (Sturgis), **Supp. XX: 227, 230, 232, 233–235**

Timber (Jonson), **II:** 16

Timberg, Scott, **Supp. XV:** 116

"Timberwolf" (Halliday), **Supp. XIX:** 91

Timbuktu (Auster), **Supp. XII:** 34, **35–36**

"Time" (Matthews), **Supp. IX: 165–166**

"Time" (Merrill), **Supp. III Part 1:** 325

"Time and Again" (Sanders), **Supp. XVI:** 269

Time and a Place, A (Humphrey), **Supp. IX:** 95, 98, **100–102**

"Time and the Garden" (Winters), **Supp. II Part 2:** 801, 809

"Time and the Liturgy" (Merton), **Supp. VIII:** 199

Time and the River (Edgell), **Supp. XXIII:** 84, 85, **91–93**

Time and Tide: A Walk through Nantucket (Conroy), **Supp. XVI:** 63, 71, **76–77**

"Time Exposure" (C. Baxter), **Supp. XVII:** 20–21

Time Exposures, by Search-Light (W. Frank), **Supp. XX:** 75

Time in the Rock (Aiken), **I:** 65

Time Is Noon, The (Buck), **Supp. II Part 1:** 129, 130–131

Time & Money (Matthews), **Supp. IX:** 155, **165–167**

"Time of Friendship, The" (Bowles), **Supp. IV Part 1:** 90–91

"Time of Her Time, The" (Mailer), **III:** 37, 45; **Retro. Supp. II:** 200

Time of Our Time, The (Mailer), **Retro. Supp. II:** 213–214

Time of the Assassins, The: A Study of Rimbaud (H. Miller), **III:** 189

Time Out of Mind (album, Dylan), **Supp. XVIII:** 28

"Time Past" (Morris), **III:** 232

"Time Present" (Morris), **III:** 232

"Times" (Beattie), **Supp. V:** 31

"Times, The" (Emerson), **II:** 11–12

Times Are Never So Bad, The (Dubus), **Supp. VII:** 87–88

Time's Arrow (Amis), **Retro. Supp. I:** 278

"Time Shall Not Die" (Chandler), **Supp. IV Part 1:** 120

Times of Melville and Whitman, The (Brooks), **I:** 257

Times They Are A-Changin', The (album, Dylan), **Supp. XVIII:** 20, 25

"Times They Are A-Changin,' The" (song, Dylan), **Supp. XVIII:** 30

"Timesweep" (Sandburg), **III:** 595–596

Time to Act, A (MacLeish), **III:** 3

Time to Be Born, A (Powell), **Supp. XIX:** 143

Time to Go (Dixon), **Supp. XII:** 147

Time to Kill (film), **Supp. IV Part 1:** 130

Time to Speak, A (MacLeish), **III:** 3

Time Will Darken It (Maxwell), **Supp. VIII:** 159, **162–164,** 169

"Timing of Sin, The" (Dubus), **Supp. VII:** 91

Tim O'Brien (Herzog), **Supp. V:** 239

Timoleon (Melville), **III:** 93; **Retro. Supp. I:** 257

Timothy Dexter Revisited (Marquand), **III:** 55, 62, 63

Timothy Findley: Stories from a Life (Roberts), **Supp. XX:** 53

Timrod, Henry, **Supp. XVIII:** 31, 33

Tin Can, The (W. J. Smith), **Supp. XIII:** 334, **Supp. XIII:** 336, 337

"Tin Can, The" (W. J. Smith), **Supp. XIII:** **337–339**

Tin Can Tree, The (Tyler), **Supp. IV Part 2:** 659–660

Tinguely, Jean, **Supp. XV:** 187

Tinker, Chauncey Brewster, **Supp. XIV:** 12

"Tinseled Bucks: A Historical Study of Indian Homosexuality"(Kenny), **Supp. XXIII:** 149

Tintern Abbey (Wordsworth), **Supp. I Part 2:** 673, 675

Tiny Alice (Albee), **I:** 81–86, 87, 88, 94

"Tiny Mummies! The True Story of the Ruler of 43rd Street's Land of the Walking Dead" (Wolfe), **Supp. III Part 2:** 573, 574

Tip on a Dead Jockey and Other Stories (Shaw), **Supp. XIX:** 251

"Tip-Top Club, The" (Keillor), **Supp. XVI:** 172

"Tired" (Hughes), **Supp. I Part 1:** 331

"Tired and Unhappy, You Think of Houses" (Schwartz), **Supp. II Part 2:** 649

"Tiresias" (Garrett), **Supp. VII:** 96–97

'Tis (McCourt), **Supp. XII:** 271, **279– 286**

Tisch (Dixon), **Supp. XII:** 141, **155–156**

Titan, The (Dreiser), **I:** 497, 501, 507– 508, 509, 510; **Retro. Supp. II:** 94, 101, 102

Titian, **Supp. I Part 2:** 397, 714

"Tito's Goodbye" (García), **Supp. XI:** 190

"To a Bird, Seen Under My Window in the Garden"(J. Schoolcraft), **Supp. XXIII:** 230

To a Blossoming Pear Tree (Wright), **Supp. III Part 2:** 602–605

"To a Blossoming Pear Tree" (Wright), **Supp. III Part 2:** 604

"To Abolish Children" (Shapiro), **Supp. II Part 2:** 717

To Abolish Children and Other Essays (Shapiro), **Supp. II Part 2:** 703

"To a Caty-Did, the Precursor of Winter" (Freneau), **Supp. II Part 1:** 274–275

"To a Chameleon" (Moore), **III:** 195, 196, 215

"To a Conscript of 1940" (Read), **II:** 372–373, 377–378

"To a Contemporary Bunk Shooter" (Sandburg), **III:** 582

"To a Cough in the Street at Midnight" (Wylie), **Supp. I Part 2:** 727, 729– 730

"To a Defeated Savior" (Wright), **Supp. III Part 2:** 593–594, 596

"To a Face in the Crowd" (Warren), **IV:** 239

"To a Fish Head Found on the Beach near Malaga" (Levine), **Supp. V:** 185

"To a Friend" (Nemerov), **III:** 272

"To a Friend"(O'Hara), **Supp. XXIII:** 212

"To a Friend Whose Work Has Come to Triumph" (Sexton), **Supp. II Part 2:** 683

To a God Unknown (Steinbeck), **I:** 107; **IV:** 51, 59–60, 67

"To a Greek Marble" (Aldington), **Supp. I Part 1:** 257

"To a Locomotive in Winter" (Whitman), **IV:** 348

"To a Military Rifle" (Winters), **Supp. II Part 2:** 810, 811, 815

"To a Mouse" (Burns), **Supp. IX:** 173

"To an American Workman Dying of Starvation" (Taggard), **Supp. XXII:** 282

"To an Athlete Dying Young" (Houseman), **Supp. XVII:** 121

"To a Negro Jazz Band in a Parisian Cabaret" (Hughes), **Supp. I Part 1:** 325

"To an Old Philosopher in Rome" (Stevens), **III:** 605; **Retro. Supp. I:** 312

"To an Old Poet in Peru" (Ginsberg), **Supp. II Part 1:** 322

"To a Now-Type Poet" (X. J. Kennedy), **Supp. XV:** 161

"To Answer Your Question" (Jarman), **Supp. XVII:** 114–115

"To Any Would-Be Terrorists" (Nye), **Supp. XIII:** 285, 286

"To a Poet" (Rich), **Supp. I Part 2:** 571; **Supp. XIX:** 83

"To a Prize Bird" (Moore), **III:** 215

"To a Republican, with Mr. Paine's Rights of Man" (Freneau), **Supp. II Part 1:** 267

"To a Shade" (Yeats), **III:** 18

"To a Skylark" (Shelley), **Supp. I Part 2:** 720; **Supp. X:** 31

"Toast to Harlem, A" (Hughes), **Supp. I Part 1:** 338

"To Aunt Rose" (Ginsberg), **Supp. II Part 1:** 320

"To Autumn" (Keats), **Supp. IX:** 50

"To a Waterfowl" (Bryant), **Supp. I Part 1:** 154, 155, 162, 171

"To a Young Poet" (X. J. Kennedy), **Supp. XV:** 161

"To a Young Writer" (Stegner), **Supp. X:** 24

Tobacco Road (Caldwell), **I:** 288, 289, 290, 295–296, 297, 298, 302, 307, 309, 310; **IV:** 198; **Supp. XXII:** 196

"To Be a Monstrous Clever Fellow" (Fante), **Supp. XI:** 167

"To Become Music or Break" (Jauss), **Supp. XXI:** 133

To Bedlam and Part Way Back (Sexton), **Retro. Supp. II:** 245; **Supp. II Part 2:** 672–678; **Supp. IV Part 2:** 441; **Supp. XI:** 317

"To Beethoven" (Lanier), **Supp. I Part 1:** 364

To Begin Again: Stories and Memoirs, 1908–1929 (M. F. K. Fisher), **Supp. XVII:** 92

Tobey, Mark, **Supp. X:** 264

To Be Young, Gifted, and Black: Lorraine Hansberry in Her Own Words (Nemiroff), **Supp. IV Part 1:** 372, 374

"To Big Mary from an Ex-Catholic" (Mora), **Supp. XIII:** 217, 224, 228

"Tobin's Palm" (O. Henry), **Supp. II Part 1:** 408; **Supp. XV:** 40

Tobit (apocryphal book), **I:** 89

"To Build a Fire" (London), **II:** 468

Toby Tyler: or, Ten Weeks with a Circus (Otis), **III:** 577

"To Change in a Good Way" (Ortiz), **Supp. IV Part 2:** 511

"To Charlotte Cushman" (Lanier), **Supp. I Part 1:** 364

"To Cole, the Painter, Departing for Europe" (Bryant), **Supp. I Part 1:** 157, 161

Tocqueville, Alexis de, **III:** 261; **IV:** 349; **Retro. Supp. I:** 235; **Supp. I Part 1:** 137; **Supp. I Part 2:** 659, 660; **Supp. II Part 1:** 281, 282, 284; **Supp. XIV:** 306, 312

"To Crispin O'Conner" (Freneau), **Supp. II Part 1:** 268

"To Da-Duh, In Memoriam" (Marshall), **Supp. XI:** 276

"TODAY" (Baraka), **Supp. II Part 1:** 55

"Today" (Ginsberg), **Supp. II Part 1:** 328

"Today Is a Good Day To Die" (Bell), **Supp. X:** 7

"Today"(O'Hara), **Supp. XXIII:** 210–211

"Today Will Be a Quiet Day" (Hempel), **Supp. XXI:** 117,**Supp. XXI:** 118

Todd, Mabel Loomis, **I:** 454, 470; **Retro. Supp. I:** 33, 34, 35, 39, 47

"To Death" (Levertov), **Supp. III Part 1:** 274

"To Delmore Schwartz" (Lowell), **II:** 547; **Retro. Supp. II:** 188

"to disembark" (Brooks), **Supp. III Part 1:** 86

"To Dorothy on Her Exclusion from The Guinness Book of Records" (X. J. Kennedy), **Supp. XV:** 166

"To Dream of Bears" (Gallagher), **Supp. XXIV:** 176

"To Dr. Thomas Shearer" (Lanier), **Supp. I Part 1:** 370

"To Earthward" (Frost), **II:** 154

"To Edwin V. McKenzie" (Winters), **Supp. II Part 2:** 801

"To Eleonora Duse" (Lowell), **II:** 528

"To Elizabeth Ward Perkins" (Lowell), **II:** 516

"To Elsie" (W. C. Williams), **Retro. Supp. I:** 419

"To Emily Dickinson" (H. Crane), **Retro. Supp. II:** 76

"To E. T." (Frost), **Retro. Supp. I:** 132

To Feel These Things (L. Michaels), **Supp. XVI:** 205, **213–214**

"To Feel These Things" (L. Michaels), **Supp. XVI:** 214

Toffler, Alvin, **Supp. IV Part 2:** 517

"To Fill" (Moore), **Supp. X:** 168, 169

"To Gabriela, a Young Writer" (Mora), **Supp. XIII:** 220

To Have and Have Not (film), **Supp. XV:** 347

To Have and Have Not (Hemingway), **I:** 31; **II:** 253–254, 264; **Retro. Supp. I:** 182, **183,** 187

"To Helen" (Poe), **III:** 410, 411, 427; **Retro. Supp. II:** 102

"To Hell With Dying" (Walker), **Supp. III Part 2:** 523

"To His Coy Mistress"(Marvell), **Supp. XXIII:** 62

"To His Excellency General Washington" (Wheatley), **Supp. XX: 289**

"To His Father" (Jeffers), **Supp. II Part 2:** 415

Toilet, The (Baraka), **Supp. II Part 1:** 37, 40–42

"To James Russell Lowell" (Holmes), **Supp. I Part 1:** 311

To Jerusalem and Back (Bellow), **Retro. Supp. II:** 29

"To Jesus on His Birthday" (Millay), **III:** 136–137

"To John Keats" (Lowell), **II:** 516

"To Judge Faolain, Dead Long Enough: A Summons" (McCarriston), **Supp. XIV:** 264–265

"To Justify My Singing" (Wright), **Supp. III Part 2:** 590

"To Kill a Deer" (C. Frost), **Supp. XV:** 102

To Kill a Mockingbird (film), **Supp. VIII:** 128–129

To Kill a Mockingbird (Lee), **Supp. VIII: 113–129; Supp. XVI:** 259; **Supp. XIX:** 142

"*To Kill a Mockingbird:* Harper Lee's Tragic Vision" (Dave), **Supp. VIII:** 126

To Kill a Mockingbird: Threatening Boundaries (Johnson), **Supp. VIII:** 126

Toklas, Alice B., **IV:** 27; **Supp. IV Part 1:** 81, 91; **Supp. XVI:** 187

"Tokyo Story" (Wasserstein), **Supp. XV:** 328

"To Larry Rivers"(O'Hara), **Supp. XXIII:** 212

"To Light" (Hogan), **Supp. IV Part 1:** 402

"To Ligurinus" (Horace; Ferry, trans.), **Supp. XXIV:** 155

"To Ligurinus" (Horace; Howard, trans.), **Supp. XXIV:** 155

"To Live and Diet" (Wasserstein), **Supp. XV:** 328

Tolkien, J. R. R., **Supp. V:** 140

Tolkin, Michael, **Supp. XI:** 160

Toller, Ernst, **I:** 479

"To Lose the Earth" (Sexton), **Supp. II Part 2:** 684, 685

Tolson, Melvin, **Retro. Supp. I:** 208, 209, 210

Tolstoy, Leo, **I:** 6, 7, 58, 103, 312, 376; **II:** 191–192, 205, 271, 272, 275, 276, 281, 285, 286, 320, 407, 542, 559, 570, 579, 606; **III:** 37, 45, 61, 323, 467, 572; **IV:** 17, 21, 170, 285; **Retro. Supp. I:** 91, 225; **Retro. Supp. II:** 299; **Supp. I Part 1:** 2, 3, 6, 20; **Supp. IV Part 1:** 392; **Supp. V:** 277, 323; **Supp. IX:** 246; **Supp. XI:** 68; **Supp. XII:** 310, 322; **Supp. XIV:** 87, 97, 98; **Supp. XIX:** 241; **Supp. XXIII:** 4, 11, 275; **Supp. XXIV:** 132

"To Lu Chi" (Nemerov), **III:** 275

"To Lydia" (Horace; Ferry, trans.), **Supp. XXIV:** 154

"To Lydia" (Horace; McHugh, trans.), **Supp. XXIV:** 154

Tom (Cummings), **I:** 430

"Tom" (Oliver), **Supp. VII:** 232

"Tom, Tom, the Piper's Son" (Ransom), **Supp. X:** 58

"To M, with a Rose" (Lanier), **Supp. I Part 1:** 364

To Make a Prairie (Kumin), **Supp. IV Part 2:** 440, 441

"To Make Words Disappear" (Simpson), **Supp. IX:** 265–266

Tomás and the Library Lady (Mora), **Supp. XIII:** 216, 221

"Tomatoes" (Francis), **Supp. IX:** 82

"Tom Ball's Barn" (Kooser), **Supp. XIX:** 119

"Tom Brown at Fisk" (Du Bois), **Supp. II Part 1:** 160

Tom Brown's School Days (Hughes), **Supp. I Part 2:** 406

"Tomb Stone" (Dickey), **Supp. IV Part 1:** 185

"Tombstone Blues" (song, Dylan), **Supp. XVIII:** 30

Tomcat in Love (O'Brien), **Supp. V:** 238, 240, 243, 252–254

"Tomcat's Wife, The" (C. Bly), **Supp. XVI:** 40

Tomcat's Wife and Other Stories, The (C. Bly), **Supp. XVI:** 40–41

"Tom Fool at Jamaica" (Moore), **III:** 215

To Mix with Time (Swenson), **Supp. IV Part 2:** 637, 643–645, 645

Tom Jones (Fielding), **I:** 131; **Supp. V:** 127

Tomlinson, Charles, **Supp. XVI:** 284

Tommy Gallagher's Crusade (Farrell), **II:** 44

Tommyknockers, The (King), **Supp. V:** 139, 144

"Tommy's Burglar" (Henry), **Supp. II Part 1:** 399, 401

"Tommy Stames" (Budbill), **Supp. XIX:** 8

Tomo Cheeki (pseudonym). *See* Freneau, Philip

Tomorrow Is Another Day (E. P. Jones), **Supp. XXII:** 252

Tomorrow is Another Day (film, Feist), **Supp. XVII:** 62

"Tomorrow the Moon" (Dos Passos), **I:** 493

Tomorrow Will Be Better (B. Smith), **Supp. XXIII:** 258, **264–267**

"Tom Outland's Story" (Cather), **I:** 325–326

Tompkins, Jane, **Supp. XVI:** 89; **Supp. XVIII:** 258, 259, 263

Tompson, Benjamin, **Supp. I Part 1:** 110, 111

"Tom-Rock Through Eels" (Hempel), **Supp. XXI:** 116, 118, **123–124**

Tom Sawyer (musical) (Gurney), **Supp. V:** 96

Tom Sawyer (Twain). *See Adventures of Tom Sawyer, The* (Twain)

Tom Sawyer Abroad (Twain), **II:** 482; **IV:** 19, 204

Tom Sawyer Detective (Twain), **IV:** 204

"Tom's Husband" (Jewett), **Retro. Supp. II:** 132, 141

Tom Swift (Stratemeyer), **III:** 146

Tom-Walker, The (Sandoz), **Supp. XXIV:** 244, **253–255**

"Tom Wolfe's Guide to Etiquette" (Wolfe), **Supp. III Part 2:** 578

"To My Brother Killed: Haumont Wood: October, 1918" (Bogan), **Supp. III Part 1:** 58

"To My Class, on Certain Fruits and Flowers Sent Me in Sickness" (Lanier), **Supp. I Part 1:** 370

"To my ever beloved & lamented son William Henry"(J. Schoolcraft), **Supp. XXIII:** 226, 231

"To My Father's Ghost" (Everwine), **Supp. XV:** 76

"To My Ghost Reflected in the Auxvasse River" (Levis), **Supp. XI:** 265

"To My Greek" (Merrill), **Supp. III Part 1:** 326

"To My Mother" (Berry), **Supp. X:** 23

"To My Sister—Ernestine Kealoha Taggard, 1900–1943" (Taggard), **Supp. XXII:** 284

"To My Small Son, at the Photographer's" (Hay), **Supp. XIV:** 121

"To My Small Son, on Certain Occasions" (Hay), **Supp. XIV:** 121

"To My Students" (Taggard), **Supp. XXII:** 280

"To Name is to Possess" (Kincaid), **Supp. VII:** 194

Tone, Aileen, **I:** 21–22

"Tongue Is, The" (Komunyakaa), **Supp. XIII:** 113

"Tongue of the Jews" (Bukiet), **Supp. XVII:** 47

Tongues (Shepard and Chaikin), **Supp. III Part 2:** 433

Tongues of Angels, The (Price), **Supp. VI:** 265

Tongues Untied (Riggs; film), **Supp. XI:** 19, 20

"Tonight" (Lowell), **II:** 538

"Tonight Is Part of the Struggle"(Le Sueur), **Supp. XXIII: 172**

Tonight Is the Night of the Prom (Jarman), **Supp. XVII:** 110, **112–113**

"Tonight Is the Night of the Prom" (Jarman), **Supp. XVII:** 113

Tony Kushner in Conversation (Vorlicky, ed.), **Supp. IX:** 132

"Too Anxious for Rivers" (Frost), **II:** 162

"Too Blue" (Hughes), **Retro. Supp. I:** 207

"Too Damn Close: Thresholds and Their Maintenance in Rick Bass's Work" (Kerridge), **Supp. XVI:** 26

"Too Early" (Leopold), **Supp. XIV:** 186

"Too Early Spring" (Benét), **Supp. XI:** 53

"Too Far from Home" (Bowles), **Supp. IV Part 1:** 94–95

Too Far from Home: Selected Writings of Paul Bowles (Halpern, ed.), **Supp. IV Part 1:** 94, 95

Too Far to Go: The Maples Stories (Updike), **Retro. Supp. I:** 321

"Too Good To Be True": The Life and Art of Leslie Fiedler (Winchell), **Supp. XIII:** 94, 98, 99, 101

Toohey, John Peter, **Supp. IX:** 190

Toolan, David, **Supp. IV Part 1:** 308

Too Late (Dixon), **Supp. XII: 143–144**

"Too Late" (Pickering), **Supp. XXI:** 197

"Too-Late Born, The" (Hemingway), **III:** 9

Toole, John Kennedy, **Supp. XIV:** 21

"Toolless" (Pickering), **Supp. XXI:** 204

Too Many Bottles (Holding), **Supp. XXII:** 126, **134–135**

Toomer, Jean, **Retro. Supp. II:** 79; **Supp. I Part 1:** 325, 332; **Supp. III Part 2: 475–491; Supp. IV Part 1:** 16, 164, 168; **Supp. IX: 305–322; Supp. XIII:** 305; **Supp. XVIII:** 122; **Supp. XX: 73; Supp. XXII:** 6

Toomer, Nathan Eugene Pinchback. *See* Toomer, Jean

Too Much Johnson (film), **Supp. IV Part 1:** 83

"To One Who Said Me Nay" (Cullen), **Supp. IV Part 1:** 166

"Tooth, The" (Jackson), **Supp. IX:** 122

Tooth and Claw (Boyle), **Supp. XX:** 20

Tooth of Crime, The (Shepard), **Supp. III Part 2:** 432, 441–445, 447

"Too Young" (O'Hara), **III:** 369

Topaz (film), **Supp. XX:** 253

Topaz (Uris), **Supp. XX: 247, 248, 253**

"Top Israeli Official Hints at 'Shared' Jerusalem" (Nye), **Supp. XIII:** 287

"To P. L., 1916–1937" (Levine), **Supp. V:** 185

"To Please a Shadow" (Brodsky), **Supp. VIII:** 30

"Top of the Food Chain" (Boyle), **Supp. XX:** 20

"Top of the Hill" (Jewett), **II:** 406

"Topography" (Olds), **Supp. X:** 208

Topper (T. Smith), **Supp. IX:** 194

To Praise the Music (Bronk), **Supp. XXI:** 31, 32

Torah, **IV:** 19

"Torch Songs" (Wrigley), **Supp. XVIII:** 296

Torday, Daniel, **Supp. XXII:** 151

Torpedo 8: The Story of Swede Larsen's Bomber Squadron (Wolfert), **Supp. XXI:** 267

"Torquemada" (Bukiet), **Supp. XVII:** 44

"Torquemada" (Longfellow), **II:** 505; **Retro. Supp. II:** 164

Torrence, Ridgely, **III:** 507

Torrent and the Night Before, The (Robinson), **III:** 504

Torrents of Spring, The (Hemingway), **I:** 117; **II:** 250–251

Torres, Héctor A., **Supp. XIII:** 225

Torres, Louis, **Supp. IV Part 2:** 529, 530

Torres-Saillant, Silvio, **Supp. XXI:** 104, 105, 108, 109

Torsney, Cheryl, **Retro. Supp. I:** 224

Tortilla Curtain, The (Boyle), **Supp. VIII: 9–10; Supp. XX: 28–29**

Tortilla Flat (Steinbeck), **IV:** 50, 51, 61, 64

Tortilla Flats (Steinbeck), **Supp. XX: 28**

Tortured Skins, and Other Fictions (Kenny), **Supp. XXIII:** 150, 156, 157

Tory Lover, The (Jewett), **II:** 406; **Retro. Supp. II:** 144–145

"Toscana" (Dixon), **Supp. XII:** 154

"To Sestius" (Horace; Ferry, trans.), **Supp. XXIV:** 155

"To Sestius" (Horace; Lasdun, trans.), **Supp. XXIV:** 154

"To Sir Toby" (Freneau), **Supp. II Part 1:** 269

"To Sophy, Expectant" (Mumford), **Supp. II Part 2:** 475

"To Speak of Woe That Is in Marriage" (Lowell), **II:** 550

"To Statecraft Embalmed" (Moore), **III:** 197

To Stay Alive (Levertov), **Supp. III Part 1:** 280–282

"Total Eclipse" (Dillard), **Supp. VI:** 28

"Total Eclipse of the Moon"(Crooker), **Supp. XXIII:** 55

Toth, Emily, **Retro. Supp. II:** 71

Toth, Susan Allan, **Retro. Supp. II:** 138

"To the Americans of the United States" (Freneau), **Supp. II Part 1:** 271

"To the Apennines" (Bryant), **Supp. I Part 1:** 157, 164

"To the Bleeding Hearts Association of American Novelists" (Nemerov), **III:** 281

"To the Botequim & Back" (Bishop), **Retro. Supp. II:** 51

To the Bright and Shining Sun (Burke), **Supp. XIV:** 22, 25

"To the Citizens of the United States" (Paine), **Supp. I Part 2:** 519–520

"To the Dandelion" (Lowell), **Supp. I Part 2:** 424

"To the End" (Haines), **Supp. XII:** 212–213

To the Ends of the Earth: The Selected Travels of Paul Theroux, **Supp. VIII:** 324

"To the Fabulous Constellation" (Ferry), **Supp. XXIV:** 148–149

"To the Film Industry in Crisis"(O'Hara), **Supp. XXIII:** 214

To the Finland Station: A Study in the Writing and Acting of History (Wilson), **IV:** 429, 436, 443–444, 446

"To the Governor & Legislature of Massachusetts" (Nemerov), **III:** 287

To the Green Man (Jarman), **Supp. XVII:** 110, 120–121

"To the Harbormaster" (O'Hara), **Supp. XXIII:** 208, 212, 214; **Supp. XXIV:** 42

To the Holy Spirit (Winters), **Supp. II Part 2:** 810

"To the Keeper of the King's Water Works" (Freneau), **Supp. II Part 1:** 269

"To the Lacedemonians" (Tate), **IV:** 134

"To the Laodiceans" (Jarrell), **Retro. Supp. I:** 121, 140

To the Lighthouse (Woolf), **I:** 309; **II:** 600; **Retro. Supp. II:** 337; **Supp. VIII:** 155

"To the Man on Trail" (London), **II:** 466

"To the Memory of the Brave Americans Under General Greene" (Freneau), **Supp. II Part 1:** 262, 274

"To the Miscodeed"(J. Schoolcraft), **Supp. XXIII:** 230

"To the Muse" (Wright), **Supp. III Part 2:** 601

"To the Natural World: at 37" (Taggard), **Supp. XXII:** 279–280

"To the Nazi Leaders" (Hay), **Supp. XIV:** 121

"To the New World" (Jarrell), **II:** 371

"To the One of Fictive Music" (Stevens), **IV:** 89; **Retro. Supp. I:** 297, 300

"To the One Upstairs" (Simic), **Supp. VIII:** 283

"To the Peoples of the World" (Du Bois), **Supp. II Part 1:** 172

"To the Pine Tree on first seeing it on returning from Europe"(J. Schoolcraft), **Supp. XXIII:** 225, 228, 232–233

To the Place of Trumpets (B. Kelly), **Supp. XVII: 123–127;** 132

"To the Pliocene Skull" (Harte), **Supp. II Part 1:** 343–344

"To the Powers of Darkness" (Taggard), **Supp. XXII:** 279, 280

"To the Powers of Desolation" (Taggard), **Supp. XXII:** 280

"To the Queen of Heaven" (Taggard), **Supp. XXII:** 280

"To the Reader" (Baudelaire), **II:** 544–545

"To The Reader" (Jarman), **Supp. XVII:** 115

"To the Reader" (Levertov), **Supp. III Part 1:** 277

"To the Republic" (Horace; Ferry, trans.), **Supp. XXIV:** 154

"To the Right Honourable William, Earl of Dartmouth" (Wheatley), **Supp. XX: 278, 284, 287–288**

"To the River Arve" (Bryant), **Supp. I Part 1:** 163

"To the Snake" (Levertov), **Supp. III Part 1:** 277

"To the Stone-Cutters" (Jeffers), **Supp. II Part 2:** 420

"To the Unseeable Animal" (Berry), **Supp. X:** 31

"To the Western World" (Simpson), **Supp. IX:** 269, 270

To the White Sea (Dickey), **Supp. IV Part 1:** 186, 190–191

"To the Young Who Want to Die" (Brooks), **Supp. III Part 1:** 85–86

"To Tlaoc of the Rain" (Everwine), **Supp. XV:** 77

"To Train a Writer" (Bierce), **I:** 199

"Touch, The" (Sexton), **Supp. II Part 2:** 687

Touch and Go (M. F. K. Fisher and D. Parrish), **Supp. XVII:** 84

"Touching the Tree" (Merwin), **Supp. III Part 1:** 355

Touching the World (Eakin), **Supp. VIII:** 167

Touch of Danger, A (Jones), **Supp. XI:** 226, **228–229**

Touch of the Poet, A (O'Neill), **III:** 385, 401, 404

Touchstone, The (Wharton), **Retro. Supp. I:** 365

"Touch-up Man" (Komunyakaa), **Supp. XIII:** 119

Tough Guys Don't Dance (Mailer), **Retro. Supp. II:** 211

"Tough People" (Offutt), **Supp. XIX:** 170–171

Toulet, Paul Jean, **IV:** 79

Tour (McNally), **Supp. XIII:** 197

"Tour 5" (Hayden), **Supp. II Part 1:** 381

To Urania (Brodsky), **Supp. VIII:** 22, 28–29

Tourgée, Albion W., **Supp. XIV:** 63

"Tour Guide" (Komunyakaa), **Supp. XIII:** 114

"Tourist Death" (MacLeish), **III:** 12

Tourmaline (J. Scott), **Supp. XVII: 192–194,** 195

Tour of Duty (Dos Passos), **I:** 489

Touron the Prairies, A (Irving), **II:** 312–313

Toussaint L'Ouverture, **Supp. XXI:** 166

Toussaint L'Ouverture (C. L. R. James), **Supp. XXI:** 167

Tovey, Donald Francis, **Supp. XIV:** 336

"To Virgil" (Horace; Ferry, trans.), **Supp. XXIV:** 155

"To Virgil" (Horace; Wright, trans.), **Supp. XXIV:** 155

To Walk a Crooked Mile (McGrath), **Supp. X:** 117

Toward a New Synthesis (Begiebing), **Retro. Supp. II:** 210

"Toward Nightfall" (Simic), **Supp. VIII:** 277

Towards a Better Life (Burke), **I:** 270

"Towards a Chicano Poetics: The Making of the Chicano Subject, 1969–1982" (Saldívar), **Supp. IV Part 2:** 544

Towards an Enduring Peace (Bourne), **I:** 232

"Towards Morning" (Pedersen; Nelson, trans.), **Supp. XVIII:** 180

Toward the Blanched Alphabets (Sobin), **Supp. XVI:** 290

Toward the Gulf (Masters), **Supp. I Part 2:** 465–466

"Toward the Solstice" (Rich), **Supp. I Part 2:** 575–576

Toward Wholeness in Paule Marshall's Fiction (Pettis), **Supp. XI:** 276

"Tower" (Merwin), **Supp. III Part 1:** 343

"Tower Beyond Tragedy, The" (Jeffers), **Supp. II Part 2:** 429–430

Tower of Ivory (Atherton), **Supp. XXIV:** 21, 23

Tower of Ivory (MacLeish), **III:** 3–4

Towers, Robert, **Supp. IX:** 259; **Supp. XVI:** 211

"To What Red Hell" (C. Himes), **Supp. XVI:** 137

"To Whistler, American" (Pound), **III:** 465–466

"To Wine" (Bogan), **Supp. III Part 1:** 57, 58

Towle, Tony, **Supp. XXIII:** 221

Town, Caren J., **Supp. XVIII:** 195, 199

Town, The (Faulkner), **II:** 57, 73; **Retro. Supp. I:** 74, 82

Town, The (Richter), **Supp. XVIII:** 207, **214–215,** 217

Town and the City, The (Kerouac), **Supp. III Part 1:** 222–224; **Supp. XIV:** 143

"Town Crier" (Bierce), **I:** 193, 194, 195, 196

"Town Crier Exclusive, Confessions of a Princess Manqué: 'How Royals Found Me "Unsuitable" to Marry Their Larry' " (Elkin), **Supp. VI:** 56

Town Down the River, The (Robinson), **III:** 508

"Town Dump, The" (Nemerov), **III:** 272, 275, 281

Towne, Robert, **Supp. XI:** 159, 172, 174

"Townhouse Interior with Cat" (Clampitt), **Supp. IX:** 40

Townie (Dubus III), **Supp. XXIV:** 98, **108–111**

"Townies" (Dubus), **Supp. VII:** 86

Town in the Forest, The: Life Story of Richmond, New Hampshire (Boyce; Faust, ed.), **Supp. XXI:** 8

"Town of the Sound of a Twig Breaking" (Carson), **Supp. XII: 102**

"Town Poor, The" (Jewett), **Retro. Supp. II:** 138, 139, 143

Townsend, Alison, **Supp. XIII:** 222; **Supp. XXIII:** 132, 139

Townsend, Ann, **Supp. V:** 77

Townsend, Jim, **Supp. XXII:** 243

"Towns in Colour" (Lowell), **II:** 523–524

Townsman, The (Sedges), **Supp. II Part 1:** 124–125

Town Smokes (P. Benedict), **Supp. XXIII: 35–39**

"Town Smokes"(P. Benedict), **Supp. XXIII:** 37

"To World War Two" (Koch), **Supp. XV:** 184

Toys in a Field (Komunyakaa), **Supp. XIII: 121–122**

"Toys in a Field" (Komunyakaa), **Supp. XIII:** 122

Toys in the Attic (Hellman), **Supp. I Part 1:** 289–290

Toyter mentsh, Der (The dead man) (Asch), **Supp. XXIII:** 9

Tracer (F. Barthelme), **Supp. XI:** 31–32, 33

Traces of Thomas Hariot, The (Rukeyser), **Supp. VI:** 273, 274, 283

"Tracing Life with a Finger" (Caldwell), **I:** 291

Tracker (Wagoner), **Supp. IX:** 329, **336–337**

"Tracking" (Wagoner), **Supp. IX:** 329

"Track Meet, The" (Schwartz), **Supp. II Part 2:** 665

Tracks (Erdrich), **Supp. IV Part 1:** 259, 262–263, 269, 272, 273–274, 274, 275

"Tract" (W. C. Williams), **Retro. Supp. I:** 414

"Tract against Communism, A" (Twelve Southerners), **IV:** 125, 237

Tractatus (Wittgenstein), **Supp. XVII:** 143

Tracy, Benjamin, **Supp. XVIII:** 4

Tracy, D. H., **Supp. XVIII:** 178

Tracy, Lee, **IV:** 287, 288

Tracy, Steven, **Retro. Supp. I:** 195

"Trade, The" (Levine), **Supp. V:** 193

Trading Twelves (Callahan and Murray, eds.), **Retro. Supp. II:** 119

Trading Twelves: The Selected Letters of Ralph Ellison and Albert Murray (Murray and Callahan, eds.), **Supp. XIX:** 148, 158

" 'Traditional' Marriage: A Secular Affair" (P. N. Warren), **Supp. XX:** 273

"Tradition and Industrialization" (Wright), **IV:** 489–490

"Tradition and Mythology: Signatures of Landscape in Chicana Poetry" (Rebolledo), **Supp. XIII:** 214

"Tradition and the Individual Talent" (Eliot), **I:** 441, 574, 585; **Retro. Supp. I:** 59, 286

Tragedies, Life and Letters of James Gates Percival (Swinburne), **Supp. I Part 2:** 422

Tragedy of Bees, A (P. N. Warren), **Supp. XX: 261**

"Tragedy of Bees, A" (P. N. Warren), **Supp. XX: 272**

Tragedy of Don Ippolito, The (Howells), **II:** 279

"Tragedy of Error, A" (James), **II:** 322; **Retro. Supp. I:** 218

Tragedy of Pudd'nhead Wilson, The (Twain), **IV:** 206–207

Tragic America (Dreiser), **Retro. Supp. II:** 95

"Tragic Dialogue" (Wylie), **Supp. I Part 2:** 724

Tragic Ground (Caldwell), **I:** 297, 306

Tragic Muse, The (James), **Retro. Supp. I:** 227

Traherne, Thomas, **IV:** 151; **Supp. III Part 1:** 14; **Supp. V:** 208; **Supp. XV:** 212; **Supp. XVI:** 282, 288, 295

"Trail, The" (W. J. Smith), **Supp. XIII:** 342

Trailerpark (Banks), **Supp. V:** 12

"Trailing Arbutus, The" (Whittier), **Supp. I Part 2:** 691

Trail of the Lonesome Pine, The (Fox), **Supp. XIII:** 166

"Train, The" (O'Connor), **Retro. Supp. II:** 225

"Train Dreams" (Berrigan), **Supp. XXIV:** 45

"Train Ride" (Berrigan), **Supp. XXIV:** 42, 43–44

"Train Rising Out of the Sea" (Ashbery), **Supp. III Part 1:** 22

"Trains" (Banks), **Supp. V:** 8

"Train Tune" (Bogan), **Supp. III Part 1:** 64

Train Whistle Guitar (Murray), **Supp. XIX: 153–155,** 157

"Traits of Indian Character" (Irving), **II:** 303

Trakl, Georg, **Supp. XVII:** 241

Tramp Abroad, A (Twain), **IV:** 200

Tramping With a Poet in the Rockies (S. Graham), **Supp. I Part 2:** 397

Tramp's Excuse, The (Lindsay), **Supp. I Part 2:** 379, 380, 382

"Trance, The" (Taggard), **Supp. XXII:** 280

"Transaction" (Cliff), **Supp. XXII:** 75

"Transatlantic" (Toomer), **Supp. III Part 2:** 486

Transatlantic Sketches (James), **II:** 324; **Retro. Supp. I:** 219

"Transcendental Etude" (Rich), **Supp. I Part 2:** 576

"Transcontinental Highway" (Cowley), **Supp. II Part 1:** 141

"Transducer" (Ammons), **Supp. VII:** 28

"Transfiguration" (Jarman), **Supp. XVII:** 118, 119

"Transfigured Bird" (Merrill), **Supp. III Part 1:** 320–321

"Transformations" (Harjo), **Supp. XII:** 226

Transformations (Sexton), **Supp. II Part 2:** 689–691; **Supp. IV Part 2:** 447; **Supp. XIV:** 125

Transforming Madness: New Lives for People Living with Mental Illness (Neugeboren), **Supp. XVI:** 229

"Transit" (Conroy), **Supp. XVI:** 72

Transit to Narcissus, A (Mailer), **Retro. Supp. II:** 196

"Translation" (Espaillat), **Supp. XXI:** 107

"Translation and Transposition" (Carne-Ross), **Supp. I Part 1:** 268–269

"Translation of a Fragment of Simonides" (Bryant), **Supp. I Part 1:** 153, 155

"Translations" (Rich), **Supp. I Part 2:** 563

Translations of Ezra Pound, The (Kenner, ed.), **III:** 463

Translations of the Gospel Back into Tongues (Wright), **Supp. XV: 342– 343,** 346

"Translator's Task, The"(Benjamin), **Supp. XXIII:** 28

"Trans-National America" (Bourne), **I:** 229, 230

"Transparency" (X. J. Kennedy), **Supp. XV:** 159–160

"Transparent Itineraries: 1983" (Sobin), **Supp. XVI:** 287

"Transparent Itineraries: 1984" (Sobin), **Supp. XVI:** 287

"Transparent Itineraries: 1992" (Sobin), **Supp. XVI:** 289

"Transparent Itineraries" poems (Sobin), **Supp. XVI:** 290

Transparent Man, The (Hecht), **Supp. X:** 57, **69–71**

"Transparent Man, The" (Hecht), **Supp. X: 69–70**

Transparent Things (Nabokov), **Retro. Supp. I:** 266, 270, 277

"Transport" (Simic), **Supp. VIII:** 282

Transport to Summer (Stevens), **IV:** 76, 93; **Retro. Supp. I:** 309–312

Tranströmer, Thomas, **Supp. IV Part 2:** 648

"Traps for the Unwary" (Bourne), **I:** 235

Trash Trilogy (McMurtry), **Supp. V:** 225–226, 231

Traub, James, **Supp. XXIV:** 221, 222

Traubel, Horace, **IV:** 350

"Travel: After a Death" (Kenyon), **Supp. VII:** 169

Travel Alarm (Nye), **Supp. XIII:** 277

"Traveled World, The" (Pickering), **Supp. XXI:** 203

"Traveler, The" (Haines), **Supp. XII:** 203–204, 210

"Traveler, The" (Stegner), **Supp. IV Part 2:** 605

Traveler at Forty, A (Dreiser), **I:** 515

Traveler from Altruria, a Romance A, (Howells), **II:** 285, 287

Traveler's Tree, The: New and Selected Poems (W. J. Smith), **Supp. XIII:** 332, 347

"Traveling" (Paley), **Supp. VI:** 230

"Traveling Light" (Wagoner), **Supp. IX:** 329

Traveling Mercies: Some Thoughts on Faith (Lamott), **Supp. XX: 132, 140– 142**

"Traveling Onion, The" (Nye), **Supp. XIII:** 276

Traveling through the Dark (Stafford), **Supp. XI:** 311, 316, **318–321**

"Traveling through the Dark" (Stafford), **Supp. XI:** 318–320, 321, 323, 329

Travelling in Amherst: A Poet's Journal, 1931–1954, **Supp. IX:** 88–89

Travelling Standing Still: Poems, 1918– 1928 (Taggard), **Supp. XXII:** 278

Travelling Thirds, The (Atherton), **Supp. XXIV:** 23

Travels in Alaska (Muir), **Supp. IX:** 182, 185–186

"Travels in Georgia" (McPhee), **Supp. III Part 1:** 293–294

"Travels in North America" (Kees), **Supp. XV:** 133–134

Travels in the Congo (Gide), **III:** 210

"Travels in the South" (Ortiz), **Supp. IV Part 2:** 506

Travels with Charley (Steinbeck), **IV:** 52

"Travel Writing: Why I Bother" (Theroux), **Supp. VIII:** 310

Travis, Merle, **Supp. V:** 335

Travisano, Thomas, **Retro. Supp. II:** 40

Treadway, Jessica, **Supp. XXIII:** 280

Treasure Hunt (Buechner), **Supp. XII:** 52

Treasure Island (Stevenson), **Supp. X:** 230

Treasure of the Humble, The (Maeterlinck), **Supp. XX: 116**

"Treasure of the Redwoods, A" (Harte), **Supp. II Part 1:** 337

Treasury of Art Masterpieces, A: From the Renaissance to the Present Day (Craven), **Supp. XII:** 44

Treasury of English Aphorisms, A (L. P. Smith), **Supp. XIV:** 344

Treasury of English Prose, A (L. P. Smith, ed.), **Supp. XIV:** 341

Treasury of the Theatre, A (Gassner), **Supp. I Part 1:** 292

Treasury of Yiddish Stories, A (Howe and Greenberg, eds.), **Supp. I Part 2:** 432; **Supp. XXIII:** 7

Treat 'Em Rough (Lardner), **II:** 422–423

Treatise Concerning Religious Affections (Edwards), **I:** 547, 552, 554, 555, 557, 558, 560, 562

Treatise Concerning the Lord's Supper (Doolittle), **IV:** 150

"Treatise on Poetry" (Milosz), **Supp. VIII:** 20

Treatise on Right and Wrong, A (Mencken), **III:** 110, 119

"Treatise on Tales of Horror, A" (Wilson), **IV:** 438

Treatise on the Gods, A (Mencken), **III:** 108–109, 119

"Treatment" (Wright), **Supp. XV:** 343

Trece poetas del mundo azteca (León-Portilla), **Supp. XV:** 77

Tre Croce (Tozzi), **Supp. III Part 2:** 616

"Tree, a Rock, a Cloud, A" (McCullers), **II:** 587

"Tree, The" (Pound), **Retro. Supp. I:** 286; **Supp. I Part 1:** 255

"Tree, the Bird, The" (Roethke), **III:** 548

"Tree at My Window" (Frost), **II:** 155

Tree Grows in Brooklyn, A (B. Smith), **Supp. XVII:** 9; **Supp. XXIII:** 257, **259–264,** 265, 271

Tree Grows in Brooklyn, A (film; Kazan), **Supp. XVI:** 193

"Tree House at Night, The" (Dickey), **Supp. IV Part 1:** 179

"Tree House"(Thompson), **Supp. XXIII:** 301

Tree Is Older Than You Are, The (Nye, ed.), **Supp. XIII:** 280

"Tree of Laughing Bells, The" (Lindsay), **Supp. I Part 2:** 376

"Tree of Life, The" (Swados), **Supp. XIX:** 268

"Tree of Night, A" (Capote), **Supp. III Part 1:** 114, 120

Tree of Night and Other Stories, A (Capote), **Supp. III Part 1:** 114

"Trees, The" (Rich), **Supp. I Part 2:** 555

Trees, The (Richter), **Supp. XVIII: 212–213, 220**

"Trees Listening to Bach" (Merrill), **Supp. III Part 1:** 336

Tree That Came to Stay, The (Quindlen), **Supp. XVII:** 167

Tree Where Man Was Born, The (Matthiessen), **Supp. V:** 199, 203, 204

Trejo, Ernesto, **Supp. V:** 178, 180; **Supp. XIII:** 313, 316; **Supp. XV:** 73

Trelawny, Edward John, **Supp. I Part 2:** 721

"Trellis for R., A" (Swenson), **Supp. IV Part 2:** 647

Tremblay, Bill, **Supp. XIII:** 112

Tremble (Wright), **Supp. XV: 348–349**

"Trespass" (Frost), **Retro. Supp. I:** 139

Trespassing (Pickering), **Supp. XXI:** 202

"Trespassing" (Pickering), **Supp. XXI:** 202

Trethewey, Eric, **Supp. XXI:** 243, 244

Trethewey, Natasha, **Supp. XXI: 243–259**

"Tretitoli, Where the Bomb Group Was" (Hugo), **Supp. VI:** 138

Trevelyan, Robert C., **Supp. XIV:** 334

Trevor-Roper, Hugh, **Supp. XIV:** 348

Trial, The (Kafka), **IV:** 113; **Retro. Supp. II:** 20

"Trial, The" (Rukeyser), **Supp. VI:** 278

"Trial by Existence, The" (Frost), **II:** 166

"Trial for Arson, The"(Hadas), **Supp. XXIII:** 114

Trial of a Poet, The (Shapiro), **Supp. II Part 2:** 710

Trial of the Hawk, The: A Comedy of the Seriousness of Life (Lewis), **II:** 441

Trials of the Human Heart (Rowson), **Supp. XV:** 237, 239

Tribal Secrets: Recovering American Indian Intellectual Traditions (Warrior), **Supp. IV Part 1:** 329

"Tribute" (A. Finch), **Supp. XVII:** 72, 73–74

"Tribute, A" (Easton), **Supp. IV Part 2:** 461

"Tribute, The" (Doolittle), **Supp. I Part 1:** 267

"Tribute (To My Mother)" (Cullen), **Supp. IV Part 1:** 166

Tribute to Freud (Doolittle), **Supp. I Part 1:** 253, 254, 258, 259, 260, 268

Tribute to the Angels (Doolittle), **Supp. I Part 1:** 272

"Trick on the World, A" (Ríos), **Supp. IV Part 2:** 553

"Tricks" (Olds), **Supp. X:** 203–204

"Trick Scenery" (F. Barthelme), **Supp. XI:** 26

Trifler, The (Masters), **Supp. I Part 2:** 459–460

Trifles (Glaspell), **Supp. III Part 1:** 175, 178, 179, 182, 186, 187; **Supp. X:** 46; **Supp. XXI:** 12

Trifonov, Iurii V., **Retro. Supp. I:** 278

Triggering Town, The: Lectures and Essays on Poetry and Writing (Hugo), **Supp. VI:** 133, 140

Trilling, Diana, **II:** 587, 600; **Supp. I Part 1:** 297; **Supp. XII:** 126; **Supp. XXI:** 271, 275

Trilling, Lionel, **I:** 48; **II:** 579; **III:** 308, 310, 319, 327; **IV:** 201, 211; **Retro. Supp. I:** 19, 97, 121, 216, 227; **Supp. III Part 2: 493–515; Supp. V:** 259; **Supp. VIII:** 93, 98, 190, 231, 236, 243; **Supp. IX:** 266, 287; **Supp. XIII:** 100–101; **Supp. XIV:** 280, 288–289; **Supp. XV:** 20, 140, 152

Trilogy (Doolittle), **Supp. I Part 1:** 271, 272

Trilogy of Desire (Dreiser), **I:** 497, 508; **Retro. Supp. II:** 94, 96, **101–102**

Trimberger, Ellen Kay, **Supp. XVII:** 96, 106; **Supp. XXI:** 12

Trimmed Lamp, The (O. Henry), **Supp. II Part 1:** 410

"Trinc" (McGrath), **Supp. X:** 127

Trinity (Uris), **Supp. XX: 243, 244, 245, 246, 247, 248, 253, 254–255**

Trio (Baker), **Supp. I Part 1:** 277

Trio (Saroyan), **Supp. XXII:** 25

"Triolets for Triolet" (Nelson), **Supp. XVIII:** 179

"Trip" (F. Barthelme), *Supp. XI:* 26

Triple Thinkers, The: Ten Essays on Literature (Wilson), **IV:** 428, 431; **Supp. II Part 1:** 146

"Triplex" (Doolittle), **Supp. I Part 1:** 271

Tripmaster Monkey: His Fake Book (Kingston), **Supp. V:** 157, 158, 169, 170–173

Trippings in Authorland (Forrester), **Supp. XVIII:** 13

Trippings of Tom Pepper, The (Briggs), **Supp. XVIII:** 3, **13–14**

"Trip to Hanoi" (Sontag), **Supp. III Part 2:** 460–462

Trip to Parnassus, A; or, The Judgement of Apollo on Dramatic Authors and Performers (Rowson), **Supp. XV: 232–233**

"Triptych" (Eberhart), **I:** 522, 539

Tristam Shandy (Sterne), **Supp. XXII:** 267

Tristan and Iseult, **Retro. Supp. I:** 328, 329, 330, 331

Tristessa (Kerouac), **Supp. III Part 1:** 225, 227, 229

Tristram (Robinson), **III:** 521, 522, 523

Tristram Shandy (Sterne), **I:** 299; **IV:** 465–466; **Supp. V:** 127; **Supp. XVIII:** 60

"Triumph" (C. L. R. James), **Supp. XXI:** 160

"Triumphal March" (Eliot), **I:** 580; **III:** 17; **Retro. Supp. I:** 64

Triumph of Achilles, The (Glück), **Supp. V:** 79, 84–86, 92

"Triumph of a Modern, The, or, Send for the Lawyer" (Anderson), **I:** 113, 114

"Triumph of the Egg, The" (Anderson), **I:** 113

Triumph of the Egg, The: A Book of Impressions from American Life in Tales and Poems (Anderson), **I:** 112, 114

Triumph of the Spider Monkey, The (Oates), **Supp. II Part 2:** 522

Triumphs of the Reformed Religion in America (Mather), **Supp. II Part 2:** 453

Trivial Breath (Wylie), **Supp. I Part 2:** 709, 722–724

Trivia; or, the Art of Walking the Streets of London (Gay), **Supp. XIV:** 337

Trivia: Printed from the Papers of Anthony Woodhouse, Esq. (L. P. Smith), **Supp. XIV:** 336, **337–340**

"Trivia Tea" (Skloot), **Supp. XX:** 205

Trocchi, Alexander, **Supp. XI:** 294, 295, 301

Troilus and Criseyde (Chaucer), **Retro. Supp. I:** 426

Trois contes (Flaubert), **IV:** 31, 37

Trojan Horse, The: A Play (MacLeish), **III:** 21

"Trojan Women, The" (Maxwell), **Supp. VIII:** 169

Troll Garden, The (Cather), **I:** 313, 314–316, 322; **Retro. Supp. I:** 5, 6, 8, 14

"Trolling for Blues" (Wilbur), **Supp. III Part 2:** 563–564

Trollope, Anthony, **I:** 10, 375; **II:** 192, 237; **III:** 51, 70, 281, 382; **Retro. Supp. I:** 361

Trombly, Albert Edmund, **Supp. I Part 2:** 403

Trombold, John, **Supp. XVIII:** 111

"Trompe L'Oeil" (Collins), **Supp. XXI:** 60

"Troop Train" (Shapiro), **Supp. II Part 2:** 707

"Tropes of the Text" (Gass), **Supp. VI:** 88

Tropic of Cancer (H. Miller), **III:** 170, 171, 174, 177, 178–180, 181, 182, 183, 187, 190; **Supp. V:** 119; **Supp. X:** 187; **Supp. XXII:** 230, 257

Tropic of Capricorn (H. Miller), **III:** 170, 176–177, 178, 182, 183, 184, 187, 188–189, 190

"Tropic of Cuba" (di Donato), **Supp. XX: 45**

Trotsky, Leon, **I:** 366; **II:** 562, 564; **IV:** 429; **Supp. XXI:** 161, 164, 165, 167, 168

Trotter, W., **I:** 249

Troubled Air, The (Shaw), **Supp. XIX: 249–250**

Troubled Island (opera; Hughes and Still), **Retro. Supp. I:** 203

Troubled Lovers in History (Goldbarth), **Supp. XII:** 176, **192–193**

Trouble Follows Me (Macdonald, under Millar), **Supp. IV Part 2:** 466

Trouble in July (Caldwell), **I:** 297, 304–305, 306, 309

Trouble Island (Hughes), **Supp. I Part 1:** 328

"Trouble of Marcie Flint, The" (Cheever), **Supp. I Part 1:** 186

Trouble with Francis, The: An Autobiography (Francis), **Supp. IX:** 76, 77, 82, **84–85**

Trouble with God, The (Francis), **Supp. IX:** 88

"Trouble with Poetry, The" (Collins), **Supp. XXI:** 57

Trouble with Poetry and Other Poems, The (Collins), **Supp. XXI:** 55, 57, 62

"Trouble with the Stars and Stripes" (Nye), **Supp. XIII:** 277

Trouillot, Michel-Rolphe, **Supp. X:** 14–15

Troupe, Quincy, **Retro. Supp. II:** 15, 111; **Supp. X:** 242

"Trout" (Hugo), **Supp. VI:** 135

Trout Fishing in America (Brautigan), **Supp. VIII:** 43

"Trouvée" (Bishop), **Retro. Supp. II:** 49

Troy (film), **Supp. XX: 273**

"Truce" (Taggard), **Supp. XXII:** 276–277

"Truce of the Bishop, The" (Frederic), **II:** 139–140

"Truck Stop: Minnesota" (Dunn), **Supp. XI:** 145–146

Trudeau, Garry, **Supp. XXIV:** 283

True Account, The: A Novel of the Lewis & Clark & Kinneson Expeditions (Mosher), **Supp. XXII:** 206, 207, 208, **214–215**

True and False: Heresy and Common Sense for the Actor (Mamet), **Supp. XIV:** 241, 243

True Blood (television series), **Supp. XIX:** 174

Trueblood, Valerie, **Supp. XIII:** 306

True Confessions (Dunne), **Supp. IV Part 1:** 198

True Confessions (film), **Supp. IV Part 1:** 198

Trueheart, Charles, **Supp. XXI:** 238

True History of the Conquest of New Spain, The (Castillo), **III:** 13

True Intellectual System of the Universe, The (Cuddleworth), **II:** 10

"True Love" (Olds), **Supp. X:** 212

Trueman, Matthew (pseudonym). *See* Lowell, James Russell

"True Morality" (Bell), **Supp. X:** 13

"True Romance" (Everett), **Supp. XVIII:** 65

Truesdale, C. W., **Supp. XXI:** 246

True Stories (Atwood), **Supp. XIII:** 34–35

"True Stories" (Atwood), **Supp. XIII:** 34

"True Stories of Bitches" (Mamet), **Supp. XIV:** 246, 252

"Truest Sport, The: Jousting with Sam and Charlie" (Wolfe), **Supp. III Part 2:** 581–582

"True Vine" (Wylie), **Supp. I Part 2:** 723

True West (Shepard), **Supp. III Part 2:** 433, 441, 445, 447, 448

Truman, Harry, **III:** 3

Truman Capote: In Which Various Friends, Enemies, Acquaintances, and Detractors Recall His Turbulent Career (Plimpton), **Supp. XVI:**245

Truman Show, The (film), **Supp. XVI:** 271

Trumbo, Dalton, **Supp. I Part 1:** 295; **Supp. XIII:** 6; **Supp. XVII:** 63; **Supp.**

XX: 246; Supp. XXI: 45

Trumbull, John, **Supp. II Part 1:** 65, 69, 70, 268

Trump, Donald, **Supp. IV Part 1:** 393

Trumpener, Katie, **Retro. Supp. I:** 380

"Trumpet Player" (Hughes), **Supp. I Part 1:** 333

"Trumpet Player, 1963" (Halliday), **Supp. XIX:** 92

Trumpet Shall Sound, The (Wilder), **IV:** 356

Trumpet Unblown, The (Hoffman), **Supp. XVIII:** 71, **74–75**

Trunk Music (Connelly), **Supp. XXI: 72,** 75

"Truro Bear, The" (Oliver), **Supp. VII:** 234

Truscott, Lucian K., **Supp. IV Part 2:** 683

Trust (Ozick), **Supp. V:** 257–258, 259, 260–263, 270, 272

Trust Me (Updike), **Retro. Supp. I:** 322

"Trust Yourself" (Emerson), **II:** 10

"Truth" (Emerson), **II:** 6

"Truth, The" (Halliday), **Supp. XIX:** 87, 88, 94

"Truth, The" (Jarrell), **II:** 381–382

Truth About Celia, The (Brockmeier), **Supp. XXII: 53–55**

"Truth about God, The" (Carson), **Supp. XII: 105–106**

"Truth be told" (Trethewey), **Supp. XXI:** 255, 256

"Truthful James" (Harte), **IV:** 196

"Truth Is, The" (Hogan), **Supp. IV Part 1:** 401–402

"Truth Is Forced, The" (Swenson), **Supp. IV Part 2:** 652

"Truth of the Matter, The" (Nemerov), **III:** 270

Truth Serum (Cooper), **Supp. XI:** 129

"Truth the Dead Know, The" (Sexton), **Supp. II Part 2:** 681

"Trying to Evangelize a Cut Flower" (Peacock), **Supp. XIX:** 199

Trying to Find Chinatown (Hwang), **Supp. XXI:** 147

Trying to Save Piggy Sneed (Irving), **Supp. VI: 19–165**

"Trying to Talk with a Man" (Rich), **Supp. I Part 2:** 559

"Tryptich I" (Bell), **Supp. X:** 7

"Tryst, The" (Wharton), **Retro. Supp. I:** 378

"Try the Girl" (Chandler), **Supp. IV Part 1:** 125

Try! Try! (O'Hara), **Supp. XXIII:** 209, 210, 216

"Ts'ai Chih" (Pound), **III:** 466

T. S. Eliot and American Philosophy (Jain), **Retro. Supp. I:** 58

T. S. Eliot's Silent Voices (Mayer), **Retro. Supp. I:** 58

Tsuji, Shizuo, **Supp. XVII:** 90

Tsurikgekumen (The return) (Asch), **Supp. XXIII:** 5

Tsvetaeva, Marina, **Supp. VIII:** 30; **Supp. XXIII:** 168

"Tuberoses" (E. Stoddard), **Supp. XV:** 282

Tubert, Susana, **Supp. XXIII:** 203

Tucker, Benjamin R., **Supp. XXI:** 9

Tuckerman, Frederick Goddard, **IV:** 144

Tucker's People (Wolfert), **Supp. XXI:** 261, 262, 263, 267, **267–275,** 278

"Tuesday, November 5th, 1940" (Benét), **Supp. XI:** 46, 52

"Tuesday April 25th 1966" (Olson), **Supp. II Part 2:** 585

"Tuesday Night at the Savoy Ballroom" (Komunyakaa), **Supp. XIII:** 132

Tuffield, Aviva, **Supp. XVI:** 147, 148

"Tuft of Flowers, The" (Frost), **II:** 153; **Retro. Supp. I:** 126, 127

Tufts, James Hayden, **Supp. I Part 2:** 632

Tu Fu, **II:** 526; **Supp. XV:** 47

Tu Fu (Ayscough), **II:** 527

Tugwell, Rexford Guy, **Supp. I Part 2:** 645

"Tulip" (Hammett), **Supp. IV Part 1:** 356

"Tulip Man, The" (McCarriston), **Supp. XIV:** 261

"Tulips" (Nye), **Supp. XIII:** 281

"Tulips" (Plath), **Retro. Supp. II:** 252–253; **Supp. I Part 2:** 540, 542, 544

"Tulips" (Snodgrass), **Supp. VI:** 325

Tulips and Chimneys (Cummings), **I:** 436, 437, 440, 445, 447

"Tulips"(Strout), **Supp. XXIII:** 283, 285

"Tulips"(theater performance, Strout), **Supp. XXIII:** 281

Tully, Jim, **III:** 103, 109

Tumble Home (Hempel), **Supp. XXI:** 115, **124–125**

"Tumble Home" (Hempel), **Supp. XXI:** 115, 116, **124–125,** 126

Tumble Tower (Modarressi and Tyler), **Supp. IV Part 2:** 657

"Tuned in Late One Night" (Stafford), **Supp. XI:** 327–328

Tunnel, The (Gass), **Supp. V:** 44; **Supp. VI: 89–91,** 94

"Tunnel, The" (Strand), **Supp. IV Part 2:** 622

"Tunnels" (Komunyakaa), **Supp. XIII:** 123

Tuqan, Fadwa, **Supp. XIII:** 278

Tura, Cosimo, **III:** 474–475

Turandot and Other Poems (Ashbery), **Supp. III Part 1:** 3

Turco, Lewis, **Supp. XV:** 118

Turgenev, Ivan Sergeevich, **I:** 106; **II:** 263, 271, 275, 280, 281, 288, 319, 320, 324–325, 338, 407; **III:** 461; **IV:** 17, 277; **Retro. Supp. I:** 215, 222; **Supp. VIII:** 167

Turgot, Anne Robert Jacques, **II:** 103; **Supp. I Part 2:** 250

"Turkey and Bones and Eating and We Liked It" (Stein), **IV:** 44

Turman, Glynn, **Supp. IV Part 1:** 362

Turnbull, Dr. George, **II:** 113

Turnbull, Lawrence, **Supp. I Part 1:** 352

"Turned" (Gilman), **Supp. XI:** 207

Turner, Addie, **IV:** 123

Turner, Darwin, **Supp. I Part 1:** 339; **Supp. IV Part 1:** 165

Turner, Frederick Jackson, **Supp. I Part 2:** 480, 481, 632, 640; **Supp. IV Part 2:** 596

Turner, Nat, **IV:** 113–114, 115, 116, 117

Turner, Patricia A., **Supp. XIII:** 237; **Supp. XX:** 110

Turner, Russell. *See* Lacy, Ed

Turner, Victor, **Supp. IV Part 1:** 304

"Turning Away Variations on Estrangement" (Dickey), **Supp. IV Part 1:** 183

Turning Point, The (McCoy), **Supp. XIII:** 175

"Turning Thirty, I Contemplate Students Bicycling Home" (Dove), **Supp. IV Part 1:** 250

Turning Wind, A (Rukeyser), **Supp. VI:** 272–273, 279–280

Turn in the South, A (Naipaul), **Supp. XXII:** 240

Turn of the Screw, The (H. James), **Retro. Supp. I:** 219, 231; **Supp. IV Part 2:** 682

"Turn of the Screw, The" (H. James), **II:** 331–332; **Retro. Supp. I:** 228, 229, 231, 232; **Supp. XVII:** 143

Turns and Movies and Other Tales in Verse (Aiken), **I:** 65

"Turn with the Sun, A" (Knowles), **Supp. XII:** 237–238

"Turn Your Radio On" (J. W. Miller), **Supp. XX:** 169

Turow, Scott, **Supp. V:** 220; **Supp. XVII:** 213–224

"Turpentine" (Gallagher), **Supp. XXIV:** 174, 175, 176

Turpin, E. Walters, **Supp. XVIII:** 283

Turrinus, Lucius Mamilius, **IV:** 373

"Turtle" (Hogan), **Supp. IV Part 1:** 401

Turtle, Swan (Doty), **Supp. XI:** 121–122

"Turtle, Swan" (Doty), **Supp. XI:** 121–122

Turtle Island (Snyder), **Supp. VIII:** 300–303

Turtle Moon (Hoffman), **Supp. X:** 77, 87–88, 89

"Turtle Shrine near Chittagong, The" (Nye), **Supp. XIII:** 277

Turtotte, James, **Supp. XXIII:** 125

Turturro, John, **Supp. XI:** 174

Tuscan Cities (Howells), **II:** 280

Tuskegee movement, **Supp. II Part 1:** 169, 172

Tuten, Frederic, **Supp. VIII:** 75, 76; **Supp. XIII:** 237, 249

Tuten, James, **Supp. XVIII:** 195

Tuthill, Louisa Cavolne, **Supp. I Part 2:** 684

"Tutored Child, The" (Kunitz), **Supp. III Part 1:** 264

Tuttleton, James W., **Supp. IV Part 1:** 166, 168

"T.V.A." (Agee), **I:** 35

Tvedten, Brother Benet, **Supp. IV Part 2:** 505

"TV Men" (Carson), **Supp. XII:** 105, 112

Twain, Mark, **I:** 57, 103, 107, 109, 190, 192, 193, 195, 197, 203, 209, 245, 246, 247–250, 255, 256, 257, 260, 261, 292, 342, 418, 469, 485; **II:** 70, 140, 259, 262, 266–268, 271, 272, 274–275, 276, 277, 280, 285–286, 287, 288, 289, 301, 304, 306, 307, 312, 415, 432, 434, 436, 446, 457, 467, 475, 476, 482; **III:** 65, 101, 102, 112–113, 114, 220, 347, 357, 409, 453, 454, 504, 507, 554, 558, 572, 575, 576; **IV:** 190–213, 333, 349, 451; **Retro. Supp. I:** 169, 194, 195; **Retro. Supp. II:** 123; **Supp. I Part 1:** 37, 39, 44, 247, 251, 313, 317; **Supp. I Part 2:** 377, 385, 393, 410, 455, 456, 457, 473, 475, 579, 602, 604, 618, 629, 651, 660; **Supp. II Part 1:** 193, 344, 354, 385; **Supp. IV Part 1:** 386, 388; **Supp. IV Part 2:** 463, 468, 603, 607, 693; **Supp. V:** 44, 113, 131; **Supp. VIII:** 40, 189; **Supp. IX:** 14, 171; **Supp. X:** 51, 227; **Supp. XII:** 343; **Supp. XIII:** 1, 17; **Supp. XV:** 41; **Supp. XVI:** 66, 208; **Supp. XVIII:** 1, 9, 13; **Supp. XXI:** 205; **Supp. XXII:** 89, 203, 205, 206; **Supp. XXIII:** 85

"Twa Sisters, The" (ballad), **Supp. I Part 2:** 696

Twelfth Night (Shakespeare), **Supp. IV Part 1:** 83; **Supp. IX:** 14; **Supp. XXII:** 229

"12 O'Clock News" (Bishop), **Retro. Supp. II:** 48

Twelve Men (Dreiser), **Retro. Supp. II:** 94, 104

Twelve Moons (Oliver), **Supp. VII:** 231, 233–236, 238, 240

Twelve Southerners, **IV:** 125; **Supp. X:** 25

Twelve Years a Slave (Northup), **Supp. XIV:** 32

Twentieth Century Authors, **I:** 376, 527

"Twentieth Century Fiction and the Black Mask of Humanity" (Ellison), **Retro. Supp. II:** 118

Twentieth Century Pleasures (Hass), **Supp. VI:** 103, 106, 109

Twenty Drawings (Gibran), **Supp. XX:** 116

"28" (Levine), **Supp. V:** 187, 191

"Twenty-Four Poems" (Schwartz), **Supp. II Part 2:** 646, 649

"2433 Agnes, First Home, Last House in Missoula" (Hugo), **Supp. VI:** 139–140

"Twenty Hill Hollow" (Muir), **Supp. IX:** 178

Twenty Love Poems and a Song of Despair (Neruda), **Supp. XXIV:** 170

"Twenty Minutes" (Salter), **Supp. IX:** 260

"Twenty-One Love Poems" (Rich), **Supp. I Part 2:** 572–573

"Twenty-One Poems" (MacLeish), **III:** 19

Twenty Poems (Haines), **Supp. XII:** 204, 205–206

Twenty Poems of Anna Akhmatova (Kenyon), **Supp. VII:** 165–166

Twenty Questions: (Posed by Poems) (McClatchy), **Supp. XII:** 254, 259–262

27 Wagons Full of Cotton and Other One-Act Plays (T. Williams), **IV:** 381, 383

Twenty-seventh City, The (Franzen), **Supp. XX:** 83–84, 84, 85, 86–88, 88, 89, 91, 92, 95

Twenty Thousand Leagues under the Sea (Verne), **I:** 480; **Supp. XI:** 63

"Twenty Years Ago" (Lindsay), **Supp. I Part 2:** 384, 399

Twenty Years at Hull-House (Addams), **Supp. I Part 1:** 3, 4, 11, 16

Twersky, David, **Supp. XX:** 244

Twice over Lightly: New York Ten and Now (Hayes and Loos), **Supp. XVI:** 195

Twice-Told Tales (Hawthorne), **I:** 354; **II:** 224; **III:** 412, 421; **Retro. Supp. I:** 154–155, 160

Twichell, Chase, **Supp. V:** 16; **Supp. XVII:** 110, 112

Twilight (Frost), **II:** 151

"Twilight's Last Gleaming" (Burroughs and Elvins), **Supp. III Part 1:** 93, 94, 101

Twilight Sleep (Wharton), **IV:** 320–322, 324–325, 327, 328; **Retro. Supp. I:** 381

"Twin, The" (Olds), **Supp. X:** 207

"Twin Beds in Rome" (Updike), **Retro. Supp. I:** 332

"Twins of Table Mountain, The" (Harte), **Supp. II Part 1:** 355

"Twist, The" (Olson), **Supp. II Part 2:** 570

Twitch and Shout (film), **Supp. XVIII:** 143

Twitchell-Waas, Jeffrey, **Supp. XVIII:** 99; **Supp. XXII:** 163

Two Admirals, The (Cooper), **I:** 350

Two against One (F. Barthelme), **Supp. XI:** 32, 33, 36

"Two and One"(Hadas), **Supp. XXIII:** 114–115

"Two Boys" (Moore), **Supp. X:** 173

"Two Brothers, The" (Jewett), **Retro. Supp. II:** 132

Two-Character Play, The (T. Williams), **IV:** 382, 386, 393, 398

Two Citizens (Wright), **Supp. III Part 2:** 602–604

"Two Deer" (Bass), **Supp. XVI:** 24

"Two Domains, The" (Goldbarth), **Supp. XII:** 192

"Two-Eleven All Around" (Offutt), **Supp. XIX:** 170

"Two Environments, The" (Trilling), **Supp. III Part 2:** 510

"Two-Fisted Self Pity" (Broyard), **Supp. XI:** 348

Two for Texas (Burke), **Supp. XIV:** 25, 34

"Two Friends" (Cather), **I:** 332

"Two Gardens in Linndale" (Robinson), **III:** 508

Two Gentlemen in Bonds (Ransom), **III:** 491–492

Two: Gertrude Stein and Her Brother (Stein), **IV:** 43

"Two Ghosts" (Francis), **Supp. IX:** 87

"Two Hangovers" (Wright), **Supp. III Part 2:** 596

Two-Headed Poems (Atwood), **Supp. XIII:** 34

Two Hot to Handle (Lacy), **Supp. XV:** 206

Two Hours to Doom (Bryant), **Supp. XI:** 302

"Two Hundred Years in an Hour" (Boyce), **Supp. XXI:** 8

"Two Kitchens in Provence" (M. F. K. Fisher), **Supp. XVII:** 88, 91

"Two Ladies in Retirement" (Taylor), **Supp. V:** 320

Two Letters to the Citizens of the United States, and One to General Washington (Barlow), **Supp. II Part 1:** 80

"Two Lives, The" (Hogan), **Supp. IV Part 1:** 400, 402, 403, 406, 411

Two Long Poems (Stern), **Supp. IX:** 296

"Two Look at Two" (Frost), **Supp. XXI:** 26

"Two Lovers and a Beachcomber by the Real Sea" (Plath), **Supp. I Part 2:** 536

"Two Men" (McClatchy)", **Supp. XII:** 269

Two Men (E. Stoddard), **Supp. XV:** 272, 273, **283–284**

Two Men of Sandy Bar (Harte), **Supp. II Part 1:** 354

Twomey, Jay, **Supp. XVII:** 111

"Two Moods of Love" (Cullen), **Supp. IV Part 1:** 166

Two Moons (Mallon), **Supp. XIX:** 132, **138–141**

"Two Morning Monologues" (Bellow), **I:** 150; **Retro. Supp. II:** 20

"Two Nations of Black America, The" *(Frontline),* **Supp. XX:** 99

Two-Ocean War, The (Morison), **Supp. I Part 2:** 491

"Two of Hearts" (Hogan), **Supp. IV Part 1:** 410

"Two on a Party" (T. Williams), **IV:** 388

"Two or Three Things I Dunno About John Cassavetes" (Lethem), **Supp. XVIII:** 148

"Two Pendants: For the Ears" (W. C. Williams), **Retro. Supp. I:** 423

"Two Poems of Going Home" (Dickey), **Supp. IV Part 1:** 182–183

"Two Portraits" (Chopin), **Supp. I Part 1:** 218

"Two Presences, The" (R. Bly), **Supp. IV Part 1:** 65

"Two Rivers" (Stegner), **Supp. IV Part 2:** 605

Tworkov, Jack, **Supp. XII:** 198

"Two Scenes" (Ashbery), **Supp. III Part 1:** 4

Two Serious Ladies (Jane Bowles), **Supp. IV Part 1:** 82

"Two Silences" (Carruth), **Supp. XVI:** 55

"Two Sisters" (Farrell), **II:** 45

Two Sisters: A Memoir in the Form of a Novel (Vidal), **Supp. IV Part 2:** 679

"Two Sisters of Persephone" (Plath), **Retro. Supp. II:** 246

"Two Songs on the Economy of Abundance" (Agee), **I:** 28

Two Sons, The (Boyce), **Supp. XXI:** 7, 13

"Two Tales of Clumsy" (Schnackenberg), **Supp. XV:** 258

"Two Temples, The" (Melville), **III:** 89–90

Two Thousand Seasons (Armah), **Supp. IV Part 1:** 373

Two Towns in Provence (M. F. K. Fisher), **Supp. XVII:** 91

Two Trains Running (Wilson), **Supp. VIII:** 345–348

"Two Tramps in Mudtime" (Frost), **II:** 164; **Retro. Supp. I:** 137; **Supp. IX:** 261

"Two Twilights for William Carlos Williams" (Boyle), **Supp. XXIV:** 63

"Two Views of a Cadaver Room" (Plath), **Supp. I Part 2:** 538

"Two Villages" (Paley), **Supp. VI:** 227

"Two Voices in a Meadow" (Wilbur), **Supp. III Part 2:** 555

Two Weeks in Another Town (Shaw), **Supp. XIX:** 251

"Two Witches" (Frost), **Retro. Supp. I:** 135

"Two Words" (Francis), **Supp. IX:** 81

Two Worlds Walking: A Mixed-Blood Anthology (Glancy and Truesdale, eds.), **Supp. XXI:** 246

Two Years before the Mast (Dana), **I:** 351

"Tyger, The" (Blake), **Supp. XVII:** 128

Tyler, Anne, **Supp. IV Part 2: 657–675; Supp. V:** 227, 326; **Supp. VIII:** 141; **Supp. X:** 1, 77, 83, 85; **Supp. XII:** 307; **Supp. XVI:** 37; **Supp. XVIII:** 157, 195; **Supp. XXIII:** 298

Tyler, Royall, **I:** 344; **Retro. Supp. I:** 377

Tymms, Ralph, **Supp. IX:** 105

Tyndale, William, **II:** 15

Tyndall, John, **Retro. Supp. II:** 93

Typee: A Peep at Polynesian Life (Melville), **III:** 75–77, 79, 84; **Retro. Supp. I:** 245–246, 249, 252, 256

Types From City Streets (Hapgood), **Supp. XVII:** 103

"Typewriter, The" (D. West), **Supp. XVIII:** 279

Typewriter Town (W. J. Smith), **Supp. XIII:** 332

"Typhus" (Simpson), **Supp. IX:** 277

Tyranny of the Normal (Fiedler), **Supp. XIII: 107–108**

"Tyranny of the Normal" (Fiedler), **Supp. XIII:** 107–108

"Tyrant of Syracuse" (MacLeish), **III:** 20

"Tyrian Businesses" (Olson), **Supp. II Part 2:** 567, 568, 569

Tytell, John, **Supp. XIV:** 140

Tzara, Tristan, **Supp. III Part 1:** 104, 105

U

U and I (Baker), **Supp. XIII: 45–47,** 48, 52, 55

Überdie Seelenfrage (Fechner), **II:** 358

Ubik (Dick), **Supp. XVIII:** 136

Ubu Roi (Jarry), **Supp. XV:** 178, 186

Ueland, Brenda, **Supp. XVII:** 13

Uhry, Alfred, **Supp. XX: 177**

ukanhavyrfuckinciti back (Phillips), **Supp. XXIII:** 174

Ukrainian Dumy (P. N. Warren as Kilina and Tarnawsky, trans.), **Supp. XX: 261**

"Ulalume" (Poe), **III:** 427; **Retro. Supp. II:** 264, 266

Ulin, David, **Supp. XIII:** 244; **Supp. XVI:** 74

Ullman, Leslie, **Supp. IV Part 2:** 550; **Supp. XVIII:** 175

Ultimate Good Luck, The (Ford), **Supp. V:** 57, 61–62

Ultimate Punishment: A Lawyer's Reflections on Dealing with the Death Penalty (Turow), **Supp. XVII:** 220–221

Ultima Thule (Longfellow), **II:** 490; **Retro. Supp. II:** 169

"Ultima Thule" (Nabokov), **Retro. Supp. I:** 274

Ultramarine (Carver), **Supp. III Part 1:** 137, 138, 147, 148

Ulysses (Joyce), **I:** 395, 475–476, 478, 479, 481; **II:** 42, 264, 542; **III:** 170, 398; **IV:** 103, 418, 428, 455; **Retro. Supp. I:** 59, 63, 290, 291; **Retro. Supp. II:** 121; **Supp. I Part 1:** 57; **Supp. III Part 2:** 618, 619; **Supp. IV Part 1:** 285; **Supp. IV Part 2:** 424; **Supp. V:** 261; **Supp. IX:** 102; **Supp. X:** 114; **Supp. XIII:** 43, 191; **Supp. XV:** 305; **Supp. XVII:** 140, 227

"*Ulysses,* Order and Myth" (Eliot), **Retro. Supp. I:** 63

"Umbrella, The" (Peacock), **Supp. XIX:** 203–204

Unaccountable Worth of the World, The (Price), **Supp. VI:** 267

Unaccustomed Earth (Lahiri), **Supp. XXI:** 176, **181–183,** 183, 188

"Unaccustomed Earth" (Lahiri), **Supp. XXI:** 186

Unamuno y Jugo, Miguel de, **III:** 310; **Supp. XV:** 79

"Unattached Smile, The" (Crews), **Supp. XI:** 101

"Unbelievable Thing Usually Goes to the Heart of the Story, The: Magic Realism in the Fiction of Rick Bass" (Dwyer), **Supp. XVI:** 16

"Unbeliever, The" (Bishop), **Retro. Supp. II:** 43

"Unborn Song" (Rukeyser), **Supp. VI:** 274

Unbought Spirit: A John Jay Chapman Reader (Stone, ed.), **Supp. XIV:** 54

Uncalled, The (Dunbar), **Supp. II Part 1:** 200, 211, 212

Uncentering the Earth: Copernicus and The Revolutions of the Heavenly Spheres (Vollmann), **Supp. XVII:** 226

Uncertain Certainty, The: Interviews, Essays, and Notes on Poetry (Simic), **Supp. VIII:** 270, 273, 274

Uncertainty and Plenitude: Five Contemporary Poets (Stitt), **Supp. IX:** 299

"Uncle" (Levine), **Supp. V:** 186

"Uncle Adler" (Kooser), **Supp. XIX:** 120

"Uncle Christmas" (Ríos), **Supp. IV Part 2:** 552

"Uncle Jim's Baptist Revival Hymn" (Lanier and Lanier), **Supp. I Part 1:** 353

"Uncle Lot" (Stowe), **Supp. I Part 2:** 585–586

Uncle Moses (Asch), **Supp. XXIII:** 14

"Uncle Moustapha's Eclipse" (McKnight), **Supp. XX: 148**

Uncle Remus Tales (Harris), **Supp. II Part 1:** 201

"Uncle Tomitudes" (Briggs), **Supp. XVIII:** 14

Uncle Tom's Cabin (Stowe), **II:** 291; **Supp. I Part 1:** 49; **Supp. I Part 2:** 410, 579, 582, 589–592; **Supp. II Part 1:** 170; **Supp. III Part 1:** 154, 171; **Supp. IX:** 19; **Supp. X:** 246, 249, 250; **Supp. XIII:** 95; **Supp. XVI:** 82, 85, 88; **Supp. XVIII:** 14

Uncle Tom's Children (Wright), **IV:** 476, 478, 488; **Supp. II Part 1:** 228, 235; **Supp. XVIII:** 283

"Uncle Wiggily in Connecticut" (Salinger), **III:** 559–560, 563

"Unclouded Day, The" (Proulx), **Supp. VII:** 254–255

"Uncommon Visage" (Brodsky), **Supp. VIII:** 31

"Uncommon Woman: An Interview with Wendy Wasserstein" (Cohen), **Supp. XV:** 323

Uncommon Women and Others (Wasserstein), **Supp. XV:** 320–321, **322–323; Supp. XXIV:** 117

Uncompromising Fictions of Cynthia Ozick (Pinsker), **Supp. V:** 272

"Unconscious Came a Beauty" (Swenson), **Supp. IV Part 2:** 646

"Uncreation, The" (Pinsky), **Supp. VI:** 245

"Undead, The" (Wilbur), **Supp. III Part 2:** 556

"Undefeated, The" (Hemingway), **II:** 250; **Retro. Supp. I:** 180

Under a Glass Bell (Nin), **Supp. X:** 186

"Under Ben Bulben" (Yeats), **Supp. V:** 220

Undercliff: Poems 1946–1953 (Eberhart), **I:** 528, 536–537

Under Cover (Goldbarth), **Supp. XII:** 177, 180, 193

Undercover Doctor (film), **Supp. XIII:** 170

"Under Cygnus" (Wilbur), **Supp. III Part 2:** 558

"Under Forty" (Trilling), **Supp. III Part 2:** 494

Underground, The Story of a People (Tenenbaum), **Supp. XX: 253**

Underground Man, The (film), **Supp. IV Part 2:** 474

Underground Man, The (Macdonald), **Supp. IV Part 2:** 474, 475

Underground Woman, The (Boyle), **Supp. XXIV:** 62

"Under Libra: Weights and Measures" (Merrill), **Supp. III Part 1:** 328

Under Milk Wood (D. Thomas), **III:** 21

"Undersea" (Carson), **Supp. IX:** 21

Understanding Cynthia Ozick (Friedman), **Supp. V:** 273

Understanding Drama (Brooks and Heilman), **Supp. XIV:** 12

Understanding E. L. Doctorow (Fowler), **Supp. IV Part 1:** 226

Understanding Fiction (Brooks and Warren), **IV:** 279; **Supp. XIV:** 11

Understanding Fiction (Brooks and Warren, eds.), **Supp. XIX:** 246

Understanding Flannery O'Connor (Whitt), **Retro. Supp. II:** 226

Understanding Nicholson Baker (Saltzman), **Supp. XIII:** 48

Understanding Poetry: An Anthology for College Students (Brooks and Warren), **IV:** 236; **Retro. Supp. I:** 40, 41; **Supp. XIV:** 4–5

Understanding Robert Bly (W. V. Davis), **Supp. XXI: 84–85,** 88

Understanding Tim O'Brien (Kaplan), **Supp. V:** 241

Understanding To Kill a Mockingbird: A Student Casebook to Issues, Sources, and Documents (Johnson), **Supp. VIII:** 127

Under Stars (Gallagher), **Supp. XXIV:** 166, 167, 168–169, 170

Undertaker's Garland, The (Wilson and Bishop), **IV:** 427

Under Taos Mountain: The Terrible Quarrel of Magpie and Tía (Schott), **Supp. XXIII: 250–251**

Under the Banner of Heaven: A Story of Violent Faith (Krakauer), **Supp. XVIII:** 105, **114–116,** 117

"Under the Cedarcroft Chestnut" (Lanier), **Supp. I Part 1:** 364

"Under the Harbour Bridge" (Komunyakaa), **Supp. XIII:** 125

"Under the Influence" (Sanders), **Supp. XVI:** 274, 277

Under the Lilacs (Alcott), **Supp. I Part 1:** 42–43, 44

"Under the Maud Moon" (Kinnell), **Supp. III Part 1:** 246–247

Under the Mountain Wall: A Chronicle of Two Seasons in the Stone Age (Matthiessen), **Supp. V:** 202

Under the Red Flag (Jin), **Supp. XVIII:** 89, **94–95**

"Under the Rose" (Pynchon), **Supp. II Part 2:** 620

Under the Sea-Wind: A Naturalist's Picture of Ocean Life (Carson), **Supp. IX:** 19, **22–23**

Under the Shadow (Sorrentino), **Supp. XXI:** 236–237

Under the Sign of Saturn (Sontag), **Supp. III Part 2:** 451, 452, 458, 470–471

"Under the Sign of Saturn" (Sontag), **Supp. III Part 2:** 470

"Under the Sky" (Bowles), **Supp. IV Part 1:** 87

"Under the Sun"(Schott), **Supp. XXIII:** 247, 248

" 'Under the Umbrella of Black Civilization': A Conversation with Reginald McKnight" (Ashe), **Supp. XX:** 154

Under the Volcano (M. Lowry), **Supp. XVII:** 135, 139, 140

"Under the Willows" (Lowell), **Supp. I Part 2:** 416

Under the Willows and Other Poems (Lowell), **Supp. I Part 2:** 424

"Undertow" (Boyce), **Supp. XXI:** 10

Underwood, John Curtis, **Supp. XXIV:** 29

Underwood, Wilbur, **Retro. Supp. II:** 79

Underworld (DeLillo), **Supp. VI:** 2, 4–5, 6–7, 8, 9, 10, 11, **13–15; Supp. XI:** 68; **Supp. XX: 91**

Underworld, The (Wolfert). *See Tucker's World* (Wolfert)

Undine (La Motte-Fouqué), **II:** 212; **III:** 78

Undiscovered Country, The (Howells), **II:** 282

"Undressing, The" (C. Frost), **Supp. XV:** 98

Uneasy Chair, The (Stegner), **Supp. IV Part 2:** 599

"Unemployed, Disabled, and Insane, The" (Haines), **Supp. XII:** 211–212

Unending Blues (Simic), **Supp. VIII: 278–279**

Unending Dialogue: Voices from an AIDS Poetry Workshop (Hadas, Barber, et al), **Supp. XXIII:** 118, **125–126**

"Unexpected Freedom" (Peacock), **Supp. XIX:** 199

"Unexpressed" (Dunbar), **Supp. II Part 1:** 199

"Unfinished Bronx, The" (Paley), **Supp. VI:** 228

Unfinished Crime, The (Holding), **Supp. XXII:** 120, **123–124,** 135, 136

"Unfinished Poems" (Eliot), **I:** 579

"Unfinished Song" (C. Frost), **Supp. XV:** 97

Unfinished Woman, An (Hellman), **Supp. I Part 1:** 292, 293, 294; **Supp. IV Part 1:** 12, 353–354; **Supp. IX:** 196, 200–201

Unforeseen Wilderness, The: An Essay on Kentucky's Red River Gorge (Berry), **Supp. X:** 28, 29, 30, 36

Unforgotten Years (L. P. Smith), **Supp. XIV:** 333, 334, 335, 336, 347

"Unfortunate Coincidence" (Parker), **Supp. IX:** 190

Unframed Originals (Merwin), **Supp. III Part 1:** 341

Ungar, Sanford, **Supp. XI:** 228

Ungaretti, Giuseppe, **Supp. V:** 337

Unguided Tour (Sontag), **Supp. III Part 2:** 452

"Unheimliche, Das" (The Uncanny) (Freud), **Supp. XVI:** 157–158

Unholy Sonnets (Jarman), **Supp. XVII:** 109, 110, **119–120; Supp. XVIII:** 178

"Unholy Sonnets" (Jarman), **Supp. XVII:** 118, 119–120

"Unidentified Flying Object" (Hayden), **Supp. II Part 1:** 368

"Unifying Principle, The" (Ammons), **Supp. VII:** 28

"Unimportant Man, An" (D. West), **Supp. XVIII:** 280
"Union" (Hughes), **Supp. I Part 1:** 331
"Union Street: San Francisco, Summer 1975" (Carver), **Supp. III Part 1:** 138
"Unitarian Christianity" (Channing), **Supp. XXIV:** 71–73, 77
Unitarians and the Universalists, The (Robinson), **Supp. XXIV:** 70
"United"(Kenny), **Supp. XXIII:** 149
United States Army in World War II (Morison), **Supp. I Part 2:** 490
United States Constitution, **I:** 6, 283
United States Essays, 1951–1991 (Vidal), **Supp. IV Part 2:** 678, 687
"United States of Huck, The: Introduction to *Adventures of Huckleberry Finn" (Saunders), Supp. XIX:* 235
United States of Poetry, The (television series), **Supp. XIII:** 274
"Unity through Diversity" (Locke), **Supp. XIV:** 212, 213
Universal Baseball Asociation, Inc., J. Henry Waugh, Prop., The (Coover), **Supp. V:** 39, 41–42, 44, 46
Universal Passion (Young), **III:** 111
"Universe of Death, The" (H. Miller), **III:** 184
Universe of Time, A (Anderson), **II:** 27, 28, 45, 46, 48, 49
"Universities" (Emerson), **II:** 6
"Universities: A Mirage? " (Mora), **Supp. XIII:** 219
"University" (Shapiro), **Supp. II Part 2:** 704–705, 717
"University Avenue" (Mora), **Supp. XIII:** 216
"University Days" (Thurber), **Supp. I Part 2:** 605
"University Hospital, Boston" (Oliver), **Supp. VII:** 235
"University's Peril, The" (Taggard), **Supp. XXII:** 273
"Unknowable, The" (Levine), **Supp. V:** 195
"Unknown Girl in the Maternity Ward" (Sexton), **Supp. II Part 2:** 676
"Unknown Love, The" (Chandler), **Supp. IV Part 1:** 120
Unknown Rilke, The (Rilke; F. Wright, trans.), **Supp. XVII:** 244
"Unknown War, The" (Sandburg), **III:** 594
Unkown Constellations, The (Swados), **Supp. XIX:** 256
Unleashed (anthology), **Supp. XI:** 132
Unleashed: Poems by Writers' Dogs (Hempel and Shepard, eds.), **Supp. XXI:** 115
"Unlighted Lamps" (Anderson), **I:** 112
Unlit Lamp, The (Holding), **Supp. XXII:** 121, 130
Unloved Wife, The (Alcott), **Supp. I Part 1:** 33
Unmarried Woman, An (film), **Supp. IV Part 1:** 303
"Unnatural Mother, The" (Gilman), **Supp. XI:** 207
"Unnatural State of the Unicorn" (Komunyakaa), **Supp. XIII:** 119

"Unparalleled Adventure of One Hans Pfaall, The" (Poe), **III:** 424
"Unpleasant Profession of Jonathan Hoag, The" (Heinlein), **Supp. XVIII:** 149
Unprecedented Era, The (Goebbels), **III:** 560
"Unprofitable Servant, The" (O. Henry), **Supp. II Part 1:** 403
Unpublished Poems of Emily Dickinson (Bianchi and Hampson, ed.), **Retro. Supp. I:** 35
Unpunished (Gilman), **Supp. XI:** 208
Unraveling Strangeness, The (Weigl), **Supp. XIX:** 287–288
"Unreal City" (Eliot), **Supp. XV:** 218
"Unreasoning Heart" (Untermeyer), **Supp. XV:** 309
"Unsaid (Gioia), **Supp. XV:** 129
"Unseen, The" (Pinsky), **Supp. VI:** 243–244
"Unseen, The" (Singer), **Retro. Supp. II:** 307
Unseen Hand, The (Shepard), **Supp. III Part 2:** 439, 445–446
Unselected Poems (Levine), **Supp. V:** 179
Unsettling of America, The: Culture and Agriculture (Berry), **Supp. X:** 22, 26, 29, 32, 33, 35; **Supp. XIV:** 177, 179
Unspeakable Gentleman, The (Marquand), **III:** 53–54, 60, 63
Unspeakable Practices, Unnatural Acts (Barthelme), **Supp. IV Part 1:** 39
"Unspeakable Things Unspoken: The Afro-American Presence in American Literature" (Morrison), **Supp. III Part 1:** 375, 377–379
Unspoken and Other Poems, The (Bremer), **Supp. XXII:** 277
"Untelling, The" (Strand), **Supp. IV Part 2:** 629
Unterecker, John, **I:** 386
Untermeyer, Jean Starr, **II:** 530; **Supp. XV:** 294, 295, 303, 307, 308, 310
Untermeyer, Louis, **II:** 516–517, 530, 532; **III:** 268; **Retro. Supp. I:** 124, 133, 136; **Supp. III Part 1:** 2; **Supp. IX:** 76; **Supp. XIV:** 119, 123; **Supp. XV:** 293–318; **Supp. XXI:** 277
Untimely Papers (Bourne), **I:** 218, 233
"Untitled" (C. Frost), **Supp. XV:** 103
"Untitled Blues" (Komunyakaa), **Supp. XIII:** 117
Unto the Sons (Talese), **Supp. XVII:** 199–200, 206–207, 208, 209, 210
"Untrustworthy Speaker, The" (Glück), **Supp. V:** 86
"Unused" (Anderson), **I:** 112, 113
Unvanquished, The (Faulkner), **II:** 55, 67–68, 71; **Retro. Supp. I:** 84; **Supp. I Part 2:** 450
"Unvexed Isles, The" (Warren), **IV:** 253
"Unwedded" (Larcom), **Supp. XIII:** 144
"Unweepables, The" (Karr), **Supp. XI:** 243
"Unwelcome Guest, An" (Papernick), **Supp. XVII:** 50
Unwelcome Man, The (W. Frank), **Supp. XX: 70, 76**

Unwelcome Words (Bowles), **Supp. IV Part 1:** 93, 94
"Unwelcome Words" (Bowles), **Supp. IV Part 1:** 94, 95
Unwin, T. Fisher, **Supp. XI:** 202
"Unwithered Garland, The" (Kunitz), **Supp. III Part 1:** 265
Unwobbling Pivot, The (Pound, trans.), **III:** 472
"Unwritten, The" (Merwin), **Supp. III Part 1:** 352
"Unwritten Law" (Glück), **Supp. V:** 91
Up (Sukenick), **Supp. V:** 39
Up Above the World (Bowles), **Supp. IV Part 1:** 82, 91, 92
"Up and Down" (Merrill), **Supp. III Part 1:** 328
Upanishads, **IV:** 183
Up Country: Poems of New England (Kumin), **Supp. IV Part 2:** 446, 447–448, 453
"Update" (Dunn), **Supp. XI:** 150–151
Updike, John, **I:** 54; **III:** 572; **IV: 214–235; Retro. Supp. I:** 116, **317–338; Retro. Supp. II:** 213, 279, 280; **Supp. I Part 1:** 186, 196; **Supp. IV Part 2:** 657; **Supp. V:** 23, 43, 95, 119; **Supp. VIII:** 151, 167, 236; **Supp. IX:** 208; **Supp. XI:** 65, 66, 99, 140; **Supp. XII:** 140, 296, 298, 310; **Supp. XIII:** 45–46, 47, 52; **Supp. XIV:** 79, 93, 111; **Supp. XVI:** 205, 207, 220; **Supp. XX:** 17; **Supp. XXI:** 116, 226; **Supp. XXIII:** 109
Updike, Mrs. Wesley, **IV:** 218, 220
Up from Slavery (Washington), **Supp. II Part 1:** 169; **Supp. IX:** 19
Upham, Thomas Goggswell, **II:** 487
"Upholsterers, The" (Lardner), **II:** 435
"Up in Michigan" (Hemingway), **II:** 263; **Supp. XIX:** 241
Upjohn, Richard, **IV:** 312
"Upon a Spider Catching a Fly" (Taylor), **IV:** 161
"Upon a Wasp Child with Cold" (Taylor), **IV:** 161
"Upon Meeting Don L. Lee, in a Dream" (Dove), **Supp. IV Part 1:** 244
"Upon My Dear and Loving Husband His Going into England, Jan. 16, 1661" (Bradstreet), **Supp. I Part 1:** 110
"Upon My Mother's Death"(Hadas), **Supp. XXIII:** 118
"Upon Returning to the Country Road" (Lindsay), **Supp. I Part 2:** 382
"Upon the Burning of Our House, July 10th, 1666" (Bradstreet), **Supp. I Part 1:** 107–108, 122
"Upon the Sweeping Flood" (Taylor), **IV:** 161
"Upon Wedlock, and Death of Children" (Taylor), **IV:** 144, 147, 161
"Upon Westminster Bridge" (Wordsworth), **Supp. XXIV:** 148
"Upset, An" (Merrill), **Supp. III Part 1:** 336
Upstairs and Downstairs (Vonnegut), **Supp. II Part 2:** 757
Upstate (Wilson), **IV:** 447
Upton, Lee, **Supp. X:** 209

"Upturned Face" (Crane), **I:** 423
Upward, Allen, **Supp. I Part 1:** 262
Upward, Edward, **Supp. XIV:** 159, 160
"Upward Moon and the Downward Moon, The" (R. Bly), **Supp. IV Part 1:** 71
Urania: A Rhymed Lesson (Holmes), **Supp. I Part 1:** 300
"Urban Convalescence, An" (Merrill), **Supp. III Part 1:** 322–324
"Urban Renewal" (Komunyakaa), **Supp. XIII:** 113
Urdang, Constance, **Supp. XV:** 74
"Urganda and Fatima" (Rowson), **Supp. XV:** 234
Urial Accosta: A Play (Reznikoff), **Supp. XIV:** 282, 288
Urich, Robert, **Supp. V:** 228
"Uriel" (Emerson), **II:** 19
Uris, Leon, **Supp. IV Part 1:** 285, 379; **Supp. XX:** 243–258
Uroff, Margaret D., **Supp. I Part 2:** 542
Ursu, Liliana, **Supp. XXIV:** 178
"Us" (Sexton), **Supp. II Part 2:** 687
U.S. 1 (Rukeyser), **Supp. VI:** 272, 278, 283, 285
U.S.A. (Dos Passos), **I:** 379, 475, 478, 482–488, 489, 490, 491, 492, 493, 494, 495; **Retro. Supp. II:** 197; **Supp. I Part 2:** 646; **Supp. III Part 1:** 104, 105; **Supp. XIV:** 24
"U.S.A. School of Writing, The" (Bishop), **Retro. Supp. II:** 43
"U.S. Commercial Orchid, The" (Agee), **I:** 35
"Used-Boy Raisers, The" (Paley), **Supp. VI:** 218, 228
"Used Cars on Oahu" (Nye), **Supp. XIII:** 282
"Used Side of the Sofa, The" (Ríos), **Supp. IV Part 2:** 551
Useless Servants, The (Hinojosa), **Supp. XIX:** 98, 103, 104, **109–110**
Use of Fire, The (Price), **Supp. VI:** 265
"Use of Force, The" (W. C. Williams), **Retro. Supp. I:** 424
Use of Poetry and the Use of Criticism, The (Eliot), **Retro. Supp. I:** 65
Uses of Enchantment, The: The Meaning and Importance of Fairy Tales (Bettelheim), **Supp. X:** 77; **Supp. XIV:** 126
"Uses of Hell, The" (E. Hoffman), **Supp. XVI:** 154
"Uses of Hell, The: An Exchange"(Novick, Katz, and Szulc), **Supp. XVI:** 154
Uses of Literacy, The (Hoggart), **Supp. XIV:** 299
Uses of Literature, The (Calvino), **Supp. XXII:** 263
"Uses of Poetry, The" (W. C. Williams), **Retro. Supp. I:** 412
"Uses of the Blues, The" (Baldwin), **Retro. Supp. II:** 8
"Use-Unuse of Us, The" (Bronk), **Supp. XXI:** 32
"USFS 1919: The Ranger, the Cook, and a Hole in the Sky" (Maclean), **Supp. XIV:** 230, 234

Ushant: An Essay (Aiken), **I:** 49, 54, 55, 56, 57
"Usher 11" (Bradbury), **Supp. I Part 2:** 622
"Using Parrots to Kill Mockingbirds: Yet Another Racial Prosecution and Wrongful Conviction in Maycomb" (Fair), **Supp. VIII:** 128
Ustedes y Nosotros: Nuevo Mensaje a Ibero-América (W. Frank), **Supp. XX:** **79**
"Usual Objects"(Schott), **Supp. XXIII:** 248
Usual Star, The (Doolittle), **Supp. I Part 1:** 270
"Usurpation (Other People's Stories)" (Ozick), **Supp. V:** 268, 271
Utopia 14 (Vonnegut), **Supp. II Part 2:** 757

V

V. (Pynchon), **Supp. II Part 2:** 618, 620–622, 627–630; **Supp. IV Part 1:** 279
"Vacation" (Stafford), **Supp. XI:** 321, 322
Vacationland (Monson), **Supp. XXIV:** 230, 231, 234
"Vacation Trip" (Stafford), **Supp. XI:** 322
Vachel Lindsay: A Poet in America (Masters), **Supp. I Part 2:** 473, 474
"Vachel Lindsay: The Midwest as Utopia" (Whitney), **Supp. I Part 2:** 403
"Vachel Lindsay Writes to Floyd Dell" (Tanselle), **Supp. I Part 2:** 403
"Vacillation" (Yeats), **Supp. XV:** 253
Vadim, Roger, **Supp. XI:** 293, 307
"Vag" (Dos Passos), **I:** 487–488
Vagina Monologues, The (Ensler), **Supp. XIX:** 204–205
Vail, Laurence, **Supp. XXIV:** 50
Valdez, Luis, **Supp. XXIII:** 203
Valediction (Parker), **Supp. XIX:** 185
Valentine, Jean, **Supp. V:** 92
Valentine, Saint, **IV:** 396
Valentines (Kooser), **Supp. XIX:** 116, 123, **128–129**
Valentino, Rudolph, **I:** 483
Valéry, Paul, **II:** 543, 544; **III:** 279, 409, 428, 609; **IV:** 79, 91, 92, 428, 443; **Retro. Supp. II:** 187
"Valhalla" (Francis), **Supp. IX:** 77
Valhalla and Other Poems (Francis), **Supp. IX:** 76
Valiant Runaways, The (Atherton), **Supp. XXIV:** 22
Validity in Interpretation (Hirsch), **Supp. XIV:** 15
Valitsky, Ken, **Supp. XII:** 7
Vallejo, César, **Supp. V:** 332; **Supp. IX:** 271; **Supp. XIII:** 114, 315, 323; **Supp. XXI:** 132
"Valley, The" (Bass), **Supp. XVI:** 20, 22
Valley, The (Hinojosa), **Supp. XIX:** 97, 99, **100–101**
"Valley Between, The" (Marshall), **Supp. XI:** 278
Valley of Decision, The (Wharton), **IV:** 311, 315; **Retro. Supp. I:** 365–367
"Valley of the Monsters, The" (Peacock), **Supp. XIX:** 198

Valley of the Moon, The (London), **II:** 467, 481
"Valley of Unrest, The" (Poe), **III:** 411
Valli, Alida, **Supp. IV Part 2:** 520
"Valor" (Bausch), **Supp. VII:** 54
Valparaiso (DeLillo), **Supp. VI:** 4, 12
"Value of a Place, The" (Bass), **Supp. XVI:** 18
"Values and Fictions" (Toomer), **Supp. III Part 2:** 485–486
"Values and Imperatives" (Locke), **Supp. XIV:** 199, 202, 212
Values of Veblen, The: A Critical Appraisal (Rosenberg), **Supp. I Part 2:** 650
"Vampire" (Karr), **Supp. XI:** 241
Vampire Armand, The (Rice), **Supp. VII:** 290, 294–295
Vampire Chronicles, The (Rice), **Supp. VII:** 290
Vampire Lestat, The (Rice), **Supp. VII:** 290–292, 298, 299
Van Aalst, Mariska, **Supp. XIX:** 50, 51
Van Buren, Martin, **II:** 134, 312; **III:** 473
Vande Kieft, Ruth M., **IV:** 260
Vanderbilt, Cornelius, **III:** 14
Van Dine, S. S., **Supp. IV Part 1:** 341
Van Doren, Carl, **I:** 252–253, 423; **II:** 103, 111, 112; **Supp. I Part 2:** 474, 486, 707, 709, 717, 718, 727; **Supp. II Part 1:** 395; **Supp. VIII:** 96–97
Van Doren, Mark, **I:** 168; **III:** 4, 23, 589; **Supp. I Part 2:** 604; **Supp. III Part 2:** 626; **Supp. VIII:** 231; **Supp. IX:** 266, 268; **Supp. XV:** 152, 305, 307; **Supp. XXII:** 275
Vandover and the Brute (Norris), **III:** 314, 315, 316, 320–322, 328, 333, 334
Van Duyn, Mona, **Supp. IX:** 269
Van Dyke, Annette, **Supp. IV Part 1:** 327
Van Dyke, Henry, **I:** 223; **II:** 456
Van Gogh, Vincent, **I:** 27; **IV:** 290; **Supp. I Part 2:** 451; **Supp. IV Part 1:** 284; **Supp. XXII:** 171–172
Van Gogh's Room at Arles (Elkin), **Supp. VI:** **56**
"Vanilla Dunk" (Lethem), **Supp. XVIII:** 139
"Vanisher, The" (Whittier), **Supp. I Part 2:** 691
Vanishing Point (Markson), **Supp. XVII:** 135, 137, 138, 145–146
"Vanishing Point: Former City" (Monson), **Supp. XXIV:** 238
"Vanishing Point for Solo Voice" (Monson), **Supp. XXIV:** 239
Vanishing Point: Not a Memoir (Monson), **Supp. XXIV:** 230, **236–239**, 241–242
"Vanishing Point: Panera" (Monson), **Supp. XXIV:** 238
"Vanishing Red, The" (Frost), **Retro. Supp. II:** 47
"Vanity" (B. Diop), **Supp. IV Part 1:** 16
Vanity Fair (Thackeray), **I:** 354; **II:** 91; **III:** 70; **Supp. IX:** 200
"Vanity of All Wordly Things, The" (Bradstreet), **Supp. I Part 1:** 102, 119
Vanity of Duluoz (Kerouac), **Supp. III Part 1:** 221, 222

CUMULATIVE INDEX / 575

"Vanity of Existence, The" (Freneau), **Supp. II Part 1:** 262

Van Matre, Lynn, **Supp. V:** 126

Vann, Barbara, **Supp. XV:** 187

Vanquished, The (Faulkner), **I:** 205

Van Rensselaer, Stephen, **I:** 351

Van Vechten, Carl, **I:** 295; **IV:** 76; **Retro. Supp. I:** 199; **Supp. I Part 1:** 324, 327, 332; **Supp. I Part 2:** 715; **Supp. II Part 2: 725–751; Supp. X:** 247; **Supp. XVI:** 135; **Supp. XVII:** 96, 97, 101, 104; **Supp. XVIII:** 123, 131, 132, 279, 280; **Supp. XIX:** 76; **Supp. XX:** 69; **Supp. XXI:** 5, 8; **Supp. XXII:** 5, 158, 160

Van Vliet, Don, **Supp. XXIII:** 174

Vanya and Sonia and Masha and Spike (Durang), **Supp. XXIV: 127–128**

Vanzetti, Bartolomeo, **I:** 482, 486, 490, 494; **II:** 38–39, 426; **III:** 139–140; **Supp. I Part 2:** 446, 610, 611; **Supp. V:** 288–289; **Supp. IX:** 199; **Supp. XXII:** 277

"Vapor Trail Reflected in the Frog Pond" (Kinnell), **Supp. III Part 1:** 242–243

"Vapor Trails" (Snyder), **Supp. VIII:** 298

"Variation: Ode to Fear" (Warren), **IV:** 241

"Variation on a Sentence" (Bogan), **Supp. III Part 1:** 60

"Variation on Gaining a Son" (Dove), **Supp. IV Part 1:** 248

"Variation on Pain" (Dove), **Supp. IV Part 1:** 248

"Variations: The air is sweetest that a thistle guards" (Merrill), **Supp. III Part 1:** 321

"Variations: White Stag, Black Bear" (Merrill), **Supp. III Part 1:** 321

"Varick Street" (Bishop), **Supp. I Part 1:** 90, 92

Varieties of Metaphysical Poetry, The (Eliot), **Retro. Supp. I:** 65

Varieties of Religious Experience, The (William James), **II:** 344, 353, 354, 359–360, 362; **IV:** 28, 291; **Supp. IX:** 19

Variety (film), **Supp. XII:** 7

Variorum (Whitman), **Retro. Supp. I:** 406

Various Antidotes (J. Scott), **Supp. XVII: 188–189**

Various Miracles (Shields), **Supp. VII:** 318–320, 323, 324

"Various Miracles" (Shields), **Supp. VII:** 318–319, 324

Various Poems (Zach), **Supp. XV:** 86

"Various Tourists" (Connell), **Supp. XIV:** 79

"Varmint Question, The" (Leopold), **Supp. XIV:** 180–181

Varno, David, **Supp. XIX:** 205

Vasari, Giorgio, **Supp. I Part 2:** 450; **Supp. III Part 1:** 5

Vasquez, Robert, **Supp. V:** 180

Vassall Morton (Parkman), **Supp. II Part 2:** 595, 597–598

Vasse, W. W., **III:** 478

Vaudeville for a Princess (Schwartz), **Supp. II Part 2:** 661–662

Vaughan, Henry, **IV:** 151; **Supp. XV:** 251

Vaughn, Robert, **Supp. XI:** 343

"Vaunting Oak" (Ransom), **III:** 490

Vazirani, Reetika, **Supp. XIII:** 133

Veblen (Hobson), **Supp. I Part 2:** 650

Veblen, Andrew, **Supp. I Part 2:** 640

Veblen, Oswald, **Supp. I Part 2:** 640

Veblen, Thorstein, **I:** 104, 283, 475–476, 483, 498, 511; **II:** 27, 272, 276, 287; **Supp. I Part 2: 628–650; Supp. IV Part 1:** 22

Veblen, Mrs. Thorstein (Ellen Rolfe), **Supp. I Part 2:** 641

Veblenism: A New Critique (Dobriansky), **Supp. I Part 2:** 648, 650

"Veblen's Attack on Culture" (Adorno), **Supp. I Part 2:** 650

Vectors and Smoothable Curves (Bronk), **Supp. XXI: 24–26,** 32

Vedanta for Modern Man (Isherwood, ed.), **Supp. XIV:** 164

Vedanta for the Western World (Isherwood, ed.), **Supp. XIV:** 164

Vedas, **IV:** 183

Vega, Janine Pommy, **Supp. XIV:** 148

Vega, Lope de, **Retro. Supp. I:** 285; **Supp. III Part 1:** 341, 347

Vegetable, The (Fitzgerald), **Retro. Supp. I:** 105; **Supp. IX:** 57

Vegetable, The, or From President to Postman (Fitzgerald), **II:** 91

"Vegetable Love" (Apple), **Supp. XVII:** 4

"Vegetable Love"(Crooker), **Supp. XXIII:** 62

"Vegetable Wisdom" (Halliday), **Supp. XIX:** 88

Veg tsu zikh, Der (The road to one's self) (Asch), **Supp. XXIII:** 5, 11

Veinberg, Jon, **Supp. V:** 180; **Supp. XIII:** 313; **Supp. XV:** 76–77, 86

Vein of Iron (Glasgow), **II:** 175, 186, 188–189, 191, 192, 194

Vein of Riches, A (Knowles), **Supp. XII:** 249

Vein of Words (J. W. Miller), **Supp. XX:** 165

Velie, Alan R., **Supp. IV Part 2:** 486

Velocities: New and Selected Poems, 1966–1992 (Dobyns), **Supp. XIII:** 86–87, 87, 88

"Velocity" (Collins), **Supp. XXI:** 61

"Velorio" (Cisneros), **Supp. VII:** 66

"Velvet Gentleman, The" (Skloot), **Supp. XX: 201**

"Velvet Shoes" (Wylie), **Supp. I Part 2:** 711, 714

Venant, Elizabeth, **Supp. XI:** 343

Vencloca, Thomas, **Supp. VIII:** 29

Vendler, Helen H., **Retro. Supp. I:** 297; **Retro. Supp. II:** 184, 191; **Supp. I Part 1:** 77, 78, 92, 95; **Supp. I Part 2:** 565; **Supp. IV Part 1:** 245, 247, 249, 254, 257; **Supp. IV Part 2:** 448; **Supp. V:** 78, 82, 189, 343; **Supp. XII:** 187, 189; **Supp. XV:** 20, 184

"Venetian Blind, The" (Jarrell), **II:** 382–383

Venetian Glass Nephew, The (Wylie), **Supp. I Part 2:** 707, 709, 714, 717–

719, 721, 724

Venetian Life (Howells), **II:** 274, 277, 279

Venetian Vespers, The (Hecht), **Supp. X:** 57, **65–69**

"Venetian Vespers, The" (Hecht), **Supp. X:** 65, **66–67**

Venice Observed (McCarthy), **II:** 562

Ventadorn, Bernard de, **Supp. IV Part 1:** 146

"Ventriloquists' Conversations" (Gentry), **Supp. IV Part 1:** 236

"Venus, Cupid, Folly and Time" (Taylor), **Supp. V:** 322–323

Venus and Adonis (film), **Supp. IV Part 1:** 82

Venus and Don Juan (C. Frost), **Supp. XV:** 93, **102–103,** 104, 107

"Venus and Don Juan" (C. Frost), **Supp. XV:** 103

Venus Blue (Sobin), **Supp. XVI: 293–294,** 294

Venus in Sparta (Auchincloss), **Supp. IV Part 1:** 25

"Venus Pandemos" (Halliday), **Supp. XIX:** 85, 89, 90, 93

"Venus's-flytraps" (Komunyakaa), **Supp. XIII:** 126, 127

"Veracruz" (Hayden), **Supp. II Part 1:** 371, 373

Verducci, Tom, **Supp. XXII:** 209

Verga, Giovanni, **II:** 271, 275

Verghese, Abraham, **Supp. X:** 160

Verhaeren, Emile, **I:** 476; **II:** 528, 529

Verlaine, Paul, **II:** 529, 543; **III:** 466; **IV:** 79, 80, 86, 286; **Retro. Supp. I:** 56, 62; **Retro. Supp. II:** 326

"Vermeer" (Nemerov), **III:** 275, 278, 280

Vermeer, Jan, **Retro. Supp. I:** 335

"Vermont" (Carruth), **Supp. XVI:** 54

Vermont Notebook, The (Ashbery), **Supp. III Part 1:** 1

Vermont Writers: A State of Mind (Daley), **Supp. XXII:** 216

"Vernal Ague, The" (Freneau), **Supp. II Part 1:** 258

Verne, Jules, **I:** 480; **Retro. Supp. I:** 270; **Supp. XI:** 63

Vernon, John, **Supp. X:** 15

Verplanck, Gulian C., **Supp. I Part 1:** 155, 156, 157, 158

Verrazano, Giovanni da, **Supp. I Part 2:** 496, 497

Verse (Zawacki), **Supp. VIII:** 272

"Verse for Urania" (Merrill), **Supp. III Part 1:** 329, 330

Verses (Wharton), **Retro. Supp. I:** 362

Verses, Printed for Her Friends (Jewett), **II:** 406

"Verses for Children" (Lowell), **II:** 516

"Verses Made at Sea in a Heavy Gale" (Freneau), **Supp. II Part 1:** 262

"Verses on the Death of T. S. Eliot" (Brodsky), **Supp. VIII:** 19

"Version of a Fragment of Simonides" (Bryant), **Supp. I Part 1:** 153, 155

Verulam, Baron. *See* Bacon, Francis

Very, Jones, **III:** 507

"Very Hot Sun in Bermuda, The" (Jackson), **Supp. IX:** 126

Very Old Bones (W. Kennedy), **Supp. VII:** 133, 148, 150–153

"Very Old Man with Enormous Wings, A" (García Márquez), **Supp. XXIV:** 190

Very Persistent Gappers of Frip, The (Saunders), **Supp. XIX: 229–230**

"Very Proper Gander, The" (Thurber), **Supp. I Part 2:** 610

"Very Short Story, A" (Hemingway), **II:** 252; **Retro. Supp. I:** 173

"Vesalius in Zante" (Wharton), **Retro. Supp. I:** 372

Vesey, Denmark, **Supp. I Part 2:** 592

Vesey, Desmond, **Supp. XIV:** 162

"Vespers" (Auden), **Supp. II Part 1:** 23

"Vespers" (Glück), **Supp. V:** 88

"Vespers"(Dybek), **Supp. XXIII:** 78

Vestal Lady on Brattle, The (Corso), **Supp. XII:** 119, **120–121,** 134

Vested Interests and the Common Man, The (Veblen), **Supp. I Part 2:** 642

"Vesuvius at Home" (Rich), **Retro. Supp. I:** 42

"Veteran, The" (Crane), **I:** 413

"Veterans' Cemetery" (Gioia), **Supp. XV:** 117

"Veteran Sirens" (Robinson), **III:** 512, 524

"Veterinarian" (X. J. Kennedy), **Supp. XV:** 168

"Vetiver" (Ashbery), **Supp. III Part 1:** 26

Vetter, Lara, **Supp. XXII:** 166

"Via Dieppe-Newhaven" (H. Miller), **III:** 183

"Via Negativa" (Salter), **Supp. IX:** 257

Vicar of Wakefeld, The (Goldsmith), **I:** 216

Vicious Circle, The (film, Wilder), **Supp. XVII:** 62

"Vicissitudes of the Avant-Garde, The" (Gass), **Supp. VI:** 91

Vico, Giambattista, **Supp. XX: 38**

Victim, The (Bellow), **I:** 144, 145, 147, 149, 150, 151, 152, 153, 155, 156, 158, 159, 164; **IV:** 19; **Retro. Supp. II:** 21, 22, 34

"Victor" (Mumford), **Supp. II Part 2:** 476

Victoria (Rowson), **Supp. XV:** 231

Victorian in the Modern World, A (Hapgood), **Supp. XVII:** 95, 97, 100, 101, 103, 105, 106; **Supp. XXI:** 8

"Victoria's Secret" (Collins), **Supp. XXI:** 58–59

"Victories" (Untermeyer), **Supp. XV:** 300

"Victory at Sea" (television series), **Supp. I Part 2:** 490

"Victory comes late" (Dickinson), **Retro. Supp. I:** 45

"Victory of the Moon, The" (Crane), **I:** 420

Vida, Vendela, **Supp. XIX:** 49, 50, 53, 57, 58, 59, 61, 62

Vidal, Gore, **II:** 587; **IV:** 383; **Supp. IV Part 1:** 22, 35, 92, 95, 198; **Supp. IV Part 2: 677–696; Supp. IX:** 96; **Supp. X:** 186, 195; **Supp. XIV:** 156, 170, 338; **Supp. XIX:** 131, 132

Video Poems (Collins), **Supp. XXI:** 53

Viebahn, Fred, **Supp. IV Part 1:** 248

Viera, Joseph M., **Supp. XI:** 178, 186

Viereck, Peter, **Supp. I Part 2:** 403

Viertel, Berthold, **Supp. XIV:** 165

Viertel, Salka, **Supp. XVI:** 192

Viet Journal (Jones), **Supp. XI: 230–231**

Vietnam (McCarthy), **II:** 578–579

"Vietnam in Me, The" (O'Brien), **Supp. V:** 241, 252

Vietnamization of New Jersey, The (Durang), **Supp. XXIV:** 113, **117–118**

Vie unanime, La (Romains), **I:** 227

"View, The" (Roussel), **Supp. III Part 1:** 15, 16, 21

View from 80, The (Cowley), **Supp. II Part 1:** 141, 144, 153

"View from an Institution" (F. Wright), **Supp. XVII:** 244

"View from the Backyard" (W. V. Davis), **Supp. XXI:** 96

View from the Bridge, A (A. Miller), **III:** 147, 148, 156, 158, 159–160

View from the Seventh Layer, The (Brockmeier), **Supp. XXII: 59–61**

"View from the Seventh Layer, The" (Brockmeier), **Supp. XXII:** 61

View of My Own, A: Essays in Literature and Society (Hardwick), **Supp. III Part 1:** 194, 200

"View of the Capital from the Library of Congress" (Bishop), **Retro. Supp. II:** 45

View of the Soil and Climate of the United States, A (Brown, trans.), **Supp. I Part 1:** 146

"View of the Woods, A" (O'Connor), **III:** 349, 351, 358; **Retro. Supp. II:** 237

"Viewpoint" (column, Siddons), **Supp. XXII:** 240, 245

"Views of the Mysterious Hill: The Appearance of Parnassus in American Poetry" (Strand), **Supp. IV Part 2:** 631

"Vigil" (Karr), **Supp. XI:** 241

"Vigil, The" (Dante), **III:** 542

"Vigil at Heiligenkreuz" (W. V. Davis), **Supp. XXI:** 93

"Vigil"(Dybek), **Supp. XXIII:** 78

"Vignette" (Trethewey), **Supp. XXI:** 253, 254

Vigny, Alfred Victor de, **II:** 543

Vildrac, Charles, **Supp. XV:** 50

Vile Bodies (Waugh), **Supp. I Part 2:** 607

Villa, Pancho, **I:** 210; **III:** 584

"Village Blacksmith, The" (Longfellow), **Retro. Supp. II:** 167, 168; **Supp. I Part 2:** 409

Village Hymns, a Supplement to Dr. Watts's Psalms and Hymns (Nettleton), **I:** 458

"Village Improvement Parade, The" (Lindsay), **Supp. I Part 2:** 388, 389

Village Magazine, The (Lindsay), **Supp. I Part 2:** 379–380, 382

Village Virus, The (Lewis), **II:** 440

"Villanelle at Sundown" (Justice), **Supp. VII:** 119, 122–123

"Villanelle of Change" (Robinson), **III:** 524

Villard, Oswald, **Supp. I Part 1:** 332

"Villa Selene" (Simpson), **Supp. IX:** 279

Villon, François, **II:** 544; **III:** 9, 174, 592; **Retro. Supp. I:** 286; **Supp. I Part 1:** 261; **Supp. III Part 1:** 235, 243, 249, 253; **Supp. III Part 2:** 560; **Supp. IX:** 116

"Villonaud for This Yule" (Pound), **Retro. Supp. I:** 286

"Vincenzo Tailor" (Di Piero), **Supp. XIX:** 38

Vindication of the Rights of Woman (Wollstonecraft), **Supp. I Part 1:** 126; **Supp. XI:** 203

Vines, Lois Davis, **Retro. Supp. II:** 261

Vintage Book of Amnesia, The (Lethem, ed.), **Supp. XVIII:** 138

"Vintage Thunderbird, A" (Beattie), **Supp. V:** 27

Vinz, Mark, **Supp. X:** 117

Viol de Lucrèce, Le (Obey), **IV:** 356

Violence (Bausch), **Supp. VII:** 48–49, 54

Violent Bear It Away, The (O'Connor), **III:** 339, 345–348, 350, 351, 354, 355, 356, 357; **Retro. Supp. II:** 233, **234– 236**

Violent Hero, Wilderness Heritage and Urban Reality, The: A Study of the Private Eye in the Novels of Dashiell Hammett, Raymond Chandler and Ross Macdonald (Parker), **Supp. XIX:** 177

"Violent Vet, The" (O'Brien), **Supp. V:** 238

Violin (Rice), **Supp. VII:** 302

Viorst, Judith, **Supp. X:** 153

Viper Run (Karr), **Supp. XI: 248–251**

Virgil, **I:** 312, 322, 587; **II:** 133, 542; **IV:** 137, 359; **Retro. Supp. I:** 135; **Supp. I Part 1:** 153; **Supp. I Part 2:** 494; **Supp. IV Part 2:** 631

"Virgin and Child with Music and Numbers" (Bronk), **Supp. XXI:** 30

"Virgin and the Dynamo" (Adams), **III:** 396

"Virgin Carrying a Lantern, The" (Stevens), **IV:** 80

Virgin Huntress, The (Holding), **Supp. XXII:** 119, 124, **135–136**

Virginia (Glasgow), **II:** 175, 178, 181– 182, 193, 194

"Virginia" (Lindsay), **Supp. I Part 2:** 398

"Virginia Britannia" (Moore), **III:** 198, 208–209

"Virginians Are Coming Again, The" (Lindsay), **Supp. I Part 2:** 399

Virginia Reels (Hoffman), **Supp. XVIII:** 79, 86

Virgin Spain (W. Frank), **Supp. XX: 76**

"Virgins Plus Curtains Minus Dots" (Loy), **Supp. XXII:** 161

Virgin Suicides, The (Eugenides), **Supp. XXIV:** 134, **136–138,** 141, 142

Virgin Time: In Search of the Contemplative Life (Hampl), **Supp. XXII:** 82, 83–84, **90–92**

"Virgin Violeta" (Porter), **III:** 454

"Virility" (Ozick), **Supp. V:** 262, 265

Virtual Light (W. Gibson), **Supp. XVI:** 124, **129,** 130

Virtue of Selfishness, The: A New Concept of Egoism (Rand), **Supp. IV Part 2:** 527, 530–532
"Virtuoso" (Francis), **Supp. IX:** 82
Virtuous Woman, A (Gibbons), **Supp. X: 44–45,** 46, 50
Visconti, Luchino, **Supp. V:** 51
Viscusi, Robert, **Supp. XX: 46**
Visible Saints: The History of a Puritan Idea (Morgan), **IV:** 149
"Vision, A" (Olds), **Supp. X:** 214
"Vision, A" (Winters), **Supp. II Part 2:** 785, 795
"Vision and Prayer" (D. Thomas), **I:** 432
"Visionary, The" (Poe), **III:** 411
Visionary Farms, The (Eberhart), **I:** 537–539
Visioning, The (Glaspell), **Supp. III Part 1:** 175–177, 180, 187, 188
Vision in Spring (Faulkner), **Retro. Supp. I:** 79
Vision of Columbus (Barlow), **Supp. I Part 1:** 124; **Supp. II Part 1:** 67, 68, 70–75, 77, 79
Vision of Sir Launfal, The (Lowell), **Supp. I Part 1:** 311; **Supp. I Part 2:** 406, 409, 410
"Vision of the World, A" (Cheever), **Supp. I Part 1:** 182, 192
"Visions of Budhardin"(Dybek), **Supp. XXIII:** 70–71
Visions of Cody (Kerouac), **Supp. III Part 1:** 225–227
Visions of Gerard (Kerouac), **Supp. III Part 1:** 219–222, 225, 227, 229
"Visions of the Daughters of Albion" (Blake), **III:** 540
"Visit" (Ammons), **Supp. VII:** 28–29
"Visit, The" (Kenyon), **Supp. VII:** 169
"Visitant, The" (Dunn), **Supp. XI:** 147
"Visitation, The/La Visitación" (Mora), **Supp. XIII:** 217, 224, 228
"Visitation"(Kenny), **Supp. XXIII:** 157
"Visit Home, A" (Stafford), **Supp. XI:** 318
Visit in 2001, The (musical, McNally), **Supp. XIII:** 207
"Visiting My Own House in Iowa City" (Stern), **Supp. IX:** 300
"Visit of Charity, A" (Welty), **IV:** 262
"Visitors" (J. W. Miller), **Supp. XX: 167**
"Visitors" (Salinas), **Supp. XIII:** 318
"Visitors, The/Los Visitantes" (Kingsolver), **Supp. VII:** 208
"Visits to St. Elizabeths" (Bishop), **Retro. Supp. II:** 47
"Visit to a Small Planet" (teleplay) (Vidal), **Supp. IV Part 2:** 682
Visit to a Small Planet: A Comedy Akin to Vaudeville (Vidal), **Supp. IV Part 2:** 682–683
"Visit to Avoyelles, A" (Chopin), **Supp. I Part 1:** 213
"Visit to Manafon, A" (W. V. Davis), **Supp. XXI:** 96
"Vissi d'Arte" (Moore), **Supp. X: 173–174**
Vistas of History (Morison), **Supp. I Part 2:** 492
"Vita" (Stafford), **Supp. XI:** 330

"Vita Brevis" (Hull), **Supp. XXI:** 138
Vital, David, **Supp. XVI:** 160
Vital Provisions (Price), **Supp. VI:** 262–263
"Vitamins" (Carver), **Supp. III Part 1:** 138
Vita Nova (Glück), **Supp. V:** 90–92
Vitruvius, **Supp. XVI:** 292
Vittorio, the Vampire (Rice), **Supp. VII:** 295–296
Viudas (Dorfman), **Supp. IX:** 138
"Vivaldi"(Dybek), **Supp. XXIII:** 68
"Viva Vargas!" (Allen), **Supp. XV:** 15
Viviparous Quadrupeds of North America, The (Audubon and Bachman), **Supp. XVI:** 10
Vivisections (Siegel), **Supp. XXII:** 257
Vizenor, Gerald, **Supp. IV Part 1:** 260, 262, 329, 404; **Supp. IV Part 2:** 502
Vladimir Nabokov: The American Years (Nabokov), **Retro. Supp. I:** 275
Vlag, Piet, **Supp. XV:** 295
"Vlemk, the Box Painter" (Gardner), **Supp. VI:** 73
"V-Letter" (Shapiro), **Supp. II Part 2:** 707
V-Letter and Other Poems (Shapiro), **Supp. II Part 2:** 702, 706
"Vocabulary of Dearness" (Nye), **Supp. XIII:** 284
"Vocation" (Stafford), **Supp. XI:** 312, 321
Vocation and a Voice, A (Chopin), **Retro. Supp. II:** 67, 72
"Vocation and a Voice, A" (Chopin), **Retro. Supp. II:** 72; **Supp. I Part 1:** 200, 220, 224, 225
Vogel, David, **Supp. XV:** 88
Vogel, Speed, **Supp. IV Part 1:** 390
"Vogue Vista" (Peacock), **Supp. XIX:** 200
"Voice" (F. Wright), **Supp. XVII:** 245
"Voice" (Notley), **Supp. XXII:** 230
"Voice, The" (Dunn), **Supp. XI:** 152
Voiced Connections of James Dickey, The (Dickey), **Supp. IV Part 1:** 177
"Voice from the Wilderness" (Ray), **Supp. XVIII:** 202
"Voice from the Woods, A" (Humphrey), **Supp. IX:** 101
"Voice from Under the Table, A" (Wilbur), **Supp. III Part 2:** 553, 554
Voice of Reason, The: Essays in Objectivist Thought (Rand), **Supp. IV Part 2:** 527, 528, 532
"Voice of Rock, The" (Ginsberg), **Supp. II Part 1:** 313
Voice of the Butterfly, The (Nichols), **Supp. XIII:** 270
Voice of the City, The (O. Henry), **Supp. II Part 1:** 410
"Voice of the Mountain, The" (Crane), **I:** 420
Voice of the Negro (Barber), **Supp. II Part 1:** 168
"Voice of the Past, The" (Skloot), **Supp. XX: 207**
Voice of the People, The (Glasgow), **II:** 175, 176
Voice of the Turtle: American Indian Literature 1900–1970 (Gunn Allen,

ed.), **Supp. IV Part 1:** 332, 334
Voices from the Moon (Dubus), **Supp. VII:** 88–89
"Voices from the Other World" (Merrill), **Supp. III Part 1:** 331
Voices in the House (Sedges), **Supp. II Part 1:** 125
Voices of a Summer Day (Shaw), **Supp. XIX:** 251
Voices of the Night (Longfellow), **II:** 489, 493; **Retro. Supp. II:** 154, 157, 168
"Voices of Village Square, The" (Wolfe), **Supp. III Part 2:** 571–572
Voice That Is Great within Us, The (Caruth, ed.), **Supp. XIII:** 112
Void Moon (Connelly), **Supp. XXI: 73,** 74
Voigt, Ellen Bryan, **Supp. XIII:** 76
"Voir Dire" (Monson), **Supp. XXIV:** 237
Voix humaine, La (Cocteau), **Supp. XX: 236**
Volkening, Henry, **Retro. Supp. II:** 117; **Supp. XV:** 142
Vollmann, William T., **Supp. XIV:** 96; **Supp. XVII: 225–237; Supp. XX: 93**
Volney, Constantin François de Chasseboeuf, **Supp. I Part 1:** 146
Voltaire, **I:** 194; **II:** 86, 103, 449; **III:** 420; **IV:** 18; **Retro. Supp. II:** 94; **Supp. I Part 1:** 288–289; **Supp. I Part 2:** 669, 717; **Supp. XV:** 258; **Supp. XX: 285**
Voltaire! Voltaire! (Endore), **Supp. XVII:** 65
Volunteers, The (Rowson and Reinagle), **Supp. XV:** 238
Volynsky, Akim (Chaim Flekser), **Supp. XXIII:** 11
Vonnegut, Kurt, **Retro. Supp. I:** 170; **Supp. II Part 2:** 557, 689, **753–784; Supp. IV Part 1:** 227, 392; **Supp. V:** 40, 42, 237, 244, 296; **Supp. X:** 260; **Supp. XI:** 104; **Supp. XII:** 139, 141; **Supp. XVIII:** 242, 252; **Supp. XXI:** 226; **Supp. XXIII:** 42, 101, 109
Vonnegut, Kurt, Jr., **Supp. XVII:** 41, 135; **Supp. XIX:** 223
"Voracities and Verities" (Moore), **III:** 214
Vore, Nellie, **I:** 199
Vorlicky, Robert, **Supp. IX:** 132, 135, 136, 141, 144, 147
Vorse, Mary Heaton, **Supp. XVII:** 99; **Supp. XX: 76; Supp. XXI:** 5, 6, 9, 13
Vortex, The (Coward), **Supp. XXIV:** 267
"Vorticism" (Pound), **Retro. Supp. I:** 288
Vosjoli, Philippe de, **Supp. XX: 253**
Voss, Richard, **I:** 199–200
"Vow, The" (Hecht), **Supp. X:** 64
"Vowels 2" (Baraka), **Supp. II Part 1:** 51
Vow of Conversation, A: Journal, 1964–1965 (Merton), **Supp. VIII:** 206
Vox (Baker), **Supp. XIII: 47–49,** 50, 52, 53
"Voyage" (MacLeish), **III:** 15
Voyage, The (Caputo), **Supp. XIX:** 25, 27–28
"Voyage, The" (Irving), **II:** 304

Voyage, The, and Other Versions of Poems by Baudelaire (Lowell), **Retro. Supp. II:** 187

Voyage dans la Haute Pennsylvanie et dans l'état de New-York (Crèvecoeur), **Supp. I Part 1:** 250–251

Voyage of the Beagle (Darwin), **Supp. IX:** 211

Voyage Out, The (Woolf), **Supp. XV:** 65

"Voyager, The" (Everwine), **Supp. XV:** 75

"Voyages" (H. Crane), **I:** 393–395; **Retro. Supp. II:** 78, 80, 81

"Voyages" (Levine), **Supp. V:** 190

Voyages and Discoveries of the Companions of Columbus (Irving), **II:** 310

Voyage to Pagany, A (W. C. Williams), **IV:** 404; **Retro. Supp. I:** 418–419, **420–421,** 423

Voyaging Portraits (Sobin), **Supp. XVI:** 282, 287

"Voyeur, The" (Gioia), **Supp. XV:** 125

"Voz de America" (column, W. Frank), **Supp. XX:** 80

Voznesensky, Andrei, **II:** 553; **Supp. III Part 1:** 268; **Supp. III Part 2:** 560

Vrbovska, Anca, **Supp. IV Part 2:** 639

V. S. Naipaul: An Introduction to His Work (Theroux), **Supp. VIII:** 314, 318

"V. S. Pritchett's Apprenticeship" (Maxwell), **Supp. VIII:** 172

Vukelich, James, **Supp. XXIII:** 228, 233

"Vulgarity in Literature" (Huxley), **III:** 429–430

"Vultures" (Oliver), **Supp. VII:** 235

"V. V." (Alcott), **Supp. I Part 1:** 37

W

W (Viva) (Cummings), **I:** 429, 433, 434, 436, 443, 444, 447

Wabash (R. O. Butler), **Supp. XII:** 61, **68–69**

Wade, Grace, **I:** 216

"Wading at Wellfleet" (Bishop), **Retro. Supp. II:** 42, 43; **Supp. I Part 1:** 80, 85, 86

Wadsworth, Charles, **I:** 454, 470; **Retro. Supp. I:** 32, 33

Wagenknecht, Edward, **II:** 508; **Supp. I Part 2:** 408, 584; **Supp. IV Part 2:** 681

"Wages of Poetry, The" (Wright), **Supp. XV:** 337

Wagner, Erica, **Supp. XXI:** 117

Wagner, Jean, **Supp. I Part 1:** 341, 346; **Supp. IV Part 1:** 165, 167, 171

Wagner, Richard, **I:** 284, 395; **II:** 425; **III:** 396, 507; **Supp. IV Part 1:** 392

Wagner, Robert, **Supp. IX:** 250

"Wagnerians, The" (Auchincloss), **Supp. IV Part 1:** 23

"Wagner Matinee, A" (Cather), **I:** 315–316; **Retro. Supp. I:** 5, 8

Wagoner, David, **Supp. IX: 323–340; Supp. XII:** 178; **Supp. XX:** 200

Wahlöö, Per, **Supp. XX:** 87

Waid, Candace, **Retro. Supp. I:** 360, 372, 373

Waif, The (Longfellow, ed.), **Retro. Supp. II:** 155

"Waif of the Plains, A" (Harte), **Supp. II Part 1:** 354

Wain, John, **Supp. XIV:** 166

"Wait" (Kinnell), **Supp. III Part 1:** 250

"Waiter in a California Vietnamese Restaurant" (Major), **Supp. XXII:** 182

"Waiting" (Dubus), **Supp. VII:** 87

Waiting (Jin), **Supp. XVIII:** 89, **96–97,** 99

"Waiting" (W. C. Williams), **Retro. Supp. I:** 418

"Waiting, The" (L.-Y. Lee), **Supp. XV:** 218

"Waiting, The" (Olds), **Supp. X:** 209

"Waiting between the Trees" (Tan), **Supp. X:** 290

"Waiting by the Gate" (Bryant), **Supp. I Part 1:** 171

Waiting for God (Weil), **I:** 298

Waiting for Godot (Beckett), **I:** 78, 91, 298; **Supp. IV Part 1:** 368–369; **Supp. XXIII:** 213

Waiting for Lefty (Odets), **Supp. I Part 1:** 277; **Supp. II Part 2:** 529, 530–533, 540; **Supp. V:** 109; **Supp. XIX:** 242

Waiting for Sweet Betty (Major), **Supp. XXII:** 183

Waiting for Teddy Williams (Mosher), **Supp. XXII:** 205, 206, 207, 208, 209, **215–216**

Waiting for the End of the World (Bell), **Supp. X: 4–5,** 11

"Waiting for the Ladies" (L. Brown), **Supp. XXI:** 44

Waiting for the Verdict (R. H. Davis), **Supp. XVI:** 85, 89, 90

"Waiting in a Rain Forest" (Wagoner), **Supp. IX:** 329

Waiting in the Wings (Loraga), **Supp. XXIII:** 195

Waiting Room, The (Kees), **Supp. XV:** 133, 148

Waiting to Exhale (McMillan), **Supp. XIII:** 184, 185, **189–190,** 191

"Waiting to Freeze" (Banks), **Supp. V:** 5, 6

Waiting to Freeze: Poems (Banks), **Supp. V:** 6, 8

Waits, Tom, **Supp. VIII:** 12

Wait until Spring, Bandini (Fante), **Supp. XI:** 160, 161, 164, 165, **166–167**

Wait until Spring, Bandini (film), **Supp. XI:** 173

"Wake, The" (Dove), **Supp. IV Part 1:** 250

"Wakefield" (Hawthorne), **Retro. Supp. I:** 154, 159

Wakefield, Dan, **Supp. VIII:** 43; **Supp. XVI:** 220; **Supp. XIX:** 257, 258

Wakefield, Richard, **Supp. IX:** 323

"Wake Island" (Rukeyser), **Supp. VI:** 273

"Wake"(Kenny), **Supp. XXIII:** 155

Wakeman, Frederic, **Supp. IX:** 247

Wake Up and Live! (Brande), **Supp. I Part 2:** 608

"Waking" (C. Frost), **Supp. XV:** 93

Waking, The (Roethke), **III:** 541

"Waking Early Sunday Morning" (Lowell), **II:** 552; **Retro. Supp. II:** 190

"Waking in the Blue" (Lowell), **II:** 547; **Retro. Supp. II:** 180

"Waking in the Dark" (Rich), **Supp. I Part 2:** 559

"Waking Up the Rake" (Hogan), **Supp. IV Part 1:** 415–416, 416

Wakoski, Diane, **Supp. V:** 79; **Supp. XII:** 184; **Supp. XV:** 252; **Supp. XVII:** 112; **Supp. XXIII:** 52; **Supp. XXIV:** 37

Walbridge, John, **Supp. XX:** 125

Walcott, Charles C., **II:** 49

Walcott, Derek, **Supp. VIII:** 28; **Supp. X:** 122, 131; **Supp. XV:** 256; **Supp. XXIV:** 86

Walcott, Jersey Joe, **Supp. V:** 182

Wald, Alan, **Supp. XV:** 202; **Supp. XVIII:** 223; **Supp. XXI:** 261, 262, 271, 275–276, 277, 278

Wald, Lillian, **Supp. I Part 1:** 12

Walden (Thoreau), **Supp. XIV:** 177, 227; **Supp. XV:** 275; **Supp. XVIII:** 14, 80, 189; **Supp. XXIV:** 73

Walden, Daniel, **Supp. IV Part 2:** 584, 591; **Supp. V:** 272

Walden; or, Life in the Woods (Thoreau), **I:** 219, 305; **II:** 8, 142, 159, 312–313, 458; **IV:** 168, 169, 170, 176, 177–178, 179–182, 183, 187; **Retro. Supp. I:** 62; **Supp. I Part 2:** 579, 655, 664, 672; **Supp. VIII:** 296; **Supp. X:** 27, 101; **Supp. XIII:** 152

Waldman, Anne, **Supp. XIV:** 150; **Supp. XXIII:** 221; **Supp. XXIV:** 33, 41, 45

Waldmeir, Joseph, **III:** 45

Waldmeir, Joseph J., **Supp. I Part 2:** 476

Waldo (Theroux), **Supp. VIII:** 313, 314, **314–315**

Waldo Frank: A Study (Munson), **Supp. XX:** 74

Waldron, Jeremy, **Supp. XVII:** 235

Waldrop, Keith, **Supp. XV:** 153, 165

Waley, Arthur, **II:** 526; **III:** 466; **Supp. V:** 340

"Walk, A" (Snyder), **Supp. VIII:** 297

Walkabout Year: Twelve Months in Australia (Pickering), **Supp. XXI:** 199, 200

"Walk at Sunset, A" (Bryant), **Supp. I Part 1:** 155

"Walk before Mass, A" (Agee), **I:** 28–29

Walker, Alice, **Retro. Supp. I:** 215; **Supp. I Part 2:** 550; **Supp. III Part 2:** 488, **517–540; Supp. IV Part 1:** 14; **Supp. VIII:** 141, 214; **Supp. IX:** 306, 311; **Supp. X:** 85, 228, 252, 325, 330; **Supp. XIII:** 179, 185, 291, 295; **Supp. XVI:** 39; **Supp. XVIII:** 200, 283; **Supp. XX: 84, 107, 108; Supp. XXI:** 172; **Supp. XXII:** 172

Walker, Cheryl, **Supp. XI:** 145

Walker, David, **Supp. V:** 189; **Supp. XVII:** 246

Walker, Franklin D., **III:** 321

Walker, Gue, **Supp. XII:** 207

Walker, Margaret, **Supp. XVIII:** 282; **Supp. XX:** 106

Walker, Marianne, **Supp. VIII:** 139
Walker, Obadiah, **II:** 113
Walker, Scott, **Supp. XV:** 92
Walker in the City, A (Kazin), **Supp. VIII: 93–95,** 99
Walk Hard (Blum and Hill), **Supp. XV:** 194
Walk Hard-Talk Loud (Zinberg), **Supp. XV:** 194, 202
"Walking" (Hogan), **Supp. IV Part 1:** 416
"Walking" (Thoreau), **Supp. IV Part 1:** 416; **Supp. IX:** 178
"Walking Along in Winter" (Kenyon), **Supp. VII:** 167
"Walking around the Block with a Three-Year-Old" (Wagoner), **Supp. IX:** 331–332
"Walking at Noon Near the Burlington Depot in Lincoln, Nebraska" (Kooser), **Supp. XIX:** 122
"Walking Backwards into the Future" (R. Williams), **Supp. IX:** 146
Walking Down the Stairs: Selections from Interviews (Kinnell), **Supp. III Part 1:** 235, 249
"Walking Home" (Schnackenberg). *See* "Laughing with One Eye" (Schnackenberg)
"Walking Home at Night" (Ginsberg), **Supp. II Part 1:** 313
"Walking Is Almost Falling" (Peacock), **Supp. XIX:** 196, 197
Walking Light (Dunn), **Supp. XI:** 140, 141, 153
"Walking Man of Rodin, The" (Sandburg), **III:** 583
"Walking Sticks and Paperweights and Water Marks" (Moore), **III:** 215
Walking Tall (Dunn), **Supp. XI:** 140
Walking the Black Cat (Simic), **Supp. VIII:** 280, **282–284**
Walking to Gatlinburg (Mosher), **Supp. XXII:** 204, 205, 206, 207, 208, 209, 215, **216–217**
Walking to Martha's Vineyard (F. Wright), **Supp. XVII:** 240, 241, 245, 246
Walking to Sleep (Wilbur), **Supp. III Part 2:** 557–560
"Walking to Sleep" (Wilbur), **Supp. III Part 2:** 544, 557, 559, 561, 562
"Walking Wounded" (Shaw), **Supp. XIX:** 248
Walkin' the Dog (Mosley), **Supp. XIII:** 242
"Walk in the Moonlight, A" (Anderson), **I:** 114
Walk Me to the Distance (Everett), **Supp. XVIII: 55–56,** 57
Walk on the Wild Side, A (Algren), **Supp. V:** 4; **Supp. IX:** 3, **12–13,** 14
"Walks in Rome" (Merrill), **Supp. III Part 1:** 337
Walk to the River, A (Hoffman), **Supp. XVIII: 77–78**
Walk with Tom Jefferson, A (Levine), **Supp. V:** 179, 187, 190–191
"Wall, The" (Bronk), **Supp. XXI:** 31
"Wall, The" (Brooks), **Supp. III Part 1:** 70, 71, 84

Wall, The (Hersey), **IV:** 4; **Supp. XX: 251**
"Wall, The" (Roethke), **III:** 544
"Wall, The" (Sexton), **Supp. II Part 2:** 696
Wallace, Daniel, **Supp. XXII:** 49
Wallace, David, **Supp. XXI:** 277
Wallace, David Foster, **Retro. Supp. II:** 279; **Supp. X: 301–318; Supp. XVII:** 226; **Supp. XIX:** 223; **Supp. XX: 91, 93; Supp. XXII:** 260, 261
Wallace, Henry, **I:** 489; **III:** 111, 475; **Supp. I Part 1:** 286; **Supp. I Part 2:** 645
Wallace, Jim, **Supp. XX: 143**
Wallace, Mike, **Supp. IV Part 1:** 364; **Supp. IV Part 2:** 526; **Supp. XX: 102**
Wallace, Richard, **Supp. XVIII:** 101–102
Wallace Stevens (Kermode), **Retro. Supp. I:** 301
Wallace Stevens: The Poems of our Climate (Bloom), **Retro. Supp. I:** 299
Wallace Stevens: Words Chosen out of Desire (Stevens), **Retro. Supp. I:** 297
Wallach, Eli, **III:** 161
Wallant, Edward Lewis, **Supp. XVI:** 220
Wallas, Graham, **Supp. I Part 2:** 643
"Walled City" (Oates), **Supp. II Part 2:** 524
Wallenstein, Anna. *See* Weinstein, Mrs. Max (Anna Wallenstein)
Waller, Edmund, **III:** 463
Waller, Fats, **IV:** 263
Waller, Nicole, **Supp. XXII:** 78
Walling, William English, **Supp. I Part 2:** 645; **Supp. XV:** 295
"Wall of Paintings, The" (Notley), **Supp. XXII:** 230
Wall of the Sky, the Wall of the Eye, The (Lethem), **Supp. XVIII:** 139
Walls Do Not Fall, The (Doolittle), **Supp. I Part 1:** 271, 272
Walls of Jericho, The (R. Fisher), **Supp. XIX:** 65, 67, 70, **72–77,** 78
"Wall Songs" (Hogan), **Supp. IV Part 1:** 413
Wall Writing (Auster), **Supp. XII:** 23–24
Walpole, Horace, **I:** 203; **Supp. I Part 2:** 410, 714
Walpole, Hugh, **Retro. Supp. I:** 231; **Supp. XX: 232**
Walpole, Robert, **IV:** 145
Walsh, David M., **Supp. XV:** 5
Walsh, Ed, **II:** 424
Walsh, Ernest, **Supp. XXIV:** 50
Walsh, George, **Supp. IV Part 2:** 528
Walsh, Raoul, **Supp. XIII:** 174
Walsh, Richard J., **Supp. II Part 1:** 119, 130
Walsh, William, **Supp. IV Part 1:** 242, 243, 246, 248, 252, 254, 257
"Walt, the Wounded" (Di Piero), **Supp. XIX:** 37
"Walt and Will" (Apple), **Supp. XVII:** 6
Walter, Eugene, **Supp. XVI:** 230
Walter, Joyce, **Supp. XV:** 121
Walter Benjamin at the Dairy Queen: Reflections at Sixty and Beyond (McMurtry), **Supp. V:** 232
Walters, Barbara, **Supp. XIV:** 125

Walters, Marguerite. *See* Smith, Mrs. Lamar (Marguerite Walters)
"Walter T. Carriman" (O'Hara), **III:** 368
Walton, Izaak, **Supp. I Part 2:** 422
"Walt Whitman" (Kooser), **Supp. XIX:** 118
"Walt Whitman" (Masters), **Supp. I Part 2:** 458
"Walt Whitman at Bear Mountain" (Simpson), **Supp. IX:** 265
Walt Whitman Bathing (Wagoner), **Supp. IX: 331–332**
Walt Whitman Handbook (Allen), **IV:** 352
Walt Whitman Reconsidered (Chase), **IV:** 352
"Waltz, The" (Parker), **Supp. IX:** 204
"Waltzer in the House, The" (Kunitz), **Supp. III Part 1:** 258
Waltzing Matilda (Notley), **Supp. XXII:** 229–230
"Waltzing Matilda" (Notley), **Supp. XXII:** 230
Waltzing the Magpies: A Year in Australia (Pickering), **Supp. XXI:** 199, 200
Walzer, Kevin, **Supp. XII:** 202; **Supp. XV:** 118; **Supp. XVIII:** 174
Wambaugh, Joseph, **Supp. X:** 5; **Supp. XXI:** 67
Wampeters, Foma, & Granfalloons (Vonnegut), **Supp. II Part 2:** 758, 759–760, 776, 779
Wand, David Hsin-fu, **Supp. X:** 292
"Wanderer, The" (W. C. Williams), **Retro. Supp. I:** 414, 421
Wanderer, The: His Parables and His Sayings (Gibran), **Supp. XX: 116, 123–124**
"Wanderers, The" (Welty), **IV:** 273–274
"Wandering Jew, The" (Robinson), **III:** 505, 516–517
Wanderings of Oisin (Yeats), **Supp. I Part 1:** 79
Wang, Dorothy, **Supp. X:** 289
Wang Wei, **Supp. XV:** 47
Waniek, Marilyn Nelson, **Supp. IV Part 1:** 244. *See also* Nelson, Marilyn
Wanking 'Tards (Silver), **Supp. XXIV:** 265
"Wan Lee, the Pagan" (Harte), **Supp. II Part 1:** 351
"Want, The" (Olds), **Supp. X:** 210
Want Bone, The (Pinsky), **Supp. VI:** 236–237, 244–245, 247
"Wanted: An Ontological Critic" (Ransom), **III:** 498
"Wanting to Die" (Sexton), **Supp. II Part 2:** 684, 686; **Supp. XIV:** 132
"Wants" (Paley), **Supp. VI:** 219
Waples, Dorothy, **I:** 348
Wapshot Chronicle, The (Cheever), **Supp. I Part 1:** 174, 177–180, 181, 196
Wapshot Scandal, The (Cheever), **Supp. I Part 1:** 180–184, 187, 191, 196
"War" (Findley), **Supp. XX: 49**
"War" (Jin), **Supp. XVIII:** 93
"War" (Kingston), **Supp. V:** 169
"War" (Simic), **Supp. VIII:** 282
"War, Response, and Contradiction" (Burke), **I:** 283

"War and Peace" (Sanders), **Supp. XVI:** 277

War and Peace (Tolstoy), **I:** 6, 7; **II:** 191, 205, 291; **IV:** 446; **Supp. V:** 277; **Supp. XI:** 68; **Supp. XIV:** 97; **Supp. XXIII:** 11

War and Remembrance (Wouk), **Supp. XX:** 243

"War and the Small Nations" (Gibran), **Supp. XX:** 127

War and War (F. Barthelme), **Supp. XI:** 25

"War Between Men and Women, The" (Thurber), **Supp. I Part 2:** 615

War Bulletins (Lindsay), **Supp. I Part 2:** 378–379

Ward, Aileen, **II:** 531

Ward, Artemus (pseudonym). *See* Browne, Charles Farrar

Ward, Douglas Turner, **Supp. IV Part 1:** 362

Ward, Geoff, **Supp. XXIII:** 218

Ward, Henry, **Supp. I Part 2:** 588

Ward, Mrs. Humphry, **II:** 338

Ward, Leo R., **Supp. VIII:** 124

Ward, Lester F., **Supp. I Part 2:** 640; **Supp. XI:** 202, 203

Ward, Lynn, **I:** 31

Ward, Nathaniel, **Supp. I Part 1:** 99, 102, 111, 116

Ward, Susan, **Supp. XXIII:** 146

Ward, Theodora, **I:** 470; **Retro. Supp. I:** 28

Ward, William Hayes, **Supp. I Part 1:** 371

"War Debt, A" (Jewett), **Retro. Supp. II:** 138, 141

"War Diary" (Boyce), **Supp. XVII:** 104; **Supp. XXI:** 6

"War Diary, A" (Bourne), **I:** 229

War Dispatches of Stephen Crane, The (Crane), **I:** 422

"Ward Line, The" (Morris), **III:** 220

Warfel, Harry R., **Supp. I Part 1:** 366

War Games (Morris), **III:** 238

War Goes On, The (Asch), **Supp. XXIII:** 6

"Warhol / Blue Jackie"(Balakian), **Supp. XXIII:** 32

War in Heaven, The (Shepard and Chaikin), **Supp. III Part 2:** 433

War Is Kind (Crane), **I:** 409; **III:** 585

"War Is Kind" (Crane), **I:** 419

Warlock (Harrison), **Supp. VIII:** 45, **46**

Warm as Wool (Sanders), **Supp. XVI:** 269

"Warming" (Trethewey), **Supp. XXI:** 245

Warner, Anna, **Supp. XVIII:** 258–275

Warner, Charles Dudley, **II:** 405; **IV:** 198

Warner, Jack, **Supp. XII:** 160–161; **Supp. XVIII:** 249

Warner, John R., **III:** 193

Warner, Oliver, **I:** 548

Warner, Susan, **Retro. Supp. I:** 246; **Supp. XV:** 275; **Supp. XVIII:** 257–275

Warner, Sylvia Townsend, **Supp. VIII:** 151, 155, 164, 171

Warner, W. Lloyd, **III:** 60

Warner Family and the Warner Books, The (Baker), **Supp. XVIII:** 259, 267

"Warning" (Hughes), **Supp. I Part 1:** 343

"Warning" (Pound), **III:** 474

"Warning, The" (Creeley), **Supp. IV Part 1:** 150

"Warning, The" (Longfellow), **II:** 498

Warning Hill (Marquand), **III:** 55–56, 60, 68

"War of Eyes, A" (Coleman), **Supp. XI:** 93–94

War of Eyes and Other Stories, A (Coleman), **Supp. XI: 91–92**

War of the Classes (London), **II:** 466

"War of the Wall, The" (Bambara), **Supp. XI:** 15–16

"War of Vaslav Nijinsky, The" (Bidart), **Supp. XV:** 21–22, **27–29**

"War Poems" (Sandburg), **III:** 581

Warren, Austin, **I:** 265, 268, 271; **Supp. I Part 2:** 423

Warren, David, **Supp. XXIV:** 269

Warren, Earl, **III:** 581

Warren, Gabriel, **IV:** 244

Warren, Mercy Otis, **Supp. XV:** 230

Warren, Patricia Nell, **Supp. XX: 259–276**

Warren, Robert Penn, **I:** 190, 211, 517; **II:** 57, 217, 228, 253; **III:** 134, 310, 382–383, 454, 482, 485, 490, 496, 497; **IV:** 121, 122, 123, 125, 126, **236–259**, 261, 262, 279, 340–341, 458; **Retro. Supp. I:** 40, 41, 73, 90; **Retro. Supp. II:** 220, 235; **Supp. I Part 1:** 359, 371; **Supp. I Part 2:** 386, 423; **Supp. II Part 1:** 139; **Supp. III Part 2:** 542; **Supp. V:** 261, 316, 318, 319, 333; **Supp. VIII:** 126, 176; **Supp. IX:** 257; **Supp. X:** 1, 25, 26; **Supp. XI:** 315; **Supp. XII:** 254, 255; **Supp. XIV:** 1, 2, 3, 4, 11, 14, 15; **Supp. XVIII:** 77, 78–79; **Supp. XIX:** 246; **Supp. XXI:** 256

Warren, Mrs. Robert Penn (Eleanor Clark), **IV:** 244

Warren, Rosanna, **IV:** 244; **Supp. XV:** 251, 261, 262, 263; **Supp. XIX:** 34

Warren, Vincent, **Supp. XXIII:** 218, 219

Warrington Poems, The (Ríos), **Supp. IV Part 2:** 540

Warrior, Robert Allen, **Supp. IV Part 1:** 329

"Warrior, The" (Gunn Allen), **Supp. IV Part 1:** 326

"Warrior: 5th Grade" (Olds), **Supp. X:** 214

"Warrior Road" (Harjo), **Supp. XII:** 217

Wars, The (Findley), **Supp. XX: 53–54**

Warsh, Lewis, **Supp. XXIV:** 41

Warshavsky, Isaac (pseudonym). *See* Singer, Isaac Bashevis

Warshow, Robert, **Supp. I Part 1:** 51

Wars I Have Seen (Stein), **IV:** 27, 36, 477

Wartime (Fussell), **Supp. V:** 241

War Trash (Jin), **Supp. XVIII:** 89, **100–101**

"War Widow, The" (Frederic), **II:** 135–136

"Was" (Creeley), **Supp. IV Part 1:** 155

"Was" (Faulkner), **II:** 71

"Wash" (Faulkner), **II:** 72

Wash, Richard, **Supp. XII:** 14

"Washboard Wizard" (Nelson), **Supp. XVIII:** 182

"Washed in the Rain" (Fante), **Supp. XI:** 165

"Washing of Hands, A" (Kooser), **Supp. XIX:** 115

Washington, Booker T., **Supp. I Part 2:** 393; **Supp. II Part 1:** 157, 160, 167, 168, 171, 225; **Supp. XIV:** 198, 199, 201; **Supp. XVIII:** 121–122

Washington, D.C. (Vidal), **Supp. IV Part 2:** 677, 684, 686–687, 690

Washington, George, **I:** 453; **II:** 313–314; **Supp. I Part 2:** 399, 485, 508, 509, 511, 513, 517, 518, 520, 599

Washington, Mary Helen, **Supp. XVIII:** 119, 284

Washington and His Generals (Lippard), **Supp. XXIII:** 178, **185–186,** 187

Washington Crossing the Delaware (Rivers), **Supp. XV:** 186

Washington Post Book World (Lesser), **Supp. IV Part 2:** 453; **Supp. VIII:** 80, 84, 241; **Supp. X:** 282

Washington Square (James), **II:** 327, 328; **Retro. Supp. I:** 215, 220, **222–223**

"Washington Square, 1946" (Ozick), **Supp. V:** 272

Washington Square Ensemble, The (Bell), **Supp. X:** 1, **3–4**

"Washman"(P. Benedict), **Supp. XXIII:** 40

"Was Lowell an Historical Critic?" (Altick), **Supp. I Part 2:** 423

Wasserman, Earl R., **Supp. I Part 2:** 439, 440

Wasserman, Jakob, **Supp. I Part 2:** 669

Wasserstein, Wendy, **Supp. IV Part 1:** 309; **Supp. XV: 319–336;** **Supp. XXIV:** 116, 117, 119, 128

Wasson, Ben, **Retro. Supp. I:** 79, 83

"Waste Carpet, The" (Matthews), **Supp. IX: 158–159**

Waste Land, The (T. S. Eliot), **I:** 107, 266, 298, 395, 396, 482, 570–571, 572, 574–575, 577–578, 580, 581, 584, 585, 586, 587; **III:** 6–8, 12, 196, 277–278, 453, 471, 492, 586; **IV:** 122, 123, 124, 140, 418, 419, 420; **Retro. Supp. I:** 51, 60, **60–62,** 63, 64, 66, 210, 290, 291, 299, 311, 420, 427; **Retro. Supp. II:** 85, 121, 190; **Supp. I Part 1:** 272; **Supp. I Part 2:** 439, 455, 614; **Supp. II Part 1:** 4, 5, 11, 96; **Supp. III Part 1:** 9, 10, 41, 63, 105; **Supp. IV Part 1:** 47, 284; **Supp. V:** 338; **Supp. IX:** 158, 305; **Supp. X:** 125; **Supp. XIII:** 341–342, 344, 346; **Supp. XIV:** 6, 284; **Supp. XV:** 21, 181, 261, 306; **Supp. XVI:** 204; **Supp. XVII:** 140–141, 144, 227; **Supp. XVIII:** 78, 79–80; **Supp. XIX:** 288; **Supp. XXIII:** 23, 25, 79, 165; **Supp. XXIV:** 140

"Waste Land, The": A Facsimile and Transcript of the Original Drafts Including the Annotations of Ezra Pound (Eliot, ed.), **Retro. Supp. I:** 58

Waste Land and Other Poems, The (T. S. Eliot), **Supp. XV:** 305

Wat, Alexander, **Supp. XVI:** 155, 161

Watch, The (Bass), **Supp. XVI: 16–17**
"Watch, The, —" (Bass), **Supp. XVI:** 17
Watch and Ward (James), **II:** 323; **Retro. Supp. I:** 218, **219,** 220
"Watcher" (Trethewey), **Supp. XXI:** 247
"Watcher, The" (R. Bly), **Supp. IV Part 1:** 71
"Watcher by the Dead, A" (Bierce), **I:** 203
Watchfires (Auchincloss), **Supp. IV Part 1:** 23
"Watching Crow, Looking toward the Manzano Mountains" (Harjo), **Supp. XII:** 219
"Watching the Oregon Whale" (A. Finch), **Supp. XVII:** 77
"Watching the Sunset" (Coleman), **Supp. XI:** 92
Watch on the Rhine (Hellman), **Supp. I Part 1:** 276, 278, 279–281, 283–284; **Supp. IV Part 1:** 83
"Water" (Emerson), **II:** 19
"Water" (Komunyakaa), **Supp. XIII:** 132
"Water" (Lowell), **II:** 550
"Waterbird" (Swenson), **Supp. IV Part 2:** 651
"Water Borders" (Dillard), **Supp. VI:** 27
"Water Buffalo" (Komunyakaa), **Supp. XIII:** 122
"Watercolor of Grantchester Meadows" (Plath), **Supp. I Part 2:** 537
Water Cure, The (Everett), **Supp. XVIII: 64–66**
"Water Drum"(Kenny), **Supp. XXIII:** 144
"Waterfall, The" (Clampitt), **Supp. IX:** 44
Waterfront (Schulberg), **Supp. XVIII: 251–252**
"Water Hose Is on Fire, The" (Simic), **Supp. XV:** 185
Waterhouse, Keith, **Supp. VIII:** 124
"Waterlily Fire" (Rukeyser), **Supp. VI:** 285, 286
Waterlily Fire: Poems 1935–1962 (Rukeyser), **Supp. VI:** 274, 283, 285
Watermark (Brodsky), **Supp. VIII:** 29
Water-Method Man, The (Irving), **Supp. VI:** 163, **167–179,** 180
Water Music (Boyle), **Supp. VIII:** 1, 3–5, 8, 14; **Supp. XX: 20–22**
"Water Music for the Progress of Love in a Life-Raft Down the Sammamish Slough" (Wagoner), **Supp. IX:** 326
"Water People" (Burke), **Supp. XIV:** 21
"Water Picture" (Swenson), **Supp. IV Part 2:** 641
"Water Rising" (Hogan), **Supp. IV Part 1:** 400
Waters, Ethel, **II:** 587
Waters, Frank, **Supp. X:** 124
Waters, Muddy, **Supp. VIII:** 345
Watershed (Everett), **Supp. XVIII: 58–59,** 64
"Watershed" (Kingsolver), **Supp. VII:** 208
"Watershed" (Warren), **IV:** 239
"Watershed, The" (Auden), **Supp. II Part 1:** 5

Waters of Kronos, The (Richter), **Supp. XVIII:** 207, 208, **218–219,** 220
Waters of Siloe, The (Merton), **Supp. VIII:** 196, 208
Waterston, Sam, **Supp. IX:** 253
Water Street (Merrill), **Supp. III Part 1:** 321–323
"Water Walker" (Wilbur), **Supp. III Part 2:** 548, 560
Water-Witch, The (Cooper), **I:** 342–343
"Water Witch"(P. Benedict), **Supp. XXIII:** 38
Waterworks, The (Doctorow), **Supp. IV Part 1:** 218, 222, 223, 231–233, 234
"Water Works, The" (Doctorow), **Supp. IV Part 1:** 234
Watkin, E. I., **Retro. Supp. II:** 187
Watkins, Floyd C., **IV:** 452
Watkins, James T., **I:** 193, 194
Watkins, Maureen, **Supp. XVI:** 188
Watkins, Mel, **Supp. X:** 330; **Supp. XIII:** 246
Watman, Max, **Supp. XX: 92**
Watrous, Peter, **Supp. VIII:** 79
Watson, Brook, **Supp. XX: 284**
Watson, Burton, **Supp. XV:** 47
Watson, James Sibley, Jr., **I:** 261
Watson, Jay, **Supp. XVIII:** 195; **Supp. XXI:** 46
Watson, J. B., **II:** 361
Watson, Richard, **Supp. I Part 2:** 516, 517
Watson, William, **II:** 114
Watsonville: Some Place Not Here (Moraga), **Supp. XXIII:** 195, 196, 202, 203
Watt, Ian, **Supp. VIII:** 4
Watteau, Jean Antoine, **III:** 275; **IV:** 79
Watts, Emily Stipes, **Supp. I Part 1:** 115
Waugh, Arthur, **Supp. XXIV:** 30
Waugh, Evelyn, **I:** 480; **III:** 281; **Supp. I Part 2:** 607; **Supp. IV Part 2:** 688; **Supp. XI:** 305, 306; **Supp. XIX:** 131
"Wave" (Snyder), **Supp. VIII:** 299
Wave, A (Ashbery), **Supp. III Part 1:** 1, 4, 24–26
"Wave, A" (Ashbery), **Supp. III Part 1:** 9, 19, 24–25
"Wave, The" (MacLeish), **III:** 19
"Wave, The" (Untermeyer), **Supp. XV:** 300
Wave Amplitude in the Mona Passage (Schott), **Supp. XXIII: 242–243**
"Wavemaker Falters, The" (Saunders), **Supp. XIX:** 225
"Waxwings" (Francis), **Supp. IX:** 82
Way, The (Steiner and Witt, eds.), **Supp. IV Part 2:** 505
"Way Down, The" (Kunitz), **Supp. III Part 1:** 263
"Way It Is, The" (Ellison), **Supp. II Part 1:** 245
"Way It Is, The" (Jones), **Supp. XI:** 229
Way It Is, The (Stafford), **Supp. XIII:** 274
"Way It Is, The" (Strand), **Supp. IV Part 2:** 627
"Wayland" (Sanders), **Supp. XVI:** 275
Wayne, John, **Supp. IV Part 1:** 200

Way of Chuang-Tzu, The (Merton), **Supp. VIII:** 208
"Way of Exchange in James Dickey's Poetry, The" (Weatherby), **Supp. IV Part 1:** 175
Way of Life According to Laotzu, The (Bynner), **Supp. XV:** 46, 48
Way Out, A (Frost), **Retro. Supp. I:** 133
Wayside Motor Inn, The (Gurney), **Supp. V:** 96, 105, 109
"Ways of Breaking: Lynda Hull's 'Ornithology' " (Jauss), **Supp. XXI:** 139
"Ways of Talking" (Jin), **Supp. XVIII:** 93
Ways of the Hour, The (Cooper), **I:** 354
Ways of White Folks, The (Hughes), **Retro. Supp. I:** 203, 204; **Supp. I Part 1:** 329, 330, 332
Way Some People Die, The (Macdonald), **Supp. IV Part 2:** 470, 471, 472, 474
Way Some People Live, The (Cheever), **Supp. I Part 1:** 175
"Way the Cards Fall, The" (Komunyakaa), **Supp. XIII:** 117
"Way the Luck Runs, The" (Wolfert), **Supp. XXI:** 265
"Way Things Are, The" (Turow, unpub.), **Supp. XVII:** 215, 218
Way to Rainy Mountain, The (Momaday), **Supp. IV Part 2:** 485–486, 487–489, 491, 493
Way to Wealth, The (Franklin), **II:** 101–102, 110; **Supp. XX: 27**
Wayward and the Seeking, The: A Collection of Writings by Jean Toomer (Toomer), **Supp. III Part 2:** 478–481, 484, 487
Wayward Bus, The (Steinbeck), **IV:** 51, 64–65
"Way We Live Now, The" (Sontag), **Supp. III Part 2:** 467–468
"Way You'll Never Be, A" (Hemingway), **II:** 249
"W. D. Sees Himself Animated" (Snodgrass), **Supp. VI:** 327
"W. D. Sits in Kafka's Chair and Is Interrogated Concerning the Assumed Death of Cock Robin" (Snodgrass), **Supp. VI:** 319
"W. D. Tries to Warn Cock Robin" (Snodgrass), **Supp. VI:** 319
"We" (Alexander), **Supp. XVIII:** 185
Weaks, Mary Louise, **Supp. X:** 5
Weales, Gerald, **II:** 602
"Wealth," from *Conduct of Life, The* (Emerson), **II:** 2, 3–4
"Wealth," from *English Traits* (Emerson), **II:** 6
Wealth of Nations, The (A. Smith), **II:** 109
"We Are Looking at You, Agnes" (Caldwell), **I:** 309
We Are Still Married: Stories and Letters (Keillor), **Supp. XVI:** 176, 177
"We Are the Crazy Lady and Other Feisty Feminist Fables" (Ozick), **Supp. V:** 259
Weary Blues, The (Hughes), **Retro. Supp. I:** 195, 197, 198, 199, 200, 203, 205;

Supp. I Part 1: 325
"Weary Blues, The" (Hughes), **Retro. Supp. I:** 198, 199; **Supp. I Part 1:** 324, 325
"Weary Kingdom" (Irving), **Supp. VI:** 163
Weasels and Wisemen: Ethics and Ethnicity in the Work of David Mamet (Kane), **Supp. XIV:** 250
Weather and the Women Treat Me Fair, The (Everett), **Supp. XVIII:** 66
Weatherby, H. L., **Supp. IV Part 1:** 175
Weather Central (Kooser), **Supp. XIX:** 116, **123–125**
"Weathering Out" (Dove), **Supp. IV Part 1:** 248
"Weather Within, The" (M. F. K. Fisher), **Supp. XVII:** 88, 91
Weaver, Harriet, **III:** 471
Weaver, James, **Supp. XVIII:** 72
Weaver, Michael, **Supp. XVIII:** 176, 177
Weaver, Mike, **Retro. Supp. I:** 430
Weaver, Will, **Supp. XVI:** 39
"Weaving" (Larcom), **Supp. XIII:** 142, **Supp. XIII:** 144–145, 150, 151
"Web" (Oliver), **Supp. VII:** 236
Web and the Rock, The (Wolfe), **IV:** 451, 455, 457, 459–460, 462, 464, 467, 468
Webb, Beatrice, **Supp. I Part 1:** 5
Webb, Mary, **I:** 226
Webb, Phyllis, **Supp. XX: 56**
Webb, Sidney, **Supp. I Part 1:** 5
Webb, W. P., **Supp. V:** 225
Webber, A. R. F., **Supp. XXI:** 160
Weber, Brom, **I:** 383, 386
Weber, Carl, **Supp. IX:** 133, 138, 141
Weber, Max, **I:** 498; **Supp. I Part 2:** 637, 648
Weber, Sarah, **Supp. I Part 1:** 2
Weberman, A. J., **Supp. XVIII:** 27
Web of Earth, The (Wolfe), **IV:** 451–452, 456, 458, 464, 465
"Web of Life, The" (Nemerov), **III:** 282
Webster, Brenda, **Supp. XVI:** 157, 161
Webster, Daniel, **II:** 5, 9; **Supp. I Part 2:** 659, 687, 689, 690
Webster, John, **I:** 384; **Supp. I Part 2:** 422
Webster, Noah, **Supp. I Part 2:** 660; **Supp. II Part 1:** 77
Wector, Dixon, **II:** 103
Wedding, The (D. West), **Supp. XVIII:** 277, **287–289**
"Wedding, The" (Everwine), **Supp. XV:** 83
"Wedding, The" (Major), **Supp. XXII:** 185
Wedding, The (television miniseries), **Supp. XVIII:** 277, 289
"Wedding Cake" (Nye), **Supp. XIII:** 283
"Wedding Dance, The" (Di Piero), **Supp. XIX:** 47
"Wedding Day" (Boyle), **Supp. XXIV:** 56–57
Wedding Day and Other Stories (Boyle), **Supp. XXIV: 56–57**
"Wedding in Brownsville, A" (Singer), **IV:** 15
Wedding in Hell, A (Simic), **Supp. VIII:** 280, **282**

"Wedding of the Rose and Lotus, The" (Lindsay), **Supp. I Part 2:** 387
"Wedding Supper, The" (Rowson), **Supp. XV:** 243
"Wedding Toast, A" (Wilbur), **Supp. III Part 2:** 561
Wedekind, Frank, **III:** 398; **Supp. XX: 85; Supp. XXII:** 23
Wedge, The (W. C. Williams), **Retro. Supp. I:** 424
"We Didn't"(Dybek), **Supp. XXIII:** 77–78
"Wednesday at the Waldorf" (Swenson), **Supp. IV Part 2:** 647
We Don't Live Here Anymore (Dubus), **Supp. XXIV:** 97
"We Don't Live Here Anymore" (Dubus), **Supp. VII:** 78–79, 85
"Weed" (McCarriston), **Supp. XIV:** 259, 273
"Weed, The" (Bishop), **Supp. I Part 1:** 80, 88–89
"Weed, The" (Taggard), **Supp. XXII:** 284
"Weeds, The" (McCarthy), **II:** 566
"Weekend" (Beattie), **Supp. V:** 27
"Weekend" (Hempel), **Supp. XXI:** 124
Weekend, The (Cameron), **Supp. XII:** 80, 81, **86–88**
"Weekend at Ellerslie, A" (Wilson), **IV:** 431
Weekend Edition (National Public Radio), **Supp. IX:** 299; **Supp. XVII:** 240, 242
Weekend in Dinlock (Sigal), **Supp. XXIII:** 166
"Week in the Word, A" (Hampl), **Supp. XXII:** 85
Week on the Concord and Merrimack Rivers, A (Thoreau), **IV:** 168, 169, 177, 182–183; **Supp. I Part 2:** 420; **Supp. XIV:** 227
Weeks, Edward, **III:** 64
Weeks, Jerome, **Supp. VIII:** 76
"Weeping Burgher" (Stevens), **IV:** 77
"Weeping Women" (Levertov), **Supp. III Part 1:** 282
We Fished All Night (W. Motley), **Supp. XVII: 155–158,** 159, 160
We Fly Away (Francis), **Supp. IX: 79–80,** 84
We Happy Few (Hinojosa), **Supp. XIX:** 99, **111–112**
We Have Always Lived in the Castle (Jackson), **Supp. IX:** 121, 126, **127–128**
"We Have Our Arts So We Won't Die of Truth" (Bradbury), **Supp. IV Part 1:** 105
We Have Tomorrow (Bontemps), **Supp. XXII:** 6, 12
Weich, Dave, **Supp. XII:** 321; **Supp. XVIII:** 91
"Weighing In" (Espaillat), **Supp. XXI:** 111
"Weight" (Wideman), **Supp. X:** 321
"Weights" (C. Baxter), **Supp. XVII:** 16
Weigl, Bruce, **Supp. VIII:** 269, 274; **Supp. XV:** 342; **Supp. XIX: 273–290**
Weik, Alexa, **Supp. XXIV:** 64
Weil, Dorothy, **Supp. XV:** 231
Weil, James L., **Supp. XXI:** 23, 31

Weil, Robert, **Supp. IX:** 236
Weil, Simone, **I:** 298; **Supp. XV:** 259; **Supp. XXII:** 93
Weiland (C. B. Brown), **Supp. XIII:** 100
Weinauer, Ellen, **Supp. XV:** 270, 284
Weinberger, Eliot, **Supp. IV Part 1:** 66; **Supp. VIII:** 290, 292; **Supp. XVI:** 284
Weinberger, Eric, **Supp. XXII:** 264
Weinfield, Henry, **Supp. XXI:** 24, 28, 33
Weininger, Otto, **Retro. Supp. I:** 416
Weinraub, Judith, **Supp. XXI:** 39
Weinreb, Mindy, **Supp. X:** 24
Weinreich, Regina, **Supp. XIV:** 22
Weinstein, Cindy, **Supp. XVIII:** 261
Weinstein, Hinda, **IV:** 285
Weinstein, Max, **IV:** 285
Weinstein, Mrs. Max (Anna Wallenstein), **IV:** 285, 287
Weinstein, Nathan. *See* West, Nathanael
Weinstein, Selma, **Supp. XXI:** 170
Weir, Sybil, **Supp. XXIV:** 20
Weisheit, Rabbi, **IV:** 76
Weismuller, Johnny, **Supp. X:** 264; **Supp. XX: 18**
Weiss, David, **Supp. XVI:** 55
Weiss, Jane, **Supp. XVIII:** 267, 269
Weiss, Peter, **IV:** 117
Weiss, Theodore, **Supp. IV Part 2:** 440; **Supp. IX:** 96
Weissleder, Paul, **Supp. XXII:** 283
Weist, Dianne, **Supp. X:** 80
Weithas, Art, **Supp. XI:** 231
Welch, Dave, **Supp. XXI:** 118
Welch, Don, **Supp. XIX:** 119
Welch, James, **Supp. IV Part 1:** 404; **Supp. IV Part 2:** 503, 513, 557, 562; **Supp. XXIV:** 257
Welch, Lew, **Supp. V:** 170; **Supp. VIII:** 303; **Supp. XXII:** 276
"Welcome from War" (Rukeyser), **Supp. VI:** 286
"Welcome Morning" (Sexton), **Supp. II Part 2:** 696
"Welcome the Wrath" (Kunitz), **Supp. III Part 1:** 261
Welcome to Hard Times (Doctorow), **Supp. IV Part 1:** 218, 219–220, 222, 224, 230, 238
Welcome to Hard Times (film), **Supp. IV Part 1:** 236
"Welcome to New Dork" (Leonard), **Supp. XVIII:** 148
Welcome to Our City (Wolfe), **IV:** 461
Welcome to the Monkey House (Vonnegut), **Supp. II Part 2:** 758
Welcome to the Moon (Shanley), **Supp. XIV:** 318
Welcome to the Moon and Other Plays (Shanley), **Supp. XIV:** 315, **316–319**
Weld, Theodore, **Supp. I Part 2:** 587, 588
Weld, Tuesday, **Supp. XI:** 306
Welded (O'Neill), **III:** 390; **Supp. XXII:** 24
"Welfare Worker, Disenchanted, Contemplates Friday Afternoon, The" (Trethewey), **Supp. XXI:** 246
"Well, The" (Momaday), **Supp. IV Part 2:** 483

"Well Dressed Man with a Beard, The" (Stevens), **Retro. Supp. I:** 297

Wellek, René, **I:** 253, 261, 282; **II:** 320; **Supp. XIV:** 12, 14

Weller, George, **III:** 322

Welles, Gideon, **Supp. I Part 2:** 484

Welles, Orson, **IV:** 476; **Supp. I Part 1:** 67; **Supp. IV Part 1:** 82, 83; **Supp. V:** 251; **Supp. VIII:** 46; **Supp. XI:** 169, 307

"Wellfleet Whale, The" (Kunitz), **Supp. III Part 1:** 263, 269

Wellfleet Whale and Companion Poems, The (Kunitz), **Supp. III Part 1:** 263

Wellink, Yvonne, **Supp. XVIII:** 257

Wellman, Flora, **II:** 463–464, 465

"Well Rising, The" (Stafford), **Supp. XI:** 318

Wells, H. G., **I:** 103, 226, 241, 243, 253, 405, 409, 415; **II:** 82, 144, 276, 337, 338, 458; **III:** 456; **IV:** 340, 455; **Retro. Supp. I:** 100, 228, 231; **Supp. XVI:** 190; **Supp. XXI:** 8

Wellspring, The (Olds), **Supp. X:** 211–212

Well Wrought Urn, The: Studies in the Structure of Poetry (Brooks), **Supp. XIV:** 1, **8–9**, 14, 15, 16

Welsh, Mary, **Supp. XIX:** 248. *See also* Hemingway, Mrs. Ernest (Mary Welsh)

Welty, Eudora, **II:** 194, 217, 606; **IV:** **260–284**; **Retro. Supp. I:** 339–358; **Retro. Supp. II:** 235; **Supp. IV Part 2:** 474; **Supp. V:** 59, 315, 336; **Supp. VIII:** 94, 151, 171; **Supp. X:** 42, 290; **Supp. XII:** 310, 322; **Supp. XIV:** 3; **Supp. XV:** 338; **Supp. XXIV:** 223

Welty, Eurora, **Supp. XIX:** 151

Weltzien, O. Alan, **Supp. XVI:** 20–21, 28

"We miss Her, not because We see—" (Dickinson), **Retro. Supp. I:** 46

We Must Dance My Darlings (Trilling), **Supp. I Part 1:** 297

Wendell, Barrett, **III:** 507; **Supp. I Part 2:** 414; **Supp. XIV:** 197

Wendell, Sarah. *See* Holmes, Mrs. Abiel (Sarah Wendell)

Wendy Wasserstein: A Casebook (Barnett), **Supp. XV:** 323, 330

"Wendy Wasserstein's Three Sisters: Squandered Privilege" (Brewer), **Supp. XV:** 330

Wenner, Jann S., **Supp. XXIV:** 280, 283

Wept of Wish-ton-Wish, The (Cooper), **I:** 339, 342, 350

Werbe, Peter, **Supp. XIII:** 236

"We Real Cool" (Brooks), **Supp. III Part 1:** 80

"We're All Pharaohs When We Die" (Gallagher), **Supp. XXIV:** 170

We're Back! A Dinosaur's Story (screenplay, Shanley), **Supp. XIV:** 316

"We're Friends Again" (O'Hara), **III:** 372–373

"Were the Whole Realm of Nature Mine" (Watts), **I:** 458

Werewolf (M. Sommers), **Supp. XVII:** 55

Were-Wolf, The (C. Housman), **Supp. XVII:** 55

Werewolf of Paris, The (Endore), **Supp. XVII:** 55–56

Werewolves in Their Youth (Chabon), **Supp. XI:** 66, **76–77**

Werlock, Abby, **Supp. XIII:** 293

Werthman, Michael, **Supp. V:** 115

"Wer-Trout, The" (Proulx), **Supp. VII:** 255–256

Wescott, Glenway, **I:** 288; **II:** 85; **III:** 448, 454; **Supp. VIII:** 156; **Supp. XIV:** 342; **Supp. XVI:** 195

"We Shall All Be Born Again But We Shall Not All Be Saved" (Matthews), **Supp. IX:** 162

West, Anthony, **Supp. IV Part 1:** 284

West, Benjamin, **Supp. I Part 2:** 511

West, Dorothy, **Supp. XIII:** 295; **Supp. XVIII: 277–291; Supp. XIX:** 72

West, James, **II:** 562

West, Nathanael, **I:** 97, 107, 190, 211, 298; **II:** 436; **III:** 357, 425; **IV: 285–307; Retro. Supp. II: 321–341; Supp. IV Part 1:** 203; **Supp. VIII:** 97; **Supp. XI:** 85, 105, 159, 296; **Supp. XII:** 173, 310; **Supp. XIII:** 106, 170; **Supp. XVIII:** 251, 253, 254

West, Nathaniel, **Supp. XIX:** 223

West, Ray, **Supp. XV:** 142

West, Rebecca, **II:** 412, 445; **Supp. XVI:** 152, 153

Westall, Julia Elizabeth. *See* Wolfe, Mrs. William Oliver (Julia Elizabeth Westall)

"We Stand United" (Benét), **Supp. XI:** 46

"West Authentic, The: Willa Cather" (Stegner), **Supp. IV Part 2:** 608

"West Coast, The: Region with a View" (Stegner), **Supp. IV Part 2:** 608–609

"West Coast Waterfront: End of an Era" (Swados), **Supp. XIX:** 264

Westcott, Edward N., **II:** 102

"Western Association of Writers" (Chopin), **Supp. I Part 1:** 217

"Western Ballad, A" (Ginsberg), **Supp. II Part 1:** 311

Western Borders, The (Howe), **Supp. IV Part 2:** 424–425

Western Canon: The Books and Schools of the Ages (Bloom), **Supp. IX:** 146

Western Lands, The (Burroughs), **Supp. III Part 1:** 106

"Western North Carolina" (Halliday), **Supp. XIX:** 85

Western Star (Benét), **Supp. XI:** 46, 47, 57

"Westland" (C. Baxter), **Supp. XVII:** 18, 19

"West Marginal Way" (Hugo), **Supp. VI:** 131, 135

West of Eden: Writers in Hollywood, 1928–1940 (Fine), **Supp. XVIII:** 248

West of Yesterday, East of Summer: New and Selected Poems, 1973–1993 (Monette), **Supp. X:** 159

West of Your City (Stafford), **Supp. XI:** 316, **317–318**, 321, 322

Weston, Jessie L., **II:** 540; **III:** 12; **Supp. I Part 2:** 438

"West Real" (Ríos), **Supp. IV Part 2:** 539, 540

West-running Brook (Frost), **II:** 155; **Retro. Supp. I:** 136, 137

"West-running Brook" (Frost), **II:** 150, 162–164

"West Wall" (Merwin), **Supp. III Part 1:** 355

"Westward Beach, A" (Jeffers), **Supp. II Part 2:** 418

Westward Ho (Harrison), **Supp. VIII:** 51, 52

Westward the Course of Empire (Leutze), **Supp. X:** 307

"Westward the Course of Empire Takes Its Way" (Wallace), **Supp. X: 307–308; Supp. XXII:** 260

"West Wind" (Oliver), **Supp. VII:** 246

"West Wind, The" (Bryant), **Supp. I Part 1:** 155

West Wind: Poems and Prose Poems (Oliver), **Supp. VII:** 243, 246–248

"Wet Casements" (Ashbery), **Supp. III Part 1:** 18–20

We the Living (film), **Supp. IV Part 2:** 520

We the Living (Rand), **Supp. IV Part 2:** 520–521

Wetherell, Elizabeth (pseudonym). *See* Warner, Susan

Wet Parade (Sinclair), **Supp. V:** 289

Wetzsteon, Ross, **Supp. XXI:** 12

"We've Adjusted Too Well" (O'Brien), **Supp. V:** 247

Wevill, David, **Retro. Supp. II:** 247, 249

"We Wear the Mask" (Dunbar), **Supp. II Part 1:** 199, 207, 209–210

We Will Be Citizens: New Essays on Gay and Lesbian Theatre (Fischer, ed.), **Supp. XXIV:** 263

Weybright, Victor, **Supp. XIII:** 172

Weyden, Rogier van der, **Supp. IV Part 1:** 284

Whalen, Marcella, **Supp. I Part 1:** 49

Whalen, Philip, **Supp. VIII:** 289; **Supp. XXII:** 226

Whalen-Bridge, John, **Retro. Supp. II:** 211–212

"Whales off Wales, The" (X. J. Kennedy), **Supp. XV:** 163

"Whales Weep" (Boyle), **Supp. XX: 19**

"Whales Weep Not!" (D. H. Lawrence), **Supp. XVII:** 55

Wharton, Edith, **I:** 12, 375; **II:** 96, 180, 183, 186, 189–190, 193, 283, 338, 444, 451; **III:** 69, 175, 576; **IV:** 8, 53, 58, **308–330; Retro. Supp. I:** 108, 232, **359–385; Supp. IV Part 1:** 23, 31, 35, 36, 80, 81, 310; **Supp. IX:** 57; **Supp. XII:** 308; **Supp. XIV:** 337, 347; **Supp. XVI:** 189; **Supp. XVIII:** 278; **Supp. XX: 227, 229, 232, 239, 240; Supp. XXIII:** 275; **Supp. XXIV:** 29, 64

Wharton, Edward Robbins, **IV:** 310, 313–314, 319

"What" (Dunn), **Supp. XI:** 144

What a Kingdom It Was (Kinnell), **Supp. III Part 1:** 235, 238, 239

"What America Would Be Like without Blacks" (Ellison), **Retro. Supp. II:** 123

What Are Masterpieces (Stein), **IV:** 30–31

What Are Years (Moore), **III:** 208–209, 210, 215

"What Are Years?" (Moore), **III:** 211, 213

What a Way to Go (Morris), **III:** 230–232

"What a Wonder among the Instruments Is the Walloping Trombone!" (Carruth), **Supp. XVI:** 51

"What Became of the Flappers?" (Zelda Fitzgerald), **Supp. IX:** 71

"What Can I Tell My Bones?" (Roethke), **III:** 546, 549

What Century? (O'Hara), **Supp. XXIII:** 216

"What Child Is This?" (Jarman), **Supp. XVII:** 113–114, 115

"What Do We Have Here" (Carson), **Supp. XII:** 101

"What Do We See" (Rukeyser), **Supp. VI:** 282

What Do Women Want? Bread Roses Sex Power (Jong), **Supp. V:** 115, 117, 129, 130

"What Do You Do in San Francisco?" (Carver), **Supp. III Part 1:** 143

What Dreams My Come (Atherton as Frank Lin), **Supp. XXIV:** 28

What D'Ya Know for Sure (Zinberg), **Supp. XV:** 196

Whatever Happened to Gloomy Gus of the Chicago Bears? (Coover), **Supp. V:** 51, 52

Whatever Happened to Jacy Farrow? (Cleveland), **Supp. V:** 222

"What Every Boy Should Know" (Maxwell), **Supp. VIII:** 169

"What Feels Like the World" (Bausch), **Supp. VII:** 46

"What Fort Sumter Did for Me" (E. Stoddard), **Supp. XV:** 282

"What Girls Read" (Salmon), **Supp. XVIII:** 258

"What God Is Like to Him I Serve" (Bradstreet), **Supp. I Part 1:** 106–107

"What Happened Here Before" (Snyder), **Supp. VIII:** 302

"What Happened to Georgia" (Ray), **Supp. XVIII:** 194

What Happens (Herrmann), **Supp. XXII:** 277

What Have I Ever Lost by Dying? (R. Bly), **Supp. IV Part 1:** 71–72

What Have You Lost? (Nye, ed.), **Supp. XIII:** 280

What I Believe (Asch), **Supp. XXIII:** 2

"What I Believe" (Mumford), **Supp. II Part 2:** 479

"What I Call What They Call Onanism" (Goldbarth), **Supp. XII:** 175

What I Did Last Summer (Gurney), **Supp. V:** 96, 100, 107, 108

"What if God" (Olds), **Supp. X:** 208

What I Have Done with Birds: Character Studies of Native American Birds (Stratton-Porter), **Supp. XX:** 218

"What I Have to Defend, What I Can't Bear Losing" (Stern), **Supp. IX:** 286, 287, 288, 298

"What I Knew" (Nelson), **Supp. XVIII:** 178

"What I Know about Being a Playwright" (McNally), **Supp. XIII:** 195, 207

"What I Mean" (Ortiz), **Supp. IV Part 2:** 497

"What Is an Emotion" (James), **II:** 350

What Is Art? (Tolstoy), **I:** 58

"What Is Civilization? Africa's Answer" (Du Bois), **Supp. II Part 1:** 176

"What Is College For?" (Bourne), **I:** 216

"What Is Exploitation?" (Bourne), **I:** 216

What Is Found There: Notebooks on Poetry and Politics (A. Rich), **Supp. XVII:** 74

"What Is It?" (Carver), **Supp. III Part 1:** 139

What Is Man? (Twain), **II:** 434; **IV:** 209

"What Is Poetry" (Ashbery), **Supp. III Part 1:** 19

"What Is Seized" (Moore), **Supp. X:** 164, 168, 169, 172, 175

"What Is the Earth?" (Olds), **Supp. X:** 213

"What Is This Poet" (Stern), **Supp. IX:** 295

What Is To Be Done? (Lenin), **Supp. XXI:** 164

"What I Think" (Hogan), **Supp. IV Part 1:** 406

What Maisie Knew (H. James), **II:** 332; **Retro. Supp. I:** 229, **230**; **Supp. XVIII:** 160

What Makes Sammy Run? (NBC broadcast, Schulberg and Schulberg), **Supp. XVIII:** 254

What Makes Sammy Run? (Schulberg), **Supp. XIII:** 170; **Supp. XVIII:** 241, **244–247**, 248, 249, 253

"What Makes Sammy Run?" (Schulberg), **Supp. XVIII:** 241

What Moon Drove Me to This? (Harjo), **Supp. XII:** **218–220**

"What Must" (MacLeish), **III:** 18

What My Father Believed (Wrigley), **Supp. XVIII:** 298–300

"What My Father Believed" (Wrigley), **Supp. XVIII:** **298–299**

What Price Hollywood? (film), **Supp. XVIII:** 243

"What Sally Said" (Cisneros), **Supp. VII:** 63

What Saves Us (Weigl), **Supp. XIX:** 282

"What's Happening in America" (Sontag), **Supp. III Part 2:** 460–461

"What She Couldn't Tell" (Hampl), **Supp. XXII:** 92

"What's in Alaska?" (Carver), **Supp. III Part 1:** 141, 143

"What's in a Name" (H. L. Gates), **Supp. XX:** 101

What's New, Pussycat? (film; Allen), **Supp. XI:** 307; **Supp. XV:** 1, 2, 14

"What's New in American and Canadian Poetry" (R. Bly), **Supp. IV Part 1:** 67

What's O'Clock (Lowell), **II:** 511, 527, 528

What's Up, Tiger Lily? (film; Allen), **Supp. XV:** 2, **3**

"What the Arts Need Now" (Baraka), **Supp. II Part 1:** 47

"What the Bed Knows"(Schott), **Supp. XXIII:** 249

"What the Body Can Say" (Trethewey), **Supp. XXI:** 255

"What the Brand New Freeway Won't Go By" (Hugo), **Supp. VI:** 132–133

"What the Gypsies Told My Grandmother While She Was Still a Young Girl" (Simic), **Supp. VIII:** 283

"What the Prose Poem Carries with It" (R. Bly), **Supp. IV Part 1:** 64

"What They Wanted" (Dunn), **Supp. XI:** 151

What Thou Lovest Well (Hugo), **Supp. VI:** 140, 141

"What Thou Lovest Well Remains American" (Hugo), **Supp. VI:** 140, 141

What Time Collects (Farrell), **II:** 46, 47–48

What to Do? (Chernyshevsky), **Retro. Supp. I:** 269

"What to Keep, What to Discard" (Taggard), **Supp. XXII:** 280

"What to the Slave is Your Fourth of July?"(Douglass), **Supp. XXIII:** 167

What Use Are Flowers? (Hansberry), **Supp. IV Part 1:** 359, 368–369, 374

What Was Literature? (Fiedler), **Supp. XIII:** 96–97, **105–106**

What Was Mine (Beattie), **Supp. V:** 33, 35

What Was the Relationship of the Lone Ranger to the Means of Production? (Baraka), **Supp. II Part 1:** 58

"What We Came Through" (Goldbarth), **Supp. XII:** 179–180

"What Were the White Things?" (Hempel), **Supp. XXI:** 126

What We Talk About When We Talk About Love (Carver), **Supp. III Part 1:** 142–146; **Supp. XII:** 139; **Supp. XXIV:** 177

"What Why When How Who" (Pinsky), **Supp. VI:** 244

What Will Suffice: Contemporary American Poets on the Art of Poetry (Buckley and Young, eds.), **Supp. XIII:** 313

What Work Is (Levine), **Supp. V:** 181, 187, 192–193

"What You Hear from Em" (Taylor), **Supp. V:** 314, 320, 324

"What You Want" (O. Henry), **Supp. II Part 1:** 402

"What You Would Do" (Weigl), **Supp. XIX:** 288

Wheatley, Phillis, **Supp. XIII:** 111; **Supp. XVII:** 74–75; **Supp. XX: 106, 277–291**

Whedon, Tony, **Supp. XXI:** 131, 132

"Wheelchairs" (Kriegel), **Supp. XXIV:** 220

Wheeler, David, **Supp. XVI:** 277

Wheeler, John, **II:** 433

Wheeler, Monroe, **Supp. XV:** 295
Wheelock, John Hall, **IV:** 461; **Supp. IX:** 268; **Supp. XIV:** 120; **Supp. XV:** 301
Wheel of Life, The (Glasgow), **II:** 176, 178, 179, 183
Wheelwright, Philip, **Supp. XV:** 20
"When" (Olds), **Supp. X:** 207
When Boyhood Dreams Come True (Farrell), **II:** 45
"When Death Came April Twelve 1945" (Sandburg), **III:** 591, 593
"When Death Comes" (Oliver), **Supp. VII:** 241
"When De Co'n Pone's Hot" (Dunbar), **Supp. II Part 1:** 202–203
"When God First Said" (Zach; Everwine trans.), **Supp. XV:** 87
"When Grandma Died—1942" (Shields), **Supp. VII:** 311
"When Howitzers Began" (Carruth), **Supp. XVI:** 55
"When I Buy Pictures" (Moore), **III:** 205
"When I Came from Colchis" (Merwin), **Supp. III Part 1:** 343
"When I Have Fears I May Cease to Be" (Keats), **Supp. XIX:** 92
"When I Left Business for Literature" (Anderson), **I:** 101
"When I Love You" (Peacock), **Supp. XIX:** 199
"When in Rome—Apologia" (Komunyakaa), **Supp. XIII:** 120
"When It Comes" (Olds), **Supp. X:** 213
"When It's Clear and Hot" (Trethewey), **Supp. XXI:** 246
When I Was Alive (Notley), **Supp. XXII:** 228
"When I Was Alive" (Notley), **Supp. XXII:** 229
"When I Was Seventeen" (Kincaid), **Supp. VII:** 181
"When I Was Twenty-five" (Talese), **Supp. XVII:** 202
When Knighthood Was in Flower (Major), **III:** 320
"\[When\] Let by rain" (Taylor), **IV:** 160–161
"When Lilacs Last in the Dooryard Bloom'd" (Whitman), **IV:** 347–348, 351; **Retro. Supp. I:** 406; **Supp. IV Part 1:** 16; **Supp. XV:** 215
"When Malindy Sings" (Dunbar), **Supp. II Part 1:** 200, 204–205
When Peoples Meet: A Study of Race and Culture (Locke and Stern), **Supp. XIV:** 202, 213
When She Was Good (P. Roth), **Retro. Supp. II:** 282, 283, 284; **Supp. III Part 2:** 403, 405, 410–413
"When Sue Wears Red" (Hughes), **Retro. Supp. I:** 195, 204
"When the Acacia Blooms"(Crooker), **Supp. XXIII:** 60
"When the Dead Ask My Father about Me" (Olds), **Supp. X:** 210
"When the Frost Is on the Punkin" (Riley), **Supp. II Part 1:** 202
When the Jack Hollers (Hughes), **Retro. Supp. I:** 203; **Supp. I Part 1:** 328

"When the Last Riders" (Zach; Everwine, trans.), **Supp. XV:** 75, 86
"When the Light Gets Green" (Warren), **IV:** 252
"When the Model Does Not Show" (Major), **Supp. XXII:** 184
"When the Peace Corps Was Young" (Theroux), **Supp. VIII:** 314
When the Sun Tries to Go On (Koch), **Supp. XV:** 185
"When the Sun Tries to Go On" (Koch), **Supp. XV:** 179, 180
"When the World Ended as We Knew It" (Harjo), **Supp. XII:** 231
When Time Was Born (Farrell), **II:** 46, 47
"When We Dead Awaken: Writing as Re-Vision" (Rich), **Supp. I Part 2:** 552–553, 560
"When We Gonna Rise" (Baraka), **Supp. II Part 1:** 48
"When We Have To" (Salinas), **Supp. XIII:** 322–323
"WHEN WE'LL WORSHIP JESUS" (Baraka), **Supp. II Part 1:** 54
"When We Sold the Tent" (Espaillat), **Supp. XXI:** 102
"When we speak of God, is it God we speak of?" (J. Logan), **Supp. XVII:** 113
"When Women Throw Down Bundles: Strong Women Make Strong Nations" (Gunn Allen), **Supp. IV Part 1:** 328
"'When You Finally See Them': The Unconquered Eye in *To Kill a Mockingbird*" (Champion), **Supp. VIII:** 128
"When You Lie Down, the Sea Stands Up" (Swenson), **Supp. IV Part 2:** 643
"Where Blue Is Blue" (Richard), **Supp. XIX:** 221
Where Does One Go When There's No Place Left to Go? (Crews), **Supp. XI:** 103
"Where Go the Boats" (R. Stevenson), **Supp. XVII:** 69
Where Horizons Go (Espaillat), **Supp. XXI:** 99, 103, 104
"Where I Come from Is Like This" (Gunn Allen), **Supp. IV Part 1:** 319
"Where I'm Calling From" (Carver), **Supp. III Part 1:** 145
Where I'm Calling From: New and Selected Stories (Carver), **Supp. III Part 1:** 138, 148; **Supp. XXIV:** 178
"Where I Ought to Be" (Erdrich), **Supp. IV Part 1:** 265
Where Is My Wandering Boy Tonight? (Wagoner), **Supp. IX:** 335–336
"Where Is the Island?" (Francis), **Supp. IX:** 78
"Where Is the Voice Coming From?" (Welty), **IV:** 280; **Retro. Supp. I:** 355
Where Joy Resides (Isherwood), **Supp. XIV:** 156
"Where Knock Is Open Wide" (Roethke), **III:** 533–535
"Where My Sympathy Lies" (H. Roth), **Supp. IX:** 234
Where's My Money? (Shanley), **Supp. XIV:** 316, 328, **330–331**

Where the Bluebird Sings to the Lemonade Springs (Stegner), **Supp. IV Part 2:** 596, 597, 598, 600, 604, 606, 613; **Supp. XXII:** 205
"Where the Bones Move" (W. V. Davis), **Supp. XXI:** 92
Where the Cross Is Made (O'Neill), **III:** 388, 391
Where the Rivers Flow North (Mosher), **Supp. XXII:** 205, 207, 208, **210–212**
"Where the Rivers Flow North" (Mosher), **Supp. XXII:** 204, 206, 207, 208, 209, **210–211**
Where the Sea Used to Be (Bass), **Supp. XVI:** 21
"Where the Sea Used to Be" (Bass), **Supp. XVI:** 20, 21
"*Where the Sea Used to Be:* Rick Bass and the Novel of Ecological Education" (Dixon), **Supp. XVI:** 21
"Where the Soft Air Lives" (Nye), **Supp. XIII:** 275
Where the Twilight Never Ends (Haines), **Supp. XII:** 211
Where the Wild Grape Grows: Selected Writings, 1930–1950 (D. West; Mitchell and Davis, eds.), **Supp. XVIII:** 283, 286
Where the Wild Things Are (Sendak), **Supp. IX:** 207
"Wherever Home Is" (Wright), **Supp. III Part 2:** 605, 606
Where Water Comes Together With Other Water (Carver), **Supp. III Part 1:** 147, 148
"Where We Crashed" (Hugo), **Supp. VI:** 138
"Where We Must Look for Help" (R. Bly), **Supp. XXI:** 84
"Where You Are" (Doty), **Supp. XI:** 131
Where You'll Find Me, and Other Stories (Beattie), **Supp. V:** 30–31
Whicher, Stephen, **II:** 20
"Which Is More Than I Can Say for Some People" (Moore), **Supp. X:** 177, 178
Which Ones Are the Enemy? (Garrett), **Supp. VII:** 98
"Which Theatre Is the Absurd One?" (Albee), **I:** 71
"Which Way to the Future?" (Rehder), **Supp. IV Part 1:** 69
While I Was Gone (Miller), **Supp. XII:** 290, **301–303**
"While Seated in a Plane" (Swenson), **Supp. IV Part 2:** 645
While the Messiah Tarries (Bukiet), **Supp. XVII:** 43, **46–47**
While We've Still Got Feet (Budbill), **Supp. XIX:** 5, 7, **10–11**, 15
Whilomville Stories (Crane), **I:** 414
"Whip, The" (Robinson), **III:** 513
Whipple, Thomas K., **II:** 456, 458; **IV:** 427
"Whippoorwill, The" (Francis), **Supp. IX:** 90
"Whip-poor-will, The" (Thurber), **Supp. I Part 2:** 616
Whirl Asunder, A (Atherton), **Supp. XXIV:** 22

Whirlpool (film, Preminger), **Supp. XVII:** 62

"Whispering Gallery, The" (Komunyakaa), **Supp. XIII:** 132

"Whispering Leaves" (Glasgow), **II:** 190

Whispering to Fool the Wind (Ríos), **Supp. IV Part 2:** 540–541, 544, 545

"Whispers in the Next Room" (Simic), **Supp. VIII:** 278

"Whispers of Heavenly Death" (Whitman), **IV:** 348

"Whispers of Immortality" (Eliot), **Supp. XI:** 242

Whistle (Jones), **Supp. XI:** 219, 224, **231–234**

"Whistle, The" (Franklin), **II:** 121

"Whistle, The" (Komunyakaa), **Supp. XIII:** 111, 126

"Whistle, The" (Welty), **IV:** 262

Whistler, James, **I:** 484; **III:** 461, 465, 466; **IV:** 77, 369

Whistler, James Abbott McNeill, **Supp. XIV:** 335–336

"Whistling Dick's Christmas Stocking" (O. Henry), **Supp. II Part 1:** 390, 392

Whistling in the Dark (Garrett), **Supp. VII:** 111

Whistling in the Dark: True Stories and Other Fables (Garrett), **Supp. VII:** 95

Whitcher, Frances Miriam Berry, **Supp. XIII:** 152

"White" (Simic), **Supp. VIII: 275–276**

White, Barbara, **Retro. Supp. I:** 379

White, Dana, **Supp. XXII:** 251

White, E. B., **Retro. Supp. I:** 335; **Supp. I Part 2:** 602, 607, 608, 612, 619, 620, **651–681; Supp. II Part 1:** 143; **Supp. VIII:** 171; **Supp. IX:** 20, 32; **Supp. XVI:** 167

White, Elizabeth Wade, **Supp. I Part 1:** 100, 103, 111

White, Henry Kirke, **Supp. I Part 1:** 150

White, James L., **Supp. XI:** 123

White, Joel, **Supp. I Part 2:** 654, 678

White, Katharine. (Katharine Sergeant Angell), **Supp. I Part 2:** 610, 653, 655, 656, 669; **Supp. VIII:** 151, 171

White, Lillian, **Supp. I Part 2:** 651

White, Lucia, **I:** 258

White, Maria. *See* Lowell, Mrs. James Russell (Maria White)

White, Morton, **I:** 258; **Supp. I Part 2:** 647, 648, 650

White, Roberta, **Supp. XII:** 293

White, Stanford, **Supp. IV Part 1:** 223

White, Stanley, **Supp. I Part 2:** 651, 655

White, T. H., **III:** 522

White, T. W., **III:** 411, 415

White, Walter, **Supp. I Part 1:** 345; **Supp. XVIII:** 123, 127; **Supp. XIX:** 73

White, William, **Retro. Supp. II:** 326

White, William A., **I:** 252

White Album, The (Didion), **Supp. IV Part 1:** 198, 202, 205–207, 210

"White Album, The" (Didion), **Supp. IV Part 1:** 205, 206

"White Angel" (Cunningham), **Supp. XV:** 59

"White Apache" (Markson), **Supp. XVII:** 136

"White as Snow" (Boyle), **Supp. XXIV:** 58, 59

White Boys (McKnight), **Supp. XX: 155–157**

"White Boys, The" (McKnight), **Supp. XX: 155–157**

White Buildings (H. Crane), **I:** 385, 386, 390–395, 400; **Retro. Supp. II:** 77–78, **80–81**, 82, 83, 85

White Butterfly (Mosley), **Supp. XIII:** 237, 238, 240

White Center (Hugo), **Supp. VI:** 144–145

"White Center" (Hugo), **Supp. VI:** 144, 146

Whited, Stephen, **Supp. XI:** 135

White Deer, The (Thurber), **Supp. I Part 2:** 606

White Doves at Morning (Burke), **Supp. XIV:** 22–23, 32, 35–36

"White Eagle, The" (Chopin), **Retro. Supp. II:** 72

White Fang (London), **II:** 471–472, 481

Whitefield, George, **I:** 546; **Supp. XX:** 280

White-Footed Deer and Other Poems (Bryant), **Supp. I Part 1:** 157

White Goddess, The (Graves), **Supp. IV Part 1:** 280

White-Haired Lover (Shapiro), **Supp. II Part 2:** 703, 717

Whitehead, Alfred North, **III:** 605, 619, 620; **IV:** 88; **Supp. I Part 2:** 554, 647

Whitehead, Mrs. Catherine, **IV:** 116

Whitehead, Colson, **Supp. XIII:** 233, 241

Whitehead, James, **Supp. XV:** 339

Whitehead, Margaret, **IV:** 114, 115, 116

Whitehead, William, **Supp. XX: 50–51, 53**

White Heat (Walsh), **Supp. XIII:** 174

"White Heron, A" (Jewett), **II:** 409; **Retro. Supp. II:** 17

White Heron and Other Stories, A (Jewett), **II:** 396

White Horses (Hoffman), **Supp. X: 83–85**, 90, 92

"White Horses of Vienna, The" (Boyle), **Supp. XXIV: 59–60**

White Horses of Vienna, The, and Other Stories (Boyle), **Supp. XXIV: 57, 58–59**

White House Diary, A (Lady Bird Johnson), **Supp. IV Part 1:** 22

White-Jacket; or, The World in a Man-of-War (Melville), **III:** 80, 81, 84, 94; **Retro Supp. I:** 248, 249, 254; **Supp. XVIII:** 7, 9

White Lantern, The (Connell), **Supp. XIV:** 97

"White Lies" (Trethewey), **Supp. XXI:** 244, 246, 251

"White Lights, The" (Robinson), **III:** 524

"White Lilies, The" (Glück), **Supp. V:** 88

White Man, Listen! (Wright), **IV:** 478, 488, 489, 494

White Morning, The (Atherton), **Supp. XXIV:** 24, 29

"White Mulberry Tree, The" (Cather), **I:** 319; **Retro. Supp. I:** 7, 9, 17

White Mule (W. C. Williams), **Retro. Supp. I:** 423

"White Negro, The" (Mailer), **III:** 36–37; **Retro. Supp. II:** 202

"Whiteness of the Whale, The" (Melville), **III:** 84, 86

"White Night" (Oliver), **Supp. VII:** 236

"White Nights" (Auster), **Supp. XII:** 23–24

White Noise (DeLillo), **Supp. VI:** 1, 3–4, 5–7, 10, 11–12, 16; **Supp. XVIII:** 140; **Supp. XX:** 91

White Oxen and Other Stories, The (Burke), **I:** 269, 271

White Paper on Contemporary American Poetry (McClatchy), **Supp. XII:** 253, **259–260**

"White Phosphorous" (Notley), **Supp. XXII:** 232, 233

"White Pine" (Oliver), **Supp. VII:** 244

White Pine: Poems and Prose Poems (Oliver), **Supp. VII:** 243–246

White Poems, The (Crooker), **Supp. XXIII: 54–55**

White Rat (G. Jones), **Supp. XXIV:** 185

White Sail (Sorrentino), **Supp. XXI:** 228

"White Silence, The" (London), **II:** 468

"White Silk" (Nye), **Supp. XIII:** 275

"White Snake, The" (Sexton), **Supp. II Part 2:** 691

"White Spot" (Anderson), **I:** 116

"White-Tailed Hornet, The" (Frost), **Retro. Supp. I:** 138

"White Trash Cowboys of *Father and Son,* The" (Bjerre), **Supp. XXI:** 41

"White Trees, Hammer Moon" (Dubus III), **Supp. XXIV:** 101, 104

Whitfield, Raoul, **Supp. IV Part 1:** 345

Whitfield, Stephen J., **Supp. XX:** 243, 244

Whitlock, Brand, **II:** 276

Whitman (Masters), **Supp. I Part 2:** 473, 475, 476

Whitman, George, **IV:** 346, 350

Whitman, Ruth, **Supp. XXI:** 246

Whitman, Sarah Wyman, **Retro. Supp. II:** 136

Whitman, Walt, **I:** 61, 68, 98, 103, 104, 109, 219, 220, 227, 228, 242, 246, 250, 251, 260, 261, 285, 381, 384, 386, 396, 397, 398, 402, 419, 430, 459, 460, 483, 485, 486, 577; **II:** 7, 8, 18, 127, 140, 273–274, 275, 289, 295, 301, 320, 321, 373, 445, 446, 451, 457, 494, 529, 530, 552; **III:** 171, 175, 177, 181–182, 189, 203, 234, 260, 426, 430, 453, 454, 461, 505, 507–508, 511, 528, 548, 552, 555, 559, 567, 572, 576, 577, 579, 584, 585, 595, 606, 609; **IV:** 74, 169, 191, 192, 202, **331–354**, 405, 409, 416, 444, 450–451, 457, 463, 464, 469, 470, 471; **Retro. Supp. I:** 8, 52, 194, 254, 283, 284, 333, **387–410**, 412, 417, 427; **Retro. Supp. II:** 40, 76, 93, 99, 155, 156, 158, 170, 262; **Supp. I Part 1:** 6, 79, 167, 311, 314, 325, 365, 368, 372; **Supp. I Part 2:** 374, 384, 385,

387, 389, 391, 393, 399, 416, 436, 455, 456, 458, 473, 474, 475, 525, 540, 579, 580, 582, 682, 691; **Supp. III Part 1:** 6, 20, 156, 239–241, 253, 340; **Supp. III Part 2:** 596; **Supp. IV Part 1:** 16, 169, 325; **Supp. IV Part 2:** 597, 625; **Supp. V:** 113, 118, 122, 130, 170, 178, 183, 277, 279, 332; **Supp. VIII:** 42, 95, 105, 126, 198, 202, 269; **Supp. IX:** 8, 9, 15, 38, 41, 44, 48, 53, 131, 292, 298, 299, 308, 320; **Supp. X:** 36, 112, 203, 204; **Supp. XI:** 83, 123, 132, 135, 203, 321; **Supp. XII:** 132, 185, 190, 256; **Supp. XIII:** 1, 77, 115, 153, 221, 304, 335; **Supp. XIV:** 89, 312, 334, 335, 338; **Supp. XV:** 41, 93, 181, 183, 212, 213, 218, 250, 275, 301, 302, 303, 309, 352; **Supp. XVI:** 209; **Supp. XVII:** 42, 71, 112, 133; **Supp. XVIII:** 4, 194, 196, 304; **Supp. XIX:** 118, 276; **Supp. XX:** 69, 115, 116, 221; **Supp. XXI:** 169, 217, 227, 256; **Supp. XXII:** 81, 82, 86, 92; **Supp. XXIII:** 19, 109, 166, 207

"Whitman Pinch Hits, 1861" (Skloot), **Supp. XX: 203**

"Whitman: The Poet and the Mask" (Cowley), **Supp. II Part 1:** 143

Whitmarsh, Jason, **Supp. VIII:** 283

Whitmer, Peter, **Supp. X:** 264, 265

Whitney, Blair, **Supp. I Part 2:** 403

Whitney, Josiah, **Supp. IX:** 180, 181

Whitt, Margaret Earley, **Retro. Supp. II:** 226

Whittemore, Reed, **III:** 268; **Supp. XI:** 315

Whittier, Elizabeth, **Supp. I Part 2:** 700, 701, 703; **Supp. XIII:** 141, 142

Whittier, John Greenleaf, **I:** 216; **II:** 275; **III:** 52; **Retro. Supp. I:** 54; **Retro. Supp. II:** 155, 163, 169; **Supp. I Part 1:** 168, 299, 313, 317, 372; **Supp. I Part 2:** 420, 602, **682–707**; **Supp. VIII:** 202, 204; **Supp. XI:** 50; **Supp. XIII:** 140, 145; **Supp. XV:** 246; **Supp. XXIII:** 156

Whittier, Mary, **Supp. I Part 2:** 683

"Whittier Birthday Speech" (Twain), **Supp. I Part 1:** 313

"Who" (Kenyon), **Supp. VII:** 174

"Who" (Sobin), **Supp. XVI:** 284–285

"Who Am I—Who I Am" (Corso), **Supp. XII:** 134

"Who Be Kind To" (Ginsberg), **Supp. II Part 1:** 323

Who Do You Love (Thompson), **Supp. XXIII:** 289, **295–296**

"Whoever Was Using This Bed" (Carver), **Supp. III Part 1:** 148

"Whoever You Are Holding Me Now in Hand" (Whitman), **IV:** 342; **Retro. Supp. I:** 52

Who Gathered and Whispered behind Me (Goldbarth), **Supp. XII:** 181, 182

"Who in One Lifetime" (Rukeyser), **Supp. VI:** 276, 279

Who Is Witter Bynner? (Kraft), **Supp. XV:** 40, 52

"Who Is Your Mother? Red Roots of White Feminism" (Gunn Allen), **Supp. IV Part 1:** 329

Whole Hog (Wagoner), **Supp. IX: 337–338**

"Whole Mess...Almost, The" (Corso), **Supp. XII:** 135

"Whole Moisty Night, The" (R. Bly), **Supp. IV Part 1:** 69

Whole New Life, A (Price), **Supp. VI:** 265, **266,** 267

"Whole Self, The" (Nye), **Supp. XIII:** 275

"Whole Soul, The" (Levine), **Supp. V:** 192

"Whole Story, The" (Strand), **Supp. IV Part 2:** 622

Whole Town's Talking, The (Loos), **Supp. XVI:** 187

"Whole World Knows, The" (Welty), **IV:** 272; **Retro. Supp. I:** 343

Who'll Stop the Rain (film), **Supp. V:** 301

Who Lost an American? (Algren), **Supp. IX: 15–16**

Who Owns America? (symposium), **Supp. XIV:** 4

"Who Puts Together" (Hogan), **Supp. IV Part 1:** 403, 405, 412–413

"Whore of Mensa, The" (Allen), **Supp. XV:** 15

Whores for Gloria (Vollmann), **Supp. XVII:** 226, 230

Whorf, Benjamin Lee, **Supp. XVI:** 283

Who's Afraid? (Holding), **Supp. XXII:** 120, **125–126**

Who's Afraid of Virginia Woolf? (Albee), **I:** 71, 77–81, 83, 85, 86, 87, 94; **IV:** 230

Who Shall Be the Sun? Poems Based on the Lore, Legends, and Myths of the Northwest Coast and Plateau Indians (Wagoner), **Supp. IX:** 328, **329–330,** 337

"Whosis Kid, The" (Hammett), **Supp. IV Part 1:** 344

"Who Sit Watch in Daylight" (Wright), **Supp. XV:** 342

"Who's Passing for Who?" (Hughes), **Supp. I Part 1:** 330

"Who Speak on the Page?" (Sanders), **Supp. XVI:** 278

Who We Are: On Being (and Not Being) a Jewish American Writer (Rubin, ed.), **Supp. XXIV:** 3

Who Will Run the Frog Hospital?: A Novel (Moore), **Supp. X:** 163, 165, 169, **175–177**

Who Wrote the Book of Love? (Siegel), **Supp. XXII: 265–267,** 267

Why Are We in Vietnam? (Mailer), **III:** 27, 29, 30, 33, 34–35, 39, 42, 44; **Retro. Supp. II:** 205–206

"Why Bother?" (Franzen). *See* "Perchance to Dream" (Franzen)

"Why China?" (Egan), **Supp. XIX:** 51, 52

"Why Did the Balinese Chicken Cross the Road?" (Walker), **Supp. III Part 2:** 527

"Why Do the Heathens Rage?" (O'Connor), **III:** 351

"Why Do You Write About Russia?" (Simpson), **Supp. IX:** 277

"Why Have We Not More Great Novelists?" (Atherton), **Supp. XXIV:** 24

"Why I Am a Danger to the Public" (Kingsolver), **Supp. VII:** 204

Why I Am Not a Christian (Russell), **Supp. I Part 2:** 522

"Why I Am Not a Painter"(O'Hara), **Supp. XXIII:** 208

Why I Came to Judevine (Budbill), **Supp. XIX:** 2, **7–8,** 15

"Why I Do Not Wish to Float in Space"(Schott), **Supp. XXIII:** 251

"Why I Entered the Gurdjieff Work" (Toomer), **Supp. III Part 2:** 481

"Why I Like Laurel" (Patchett), **Supp. XII:** 309

"Why I Live at the P.O." (Welty), **IV:** 262; **Retro. Supp. I:** 345

"Why I Make Sam Go to Church" (Lamott), **Supp. XX: 141**

"Why Is American Literature Bourgeois?" (Atherton), **Supp. XXIV:** 24, 28

"Why Is Economics Not an Evolutionary Science?" (Veblen), **Supp. I Part 2:** 634

"Why I Write" (Didion), **Supp. IV Part 1:** 201, 203

"Why I Wrote *Phil:* An Exclusive Essay for Amazon.com" (Saunders), **Supp. XIX:** 230–231

Why Johnny Can't Read: And What You Can Do About It (Flesch), **Supp. XVI:** 105

"Why Negro Women Leave Home" (Brooks), **Supp. III Part 1:** 75

Why Poetry Matters (Parini), **Supp. XIX:** 120, 129

"Why Resign from the Human Race?" (Swados), **Supp. XIX:** 265

"Why the Little Frenchman Wears His Hand in a Sling" (Poe), **III:** 425

Why Torture Is Wrong, and the People Who Love Them (Durang), **Supp. XXIV: 126–127**

"Why We Are Forgiven" (Weigl), **Supp. XIX:** 282–283

Why We Behave Like Microbe Hunters (Thurber), **Supp. I Part 2:** 606

Why We Were in Vietnam (Podhoretz), **Supp. VIII:** 241

"Why Write?" (Updike), **Retro. Supp. I:** 317

"Wichita Vortex Sutra" (Ginsberg), **Supp. II Part 1:** 319, 321, 323–325, 327

Wickenden, Dorothy, **Supp. XXIII:** 291

Wickes, George, **Supp. XIV:** 165

Wickford Point (Marquand), **III:** 50, 58, 64–65, 69

Wicks, Robert Russell, **Supp. XII:** 49

Wide, Wide World, The (S. Warner as Wetherell), **Supp. XV:** 275; **Supp. XVIII:** 257, 260, **262–264,** 265

Wide Blue Yonder (Thompson), **Supp. XXIII:** 289, **296–298**

"Wide Empty Landscape with a Death in the Foreground" (Momaday), **Supp.**

IV Part 2: 492

Wideman, John Edgar, **Retro. Supp. II:** 123; **Supp. X:** 239, 250, **319–336;** **Supp. XI:** 245; **Supp. XIII:** 247; **Supp. XVIII:** 89; **Supp. XXI:** 246; **Supp. XXIV:** 183

Widener, Jeff, **Supp. XVIII:** 91

"Wideness" (Pickering), **Supp. XXI:** 203

"Wide Net, The" (Welty), **IV:** 266

Wide Net and Other Stories, The (Welty), **IV:** 261, 264–266, 271; **Retro. Supp. I:** 347–349, 352, 355

Widening Spell of the Leaves, The (Levis), **Supp. XI:** 258, 259, 261, **268–269,** 271

"Wide Prospect, The" (Jarrell), **II:** 376–377

Wide Sargasso Sea (Rhys), **Supp. XVIII:** 131

"Widow" (Peacock), **Supp. XIX:** 206

"Widower" (Robison), **Supp. XXI:** 118

Widow for One Year, A (Irving), **Supp. VI:** 165, **179–181**

Widow's Mite (Holding), **Supp. XXII:** **136**

Widows of Thornton, The (Taylor), **Supp. V:** 320, 321

"Widow's Wish, The" (Briggs), **Supp. XVIII:** 15

Wieland; or, The Transformation. An American Tale (Brown), **Supp. I Part 1:** 128–132, 133, 137, 140

Wiene, Robert, **Retro. Supp. I:** 268

Wiener, John, **Supp. IV Part 1:** 153

Wieners, John, **Supp. II Part 1:** 32; **Supp. XXIII:** 215

Wiesel, Elie, **Supp. XVII:** 47, 48, 49

Wiest, Dianne, **Supp. XV:** 12

"Wife, Forty-five, Remembers Love, A" (Shields), **Supp. VII:** 310

"Wifebeater, The" (Sexton), **Supp. II Part 2:** 693

"Wife for Dino Rossi, A" (Fante), **Supp. XI:** 165

"Wife of His Youth, The" (Chesnutt), **Supp. XIV: 63–66**

Wife of His Youth and Other Stories of the Color Line, The (Chesnutt), **Supp. XIV:** 62, 63

"Wife of Jesus Speaks, The" (Karr), **Supp. XI:** 250–251

"Wife of Nashville, A" (Taylor), **Supp. V:** 320

"Wife's Story, The" (R. H. Davis), **Supp. XVI:** 85, 91, 92–93

Wife's Story, The (Shields), **Supp. VII:** 316. *See also* Happenstance

"Wife-Wooing" (Updike), **IV:** 226

Wigan, Gareth, **Supp. XI:** 306

Wiget, Andrew, **Supp. IV Part 2:** 509

Wigglesworth, Michael, **IV:** 147, 156; **Supp. I Part 1:** 110, 111

Wilbur, Richard, **III:** 527; **Retro. Supp. II:** 50; **Supp. III Part 1:** 64; **Supp. III Part 2: 541–565; Supp. IV Part 2:** 626, 634, 642; **Supp. V:** 337; **Supp. VIII:** 28; **Supp. X:** 58, 120; **Supp. XII:** 258; **Supp. XIII:** 76, 336; **Supp. XV:** 51, 251, 256; **Supp. XVII:** 26; **Supp. XVIII:** 178; **Supp. XX: 199;**

Supp. XXI: 247; **Supp. XXIV:** 36, 45

Wilcocks, Alexander, **Supp. I Part 1:** 125

Wilcox, Ella Wheeler, **Supp. II Part 1:** 197

Wilcox, Kirstin, **Supp. XX: 283, 284, 285**

Wild, John, **II:** 362, 363–364

Wild, Peter, **Supp. V:** 5

Wild, Robert, **IV:** 155

"Wild, The" (Berry), **Supp. X:** 30

Wild 90 (film) (Mailer), **Retro. Supp. II:** 205

Wild and Woolly (film), **Supp. XVI:** 185

Wild Boy of Aveyron, The (Itard). *See* De l'éducation d'un homme sauvage

Wild Boys, The: A Book of the Dead (Burroughs), **Supp. III Part 1:** 106–107

Wild Card Quilt: Taking A chance on Home (Ray), **Supp. XVIII:** 189, 192, 193, 196, 198, **200–202,** 204

Wilde, Oscar, **I:** 50, 66, 381, 384; **II:** 515; **IV:** 77, 350; **Retro. Supp. I:** 56, 102, 227; **Retro. Supp. II:** 76, 326; **Supp. IV Part 2:** 578, 679, 683; **Supp. V:** 106, 283; **Supp. IX:** 65, 66, 68, 189, 192; **Supp. X:** 148, 151, 188–189; **Supp. XIV:** 324, 334; **Supp. XV:** 350; **Supp. XXIV:** 263

Wilder, Amos Parker, **IV:** 356

Wilder, Mrs. Amos Parker (Isabella Thornton Niven), **IV:** 356

Wilder, Billy, **Supp. IV Part 1:** 130; **Supp. XI:** 307

Wilder, Isabel, **IV:** 357, 366, 375

Wilder, Laura Ingalls, **Supp. XXI:** 2; **Supp. XXII: 289–303**

Wilder, Thornton, **I:** 360, 482; **IV: 355–377,** 431; **Retro. Supp. I:** 109, 359; **Supp. I Part 2:** 609; **Supp. IV Part 2:** 586; **Supp. V:** 105; **Supp. IX:** 140; **Supp. XII:** 236–237; **Supp. XX:** 50

"Wilderness" (Leopold), **Supp. XIV:** 190

Wilderness (Parker), **Supp. XIX:** 177, **188–189**

"Wilderness" (Sandburg), **III:** 584, 595

Wilderness (Warren), **IV:** 256

"Wilderness, The" (Merwin), **Supp. III Part 1:** 340, 345

"Wilderness, The" (Robinson), **III:** 524

Wilderness of Vision, The: On the Poetry of John Haines (Bezner and Walzer, eds.), **Supp. XII:** 202

Wilderness Plots: Tales about the Settlement of the American Land (Sanders), **Supp. XVI:** 267–268, 269

"Wilderness"(Thompson), **Supp. XXIII:** 301

Wilderness World of Anne LaBastille, The (LaBastille), **Supp. X: 105,** 106

Wild Flag, The (White), **Supp. I Part 2:** 654

"Wildflower, The" (W. C. Williams), **Retro. Supp. I:** 420

"Wild Flowers" (Caldwell), **I:** 310

"Wildflowers" (Minot), **Supp. VI:** 208

"Wild Geese" (Oliver), **Supp. VII:** 237

"Wild Honey Suckle, The" (Freneau), **Supp. II Part 1:** 253, 264, 266

Wild in the Country (Odets), **Supp. II Part 2:** 546

"Wild in the Woods" (Skloot), **Supp. XX: 206**

Wild Iris, The (Glück), **Supp. V:** 79, 87–89, 91

Wildlife (Ford), **Supp. V:** 57, 69–71

Wildlife in America (Matthiessen), **Supp. V:** 199, 201, 204

"Wildlife in American Culture" (Leopold), **Supp. XIV:** 190, 191

"Wild Light" (Skloot), **Supp. XX: 200**

Wild Man, The (P. N. Warren), **Supp. XX: 260, 270–272**

"Wildness" (Sanders), **Supp. XVI:** 276

Wild Old Wicked Man, The (MacLeish), **III:** 3, 20

Wild Palms, The (Faulkner), **II:** 68–69; **Retro. Supp. I:** 85

"Wild Palms, The" (Faulkner), **II:** 68

"Wild Peaches" (Wylie), **Supp. I Part 2:** 707, 712

Wild Roses of Cape Ann and Other Poems (Larcom), **Supp. XIII:** 142, 147

Wild Seed (O. Butler), **Supp. XIII:** 62, 63

"Wild Swans at Coole, The " (W. B. Yeats), **Supp. XVI:** 48

"Wild Swans at Norfolk, The" (Carruth), **Supp. XVI:** 48

"Wild Thing" (L. Brown), **Supp. XXI:** 44

Wild Thorn (Hoffman), **Supp. XVIII: 84–85**

Wild to the Heart (Bass), **Supp. XVI:** 16

"Wild Turkeys: Dignity of the Damned" (B. Kelly), **Supp. XVII:** 129

"Wildwest" (MacLeish), **III:** 14

Wiley, Catherine, **Supp. XXIII:** 199

Wiley, Craig, **Supp. VIII:** 313

Wilhelm Meister (Goethe), **II:** 291

Wilkes, John, **Supp. I Part 2:** 503, 519, 522

Wilkie, Curtis, **Supp. V:** 11

Wilkins, Roy, **Supp. I Part 1:** 345

Wilkinson, Alec, **Supp. VIII:** 164, 168, 171

Wilkinson, Max, **Supp. IX:** 251

Will, The (Swados), **Supp. XIX: 265–266**

Willard, Nancy, **Supp. XIX:** 138

Willard, Samuel, **IV:** 150

Willard Gibbs (Rukeyser), **Supp. VI:** 273, 283, 284

Willcutts, Tim, **Supp. XVII:** 239, 241, 246

Willett, Ralph, **Supp. XIV:** 27

Willey, Basil, **Retro. Supp. II:** 243

"William Butler Yeats Among the Ghosts" (Skloot), **Supp. XX: 204–205**

William Carlos Williams (Koch), **Retro. Supp. I:** 428

William Carlos Williams: An American Artist (Breslin), **Retro. Supp. I:** 430

William Carlos Williams and Alterity (Ahearn), **Retro. Supp. I:** 415

William Carlos Williams and the Meanings of Measure (Cushman), **Retro. Supp. I:** 430

William Carlos Williams: The American Background (Weaver), **Retro. Supp. I:** 430

William Ellery Channing: An Intellectual Portrait (Edgell), **Supp. XXIV:** 71
William Ellery Channing: Selected Writings (Robinson, ed.), **Supp. XXIV:** 71
William Faulkner: A Critical Study (Howe), **Supp. VI:** 119–120, 125
William Faulkner: Early Prose and Poetry (Faulkner), **Retro. Supp. I:** 80
William Faulkner: First Encounters (Brooks), **Supp. XIV:** 13
"William Faulkner's Legend of the South" (Cowley), **Supp. II Part 1:** 143
"William Faulkner: The Stillness of *Light in August*" (Kazin), *Supp. VIII:* 104
William Faulkner: The Yoknapatawpha Country (Brooks), **Supp. XIV: 12–13,** 16
William Faulkner: Toward Yoknapatawpha and Beyond (Brooks), **Supp. XIV:** 13
"William Humphrey, 73, Writer of Novels about Rural Texas" (Gussow), **Supp. IX:** 93
William Humphrey, Destroyer of Myths (Almon), **Supp. IX:** 93
William Humphrey. Boise State University Western Writers Series (Winchell), **Supp. IX:** 109
"William Humphrey Remembered" (Masters), **Supp. IX:** 96
William Humphrey. Southwestern Series (Lee), **Supp. IX:** 109
"William Ireland's Confession" (A. Miller), **III:** 147–148
William James and Phenomenology: A Study of the "Principles of Psychology" (Wilshire), **II:** 362
William Lloyd Garrison (Chapman), **Supp. XIV:** 46–51, 52, 53, 55
William Maxwell Portrait, A: Memories and Appreciations (C. Baxter, Collier, and Hirsch, eds.), **Supp. XVII:** 23
Williams, Annie Laurie, **Supp. IX:** 93
Williams, Blanch Colton, **Supp. XVIII:** 279
Williams, Cecil, **II:** 508
Williams, Charles, **Supp. II Part 1:** 15, 16
Williams, C. K., **Supp. XIII:** 114; **Supp. XVII:** 112
Williams, Cratis, **Supp. XX: 163**
Williams, Dakin, **IV:** 379
Williams, David Reichard, **Supp. XIII:** 162
Williams, Edward, **IV:** 404
Williams, Edwina Dakin, **IV:** 379
Williams, Eric, **Supp. XXI:** 166, 170, 171
Williams, Esther, **Supp. XII:** 165
Williams, Fannie Barrier, **Supp. XIV:** 201
Williams, Garth, **Supp. XXII:** 301
Williams, George, **Supp. V:** 220
Williams, Henry Sylvester, **Supp. XXI:** 166
Williams, Horace, **IV:** 453
Williams, Joan, **Supp. IX:** 95
Williams, John A., **Supp. XVI:** 143
Williams, John Alexander, **Supp. XXIII:** 39
Williams, John Sharp, **IV:** 378

Williams, Jonathan, **Supp. XXII:** 168
Williams, Kenny J., **Supp. XX: 281, 286**
Williams, Lyle, **Supp. XIV:** 22
Williams, Michael, **Supp. V:** 286
Williams, Miller, **Supp. XIV:** 126; **Supp. XV:** 339; **Supp. XVIII:** 177
Williams, Paul, **IV:** 404
Williams, Raymond, **Supp. IX:** 146
Williams, Roger, **Supp. I Part 2:** 699; **Supp. XXIII:** 15
Williams, Rose, **IV:** 379
Williams, Sherley Anne, **Supp. V:** 180
Williams, Solomon, **I:** 549
Williams, Stanley T., **II:** 301, 316; **Supp. I Part 1:** 251
Williams, Stephen, **IV:** 148
Williams, Ted, **IV:** 216; **Supp. IX:** 162
Williams, Tennessee, **I:** 73, 81, 113, 211; **II:** 190, 194; **III:** 145, 147; **IV:** 4, **378–401; Supp. I Part 1:** 290, 291; **Supp. IV Part 1:** 79, 83, 84, 359; **Supp. IV Part 2:** 574, 682; **Supp. IX:** 133; **Supp. XI:** 103; **Supp. XIII:** 331; **Supp. XIV:** 250, 315; **Supp. XVI:** 194; **Supp. XXIV:** 113
Williams, Terry Tempest, **Supp. XIII:** 16; **Supp. XVIII:** 189
Williams, Walter L., **Supp. IV Part 1:** 330, 331
Williams, William, **IV:** 404, 405
Williams, William Carlos, **I:** 61, 62, 229, 255, 256, 261, 285, 428, 438, 446, 539; **II:** 133, 536, 542, 543, 544, 545; **III:** 194, 196, 198, 214, 269, 409, 453, 457, 458, 464, 465, 591; **IV:** 30, 74, 75, 76, 94, 95, 286, 287, **402–425; Retro. Supp. I:** 51, 52, 62, 209, 284, 285, 288, 296, 298, **411–433; Retro. Supp. II:** 178, 181, 189, 250, 321, 322, 326, 327, 328, 334, 335; **Supp. I Part 1:** 254, 255, 259, 266; **Supp. II Part 1:** 9, 30, 308, 318; **Supp. II Part 2:** 421, 443; **Supp. III Part 1:** 9, 147, 239, 271, 275, 276, 278, 350; **Supp. III Part 2:** 542, 610, 613, 614, 615, 616, 617, 621, 622, 626, 628; **Supp. IV Part 1:** 151, 153, 246, 325; **Supp. V:** 180, 337; **Supp. VIII:** 195, 269, 272, 277, 292; **Supp. IX:** 38, 268, 291; **Supp. X:** 112, 120, 204; **Supp. XI:** 311, 328; **Supp. XII:** 198; **Supp. XIII:** 77, 90, 335; **Supp. XIV:** 280, 284, 285, 293; **Supp. XV:** 42, 51, 182, 250, 306, 307; **Supp. XVI:** 48, 282; **Supp. XVII:** 36, 113, 227, 243; **Supp. XIX:** 1, 42, 117, 119, 121; **Supp. XXI:** 226, 227, 230, 233; **Supp. XXII:** 162, 165, 168, 226, 227, 228; **Supp. XXIII:** 164, 207, 211; **Supp. XXIV:** 39, 41, 52, 63
Williams, Mrs. William Carlos (Florence Herman), **IV:** 404
Williams, Wirt, **Supp. XIV:** 24
Williamson, Alan, **Retro. Supp. II:** 185; **Supp. XIX:** 91
Williamson, J. W., **Supp. XX: 164**
William Styron's Nat Turner: Ten Black Writers Respond (Clarke, ed.), **IV:** 115
Williams-Walsh, Mary Ellen, **Supp. IV Part 2:** 611

William the Conqueror, **Supp. I Part 2:** 507
William Wetmore Story and His Friends (James), **Retro. Supp. I:** 235; **Supp. XX: 228**
William Wilson (Gardner), **Supp. VI:** 72
"William Wilson" (Poe), **II:** 475; **III:** 410, 412; **Retro. Supp. II:** 269; **Supp. IX:** 105
"Willie" (Angelou), **Supp. IV Part 1:** 15
Willie Masters' Lonesome Wife (Gass), **Supp. VI:** 77, **84–85, 86–87**
"Willing" (Moore), **Supp. X:** 178
Willingly (Gallagher), **Supp. XXIV:** 166, 168, 169, 170, 176
Willis, Bruce, **Supp. IV Part 1:** 236
Willis, Dail, **Supp. XXIII:** 298
Willis, Gordon, **Supp. XV:** 7
Willis, Mary Hard, **Supp. V:** 290–291
Willis, Nathaniel Parker, **II:** 313; **Supp. I Part 2:** 405; **Supp. XVIII:** 12
Williwaw (Vidal), **Supp. IV Part 2:** 677, 680, 681
"Willow Woman" (Francis), **Supp. IX:** 78
Wills, Garry, **Supp. I Part 1:** 294; **Supp. IV Part 1:** 355
Wills, Ridley, **IV:** 122
Wills, Ross B., **Supp. XI:** 169
"Will to Believe, The" (James), **II:** 352; **Supp. XIV:** 50
Will to Believe, The, and Other Essays in Popular Philosophy (James), **II:** 356; **IV:** 28
Will to Change, The: Poems, 1968–1970 (Rich), **Supp. I Part 2:** 551, 557–559
"Will We Plug Chips into Our Brains?" (W. Gibson), **Supp. XVI:** 117–118
Will You Please Be Quiet, Please? (Carver), **Supp. III Part 1:** 138, 140, 144
"Will You Please Be Quiet, Please?" (Carver), **Supp. III Part 1:** 137, 141
"Will You Tell Me?" (Barthelme), **Supp. IV Part 1:** 42, 47
Wilsdorf, Anne, **Supp. XVI:** 177
Wilshire, Bruce, **II:** 362, 364
Wilshire, Gaylord, **Supp. V:** 280
Wilson, Adrian, **Supp. XV:** 147
Wilson, Alexander, **Supp. XVI:** 4, 6
Wilson, Angus, **IV:** 430, 435
Wilson, August, **Supp. VIII: 329–353; Supp. XIX:** 132
Wilson, Augusta Jane Evans, **Retro. Supp. I:** 351
Wilson, Earl, **Supp. X:** 264
Wilson, Edmund, **I:** 67, 185, 236, 247, 260, 434, 482; **II:** 79, 80, 81, 86, 87, 91, 97, 98, 146, 276, 430, 530, 562, 587; **III:** 588; **IV:** 308, 310, **426–449; Retro. Supp. I:** 1, 97, 100, 101, 103, 104, 105, 115, 274; **Retro. Supp. II:** 321, 327, 329; **Supp. I Part 1:** 372; **Supp. I Part 2:** 407, 646, 678, 709; **Supp. II Part 1:** 19, 90, 106, 136, 137, 143; **Supp. III Part 2:** 612; **Supp. IV Part 2:** 693; **Supp. VIII:** 93, 95, 96, 97, 98–99, 100, 101, 103, 105, 162; **Supp. IX:** 55, 65, 190; **Supp. X:** 186; **Supp. XI:** 160; **Supp.**

XIII: 170; **Supp. XIV:** 338; **Supp. XV:** 142, 308; **Supp. XVI:** 194; **Supp. XX: 76, 81; Supp. XXII:** 278; **Supp. XXIII:** 104–105, 106; **Supp. XXIV:** 62, 217, 222, 281

Wilson, Edmund (father), **IV:** 441

Wilson, E. O., **Supp. X:** 35

Wilson, Harriet, **Supp. XX: 105**

Wilson, Henry, **Supp. XIV:** 48

Wilson, Reuel, **II:** 562

Wilson, Robert, **Supp. XI:** 144

Wilson, Robley, **Supp. XXIII:** 290

Wilson, Sloan, **Supp. IV Part 1:** 387

Wilson, Thomas, **IV:** 153

Wilson, Tracy, **Supp. XVIII:** 101

Wilson, Victoria, **Supp. X:** 166

Wilson, Woodrow, **I:** 245, 246, 490; **II:** 183, 253; **III:** 105, 581; **Supp. I Part 1:** 21; **Supp. I Part 2:** 474, 643; **Supp. V:** 288

Wilton, David, **IV:** 147

Wiman, Christian, **Supp. XV:** 251, 253, 264; **Supp. XVII:** 74; **Supp. XVIII:** 173, 174

Wimberly, Lowry, **Supp. XV:** 136, 137

"Wimp, The" (Gallagher), **Supp. XXIV:** 174

Wimsatt, William K., **Supp. XIV:** 12

Winch, Terence, **Supp. XXIII:** 291

Winchell, Mark, **Supp. VIII:** 176, 189

Winchell, Mark Royden, **Supp. VIII:** 241; **Supp. IX:** 97, 98, 109; **Supp. XIII:** 94, 98, 99, 101; **Supp. XIV:** 103, 106, 111

Winckelmann, Johann Joachim, **Supp. XII:** 178

Wind, Sand, and Stars (Saint-Exupéry), **Supp. IX:** 247

Wind Across the Everglades (film, Ray), **Supp. XVIII:** 253

Wind Chrysalid's Rattle (Sobin), **Supp. XVI:** 283

"Windfall" (B. Kelly), **Supp. XVII:** 132

Windflower Home Almanac of Poetry, The (Kooser, ed.), **Supp. XIX:** 119

Windham, Donald, **IV:** 382

"Windhover" (Hopkins), **I:** 397; **II:** 539; **Supp. IX:** 43

Winding Stair and Other Poems, The (Yeats), **Supp. XV:** 253

"Winding Street, The" (Petry), **Supp. XI:** 6

"Window" (Pinsky), **Supp. VI:** 237, 247

"Window, The" (Hull), **Supp. XXI:** 140–141

Windows (Creeley), **Supp. IV Part 1:** 157, 158

"Windows" (Jarrell), **II:** 388, 389

"Window Seat, A" (Goldbarth), **Supp. XII:** 185

Wind Remains, The (opera) (Bowles), **Supp. IV Part 1:** 83

"Winds, The" (Welty), **IV:** 265; **Retro. Supp. I:** 348, 350

"Winds and Clouds over a Funeral" (Jin), **Supp. XVIII:** 94

Winds of War (Wouk), **Supp. XX: 243**

"Wind up Sushi" (Goldbarth), **Supp. XII:** 186–187

"Windy Day at the Reservoir, A" (Beattie), **Supp. V:** 33

Windy McPherson's Son (Anderson), **I:** 101, 102–103, 105, 111

"Wine" (Carver), **Supp. III Part 1:** 138

"Wine Menagerie, The" (H. Crane), **I:** 389, 391; **Retro. Supp. II:** 82

Wine of the Puritans, The: A Study of Present-Day America (Brooks), **I:** 240

"Wine of Wizardry, A" (Sterling), **I:** 208

Winer, Linda, **Supp. IV Part 2:** 580; **Supp. XV:** 332

Winesburg, Ohio: A Group of Tales of Ohio Small Town Life (Anderson), **I:** 97, 102, 103, 104, 105–108; **III:** 112, 113, 114, 116, 224, 579; **Supp. V:** 12; **Supp. IX:** 306, 308; **Supp. XI:** 164; **Supp. XVI:** 17; **Supp. XXII:** 282; **Supp. XXIV:** 281

Winfrey, Oprah, **Supp. XIX:** 194, 204; **Supp. XX: 83, 93**

Wing-and-Wing, The (Cooper), **I:** 350, 355

Winged Seed, The: A Remembrance (L.-Y. Lee), **Supp. XV:** 211, **220–223**

Winged Words: American Indian Writers Speak (Coltelli), **Supp. IV Part 2:** 493, 497

"Wingfield" (Wolff), **Supp. VII:** 341–342

"Wings, The" (Doty), **Supp. XI:** 124

Wings of the Dove, The (James), **I:** 436; **II:** 320, 323, 333, 334–335; **Retro. Supp. I:** 215, 216, 217, 232, **233–234;** **Supp. II Part 1:** 94–95; **Supp. IV Part 1:** 349

"Wink of the Zenith, The" (Skloot), **Supp. XX: 207**

Wink of the Zenith, The: The Shaping of a Writer's Life (Skloot), **Supp. XX: 195, 196, 207**

"Winkte"(Kenny), **Supp. XXIII:** 148–149

"Winky" (Saunders), **Supp. XIX:** 228–229, 229

Winner Names the Age, The: A Collection of Works by Lillian Smith (Cliff, ed.), **Supp. XXII:** 67

Winner Take Nothing (Hemingway), **II:** 249; **Retro. Supp. I:** 170, 175, 176, 181

"Winnie" (Brooks), **Supp. III Part 1:** 86

Winokur, Maxine. *See* Kumin, Maxine

Winslow, Art, **Supp. XVIII:** 102

Winslow, Devereux, **II:** 547

Winslow, Harriet, **II:** 552–553

Winslow, Ola Elizabeth, **I:** 547

Winslow, Warren, **II:** 540

Winston, Andrew, **Supp. XII:** 189

Winston, Michael R., **Supp. XIV:** 197

Winter, Douglas, **Supp. V:** 144

Winter, Johnny and Edgar, **Supp. V:** 334

Winter, Kate, **Supp. X:** 104

"Winter Branch, A" (Irving), **Supp. VI:** 163

"Winter Burial, A" (Clampitt), **Supp. IX:** 48

Winter Carnival (film), **Retro. Supp. I:** 113

"Winter Concert"(Strout), **Supp. XXIII:** 283

"Winter Daybreak at Vence, A" (Wright), **Supp. III Part 1:** 249–250

Winter Diary, A (Van Doren), **I:** 168

"Winter Dreams" (Fitzgerald), **II:** 80, 94; **Retro. Supp. I:** 108

"Winter Drive, A" (Jewett), **Retro. Supp. II:** 147

"Winter Eden, A" (Frost), **Retro. Supp. I:** 137

"Winter Father, The" (Dubus), **Supp. VII:** 83, 87

Winter Hours: Prose, Prose Poems, and Poems (Oliver), **Supp. VII:** 230, 247

"Winter in Dunbarton" (Lowell), **II:** 547; **Retro. Supp. II:** 187

"Wintering" (Plath), **Retro. Supp. II:** 255

Winter Insomnia (Carver), **Supp. III Part 1:** 138

Winter in the Blood (Welch), **Supp. IV Part 2:** 562

"Winter Landscape" (Berryman), **I:** 174; **Retro. Supp. I:** 430

Winter Light (W. V. Davis), **Supp. XXI: 92, 93**

"Winter Light" (W. V. Davis), **Supp. XXI:** 90, 92

Winter Lightning (Nemerov), **III:** 269

Winter Morning Walks: One Hundred Postcards to Jim Harrison (Kooser), **Supp. XIX:** 116, **125–126**

Winter News (Haines), **Supp. XII:** 199, **201–204,** 207–208, 208

Winternitz, Mary. *See* Cheever, Mrs. John (Mary Winternitz)

Winter: Notes from Montana (Bass), **Supp. XVI:** 17–18

Winter of Our Discontent, The (Steinbeck), **IV:** 52, 65–66, 68

"Winter on Earth" (Toomer), **Supp. III Part 2:** 486

"Winter Piece, A" (Bryant), **Supp. I Part 1:** 150, 155

"Winter Rains, Cataluña" (Levine), **Supp. V:** 182

"Winter Remembered" (Ransom), **III:** 492–493

"Winter Roses" (W. V. Davis), **Supp. XXI:** 94

Winterrowd, Prudence, **I:** 217, 224

Winters, Jonathan, **Supp. XI:** 305

Winters, Yvor, **I:** 59, 63, 386, 393, 397, 398, 402, 471; **III:** 194, 498; **IV:** 153; **Retro. Supp. II:** 76, 77, 78, 82, 83, 85, 89; **Supp. I Part 1:** 268; **Supp. II Part 2:** 416, 666, **785–816; Supp. IV Part 2:** 480; **Supp. V:** 180, 191–192; **Supp. XIV:** 287; **Supp. XV:** 74, 341

"Winter Sacrament" (Bronk), **Supp. XXI:** 33

"Winter Scenes" (Bryant). *See* "Winter Piece, A"

Winterset (Anderson), **III:** 159

"Winter Shrub, A" (Bronk), **Supp. XXI:** 28

"Winter Skyline Late" (F. Wright), **Supp. XVII:** 245

"Winter Sleep" (Wylie), **Supp. I Part 2:** 711, 729

Winter's Night (Boyce), **Supp. XXI:** 7, **12–13**

Winter's Tale, The (Shakespeare), **Supp. XIII:** 219

Winter Stars (Levis), **Supp. XI:** 259, **266–268**

"Winter Stars" (Levis), **Supp. XI:** 267–268

Winter Stop-Over (Everwine), **Supp. XV:** 74, 76

"Winter Stop-Over" (Everwine), **Supp. XV:** 76

Winter Studies and Summer Rambles in Canada (Jameson), **Supp. XXIII:** 225, 226

"Winter Swan" (Bogan), **Supp. III Part 1:** 52

"Winter Thunder" (Sandoz), **Supp. XXIV:** 255

"Winter Thunder" (X. J. Kennedy), **Supp. XV:** 167

"Winter Thunder" (X. J. Kennedy), **Supp. XV:** 169

"Winter Trees" (Pedersen; Nelson, trans.), **Supp. XVIII:** 180

Winter Trees (Plath), **Retro. Supp. II:** 257; **Supp. I Part 2:** 526, 539, 541

"Winter Walk" (W. V. Davis), **Supp. XXI:** 92

"Winter Weather Advisory" (Ashbery), **Supp. III Part 1:** 26

"Winter Wheat" (Hoffman), **Supp. XVIII:** 86, 87

"Winter without Snow, The" (C. Frost), **Supp. XV:** 96, 105–106

"Winter Words" (Levine), **Supp. V:** 192

Winthrop, John, **Supp. I Part 1:** 99, 100, 101, 102, 105; **Supp. I Part 2:** 484, 485

Winthrop Covenant, The (Auchincloss), **Supp. IV Part 1:** 23

"Wires of the Night, The" (Collins), **Supp. XXI:** 64

Wirt, William, **I:** 232

Wirth, Louis, **IV:** 475

Wisconsin Death Trip (Levy), **Supp. XIX:** 102

"Wisdom Cometh with the Years" (Cullen), **Supp. IV Part 1:** 166

Wisdom of the African World (McKnight, ed.), **Supp. XX:** 157–158

Wisdom of the Desert, The: Sayings from the Desert Fathers of the Fourth Century (Merton), **Supp. VIII:** 201

Wisdom of the Heart, The (H. Miller), **III:** 178, 184

Wise Blood (O'Connor), **III:** 337, 338, 339–343, 344, 345, 346, 350, 354, 356, 357; **Retro. Supp. II:** 219, 221, 222, 223, **225–228**

Wise Men, The (Price), **Supp. VI:** 254

"Wiser Than a God" (Chopin), **Retro. Supp. II:** 61; **Supp. I Part 1:** 208

Wishes, Lies, and Dreams: Teaching Children to Write Poetry (Koch), **Supp. XV:** 176, 189

"Wish for a Young Wife" (Roethke), **III:** 548

Wishful Thinking: A Theological ABC (Buechner), **Supp. XII:** 53

Wishing Tree, The: Christopher Isherwood on Mystical Religion (Adjemian,

ed.), **Supp. XIV:** 164, 173

Wismer, Helen Muriel. *See* Thurber, Mrs. James (Helen Muriel Wismer)

Wisse, Ruth, **Supp. XII:** 167, 168

Wister, Owen, **I:** 62; **Retro. Supp. II:** 72; **Supp. XIV:** 39

Wit (Edson), **Supp. XVIII:** 35–36, 37, **38–51**

"Witchbird" (Bambara), **Supp. XI:** 11

"Witch Burning" (Plath), **Supp. I Part 2:** 539

Witchcraft of Salem Village, The (Jackson), **Supp. IX:** 121

"Witch Doctor" (Hayden), **Supp. II Part 1:** 368, 380

Witches of Eastwick, The (Updike), **Retro. Supp. I:** 330, 331

Witch from Castile, The (Asch), **Supp. XXIII:** 6, 10

Witching Hour, The (Rice), **Supp. VII:** 299–300

"Witch of Coös, The" (Frost), **II:** 154–155; **Retro. Supp. I:** 135; **Retro. Supp. II:** 42

"Witch of Owl Mountain Springs, The: An Account of Her Remarkable Powers" (Taylor), **Supp. V:** 328

"Witch of Wenham, The" (Whittier), **Supp. I Part 2:** 694, 696

Witek, Terri, **Supp. XVII:** 117

"With a Little Help from My Friends" (Kushner), **Supp. IX:** 131

With Bold Knife and Fork (M. F. K. Fisher), **Supp. XVII:** 89, 91

"With Che at Kitty Hawk" (Banks), **Supp. V:** 6

"With Che at the Plaza" (Banks), **Supp. V:** 7

"With Che in New Hampshire" (Banks), **Supp. V:** 6

"With Child" (Taggard), **Supp. XXII:** 276, 278

"Withdrawal Symptoms" (Mora), **Supp. XIII:** 216

"Withered Skins of Berries" (Toomer), **Supp. III Part 2:** 485; **Supp. IX:** 320

Withers, Harry Clay, **Supp. XIII:** 161

Witherspoon, John, **Supp. I Part 2:** 504

With Eyes at the Back of Our Heads (Levertov), **Supp. III Part 1:** 276–277

With Her in Ourland (Gilman), **Supp. XI:** 208–209

With His Pistol in His Hand (Paredes), **Supp. XIII:** 225; **Supp. XIX:** 98

"Within the Words: An Apprenticeship" (Haines), **Supp. XII:** 197

"With Kit, Age 7, at the Beach" (Stafford), **Supp. XI:** 323

With Love to Lesbia (Kenny), **Supp. XXIII:** 145

"With Mercy for the Greedy" (Sexton), **Supp. II Part 2:** 680

With My Trousers Rolled (Epstein), **Supp. XIV:** 101, 105

Without a Hero (Boyle), **Supp. VIII:** 16; **Supp. XX:** 20

Without Feathers (Allen), **Supp. XV:** 3, 14, 15

Without Stopping (Bowles), **Supp. IV Part 1:** 79, 81, 85, 90, 91, 92

"Without Tradition and within Reason: Judge Horton and Atticus Finch in Court" (Johnson), **Supp. VIII:** 127

With Shuddering Fall (Oates), **Supp. II Part 2:** 504–506

"With the Dog at Sunrise" (Kenyon), **Supp. VII:** 170

With the Empress Dowager of China (Carl), **III:** 475

"With the Horse in the Winter Pasture" (McCarriston), **Supp. XIV:** 262

With the Old Breed: At Peleliu and Okinawa (Sledge), **Supp. V:** 249–250

"With the Violin" (Chopin), **Retro. Supp. II:** 61

"Witness" (Clampitt), **Supp. IX:** 42–43, 45, 46

"Witness" (Dubus), **Supp. VII:** 89

"Witness" (Harjo), **Supp. XII:** 227–228

Witness (McNally), **Supp. XIII:** 197

"Witness" (Nelson), **Supp. XVIII:** 186

"Witness, The" (Porter), **III:** 443–444

"Witness for Poetry, A" (Stafford), **Supp. XI:** 324

"Witness for the Defense" (Hay), **Supp. XIV:** 124

"Witnessing My Father's Will" (Karr), **Supp. XI:** 241

"Witnessing to a Shared World" (Sanders), **Supp. XVI:** 278

Witness to the Times! (McGrath), **Supp. X:** 118

Witness Tree, A (Frost), **II:** 155; **Retro. Supp. I:** 122, 137, 139

Wit's End: Days and Nights of the Algonquin Round Table (Gaines), **Supp. IX:** 190

Wits Recreations (Mennes and Smith), **II:** 111

Witt, Shirley Hill, **Supp. IV Part 2:** 505

Witte, John, **Supp. XX: 200**

Wittels, Anne F., **Supp. XV:** 59

Wittenberg, Judith Bryant, **Retro. Supp. II:** 146

Wittgenstein, Ludwig, **Retro. Supp. I:** 53; **Supp. I Part 2:** 626–627; **Supp. X:** 304; **Supp. XII:** 21; **Supp. XV:** 344, 346

Wittgensteins' Mistress (Markson), **Supp. XVII:** 135, 142, 143, 145

Wittliff, William, **Supp. V:** 227

"Witty War, A" (Simpson), **Supp. IX:** 268

Witz (Cohen), **Supp. XXII:** 268

"Wives and Mistresses" (Hardwick), **Supp. III Part 1:** 211–212

Wizard of Loneliness, The (Nichols), **Supp. XIII:** 259, 263, 264

Wizard of Oz, The (Baum), **Supp. IV Part 1:** 113

Wizard of Oz, The (film), **Supp. X:** 172, 214

Wizard's Tide, The: A Story (Buechner), **Supp. XII:** 54

"WLT (The Edgar Era)" (Keillor), **Supp. XVI:** 172

WLT: A Radio Romance (Keillor), **Supp. XVI:** 176

Wobegon Boy (Keillor), **Supp. XVI:** 177

Wodehouse, P. G., **Supp. IX:** 195; **Supp. XXI:** 204–205

Woiwode, Larry, **Supp. VIII:** 151; **Supp. XVI:** 206

Wojahn, David, **Supp. IX:** 161, 292, 293; **Supp. XXI:** 130, 131, 132, 138, 139, 141

Wolcott, James, **Supp. IX:** 259

Wolf, Christa, **Supp. IV Part 1:** 310, 314

Wolf, Daniel, **Retro. Supp. II:** 202

Wolf, Robert L., **Supp. XXII:** 274, 277, 279, 280

Wolf: A False Memoir (Harrison), **Supp. VIII:** 40, **41–42,** 45

Wolfe, Ben, **IV:** 454

Wolfe, Gregory, **Supp. XIV:** 307

Wolfe, James, **Supp. I Part 2:** 498

Wolfe, Linnie, **Supp. IX:** 176

Wolfe, Mabel, **IV:** 454

Wolfe, Thomas, **I:** 288, 289, 374, 478, 495; **II:** 457; **III:** 40, 108, 278, 334, 482; **IV:** 52, 97, 357, **450–473; Retro. Supp. I:** 382; **Supp. I Part 1:** 29; **Supp. IV Part 1:** 101; **Supp. IX:** 229; **Supp. X:** 225; **Supp. XI:** 213, 216, 217, 218; **Supp. XIII:** 17; **Supp. XIV:** 122; **Supp. XVIII:** 78; **Supp. XX:** 163

Wolfe, Tom, **Supp. III Part 2: 567–588; Supp. IV Part 1:** 35, 198; **Supp. V:** 296; **Supp. X:** 264; **Supp. XI:** 239; **Supp. XV:** 143; **Supp. XVII:** 202; **Supp. XVIII:** 72, 117; **Supp. XXIV:** 282, 283

Wolfe, William Oliver, **IV:** 454

Wolfe, Mrs. William Oliver (Julia Elizabeth Westall), **IV:** 454

"Wolfe Homo Scribens" (Cowley), **Supp. II Part 1:** 144

Wolfert, Ira, **Supp. XXI: 261–279**

Wolfert's Roost (Irving), **II:** 314

Wolff, Cynthia Griffin, **Retro. Supp. I:** 379; **Supp. IV Part 1:** 203

Wolff, Donald, **Supp. XIII:** 316, 317, 326

Wolff, Geoffrey, **Supp. II Part 1:** 97; **Supp. XI:** 239, 245, 246; **Supp. XXII:** 206, 211

Wolff, Tobias, **Retro. Supp. I:** 190; **Supp. V:** 22; **Supp. VII: 331–346; Supp. X:** 1; **Supp. XI:** 26, 239, 245, 246, 247; **Supp. XV:** 223; **Supp. XVI:** 39, 41, 63, 70, 77; **Supp. XXIII:** 289

"Wolf in the Bed, The"(Hadas), **Supp. XXIII:** 118

Wolfreys, Julian, **Supp. XVIII:** 61

Wolfson, P. J., **Supp. XIII:** 172

"Wolf Town" (Carson), **Supp. XII: 102**

Wolf Willow: A History, a Story, and a Memory of the Last Plains Frontier (Stegner), **Supp. IV Part 2:** 595, 596, 597, 598, 599, 600, 601, 604, 606, 611, 613, 614

Wolitzer, Hilma, **Supp. XV:** 55; **Supp. XXIII:** 108

Wolitzer, Meg, **Supp. XV:** 65

Wolkomir, Richard, **Supp. XXII:** 218

Wollaston, William, **II:** 108

Wollstonecraft, Mary, **Supp. I Part 1:** 126; **Supp. I Part 2:** 512, 554

"Wolves in the Marsh" (Dubus III), **Supp. XXIV:** 99–100

Womack, Craig, **Supp. XXIII:** 147, 153, 154–155

"Woman" (Bogan), **Supp. X:** 102

"Woman, I Got the Blues" (Komunyakaa), **Supp. XIII:** 117

"Woman, Why Are You Weeping?" (Kenyon), **Supp. VII:** 174–175

"Woman, Young and Old, A" (Paley), **Supp. VI:** 222, 225

Woman Aroused, The (Lacy), **Supp. XV:** 199–200

Woman at the Washington Zoo, The (Jarrell), **II:** 367, 386, 387, 389

Woman Before an Aquarium (Hampl), **Supp. XXII:** 83, 86, 98

"Woman Before an Aquarium" (Hampl), **Supp. XXII:** 85, 98

"Womand and the Woman's Movement" (Briggs), **Supp. XVIII:** 14

"Woman Dead in Her Forties, A" (Rich), **Supp. I Part 2:** 574–575

Woman Driver, The (Thompson), **Supp. XXIII:** 291, **294–295**

"Woman Enough" (Gallagher), **Supp. XXIV:** 169

"Woman Hanging from the Thirteenth Floor Window, The" (Harjo), **Supp. XII:** 216, 221

"Woman Hollering Creek" (Cisneros), **Supp. VII:** 70

Woman Hollering Creek and Other Stories (Cisneros), **Supp. VII:** 58, 68–70

"Womanhood" (Brooks), **Supp. III Part 1:** 77

"Woman in Rain" (X. J. Kennedy), **Supp. XV:** 168

Woman in the Dark (Hammett), **Supp. IV Part 1:** 343

"Woman in the House, A" (Caldwell), **I:** 310

Woman in the Nineteenth Century (Fuller), **Retro. Supp. I:** 156; **Supp. II Part 1:** 279, 292, 294–296; **Supp. XI:** 197, 203; **Supp. XVIII:** 3, 11

"Woman in the Shoe, The" (Ryan as Quin), **Supp. XVIII:** 231

Woman in White, The (Collins), **Supp. I Part 1:** 35, 36

"Woman Is Talking to Death, A"(Grahn), **Supp. XXIII:** 195

"Womanizer, The" (Ford), **Supp. V:** 71, 72

"Woman Like Yourself, A" (C. Frost), **Supp. XV:** 107

Woman Lit by Fireflies, The (Harrison), **Supp. VIII: 50–51**

"Woman Loses Cookie Bake-Off, Sets Self on Fire" (R. O. Butler), **Supp. XII:** 72

Woman of Andros, The (Wilder), **IV:** 356, 363–364, 367, 368, 374

Woman of Means, A (Taylor), **Supp. V:** 319–320

"Woman of Tomorrow, The" (Atherton), **Supp. XXIV:** 29

Woman on the Edge of Time (Piercy), **Supp. XIII:** 29

Woman on the Porch, The (Gordon), **II:** 199, 209–211

"Woman on the Stair, The" (MacLeish), **III:** 15–16

"Woman's Dream, A" (E. Stoddard), **Supp. XV:** 278

Woman's Fiction: A Guide to Novels By and About Women in America, 1820–1870 (Baym), **Supp. XVIII:** 258

"Woman's Heartlessness" (Thaxter), **Retro. Supp. II:** 147

Woman's Honor (Glaspell), **Supp. III Part 1:** 179

"Woman Singing" (Ortiz), **Supp. IV Part 2:** 513

Woman's Place, A (C. L. R. James and Weinstein), **Supp. XXI:** 170

Woman's Share in Primitive Culture (Mason), **Supp. I Part 1:** 18

"Woman Struck by Car Turns into Nymphomaniac" (R. O. Butler), **Supp. XII:** 72

"Woman's Work" (Alvarez), **Supp. VII:** 4

"Woman Taken in Adultery, A"(Thompson), **Supp. XXIII:** 300

"Woman Uses Glass Eye to Spy on Philandering Husband" (R. O. Butler), **Supp. XII:** 70, 72

Woman Warrior (Kingston), **Supp. IV Part 1:** 12; **Supp. V:** 157, 158, 159, 160–164, 166, 169; **Supp. X:** 291–292; **Supp. XIV:** 162

Woman Warrior, The (Kingston), **Supp. XV:** 220

Woman Who Fell from the Sky, The (Harjo), **Supp. XII: 226–228**

"Woman Who Fell From the Sky, The" (Iroquois creation story), **Supp. IV Part 1:** 327

Woman Who Owned the Shadows, The (Gunn Allen), **Supp. IV Part 1:** 320, 322, 326, 327–328

"Woman Who Plays Trumpet Is Deported, A" (Cliff), **Supp. XXII:** 74

"Woman Who Prayed, The" (Gallagher), **Supp. XXIV:** 175

"Woman Who Raised Goats, The" (Gallagher), **Supp. XXIV:** 168

"Woman Who Went Backwards, The"(Schott), **Supp. XXIII:** 241

Woman Within, The (Glasgow), **II:** 183, 190–191

"Womanwork" (Gunn Allen), **Supp. IV Part 1:** 326

Women (Bukowski), **Supp. XI:** 172

"Women" (Didion), **Supp. IV Part 1:** 205

"Women" (Swenson), **Supp. IV Part 2:** 647

Women, The (Boyle), **Supp. XX: 24, 26–27**

Women, The (film), **Retro. Supp. I:** 113

Women, The (film; Cukor), **Supp. XVI:** 181, 192

"Women and Children First" (Prose), **Supp. XVI:** 254

Women and Children First: Stories (Prose), **Supp. XVI:** 254

Women and Economics (Gilman), **Supp. I Part 2:** 637; **Supp. V:** 284; **Supp. XI:** 200, **203–204,** 206

"Women and Poetry" (Notley), **Supp. XXII:** 236

Women and Thomas Harrow (Marquand), **III:** 50, 61, 62, 66, 68, 69–70, 71

Women and Vodka (Markson as Merrill, ed.), **Supp. XVII:** 136

Women and Wilderness (LaBastille), **Supp. X:** 97, **102–104**

"Women as They Are" (Rowson), **Supp. XV:** 243

Women at Point Sur, The (Jeffers), **Supp. II Part 2:** 430–431

Women Authors of Our Day in Their Homes (Halsey), **Supp. XXIV:** 20

Women in Love (Lawrence), **III:** 27, 34; **Supp. XXIV:** 58

Women in Praise of the Sacred: 43 Centuries of Spiritual Poetry by Women (Hirshfield, ed.), **Supp. XXIII:** 136, 137

"Women of Auschwitz, The" (Gallagher), **Supp. XXIV:** 171

Women of Belize: Gender and Change in Central America (McClaurin), **Supp. XXIII:** 84

Women of Brewster Place, The: A Novel in Seven Stories (Naylor), **Supp. VIII:** 213, **214–218**

Women of Manhattan: An Upper West Side Story (Shanley), **Supp. XIV:** 315, **326–327**

"Women of My Color" (Coleman), **Supp. XI:** 88–89

Women of Trachis (Pound, trans.), **III:** 476

"Women on the Breadlines"(Le Sueur), **Supp. XXIII:** 166, 167

Women on the Wall, The (Stegner), **Supp. IV Part 2:** 599, 605, 606

Women Poets in English (Stanford, ed.), **Retro. Supp. I:** 41

"Women Reformers and American Culture, 1870–1930" (Conway), **Supp. I Part 1:** 19

"Women's Movement, The" (Didion), **Supp. IV Part 1:** 206

"Women Waiting" (Shields), **Supp. VII:** 320

"Women We Love Whom We Never See Again" (R. Bly), **Supp. IV Part 1:** 66

"Women We Never See Again" (R. Bly), **Supp. IV Part 1:** 66

Women with Men (Ford), **Supp. V:** 57, 71–72

"Wonder" (Olds), **Supp. X:** 210

Wonder Boys (Chabon), **Supp. XI:** 67, **73–75,Supp. XI:** 78; **Supp. XVI:** 259

Wonder Boys (film), **Supp. XI:** 67

Wonderful O, The (Thurber), **Supp. I Part 2:** 612

"Wonderful Old Gentleman, The" (Parker), **Supp. IX:** 197

"Wonderful Pen, The" (Swenson), **Supp. IV Part 2:** 650

Wonderful Words, Silent Truth: Essays on Poetry and a Memoir (Simic), **Supp. VIII:** 270

Wonderland (Oates), **Supp. II Part 2:** 511, 512, 514–515

Wonders Hidden (Sanders), **Supp. XVI:** 269

Wonders of the African World (television series), **Supp. XX: 99**

Wonders of the Invisible World, The (Mather), **Supp. II Part 2:** 456–459, 460, 467

Wonder-Working Providence (Johnson), **IV:** 157

Wong, Hertha, **Supp. IV Part 1:** 275

Wong, Jade Snow, **Supp. X:** 291

Wong, Nellie, **Supp. XVII:** 72

Wong, Shawn, **Supp. XV:** 221

Wong, Timothy, **Supp. XVIII:** 94

"Wood" (Nye), **Supp. XIII:** 276

Wood, Audrey, **IV:** 381

Wood, Charles Erskine Scott, **Supp. XV:** 301

Wood, Clement, **Supp. XV:** 298

Wood, Clement Biddle, **Supp. XI:** 307

Wood, Gaby, **Supp. XXIV:** 166

Wood, Harrison, **Supp. XXII:** 283

Wood, Mrs. Henry, **Supp. I Part 1:** 35

Wood, James, **Supp. XIV:** 95–96; **Supp. XIX:** 138

Wood, Mabel, **I:** 199

Wood, Michael, **Supp. IV Part 2:** 691

Wood, Norman Barton, **Supp. XIV:** 201

Wood, Susan, **Supp. XVI:** 123

Woodard, Calvin, **Supp. VIII:** 128

Woodard, Charles L., **Supp. IV Part 2:** 484, 493

Woodard, Deborah, **Supp. XIII:** 114

Woodberry, George Edward, **III:** 508

Woodbridge, Frederick, **I:** 217, 224

Woodbridge, John, **Supp. I Part 1:** 101, 102, 114

"Wood-Choppers, The" (Chopin), **Retro. Supp. II:** 72

Woodcock, George, **Supp. XIII:** 33

Woodcome, Beth, **Supp. XVII:** 240

"Wood Dove at Sandy Spring, The" (MacLeish), **III:** 19

"Wooden Spring" (Rukeyser), **Supp. VI:** 285

"Wooden Umbrella, The" (Porter), **IV:** 26

Woodhull, Victoria, **Supp. XVIII:** 4

"Woodnotes" (Emerson), **II:** 7, 19

"Wood-Pile, The" (Frost), **Retro. Supp. I:** 128; **Supp. IV Part 2:** 445

Woodrow, James, **Supp. I Part 1:** 349, 366

"Woods, Books, and Truant Officers, The" (Maclean), **Supp. XIV:** 221, 225

"Woods, New York, The" (Bronk), **Supp. XXI:** 27

Woods, Paula L., **Supp. XXI:** 70

Woods, Robert A., **Supp. I Part 1:** 19

Woods, The (Mamet), **Supp. XIV:** 241, 254–255

Woodswoman (LaBastille), **Supp. X:** 95, **96–99**, 108

Woodswoman III: Book Three of the Woodswoman's Adventures (LaBastille), **Supp. X:** 95, **106–107**

"Wood Thrush" (Kenyon), **Supp. VII:** 172

Woodward, C. Vann, **IV:** 114, 470–471; **Retro. Supp. I:** 75, 76; **Supp. XIX:** 152; **Supp. XXII:** 194

"Woof: A Plea of Sorts" (Saunders), **Supp. XIX:** 235

"Wooing the Inanimate" (Brodsky), **Supp. VIII:** 32

Woolcott, Alexander, **Supp. IX:** 197

Wooley, Bryan, **Supp. V:** 225

Woolf, Douglas, **Supp. XXIII:** 174

Woolf, Leonard, **Supp. IX:** 95

Woolf, Virginia, **I:** 53, 79, 112, 309; **II:** 320, 415; **IV:** 59; **Retro. Supp. I:** 59, 75, 170, 215, 291, 359; **Supp. I Part 2:** 553, 714, 718; **Supp. IV Part 1:** 299; **Supp. V:** 127; **Supp. VIII:** 5, 155, 251, 252, 263, 265; **Supp. IX:** 66, 109; **Supp. XI:** 134, 193; **Supp. XII:** 81, 98, 289; **Supp. XIII:** 305; **Supp. XIV:** 341–342, 342, 343, 346, 348; **Supp. XV:** 55, 65; **Supp. XIX:** 134; **Supp. XXIII:** 275

Woollcott, Alexander, **IV:** 432; **Retro. Supp. I:** 327; **Supp. I Part 2:** 664; **Supp. IX:** 190, 194

Woolley, Leonard, **Supp. XXIII:** 33

Woollstonecraft, Mary, **Supp. XVI:** 184

"Woolly Mammoth" (X. J. Kennedy), **Supp. XV:** 163–164

Woolman, John, **Supp. VIII:** 202, 204, 205

Woolson, Constance Fenimore, **Retro. Supp. I:** 224, 228

Woolverton, Linda, **Supp. XXI:** 148

Wooster, David, **Supp. XX: 288**

Worcester, Samuel, **I:** 458

Word and Idioms: Studies in the English Language (L. P. Smith), **Supp. XIV:** 343

"Word by Word" (column, Lamott), **Supp. XX: 140**

Word of God and the Word of Man, The (Barth), **Retro. Supp. I:** 327

"Word out of the Sea, A" (Whitman), **IV:** 344

Words (Creeley), **Supp. IV Part 1:** 139, 150–153, 154, 155, 158

"Words" (Creeley), **Supp. IV Part 1:** 152

"Words" (Gioia), **Supp. XV:** 125

"Words" (Merwin), **Supp. III Part 1:** 352

"Words" (Plath), **Supp. I Part 2:** 547

"Words" (Shields), **Supp. VII:** 323

"Words, The" (Wagoner), **Supp. IX:** 326

"Words above a Narrow Entrance" (Wagoner), **Supp. IX:** 325

"Words for a Bike-Racing, Osprey-Chasing Wine-Drunk Squaw Man" (Gunn Allen), **Supp. IV Part 1:** 325

Words for Dr. Y (Sexton), **Supp. II Part 2:** 698

"Words for Hart Crane" (Lowell), **I:** 381; **II:** 547; **Retro. Supp. II:** 188

"Words for Love" (Berrigan), **Supp. XXIV:** 35

"Words for Maria" (Merrill), **Supp. III Part 1:** 327

"Words for My Grandmother"(Balakian), **Supp. XXIII:** 19, 20

Words for the Chisel (Taggard), **Supp. XXII: 276–277**

"Words for the Unknown Makers" (Kunitz), **Supp. III Part 1:** 264

Words for the Wind (Roethke), **III:** 529, 533, 541, 543, 545

"Words for the Wind" (Roethke), **III:** 542–543

Words in the Mourning Time (Hayden), **Supp. II Part 1:** 361, 366, 367

"Words in the Mourning Time" (Hayden), **Supp. II Part 1:** 370–371

"Words into Fiction" (Welty), **IV:** 279

"Words into Worlds Won't Go" (Major), **Supp. XXII:** 174

"Words Like Freedom" (Hughes), **Retro. Supp. I:** 207

"Words of a Young Girl" (Lowell), **II:** 554

Words under the Words: Selected Poems (Nye), **Supp. XIII:** 277

Wordsworth, Dorothy, **Supp. IX:** 38

Wordsworth, William, **I:** 283, 522, 524, 525, 588; **II:** 7, 11, 17, 18, 97, 169, 273, 303, 304, 532, 549, 552; **III:** 219, 263, 277, 278, 511, 521, 523, 528, 583; **IV:** 120, 331, 343, 453, 465; **Retro. Supp. I:** 121, 196; **Supp. I Part 1:** 150, 151, 154, 161, 163, 312, 313, 349, 365; **Supp. I Part 2:** 375, 409, 416, 422, 607, 621, 622, 673, 674, 675, 676, 677, 710–711, 729; **Supp. II Part 1:** 4; **Supp. III Part 1:** 12, 15, 73, 279; **Supp. IV Part 2:** 597, 601; **Supp. V:** 258; **Supp. VIII:** 273; **Supp. IX:** 38, 41, 265, 274; **Supp. X:** 22, 23, 65, 120; **Supp. XI:** 248, 251, 312; **Supp. XIII:** 214; **Supp. XIV:** 184; **Supp. XV:** 93, 250; **Supp. XIX:** 1; **Supp. XX: 108, 116; Supp. XXI:** 131; **Supp. XXIV:** 74, 159

" 'Word Which Made All Clear, The': The Silent Close of *The House of Mirth*" (Benstock), **Supp. XX:** 240

Work (Alcott), **Supp. I Part 1:** 32–33, 42

Work (Dixon), **Supp. XII:** 141, **143**

"Work" (Halliday), **Supp. XIX:** 85

"Work" (Oliver), **Supp. VII:** 243

Work and Love (Dunn), **Supp. XI:** 147–**148**

"Worker" (Coleman), **Supp. XI:** 89

Worker Writers (Le Sueur), **Supp. XXIII:** 165

Working a Passage; or, Life on a Liner (Briggs), **Supp. XVIII:** 2, **9–10**

Working Class Movement in America, The (E. Marx and E. Aveling), **Supp. XVI:** 85

Working Papers: Selected Essays and Reviews (Carruth), **Supp. XVI:** 46

"Working Roots: A Collection of Poetry and Prose" (Trethewey), **Supp. XXI:** 245

"Working the Landscape" (Dunn), **Supp. XI:** 151

Working Through: A Teacher's Journey in the Urban University (Kriegel), **Supp. XXIV: 222–223**

Workin' on the Chain Gang: Shaking Off the Dead Hand of History (Mosley), **Supp. XIII:** 247, 248

"Work Notes '66" (Baraka), **Supp. II Part 1:** 47

Work of Art (Lewis), **II:** 453–454

"Work of Shading, The" (Simic), **Supp. VIII:** 277–278

Work of Stephen Crane, The (Follett, ed.), **I:** 405

"Work on Red Mountain, The" (Harte), **Supp. II Part 1:** 339

"Workshop" (Espaillat), **Supp. XXI:** 105

Works of Love, The (Morris), **III:** 223–224, 225, 233

Works of Witter Bynner, The (Kraft, ed.), **Supp. XV:** 52

"World, The" (Bronk), **Supp. XXI:** 32

"World, The" (Simic), **Supp. VIII:** 282

"World, the Flesh, and the Devil, The"(P. Benedict), **Supp. XXIII:** 48

World, the Worldless, The (Bronk), **Supp. XXI: 29–31**

World According to Garp, The (Irving), **Supp. VI:** 163, 164, **170–173**, 181

World and Africa, The: An Inquiry into the Part Which Africa Has Played in World History (Du Bois), **Supp. II Part 1:** 184–185

"World and All Its Teeth, The" (Nye), **Supp. XIII:** 282

"World and the Door, The" (O. Henry), **Supp. II Part 1:** 402

"World and the Jug, The" (Ellison), **Retro. Supp. II:** 112, 119, 123

"World as We Know It, The" (Barresi), **Supp. XV:** 100

World Authors 1950–1970, **Supp. XIII:** 102

World Below, The (Miller), **Supp. XII: 303–304**

World Below the Window, The: Poems 1937–1997 (W. J. Smith), **Supp. XIII:** 332, 340, 345

World Doesn't End, The (Simic), **Supp. VIII:** 272, **279–280**

World Elsewhere, A: The Place of Style in American Literature (Poirier), **I:** 239

"World Ends Here, The" (Harjo), **Supp. XII:** 227–228

World Enough and Time (Warren), **IV:** 243, 253–254

World Gone Wrong (album, Dylan), **Supp. XVIII:** 28

"World I Live In, The" (T. Williams), **IV:** 388

World I Never Made, A (Farrell), **II:** 34, 35, 424

World in the Attic, The (Morris), **III:** 222–223, 224

World in the Evening, The (Isherwood), **Supp. XIV:** 157, 164, 165, **166–167**, 170

World Is a Wedding, The (Schwartz), **Supp. II Part 2:** 643, 654–660

"World Is a Wedding, The" (Schwartz), **Supp. II Part 2:** 655–656, 657

"World Is Too Much with Us, The" (Wordsworth), **Supp. I Part 1:** 312

Worldly Hopes (Ammons), **Supp. VII:** 34

Worldly Philosophers, The (Heilbroner), **Supp. I Part 2:** 644, 650

World of Apples, The (Cheever), **Supp. I Part 1:** 191, 193

World of David Wagoner, The (McFarland), **Supp. IX:** 323

"World of Easy Rawlins, The" (Mosley), **Supp. XIII:** 234, 236

World of Gwendolyn Brooks, The (Brooks), **Supp. III Part 1:** 83, 84

World of H. G. Wells, The (Brooks), **I:** 240, 241, 242

World of Light, A (Skloot), **Supp. XX: 196, 205, 206–207**

"World of Light, A" (Skloot), **Supp. XX: 194, 207**

World of Light, A: Portraits and Celebrations (Sarton), **Supp. III Part 1:** 62; **Supp. VIII:** 249, 253, 262

World of Our Fathers: The Journey of the Eastern European Jews to America and the Life They Found and Made (Howe), **Supp. VI:** 113, 114, 116, 118, 119, **120–125**; **Supp. XIV:**104; **Supp. XXIII:** 3; **Supp. XXIV:** 220–221

"World of Pure Experience, A" (James), **II:** 356–357

World of Raymond Chandler, The (Spender), **Supp. IV Part 1:** 119

World of Sex, The (H. Miller), **III:** 170, 178, 187

"World of the Perfect Tear, The" (McGrath), **Supp. X:** 116, 118

World of the Ten Thousand Things, The: Selected Poems (Wright), **Supp. V:** 333

"World of Tomorrow, The" (White), **Supp. I Part 2:** 663

World of Washington Irving, The (Brooks), **I:** 256–257

World Over, The (Wharton), **Retro. Supp. I:** 382

World Revolution (C. L. R. James), **Supp. XXI:** 167

"Worlds" (Goldbarth), **Supp. XII:** 183, 189

World's Body, The (Ransom), **III:** 497, 499; **Supp. II Part 1:** 146

World's End (Boyle), **Supp. VIII:** 11–12; **Supp. XX: 22–23**

World's End and Other Stories (Theroux), **Supp. VIII:** 322

"World's Fair" (Berryman), **I:** 173

World's Fair (Doctorow), **Supp. IV Part 1:** 217, 224, 227–229, 234, 236–237

World's Fair, The (Fitzgerald), **II:** 93

Worlds of Color (Du Bois), **Supp. II Part 1:** 185–186

"Worlds of Color" (Du Bois), **Supp. II Part 1:** 175

World So Wide (Lewis), **II:** 456

"World's Worst Boyfriends, The" (Wasserstein), **Supp. XV:** 328

"World-Telegram" (Berryman), **I:** 173

World to Come, The (D. Horn), **Supp. XVII:** 50

"World Trade Center / Mail runner / '73"(Balakian), **Supp. XXIII:** 32–33

World View on Race and Democracy: A Study Guide in Human Group Relations (Locke), **Supp. XIV:** 205, 206

World within the Word, The (Gass), **Supp. VI:** 77

"World Without Objects Is a Sensible Place, A" (Wilbur), **Supp. III Part 2:** 550

"World Without Rodrigo, The" (Cisneros), **Supp. VII:** 68

"Worm Moon" (Oliver), **Supp. VII:** 234

Wormser, Baron, **Supp. XXIII:** 57

"Worn Path, A" (Welty), **IV:** 262; **Retro. Supp. I:** 345–346

"Worsening Situation" (Ashbery), **Supp. III Part 1:** 17–18

"Worship" (Emerson), **II:** 2, 4–5

"Worship and Church Bells" (Paine), **Supp. I Part 2:** 521

Worster, Donald, **Supp. IX:** 19

Worthington, Marjorie, **Supp. XII:** 13

Wouk, Herman, **Supp. XX:** 243

Wouldn't Take Nothing for My Journey Now (Angelou), **Supp. IV Part 1:** 10, 12, 14, 15, 16

"Wound" (Pedersen; Nelson, trans.), **Supp. XVIII:** 180

Wound and the Bow, The: Seven Studies in Literature (Wilson), **IV:** 429; **Supp. XXIV:** 217

Wounded (Everett), **Supp. XVIII:** 54, **64, 65**

Wounds in the Rain (Crane), **I:** 409, 414, 423

Woven Stone (Ortiz), **Supp. IV Part 2:** 501, 514

Woven Stories (Ortiz), **Supp. IV Part 2:** 503

"Wraith, The" (Roethke), **III:** 542

"Wrath of God, The" (Fante), **Supp. XI:** 160, 164

"Wreath for a Bridal" (Plath), **Supp. I Part 2:** 537

"Wreath for Emmet Till, A" (Nelson), **Supp. XVIII:** 177

Wreath for Emmett Till, A (Nelson), **Supp. XVIII:** 171, 173, 175, 181, **183–185**

Wreath for Garibaldi and Other Stories, A (Garrett), **Supp. VII:** 99–101

"Wreath of Women" (Rukeyser), **Supp. VI:** 280

Wreckage (Jin), **Supp. XVIII: 98–99**

Wreckage of Agathon, The (Gardner), **Supp. VI:** 63, **65–66**

Wrecking Crew (Levis), **Supp. XI:** 259–260

Wrecking Yard, The (Benedict), **Supp. XXIII:** 35, **39–41**

"Wrecking Yard, The" (P. Benedict), **Supp. XXIII:** 39–40

"Wreck of Rivermouth, The" (Whittier), **Supp. I Part 2:** 694, 696–697

"Wreck of the Deutschland" (Hopkins), **Supp. X:** 61

"Wreck of the Hesperus, The" (Longfellow), **Retro. Supp. II:** 168, 169

Wrestler's Cruel Study, The (Dobyns), **Supp. XIII: 82–83**

"Wrestler with Sharks, A" (Yates), **Supp. XI:** 341

"Wrestling with Augie March" (Kriegel), **Supp. XXIV:** 220

Wright, Bernie, **I:** 191, 193

Wright, C. D. (Carolyn Doris), **Supp. XV: 337–355**

Wright, Charles, **Supp. V:** 92, **331–346; Supp. VIII:** 272; **Supp. XIII:** 114; **Supp. XVII:** 71; **Supp. XXI:** 95, 255; **Supp. XXIV:** 155

Wright, Chauncey, **II:** 344

Wright, Conrad, **Supp. XXIV:** 71, 72

Wright, Frank Lloyd, **I:** 104, 483

Wright, Franz, **Supp. XVII: 239–249**

Wright, George, **III:** 479

Wright, Harold Bell, **II:** 467–468

Wright, Holly, **Supp. VIII:** 272

Wright, James, **I:** 291; **Supp. III Part 1:** 249; **Supp. III Part 2:** 541, **589–607; Supp. IV Part 1:** 60, 72; **Supp. IV Part 2:** 557, 558, 561, 566, 571, 623; **Supp. V:** 332; **Supp. IX:** 152, 155, 159, 265, 271, 290, 293, 296; **Supp. X:** 69, 127; **Supp. XI:** 150; **Supp. XII:** 217; **Supp. XIII:** 76; **Supp. XV:** 79, 93, 212; **Supp. XVII:** 239, 241, 243, 244; **Supp. XIX:** 122, 273

Wright, Nathalia, **IV:** 155

Wright, Philip Green, **III:** 578, 579, 580

Wright, Richard, **II:** 586; **IV:** 40, **474–497; Retro. Supp. II:** 4, 111, 116, 120; **Supp. I Part 1:** 51, 52, 64, 332, 337; **Supp. II Part 1:** 17, 40, 221, 228, 235, 250; **Supp. IV Part 1:** 1, 11, 84, 374; **Supp. VIII:** 88; **Supp. IX:** 316; **Supp. X:** 131, 245, 254; **Supp. XI:** 85; **Supp. XII:** 316; **Supp. XIII:** 46, 233; **Supp. XIV:** 73; **Supp. XVI:** 135, 139, 141, 143; **Supp. XVIII:** 277, 282, 286; **Supp. XXI:** 169; **Supp. XXIII:** 166

Wright, Mrs. Richard (Ellen Poplar), **IV:** 476

Wright, Sarah, **Supp. IV Part 1:** 8; **Supp. XIII:** 295

Wright, William, **Retro. Supp. II:** 76, 77

Wrigley, Robert, **Supp. XVIII: 293–308**

"Writer" (Sanders), **Supp. XVI:** 277

"Writer, The" (Wilbur), **Supp. III Part 2:** 561, 562

"Writer as Alaskan, The" (Haines), **Supp. XII:** 199

Writer in America, The (Brooks), **I:** 253, 254, 257

Writer in America, The (Stegner), **Supp. IV Part 2:** 597, 599, 607

"Writers" (Lowell), **II:** 554

Writer's Almanac, The (Keillor, radio program), **Supp. XIII:** 274; **Supp. XVI:** 178; **Supp. XXIII:** 138

Writer's America, A: Landscape in Literature (Kazin), **Supp. VIII:** 106

Writers and Their Craft (Delbanco, ed.), **Supp. XXII:** 204

"Writer's Bed, A" (Mirvis), **Supp. XX:** 179

Writer's Capital, A (Auchincloss), **Supp. IV Part 1:** 21, 23, 24, 31

"Writer's Credo, A" (Abbey), **Supp. XIII:** 1, 17

Writer's Eye, A: Collected Book Reviews (Welty), **Retro. Supp. I:** 339, 354, 356

Writers in America (Schulberg), **Supp. XVIII:** 242, 243, 250, 254

Writers in Revolt (Southern, Seaver, and Trocchi, eds.), **Supp. XI:** 301

Writer's Life, A (Talese), **Supp. XVII:** 208–209, 210

Writer's Notebook, A (Maugham), **Supp. X:** 58

Writers on America (U.S. Department of State, ed.), **Supp. XIII:** 288

Writers on the Left (Aaron), **IV:** 429; **Supp. II Part 1:** 137

Writers on Writing (Prose), **Supp. XVI:** 259

"Writer's Prologue to a Play in Verse" (W. C. Williams), **Retro. Supp. I:** 424

"Writer's Quest for a Parnassus, A" (T. Williams), **IV:** 392

Writers' Workshop (University of Iowa), **Supp. V:** 42

"Writers Workshop, The" (Conroy), **Supp. XVI:** 76

"Writing" (Nemerov), **III:** 275

"Writing About the Universe" (Mosley), **Supp. XIII:** 247

"Writing American Fiction" (P. Roth), **Retro. Supp. II:** 279; **Supp. I Part 1:** 192; **Supp. I Part 2:** 431; **Supp. III Part 2:** 414, 420, 421; **Supp. V:** 45

"Writing and a Life Lived Well" (Patchett), **Supp. XII:** 308

"Writing and Writers: *Disjecta Membra*" (Sorrentino), Supp. XXI: 235

Writing a Woman's Life (Heilbrun), **Supp. IX:** 66

"Writing Between Worlds" (Mirvis), **Supp. XX: 177, 178, 179**

Writing Brave and Free: Encouraging Words for People Who Want to Start Writing (Kooser and Cox), **Supp. XIX:** 116, 128

Writing Chicago: Modernism, Ethnography, and the Novel (Cappetti), **Supp. IX:** 4, 8

Writing Creative Nonfiction: The Literature of Reality (Talese and Lounsberry, eds.), **Supp. XVII:** 208

Writing Dylan: The Songs of a Lonesome Traveler (Smith), **Supp. XVIII:** 22

Writing from the Center (Sanders), **Supp. XVI:** 266, 275–276

"Writing from the Inside Out: Style Is Not the Frosting; It's the Cake" (Robbins), **Supp. X:** 266

"Writing here last autumn of my hopes of seeing a hoopoe" (Updike), **Retro. Supp. I:** 335

Writing Home (Crooker), **Supp. XXIII:** 54

Writing in Restaurants (Mamet), **Supp. XIV:** 246

"Writing Lesson, The" (Gordon), **Supp. IV Part 1:** 306

Writing Life, The (Dillard), **Supp. VI:** 23, 31

"Writing of Apollinaire, The" (Zukofsky), **Supp. III Part 2:** 616, 617

"Writing of *Fearless Jones,* The" (Mosley), **Supp. XIII:** 242

Writing on the Wall, The, and Literary Essays (McCarthy), **II:** 579

Writings to an Unfinished Accompaniment (Merwin), **Supp. III Part 1:** 352

"Writing the Universe-Mind" (Tabios), **Supp. XV:** 225

Writing the World (Stafford), **Supp. XI:** 314

"Writing to Save Our Lives" (Milligan), **Supp. XIII:** 274

Writing Vietnam, Writing Life: Caputo, Heinemann, O'Brien, Butler (Herzog), **Supp. XXII:** 116

Writin' Is Fightin' (Reed), *Supp. X:* 241

"Writ on the Eve of My 32nd Birthday" (Corso), **Supp. XII:** 129–130

"Written History as an Act of Faith" (Beard), **Supp. I Part 2:** 492

"Written on the Land" (J. W. Miller), **Supp. XX:** 170

"Wrong Man, The" (Larsen), **Supp. XVIII:** 124

"Wrong Notes" (S. Kauffmann), **Supp. XVI:** 74

"Wrought Figure" (McCarriston), **Supp. XIV:** 272

Wrozynski, Henryk, **Supp. XXIII:** 64

"Wunderkind" (McCullers), **II:** 585

Wunderlich, Mark, **Supp. XI:** 119, 132

Wundt, Wilhelm, **II:** 345

Wurster, William Wilson, **Supp. IV Part 1:** 197

WUSA (film), **Supp. V:** 301

Wuthering Heights (E. Brontë), **Supp. V:** 305; **Supp. X:** 89

WWII (Jones), **Supp. XI:** 219, 231

Wyandotté (Cooper), **I:** 350, 355

Wyatt, Robert B., **Supp. V:** 14

Wyatt, Thomas, **Supp. I Part 1:** 369

Wycherly Woman, The (Macdonald), **Supp. IV Part 2:** 473

Wych Hazel (S. and A. Warner), **Supp. XVIII:** 267, **268–269**

Wydra, Ewa. *See* Hoffman, Eva

Wyeth, Andrew, **Supp. XIX:** 117

Wyler, William, **Supp. XV:** 195

Wylie, Elinor, **IV:** 436; **Supp. I Part 2:** **707–730;** **Supp. III Part 1:** 2, 63, 318–319; **Supp. XI:** 44; **Supp. XIV:** 127; **Supp. XV:** 307

Wylie, Horace, **Supp. I Part 2:** 708, 709

Wylie, Philip, **III:** 223

Wyllys, Ruth. *See* Taylor, Mrs. Edward (Ruth Wyllys)

"Wyoming Valley Tales" (Crane), **I:** 409

Wyzewa, Théodore de, **Supp. XIV:** 336

X

Xaipe (Cummings), **I:** 430, 432–433, 447

Xarque and Other Poems (G. Jones), **Supp. XXIV:** 194

Xenogenesis trilogy (O. Butler), **Supp. XIII: 63–66,** 69

Xenophon, **II:** 105

X Factor, The: A Quest for Excellence" (Plimpton), *Supp. XVI:* 241

X Files (television series), **Supp. XVI:** 125

Xiaojing, Zhou, **Supp. XV:** 214

Xicana Codex of Changing Consciousness, A: Writings, 2000–2010 (Moraga), **Supp. XXIII:** 197

Xingu and Other Stories (Wharton), **IV:** 314, 320; **Retro. Supp. I:** 378

Xionia (Wright), **Supp. V:** 333

XLI Poems (Cummings), **I:** 429, 432, 440, 443

Y

Yabroff, Jennie, **Supp. XIX:** 50, 58, 61

Yacoubi, Ahmed, **Supp. IV Part 1:** 88, 92, 93

Yage Letters, The (Burroughs), **Supp. III Part 1:** 94, 98, 100

Yagoda, Ben, **Supp. VIII:** 151

Yamamoto, Isoroku, **Supp. I Part 2:** 491

Yancey's War (Hoffman), **Supp. XVIII:** 71, **75–76**

Yankee City (Warner), **III:** 60

Yankee Clipper (ballet) (Kirstein), **Supp. IV Part 1:** 82

Yankee in Canada, A (Thoreau), **IV:** 188

Yankey in London (Tyler), **I:** 344

"Yánnina" (Merrill), **Supp. III Part 1:** 329

"Yanosz Korczak's Last Walk" (Markowick-Olczakova), **Supp. X:** 70

Yarboro, Chelsea Quinn, **Supp. V:** 147

Yarbro-Bejarano, Yvonne, **Supp. XXIII:** 196, 201

Yardley, Jonathan, **Supp. V:** 326; **Supp. XI:** 67; **Supp. XXIII:** 97, 99, 103, 104, 107, 108, 109

"Yard Sale" (Kenyon), **Supp. VII:** 169

Yates, Richard, **Supp. XI: 333–350;** **Supp. XXIII:** 289; **Supp. XXIV:** 97

"Year, The" (Sandburg), **III:** 584

Year at the Races, A (Parker and Parker), **Supp. XIX:** 187

Year Before Last (Boyle), **Supp. XXIV: 52–53**

"Year Between, The" (Neugeboren), **Supp. XVI:** 226

Year in Provence, A (Mayle), **Supp. XVI:** 295

Yearling, The (Rawlings), **Supp. X:** 219, **230–231,** 233, 234; **Supp. XXII:** 195

"Year of Grace" (Swados), **Supp. XIX:** 262–263

Year of Happy, A (Goldbarth), **Supp. XII:** 180

"Year of Mourning, The" (Jeffers), **Supp. II Part 2:** 415

Year of Silence, The (Bell), **Supp. X:** 1, **5–6,** 7

"Year of Silence, The" (Brockmeier), **Supp. XXII:** 59

"Year of the Double Spring, The" (Swenson), **Supp. IV Part 2:** 647

Year's Best Fantasy and Horror, 2004, **Supp. XXII:** 55

Year's Best Science Fiction, The (Merril, ed.), **Supp. XVI:** 123

Year's Life, A (Lowell), **Supp. I Part 2:** 405

"Years of Birth" (Cowley), **Supp. II Part 1:** 149

Years of Conscience: The Muckrakers: An Anthology of Reform Journalism (Swados, ed.), **Supp. XIX:** 264

Years of My Youth (Howells), **II:** 276

"Years of Wonder" (White), **Supp. I Part 2:** 652, 653

"Years Without Understanding, The" (Weigl), **Supp. XIX:** 282–283

Years With Ross, The (Thurber), **Supp. I Part 2:** 619

Year We Left Home, The (Thompson), **Supp. XXIII:** 301, **302–303**

Yeats, Jack, **Supp. XVI:** 190

Yeats, Jack B., **Supp. XX: 201**

Yeats, John Butler, **III:** 458; **Supp. XX: 69**

Yeats, William Butler, **I:** 69, 172, 384, 389, 403, 434, 478, 494, 532; **II:** 168–169, 566, 598; **III:** 4, 5, 8, 18, 19, 20, 23, 29, 40, 205, 249, 269, 270–271, 272, 278, 279, 294, 347, 409, 457, 458–460, 472, 473, 476–477, 521, 523, 524, 527, 528, 533, 540, 541, 542, 543–544, 591–592; **IV:** 89, 93, 121, 126, 136, 140, 271, 394, 404; **Retro. Supp. I:** 59, 66, 127, 141, 270, 283, 285, 286, 288, 290, 311, 342, 350, 378, 413; **Retro. Supp. II:** 185, 331; **Supp. I Part 1:** 79, 80, 254, 257, 262; **Supp. I Part 2:** 388, 389; **Supp. II Part 1:** 1, 4, 9, 20, 26, 361; **Supp. III Part 1:** 59, 63, 236, 238, 253; **Supp. IV Part 1:** 81; **Supp. IV Part 2:** 634; **Supp. V:** 220; **Supp. VIII:** 19, 21, 30, 155, 156, 190, 239, 262, 292; **Supp. IX:** 43, 119; **Supp. X:** 35, 58, 119, 120; **Supp. XI:** 140; **Supp. XII:** 132, 198, 217, 266; **Supp. XIII:** 77, **Supp. XIII:** 87; **Supp. XIV:** 7; **Supp. XV:** 36, 41, 181, 186; **Supp. XVI:** 47–48, 159; **Supp. XVII:** 36; **Supp. XXI:** 61

Yee, Amy, **Supp. XVIII:** 93, 94

Yellin, Jean Fagan, **Supp. XVI:** 88, 89

Yellow Back Radio Broke-Down (Reed), **Supp. X:** 240, 242, **243–245**

"Yellow Dog Café" (Komunyakaa), **Supp. XIII:** 126

Yellow Face (Hwang), **Supp. XXI:** 143, 148, **154–156**

"Yellow Girl" (Caldwell), **I:** 310

Yellow Glove (Nye), **Supp. XIII:** 275, **276–277**

"Yellow Glove" (Nye), **Supp. XIII:** 276

"Yellow Gown, The" (Anderson), **I:** 114

Yellow House on the Corner, The (Dove), **Supp. IV Part 1:** 244, 245, 246, 254

"Yellow Raft, The" (Connell), **Supp. XIV: 85–86**

"Yellow River" (Tate), **IV:** 141

"Yellowstone, The" (Kenny), **Supp. XXIII:** 155

"Yellow Violet, The" (Bryant), **Supp. I Part 1:** 154, 155

"Yellow Wallpaper, The" (Gilman), **Supp. XI: 198–199,** 207; **Supp. XVI:** 84

"Yellow Woman" (Keres stories), **Supp. IV Part 1:** 327

"Yellow Woman" (Silko), **Supp. IV Part 2:** 567–568

Yelverton, Theresa, **Supp. IX:** 181

Yenser, Stephen, **Supp. X:** 207, 208; **Supp. XV:** 113–114

"Yentl the Yeshiva Boy" (Singer), **IV:** 15, 20

Yerkes, Charles E., **I:** 507, 512

Yerma (opera) (Bowles), **Supp. IV Part 1:** 89

Yertle the Turtle and Other Stories (Geisel), **Supp. XVI:** 109

"Yes" (Stafford), **Supp. XI:** 329

Yes, Mrs. Williams (W. C. Williams), **Retro. Supp. I:** 423

Yes, Yes, No, No (Kushner), **Supp. IX:** 133

"Yes and It's Hopeless" (Ginsberg), **Supp. II Part 1:** 326

"Yes" (Crooker), **Supp. XXIII:** 62

Yesenin, Sergey, **Supp. VIII:** 40

"Yes: I Mean So OK–Love" (Bronk), **Supp. XXI:** 31

"Yes! No!" (Oliver), **Supp. VII:** 243–244

Yesterday and Today: A Comparative Anthology of Poetry (Untermeyer, ed.), **Supp. XV:** 309

Yesterday's Self: Nostalgia and the Immigrant Identity (Ritivoi), **Supp. XVI:** 148

Yesterday Will Make You Cry (C. Himes), **Supp. XVI:** 137

"Yet Another Example of the Porousness of Certain Borders" (Wallace), **Supp. X:** 309

"Yet Do I Marvel" (Cullen), **Supp. IV Part 1:** 165, 169

Yet Other Waters (Farrell), **II:** 29, 38, 39, 40

"Yevtushenko" (Kooser), **Supp. XIX:** 124

Yevtushenko, Yevgeny, **Supp. III Part 1:** 268

Yezzi, David, **Supp. XII:** 193

Yiddish Policemen's Union, The (Chabon), **Supp. XXII:** 49

Yizkor Book, **Supp. XVI:** 154

...*y no se lo tragó la tierra* (Rivera), **Supp. XIX:** 99, 101

Y no se lo trago la tierra (And the Earth Did Not Cover Him) (Rivera), **Supp. XIII:** 216

¡Yo! (Alvarez), **Supp. VII:** 1, 15–17

"Yogurt of Vasirin Kefirovsky, The" (Apple), **Supp. XVII:** 3, 4

Yohannan, J. D., **II:** 20

"Yoke, The" (Bidart), **Supp. XV:** 33

Yonge, Charlotte, **II:** 174

"Yonnondio" (Whitman), **Supp. XIII:** 304

Yonnondio: From the Thirties (Olsen), **Supp. XIII:** 295, 295, **Supp. XIII:** 292, 296, **303–304,** 305

"Yore" (Nemerov), **III:** 283

York, Jake Adam, **Supp. XXI:** 257

York, Lorraine, **Supp. XX: 51**

"York Beach" (Toomer), **Supp. III Part 2:** 486

Yorke, Dorothy, **Supp. I Part 1:** 258

Yorke, Henry Vincent. *See* Green, Henry

"York Garrison, 1640" (Jewett), **Retro. Supp. II:** 141

Yosemite, The (Muir), **Supp. IX:** 185

"Yosemite Glaciers: Ice Streams of the Great Valley" (Muir), **Supp. IX:** 181

Yoshe Kalb (Singer), **IV:** 2

"You, Andrew Marvell" (MacLeish), **III:** 12–13

"You, Dr. Martin" (Sexton), **Supp. II Part 2:** 673

You, Emperors, and Others: Poems 1957–1960 (Warren), **IV:** 245

"You, Genoese Mariner" (Merwin), **Supp. III Part 1:** 343

"You, Reader" (Collins), **Supp. XXI:** 55

"You All Know the Story of the Other Woman" (Sexton), **Supp. II Part 2:** 688

"You Are Gorgeous and I'm Coming" (O'Hara), **Supp. XXIII:** 219

You Are Happy (Atwood), **Supp. XIII:** 34

"You Are Happy" (Atwood), **Supp. XIII:** 34

"You Are in Bear Country" (Kumin), **Supp. IV Part 2:** 453, 455

"You Are Not I" (Bowles), **Supp. IV Part 1:** 87

"You Begin" (Atwood), **Supp. XIII:** 34

You Bright and Risen Angels (Vollmann), **Supp. XVII:** 225, 226

"You Bring Out the Mexican in Me" (Cisneros), **Supp. VII:** 71

You Came Along (film), **Supp. IV Part 2:** 524

"You Can Go Home Again" (TallMountain), **Supp. IV Part 1:** 324–325

"You Can Have It" (Levine), **Supp. V:** 188–189

You Can't Go Home Again (Wolfe), **IV:** 450, 451, 454, 456, 460, 462, 468, 469, 470

You Can't Keep a Good Woman Down (Walker), **Supp. III Part 2:** 520, 525, 531

You Can't Pet a Possom (Bontemps), **Supp. XXII:** 4, 12

You Can't Take It with You (Kaufman and Hart), **Supp. XIV:** 327

"You Can't Tell a Man by the Song He Sings" (P. Roth), **Supp. III Part 2:** 406

"You Don't Know What Love Is" (Carver), **Supp. III Part 1:** 147

You Don't Love Me Yet (Lethem), **Supp. XVIII: 149–150**

"You Have Left Your Lotus Pods on the Bus" (Bowles), **Supp. IV Part 1:** 91

You Have Seen Their Faces (Caldwell), **I:** 290, 293–294, 295, 304, 309

You Know Me, Al: A Busher's Letters (Lardner), **Supp. XVI:** 189

You Know Me Al (comic strip), **II:** 423

You Know Me Al (Lardner), **II:** 26, 415, 419, 422, 431

"You Know More Than You Think You Do" (Hadas), **Supp. XXIII:** 124

"You Know What" (Beattie), **Supp. V:** 33

"You Know Who You Are" (Nye), **Supp. XIII:** 275

You Might As Well Live: The Life and Times of Dorothy Parker (Keats), **Supp. IX:** 190

"You Must Relax!" (J. Scott), **Supp. XVII:** 189

You Must Revise Your Life (Stafford), **Supp. XI:** 312–313, 313–314, 315

"Young" (Sexton), **Supp. II Part 2:** 680

Young, Al, **Supp. X:** 240

Young, Art, **IV:** 436

Young, Barbara, **Supp. XX: 119, 123**

Young, Brigham, **Supp. IV Part 2:** 603

Young, Courtland, **Supp. XXII:** 21

Young, David, **Supp. XIX:** 276

Young, Dianne, **Supp. XXII:** 252

Young, Edward, **II:** 111; **III:** 415, 503

Young, Gary, **Supp. XV:** 88

Young, Hershini Bhana, **Supp. XXIV:** 189

Young, Mary, **Supp. XIII:** 236, 238, 239, 240

Young, Philip, **II:** 306; **Retro. Supp. I:** 172

Young, Stark, **Supp. XXII:** 193

Young Adventure (Benét), **Supp. XI:** 44

"Young America" (Brooks), **Supp. XV:** 298

"Young Child and His Pregnant Mother, A" (Schwartz), **Supp. II Part 2:** 650

Young Christian, The (Abbott), **Supp. I Part 1:** 38

"Young Dr. Gosse" (Chopin), **Supp. I Part 1:** 211, 216

Younger Choir, The (anthology), **Supp. XV:** 294

Younger Quire, The (Untermeyer), **Supp. XV:** 294, 297

"Young Folks, The" (Salinger), **III:** 551

Young Folk's Cyclopaedia of Persons and Places (Champlin), **III:** 577

"Young Girl's Lament, A" (Jin), **Supp. XVIII:** 99

"Young Goodman Brown" (Hawthorne), **II:** 229; **Retro. Supp. I:** 151–152, 153, 154; **Supp. XI:** 51; **Supp. XIV:** 48, 50

Young Harvard: First Poems of Witter Bynner (Bynner), **Supp. XV:** 41

Young Hearts Crying (Yates), **Supp. XI:** 348

"Young Housewife, The" (W. C. Williams), **Retro. Supp. I:** 415

Young Immigrants, The (Lardner), **II:** 426

"Young Lady's Friend, The: Verses, Addressed to a Young Lady, on Her Leaving School" (Rowson), **Supp. XV:** 234

"Young Lions" (E. P. Jones), **Supp. XXII:** 145

Young Lions, The (Shaw), **Supp. XIX: 248–249**

Young Lonigan: A Boyhood in Chicago Streets (Farrell), **II:** 31, 41

Young Manhood of Studs Lonigan, The (Farrell), **II:** 31, 34

"Young Man on the Go" (column, Siddons), **Supp. XXII:** 244

Young Men and Fire (Maclean), **Supp. XIV:** 221, **231–233**

Young People's Pride (Benét), **Supp. XI:** 44

Young Poet's Primer (Brooks), **Supp. III Part 1:** 86

Youngren, J. Alan, **Supp. XVI:** 174

"Young Sammy's First Wild Oats" (Santayana), **III:** 607, 615

"Young Sor Juana, The" (Mora), **Supp. XIII:** 218

"Your Arkansas Traveler" (Schulberg), **Supp. XVIII:** 252

"Your Dailiness" (Notley), **Supp. XXII:** 227

"Your Death" (Dove), **Supp. IV Part 1:** 250

"You're History" (Hampl), **Supp. XXII:** 84, 95

You're Only Old Once! (Geisel), **Supp. XVI:** 111

"You're Ugly, Too" (Moore), **Supp. X:** 171

"Your Face on the Dog's Neck" (Sexton), **Supp. II Part 2:** 686

"Your Hand, Your Hand" (Hoffman), **Supp. XVIII:** 79

Your Job in Germany (film, Capra), **Supp. XVI:** 102

Your Job in Japan (film, Capra), **Supp. XVI:** 102

"Your Life" (Stafford), **Supp. XI:** 329

"Your Mother's Eyes" (Kingsolver), **Supp. VII:** 209

"You Take a Train through a Foreign Country" (Dobyns), **Supp. XIII:** 90

"Youth" (Hughes), **Supp. I Part 1:** 321; **Supp. XXII:** 12

"Youth" (Huncke), **Supp. XIV:** 145

Youth and Life (Bourne), **I:** 217–222, 232

Youth and the Bright Medusa (Cather), **I:** 322; **Retro. Supp. I:** 14

"Youthful Religious Experiences" (Corso), **Supp. XII:** 117

Youth of Parnassus, and Other Stories, The (L. P. Smith), **Supp. XIV:** 336

Youth's First Steps in Geography (Rowson), **Supp. XV:** 243

You Touched Me! (Williams and Windham), **IV:** 382, 385, 387, 390, 392–393

"You Touch Me" (X. J. Kennedy), **Supp. XV:** 166

You Went Away (Findley), **Supp. XX: 49**

"You Who Sleep Soundly Through Our Bleakest Hour" (Espaillat), **Supp. XXI:** 110

Yurchenco, Henrietta, **Supp. XVIII:** 20

Yurka, Blanche, **Supp. I Part 1:** 67

Yutang, Adet, **Supp. X:** 291

Yutang, Anor, **Supp. X:** 291

Yutang, Lin, **Supp. X:** 291; **Supp. XVI:** 190

Yutang, Mei-mei, **Supp. X:** 291

Yvernelle: A Legend of Feudal France (Norris), **III:** 314

Y & X (Olson), **Supp. II Part 2:** 556

Z

Zabel, Morton Dauwen, **II:** 431; **III:** 194, 215; **Supp. I Part 2:** 721

Zach, Natan, **Supp. XV:** 75, 82, 85

Zaehner, R. C., **Supp. XXII:** 258

Zagajewski, Adam, **Supp. XVII:** 241

Zagarell, Sandra, **Supp. XV:** 269, 270, 278, 281, 282

Zagarell, Sandra A., **Retro. Supp. II:** 140, 143

"Zagrowsky Tells" (Paley), **Supp. VI:** 229

Zaino, Nick, **Supp. XXII:** 207

Zakrzewska, Marie, **Retro. Supp. II:** 146

Zaleski, Jeff, **Supp. XI:** 143; **Supp. XIX:** 54

Zall, Paul, **Supp. XIV:** 156

Zaltzberg, Charlotte, **Supp. IV Part 1:** 374

"Zambesi and Ranee" (Swenson), **Supp. IV Part 2:** 647

Zamir, Israel, **Retro. Supp. II:** 303, 317

Zamora, Bernice, **Supp. IV Part 2:** 545

Zamoyski, Adam, **Supp. XV:** 257

Zangwill, Israel, **I:** 229; **Supp. XX:** 2

Zanita: A Tale of the Yosemite (Yelverton), **Supp. IX:** 181

Zanuck, Darryl F., **Supp. XI:** 170; **Supp. XII:** 165

Zapata, Emiliano, **Supp. XIII:** 324

"Zapatos" (Boyle), **Supp. VIII:** 15

Zapruder, Matthew, **Supp. XVI:** 55

Zarathustra, **III:** 602

Zawacki, Andrew, **Supp. VIII:** 272

"Zaydee" (Levine), **Supp. V:** 186

Zebra-Striped Hearse, The (Macdonald), **Supp. IV Part 2:** 473

Zechariah (biblical book), **IV:** 152

Zeidner, Lisa, **Supp. IV Part 2:** 453; **Supp. XXIII:** 297

"Zeitl and Rickel" (Singer), **IV:** 20

Zeke and Ned (McMurtry and Ossana), **Supp. V:** 232

Zeke Proctor, Cherokee Outlaw (Conley), **Supp. V:** 232

Zelazo, Suzanne, **Supp. XXII:** 158, 167

Zelda: A Biography (Milford), **Supp. IX:** 60

"Zelda and Scott: The Beautiful and Damned" (National Portrait Gallery exhibit), **Supp. IX:** 65

Zelig (film; Allen), **Supp. XV:** 4, 6, **8–9**

Zeller, Maya Jewell, **Supp. XXIV:** 167

Zen and the Birds of Appetite (Merton), **Supp. VIII:** 205–206, 208

Zend-Avesta (Fechner), **II:** 358

Zeno, **Retro. Supp. I:** 247

Zero db and Other Stories (Bell), **Supp. X:** 1, 5, 6

"Zeus over Redeye" (Hayden), **Supp. II Part 1:** 380

Zevi, Sabbatai, **IV:** 6

Ziegfeld, Florenz, **II:** 427–428

Ziegler, Cyd, **Supp. XX:** **273**

Ziegler, Heidi, **Supp. XXII:** 260

Ziggurat (Balakian), **Supp. XXIII:** 19, **32–33**

Zigrosser, Carl, **I:** 226, 228, 231

Zilles, Klaus, **Supp. XIX:** 112

Zimmerman, Paul D., **Supp. IV Part 2:** 583, 589, 590

Zimmerman, Robert. *See* Dylan, Bob

Zimmerman, Robert Allen. *See* Dylan, Bob

Zinberg, Leonard S. *See* Lacy, Ed

Zinman, Toby Silverman, **Supp. XIII:** 207–208, 209

Zinn, Howard, **Supp. V:** 289; **Supp. XXIV:** 87

Zinovyev, Grigory, **Supp. XXI:** 167

Zinsser, Hans, **I:** 251, 385

Zip: A Novel of the Left and Right (Apple), **Supp. XVII:** **4–5**

Zipes, Jack, **Supp. XIV:** 126

"Zipper, The" (L. Michaels), **Supp. XVI:** 214

"Zizi's Lament" (Corso), **Supp. XII:** 123

Zodiac, The (Dickey), **Supp. IV Part 1:** 178, 183–184, 185

"Zog-19: A Scientific Romance"(P. Benedict), **Supp. XXIII:** 49

Zola, Émile, **I:** 211, 411, 474, 500, 502, 518; **II:** 174, 175–176, 182, 194, 275, 276, 281, 282, 319, 325, 337, 338; **III:** 315, 316, 317–318, 319–320, 321, 322, 323, 393, 511, 583; **IV:** 326; **Retro. Supp. I:** 226, 235; **Retro. Supp. II:** 93; **Supp. I Part 1:** 207; **Supp. II Part 1:** 117

Zolotow, Maurice, **III:** 161

"Zone" (Bogan), **Supp. III Part 1:** 60–61

Zone Journals (Wright), **Supp. V:** 332–333, 342–343

"Zooey" (Salinger), **III:** 564–565, 566, 567, 569, 572

"Zoo Revisited" (White), **Supp. I Part 2:** 654

Zoo Story, The (Albee), **I:** 71, 72–74, 75, 77, 84, 93, 94; **III:** 281

Zorach, William, **I:** 260

Zuccotti, Susan, **Supp. XVI:** 154

Zuckerman Bound: A Trilogy and Epilogue (P. Roth), **Supp. III Part 2:** 423

Zuckerman Unbound (P. Roth), **Retro. Supp. II:** 283; **Supp. III Part 2:** 421–422

Zueblin, Charles, **Supp. I Part 1:** 5

Zuger, Abigail, **Supp. X:** 160

Zukofsky, Celia (Mrs. Louis), **Supp. III Part 2:** 619–621, 623, 625, 626–629, 631

Zukofsky, Louis, **IV:** 415; **Retro. Supp. I:** 422; **Supp. III Part 2:** **619–636**; **Supp. IV Part 1:** 154; **Supp. XIV:** 279, 282, 285, 286–287

Zukofsky, Paul, **Supp. III Part 2:** 622, 623–626, 627, 628

Zuleika Dobson (Beerbohm), **Supp. I Part 2:** 714

Zulus (Everett), **Supp. XVIII:** 54, **56–57**

"Zuni Potter: Drawing the Heartline" (Bierds), **Supp. XVII:** 26

Zverev, Aleksei, **Retro. Supp. I:** 278

Zwinger, Ann, **Supp. X:** 29

Zyda, Joan, **Retro. Supp. II:** 52